CHILTON'S TRUCK REPAIR MANUAL 1961-1971

Editorial Director	Alan F. Turner
Executive Editor	Kerry A. Freeman, S.A.E.
Senior Editor	Richard J. Rivele, S.A.E.
Editorial Staff	John M. Baxter
	Tony Molla
	W. Calvin Settle, Jr.
	Richard T. Smith
	Ron Webb
Production Manager	John J. Cantwell
Manager, Editing and Design	Dean F. Morgantini, S.A.E.
Art & Production Coordinator	Robin S. Miller
Mechanical Paste-Up Supervisor	Margaret A. Stoner
Mechanical Artists	Cynthia Fiore
	William Gaskins
OFFICERS	
President	Lawrence A. Fornasieri
Vice-President & General Manager	John P. Kushnerick

CHILTON BOOK COMPANY
Chilton Way, Radnor, PA 19089

Manufactured in USA

ISBN 0-8019-6198-X
Library of Congress Card No. 70-153137

11 12 13 15 432109876

CONTENTS

Truck Service Section

General Repair Section

Transmission Section

Chevrolet and Chevy Van

Index

Rear Axles

Rear Suspension

Specifications

Steering—Manual

Steering—Power

Transfer Case

Transmissions—Automatic

Transmissions—Manual

TUNE-UP SPECIFICATIONS

CU. IN. DISPLACEMENT	YEAR	SPARK PLUG GAP	DISTRIBUTOR POINT DWELL	DISTRIBUTOR POINT GAP	IGNITION TIMING DEGREES	CRANKCASE COMP. PRESSURE	VALVE CLEARANCE IN LOT EXTEN.	GOV. R.P.M. NO LOAD	FUEL PUMP PRESS	IDLE SPEED STD.	IDLE SPEED AUTO.
FOUR CYLINDER											
153	1963-65	.035	31-34	.019	4B	130	0+1 Turn	—	3½-4½	500	—
SIX CYLINDER											
194	1964-65	.035	31-34	.019	8B	130	0+1 Turn	—	3½-4½	500	—
	1966-67	.035	31-34	.019	8B[1]	130	0+1 Turn	—	3-4½	700•	600•
230	1963-65	.035	31-34	.019	4B	130	0+1 Turn	—	3½-4½	500	450
	1966	.035	31-34	.019	6B[2]	130	0+1 Turn	—	3½-4½	700•	600•
	1967	.035	31-34	.019	4B	130	0+1 Turn	—	3-4½	700•	500•
	1968-69	.035	31-34	.019	4B[3]	130	0+1 Turn	—	3½-4½	700•	550•
235	1961-62	.035	28-33	.019	5B	130	.006H-.018H	—	3½-4½	500	•
250	1966	.035	31-34	.019	6B	150	0+1 Turn	4000	3-4½	700•	600•
	1967	.035	31-34	.019	4B	130	0+1 Turn	—	3-4½	700•	500•
	1968-71	.035	31-34	.019	4B[3]	130	0+1 Turn	4000	3-4½	700	500
261	1961-62	.035	28-33	.019	TDC	130	.006H-.018H	—	3½-4½	500	450
292	1963-65	.035	31-34	.019	4B	130	0+1 Turn	—	3½-4½	500	450
	1966	.035	31-34	.019	4B[4]	140	0+1 Turn	3900	3-4½	700•	600•
	1967	.035	31-34	.019	4B[5]	130	0+1 Turn	3900	3-4½	700•	600•
	1968	.035	31-34	.019	4B[3]	130	0+1 Turn	3900	3-4½	700•	600•
	1969-71	.035	31-34	.019	TDC[6]	130	0+1 Turn	3900	3-4½	700	550
401 (V6)	1966-68	.035	31-34	.019	5B	130	.012H-.018H	3700	5-6½	500	—
478 (V6)	1966-68	.035	31-34	.019	2½B	130	.012H-.018H	3400	5-6½	500	—
EIGHT CYLINDER											
283	1961	.035	28-32	.019	4B	150	0+¾ Turn	3700	5¼-6½	500	•
	1962	.035	28-32	.019	4B	150	0+1 Turn	3700	5½-6½	500	•
	1963-66	.035	28-32	.019	4B	160	0+1 Turn	4000	5-6½	500	•
	1967	.035	28-32	.019	4B[7]	150	0+1 Turn	4000	5-6½	700•	600•
307	1968-69	.035	28-32	.019	2B	150	0+1 Turn	4000	5-6½	700•	600•
	1970-71	.035	28-32	.019	2B[8]	150	0+1 Turn	4000	5-6½	700	600
327	1962-65	.035	28-32	.019	8B	150	0+1 Turn	4000	5-6½	500	•
	1966	.035	28-32	.019	2B[9]	150	0+1 Turn	4000	5-6½	700•	600
185 H.P.	1967	.035	28-32	.019	8B	150	0+1 Turn	4000	5-6½	500	•
220 H.P.	1967	.035	28-32	.019	2B[10]	150	0+1 Turn	4000	5-6½	700•	600•
348	1961-62	.035	28-32	.019	4B	125	0+1 Turn	3700	5¼-6½	500	•
	1963-65	.035	28-32	.019	8B	140	0+1 Turn	4000	5¼-6½	500	•
350 215 H.P.	1969-71	.035	28-32	.019	4B	150	0+1 Turn	4000	5-6½	500	500
255 H.P.	1969-71	.035	28-32	.019	TDC[6]	150	0+1 Turn	4000	5-6½	700	600
366	1966-71	.035	29-31	.019	6B	130	0+1 Turn	4000	5-6½	500	500
396	1968-69	.035	29-31	.019	4B	150	0+1 Turn	4000	5-6½	700	600
409	1962-65	.035	28-32	.019	4B	140	0+1 Turn	4000	5-6½	500	•
427	1968-71	.035	28-32	.019	6B	150	0+1 Turn	4000	5-6½	500	500

WITH AIR INJECTION REACTOR SYSTEM

1—Std. Trans. 3° BTC.
2—Std. Auto. Trans. 4° BTC.
3—Std. TDC.
4—Std. 1° BTC.
5—Std. 2° BTC.
6—Auto. 4° BTC.
7—Std. 6° ATC.
8—Auto. 8° BTC.
9—Std. 8° BTC.
10—All TDC.

•—w/out A.I.R. Std. Trans. 500, Auto. Trans. Set As Low As Possible To Obtain A Good Idle.

GENERAL ENGINE SPECIFICATIONS

CU. IN. DISPLACEMENT	YEAR	BORE AND STROKE	FIRING ORDER	DEVELOPED HORSE POWER @ R.P.M.	DEVELOPED TORQUE @ R.P.M.	COMPRESSION RATIO	CARBURETOR	VALVE LIFTER TYPE	NORMAL OIL PRESSURE
FOUR CYLINDER									
153	1963-65	3.875x3.250	1-3-4-2	90@4000	152@2400	8.5	1V	Hyd.	40-60

FIRING ORDER AND ROTATION

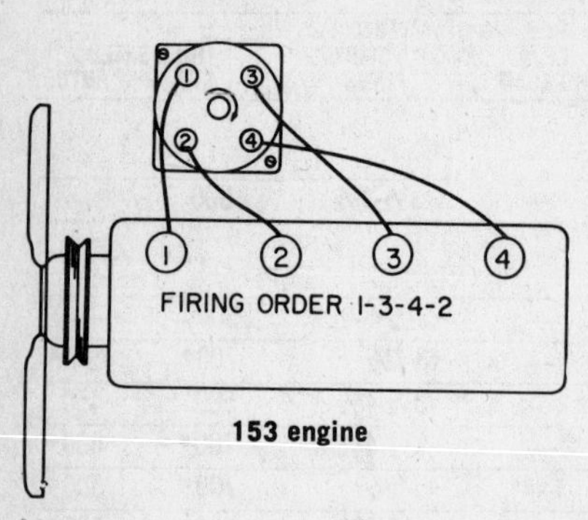

153 engine

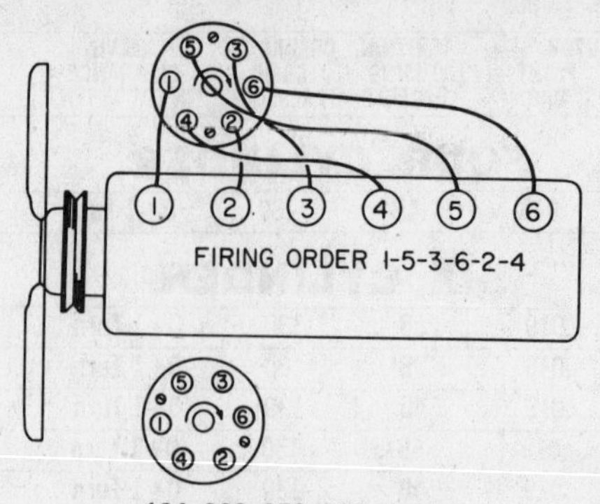

194, 230, 250, 292 engines

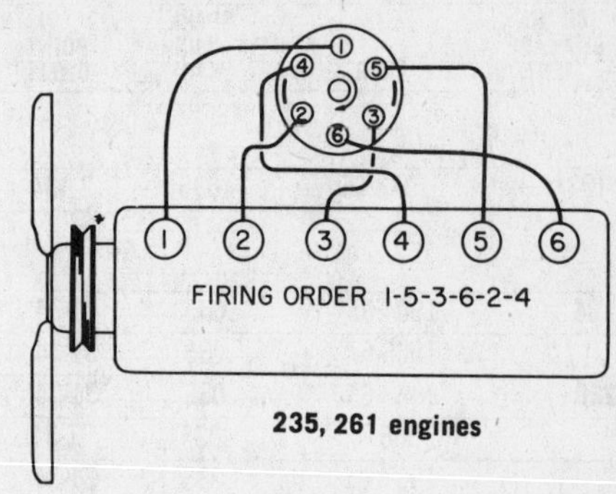

235, 261 engines

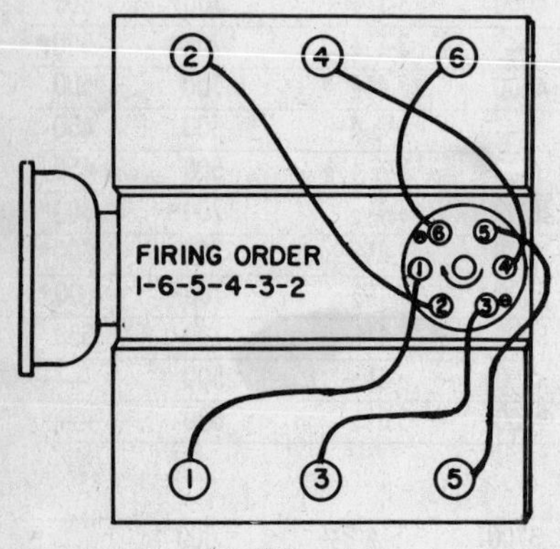

401, 478 engines

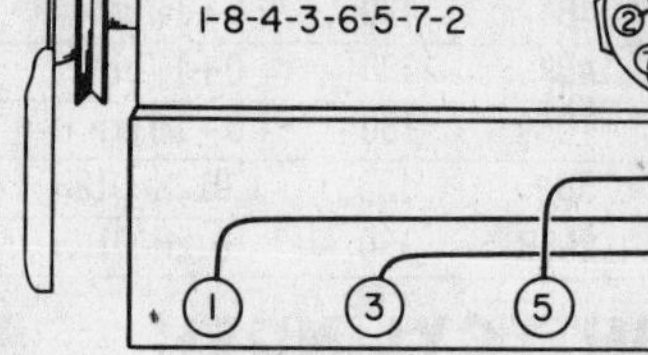

407, 348 engines

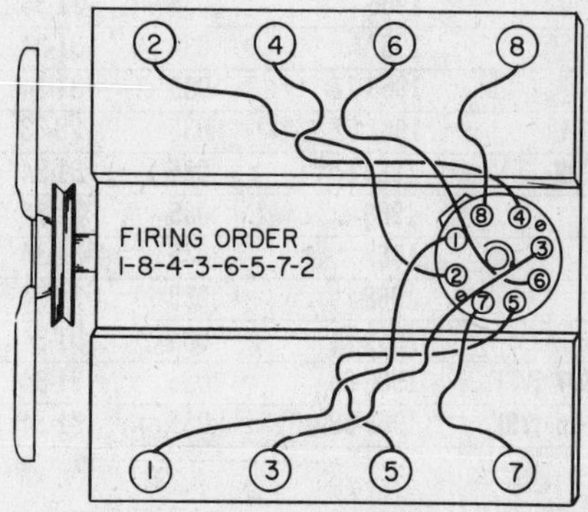

283, 307, 327, 350, 366, 396, 427 engines

GENERAL ENGINE SPECIFICATIONS, continued

CU. IN. DISPLACE-MENT	YEAR	BORE AND STROKE	FIRING ORDER	DEVELOPED HORSE POWER @ R.P.M.	DEVELOPED TORQUE @ R.P.M.	COM-PRESSION RATIO	CARBUR-ETOR	VALVE LIFTER TYPE	NORMAL OIL PRESSURE
SIX CYLINDER									
194	1964-67	3.5625x3.250	1-5-3-6-2-4	120@4400	177@2400	8.5	1V	Hyd.	40-60
230 125 H.P.	1963-65	3.875x3.250	1-5-3-6-2-4	125@3400	210@1600	8.5	1V	Hyd.	40-60
140 H.P.	1963-65	3.875x3.250	1-5-3-6-2-4	140@4400	220@1600	8.5	1V	Hyd.	40-60
	1966-69	3.875x3.250	1-5-3-6-2-4	140@4400	220@1600	8.5	1V	Hyd.	40-60
235	1961-62	3.5625x3.937	1-5-3-6-2-4	135@4000	217@2000	8.25	1V	Mech.	35
250	1966	3.875x3.530	1-5-3-6-2-4	150@4200	235@1600	8.5	1V	Hyd.	40-60
	1967-71	3.875x3.530	1-5-3-6-2-4	155@4200	235@1600	8.5	1V	Hyd.	40-60
261	1961-62	3.750x3.937	1-5-3-6-2-4	150@4000	235@2000	8.0	1V	Mech.	35
292	1963-71	3.875x4.125	1-5-3-6-2-4	170@4000	275@1600	8.0	1V	Hyd.	40-60
401 (V6)	1967-68	4.87x3.58	1-6-5-4-3-2	237@4000	372@1600	7.5	2V	Mech.	60
478 (V6)	1967-68	5.125x3.86	1-6-5-4-3-2	254@3700	442@1400	7.5	2V	Mech.	60
EIGHT CYLINDER									
283	1961-62	3.875x3.00	1-8-4-3-6-5-7-2	160@4200	270@2000	8.5	2V	Hyd.	30
	1963-65	3.875x3.00	1-8-4-3-6-5-7-2	175@4400	275@2400	8.5	2V	Hyd.	30
Hi-Torque	1966-67	3.875x3.00	1-8-4-3-6-5-7-2	175@4400	275@2400	9.0	2V	Hyd.	30-35
Turbo-Fire	1966-67	3.875x3.00	1-8-4-3-6-5-7-2	195@4800	285@2400	9.25	2V	Hyd.	30-35
Turbo-Fire	1966-67	3.875x3.00	1-8-4-3-6-5-7-2	220@4800	295@3200	9.25	4V	Hyd.	30-35
307 180 H.P.	1968	3.875x3.25	1-8-4-3-6-5-7-2	180@4400	285@2400	8.25	2V	Hyd.	30-35
200 H.P.	1968-71	3.875x3.25	1-8-4-3-6-5-7-2	200@4600	300@2400	9.0	2V	Hyd.	30-35
327	1962-68	4.000x3.25	1-8-4-3-6-5-7-2	185@4400	305@2000	8.0	2V	Hyd.	30
Hi-Torque	1966-68	4.000x3.25	1-8-4-3-6-5-7-2	220@4400	320@2800	8.5	4V	Hyd.	30-35
348 185 H.P.	1961	4.125x3.25	1-8-4-3-6-5-7-2	185@4400	325@2600	8.0	4V	Hyd.	35
230 H.P.	1961	4.125x3.25	1-8-4-3-6-5-7-2	230@4400	325@2600	8.0	4V	Hyd.	35
220 H.P.	1962	4.125x3.25	1-8-4-3-6-5-7-2	220@4400	325@2600	7.75	4V	Hyd.	35
	1963-65	4.125x3.25	1-8-4-3-6-5-7-2	175@4000	315@2200	7.75	2V	Hyd.	35-40
	1963-65	4.125x3.25	1-8-4-3-6-5-7-2	220@4400	325@2600	7.75	4V	Hyd.	35-40

GENERAL ENGINE SPECIFICATIONS, continued

CU. IN. DISPLACE-MENT	YEAR	BORE AND STROKE	FIRING ORDER	DEVELOPED HORSE POWER @ R.P.M.	DEVELOPED TORQUE @ R.P.M.	COM-PRESSION RATIO	CARBUR-ETOR	VALVE LIFTER TYPE	NORMAL OIL PRESSURE
350	1969-70	4.00x3.48	1-8-4-3-6-5-7-2	215@4400	320@2400	8.0	2V	Hyd.	30
	1969-70	4.00x3.48	1-8-4-3-6-5-7-2	255@4600	355@3000	9.0	4V	Hyd.	30
366	1966-67	3.937x3.76	1-8-4-3-6-5-7-2	220@4000	345@2400	8.0	2V	Hyd.	50-75
	1968-71	3.937x3.76	1-8-4-3-6-5-7-2	235@4000	345@2600	8.0	4V	Hyd.	50-75
396	1968	4.094x3.76	1-8-4-3-6-5-7-2	325@4800	410@3200	10.25	4V	Hyd.	50-75
	1969-71	4.094x3.76	1-8-4-3-6-5-7-2	310@4800	400@3200	9.0	4V	Hyd.	50-75
409	1962-65	4.3125x3.50	1-8-4-3-6-5-7-2	252@4000	390@2400	7.75	4V	Hyd.	35
427	1968-71	4.250x3.76	1-8-4-3-6-5-7-2	260@4000	405@2600	8.0	4V	Hyd.	50-75

CRANKSHAFT BEARING JOURNAL SPECIFICATIONS

CU. IN. DISPLACE MENT	YEAR	MAIN BEARING JOURNALS: JOURNAL DIAMETER	OIL CLEARANCE	SHAFT END PLAY	THRUST ON NO.	CONNECTING ROD BEARING JOURNALS: JOURNAL DIAMETER	OIL CLEARANCE	END PLAY
				FOUR CYLINDER				
153	1963-65	2.2983-2.2993	.0003-.0019[8]	.002-.006	Rear	1.997-2.000	.0007-.0028	.008-.014
				SIX CYLINDER				
194	1964-67	2.2983-2.2993	.0008-.004	.002-.006	Rear	1.999-2.000	.0007-.0028	.008-.014
230	1963-65	2.2983-2.2993	.0003-.0019[8]	.002-.006	Rear	1.999-2.000	.0007-.0028	.0085-.0135
	1966-69	2.2983-2.2993	.0003-.0029	.002-.006	Rear	1.999-2.000	.0007-.0027	.0085-.0135
235	1961-62	[1]	.0008-.0026	.003-.009	3	2.311-2.312	.001-.003	.005-.012
250	1966-71	2.2983-2.2993	.0003-.0029	.002-.006	Rear	1.999-2.000	.0007-.0027	.0085-.0135
261	1961-62	[1]	.0008-.0026	.003-.009	3	2.311-2.312	.001-.003	—
292	1963-71	2.2983-2.2993	.0008-.0034	.002-.006	5	2.099-2.100	.0007-.0028	.0085-.0135
401 (V6)	1966-68	3.1237-3.1247[2]	.0013-.0039	.003-.008	3	2.8112-2.8122	.0013-.0039	.006-.011
478 (V6)	1966-68	3.1237-3.1247[2]	.0013-.0039	.003-.008	3	2.8112-2.8122	.0013-.0039	.006-.011
				EIGHT CYLINDER				
283	1961-67	2.2978-2.2988	.0007-.0028	.002-.006	5	1.999-2.000	.0007-.0027	.009-.013
307	1968-69	2.4484-2.4493[3]	.0008-.0024[10]	.003-.011	5	2.0990-2.100	.0007-.0027	.009-.013
	1970-71	2.4484-2.4493[3]	[11]	.002-.006	5	2.0990-2.100	.0007-.0028	.009-.013
327	1962-67	2.2983-2.2993	.0008-.0024[10]	.003-.011	5	1.999-2.100	.0007-.0028	.009-.013
	1968	2.4484-2.4493[3]	.0008-.0024[10]	.003-.011	5	2.0990-2.100	.0007-.0028	.009-.013
348	1961	2.498-2.499	.0008-.0034[12]	.002-.006	5	2.199-2.200	.001-.003	.008-.014
	1962-65	2.498-2.499	.001-.003	.006-.016	5	2.199-2.200	.0007-.0028	.008-.014
350	1969	2.4484-2.4493[3]	.0008-.0024[10]	.003-.011	5	2.099-2.100	.0007-.0028	.008-.014
	1970-71	2.4484-2.4493[3]	[11]	.002-.006	5	2.099-2.100	.0007-.0028	.008-.014
366	1966-69	2.7481-2.7490[4]	.0013-.0025[13]	.006-.010	5	2.1988-2.1998	.0007-.0028	.019-.025
	1970-71	2.7481-2.7490[5]	.0013-.0025[14]	.006-.010	5	2.1988-2.1998	.0014-.0030	.019-.025
396	1966-69	2.7481-2.7490[4]	.0013-.0025[13]	.006-.010	5	2.1988-2.1998	.0007-.0028	.015-.021
	1970-71	2.7481-2.7490[5]	.0013-.0025[14]	.006-.010	5	2.199-2.200	.0009-.0025	.015-.021
409	1962-65	2.498-2.499	.0008-.0034[12]	.004-.012	5	2.199-2.200	.001-.003	.016-.020
427	1968-69	2.7481-2.7490[4]	.0013-.0025[13]	.006-.010	5	2.199-2.1998	.0007-.0028	.019-.025
	1970-71	2.7481-2.7490[5]	.0013-.0025[14]	.006-.010	5	2.199-2.1998	.0014-.0030	.019-.025

1—No. 1—2.6835-2.6845, No. 2—2.7145-2.7155, No. 3—2.7455-2.7465, No. 4—2.7765-2.7775.
2—Rear—3.1239-3.1249.
3—Rear—2.4479-2.4488.
4—Rear—2.7478-2.7488.
5—Rear—2.7473-2.7483.
8—Rear—.0008-.0024.
10—Rear—.0010-.0026.
11—No. 1—.0003-.0015, No. 2, 3, 4—.0006-.0018, No. 5—.0008-.0023.
12—Rear—.0018-.0034.
13—Rear—.0015-.0031.
14—Rear—.0029-.0045.

VALVE SPECIFICATIONS

CU. IN. DISPLACE-MENT	YEAR	LASH (HOT) INCHES INT.	EXH.	ANGLE DEGREE FACE	SEAT	STEM DIA. INCHES INT.	EXH.	STEM CLEARANCE INTAKE	EXHAUST	VALVE LIFT INCHES	VALVE SPRING LBS @ INCHES OPEN	CLOSED	FREE LENGTH INCH
						FOUR CYLINDER							
153	1963-65	0+1	Turn	45	46	.341	.341	.001-.003	.002-.004	.397	175@1.26	82@1.66	2.08
						SIX CYLINDER							
194	1964-67	0+1	Turn	45	46	.341	.341	.001-.003	.002-.004	.335	171@1.33	82@1.66	1.92
230	1963-69	0+1	Turn	45	46	.341	.341	.001-.003	.002-.004	.335	171@1.33	60@1.66	2.03
235	1961-62	.006	.018	[1]	[2]	.341	.341	.001-.003	.001-.003	[3]	163@1.52	65@1.84	2.16

VALVE SPECIFICATIONS, continued

CU. IN. DISPLACEMENT	YEAR	LASH (HOT) INCHES INT.	EXH.	ANGLE DEGREE FACE	SEAT	STEM DIA. INCHES INT.	EXH.	STEM CLEARANCE INTAKE	EXHAUST	VALVE LIFT INCHES	VALVE SPRING LBS @ INCHES OPEN	CLOSED	FREE LENGTH INCH
250	1966-71	0+1	Turn	45	46	.341	.341	.001-.003	.002-.004	.390	186@1.27	60@1.66	2.08
261	1961-62	.006	.020	[1]	[2]	.341	.341	.001-.003	.001-.003	[4]	192@1.46	78@1.84	2.25
292	1963-71	0+1	Turn	[5]	46	.341	.341	.001-.003	.001-.003	.400	179@1.30	89@1.69	1.90
401 (V-6)	1966-69	.012H	.018H	[2]	[2]	.373	.434	.001-.003	.002-.004	.442	204@1.49	80@1.92	2.27
478 (V-6)	1966-69	.012H	.018H	[2]	[2]	.373	.434	.001-.003	.002-.004	.442	204@1.49	80@1.92	2.27
EIGHT CYLINDER													
283	1961-62	0+¾	Turn	45	46	.341	.341	.001-.003	.001-.003	.333	168@1.33	71@1.70	2.03
	1963-67	0+1	Turn	45	46	.341	.341	.001-.003	.001-.003	.398	175@1.26	82@1.66	2.08
307	1968-69	0+1	Turn	45	46	.341	.341	.001-.003	.001-.003	[6]	174@1.26	82@1.66	2.08
	1970-71	0+1	Turn	45	46	.341	.341	.001-.003	.001-.003	[6]	200@1.25	80@1.70	2.03
327	1962-68	0+1	Turn	[5]	46	.341	.341	.001-.003	.001-.003	.398	175@1.26	82@1.66	2.08
348	1961-65	0+1	Turn	45	46	.341	.341	.001-.003	.002-.004	[4]	190@1.23	82@1.63	2.00
350	1969	0+1	Turn	[5]	46	.341	.341	.001-.003	.001-.003	[6]	174@1.26	92@1.66	2.08
	1970-71	0+1	Turn	45	46	.341	.341	.001-.003	.001-.003	[6]	200@1.25	80@1.70	2.03
366	1966-69	0+1	Turn	[5]	46	.371	.371	.001-.003	.002-.004	.400	220@1.40	90@1.80	2.05
	1970-71	0+1	Turn	45	46	.371	.371	.001-.003	.002-.004	.400	220@1.40	90@1.80	2.05
396	1968-69	0+1	Turn	[5]	46	.341	.371	.001-.003	.001-.003	.398	315@1.38	100@1.88	2.09
	1970-71	0+1	Turn	45	46	.371	.371	.001-.002	.001-.002	.398	315@1.38	100@1.89	2.09
409	1962-65	0+1	Turn	[5]	46	.372	.371	.001-.003	.002-.004	[8]	190@1.23	82@1.63	2.00
427	1968-69	0+1	Turn	[5]	46	.371	.371	.001-.003	.001-.003	[7]	220@1.40	90@1.80	2.05
	1970-71	0+1	Turn	45	46	.371	.371	.001-.003	.001-.003	[7]	220@1.40	90@1.80	2.05

1—Intake 31, Exhaust 46.
2—Intake 31, Exhaust 45.
3—Intake .310, Exhaust .332.
4—Intake 405, Exhaust 414.
5—Intake 45, Exhaust 46.
6—Intake 390, Exhaust 410.
7—Intake 398, Exhaust 430.
8—Intake 400, Exhaust 411.

TORQUE SPECIFICATIONS

CU. IN. DISPLACEMENT	YEAR	CYLINDER HEAD BOLTS FT. LBS.	ROD BEARING BOLTS FT. LBS.	MAIN BEARING BOLTS FT. LBS.	CRANKSHAFT BALANCER BOLT FT. LBS.	FLYWHEEL TO CRANKSHAFT BOLTS FT. LBS.	MANIFOLD FT. LBS. INTAKE	EXHAUST
FOUR CYLINDER								
153	1963-65	90-95	30-35	60-70	Pressed on	55-65	[1]	[1]
SIX CYLINDER								
194	1964-67	90-95	30-35	60-70	Pressed on	55-65	[1]	[1]
230	1963-69	90-95	35-45	60-70	Pressed on	55-65	[1]	[1]
235	1961-62	90-95	35-45	100-110	Pressed on	55-65	30	[1]
250	1966-71	90-95	35-45	60-70	Pressed on	60	[1]	[1]
261	1961-62	90-95	35-45	100-110	Pressed on	55-65	30	[1]
292	1963-71	90-95	30-35	60-70	Pressed on	55-65	[1]	[1]
401 (V6)	1966-68	65-72	50-55	130-140[6]	200-210	100-105	20-25	15-20
478 (V6)	1966-68	65-72	50-55	130-140[6]	200-210	100-105	20-25	15-20
EIGHT CYLINDER								
283	1961-71	60-70	30-35	60-70	Pressed on	55-65	25-35	18-22
307	1968-71	65	45	70[4]	Pressed on	60	30	20[2]
327	1962-68	60-70	30-35	80	Pressed on	60	30	20
348	1961-65	60-70	35-45	95-105	Pressed on	60	30	25[3]
350	1969-71	65	45	70[8]	Pressed on	60	30	20[2]
366	1966-71	60-70	45-55	110[5]	85	65	30	20
396	1968-71	60-70	45-55	110	85	65	30	20
409	1962-65	65	35-45	95-105	Pressed on	60	30	20[2]
427	1968-71	60-70	45-55	90-100	85	65	30	20

1—Outer 20 Ft. Lbs., Others 30 Ft. Lbs.
2—Inside Bolts 30 Ft. Lbs.
3—Center Clamp, Others 20 Ft. Lbs.
4—1968, 80 Ft. Lbs.
5—1966-67, 115 Ft. Lbs.
6—Rear 55-65 Ft. Lbs.
8—Outer Bolts On Engines With 4 Bolt Caps. 65 Ft. Lbs.

WHEEL ALIGNMENT SPECIFICATIONS

YEAR	MODEL	CASTER (Deg.)	CAMBER (Deg.)	TOE-IN (In.)	KING PIN INCLINATION (Deg.)
1963-66	C10 Series	+2½	+¼	3/16	—
1963-65	P13, C25, C36 Series	+2½	+¼	3/16	—
1963-65	CLS 50[1]	+3¾	+1½	⅛-3/16	7⅕
1963-65	CLS 50; CDLS 60[2]	+3¾	+1½	⅛-3/16	7⅕
1963-65	CDLS 60[3]	+3¾	+1½	⅛-3/16	7⅕
1963-65	S69; T60; CLMETU 80[3]	+3¾	+1½	⅛-3/16	7⅕
1963-65	CLMETU 80[4]	+3¾	+1	⅛-3/16	5
1963-65	CLMETU 80[5]	+3¾	+1	⅛-3/16	5
1963-65	P20, P30	+2	+1½	¼-5/16	7½
1964-66	Chevy Van	+3⅓	+1½	1/16-⅛	7⅙
1966	P20, P30	+2½	+1½	⅛-3/16	7⅙
1966	CPD; L-S 50[1]	+3¾	+1½	⅛-3/16	7⅙
1966	CDLN; VXY; T50; M-S-T60[2]	+3¾	+1½	⅛-3/16	7⅙
1966	CDLS; T60H; Y60; S69[3]	+3¾	+1½	⅛-3/16	7⅙
1966	CLMTU[4 5]	+3¾	+1	⅛-3/16	5
1967	CA-PA-SA-TA40	+1½	+1½	1/32-3/32	7¼
1967	MASO, SA531,TD50,TA60[3]	+1½	+1½	1/32-3/32	7¼
1967	TE-TG-TS50	+1½	+1½	1/32-3/32	7¼
1967	CA-SA50[6]	+1½	+1½	1/32-3/32	7¼
1967	CA-MA-SA60	+1½	+1½	1/32-3/32	7¼
1967	CA-MA-TA60[4]	+2¼	+1	1/32-3/32	5
1967	MA60	+2½	[9]	1/32-3/32	[8]
1967	G-K 10, 20	+3¼	+1½	1/16-⅛	7¼

YEAR	MODEL	CASTER (Deg.)	CAMBER (Deg.)	TOE-IN (In.)	KING PIN INCLINATION (Deg.)
1967	CA-PA 10	+2½	+¾	1/32-3/32	—
1967	CA 20, 30	+3¼	+1¾	1/32-3/32	—
1967	PA 20, 30	+2	+1½	1/16-3/16	7¼
1968	C-P 10	+2½	+¾	⅛-¼	—
1968	C-P 20, 30	+3¼	+1½	3/32-3/16	7¼
1968	G-K 10, 20	+3¼	+1½	3/32-3/16	7¼
1968	P-40; C-S 40, 50	+1½	+1½	3/32-3/16	7¼
1968	S531; T40; MT50	+1½	+1½	3/32-3/16	7¼
1968	C-S-M-T 60[3]	+1½	+1½	3/32-3/16	7¼
1968	C-M-T 60[4 5]	+2	+1½	3/32-3/16	5¾
1969	G-K10, 20	+3¼	+1	3/32-3/16	7¼
1970	K10, 20	+3¼	+1	3/32-3/16	8½
1969-70	C-P 10, 20, 30	0	+¼	⅛-¼	—
1969-70	C-P 60; C-S 50[2]	+2½	+1	3/32-3/16	7¼
1969-70	M50; C-S 60	+2½	+1	3/32-3/16	7¼
1969-70	S531; T50, 60[3]	+1¾	+1	3/32-3/16	7¼
1969-70	P40[1]	+1½	+1	⅛-3/16	7¼
1969-70	C-M-T 60[4 5]	+2½	[7]	⅛-7/32	[8]
1969-70	Blazer 2 WD	+3¼	+1	3/32-3/16	8½
1969-70	Blazer 4 WD	+3¼	+1½	3/32-3/16	8½
1964	El Camino	+¼ ±½	+¾ ±½	0-⅛	8¼
1965-70	El Camino	−½ ±½	+½ ±½	⅛-¼	8¼

1—4000 lbs. capacity.
2—5000 lbs. capacity.
3—7000 lbs. capacity.
4—9000 lbs. capacity.
5—11,000 lbs. capacity.
6—5000, 5500 lbs. axles.
7—Left Side +¼°, Right Side −¼°.
8—Left Side +5¾°, Right Side +6¼°.

TRUCK MODELS AND ENGINE APPLICATION

IDENTIFICATION PLATE: Located inside of drivers compartment. Engine identification and other unit data on plate designates equipment in vehicle when shipped from factory.

CONVENTIONAL GASOLINE ENGINES

STANDARD ENGINES	YEARS	MODELS	ENGINE MAKE
SIX CYLINDER			
6-194	1964-66	El Camino	Own
6-230	1961-65	C-10-20-30	Own
	1966-67	C-10-20-30	Own
	1967	El Camino	Own
	1968-69	El Camino	Own
	1963-65	C-50	Own
6-235	1961-62	El Camino	Own
	1961-63	C-50	Own
6-250	1968-70	CS-10-20-30	Own
	1967-70	CS-40	Own
	1966	C-50	Own
	1969-70	Blazer	Own
6-261	1961-62	C-60-C60H	Own
6-292	1967-70	CS-50	Own
	1963-66	C-60-C60H	Own
	1967-68	CS-60	Own
EIGHT CYLINDER			
V8-283	1961-67	El Camino	Own
	1967	C-10-20-30	Own
	1967	CE-40	Own
V8-307	1968-69	El Camino	Own
	1986-70	CE-10-20-30	Own
	1968	CE-40	Own
	1969-70	Blazer	Own
V8-327	1967-68	CE-50	Own
	1967-68	CE-60	Own
V8-348	1961-62	C-70	Own

STANDARD ENGINES	YEARS	MODELS	ENGINE MAKE
	1961-65	C-80	Own
V8-350	1969-70	CE-40	Own
	1969-70	CE-50	Own
V8-366	1969	CE-60	Own
	1966	C-80	Own
V8-396	1968	El Camino	Own
V-6 ENGINES			
V6-401	1966	HM7000	G.M.C.
	1966	HM8000	G.M.C.
	1967-68	HM70	G.M.C.
	1969-70	HM80	G.M.C.

FOUR WHEEL DRIVE

STANDARD ENGINES	YEARS	MODELS	ENGINE MAKE
SIX CYLINDER			
6-230	1964-65	K-10-20	Own
6-235	1961-63	K-10-20	Own
6-250	1966-67	K-10-20	Own
	1968-70	KS-10-20	Own
EIGHT CYLINDER			
V8-283	1967	K-10-20	Own
V8-307	1968-70	KE10-20	Own

LOW CAB FORWARD

STANDARD ENGINES	YEARS	MODELS	ENGINE MAKE
SIX CYLINDER			
6-230	1963-65	L50	Own
6-235	1961-62	L50	Own
6-261	1961-62	L60-60H	Own
6-292	1963-66	L60-60H	Own

STANDARD ENGINES	YEARS	MODELS	ENGINE MAKE
EIGHT CYLINDER			
V8-348	1961-65	L80	Own
V8-366	1966	L80-T80	Own
V-6 ENGINES			
V6-401	1966	TM70000	Own
	1966	TM80000	Own
	1966	WM80000	Own

TILT CAB SERIES

STANDARD ENGINES	YEARS	MODELS	ENGINE MAKE
SIX CYLINDER			
6-230	1965	T50	Own
6-250	1967-68	TS40	Own
	1966	T50	Own
6-261	1961-62	T60-60H	Own
6-292	1963-66	T60-60H	Own
	1967-70	TS50	Own
	1967-68	TS60	Own
EIGHT CYLINDER			
V8-307	1968	TE40	Own
V8-327	1967-68	TE50	Own
	1967-68	TE60	Own
V8-348	1961	T70	Own
	1961-65	T80	Own
V8 350	1969-70	TE50	Own
V8-366	1969-70	TE60	Own
V-6 ENGINES			
V6-401	1967-68	TM70	G.M.C.
	1967-70	TM80	G.M.C.

TRUCK MODELS AND ENGINE APPLICATION

IDENTIFICATION PLATE: Located inside of drivers compartment. Engine identification and other unit data on plate designates equipment in vehicle when shipped from factory.

STEP VAN & FORWARD CONTROL SERIES

STANDARD ENGINES	YEARS	MODELS	ENGINE MAKE
	FOUR CYLINDER		
4-153	1964-65	G1205	Own
	1963-65	P10	Own
	SIX CYLINDER		
6-194	1966	G1205	Own
	1966	P10	Own
6-230	1967	G10-20	Own
	1968-69	GS10-20	Own
	1967	P10	Own
	1968-69	PS10	Own
	1963-65	P20-30	Own
	1965	P50	Own
6-235	1962	P10	Own
	1961-62	P-20-30	Own
6-250	1970	P10	Own
	1966-67	P-20-30	Own
	1968-70	PS20-30	Own
	1967	P40	Own
	1968-70	PS40	Own
	1966	P50	Own
	EIGHT CYLINDER		
V8-283	1967	G10-20	Own
V8-307	1968-69	GE10-20	Own
	1968-70	PE20-30	Own

CONVENTIONAL DIESELS

3-53N	1965-66	D50	Detroit
	1968-70	JV70	Detroit
	1962-65	E80	Detroit
4-53N	1967-70	CD50	Detroit
	1967-68	CD60	Detroit
	1962-66	D60-60H	Detroit
	1965-66	X60	Detroit
6V-53N	1967-70	HV70	Detroit
	1962-65	E80	Detroit
	1966	HV70000	Detroit
	1966	JV70000	Detroit
6-71N	1970	H190	Detroit
	1970	J190	Detroit
	1970	M190	Detroit
8V-71N	1970	MH90	Detroit
D351	1965-66	Q50	G.M.C.
D-478	1967-70	CG50	G.M.C.
	1965-66	A60-60H	G.M.C.
	1967	CG60	G.M.C.
	1965-66	Q60-60H	G.M.C.
	1965-66	V-60	G.M.C.
DH-478	1968	HG70	G.M.C.
	1968	JG70	G.M.C.
	1965	A80	G.M.C.
	1965	N80	G.M.C.
	1965	080	G.M.C.
	1966	HG70000	G.M.C.
	1966	JG70000	G.M.C.
D-637	1967-68	HJ70	G.M.C.
	1968	JJ70	G.M.C.
	1966	HJ70000	G.M.C.
	1966	JJ70000	G.M.C.
HNC-250	1970	HN90	Cummins
	1970	JN90	Cummins

TILT CAB DIESELS

3-53N	1967	TT40	Detroit
	1967-70	TV70	Detroit
	1962-66	U80	Detroit
4-53N	1967-68	TD50	Detroit
	1967-68	TD60	Detroit
	1965-66	Y60-60H	Detroit
D-351	1965-66	N50	G.M.C.
D-478	1967-68	TG50	G.M.C.
	1965-66	N60-60H	G.M.C.
	1967-68	TG60	G.M.C.
DH-478	1968	TG70	G.M.C.
	1966	TG70000	G.M.C.
D-637	1967-68	TJ70	G.M.C.
	1966	TJ70000	G.M.C.
6-71N	1970	F190	Detroit
	1970	D190	Detroit
8V-71N	1970	FH190	Detroit
	1970	DH90	Detroit
D-637	1967-68	TJ70	G.M.C.
NHC-250	1970	FN90	Cummins
	1970	DN90	Cummins
NHCT270	1970	FC90	Cummins
	1970	DC90	Cummins

Distributor

Reference

Detailed information on distributor drive, direction of distributor rotation, cylinder numbering, firing order, point gap, cam dwell, timing mark location, spark plugs, spark advance, ignition resistor location and idle speed will be found in the Specifications tables.

A professional approach to engine diagnosis is treated in the General Repair Section.

General Information

In Line Engines

Distributor design, (except for number of cam lobes and distributor cap) is similar for the unit used on the L4 and L6 engines. Mounting is on the forward right side of the engine. Both units use centrifugal and cacuum controlled advance mechanism. Direction of rotation (as viewed from the top) is clockwise for both models. Other pertinent distributor specifications can be found in the tune-up and distributor charts.

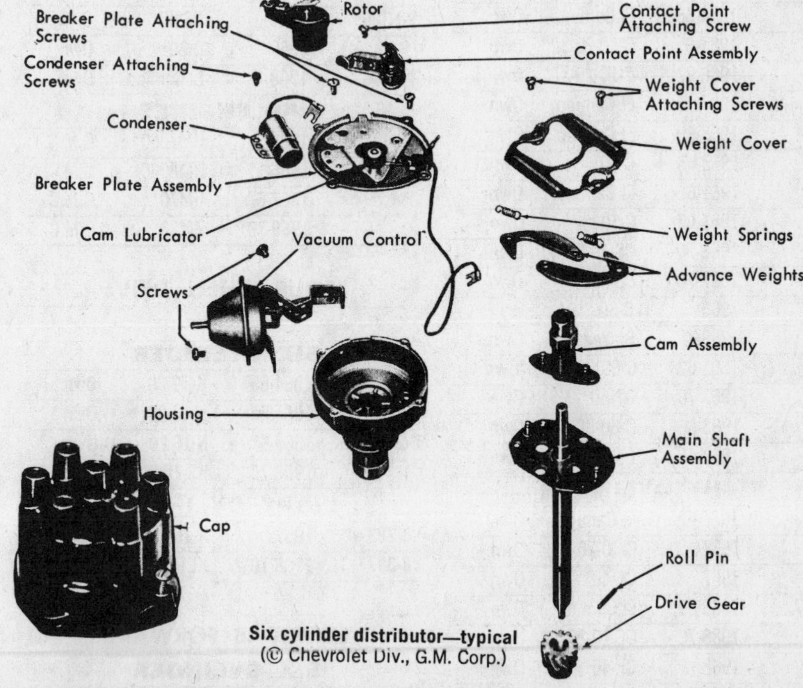

Six cylinder distributor—typical
(© Chevrolet Div., G.M. Corp.)

Distributor Removal

In Line Engines

1. Remove distributor cap, primary wire and vacuum line.
2. Scribe a mark on the distributor body, locating the position of the

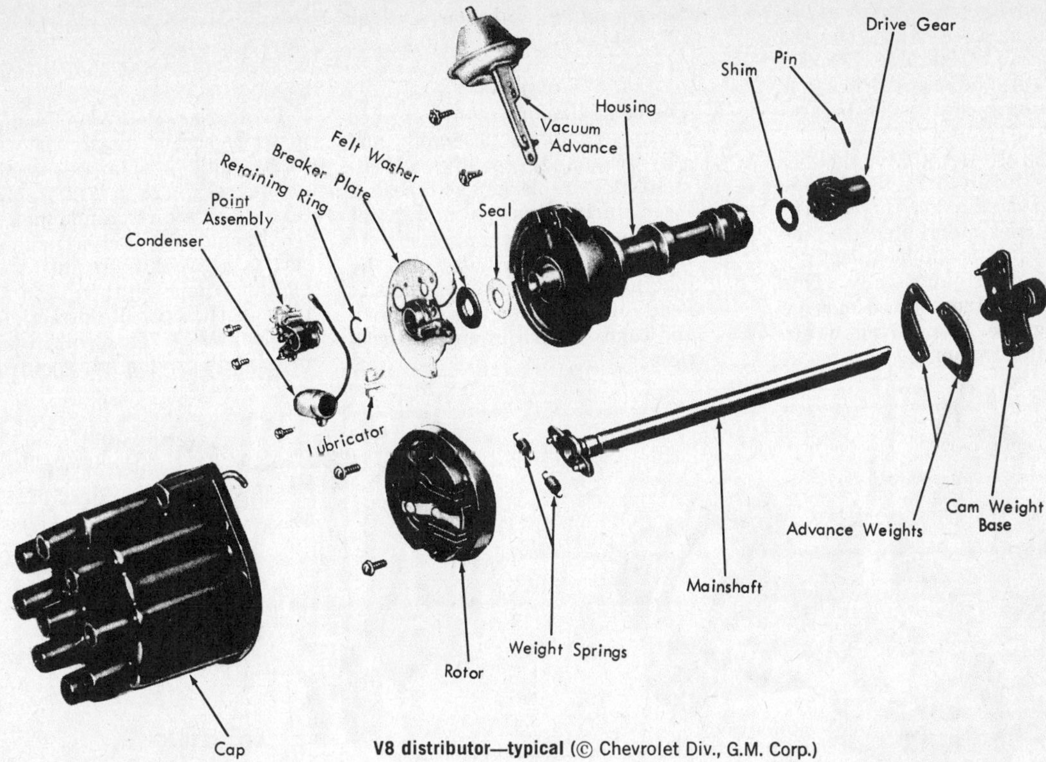

V8 distributor—typical (© Chevrolet Div., G.M. Corp.)

rotor. Scribe another mark on the distributer body and engine block, showing the position of the body in the block.

3. Remove the distributor hold-down screw and lift the distributor up and out of the engine.

NOTE—As the distributor is removed from engine, the rotor will turn counterclockwise slightly. When reinstalling be sure to allow for this.

Distributor Installation

In-line Engines

1. If the crankshaft was rotated, turn the engine until the piston of No. 1 cylinder is at the top of its compression stroke.
2. Position the distributor to the block so that the vacuum control unit is in its normal postion.
3. Position the rotor to point toward the front of the engine (with distributor held out of the block, but in installed position). Turn rotor counterblockwise about one-eighth turn and push distributor down to engage camshaft drive. It may be necessary to move the rotor one way or the other to mesh the drive and driven gears properly.
4. While holding the distributor down in place, kick the starter a few times to make sure the oil pump shaft is engaged. Install hold-down clamp and bolt and snug up the bolt.
5. Once again, rotate the crankshaft until No. 1 cylinder is on the compression stroke and the harmonic balancer mark is on 0°.
6. Turn distributor body slightly until points open. Tighten distributor clamp bolt.
7. Place distributor cap in postion and see that the rotor lines up with the terminal for the No. 1 spark plug.
8. Install cap, distributor primary wire, and double check plug wires in the cap towers.
9. Start engine and set timing according to the Tune-up chart.
10. Reconnect vacuum hose to vacuum control assembly.

CAUTION: When using an auxiliary starter switch for bumping the engine into position for timing or compression test, the primary distributor lead must be disconnected from the negative post of the ignition coil and the ignition switch must be on. Failure to do this may cause damage to the grounding circuit in the ignition switch. This will also prevent the sudden starting of engine and possible serious injury.

V8 Engines

The distributor is located between the two banks of cylinders at the back of the block.

Distributor Removal

V8 Engines

The drive gear is attached to the distributor shaft. If it becomes necessary to remove the distributor, carefully mark the position of the rotor so that, if the engine is not turned after the distributor is taken out, the rotor can be returned to the position from which it was removed without difficulty.

To remove the distributor, take off the carburetor air cleaner, disconnect the coil primary wire and the vacuum line, remove the distributor cap, take out the single hold-down bolt located under the distributor body. With a pencil, mark the position of the body relative to the block, and then work the distributor up out of the block.

NOTE: If necessary, remove secondary leads from cap after first marking cap tower for No. 1 lead.

Distributor Installation

V8 Engines

Remove No. 1 spark plug and, with finger on plug hole, crank the engine until compression is felt in No. 1 cylinder. Continue cranking until pointer lines up with the timing mark on the crankshaft pulley.

Position distributor in opening of the block in normal installed attitude; have rotor pointing to front of engine.

Turn the rotor counterclockwise about one-eighth of a turn (from straight front toward the left cylinder bank). Push the distributor down to engage the camshaft and while holding, turn the engine with the starter so that distributor shaft engages the oil pump shaft.

Return engine to compression stroke of No. 1 piston with timing mark on pulley aligned with the pointer. Adjust the distributor so that the points are opening. Install the cap being sure the rotor points to the contact for No. 1 spark plug. Connect the timing light and check that spark occurs as timing mark and pointer are aligned.

CAUTION: On the V8, the distributor body is involved in the engine lubricating system. The lubricating circuit can be interrupted to the right bank valve train by misalignment of the distributor body. This can cause serious trouble and may be hard to diagnose. See Firing Order and Timing illustrations.

12. Start engine and check dwell (31°-34°).

V8 Engines

1. The contact point set is replaced as one complete assembly and only dwell angle requires adjustment after replacement. Breaker lever spring tension and point alignment are factory set.
2. Remove the distributor cap by placing a screw driver in the slot head of the latch, press down and turn ¼ turn in either direction.

raising the window provided in the cap and inserting a "Hex" type wrench into the adjusting screw head.

Preferred Method—Turn the adjusting screw until the specified dwell angle is obtained as measured in degrees (28° to 32°, 30° preferred) by a dwell angle meter.

Alternate Method—Turn adjusting screw in (clockwise) until the engine begins to misfire, then turn screw ½ turn in the opposite direction (counterclockwise). This will give the approximate dwell angle required. (Use

Adjusting contact points
(© Chevrolet Div., G.M. Corp.)

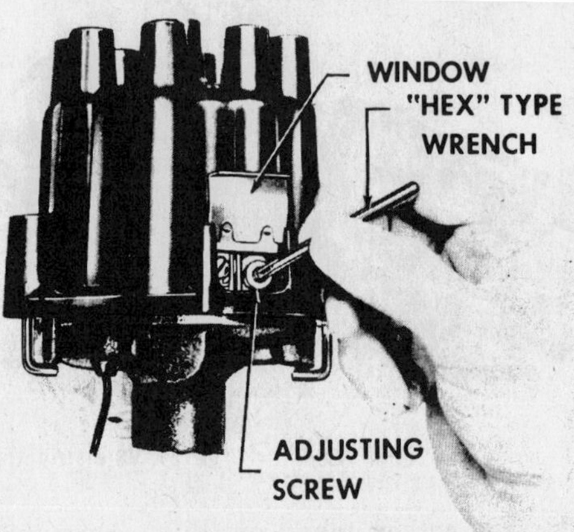

Thru cap point adjustment
(© Chevrolet Div., G.M. Corp.)

Contact Point Replacement

In Line Engines

1. Release distributor cap hold-down screws, remove cap.
2. Remove rotor.
3. Pull primary and condenser lead wires from contact point quick disconnect terminal.
4. Remove condenser hold-down screw and replace condenser.
5. Remove contact set attaching screw, lift contact point set from breaker plate.
6. Clean breaker plate of oil and dirt.
7. Place new contact point assembly in position on breaker plate, install attaching screw.

CAUTION: Carefully wipe protective film from point set prior to installation.

NOTE: Pilot on contact set must engage matching hole in breaker plate.

8. Connect primary and condenser lead wires to quick disconnect terminal on contact point set.
9. Check and adjust points for proper alignment and breaker arm spring tension. Use an aligning tool to bend *stationary contact support* if points need alignment.
10. Set point opening (.019" for new points).
11. Reinstall rotor, position and lock distributor cap to housing.

3. Remove the two attaching screws which hold the base of the contact set assembly in place.
4. Remove the primary and condenser leads from their nylon insulated connection in contact set.
5. Reverse Steps 2, 3 and 4 to install new contact set.

CAUTION: Install the primary and condenser leads as shown. Improper installation will cause lead interference between the cap, weight base and breaker advance plate.

6. Start engine and check point dwell.

With the engine running at idle and operating temperatures normalized, the dwell is adjusted by first

only when meter is not available).

AC Generator (Delcotron)

Reference

Delcotron, the AC generator by Delco-Remy is available on Chevrolet trucks. These units are furnished in two service types with companion voltage regulators. A three-unit regulator will be used with vehicles having a 42 or 52 ampere Delcotron.

Repair and test details on the Delcotron and its regulators are covered in the General Repair Section.

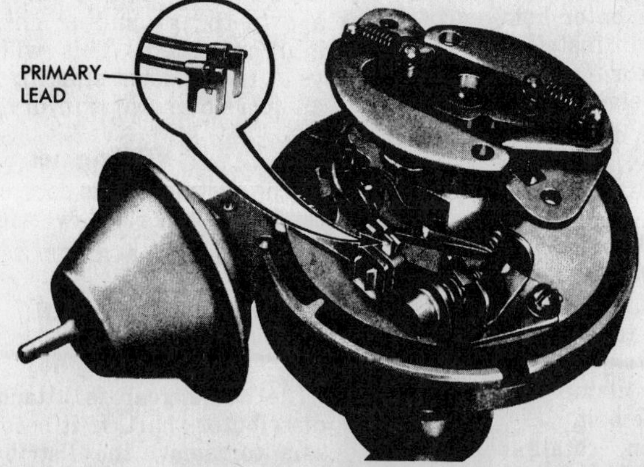

Distributor head arrangements
(© Chevrolet Div., G.M. Corp.)

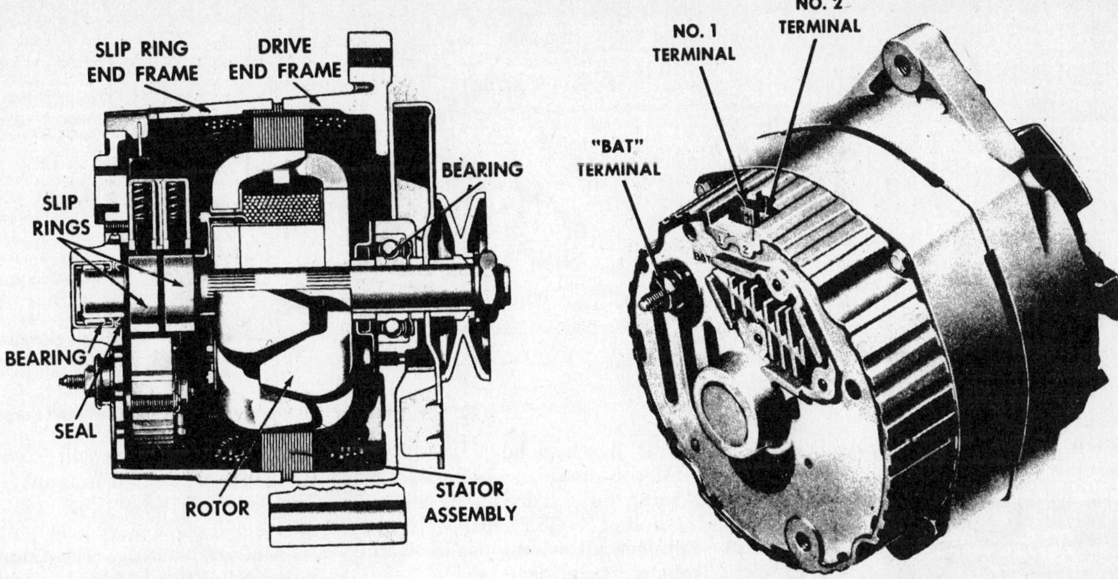

Cross section of alternator (© Chevrolet Div., G.M. Corp.)

Alternator wiring terminals (© Chevrolet Div., G.M. Corp.)

Delcotron Removal and Installation

1. Disconnect the battery ground strap at battery to prevent damaging diodes or wiring harness (also prevents accidentally reversing polarity).
2. Disconnect wiring leads at Delcotron.
3. Remove generator brace bolt, (if power steering equipped, loosen pump brace and mount nuts) then detach drive belt (belts).
4. Support the generator and remove generator mount bolt (6.2" Delcotron uses 2 mount bolts) or bolts and remove from vehicle.
5. Reverse the removal procedure to install, then adjust drive belt (belts).
6. If no belt tension tool is available, force generator away from the engine until fan belt has 5/16 in. deflection when forced downward from normal position with light pressure applied between the generator and the fan.

NOTE: If belt tension tool is used, a strand tension of 75lbs. is correct for new belts (under 1,000 mile service) and 50 lbs. for used belts.

CAUTION: Since the Delcotron and regulator are designed for use on a single polarity system, the following precautions must be observed:

1. The polarity of the battery, generator, and regulator must be matched and considered before making any electrical connections in the system.
2. When connecting a booster battery, be sure to connect the negative battery terminals with one another, and the positive battery terminals with one another.
3. When connecting a charger to the battery, connect the charger positive lead to the battery positive terminal. Connect the charger negative lead to the battry negative terminal.
4. Never operate the Delcotron on uncontrolled open circuit. Be sure that all connections in the circuit are clean and tight.
5. Do not short across or ground any of the terminals on the Delcotron regulator.
6. Do not attempt to polarize the Delcotron.
7. Do not use test lamps of more than 12 volts for checking diode continuity.
8. Avoid long soldering times when replacing diodes or transistors. Prolonged heat is damaging to these units.
9. Disconnect the battery ground terminal when servicing any AC system. This will prevent the

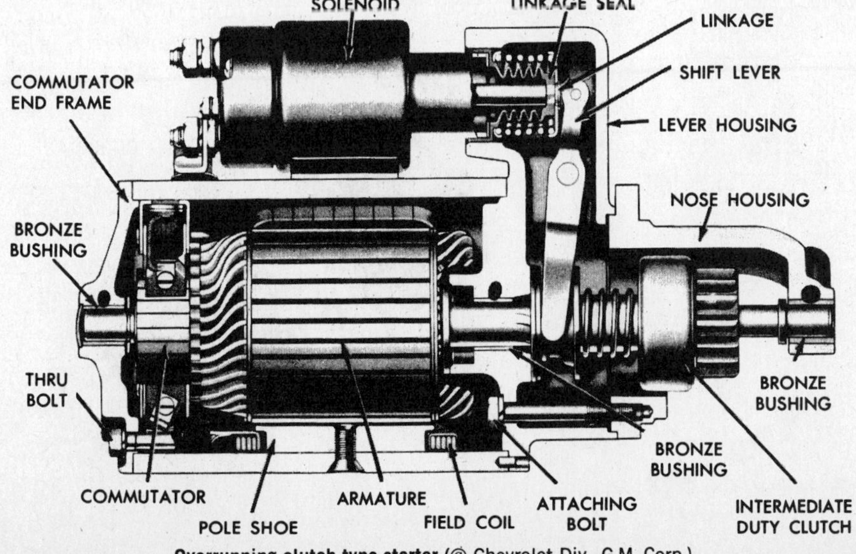

Overrunning clutch type starter (© Chevrolet Div., G.M. Corp.)

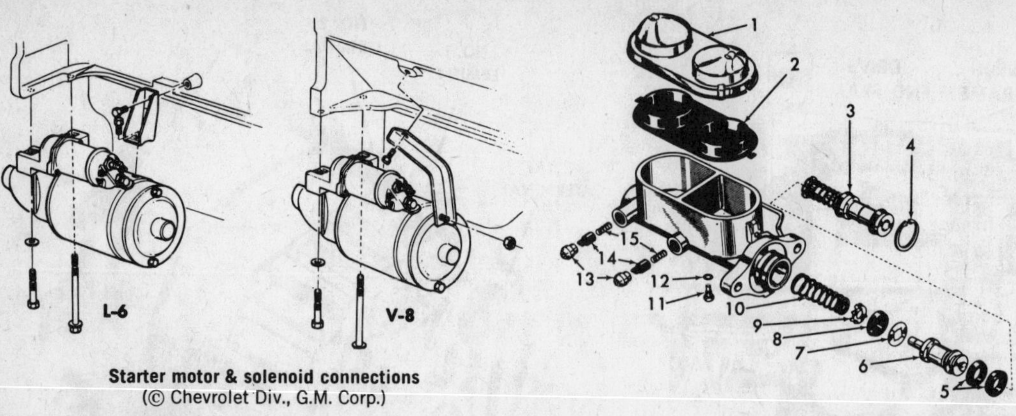

Starter motor & solenoid connections (© Chevrolet Div., G.M. Corp.)

Dual type master cylinder (© Chevrolet Div., G.M. Corp.)

possibility of accidentally reversing polarity.

Starter

Starter Motor Removal and Installation

The following procedure is a general guide for all vehicles and will vary slightly depending on the truck series and model. (On Forward Control Vans, vehicle must be raised and supported.)

1. Disconnect battery ground cable at the battery.
2. Disconnect engine wiring harness and battery leads at solenoid terminals.
3. Remove starter mounting bolts and retaining nuts and disengage starter assembly from the flywheel housing. Light duty gasoline powered engines use conventional nose housing or pad mounting. Intermediate and heavy duty use conventional flange. On these, scribe mark on flange and flywheel housing a nose housing can be mounted in several positions.
4. Position starter motor assembly to the flywheel housing and install the mounting bolts and retaining nuts. Torque the moun ing bolts 25 - 35 ft. lbs.
5. Connect all wiring leads at the solenoid terminals.
6. Connect the battery ground cable and check operation of the unit.

Brakes

Reference

Specific information will be found in General Brake Section on adjustments, bleeding, master cylinder and wheel cylinder overhaul procedures and trouble shooting.

Refer to Power Brake Section for details concerning power brakes.

Master Cylinders

Standard

A twin master cylinder, one side for brakes and the other for clutch operations, was used on some light duty trucks. Starting in 1964 a conventional single piston cylinder is used. A dual master cylinder is introduced in 1967 on small trucks. This one designed to be used with separate hydraulic systems for front and rear brakes. This new type cylinder has two separate reservoirs and outlets in a single casting. The front reservoir and outlet is for the front wheel brakes.

Twin (Brake & Clutch) Type

Master Cylinder Removal

1. Disconnect clutch and brake pedal return springs.
2. Detach push rod boots from cylinders.
3. Remove clutch and brake hydraulic lines.
4. Remove three bolts holding cylinder to dash and slide cylinder off push rod.

NOTE: Wipe hydraulic fittings clean and place dry cloth under lines to absorb any fluid spillage. Cover fittings and lines to prevent any foreign matter from entering system.

Installation

1. Place new gaskets and push rod boots over cylinder tubes.
2. Hold cylinder next to dash and insert push rods, making sure they are centered.
3. Bolt assembly loosely to dash.

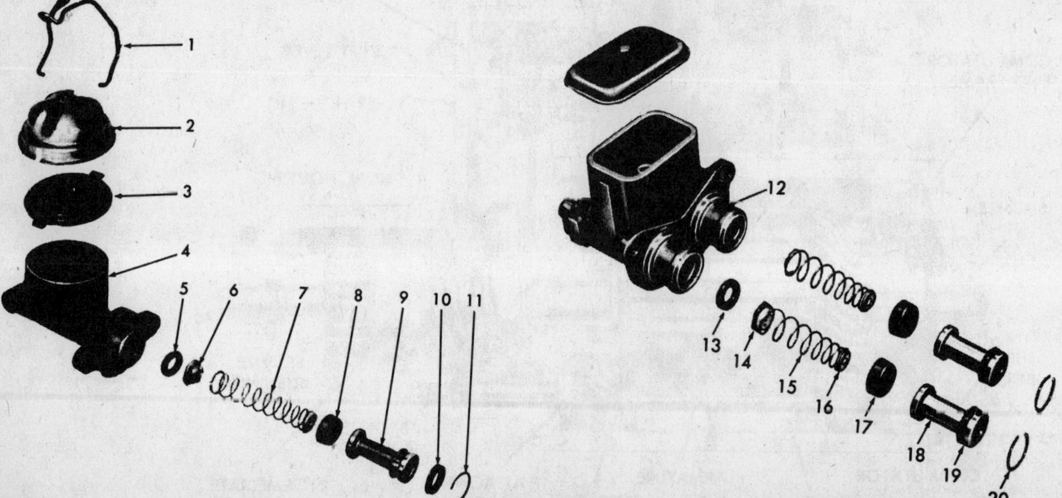

Single & clutch assist type cylinders (© Chevrolet Div., G.M. Corp.)

This freedom of assembly will allow hydraulic lines to be started in cylinder without stripping fittings.

4. Tighten assembly and hydraulic lines securely.
5. Replace pedal return springs.
6. Fill reservoir and bleed both clutch and brake cylinders.
7. Check pedal free play and opera-leakage.

Standard Conventional Single

Master Cylinder Removal

1. Clean area at fitting and place dry cloth under line to absorb leakage.
2. Disconnect hydraulic line at cylinder and cover ends with clean cloth to prevent any foreign matter from entering system.
3. Disconnect push rod from pedal.
4. Remove the two nuts and washers holding cylinder to firewall. Remove Cylinder.

Installation

1. Position cylinder at dash, align push rod through boot and secure loosely. This freedom of assembly will allow hydraulic line and push rod to be installed with minimum of effort.
2. Tighten nuts and line. Check free play.
3. Fill cylinder and bleed. Bleeding can be accomplished by slowly pressing down on brake pedal and at same time tightening the hydraulic line fitting. Any air still trapped in line at fitting can be expelled by pressing hard on brake pedal to a point of just below free. play. By having a slight pressure on pedal, the piston is held forward enough to clear ports in reservoir and check valve is held off its seat, so air can be released.
4. Final check of fluid and brake operation.

Standard Dual

Master Cylinder Removal

1. Clean area at fittings and place dry cloth under lines to absorb leakage.
2. Disconnect both lines at cylinder and cover to prevent foreign matter from entering system.
3. Disconnect any stop light or brake warning light wires.
4. Unbolt cylinder and remove, allowing push rod to fall loose.

Installation

1. Install new boot on push rod.
2. Position cylinder making certain push rod and boot are in proper position and fasten loosely to firewall. This freedom of assembly will allow both hydraulic lines to be started easily.
3. Tighten mounting nuts and lines. Check free play.
4. Connect any stop light or brake warning light wires.
5. Fill reservoir and bleed. Test brakes before moving truck.

NOTE: Front reservoir and outlet is connected to front wheel brakes.

Wheel Cylinders

Four types of cylinders are used, identified by type of brake system used.

Duo servo—One double-end cylinder mounted at toe ends of shoes.

Twinplex—Two double-end cylinders mounted between shoes at toe and heel.

Wagner F (FA)—Two single end cylinders (single piston, single direction) mounted so as to be an anchor for one and powering other.

Wagner FR3 (FR3A)—Two double-end cylinders mounted between shoes.

Wheel Cylinder Removal

1. Jack up axle and support. Remove wheel and drum.

NOTE: To remove drum it may be necessary to back off brake adjustment, also if rear drum, release hand brake cable if so equipped.

CAUTION: Starting in 1964 to gain access to adjusting starwheel, a knockout lanced area is located in web of drum. After knocking out metal be sure to clean all metal particles from brake compartment. A new

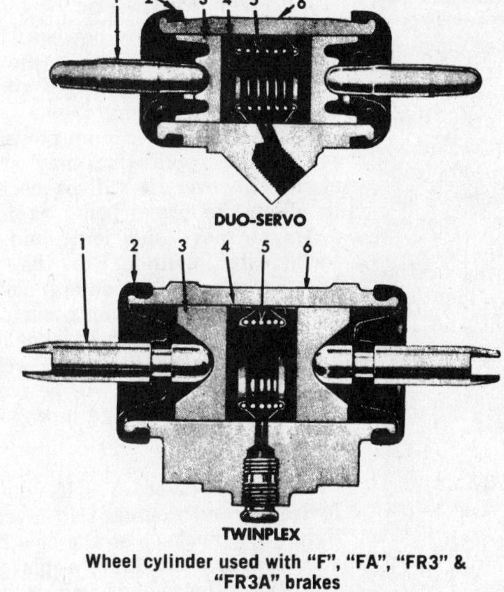

1 Push rod
2 Boot
3 Piston
4 Piston cup
5 Spring
6 Housing

Wheel cylinder used with "F", "FA", "FR3" & "FR3A" brakes
(© Chevrolet Div., G.M. Corp.)

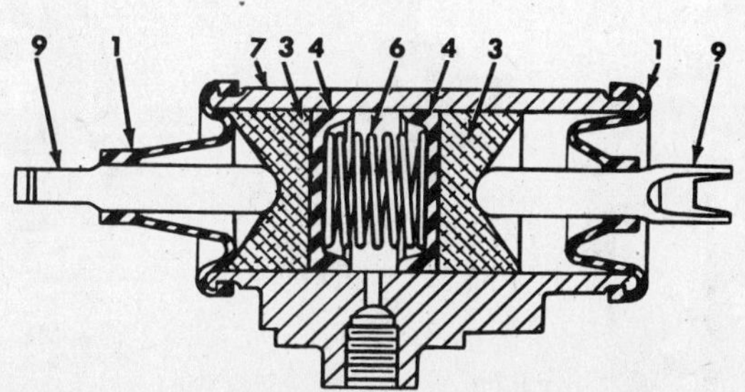

1 Boot
2 Brake shoe guide
3 Piston
4 Piston cup
5 Cup filler
6 Piston spring
7 Cylinder
8 Brake shoe anchor slot
9 Push rod

Duo servo and Twin Plex cylinders
(© Chevrolet Div., G.M. Corp.)

cover plug must be installed.

2. Release shoe return springs and spread shoes to clear wheel cylinder links. Make sure any lubricant or brake fluid does not get on facings by covering same.
3. At front—Disconnect metal line from flexible hose and remove hose if accessible or remove hose later after cylinder is removed. At rear—Disconnect metal line from cylinder.
4. Remove shield over cylinder and connecting line between cylinders, if so equipped.
5. Remove cap screws and washers holding cylinder to backing plate. Remove cylinder being careful of any fluid spillage.

Installation

1. Clean mounting surface and reverse above procedures.
2. Bleed and readjust brakes. Check pedal before moving vehicle.

NOTE: *Twinplex*—Upper and lower cylinders are not interchangeable due to position of connector tube openings. Upper cylinder has threaded bleeder valve opening drilled at outer edge of bore.

Wagner F & FA—Two wheel cylinders (upper and lower) are identical, however cylinders on right and left brakes have opposite castings.

Wagner FR3 & FR3A—Upper and lower cylinders on both right and left brakes are interchangeable.

Power Brakes

(Power -Hydraulic)

Reference

Specific information will be found in Power Brake Section on adjustments, bleeding, overhaul and trouble shooting.

General Description

Various vacuum-hydraulic or air-hydraulic brake systems are used, although sizes and shapes differ the basic function is the same.

Hydrovac (Early-piston Type)

When driver presses the brake pedal, brake fluid is compressed in master cylinder and acts to open a valve which allows a power source (air or vacuum) to exert a greater pressure in a second cylinder.

In event of loss of power (reservoir tank empty), the foundation brakes will stop the vehicle but with greater driver pedal effort.

Master-Vac Moraine

Starting in 1963 the master-vac is used. It is a single unit, containing both hydraulic and vacuum systems, using manifold vacuum and atmospheric pressure. It is usually mounted on engine side of firewall. This is also true of the moraine.

Hy-Power Multi-Vac

Bigger and more powerful units such as these are frame mounted. Some are single diaphragm and others double diaphragm.

In the event of vacuum power failure, brake application may still be made. However, it will be necessary to pump the brake pedal rapidly in order to move sufficient fluid from the master cylinder to the wheel brake system for the emergency stop. The amount of pumping required will depend upon the brake shoe clearances. If brakes are kept well adjusted, less pumping will be required in the event of power failure.

Master-Vac

The master-vac, a self contained hydraulic and vacuum unit is used on light duty trucks, also the new hydrovac, starting in 1966, replaces the multi-vac. This hydrovac is of the diaphragm type. The multi-vac unit was designed for use with the low input-high output system, while the newer hydrovac is used in equal displacement system. In equal displacement hydraulic system the fluid displaced by the master cylinder is equal to the fluid displaced by the power cylinder. Vacuum powered cylinders on 40-50-60 series, with hydraulic brakes, are either single or tamden diaphragms. The tamden diaphragm unit is used with single master cylinder. Single diaphragm units, two used, are on dual cylinder units. One for each system.

Air-Pak

Air-pak is a self contained hydraulic-air pressure power unit for use on trucks with an air compressor, reservoir, regulator and check valve. It consists of three elements.

1. An air cylinder, consisting of a cylinder, a piston and a push rod that connects power piston to hydraulic piston.
2. A hydraulic cylinder, consists of a hydraulic piston with built in check valve, a residual check valve and a compensating check valve.
3. An air pressure control valve, which controls the power output of the air pressure cylinder in relation to the hydraulic pressure in the master cylinder.

The operation of the air-pak is similar to the multi-pak unit. The difference between units is that the air-pak is designed to operate in equal displacement hydraulic systems. The multi-pak is made to work in the low-input, high-output systems. In the equal displacement system, the fluid output of the master cylinder is equal to the fluid output of the power cylinder.

NOTE: The correct master cylinder MUST be used with the proper power unit. Air-pak and multi-pak units ar NOT interchangeable.

Power Brakes

(Power-Vacuum)

Unit Removal

NOTE: Wipe hydraulic fittings clean, place dry cloth under lines to absorb any fluid leakage, cover lines to keep system clean.

1. Disconnect push rod clevis at pedal, if clearance hole in dash is not large enough, remove clevis. (mark position)
2. Remove vacuum hose from unit. (check valve)

Piston type hydro vac unit
(© Chevrolet Div., G.M. Corp.)

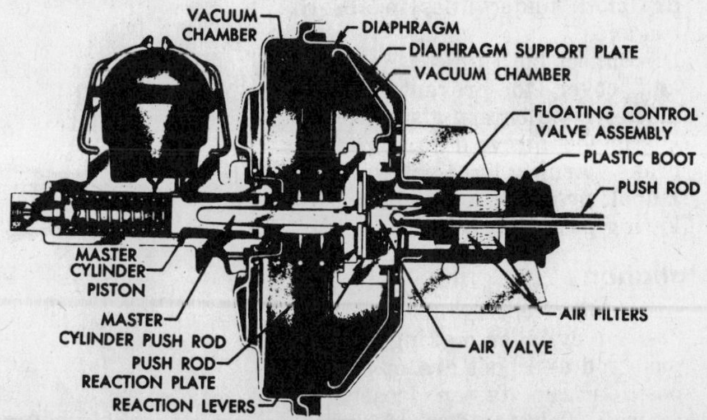

Moraine unit (© Chevrolet Div., G.M. Corp.)

Bendix master vac unit
(© Chevrolet Div., G.M. Corp.)

Hy-Power vacuum booster unit
(© Chevrolet Div., G.M. Corp.)

3. Disconnect hydraulic lines.
4. Remove any stop light wires.
5. Remove 4 nuts and washers holding unit to firewall, remove unit (and bracket)

Unit Installation

1. Mount unit in place and install loosely (freedom of assembly will allow easy starting of fittings), secure push rod to pedal and check free-play.
2. Tighten mounting nuts and hydraulic lines.
3. Install vacuum line.
4. Connect any stop light wire.
5. Bleed brakes, (bench-bleed unit before installing, units with 2 bleeder valves bleed valve nearest to shell first).

CAUTION: Pressure bleeding must be done with engine off (no vacuum). Manual bleeding use engine (start engine, allow vacuum to build up).

6. Check brakes and stoplight before moving vehicle.
7. Units requiring lubrication, remove 1/8 inch pipe plug in front end of shell (engine off). Fill with vacuum cylinder oil until oil runs out filler hole.

Air Brakes

Reference

Specific information will be found in Power Brake Section on adjustments, overhauling and troubleshooting.

General Description

Full air brakes completely replace ALL hydraulic parts with more durable components, capable of producing and using greater braking energy.

Brakes are applied by pushing on the pedal, which controls the application valve. Varying amounts of pressurized air will fill the brake chambers depending on brake pedal travel. Cam type shoe actuators (wedge type on stopmaster) are connected to push rods attached to diaphragms in the brake chamber. When air pressure is passed to brake chambers, the diaphragm then converts air pressure energy to mechanical force, the pressured diaphragms move the cam type actuators (wedge type on stopmaster) spreading the brake shoes and thereby applying brakes.

When the brake pedal (application valve) is released, a rapid discharge of air pressure from brake chambers is necessary to speed brake shoe release. A front and rear quick release valve aids in this function.

Many safety devices are used. A low air pressure warning buzzer sounds when pressure falls below a safe level. An air pressure gauge on dash shows the air pressure in system. Normal air pressure, for brake application, is at least 70 lbs. "Wet" and "dry" reserve tanks (also called primary and secondary) serve to remove moisture from air and also to provide a reserve of braking power. Drain cocks in tanks are provided to drain condensation. A pressure relief valve on the "wet" tank will release pressures over 150 lbs. A check valve located ahead of "wet" tank will retain air pressure in event of compressor failure or leaks.

Components

Compressor

Belt driven on gas engines and usually gear driven on diesel.

The air compressor serves only to supply and maintain sufficient pressure for brakes and air operated accessories. When pressure in system reaches top of normal range, an unloading valve opens and nullifies compressor action.

The average compressor is a single stage reciprocating piston type, usually one cylinder. Larger units are two cylinders. Compressors are lubricated by the engine system.

NOTE: Water cooled compressors, in event of freezing weather, must be drained as well as engine block.

Governor

Controls load and unload mechanism to automatically maintain maxi-

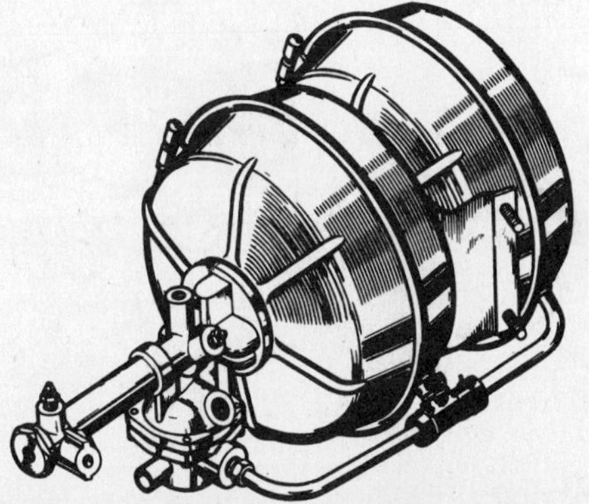
Dual vacuum rooster unit
(© Chevrolet Div., G.M. Corp.)

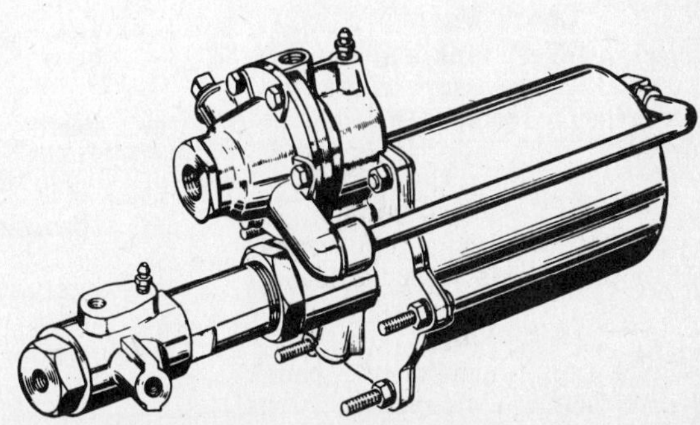
Air-Pak unit (© Chevrolet Div., G.M. Corp.)

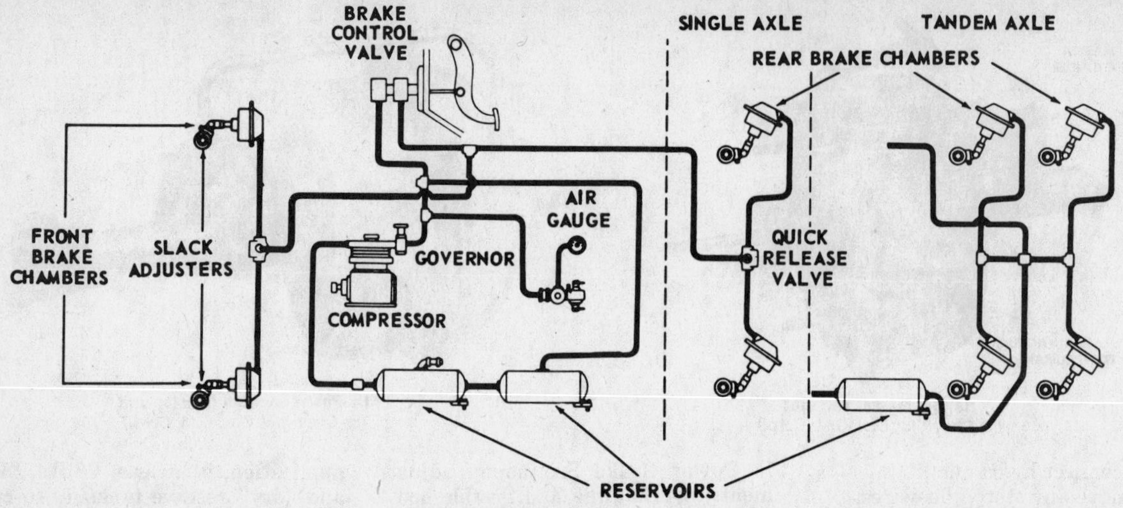

FULL-AIR BRAKE SYSTEM

Full air brake system (© Chevrolet Div., G.M. Corp.)

mum and minimum air pressures in reservoirs. Pressure ranges or settings are adjustable. The governor, by regulating the load and unloading mechanism, establishes an intermittent compressor pumping cycle.

Brake Control (Application) Valve (Foot Operated)

Provides quick and sensitive control of air pressure (FORCE) from reservoir to brake chambers. The amount of force applied to brakes is proportional to the amount of pedal depression.

Reservoir(s)

"Wet and Dry" tanks serve to remove moisture and provide a sufficient reserve of air under pressure for several brake applications (safety factor). Drain cocks are provided to drain condensed moisture. A dash mounted gauge will show amount of reservoir pressure.

Safety Valve

Usually mounted on reservoir, allows air to escape when air pressure exceeds a predetermined setting (adjustable).

Check Valve

Between "Wet" tank and compressor to retain air pressure in the event of compression (compressor or lines) failure.

Low Pressure Signal

A safety device (buzzer) sounds when air pressure is absent or low.

Air Guage

Located on instrument panel, shows air pressure in system, works in conjunction with low pressure switch to warn of low pressure.

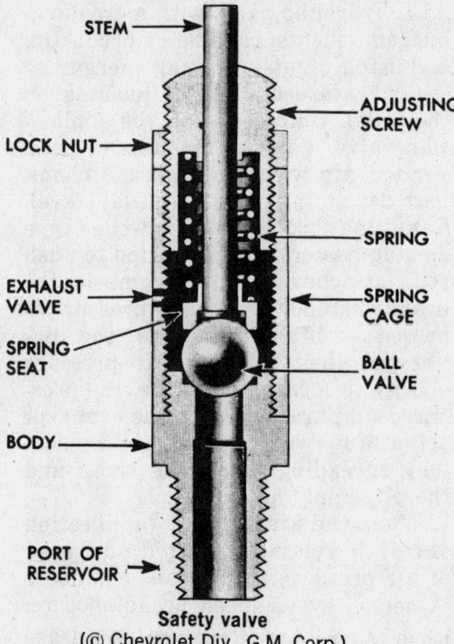

Safety valve
(© Chevrolet Div., G.M. Corp.)

Pressure Protection Valve

Usually at junction of main (brake) and auxiliary systems. Its function is to close auxiliary system in event of loss of air pressure.

Relay Valve

A relay station to speed the application and release of brakes because of long air lines and volume of air necessary. A relay valve is usually at rear wheels. It is connected to application valve and meters air directly to rear brake chambers from an auxiliary reservoir.

Quick Release Valve

When brake pedal is released, a rapid discharge of air is necessary to speed the return of brake shoes. Two valves are used, one with front brake chambers and one with rear chambers.

Brake Chambers

Converts energy of compressed air into mechanical force required for

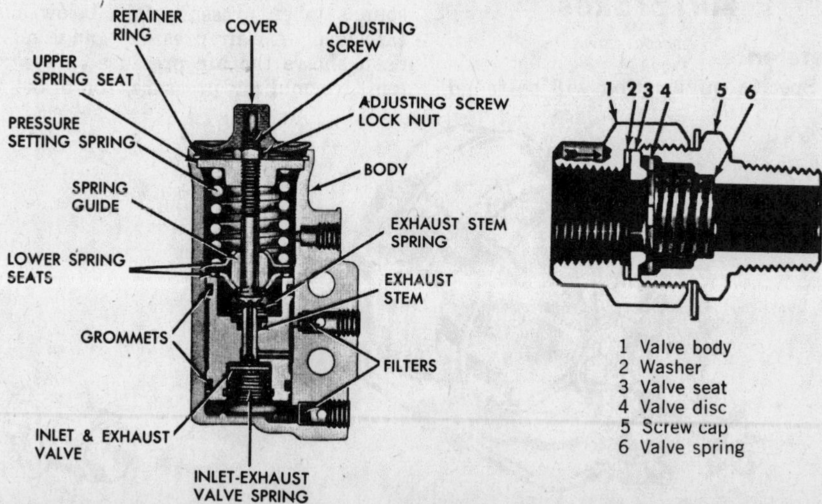

Governor assembly (© Chevrolet Div., G.M. Corp.)

Air tank check valve
(© Chevrolet Div., G.M. Corp.)

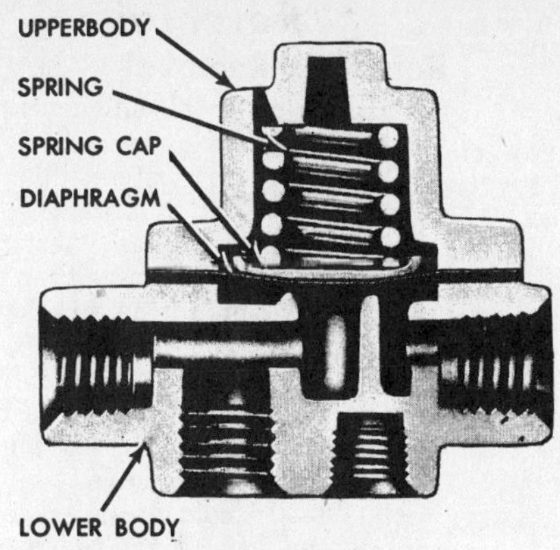

Pressure protection valve
(© Chevrolet Div., G.M. Corp.)

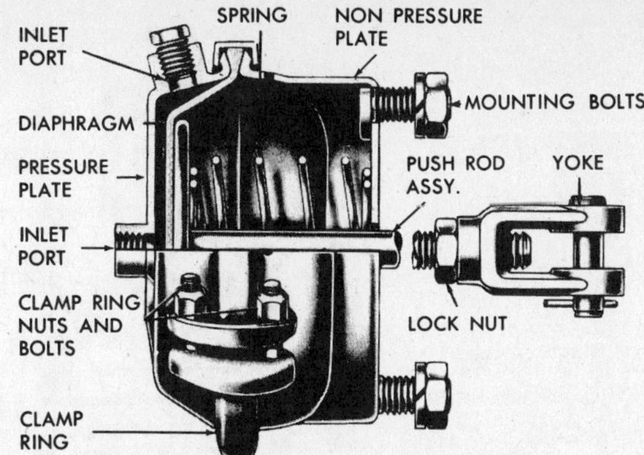

Air brake chamber (© Chevrolet Div., G.M. Corp.)

brake application.

Cam Type

Air, admitted by control valve, enters brake chamber and pressurizes diaphragm with attached push rod. Push rod rotates lever arm of slack adjuster exerting a turning force on camshaft with an "S" design on end. This "S" cam operates between rollers on free ends of brake shoes and serves to expand shoes. Adjustment is manual at slack adjusters.

Wedge Type

Features two brake chambers per wheel. Wedge type actuators, operating between roller assemblies, forces *each* shoe evenly against drum. Stopmaster brakes have automatic adjusters and do not need slack adjusters. *Fail-Safe* and *Super Fail-Safe* can be operated by either air or spring pressure, with additional features such as spring applied parking brake and is a safety factor in event of air brake failure.

NOTE: These units have a manual release bolt, in center of chamber cap, to permit safe handling for service. See note and caution under R&R.

Slack Adjusters

Used with cam type brakes to provide convenient means of adjustment for brake lining wear. With brakes APPLIED the angle formed by slack adjuster lever and brake chamber push rod should be approximately 90 degrees, and all adjusters to be about the same angle. Excessive travel of push rod shortens the life of chamber diaphragms and also results in slow braking response. Some slack adjusters have a locking sleeve, which engages head of worm shaft adjusting bolt, that must be pushed in to clear bolt head in order to make brake adjustments. Re-engage sleeve when finished.

Compressor (Belt Driven)

Compressor Removal

1. Block or hold vehicle by means other than air brakes.
2. Drain air from system, usually at reservoirs.
3. If water cooled, drain cooling system.
4. Disconnect ALL lines. (air, water and oil).
5. Loosen belt adjusting stud and remove drive belt.
6. Remove mounting bolts, remove compressor.

Compressor Installation

1. Run engine briefly to clear and check oil supply lines. Clean oil return lines and passages. Check coolant supply and lines (if used).
2. Clean mounting surface and replace gasket, be sure oil holes in gasket are aligned.
3. Install compressor with mounting cap screws loose, compressor will be moveable to allow fittings on lines to be started.
4. Make sure air cleaner is cleaned and properly installed.
5. Align compressor, check drive belt.
6. Tighten mounting bolts and adjust belt tension.
7. Tighten all lines, fill cooling system if drained.
8. Run engine and check compressor for noises, leaks and output. Soapy water will help pin-point any air leaks. Check build-up

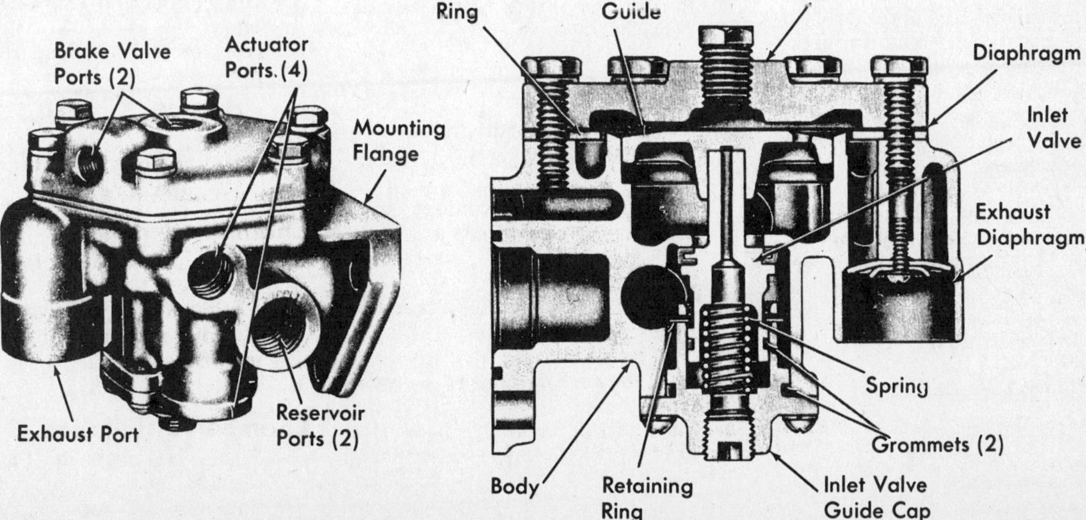

Relay valve compone s (© Chevrolet Div., G.M. Corp.)

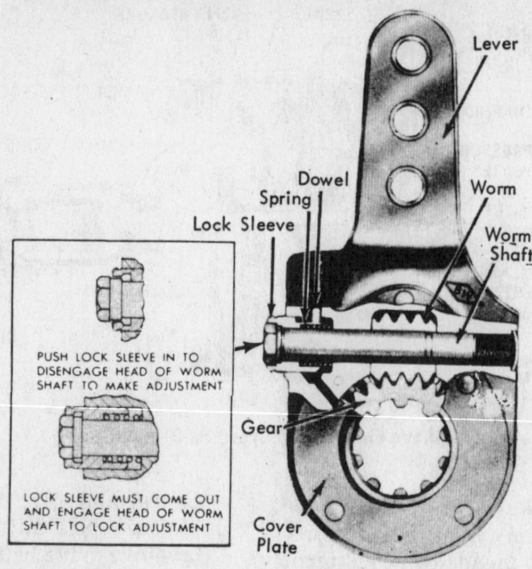

Slack adjusters (© Chevrolet Div., G.M. Corp.)

time and governor.

Compressor (Gear Driven)

Compressor Removal

1. Block or hold vehicle by means other than air brakes.
2. Drain air from system.
3. Drain engine block.
4. Disconnect ALL lines (air, water, oil).
5. Remove four nuts and washers from mounting studs, pull compressor back off studs and remove.

Compressor Installation

1. Run engine briefly to clear and check oil supply lines. Check oil return lines and passages. Check coolant supply and lines. Inspect drive gears and coupling.
2. Clean mating surfaces of compressor and housing are clean. Place new gasket on studs.
3. Install drive coupling on hub and position compressor on mounting studs. Guide compressor into mesh with driven disc, making sure coupling teeth engage disc. Install nuts and washers and torque to 65 foot pounds.
4. Connect water, air and oil lines securely, fill cooling system.
5. Run engine and check compressor for noise, leaks and output. Check build-up time and governor action.

Governor

Governor Removal

1. Block or hold vehicle by means other than air brakes.
2. Drain air system.
3. Remove dirt and grease from air line fittings, disconnect air lines.
4. Remove mounting bolts, remove governor.

Governor Installation

1. Make sure both air lines, to governor, are clean and open.
2. Place governor in position with exhaust port towards ground, tighten bolts finger-tight allowing unit to move. Start fittings.
3. After fittings are started, tighten governor mounting bolts then securely tighten fittings.
4. Test governor and check for leaks.

Brake Control (Application) Valve

Control Valve Removal

1. Block or hold vehicle by means other than air brakes.
2. Exhaust air system.
3. Remove all lines and wires.
4. Remove pedal clevis pin and pedal.
5. Remove mounting bolts, remove valve.

Control Valve Installation

1. Mount valve in position, fasten loosely.
2. Start all fittings, connect stop lite wires. NOTE. Keep any sealant compound off first two threads of fittings.
3. Tighten mounting bolts, then securely tighten all lines.
4. Replace pedal.
5. Run engine and charge air system.
6. Check all fittings with pedal depressed with soapy water solution.
7. Check (and adjust) pedal free play.
8. Check valve action.

Reservoirs

Reservoir Removal

1. Block or hold vehicle by means other than air brakes.
2. Exhaust air system, open drain cocks.
3. Disconnect all air lines, remove drain cock and valves.
4. Remove mounting bracket bolts and nuts, remove tank.

CAUTION: Where inside of reservoir is sludged and steam is used to clean, do not plug up reservoir or use excessive steam pressure.

NOTE—In cold weather, more attention should be given to draining of moisture.

Reservoir Installation

1. Install reservoir in place loosely.
2. Start all fittings, valves and drain cock.
3. Tighten all mounting bolts and nuts to make sure reservoir does not vibrate in service. (Vibration causes premature line failures).
4. Securely tighten all lines, drain cock and valves.
5. Run engine, charge air system.
6. Check for leaks.

Valves, Signals and Gauges

Removal

1. Block or hold vehicle by means other than air brakes.
2. Exhaust air system, make certain ignition is off.
3. Clean work area, remove any wires, air lines and brackets. Remove unit.

Installation

1. Position replacement unit in system, making certain of any markings showing air flow direction, and secure.
2. Connect any wires and air lines.
3. Run engine and charge air system.
4. Test for leaks and operation of unit.

Brake Chamber

Cam type (uses slack adjusters one per wheel.)

Chamber Removal

1. Disconnect air hose from chamber.
2. Remove clevis pin from yoke.
3. Remove nuts and washers from mounting studs.
4. Remove chamber.

Chamber Installation

1. Place chamber on mounting bracket and secure with stud nuts and lock washers.
2. Connect air hose.
3. Install slack adjuster yoke clevis

pin, after adjusting for minimum travel. (Angle made by push rod and slack adjuster lever should *not* be less than 90°, brakes applied). Lock yoke with locking nut. Push rod travel should be as short as possible without brakes dragging.

4. Check for leaks, and possible brake shoe adjustment.

Wedge Type (two per wheel) see note and caution below

Chamber Removal

1. Block or hold vehicle by means other than air brakes.
2. Disconnect air hose from chamber.
3. Remove lock washer tangs from notches in spanner nut and spider housing.
4. Loosen spanner nut and unscrew air chamber from housing.

Chamber Installation

1. Screw air chamber in spider housing until it "bottoms", then back off (no more than one turn) until chamber air port aligns with air hose. The plastic guide will assure proper position of wedge. Lock brake chamber in position with spanner nut and lock washer.
2. Start engine, charge air system check for leaks. Pump brake pedal to allow automatic adjusters to adjust brakes.

NOTE: When brakes are equipped with "fail-safe" brake chambers, cage power spring before starting any disassembly or removal of wheels or drums to avoid possible injury. When a vehicle is disabled, due to low or lost air pressure, cage power spring before attempting to move the vehicle. Cage the power spring by rotating the release bolt approximately 18 to 21 turns clockwise. Caging and uncaging can be made easier by applying air pressure, 65 lbs needed (if possible). This takes spring load off release bolt.

CAUTION: Before removing or caging brake chamber, block wheels since parking brake will not be applied.

Slack Adjusters

Adjuster Removal

1. Remove clevis pin at lever.
2. Remove lock ring and washer on splined camshaft (some front slack adjusters are held on by a retaining screw).
3. Slide adjuster off splined shaft.

Adjuster Installation

1. Make sure spacer washers are in place (if used).
2. Slide slack adjuster on splined camshaft, lock in place with snap ring and washer. If held on by retaining screw, allow .010" end play. Stake edge of screw to lock.
3. Connect yoke clevis pin. Angle made by push rod and slack adjuster lever should NOT be less than 90° brakes applied. Push rod travel should be as short as possible without brakes dragging.
4. Lubricate adjuster.

Parking Brakes

NOTE: Except in case of an emergency, set parking brake only after vehicle is brought to a complete stop. Parking brakes are not designed to take the place of service brakes.

Propeller Shaft—Band type.

This type, using external band and drum mounted on rear of transmission, provides a hand controlled brake independent of service brakes. Band, with lining, is centered on transmission bracket (anchor) and both sides are arranged to contract equally. Brake is actuated by lever and rod, or cable, to a cam and "J" bolt.

Adjustment

1. Block wheels and release hand brake.
2. Remove locking wire from anchor bolt and adjust to obtain .010" clearance between lining and drum—rewire anchor.
3. Loosen lock nut on locating bolt and tighten adjusting nut until there is a clearance of .020" between lining and drum. Measure

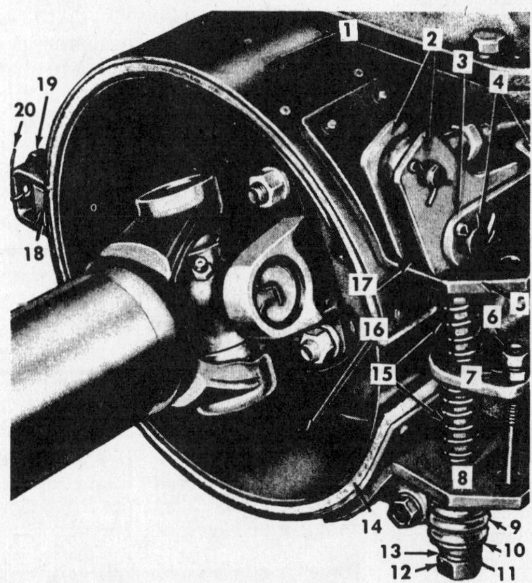

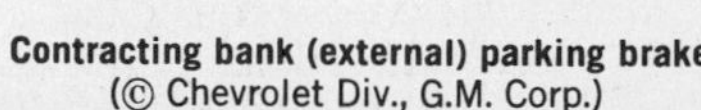

1 Brake band
2 Cams
3 Links
4 Clevis pins
5 Cam shoe
6 Lock nut
7 Adjusting nut
8 Locating bolt
9 Tension spring
10 Washer
11 Adjusting nut
12 Lock nut
13 Lock washer
14 Brake lining
15 Release spring
16 Brake drum
17 Adjusting bolt
18 Anchor bar
19 Anchor screw
20 Lock wire

Contracting bank (external) parking brake
(© Chevrolet Div., G.M. Corp.)

1 Brake cable
2 Adjustable clevis
3 Connecting lever
4 Return spring
5 Link
6 Lock nut
7 Operating lever
8 Inner shoe
9 Outer shoe
10 Brake drum
11 Adjusting nut
12 Lock nut
13 Adjusting bolt
14 return spring
15 Adjuster bracket

Two shoe (Duo Grip) parking brake
(© Chevrolet Div., G.M. Corp.)

Internal expanding type adjustment
(© Chevrolet Div., G.M. Corp.)

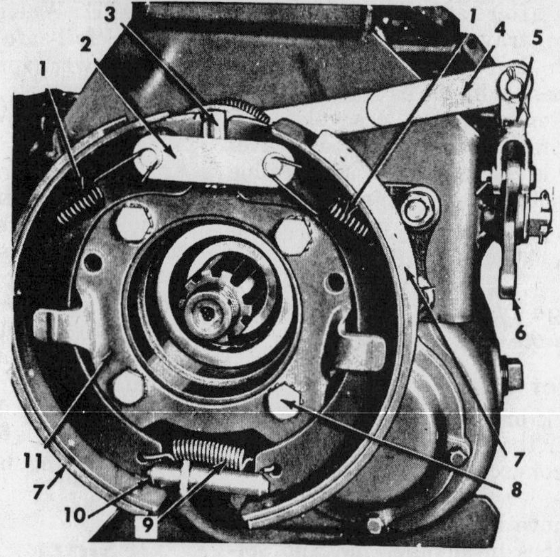

1 Return springs
2 Anchor pin link
3 Camshaft
4 Control lever
5 Link
6 Relay lever
7 Brake shoe
8 Plate bolt
9 Adjusting screw spring
10 Adjusting screw
11 Support plate

Internal expanding type brake—installed
(© Chevrolet Div., G.M. Corp.)

clearance about 1 inch from end of lining. Tighten lock nut.

4. Loosen lock nut on adjusting "J" bolt and tighten adjusting nut to obtain a clearance of .020" approximately 1 inch from end of lining. Tighten lock nut.
5. Check hand brake operation by applying lever. If more than ½ the number of notches on sector are needed to lock the propeller shaft, make final adjustment on lever rod, at clevis end. Remove blocks.

Propeller Shaft—Shoe Type

Hand brake drum is mounted on rear of transmission with internal and external shoes (duo-grip) or with two internal expanding shoes. Shoes are forced against drum by lever and cam actuated by cable. Propeller shaft brakes lock the driveline for parking.

Adjustment—Duo-Grip

1. Block wheels and release hand brake.
2. Loosen lock nut and tighten adjusting bolt to obtain .010" clearance between outer shoe lining and drum at this point. Hold bolt and lock nut securely.
3. Loosen lock nut and tighten adjusting nut to obtain .010" between inner shoe lining and drum, at center of shoe. Hold nut and tighten nut.

NOTE: Some vehicles, such as tilt cab, use a compound hand brake lever with flexible cable that features a cable adjustment. This allows the operator to adjust the "over-center" position of lever required to lock parking brake.

Adjustment—Two Shoe Internal Expanding

1. Block wheels and release hand brake, it may be necessary to remove clevis pin to assure full release of shoes.
2. Align slot in drum with star wheel adjuster. Knock out lanced area in drum, if necessary to gain access to star wheel. Be sure to remove all metal from brake compartment.
3. Engage star wheel with brake spoon and rotate star wheel to obtain a .010" clearance between lining and drum. Moving handle end of spoon down expands shoes. Check with .010" feeler gauge rotating drum. Shoes can be expanded so as to lock drum then backed off 10 notches similar to a wheel adjustment. Check drum, jack up one rear wheel, for free rotation.
4. Replace clevis, install drum hole cover, remove jack and blocks.

Rear Wheel—Cable Type

Hand lever or foot pedal operated, cable actuated, rear wheel service brakes are used for parking brakes.

Adjustment

1. Block front wheels and apply hand brake two notches from released position.
2. Jack up both rear wheels.
3. All cables and linkage connected, pull back spring in place, loosen cable adjusting lock nut and tighten adjusting nut until a drag is felt when rotating rear wheels. Tighten lock nut.
4. Fully release parking brake and check both rear wheels. No drag should be present.
5. Remove jack and blocks.

NOTE: Adjustment of cable should only be made when service brakes are in full adjustment. Cable should be lubricated when rear drums are off.

Rear Wheel—Air Brake

NOTE: For stopmaster fail-safe and super fail-safe information see brake chamber section. (automatic adjusters)

Anchorlok

Anchorlok chamber is mounted "piggy back" on service chamber. It contains a diaphragm under air pressure (60 pounds or more) to contain a powerful spring in compression in normal opration. When air pressure drops below 60 pounds, the coiled spring starts to move out. If air pressure continues to drop, the spring will keep expanding to apply brakes until at approximately 30 pounds the spring will have applied the brakes sufficiently to bring the vehicle to a safe, even stop.

To permit moving vehicle, when air pressure is not available to compress spring, a caging tool consisting of a stud and nut will be found stored on service chamber housing. Remove rubber plug in center of anchorlok and insert stud ¼ turn. Turning nut on stud will cage spring.

CAUTION: Cage spring before removing or servicing anchorlok.

Fuel System

Reference

This section contains brief information on removal, installation and minor external adjustments. For more detailed information and major service operations see carburetor general section.

Data on capacity of the gas tank

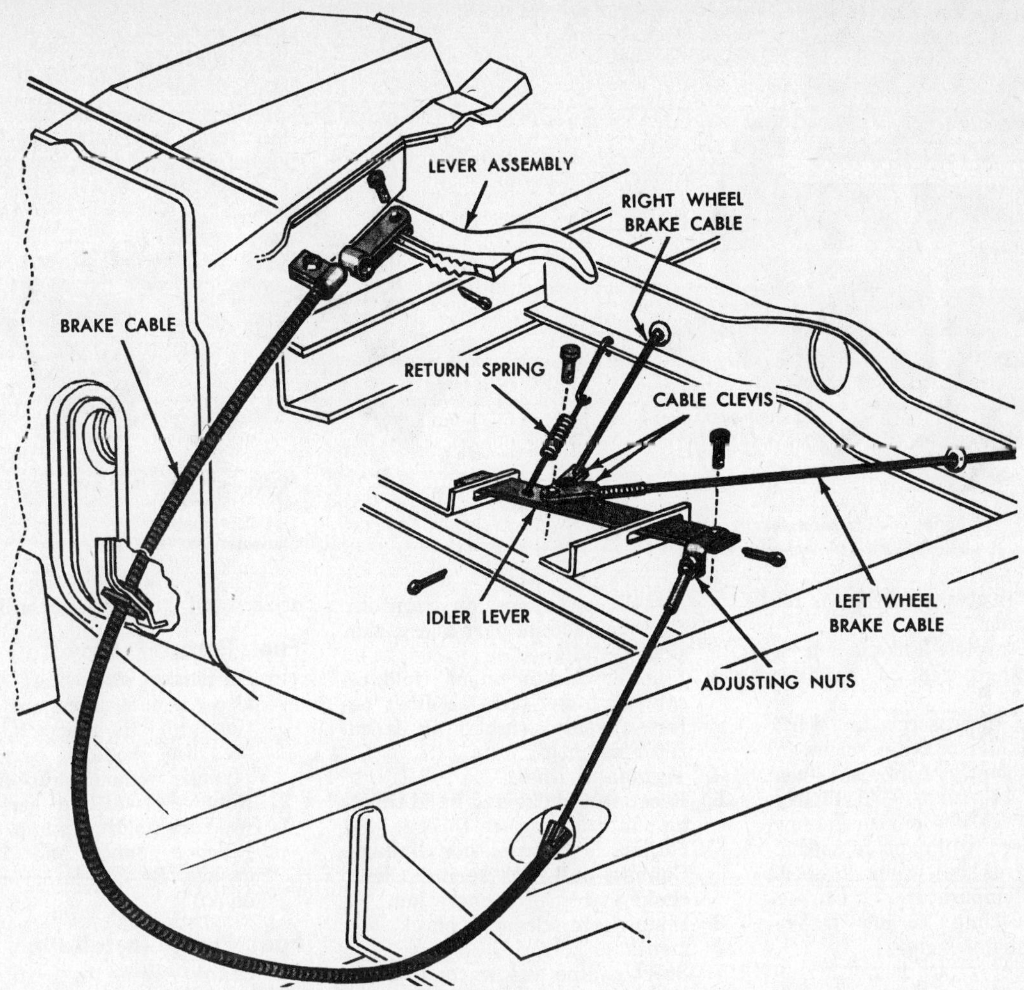

Parking brake (cable type) linkage (© Chevrolet Div., G.M. Corp.)

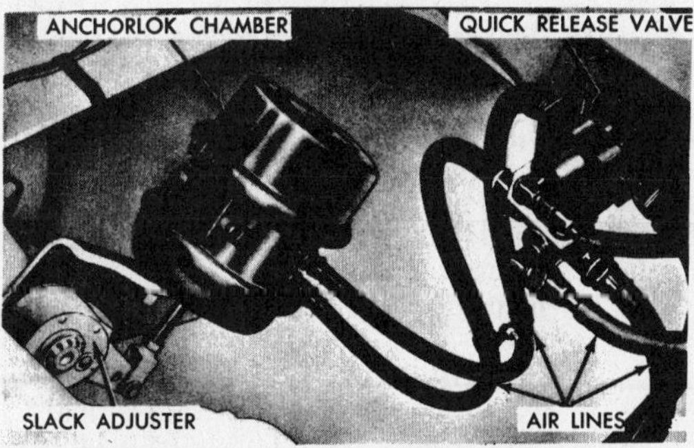

"Anchor Lock" brake chamber—installed
(© Chevrolet Div., G.M. Corp.)

will be found in the Capacities table. Data on correct engine idle speed and fuel pump pressure will be found in the Tune-up Specifications table. Both can be found at the start of this section.

Carburetors

Two basically different types of carburetors are used, downdraft and carburetor used is updraft, all others updraft. Due to construction of forward control trucks (C.O.E.) the are downdraft. All carburetors have conventional float, idle, low speed, power or high speed and accelerating circuits with either manual or automatic chokes and are designed to meet particular requirements of engines, transmissions and vehicle type.

NOTE: Some symptoms indicate carburetor trouble but in reality are ignition. Before any extensive repairs on carburetor, check first—heat riser, intake manifold and ignition.

Updraft Carburetor

Removal

1. Disconnect pedal linkage and stop lite wires.
2. Remove toe pan.
3. Remove air cleaner.
4. Disconnect choke cable (and throttle cable if used).
5. Remove fuel line and cap.
6. Remove vacuum line.
7. Disconnect throttle linkage at carburetor lever, remove pullback spring.
8. Remove two stud nuts and washers. Remove carburetor and drain. Discard gasket.

Installation

1. Install new flange gasket on carburetor making sure vacuum port is clear and manifold flange is clean. (No gasket sealant).
2. Install carburetor on manifold finger tight.
3. Connect fuel line using flexibility of carburetor to insure against crossing fitting threads
4. Connect vacuum line, check first for restrictions.
5. Tighten carburetor flange nuts, then fuel and vacuum lines.
6. Connect choke cable (and throttle), make sure control knobs are flush with instrument panel. Check operation of choke.

Spring compressor assembly
(© Chevrolet Div., G.M. Corp.)

7. Replace air cleaner. Clean or replace element.
8. Connect throttle linkage, check for binding. Replace pullback spring.
9. Turn idle speed screw in 1 turn and turn idle mixture screw in until it gently bottoms. Then back out 1½ turns. CAUTION: Do not force idle mixture screw against seat, will damage needle.
10. Start engine and warm to operating temperature. During warm-up time, torque intake manifold bolts or nuts.
11. Turn idle mixture screw in slowly until motor starts to idle roughly, then turn out slowly until motor runs smooth. Back off idle speed screw until desired curb idle is obtained. (Be sure choke is fully open.)
12. Replace toe pan, connect accelerator pedal and stop lite wires.

NOTE: If possible (safely), fill carburetor bowl before installing, will save time and battery drain. Also reduce possible backfiring. Dirt is greatest troublemaker for carburetors, check filters.

Downdraft Carburetor

Removal

1. Remove air cleaner.
2. Disconnect fuel, vacuum, spark control and governor lines.
3. Disconnect choke and hand throttle controls.
4. Disconnect throttle and automatic transmission linkage at carburetor. Remove pull back spring.
5. Remove mounting nuts and washers.
6. Lift carburetor off manifold and drain. Discard gasket.

Installation

1. Clean carburetor mounting surface.
2. Install new gasket on manifold. Be sure vacuum port and gasket slots are aligned.
3. Place carburetor on manifold, reconnect finger-tight all lines before (evenly) tightening carburetor mounting nuts.
4. Tighten all lines.
5. Reconnect choke and hand throttle controls, replace throttle and automatic transmission linkage. Connect pull back spring. Check choke and throttle operation.
6. Install air cleaner, check element.
7. Start engine and warm to operating temperature. During warm-up time, torque intake manifold.
8. Adjust idle mixture and idle speed screws, be sure choke is fully open.

CAUTION: Do not force idle mixture screw against seat, will damage needle. On transmission controlled spark engines (TSC), fast idle adjustment must be set with electrical leads disconnected at solenoid and transmission in neutral.

NOTE: If possible (safely), fill carburetor bowl before installing, will save time and battery drain as well as reducing possible backfiring. Dirt is greatest troublemaker for carburetors, check all filters. Use starter briefly to clear fuel lines (before reconnecting) or any metal flakes that are always present when fuel lines (metal) are disturbed.

Fuel Pumps

Description

Two types of pumps are used, mechanical and electric. Mechanical pump is diaphragm type, consisting of a single fuel chamber or a combination fuel and vacuum chambers. In-line engines the pump is actuated by an eccentric lobe on camshaft, V6 eccentric is attached to front of camshaft, V8 engines use a push rod between eccentric lobe on camshaft and pump rocker arm. The single pump is non-serviceable while the combination pump is rebuildable. Electrical pumps are used with step fuel tanks

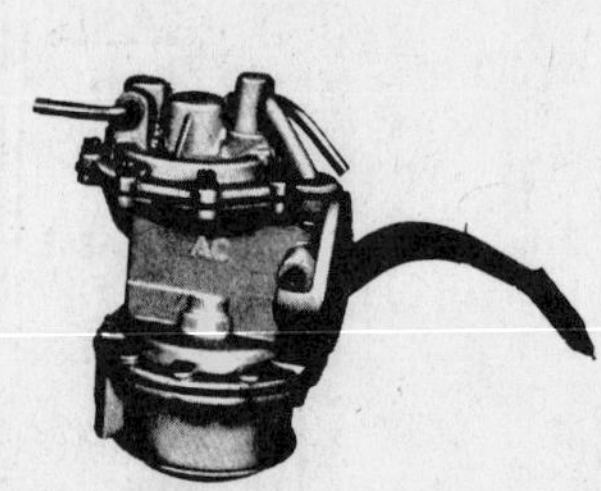

Mechanical fuel pump
Single
Combination
(© Chevrolet Div., G.M. Corp.)

or as stand-by emergency units.

Fuel Pump Removal

1. Disconnect fuel lines at pump, also vacuum lines on combination unit. Be ready to cap gas feed line should it be necessary (trucks without shut-off valve).
2. Remove two cap screws and washers holding pump to block. Remove pump and mounting gasket. Be careful of push rod on V8's.

Fuel Pump Installation

1. Crank engine to position camshaft lobe on lowest point.
2. Check feed line for restrictions.
3. On V8s—place heavy grease on one end of push rod and slide into position.
4. Hold fuel pump, with new gasket, in position and start two cap screws finger tight. CAUTION: Be sure rocker arm contacts eccentric in correct position.
5. Start fuel line fittings, using flexibility of pump to insure against crossing threads, also start vacuum lines if dual pump.
6. Tighten mounting bolts and lines. Start engine and check for leaks. (open shut-off valve if closed)

CAUTION: When engine is cranked at starter with jumper cable, remove distributor lead from negative post on coil and ignition switch

Electric fuel pump
(© Chevrolet Div., G.M. Corp.)

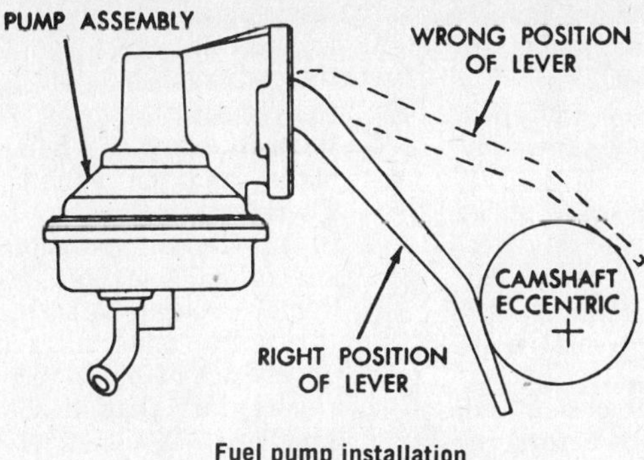

Fuel pump installation
(© Chevrolet Div., G.M. Corp.)

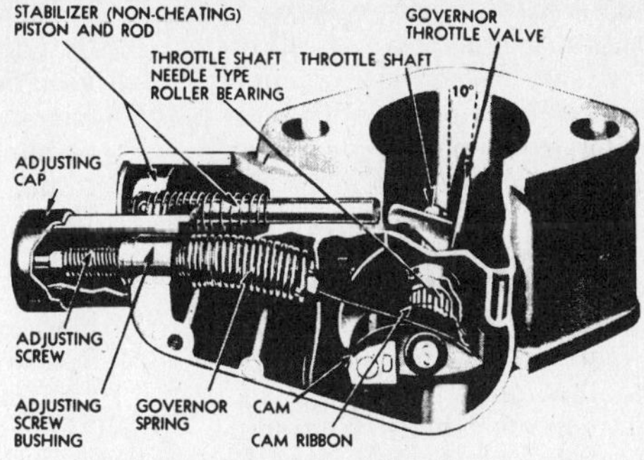

Diagrammatic view of governor
(© Chevrolet Div., G.M. Corp.)

must be on. Failure to do this can result in damage to the ground circuit of ignition switch.

Fuel Tank

Description

Various types and designs of gas tanks are used due to complexity of engine body and chassis combinations. On ½ ton and ¾ ton the tank is located in rear behind drive axle. Larger vehicles use frame mounted tanks on right side, frame side rail. Cab models, except tilt cab, tank is behind seat in cab. Increased fuel capacity is available by using optional tanks. Tanks may be cylindrical, step, saddle or round. All tanks are equipped with a vented filler neck cap. A large fine-mesh, self cleaning screen is used on bottom of fuel pickup pipe.

Following procedure is intended only as a guide. It will vary according to truck model and tank type.

Fuel Tank Removal and Installation

1. On trucks with dual tanks check shut-off valve position.
2. Be sure ignition switch is off or battery ground is disconnected.
3. Remove seat back rest if cab mounted.
4. Drain tank. If tank does not have a drain plug, disconnect gas line and use opening to drain tank. If not accessible, siphon fuel. Do not siphon by mouth, use equipment for that purpose or make a siphon hose as shown below and use air pressure if available.
5. Remove filler neck, cap and vent hose.
6. Disconnect tank gage wire and any ground lead.
7. Remove tank support straps or mounting bolts. Remove tank.
8. Clean all lines, check filters. (Blow clean only after disconnecting other end of line).
9. To install, reverse removal procedures.

CAUTION: Do not use drop cord in area. A bulb breakage could have disastrous effects. Use only safety cans for fuel storage. Do not overtighten lines, could distort or twist and lead to leaks.

Governors

Velocity Type

Governor is mounted between carburetor and intake manifold and automatically governs the maximum speed of engine which in turn limits maximum speed of vehicle.

Operation

Governor is operated by vacuum intake manifold opposing a calibrated (adjusting) spring, which in turn is connected to a throttle shaft and valve. Velocity of gas mixture from carburetor tends to close valve but this action is opposed by governor spring tension. The calibration of velocity versus spring tension is very sensitive.

Adjustment

Adjustment of spring pull is accomplished by number of spring coils operating (active). Turn adjusting cap counter-clockwise for higher speeds. If too sensitive use special hollow wrench to turn adjusting screw nut. Caps are usually wire locked and sealed.

Vacuum Spinner Type

Governor consists of two components connected by tubing. One is in distributor housing and other on carburetor throttle body. This type permits full horsepower usage without excessive engine speeds. An overspeed warning device is usually incorporated in system. A system of calibration of vacuum versus spring tension.

Operation

To limit engine speed while permitting greater throttle openings when additional power is required.

Vacuum is applied to diaphragm in carburetor chamber on throttle housing by internal passages. This vacuum is controlled by distributor air valve thru inter-connecting tube. Distributor centrifugal air valve, by spring pressure, remains open until desired governor speed is reached. Then adjustable centrifugal weight will close air valve in opposition to spring, thereby allowing vacuum to be applied to diaphragm which in turn acts to close throttle valve in opposition to carburetor governor tension.

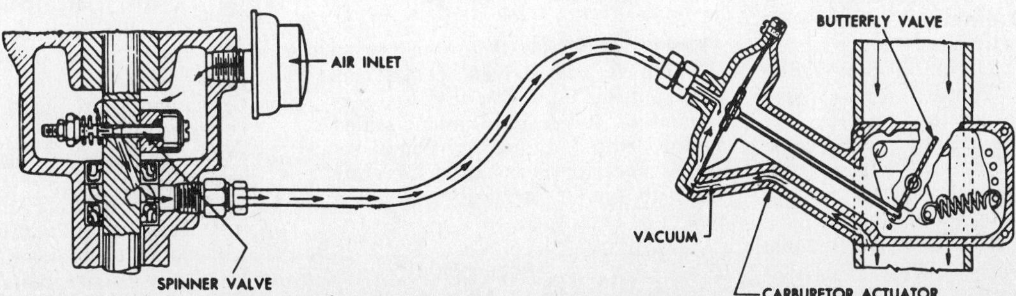

Spinner type governor installation (© Chevrolet Div., G.M. Corp.)

Increased engine load results in lower distributor speed which allows air valve to open, permitting vacuum to drop, which will in turn allow governor spring to open throttle wider, increasing engine power to meet load increase.

Adjustment

Since governor speed is a function of both distributor and carburetor the best method of setting speed is to adjust spinner on vehicle. The spinner mechanism can be adjusted by holding slotted end of ballast weight with screw driver and turning adjusting nut on other end.

Increase speed by turning nut clockwise, decrease — counter-clockwise.

NOTE: Efficiency of governor depends on keeping all passageways clean and tight, also distributor air filter clean.

Cooling System

Reference

Detailed information on cooling system capacity can be found in the Capacities table.

Type—Description

All models have pressurized cooling system, thermostatically controlled bypass, sealed by radiator cap. System is designed to operate with coolant's boiling point raised which increases efficiency of radiator. Pressure cap contains both pressure and vacuum relief valves, spring loaded. Pressure valve allows excess pressure out overflow and vacuum valve relieves when system cools off. Thermostat is pellet or poppet construction designed to open and close at predetermined temperatures, and incorporates a by-pass Two types of cores are used, down-flow and cross-flow, according to vehicle needs and design.

NOTE: Due to various body and chassis designs the following procedures are typical.

Radiator Removal

1. Drain radiator. NOTE: When draining, use short piece of ⅜ hose over draincock to save coolant or anti-freeze.
2. Remove radiator, heater, radiator filler and overflow hoses, also oil cooler lines (and plug).
3. Disconnect battery ground cable at battery. Remove wiring from front-end sheet metal, remove hood on cab-over-engines.
4. Remove grille, lower panel, baffle plates and air duct hoses on step-vans.
5. Remove heater from firewall and raise out of way, remove inspection plate on firewall above engine box on step-vans.
6. Remove shroud, if so equipped, or hang over fan blades for additional clearance.
7. Remove finger guard and surge tank, if so equipped.
8. Loosen fan belt and remove fan blades if necessary.
9. Remove radiator (support) bolts and any braces.

NOTE: On larger vehicles attach hoist to support assembly before removing bolts as support assembly of core, grille, shroud, surge tank and air cleaner ducts will be removed as a unit.

10. Conventional vehicles—Lift up core to remove, on step-vans and forward control units it may be necessary to raise vehicle and remove from below.

Radiator Installation

Install in reverse order of removal —fill system and check for leaks, adjust fan belt if necessary.

Tests

Test radiator by warming engine to operating temperature, then turning off and feeling core. Radiator should be hot at top and warm at bottom, an even temperature drop from top to bottom. A cool spot indicates stoppage. All radiator fins should be straight and free of bugs and any dirt that might restrict air flow.

CAUTION: Radiator coolant level should be checked when engine is cool otherwise, unless precautions are taken, serious personal injury may result. The radiator cap removal, when system is at operating temperature, will cause the pressure in system to drop to atmospheric pressure. Since operating temperatures are as high as 247°F., steam pockets will form in system and blow coolant out of radiator. It is important that coolant level be maintained either 1″ below filler neck or at level indicated on radiator.

CAUTION: Do not pour cold water in radiator while engine is hot. Wait until boiling ceases, start engine and while engine is idling then add water slowly.

Water Pump

Types—Description

Pump is belt driven, centrifugal vane impeller type. Bearings are permanently lubricated and sealed against water and dirt. Pump requires no care other than keeping air vent, on top of housing, and drain hole in bottom, open.

Water Pump Removal

1. Drain system.
2. Remove lower radiator and heater hoses.
3. Loosen alternator and remove fan belt (and idler belt if so equipped).
4. Remove fan blade bolts, remove blades and pulley. CAUTION—Thermostatic fans are to be kept in "on the car" position to avoid loss of silicone fluid.
5. Remove pump attaching bolts (or nuts) and pull pump cautiously out of block recess, avoid any contact that might damage impeller.

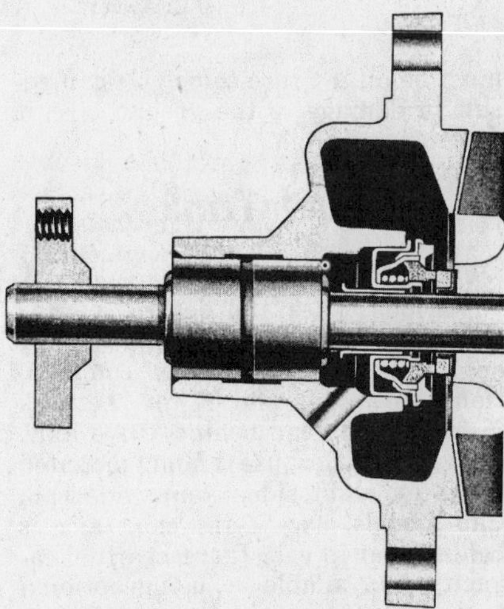

Water pump—typical inline engines
(© Chevrolet Div., G.M. Corp.)

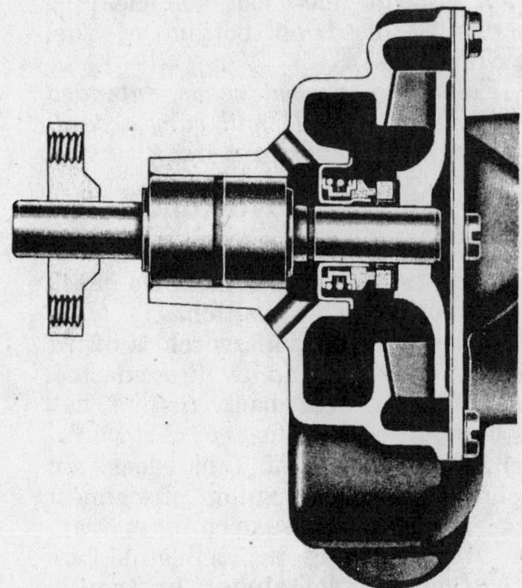

Water pump—typical V8 engines
(© Chevrolet Div., G.M. Corp.)

Water Pump Installation

1. Clean gasket surface on block and install new pump-to-block gasket, sealed on *both* sides.
2. Guide pump into position and secure evenly.
3. Connect all hoses, use a good sealer.
4. Replace fan blades and pulley.
5. Install fan belt and adjust.
6. Fill cooling system and check for leaks, check heater operation.

NOTE: A 5/16 x 1″ sae cap screw (with head removed) will make a guide stud to help align fan blades, pulley and hub.

Tests

Water pump operation may be checked by accelerating engine while squeezing top hose. A pressure surge should be felt. *Under safe conditions* this will also be apparent in top tank of radiator. Do not confuse surge in top tank with gas bubbles due to cylinder head (gasket) leakage.

NOTE: Consult index for procedures on GMC V6 engines.

Engine

Reference

In the specifications tables of this section are listed most of the service references needed by the mechanic.

Where different sized engines are used, identification can be made by refering to Serial Number Location and Engine Identification, near the beginning of this section.

Exhaust Emission Control

Beginning 1966, the California inspired Air Injection System (K-19) is used on all General Motors built trucks (with a few design exceptions) for delivery into that state. This Emission Control System, in some cases, involves removal and installation procedures more complicated than standard R&R procedures. This situation is especially true in the area of Manifolds, Cylinder Heads, or Engine R&R.

Beginning 1968

In compliance with anti-pollution laws involving all of the continental United States, the General Motors Corporation has adopted a special system of terminal exhaust treatment. This plan supersedes (in most cases) the method used to conform to 1966-67 California laws. The new system replaces (except with stick shift and special purpose engine applications) the use of the A.I.R. method previously used.

The new concept, Combustion Control System (C.C.S.) utilizes engine modification, with emphasis on carburetor and distributor changes. Any of the methods of terminal exhaust treatment requires close and frequent attention to tune-up factors of engine maintenance.

Since 1968, all manufacturers post idle speeds, and other pertinent data relative to the specific engine application, in a conspicuous place in the engine compartment.

For more detailed information refer to the General Section.

NOTE: Engine details for V6 see GMC

Engine Removal

Conventional Cab, Pickups, Panel and 4 Wheel Drive

1. Disconnect and remove battery.
2. Drain cooling system.
3. Drain engine oil.
4. Remove air cleaner and ducts.
5. Remove hood and radiator (also shroud if equipped) on larger models (1½ ton and up) it will be necessary to remove front end sheet metal. NOTE: Scribe alignment marks on hood hinges.
6. Disconnect wires at:
   Starter solenoid.
   Delcotron.
   Temperature switch.
   Oil Pressure switch.
   Transmission controlled spark solenoid.
   Coil.
   Neutral safety switch.
7. Disconnect:
   Accelerator linkage.
   Choke cable at carburetor (if so equipped).
   Fuel line to fuel pump. (capline).
   Heater hoses.
   Transmission dipstick and tube, plug hole (if so equipped).
   Oil pressure line to gauge. (if so equipped).
   Oil fill tube (and dipstick).
   Vacuum or air lines.
   Parking brake cable (if used).
   Power steering lines (if so equipped).
   Engine ground straps.
   Exhaust pipe (support if necessary).
8. Loosen fan belt, remove fan blades and pulley.
9. Remove clutch cross-shaft or disconnect clutch slave cylinder (if so equipped).
10. Remove road draft tube (if so equipped).
11. Remove rocker arm cover (s) and attach engine lifting tool. Take engine weight off mounting bolts.
12. Remove propeller shaft and plug end of transmission housing on light trucks. On 1½ ton and up, support transmission and disconnect from engine.
13. On light duty trucks, disconnect speedometer cable at transmission, shift linkage and any clutch linkage as required.
14. Disconnect transmission cooler lines (if so equipped).
15. On light trucks equipped with automatic or 4 speed transmission, remove rear engine mount bolts and rear crossmember.
16. Remove front engine mount bolts. CAUTION: Make final check that all necessary disconnects have been made.
17. On light trucks, raise engine and transmission and pull forward until removed. Larger trucks remove rear mounting bolts,

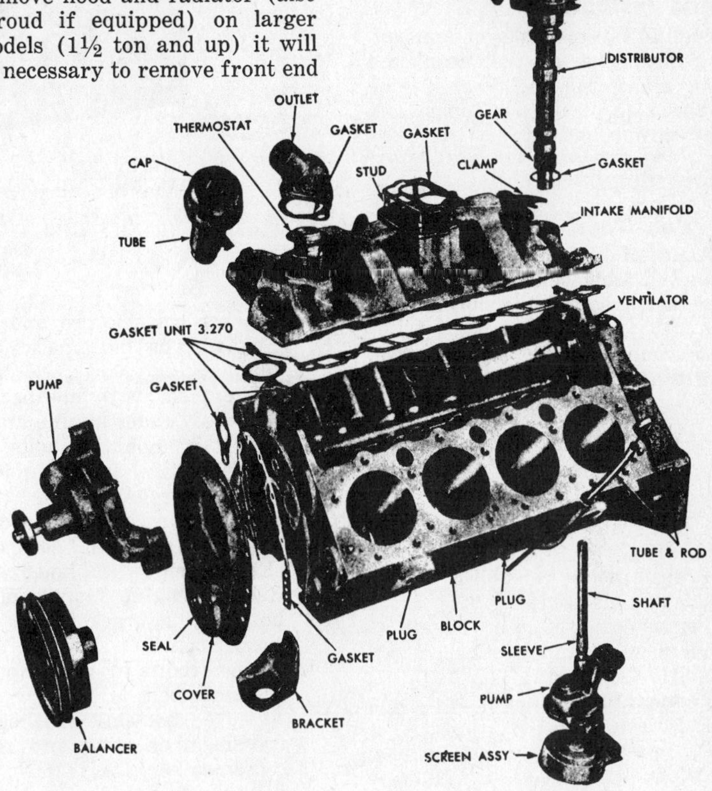

Exploded view—V8 engine typical (© Chevrolet Div., G.M. Corp.)

raise engine and pull forward until disconnected from transmission continue to raise engine until removed from vehicle. Be careful not to damage clutch disc.

Engine Installation

Install in reverse order of removal, fill cooling system and crankcase (check transmission). Start engine and check for leaks and operation. Adjust carburetor and road test.

Engine Removal

Van (Panel and Sport)

Because of its location, the engine is removed from below and both engine and transmission removed as a unit.

1. Disconnect battery ground cable.
2. Drain cooling system.
3. Raise engine cover and secure.
4. Disconnect:
   Air cleaner, extensions and heat tubes.
   Accelerator linkage.
   Choke cable at carburetor (if used).
   Transmission controlled spark solenoid (if used)
   Primary wire at coil.
   Oil fill tube (and dipstick).
   Starter solenoid.
   Temperature sender at unit.
   Delcotron.
   Oil pressure line or sender switch.
   Transmission dipstick and tube, plug hole (if so equipped).
5. Remove upper radiator hose and heater hoses.
6. Loosen fan belt, remove blades, pulley and shroud (if used).
7. Remove distributor cap and spark plug wiring harness. NOTE: Disconnect any wiring harness retaining clips.
8. Raise vehicle on hosit, drain crankcase and disconnect:
   Engine splash shields (if used).
   Lower radiator hose.
   Neutral safety switch, at transmission (if equipped).
   Fuel line to fuel pump. (capline).
   Transmission controlled spark switch, at transmission (if used).
   Transmission cooler lines (if used).
   Speedometer cable at transmission (and plug).
   Power steering hoses (if equipped).
   Parking brake cable (if used).
9. Disconnect exhaust pipe, support if necessary or block out of way.
10. Remove propeller shaft at transmission and plug extension housing to prevent oil leakage.
11. On manual transmissions, disconnect shift levers and clutch linkage; on automatics, shift linkage.
12. Place jack, with engine cradle attached, under engine and take weight off mounting bolts. CAUTION: Place cradle under engine as far as possible, (to the fifth oil pan cap screw from flywheel at least) and secure with chain over flywheel housing.
13. Remove engine front mounting bolts (and brackets for additional room).
14. Remove bolts at rear mount to crossmember.
15. Remove transmission support crossmember bolts and remove crossmember. CAUTION: Make final check that all necessary disconnects have been made.
16. Lower engine and transmission assembly slowly, pulling to rear to clear front crossmember, and move unit out from under vehicle.

Engine cradle under engine
(© Chevrolet Div., G.M. Corp.)

Engine Installation

Van (Panel and Sport)

Install in reverse order of removal, fill cooling system and crankcase (check transmission). Start engine and check for leaks and operation. Adjust carburetor and road test.

Engine Removal

Step Vans

1. Disconnect battery and remove.
2. Drain cooling system, drain engine oil.
3. Remove engine box, drivers seat, floor panels at stepwells, floor panel around steering column and pedals, and inspection plate on firewall above engine box.
4. Remove air cleaner (and any ducts).
5. Remove radiator and shroud.
6. Loosen fan belt and remove fan blades.
7. Remove engine splash pans (if used).
8. Disconnect neutral safety wire at converter (if used).
9. Remove upper and lower radiator hoses.
10. Disconnect wires at:
    Starter solenoid.
    Delcotron.
    Transmission controlled spack solenoid (if used).
    Temperature switch.
    Oil pressure switch.
    Coil.
11. Disconnect:
    Accelerator Linkage.
    Choke cable at carburetor (if so equipped).
    Fuel line to pump.
    Heater hoses.
    Oil pressure gauge line (if so equipped).
    Parking brake cable (if used).
    Vacuum or airlines.
    Power steering lines (if so equipped).
    Engine ground straps.
    Exhaust pipe (support if necessary).
12. Remove clutch cross-shaft or disconnect clutch slave cylinder (if so equipped).
13. Remove oil fill tube and dipstick also transmission dipstick and tube, plug holes (if used)
14. Remove rocker arm cover (s) and attach engine lift tool.
15. Push arm of engine lift crane in right side door opening. Attach to lifting device or sling and take engine weight off mounts. CAUTION: Make final check that all necessary disconnects have been made.
16. Support transmission and remove shift controls (cover opening), speedometer cable (plug hole), transmission spark control switch wire and oil cooler lines (if used).
17. Remove propeller shaft at transmission. Plug extension housing to prevent leakage.
18. Remove 2 top transmission to clutch housing cap screws and insert 2 guide pins. NOTE: Take 2 bolts, the same diameter and threads as just removed, but

at least 4" long and cut heads of bolts off. Using a hack saw, slot ends just cut for screwdriver and use for guides.

19. Remove 2 lower transmission to clutch housing cap screws and slide transmission back until clear of clutch disc. When transmission is free from engine, lower and remove from under vehicle.
20. Remove engine mounting bolts, front and rear.
21. Raise engine slightly and push forward to clear crossmember, then lift up and remove engine through door opening.

Engine Installation

Step Vans

A careful check of clutch components should be made. Install in reverse order of removal, fill cooling system and crankcase (check transmission). Start engine and check for leaks and operation. Adjust carburetor and road test.

Engine Removal

Tilt Cab

1. Tilt cab to expose engine area and secure.
2. Block wheels and exhaust air (if so equipped).
3. Disconnect battery ground cable.
4. Drain cooling system.
5. Drain crankcase.
6. Remove air cleaner and any ducts.
7. Remove radiator and heater hoses.
8. Remove radiator support and shroud assembly.
9. Disconnect hoses and remove surge tank.
10. Disconnect choke cable at carburetor.
11. Disconnect hand throttle at carburetor.
12. Disconnect shift linkage at control island.
13. Remove control island bolts and swing island out of way.
14. Remove both right and left island supports.
15. Disconnect cab safety lock and remote cab support.
16. Disconnect emergency brake cable.
17. Remove any engine splash shields.
18. Disconnect wires at:
    Starter solenoid.
    Delcotron.
    Temperature sender.
    Oil pressure sender.
    Coil.
    Governor speed warning.
    Transmission controlled spark solenoid at carburetor.
19. Remove:
    Accelerator linkage.
    Fuel line to pump.
    Lines or wires to dash guages.
    Vacuum or air lines at engine.
    Power steering lines at pump (if equipped).
    Engine ground straps.
    Exhaust pipe or crossover pipe (support if necessary).
20. Remove fan blades, pulley and support bracket assembly.
21. Remove clutch cross-shaft or disconnect clutch slave cylinder.
22. Remove rocker arm covers and install lift tool or sling.
23. Hoist engine and take engine weight off motor mounts.

NOTE: According to work to be performed select either of the following.

Removal of Engine and Transmission as a Unit

24. Disconnect speedometer (and plug).
25. Disconnect shift linkage at transmission (cover opening).
26. Disconnect any clutch linkage not yet removed.
27. Disconnect and drop propeller shaft at transmission, also any power take-off or auxiliary transmission couplings (cover or plug all openings).
28. Disconnect oil cooler lines or transmission spark control switch (if so equipped).
29. On Roadrangers remove air lines and parking brake drum (if used).
30. Remove all engine mounting bolts and raise slightly to support transmission weight. CAUTION: Make final check that all necessary disconnects have been made.
31. Remove any transmission to support bolts.
32. Raise engine and transmission assembly out of chassis as a unit.

Removal of Engine Only

24. Support transmission, remove flywheel under-pan, and disconnect from engine. NOTE: If possible, install transmission guide pins in top (transmission to clutch housing) holes to allow engine to slide forward to clear clutch disc splines. This will prevent bending clutch hub.
25. Remove all engine mounting bolts. CAUTION: Make final check that all necessary disconnects have been made.
26. Raise slightly and pull forward until clear of transmission.
27. Continue to raise engine until high enough to clear chassis.

Engine Installation

Tilt Cab

Install in reverse order of removal, fill cooling system and crankcase (check transmission). Start engine and check for leaks and operation. Make any minor adjustments and road test.

Engine Manifolds

Reference

Due to various body and chassis designs, it will be necessary to expose engine areas such as raising tilt cabs, hoods and removing engine boxes on vans.

NOTE: The use of a good chemical solvent on exhaust manifold bolts and nuts will facilitate the operation.

CAUTION: Pay particular attention to heat risers, their failure increases warm-up time and failure to open can cause lean mixtures at higher speeds.

In-line Engines (Combination Manifold)

Removal

1. Remove air cleaner (and any ducts).
2. Disconnect throttle controls, rods, linkage and return spring.
3. Disconnect fuel and vacuum lines at carburetor, also choke cable or control (if used).
4. Disconnect crankcase ventilation valve, vacuum brake or transmission spark control hoses (if used).
5. Remove carburetor.
6. Remove oil filter support bracket and swing filter to one side (if so equipped).
7. Disconnect exhaust pipe at flange and support if necessary (discard gasket or packing).
8. Remove manifold attaching bolts and clamps, remove manifold assembly (be careful of locating rings). Discard gaskets.

Installation

Reverse removal procedures after cleaning all gasket surfaces, checking for cracks, check heat riser and alignment. Lay straight edge on manifold to head surface to check. If intake and exhaust are not in line, loosen center bolts where they are joined and do not tighten until assembly is bolted to head, then retighten). Install finger-tight, check that pilot or locating rings and gaskets are in place, then torque to specifications in proper sequence. Torque on end bolts is 15 to 20 ft. lbs., all others are 20-30 ft. lbs.

Warm engine, adjust idle and check for leaks.

V Engines—Intake Manifold

Removal

1. Drain radiator, remove top hose at thermostat housing also any

Manifold torque (typical)
(© Chevrolet Div., G.M. Corp.)

bypass or heater hoses.
2. Remove battery ground cable.
3. Remove carburetor air cleaner and any ducts.
4. Remove oil fill tube and cap.
5. Disconnect gas line, all vacuum hoses, throttle linkage and return spring, choke cable and crankcase ventilation valve.
6. Disconnect wires to temperature sender, coil and transmission spark controlled solenoid (if so equipped).
7. Remove carburetor.
8. Remove distributor cap and mark position of rotor. Remove distributor.
9. Exhaust air and remove air compressor, disconnect oil drain line at manifold (if so equipped and interferes).
10. Remove manifold attaching bolts, remove manifold.

NOTE: If manifold is not to be replaced, some components can be left on such as carburetor, oil fill tube, thermostat housing and temperature sender.

Installation

Clean gasket and seal surfaces on manifold, block and heads. Install new gaskets and seals, coated with a good sealer particularly at water passages. Position manifold, use guide pins to prevent gaskets moving, and check mating angle at heads. (Angle could be incorrect due to excessive cylinder head resurfacing)

Install bolts finger tight, then torque to specifications in proper sequence. Reverse the removal procedures fill radiator, warm engine, adjust timing and carburetor idle if necessary and check for leaks.

V Engines—Exhaust Manifold

Removal

1. Use a good liquid penetrant freely on attaching bolts and nuts.
2. Remove exhaust pipe (support if necessary).
3. Open french locks and remove manifold attaching bolts. NOTE: A 9/16", thin wall, 6 point socket sharpened at leading edges, placed over head of bolt then tapped with hammer will speed the opening of french locks.
4. Remove Delcotron (on left side), remove manifold.

Installation

Clean mating surfaces, install new gaskets where used, check heat riser and check for cracks. Reverse removal procedures. Start engine and check for leaks.

Cylinder Head

Reference

Due to many types of vehicles it will be necessary to remove various access covers to expose engine area.

In-line Engines

Removal

1. Drain cooling system and remove battery ground strap at head.
2. Remove air cleaner and any ducts.
3. Remove choke cable, accelerator rod and return spring, fuel and vacuum lines at carburetor.
4. Remove manifold to head bolts and clamps, pull manifold and carburetor assembly clear of head and support.
5. Remove fuel and vacuum lines from retaining clip at thermostat housing.
6. Disconnect temperature sender wire, remove wiring harness from rocker cover clip. Remove coil wires and coil.
7. Remove top radiator hose, at thermostat housing.
8. Remove spark plug wires and distributor cap.
9. Remove rocker arm cover. CAUTION: Never pry rocker arm cover loose—bump cover rearward in a gasket shearing manner.
10 Engines with rocker arm shafts, back off adjusting nuts, rotate rocker arm to clear push rod and remove push rods. Engines using pedestal rocker arms, remove rocker arm ball nuts, arms and push rods.
11. Remove push rod cover.
12. Remove cylinder head bolts, cylinder head and discard gasket.

NOTE: Place rocker arm mechanism and cylinder head bolts in a rack so they can be re-installed in same locations. (mated)

Check cylinder head for warpage with a straight edge. Inspect for cracks and burnt valves.

Installation

Reverse removal procedures and adjust valves after cleaning gasket surfaces. Engines using a steel (shim) gasket, coat both sides with a good sealer, bead side up. Do not reuse gaskets. Cylinder head bolt threads in block and threads on bolts must be clean. Coat threads on bolts with sealer before installing. Tighten each cylinder head bolt a little at a time, in correct sequence, until specified torque is reached. Engines using composition (steel asbestos) gaskets

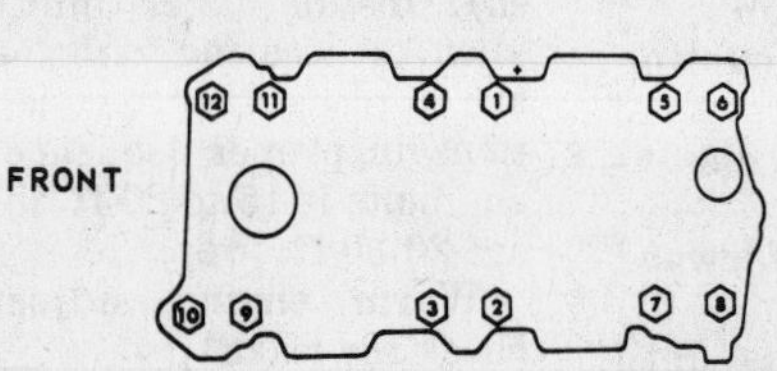

"SMALL V8"

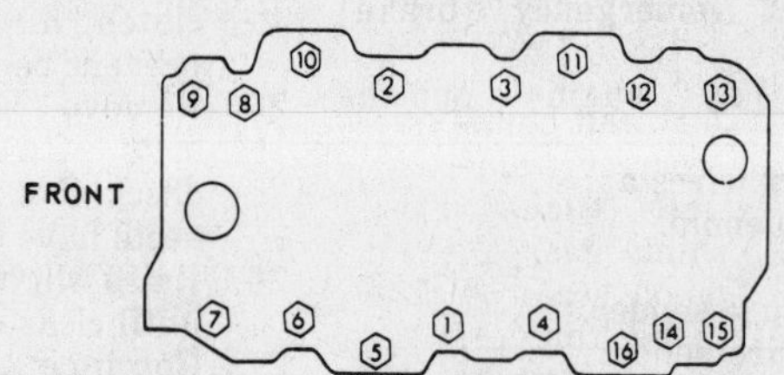

"MARK IV V8"

Intake manifold bolt torque sequence (© Chevrolet Div., G.M. Corp.)

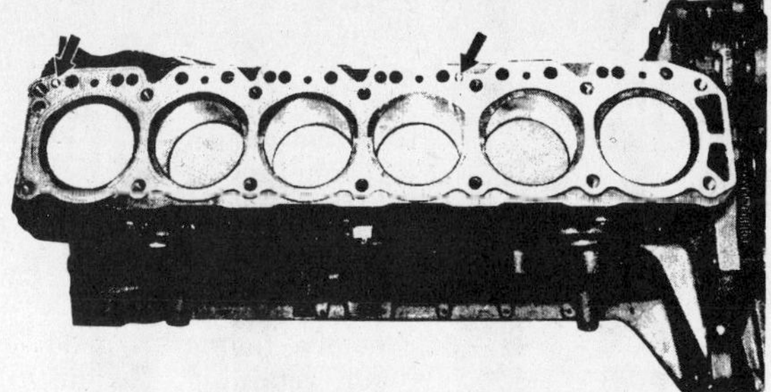

Installing head gasket (typical)
(© Chevrolet Div., G.M. Corp.)

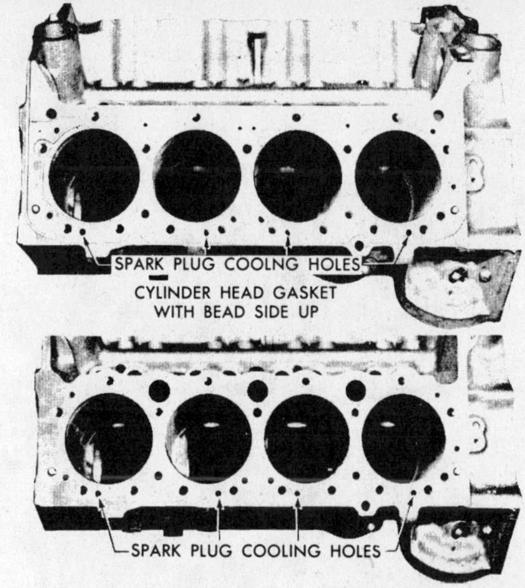

Cylinder block spark plug cooling holes
(© Chevrolet Div., G.M. Corp.)

must have heads retorqued after warm-up. (retightening heads effects valve lash) Refer to specifications at beginning of this section for nut tightening sequence.

V Engines

Removal

1. Remove intake manifold (with carburetor) and exhaust manifold—see manifolds R & R. NOTE: If only one head is to be R & R, remove inlet manifold bolts on that side only and leave inlet manifold assembly in place.
2. Loosen belt and remove power steering pump (if so equipped).
3. Remove rocker arm covers. CAUTION: Never pry rocker arm cover loose—bump cover rearward in a gasket shearing manner.
4. Loosen rocker arm adjusting nut, turn rocker arm to clear push rods and remove push rods. Exhaust push rods are longer than intake push rods in some engines so to be sure—place in sequence so that they can be installed in same location (mated).
5. Remove cylinder head bolts, cylinder head and discard gasket.
6. Check cylinder head for warpage with a straight edge. Inspect for cracks and burnt valves.

Installation

Reverse removal procedures and adjust valves, after cleaning gasket surfaces. If heads are to be resurfaced check alignment at intake manifold. Cylinder head bolt threads in block and threads on bolts must be clean, coat threads with sealer. Tighten each cylinder head bolt a little at a time, in correct sequence, until specified torque is reached. Engines using steel (shim) gasket, coat both sides with a good sealer, bead side up. Engines using composition (steel asbestos) gaskets must be retorqued after warm-up (retightening heads effects valve lash).

Refer to specifications at beginning of this section for nut tightening sequence.

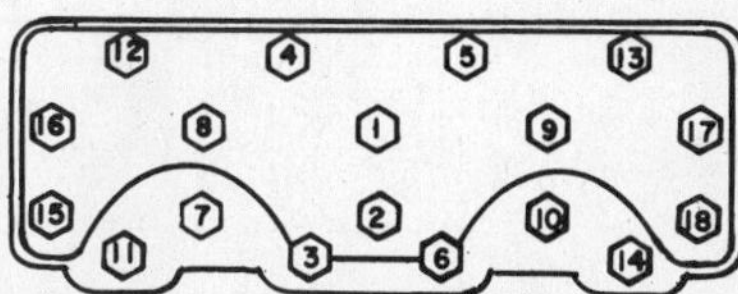

Cylinder head bolt tightening sequence V8 —345 & 409 engines

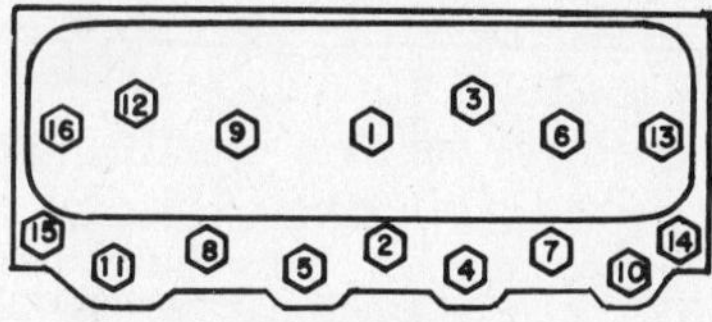

V8—366, 396 & 427 engines

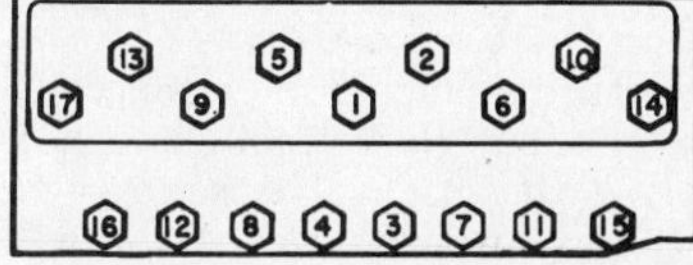

V8—283, 307, 327 & 350 engines

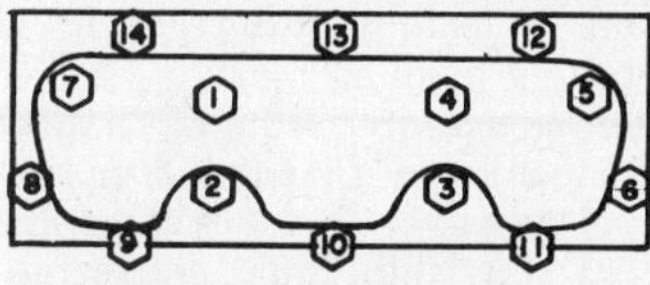

V6—401 & 478 engines

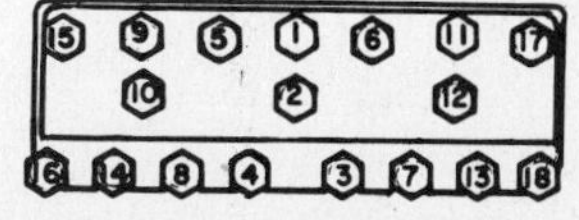

6—235 & 261 engines

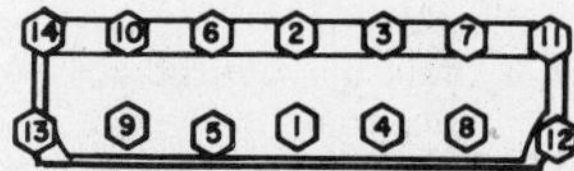

6—194, 230, 250 & 292 engines

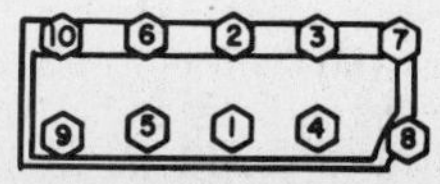

4—153 engine

Valve System

Adjustments—Hydraulic lifters

Engine Running

1. Run engine to normalize (stabilize oil temperature), remove rocker cover (s) bump off—do not pry off). Leave old gasket on head to aid against oil overflow or use oil deflector clips.
2. Reduce engine idle as low as possible, tighten cylinder head bolts (and rocker supports if used). Check camshaft lobe lift.
3. Back off rocker arm adjusting nut until rocker arm starts to clatter, then turn nut down slowly until clatter stops. This is zero lash position.
4. Turn adjusting nut down ¼ turn and pause 10 seconds until engine runs smoothly. Repeat operation 3 more times until 1 full turn down from zero lash position is reached. NOTE: This 1 turn pre-load adjustment must be done slowly and in stages to allow hydraulic lifter to adjust itself to prevent possibility of internal interference or bent push rods.
5. Repeat for each valve, the use of a vacuum gauge is recommended.
6. Install new rocker cover gaskets and torque rocker covers. Reset engine idle.

Engine Not Running

1. Remove rocker cover (s) (bump off—do not pry off).
2. Tighten cylinder head bolts (and rocker arm supports if used).
3. Disconnect primary wire at negative terminal of coil.
4. Mark distributor housing with chalk at each spark plug tower

Valve adjustment (© Chevrolet Div., G.M. Corp.)

(double mark no. 1 cylinder).

5. Remove distributor cap and crank engine until rotor points to No. 1 chalk mark. (No. 1 cylinder is approximately at TDC and both valves can be adjusted). Valve adjustment is made by backing off rocker arm nut until push rod can be rotated and then slowly tightened until push rod does not turn. This is zero lash position. Turn adjusting nut down 1 full turn to complete adjustment.
6. Adjust the remaining valves, one cylinder at a time (following firing order) in same one cylinder at a time (following firing order) in same manner.
7. Install distributor cap.
8. Install new rocker cover gasket (s) and torque rocker cover (s).

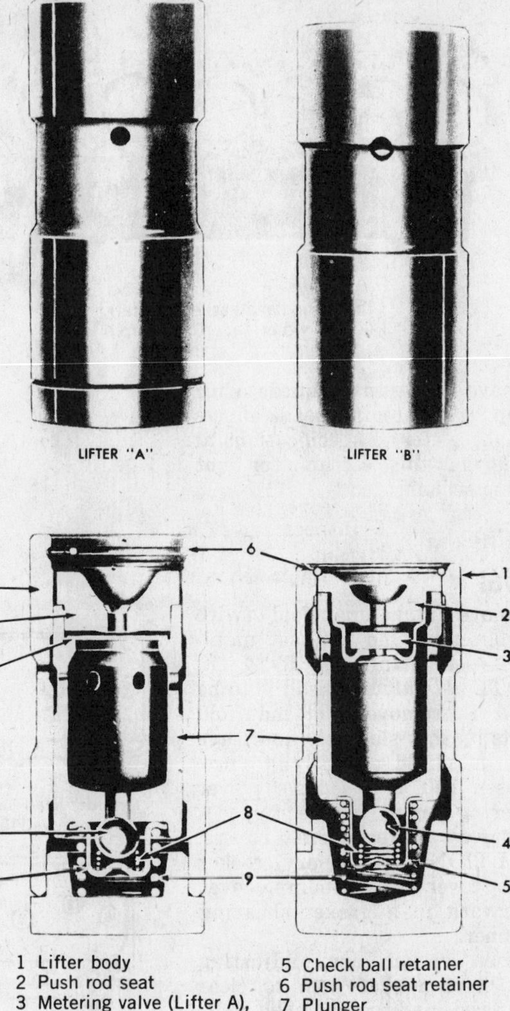

1 Lifter body
2 Push rod seat
3 Metering valve (Lifter A), inertia valve (Lifter B)
4 Check ball
5 Check ball retainer
6 Push rod seat retainer
7 Plunger
8 Check ball spring
9 Plunger spring

Hydraulic valve lifters (© Chevrolet Div., G.M. Corp.)

Noisy Lifters

Locate a noisy lifter by using a mechanic's stethoscope or hose, can also be detected by placing finger on valve spring retainer (a distinct shock will be felt each time valve returns to seat). Forcing push rod down will cause lifter check valve to unload and remain open. A noisy or defective push rod is usually indicated by a free-spinning push rod.

Rocker arms are trough shaped, pressed steel levers that transfer lifter motion to valves. Rocker arms are supported on individual pedestals and have an oval hole in center to fit over stud and pivot on ball seats. Oil is fed to rocker arms by means of hollow push rods. Whenever arms or ball seats are being installed, coat all bearing surfaces with engine oil.

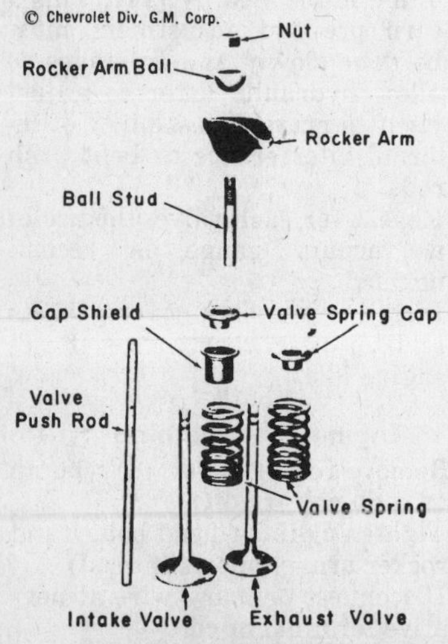

V8 engine—valve system (© Chevrolet Div., G.M. Corp.)

Rocker Arms

Rocker arm studs are pressed in cylinder head and are available in oversize for replacement.

CAUTION: Do not try to press oversize stud in head without reaming stud hole first.

Pressed in studs can be replaced by a stud threaded on both ends. Head is to be threaded in stud hole to accept threaded stud.

Timing Gears and Chain

Crankshaft Pulley or Damper

Removal

1. Drain radiator; remove hoses.
2. Remove radiator—See Radiator R & R
3. Loosen fan belt and remove any accessory drive.
4. Use puller to remove pulley or damper.

NOTE: On some early models, pulley is bolted to Hub. Remove pulley first then, using pulley holes, remove hub. More recent models have the hub bonded to inertia weight. Care must be exercised when using a puller.

Installation

1. Clean area, inspect oil seal in cover. (Now would be good time to install new seal even if just for preventative maintenance).

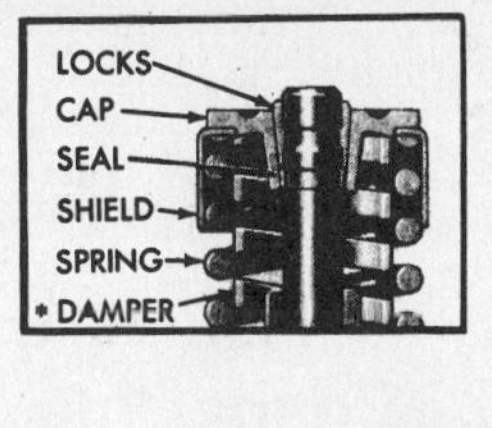

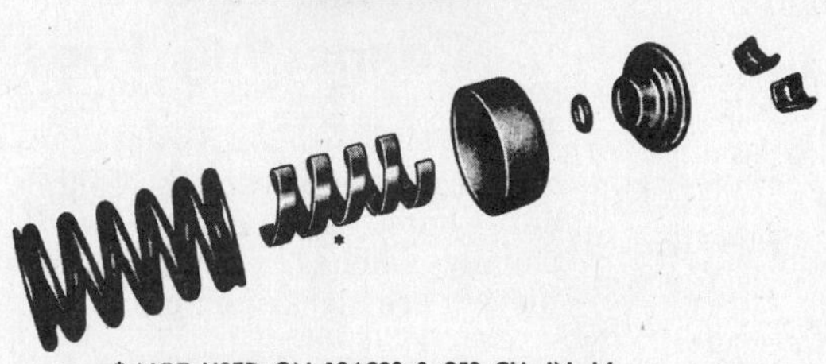

* NOT USED ON 194,230 & 250 CU. IN. L6

Valve spring installation (inline & small V8 engines)
(© Chevrolet Div., G.M. Corp.)

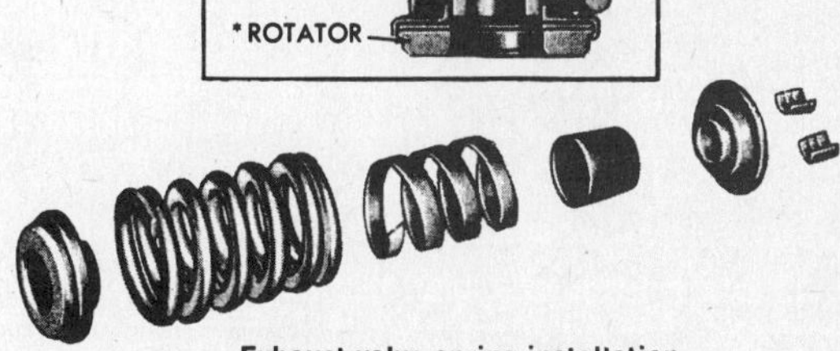

Exhaust valve spring installation (Mark IV V8 truck, 366 and 427 engines)
(© Chevrolet Div., G.M. Corp.)

2. Coat timing case cover oil seal with light oil, inspect hub for seal (grooved) wear.
3. Position damper (or hub) on crankshaft, aligning keyway, and tap lightly into position.
4. Pull damper (or hub) into position with damper retaining bolt and washer. (Make sure damper retaining bolt has good thread engagement before applying force). Torque to specifications.
5. Reverse balance of removal steps.

Timing Cover Oil Seal Replacement

With Cover On (To Remove Cover Means Removing Oil Pan)

1. Remove torsional damper—see damper R & R.
2. Pry old seal out, be careful not to mar crankshaft or bend cover.
3. Install new seal (lip of seal toward block), tap lightly into position. Coat seal with oil.
4. Reverse removal procedures.

Timing Gear Replacement

NOTE: When necessary to install a new camshaft gear the camshaft should be removed. However gear can be removed from camshaft without removing camshaft from engine. Cam gear can be split and hub section pulled off but extreme care must be taken not to allow any impart, either removing or installing gear on shaft. Camshaft must be totally blocked so as not to allow any movement to disturb oil sealing welsh plug at camshaft rear bearing.

Removal (Pulling Camshaft)

1. Drain and remove radiator.
2. Remove front end sheet metal or grille.
3. Remove damper or pulley.
4. Remove oil pan (See Oil Pan R & R).
5. Remove timing case cover (2 bolts inside oil pan at front main bearing cap).
6. Remove rocker arm cover(s). Pivot rocker arms to relieve lifters.
7. Remove fuel pump and distributor (mark position of rotor).
8. Align timing gear marks (check rotor mark) then remove 2 thrust plate screws by reaching through 2 holes in camgear.
9. Remove camshaft and rear assembly by pulling and turning shaft carefully so lobes will not mar bearings and clear lifters.
10. Use press to remove cam gear using caution not to damage thrust plate by woodruff key.
11. Clean all gasket surfaces and inspect.
12. Check camshaft alignment and lobes for wear. Check camshaft bearings in block, check crank gear and oil spray nozzle.

Installation

1. Support camshaft at back end of front bearing in a press, place thrust plate over end of shaft, install woodruff key in key way, align camgear with key and press gear on shaft until clearance at thrust plate (and front end of front bearing) is .001-.003".
2. Install camshaft and gear assembly in block, turning shaft carefully so lobes clear lifters and bearings, until it almost bottoms. NOTE: Coat lobes and bearing surfaces with engine oil.
3. Turn camshaft and mesh timing marks, tighten thrust plate.
4. Check cam gear for runout (should not exceed .005").
5. Check backlash at gears. (.004-.006").
6. Reverse remaining removal procedures.
7. Fill radiator, and oil and start

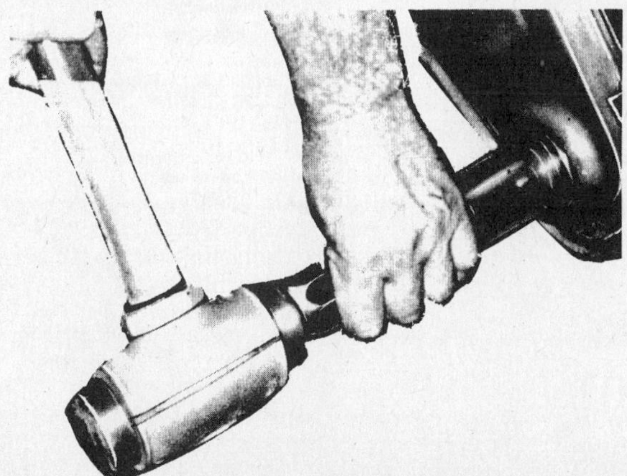

Installing oil seal (cover installed)
(© Chevrolet Div., G.M. Corp.)

Removing torsional damper
(© Chevrolet Div., G.M. Corp.)

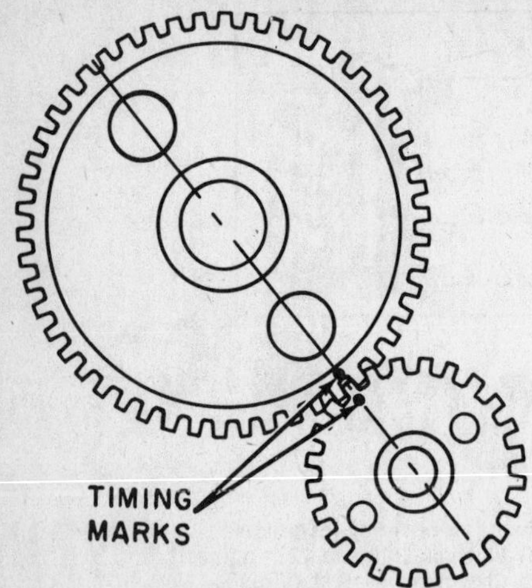

Timing mark alignment 366 & 427 engines

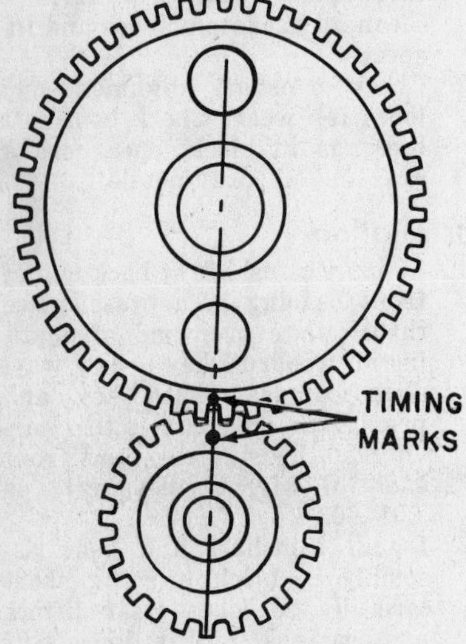

Timing mark alignment inline engines

engine. Adjust valves, check timing and inspect for leaks.

Timing Chain

Removal

1. Drain and remove radiator.
2. Remove torsional damper.
3. Remove oil pan (see oil pan R & R).
4. Remove water pump or pulley if necessary.
5. Remove timing case cover.
6. Align timing marks.
7. Remove (3) camshaft sprocket bolts.
8. Remove sprocket and chain. NOTE: sprocket is a light press fit on-camshaft, especially at dowel pin. If sprocket is tight, tap lightly with plastic hammer on lower edge of sprocket.
9. Clean all gasket and seal areas and inspect.
10. Check teeth on both sprockets for wear.

Installation

1. Suspend chain on camshaft sprocket with timing mark in approximate position.
2. Place chain over crankshaft sprocket and position camshaft sprocket on dowel. Recheck timing marks.

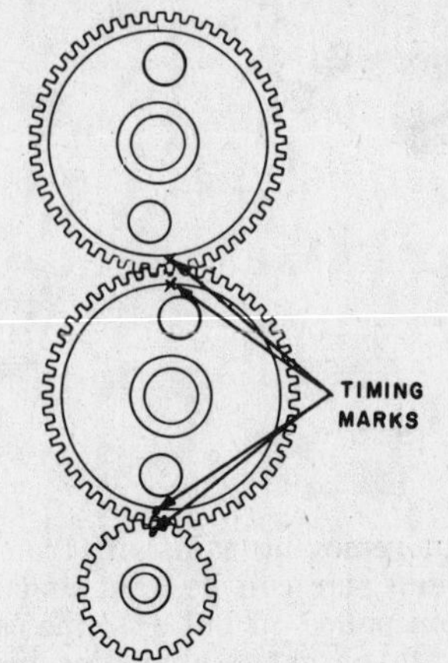

Timing mark alignment V6 401 & 478 engines

3. Draw camshaft sprocket in place using the three mounting bolts. Torque to specifications. CAUTION: do not drive sprocket on camshaft as welsh plug at rear of camshaft can be dislodged.
4. Lubricate chain with engine oil, make sure oil slinger is in place.
5. Reverse removal procedures.
6. Fill radiator, add engine oil and start engine. Check for leaks.

Check for Worn Chain

1. Check fan belt tension, adjust if too loose.
2. Remove distributor cap, loosen spark plugs.
3. Move fan blades until rotor moves. Mark distributor housing and balancer at pointer.
4. Move fan in opposite direction until rotor moves, remark both units.
5. Marks in excess of 4° apart, 2 graduations (usually) on balancer, indicate excess wear.

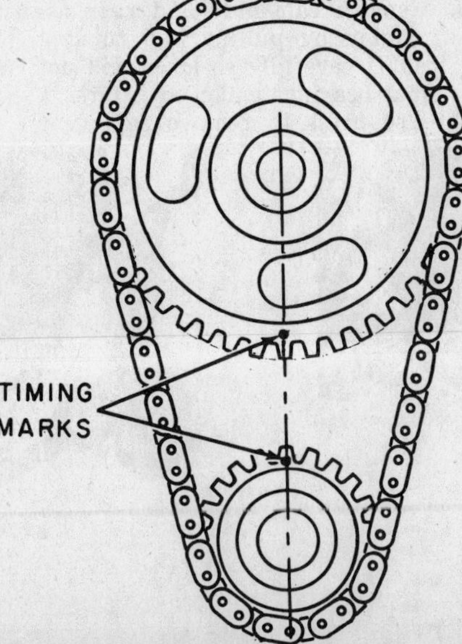

Valve timing—V8 engines

Pistons and Connecting Rods

Pistons

Pistons are of various designs, flat, cup, hump and dome. Heads are usually notched to indicate front or pistons are marked on pin boss.

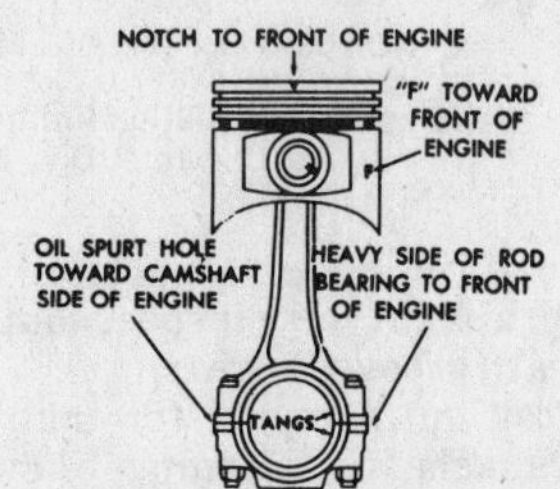

Correct relation of piston & rod 153, 194, 230 & 250 engines

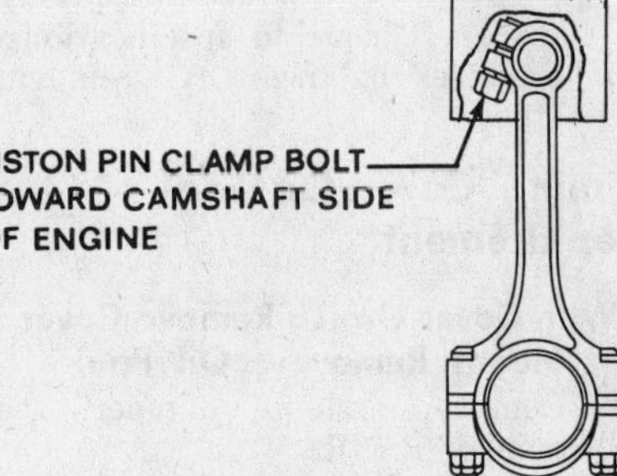

Correct relation of piston & rod 235 & 261 engines

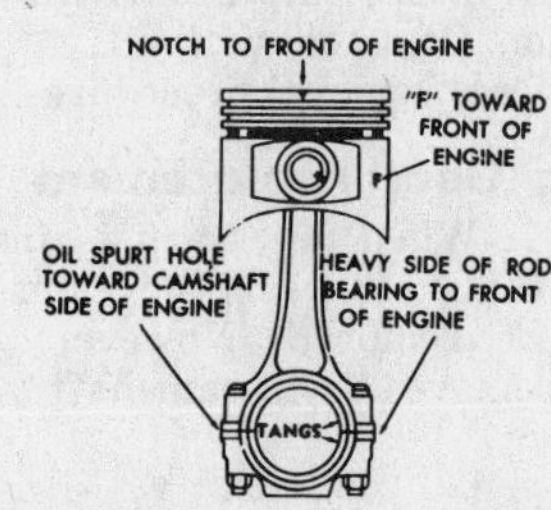

Correct relation of piston & rod 6—292 engine

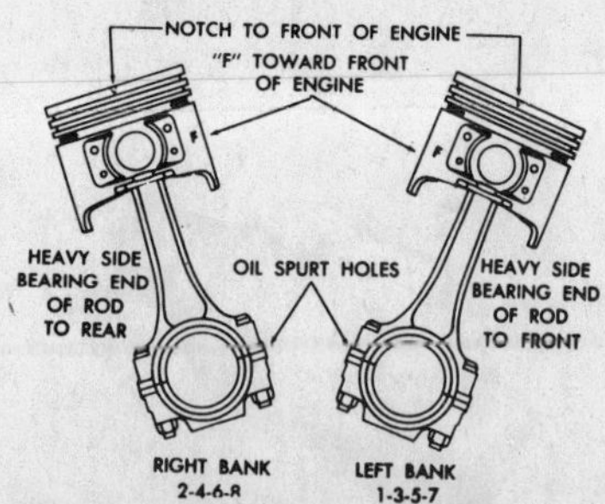

Correct relation of piston to rod 293, 307 & 350 engines

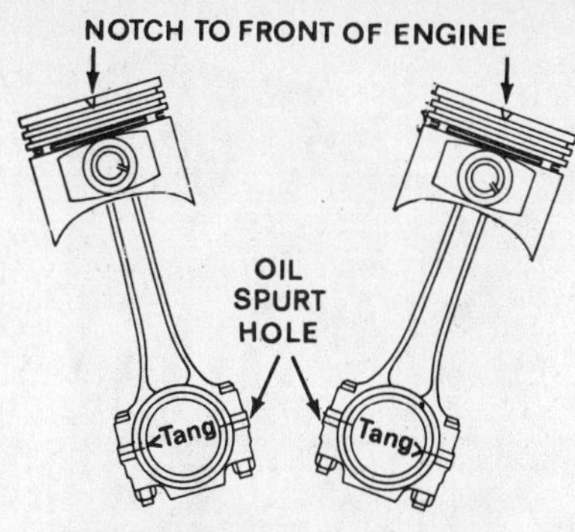

Correct relation of piston & rod 327 engine

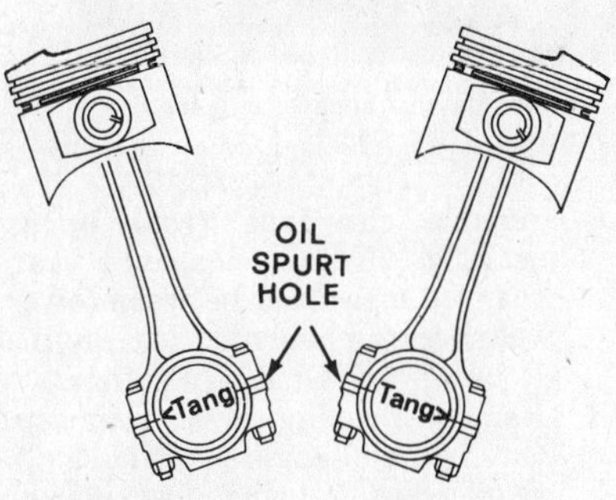

Correct relation of piston & rod 348 & 409 engines

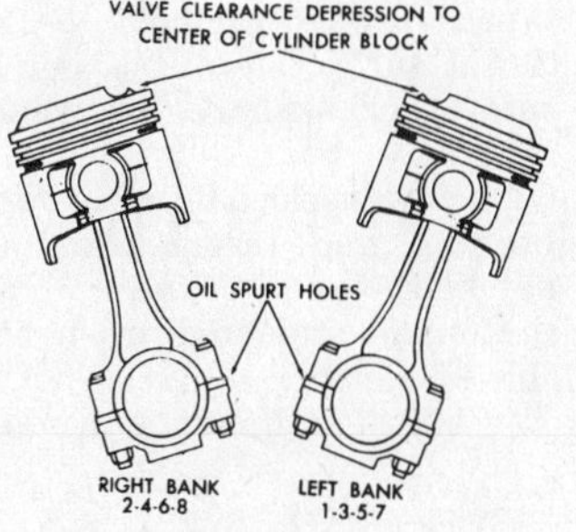

Correct relation of piston & rod 396 engine

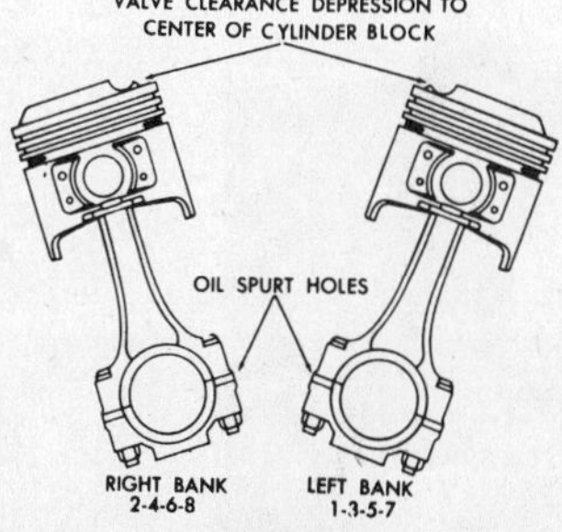

Correct relation of piston & rod 366 & 427 engines

Connecting Rods

Rod forging and cap have mating numbers and must be on same side when installed or cap is on "backwards." Rod number on in-line engines go to camshaft side. Numbers on "V" engines go to outside of block. The oil spurt (cylinder wall oiling) hole goes toward camshaft. On in-line engines the spurt hole and number are both on camshaft side. On "V" engines the spurt hole is in center, toward camshaft, and numbers to outside.

Piston and Rod Removal

1. Drain cooling system and remove cylinder head(s). See cylinder head removal.
2. Drain crankcase oil and remove oil pan. See Oil Pan Removal.
3. Remove any ridge and/or deposits from upper end of cylinder bores with a ridge reamer. NOTE: Move piston to bottom of its travel and place a cloth on top of piston to collect cuttings. After ridge and/or deposits are removed turn crankshaft until piston is at top of its stroke and carefully remove cloth with its cuttings.
4. Check connecting rods and pistons for cylinder number identification and if necessary, mark them.
5. Remove conecting rod nuts and caps. Push rods away from crankshaft and install caps and nuts loosely to their respective rods.
6. Push piston and rod assemblies away from crankshaft and out of cylinders. See Engine Rebuilding—General Section.

Piston and Rod Installation

1. Lightly coat pistons, rings and cylinder walls with light engine oil.
2. With bearing caps removed, and ring compressor tool installed, install each piston in its respective bore.
3. Install bearing caps and check bearing clearance. See Engine Rebuilding—General Section.
4. Install oil pan gaskets, seals and oil pan. See Oil Pan Installation.
5. Install cylinder head gasket(s) and head(s). See Cylinder Head Installation.
6. Refill crankcase and cooling system and check for leaks.

Install piston & rod assemblies
(© Chevrolet Div., G.M. Corp.)

Piston Rings

Piston rings are available in standard size as well as .020", .030", and .040" oversizes.

Piston Ring Removal

1. With pistons removed from cylinders, remove piston rings by expanding them and sliding them off piston.
2. Clean piston ring grooves by removing all particles of carbon. Check for burrs or nicks that might cause rings to hang up.

Piston Ring Installation

See Engine Rebuilding—General Section.

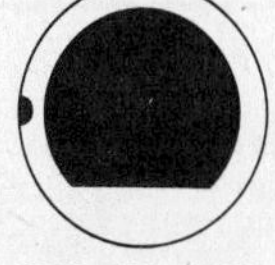

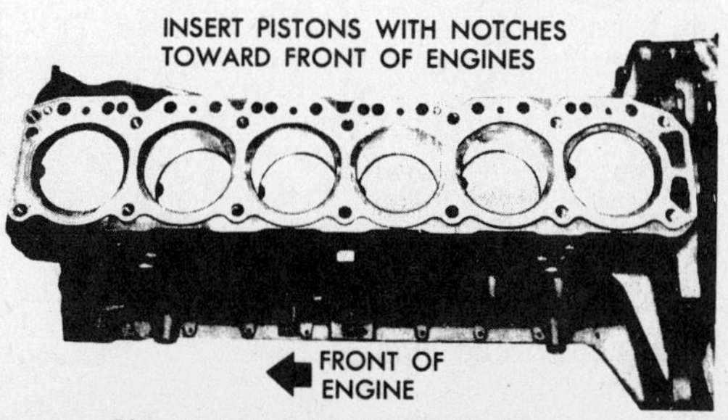

Pistons installed (inline engines)
(© Chevrolet Div., G.M. Corp.)

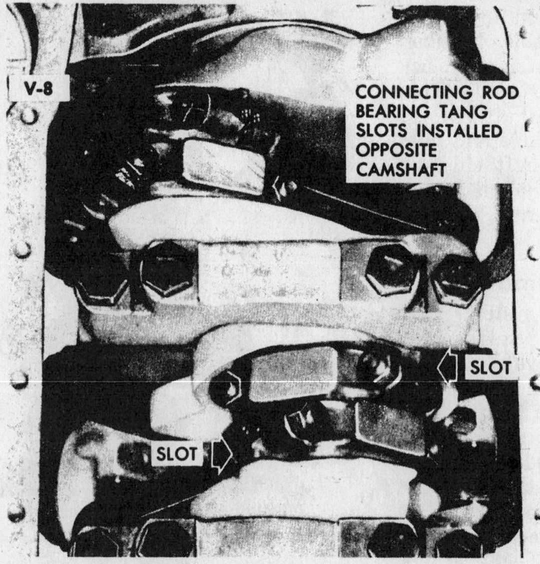

Connecting rods installed V8 engines

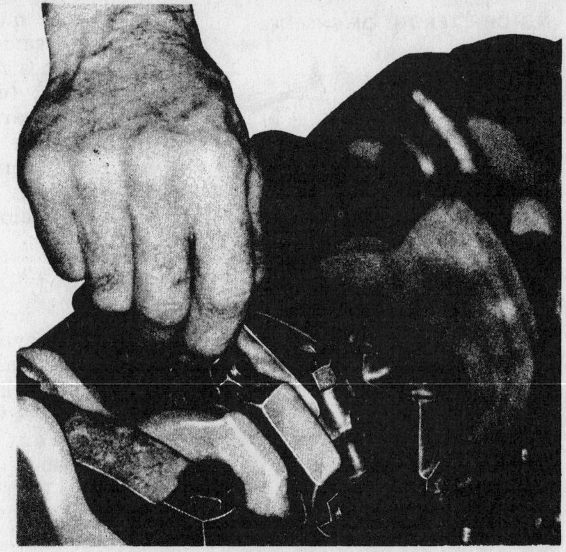

Measuring connecting rod side clearance V8 engines
(© Chevrolet Div., G.M. Corp.)

Main and Rod Bearings

Main bearings and connecting rod bearings are replaceable inserts, precision fit and held in place by locking tangs. Excessive bearing clearances reduce oil pressure. Never replace the lower half of any bearing without replacing the upper half. Do not file any bearing cap. Make sure, on main bearings, the upper half oil hole is aligned. Be certain oil passages in the crankshaft are open. Mark rod caps and upper forgings, also main caps and block, in numerical order to aid in reassembly. Rod bearings are available in standard size as well as .001″, .002″, .010″ and .020″ undersizes. Main bearings are furnished in standard size and .001″, .002″, .009″, .010″, .020″ and .030″ undersizes.

Rod Bearing Replacement

1. Drain crankcase oil and remove oil pan. See Oil Pan Removal.
2. Remove connecting rod bearing cap.
3. Wipe bearing shell and crankpin clean of oil.
4. Inspect bearings for evidence of wear or damage. (Bearings showing the above should not be installed).
5. Measure crankpin for out-of-round or taper with a micrometer. If within specifications measure bearing clearance with plastigage or its equivalent. See Engine Rebuilding—General Section.
6. Install bearing in connecting rod and cap.
7. Coat bearing surface with oil, install rod cap and torque nuts to specifications.
8. Rotate crankshaft after bearing adjustment to be sure bearings are not too tight. Check side clearance.
9. Install oil pan gaskets, seals and oil pan. See Oil Pan Installation.

Main Bearing Replacement

NOTE: Main bearings may be replaced with or without removing crankshaft.

(Engine in Vehicle)

1. Drain crankcase oil and remove oil pan. See Oil Pan Removal.
2. Remove oil pump.
3. Loosen or remove spark plugs for easier crankshaft rotation.
4. Starting with rear main bearing, remove bearing cap and wipe oil from journal and cap.
5. Inspect bearings for evidence of wear or damage.
6. Measure bearing clearance with plastigage or its equivalent. The crankshaft should be supported at damper and flywheel to remove clearance from upper bearing. Total clearance can then be measured between lower bearing and journal. See Engine Rebuilding—General Section.
7. Remove bearing shell from cap.
8. On in-line engine crankshaft, rear main bearing has no oil hole. Replace rear main bearing upper half as follows:
   a. Use a small drift punch and hammer to start upper bearing half rotating out of block.
   b. Use a pair of pliers (with taped jaws) to hold bearing thrust surface to oil slinger and rotate crankshaft to remove bearing.
   c. Oil new selected size upper bearing and insert plate (unnotched) and between crankshaft and indented or notched side of block.
   d. Use pliers as in removing to ro-

Rear main bearing removal (upper half)
(© Chevrolet Div., G.M. Corp.)

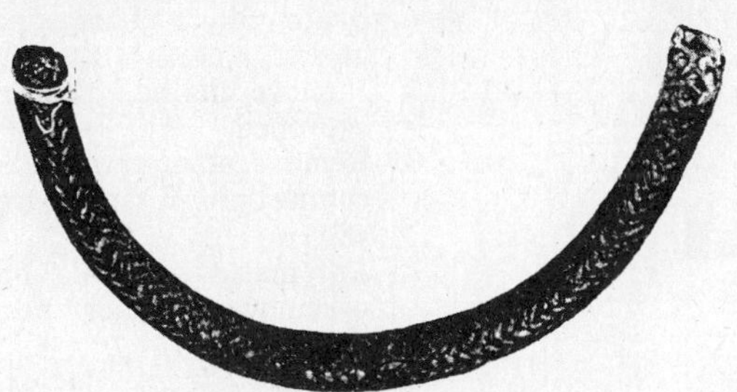

Wire attached on oil seal
(© Chevrolet Div., G.M. Corp.)

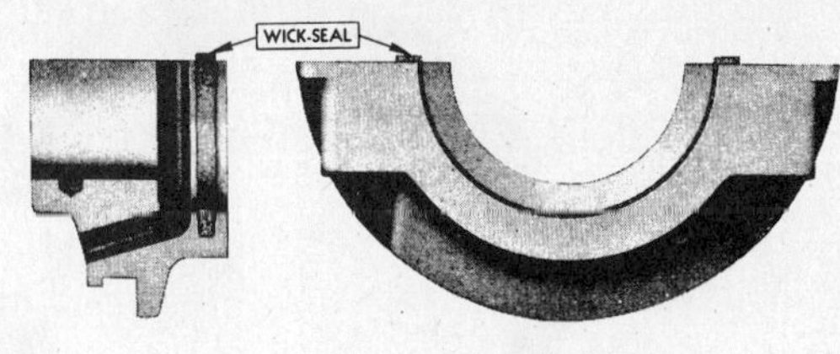

Rear main oil seal installation
(© Chevrolet Div., G.M. Corp.)

tate bearing into place. The last ¼ movement may be done by holding just the slinger with pliers or tap in place with a drift punch.

9. All other crankshaft journals (in-line and "V" models) have oil holes. Replace main bearing upper half as follows:
   a. Install a main bearing removing and installing tool in oil hole in crankshaft journal. NOTE: If such a tool is not available, a cotter pin (with head flattened) may be used.
   b. Rotate crankshaft clockwise as viewed from front of engine. This will roll upper bearing out of block.
   c. Oil new selected size upper bearing and insert plain (unnotched) end between crankshaft and indented or notched side of block. Rotate bearing into place and remove tool from oil hole in crankshaft journal.
10. Oil new lower bearing and install in bearing cap.
11. Install main bearing cap according to markings. Torque bearing cap bolts to specifications.
12. Install oil pump and oil pan. Refill crankcase. Install and tighten spark plugs.

Rear Main Bearing Oil Seal Replacement (Engine in Vehicle)

1. Raise vehicle and drain oil.
2. Remove oil pan and oil pump. See oil pan and oil pump removal.
3. Remove rear main cap and discard seal.
4. Loosen all mains (except no. 1) and block crankshaft down for maximum clearance at rear main.
5. Use wooden dowel, so as not to mar journal, tap lightly until seal can be gripped and removed. Rotating shaft may help.
6. Wick type seal: Use "Chinese Finger" type of tool, or insert a piece of soft wire through seal approximately ¼ from end, then wrap end with wire. Insert wire through seal opening in crankcase and around crankshaft. Start upper half of seal in place, lubricated with light sealer. Pull seal into place (rotating shaft may help) until centered. Cut each end of seal so that ¼″ protrudes. Install new lower half of oil seal in cap and roll or pack into position. Cut ends flush with cap parting face. Replace cap. Molded type seal: Insert new upper half, lubricated with light sealer, into channel and apply firm pressure with hammer handle until seal is centered. (Lip of seal facing toward front of engine.) Install lower half of oil seal in cap (lip toward front), lubricate lip with oil and install cap.
7. Torque all mains, check for drag.
8. Replace oil pump, oil pan and add oil.
9. Start engine and check for leaks.

Engine Lubrication

Oil Pan Removal and Installation

1961-1962

1. Raise front of vehicle and support on stands.
2. Remove road dirt at oil pan bolts and drain plug.
3. Drain oil (install new drain plug gasket).
4. On V8—Remove oil level dipstick and tube.
5. Remove oil pan bolts and screws, remove oil pan. CAUTION: On 6 cylinder—crankshaft may have to be turned to allow clearance at crossmember.
6. Reverse removal steps after cleaning gasket and seal surfaces. Install pan side gaskets on block, using a good sealer as a retainer. End seals go into

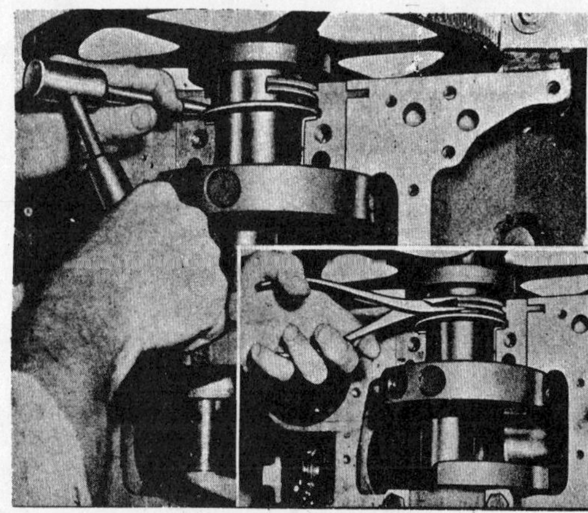

Rear main oil seal removal
(© Chevrolet Div., G.M. Corp.)

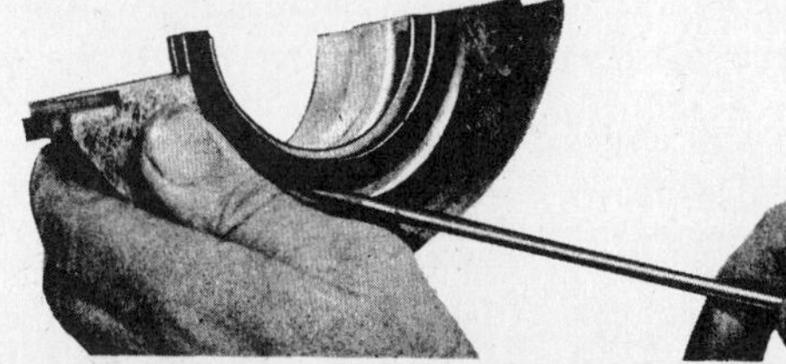

Removing lower half—rear oil seal
(© Chevrolet Div., G.M. Corp.)

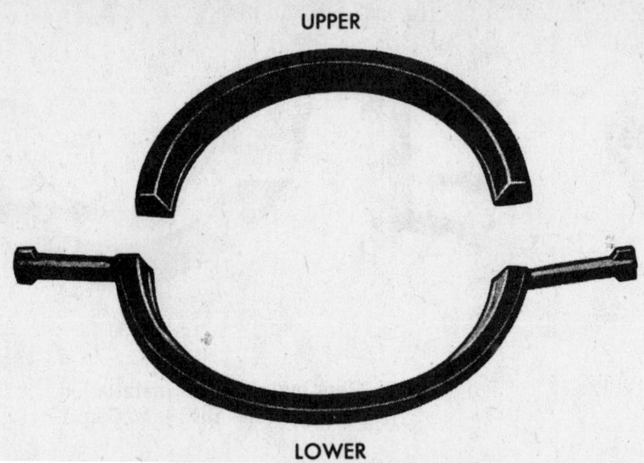

Rear main oil seal 6 cyl. engines
(© Chevrolet Div., G.M. Corp.)

grooves and butt side gaskets, use sealer especially at corners. Install corner bolts first (12-15 ft. lb.), then side rail screws (6-8 ft. lb).

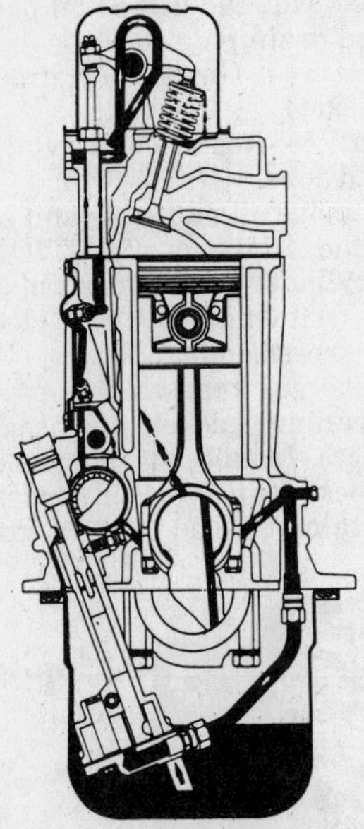

Engine lubrication 6 cyl.
235 & 261 engines
(© Chevrolet Div., G.M. Corp.)

7. Lower vehicle, fill crankcase to mark, start engine and check for leaks.

1963-1965 (Except Vans)

1. Raise front of vehicle and support on stands.
2. Remove road dirt at oil pan bolts and drain plug.
3. Drain oil, replace drain plug gasket.
4. Remove engine splash shields (if used).
   a. Automatic Transmission — Disconnect battery ground cable, remove starter (leave electrical connections intact and swing out of way), remove oil cooler lines, and flywheel pan.
   b. V8 Remove oil level stick and tube.
   c. 292 engine in 10-30 series—drain radiator, remove radiator and shroud, remove front motor mount bolts, using suitable jack with a flat block of wood (to

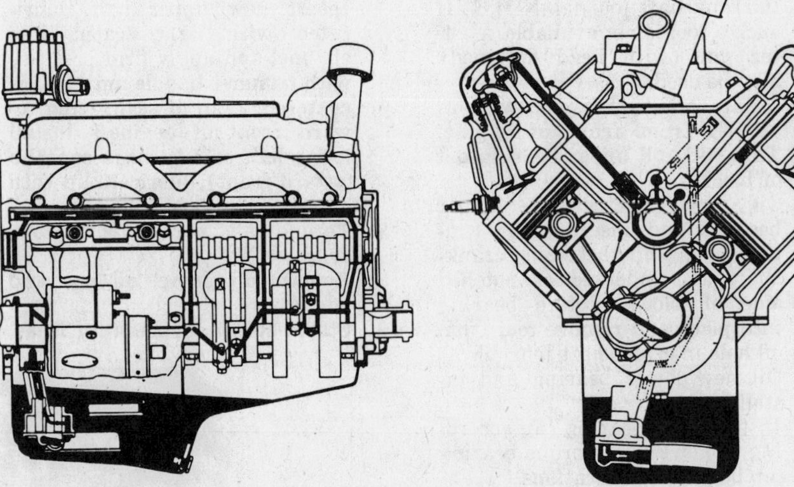

Engine lubrication 283, 327 & 350 engines (© Chevrolet Div., G.M. Corp.)

protect pan), raise engine and insert 2x4 blocks at motor mount.

5. Remove oil pan bolts and oil pan.
6. Reverse removal steps after cleaning gasket and seal surfaces.
7. Lower vehicle, fill crankcase to mark, fill cooling system (if drained), start engine and check for leaks.

NOTE: Bolts in front cover should be installed last because of alignment. Use gasket sealer as a retainer to hold side gaskets in place on block.

1963 and Up—Vans

1. Disconnect battery ground cable, loosen fan belt and remove radiator shroud top belt.
2. Remove radiator fan and pulley.
3. Raise vehicle, clean road dirt from oil pan.
4. Drain oil, replace drain plug gasket.
5. Remove engine splash shields if equipped.
6. Remove starter, leave electrical connections intact, swing out of way.
7. Automatic transmission models —remove oil cooler lines and converter pan.
8. Remove front motor mount bolts.
9. Remove accessory drive pulley (if used).
10. Engines with radiator shroud—drain radiator, remove lower radiator hose, remove lower shroud bolts and lower shroud out of way.
11. Using a jack, raise and support front of engine.
12. Remove crossmember to frame bolts, remove crossmember.
13. Remove oil pan bolts, remove oil pan. CAUTION: If any prolonged operations are planned (with pan off), it would be safer to re-install crossmember and lower engine on mounts.
14. Reverse removal steps to install after cleaning gasket and seal surfaces.
15. Lower vehicle, fill crankcase and radiator, start engine and check for leaks. NOTE: Use gasket sealer as a retainer to hold side gaskets in place on block. Bolts in front cover should be installed last. They are installed at an angle and holes line up after rest of pan bolts are tightened.

1966-1967 (Except Vans)

1. Raise front of vehicle and sup-

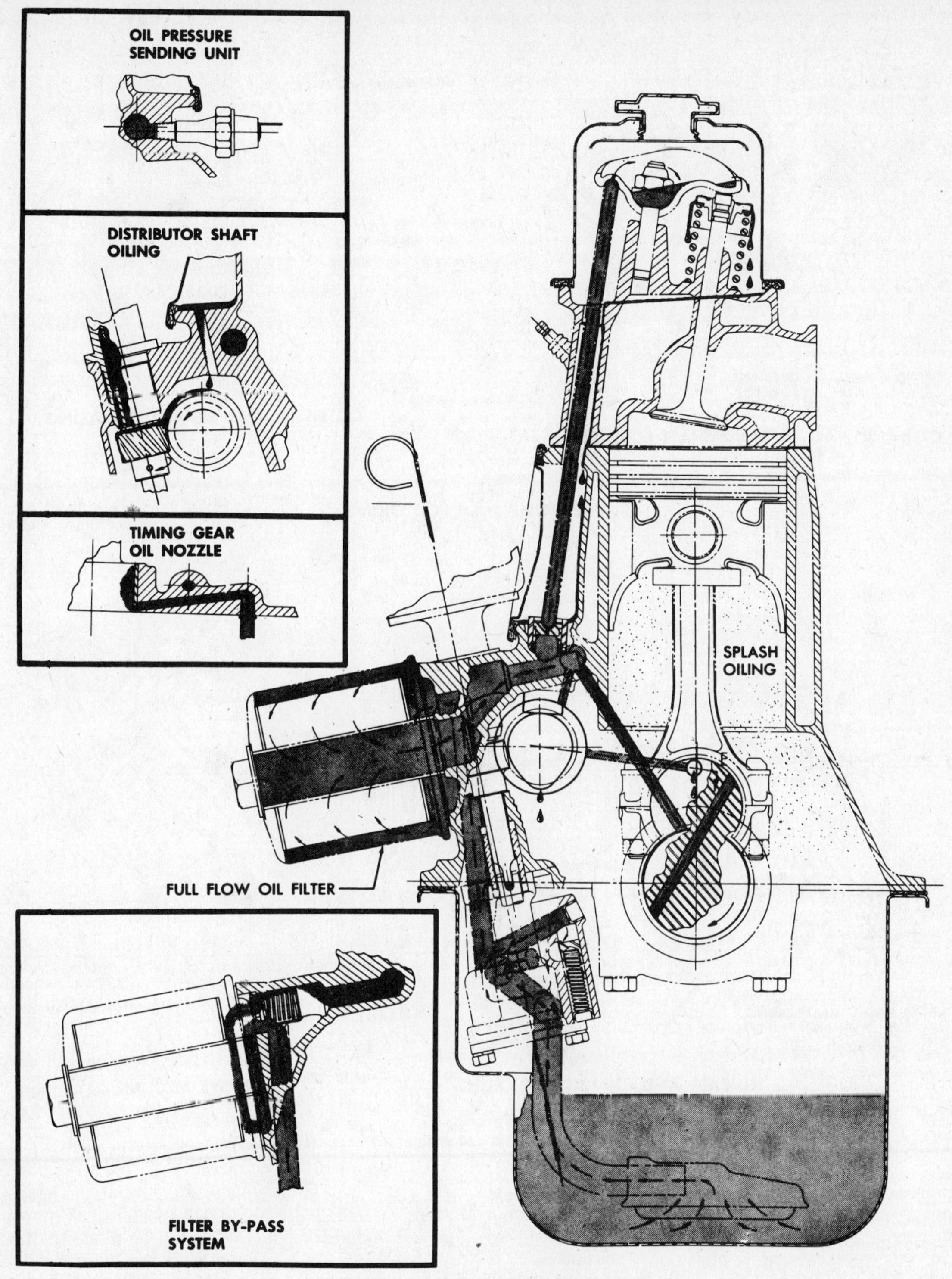

Engine lubrication 4 cyl. 153 engine
6 cyl. 194, 230, 250 & 292 engines
(© Chevrolet Div., G.M. Corp.)

port on stands.

2. Remove road dirt from pan and drain plug.
3. Drain oil, install new drain plug gasket.
4. Remove flywheel (converter) pan on automatic transmissions.
   a. V8—Remove oil dipstick and tube, remove exhaust crossover pipe.
   b. L6—Remove battery ground cable, remove starter.
   c. L6 — (C10-30) — Remove front motor mount bolts, using a block of wood under oil pan, raise engine with a jack high enough to insert blocks at motor mounts.
5. Remove oil pan and discard gaskets and seals.
6. Reverse removal steps to install after cleaning gasket and seal surfaces.
7. Lower vehicle, fill crankcase to mark, start engine and check for leaks.

NOTE: Use gasket sealer as a retainer to hold side gaskets in place on block. On 366 engine, start (3) bolts into front cover before tightening any other bolts or screws.

1968 and Up (Except Vans)

1. Raise front of vehicle and sup-

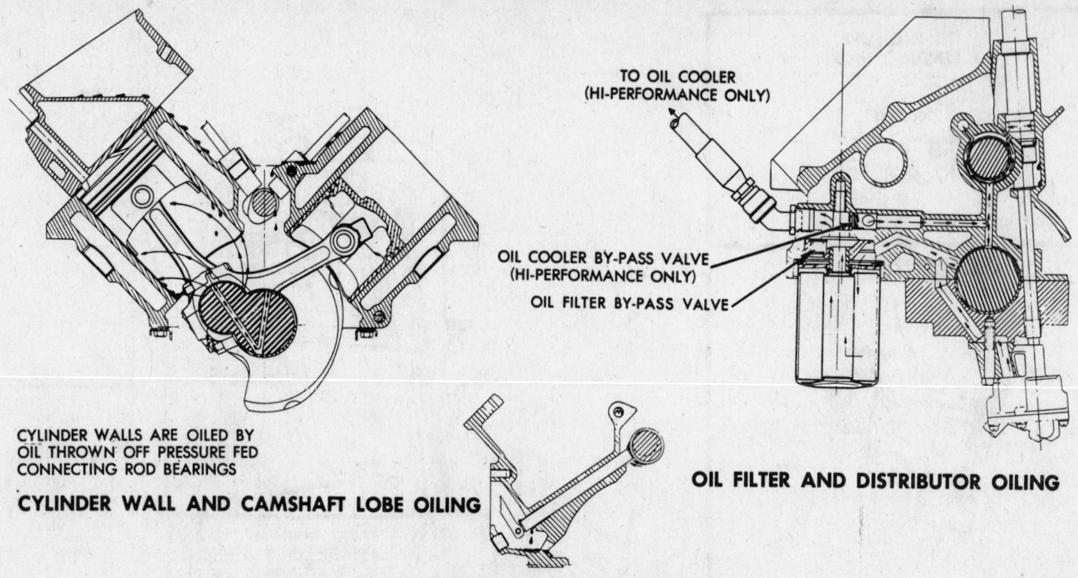

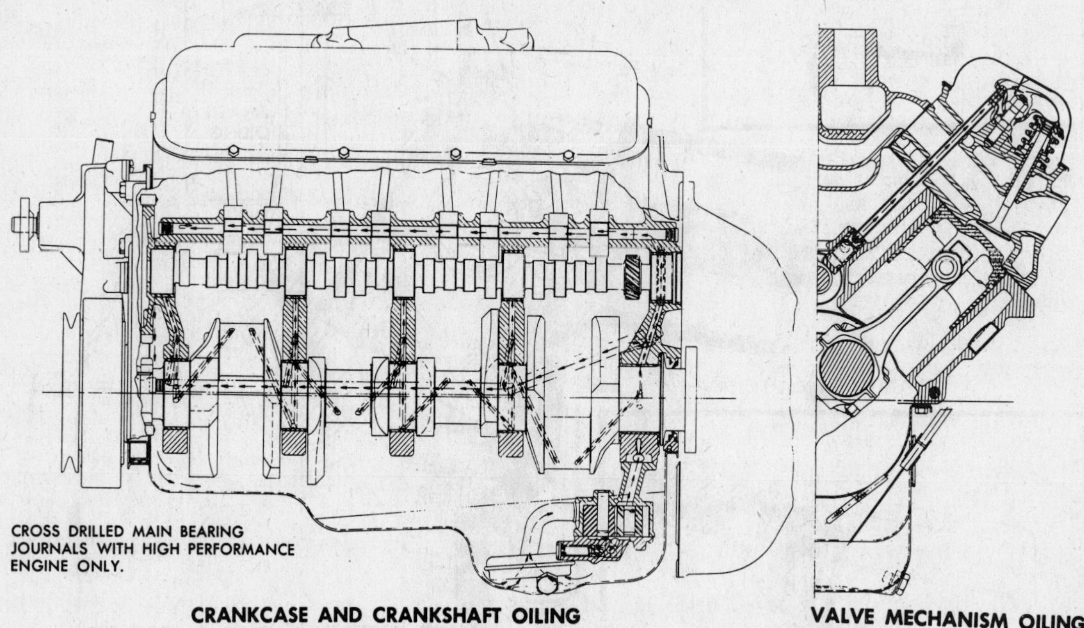

Engine lubrication 348, 366, 396, 409 & 424 engines (© Chevrolet Div., G.M. Corp.)

port on stands.
2. Remove road dirt from pan and drain plug.
3. Drain oil, replace drain plug gasket.
4. Remove converter pan on automatic transmission.
5. Remove battery ground cable, remove starter (leave electrical connections intact and swing aside).
6. V8—Remove dipstick and tube, remove exhaust crossover pipe.
7. C10-30—Remove front motor mount bolts, using a block of wood under oil pan, raise engine with a jack high enough to insert blocks at motor mounts.
8. Remove oil pan and discard gaskets and seals.
9. Reverse removal steps to install after cleaning all gasket and seal surfaces.
10. Lower vehicle, fill crankcase to level, start engine and check for leaks.

NOTE: Use gasket sealer as a retainer to hold side gaskets in place on block.

Oil Filters

Oil filters are related to oil change periods, which in turn are related to quality of oil used, type of service and operating conditions. Severe conditions such as frequent and prolonged idle periods may warrant more changes. Heavy sludge in pan or filter indicates oil change intervals should be shortened. Filter replacements should be made at time of oil change. It is recommended that filter be replaced with initial oil change and every second oil change thereafter.

Filters on in-line engines are located at right front of engine, "V" engines at left rear.

Replacement—Element Type

1. Remove drain plug (some models) in shell and drain, replace drain plug (if used).
2. Remove center stud, withdraw shell and empty (if no drain plug).
3. Lift out element and clean inside

of shell thoroughly.
4. Clean base and replace shell gasket, check bypass valve.
5. Install new element (with element gasket) in shell.
6. Install shell on base, drain plug away from engine, and tighten retaining bolt to engine and check for leaks, check oil level.

Replacement-Disposable (Spin-on) type

1. Turn filter from mounting base and discard.
2. Clean base and inspect gasket area.
3. Apply oil film to gasket and turn filter on stud until gasket seats then tighten ½ turn more.
4. Run engine, check for leaks, check oil level.

NOTE: On some vans the right hand engine splash shield will have to be removed.

Oil Pump

The pumps used are distributor driven gearm type. Oil pump consists of two spur gears and a relief valve in a two piece housing. On in-line engines, pump is mounted on cylinder block while on "V" engines pump is mounted on rear main cap inside oil pan. Pump gears and body are not serviced separately, replace pump as a unit. A baffle, incorporated on screen, eliminates oil pressure loss due to surging.

Removal and Installation

1. Remove oil pan—see oil pan removal.
2. In-line engines—Remove oil suction pipe at housing. CAUTION: Do not disturb screen on pick up pipe.
3. Remove two flange mounting bolts, remove pump.
4. Reverse removal steps to install, using new pan gasket, watch slot alignment with distributor tang. NOTE: Pump should slide easily into place, if not remove and relocate slot.
5. Refill with oil, start engine and check for leaks.

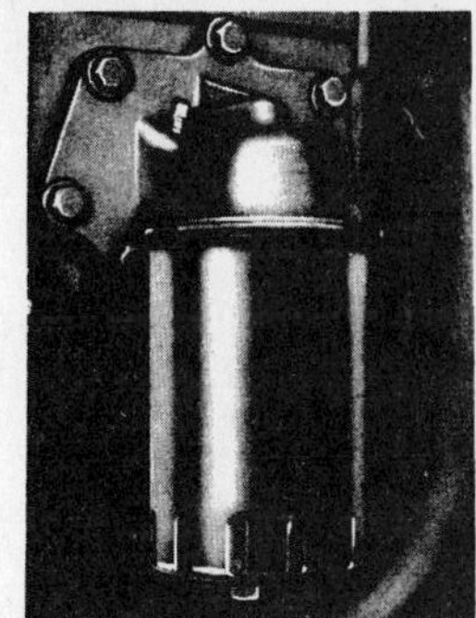

THROW-AWAY TYPE   REPLACEABLE ELEMENT TYPE

Engine oil filters (© Chevrolet Div., G.M. Corp.)

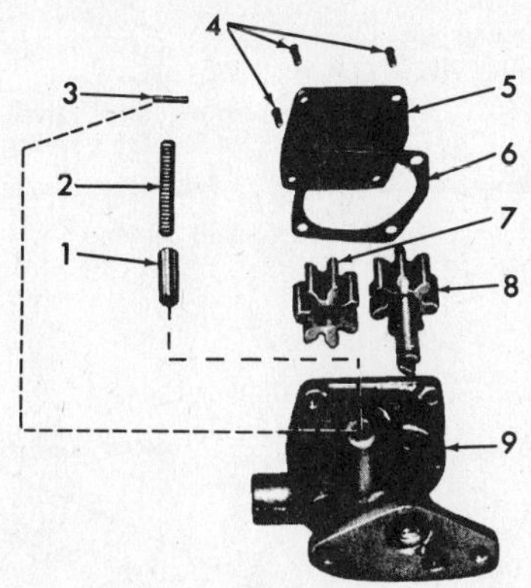

1 Pressure regulator valve
2 Pressure regulator spring
3 Retaining pin
4 Screws
5 Pump cover
6 Cover gasket
7 Idler gear
8 Drive gear and shaft
9 Pump body
10 Pickup screen and pipe

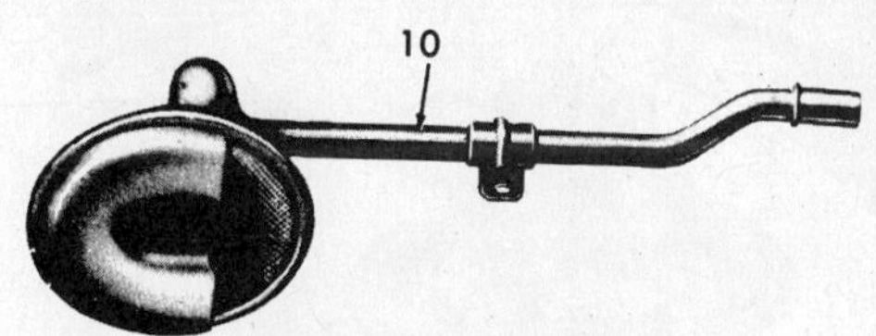

Oil pump inline engines
(© Chevrolet Div., G.M. Corp.)

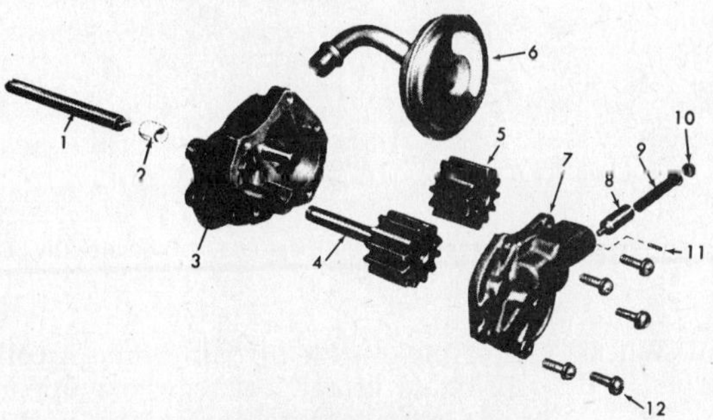

1 Shaft extension
2 Shaft coupling
3 Pump body
4 Drive gear and shaft
5 Idler gear
6 Pickup screen and pipe
7 pump cover
8 Pressure regulator valve
9 Pressure regulator spring
10 Washer
11 Retaining pin
12 Screws

Oil pump V8 engines
(© Chevrolet Div., G.M. Corp.)

Front Suspension

References

General instructions covering the front suspension and how to repair and adjust it, together with information on installation of front wheel bearings and grease seals, are given in the General Repair Section.

Definitions on the points of steering geometry are covered in the General Repair Section. This article also covers troubleshooting front end geometry and irregular tire wear.

Figures covering the caster, camber, toe-in, kingpin inclination, and turning radius can be found in the Wheel Alignment table of this section.

Types

1961-62

All trucks except 4 wheel drive have independent torsion bar front suspension with ball joints, using short and long type upper and lower control arms. On 19-40 series the torsion bar is connected to the lower control arm. The rear end of torsion bar is supported in an adjustable anchor, connected to a bracket or crossmember. Torsion bars are right and left hand, and must be installed on correct side for proper vehicle height. Bars are identified by colored

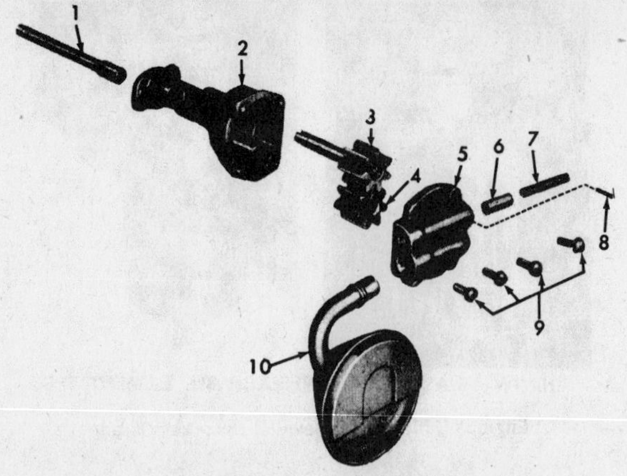

Oil pump (small V8 engines)
(© Chevrolet Div., G.M. Corp.)

1 Shaft extension
2 Pup body
3 Drive gear and shaft
4 Idler gear
5 Pump cover
6 Pressure regulator valve
7 Pressure regulator spring
8 Retaining pin
9 Screws
10 Oil pickup screen

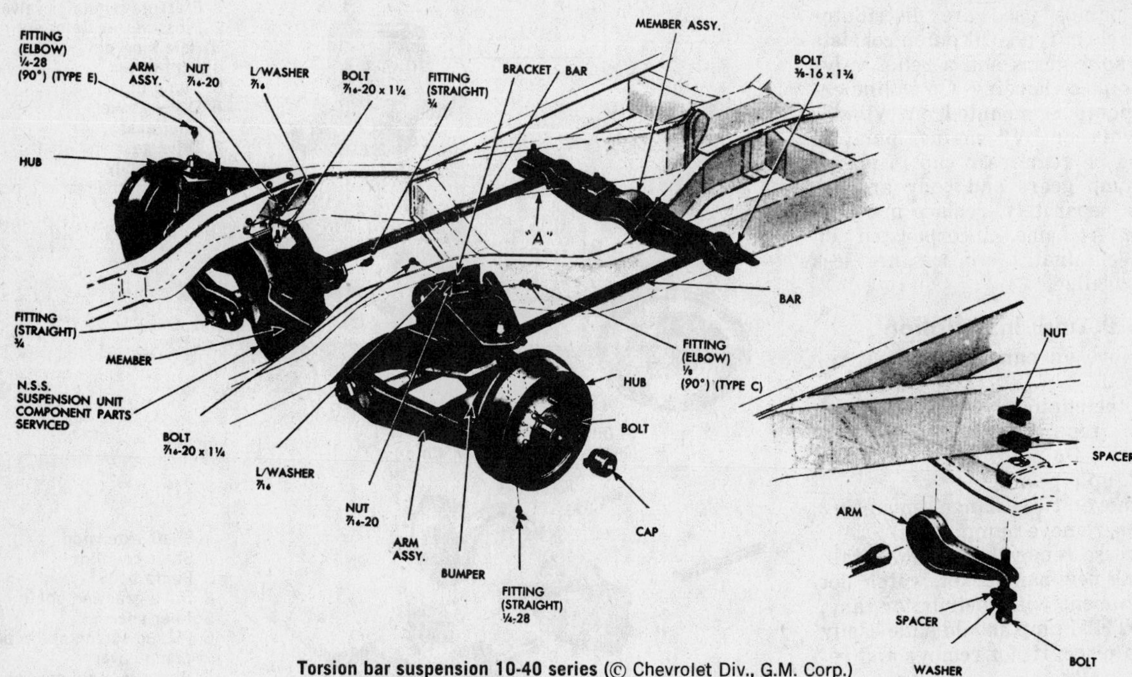

Torsion bar suspension 10-40 series (© Chevrolet Div., G.M. Corp.)

bands about 6″ from hex end. Whenever bar is adjusted, front end alignment must be checked.

1963 and Up

Two different types of front end suspension are used, independent coil spring and I-beam with leaf spring. Four wheel drive series uses a driving axle with tapered leaf springs.

Coil Spring Type

This suspension consists of upper and lower control arms, pivoting on steel threaded bushings on upper and lower control arm inner shafts which are attached to the crossmember. Control arms are connected to the steering knuckle by ball joints. A coil spring is seated between the upper and lower control arms, thus the lower control arm is the load carrying member.

I Beam Type

Front axle is the conventional reverse Elliott type with king pins that use full floating bushings up to approximately 7,000 lb. Front leaf spring is semi-elliptical, steel bushed at front eye, shackled at rear and seated on top of axle.

Spring Replacement 1961-62

Torsion bars, no springs except on four wheel drive vehicles.

Coil Spring

1963 and Up

1. Raise vehicle and place (high) stands under frame allowing control arm to hang free.
2. Disconnect shock absorber (and stabilizer if used) at lower end.
3. Using a floor jack, under center of lower control arm inner shaft, raise and remove tension from shaft. CAUTION: Install a safety chain through spring.
4. Remove both clamps or "U" bolts securing inner shaft to crossmember.
5. Release jack very cautiously, slowly lowering arm with spring until spring is free. Remove safety chain, remove spring.
6. Inspect front end especially at ball joints and both upper and lower control arm inner shaft bushings.
7. Reverse removal steps to install, use a long tapered drift to align holes of inner control arm shaft and crossmember while showly jacking arm into place.

Leaf Spring

1963 and Up

1. Wire brush all road dirt from threaded areas on U bolts, shock absorbers and stabilizer links, apply a good penetrant on threads.
2. Disconnect shock and stabilizer link at lower bracket.

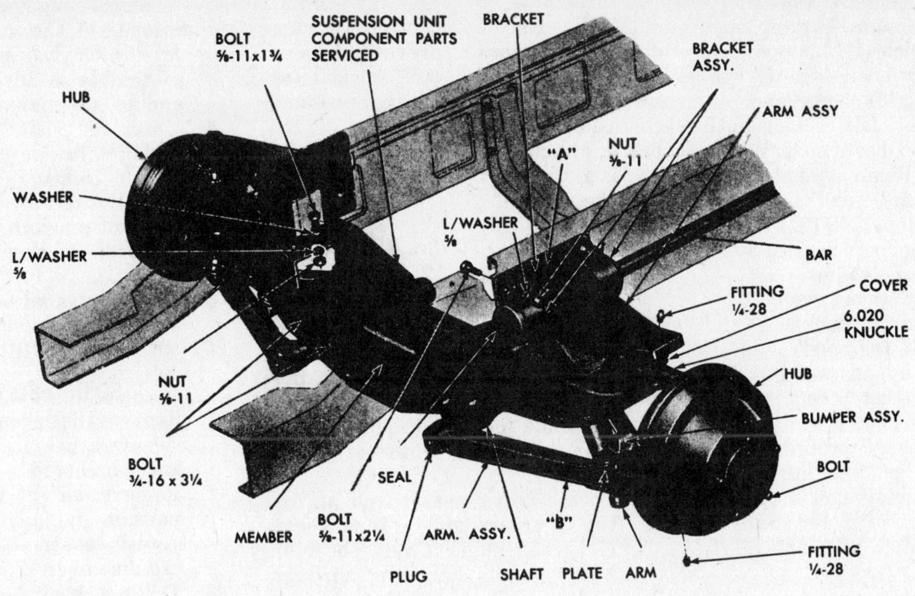

Torsion bar suspension 50-80 series (© Chevrolet Div., G.M. Corp.)

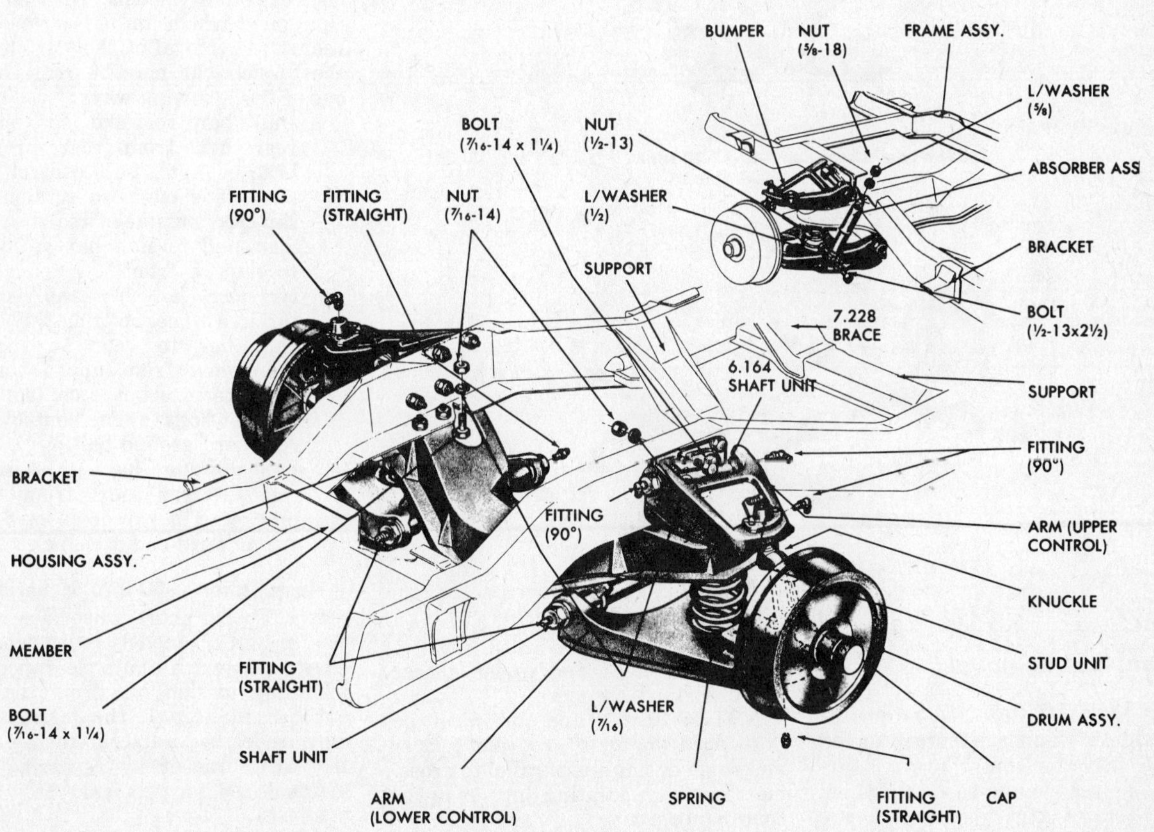

Coil spring type suspension (© Chevrolet Div., G.M. Corp.)

3. Loosen both spring U bolts.
4. Using jack under I-beam, raise front of vehicle and support at frame side rail with stand. Finish removing U bolts and rebound bumper. Lower jack until spring clears I-beam or tire rests on ground. Remove any caster wedges (shims) and set aside for installation. NOTE: Thick end of shim goes to rear of vehicle for increased caster.
5. Remove front spring eye bolt.
6. Remove rear shackle (and hanger cam if equipped).
7. Remove spring, inspect hangers and spring seat (center bolt index).
8. Reverse removal procedures to install after placing spring on axle with center bolt head indexed in seat and caster shims in place. Torque all nuts and lubricate.

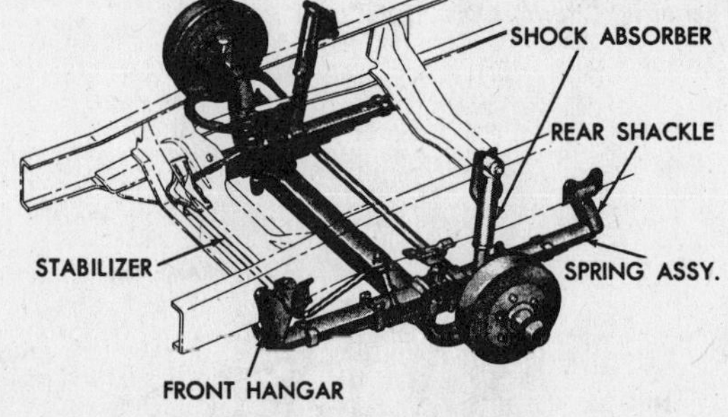

I beam type suspension P-20—P-20 series
(© Chevrolet Div., G.M. Corp.)

I beam type suspension 40, 50 and 60 series
(© Chevrolet Div., G.M. Corp.)

Torsion Bar Removal

1961-62 10 thru 40 Series

1. Remove upper control arm bumper from control arm.
2. Raise vehicle and support frame so control arms are at full rebound position (under no load).
3. Back off adjusting bolt to unwind torsion bar until bolt and lower spacer can be slipped out of anchor arm then pull anchor arm rearward off bar.
4. Pull torsion bar rearward out of front socket and away from vehicle.

NOTE: Exercise caution in handling torsion bars to prevent nicks or scratches. If bars are nicked or scratched, stress concentrations and corrosion can lead to failure of the bar in operation. Whenever a torsion bar is replaced, front end alignment must be checked.

Installation—10 thru 40 Series 1961-62

1. Prior to assembly of the rebound bumper, and with the front suspension in full rebound position, install front hex of torsion bar into lower control arm socket and slide forward to position the rear of bar at center of crossmember.
2. Locate upper spacer and nut on top of crossmember. Install special washer and lower spacer on bolt, insert bolt up through crossmember and upper spacer and start into nut.

NOTE: Spacer and nut must be positioned so rocker groove of spacer and ridge of nut are parallel to crossmember, with locating lug on lower spacer inboard.

CAUTION: The spacer must be properly positioned with lug inboard or convex on spacer will not seat in mating curvature of the torsion bar control arm.

3. Assemble torsion bar arm to rear hex of torsion bar so spacer and bolt can be slipped into arm when bolt engages about half the threads of the nut. Position the arm to the bar so the rear face of the bar is flush with the rear end of the bar within ±3/32".
4. Check the position of spacer and nut to be certain the lower spacer locating lug is inboard, then tighten torsion bar adjusting bolt on each side until vehicle assumes normal vehicle curb height.
5. Install rebound bumper.

Torsion Bar Removal

50 thru 80 Series

1. Remove the rebound bumper and remove shock absorber bolt from lower ball stud support.
2. Remove weight from front suspension by jacking frame until upper control arm contacts crossmember.
3. Drive lock pin up out of torsion bar rear bracket.
4. Pull torsion bar to the rear and out of control arm box and bracket hex.
5. Pull torsion bar out through rear bracket.

NOTE: On short wheelbase models, or other models with special equipment which limits clearance for rearward removal of the torsion bar, the torsion bar may be removed in one of the following ways:

a. Pull bar forward to remove rear hex from rear bracket. bracket nuts, pull control arm out far enough so torsion bar can clear outside of rear bracket, then pull torsion bar rearward to remove front hex from control arm. Tilt bar and remove through wheel opening.
b. Pull bar to rear to remove front hex from upper control arm. Remove upper control arm bracket bolts, swing control arm rearward around ball joint, then pull torsion bar forward to remove rear hex from rear bracket. Tilt bar downward and out forward end of vehicle.

Installation—50 thru 80 Series

NOTE: On short wheelbase models, or other models with special equipment which limits clearance for installing torsion bar from rear as outlined in Step 1, the torsion bar may be located adjacent to the control arm bracket by reversing the method used for removal (Step a or b, above).

1. Pass forward end of bar (end not notched) through bracket and place adjacent to the control arm.
2. Align the notched corner on rear hex of bar with drilled corner of bracket hex.
3. Slide bar into control arm and

Unloading torsion bar (© Chevrolet Div., G.M. Corp.)

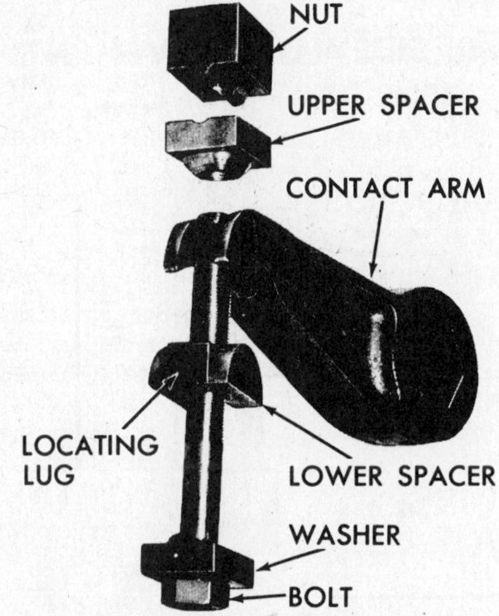

Torsion bar anchor bolt (© Chevrolet Div., G.M. Corp.)

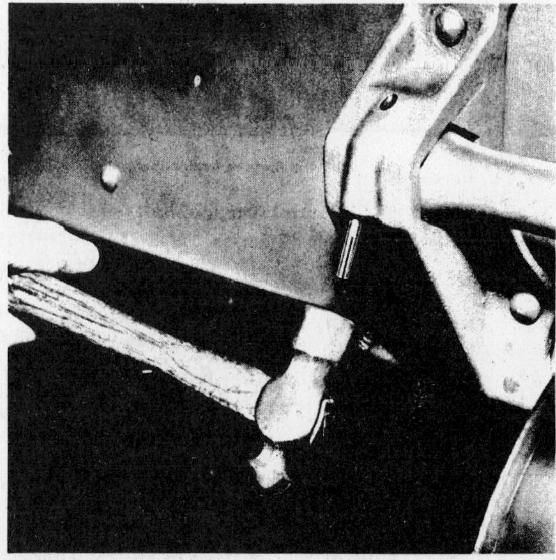
Installing torsion bar lock pin 50-80 series (© Chevrolet Div., G.M. Corp.)

bracket hexes, align notch in bar with lock pin hole in bracket and start lock pin into top of hole.

4. Drive lock pin into bracket flush with surface.
5. Allow weight of vehicle to rest on suspension and lubricate control arm.
6. Install shock absorber lower mounting bolt and rebound bumper.

Ball Joint Replacement

Torsion Bar Suspension—Upper and Lower

1. Remove torsion bar—see torsion bar R&R.
2. Remove wheel, tire and drum assembly.
3. Remove ball stud nut, release stud by rapping sides of steering knuckle at flats adjacent to stud. Separate stud from knuckle and remove seal.
4. Cut rivet heads with chisel and punch out rivets.
5. Install new ball joint with bolts and nuts furnished with joint. CAUTION: Do not substitute regular (soft) hardware in place of hardened bolts and nuts furnished.
   NOTE: On lower ball joint, 50-80 series, remove two joint-to-arm bolts, spread arms (watch special washers) and replace joint.
6. Reverse remaining removal steps to complete installation.

Coil Spring Suspension

Upper

1. Place jack under lower control arm, at coil spring, and raise vehicle until tire clears floor.
2. Remove tire, wheel and drum assembly.
3. Remove upper ball stud nut and break the stud taper from the steering knuckle by rapping sides of knuckle flats at stud. Separate stud from knuckle.
4. Remove rivets and bolt in new ball joint. Rivets can be chisled off, ground off or drilled out. CAUTION: Use special hardened bolts only when installing joint (furnished with joint).
5. Reverse remaining removal steps to complete installation.

Coil Spring Suspension

Lower

1. Jack vehicle at lower control arm spring seat and remove tire, wheel and drum assembly.
2. Remove coil spring, see coil spring R&R.
3. Remove ball stud nut at knuckle, use stud jack or rap stud loose from knuckle.

4. Remove lower control arm assembly.
5. Press out ball joint. Press new ball joint into arm. Make sure ball joint assembly is fully seated and square with arm. Check inner shaft bushings.
6. Reverse remaining removal steps to complete installation.

Description

The front axle is a Spicer hypoid gear axle unit equipped with steering knuckles. Axle assembly number and production date are stamped on left tube of assembly.

Conventional truck service brakes are provided on all 4-wheel drive units.

Transfer Case

The transfer case, also known as a drop gear box, is the unit which transmits power from the transmission to the rear and/or front axles and power take-off. Engagement of front wheel drive, power take-off or speed range is accomplished through control levers in the cab. The case is mounted to an adapter at the rear of the transmission.

Model number, ratio and production date are stamped on a plate located on top of the transfer case.

For service on transfer case refer to General Repair Section.

Front Drive Axle

Front Axle Assembly

Removal and Installation

1. Disassemble propeller shaft from front axle differential.
2. Raise front of vehicle until weight is removed from front springs.
3. Disconnect connecting rod from steering arm.
4. Disconnect brake hoses from frame fittings.
5. Disconnect shock absorbers from axle brackets.
6. Dismount "U" bolts from axle to separate axle from trunk springs.
7. Roll front axle out from under truck.
8. To install axle, reverse removal procedures.

Front Axle Shaft Assembly Removal and Installation

1. Support vehicle with front wheel free.
2. Place drain pan under wheel and hub grease cap.
3. Remove snap ring from axle shaft.
4. Remove drive flange as follows:

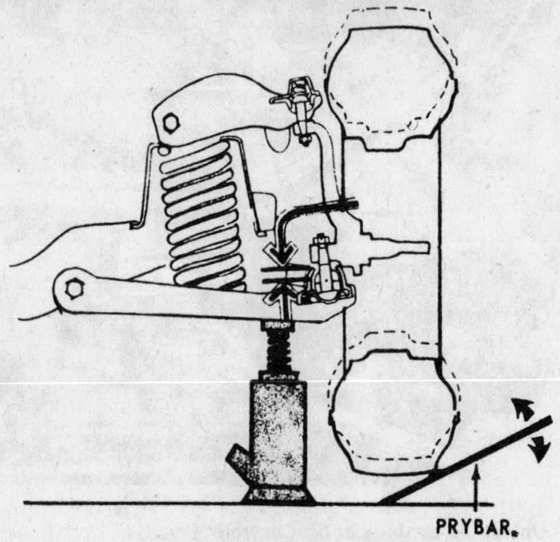

Ball joint check—unloaded
(© Chevrolet Div., G.M. Corp.)

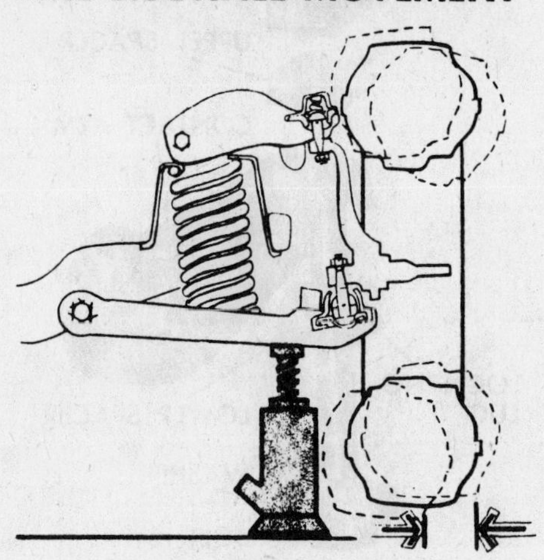

Ball joint check—unloaded
(© Chevrolet Div., G.M. Corp.)

a. On K10 and K14 models, pull splined drive flange from shaft and hub and remove spacer from hub.
b. On K20 and K25 models remove stud nuts and washers, remove drive flange and gasket.

5. Remove bearing lock nut and lock ring and remove adjusting nut.
6. Remove wheel, hub and drum as an assembly.
7. Remove bolts and lockwashers holding brake flange plate and spindle to steering knuckle.
8. Remove flange plate from steering knuckle and support the plate so brake hose will not be damaged.
9. Slide spindle from shaft.
10. Remove axle shaft and joint assembly.
11. To install, reverse removal procedures. Adjust bearings by tightening nut snug while rotating drum. Loosen nut 1/8 turn and assemble lock-washer by loosening nut to nearest hole, then assemble outer nut. Tighten nut to 40 ft. lbs. minimum.

Kingpin Trunnion

Adjustment

Front axle trunnion adjustment is generally necessary only when there is excessive play in steering, irregular wear on tires or persistent loosening of the tie rod.

1. Raise front end of vehicle, then place jack stands just inside of front springs.
2. Disconnect connecting rod and tie rod to allow independent movement of each steering knuckle.
3. Remove all cap screws which attach knuckle seal retainers, then move seals and retainers free of the knuckle.
4. At top of knuckle, apply torque wrench to one of the steering arms attaching stud nuts, then

FOUR WHEEL DRIVE

Four wheel drive components (© Chevrolet Div., G.M. Corp.)

check torque necessary to turn the steering knuckle.

Starting torque should be:

5 to 10 in. lbs.—Axle 44-5F

15 to 35 lbs.—Axle 44-5HDF

NOTE: Knuckle should turn smoothly through turning arc but have no vertical end play.

IMPORTANT: Temperature will affect turning torque considerably.

Steering Knuckle

Removal

1. Remove axle shaft and joint assembly.
2. Disconnect steering connecting rod from steering arm.
3. Disconnect the tie rod from steering knuckle.
4. Remove the seal retainers (2 pieces) from knuckle.
5. Remove the felt seal, rubber seal and the seal ring from knuckle and let them hang on axle housing.
6. Remove upper and lower bearing retainers and shims from knuckle.
7. Remove knuckle from housing and remove bearing cones from axle housing.

NOTE: On K20 HD models the upper kingpin bearing consists of a cup and bushing assembly. The kingpin and bushing are slotted to receive a key which acts to connect the two components so that they will pivot together. Removal procedure for this installation is as listed above.

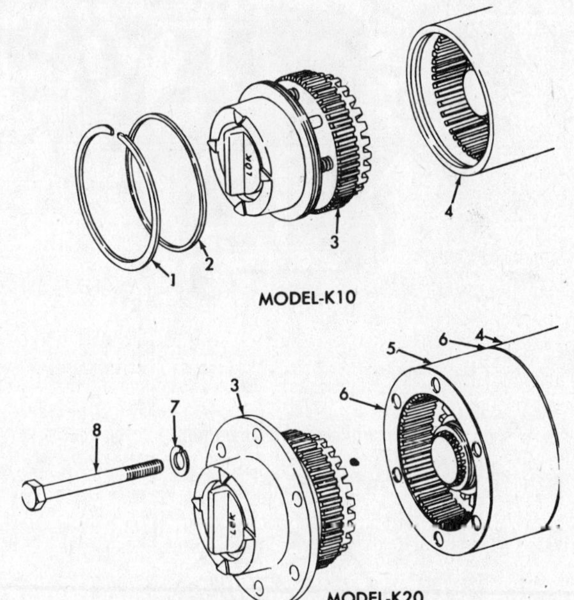

1 Lock ring
2 "O" ring seal
3 Hub assembly
4 Wheel hub housing
5 Extension housing
6 Gaskets
7 Bolts (6)
8 Lock washer (6)

Locking front hub installation
(© Chevrolet Div., G.M. Corp.)

Free Wheeling Hub

Reference

Free-wheeling hubs are available for the front wheels of four wheel drive vehicles. The purpose of these hubs is to reduce friction and wear by disengaging the front axle shafts, differential and drive line from the front wheels when the vehicle is operated under conditions where front wheel drive is not needed.

The engagement and disengagement of free-wheeling hubs is a manual operation which must be performed at each front wheel. The transfer case control lever must be in 2-wheel drive position when locking or unlocking hubs. Both hubs must be in the fully locked or fully unlocked position. They must not be in the free-wheeling position when low all wheel drive is used as the additional torque output in this position can subject the rear axle to severe strain and rear axle failure may result.

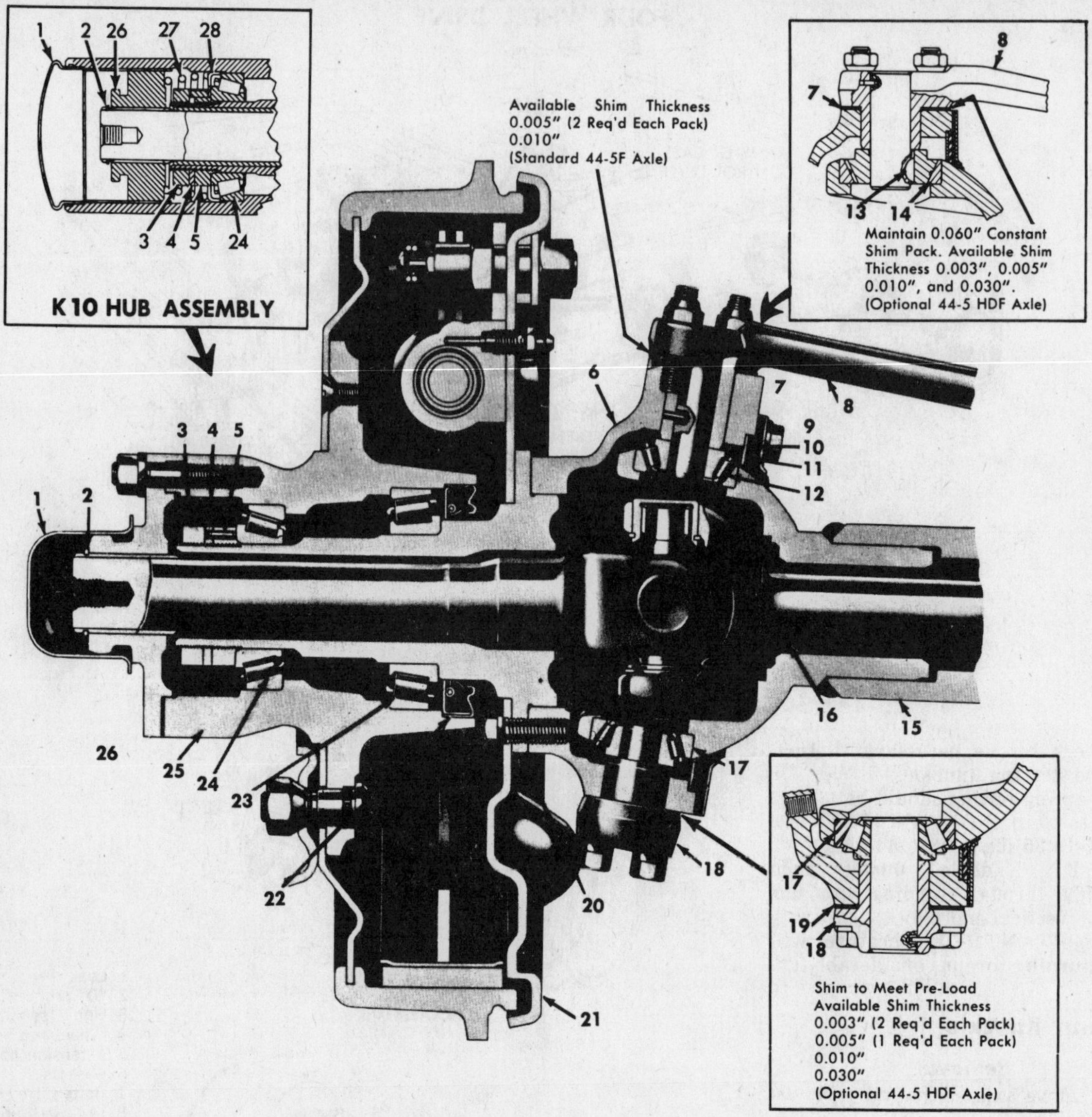

K10 HUB ASSEMBLY
Available Shim Thickness
0.005" (2 Req'd Each Pack)
0.010"
(Standard 44-5F Axle)
Maintain 0.060" Constant
Shim Pack. Available Shim
Thickness 0.003", 0.005"
0.010", and 0.030".
(Optional 44-5 HDF Axle)
Shim to Meet Pre-Load
Available Shim Thickness
0.003" (2 Req'd Each Pack)
0.005" (1 Req'd Each Pack)
0.010"
0.030"
(Optional 44-5 HDF Axle)

Steering knuckle and wheel hub (© Chevrolet Div., G.M. Corp.)

1 Hub cap
2 Snap ring
3 Lock nut
4 Lock ring
5 Adjustig nut
6 Steering knuckle
7 Upper adjusting shims
8 Steering arm
9 Seal retainer
10 Seal ring
11 Rubber seal
12 Knuckle bearing (upper)
13 Bushing Woodruff key (H.D.)
14 Knuckle bushing (H.D. K20)
15 Axle housing
16 Axle shaft
17 Knuckle bearing (lower)
18 Bearing retainer
19 Lower adjusting shims (H.D. K20)
20 Spindle
21 Brake flange plate
22 Wheel bearing seal
23 Wheel bearing (inner)
24 Wheel bearing (outer)
25 Wheel hub
26 Drive flange
27 Spring
28 Retainer

ADAPTER ASM
TRANSFER CASE ASM
TRANSMISSION

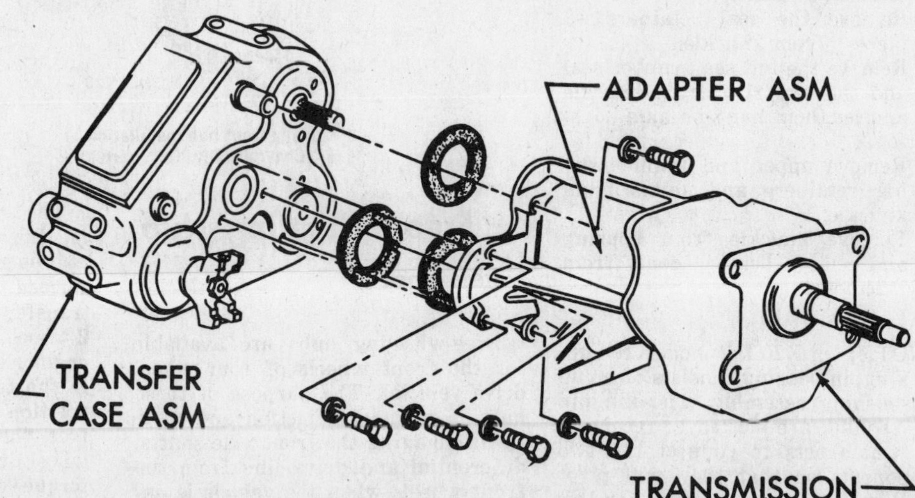

Transfer Case Assembly (Typical)

Removal

K10 Series through 1967 & All K20 Series

1. Turn hub key to set hub to *"free"* or *"disengage"* position.
2. Remove outer clutch ring, cap and cam assemblies as follows:
   a. On K10 and K14 models remove internal snap ring from hub and pull assembly out of hub.
   b. On K20 and K25 models remove bolts retaining hub cap assembly to wheel hub, pull assembly and extension housing away from hub and remove gasket.
3. Remove snap ring from end of axle shaft.
4. Pull bushing and inner clutch ring assembly shaft.

Installation

1. Place bushing and inner clutch ring over axle spline with clutch teeth outward. Slide on until bushing bottoms in wheel hub and install snap ring in axle shaft.
2. Install outer clutch ring, cap and cam assembly as follows:
   a. On K10 and K14 models, start assembly straight into hub taking care to work "O" ring seal past the snap ring groove in hub. Install snap ring in hub.
   b. On K20 and K25 models, place gasket on hub, align mounting holes in clutch ring and cap with holes in hub and install bolts and lockwashers.
3. Turn knob to check for proper locking.

Removal

K10 Series 1968 and Up

1. Turn actuator lever to set hub to "lock" position and raise vehicle.
2. Remove retaining plate bolts and remove retaining plate actuating knob and "O" ring.
3. Remove internal snap ring, outer clutch retaining ring and actuating cam body.
4. Remove axle shaft snap ring.
5. Remove axle shaft sleeve and clutch ring assmbly and inner clutch ring and bushing assembly.
6. Remove pressure spring and spring retainer plate.

Installation

1. Lubricate all parts. Install spring retainer plate (flange side facing bearing) over spindle nuts and seat retainer against bearing outer cup.
2. Install pressure spring into position. Large O.D. seats against spring retaining plate. NOTE: When spring is seated, spring extends past the spindle nuts by approximately ⅞".
3. Place inner clutch ring and bushing assembly into axle shaft sleeve and clutch ring assembly and install as an assembly into the axle shaft. Press in on assembly and install axle shaft snap ring. NOTE: Install 7/16x20 bolt in axle shaft end and pull outward on axle shaft to aid in installing snap rings.
4. Install activating cam body (cams facing outward), outer clutch retaining ring and internal snap ring.
5. Install "O" ring on retaining plate and install activating knob and retaining plate. NOTE: Install activating knob with knob in "lock" position, grooves in knob must fit into activator cam body.
6. Install cover bolts and seals.
7. Turn knob to *"free"* position to check for proper operation.
8. Lower vehicle.

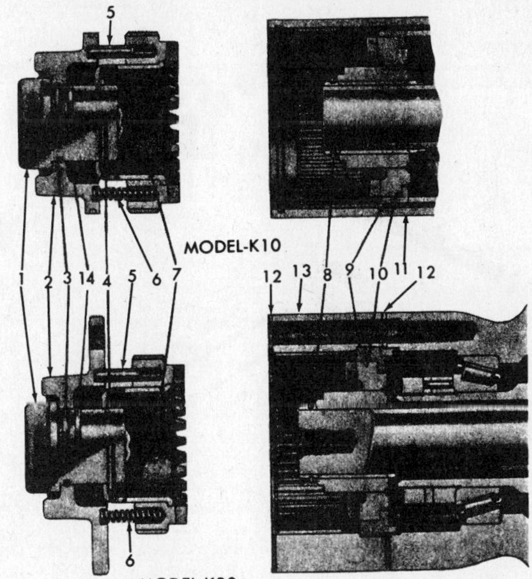

1 Key knob
2 Retainer cap
3 Key knob seal
4 Key knob retainer pin
5 Cap aligning pin
6 Spring
7 Outer clutch gear assembly
8 Axle shaft lock ring
9 Collar (bushing) internal clutch gear
10 Internal clutch gear
11 Wheel hub housing
12 Extension housing gaskets
13 Extension housing
14 Snap ring

Hub assembly (© Chevrolet Div., G.M. Corp.)

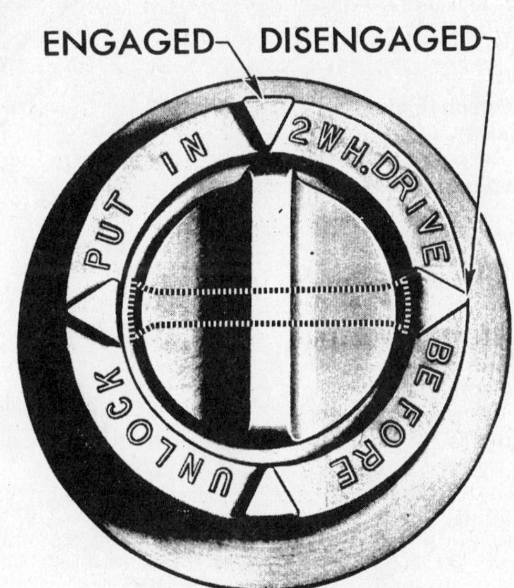

Locking front hub key positions
(© Chevrolet Div., G.M. Corp.)

Steering Gear

Manual Steering Gear

Instructions covering the overhaul of the steering gear will be found in the General Repair Section.

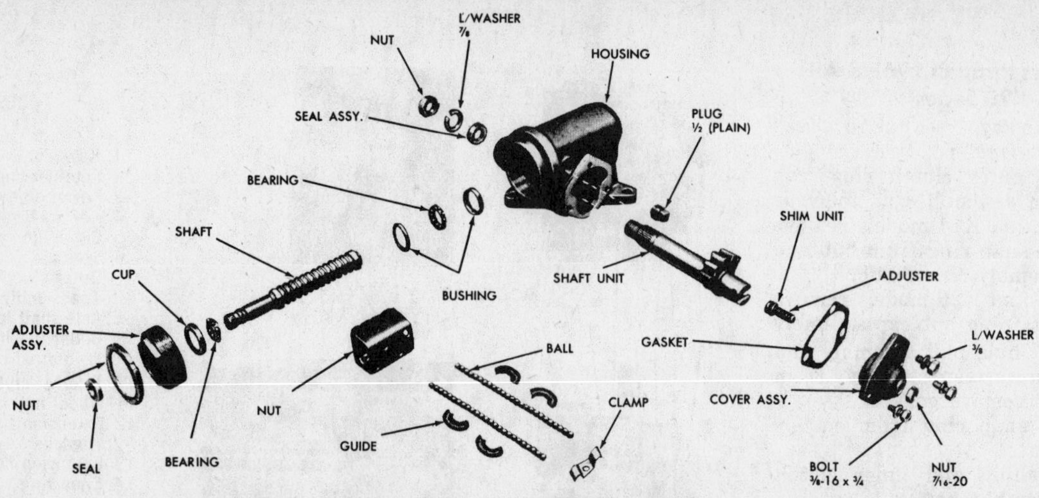

Manual steering gear (© Chevrolet Div., G.M. Corp.)

Power Steering Gears

Troubleshooting and repair instructions covering power steering gears are given in the General Repair Section.

Type

Steering Gear is recirculating ball device with several types of linkag used, on power steering units the power assist is supplied by an enginc driven, valve type pump. An oil cooler is used on large trucks.

Steering Gear Replacement

Except Van and Forward Control

1. Set wheels in straight ahead position. Mark alignment of upper and lower steering shafts. Loosen champ bolt at coupling (coupling is splined), or separate at joint. On some models to remove coupling, either lower steering gear or raise mast jacket assembly.
2. Mark pitman arm and sector shaft, for reassembly, and using puller remove pitman arm, or remove drag link from pitman arm if sufficient room between drag link stud and frame rail. If clamp type pitman arm is used, spread just enough to remove.
3. Remove power steering hoses from gear assembly, cap lines and plug openings (if equipped). from vehicle.
4. Remove gear housing to frame rail bolts (watch shims), remove from vehicle.
5. Reverse removal steps to install. NOTE: Do not hammer pitman arm on sector shaft, use nut to pull into position. On power steering vehicles, raise front when bleeding.

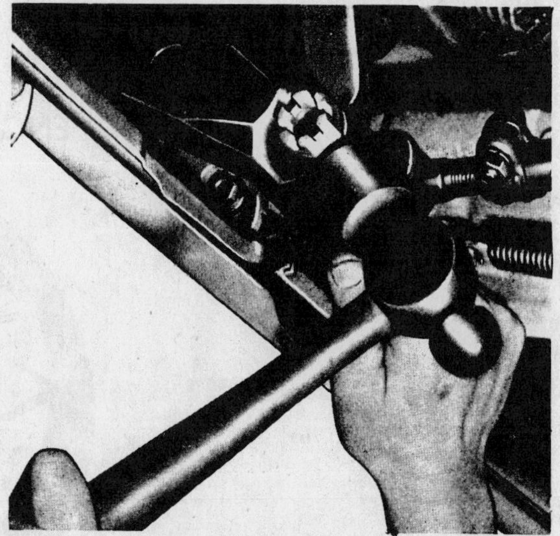
Ball stud removal (typical)
(© Chevrolet Div., G.M. Corp.)

K-10-20 steering linkage
(© Chevrolet Div., G.M. Corp.)

Steering Gear Replacement

Van and Forward Control

1. Disconnect turn signal harness from chassis harness at connector.
2. Remove horn button, cup, spring, bushing and horn wire.
3. Remove tube and worm nut and washer.
4. Use puller to remove steering wheel (mark position for reinstalling).
5. Disconnct brake pedal from pedal assembly (Van).
6. Pull back floor mat and disconnect toe-pan seal, remove toe-pan cover.
7. Remove mast jacket bracket from support.
8. Remove power steering hoses from gear assembly, cap lines and plug openings (if equipped).
9. Hoist vehicle or raise by jack and support (Van).
10. Remove deflector and extension (Van).
11. Use puller to remove pitman arm (mark position for reassembly). Insufficient room between drag link ball stud and frame rail requires pulling pitman arm. If clamp type pitman arm is used, spread just enough to remove.
12. Disconnect transmission shift linkage from levers (Van).
13. Remove steering gear to frame bolts.
14. Remove steering gear with mast jacket (and shift linkage—Van).
15. Reverse removal steps to install.

NOTE: Do not hammer pitman arm on sector shaft, use nut to pull into position. Directional signal control must be in neutral position when installing steering wheel to prevent damage to cancelling cam.

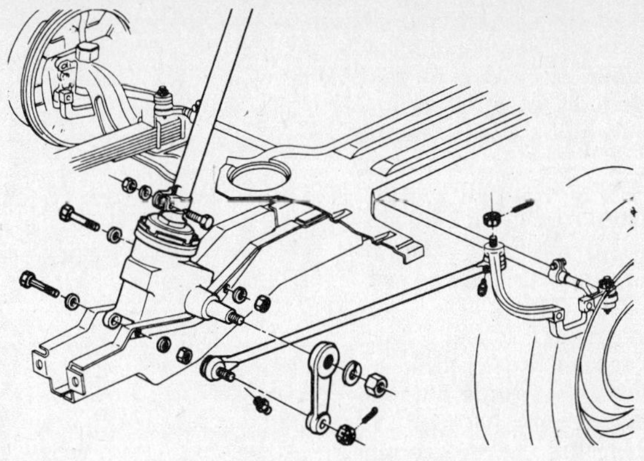

(© Chevrolet Div., G.M. Corp.)
Chevy Van steering gear mounting

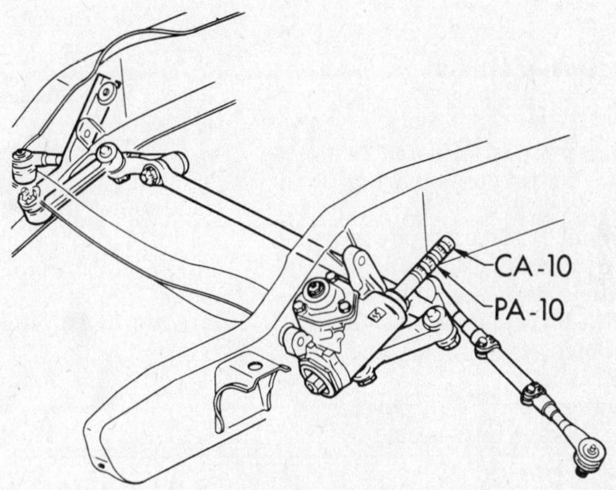

C-10-20-30 steering linkage
(© Chevrolet Div., G.M. Corp.)

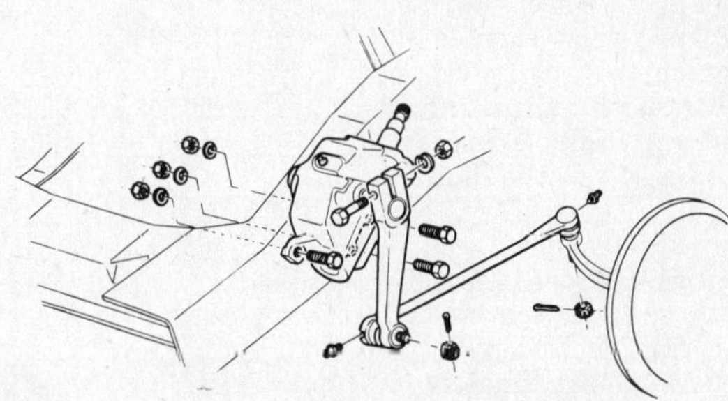

20-40-50-60 ser. steering linkage (typical)
(© Chevrolet Div., G.M. Corp.)

Adjustments (on Vehicle)

Manual Steering

1. Check tire pressure and inspect steering linkage.
2. Check gear housing for lubricant, tighten cover side plate.
3. Check steering gear housing to frame rail bolts.
4. Set wheels in straight ahead position.
5. Disconnect drag link from pitman arm, remove pitman arm on Vans.
6. Loosen sector (cross) shaft lock nut and back off lash adjuster. This lessens steering worm bearing load by reducing tooth mesh contact.
7. Check load on steering gear by measuring pull on steering wheel with scale. Pull is measured at rim of wheel with scale tangent to rim of wheel (½ to 3 lb. pull according to size of truck).
8. If pull is not within limits, adjust worm bearings. Loosen worm bearing lock nut and turn adjusting nut in until there is no perceptible end play. Tighten lock nut. Using an inch-pound torque wrench and socket on steering wheel nut (remove horn wire and button), measure torque (3 inch pounds to 14 inch pounds according to size of truck). A rough feeling when rotating steering wheel indicates defective worm bearings. Some early heavy duty steering gears use shims under steering gear housing top cover, and also use a back-up adjuster. Removal of shims decreases worm bearing end play. Back-up adjuster setting is made last. After adjusting worm bearings and lash, then tighten back-up adjuster until adjuster bottoms against ball nut return guide clamp, then back-off adjuster ⅛ to ¼ turn and secure with lock nut.
9. After proper adjustment of worm bearings is obtained, center steering wheel by turning wheel gently from one stop to the other, counting the number of turns. Turn wheel back exactly half way to center position (high point). Mark steering

wheel rim at top or bottom center with tape. Turn lash (slotted) adjuster clockwise to take out all lash in gear teeth and tighten lock nut. Check steering free play. NOTE: If maximum adjustment is exceeded, turn lash adjuster screw back (counter-clockwise) and then come in (clockwise) slowly on adjustment. CAUTION: Do not bounce steering wheel hard against stops with drag link removed, worm ball guide damage can result.

10. Connect drag link or replace pitman arm, road test and check steering.

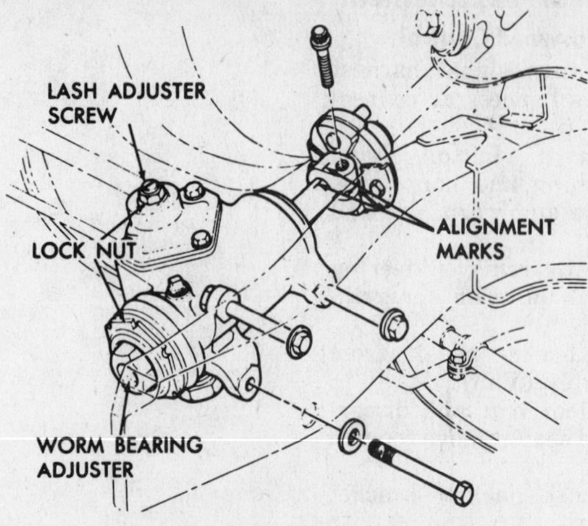

Steering gear adjustment points (typical)
(© Chevrolet Div., G.M. Corp.)

Adjustments (on Vehicle)

Power Steering

Power steering gear is adjusted in the same manner as manual steering gear, however starting in 1967, sector lash adjustment is the only power steering gear adjustment that can be made on the vehicle. In order to make this adjustment, it is necessary to check the combined valve drag and worm bearing preload.

1. Check power steering fluid level, check belt tension and hose for leaks or kinks.
2. Remove drag link from pitman arm.
3. Disconnect horn wire, remove horn button assembly.
4. Center steering wheel—turn through its full travel then locate wheel at center of its travel.
5. Loosen sector lash adjusting screw locknut and back off (slotted) adjusting screw to the limit of its travel.
6. Check combined valve drag and worm bearing preload with inch-pound torque wrench and socket on steering shaft nut, by rotating wheel approximately 20° in each direction. Note highest reading.
7. Tighten sector lash adjusting screw until torque at steering wheel meets specifications (4 to 18 inch pounds according to truck size). Secure lock nut. NOTE: If maximum adjustment is exceeded, turn lash adjuster screw back (counter-clockwise) and then come in (clockwise) slowly on adjustment. CAUTION: Do not bounce steering wheel hard against stops with drag link removed, worm ball guide damage can result. When bleeding hydraulic system, raise front of vehicle.
8. Replace drag link, horn button assembly and connect horn wire.
9. Road test and check steering.

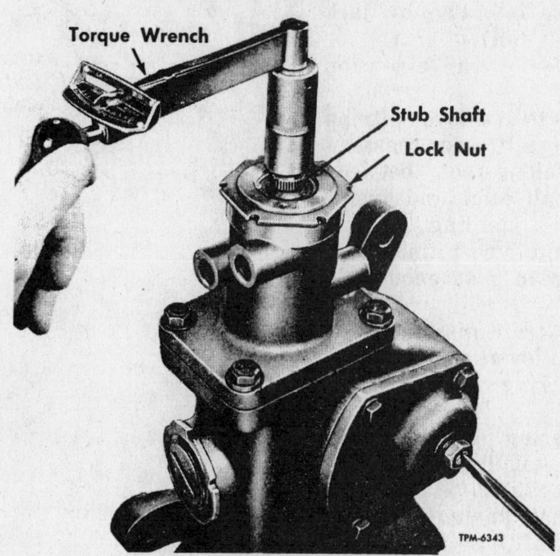

Adjusting sector shaft preload
(© Chevrolet Div., G.M. Corp.)

40-50-60 series power steering gear and central valve (typical)
(© Chevrolet Div., G.M. Corp.)

Idler Arm

Removal

1. Jack up front of vehicle and support or raise on hoist.
2. Remove cotter pin and castellated nut from ball stud at relay rod. Remove ball stud from relay rod by using a tapered driver or tapping on relay rod boss. Support relay rod so impact will center on ball stud.
3. Remove idler arm to frame bolts, remove idler arm.

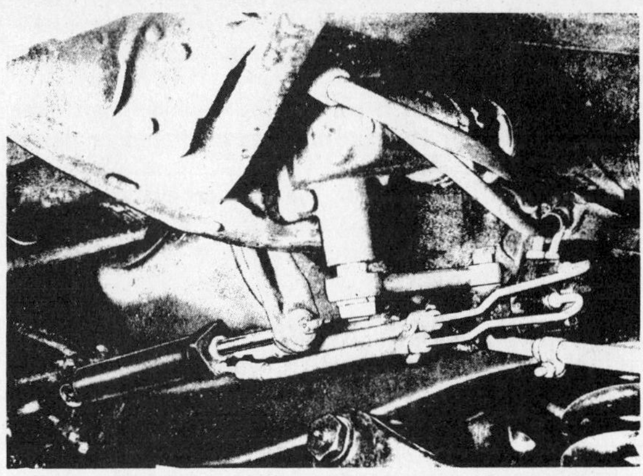

C-10-20-30 series control valve and power cyl. installed
(© Chevrolet Div., G.M. Corp.)

Installation

1. Position idler arm on frame and install mounting bolts. (special plain washers under bolt heads). Torque nuts.
2. Make sure threads on ball stud and in ball stud nut are good—ball stud may turn in sket if threads are damaged. Check ball and seal.
3. Install idler arm ball stud in relay rod (seal in place) and install castellated nut and cotter pin. Torque nut to specifications.
4. Lower vehicle or remove from hoist.

Clutch

Description—Types

Clutches used on inline engines are single (driven) disc with either of two types of pressure (drive) plates, diaphragm or coil spring. "V" engines use a single disc with coil spring pressure plate. Heavy duty clutches use two discs. The two plate clutch consists of three basic assemblies, the cover with rear pressure plate assembly, front pressure plate and two discs. The front pressure plate, located between the two driven discs, has two friction surfaces and is coupled to rear pressure plate through steel drive straps bolted at each of its four driving bosses. Diaphragm spring covers operate with light pedal pressure while coil spring levers combine operating ease and high torque capacity. The operating controls are either mechanical or hydraulic. Discs have torsion spring centers.

Adjustments

Free Pedal Travel

This adjustment is for the amount of pedal travel (measured at pedal) before clutch release bearing contacts the levers, or fingers of a coil spring cover or the diaphragm spring of a diaphragm clutch cover. This is called free-play. With normal clutch wear the amount of free-play is reduced and in time this will cause the release bearing to be in constant contact with the cover. This in turn will cause clutch disc slippage resulting in premature failure of disc and release bearing. It is necessary to maintain sufficient free pedal travel for clutch efficiency and long life.

Mechanical Linkage

1. Check linkage for excessive wear (will create false free play).
2. Disconnect fork arm return spring.
3. Back off locknut "A" at least ½" from swivel.
4. Hold fork push rod against fork to keep release bearing touching fingers (or diaphragm). Push rod will slide through swivel at cross shaft.
5. Adjust nut "B" to obtain approximately 3/16" to ¼" clearance between nut "B" and swivel.
6. Release push rod, connect pull back spring at fork and tighten nut "A" to lock swivel against nut "B".
7. Check free play at pedal for ¾" to 1" clearance.

Hydraulic Controls

1. Check master cylinder, cylinder must be filled and no air in system.
2. 1961-62—Loosen lock nut on master cylinder push rod and turn eccentric bolt to obtain ¼" free pedal travel, tighten lock nut.
3. 1963 and Up—Loosen lock nut on slave cylinder push rod and turn adjusting nut at fork arm to obtain ¼" free pedal travel, tighten lock nut (3/16" at fork arm).

NOTE: This should insure master cylinder piston moving sufficiently to uncover port in master cylinder reservoir.

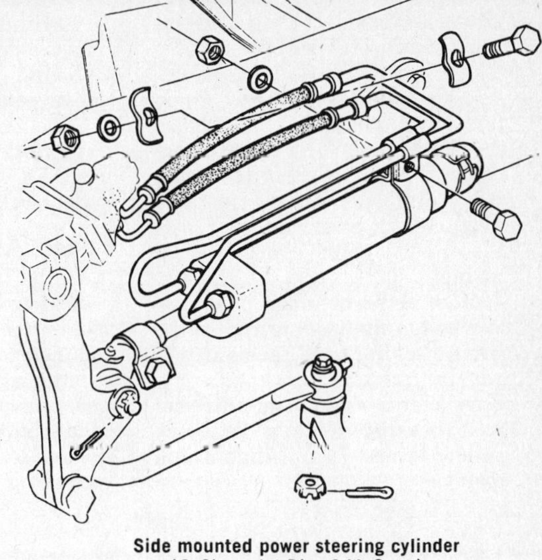

Side mounted power steering cylinder
(© Chevrolet Div., G.M. Corp.)

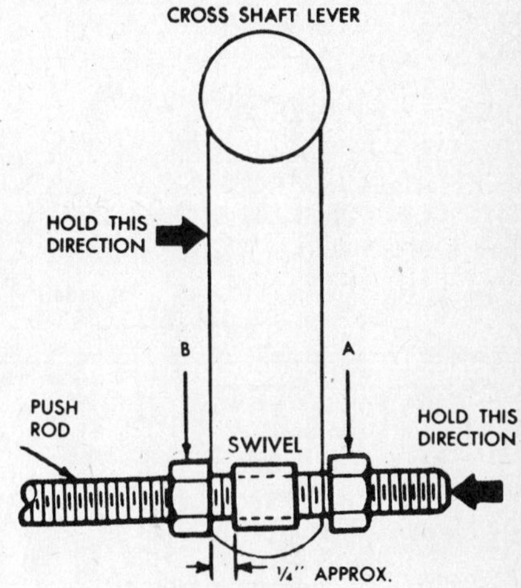

Free travel adjustment
(© Chevrolet Div., G.M. Corp.)

Total Pedal Travel

Mechanical Linkage

1. Check linkage for excessive wear.
2. Loosen lock nut on adjustable pedal stop. (conventional pedal —on pedal support bracket under dash).
3. Turn adjustment bolt until clutch pedal is equal in height to brake pedal.
4. Tighten lock nut.
5. Pedal Free Travel must be made after this adjustment.

NOTE: Inverted pedal—additional pedal travel will be gained by cutting rubber bumper stop. Since shortening the bumper increases free play, the lash must be reduced to gain the additional pedal travel. Insufficient clutch release leads to low and reverse gear clash.

Hydraulic Controls

1. Locate clutch pedal bumper so clutch pedal, in fully released position, is even with brake pedal (if equipped with adjustable stop). Check reservoir.
2. Disconnect clutch fork return spring.
3. Bottom slave cylinder push rod and piston by pushing rod to the front of cylinder as far as it will go.
4. Move clutch fork arm until release bearing contacts pressure plate levers (or diaphragm spring).
5. Adjust clearance between slave cylinder push rod fulcrum (wedge) by adjusting nut behind it to 3/16" clearance between wedge and nut (hold wedge against fork arm).
6. Check pedal free play.

NOTE: Clearance can be checked with shank of 3/16 drill.

Cover Assemblies

While no wear adjustment is needed (except Spicer), original settings at time of manufacture must be retained for good clutch operation. If a diaphragm clutch cover fails to release properly, after first checking pedal travel and pedal lash and linkage for looseness, replace diaphragm retracting springs. This can be done in the vehicle. If trouble still persists the diaphragm is probably overstressed.

With coil spring covers, the finger or lever adjusting screw nut is locked (staked) at time of manufacture and should not be disturbed unless rebuilding. Some Spicer heavy duty covers are internally adjusted for wear.

Clutch Replacement

1. Remove transmission (see transmission R & R).
2. Block clutch fingers down on coil spring covers for additional clearance. On heavy duty clutches use blocks between release bearing and spring plate hub. On Lipe-Rollaway use bolts

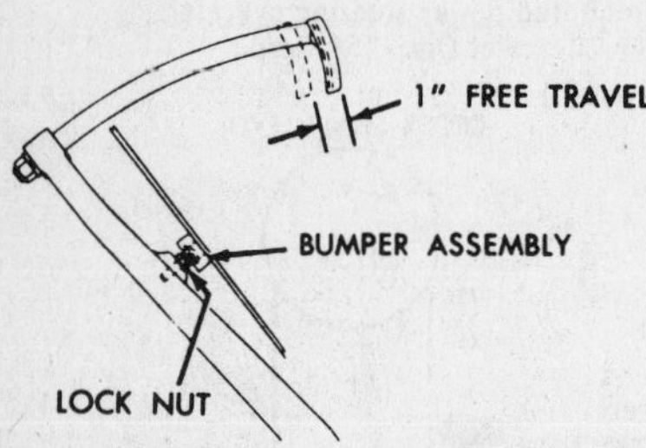

Pedal height adjustment (conventional pedal)
(© Chevrolet Div., G.M. Corp.)

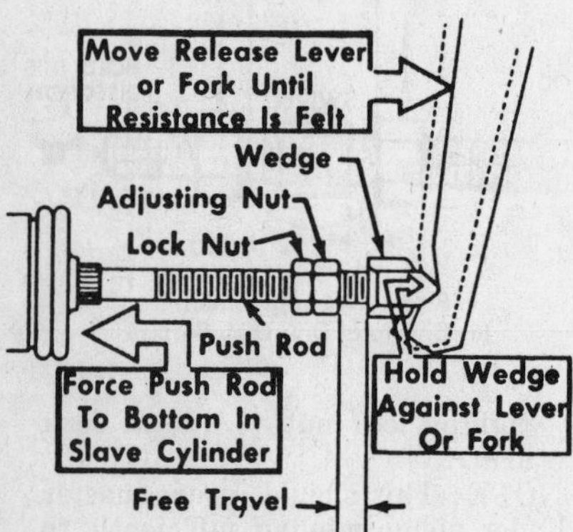

Clutch slave cylinder adjustment
(© Chevrolet Div., G.M. Corp.)

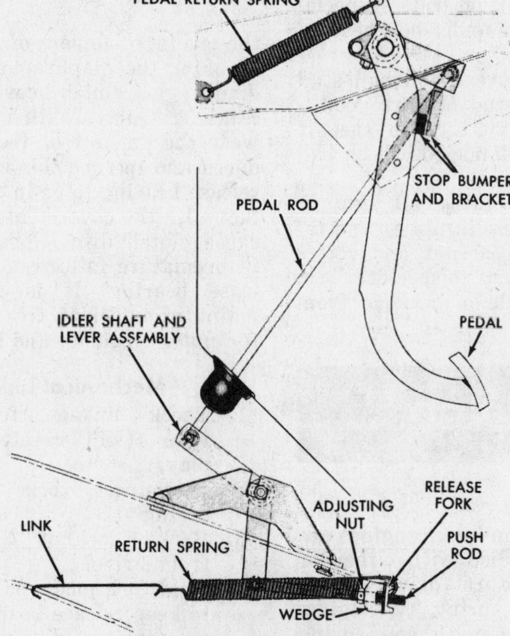

Mechanical linkage (inverted pedal)
(© Chevrolet Div., G.M. Corp.)

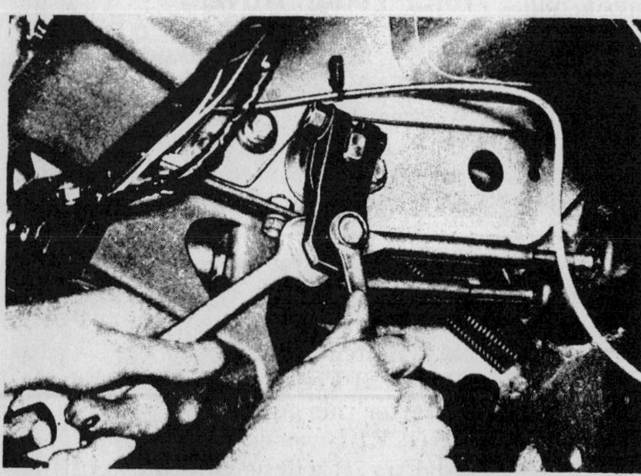

Adjusting clutch push rod (eccentric method)
(© Chevrolet Div., G.M. Corp.)

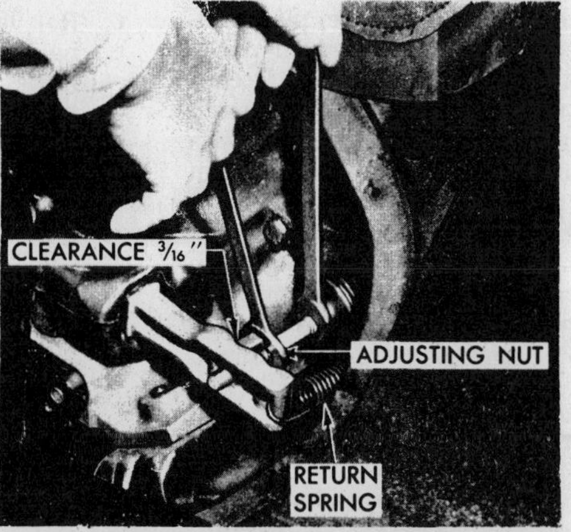

Adjusting slave cylinder push rod
(© Chevrolet Div., G.M. Corp.)

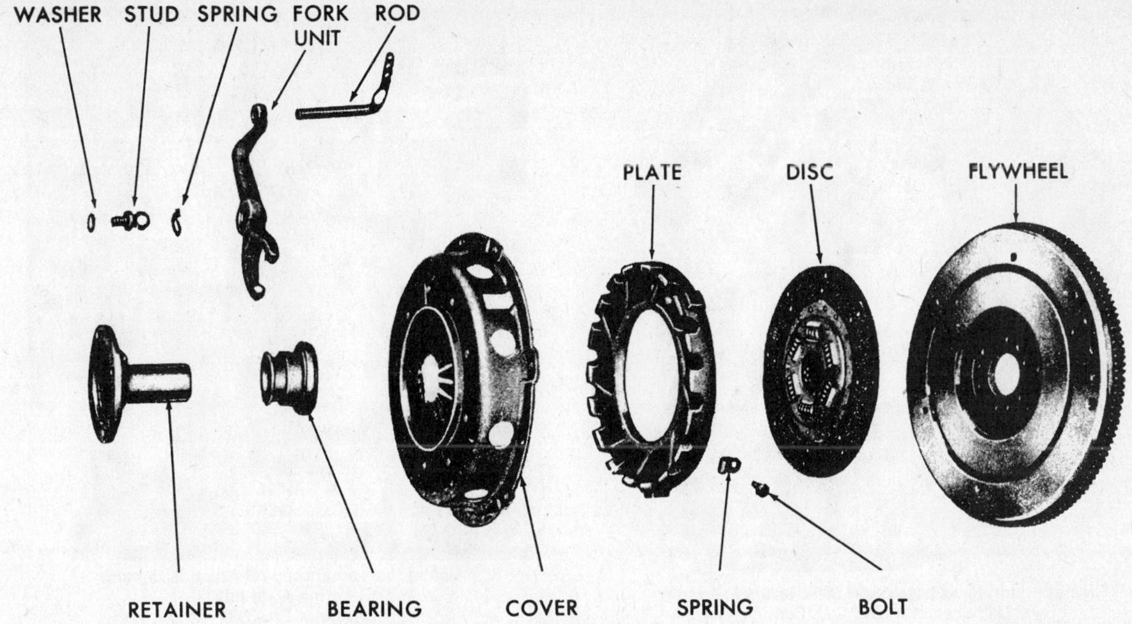

101 Diaphragm spring type clutch parts (typical) (© Chevrolet Div., G.M. Corp.)

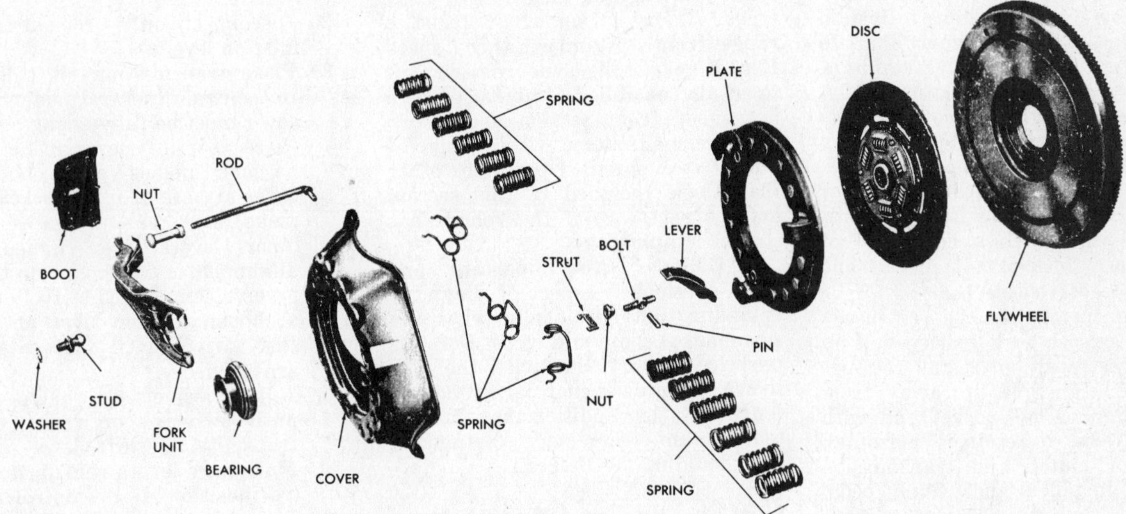

Coil spring clutch parts (typical) (© Chevrolet Div., G.M. Corp.)

and washer in three holes provided
3. Disconnect pedal linkage and fork arm pull back springs.
4. Disconnect slave cylinder from fork arm (if equipped).
5. Remove release bearing from fork arm or disconnect grease hose and remove bearing assembly from yoke.
6. Remove fork arm from ball stud or remove yoke and shaft.
7. Fork arm ball stud can be removed if necessary.
8. Punch mark cover and flywheel for alignment if cover assembly is to be re-used.
9. Loosen cover bolts a turn or two at a time to prevent cover distortion. Support cover and disc with pilot tool (or sling) to prevent damage to clutch when last cover bolt is removed. A good practice on heavy units is to remove one cover bolt and install a support stud. Rotate flywheel and locate stud at top, loosen all other bolts evenly until pressure is released from disc(s). Disc(s) can be removed and marked for positions. Remove remaining cover bolts and slide cover assembly off stud. Stud will also aid in installation.
10. Clean flywheel and pressure plates, check for scores and heat cracks. Excessive bluing indicates abnormally high operating temperatures. Torque flywheel bolts.
11. Check pilot bearing or bushing (lubricate sparingly), check splines on clutch shaft, check release bearing (do not wash bear-

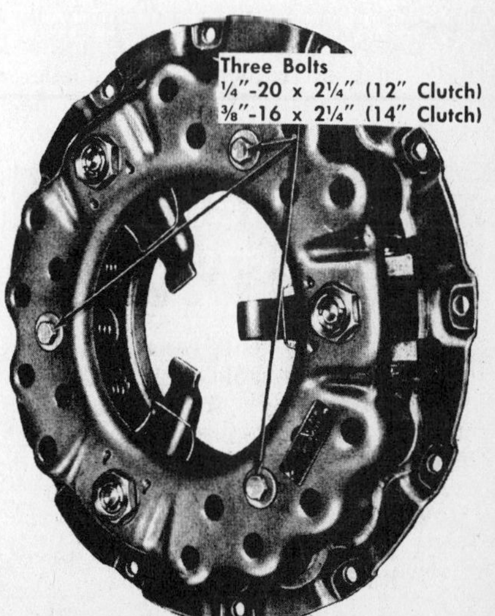

Lipe clutch hold-down bolts installed (typical)
(© Chevrolet Div., G.M. Corp.)

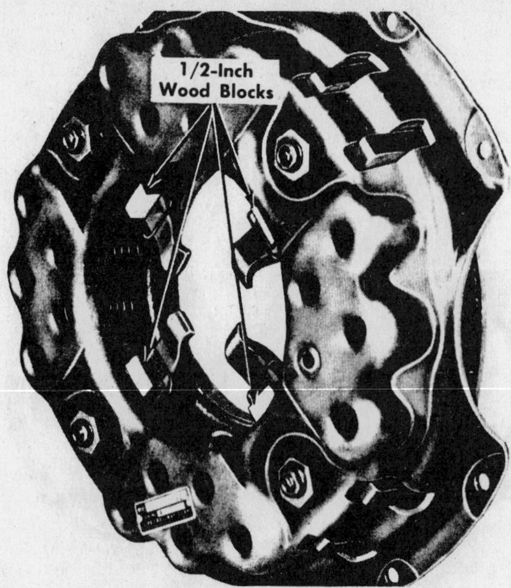

Use of wood blocks between release levers and cover
(© Chevrolet Div., G.M. Corp.)

Use of blocks between release bearing and spring plate hub
(© Chevrolet Div., G.M. Corp.)

ing).

12. Reverse removal steps to install. Use pilot tool or dummy shaft to align disc(s). Be certain of disc's position in relation to flywheel. Tighten cover bolts evenly. Do not try to pull clutch into place with impact wrench. This procedure can crack or break pilot shoulders on bolts. Lubricate with a light coat of grease, fork arm ball seat and inside of release bearing. Make sure spring retainer (if used) for release fork ball stud is in correct position. Install retainer with high side up, away from bottom of ball socket and with open end of retainer horizontal. After clutch and transmission are installed and clutch pedal free travel adjusted, check disc(s) for release. This can be done by putting transmission in gear and pulling down slowly on clutch pedal while applying torque to transmission propeller shaft flange. If release can be felt, then complete installation.

Standard Transmission

Transmission refill capacities are in the Capacities table of this section.

Troubleshooting and repair of manual transmissions are covered in the General Repair Section.

Types

The transmission is used to provide suitable gear ratios between engine and rear wheels for all driving conditions. Various types and designs of transmissions are used due to complexity of engines, chassis and body types. Transmission characteristics range from a standard three speed Helical gear, fully synchronized unit to an air controlled combination of a five speed front section and a two speed rear auxiliary, with a range of ten forward speeds. Operations other than those included in this section may be necessary if the vehicle has special equipment.

CAUTION: An important and often overlooked aspect of diagnosis is finding out specifically what the customer is complaining of. For this purpose a short ride with the customer will prove beneficial. It may be found that the condition that the customer wants corrected is standard and should not be altered.

Shift Linkage and Adjustments

3 Speed Column Shift

1. Raise vehicle and support on stands.
2. Disconnect control rods at transmission levers.
3. Place transmission shift levers in neutral (neutral detents in cover must be fully engaged).
4. Place gearshift lever in neutral, on early models remove housing cover at base of mast jacket and make sure shifter gates and inner levers are aligned. If alignment is off, loosen first and reverse control rod swivel clamp at housing outer lever and adjust swivel until shifter gates are aligned.
5. Adjust swivels on control rods until swivels (or rods) enter transmission shift lever holes. Make sure levers remain in neutral position. Lock control rods.
6. Lower vehicle and move gearshift lever through all gear positions to check (keep clutch pedal depressed to aid shifting).

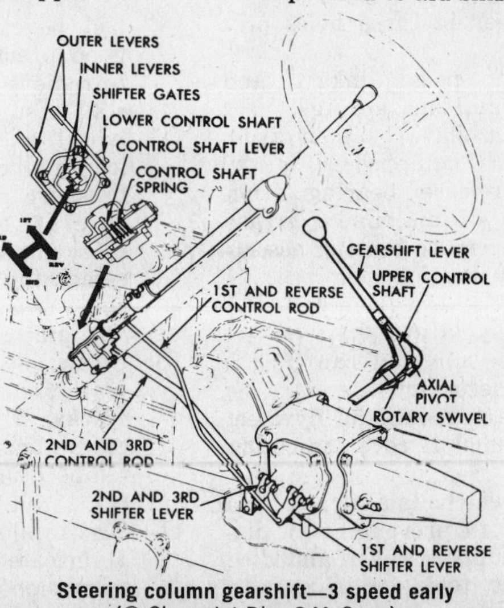

Steering column gearshift—3 speed early
(© Chevrolet Div., G.M. Corp.)

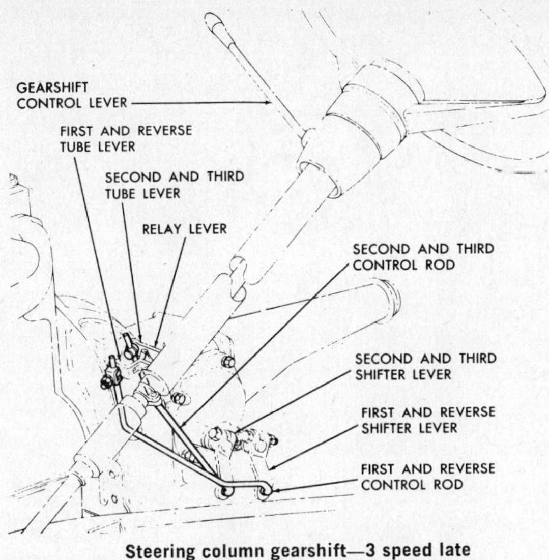

Steering column gearshift—3 speed late
(© Chevrolet Div., G.M. Corp.)

4 Speed Column Shift

1. Place gearshift lever in neutral. Raise vehicle on hoist.
2. Disconnect first and second shift rod from cross shaft lever. Disconnect third and fourth shift rod from transmission lever. Disconnect reverse cable from reverse lever by removing "C" clip. Manually shift all transmission controls into neutral, including reverse lever.
3. Remove engine splash shield. Install a fabricated pin (see illustration for details) through upper control shaft bracket into cutouts in shift levers and into hole provided at base of control shaft as shown.
4. Adjust swivel on end of first and second rod to freely enter cross shaft lever hole. Reconnect rod to lever.
5. Adjust swivel on end of third and fourth rod to freely enter transmission lever. Reconnect rod to lever.
6. Adjust swivel on end of reverse cable to freely enter reverse lever hole. If more adjustment is needed at swivel, adjust cable assembly by using cable to bracket attaching nuts. Install washer and "C" clip. Tighten swivel lock nut.
7. Remove fabricated pin, replace splash shield, lower vehicle and move gearshift lever through all gear positions to check. Depressing clutch pedal will aid in shifting.

Van Column Shift

1. Raise vehicle and support on stands.
2. Remove control rods at transmission levers.
3. Move both transmission levers until transmission is in neutral. Neutral detents must be fully engaged.
4. Move gearshift lever into neutral position, align shifter relay levers on mast jacket, install pin in holes of levers to hold levers in alignment and in neutral position.
5. Adjust swivel on end of low and reverse control rod until swivel enters transmission lever freely, lock with retaining ring, tighten swivel locknut.
6. Similarly, install second and third control rod, be sure levers remain in neutral.
7. Lower vehicle and move gearshift lever through all gear positions to check. Keep clutch pedal depressed to aid in shifting.

Floor Shift (and Related Controls)

Removal of gearshift lever, remote control and control island and any linkage adjustments are carried in transmission removal and installation section.

Transmission Removal

3 Speed Except Van and Blazer with 4 Wheel Drive

1. Raise and support vehicle on stands or hoist.
2. Drain transmission.
3. Disconnect speedometer cable at transmission.
4. Disconnect shift control levers at transmission.
5. Disconnect propeller shaft at transmission (align mark).
6. Disconnect parking brake, back up lamp and T.S.C. switch (if used).
7. Remove two top transmission to housing bolts and install two guide pins. NOTE: The use of transmission guide pins will not only support and align transmission but will also prevent damage to clutch disc. Guide pins can be made by taking two bolts, same as ones just removed only longer, and cutting off heads (slot for screwdriver).
8. Remove two lower mounting bolts (on heavy duty transmission—remove flywheel pan to reach).
9. Visually inspect to determine if

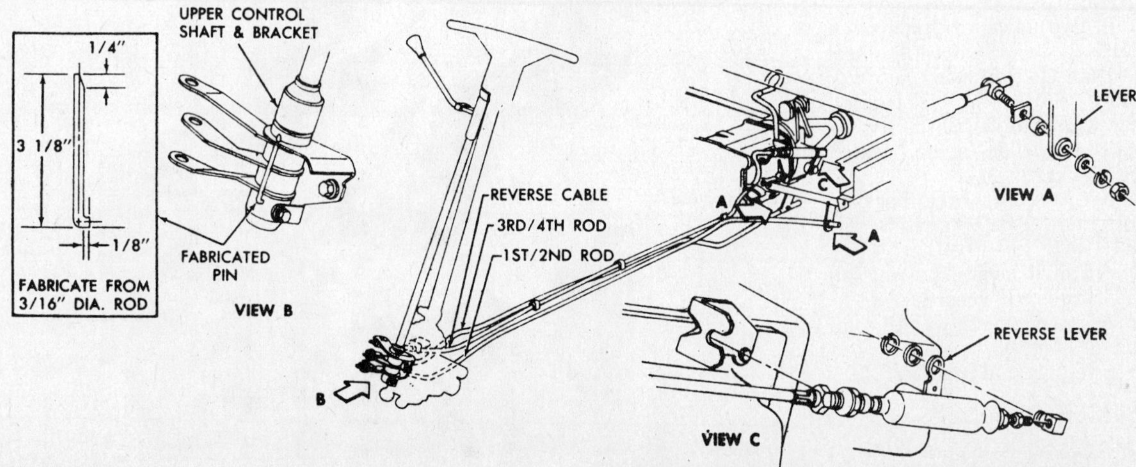

Steering column gearshift—4 speed (© Chevrolet Div., G.M. Corp.)

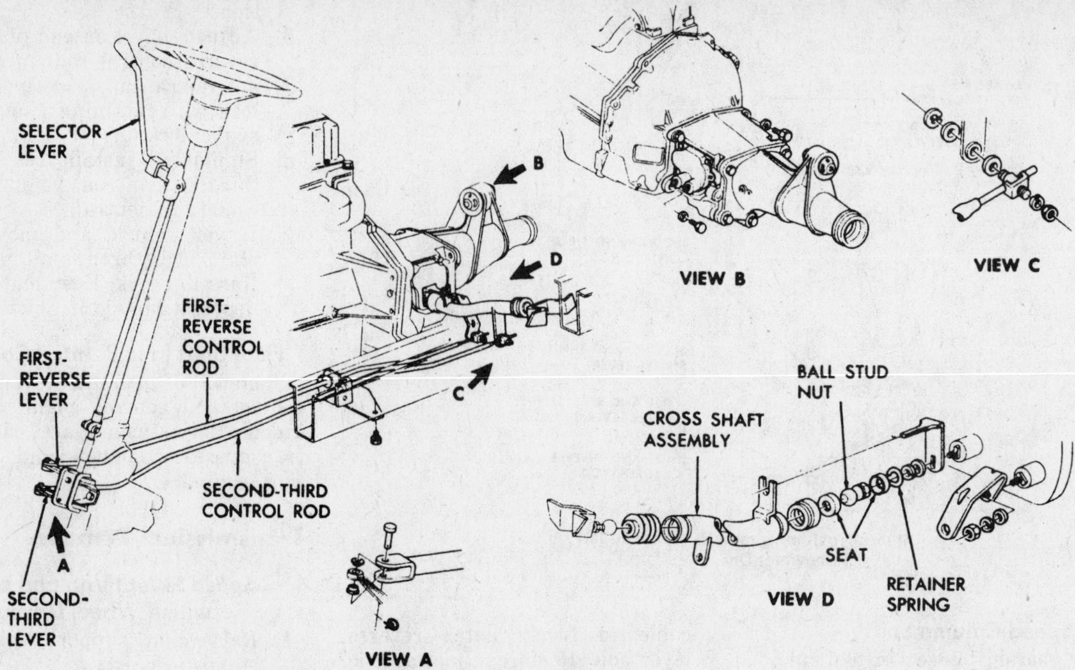

Column shift linkage—vans (© Chevrolet Div., G.M. Corp.)

other equipment or lines must be removed.

10. Slide transmission back on guide pins until clear. Be sure to support clutch release bearing during removal.
11. When transmission is free from engine, move from under vehicle.

Transmission Installation

3 Speed Except Van and Blazer with 4 Wheel Drive

1. Place transmission on guide pins, slide forward starting main drive gear into clutch disc's splines. NOTE: Place transmission in gear and rotate transmission flange or output yoke to aid entry of main drive gear into disc's splines. Make sure clutch release bearing is in position.
2. Install two lower transmission mounting bolts, and flywheel lower pan (if equipped).
3. Remove guide pins and install upper mounting bolts.
4. Install propeller shaft, watch align marks.
5. Connect parking brake, back-up lamp and T.S.C. switch (if used).
6. Connect shift levers, see section on adjustment if needed.
7. Connect speedometer cable, refill transmission.
8. Lower vehicle and road test.

Transmission Removal

Vans

1. Place heavy cardboard between radiator core and fan blades as a precautionary measure.
2. Raise and support vehicle on stands or hoist, drain transmission.
3. Disconnect speedometer cable at transmission.
4. Disconnect parking brake, back-up lamp and T.S.C. switch (if used).
5. Disconnect propeller shaft and power take off (if equipped).
6. 3 Speed (Column Shift)
   a. Remove shift controls from transmission.

   4 Speed (Floor Shift)
   a. Remove floor mat.
   b. Remove floor pan.
   c. Place transmission in neutral and remove gearshift lever by sliding open side of tool over lever, engage lugs of tool in the open slot of retainer, press down on tool and turn to left to disengage the lugs on retainer. Cover transmission opening. Be careful of pivot pin.
   d. Remove reverse lever cable and bracket at transmission.

   4 Speed (Column Shift)
   a. Remove shift controls from levers.
   b. Remove reverse lever cable and bracket at transmission.
7. Remove clutch shaft frame bolts and accelerator linkage at manifold bellcrank.
8. Place jack under bell housing and raise enough to relieve weight at transmission rear support.
9. Remove transmission rear support crossmember or on early models, remove support bolt and lower engine carefully to allow transmission rear mount to clear

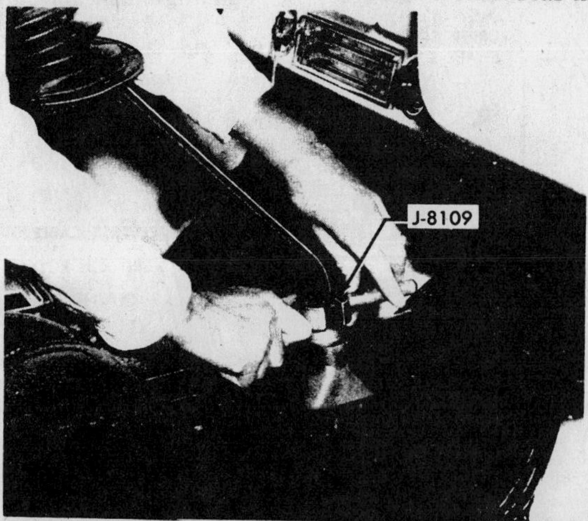

Replacing transmission gearshift lever—floor shift (© Chevrolet Div., G.M. Corp.)

support bracket.

10. Position jack under transmission and adjust to carry weight of transmission (if 4 speed).
11. Remove 2 top transmission to bell housing bolts and install 2 guide pins to prevent damaging clutch disc.
12. Remove two lower transmission mounting bolts.
13. Visually inspect to determine if other equipment or lines need to be removed.
14. Slide transmission back on guide pins, four speed units aided by jack (support release bearing), until transmission clears engine. Remove transmission from under vehicle.

CAUTION: If other work is to be performed support engine more securely after transmission is removed.

Transmission Installation

Vans

1. Clean bell housing and transmission mating surfaces, lightly lubricate main drive gear bearing retainer and clutch pilot bushing or bearing. Make sure release bearing is in position.
2. Move transmission into position on guide pins, shift transmission into any gear.
3. Slide transmission forward rotating transmission flange or yoke to aid entry of main drive gear into clutch disc splines.
4. Install two lower transmission mounting bolts. Remove guide pins and install two upper mounting bolts. Remove transmission jack.
5. Carefully raise engine and transmission to normal position and install transmission rear mounting bolt or crossmember. Remove jack from under bell housing. Remove cardboard from radiator.
6. Connect speedometer cable, parking brake, back-up light and T.S.C. switch (if equipped).
7. Connect propeller shaft and power take off (if equipped).
8. Connect clutch shaft and accelerator linkage.
9. Reinstall shift controls on transmission or gearshift lever on four speed. Install reverse cable and bracket. See section on shift linkage adjustment if needed.
10. Replace floor mat and floor pans on four speed units.
11. Refill transmission, lower vehicle and road test.

Transmission Removal and Installation

4 Wheel Drive (Including Blazer)

1. Floor shift models.
   a. Remove shift lever boots and retainers on both transfer case and transmission.
   b. Remove floor mat or carpet, seat and accelerator pedal.
   c. Center console models: remove center outlet from heater distributor duct and remove console.
   d. Remove transmission floor cover, shift transfer case lever into neutral and rotate floor cover approximately 90° while lifting to clear transfer case lever.
   e. Slide open side of tool over transmission gearshift lever, engage lugs of tool in open slot of retainer, press down and turn counter-clockwise to remove lever. Do same for transfer case lever. Be careful of any pivot pins. Cover transmission openings.
2. Raise vehicle and support on stands or hoist vehicle.
3. Drain transmission and transfer case.
4. Disconnect back-up light and T.S.C. switches (if equipped).
5. Disconnect parking brake.
6. Disconnect speedometer cable (at transfer case on some models).
7. Disconnect front and rear auxiliary drive shafts at transfer case and tie up out of work area.
8. 1961-66—Disconnect propeller shaft joint "U" bolts and remove propeller shaft. Disconnect auxiliary shift rod.

   1967 and Up—Remove bolts attaching transfer case to adapter (remove side access cover to reach two bolts).
9. Support rear of engine with jack.
10. Support transfer case on cradle or dolly. Remove two transmission adapter mounting bolts.
11. Remove transfer case mounting bolts, remove transfer case (all except Blazer).
12. Column Shift Models:
    a. Disconnect shift control rods from levers at transmission.
    b. On 4 speed, remove reverse cable and bracket at transmission.
13. Remove two upper transmission mounting bolts and install two guide pins (longer bolts with heads cut off and slotted). Use of guide pins will prevent damage to clutch disc.
14. Remove flywheel under pan and remove two lower transmission mounting bolts.
15. On V-8 engines, remove exhaust crossover pipe.
16. On Blazer, remove transmission frame crossmember bolts. Remove crossmember (rotating to clear frame rails).
17. Visually inspect to determine if other equipment or lines need to be removed.
18. Slid transmission and adapter (transmission with transfer case on Blazer) back on guide pins, aided by transmission dolly, until main drive gear clears clutch (watch clutch release bearing), remove from under vehicle.
19. Luricate pilot bushing or bearing, make sure clutch release bearing is in position, use guide pins to align transmission and rotate main drive gear to enter clutch disc splines without forcing. Reverse removal procedures to install.

4 and 5 Speed Heavy Duty Transmissions

The procedures required to remove

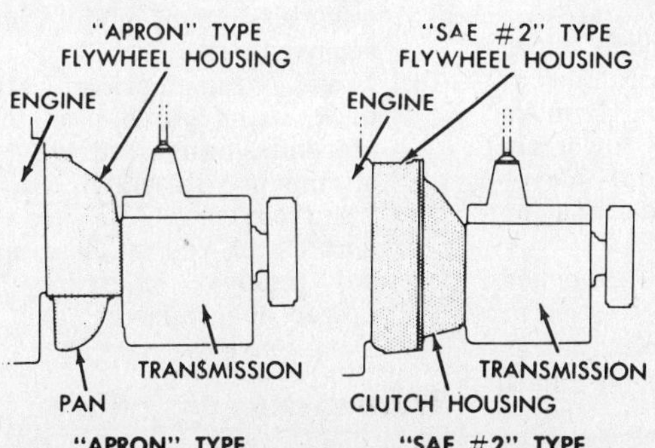

Replacing transfer case gearshift lever
(© Chevrolet Div., G.M. Corp.)

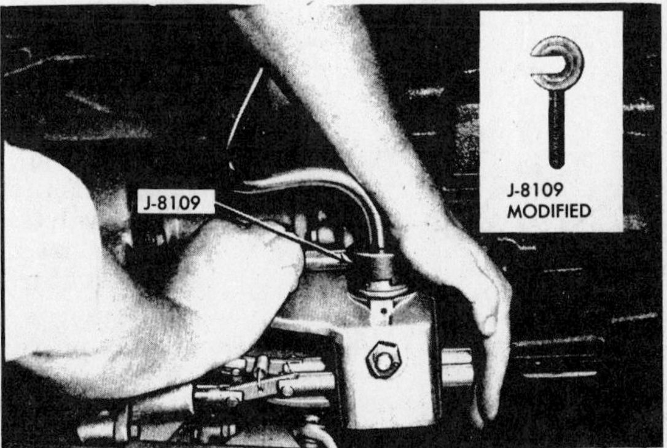

Flywheel housing identification
(© Chevrolet Div., G.M. Corp.)

and install the transmissions covered in this section are dependent upon types of cabs, engines and chassis used, also what equipment is available in repair shop. Other operations may be necessary if vehicle has special equipment, therefore, procedures contained herein will serve only as a guide. It is important to note that vehicles covered in this section will have either an "apron" or "S.A.E. 2" type of flywheel housing. The apron type is identified by sheet metal pan, also note it is a one piece housing. The "S.A.E. 2" type completely surrounds the flywheel. A separate clutch housing is used in addition to the flywheel housing. Transmission replacement procedures are different for each type of flywheel housing used.

Transmission Removal

1. Drain transmission.

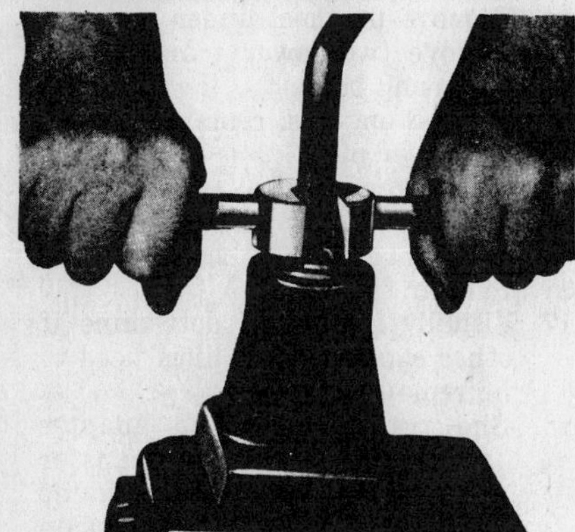

Removing gearshift lever
(© Chevrolet Div., G.M. Corp.)

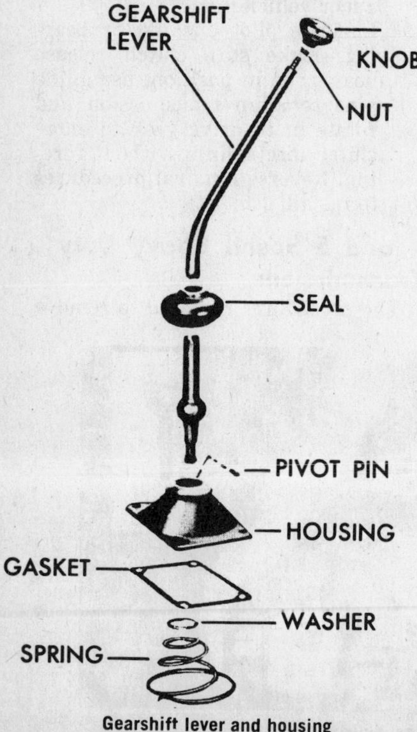

Gearshift lever and housing
(© Chevrolet Div., G.M. Corp.)

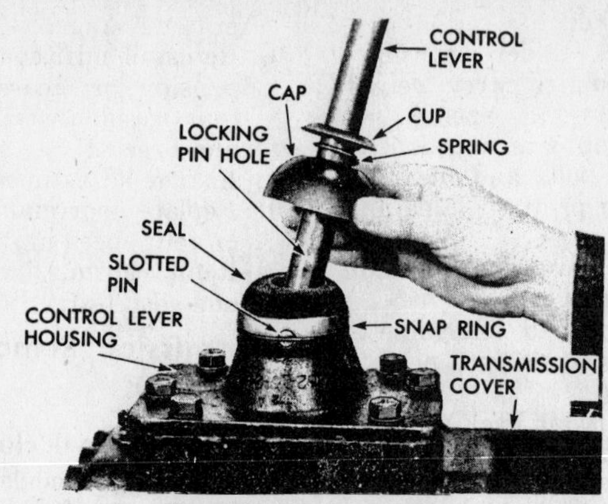

Gearshift lever installation
(© Chevrolet Div., G.M. Corp.)

2. On transmission equipped with remote controls.
   a. Disconnect control rods from shift levers at transmission.
3. On transmissions with a conventional floor gearshift lever.
   a. Remove steering jacket grommet from floor and slide grommet up mast jacket out of way (if used).
   b. Remove floor mat and accelerator pedal.
   c. Disconnect and remove parking brake lever.
   d. Remove transmission floor pan (s), place gearshift lever in neutral.
   e. Remove gearshift lever (and control tower on some models).

NOTE: On models with New Process Transmissions remove lever by sliding open side of tool over lever. Engage lugs of tool in open slot of retainer, press down on tool and turn to left to disengage lugs on retainer. Lift lever out of cover, be careful of pivot pin. Cover opening in transmission.

On spicer models, press down on shift lever cup and drive locking pin out of lever. Lift off cup, spring, cap and seal. Remove snap ring from groove on lever housing and tap out slotted pin. Lift lever out of housing and cover opening.

On Clark models remove shift lever housing cover to transmission bolts. Lift lever and control tower from transmission. Cover transmission opening.

On Air Control Shift models, bleed air tanks, remove range shift lines at air valve on transmission. Remove gearshift lever and control tower assembly from transmission. Cover transmission opening and tape or plug air valves.

4. Disconnect and drop propeller shaft at transmission.
5. If unit is equipped with power take-off, disconnect drive shaft and controls.
6. Remove reverse shift control cable and bracket on 4 speed units.
7. Disconnect any clutch control linkage on transmission.
8. Disconnect speedometer cable at transmission.
9. Remove engine ground strap, back up lamp switch and "T.S.C." switch (if used).
10. Place transmission jack into position and adjust to carry weight of transmission. Use locking chain to secure transmission to jack. NOTE: On vehicles which have rear engine mountings attached to the clutch housing (except "apron" type flywheel housing models), position a jack under flywheel housing and adjust to carry the weight of the engine. Remove rear engine mounts.
11. Remove bolts attaching transmission to rear crossmember support brackets (if used).
12. Remove clutch housing-to-flywheel housing bolts. (except on "apron" type flywheel housing models) NOTE: On models with "apron" type flywheel housing, remove flywheel housing under pan (also access panel on Spicer) and transmission to flywheel housing bolts. The use of guidepins in two top holes of "apron" type flywheel housing or in two top side holes on "S.A.E." type will maintain alignment during both removal and installation of transmission.
13. Visually inspect to determine if other equipment or lines must be removed.
14. Move transmission straight back, using guide pins to keep transmission main drive gear in alignment with clutch disc, until free from engine. Be sure to support clutch release bearing during removal of transmission. Lower transmission and move from under the vehicle.

Transmission Installation

1. Clean transmission mating surfaces and apply a light film of grease to main drive gear bearing retainer and clutch pivot

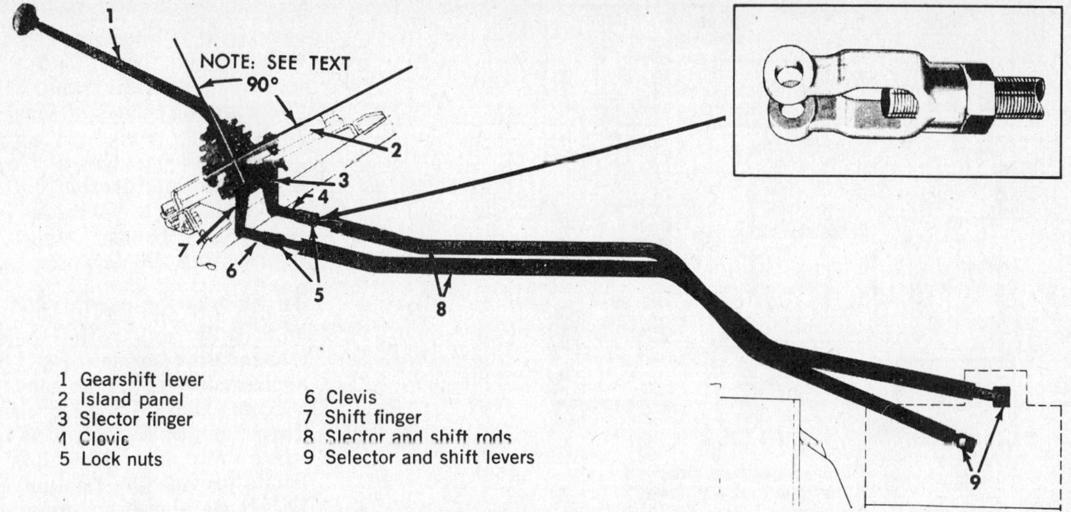

Tilt cab transmission control linkage (© Chevrolet Div., G.M. Corp.)

bearing.

2. Place transmission on jack and move into position.
3. On "apron" type, place clutch release bearing and support assembly inside flywheel housing. Be sure clutch fork engages bearing. On "S.A.E. 2" type, make sure clutch release bearing is in position.
4. Using guide pins to align transmission main drive gear with clutch disc, move transmission forward rotating main drive gear so gear can enter clutch disc splines without forcing.
5. Reverse removal procedures to install.

NOTE: On transmissions having remote controls make the following control island shift mechanism adjustments if necessary.

1. Place transmission selector and shift levers in neutral.
2. Adjust selector and shift rods to provide 90° angle at the lower end of the gearshift lever to the control island panel. Adjustment is made by rotating the adjustable clevis at either the control island or transmission end of the selector and shift rods. Tighten lock nuts.
3. Check adjustments by moving gearshift lever through shift pattern.

NOTE: On 4 speed transmissions with reverse idler eccentric. To adjust the position of the reverse idler gear, the transmission must be fully assembled except for power take-off cover. Then proceed as follows:

1. Loosen the eccentric nut and rotate the eccentric, using a screwdriver in the slot with end of electric, until slot with dot on end is to the rear. This places the reverse idler in its extreme rear position and will provide for maximum engagement when the transmission is shifted into reverse.
2. Shift transmission into second. Check for interference between reverse idler and first and reverse gear. If interference exists, rotate eccentric in a counter-clockwise direction to obtain approximately 1/32" clearance This clearance can be checked through the power take-off opening.
4. Shift transmission into reverse and check clearance between reverse idler gear and transmission case. If necessary, rotate the eccentric an additional amount, in counter-clockwise direction, to obtain running clearance at this point.
5. Tighten eccentric nut and lock.
6. Install power take-off cover and new gasket.

Overdrive

Reference

Reverse idler gear and adjustment (© Chevrolet Div., G.M. Corp.)

The overdrive unit is essentially a two-speed planetary transmission attached to the rear of a conventional three speed transmission. In overdrive, engine speed is approximately thirty per cent slower at a given road speed since the drive train includes planetary gears which provide a lower overall gear ratio than that obtained in high gear with the conventional transmission.

The electrical equipment which controls the automatic action of the mechanical portion of the overdrive unit consists of a solenoid, a governor switch, a relay and a kickdown switch. The circuit including this equipment makes it possible to operate in overdrive above a pre-set cut-in speed, or in conventional drive at any speed.

Repairs to the overdrive housing, output shaft, ring gear assembly, clutch cam, roller retainer, pinion cage, sun gear, shift rail, sun gear control plate, output shaft bearing, oil seal, speedometer drive gear, solenoid pawl and interlock plunger may be performed underneath the vehicle, by removing the overdrive housing without disturbing the transmission.

If the transmission mainshaft overdrive adaptor or transmission rear bearing which is retained in the adaptor require replacement the entire transmission and overdrive assembly should be removed.

Governor Switch

To remove governor switch disconnect wires at switch and screw governor out of housing.

Solenoid

Remove solenoid by taking out the two mounting bolts and lockwashers. Turn solenoid ¼ turn and pull solenoid plunger out of adapter.

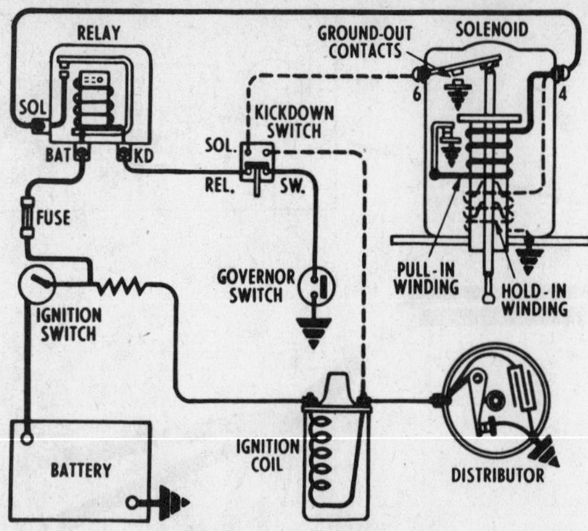

Overdrive electrical circuit
(© Chevrolet Div., G.M. Corp.)

Automatic Transmission

Reference

See specific chapter in general section for overhaul procedures for each make.

Types

Transmissions basically used are powerglide, Powermatic (Allison) and Turbo Hydra-matic 350 and 400.

Powerglide

Available for light trucks consisting of a 3 element torque converter (a welded unit), and a two speed planetary transmission automatically shifted by a hydraulic control system, in a one piece aluminum case with a single shift occurring between Low and Drive. A forced downshift provides a passing gear by returning transmission to Low range. When gearshift lever is placed in Drive position, the transmission automatically shifts to Low range for initial vehicle movement. As the vehicle gains speed, depending on load and throttlé position, an automatic shift is made to high gear.

Powermatic (Allison)

Powermatic or Allison automatic transmissions are designed for medium and heavy duty trucks. It is a torque converter type, using planetary gearing for full power shifting, with 6 speeds forward and one reverse and with automatic lock-up for direct drive from engine to the range gearing. An outstanding feature is the integral hydraulic retarder for controlling truck speed downhill. It is also equipped with two power take-off mounting openings, one on each side of housing.

NOTE: Do not apply hydraulic retarder while checking oil level, it will aerate the oil making an accurate oil level check impossible.

CAUTION: Do not tow or push Powermatic. Disconnect drive line or pull axles.

Turbo Hydra-matic 350

A fully automatic 3 speed transmission in a two piece aluminum casting, consisting primarily of a torque converter and a compound planetary gear set. Four multiple disc clutches, two roller clutches and one band provide the friction elements. The compound planetary gear set produces three forward speeds and one reverse. The cable operated detent system is designed to ensure positive part throttle or full throttle downshifting, depending on throttle position.

NOTE: Do not overfill, with oil level at the full mark on the dipstick it is just slightly below the planetary gear unit. If additional oil is added, bringing oil level above the full mark, the planetary unit will run in oil, foaming and aerating the oil. Aerated oil, carried through various oil pressure passages and converter, may cause malfunction of transmission resulting in cavitation noises in converter, bands and clutches. Overheating will also occur.

Power Glide and Turbo Hydramatic 350 identification number located on right rear vertical surface of oil pan
(© Chevrolet Div., G.M. Corp.)

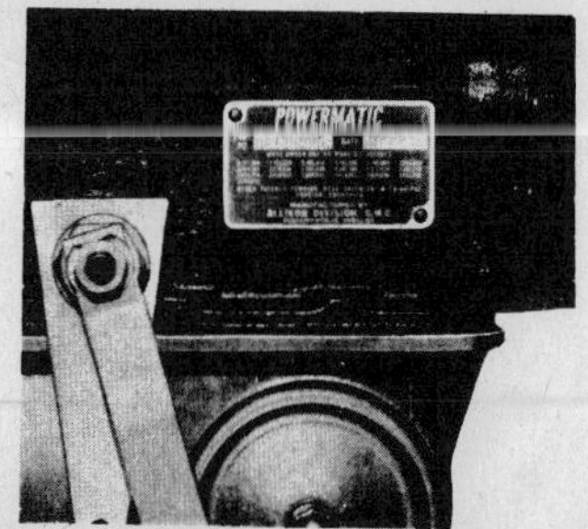

Power Matic (Allison) transmission number and production date on tag left side of case
(© Chevrolet Div., G.M. Corp.)

Turbo Hydra-matic 400

A fully automatic three speed transmission consisting primarily of a three element torque converter and a compound planetary gear set. Three multiple disc clutches, one sprag unit, one roller clutch and two bands provide the friction elements. The three element torque converter consists of a pump (driving member), a turbine (driven member) and a stator mounted on a one-way (clockwise) roller clutch.

The detent solenoid is activated by an electric switch on the carburetor. When the throttle is fully opened, the switch on the carburetor is closed, activating the detent solenoid, causing transmission to downshift for passing speeds.

NOTE: Park position is not provided for 30 series.

CAUTION: Do not overfill, this transmission is very sensitive to oil level. If fluid is too low, especially when cold, complete loss of drive may result.

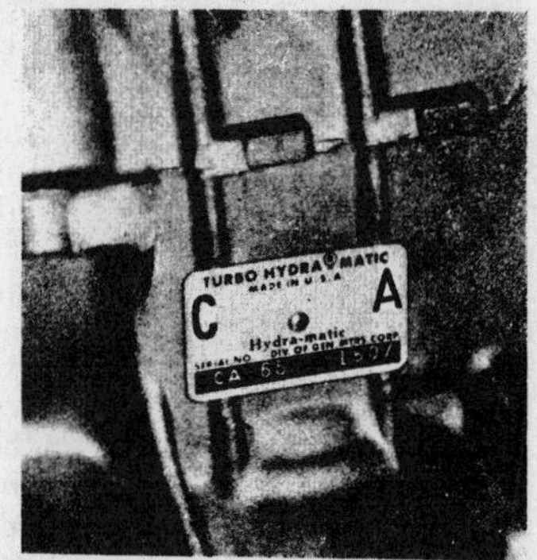

Turbo Hydra Matic 400 transmission ser. no. is located on plate on right side of transmission
(© Chevrolet Div., G.M. Corp.)

Powerglide Transmission

Shift Linkage and Adjustments

Manual linkage adjustment and neutral safety switch are important from a safety stand point. The neutral safety switch should be adjusted so that the engine will start in Park and Neutral positions only. With selector lever in Park position, the parking pawl should freely engage and prevent the vehicle from moving. The pointer on the indicator quadrant should line up with the range indicators in all ranges.

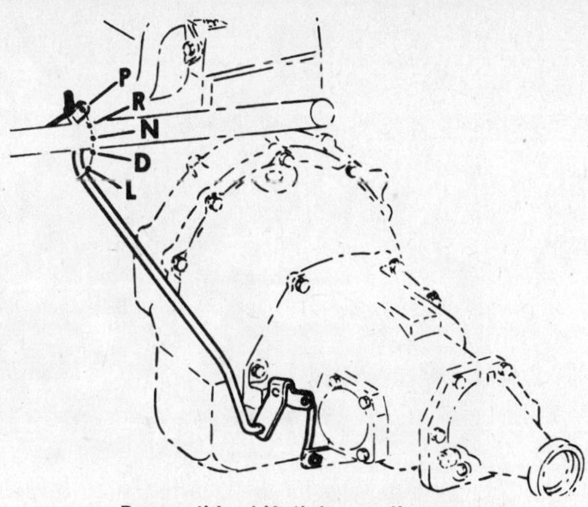

Power glide shift linkage adjustment
(© Chevrolet Div., G.M. Corp.)

Powerglide 1961-62

Check for adjustment.

With engine off, lift up on gearshift lever and move lever to the position where transmission Drive (D) detent is felt. Slowly release lever to feel if the shaft lever tang freely enters the lock plate. Check reverse range in a similar manner. If tang does not freely enter lock plate in BOTH drive and reverse ranges, it will be necessary to adjust linkage.

Linkage Adjustment

1. Place gearshift lever in drive position.
2. Disconnect swivel on shift control rod at lever on mast jacket by loosening lock nut.
3. Position transmission lever in drive detent. NOTE: Drive detent in transmission is the first clockwise detent position from the fully counter-clockwise (L) detent position.
4. Adjust swivel on control rod for free entry into mast jacket lever. Lock swivel nut.
5. Test transmission shifts in all ranges.

Shift Linkage and Adjustments

Powerglide 1964 & Up

Check for adjustment. With engine off, lift gearshift lever towards steering wheel, allow gearshift lever to be positioned in Drive (D) by the transmission detent. DO NOT use the indicator pointer to position the gearshift lever. Pointer is adjusted (or set) after linkage adjustment is made. Gearshift lever now won't engage reverse range unless lifted. A properly adjusted linkage will prevent the gearshift lever from moving beyond the Neutral detent and drive detent unless lever is raised to pass over mechanical stop in steering column.

Linkage Adjustment

1. Place the gearshift lever in Drive (D) position, as determined by detent.
2. Loosen adjustment swivel at mast jacket lever and rotate transmission lever so that it contacts the Drive stop in the steering column.
3. Tighten the swivel and recheck the adjustment.
4. Readjust indicator pointer, if necessary, to agree with transmission detent positions.
5. Readjust neutral safety switch, if necessary.

Low Band Adjustment

Adjustments should be made at periodical intervals or sooner if necessary, determined by operating performances.

1. Raise vehicle and support on stands.
2. Place gearshift lever in Neutral.
3. Remove protective cap from adjustment screw on transmission. NOTE: On some models it may be necessary to remove rear mounting bolts from crossmember and move transmission slightly to passenger side for additional clearance.
4. Loosen adjusting screw locknut $\frac{1}{4}$ turn and hold in this position during adjusting procedure.
5. Using an inch-pound torque wrench, adjust band to 70 inch pounds and back off four complete turns for a band which has been in service for 6000 miles or more, or three full turns for one with less than 6000 miles.
6. Tighten adjusting screw locknut to specified torque.

CAUTION: The back-off amount is not an approximate figure, it must be exact.

Throttle Linkage Adjustments

NOTE: Powerglide throttle linkage adjustments are made when carburetor throttle valve(s) is in closed position (hot idle) and transmission throttle lever is back against its internal stop. If shift occurs too early, shorten rod a turn or two and road test. If shift occurs too late, lengthen rod.

Powerglide (1961-62 6 Cylinder)

1. Loosely assemble lever (B) to clamp (A).

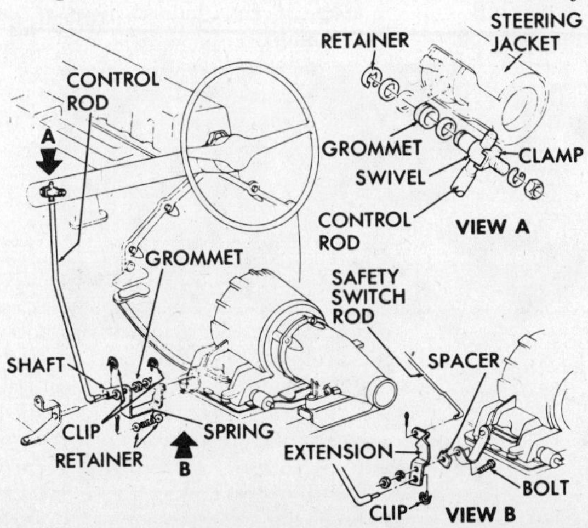

Powerglide shift linkage
(© Chevrolet Div., G.M. Corp.)

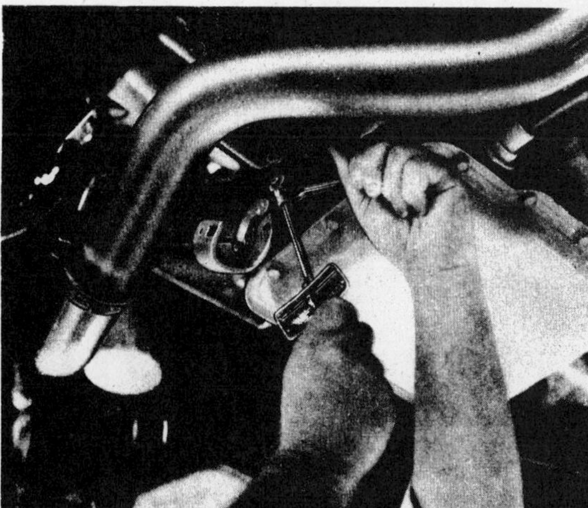
Adjusting low band (© Chevrolet Div., G.M. Corp.)

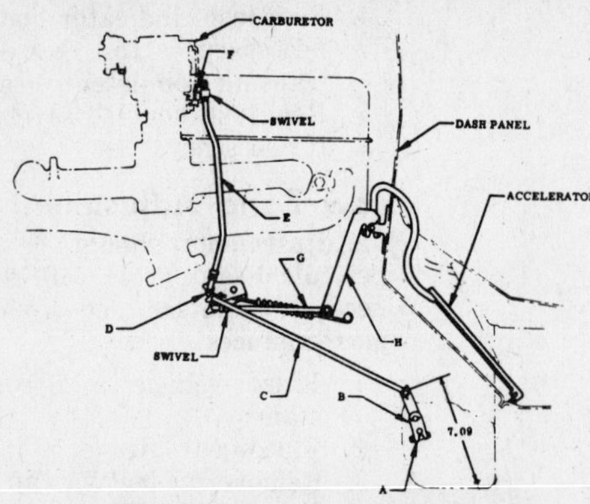

Powerglide throttle valve linkage adjustment —6 cyl.
(© Chevrolet Div., G.M. Corp.)

Throttle valve linkage adjustment (using special tool)
(© Chevrolet Div., G.M. Corp.)

2. Insert gauge between transmission left hand side cover lower rear bolt and hole in lever (B). Dimension between bolt and hole center lines is 7.09″. With gauge in place and holding clamp (A) counter clockwise in full detent position, tighten lever (B) to clamp (A). Remove gauge.
3. Install rod (C).
4. Install rod (E) in lever (D). Placelever (F) in wide open position and pull rod (E) up until it is stopped by transmission internal stop. Adjust swivel in rod (E) for free entry in lever (F) before fixing swivel in lever (F).
5. Check adjustment by placing linkage in idle position then return to wide open position by rotating lever (F). Push upward on lever (B) to see if rod (C) deflects, meaning transmission is not on internal stop. If rod deflects, or lever (F) will not reach wide open position, repeat adjustment 4.
6. With accelerator pedal depressed until lever (H) contacts stop and lever (D) rotated to wide open position, adjust swivel or rod (G) for free entry into lever (D) before fixing swivel to lever (D).
7. Check adjustment by releasing then depressing accelerator pedal. Check lever (F) for wide open position. If lever (F) will not reach wide open position, repeat step 6.

Powerglide (1961-62 V8)

1. Loosely assemble lever (B) to clamp (A).
2. Insert gauge between transmission left hand side cover lower front bolt and hole in lever (B). Distance between hole center lines is 3.60″. With gauge in place and holding clamp (A) counterclockwise in full detent position, tighten lever (B) to clamp (A).
Remove gauge.
3. Install rod (C).
4. Install rod (E) and cross shaft (D). Place lever (F) in wide open throttle position and adjust rod swivel on rod (E) for free entry in throttle bellcrank. Fasten swivel in bellcrank.
5. Check the adjustment by releasing linkage to its idle position, then rotate throttle bellcrank (F) to the wide open position. While holding linkage in this attitude, press downward on transmission outer TV lever (B) and check for deflection. If rod (C) deflects, repeat step 4.
6. Place a ½″ wood block beneath the accelerator pedal rod, depress and hold the accelerator to the block, and then adjust swivel on rod (G) for free entry into the throttle bellcrank (F) with the throttle bellcrank held fully wide open.
7. Remove the wood block and depress the accelerator pedal by hand to check for detent feel and check that throttle bellcrank (F) reaches the wide open position. Repeat step 6 if adjustment is not satisfactory.

Powerglide 1963-66 (6 Cylinder Except Forward Control)

1. Install rod (E) to levers (D) and (F).
2. Install rod (L) to lever (A) and with lever (F) in wide open position adjust swivel (H) on rod (L) and install, for free entry, in lever (D).
3. Check adjustment by placing linkage in idle position, then return to wide open position by rotating lever (F). Push downward on lever (A) and note if rod (L) deflects, meaning transmission is not on internal stop. If rod deflects, repeat adjustment 2.

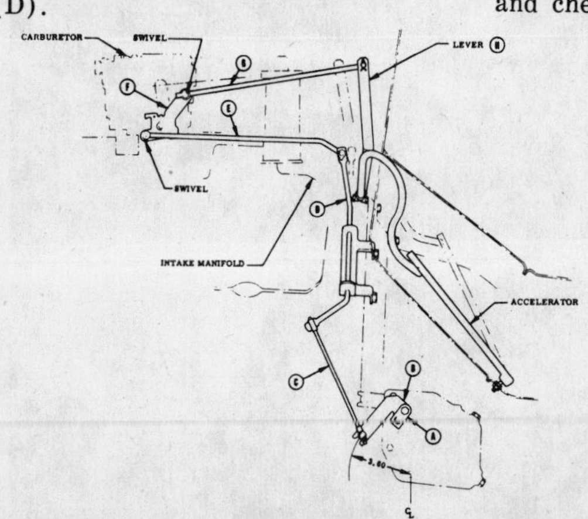

Throttle valve linkage adjustment—V8 engines
(© Chevrolet Div., G.M. Corp.)

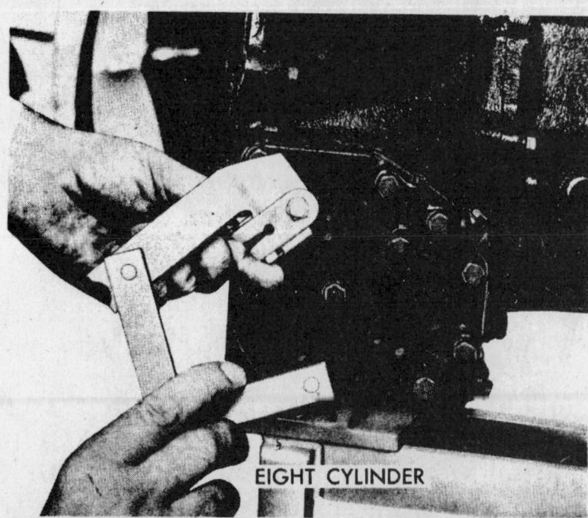

Throttle valve linkage adjustment (using special tool)
(© Chevrolet Div., G.M. Corp.)

4. With accelerator depressed, .10 from toe pan, and lever (D) rotated in wide open position, adjust swivel (G) on rod (J) for free entry into lever (D) before fixing swivel to lever (D).
5. Check adjustment by releasing then depressing accelerator pedal. Check lever (F) for wide open position; if lever (F) will not reach wide open position, repeat step 4.

Powerglide 1963-66 (P-10 4 and 6 Cylinder)

1. Install rod (F) to levers (E) and (D).
2. Install rod (K) to levers (L) and (J).
3. Thread rod (G) approximately halfway through swivel (H), install swivel in (cross shaft) assembly (J). Place lever (E) in wide open position and pull rod (G) forward until it is stopped by transmission internal stop. Adjust rod (G) by twisting in swivel until rod end freely enters lever (D). Fix rod in lever (D).
4. Check adjustment by placing linkage in idle position, then return to wide open position by rotating lever (E). Push downward on lever (L) and note if rod (G) deflects, meaning transmission is not on internal stop. If rod deflects, or lever (E) will not reach wide open position, repeat adjustment 3.
5. With accelerator pedal fully depressed and lever (E) rotated to wide open position, adjust swivel (B) on rod (C) for free entry into levers (D) and (A) before fixing swivel to lever (A).
6. Check adjustment by releasing, then depressing accelerator pedal. Check lever (E) for wide open position: if lever (E) will not reach wide open position, repeat step 5.

Powerglide 1963-66 (P-20 Models)

1. Assemble rod (K) to transmission throttle valve lever (L).
2. With throttle valve (L) rotated in a counter-clockwise direction to stop in transmission and with lever (M) rotated clockwise to wide open throttle at carburetor adjust swivel on rod (K) for free entry into lever (M). Rotate swivel one turn to shorten rod (K) by that amount. Assemble swivel to lever (M).
3. Check adjustment by returning linkage to idle position of carburetor then open to wide open throttle by rotating lever (M). With lever (M) held in wide open position attempt to rotate lever (L) at transmission counter-clockwise. If rotation is possible transmission is not on internal stop in which case disassemble swivel from lever (M) and shorten rod (K) by one turn of swivel. Reassemble swivel to lever (M).

Powerglide 1963-66 (V8 Models)

1. Install rod assy. (B).
2. Thread rod (D) approximately halfway through swivel, install swivel in (cross shaft) assembly (C). Place lever (E) in wide open position and pull rod (D) forward until it is stopped by transmission internal stop, adjust rod (D) by twisting in swivel until rod end freely enters lever (E). Fix rod end in lever (E).
3. Check adjustment by placing linkage in idle position, then return to wide open position by rotating lever (E). Push downward on lever (A) and note if rod (D) deflects, meaning transmission is not on internal stop. If rod deflects, or lever (E) will not reach wide open position, repeat adjustment 2.
4. With accelerator pedal de-

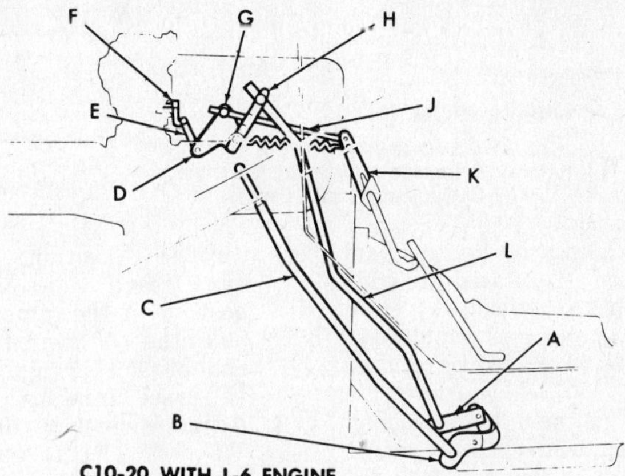

Throttle valve linkage adjustments L-6 engines
(© Chevrolet Div., G.M. Corp.)

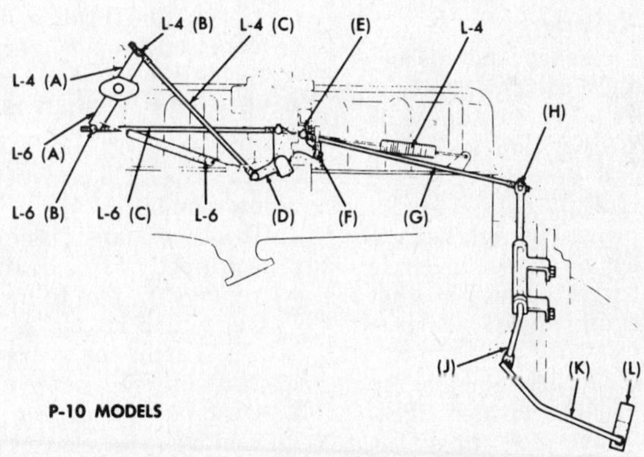

Throttle valve linkage adjustments—P-10 models
(© Chevrolet Div., G.M. Corp.)

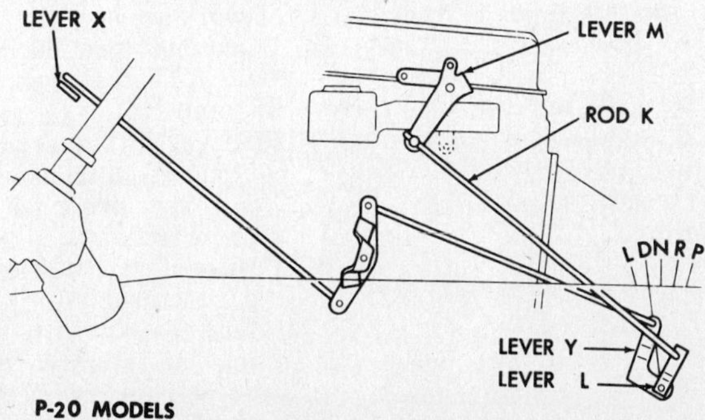

Throttle valve linkage adjustments—P20 models
(© Chevrolet Div., G.M. Corp.)

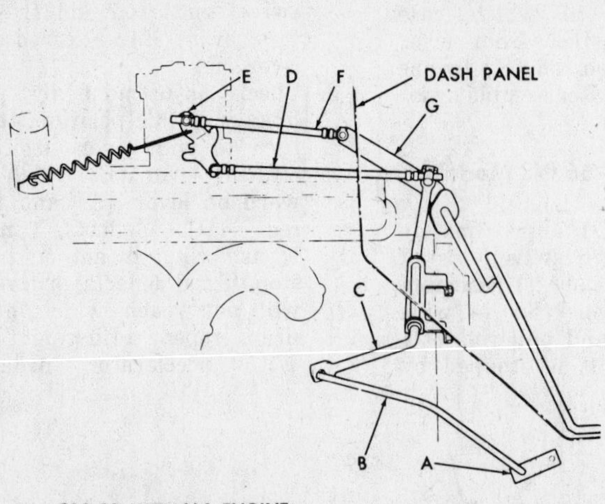

Throttle valve linkage adjustments V8 engines
(© Chevrolet Div., G.M. Corp.)

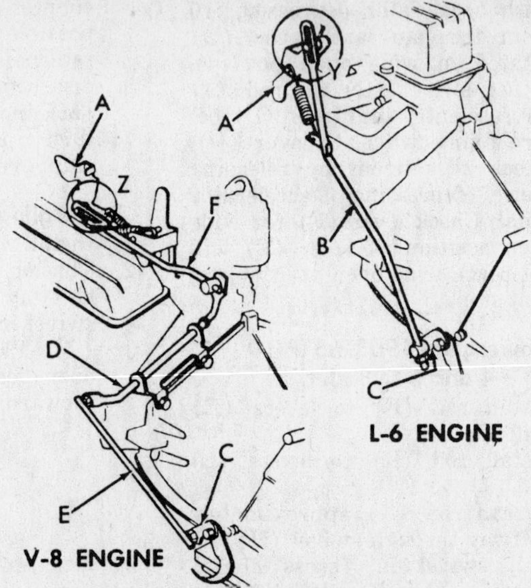

Powerglide throttle valve linkage adjustment
(© Chevrolet Div., G.M. Corp.)

pressed, .10 from the toe pan, and lever (E) rotated to wide open position, adjust swivel in rod (F) for free entry into lever (E) before fixing swivel to lever (E).

5. Check adjustment by releasing, then depressing accelerator pedal. Check lever (E) for wide open position; if lever (E) will not reach wide open position, repeat step 4.

Powerglide 1967 and Up (6 Cylinder)

1. Remove air cleaner and disconnect carburetor return spring.
2. Rotate lever (A) to the wide open throttle position and T.V. lever through detent. (Depress accelerator fully).
3. Hold slot on rod (B) against pin on lever (A) as shown in circle Y—adjust swivel on rod so that it freely enters hole on lever (C).
4. Hold rod (B) perpendicular to pin on lever (A) and then tighten swivel nut. Rod must be 1/64"-1/16" off lever stop with transmission lever against internal stop. Connect carburetor return spring.
5. Check for throttle linkage freedom and proper operation.

Powerglide 1967 and Up (V8 Models)

1. Remove air cleaner.
2. Disconnect accelerator linkage at carburetor.
3. Disconnect accelerator return and throttle valve rod return springs.
4. With right hand, pull T.V. upper rod (F) forward until transmission lever (C) is through detent. With left hand, rotate carburetor lever (A) to wide open throttle position. Carburetor must reach wide open throttle position at the same time pin or ball stud on lever (A) contacts end of slot in upper T.V. rod (F)—see circle Z.
5. Adjust swivel on upper end of T.V. rod (F) to obtain setting described in step 4 (approximately 1/32").
6. Connect and adjust accelerator linkage. Connect carburetor return springs.
7. Check for throttle linkage freedom and proper operation.

Powerglide Transmission Removal

1. Raise vehicle on hoist or support on stands.
2. Drain transmission oil if equipped with drain plug (or remove oil pan to drain, then replace pan using several bolts). Oil can be drained after transmission removal, if desired.
3. On models with long oil fill pipe, remove dipstick and pipe.
4. Disconnect oil cooler lines (if equipped), vacuum modulator hose and speedometer cable at transmission. Support lines out of work area.
5. Disconnect ground cable, T.S.C. switch, neutral switch and back-up lamp switch (if used).
6. Remove shift and throttle valve controls from transmission.
7. Disconnect propeller shaft from rear of transmission.
8. Position transmission jack and secure transmission to jack with safety chain.
9. Raise jack slightly to relieve engine rear mount on transmission extension and remove transmission support crossmember (Vans—remove thru-bolt).

   NOTE: Use care to remove any shims (if used) at crossmember. It is vital that exactly the same number be reinstalled.
10. Remove flywheel cover or converter under pan, scribe flywheel-converter marks for reassembly, remove flywheel to converter attaching bolts.
11. Support engine at oil pan rail with a jack to support engine weight when transmission is removed.
12. Vans—Remove linkage cross shaft frame bolts and accelerator linkage at bellcrank before lowering engine. Lower engine to allow rear mount housing to clear support bracket.
13. Lower rear of transmission slightly so that the upper transmission to engine bolts can be reached using a universal socket and a long extension. Remove upper bolts. CAUTION: On V8 engines do not lower too far becuuse of distributor—firewall interference.
14. Remove remaining transmission mounting bolts.
15. Remove transmission by moving it slightly to the rear and downward, remove from under vehicle.

NOTE: Watch converter when moving transmission back. If it does not move with transmission pry it free of flywheel before proceeding.

CAUTION: Keep front of transmission up to prevent the converter from falling out. Install a converter hold tool or improvise.

For Overhaul Procedures—See General Repair Section

Installation

1. Reverse removal procedures. NOTE: If reusing converter

align scribed marks, if not through flywheel cover opening align as closely as possible the white stripe painted on engine side of flywheel outer rim (heavy side) with the blue stripe painted on end of converter (light side) to maintain balance.

2. Refill transmission and check for proper operation and leaks.

Powermatic Transmission

Shift Linkage and Adjustments (Range Selector)

The range selector shift control cable is designed so the only adjustment is on the lower clevis at the transmission shift lever.

1. Place gearshift lever (at tower) in "Lo" position, disconnect control cable at transmission lever.
2. Place transmission shift lever in full rearward position.
3. Adjust clevis on cable so that clevis pin freely enters hole in transmission shift lever.
4. Shift slowly several times to insure that the shift lever is not at the end of its travel (at either end of slot) before the detent acts.

Hydraulic Retarder Linkage Adjustment

Adjustment is same fundamentally as the hydraulic clutch pedal adjustment. Hydraulic retarder pedal free play is 1/8". Once the pedal is adjusted make final adjustment at slave cylinder which actuates the hydraulic retarder valve at the powermatic. To adjust slave cylinder, fully depress the slave cylinder push rod into the cylinder, then adjust the clevis on push rod for free entry of clevis pin into the hydraulic retarder valve lever on transmission.

Throttle Linkage Adjustments

1961-62 (Except Tilt Cab)

1. Insert a 1/4" diameter steel pin approximately 3" long through point "A". This pin must pass through bosses on both sides of the lever and a boss on the support bracket.
2. Place carburetor on HOT idle stop and position TV rod full rearward against internal stop in transmission. To hold this rod in position a retaining wire must be inserted through the TV lever on the transmission and into a small hole on the transmission pan.
3. Insert swivel "B" on rod "X" into the accelerator control outer lever, and then tighten compression nut. NOTE: Use the upper hole in control outer lever for four barrel carburetor and the lower hole for the two barrel carburetor.
4. Insert swivel "C" on the TV rod into the accelerator inner lever, then tighten compression nut.
5. If installed, remove the retaining wire from TV lever on transmission. Rotate the accelerator control levers through detent. Adjust accelerator pedal rod at "D" so that surface "E" comes in full contact with floor mat. The L.C.F. accelerator rod attaches at rearmost hole on the inboard arm or the inner lever. All others attach at the lower hole of outboard arm of inner control lever.

NOTE: If after adjusting linkage engine idles too fast, recheck linkage adjustment. Be sure carburetor idle speed screw is fully off the fast idle cam throughout adjustment.

Throttle Linkage Adjustments

1961-62 (Tilt Cab Models)

1. Insert 3" long pin of 1/4" diameter through two holes and notch indicated to retain linkage in proper position.
2. With the carburetor-to-lever rod clamp nut loose, place carburetor on normal idle stop and tighten clamp nut.
3. With clamp nut loose on transmission throttle valve rod and the TV lever on the transmission held fully to the rear, tighten the TV rod clamp nut.

Powermatic 1964-66 (Gasoline Engines)

1. With pull back spring in place as shown and carburetor throttle valve lever held in hot idle position (carburetor lever idle speed adjust screw against low position of cam) install rod assembly (A) by aligning swivel pin and top hole of accelerator control lever. Snap clips into place over rod assembly ends.
2. If new assembly, remove shipping wire from lever (B) with joint assembly, sleeve and nut loosely mounted at top of rod assembly (C). Install lower (clevis) end of rod assembly (C) to lever (B). Install ball assembly in proper hole in lever (D) with lever (B) held firmly rearward against internal stop. Then tighten nut (E).

1964-66 (Diesel Engines)

1. Position lever H by inserting 1/4" diameter rod thru gage hole J (hole in lever H and slot in bracket (K).
2. With lever assembly C at idle position, install rod assembly L by loosening nut M and installing ball joint assemblies in respective levers, as shown. Then tighten nut M.
3. Install ball joint assembly N loosely on rod assembly P.
4. Install lower end (clevis end) of rod assembly P to lever R. Then install ball joint assembly in hole T of lever H. Then tighten nut S.
5. Remove 1/4" diameter rod from gage holes J and remove shipping wire from lever R if new assembly.

Transmission Removal

1. Loosen or remove spark plugs and disconnect battery ground strap.

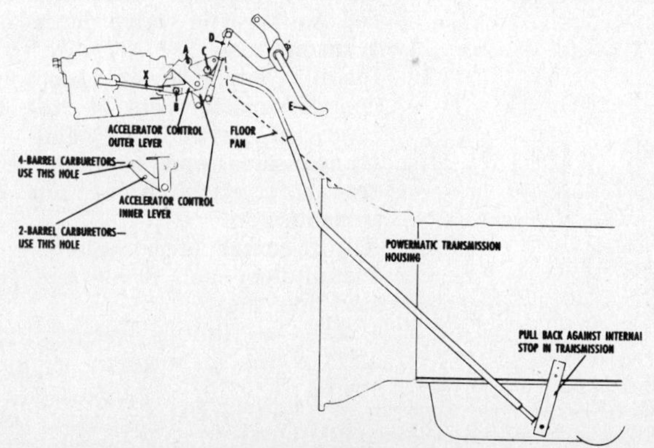

Linkage adjustment (typical)
(© Chevrolet Div., G.M. Corp.)

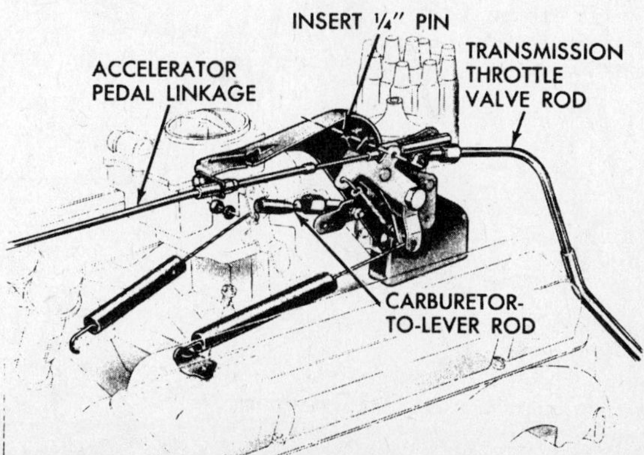

Linkage adjustment (tilt cab)
(© Chevrolet Div., G.M. Corp.)

2. Place an oil receptacle beneath filter, then loosen bolt from filter cover to allow oil to drain. Remove cover and seal ring, then pull retainer and cartridge from transmission oil pan.
3. Remove control tower as follows:
   a. Remove floor mat and remove transmission floor pan cover.
   b. Remove control tower bracket-to-transmission bolts.
   c. Disconnect neutral safety switch wires at top of transmission.
   d. Disconnect control rod (long) from lever at left front of transmission.
   e. Lift control tower assembly from transmission.
4. Disconnect throttle valve control rod from control lever.
5. Remove hydraulic retarder slave cylinder mounting bracket.
6. Remove oil level gauge, disconnect tube at right side of oil pan, disconnect vent hose at upper left side of transmission, remove tube clamp at right front of transmission and lift out tube and hose assembly.
7. Disconnect oil cooler lines at retarder valve body and disconnect warning signal wire from sender at top of oil line tee.
8. Disconnect speedometer driven shaft fitting from adapter.
9. Remove propeller shaft and bearing support and remove propeller shaft brake assembly.
10. Remove flywheel underpan and, turning flywheel as necessary, remove flywheel-to-converter pump cover stud nuts.
11. Support rear of engine and remove converter housing-to-flywheel housing bolts and lockwashers.
12. Support transmission in suitable cradle and remove transmission mounting bolts.
13. Remove transmission rear support from frame, move transmission to rear slightly and lower from under vehicle.

For overhaul procedures—see General Repair Section

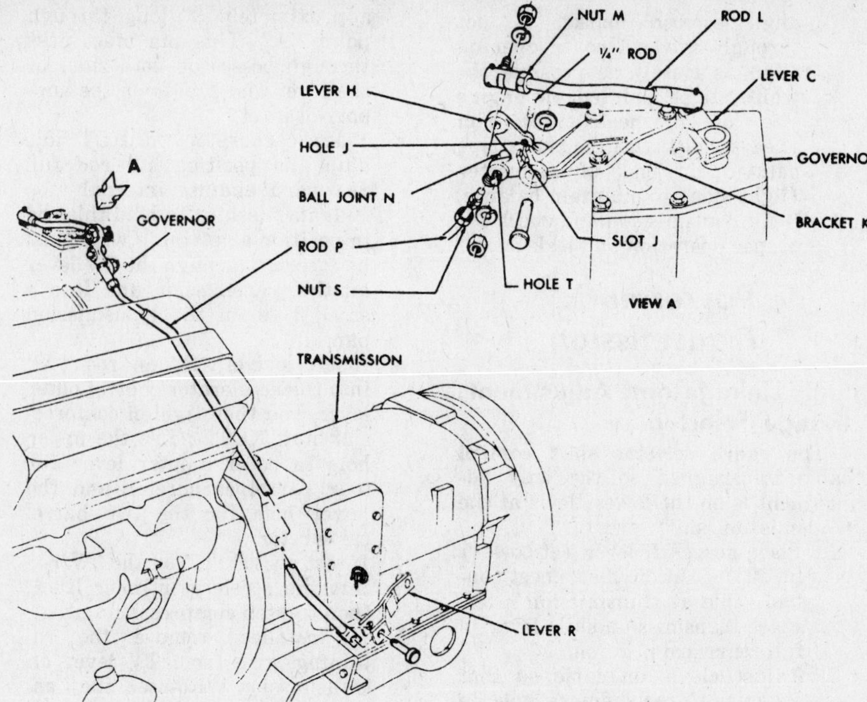

Powermatic throttle valve control (diesel engines) (© Chevrolet Div., G.M. Corp.)

Transmission Installation

1. Support transmission in suitable cradle and move it into positoin under vehicle with converter housing in approximate alignment with flywheel housing. NOTE: Make sure proper stud shims are installed if required.
2. Align studs in converter pump cover with holes in flywheel, move transmission into position and install converter housing-to-flywheel housing bolts and lockwashers.
3. Install flywheel - to - converter pump cover stud nuts and install flywheel underpan.
4. Install propeller shaft bearing support and propeller shaft brake assembly.
5. Install speedometer adapter and connect speedometer shaft to adapter.
6. Connect Oil cooler lines at brake valve body and attach warning signal wire to sender at top of tee.
7. Install oil level gauge tube and vent hose assembly and install gage.
8. Connect retarder pedal rod to lever at left front of transmission and install return spring between shaft and engine rear support.
9. Connect throttle valve control rod to throttle valve lever on transmission.
10. Install control tower assembly, connect selector control cable to lever at left front end of transmission and connect neutral safety switch at top of transmission.
11. Adjust control lever cable.
12. Install floor pan cover and install floor mat.
13. Install or tighten spark plugs and connect battery ground strap.
14. Fill with lubricant as recommended and check for proper operation and leaks.

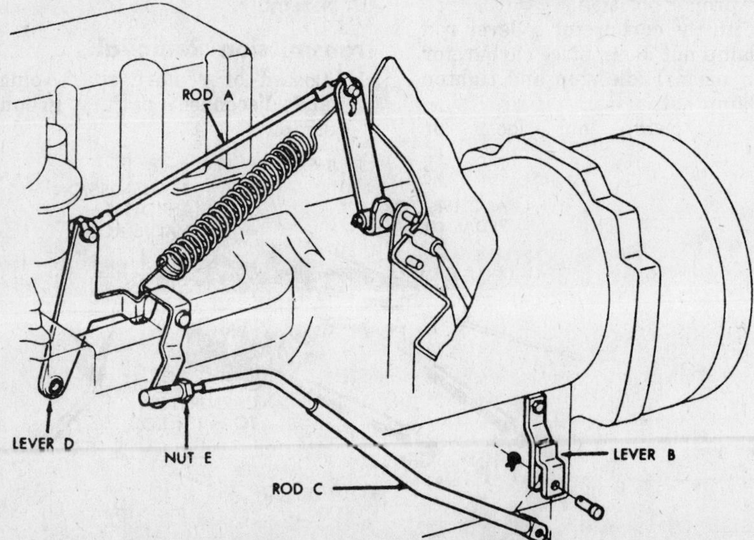

Powermatic throttle valve control (gasoline engines) (© Chevrolet Div., G.M. Corp.)

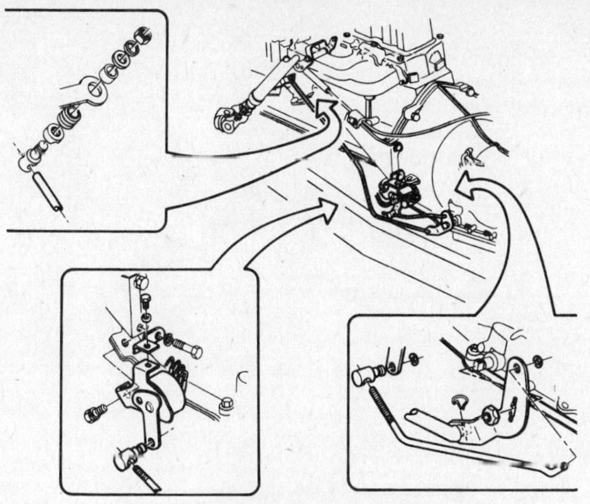

Turbo Hydra Matic control rod linkage (except forward control) (© Chevrolet Div., G.M. Corp.)

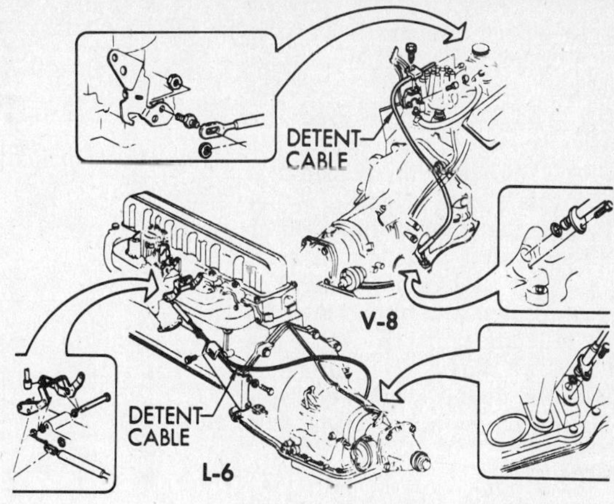

Vacuum modulator assembly (© Chevrolet Div., G.M. Corp.)

Turbo-Hydramatic

Shift Linkage

Check for adjustment with engine off, lift gearshift lever towards steering wheel, allow gearshift lever to be positioned in Drive (D) by the transmission detent. DO NOT use the indicator pointer to position the gearshift lever. Pointer is adjusted (or set) after linkage adjustment is made. Release gearshift lever. Lever must drop back into position, with no restriction, and be inhibited from engaging low range (unless lifted). Lift gearshift lever towards steering wheel and allow the lever to be positioned in Neutral (N) by the transmission detent. Release gearshift lever. The lever should now be inhibited from engaging reverse range (unless lifted). A properly adjusted linkage will prevent the gearshift lever from moving beyond both the Neutral detent and the Drive detent unless lever is lifted to pass over the mechanical stop in steering column.

Linkage Adjustment (Except Forward Control)

1. Place gearshift lever in Drive (D), as determined by transmission detent. Obtain Drive position by rotating transmission lever (A) counterclockwise to low detent, then clockwise two detent positions to Drive.
2. Loosen adjustment swivel at mast jacket lever (B) and rotate transmission lever (A) so that it contacts the Drive stop in the steering column.
3. Tighten swivel and recheck adjustment.
4. Readjust indicator pointer, if necessary, to agree with transmission detent positions.
5. Readjust Neutral safety switch if necessary (C).

Linkage Adjustment (Forward Control)

1. Set transmission lever (E) in Drive position. Obtain Drive position by rotating transmission lever (E) counter-clockwise to Low detent, then clockwise two detent positions to Drive.
2. Attach control rod (D) to lever (E) and shaft assembly (B) with retainers.
3. Assemble ring, washers, grommet, swivel, retainer and nut loosely on shaft (B).
4. Insert control rod (C) in swivel and retainer, attach opposite end to tube and lever assembly.
5. Set tube lever assembly in Drive position and tighten nut (F).

NOTE: When above procedure is adhered to, the following conditions must be met by manual operation of the gearshift lever. From Reverse to Drive position travel, the transmission detent feel must be noted and related to indicated position on dial. When in Drive and Reverse position, pull lever toward steering wheel and then release. It must drop back into position with no restriction.

CAUTION: Any inaccuracies in the above adjustments may result in premature failure of the transmission due to operation without controls in full detent position. Such operation results in reduced oil pressure and partial engagement of clutches.

Detent Switch

Turbo Hydra-matic 350

A hydraulic system, pressurized by

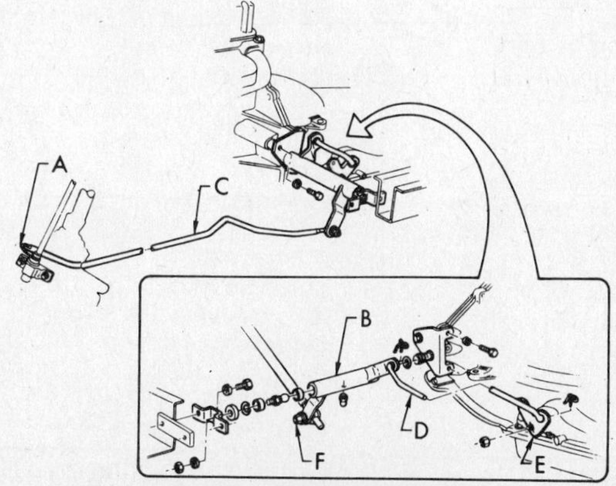

Turbo Hydra Matic control rod adjustment (forward control models) (© Chevrolet Div., G.M. Corp.)

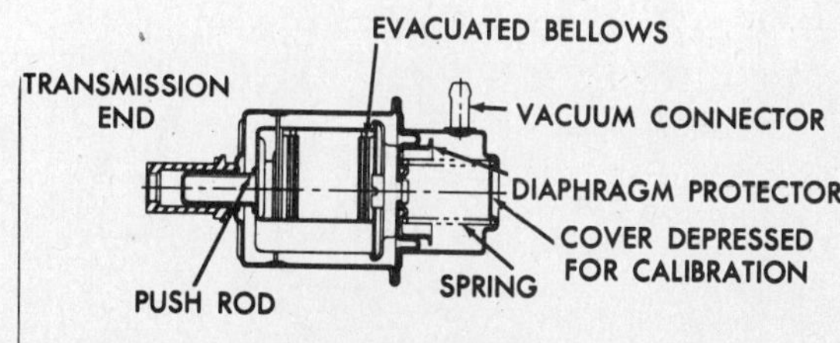

Detent cable adjustment (© Chevrolet Div., G.M. Corp.)

a gear pump, provides the working pressure required to operate the friction elements and automatic controls. The vacuum modulator is of the aneriod type and is used to automatically sense any change in torque input to the transmission. It transmits this signal to the pressure regulator, to the intermediate clutch accumulator valve and to the shift valves so that all torque and shift speed requirements of the transmission are met and smooth shifts are obtained at all throttle openings. A cable operated detent system controls downshifting for passing speeds.

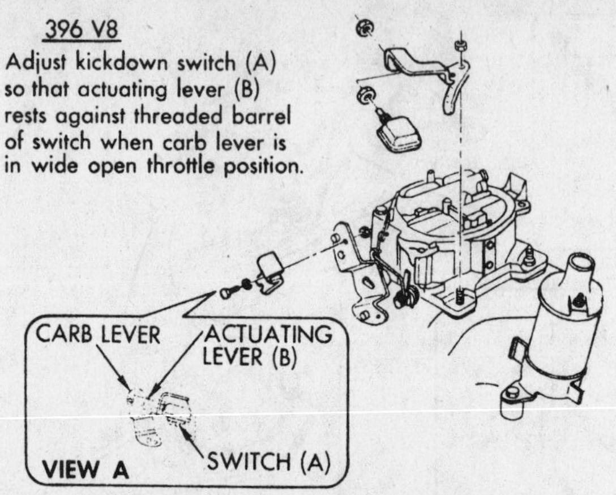

Detent switch adjustment (396 engine)
(© Chevrolet Div., G.M. Corp.)

Adjustment

1. Remove air cleaner.
2. Loosen detent cable screw.
3. With choke off and accelerator linkage properly adjusted, position carburetor lever in wide open throttle position.
4. Pull detent cable rearward until wide open throttle stop in transmission is felt. NOTE: Cable must be pulled through detent position to reach wide open throttle stop in transmission.
5. Tighten detent cable screw and check linkage for proper operation.

Turbo Hydra-matic 400

A hydraulic system pressurized by a gear pump provides the working pressure required to operate the friction elements and automatic controls. A vacuum modulator is used to automatically sense any change in torque input to the transmission. The vacuum modulator transmits this signal to the pressure regulator for line pressure control, to the 1-2 accumulator valve, and to the shift valves so that all torque requirements of this transmission are met and smooth shifts are obtained at all throttle openings. A detent solenoid, activated by an electrical switch on carburetor, controls downshift for passing speeds.

Neutral Safety Switch Adjustment

Mast Jacket Mounted

1. Place gearshift lever in Neutral (N).
2. Loosen retainer screws holding switch, install 3/32" drill (or pin) through hole in lower switch arm and bracket. Adjust position of switch until engine turns over (with ignition switch in start).

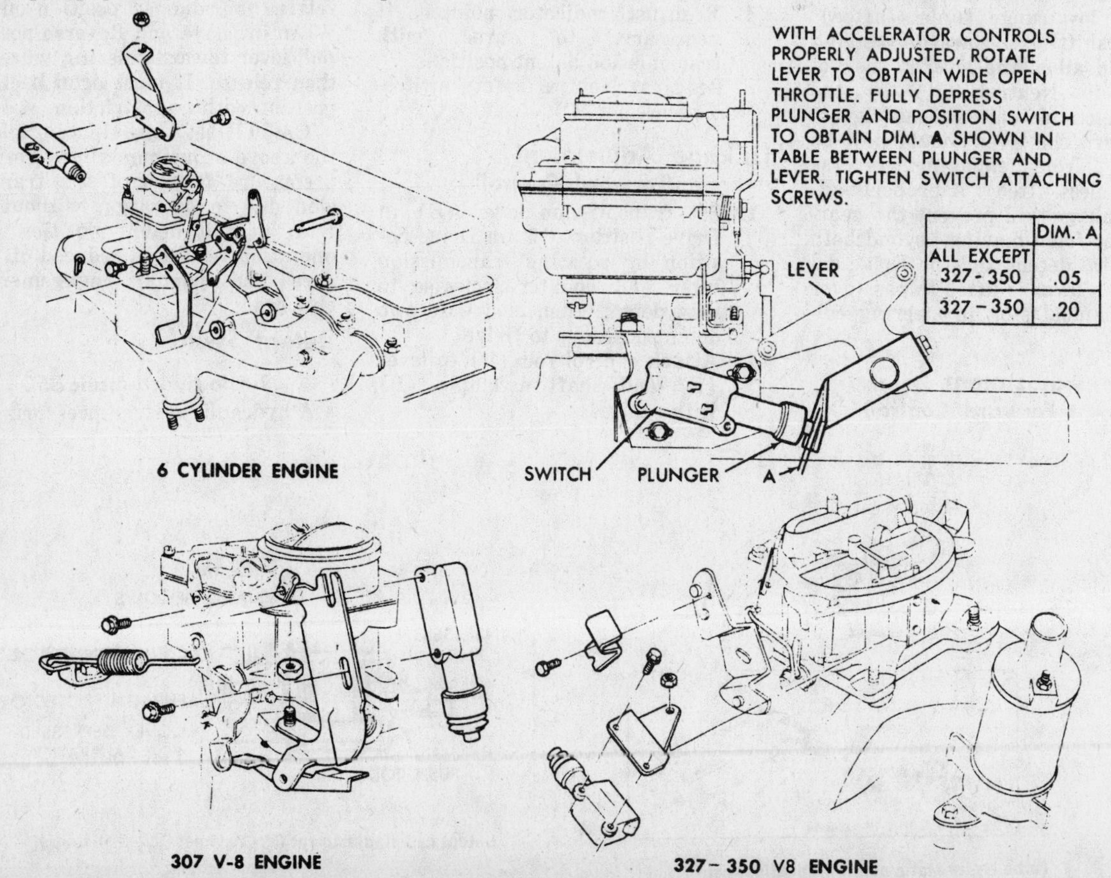

	DIM. A
ALL EXCEPT 327-350	.05
327-350	.20

Detent switch adjustment (© Chevrolet Div., G.M. Corp.)

Transmission Mounted

1. Place gearshift lever in Neutral (N), loosen transmission lever extension bolt.
2. Pin switch lever in Neutral position with 3/32″ drill or pin.
3. Install rod into switch lever, adjust swivel on rod to allow free entry of rod into lever.
4. Secure rod with retainer, tighten transmission lever extension bolt.
5. Check adjustment by testing for cranking in both Neutral and Park.

Transmission Removal

Turbo Hydra-matic 350 (Except 4 Wheel Drive)

1. Place vehicle on hoist and remove oil pan drain plug to drain oil. NOTE: If desired, the oil may be drained after transmission removal.
2. Disconnect the vacuum modulator line and the speedometer drive cable fitting at the transmission. Tie lines out of the way.
3. Disconnect manual control lever rod and detent cable from transmission.
5. Install suitable transmission lift equipment to jack or other lifting device and attach on transmission.
6. Disconnect engine rear mount on transmission extension, then remove the transmission support crossmember.
7. Remove converter underpan, scribe flywheel-converter relationship for assembly, then remove the flywheel-to-converter attaching bolts.
8. Support engine at the oil pan rail with a jack or other suitable brace capable of supporting the engine weight when the transmission is removed.
9. Lower the rear of the transmission slightly so that the upper transmission housing-to-engine attaching bolts can be reached using a universal socket and a long extension. Remove upper bolts. CAUTION: It is best to have an assistant observe clearance of upper engine components while the transmission rear end is being lowered.
10. Remove remainder of transmission housing-to-engine attaching bolts.
11. Remove the transmission by moving it slightly to the rear and downward, then remove from beneath the vehicle.

NOTE: Observe converter when moving the transmission rearward. If it does not move with transmission, pry it free of flywheel before proceeding.

CAUTION: Keep front of transmission upward to prevent the converter from falling out. Install suitable converter holding tool after removal from the engine. For overhaul procedures—see General Repair Section

Transmission Installation

Turbo Hydra-matic 350 (Except 4 Wheel Drive)

1. Mount transmission on transmission lifting equipment installed on jack or other lifting device.
2. Remove converter holding tool. CAUTION: Do not permit converter to move forward after removal of holding tool.
3. Raise transmission into place at rear of engine and install transmission case to engine upper mounting bolts, then install remainder of the mounting bolts.
4. Remove support from beneath engine, then raise rear of transmission to final position.
5. If scribed during removal, align scribe marks on flywheel and converter cover. Install converter to flywheel attaching nuts and bolts.
6. Install converter underpan.
7. Reinstall transmission support crossmember to transmission and frame.
8. Remove transmission lift equipment.
9. Connect propeller shaft to transmission.
10. Connect manual control lever rod and detent cable to transmission.
11. Connect vacuum modulator line, and speedometer drive cable to transmission.
12. Lower vehicle.
13. Refill transmission.
14. Check transmission for proper operation and for leakage. Check and, if necessary, adjust linkage.
15. Remove vehicle from hoist.

Transmission Removal

Turbo Hydra-matic 350 (4 Wheel Drive)

1. Raise vehicle on hoist and remove oil pan drain plug to drain oil. NOTE: If desired, the oil may be drained after transmission removal.
2. Remove transfer case shift lever and rod.
3. Disconnect the vacuum modulator line and the speedometer drive cable at the transmission. Tie lines out of the way.
4. Disconnect manual control lever rod and detent cable from transmission.
5. a. Disconnect front and rear axle propeller shafts at transfer case.
   b. Remove transmission to adapter case attaching bolts and place suitable support under transfer case.
   c. Install suitable transmission lift equipment to lifting device and attach to transmission.
6. Remove transfer case to frame bracket attaching bolts and remove transfer case.
7. Remove exhaust system crossover pipe on vehicles with V8 engine.
8. Remove the transmission support rear crossmember.
9. Remove converter under pan (scribe flywheel to converter relationship for assembly), then remove flywheel to converter attaching bolts.
10. Support engine at the oil pan rail with a jack or other suitable brace capable of supporting the engine weight when the transmission is removed.
11. Lower rear of the transmission slightly so that the upper transmission housing-to-engine attaching bolts can be reached using a universal socket with a long extension. Remove upper bolts. CAUTION: It is best to have an assistant observe clearance of upper engine components while the transmission rear end is being lowered.
12. Remove remainder of transmission housing-to-engine attaching bolts.
13. Remove transmission by moving it slightly to the rear and downward, then remove from beneath vehicle and transfer to work bench.

NOTE: Observe converter when moving the transmission rearward. If it does not move with the transmission, pry it free of flywheel before proceeding.

CAUTION: Keep front of transmission upward to prevent the converter from falling out. Install suitable converter holding tool after removal from engine.

Transmission Installation

Turbo Hydra-matic 350 (4 Wheel Drive)

1. Mount transmission on transmission lifting equipment installed on jack or other lifting device.
2. Remove converter holding tool.

   CAUTION: Do not permit converter to move forward after removal of holding tool.
3. Raise transmission into place at rear of engine and install transmission case to engine upper mounting bolts, then install remainder of the mounting bolts.
4. Remove support from beneath

engine, then raise rear of transmission to final position.

5. If scribed during removal, align scribe marks on flywheel and converter cover. Install converter to flywheel attaching bolts.
6. Install flywheel cover.
7. Place transfer case and adapter assembly at rear of transmission on suitable lift equipment and install transfer case to frame bracket attaching bolts.
8. Reinstall transmission to transfer case adapter attaching bolts and remove lift equipment.
10. Connect front and rear axle propeller shafts to transfer case.
11. Install exhaust system cross pipe.
12. Connect manual control lever rod and detent cable to transmission.
13. Connect vacuum modulator line and speedometer drive cable to transmission.
14. Assemble rod on transfer case shift lever before installing rod to transfer case shift linkage.
15. Lower vehicle.
16. Refill transmission.
17. Check transmission for proper operation and for leakage. Check, and if necessary, adjust linkage.
18. Remove from hoist.

Removal and Installation

Turbo Hydra-matic 400

Before raising the truck, disconnect the battery and release the parking brake.

1. Raise truck on hoist.
2. Remove propeller shaft.
3. Disconnect speedometer cable, electrical lead to case connector, vacuum line at modulator, and oil cooler pipes.
4. Disconnect shift control linkage.
5. Support transmission with transmission jack.
6. Disconnect rear mount from frame crossmember.
7. Remove two bolts at each end of frame crossmember and remove crossmember.
8. Remove converter under pan.
9. Remove converter to flywheel bolts.
10. Loosen exhaust pipe to manifold bolts approximately ¼ inch, and lower transmission until jack is barely supporting it.
11. Remove transmission to engine mounting bolts and remove oil filler tube at transmission.
12. Raise transmission to its normal position, support engine with jack and slide transmission rearward from engine and lower it away from vehicle.

CAUTION: Use converter holding tool when lowering transmission or keep rear of transmission lower than front so as not to lose converter.

The installation of the transmission is the reverse of the removal with the following additional steps.

Before installing the flex plate to converter bolts, make certain that the weld nuts on the converter are flush with the flex plate and the converter rotates freely by hand in this position. Then, hand start all three bolts and tighten finger tight before torquing to specification. This will insure proper converter alignment.

NOTE: After installation of transmission check linkage for proper adjustment and check for leaks.

U Joints, Drive Lines

Description

Tubular type propeller shafts and needle bearing type universal joints are used on all model trucks. An internally splined sleeve which compensates for variation in distance between rear axle and transmission is located at the forward end of single or rear propeller shafts.

The number of propeller shafts used is dependent upon the wheel base of the vehicle. On vehicles which use two or more propeller shafts, each shaft (except the rear) is supported near its splined end in a rubber cushioned ball bearing which is mounted in a bracket attached to a frame cross member. The ball bearing is a permanently sealed and lubricated type.

An extended-life universal joint, which does not require periodic inspection and lubrication, has been incorporated in several applications on the 10 and 20 series vehicles.

This extended-life universal joint is identified by the absence of the lubrication fitting, which is present on all trunnions not equipped with the exteneded-lift feature.

A lubrication fitting is also provided on each sliding sleeve to lubricate the splines. A plug is staked into the yoke end of sleeve to retain lubricant and a small hole is drilled in the end of this plug to relieve trapped air. The opposite end of the sleeve is sealed by means of a cork packing in a retainer which screws on the end of the sleeve.

Shaft Removal

Single or Rear

Remove rear trunnion "U" clamps, lower the rear of propeller shaft and pull back to disengage the sleeve at front of shaft. Remove shaft from under vehicle.

Front

Remove four front flange nuts at transmission and, if equipped with intermediate propeller shaft, remove the rear trunnion "U" clamps. Remove nuts and lock washers attaching bearing support to frame crossmember and pull shaft assembly from vehicle.

Intermediate or Rear Intermediate Shaft

Remove the front trunnion "U" clamps and the bearing support mounting bolt nuts and lock washers. Lower the front of the shaft and pull forward to disengage splines at rear of shaft. Remove shaft and bearing support assembly from under vehicle.

Front Intermediate Shaft

Remove the front and rear trunnion "U" clamps and the bearing support mounting bolt nuts and lock washers. Lower shaft and bearing support assembly from vehicle.

Inspection

Wash ends of propeller shaft in cleaning solvent, inspect for damage and excessive wear on splines, trunnions and bearings. Examine sleeve seal, washer and retainer for damage or deterioration.

CAUTION: When trunnion bearing "U" clamps are removed to remove the propeller shaft, tape the bearings to keep them clean and from becoming damaged. Propeller shaft guards may be removed, if necessary, by removing nut at each end of the guard.

Shaft Installation

Propeller shafts may be installed by reversing the procedure used in removal when the following notes are observed.

NOTE 1: Before installing a rear propeller shaft and sleeve assembly, slide seal retainer, steel washer and cork seal on spline of mating shaft. Assemble these parts to sleeve by turning retainer onto sleeve after rear propeller shaft is installed.

NOTE 2: Over torquing "U" clamp nuts will result in bearing cap distortion which will reduce roller bearing life.

NOTE 3: To prevent excessive driveline vibration on some models, the rear propeller shaft must be installed so that centerline of sleeve yoke is positioned from vertical to 7 splines clockwise from vertical. The centerline of either yoke at the transmissoin end is perpendicular to the ground.

NOTE 4: The propeller shaft to pinion flange fastener is an important attaching part in that it could affect the performance of vital components and systems, and/or could result in major repair expense. It must be replaced with one of the same part number or with an equiva-

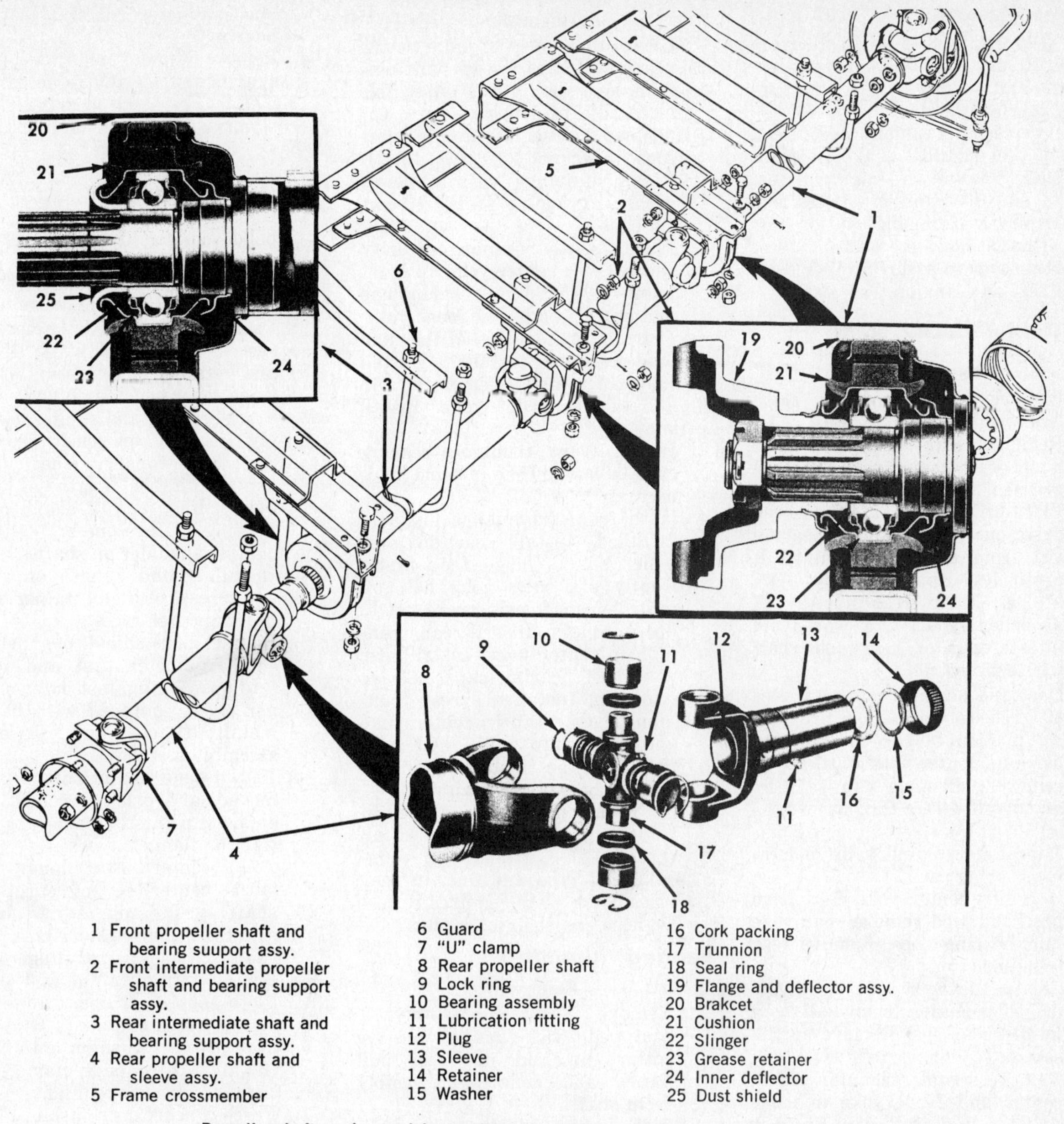

1 Front propeller shaft and bearing suuport assy.
2 Front intermediate propeller shaft and bearing support assy.
3 Rear intermediate shaft and bearing support assy.
4 Rear propeller shaft and sleeve assy.
5 Frame crossmember
6 Guard
7 "U" clamp
8 Rear propeller shaft
9 Lock ring
10 Bearing assembly
11 Lubrication fitting
12 Plug
13 Sleeve
14 Retainer
15 Washer
16 Cork packing
17 Trunnion
18 Seal ring
19 Flange and deflector assy.
20 Brakcet
21 Cushion
22 Slinger
23 Grease retainer
24 Inner deflector
25 Dust shield

Propeller shafts, universal joints and bearing supports (© Chevrolet Div., G.M. Corp.)

lent part if replacement becomes necessary. Do not use a replacement part of lesser quality or substitute design. Torque values must be used as specified during reassembly to assure proper retention of this part.

Universal Joint R&R

Disassembly

1. Remove trunnion bearings from propeller shaft yoke as follows:
   a. Remove lock rings from yoke and lubrication fitting from trunnion.
   b. Support yoke in a bench vise.
   c. Using soft drift and hammer, drive on one trunnion bearing to drive opposite bearing from yoke.

NOTE: The bearing cap cannot be driven completely out.

   d. Grasp cap in vise and work out.
   e. Support other side of yoke and drive other bearing cap from yoke and remove as in step d.
   f. Remove trunnion from propeller shaft yoke.
2. If equipped with sliding sleeve, remove trunnion bearings from sleeve yoke in the same manner as above. Remove seal retainer from end of sleeve and pull seal and washer from retainer.

Assembly

1. Assemble trunnion bearings to propeller shaft as follows:
   a. On extended life universal joints when performing service operations that require disassembly of the universal joint, repack bearings with grease as outlined in NOTE below and replace trunnion assembly dust seals.
   b. On all other universal joints lubricate trunnion bearing rollers and install new seal rings.
   c. Insert trunnion in propeller shaft yoke and press bearings into yoke and over trunnion hubs far enough to install lock rings.
   d. Hold trunnion in one hand and tap propeller shaft yoke lightly to seat bearings against lock rings.
2. On rear propeller shafts, install sleeve yoke over trunnion hubs and install bearings in the same manner as above.

NOTE: In addition to packing the bearings, make sure the lubricant reservoir at the end of each trunnion is completely filled with lubricant. In filling these reservoirs, pack lubricant into the hole so as to fill from the bottom. This will prevent air pockets and ensure an adequate supply of lubricant.

To replace trunnion dust seal, remove the old dust seal and place new seal on trunnion—cavity of seal toward end of trunnion—Press seal onto trunnion exercising caution during installation to prevent seal distortion and to assure proper seating of seal on trunnion.

Constant Velocity Joint

Disassembly

1. Remove front propeller shaft from vehicle.
2. Remove rear trunnion snap rings from center yoke. Remove grease fitting.
3. Place propeller shaft in vise and drive one rear trunnion bearing cap from center yoke until it protrudes approximately 3/8". NOTE: Keep rear portion of propeller shaft up to avoid interference of rear yoke half with center yoke.
4. Once the bearing cap protrudes 3/8", release vise. Grasp protruding portion of cap in vise and drive on center yoke until cap is removed. Remove cap seal by prying off with a thin screwdriver.
5. Repeat steps 3 and 4 for remaining bearing caps.
6. Once the center yoke caps have been removed remove rear yoke half bearing caps. Remove rear trunnion.
7. Gently pull rear yoke half from propeller shaft. Remove all loose needle bearings. Remove spring seal.
8. Remove front trunnion from center and front yoke in same manner as described in Steps 2, 3 & 4.

NOTE: Before front trunnion can be removed all four (4) bearing caps must be removed.

Assembly

1. Clean and inspect all needle bearings, caps, seals, fittings, trunnions and yokes. Assemble all needle bearings in caps (27 per cap); assemble needle bearings in front yoke (28 total). Retain bearings with a heavy grease. Assemble seals to bearing caps.
2. Place front trunnion in drive shaft. Place center yoke on front trunnion. Install one bearing cap and seal assembly in front yoke. Drive in to a depth that the snap ring can be installed. Install snap ring. Install remaining cap and seal in front yoke. Install snap ring.
3. Install front trunnion bearing caps in center yoke in same manner.
4. With front trunnion completely installed, install seal on propeller shaft (large face first). Gently slip rear yoke half on propeller shaft using care not to upset rollers. Insert rear trunnion in center yoke. Install rear yoke half bearing caps on rear trunnion. Install one rear trunnion bearing cap in center yoke and press into yoke until snap ring can be installed. Install remaining cap and snap ring.
5. Before assembly is reinstalled in vehicle, grease universal at all three (3) fittings (2 conventional type and one, in rear yoke half), that requires a needle nose grease gun adapter.

Bearing Support

Removal

1. Remove dust shield, or, if equipped with flange, remove cotter pin and nut and pull flange and deflector assembly from shaft.
2. Pull support bracket from rubber cushion and pull cushion from bearing.
3. Pull bearing assembly from shaft. Remove grease retainers and slingers (if used) from bearing.
4. Remove inner deflector from shaft if replacement is necessary.

NOTE: The ball bearing is a permanently sealed and lubricated type.

Installation

1. Install inner deflector on propeller shaft, if removed, and prick punch deflector at two opposite points to make sure it is tight on shaft.
2. Pack retainers with grease. Insert a slinger (if used) inside one retainer and press this retainer over bearing outer race.
3. Start bearing and slinger assembly straight on shaft journal. Support propeller shaft and, using suitable length of pipe over splined end of shaft, press bearing and inner slinger against shoulder on shaft.
4. Install second slinger on shaft and press second retainer over bearing outer race.
5. Install dust shield over shaft, small diameter first and press into position against outer slinger or, if equipped with flange, install flange and deflector assembly as follows:
   a. Install deflector on flange, if removed, and prick punch at two opposite points to make sure it is tight on flange.
   b. Align centerline of flange yoke with centerline of propeller shaft yoke and start flange straight on splines of shaft with end of flange against slinger.
   c. Install retaining nut and tighten to 160-180 ft. lbs. torque. Install cotter pin.
6. Force rubber cushion onto bearing and coat outside diameter of cushion with brake fluid.
7. Force bracket onto cushion.

Drive Shaft Alignment

Correct drive line angles are necessary to prevent excessive torsional vibrations, especially tandem

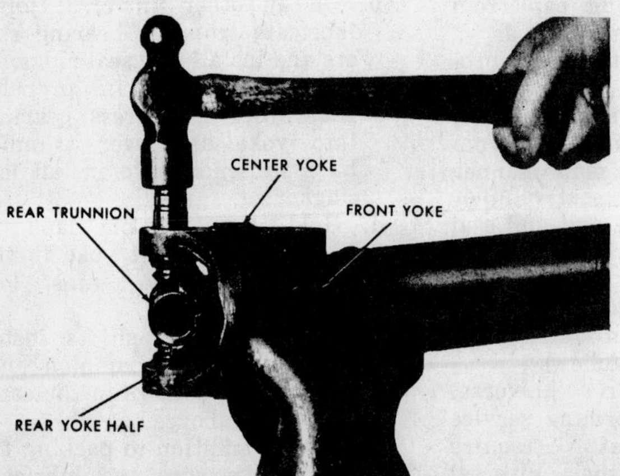

Driving out U-joint bearing cups
(© Chevrolet Div., G.M. Corp.)

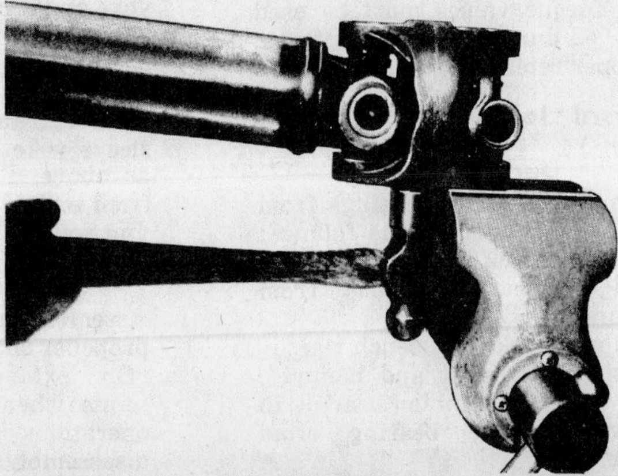
Removing U-joint bearing cups
(© Chevrolet Div., G.M. Corp.)

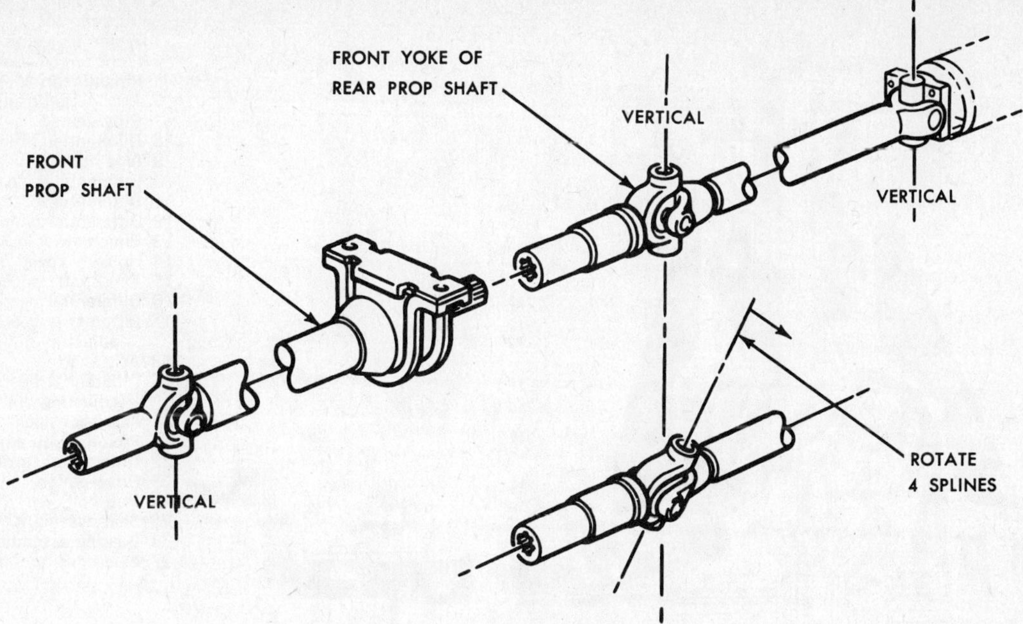

Aligning universal joints (© Chevrolet Div., G.M. Corp.)

rear axle models. On some vehicles adjustable auxiliary transmission mountings are provided for adjusting the angle of the various drive line components. On vehicles not having adjustable auxiliary transmission mountings and adjustable torque rods at rear axles, proper adjustment of the angle of the drive line components must be accomplished by the use of spacers or shims at the frame crossmember or hangers. All angles must be checked with a maximum amount of exactness. The use of a bubble level is not sufficient, a bevel protractor must be used. The vehicle should be checked on a reasonably flat surface.

Clean machined surface at rear of (main) tranmission to check engine (and transmission) angle. This is key angle and auxiliary transmission (if equipped) and rear axle pinion must be set to this angle. Make sure all drive line components from (main) transmission to rear axle are properly centered. Clean dirt and paint off machined surface of propeller shaft yoke, make sure surface is free of nicks or burrs. Set bevel protractor to zero, place protractor on yoke surface at right angle to propeller shaft and rotate shaft until bubble is centered in glass. Reposition protractor on yoke, in-line with propeller shaft, and note shaft angle.

Shaft angle must be held within a maximum of 1° less than engine. Check rear axles on machined surfaces on differential carrier housing, at right angle to pinion shaft. Make sure protractor is held straight up to get correct angle. On rear axles that do not have a machined surface it will be necessary to remove propeller shaft. Rotate the pinion yoke into a vertical position, clean the four machined ends of yoke of dirt, paint, nicks and burrs. Place the protractor across ends of yoke, on either side, and in as close as possible to a vertical position. Rear axle angle should be same as engine.

Rear Axle

Chevrolet Semi Floating Single Speed

Description

Two types of rear axles are used. The removable carrier type thru 1962 with Hotchkiss drive and the Salisbury type from 1963 with an integral carrier.

The following applies to both rear axles except where noted.

The drive pinion is mounted on two preloaded taper roller bearings. The ring gear is bolted to the differential case which is mounted on preloaded taper roller bearings. There are two side gears and two differential pinion gears.

Axle Shaft Removal

1. Remove the brake drum.
3. Drain lubricant from the differential and remove the housing cover.
4. Remove the differential pinion shaft lock screw, pinion shaft and axle shaft spacer.
5. Push the axle shaft in and remove the "C" washer from the inner end of the axle shaft.
6. Remove the axle shaft from the housing.

Installation

NOTE: If a new axle shaft is to be installed.

1. Position the axle shaft gasket to

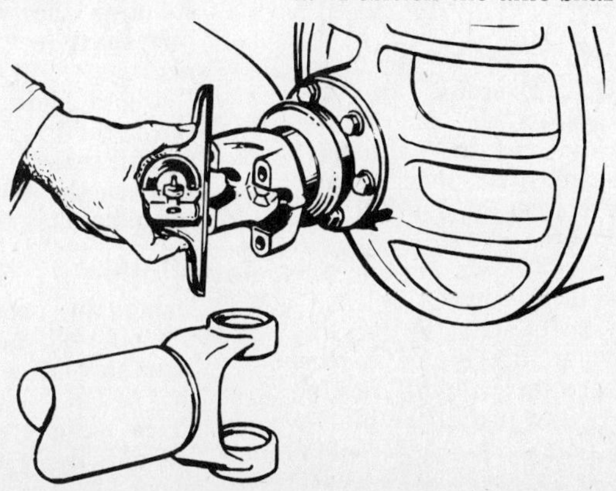

Checking pinion angles
(© Chevrolet Div., G.M. Corp.)

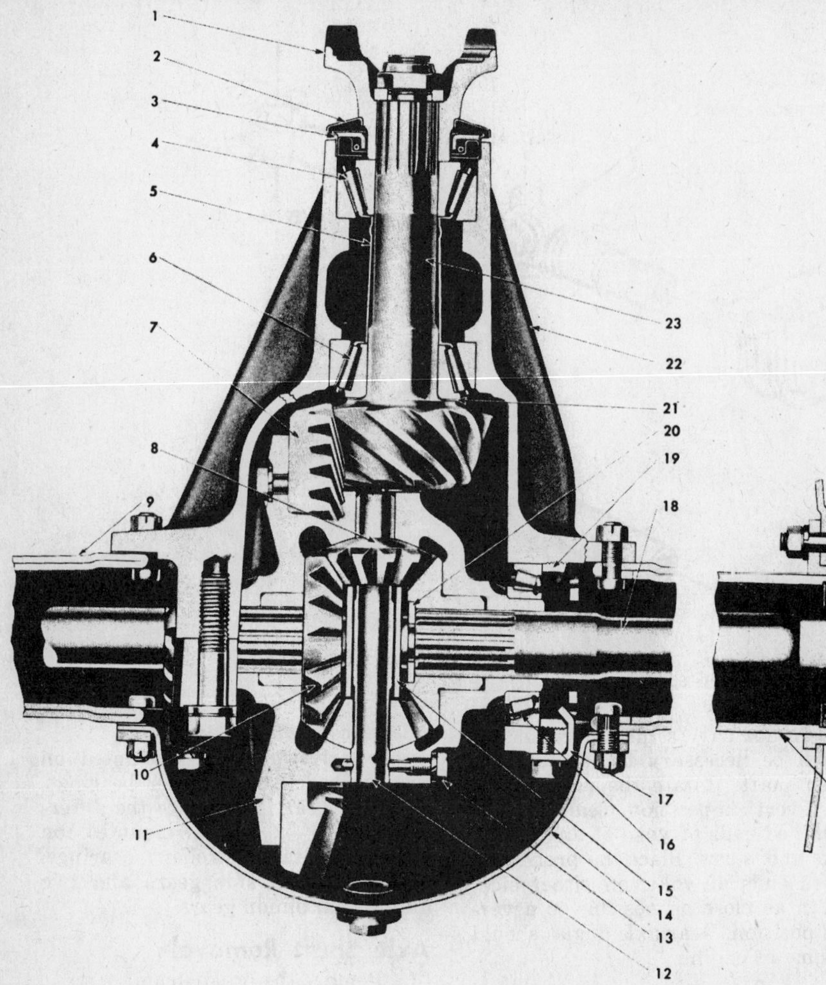

1 Pinion flange
2 Oil deflector
3 Pinion flange oil seal
4 Front pinion bearing
5 Pinion bearing spacer
6 Rear pinion bearing
7 Ring gear
8 Differential pinion
9 Axle housing
10 Differential side gear
11 Differential case
12 Differential pinion shaft
13 Pinion shaft lock screw
14 Housing cover
15 Axle shaft spacer
16 Differential bearing
17 Differential bearing adjusting nut lock
18 Axle shaft
19 Differential bearing adjusting nut
20 Axle shaft lock
21 Pinion depth adjusting shim
22 Differential carrier
23 Drive pinion
24 Hub bolt
25 Seal assembly
26 Bearing assembly
27 Axle housing

½ ton axle shaft and differential assembly (© Chevrolet Div., G.M. Corp.)

the axle shaft flange.

2. Apply heavy shellac or paint to both sides of the gasket and axle shaft oil deflector.
3. Install the axle shaft oil deflector over the gasket aligning the oil pocket with the notch in the flange.
4. Insert six special axle shaft bolts and force the heads down to the deflector.
5. Peen the end of the shoulder on the bolts into the countersink around the bolt holes in the flange.
6. Slide the axle shaft into place. CAUTION: Exercise care that the splines on the end of the shaft do not cut the axle shaft oil seal and that they engage with the splines of the differential side gears.
7. Install the "C" washer on the inner end of the shaft.
8. Pry the shafts apart so that the "C" washers are seated in the counterbore in the differential side gears and install the pinion gears.
9. Select the proper axle shaft spacer to give free fit to .014" maximum clearance between the end of the axle shaft and the spacer.
10. Install the spacer and pinion shaft, locking in place with the special screw.
11. Install the axle housing cover and gasket and refill the differential.
12. Install the drum and wheel.
13. Road test for leaks and noise.

Axle Shaft Bearing or Oil Seal Removal

1. Remove the wheel, drum and axle shaft (see axle shaft removal).
2. Using a slide hammer, remove the bearing, bearing retainer and oil seal.
3. Inspect the bore and dress out the old stake points.

Installation

1. Using the proper driver, place the oil seal, bearing and inside bearing retainer on the driver in that order.
2. Place a light coat of sealer on the outside of the seal to insure proper sealing of the seal in the housing bore.
3. Start the bearing into the axle housing and tap the tool with a hammer to seat the parts.
4. Remove the driver and stake the oil seal in place with a punch.
5. Assemble the axle shafts (see Axle Shaft Installation).

Pinion Flange, Oil Deflector and/or Oil Seal Replacement

1. Raise the vehicle and support the frame on stand jacks, allow the axle to drop for clearance and expand the brake shoes on one wheel to lock the wheel.
2. Check the free wheel for freedom of rotation.
3. Separate the rear universal, tape the trunnion bearings to the joint and lower the rear of the propeller shaft.
4. Using a one inch torque wrench, and proper socket on the pinion flange nut, rotate the pinion through several complete revolutions and record the torque required to keep the pinion turning. If the old flange is to be installed, mark the pinion and flange for reassembly in the same relative position.
5. Hold the pinion flange, remove the pinion flange nut and special

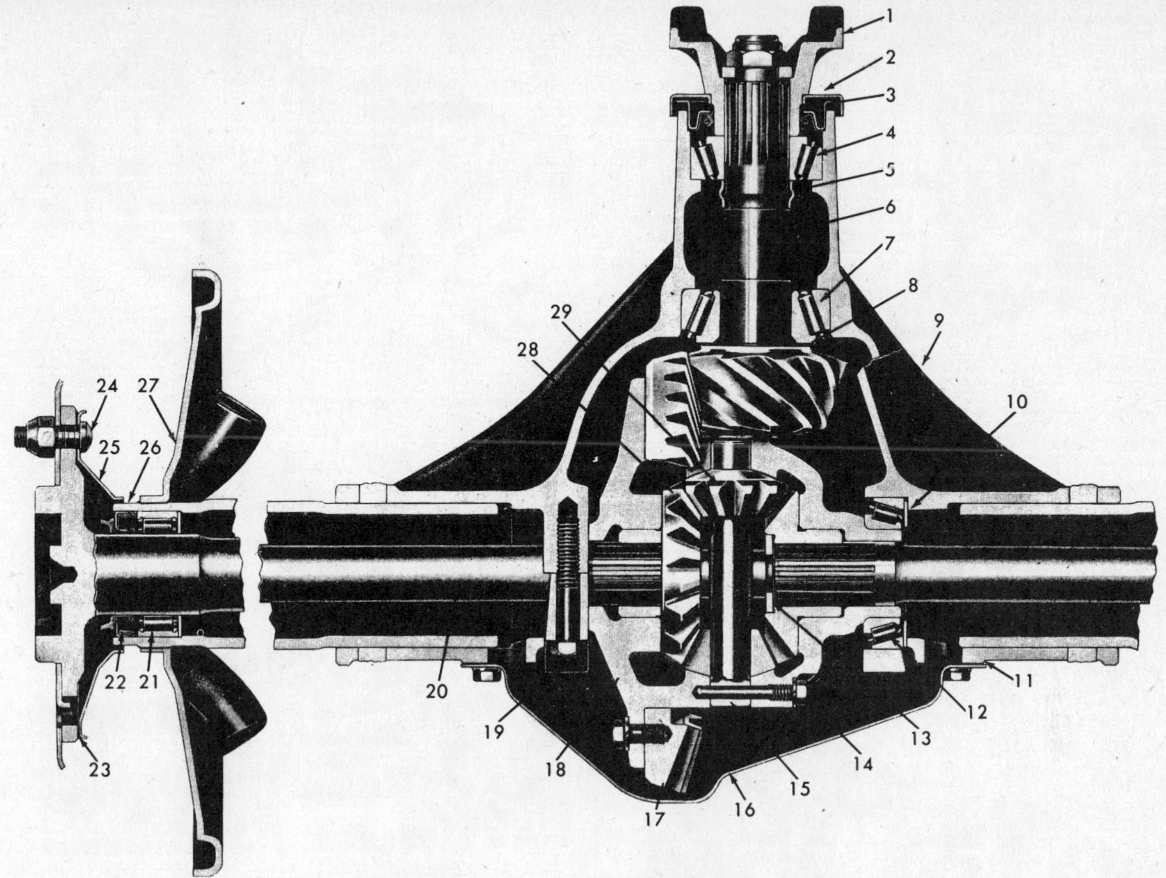

1 Companion flange
2 Deflector
3 Pinion oil seal
4 Pinion front bearing
5 Pinion bearing spacer
6 Drive pinion
7 Pinion rear bearing
8 Shim
9 Differential carrier
10 Shim
11 Gasket
12 Differential bearing
13 "C" lock
14 Differential pinion shaft lock bolt
15 Differential pinion shaft
16 Cover
17 Ring gear
18 Differential case
19 Bearing cap
20 Axle shaft
21 Wheel bearing
22 Oil seal
23 Gasket
24 Wheel bolt
25 Oil deflector
26 Axle shaft housing
27 Brake flange plate
28 Differential side gear
29 Differential pinion

3300 and 3500 lb. capacity axle—cross section (© Chevrolet Div., G.M. Corp.)

Bearing and oil seal removal (© Chevrolet Div., G.M. Corp.)

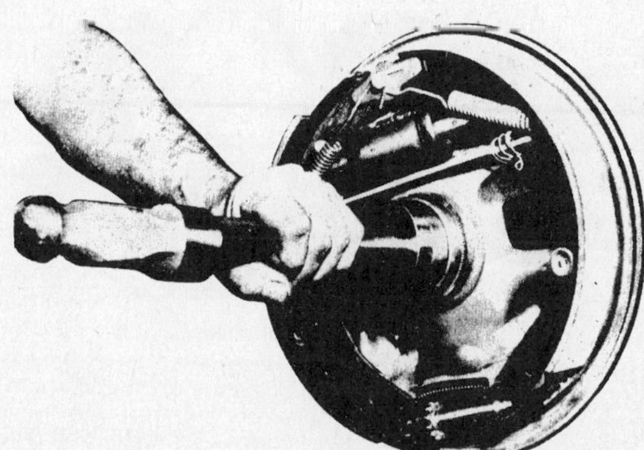

Bearing and/or oil seal installation (© Chevrolet Div., G.M. Corp.)

washer. Discard the nut and use a new one upon reassembly.

6. Remove the pinion flange. Pry the old oil seal out of the case.
7. Inspect the pinion flange for smooth oil seal surface or worn drive splines. Replace if necessary.
8. Install a new flange oil deflector if the deflector is damaged.
9. Soak the new seal in light engine oil before installation. Wipe the outside of the seal and coat the outside with sealer.
10. Install the new seal using the

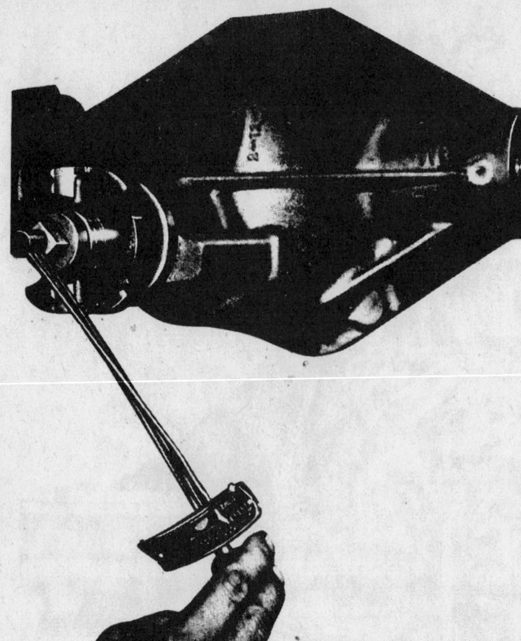
Measuring pinion bearing preload (© Chevrolet Div., G.M. Corp.)

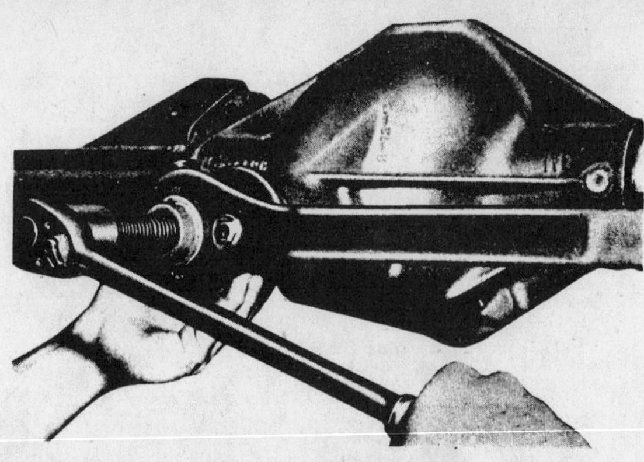
Pinion flange removal (© Chevrolet Div., G.M. Corp.)

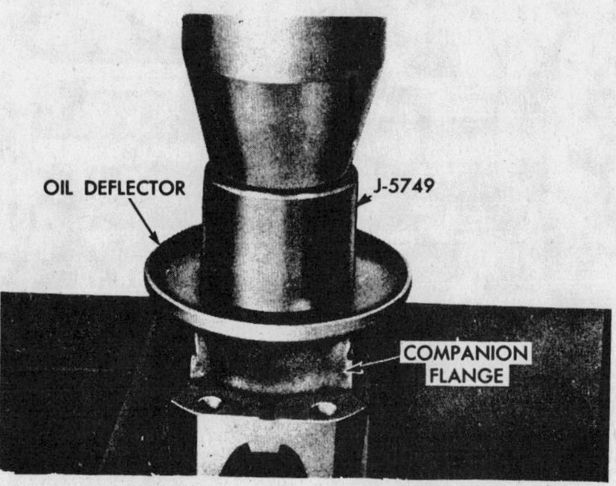

Pinion flange deflector installation (© Chevrolet Div., G.M. Corp.)

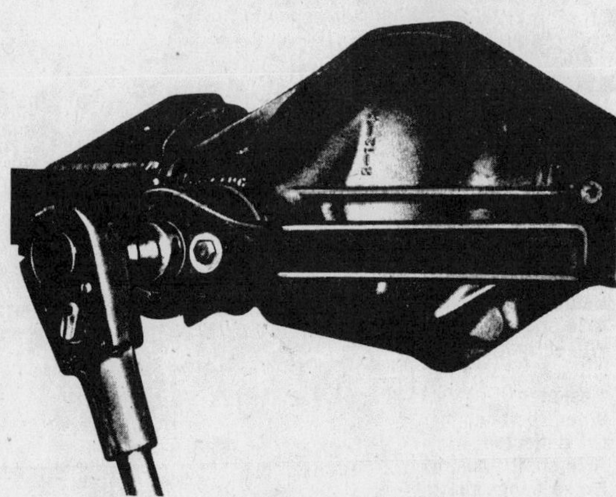
Drive pinion nut removal (© Chevrolet Div., G.M. Corp.)

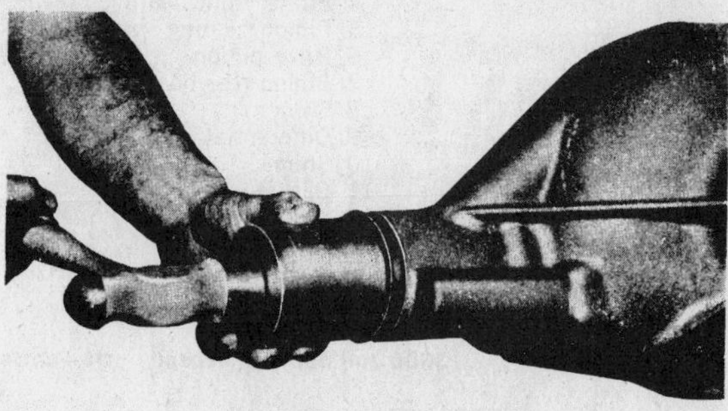
Pinion flange oil seal installation (© Chevrolet Div., G.M. Corp.)

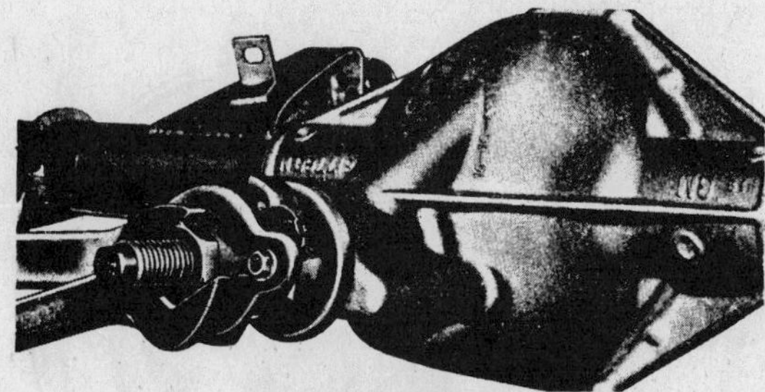
Pinion flange installation (© Chevrolet Div., G.M. Corp.)

proper driver.

11. Install the pinion flange, aligning the marks on the pinion and flange if the old flange is being used. If the flange does not go on the shaft easily, pull the flange on the shaft using a special tool. Remove the special tool and install the special washer and new nut.
12. Tighten the nut to remove end play and continue alternately tightening and checking preload with an inch pound torque wrench until it is the same as recorded in step 4.
13. Readjust the brake on the locked wheel.
14. Connect the propeller shaft, lower the vehicle and road test for leaks and noise.

Removable Carrier Differential Removal

1. Remove the wheel, drum and axle shafts (see Axle Shaft Removal).
2. Reinstall the axle shaft spacer, pinion shaft and lock screw to retain assembly for removal

from the vehicle.
3. Separate the rear universal, tape the trunnion bearings to the joint and lower the rear of the propeller shaft.
4. Remove the nuts which attach the differential carrier to the axle housing, separate the carrier from the housing and remove the carrier from the vehicle.

For overhaul—see general section.

Installation

1. Clean the axle housing and differential gasket surfaces and install a new gasket.
2. Position the differential carrier to the axle housing, install the nuts and tighten securely.
3. Connect the rear universal joint.
4. Assemble the axle shafts (see Axle Shaft Installation).

Salisbury Differential Removal

1. Remove the wheel, drum and axle shafts (see Axle Shaft Removal).
2. Roll out the differential pinion and thrust washers, then remove the side gears and thrust washers. Mark the pinions and side gears so that they can be reassembled in the original position.
3. Mark one bearing cap and housing for reassembly in the same position. Remove the bearing cap bolts and bearing caps, tap the surface of the bearing caps to loosen. CAUTION: Do not pry the caps off as this may damage the machined face of the caps.

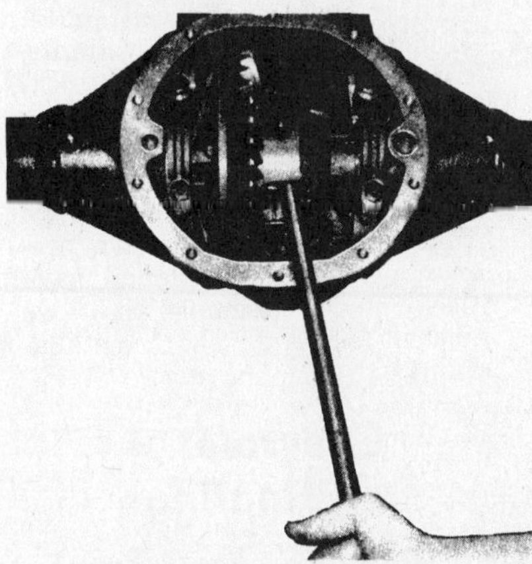

Differential case removal
(© Chevrolet Div., G.M. Corp.)

4. Using a pry bar, pry the differential case out of the carrier. NOTE: Exercise caution in prying on the case and gasket sealing surface. If the bearings are preloaded, the case will suddenly fall free when it is pried past a certain point. Make sure the case is properly supported to prevent damage.
5. Place the left and right bearing cups, caps and shims so that they may be reinstalled in the original positions.

Salisbury Drive Pinion Removal

1. Remove the differential as previously outlined.
2. Remove the propeller shaft.
3. Remove the pinion flange nut and washer. Discard the nut and use a new one upon reassembly.
4. Remove the pinion flange. Pry the oil seal out of the bore.
5. Remove the drive pinion by tapping on the front end with a soft faced hammer.
6. Remove the pinion front bearing from the carrier bore. Discard the pinion bearing spacer and use a new one upon reassembly.
7. Clean all gears and bearings and inspect all bearing cups, races and rollers for scoring, chipping or excessive wear. Inspect pinion splines and flange splines. Inspect the ring gear and pinion teeth.

Salisbury Pinion and/or Bearing Replacement

1. If necessary to replace the pinion bearings, tap the old cups out of the carrier using a brass drift.
2. Position the new cup in the carrier, thick edge of the cup toward the shoulder of the carrier. Using a cup installer, tap the cup into the carrier until it is fully seated against the shoulder.

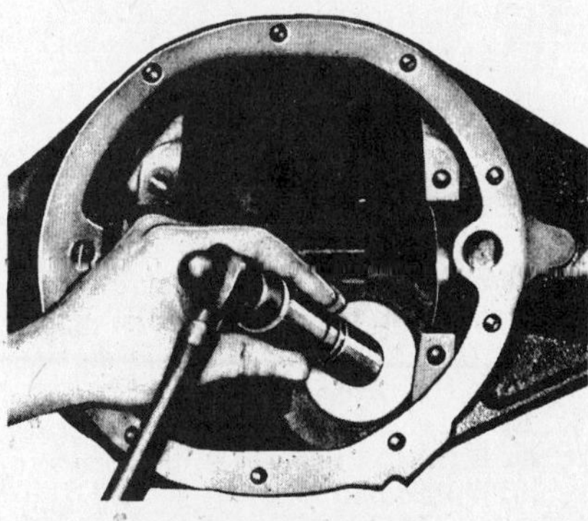

Installing bearing cap
(© Chevrolet Div., G.M. Corp.)

3. Press the rear bearing cone and roller assembly from the pinion and note the shim between the bearing cone and pinion head.
4. When the ring gear and pinion or the pinion rear bearing assembly are replaced, the correct shim thickness must be determined by using special gauges or the trial and error method according to tooth pattern.
5. Position the shim selected on the pinion shaft against the pinion head.
6. Press the new cone and roller assembly on the pinion.

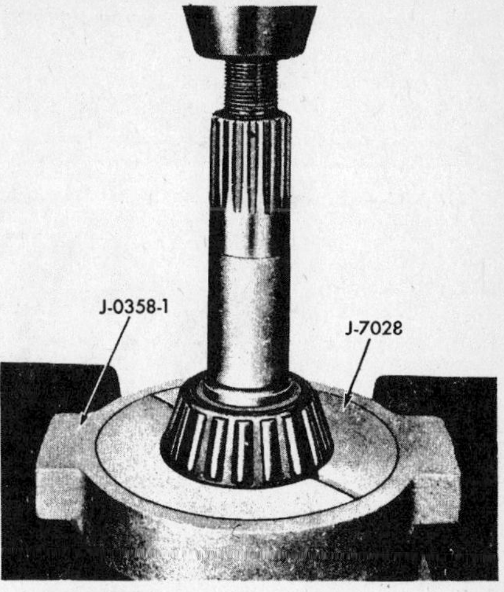

Pinion cone & roller assembly removal
(© Chevrolet Div., G.M. Corp.)

Salisbury Drive Pinion Installation

1. Position the drive pinion and rear bearing cone and roller assembly in the carrier, install a new pinion bearing spacer on the pinion shaft and install the pinion front bearing cone and roller assembly.
2. Soak the new seal in light engine oil before installation. Wipe the outside of the seal and coat the outside with sealer.
3. Install the new seal using the proper driver.
4. Install the pinion flange. If the flange does not go on the shaft easily, pull the flange on the shaft using a special tool. Remove the special tool and pack the cavity between the end of the pinion splines and pinion flange with a non-hardening sealer.
5. Install the pinion flange washer and new nut. Tighten the nut to remove end play and continue alternately tightening and checking preload with an inch pound torque wrench until torque required to rotate the pinion is 20-25 in. lbs. for new bearings and seal, or 5-10 in. lbs. when used parts are installed.

Salisbury Differential Bearing Replacement

1. Using a bearing puller, remove the bearings from the case.
2. Place the new bearing on the hub of the case, thick side of inner race toward case. Using a

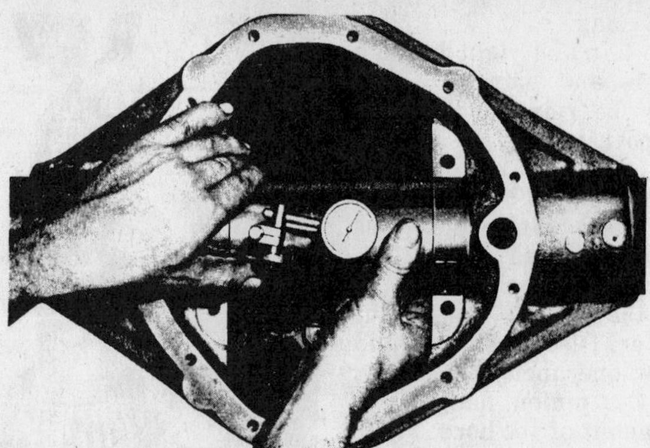

PINION SHIM IDENTIFICATION

Thickness	Identification Notches
.021	None
.024	1
.027	2
.030	3
.033	4

Measuring pinion shim requirement
(© Chevrolet Div., G.M. Corp.)

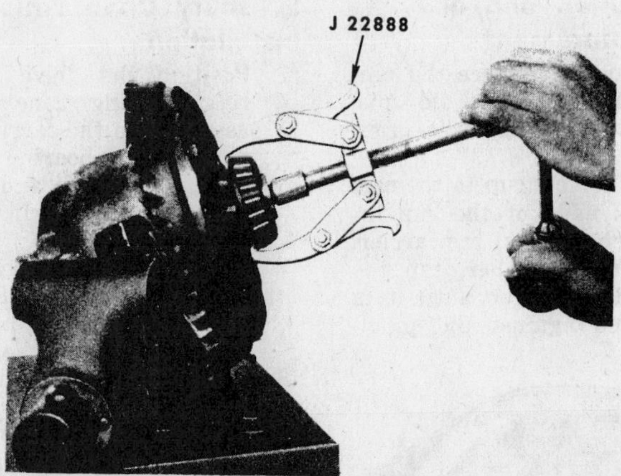

Differential bearing removal
(© Chevrolet Div., G.M. Corp.)

bearing driver, drive the bearing into place.

3. Before installing the bearing on the opposite hub, support the case on an adapter. This allows the case to rest on the adapter instead of the bearing cage which has already been installed. Install the remaining bearing.

Salisbury Ring Gear Replacement

1. Remove the ring gear bolts and lock washers and, using a soft faced hammer, tap the ring gear off the case.
2. Install five guide pins, made from 3/8"—24x1½" long cap screws with the heads cut off and ends slotted, to the ring gear.
3. Position the ring gear on the case. Install every other ring gear bolt and lock washer, then draw them up evenly and snugly so that the gear face is flush with the case.
4. Remove the guide pins and install the remaining bolts, torque all bolts to 50 ft. lbs.

Salisbury Differential Bearing Preload

1. Place the differential case and bearing assembly in the carrier. If the same bearings and case are used, select new right and left adjusting shims each 0.002" thicker than the original shim. If new bearings and/or case are being installed, loosely install the left bearing cap and select the preload shim as follows:
   a. Select two shims of known thickness and position them between the right bearing cup and the cup seat in the carrier. (select shims with a total thickness that will permit a feeler gauge of at least .010" to be inserted between the shim and cup seat in the carrier) Make sure the left bearing cup and case are against the left cup seat. Using a feeler gauge, determine the distance between the shim and cup seat.
   b. Add .010" to the total of both shims and feeler gauge thickness used in step a, then select two shims of equal thickness which in total are equal to the value obtained in step a plus the additional .010".

NOTE: Use only one shim at each side.

2. Remove the left bearing cap and position the shim between the bearing cup and cup seat. Wedge the right shim between the bearing cup and cup seat (position the shim so that the chamfered side is outward or next to the cup seat). Tap the shim into position, using a soft faced hammer, while rotating the differential case.
3. Install the bearing caps and torque them alternately to 50-60 ft. lbs.

Salisbury Ring Gear and Pinion Adjustment

1. Mount a dial indicator on the carrier and check the backlash between the ring gear and pinion. The backlash should be within .003"-.010" with .005"-.008" preferred. Check gear lash at four equally spaced positions around the gear. Variations in reading should not exceed .001".
2. If gear lash is not within limits, correct by decreasing shim thickness on one side and increasing thickness of the other shim the same amount. Total shim thickness must be maintained at all times to maintain proper preload. After adjustments have been made, assemble the axle shafts (see Axle Shaft Installation).

Chevrolet Full Floating

Description

Single Speed

The rear axle is a full floating type with hypoid ring gear and pinion. The full floating construction enables removal of the axle shafts without removing the truck load or jacking up the rear axle. The drive pinion is straddle mounted being supported at the rear end on a roller bearing and at the front end on a double row bearing.

Measuring differential shim requirement
(© Chevrolet Div., G.M. Corp.)

Checking ring gear backlash
(© Chevrolet Div., G.M. Corp.)

Installing differential shim
(© Chevrolet Div., G.M. Corp.)

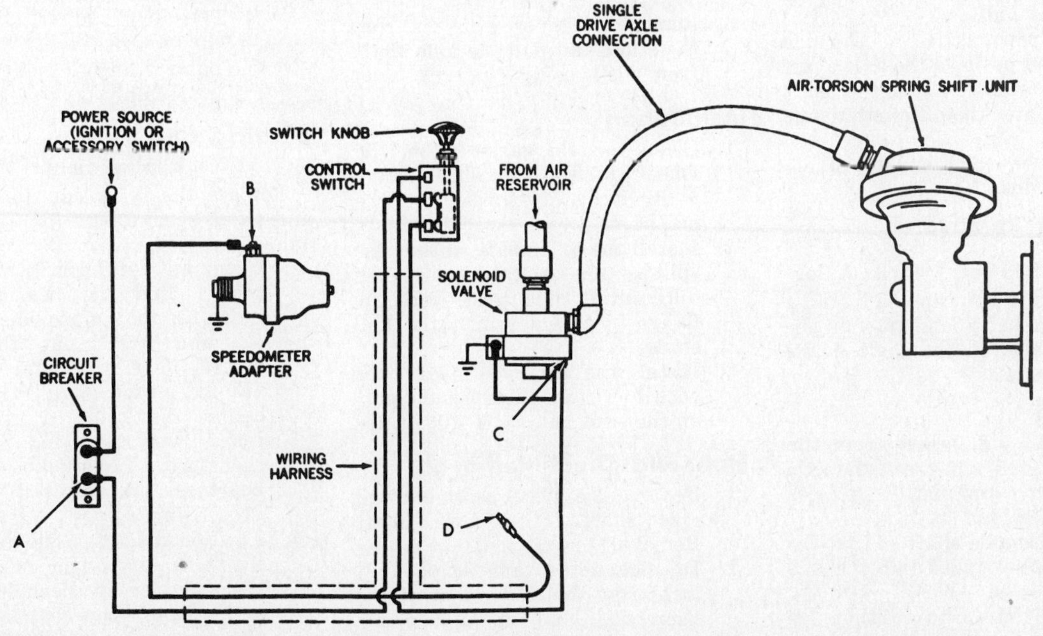

Vacuum shift system (© Chevrolet Div., G.M. Corp.)

The ring gear is bolted to the differential case and some models are provided with a ring gear thrust pad to prevent distortion when starting under heavy loads.

Some models have a two pinion differential while others have a four pinion differential.

Description

Two-Speed

The Chevrolet two-speed axle is available in the 15,000 and 17,000 lb. capacity. In low gear, torque is transmitted to the differential case through the planetary pinions. The straddle mounted drive pinion and the ring gears operate to produce the high range reduction, the planet and sun gears being locked to revolve with the ring gear.

Early models have a two way vacuum system for axle shifts. Later models use an electric shift system.

Maintenance and adjustments for the two speed axle are performed the same as those outlined for the Chevrolet single-speed axles.

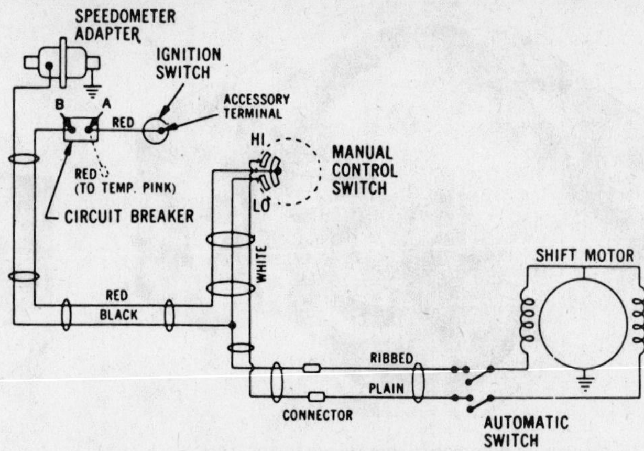

Electric shift system—wiring
(© Chevrolet Div., G.M. Corp.)

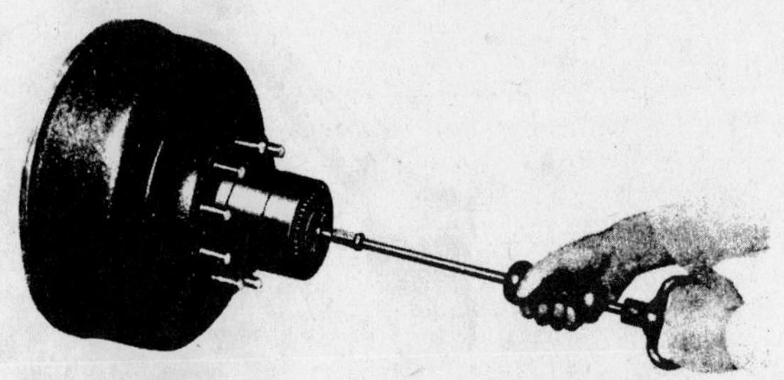

Removing axle shaft—11,000, 13,500 and 15,000 lb. axle
(© Chevrolet Div., G.M. Corp.)

Axle Shaft Removal

5200 and 7200 lb. Axles

1. Remove the bolts and lockwashers that attach the axle shaft flange to the wheel hub.
2. Install two ½" - 13 bolts in the threaded holes provided in the axle shaft flange. By turning these bolts alternately the axle shaft may be started and then removed from the housing.

Installation

1. Clean both the axle flange and the wheel hub.
2. Place a new gasket over the axle shaft and position the axle shaft in the housing so that the shaft splines enter the differential side gear.
3. Install the bolts and torque to 85-95 ft. lbs.

Axle Shaft Removal

11,000-13,500 and 1500 lb. Axles

1. Remove the hub cap and install a slide hammer and adapter in the tapped hole on the shaft flange
2. Remove the axle shaft.

Installation

1. Clean the old gasket from the hub and hub cap. Clean the axle shaft flange and mating surfaces in the wheel hub.
2. Install the axle shaft so that the shaft splines index into the hub splines.
3. Tap the shaft into position. Install a new hub cap gasket, position the hub cap to the hub and install the attaching bolts. Torque the bolts to 11-18 ft. lbs.

Axle Shaft Removal

17,000 lb. Axle

1. Remove the axle shaft flange—to—hub nuts.
2. Strike the flange with a lead hammer to loosen the flange and dowels.
3. Remove the tapered dowels from the studs and pull the axle shaft from the housing.

Installation

1. Clean the old gasket from the wheel hub and axle shaft flange and install a new gasket over the hub studs.
2. Install the axle shaft so that the splines are aligned with the differential side gear and the flange holes index over the hub studs.
3. Install the tapered dowel over each hub stud. Install and tighten the stud nuts to 80-100 ft. lbs

Hub and Drum Removal

1. Remove the wheel assembly and axle shaft. (See Axle Shaft Removal)
2. Disengage the tang of the nut lock from the slot or flat of the lock nut. Using an appropriate tool, remove the lock nut from the housing.
3. Disengate the tang of the nut lock from the slot or flat of the adjusting nut and remove the nut lock. Using an appropriate tool, remove the adjusting nut. NOTE: On 5200 through 15,000 lb. axles, remove the thrus washer from the housing tube.
4. Pull the hub and drum assembly straight off the axle housing. NOTE: On 11,000 through 17,000 lb. axles avoid dropping the outer bearing inner race and roller assembly.

Bearing and Bearing Cup

Replacement

Replace the inner cup (all axles) and outer bearing cup for 17,000 lb. axle as follows:

1. Place an appropriate press-out tool behind the bearing cup, index the tool in provided notches, and press out the cup. NOTE: The hub outer bearing (all axles except 17,000 lb. axle) cannot be replaced with the inner bearings in position; therefore, replace the outer bearings (if required) before proceeding.
2. Position the cup in the hub, with the thick edge of the cup toward the shoulder of the hub. Using an applicable cup installer, press the cup into the hub until it seats on the hub shoulder.

Replace the outer bearing assembly (all axles except 17,000 lb.) as

Removing bearing adjusting nut (typical)
(© Chevrolet Div., G.M. Corp.)

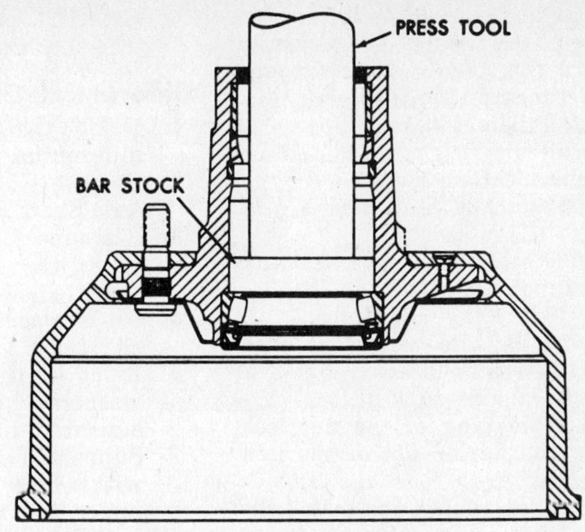

Removing hub inner bearing cup
(© Chevrolet Div., G.M. Corp.)

follows:

NOTE: The inner bearing assembly must be removed before attempting to replace the outer bearing.

1. Using a punch, tap the bearing outer race away from the bearing retaining ring. Then remove the retaining ring from the hub.
2. On 5,200 and 7,200 lb. axles, remove the outer bearing by using a brass drift. On 11,000, 13,500 and 15,000 lb. axles, remove the bearings by driving on the axle spacer, using the splined flange cut from an old axle.
3. On 11,000, 13,500 and 15,000 lb. axles place the axle shaft spacer in the hub first. Place the inner race and roller assembly in the hub, larger O.D. towards the outer end of the hub. Position the bearing cup in the hub, then end of the cup toward the outer end of the hub. Press the cup into the hub, install the retainer ring, then press the cup into positive contact with the retainer ring.

NOTE: The bearing cup to retainer ring seating is essential to assure accurate wheel bearing adjustment.

Wheel Hub Oil Seal

Replacement

Pry out the old seal from the hub bore. Pack the cavity between the new seal lips with wheel bearing grease. Position the seal in the hub bore and press the seal into the bore until it is properly seated.

With the exception of the 15,000 lb. axle with 15x4 inch brakes, the seal should be installed flush with the end of the hub. On the 15,000 lb. axle with 15x4 inch brakes the seal should be installed so that it makes contact with the bearing eace.

Hub and Drum Installation

On the 15,000 lb. axle with 4 inch brakes, install the inner bearing oil seal in the inner bearing race and position the bearing race on the axle housing.

1. Using a smooth cup grease, pack the bearings and apply a light coat of grease to the inside of the bearing hub and the outside of the axle housing tube.
2. Install the hub and drum assembly on the axle housing, exercise care so as not to damage the oil seal or dislocate other internal componants.
3. On the 11,000, 13,500, 15,000 with 15x4 inch brake, and the 17,000 lb. (single speed) axles, place the outer bearing on the axle housing and press firmly into the hub.
4. On 5,200 through 15,000 lb. with 4 inch brake axles, install the thrust washer so that the tang is in the keyway on the axle housing.
5. Install the adjusting nut and adjust the bearings.

Bearing Adjustment

Before checking the bearing adjustment, make sure the brakes are fully released and do not drag. Check bearing play by grasping the tire at the top and pulling back and forth, or by using a pry bar under the tire. If the bearings are properly adjusted, movement of the brake drum in relation to the brake flange plate will be barely noticeable and the wheel will turn freely. If movement is excessive, adjust the bearings as follows:

1. Remove the axle shaft and raise the vehicle until the wheel is free to rotate. (See Axle Shaft Removal)
2. Disengage the nut lock from the lock nut and remove them from the axle housing tube.
3. Using an appropriate tool, tighten the adjusting nut to specifications, at the same time rotating the hub.
   5,200 and 7,200 lb. axles—55 ft. lbs.
   11,000 and 13,500 lb. axles—90 ft. lbs.
   15,000 lb. axle
   4 inch brakes—90 ft. lbs.
   5 inch brakes—50 ft. lbs.

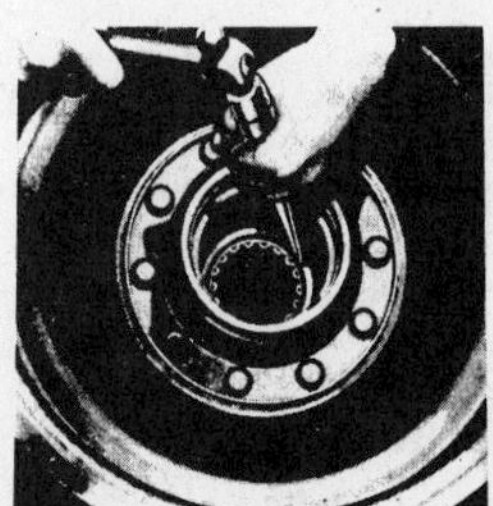

Removing bearing rotation ring 5200 and 7200 lb. axle
(© Chevrolet Div., G.M. Corp.)

Tightening wheel hub bearing nut
(© Chevrolet Div., G.M. Corp.)

17,000 lb. axle—65 ft. lbs.
Then back the nut off ½ turn to align the nearest slot with the short tang on the nut lock.
3. Install the nut lock.
4. Install the lock nut and tighten to specifications.
5,200 and 7,200 lb. axles—175 ft. lbs.
11,000 and 15,000 lb. axles with 15x4 inch brake—250 ft. lbs.
13,500 lb. axle—135 ft. lbs.
15,000 lb. axle with 15x5 inch brake—135 ft. lbs.
17,000 lb. axle—135 ft. lbs.
5. Bend the tang of the nut lock over the flat or slot of the lock nut.
6. Lower the vehicle and install the axle shaft. (See Axle Shaft Installation)

Drive Pinion Oil Seal Replacement

1. Disconnect the propeller shaft and remove the pinion flange and deflector.
2. Remove the bolts retaining the oil seal retainer to the carrier, and withdraw the retainer from the pinion.
3. Pry the old seal from the bore.
4. Clean all foreign matter from the retainer.
5. Pack the cavity of the new seal with a high melting point bearing lubricant, position the seal on an installer.
6. Press the seal into the retainer until it bottoms against the shoulder.
7. Position the seal retainer over the pinion. Install and tighten the retaining bolts.
8. Reinstall the pinion flange and propeller shaft.

Differential Carrier Removal

1. Drain the lubricant from the differential.
2. Remove the axle shafts. (See Axle Shaft Removal)
3. Disconnect the rear universal joint and swing the propeller shaft to one side.
4. On two speed axles, remove the electric or vacuum lines.
5. Remove the bolts and lockwashers which retain the carrier assembly to the axle housing. Support the differential housing with a floor jack and roll it from under the truck.

For overhaul—see General Section.

Installation

1. Clean the axle housing and differential housing gasket surfaces and place a new gasket over the axle housing.
2. Assembly the carrier to the axle housing, install the lockwashers and bolts and tighten securely.
3. Assemble the rear universal joint.
4. On two speed axles, connect the electric or vacuum lines.
5. Install the axle shafts. (See Axle Shaft Installation)
6. Fill with lubricant and road test for proper operation.

Eaton Full Floating

Description Single Speed

This axle is equipped with a straddle mounted drive pinion. Pinion bearings are of the opposed tapered roller bearing type.

A straight roller type pilot bearing is pressed onto the inner end of the drive pinion and seats in the bore of the differential case.

The differential carrier assembly may be removed, while the axle is still installed in the truck, after the axle shafts have been removed.

The differential is a conventional four pinion type. On early models the ring gear is riveted to the differential case. On later models the ring gear is bolted to the differential case.

Some models have a thrust pad mounted on the end of an adjusting screw which is threaded into an opening in the differential carrier. This thrust pad limits the deflection of the drive gear under severe loads.

Axle shaft, oil seal, wheel bearings, pinion seal and differential removal and installtion are performed the same as those outlined for Chevrolet axles. Refer to Rear Axle (Chevrolet).

For overhaul—see General Section.

Description Two Speed

The differential and planetary assembly is installed in a two-piece support case. The ring gear is installed between the halves of the support case and retained in place by the same bolts which fasten the support case halves together.

The planetary assembly is composed of a high speed clutch plate, and four planetary pinions.

An electric power shifting arrange-

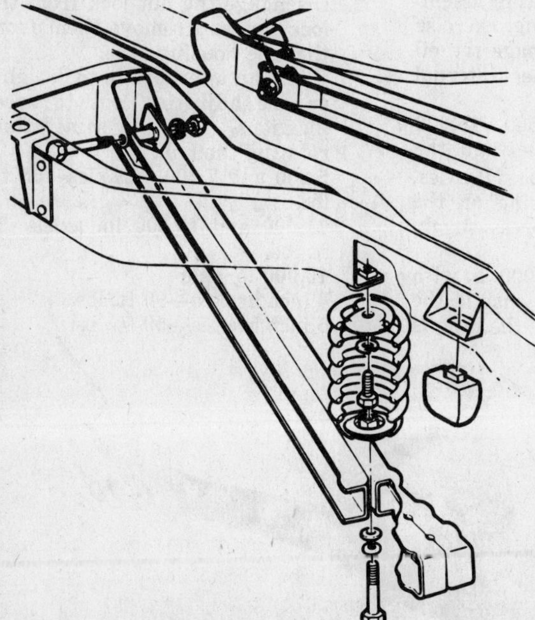

Control arm and spring details C-P10 & P-20 series
(© Chevrolet Div., G.M. Corp.)

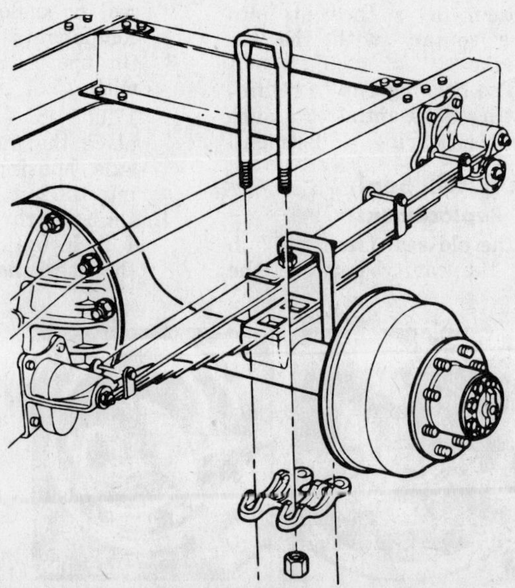

Rear suspension series P-20 and C-P-30
(© Chevrolet Div., G.M. Corp.)

ment is used to assist in making ratio changes. For schematic of Electric Shift see Chevrolet Two Speed Axle.

Axle shaft, oil seal, wheel bearings, pinion seal and differential removal and installation are performed the same as those outlined for Chevrolet Axles. Refer to Rear Axle (Chevrolet).

For overhaul—see General Section.

Rear Suspension

Coil Spring Type

Control Arm Removal

1. Remove the load from the spring by jacking at the frame.
2. Disconnect the parking brake cable from the control arm.
3. Remove the spring clamp bolt from the underside of the control arm.
4. Remove the "U" bolt nuts and separate the shock absorber bracket from the control arm. Separate the control arm from the "U" bolts and lower the rear of the arm.
5. Remove the pivot bolt and remove the arm from the vehicle.

Installation

1. Position the bushed end of control arm and insert the pivot bolt. Place the nut on the bolt finger tight.
2. Position the clamp inside the spring, raise the control arm, then pass the bolt, with the flat washer installed, up through the control arm and clamp. Install the lock washer and nut. Torque from 40 to 50 ft. lbs.
3. Place the arm adjacent to the axle. Pass the "U" bolt over the axle and through the holes in the arm.
4. Place the shock absorber bracket on the "U" bolt, install the nuts and torque from 200 to 320 ft. lbs.
5. Lower the vehicle to put full weight of the unloaded vehicle on the front and rear suspension, torque the control arm pivot bolt from 125 to 165 ft. lbs.

Coil Spring Removal

1. Raise the vehicle and adjust the axle to frame height so that the spring is not under tension.
2. Remove the shock absorber bolt from the mounting bracket at the control arm.
3. Remove the upper and lower clamps from the spring.
4. Lower the control arm suffi-

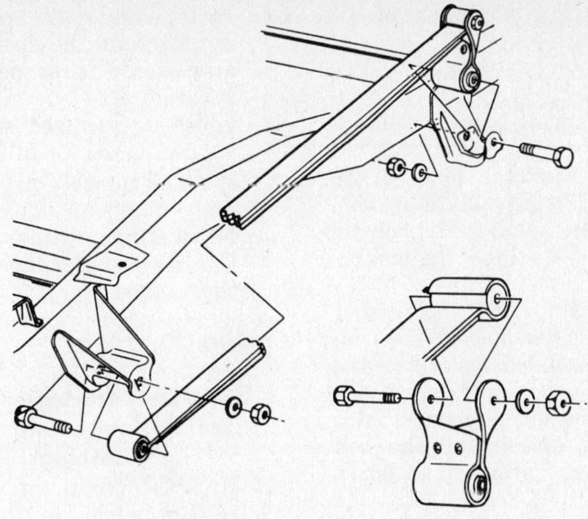

Spring shackle K-10 and K-20 series
(© Chevrolet Div., G.M. Corp.)

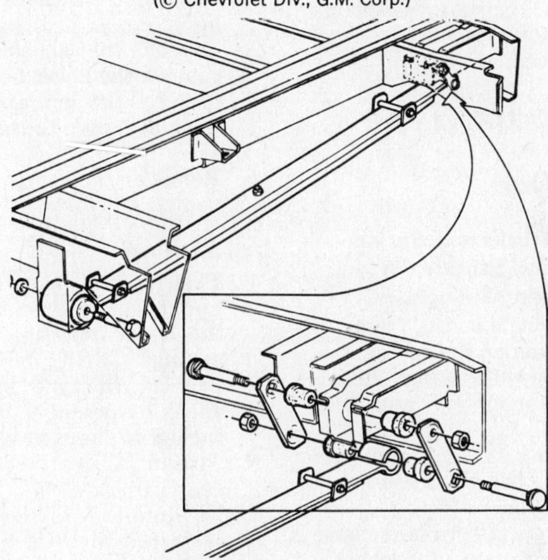

Spring shackle G-10 and G-20 series
(© Chevrolet Div., G.M. Corp.)

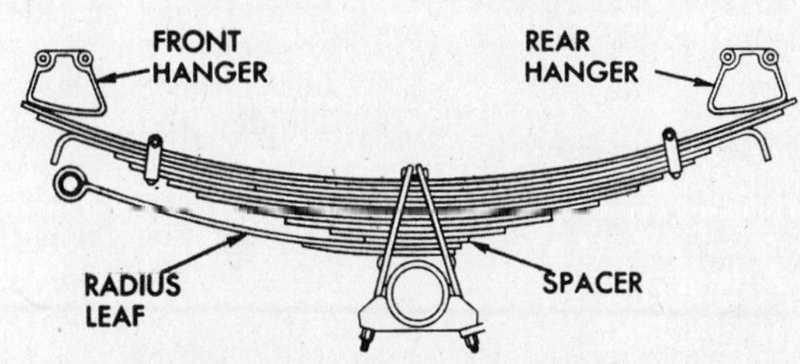

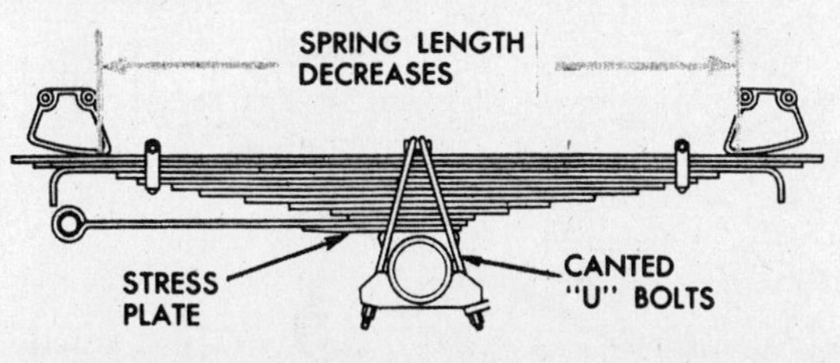

Rear suspension 50, 60 and 80 series
(© Chevrolet Div., G.M. Corp.)

ciently to permit removal of the spring.

Installation

1. Place the spring lower clamp inside the spring. Position the clamp so that the end of the spring coil is within the notch. Locate the spring and clamp over the bolt hole in the control arm.
2. Pass the clamp bolt and washer up through the hole in the control arm and loosely install the nut.
3. Position the upper clamp inside the spring and install the bolt and washer. Torque to 45-55 ft. lbs.
4. Connect the shock absorber. Torque the nut to 110-150 ft. lbs.
5. Torque the spring lower clamp bolt to 40-50 ft. lbs.
6. Lower the vehicle.

Leaf Spring Type

Spring Removal

(Light Duty Trucks with Spring Hanger and Shackle Pin Lubricating Fittings)

1. Jack the vehicle at the frame to relieve tension on the spring.
2. Remove the lubrication fitting from the spring eye and rear shackle pin.
3. Remove the lock bolts and nuts or pins from the shackle pin and spring eye pin.
4. Using appropriate tools, remove the spring eye pin and shackle pin.
5. Remove the "U" bolt nuts, withdraw the "U" bolts and remove the spring from the vehicle.

Installation

1. Position the spring assembly on the axle housing. Install the spacer assembly between the axle housing and spring, if so equipped, then install the "U" bolts.
2. Install the "U" bolt retaining nuts, torque the nuts alternately and evenly to properly seat the spring.
3. Jack as required to align the spring eyes; install the spring eye and shackle pins, lock bolts and nuts or lock pins and lubricating fittings. Lubricate the spring bushings and lower the vehicle.

Spring Removal

(Light Duty Trucks with Rubber Spring Hanger and Shackle Bushings)

1. Jack the vehicle at the frame to relieve tension on the spring.
2. Remove the "U" bolt retaining nuts and withdraw the "U" bolts.
3. Loosen the shackle bolts and remove the lower bolt.
4. Remove the nut and bolt securing the spring to the front hanger.
5. Remove the spring from the vehicle.

Installation

1. Position the spring assembly, and spacers if so equipped, on the axle housing. NOTE: On springs with metal encased pressed in type bushings, the shackle assembly must be attached to the rear spring eye before installing the shackle to the rear hanger.
2. Position the "U" bolts and loosely install the "U" bolt retaining nuts.
3. Jack as required to align the spring eyes with the front hanger and rear shackle, install the eye bolts.
4. Lower the vehicle.
5. Tighten the "U" bolt retaining nuts alternately and evenly to properly seat the spring, and tighten the front hanger and rear shackle bolts.

Spring Removal

(Medium Duty Trucks)

CAUTION: Do not jack under the radius leaf.

1. Jack the vehicle at the frame so that the weight is off the spring.
2. Straighten the tabs on the rebound stop pin retainers at the front and rear hangers and remove the retainer bolts and rebound pins.
3. Install a "C" clamp on the radius leaf to relieve the load on the spring eye bolt. Remove the eye bolt and slowly release tension on the radius leaf.
4. Remove the "U" bolt nuts, "U" bolts and spacer plate. Note the position of the caster shim.
5. Remove the spring and caster shim from the vehicle.

Installation

1. Install the caster shim in the same position as noted in step 4 of "Removal" procedures.
2. Place the spring on the shim with the center bolt indexed in the pad center hole and the spring end positioned in the hangers.
3. Seat the "U" bolts in the spacer and secure the spring to the axle by installing the anchor plate and nuts on the "U" bolts. Torque the nuts alternately and evenly to 300 ft. lbs.
5. Lower the frame so the ends of the spring enters the hanger and the top of the spring touches the cam surface of the hanger. Compress the radius leaf with a "C" clamp until the pivot bushing and hanger holes are aligned. Insert the retainer bolt and torque to 85 ft. lbs.
6. Remove the "C" clamp from the radius leaf, lower the vehicle and install the rebound pins at the front and rear hangers. Install the rebound pin locks, secure the locks with bolts and bend the tab of the lock over the flat of the bolt.

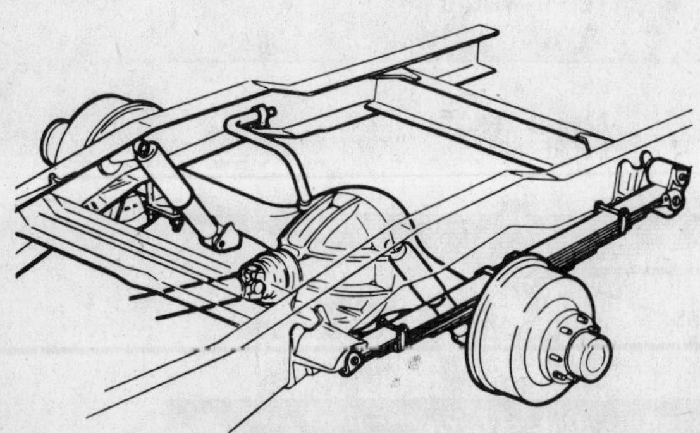

Series P20 and C-P30 Rear Suspension

Series K10 and K20 Rear Suspension

Dodge

Index

TUNE-UP SPECIFICATIONS

CU. IN. DISPLACE-MENT	YEAR	SPARK PLUG GAP	DISTRIBUTOR POINT DWELL	DISTRIBUTOR POINT GAP	IGNITION TIMING DEG. BTC	CRANKING COMP. PRESS.	VALVE CLEARANCE IN LOT	VALVE CLEARANCE EXHAUST	GOV. R.P.M. NO LOAD	FUEL PUMP PRESS	IDLE SPEED STD.	IDLE SPEED AUTO.
SIX CYLINDER												
170	1961-65	.035	40-45	.020	2½B	140	.012H	.024H	3500	3½-5	550	550N
wo/Exh. Em.	1966	.035	40-45	.020	5B	145	.012H	.024H	3500	3½-5	550	550N
w/Exh. Em		.035	40-45	.020	5A	145	.012H	.024H	3500	3½-5	700	650N
Std. Tr.	1967-69	.035	40-45	.020	5A	150	.012H	.024H	3500	3½-5	700	—
Aut. Tr.		.035	40-45	.020	2½A	130	.012H	.024H	3500	3½-5	—	700
198	1970-71	.035	40-45	.020	TDC	—	.012H	.024H	—	—	550	650N
225	1961-65	.035	40-45	.020	2½B	140	.012H	.024H	3900	3½-5	550	550N
wo/Exh. Em.	1966	.035	40-45	.020	2B	145	.012H	.024H	3900	3½-5	550	550N
w/Exh. Em.		.035	40-45	.020	5A	145	.012H	.024H	3900	3½-5	650	650N
wo/Exh. Em.	1967-68	.035	40-45	.020	5B	145	.012H	.024H	3900	3½-5	550	550N
w/Exh. Em.		.035	40-45	.020	TDC	145	.012H	.024H	3900	5-7	650	600N
	1969-71	.035	42-47	.020	TDC	125	.012H	.024H	3500	3½-5	650	650N
251	1961-68	.035	36-42	.020	5B	135	.010H	.014H	3200	3½-5	550	550N
EIGHT CYLINDER												
273 Std. Tr.	1964-66	.035	28-32	.017	5B	135	.013H	.021H	—	3½-5	500	—
Aut. Tr.		.035	28-32	.017	10B	135	.013H	.021H	—	3½-5	—	500N
w/Exh. Em.		.035	28-32	.017	5A	135	.013H	.021H	—	3½-5	700	650N
318	1961-65	.035	27-32	.017	10B	140	.010H[1]	.018H	3900	5-7	500	500N
wo/Exh. Em.	1966	.035	28-32	.017	10B	140	.012H[1]	.022H	3900	5-7	500	500N
w/Exh. Em.		.035	28 32	.017	5A	140	.012H[1]	.022H	3900	5-7	700	650N
318-3		.035	28-32	.017	12½B	110	.012H[1]	.022H	3800	5-7	500	500N
LA-318 Std. Tr.	1967-71	.035	28-32	.017	5B	140	[1]		3900	5-7	500	—
LA-318 Aut. Tr.		.035	28-32	.017	10B	140	[1]		3900	5-7	—	500N
LA-318 w/Exh. Em.		.035	28-32	.017	5A	140	[1]		3800	5-7	650	600N
318-1		.035	28-32	.017	5B	140	[1]		3800	5-7	500	500N
318-3		.035	28-32	.017	12½B	110	[1]		3800	5-7	500	500N
361	1961-62	.035	27-32	.017	12B	130	[1]		3600	3½-5	500	500N
	1963	.035	27-32	.017	5B	130	[1]		3600	3½-5	500	500N
361 2	1964-66	.035	28-33	.017	10B	115	[1]		3600	3½-5	500	500N
361-3, 4		.035	28-33	.017	5B	120	[1]		3600	3½-5	500	500N
	1967	.035	28-33	.017	5B	120	[1]		3600	3½-5	500	500N
361-2	1968	.035	28-33	.017	10B	120	[1]		3600	3½-5	500	500N
361-3, 4		.035	28-33	.017	5B	120	[1]		3600	3½-5	500	500N
	1969-71	.035	28-32	.016	5B	120	[1]		3600	3½-5	500	—
383 wo/Exh. Em.	1966	.035	28-33	.017	12½B	140	[1]		—	3½-5	500	500N
w/Exh. Em. Std.		.035	28-33	.017	5A	140	[1]		—	3½-5	650	—
w/Exh. Em. Aut.		.035	28-33	.017	TDC	140	[1]		—	3½-5	—	600N
wo/Exh. Em.	1967	.035	28-33	.017	12½B	140	[1]		—	3½-5	550	550N
w/Exh. Em. Std.		.035	28-33	.017	TDC	140	[1]		—	3½-5	650	—
wo/Exh. Em. Aut.		.035	28-33	.017	5B	140	[1]		—	3½-5	—	600N
Std.	1968-71	.035	28-33	.017	TDC	140	[1]		—	3½-5	650	—
Aut.		.035	28-33	.017	7½B	140	[1]		—	3½-5	—	600N
413	1961-71	.035	27-32	.017	5B	130	[1]		3600	3½-5	500	500N
478		.030	25-29	.016	10B	140	[1]		3400	4-4¾	500	500N
549		.030	25-29	.016	7B	140	[1]		3200	4-4¾	500	500N

FIRING ORDER AND ROTATION

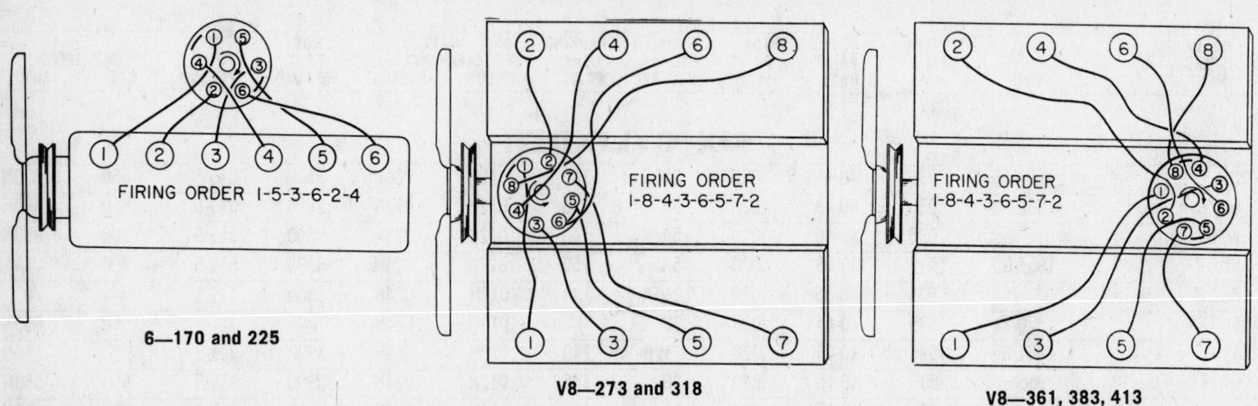

6—170 and 225 | V8—273 and 318 | V8—361, 383, 413

GENERAL ENGINE SPECIFICATIONS

CU. IN. DISPLACE-MENT	YEAR	BORE & STROKE	FIRING ORDER	DEVELOPED H.P. @ R.P.M.	DEVELOPED TORQUE @ R.P.M.	COMPRESSION RATIO	CARBUR-ETOR	VALVE LIFTER TYPE	NORMAL OIL PRESSURE
SIX CYLINDER									
170	1961-66	3.40x3.12	1-5-3-6-2-4	88@3600	136@1600	8.2	1V	Mech.	45-65
	1967-69	3.40x3.12	1-5-3-6-2-4	101@4000	145@1600	8.5	1V	Mech.	50
198	1970-71	3.406x3.64	1-5-3-6-2-4	130@4000	182@1600	—	—	—	50
225	1961-65	3.40x4.12	1-5-3-6-2-4	127@3900	201@2000	8.4	1V	Mech.	50
	1966-71	3.40x4.12	1-5-3-6-2-4	140@3900	215@1600	8.4	1V	Mech.	50
251	1961-66	3.437x4.50	1-5-3-6-2-4	115@3600	207@1600	7.0	1V	Mech.	40
	1967-68	3.437x4.50	1-5-3-6-2-4	125@3600	216@1600	7.1	1V	Mech.	40
EIGHT CYLINDER									
273	1964-66	3.625x3.31	1-8-4-3-6-5-7-2	140@3900	230@2000	8.8	2V	Mech.	45-65
318	1961	3.91x3.312	1-8-4-3-6-5-7-2	165@3900	260@2200	8.25	2V	[1]	45
318-1	1962-66	3.91x3.312	1-8-4-3-6-5-7-2	164@3900	258@2200	8.25	2V	Hyd.	50
318-2, 3	1962-66	3.91x3.312	1-8-4-3-6-5-7-2	165@3900	260@2200	7.5	2V	—	50
318-3	1967	3.91x3.312	1-8-4-3-6-5-7-2	202@3900	288@2400	7.5	2V	Hyd.	70
LA-318-3	1968-71	3.91x3.312	1-8-4-3-6-5-7-2	212@4000	322@2800	8.0	2V	Hyd.	70
318	1967-69	3.91x3.312	1-8-4-3-6-5-7-2	210@4000	318@2800	8.5	2V	Hyd.	60
361	1961	4.125x3.375	1-8-4-3-6-5-7-2	186@3600	325@2400	7.5	2V	Hyd.	50-60
361-2	1962-66	4.125x3.375	1-8-4-3-6-5-7-2	166@3600	290@2400	7.5	2V	Hyd.	50-60
361-3		4.125x3.375	1-8-4-3-6-5-7-2	181@3600	304@2400	7.5	2V	Hyd.	50-60
361-4		4.125x3.375	1-8-4-3-6-5-7-2	185@3600	325@2400	7.5	2V	Hyd.	50-60
361-2	1967-71	4.125x3.375	1-8-4-3-6-5-7-2	186@4000	300@2400	7.5	2V	Hyd.	70
361-3		4.125x3.375	1-8-4-3-5-5-7-2	194@3600	310@2400	7.5	2V	Hyd.	70
361-4		4.125x3.375	1-8-4-3-6-5-7-2	204@3600	335@2400	7.5	2V	Hyd.	70
383	1965-71	4.25x3.38	1-8-4-3-6-5-7-2	258@4400	375@2800	9.2	2V	Hyd.	45-65
413-3	1961-66	4.188x3.75	1-8-4-3-6-5-7-2	205@3600	380@2200	7.5	4V	Hyd.	50-60
413-2		4.188x3.75	1-8-4-3-6-5-7-2	200@3600	362@2000	7.5	2V	Hyd.	50-60
413-2	1967-68	4.188x3.75	1-8-4-3-6-5-7-2	217@3600	373@2000	7.5	2V	Hyd.	70
413-3		4.188x3.75	1-8-4-3-6-5-7-2	228@3600	400@2000	7.5	2V	Hyd.	70
413-2	1969-71	4.188x3.75	1-8-4-3-6-5-7-2	220@3600	386@2200	7.5	2V	Hyd.	70
413-3		4.188x3.75	1-8-4-3-6-5-7-2	238@3600	407@2000	7.5	4V	Hyd.	70
478	1970-71	4.50x3.75	1-8-7-3-6-5-4-2	—	—	—	2V	Hyd.	50-70
549	1970-71	4.50x4.312	1-8-7-3-6-5-4-2	—	—	—	4V	Hyd.	50-70

CRANKSHAFT BEARING JOURNAL SPECIFICATIONS

CU. IN. DISPLACE-MENT	YEAR	MAIN BEARING JOURNALS JOURNAL DIAMETER	OIL CLEARANCE	SHAFT END PLAY	THRUST ON NO.	CONNECTING ROD BEARINGS JOURNALS JOURNAL DIAMETER	OIL CLEARANCE	END PLAY
SIX CYLINDER								
170	1961-69	2.7495-2.7505	.0005-.0015	.004-.008	3	2.1865-2.1875	.0005-.0015	——
198	1970-71	2.7495-2.7505	.0005-.0015	.004-.008	3	2.1865-2.1875	.0005-.0015	——
225	1961-71	2.7495-2.7505	.0005-.0015	.004-.008	3	2.1865-2.1875	.0005-.0015	.006-.012
251	1961-68	2.499-2.500	.0005-.0015	.003-.007	Rear	2.124-2.125	.0005-.0015	——
EIGHT CYLINDER								
273	1964-66	2.499-2.500	.0015-.0025	.002-.007	3	2.249-2.250	.001-.002	——
318	1961-71	2.4995-2.5005	.0005 .0015	.002-.007	3	2.124-2.125	.0005-.0015	.006-.014
361	1961-71	2.6245-2.6255	.0005-.002	.002-.007	3	2.374-2.375	.001-.002	.009-.017
383	1961-71	2.6245-2.6255	.0005-.0015	.002-.007	3	2.374-2.375	.0005-.0015	——
413	1961-71	2.7495-2.7505	.0005-.002	.002-.007	3	2.374-2.375	.0005-.002	.004-.017
478	1970-71	3.123-3.124	.0014-.0044	.004-.009	3	2.623-2.624	.0017-.0042	.010-.018
549	1970-71	3.123-3.124	.0014-.0044	.004-.009	3	2.623-2.624	.0017-.0042	.010-.018

VALVE SPECIFICATIONS

CU. IN. DISPLACE-MENT	YEAR	LASH (HOT) INCHES INT.	EXH.	ANGLE DEGREE FACE	SEAT	STEM DIA. INCHES INT.	EXH.	STEM CLEARANCE INTAKE	EXHAUST	VALVE LIFT INCHES	VALVE SPRING LBS. @ INCHES OPEN	CLOSED	FREE LENGTH INCH
SIX CYLINDER													
170	1961-62	.012	.024	45	45	.372	.371	.001-.003	.002-.004	.375	144@$1\frac{5}{16}$	83@1.69	1.92
	1963	.012	.024	[1]	[1]	.372	.371	.001-.003	.002-.004	.375	144@$1\frac{5}{16}$	53@1.69	1.92
	1964-69	.012	.024	[2]	[2]	.372	.371	.001-.003	.002-.004	.395	144@$1\frac{5}{16}$	53@1.69	1.92
198	1970-71	.012	.024	[2]	[2]	.372	.371	.001-.003	.002-.004	.395	144@$1\frac{5}{16}$	53@1.69	1.92
225	1961-62	.012	.024	45	45	.372	.371	.001-.003	.002-.004	[4]	144@$1\frac{5}{16}$	53@1.69	1.92
	1963-71	.012	.024	[2]	[2]	.372	.371	.001-.003	.002-.004	[4]	144@$1\frac{5}{16}$	53@1.69	1.92
251	1961-69	.010	.014	45	45	.340	.340	.001-.003	.002-.004	.379	115@$1\frac{3}{8}$	43@1.75	[3]
EIGHT CYLINDER													
273	1964-66	.013	.021	45	45	.372	.371	.001-.003	.002-.004	[5]	144@$1\frac{5}{16}$	53@1.68	1.92
318	1961-66	.010*	.018*	45	45	.372	.371	.001-.003	.002-.004	.380	144@$1\frac{5}{16}$[6]	53@1.68	——
LA-318-1, 3	1967-69	0+1	Turn	[2]	[2]	.372	.371	.001-.003	.002-.004	.390	177@$1\frac{5}{16}$	83@1.68	2.00[13]
361	1961-71	0+1	Turn	45	45	.372	.433	.001-.003	.003-.005	.360	[7]	[8]	2.312[14]
383	1961-71	0+1	Turn	45	45	.372	.371	.001-.003	.002-.004	[9]	200@$1\frac{7}{16}$	125@1.86	2.625
413	1961-71	0+1	Turn	45	45	.372	.433	.001-.003	.003-.005	.360	[7]	[8]	2.312[14]
478	1970-71	0+1	Turn	15[10]	14[11]	.434	.433	.0015-.004	.0025-.005	—	83@$1\frac{17}{32}$[12]	——	2.281[15]
549	1970-71	0+1	Turn	15[10]	14[11]	.434	.433	.0015-.004	.0025-.005	—	83@$1\frac{17}{32}$[12]	——	2.281[15]

*—With Hydraulic Lifters—Zero.
1—Intake 45, Exhaust 47.
2—Intake 45, Exhaust 43.
3—Intake 2.00, Exhaust 1.875.
4—Intake .397, Exhaust .392.
5—Intake .395, Exhaust .405.
6—Hydraulic Lifters—Intake, Exhaust 185 @ $1\frac{5}{32}$.
7—Intake 180 @ $1\frac{5}{32}$, Exhaust Outer 115 @ $1\frac{3}{8}$, Inner 49 @ $1\frac{11}{64}$.
8—Intake 80 @ $1\frac{55}{64}$, Exhaust 57 @ $1\frac{47}{64}$.
9—Intake .425, Exhaust .435.
10—Intake, Exhaust 45.
11—Intake, Exhaust 44.
12—Inner, Outer 116.5
13—Intake, Exhaust 1.890.
14—Intake, Exhaust (Outer) 2.125, (Inner) 1.875.
15—Inner, Outer 2.562,

TORQUE SPECIFICATIONS

CU. IN. DISPLACE-MENT	YEAR	CYLINDER HEAD BOLTS (FT. LBS.)	ROD BEARING BOLTS (FT. LBS.)	MAIN BEARING BOLTS (FT. LBS.)	CRANKSHAFT BALANCER BOLT (FT. LBS.)	FLYWHEEL TO CRANKSHAFT BOLTS (FT. LBS.)	MANIFOLD (FT. LBS.) INTAKE	MANIFOLD (FT. LBS.) EXHAUST
SIX CYLINDER								
170	1961-71	65	45	85	Press	55	10	10
225	1961-71	65	45	85	Press	55	10	10
230	1961	70	45	85	135	60	20	20
251	1961-68	65	45	85	135	60	20	20
265	1961	70	45	85	135	60	20	20
EIGHT CYLINDER								
273	1965-66	85	45	85	135	60	30	15
318	1961-71	85	45	85	135	60	30	25
361	1961-71	70	45	85	135	60	40	30
383	1965-69	70	45	85	135	60	50	30
413	1961-71	70	45	85	135	60	40	30
478	1970-71	90-100	60-70	100-110	—	90-100	—	30
549	1970-71	90-100	60-70	100-110	—	90-100	—	30

WHEEL ALIGNMENT SPECIFICATIONS

YEAR	MODEL	CASTER (Deg.)*	CAMBER (Deg.)	TOE-IN (In.)	KING PIN INCLINATION (Deg.)
1963-70	A1000	6	1½	0-⅛	4
1963-70	D100	1½-2½	1½	0-⅛	4
1963-70	W100	3	1½	0-⅛	7½
1963-70	D200	1½	2	0-⅛	4
1968-70	D200 crew cab	1½	1½	0-⅛	7
1963-70	P200	1½	1½	0-⅛	4
1963-70	W200	3	1½	0-⅛	7½
1963-67	D300	1½	1½	0-⅛	7
1968-70	D300	1½	2	0-⅛	7
1963-67	P300	1½	1½	0-⅛	7
1968-70	P300, M300	1½	2	0-⅛	7
1963-67	W300	3½	1½	0-⅛	8
1968-70	W300	1½	3½	0-⅛	8
1963-67	WM300	½	1½	0-⅛	8
1968-70	WM300	1½	½	0-⅛	8
1968-70	M375	1½-2½	2	0-⅛	7
1963-70	D400, P400[1]	1½-2½	2	0-⅛	7
1963-67	D400, P400[2]	½-1½	2	0-⅛	7
1963-67	S400	1½-2½	2	0-⅛	7

*—No load.
1—4000 lb. axle.
2—5000 lb. axle.

YEAR	MODEL	CASTER (Deg.)*	CAMBER (Deg.)	TOE-IN (In.)	KING PIN INCLINATION (Deg.)
1963-67	C500	0-1	2	0-⅛	7
1963-70	C500, D500, S500[2]	½-2	2	0-⅛	7
1968-70	S500	0-1	1	0-⅛	5½
1963-68	W500	2½	¾	0-⅛	8
1963-67	C600[2]	0-1	2	0-⅛	7
1968-70	C600[2]	½-2	2	0-⅛	7
	C600[3]	½-1	2	0-⅛	7
1963-67	D600[2]	1-2	2	0-⅛	7
1963-67	D600[3]	0-1	2	0-⅛	7
1968-70	D600[2]	½-2	2	0-⅛	7
1963-70	C700, CT700	1[4]	1	0-⅛	5½
1963-70	D700[2]	½-2	2	0-⅛	7
1963-67	D700[3]	0-1	2	0-⅛	7
1963-70	800 All	0-1[4]	1	0-⅛	5½
1968-70	850	1[3]	1	0-⅛	5½
1963-70	900 All	0-1[4]	1	0-⅛	5½
1963-70	1000 All	0-1[4]	1	0-⅛	5½

3—7000 lb. axle.
4—With power steering 4-5 degree. Caster should be checked with vehicle loaded.

TRUCK MODELS AND ENGINE APPLICATION

ENGINE NUMBER LOCATION: The engine serial number is located on a machined surface on the cylinder block. The engine serial number prefix denotes the series, followed by engine model, followed by serial number.

COMPACT MODELS

STANDARD ENGINES	YEARS	MODELS	ENGINE MAKE
SIX CYLINDER			
6-170	1964-66	S6-A100	Own
	1967-70	A100	Own
6-198	1970	A100	Own
EIGHT CYLINDER			
V8-273	1961	S8-A100	Own

FORWARD CONTROL MODELS

6-170-225	1961	R6-P200	Own
	1961	R6-P300	Own
	1961	R6-P400	Own
6-225	1962-65	S6-P100	Own
	1962-66	S6-P200	Own
	1962-66	S6-P300	Own
	1963-66	S6-P500	Own
	1967-70	P200	Own
	1967-70	P300	Own
	1967-70	P400	Own
6-251	1962	S6-400	Own

PICK UP & SPORTSMAN MODELS

6-170	1967-68	D100	Own
6-225	1967-68	D100	Own
	1967-68	D200	Own
	1967-68	D300	Own

FOUR WHEEL DRIVE MODELS

6-225	1967-68	W100	Own
	1967-68	W200	Own
	1967-68	W300	Own
	1967-68	W500	Own
6-251	1967-68	WM300	Own

TRUCK MODELS AND ENGINE APPLICATION

ENGINE NUMBER LOCATION: The engine serial number is located on a machined surface on the cylinder block. The engine serial number prefix denotes the series, followed by engine model, followed by serial number.

CONVENTIONAL GASOLINE ENGINES

STANDARD ENGINES	YEARS	MODELS	ENGINE MAKE
SIX CYLINDER			
6-170	1961	R6-D100	Own
	1961	R6-D200	Own
	1961	R6-D300	Own
6-225	1961	R6-D100	Own
	1961	R6-D200	Own
	1961	R6-D300	Own
	1962-66	S6-D100	Own
	1962-66	S6-D200	Own
	1962-66	S6-D300	Own
	1963-66	S6-D400	Own
	1963-66	S6 D500	Own
	1967-70	D100-200	Own
	1967-70	D300-400	Own
	1967-70	D500	Own
	1969-70	W100-200	Own
	1969-70	W300-500	Own
6-251	1961	R6-D400	Own
	1961	R6-D500	Own
	1962	S6-D400	Own
	1962	S6-D500	Own
EIGHT CYLINDER			
V8-318	1961	R8-D100	Own
	1961	R8-D200	Own
	1961	R8-D300	Own
	1961	R8-D400	Own
	1961	R8-D500	Own
	1962	S8-D100	Own
	1966	S8-D100	Own
	1962-66	S8-D200	Own
	1962-66	S8-D300	Own
	1962-66	S8-D400	Own
	1962-66	S8-D500	Own
	1962-66	S8-D700	Own
V8-361	1962-66	S8-D700	Own

CAB FORWARD MODELS EIGHT CYLINDER

V8-318	1961	S8-C500	Own
	1962-66	R8-C500	Own
V8-361	1961	R8-C600	Own
	1961	R8-C700	Own
	1961	R8-C800	Own
	1961	R8-CT700	Own

STANDARD ENGINES	YEARS	MODELS	MAKE ENGINE
	1961	R8-CT800	Own
	1961	R8 CT900	Own
	1962-66	S8-C600	Own
	1962-66	S8-C700	Own
	1962-66	S8-C800	Own
	1962-66	S8-CT700	Own
	1962-66	S8-CT800	Own
V8-413	1961	R8-C900	Own
	1961	R8-C1000	Own
	1961	R8-CT900	Own
	1962-66	S8-C900	Own
	1962-66	S8-C1000	Own
	1962-66	S8-CT900	Own

4 x 4 MODELS

SIX CYLINDER			
6-170-225	1961	R6-W100	Own
	1961	R6-W200	Own
6-225	1963-66	S6-W300	Own
	1963-66	S6-W500	Own
6-251	1961	R6-W300	Own
	1961	R6-WM300	Own
	1961	R6W500	Own
	1962-66	S6-W100	Own
	1962-66	S6-W200	Own
	1962	S6-W300	Own
	1962-66	S6-WM300	Own
	1962	S6-W500	Own
EIGHT CYLINDER			
V8-318	1961	R8-W100	Own
	1961	R8-W200	Own
	1961	R8-W300	Own
	1961	R8-W500	Own
	1962-66	S8-W100	Own
	1962-66	S8-W200	Own
	1962-66	S8-W300	Own
	1962-66	S8-W500	Own

GASOLINE ENGINES CHASSIS CAB AND COWL MODELS

SIX CYLINDER			
6-225	1967-68	D100	Own
	1967-68	D200	Own
	1967-68	D300	Own
	1967-68	D400	Own
	1967-68	D500	Own
	1967-68	L600	Own
V8-318	1967-68	D600	Own
	1967-68	C500	Own
V8-361	1967-68	D700	Own
	1967-68	D800	Own
	1967-68	L700	Own
	1967-68	C600	Own
	1967-68	C700	Own
	1967-68	C850	Own
	1967-68	CT700	Own
	1967-68	CT800	Own
V8-413	1967-68	CT900	Own

DIESEL ENGINES

CHASSIS CAB MODELS			
6-354	1967	PD500	Perkins
	1967	PC500	Perkins
	1967	PD600	Perkins
	1967	PC600	Perkins
NH-180	1967	CN900	Cummins
	1967	CNT900	Cummins
NHE-195	1967	LN1000	Cummins
	1967	LNT1000	Cummins
NH-230	1968	CN900	Cummins
	1968	CNT900	Summins
	1968	LN1000	Cummins
	1968	LNT1000	Cummins
V8E-235	1967	LV1000	Cummins
	1968	LTV1000	Cummins
TILT CAB MODELS			
6-225	1967-70	L600	Own
NH-230	1969-70	LN1000	Cummins
	1969-70	LNT1000	Cummins
V8-361	1969-70	L700	Own
8V-7INE	1969-70	LV100	Detroit
	1969-70	LVT1000	Detroit
L.C.F. CAB MODELS			
V8-318	1969-70	C500	Own
V8-361	1969-70	C600	Own
	1969-70	C700	Own
	1969	CT700	Own
	1969-70	C800	Own
	1969-70	CT800	Own
NH-230	1969-70	CN900	Cummins
	1969-70	CNT900	Cummins
V8-413	1969-70	CT900	Own
	1969-70	C1000	Own

Distributor

Distributor Removal

1. Disconnect primary lead wire at coil.
2. Disconnect vacuum hose at distributor.
3. On the Holley distributor, disconnect tachometer drive and governor inlet and outlet lines.
4. Unfasten distributor cap retaining clips and remove distributor cap.
5. Scribe a line on the distributor housing to indicate positioning of rotor.
6. Remove distributor hold-down clamp or arm screw.
7. Carefully lift out distributor assembly.

NOTE: Do not disturb engine position.

Installation

1. Clean top of cylinder block to insure a good seal between distributor base and block.
2. If the crankshaft has not been rotated, insert distributor into block with the rotor aligned to the previously scribed mark on the distributor housing. Make sure O-ring seal is in groove of shank. NOTE: Distributors on 6 cylinder engines have the drive gear mounted on the bottom of the distributor shaft and a slight rotation will occur when installing. Allow for this rotation when aligning rotor with scribed line on housing.

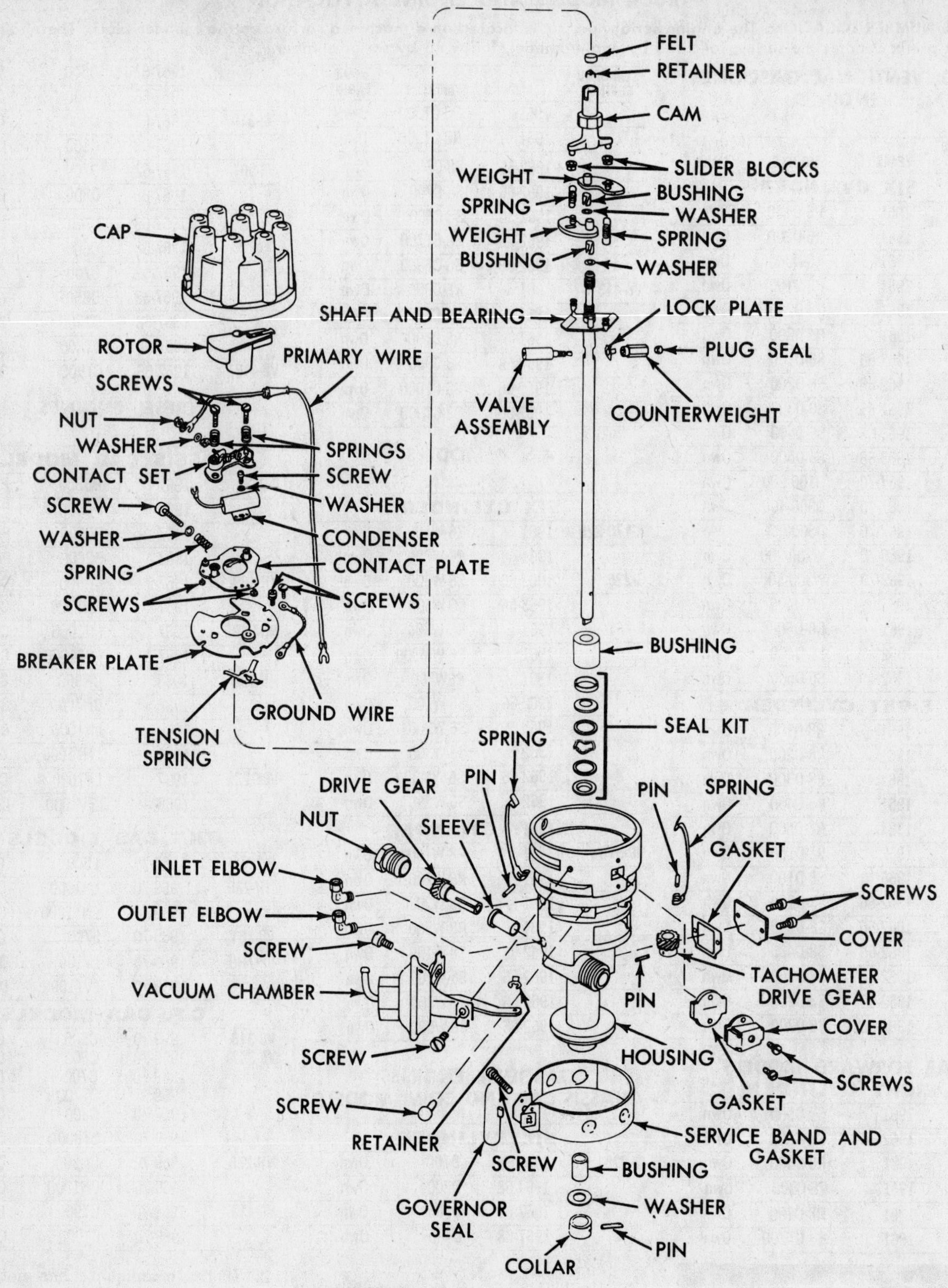

Holley distributor—V8 engines (© Chrysler Corp.)

3. If engine has been cranked while distributor was removed, it will be necessary to correctly time the distributor with the camshaft. This is done by rotating the crankshaft until No. 1 piston is at top dead center of compression stroke. With rotor in No. 1 cylinder firing position with respect to the distributor cap, insert d stributor into engine.
4. Connect primary lead to terminal at coil.
5. Install distributor cap and check that all high tension leads are securely in position.
6. On the Holley distributor, connect governor lines and tachometer drive cable.
7. Set ignition timing.
8. Tighten distributor arm or clamp screw.
9. Connect vacuum advance line.

Ignition Timing

Reference

Ignition breaker point replacement, gap (dwell) setting, point alignment and timing procedures are conventional and may be found in the Electrical Diagnosis Section in the General Repair Section. See Specifications at the beginning of this section for point dwell and point gap settings.

Ignition Timing Marks

On all engines the timing plate is located on the timing case (front) cover and the timing mark is on the crankshaft pulley damper. On all models the ignition is timed to the No. 1 cylinder spark plug. Always remove vacuum advance line when setting ignition timing.

Holley Distributor

Dwell setting may be adjusted externally with the use of an 1/8" Allen wrench. See Specifications for correct dwell angle. Disconnect vacuum advance line and connect dwell meter. Insert wrench while engine is running and turn adjusting screw until correct dwell angle reading is obtained.

Alternator

Reference

For voltage regulator circuit tests and adjustments and for alternator off-the-vehicle service, see The Electrical Diagnosis Section.

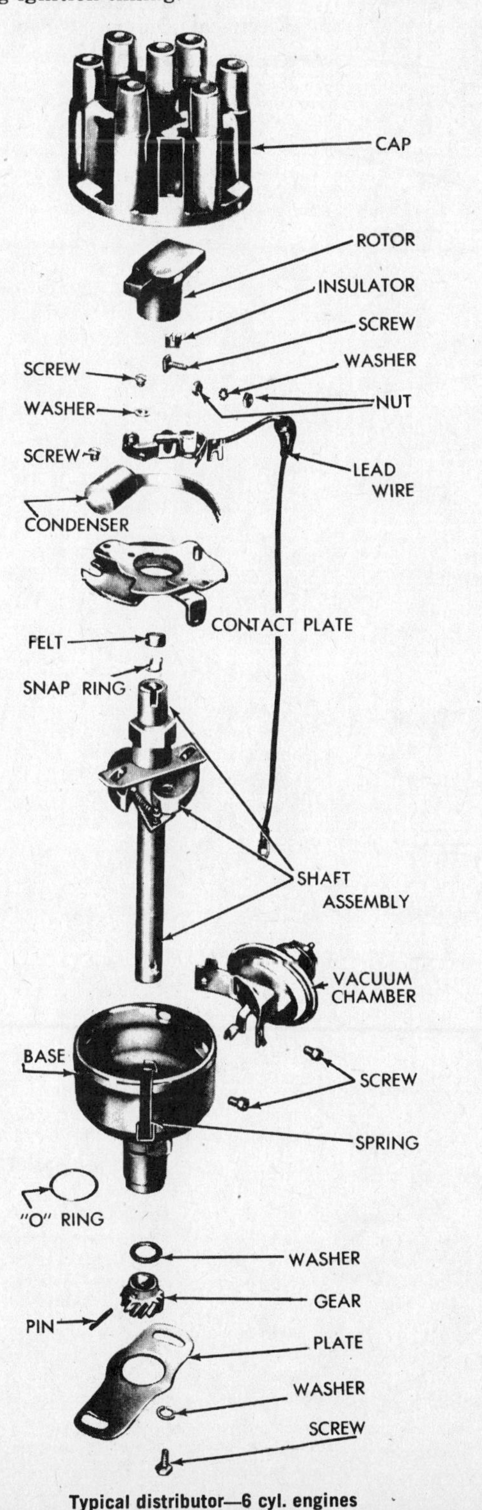

Typical distributor—6 cyl. engines
(© Chrysler Corp.)

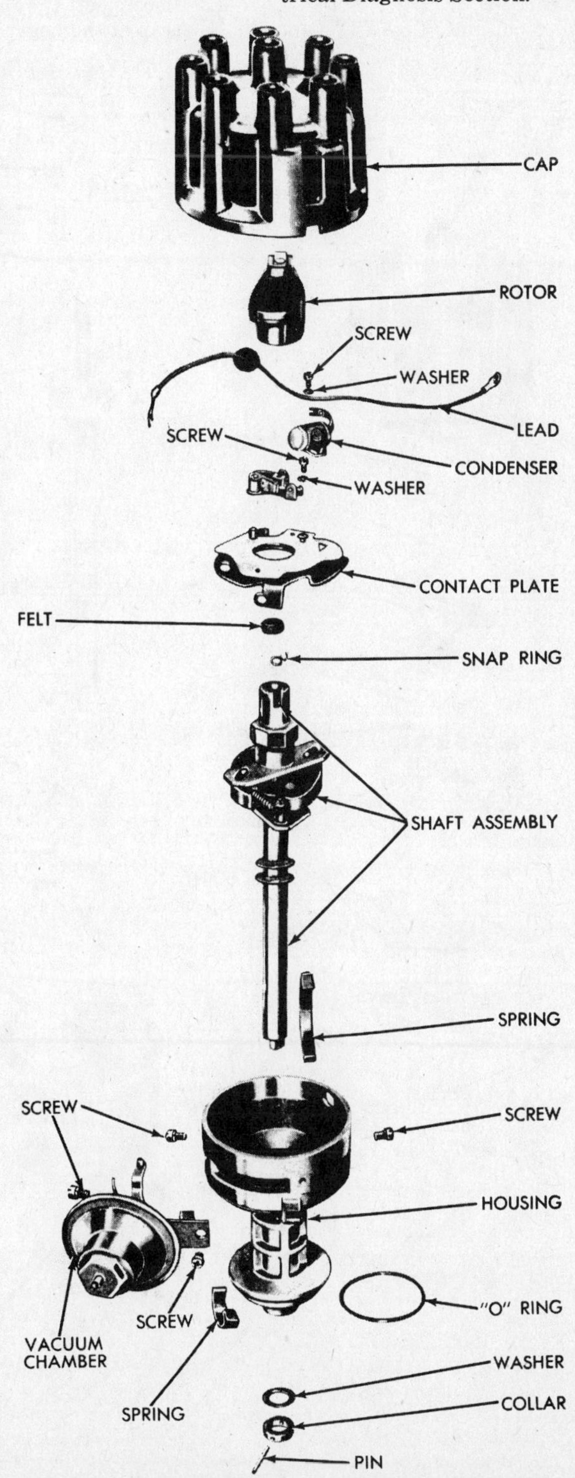

Chrysler built distributor—V8 engines
(© Chrysler Corp.)

Alternator Removal

1. Disconnect battery ground cable at the negative terminal.
2. Disconnect alternator output "BATT" and field "FLD" leads and disconnect ground wire.
3. Remove mounting bolts and remove alternator.

Installation

1. Install alternator and adjust drive belt.
2. Connect output "BATT" and field "FLD" leads and connect ground wire.
3. Connect battery ground cable.
4. Start engine, and observe alternator operation.
5. Test current output and adjust regulator voltage setting, if necessary. See Electrical Diagnosis Section.

Delcotron A.C. Generator

Removal

1. Disconnect the battery ground strap at the negative post.
2. Disconnect the generator to battery, relay and ground leads.
3. Remove the generator brace bolt, push the generator toward the engine, detach the belt and lower the generator.
4. Remove the generator to support bracket bolts and remove the generator. Repair and test details for the Delcotron and its regulators are described in the Electrical Diagnosis Section.

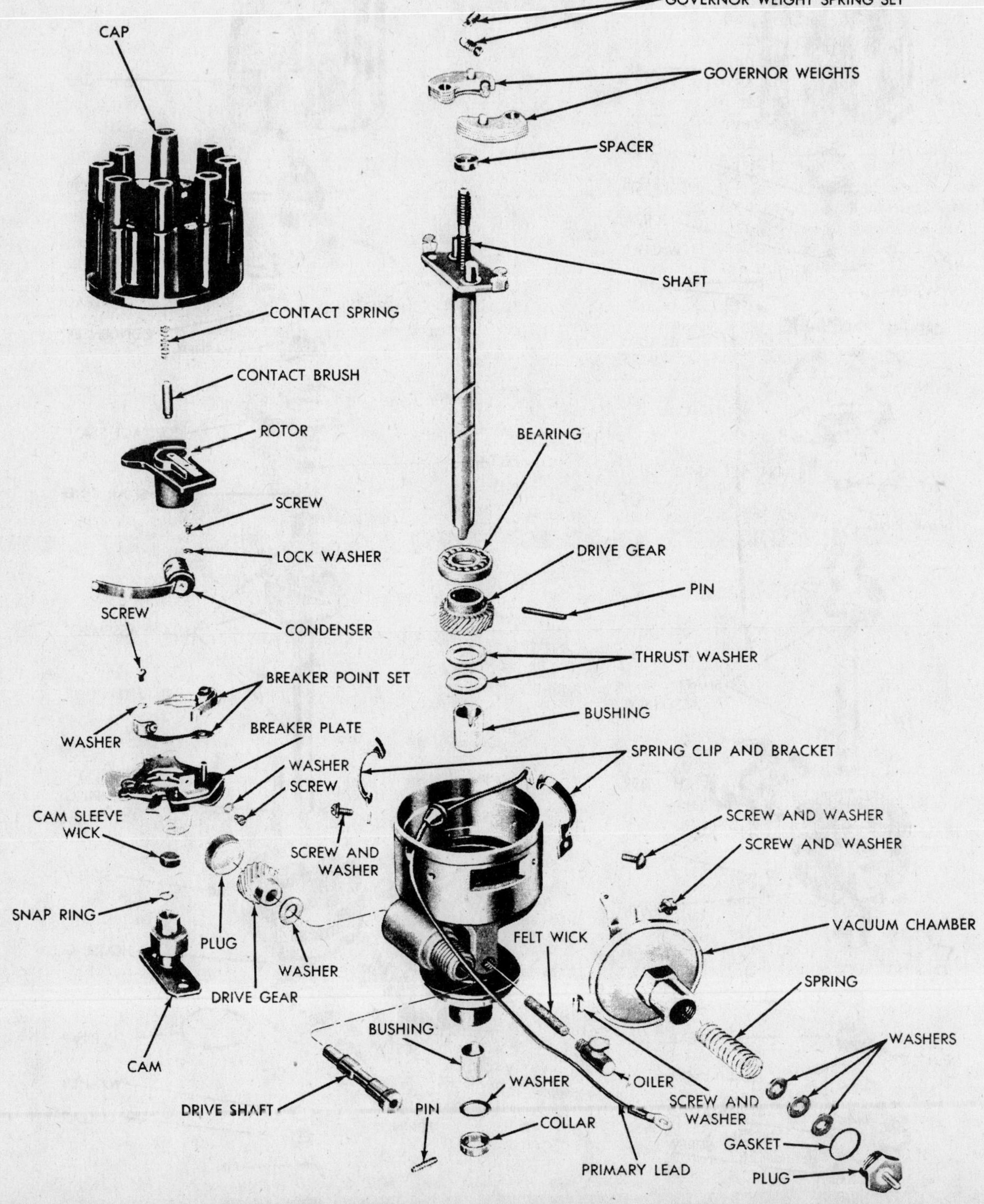

Prestolite distributor—V8 engines (© Chrysler Corp.)

5. Reverse the removal procedure to install. Adjust drive belt(s).
6. If no belt tension tool is available, force generator away from the engine until fan belt has 5/16" deflection when forced downward from normal position.

NOTE: If belt tension tool is used, a tension of 75 lbs. is correct for new belts (under 1000 miles service) and 50 lbs. for used belts.

CAUTION: Since the Delcotron and regulator are designed for use on a single polarity system, the following precautions must be observed:

The polarity of the battery, generator and regulator must be matched and considered before making any electrical connections in the system.

When connecting a booster battery, be sure to connect the negative terminals with one another and the positive terminals to one another.

When connecting a charger to the battery, connect the charger positive lead to the battery positive terminal, connect the charger negative lead to the battery negative terminal.

Never operate the Delcotron on controlled open circuit. Be sure that all connections in the circuit are clean and tight.

Do not short across or ground any of the terminals on the Delcotron regulator.

Do not attempt to polarize the Delcotron.

Do not use lamps of more than 12 volts for checking diode continuity.

Avoid long soldering times when replacing diodes or transistors as heat will damage these components.

Disconnect the battery ground terminal when servicing any A.C. system. This will prevent the possibility of accidentally reversing polarity.

Voltage Regulator

Removal and Installation

1. Disconnect the battery ground cable at battery negative terminal.
2. Disconnect the field lead from alternator and ignition lead from regulator terminals.
3. Remove three regulator assembly mounting screws and remove regulator.
4. Installation is the reverse of the above procedure. Adjust drive belt tension.

Fusible Wire

Replacement

Excessive current loads through the two fusible wires will cause them to melt and break the circuit. Remove what is left of the old wire and solder new fusible wire to terminals, using only resin core solder. See illustration for fusible wire position. See Electrical Diagnosis Section for service and testing of alternator systems.

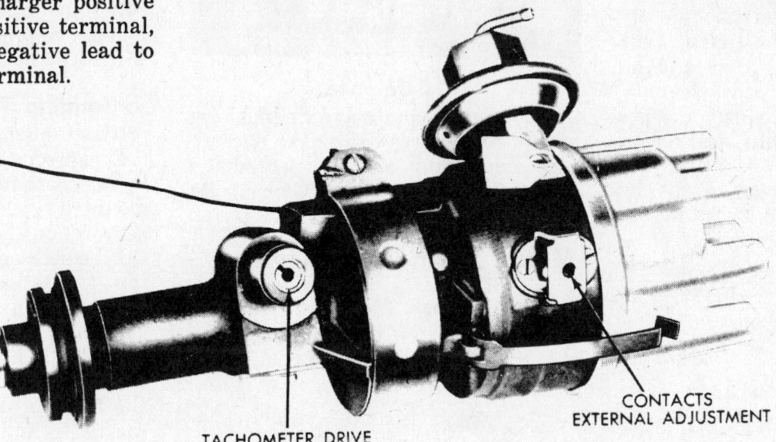

External point gap adjustment (© Chrysler Corp.)

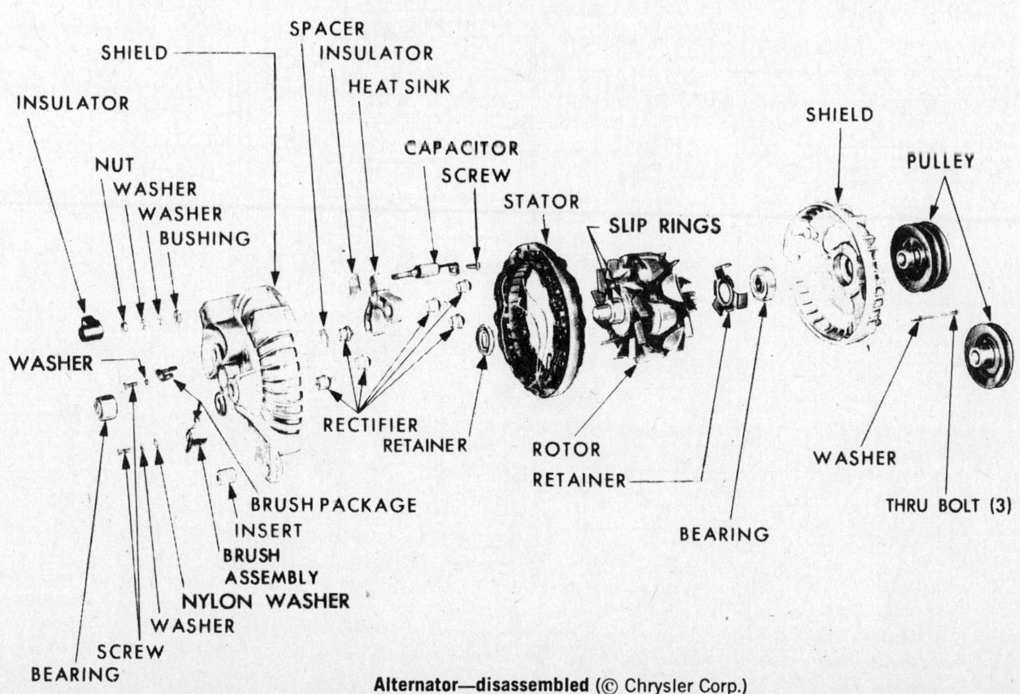

Alternator—disassembled (© Chrysler Corp.)

Starter

Reference

For starter motor overhaul procedures see Electrical Diagnosis Section.

Starter Removal

1. Disconnect the battery ground cable.
2. Remove the cable at the starter.
3. If the solonoid is mounted on the starter, disconnect the wires at the solonoid terminals. On Diesel engine starters, record the wiring harness color coding at the solonoid to insure proper installation.
4. Remove the starter to flywheel housing mounting bolts and remove the starter and removable seal if so equipped.
5. Before installing the starter, make sure the starter and flywheel housing mounting surfaces are free of dirt and oil. These surfaces must be clean.
6. Install the starter to flywheel housing removable seal if so equipped.
7. Position the starter to the flywheel housing and install mounting bolts. Tighten securely.
8. If the solonoid is mounted on the starter, connect the wires to the solonoid terminals.
9. Connect the cable to the starter terminal.

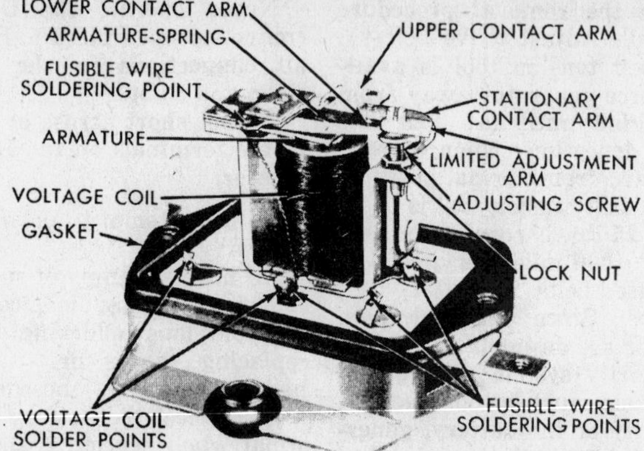

Voltage regulator (cover removed) (© Chrysler Corp.)

10. Connect the battery ground cable and test operation of the starter for proper engine cranking.

Brakes

Reference

For master and slave cylinder overhaul procedures and brake shoe replacement and service procedures, see Brake Section of the General Repair Section.

Master Cylinder Removal

Dash Mounted

1. From within the cab, disconnect push rod from brake pedal.
2. Disconnect hydraulic line from master cylinder.
3. Remove four nuts and washers from master cylinder mounting studs and remove master cylinder assembly.
4. Installation is the reverse of the above procedure.
5. Bleed hydraulic system.

Tandem Type Dual Cylinder

The tandem master cylinder is of the compensating type with reservoirs cast integrally on the dash mounted type and with removable reservoirs on the booster mounted type. Both consist of a front and rear piston (in tandem) with two outlets, each containing a residual pressure valve and spring.

The dual hydraulic brake system is basically a safety system in which the front brakes are actuated by one master cylinder and the rear brakes

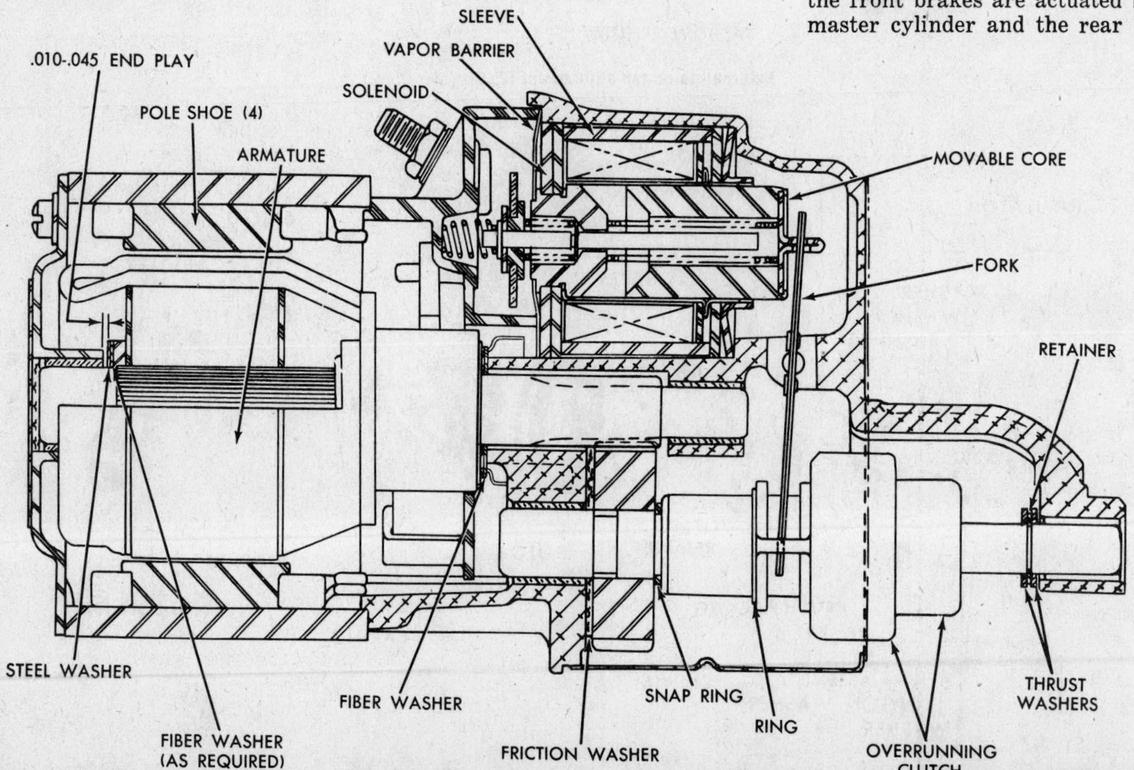

Starter motor (reduction gear type) (© Chrysler Corp.)

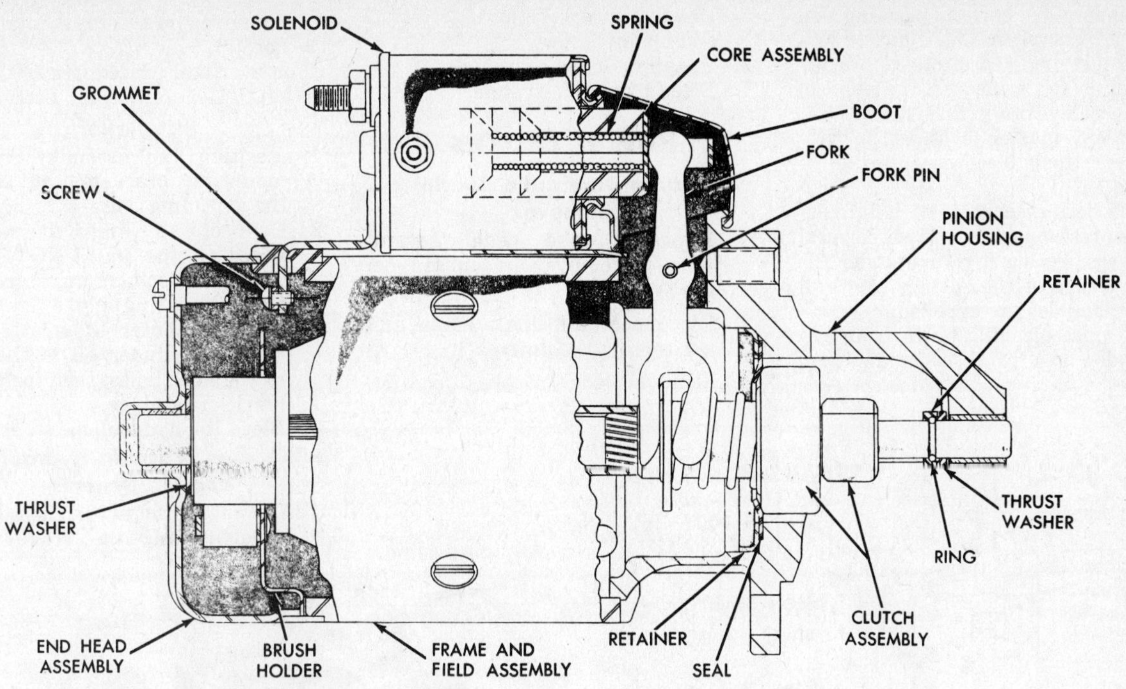

Starter motor (direct drive type) (© Chrysler Corp.)

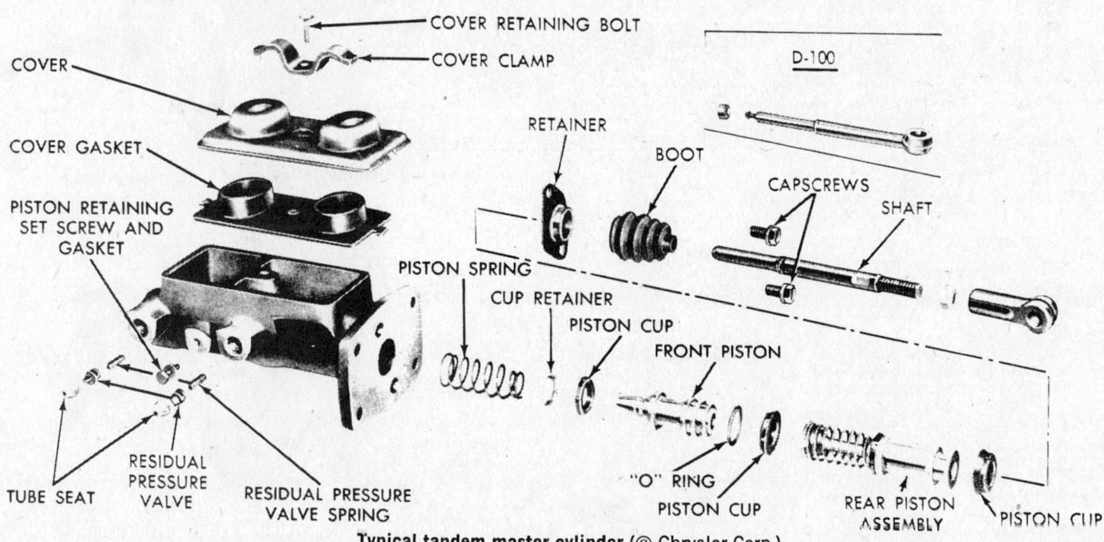

Typical tandem master cylinder (© Chrysler Corp.)

by the other. A hydraulic safety switch closes a warning light circuit whenever unequal pressure exists between the two systems whenever a pressure failure occurs in either.

The procedure for removing and installing dual master cylinders is the same as that for single master cylinders as described above.

Booster Mounted Type Removal

1. Disconnect both hydraulic lines at master cylinder outlets.
2. Remove capscrew holding lower support strap to cylinder.
3. Remove master cylinder to booster mounting nuts and lift cylinder from vehicle.

Installation

1. Position seal ring in groove on master cylinder body mounting flange, then install unit on power booster. Tighten mounting nuts to 18-20 ft. lbs. torque.
2. Install capscrew holding lower support strap to cylinder.
3. Connect and tighten both hydraulic brake lines at cylinder outlet.
4. Bleed entire brake system.

Frame Mounted Type (Van) Removal

1. Remove bolts and screws that attach the airscoop to the frame.
2. Slide scoop out (toward front) from under vehicle.
3. Disconnect brake tube at rear of master cylinder.
4. Disconnect stop light switch wires.
5. Remove bolts and nuts that attach master cylinder to frame bracket.
6. Slide unit toward rear to clear push rod and remove from under vehicle.
7. Installation is the reverse of the above procedure.

Bleeding Hydraulic Brakes

Bleed brakes in the conventional manner. Be sure to fill fluid reservoir and to check frequently during bleeding. Start with right rear wheel. Bleed power units first.

Dual Master Cylinder Bleeding

Before installing master cylinder

on vehicle or before bleeding the wheel cylinders, the dual master cylinder must be bled first. If master cylinder is to be bled on the vehicle, disconnect hydraulic lines first.

1. Clamp master cylinder in vise and attach bleeding tubes as illustrated.
2. Fill both reservoirs with fluid.
3. Depress push rod slowly several times, letting it return under the pressure of the springs, until all air bubbles are expelled.
4. Remove bleeding tubes from cylinder and install cover and gasket.
5. Install cover retaining clamp and clamp screw.
6. Install cylinder on vehicle.
7. Bleed hydraulic system.

Power Brakes

Vacuum-Hydraulic Booster

Removal

1. Depress brake pedal several times to remove all vacuum from the system.
2. Disconnect all lines, hoses and wires from the unit.
3. Remove the brake booster mounting brackets, then remove booster.

For overhaul procedures see Brake Section in General Repair Section.

Installation

1. Position the assembly on the mounting brackets, and install the attaching bolts.
2. Connect all lines, hoses and wires to the unit. NOTE: On Tandem Booster units, remove the lubricating plugs from the end and center the plates. Add vacuum cylinder oil to the level of the filler holes, then install the lubricating plugs.
3. Bleed the hydraulic system.

Bleeding Vacuum-Hydraulic Booster Systems

1. Eliminate vacuum in the booster by depressing the brake pedal

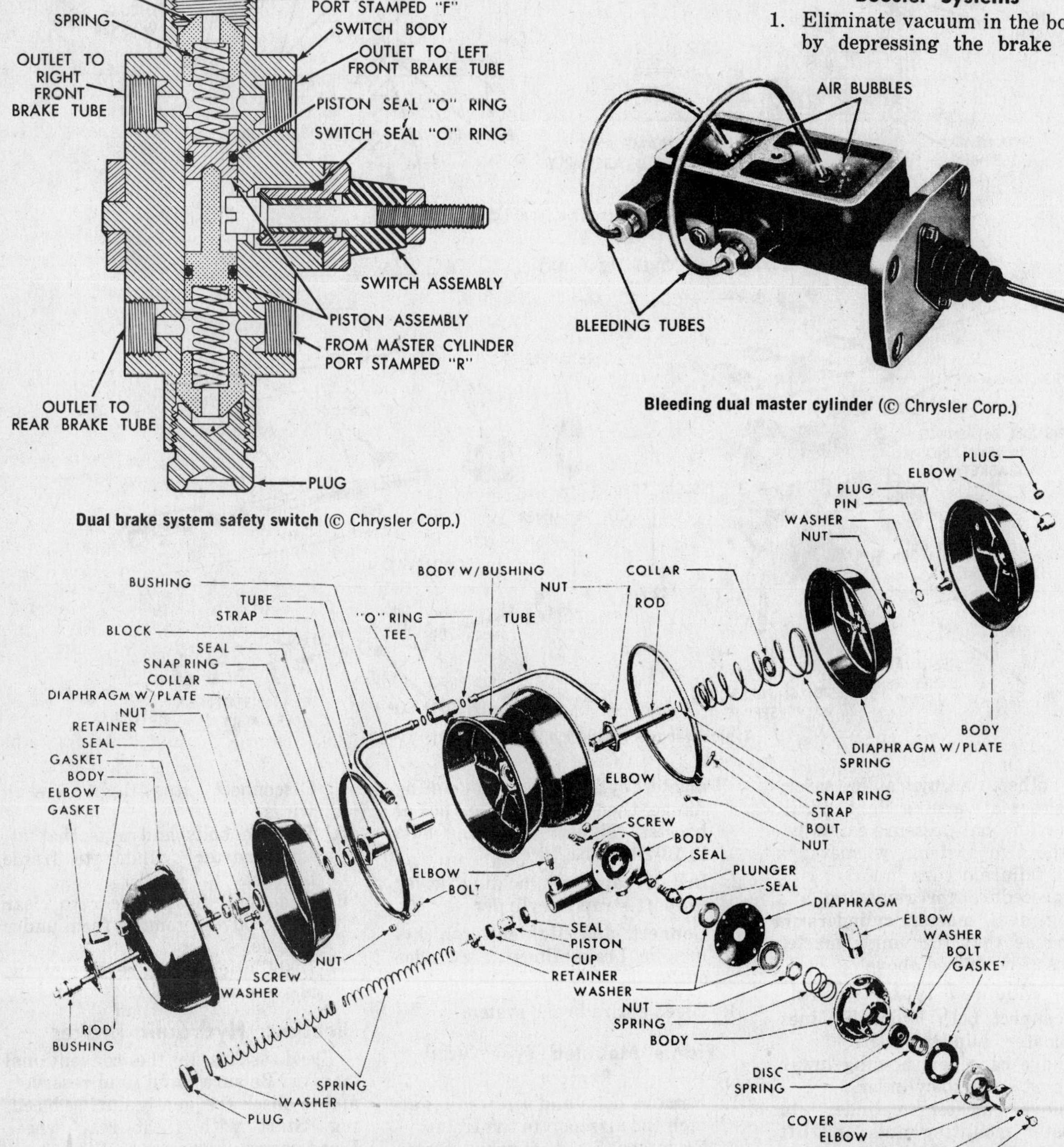

Dual brake system safety switch (© Chrysler Corp.)

Bleeding dual master cylinder (© Chrysler Corp.)

Double diaphragm power brake unit (© Chrysler Corp.)

several times while the engine is not running.

2. On trucks not equipped with reservoir tanks, disconnect the manifold tube at the booster side of the manifold check valve (engine not running).
3. Alternately loosen the brake tube at each unit until all air is expelled. Booster slave cylinder is bled first.

CAUTION: Where air pressure brake bleeding equipment is used to bleed brakes, do not use more than 25-30 psi.

NOTE: A piston stop is provided in the slave cylinder to eliminate the possibility of damaging the return spring while bleeding the system. This damage occurs only when bleeding the brakes with a vacuum present in the booster system.

Parking Brakes

Reference

The external type parking brake consists of a brake drum bolted to the transmission mainshaft companion flange, and an external contracting type band mounted on the rear of the transmission.

External Contracting Type

Removal

1. Disconnect brake cable.
2. Remove adjusting bolt nut.
3. Remove guide bolt adjusting lock nuts.
4. Remove anchor adjusting screw.
5. Pull band assembly away from transmission and off propeller shaft.

Installation

1. Position brake band and lining assembly over propeller shaft and on brake drum.
2. Install brake band anchor adjusting screw and adjusting guide bolt nut and lock nuts.
3. Connect brake cable.

Internal Expanding Type

Removal

1. Disconnect propeller shaft at transmission.
2. Remove companion flange nut, lockwasher and flatwasher.
3. Install puller tool C-452 on companion flange and remove flange and brake drum while using a holding tool to prevent rotation.
4. Disengage ball end of cable from operating lever.
5. Separate shoes at bottom, allowing brake shoe adjusting nut screws, and sleeve to drop out and release shoes.
6. Pry brake shoe return spring up and over to the right and brake shoe in.
7. Then, work spring out of assembly.
8. Pry out brake shoe retaining washer and remove outer guide.
9. Slide each shoe out from under guide spring. (as shoes are removed, the operating lever strut will drop out of place)
10. Separate the operating lever from the right hand brake shoe by removing nut, lockwasher and bolt.

Installation

1. Assemble operating lever to right hand brake shoe.
2. Slide the right and left parking brake shoes under guide.
3. Spread shoes and insert operating lever.
4. Work return spring under guide spring and upward to engage retaining pin on left hand shoe.
5. Force the other end of return spring upward and over retaining pin on right hand shoe.
6. Install adjusting nut, screw and sleeve.
7. Place outer anchor guide over anchor and secure shoes with retaining washer.
8. Turn shoe adjusting nut until shoes are in a released position and install brake drum.
9. Adjust brake shoe and control cable.

Typical external contracting type parking brake (© Chrysler Corp.)

2 Parking brake adjusting bolt
3 Parking brake rod yoke nut
4 Parking brake band guide bolt nuts
5 Parking brake adjusting bolt nut

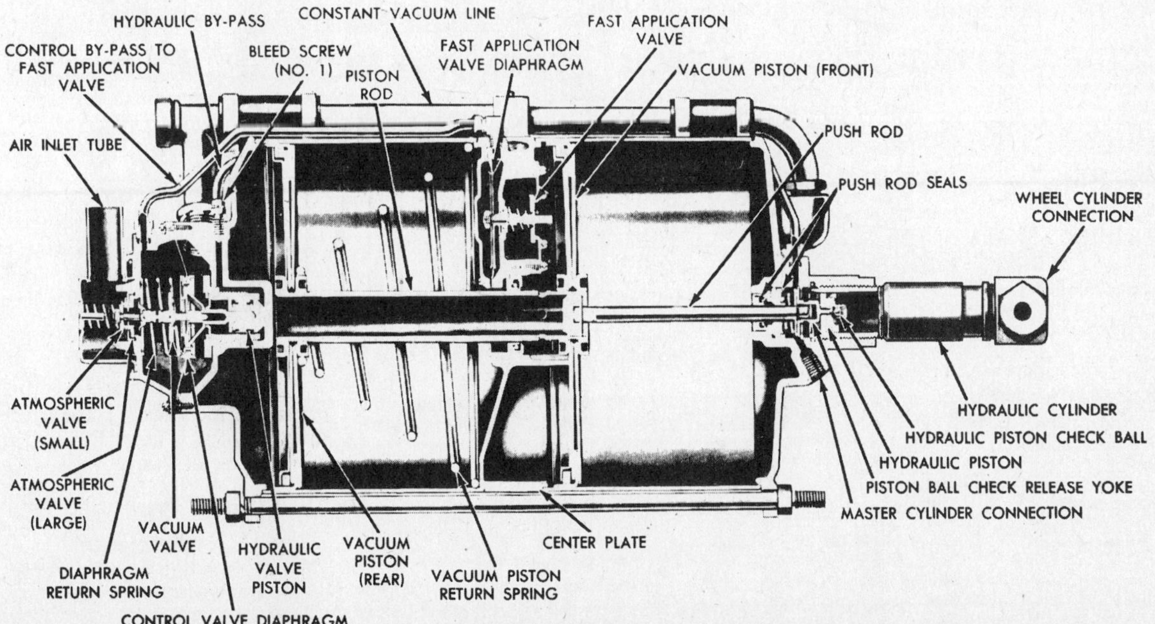

Tandem power brake unit (© Chrysler Corp.)

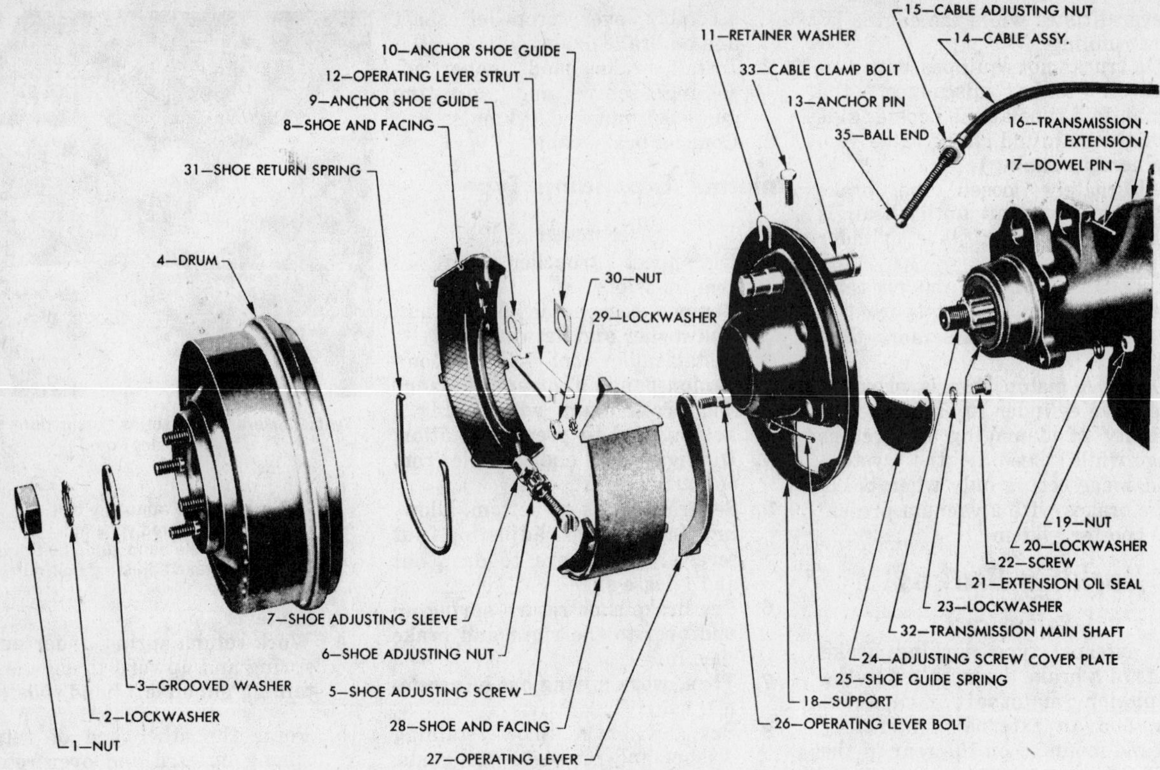

Typical internal expanding type parking brake (© Chrysler Corp.)

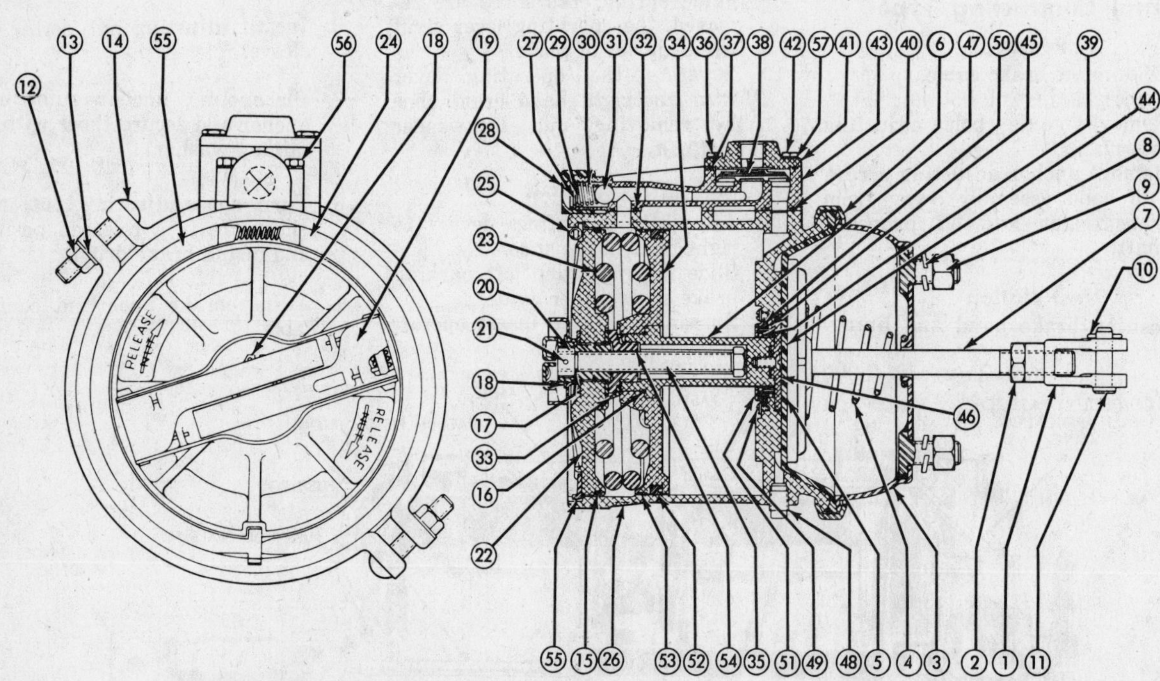

Spring type parking brake (© Chrysler Corp.)

1 Yoke
2 Jam nut
3 Non press housing
4 Spring
5 Diaphragm
6 Clamp band
7 Push rod
8 Lockwasher
9 Nut
10 Cotter pin
11 Clevis pin
12 Nut
13 Washer
14 Carriage bolt
15 O-ring
16 O-ring
17 O-ring
18 Snap ring
20 Nut
19 Handle
21 Pin
22 Cover plate-sub assembly
23 Spring
24 Retaining ring
25 Spring
26 Cylinder
27 Snap ring
28 Boot
29 Washer
30 Spring
31 Ball
32 O-ring
33 Tooth washer
34 Piston
35 Release bolt
36 Screw
37 O-ring
38 Diaphragm
39 Screw
40 O-ring
41 Cap
42 Screw
43 Body
44 O-ring
45 O-ring
46 Plunger
47 Piston shaft
48 Pipe Plug
49 Screw
50 Bushing
51 Cap
52 O-ring
53 Ring
54 Piston nut
55 Retaining ring
56 Screw
57 Lock washer

CAUTION: If parking brake is adjusted incorrectly, the automatic shifting of the Load-Flite Transmission will be affected.

Air Spring Type

Reference

The air spring type parking brake is air actuated and is operated in conjunction with the rear wheel service brake air chamber. The spring is held in the retracted (or off) position by

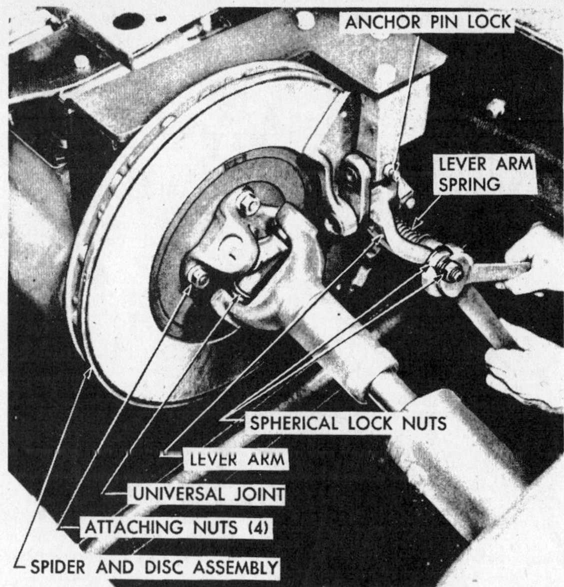

Disc type parking brake (© Chrysler Corp.)

air pressure from a protected third air reservoir. As the air pressure is released from the cylinder housing, the spring is released thereby actuating the service brake push rod and applying the brakes.

Air Spring Type—Removal

1. Back off slack adjuster adjusting screw.
2. Disconnect brake chamber push rod by removing clevis pin.
3. Disconnect air lines.
4. Remove nuts and washers from mounting bolts, remove brake chamber and spring brake assembly.
5. To install reverse the above procedure, and adjust brakes.

Quick Release Valve—Removal

1. Relieve air pressure. Disconnect air line.
2. Remove four capscrews and remove cap.
3. Remove remaining two capscrews holding release valve to body.
4. Remove boot from small end of body, clean all parts with solvent and blow dry with compressed air. All "O" rings and rubber parts must be replaced.
5. To install, reverse the above procedure. Tighten all six capscrews to 15 ft. lb. Connect air line pressurize system and check for leaks.

Disc Type

Reference

The disc type parking brake consists of a spider and spacers located between two disc plates and brake shoe assemblies. The disc assembly is mounted to drive line between companion flange and universal joint. The spider and spacers separate disc plates and insure adequate cooling and prevent warpage during continuous heavy duty operation.

Removal and Installation

1. Disconnect brake cable at brake operating lever.
2. Remove locking and adjusting nuts from adjusting rod.
3. Remove cotter and clevis pins from the lower end of operating arm.
4. Remove the operating lever and adjusting rod assembly from the brake shoe levers.
5. Remove brake lever spring and washers from between brake shoe levers.
6. Remove small brake shoe retracting spring.
7. Remove rear brake shoe pivot locking bolt and clamp.
8. Remove rear brake shoe pivot pin and brake shoe from the lever assembly.
9. Remove the front brake shoe pivot locking bolt and clamp.
10. Remove the front brake shoe pivot pin and brake shoe. Clean and inspect all linkage for worn parts, pivot pins operate on teflon bushings and need no lubrication. If inspection shows worn pins or bushings replace both pin and bushing. Bushings are a prefit size and need no fitting.
11. Install in reverse of the above procedure.

Fail-Safe

Reference

This unit is mounted "Piggy Back" on the air chamber non-pressure housing of the stopmaster brake. The power spring is held in a compressed position as long as the air pressure is 65 PSI or more. Anytime the air pressure drops below 65 PSI the power spring pushes the piston against the diaphragm plate, forcing the wedge head between the rollers, which spreads the plungers apart and applies the brake.

Fail-Safe—Removal

1. Cage power spring. Relieve air pressure and remove air lines from unit.
2. Mark non-pressure housing, pressure housing and cap with punch or chisel to aid in alignment at reassembly. Loosen or remove clamp ring and remove unit from non-pressure housing.

Installation

1. Align cap and housing with marks made during removal.
2. Position unit on non-pressure housing and install clamp ring and bolt.
3. Connect air lines and apply air pressure. Uncage power spring and check operation of system.

Shortstop Spring Brake

Reference

This spring type parking brake assembly is used in conjunction with the wedge type air brakes.

Removal

1. Bleed air from system. Disconnect air lines (mark lines for proper assembly).
2. Remove breather cap. Using a 9/16" deep socket, unscrew release bolt completely.
3. Mark clamp ring, spring brake housing and service brake housing to aid in proper alignment at assembly. Remove bolt from clamp ring. Spring brake is now free for further work.

Installation

1. Align service brake housing, spring brake housing and clamp ring. Install and tighten clamp bolt.
2. Connect and tighten air lines using marks made during removal.
3. Charge system with air, screw release bolt down.
4. Check for air leaks, clean and replace breather cap.

Adjustment—Internal

Disconnect front end of propeller shaft to permit turning brake drum by hand.

1. Remove adjusting screw cover plate, loosen brake cable clamping bolt and back off the cable adjusting nut.
2. Turn adjusting nut to decrease shoe-to-drum clearances, until a

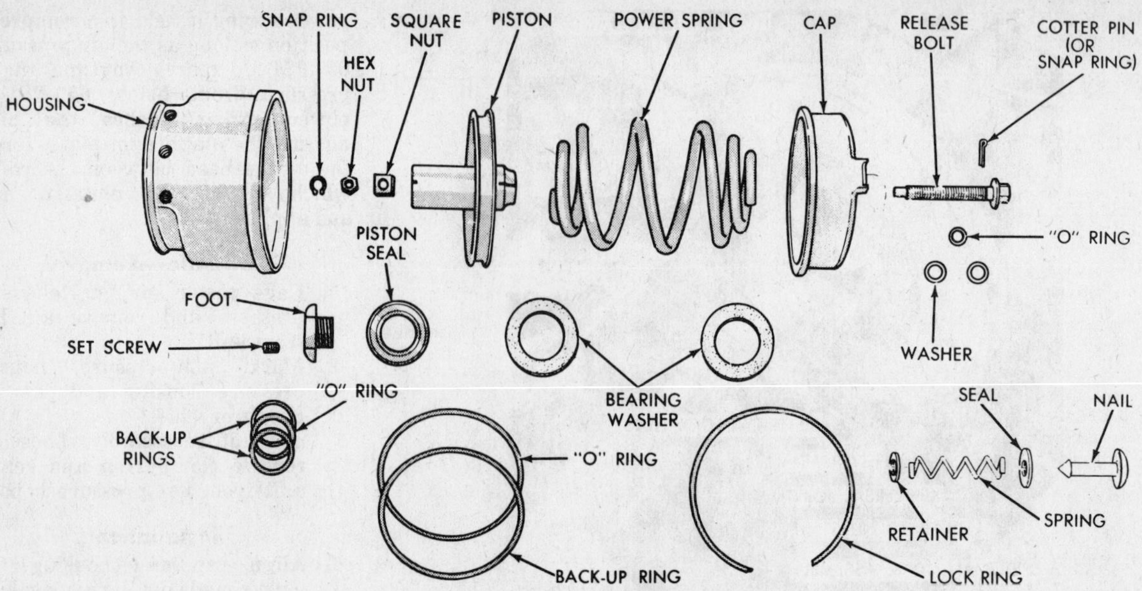

Fail safe unit (© Chrysler Corp.)

slight drag is felt on drum.

3. Back off adjusting nut at least one full notch, using spanner wrench. CAUTION: Make sure the two raised shoulders on adjusting nut are seated in the grooves on the adjusting sleeve.
4. The cable length adjusting nut should be positioned against cable housing so there is at least .005 inch but no more than .010 inch clearance, between the operating lever and brake shoe cable. To lock adjustment, tighten cable housing clamp securely.
5. Tighten cable adjusting nut against the housing.
6. Check parking brake lever for travel.
7. Install adjusting screw cover plate and connect propeller shaft.
8. With rear wheels off the floor, start engine, apply brakes a few times, check for binding and proper adjustment.

Adjustment (External Type)

With the parking brake lever in a fully released position, check the lever cam to be sure that the flat "Foot," portion is resting squarely on the brake band bracket. If the "Foot," is not resting squarely on the bracket proceed as follows:

a. Loosen cable clevis lock nut. Remove cotter key and clevis pin.

b. With "Foot" of lever cam resting squarely on brake band bracket, adjust clevis in or out so that clevis pin will slide smoothly through clevis and lever. Install clevis pin and cotter key. Tighten lock nut securely, and proceed as follows:

(1) Remove the lockwire from the anchor adjusting screw.

(2) Using a feeler gauge between drum and lining tighten or loosen adjusting screw to give .015 to .020 inch clearance. Install lock wire. CAUTION: The lockwire which retains anchor screw must not be drawn up tight. It will cause uneven wear and poor brake application.

(3) Loosen lock nut on adjusting screw for lower half of brake band, adjust screw to .015 to .020 inches, tighten lock nut.

(4) Loosen lock nut on guide bolt, loosen or tighten adjusting nut to .015 to .020 inches then tighten lock nut.

Adjustment (Disc)

1. Remove brake cable from the operating lever.
2. Disconnect universal joint from flange so disc is free to turn.
3. Adjust both brake anchor screws so that a slight drag may be felt when passing a .030 inch feeler gauge between top end of brake shoe and disc, with feeler gauge in this position tighten spherical adjusting nut until a slight drag may be felt on a .030 inch feeler inserted at lower end of both brake shoes.
4. Holding adjusting nut, tighten lock nut.
5. Remove all feeler stock and revolve brake disc and check for dragging.
6. Reinstall universal joint.

Handle and Cable Adjustment (Disc)

1. With brake cable disconnected at the operating lever and the lever handle in the off position, turn the knob of the brake lever handle counter-clockwise to the completely relaxed or off position.
2. Align the brake cable with the brake operating lever and adjust the cable by tightening or turning the brake lever knob clockwise until there is approximately 1/32 inch movement of the brake cable before the operating lever starts to apply the brake.
3. Attach brake cable to the brake operating lever, then operate the brake several times and check for dragging.

Fuel System

Fuel Tank

Removal—Exc. A-100 Series

1. Disconnect battery.
2. Drain fuel tank.
3. Disconnect fuel tank gauge unit wire.
4. Disconnect fuel line.
5. Remove support strap nuts and studs, remove tank.
6. Remove gauge unit. using tool C-3582.

Installation

1. Install gauge unit using tool C-3582.
2. Position tank, install support straps and studs and nuts.
3. Connect fuel line.
4. Connect gauge wire.
5. Connect battery.

Removal—A-100 Series

1. Raise vehicle on hoist.
2. Disconnect fuel gauge electrical wire, then remove fuel tank gauge unit, using too C-3582.
3. Drain tank, using siphon tube through gauge unit opening.
4. Remove fill tube elbow hose

clamps and disconnect hose from tank.
5. Remove fuel tank vent tube hose clamps and disconnect vent tube from tank.
6. Remove fuel tank retaining strap and lower tank from under vehicle.

Installation—A-100 Series

1. Position tank under vehicle and raise into position, install retaining strap and tighten belt securely.
2. Install fuel tank vent tube hose and secure with clamps.
3. Install filler tube elbow hose to tank and install clamps.
4. Install fuel gauge tank unit and tighten securely, using tool C-3582. Reconnect fuel gauge electrical wire to gauge terminal.
5. Lower vehicle and fill fuel tank and check for leaks.

Carburetor

Reference

For off-the-vehicle and overhaul procedures of carburetors see the Carburetor Section of the General Repair section. For idle speeds see the Specifications at the beginning of this section.

Well Type Automatic Choke

This choke requires no servicing as the unit is set when manufactured. Move the choke rod up and down to check for free movement in the pivot. If the unit binds, a new choke unit must be installed. NOTE: Do not attempt to repair or change the setting. When installing the well type choke unit, be certain that the coil housing does not contact the sides of the well in the exhaust manifold.

Idle Speed Adjustment

CAS or CAP Carburetors

Clean Air System carburetors are identified by a green tag attached over the model identification tag. A reliable exhaust analyzer should be used.

1. Set ignition timing as described in Electrical Diagnosis Section. Leave engine running until normal operating temperature is reached.
2. With engine running, air cleaner installed, automatic transmission in neutral position (not park), ignition tachometer connected and headlights turned on high beam (6 cylinder engines only), insert exhaust analyzer into tailpipe 24". Probe and tubing must be free of leaks. A plenum chamber or other means of reducing pressure must be used if a garage exhaust system is conducting gases away.
3. Connect exhaust analyzer, warm up and calibrate according to manufacturer's instructions.
4. Place clamp on hose between distributor and intake manifold.
5. Set idle speed to specified value for specific engine-transmission combination (see Specifications) as follows:

IMPORTANT: When adjusting mixture screw to obtain fuel/air ratio specified for CAS, do not turn mixture screw more than 1/16 turn at a time. The combustion analyzer is so sensitive that the ratio must be changed in very small increments if accurate readings are to be obtained.

a. Adjust screw 1/16 turn richer (counterclockwise) and wait 10 seconds before reading meter. Repeat this step until a definite increase in richness is indicated on meter. This is important because meter reverses readings and indicates a richer mixture as carburetor is leaned out if the initial setting is very lean.
b. When it is established that meter is indicating a lower reading (richer mixture) when idle mixture screws are turned in richer direction, proceed to adjust carburetor to give 14.2 air-fuel ratio, turning screws counterclockwise (richer) to lower meter reading and clockwise (leaner) to increase meter reading.
c. If idle speed changes as mixture screw is turned, adjust speed to specified value and readjust mixture as required so that 14.2 air/fuel mixture is obtained at specified idle speed.
d. If idle is rough, screw may be adjusted independently to achieve smooth idle, provided air/fuel ratio is held to 14.2 value.
e. Remove clamp from distributor hose.

Distributor Vacuum Control Valve Adjustment

1. Warm up engine, connect a tachometer and connect a vacuum gauge (0-30 in. Hg.) to the distributor vacuum tube with a tee.
2. If carburetor has a dashpot (automatic transmission), adjust it so that it does not contact throttle lever at curb idle.
3. Clamp closed the vacuum tube that connects vacuum valve to manifold vacuum.
4. Remove distributor vacuum tube at distributor and clamp tube closed.
5. Set basic ignition timing and idle speed, adjusting carburetor to specified exhaust emission level. The distributor vacuum must be below 6 in. Hg. at curb idle.
6. Remove clamps from vacuum lines and reconnect vacuum tube to distributor.
7. Remove vacuum valve cover. Speed engine up to 2000 rpm and hold for 5 seconds. Release throttle and observe distributor vacuum. It should increase to 16 in. Hg. and hold there for 1 second, then fall to 6 in. Hg. within 3 seconds after throttle is released.
8. Adjustment is made by turning spring end adjusting screw counterclockwise to increase time that distributor vacuum remains above 6 in. Hg. after throttle is released. One turn of adjusting screw will change valve setting approximately ½ in. Hg. If valve cannot be adjusted to function properly, replace valve.
9. Replace vacuum valve cover, reset carburetor dashpot, and recheck valve performance as described in Step 7. If distributor vacuum does not fall below 6 in. Hg. within 4 seconds after throttle is released, readjust or replace dashpot.

Carburetor Removal

1. Remove air cleaner.
2. Disconnect fuel line, distributor vacuum line, throttle linkage and, if so equipped, manual choke cable, governor lines, anti-icing lines and crankcase ventilation hose.
3. Remove carburetor mounting stud nuts and washers.
4. Remove carburetor.
5. Installation is the reverse of the above procedure. Be sure to thoroughly clean carburetor to manifold mating surfaces and to use a new manifold flange gasket. Tighten mounting stud nuts in an alternating pattern to insure a good flange seal.

Carter BBS and BBD Float Lever Adjustment

1. Remove air horn (top of carburetor), installing two short screws to hold main body to throttle body.
2. Remove accelerator pump rod and twist air horn to disengage fast idle cam link when lifting off air horn.
3. Remove gasket and carefully add fuel to the bowl until needle valves are held shut.
4. Measure distance between float crown and top edge of bowl. It should be ¼". Carefully bend float lip (part which presses against needle) while holding down float until the correct setting is obtained. CAUTION: Do not exert pressure on needle

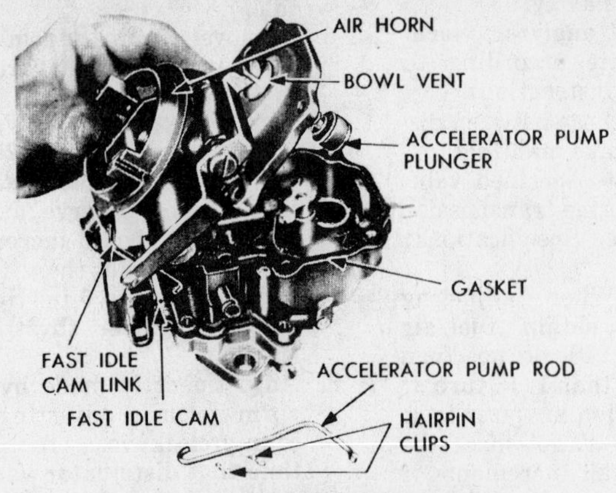

Removing air horn BBS & BBD carburetor (© Chrysler Corp.)

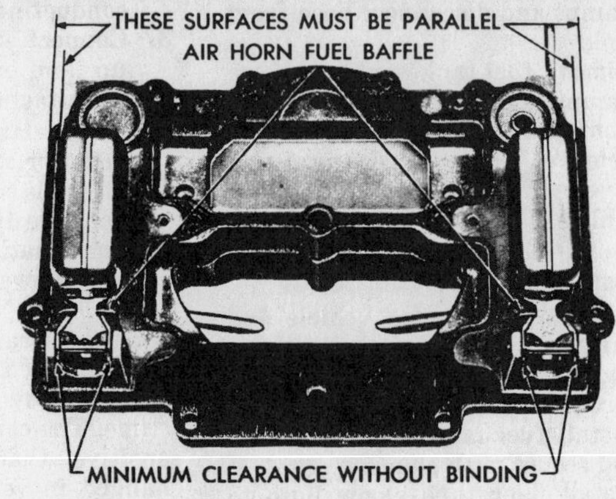

Checking float alignment (© Chrysler Corp.)

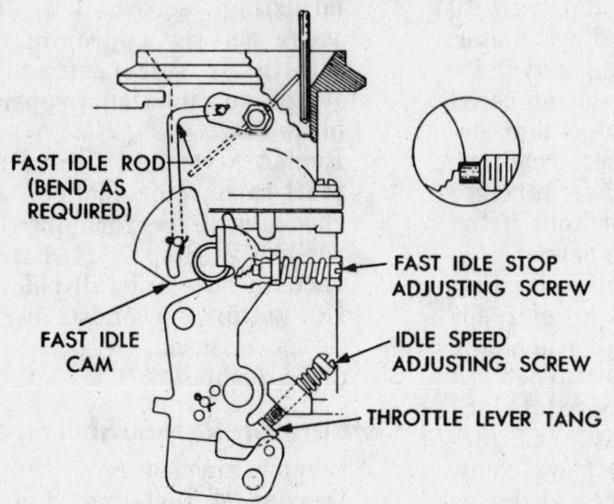

Fast Idle adjustment (© Chrysler Corp.)

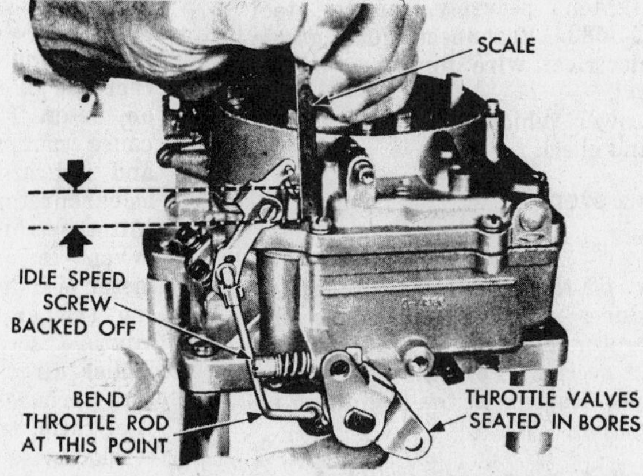

Measuring pump travel (© Chrysler Corp.)

valve as the seat is easily ruined. Float lip should always be perpendicular to needle valve to avoid binding.

5. Reassemble air horn, reconnecting fast idle cam link and accelerator pump rod.

Carter BBS and BBD Idle Speed Adjustment

1. After thoroughly warming up engine, connect a tachometer and, on 6 cylinder engines, turn on high-beam headlights.
2. Turn idle speed screw in or out to obtain 550 rpm (be sure that choke is fully off and that fast idle adjusting screw is not contacting cam).
3. Adjust each idle mixture screw for maximum engine rpm, then turn screw clockwise (leaner) until engine speed starts to drop. Turn back screw (counterclockwise) just enough to regain speed that was lost.
4. Readjust speed screw to obtain correct idle speed, then repeat Steps 2 and 3.

Carter AFB Float Level Setting

1. Remove carburetor from engine.
2. Disconnect accelerator pump rod.
3. Holding step-up piston cover plate so that pistons, rods and springs do not fly out, remove cover plate screws and step-up piston components.
4. Remove ten air horn attaching screws and lift air horn straight up, being careful not to bend or damage floats.
5. Set air horn upside-down on a flat surface and measure distance between float and air horn gasket. It should be 7/32". If necessary, bend float arm to obtain correct setting.
6. To reassemble and install, reverse Steps 1 through 4.

Carter AFB Accelerator Pump Adjustment

1. Back off idle adjusting screw until throttle valves are seated in bore.
2. Measure how far the plunger shaft protrudes from the air horn, which should be 7/16". Adjustment is made by bending pump rod at the lower angle.

Carter AFB Idle Adjustment

1. Run engine until normal operating temperature is reached. Make sure choke is completely off.
2. Using a tachometer, set idle speed screw for an engine speed of 500 rpm.
3. Adjust idle mixture screws until engine idles smoothly, then reset idle to 500 rpm.

Stromberg WW3 Carburetor Adjustment

The following adjustments must be made in the sequence presented here, that is: fast idle cam position, vacuum kick, unloader, accelerator pump travel and fast idle speed. The idle mixture adjustment may be made at any time.

Fast Idle Cam Position 1961-1963

1. Screw idle speed adjusting screw out to clear throttle lever tang when throttle valves are closed.
2. Hold throttle valve closed and turn fast idle adjusting screw out until fast idle cam can be positioned as illustrated.
3. Turn fast idle screw 7½ turns from the point of initial contact of Step 2.
4. Holding fast idle screw and cam as illustrated, choke valve plate should have 13/64" clearance from horn wall (use a 13/64" drill as a gauge). Bend fast idle rod at angle to achieve required choke valve to horn wall clearance.

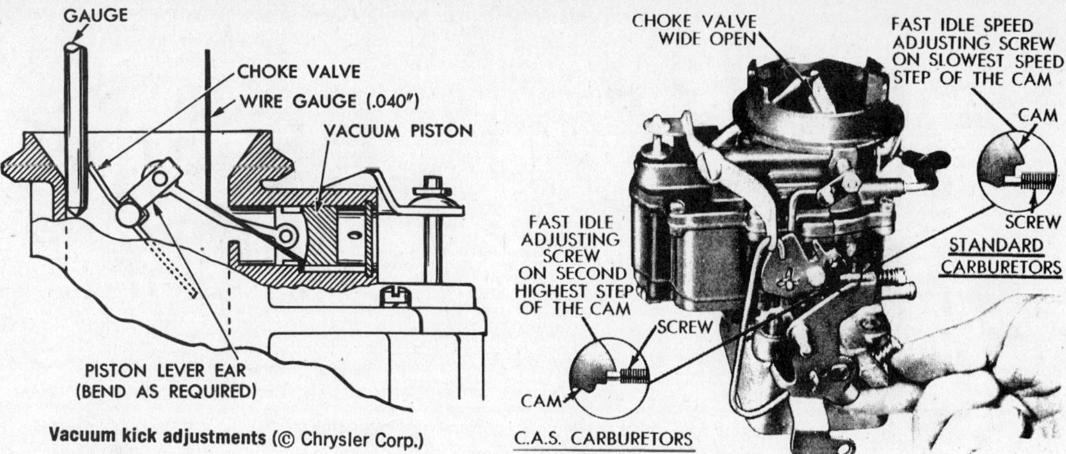

Vacuum kick adjustments (© Chrysler Corp.)

Fast idle speed adjustment (on vehicle) (© Chrysler Corp.)

Fast Idle Cam Position 1964-1971

1. While holding fast idle screw in second highest speed step on fast idle cam, choke valve should have #20 drill (gauge) clearance between plate and air horn, as illustrated.
2. Bend fast idle rod at upper angle to achieve correct adjustment.

Vacuum Kick Adjustment (1961-63)

1. While holding a .040" wire (bent as illustrated) in slot at bottom of vacuum piston bore, the choke valve should be open enough to insert a 19/64" drill between choke valve and air horn.
2. Bend piston lever ear to obtain required setting.

Vacuum Kick Adjustment 1964-1971

1. Disconnect fast idle linkage.
2. Connect diaphragm hose to a vacuum source of at least 10 in. Hg. (another running engine will do).
3. Hold diaphragm gently bottomed and check choke valve to air horn clearance. Clearance should be #2 on WW3-287, #42 on WW3-298 an A on WW3-299 and WW3-301.
4. Shorten or lengthen diaphragm link to obtain correct setting. Be careful not to apply force to diaphragm stem.

Choke Unloader Adjustment 1961-1963

1. Open throttle valves wide-open while gently holding choke valve closed. Choke valve to air horn clearance should be 15/64" (#1 drill.
2. To adjust, bend tang on throttle lever as illustrated.
3. Check for bind in choke mechanism. All linkage should work freely.

Choke Unloader Adjustment 1964-1971

1. Holding throttle wide open, insert 5/16" drill (15/64" drill on WW3-287) between choke valve and air horn. There should be a slight drag when drill is withdrawn.
2. Adjust to proper clearance by bending tang on throttle lever.

Accelerator Pump and Bowl Vent Adjustment

1. Accelerator pump travel is automatically adjusted when correct bowl vent is obtained.
2. With horseshoe clip in the middle slot on the pump plunger rod and pump rod in middle stroke hole on throttle lever, back off idle speed adjusting screw and open choke valve so that when throttle valves are closed the fast idle adjusting screw will not contact fast idle cam.
3. Hold throttle tightly closed and insert 5/64" drill (.060" for 1964-1971 Standard and .050" for 1964-70 CAP carburetors) between bowl vent and vent seat as illustrated.
4. Adjustment is made by bending pump rod at lower angle.

Fast Idle Speed Adjustment

WW3-227 (1961-1963)

With warmed-up engine running, and fast idle adjusting screw in contact with top (fastest) step of the fast idle cam, turn fast idle adjusting screw until an engine speed of 1250 rpm is achieved.

1964-1971

1. Warm up engine, attach tachometer and place transmission in park or neutral.
2. On standard carburetors the fast idle screw should rest on the slowest speed step of the fast idle cam when throttle is closed after choke has been set at 20-degree closed position. On CAP carburetors, close choke valve until fast idle screw can be positioned on second-highest speed step of fast idle cam.
3. Start engine without disturbing throttle and adjust fast idle screw for 500 rpm (1350 rpm for CAP carburetors).

Holley 1920 Carburetor

Checking Wet Fuel Level

1. Remove economizer diaphragm assembly.
2. With vehicle on level floor and engine running, insert a scale to the exact level of fuel. Distance from fuel level to machined surface of opening should be 27/32".
3. If fuel level is not correct, remove bowl and adjust by bending float tab with needle nosed pliers.
4. Reassemble bowl and check level. Readjust if necessary.
5. Install economizer diaphragm assembly.

Dashpot Adjustment (CAP Carburetors)

1. Set curb idle speed and mixture and install tachometer.
2. With engine running, open throttle until actuating tab on throttle lever is just barely touching stem of dashpot but not depressing it. Tachometer should read 2500 rpm at this point.
3. To adjust, loosen locknut on dashpot and screw dashpot in or out until correct setting is obtained. Tighten locknut.
4. See CAP Idle Speed Adjustment above for setting idle speed on CAS or CAP carburetors.

Curb Idle Speed (Standard Carburetors)

1. Warm up engine, attach tachometer, place transmission in neutral and, on 6 cylinder engines, turn headlights on bright.

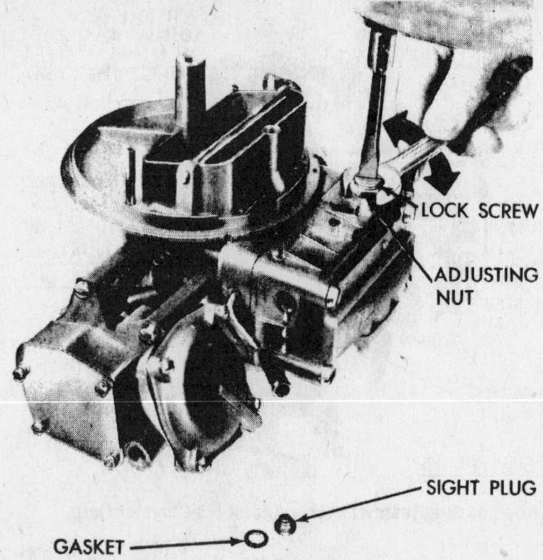

Adjusting float bowl fuel level—Holley
(© Chrysler Corp.)

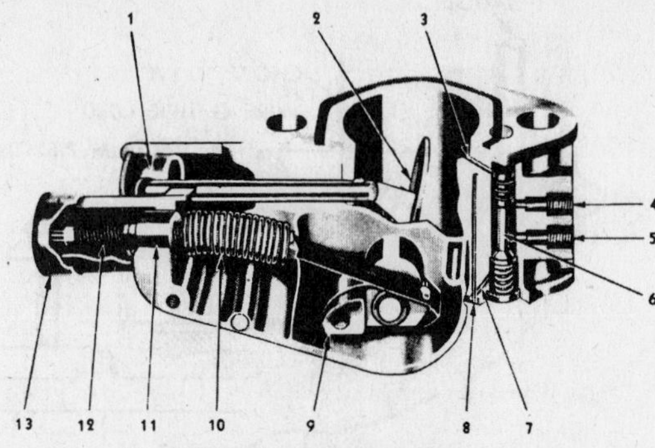

Sandwich velocity type governor
(© Chrysler Corp.)

1 Non-cheating stabilizer piston
2 Throttle valve
3 Passage to transfer valve chamber
4 Carburetor vacuum connection (not used)
5 Ignition distributor vacuum connection (not used)
6 Vaccum transfer valve plunger
7 Vacuum passage
8 Vacuum by-pass passage
9 Cam and valve shaft assembly
10 Control spring and ribbon assembly
11 Calibrating nut
12 Adjusting screw
13 Adjusting screw cap assembly

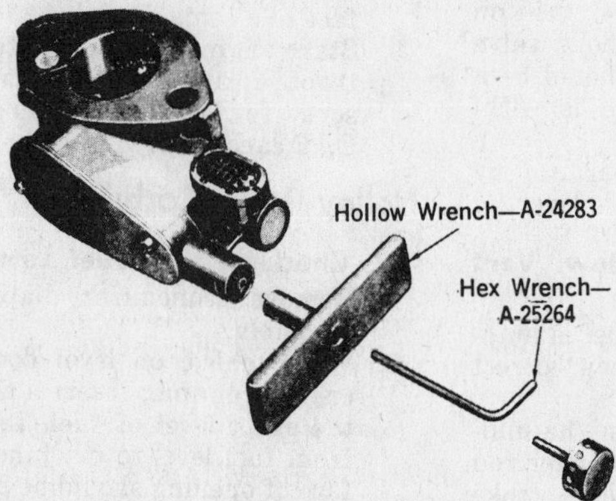

Sandwich governor surge adjustment
(© Chrysler Corp.)

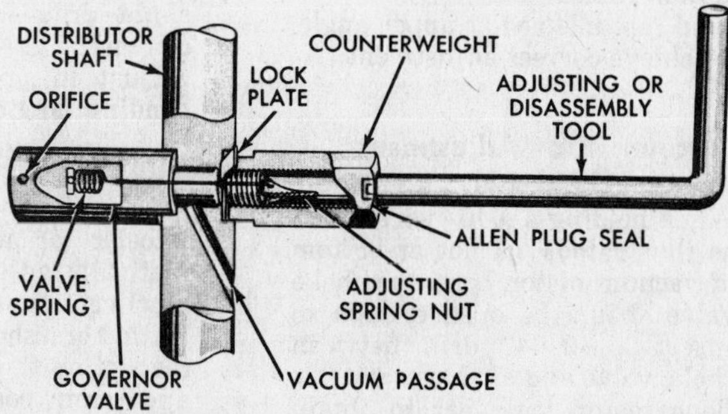

Governor valve and weights (© Chrysler Corp.)

2. Turn idle speed screw in or out for an idle of 550 rpm.
3. Adjust idle mixture screw to obtain highest rpm, then turn screw clockwise (leaner) until rpm begins to drop. Turn screw back counterclockwise (richer) just far enough to recover speed that was lost.
4. Readjust idle speed screw for 550 rpm.

Holley 2300G and 4150G Carburetors

Curb idle speed and mixture adjustment procedures are described in CAS and CAP Carburetor Idle Speed Adjustment above. Dashpot adjustment procedure is the same for these carburetors as for the Holley model 1920 described above. Fuel level can be checked by removing sight plug on float bowl. Fuel level should just be high enough so that a slight amount dribbles out sight hole. Float level may be adjusted by loosening lockscrew and turning adjusting nut on the top of the float bowl as illustrated.

Governors

Sandwich Velocity Type Governor

Speed Adjustment

1. See Specifications at the beginning of this section for engine no load governed rpm.
2. Remove seal.
3. Turn speed screw adjusting cap, one-half turn at a time, counterclockwise to increase speed and clockwise to decrease speed. Each ½ turn equals approximately 150 rpm. More than two complete counterclockwise turns from factory setting is not recommended.

Surge Adjustment

1. Remove adjusting screw cap assembly and locate special hollow wrench in calibrating nut.
2. Locate hex wrench through hollow wrench into adjusting screw.
3. Block throttle linkage to produce surge at governed speed.
4. Turn calibrating nut clockwise ¼ turn at a time while holding adjusting screw with hex wrench until surge is minimized.
5. Reinstall adjusting screw cap assembly and reset governor speed if necessary.

Slow Action Adjustment

If governor does not cut in quickly at maximum speed or does not open promptly at governed speed when load is applied, governor is said to be slow acting. This is corrected by the same procedure as that described for surge adjustments above, except that the calibrating nut is turned counterclockwise.

Holley Governors

Adjustment

1. Connect tachometer to engine.
2. After engine has warmed up, race it momentarily at wide open throttle and note engine speed registered on tachometer.
3. If adjustment is required, remove the cover band from the governor housing of the distrib-

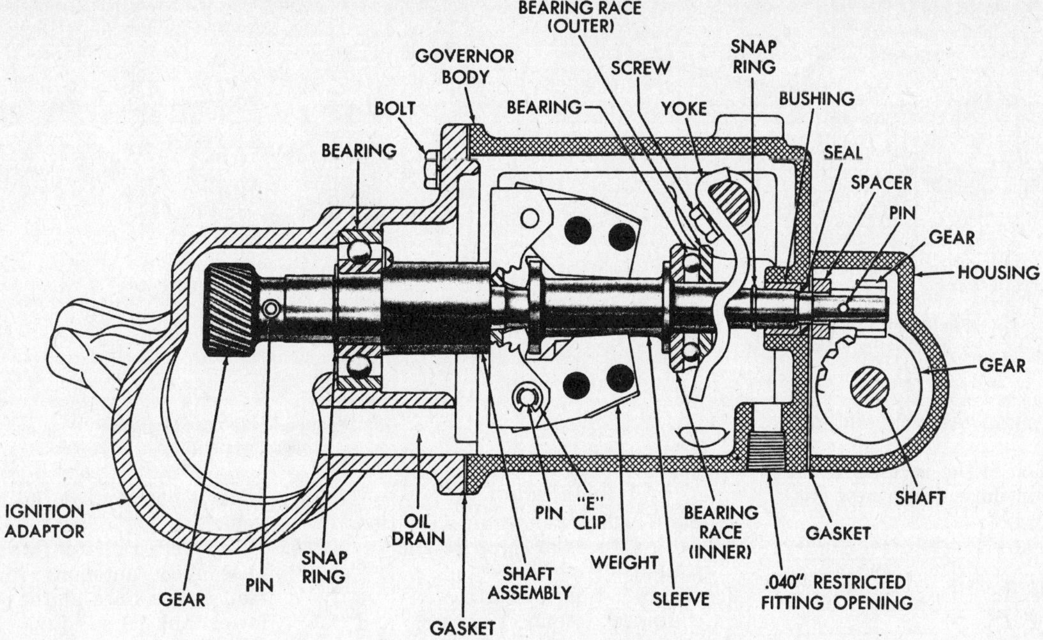

Pierce governor assembly (© Chrysler Corp.)

utor and turn centrifugal valve adjusting nut while holding opposite end of shaft with a screwdriver. A bent screwdriver may be required. Rpm is increased by turning adjusting nut clockwise.

4. Replace cover band, being sure it covers openings and is tight enough to prevent the entrance of any dirt.

Pierce Governor

Models GC-4917 and 4922

Removal

1. Remove distributor.
2. Disconnect oil line, linkage to carburetor and tachometer cable.
3. Remove hold-down bolt at lower end of support housing that also holds down distributor.
4. Remove ignition distributor adapter and governor from engine as an assembly.

Installation

1. With distributor intermediate drive shaft in proper mesh with camshaft gear, install adapter on engine and install hold-down bolt.
2. Install ignition distributor.
3. Connect oil line and tachometer cable.
4. Adjust linkage to proper length and connect to governor (see throttle linkage).
5. Connect governor adjusting spring.
6. Start and run engine to operating temperature.
7. Adjust tension on governor adjusting spring to control engine speed to specification.

Fuel Pump

On all models the fuel pump is located on the right side of the engine block immediately behind the timing case. Mechanical fuel pumps are actuated by one of the lobes of the camshaft.

Pressure Test

1. Check fuel system for leaks.
2. Insert a "T" fitting in fuel line at carburetor as illustrated.
3. Connect a 6" piece of hose between "T" fitting and pressure gauge. Do not use a hose longer than 6".
4. Vent pump by cranking engine while cracking hose connection at gauge just enough to let air escape. Unless air is bled a low pressure reading will result.
5. Connect a tachometer and run engine at 500 rpm. Correct pressure values are found in the Tune-Up Specifications at the beginning of this Section.

Volume Test

Disconnect the outlet line and measure expelled fuel while engine is idling. Fuel pump should supply 1 quart of fuel in 1 minute or less at 500 rpm.

Inlet Valve Test

1. Connect a vacuum gauge on inlet fitting while line is disconnected.
2. Start engine or turn over with starter motor.
3. There should be noticeable vacuum present, with no alternating blowback. If blowback is present, inlet valve(s) are not seating properly and must be cleaned or replaced.

Fuel Pump Removal and Installation

1. Disconnect inlet and outlet lines.
2. Remove belts which secure pump to engine block.

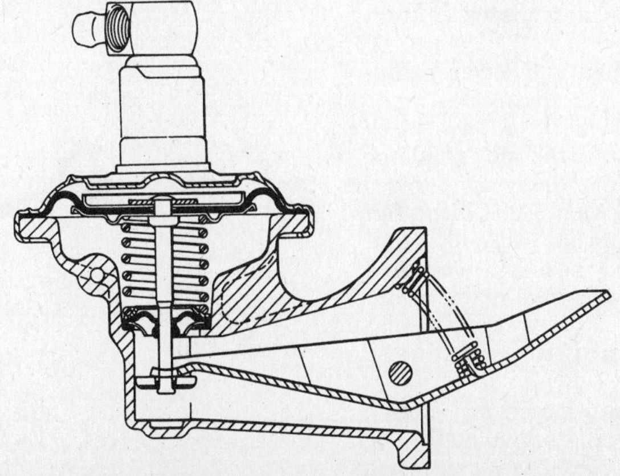

Fuel pump 225 engine (© Chrysler Corp.)

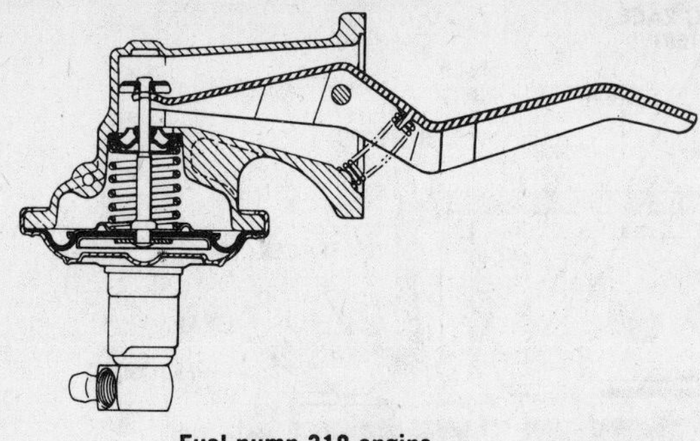

Fuel pump 318 engine
(© Chrysler Corp.)

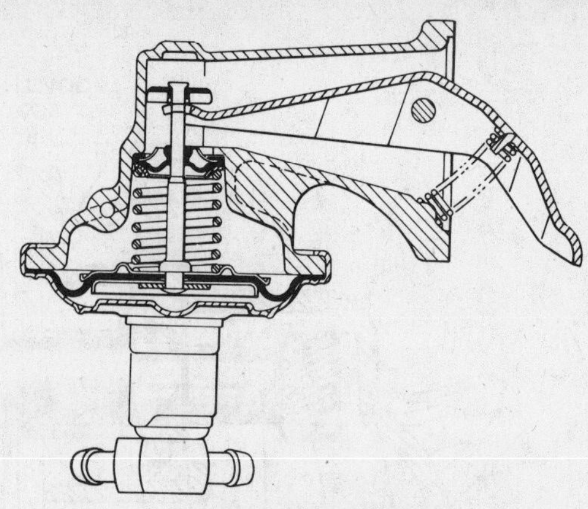

Fuel pump 361 & 413 engine
(© Chrysler Corp.)

3. Remove pump assembly and gasket.
4. Installation is the reverse of the above procedure. Use a new gasket.

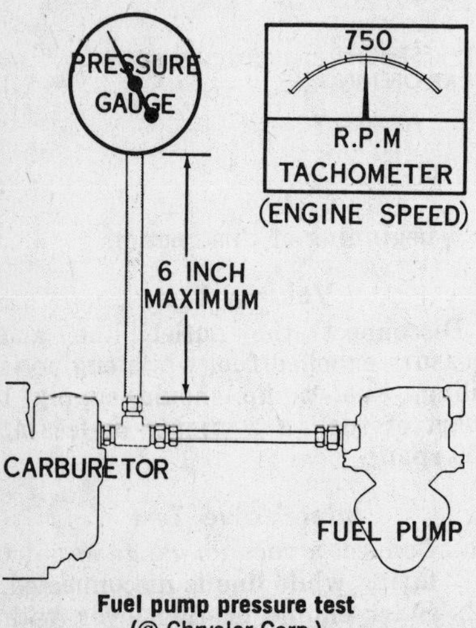

Fuel pump pressure test
(© Chrysler Corp.)

Cooling System

Radiator Removal

Conventional Models

1. Drain cooling system.
2. On vehicles with automatic transmission, disconnect oil cooler lines at radiator bottom tank.
3. Remove upper and lower radiator hoses.
4. On vehicles with a two piece shroud remove the lower half of the shroud.
5. On vehicles with a one piece fan shroud, separate shroud from radiator and position rearward on engine for maximum clearance.
6. Remove radiator attaching screws.
7. Remove radiator from engine compartment. Care should be taken not to damage cooling fins or water tubes during removal.

Installation

1. Slide radiator down into position behind radiator support and install attaching screws.
2. Install fan shroud (if so equipped) connect hoses, and connect transmission oil cooler lines, if so equipped.
3. Fill cooling system as required. After warm-up re-check coolant level.
4. On vehicles with automatic transmission, measure transmission level after warm-up and add oil as required.

Radiator Removal

A-100 Series

1. Drain cooling system and remove upper radiator hose. Remove the upper bolts securing the core to yoke.
2. Raise the vehicle on a hoist.
3. Remove bolts from front end of air scoop (behind the bumper) and from both sides of air scoop. Remove one bolt from left rear of air scoop, pry scoop downward and remove bolt attaching horizontal reinforcement to vertical bracket. Remove one bolt from right rear of air scoop, attaching the scoop and reinforcement to the vertical bracket.
4. Lower front end of air scoop and slide it out toward the front of vehicle.
5. Disconnect radiator lower hose. Disconnect automatic transmission cooler lines at the radiator lower tank (if so equipped).
6. While holding core in place, remove lower bolts securing the core to the yoke. Then lower the core down out of the yoke.

Installation

1. Slide core up into yoke and install lower core to yoke bolts.
2. Connect the radiator lower hose. Connect transmission cooler lines to the radiator lower tank (if so equipped).
3. Slide the air scoop into position and install scoop retaining bolts. Make sure no large gap occurs between the scoop and core or poor cooling may result.
4. Lower the vehicle and install upper core to yoke bolts. Install upper radiator hose.
5. Fill cooling system to 1¼ inches below the filler neck.
6. Measure transmission fluid level (after warm-up) and add fluid as required.

Water Pump

Removal—All Engines

1. Drain cooling system and

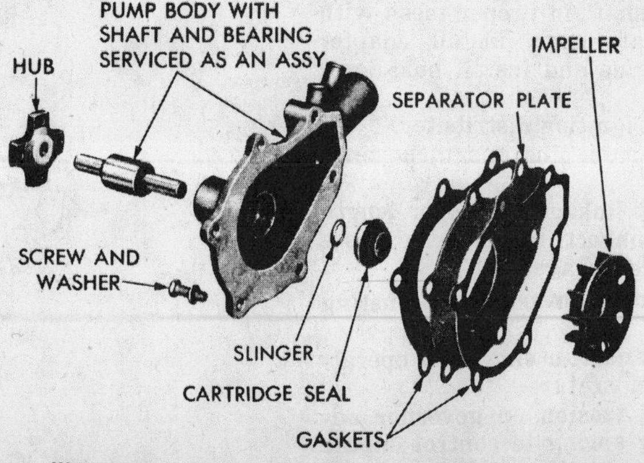

Water pump—6 cyl .engines (© Chrysler Corp.)

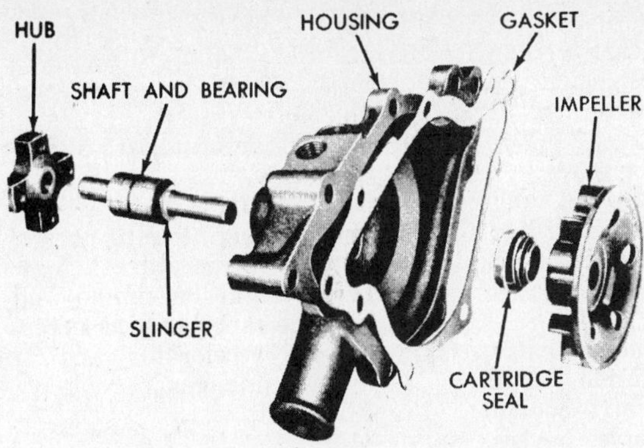

Water pump—318 engines (© Chrysler Corp.)

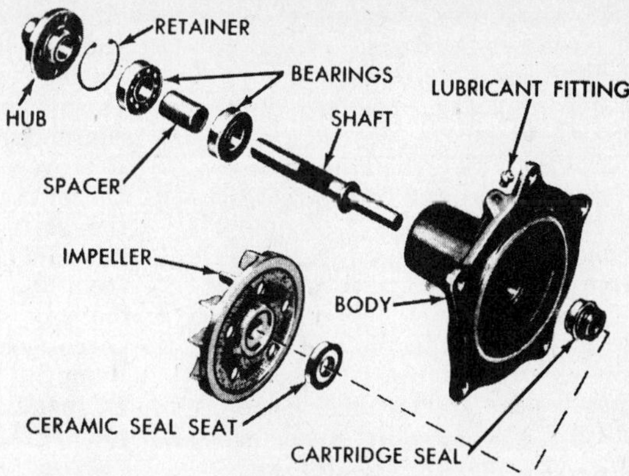

Water pump—361 & 413 engines (© Chrysler Corp.)

remove the fan belt.
2. Unscrew fan blade bolts and remove fan blade, spacers and bolts as an assembly.
3. Position both hose clamps in the center of the by-pass hose. Disconnect or remove heater and radiator hoses.
4. Remove water pump retaining bolts and remove water pump assembly.

Installation

1. Install a new by-pass hose if necessary, with clamps positioned in the center of the hose.
2. Use a new gasket and install water pump. Install and tighten pump retaining bolts to 30 foot pounds. Position by-pass hose clamps. Install the heater and radiator hoses.
3. Install fan blade, spacer and bolt assembly. Start all bolts, then tighten to 15-18 foot pounds.
4. Install fan belt and adjust belt tension. Fill cooling system.

Thermostat Removal

1. Drain cooling system down to thermostat level or below.
2. Remove upper radiator hose from thermostat housing.
3. Remove thermostat housing bolts and remove thermostat and housing.
4. Installation is the reverse of the above procedure. Use a new gasket.

Engine

Exhaust Emission Control

Reference

For service and adjustment of the CAS and CAP systems, see Exhaust Emission Systems of General Repair Section.

Engine Removal

Conventional, Forward Control and 4x4 Six Cylinder

1. Drain coolant from radiator and block.
2. Disconnect battery and fuel pump flexible line at pump. Cap the line.
3. Disconnect headlamp wires and upper and lower radiator hoses.
4. Remove front sheet metal and radiator as a unit.
5. Remove the floor mat and floor boards from the driver's compartment.
6. Disconnect the propeller shaft at the front universal joint.
7. Remove the transmission. (See Index For Transmission R&R.)
8. Disconnect the clutch yoke by removing the cotter key and pin.
9. Disconnect the exhaust pipe at the manifold, throttle and choke controls, heat indicator wire and oil gauge line.
10. Disconnect the starter cable, coil wires, alternator wires, carburetor to brake booster line (if so equipped), air lines at air brake compressor (if so squipped), and horn wires.
11. Remove the air cleaner, carburettor, closed vent system and ignition coil.
12. Install a suitable engine lifting bracket on the engine and attach a chain hoist hook to the bracket.
13. Remove the front and rear engine support bolts and lift the engine from the truck.

Installation

Install in the reverse order of removal. Fill cooling system and crankcase. Check transmission lubricant. Start the engine and check for leaks and operation. Adjust the carburetor and timing. Road test.

Engine Removal

Medium Duty Tilt Cab—All Engines

1. Tilt cab and lock in the lift position.
2. Drain coolant from the radiator and block, disconnect the battery. NOTE: Removal of the right or left front wheel depending on engine application will facilitate engine removal.
3. Remove the splash shield and fender skirt. Disconnect the flexible fuel line and cap the line.
4. Disconnect the electrical con-

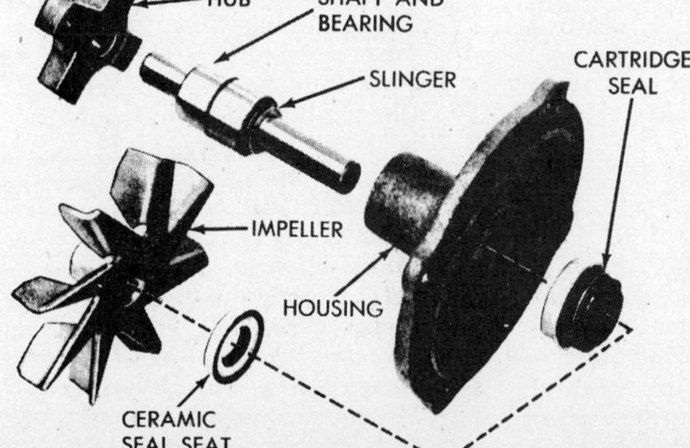

Water pump—383 engines (© Chrysler Corp.)

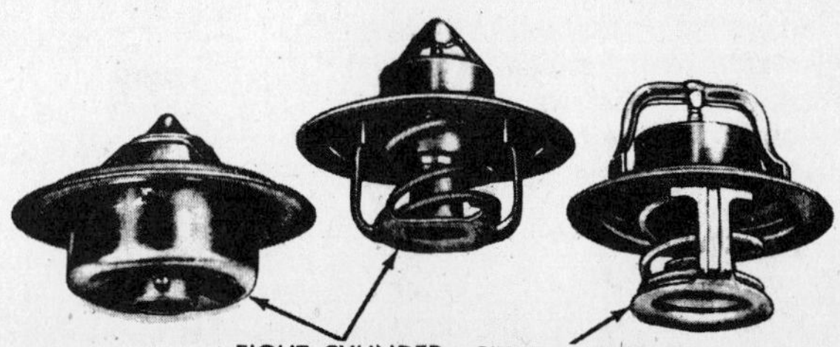

Thermostats (© Chrysler Corp.)

nections at the alternator, coil, temperature and oil pressure sending units (oil gauge line if so equipped), starter and ground wires.

5. Disconnect the radiator hoses, heater hoses and ether quick start, if so equipped.
6. Remove the fan and adaptor from the crankshaft to prevent damage.
7. Remove the radiator and support as an assembly. NOTE: On some model applications, removal of the cab locking yoke, instead of removing radiator with support will facilitate engine removal.
8. Disconnect the exhaust system from the engine and tie out of the way.
9. Disconnect the power steering hoses from the pump, air lines from the air compressor or vacuum brake lines from the engine, if so equipped. Cap all openings.
10. Remove the air cleaner, carburetor and necessary linkage. Install engine lifting fixture.
11. Attach a chain hoist or hydrocrane to lifting fixture, raise the engine enough to take the weight off the mounts.
12. With the transmission jack in place, remove the transmission to clutch housing bolts.
13. Disconnect the clutch linkage and torque shaft.
14. Remove the motor mount attaching bolts. Raise engine with a lifting tool, remove the rear motor mounts, remove the engine.

Installation

Install in the reverse order of removal. Fill the cooling system, power steering pump and crankcase. Check the transmission lubricant. Start the engine and check for leaks and operation. Adjust the carburetor (see Carburetor for adjustment procedure) and ignition timing.

Engine Removal

A-100 Series

1. Drain coolant from radiator and cylinder block.
2. Disconnect battery, remove air cleaner, radiator and heater hoses.
3. Disconnect throttle linkage, electrical connections at the alternator, distributor, body ground to engine, temperature and oil pressure sending units (oil gauge line on units so equipped).
4. Remove right inner valve cover nuts to remove wiring harness. Remove distributor cap and rotor.
5. Remove carburetor.
6. Raise vehicle on a hoist, drain engine and transmission oil (also torque converter if so equipped).
7. Remove starter motor wires.
8. Disconnect battery ground cable, the shift linkage at the transmission and anti-rattle block from body sill. Tie linkage out of the way.
9. Disconnect speedometer cable. Remove clutch torque shaft (transmission gearshift control rod, parking lock cable, neutral starting switch wire and oil cooler lines at radiator if so equipped).
10. Disconnect exhaust pipe at the manifold and muffler, driveshaft from transmission and tie out of the way.
11. Disconnect fuel inlet line at fuel pump and cap line.
12. Support engine and transmission as an assembly on a suitable jack stand. Remove transmission rear support bolt, front engine mount lower stud nuts and washers.
13. Remove right engine support bracket from body sill and, on V8 engine, left front motor mount from engine bracket.
14. Lower transmission and engine as an assembly.
15. Remove transmission (torque converter and flex plate if so equipped), and place engine in repair stand.

Installation

1. With vehicle on a hoist and engine with transmission on a suitable jack stand, raise engine and transmission into position.
2. Install transmission rear support bolt, left front motor mount to engine bracket (V8 engines), right engine support bracket to body sill, both front lower stud washers and nuts. Remove jack stand.
3. Install battery ground cable and starter motor wires.
4. Install transmission and clutch linkage, speedometer cable (oil cooler lines at radiator, neutral starting switch wire, transmission gearshift control rod, parking lock cable and adjust if so equipped).
5. Install driveshaft, exhaust pipe and connect fuel line to fuel pump.
6. Lower vehicle, install throttle linkage, electrical connections at distributor, starter motor, temperature and oil pressure sending units, oil gauge line on units so equipped, and body ground to engine.
7. Install electrical connections at alternator and wire harness clips to right valve cover.
8. Install radiator and heater hoses. Close all drain cocks and fill cooling system.
9. Fill engine crankcase and transmission.
10. Connect battery, start engine and run engine until normal operating temperature is reached.
11. Inspect ignition timing and adjust the carburetor as necessary.
12. Adjust accelerator and transmission linkages.
13. Road test.

Manifolds

Removal and Installation

6 Cylinder Engines

1. Remove air cleaner.
2. Disconnect vacuum control tube at carburetor.
3. Disconnect fuel line at carburetor.
4. Disconnect crankcase ventilation tube at carburetor.
5. Disconnect automatic choke rod at carburetor and remove choke from intake manifold.
6. Disconnect throttle linkage at carburetor.
7. Remove carburetor from intake manifold.
8. Disconnect exhaust pipe at exhaust manifold flange.
9. Remove nuts and washers securing manifold assembly to cylinder head.
10. Remove manifold from cylinder head.
11. Remove three screws securing intake manifold to exhaust manifold.
12. Separate intake and exhaust manifolds and discard gasket.
13. Clean all gasket surfaces on manifolds in solvent and blow dry with compressed air.
14. Clean manifold gasket surfaces on cylinder head, wash with solvent and blow dry with compressed air.
15. Check mating surfaces of manifolds for parallelism with straightedge. Surfaces should be flat within .008″.
16. Inspect manifolds for cracks or distortion.
17. Check operation of manifold heat control valve. If necessary to free up operation, apply a manifold heat control valve solvent.
18. To install, first install a new gasket between the two manifolds.
19. Install three long screws securing the two manifolds. *Do not tighten screws at this time.*
20. Position manifold assembly on cylinder head, using a new gasket.
21. Install triangular washers and

nuts on upper studs and on the four lower studs opposite numbers 2 and 5 cylinders. The eight triangular washers should be positioned squarely on the machined surfaces of both intake and exhaust manifold retaining pads. These washers must be installed with *cup side* against manifold. Install nuts and washers only when engine is cold. On 251 cu. in. engine, be sure conical nuts are used on forward and rear extreme ends of exhaust manifold.

22. Install steel conical washers with cup side to manifold, one on center upper stud and two on center lower studs. Install nuts with flat side away from washers. Tighten nuts to 10 ft. lbs. CAUTION: *Do not over-tighten.*
23. Tighten three screws securing intake manifold to exhaust manifold to 15 ft. lbs., starting with inner screw.
24. Attach exhaust pipe to manifold flange, using a new gasket and tighten bolt nuts to 35 ft. lbs.
25. Install carburetor and connect automatic choke rod and throttle linkage. Assemble crankcase ventilation hose, vacuum control tube and fuel line to carburetor. Install carburetor air cleaner, and connect closed breather cap hose to air cleaner inlet tube, if used.

Intake Manifold Removal

V8 Engines

1. Drain cooling system and disconnect battery.
2. Remove alternator, carburetor air cleaner, and fuel line.
3. Disconnect accelerator linkage.
4. Remove vacuum control between carburetor and distributor.
5. Remove distributor cap and wires.
6. Disconnect coil wires, temperature sending unit wire, heater hoses and bypass hose.
7. Remove intake manifold, ignition coil and carburetor as an assembly.

Installation

Installation is the reverse of the above procedure. Tighten the intake manifold to head bolts in the sequence illustrated, from center alternating out. Tighten manifold mounting bolts to torque listed in Specifications, tightening in 15 ft. lb. increments.

Exhaust Manifold Removal

318 Cu. In. Engines

1. Remove bolts and nuts attaching exhaust pipe to manifold.
2. Remove bolts, nuts and washers

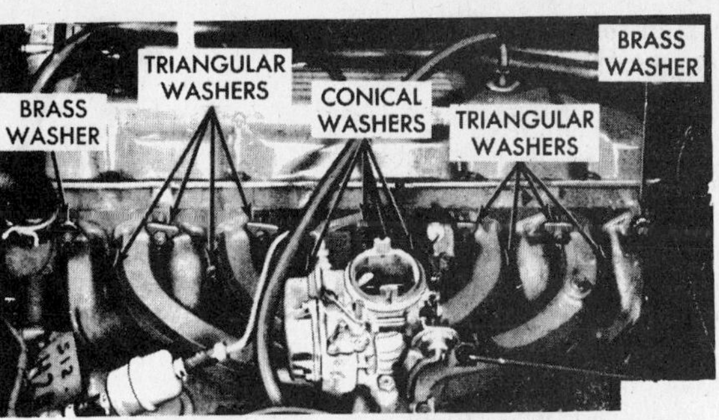

Intake & exhaust manifold installation 170 & 225 engines (© Chrysler Corp.)

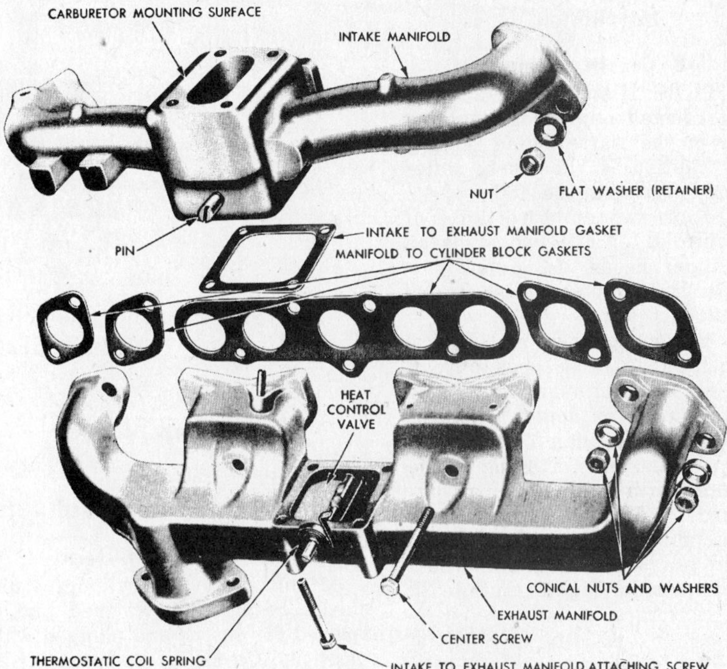

Intake & exhaust manifold 251 engine (© Chrysler Corp.)

Intake manifold bolt tightening sequence (© Chrysler Corp.)

Installing exhaust manifold 318 engines (© Chrysler Corp.)

attaching manifolds to cylinder heads. Remove manifolds from cylinder heads.

383 Cu. In. Engines

1. Remove spark plugs and disconnect battery.
2. Remove alternator.
3. Disconnect exhaust pipe at exhaust manifolds.
4. Remove stud nuts attaching exhaust manifolds to cylinder heads. Slide manifold off studs and away from cylinder heads.

Installation

318 Cu. In. Engines

CAUTION: If studs came out with the nuts, install new studs, applying a sealer on the coarse thread ends. If this precaution is not taken, water leaks may develop at the studs.

1. Position two outboard arms of manifolds on the two studs on cylinder heads, using new gaskets. Install conical washers and nuts on studs.
2. Install two screws and conical washers at inner ends of outboard arms of manifold. Install two screws *without* washers on center arm of manifold. Tighten screws and nuts, starting at the center arm and working outward, to 15 ft. lbs. torque.
3. Assemble exhaust pipe to manifold, and secure with bolts, nuts and washers. Tighten nuts to 35 ft. lbs. torque.

Installation

383 Cu. In. Engines

1. If studs came out with the manifold mounting nuts, install new studs, applying a sealant to prevent possible water leakage.
2. Install stud nuts to 30 ft. lbs. torque, from center out.
3. Install alternator and adjust belt tension.
4. Install spark plugs, and connect battery.

Manifold Heat Control Valve

Inspect operation of manifold heat control valve by racing engine momentarily to wide open throttle. The counterweight should respond by moving clockwise about ½" on 6 cylinder and 318 cu. in. engines and counterclockwise on the 383 cu. in. engines. If it does not move it may be frozen with deposits or the thermostatic spring may be weak or broken. Use a manifold heat control valve solvent to loosen valve shaft at bushings. CAUTION: Be sure that manifold is *cool* when applying solvent and let it soak for a few minutes before attempting to free the valve.

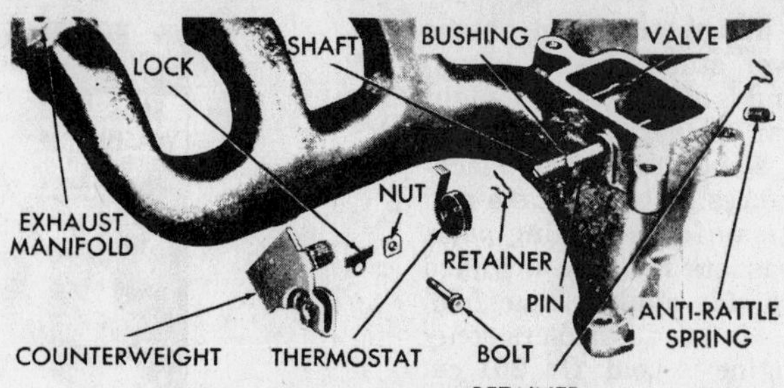

Manifold heat control valve 225 engine
(© Chrysler Corp.)

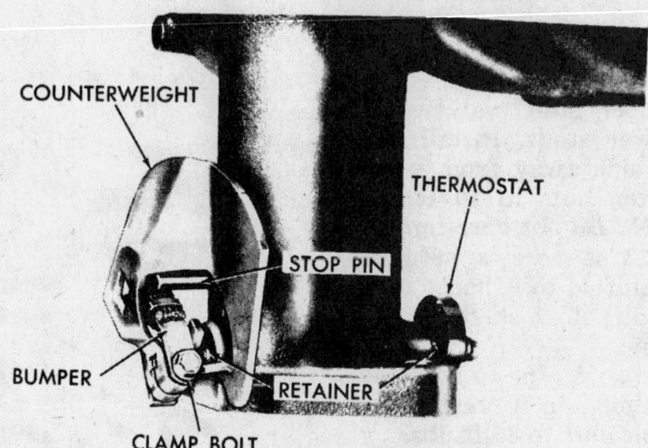

Manifold heat control valve 383 engine
(© Chrysler Corp.)

Cylinder Head

Cylinder Head Removal

251 Cu. In. L-Head

After removal cylinder head should be carefully cleaned and inspected for cracks and plugged water passages. Check for warpage with a good straightedge. If head is more than .024" out lengthwise or .006" out cross-wise, it cannot safely be used. It is possible to plane up to 0.20" from head to eliminate warpage.

Installation

1. Always use a new head gasket and coat it with a suitable sealing compound.

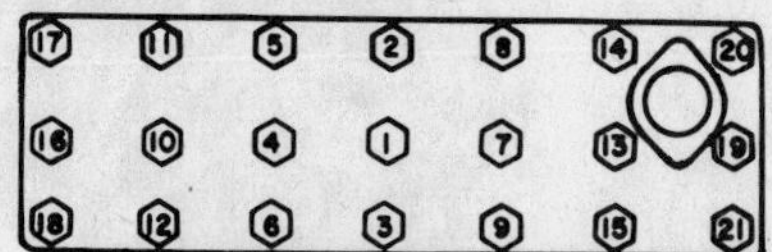

Cylinder heat bolt tightening sequence
6 cyl. engines (21 bolt side)
(© Chrysler Corp.)

2. Tighten cylinder head bolts to 65-70 ft. lbs. torque in the sequence illustrated (hot). Retighten to same torque (hot) after 500 miles of operation.

Cylinder Head Removal

6 Cyl. OHV

1. Drain cooling system.
2. Remove air cleaner and fuel line.
3. Remove vacuum line at carburetor and distributor.
4. Disconnect accelerator linkage.
5. Disconnect spark plug wires by pulling straight out in line with plugs.
6. Disconnect heater hose and bypass hose clamp.

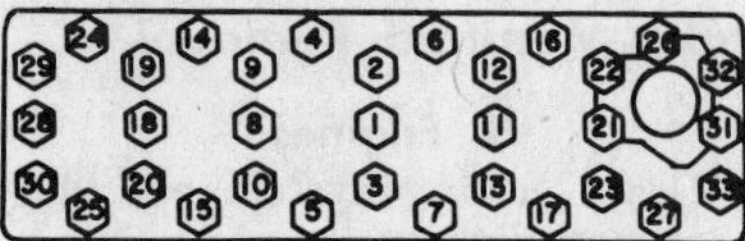

Cylinder head bolt tightening sequence
6 cyl. engines (33 bolt side)
(© Chrysler Corp.)

7. Disconnect temperature sending wire.
8. Disconnect exhaust pipe at exhaust manifold flange.
9. Remove intake and exhaust manifolds as described above.
10. Remove closed vent system (PCV) and rocker cover.
11. Remove rocker shaft assembly. See Rocker Arm Assembly Removal.
12. Remove pushrods in sequence and mark them in such a way that they may be put back into their original positions.
13. Remove head bolts.
14. Remove spark plugs and tubes.
15. To install, clean all gasket surfaces of cylinder block and cylinder head and install spark plugs.
16. Check all surfaces with a

Cylinder head bolt tightening sequence
6 cyl. OHV engine
(© Chrysler Corp.)

straightedge if there is any reason to suspect leakage.

17. Install gasket and cylinder head.
18. Install cylinder head attaching bolts. Tighten all bolts in the sequence illustrated to 50 ft. lbs. torque, then repeat tightening sequence torquing to 65 ft. lbs.
19. Install rocker arms and shaft assembly with "FLAT" end of the rocker shaft "ON TOP" and pointing toward front of engine, as illustrated, to insure proper lubrication of rocker assemblies. Install rocker shaft retainers between rocker arms so they seat on rocker shaft and not on extended bushing of rocker arm. Be sure to install long retainer in center position only. Tighten bolts to 25 ft. lbs.

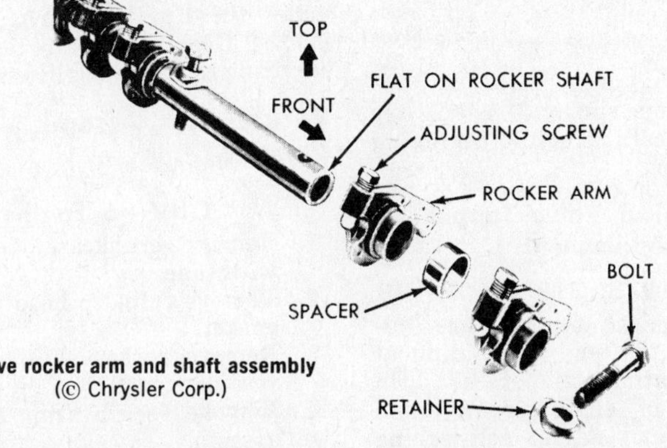

Valve rocker arm and shaft assembly
(© Chrysler Corp.)

20. Loosen the 3 bolts holding intake manifold to exhaust manifold. This is necessary for proper alignment.
21. Install intake and exhaust manifold and carburetor assembly to cylinder head with the cap side of conical washers against manifolds. Tighten to 10 ft. lbs.
22. Tighten the 3 bolts holding intake manifold to exhaust manifold to 15 ft. lbs. Tighten inner bolt first, then two outer bolts.
23. Connect heater hose and by-pass hose clamp.
24. Connect heat indicator sending unit wire, the accelerator linkage and spark plug wires.
25. Install the vacuum control tube from carburetor to distributor.
26. Connect exhaust pipe to exhaust manifold flange.
27. Install fuel line and carburetor air cleaner.
28. Fill cooling system, start and warm up engine, and adjust valve tappet clearance.
29. Install valve cover using new gasket, tightening retaining nuts to 3-4 ft. lbs.
30. Install crankcase ventilation system.

Cylinder Head Removal

V8 Engines

1. Drain cooling system and disconnect battery. On vehicles with 361 cu. in. engines, remove battery.
2. Remove alternator, air cleaner and fuel line.
3. Disconnect accelerator linkage.
4. Remove vacuum control hose between carburetor and distributor.
5. Remove cooling and heater hoses from head and, if so equipped, remove air compressor.
6. Remove distributor cap and high tension leads as an assembly.
7. Remove heat indicator sending unit wire.
8. Remove crankcase ventilation system and valve covers.
9. Remove spark plugs and, on 361, 413 cu. in. engines, remove distributor and governor.
10. Remove intake manifold, carburetor and, if attached to manifold, ignition coil as an assembly.
11. Remove tappet chamber cover.
12. On 361, 413 cu. in. engines, remove the bolts that secure water pump housing to each cylinder head.
13. Remove exhaust manifolds. On the 361, 413 cu. in. engines, tag the center bolts for reinstallation in same hole.
14. Remove rocker arms and shaft assemblies.
15. Remove pushrods and *identify to insure installation in original location.*
16. Remove cylinder head bolts and cylinder heads.
17. Before installing cylinder heads, clean all gasket surfaces of block and heads.
18. Inspect all surfaces with a straightedge if there is any indication of leakage.
19. Coat new head gaskets with sealant and install on block.
20. Install cylinder head and head bolts. Tighten bolts in the sequence illustrated, first to 50 ft. lbs. torque, then in sequence again to the specified torque (see Specifications at the beginning of this section). CAUTION: Do not retighten cylinder head bolts after engine has been operated if embossed steel head gaskets are used.

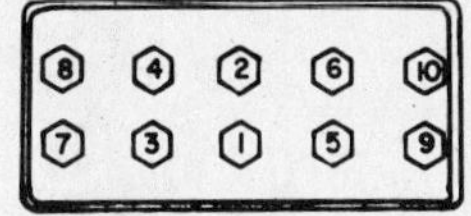

Cylinder head bolt tightening sequence
V8 engine (2 rocker shafts)
(© Chrysler Corp.)

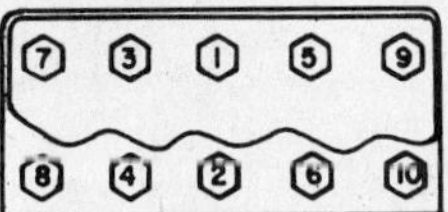

Cylinder head bolt tightening sequence
V8 engine (1 rocker shaft)
(© Chrysler Corp.)

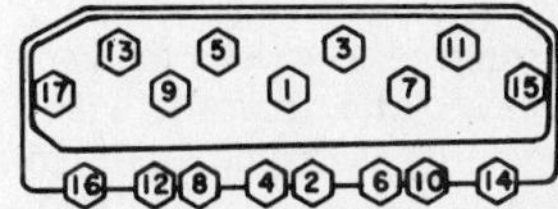

Cylinder head bolt tightening sequence
V8-361, 383, 413 engines
(© Chrysler Corp.)

21. Inspect pushrods for wear or bending and install in original positions. Use an aligning rod.
22. Install rocker shaft assembly, making sure long stamped steel retainers are in the No. 2 and No. 4 positions. Tighten rocker shaft mounting bolts to 25 ft. lbs. (15 ft. lbs on 318 cu. in. engine) torque. On the 318 cu. in. engines, make sure the "NOTCH" end of the rocker assemblies are pointing toward the centerline of the engine and toward the front on the left bank and toward the rear on the right bank.
23. Install tappet chamber cover. On the 361, 413 cu. in. engines, make sure the 1/8" bleed hole at the crossover is on the right side of the engine. Tighten bolts to 7-8 ft. lbs. torque.
24. Install engine manifolds. Use new gaskets on the 318 cu. in engine, the extended shield going on the left side. On the 361, 413 cu. in engines, be sure center bolt is inserted in its original position. Tighten bolts to 30 ft. lbs. torque.
25. Set correct gap on spark plugs (see Tune-Up Specifications at the beginning of this section) and install, tightening to 30 ft. lbs. torque.
26. Install intake manifold and carburetor assembly, tightening bolts from center outward, first to 25 ft. lbs. torque, then again to correct torque (see Torque Specifications at the beginning of this section). On the 318 cu.

Installing push rods (© Chrysler Corp.)

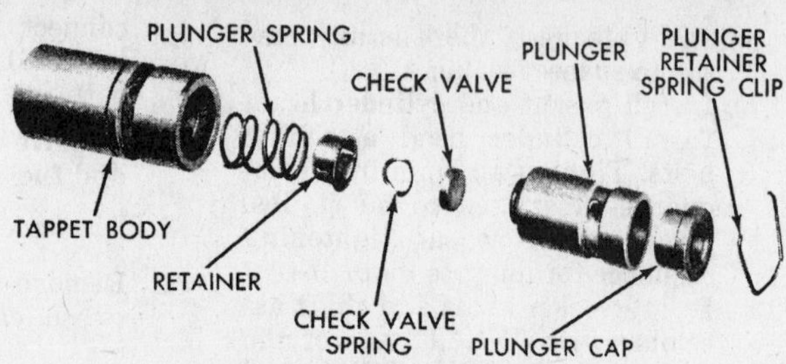

Typical hydraulic tappet (© Chrysler Corp.)

in. engine, coat the gaskets with sealant and install with bead down, locking end seals in tang of head gasket and adding a drop of sealant in the "V" notches of side seals after installation.

27. If they were removed, install distributor and governor.
28. Install distributor cap and high tension leads.
29. Connect vacuum control hose between distributor and carburetor, throttle linkage, heat indicator sending unit wire, heater and coolant hoses, fuel line and, if so equipped, manual choke cable.
30. On the 361, 413 cu. in. engines, install bolts which secure water pump housing to each cylinder head.
31. Install rocker cover, using new gasket. Tighten bolts to 3-4 ft. lbs. torque.
32. Install crankcase ventilation system and air cleaner.
33. Install alternator and drive belts. Install air compressor if so equipped.
34. Fill cooling system and install or connect battery.

Valve System

Reference

For complete instructions for servicing valves and valve train see the Engine Overhaul Section of the General Repair Section.

For valve angles, stem dimensions, clearances and spring tensions see Valve Specifications at the beginning of this section.

Mechanical Valve Tappet Adjustment

6 Cyl. and 273, 318 Cu. In. V8

All mechanical tappets are adjusted when the engine is idling at normal operating temperature. On the 251 cu. in. engine, remove the valve cover and adjust self-locking type (no lock nuts) valve tappet screws. NOTE: sodium filled exhaust valves should be set at .018" clearance and never set less than this limit.

Adjustment of valves on OHV 8 and 6 cylinder engines is made by loosening the locknut on the adjusting screw, then turning adjusting screw while feeling the clearance with a feeler gauge. Tighten locknut and recheck clearance. Valve tappet clearance should be checked and readjusted if necessary after 15-20 hours of operation.

Hydraulic Lifters

See the Engine Overhaul Section in the General Repair Section for servicing of hydraulic lifters.

Rocker Arm Assembly Removal

OHV—6 Engine

1. Remove crankcase vent valve with tube.
2. Remove cylinder head cover and gasket.
3. Remove rocker shaft bolts and retainers.
4. Remove rocker arms and shaft assembly.
5. When installing rocker shaft assembly, be sure that the flat on the end of the rocker shaft is on top and points toward front of engine.
6. Install long retainer in center position only. Install rocker shaft retainers so that they seat on rocker shaft and not on ex-

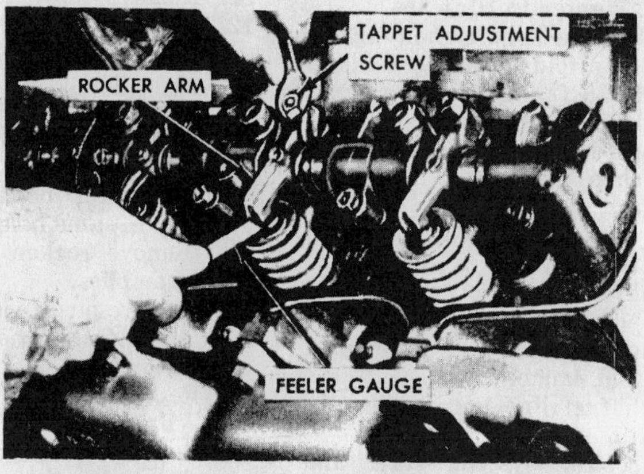

Adjusting mechanical tappets (© Chrysler Corp.)

E—EXHAUST I—INTAKE

Valve arrangefent 251 engines (© Chrysler Corp.)

tended bushing of rocker arm.

7. Install rocker shaft bolts, the long bolt at the rear of the engine. Tighten to 25 ft. lbs.
8. Adjust tappets as described above.
9. Install rocker cover, using new gasket and tightening nuts to 3-4 ft. lbs.
10. Install crankcase ventilation system.

Rocker Arm Assembly Removal

318 Cu. In. Engine

1. Disconnect spark plug wires.
2. Disconnect closed vent system from cylinder head (rocker) cover.
3. Remove cylinder head cover and gasket.
4. Remove five rocker shaft bolts and retainers.
5. Remove rocker arms and shaft assembly.
6. When installing, the "NOTCH" on end of rocker shaft points toward centerline of engine and toward the front of engine on the leftbank and toward the rear of engine on the right bank. Long stamped steel retainers belong in No. 2 and No. 4 positions. Tighten to 15 ft. lbs. torque.
7. Install cylinder head cover and tighten to 3-4 ft. lbs. torque.
8. Install closed crankcase ventilation system.

Rocker Arm Assembly Removal

361, 413 and 383 Cu. In. Engines

1. Remove cylinder head cover and gasket.
2. Remove bolts which attach rocker arm assemblies to head.
3. Remove rocker arms and shaft as an assembly.
4. If rocker assemblies are disassembled, refer to illustration for correct assembly. Note that stamped steel arms are right or left handed depending upon location of pushrod well.
5. Install rocker shaft so that the 3/16" shaft lubrication holes point downward into the rocker arm at an angle 15 degrees LOWER than centerline of shaft mounting bolts.
6. Install rocker arms and shaft assembly, making sure that the long stamped steel retainers are in the No. 2 and No. 4 positions as illustrated. Tighten bolts to 25 ft. lbs. torque.
7. Install rocker cover, using a new gasket and tightening nuts to 3-4 ft. lbs. torque.

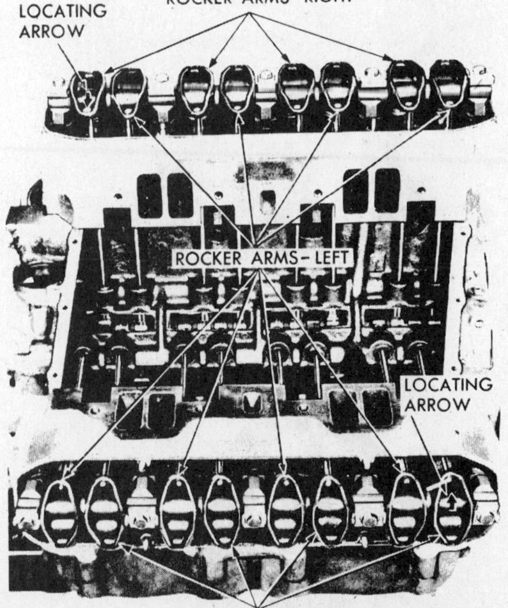

Rocker arms installed 361, 413 engines
(© Chrysler Corp.)

Timing Case

Front Cover Removal

1. Drain cooling system.
2. Remove radiator, fan and, on 318 and 383 cu. in. engine, water pump housing.
3. Remove drive belt, pulley and vibration damper attaching bolt.
4. Using a suitable puller, remove vibration damper.
5. On the 251 cu. in. engine, remove front engine mounting bracket.
6. On 361 and 413 cu. in. engines, remove front engine mount and jack up engine.
7. On 318 cu. in. engine, remove fuel lines and fuel pump.
8. On all V8 engines, loosen the oil pan bolts and remove the front two bolts.
9. Remove front cover attaching bolts, front cover and gasket.
10. Slide oil slinger off end of crankshaft.

Front Cover Installation

251 Cu. In. Engine

1. Lubricate oil seal with lubriplate.
2. Install timing cover using a new gasket, tightening bolts finger tight.
3. Install centering tool on crankshaft, tapered and against housing.

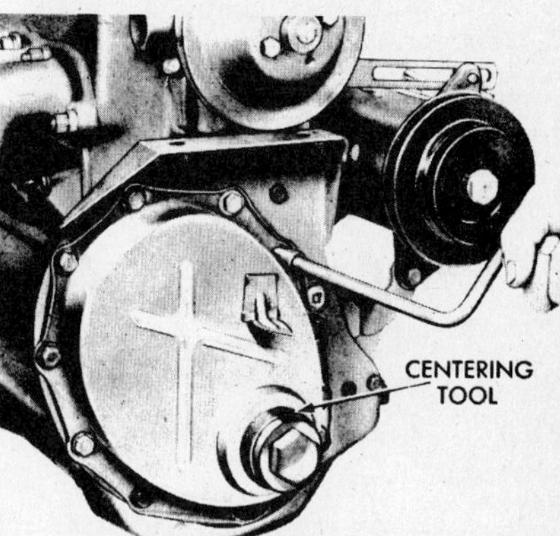

Centering chain case cover oil seal
(© Chrysler Corp.)

4. Install starting jaw nut and tighten finger tight.
5. Tighten cover bolts, frequently tightening jaw nut to maintain tension between centering tool and seal.
6. Remove jaw nut and centering tool.
7. Reinstall jaw nut and tighten to 108 ft. lbs. torque.
8. Install vibration damper, pulley,

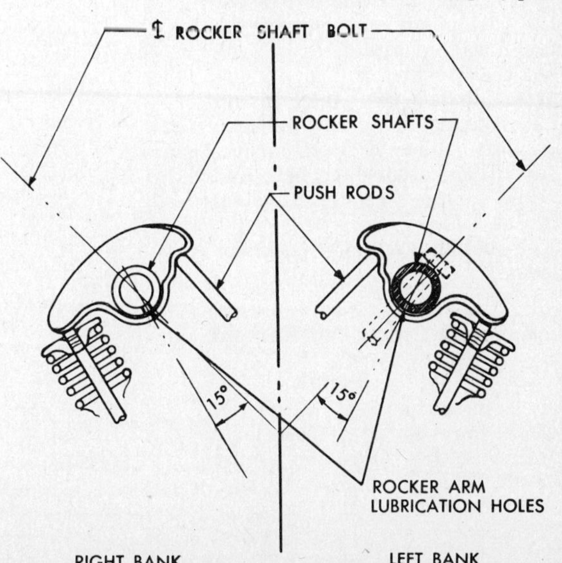

Rocker arm lubrication holes (© Chrysler Corp.)

belt, fan and radiator.
9. Fill cooling system.

Front Cover Installation

OHV—6 and V8

1. Clean and remove burrs from mating surfaces of block and cover.
2. Lubricate oil seal with lubriplate.
3. Using a new gasket, slide case cover over locating dowels and install attaching bolts. Tighten bolts to 15 ft. lbs. (30 ft. lbs. on the 318 cu. in. engine). Tighten oil pan bolts to 15 ft. lbs.
4. On the 361 cu. in. engine, install front engine-mount using lower four holes. Be sure to use special hardened bolts with Bellville washers. Tighten to 40 ft. lbs. torque.

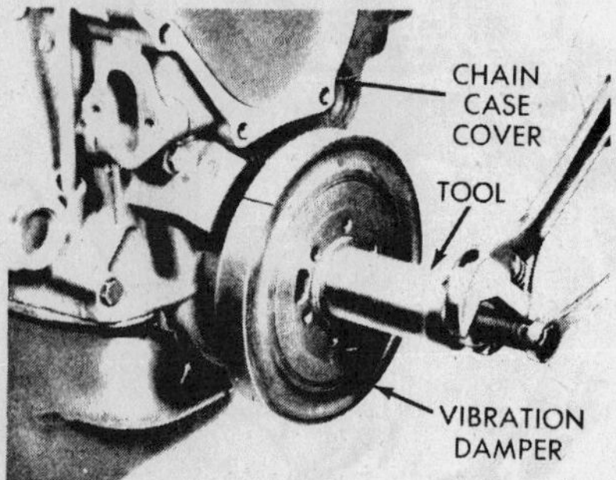

Installing vibration damper (© Chrysler Corp.)

5. Slide vibration damper hub onto crankshaft and press on using a suitable installing tool. On the OHV-6 and 318 and 383 cu. in. engines position hub slot key onto crankshaft before installing hub.
6. Install retainer washer and bolt, tightening to 135 ft. lbs. torque.
7. Install pulley on hub, tighten bolts to 15 ft. lbs. torque.
8. On the 318 cu. in. engine, install the fuel pump and connect the fuel lines to pump.
9. On the 318 and 361 cu. in. engines, install the water pump and housing, using new gaskets. Tighten bolts to 30 ft. lbs. torque.
10. Install radiator, fan, belt and hoses. Close cooling system drains.
11. Fill cooling system. Check for leaks.

Front Cover Oil Seal Replacement

251 Cu. In. Engine

The front oil seal is a spring-backed seal in a stamped steel housing and is a press fit in the timing case cover. When installing the timing case cover, care must be exercised to assure centering the seal on the crankshaft before tightening the cover. See Front Cover installation—251 Cu. In. Engine for correct centering procedure.

OHV—6 and V8 Engines

1. Remove front cover as described above.
2. Position removing screw and puller blocks of Tool C-3506 as illustrated and force the angular lip between the neoprene and flange of the seal retainer.
3. Place washer and nut on remover screw. Tighten nut forcing the blocks into the gap to a point of distorting the seal retainer lip. NOTE: Remover is only positioned at this point.
4. Place sleeve over retainer and place removing and installing plate onto sleeve.
5. Place flat washer and nut on remover screw. Hold tool center

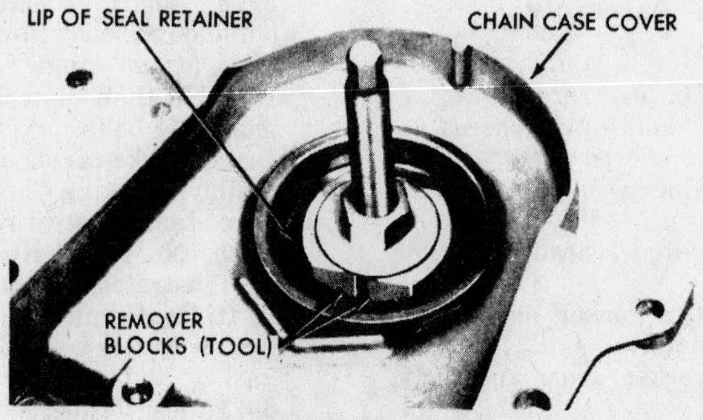

Oil seal remover tool installed (© Chrysler Corp.)

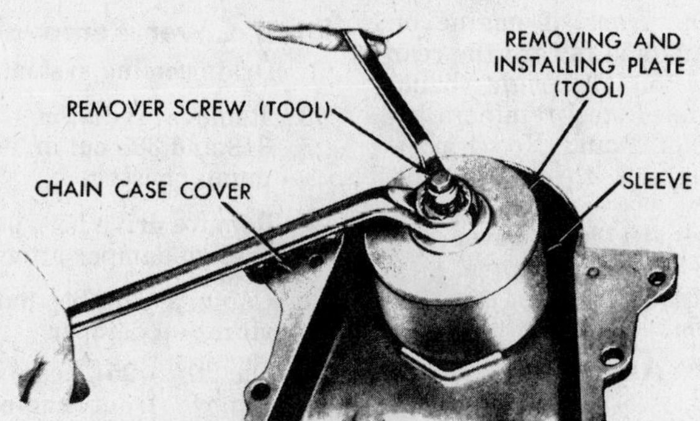

Removing cover oil seal (© Chrysler Corp.)

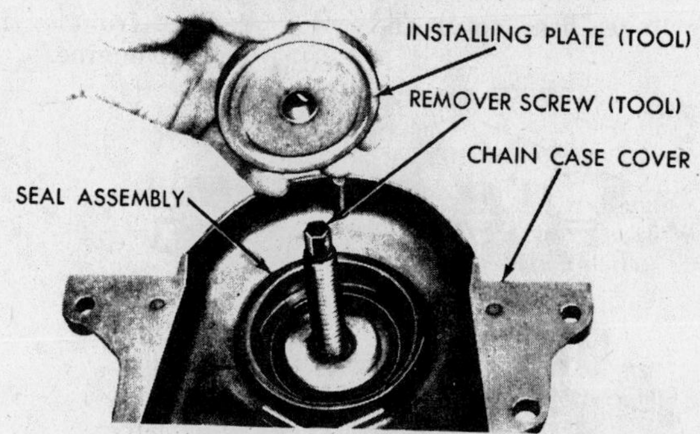

Positioning seal installer plate (© Chrysler Corp.)

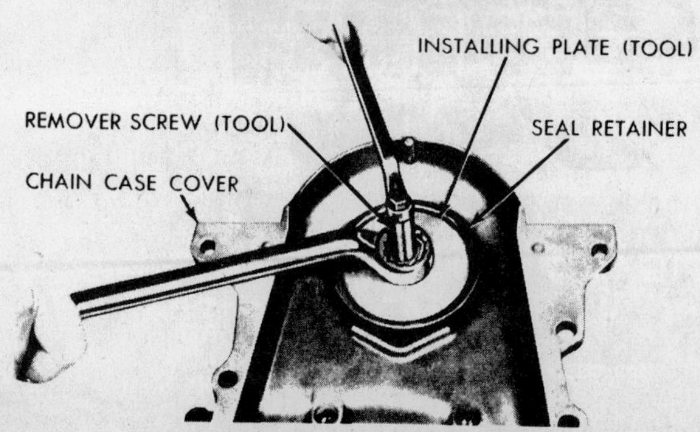

Installing oil seal (© Chrysler Corp.)

screw and tighten tool lock nut to remove seal.

6. Insert remover screw through removing and installing plate so that the thin shoulder will be facing up.
7. Insert remover screw with plate through the seal opening (inside of case cover facing up).
8. Place seal in the cover opening, with neoprene down. Place the seal installing plate into the new seal, with protective recess toward lip of seal retainer as illustrated.
9. Install flat washer and nut in remover screw, hold screw and

Inspection of oil seal for proper seating
(© Chrysler Corp.)

tighten the nut.

10. Seal is properly installed when neoprene is tight against face of cover. Try to insert a .0015" feeler gauge between neoprene and cover. If the seal is installed properly, the feeler gauge cannot be inserted.
11. Install front cover as described above.

Measuring Timing Chain Stretch

On OHV-6 and 318, 383 cu. in. V8 engines, the timing chain should be replaced if play is more than 3/16". Measure play by applying 30 (15 with head removed) ft. lbs. with a torque wrench to camshaft sprocket bolt in each direction. It may be necessary to block crankshaft to prevent rotation. Use a scale to measure play. Camshaft is replaced by removing camshaft retaining bolt and removing sprocket with a suitable puller. On V8 engines use Tool C-3509 (insert in distributor drive position) to prevent camshaft from being pushed back too far where it could knock out welch plug at rear of engine block.

Timing Gear/Chain Alignment

Timing gears or sprockets must be aligned upon reinstallation. Position marks as illustrated. Tighten camshaft gear/sprocket retaining bolt to 35-40 ft. lbs. torque. Note that timing gears and sprockets are located on shaft with either a slot key or locating pin.

Camshaft Removal

251 Cu. In. Engine

1. Drain cooling system and remove radiator.

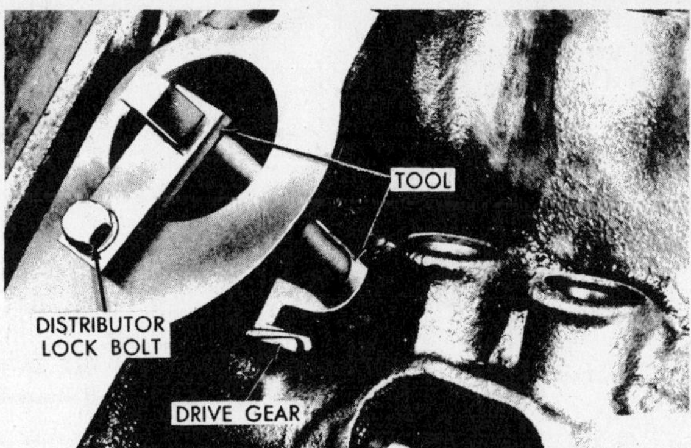

Camshaft holding tool (© Chrysler Corp.)

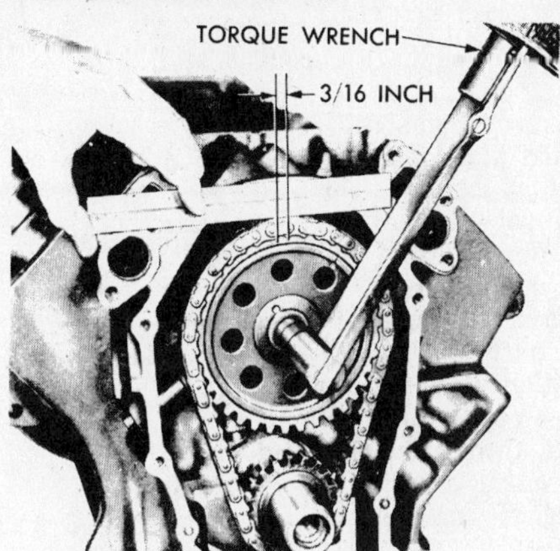

Measuring timing chain stretch
(© Chrysler Corp.)

2. Remove front cover as described above. Note that front engine mounting bracket must be removed. Disconnect and remove fuel pump.
3. Remove cylinder head (see Cylinder Head Removal—251 Cu. In. Engine).
4. Lift valves with lifting tool and place blocks of wood of the same thickness at opposite sides of the valve between valve and valve seat.
5. Lift tappets and secure in full travel position with clothes pins.

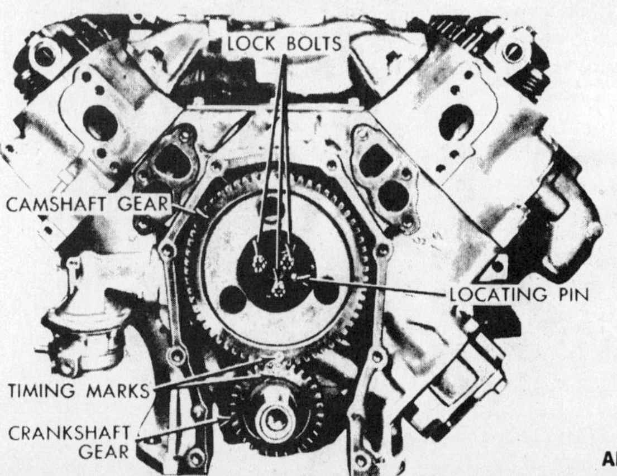

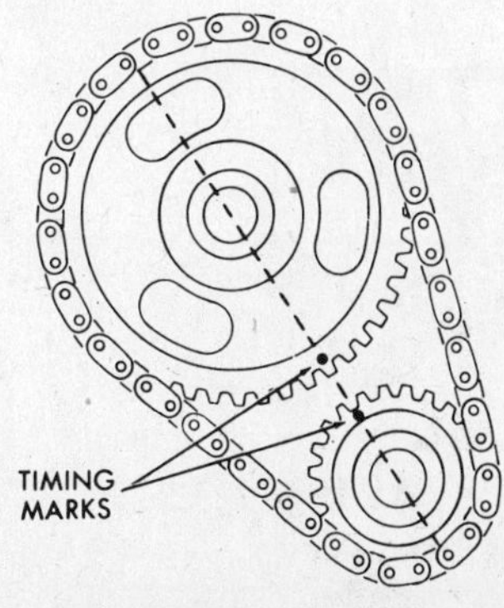

Alignment of timing gear marks 6 cyl. engines
(© Chrysler Corp.)

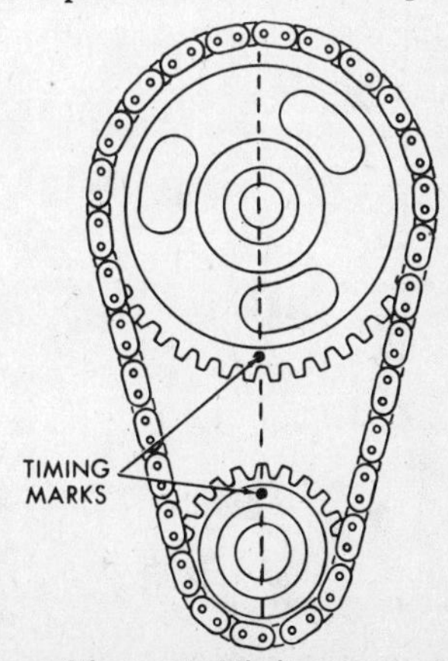

Alignment of timing gear marks
318 & 383 engines
(© Chrysler Corp.)

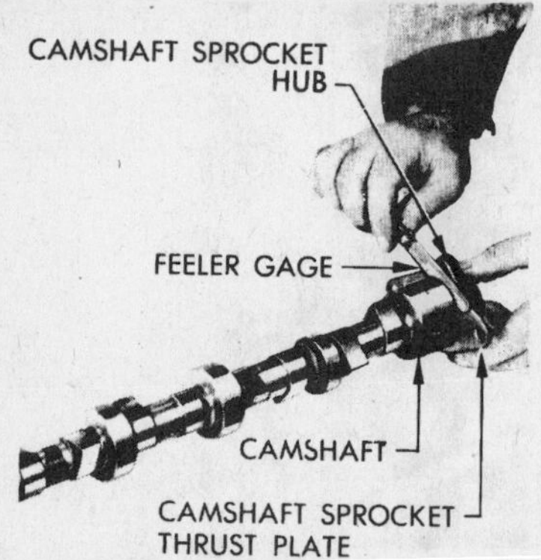

Measuring camshaft end play
(© Chrysler Corp.)

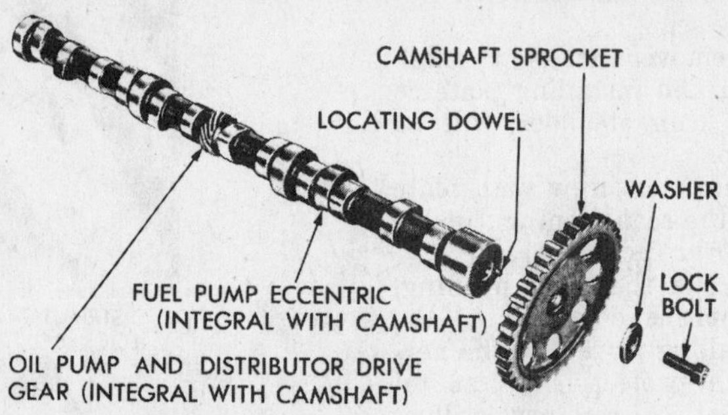

Camshaft OHV 6 cyl. engines (© Chrysler Corp.)

6. Remove camshaft sprocket and timing chain.
7. Measure camshaft end play. Thrust plate must be replaced if end play exceeds .006".
8. Remove camshaft thrust plate retaining bolts.
9. Pull out camshaft. Extreme care must be taken not to damage camshaft bearings.
10. Installation is the reverse of the above procedure. Be sure to align timing marks and check alignment after rotating crankshaft two complete turns.

Camshaft holding tool (© Chrysler Corp.)

OHV—6 Engine

1. On models where there is enough forward clearance to remove the camshaft with the engine still in the vehicle, drain cooling system and remove radiator and fan.
2. Remove cylinder head cover, timing cover and timing chain.
3. Remove rocker arm shaft assembly and pushrods, identifying pushrods so that they may be reinstalled in their original locations.
4. Remove tappets, fuel pump, distributor and oil pump.
5. When removing and installing camshaft, be careful not to damage the bearing journals with the lobes. Inspect tappets for wear, replacing any that are dished. Lubricate lobes, and use a break-in oil additive whenever any new cam components are installed.
6. Reinstall all engine components in reverse order of removal.

V8 Engines

Removal and installation of camshafts on V8 engines is essentially the same process as that described above for the OHV-6 engine. Note that on the 318 cu. in. engine, however, the fuel pump eccentric is not integral with the camshaft and is installed in front of the sprocket, and that the camshaft must be held secure (use tool C-3509) during sprocket and chain installation.

Distributor and oil pump shaft must be timed to the camshaft upon reinstallation. Rotate crankshaft until No. 1 cylinder is at top dead center of compression stroke. Timing line on vibration damper (crankshaft drive pulley) should be aligned with the "O" on the timing indicator. On the 318 cu. in. engine, install shaft so that after gear spirals into place, the slot in top of drive gear will point to the first intake manifold bolt on the left side of engine as illustrated. On the 361, 383 and 413 engines, install shaft so that after gear spirals into place, the slot in the top of the gear will be parallel to center line of crankshaft and offset to the bottom.

Distributor drive gear installation 318 engine
(© Chrysler Corp.)

Distributor drive gear installation 361, 383 & 413 engines
(© Chrysler Corp.)

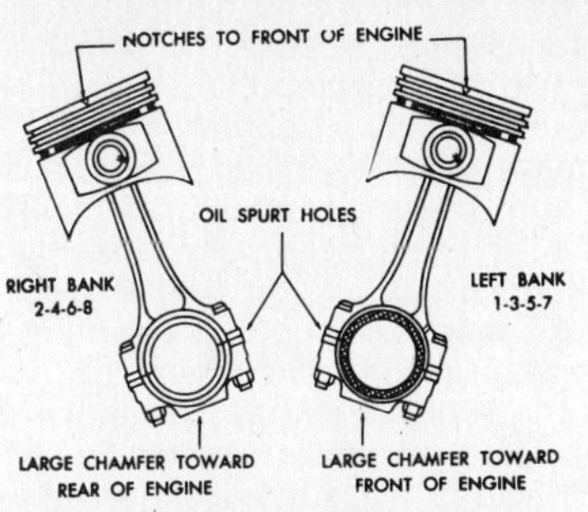

Relation of piston to rod V8 engines
(© Chrysler Corp.)

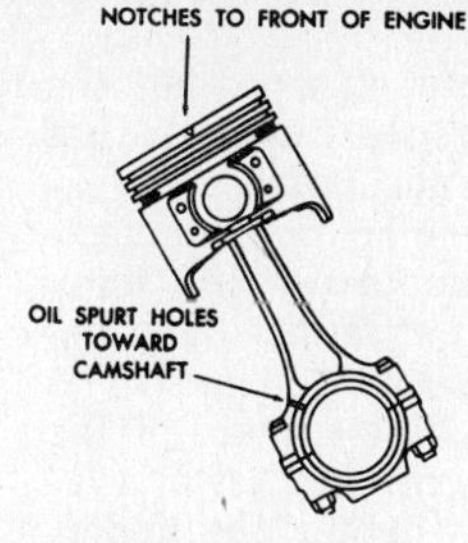

Relation of piston to rod OHV 6 engines
(© Chrysler Corp.)

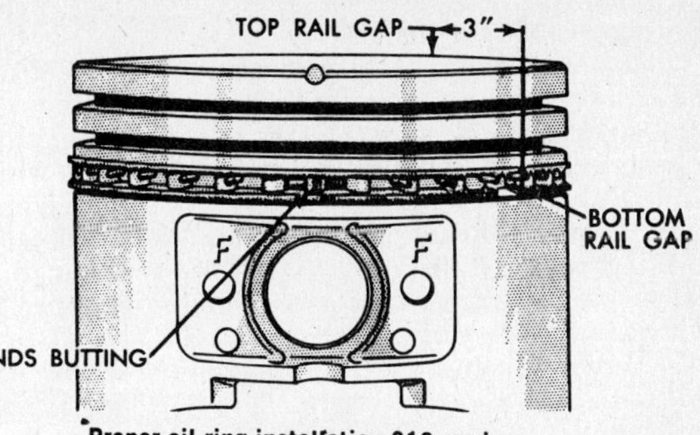

Proper oil ring installation 318 engine
(© Chrysler Corp.)

Pistons and Connecting Rods

Reference

For ring fitting, piston and rod assembly and rod bearing installation procedures see the Engine Rebuilding Section.

Piston Assembly Installation

On the 251 cu. in. engine, install piston and rod assembly so that the slot in the piston is facing away from the valve side and the oil hole in the rod is toward the valve side.

On the 170 and 225 cu. in. slant six engines, the pistons are installed with the notch on the top edge of the piston toward the front of the engine and the oil hole in the connecting rod toward the right (camshaft) side of the engine.

On the 318 cu. in. V8 engine, install pistons with the oil ring situated so that the expander ends butt and face toward the front of the engine and the oil ring rail gaps have a 3" distance between them which centers towards the inside of the engine "V." Compression ring gaps are staggered with respect to the oil ring gaps.

On the 361, 413 and 383 cu. in. V8 engines, the oil ring expander faces toward the outside of the engine "V" with the top and bottom oil ring rail gaps opposite each other above the piston pin holes. Stagger compression rings.

On all V8 engines the notch on the top edge of the piston faces the front of the engine and rods and the oil squirt hole faces the inside of the engine. Make sure the "V" groove across the parting faces of lower bearing shell is in line with the "V" groove of the bearing cap. Right and left bank connecting rods are not interchangeable. The larger chamfer of connecting rod bore must be installed toward the crank pin journal fillet.

Piston Ring Specifications

Ring End Gap (in.)

Year and Engine	*Top Compression*	*Bottom Compression*	*Oil Control*
1961-68 251	0.010-0.020	0.010-0.020	0.010-0.020
1964-65 OHV-6	0.010-0.020	0.010-0.020	0.015-0.062
1964 318	0.010-0.020	0.010-0.020	0.010-0.020
1966-71 OHV-6	0.010-0.020	0.010-0.020	0.015-0.055
1965-71 273, 318	0.010-0.020	0.010-0.020	0.015-0.055
1964-65 big V8s	0.013-0.025	0.013-0.025	0.013-0.025
1966-67 big V8s	0.013-0.025	0.013-0.025	0.015-0.055
1968-71 big V8s	0.013-0.023	0.013-0.023	0.015-0.055

Ring Side Clearance (in.)

Year and Engine	*Top Compression*	*Bottom Compression*	*Oil Control*
1961-68 251	0.0020-0.0035	0.0020-0.0035	0.0015-0.0030
1964-65 OHV-6	0.0015-0.0040	0.0015-0.0040	0.009 max.
1964-65 all V8	0.0015-0.0030	0.0015-0.0040	0.009 max.
1966-71 OHV-6, 273, 318 V8s	0.0015-0.0040	0.0015-0.0040	0.0002-0.0050
1966 361, 383, 413	0.0015-0.0040	0.0015-0.0040	0.0002-0.0050
1967-71 383, V8	0.0015-0.0040	0.0015-0.0040	0.0000-0.0050

Main Bearings

Reference

Detailed procedures for fitting main and rod bearings can be found in the Engine Rebuilding Section.

Main Bearing Replacement (Engine in Vehicle)

251 Cu. In. Engine

1. Drain engine oil.
2. Remove clutch housing pan, oil pan, oil suction pipe and screen assembly. (For removal procedures of these components see the various paragraphs under their individual headings.)
3. Check crankshaft end play. Permissible end play is between .003-007".
4. Remove bearing cams one at a time and inspect shell for scoring, chipping or etching. Check bearing clearance and replace if the clearance exceeds .002".

   NOTE: Always replace bearing inserts in pairs.
5. To remove upper bearing inserts use tool C-584 as illustrated. Use

tool C-584 to install new upper bearing insert, rotating crankshaft slowly in counterclockwise direction to be sure that the tang enters the groove in engine block.

6. Torque bearing cap retaining bolts to 85 ft. lbs.
7. Install oil pump suction pipe and screen assembly, oil pan and clutch housing pan. Add engine oil.

Installing upper bearing shell
(© Chrysler Corp.)

OHV—6 Engine

The procedure for replacement of main bearings is the same as that described for the 251 cu. in. side-valve engine above. The maximum allowable bearing clearance is.0015″. No. 1, No. 2 and No. 4 lower inserts are interchangeable. No. 2 and No. 4 upper inserts are interchangeable. No. 1 upper insert has a chamfer on the tab side for timing chain oiling and is identified by the red mark on the edge of the insert. No. 3 upper and lower inserts are flanged. Bearing caps are not interchangeable and are numbered for correct installation. Maximum end play is .007″. Replace No. 3 (thrust) bearing if end play exceeds that amount. Tighten bearing cap retaining bolts to 85 ft. lbs. torque.

V8 Engines

A Maltese Cross stamped on the engine numbering pad indicates that the engine is equipped with a crankshaft which has one or more connecting rods and/or main bearing journal finished .001″ undersize. The position of the undersize journal(s) is stamped on a machine surface of the No. 3 counterweight. The letter "R" or "M" signifies whether the undersize journal is a rod or main, and the number following the letter indicates which one it is. A Maltese Cross with an "X" indicates that the journals are .010″ undersize.

Upper and lower bearing inserts are not interchangeable on any of the V8 engines due to oil hole and V-groove in the uppers. On the 318 cu. in. engine lower bearing halves No. 1, No. 2 and No. 4 are interchangeable; No. 1, No. 2 and No. 4 upper bearing halves are interchangeable. No. 3 bearing is the thrust bearing and No. 5 is the wider rear main bearing. On 361, 383 and 413 cu. in. engines the No. 1, No. 2, No. 4 and No. 5 lower bearing halves are interchangeable; No. 2, No. 4 and No. 5 upper bearing halves are interchangeable. No. 1 upper insert has a chamfer on the tab side for timing chain oiling and is identified by the red marking on the edge. No. 3 bearing is a thrust bearing and should be replaced if end play exceeds .007″.

Remove main bearing caps one at a time and check clearance. Use tool C-3059 to remove upper inserts. Check number of cap for proper location. All main bearing cap retaining bolts are torqued to 85 ft. lbs.

On the 361, 383 and 413 cu. in. engines, the rear main bearing lower seal is held in place by a seal retainer. On the 318 cu. in. engine, the rear main bearing lower seal is held in place by the rear main bearing cap. Note that the oil pump is mounted on this cap and that there is a hollow dowel which must be in place when the cap is installed.

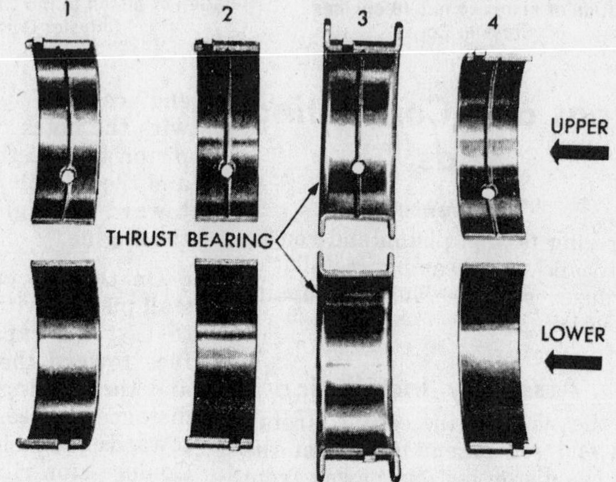

Main bearing identification OHV 6 engine
(© Chrysler Corp.)

Positioning oil pick up screen measurement —1⅛″
(© Chrysler Corp.)

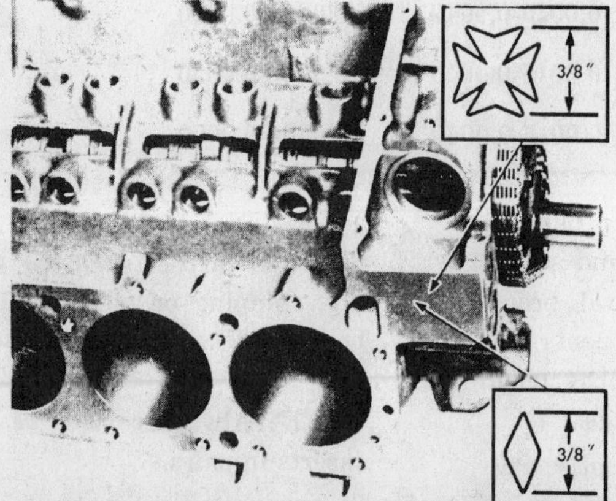

Engine numbering pad—V8 (© Chrysler Corp.)

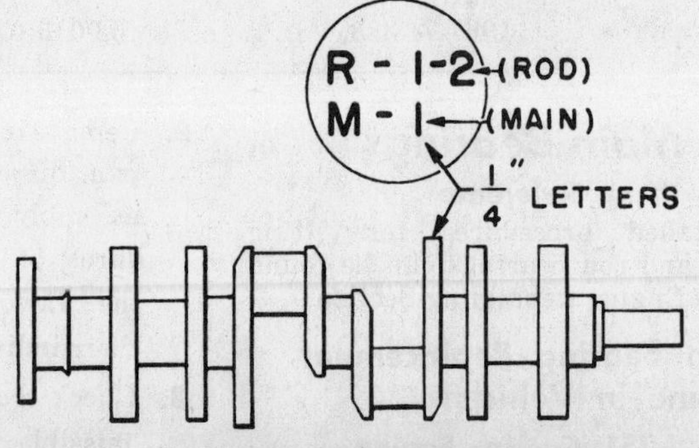

Location of markings on counterweight
(© Chrysler Corp.)

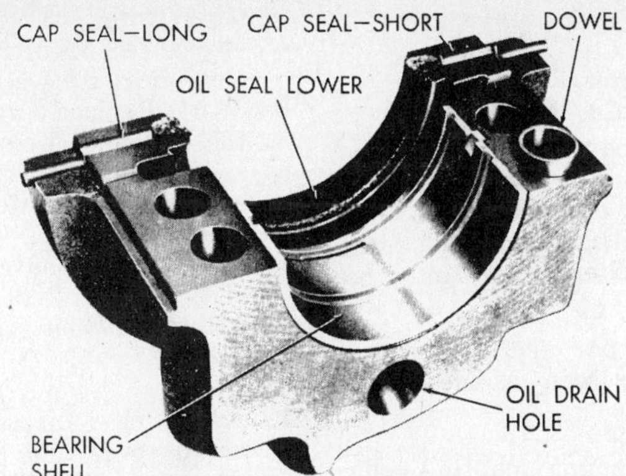

Rear main bearing cap (© Chrysler Corp.)

Rear main bearing oil seal retainer side seals are made from a material that expands quickly when oiled.

When installing, pre-oil in mineral spirits or diesel fuel and quickly insert into groove of seal retainer. Install retainer and tighten screws to 30 ft. lbs.

Engine Lubrication

Oil Pan Removal

Sportsman Van Compact-models—B-100,200,300 (Six Cylinder—198, 225 Cu. Inch)

1. Disconnect the battery and remove dipstick.
2. Remove the engine cover, air cleaner and the starter.
3. Raise the vehicle on a hoist. Drain crankcase oil.
4. Install an engine lifting fixture.
5. Disconnect the propeller shaft, transmission shift rods, and exhaust pipe from manifold and tie out of way.
6. Remove the clutch torque shaft (shifter torque shaft and oil cooler lines if so equipped)
7. Disconnect the speedometer cable and electrical connections to the transmission.
8. Remove the support bracket, inspection plate (drive plate to converter attaching screws if so equipped).
9. Remove the engine rear support crossmember and position transmission jack.
10. Remove the bolts attaching the transmission to clutch housing and remove transmission or remove bell housing bolts. Move the transmission and converter rearward off engine block dowels and disengage converter hub from end of crankshaft if so equipped.
11. Support right rear corner of cylinder block with transmission jack and remove the engine support fixture.
12. Remove the oil pan attaching bolts and lower the oil pan. Position crankshaft so that counterweight will clear the oil pan. Rotate oil pan to steering gear side to clear the oil pump pick up tube, remove the oil pan.

Installation

Reverse the removal procedure. Check the position of the oil pick up tube and screen. Hold a rule against the flat surface inside the block and measure from the edge of the rule to edge of oil screen. Use new gaskets and seals, tighten oil pan attaching screws to 200 inch pounds.

Oil Pan Removal

(V8—318 Cu. Inch)

1. Drain the cooling system and disconnect the battery.
2. Disconnect the shroud and position back on engine.
3. Disconnect the radiator hoses.
4. Disconnect the exhaust pipes. Remove the left exhaust manifold, oil dip stick and tube.
5. Raise vehicle on hoist. Drain the crankcase.
6. Remove the clutch dust pan, inspection plate and engine to torque converter left housing strut.
7. Remove the starter assembly and clutch torque shaft or shifter torque shaft.
8. Disconnect the fuel supply line from fuel pump and cap.
9. Remove the front engine mount insulated top nut and washer.
10. Loosen the transmission mount through bolt, jack up the engine and install wooden blocks between the insulator and motor brackets.
11. Remove the engine lifting fixture.
12. Remove the oil pan attaching screws.
13. Position crankshaft so that counter-weight will clear the oil pan.
14. Remove the oil pan.

Installation

Reverse the removal procedure.

Oil Pan Removal

Van and Pickup Compact-models—A-100 (Six Cylinder—170, 225 Cu. Inch) (V8—273, 318 Cu. Inch)

1. Disconnect the battery cable and remove dipstick.
2. Raise the vehicle on a hoist.
3. Drain crankcase oil. (Remove torque converter or clutch housing brace, exhaust pipes if so equipped)
4. Remove the oil pan bolts, remove oil pan.

Installation

Reverse the removal procedure.

Oil Pan Removal

"S" Series Conventional, Forward Control 4x4, Low Cab Forward Models—100-600 (Except Compact Van and Pick Up)

1. Raise vehicle on a hoist.
2. Remove the two front engine mounting bolts.
3. Remove the left side support, connecting the converter hous-

Installing wood blocks 318 engine (© Chrysler Corp.)

ing and cylinder block.

4. Raise the engine approximately two inches.
5. Drain oil.
6. Remove the oil pan bolts, lower pan down and to the rear. (Do not turn oil pickup out of position)

Installation

Reverse the removal procedure.

Oil Pan Removal

Except "S" Series and Compact Van and Pickup

Conventional Cab
Low Cab Forward
Tilt Cab
Models 100-700

1. Raise the vehicle on a hoist. Jack vehicle at the frame to drop the front axle.
2. Drain the oil pan.
3. Remove the frame reinforcement if so equipped and the left bellhousing brace.
4. Remove the oil pan attaching bolts, lower pan down and toward the front.
5. Remove the oil pick-up tube and screen.

Installation

Reverse the removal procedure. Check the position of the oil pickup tube and screen. Hold a rule against the flat surface inside the block and measure from the edge of the rule to edge of oil screen. Use new gaskets and seals. Tighten oil pan attaching screws to 200 in. lbs.

Oil Pump

Oil Pump Removal 170, 225 Cu. In. Engines

The rotor type oil pump is externally mounted on the rear right-hand (camshaft) side of the engine and is gear driven (helical) from the camshaft. The oil filter screws into the pump body.

1. Remove oil pan and oil pick up tube and screen as described above.
2. Remove oil pump mounting bolts and remove pump and filter assembly from engine.
3. Disassemble oil pump (drive gear must be pressed off) and inspect the following clearances: maximum cover wear is .0015"; outer rotor to body maximum clearance is .012"; maximum clearance between rotors is .010". Replace any parts where the clearance exceeds the above specifications. Inspect the pressure relief valve for scoring and free operation. Relief valve spring should have a free length of 2-9/32" to 2-19/64" and a 15 lb. test when compressed to 1-19/32".
4. Install new oil seal rings between cover and body, tightening cover attaching bolts to 11 ft. lbs.
5. Install oil pump to engine block using a new gasket and tightening mounting bolts to 16-17 ft. lbs.

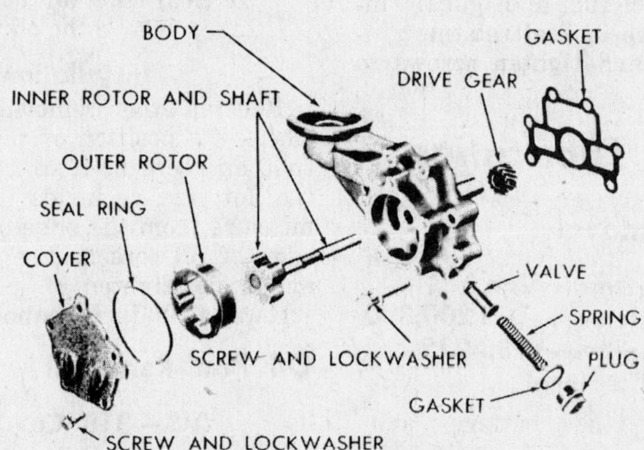

Oil pump 170, 225 engines (© Chrysler Corp.)

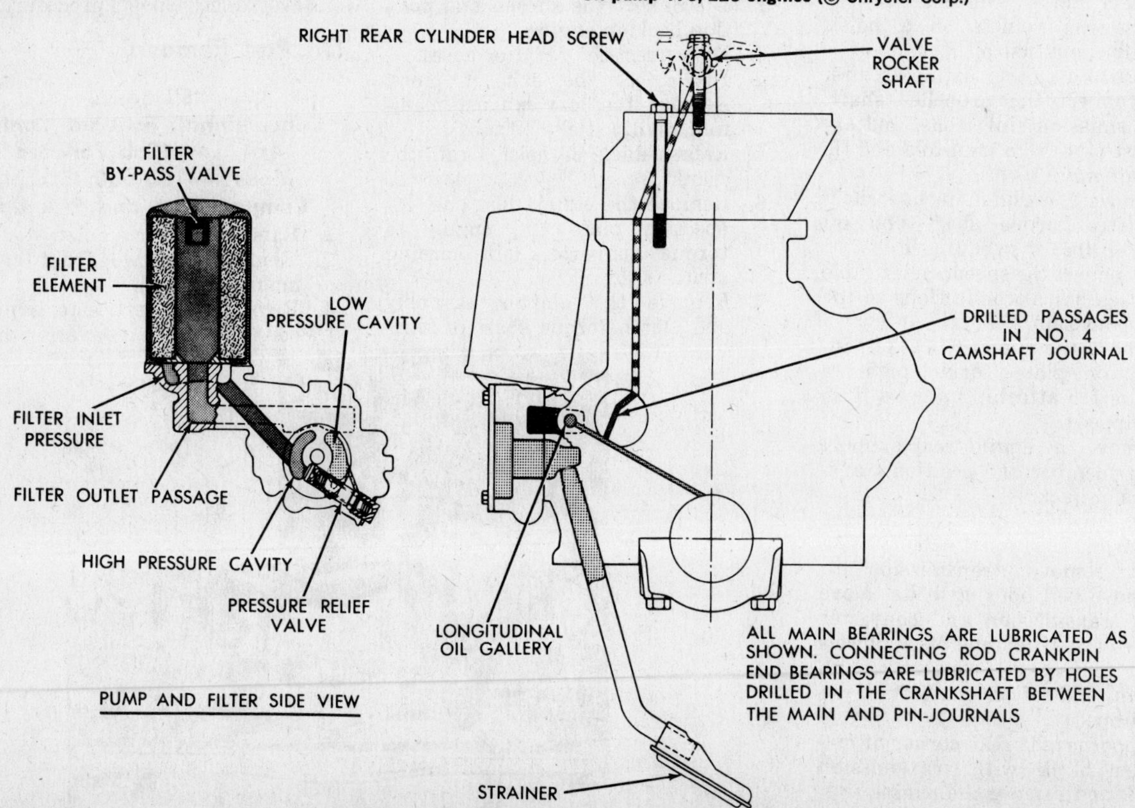

Engine oiling system 170, 225 engines (© Chrysler Corp.)

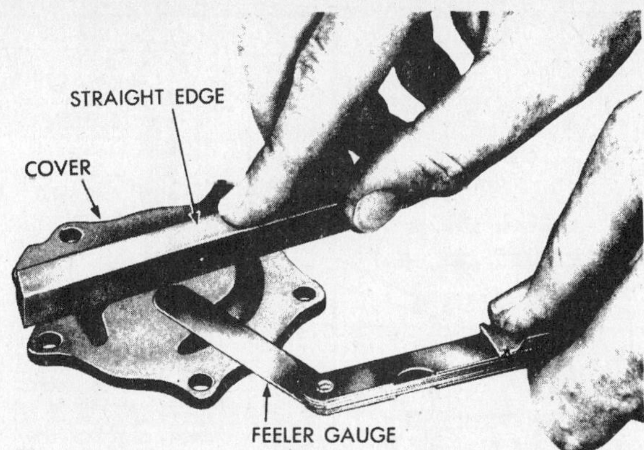

Measuring oil pump cover wear (© Chrysler Corp.)

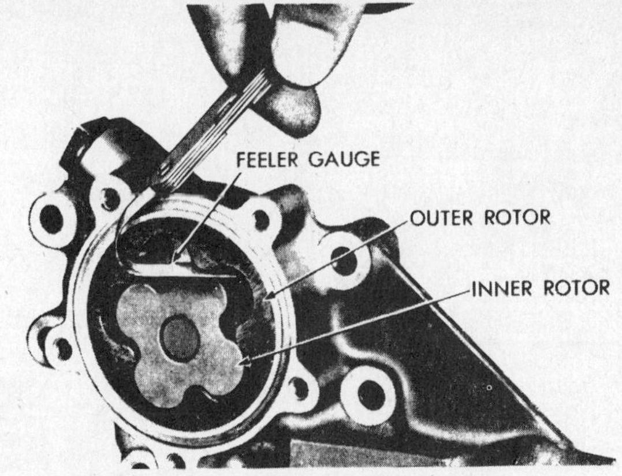

Measuring clearance between rotors (© Chrysler Corp.)

Oil Pump Removal
251 Cu. In. Side-Valve Engine

1. Lift off distributor cap and rotate the crankshaft until the distributor rotor is in firing position for the No. 1 cylinder. NOTE: Keep engine in this position while the pump is removed.
2. Drain engine oil and remove oil pan as described above.
3. Remove the mounting bolts from pump body and remove pump from engine.
4. Oil pump is disassembled by removing the cover and driving out the pin which holds the drive gear to the shaft. Rotor to rotor clearance should be less than .010/. Clearance between straightedge placed over end of pump body should be less than .004″. Outer rotor to body clearance should not exceed .012″. Cover should be smooth; replace if scored or grooved. Replace pump components which are worn beyond these limits.
5. When assembling pump, drive gear is pressed on until end play of shaft is .003-.005″. Use a new cover seal ring.
6. Use a new seal ring when installing the pump. If the engine was moved during the time when the pump was off, rotate the engine until No. 1 cylinder is in firing position.
7. Set the distributor rotor in the No. 1 cylinder firing position and install the oil pump.
8. Install the oil pan and check ignition timing, refering to the Tune-Up Specifications at the beginning of this section.
9. Test drive truck. Normal oil pressure is 30-45 psi at speeds above 30 mph. Low or high oil pressure may be the result of a weak or strong oil pressure relief valve spring. Lighter tension springs are painted red and heavier tension springs are painted green.

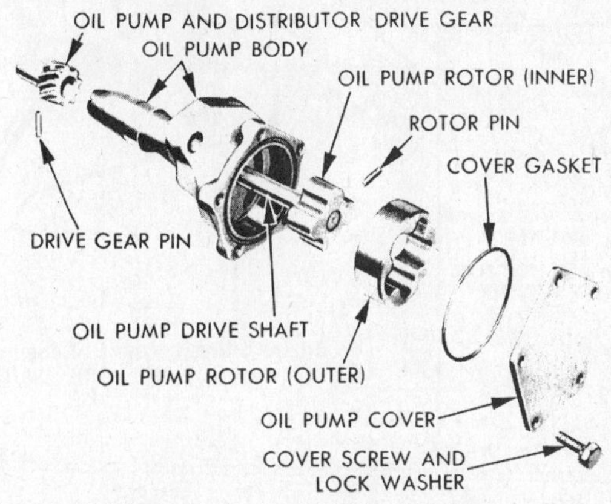

Oil pump 251 engine (© Chrysler Corp.)

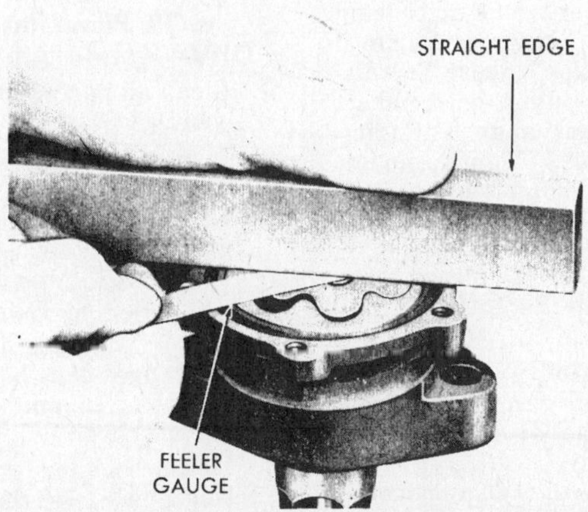

Measuring clearance over rotors (© Chrysler Corp.)

Oil Pump Removal
318 Cu. In. V8 Engine

The rotor type oil pump is gear (helical) driven from the camshaft and is mounted on the rear main bearing CAP.

1. Drain engine oil and remove oil pan as described above.
2. Remove oil pump mounting bolts and remove pump from rear main bearing cap.
3. Dissasemble pump. Drive gear is pressed on. Measure clearances as described below and replace any components which exceed specified tolerances. Be sure to use new oil seal ring between cover and body. Tighten cover bolts to 10 ft. lbs. torque.
4. The pressure relief valve cap is pressed in and is destroyed when removed. Remove cotter pin first, then drill cap and use a self-tapping sheet metal screw to get a grip on the cap. Free length of spring is 2-1/32″ to 2-3/64″. Spring should test to 17 lbs. when compressed to 1-11/32″.

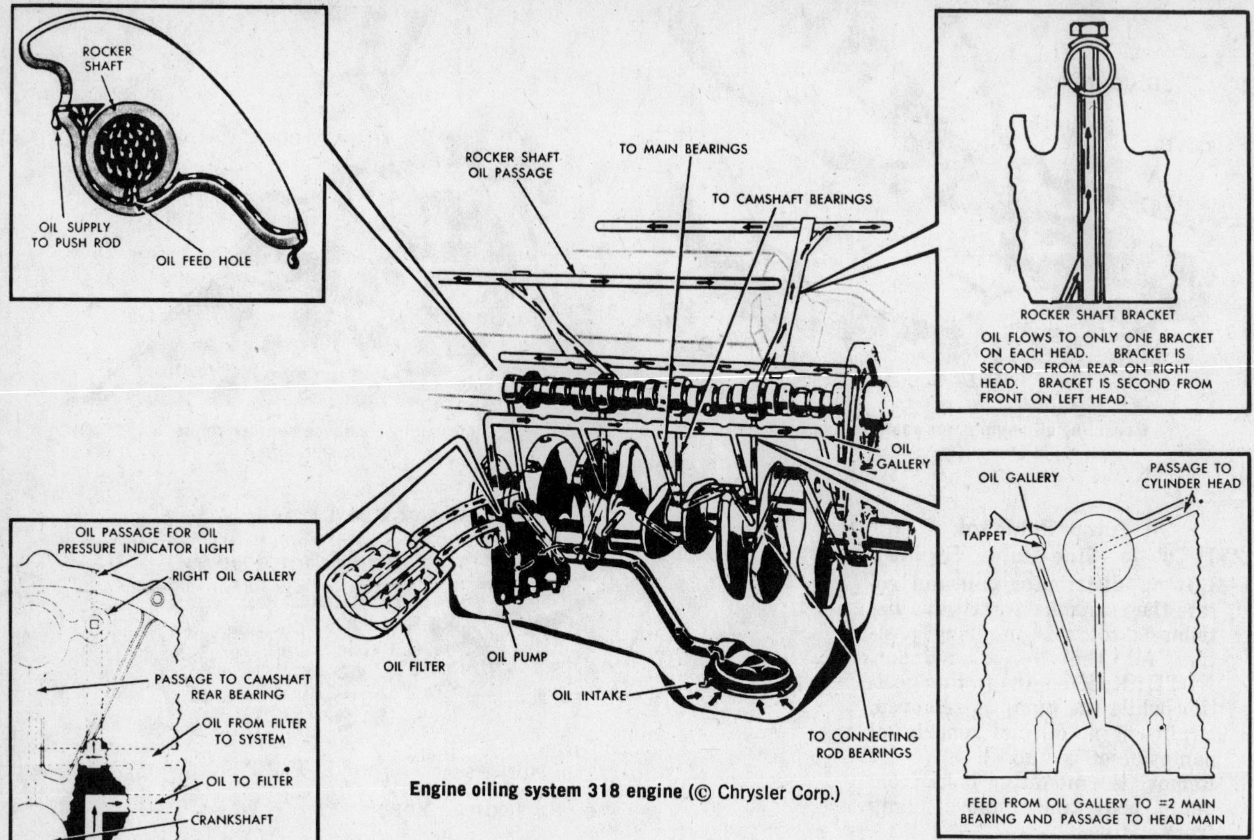

Engine oiling system 318 engine (© Chrysler Corp.)

5. When assembling pump, use a new oil seal ring between cover and body. Prime pump before installing onto rear main bearing cap. See "Camshaft Removal and Installation" above for distributor/oil pump drive shaft installation and alignment (timing) procedures. Tighten mounting bolts to 35 ft. lbs. torque. Use new gaskets when installing oil pan.

Oil Pump Removal
361, 383, 413 Cu. In. V8 Engines

The rotor type oil pump is externally mounted and gear driven from the camshaft. The oil filter screws into the pump body.

1. Drain engine oil and remove oil pan as described above.
2. Remove oil pick up tube and screen.
3. Remove oil pump and filter assembly.
4. Disassemble and inspect pump components for wear as described below. Replace appropriate parts if specified clearances are exceeded. Use new oil seal rings between filter base and body. Tighten bolts to 10 ft. lbs. Use a new "O" ring seal on pilot of oil pump before attaching pump to engine block.
5. Install oil pump on engine using new gasket and tightening bolts to 30 ft. lbs.
6. Install oil pan and fill crankcase with oil.

Oil Pump Inspection
OHV—6 and All V8 Engines

1. Clean all parts thoroughly in solvent.
2. Inspect mating surface of oil pump cover. Mating face should be smooth with no scratches or grooving. Replace if scratched or grooved.
3. Lay straight edge across oil pump cover face. If 0.0015" feeler gauge can be inserted between cover and straight edge, replace cover.
4. Measure outer rotor. If rotor length is less than 0.649" for OHV-6, 0.825" for 273,318 cu. in. V8 or 0.943" for 361,383,413 cu. in. V8 engines, replace rotor. If rotor diameter is less than 2.469" for any engine, replace rotor.

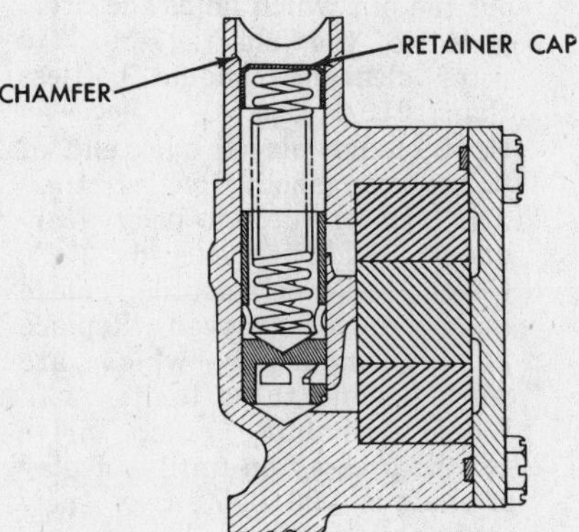

Pump relief valve (© Chrysler Corp.)

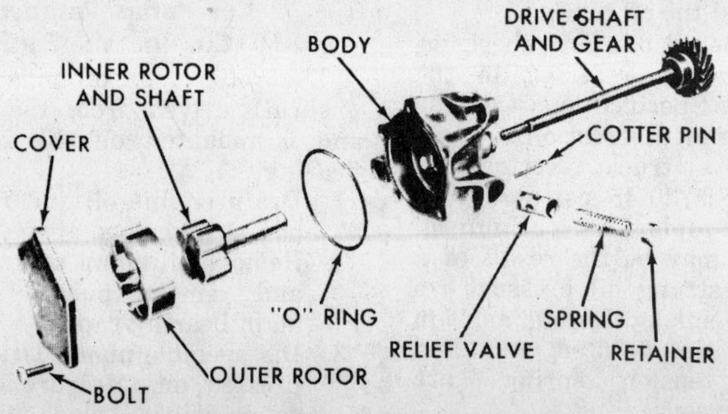

Oil pump 318 engine (© Chrysler Corp.)

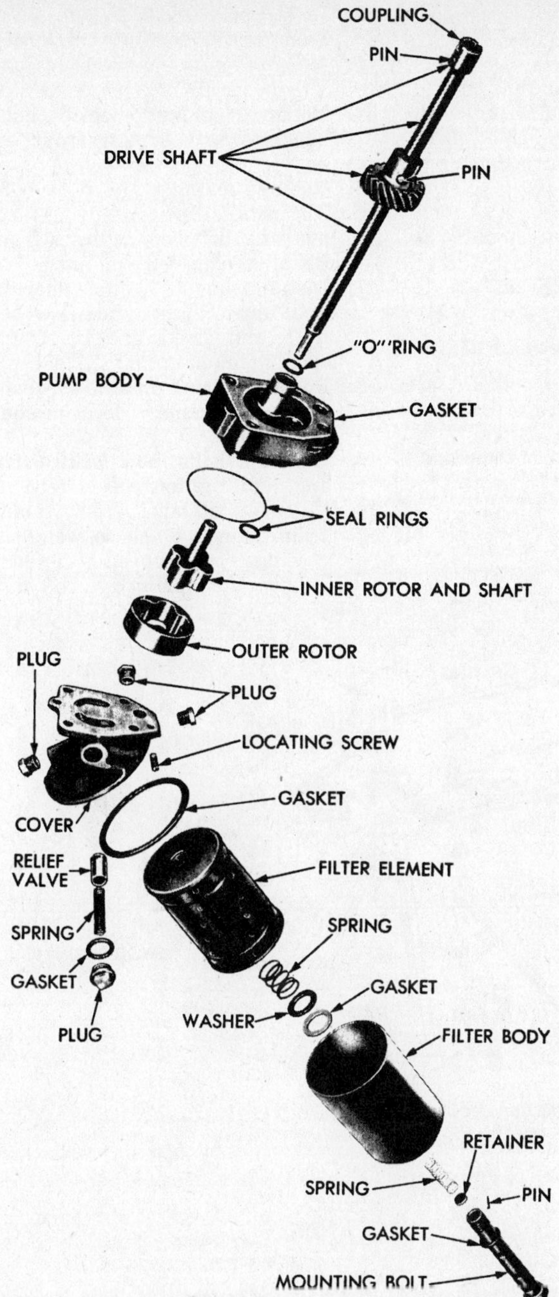

Oil pump & filter assy. 361, 383 & 413 engines
(Chrysler Corp.)

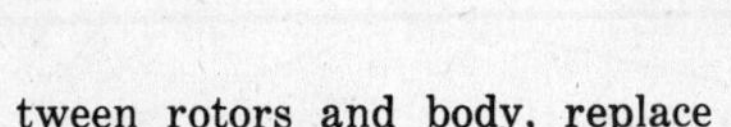

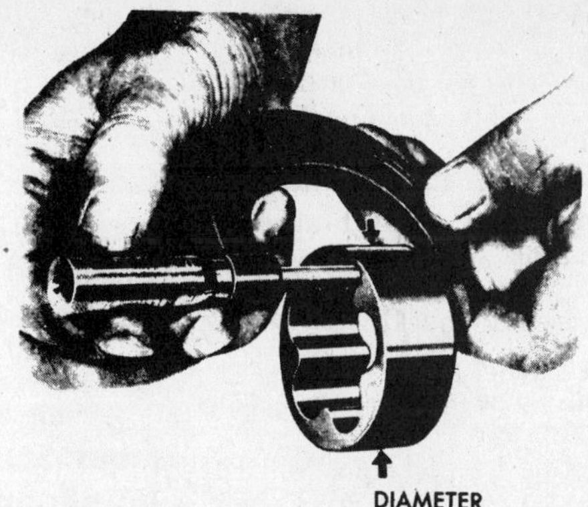

Measuring outer rotor clearance
(© Chrysler Corp.)

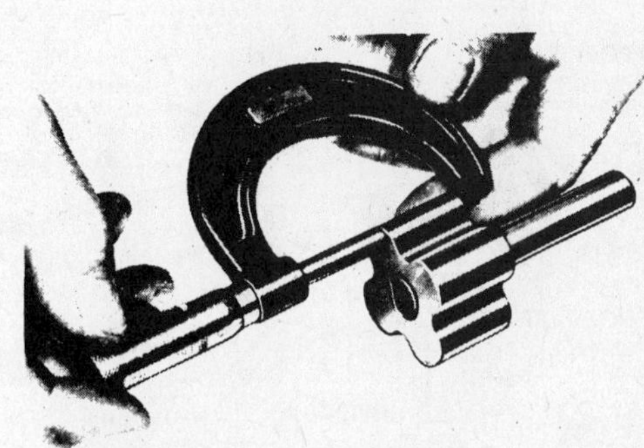

Measuring inner rotor clearance
(© Chrysler Corp.)

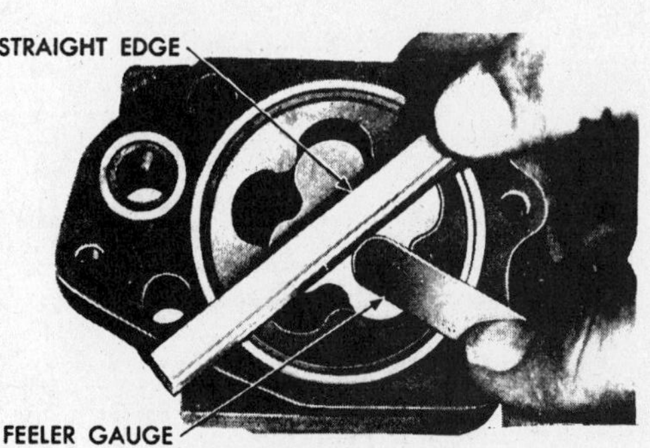

Measuring clearance over rotors
(© Chrysler Corp.)

5. Measure inner rotor. If rotor length is less than 0.649 for OHV-6, 0.825″ for 273,318 cu. in. V8, or 0.942″ for 361, 383, 413 cu. in. V8 engines, replace inner rotor.
6. Install outer rotor in pump body and holding against one side of body measure clearance between rotor and body. If clearance is greater than 0.014″, replace oil pump body.
7. Install inner rotor into pump body and place straight edge across pump body between bolt holes. If feeler gauge greater than 0.004″ can be inserted between rotors and body, replace oil pump body.
8. Measure clearance between tips of inner and outer rotor where they are opposed. If clearance exceeds 0.010″, replace inner and outer rotors.

Oil Filter

Oil Filter Replacement

The oil filter is located at the left side of the engine and is the throw-away-type. It is only necessary to unscrew the filter from the base by hand and discard.

Screw on the new filter until the gasket contacts the base, then tighten at least ½ more turn. Run the engine and check for leaks.

Front Suspension

Solid Front Axle

King Pin and Bushing Removal and Installation

1. Block brake pedal to prevent its being depressed and forcing out brake wheel cylinder cups and fluid necessitating bleeding of brakes.
2. Remove brake support attaching bolts or screws.

3. Lift complete brake shoe and support assembly from steering knuckle (brake hose attached) and wire to frame (don't let it dangle by hose). Check hose for deterioration. Replace hose if necessary and bleed brakes if hose is replaced.
4. Remove steering knuckle arm from steering knuckle.
5. Remove pivot pin locking screw or pin. Some models have two locking screws.
6. Remove upper pivot pin oil seal plug (steel disc) and drive pivot pin down forcing the lower seal plug (steel disc) from assembly.
7. Remove pivot thrust bearing.
8. To remove king pin bushings, use tool C-328A.
9. To install bushings, use tool C-328A. Make sure that grease holes in bushings line up with the grease fitting hole. Line ream bushings. Pack bushings with grease.
10. Install king pin.
11. Expansion plugs should be staked as illustrated.
12. Reverse Steps 1 through 5 to complete assembly.

Front Spring Removal and Installation

1. Hoist from toe eyes or at frame attachment, raising truck until weight is removed from springs.
2. Install stands under side frame members as a safety precaution.
3. Remove nuts, lockwashers and U-bolts securing spring to axle.
4. Remove spring shackle bolts, shackles and spring front eye bolt.
5. Remove spring.
6. To install, line up spring fixed eye with bolt hole in bracket and install spring bolt and nut.
7. Install shackle bolts, shackles and nuts. Tighten shackle bolt nuts and fixed eye bolt until slack is taken up.
8. Position spring on axle so spring center bolt enters locating hole in axle pad.
9. Install U-bolts, new lockwashers and nuts, tightening securely.
10. Remove stands from under frame, lower truck so weight is resting on wheels. Tighten U-bolt nuts, spring eye bolt nuts

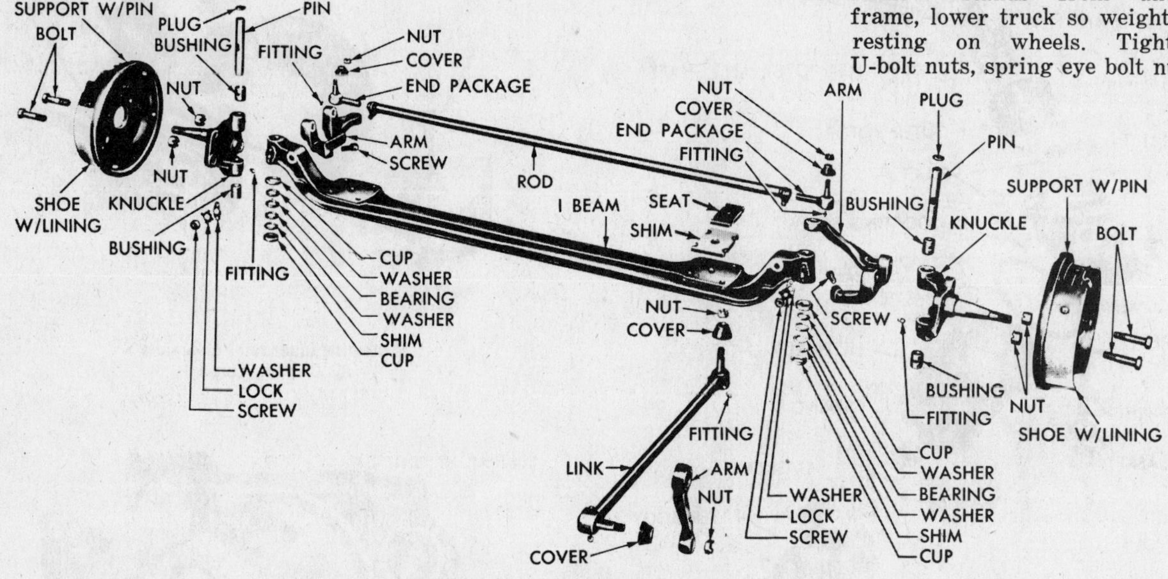

Front axle A-100 series (© Chrysler Corp.)

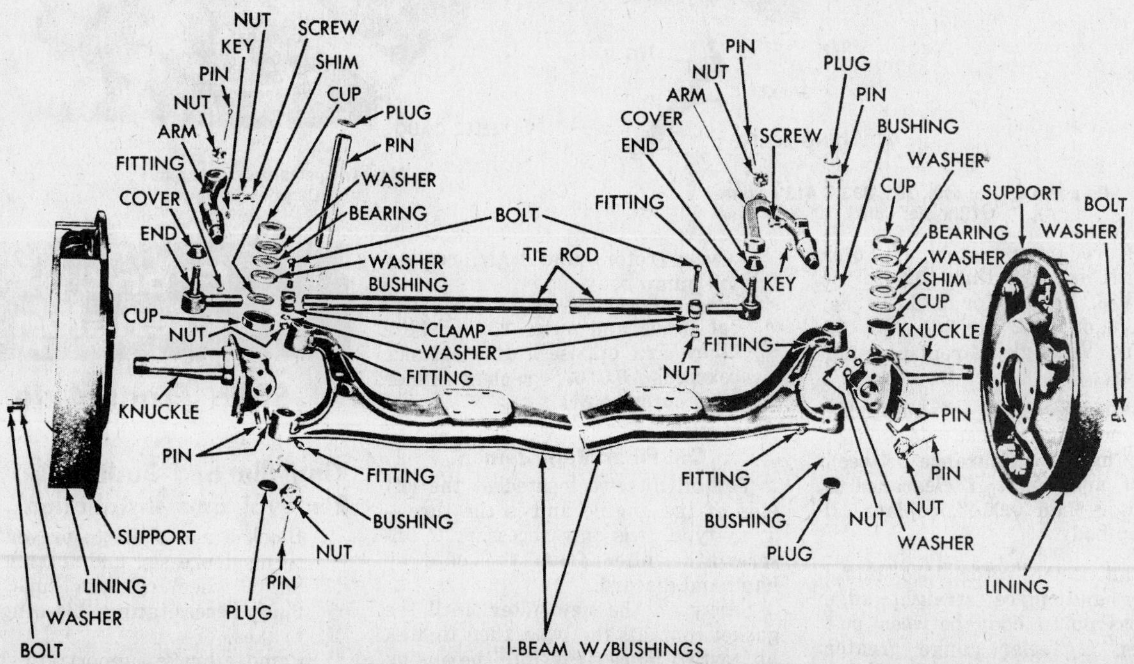

Front axle 4000 lb. Elliott type (© Chrysler Corp.)

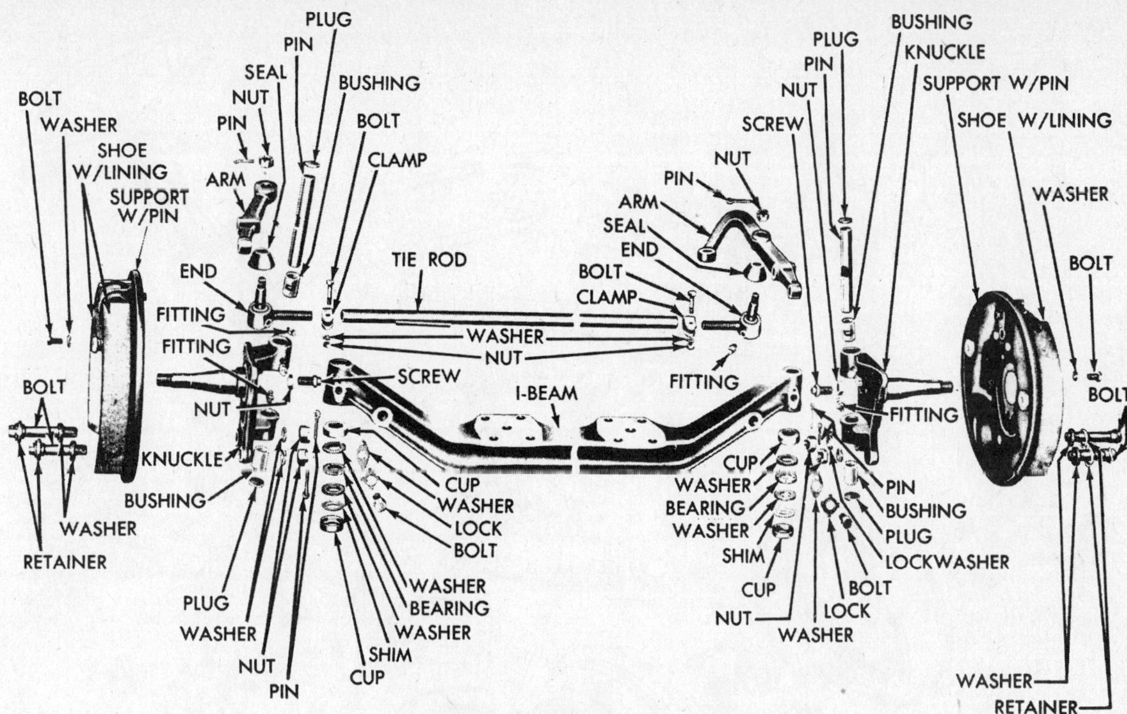

Front axle 2800 lb. Reverse Elliott type (© Chrysler Corp.)

and shackle bolt nuts to specifications given below.

11. Lubricate spring bolts and shackle bolts with chassis lubricant if equipped with pressure fittings. *Do not lubricate rubber bushings.*

Tightening Specifications—Springs

	Thread Size	*Torque (ft. lbs.)*
Spring U-bolt nuts	1/2-20	62-70
	9/16-18	120-130
	5/8-18	175-200
	3/4-16	350-400
Spring shackle bolt nuts	13/32-20	35-40
	7/16-20	45-50
Spring bolt	5/8-18	150-175
Spring center bolt	5/16	15
	3/8	30
	7/16	50
	1/2	75

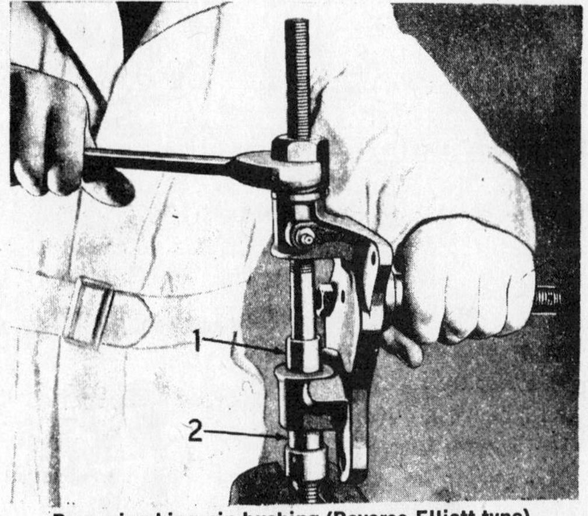

Removing king pin bushing (Reverse Elliott type) (© Chrysler Corp.)

Front Drive Axle

Reference

For front differential overhaul procedures, see General Section.

Description

The drive pinion and differential case with drive gear are mounted directly in the carrier section of assembly. Shims are used to adjust differential bearings. The front axle drive shaft outer end connects through a splined slip joint flange to the wheel hub. The inner and outer axle shafts are connected through universal joints, which revolve in the steering knuckle. Some service part replacements can be made without complete removal of the axle assembly. However it is generally desirable to remove assembly for complete disassembly and inspection in connection with any major assembly repairs. Caster and camber is built into the axle and cannot be changed.

Axle Assembly Removal

W100, W200, W300, WM300 (Power Wagon)

1. Raise front end of vehicle until wheels clear ground and block up frame at rear of front springs.
2. Disconnect front driveshaft at drive pinion yoke.
3. Disconnect steering linkage at drag link. On WM300, remove steering arm from left flange assembly.
4. Disconnect front shock absorbers and brake line at frame. On WM300, disconnect brake line from the "T" on top of the axle housing.
5. Remove nuts from the spring hold down bolts and remove axle assembly from under vehicle.
6. To install, place axle assembly under vehicle and line up spring center bolts with locating hole in axle housing pad.
7. Install spring clips or spring U-bolts, new lock washer and nuts. Tighten to torque specified in "Tightening Specifications—Springs" above.
8. Connect shock absorbers.
9. Connect brake line at frame. On WM300, connect brake line to "T". Bleed hydraulic brake system.

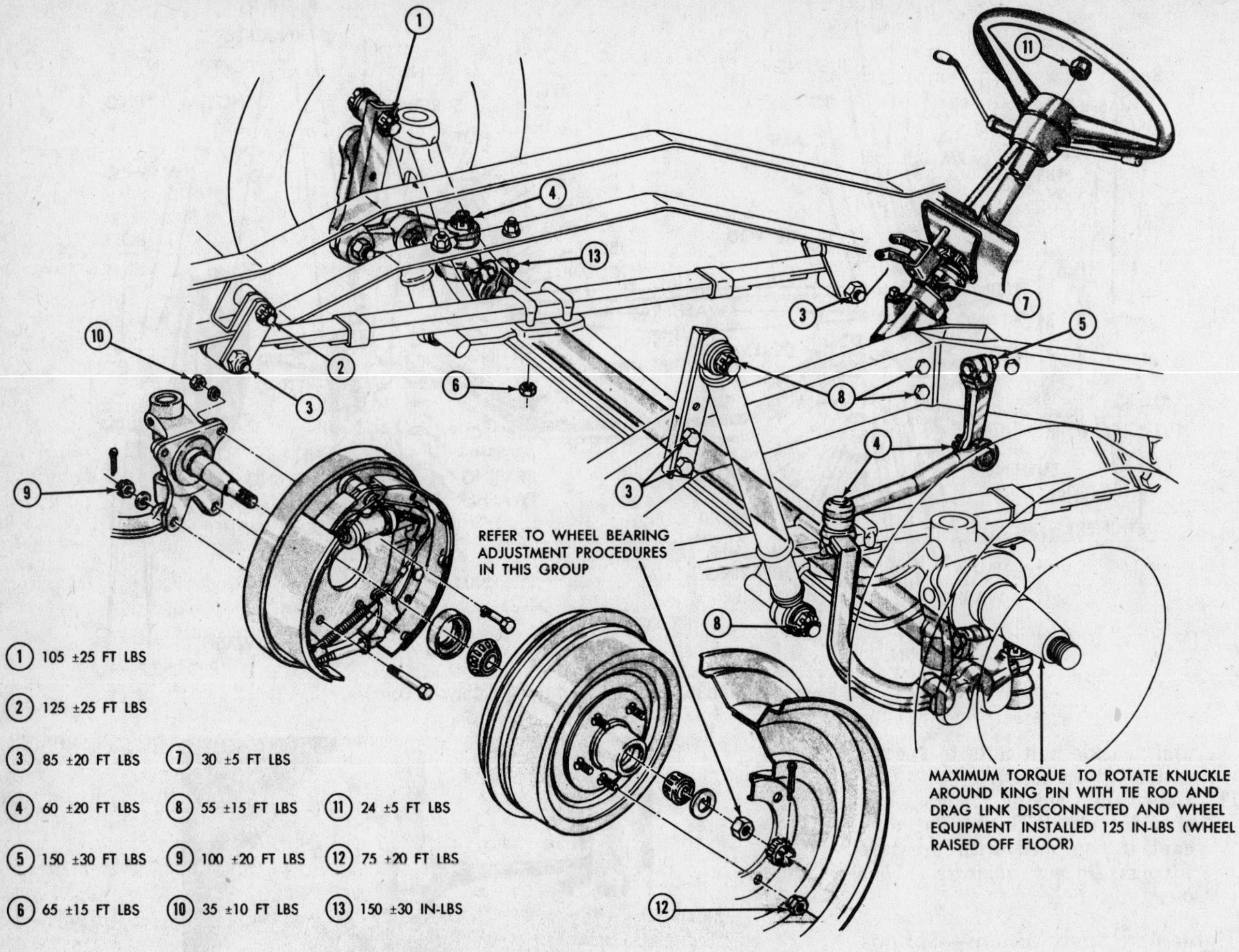

REFER TO WHEEL BEARING ADJUSTMENT PROCEDURES IN THIS GROUP

MAXIMUM TORQUE TO ROTATE KNUCKLE AROUND KING PIN WITH TIE ROD AND DRAG LINK DISCONNECTED AND WHEEL EQUIPMENT INSTALLED 125 IN-LBS (WHEEL RAISED OFF FLOOR)

(1) 105 ±25 FT LBS
(2) 125 ±25 FT LBS
(3) 85 ±20 FT LBS
(4) 60 ±20 FT LBS
(5) 150 ±30 FT LBS
(6) 65 ±15 FT LBS
(7) 30 ±5 FT LBS
(8) 55 ±15 FT LBS
(9) 100 +20 FT LBS
(10) 35 ±10 FT LBS
(11) 24 ±5 FT LBS
(12) 75 +20 FT LBS
(13) 150 ±30 IN-LBS

Steering and front end torque data (© Chrysler Corp.)

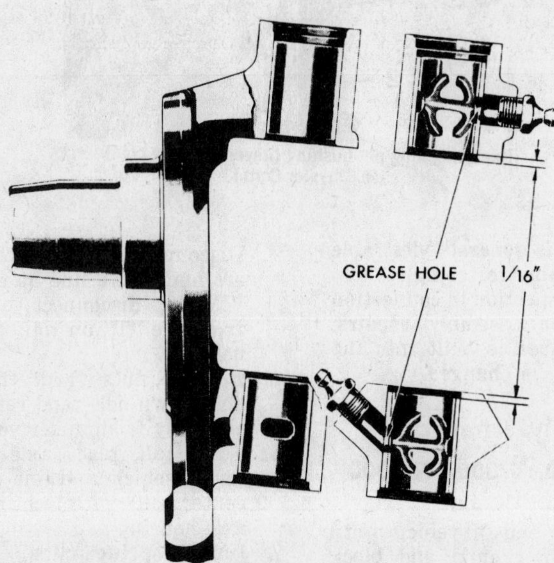

King pin bushing installed (Reverse Elliott type) (© Chrysler Corp.)

10. Connect steering linkage to drag link. On WM300, connect steering linkage to steering arm on left flange assembly.
11. Connect driveshaft to drive pinion yoke.
12. Lubricate all necessary points on the axle.
13. Lower vehicle and check front wheel alignment.

Axle Assembly Removal—W500

1. Disconnect drag link from axle steering knuckle arm.
2. Disconnect driveshaft at differential yoke.
3. Disconnect shock absorbers, brake tube at frame and axle housing from springs.
4. Raise front end of truck and block up with stands.
5. Roll axle assembly from under vehicle.
6. To install, position axle assembly, seating springs on housing pads. Securely attach spring clips, torquing nuts to 62-69 ft. lbs.
7. Connect shock absorbers and driveshaft.
8. Connect steering drag link to steering arm.
9. Attach brake line, bleed and adjust brakes.
10. Completely lubricate all points of axle assembly and steering linkage, then check alignment.

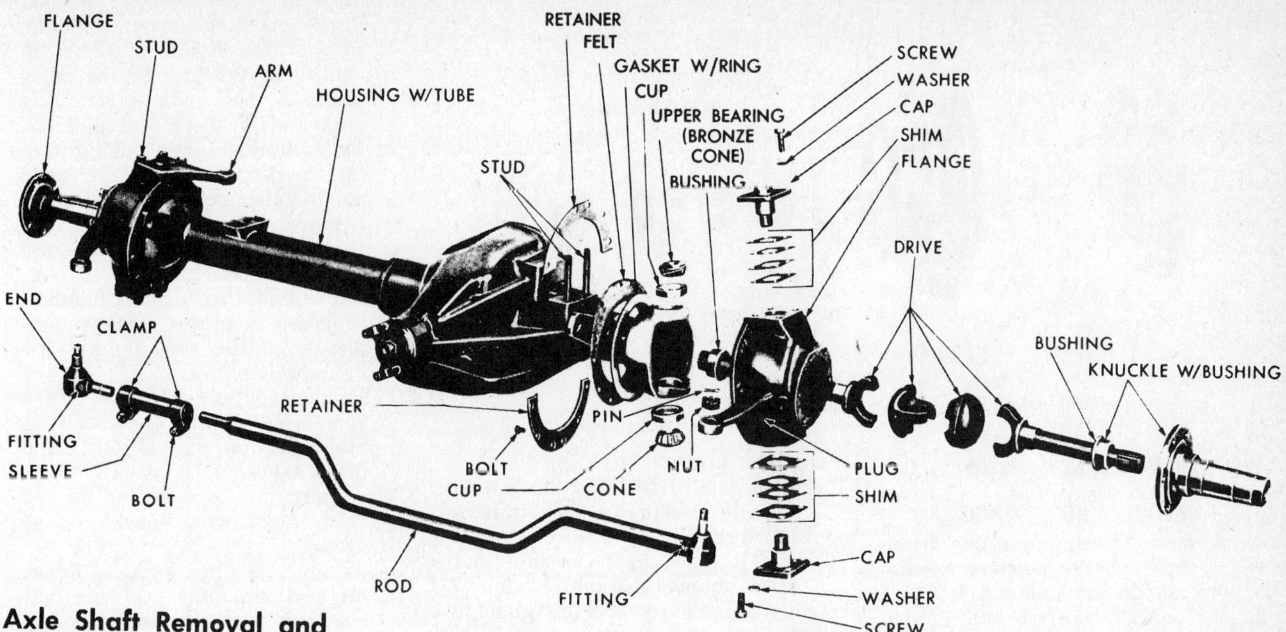

70F axle & steering knuckle (W-300) (© Chrysler Corp.)

Axle Shaft Removal and Installation

W100, W200, W300

1. After removing wheel assembly, remove grease cap from drive flange.
2. Remove drive flange bolts and snap ring. Then, using a suitable puller, remove drive flange.
3. Remove locknut, lockwasher and adjusting nut.
4. Remove wheel hub and brake drum assembly, being careful not to damage oil seal.
5. Remove brake assembly and wire to frame, leaving hydraulic line connected.
6. Tap end of spindle with a soft hammer and remove spindle.
7. Inspect spindle and bushing for wear. Bushing is pressed on and requires no reaming for proper fit.
8. Remove axle shaft assembly. Inspect universal joint. Disassemble and replace any worn components.
9. Install axle assembly, being careful not to damage inner oil seal.
10. Lubricate flanged bushing and install spindle and brake support assembly.
11. Remove, clean, inspect and repack inner and outer wheel bearings.
12. Install inner wheel bearing, position hub, drum and wheel assembly on spindle, then install outer bearing, washer and adjusting nut.
13. Adjust bearing by tightening adjusting nut to 50 ft. lbs. torque, then back off 1/4 turn (1/8 turn on 44F axles). Tighten locknut and bend tab of lockwasher.
14. Install drive flange, retaining nuts, snap ring and grease cup.

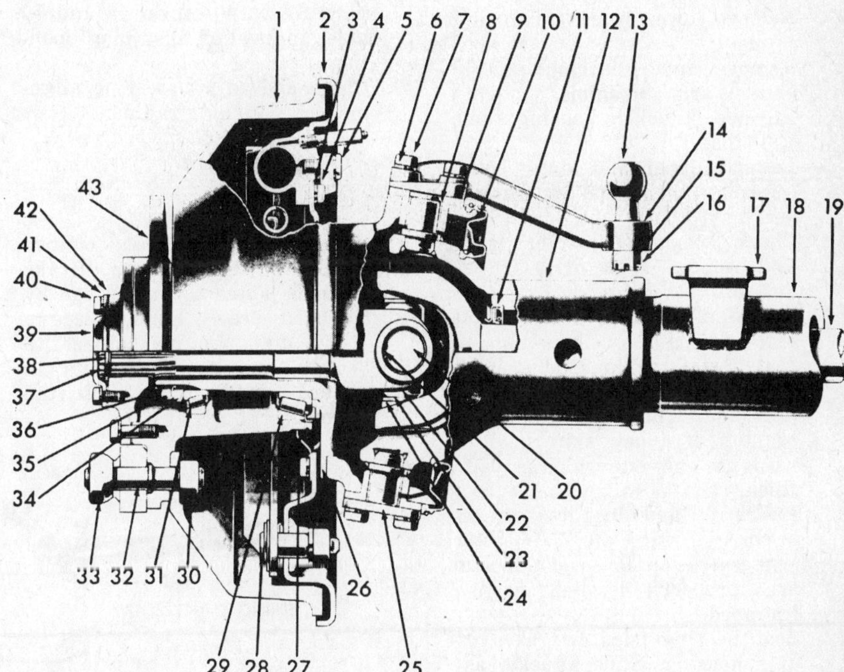

Axle housing (W-500) (© Chrysler Corp.)

1 Drum
2 Backing plate
3 Backing plate lockwasher
4 Backing plate nut
5 Brake cylinder
6 Sterring arm capscrew
7 Steering arm capscrew
8 Trunnion pin bushing
9 Trunnion pin bushing retainer
10 Steering knuckle boot
11 Oil seal assembly
12 Sterring knuckle socket
13 Sterring ball
14 Steering arm
15 Sterring arm nut
16 Steering arm cotter
17 Spring seat
18 Housing tube
19 Cardon joint axle shaft
20 Cardon joint needle bearing cap
21 Bearing cap retaining ring
22 Cardon joint cross
23 Needle bearing retainer
24 Needle bearing cap
25 Lower steering knuckle plate
26 Steering knuckle spindle
27 Oil slinger
28 Anchor pin
29 Inner cup and cone
30 Hub and drum inner stud nut
31 Outer cup and cone
32 Hub and drum stud
33 Outer hub and drum stud nut
34 Wheel bearing jam nut
35 Jam nut retainer
36 Wheel bearing adjusting nut
37 Outer cardon joint axle shaft
38 Axle shaft retaining ring
39 Hub cap
40 Hub cap capscrew
41 Hub cap lockwasher
42 Drive flange
43 Hub

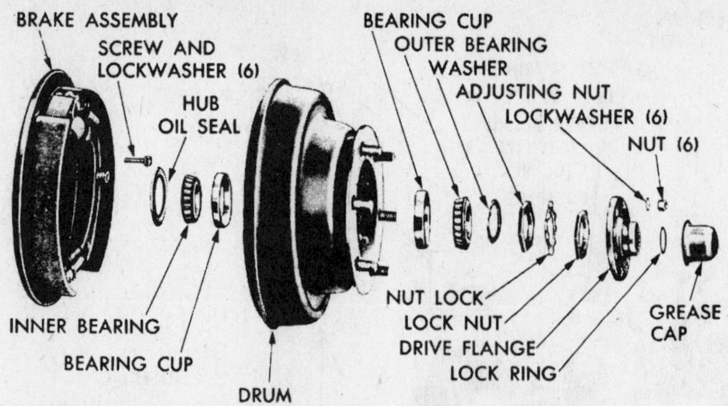

Typical brake hub and drum assembly (© Chrysler Corp.)

Steering Knuckle Service

W100, W200, W300

1. Remove, wheel, hub, brake drum assembly, brake support assembly, spindle and axle shaft.
2. Disconnect tie rod ends from steering knuckles and drag link from steering knuckle arm.
3. Remove steering knuckle felt and oil seal retainers.
4. Remove lower bearing cap and shims.
5. Remove upper bearing cap or knuckle arm and shims.
6. Remove knuckle housing, felt and oil seal.
7. Remove upper and lower bearing cones, then clean and inspect bearings.
8. Check bearing cups for wear and remove with drift if required.
9. To assemble, place felt and oil seal over end of axle housing.
10. Install steering knuckle arm or upper bearing cap and shim pack and tighten retaining bolts or nuts. If a new shim pack is used, use *only* one which is .060" thick.
11. Lubricate and install cone on upper bearing pivot, making sure serration or key and slot are properly located, if so equipped.
12. Seat bearing cups in yokes of axle housing. Slide knuckle assembly over yoke and enter bronze cone in its cup.
13. Lubricate and insert lower bearing cone, tilting knuckle to provide access. Install lower bearing cap and shim pack. If a new pack is required, use *only* .025" thick pack for 44-3F axle or .055" thick pack for 44-3HF or 70F axle.
14. Using a torque wrench on a top outer knuckle bearing cap retaining bolt or nut, measure bearing preload as knuckle is turning. It must read 5-15 ft. lbs. for 44-3F axle and 15-35 ft lbs. for the 44-3HDF or 70-F axles. Remove or add shims to adjust preload.
15. Attach oiled felt and oil seal to knuckle housing with retainers and screws.
16. Install axle shaft, spindle and brake support assembly, tightening spindle to steering knuckle flange bolts.
17. Install hub, brake drum and wheel assembly.
18. Fill steering knuckle housing with SAE 140 oil on 44 and 70 axles to level of filler plug opening.
19. Check and adjust steering alignment and turning radius.

Front Axle Service

WM300

1. Raise front of truck and remove wheel and brake drum. Brake drum is bolted to hub flange by flat-head screws. Remove screws (they may require impact to loosen) and use 3/8" bolts in puller bolt holes to pull the drum.
2. Punch mark the flange and hub so that the flange may be installed on the hub in the same position, then remove retaining nuts and washers and pull the flange by installing and tightening puller bolts in threaded flange puller holes.
3. Remove wheel bearings.
4. Remove brake backing plate and wire it to frame.
5. Tap spindles with a soft hammer to loosen them and remove spindles from the steering knuckle flange assemblies.
6. Remove outer axle shaft and female section of U-joint, then male section of U-joint and inner axle shaft.
7. Disconnect the steering tie rod from the steering knuckle flange arm.
8. Remove steering knuckle flange oil seal assembly. On the left side, it is necessary to disconnect the drag link from the steering arm.
9. Due to the fact that the upper and lower halves of each steering knuckle are machined as an assembly, it is imperative that they be reassembled as such. Be sure to mark pairs so that they may be assembled correctly. Remove dowel pins and bolts. Remove two sections of steering knuckle flange assembly from axle housing.
10. If replacement is necessary, remove the bearing cones from the front axle housing trunnion pins.
11. Remove steering arm from steering knuckle flange assembly, or the upper bearing cap from the right side.

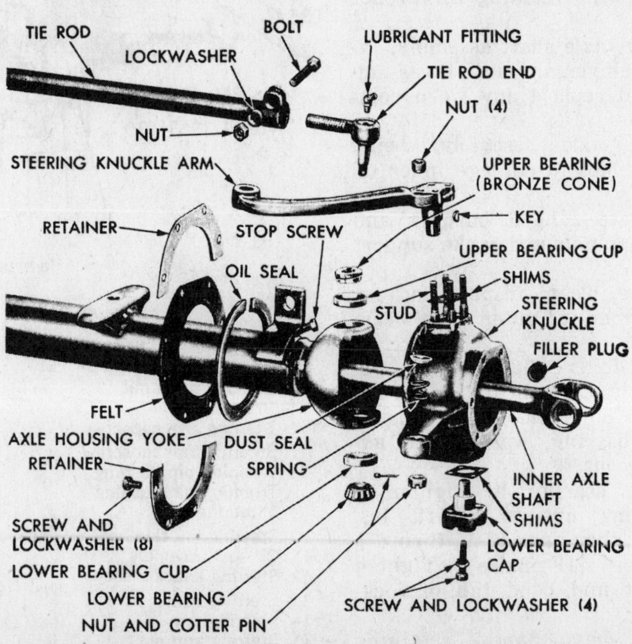

Steering knuckle (W-100 & W-200) (© Chrysler Corp.)

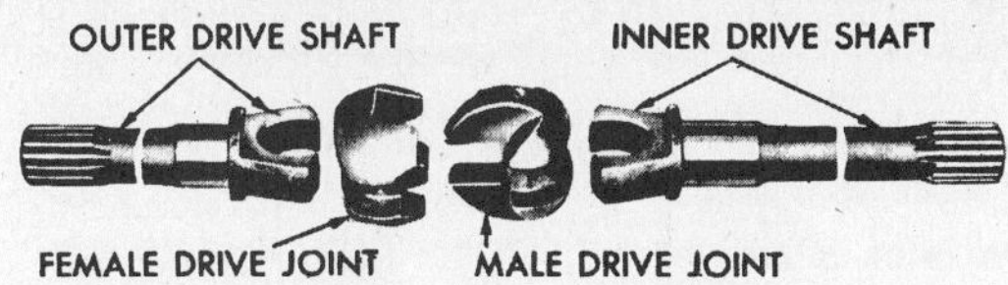

Front drive axle U-joint (WM-300)
(© Chrysler Corp.)

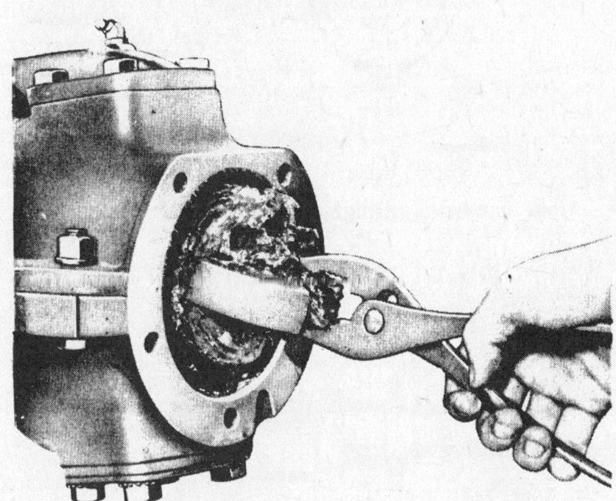

Removing male drive joint (© Chrysler Corp.)

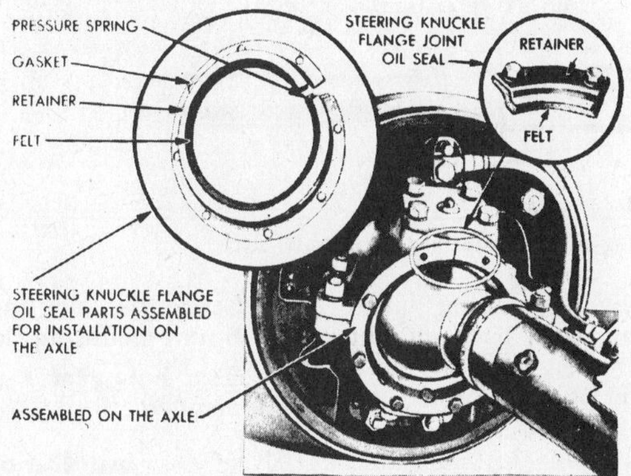

Steering knuckle flange oil seal (© Chrysler Corp.)

12. Remove flange lower bearing cap and gasket.
13. Remove bushing and oil seal from axle housing end.
14. Thoroughly clean and inspect all components.
15. Differential carrier may be removed and serviced in the same manner as the rear axle.
16. Before assembling front axle, check trunnion sockets and ball ends of steering knuckle for damage, cleaning surfaces with abrasive cloth if they are scored.
17. Check steering knuckle trunnion bearings and replace cones if necessary.
18. Inspect bronze axle bushings (8 and 27) in steering knuckle and axle housing for wear or scoring and replace if condition is questionable. These bushings must be in good condition. If badly worn, it is likely that the wheel bearings were too loose.
19. Check front axle housing alignment. See illustration.
20. Install bronze bushings in axle housing and spindle, and new oil seal in axle housing, lip (leather edge) toward differential, using suitable drift.
21. Install woodruff key in axle housing upper trunnion pins.
22. Lubricate bearing cones and install bronze cone on the upper trunnion pin and the roller bearing on the lower trunnion pin.
23. Install upper and lower steering knuckle flanges in their original positions on axle housing and install bolts, washers and nuts.
24. Install dowel pins and tighten nuts.
25. Install flange lower bearing caps and gaskets.
26. Place shims on the top of steering knuckle flange assemblies, and install steering arm (left side) or top bearing cap (right side.
27. Using a torque wrench on an outer upper bearing cap bolts, measure bearing preload while flange is being moved with wrench. The reading should be 25-27½ ft. lbs. Add or remove shims to correct preload.
28. Install steering knuckle flange oil seal assemblies, using new felt seals and gaskets. Open ends are at the top. Clean sealing surfaces. Saturate felt seal with oil and put it in retainer ring with the ends even with retainer ends. Install pressure spring.
29. Assemble tie rod to steering knuckle flange arms and connect drag link to left steering arm.
30. Assemble the axle shaft and universal joint assembly. Male and female sections usually each have the numbers 1, 2, 3 and 4 etched on them so that they may be matched.
31. Pack universal joint with grease and carefully insert axle assembly into axle housing, long shaft first. Do not damage oil seal.
32. Install spindles and brake backing plate.
33. Pack wheel bearings, lubricate inside of hub and install hub assembly.
34. Adjust wheel bearings by turning adjusting nut up tight, then backing off 1/6 turn.
35. Install adjusting nut lock, making certain the dowel pin in the inner nut enters one of the holes in the lock. It may be necessary to reverse the lock, or turn the inner adjusting nut slightly to permit the dowel pin to engage with the nut.
36. Install the outer nut and tighten it securely.
37. Install drive flanges in their original locations with new gaskets.
38. Before installing the brake drums, coat the contact surfaces of the wheel nut flange of both the drum and hub with water pump lubricant to facilitate future removal.
39. Install wheel and tire assembly.
40. Align the front wheels. Check and adjust steering radius.

W500 Axle

General Information

The front driving axle is composed of the outer drive assemblies, the differential carrier and sleeve assemblies (axle housings), the differential pinion and cage assembly and the differential. Several units can be removed without complete disassembly to make parts replacements and these will be indicated with the complete disassembly to cover replacements which are required most frequently as a result of wear or breakage.

Some service parts replacements such as a broken axle shaft, outer drive assembly, wheel bearings, oil seals and brake parts can be made without complete removal of the axle assembly. However, it is generally desirable to remove the assembly for complete disassembly and inspection in connection with any major assembly repairs. The angles that control front wheel alignment are built into the axle. Damage to parts causing misalignment of caster or camber angles must be replaced, as these parts cannot be readjusted to original specifications. Toe-in set by turning the tie rod ends.

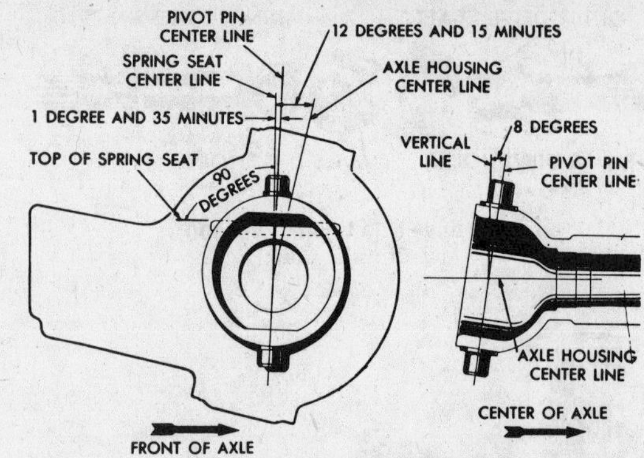

Front axle housing alignment (© Chrysler Corp.)

Axle Housing Service

W500

1. Remove hub cap and shims, wiring shim pack together to aid reassembly.
2. Remove snap ring from splined shaft.
3. Remove drive flange and gasket.
4. Straighten tab on locknut washer and remove locknut, washer and adjusting nut.
5. Remove hub, drum and outer wheel bearing.
6. Remove brake backing plate and spindle.
7. Slide out axle and universal joint assembly, being careful not to damage inner oil seal.
8. Remove steering knuckle boot.
9. Remove bearing caps and bearing sleeves from knuckle and remove steering knuckles from axle housing.
10. Check all parts for damage and wear. Replace all oil seals.
11. Universal joint is serviced in the conventional manner. For details of universal joint overhaul procedure, see Driveshaft and Universal Joint section below.
12. Make sure that axle shaft inner oil seal is installed.
13. Position steering knuckle and install lower bearing and cap.
14. Install upper bearing.
15. Place spacer in position and lay a short piece of plastic gauge material on the spacer. Install cap and tighten both upper and lower bolts securely. Remove upper cap and measure gauge material. Clearance should be .005-.013″. Install spacers to correct clearance if necessary.
16. Install steering knuckle boot.
17. Install axle, universal and spindle assembly.
18. Position brakes and oil slinger on spindle and attach with bolts and lockwashers. Drain hole on backing plate must be on the bottom.
19. Position hub and drum on spindle, and install outer wheel bearing cone and adjusting nut. Adjust nut by tightening until there is drag, then back off nut until hub turns easily with just a slight amount of end play.
20. Install locknut and tabbed lock washer. Tighten locknut and bend tab of lockwasher. Check bearing preload again.
21. Install drive shaft flange with a new gasket.
22. Install lock (snap) ring in groove of splined shaft.
23. Position shims between flange and hub cap, using original shims removed during disassembly.
24. Install hub cap.

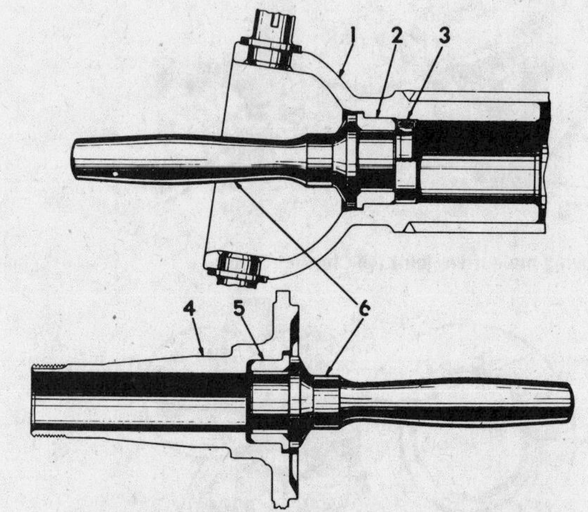

1 Housing assembly
2 Trunnion socket bushing
3 Shaft oil seal
4 Steering knuckle
5 Steering knuckle bushing
6 Drift

Installing oil seal & bushing (© Chrysler Corp.)

Warn Selective Drive Hubs

General Information

The Warn Hub is designed for use in the W200, "300 front axle drive vehicles. With hubs in lock position the vehicle operated in 4-wheel drive the same as before installing hubs. With hubs in the free position the vehicle will operate as two wheel drive but without front end drag, gear whine or front wheel shimmy.

Removal

1. Raise wheel until it clears floor.
2. Straighten lock tabs and remove 6 hub mounting bolts.
3. Tap hub gently with mallet to remove.

Installation

1. Position hub assembly over end of axle.
2. Replace 6 hub mounting bolts and tighten to 30 to 35 foot-pounds. Bend lock washer tabs to anchor bolts.
3. Lower vehicle.

Disassembly

1. Remove hub assembly from vehicle.
2. Separate clutch assembly from body assembly.
3. Remove snap-ring from rear of body assembly using snap-ring pliers. Slip axle shaft hub out of body from the front.
4. Remove allenscrew from inner side of clutch.
5. Remove bronze dial assembly from front of clutch housing assembly.
6. Remove clutch assembly from rear of housing complete with 12 roller pins.
7. Wash all parts for burrs, chips, wear, flat spots or cracks. Replace necessary parts.

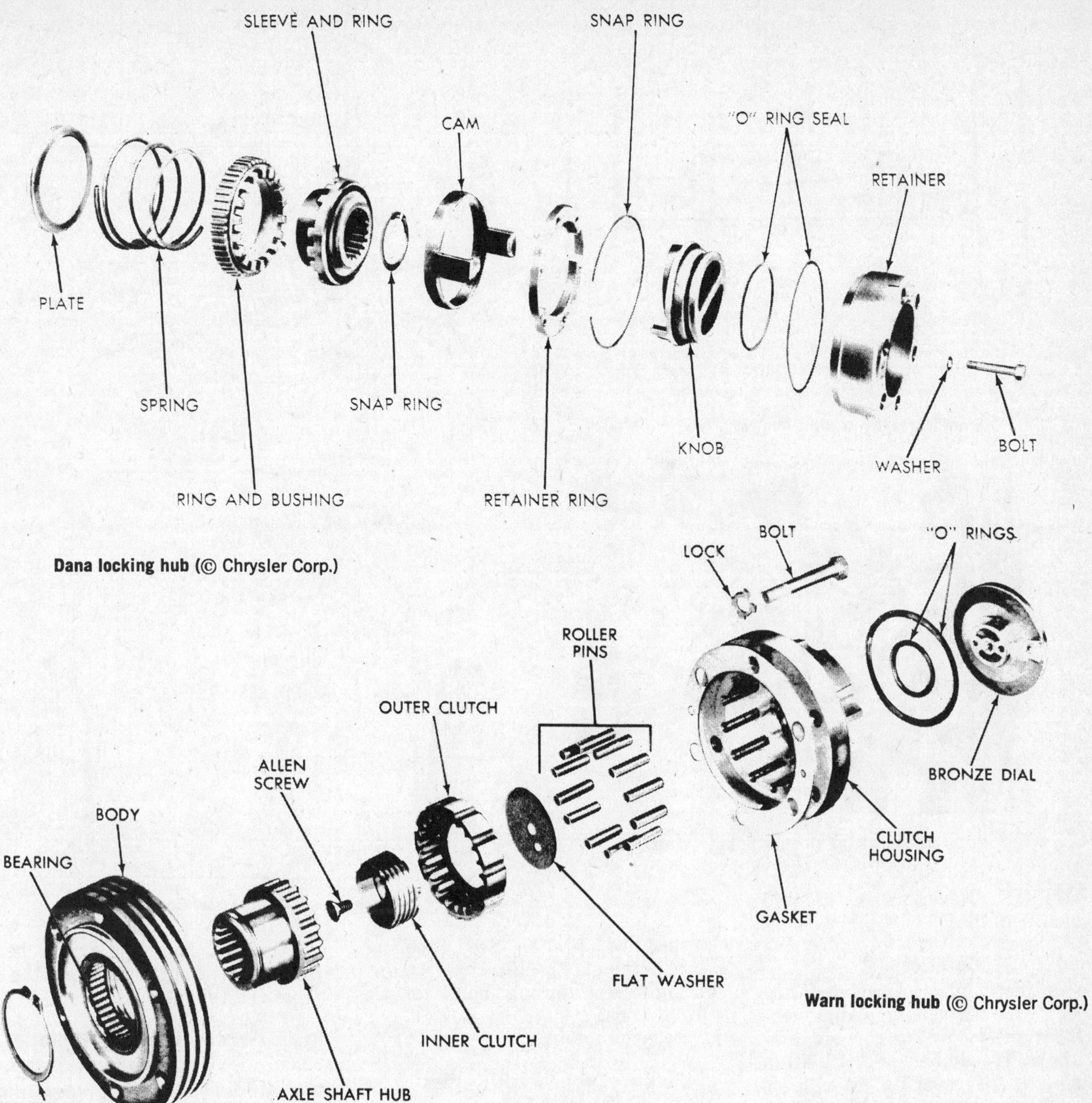

Dana locking hub (© Chrysler Corp.)

Warn locking hub (© Chrysler Corp.)

Assembly

1. Coat moving parts with a suitable oil.
2. Slide axle shaft hub into body from front. Replace snap-ring.
3. Replace bronze dial assembly and inner clutch tighten allenscrew. Stake edge of screw with center punch to prevent loosening.
4. With dial in FREE position rotate outer clutch body into inner assembly until it bottoms in housing, back it up to nearest hole, then insert roller pins.
5. Position hub and clutch assembly together with new gasket in between.
6. Install complete assembly on vehicle with new gasket. Follow installation procedure.

Dana Locking Hub

Removal and Disassembly

1. Place hub in lock position. Remove allen head mounting screws and washers.
2. Carefully remove retainer, "O" ring seal and knob. Separate knob from retainer.
3. Remove large internal snap-ring. Slide retainer ring and cam from hub.
4. While pressing against sleeve and ring assembly, remove axle shaft snap-ring. Relieve pressure and remove sleeve and ring, ring and bushing, spring and plate.
5. Wash all parts in a suitable solvent, inspect all parts for wear, nicks and burrs. Replace all parts which appear questionable.

Assembly and Installation

1. Slide plate and spring (large coils first) into wheel hub housing.
2. Assemble ring and bushing and sleeve and bushing. Slide complete assembly into housing.
3. Compress spring and install axle shaft snap-ring.
4. Position cam and retainer in housing and install large internal snap-ring.
5. Place small "O" ring seal on knob, lubricate with Moly X-L or equivalent and install in retainer at lock position.
6. Place large "O" ring seal on retainer. Align retainer and retainer ring and install washers and Allen head mounting screws.
7. Check operation.

Steering Linkage

Disconnecting Linkage Joints

1. Remove cotter pin and loosen castellated nut.
2. Applying pressure with a pry bar to female member, strike the female member with a hammer to dislodge tapered stud.

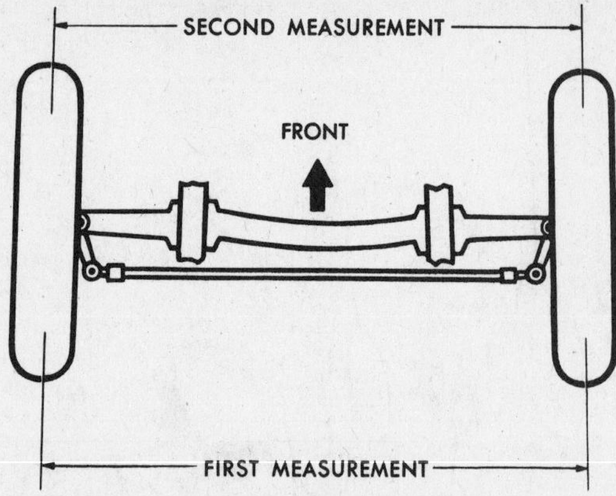

Front wheel toe in adjustment (© Chrysler Corp.)

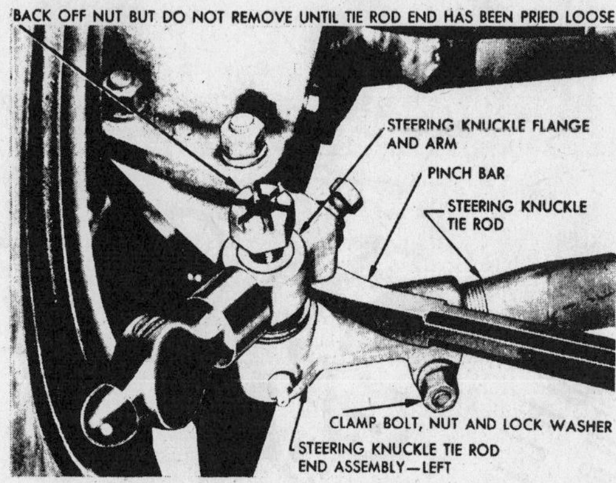

Disconnecting steering linkage joints (© Chrysler Corp.)

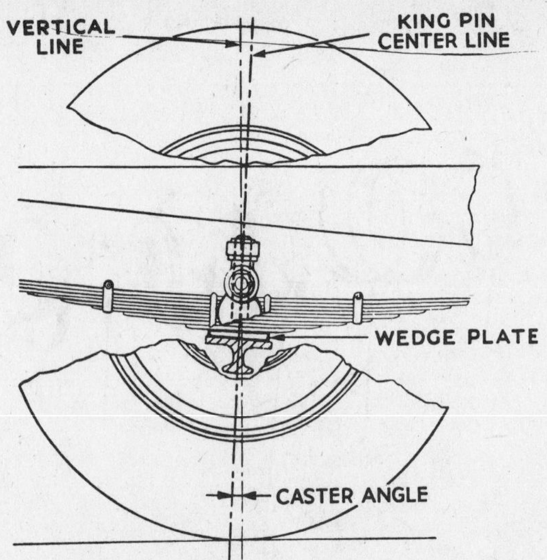

Castor angle (© Chrysler Corp.)

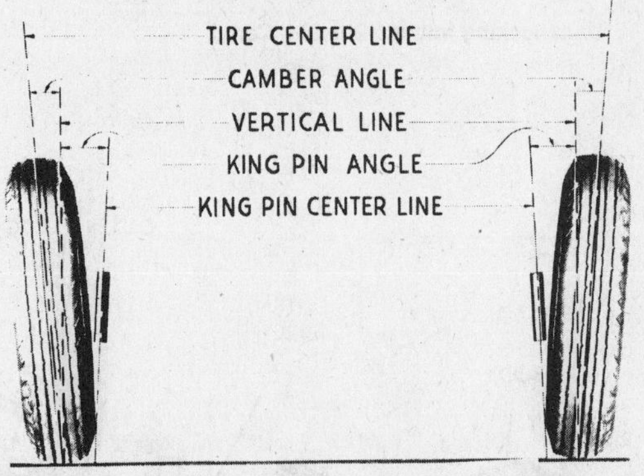

Camber angle (© Chrysler Corp.)

CAUTION: Never strike the stud half of the joint.

Camber

No adjustment is provided for camber. See Steering Alignment Specifications below for correct camber angle. If camber is not within limits, axle or steering knuckle is bent and should be replaced.

Caster Adjustment

Check camber before attempting to check or adjust caster. See Steering Alignment Specifications below for correct caster angle. If caster is not within the specified limits, adjust caster by inserting a wedge between the spring and axle, the thick part of the wedge toward the rear of the vehicle to increase caster or the thick part of the wedge toward the front of the vehicle to decrease caster. Excessive negative or positive caster indicates bent or worn spring. Check contour of spring and replace if necessary.

Toe-In Adjustment

Solid (I-Beam) Type Front Axles

1. Center steering.
2. Loosen clamping bolts on both ends of tie rod.
3. Turn tie rod in the direction necessary to bring toe-in within specified limits. See Steering Alignment Specifications below.
4. Tighten clamping bolts on tie rod ends.
5. Recheck toe-in.

Front Drive Type Axles

1. Center steering.
2. Disconnect left tie rod end from steering knuckle as described above.
3. Turn tie rod end assembly in the direction necessary to correct toe-in.
4. Connect left tie rod end to steering knuckle.
5. Tighten clamping bolt on tie rod end.
6. Recheck toe-in.

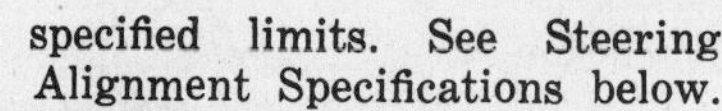

Adjustments, Gear in Vehicle

Before making any adjustments, inspect steering linkage for lash and wheel bearing adjustment, raising front of truck with a jack. Ross and Saginaw steering gears, except the model 24-J Ross, may be adjusted for cross shaft lash and worm bearing preload without removing the gear from the vehicle.

Worm Bearing Preload Adjustment Model 525D Saginaw and All Ross Except Model 24-J

1. On Ross gears, remove the horn button and spring.
2. Remove the steering arm from the steering gear cross (sector) shaft. Mark relation of steering arm to shaft before removing.
3. On long worm shaft type gears, check steering column for alignment.
4. Loosen cross (sector) shaft adjusting screw and back out adjusting screw about two turns.
5. Turn steering wheel two complete turns from the straight-ahead position. CAUTION: Do not turn steering wheel hard against the stops as this may damage gear.
6. Using a torque wrench on the steering wheel nut, rotate steering wheel through "lash" area toward straight-ahead position. Torque required to keep wheel moving indicates worm bearing preload. This should read be-

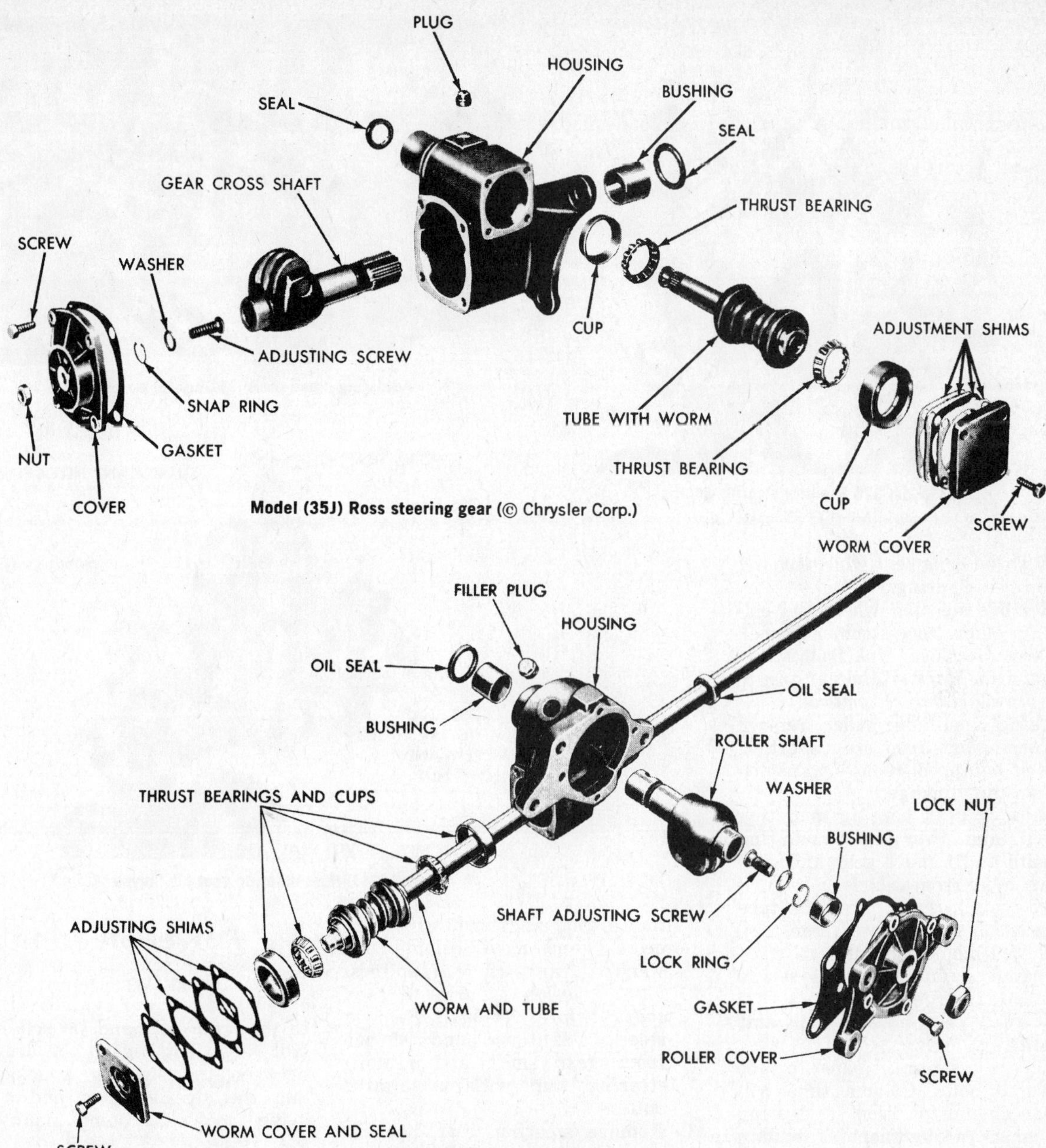

Model (35J) Ross steering gear (© Chrysler Corp.)

Model (Y4D-335) Ross steering gear (© Chrysler Corp.)

tween 7 and 14 in. lbs.

7. If preload is not within limits, remove or add shims beneath the lower worm bearing cover on Ross gears. Cover retaining bolts are tightened to 20 ft. lbs. torque. Preload on the Saginaw gear is made by turning the large adjuster. Adjuster locknut is tightened to 85 ft. lbs. torque.
8. Recheck preload, adjusting again if necessary.

Cross or Sector Gear Mesh Adjustment

Model 525-D Saginaw and All Ross Except Model 24-J

This adjustment is made only after worm bearing preload is adjusted as described above. Steering arm is still removed from cross (sector) shaft.

1. Center steering wheel (worm-shaft) by counting turns from full right to full left and counting back exactly half way.
2. Loosen locknut on cross (sector) shaft adjusting screw and turn adjusting screw in until all lash is gone. Tighten locknut to 20 ft. lbs. torque.
3. Check torque required to move steering wheel (torque wrench on steering wheel nut through high-spot (center) position. Overcenter torque should be 20-25 in. lbs.
4. Readjust if necessary and retighten locknut.
5. Reinstall steering arm on cross (sector) shaft and tighten clamp bolt to 85 ft. lbs. torque.

Worm Bearing Preload Adjustment Model 24-J Ross

This gear must be removed to adjust the worm bearing preload. Torque required to keep the worm shaft moving through "lash" (center position) should be 5-10 in. lbs. Adjustment is made by removing or adding shims between the worm shaft cover plate and the gear body. Tighten cover bolts to 18-20 ft. lbs. torque. Perform cross shaft adjustment after worm gear preload is adjusted.

Manual Steering Gear Removal

Models With Long Worm Shaft

1. Disconnect battery negative cable at battery, horn wire at connector and any gear shift linkage or directional signal controls that are attached to steering column jacket.
2. Remove horn button by pressing

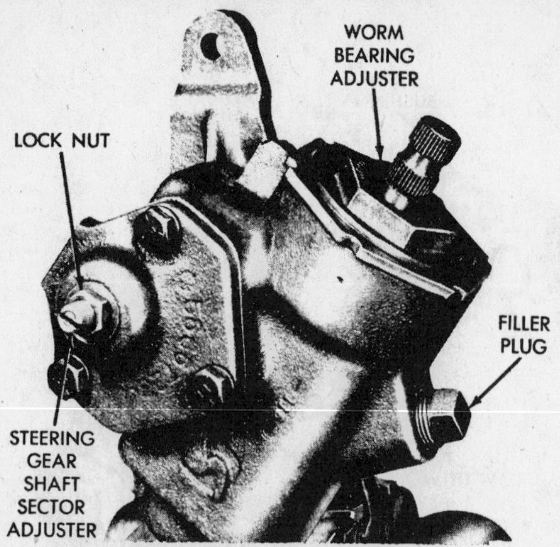

Model 325 Saginaw steering gear (© Chrysler Corp.)

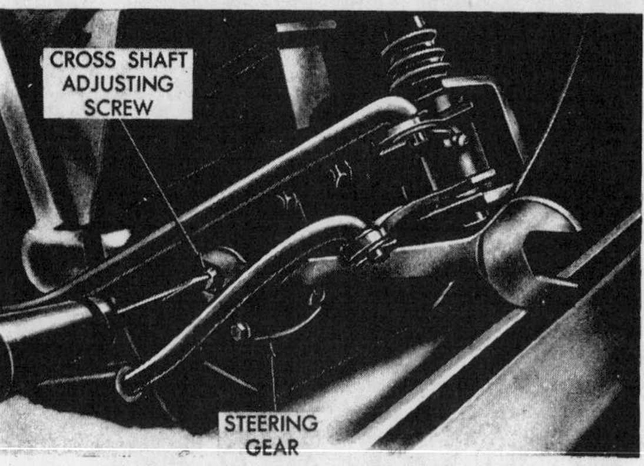

Adjusting cross shaft (© Chrysler Corp.)

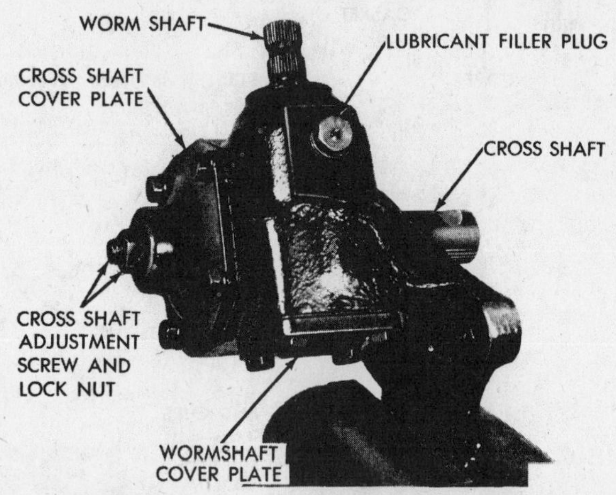

Model (24J) Ross steering gear (© Chrysler Corp.)

down on ornament while turning to release spring.

3. Remove steering wheel and column clamp to instrument panel.
4. Disconnect drag link from steering arm. *Mark relation of arm to cross shaft before removal.*
5. Using a suitable puller, remove steering arm from cross shaft.
6. If so equipped, remove transmission shift linkage.
7. Remove gear housing mounting bolts and lower jacket mounting bolts and remove gear and tube assembly from vehicle.
8. To install, insert gear and tube assembly from below frame.
9. Install mounting bolts.
10. Install clamp bolts and secure tube to instrument panel.
11. Tighten gear housing to frame bolts.
12. Loosen instrument panel to tube clamp bolts. Column tube will not change position if steering gear is in alignment. If column tube shifted position when clamp was loosened, relocate column tube bracket before tightening clamp.
13. Install spring, retainer, steering wheel, horn button spring, retainer and wheel nut, tightening nut to 24 ft. lbs. torque.
14. If so equipped, attach directional signal switch.
15. Install spring, contact plate, horn wire spring and horn button.
16. Connect and adjust shift linkage (see "Manual Transmissions") if so equipped.
17. Install steering arm and drag link, tighten steering arm clamp bolt to 85 ft. lbs. torque.

Models With Short Worm Shaft

1. Remove bolt from column coupling clamp at upper end of steering worm shaft. Disconnect turn signal and horn wire connectors and move column upward to clear worm shaft splines.
2. *Mark relation of arm to gear shaft before removal.* Remove steering arm nut and washer from gear shaft and remove steering arm with a suitable puller.
3. Remove steering gear housing mounting bolts. On 6D-400 models, remove two bolts at trunnion cap.
4. Remove steering gear from vehicle.
5. To install, center gear and install in frame, aligning housing with frame. Tighten 7/16" and ½" mounting bolts to 70 ft. lbs. torque and 9/16" bolts to 100 ft. lbs. torque.
6. Install universal joint clamp to worm shaft and tighten to 30 ft. lbs. torque. On pot type joint, center the steering column shaft in the joint to insure adequate travel.
7. Set front wheels straight ahead.
8. Install steering arm in gearshaft (use marks made during removal to position arm in original location). Tighten bolt clamp to 170 ft. lbs. torque and cross shaft nut to 250 ft. lbs. torque.

Power Steering

The linkage type power steering consists of a power cylinder attached to the front axle and tie rod, a control valve installed on the drag link between the steering knuckle arm and the steering arm and a belt-driven hydraulic pump mounted on the engine.

Power Steering Pump Pressure Test

Model .94

1. Fill fluid reservoir and check drive belt tension.
2. Disconnect the high pressure hydraulic line going to the control valve at the control valve and install a pressure gauge and valve, connecting the gauge end to the pump and the valve end to the control valve.
3. After warming up the fluid to 150-170° (let engine run and turn steering back and forth), note pressure reading while turning steering wheel to extreme in either direction as engine idles at 600 rpm. Maximum pressure should be at least 900 psi.
4. If maximum pressure is below

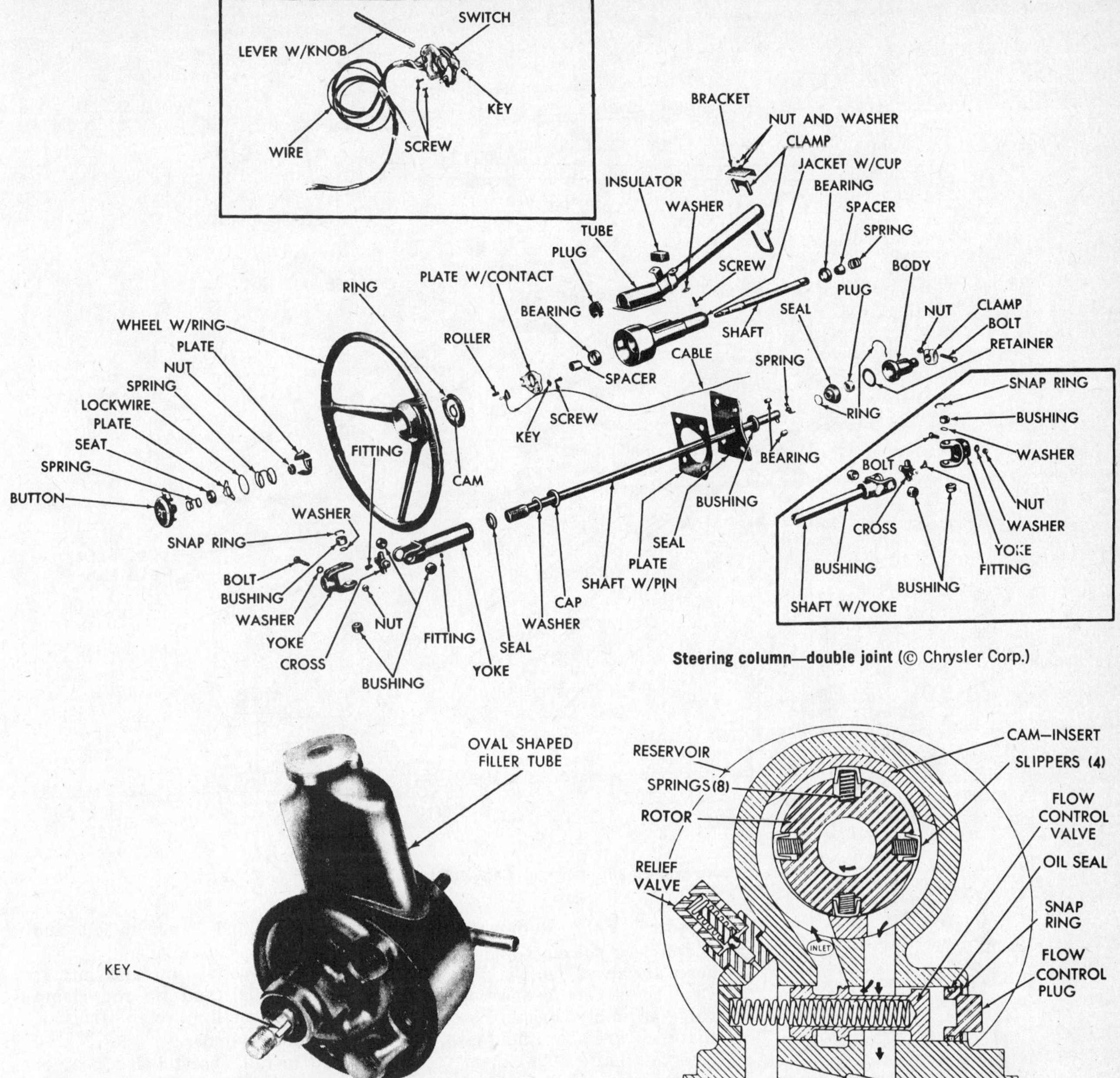

Steering column—double joint (© Chrysler Corp.)

Model .94 power steering pump (© Chrysler Corp.)

Slipper type power steering pump (© Chrysler Corp.)

900 psi, momentarily close valve and note maximum pressure reading. If pressure was less than 1000 psi, the pump is faulty. If pressure was at least 1000 psi, then either the control valve or the power cylinder is faulty.

5. When removing test gauge and valve, be sure to reinstall high pressure line in its original position to avoid interference with engine or sheet metal.
6. For power steering pump overhaul procedures, see "Power Steering" in the General Repair Section.

Model 1.2

The pressure test procedure is the same as that described for the model .94 above. In this test, however, the engine idles at 500 rpm. It is possible with this pump that the pressure relief valve may be faulty if the test indicated that the pump was faulty. Before removing pump and overhauling pump, retest with a new pressure relief valve.

Oil Pump

Reference

See "Power Steering" in General Repair Section for power steering pump overhaul procedures.

Oil Pump Removal

1. Loosen pump lower mounting and locking bolts and remove the belt.
2. Place a container under pump and disconnect both pump hoses.
3. Remove mounting and locking bolts and remove pump and brackets.
4. To install, position pump on engine and install retaining and locking bolts.
5. Install drive belt and adjust. Tighten pump brackets to 30 ft. lbs. torque.
6. Connect pressure and return hoses, routing them in the same position they were in before removal.
7. Fill pump reservoir.

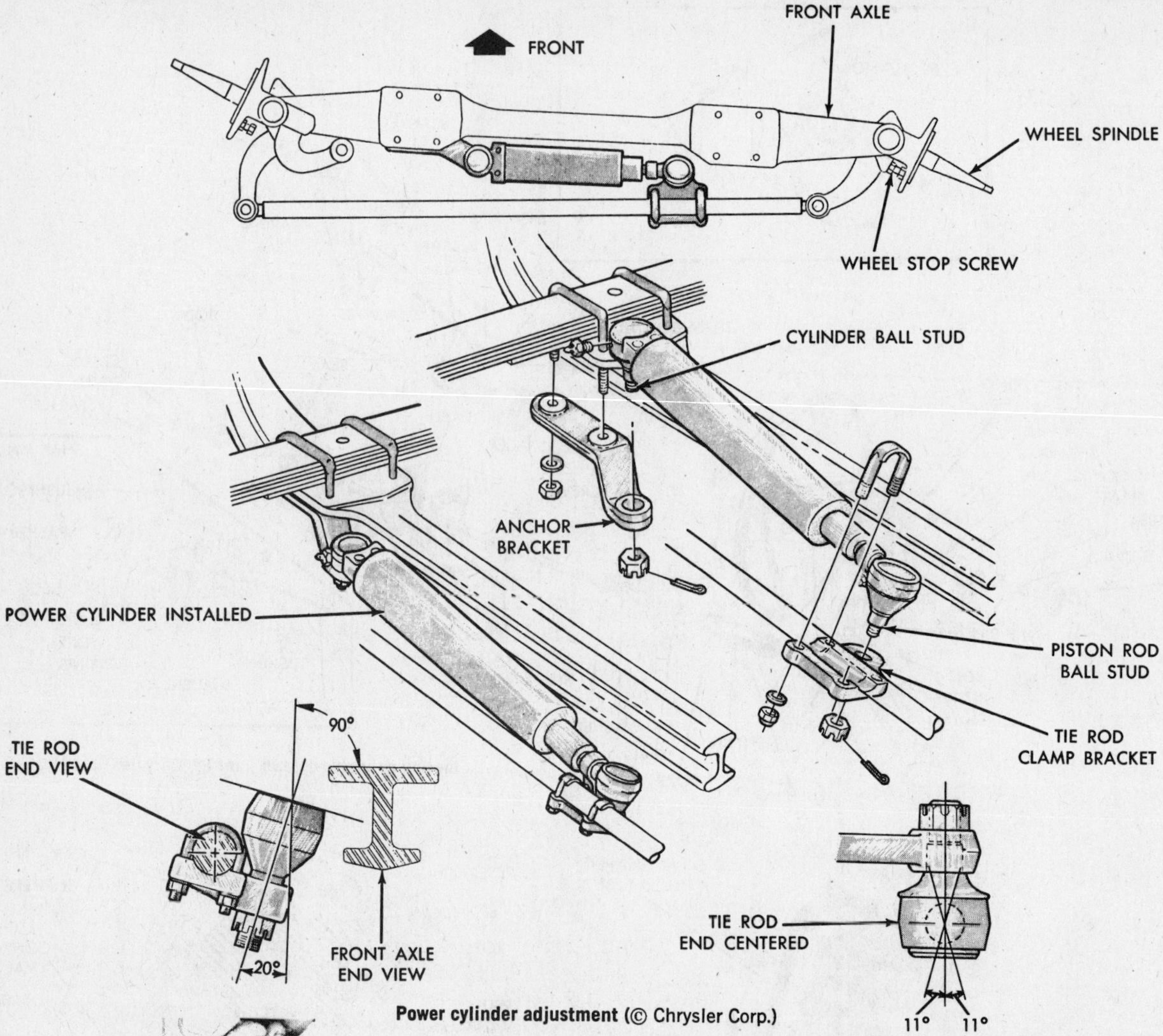

Power cylinder adjustment (© Chrysler Corp.)

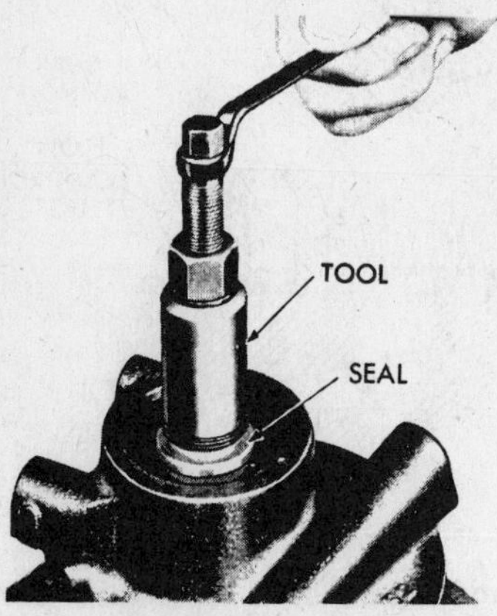

Removing pump oil seal
(© Chrysler Corp.)

8. Start engine and turn steering wheel all the way left and right to bleed the system. Stop engine and recheck fluid level, refilling if necessary.

Control Valve

Reference

See "Power Steering" in the General Repair Section for control valve overhaul and service procedures.

Control Valve Removal

1. Disconnect pressure and return hoses at valve assembly.
2. Cap hoses and connections at valve assembly. Fasten hoses so that ends are above fluid level in reservoir and tag them for reinstallation identification.
3. Disconnect ball ends at steering arm and steering knuckle arm and remove control valve and drag link assembly.
4. To install, connect control valve sliding sleeve end at steering arm and install nut and cotter pin.
5. Connect drag link end to steering knuckle arm and install nut and cotter pin.
6. Connect pressure and return hydraulic lines at valve assembly, tightening securely.
7. Refill pump reservoir.
8. Bleed system by turning steering wheel back and forth several times while the engine is idling.
9. Recheck fluid level and refill if necessary.

Power Cylinder Removal

1. Disconnect hydraulic lines at power cylinder and cap ends and connections at cylinder.
2. Remove cotter pin and nut at ball studs (and tie rod clamp U-bolts on lightweight trucks). Remove cylinder.
3. To install, insert ball stud into place on axle bracket and install nut and cotter pin, tighten nut securely.
4. Rotate steering wheel to extreme right turn position.
5. Install tie rod clamp loosely (on medium weight trucks loosen tie rod clamp and install ball stud and nut).
6. Position cylinder piston rod in fully retracted position and tighten U-bolt clamps on tie rod. On medium weight trucks the ball stud will have to be connected to tie rod clamp bracket before tightening clamp bolts. Clamp should be mounted on tie rod at a 20° angle as illustrated. Nuts on U-bolts are torqued to 40 ft. lbs.
7. Connect hydraulic lines to power cylinder in their original positions.
8. Bleed system as described in

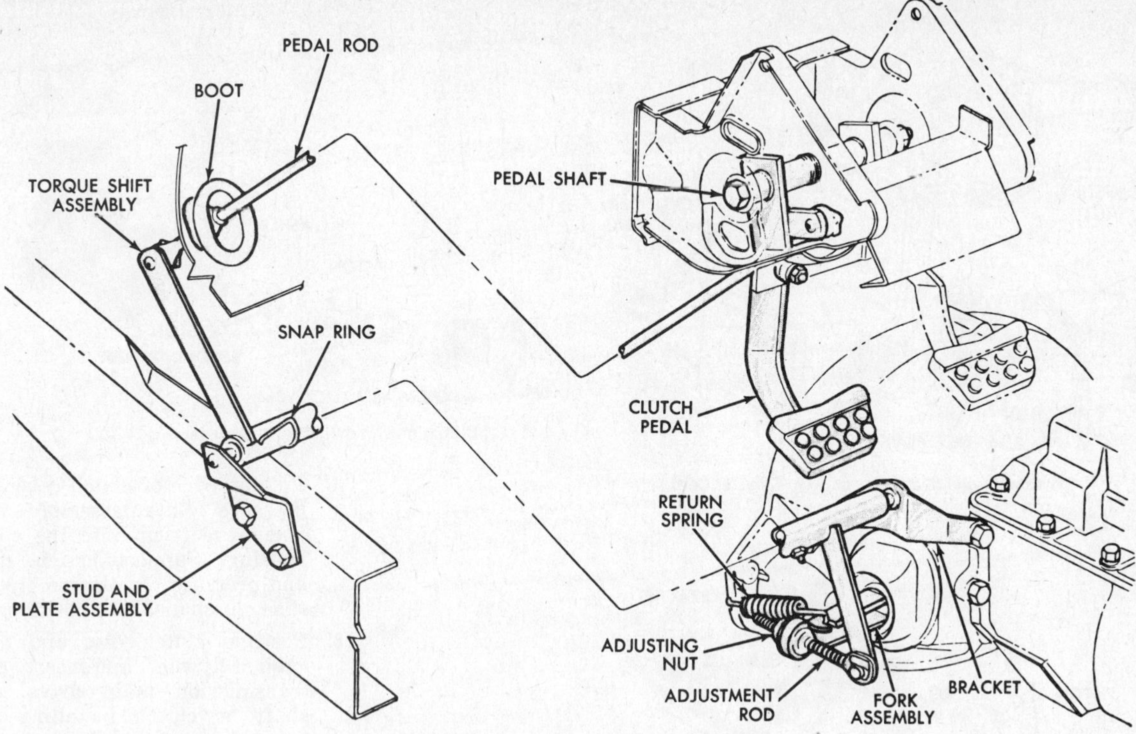

Clutch linkage typical (D-300 & W-300) (© Chrysler Corp.)

Step 8 of "Control Valve Removal and Installation."

Clutch

Mechanical Clutch Linkage Adjustment

1969-1971 100, 200, 300 Models

The only adjustment required for the clutch is the pedal free play. Adjust fork rod by turning self-locking nut to provide 1/8" (3/16" on "B" series compacts) free movement at the end of the fork. This movement will provide the prescribed 1-1/2" (1" on "B" series compacts) free play at the pedal.

Hydraulic Clutch Adjustment

1. Inside the cab, adjust clutch pedal free play by turning adjusting nut to allow. .010" free play between push rod and master cylinder piston.
2. At the slave cylinder, adjust clutch linkage free play at clutch fork pivot pin to 3/16". Total pedal free play should then be approximately 1-1/2". This figure should be used as a check and not for setting free play.
3. Inside the cab, check clutch pedal reserve. This is that portion of pedal travel remaining after free play and complete clutch disengagement. There should be a minimum of 1" pedal reserve. If there is insufficient pedal reserve, bleed the hydraulic system as described below. Extremely low reserve indicates excessive wear in either of the cylinders.
4. Check for binding, incorrect parts or improperly installed parts and make corrections, repeating Steps 1 through 3 if necessary.
5. Over center spring tension (pedal return) is increased by backing off end nut on rod at top of clutch pedal.

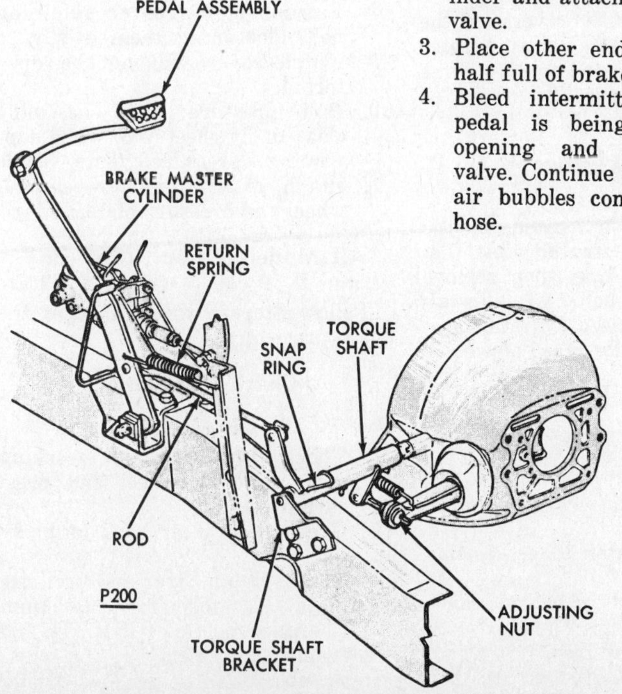

Clutch linkage P-200 & 300 (© Chrysler Corp.)

Bleeding Hydraulic Clutch System

1. Clean away dirt from around master cylinder reservoir filler cap, remove cap and fill reservoir. Make sure to check reservoir frequently during bleeding process and fill when necessary.
2. Clean bleeder valve on slave cylinder and attach bleeder hose to valve.
3. Place other end of hose in jar half full of brake fluid.
4. Bleed intermittently as clutch pedal is being depressed by opening and closing bleeder valve. Continue bleeding until no air bubbles come from bleeder hose.

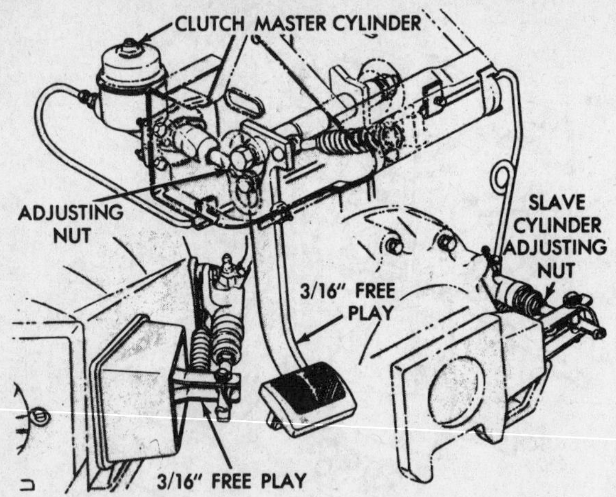

Hydraulic clutch adjustments (© Chrysler Corp.)

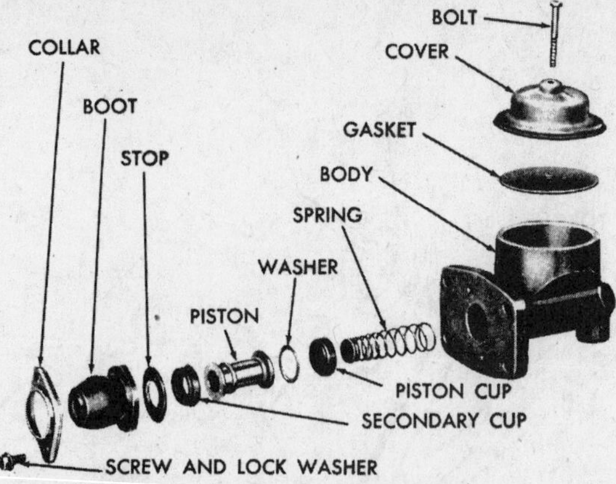

Clutch master cylinder (© Chrysler Corp.)

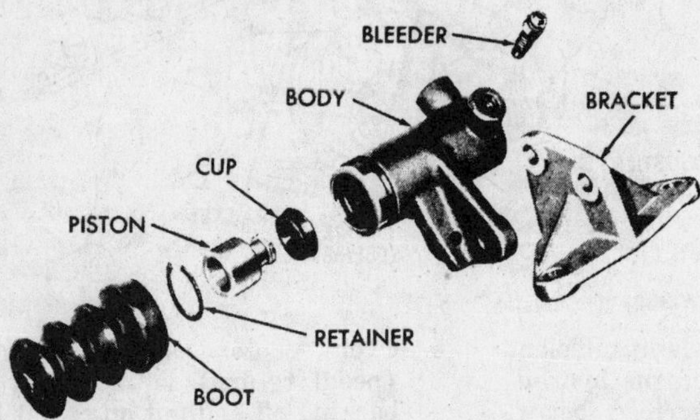

Clutch slave cylinder (© Chrysler Corp.)

Clutch Master Cylinder Removal

1. Remove pedal return spring.
2. Disconnect push rod end at clutch pedal and hydraulic fluid line at master cylinder.
3. Unbolt master cylinder from dash panel.
4. Installation is the reverse of the above procedure. Adjust master cylinder push rod to .010" free play. Bleed hydraulic system as described above.

Clutch Slave Cylinder Removal

Slave cylinder is located on the right side of the clutch housing. Disconnect hydraulic line, then remove cylinder mounting bolts. After installation, be sure to bleed hydraulic system and adjust as described above.

Clutch Removal

1969 and Later D, P, W—100, 200, 300 Models

1. Support engine on a suitable jack.
2. Remove insulator to crossmember bolts.
3. Remove crossmember to frame bracket mounting bolts.
4. Remove crossmember.
5. Remove transmission as described in "Transmission Removal and Installation" below.
6. Remove clutch housing pan if so equipped.
7. Remove clutch fork, clutch bearing and sleeve assembly if not removed with transmission.
8. Mark clutch cover and flywheel, with a prick punch, to assure correct reassembly.
9. Remove clutch cover retaining bolts, loosening them evenly so clutch cover will not be distorted.
10. Pull pressure plate assembly clear of flywheel and, while supporting pressure plate, slide clutch disc from between flywheel and pressure plate.

All Models Except 1969 and Later D, P, W—100, 200, 300

Follow Steps 5 through 10 of the above procedure.

Clutch Installation

All Models

1. Thoroughly clean all working surfaces of flywheel and pressure plate.
2. Grease radius at back of bushing.
3. Rotate clutch cover and pressure plate assembly for maximum clearance between flywheel and frame crossmember if crossmember was not removed during clutch removal.
4. Tilt top edge of clutch cover and pressure plate assembly back and move it up into the clutch housing. Support clutch cover and pressure plate assembly and slide clutch disc into position.
5. Position clutch disc and plate against flywheel and insert spare transmission main drive gear shaft or clutch installing tool through clutch disc hub and into main drive pilot bearing.
6. Rotate clutch cover until the prick punch marks on cover and flywheel line up.
7. Bolt cover loosely to flywheel. Tighten cover bolts a few turns at a time, in progression, until tight. Then tighten bolts to 20 ft. lbs. torque.
8. Install transmission as described in "Transmission Installation" below.
9. On D, P, W-100, 200, 300 models, install frame crossmembers and insulator, tighten all bolts.

Replacing Clutch Release (Throwout) Bearing

1. Remove transmission. See "Transmission Removal" below.
2. Disconnect clutch linkage from clutch fork.
3. Unhook release bearing return spring.
4. Remove release bearing.
5. To install, position release bearing on clutch fork shaft.
6. Connect return spring.
7. Position and secure transmission.
8. Place clutch linkage in position and secure.
9. Adjust clutch pedal free travel as described above.

Manual Transmission

Reference

For Manual Transmission overhaul procedures see "Manual Transmission" in General Section.

3-Speed Transmission Removal

All 100, 200, 300 Models

1. Drain lubricant.
2. Disconnect driveshaft. On the sliding spline type, disconnect driveshaft at the rear universal joint, then carefully pull the shaft yoke out of the transmission extension housing. Do not nick or scratch splines.
3. Disconnect gearshift control rods and speedometer cable.
4. Remove backup light switch if so equipped.
5. Support engine with a suitable fixture.
6. On 1969 and later D, P, W-100, 200, 300 models, remove crossmember and rubber insulator. See illustration in "Clutch Removal" of preceding section. Support transmission with a suitable jack. On all other models, remove belts securing rear transmission housing to underbody bracket.
7. Remove transmission to clutch housing bolts.
8. Slide transmission rearward until pinion shaft clears clutch completely, then lower transmission from vehicle.
9. Installation is the reverse order of the above procedure. Before inserting transmission drive shaft into clutch, make sure clutch housing bore, disc and face are aligned. Tighten clutch housing to transmission bolts to 50 ft. lbs. torque.
10. Fill with lubricant.
11. Adjust shift linkage.
12. Road test.

4-Speed Transmission Removal

Except 433D

1. Shift transmission into any gear.
2. Disconnect universal joint and loosen yoke retaining nut.
3. Disconnect parking brake (if so equipped) and speedometer cables at transmission.
4. Remove lever retainer by pressing down, rotating retainer counter-clockwise slightly, then releasing.
5. Remove lever and its springs and washers.
6. Remove transmission to clutch bell housing retaining bolts and pull transmission rearward until drive pinion clears clutch, then remove transmission.
7. To install, place ½ teaspoon of short fibre grease in pinion shaft pilot bushing, taking care not to get any grease on flywheel face.
8. Align clutch disc and backing plate with a spare drive pinion shaft or clutch aligning tool, then carefully install transmission.
9. Install transmission to bell housing bolts, tightening to 50 ft. lbs. torque.
10. Install gear shift lever, shift into any gear and tighten yoke nut to 95-105 ft. lbs. torque.
11. Install universal joint, speedometer cable and brake cable.
12. Adjust clutch as described in "Clutch" above.
13. Install transmission drain plug and fill transmission with lubricant.
14. Road test.

5-Speed and 433D Transmission Removal

1. Drain lubricant.
2. Remove gearshift lever, floor mat and floor cover over transmission.
3. Disconnect parking brake cable, speedometer cable and driveshaft.
4. Loosen flange nut and drop center bearing if so equipped.
5. Position a transmission jack under transmission and remove clutch housing to transmission bolts.
6. Slide transmission rearward until pinion shaft clears clutch (about 6"), then lower jack slightly. Move transmission to the left just enough for the main drive pinion to clear clutch housing, then lower transmission.
7. Installation is the reverse order of the above procedure. Align clutch backing plate and disc with a spare drive pinion shaft or clutch aligning tool before inserting transmission drive pinion and be sure splines on shaft align with clutch hub splines before inserting. Tighten bell housing to transmission bolts to 100 ft. lbs. torque and driveshaft flange nut to 125 ft. lbs. torque.
8. Fill with lubricant and adjust clutch.
9. Road test.

Gearshift Linkage Adjustment

1970-71 B Series 3-Speed (Top Cover)

1. Remove both shift rod swivels from transmission shift levers. Make sure transmission shift levers are in neutral (middle detent) position.
2. Move shift lever to line up locating slots in bottom of steering column shift housing and bearing housing. Install suitable tool in slot and lock ignition switch.
3. Place screwdriver or suitable tool between crossover blade and second-third lever at steering column so that both lever pins are engaged by cross-over blade.
4. Set first-reverse lever on transmission to reverse position (rotate clockwise).
5. Adjust first-reverse rod swivel by loosening clamp bolt and sliding swivel along rod so it will enter first-reverse lever at transmission. Install washers and clip. Tighten swivel bolt to 100 in. lbs.
6. Remove gearshift housing locating tool, unlock ignition switch, and shift column lever into neutral position.
7. Adjust second-third rod swivel by loosening clamp bolt and sliding swivel along rod so it will enter second-third lever at transmission. Install washers and clip. Tighten swivel bolt to 100 in. lbs.
8. Remove tool from crossover blade at steering column, and shift through all gears to check adjustment and cross-over smoothness.

Gearshift Interlock Adjustment

1970-71 B Series All Synchromesh 3-Speed (Side Cover)

1. Inspect condition of clutch pedal rubber stop. If stop is damaged, install new stop.
2. On six cylinder models disconnect the interlock rod by loosening rod swivel screw.
3. Adjust fork rod by turning self-locking self-adjusting nut to provide 3/32" free movement at end of fork. This movement will provide prescribed one inch play at pedal.
4. Place transmission in neutral. The interlock pawl will enter slot in first-reverse lever.
5. Loosen swivel clamp bolt and slide swivel on rod to enter pawl. Install washers and clip. Hold interlock pawl forward and tighten swivel clamp bolt to 100 in. lbs. Clutch pedal must be in full return position during the adjustment.
6. Disengage clutch and shift half way to first or reverse. Clutch should now be held down by interlock to within one or two in. of floor.

3-Speed Linkage Adjustment

All Models 1969

1. With the second and third control rod disconnected from the lever on the column, and first and reverse control rod disconnected at the transmission lever, position both transmission levers in neutral.
2. Check for axial freedom of the shift levers in the column. If the

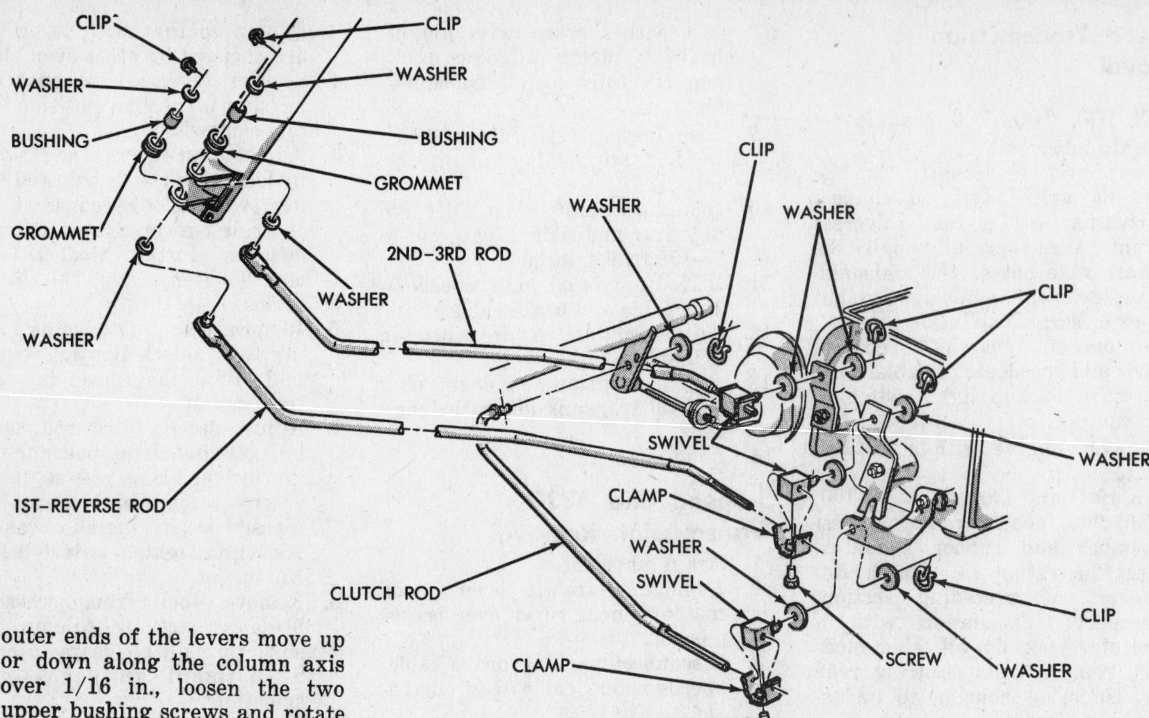

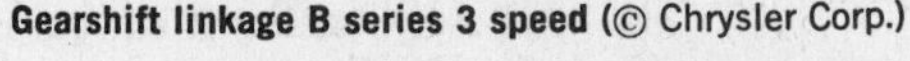
Gearshift linkage B series 3 speed (© Chrysler Corp.)

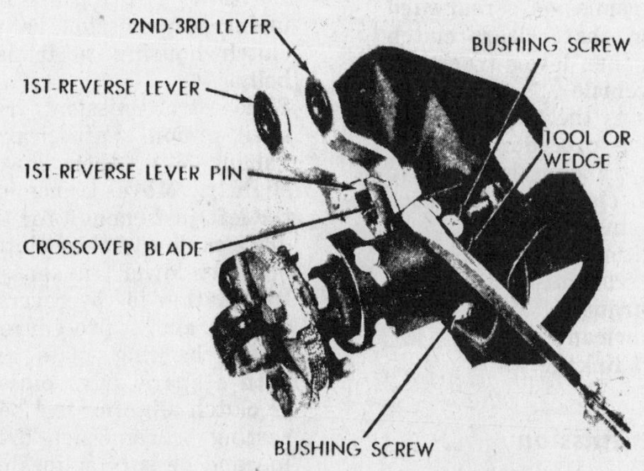

Gearshift lever adjustment (© Chrysler Corp.)

outer ends of the levers move up or down along the column axis over 1/16 in., loosen the two upper bushing screws and rotate the plastic bushing, downward, until all of the axial play is eliminated. Retighten bushing screws.

3. Wedge a screwdriver between the crossover blade and the second and third lever, so that the crossover blade is engaged with both lever crossover pins.
4. Adjust the swivel on the end of second and third rod until the stub shaft of the swivel enters the hole in the column lever. Install washers and clip. Tighten swivel lock nut to 70 in. lbs.
5. Slide the clamp and swivel on the end of the first and reverse control rod until the swivel stub shaft enters the hole in the transmission lever. Install washers and clip. Tighten the swivel clamp bolt to 100 in. lbs.

All Models 1961-68

1. If shift lever does not move smoothly through neutral from the second/third position to the first/reverse position, the cross-over must be adjusted. With transmission in neutral, loosen first/reverse control rod swivel at shift lever. Move lever until notches in both levers are aligned, then tighten control rod swivel nut.
2. To adjust control rods, place transmission in neutral, then loosen and back off both adjusting nuts at control rod adjusting swivels.
3. Move cross-over pin into engagement with second/third lever slot. Without moving second-/third shift lever, adjust and tighten second/third shift rod swivel nuts to 70 in. lbs. torque.
4. Move shift lever to line up slots in lever hubs (first/reverse side neutral), then, without moving first/reverse lever, adjust and tighten first/reverse swivel nuts to 70 in. lbs. torque.
5. Road test truck. If shift from first to second or from third to reverse is not smooth, readjust the first/reverse rod swivel nuts to eliminate difficulty.

Transfer Case

Reference

See General Section for overhaul procedures.

Transfer Case Removal and Installation

1968 and Earlier W100, 200, 300

1. Drain lubricant from transfer case.
2. Disconnect shift rod and de-clutch rod at the transfercase.
3. Disconnect input and output driveshafts from the transfer case, securing them to the frame.
4. If equipped with a power take-off, disconnect power take-off output shaft.
5. Disconnect control cable at top of power take-off housing by loosening locknut where cable enters shift plug on power take-off.
6. Turn power take-off control handle (in cab) counter-clockwise to unscrew control cable from power take-off shift plug.
7. Remove speedometer drive cable from speedometer sleeve assembly.
8. Disconnect parking brake cable at parking brake cam levers.

9. Support transfer case with suitable blocks or jack.
10. Remove transfer case to bracket bolts at right side of case.
11. Remove cotter pins and stud nuts securing transfer case to frame crossmember. Carefully lower transfer case and remove from truck. NOTE: To prevent damage to power take-off oil pump suction tube and to assure correct alignment of power take-off unit with transfer case, it is recommended that the power take-off be removed intact with the transfer case.
12. To install, use a jack to guide transfer case into proper position. If power take-off was removed, reinstall and align.
13. Position transfer case under crossmember, align mounting studs at top left of transfer case with mounting holes in crossmember.
14. Align right side of transfer case with mounting bracket and install bolts through mounting bracket and into transfer case, but do not tighten at this time.
15. Install washers and nuts on mounting studs and carefully tighten bolts and studs in an alternate manner until transfer case is properly located. Tighten bolts and nuts to 35 ft. lbs. torque.
16. Secure stud nuts with cotter pins and mounting bolts with lockwires.
17. Connect parking brake and speedometer cables.
18. Connect driveshafts, tightening to 300-400 ft. lbs. torque.
19. Connect power take-off output shaft and control cable.
20. Adjust power take-off cable by turning cable (or handle from inside cab) clockwise into the shift plug, after pushing shift plug into its housing until detent ball is fully seated in detent. Adjustment is correct when plug is fully retracted and control handle is fully pushed in. Tighten locknut.
21. Connect stabilizer to bracket.
22. Connect de-clutch and shift rods. Be sure spacer is installed at stabilizer red yoke. Fill with lubricant.

Transfer Case Removal and Installation

1969 and Later W100, 200, 300

1. Drain lubricant.
2. Disconnect speedometer cable.
3. Disconnect input and output shafts, securing driveshafts to frame.
4. Remove shift rod from shift rail link.
5. Using a suitable jack, support transfer case while removing frame crossmember.
6. Remove mounting bolts and lower transfer case from truck.
7. Installation is the reverse of the above procedure. Tighten mounting bolts to 35 ft. lbs. and driveshaft yoke bolts to 300-400 ft. lbs. torque.

Transfer Case Linkage Adjustment

1968 and Earlier W100, 200, 300 and All W500

1. Engage front axle drive and shift transfer case into low range.
2. Disconnect de-clutch and shift rods at shift levers.
3. Adjust the de-clutch rod length by turning adjusting yoke. When de-clutch lever clears rear end of slot in cab underbody by 5/8"., tighten locknut and install cotter pin.
4. Adjust transfer case shift rod length by rotating adjusting yoke until distance "A" between levers is 1/4". Install clevis pin, washer and cotter pin. Tighten locknut.
5. Road test vehicle to check operation of transfer case shift linkage.

Transfer Case Removal and Installation

All W500

1. Drain lubricant.
2. Disconnect speedometer and parking brake cables.
3. Disconnect input and output shafts. *Do not allow shafts to hang.*
4. Remove clevis pins, disconnecting de-clutch and shift control rods from transfer case rails. Secure rods out of the way.
5. Using a suitable jack, support transfer case while removing support bracket bolts.
6. Carefully lower transfer case from truck.
7. To install, raise transfer case with a suitable jack and align threaded mounting bolt holes in transfer case with holes in support brackets. Install bolts and tighten securely.
8. Connect speedometer cable and parking brake cable, adjusting parking brake as described in "Parking Brake" above.
9. Install and adjust transfer case shift and de-clutch rods as described above.
10. Connect driveshafts, tightening bolts. to 300-400 ft. lbs. torque.

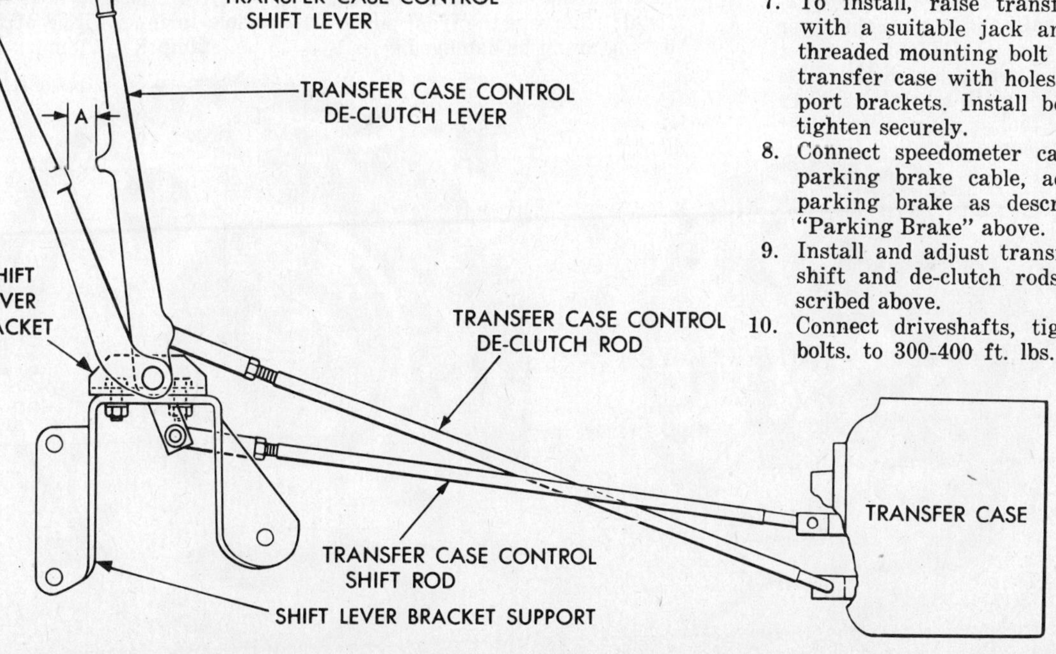

Transfer case linkage adjustment (© Chrysler Corp.)

Automatic Transmission

Reference

For complete overhaul procedures see "Automatic Transmission" section of the General Repair Section. The Dodge "Torqmatic" 6-speed transmission is the Allison automatic transmission.

Loadflite Transmission Removal

1. Remove the transmission and converter as an assembly; otherwise the converter drive plate, pump bushing, and oil seal will be damaged. The drive plate will not support a load. Therefore, none of the weight of transmission should be allowed to rest on the plate during removal.
2. Attach a remote control starter switch to the starter solenoid so the engine can be rotated from under the vehicle.
3. Disconnect high tension cable from the ignition coil.
4. Remove cover plate from in front of converter assembly to provide access to the converter drain plug and mounting bolts.
5. Rotate engine to bring drain plug to "6 o'clock" position. Drain the converter and transmission.
6. Mark converter and drive plate to aid in reassembly.
7. Rotate the engine with the remote control switch to locate two converter to drive plate bolts at "5 and 7 o'clock" positions. Remove the two bolts, rotate engine again and remove the other two bolts. CAUTION: Do not rotate converter on drive plate by prying with a screwdriver or similar tool as drive plate might become distorted. Also the starter should never be engaged if drive plate is not attached to converter with at least one bolt or if transmission case to engine block bolts have been loosened.
8. Disconnect battery ground cable.
9. Remove the starter.
10. Remove wire from the neutral starting switch.
11. Remove gearshift cable from the transmission and the lever.
12. Disconnect the throttle rod from bellcrank at left side of transmission bell housing.
13. Disconnect the oil cooler lines at transmission and remove the oil filler tube. Disconnect the speedometer cable.
14. Disconnect the front universal joint (A-100 models with 146″ wheel base) and tie the propeller shaft out of the way.
15. Disconnect the propeller shaft at the rear universal joint (models with 128″ wheelbase) and carefully pull the shaft assembly out of the extension housing.
16. Install engine support fixture that will support fixture hooks to the front spring rear shackles.
17. On A-100 models loosen horizontal bolt at the upper end of extension housing support bracket.
18. Raise transmission slightly with jack to relieve load and remove support bracket or crossmember. Remove all bell housing bolts and carefully work transmission and converter rearward off engine dowels and disengage converter hub from end of crankshaft. CAUTION: Attach a small "C" clamp to edge of bell housing to hold converter in place during transmission removal; otherwise the front pump bushing might be damaged.
19. Lower front end of transmission (models D-100, D-200, P-200) below the rear end of engine, carefully move assembly forward sliding extension housing over crossmember and remove from under vehicle.
20. On D-300, P-300 models, remove the crossmember and lower the transmission and remove the assembly.

Installation

1. Install transmission and converter as an assembly. The drive plate will not support a load. Do not allow weight of transmission to rest on the plate during installation.
2. Rotate pump rotors until the two small holes in handle of tool C-3881 are vertical.
3. Carefully slide converter assembly over input shaft and reaction shaft. Make sure converter impeller shaft slots are also vertical and fully engage front pump inner rotor lugs.
4. Use a "C" clamp on edge of converter housing to hold converter in place during transmission installation.
5. Converter drive plate should be free of distortion and drive plate to crankshaft bolts tightened to 55 ft. lbs. torque. Grease converter hub hole in crankshaft.
6. Using a suitable jack, position transmission and converter assembly in alignment with engine.
7. Rotate converter so mark on converter (made during removal) will align with mark on drive plate. The offset holes in plate are located next to the 1/8″ hole in inner circle of the plate. A stamped "V" mark identifies

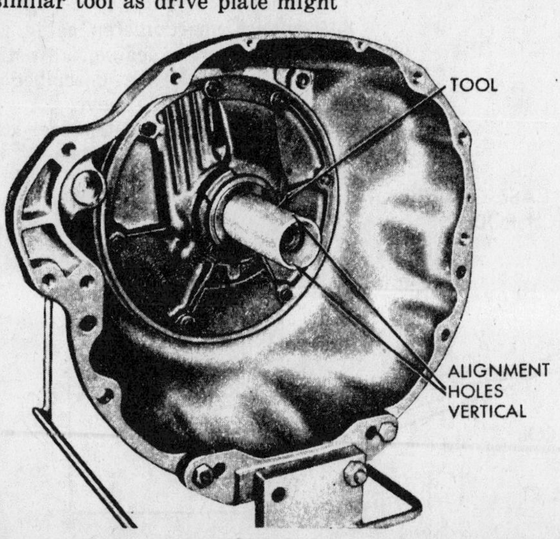

Aligning pump rotors (© Chrysler Corp.)

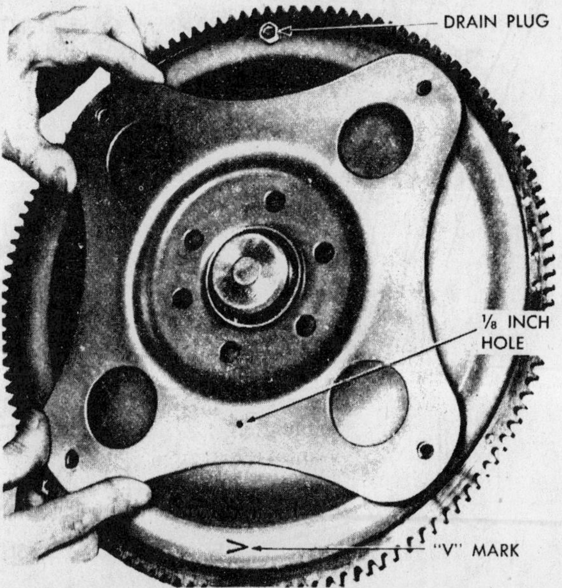

Converter & drive plate markings (© Chrysler Corp.)

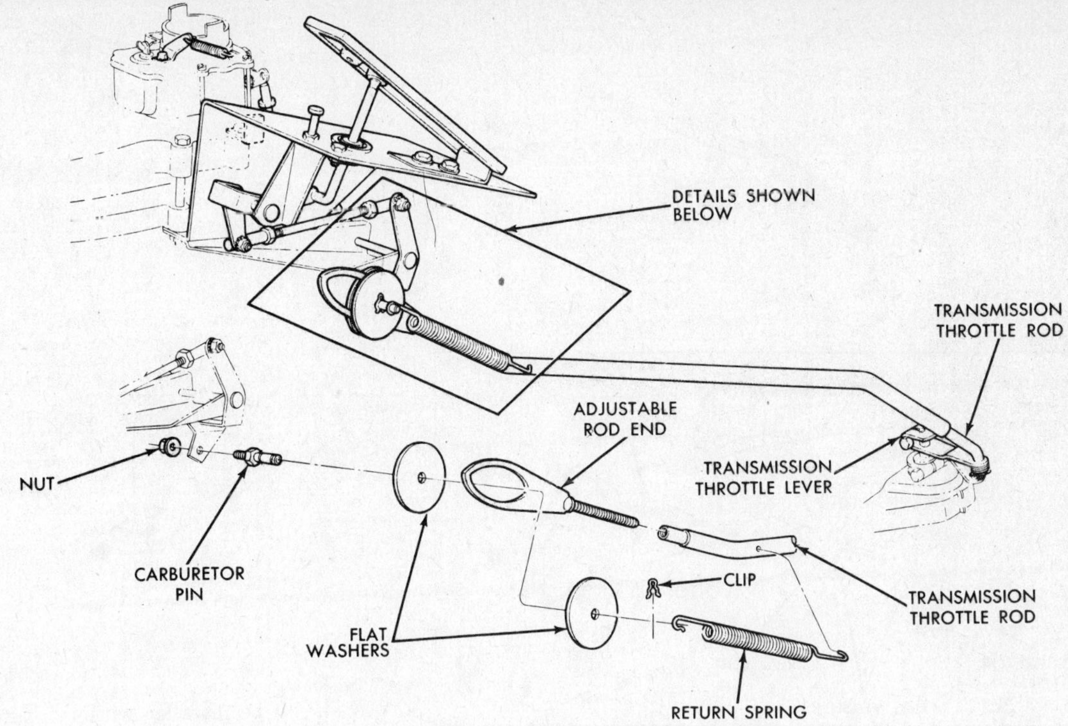

Transmission throttle linkage 225 eng. (P-200 & 300) (© Chrysler Corp.)

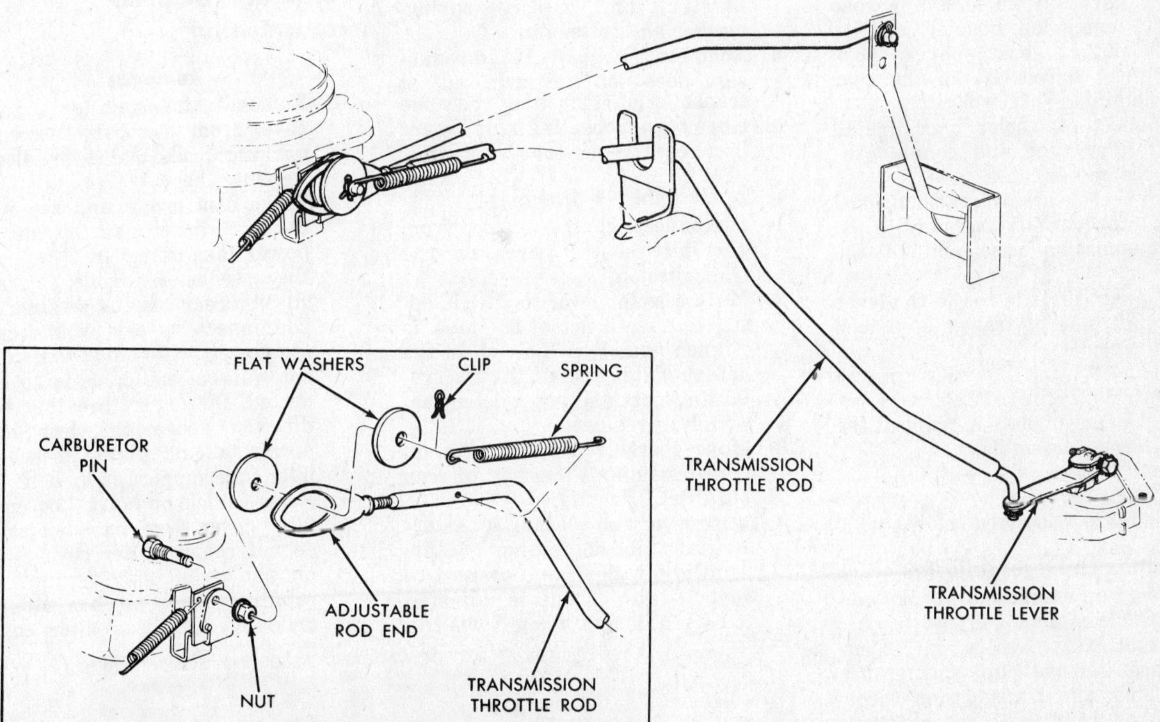

Transmission throttle linkage 383 eng. (D-100, D-200, D-300) (© Chrysler Corp.)

the offset hole in converter front cover. Carefully work transmission assembly forward over engine block dowels with converter hub entering the crankshaft opening.

8. Install converter housing to engine bolts and tighten to 28 ft. lbs.
9. Install the two lower drive plate to converter bolts and tighten to 270 in. lbs. torque.
10. Install starting motor and connect battery ground cable.
11. Rotate engine and install two remaining drive plate to converter bolts.
12. Install crossmember and tighten attaching bolts to 90 ft. lbs. torque. Lower transmission so that extension housing is aligned and rests on the rear mount. Install bolts and tighten to 40 ft. lbs. torque.
13. Remove transmission jack and engine support fixture, then install tie-bars under the transmission.
14. On models with short extension housing, connect the driveshaft to the parking brake drum flange or transmission flange. On models with long extension hous-

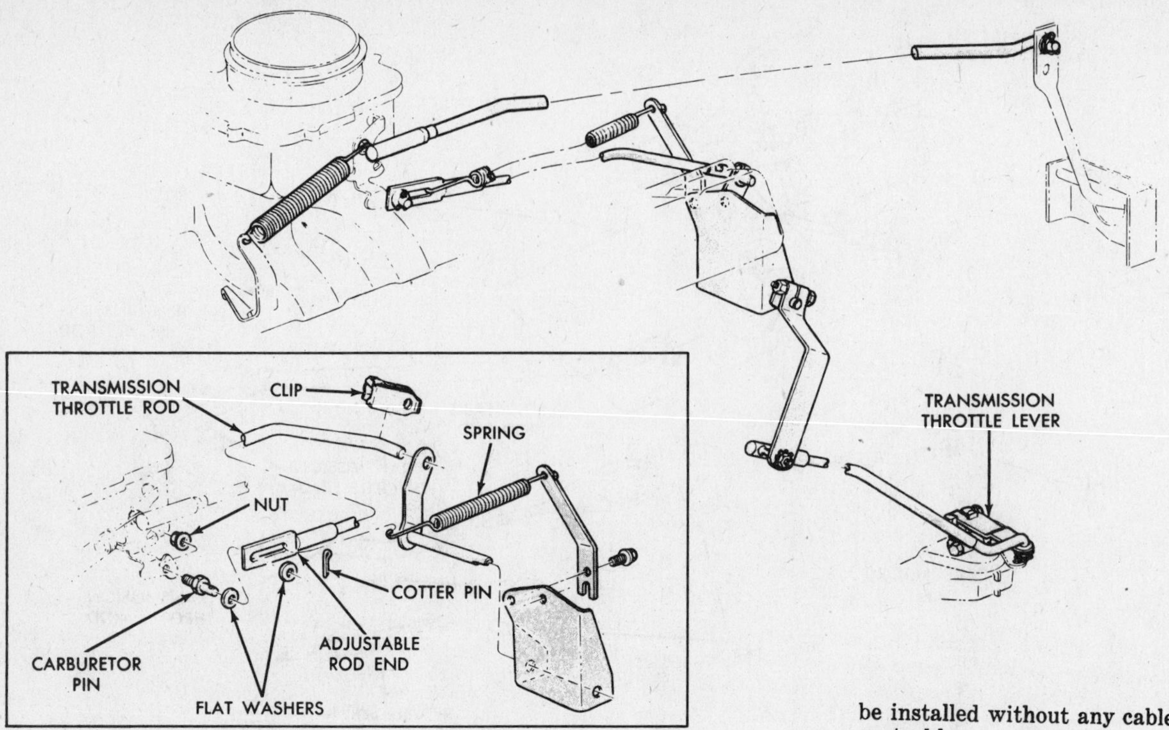

Transmission throttle linkage 318 eng. (© Chrysler Corp.)

ing, carefully guide sliding yoke into extension housing and on the output shaft splines. Then connect driveshaft to the rear axle pinion shaft yoke.

15. Connect oil cooler lines, install oil filler tube and connect the speedometer cable.
16. Connect gearshift cable or rod and torqueshaft assembly to the transmission case and to the lever.
17. Connect throttle rod to the lever at left side of transmission bell housing.
18. Connect wire to back-up and neutral starting switch.
19. Install cover plate in front of the converter assembly.
20. Refill transmission with fluid.
21. Adjust throttle and gearshift linkage as described below

Throttle Linkage Adjustment

1. Warm up engine until choke and fast idle cam are released.
2. On all except 318 cu. in. V8 engines, remove clip, spring, flat washer and transmission throttle rod from the carburetor pin. Holding transmission throttle lever forward against its stop, adjust rod end so rear of slot contacts carburetor pin. Reinstall washer, spring and clip.
3. On 318 cu. in. engine, remove cotter pin, washer and transmission throttle rod from carburetor pin. Unhook spring from adjustable rod end. Hold transmission throttle lever forward against its stop and adjust rod end so front of slot contacts carburetor pin. Replace spring, washer and cotter pin.
4. Road test vehicle. If transmission does not kickdown, adjust transmission throttle rod one more turn, repeating adjustment if necessary one turn at a time.

Gearshift Adjustment

1. Disconnect control cable from gearshift control lever on the transmission.
2. Move selector lever to PARK position to see if detent assembly is aligned with PARK notch in the detent plate. Loosen the two retaining nuts and align detent assembly if required.
3. Move gearshift control lever on transmission all the way to rear (in PARK detent).
4. With lever and selector set as described above, adjust cable length with clevis and connect to control lever. Cable is adjusted to correct length when clevis can be installed without any cable or control lever movement.

Torqmatic 6-Speed Transmission

Removal

1. Remove transmission access cover from floor pan. Disconnect parking brake cable by disconnecting the cable clevis of the brake cam levers and removing cable bracket at right-hand power take-off cover. Disconnect the speedometer cable at transmission rear bearing retainer.
2. Disconnect battery around cable at power take-off cover (left side) if battery cable is so connected. Disconnect breather hose directly above the left hand power take-off plate. Loosen oil filler tube support strap belt.
3. Raise vehicle on hoist. Loosen oil filter cover. Drain transmission, do not remove filter cover from oil pan as oil may "dump" too rapidly. When oil has stopped draining, retighten filter cover.

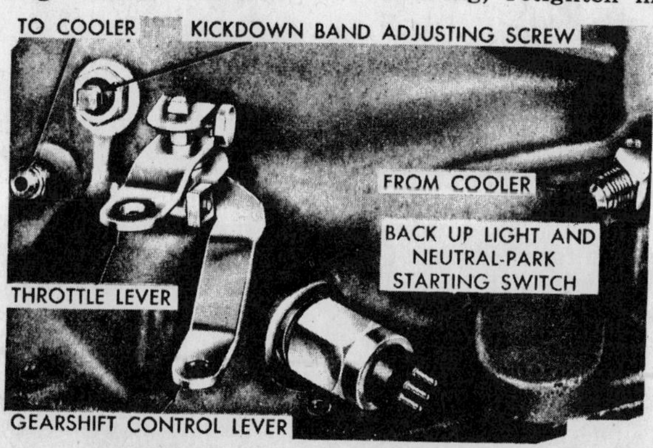

Load flite external controls (© Chrysler Corp.)

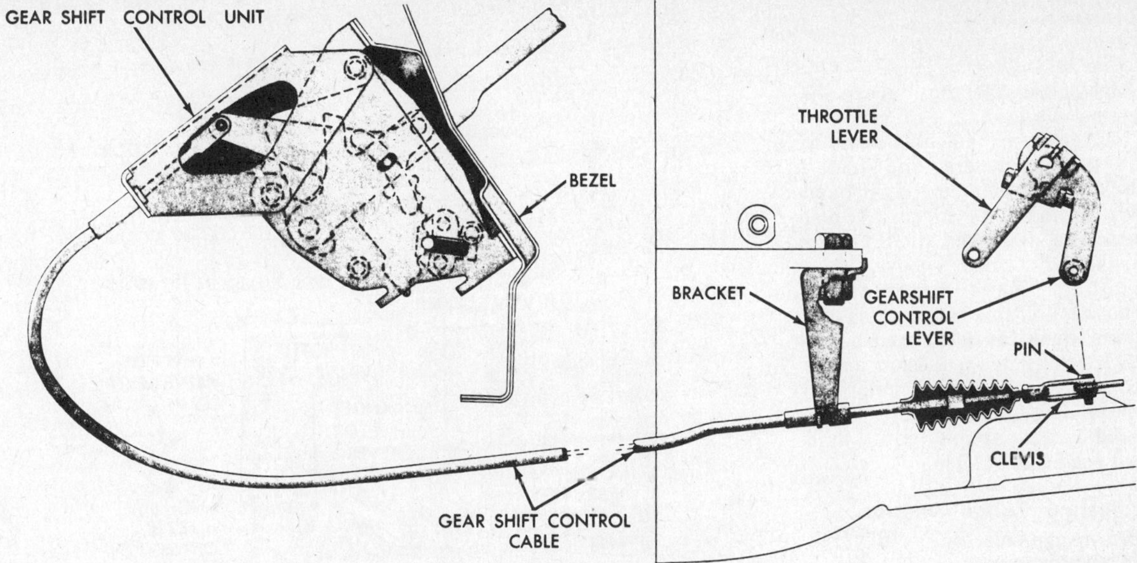

Loadflite gearshift control cable (© Chrysler Corp.)

4. Disconnect driveshaft at flange assembly. Disconnect filler tube at oil pan.
5. Remove cotter pins from the throttle control rod swivel and range selector lever cable (at levers on the left side of transmission). Remove range selector lever cable bracket from the transmission housing.
6. Remove the retarder slave cylinder with brackets from the power take-off mounting as an assembly.
7. Remove oil temperature warning light switch wire and switch from retarder on the right side of transmission.
8. Disconnect oil cooler lines, plug lines before removing converter and transmission. Through the access hole, at front of drive plate adapter, remove the six self-locking nuts which attach converter pump cover to the engine drive plate. CAUTION: Ignition system should be disconnected before removing nuts, to prevent accidental starting of the engine.
9. Straighten locking tabs on crossmember to converter support bolts, remove bolts.
10. Cut lockwire and remove crossmember to transmission rear support bolt.
11. Support rear end of engine with a suitable holding fixture. Support the transmission with a hydraulic jack placed so that oil pan does not support entire weight of transmission.
12. Remove both crossmembers, remove bolts and lockwashers which attach converter housing to engine drive plate adapter housing. Carefully move converter and transmission assembly back from the engine, lower and remove from under vehicle.

Installation

1. Position transmission assembly in alignment with drive plate.
2. Align studs in converter cover with the stud holes in the drive plate then push transmission assembly forward until studs fully enter holes in drive plate.
3. Install bolts and lockwashers on studs and tighten to 42-50 ft. lbs. torque.
4. Install converter pump cover to engine drive plate adapter housing locknuts and tighten to 19-23 ft. lbs. torque.
5. Install crossmembers and tighten bolts to 75-85 ft. lbs. torque.
6. Lower jack and engine support. Install bolts and nuts which secure converter housing to frame crossmember, tightening to 42-50 ft. lbs. torque. CAUTION: Be sure to bend lock taps on crossmember to converter housing bolt washers and to install lockwire at rear crossmember to transmission support bolt.
7. Connect oil cooler lines and install oil temperature warning light switch.
8. Install retarder slave cylinder and brackets to power take-off mounting as an assembly, making sure that bell crank engages valve pin. Connect control rod to lever.
9. Install range selector lever cable bracket on left hand side of transmission. Connect range selector lever cable and throttle control rod to their respective levers. Throttle control rod must be installed in outer hole of lever.
10. Adjust all linkages as described below. Connect driveshaft at parking brake drum and flange assemblies.
11. Connect oil filler tube to transmission oil pan. Tighten tube connector and support strap bolt

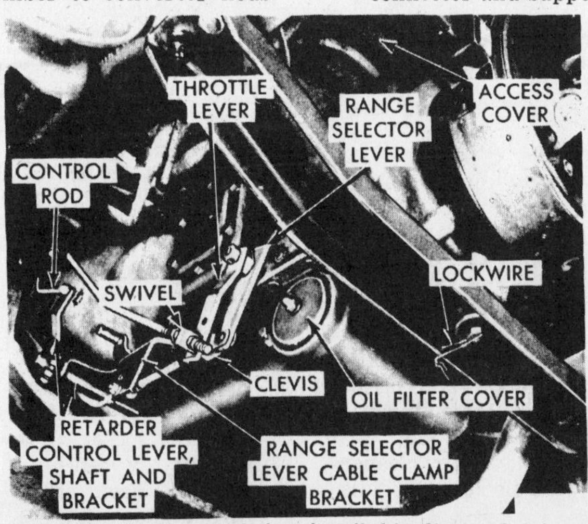

Torquematic transmission—installed (© Chrysler Corp.)

securely.

12. Connect battery ground cable to power take-off cover.
13. Connect breather hose above the left hand power take-off cover.
14. Connect the brake cable clevis to brake cam levers and install cable bracket on right-hand power take-off cover. Adjust brake as described in "Parking Brake Adjustment" above.
15. Connect speedometer cable. Check all oil line connections and filter cover for leaks and tightness. Install transmission access cover and replace floor mat.
16. Install new filter element.
17. Refill transmission with fluid and road test vehicle.

Adjusting Range Selector

1. Place range selector in "R" (reverse) position.
2. Remove cotter pin and disconnect cable from selector lever on transmission and move transmission lever all the way forward.
3. Place range selector lever (in cab) in R (reverse) position. Alignment is correct when the pin in cable connector is aligned with hole in transmission range selector lever. Adjustment is made by loosening locknut at connector and turning connector in or out until connector pin can be installed without moving cable or lever.
4. Install connector pin and cotter pin. Tighten locknut.
5. Test operation of selector in all positions.

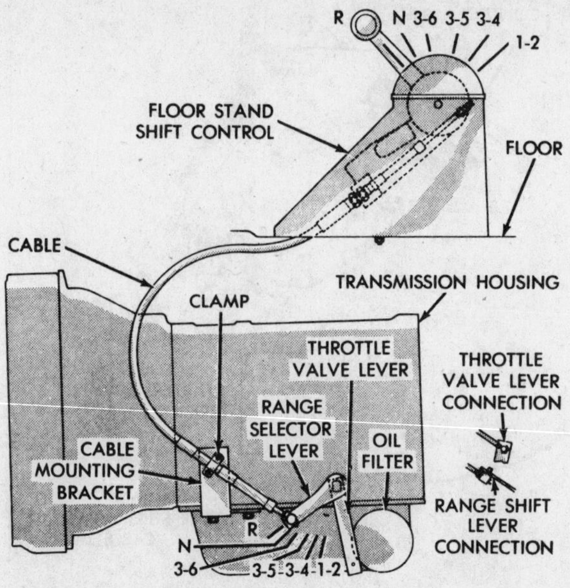

Typical range selector installed (© Chrysler Corp.)

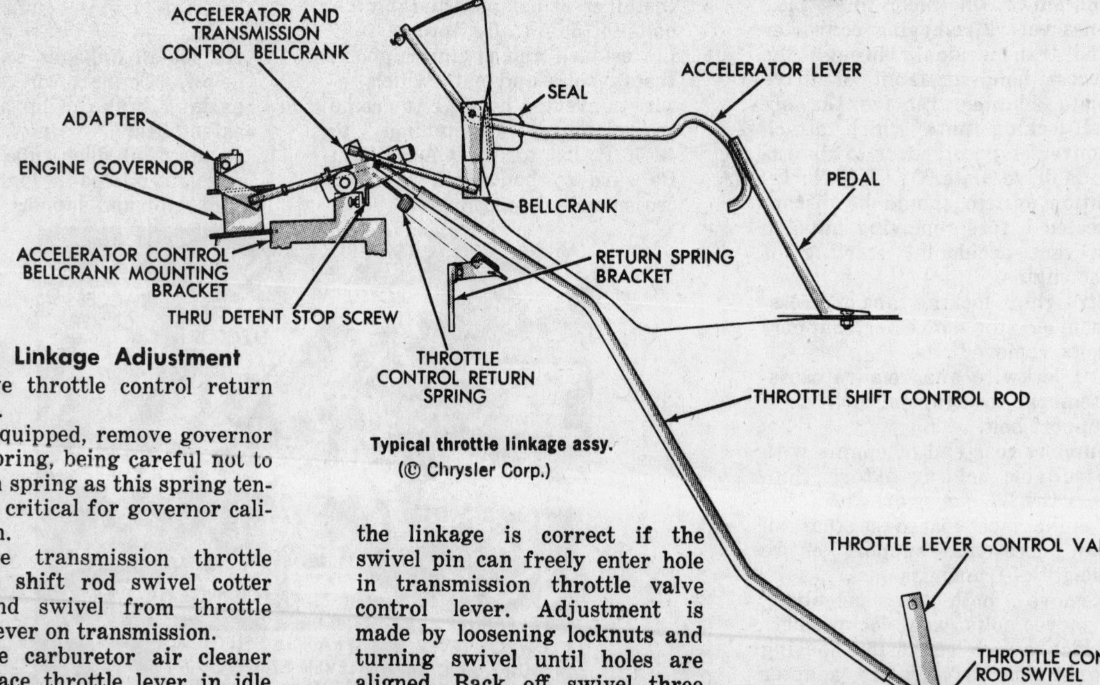

Typical throttle linkage assy. (© Chrysler Corp.)

Throttle Linkage Adjustment

1. Remove throttle control return spring.
2. If so equipped, remove governor arm spring, being careful not to stretch spring as this spring tension is critical for governor calibration.
3. Remove transmission throttle control shift rod swivel cotter pin and swivel from throttle valve lever on transmission.
4. Remove carburetor air cleaner and place throttle lever in idle position.
5. Adjust throttle control rod so that accelerator control bell crank stop is against bracket. Tighten nuts on throttle control rod.
6. Move carburetor throttle lever to wide open position.
7. Adjust wide open throttle stop bolt so that the bolt head contacts the bell crank when lever is wide open.
8. Push throttle control shaft upward until the travel of rod is stopped by wide open throttle stop. Rotate transmission throttle control lever at the transmission forward until lever is firm against internal stop in the transmission. At this position, the linkage is correct if the swivel pin can freely enter hole in transmission throttle valve control lever. Adjustment is made by loosening locknuts and turning swivel until holes are aligned. Back off swivel three turns, then tighten front and rear locknuts.
9. Adjust thru detent stop screw by turning stop screw to contact bracket on bellcrank when the transmission valve lever contacts its stop in the transmission. Back off 1/16" and tighten locknut.

Neutral Safety Switch Adjustment

1. Try starting engine in all range selector positions. The engine should start only in N (neutral) position.
2. If adjustment is required, loosen switch to bracket screws and rotate switch clockwise until starter circuit functions only when range selector is in neutral.

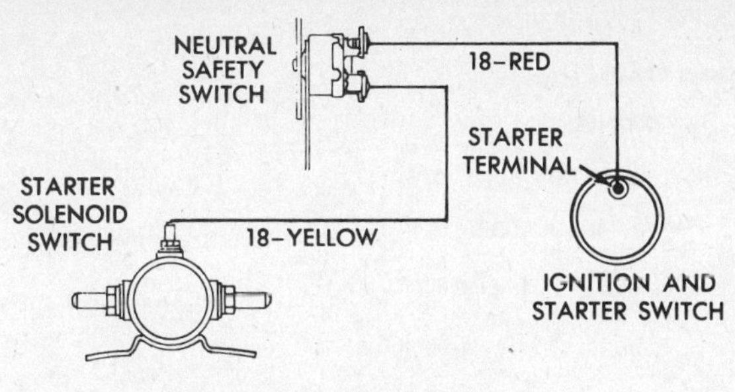

Neutral safety switch circuit diagram (© Chrysler Corp.)

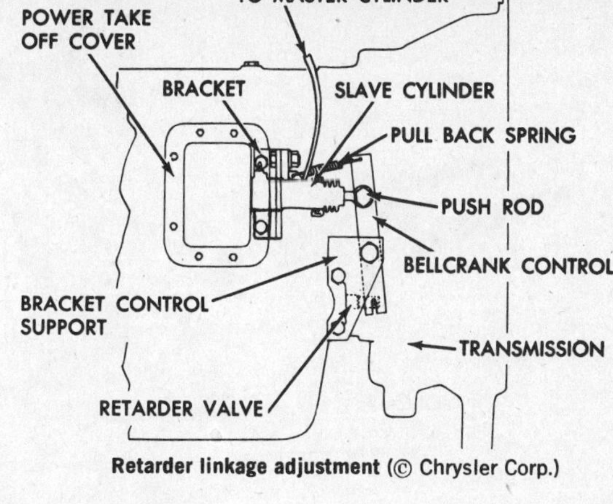

Retarder linkage adjustment (© Chrysler Corp.)

3. If starter does not engage at all, check for circuit continuity with a test lamp.

Retarder Linkage Adjustment

1. Adjust master cylinder push rod so there is a .010" free play (1/16" at pedal) between push rod and master cylinder, when piston is in fully returned position. NOTE: The system should be free of air and master cylinder reservoir filled to ½" of top.
2. Push rod on slave cylinder should travel ½" for full retarder action.

Drive Shaft, U Joints

Universal Joint Replacement

Lock Ring Type

Remove snap ring bushing retainers, then drive bushing out by tapping on yoke next to bushing opening. Pull out bearings then work cross up and out of yoke. To install, first position washer retainers (use new seals) on cross, then position cross in driveshaft yoke with grease fitting approximately parallel to other fittings on shaft. Grease rollers and tap bearings into place. Install snap rings. Lubricate slip joint.

Strap Clamp Type (Rear Axle Yoke)

Unbolt strap bolts and remove straps, bushings, seals and washer retainers. Install new components as required. When assembling, grease bearings. Install with grease fitting parallel to other fittings in drive train. Tighten strap bolts to 20 ft. lbs. torque.

Slip Joints

When reassembling slip joints make sure that arrows stamped on each side are matched as illustrated. This will assure proper universal joint alignment.

Center Bearings

Two and three piece driveshafts are supported in the center by a rubber mounted center bearing. On 500 and 600 models, note that the yoke cap behind center bearing is secured with tabs that are bent or straighten to secure or remove center bearing assembly. On all other models, the cap screws onto the yoke. The bearings are sealed type and cannot be lubricated. Grease retainers on both sides of bearing, however, to provide protection against dust and water. Coat slip joint splines with grease before assembly.

Vibration may result as a result of incorrect center bearing mounting. Loosen center bearing bracket mounting bolts. Jack up truck and let engine drive wheels. This will allow center bearing to seek its own alignment. Tighten mounting bolts to 35 ft. lbs. torque.

Rear Axles

Rear Axle Assembly Removal

1. Raise vehicle and support at front of rear springs.
2. Block brake pedal in the up position.
3. Remove rear wheels.
4. Disconnect hydraulic brake hose at "T" fitting or at each wheel.
5. Disconnect parking brake cable. NOTE: To insure proper drive line balance when reassembling, make scribe marks on the driveshaft universal joint and differential pinion flange before removal.
6. Disconnect driveshaft at rear universal joint bearing clamps and secure with wire to prevent damage to front universal joint.
7. Disconnect shock absorbers and remove rear spring nuts and U-bolts.
8. Remove assembly from vehicle.
9. To install, position rear axle assembly spring pads over the spring center bolts.
10. Install U-bolts and tighten nuts securely: to 50-80 ft. lbs. torque on 100 series trucks, 100-150 ft. lbs. torque on 200, 300 and all W series trucks, 400 ft. lbs. torque on 400 to 700 models.
11. Connect shock absorbers.
12. Connect parking brake cable.
13. Connect hydraulic brake lines. Install brake drums and adjust. Bleed hydraulic brake system.
14. Connect driveshaft universal joint in its original position, matching scribe marks made during removal. Tighten universal joint clamp bolts to 15 ft. lbs. torque.

Differential Service

For service and overhaul procedures for Eaton, Spicer and Dodge differentials and for locking type dif-

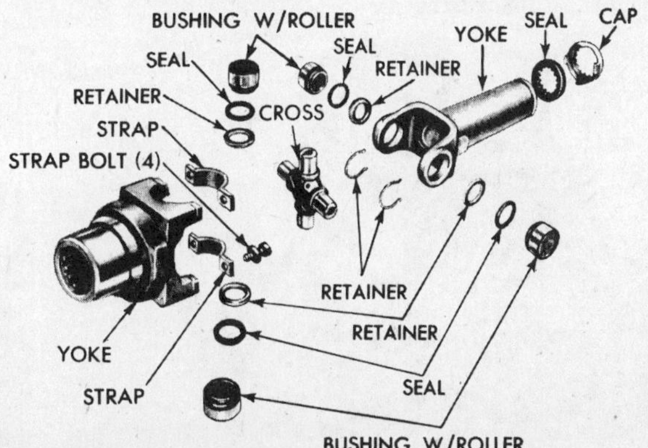

Strap clamp type universal joint (© Chrysler Corp.)

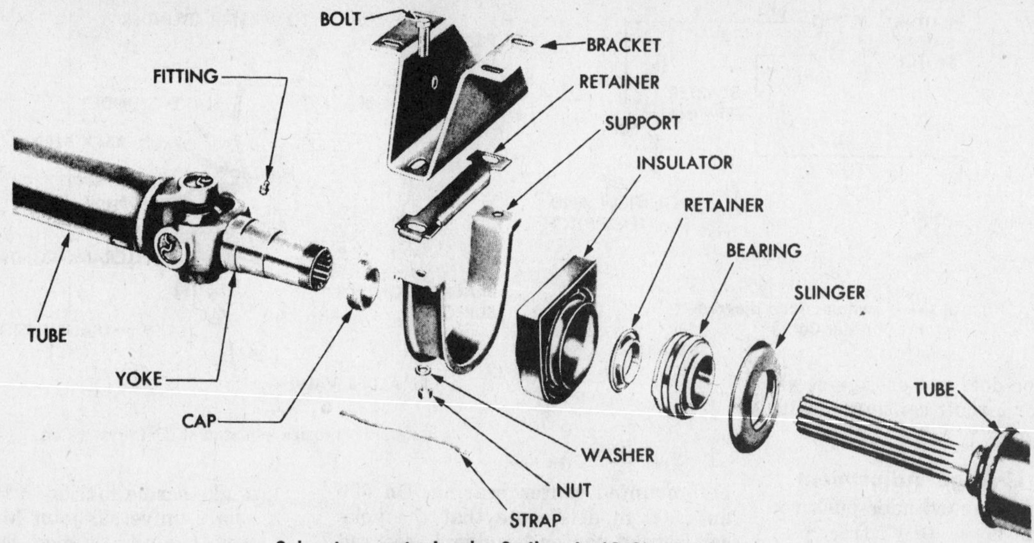

Spicer type center bearing & slip yoke (© Chrysler Corp.)

ferentials, see "Rear Axle" in the General Repair Section.

Rear Axle Shaft Removal and Installation

1970-71 Models

1. Raise vehicle and remove wheels and brake drums.
2. Drain lubricant and remove housing cover.
3. Turn differential case until pinion shaft lock bolt can be removed, then remove lock bolt and pinion shaft.
4. Push axle shaft in and remove "C" snap ring retainers from groove.
5. Carefully remove axle shaft.
6. Remove axle shaft bearing and seal from housing with a suitable puller.
7. When installing, use a new axle shaft seal. Use a new bearing if there is any question of axle shaft bearing. Wipe bearing cavity of housing and remove any burrs. Install bearing and seal using suitable installing tool.
8. Slide axle shaft into place being careful not to damage seal.
9. Install "C" snap ring retainers in groove of shaft and pull outward on shaft to insure that retainer seats in counter bore of side gear.
10. Install pinion shaft through case and pinions, aligning hole with lock bolt hole. Install lock bolt and tighten securely.
11. Clean housing and cover gasket surfaces and install housing cover, using a new gasket. Tighten cover bolts to 15-25 ft. lbs. torque. Install ratio identification tag under one of the bolts.
12. Fill housing with lubricant.
13. Install brake drum and wheel. Lower vehicle.

1964-69 100 Models—RA30, RA36 Axle

1. Remove wheel, drum retaining clips and drum.
2. Through hole in axle shaft flange, remove five nuts from axle shaft retainer plate. There is a lock under one of the nuts of the right hand retainer plate (adjusting) which is removed at this time.
3. Using a suitable puller, remove axle shaft.
4. Remove inner seal and install a new one.
5. Remove bearing retainer collar.

Replacement of bearing is accomplished by first grinding off a portion of the inner cone flange and chiselling off bearing roller retainer, then removing rollers and the rest of roller retainer. Use special puller tool C-3971 to remove inner cone.

6. Install a new seal in retainer plate. Use tool C-3971 to install a new axle bearing, first packing it with grease.
7. To install axle shafts, install new rubber asbestos gasket on left axle housing studs, then brake backing plate. Apply grease to outside diameter of bearing cup. Install foam gasket on studs of axle housing, then carefully slide axle shaft into position, tightening retainer plate nuts to 30-35 ft. lbs. torque.
8. Install rubber asbestos gasket and brake backing plate and bearing cup on right hand side of housing.
9. Measure and set axle shaft end play (both rear wheels off ground) as follows: Back off threaded adjuster on right hand side of housing until its inner face is flush with inner face of retainer plate. Carefully insert

Removing roller retainer (© Chrysler Corp.)

Flange ground off inner cone (© Chrysler Corp.)

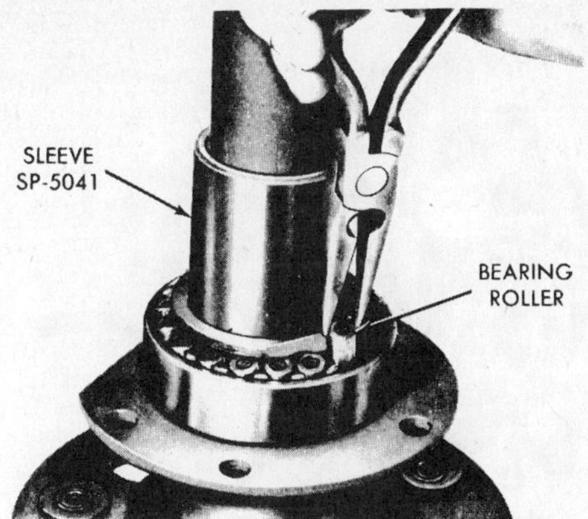

Removing bearing rollers
(© Chrysler Corp.)

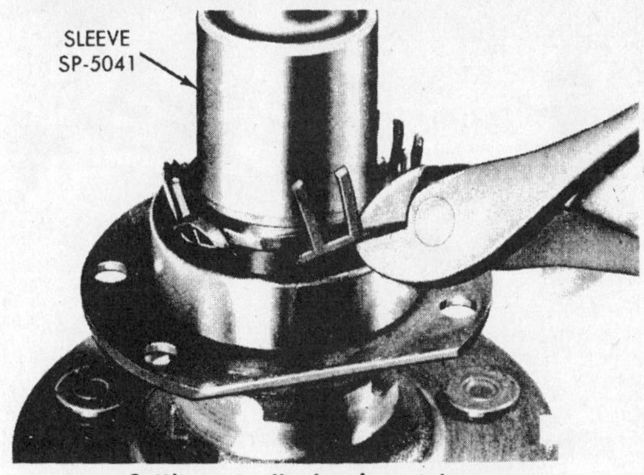

Cutting out roller bearing retainer
(© Chrysler Corp.)

Installing new bearing & collar
(© Chrysler Corp.)

Removing bearing inner cone
(© Chrysler Corp.)

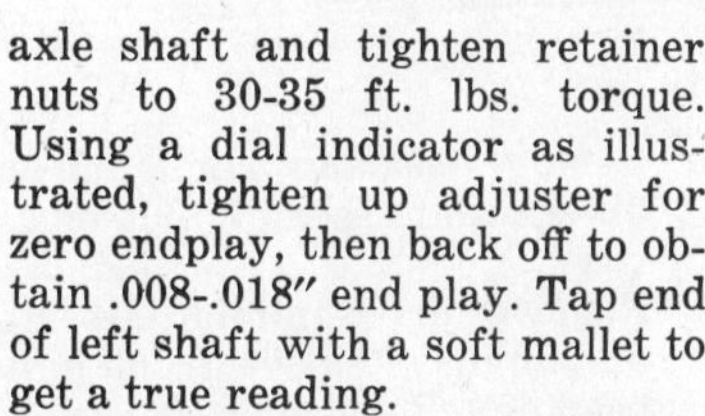

axle shaft and tighten retainer nuts to 30-35 ft. lbs. torque. Using a dial indicator as illustrated, tighten up adjuster for zero endplay, then back off to obtain .008-.018″ end play. Tap end of left shaft with a soft mallet to get a true reading.

10. Remove one retainer nut and install adjustor lock. Recheck end play, readjusting if necessary.
11. Remove dial indicator and install brake drum, drum retaining clips and wheel.

Rear Axle Shaft Removal and Installation

1961-64 100 Models—RA30, RA36 Axle

1. Remove wheel hub and drum assembly using tool C-319 or C-845.
2. Remove axle shaft key.
3. Disconnect brake line at wheel cylinder.
4. Remove dust shield and brake backing plate.
5. Remove axle bearing adjusting shims, axle shaft and bearing cup.
6. When installing, use a shim pack totalling .040″ on one side of axle housing, after greasing bearing and installing axle shaft.
7. Drive in bearing.
8. Install brake backing plate and dust shield, tightening nuts to 30-35 ft. lbs. torque.
9. On the opposite side of the axle housing, lubricate shaft bearing and install shaft.
10. Drive in bearing cup just far enough to eliminate end play.
11. Check clearance betwen installing tool and housing flange. Add .013-.018″ to this measurement to estimate shim pack thickness and install shim pack on end of axle housing.
12. Carefully install brake backing plate and dust shield, tightening retaining nuts to 30-35 ft. lbs. torque.
13. Check end play and add or remove shims to achieve .013-.018″ end play if necessary.
14. Install axle keys, hub and drum assemblies and wheels.
15. Connect brake lines and bleed hydraulic brake system.

Measuring drive axle end play
(© Chrysler Corp.)

RA115, Spicer Model 60 and 70 —All 200, 300, 400 Series

1. Remove axle drive shaft flange nuts.
2. Rap center of axle shaft flange with a hammer to loosen shafts, then remove shafts.
3. When installing shafts, use a new gasket and tighten flange nuts to 30-35 ft. lbs. torque.

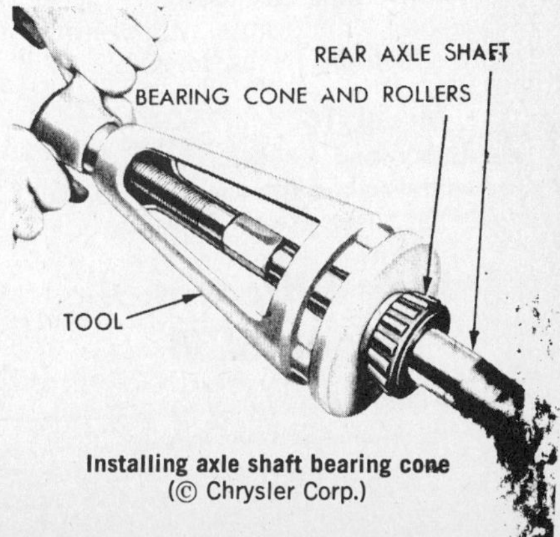

Installing axle shaft bearing cone
(© Chrysler Corp.)

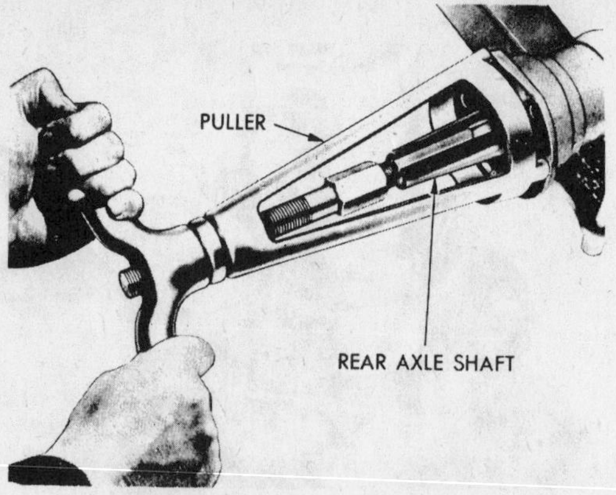

Removing axle shaft (© Chrysler Corp.)

Determining run out & zero end play (© Chrysler Corp.)

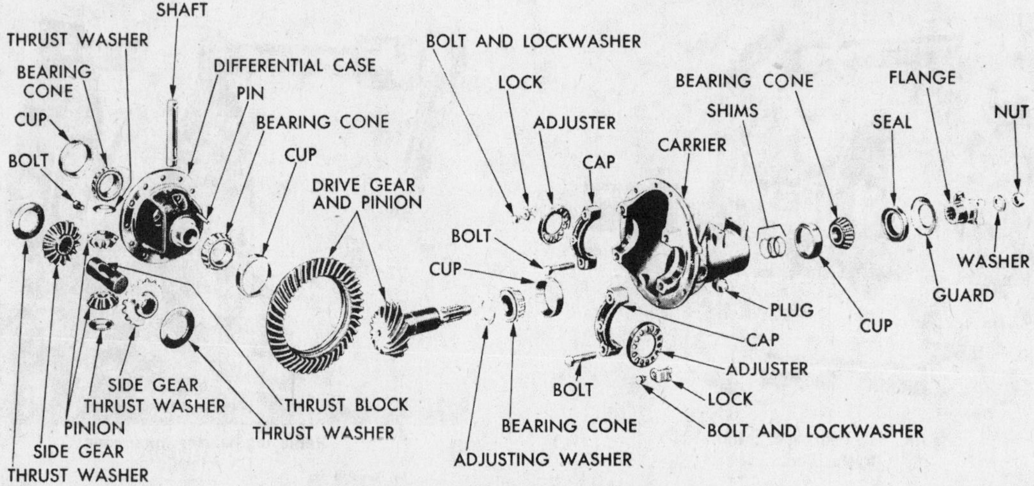

Differential carrier components (© Chrysler Corp.)

F147, H141 and Eaton 2-Speed Axles

1. Remove axle shaft flange nuts and washers.
2. Rap axle shafts sharply in center of flange with hammer to free dowels.
3. Remove tapered dowels and axle shafts.
4. Clean gasket contact area with suitable solvent and install a new flange gasket.
5. Install axle shaft into axle housing.
6. On axles having an outer wheel bearing seal, install new gaskets on each side of seal mounting flange.
7. Install tapered dowels, lock washers and nuts, tightening nuts to 40-50 ft. lbs. torque.

Model 1614, 1790A

Removal and installation is the same as described for the F147 above except that there are no dowels.

Dodge Differential Model RA36

IMPORTANT: Before proceeding with disassembly, consult the "General Axle Service" section for instructions on important pre-assembly inspections and checks.

Disassembly

1. Thoroughly clean carrier assembly.
2. Check drive gear runout (use a dial indicator) and, if more than .003 inch, replace gear and/or case.
3. Remove nut from drive pinion shaft and remove companion flange.
4. Remove drive pinion oil seal.
5. Punch-mark both differential bearing adjusters and caps. Remove adjuster locks, loosen cap bolts and adjusters to relieve bearing pre-load before removing bearing caps.

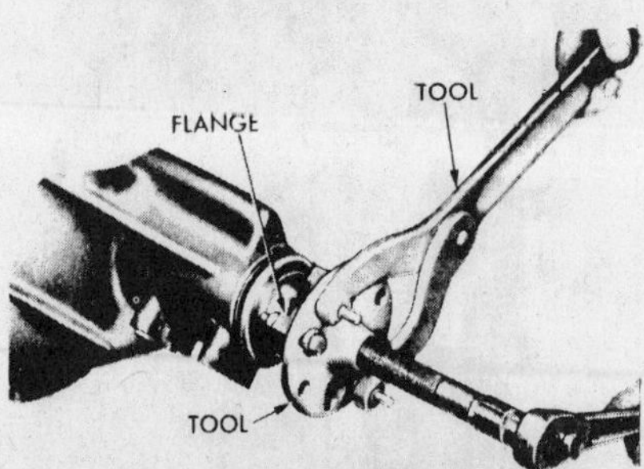

Companion flange removal (© Chrysler Corp.)

6. Remove bearing caps and lift differential assembly out of carrier.
7. Remove drive pinion assembly and shims. Remove front pinion bearing. Remove rear bearing from pinion shaft.
8. Remove drive gear bolts and gear from differential case. If drive gear runout exceeded .003 inch, mount differential case in carrier. Adjust differential bearings with adjusters to remove excessive play, then check runout of drive gear mounting flange. Replace the differential case if runout is greater than .003 inch.
9. Remove bearings from differential case.
10. Drive out differential pinion shaft lock pin from left side of case (drive gear side), then remove pinion shaft, pinions, side gears and thrust washers.
11. Clean all parts in a solvent and dry with compressed air. Bearings should be cleaned in clean solvent and rotated by hand until clean. After cleaning, blow dry with compressed air. *Do not spin bearings with air pressure as they might score due to absence of any lubrication.*

Inspect bearings and cups for wear

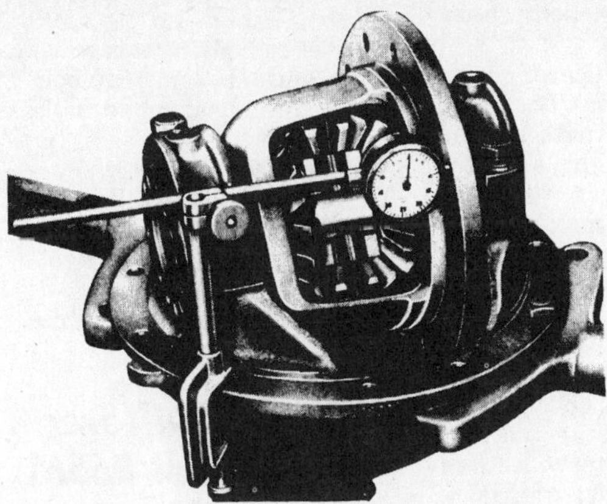

Determining runout on drive gear mounting plate (© Chrysler Corp.)

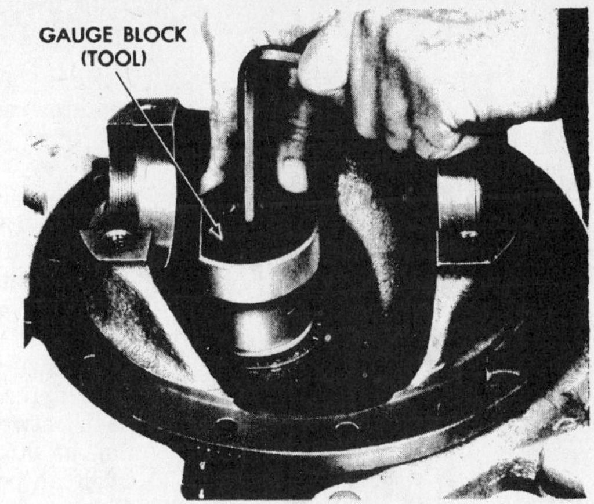

Installing gauge block on tool (© Chrysler Corp.)

or defects.

Check all machined surfaces for defects.

Replace axle shafts having twists or worn or distorted splines.

Assembly

A rear axle setting gauge set is required to properly adjust drive gear and pinion.

1. Position both pinion bearing cups in carrier housing.
2. Slide sleeve on main body, place rear pinion bearing on tool, and insert assembly in housing.
3. Place front pinion bearing on tool followed by compression sleeve, centralizing washer, and compression nut. Press bearing cups into place by tightening compression nut. Allow tool to rotate slightly so as not to damage bearings or cups during procedure. Correct pinion bearing pre-load is very important. When adjusting a differential, the proper pre-load will appear to be too tight, but it will correct itself to the specified pre-load when it reaches operating temperature.
4. Disassemble tool and lubricate the bearings with axle lubricant.
5. Place spacer on tool main body, followed by drive pinion rear bearing, sleeve and shims. Place assembly in housing, and place front bearing, compression sleeve, centralizing washer and compression nut on tool.
6. Tighten compression nut 180-200 foot-pounds and rotate tool while tightening. Turn tool with a speed wrench to allow bearings to seat properly.
7. Check bearing pre-load by revolving tool with an inch-pound torque wrench. Torque reading should be 20 to 30 inch-pounds, and uniform throughout full rotation of the tool.
8. Obtain proper pre-load torque by adding or removing shims (available in .014, .016, .018, 0.20, .024, .026 inch thickness). After correct preload is obtained, leave tool in place with compression nut properly torqued. This is necessary to obtain correct pinion setting.
9. Attach gauge block to end of tool.
10. Place arbor in carrier pedestals. Install bearing caps over arbor with a .002 inch feeler between the caps and arbor and torque caps to 5-10 foot-pounds.
11. Select a pinion spacer washer to fit between gauge block and arbor. The spacer selected in this way fits this carrier, and would be used with a zero (0) marked pinion. (Spacers are available in .002 graduations from .084 to .100 inch). Pinions are etched with a plus (+) or minus (—) sign, followed by a number (ranging from 1 to 4) or may be marked zero (0). If pinion is marked (+2), a .002 inch thinner spacer will be necessary. If pinion was marked (—2), a thicker spacer must be used. Therefore, as a general rule, pinions marked (+) use a thinner spacer while pinions marked (—) require a thicker spacer.
12. Place spacer washer on pinion shaft with chamfered bore facing gear teeth. Press rear bearing onto pinion shaft.
13. Slide shim pack selected during pre-load procedure over pinion shaft.
14. Lubricate pinion bearings with axle lubricant. Slide pinion shaft assembly into housing and place front bearing on shaft.
15. Lightly coat a seal with sealer and install in housing counterbore. Soak leather seals in thin oil for about 30 minutes, then work soft and pliable by rolling with a smooth bar. Synthetic rubber seals require only initial lubrication.
16. Install companion flange on pinion shaft and tighten nut 180-200 foot-pounds.
17. Install differential side gears and thrust washers.
18. Position two pinions with thrust washers to engage with side gears, and roll them into alignment with pinion shaft hole in

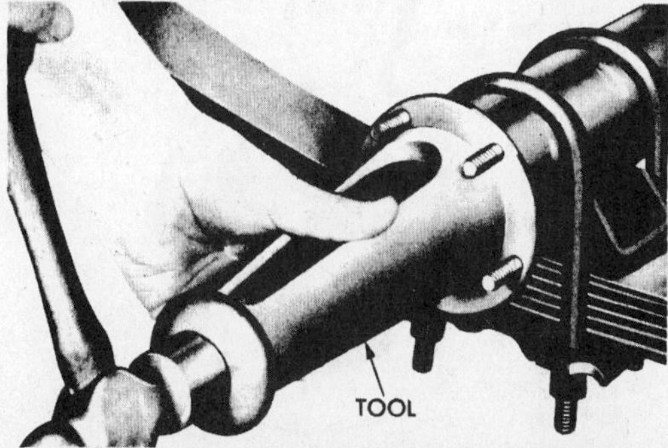

Installing bearing cup in housing (© Chrysler Corp.)

Installation of arbor in carrier (© Chrysler Corp.)

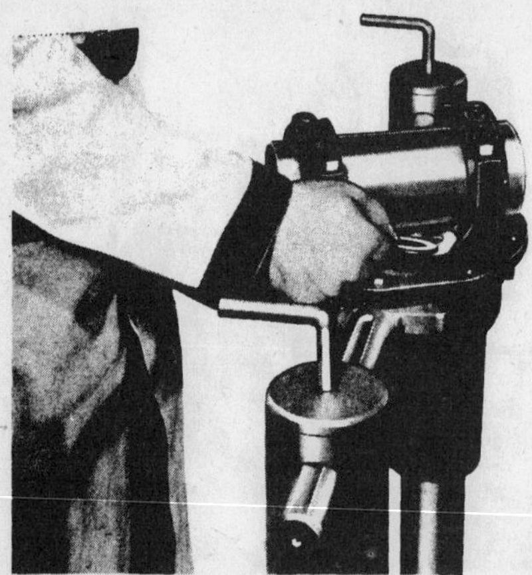

Determining spacer thickness
(© Chrysler Corp.)

case.

19. Lubricate gears in differential.
20. Push pinion shaft through first thrust washer and pinion, insert through thrust block and complete with other pinion and thrust washer.
21. Insert lock pin into case from right side (tooth side of drive gear) and into pinion shaft. Peen metal of case cover over pin to hold pin in place.
22. Place drive gear on differential flange and install and torque retaining bolts to 40-45 foot-pounds.
23. Install lubricated bearing cones on different hubs.
24. Place bearing cups on cones and position assembly in pedestals of carrier.
25. Screw in adjusters in both sides, matching identification marks with those on the pedestals. Adjusters should fully contact bearing cups. Finger-tighten bearing caps on pedestals with identifying marks matched. Adjusters can then be turned by hand when caps are snug to pedestals and properly located.
26. Turn bearing adjusters to create excessive gear lash. Tighten lower pedestal bolts 85-90 foot-pounds leaving top bolts hand tight.
27. Attach a dial indicator with pointer resting against back face of drive gear. Eliminate all end play by turning right adjuster clockwise. Also check for gear runout (.003 inch maximum).
28. Position dial indicator on carrier with pointer resting against face of drive gear tooth. Proper positioning of pointer is necessary to measure exact backlash. Rotate drive gear and check backlash between drive gear and pinion at 90 degree intervals, then stop at point of least backlash.
29. Turn left adjuster (drive gear side) clockwise to create .001 inch backlash between drive gear and pinion. Always move both adjusters the same amount in same direction to maintain zero end play. Correct bearing preload will be obtained in Step 31 by spreading pedestals apart enough to increase backlash to .006-.009 inch.
30. Install left adjuster lock and tighten left bearing cap upper bolt 85-90 foot-pounds.
31. Turn right adjuster clockwise until backlash reading is .006-.008 inch. This procedure forces pedestals apart creating bearing pre-load. Install adjuster lock.
32. Tighten right bearing cap upper bolt 85-90 foot-pounds and retorque other cap bolts.

If all adjustments have been correct, gears will be properly meshed and quiet in operation. Proper tooth contact is essential for quiet operation and long life; therefore, check tooth contact with red lead before installing in carrier assembly axle housing. See "General Axle Service" section for details on checking tooth contact.

Torque Chart

Axle drive shaft nut (cotter key type)	175-250
Axle drive shaft flange nut	30-35
Axle drive shaft bearing retainer bolt	30-35
Carrier to housing screw	40
Differential bearing cap bolt	85-90
Differential bearing adjuster lock bolt	20
Differential case bolt	45
Drive gear bolts to differential case (anti-spin)	40-45
Drive pinion yoke nut (two bearing pinion)	180-200
Drive pinion yoke nut (three bearing pinion)	325

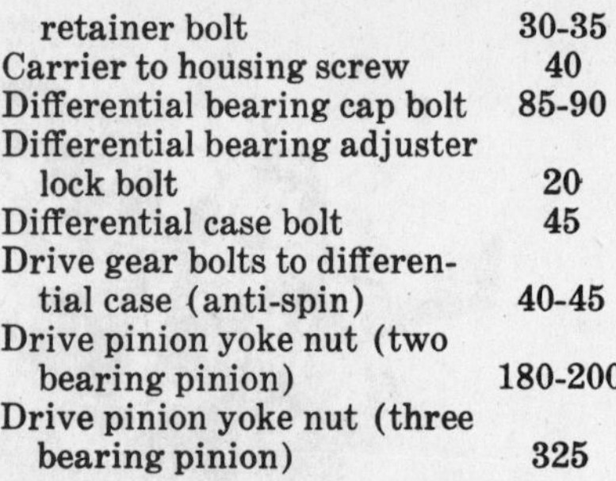

Dodge Differential Model R65M

Differential Case Pinions and Side Gears

After removing differential assembly from carrier, remove the drive gear thrust block from the drive gear side of carrier housing. Break weld on thrust block screw lock nut and remove the screw.

IMPORTANT: Before proceeding with disassembly, consult the "General Axle Service" section for instructions on important pre-assembly inspections and checks.

Disassembly

1. Drill out differential case cap locking pins.
2. Heat outside of case (not cap) with a torch and test temperature with a piece of solder. When solder just begins to melt, case is heated to proper temperature. *If case is heated beyond this temperature, inside washers may be damaged.*
3. Unscrew cap. Remove side gear and thrust washer.
4. Using a punch, remove pinion shaft lock pins.
5. Remove pinion shafts, thrust blocks, pinions, side gear and thrust washers.

Assembly

1. Install side gear and thrust washer in differential case.
2. Drive long pinion shaft into case

Checking backlash between drive gear & pinion
(© Chrysler Corp.)

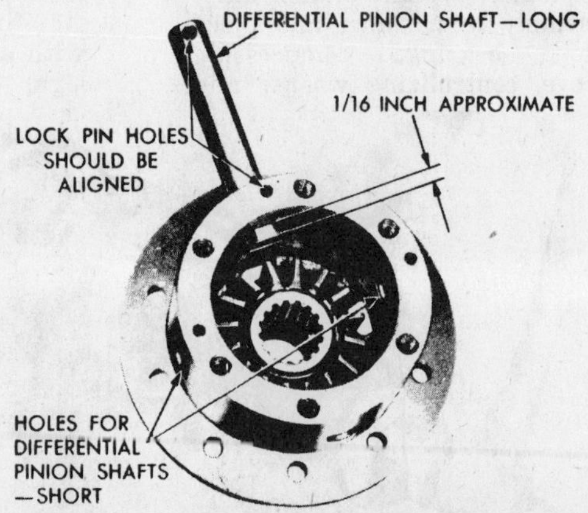

Proper installation of long pinion shaft in case
(© Chrysler Corp.)

until lock pin holes in shaft and case align.
3. Place washer and pinion on the end of long shaft protruding through case. Tap in shaft until flush with bottom of pinion.
4. Insert pinion shaft thrust block into axle drive shaft thrust block with long pinion holes aligned, and prick punched faces toward short pinion holes. Install this assembly in case, then drive shaft through blocks just flush with bottom of blocks.
5. Drive shaft through next thrust washer and pinion, making sure locking pin holes are lined up.
6. Drive one of short pinion shafts into case with lock pin hole aligned with lock pin hole in case.
7. Position a thrust washer and pinion on end of shaft; then drive shaft through pinion and into pinion shaft block. Install other short pinion shaft, thrust washer and pinion in same manner.
8. Drive three new locking pins, to a depth 1/16 inch below machined face of case. Peen case to secure them.
9. Install a thrust washer on remaining side gear hub; then place gear and washer in case.
10. Heat case to recommended temperature and install and tighten cap. Drill new 1/4 inch holes through case and cap; then install new locking pins.

Install drive gear thrust block before installing differential assembly in carrier housing. Thread thrust block screw through carrier having one thread visible inside carrier. Use heavy grease to hold block on screw.

Drive Gear Thrust Adjustment ....

Turn in thrust block screw about four turns to force block against back face of drive gear. Install lock nut on screw, back out screw 1/8 turn to create .006-.008 inch clearance: then tighten lock nut securely. Spot-weld lock nut to carrier and screw.

Torque Chart

Axle drive shaft nut (cotter key type)	175-250
Axle drive shaft flange nut	30-35
Axle drive shaft bearing retainer bolt	30-35
Carrier to housing screw	40
Differential bearing cap bolt	85-90
Differential bearing adjuster lock bolt	20
Differential case bolt	45
Drive gear bolts to differential case (anti-spin)	40-45
Drive pinion yoke nut (two bearing pinion)	180-200
Drive pinion yoke nut (three bearing pinion)	325

Dodge Differential Model RA115

Description

The RA115 is a full-floating rear axle with hypoid drive gear and pinion and uses a two-pinion differential assembly. The drive pinion shaft is supported by three tapered roller bearings (two front and one rear).

IMPORTANT: Before proceeding with disassembly, consult the "General Axle Service" section for instructions on important pre-assembly inspections and checks.

Axle Drive Pinion

After removing differential assembly from the carrier, remove the drive gear thrust block from the drive gear side of carrier housing. Break weld and remove thrust block adjusting screw.

Disassembly

1. Unscrew nut from drive pinion shaft and remove companion yoke.
2. Remove drive pinion oil seal.
3. Loosen drive pinion front bearing retainer lock screw and remove bearing.
4. Remove drive pinion shaft as-

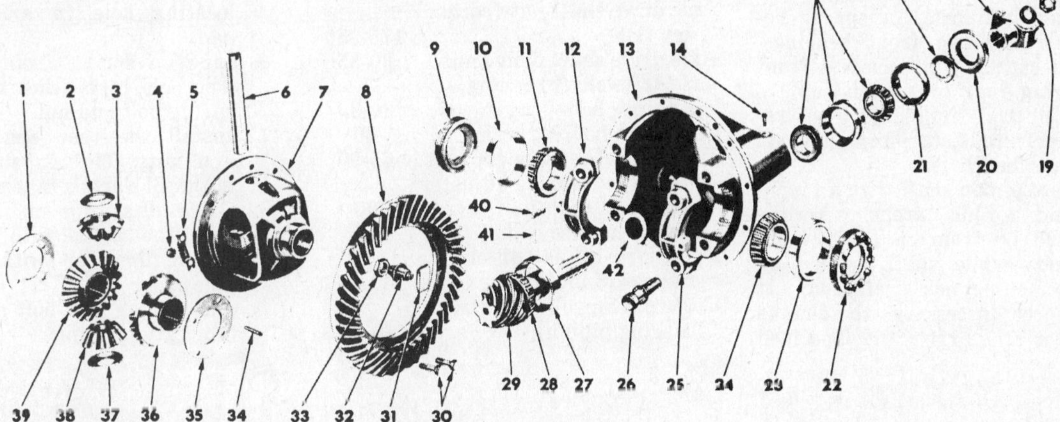

1 Differential side gear thrust washer
2 Differential pinion thrust washer
3 Differential pinion
4 Rear axle drive gear bolt nut
5 Rear axle drive gear bolt nut lock
6 Differential pinion shaft
7 Differential case
8 Rear axle drive gear
9 Differential bearing adjuster
10 Differential bearing cup
11 Differential bearing cone and rollers
12 Differential bearing cup
13 Differential carrier
14 Rear axle drive pinion front bearing retainer nut lock screw
15 Rear axle drive pinion front bearing assembly
16 Rear axle drive pinion front bearing washer
17 Rear axle drive pinion companion yoke
18 Rear axle drive pinion companion yoke nut
19 Rear axle drive pinion companion yoke nut washer
20 Rear axle drive pinion bearing oil seal
21 Rear axle drive pinion front bearing retainer nut
22 Differential bearing adjuster
23 Differential bearing cup
24 Differential bearing cone and rollers
25 Differential bearing cap
26 Differential bearing cap screw and lock washer
27 Rear axle drive pinion rear bearing cup
28 Rear axle drive pinion rear bearing cone and rollers
29 Rear axle drive pinion
30 Rear axle drive gear bolts
31 Rear axle drive gear thrust pad
32 Rear axle gear thrust screw
33 Rear axle drive gear thrust screw nut and lock washer
34 Differential pinion shaft lock pin
35 Differential side gear thrust washer
36 Differential side gear
37 Differential pinion thrust washer
38 Differential pinion
39 Differential side gear
40 Differential bearing adjuster lock pin
41 Differential bearing adjuster lock pin cotter pin
42 Rear axle drive pinion bearing spacer

Differential assembly model RA115 (© Chrysler Corp.)

sembly and front bearing forward cone from carrier.

5. Remove front bearing rear cone and pre-load spacer from pinion shaft, then pull rear bearing from shaft.
6. Complete disassembly by driving cups out of carrier.

Assembly

1. Install pinion bearing cups in carrier, making sure they are seated evenly. The front bearing cup is designed so that front bearing cones are seated in taper of cup from opposite sides. The cup is marked with the letter "Y", which must face toward the front (engine side). The front bearing cone that operates in this cup is also marked "Y". The cone must be assembled with corresponding marks mated together.
2. Press rear bearing on pinion shaft. Install front bearing rear cone on shaft.
3. Lubricate bearing cones and cups with axle lubricant and insert shaft assembly into carrier. Adjustment of pinion bearing preload is required whenever a change is made in pinion or bearings. Adjustment is made with spacers available in .020 inch graduations from .1790 to .1930 inch.
4. Select and install a spacer between the two front bearings. This spacer will separate front bearing rear cone from cup.
5. Install and tighten bearing retainer nut. Rotate pinion shaft to seat bearings.
6. Rotate pinion shaft with an inch-pound torque wrench. Torque should be from 35 to 70 inch-pounds while shaft is turning (40 inch-pounds preferred). It may be necessary to change spacer to arrive at specified torque.
7. Remove spacer from between two front bearings and install it in its proper location. After tightening bearing retainer nut, recheck bearing pre-load. Torque should be from 60 to 95 inch-pounds while rotating pinion (70 to 80 inch-pounds preferred). Tighten front bearing retainer nut lock screw.
8. Place front bearing washer on pinion shaft and install new oil seal.
9. Install companion yoke, washer and nut and tighten nut to 325 foot-pounds. Install cotter key.

Install drive gear thrust block before installing differential assembly in carrier. Thread thrust block adjusting screw through carrier with one thread inside carrier. Hold thrust block on screw with heavy grease.

Drive Gear Thrust Block ....

Adjustment ....

Turn in thrust block screw approximately four turns to force block against back face of drive gear. Install lock nut on screw, back out screw 1/8 turn to provide .006-.008 inch clearance, then tighten lock nut securely. Spot-weld lock nut to carrier and screw.

Torque Chart

Axle drive shaft nut (cotter key type)	175-250
Axle drive shaft flange nut	30-35
Axle drive shaft bearing retainer bolt	30-35
Carrier to housing screw	40
Differential bearing cap bolt	85-90
Differential bearing adjuster lock bolt	20
Differential case bolt	45
Drive gear bolts to differential case (anti-spin)	40-45
Drive pinion yoke nut (two bearing pinion)	180-200
Drive pinion yoke nut (three bearing pinion)	325

Locking Differentials

See General Repair Section for overhaul and service procedures for Dana and Sure-Grip locking differentials.

Rear Suspension

Rear Spring Removal and Installation

100, 200, 300 Series

1. Raise rear of truck with chain hoist of hydraulic crane until weight is removed from springs, wheels just touching the floor. NOTE: Truck must be lifted by jack or hoist under frame side rail at crossmember behind the axle being careful not to bend flange of side rail.
2. Place stands under side frame members as a safety precaution.
3. Remove nuts, lockwashers and U-bolts securing spring to axle.
4. Remove spring shackle bolts, shackle and spring front bolt, then remove spring.
5. To install, position spring on axle so spring center bolt enters locating hole in axle housing pad.
6. Line up spring front eye with bolt hole in bracket and install spring bolt and nut.
7. Install the rear shackle, bolts and nuts. Tighten shackle bolt nut until slack is taken up.
8. On headless type spring bolts install the bolts with lock bolt groove lined up with lock bolt hole in bracket. Install lock bolt and tighten lock bolt nut. Install lubrication fittings.

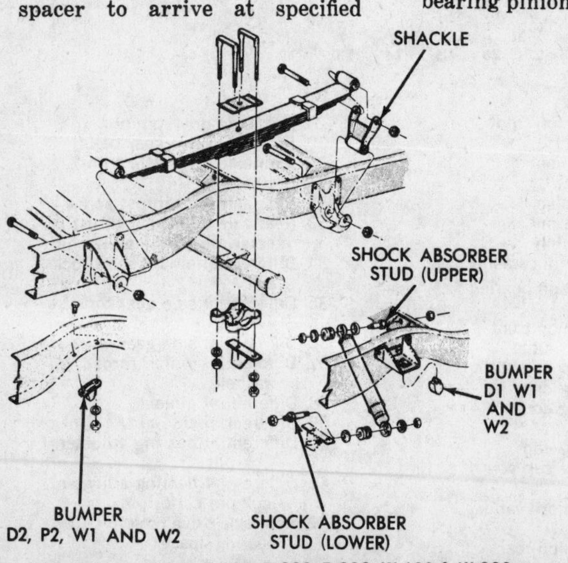

Rear spring models D-100, D-200, P-200, W-100 & W-200
(© Chrysler Corp.)

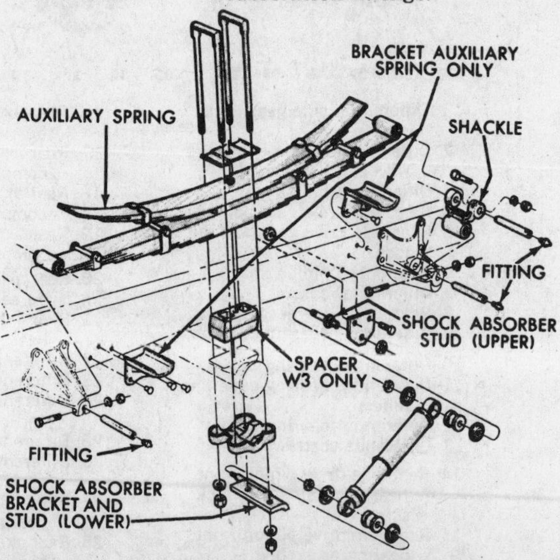

Rear spring models D-300, P-300 & W-300
(© Chrysler Corp.)

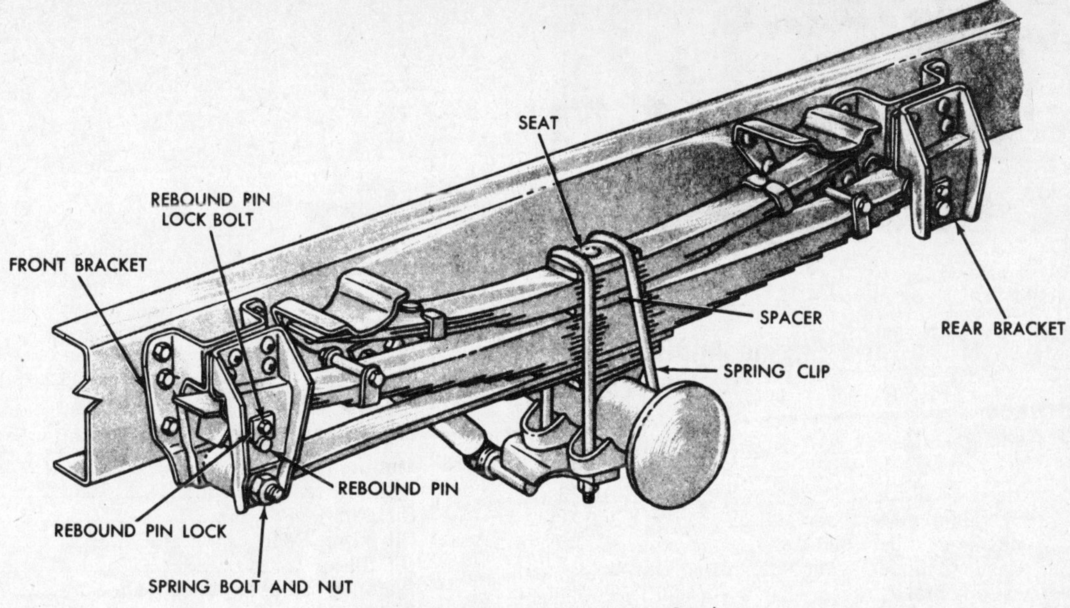

Vari rate suspension (© Chrysler Corp.)

9. Install U-bolts, new lockwashers and nuts, tightening until nuts push lockwashers against axle. Align auxiliary spring parallel with main spring.
10. Remove stands from under vehicle, lower truck so weight is resting on wheels. Tighten U-bolt nuts, spring eye nuts and shackle bolt nuts to specifications listed below.
11. Lubricate spring bolts and shackle bolts with chassis lubricant when equipped with lubrication fittings.

Installing New Leaf

1. Clamp spring in a vise, remove center bolt and bend clamp type clips back from spring leaves.
2. Insert long drift in center bolt hole and release vise slowly.
3. Remove assembly from vise and replace broken leaf.
4. Place spring assembly in vise, slowly tightening vise while holding spring leaves in alignment with drift.
5. Remove drift and install new center bolt.
6. Install nut, tightening to 15 ft. lbs. torque.
7. Remove spring from vise.

Variable Rate Spring Removal and Installation

1. Raise truck frame until weight is off rear springs with wheels still touching the ground.
2. Remove nuts from spring clips and remove spring clip plate. Remove spring clips.
3. If truck is so equipped, remove the auxiliary spring and spacer.
4. Install a "C" clamp on radius leaf to relieve load on spring eye bolt. Remove front eye bolt retaining nut.
5. Remove spring eye bolt and slowly release tension on radius leaf.
6. Remove rebound pin retaining lock from front bracket. Remove spring rebound pin. Repeat for rear rebound pin.
7. Remove rear spring.
8. If necessary, replace radius leaf eye rubber bushing.
9. To install, position spring in front bracket and install rebound pin. Install retaining lock.
10. Position spring in rear bracket, and install rebound pin. Install retaining lock.
11. Align spring eye and install spring eye bolt and nut. It may be necessary to draw the radius leaf eye into position with a "C" clamp.
12. Install auxiliary spring assembly if so equipped.
13. Install spring U-bolt plate and U-bolt seat. Install spring clips and nuts and washers, tightening nuts until they are snug.
14. Lower truck to the floor and tighten spring U-bolts to 400 ft. lbs. torque.

Spring Tightening Specifications (ft. lbs.)

Rear spring U-bolt nuts	D100	50-80
	W100, all 200, 300	100-150
Rear spring U-bolt nuts, VariRate	D400, 500, 600, 700	400
Rear spring shackle and eye bolt nuts	D100	65-105
	W100, all 200, 300	125-175

Ford and Ford Bronco

Index

Rear Axle

Rear Suspension

Specifications

Steering—Manual

Steering—Power

Transfer Case

Transmission—Automatic

Transmission—Manual

TUNE-UP SPECIFICATIONS

CU. IN. DISPLACEMENT	YEAR	SPARK PLUG GAP	DISTRIBUTOR POINT DWELL	DISTRIBUTOR POINT GAP	IGNITION TIMING DEGREES	CRANKING COMP. PRESSURE	VALVE CLEARANCE INLET	VALVE CLEARANCE EXHAUST	GOV. R.P.M. NO LOAD	FUEL PUMP PRESS.	IDLE SPEED STD.	IDLE SPEED AUTO.
SIX CYLINDER												
144	1961	.034	37-42	.025	4	170	.018H	.018H	—	4-6	550	—
	1962	.035	37-42	.025	6	170	.018H	.018H	—	4-6	550	—
Std. Tr.	1963-64	.035	37-42	.025	4	170	.018H	.018H	—	4-6	585	—
Auto. Tr.	1963-64	.035	37.42	.025	8	170	.018H	.018H	—	4-6	—	565D
170	1961	.035	35-38	.025	4	170	.018H	.018H	—	4-6	585	—
	1962	.035	35-38	.025	4	170	.018H	.018H	—	4-6	585	565D
Std. Tr.	1963-67	.035	37-42	.025	4[1]	175	.018H	.018H	—	4-6	585	—
Auto. Tr.	1963-67	.035	37-42	.025	8[1]	175	.018H	.018H	—	4-6	—	565D
	1968-71	.034	35-40	.027	6	175	.018H	.018H	—	4-6	525	—
200 Std. Tr.	1965	.034	37-42	.025	6	175	Zero		—	4-6	585	—
Auto. Tr.	1965	.034	37-42	.025	10	175	Zero		—	4-6	—	510
223 Std. Tr.	1961	.030	37-42	.025	4	150	.019H	.019H	—	3½-5½	500	—
Auto. Tr.	1961	.030	37-42	.025	6	150	.019H	.019H	—	3½-5½	—	500D
	1962	.030	37-42	.025	6	150	.019H	.019H	—	3½-5½	500	500D
	1963-64	.030	37-42	.025	4	150	.019H	.019H	—	3½-5½	500	500D
240 Std. Tr.	1965	.034	37-42	.025	6	175	Zero		4000	4-6	500	—
Auto. Tr.	1965	.034	37-42	.025	8	175	Zero		4000	4-6	—	500D
Std. Tr.	1966-67	.032	37-42	.025	6[2]	175	Zero		4000	4-6	500	—
Auto. Tr.	1966-67	.034	37-42	.025	10[2]	175	Zero		4000	4-6	—	500D
Std. Tr.	1968	.034	37-42	.025	6	175	Zero		4000	4-6	525	500D
Auto. Tr.	1968	.030	37-42	.025	10	175	Zero		4000	4-6	525	—
	1969-71	.034	37-42	.025	6	175	Zero		4000	4-6	600	525D
262	1961-64	.030	37-42	.025	2	150	.019H	.019H	—	3½-5½	500	500D
300 Std. Tr.	1965	.032	37-42	.025	6	175	Zero		3600	4-6	500	—
Auto. Tr.	1965	.032	37-42	.025	10	175	Zero		3600	4-6	—	500D
Std. Tr.	1966-67	.032	37-42	.025	6[2]	175	Zero		3600	4-6	500	—
Auto. Tr.	1966-67	.030	37-42	.025	10[2]	175	Zero		3600	4-6	—	500D
Std. Tr.	1968	.032	35-40	.027	6	175	Zero		3600	4-6	525	—
Auto. Tr.	1968	.032	37-42	.025	10[3]	175	Zero		3600	4-6	—	500
	1969-71	.034	35-40	.027	6	175	Zero		3600	4-6	600	525
EIGHT CYLINDER												
289	1966	.034	26-31	.017	6[2]	150	Zero		—	4-6	—	—
	1967	.034	26-31	.017	6	150	Zero		—	4-6	—	—
	1968	.034	24-29	.021	6	150	Zero		—	4-6	625	500
292	1961	.030	26-31	.017	6	150	.019	.019	3800	3½-5½	500	500D
	1962	.030	26-31	.017	8	150	.019	.019	3800	3½-5½	500	500D
2 Bbl.	1963	.030	26-31	.017	6	150	.019	.019	3800	4-6	500	500D
4 Bbl.	1963	.030	26-31	.017	8	150	.019	.019	3600	4-6	500	500D
	1964	.030	26-31	.017	6	150	.019	.019	3900	4-6	500	500D
302	1961-63	.030	26-31	.017	8	150	.020	.020	3600	3½-6½	500	500D
	1968-71	.030	24-29	.021	6	150	Zero		—	5	625	550D
330	1964-71	.030	26-31[4]	.017[5]	12[6]	140	Zero		3900	4½-6½	525	500D
332	1961	.030	26-31	.017	8	140	.020	.020	3600	3½-6½	500	500D
2 Bbl.	1962-63	.030	26-31	.017	2	150	.020	.020	3600	4-6	500	500D
4 Bbl.	1962-63	.030	26-31	.017	8	150	.020	.020	3600	4-6	500	500D
352	1965-67	.034	26-31	.017	6[2]	140	Zero		—	5-6	550	475D
360	1968-71	.034	26-31	.017	6[7]	140	Zero		—	4½-6½	625	550
w/Exh. Em.	1968-71	.034	24-29	.021	6	140	Zero		—	4½-6½	625	550
361	1964	.030	26-31[4]	.017[5]	10	140	Zero		3800	4½-6½	525	500D
	1965	.030	26-31[4]	.017[5]	12	140	Zero		3800	4½-6½	525	500D
	1966-68	.030	26-31[4]	.017[5]	10	140	Zero		3800	4½-6½	525	500D
	1969-71	.030	26-31[4]	.017[5]	6	140	Zero		3800	4½-6½	525	500
390	1968-71	.034	26-31	.017	10	140	Zero		3800	4½-6½	625	550
w/Exh. Em.	1968-71	.034	24-29	.021	6	140	Zero		3800	4½-6½	625	550
391	1964	.030	26-31[4]	.017[5]	8	140	Zero		3800	4½-6½	525	500D
	1965	.030	26-31[4]	.017[5]	10	140	Zero		3800	4½-6½	525	500D
	1966-68	.030	26-31[4]	.017[5]	8	140	Zero		3800	4½-6½	525	500

TUNE-UP SPECIFICATIONS, continued

CU. IN. DISPLACE-MENT	YEAR	SPARK PLUG GAP	DISTRIBUTOR POINT DWELL	DISTRIBUTOR POINT GAP	IGNITION TIMING DEGREES	CRANKING COMP. PRESSURE	VALVE CLEARANCE INLET	VALVE CLEARANCE EXHAUST	GOV. R.P.M. NO LOAD	FUEL PUMP PRESS.	IDLE SPEED STD.	IDLE SPEED AUTO
EIGHT CYLINDER												
	1969-71	.030	26-31[4]	.017[5]	6	140	Zero		3800	4½-6½	550	500
401	1961	.030	26-31	.017	8	150	.020	.020	3400	[8]	525	500D
	1962-71[1]	.030	26-31[4]	.017[5]	8	150	.020	.020	3400	[8]	525	500D
477	1961-71	.030	26-31[4]	.017[5]	8	150	.020	.020	3200	[8]	525	500D
534	1961-68	.030	26-31[4]	.017[5]	8	150	.020	.020	3200	[8]	525	500D
	1969-71	.030	22-24	.020	8	150	.020	.020	3000	[8]	550	500

1—1967, With Exhaust Emission, Std. Trans. 3B, Auto. Trans. 5B.
2—With Exhaust Emission TDC.
3—With Exhaust Emission 6B.
4—Transistor Ignition 22-24.
5—Transistor Ignition .020.
6—Heavy Duty—1964-68. 10, 1969-70 6.
7—Auto. Trans. Without Exhaust Emission 10.
8—Electric.

FIRING ORDER AND ROTATION

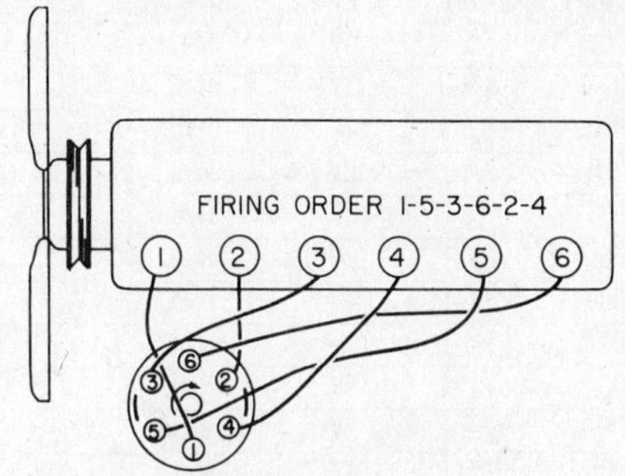

Six—144, 170 & 200 engines

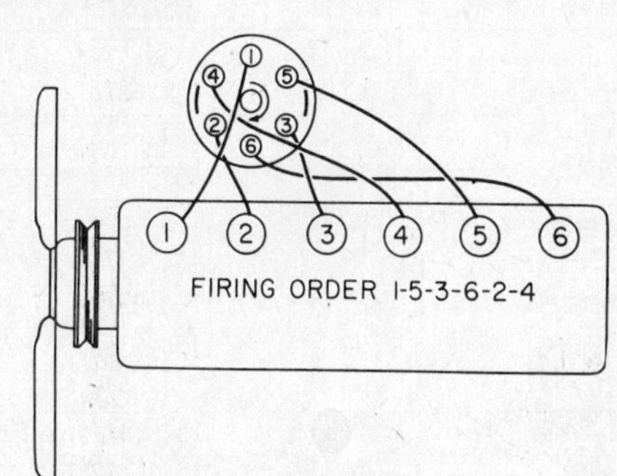

Six 223 & 262 engines

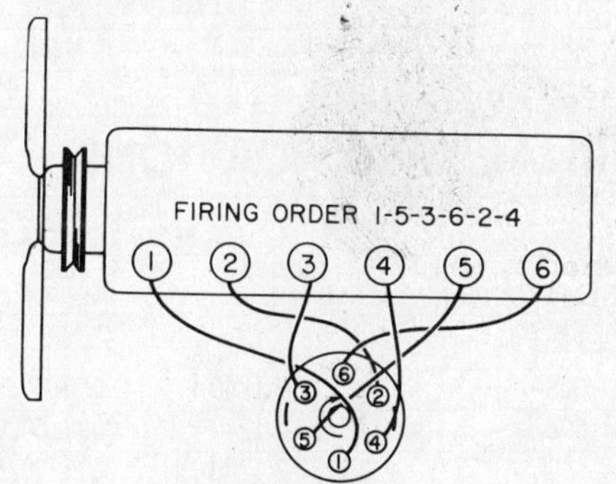

Six—240 & 300 engines

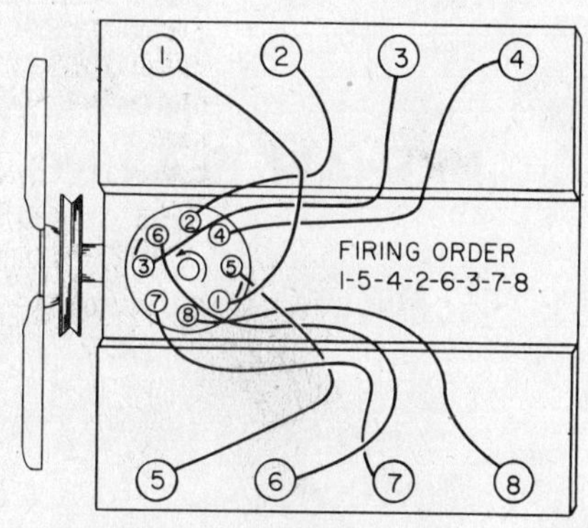

V8—all

GENERAL ENGINE SPECIFICATIONS

CU. IN. DISPLACE-MENT	YEAR	BORE AND STROKE	FIRING ORDER	DEVELOPED HORSE POWER @ R.P.M.	DEVELOPED TORQUE @ R.P.M.	COM-PRESSION RATIO	CARBUR-ETOR	VALVE LIFTER TYPE	NORMAL OIL PRESSURE
SIX CYLINDER									
144	1961-64	3.500x2.50	153624	85@4200	134@2000	8.7	1V	Mech.	35-55
170	1961-63	3.500x2.94	153624	101@4400	152@2000	8.7	1V	Mech.	35-55
	1964-67	3.500x2.94	153624	105@4400	158@2400	9.1	1V	Mech.	35-55
	1968-71	3.500x2.94	153624	100@4000	156@2200	8.7	1V	Mech.	35-55
200	1965	3.68x3.126	153624	120@4400	190@2400	9.2	1V	Hyd.	35-55
223	1961-63	3.625x3.60	153624	114@3600	186@1600	8.4	1V	Mech.	35-55
	1964	3.625x3.60	153624	135@4000	200@1800	8.1	1V	Mech.	35-55
240	1965	4.000x3.18	153624	150@4000	234@2200	8.75-1	1V	Hyd.	35-55
	1966-71	4.000x3.18	153624	150@4400	234@2200	9.2-1	1V	Hyd.	35-55
262	1961-63	3.718x4.03	153624	132@3600	224@1300	8.0-1	1V	Mech.	35-60
	1964	3.718x4.03	153624	152@4000	238@1400	7.9-1	1V	Mech.	35-55
300	1965	4.000x3.98	153624	170@3600	213@2000	8.0-1	1V	Hyd.	35-60
	1965	4.000x3.98	153624	170@3600	213@2000	8.4-1	1V	Hyd.	35-60
	1966	4.000x3.98	153624	170@3600	283@1900	8.0-1	1V	Hyd.	35-60
	1967	4.000x3.98	153624	170@3600	283@1400	8.0-1	1V	Hyd.	40-50
	1968-71	4.000x3.98	153624	165@3600	284@2000	8.8-1	1V	Hyd.	35-60

GENERAL ENGINE SPECIFICATIONS, continued

CU. IN. DISPLACEMENT	YEAR	BORE AND STROKE	FIRING ORDER	DEVELOPED HORSE POWER @ R.P.M.	DEVELOPED TORQUE @ R.P.M.	COMPRESSION RATIO	CARBURETOR	VALVE LIFTER TYPE	NORMAL OIL PRESSURE
EIGHT CYLINDER									
289	1966-68	4.000x2.87	15426378	200@4400	282@2400	9.3-1	2V	Hyd.	35-55
292	1961-64	3.7500x3.30	15486372	160@4000	270@2600	8.0-1	2V	Mech.	35-55
	1961-64	3.7500x3.30	15486372	173@4000	274@2600	8.0-1	4V	Mech.	35-55
302	1961	3.6250x3.66	15486372	163@3600	262@2200	7.5-1	4V	Mech.	35-55
	1962-63	3.6250x3.66	15486372	159@3800	262@2200	7.5-1	2V	Mech.	35-55
	1962-63	3.6250x3.66	15486372	163@3600	262@2200	7.5-1	4V	Mech.	35-55
	1968-71	4.00x3.00	15426378	205@4600	300@2600	8.6-1	2V	Hyd.	35-60
330	1964-65	3.875x3.50	15426378	186@4000	300@2000	7.6-1	2V	Hyd.	45-70
	1966-71	3.875x3.50	15426378	190@4000	306@2000	7.4-1	2V	Hyd.	45-70
332	1961	3.800x3.66	15426378	173@3600	260@2600	7.5-1	4V	Mech.	35-55
	1962-63	3.800x3.66	15426378	192@4000	302@2600	7.5-1	2V	Mech.	35-55
		3.800x3.66	15426378	205@3800	312@2600	7.5-1	4V	Mech.	35-55
352	1965-67	4.000x3.50	15426378	208@4400	315@2400	8.9-1	2V	Hyd.	35-55
360	1968-71	4.05x3.50	15426378	215@4400	327@2600	8.4-1	2V	Hyd.	35-60
361	1964-65	4.05x3.50	15426378	203@4000	330@2000	7.6-1	2V	Hyd.	45-70
	1966-71	4.050x3.50	15426378	210@4000	345@2000	7.4-1	2V	Hyd.	45-70
390	1968-71	4.050x3.78	15426378	255@4400	376@2600	8.6-1	2V	Hyd.	35-60
391	1964-65	4.050x3.78	15426378	235@4000	372@2000	7.6-1	4V	Hyd.	45-70
	1966-67	4.050x3.78	15426378	235@4000	372@2000	7.4-1	4V	Hyd.	45-70
	1968-71	4.050x3.79	15426378	235@4000	372@2000	7.2-1	4V	Hyd.	35-60
401	1961-67	4.1250x3.75	15486372	206@3600	341@1700	7.5-1	2V	Mech.	35-65
	1961-71	4.1250x3.75	15486372	226@3600	343@2300	7.5-1	4V	Mech.	35-65
477	1961-71	4.5000x3.75	15486372	231@3400	412@1600	7.5-1	2V	Mech.	35-65
	1961-71	4.5000x3.75	15486372	253@3400	415@2300	7.5-1	4V	Mech.	35-65
534	1961-71	4.5000x4.20	15486372	266@3200	481@1700	7.5-1	4V	Mech.	35-65

CRANKSHAFT BEARING JOURNAL SPECIFICATIONS

CU. IN. DISPLACEMENT	YEAR	MAIN BEARING JOURNALS				CONNECTING ROD BEARING JOURNALS		
		JOURNAL DIAMETER	OIL CLEARANCE	SHAFT END PLAY	THRUST ON NO.	JOURNAL DIAMETER	OIL CLEARANCE	END PLAY
SIX CYLINDER								
144	1961-64	2.2482-2.2490	.0007-.0026	.004-.008	3	2.1232-2.1240	.0006-.0026	.004-.008
170	1962-71	2.2482-2.2490	.0007-.0026	.004-.008	3	2.1232-2.1240	.0006-.0026	.0035-.0105
200	1965	2.2486-2.2490	.0007-.0026	.004-.008	5	2.1232-2.1240	.0006-.0026	.004-.008
223	1961-64	2.4980-2.4988	.0009-.0033	.004-.008	3	2.2980-2.2988	.0008-.0028	.005-.011
240	1965-71	2.3982-2.3990	.0005-.0022	.004-.008	5	2.1228-2.1236	.0008-.0024	.006-.013
262	1961-64	2.4976-2.4984	.0010-.0033	.004-.008	3	2.2980-2.2988	.0006-.0025	.005-.011
300	1965	2.3982-2.3990	.0006-.0026	.004-.008	5	2.1228-2.1236	.0006-.0022	.006-.013
	1966-71	2.3982-2.3990	.0009-.0028	.004-.008	5	2.1228-2.1236	.0009-.0027	.006-.013
EIGHT CYLINDER								
289	1961-68	2.2482-2.2490	.0005-.0015	.004-.008	3	2.1228-2.1236	.0010-.0015	.010-.020
292	1961-64	2.4980-2.4988	.0006-.0032	.004-.008	3	2.1880-2.1888	.0005-.0024	.006-.016
302	1961-63	2.6230-2.6238	.0012-.0032	.004-.008	3	2.2482-2.2490	.0006-.0027	.006-.014
	1968-71	2.2482-2.2490	.0005-.0015	.004-.008	3	2.1228-2.1236	.0010-.0015	.010-.020
330	1964	2.7479-2.7487	.0012-.0033	.004-.008	3	2.4377-2.4385	.0012-.0033	.006-.016
MD.	1965-71	2.7484-2.7492	.0011-.0031	.004-.008	3	2.4380-2.4388	.0006-.0023	.010-.020
HD.	1965-71	2.7479-2.7487	[1]	.004-.010	3	2.4377-2.4385	.0009-.0027	.010-.020
332	1961-63	2.6230-2.6238	.0012-.0032	.004-.008	3	2.2482-2.2490	.0006-.0027	.006-.014
352	1965	2.7484-2.7492	[2]	.004-.010	3	2.4380-2.4388	.0007-.0028	.010-.020
	1966-67	2.7484-2.7492	.0005-.0025	.004-.010	3	2.4380-2.4388	.0008-.0026	.010-.020
360	1968-71	2.7484-2.7492	.0005-.0024	.004-.010	3	2.4380-2.4388	.0008-.0026	
361	1964	2.7479-2.7487	.0012-.0033	.004-.008	3	2.4377-2.4385	.0012-.0033	.006-.016
	1965-71	2.7479-2.7487	[1]	.004-.010	3	2.4377-2.4385	.0010-.0029	.010-.020
390	1968-71	2.7484-2.7492	.0005-.0024	.004-.010	3	2.4380-2.4388	.0008-.0026	.010-.020
391	1964-71	2.7479-2.7487	.0012-.0033	.004-.008	3	2.4377-2.4385	.0012-.0033	.006-.016
401	1961-71	3.1246-3.1254	.0018-.0039	.004-.008	3	2.7092-2.7100	.0017-.0036	.006-.014

CRANKSHAFT BEARING JOURNAL SPECIFICATIONS

CU. IN. DISPLACEMENT	YEAR	MAIN BEARING JOURNALS: JOURNAL DIAMETER	MAIN BEARING JOURNALS: OIL CLEARANCE	MAIN BEARING JOURNALS: SHAFT END PLAY	MAIN BEARING JOURNALS: THRUST ON NO.	CONNECTING ROD BEARING JOURNALS: JOURNAL DIAMETER	CONNECTING ROD BEARING JOURNALS: OIL CLEARANCE	CONNECTING ROD BEARING JOURNALS: END PLAY
EIGHT CYLINDER								
477	1961-71	3.1246-3.1254	.0018-.0039	.004-.008	3	2.7092-2.7100	.0017-.0036	.006-.014
534	1961-71	3.1246-3.1254	.0018-.0039	.004-.008	3	2.7092-2.7100	.0017-.0036	.006-.014

MD—Medium Duty.
HD—Heavy Duty.

1—No. 1, 3 .0012-.0036, No. 2, 4, 5 .0010-.0033.
2—No. 1. .0007-.0031, others .0005-.0028.

VALVE SPECIFICATIONS

CU. IN. DISPLACEMENT	YEAR	LASH (HOT) INCHES INT.	LASH (HOT) INCHES EXH.	ANGLE DEGREE FACE	ANGLE DEGREE SEAT	STEM DIA. INCHES INT.	STEM DIA. INCHES EXH.	STEM CLEARANCE INTAKE	STEM CLEARANCE EXHAUST	VALVE LIFT INCHES	VALVE SPRING LBS. @ INCHES OPEN	VALVE SPRING LBS. @ INCHES CLOSED	FREE LENGTH INCH
SIX CYLINDER													
144	1961-64	.018	.018	44	45	.3104	.3098	.0008-.0025	.0018-.0035	.2405[4]	117@1.222	52@1.585	2.00
170*	1962-71	.018	.018	44	45	.3104	.3102	.0008-.0025	.0010-.0027	.2405[4]	117@1.222	52@1.585	2.00
200	1965	.066	.216	44	45	.3104	.3098	.0008-.0025	.0018-.0035	.2450	150@1.222	54@1.590	1.79
223	1961-64	.019	.019	44	45	.3420	.3402	.0010-.0024	.0028-.0042	.2730	169@1.390	75@1.78	2.09
240	1965-71	.082	.152	44	45	.3420	.3420	.0010-.0027	.0010-.0027	.2330[5]	197@1.300	80@1.70	1.99
262	1961-64	.019	.019	44	45	.3715	.3698	.0008-.0025	.0025-.0042	.2730	169@1.260	75@1.65	1.96
300	1965-71	.082	.152	44	45	.3420	.3420	.0010-.0027	.0010-.0027	.2490	192@1.180	80@1.58	1.87
MD.	1965-71	.082	.152	44	45	.3420	.3420	.0010-.0024	.0028-.0042	.2490	1	2	3
EIGHT CYLINDER													
289	1966	.082	.152	44	45	.3420	.3420	.0010-.0027	.0020-.0037	.230[6]	169@1.390	75@1.78	2.09
	1967	.067	.167	44	45	.3420	.3420	.0010-.0027	.0010-.0027	.230[6]	166@1.250	60@1.64	1.86
	1968	.067	.167	44	45	.3420	.3420	.0010-.0027	.0010-.0027	.230[6]	180@1.230	75@1.66	1.97
292	1961-64	.019	.019	44	45	.3420	.3420	.0010-.0024	.0028-.0042	.263	169@1.390	75@1.65	2.09
302	1961-63	.020	.020	44	45	.3420	.3420	.0010-.0024	.0028-.0042	.244[7]	169@1.390	75@1.65	2.09
	1968-70	.067	.167	44	45	.3420	.3420	.0010-.0027	.0010-.0027	.244[7]	180@1.230	75@1.66	1.97
330	1964	.078	.178	44	45	.3715	.4343	.0010-.0024	.0020-.0037	.2446[8]	185@1.240	80@1.67	2.00
MD.	1965-67	.050	.150	44	45	.3715	.3705	.0010-.0024	.0028-.0042	.2446[8]	189@1.420	99@1.82	2.26
HD.	1965-67	.050	.150	44	45	.3715	.4343	.0010-.0024	.0020-.0037	.2446[8]	185@1.240	80@1.67	2.00
MD.	1968-71	.100	.200	44	45	.3715	.3705	.0010-.0024	.0028-.0042	.2446[8]	189@1.420	99@1.82	2.26
H.D.	1968-71	.100	.200	44	45	.3715	.4343	.0010-.0024	.0020-.0037	.2446[8]	185@1.240	80@1.67	2.00
332	1961-63	.020	.020	44	45	.3420	.3402	.0010-.0024	.0028-.0042	.244[7]	169@1.390	75@1.65	2.09
352	1965-67	.050	.150	44	45	.3715	.3705	.0010-.0024	.0020-.0043	.232	189@1.420	91@1.82	2.26
360	1968-71	.100	.200	44	45	.3715	.3715	.0010-.0024	.0020-.0034	.248	220@1.380	90@1.82	2.12
361	1964-67	.050	.150	44	45	.3715	.4343	.0010-.0024	.0020-.0037	.2448	185@1.240	80@1.67	2.00
	1968-71	.100	.200	44	45	.3715	.4343	.0010-.0024	.0020-.0037	.2448	185@1.240	80@1.67	2.00
390	1968-71	.100	.200	44	45	.3715	.3715	.0010-.0024	.0020-.0034	.248	220@1.380	90@1.82	2.12
391	1964-67	.050	.150	44	45	.3715	.4343	.0010-.0024	.0020-.0037	.2448	185@1.240	80@1.67	2.00
	1968-71	.100	.200	44	45	.3715	.4343	.0010-.0024	.0020-.0037	.2448	185@1.240	80@1.67	2.00
401	1961-71	.020	.020	44	45	.4354	.4340	.0010-.0026	.0024-.0040	.278	185@1.280	77@1.70	2.07
477	1961-67	.020	.020	44	45	.4354	.4340	.0010-.0026	.0024-.0040	.278	185@1.280	77@1.70	2.07
534	1961-71	.020	.020	44	45	.4354	.4340	.0010-.0026	.0024-.0040	.278	185@1.280	77@1.70	2.07

*—1968, Hydraulic Lifters.
HD—Heavy Duty.
MD—Medium Duty.
1—Intake 197 @ 1.30, Exhaust 192 @ 1.18.
2—Intake 80 @ 1.70, Exhaust 81 @ 1.58.
3—Intake 1.99, Exhaust 1.87.

4—Exhaust .2395.
5—Exhaust .2490.
6—Exhaust .237.
7—Exhaust .265.
8—Exhaust .2329.

TORQUE SPECIFICATIONS

CU. IN. DISPLACEMENT	YEAR	CYLINDER HEAD BOLTS (FT. LBS.)	ROD BEARING BOLTS (FT. LBS.)	MAIN BEARING BOLTS (FT. LBS.)	CRANKSHAFT BALANCER BOLT (FT. LBS.)	FLYWHEEL TO CRANKSHAFT BOLTS (FT. LBS.)	MANIFOLD (FT. LBS.) INTAKE	MANIFOLD (FT. LBS.) EXHAUST
SIX CYLINDER								
144	1961-64	70-75	19-24	60-70	85-100	75-85	—	13-18
170	1962-71	70-75	19-24	60-70	85-100	75-85	—	13-18
200	1965	70-75	19-24	60-70	85-100	75-85	—	13-18

WHEEL ALIGNMENT SPECIFICATIONS

YEAR	MODEL	CASTER (Deg.)	CAMBER (Deg.)	TOE-IN (In.)	KING PIN INCLINATION (Deg.)
1963	Econoline	5	1	1⁄16-⅛	7½
	F100, 200	3	1	1⁄16-3⁄16	4
	F100, 200 F.W.D.	4	1½	1⁄16-3⁄16	7½
	P100, 400, 500	3	1	1⁄16-3⁄16	4
	P500 w/154" W.B.	3½	1	1⁄16-3⁄16	4
	BF-350, 500, 600	4	1	1⁄16-3⁄16	4
	P350	4½	1	1⁄16-3⁄16	4
	B-F-T700, 750	4	1	1⁄16-3⁄16	5½
	C550 Thru 800	3	1	1⁄16-3⁄16	5½
	F-T800	4	1	1⁄16-3⁄16	5½
	F-T800, 15.000 Axle	3¼	1	1⁄16-3⁄16	8
	850 Thru 1100	3¼	1	1⁄16-3⁄16	5½
1964	E100 Econoline	5	⅜	1⁄16-⅛	7½
	F100, 250	3	1	⅛	4
	F100, 250 F.W.D.	4	1½	⅛	7½
	P100, 400, 4000	3	1	1⁄16-3⁄16	4
	F350	4	⅜	1⁄16-3⁄16	4⅝
	P350, 3500	4½	⅝P	1⁄16-3⁄16	4
	P500, 5000	3	½P	1⁄16-3⁄16	4
	B-F500, 600	4	½P	1⁄16-3⁄16	4
	N500 Thru 7000[1]	3½	1	1⁄16-3⁄16	4
	C550 Thru 7000	3	1	1⁄16-3⁄16	5½
	F-B700, 750[1]	3½	1	1⁄16-3⁄16	4
	C-CT700, 750	3¼	1	1⁄16-3⁄16	5½
	C-CT700, 750[2]	—1	1	1⁄32-5⁄32	0
	800 Thru 1100[2]	3¼	1	1⁄16-3⁄16	5½
1965	E100 Econoline	5	⅜	1⁄16-⅛	7½
	F100, 250	5	⅝	⅛	—
	F100, 250 F.W.D.	4	⅝	1⁄16-¼	7½
	P100, 400, 4000	3	1	1⁄16	4
	F350	4	1	1⁄16	4
	B-F500, 600	4	1	1⁄16	4[3]
	P360, 3500	4½	1	1⁄16	4
	P500, 5000	4½	1	1⁄16	4
	N500 Thru 7000[1]	3½	1	1⁄16	4
	C550 Thru 7000	3	1	1⁄16	5½
	B-F700, 750[1]	3½	1	1⁄16	4
	T-TC700, 750	3½	1	1⁄16	5½
	T-TC700, 750[4]	—1	1	3⁄32	0
	800, 850	3¼	1	3⁄32	5½
	800, 850[4]	—1	1	3⁄32	0
	800, 850[5]	3¼	1	1⁄16	8
1966	E100 Econoline	+5¼	⅜	3⁄32	7½
	F100, 250	5	⅜	⅛	4
	F100 4x4	—	—	⅛	—
	F250 4x4	4	—	⅛	—
	P100	3½	⅜	⅛	4⅝
	F350	4	⅜	⅛	4⅝
	P350, 3500	4½	⅝	⅛	4⅜
	P400, 500, 4000, 5000	3½	½	⅛	4½
	F-B-N-500 Thru 750	3½	¾	⅛	4
	C550 Thru 750	3	¾	⅛	5½
	C6000, 7000	3	¾	⅛	5½
	N6000, 7000	3½	¾	⅛	5½
	700 Thru 1000[6]	3	¾	⅛	5½
	700 Thru 1000[7]	3¼	—	⅛	L½ - R¼
1967-69	E100, 200, 300	5	½	3⁄32	7½
	Twin I-Beam	5	½	⅛	4
	F100, 250	4	1	⅛	4
	F100 4x4	—	—	⅛	—
	F250 4x4	4	—	⅛	—
	P100	3½	⅜	⅛	4⅝
	F350	5	½	⅛	4
	P350, 3500	4½	⅝	⅛	4½
	P400, 4000	3½	½	⅛	4½
	P500, 5000	3½	½	⅛	4½
	F-B-N-500, 750	3⅝[8]	1	⅛	4
	F,N6000, 7000 D[9]	3⅝[8]	1	⅛	4
	F,N6000, 7000 D[10]	4[11]	1	⅛	5½
	C550, 750, 6000, 7000	3¼	1	⅛	5½
	T700, 750-6-7000 lb. Axle	3¼	1	⅛	5½
	F,N800-950, 950-D	—	—	—	—
	6000-7000 lb. Axle	3¼	1	⅛	5½
	9000-12000 lb. Axle	3¼	L+¼ R–¼	⅛	5½
	Center Point Strg.	—1	L+¼ R–¼	3⁄32	0
	15000 lb. Axle	3¼	1	⅛	8
	18000 lb. Axle	3¼	1	⅛	5
1970	Econoline	5	½	⅛	—
	F100 4x4	3½	1½	⅛	8½
	F250 4x4	4	1½	⅛	7½
	F100, 250	4	1	⅛	4
	F350	5	½	⅛	4
	P350	4½	⅝	⅛	4½
	P400, 500	3½	½	⅛	4½
	P4000, 5000	3½	½	⅛	—
	F,B500, 750	3½	9⁄16	¼	4
	F,B500-750 Pow. Strg.	6½	9⁄16	¼	4
	C500-750[6]	3	9⁄16	¼	5½
	C750[7]	3	⅜	¼	5½
	L,800-900[6]	3¾	9⁄16	¼	5½
	L,800-900[7]	4	L+⅜ R⅞	⅜	—
	LN500[12]	4½	9⁄16	¼	5½
	Center Point Strg.	0	L+½ R.O.	[illegible]	0

1—6000, 7000 Lb. Axle—Caster 4°, King Pin Inclination 5½°.
2—11.000 Lb. Axle.
3—6000 Lb. Axle 5½°.
4—11,000 Lb. Axle.
5—15.000 Lb. Axle.
6—6-7000 Lb. Axle.
7—9-12,000 Lb. Axle.
8—Power Steering 6⅝.
9—5-5500 Lb. Axle.
10—6-7000 Lb. Axle, Manual Steering.
11—Power Steering 7.
12—Power Steering 7½.

BRONCO

YEAR	MODEL	CASTER (Deg.)	CAMBER (Deg.)	TOE-IN (In.)	KING PIN INCLINATION (Deg.)
1966		①	①	3⁄32	—
1967-69		3½①	1½①	⅛	—
1970-71		3½①	1½①	⅛	8½

①—The Caster and Camber angles are designed into the front axle and can not be adjusted.

TORQUE SPECIFICATIONS, continued

CU. IN. DISPLACEMENT	YEAR	CYLINDER HEAD BOLTS (FT. LBS.)	ROD BEARING BOLTS (FT. LBS.)	MAIN BEARING BOLTS (FT. LBS.)	CRANKSHAFT BALANCER BOLT (FT. LBS.)	FLYWHEEL TO CRANKSHAFT BOLTS (FT. LBS.)	MANIFOLD (FT. LBS.) INTAKE	EXHAUST
SIX CYLINDER								
223	1961	95-105	40-45	95-105	70-90	75-85	23-28	23-28
	1962-64	105-115	40-45	90-105	70-90	75-85	23-28	23-28
240	1965	70-75	40-45	60-70	130-145	75-85	20-25	20-25
	1966-70	70-75	40-45	60-70	130-150	75-85	23-28	23-28
262	1961	105-115	40-45	105-115	70-90	75-85	23-28	23-28
	1962-64	105-115	40-45	95-105	140-150	75-85	23-28	23-28
300	1965-71	70-75	40-45	60-70	130-145	75-85	20-25	20-25
EIGHT CYLINDER								
289	1966-71	65-72	19-24	60-70	70-90	75-85	20-23	15-22
292 MD.	1961-64	65-75	40-45	80-90	70-90	75-85	23-28	23-28
HD.		70-85	40-45	80-90	70-90	75-85	23-28	23-28
302	1961-63	100-115	40-45	120-130	130-145	75-85	23-28	12-15
	1966-71	65-75	19-24	60-70	70-90	75-85	20-22	15-20
330	1964	80-90	40-45	95-105	130-145	75-85	32-35	23-28
MD.	1965-71	80-90	40-45	95-105	70-90	75-85	32-35	23-28[1]
HD.	1965-71	80-90	40-45	95-105	150-175	75-85	32-35	23-28[1]
332	1961-63	105-115	40-45	120-130	130-145	75-85	23-28	12-15
352	1965-67	80-90	40-45	95-105	70-90	75-85	32-35	12-18
360	1968-71	80-90	40-45	95-105	70-90	75-85	32-35	12-18
361	1964	80-90	40-45	95-105	130-145	75-85	32-35	23-28
	1965	80-90	40-45	95-105	150-175	75-85	32-35	23-28
	1966-71	80-90	40-45	95-105	150-175	75-85	32-35	18-24
390	1968-71	80-90	40-45	95-105	70-90	75-85	32-35	12-18
391	1964	80-90	40-45	95-105	130-145	75-85	32-35	23-28
	1965	80-90	40-45	95-105	150-175	75-85	32-35	23-28
	1966-71	80-90	40-45	95-105	150-175	75-85	32-35	18-24
401	1961-63	130-150	60-65	150-165	130-145	100-110	23-28	23-28
	1964-66	170-180	60-65	150-165	130-145	100-110	23-28	23-28
	1967-71	170-180	60-65	130-150	130-145	100-110	23-28	23-28
477	1961-63	130-150	60-65	150-165	130-145	100-110	23-28	23-28
	1964-65	170-180	60-65	150-165	130-145	100-110	23-28	23-28
	1966-71	170-180	60-65	130-150	130-145	100-110	23-28	23-28
534	1961-63	130-150	60-65	150-165	130-145	100-110	23-28	23-28
	1964-65	170-180	60-65	150-165	130-145	100-110	23-28	23-28
	1966-71	170-180	60-65	130-150	130-145	100-110	23-28	23-28

MD—Medium Duty. **HD—Heavy Duty.** **1—1966-70, 18-24.**

TRUCK MODELS AND ENGINE APPLICATION

IDENTIFICATION PLATE: On light and medium cowl and windshield vehicles, the Rating Plate is mounted on the right side of the cowl top panel or upper cowl panel under the hood. On Parcel Delivery vehicles, the rating plate is mounted on the right side of the radiator support. On Bronco models, the plate is mounted on the inside panel of the glove compartment door. On all other vehicles, the Rating Plate is mounted on the rear face of the left front door.

All identifications designate equipment on the vehicle when it was shipped from the factory.

CONVENTIONAL GASOLINE ENGINES

STANDARD ENGINES	YEAR	MODELS	ENGINE MAKE
SIX CYLINDER			
6-144	1961-64	Econoline	Own
6-170	1965-67	Econoline	Own
	1968-70	Econoline	Own
	1966-70	Bronco	Own
6-223	1961-64	F-100	Own
	1961-64	F-250	Own
	1961-64	F-350	Own
	1961-64	F-500	Own
	1963-64	N-500	Own
	1961-64	F-600	Own
	1963-64	N-600	Own
6-240	1965-70	F-100	Own
	1965-70	F-250	Own
	1965-70	F-350	Own
	1965-70	F-500	Own
	1965-69	N-500	Own
	1965-67	F-600	Own
	1965-67	N-600	Own
6-300	1968-69	N-600	Own
	1968-70	F-600	Own
EIGHT CYLINDER			
V8-292	1961-63	F-700	Own
	1963	N-700	Own
V8-302	1961-63	F-750	Own
V8-330	1964-69	N-700	Own
	1964-70	F-700	Own
V8-332	1963	N-750	Own
	1961-63	F-800	Own
V8-361	1964-67	N-750	Own
	1964-70	F-800	Own
	1964-70	F-750	Own
V8-391	1968-69	N-750	Own
V8-401	1961-69	F-850	Own
	1963-69	N-850	Own
	1961-69	F-950	Own
V8-477	1961-69	F-1000	Own
	1963-69	N-1000	Own

TRUCK MODELS AND ENGINE APPLICATION

ENGINE NUMBER LOCATION: The engine serial number is located on a machined surface on the cylinder block. The engine serial number prefix denotes the series, followed by engine model, followed by serial number.

TILT CAB GASOLINE MODELS

STANDARD ENGINES	YEAR	MODELS	ENGINE MAKE
SIX CYLINDER			
6-262	1961-64	C-550	Own
	1961-64	C-600	Own
6-300	1965-69	C-550	Own
	1965-70	C-600	Own
EIGHT CYLINDER			
V8-292	1961-63	C-700	Own
V8-302	1961-62	C-750	Own
V8-330	1964-70	C-700	Own
V8-332	1963	C-750	Own
	1961-63	C-800	Own
	1961-62	C-900	Own
V8-354	1961-62	H-950	Own
V8-361	1964-70	C-750	Own
	1964-70	C-800	Own
V8-401	1961-69	C-850	Own
	1970	C-900	Own
	1961-64	H-1000	Own
V8-477	1961-69	C-1000	Own
	1965-66	H-1000	Own
	1961-65	C-1100	Own

PARCEL DELIVERY GASOLINE ENGINES

SIX CYLINDER			
6-170	1966-67	P-100	Own
6-223	1964	P-350	Own
	1961-64	P-400	Own
	1961-64	P-500	Own
6-240	1965-69	P-350	Own
	1965-69	P-400	Own
	1965-69	P-500	Own

LOUISVILLE GASOLINE ENGINES

SIX CYLINDER			
6-240	1970	LN-500	Own
6-300	1970	LN-600	Own
EIGHT CYLINDER			
V8-330	1970	LN-700	Own
	1970	LT-800	Own
	1970	LNT-800	Own
V8-361	1970	LN-750	Own
	1970	LN-800	Own
	1970	LT-800	Own
V8-401	1970	L-900	Own
	1970	LN-900	Own

FORD DIESEL MODELS

STANDARD ENGINES	YEARS	MODELS	ENGINE MAKE
6V-53N	1968-69	N-8000	Detroit
V-150	1970	C-6000	Caterpillar
	1970	F-6000	Caterpillar
CF-160	1968-69	C-8000	Cummins
	1968-69	F-8000	Cummins
	1968-69	T-8000	Cummins
V-175	1970	C-7000	Caterpillar
	1970	F-7000	Caterpillar
	1970	CT-8000	Caterpillar
NHE-195	1968-69	NT-850D	Cummins
	1968-69	NT-950-D	Cummins
	1968-69	N-1000-D	Cummins
	1968-69	W-1000-D	Cummins
	1968-69	WT-1000-D	Cummins
V6E-195	1968-69	T-850-D	Cummins
	1968-69	F-950-D	Cummins
	1968-69	T-950-D	Cummins
	1968-69	F-1000-D	Cummins
V-200	1970	C-8000	Caterpillar
4-220	1963-66	P-3500	Own
	1963-66	P-4000	Own
	1963-66	P-5000	Own
NH-230	1970	W-9000	Cummins
	1970	WT-9000	Cummins
NH-242	1967-69	P-3500	Own
	1967-69	P-4000	Own
	1967-69	P-5000	Own
6-330	1963-66	C-6000	Own
	1965-66	N-6000	Own
	1963-66	C-7000	Own
	1963-66	N-7000	Own
6-363	1963-64	C-6000	Own
	1967-69	C-6000	Own
	1967-69	N-6000	Own
	1967-69	B-7000	Own
	1967-69	C-7000	Own
	1967-69	F-7000	Own
	1967-69	N-7000	Own

LOUISVILLE DIESEL MODELS

V-150	1970	LN-6000	Caterpillar
V-175	1970	LN-7000	Caterpillar
	1970	L-8000	Caterpillar
	1970	LN-8000	Caterpillar
	1970	LT-8000	Caterpillar
	1970	LNT-8000	Caterpillar
NH-230	1970	L-9000	Cummins
	1970	LN-9000	Cummins
	1970	LT-9000	Cummins
	1970	LNT-9000	Cummins

Distributor

General Information

All 1961-65 6-cylinder and some 1966-69 6-cylinder engines on light duty models are equipped with the Loadomatic distributor which has vacuum advance only. 1966-69 Medium duty and all 1970-71 6-cylinder engines are equipped with Autolite dual advance distributors. All V8 engines have Autolite dual advance distributors. 1968-71 model Autolite distributors may have the dual diaphragm vacuum advance mechanism, depending on which exhaust emission control system is utilized. See "Exhaust Emission Controls" below in this section or "Exhaust Emission Controls" in the General Repair Section for detailed information on emission control systems. Rotation is clockwise on 6-cylinder engines and counterclockwise on V8 engines.

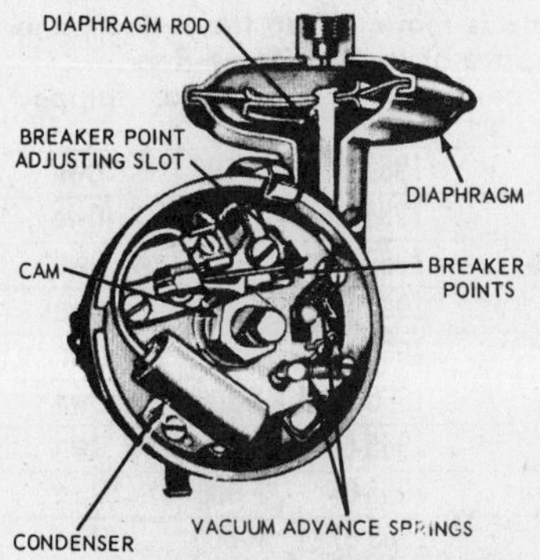

Loadomatic distributor spark advance mechanism
(© Ford Motor Co.)

For information on governors, see "Governors" below.

Distributor Removal

1. On a conventional ignition system, disconnect the primary wire at the coil. On a transistor ignition system, disconnect the primary wire from the quick disconnect.
2. Disconnect the vacuum line(s) at the distributor.
3. Remove the distributor cap.
4. Scribe a mark on the distributor body, indicating the position of the rotor. Scribe another mark

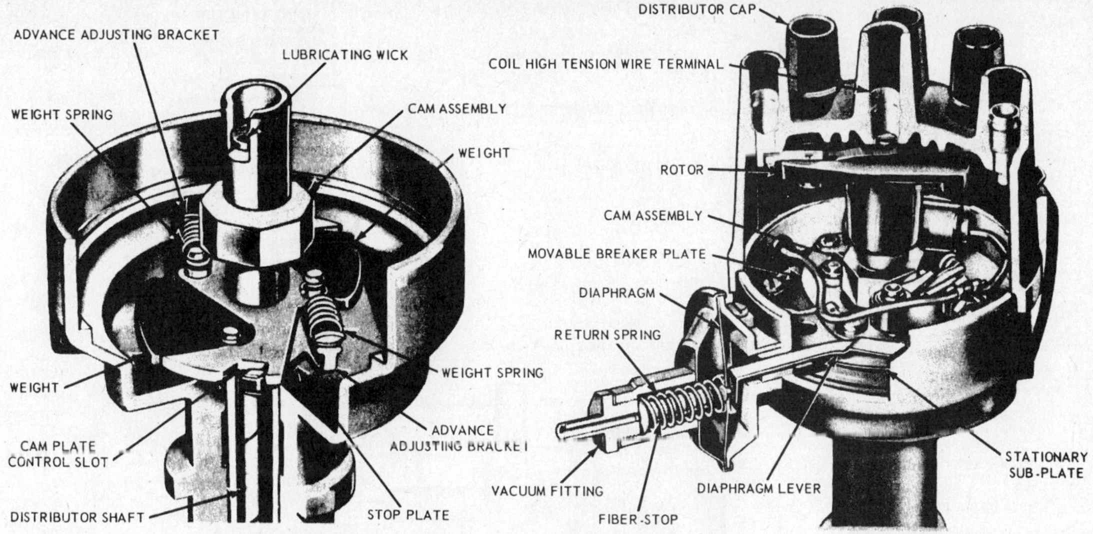

Autolite dual advance distributor w/single diaphragm (© Ford Motor Co.)

on the body and engine block, indicating the position of the body in the block. These marks will insure that the distributor will be correctly timed when it is reinstalled.

5. Remove hold down bolt and clamp or retaining bolt and lockwasher and lift the distributor out of the block. NOTE: Do not rotate the crankshaft while the distributor is removed, or it will be necessary to time the engine.
6. To install, position the distributor in the block with the rotor aligned to the mark previously scribed on the distributor and the marks on the distributor and block aligned.
7. If the crankshaft has been rotated while the distributor was removed, the distributor must be timed with respect to the crankshaft. Rotate engine until No. 1 piston is at top dead center of compression stroke. Position the distributor in the block with the rotor in No. 1 firing position. Rotate the distributor until points are just about to open. NOTE: Make sure the oil pump intermediate shaft properly engages (Autolite dual advance) the distributor shaft. It may be necessary to crank the engine with the starter, after the distributor gear is engaged, in order to engage the oil pump intermediate shaft.
8. Install retaining clamp and bolt or retaining bolt and lockwasher, but do not tighten.
9. Connect primary wire and install distributor cap.
10. Check and reset ignition timing as described below.
11. Tighten hold down clamp bolt or retaining bolt.

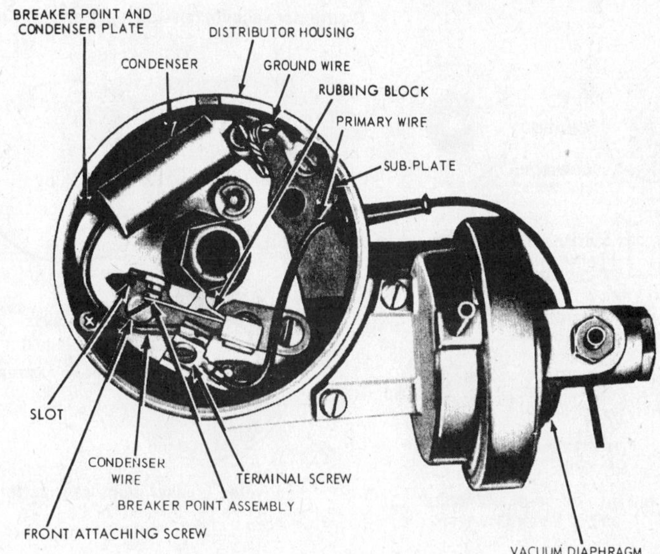

Autolite dual diaphragm distributor—6 cyl. (© Ford Motor Co.)

12. Connect vacuum hose(s).

Setting Ignition Timing

Before checking and adjusting the ignition timing, inspect the breaker points for alignment and adjust if necessary. Rotate the distributor until breaker rubbing block rests on the peak of a cam lobe and check the breaker point gap, adjusting if necessary. See Specifications at the beginning of this section for correct gap setting.

1. Clean and mark timing marks. All timing marks are on the crankshaft belt drive pulley, except on the 240 cu. in. engine in Econoline models and 240 and 300 cu. in. engines in P series models, where the marks are on the flywheel or flexplate (automatic transmission).
2. Disconnect vacuum line(s) and plug the disconnected line(s).
3. Connect a timing strobe light to the No. 1 spark plug lead and install a tachometer.
4. Start engine and set idle speed at 600 rpm.
5. Loosen hold down clamp bolt or retainer bolt and rotate distributor housing until timing is correctly set. See Tune-up Specifications at the beginning of this section for correct timing setting.
6. Check the operation of the centrifugal advance by accelerating the engine to 2000 rpm. If the timing does not advance 9-14 degrees, the mechanical advance mechanism is faulty and must be removed for service.
7. Unplug vacuum line(s) and con-

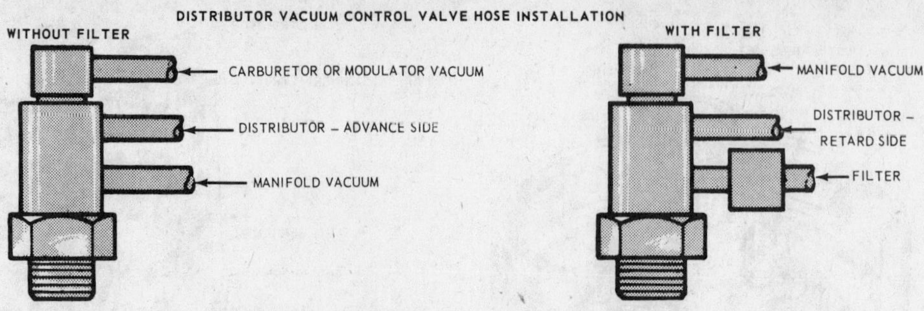

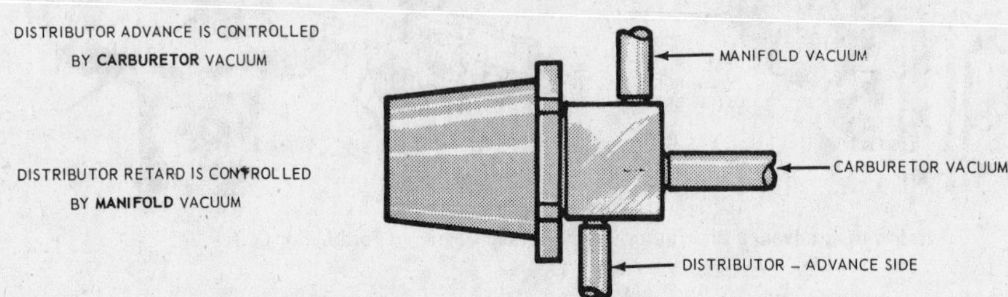

Distributor vacuum hose connections (© Ford Motor Co.)

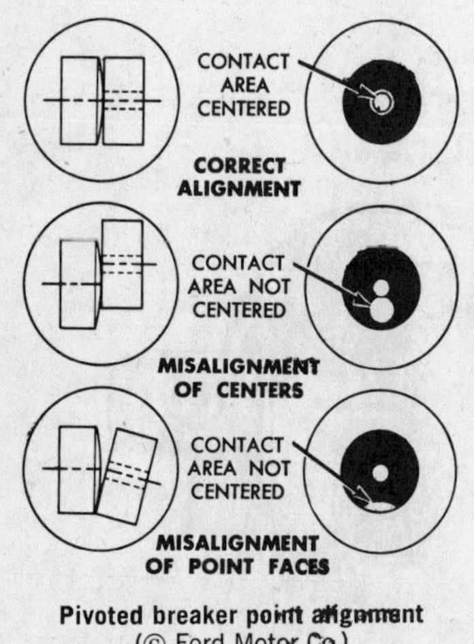

Pivoted breaker point alignment (© Ford Motor Co.)

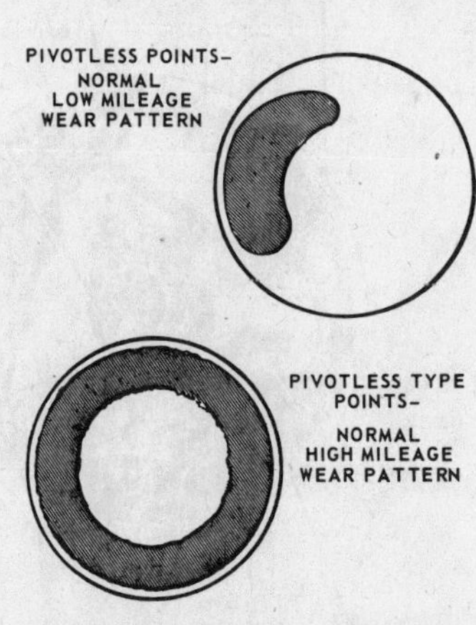

Pivoted breaker point wear pattern (© Ford Motor Co.)

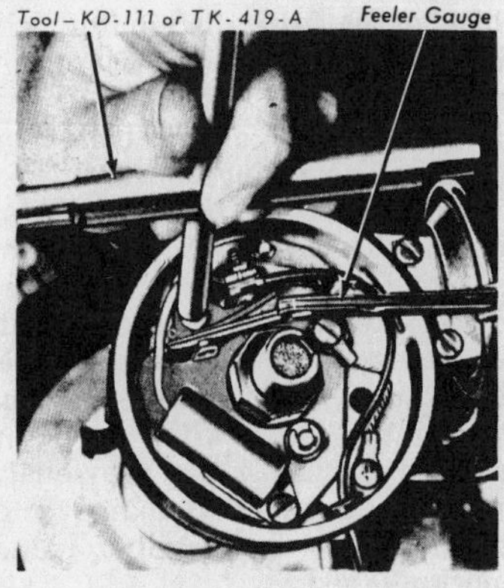

Adjusting breaker points (© Ford Motor Co.)

Typical engine timing marks—pointer mounted (© Ford Motor Co.)

Typical engine timing marks—pulley mounted (© Ford Motor Co.)

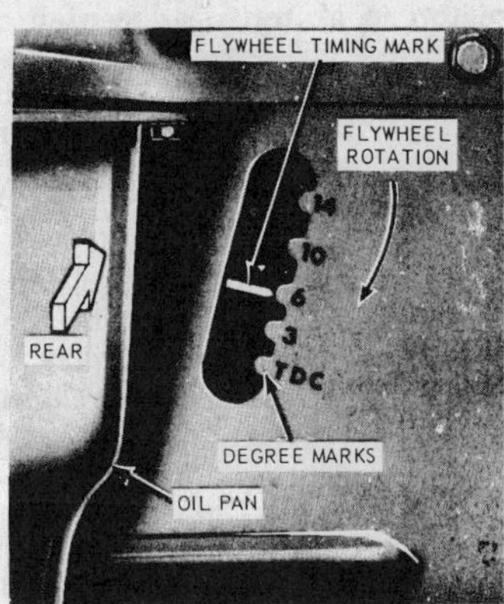

Timing marks—Econline & P series (© Ford Motor Co.)

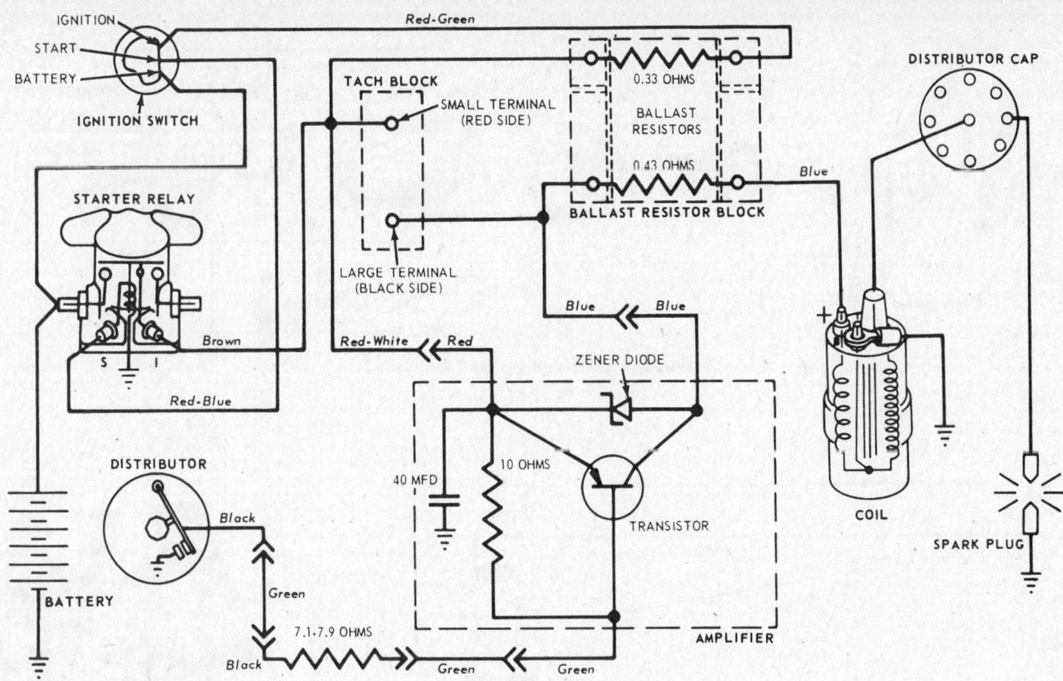

Transistor ignition system (© Ford Motor Co.)

nect to distributor diaphragm. Momentarily accelerate engine to 2000 rpm and note timing advance. If it is not considerably more than the mechanical advance alone, the disphragm must be replaced.

8. Remove timing light and tachometer. Reset idle to correct speed.

Breaker Point Replacement

1. Remove the distributor cap and rotor.
2. Disconnect the primary and condenser wires from breaker point assembly.
3. Remove the breaker point assembly and condenser retainer screws and lift the breaker point assembly and condenser out of the vehicle.
4. To install, place breaker point assembly and condenser in position and install retaining screws. Be sure to place the ground wire under the breaker point assembly screw farthest from the breaker point contacts on V8 engine distributor or under the condenser retaining screw on 6-cylinder engine distributor.
5. Align and adjust the breaker points as described above.
6. Connect primary and condenser wires to the breaker point assembly.
7. Install rotor and distributor cap.
8. Set ignition timing as described above.

Reference

For detailed service procedures ignition systems and components see the Electrical Diagnosis Section and Trouble Shooting Section in the General Repair Section.

Transistor Ignition System

The tachometer block is used to connect a tachometer or other test equipment into the circuit.

CAUTION: Do not connect test equipment into the circuit in any other manner, or reading will be inaccurate and damage may occur to the resistor, or change its operating characteristics.

Connect the tachometer red lead to the tachometer block small terminal and black lead to the large terminal when making tests.

Ignition timing and breaker point gap are set in the conventional manner as described above.

DC Generator, Regulator

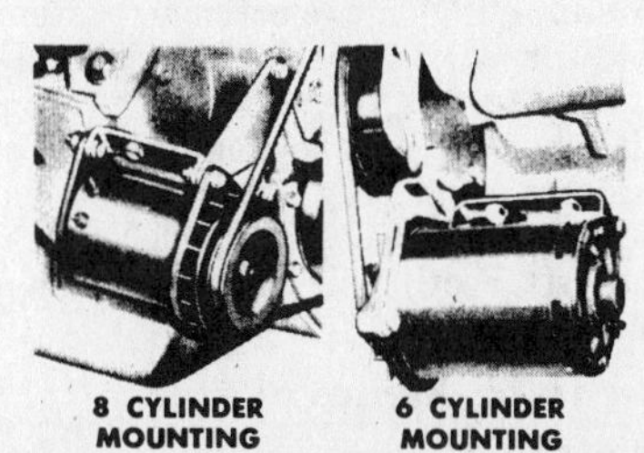

Generator mountings
(© Ford Motor Co.)

DC Generator

1961-64

The DC generator system is a negative ground (—) system. Output is controlled by a regulator which is connected between the armature and field. The standard generator field is grounded internally as illustrated. The field of the 40 ampere Autolite generator is externally grounded through the regulator. For detailed charging system test procedures and charging system component service procedures see the Electrical Diagnosis Section in the General Repair Section.

Generator Removal and Installation

1. Disconnect the armature, field and ground wires at the generator.
2. Remove the adjustment arm to generator bolt, generator drive belt and the two pivot bolts from the mounting bracket.
3. Remove generator.
4. To install, first clean the mating surfaces of the generator frame and mounting bracket. Install the generator in the bracket with the two pivot bolts and lockwashers. Install the generator drive belt and the adjustment arm to generator bolt.
5. Adjust the belt tension and tighten all bolts securely. Install the armature, field and ground leads on the generator terminals.
6. Start engine and check the generator operation.

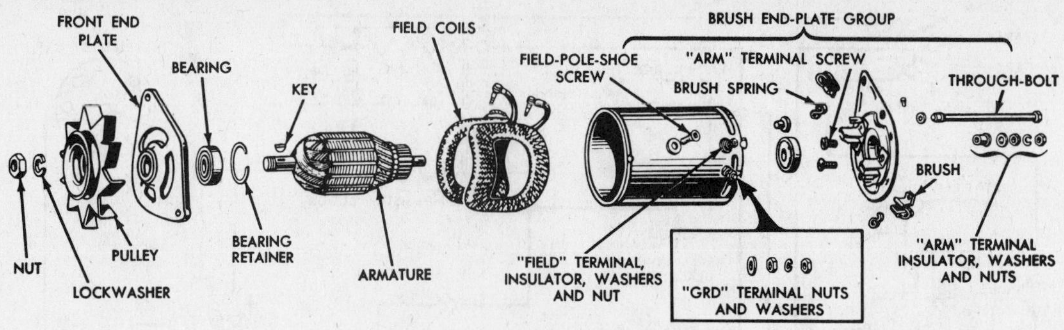

Typical D.C. generator (© Ford Motor Co.)

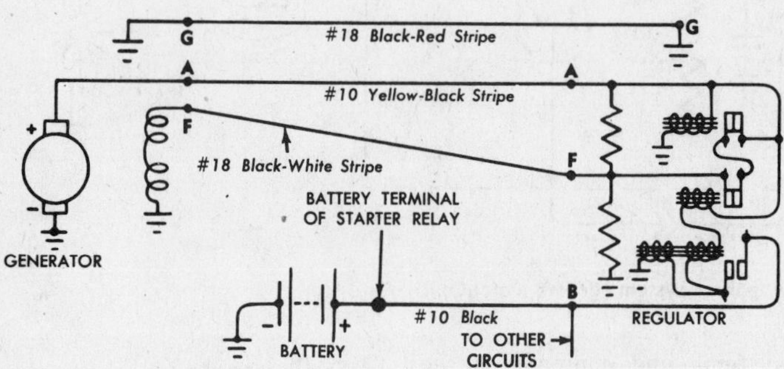

Typical generating system (© Ford Motor Co.)

D.C. regulator (© Ford Motor Co.)

Voltage Regulator Adjustments

If voltage regulator and circuit tests indicate that regulator adjustment is necessary, remove two cover screws and adjust as described below.

1. To adjust cut-in voltage, bend the adjusting arm upward (increase voltage) or downward (decrease voltage). On the heavy-duty regulator, bend spring adjusting arms, upward to decrease and downward to increase cut-in voltage.
2. Voltage limit adjustment is made in the same way as voltage cut-in adjustment described above.
3. Current limit is adjusted by bending the adjusting arm upward (increase current limit) or downward (decrease current limit). On the heavy-duty regulator, bend spring adjusting arm either upward (decrease current limit) or downward (increase current limit).

Regulator Removal and Installation

1. Disconnect battery ground cable.
2. Disconnect ARM, FIELD and GEN leads at the regulator terminals. NOTE: Always disconnect a battery cable when working on the regulator to prevent an accidental short circuit of the BAT lead to the ground.
3. Remove the mounting screws and the regulator.
4. To install the regulator, place it in position and install the mounting screws. Mount the ground wire terminal under the mounting screw closest to the ARM terminal.
5. Connect the ARM, FIELD and BAT wire leads to the regulator.
6. Connect the battery ground cable.

Alternator

The alternator charging system is a negative (—) ground system consisting of an alternator, regulator, charge indicator, storage battery and associated wiring. The belt-driven alternator produces power in the form of alternating current which is rectified to direct current by six diodes (eight diodes in 61 ampere alternators) for use in charging the battery and supplying the electrical system. The alternator is self current limiting and there is therefore no current limiting relay in the regulator. For alternator and regulator electrical testing procedures see the Electrical Diagnosis Section in the General Repair Section.

Alternator Removal and Installation

1. Disconnect battery ground cable.
2. Loosen the alternator mounting bolts and remove the adjustment arm to alternator attaching bolt.
3. Remove the electrical connectors from the alternator. The stator and field connectors are of the push-on type and should be pulled straight off to prevent damage to the terminal studs.
4. Disengage the alternator belt.
5. Remove the alternator mounting bolt and alternator.
6. To install, first install the wiring harness, then position the alternator on engine, installing spacer (if used) and mounting bolt. Tighten bolt only finger tight.
7. Install the adjustment arm to alternator attaching bolt.
8. Adjust belt tension as described

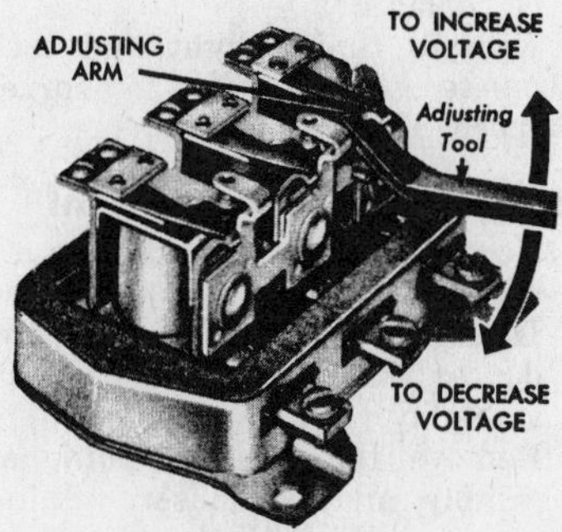

Adjusting D.C. regulator (© Ford Motor Co.)

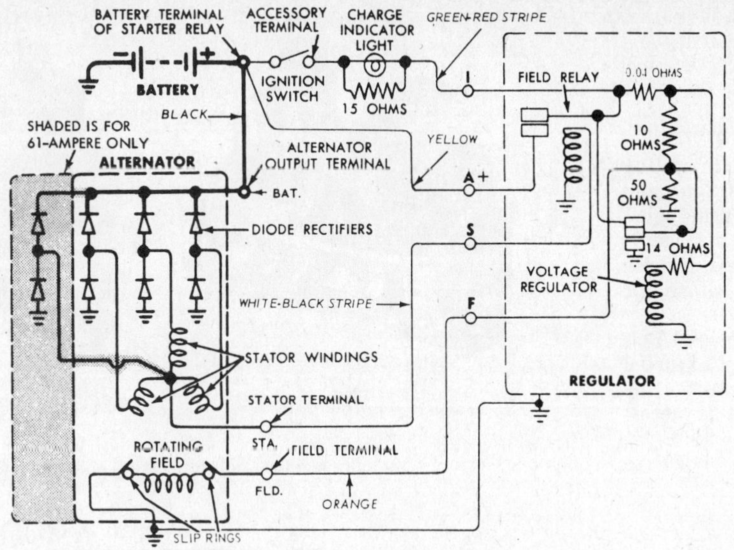

Autolite alternator system (© Ford Motor Co.)

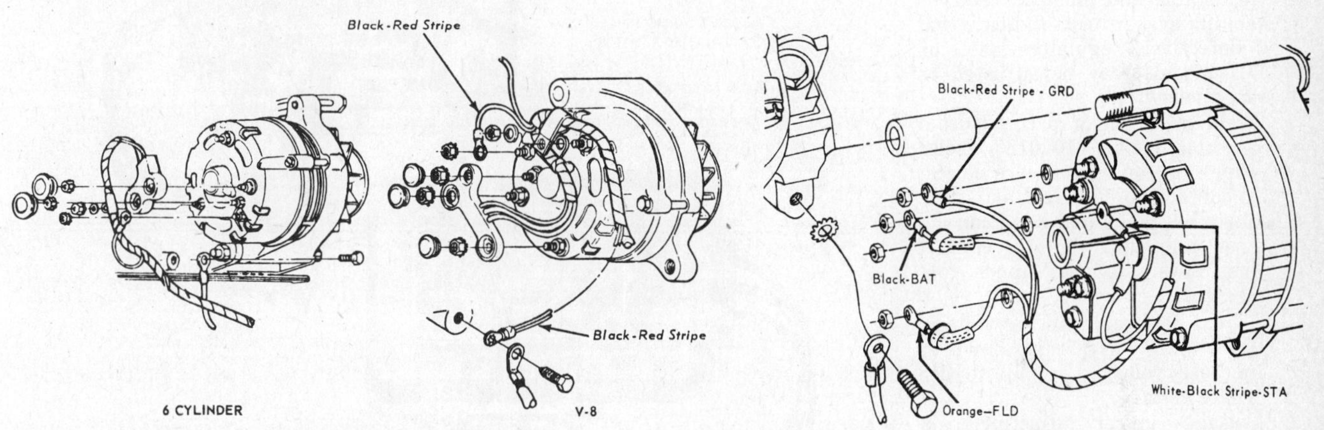

Wiring connections—exc. 65 and 85 amp. alternators
(© Ford Motor Co.)

Wiring connections 65 and 85 amp. alternators
(© Ford Motor Co.)

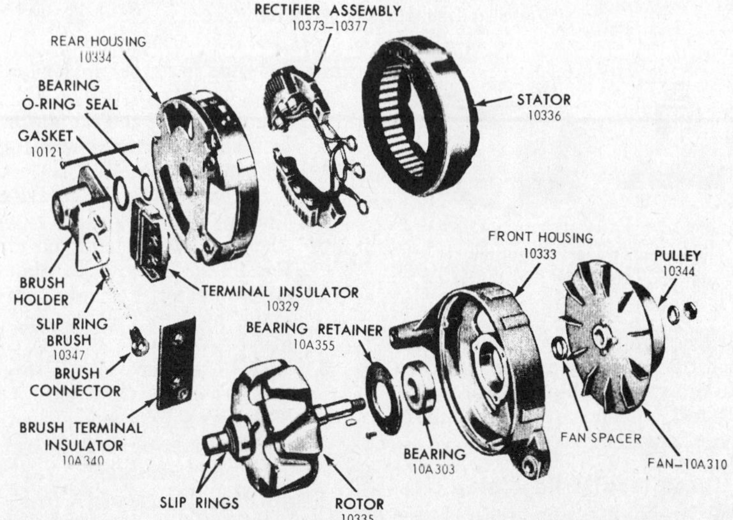

65 amp. Leece Neville alternator (© Ford Motor Co.)

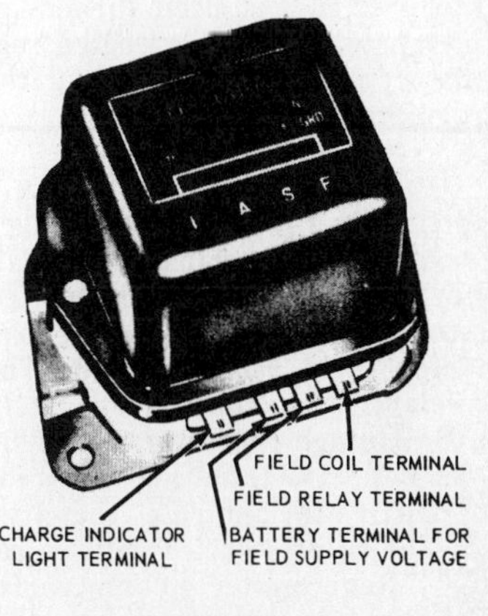

Autolite regulator wiring
(© Ford Motor Co.)

below.
9. Tighten adjusting arm bolts and mounting bolt to 22-32 ft. lbs. torque.

Alternator Belt Adjustment

1. Loosen the alternator mounting bolt to a snug position and loosen the adjusting arm bolt.
2. *Apply pressure on the alternator front housing only* and tighten the adjusting arm to alternator bolt.
3. Check for correct tension. Belt tension is correctly adjusted when belt can be deflected by hand 1/2-3/4". Readjust if necessary.
4. Tighten all mounting bolts to 22-32 ft. lbs. torque.

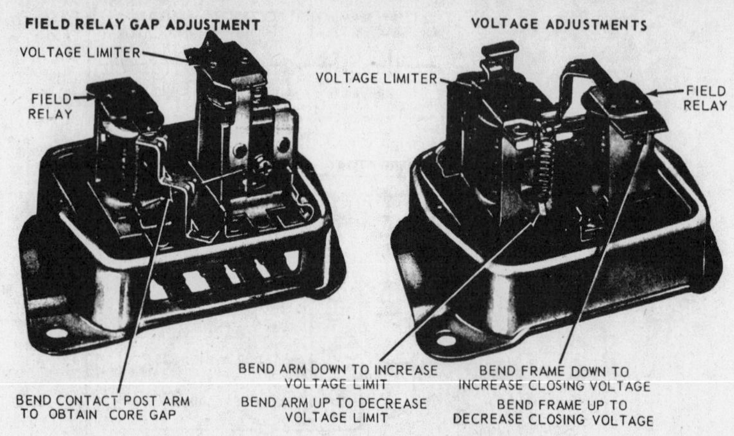

Autolite regulator adjustments (© Ford Motor Co.)

Regulator Adjustments

Autolite

The Autolite electro-mechanical regulator used in 1968-71 models is not adjustable and must be replaced if charging system tests indicate that it is defective. Regulators used on 1962-67 models may be adjusted as described below.

1. Field relay air gap is adjusted by placing a .010-.018" feeler gauge on top of coil core closest to contact points. Hold armature down on gauge and bend contact post arm until bottom contact just barely touches upper contact.
2. Adjust field relay closing voltage by bending relay frame down to increase voltage and up to decrease voltage.
3. Voltage limiter adjustment is made on test stand at normal operating temperature. Bend voltage limiter spring arm down to increase voltage and up to decrease voltage. Adjust while alternator is not turning and ignition switch has been turned on momentarily to de-energize regulator circuits, thus cycling the regulator.

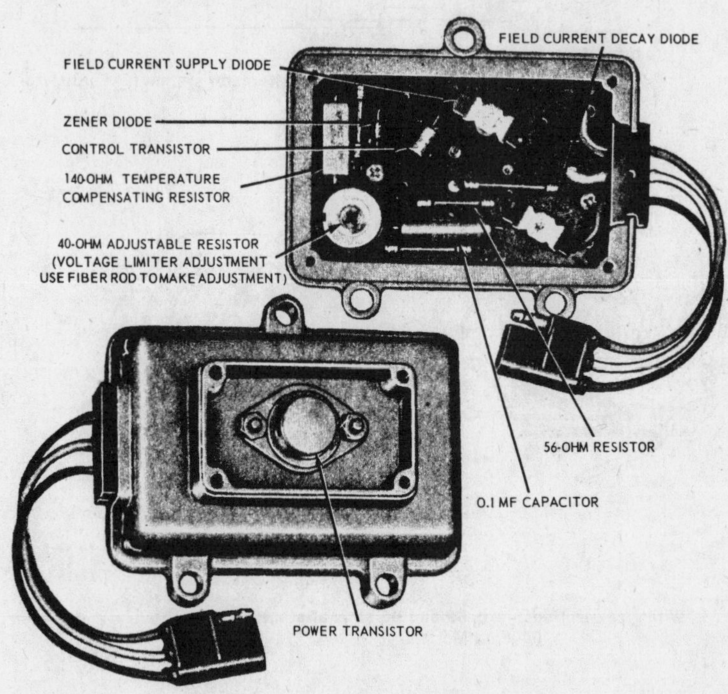

Transistorized regulator (© Ford Motor Co.)

Transistorized Regulator

Starting in 1966, some models were equipped with transistorized alternator regulators. In transistorized regulator circuits the electro-mechanical field relay is used. The field relay is mounted separately from the voltage regulator. The field relay is not adjustable and must be replaced if testing indicates that it is faulty. The transistorized voltage regulator voltage limiter 40 ohm variable resistor may be adjusted as described below.

1. Remove regulator mounting screws and regulator.
2. Remove bottom cover from regulator.
3. With regulator at normal operating temperature, use a fiber rod as a screwdriver to turn 40-ohm adjustable resistor.
4. Install bottom cover and mount regulator.

Field relay transistor ignition (© Ford Motor Co.)

Leece Neville Regulator

Used in conjunction with Leece Neville alternators on some 1964-69 models, the electro-mechanical Leece Neville regulator is adjusted by bending the adjusting arms in 1964 models and, in later models, as follows:

1. Final check of the regulator must be made at normal operating temperature. Regulator is temperature compensated. Remove cover.
2. Voltage limiter contact gap is adjusted before the core gap. Loosen lockscrews to make gap adjustments. Voltage setting is made by bending the adjusting arm.
3. Adjust the core gap before contact gap on the field relay. Loosen lockscrews to make adjustment. Bend adjusting arm to set field relay cut-in voltage.

Regulator Removal and Installation

1. Remove battery ground cable.
2. Remove the regulator mounting screws.

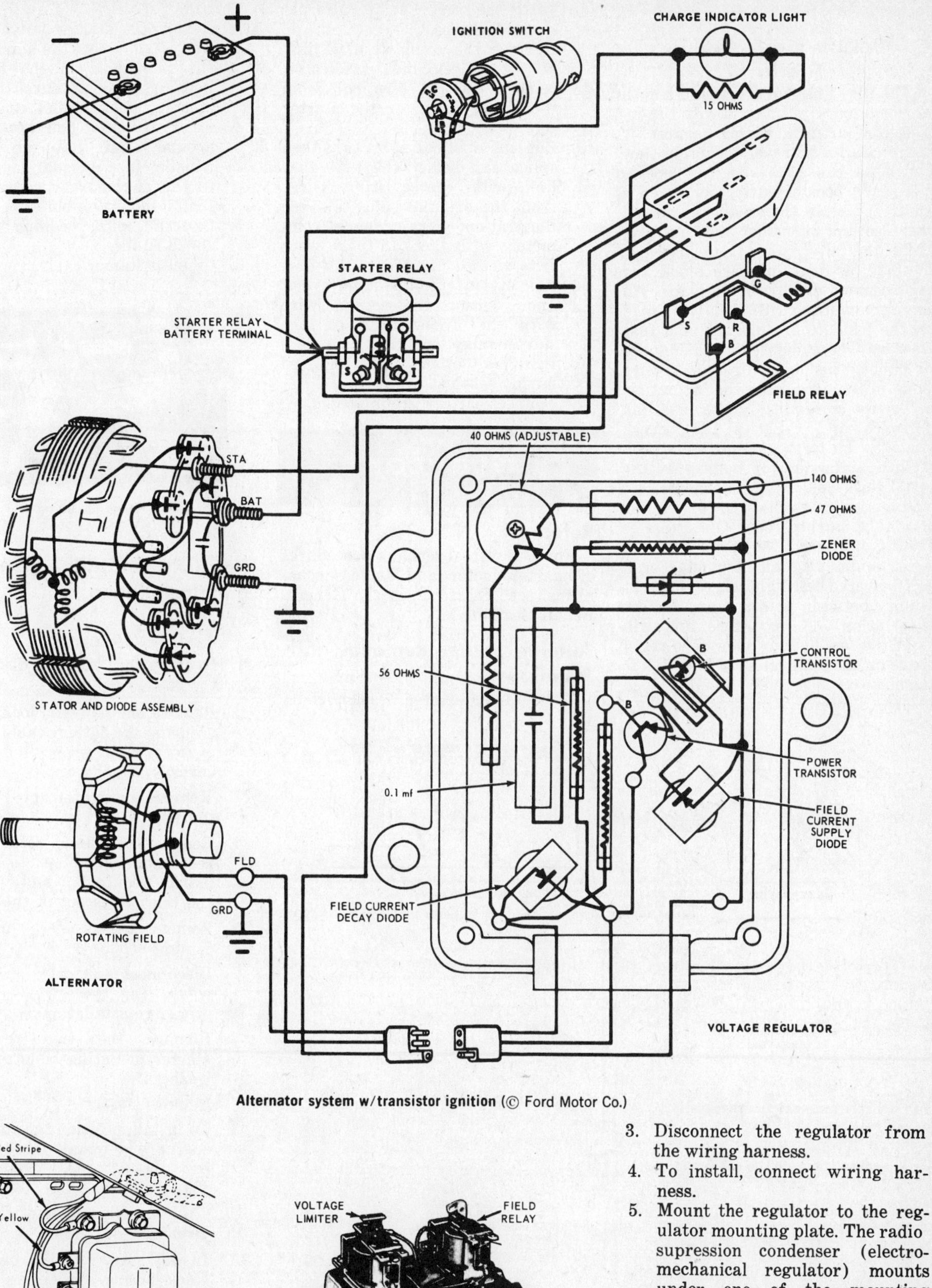

Alternator system w/transistor ignition (© Ford Motor Co.)

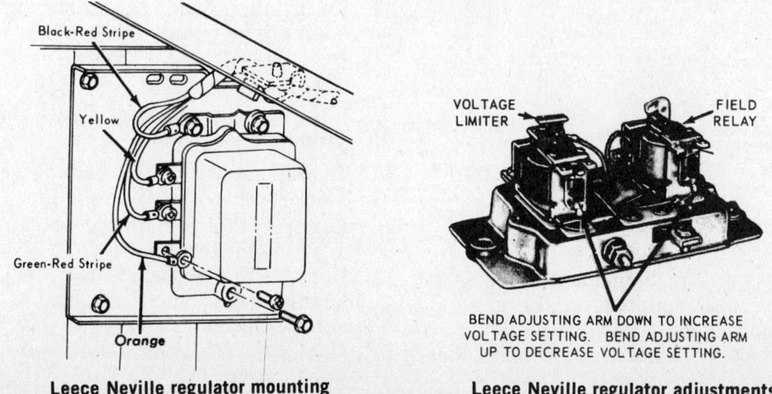

Leece Neville regulator mounting (© Ford Motor Co.)

Leece Neville regulator adjustments (© Ford Motor Co.)

3. Disconnect the regulator from the wiring harness.
4. To install, connect wiring harness.
5. Mount the regulator to the regulator mounting plate. The radio supression condenser (electromechanical regulator) mounts under one of the mounting screws. The ground lead mounts under the other mounting screw.
6. Connect battery ground cable and test the charging system for proper voltage regulation. See Electrical Diagnosis Section in the General Repair Section for testing procedures.

Fuse Link

1970-71 Bronco, P-Series, F-Series LD

The fuse link is a short thin length of insulated wire integral with the engine compartment wiring harness. If there is a heavy reverse current flow (such as caused by an improperly connected booster battery or when a short occurs in the wiring harness), the fuse link burns out and thus protects the alternator from damage. Production fuse links are black and replacement are green or black. All have the words FUSE LINK printed on the insulation. Burn-out of a fuse link may be evidenced by disfigured or bubbled insulation or by bare wire ends protruding from the insulation.

To test continuity of the fuse link (Bronco and F-Series LD) check that the battery is OK, then check with a voltmeter for voltage at the BAT terminal of the alternator. No voltage indicates that the fuse link is probably burned out. On P-Series trucks, disconnect the battery ground cable and, using an ohmmeter or a self-powered test light, check for continuity between points A and B (see illustration). A good fuse link will light the test bulb or show zero resistance on the ohmmeter. If fuse link is burned out, replace as described below.

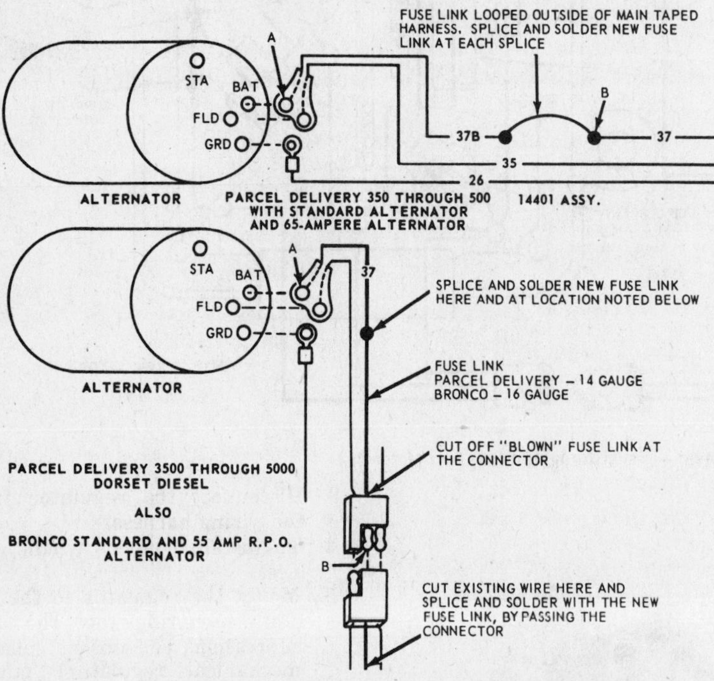

Fusible link installation (© Ford Motor Co.)

Fuse Link Replacement

1. If the 5/16" eyelet terminal is not required, cut it off as close to the terminal as possible.
2. Disconnect battery ground cable.
3. Disconnect the fuse link terminal at the starter relay (alternator on P-Series).
4. Remove the complete fuse link at the splice, when applicable, remove the old terminal from the battery stud of the starter relay.
5. Cut out original splice(s), then splice and solder the new fuse link with the existing wires from the original splice(s). See illustration. Wrap splice completely with tape. If there were two wires connected to the fuse link eyelet, cut link from eyelet and position the second wire with the eyelet back on the starter relay terminal.
6. Install all other wires removed during service.
7. Connect battery ground cable.

Starter

Reference

For complete overhaul procedures of starter motor and drive mechanisms, see "Starters" in the General Repair Section.

Autolite Starter Removal and Installation

This starter utilizes a solenoid integral positive-engagement drive. All starters are mounted on the engine block and flywheel housing.

1. Disconnect starter cable at the starter terminal.
2. Remove the starter mounting bolts.
3. Remove the starter assembly.
4. To install, insert the starter into the pilot hole in the flywheel housing, making sure that the starter housing pilot completely enters the pilot hole all the way around, and that the starter housing face is square and tight to the engine rear cover plate. Install mounting bolts.
5. Snug all bolts, torquing them to 23–28 ft. lbs.
6. Connect starter cable.

Starter mounting
(© Ford Motor Co.)

Delco Remy Starter Removal and Installation

1966-71

1. Open battery box and disconnect the battery cables.
2. Remove one bolt and lockwasher securing the battery cable retainer to the right rear cylinder head cover.
3. Remove the starter upper mounting bolt.
4. Remove the clamps securing the resonator inlet pipes to the exhaust manifolds, and position the inlet pipes out of the way.
5. Remove the starter shield retaining bolts.
6. Disconnect starter and solenoid wires. Tag the wires to insure proper reinstallation.
7. Remove the two remaining starter mounting bolts and lockwashers.
8. Remove starter.
9. To install, position the starter on engine and install three mounting bolts and lockwashers. Tighten to 23–28 ft. lbs. torque.
10. Connect solenoid wire to starter terminal.
11. Install starter shield on engine block with two retaining bolts.
12. Connect the remaining starter wires to the terminals.
13. Connect the resonator inlet pipes to the exhaust manifolds, and secure with clamps.
14. Connect the battery cables and close battery box.
15. Check operation of starter.

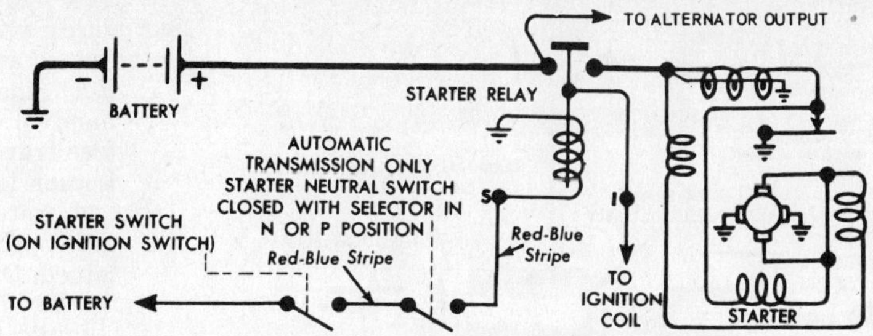

Typical starting circuit (© Ford Motor Co.)

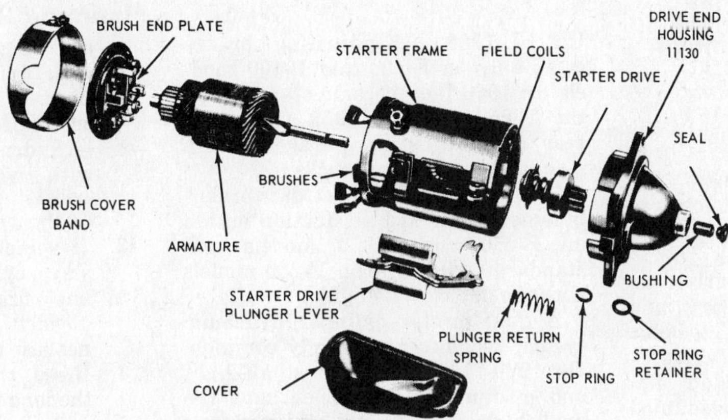

Autolite starter—disassembled (© Ford Motor Co.)

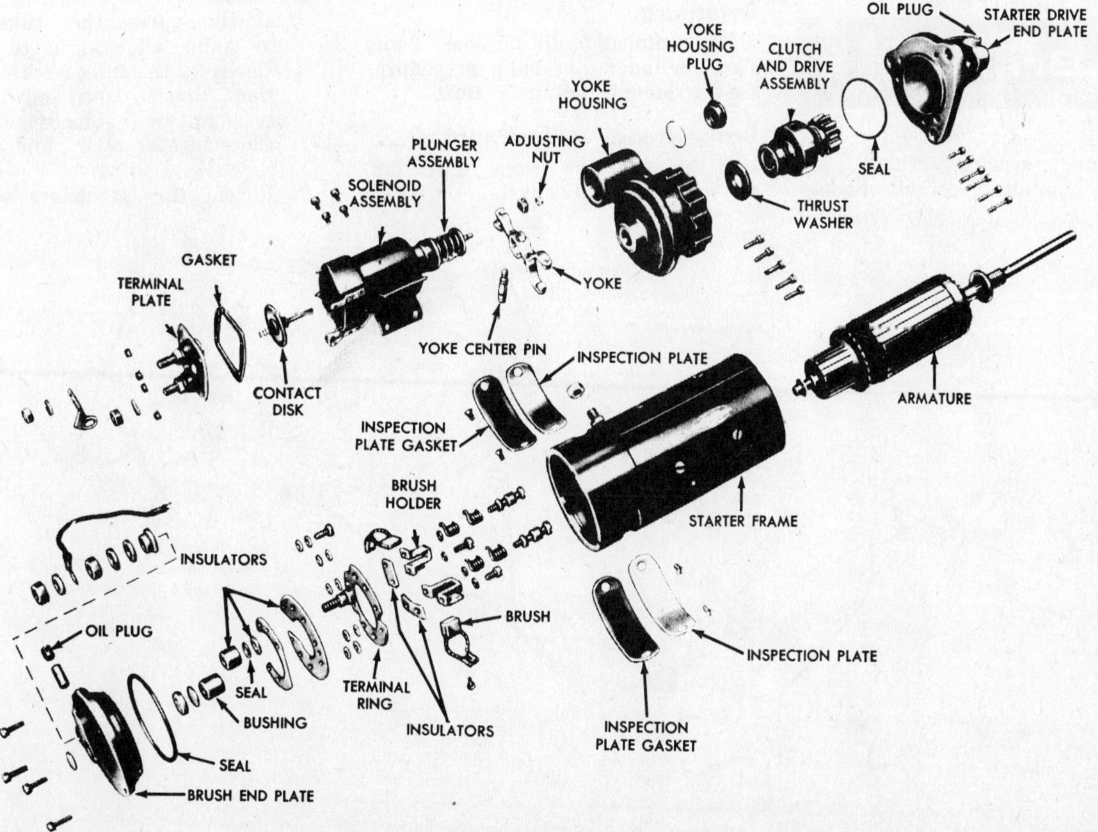

Delco starter—typical—1966-71 (© Ford Motor Co.)

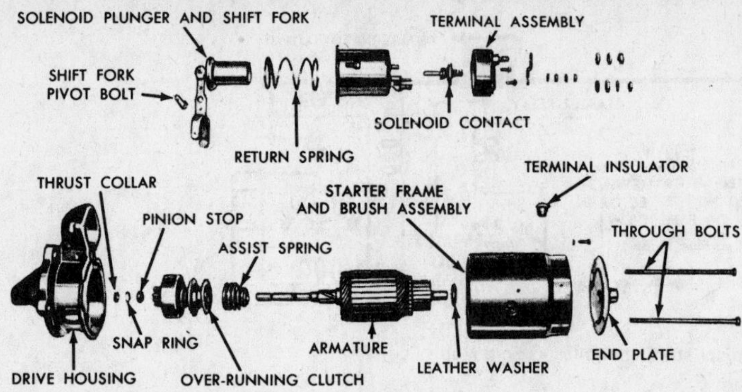

Delco starter—typical—1961-65 (© Ford Motor Co.)

Delco Remy Starter Removal and Installation

1961-65

1. Disconnect starter cable at starter terminal.
2. Remove the flywheel housing to starter retaining bolts.
3. Remove starter assembly.
4. To install, position starter assembly to flywheel housing, and start the starter retaining bolts. On trucks with automatic transmission, the transmission dipstick tube bracket is mounted under the starter side mounting bolt.
5. Tighten mounting bolts to 5-20 ft. lbs. torque.
6. Connect starter cable.

Brakes

Hydraulic

Hydraulic service brakes are standard equipment on all models. Up to 1965, self-adjusting brakes came only on F-100 and P-100 models. In 1966 they became standard on the F-250, and by 1969 front and rear self-adjusting brakes were standard on all Ford trucks.

Starting in 1968, front disc brakes became a standard production option on F-250 and F-350 models and standard equipment on F-250 models with the 390 cu. in. engine.

A dual master cylinder hydraulic system became increasingly common. On 1970-71 models, almost all light and medium duty vehicles have the dual hydraulic system as standard equipment.

Vacuum assist is optional equipment on most 1961-71 models.

Reference

For complete hydraulic master and slave cylinder overhaul procedures see the General Repair Section.

Brake Pedal Adjustment

If the pedal free travel in a standard hydraulic brake system or frame mounted hydraulic booster system is not within 3/16–3/8″, the pedal should be adjusted as follows:

1. Push the brake pedal down by hand pressure, and check the free travel.
2. Loosen locknut on eccentric bolt, and rotate the eccentric bolt until proper free travel is obtained. On P-series trucks rotate the hex head of the push rod to obtain correct free travel.
3. Hold the bolt securely and torque locknut to 30–35 ft. lbs.
4. Recheck brake pedal free travel.

Bleeding Conventional Hydraulic Brake System

1. Fill master cylinder reservoir with fluid. Check level of fluid frequently during bleeding procedure.
2. If hydraulic system is equipped with a vacuum booster, bleed the booster before bleeding the rest of the system.
3. If vehicle is equipped with dual slave cylinders, bleed the upper one first. If there are two bleeder screws, bleed the one nearest the power chamber first.
4. Bleed the wheel cylinder with the longest hydraulic line first.
5. Attach bleeder tube to bleeder screw and place other end of tube in a container partially filled with fluid.
6. Loosen bleeder screw, then slowly depress the brake pedal by hand, allowing it to return slowly to the fully-released position. Repeat until all bubbles cease to flow fom bleeder tube.
7. Close bleeder screw and remove tube.
8. Repeat this procedure at each

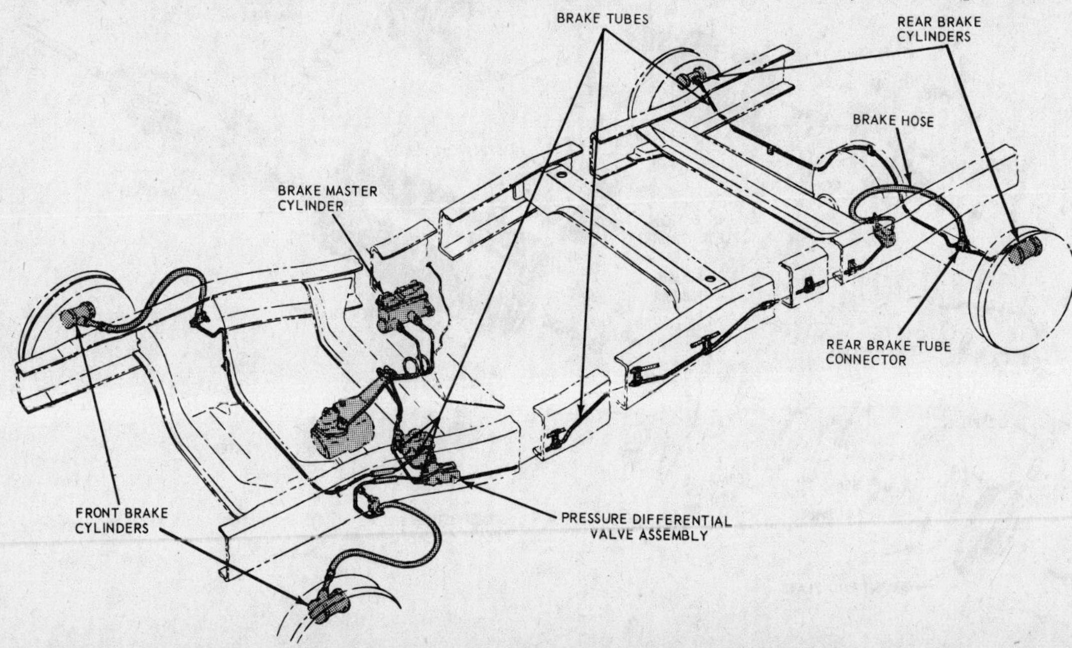

Typical dual master cylinder brake system (© Ford Motor Co.)

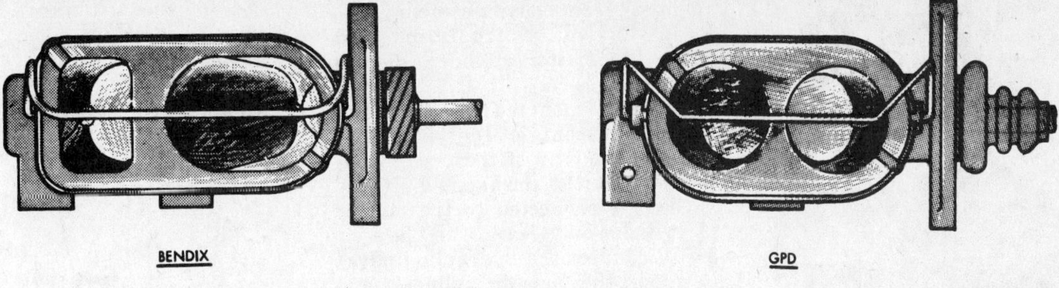

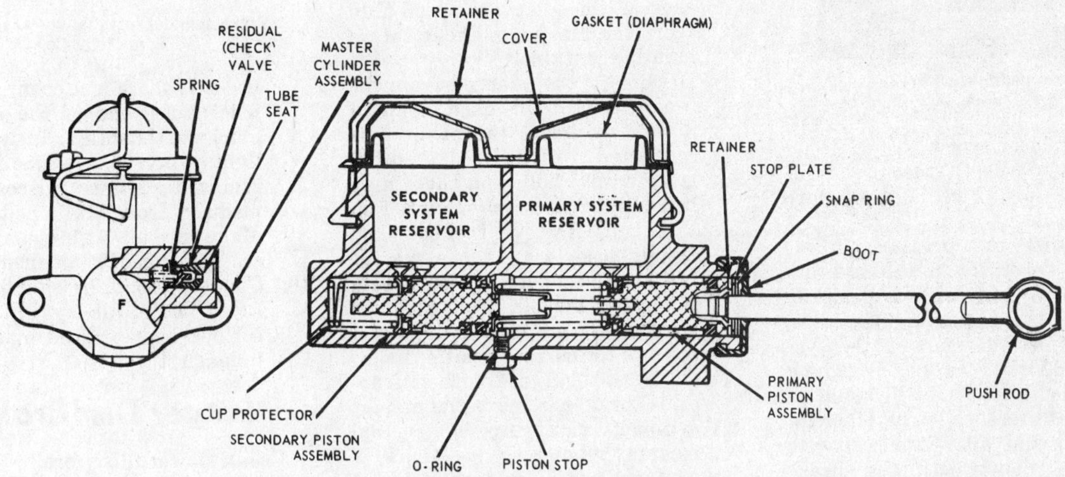

Typical dual master cylinder (© Ford Motor Co.)

wheel until system is completely free of air bubbles.

Bleeding Dual Hydraulic Brake Systems

The primary and secondary hydraulic brake system are individual systems and are bled separately. Bleed the longest line first on the individual system being serviced. Be sure to keep reservoir filled during bleeding operation.

After bleeding it is necessary to centralize the pressure differential valve. On 1970-71 500-950 series trucks, remove the brake warning light switch from the pressure differential valve to prevent damage to the switch assembly.

1. Bleed master cylinder at the outlet port side of the system being serviced. If there are no bleed screws, loosen the hydraulic line nut. Do not use the secondary piston stop screw located on the bottom of the master cylinder—the stop screw or piston could easily be damaged.
2. Operate pedal slowly until fluid is free of air bubbles, then

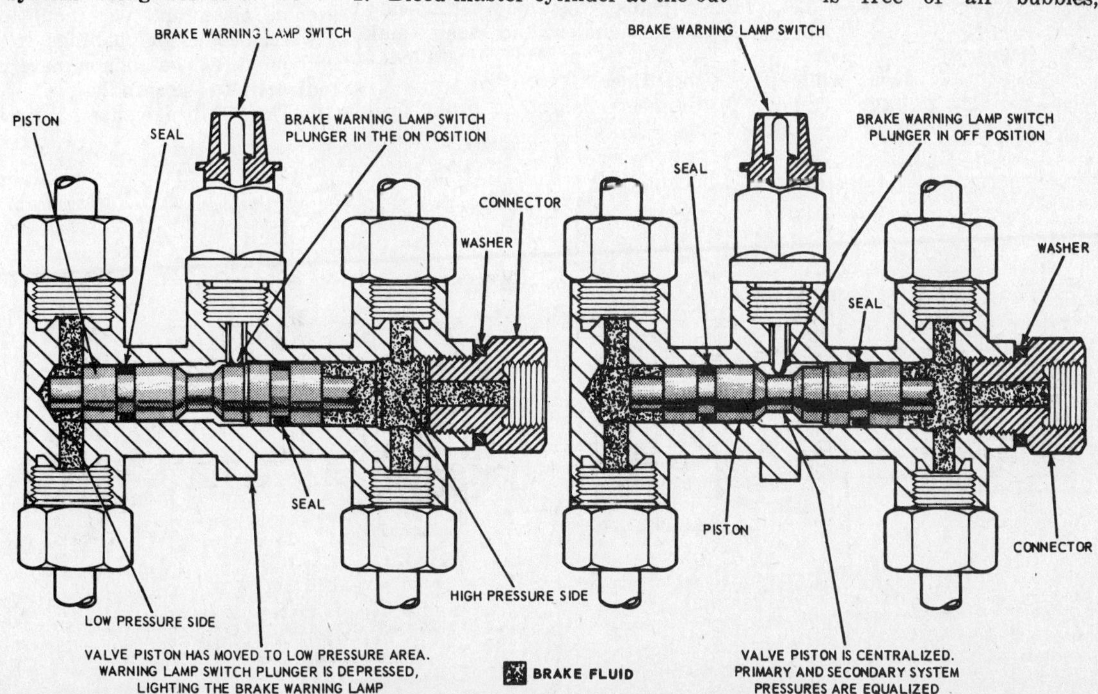

Brake differential valve—100-400 series (© Ford Motor Co.)

Brake pedal free travel
(© Ford Motor Co.)

tighten bleed screw.

3. Follow Steps 1 through 8 of Conventional Bleeding procedure above.
4. Centralize the pressure differential valve. Turn the ignition switch to ACC or ON position. Loosen the pressure differential valve inlet tube nut on the system opposite the system which was bled last. This will result in unequal pressure in the other direction and allow the valve to center. Slowly depress brake pedal until light goes out. Tighten inlet tube nut. On 1970-71 500-900 series trucks, disconnect wires from warning light switch on the differential valve, remove switch. Springs inside valve will center valve. Replace switch and wire.
5. Check fluid level in reservoir and fill to within ¼″ of top.

Master Cylinder Removal and Installation

On models equipped with power boosters, depress brake pedal while engine is not running to expell vacuum or air from booster system.

1. If stoplight switch is mounted on the master cylinder, disconnect wires.
2. On dash-mounted master cylinders, disconnect the dust boot from the rear of the master cylinder at the dash panel. If the boot is connected to the master cylinder only, leave it in place.
3. Disconnect the hydraulic line(s) from the master cylinder and pump the brake pedal all the way several times to evacuate all fluid from the master cylinder into a suitable container.
4. Disconnect the pushrod from the brake pedal. On dash-mounted master cylinders the pushrod is connected to the brake pedal lever with a bolt, and there may be a stoplight switch mounted by that bolt. Remove the bolt and stoplight switch. If the master cylinder is under the floorboard, remove clevis pin from pushrod yoke. Mark or tag bushings and spacers for correct position.
5. On trucks equipped with conventional brakes, remove the master cylinder mounting bolts and master cylinder. If the truck is equipped with a dash-mounted booster, remove the retaining nuts and washers and pull master cylinder off mounting studs.
6. To install, position master cylinder so that mounting bolts or retainer nuts may be installed. Tighten mounting bolts or nuts securely.
7. Connect hydraulic lines(s) loosely to master cylinder fitting(s).
8. If rubber dust boot attaches to both cylinder and dash, make sure it is properly installed at this time.
9. Connect pushrod to brake pedal lever. If there is a bushing in the hole at the end of the pushrod, lubricate bushing. Install stoplight switch at this time if it was removed when disconnecting pushrod from brake pedal lever. Make sure all bushings and spacers are properly installed.
10. Connect stoplight switch wires.
11. Bleed hydraulic system as described above. Bleed master cylinder first.

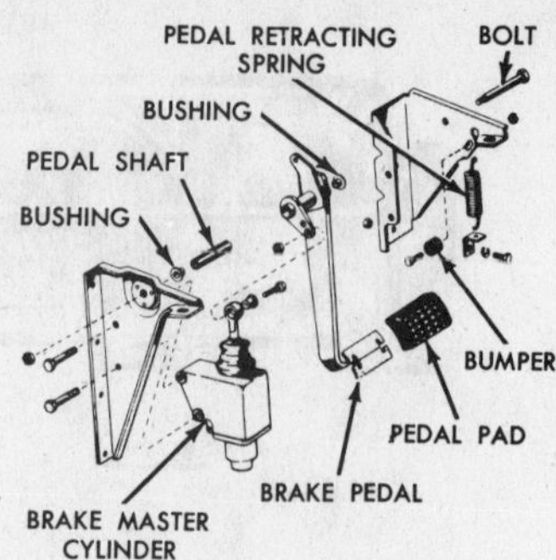

Brake cylinder installation—C series
(© Ford Motor Co.)

Power Disc Brake

Front power disc brakes became available as an option on F-250 and F-350 models in 1968. The brake system consists of a dual master cylinder coupled to a dash-mounted vacuum booster. Both primary and secondary hydraulic lines run to a differential valve and warning light switch unit. A metering valve is located in the front brake line between the pressure differential valve and the disc brake calipers. The double piston housing is mounted to the anchor plate on two mounting pins which travel in bushings in the anchor plate. The anchor plate is bolted directly to the spindle.

The disc brake shoe requires no ad-

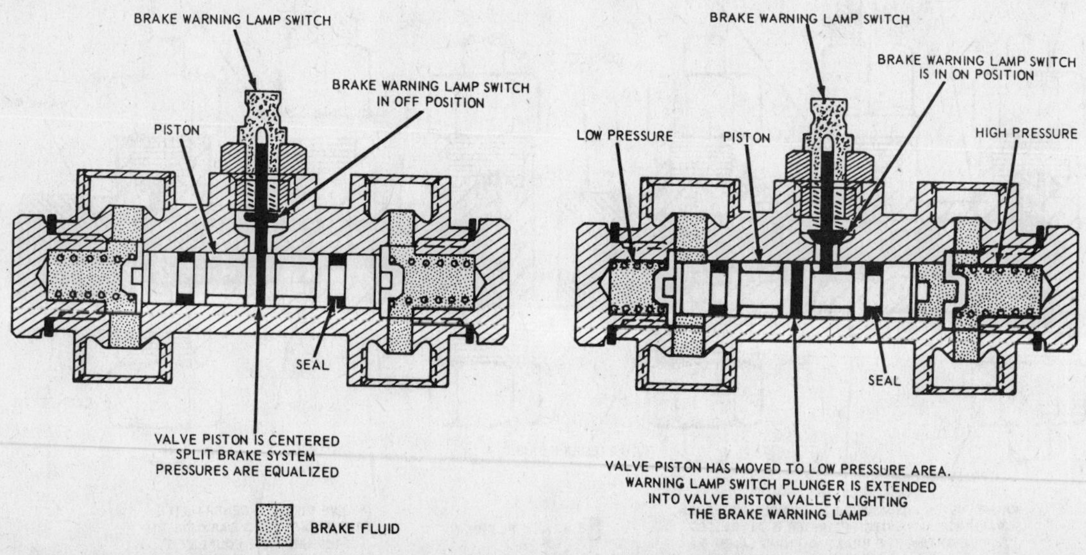

Brake differential valve—500-900 series w/split hydraulic brakes (© Ford Motor Co.)

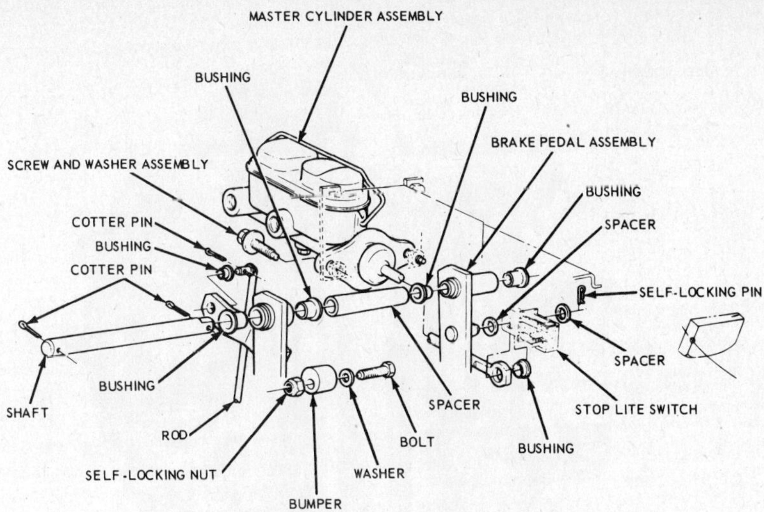

Typical dash mounted master cylinder (© Ford Motor Co.)

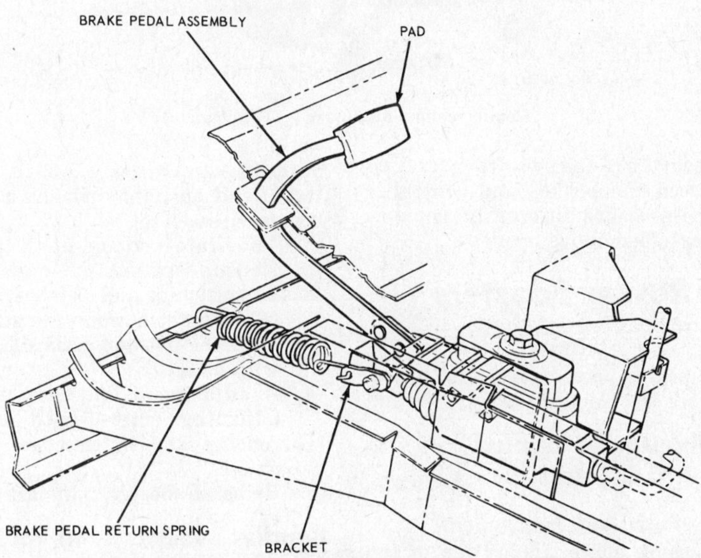

Brake cylinder installation—early Econoline models (© Ford Motor Co.)

justment as the unit is designed so that it is inherently self-adjusting.

Bleeding Disc Brake Hydraulic System

The hydraulic system may be bled in the conventional manner, with the following additional steps.

1. First bleed master cylinder, then rear brake cylinders (longest line first).
2. On front disc brakes, the bleeder button on the metering valve must be depressed to allow the brake fluid to reach the caliper assemblies. When the bleeding operation is complete, fill the reservoir to within ¼″ of top.
3. Centralize the pressure differential valve as described above in "Bleeding Dual Hydraulic Brake Systems".

Shoe and Lining Removal and Installation

Replace shoe and lining assembles when lining is worn to a minimum of 1/16″ in thickness (combined thickness of shoe and lining: ¼″ minimum).

1. Remove shoe and lining mounting pins, anti-rattle springs and old shoe and lining assemblies.
2. To install, remove the master cylinder cover.
3. Loosen the piston housing to caliper mounting bolts sufficiently to permit the installation of new shoe and lining assemblies. CAUTION: Do not move pistons.
4. Install new shoe and lining assemblies. Install the brake shoe mounting pins and anti-rattle springs. Be sure that the spring tangs are located in the holes provided in the shoe plates.

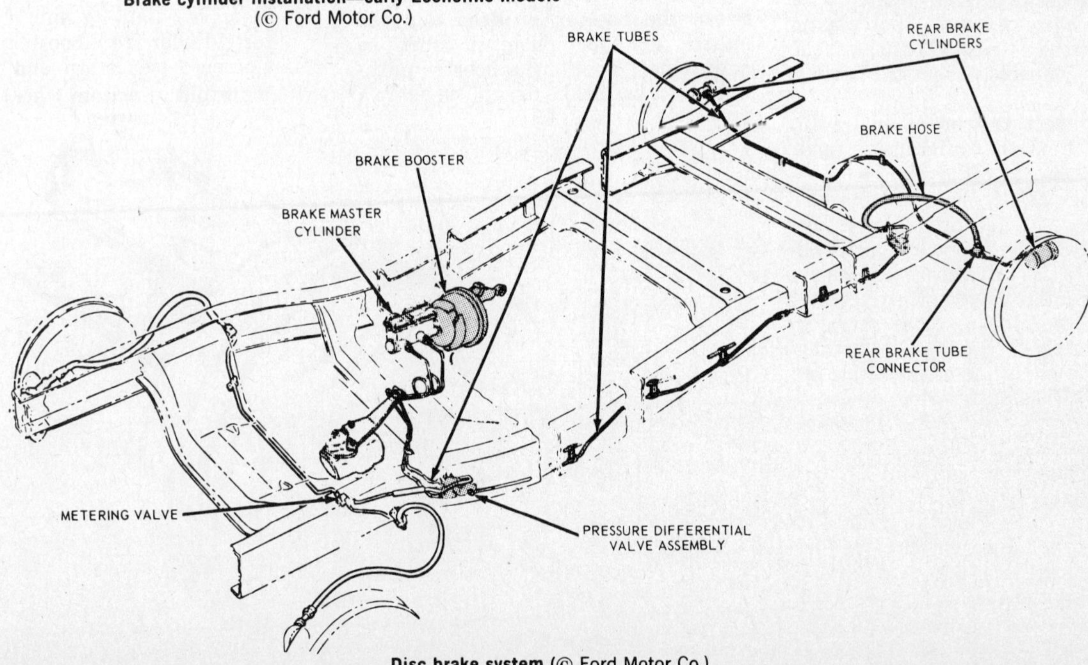

Disc brake system (© Ford Motor Co.)

Brake metering valve (© Ford Motor Co.)

5. Torque the brake shoe mounting pins to 17-23 ft. lbs.
6. Reset the pistons to the correct location in the cylinders by placing shims or feeler gauges of .023-.035" thickness between the shoe plate of the outboard shoe and lining assembly and the caliper.
7. Retighten the piston housing to caliper mounting bolts. Be sure to keep the cylinder housing square with the caliper. Check master cylinder for brake fluid overflow.
8. Loosen piston housing to caliper mounting bolts and remove the shims or feeler gauge.
9. Torque the piston housing to caliper mounting bolts to 155-185 ft. lbs.
10. Check master cylinder reservoirs, refilling if necessary to within ¼" of top.

Differential Valve Removal and Installation

1. Raise the vehicle on a hoist.
2. Disconnect the brake warning light from the pressure differential valve assembly switch. CAUTION: To prevent damage to the brake warning switch wire connector, expand the plastic lugs to allow removal of the shell-wire connector from the switch body.
3. Disconnect the brake hydraulic lines from the differential valve assembly.
4. Remove the screw retaining the pressure differential valve assembly to the frame side rail and remove the valve assembly.
5. Differential valve and switch are separate units and are serviced separately. Remove warning light switch from valve to replace either unit.
6. To install, mount the pressure differential valve assembly on the frame side rail and tighten the attaching bolt.
7. Connect the brake hydraulic lines to the differential valve and tighten the tube nuts securely.
8. Connect the shell-wire connector to the brake warning light switch. Make sure plastic lugs on the connector hold the connector securely to the switch.
9. Bleed the brakes and centralize the pressure differential valve as described above.

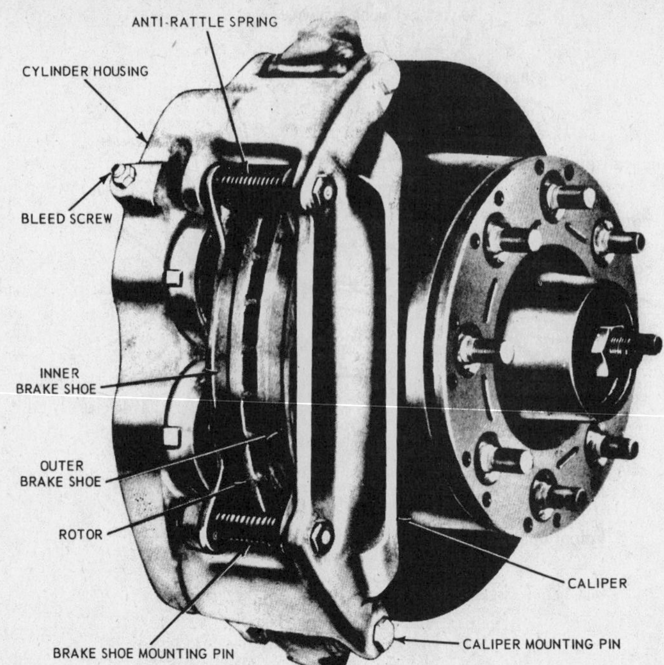

Floating caliper disc brake (© Ford Motor Co.)

Power Boosters

Reference

For power booster overhaul procedures see the General Repair Section.

Bendix Dash-Mounted Vacuum Booster

Push Rod Adjustment

To assure correct operation of the vacuum booster, proper clearance between the booster pushrod and the master cylinder pushrod must be maintained. Too long a booster pushrod can cause brake drag. Too short a pushrod can cause excessive pedal travel and an annoying clunk in the booster area.

1. Fabricate a gauge of the dimensions illustrated.
2. Unbolt nuts and remove master cylinder from mounting studs.
3. Measure booster pushrod length with gauge.
4. If adjustment is necessary, turn adjusting screw until it just touches the inner edge of the gauge.
5. Reinstall master cylinder.

Bendix Booster Removal and Installation

1. Remove retaining nuts and master cylinder from booster.
2. Loosen hose clamp and remove manifold vacuum hose from

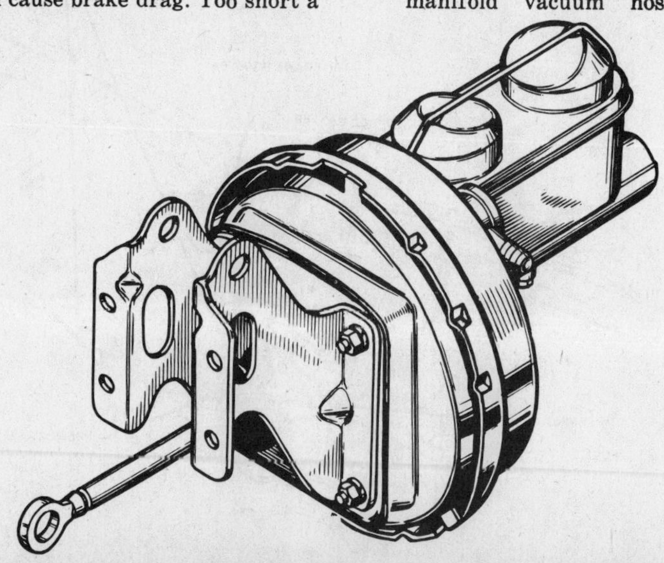

Bendix dash mounted vacuum booster (© Ford Motor Co.)

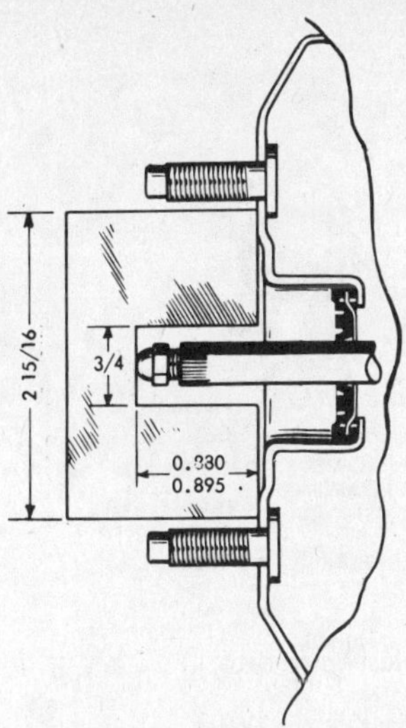

Bendix booster push rod adjustments (© Ford Motor Co.)

booster.

3. From inside the cab, remove the attaching bolt, nut and plastic bushings and disconnect the booster pushrod from the brake pedal.
4. Remove nuts that retain the booster mounting bracket to the dash panel.
5. Remove the booster assembly from engine compartment.
6. To install, mount the booster and bracket assembly to the engine side of the dash panel by sliding the bracket mounting bolts and valve operating rod in through the holes in the dash panel.
7. From inside the cab, install the booster mounting bracket to dash panel retaining nuts.
8. Position the master cylinder to the booster assembly and install the retaining nuts.
9. Connect the manifold vacuum hose to the booster and secure with clamp.
10. From inside the cab connect the booster valve operating rod to the brake pedal with the attaching bolt, nut and plastic bushings.
11. Start engine and check operation of the brake system.

Midland-Ross Dash-Mounted Vacuum Booster

Pushrod Adjustment

Checking the adjustment of the pushrod length on the dash-mounted Midland-Ross vacuum brake booster is the same as that described for the Bendix above, with the exception of the gauge dimensions.

Midland-Ross Booster Removal and Installation

Removal and installation procedure for the Midland-Ross booster is the same as that described for the Bendix booster above.

Parking Brakes

Adjustment

Orscheln Lever

The Orscheln parking brake is the over center locking type. It is adjusted (in the fully released position) by turning the lever knob. When properly adjusted, it pulls over center with a distinct click. No other adjustment is normally required.

Cable Actuated Rear Wheel Type

Adjust service breaks before attempting to adjust the parking brake cables. Place parking brake lever in fully released position, then check for slack in the parking brake two rear cables. Cables are properly adjusted when the rear brake shoes are fully applied when parking brake is applied, and the brake shoes fully release when the parking brake lever is released.

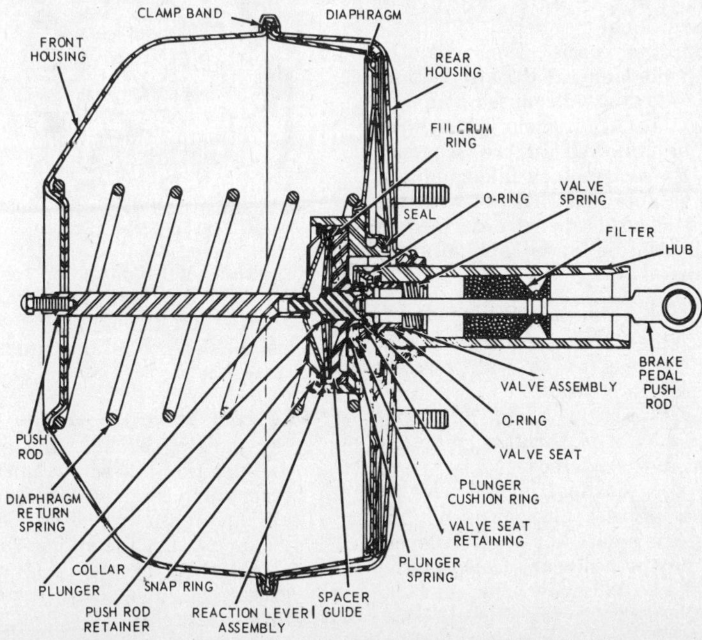

Midland Ross dash mounted vacuum booster (© Ford Motor Co.)

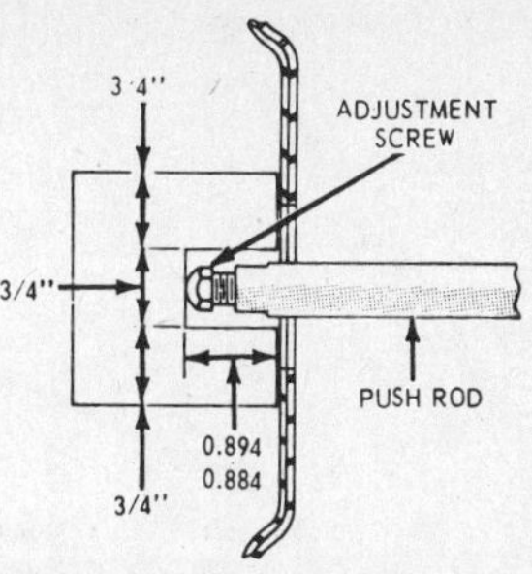

Midland Ross booster push rod adjustments (© Ford Motor Co.)

To tighten cables, loosen locknut and tighten adjusting nut on equalizer. Tighten locknut when proper adjustment is obtained.

External Band Type

1. On cable controlled parking brakes, move the parking brake lever to the fully released position. On a vehicle with a rod type linkage, set the lever at the first notch.
2. Check the position of the cam to make sure that the flat portion is resting on the brake band bracket. If the cam is not flat with the bracket, remove the clevis pin from the upper part of the cam and adjust the clevis rod to allow the flat portion of the cam to rest on the brake band bracket. Install the clevis pin and cotter pin.
3. Remove the lock wire from the anchor adjusting screw, and turn the adjusting screw clockwise until a clearance of 0.100" is obtained between the brake lining and the brake drum at the anchor bracket. Install the lock wire in the anchor adjusting screw.
4. Adjust the clearance on the upper and lower halves of the band in a similar manner. See illustration for location of adjusting screws. Adjust for a 0.010" clearance between band and drum.

Internal Shoe Type 9" Drum

1. Release parking brake lever.
2. Remove cotter pin from the parking brake linkage adjusting clevis pin and remove the clevis pin.
3. Lengthen or shorten adjusting link by turning the clevis. There

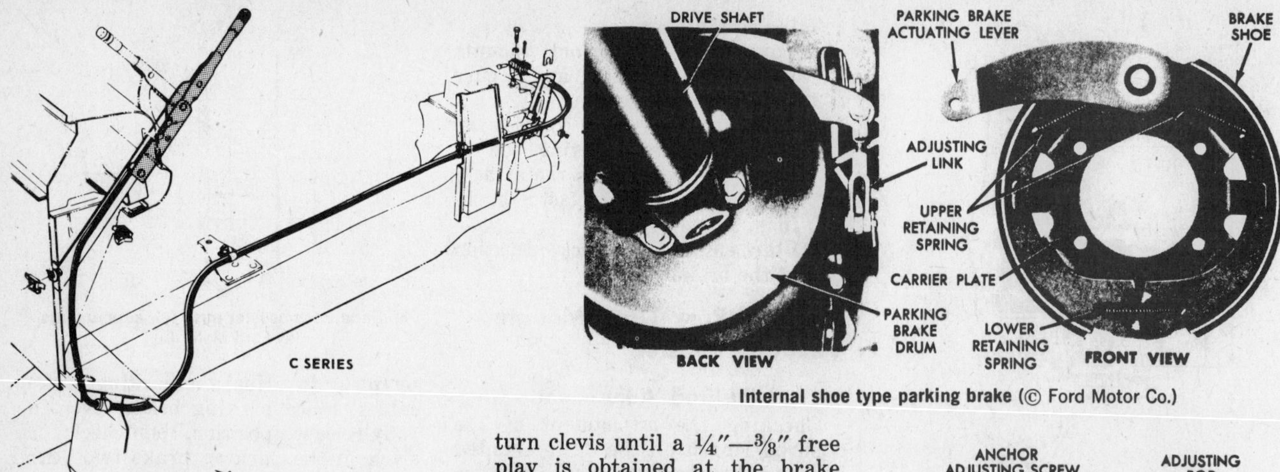

Internal shoe type parking brake (© Ford Motor Co.)

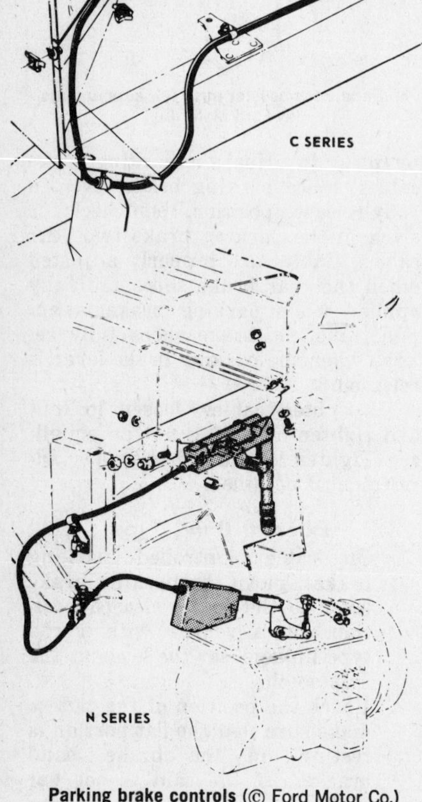

Parking brake controls (© Ford Motor Co.)

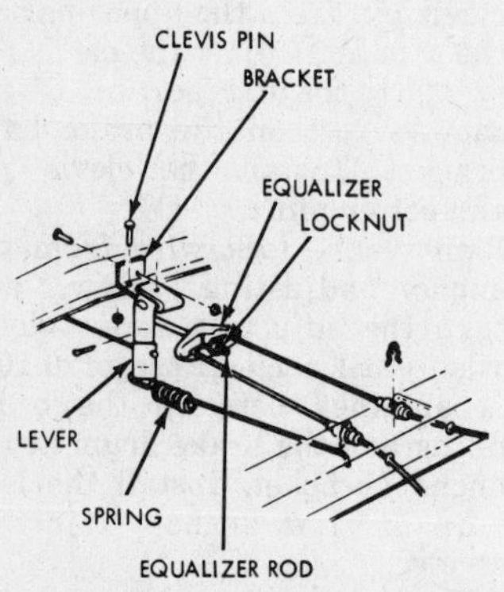

Parking brake cable adjustment (© Ford Motor Co.)

should be a 0.010″ clearance between the drum and the band all the way around when the clevis pin is installed.

4. Install a new cotter pin in the clevis pin and check brake operation.

12″ Drum

There is no internal adjustment on this brake. Adjust the linkage as follows:

1. Remove clevis pin, loosen the nuts on the adjusting rod and turn clevis until a ¼″—⅜″ free play is obtained at the brake lever with pin installed.
2. Tighten locknuts on adjusting rod and reinstall clevis pin.

Fuel System

On models 1968 and later, all carburetors on Ford trucks are equipped with fuel mixture adjusting limiters. The external type plastic idle limiter cap is installed on the head of the idle fuel mixture adjusting screw(s). The cap limits the maximum idle fuel richness and helps prevent unauthorized persons from making overly rich idle adjustments.

On the Autolite 2-barrel, the limiter stops must be installed under the power valve cover in order that the limiters have positive stops.

If all other engine systems are operating within specifications, a satisfactory idle should be obtainable within the range of idle adjusting limiters. Carburetors on models 1967 and earlier are, of course, adjusted in the conventional manner.

Carburetor specifications may be found in the General Repair Section.

The following idle speed and idle fuel mixture adjustment procedures should be followed in the sequence given. If a satisfactory idle condition cannot be obtained, proceed with the checks and adjustments described in "Additional Idle Speed and Mixture Procedures".

Idle Fuel Settings—Engine Off

1. Set idle mixture screw(s) and limiter cap(s) to full counterclockwise position.
2. Back off idle speed adjusting screw until throttle plate(s) seat in throttle bore(s).
3. Be sure dashpot or solenoid (if so equipped) plunger is not interfering with the throttle lever. It may be necessary to loosen the dashpot to allow the throttle plate to seat in the throttle bore.
4. Turn the idle speed adjusting screw inward until it just makes contact with stop on throttle shaft and lever assembly, then turn screw inward 1½ turns to establish a preliminary idle speed adjustment.

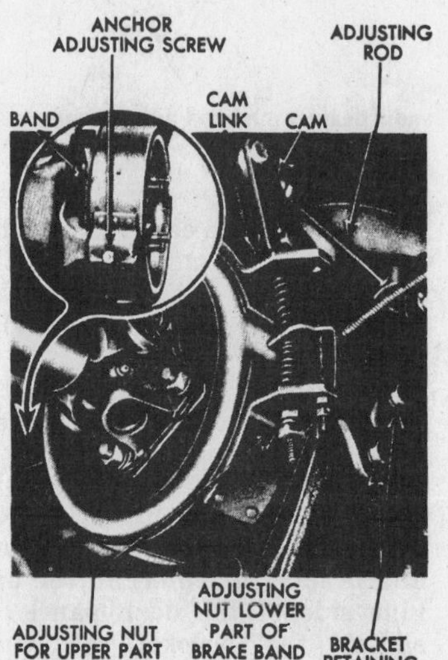

External band type parking brake (© Ford Motor Co.)

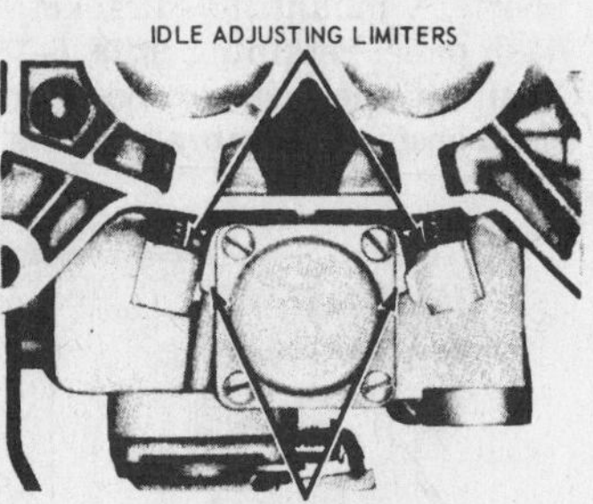

Idle adjusting limiters & stops—Autolite (© Ford Motor Co.)

Idle Fuel Settings—Engine On

1. Set parking brake, start engine and position idle screw on the intermediate step of the fast idle cam to obtain an engine speed of 1500 rpm. Let the engine run for at least 20 minutes so that engine and underhood temperatures are stabilized.
2. Check ignition timing and advance as described above in this

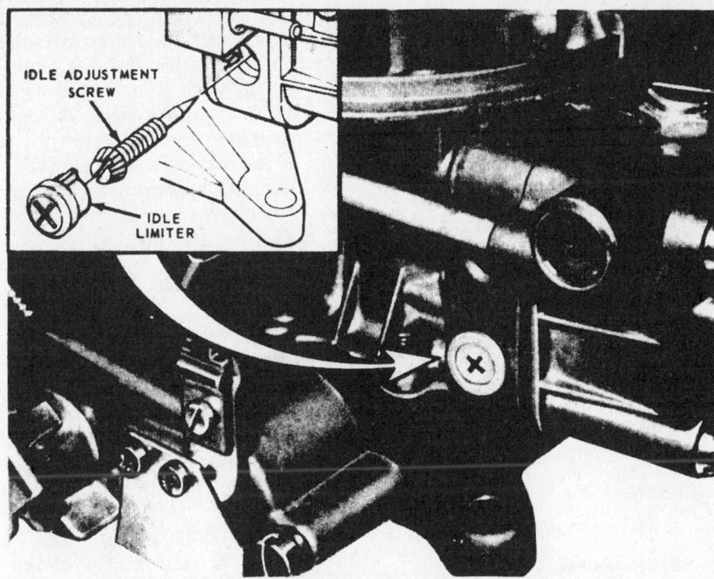

Idle fuel mixture limiter—Holley 4 BBL (© Ford Motor Co.)

section. These settings must be accurate.

3. On manual transmission model, idle setting is made with transmission in *neutral.* On automatic transmission models, set selector lever in DRIVE position and parking brake on, except as noted when using an exhaust gas analyzer.
4. Be sure choke plate is in full open position.
5. On carburetors equipped with a hot idle compensator or where the idle compensator is in the crankcase ventilation hose, be sure the compensator is seated to allow for proper idle adjustment.
6. Turn headlights on so that alternator is under load.
7. Turn air conditioner OFF for final idle speed adjustment, except on 1968 models, where the air conditioner is turned on to maximum cooling.
8. Adjust curb idle rpm to specifications (see Specifications at the beginning of this section or in the Carburetor section of the General Repair Section). Use a tachometer and leave the air cleaner on. On Carter model YF IV with solenoid throttle modulator, turn solenoid plunger screw to obtain correct curb idle. Disconnect solenoid lead wire at bullet connector near the loom (*not* at solenoid), then adjust the throttle stop screw for 500 rpm. Reconnect solenoid lead wire and open throttle by hand: the throttle plunger should follow the throttle lever and remain in the fully extended position as long as the ignition is on and the solenoid energized. If it is impossible to idle speed with the air cleaner on, remove it to adjust, then reinstall it and check speed, repeating the process until correct idle speed is obtained.
9. Turn idle mixture adjusting screw(s) inward to obtain the smoothest possible idle within range of limiter(s). On 2- and 4-barrel carburetors, turn idle mixture limiters and equal amount. Check for smoothness only with the air cleaner installed.

Additional Idle Speed and Mixture Procedures

If a satisfactory idle is not obtained with the above normal procedures, make the following checks, making corrections if necessary:

1. Vacuum leaks, ignition wiring continuity, spark plugs, breaker point dwell angle, breaker point gap and initial ignition timing.
2. If a satisfactory idle condition is still not obtained with the checks and corrections of Step 1 above, check: fuel level, crankcase ventilation system, valve clearance and engine compression.
3. If the above procedures fail to produce a satisfactory idle condition, it may be due to a lean idle mixture. Check air-fuel mixture with an exhaust analyzer and adjust as described below.

Use of Exhaust Gas Analyzer

1. Connect analyzer in accordance with manufacturer's instructions. All exhaust gas analyzers must be checked for calibration.
2. Observe reading with *air cleaner installed.* Refer to specifications below for correct air-fuel ration.
3. Turn idle mixture adjusting screw(s) to obtain specified air-fuel ratio. On 2- and 4-barrel carburetors, turn the idle limiters equal amounts. Be sure to check idle speed frequently, correcting if necessary. Allow at least 10 seconds after each mixture adjustment for the analyzer to properly respond and stabilize.
4. If the air-fuel ratio is not to specifications, as shown by analyzer reading, it may be corrected by altering the controlled limits of the idle mixture system. See following paragraph for limiter cap replacement procedure.

Replacing Idle Limiter Caps

1. Cut plastic cap with a knife or side-cutter pliers, then carefully pry limiter apart. On some carburetors it may be necessary to remove the carburetor to remove the limiters. On Holley 4-barrel carburetors, pry limiters out of metering block with a screwdriver.
2. After limiters are removed, set the carburetor to the correct fuel-ratio, using exhaust gas analyzer.
3. When air-fuel ratio is within specified value, install limiter caps. Install cap so that it is the maximum counterclockwise position with the tab of the limiter against the stop on the carburetor. Be careful not to turn the screw, installing cap with a straight, forward push.
4. Recheck air-fuel ratio with the analizer.

Carter YF 1-Barrel

Fast Idle Adjustment Manual Choke

1. Open the throttle plate and hold the choke plate fully closed to allow the fast idle cam to revolve to the fast idle position.
2. To adjust the fast idle, bend the choke connector rod until there is light contact between the fast idle arm and the stop on the carburetor body.

Carter YF-1V with solenoid throttle modulator (© Ford Motor Co.)

Air Fuel Ratio

Engine	Year	Model	Transmission	Ratio (air/fuel)
		6-CYLINDER		
170 cu. in.	1969	Bronco, E-series	manual	13.8
	1970-71	Bronco, E-series	manual	14.4
240 cu. in.	1968	(Imco emission)	manual	13.75
	1968	(Thermactor emission)	auto	13.9
	1969	All models	man'l/auto	13.91
	1970-71	F, B, N-500	manual	13.66
	1970-71	P-350, 400, 500	man'l/auto	13.65
	1970	F-250 (4x2)	man'l/auto	13.9
	1970	F-250 (4x4)	manual	14.7
	1970	F-350	man'l/auto	13.9
	1970	E-100	manual	14.7
	1970	E-100, 200, 300 bus	manual	14.7
	1970	F-100 (4x4, 4x2)	manual	14.7
	1970	E-100, 200, 300 bus	auto	14.4
	1970	F-100 (4x2)	auto	14.7
	1971	All models except:	man'l/auto	greater than 14.5
	1971	F, B, N-500 and P-350, 400, 500		
300 cu. in	1968-69	(Imco emission)	man'l/auto	13.91
	1968	(Thermactor emission)	man'l/auto	13.75
	1970	All except F-100	man'l/auto	13.5
	1970	F-100	man'l/auto	14.2
	1971	F-100	man'l/auto	greater than 14.5
	1971	F-250, 350	man'l/auto	13.7
	1971	C-500, 600 P-350, 400, 500 F, B, LN-500, 600	man'l/auto	13.65
		8-CYLINDER		
302 cu. in.	1969	Bronco, E-series	manual	14.0
		E-series	auto	13.81
	1970	Bronco	manual	14.0
	1970-71	E-100, 200, 300, F-100	manual	14.0
	1970-71	E-100, 200, 300, F-100	auto	13.8
330 cu. in.	1969	MD models	man'l/auto	14.5
	1970	MD with Autolite carb	manual	13.0
	1970	MD with Holley carb	man'l/auto	14.5
	1971	All models	man'l/auto	14.5
360 cu. in.	1968	(Imco emission)	man'l/auto	14.7
	1968	(Thermactor emission)	man'l/auto	13.2
	1969-71	Autolite carb	man'l/auto	14.1
361 cu. in.	1969-71	MD models	man'l/auto	14.5
390 cu. in.	1968	(Imco emission)	man'l/auto	14.7
	1968	(Thermactor emission)	man'l/auto	13.2
	1969	Autolite carb	man'l/auto	14.1
	1970-71	Autolite carb	manual	14.1
	1970-71	Autolite carb	auto	14.4

Automatic Choke 1971 Models

1. Adjust curb idle speed and mixture.
2. Warm up engine, remove air cleaner and attach tachometer.
3. Manually rotate fast idle cam until the fast idle adjusting screw rests on the specified step of the cam.
4. Turn fast idle adjusting screw in or out to obtain specified fast idle rpm.

1970 Model

1. Remove carburetor from engine. See instructions below for removal procedure.
2. Open throttle plate and hold choke plate fully closed to allow the fast idle cam to revolve to the fast idle position.
3. Close the throttle and use a drill to check clearance between throttle plate and throttle body bore. Use a 0.038" drill on Bronco and Econoline with 170 cu. in. engine, a 0.036" drill on any 240 cu. in. engine, a 0.031" drill on manual shift F-100 and F-250, 350 trucks and a 0.039" drill on F-100 with automatic transmission.
4. If clearance needs adjusting, bend the choke connector rod to open or close as required.

Dashpot Adjustment

1. Adjust engine idle speed and mixture.
2. Remove air cleaner.
3. Loosen the locknut on the dashpot.
4. With choke plate open and holding the throttle plate closed, check the clearance between the throttle lever and dashpot plunger tip with a feeler gauge (3/32-1/8") *Plunger must be fully depressed.*
5. If adjustment is required, turn dashpot assembly either in or out to achieve correct clearance.
6. Tighten locknut.

Carter YF and Autolite 1101 and 2100

Removal and Installation

1. Remove air cleaner.
2. Disconnect vacuum hose from carburetor, accelerator linkage, fuel line and, if so equipped, the choke clean air line from the air horn.
3. Disconnect either the choke cable or automatic choke heat tube at the carburetor.
4. Remove carburetor retaining nuts and carburetor. Remove gasket and, if so equipped, spacer and lower gasket.
5. To install, clean manifold, spacer and carburetor mating surfaces and install carburetor on manifold using new gaskets.
6. Install retaining nuts, tightening in an alternating pattern to insure an even seal.
7. Connect choke cable or heat tube, clean air line, fuel line, accelerator linkage and vacuum hose.
8. Adjust engine idle speed and mixture. Adjust dashpot if so equipped.
9. Install air filter.

Autolite 1101 1-Barrel and 2100 2-Barrel

Fast Idle Adjustment

1. This adjustment is made after the idle speed and mixture have been adjusted at normal operating temperature.
2. Warm up engine, remove air cleaner and install a tachometer.
3. Rotate fast idle cam by hand

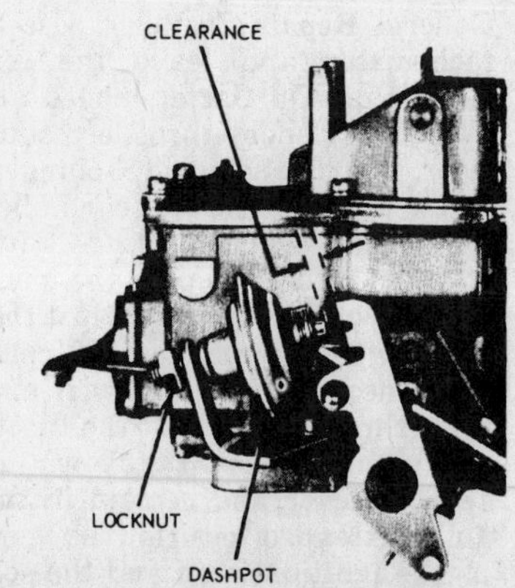

Adjusting anti-stall dashpot
(© Ford Motor Co.)

until adjusting screw rests on the center step on the cam.

4. Start engine and turn adjusting screw to obtain adequate fast idle speed.
5. Remove tachometer and install air filter.

Dashpot Adjustment

1. Adjust idle speed and mixture, warm up engine and remove air cleaner.
2. Loosen locknut on dashpot stud mounting.
3. Hold throttle in closed position and depress plunger with a screwdriver.
4. Measure clearance between dashpot plunger and throttle lever. On the 1-barrel the clearance should be .080-.100″ and on the 2-barrel the clearance should be .125″.
5. If adjustment is required, rotate dashpot unit to obtain the proper clearance.
6. Tighten locknut and recheck clearance.
7. Install air cleaners.

Holley 2-Barrel

Fast Idle Adjustment

1. Adjust the idle (hot engine) speed and mixture before making the fast (cold engine) idle speed adjustment.
2. Push the dash-mounted hand throttle control knob all the way in.
3. Start engine and let it warm up to normal, stabilized operating temperature.
4. Attach a tachometer.
5. Disconnect the choke cable housing from the choke cable bracket clamp.
6. Pull the choke cable housing rearward until the choke cable housing is against the stop on the choke cable bracket. Hold the choke plate open to the choke pulldown limit, to keep the engine running.
7. If engine speed is not 2300 rpm, turn fast (cold) idle screw with a 3/16″ wrench until correct speed is obtained.
8. Turn off engine and remove tachometer.
9. Push choke lever, cable and housing forward to full choke position and clamp the choke cable housing to the choke cable bracket.
10. Install the air cleaner.

Holley 2-Barrell Fuel

Enrichment Adjustment

This adjustment is to be made if the engine backfires.

1. Warm engine up to normal operating temperature then turn it

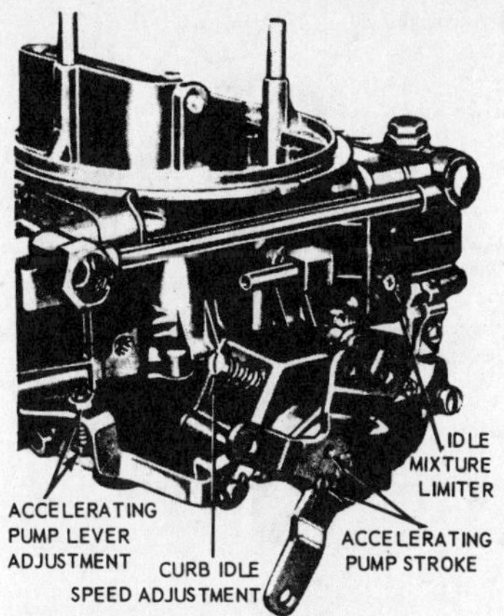

Typical adjustments for Holley 4V
(© Ford Motor Co.)

off.

2. Remove air filter, then install a tachometer and a manifold vacuum gauge.
3. Turn the fuel enrichment piston adjusting screw in (clockwise) until the head of the screw is flush with the cast boss as illustrated. This insures that the piston is in the open position.
4. Start engine and adjust the idle mixture and speed for the highest possible manifold vacuum and smoothest running.
5. Slowly turn fuel enrichment adjusting screw out (counterclockwise) until the manifold vacuum starts to drop and/or the engine begins to run rough.
6. Turn the adjusting screw in an additional number of turns, as specified in the table below, according to the maximum manifold reading obtained in Step 4.

Vacuum Reading	*No. of Turns on Screw*
17.0	2½
17.5	2
18.0	1½
18.5	1
19.0	½
above 19.0	½

7. Remove the vacuum gauge and tachometer, install the air cleaner and road test the truck. Decelerate the engine from a very fast speed down to 20 mph in high gear. If popping is still evident, turn adjusting screw outward (counterclockwise) in increments of ¼-turn, repeating test after each adjustment. If the engine still pops the trouble is elsewhere in the exhaust or carburetor metering systems. *Do not turn back the adjusting screw far enough to effect engine idle.*

Holley 2-Barrel and 4-Barrel

Fuel Level Adjustment

Before performing the following adjustment, test the fuel pump to insure that pump pressure and volume are within the proper specifications.

1. Warm up engine and place truck on level surface.
2. Remove air filter.
3. Holding a suitable container to catch any runover, remove float chamber sight plug and check fuel level in bowl. Correct level is just barely to the bottom edge of the sight hole.
4. If fuel level is too high or to low, reinstall plug and gasket and drain bowl by loosening one of the retaining bolts and letting the fuel run out into a suitable container. Start engine to refill the bowl. This draining is done to check the possibility that dirt or water may have been affecting the fuel level. If level does not stabilize at the correct point, proceed to raise or lower level as described below.
5. To lower fuel level, loosen the lockscrew on top of the bowl and turn adjusting nut ½-turn in. Tighten lock screw and start engine to stabilize the fuel level. CAUTION: Do not attempt to adjust the fuel level with the sight plug out and the engine running. The pressure will spray fuel out the sight hole and create a fire hazard. The fuel level should now be below the sight hole. If it is not, repeat the above procedure until the level falls below the sight hole lower edge. Adjustment of level is always made by *raising* the level.
6. Turning the adjusting nut out in increments of no more than 1/6-turn, raise the level in the bowl until it just reaches the sight hole, reinstalling sight plug and gasket and starting engine to stabilize the fuel level each time.
7. When correct fuel level is achieved, firmly tighten the sight plug, tighten lock screw on adjusting nut and install air filter.

Fast Idle Speed Adjustment

Fast idle speed is adjusted with the hand throttle knob pushed fully inward. The idle mixture and speed must be adjusted (see "Idle Fuel Settings" above) before the fast idle speed can be adjusted.

391 Cu. In. Engine

1. Warm up engine until stabilized operating temperature is obtained.
2. Attach a tachometer.
3. With engine running, disconnect the choke cable housing from the choke cable bracket clamp.
4. Pull the choke cable housing rearward until the choke plate operating lever is against the

stop on the choke cable bracket. Hold choke plate open all the way to keep the engine running.

5. Correct fast idle speed is 2300 rpm. If fast idle speed is not correct, the fast idle adjusting screw (located in governor housing) is turned in (clockwise) to decrease rpm or out (counterclockwise) to increase engine rpm. Use a 3/16″ wrench *with a 90-degree head.*
6. Turn off engine and remove tachometer.
7. Push choke lever, cable and housing forward to the full choke position and clamp the choke cable housing to the choke cable bracket.
8. Install air cleaner assembly.

401, 477, 534 Cu. In. Engine

1. Run engine until stabilized normal operating temperature is reached.
2. With choke in the wide open position, turn fast idle adjusting screw (left side of carburetor) in until it just touches the cam, then back it off 1/8 to 1/4-turn.

Holley 2-Barrel and 4-Barrel

Removal and Installation

1. Remove air cleaner from the carburetor and throttle rod from the throttle lever.
2. Disconnect choke control cable, hand throttle control cable, the distributor vacuum line and the fuel line.
3. Disconnect the governor throttle control lines or rod at the carburetor.
4. Remove carburetor retaining nuts, then carburetor, spacer and gaskets.
5. To install, thoroughly clean manifold, spacer and carburetor mating surfaces, then place new gaskets and spacer on manifold.
6. Position carburetor, then install retaining nuts and lockwashers. Tighten nuts securely in an alternating pattern to insure a good seal.
7. Connect throttle rod and choke control cable. Be sure to bend the end of the choke cable downward to keep it from hitting the bottom of the air cleaner.
8. Connect the hand throttle control cable, the distributor vacuum hose, the fuel line, and the governor lines or control rod.
9. Adjust the idle speed, primary (and secondary) fuel level(s), idle fuel mixture and governor control rod.
10. Install air cleaner.

Fuel Pump

All engines except the 401, 477 and 534 cu. in. are equipped with mechanical fuel pumps which are driven by an eccentric on the camshaft. On 6-cylinder engines it is located on the lower, left center of the block. On V-8 engines mechanical pumps are mounted on the lift side of the cylinder front cover. Some fuel pumps have an integral filter. Other models have an in-line filter assembly. Filters are replaced (see owner's manual for specified replacement interval) by unscrewing the filter housing and replacing the old filter.

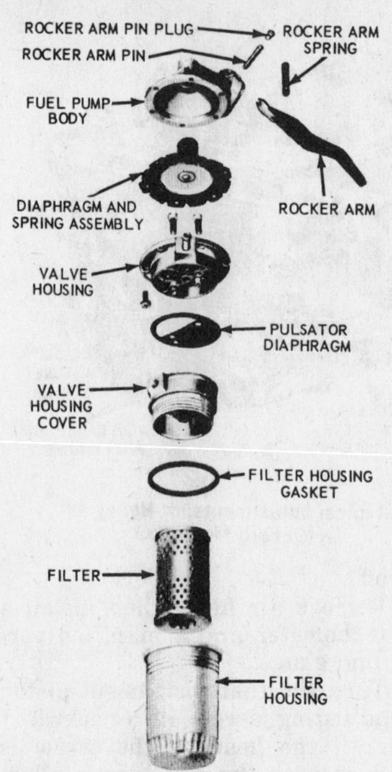

Typical Carter fuel pump (© Ford Motor Co.)

Testing Mechanical Fuel Pump

Install a new filter element before making the following tests. Tests are made with the fuel pump installed on the engine, with the engine warmed up to normal operating temperature, and with the engine idling at proper idle speed.

1. Remove air cleaner assembly and disconnect fuel inlet line at the carburetor.
2. Connect pressure gauge and fitting, flexible hose and restrictor clamp as illustrated.
3. Operate engine at idle speed. Momentarily open restrictor clamp to bleed system of air.
4. Close restrictor and note reading after pressure has stabilized. See Tune-Up Specifications at the beginning of this section for correct fuel pump pressure. If pressure is below specified value, fuel pump must be replaced or rebuilt.
5. If fuel pump is producing correct pressure, leave engine idling and proceed with volume test.
6. Open restrictor clamp and note time required to expell one pint into the container. It should take no more than 30 seconds.
7. If it takes more than 30 seconds, check for restriction in the fuel line from the tank by connecting pump to an external fuel source. If the volume test still takes more than 30 seconds per pint, then the fuel pump must be replaced.

Testing Electric Fuel Pump

1. Remove air filter and disconnect

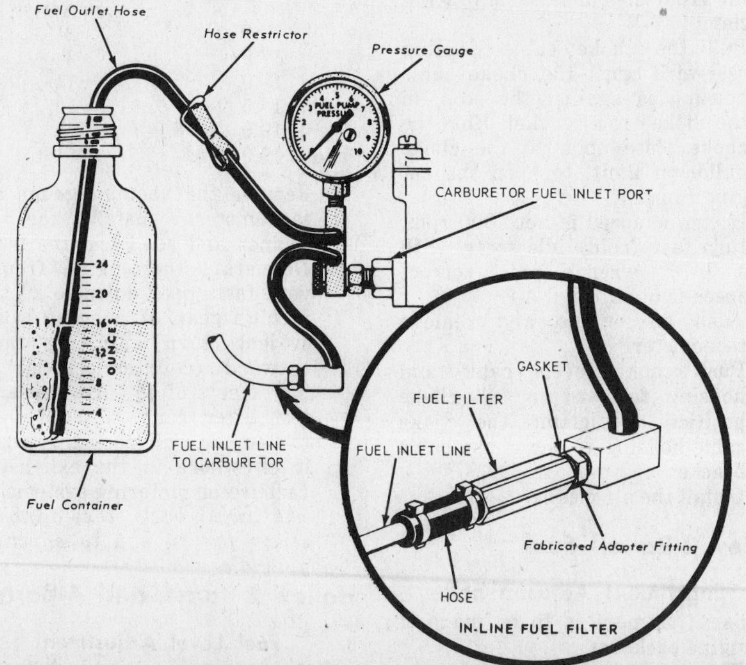

Testing mechanical fuel pump (© Ford Motor Co.)

Testing electrical fuel pump (© Ford Motor Co.)

the fuel inlet line at the carburetor.

2. Using ¼″ pipe fittings (smaller diameter will restrict the flow), connect the pressure gauge, gate valve and flexible hose as illustrated. Use a suitable container to collect expelled fuel.
3. Operate fuel pump with primer switch. *Be sure the battery is fully charged.* Adjust gate valve for a reading of 2 psi, then note time required to expell 1 quart of fuel.
4. If the time required to expell one quart exceeds that specified in the table below, repeat the same test at the outlet at the tank to establish whether or not there is restriction in the fuel line.

Engine	*Time (Sec.)*
330	40
361	37
391	34
401	36
477	33
534	30

5. If the fuel pump does not fill the quart container fast enough, the pump must be replaced as a unit.
6. Remove test equipment, connect fuel line and install air cleaner.

Mechanical Fuel Pump

Removal and Installation

1. Disconnect inlet and outlet lines

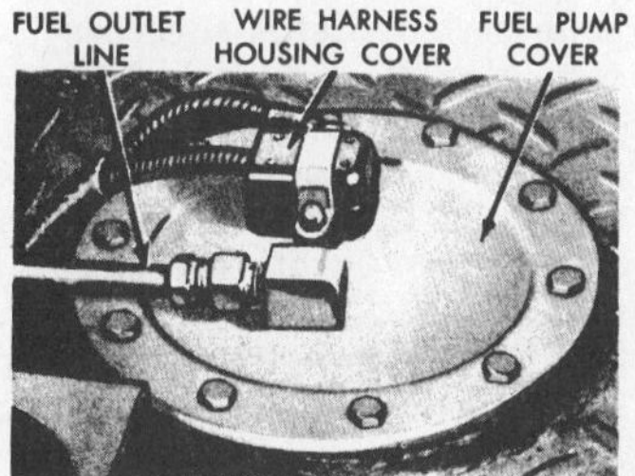

Electric fuel pump wiring (© Ford Motor Co.)

from pump.

2. Remove pump mounting bolts and remove pump and gasket. Discard gasket.

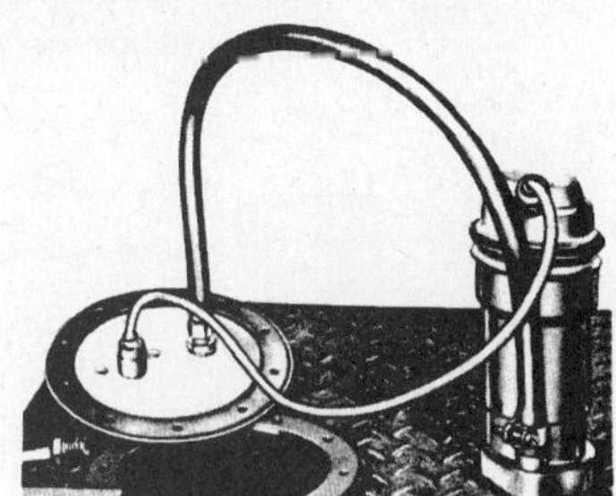
Electric fuel pump installation (© Ford Motor Co.)

3. To install, clean away all gasket material from mounting pad and pump flange. Apply sealant to new gasket and threads of bolts.
4. Position pump and gasket on the mounting pad, being sure the rocker arm is riding on the cam eccentric. Turn engine over until eccentric is on low side of stroke.
5. Install mounting bolts and tighten securely.
6. Connect fuel lines.
7. Operate engine and check for leaks.

Electric Fuel Pump

Removal and Installation

1. Disconnect the battery.
2. Disconnect the fuel outlet line at the pump cover.
3. Remove wire harness housing cover from the fuel pump cover and disconnect the wires.
4. Remove fuel pump cover and reach down into the tank and disconnect the toggle clamp which secures the pump in the retaining bracket and remove the fuel pump.
5. Disconnect the fuel outlet tube and the wire assembly at the cover and at the pump.
6. To install, remove the old gasket from the cover and install a new gasket.
7. Connect the fuel outlet tube and the wire assembly to the pump cover and to the pump.
8. Install fuel pump in the bracket in the tank and fasten the toggle clamp.
9. Position the pump cover assembly on the tank and install the attaching bolts and wire clamps.
10. Connect the fuel line to the fitting on the cover.
11. Position the wiring harness in its housing on the cover and install the wire harness housing cover.
12. Connect the battery and operate the pump and truck engine to check for leaks.

Governors

There are three types of governors used on Ford truck engines. The velocity governor (used on 240, 300, 360, 390 cu. in. engines) is a single unit mounted between the carburetor and the intake manifold. There is not provision for repair of this governor and it must be replaced as a unit when damaged. Some velocity governors are equipped with a coolant passage so that they are also used as a heated carburetor spacer. The velocity governor on the MD 330 V-8 engine may be adjusted for specific alti-

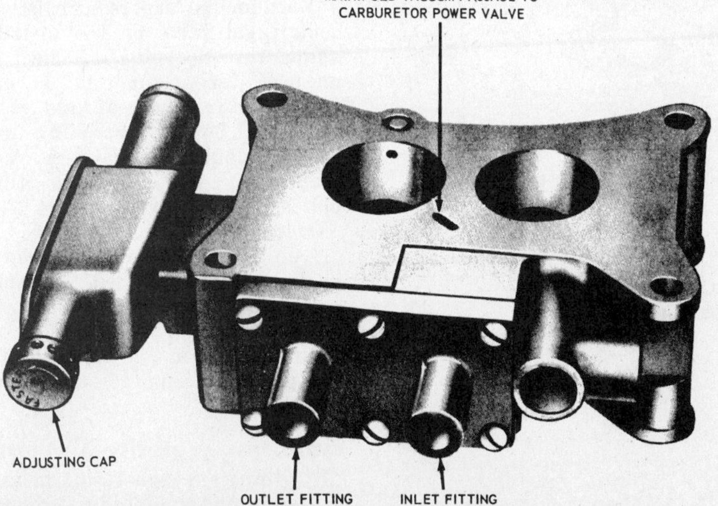

Coolant heated velocity governor (© Ford Motor Co.)

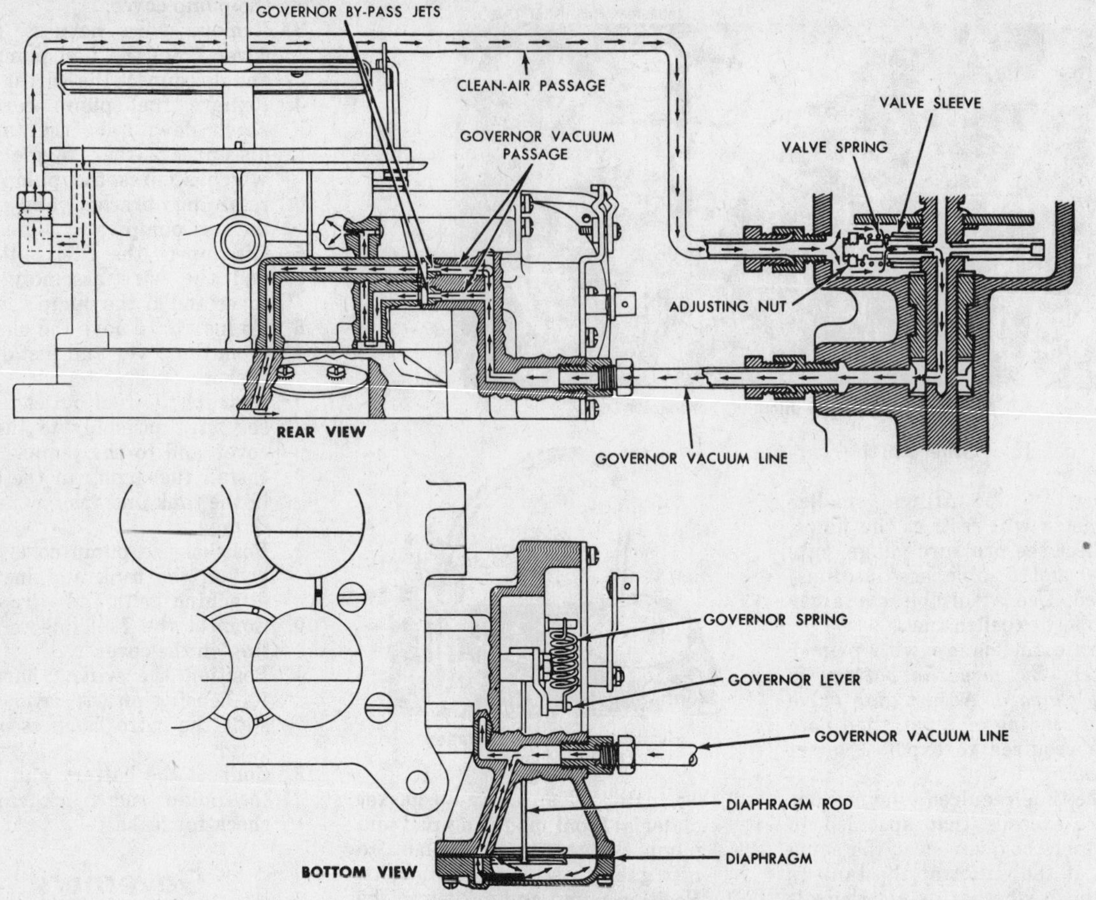

Vacuum governor system (© Ford Motor Co.)

Altitude compensation adjustment (© Ford Motor Co.)

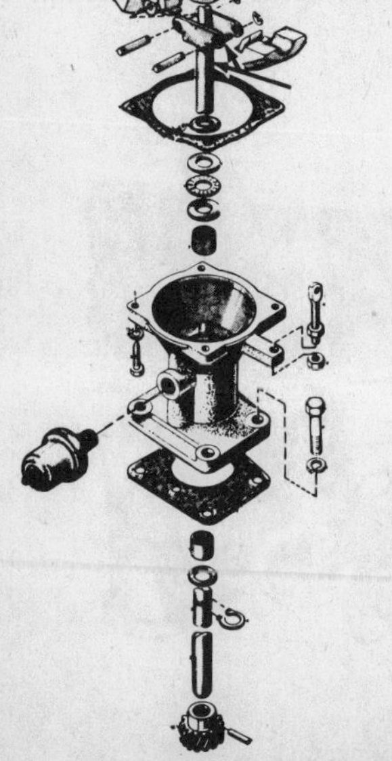

Mechanical governor (© Ford Motor Co.)

tude.

Vacuum governors consist of a centrifugal valve on the distributor and a throttle actuating mechanism on the carburetor. At governing speed venturi and manifold vacuum, controlled by the controlling unit on the distributor, operates a vacuum diaphragm to close the throttle plates.

Mechanical governors are gear-driven off the camshaft. When governing speed is reached, the centrifugal force of the flyweights pivoted on the governor shaft overcomes the spring retention and close the throttle plates through linkage to the throttle shaft.

Adjusting Velocity Governors

1. Connect a tachometer to the engine, warm up the engine then read engine rpm at wide-open throttle. If governed speed is not within the range stamped on the governor plate, adjustment is required.
2. Remove the governor seal.
3. To increase rpm, turn the cap counterclockwise; to decrease the rpm turn it counterclockwise.
4. If the truck is to be operated at a consistent altitude, cut the seal wire and remove the adjusting cap. *Do not rotate the cap during removal.* Use a mirror and light to observe the position of the slots in the adjusting bushing. *Do not disturb the center post or adjusting bushing*—if the tool does not engage the slots easily, remove the tool and realign it. For an increase in the average altitude of operation rotate the inserted tool the amount specified in the table below in

the counterclockwise direction.

Aver. Operating Altitude—Feet	*Amount of Tool Rotation*
2000	1/3 turn (120°)
3000	1/2 turn (180°)
4000	2/3 turn (240°)
5000	5/6 turn (300°)
6000	1 1 turn (360°)

60° or 1/6 turn rotation is equivalent to one flat of the tool hex head.

5. Remove tool and install cap, but *do not turn the adjusting cap.*
6. Install a tachometer and check and adjust the no-load setting. It should be 3900 for no-load at altitude and 3600 for load at altitude. Load and no-load speed should be slightly above these speeds if the governor is being adjusted above anticipated operating altitude and slightly below if it is being adjusted below anticipated operating altitude.
7. If load rpm is below 3600 rpm at operating altitude, repeat Step 4 turning the tool counterclockwise. If load governed speed is above 3600 rpm, repeat Step 4 turning the tool clockwise.
8. Seal adjusting cap to the governor body using service governor seal wire.
9. If the engine is to be operated at varying altitudes, adjust the governor for 3800 rpm no-load for sea-level. Using the adjusting cap only, adjust the no-load speed for 4100 rpm at the anticipated altitude by turning the adjustment cap ¼-turn (clockwise) for each 1000′ difference between the adjusting and anticipated altitudes. If the maximum operating altitude of the truck is lower than the altitude at which the adjustment is being made, adjust the no-load speed to 4100 rpm with the adjusting cap.

Adjusting Mechanical Governor

1. Disconnect the throttle control rod at the carburetor.
2. Loosen the top nut on the primary spring adjusting eye bolt.
3. Tighten the bottom nut finger tight, then turn it in two additional turns to pre-load the spring. Tighten the top nut.
4. Move the throttle to the wide-open position and connect the governor throttle control rod to the carburetor control arm.
5. Adjust the governor throttle control rod so that the governor throttle control auxiliary lever is full forward, then back off (shorten) the rod one full turn.
6. Check the throttle linkage to be sure that the throttle is wide-open when pedal is depressed to the floor.
7. Check operation of choke plate for proper adjustment. On C- AND W-Series trucks the choke plate does not completely close when the dash knob is fully out.
8. To adjust speed, operate the engine (parking brake on) until normal operating temperature is reached. With throttle wide-open, adjust main spring (higher tension increases rpm and lower tension decreases rpm). Sensitivity of the governor can be sharpened by installing the governor spring in the hole closest to the lower arm pivot. Adjust governed speed after changing spring position.

Adjusting Vacuum Governor

1. Warm up the engine until normal operating temperature is reached, then connect a tachometer.
2. Momentarily operate engine at wide-open throttle (governed speed) and note rpm reading.
3. If governed speed is not at the correct value (see Tune-Up Specifications at the beginning of this section), turn off the ignition switch and remove adjusting hole cover from the controlling unit (distributor).
4. Crank engine by hand until adjusting nut is aligned with access hole.
5. Turn adjusting nut clockwise to increase speed and counterclockwise to decrease speed. One full turn equals about 150 rpm.
6. Repeat above procedure until proper govern speed is obtained.
7. Install adjusting access hole cover and tighten securely.
8. Install new locking wire and lead seal.

Cooling System

Radiator Removal and Installation

To remove radiator, drain coolant and disconnect all hoses at the radiator. Fiberglass shrouds are retained to the radiator support with bolts having flat washers between the bolt head and the fiberglass and should always be assembled in this manner. Remove shrouding. On trucks equipped with a fan shroud, remove the fan, spacer, water pump pulley and drive belt.

When replacing radiator with a new one, remove the drain cock from the old one and install it in the new radiator using a sealing compound. If

Radiator installation—typical—F100-350 (© Ford Motor Co.)

necessary, transfer hose fittings also.

On engines equipped with coolant recovery systems, fill the radiator through the filler cap opening of the radiator upper tank, completely full. The cap may be removed by turning to the stop and, forcing down on the cap, force the cap past the *stop* tangs on the the filler neck. Engine should be running at idle speed to circulate coolant and eliminate any trapped air in the system. Install the radiator cap. Fill coolant reservoir with one quart of coolant and operate vehicle until normal operating temperature is reached. Check coolant reservoir to see if coolant level is noted at the "Engine Hot" level. Add coolant if necessary.

Always check for leaks in the engine and, if so equipped, transmission cooling lines.

On P-Series trucks the hood, grill and headlights must be removed in order to replace radiator.

On C-Series trucks remove the tachometer cable clamp from the radiator and disconnect the accelerator linkage to remove radiator.

Water Pump Removal and Installation

6-Cylinder Engines

1. Drain cooling system.
2. Disconnect radiator lower hose and heater hose at the water pump.
3. On 223 and 262 cu. in. engines, remove the radiator.
4. Remove fan belt, fan and water pump pulley.
5. On trucks equipped with air compressors, remove the air compressor belt.

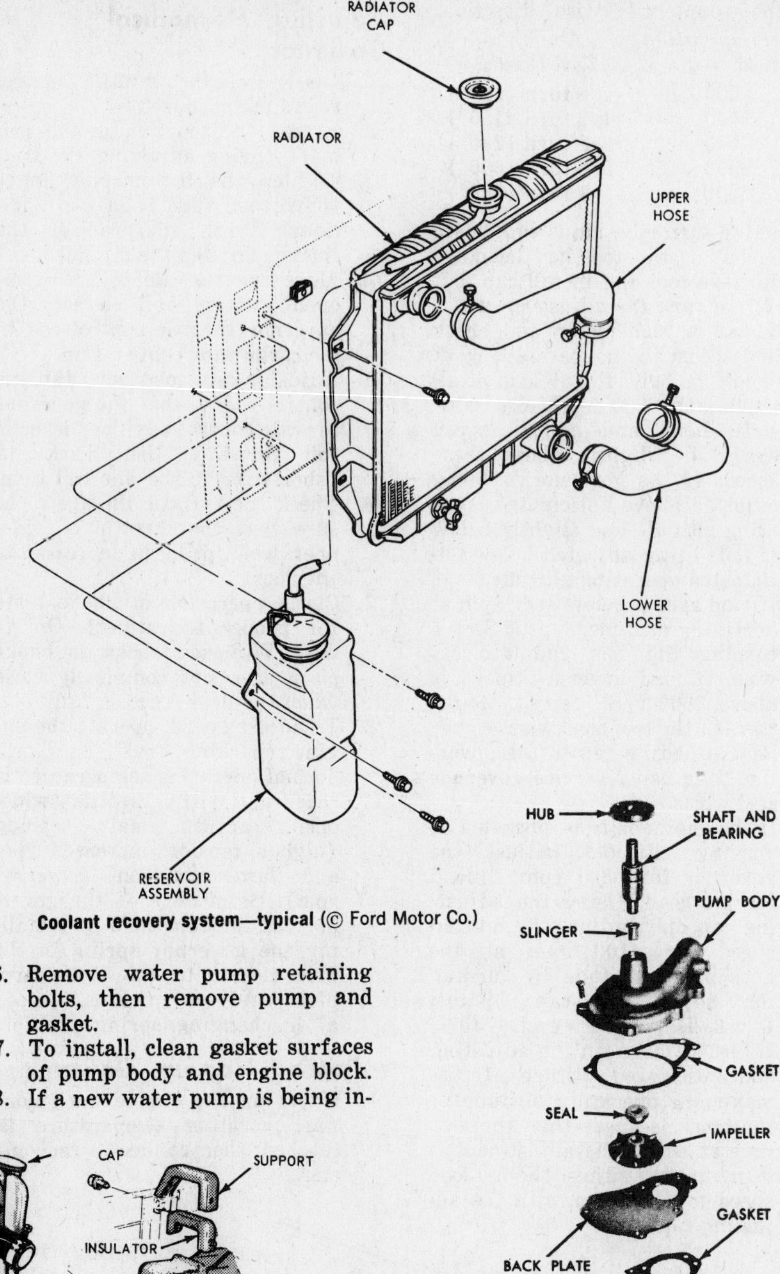

Coolant recovery system—typical (© Ford Motor Co.)

Water pump 223 six cyl. (© Ford Motor Co.)

6. Remove water pump retaining bolts, then remove pump and gasket.
7. To install, clean gasket surfaces of pump body and engine block.
8. If a new water pump is being installed, remove the fittings from the old pump and install them on the new pump.
9. Coat new gasket with water-resistant sealer on both sides and install gasket and pump on engine. Tighten mounting bolts securely. On the 223 cu. in. engine the generator adjusting arm is retained by one of the water pump mounting bolts.
10. Install water pump pulley, fan and fan belt, adjusting fan belt tension.
11. If so equipped, install air compressor belt.
12. On 223 and 262 cu. in. engines, install the radiator.
13. Connect radiator and heater

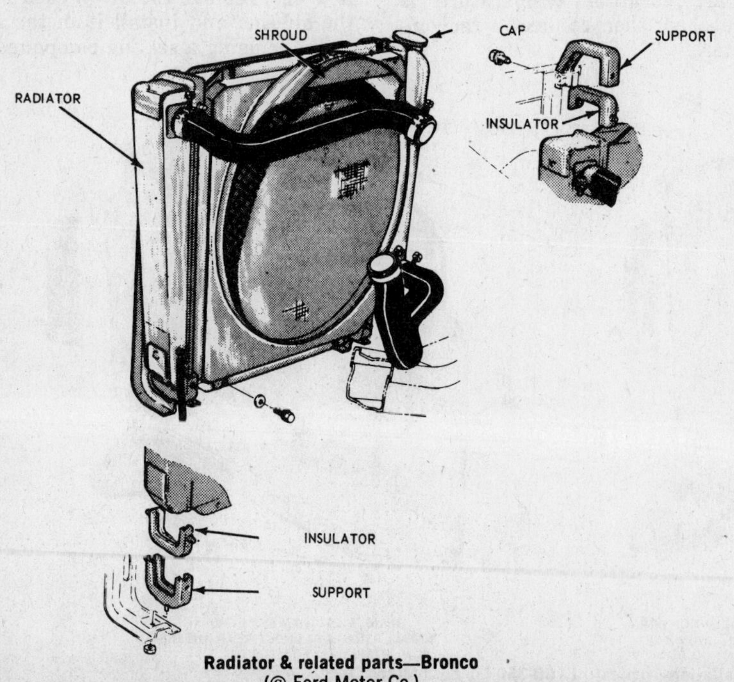

Radiator & related parts—Bronco (© Ford Motor Co.)

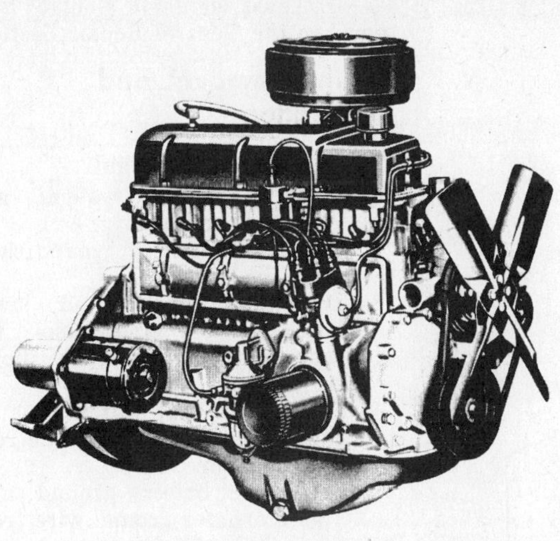
223 six cylinder engine (© Ford Motor Co.)

330 V8 engine (© Ford Motor Co.)

hoses.

14. Fill cooling system and operate engine to bleed air. Check for leaks and recheck coolant level.

V-8 Engines

Removal and installation of water pumps on V-8 engines are essentially the same as described for 6-cylinder engines. On V-8 equipped Econolines, the radiator must be removed in order to replace the water pump. On late model F-100 and Bronco vehicles, there may be a radiator shroud which must be unbolted and hung on the fan to permit access to the lower radiator hose. Remove lower radiator hose, then shroud.

Engine

Description

All Ford truck engines are of the conventional overhead valve design, either of six-cylinder in-line or V-8 configuration.

The 223 and 262 cu. in. 6-cylinder engines (1961-64) are very similar, both having the unusual/exhaust manifold location on the left side of the engine. The 233 cu. in. engine has a chain driven camshaft whereas the 262 cu. in. engine has timing gears.

The 144 cu. in. (1962-64), 200 cu. in. (1965 and 1967) and 170 cu. in. (1962-71) small block engines are essentially the same engines except for bore and stroke. These are the standard light duty engines for P-series, Econoline and Bronco vehicles.

The 240 cu. in. and 300 cu. in. 6-cylinder engines (1965-71) are the large block units found in most medium and some heavy duty trucks. The 300 HD Six has a lower compression ratio to meet the higher torque requirements of heavier vehicles. These are the most common Ford power units.

The 292 cu. in. V-8 used in 1961-64 medium and heavy duty trucks feature the sturdy Y-block design. The early 332 and 302 cu. in. V-8's were only used in heavy duty trucks and will not be considered here.

Starting in 1964, the 330 cu. in. engine became the most popular V-8 option in medium and heavy duty trucks. The difference between the medium and heavy duty models is that the HD has a longer crankshaft in front.

The popular 289 Challenger engine was the optional V-8 for Broncos in 1967 and 1968. Its stroked bigger brother, the 302 cu. in., was the Econoline V-8 for both Econoline and Bronco models.

The large block 360, 361, 390 and 391 cu. in. and the Super Duty 401, 477 and 534 cu. in. V-8 engines are used mainly in heavy duty trucks and will not be considered here.

Reference

Tune-up and general specifications for Ford truck engines may be found at the beginning of this section.

Emission Control Systems

Some 1961-62 models have positive crankcase ventilation systems. Starting in 1963 all Ford truck engines were equipped with positive crankcase ventilation systems. PCV systems route crankcase vapors to the intake manifold instead of discharging them into the atmosphere. Usually, an air hose runs from the rocker cover to the intake manifold. A regulator (PCV) valve allows the flow to move in only one direction.

In 1966 the Thermactor exhaust emission control system became available on Ford truck engines. It was discontinued in 1970. The system reduced unburnt hydrocarbons in the exhaust by injecting air into the hot exhaust ports, allowing for spontaneous combustion of unburnt gases. A fan-belt driven air pump is used to supply a constant supply of air to the manifold injectors. A check valve prevents backflow into the pressure system whenever manifold pressure exceeds that of the Thermactor system.

240 six cylinder engine (© Ford Motor Co.)

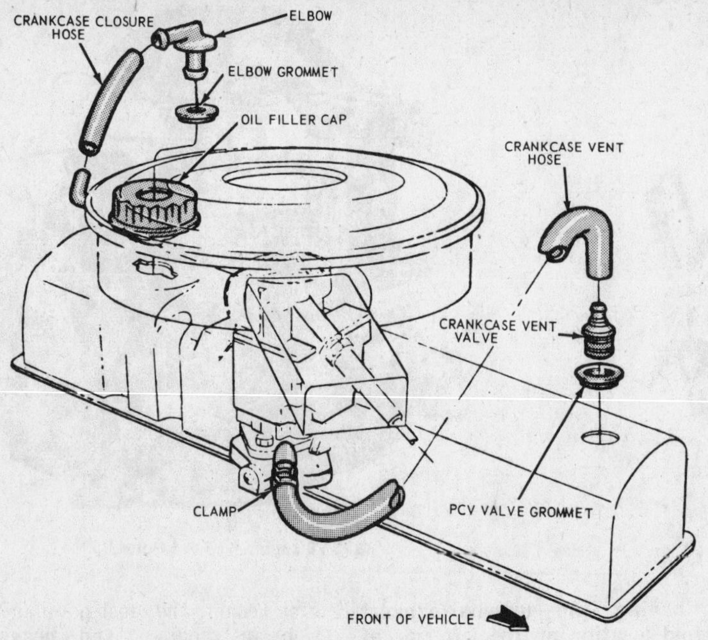

Closed crankcase ventilation system (© Ford Motor Co.)

Starting with 1968 models, the IMCO (improved combustion) exhaust emission control system was available on many models. The IMCO system uses a specially calibrated carburetor and distributor in conjunction with retarded ignition timing at idle speeds to reduce unburnt exhaust contaminants. The carburetor is maintained at a lean state of tune and ignition timing is regulated by either a deceleration vacuum control valve, distributor vacuum control valve or an electronic distributor modulator or a combination of these components.

For a more detailed discussion of these emission control systems and adjustment and service procedures see "Exhaust Emission Control Systems" in the General Repair Section.

Engine Removal and Installation

Bronco 6-Cylinder

1. Drain cooling system and remove air cleaner.
2. Disconnect battery ground cable from the battery.
3. Disconnect upper and lower hoses at the engine, remove the four radiator mounting bolts, then remove radiator.
4. Disconnect the heater hose at the water pump and at the rear of the carburetor spacer.
5. Disconnect battery ground cable and alternator ground wire from the cylinder block.
6. Remove fan belt and alternator.
7. Disconnect the starter cable at starter, then remove the starter.
8. Remove U-clamp holding exhaust head pipe to the block, remove manifold stud retaining

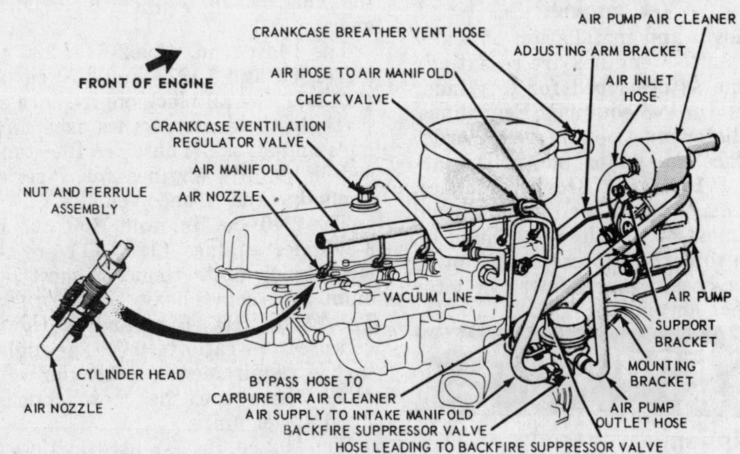

Thermactor system—installation (© Ford Motor Co.)

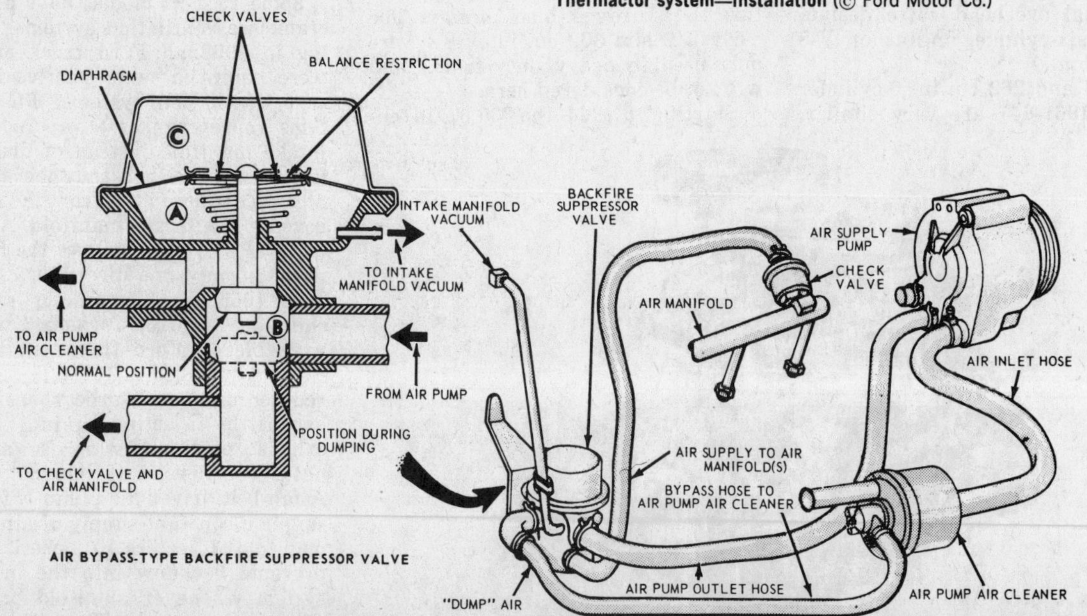

Thermactor exhaust emission control system (© Ford Motor Co.)

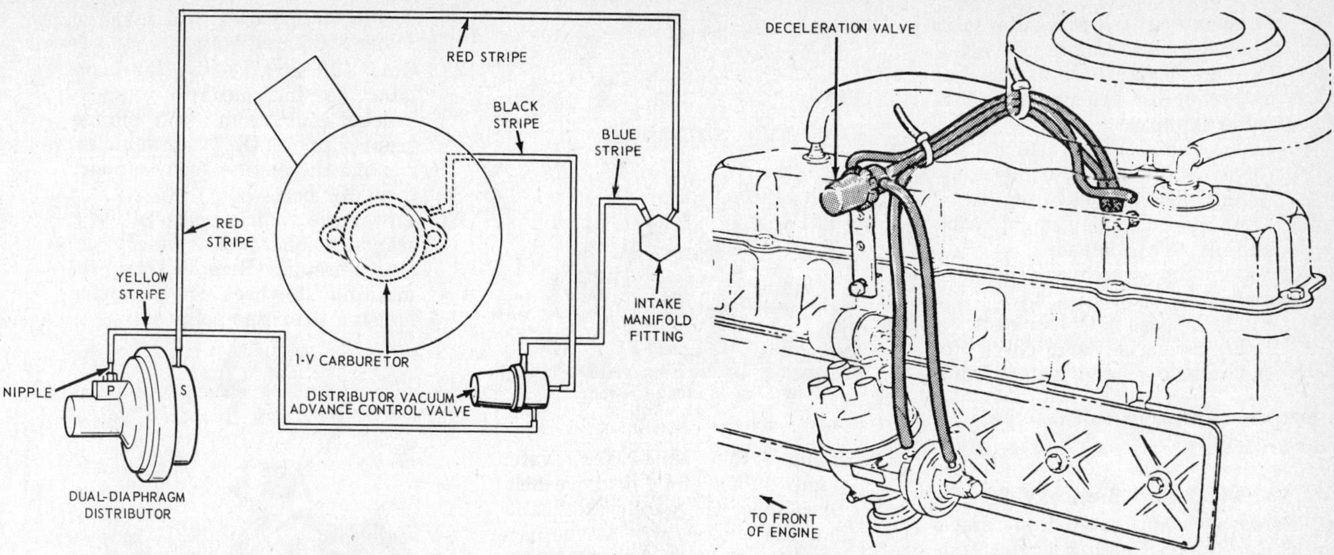

Ignition vacuum system with Imco emission (© Ford Motor Co.)

Typical deceleration valve installation (© Ford Motor Co.)

nuts, and remove pipe from the exhaust manifold.
9. Disconnect wiring at the coil and oil and temperature sending units.
10. Disconnect throttle and choke cables from the carburetor.
11. Remove windshield wiper vacuum hose from fuel pump.
12. Remove the crimped clamp, then the flex line from fuel pump.
13. Remove the retaining screws from the equalizer shaft bracket at the block and clutch housing, and remove the bracket.
14. Remove nut and washer from each of the engine mounts.
15. Loosen clutch housing to block bolts just enough so that they may be hand removed later.
16. Remove clutch housing cover retaining bolts.
17. Lower vehicle to the floor.
18. Position a jack under the transmission, and remove the clutch housing to block bolts.
19. Carefully remove engine.
20. To install, lower engine assembly carefully aligning the transmission shaft with the clutch disc splines.
21. Remove hoisting equipment and transmission jack.
22. Raise vehicle on a hoist.
23. Install lower clutch housing to block bolts securely.
24. Install clutch housing cover to clutch housing retaining bolts.
25. Install engine mount washers and retaining nuts, tightening securely.
26. Lubricate the clutch equalizer shaft and bracket and position the bracket and install the retaining bolts.
27. Lower vehicle.
28. Connect flex line (use a new clamp) and vacuum line to fuel pump.
29. Connect and adjust choke and throttle cables.
30. Connect the wiring at the coil and at the oil and temperature sending units.
31. If they were removed, install the water pump pulley, spacer and fan.
32. Place a new gasket on the exhaust inlet pipe, connect the pipe to the exhaust manifold, install the reaining nuts and tighten securely.
33. Install the U-bolt clamp to retain the inlet pipe to the bolck.
34. Install the starter and starter cable.
35. Install alternator and belt. Adjust belt.

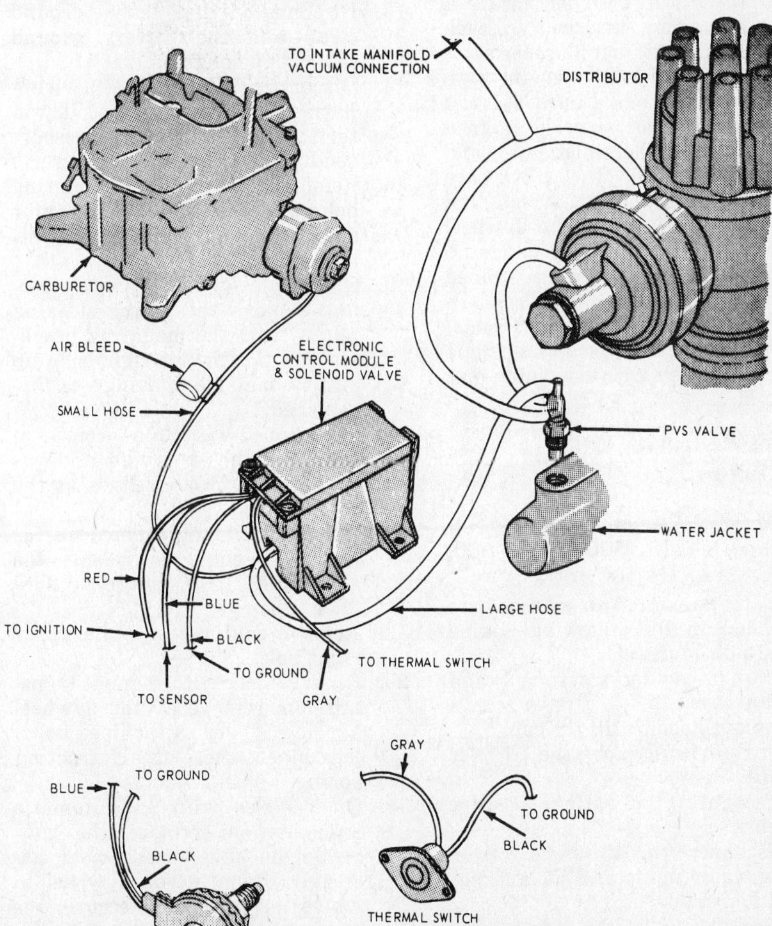

Distributor modulator schematic (© Ford Motor Co.)

36. Connect battery and alternator ground cables to block.
37. Connect heater hose at the rear of carburetor spacer and at the water pump.
38. Install radiator and, using a water-resistant sealer, connect upper and lower hoses to engine.
39. Connect battery ground cable and install air cleaner.
40. Fill cooling system and bleed all air.
41. Fill crankcase with lubricant.
42. Operate engine and check for fuel, lubricant and coolant leaks.

Engine Removal and Installation

F-100 and Bronco V-8

Removal and installation procedure for the V-8 engine is the same as that for the 170 cu. in. 6-cylinder described above except for the following.

1. Transmission shift rod must be disconnected and retracting spring removed.
2. A left and a right lifting bracket are used, the left bracket on the front of the left cylinder head and the right bracket on the rear of the right cylinder head. A sling is then attached to each bracket to lift out the engine.
3. When lowering the engine into the vehicle, make sure exhaust manifolds are properly aligned with the muffler inlet pipes and the dowels in the block are through the rear cover plate and engage the holes in the flywheel housing. If the engine hangs up after the transmission splined shaft enters the clutch disc, turn the crankshaft slowly (transmission in gear) until the shaft splines mesh with the clutch disc splines.

Engine Removal and Installation

240, 300 Cu. In. 6-Cylinder Econoline, P-350, 500, F-100-600, C, B, LN-500, 600

The engine and transmission are disattached in the following engine removal procedure.

1. Drain cooling system and crankcase.
2. Remove hood or tilt the cab.
3. On C-series, remove the oil filler tube.
4. Disconnect the battery positive cable.
5. Disconnect the heater hose from the water pump and coolant outlet housing.
6. Disconnect flexible fuel line from the fuel pump.
7. Remove the radiator following procedure described above.

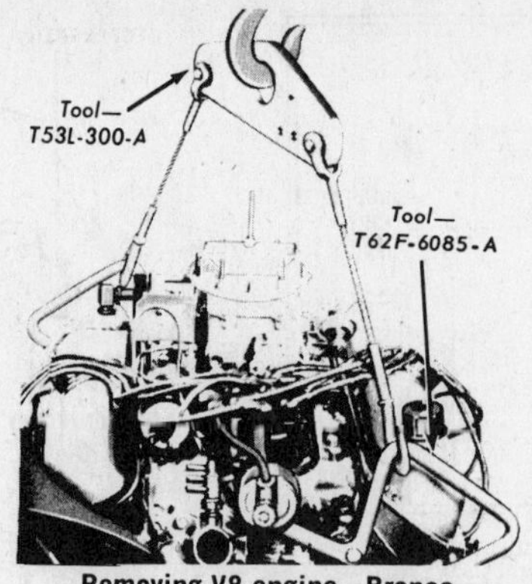

Removing V8 engine—Bronco (© Ford Motor Co.)

8. Remove the cooling fan, water pump pulley and fan drive belt.
9. Disconnect the accelerator cable and the choke cable at the carburetor. Remove the cable retracting spring.
10. On a vehicle with power brakes, disconnect the vacuum line at the intake manifold.
11. On a vehicle with automatic transmission, disconnect the transmission kickdown rod at the bellcrank assembly.
12. Disconnect exhaust manifold from the muffler inlet pipe.
13. Disconnect the body ground strap and the battery ground cable at the engine.
14. Disconnect the engine wiring harness at the ignition coil, water temperature and oil pressure sending units.
15. Remove alternator mounting bolts and position the alternator out of the way, leaving wires attached.
16. On a vehicle with power steering, remove the power steering pump from the mounting brackets and position it right side up and to one side, leaving the line attached.
17. If equipped with an air compressor, bleed the air system and disconnect the two air lines at the compressor.
18. Raise vehicle and remove starter and, if so equipped, remove the automatic transmission fluid filler tube.
19. Remove engine rear plate upper right bolt.
20. On a vehicle with manual transmission, remove all the flywheel housing lower attaching bolts. Disconnect the clutch retracting spring.
21. On vehicles with an automatic transmission, remove the converter housing access cover assembly. Remove the flywheel to converter nut and secure the converter assembly in the housing. Remove the transmission oil cooler lines from the retaining clip at the engine. Remove the converter housing to engine lower attaching bolts.
22. On F-100, 250, remove the insulator to intermediate support bracket nut from each engine front support. On other vehicles, remove the engine from support insulator bolt.
23. Lower the vehicle and position a transmission jack under the transmission. Remove the remaining flywheel or converter housing to engine bolts.

Removing six cylinder engine (© Ford Motor Co.)

24. Attach engine lifting hook and raise the engine slightly and carefully pull it from the transmission. Lift engine out of the chassis.
25. To install, place a new gasket on the muffler inlet pipe.
26. Lower engine carefully into chassis. Make sure the studs on the exhaust manifold are aligned with the holes in the muffler inlet pipe and the dowels in the block engage the holes in the flywheel or converter housing.
27. On a vehicle with an automatic transmission, start the converter pilot into the crankshaft. Remove the retainer securing the converter in the housing.
28. On a vehicle with standard transmission, start the transmission input shaft into the clutch disc. It may be necessary to adjust the position of the transmission with relation to the engine if the transmission input shaft will not enter the clutch disc. If the engine hangs up after the shaft enters, turn the crankshaft slowly (with transmission in gear) until the shaft splines mesh with the clutch disc splines.
29. Install the converter or flywheel housing upper attaching bolts. Remove the transmission jack.
30. Lower the engine until it rests on the engine support(s) and remove the lifting hook.
31. On the F-100, 250, install engine left and right support insulator to intermediate support bracket

retaining nuts, tightening securely. Install the front engine mount bolt and nut on other vehicles.
32. Install the transmission oil cooler lines bracket, if so equipped.
33. Install remaining converter or flywheel housing attaching bolts.
34. Connect clutch return spring.
35. Install starter and connect cable.
36. If so equipped, install transmission fluid filler tube bracket.
37. On a vehicle with automatic transmission, install transmission oil cooler lines in the bracket at the engine block.
38. Install exhaust pipe to exhaust manifold, tightening bolts securely.
39. Connect engine ground strap and battery ground cable.
40. On a vehicle with automatic transmission, connect the kickdown rod to the bellcrank assembly on the intake manifold.
41. Connect the accelerator linkage to the carburetor and install the retrackting spring. Connect the choke cable to the carburetor and hand throttle if so equipped.
42. On a vehicle with power brakes, connect the brake vacuum line to the intake manifold.
43. On a C-series vehicle, install the oil filler tube.
44. Connect coil primary wire, oil pressure and water temperature sending units, flexible fuel line, heater hoses and battery positive cable.
45. Install alternator on mounting bracket. On a vehicle with power steering, install the power steering pump on the mounting brackets.
46. Install water pump pulley, spacer, cooling fan and drive belt, tightening bolts securely.
47. Install radiator.
48. Connect air compressor lines.
49. If so equipped, connect oil cooler lines.
50. Install and adjust hood.
51. Fill and bleed cooling system, checking for leaks.
52. Adjust the carburetor idle speed and mixture.
53. Adjust clutch pedal free travel or automatic transmission control linkage and check transmission fluid level.
54. Install air cleaner.

Engine Removal and Installation

302 Cu. In. V-8

Econoline

In this procedure the engine is removed without the transmission attached.

1. Remove engine cover.
2. Remove right front seat.
3. Drain cooling system.
4. Remove air cleaner and intake duct assembly (later models), including crankcase ventilation hose.
5. Disconnect battery and alternator ground cables at block.
6. Remove oil filler tube at dash panel and disconnect at the rocker arm cover.
7. Disconnect radiator upper and lower hoses at the radiator and automatic transmission cooler lines (if so equipped).
8. Remove radiator.
9. Disconnect heater hoses at the engine.
10. Remove fan, spacer, pulley and drive belt.
11. Disconnect accelerator linkage at accelerator shaft assembly on the left cylinder head.
12. Disconnect automatic transmission kickdown rod at the carburetor and vacuum line at the intake manifold, if so equipped.
13. Disconnect wiring harness from left rocker arm cover.
14. Remove upper nut attaching right exhaust manifolds to exhaust pipe.
15. Raise vehicle on hoist.
16. Drain crankcase and remove filter.
17. Disconnect fuel pump inlet line at the pump.
18. Disconnect oil dipstick tube bracket from exhaust manifold and oil pan.
19. On vehicles with standard transmission, remove bolts attaching the equalizer arm bracket to cylinder block and clutch housing (this includes clutch linkage disconnection and retracting spring).
20. Disconnect starter cable at starter and remove starter.
21. On a vehicle with standard transmission, disconnect driveshaft at the rear axle and remove driveshaft. Install plug in transmission end.
22. On a vehicle with automatic transmission, disconnect driveshaft at companion flange.
23. Disconnect speedometer cable and transmission linkage at transmission.
24. Position a transmission jack under transmission. Raise transmission and remove bolts attaching crossmember to chassis. Lower transmission slightly and remove bolt which attaches rear engine support to frame crossmember. Remove crossmember.
25. On a vehicle with standard transmission, remove bolts attaching transmission to clutch housing. Remove transmission.
26. On a vehicle with automatic transmission, remove the lower front cover from converter housing. Remove transmission dipstick tube and drain transmission. Install plastic bag in transmission oil pan. Remove nuts attaching transmission converter to flywheel. Disconnect oil cooler lines and vacuum lines at transmission. Remove remaining bolts fastening transmission to engine. Remove transmission.
27. Position engine support bar (tool T65E-6000-J) to engine and chassis, or improvise a suitable support.
28. Disconnect exhaust pipes at exhaust manifold.
29. Remove front engine mount attaching nuts and washers.
30. Remove bellcrank bolt from side of engine block and position bellcrank aside.
31. Lower vehicle.
32. Remove bolts which fasten alternator and adjusting arm to the block and water pump. Set alternator aside.
33. Remove carburetor air horn stud. Disconnect fuel line at fuel pump.
34. Install engine lifting apparatus and remove engine through side door.
35. On vehicle with standard transmission, remove bolts which fasten adapter plate to clutch housing. Remove clutch housing from block.
36. To install, connect fuel line to fuel pump.
37. On models with manual transmission, position clutch housing to block and install mounting bolts. Install adapter plate to clutch housing.
38. Position alternator and adjusting arm to cylinder block and water pump. Install and tighten attaching bolts.
39. Lift engine and position to chassis and supporting tool.
40. Raise vehicle on hoist.
41. Install front engine support retaining nuts and washers, tightening securely.
42. On vehicle with automatic transmission, position bellcrank assembly to engine block and install attaching bolt, tightening securely. Position transmission to engine and install attaching bolts, tightening securely.
43. On vehicle with standard transmission, position transmission to clutch housing and install attaching bolt, tightening securely.
44. Remove engine support bar.
45. Position rear engine support crossmember to chassis and install retaining bolts. Position transmission with rear engine support attached to crossmember. Install bolt and nut. Tighten all bolts and nuts securely.
46. On vehicle with automatic trans-

mission, install and tighten converter-to-flywheel attaching nuts. Connect oil cooler and vacuum lines at transmission. Install transmission dipstick tube in pan. Install dipstick tube and vacuum line retaining bracket bolt to engine block.

47. Connect transmission shift linkages and speedometer cable.
48. On vehicle with automatic transmission, connect driveshaft to transmission companion flange.
49. On vehicle with standard transmission, remove plug from transmission and install driveshaft yoke into transmission. Connect rear end of driveshaft at rear axle.
50. Install starter and connect cable to starter.
51. Install the exhaust pipe to exhaust manifold, installing all bolts except upper nut on right exhaust manifold.
52. On a standard transmission, install the bolts connecting equalizer arm bracket to block and clutch housing (including clutch linkage connection and retracting spring).
53. Install oil filter, then oil dipstick tube bracket to oil pan and exhaust manifold.
54. Connect fuel line at fuel pump.
55. Lower the vehicle.
56. Install upper nut attaching right exhaust manifold to exhaust pipe.
57. Connect engine wire harness at left rocker arm cover.
58. Connect battery and alternator ground cables at block.
59. If applicable, connect automatic transmission vacuum line at intake manifold and transmission kickdown rod at carburetor.
60. Connect accelerator linkage at accelerator shaft assembly on left cylinder head.
61. Install drive belt, pulley, spacer and fan.
62. Connect heater hoses at engine, then install radiator and connect hoses.
63. Install oil filler tube by connecting to left rocker arm cover and dash panel.
64. Install air cleaner and intake duct assembly, including the crankcase ventilation hose.
65. Fill and bleed cooling system.
66. Fill crankcase and automatic transmission (if so equipped).
67. Install right front seat and engine cover.
68. Operate engine at fast idle and check for leaks.

Engine Removal and Installation

330, 360, 361, 390, 391 Cu. In. V-8—All Models

1. On B, F and FT series trucks, remove engine hood assembly from vehicle; on C and CT vehicles, release cab lock and tilt the cab forward. On N and NT series vehicles, position a suitable support in front of the truck to accept the hood and fender assembly when it is fully forward, then raise the hood and fender assembly.
2. Disconnect the ground cable from the battery. On N and NT series trucks, disconnect and remove the battery.
3. Drain cooling system and crankcase.
4. On N and NT series trucks, disconnect the check cable assemblies and let the hood swing forward out of the way, resting on the support. Remove radiator to cowl support rod, disconnect water hoses and unbolt and remove radiator.
   On C and CT series trucks, remove the heater hoses from the radiator, transmission oil cooler lines (automatic transmission), disconnect upper and lower radiator hoses, disconnect and remove vent line between radiator and supply tank and hose between water outlet housing and supply tank, remove fan (leaving it lay in the shroud), then remove the radiator, shroud and fan as an assembly. Remove radiator supply tank from cab rear support.
   On B, F and FT series trucks, disconnect the upper and lower hoses from the engine and water pump, remove the fan, disconnect the transmission oil cooler hoses (if applicable), then unbolt and remove radiator.
5. On a vehicle with power steering, disconnect the power steering pressure line from the pump reservoir and return line from the pump housing. Drain oil, then loosen and remove the power steering drive belt.
6. On N and NT series trucks, remove fan.
7. On N, NT, C and CT series truck, disconnect heater hoses at engine.
8. Remove air cleaner and, if applicable, vent hose from carburetor.
9. Disconnect choke and throttle cables and accelerator linkage.
10. Disconnect tachometer cable (and bracket, if so attached) and position out of the way.
11. Remove ignition coil.
12. On a vehicle with an air compressor, relieve pressure from the system and disconnect main line from the compressor and treadle valve. Remove drive belt if it is still in place.
13. Disconnect fuel line (from tank) at the fuel pump and cap line.
14. Disconnect wires from the alternator and remove wiring harness from engine (or disconnect from junction block).
15. Disconnect cable from starter and remove starter. Remove flywheel lower housing attaching bolts first on L and LT truck. Disconnect engine-to-body ground strap.
16. Unbolt exhaust pipes from right and left exhaust manifolds.
17. Disconnect vacuum lines from intake manifold.
18. Remove clutch return spring and hydraulic clutch slave cylinder attaching bolts on C and CT trucks.
19. Remove driveshaft center bearing retainer (except on C and CT series) and position a jack under transmission.
20. Remove flywheel housing cover.
21. On B, F and FT series trucks, remove lower clutch housing attaching bolts. Secure lifting apparatus. Remove front engine mount nuts. Remove remaining clutch housing bolts. Raise engine high enough to remove the bolts that attach the engine front mount bracket to the upper insulator. Carefully lift engine away from the transmission and chassis. On C and CT vehicles, remove flywheel housing to engine attaching bolts. Remove nuts and bolts from front engine mount and upper insulator. Attach lifting apparatus and remove engine from chassis. On N and NT trucks, remove flywheel upper housing to engine attaching bolts. Remove the bolt(s) attaching the front engine mounting plate to the front engine mount. Attach lifting apparatus. Raise engine sufficiently to remove the front support bracket-to-upper insulator bolt and nuts. Remove engine.
22. To install, carefully lower engine into chassis, aligning clutch disc splines with transmission shaft and aligning front engine mount bracket with upper insulator.
23. Install flywheel housing to engine attaching bolts, tightening securely.
24. Install flywheel housing cover.
25. Lower engine and remove jack from under transmission, being careful to keep front engine mounting aligned.
26. Install and tighten front engine mount bolts and nuts. On N and NT trucks, install front engine mount to mounting plate.
27. Remove lifting apparatus.
28. Install driveshaft center bearing support to frame crossmember.
29. On vehicle with power steering,

install power steering unit if it was removed.
30. Install starter motor and starter cable, attaching engine-to-frame ground cable if applicable.
31. Install left and right exhaust pipes to exhaust manifolds, using new gaskets.
32. Connect alternator wires and engine wiring harness wires. Secure engine wiring harness to bracket on engine.
33. On C and CT trucks, install hydraulic clutch slave cylinder to the flywheel housing and attach the clutch return spring.
34. Secure coil and bracket to cylinder head and connect all leads.
35. Connect vacuum line(s) to intake manifold.
36. Connect fuel line to fuel pump.
37. On C and CT trucks install radiator supply tank to cab rear support.
38. Connect accelerator linkage, choke and throttle cables and tachometer cable. Adjust linkage and cables if necessary.
39. Connect heater hoses.
40. On vehicles equipped with air system, install and connect all components.
41. Connect engine-to-body ground strap.
42. On N and NT series trucks, install fan. On B, F, FT, C and CT trucks, place fan in radiator, shroud, then install radiator, shroud and fan (loose) in vehicle. Secure all attaching bolts, insulators and radiator supports. Make sure belts are ready to be installed. Install fan and belts.
43. Connect radiator upper and lower hoses. On C and CT series trucks, connect hoses to radiator supply tank.
44. On vehicle with automatic transmission, connect transmission oil cooler lines to radiator lower tank.
45. On vehicle with power steering, install and tighten the drive belt and connect power steering pressure line to the pump reservoir and return line to the pump housing.
46. On C and CT series trucks, attach the heater hoses, throttle cable, choke cable and tachometer cable to the radiator.
47. Install air cleaner.
48. Install (if removed) and connect battery cables.
49. Fill crankcase and cooling system.
50. On B, F and FT series trucks, install the hood.
51. On N and NT series trucks, raise hood and connect check cables.
52. Adjust clutch as required.
53. Operate engine and check for lubricant and coolant leaks.

Manifolds

Exhaust Manifold Removal and Installation

144, 170, 200 Cu. In. 6-Cylinder F-100, Econoline and Bronco

1. Remove air cleaner and, if so equipped (later models), hot air duct.
2. Disconnect exhaust pipe from manifold.
3. Remove retaining bolts and manifold.
4. To install, clean mating surfaces of head and manifold and scrape gasket material from manifold exhaust pipe flange and pipe.
5. Apply graphite grease to the mating surface of the exhaust manifold.
6. Install manifold, retaining bolts and tab washers, tightening bolts from the center out to 13-18 ft. lbs. Bend tabs to lock bolts.
7. Install exhaust pipe on manifold, using new gasket.
8. Install air cleaner and hot air duct.
9. Start engine and check for exhaust leaks.

289 and 302 Cu. In. V-8 1967-71 F-100, Econoline and Bronco

1. Remove air cleaner, intake duct and crankcase ventilation hose as an assembly.
2. Remove air cleaner inlet duct attaching bolts (Bronco and F-100) and oil dipstick tube bracket on right exhaust manifold.
3. Disconnect exhaust pipes from manifolds.
4. Remove bolts, washers and manifolds.
5. To install, clean mating surfaces of cylinder head and manifolds. Clean out exhaust pipe flange of manifolds and exhaust pipe.
6. Apply graphite grease to mating surfaces of manifolds.
7. Install manifolds, tab washers, and bolts, tightening from the center out to 12-16 ft. lbs. torque. Bend tabs to lock bolts.
8. Install exhaust pipe to flange on manifold, using a new gasket.
9. Install air cleaner inlet duct (Bronco and F-100) and oil dipstick tube bracket on the right exhaust manifold.
10. Install air cleaner and intake duct, including crankcase ventilation hose.

330, 360, 361, 390 and 391 Cu. In. V-8—All Models

1. Remove air cleaner and disconnect exhaust pipes from manifolds.
2. Disconnect the power steering pump bracket from the cylinder block and move it out of the way. Position the pump so that the oil will not drain out.
3. Remove dipstick and tube assembly.
4. Remove attaching bolts, washers of cylinder head, manifold, manifold pipe flange and exhaust pipe.
5. To install, clean mating surfaces.
6. Apply graphite grease to mating surface of manifold, then install manifold, tab washers and bolts. Tighten bolts from the center

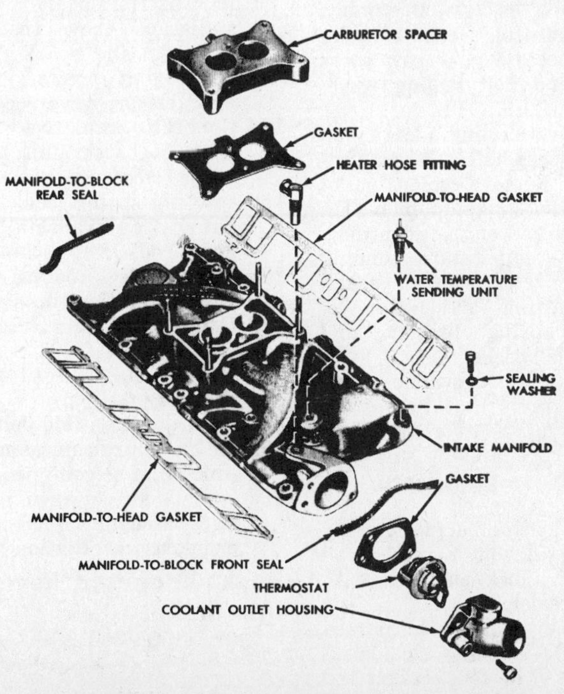

Intake manifold—289, 302 V8 engines (© Ford Motor Co.)

out to 18-24 ft. lbs. on 330, 360, and 390 cu. in. and 12-18 ft. lbs. on 361 and 391 cu. in. Bend tabs to lock bolts.

7. Install dipstick and tube assembly.
8. Install power steering pump bracket and adjust belt tension.
9. Connect exhaust pipes to manifolds, using new gaskets.
10. Install air cleaner.

Intake Manifold Removal and Installation

289 and 302 Cu. In. V-8 1967-71 F-100, Econoline and Bronco

1. Drain cooling system.
2. Remove air cleaner and intake duct assembly, including crankcase ventilation hose.
3. Disconnect accelerator rod, choke cable and automatic transmission kickdown rod (if applicable) at the carburetor.
4. Disconnect high tension lead and wires from the coil.
5. Remove spark plug wire from plugs and harness brackets, then remove distributor cap and spark plug wire assembly.
6. Disconnect fuel inlet line at carburetor.
7. Disconnect distributor vacuum hoses and remove distributor.
8. Remove heater hose, radiator hose and water temperature sending unit wire from manifold.
9. Remove water pump bypass hose from coolant outlet housing.
10. Disconnect crankcase ventilation hose from valve rocker cover.
11. Remove intake manifold and carburetor as an assembly, prying manifold from cylinder head if necessary. Throw away gaskets and bolt sealing washers.
12. When disassembling, identify all vacuum hoses before disconnecting them. Remove coolant outlet housing and gasket. Remove ignition coil and engine identification tag, temperature sending unit, carburetor, spacer, gasket, vacuum fitting, accelerator retracting spring bracket and choke cable bracket.
13. To install, first assemble manifold/carburetor unit by installing all components removed in Step 12 above, making sure vacuum lines are positioned correctly.
14. Clean all mating surfaces, using a suitable solvent to remove all oil. Apply block surfaces with adhesive sealer.
15. Position new gaskets and front and rear seals, using a nonhardening sealer at four gasket-seal junctions. Interlock gaskets with seal tabs and be sure all holes are aligned.

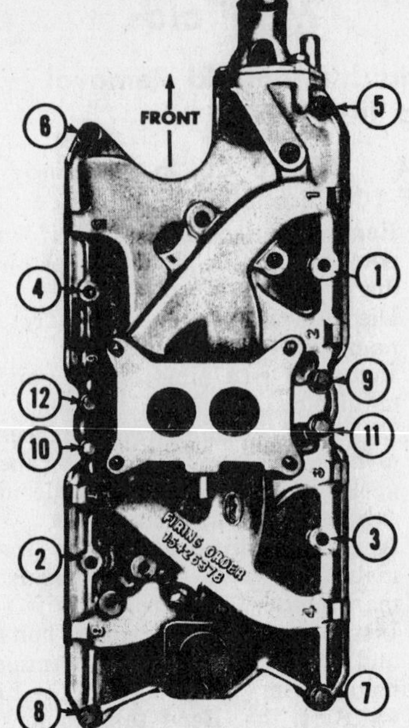

Intake manifold tightening sequence—289, 302 engines
(© Ford Motor Co.)

16. Carefully position manifold, making sure that gaskets and seals do not shift. Install bolts and new bolt seal washers, tightening in the sequence illustrated. *Retighten after engine has been operated until warmed up.* Torque bolts to 23-25 ft. lbs.
17. Install water bypass hose to coolant outlet housing, radiator upper hose and heater hose.
18. Install distributor as described in "Distributor Removal and Installation" above. Install distributor cap and spark plug wires, positioning wires in harness brackets on valve rocker covers.
19. Connect crankcase ventilation hose, high tension lead and coil wires, accelerator rod and retracting spring, choke cable and automatic transmission kickdown rod (if applicable).
20. Fill and bleed cooling system.
21. Adjust ignition timing.
22. Connect vacuum hoses at distributor.
23. Operate engine until warmed up, checking for leaks.
24. Retorque manifold bolts.
25. Adjust transmission throttle linkage, if so equipped.
26. Install air cleaner and intake duct assembly including closed crankcase ventilation hose.

Intake Manifold Removal and Installation

330, 360, 361, 390 and 391 Cu. In. V-8—All Models

1. Drain cooling system.
2. Remove air cleaner and crankcase vent hose(s).
3. Disconnect accelerator linkage at the carburetor.
4. If so equipped, remove the accelerator cross shaft bracket from the intake manifold.
5. Disconnect fuel line and distributor vacuum line at the carburetor.
6. Disconnect all leads at the coil and oil pressure and water temperature sending units.
7. Remove wiring harness from the retaining clips on the left valve rocker cover.
8. Disconnect spark plug wires, remove wires from harness brackets, remove distributor cap and spark plug wire assembly.
9. Disconnect and remove distributor vacuum line.
10. Remove distributor.
11. Disconnect radiator upper hose(s) at the water outlet housing, heater hoses and, on C series vehicle, the coolant supply tank hose at the water outlet housing.
12. Disconnect water pump bypass hose(s) at the water pump.
13. Remove valve rocker covers and crankcase ventilation hoses.
14. Remove valve rocker shaft assembly as described below in the section, "Rocker Arm Shaft Assembly Removal and Installation."
15. Remove and identify pushrods so that they can be put back in their original positions.
16. Remove manifold attaching bolts.
17. Install eyebolts (5/16-18 thread) in the left front and right rear rocker arm cover screw holes and attach lifting sling.
18. Carefully lift out intake manifold, then remove seals and gaskets.
19. Remove water pump bypass hoses (s), water outlet housing, carburetor, gaskets spacer and water temperature sending unit.
20. Before installing, assemble com-

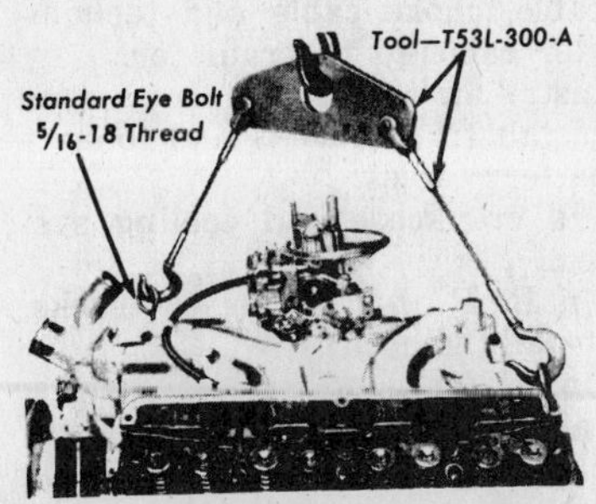

Removing or installing intake manifold—typical
(© Ford Motor Co.)

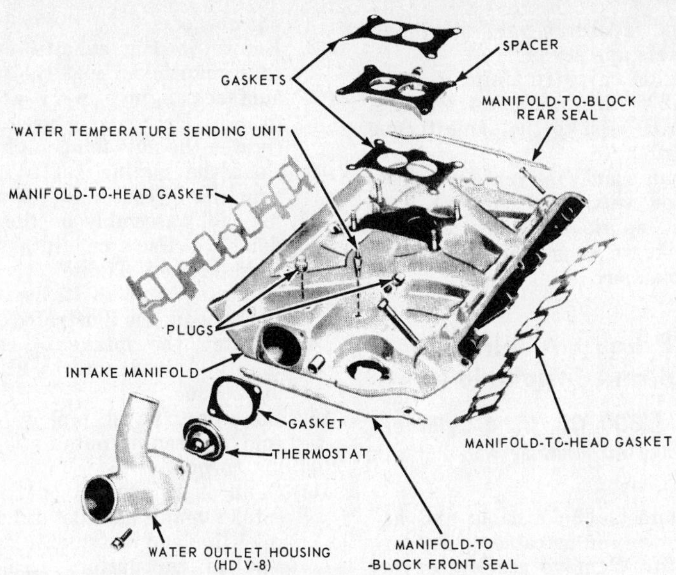

Typical V8 intake manifold (© Ford Motor Co.)

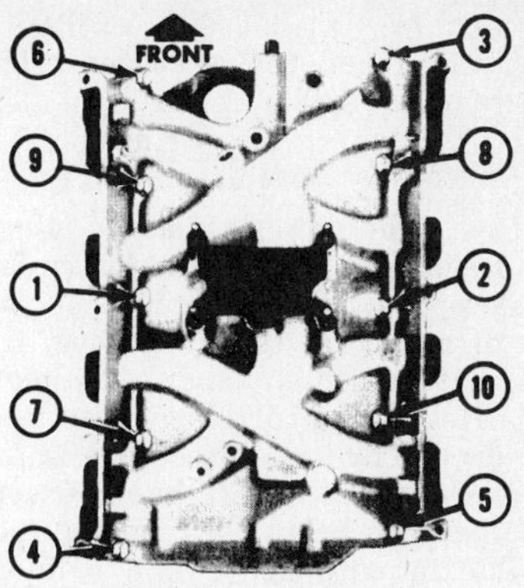

Intake manifold tightening sequence—V8 engines exc. 289 & 302 (© Ford Motor Co.)

ponents removed in Step 19. Use a new gasket and sealing compound when installing water outlet (thermostat) housing. Use electrical-conductive sealer when installing water temperature sending unit.

21. Thoroughly clean all manifold, cylinder head and block mating surfaces (use solvent to remove all traces of oil). Coat block seal surfaces with quick-setting seal adhesive and coat mating surfaces of cylinder heads and block with non-hardening Oil-resistant sealer. Position new seals on block and cylinder heads, *making sure they are properly aligned.* Position manifold gasket slots over the end tabs on the seals and coat these junctions with non-hardening sealer.
22. Install eyebolts in intake manifold and attach lifting sling, then carefully lower manifold onto engine. Position manifold by inserting distributor and check that seals and gaskets are still properly aligned and that all holes line up.
23. Install manifold attaching bolts, coating under side of bolt heads with non-hardening sealer. Tighten bolts to 32-35 ft. lbs. torque in the sequence illustrated. Retorque bolts after engine has been run and warmed up. Remove distributor, lifting sling and eyebolts.
24. Connect water pump bypass hose (s) to water pump, radiator upper hose, heater hoses, water temperature sending unit and, on C series trucks, coolant supply tank hose.
25. Apply lubriplate to both ends of pushrods and install them in their original positions. Install valve rocker shaft as described in "Rocker Arm Shaft Assembly Removal and Installation" below.
26. Install the distributor as described in "Distributor Removal and Installation" above.
27. Install rocker covers, using new gasket and sealer, tightening to 10-12 ft. lbs., waiting two minutes then torquing again.
28. Connect crankcase ventilation hoses.
29. Install carburetor fuel inlet line, spark plug wires, wiring harness, distributor vacuum line and distributor cap.
30. Connect oil pressure sending unit wire and coil wire and lead.
31. Install accelerator cross shaft bracket (if applicable) and accelerator rod.
32. Fill and bleed cooling system.
33. Install air cleaner and vent hose.
34. Start engine, then check ignition timing idle speed and idle fuel mixture, then let engine warm up.
35. Retorque intake manifold bolts to 32-35 ft. lbs.

Valve Rocker Arm Shaft Assembly Removal and Installation

330, 369, 361, 390 and 391 Cu. In. Engine

1. Remove air cleaner, disconnect spark plug leads and remove leads from bracket on the valve rocker cover.

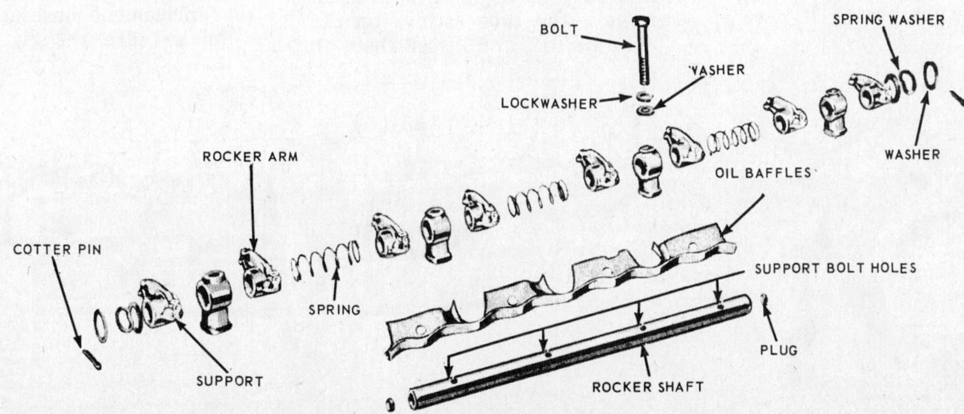

Valve rocker arm shaft assembly V8—typical (© Ford Motor Co.)

2. Remove crankcase ventilation hose from rocker cover, then remove rocker cover. On left rocker cover the wiring harness must be removed.
3. On right side, start at No. 4 cylinder (rearmost) and loosen the support bolts in sequence, two turns at a time. Remove the shaft assembly and baffle plate after all the bolts have been loosened. The same procedure is followed on the left bank, except that the bolt-loosening sequence starts with the No. 5 cylinder (foremost). CAUTION: The above bolt-loosening procedure must be followed to avoid damage to the rocker arm shaft.
4. To install, apply Lubriplate to the pad end of the rocker arms, to the tip of the valve stems and to both ends of the pushrods.
5. Rotate engine to 45 degrees *past* No. 1 cylinder TDC.
6. With the pushrods in place, position rocker arm shaft assembly and baffle plate on the cylinder head such that *oil holes are on the bottom and identification notch is down and toward the front on the right bank and toward the rear on the left bank.* Tighten support bolts finger tight.
7. On the right bank, start at No. 4 cylinder and tighten the support bolts two turns at a time in sequence (4-3-2-1) until the supports are fully in contact with the cylinder head. Then tighten the support bolts to 40-45 ft. lbs. torque. The same procedure is followed on the left valve rocker arm shaft support bolts, starting with the No. 5 cylinder. This procedure allows time for the hydraulic lifter leakdown and thus prevents damage to pushrods, valves and rocker arms.
8. Check valve clearances as described below, adjusting if necessary.
9. Install rocker cover, using new gaskets and sealer.
10. Tighten cover retaining bolts to 10-12 ft. lbs, wait two minutes, then tighten to the same torque again.
11. Install crankcase ventilation regulator valve and hose(s), connect spark plug wires and crankcase vent hose, and install air cleaner.

Intake/Exhaust Manifold Removal and Installation

240 and 300 Cu. In. 6-Cylinder

1. Remove air cleaner and hot air ducts.
2. Disconnect choke cable and accelerator rod or cable at the carburetor. Remove accelerator retracting spring.
3. On LN series vehicles, disconnect the battery and remove the alternator.
4. On vehicle with an automatic transmission, remove the kickdown rod retracting spring and remove the accelerator rod bellcrank assembly.
5. On C series vehicle, remove the engine oil dipstick and tube.
6. Disconnect fuel inlet line and distributor vacuum line from the carburetor, exhaust pipe from the manifold and, if so equipped, power brake vacuum line.
7. Remove manifold attaching bolts and lift manifolds from engine.
8. To separate manifolds, remove the nuts joining the intake and exhaust manifolds. Discard all gaskets.
9. If the exhaust control valve requires replacement, see "Exhaust Control Valve Removal and Installation" below.
10. To install, clean the mating surfaces of cylinder head and manifolds.
11. If a new manifold is to be used, remove the tube fittings on the old manifold and install them on the new one.
12. Before joining exhaust and intake manifolds, coat the mating surfaces lightly with graphite grease. Use a new gasket and tighten the nuts finger tight.
13. Coat the mating surfaces with graphite grease and install the manifold assembly on the cylinder head. Use a new intake manifold gasket. Tighten the bolts and nuts to 23-28 ft. lbs. torque in the sequence illustrated.
14. Tighten the intake to exhaust manifold stud nuts to 28-33 ft. lbs. torque.
15. Connect exhaust pipe to manifold, tightening nuts to 25-30 ft. lbs. torque.
16. Connect crankcase vent hose to intake manifold inlet tube, fuel inlet line and distributor vacuum line to carburetor, accelerator rod or cable and choke cable to carburetor. Install the accelerator retracting spring.
17. On LN series trucks, install the alternator and belts and connect the battery.
18. On C series trucks, install the dipstick and tube.
19. On a vehicle with an automatic transmission, install the bellcrank assembly and kickdown rod retracting spring. Adjust the transmission control linkage.
20. Install the air cleaner and hot air duct.
21. Adjust idle speed and idle fuel mixture.

Exhaust Control Valve Removal and Installation

240 and 300 Cu. In. 6-Cylinder

1. Separate intake and exhaust manifolds.
2. Remove valve tension spring, thermostatic spring and stop pin.
3. The valve shaft must be cut with a torch on each side of the valve plate. Remove valve plate and expansion plug.
4. Remove bushings and install new ones. There are two sizes of replacement bushings (OD) so make sure the right ones are

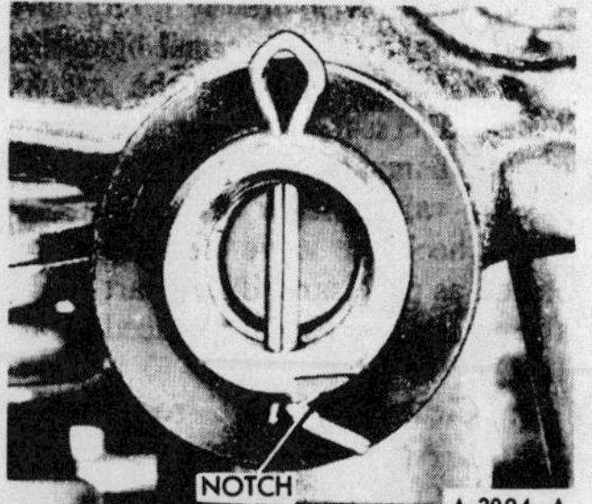

Rocker arm shaft identification notch
(© Ford Motor Co.)

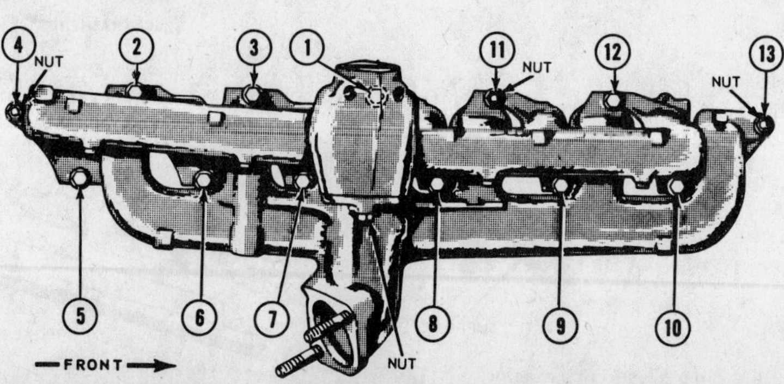

Manifold tightening sequence—240 & 300 engines (© Ford Motor Co.)

used. Ream the ID of bushings to 0.51-0.253". The shorter bushing (front) is installed 0.010-0.015" below inside surface of the manifold and the longer bushing (rear) protrudes into the manifold cavity 0.020" (note that beveled end points inward).

5. Slide new shaft into the bushings, flat washer and valve plate. Note that the flat washer is between the valve plate and the long (rearward) bushing. Install a new stop pin spring on the stop pin.
6. Rotate the counterweight and shaft assembly clockwise until the counterweight contacts the stop pin spring, then place a 0.030" feeler gauge between the counterweight and the manifold to maintain the specified clearance. Hold the valve plate at a 84 degree angle to the top surface of the manifold as illustrated and tack-weld the plate to the shaft, *using stainless steel welding rod.*
7. Check for free movement of the valve and install expansion plug in the bushing bore.
8. Install the thermostatic spring, positioned so that it will be necessary to wind the spring ½ turn clockwise to hook it over the stop pin.
9. Install a new valve tension spring on the exhaust control valve shaft and the stop pin.

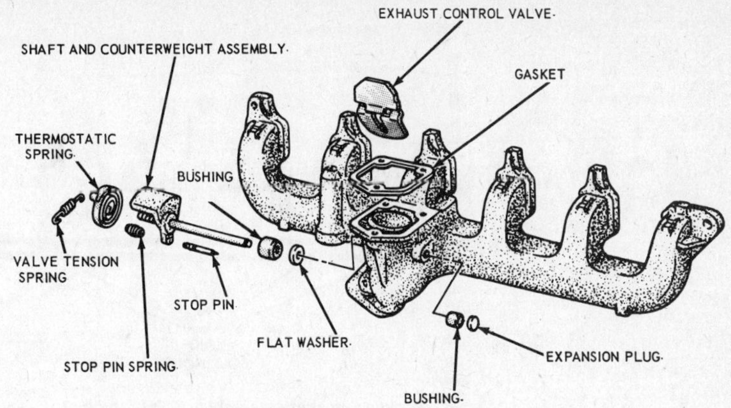

Exhaust control valve assy.—240 & 300 engines (© Ford Motor Co.)

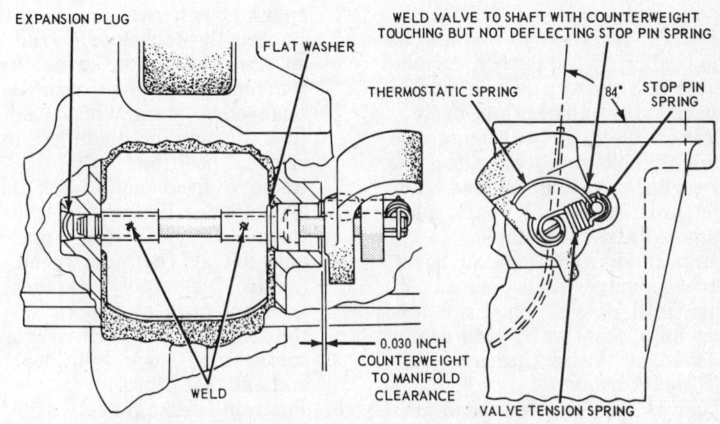

Exhaust valve plate position & counterweight clearance (© Ford Motor Co.)

Cylinder Head

Cylinder Head Removal and Installation

144, 170, 200 Cu. In. 6-Cylinder F-100, Econoline and Bronco

1. Drain cooling system, remove the air cleaner and oil filler tube, and disconnect the battery cable at cylinder head.
2. Disconnect exhaust pipe from manifold.
3. Disconnect accelerator rod retracting spring, choke control cable and accelerator rod at the carburetor, transmission kickdown rod (automatic transmission), accelerator linkage at bellcrank, fuel inlet line at fuel filter hose, distributor vacuum line at the carburetor and other vacuum lines as necessary for accessibility (identify them for proper reinstallation).
4. Remove upper radiator hose at the coolant outlet housing.
5. Disconnect the distributor vacuum line at the distributor and carburetor fuel inlet line at the fuel pump.
6. Disconnect spark plug wires at the plugs and temperature sending unit wire at the unit.
7. Remove PCV valve and hose from valve rocker cover and disconnect the other end of the hose from the intake manifold.
8. Remove the valve rocker arm cover, then remove the rocker arm shaft support bolts by loosening them two turns at a time in sequence.
9. Lift off rocker arm shaft.
10. Remove cylinder head bolts and cylinder head. *Do not pry.*
11. Before installing, clean gasket surfaces of cylinder head and engine block, install guide studs at each end of block, apply cylinder head gasket sealer evenly to both sides of the head gasket, and run the gasket down the guide studs into position on the engine block.
12. Put a new gasket on the flange of the exhaust pipe, then carefully lower the head down the guide studs onto the block, guiding the exhaust manifold studs into the exhaust pipe.
13. Coat the threads of the cylinder head right side end bolts (Nos. 12 and 13 in the illustration) and install them finger tight to hold the head and gasket in position. Install the rest of the head bolts finger tight, then tighten in steps to 55 ft. lbs, 65 ft. lbs. and 70-75 ft. lbs., following the sequence illustrated for each step.
14. Apply Lubriplate to both ends of their original locations.
15. Apply Lubriplate to the rocker arm follower pads and to the valve stem tips, then position rocker arm shaft assembly on the head.
16. Install the rocker arm shaft support bolts and tighten them in sequence two turns at a time until they are torqued to 30-35 ft. lbs.
17. Check and adjust the preliminary (cold) lash as described in "Valve Clearance Adjustment" below.
18. Install lockwashers and nuts to exhaust manifold to exhaust pipe studs and tighten to 25-35 ft. lbs. torque.
19. Connect radiator upper hose at the coolant outlet housing.

Cylinder head bolt tightening sequence—6 cyl.—144, 170 & 200 engines
(© Ford Motor Co.)

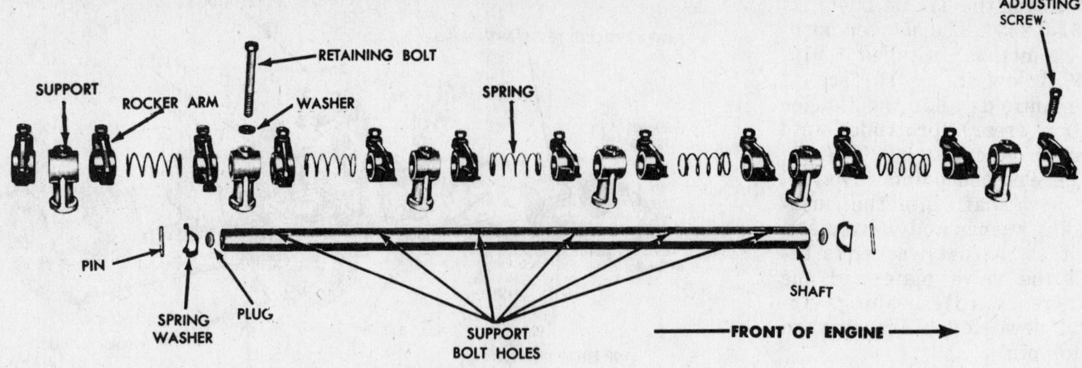

Rocker arm shaft assembly—6 cyl.—typical (© Ford Motor Co.)

20. Install vacuum lines (s) and fuel line.
21. Connect accelerator linkage at the bellcrank assembly, transmission kickdown rod, accelerator rod retracing spring, battery cable at the cylinder head, choke control cable and accelerator rod at carburetor, temperature sending unit wire and spark plug leads. Adjust choke cable.
22. Temporarily install rocker cover and PC valve, then operate engine until it is warmed up. Adjust final (hot) valve lash as described in "Valve Clearance Adjustment" below.
23. Clean rocker cover and head gasket surfaces and install cover using a new seal coated on both sides with oil-resistant sealer. Tighten cover retaining bolts to 3-5 ft. lbs. torque, wait two minutes, then retorque to the same value.
24. Connect one end of the crankcase vent hose to the carburetor spacer and the valve end to the rocker cover.
25. Install oil filler tube and air cleaner.
26. Start engine and check for coolant and oil leaks.

Cylinder Head Removal and Installation

240 and 300 Cu. In. 6-Cylinder

1. Drain cooling system and remove air cleaner and crankcase ventilation valve.
2. Disconnect the following: the vent hose at the intake manifold inlet tube, carburetor fuel inlet line, distributor vacuum line, choke cable, accelerator cable and heater hose at the coolant outlet elbow. Remove accelerator cable retracting spring.
3. On a vehicle with automatic transmission, disconnect the kickdown rod at the carburetor.
4. Disconnect upper radiator hose and exhaust pipe.
5. Remove the coil and the valve rocker cover and disconnect spark plug wires.
6. Loosen the rocker arm stud nuts so that the rocker arms can be twisted aside, then remove the pushrods, identifying each so that it may be installed in its original position.
7. Remove head bolts and install eyebolts for lifting (see illustration). Attach lifting apparatus and lift off cylinder head and manifold assembly. *Do not pry between head and block.*
8. Before installing, clean mating surfaces of block, cylinder head and exhaust pipe.
9. Position new gasket over the dowel pins on the cylinder block, then carefully lower head into place on the block. Remove lifting apparatus.
10. Oil the threads and install head bolts. Tighten the bolts in three steps, following the sequence illustrated in each step: first to 50-55 ft. lbs., then to 60-65 ft. lbs, and finally to 70-75 ft. lbs.
11. Connect exhaust pipe to manifold flange, using a new gasket and tighten the nuts to 25-30 ft. lbs.
12. Apply Lubriplate to both ends of the pushrods and install them in their original positions.
13. Apply Lubriplate to both the rocker arm fulcrum seat and the fulcrum seat socket of each rocker arm and install the rocker arms, tightening the stud nuts just enough to hold the pushrods. Adjust the valve lash as described in "Valve Clearance Adjustment" below.
14. Install the rocker cover, using oil-resistant sealer and a new gasket. Tighten the retaining bolts to 4-7 ft. lbs.

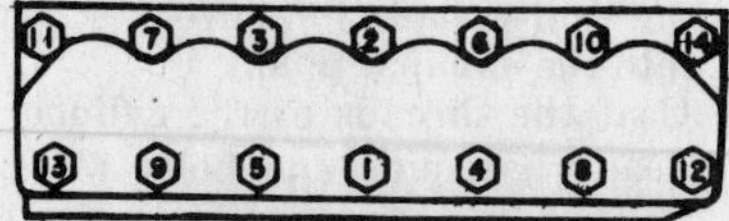

Cylinder head bolt tightening sequence—6 cyl.—240 & 300 engines
(© Ford Motor Co.)

15. Connect the spark plug wires to the plugs, crankcase vent hose to the intake manifold, PCV valve in the valve rocker cover, fuel inlet line, distributor vacuum hose, accelerator cable and choke cable. Install accelerator cable retracting spring.
16. On a vehicle with automatic transmission, connect the kickdown rod to the carburetor.
17. Connect radiator upper hose to the coolant outlet housing and the heater hose to the coolant outlet housing, leaving the clamp loose.
18. Fill the cooling system and bleed. Then tighten the heater hose clamp.
19. Operate the engine until it is warmed up, checking for leaks.
20. Adjust engine idle speed and idle fuel mixture.

Cylinder Head Removal and Installation

289 and 302 Cu. In. V-8

1. Remove the intake manifold and carburetor as an assembly as described in "Intake Manifold Removal and Installation" above.
2. Remove rocker arm cover.
3. To remove right cylinder head, loosen alternator adjusting arm bolt and remove the alternator mounting bracket bolt and spacer. Swing alternator down out of the way. On Bronco and Econoline trucks, remove the coil and air cleaner inlet duct from the right head. To remove left cylinder head, remove accelerator shaft fastening bolts at the front of the head.
4. Disconnect exhaust pipe from the manifold.
5. Loosen rocker arm stud nuts and twist rocker arms so that the pushrods may be removed. Identify the pushrods when removing so that they may be reinstalled in their original locations.
6. Remove exhaust valve stem caps.

7. Install cylinder head holding fixtures, remove head bolts and lift off head.
8. To install, clean all gasket surfaces of block, head and rocker cover. Position new head gasket over the dowels onto the block (do *not* use sealer on this composition gasket). Install head and remove holding fixture.
9. Install head bolts and tighten in three steps: first to 50 ft. lbs, then to 60 ft. lbs, and finally to 65-72 ft. lbs. Tighten in the sequence illustrated for each step.
10. Clean pushrods, blowing out oil passage, and check them for straightness. Lubricate pushrod ends, valve stem tips and rocker arm cups, fulcrum seats and followers. Install pushrods in their original positions, install exhaust stem caps and install rocker arms. Adjust the valve clearance as described in "Valve Clearance Adjustment" below.
11. Connect the exhaust pipe to the manifold, using new gasket and tightening nuts to 25-35 ft. lbs. torque.
12. On right cylinder head, position the alternator and install the attaching bolt and spacer, ignition coil (Bronco and Econoline) and air cleaner inlet duct. Adjust drive belt tension. On left cylinder head, install accelerator shaft assembly.
13. Install rocker cover using new gasket and tightening cover bolts to 3-5 ft. lbs.
14. Install intake manifold and carburetor assembly as described in "Intake Manifold Removal and Installation" above.

Cylinder Head Removal and Installation

330, 360, 361, 390 and 391 Cu. In. V-8

Removal and installation of cylinder heads on the larger V 8's is essentially the same procedure as that described above for the 289 and 302 cu. in. engines. The intake manifold and carburetor assembly and rocker arm shaft assembly are removed first (see "Intake Manifold Removal and Installation" above). When installing new head gasket, note the word "front" on the gasket and install accordingly. The head bolts are tightened in three steps, first to 70 ft. lbs., then to 80 ft. lbs., and finally to 85-90 ft. lbs. Tighten in the sequence illustrated for each step.

Valve Train

Valve Clearance (Lash) Adjustment

Reference

For cylinder head overhaul procedures see General Repair Section.

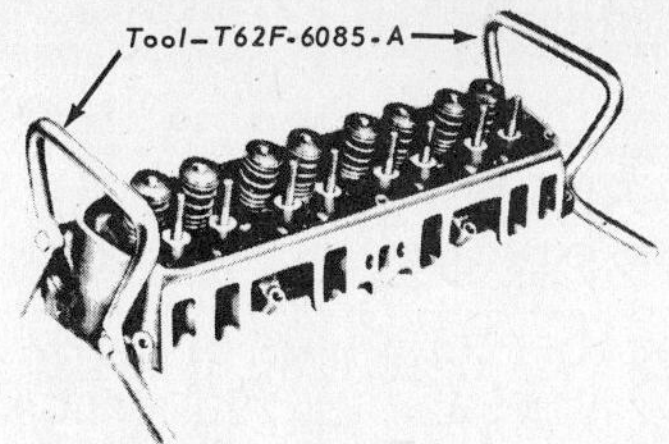

Cylinder head holding fixture—6 cyl.
(© Ford Motor Co.)

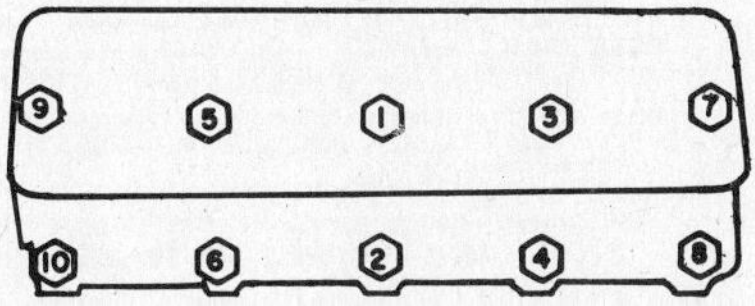

Cylinder head bolt tightening sequence—all V8 engines

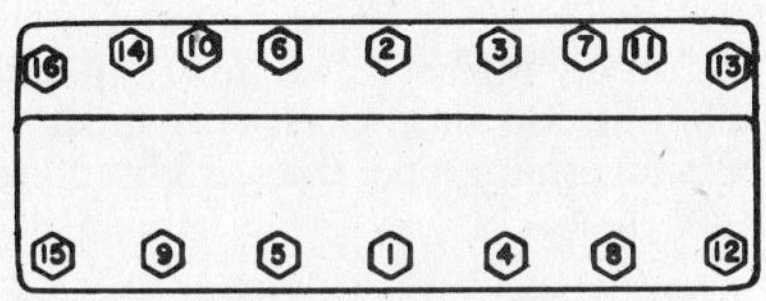

Cylinder head bolt tightening sequence—6 cyl.—223 & 262 engines

STEP 1—SET NO. 1 PISTON ON T.D.C. AT END OF COMPRESSION STROKE, ADJUST NO. 1 INTAKE & EXHAUST.
STEP 4—ADJUST NO. 6 INTAKE & EXHAUST.

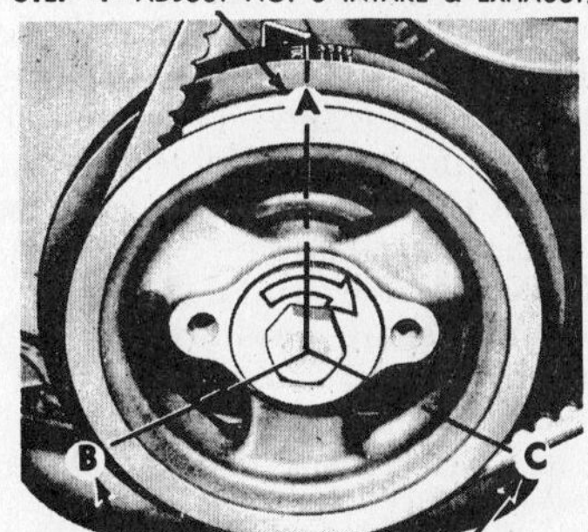

STEP 2 ADJUST NO. 5 INTAKE & EXHAUST.
STEP 5 ADJUST NO. 2 INTAKE & EXHAUST.
STEP 3-ADJUST NO. 3 INTAKE & EXHAUST.
STEP 6 ADJUST NO. 4 INTAKE & EXHAUST.

Preliminary valve adjustment
(© Ford Motor Co.)

Adjusting valves (hot)
(© Ford Motor Co.)

Preliminary (Cold) Lash Adjustment Final (Hot) Lash Adjustment

This adjustment is made when the rocker arm shaft assembly has been removed and installed. This adjustment is only a preliminary one and final (hot) adjustment must be made after the engine has run until warmed up.

1. Turn all adjusting screws in until interference is felt. Check the torque required to turn each beyond this point. If it's less than 7 ft. lbs, a new oversize self-locking adjusting screw must be used. If this is loose (torque required less than 7 ft. lbs.), then the rocker arm must be replaced.
2. Make two 120-degree marks on the crankshaft damper as illustrated.
3. Rotate crankshaft until No. 1 piston is at TDC of compression stroke (both valve closed and timing marks are aligned with timing pointer). Valves for each cylinder are adjusted when the piston is at TDC of compression stroke.
4. Holding a feeler gauge of the specified clearance between the rocker arm and the valve stem tip, turn adjusting screw until the correct lash is obtained. Adjust both valves. See Tune-Up Specifications at the beginning of this section for correct valve lash settings.
5. Repeat Step 4 for each of the remaining cylinders, following the order 1-5-3-6-2-4 and rotating the crankshaft 120 degrees (1/3 turn to the next mark on the damper). Two complete turns of the crankshaft are required.

Final (Hot) Lash Adjustment

1. Operate the engine until it is warmed up.
2. With engine idling, set the valve lash *using a step-type feeler gauge only (go or no go).*

240 and 300 Cu. In. 6-Cylinder

1. Mark the crankshaft pulley damper with two 120-degree marks as illustrated in the preceding (144, 170, 200 cu. in.) paragraph.
2. Rotate crankshaft until No. 1 piston is at TDC.
3. Check the breakaway torque (torque necessary to turn nut in counterclockwise direction) of each stud nut of No. 1 cylinder rockers. If it is not 4.5-15 ft. lbs., replace the nut. If the breakaway torque is still not within specification, replace the stud.

4. Loosen rocker nuts until there is definite clearance, then adjust nut until zero clearance is obtained (this can be felt when it becomes difficult to turn pushrod). Then tighten stud nut one additional turn.
5. Repeat Steps 3 and 4 for the rest of the valves, rotating the crankshaft 1/3 for each cylinder in the sequence 1-5-3-6-2-4.
6. Operate engine and check for rough idle or noisy lifters. Rough idle indicates that valve clearance is set too tight and noisy lifters indicates that valve clearance is set too loose.

With No. 1 at TDC at end of compression stroke make a chalk mark at points B and C approximately 90 degrees apart.

TIMING POINTER

TDC

A

B

C

POSITION A – No. 1 at TDC at end of compression stroke.
POSITION B – Rotate the crankshaft 180 degrees (one half revolution) clockwise from POSITION A.
POSITION C – Rotate the crankshaft 270 degrees (three quarter revolution) clockwise from POSITION B.

Position of crankshaft for adjusting valve clearance (© Ford Motor Co.)

Final (Hot) Lash Adjustment 289 and 302 Cu. In. V-8

Excessive dimension variation in the valve train is compensated for by the substitution of the pushrod with a 0.060″ over- or under-size pushrod. These are a standard replacement part. Valve rocker clearance is checked with the hydraulic lifter completely collapsed.

To check clearance, first rotate the crankshaft to No. 1 piston TDC. Mark the crankshaft pulley at points B and C as illustrated.

Position a hydraulic lifter collapsing tool on the rocker arm and slowly apply pressure to bleed down the hydraulic lifter until plunger is completely bottomed (see illustration). Holding the lifter in this position, check clearance between rocker arm and valve stem tip (feeler gauge must be narrower than ⅜″). See Tune-Up Specifications for correct clearance. If the clearance is greater than specified limit, install a longer pushrod. If clearance is less than specified limit, install a shorter pushrod.

The following valves may be checked with crankshaft pulley in No. 1 cylinder TDC (position "A"):

No. 1 intake No. 1 exhaust
No. 7 intake No. 5 exhaust
No. 8 intake No. 4 exhaust

Rotate the crankshaft (clockwise) to position "B" and check clearance on the following valves:

No. 5 intake No. 2 exhaust
No. 4 intake No. 6 exhaust

Rotate the crankshaft (clockwise) to position "C" and check clearance on the following valves:

No. 2 intake No. 7 exhaust
No. 3 intake No. 3 exhaust
No. 6 intake No. 8 exhaust

The only valve lash adjustment, besides replacement of worn parts, is the correct tightening of the rocker stud nut. Remove each rocker stud nut as the crankshaft is at the correct positions "AK", "B" and "C" and inspect it for wear. If the inside bevel wear is too great or the nut is fractured, release the nut. Install each nut, turning clockwise until it contacts the stop, then tighten to 18-20 ft. lbs.

Final (Hot) Lash Adjustment 330, 360, 361, 390 and 391 Cu. In. V-8

Longer (0.060″) and shorter (0.060″) pushrods are available as standard replacement parts to accommodate dimensional changes in the valve train. Valve clearance is measured with the hydraulic lifter collapsed. If clearance is not within specified limits (see Valve Specifications at the beginning of this section), replace pushrod.

Valve clearances are measured at two crankshaft positions. Rotate crankshaft until No. 1 piston is at TDC at the end of the compression stroke and check the following valves:

No. 1 intake No. 1 exhaust
No. 3 intake No. 4 exhaust
No. 7 intake No. 5 exhaust
No. 8 intake No. 8 exhaust

Rotate the crankshaft 360 degrees to position No. 6 piston on TDC and check the following valves:

No. 2 intake No. 2 exhaust
No. 4 intake No. 3 exhaust
No. 5 intake No. 7 exhaust
No. 6 intake No. 6 exhaust

Valve Overhaul

See the General Repair Section for complete valve overhaul procedures. All valves are removed by compressing the spring with a valve spring compressing tool, then removing the keepers from the end of the valve stem. Most models utilized an O-ring or cup type oil seal as illustrated. Valve spring, stem and seal specifications may be found in the Valve Specifications Table at the beginning of this section.

Valve rocker arm shaft assembly

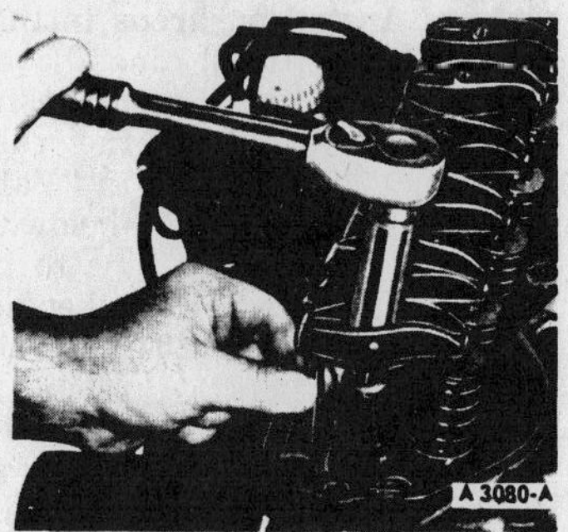

Feeling zero lash 240 & 300 engines (© Ford Motor Co.)

Tool – 6513-AC

Checking valve clearance—hydraulic lifters (© Ford Motor Co.)

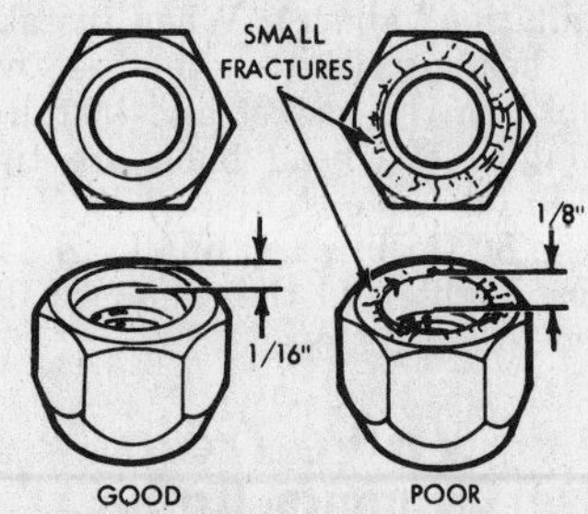

Rocker arm stud nut—inspection (© Ford Motor Co.)

removal and installation procedures may be found immediately following "Intake Manifold Removal and Installation" above (330, 360, 361, 390 and 391 cu. in. V-8) and under "Cylinder Head Removal and Installation" (144, 170 and 200 cu. in. 6-cylinder).

Timing Gears and Chain

Timing (Front) Cover and Seal Removal and Installation

144, 170 and 200 Cu. In. 6-Cylinder

1. Drain cooling system, disconnect the radiator upper hose at the coolant outlet elbow and remove the two radiator upper attaching bolts.
2. Raise vehicle and drain crankcase.
3. Remove splash shield (if applicable) and radiator as described above.
4. Remove drive belts, fan, pulley and crankshaft damper (use a suitable puller).
5. Remove front cover attaching bolts. Before removing the cover, cut the oil pan gasket. Remove cover.
6. Check timing chain deflection and camshaft endplay as described below. Endplay should be within 0.001-0.007" and chain deflection should not exceed 0.500".
7. Rotate crankshaft until sprocket timing marks are aligned, then remove camshaft sprocket attaching bolt and washer. Slide off sprockets and chain.
8. Drive out the old seal with a pin punch and clean out seal recess.
9. Coat new seal with grease and install using a suitable installing tool.
10. Clean and oil chain and sprockets, then install as an assembly with timing marks aligned as illustrated. Install camshaft sprocket retaining bolt and washer, tightening to 34-45 ft. lbs.
11. Cut and install a piece of new gasket to go between front cover and oil pan, using sealer on all surfaces.
12. Install front cover and new seal, coating all surfaces with sealer. It may be necessary to force the cover downward to compress the new piece of oil pan gasket. Coat threads of cover attaching screws with oil-resistance sealer and install them finger-tight. While holding the front cover in alignment (using an aligning tool if available), tighten oil pan to cover attaching to 7-9 ft. lbs. Tighten the rest of the mounting bolts to the same torque.
13. Apply Lubriplate to the hub of the crankshaft and install damper, tightening attaching bolt to 85-100 ft. lbs.
14. Install fan, pulley, drive belt (adjust), radiator, radiator lower hose and splash shield.
15. Lower the vehicle and connect upper hose.
16. Fill and bleed cooling system.
17. Fill crankcase.
18. Operate engine and check for leaks.

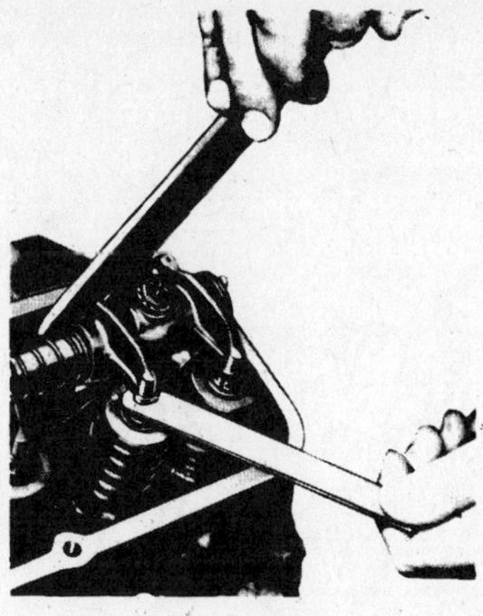

Checking valve lash—330 engine
(© Ford Motor Co.)

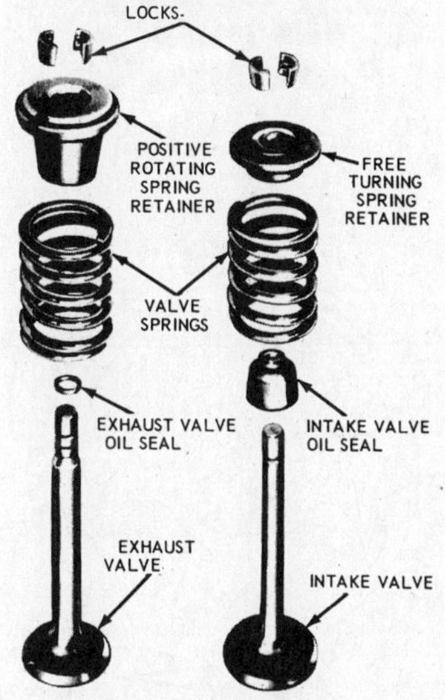

Typical valve layout
(© Ford Motor Co.)

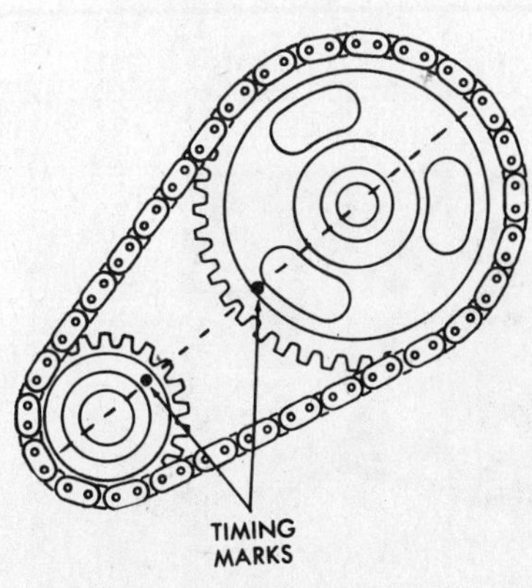

Timing mark alignment—
6 cyl.—144, 170 & 200 engines

Timing Cover and Seal Removal and Installation

240 and 300 Cu. In. 6-Cylinder

Drain cooling system and crankcase then remove in order: radiator (see "Radiator Removal and Installation" above), alternator adjusting arm bolt, drive belt (swing alternator out of the way), fan, pulley, air compressor and/or steering pump belt, damper cam screw, washer, damper, oil level dipstick, oil pan (see "Oil Pan Removal and Installation" above) and oil pump screen and inlet tube assembly.

Remove front cover retaining bolts and front cover. Discard old seal and gasket and clean out seal recess in cover. New seal is pressed in from the inside of cover.

Check camshaft endplay (0.003-0.007"), gear backlash (0.002-0.004") and timing gear runout (0.006" for camshaft gear and 0.003" and 0.006" for the 240 and 300 crankshaft gears respectively). Replace worn parts.

Before pulling gears, rotate crankshaft until timing marks are aligned. Metal camshaft gear (300 HD) and crankshaft gear may be removed with a puller. *Do not rotate crankshaft while gears are removed.* Fiber camshaft gear (240 and 300 LD) may only be separated from the camshaft after the camshaft has been removed. See "Camshaft Removal and Installation" below. Fiber gear is removed with an arbor press. Camshaft, spacer and thrust plate are installed before the gear (metal or fiber) is installed with special tools as illustrated. Be sure to install key in slot and to align timing marks before installing gear. Install thrust plate bolts, tightening to 19-20 ft. lbs.

When installing front cover, use a new gasket and be sure to align the cover before tightening cover retaining bolts to 15 ft. lbs. Lubricate the rubbing surface of the oil seal and damper, then install key and damper. Install oil pan using new gaskets and sealer. Install in reverse order all the other componants which were removed. Fill cooling system and crankcase.

Timing Cover and Seal Removal and Installation

289 and 302 Cu. In. V-8

Drain cooling system and crankcase. Remove the following: alternator pivot and adjusting arm bolts, fan shroud, fan, spacer, pulley, drive belts, crankshaft pulley and damper (use a puller), fuel pump (disconnect fuel and vacuum lines), dipstick and dipstick tube. Disconnect the radiator lower hose and heater hose at the water pump. On Econoline models, remove the air cleaner and intake duct assembly, including the crankcase ventilation hose. Then remove the radiator.

In addition to the four front cover to block attaching bolts, the four front oil pan bolts must be removed to get the front cover off. Cut the oil pan gasket flush with the block with a thin-bladed knife before removing front cover. Check the deflection of the timing chain. If the chain deflection exceeds 0.500″, the chain must be replaced. To remove chain and sprocket, first rotate crankshaft until the timing marks are aligned, then remove camshaft sprocket bolt, washers, crankshaft oil slinger and fuel pump eccentric. Slide off sprockets and chain as an assembly.

Always install a new front seal when the front cover is removed. Drive out old seal with a pin punch. Coat new seal with grease, then drive in seal until it is fully seated. Check spring position.

Install timing chain and sprockets as an assembly, making sure timing marks are aligned. Install fuel pump eccentric, washers and camshaft sprocket bolt, tightening 40-45 ft. lbs. Install oil slinger on crankshaft. Lubricate chain and sprockets with heavy engine oil.

Using a new front cover gasket and a piece of oil pan gasket cut to size, install front cover, tightening bolts finger tight. Use oil-resistant sealer on gaskets and bolt threads. It may be necessary to force the cover downward to compress the section of oil pan gasket. Align the front cover with respect to the crankshaft (it is best to use an aligning tool). Tighten front cover and front oil pan bolts to 12-15 ft. lbs, oil pan bolts first.

Apply Lubriplate to oil seal to damper rubbing surface, then install key, damper, washer and retaining bolt, tightening bolt to 100-130 ft. lbs.

Install in reverse order all the rest of the components previously removed. Fill and bleed cooling system. Fill crankcase. Operate engine and check for leaks.

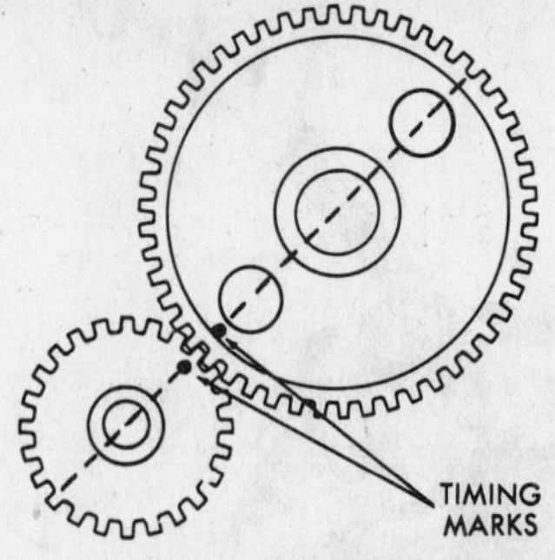

Timing mark alignment—6 cyl.—240 & 300 engines

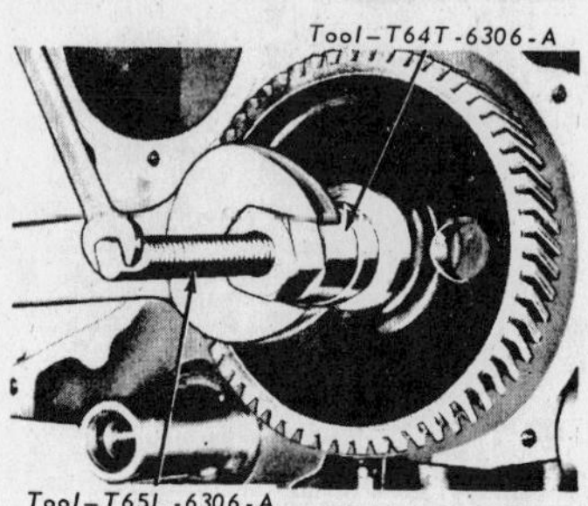

Installing camshaft gear
(© Ford Motor Co.)

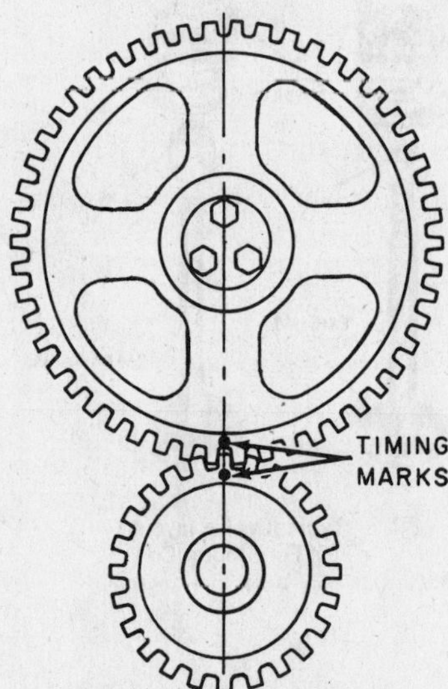

Timing mark alignment—V8—302, 332, 401, 477 & 534 engines

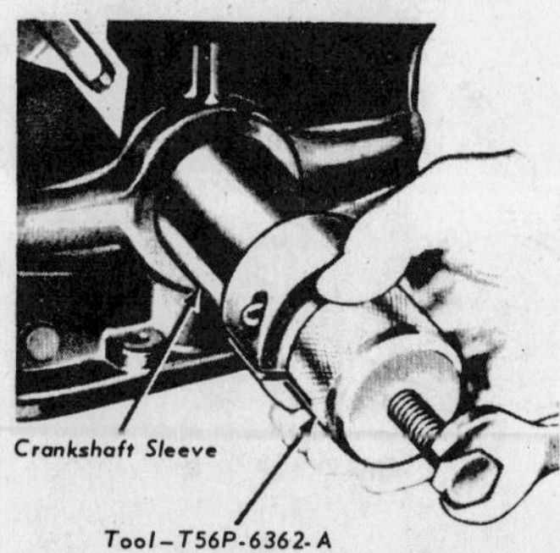

Removing crankshaft sleeve—330 engine
(© Ford Motor Co.)

Timing Cover and Seal Removal and Installation

330, 360, 361, 390 and 391 Cu. In. V-8

Drain the cooling system and crankcase. Disconnect battery ground cable and distributor vacuum line. Remove the following in the order given: air cleaner, radiator (see "Radiator Removal and Installation"), water pump bypass hose, fan, fan drive belt, power steering pump, air compressor, alternator, water pump, crankshaft damper retaining bolt, damper, fuel pump (leave flex line attached) and crankshaft sleeve (use puller).

Remove all front cover attaching bolts (to oil pan and block). Before removing cover, cut the oil pan gasket flush with the block. Remove front cover, alternator support bracket and adjusting arm bracket, engine front mount bracket and oil slinger. Check timing chain deflection (0.500″ for 360 and 390, 0.680″ for 330, 361, 391) and camshaft endplay (0.001-0.007″). Rotate crankshaft until timing marks are aligned. Remove camshaft sprocket bolt and fuel pump eccentric, then slide off sprockets and chain as an assembly.

Replace front oil seal by driving out old one with a pin punch, cleaning seal recess, then driving greased new seal into cover (it is best to use a seal installing tool). Make sure the spring is properly seated in seal.

Install camshaft spacer, then timing chain and sprockets as an assembly, making sure slotted spacer is aligned with dowel and timing marks are aligned. Install fuel pump eccentric and spocket bolt on camshaft, tightening bolt to 34-45 ft. lbs. Check endplay if new camshaft thrust plate was installed. Install oil slinger on crankshaft.

Cut a piece of gasket material to replace the section of oil pan gasket and install front cover, cover gasket and oil pan gasket, using oil-resistant sealer on all surfaces. Align cover (use an aligning tool), position front engine mount bracket and install attaching bolts, tightening 3/8-16 bolts to 23-28 ft. lbs. or 5/16-18 bolts to 12-15 ft. lbs.

Lubricate the rubbing surface with grease and insert the crankshaft sleeve. Use a new sleeve if the old one is nicked or worn, for seal is easily damaged. Install key, damper and retaining bolt, tightening to 75-85 ft. lbs. torque. Install in reverse order all components which were removed. Fill crankcase. Fill and bleed cooling system. Operate engine and check for leaks.

Checking Timing Chain Deflection

To measure timing chain deflection, rotate crankshaft clockwise to take up slack on the left side of chain. Choose a reference point and measure distance from this point and the chain. Rotate crankshaft in the opposite direction to take up slack on the right side of the chain. Force the left (slack) side of the chain out and measure the distance to the reference point chosen earlier. The difference between the two measurements is the deflection.

Timing chain should be replaced if deflection measurement exceeds specified limit.

Camshaft Endplay Measurement

The fiber camshaft gears used on some engines is easily damaged if pried upon while the valve train load is on the camshaft. Loosen rocker arm nuts or rocker arm shaft support bolts before checking camshaft endplay.

Push camshaft toward rear of engine, install and zero a dial indicator, then pry between camshaft gear and block to pull the camshaft forward. If endplay is excessive, check for correct installation of spacer. If spacer is installed correctly, then replace thrust plate.

Measuring Timing Gear Backlash

Use a dial indicator installed on block to measure timing gear backlash. Hold gear firmly against the block while making measurement. If excessive backlash exists, replace both gears.

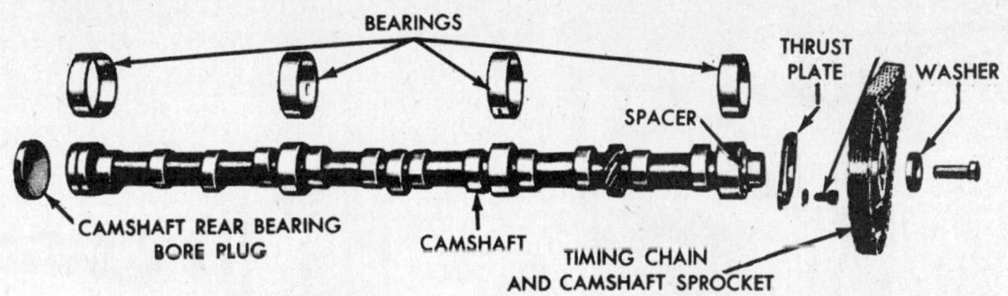

Camshaft—6 cyl.—170 engine (© Ford Motor Co.)

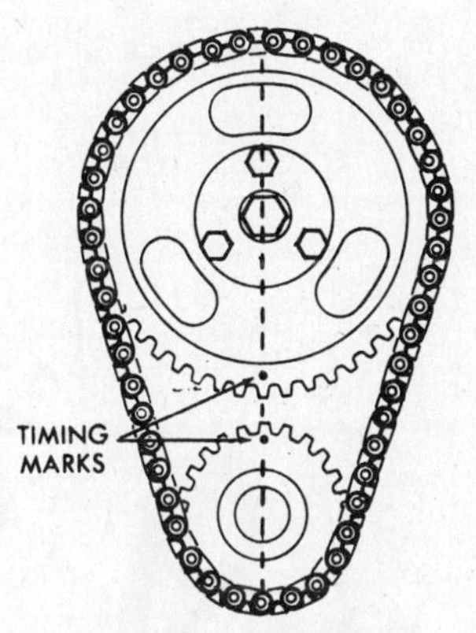

Timing mark alignment—V8—330, 352, 360, 361, 390 & 391 engines

TAKE UP SLACK ON LEFT SIDE, ESTABLISH REFERENCE POINT. MEASURE DISTANCE **A.** TAKE UP SLACK ON RIGHT SIDE. FORCE LEFT SIDE OUT. MEASURE DISTANCE **B.** DEFLECTION IS **A** MINUS **B.**

Checking timing chain deflection (© Ford Motor Co.)

1. PUSH CAM TO REAR OF ENGINE
2. SET *Dial* ON ZERO
3. PULL CAM FORWARD AND RELEASE

Measuring camshaft end play (© Ford Motor Co.)

Checking timing gear backlash (© Ford Motor Co.)

Camshaft

Camshaft Removal and Installation

144, 170 and 200 Cu. In. 6-Cylinder

1. Remove in order front cover, timing chain, cylinder head, distributor and fuel pump. Detailed removal and installation procedures for these components may be found in this section under each component heading.
2. Remove tappets with a magnet.
3. Remove dipstick, headlights, parking lights and the grill and hoodlock assembly.
4. Remove camshaft thrust plate and carefully slide camshaft from block.
5. Blow out rocker arm oil supply passages in the block with compressed air. Oil camshaft journals and apply Lubriplate to lobes. If a new camshaft is being used, transfer the spacer and dowel from old camshaft. Carefully slide camshaft into place.
6. Install thrust plate, tightening bolts to 12-15 ft. lbs.
7. Install timing sprockets, chain and all related front cover components as described in front cover removal and installation procedures above. Be sure to install a new front cover oil seal.
8. Install in reverse order all components removed, following instructions for each component group described topically in this section.
9. Start engine, adjust ignition timing, set idle speed and check for leaks.

Camshaft Removal and Installation

240 and 300 Cu. In. 6-Cylinder

1. Remove the front cover following procedure described in "Front Cover Removal and Installation" above.
2. Remove air cleaner and crankcase vent tube at the rocker cover.
3. Disconnect accelerator cable, choke cable and hand throttle cable (if so equpped). Remove accelerator cable retracting spring.
4. If applicable, remove air compressor and power steering belts.
5. Disconnect oil filler hose from rocker cover.
6. Remove distributor cap and wiring as an assembly, then disconnect vacuum line and primary wire and remove distributor.
7. Remove fuel pump.
8. Remove valve rocker cover, loosen rocker arm stud nuts and move rocker arms to one side. Remove pushrods, identifying each so that they may be installed in their original loca-

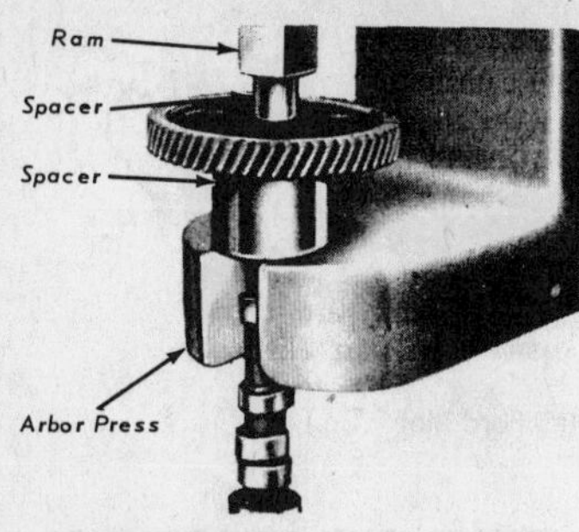

Removing fibre camshaft gear
(© Ford Motor Co.)

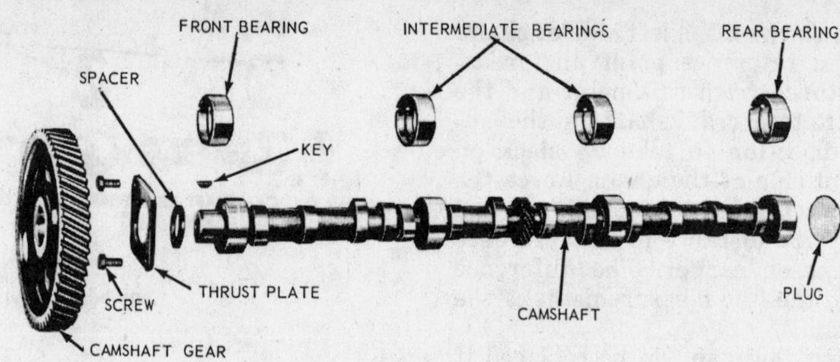

Camshaft—6 cyl.—240 & 300 engines (© Ford Motor Co.)

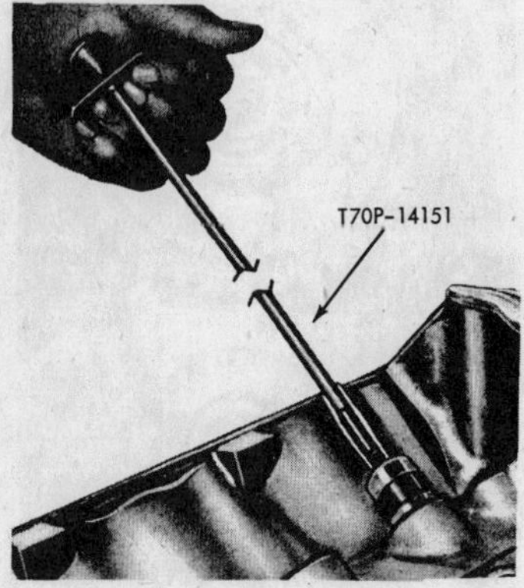

Removing valve lifters
(© Ford Motor Co.)

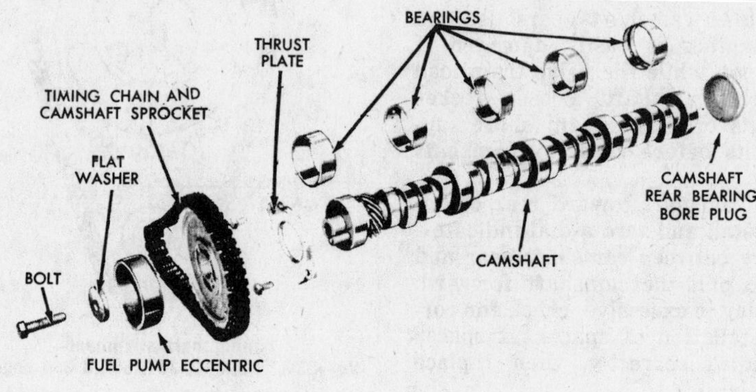

Typical camshaft—V8 engines (© Ford Motor Co.)

tions.

9. Remove pushrod cover and valve lifters, identifying the position of each.
10. Turn crankshaft to align timing marks, remove camshaft thrust plate bolts and carefully pull camshaft and gear from block. Metal camshaft gear (300 HD) is bolted onto camshaft and fiber gear (240 and 300 LD) is pressed on and must be removed with an arbor press.
11. To install camshaft, oil journals and apply Lubriplate to lobes, then carefully install camshaft, spacer, thrustplate and gear as an assembly, making sure timing marks are aligned, then tighten-ing thrustplate bolts to 19-20 ft. lbs. Do not rotate crankshaft until distributor is installed.
12. Install front cover, referring to "Front Cover Removal and Installation" for correct procedure.
13. Install valve lifters, then the pushrods in their original locations. Apply heavy engine oil to the lifters and Lubriplate to the pushrods.
14. Install in order the following components, referring to appropriate sections by topic for detailed instructions if necessary and using new gaskets with sealer: pushrod cover, valve rocker cover (adjust valve lash first), distributor (rotor in No. 1. cylinder firing position), fuel pump, distributor cap and wiring assembly, crankcase ventilation valve (in rocker cover), oil filler hose, accelerator cable and retracting spring, choke cable, hand throttle cable, water pump pulley, fan, belt, air compressor and power steering belts, radiator, hood latch, grill and air cleaner.
15. Fill crankcase.
16. Fill and bleed cooling system, checking for leaks.
17. Set the ignition timing, then connect distributor vacuum line.
18. Adjust carburetor idle speed and idle fuel mixture.

Camshaft Removal and Installation

289 and 302 Cu. In. V-8

To get at the camshaft for removal, the front cover, timing chain and intake manifold must be removed. See "Front Cover Removal and Installation" and "Intake Manifold Removal and Installation" above for detailed instructions. After work with the camshaft has been completed, refer to these sections for installation procedures.

Remove the rocker arm cover and loosen the rocker arm stud nuts so that the rocker arms may be rotated to one side and the pushrods removed. Be sure to identify each pushrod with its location so that it may be reinstalled in the same place. Remove the valve lifters and identify them also. Remove camshaft thrust plate, then carefully pull camshaft out of block.

When installing camshaft, apply Lubriplate to the lobes and heavy oil to the journals and thrust plate. Tighten thrust plate bolts to 9-12 ft. lbs. Lubricate lifters and pushrods with heavy engine oil before installing them in their original locations. Apply Lubriplate to the valve stem tips.

Adjust valve lash as described in "Valve Lash Adjustment" above and note the correct rocker cover installation procedure. Use new gaskets with sealer when installing the intake manifold and front cover.

Camshaft Removal and Installation

330, 360, 361, 390 and 391 Cu. In. V-8

Remove the valve rocker arm shaft assembly and intake manifold assembly, referring to the instructions for each given above. Remove the valve lifters, identifying the location of each for correct reinstallation. Remove the front cover and timing chain following the procedure given in "Front Cover Removal and Installation" above. Remove the camshaft thrust plate and carefully pull camshaft from block.

To install, apply Lubriplate to the lobes and heavy oil to the bearing journals. Tighten thrust plate bolts to 12-15 ft. lbs. Be sure the thrust

Camshaft thrustplate & spacer—330 engine
(© Ford Motor Co.)

plate and spacer are positioned correctly with respect to the dowel pin as illustrated.

Following when necessary instructions referred to above, install in order: timing chain and sprockets, fuel pump eccentric, oil slinger, front cover, valve lifters, intake manifold assembly, rocker arm shaft assembly, distributor (No. cylinder rotor location timed to No. 1 piston TDC compression stroke) and distributor cap with high tension lead. Adjust ignition timing and fast idle.

Camshaft Bearings and Valve Lifters

Reference

For detailed procedures for camshaft bearing replacement and hydraulic lifter service see the General Repair Section.

Pistons and Connecting Rods

Reference

Instructions for fitting of rings and rod bearings, ridge reaming and cylinder honing may be found in the General Repair Section.

Piston and Rod Removal and Installation

All Models

1. Drain cooling system and crankcase.
2. Remove the cylinder head.
3. Remove oil pan, oil pump pick-up tube and screen assembly and oil pump.
4. Turning crankshaft so that piston is at the bottom of its stroke, then ridge ream the top of the cylinder. *Never cut into the ring travel area in excess of 1/32" when removing ridges.*
5. Mark each rod bearing cap before removal so that it can be installed in its original location, then remove cap. Caps and rods are numbered on some models.
6. Push connecting rod and piston assembly out the top of the cylinder.
7. Make sure piston is assembled in correct relation to the connecting rod, that is, that the notch on the top of the piston and the oil hole in the rod are positioned as illustrated. Align ring gaps as illustrated and oil the piston rings, pistons and cylinder walls.
8. Install a ring compressor and push the piston and rod assembly into the cylinder (if reinstalling an old piston, make sure it is in the same cylinder). On all but the 330, 360, 361, 390 and 391 cu. in. V-8 engines the piston is installed with the notch on the crown toward the front of the engine. On the 330, 360, 361, 390 and 391 cu. in. engines the notch faces in (toward "V").
9. Fit rod bearings, apply oil to journals and bearings, then install bearings and cap, tightening cap bolts to specified torque (see Specifications at the beginning of this section).
10. Check rod bearing side clearance.
11. Thoroughly clean oil pump assembly, then prime it by filling and rotating shaft until pump is full. Install pump assembly.
12. Install oil pan, cylinder head and intake manifold (V-8 engines).
13. Fill and bleed cooling system.
14. Fill crankcase.
15. Set ignition timing and operate engine to check for leaks.
16. Make final (hot) valve lash adjustment.

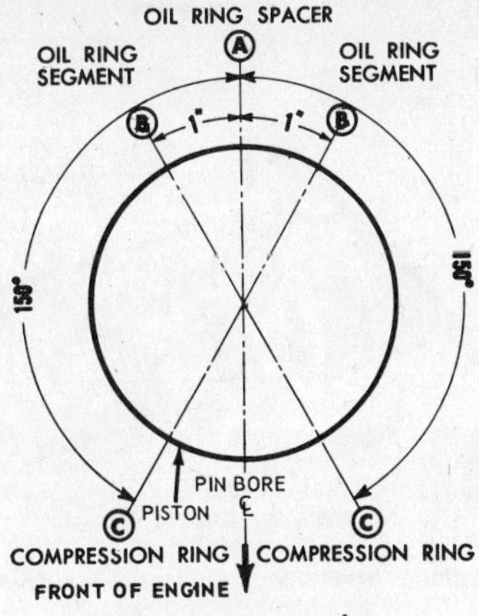

Piston ring gap spacing
(© Ford Motor Co.)

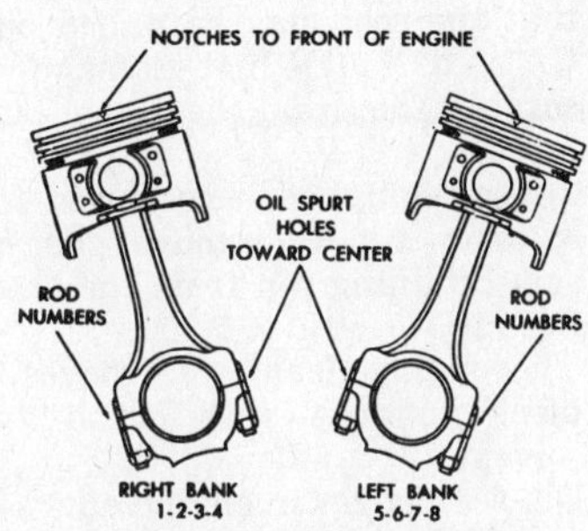

Correct relation of piston to rod—
V8—292, 302, 332 & 352 engines

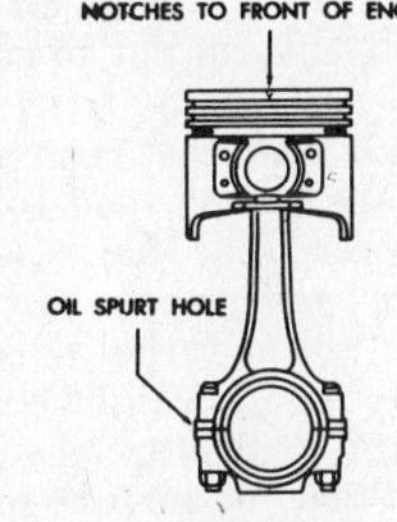

Correct relation of piston to rod—
6 cyl.—144, 170 & 200 engines

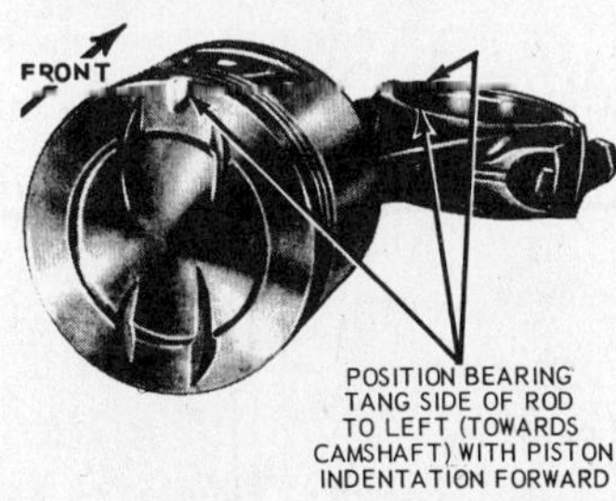

Correct relation of piston to rod—
6 cyl.—240 & 300 engines

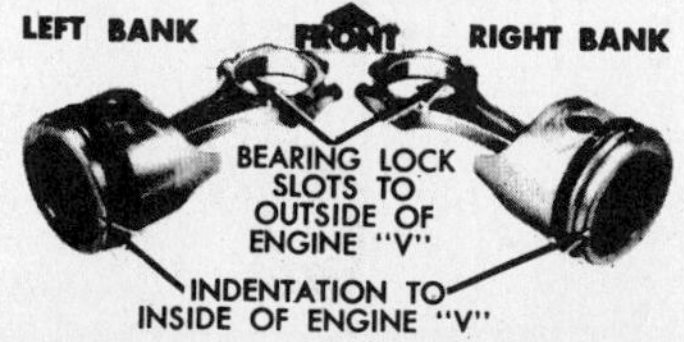

Correct relation of piston to rod—
V8—330 engines

Main Bearings

Main Bearing Removal and Installation

All main bearings may be replaced with the engine in the vehicle with the exception of the 240 and 300 cu. in. rear main bearing. See the General Repair Section for main bearing fitting procedure.

Remove oil pan and oil pump assembly (see Engine Lubrication System below). Replace one bearing at a time. Remove cap and insert special Ford tool #6331 (-E) or similar bearing removing tool into the crankshaft journal oil hole. Slowly rotate crankshaft in its running direction to force upper bearing insert out of its seat. Fit new bearings (0.001" and 0.002" undersize available) for specified main bearing clearance, then oil journal and bearings and install cap, tightening cap bolts to specified torque (see Specifications).

To seat thrust bearing (No. 3 on

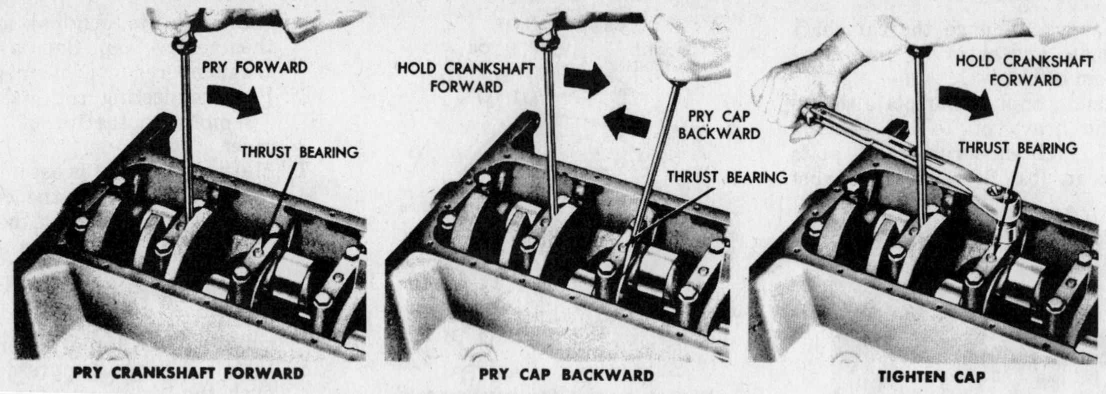

Aligning thrust bearing (© Ford Motor Co.)

144, 170, 200 Six and V-8's; No. 5 on 240, 300 Six), fit bearing inserts, then install bearings and cap, tightening cap bolts finger-tight. While prying crankshaft forward and bearing cap rearward (see illustration), tighten the cap bolts to specified torque.

If the rear main bearing is replaced, install a new rear oil seal as described below.

Rear Oil Seal Removal and Installation

144, 170, 200 Cu. In. Six and 289, 302, 330, 360, 361, 390 and 391 V-8

On all models, remove the oil pan as described below. In some cases it may be necessary to remove the oil pump pick-up and screen or the whole pump assembly.

Use only the split-lip type crankshaft rear oil seal as a replacement.

1. Loosen all main bearing caps, lowering the crankshaft slightly, but not more than 1/32".
2. Remove the rear main bearing cap.
3. Remove the seal halves from cap and block. Use a seal removing tool on the block half or install a small metal screw in one end so that the seal may be pulled out. CAUTION: Do not damage or scratch the crankshaft seal surfaces.
4. If so equipped (not used on split-lip type), remove the oil seal retaining pin from the bearing cap.
5. Thoroughly clean seal grooves in block and cap with brush and solvent.
6. Dip seal halves in engine oil.
7. Carefully install upper half of seal with the lip facing toward the *front* of the engine until ⅜" is left protruding below parting surface. Be careful not to scrape seal.
8. Tighten all but the rear main bearing caps to specified torque.
9. Install lower seal half in the rear main bearing cap with the lip facing toward the *front* of the engine. Apply a light coat of oil-resistant sealer to the rear of the top mating surface of the cap. Do not apply sealer to the area forward of the side seal groove.
10. Install rear main bearing cap and tighten bolts to specified torque.
11. Install side seals on the 330, 360, 361, 390 and 391 cu. in. V-8. Dip side seals in oil (do not use sealer as these seals expand when in contact with oil and sealer would retard or stop the expansion). Install seals in grooves, lightly tapping them if necessary. Do not cut off projecting ends. After allowing sufficient time for the seals to expand, squirt oil over the seal end and blow compressed air against the seals from inside the block to check for leakage.
12. Install oil pump and oil pan.
13. Fill crankcase and operate engine to check for leaks.

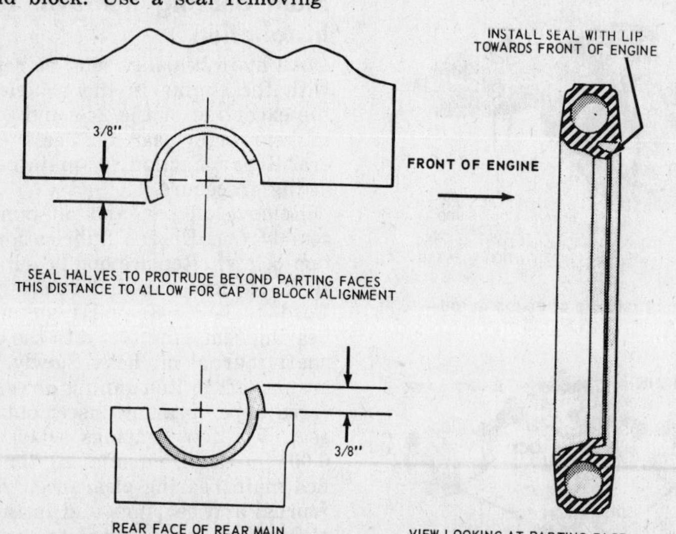

Crankshaft rear oil seal installation (© Ford Motor Co.)

Rear Oil Seal Removal and Installation

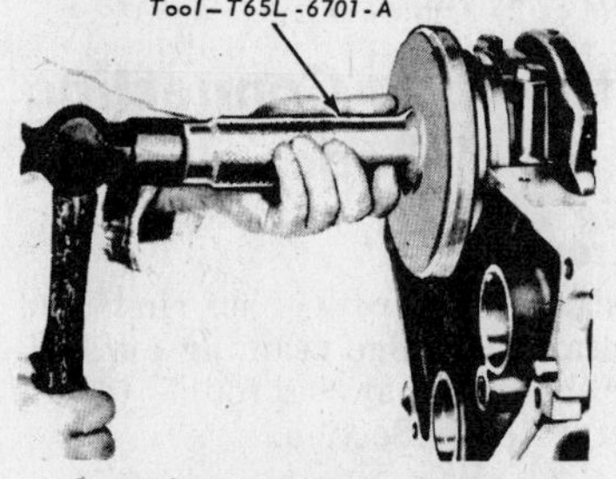

Installing crankshaft rear oil seal (© Ford Motor Co.)

24 and 300 Cu. In. 6-Cylinder

1. Remove the starter.
2. Remove the transmission (see Transmission Removal and Installation). On standard transmission, remove pressure plate and cover assembly and the clutch disc.
3. Remove flywheel and engine rear cover plate.
4. Punch two holes with an awl on each side of the crankshaft just above the bearing cap to cylinder block splint line.
5. Install two sheet metal screws,

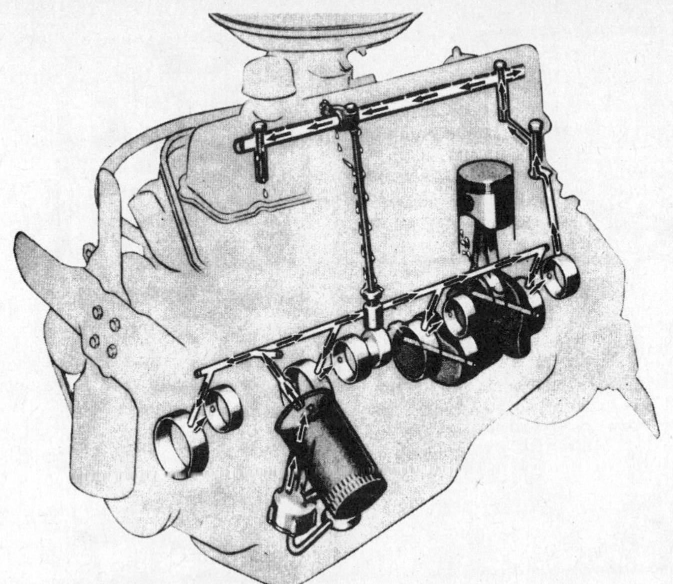

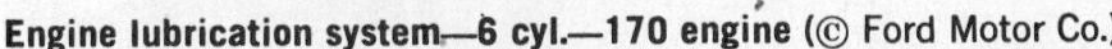

Engine lubrication system—6 cyl.—170 engine (© Ford Motor Co.)

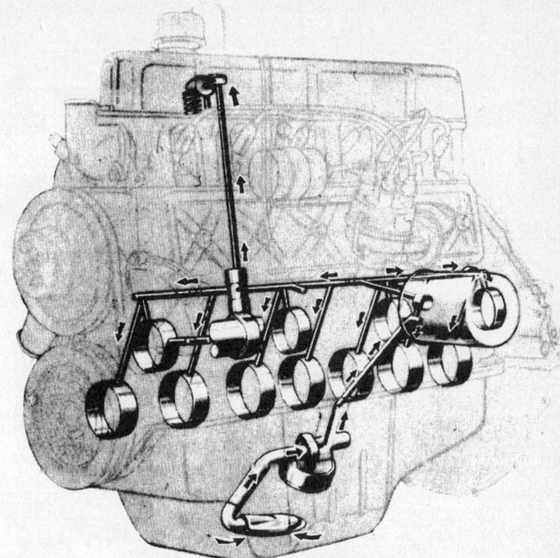

Engine lubrication system—240 & 300 engines (© Ford Motor Co.)

then pry on both at once to remove seal. Be careful not to damage or scratch oil seal surface. Clean out seal recess in cap and block.

6. Lightly oil crankshaft and seal, then install seal with tool as illustrated. Carefully drive the seal straight in.
7. Install engine rear cover plate and flywheel. Coat the flywheel attaching bolt threads with oil-resistant sealer and torque to 75-85 ft. lbs.
8. On standard transmission, install the clutch disc and pressure plate assembly (see Clutch Removal and Installation).
9. Install transmission.

Engine Lubrication System

All models are equipped with rotor type oil pumps, helical gear-driven from the camshaft. The oil flow is from the pan, through the pump, to the oil filter, then crankshaft and bearings and rockers.

Oil Pan Removal and Installation

144, 170, and 200 Cu. In. 6-Cylinder

On some earlier models there is no frame crossmember under the oil pan. Therefore, some of the steps of the following procedure will not be applicable in certain cases.

1. Drain crankcase and cooling system and remove dipstick.
2. Remove fan and water pump pulley.
3. Disconnect the radiator upper and lower hoses, flex fuel line at the fuel pump and starter cable at the starter.
4. Remove the starter.
5. Remove nuts from both front engine support insulators and raise the front of the engine with a transmission jack and wood block. Remove crossmember from beneath the pan and install blocks between front support insulators and side rails. Lower

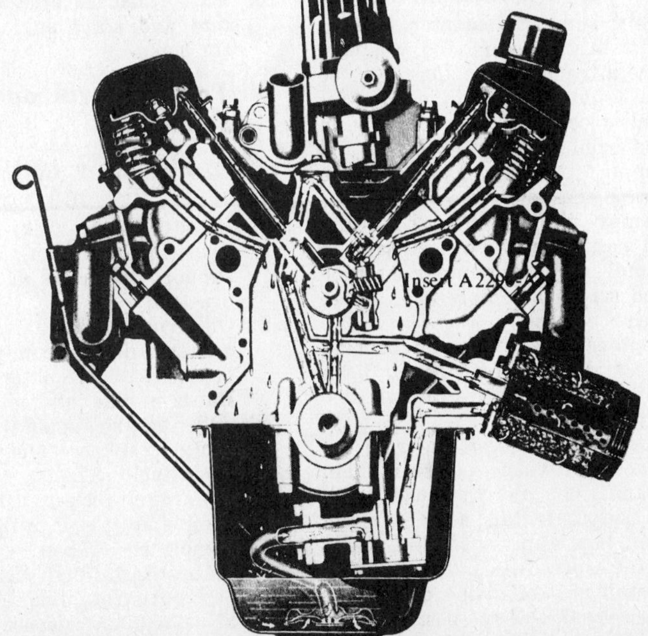

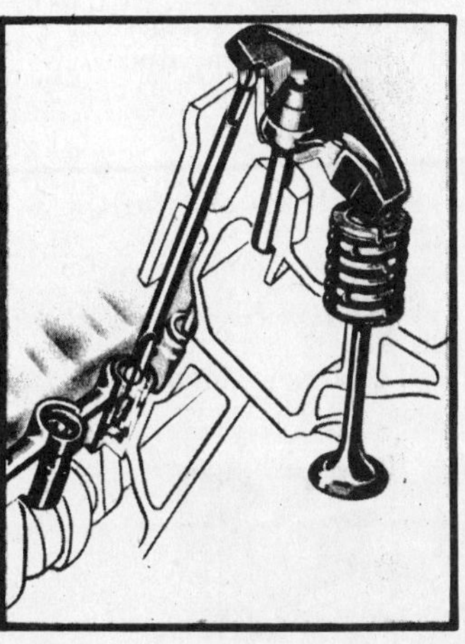

Engine lubrication system—289 & 302 engines (© Ford Motor Co.)

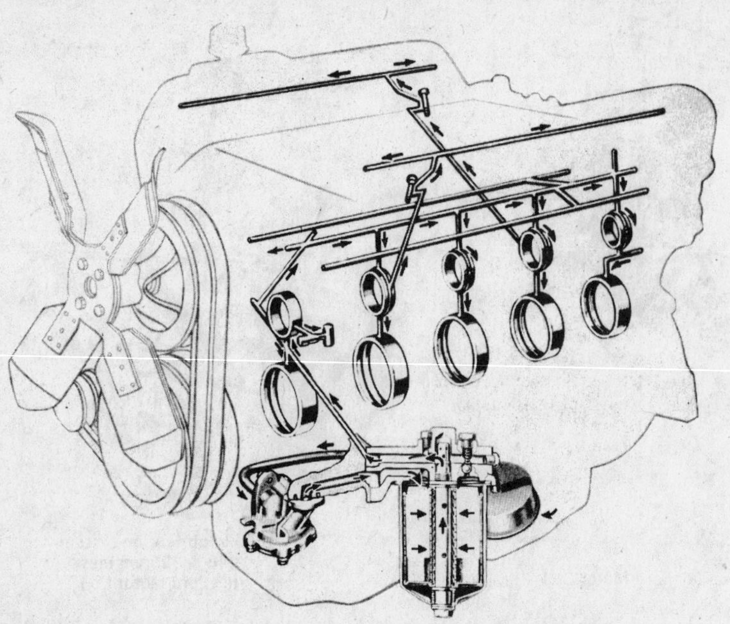

Engine lubrication system—330, 361 & 391 engines (© Ford Motor Co.)

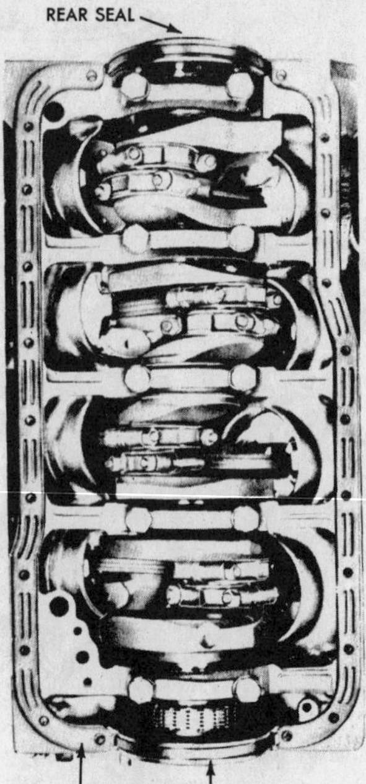

Oil pan gasket & seals installed—289 & 302 engines (© Ford Motor Co.)

and remove jack.

6. Remove the oil pan attaching bolts and pan.
7. Clean all gasket surfaces and remove seals from their grooves in the front cover and rear main bearing cap.
8. Position oil pan gasket, then pan front seal on front cover, making sure that the tabs on the seal are over the oil pan gasket. Position oil pan rear seal on the rear main bearing cap, making sure the tabs on the seal are over the oil pan gasket.
9. Install oil pan, tightening bolts to 7-9 ft. lbs.
10. Raise the engine with a transmission jack and remove the blocks. Install crossmember and lower the engine. Install washers and nuts on the insulator studs and tighten to 30-40 ft. lbs.
11. Install starter and connect starter cable.
12. Connect radiator hoses and fuel pump flex line.
13. Install water pump pulley, fan and drive belt. Adjust belt.
14. Install dipstick.
15. Fill and bleed cooling system.

Installing oil pan seal—240 & 300 engines (© Ford Motor Co.)

16. Fill crankcase.
17. Operate the engine and check for leaks.

Oil Pan Removal and Installation

240 and 300 Cu. In. 6-Cylinder

1. Drain the crankcase.
2. On the F-100-250, also drain the cooling system.
3. Remove radiator from F-100-250 vehicles.
4. Raise vehicle on a hoist. On F-100-250 trucks disconnect and remove the starter.
5. On F-100-250, remove engine front support insulator to support bracket nuts and washers. Use a transmission jack to raise the front of the engine, then install blocks (1" thick) between the front support insulators and support brackets. Lower engine onto blocks and remove jack.
6. Remove the attaching bolts and oil pan. It may be necessary to remove the oil pump inlet tube and screen assembly in order to free the pan.
7. Remove the rear main bearing cap and front cover seals. Clean out the seal grooves and all gasket surfaces.
8. Apply oil-resistant sealer in the spaces between the rear main bearing cap and the block as illustrated. Install new rear cap seal, then apply a bead of sealer to the tapered ends of the seal.
9. Install new oil pan side gaskets with sealer and position the front cover seal.
10. Clean oil pump pick-up assembly and place it in the pan.
11. Position pan under the engine and install pick-up assembly.
12. Install pan and attaching bolts, tightening to 10-12 ft. lbs.
13. Raise engine enough with a jack and remove wood blocks. Lower engine and install washers and nuts on the support insulator studs, tightening to 40-60 ft. lbs. on LD trucks and 110-150 ft. lbs. on MD and HD trucks.
14. Install starter and starter cable on F-100-250 trucks.
15. Lower vehicle and install radiator if it was removed.
16. Fill crankcase and cooling system and start engine to check for leaks.

Oil Pan Removal and Installation

289 and 302 Cu. In. V-8 F-100

1. Remove oil dipstick, fan shroud (position over fan) and engine support insulators at the chassis bracket.
2. On trucks with an automatic transmission, disconnect oil cooler lines at the radiator.
3. Raise engine and place blocks under engine supports.
4. Drain crankcase and remove oil pan attaching bolts.
5. Remove oil pick-up tube from oil pump and leave it in the pan.
6. Remove the oil pan.
7. Before installing, clean the oil pan and straighten if necessary.
8. Position new gasket and end seals.
9. With oil pan lying on the cross-

member, install the oil pump pick-up assembly.

10. Install the oil pan and attaching bolts, tightening to 9 ft. lbs.
11. Raise the engine, remove the blocks, then lower engine and install the insulator-to-chassis bracket nuts and washers, tightening to 55-65 ft. lbs.
12. Connect automatic transmission oil cooler lines, if applicable.
13. Install fan shroud.
14. Fill the crankcase, install dipstick and start the engine to check for leaks.

Bronco

1. Remove air cleaner, air cleaner duct and oil dipstick tube.
2. Drain the crankcase.
3. Remove the oil pan attaching bolts, oil pan, gaskets and seals.
4. Clean all gasket and seal surfaces.
5. Install new oil pan gaskets and end seals.
6. Install the oil pan and attaching bolts, tightening to 9 ft. lbs.
7. Install oil dipstick tube, air cleaner and air cleaner duct.
8. Fill crankcase and start engine to check for leaks.

Engine support tools—Econoline
(© Ford Motor Co.)

Econoline

1. Raise vehicle on a hoist and remove the oil dipstick tube.
2. Drain the crankcase and remove oil filter, then disconnect the steering rod end at the idler arm.
3. Remove attaching nuts from front engine supports and crossmember, jack up the engine, then remove the engine support crossmember.
4. Install engine support tools (T68E-6038-A) and remove jack.
5. Remove oil pan attaching bolts and oil pan.
6. Clean all gasket and seal surfaces, then install new gaskets and end seals.
7. Install oil pan and attaching bolts, tightening to 9 ft. lbs.
8. Position jack under the damper and raise engine so that the engine support tools may be removed.
9. Install the crossmember to side rails (torque bolts to 35-50 ft. lbs.), then lower engine and remove the jack.
10. Install the engine support nuts and washers, tightening to 45-55 ft. lbs.
11. Connect the steering rod end to idler arm.

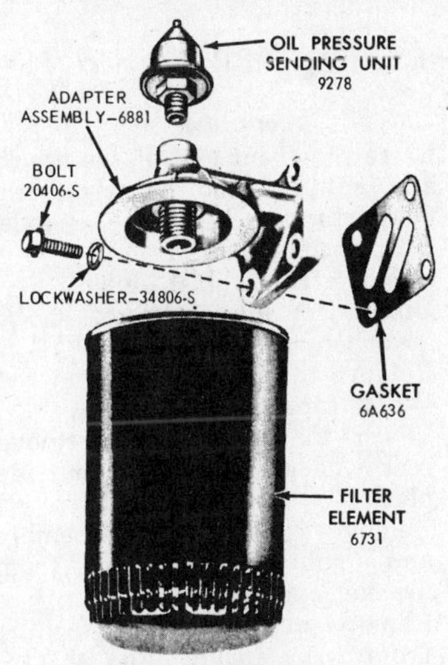

Screw on type oil filter
(© Ford Motor Co.)

12. Install oil dipstick tube and oil filter.
13. Fill the crankcase and start the engine to check for leaks.

330, 360, 361, 390 and 391 Cu. In. V-8

1. Drain the crankcase and remove the oil dipstick tube.
2. Remove oil pan bolts and let the pan rest on the front axle.
3. Remove the oil pump and set it in the pan.
4. Rotate the crankshaft so that the pan will clear the counterweights, and remove the oil pan.
5. Clean all gasket surfaces and position a new gasket on the pan.
6. Clean oil pump and pick-up tube assembly, then prime it and place it in the pan.
7. Install the oil pump using a new gasket. It may be necessary to locate the drive gears.
8. Install oil pan and bolts, tightening to 10-11 ft. lbs. from the center outward.
9. Install dipstick tube and replace the oil filter element.
10. Fill crankcase and operate engine to check for leaks.

Replacing Oil Filter

All engines are equipped with either a screw-on oil filter assembly or a cartridge type filter element.

To change the screw-on type, rotate the filter counter clockwise. Clean the gasket surfaces and oil the new gasket before installation. Hand tighten until the gasket contacts the adapter face, the advance ½-turn.

Cartridge type filter elements are removed by unscrewing the long center bolt. Remove both the large and small gasket. Install new filter element, position new gaskets and install the filter assembly. Tighten center bolt to 20-25 ft. lbs.

Operate engine to check for leaks.

Oil Pump Removal and Installation

To remove oil pump, remove oil pan as described above. Remove oil pump attaching bolts, then pull pump shaft from engine.

Thoroughly clean all parts in solvent and dry with compressed air. Check the inside of the pump housing for obvious wear or scoring. Check mating surfaces of pump cover and rotors, replacing the cover if it is scored or grooved.

Measure outer race to housing clearance and clearance (rotor endplay) between a straightedge and the rotor. The outer race, shaft and rotor are replaceable only as an assembly.

Measure the driveshaft to housing clearance by comparing shaft OD to housing bearing ID.

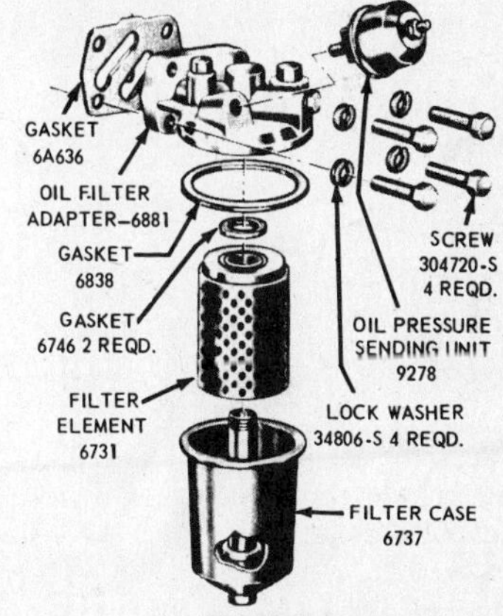

Cartridge type oil filter
(© Ford Motor Co.)

Oil Pump Specifications

Relief spring tension (lbs. @ specified length)	144, 170, 200 Six	9.0-10.1 @ 1.078
	240, 300 Six	20.6-22.6 @ 2.490
	289, 302 V-8	11.15-11.75 @ 1.704
	330 MD, 360, 390 V-8	9.0-9.6 @ 1.530
	330 HD, 361, 391 V-8	11.1-11.8 @ 1.560
Driveshaft to housing bearing clearance		0.0015-0.0029″
Rotor assembly end clearance		0.0011-0.0041″
Outer race to housing clearance		0.006-0.012″

Inspect relief valve spring for collapsed or worn condition. Check the spring tension. Replace the spring if weak or worn.

Check relief valve piston and bore for scores and free operation.

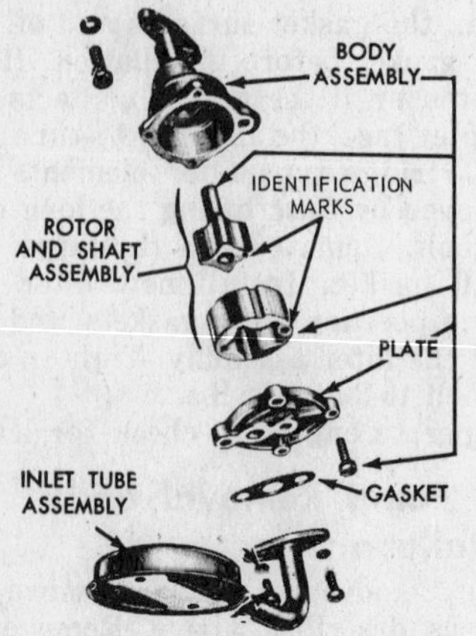

Typical oil pump assembly
(© Ford Motor Co.)

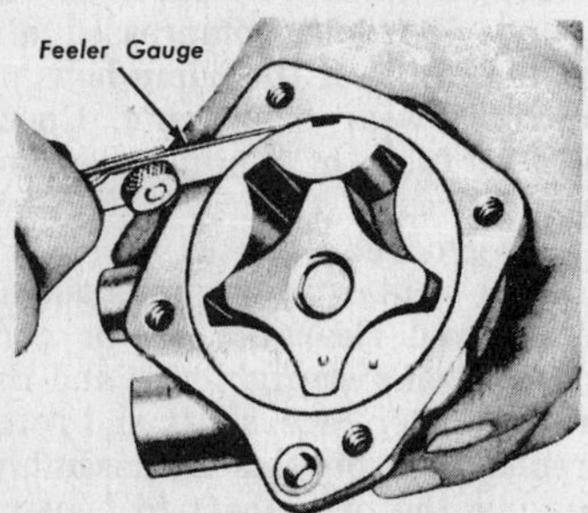

Checking outer race to housing clearance
(© Ford Motor Co.)

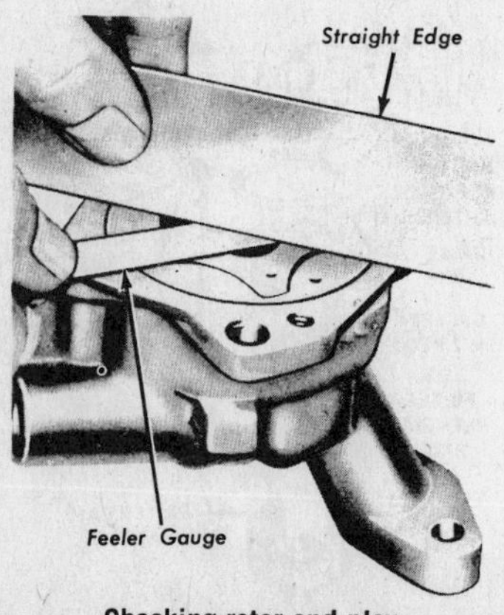

Checking rotor end play
(© Ford Motor Co.)

Front Axle, Suspension

Solid I-Beam

Description

Spindles, held in place by bolts, are mounted at each end of the axle. Steel-backed bronze or delrin bushings provide bearing surfaces for the spindle bolt.

Thrust bearings at the lower ends of the axle help support the load. Semi-elliptic, leaf-type springs are mounted parallel to the frame side rails by U-bolt and shackle assemblies.

Front Spring R&R

Econoline

1. Raise the front end of the truck and support the chassis with floor stands. Support the axle with a jack or hoist.
2. Remove front splash shield.
3. Disconnect lower end of shock absorber.
4. Remove the two U bolts and the U-bolt (spring clip) plate.
5. Lower the spring, then remove rear shackle nuts and outside plate.
6. Remove rear shackle assembly and rubber bushings from bracket and spring.
7. Remove nut and bolt attaching front of spring to shackle bracket. Remove spring.

Installation is a reversal of the removal procedure, in addition to noting the following:

1. Install new rubber bushings in the rear shackle bracket and rear spring eye.
2. Do not tighten attaching bolts and nuts until after connecting shock absorber.

Front Spring R&R

F-100, F-250, P Series

1. Raise truck until weight is off front springs, but with wheels still touching ground.
2. Remove spring clips (U-bolts) and spring clip plate.
3. Remove attaching nut, then drive out spring to frame bracket bolt with a brass drift.
4. Remove attaching nut, then drive out lower shackle bolt.
5. Remove lubrication fittings (if so equipped).

Installation is a reversal of the removal procedure, in addition to noting the following:

1. Replace bushings in spring and shackle bracket.
2. Install caster wedge (if so equipped) pointing in same direction as before removal.
3. Position bolt through bracket and spring eye with head toward inside. NOTE: Install bolt with head toward outside on P Series trucks.
4. Install attaching nuts and bolts, but do not fully tighten until truck has been lowered to floor.

Front Spring R&R

F-350

1. Raise truck until weight is off front springs, but with wheels still touching ground.
2. Disconnect lower end of shock absorber.
3. Remove spring clips (U-bolts) and plate.
4. Remove attaching nut, then drive out rear bracket bolt with a brass drift.
5. Support spring; then, remove cotter pin, rebound pin and rubber bushing from front bracket.
6. Remove spring, noting position of caster wedge (if so equipped).

Installation is a reversal of the removal procedure, in addition to noting the following:

1. Install caster wedge (if so equipped) pointing in same direction as before removal.
2. Install attaching nuts and bolts, but do not fully tighten until truck has been lowered to floor.

Front Spring R&R

N-500, N-600
Early Model F-500 Thru 750

NOTE: On F Series trucks, the locking bracket is at the rear end of the spring and the supporting bracket at the front. On N Series trucks, the bracket positions are reversed.

1. Raise truck until weight is off spring.
2. Remove attaching locking bolt and nut, then drive shackle pin out of locking bracket.
3. Remove shackle pin lubrication fitting.
4. Support spring, then remove supporting bracket cotter pin, rebound pin and rubber bushing.
5. Remove attaching nuts and spring clips (U-bolts), then remove spring and caster wedge (if so equipped).

Installation is a reversal of the removal procedure, in addition to noting the following:

1. Install shackle pin with lubricator opening facing outward.
2. Install caster wedge (if so equipped) pointing in same direction as before removal.
3. Fully tighten attaching nuts and bolts only after truck has been lowered to ground.

Front Spring R&R

Late Model F-500 Thru 750

1. Raise truck until weight is off front springs, but with wheels still touching ground.
2. Support front axle.
3. Remove attaching nuts and U-bolts.
4. Remove rear hanger cotter pin, nut, washers and bolt.
5. Remove securing cotter pin, then remove spring front hanger pin.
6. Remove spring.

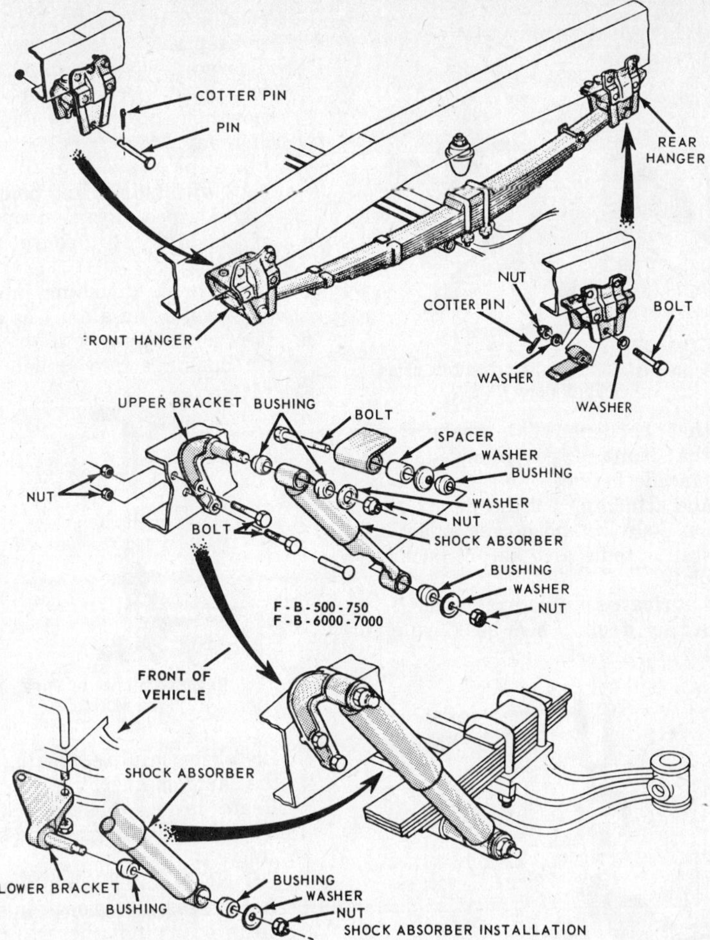

Front spring installation—F-B 500-750 (© Ford Motor Co.)

Installation is a reversal of the removal procedure, in addition to noting the following:

1. Make certain that front U-bolt enters shock absorber lower bracket.
2. Raise or lower axle to align spring eye with bolt hole in rear hanger. Install bolt and one washer on each side of bracket; then, with the weight of the truck on the springs, tighten rear hanger bolt nut and install cotter pin.

NOTE: Do not back-off nut to align castellation with cotter pin hole. If necessary, tighten nut.

Front Spring R&R

C Series

1. Raise truck until weight is off front springs, but with wheels still touching ground.
2. Remove attaching nuts, then drive out front and rear mounting studs.
3. Remove attaching nuts, spring clips, plate, shock absorber lower mounting bracket and spring. Note position of caster wedge and spacer (if so equipped).
4. Installation procedure is given in Steps 5 through 11.
5. Position spring on seat and align front eye with bracket.
6. Remove lubrication fitting from front stud, then drive stud (lubricator opening facing outward) through bracket and front eye. Install nut and tighten snugly; then, back off 1/3 turn. Install cotter pin at inner end of stud and lubrication fitting at outer end.
7. Align rear spring eye with shackle bars.
8. Repeat Step 6 at the rear mounting stud and bracket.
9. Install caster wedge (if so equipped) pointing in same direction as before removal.
10. Install shock absorber lower bracket. Secure with lockwasher and nut.
11. Lower the truck, then fully tighten all attaching nuts and bolts. Lubricate stud fittings.

Spindle R&R

Econoline

1. Raise truck and support frame with floor stands. Do not use a bumper jack.
2. Remove front wheel hub and drum assembly.
3. Remove attaching bolts and brake backing (carrier) plate. Secure plate to frame with wire.
4. Remove spindle arm attaching nut, then drive arm off spindle with a soft-faced hammer. NOTE: If removing left spindle, disconnect steering drag link.
5. Drive out spindle bolt locking pin.
6. Remove threaded caps from top and bottom of spindle.
7. Drive bolt out of spindle and axle, then remove spindle and bearing.

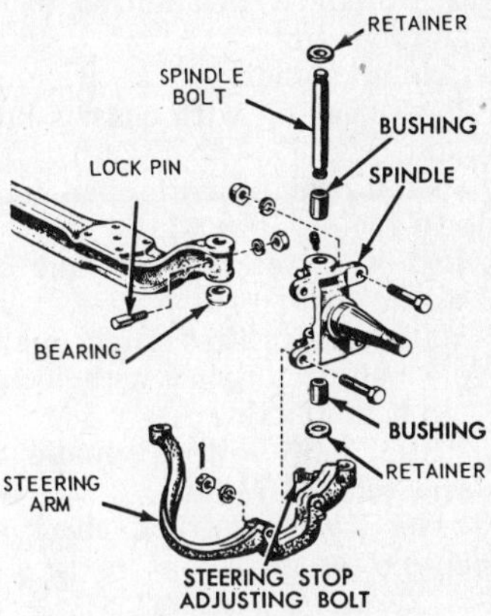

Spindle installation—P-Series
(© Ford Motor Co.)

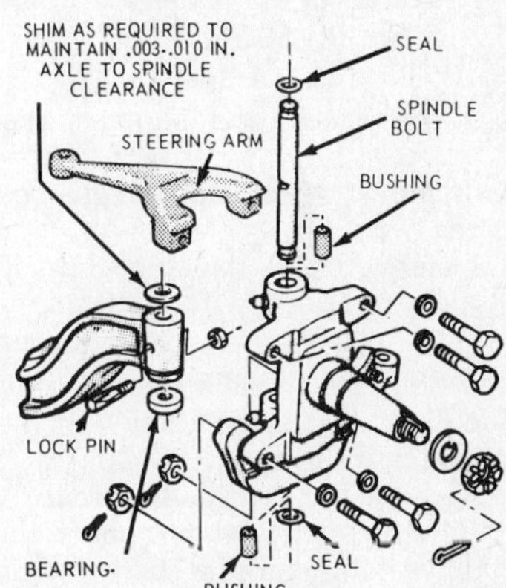

Spindle installation—5000-5500 lb. axles
(© Ford Motor Co.)

Installation is a reversal of the removal procedure, in addition to noting the following:

1. Make certain that notch in spindle bolt is correctly aligned with locking pin hole in axle.
2. Lubricate spindle fittings. Adjust brakes and front wheel bearings.
3. After lowering truck, adjust toe-in and tighten spindle connecting rod clamps.

Spindle R&R

P Series, Early Model C, F, N Series

1. Raise truck until wheels clear

floor. Place a support under axle.
2. Remove wheel, drum, bearing and hub assembly. NOTE: It may be necessary to back-off brakes adjustment in order to remove drum.
3. Remove brake backing (carrier) plate, then remove spindle arm bolt and nut. Tie plate and arm to frame with wire.
4. Remove attaching nut, lockwasher and spindle bolt locking pin.
5. Remove top spindle bolt seal, then drive bolt out from top of axle.

Installation is a reversal of the removal procedure, in addition to noting the following:

1. Coat all spindle parts with oil.
2. Pack bearing with chassis lubricant.
3. Install bearing with open end of seal facing downward.
4. Install a new top spindle bolt seal.
5. Make certain that notch in spindle bolt is aligned with locking pin hole in axle.
6. Install new bottom spindle bolt seal (except F-350).
7. After lowering truck, check and adjust toe-in.

Spindle R&R

Late Model C, F, N Series (5000, 5500, 6000, 7000 Lb. Axles)

1. Raise truck and support front axle.
2. Remove wheel, hub, drum bearing.
3. Remove brake backing plate. Tie plate to frame with wire.
4. Disconnect spindle arm. NOTE: F-250 and F-350 models with BX or disc brakes have an integral spindle arm.
5. Remove top spindle bolt seal.
6. Remove attaching nut, then drive out spindle bolt locking pin.
7. Using a suitable drift, drive out spindle bolt from top of axle.
8. Remove spindle assembly.

Installation is a reversal of the removal procedure, in addition to noting the following:

1. Install thrust bearing with seal (retainer) lip downward.
2. Late model trucks, excluding F Series, are equipped with shims between top of axle and spindle. A clearance of .003-010" between axle and spindle must be maintained on all models.
3. Excluding F Series, install spindle bolt with letter "T" upward.
4. Install new top and bottom spindle bolt seals.
5. On 5000 and 5500 lb. axles. excluding F Series, make certain

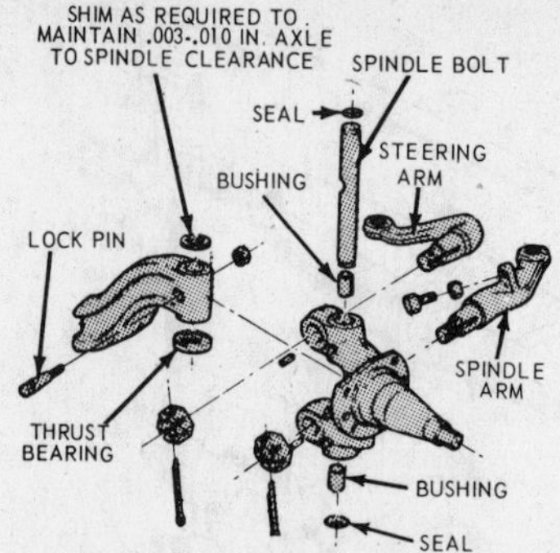

Spindle installation—6000-7000 lb. axles
(© Ford Motor Co.)

that hardened flat washers, of the same type removed, are placed between backing plate and attaching bolt heads.
6. On 6000 lb. and larger axles, install spindle arm before backing plate.
7. Lubricate spindle bushings.
8. Adjust front wheel bearings and toe-in.

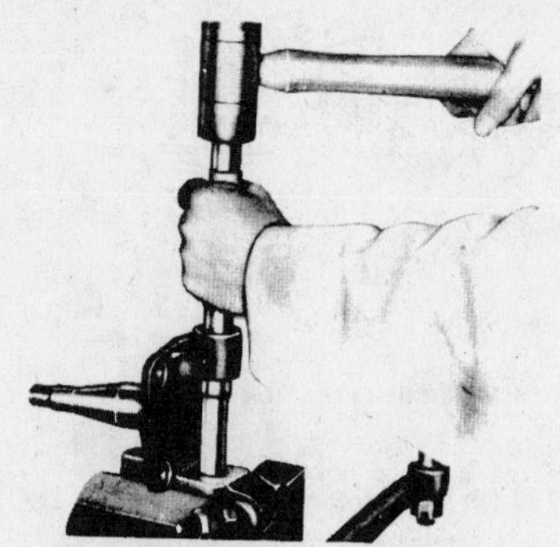
Removing bronze bushing
(© Ford Motor Co.)

Spindle Bushing Replacement

1. Remove bronze bushings by driving them out with a drift slightly smaller than spindle bore. If a drift is not available, carefully drive a small center punch between the bushing and the spindle bore. Collapse the bushing, then remove.
2. Remove Delrin bushings, using a

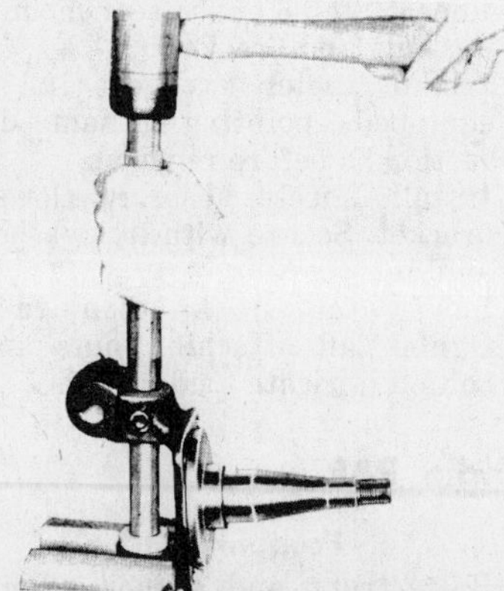
Installing bronze bushing
(© Ford Motor Co.)

small center punch as described in Step 1.
3. Thoroughly clean spindle bores and make certain that lubrication holes are not obstructed in any way.
4. Place new bushing in spindle bore with lubricating holes properly aligned. Position open end of bushing oil groove toward axle.
5. Drive bronze bushing into spindle bore, using a drift as a pilot.
6. It is not necessary to drive Delrin bushings into spindle bores.

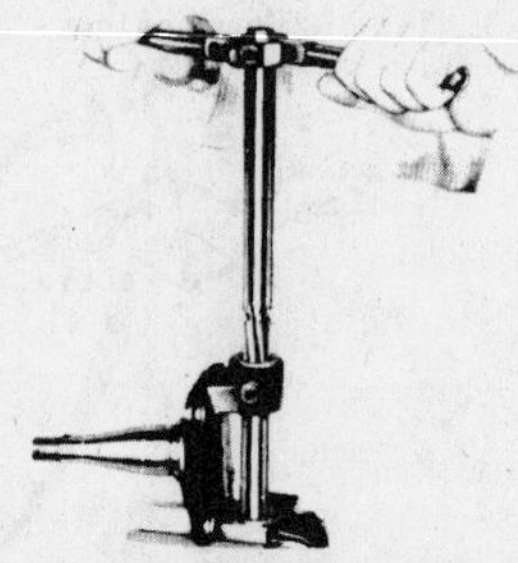
Reaming bronze bushing
(© Ford Motor Co.)

7. Install remaining bushing(s) in the same manner.
8. Ream bronze bushings .001 to .003" larger than spindle bolt diameter.
9. DO NOT ream Delrin bushings.
10. After reaming bronze bushings, clean out spindle bore to remove metal shavings.
11. Apply a light coat of oil to all bushings before spindle assembly and installation.

Twin I-Beam

Description

One end of each axle is attached to a spindle and radius arm; the other end is attached to a frame pivot bracket on the opposite side of the truck. Each spindle is held in place by a bolt, which pivots in steel-backed bronze bushings. A thrust bearing, between the spindle and the lower end of the axle, helps support the load. An arm is bolted to the spindle for attachment to the steering linkage.

NOTE: F-100 and F-250 models with standard brakes utilize Drlin spindle bolt bushings.

NOTE: F-250, F-350 and E-300 models with BX or disc brakes are equipped with an integral arm and spindle.

Front Coil Spring R&R

Econoline

1. Remove floor mat retainer from lower end of door opening.
2. Fold mat to one side, then remove attaching screws and shock absorber cover plate.

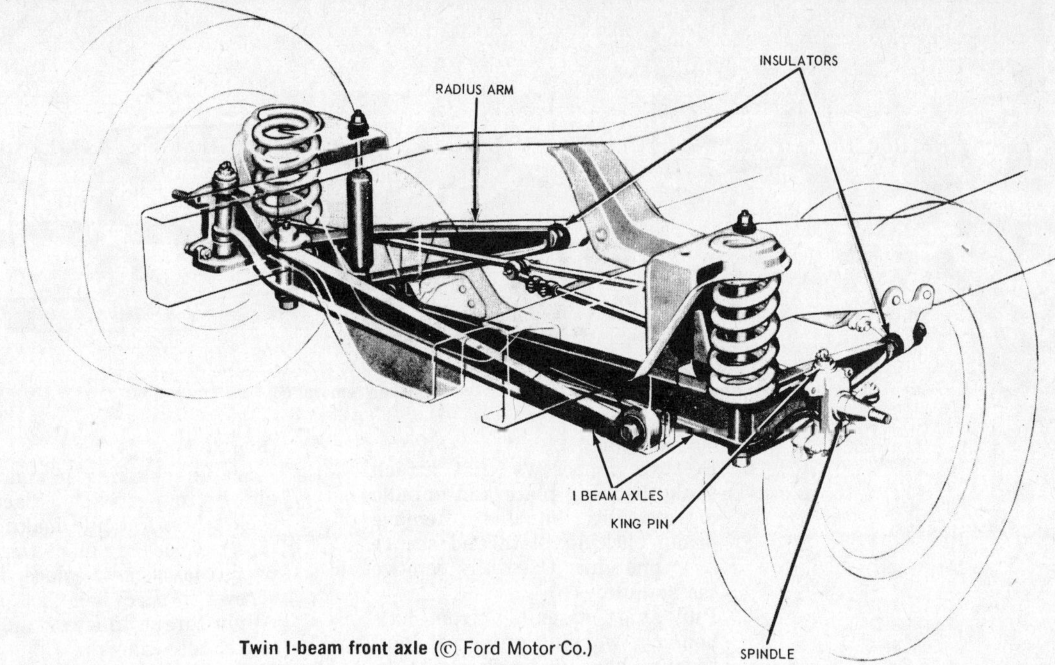

Twin I-beam front axle (© Ford Motor Co.)

3. Remove spring upper retainer attaching screws, insulator and clamp.
4. Support frame side rails with a jack stand.
5. Position a floor jack under axle, then remove lower retainer attaching bolt, retainer and spring support.
6. Slowly lower axle to release tension, then remove spring.
7. Installation procedure is given in steps 8-14.
8. Position spring on axle with pigtails toward rear end of truck.
9. Position spring lower support and retainer. Install attaching bolt loosely.
10. Place upper insulator on spring.
11. Raise jack to apply light spring pressure.
12. Install upper retainer and clamp. NOTE: Make certain that all upper retainer parts are correctly seated.
13. Remove jack stand.
14. Install shock absorber cover plate and floor mat retainer.

Front Spring R&R

F-100, 250, 350

1. Raise front end of truck and support frame with floor stands.
2. Position a jack under axle.
3. Disconnect shock absorber from lower bracket.
4. Remove attaching bolt, nut and rebound bracket.
5. On pre-1966 F-100 and F-250, lower axle and remove spring.
6. On 1966-71 F-100 and F-250, perform the following:
   a. Remove attaching bolts and retainer.
   b. Remove attaching nut and lower spring retainer.
   c. Lower axle and remove spring.
7. On F-350, perform the following:
   a. Remove bolts attaching upper spring clip to seat. Remove clip.
   b. Remove attaching nut and lower spring retainer.
   c. Lower axle and remove spring.

Installation is a reversal of the removal procedure.

Radius Arm R&R

All Models

1. Raise front end of truck and support frame with floor stands.
2. Position a jack under axle or appropriate wheel.
3. Remove coil spring.
4. Disconnect steering rod from spindle arm.
5. Remove coil spring lower seat and shim.
6. Remove radius arm front attaching bolt and nut.
7. Remove cotter pin, nut and washer from radius arm rear attachment.
8. Remove bushing (insulator) from rear end of arm.
9. Remove radius arm.
10. Remove inner bushing (insulator).

Installation is reversal of the removal procedure.

Refer to Wheel Alignment Specifications for toe-in, caster, camber and kingpin (spindle bolt) inclination values.

Front Drive Axle

Description

Bronco

The Dana Model 441F drive axle is used on Bronco trucks. The axle has an open yoke welded to the outer ends of the axle housing. Cardan-type universal joints transmit power to the front driving wheels.

NOTE: Early Bronco models used the Dana Model 30F, utilizing kingpins rather than ball joints, as on the Model 441F. This is the only significant difference between the two models.

F-100

The Dana Model 44-7F drive axle is used on F-100 four wheel drive trucks. The axle has an open spindle assembly, utilizing Cardan-type universal joints to transmit power to the front drive wheels.

NOTE: Early model F-100 trucks were equipped with a Spicer 2559 drive axle. Follow repair procedures given for F-250.

F-250

Dana Models 44-6BF and 44-7BF-HD are used on F-250 four wheel drive trucks. The axle has a spherical, closed spindle and enclosed universal joint, as in the early F-100 and F-250 models.

NOTE: Early model F-250 trucks were equipped with a Spicer 2559 or optional Spicer 2558. Follow repair procedures given for F-250 with Dana drive axle.

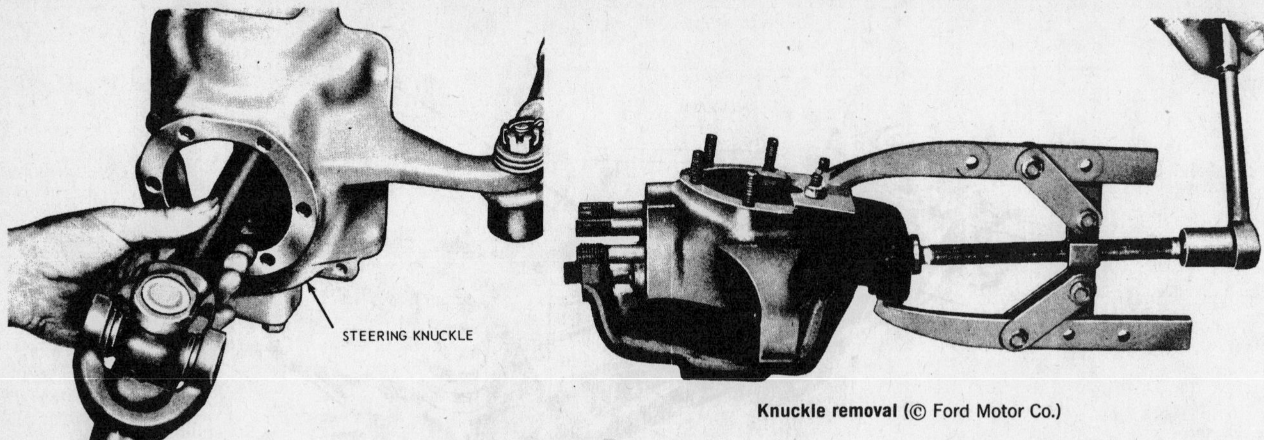

Removing axle shaft (© Ford Motor Co.)

Knuckle removal (© Ford Motor Co.)

F-600

The Rockwell-Standard Single-Reduction Final Drive Axle was made available on 1971 F-600 trucks. The axle has a heavy duty spiral bevel or hypoid pinion and gear. The differential and gear assembly is carried in tapered roller bearings.

Refer to the General Repair Section for complete overhaul procedures on the front wheel drive axles.

With the exception of specialized components required for front drive application, the Dana and Rockwell-Standard models are identical to their rear axle counterparts (i.e. Dana 44-7F—Dana Model 44, Rockwell - Standard Single - Reduction—same, etc.). Spicer and Dana front drive axles are identical. The Dana Model 44IF, used on Bronco models, is similar to the other Dana axles except in size.

Axle Shaft and Steering Knuckle R&R

Bronco

1. Raise vehicle on a hoist.
2. Remove front hub grease cap. Remove driving hub retaining snap-ring, then slide splined driving hub from between axle shaft and wheel hub.
3. Remove driving hub spring. NOTE: If equipped with free-wheeling hubs, see hub removal.
4. Remove lock nut, washer, and wheel bearing adjusting nut from spindle. Remove wheel, hub and drum as an assembly. The wheel outer bearing will be forced off the spindle at the same time. Remove wheel inner bearing cone.
5. Remove capscrews that attach brake backing plate and spindle to steering knuckle. Remove brake backing plate and secure it to one side. Carefully remove the spindle.
6. Pull shaft assembly from axle housing, working universal joint through bore in steering knuckle.
7. To remove steering knuckle (housing), disconnect the steering connecting rod end from the steering knuckle and remove the bearing caps. Remove the steering knuckle.
8. Remove the three retaining nuts and remove the steering arm. Remove the cotter key from the upper ball socket.
9. Remove the nut from the upper ball socket. Remove the nut from the lower ball socket. NOTE: Discard the nut from the bottom socket.
10. Remove the knuckle from the yoke. If the top socket remains in the yoke it can be dislodged with a rawhide hammer.

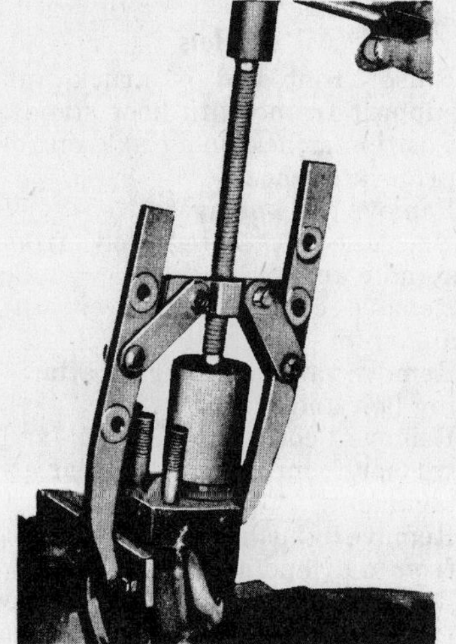

Top socket assembly (© Ford Motor Co.)

11. Remove the bottom socket, the adjusting sleeve and the top socket from the knuckle.
12. Installation is given in steps 13 thru 30.
13. Place knuckle in vise and assemble bottom socket. Place new socket into knuckle making sure it is not cocked; place the driver over the socket; place forcing screw into driver as shown. Apply torque to screw and force socket into knuckle.
14. Make sure socket shoulder is seated against knuckle. Use a .0015″ feeler gauge between socket and knuckle. Feeler gauge is not to enter at minimum area of contact.
15. Assemble top socket into knuckle. Assemble holding plate onto backing plate screw. Tighten nuts snug. Place new socket into knuckle. Be sure socket is straight and not in a cocked position. Place driver over socket.
16. Make sure socket shoulder is seated against knuckle. Use a .0015″ feeler gauge between socket and knuckle. Feeler gauge is not to enter at minimum area of contact.
17. Assemble new adjusting sleeve into top of yoke. Leave approximately two threads exposed. This will protect the threads in the yoke.
18. Assemble knuckle with sockets to yoke. Assemble new nut to bottom socket. Tighten nut finger loose. This will serve as a holding device.
19. Place spanner wrench and step plate over adjusting sleeve. Position puller, and turn forcing screw. This will pull the knuckle assembly into the yoke. With torque still applied, tighten the bottom nut on the socket. Torque nut to 70-90 ft. lbs. NOTE: If the bottom stud should turn with the nut, add more torque to the puller forcing screw.
20. Torque adjusting sleeve to 50 ft. lbs. Remove spanner wrench.
21. Assemble top socket nut. Torque to 100 ft. lbs. Line up cotter key hole of stud with the castellation or slot of the nut. Tighten nut

when it is being lined up with the hole of the stud. Do not loosen nut. Assemble cotter key.

22. Assemble steering arm, three stud adapters, and three nuts. Torque nuts to 80-100 ft. lbs.
23. Assemble the tie rod to the knuckle arm. Torque the nut to specifications and install the cotter key.
24. Assemble the protective inner slinger on to the axle shaft. The outer wheel bearing spindle nut will serve as a guide to assemble the slinger. Place the nut in a vise and the slinger on the end of the shaft. Tap on the shaft with a rawhide hammer until the slinger is seated.
25. Assemble the protective outer slinger on to the shaft. One of the wheel spindles will serve as a guide. Place the spindle in a vise. Do not clamp on the bearing diameters. Place the slinger on the shaft. Tap on the end of the shaft with a rawhide hammer until the slinger is seated. NOTE: Take care not to damage the seal diameter of the slinger.
26. Assemble the axle shaft joint assembly into the housing.
27. Place the spindle in a vise and install the needle roller bearings, using driver and rawhide hammer.

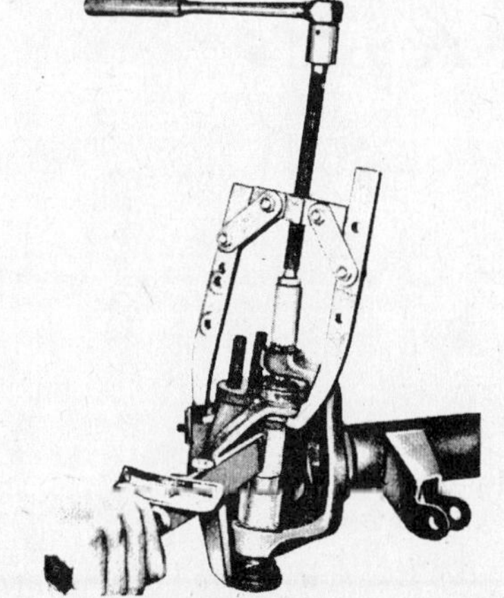

Final assembly of knuckle & sockets to yoke (© Ford Motor Co.)

28. Assemble the grease seal into the spindle, flush with the spindle face.
29. After assembly of the needle bearing and oil seal, pack wheel bearing grease around the needle bearing and lip of the seal.
30. Assemble the axle shaft joint assembly, bronze spacer and spindle to the knuckle.

NOTE: The chamfer of the spacer should be inboard against the shaft.

Axle Shaft and Steering Knuckle R&R

F-100

1. Raise the vehicle on a hoist.

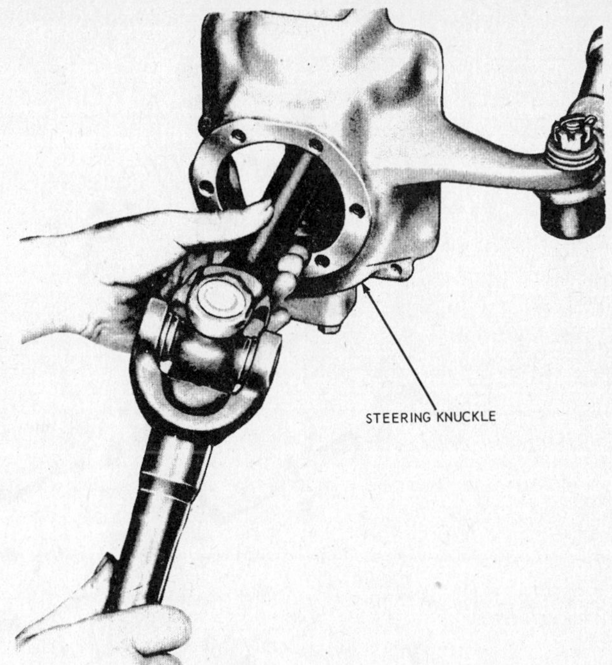

Removing axle shaft—F-100 (© Ford Motor Co.)

2. Drain the lubricant from the axle.
3. Remove the front hub grease cap. Remove the driving hub retaining snap-ring and slide the splined driving hub from between the axle shaft and the wheel hub. Remove the driving hub spacer. NOTE: If equipped with free-wheeling hubs, see hub removal.
4. Remove the lock nut, washer, and wheel bearing adjusting nut from the spindle. Remove the wheel, hub and drum as an assembly. The wheel outer bearing will be forced off the spindle at the same time. Remove the wheel inner bearing cone.
5. Remove the capscrews that attach the brake backing plate and the spindle to the steering knuckle. Remove the brake backing plate and secure it to one side to avoid damaging the brake hose. Carefully remove the spindle.
6. Pull the axle shaft assembly from the axle housing, working the universal joint through the bore of the steering knuckle.
7. To remove the steering knuckle (housing), disconnect the steering arm from the steering knuckle and remove the bearing caps. Remove the king pin.
8. Replace king pin bearing if necessary.
9. Remove the king pin bearing inner dust caps by inserting a small diameter drift through the bearing bore, and driving the cap toward the inside of the yoke.
10. Remove the king pin bearing cup, bearing and seal by driving on the bearing cup from inside the yoke, using a longer small-diameter drift and a suitable wrench socket.
11. Installation is given in steps 12 thru 24.
12. Install the king pin bearing cup in the steering knuckle bore using a suitable wrench socket. Position the bearing in the cup and install the bearing seal using a larger wrench socket or suitable seal driver. Coat the outer edge of the seal with non-hardening sealer before installation.
13. Install one bearing dust cap by using a long drift and socket. Install the remaining dust cap by using a C-clamp and wood block, squeezing the cap into position.
14. If the steering knuckle was removed, position it to the axle housing and install the king pin bearings and caps, placing the shims in their original position. Torque the attaching cap-screws to 24-40 ft. lbs.
15. Install an inch-pound torque wrench on one king pin bearing cap retaining capscrew and check the torque required to turn the steering-knuckle. Adjust this turning torque by varying the shims under the bearing caps until the turning torque (bearing preload) is the correct value (5-10 ft. lbs.)
16. Connect the steering connecting rod end to the steering arm and torque the attaching nut to 35-55

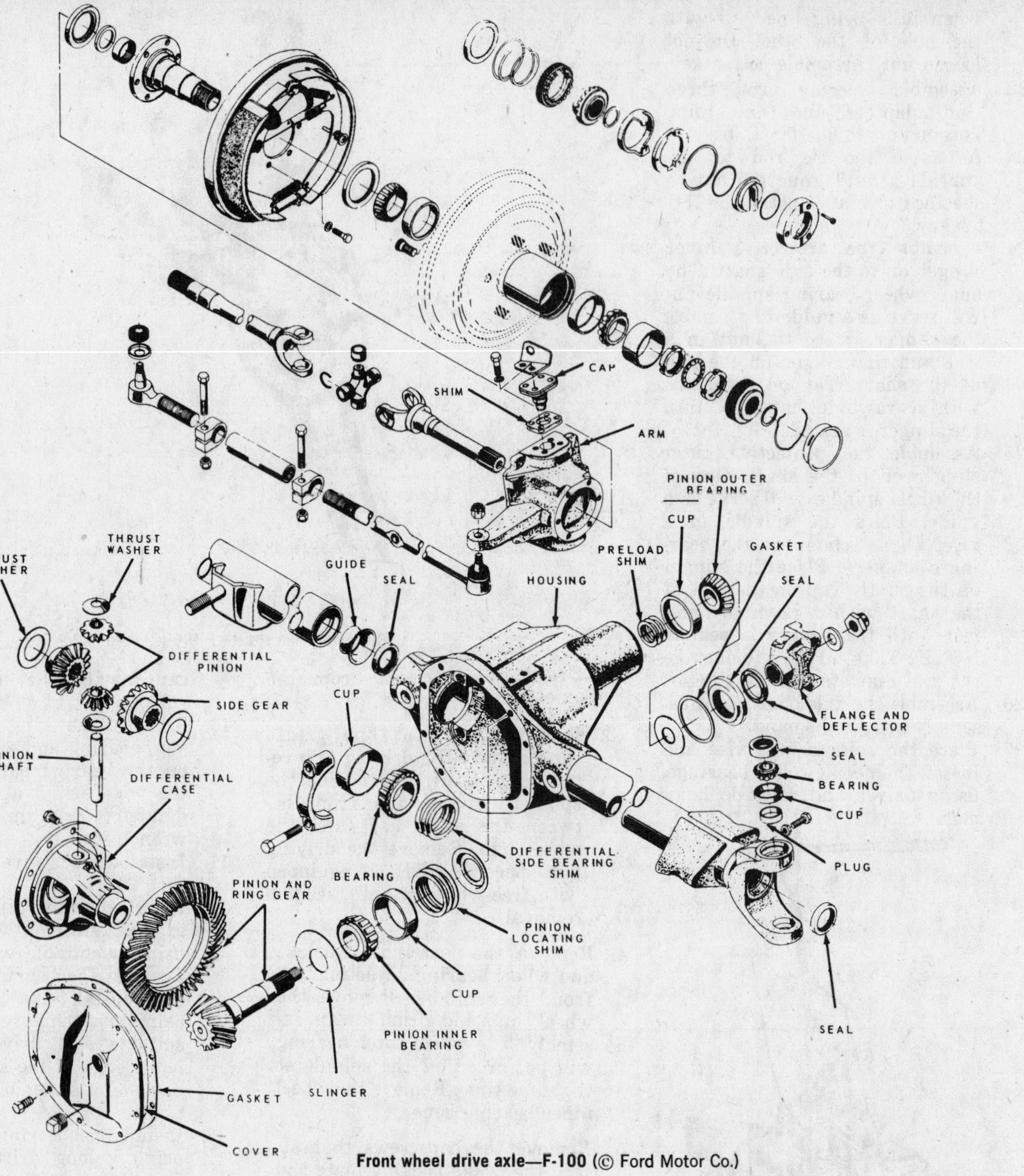

Front wheel drive axle—F-100 (© Ford Motor Co.)

ft. lbs.

17. If a new outer seal is to be installed in the axle housing, remove the seal.
18. Install the new axle housing outer seal.
19. If a new seal is to be installed in the spindle inner bore, coat the outer seating edge of the new seal with non-hardening sealer prior to installation.
20. Extra care should be used in inserting the axle shaft into the axle housing, because of the inner grease seal. This seal seats on a ground surface of the axle shaft and a bell-shaped guide is installed in the housing ahead of the seal to assist in piloting the shaft into the seal and the differential side gear.
21. Be sure that the roller bearing in the inner bore of the spindle is packed full of the specified lubricant, slide the spindle over the axle shaft and into position on the steering knuckle.
22. Position the brake backing plate

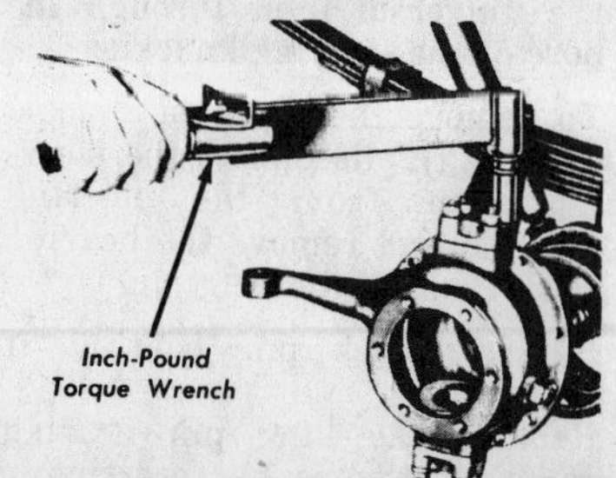

Checking steering knuckle bearing preload (© Ford Motor Co.)

to the spindle and install and tighten the attaching bolts.

23. Pack the front wheel bearings with the specified lubricant, if required. Position the wheel bearing inner cone and install the wheel, tire and brake drum on the spindle.
24. Install the outer wheel bearing cone and adjusting nut. Adjust the front wheel bearings.

Axle Shaft and Steering Knuckle R&R

F-250

1. Raise the vehicle on a hoist.
2. Remove the hub grease cap. Remove the hub retaining snap-ring, and slide the splined driving hub from between the

axle shaft and the wheel hub. Remove the driving hub spacer.

3. Remove the lock nut, washer, and wheel bearing adjusting nut from the spindle. Remove the wheel, hub and drum as an assembly. The wheel outer bearing will be forced off the spindle at the same time. Remove the wheel inner bearing cone.
4. Place a drain pan under the steering knuckle assembly. Remove the oil baffle from the brake backing plate.
5. Remove the cap screws which retain the brake backing plate and spindle to the steering knuckle. Remove the brake backing plate and spindle. It is not necessary to disconnect the hydraulic brake flex line before removing the brake backing plate from the spindle. NOTE: Support the brake backing plate so that the brake hose is not damaged.

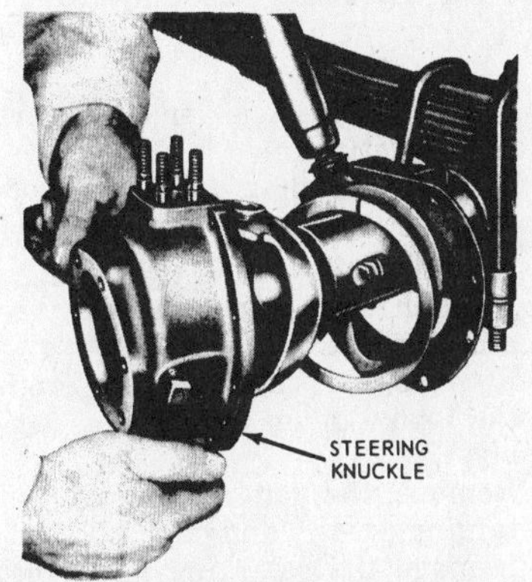

Removing or installing steering knuckle—F-250
(© Ford Motor Co.)

6. Remove the axle shaft.
7. Disconnect the steering drag link from the steering knuckle.
8. Disconnect the spindle connecting rod at both ends.
9. Remove the seal retainer from the steering arms. Remove the felt, rubber and steering retainer assembly from the steering knuckle and place it on the axle housing tubes.

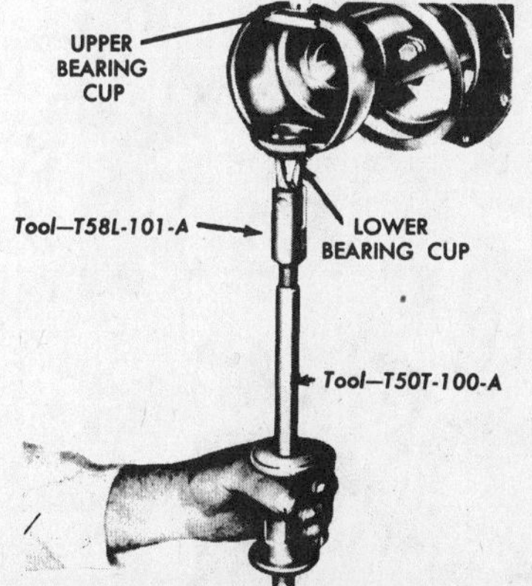

Removing king pin bearing cup
(© Ford Motor Co.)

10. Remove the upper and lower king pin bearing caps and shims.
11. Remove the steering knuckle from the housing Remove the bearing cones.
12. Remove bearing cups, if necessary.
13. Installation is given in steps 14 thru 26.
14. If new seals are to be installed at the steering knuckle, place the new seal assembly on the axle housing tube. The combination seal and steel retainer assembly should be installed with the split up to prevent lubricant leakage.
15. Install the upper and lower king pin bearing cups in the axle housing yoke.
16. Place the king pin bearing cones in the cups. Retain the lower bearing in place with grease.
17. Place the steering knuckle over the yoke, then install the lower and upper bearing caps. Install the old shims for a trial build-up. Torque the bearing cap bolts or stud nuts to 25 ft. lbs.
18. Check the steering knuckle bearing preload. It should be 60-120 in. lbs. Adjust the shim thickness at the bearing caps, as required, to obtain the proper preload.
19. Install the oil seal rings.
20. Connect the spindle connecting rod and the drag link.
21. Install the axle shaft
22. Position the spindle and the brake backing plate on the steering knuckle, and then install the retaining cap screws. Install the oil baffle.

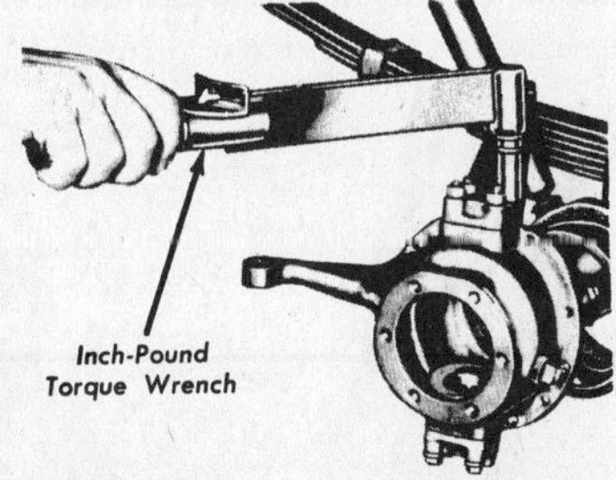

Checking steering knuckle bearing preload
(© Ford Motor Co.)

23. Install the wheel inner bearing cone on the spindle. Install the wheel hub and drum. Install the driving hub spacer, then the wheel outer bearing cone and adjusting nut.
24. Rotate the wheel in both directions and at the same time tighten the bearing adjusting nut to bring the bearing rollers into proper contact. After the bearings are firmly seated, torque the adjusting nut to 40 ft. lbs. and back off the nut ¼ turn. Place the bearing adjusting lockwasher on the spindle. Assemble the lockwasher by turning the adjusting nut to the nearest hole in the washer to lock. Install the locknut and torque to 40 ft. lbs.
25. Install the driving hub and snap-ring. Coat the edge of the grease cap with a non-hardening sealer and install the grease cap.
26. Fill the steering knuckle with the proper grade and amount of lubricant.

Front Drive Axle R&R

Bronco

1. Raise the vehicle on a hoist or jack and install safety stands under the radius arm brackets.
2. Follow the procedure given in Axle Shaft and Steering Knuckle Removal and remove the front wheels, tires, brake drums, brake backing plates, spindles and axle shaft.
3. Remove the hydraulic brake line brackets from each end of the axle without breaking the hydraulic connection. Disengage the hydraulic lines from the axle clips. Tie the lines to the frame to keep them out of the working area.
4. Disconnect the steering tie rod at the knuckle connecting rod ends and tie it out of the working area. Disconnect the axle stablizer bar.
5. Disconnect the front drive shaft at the pinion companion flange and universal joint. Secure the drive shaft out of the working area.
6. Lower the vehicle onto the safety stands and place a jack under the axle to support it while disconnecting it from the radius arms.
7. Each radius arm and cap is numbered from 1 through 100 for proper assembly, since they are manufactured as matched pairs. Remove the bolts attaching the radius arms to the radius arm caps. Remove the rubber insulators and roll the axle form under the vehicle.
8. Installation is given in steps 9 thru 15.
9. Position the front drive axle under the vehicle, using a floor jack, and install the radius arms, insulators and caps to the axle. The numbers enscribed on cap and arm should be matched. Torque the attaching bolts to specifications, tightening them diagonally in pairs.
10. Raise the vehicle to working height and install the drive shaft to the pinion companion flange at the universal joint. Torque

the universal joint U-bolt nuts to specifications.

11. Connect the axle stabilizer bar. Connect the steering tie rod to the steering knuckle by the steering connecting rod ends. Torque the attaching nuts to specifications, then install cotter pins.
12. Follow the procedure detailed in Axle Shaft and Steering Knuckle Installation and install the axle shafts, spindles and brake backing plates.
13. Position the hydraulic brake lines and brackets, then install the retaining clips.
14. Install the front brake drums, wheels and tires. Adjust the front wheel bearings. Install the dust cap or locking hub cap and the wheel cover on each front wheel.
15. Lower the truck and fill the axle housing with the specified lubricant.

Front Drive Axle R&R

F-100

1. Raise the vehicle on a hoist or jack and install safety stands under the radius arm brackets.
2. Follow the procedure detailed in Axle Shaft and Steering Knuckle Removal and remove the front wheels, tires, brake drums, brake carrier plates, spindles and axle shafts.
3. Remove the hydraulic brake line brackets from each end of the axle without breaking the hydraulic connection. Disengage the hydraulic lines from the axle clips. Tie the lines to the frame.
4. Disconnect the steering tie rod at the spindle connecting rod ends. Disconnect the axle stabilizer bar.
5. Disconnect the front drive shaft at the pinion companion flange and universal joint. Secure the drive shaft out of the working area.
6. Lower the vehicle onto the safety stands and place a jack under the axle to support it while disconnecting it from the radius arms.
7. Each radius arm and cap is marked, since they are manufactured as matched pairs (parts are numbered 1 through 100). Remove the bolts attaching the radius to the radius arm caps. Remove the rubber insulators and roll the axle from under the truck.
8. Installation is given in steps 9 thru 15.
9. Position the front drive axle under the vehicle, using a floor jack, and install the radius arms, insulators and caps to the axle. Numbers on radius arm and cap should be matched. Torque the attaching bolts to specifications, tightening them diagonally in pairs.
10. Raise the vehicle to working height and install the drive shaft to the pinion companion flange at the universal joint. Torque the universal joint U-bolt nuts to specifications.
11. Connect the axle stablizer bar. Connect the steering tie rod to the spindle arms by means of the steering connecting rod ends. Torque the attaching nuts to specifications, then install the cotter pins.
12. Follow the procedure detailed in Axle Shaft and Spindle Arm Installation and install the axle shafts, spindles and brake backing plates.
13. Position the hydraulic brake lines and brackets, then install the retaining clips.
14. Install the front brake drums, wheels and tires. Adjust the front wheel bearings. Install the dust cap or locking hub cap and the wheel cover on each front wheel. NOTE: If a dust cap is used, install it with a coat of non-hardening sealer on the sealing surface.
15. Lower the truck and fill the axle housing with the specified lubricant.

Front Drive Axle R&R

F-250

1. Raise the vehicle on a hoist so that no weight is supported by the front axle.
2. Remove the hubs, brake carrier plates, axle shafts and steering knuckle as given in Axle Shaft and Steering Arm.
3. Disconnect both front axle shock absorbers at their lower ends.
4. Disconnect the front axle drive shaft at the pinion flange.
5. Support the front axle on a transmission jack, then remove the spring clip (U-bolt) nuts and the spring seats.
6. Lower the axle assembly and roll it from under the truck.
7. Installation is given in steps 8 thru 11.
8. Position axle under truck and raise it so that the spring clips and spring seats can be installed.
9. Connect the front axle shock absorbers.
10. Connect the front axle drive shaft.
11. Complete the assembly as given in Axle Shaft and Steering Knuckle Installation.

Steering Knuckle R&R

F-600

1. Raise the vehicle and support with safety stands.
2. Remove the plug from the bottom of the axle housing and drain the lubricant.
3. Disconnect the driveshaft at the pinion shaft.
4. Remove one front wheel from the brake drum and hub assembly.
5. Remove the outer hub cap retaining screws and cap.
6. Remove the retaining lock ring.
7. Remove the retaining screws and the splined drive plate.
8. Bend the tab of the lockwasher from the locknut, then remove

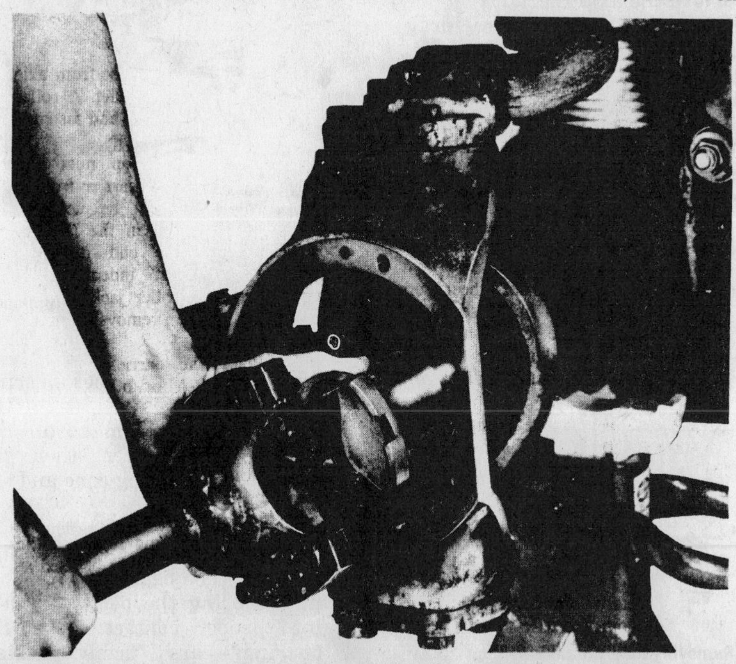

Axle shaft removal—F-600 (© Ford Motor Co.)

the locknut.
9. Remove lockwasher and discard. Remove the adjusting nut.
10. Remove the drum and hub assembly from the spindle.
11. Remove the brake backing plate retaining screws and carefully lift out the backing plate and wire it out of the way.
12. Remove the spindle positioning screw and spindle.
13. Remove the axle shaft from the housing.
14. Repeat steps 4 thru 13 to remove the opposite axle shaft.
15. Remove the carrier to housing stud nuts and washers. Loosen two top nuts and leave on studs to prevent carrier from falling.
16. Break carrier loose from axle housing with rawhide mallet. NOTE: A roller jack should be positioned and fastened to the carrier at this point.
17. Remove the top nuts and washers, then work the carrier free. A small pinch bar may be used to straighten the carrier in the housing bore. However, the end must be rounded to prevent identing the carrier flange. A roller jack may be used to facilitate removal of the carrier.
18. Installation is given in steps 21 thru 39.
19. Remove all traces of old gasket material from the carrier and housing surfaces, then position a new gasket over the housing mounting studs.
20. Using a roller jack, ease the carrier into position in the housing bore.
21. Position two washers and run two nuts part way on to the studs to hold the carrier; then align it properly with the housing.
22. Install the housing stud nuts and torque them to specifications.
23. Install one axle shaft in the housing.
24. Install the spindle and secure it with the positioning screw.
25. Position the brake backing plate, install the retaining screws and torque to specifications.
26. Carefully position the drum and hub assembly on the axle spindle, and tighten the adjusting nut.
27. Adjust wheel bearing. Position a new lockwasher against the adjusting nut and apply a film of oil to the outer face of the lockwasher.
28. Run the lock nut against the lockwasher, then torque it to specifications.
29. Bend one tab of the lockwasher over the adjusting nut.
30. Bend other tab of the lockwasher (in the opposite direction) over the lock nut.

Spindle in position
(© Ford Motor Co.)

31. Apply Silastic Sealer to the front and rear mounting faces of the splined drive plate. Position the drive plate and install the plate retaining screws, then torque to specifications.
32. Install the retaining lock ring.
33. Position the outer hub cap and install the retaining screws, then torque to specifications.
34. Install the front wheel.
35. Connect the drive shaft at the pinion shaft.
36. Repeat steps 23 through 34 for the other axle shaft assembly.
37. Make sure that the housing drain plug has been installed.
38. Fill the axle housing with the correct grade and quantity of lubricant.
39. Lower the vehicle.

Drive Pinion Oil Seal Replacement

Bronco, F-100, F-250

The drive pinion oil seal can be replaced without removing the axle assembly from the vehicle. If the new seal is of leather construction, it must be soaked in light engine oil for thirty minutes before installation. Compounded or synthetic rubber seals do not require soaking.

1. Raise the front end of the vehicle with a jack. Install safety stands under the frame rails, then lower the jack far enough to allow the axle to drop into the rebound position for working clearance.
2. Scribe marks on the companion flanges and U-joints, then remove the drive shaft.
3. Remove the pinion shaft nut.
4. Remove the companion flange.
5. Using a suitable puller, in combination with a slide hammer, remove the pinion oil seal.
6. Clean the pinion oil seal seat. Coating the sealing edge of the new seal with a small amount of oil resistant sealer. NOTE: Do not put sealer on the sealing lip. Drive the seal into the housing.
7. Coat the inside of the pinion flange with a small quantity of lubricant, then install on the pinion shaft.
8. Install the pinion attaching nut on the shaft and torque to 200-220 ft. lbs.
9. Position the drive shaft in the original position, matching the previously made scribe marks. Install the attaching parts.
10. Torque the universal joint U-bolt nuts to 15-20 ft. lbs.
11. Raise the truck, remove the safety stands, then lower.

Wheel Bearing Adjustment

Bronco, F-100, F-250

NOTE: On 1971 Bronco and F-100 models, the hub spacer has been replaced with a pressure spring.

1. Raise the vehicle and support with safety stands.
2. Back off the brake adjusting screw, if necessary. Remove the wheel cover.
3. Remove the front hub grease cap. Remove the driving hub retaining snap-ring and slide the splined driving hub from between the axle shaft and the wheel hub. Remove the driving hub spacer. NOTE: If equipped with free-wheeling hubs, see Free-Wheeling Hub Removal.
4. Remove lock nut and lock ring from the spindle.
5. Tighten the bearing adjusting nut to 50 ft. lbs., while rotating the wheel back and forth to seat the bearings.
6. Continue rotating the wheel and then, loosen and re-torque the adjusting nut to 30-40 ft. lbs.
7. Back the adjusting nut off approximately ¼ turn (90 degrees). Assemble the lock ring by turning the nut to the nearest notch where the dowel pin will enter.
8. Install the outer lock nut and torque to 50 ft. lbs. Final endplay of the wheel on the spindle should be 0.001 to 0.010.
9. Install the driving hub, spacer, snap-ring and hub grease cap. Apply a thin coat of nonhardening sealer to the seating edge of the grease cap before installation. NOTE: If equipped with free-wheeling hubs, installation refer to Free-Wheeling Hub.
10. Adjust the brake.
11. Remove safety stands and lower the vehicle.

Wheel Bearing Adjustment

F-600

1. Remove the outer hub cap retaining screws, then remove the

cap.
2. Remove the retaining lock ring.
3. Remove the retaining screws and the splined drive plate.
4. Bend the tab of the lockwasher away from the locknut, then remove the locknut.
5. Remove the lockwasher and discard.
6. While rotating the wheel back and forth to correctly seat the bearings, torque the adjusting nut to 50 ft. lbs.
7. Back-off the adjusting nut from ¼ to 1/3 turn.
8. Position a new lockwasher against the adjusting nut and apply a film of oil to the outer face of the lockwasher.
9. Run the lock nut up against the lockwasher, then torque it to 100-150 ft. lbs.
10. Bend one tab of the lockwasher over the adjusting nut.
11. Bend other tap (in the opposite direction) over the lock nut. NOTE: Use a blunt tool when bending the tabs.
12. Apply Silastic Sealer to the front and rear mounting faces of the spined drive plate.
13. Position the drive plate, install the retaining screws and torque to specifications.
14. Install the retaining lock ring.
15. Position the outer hub cap and install the retaining screws. Torque to specifications.

Free-Wheeling Lock-out Hubs

Description

Free-Wheeling lock-out hubs are available on Bronco, F-100 and F-250 front wheel drive models. An internal design hub is used on Bronco and F-100 trucks; an external type on F-250 trucks.

Operation
Bronco and F-100

Locked Position: When the transfer case is to be shifted into position for driving the front axle, turn the actuating knob so that it is aligned 180 degrees opposite F position (with arrow toward ("LOCK" on Bronco). If the clutch teeth do not engage with the knob turned to this position, the teeth are butted and a slight movement of the wheel in either direction will complete the lock.

Free-Wheel Position: When the transfer case is to be shifted into position for driving the rear axle only, turn the actuating knob so that it is aligned with the letter F (with arrow toward "FREE" on Bronco). This will disengage the clutch teeth and unlock the wheel hub from the axle shaft.

CAUTION: Make certain that transfer case is in 2-wheel drive before disengaging Hub/Lok.

Operation
F-250

Locked Position: When the transfer case is to be shifted into position for driving the front axle, turn the actuating knob ¼ turn in either direction, so that it is aligned with the letter L stamped on the inward pointing arrow heads. If the clutch teeth do not engage with the knob turned to this position, the teeth are butted and a slight movement of the wheel in either direction will complete the lock.

Free-Wheel Position: When the transfer case is to be shifted into position for driving the rear axle only, turn the actuating knob ¼ turn in either direction, so that it is aligned with the letter F stamped in the outward pointing arrow heads. This will disengage the clutch teeth and unlock the wheel hub from the axle shaft.

CAUTION: Make certain transfer case is in 2-wheel drive before disengaging hub. Do not drive truck with one hub engaged and the other disengaged.

Free Wheeling Hub R&R

Bronco and F-100

1. Remove the three screws (six screws on Bronco) attaching the lock-out actuating knob and retaining plate assembly to the wheel hub. Remove the actuating knob and retaining plate assembly and large O-ring.
2. Remove the large internal snap-ring, the outer clutch retaining ring and the actuating cam body.
3. While pressing inward against the axle shaft sleeve and ring assembly, remove the snap-ring that secures the axle sleeve and ring assembly to the axle shaft.
4. Remove the axle shaft sleeve and ring assembly and the inner clutch and bushing assembly.
5. Remove the pressure spring (or spacer) and spring retainer plate.
6. Installation is given in steps 7 thru 13.
7. Insert the spring retainer plate into the wheel hub with the flange side facing inward. Be sure spring retainer plate bottoms against the outer wheel hub bearing cap.
8. Position the pressure spring (or spacer), with the large end seating against the spring retainer plate, inside the wheel hub.
9. Assemble the inner clutch ring and bushing assembly to the axle shaft sleeve and ring assembly, sliding both assemblies as a unit on to the axle shaft splines. Using a new axle shaft snap-ring, lock the axle shaft sleeve and ring assembly to the shaft.
10. Place the actuating cam body in position against the axle shaft sleeve and ring assembly, inside

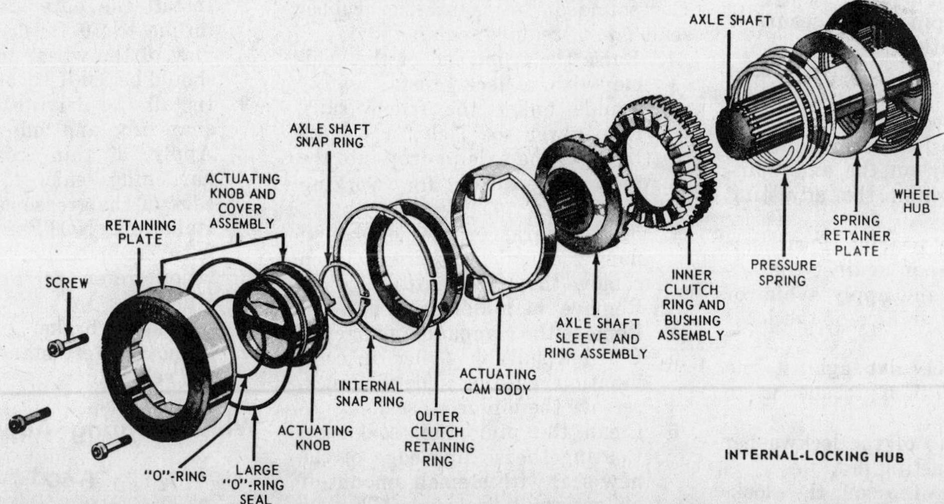

Internal lock-out hub—disassembled (© Ford Motor Co.)

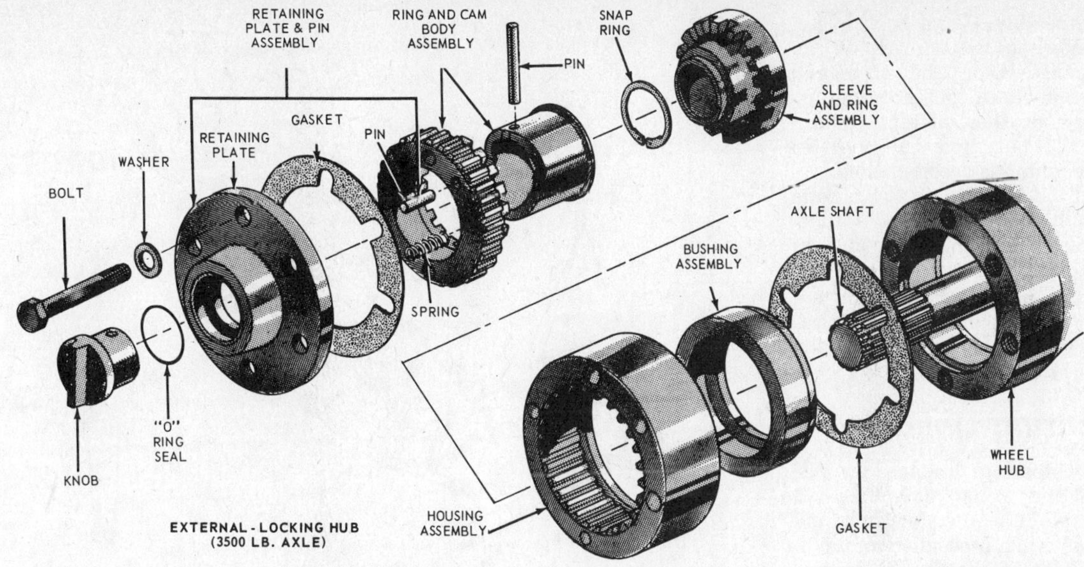

External lock-out hub—disassembled (© Ford Motor Co.)

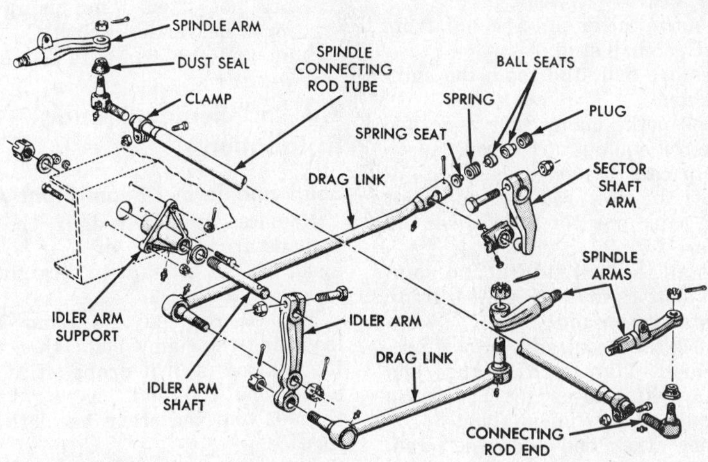

Typical steering linkage—F100, 250, 350 & 4x2 (© Ford Motor Co.)

the wheel hub.

11. Install the outer clutch retaining ring and the internal snap-ring into position in the wheel hub. Make certain the snap-ring is well seated in the groove on the inside diameter of the hub.
12. Coat the large O-ring seal with O-ring lubricant. Install the large O-ring seal onto the actuating knob and retaining plate and place the know and retaining plate assembly into position in the wheel hub.
13. Install the three (six on Bronco) knob and retaining plate assembly attaching screws and copper washers. Tighten screws securely.

Free-Wheeling Hub R&R

F-250

1. Remove the six bolts attaching the actuating knob, retaining plate, ring and cam body and housing assembly to the wheel hub.
2. Remove the actuating knob, retaining plate, ring and cam body and housing assembly as one unit.
3. Remove the inner sleeve and ring assembly retaining snap-ring from the axle shaft.
4. Remove the inner sleeve and ring assembly.
5. Remove the inner sleeve and ring bushing from the wheel hub.
6. Installation is given in steps 7 thru 13.
7. Place the inner sleeve and ring bushing into the wheel hub with the flange outward. Be sure that the bushing buttoms on the offset in the wheel hub.
8. Slide the inner sleeve and ring assembly onto the axle shaft splines with the clutch teeth facing outward. Push the clutch ring inward until it seats in the inner bushing. Lock the inner clutch ring to the axle shaft with a new snap-ring.
9. Position a new gasket on the wheel hub and align bolt holes.
10. Position a new gasket between the retaining plate and the hous-

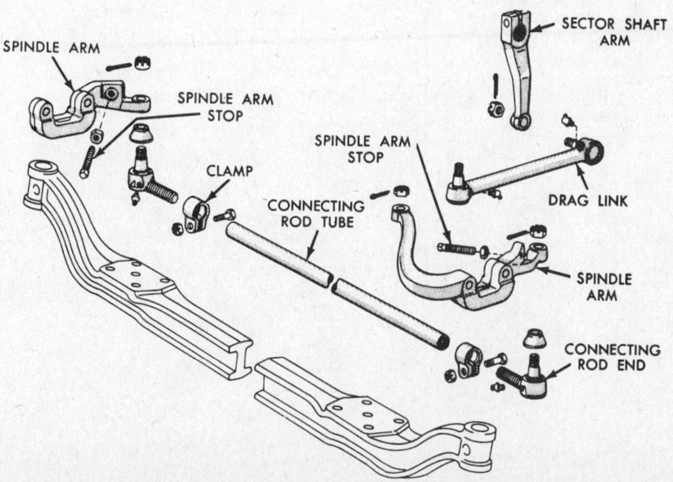

Typical steering linkage with bolt on steering arms (© Ford Motor Co.)

ing assembly. Align bolt holes.
11. Assemble the actuating knob end retaining plate, the ring and cam body and the housing assembly together, making certain that the bolt holes align after spline match is accomplished.
12. Insert and start two bolts through the housing and retaining plate assemblies for use in positioning to the wheel hub.
13. Insert remaining bolts, then securely attach housing and retaining plate assemblies to the wheel hub.

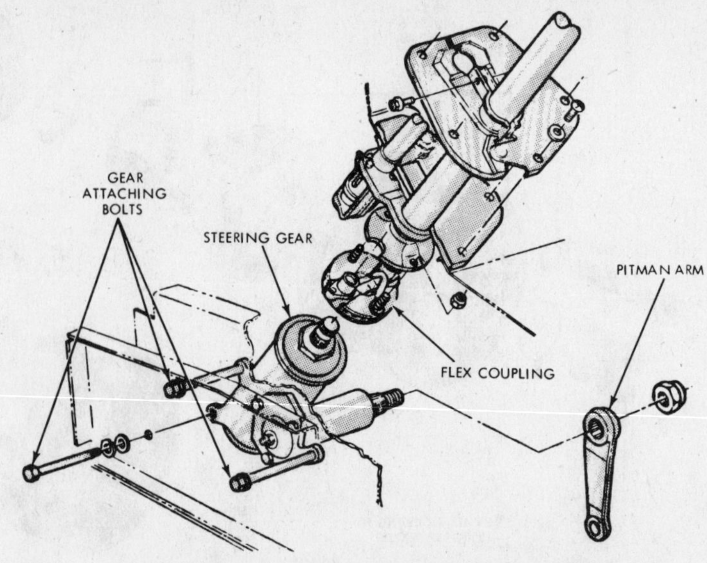

Steering gear installation—Econoline (© Ford Motor Co.)

Steering Linkage

Typical steering linkage on the Econoline and F-100, 250, 350 4x2 trucks employs a double drag link with a frame-mounted idler and support. The rest of the linkage is conventional in design with pitman arm, tie rod, steering arms and idlers. A manual recirculating ball type steering gear is used. Optional power steering on these vehicles is the Ford integral power steering gear.

On other trucks a simpler steering linkage system is employed. These systems may have tapered or bolt-on spindle arms as illustrated. The manual steering gear used on these trucks is the gear-worm and roller.

Reference

Front wheel and steering alignment procedures may be found in the General Repair Section.

Tie Rod End Replacement

All Models

The tie rod end should be replaced if there is excessive wear.

1. Remove cotter pin and nut from rod end ball stud.
2. Remove ball stud from the spindle arm.
3. Loosen the clamp bolt and turn the rod end out of the rod.
4. Lubricate the threads, then install the new rod end to about the same position as was the old one.
5. Install the ball stud in the spindle arm, tightening nut securely. Install cotter pin.
6. Check the toe-in, adjusting if necessary. Tighten the rod end clamp after adjusting. The clamp should be positioned about 3/16" from the end of the rod, with the clamp bolt at right angles to the slot in the rod if they are not fixed. The clamp bolt must be vertical, with the head up and the clamp facing downward.

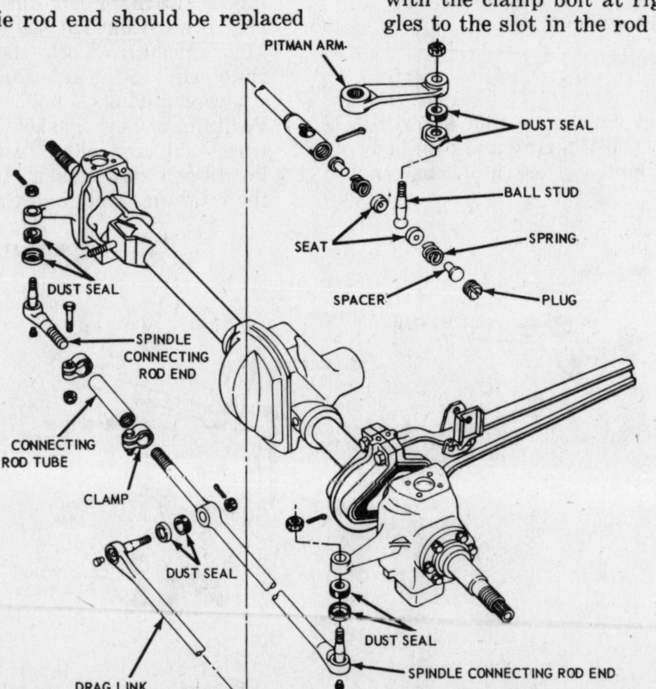

Steering linkage—F100 & 4x4 Bronco (© Ford Motor Co.)

Tie Rod Removal and Installation

Solid and Twin I-Beam Front Axles

Replace the tie rod if the end threads are stripped or if it is damaged. Do not attempt to straighten a tie rod.

The tie rod may be removed by loosening the clamp bolts, then turning the rod until it drops off at both ends. One rod end has right-hand threads and the other has left-hand threads.

Install new rod after coating threads with oil. Start one end about one thread, then start the other end. Turn the tie rod until the ends have entered the rod about the same distance as into the old rod.

Check and adjust the toe-in. Be sure to tighten the rod end bolt clamps.

F-100 (4x4) and Bronco

In the following procedure the tie rod is referred to at the "connecting rod," composed of two spindle connecting rod ends and the connecting rod tube (see illustration).

1. Raise the vehicle on a hoist and disconnect the drag link from the spindle connecting rod end.
2. Disconnect the right spindle connecting rod end from the right spindle arm.
3. Disconnect the left spindle connecting rod end from the left spindle arm and remove the spindle connect rod ends from the vehicle.
4. Position the connecting rod ends in a vise and loosen the connecting rod tube clamps.
5. Remove the right (short) rod

end from the connecting rod tube and remove the tube from the left (long) connecting rod end.
6. Clean and oil all threads on components that are to be re-used.
7. Install the connecting rod tube and clamps on the left spindle connecting rod end. Do not tighten the clamps.
8. Install the right connecting rod end in the tube and remove the assembly from the vise.
9. Position new dust seals on the left spindle connecting rod end and position the end to the left spindle arm.
10. Install the connecting rod end attaching nut and tighten it securely. Continue to tighten the nut until the slots on the nut are aligned with the hole in the ball stud and install the cotter pin.
11. Position new dust seals on the right spindle connecting rod end and position the end to the right spindle arm. Install the attaching nut and tighten it securely. Continue to tighten the nut until the nut castellations are aligned with the hole in the ball stud and install the cotter pin.
12. Position new seals on the drag link ball stud and position the drag link to the spindle connecting rod end. Install the attaching nut and tighten it securely. Continue to tighten the nut until the nut castellations are aligned with the hole in the ball stud and install the cotter pin.
13. Lubricate the spindle connecting rod ends and the drag link.
14. Lower the vehicle, then check and adjust the toe-in. Tighten the connecting rod tube clamps securely.

Steering Gear

Manual Steering Gear

Steering Gear R&R

Econoline

1. Raise the vehicle on a hoist.
2. Remove the flex coupling lower attaching bolt.
3. Disconnect the pitman arm from the drag link.
4. Remove the three attaching bolts and remove the gear.
5. Remove the pitman arm attaching nut and remove the pitman arm.
6. To install, center the input shaft (approximately three turns from either stop).
7. Install pitman arm pointing downward, tightening attaching nut securely.

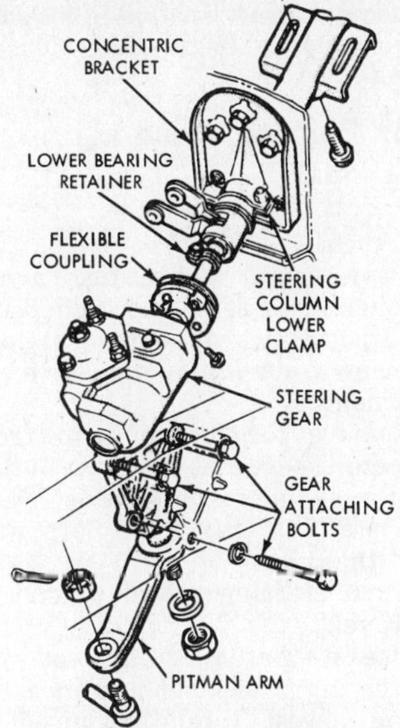

Steering gear installation—F100, 250 & 350, 4x2 (© Ford Motor Co.)

8. Fill the steering gear to the proper level with lubricant.
9. Position the steering gear in the truck, aligning the input shaft splines to engage the flexible coupling. Install and tighten the three steering gear mounting bolts.
10. Connect drag link to pitman arm. Install attaching bolt and tighten securely. Install cotter pin.
11. Install flexible coupling attaching bolt and tighten securely.
12. Lower vehicle.

F-100, 250, 350 (4x2)

1. Remove flex joint attaching bolt and remove the brake line bracket.
2. Raise the front of the vehicle.
3. Disconnect the pitman arm from the sector shaft.
4. Remove the steering gear attaching bolts and the gear.
5. Before installing gear, align the wheels and the sector shaft to the straight-forward position.
6. Install steering gear, tightening attaching bolts securely.
7. Install the brake line bracket to the gear cover studs.
8. Connect the pitman arm to the sector shaft.
9. Install and tighten flex coupling bolt.
10. Remove the steering gear filler plug and housing lower cover bolt. Turn the steering wheel to the left to move the ball nut away from the filler hole. Fill the steering gear with lubricant

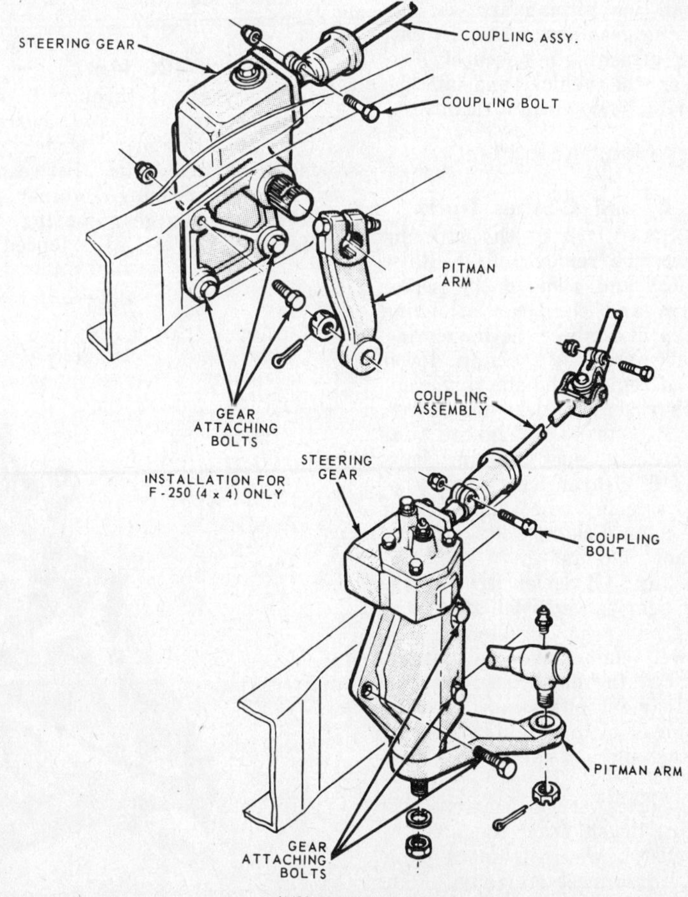

Steering gear installation—F100, 250 & Bronco 4x4 (© Ford Motor Co.)

(until lubricant comes out of the housing cover lower bolt hole). Install filler plug and cover bolt.

Steering Gear R&R

Bronco and F-100, 250 (4x4)

1. Raise the vehicle on a hoist.
2. Remove the pitman arm.
3. Remove the three gear to frame attaching bolts, then lower the vehicle.
4. Remove the flex coupling clamp bolt at the steering gear input shaft and loosen the other clamp bolt (steering column). Remove the coupling from the steering gear input shaft. Discard clamp, bolt and nut.
5. Remove the steering gear from the vehicle.
6. When installing, first mount the steering gear to the frame, but do not tighten attaching bolts.
7. Install steering shaft flex coupling to the gear input shaft using a new clamp and bolt. Tighten bolt securely.
8. Install the flex coupling to the steering column shaft with a new clamp and bolt. Tighten bolt securely.
9. Raise the vehicle and tighten the steering gear attaching bolts securely.
10. Install the pitman arm on the steering gear sector shaft, tightening attaching nut securely.
11. Lower the vehicle and fill the steering gear with lubricant.

Steering Gear R&R

P, F, B, and C-Series Trucks

On P-Series trucks the steering wheel must be removed first. Raise the vehicle and remove the sector shaft arm and the gear attaching bolts, then disconnect the horn wire, loosen the steering column lower clamp and remove the steering gear. Install in reverse order of removal, leaving all bolts loose. Tighten bolts in this order: upper steering bolts (leave 1/16" clearance between top of tube and steering wheel hub), lower steering column clamp bolts, steering gear attaching bolts.

On F and B-Series trucks the steering gear is removed after first loosening and removing steering column lower clamp and the pitman arm. Install in this order: steering gear in frame (bolts loose), steering column lower clamp, tighten steering gear attaching bolts, install pitman arm.

On C-Series trucks remove the horn wire brush from the steering column just below instrument panel bracket, disconnect universal joint from steering gear, turn the wheels to the right, remove the pitman arm from the steering gear, then remove the steering gear. Install in reverse order of removal, tightening bolts as you go.

Worm Bearing Preload Adjustment

F-100, 250, 350 (4x2)

Always check and adjust worm and roller mesh after check checking and adjusting worm bearing preload (see below for worm and roller mesh adjustment).

1. Remove the pitman arm from sector shaft and the horn button and spring from the steering wheel. Disconnect the horn wire at the relay.
2. Turn steering wheel to end of travel.
3. Use a torque wrench on the steering wheel nut and measure the lowest torque required to move the wheel at a constant speed. This torque is the worm bearing preload.
4. If the preload is not 4-5 in. lbs (manual) or 3-4 in. lbs. (power assist), adjust the preload as follows: loosen the steering shaft bearing adjuster locknut and turn adjuster to set the preload.
5. Tighten bearing adjuster locknut, install the pitman arm and horn components.

F-100 (4x4)

Follow Steps 1 through 3 of the procedure for F-100, 250, 350 (4x2) above. If adjustment is necessary, remove or add shims between the worm shaft bearing retainer cover and the steering gear housing. If erratic readings are experienced, disconnect the steering shaft joint at the steering gear and check torque required to rotate the steering shaft. If that torque is measurable, add it to the preload specification.

Bronco

Remove the gear from the vehicle, loosen locknut and back off the mesh and roller adjusting nut. Check the torque required to rotate the input shaft 1½ turns either side of center. If bearing preload is not 5-10 in. lbs., add or remove shims between the worm shaft bearing retainer cover and the steering gear housing until proper preload is obtained.

F and C-Series

Remove the steering gear and use a 12-point socket and torque wrench on the lower steering serrated shaft to measure preload at a constant speed rotation. If bearing preload is not within 9-11 in. lbs. (C-series) or 5-9 in. lbs. (F-series), add or remove gasket shims between the worm shaft bearing retainer and the gear housing. Adjust the worm and roller mesh preload. Install steering gear in vehicle.

Worm and Roller Mesh Adjustment

Always check and adjust worm bearing preload before making the mesh adjustment (see above).

1. Remove the steering gear from the vehicle.
2. Measure the torque required to move the gear through middle (straight-ahead) position with a torque wrench on the input shaft. The highest reading is used. If it is not 24-29 in. lbs.

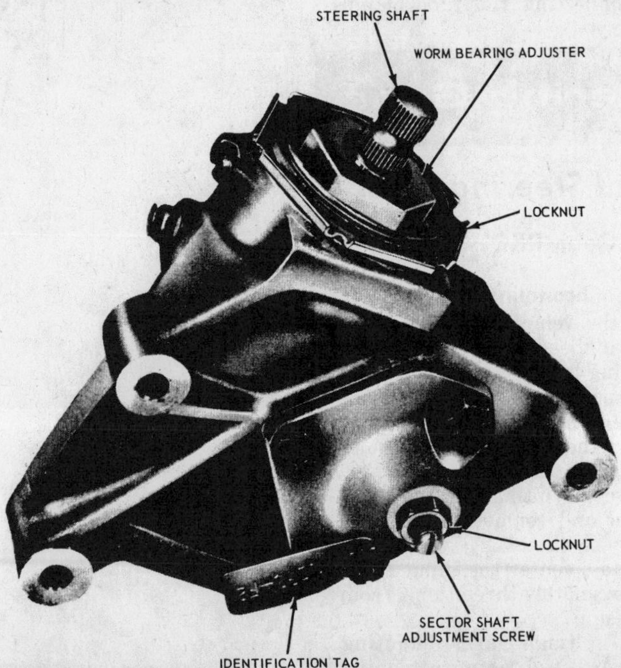

Recirculating ball type steering gear—Econoline (© Ford Motor Co.)

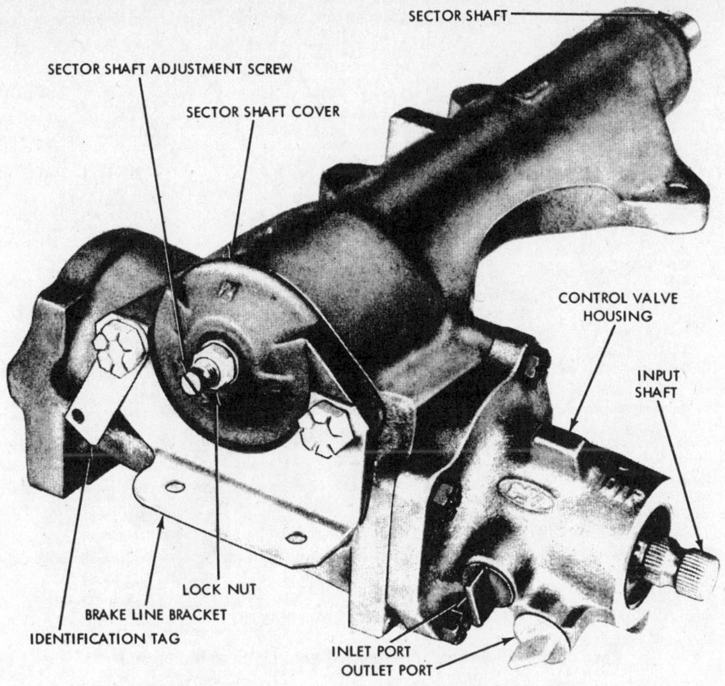

Ford integral power steering gear (© Ford Motor Co.)

(C-series), 14-22 in. lbs. (F-500-750) or 12-21 in. lbs. (F-100 4x4 and Bronco), loosen locknut and turn adjusting screw until correct mesh load is obtained. Tighten locknut.

3. Recheck mesh load, install steering gear in vehicle and fill gear with lubricant.

Steering Worm and Sector Adjustment

Econoline

1. Remove the steering gear from the vehicle.
2. Loosen locknut on the sector shaft adjusting screw and turn adjusting screw out (counterclockwise) approximately three turns.
3. Using a torque wrench on the input shaft, rotate shaft about $1\frac{1}{2}$ turns either side of center. If the preload is not 4-5 in. lbs. (manual) or 3-4 in. lbs. (power assist), loosen input shaft bearing adjuster locknut and tighten or loosen bearing adjuster to obtain the correct bearing preload. Tighten locknut and recheck preload.
4. Center the input shaft (turn against stops gently as it is easy to damage the ball return guides).
5. Turn sector shaft adjusting screw clockwise until an over-center meshload of 9-10 in. lbs. (manual) or 8-9 in. lbs. (power assist) is obtained (measured at input shaft). Tighten the locknut.
6. Check the total gear lash by holding the sector shaft solid in the center position and pulling with the torque wrench 15 in. lbs. in each direction. If the travel of the wrench exceeds $1\frac{1}{4}$", then the whole gear must be replaced.
7. Recheck total over-center preload, then install steering gear in vehicle.

Power Steering Gear

Reference

For power steering gear overhaul procedures, see the General Repair Section.

Ford Integral Power Steering Gear

F-100, 250, 350 (4x2)

This torsion-bar type power assist unit consists of a worm and one-piece rack piston, a hydraulic valve, valve actuator, input shaft and torsion bar assembly. The double acting power cylinder is integral with the housing. The hydraulic pump is belt driven with integral reservoir.

Over Center Preload

1. Disconnect pitman arm from the sector shaft.
2. Disconnect the fluid return line at the reservoir and cap the reservoir return line.
3. Place the end of the return line in a clean container and cycle the steering wheel in both directions to discharge the fluid from the gear.
4. Turn the steering wheel to 45-degrees from the left stop and measure the torque (at the steering wheel nut) required to turn $\frac{1}{8}$-turn from there.
5. Determine the torque required to turn the steering gear through center position. Loosen adjusting screw locknut and turn adjusting screw to obtain a torque reading 11-12 in. lbs. greater than the torque 45-degrees from the stop.
6. Hold adjusting screw while tightening locknut.
7. Install the pitman arm and steering wheel hub cover.
8. Connect the fluid return line and fill reservoir with fluid.

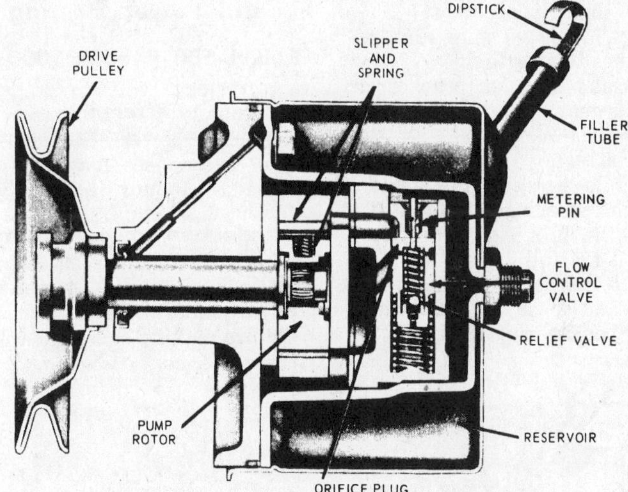

Power steering pump—typical (© Ford Motor Co.)

Steering Gear Removal and Installation

1. Disconnect pressure and return lines from the steering gear, *being sure to tag them for identification.* Plug lines and ports.
2. Remove brake lines attached to bracket on the steering gear.
3. Remove the two bolts that secure

the flex coupling to the steering gear and to the column steering shaft assembly.
4. Raise the vehicle.
5. Remove the pitman arm from the sector shaft, using a puller if necessary.
6. If vehicle has a standard transmission, remove the clutch release lever retracting spring.
7. Remove the steering gear attaching bolts and steering gear, working the steering gear free of the flex coupling.
8. To install, slide the flex coupling into place on the bottom of the steering shaft.
9. Set the steering wheel so that the spokes are horizontal and center the steering gear input shaft.
10. Slide the steering gear input shaft into the flex coupling. Install the three steering gear attaching bolts and tighten them securely.
11. With wheels in the straight ahead position, install the pitman arm on the sector shaft.
12. Install the flex coupling and tighten the bolts securely.
13. Connect fluid pressure and return lines to steering gear. Reinstall brake lines on bracket on steering gear.
14. Remove the coil wire, fill the power steering pump reservoir and, while engaging the starter, cycle the steering wheel to distribute the fluid. Add fluid if reservoir is not full.
15. Connect the coil wire, start the engine and check for leaks while cycling the steering wheel.

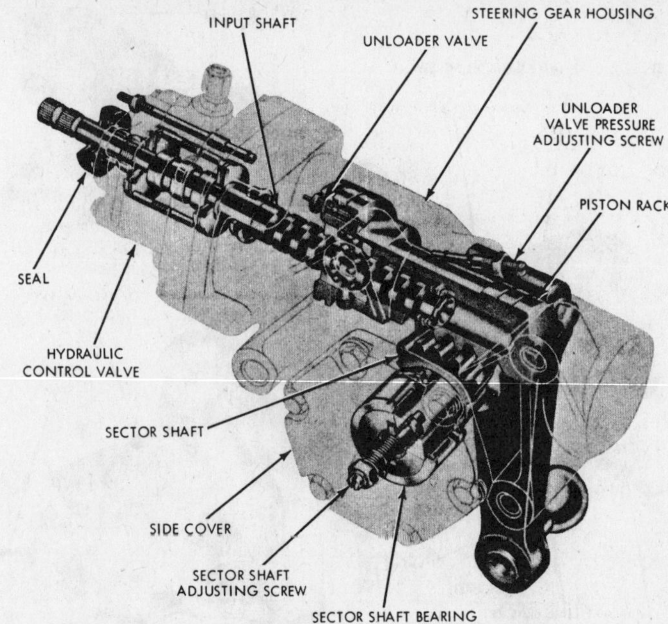

Ross model HF-64 integral steering gear (© Ford Motor Co.)

Ross HF-54 and HF-64 Integral Power Steering Gears

F, B, L-500 through 9000 Series

Reference

Complete power steering gear overhaul procedures may be found in the General Repair Section.

Unloader Valve Adjustment

This adjustment is made for *right turn only* on the HF-54 gear and for *both turns* on the HF-64 gear.

Before making this adjustment, establish the straight-forward center of the steering system by driving the truck forward with hands off the wheel until the steering finds its own center. Stop the truck and mark the steering column to steering wheel with chalk or masking tape.

1. With wheels straight ahead engine warm and idling, turn the steering wheel 1¾ turns to the right (HF-54), 1½ turns (2 port HF-64) or 1¼ turns (4 port HF-64). Hold this position.
2. Loosen locknut and turn the unloader valve pressure adjusting screw until an audible hiss is heard. Tighten locknut.
3. While vehicle is moving, let the steering wheel center (straight-forward), then stop the truck and turn the wheel the prescribed number of turns (Step 2 above) and listen for audible hiss. Repeat Step 2 if necessary. NOTE: The pitman arm on the HF-64 must not contact the stop cast on the gear housing prior to contacting the unloader valve. The distance between the pitman arm and the stop should be 1/16" to ⅛" when the hiss is heard.
4. To adjust the unloader valve for left turn (HF-64 ONLY), repeat Steps 1 through 3 above turning the steering wheel to the left.

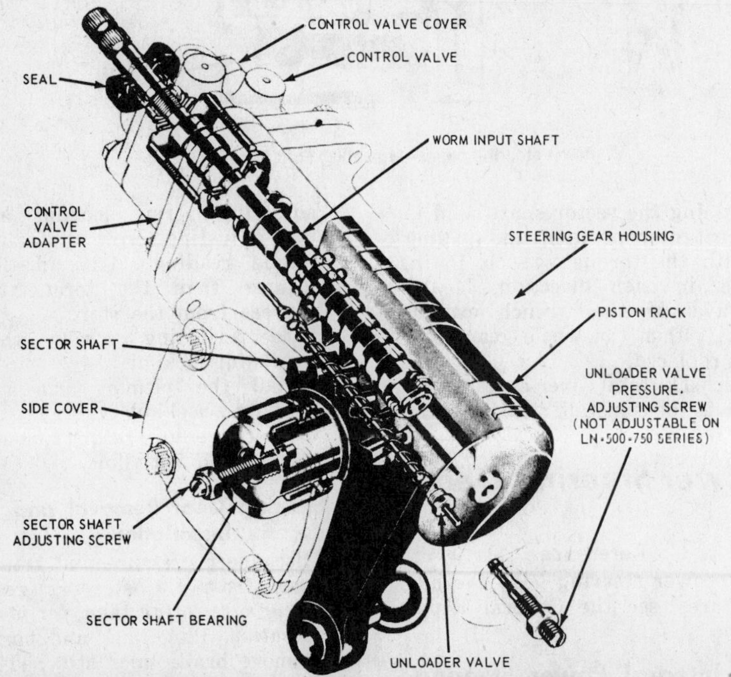

Ross model HF-54 integral steering gear (© Ford Motor Co.)

Sector Shaft Adjustment

1. Disconnect the drag link from the pitman arm and center the steering wheel. Check for lash between the sector shaft and the rack piston by moving the pitman arm. If there is noticeable lash, remove the gear from the vehicle.
2. Loosen the sector shaft adjust-

ment screw locknut on the side cover.

3. Rotate the input shaft through its full travel at least five times, then adjust the sector shaft adjusting screw for a 15–20 in. lb. torque as shaft is rotated 90 degrees each side of center.
4. Back off adjusting screw one turn and note torque required to move the input shaft 90 degrees each side of center. Move the adjusting screw in to provide for an increase of 2–4 in. lbs. at a point within 45 degrees each side of center after locknut is first tightened snugly. Torque locknut to 20–25 ft. lbs.
5. Input torque of assembled gear (no fluid) should not exceed 15 in. lbs. over the full travel of output shaft.
6. Install steering gear in the vehicle.
7. Connect the drag link to the pitman arm.
8. Connect the pump lines and fill the system with fluid.

Steering Gear R&R

1. Position a drain pan under the steering gear and disconnect the pressure line from the gear, the return line from the gear and the turning hoses if so equipped. Mark all lines for identification.
2. Remove the pitman arm from the sector shaft.
3. Disconnect the universal joint from the input shaft of the gear, sliding it up and off the shaft.
4. Remove the steering gear attaching bolts and remove the gear.
5. To install, first position gear in vehicle and install and tighten attaching bolts.
6. Connect universal joint to the steering gear input shaft.
7. Install pitman arm on the sector shaft.
8. Connect all hydraulic lines in their original locations.
9. Fill power steering hydraulic system, start engine and check for leaks.

Clutch

Mechanical Clutch Linkage Adjustment

The clutch pedal free travel is the distance between the clutch pedal in the fully released position and the pedal position at which the clutch release fingers contact the clutch release bearing (this can be felt).

The clutch pedal total travel is the distance between the floor pan and the top of the pedal when the clutch is in the fully released position.

Only the clutch pedal free travel is adjusted. If the pedal free travel is not within 11/16″ to 1⅛″, adjust the clutch release rod until correct free travel is obtained.

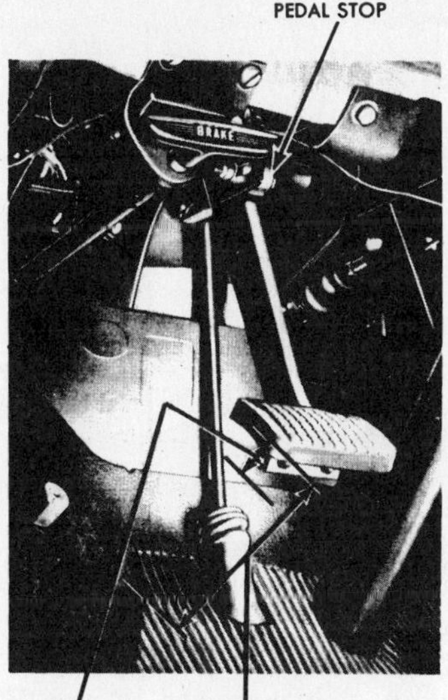

Clutch pedal travel
(© Ford Motor Co.)

1968-71 Econoline

First the clutch pedal total travel is adjusted. It should be between 7½″ and 7¾″. Adjustment is made by loosening the locknut on the pedal stop eccentric bolt and turning the eccentric bolt until correct total travel is obtained. Tighten locknut.

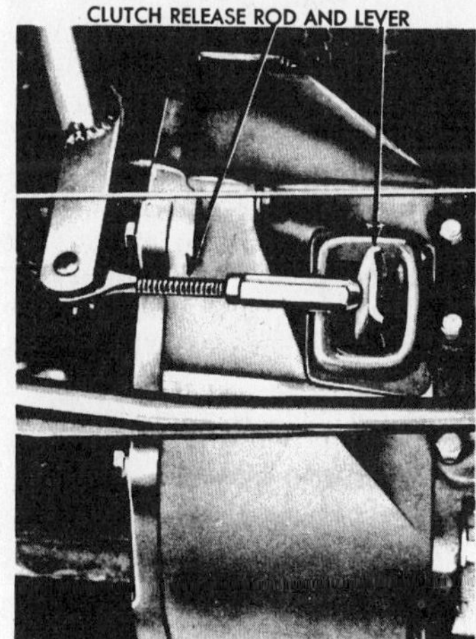

Clutch adjustment—Econoline
(© Ford Motor Co.)

Check the clutch pedal free travel. It should be 1⅛″ to 1⅜″. Adjustment is made at the clutch release rod turnbuckle.

Bronco

If the clutch pedal total travel is not within 6⅝″ and 6⅞″ (1966–69) or 6-43/64″ and 6-11/16″ (1970) or 6-11/16″ and 6-15/16″ (1971), move the clutch pedal bumper and bracket up or down to obtain required free travel.

Check and adjust pedal free travel. For 1966–69 Bronco's the free travel should be 1-3/16″ to 1⅜″ and for 1970–71 Bronco's it is 1-7/32″ to 1-27/64″. Adjustment is made at the clutch release rod turnbuckle.

F- and N-Series

Total pedal travel is adjusted at the pedal bumper stop. Pedal free travel is made at the clutch release rod.

Hydraulic Actuated Clutch Adjustment

Before adjusting hydraulic clutch, check the level of fluid in the master cylinder reservoir, filling to within ½″ of the top if necessary. Bleed the hydraulic system as described below.

Bleeding Hydraulic Clutch

1. Attach a funnel to the bleeder screw of the slave cylinder by means of a transparent bleeder hose. The funnel must be higher than the master cylinder.
2. Pour fluid into the funnel as the system is filling, *being careful not to pour bubbles in the fluid.* Bleeder screw must be open.
3. Close the bleeder screw when master cylinder reservoir is full.
4. Check the slave cylinder pushrod total travel which should be 1⅛″.
5. The clutch master cylinder relief port must be open in order to bleed the system. Clutch master

Mechanical Clutch Linkage Adjustments

Model	*Year*	*Total Pedal Travel (inches)*	*Pedal Free Travel (inches)*
F-100-700	1961–63	8-1/16–8-5/16	1-3/8 –1-1/2
F-100-250	1964	6-3/16–7-1/16	1-1/8 –1-3/8
F-350	1964	8-1/16–8-5/16	1-1/8 –1-3/8
F-100-250, P-series with suspended pedal	1965–67	6-5/8 –6-7/8	1-1/16–1-1/4
F-100-250 4x4, F-350	1965–67	8-3/16–8-3/8	1-1/8 –1-3/8
N, F-500-700	1965–67	8-1/16–8-5/16	1-1/8 –1-3/8
F-100-250, P-series with suspended pedal	1968	7-3/8 –7-3/4	1-1/16–1-1/4
F-100-250 4x4, F-350	1968	7-3/8 –7-3/4	1-1/8 –1-3/8
F, N-500-700	1968	8-1/16–8-5/16	1-1/8 –1-3/8
F-100-250, P-series with suspended pedal	1969	7-3/8 –7-3/4	1-1/8 –1-3/8
F, N-500-700	1969–71	8-1/16–8-5/16	1-1/8 –1-3/8
F-100-350, P-series with suspended pedal	1970–71	7-3/8 –7-3/4	1-1-1/2

cylinder pushrod lash of ¼″ is required on the P-500 and 5000 series vehicles to permit the conventional type master cylinder piston to return to the piston stop ring and open the relief port. The clutch master cylinder cannot be adjusted on the P-350, 400, 3500 and 4000 series vehicles. In the case of tilt-cab (C-series) master cylinder, the O-ring seal on the end of the pushrod must not seat against the piston. Uncovering of the piston port is accomplished by adjustment of the pushrod to a piston lash of ¼″. Forcing the clutch pedal to compress the pedal bumper more than normal by jamming a screwdriver between the pedal pad and the floor insures a complete uncovering of the relief port.

Hydraulic Clutch Adjustment

There are two adjustments for obtaining clutch pedal free travel. The initial pedal free travel should be ¼″ for all models. On F, N, NT, and T Series vehicles the pedal height is first adjusted to 8-1/16″ to 8-3/16″ at the pedal stop (10⅜″ on H, HT and 1962–65 N Series). Turn eccentric

Hydraulic slave cylinder push rod adjustment (© Ford Motor Co.)

bolt on pedal to obtain an initial pedal free travel of 3/16″ to ⅜″. Remove retracting spring, push slave cylinder pushrod as far forward as possible and release lever back until it contacts the release fingers. Adjust the nut on the pushrod for a clearance of ¼″ between pushrod adjusting nut and release lever. A total pedal travel of at least 2″ should result.

On P and C Series trucks, the initial pedal free travel is that distance of pedal travel before the master cylinder pushrod contacts the piston. On C Series vehicles this adjustment is made with the eccentric bolt and on P Series it is made by rotating the master cylinder pushrod. Obtain an initial pedal free travel of ¼″. With the retracting spring removed, the

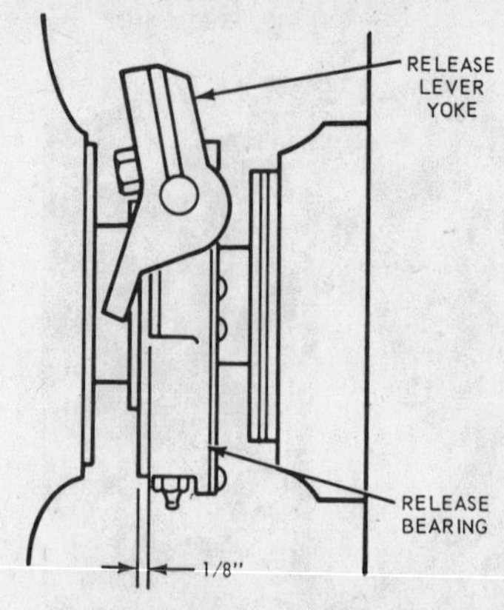

Spicer clutch adjustment (© Ford Motor Co.)

slave cylinder pushrod held completely forward and the release lever held in contact with the release fingers, turn adjusting nut on the slave cylinder pushrod to obtain a final pedal free travel of approximately 2″.

Internal Clutch Adjustment

1. Remove inspection cover from the bottom of the clutch housing.
2. Disconnect the retracting spring and hold the release lever against the throwout bearing. Measure the distance between the throwout bearing and the clutch spring hub (synchromatic transmission) or clutch brake (non-synchromatic transmission). On vehicles with the 14″ single plate clutch, this distance should be 11/32″ to 13/32″. On all Spicer clutches, also adjust the adjusting ring to obtain a ⅛″ clearance between release yoke fingers and the throwout bearing.
3. If adjustment is necessary, rotate the clutch assembly to get at the adjusting lockring and bolt. Remove the bolt and lockring.
4. With clutch pedal held or blocked in the released position, rotate the adjusting ring (use a pry bar) clockwise to move the throwout bearing toward the flywheel or counterclockwise to move the throwout bearing away from the flywheel. Rotating the adjusting ring one lug position moves the throwout bearing about 1/32″.
5. Let clutch pedal return to engage the clutch, then recheck clearance.
6. Install lock and bolt.
7. Adjust clutch linkage.
8. Connect the retracting spring and replace the clutch housing cover.

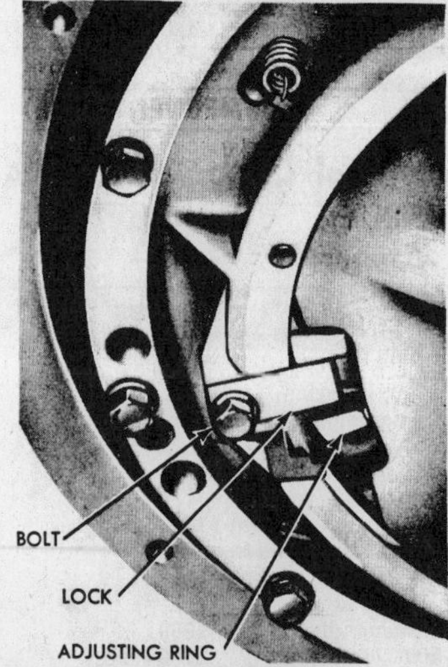

Internal clutch adjustment (© Ford Motor Co.)

Clutch Removal and Installation

9.37″, 10″, 11″, 11.5″, 12″ and 13″ Single Disc

1. Disconnect the release lever retracting spring and pushrod at the lever.
2. If so equipped, remove the slave cylinder attaching bolts.
3. Remove the transmission.
4. If there is no dust cover on the flywheel housing remove the starter. Remove the release lever and bearing.
   If the flywheel housing has a dust cover, remove the dust cover, release lever and bearing.
5. Mark the pressure plate and cover assembly and the flywheel so that they may be assembled in the same relative position.
6. Loosen the pressure plate attaching bolts evenly until the springs are loose then remove the bolts, pressure plate assembly and clutch disc. Do not remove the pilot bushing unless it is to be replaced.
7. To install, position the disc on the flywheel and install a pilot tool or spare transmission spline shaft.
8. Install the pressure plate assembly over the aligning tool and align the marks made during removal. Install the retaining bolts, tightening securely.
9. Remove pilot tool and apply a light coat of lithium-base grease to the hub splines of the clutch disc.
10. Apply lithium-base grease to the sides of the driving lugs.
11. Position throwout bearing and bearing hub on the release lever and install release lever on the trunnion in the flywheel housing.
12. Apply a light film of lithium-base grease to the release lever fingers and to the lever trunnion or fulcrum. Fill the angular groove of the release bearing hub with grease.
13. If removed, install the flywheel

Pressure plate lubrication point
(© Ford Motor Co.)

housing, tightening bolts securely.
14. Install the starter motor if it was removed.
15. Apply a light film of lithium-base grease to the transmission front bearing retainer and install the transmission assembly on the clutch housing, tightening attaching bolts securely.
16. Install the slave cylinder, if applicable.
17. Adjust the clutch linkage and install the clutch housing dust cover.

Clutch Removal and Installation

14″ Single Plate Clutch

1. Disconnect the clutch pedal assist spring, removing the left-hand exhaust pipe from the manifold if necessary.
2. Disconnect the release lever retracting spring and remove the slave cylinder attaching bolts, if applicable.
3. Remove the transmission.
4. Insert two ¾″ wood blocks between the throwout bearing housing and the rear surface of the pressure plate assembly.
5. Remove the clutch to flywheel bolts and remove the flywheel ring and pressure plate assembly. Remove the clutch disc.
6. To install, position the clutch disc and pressure plate assembly on the flywheel and start the bolts. NOTE: the long hub of the clutch disc faces the rear.
7. Insert a spare transmission splined shaft or a disc aligning tool through the disc and into the pilot bushing. Tighten pressure plate bolts evenly and securely.
8. Remove the wood blocks and aligning tool or shaft.
9. Install the transmission.
10. Install the clutch slave cylinder.
11. Connect the release lever retracting spring and exhaust pipe.
12. Connect the clutch pedal assist spring.
13. Check internal clutch adjustment, linkage adjustment and correct if necessary.

Manual Transmission

Reference

For complete manual transmission overhaul procedures see the General Repair Section. Overhaul procedures for the Ford 3.03 3-speed are described in this section below.

Transmission R&R

Ford 3.03 3-Speed

1. Raise vehicle.
2. Support the transfer case shield with a jack and remove the bolts that attach the shield to the frame side rails. Remove the shield.
3. Drain transmission and transfer case lubricant. To drain the transmission lubricant, remove the transmission drain plug if the vehicle is so equipped. For models without drain plugs, remove the lower extension housing-to-transmission bolt.
4. Disconnect the front and rear drive shafts at the transfer case.
5. Disconnect the speedometer cable at transfer case.
6. Disconnect the shift rods from the transmission shift levers. Place the first-reverse gear shift lever into the first gear position and insert the fabricated tool. This tool will prevent the input shaft roller bearings from dropping into the transmission case when separating the transfer case from the transmission and output shaft.
7. Cut the lock wire and remove two bolts, washers, plates and insulators that secure the crossmember to the transfer case adapter.
8. Remove the crossmember-to-frame side support attaching bolts.
9. Raise the transmission and remove the upper insulators from the crossmember. Remove the crossmember.
10. Remove the two lower bolts attaching transmission to the flywheel housing.
11. Disconnect the shift rod from the transfer case shift lever bracket.
12. Remove the bolt that attaches the shift lever bracket to the transfer case adapter, and allow the assembly to hang by the shift lever.
13. Reposition the transmission jack under the transmission and secure with the chain.
14. Remove the two upper bolts securing the transmission to the flywheel housing. Move the transmission and transfer case rearward and downward out of the vehicle.
15. Move the assembly to a bench and remove the transfer case-to-transmission attaching bolts.
16. Slide the transmission assembly off the transfer case.
17. To install, position transfer case to transmission and install attaching bolts.
18. Position the transmission and transfer case on a transmission jack and secure with the safety chain.
19. Raise the transmission and transfer case assembly into position and install the transmission case to the flywheel housing.
20. Install the two upper and two lower transmission attaching bolts.
21. Position the shift lever to the transfer case adapter and install the attaching bolt.
22. Connect the shift rod to the shift lever bracket and secure with the spring washer, flat washer and cotter pin.
23. Raise the transmission and transfer case high enough to provide clearance for installing the cross-member. Position the upper insulators to the cross-member and install the cross-member-to-frame side support attaching bolts.
24. Align the bolt holes in the transfer case adapter with those in the crossmember, then lower the jack.
25. Install the crossmember-to-transfer case adapter bolts, insulators, plates and washer. Secure the bolts with lock wire.
26. Remove the fabricated tool and connect each shift rod to its respective lever on the transmission with a spring washer, flat washer and cotter pin.
27. Connect the speedometer cable.
28. Install the rear axle drive shaft to the transfer case.
29. Install the front wheel drive shaft to the transfer case.
30. Fill the transmission and transfer case to the bottom of the filler hole with the recommended lubricant.
31. Position the transfer case shield to the frame side rails and install the attaching bolts.

Transmission R&R

Econoline

1. Raise the vehicle on a hoist and drain the lubricant from the transmission by removing the

drain plug if the vehicle is so equipped. For models without drain plugs, remove the lower extension housing-to-transmission bolt.

2. Disconnect the drive shaft from the flange at the transmission. Secure the front end of the drive shaft out of the way with lock wire.
3. Disconnect the speedometer cable from the extension housing and disconnect the gear shift rods from the transmission shift levers.
4. Position a transmission jack under the transmission. Secure the transmission to the jack.
5. Raise the transmission slightly and remove the four bolts retaining the transmission support crossmember to the frame side rails. Remove the bolt retaining the transmission extension housing to the crossmember.
6. Remove the four transmission-to-flywheel housing bolts.
7. Position engine support bar (Tool T65E-6000-J) to the frame.
8. Lower the transmission.
9. To install, make certain that the machined surfaces of the transmission case and the flywheel housing are free of dirt, paint and burrs.
10. Install a guide pin in each lower mounting bolt hole.
11. Start the input shaft through the release bearing. Align the splines on the input shaft with the splines in the clutch disc. Move the transmission forward on the guide pins until the input shaft pilot enters the bearing or bushing in the crankshaft. If the transmission front bearing retainer binds up on the clutch release bearing hub, work the release bearing lever until the hub slides onto the transmission front bearing retainer. Install the two transmission-to-flywheel housing upper mounting bolts and lock washers. Remove the two guide pins and install the lower mounting bolts and lock washers.
12. Raise the jack slightly and remove the engine support bar.
13. Position the support crossmember on the frame side rails and install the retaining bolts. Install the extension housing-to-crossmember retaining bolt.
14. Connect the gear shift rods and the speedometer cable.
15. Install the drive shaft and torque the attaching bolts to specification.
16. Fill the transmission to the bottom of the filler hole with the recommended lubricant.
17. Adjust the clutch pedal free travel and shift linkage as required.

Transmission R&R

F-100-250

1. Raise the vehicle and position safety stands.
2. Drain the transmission lubricant by removing the drain plug if the vehicle is so equipped. For models without drain plugs, remove the lower extension housing-to-transmission bolt.
3. Position a transmission jack under the transmission.
4. Disconnect the gear shift linkage at the transmission.
5. If the vehicle has a four-wheel drive, remove the transfer case shift lever bracket from the transmission.
6. Disconnect the speedometer cable.
7. Disconnect the drive shaft from the transmission as detailed.
8. Remove the transmission-to-clutch housing attaching bolts.
9. Move transmission to the rear until the input shaft clears the clutch housing and lower the transmission. *Do not depress the clutch pedal while the transmission is removed...*
10. Before installing the transmission, apply a light film of lubricant to the clutch disc splines, release bearing inner hub surfaces, release lever fulcrum and fork and the transmission front bearing retainer. Exercise care to avoid contaminating the clutch disc with excessive grease.
11. Place the transmission on a transmission jack. Raise the transmission until the input shaft splines are in line with the clutch disc splines. The clutch release bearing and hub must be properly positioned in the release lever fork.
12. Install a guide stud in each lower clutch housing-to-transmission case mounting bolt and align the splines on the input shaft with the splines on the clutch disc.
13. Slide the transmission forward on the guide studs until it contacts the clutch housing.
14. Install the two transmission to flywheel housing upper mounting bolts and nuts. Remove the two guide studs and install the lower mounting bolts.
15. Connect the speedometer cable and the driven gear.
16. Install the drive shaft as detailed.
17. Connect each shift rod to its respective lever on the transmission.
18. If the vehicle is equipped with four-wheel drive, install the four-wheel drive shaft bracket.
19. Fill the transmission to the proper level with an approved lubricant.
20. Adjust the clutch pedal free travel and shift linkage as required.

Warner T85N 3-Speed With Overdrive

Transmission R&R

F-100

The overdrive unit cannot be removed from the vehicle as a separate assembly. Drain both the transmission and the overdrive unit, and then remove the transmission and overdrive as a unit.

To remove the overdrive transmission, follow the same procedure as that for the standard three-speed transmission plus the following:

1. Disconnect the solenoid and governor wires at the connectors near the solenoid.
2. Remove the overdrive wiring harness from its clip on the transmission.
3. Disconnect the overdrive control cable.

To install the overdrive transmission, follow the same procedure as that for the standard transmission, plus the following:

1. Connect the overdrive control cable so that there is 1/4" clearance between the handle shank and dash bracket when the lever at the overdrive housing is against its rear stop.
2. Connect the solenoid and governor wires, and replace the overdrive wiring harness in its clip.
3. Fill only the transmission with lubricant.

Warner T-18 4-Speed

Transmission R&R

F-100, 250 (4x2), F-350, P-3500 through 500

1. Disconnect the back-up light switch located at the rear of the gearshift housing cover.
2. Remove the rubber boot, floor mat, and the body floor pan cover, and remove the transmission shift lever. Remove the weather pad and pad retainer.
3. Raise the truck and position safety stands. Position a transmission jack under the transmission, and disconnect the speedometer cable.
4. If the truck is equipped with band-type parking brake, disconnect the brake cable clevis at the cam. Remove the brake cable conduit clamp.
5. Remove the front U-joint flange

attaching bolts. Remove the bolts that attach the coupling shaft center support to the crossmember and wire the coupling shaft and drive shaft to one side. On F-100-350 Series trucks, remove the transmission rear support.

6. Remove the transmission attaching bolts.
7. Move the transmission to the rear until the input shaft clears the clutch housing, and lower the transmission.

Before installing the transmission, apply a light film of lubricant to the clutch disc splines, release bearing inner hub surfaces, release lever fulcrum and fork, and the transmission front bearing retainer. Care must be exercised to avoid excessive grease from contaminating the clutch disc.

8. Place the transmission on a transmission jack, and raise the transmission until the input shaft splines are aligned with the clutch disc splines. The clutch release bearing and hub must be properly positioned in the release lever fork.
9. Install guide studs in the clutch housing and slide the transmission forward on the guide studs until it is in position on the clutch housing. Install the attaching bolts and nuts. Remove the guide studs and install the two lower attaching bolts.
10. Connect the speedometer cable and driven gear and parking brake clevis. Install the brake cable conduit clamp, and shift linkage.
11. Install the bolts attaching the coupling shaft center support to the crossmember.
12. Install the bolts attaching the front U-joint flange to the transmission output shaft flange. On F-100-350 Series trucks, install the transmission rear support.
13. Connect the back-up light switch.
14. Install the shift lever and lubricate the spherical ball seat with lubricant.
15. Install the weather pad and pad retainer. Install the floor pan cover, floor mat and boot.

New Process 435 4-Speed

Transmission R&R

F-100, 250, 350 (4x2), F-100, 250 (4x4), P-350 through 500, F, B, C, LN-500 through 700

1. On F-, LN- or B-Series truck, remove the rubber boot and floor mat.
2. On a F-, LN- or B-Series truck, remove the floor pan transmission cover plate. Remove the weather pad and pad retainer. It may be necessary first to remove the seat assembly.
3. Disconnect the back-up light switch located in the rear of the gearshift housing cover.
4. Raise the truck and position safety stands. Position a transmission jack under the transmission, and disconnect the speedometer cable.
5. Disconnect the parking brake lever from its linkage, and remove the gearshift housing. On a C-Series truck, disconnect parking brake cable and bracket at the transmission.
6. Disconnect the drive shaft. Remove the bolts that attach the coupling shaft center support to the cross-member and wire the coupling shaft and drive shaft to one side. In F-100-350 Series Trucks, remove the transmission rear support.
7. Remove the two transmission upper mounting nuts at the clutch housing.
8. Remove the transmission attaching bolts at the clutch housing, and remove the transmission.
9. Before installing the transmission, apply a light film of lubricant to the clutch disc splines, release bearing inner hub surfaces, release lever fulcrum and fork, and the transmission front bearing retainer. Care must be exercised to avoid excessive grease from contaminating the clutch disc.
10. Place the transmission on a transmission jack, and raise the transmission until the input shaft splines are aligned with the clutch disc splines. The clutch release bearing and hub must be properly positioned in the release lever fork.
11. Install guide studs in the clutch housing and slide the transmission forward on the guide studs until it is in position on the clutch housing. Install the attaching bolts and nuts. Remove the guide studs and install the two lower attaching bolts.
12. Install the bolts attaching the coupling shaft center support to the crossmember.
13. Connect the drive shaft and the speedometer cable. On F-100-350 Series trucks, install the transmission rear support.
14. Connect the parking brake to the transmission.
15. Connect the back-up light switch.
16. On an F-, LN- or B-Series truck, install the weather pad, the pad retainer and the transmission cover plate. Install the seat assembly if it was removed.
17. On an F-, LN- or B-Series truck, install the weather pad, the pad retainer, the floor mat and rubber boot.

Gearshift Linkage Adjustment

Ford 3.03 3-Speed

F-100, 250 and F-250 (4x4)

1. Check the operation of the gear shift linkage for smooth crossover operation.
2. To adjust the gear shift linkage, move the selector lever to the neutral position.
3. When in the neutral position, the selector lever should be as shown.
4. If the selector lever position must be changed, disconnect both connecting rods at the transmission shift levers and be certain the shift levers are in the neutral detent.
5. Install the gauge rod through the steering column gauge bracket and shift levers.
6. Position the sleeves on the rods so that the ends enter the levers freely. On 4 x 4 trucks, adjust the adjusting nut and the lock nut as required.
7. Lengthen each rod seven turns.
8. Remove the gauge rod and attach the rods to levers.
9. The gear shift tube shift arms should be approximately parallel with each other.
10. Move the selector lever through all shift positions as a final check for smooth operation.
11. If there is interference, adjust the position of the steering column tube.

Econoline

Move the selector lever through all shift positions to see if cross-over operation is smooth. If cross-over operation is not smooth, adjust the gear shift levers.

1. Place the gear shift lever in the neutral position.
2. Disconnect the gear shift rods at the transmission shift levers. Be sure shift levers are in neutral detent.
3. Insert a 1/4″ rod through the pilot hole in the shift tube floor-mounted bracket until it enters the adjustment hole of both the upper and lower shift lever.
4. Adjust the position of each shift rod adjustment sleeve so that it enters the transmission lever freely. Then, run the sleeves out four turns and secure the sleeves to the levers with the lock nuts.
5. Remove the ¼″ rod from the pilot hole and check the operation of the selector lever in all shift positions.

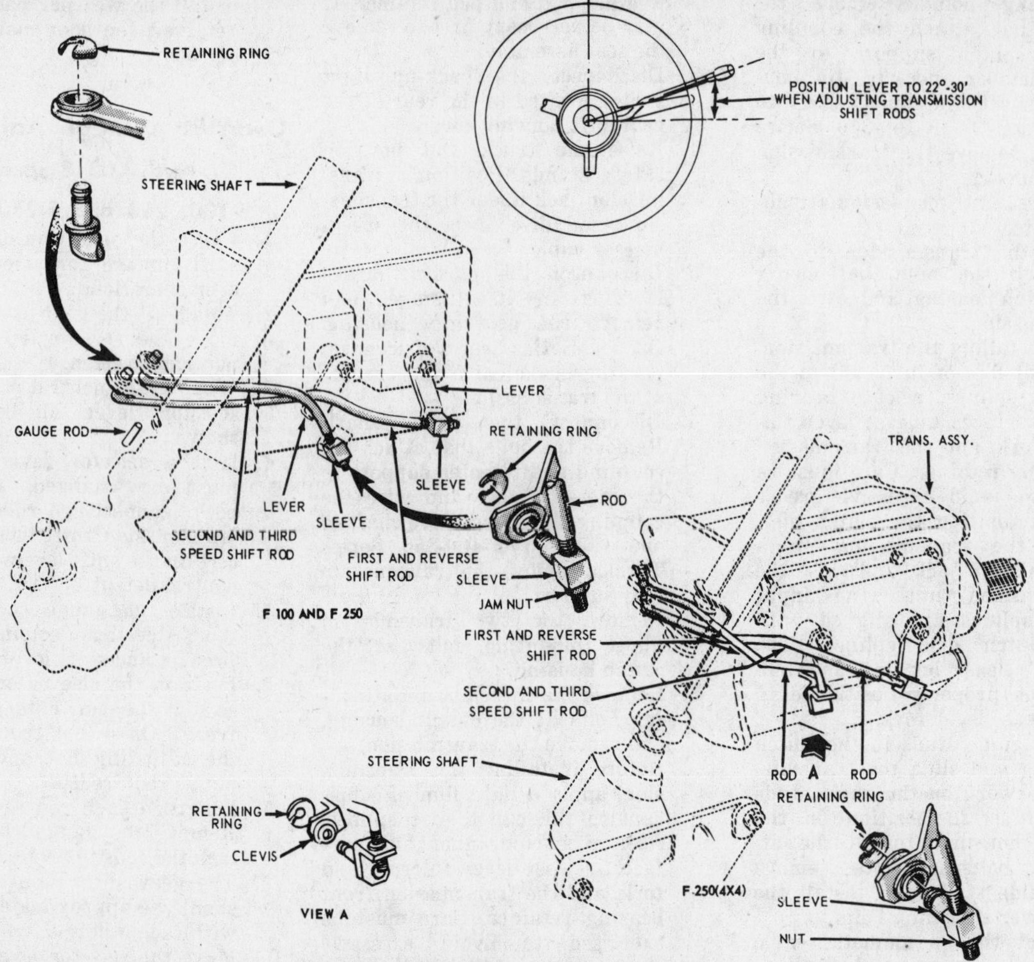

Gearshift linkage adjustment (© Ford Motor Co.)

Gearshift Linkage Adjustment

Bronco

1. Place the gear shift lever in the neutral position.
2. Insert a 3/16″ diameter alignment pin through the steering column bracket and shift levers. It may be necessary to align the levers to insert the pin.
3. Disconnect the gearshift rods at the transmission shift levers.
4. Adjust the position of each shift rod adjustment sleeve so that it enters the transmission lever freely. Run the sleeves out four turns and secure the adjustments with the lock nut.
5. Remove the alignment pin from the levers.
6. Secure the gearshift rods to the transmission levers with the retaining clip.
7. Start the engine and shift the selector lever to each position to make sure it operates freely.

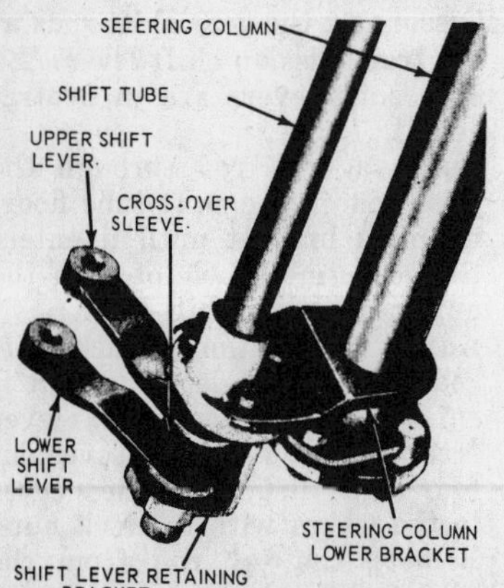

Gearshift linkage adjustment—Econoline (© Ford Motor Co.)

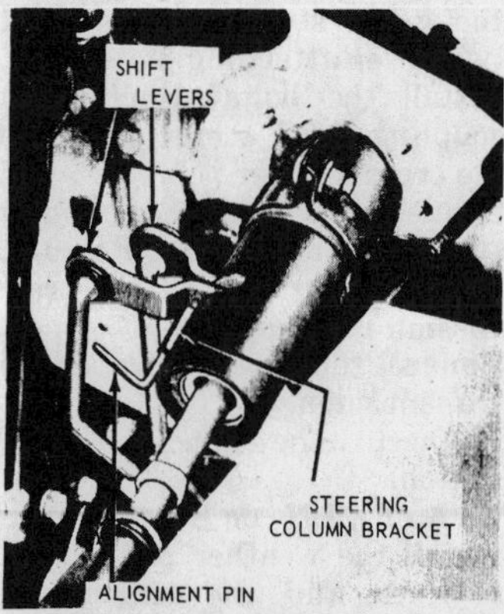

Gearshift linkage adjustment—Bronco (© Ford Motor Co.)

Warner T85N 3-Speed With Overdrive

1. Check the operation of the gear shift linkage for smooth operation.
2. To adjust the gear shift linkage, move the selector lever to the neutral position.
3. If the selector lever position must be changed, disconnect the adjustable rods at the transmission, and install the gauge pin.
4. Loosen the lock nuts and adjust the swivels on the rods so that ends enter the levers freely, but do not put them in. Now adjust the swivels 7 turns to lengthen the rods by that amount. Connect the rods and lock the lock nuts.
5. Move the selector lever through all shift positions as a final check for smooth operation.
6. Adjust the position of the steering column tube if there is interference.

Overdrive Control Cable Adjustment

1. Loosen the overdrive cable lock nut at the overdrive control lever.

2. Position the overdrive cable until there is 1/4″ clearance between the cable control handle and bezel.
3. Move the overdrive control lever to the rear against the stop. When moving the lever, be careful not to move the cable out of position.
4. Tighten the control cable lock nut on the overdrive.

Overdrive Kickdown Switch Adjustment

1. With the accelerator shaft held in the full throttle position, slide the switch up or down on the elongated slots until the accelerator shaft is just touching the switch plunger. If at the closest position the plunger is still not touching the shaft, an adjustment not exceeding 4 turns counterclockwise may be made at the switch plunger.
2. The accelerator shaft can now be returned to the normal position and an additional adjustment of 5 turns counterclockwise performed at the switch plunger.

Transmission Overhaul

Ford 3.03 3-Speed

Disassembly

1. Drain the lubricant, then remove the cover bolts and the case cover.
2. Remove the five attaching screws, then remove the extension housing from the transmission case.
3. Remove the four attaching screws, then remove the front bearing retainer from the case.
4. Remove the filler plug. Working through the filler plug hole, drive the roll pin out of the case and countershaft with a small punch.
5. With a dummy shaft, push the countershaft out of the rear of the case until the countershaft cluster gear can be lowered to the bottom of the case. Remove the countershaft from the rear of the case.
6. Remove the snap-ring. Lift the input gear and shaft from the front of the case. Press the shaft out of the bearing.
7. Remove the snap-ring that holds the speedometer gear onto the shaft. Slide the speedometer gear off the output shaft. Remove the speedometer gear lock ball.
8. Remove the snap-ring that holds the output shaft bearing on the shaft. With a puller, remove the bearing from both the case and shaft.
9. Place both shaft levers in the neutral position.
10. Remove the set screw that holds the detent springs and plugs in the case. Remove a detent spring and plug from the case.
11. Remove the set screw that holds the first and reverse shift fork to the shift rail. Slide first and reverse shift rail out through the rear of the case.
12. Rotate the first and reverse shift fork upward, then lift it from the case.
13. Remove the set screw that holds the second and third shift fork to the shift rail. Rotate the shift rail 90°.
14. With a magnet, lift the interlock plug from the case.
15. Tap on the inner end of the second and third shift rail to remove the expansion plug from the front of the case. Remove the shift rail.
16. Remove second and third detent plug and spring from the detent bore.
17. Rotate the second and third shift fork upward, then lift it from the case.
18. Lift the output shaft out through the top of the case.
19. Working through the front bearing opening, drive the reverse idler shaft out through the rear of the case.
20. Lift the reverse idler gear and two thrust washers from the case.
21. Lift the countershaft gear and thrust washers from the case.
22. Remove the countershaft-to-case retaining pin and any needle bearings which may have fallen into the case.
23. Remove the shift levers and

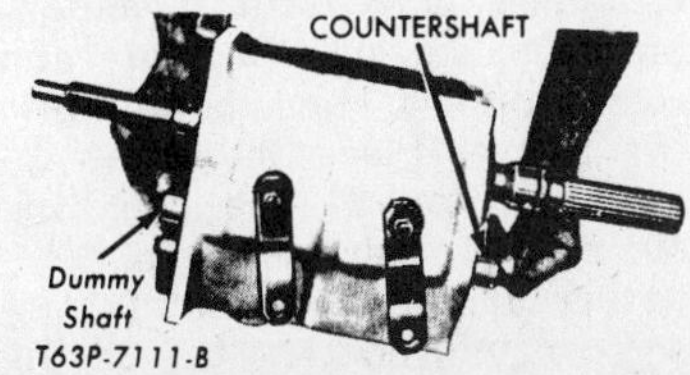

Removing countershaft (© Ford Motor Co.)

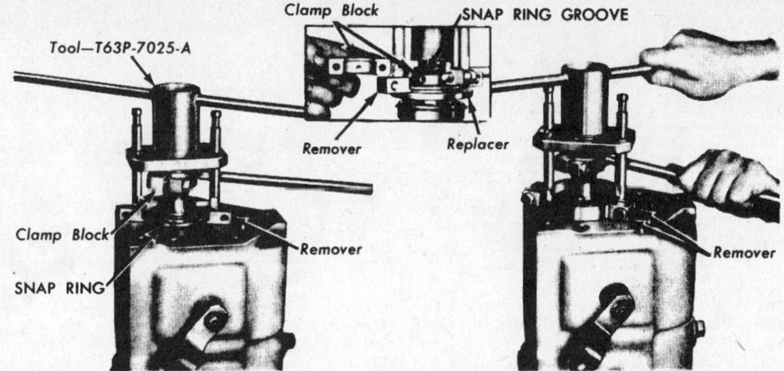

Removing output shaft bearing (© Ford Motor Co.)

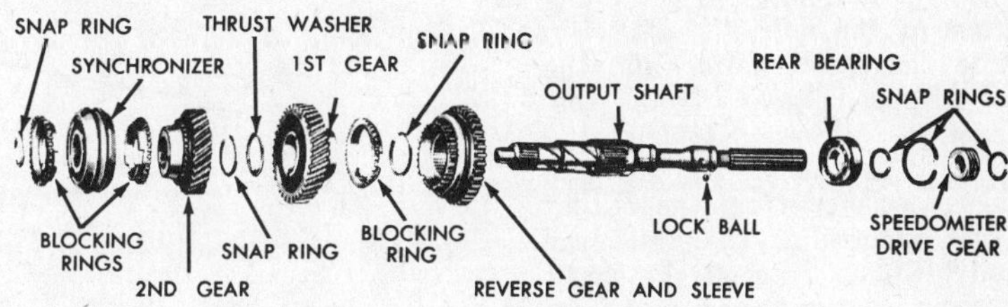

Output shaft disassembled (© Ford Motor Co.)

Rotating second and third speed shift rail (© Ford Motor Co.)

Removing countershaft roll pin (© Ford Motor Co.)

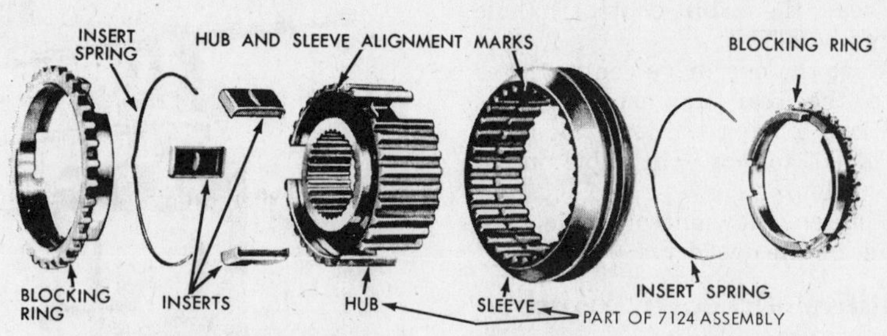

Second and third synchronizer disassembled (© Ford Motor Co.)

shafts from the case. Discard the O-rings.

24. Remove the snap-ring from the front of the output shaft, then slide the synchronizer and the second-speed gear from the shaft.
25. Remove the next snap-ring and thrust washer from the output shaft, then slide the first gear and blocking ring off the shaft.
26. Remove the next snap-ring from the output shaft, then press off the first-reverse synchronizer hub from the shaft.
27. Remove the dummy shaft, 50 bearing rollers and the two retainer washers from the counter-shaft gear.
28. Disassemble the synchronizers.

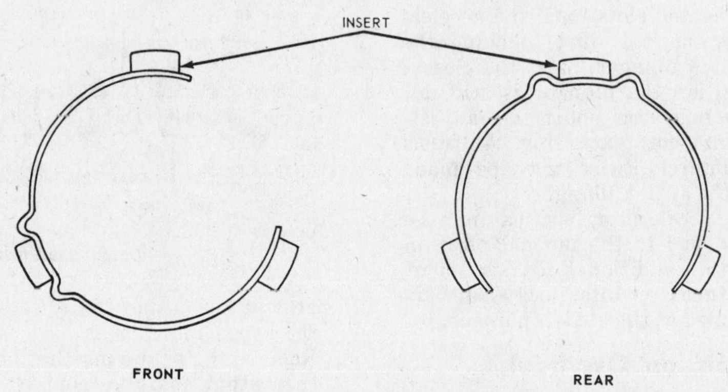

First and reverse synchronizer insert spring (© Ford Motor Co.)

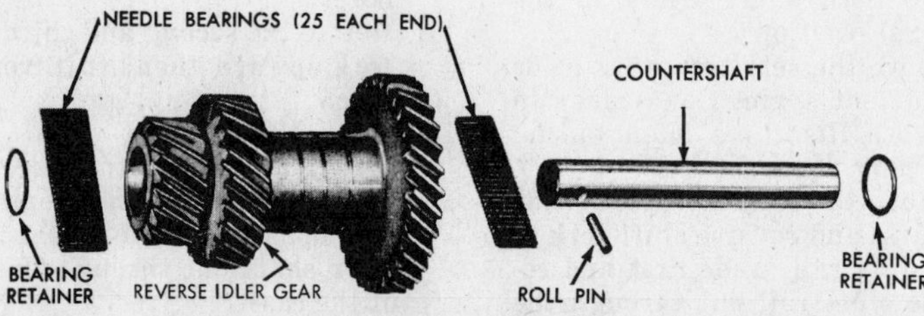

Countershaft gear disassembled (© Ford Motor Co.)

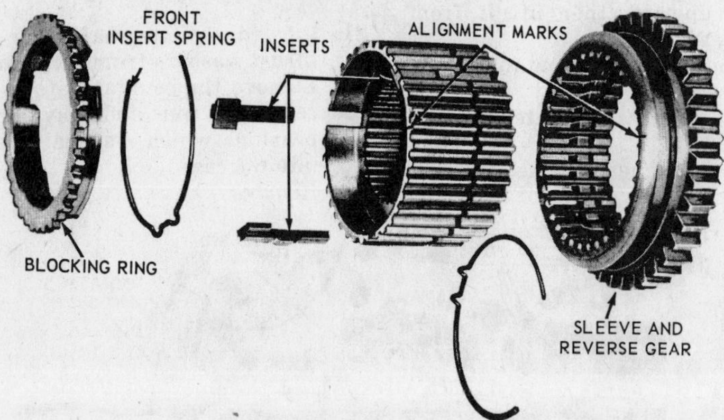

First and reverse synchronizer disassembled (© Ford Motor Co.)

Assembly

1. Coat the bore in each end of the countershaft gear with grease. Hold the dummy shaft in the gear and install 25 bearing rollers and a retainer washer in each end of the gear. Install the countershaft gear, thrust washers and dummy shaft in the case. End-play is controlled with variable thickness thrust washers to .004-.018 in. Let the gear cluster assembly lie in the bottom of the case.
2. Install the idler gear, thrust washers and shaft in the case. Make sure that the thrust washer with the flat side, is at the web end and that the spur gear is toward the rear of the case. Idler gear end-play should be .004-018 in.
3. Install an insert spring into the groove of the first and reverse synchronizer hub. Be sure that the spring covers all insert grooves. Start the hub in the sleeve, being sure the alignment marks are properly indexed. Position the three inserts in the hub and be sure the small end is over the spring and that the shoulder is on the inside of the hub. Slide the sleeve and reverse gear onto the hub until the detent is engaged. Install the other insert spring in the front of the hub to hold the inserts against it.
4. Install one insert spring into a groove of the second-third synchronizer hub. With the alignment marks on the hub and sleeve aligned, start the hub into the sleeve. Place the three inserts on top of the retaining spring and push the assembly together. Install the remaining insert spring, so that the spring ends cover the same slots as do the other springs. Do not stagger

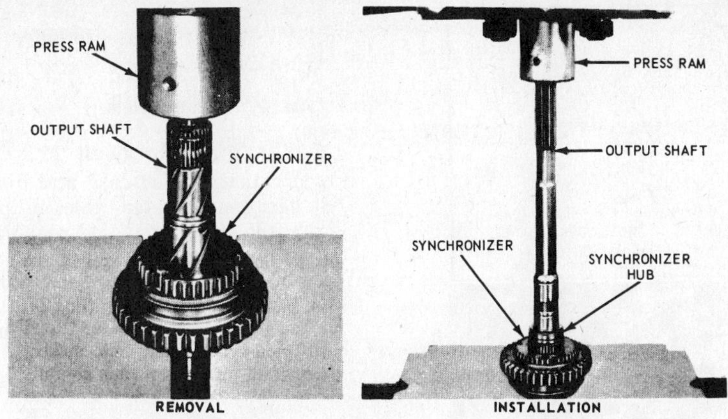

Removing and installing first and reverse synchronizer (© Ford Motor Co.)

the springs. Place a synchronizer blocking ring in each end of the synchronizer sleeve.

5. Lubricate the output shaft splines and machined surfaces with transmission lubricant.
6. Press the first and reverse synchronizer hub onto the output shaft, with the teeth end of the gear facing toward the rear end of the shaft. Secure it with the snap-ring.
7. Place the blocking ring on the tapered machined surface of the first gear.
8. Slide the first gear onto the output shaft, with the blocking ring toward the rear of the shaft. Rotate the gear to engage the three notches in the blocking ring with the synchronizer inserts. Secure the first gear with the thrust washer and snap-ring.
9. Slide the blocking ring onto the tapered, machined surface of the second gear. Slide the second gear, with blocking ring and the second and third gear synchronizer, onto the mainshaft. The tapered machined surface of the second gear must be toward the front of the shaft. Secure the synchronizer with a snap-ring.
10. Install new O-rings onto the two shift lever shafts. Lubricate the shafts with transmission fluid and install them into the case. Secure each shift lever onto its shaft.
11. Coat the bore of the input shaft with a light coat of grease. Install the 15 bearing rollers into the bore.
12. Position the output shaft assembly in the case.
13. Place a detent plug spring and a plug in the case. Place a second and third-speed shift fork in the synchronizer groove. Rotate the fork into position and install the second and third-speed shift rail. Move the rail inward until the detent plug engages the forward notch (second). Secure the fork to the shaft with a set screw. Move the synchronizer to the neutral position.
14. Install the interlock plug in the case.
15. Place first and reverse shift fork in the groove of the first and reverse synchronizer. Rotate the fork into position and install the first and reverse shift rail. Move the rail inward until the center notch is aligned with the detent bore. Secure the fork to the shaft with a set screw. Install the remaining detent plug and spring. Secure the detent spring with the slotted head set screw. Tighten set screw until the head is flush with the case.
16. Install a new expansion plug in the case front.
17. Install the input shaft and gear in the front of the case.
18. Place front bearing retainer (with new gasket in place) on the case with the oil return groove at the bottom. Torque attaching screws to 30 ft. lbs.
19. Install the large snap-ring on the rear bearing. Place the bearing on the output shaft, with the snap-ring end toward the rear of the shaft. Press bearing into place and secure with a snap-ring.
20. Hold the speedometer drive gear lock ball in the detent and slide the speedometer gear into place.
21. Lift the countershaft gear cluster up into place, and, by entering the countershaft at the rear of the case, push the dummy shaft out of the gear and transmission case. Before the countershaft is completely in place, align the roll pin hole in the shaft with the hole in the case.
22. Working through the filler hole, install a roll pin into the case and countershaft.
23. Install filler and drain plugs in the case.
24. Coat a new extension housing gasket with sealer and install it on the case.

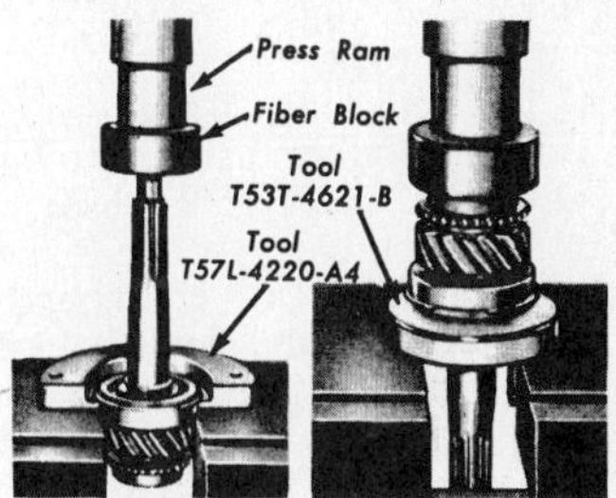

Replacing input shaft bearing (© Ford Motor Co.)

25. Apply sealer to attaching screws and secure extension housing to the case by torquing the screws to 42 to 50 ft. lbs.
26. With transmission in gear, pour lubricant over the entire gear train while rotating the input or output shaft.
27. Install the transmission cover, with a new sealer-coated gasket in place, and torque the nine attaching screws to 14-19 ft. lbs.
28. Check operation of transmission in all of the gear positions.

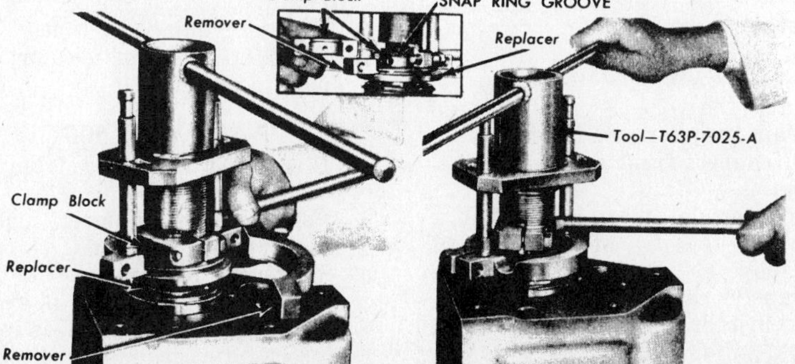

Installing output shaft rear bearing (© Ford Motor Co.)

Transfer Case

Reference

For transfer case overhaul procedures see the General Repair Section.

Transfer Case R&R

Bronco (Dana 20)

1. Raise vehicle, support transfer case shield, then remove shield.

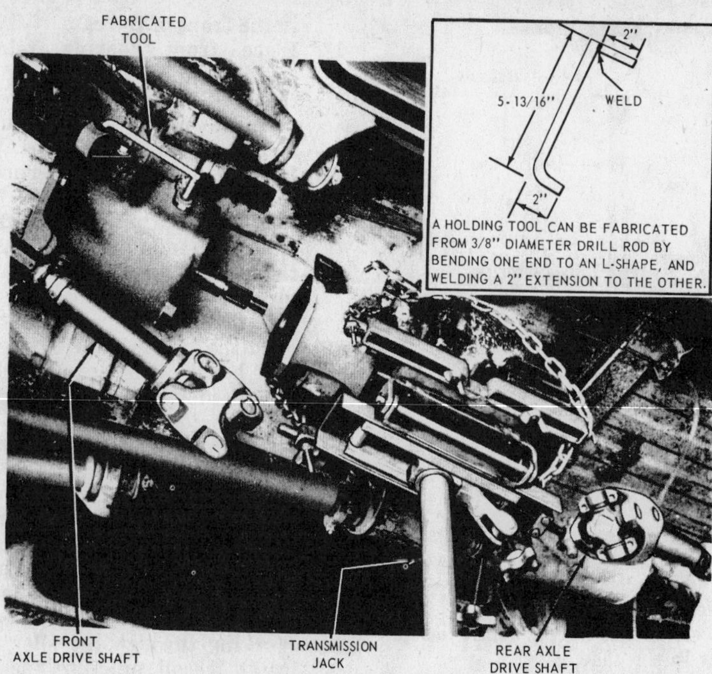

Removing or installing transfer case—Bronco (© Ford Motor Co.)

2. Drain the transmission and transfer case lubricant then disconnect driveshafts from transfer case.
3. Disconnect speedometer cable and shift rods.
4. A tool must be placed in the transmission shift levers to keep the input shaft roller bearings from falling out.
5. Remove the frame crossmember from side frame and transfer case, first raising transmission and removing adapter insulators.
6. Disconnect the shift rod from the transfer case shift lever bracket.
7. Remove the shift lever bracket to transfer case adapter bolt and let the assembly hang.
8. Position a transmission jack under the transfer case, remove the transfer case to transmission attaching bolts, then pull the transfer case back until it clears the transmission output shaft.
9. To install, place the transfer case in position and install the attaching bolts, tightening securely.
10. Install the shift lever to transfer case adapter. Connect the shift rod to the shift lever bracket.
11. Raise the transmission and transfer case high enough to provide clearance for installing the crossmember. Position the upper insulators on the crossmember, install the crossmember, then lower the transmission and install the bolts, tightening securely.
12. Remove fabricated tool from shift levers and install the shift rods.
13. Connect the speedometer cable.
14. Install the forward and rear driveshafts.
15. Fill the transmission and transfer case with lubricant.
16. Install transfer case shield.

Transfer Case R&R

F-100 (4x4) (Dana 21)

1. Raise the vehicle on a hoist and disconnect the front and rear driveshafts.
2. Disconnect the shift rod from transfer case shift lever.
3. Remove transmission extension housing to transfer case attaching bolts and remove the transfer case.
4. To install, position transfer case and new gasket to extension housing and install attaching bolts.
5. Connect shift rod to shift lever.
6. Connect the front and rear driveshafts.
7. Lower vehicle and check for proper operation.

Transfer Case R&R

F-250 (4x4) (Dana 24)

1. Raise the vehicle on a hoist and drain transfer case lubricant.
2. Disconnect front and rear driveshafts.
3. Position a transmission jack under the transfer case and remove mounting bolts. Remove transfer case.
4. To install, raise transfer case on the jack and install nuts on mounting studs.
5. Connect shift rod and speedometer cable.
6. Fill transfer case to filler plug with lubricant.

Transfer Case R&R

F-600 (4x4) (Rockwell 223-C9)

1. Drain transfer case and disconnect speedometer cable.
2. Disconnect front and rear driveshafts and secure with wire or rope *so that they do not hang.*
3. Disconnect parking brake at the bellcrank and secure rod out of the way.
4. Disconnect de-clutch and shift rods.
5. Support the transfer case with a transmission jack and remove the support bracket bolts. Remove transfer case.
6. Install with the use of a transmission jack. Install and tighten mounting bolts.
7. Connect and adjust parking brake rod at the bellcrank.
8. Connect de-clutch and shift rods.
9. Connect front and rear driveshafts.
10. Connect speedometer.
11. Fill transfer case with lubricant.

Automatic Transmission

Reference

For complete automatic transmission overhaul procedures see the General Repair Section.

Shift Linkage Adjustment

F-100, 250, 350

1. Remove and discard shift rod trunnion retainer clip and grommet.
2. Install a new grommet and position selector lever against stop in D position.
3. Shift lever on transmission in D position (third from rear).
4. Adjust shift rod length until trunnion fits easily into the column shift lever, then lengthen rod seven additional turns.
5. Install trunnion in column shift lever and secure with new retainer clip.
6. Tighten trunnion locknut.
7. Check operation of selector lever in all positions.

P-350, 400, 500

1. Disconnect shift rod from column shift lever.
2. Position selector lever against the stop in N position.
3. Shift lever on transmission to N position (fourth from the rear).
4. Rotate trunnion until it is easily inserted in column lever, then turn trunnion two full turns to lengthen rod.

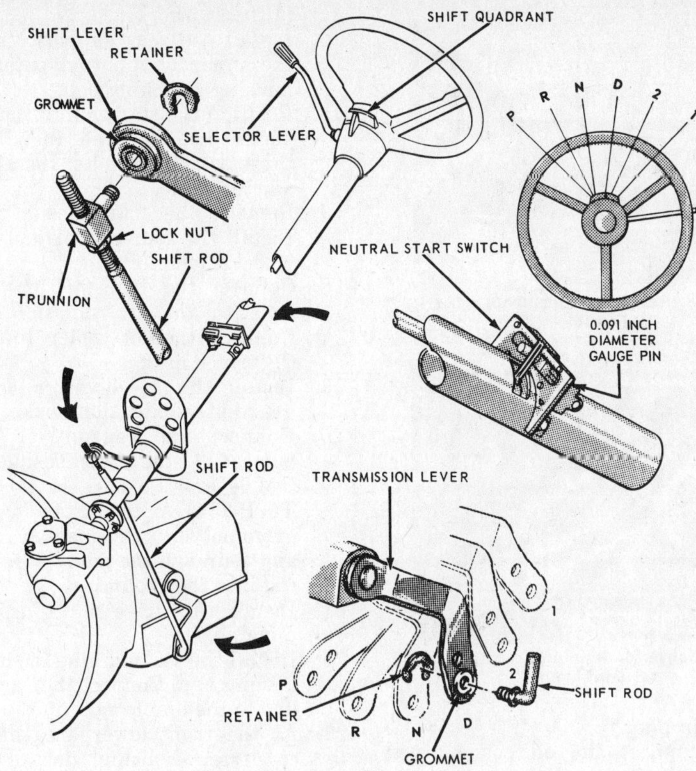

Manual linkage adjustment F-100-250-350 (© Ford Motor Co.)

5. Connect trunnion to column lever.
6. Check operation in all shift positions, adjusting trunnion one turn at a time if necessary. Relocate quadrant to selector indicator if necessary.

Econoline

1. Position selector lever in drive position.
2. Loosen the locknut on the shift rod at the transmission and disconnect the manual shift rod.
3. Place transmission lever in drive position (third from rear).
4. Adjust trunnion so that it fits into the lower column lever, then rotate the trunnion four additional turns to lengthen rod.
5. Connect trunnion and tighten the locknut.
6. Check operation of linkage in all positions, adjusting the rod length one turn at a time if necessary.
7. Adjust selector indicator to quadrant if necessary.

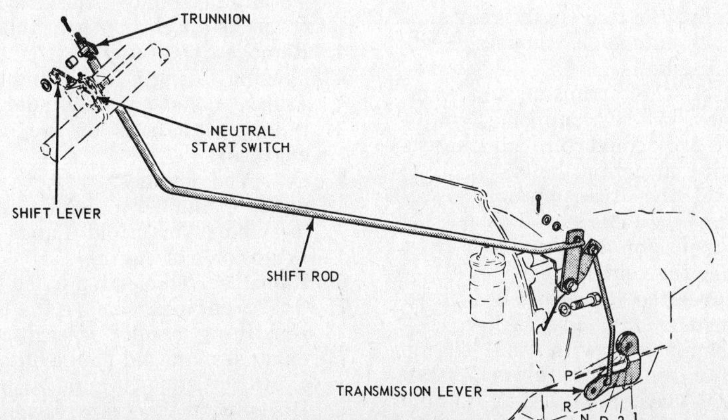

Manual linkage adjustment P-350-400-500 (© Ford Motor Co.)

C4 Automatic Transmission

Econoline, F-100, 250

Intermediate Band Adjustment

1. Clean adjusting screw, apply penetrating lubricant and remove and discard locknut.
2. Install a new locknut (loosely) and torque adjusting screw to 10 ft. lbs., then *back off 1 3/4 turns.*
3. Hold adjusting screw and tighten locknut.

Low-Reverse Band Adjustment

The adjusting procedure is exactly the same as that described for the intermediate band above except the *adjusting screw is backed off 3 full turns.*

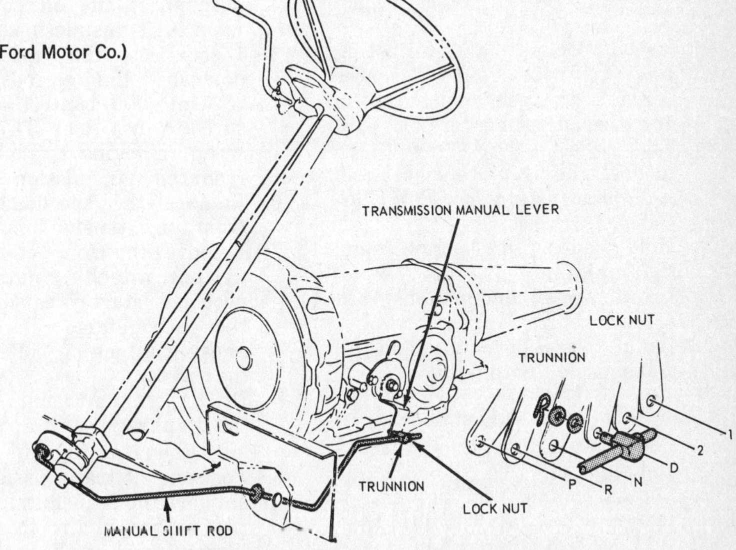

Manual linkage adjustment—Econoline (© Ford Motor Co.)

C-6 Automatic Transmission

Intermediate Band Adjustment

F-100, 250, 350

The adjusting procedure is exactly the same as that described for the C4 intermediate band adjustment above except that the adjusting screw is *backed off 1 1/2 turns.*

MX-HD Automatic Transmission

P-350, 400, 500 and F-350

Front Band Adjustment

1. Disconnect filler tube and drain fluid.

Adjusting intermediate band
(© Ford Motor Co.)

Adjusting low-reverse band
(© Ford Motor Co.)

2. Remove and clean transmission pan and screen. Discard pan gasket.
3. Loosen locknut and adjusting screw, then insert a 1/4″ spacer between the servo piston stem and the adjusting screw.
4. Tighten adjusting screw to 10 in. lbs., then remove spacer and *tighten adjusting screw an additional 3/4 turn.*
5. Hold adjusting screw and tighten locknut.
6. Install screen and pan using a new gasket.
7. Install the filler tube and fill transmission with fluid.

Rear Band Adjustment

1. Clean adjusting screw threads and apply oil.
2. Loosen locknut and tighten adjusting screw to 10 ft. lbs., then *back off adjusting screw 1 1/2 turns.*
3. Hold adjusting screw and tighten locknut.

C4 Automatic Transmission R&R

F-100, 250

1. Raise the vehicle and disconnect the transmission fluid filler tube from the pan. Drain the transmission fluid.
2. At the front lower edge of the converter housing, remove the cover attaching bolts and remove the dust cover. Remove the splash shield at the control levers.
3. Remove the drive shaft or coupling shaft. Remove the converter drain plug. Allow the converter to drain and install the drain plug.

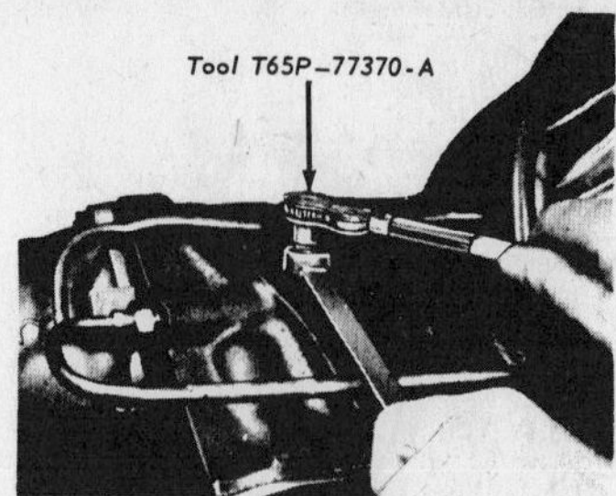

Rear band adjustment
(© Ford Motor Co.)

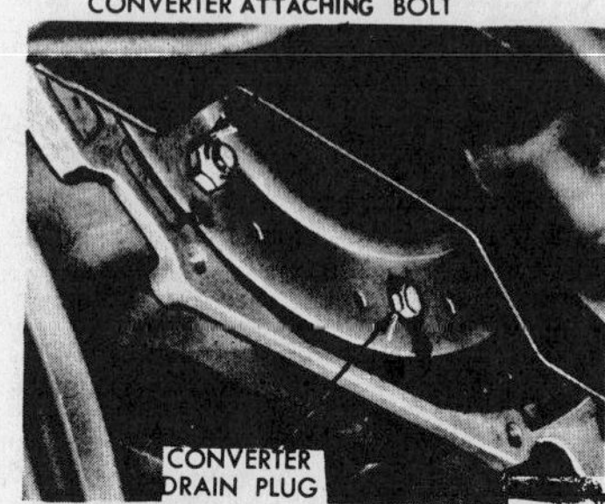

Converter drain plug location
(© Ford Motor Co.)

4. Disconnect the oil cooler lines from the transmission.
5. Disconnect the manual and downshift linkage rods from the transmission control levers. Be sure to use tool T67P-7341-A when removing the manual rod from the transmission lever.
6. Remove the speedometer gear from the extension housing.
7. Remove the four converter to flywheel attaching nuts. Disconnect the starter cable. Remove the three starter to converter housing attaching bolts. Remove the starter.
8. Disconnect the vacuum line from the diaphragm unit and the vacuum line retaining clip.
9. Position the transmission jack to support the transmission. Install the safety chain to hold the transmission on the jack.
10. Remove the two engine rear support crossmember-to-frame attaching bolts.
11. Remove the two engine rear support-to-extension housing attaching bolts.
12. Raise the transmission and remove the rear support. Remove the six converter housing-to-engine attaching bolts.
13. Move the transmission away from the engine. Lower the transmission and remove it from under the vehicle.
14. Secure the transmission in a transmission jack. Align the transmission with the engine and move it into place. Install the converter housing-to-engine attaching bolts. Make sure that the converter studs are entered in the flywheel.
15. Install the rear support. Install the rear support-to-extension housing attaching bolts.
16. Position the starter into the converter housing and install the three attaching bolts. Install the starter cable.
17. Remove the transmission jack. Install the four converter to flywheel attaching nuts.
18. Connect the transmission filler tube to the transmission pan. Connect the oil cooler lines to the transmission.
19. Install the speedometer driven gear in the extension housing.
20. Connect the transmission linkage rods to the transmission control levers. Be sure to use tool T67P-7341-A to install a new grommet into the manual lever, and to install the manual linkage rod into the ground.
21. Install the drive shaft or coupling shaft.
22. Install the vacuum line in the retaining clip. Connect the vacuum line to the diaphragm unit.
23. At the front lower area of the converter housing, install the lower cover and the control lever dust shield. Install the attaching bolts.
24. Secure the fluid filler tube to the pan.
25. Lower the vehicle.
26. Fill the transmission to the proper level.
27. Raise the vehicle and check for transmission fluid leakage. Lower the vehicle and adjust the throttle and manual linkage.

C4 Automatic Transmission R&R

Econoline

1. Working from inside the vehicle, remove the engine compartment cover.
2. Disconnect the neutral start switch wires at the plug connector.
3. If the vehicle is equipped with a V8 engine, remove the flex hose from the air cleaner heat tube.
4. Remove the upper converter housing-to-engine attaching bolts (three bolts on 6-cylinder engines; four bolts on 8-cylinder engines).
5. On V8 engines, remove the upper muffler inlet pipe-to-exhaust manifold flange nut (right side of engine).
6. Raise the vehicle on a hoist.
7. On V8 engines, remove the three remaining muffler inlet pipe-to-exhaust manifold flange nuts and allow the exhaust pipe to hang.
8. Disconnect the transmission filler tube at the pan and drain the transmission fluid.

9. At the front lower edge of the converter housing, remove the dust cover attaching bolts and remove the cover.
10. Remove the converter-to-flywheel attaching nuts. As the flywheel is being rotated, remove the converter drain plug and drain the fluid from the converter.
11. Disconnect the drive shaft from the transmission companion flange and position it out of the way.
12. Remove the bolt retaining the fluid filler tube to the engine and remove the tube.
13. Disconnect the starter cable at the starter. Remove the starter-to-converter housing attaching bolts and remove the starter.
14. Position the engine support bar (Tool T65E-6000-J) to the side rail and engine oil pan flanges.
15. Disconnect the cooler lines from the transmission. Disconnect the vacuum line from the vacuum diaphragm unit.
16. Remove the speedometer driven gear from the extension housing.
17. Disconnect the manual and downshift linkage rods from the transmission control levers.
18. Install the converter drain plug. If the converter is not going to be cleaned, torque the drain plug to specification.
19. Position a transmission jack to support the transmission. Install the safety chain to hold the transmission on the jack.
20. Remove the bolt and nut securing the rear mount to the crossmember. Remove the four bolts retaining the crossmember to the side rails. Then, with the transmission jack, raise the transmission and remove the crossmember.
21. Remove the remaining converter housing-to-engine attaching bolts. Lower the transmission and remove it from under the vehicle.
22. Position the transmission on the jack and secure the transmission and converter to the jack with the safety chain.
23. Raise the transmission and guide the transmission and converter into position. The converter-to-flywheel retaining studs must line up with the holes in the flywheel. The converter hub must enter the end of the crankshaft.
24. Install the converter engine attaching bolts. Install the converter-to-flywheel attaching nuts.
25. Install the crossmember. Install the rear mount-to-crossmember attaching bolt and nut.
26. Remove the safety chain and remove the jack from under the vehicle. Remove the engine support bar.
27. Connect the cooler lines to the transmission. Connect the vacuum line to the vacuum diaphragm unit.
28. Install the speedometer driven gear into the extension housing.
29. Connect the transmission linkage rods to the transmission control levers.
30. Connect the transmission filler tube to the transmission pan. Secure the tube to the engine with the attaching bolt.
31. Install the converter dust cover.
32. Position the starter into the convertor housing and install the attaching bolts. Install the starter cable.
33. Install the drive shaft.
34. If equipped with a V8 engine, install the muffler inlet pipe on the exhaust manifolds and install and torque the three retaining nuts.
35. Lower the vehicle.
36. On V8 engines, install and torque the upper muffler inlet pipe-to-exhaust manifold flange nut.
37. Install the upper converter housing-to-engine attaching bolts.
38. On V8 engines, install the flex hose to the air cleaner heat tube.
39. Connect the neutral start switch wires at the plug connector.
40. Fill the transmission to the proper level with the specified fluid.
41. Raise the vehicle and check for transmission fluid leakage. Lower the vehicle and adjust the throttle and manual linkage.
42. Install the engine compartment cover.

C-6 Automatic Transmission R&R

F-100, 250, 350

1. Drive the vehicle on a hoist, but do not raise at this time.
2. Remove the two upper converter housing-to-engine bolts.
3. Remove the bolt securing the fluid filler tube to the engine cylinder head.
4. Raise the vehicle and drain the fluid from the transmission and converter.
5. Disconnect the coupling shaft or driveshaft from the transmission companion flange and position it out of the way.
6. Disconnect the speedometer cable from the bearing retainer.
7. Disconnect the throttle and manual linkage rods from the levers at the transmission.
8. Disconnect the oil cooler lines from the transmission.
9. Remove the vacuum hose from the vacuum unit. Remove the vacuum line retaining clip.
10. Disconnect the cable from the terminal on the starter motor. Remove the three attaching bolts and remove the starter motor.
11. Remove the four flywheel attaching nuts. Place a wrench on the crankshaft pulley attaching bolt to turn the converter to gain access to the nuts.
12. Remove the two engine rear support crossmember-to-frame attaching bolts.
13. Remove the two engine rear support-to-extension housing attaching bolts.
14. Remove the eight bolts securing the No. 2 crossmember to the frame side rails.
15. Raise the transmission with a transmission jack and remove both crossmembers.
16. Secure the transmission to the jack with the safety chain.
17. Remove the remaining converter housing-to-engine attaching bolts.
18. Move the transmission away from the engine. Lower the transmission and remove it from under the vehicle.
19. Install the converter on the stator support.
20. Secure the transmission to the jack with the safety chain.
21. Rotate the flywheel to place the two converter mounting stud holes in a vertical position.
22. Rotate the converter so that studs and drain plug are in alignment with those in the flywheel.
23. Move the transmission toward the cylinder block until they are in contact. Install attaching bolts.
24. Remove the transmission jack safety chain from around the transmission.
25. Position the No. 2 crossmember to the frame side rails. Install the attaching bolts.
26. Position the engine rear support crossmember to the frame side rails. Install the rear support to extension housing mounting bolts.
27. Lower the transmission and remove the jack.
28. Secure the engine rear support crossmember to the frame side rails with the attaching bolts.
29. Connect the vacuum line to the vacuum diaphragm making sure that the metal tube is secured in the retaining clip.
30. Connect the oil cooler lines to the transmission.
31. Connect the throttle and manual linkage rods to their respective levers on the transmission.
32. Connect the speedometer cable to the bearing retainer.
33. Secure the starter motor in place with the attaching bolts. Con-

nect the cable to the terminal on the starter.
34. Install a new O-ring on the lower end of the transmission filler tube and insert the tube in the case.
35. Secure the converter-to-flywheel attaching nuts. Use a wrench on the crankshaft pulley attaching nut to rotate the flywheel. Do not use a wrench on the converter attaching nuts to rotate it.
36. Install the converter housing dust shield and secure it with the attaching bolts.
37. Connect the coupling shaft drive shaft.
38. Adjust the shift linkage.
39. Lower the vehicle. Then install the two upper converter housing-to-engine bolts.
40. Position the transmission fluid filler tube to the cylinder head and secure with the attaching bolt.
41. Fill the transmission to the correct level with the specified lubricant. Start the engine and shift the transmission thru all ranges, then re-check the fluid level.

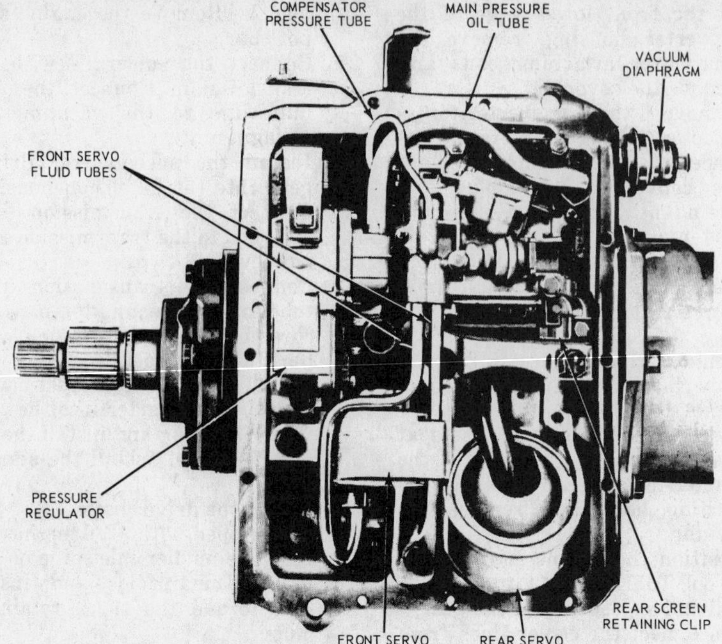

Hydraulic cohtrol system—typical (© Ford Motor Co.)

MX-HD Automatic Transmission R&R

P-350, 400, 500 and F-350

1. Drive the vehicle onto a hoist, but do not raise it at this time.
2. After removing the converter access hole covers, remove the two upper bolts and lockwashers which attach the converter housing to the engine.
3. Raise the vehicle, and remove the cover from the lower front side of the converter housing.
4. Remove the converter drain plug. Drain the converter and reinstall the plug. If desired, the converter may be drained after the unit has been removed from the vehicle.
5. Disconnect the fluid filler tube from the transmission pan.

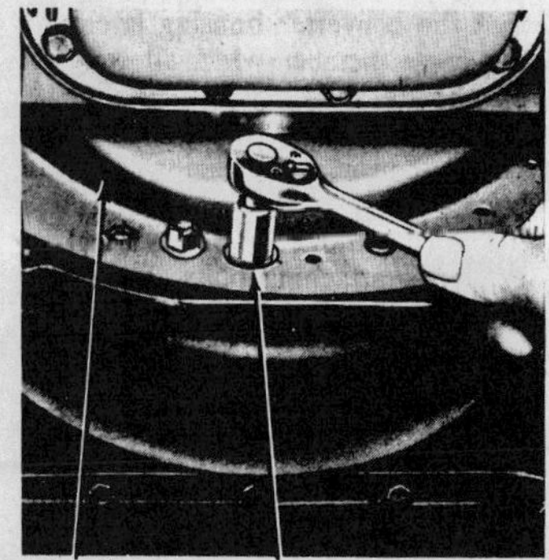

Converter drain plug location (© Ford Motor Co.)

6. When the fluid has stopped draining from the transmission, remove the flywheel to converter bolts. Wedge the converter to hold it in place when the transmission is removed.
7. Disconnect the starter cable from the starter, and disconnect the transmission to body ground cable from the transmission. Remove the starter.
8. On a transmission that has an oil cooler in the radiator, disconnect the fluid lines. On models equipped with a sidemounted cooler, disconnect the radiator-to-cooler coolant lines at the cooler. Plug the lines to prevent coolant loss from the radiator.
9. Disconnect the manual and throttle linkages from the transmission.
10. Remove the vacuum hose from the vacuum unit. Remove the vacuum line retaining clip.
11. Disconnect the speedometer cable from the extension housing, and remove the drive shaft and/or coupling shaft.
12. Remove both engine rear support bolts.
13. With the transmission jack, raise the engine and transmission high enough to remove the engine rear supports.
14. Lower the engine against a floor stand or engine support bar so that the converter housing is clear of the cross member when all weight is off the transmission jack.
15. Remove the remaining converter housing to engine attaching bolts.
16. Remove the flywheel to converter attaching bolts. Then move the assembly toward the rear and lower it, leaving the flywheel attached to the crankshaft. If additional clearance is needed, tilt the rear of the assembly upright slightly and to the rear (enough to allow removal of the six flywheel to crankshaft bolts). Move the assembly to the rear, and remove it.
17. If the converter has been removed from its housing, position the converter in the housing, and install a wedge to prevent the converter from slipping out of the housing.
18. Rotate the converter until the studs are in the vertical position. Position the flywheel on the crankshaft flange and install the six attaching bolts.
19. Raise the transmission and converter with the jack to align it with the engine. Remove the wedge from the converter housing. Carefully move the transmission toward the engine and at the same time engage the converter studs with the holes in the flywheel.
20. Install the converter engine lower bolts.
21. Raise the engine and transmission with the transmission jack, and remove the engine support stand or support bar.
22. Place the engine rear supports in position on the cross member.
23. Lower the engine and transmission against the supports, and at the same time install the support bolts.
24. Rotate the flywheel, and tighten the attaching bolts.

25. Install the four converter-to-flywheel attaching nuts. Install the converter drain plug and the access plate.
26. Connect the oil cooler inlet and outlet lines to the transmission or side-mounted cooler.
27. Install the vacuum line and retaining clip. Install the vacuum hose on the vacuum unit.
28. Coat the universal joint knuckle with transmission fluid, and install the drive shaft and/or coupling shaft.
29. Connect the speedometer cable to the transmission.
30. Connect the manual linkage rod to the transmission manual lever.
31. Connect the throttle linkage to the transmission throttle lever.
32. Install the linkage splash shield.
33. Install the starter motor. Connect the transmission to frame ground cable to the transmission.
34. Connect the fluid filler tube to the pan.
35. Lower the hoist. Then install the upper two converter housing-to-engine bolts.
36. Install the access hole covers, and position the floor mat.
37. Fill the transmission with fluid.
38. Check the transmission, converter assembly, and oil cooler lines for fluid leaks. Then adjust the transmission control linkage.

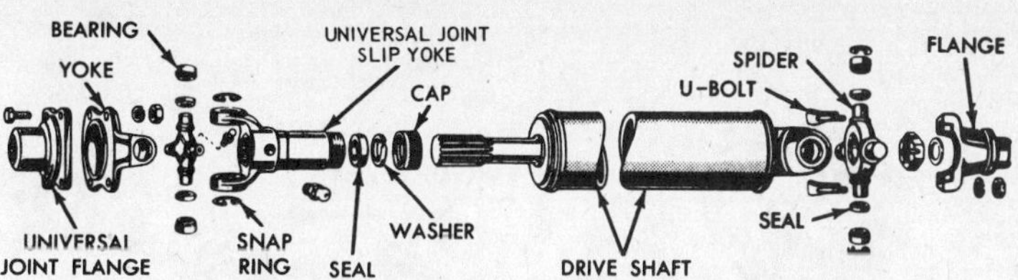

Drive shaft components—115″ wheelbase (© Ford Motor Co.)

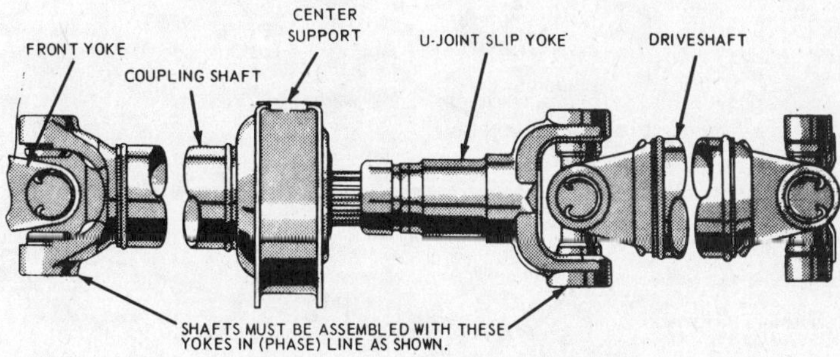

Drive shaft components—132″ wheelbase (© Ford Motor Co.)

Drive Shaft, U Joints

Driveshaft R&R

Except Bronco

1. Disconnect the driveshaft from the rear axle flange.
2. On a 115″ wheelbase vehicle, disconnect the driveshaft rear flange from the flange on the rear axle.
3. If vehicle has a coupling shaft, slide the driveshaft off the coupling splines.
4. Working from the center support nearest to the rear of the vehicle, remove the two attaching bolts and support the bearing.
5. On a vehicle with more than one coupling shaft, disconnect the rear shaft from the front one.
6. Remove the remaining center support attaching bolts and support the bearing.
7. Remove the transmission coupling shaft flange attaching nuts and remove the shaft and center bearing(s) as an assembly.
8. Thoroughly clean all driveshaft components before installing.
9. To install, connect the front flange or joint to the transmission flange.
10. Secure the center bearing to the frame bracket, tightening the bracket attaching bolts securely.
11. If vehicle has more than one coupling shaft, connect the rear shaft to the forward one, then install the remaining center support.
12. Connect the rear universal to the rear axle flange, tightening nuts or bolts securely.
13. Be sure all driveshaft and coupling shaft yokes are in phase.

Driveshaft R&R

Bronco

1. Disconnect the double cardan joint from the transfer case flange and at the rear axle. Remove axle.
2. Remove the front axle by disconnecting the double cardan joint from the flange at the transfer case and the universal joint flange at the front axle. Remove the driveshaft.
3. Install axles connecting the universal joint ends before the cardan ends.

Rear Axles, Suspension

Ford Integral Carrier Axle R&R

1. Loosen the wheel stud nuts and the axle shaft retaining bolts.
2. Disconnect the rear shock absorbers from the spring seat caps. Then raise the rear end of the vehicle frame until the weight is off the rear springs. Place safety stands under the frame in this position.
3. Disconnect the flexible hydraulic line at the frame and disconnect the axle vent hose at the axle connection.
4. Disconnect the parking brake

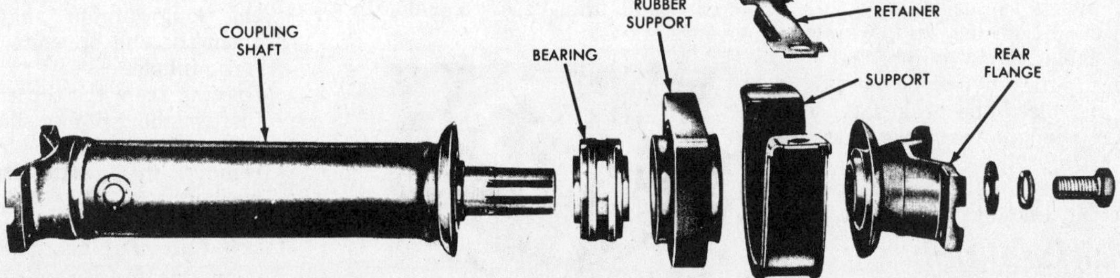

Fig. 227

Coupling shaft and center support bearing (© Ford Motor Co.)

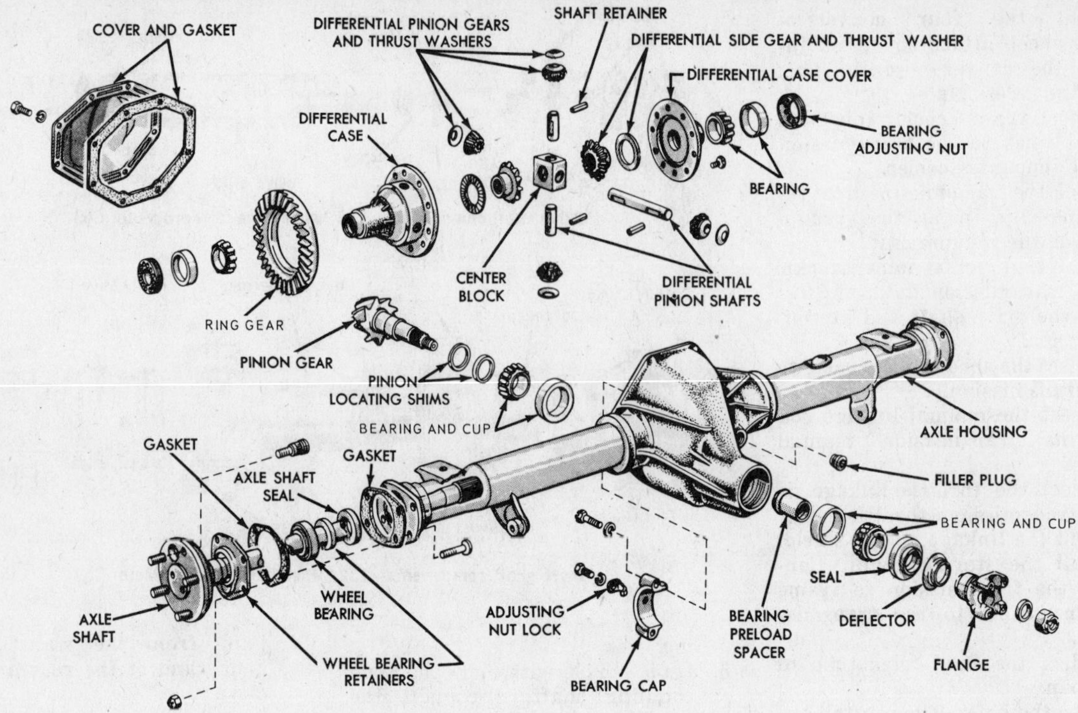

Ford integral carrier differential (© Ford Motor Co.)

cable (if so equipped) at the equalizer, and remove the cables from the cable support brackets.

5. Disconnect the drive shaft from the rear U-joint flange.
6. Remove the nuts from the spring clips (U-bolts), and remove the spring seat caps.
7. Roll the axle from under the vehicle, and drain the lubricant. Remove the wheels. Mount the axle in a work stand.
8. Replace the hub inner grease seal. Install the axle shafts through the housing ends so that they will spline to the differential side gears. Install the shaft retaining bolts and lock washers.
9. After installing rear wheels, roll the axle assembly under the vehicle.
10. Install the spring clips (U-bolts) and spring seat caps. Torque the nuts to 165-185 ft-lbs.
11. Connect the rear shock absorbers.
12. Lower the vehicle to the floor. Connect the drive shaft to the rear universal joint flange.
13. Connect and adjust the parking brake cables (if so equipped).
14. Connect the hydraulic brake hose and bleed the brakes. Also connect the axle vent hose to the axle fitting.
15. Fill the axle with the proper grade and amount of lubricant.

Differential

Description

The integral carrier type differential has hypoid gearing with the centerline of the pinion set below the ring gear centerline. Bearing pre-load and ring gear backlash can be changed by adjusting nuts located behind each differential bearing cup. Pinion bearing pre-load is adjusted by a collapsible spacer on the pinion shaft. Ring and pinion tooth contact is adjusted by adding or removing shims from the area between the rear bearing cone and pinion gear. The differential assembly and drive pinion can be inspected or removed through the housing without having to remove the housing from the truck.

IMPORTANT: Before proceeding with disassembly, perform an inspection as described in the "General Axle Service" section.

Differential Removal

1. Remove the carrier cover and drain the lubricant.
2. Remove the differential bearing adjusting nut locks.
3. Mark one differential bearing cap and the case to help in proper reassembly.
4. Remove the differential bearing caps.
5. Remove the differential case and bearing cups.
6. Remove the pinion nut and pinion flange.
7. Drive the pinion out of the front bearing cone and remove it through the rear of the carrier.
8. Drive the pinion flange seal and the front bearing cone out of the front of the carrier.
9. Remove the pinion rear bearing cone.
10. Measure and record the shim thickness which is found under the bearing cone.

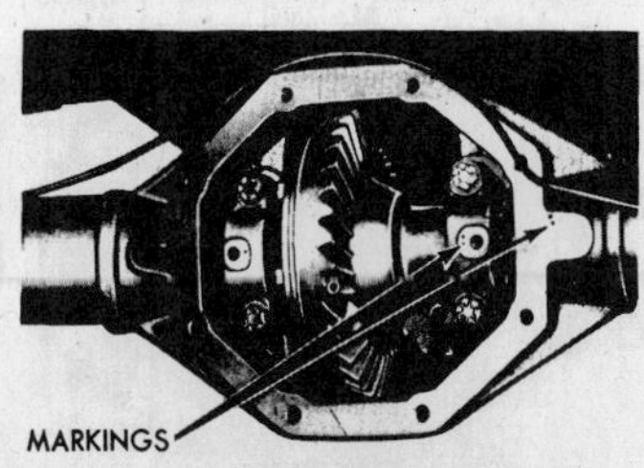

Bearing cap markings
(© Ford Motor Co.)

Disassembly of 4-Pinion Differential Case

1. Remove the old bearings.
2. Press or tap the ring gear from the case.
3. Drive out the three differential pinion shaft lock pins, and separate the differential case.
4. Using a brass drift, drive out the long pinion shaft. Drive from the end opposite the shaft lock pinhole.
5. Driving from the center, remove the two short pinion shafts.
6. Lift out the center block; then remove the gears and thrust washers.

Parts Replacement

Follow cleaning and inspection procedures in the "General Axle Service" section and then determine which parts need replacement. The following information describes replacement operations.

Pinion Bearing Cups

Remove the pinion bearing cups only if worn or damaged.

If the pinion bearing cups are to be replaced, remove them from carrier. Make sure that the new cups are properly seated in their bores. If a 0.0015-inch feeler gauge can be inserted between a cup and the bottom of its bore at any point around the cup, the cup is improperly seated.

When replacing cups, the cone and roller assemblies should also be replaced.

Drive Pinion and Gear Set

A shim is required between the pinion rear bearing cone and the pinion gear in order to align the pinion for correct tooth contact with the ring gear. Each pinion gear is marked with an adjustment number to aid in shim pack selection for that specific gear set.

When installing a new ring and pinion, select the correct shim thickness as follows:

1. Measure the thickness of the original shim with a micrometer.
2. Note the shim adjustment number on both the old and new pinions.
3. Refer to the shim change table. The amount shown in the table under the old pinion number and in line with the new pinion number is the amount of change that should be made to the original shim thickness.

For example, if the old pinion is marked +4, and the new pinion is marked −2, the table indicates that 0.006 inch of shim stock should be added to the original shim pack.

If the original shim pack was lost or if a new carrier casting is being installed, substitute a nominal 0.018 inch shim for the original, and follow the preceding procedure for a trial build-up. If any further shim change is necessary, it will be apparent in the tooth pattern check.

A new ring gear and pinion should always be installed as a matched set (never separately). Be sure that both the drive pinion and the ring gear have the same number.

4. After determining the correct shim thickness, install the new pinion and ring gear as explained later. Differential case, Bearings, and Drive Gear.

If the ring gear runout check (made before disassembly) exceeded specifications, the condition may be caused by a warped gear, a defective case, or excessively worn differential bearings.

To determine the cause of excessive runout, perform the following:

1. Assemble the two halves of the differential case together without the ring gear, and press the two differential side bearings on the case hubs.
2. Position the bearing cups and place the differential case in the carrier.
3. Install the bearing caps and adjusting nuts as described in steps 11 thru 14 under "Installation of Drive Pinion and Differential Case" in this section.
4. IMPORTANT: Tighten the right-hand nut two notches beyond the position where it first contacts the bearing cup. Rotate the differential case several revolutions in each direction while the bearings are loaded to seat the bearings in their cups.
5. Again loosen the right nut to release the preload and make sure that the left nut contacts the bearing cup. Then set a preload of 2 to 3 notches tight at the right nut.
6. With a dial indicator, check the differential case flange runout. If the runout does not now exceed specifications, install a new drive gear. If the runout still exceeds specifications, the ring gear is true and the trouble is caused by defective case or worn bearings.
7. Remove the differential case from the carrier and remove the side bearings from the case.
8. Install new bearings on the case hubs, and again install the differential assembly in the carrier without the ring gear.
9. Check the case runout again with the new bearings and if it is now correct then the old bearings were badly worn. Use the new bearings for assembly. If the runout is still excessive, the case should be replaced.

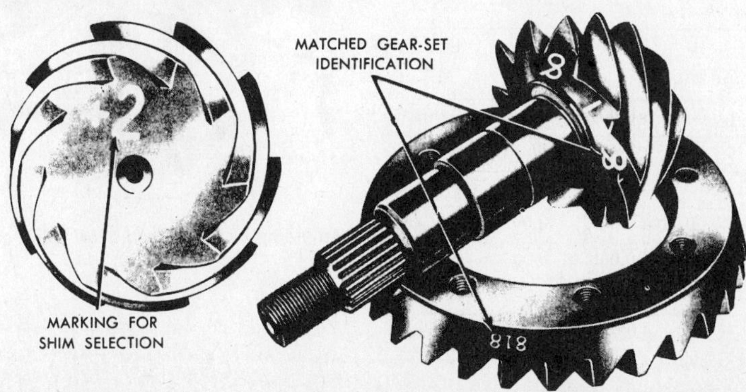

Gear set markings (© Ford Motor Co.)

Assembly of Differential Case

Refer to "General Axle Service" section before proceeding with assembly.

Assembly of 4-Pinion Differential Case

Lubricate all parts thoroughly with axle lubricant during assembly.

1. Place a thrust washer and side gear in the differential case bore.
2. Install the four thrust washers, and place the pinion gears on the side gear. Align the washers and pinion gears with the pinion shaft holes in the case.

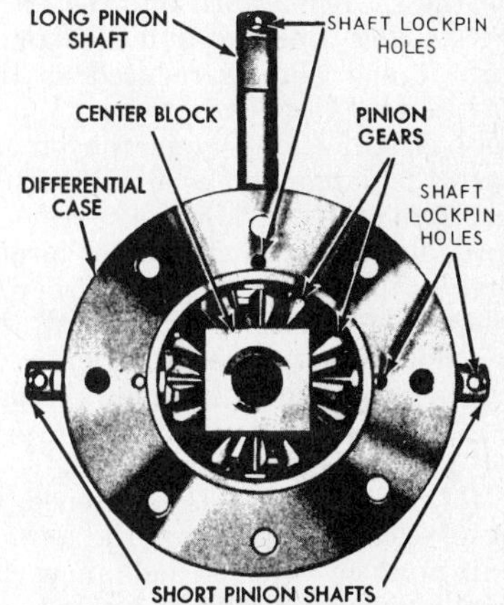

Differential case assembly
(© Ford Motor Co.)

3. Install the center block so that it is aligned with the pinion gear holes and with the holes in the case.
4. Drive in the two short pinion shafts from case exterior. Be sure to align the shaft lock pin holes as each shaft is being driven into place.
5. Drive the long pinion shaft into place from the lock pin hole end of the case.
6. Place the second side gear and thrust washer on top of the four pinion gears, then position the differential case cover so that the three shaft lock pin holes in the cover are aligned with the case holes.
7. Install the three shaft lock pins. Insert a pinion or axle shaft spline in the side gear spline to check for free rotation of the differential case.
8. Install the ring gear on the differential case.
9. Press on the differential bear-

ings.

10. Fill the case with the specified lubricant!

Installation of Drive Pinion and Differential Case

1. Press the shim and pinion rear bearing cone on the pinion shaft.
2. Place a new pinion bearing preload spacer on the pinion shaft.
3. Lubricate the pinion front bearing with axle lubricant.
4. Lubricate and install the pinion front bearing cone.
5. Coat the outside edge of a new oil seal with an oil resistant sealer and install it in the carrier.
6. Insert the drive pinion shaft flange into the seal and hold it firmly against the pinion front bearing cone. Insert the pinion shaft into the flange.
7. Install and tighten a new integral nut and washer on the pinion shaft. As nut is tightened, the shaft is pulled into the front bearing cone and into the flange.

Shaft end play is reduced as the shaft enters the bearing cone. While there is still end play in the pinion shaft, the flange and cone will be felt to bottom on the collapsible spacer.

At this time a much greater torque must be applied to the nut in order to collapse the spacer. At this point, the nut should be tightened very slowly and the pinion shaft end play checked often, so that the pinion bearing preload does not exceed the limits.

If the shaft nut is tightened to cause excessive preload, the pinion shaft must be removed and a new collapsible spacer installed. Do not decrease the preload by loosening the pinion shaft nut. This will remove the compression between the pinion front and rear bearing cones and the collapsible spacer and may cause the front bearing cone to turn on the pinion shaft.

PAINT MARKING INDICATES POSITION IN WHICH GEARS WERE LAPPED

Gear set timing marks (© Ford Motor Co.)

8. As soon as there is preload on the bearings, seat the bearing rollers by turning the pinion shaft in both directions several times.
9. Adjust the bearing preload to specification.
10. Lightly lubricate the bearing bores.
11. Place the cups on the bearings and set the case assembly in the carrier.

If the gear set is of the non-hunting or partial non-hunting type, assemble the differential case and ring gear assembly in the carrier so that the marked tooth on the pinion and the marked teeth on the ring gear coincide. If this is not done, the noise level would be obvious and failure might soon result.

When installing the hunting type gear set (no "timing marks"), assemble the differential case and ring gear assembly in the carrier without having to match any specific gear teeth.

12. Slide the case assembly along the bores until a slight amount of backlash is felt between the gear teeth. Hold the differential case in place.
13. Position the adjusting nuts in the bores so that they just contact the bearing cups.
14. Carefully position the bearing caps on the carrier casting and while tightening the bolts, turn the adjusting nut.
15. If the adjusting nuts do not turn easily as the cap bolts are tightened, remove the caps and again inspect for damaged threads or incorrectly positioned caps. Loosen the cap bolts, and torque them to only 5 ft-lbs. before making adjustments. See "General Axle Service" section for backlash and preload adjustment.

Drive Pinion Adjusting Shim Thickness Changes—Inches—Removable Carrier Type

New Pinion Marking	*Old Pinion Marking*								
	−4	*−3*	*−2*	*−1*	*0*	*+1*	*+2*	*+3*	*+4*
+4	+0.008	+0.007	+0.006	+0.005	+0.004	+0.003	+0.002	+0.001	0
+3	+0.007	+0.006	+0.005	+0.004	+0.003	+0.002	+0.001	0	−0.001
+2	+0.006	+0.005	+0.004	+0.003	+0.002	+0.001	0	−0.001	−0.002
+1	+0.005	+0.004	+0.003	+0.002	+0.001	0	−0.001	−0.002	−0.003
0	+0.004	+0.003	+0.002	+0.001	0	−0.001	−0.002	−0.003	−0.004
−1	+0.003	+0.002	+0.001	0	−0.001	−0.002	−0.003	−0.004	−0.005
−2	+0.002	+0.001	0	−0.001	−0.002	−0.003	−0.004	−0.005	−0.006
−3	+0.001	0	−0.001	−0.002	−0.003	−0.004	−0.005	−0.006	−0.007
−4	0	−0.001	−0.002	−0.003	−0.004	−0.005	−0.006	−0.007	−0.008

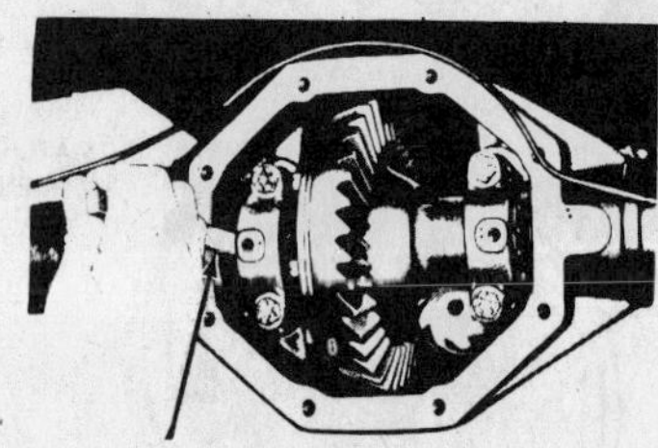

Adjusting back lash and bearing preload (© Ford Motor Co.)

Rear Axle Adjustments—Ford

Rear Axle Type	*Integral Carrier 2300 lbs. Inches*
Backlash Between Ring Gear and Pinion	0.008-0.012
Backlash Variation between Teeth	Max 0.002
Runout of Backface of Ring Gears as Assembled	Max 0.002
Thickness: Differential Side Gear Thrust Washers	0.030-0.032
Differential Pinion Gear Thrust Washers	0.030-0.032
Ring Bearing Cone to Pinion Gear Nominal Shim Shims Available	0.017 0.008-0.024

Torque Chart

Rear Axle Type	*Integral Carrier 2300 lbs. Foot-Pounds*
Rear Cover Bolts	10-17
Differential Bearing Cap Screws	40-55
Differential Bearing Adjusting Nut Lock Bolts	12-20
Universal Joint Flange Axle End to Universal Joint Bearing Assembly Nuts	10-14
Ring Gear Attaching Cap Screws	40-55
Rear Axle Shaft Bearing Retaining Nuts	30-35
Minimum Torque Required to Tighten Pinion Flange Lock Nut to Obtain Correct Pinion Bearing Preload	140
Pinion Bearing Preload (Inch-Pounds) New Bearings Used Bearings	 17-27 8-12
Differential Bearing Preload	2-3 Notches Tight
Carrier to Housing Stud Nuts	—
Pinion Retainer to Carrier Bolts	—

Ford Removable (Banjo Type) Carrier Axle

Carrier Assembly R&R

1. Raise the vehicle on a hoist and remove the two rear wheel and tire assemblies.
2. Remove the two brake drums (3 Tinnerman nuts at each drum) from the axle shaft flange studs. If difficulty is experienced in removing the drums, back off the brake shoes.
3. Working through the hole provided in each axle shaft flange, remove the nuts that secure the rear wheel bearing retainer plate. Pull each axle shaft assembly out of the axle housing using axle shaft remover, Tool 4235-C. Care must be exercised to prevent damage to oil seal, if so equipped. Any roughing or cutting of the seal element during removal or installation can result in early seal failure. Install a nut on one of the brake carrier plate attaching bolts to hold the plate to the axle housing after the shaft has been removed. Whenever a rear axle shaft is replaced, the wheel bearing oil seals must be replaced. Remove the seals with tool 1175-AB.
4. Make scribe marks on the drive shaft end yoke and the axle U-joint flange to insure proper position at assembly. Disconnect the drive shaft at the rear axle U-joint, remove the drive shaft from the transmission extension housing. Install oil seal replacer tool T57P-7657-A in the housing to prevent transmission leakage.
5. Place a drain pan under the carrier and housing, remove the carrier attaching nuts, and drain the axle. Remove the carrier assembly from the axle housing.
6. Synthetic wheel bearing seals must not be cleaned, soaked or washed in cleaning solvent. Clean the axle housing and shafts using kerosene and swabs. To avoid contamination of the grease in the sealed ball bearings, do not allow any quantity of solvent directly on the wheel bearings. Clean the mating surfaces of the axle housing and carrier.
7. Position the differential carrier on the studs in the axle housing using a new gasket between carrier and housing. Install the carrier-to-housing attaching nuts.
8. Remove the oil seal replacer tool from the transmission extension housing. Position the drive shaft so that the front U-joint slip yoke splines to the transmission output shaft.
9. Connect the drive shaft to the axle U-joint flange, aligning the scribe marks made on the drive shaft end yoke and the axle U-joint flange during the removal procedure. Install the U-bolts and nuts and torque to specifications.
10. Wipe a small amount of an oil-resistant sealer on the outer edge of each seal before it is installed. Do not put any of the sealer on the sealing lip. Install the oil seals in the ends of the rear axle housing with tool shown in illustration.
11. Install the two axle shaft assemblies in the axle housing. Care must be exercised to prevent damage to the oil seals. The shorter shaft goes into the left side of the housing. When installing an axle shaft, place a new gasket between the housing flange and the brake backing plate, and carefully slide the axle shaft into the housing so that the rough forging of the shaft will not damage the oil seal. Start the axle splines into the differential side gear, and push the shaft in until the bearing bottoms in the housing.
12. Install the bearing retainer plates on the attaching bolts on the axle housing flanges. Install and tighten the nuts on the bolts.
13. Install the two rear brake drums and the drum attaching nuts.
14. Install the rear wheel and tire assemblies.
15. If the rear brake shoes were backed off, adjust the brakes.
16. Fill the rear axle with lubricant.

Axle Housing R&R

1. Remove the carrier assembly from the axle housing as outlined in the foregoing procedure.
2. Position safety stands under the rear frame members, and support the axle housing with either a floor jack or hoist.
3. Disengage the brake line from the clips that retain the line to the axle housing.
4. Disconnect the vent tube from the rear axle housing.
5. Remove the brake backing plate assemblies from the axle housing, and support them with wire. Do not disconnect the brake line.
6. Disconnect each rear shock absorber from the mounting bracket stud on the axle housing.
7. Lower the rear axle slightly to reduce some of the spring tension. At each rear spring, remove the spring clip (U-bolt) nuts, spring clips, and spring seat caps.

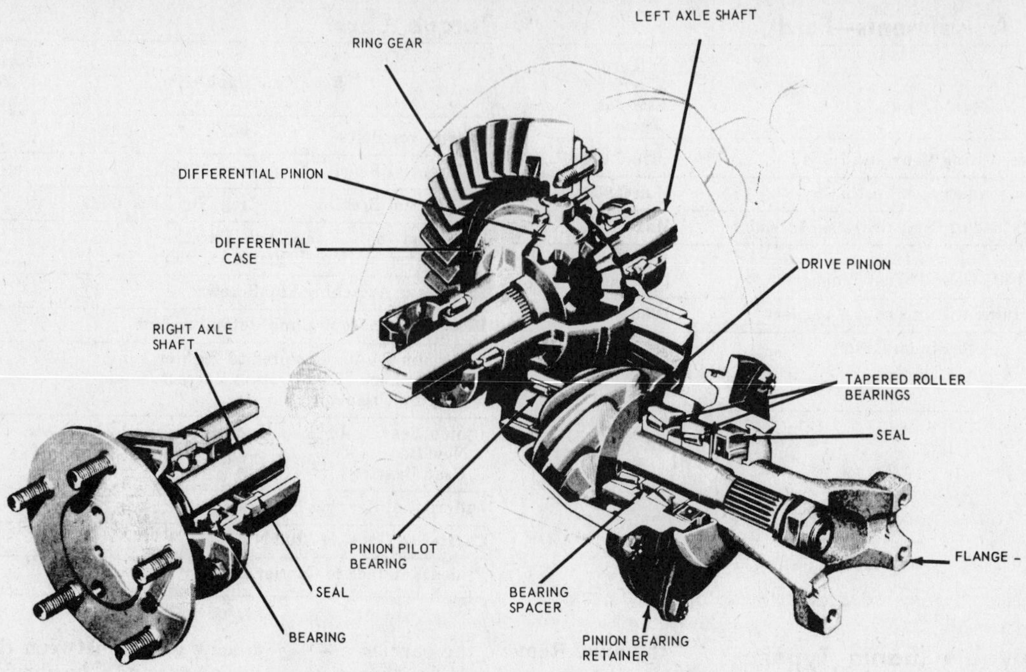

Ford banjo (removable carrier) type differential (© Ford Motor Co.)

8. Remove the rear axle housing from under the vehicle. If the axle housing is new, install a new vent. The hose attaching portion must face toward the front of the vehicle.
9. Install new rear wheel bearing oil seals in the ends of the rear axle housing. If leather-type wheel bearing service seals are to be installed, soak the new rear wheel bearing oil seals in SAE 10 oil for ½ hour before installation.
10. Position the rear axle housing under the rear springs. Install the spring clips (U-bolts), spring seat caps, and nuts. *Torque the spring clip nuts evenly.*
11. If a new axle housing is being installed, remove the bolts that attach the carrier plate and bearing retainer from the old housing flanges. Position the bolts in the new housing flanges to hold the brake backing plates in position. Install the backing plates with new gaskets between the housing flange and the brake backing plate.
12. Connect the vent tube to the axle housing.
13. Position the brake line to the axle housing, and secure with the retaining clips.
14. Raise the rear axle housing and springs enough to allow connecting the rear shock absorbers to the mounting bracket studs on the axle housing.
15. Install the carrier assembly and the two axle shaft assemblies in the axle housing as outlined in this section.

Differential

Description

This differential has a banjo (removable carrier) type housing in which the pinion is mounted below the ring gear centerline.

The pinion gear and bearings are connected to a pinion retainer which is bolted to the carrier. The pinion shaft is supported in front of the gear by two roller bearings and a spacer—a collapsible spacer for a 8¾ or 9 inch ring gear and solid spacer used with the 9⅜ inch ring gear. Tooth contact of the ring and pinion can be changed by adding or removing shims from between the pinion retainer and the carrier housing.

Do not attempt to interchange axle shafts, since the left is shorter than the right.

Disassembly of Differential

IMPORTANT: Before proceeding with disassembly consult the "General Axle Service" section for instructions on pre-assembly inspections and checks.

1. Punch-mark differential bearing cap and its corresponding support and a bearing adjusting nut and the carrier to aid in proper reassembly.
2. Remove the differential assembly from the carrier.
3. Remove the differential bearings.

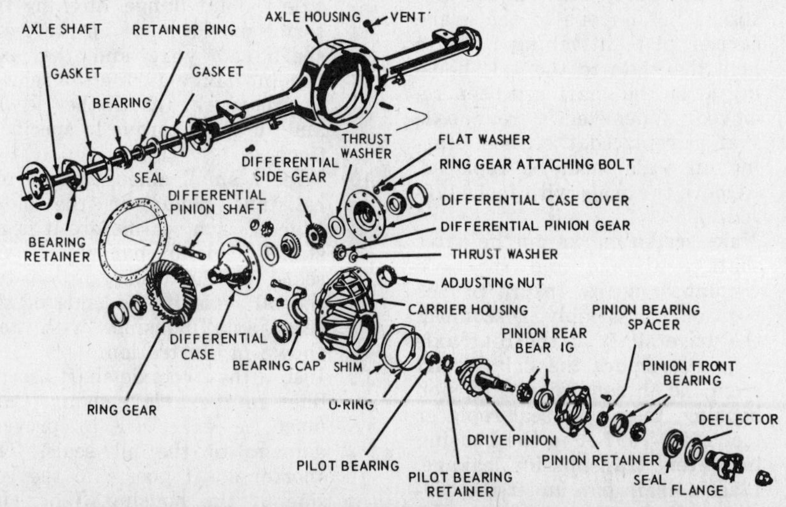

Ford banjo type differential—exploded view (© Ford Motor Co.)

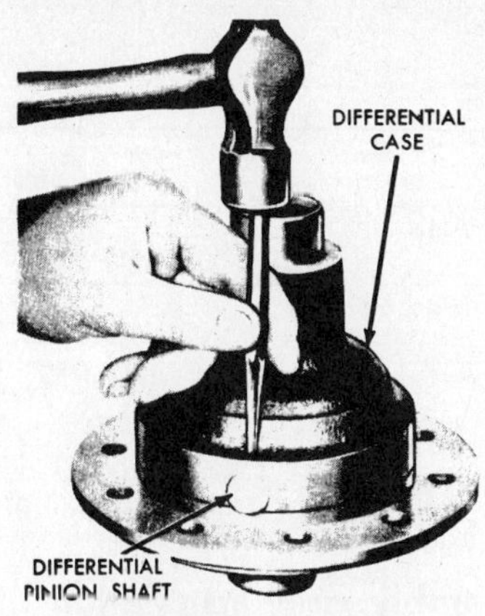

Pinion shaft lockpin removal
(© Ford Motor Co.)

4. Mark the differential case, cover, and ring gear for assembly in the original position.
5. Remove the ring gear from the case.
6. Drive out the differential pinion shaft lock pin and separate the 2-piece differential case.
7. Remove the pinion shaft.
8. Remove the gears and thrust washers.

Removal and Disassembly of Drive Pinion and Bearing Retainer

1. Remove the pinion shaft nut and U-joint flange.
2. Remove the pinion seal, pinion, bearing, and retainer assembly from the carrier. Measure and record the shim thickness with a micrometer. If a new gear set is installed, a new shim will be necessary. Be very careful to avoid damage to the MOUNTING surfaces of the retainer and carrier.
3. Place a protective sleeve (hose) on the pinion pilot bearing surface. Press the pinion shaft out of the front and rear bearing cones.

Pilot Bearing

1. Drive out the pilot bearing and bearing retainer together.
2. Drive in the new bearing until it bottoms.
3. Install a new pilot bearing retainer with the concave side up.

Pinion Bearing Cups

Replace the pinion bearing cups from the retainer only if they are worn or damaged.

After installing new cups, make sure they are seated in the retainer by trying to insert a 0.0015-inch feeler gauge between the cup and the bottom of the bore. When replacing the cups, the cone and roller assemblies should also be replaced.

Assembly

Drive Pinion and Gear Set

When replacing a ring gear and pinion, note that the original factory installed shim is of the correct thickness to adjust for individual variations in both the carrier housing dimension and in the original gear set dimension. Therefore, to select the correct shim thickness for the new gear set to be installed, follow these steps:

1. Using a micrometer, measure original shim thickness and duplicate this thickness when installing and use the replacement carrier assembly or drive pinion. If further shim change is necessary, it will show up in tooth pattern check (see "General Axle Service" section). Check the shim adjustment number on the new and old pinions and refer to the chart to determine the amount of shim thickness change.
2. If the original shim is lost, substitute a nominal shim for the original and check tooth pattern to decide if another shim change is necessary (see axle adjustment chart for specifications). A new ring gear and pinion should always be installed as a matched set (never separately). Be sure the same identifying (matching) number, painted in white, appears on the ring gear and on the drive pinion head.
3. After determining the correct shim thickness, install the new ring and pinion.

Assembly and Installation of Drive Pinion and Bearing Retainer

Collapsible Spacer

1. Install the pinion rear bearing cone and a new spacer on the pinion shaft.

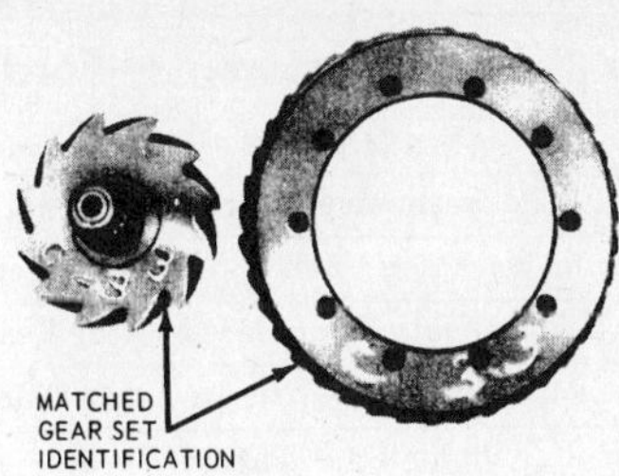

Pinion and ring gear markings
(© Ford Motor Co.)

2. Place the bearing retainer on the pinion shaft, and install the front bearing cone and roller. Press the front bearing cone and roller into position. Don't crush the bearing spacer.
3. Lubricate the O-ring with axle lubricant and snap it into the pinion retainer. Be careful not to twist it. Also lubricate both pinion bearings.
4. Place the proper pinion locating shim on the carrier housing and install the pinion and retainer assembly, being careful not to pinch the O-ring (see "General Axle Service" section for pinion selection).
5. Install and torque the pinion retainer attaching bolts.
6. Install a new pinion oil seal in the bearing retainer.
7. Install the U-joint flange.
8. Start a new integral nut (lubricated) and washer on the pinion shaft.
9. Hold the flange and torque the pinion shaft nut *no tighter than 175 ft.-lbs.*
10. Check the pinion bearing preload. Correct preload occurs when the torque required to rotate the pinion in the retainer meets specifications. If the torque required to rotate the pinion is less than specified, tighten the pinion shaft nut a little at a time until the proper preload is created. Do not overtighten the nut. If excessive pre-load is obtained as a result of overtightening, replace the collapsible bearing spacer.

Do not back off the pinion shaft

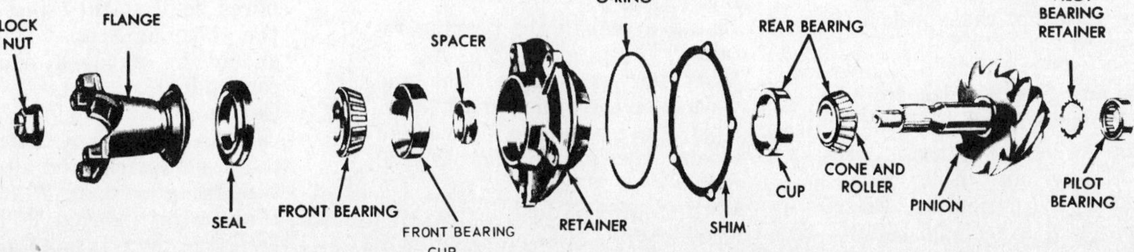

Pinion and bearing retainer components (© Ford Motor Co.)

Rear Axle Adjustments—Ford

Description	Inch
Backlash Between Ring Gear and Pinion	0.008–0.012
Maximum Backlash Variation Between Teeth	0.003
Maximum Runout of Backface of Ring Gear	0.003
Differential Side Gear Thrust Washer Thickness	0.030–0.032
Differential Pinion Gear Thrust Washer Thickness	0.030–0.032

Description	Inch
Nominal Locating Shim Removable Carrier	0.015
Shims Available (Steps of 0.001) Removable Carrier	0.010–0.029
Differential Bearing Preload (Case Spread) New Bearings	0.008–0.012
Original Bearings	0.003–0.005

nut to establish pinion bearing preload. If the torque on the pinion shaft nut is less than 175 ft-lbs. after bearing preload is established, a new collapsible spacer must be used.

Axle with Solid Pinion Bearing Spacer

A vehicle having a large engine and standard transmission will usually require a solid spacer between the pinion bearings. Selecting the right size spacer is necessary in obtaining correct preload. The following procedure describes proper spacer selection:

1. Install the drive pinion rear bearing cone and roller assembly on the pinion shaft.
2. Select a new solid spacer of a larger size (0.485 inch thick), and slide it over the pinion shaft against the rear bearing. The pinion bearing preload can be accurately measured only when the pinion shaft nut is torqued to 180-220 ft-lbs. This much torque would damage the bearings if a smaller spacer were used; therefor, try the largest spacer first. Then, if the bearings are too loose, the size of the spacer can be decreased until the correct preload is obtained.
3. Position the bearing retainer and cup assembly on the shaft and press on the front bearing cone and roller.
4. Mount the retainer in a holding fixture and place the slinger over the pinion shaft and against the front bearing.
5. Install the U-joint flange.
6. Hold the flange and install and torque the old pinion shaft nut to 180-220 ft-lbs. While tightening the nut, determine bearing preload by rotating the bearing retainer—if a slight drag exists in the rotation, then preload is present.

Determining Spacer Size from Preload Reading

1. If bearing drag indicates preload, apply an in-lb. torque wrench to the pinion nut. Effort to turn the shaft should be 12½ to 32½ in-lbs.
2. If preload is correct, continue with assembly procedure.
3. If preload exists, but is below specification, select the correct spacer from the list and complete assembly.

Determining Spacer Size from End Play Reading

1. If no perceptible preload is felt when rotating the pinion shaft, install a dial indicator with the point resting on the end of the pinion gear shaft (companion flange end).
2. Use both hands to squeeze the pinion shaft and the bearing retainer together and record the end-play reading.
3. Disassemble the pinion shaft and retainer and install the correct spacer.
4. Proceed with assembly of the pinion shaft and retainer.

Final Assembly of Pinion and Retainer

1. Install the drive pinion rear bearing cone and roller assembly on the pinion shaft.
2. Slide the correct spacer against the rear bearing.
3. Position the bearing retainer and cup assembly on the pinion shaft and press on the front bearing cone and roller.
4. Lubricate a new O-ring with axle lubricant and snap it onto the pinion retainer taking care not to twist it.
5. Place the proper shim on the carrier housing and install the pinion and retainer assembly, being careful not to pinch the O-ring.
6. Install and torque the pinion retainer bolts.
7. Place the slinger over the pinion shaft and against the front bearing.
8. Install a seal in the bearing retainer.
9. Start a new integral nut and washer on the pinion shaft.
10. Hold the companion flange and torque the pinion nut to 200 ft-lbs.
11. With a new seal installed, pinion bearing preload should now read 17 to 32 in-lbs. for new pinion bearings and new seal, or 8 to 14 in-lbs. for original bearings and a new seal.

Assembly and Installation of Differential Case

1. Place a side gear and thrust washer in the differential case bore. Lubricate all differential parts liberally with axle lubricant during assembly.
2. Carefully drive the pinion shaft into the case only far enough to hold a pinion thrust washer and pinion gear.
3. Place the second pinion and thrust washer in position, and drive the pinion shaft into place. Carefully line up the pinion shaft lock pin holes.
4. Place the second side gear and thrust washer in position and install the differential case cover. Install the pinion shaft lock pin. Free rotation of the differential gears can be checked by inserting an axle or pinion shaft spline in the side gear spline.
5. Insert two 7/16 (N.F.) bolts two inches long through the differential case flange, and turn them three or four times into the ring gear as a guide in aligning the ring gear bolt holes. Press or tap the ring gear into position.
6. Install and alternately tighten the ring gear bolts evenly.
7. Press on the differential bearings.
8. Apply a thin coating of lubricant on the carrier bearing bores. Place the cups on the bearings and set the differential case assembly in the carrier.
9. Slide the assembly along the bores until a slight amount of backlash is felt between the gear teeth.
10. Set the adjusting nuts in the bores so that they just contact the bearing cups. The nuts should be engaged equally on each side.
11. Carefully position the bearing caps on the carrier, matching up the punch-marks and alternately tightening bolts to 70-80 ft-lbs.
12. If the adjusting nuts do not turn freely as the cap bolts are tightened, remove the bearing caps and inspect for damaged threads

Ford Axle Torque Limits (Ft. Lbs.)

Description	Ft-Lbs
Differential Bearing Cap Bolts	70-85
Differential Bearing Adjusting Nut Lock	12-25
Carrier to Housing Stud Nuts	30-40
Pinion Retainer to Carrier Bolts	30-45
Ring Gear Attaching Bolts	65-80
Rear Axle Shaft Bearing Retainer Bolts Light Duty	30-40
Heavy Duty	50-70

[1] This rotating torque may fluctuate up to 40 ft. lbs.

Description	Ft-Lbs
Minimum torque required to turn axle shaft and side gear with one wheel on the ground (Traction-Lok)	40
Bench Check with new plates	100 to 250[1]
Original plates (Traction-Lok)	40 Minimum
Minimum Torque Required to Tighten Pinion Nut to Obtain Correct Pinion Bearing Preload	175
Pinion Bearing Preload (Inch-Pounds) New Bearings	22-32
Used Bearings	8-14
Oil Filter Plug	25-50

or incorrectly positioned caps.

13. Adjust the backlash between the ring gear and pinion and the differential bearing preload.

Backlash and Differential Bearing Preload Adjustment

1. Loosen the cap bolts, then tighten them to only 35 ft-lbs torque before making adjustments. The left adjusting nut is on the ring gear side of the carrier. The right nut is on the pinion side. Tightening the left nut moves the ring gear into the pinion to decrease backlash, and tightening the right nut moves the ring gear away.
2. Loosen the right nut until it is away from the cup. Tighten the left nut until the ring gear is just forced into the pinion with no backlash. (Recheck the right nut at this time to be sure it is still loose). Tighten the right nut two notches beyond the position where it first contacts the cup. Rotate the ring gear several times in each direction while the bearings are loaded to seat the bearings in their cups. This step is important.
3. Again loosen the right nut to release the preload. If there is any backlash between the gears, tighten the left nut just enough to remove this backlash. Install a dial indicator and carefully tighten the right nut until it just contacts the cup. Set preload of 0.008 to 0.012 for new bearings and .005 to .008 for used bearings by spreading the case using the right nut. As preload is applied from the right-hand side, the ring gear is forced away from the pinion and often results in the correct backlash The specified backlash for all gears is 0.008 to 0.012 inch. Tighten the differential cap bolts to the specified 75-80 ft-lbs torque.
4. Measure the backlash on several teeth around the ring gear and if it varies more than 0.003 inch, there is excessive runout in the gears or their mountings, which must be corrected to obtain proper operation. If the backlash disagrees with specification, loosen one adjusting nut and tighten the opposite nut an equal amount, to move the ring gear away from or toward the pinion. When the adjusting nuts are moved, the final movement should always be made in a tightening direction.
5. Check the gear tooth contact.

Solid Spacer Selection Chart

As end play reads (10/1000 inch) in left col. use spacer in right col.

0	0.481
1	0.480
2	0.479
3	0.478
4	0.478
5	0.476
6	0.474
7	0.474
8	0.472
9	0.472
10	0.470
11	0.470
12	0.468
13	0.468
14	0.466
15	0.465

If there is no end play and preload on the bearings exists:

If preload reads (in.-lbs.) in left col. use spacer in right col.

2-11	0.482
12-20	0.483
21-30	0.484
31-45	0.485

Locking Differentials

For overhaul procedures see the General Repair Section.

Removal and installation of locking differentials is basically the same as those described for the conventional differentials above.

Rear Spring

Rear Spring R&R

F-100, 250

1. Raise the vehicle frame until the weight is off the rear spring, with the wheels touching the floor.
2. Remove the nuts from the spring clips (U-Bolts) and drive the clips out of the spring seat cap. If so equipped, remove the auxiliary spring and spacer.
3. Remove the spring to bracket nut and bolt at the front of the spring.
4. Remove shackle lower nut and bolt at the rear of the spring, and remove the spring and shackle assembly from the rear bracket. Remove the spring and compensating shackle from the rear bracket.
5. Remove the shackle from the spring. If the bushing in the spring or the bushing in the shackle are worn or damaged, remove them.
6. If required, install new bushings in the spring and the shackle.
7. Position the spring in the shackle, and install the upper shackle to spring bolt and nut with the bolt head facing outboard.
8. Position the front end of the spring in the bracket and install the bolt and nut.
9. Position the shackle in the rear bracket and install the bolt and nut.
10. Position the spring on top of the axle with the spring tie bolt centered in the hole provided in the seat. If so equipped, install the auxiliary spring and spacer.
11. Install the spring clips, spring seat cap, and nuts.
12. Lower the vehicle to the floor, tighten the spring bolt nuts and spring clip nuts (U-bolts), tighten the front spring bolt and nut, the rear shackle bolt and nut and the compensating

shackle bolt and nut.

E-100, 200

1. Raise the rear end of the vehicle and support the chassis with safety stands. Support the rear axle with a floor jack or hoist.
2. Disconnect the lower end of the shock absorber from the bracket on the axle housing.
3. Remove the two U-bolts and plate.
4. Lower the axle and remove the upper and lower rear shackle bolts.
5. Pull the rear shackle assembly and rubber bushings from the bracket and spring.
6. Remove the nut and mounting bolt that secures the front end of the spring. Remove the spring assembly from the front shackle bracket.
7. Install new rubber bushings in the rear shackle bracket and in the rear eye of the replacement spring.
8. Position the spring assembly and connect the front eye of the spring to the front shackle bracket by installing the front mounting bolt and nut. Do not tighten the nut.
9. Mount the rear end of the spring by inserting the upper bolt of the rear shackle assembly through the eye of the spring and lower bolt through the rear spring hanger.
10. Position the spring center bolt to the pilot hole in the axle and install the plate. Install the U-bolts through the plate. Do not tighten the attaching nuts at this time.

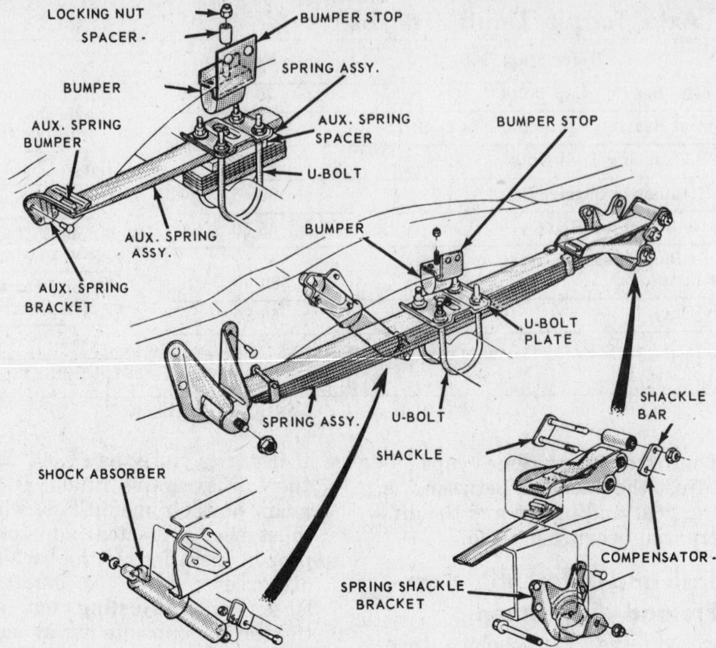

Rear spring F-100-250 (© Ford Motor Co.)

11. Raise the axle with a floor jack or hoist until the vehicle is free of the stands and connect the lower end of the shock absorber to the bracket on the axle housing.
12. Tighten the spring front mounting bolt and nut, the rear shackle nuts and the U-bolt nuts.
13. Remove the safety stands and lower the vehicle.

E-300

1. Raise the rear end of the vehicle and support the chassis with safety stands. Support the rear axle with a floor jack or hoist.
2. Disconnect the lower end of the shock absorber from the bracket on the axle housing.
3. Remove the two spring clips (U-bolts) and the spring clip cap.
4. Lower the axle and remove the spring front bolt from the hanger.
5. Remove the two attaching bolts from the rear of the spring. Remove the spring and the shackle.
6. Assemble the upper end of the shackle to the spring with the

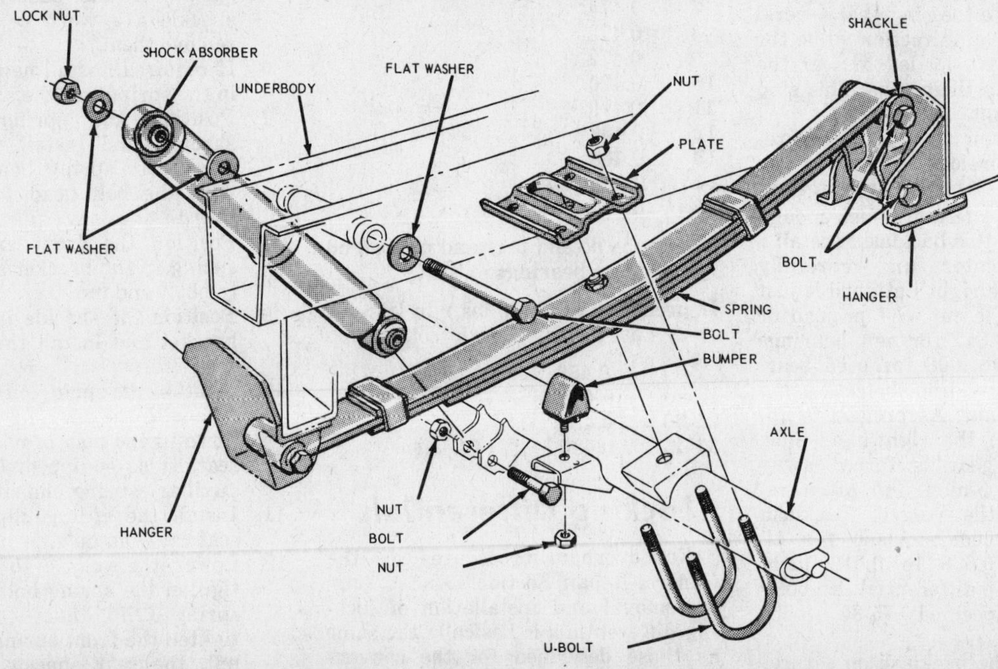

Rear spring E-100—E-200 (© Ford Motor Co.)

attaching bolt.

7. Connect the front of the spring to the front bracket with the attaching bolt.
8. Assemble the spring and shackle to the rear bracket with the attaching bolt.
9. Place the spring clip plate over the head of the center bolt.
10. Raise the axle with a jack and guiding it so that the center bolt enters the pilot hole in the pad on the axle housing.
11. Install the spring clips, cap and attaching nuts. Tighten the nuts snugly.
12. Connect the lower end of the shock absorber to the lower bracket.
13. Tighten the spring front mounting bolt and nut, the rear shackle nuts and spring clip nuts.
14. Remove the safety stands and lower the vehicle.

Rear Spring R&R

F-100, F-250 4-Wheel Drive and P-Series

1. Raise the vehicle frame until the weight is off the rear springs with the wheels still touching the floor.
2. Remove the nuts from the spring clips (U-bolts) and drive the clips out of the spring seat cap and remove the spring clip plate. If the truck is so equipped, remove the auxiliary spring and spacer.
3. Remove the shackle pin locking bolts from each end of the spring (bolt and nut on F-250 4 x 4 front eye).
4. Working from the inner side of the frame, insert a drift in the hole provided in the frame for removing the shackle pin. Drive the shackle pin out of each spring bracket (bolt on F-250 4 x 4 front eye).
5. Remove the spring and shackle from the vehicle. On F-100-250 4 x 4 models, remove the spring to axle spacer.
6. Drive out the remaining shackle pin from the rear spring eye and remove the shackle from the spring.
7. Position the shackle to the rear spring eye.
8. Install the shackle pin through the shackle and spring eye with the lubricator fitting on the shackle pin facing outward.
9. Line up the shackle pin lock bolt groove with the lock bolt hole in the shackle. Install the lock bolt, lock washer, and nut.
10. Position the spring on the axle, making sure that the spring tie bolt is in the hole provided in the axle spring seat or spacer. On F-100-250 4 x 4 models, first install the spacer between the spring seat and the spring, making sure the spacer dowel is positioned in the pilot hole of the axle spring seat.
11. Install a shackle pin through the shackle and rear bracket, with the lubricating fitting on the shackle pin facing outward. Line up the pin groove with the lock bolt hole in the bracket, and install the lock bolt, lock washer, and nut as before.
12. Repeat this operation to install a shackle pin at the front bracket and spring eye (bolt on F-250 4 x 4).
13. If so equipped, install the auxiliary spring and spacer. Place the spring clip plate on top of the spring at the tie bolt, and put the spring clips over the spring assembly and axle.
14. Position the spring seat cap, and install the nuts on the spring clips.
15. Lower the vehicle to the floor and tighten the spring clip nuts. Lubricate the fittings on the shackle pins.

Bronco

1. Raise the vehicle by the axles and install safety stands under the frame.
2. Disconnect the shock absorber from the axle.
3. Remove the U-bolt attaching nuts and remove the 2 U-bolts and the spring clip plate.
4. Lower the axle to relieve spring tension and remove the nut from the spring front attaching bolt.
5. Remove the spring front attaching bolt from the spring and hanger with a drift.
6. Remove the nut from the shackle to hanger attaching bolt and drive the bolt from the shackle and hanger with a drift and remove the spring from the vehicle.
7. Remove the nut from the spring rear attaching bolt. Drive the bolt out of the spring and shackle with a drift.
8. Position the shackle (closed section facing toward front of vehicle) to the spring rear eye and install the bolt and nut.
9. Position the spring front eye and bushing to the spring front hanger, and install the attaching bolt and nut.
10. Position the spring rear eye and bushing to the shackle, and install the attaching bolt and nut.
11. Raise the axle to the spring and install the U-boats (when an axle cap is not used, the U-bolt shank should contact the leaf edges) and spring clip plate. Align the spring leaves.
12. Tighten the U-bolt nuts and the spring front and rear attaching bolt nuts. The U-bolts should contact the spring assembly edges or axle seat.
13. Connect the shock absorber to the axle and tighten the nut.
14. Remove the safety stands and lower the vehicle.

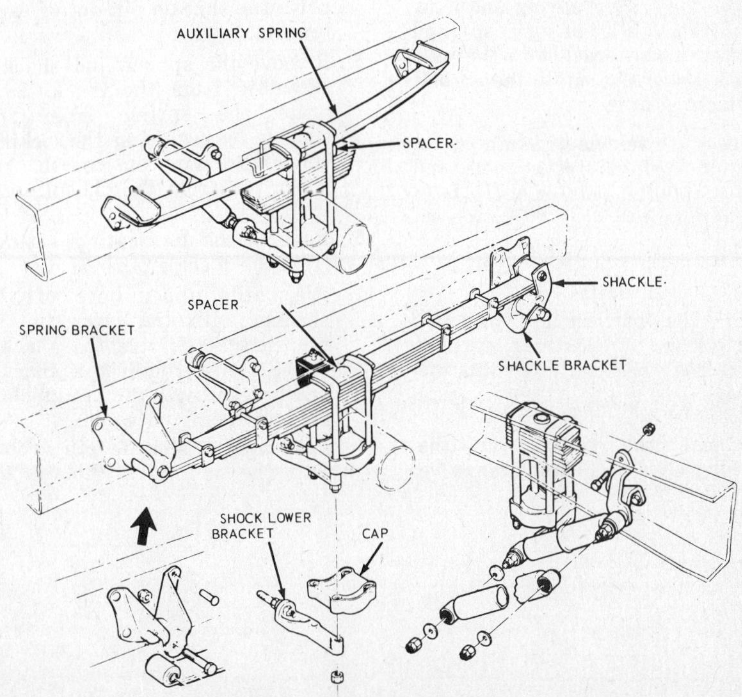

Rear spring F-350 (© Ford Motor Co.)

F-350

1. Raise the vehicle frame until the weight is off the rear springs with the wheels still touching the floor.
2. Remove the nuts from the spring U-bolts.
3. Drive the U-bolts out of the shock absorber lower bracket and the spring cap and remove the U-bolts.
4. Remove the spacer from the top of the spring.
5. If equipped with auxiliary springs, remove the auxiliary spring and spacer.
6. Remove the shackle to bracket bolt and nut from the rear of the spring.
7. Remove the spring to hanger bolt and nut from the front of the spring and remove the spring.
8. Remove the shackle to spring bolt and nut and remove the shackle from the spring.
9. Position the shackle to the spring and install the attaching bolt and nut. The bolt must be installed so the nut is away from the frame.
10. Position the spring to the spring front hanger and install the attaching bolt and nut.
11. Position the shackle to the bracket and install the attaching bolt and nut.
12. Align the spring toe bolt with the pilot hole in the axle spring seat and, if so equipped, install the auxiliary spring and spacer.
13. Position the spacer on top of the spring and install the U-bolts over the spacer, spring and axle.
14. Position the spring cap and shock lower bracket to the axle and U-bolts. Install the U-bolt attaching nuts.
15. Lower the vehicle and tighten the front spring bracket bolt and nut and the rear shackle bolts and nuts.

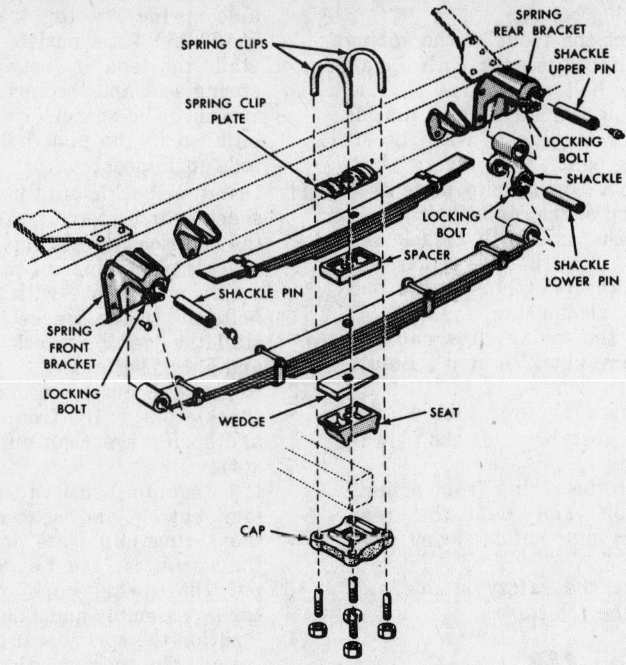

Rear spring C-series (© Ford Motor Co.)

C-Series

1. Raise the vehicle frame until the weight is off the rear springs with the wheels still touching the floor.
2. Remove the nuts from the spring clips (U-bolts) and drive the clips out of the spring seat cap. If so equipped, remove the auxiliary spring and spacer.
3. Remove the shackle pin locking bolts from each spring bracket.
4. A hole is provided in the frame opposite each spring bracket for removing the shackle pin. Insert a drift from the inside of the frame through these holes and drive the shackle pin out of each bracket.
5. Remove the spring and shackle assembly from the truck. Separate the spring from the shackle by removing the locking bolt and driving out the shackle lower pin from the shackle and spring eye.
6. Remove the lubricating fittings from the shackle pins.
7. Align the upper bore of the shackle with the holes in the rear bracket. Drive the shackle upper pin through the shackle and bracket with the pin lubricator hole facing outward.
8. Line up the shackle pin groove with the locking bolt hole in the bracket and install the locking bolt, washer and nut.
9. Install the spring seat and the wedge (if so equipped) between the axle and the spring. Position the spring on the axle, being sure that the spring tie bolt is in the hole provided in the axle or spring seats. If so equipped, install the auxiliary spring and spacer.
10. Drive the shackle lower pin through the shackle and spring rear eye. Install the locking bolt, washer and nut as before. Repeat the operation to install the shackle pin through the spring front bracket and eye.
11. Place the spring clip plate on top of the spring at the tie bolt, and put the spring clips over the spring assembly and the axle.
12. Install the spring seat cap on the spring clips and install the spring clip nuts on the clips.
13. Lower the vehicle to the floor and tighten the spring clip nuts.

GMC Trucks

Index

TUNE-UP SPECIFICATIONS

CU. IN. DISPLACE-MENT	YEAR	SPARK PLUG GAP	DISTRIBUTOR POINT DWELL	DISTRIBUTOR POINT GAP	IGNITION TIMING DEGREES	CRANKING COMP. PRESSURE	VALVE CLEARANCE IN. EXH.	GOV. R.P.M. NO LOAD	FUEL PUMP PRESS.	IDLE SPEED STD.	IDLE SPEED AUTO.
FOUR CYLINDER											
153	1963-65	.035	31-34	.019	4B	150	0 + 1 Turn	—	3½-4½	475	450N
SIX CYLINDER											
194	1963-66	.035	31-34	.019	4B	130	0 + 1 Turn	—	3½-4½	475	475D
230	1963-69	.035	31-34	.019	4B[1]	130	0 + 1 Turn	—	3½-4½	500[2]	500
250	1966	.035	31-34	.019	6B	130	0 + 1 Turn	—	3-4½	475[3]	475[3]
	1967	.035	31-34	.019	4B	130	0 + 1 Turn	—	3-4½	500[3]	500[3]
	1968-70	.035	31-34	.019	4B[1]	130	0 + 1 Turn	—	3-4½	500[3]	500[3]
270	1961-62	.030	31-34	.016	Ball	135	.012H-.020H	3850	4½-6	—	—
292	1964-66	.035	31-34	.019	4B[4]	130	0 + 1 Turn	—	3½-4½	475	475
	1967	.035	31-34	.019	4B	130	0 + 1 Turn	—	3½-4½	500	500
W/AIR	1967	.035	31-34	.019	2B	130	0 + 1 Turn	—	3½-4½	700	600
	1968-70	.035	31-34	.019	4B[1]	130	0 + 1 Turn	—	3-4½	500[3]	500[3]
V-6 ENGINES											
305	1961-66	.030	31-34	.016	7½B[5]	125	.012H-.018H	3600	5-6	525[6]	—
	1967-70	.035	31-34	.019	7½B[7]	125	.012H-.018H	3600	5-6	525[8]	—
351	1961-66	.030	29-33	.016	5B	125	.012H-.018H	—	5-6	525	—
	1967-70	.030	31-34	.016	10B[7]	125	.012H-.018H	—	5-6	525[8]	—
401	1961-65	.030	29-33	.016	5B	125	.012H-.018H	3700	5-6	—	—
	1966-70	.035	31-34	.019	10B	125	.012H-.018H	3700	5-6	—	—
478	1962	.030	29-33	.016	TDC	125	.012H-.018H	3500	5-6	—	—
	1963-64	.030	29-33	.016	2½B	125	.012H-.018H	3500	5-6	—	—
	1965	.030	31-34	.019	2½B	125	.012H-.018H	3500	5-6	—	—
	1966-70	.035	31-34	.019	10B	125	.012H-.018H	3500	5-6	—	—
EIGHT CYLINDER											
283	1966-67	.035	28-32	.019	4B[9]	150	0 + 1 Turn	—	5¼-6½	475	475
307	1968-70	.035	28-32	.019	2B[10]	150	0 + 1 Turn	—	5-6½	700	600
327	1967	.035	28-32	.019	TDC[11]	150	0 + 1 Turn	—	5¼-6½	700	600
	1968	.035	28-32	.019	4B[12]	150	0 + 1 Turn	—	5¼-6½	700	600
350	1969-70	.035	28-32	.019	4B[12]	150	0 + 1 Turn	—	5-6½	700	600
366	1969-70	.035	28-32	.019	6B	150	0 + 1 Turn	—	5-6½	700	600
396	1968-70	.035	28-32	.019	4B	150	0 + 1 Turn	—	5-6½	700	600
427	1969-70	.035	28-32	.019	6B	150	0 + 1 Turn	—	5-6½	500	500
637	1966-70	.035	28-32	.019	10B	125	.010H-.018H	3100	5½-7	425	—
V-12 ENGINES											
702	1961	.030	47	.016	5B	130	Zero-Zero	—	5-6	—	—
	1962	.030	42	.018	TDC	130	Zero-Zero	2700	5-6	—	—
	1963-65	.030	42	.016	7½B	130	Zero-Zero	2700	5-6	—	—

1—1968-69 w/A.I.R. and Std. Trans. T.D.C.
2—1968-69 w/A.I.R. and Std. Trans. 700
3—Std. w/A.I.R. 700, Auto. 600
4—1966 Std. Trans. w/A.I.R. 1 dec. A.T.D.C.
5—Heavy Duty 5B.
6—Heavy Duty 400-450.
7—w/A.I.R. 2½A.
8—w/A.I.R. 650.

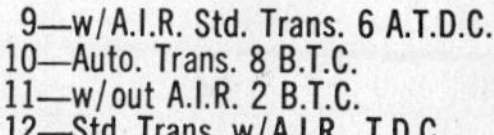

9—w/A.I.R. Std. Trans. 6 A.T.D.C.
10—Auto. Trans. 8 B.T.C.
11—w/out A.I.R. 2 B.T.C.
12—Std. Trans. w/A.I.R., T.D.C.

FIRING ORDER AND ROTATION

4 Cyl-153 engines

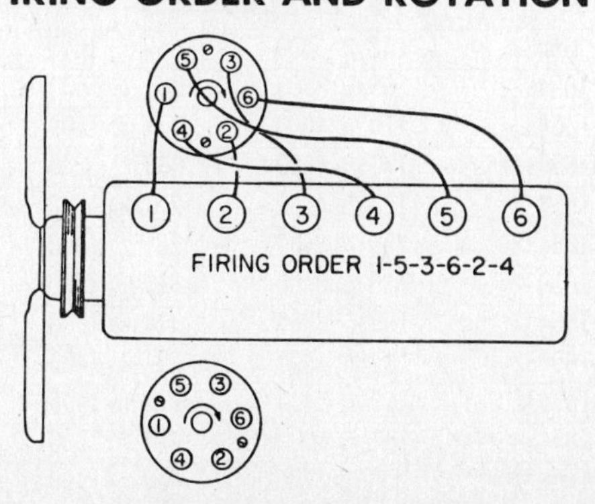

6 Cyl-194, 230, 250 & 292 engines

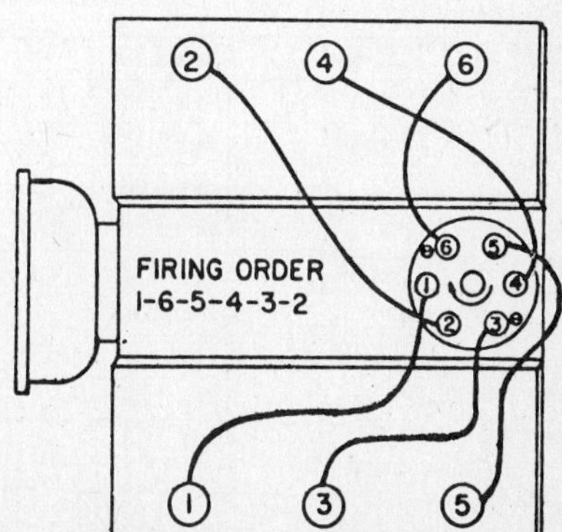

V6-engines

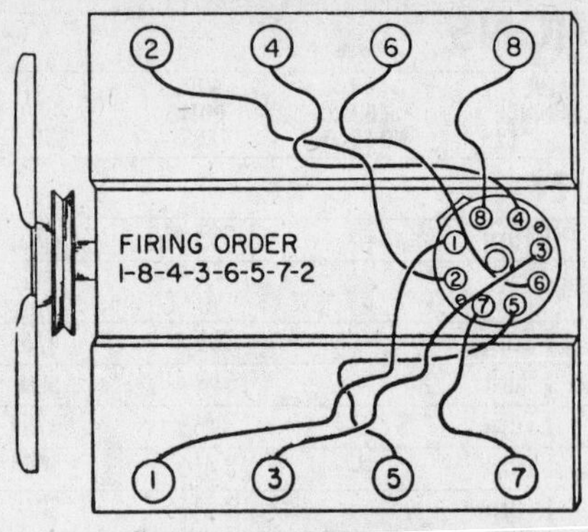

V8-283, 307, 327 & 396 engines

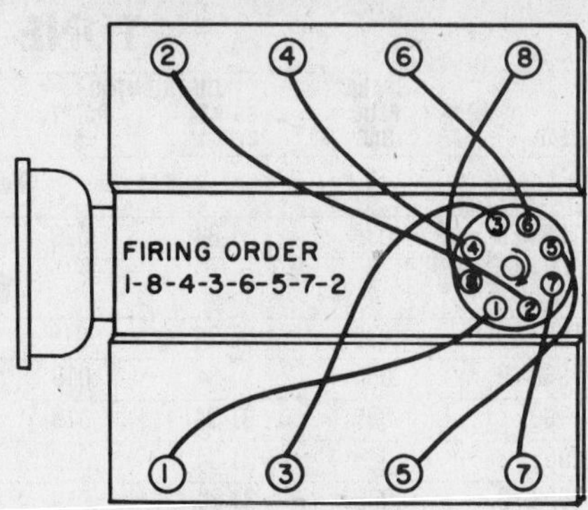

V8-637 engines

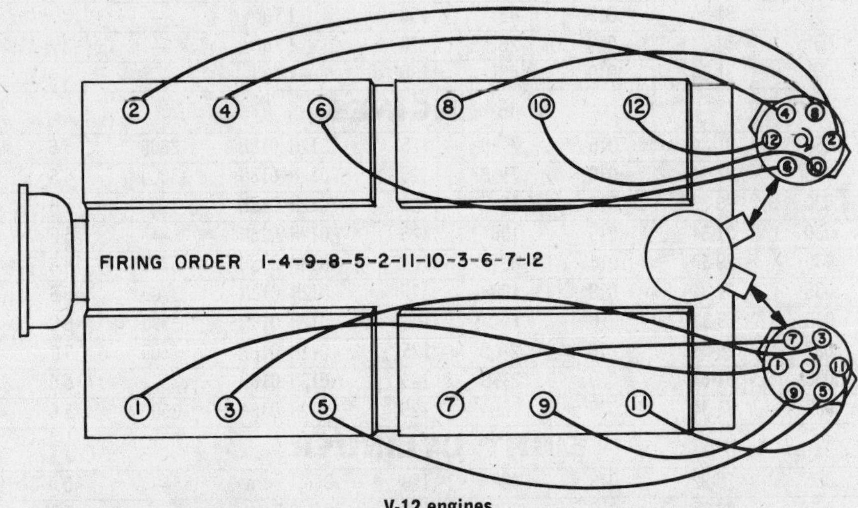

V-12 engines

GENERAL ENGINE SPECIFICATIONS

CU. IN. DISPLACE-MENT	YEAR	BORE AND STROKE	FIRING ORDER	DEVELOPED HORSEPOWER @ R.P.M.	DEVELOPED TORQUE @ R.P.M.	COM-PRESSION RATIO	CARBU-RETOR	VALVE LIFTER TYPE	NORMAL OIL PRESSURE
				FOUR CYLINDER					
153	1963-64	3⅞ x 3.25	1-3-4-2	75 @ 4000	144 @ 2000	8.5-1	1V	Hyd.	40-60
	1965	3⅞ x 3.25	1-3-4-2	90 @ 4000	152 @ 2400	8.5-1	1V	Hyd.	30-45
				SIX CYLINDER					
194	1963-66	$3\frac{9}{16}$ x 3¼	153624	120 @ 4400	177 @ 2400	8.5-1	1V	Hyd.	40-60
230	1963-64	3⅞ x 3¼	153624	120 @ 3600	205 @ 1600	8.5-1	1V	Hyd.	40-60
	1965-69	3⅞ x 3¼	153624	140 @ 4400	220 @ 1600	8.5-1	1V	Hyd.	40-60
250	1966-70	3⅞ x $3\frac{17}{32}$	153624	150 @ 4200	235 @ 1600	8.5-1	1V	Hyd.	40-60
270	1961-62	$3\frac{25}{32}$ x 4.0	153624	133 @ 3600	244 @ 1300	7.75-1	1V	Mech.	35-40
292	1964-70	3⅞ x 4⅛	153624	170 @ 4000	275 @ 1600	8.0-1	1V	Hyd.	40-60
				V-6 ENGINES					
305	1961-64	4¼ x 3.58	165432	142 @ 3800	260 @ 1600	7.75-1	2V	Mech.	60
	1965	4¼ x 3.58	165432	165 @ 3800	280 @ 1600	7.75-1	2V	Mech.	60
	1966-68	4¼ x 3.58	165432	170 @ 4000	277 @ 1600	7.75-1	2V	Mech.	60
	1969	4¼ x 3.58	165432	170 @ 4000	263 @ 1600	7.75-1	2V	Mech.	60
	1970	4¼ x 3.58	165432	170 @ 4000	277 @ 1600	7.75-1	2V	Mech.	60
351	1961-64	$4\frac{9}{16}$ x 3.58	165432	155 @ 3400	288 @ 1400	7.5-1	2V	Mech.	60
	1965	$4\frac{9}{16}$ x 3.58	165432	180 @ 3400	312 @ 1800	7.5-1	2V	Mech.	60
	1966-70	$4\frac{9}{16}$ x 3.58	165432	195 @ 3600	314 @ 1600	7.5-1	2V	Mech.	60
401	1961-64	4⅞ x 3.58	165432	182 @ 3400	351 @ 1400	7.5-1	2V	Mech.	60
	1965	4⅞ x 3.58	165432	210 @ 3400	377 @ 1400	7.5-1	2V	Mech.	60
	1966-70	4⅞ x 3.58	165432	237 @ 4000	372 @ 1600	7.5-1	2V	Mech.	60
478	1961-64	5⅛ x 3.86	165432	206 @ 3200	400 @ 1400	7.5-1	2V	Mech.	60
	1965	5⅛ x 3.86	165432	235 @ 3200	440 @ 1400	7.5-1	2V	Mech.	60
	1966-70	5⅛ x 3.86	165432	254 @ 3700	442 @ 1400	7.5-1	2V	Mech.	60

GENERAL ENGINE SPECIFICATIONS, continued

CU. IN. DISPLACEMENT	YEAR	BORE AND STROKE	FIRING ORDER	DEVELOPED HORSEPOWER @ R.P.M.	DEVELOPED TORQUE @ R.P.M.	COMPRESSION RATIO	CARBURETOR	VALVE LIFTER TYPE	NORMAL OIL PRESSURE
EIGHT CYLINDER									
283	1966-67	3⅞ x 3.00	18436572	175 @ 4400	275 @ 2400	9.0-1	2V	Hyd.	30
307	1968-70	3⅞ x 3.25	18436572	200 @ 4600	300 @ 2400	9.0-1	2V	Hyd.	30
327	1967-68	4.0 x 3.25	18436572	220 @ 4400	320 @ 2800	8.5-1	4V	Hyd.	30
350	1969[1]	4.0 x 3.48	18436572	200 @ 4000	325 @ 2000	8.0-1	2V	Hyd.	30
	1969-70[2]	4.0 x 3.48	18436572	215 @ 4000	335 @ 2800	8.0-1	2V	Hyd.	30
	1969-70	4.0 x 3.48	18436572	255 @ 4600	355 @ 3000	9.0-1	4V	Hyd.	30
366	1969-70	3 15/16 x 3.76	18436572	235 @ 4000	345 @ 2600	8.0-1	4V	Hyd.	50-75
396	1966-68	4 3/32 x 3.76	18436572	275 @ 4400	390 @ 2800	9.0-1	2V	Hyd.	50-75
	1966-70	4 3/32 x 3.76	18436572	310 @ 4800	400 @ 3200	9.0-1	4V	Hyd.	50-75
427	1969-70	4.25 x 3.76	18436572	260 @ 4000	405 @ 2600	8.0-1	4V	Hyd.	50-75
637	1966-70	5⅛ x 3.86	18436572	275 @ 2400	600 @ 1600	8.0-1	2V	Mech.	60
V-12 ENGINES									
702	1961-64	4 9/16 x 3.58	[3]	250 @ 2400	585 @ 1600	7.5-1	2-2V	Hyd.	60
	1965	4 9/16 x 3.58	[3]	275 @ 2400	630 @ 1600	7.5-1	2-2V	Hyd.	60

1—w/A.I.R. 2—w/o A.I.R. 3—1, 4, 9, 8, 5, 2, 11, 10, 3, 6, 7, 12

CRANKSHAFT BEARING JOURNAL SPECIFICATIONS

CU. IN. DISPLACEMENT	YEAR	MAIN BEARING JOURNALS: JOURNAL DIAMETER	MAIN BEARING JOURNALS: OIL CLEARANCE	MAIN BEARING JOURNALS: SHAFT END PLAY	MAIN BEARING JOURNALS: THRUST ON NO.	CONNECTING ROD BEARING JOURNALS: JOURNAL DIAMETER	CONNECTING ROD BEARING JOURNALS: OIL CLEARANCE	CONNECTING ROD BEARING JOURNALS: END PLAY
FOUR CYLINDER								
153	1963-65	2.2983-2.2993	.0003-.0019[1]	.002-.006	Rear	1.999-2.000	.0007-.0028	.008-.014
SIX CYLINDER								
194	1963-66	2.2983-2.2993	.0008-.004	.002-.006	Rear	1.999-2.000	.0007-.0028	.008-.014
230	1963-70	2.2983-2.2993	.0003-.0019[1]	.002-.006	Rear	1.999-2.000	.0007-.0028	.0085-.0135
250	1966-70	2.2983-2.2993	.0003-.0029	.002-.006	Rear	1.999-2.000	.0007-.0027	.0085-.0135
270	1961-62	[2]	.0007-.0033[3]	.003-.008	3	2.311-2.312	.0004-.0025	—
292	1964-70	2.2983-2.2993	.0008-.0024	.002-.006	Rear	2.099-2.100	.0007-.0028	.0085-.0135
V-6 ENGINES								
305	1961-70	3.1237-3.1247[4]	.0013-.0039	.003-.008	3	2.8112-2.8122	.0013-.0039	.006-.011
351	1961-70	3.1237-3.1247[4]	.0013-.0039	.003-.008	3	2.8112-2.8122	.0013-.0039	.006-.011
401	1961-70	3.1237-3.1247[4]	.0013-.0039	.003-.008	3	2.8112-2.8122	.0013-.0039	.006-.011
478	1962-70	3.1237-3.1247[4]	.0013-.0039	.003-.008	3	2.8112-2.8122	.0013-.0039	.006-.011
EIGHT CYLINDER								
283	1966-67	2.2978-2.2988	.0007-.0028	.002-.006	5	1.999-2.000	.0007-.0027	.009-.013
307	1968-70	2.4484-2.4493[5]	.0008-.0024[7]	.003-.011	5	2.099-2.100	.0007-.0028	.009-.013
327	1967	2.2983-2.2993[6]	.0008-.0024[7]	.003-.011	5	1.999-2.000	.0007-.0028	.009-.013
	1968-70	2.4484-2.4493[5]	.0008-.0024[7]	.003-.011	5	2.099-2.100	.0007-.0028	.009-.013
350	1969	2.4484-2.4493[5]	.0008-.0024[7]	.003-.011	5	2.099-2.100	.0007-.0028	.008-.014
	1970	2.4484-2.4493[5]	[8]	.002-.006	5	2.099-2.100	.0007-.0028	.008-.014
366	1969-70	2.7481-2.7490[9]	.0013-.0025[10]	.006-.010	5	2.1988-2.1998	.0007-.0030	.019-.025
396	1968-70	2.7481-2.7490[9]	.0013-.0025[10]	.006-.010	5	2.1988-2.1998	.0007-.0028	.019-.025
427	1969-70	2.7481-2.7490[11]	.0013-.0025[12]	.006-.010	5	2.1988-2.1998	.0007-.0028	.019-.025
637	1966-70	3.1237-3.1247	.0013-.0039	.003-.008	4	2.8112-2.8122	.0010-.0031	.006-.011

1—Rear .0008-.0024.
2—No. 1—2.6835-2.6845, No. 2—2.7145-2.7155, No. 3—2.7455-2.7465, No. 4—2.7765-2.7775.
3—Rear .0011-.0037
4—Rear No. 4—3.1229-3.1239.
5—Rear 2.4478-2.4488.
6—Rear 2.2978-2.2988.
7—Rear .0010-.0026.
8—No. 1—.0003-.0015, No. 2, 3, 4—.0006-.0018, No. 5—.0008-.0023.
9—Rear 2.7478-2.7488.
10—Rear .0015-.0031.
11—Rear 2.7473-.2.7483
12—1969 Rear .0015-.0031, 1970—.0029-.0045.
13—Rear 3.1229-3.1239.

VALVE SPECIFICATIONS

CU. IN. DISPLACEMENT	YEAR	LASH (HOT) INCHES INT.	LASH (HOT) INCHES EXH.	ANGLE DEGREES FACE	ANGLE DEGREES SEAT	STEM DIA. INCHES INT.	STEM DIA. INCHES EXH.	STEM CLEARANCE INTAKE	STEM CLEARANCE EXHAUST	VALVE LIFT INCHES	VALVE SPRING LBS. @ INCHES OPEN	VALVE SPRING LBS. @ INCHES CLOSED	FREE LENGTH INCH
FOUR CYLINDER													
153	1963-65	0 + 1 Turn		45	46	.341	.341	.001-.003	.002-.004	.397	175 @ 1.26	82 @ 1.66	2.08

VALVE SPECIFICATIONS, continued

CU. IN. DISPLACEMENT	YEAR	LASH (HOT) INCHES INT.	LASH (HOT) INCHES EXH.	ANGLE DEGREES FACE	ANGLE DEGREES SEAT	STEM DIA. INCHES INT.	STEM DIA. INCHES EXH.	STEM CLEARANCE INTAKE	STEM CLEARANCE EXHAUST	VALVE LIFT INCHES	VALVE SPRING LBS. @ INCHES OPEN	VALVE SPRING LBS. @ INCHES CLOSED	FREE LENGTH INCH
SIX CYLINDER													
194	1963-66	0 + 1 Turn		45	46	.341	.341	.001-.003	.002-.004	.335	171 @ 1.33	82 @ 1.66	1.92
230	1963-70	0 + 1 Turn		45	46	.341	.341	.001-.003	.002-.004	.335	171 @ 1.33	82 @ 1.66	2.03
250	1966-70	0 + 1 Turn		45	46	.341	.341	.001-.003	.002-.004	.390	186 @ 1.27	60 @ 1.66	2.08
270	1961-62	.012H	.020H	29	30	.341	.340	.001-.003	.002-.004	—	134 @ 1.50	—	—
292	1964-70	0 + 1 Turn		[1]	46	.341	.341	.001-.003	.001-.003	.400	179 @ 1.30	89 @ 1.69	1.90
V-6 ENGINES													
305	1961-70	.012H	.018H	[7]	[7]	.341	.340	.001-.003	.002-.004	—	204 @ 1.50	—	—
351	1961-70	.012H	.018H	[7]	[7]	—	—	.001-.003	.002-.004	—	204 @ 1.50	—	—
401	1961-70	.012H	.018H	[2]	[3]	.373	.434	.001-.003	.002-.004	.442	204 @ 1.49	80 @ 1.92	2.27
478	1962-70	.012H	.018H	[2]	[3]	.373	.434	.001-.003	.002-.004	.442	204 @ 1.49	80 @ 1.92	2.27
EIGHT CYLINDER													
283	1966-67	0 + 1 Turn		45	46	.341	.341	.001-.003	.001-.003	.398	175 @ 1.26	82 @ 1.66	2.08
307	1968-69	0 + 1 Turn		45	46	.341	.341	.001-.003	.001-.003	[4]	174 @ 1.26	82 @ 1.66	2.08
	1970	0 + 1 Turn		45	46	.341	.341	.001-.003	.001-.003	[4]	200 @ 1.25	80 @ 1.70	2.03
327	1967-68	0 + 1 Turn		[1]	46	.341	.341	.001-.003	.001-.003	.398	174 @ 1.26	82 @ 1.66	2.08
350	1969-70	0 + 1 Turn		[1]	46	.341	.341	.001-.003	.001-.003	[4]	174 @ 1.26	92 @ 1.66	2.08
366	1969-70	0 + 1 Turn		[1]	46	.371	.371	.001-.003	.001-.003	.400	220 @ 1.40	90 @ 1.80	2.05
396	1968-69	0 + 1 Turn		[1]	46	.371	.371	.001-.003	.001-.003	.398	315 @ 1.38	100 @ 1.88	2.09
427	1969-70	0 + 1 Turn		[5]	46	.371	.371	.001-.003	.001-.003	[6]	220 @ 1.40	90 @ 1.80	2.05
637	1966-70	.010H	.018H	45	45	.373	.434	.001-.003	.002-.004	—	154 @ 1.60	—	—
V-12 ENGINES													
702	1961-65	Zero		[2]	[7]	.373	.434	.001-.003	.002-.004	—	204 @ 1.49	80 @ 1.92	2.70

1—Intake 45, Exhaust 46.
2—Inlet 29, Exhaust 44.
3—Inlet 30, Exhaust 44.
4—Intake .390, Exhaust .410.
5—1969 Intake 45, Exhaust 46. 1970 Intake and Exhaust 46.
6—Intake .398, Exhaust .430.
7—Inlet 30, Exhaust 45.

TORQUE SPECIFICATIONS

CU. IN. DISPLACEMENT	YEAR	CYLINDER HEAD BOLTS FT. LBS.	ROD BEARING BOLTS FT. LBS.	MAIN BEARING BOLT FT. LBS.	CRANKSHAFT DAMPER BALANCER BOLT FT. LBS.	FLYWHEEL TO CRANKSHAFT BOLTS FT. LBS.	MANIFOLD INTAKE FT. LBS.	MANIFOLD EXHAUST FT. LBS.
FOUR CYLINDER								
153	1963-65	90-95	30-35	60-70	Pressed on	55-65	[1]	[1]
SIX CYLINDER								
194	1963-66	90-95	30-35	60-70	Pressed on	55-65	[1]	[1]
230	1963-69	90-95	35-45	60-70	Pressed on	55-65	[1]	[1]
250	1966-70	90-95	35-45	60-70	Pressed on	55-65	[1]	[1]
270	1961-62	90-100	40-45	90-100	115-125	102-107	—	—
292	1964-70	90-95	30-35	60-70	Pressed on	55-65	[1]	[1]
V-6 ENGINES								
305	1961-70	65-72	50-55	130-140[3]	200-210	100-105	20-25	15-20
351	1961-70	65-72	50-55	130-140[3]	200-210	100-105	20-25	15-20
401	1961-70	65-72	50-55	130-140[3]	200-210	100-105	20-25	15-20
478	1962-70	65-72	50-55	130-140[3]	200-210	100-105	20-25	15-20
EIGHT CYLINDER								
283	1961-67	60-70	30-35	60-70	Pressed on	60	30	20
307	1968-70	65	35	70	Pressed on	60	30	20
327	1967-68	60-70	35	80	Pressed on	60	30	20
350	1969-70	65	35	80	Pressed on	60	30	20
366	1969-70	60-70	45-55	90-100	85	65	—	—
396	1968-70	60-70	45-55	90-100	85	65	30	20
427	1969-70	60-70	45-55	90-100	85	100-105	30	20
637	1966-70	130-135	55-65	170-180[2]	200-210	100-105	25	20
V-12 ENGINES								
702	1961-65	65-72	55-65	130-140[3]	135-145	100-105	25	20

1—Outer 20, others 30.
2—Rear and side ½", 90-100.
3—Rear 55-65.

WHEEL ALIGNMENT SPECIFICATIONS

YEAR	MODEL	CASTER (Deg.)	CAMBER (Deg.)	TOE-IN (In.)	KING PIN INCLINATION (Deg.)
1963	P1000, PB1000[1]	+2½	+¼	3/16	—
1963	P1500, 2500, PB1500, 2500[1]	+2	+¼-1¾	3/16	7½
1963	1000, 1500, 2500[2]	—	—	3/16-¼	—
1963	3500, B3500, 4000[3]	+3¼-4¼	+1-2	⅛-¼	—
1963	SP5000, W5000[3]	0-+½[4]	+½-1½	⅛-¼	—
1963	All Other 5000[3]	+3¼-4¼	+1-2	⅛-¼	—
1963-65	5500-7100[3]	0-+½[4]	+½-1½	⅛-¼	—
1963-65	DBWI 7000	+2-3	+½-1½	⅛-¼	—
1964-66	1000, 1500, 2500[2]	—	—	3/16-¼	—
1964-66	Handi-Van[3]	+3⅓	+1½	1/16-⅛	7/16
1964-66	P1500, PB1500, P2500, PB2500[3]	+2	+1¼-1¾	¼-5/16	7/16
1964-66	3500, B3500	+3¼-4¼	+1¼-1¾	⅛-¼	7/16
1964-66	4000, B4000, S4000[3]	3¼-4¼	+1¼-1¾	⅛-¼	7/16
1964-66	L4000, LH4000[3]	+4¾-5¾	1¼-1¾	⅛-¼	7/16
1964-66	L5000, LH5000[3]	+4¾-5¾	+1¼-1¾	⅛-¼	7/16
1964-66	5000, B5000, S5000[3]	+4¾-5¾	+1¼-1¾	⅛-¼	7/16
1964-66	H5000, BH5000[3]	+4¾-5¾	+1¼-1¾	⅛-¼	7/16
1964-66	W5000[3]	0-+½[4]	+½-1½	⅛-¼	5
1964-66	SP5000[3]	+2-3	+½-1½	⅛-¼	5
1966	5500	+2⅓	+1-2	⅛-¼	7/16
1966	H&J7500	+2¼-3¼	+1-2	⅛-¼	7/16
1966	RG, RM7500	+2½-3½	+1-2	⅛-¼	L-5¾, R-6¼
1966	T7500	+¾-1¾	+1-2	⅛-¼	7/16
1966	HM8500	+2¼-3¼	+1-2	⅛-¼	7/16
1966	JM8500	+½-1½	[5]	⅛-¼	L-5¾, R-6¼
1966	TM, WM8500	0-+½	[5]	⅛-¼	L-5¾, R-6¼
1966	HE, HJ8500	+2¼-3¼	+1-2	⅛-¼	7/16
1966	JJ, JE, HI, JE9500	+½-1½	[5]	⅛-¼	L-5¾, R-6¼
1966	[6]	0-+½	[5]	⅛-¼	L-5¾, R-6¼
1966		0-+½[8]	[5]	⅛-¼	L-5¾, R-6¼
1966	MH, MI9501	+½-1½	[9]	⅛-¼	L-6, R-7
1967-68	CP1500	—	—	1/32-3/32	—
1967-68	C2500, C3500	—	—	1/32-3/32	—
1967-68	G1500, G2500	+2¼-4¼	+1¼-1¾	1/16-⅛	7¼
1967-68	K1500, K2500	+1½	+1½	1/16-⅛	7¼
1967-68	P2500, P3500	+2	+1¼-1¾	1/16-3/16	7¼
1967-68	L3500, LI3500	+¾-1¾	+1-2	⅛-¼	7⅛
1969	C, P1500	—	—	⅛-¼	—
1969	C2500, 3500	—	—	⅛-¼	—
1969	G&K1500, G&K2500	+3¼	+½-1½	3/32-3/16	7¼
1969	P2500, 3500	—	—	⅛-¼	—
1967-69	EG, EM, ES4500	+2¼-3¼	+1-2	⅛-¼	7⅛
1967-69	PS4500	+1½	+1½	⅛-3/16	7⅛
1967-69	[10]	+2¼-3¼	+1-2	⅛-¼	7⅛
1967-69	4000 Series	+¾-1¾	+1-2	⅛-¼	7⅛
1967-69	EG, EM, ES, SM6500	+2¼-3¼	+1-2	⅛-¼	7⅛
1967-69	HG, HJ, HM, HV7500	+2¼-3¼	+1-2	⅛-¼	7⅛
1967-69	HG, HJ, HM, HV7500[11]	+½-1½	[12]	⅛-¼	L-5¾, R-6¼
1967-69	HJ, HV7500	+½-1½	[12]	⅛-¼	L-5¾, R-6¼
1967-69	JG, JJ, JM, JV760	+2¼-3¼	+1-2	⅛-¼	7⅛
1967-69	JG, JJ, JM, JV7500[11 12]	+½-1½	[12]	⅛-¼	L-5¾, R-6¼
1967-69	RG, RM7500[11]	+2½-3½	−¼-+¾	⅛-¼	L-5¾, R-6¼
1967-69	TG, TJ, TM7500[14]	+¾-1¾	+1-2	⅛-¼	7⅛
1967-69	TG, TJ, TM7500[11 15]	+¾-1¾	[12]	⅛-¼	L-5¾, R-6¼
1967-69	HM8500[14]	+¼-3¼	+1-2	⅛-¼	7⅛
1967-69	HM, JM8500[11 13]	+½-1½	[12]	⅛-¼	L-5¾, R-6¼
1967-69	JM8500[16]	+½-1½	+½-1½	⅛-¼	8
1967-69	TM, WM8500[11 15]	0-+½	[12]	⅛-¼	L-5¾, R-6¼
1967-69	WM8500[17]	0-+½	+½-1½	⅛-¼	L-5¾, R-6¼
1967-69	CE, CH, CI, CJ9500[11 13]	+½-1½	[12]	⅛-¼	L-5¾, R-6¼
1967-69	CE, CH, CI, CJ9500[16]	+½-1½	+½-1½	⅛-¼	8
1967-69	DE, DH9500[18]	0+0-1	+½-1½	0-¼	1
1967-69	DE, DH9500[11 15]	−½ to +½	[12]	⅛-¼	L-5¾, R-6¼
1967-69	DJ, DW9500[11 15]	−½ to +½[8]	[12]	⅛-¼	L-5¾, R-6¼
1967-69	FH, FI9500[18]	0 to −1	+½-1½	0-¼	1
1967-69	FH, FI9500[11 15]	−½ to +½	[12]	⅛-¼	L-5¾, R-6¼
1967-69	FE, FJ, FW9500[11 15]	−½ to +½[8]	[12]	⅛-¼	L-5¾, R-6¼
1967-69	HE, HJ9500[14]	+2¼-3¼	+1-2	⅛-¼	7⅛
1967-69	HE, HI, HJ9500[11 13]	+½-1½	[12]	⅛-¼	L-5¾, R-6¼
1967-69	HI9500[16]	+½-1½	+½-1½	⅛-¼	8
1967-69	JE, JI, JJ9500[11 13]	+½-1½	[12]	⅛-¼	L-5¾, R-6¼
1967-69	JE, JI, JJ9500[16]	+½-1½	+½-1½	⅛-¼	8
1967-69	ME, MI, MJ, MH9500[11 13]	+½-1½	[12]	⅛-¼	L-5¾, R-6¼
1967-69	ME, MI, MJ, MH9500[16]	+½-1½	+½-1½	⅛-¼	8
1967-69	TE, TJ9500[11 15]	−½-+½	[12]	⅛-¼	L-5¾, R-6¼
1967-69	TW9500[15]	−½-+½[8]	[12]	⅛-¼	L-5¾, R-6¼
1967-69	TW9500[17]	−½-+½[8]	+½-1½	⅛-¼	8
1967-69	WE, WJ9500[11]	−½-+½	[12]	⅛-¼	L-5¾, R-6¼
1967-69	WE, WJ9500[17]	−½-+½	+½-1½	⅛-¼	8
1967-69	WW9500[15]	−½-+½[8]	[12]	⅛-¼	L-5¾, R-6¼
1967-69	WW9500[17]	−½-+½[8]	+½-1½	⅛-¼	8
1967-68	MH, MI9501[19]	+½-1½	L+½, R−½	⅛-¼	L-6, R-7
1967-68	MH, MI9501[16]	+½-1½	+½-1½	⅛-¼	8
1969	9502[13]	+½-1½	−¼-+¾	⅛-¼	L-5¾, R-6¼
1969	9502[16]	+½-1½	+½-1½	⅛-¼	8
1970-71	C1550—Jimmy	—	—	—	—
1970-71	K1550—Jimmy	—	—	—	—
1970-71	G&K1500, G&K2500	+3¼	+½-1½	3/32-3/16	7¼
1970-71	G3500	—	—	—	—
1970-71	G1530	—	—	—	—
1970-71	G2530	—	—	—	—
1970-71	G3530	—	—	—	—
1970-71	CP1500	—	—	⅛-¼	—
1970-71	P2500, 3500	—	—	⅛-¼	—
1970-71	P4500	—	—	⅛-3/16	—
1970-71	C2500, 3500	—	—	⅛-¼	—
1970-71	C4500	—	—	—	—
1970-71	C5500	—	—	—	—
1970-71	C5500	—	—	—	—
1970-71	C6500	—	—	⅛-7/32	—
1970-71	M6500	—	—	⅛-7/32	—
1970-71	H7500	—	—	⅛-¼	—
1970-71	H7500	—	—	⅛-¼	—
1970-71	H9500	—	—	⅛-¼	—
1970-71	J7500	—	—	⅛-¼	—
1970-71	J7500	—	—	⅛-¼	—
1970-71	J9500	—	—	⅛-¼	—
1970-71	J9500	—	—	⅛-¼	—
1970-71	M9500	—	—	⅛-¼	—
1970-71	T5500	—	—	⅛-¼	—
1970-71	T5500	—	—	⅛-¼	—
1970-71	T6500	—	—	⅛-¼	—
1970-71	T7500	—	—	⅛-¼	—
1970-71	T7500	—	—	⅛-¼	—
1970-71	T9500	—	—	⅛-¼	—
1970-71	W7500	—	—	⅛-¼	—
1970-71	F9500	—	—	⅛-¼	—
1970-71	D9500	—	—	⅛-¼	—

1—"G" Series.
2—With Coil Springs.
3—With Leaf Springs.
4—Model 5500-6500 with Power Steering +2-3.
5—Left Side—¼ to +¾, Right Side— ¾ to +¾.
6—FH, DH, TJ, TE, WJ, WE, FI, DI 9500.
7—FW, DW, FT, DJ, FE, DF, TW, WW 9500.
8—With Power Steering, +2½ to +3½.
9—Left Side 0 to +1½, Right Side 0 to −½.
10—HG, HM, EG, EM, ES, SG, SM, SS 5500.
11—With Front Axle #F090.
12—Left Side +¼ ±½, Right Side −¼.
13—With Front Axle #FR0.
14—With Front Axle #F070.
15—With Front Axle #F110.
16—With Front Axle #F160.
17—With Front Axle #F150.
18—With Front Axle #FE970.
19—With Front Axle #FE900.

ENGINE IDENTIFICATION—The identification plate is located inside the cab or on the firewall. The plate shows the model of engine, transmission, auxiliary transmission, brakes, front and rear axles. All identifications are for equipment on the vehicle when it was shipped from the factory.

CONVENTIONAL MODELS (2 AXLE)

STANDARD ENGINE	YEAR	MODELS	ENGINE MAKE
	SIX CYLINDER		
6-230	1964-65	I-1000	Chevrolet
	1964-65	I-1500	Chevrolet
	1964-65	I-2500	Chevrolet
6-250	1966	I-1000	Chevrolet
	1967-70	CS-1500	Chevrolet
	1966	I-1500	Chevrolet
	1967-70	KS-1500	Chevrolet
	1970	CS-1550	Chevrolet
	1970	KS-1550	Chevrolet
	1967-70	CS-2500	Chevrolet
	1966	I-2500	Chevrolet
	1968-70	KS-2500	Chevrolet
	1967-70	CS-3500	Chevrolet
	1966	I-3500	Chevrolet
	1970	CS-4500	Chevrolet
	1967-69	ES-4500	Chevrolet
6-292	1966	HI-4000	Chevrolet
	1970	CS-5500	Chevrolet

	1967-69	ES-5500V	Chevrolet
	1967-69	ES 5500M	Chevrolet
	1967	ES-5500A	Chevrolet
	1967	ES-5500Y	Chevrolet
	1967-68	ES-6500	Chevrolet
	1967-68	I-4000	Chevrolet

EIGHT CYLINDER

V8-283	1967	CE-1500	Chevrolet
V8-307	1968-70	CE-1500	Chevrolet
	1968-70	KE-1500	Chevrolet
	1970	CE-1550	Chevrolet
	1970	KE-1550	Chevrolet
	1970	CE-2500	Chevrolet
	1970	KE-2500	Chevrolet
	1968-70	CE 2500	Chevrolet
	1968-70	CE-3500	Chevrolet
V8-350	1970	CE-5500	Chevrolet
	1969-70	CE-4500	Chevrolet
V8-366	1970	CE-6500	Chevrolet
V8-637	1967-68	CJ-9500A	Own
	1966-70	HE-9500A	Own
	1967-68	CE-9500A	Own
V8-637D	1966-70	HJ-7500A	Own
	1966-70	HJ-9500A	Own

V-6 MODELS

V6-305A	1961	1000	Own
	1961	K-1000	Own
	1961	1500	Own
	1961	K-1500	Own
	1961	2500	Own
	1961	V-3000	Own
	1961	V-3500	Own
V6-305D	1962	1000	Own
	1962	K-1000	Own
	1962	1500	Own
	1962	K-1500	Own
	1962	2500	Own
	1962	V-3000	Own
	1962	V-3500	Own
V6-305E	1963-66	1000	Own
	1963-66	K-1000	Own
	1963-66	1500	Own
	1967-70	CM-1500	Own
	1963-66	K-1500	Own
	1963-66	2500	Own
	1967-69	CM-2500	Own
	1967-69	KM-2500	Own
	1963-65	B-3500	Own
	1963-66	3500	Own
	1967-69	CM-3500	Own
	1967-69	CM 4500	Own
	1967-69	RM-1500	Own
V6-350C	1963-65	B-4000	Own
	1962-63	BA-4000	Own
	1963-65	BH-4000	Own
	1962-63	BV-4000	Own
	1962-66	4000	Own
	1966	H-4000	Own
	1964-66	KV-4000	Own
	1970	CM-5500	Own
	1967-69	EM-5500M	Own
	1967-69	EM-5500V	Own
	1967-69	EM-5500A	Own
	1967	EM-5500Y	Own
	1966-67	HM-5500V	Own
	1966-67	HM-5500A	Own
	1967-69	EM-6500	Own
V6-305B	1961	BA-4000	Own
	1961	BU-4000	Own
	1961	4000	Own
V6-351	1966	D-3500	Own
	1961-65	5000	Own
	1961-65	W5000	Own
	1961-65	B-5000	Own
	1961	BA-5000	Own
	1961	BV-5000	Own
	1961-63	BW-5000	Own
	1961	BWA-5000	Own
	1961	BWV-5000	Own
	1970	CM-6500	Own
V6-351C	1966-69	HM-7500	Own
V6-351M	1966-69	HM-8500A	Own
V6-401	1961-65	H-5000	Own
	1963-65	BH-5000	Own
	1961-65	WA-5500	Own
	1961-65	WV-5500	Own
	1961-65	B-5500	Own
	1961	BA-5500	Own
	1961	BV-5500	Own
	1961-65	BWA-5500	Own
	1961	BWV-5500	Own
	1963-65	A-6000	Own
	1961-63	B-6000	Own
	1961-65	BA-6000	Own
	1970	HM-7500	Own
V6-478D	1966	D-4000	Own
	1967-69	EG-5500V	Own
	1967-69	EG-5500A	Own
	1966-67	HG-5500A	Own
	1966-67	HG-5500V	Own
	1962-65	A-6500	Own
	1967-69	EG-6500	Own
	1962-65	WA-6500	Own
	1962-65	BA-6500	Own
V6-478DH	1966-69	HG-7500	Own

V-12 MODELS

V-12-702	1961-65	B-7000	Own
	1961-65	BW-7000	Own
	1961	BW-9000	Detroit

OTHER DIESELS

4-53	1966	D-4100	Detroit
6-71NE	1967-69	CI-9500A	Detroit
	1966-70	HI-9500A	Detroit
6V-53N	1966-70	HV-7500A	Detroit
NHC-250	1970	HN-9500	Cummins
8V-71NE	1967-69	CH-9500A	Detroit

CONVENTIONAL MODELS (3 AXLE)

STANDARD ENGINES	YEAR	MODELS	ENGINE MAKE
		V-6 MODELS	
V6-351C	1966-69	JM-7500	Own
V6-366	1970	ME-6500	Chevrolet
V6-401	1970	JM-7500	Own
	1966	JM-8500	Own
V6-401M	1967-69	JM-8500A	Own
V6-478DH	1966-69	JG-7500	Own
V6-637D	1966-70	JJ-7500A	Own

EIGHT CYLINDER

V8-637	1966-70	JE-9500A	Own
	1966-70	JJ-9500A	Own
	1966-68	ME-9500A	Own
V8-637D	1966-68	MJ-9500A	Own

OTHER DIESELS

6V-53N	1966-70	JV-7500A	Detroit
6-71NE	1966-70	JI-9500A	Detroit
	1966-70	MI-9500A	Detroit
	1966-68	MI-9501A	Detroit
8V-71NE	1966-70	MH-9500A	Detroit
	1966-68	MH-9501A	Detroit
NHC-250	1970	JN-9500	Cummins

TILT CAB MODELS (2 AXLE)

SIX CYLINDER

6-250	1966	LI-3500	Chevrolet
6-292	1966-69	LVI-4000	Chevrolet
	1966-68	LVHI-4000	Chevrolet
	1970	TS-5500	Chevrolet

V-6 ENGINES

V6-305E	1965-66	L-3500	Own
V6-305C	1963-68	L-4000	Own
	1962-69	LA-4000	Own
	1963-67	LH-4000	Own
	1962-69	LV-4000	Own
	1970	TM-5500	Own
V6-351B	1961	LA-4000	Own
	1961	LV-4000	Own
V6-351D	1964-65	D-3500	Own
V6-351	1961-65	L-5000	Own
	1961	LA-5000	Own
	1961	LV-5000	Own
	1961	LWA-5000	Own
	1961	LWV-5000	Own
	1966	TM-7500	Own
V6-351C	1970	TM-6500	Own
	1967-70	TM-7500	Own
V6-401	1961-65	L-5500	Own
	1961	LA-5500	Own
	1961	LV-5500	Own
	1961-65	LWA-5500	Own
	1961-65	LA-6000	Own
	1963-65	LH-5000	Own
V6-478D	1964-65	D-4000	Own
	1964-69	DL-4000	Own
V6-478DH	1964-65	DH-5000	Own
	1964-65	DLH-5000	Own
	1964-65	DW-5000	Own
	1970	TG-5500	Own
	1966-69	TG-7500	Own
V6-478	1962-65	LA-6500	Own

EIGHT CYLINDER

V8-350	1970	TE-5500	Chevrolet
V8-366	1970	TE-6500	Chevrolet
V8-637D	1966-68	TJ-7500A	Own
	1966-68	TJ-9500A	Own
V8-637	1966-70	TE-9500A	Own

V-12 MODELS

V12-702	1961-65	L-7000	Own
	1961-63	LW-7000	Own

OTHER DIESELS

4-53	1966	DL-4100	Detroit
	1966-70	TV-7500A	Detroit
6V-53N	1965	DLA-5900	Detroit
6V-71	1961-65	DF-7000	Detroit
	1961-63	DFW-7000	Detroit
	1961-63	DL-7000	Detroit
	1963	DLW-7000	Detroit
	1961-63	DFR-8000	Detroit
6V-71N	1964-65	DFI-7000	Detroit
	1964-65	DFW-7000	Detroit
	1964-65	DLW-7000	Detroit
	1964-65	DFWI-7000	Detroit
	1964-65	DL-7000	Detroit
6V-71NE	1966-67	TW-9500A	Detroit
6V-71SE	1961-63	DLR-8000	Detroit
8V-71	1961-63	DF-7100	Detroit
	1961-63	DFW-7100	Detroit
	1961-63	DFR-8100	Detroit
8V-71N	1964-65	DF-7100	Detroit
	1964-65	DFW-7100	Detroit

CHASSIS FORWARD CONTROL

FOUR AND SIX CYLINDER

4-153	1963-65	P-1000	Chevrolet
6-194	1966	P-1000	Chevrolet
6-230	1963-65	P-1500	Chevrolet
	1967	P-1500	Chevrolet
	1967-69	PS-1500	Chevrolet
	1963-65	P-2500	Chevrolet
	1967	PS-2500	Chevrolet
	1965	P-3500	Chevrolet
6-250	1966	P-1500	Chevrolet
	1970	P-1500	Chevrolet
	1966	P-2500	Chevrolet
	1968-70	PS-2500	Chevrolet
	1966	P-3500	Chevrolt
	1967-70	PS-3500	Chevrolet
	1967-70	PS-4500	Chevrolet
6-270	1961-62	P-1500	Own
	1961-62	P-2500	Own

EIGHT CYLINDER

V8-307	1968-70	PE-2500	Chevrolet
	1968-70	PE-3500	Chevrolet

DIESEL MODELS

3-53N	1967-68	PT-2500	Detroit
	1967-69	PT-3500	Detroit

TILT CAB MODELS (2 AXLE)

6-7INE	1966-70	FI-9500A	Detroit
6V-7INE	1966-67	FW-9500A	Detroit
8V-7INE	1966-70	FH-9500A	Detroit
V8-637	1966-67	FE-9500A	Own
V8-637D	1966-69	FJ-9500A	Own
NHC-250	1970	FN-9502	Cummins
NHCT-270	1970	FC-9502	Cummins

TILT CAB MODELS (3 AXLE)

V6-401	1970	WM-7500A	Own
	1966-69	WM-8500A	Own
V8-637	1966-69	WE-9500A	Own
V8-637D	1966-69	WJ-9500A	Own
6V-7INE	1966-67	WW-9500A	Detroit

FORWARD TILT CAB MODELS (3 AXLE)

V8-637	1966-67	DE-9500A	Own
V8-637D	1966-67	DJ-9500A	Own
6-7INE	1966-70	DI-9500A	Detroit
6V-7INE	1966-67	DW-9500A	Detroit
8V-7INE	1966-70	DH-9500A	Detroit
NHC-250	1970	DN-9502	Cummins
NHCT-270	1970	DC-9502	Cummins

UNITIZED FORWARD CONTROL MODELS

4-153	1964-65	G-1000	Chevrolet
6-194	1966	G-1011	Chevrolet
	1966	G-1021	Chevrolet
6-230	1966	G-1031	Chevrolet
	1967-69	GS-1500	Chevrolet
	1967	GS-2500	Chevrolet
	1968-69	GS-2500	Chevrolet
6-250	1970	GS-1500	Chevrolet
	1970	GS-2500	Chevrolet
V8-283	1967	GE-1500	Chevrolet
	1967	GE-2500	Chevrolet
V8-307	1968-70	GE-1500	Chevrolet
	1968-70	GE-2500	Chevrolet

CONVENTIONAL DIESEL MODELS

8V-53	1965	DBA5900	Detroit
6V-53N	1965	DBWA5900	Detroit
6-71SE	1961-62	D860	Detroit
6V-71	1961-63	DB7000	Detroit
	1961-63	DBW7000	Detroit
	1961	DBW9000	Detroit
6V-71N	1964-65	DB7000	Detroit
	1964-65	DBI-7000	Detroit
	1964-65	DBW-7000	Detroit
	1964-65	DBWI-7000	Detroit
V6-478D	1964-65	DB4000	Own
V6-478DH	1964-65	DBH5000	Own

Distributor

General Information

Distributor used on in-line engines is driven from the engine camshaft by spiral cut gears and is located on the right side of the engine. A gasket is used between the distributor flange and cylinder block. The distributor is held in place by a hold-down clamp and cap screw. The lower end of the distributor shaft is tongued and fits a slot in the upper end of the oil pump shaft to drive the oil pump.

Distributor used on V6 and V8 engines is mounted on top center of cylinder block at the rear end, and is driven from the camshaft by spiral cut gears. A gasket is used between distributor flange and engine block. The distributor is held in place by a hold-down clamp and cap screw. The lower end of the distributor shaft has a hexagonal opening that fits the end of the oil pump shaft to drive the oil pump. Model number is stamped on distributor housing.

Distributor Removal

In Line, V6 Engines

1. Locate and mark the No. 1 cylinder spark plug wire position on distributor cap and on adjacent distributor housing.
2. Release distributor cap hold-down screws, remove and place cap clear of work area.
3. Disconnect distributor primary wire from coil terminal.
4. Disconnect vacuum line from distributor, noting vacuum advance mechanism position relative to engine. Mark rotor position on distributor body.
5. Remove distributor.
6. Set distributor in upright position to prevent oil on distributor shaft from contacting breaker plate and points.

(V8 Engines) Models 1000-5000

1. Locate and mark the No. 1 cylinder spark plug wire position on distributor housing.
2. Disconnect distributor primary wire from coil terminal.
3. Disconnect vacuum line and remove distributor cap.
4. Remove single hold-down bolt located under the distributor body.
5. Mark position of distributor body relative to block, then remove distributor.
6. Set distributor in upright position to prevent oil on distributor shaft from contacting breaker plate and points.

(Inline, V6, V8 Engines) Models 5500-7500

1. Locate and mark the No. 1 cylinder spark plug wire position on distributor cap and on adjacent distributor housing.
2. Release distributor cap hold-down screws, remove and place cap clear of work area.
3. Disconnect distributor primary wire from coil terminal.
4. Operate starter intermittently until crankshaft pulley timing mark aligns with pointer or timing tab. With pointer and timing mark properly aligned, rotor should point towards mark made in Step (1). If rotor points 180° from mark, rotate engine one complete revolution and re-align timing mark with tab.

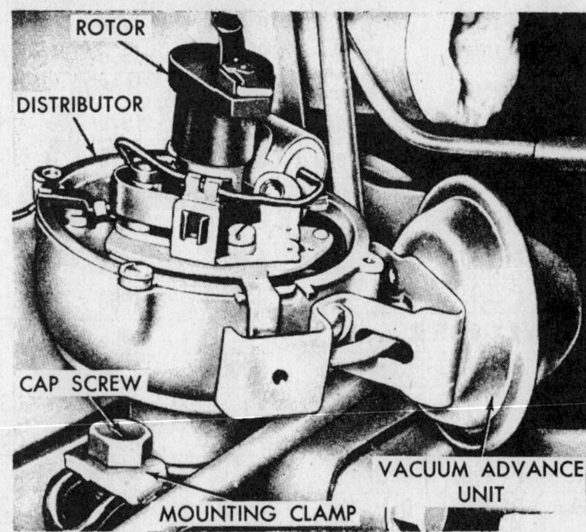

Distributor with cover removed—inline engine (typical)
(© G.M.C.)

5. Disconnect vacuum line, drive cable, etc. Remove cap screw and mounting clamp. Lift distributor straight up until spiral gear disengages from camshaft gear. Rotor will move clockwise as the gears disengage. Mark this position on distributor housing. Also note position of vacuum advance mechanism relative to engine. To complete removal, lift distributor straight up and remove cylinder block to distributor flange gasket.
6. Set distributor in upright position to prevent oil on distributor shaft from contacting breaker plate and points.

Distributor Installation

(Inline Engines) Engine Has Not Been Cranked

1. Turn rotor in clockwise direction ⅛ turn past previously marked rotor position on distributor housing.
2. Lubricate distributor drive gear with engine oil and place new distributor flange to cylinder gasket on block.
3. Push distributor down into engine block to the "normal" position. It may be necessary to move rotor a few degrees to mesh with camshaft gear; however, rotor will align with mark on distributor housing when properly in place.
4. Install cap screw and hold-down clamp, tightening clamp bolt firmly. Connect vacuum line and primary wire to coil terminal. Install No. 1 spark plug wire in socket adjacent to No. 1 firing position mark on distributor housing. Continue installing spark plug wires clockwise around cap in correct firing sequence.

(V6, V8 Engines) Engine Has Not Been Cranked

1. From old distributor, locate No. 1 firing position and mark made on housing after gears were disengaged.
2. Lubricate distributor drive gear with engine oil and place new distributor flange to cylinder gasket on block.
3. Turn rotor to point toward mark made after gears were disengaged. As distributor is inserted into place, spiral gear will cause rotor to turn counter-clockwise. It may be necessary to insert the assembly several times in order to find the correct position to bring rotor to No. 1 firing position.
4. Install cap screw and hold-down clamp, tightening clamp bolt firmly. Install No. 1 spark plug wire in socket adjacent to No. 1 firing position mark on distributor housing. Continue installing spark plug wires clockwise around cap in correct firing sequence.
5. Connect vacuum line and primary wire to coil terminal.

(Inline Engines) Engine Has Been Cranked

1. Locate No. 1 cylinder firing position by one of two methods below:
   a. Remove No. 1 spark plug, put finger over hole and crank engine until compression is felt. Continue cranking until timing mark on crankshaft pulley aligns with timing tab.
   b. Remove rocker arm cover and crank engine until No. 1 intake valve begins to close. Continue cranking very slowly until timing mark on crankshaft pulley aligns with timing tab.
2. Place new distributor flange gasket on cylinder block and position distributor at the opening. Note position of vacuum advance mechanism.
3. Turn rotor to point toward front of engine (distributor held in "installed" attitude), then turn rotor ⅛ turn counter-clockwise

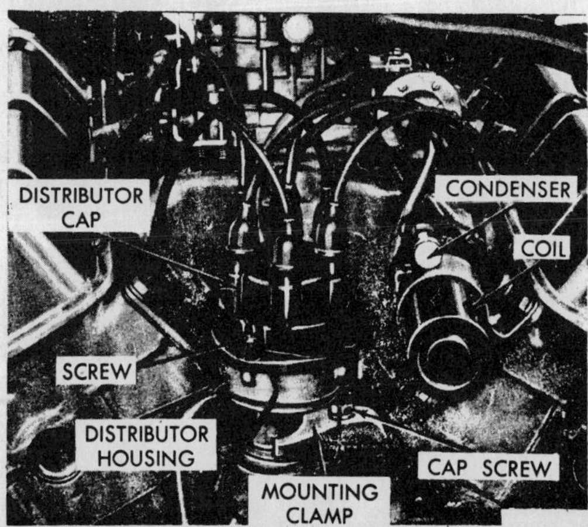

Distributor and coil—V6 engine (typical)
(© G.M.C.)

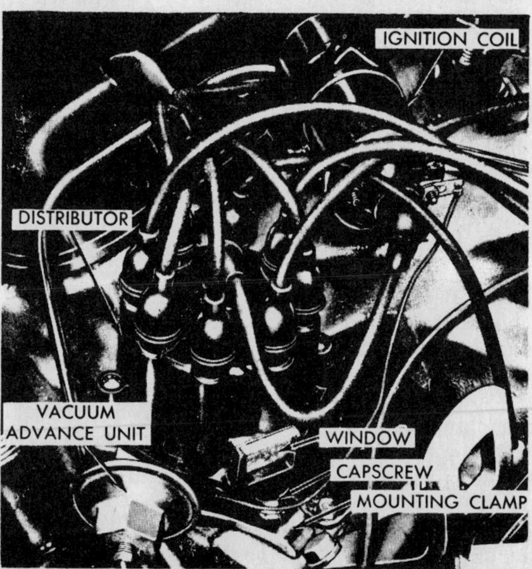

Distributor and coil—V8 engine (typical)
(© G.M.C.)

and push distributor down. It may be necessary to move rotor slightly until gears engage.

4. Press down on distributor and engage starter several times to make certain oil pump shaft is engaged. Install hold-down clamp and bolt.
5. Rotate distributor body slightly until points just begin to open, then tighten clamp boot.
6. Install distributor cap, aligning rotor with terminal for No. 1 spark plug wire.
7. Install No. 1 spark plug wire in socket adjacent to No. 1 firing position mark on distributor housing. Proceed installing spark plug wires clockwise around cap in correct firing sequence.
8. Connect vacuum line and then primary wire to negative (-) terminal on ignition coil.

("P/PB" Models)

Use same procedure as for other inline models except time to No. 2 cylinder, piston, spark plug, and intake valve instead of No. 1.

Distributor Installation

(V6, V8 Engines) Engine Has Been Cranked

1. Remove left side rocker arm cover. Intermittently operate starter and observe No. 1 intake valve as it begins to close. Continue cranking until timing mark on crankshaft pulley or damper aligns with timing tab.
2. Install distributor as previously described. It may be necessary to rotate oil pump drive shaft to engage distributor drive gear.
3. Install distributor hold-down clamp, cap screw and cap.
4. Install No. 1 spark plug wire in socket adjacent to No. 1 firing position mark on distributor housing. Continue installing spark wires clockwise around cap in correct firing order.
5. Connect vacuum line and then primary wire to negative (-) terminal on ignition coil.

Contact Point Replacement

Cleaning

Dirty breaker points should be cleaned with a few strokes of a fine-cut contact file. File should be kept free of grease, dirt and should not be used on other metals. Never use emery cloth to clean breaker points. Do not attempt to file point surface smooth, just remove scale or dirt.

NOTE: Highly pitted or burnt points are often caused by improper condenser capacity.

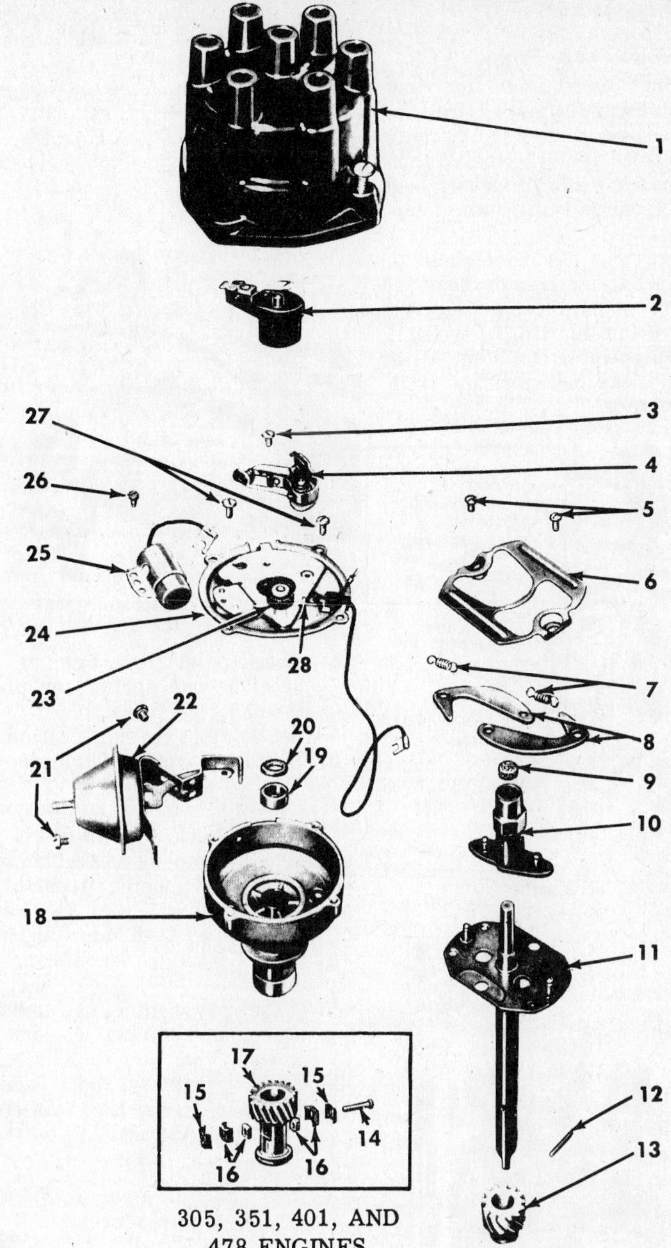

Distributor assembly—inline, V6 engines (typical)
(© G.M.C.)

1 Distributor cap
2 Rotor
3 Contact point attaching screw
4 Contact point assy.
5 Weight cover attaching screws
6 Weight cover
7 Weight springs
8 Advance weights
9 Wick (felt)
10 Cam assy.
11 Main shaft assy.
12 Roll pin
13 Drive gear
14 Pin
15 Washer
16 Cushion assy.
17 Drive gear
18 Housing
19 Oil seal—292, 351, and 401 engines
20 Flat washer—292 eng.
21 Vacuum control attaching screws
22 Vacuum control assy.
23 Oil wick
24 Breaker plate assy.
25 Condenser
26 Condenser attaching screw
27 Breaker plate attaching screws
28 Tension spring

Removal—Inline, V6 Engines

1. Remove distributor cap and place it away from work area.
2. Lift off rotor.
3. Pull primary and condenser lead wires from quick-disconnect terminal.
4. Remove attaching screws and lift breaker point set from plate.
5. Remove oil, dirt and smudge

from breaker plate.

Removal V8 Engines

1. Remove distributor cap and place it away from work area.
2. Remove two screws attaching rotor to weight assembly, then pull primary and condenser lead wires from quick-disconnect terminal.
3. Remove two screws holding point set to distributor housing, and lift out set. Clean housing.
4. Remove cam lubricating wick, if so equipped, with long nose pliers. Clean old lubricant from cam surface.

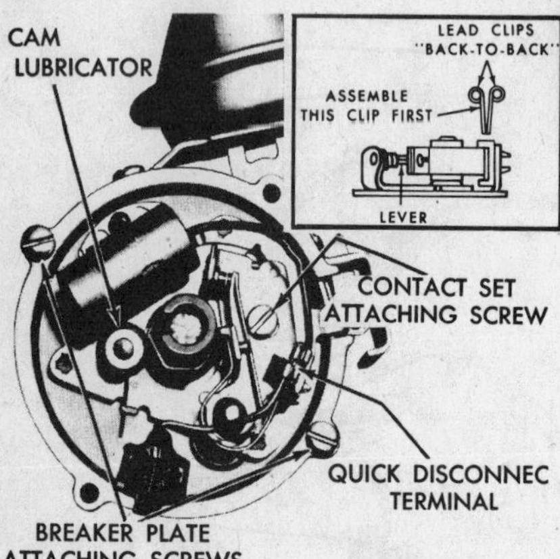

Breaker plate parts
(© G.M.C.)

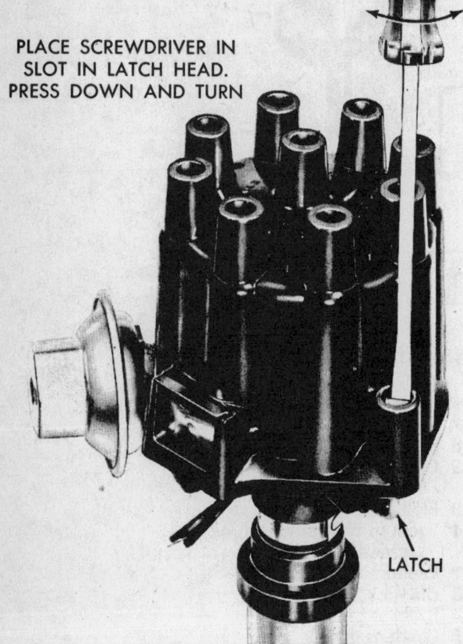

Removing distributor cap—V8 engine (typical)
(© G.M.C.)

Installation—Inline, V6 Engines

1. Carefully remove protective covering from points and place set on breaker plate. Install attaching screw.
2. Connect primary and condenser leads to terminals. Assemble clips "back to back". Do not push on spring.
3. Apply slight amount of petroleum jelly to breaker cam and a few drops of S.A.E. #20 oil to top of shaft.

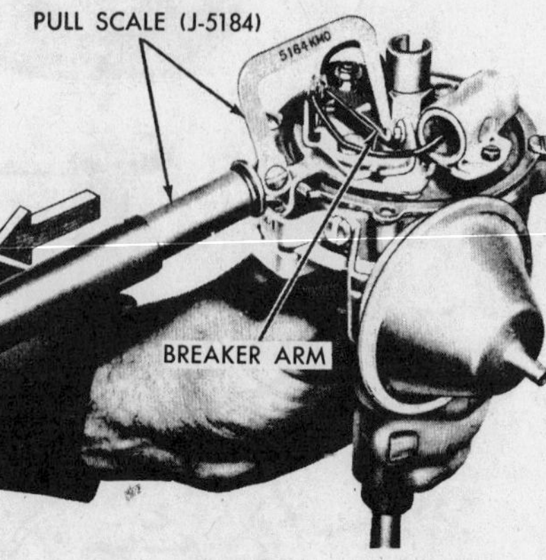

Checking breaker arm spring tension
(© G.M.C.)

4. Check points for alignment and breaker arm spring for proper tension.
5. Set point gap to specifications.
6. Install rotor and distributor cap.

Installation V8 Engines

NOTE: Breaker point set is replaced as a complete assembly; point alignment and spring tension are pre-adjusted.

1. If equipped with cam lubricator, adjust wick to touch cam lobe only.
2. Install new contact set assembly on housing and attach with two screws.
3. Connect primary and condenser leads to terminals. Assemble clips "back to back".

Distributor point set replacement
(© G.M.C.)

4. Install rotor on weight assembly with two screws and washers.
5. Install distributor cap and lock into position with screw latches.

Ignition Timing

NOTE: To use a timing light, disconnect vacuum advance line to carburetor and tape open end. Carburetor trouble can affect ignition timing adjustments. Without a power timing unit, an accurate method of setting timing with engine stopped is by using a jumper light.

1. Remove distributor cap and rotor, set breaker gap to specifications.
2. Rotate engine until No. 1 cylin-

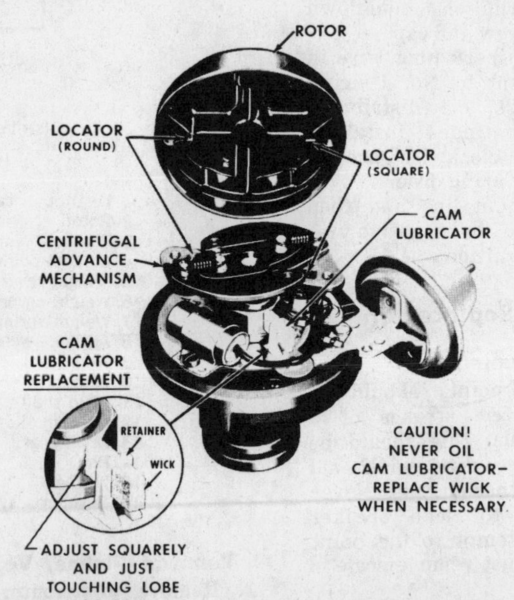

Distributor view—V8 engine (typical)
(© G.M.C.)

der is at firing position (timing mark on crankshaft pulley aligned with timing tab).
3. Connect jumper light between distributor ignition terminal and ground.
4. Turn on ignition.
5. Loosen distributor and move in normal rotation until light goes out (points closed), then slowly turn distributor back until light just comes on. Tighten distributor.

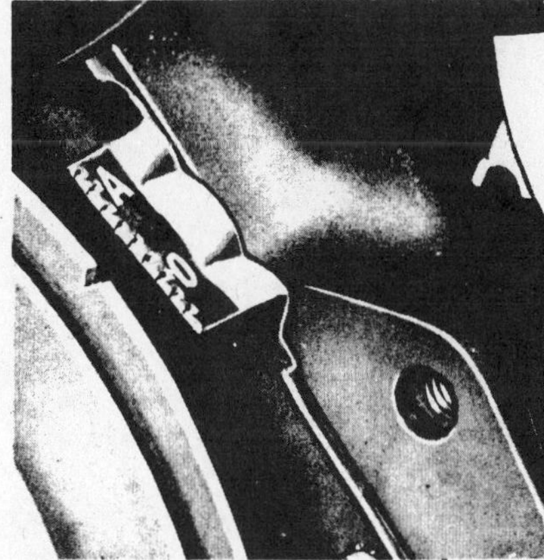

Timing marks—inline engine (typical)
(© G.M.C.)

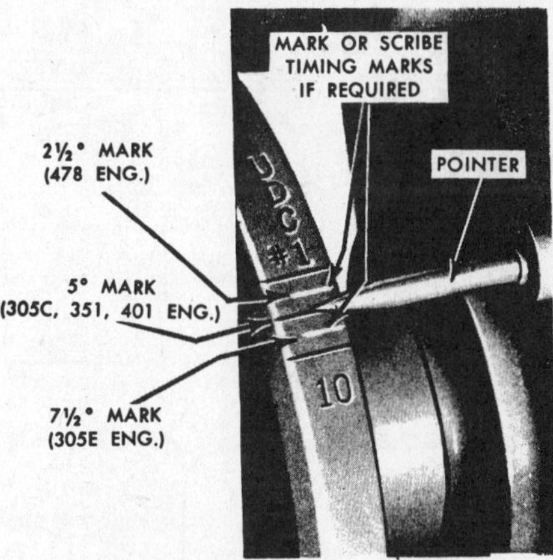

Timing marks—V6 engine (typical)
(© G.M.C.)

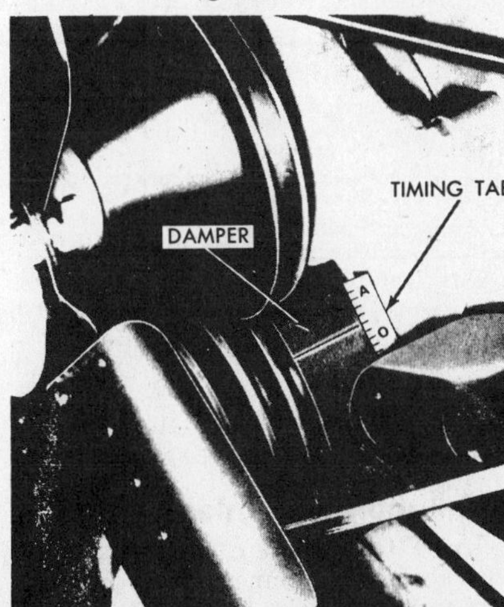

Timing marks—V8 engine (typical)
(© G.M.C.)

Refer to Troubleshooting section for ignition problem analysis.

Generator, Regulator

Direct Current Generator

All generators used are of the two brush shunt type, with external regulation. Drive and commutator ends are mounted in ball bearings. Oilers are provided on all models. Generators are designed to operate only with a certain type regulator; check model specifications.

D.C. Generator Removal

1. Remove screw attaching regulator ground wire to field frame; also disconnect wires from generator terminals. Tag for identification.
2. Loosen adjusting arm cap screw and generator mounting bolts to loosen drive belt (s).
3. Remove drive belt (s).
4. Remove adjusting arm cap screw and generator mounting bolts; lift generator assembly from engine.
5. If a new unit is to be installed, remove fan and pulley for replacement unit.

D.C. Generator Installation

1. Position generator at mounting bracket and install bolts, nuts, and lock washers.
2. Place belt (s) in generator pulley and attach adjusting arm to generator frame with cap screw and washers.
3. Adjust belt tension to specifications and then tighten cap screw and generator mounting bolts.
4. Connect wires to correct generator terminals.
5. Polarize generator by shorting "GEN" and "BAT" terminals on regulator for approximately one second (count one, two, three). This connection allows a surge of current from the battery to reach generator fields and polarize them correctly with respect to the battery.

Alternating Current Generator

(Integral and non-integral)

All generators used are the self-rectifying, alternating current type with a direct current output. The generator consists of a stator and a rotor. The rotor revolves within the stator (a large number of windings

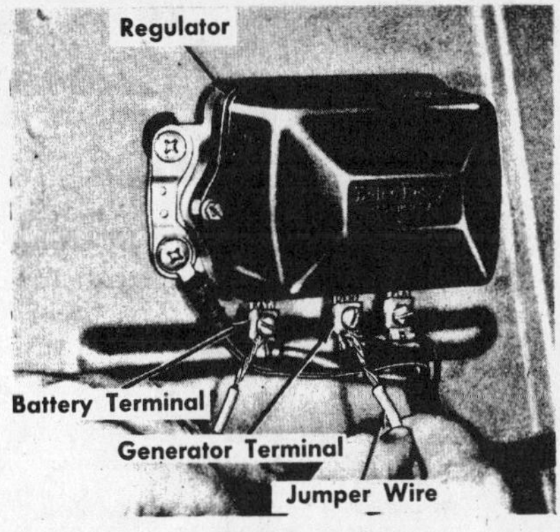

Polarizing generator
(© G.M.C.)

within a laminated core) and is carried in bearings at either end of the generator frame. Two brushes carry current through slip rings to the field coils which are wound concentric with the rotor shaft.

Due to design and equipment variations, the removal and installation procedures will vary accordingly. Additional operations may be required to permit access to generator, belts and mounting bolts. The following procedures are intended as a guide.

A.C. Alternator Removal

1. Disconnect negative (-) cable from battery. CAUTION: Generator will be damaged if terminals or wiring is accidentally shorted or grounded with negative (-) cable connected to battery.
2. Depress lock and pull connector out of socket on generator. Remove rubber boot from "BAT" terminal and remove terminal nut. Disconnect wire from "GRD" terminal and remove clip. NOTE: On 130 amp generator, remove nuts and washers from harness leads at generator terminals. Remove harness clip from generator, then pull leads from terminals.
3. Loosen generator mounting bolts and adjusting arm pivot bolt, then remove drive belt (s).
4. Remove generator mounting bolts and adjusting arm pivot bolt. Lift generator assembly from engine.

A.C. Generator Installation

CAUTION: Make certain negative (-) cable is disconnected from battery.

1. Attach generator to mounting bracket and install adjusting arm. Tighten lock nuts.
2. Install drive belt (s) and adjust to specifications. Torque lock nuts and mounting bolts to specifications.
3. Push connector into socket, making certain that it locks; place

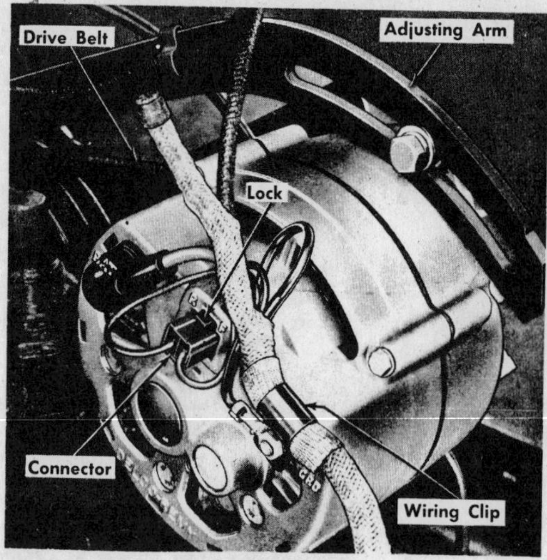

AC generator installed (typical)
(© G.M.C.)

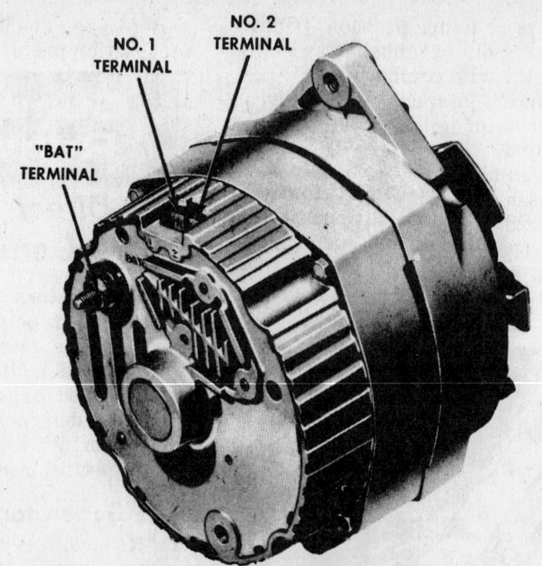

Integral AC generator (typical)
(© G.M.C.)

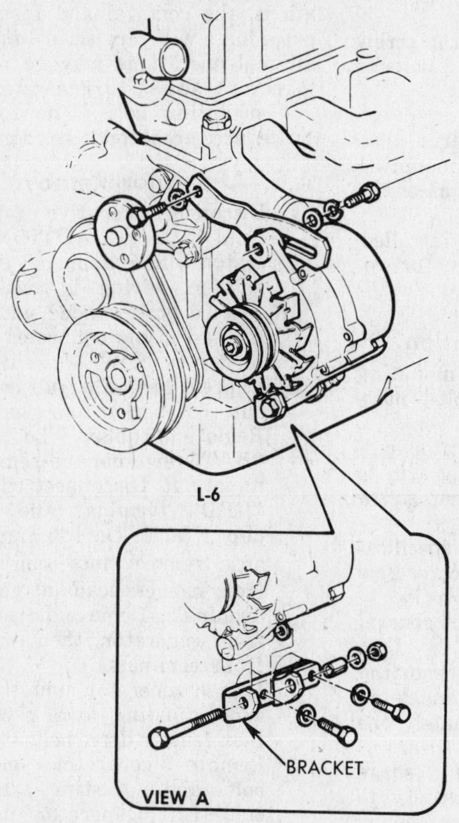

Delcotron installation
(© G.M.C.)

clip on "GRD" terminal and connect ground wire. NOTE: On 130 amp generator, connect leads to respective terminals, install attaching nuts and washers.

4. Install harness clip.
5. Attach red wire to "BAT" terminal on generator and fit rubber boot.

Voltage Regulator

Removal-Non-Integral

1. Disconnect negative (-) cable from battery.
2. Carefully remove wiring harness connector from regulator.
3. Remove regulator mounting screws; lift off regulator assembly.

Installation-Non-Integral

CAUTION: Make certain negative (-) cable is disconnected from battery.

1. Place regulator ground wire on mount and install attaching

screws.
2. Lift regulator terminal latch and insert wiring harness connector. Make certain connector is locked.
3. Connect negative (-) cable to battery.

Adjustment-Non-Integral

1. Connect (POS) voltmeter lead to battery (POS) terminal on regulator and (NEG) voltmeter lead to ground on regulator.
2. Adjust engine speed to approximately 1500 rpm, turn heater to medium speed and turn all other electrical load "OFF." Disconnect negative cable from battery.
3. Place a thermometer approximately 1/4" from regulator cover and operate engine 15 minutes.
4. Compare voltmeter reading with those given in specifications.
5. If voltmeter is not within limits listed in specifications, remove plug from regulator cover and insert thin-bladed screwdriver into adjustment screw. NOTE: After two notches in either direction there is a positive stop. CAUTION: Forcing screw beyond normal stop will destroy regulator.
6. For an undercharged battery, turn adjusting screw one notch clockwise.
7. For an overcharged battery, turn adjusting screw one notch counterclockwise.
8. Check battery condition after a service period of reasonable length.
9. If regulator cannot be adjusted to within limits listed in specifications, repair or replace the regulator.

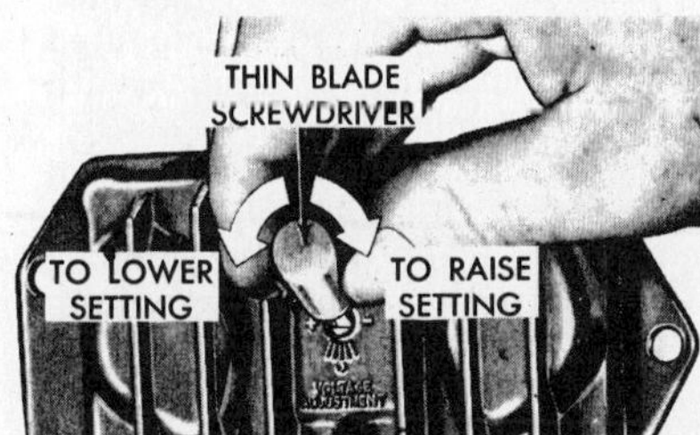

Adjusting voltage setting (typical) (© G.M.C.)

Refer to General Section for generator/voltage regulator overhaul.

Battery, Starter

Starter Motor used on all models is the over-running clutch type, having an enclosed shift lever. Entire shift lever mechanism and solenoid plunger are enclosed in the extended drive end housing. A compression type lever return spring is used to operate the over-running clutch. Oil saturated wicks lubricate armature shaft through bronze bushings in the drive end, commutator end and nose housing.

Starter Motor Removal

1. Remove ground strap from negative (-) post on battery.
2. Disconnect wires from terminals on starter solenoid.
3. Remove bolts, nuts and washers attaching starter to flywheel housing.
4. Remove starter and spacer (when used).

Starter Motor Installation

1. Install spacer (when used) and position starter against flywheel housing.
2. Install bolts, nuts and washers and torque to specifications.
3. Connect wires to proper terminals on starter solenoid and tighten attaching nuts.
4. Connect ground strap to negative (-) post on battery.

Refer to General Section for starter motor overhaul.

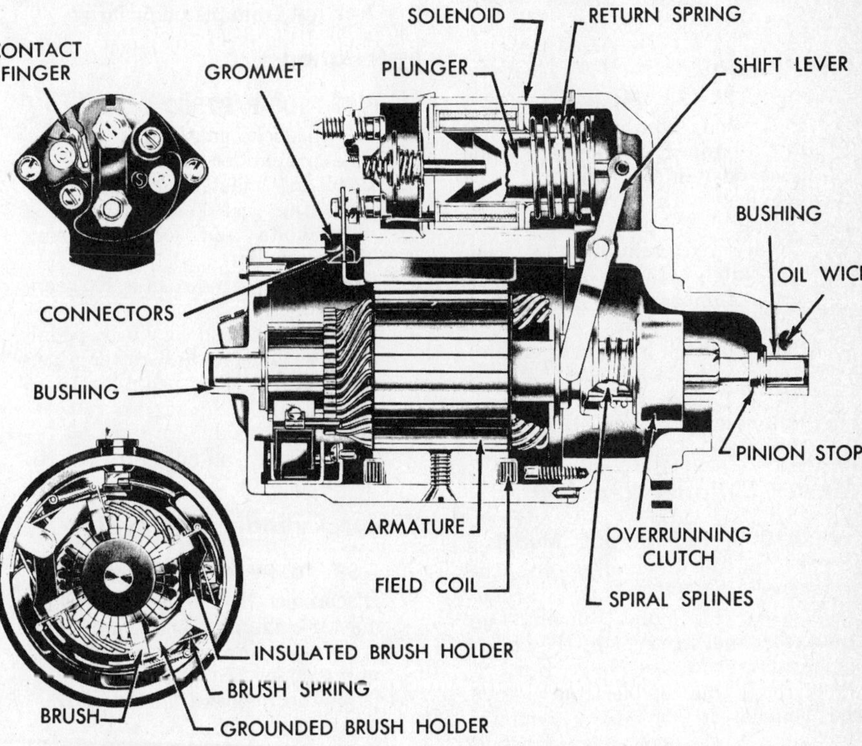

Over-running clutch type starter motor (typical) (© G.M.C.)

Brakes

Master Cylinder

Three different types of master cylinders are used on GMC trucks covered by this manual: double-barrel dash mounted type, single-barrel dash mounted type and single-barrel frame mounted type.

Removal

Standard Models

1. Hold container under master cylinder to catch fluid when hydraulic lines are disconnected. *Do not re-use this fluid.*
2. Disconnect hydraulic lines from outlets of brake and clutch cylinders. Disconnect compensating line (when used) from master cylinder reservoir.
3. Pull pushrod boots off master cylinder tubes. Boots will remain on pushrods when master cylinder is removed.
4. Remove three bolts and lock washers attaching master cylinder to dash.
5. Remove master cylinder assembly.

Installation

Standard Models

1. Place gasket over each cylinder tube. Position assembly at dash while assistant inside cab guides pushrods into pistons. Attach cylinder to dash with three bolts and lock washers.
2. Connect hydraulic lines to brake and clutch cylinder outlets. Connect compensating line (when used) to reservoir.
3. Place pushrod boots over ends of cylinder tubes.

4. Adjust pushrods.
5. Fill reservoir and bleed brake system.

Removal

Tilt Cab Models

1. Hold container under master cylinder to catch fluid when hydraulic lines are disconnected. *Do not re-use this fluid.*
2. Disconnect hydraulic lines from brake and clutch cylinders. Disconnect compensating line (when used) from master cylinder reservoir.
3. Pull pushrod boots off master cylinder. Boots will remain on pushrods when master cylinder is removed.
4. Remove three bolts attaching master cylinder to support bracket.
5. Remove master cylinder assembly.

Installation

Tilt Cab Models

1. Position master cylinder assembly at support bracket and guide pushrods into pistons. Attach cylinder with three bolts and tighten.
2. Connect hydraulic lines to brake and clutch cylinder outlets. Connect compensating line (when used) to reservoir.
3. Place pushrod boots over ends of master cylinder brackets.
4. Adjust pushrods.
5. Fill reservoir and bleed brake system.

Master Cylinder Removal

P/PB1000, P3500-7500 Models

The master cylinder on the P/PB1000 and P3500-7500 is a double barrel cylinder and is mounted on the dash panel in front of the clutch and brake pedal assemblies. Since it 's not readily accessible from outside the vehicle, it should be removed through access door above instrument panel.

1. Hold container beneath cylinder to catch fluid. *Do not re-use this fluid.*
2. Disconnect hydraulic lines from brake and clutch cylinders.
3. Pull pushrod boots off master cylinder. Boots will remain on pushrods when master cylinder is removed.
4. Remove three bolts which fasten master cylinder to dash panel. Remove master cylinder through access door.

Installation

P/PB1000, P3500-7500 Models

1. Insert master cylinder through access door.
2. Install three bolts which fasten cylinder to dash panel. Make certain pushrods are in proper location.
3. Install pushrod boots on master cylinder.
4. Connect hydraulic lines to brake and clutch cylinder outlets.

Master Cylinder Removal

P/PB1500-P/P2500 Models

1. Disconnect brake pedal return spring.
2. Disconnect hydraulic line from master cylinder head nut.
3. Remove pin connecting pushrod clevis to pedal lever.
4. Remove bolts and lock washers attaching master cylinder to mounting bracket. Remove master cylinder assembly.
5. Remove adjustable clevis and lock nut from piston pushrod.

Installation

P/PB1500-P/P2500 Models

1. Install lock nut and clevis on master cylinder pushrod.
2. Position master cylinder at mounting bracket and attach with bolts and lock washers. Tighten bolts.
3. Connect hydraulic line to head nut.
4. Connect pushrod clevis to pedal lever with clevis and cotter pins.
5. Connect brake pedal return spring.
6. Adjust pushrod.
7. Fill master cylinder and bleed brake system.

Master Cylinder Removal

SPV/DSPV5000 Models

1. Disconnect hydraulic lines from master cylinder head nut and from reservoir port at inner side of mounting bracket.
2. Disconnect brake pedal return spring.
3. Remove eccentric bolt attaching piston pushrod to pedal lower half.
4. Remove nuts, lock washers, and flat washers from master cylinder mounting bolts.
5. Remove shaft from pedal and supports, then drop pedal down.
6. Remove mounting bolts and master cylinder assembly.

Installation

SPV/DSPV5000 Models

1. Position master cylinder assembly at mounting bracket and insert bolts from inner side of bracket through master cylinder housing.
2. Position pedal lower half between supports and install shaft.

   NOTE: Shaft must be installed with milled notch at outer side of bracket, facing rearward.
3. Install retaining bracket on mounting bolts, with forward end of bracket engaging notch in pedal shaft. Install flat washer, lock washer, and nut on each mounting bolt and tighten.
4. Connect hydraulic lines to master cylinder head nut and reservoir port.
5. Install bolt connecting piston pushrod to pedal lower half. Adjust pedal to toeboard clearance.
6. Fill master cylinder and bleed brake system.

Air Brakes

Application Valve Removal

1. Relieve air pressure from system.
2. Disconnect all air lines from valve. On "L" models, disconnect hose from exhaust tube.
3. Remove valve as follows:

All Except SPA5000

Remove three attaching bolts and valve assembly.

SPA5000

Remove bolts attaching valve and treadle mounting plate to toeboard and then remove the complete assembly from the truck. Remove three bolts attaching valve to mounting plate and remove valve.

Installation

Except SPA5000 Models

Position valve assembly on mounting bracket with pushrod inserted into piston cup. On dash mounted units, the exhaust opening (with filter screen) must be down; on "L" models, exhaust tube must be toward right side of cab. Attach valve to mounting bracket with three bolts. Check pushrod or stop screw adjustment and correct if necessary.

Installation

SPA5000 Models

Connect valve assembly to mounting plate, with pushrod inserted into plate. Attach with three bolts and lock washers. Check for free travel between end of pushrod and piston cup. If necessary, remove treadle pin, then remove treadle stop bumper and add shims under bumper as necessary to remove clearance. Install treadle pin and secure with cotter pin. Install the complete assembly on toeboard and attach with three bolts, lock washers, and nuts.

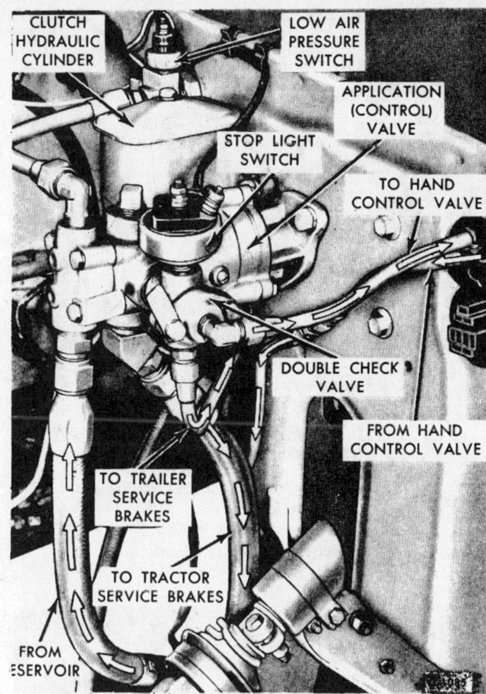

Application valve—models 1000-4500 (typical)
(© G.M.C.)

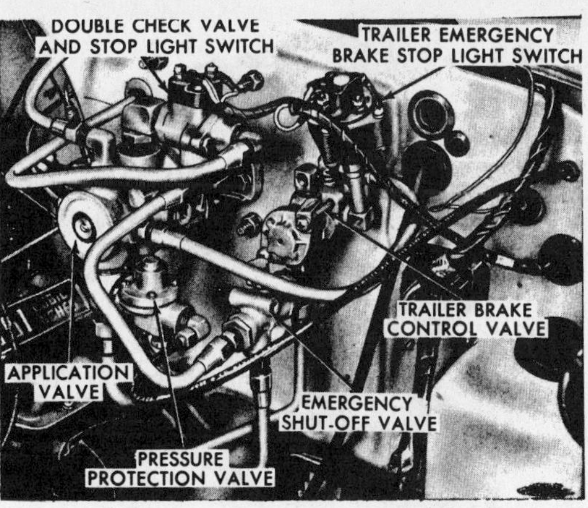

Application valve—model 6500 (typical)
(© G.M.C.)

All Models

Connect air lines to valve. When installing connector fittings in valve, use sealing compound on threads. *Keep sealing compound off first two threads of fittings.* Sealing compound inside the valve could foul valve seats and block compensating port. On "L" models, connect hose to exhaust tube. Build up air pressure in system and test application valve operation.

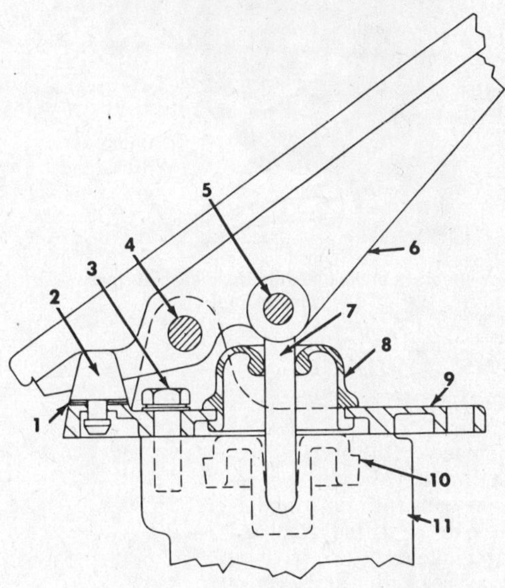

Brake treadle installation (SPA5000)
(© G.M.C.)

1 Shims
2 Treadle stop bumper
3 Mounting plate to application valve bolt
4 Treadle pin
5 Push rod pin
6 Treadle
7 Push rod
8 Push rod boot
9 Mountain plate
10 Application valve piston cup
11 Application vlave

Bleeding Brakes

Pressure Brakes

CAUTION: Stop engine and relieve vacuum or exhaust pressure from system before following procedures.

1. Make certain lever in pressure tank is up to petcock above outlet and that tank is charged with 40 to 50 psi.
2. Clean dirt from around master cylinder filler cap. Connect pressure tank hose to filler cap or cover opening. Bleed air from hose before tightening connection. Open valves at both ends.
3. Bleed slave cylinder and control valve first. (when used). Slip end of bleeder hose over bleeder valve No. 1 and place other end in glass jar containing enough hydraulic fluid to cover end of hose. Open bleeder valve with wrench and observe flow of fluid. On Models 4000 and 5000, start engine and make at least two power brake applications with bleeder valve open to force air out of slave cylinder. Close bleeder valve as soon as bubbles stop and fluid flows in solid stream. Stop engine and relieve vacuum from system.
4. Bleed valve No. 2 (on power cylinder control valve), then bleed wheel cylinders in sequence. Repeat bleeding operations at power cylinder. On Models 4000 and 5000, repeat power brake applications with engine running as in Step (3).
5. If, after bleeding, the pedal "feel" is not satisfactory, inspect residual check valve in the master cylinder and the check valve in the power cylinder piston. Improper operation of either or both of these valves will result in same pedal "feel" as air in the system, since malfunction permits recirculation of fluid through compensating line and back to master cylinder reservoir. Refer to applicable procedures for repair.

Manual Bleeding

Manual bleeding follows the same procedures as pressure bleeding, except that brake fluid is forced through lines by pumping the brake pedal instead of by air pressure.

Fluid in master cylinder must be replenished after bleeding at each valve. Brake pedal should be pumped up and down slowly, and should be on downstroke as valve is closed.

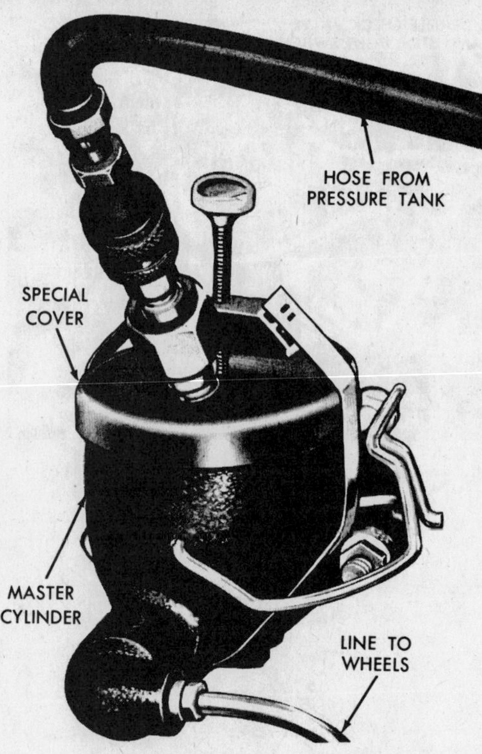

Pressure brake bleeding using special cover
(© G.M.C.)

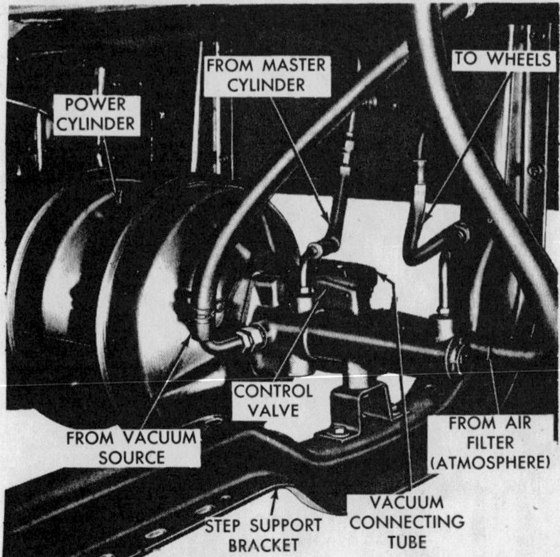

Power cylinder (conventional)
(© G.M.C.)

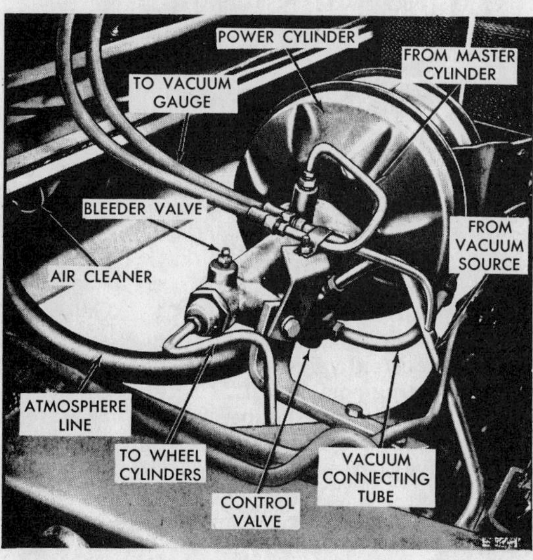

Power cylinder (tilt cab)
(© G.M.C.)

Power Cylinder

Removal

1. For easier accessibility, it is recommended that cab step be removed on conventional models and that cab be tilted forward on tilt cab models.
2. Clean away road dirt and grease to prevent contamination of vacuum or hydraulic systems.
3. Have a container available to catch hydraulic brake fluid which will flow from system. *Do not re-use this fluid.*
4. Disconnect all hydraulic, vacuum and atmospheric lines and hoses from power cylinder.
5. Remove bolts and nuts fastening cylinder to frame and support brackets.
6. Remove power cylinder.

Installation

1. Place power cylinder in position and fasten with nuts and bolts to frame and support brackets.
2. Connect all hydraulic, vacuum, and atmospheric lines and hoses to power cylinder.
3. Bleed master cylinder and vacuum power cylinder as directed under "Bleeding Brakes." If ONLY the power cylinder has been removed, it should not be necessary to bleed the wheel cylinders IF the master cylinder and power cylinders are bled first AND lines to wheel cylinder have not been disturbed.

Parking Brakes

Adjustments

Foot Pedal Type

1. Jack up rear wheels.
2. Apply parking brake 1 notch from fully released position.
3. Loosen equalizer check nut and tighten the adjusting nut until moderate drag is felt when rear wheels are rotated.
4. Tighten check nut securely.
5. Fully release parking brake and rotate rear wheels. No drag should be present.

Orscheln Lever Type

1. Turn adjusting knob on parking brake lever counter-clockwise to stop.
2. Apply parking brake.
3. Jack up rear wheels.
4. Loosen lock nut at intermediate cable equalizer and adjust front nut to give light drag at rear wheels.
5. Re-adjust parking brake lever knob to give definite snap-over-center feel.
6. Fully release parking brake and rotate rear wheels. No drag should be present.

Driveshaft Type (Drum On)

1. Jack up at least one rear wheel. Block wheels and release hand brake.
2. Remove cotter pin and clevis pin connecting pull rod to relay lever. NOTE: It may be necessary to knock out lanced area in brake drum with punch and hammer to gain entry to adjusting screw through brake drum.
3. Rotate brake drum to bring an access hole into line with adjusting screw at bottom of shoes.
4. Expand shoes by rotating adjusting screw with screw driver.

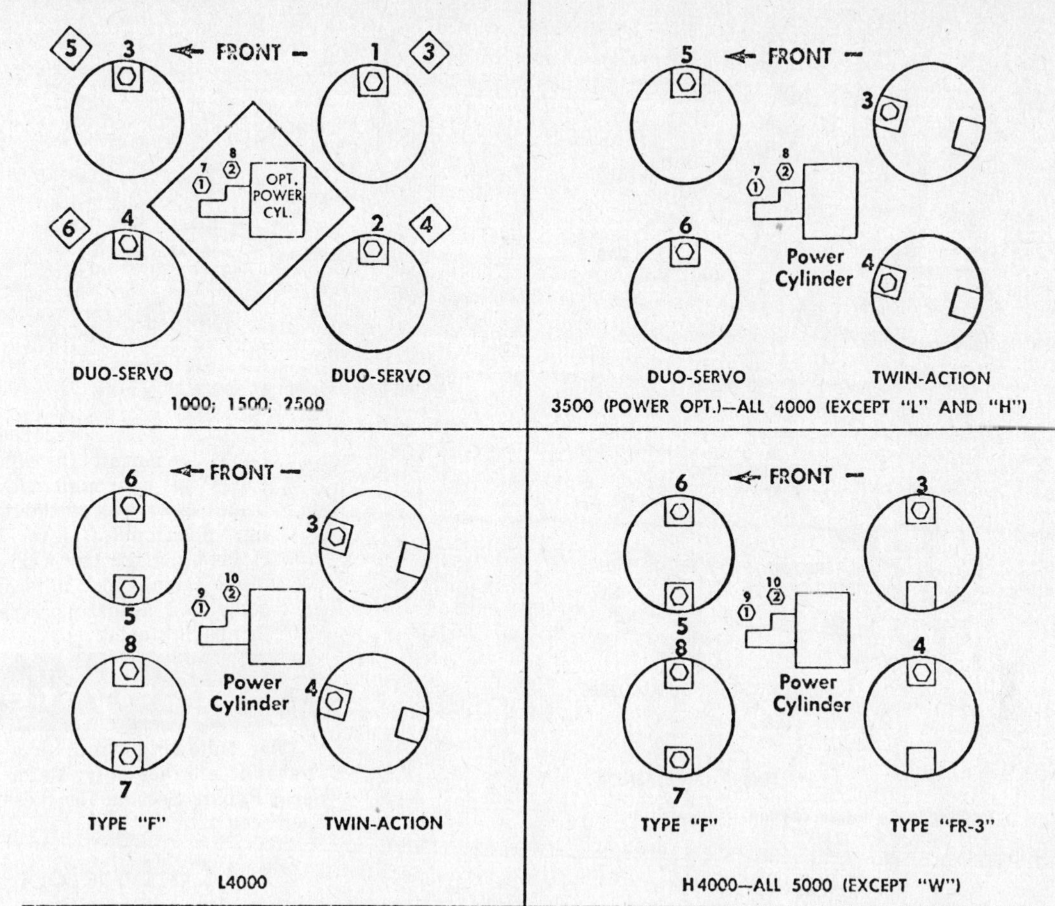

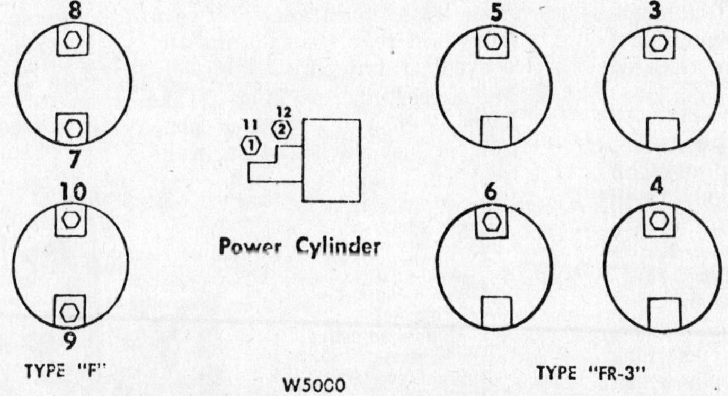

Brake bleeding sequence (© G.M.C.)

Move outer end of screw driver away from drive shaft. Continue adjustment until shoes are tight against drum and drum cannot be rotated by hand. Back off adjustment ten notches and check drum for free rotation.

5. Place parking brake lever in fully released position. Take up slack in brake linkage by pulling back on cable just enough to overcome spring tension. Adjust clevis of pull rod or front cable to line up with hole in relay levers.
6. Insert clevis pin and cotter pin, tighten clevis locknut.
7. Install new hole cover in drum to prevent dirt contamination.
8. Lower rear wheels. Remove jack and wheel blocks.

Driveshaft Type (Drum Off)

1. With parking brake drum off, check diameter of drum clearance surface.
2. Turn tool to the opposite side and fit over brake shoes by turning star wheel until gauge just slides over linings.
3. Rotate gauge around brake shoe lining surface to insure proper clearance.
4. Install driveshift flange at mainshaft.
5. Lower rear wheels. Remove jack and wheel blocks.

Stopmaster "Fail-Safe" Type

Stopmaster "Fail-Safe" parking brakes are used as standard equipment on some models and as optional equipment on others. When Stopmaster service brakes with "Fail-Safe" feature are used, no other parking

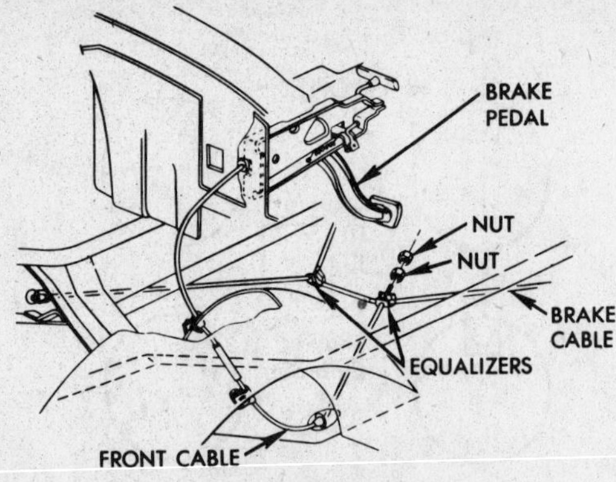

Parking brake system ("C"-"K" models)
(© G.M.C.)

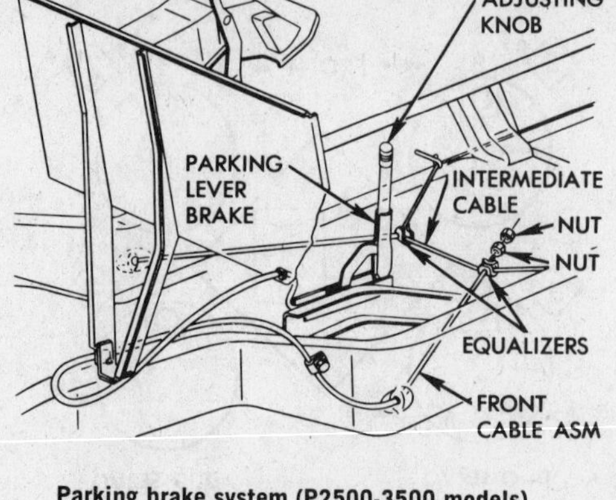

Parking brake system (P2500-3500 models)
(© G.M.C.)

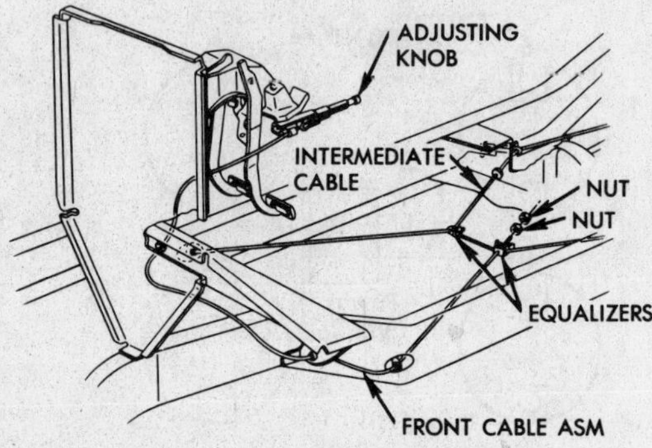

Parking brake system (P1500 models)
(© G.M.C.)

brake system is required.

Anchorlok Type

The "Anchorlok" brake chamber is used as optional equipment on some models. This chamber incorporates a spring applied, air pressure released parking/emergency brake.

Tru-Stop (Disc) Type

This type brake is used only on "W" models when equipped with 3-speed or 4-speed auxiliary transmission. The ventilated brake disc is mounted between propeller shaft flange and auxiliary transmission shaft companion flange. Brake shoes are mounted in opposed positions with brake disc between, as shown in illustration. When brake is applied, the shoes are forced against disc. Brake should be adjusted before a full application requires parking brake lever to be pulled to travel limit.

1. Disconnect brake cable clevis (5) from brake lever (6).
2. Tighten adjusting nut (16) until spring (14) exerts enough pressure to bring lever (6) against front lever arm (11).
3. Insert a 1/32" shim between rear shoe lining and brake disc.
4. Tighten adjusting nut (16) until front shoe lining is firmly against disc, yet allowing removal of shim.
5. Make certain tension spring (13) is in place. Turn adjusting screws (2) so that both linings are parallel with disc. This provides 16¼" clearance between front and rear shoe linings and brake disc at all points.
6. Make certain parking brake lever is in fully released position. Adjust clevis (5) on brake cable to permit installation of clevis pin through clevis and brake lever (6) without changing position of lever. Install clevis pin and cotter pin.
7. Make certain lock nuts on brake cable and adjusting screws are firmly tightened.

Fuel System

The following procedures are for gasoline engines only. Refer to General Repair Section for diesel engine service.

Carburetors

GMC trucks models 1000-7500 utilize Carter, Rochester, Holley and Bendix-Stromberg carburetors.

Removal—Carter Carburetor

1. Remove air cleaner.
2. Disconnect fuel and vacuum advance lines at carburetor.
3. Disconnect accelerator linkage at carburetor throttle lever.

1 Brake support bracket
2 Parallel adjusting screws
3 Front lever arm pin
4 Pin retaining screw
5 Brake cable clevis
6 Brake lever
7 Brake shoe pin retainer
8 Brake shoe pin
9 Front brake shoe
10 Rear brake shoe
11 Front lever arm
12 Brake disc
13 Tension spring
14 Spring
15 Rear lever arm
16 Adjusting nut
17 Tie Rod

Tru-stop (disc) parking brake
(© G.M.C.)

4. Loosen choke cable clamp screw at bracket on carburetor and disconnect wire lever.
5. Remove carburetor flange-to-manifold adapter and nuts; lift carburetor from adapter.

Installation

1. Install new manifold adapter to carburetor flange gasket.
2. Position carburetor over manifold studs, install nuts and tighten securely.
3. Connect fuel line and vacuum advance tube at carburetor.
4. Connect choke cable assembly and adjust.
5. Connect accelerator linkage at carburetor throttle lever and check adjustment.
6. Install air cleaner.
7. Adjust idle speed and mixture.

Adjustments

Idle speed and mixture adjustment

1. Disconnect spark advance tube at distributor and tape open end.
2. Connect tachometer at coil.
3. Connect vacuum gauge to manifold.
4. Adjust idle to 500 rpm with engine running, choke open.
5. Adjust mixture screw for highest steady vacuum. CAUTION: Do not turn idle mixture screw tightly against seat.

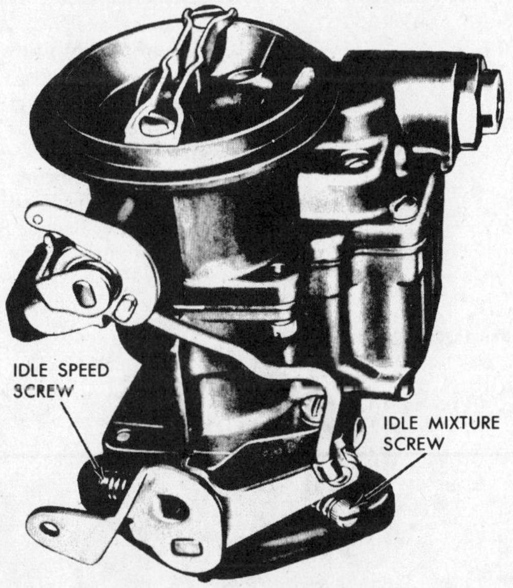

Idle speed and mixture adjustments (Carter)
(© G.M.C.)

Choke Adjustment

1. Move hand choke knob to within 1/8″ from dash.
2. Loosen choke wire clamp at carburetor bracket and adjust until choke is wide open.
3. Tighten cable clamp.

Idle Vent Adjustment

Set clearance between cover and vent at 0.030″ with throttle at normal idle.

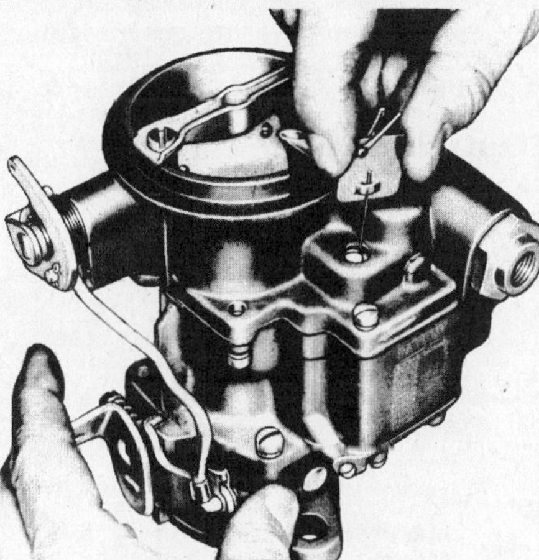

Idle vent adjustment (Carter)
(© G.M.C.)

Fast Idle Rod Adjustment

1. Remove air cleaner tube adapter.
2. With choke valve in wide open position, tang on fast idle lever should just contact stop boss on carburetor body.
3. If necessary to adjust, bend rod at offset to establish this relationship.
4. Install air cleaner tube adapter.

Rochester Carburetor

Removal

1. Remove air cleaner and gasket.
2. Disconnect fuel and vacuum lines from carburetor.
3. Disconect choke cable or rod.
4. Disconnect accelerator linkage.
5. If equipped with Automatic transmission (MT Models), disconnect TV linkage.
6. Remove carburetor attaching nuts and remove carburetor. NOTE: Fill the carburetor bowl before installing the carburetor. This reduces the strain on the starter motor and battery and reduces the possibility of backfiring while attempting to start the engine.

Installation

1. Be certain throttle body and intake manifold sealing surfaces are clean.
2. Install new carburetor to manifold flange gasket.
3. Install carburetor over manifold studs.
4. Start vacuum and fuel lines at carburetor.
5. Install attaching nuts and tighten securely.
6. Tighten fuel and vacuum lines.
7. Connect and adjust accelerator and TV linkage (when used).
8. Connect choke cable.

Adjustments

Idle and Mixture Adjustment

1. Have engine at operating temperature, choke open, and air cleaner installed.
2. Air conditioning (when used) must be turned ON. Hot idle compensator must be held closed.
3. When equipped with automatic transmission, apply parking brake and block driving wheels.
4. Check the distributor dwell reading.
5. Adjust idle speed and mixture as follows: NOTE: When setting ignition timing, the term BTDC means BEFORE TOP DEAD CENTER.

Inline Engines

1. Turn misture screw IN until it lightly contacts seat, then back screw OUT 4 full turns.
2. Disconnect and plug distributor vacuum line. Set ignition timing:
   Manual Transmission 4° BTDC
   Automatic Trans. 4° BTDC
3. Connect distributor vacuum line.
4. Adjust idle speed screw to 600 rpm (manual transmission in neutral) or 530 rpm (automatic transmission in drive).
5. Adjust mixture screw IN to obtain 550 rpm (manual transmission in neutral), or 500 rpm (automatic transmission in drive).

350 V8 Engine

1. Adjust the mixture screws for maximum steady idle speed.
2. Disconnect and plug distributor vacuum advance line. Set ignition timing as follows:
   Manual Transmission 4° BTDC

Automatic Trans. 4° BTDC
3. Connect distributor vacuum line.
4. Adjust idle speed screw to 500 rpm.
5. Adjust mixture screws IN for a 20 rpm drop.
6. Adjust each mixture screw out ¼ turn.
7. Check idle speed and re-adjust screw to 500 rpm.

Choke Adjustment

Model 2G Carburetor

1. Remove air cleaner.
2. Move hand choke knob to within ⅛″ of dash panel.
3. Loosen choke clamp at carburetor or bracket and adjust cable until choke is wide open.
4. Tighten cable clamp at carburetor bracket and check operation of choke valve to ensure full closed and wide open position.
5. Install air cleaner.

Fast Idle Adjustment

Model M Carburetor

1. Adjust idle speed.
2. Rotate fast idle cam clockwise to its highest position.
3. With tang held against cam, check clearance between end of slow idle screw and idle stop tang on throttle lever.
4. Set clearance to 0.1″.
5. Check fast idle rpm with specifications.

Holley Carburetor

Removal

1. Remove air cleaner and gasket.
2. Disconnect fuel and vacuum lines from carburetor.
3. Disconnect choke cable or rod.
4. Disconnect accelerator linkage.
5. If equipped with automatic transmission, disconnect TV linkage.
6. Remove carburetor attaching nuts.
7. Remove carburetor.

Installation

1. Be certain throttle body and intake manifold sealing surfaces are clean.
2. Install new carburetor to manifold flange gasket.
3. Install carburetor over manifold studs.
4. Start vacuum and fuel lines at carburetor.
5. Install attaching nuts and tighten.
6. Tighten fuel and vacuum lines.
7. Connect and adjust accelerator and TV linkage (when used).
8. Connect choke cable or rod.

Adjustments

Idle Speed and Mixture Adjustment

1. Check dwell reading. NOTE: The dwell reading should be 28 to 32 degrees. Readjust if necessary.
2. Set ignition timing as follows:
Manual Transmission 8° BTDC
Automatic Trans. 8° BTDC
3. Set the engine idle speed to 500 rpm.

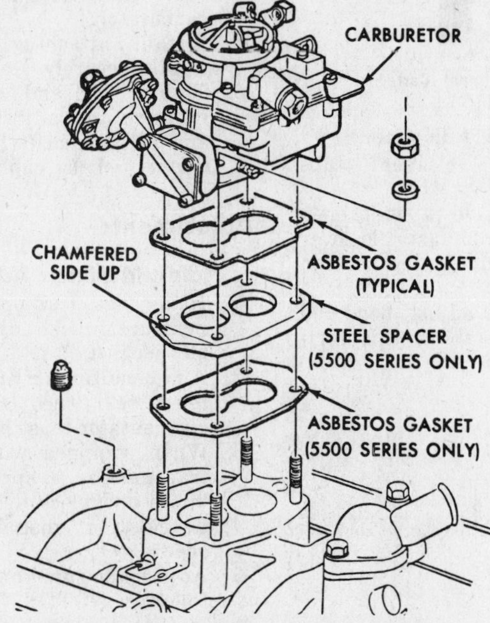

Carburetor installation (Rochester 2G) (© G.M.C.)

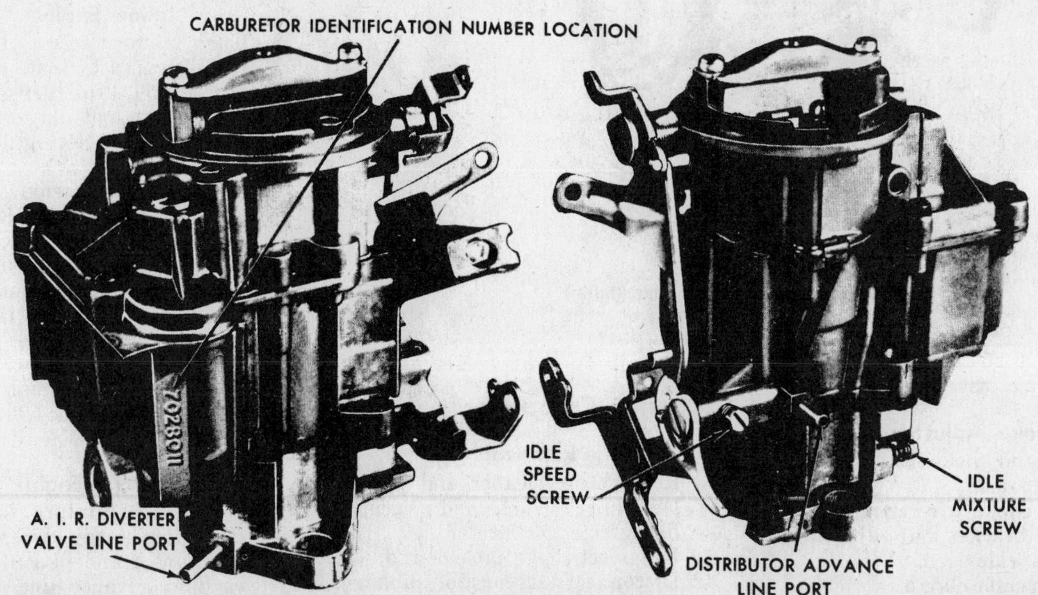

Rochester M carburetor (© G.M.C.)

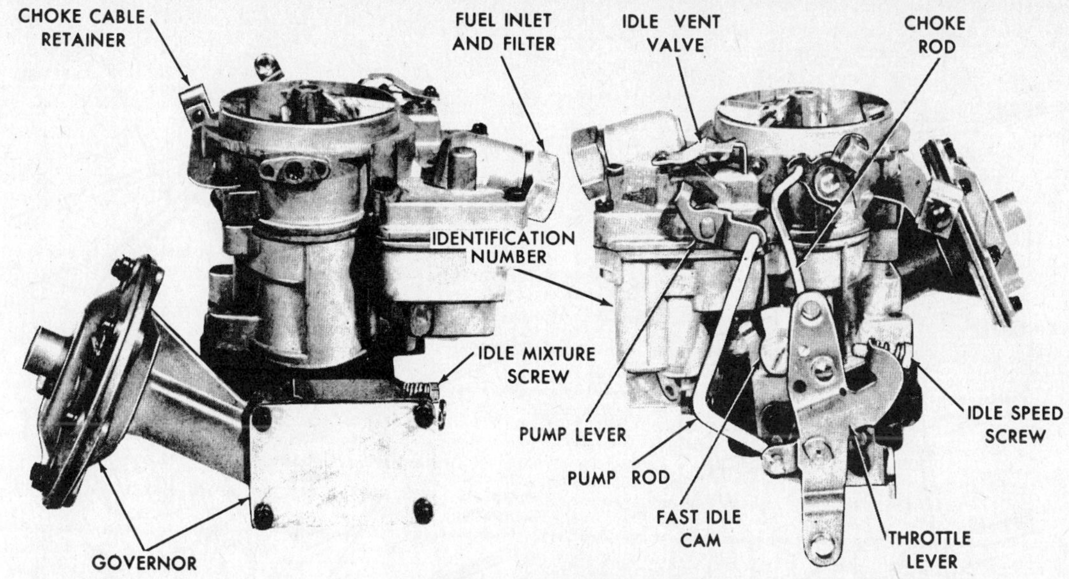

Rochester 2G carburetor (© G.M.C.)

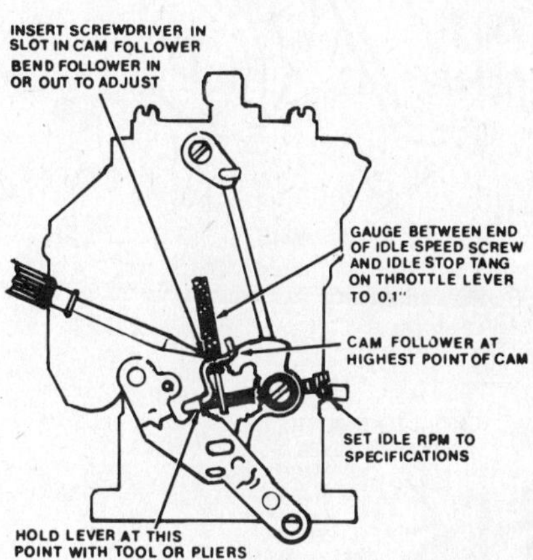

Fast idle adjustment (Rochester M) (© G.M.C.)

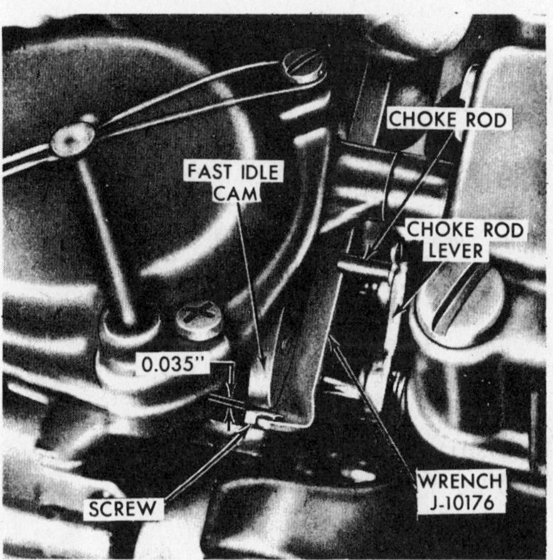

Fast idle adjustment (Holley) (© G.M.C.)

4. Adjust mixture screws for maximum steady idle speed.
5. Adjust each carburetor mixture screw to obtain a 20 rpm drop (lean roll).
6. Adjust each mixture screw out ¼ turn.
7. Check idle speed and re-adjust to 500 rpm.

Choke Adjustment

Choke adjustments on the Holley carburetor are the same as on the Rochester carburetor.

Rochester Carburetor

Fast Idle Adjustment

1. With engine "OFF" and air cleaner removed, disconnect throttle return spring.
2. With throttle lever in wide open position and choke fully closed, measure gap between fast idle cam and screw. Gap should be 0.035".
3. If necessary, adjust fast idle screw to provide correct gap.
4. Connect throttle return spring and install air cleaner.

Adjustment—Bendix—Stromberg Carburetor

Idle Speed and Mixture Adjustment

All V6 Engines

1. Dwell reading on all V6 engines should be 31 to 34 degrees.
2. Disconnect and plug distributor vacuum lines.
3. Set ignition timing to:
   305C Engine ....7½° BTDC
   351C Engine ....5° BTDC
4. Connect distributor vacuum lines except to vacuum idle stop.
5. With engine running, vacuum idle stop disconnected, check reduced engine rpm. The engine speed should be 400 rpm. If necessary, readjust.
6. Connect vacuum line from carburetor to vacuum idle stop. With engine running, vacuum idle stop connected, idle speed should be 550 rpm. If necessary to readjust, perform the following:
   a. Place a ¼" open end wrench on diaphragm extension of vacuum idle stop to prevent its rotation while adjusting plunger.
   b. Adjust the plunger with a ⅜" open end wrench until the face of the plunger hex contacting the carburetor throttle lever results in an idle speed of 550 rpm.
7. Adjust the idle mixture screws. With engine running and idling speed set, turn each mixture screw "in" until engine begins to slow down or run unevenly, then back out screws until engine runs smoothly with highest vac-

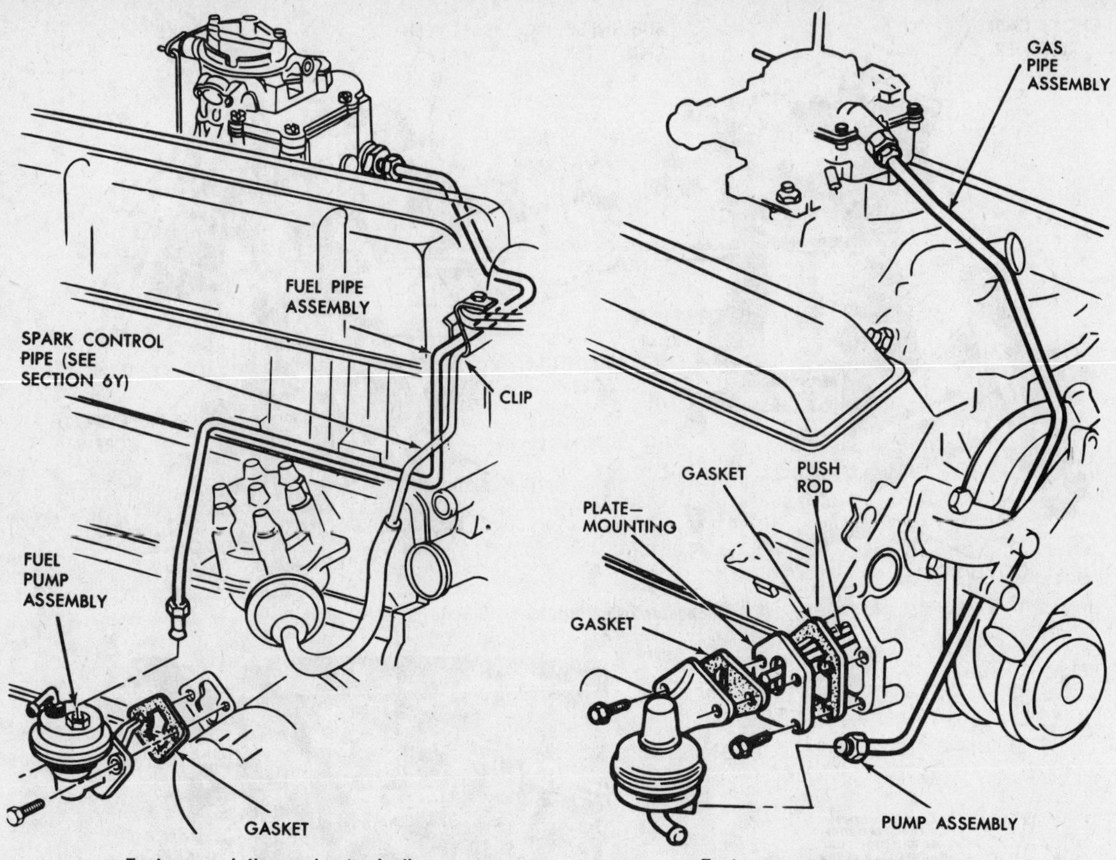

Fuel pump—inline engine (typical)
(© G.M.C.)

Fuel pump—V6 engine (typical)
(© G.M.C.)

uum gauge reading.

8. Reset the engine idle speed to 575 rpm, by adjusting plunger on vacuum idle stop as previously described.
9. Turn "in" idle mixture screws equally to reduce idle speed to 550 rpm.

Manual Choke Adjustment

1. Loosen choke wire screw at carburetor.
2. Move choke control knob to within 1/8" from instrument panel.
3. Move choke lever to fully open position and tighten screw.

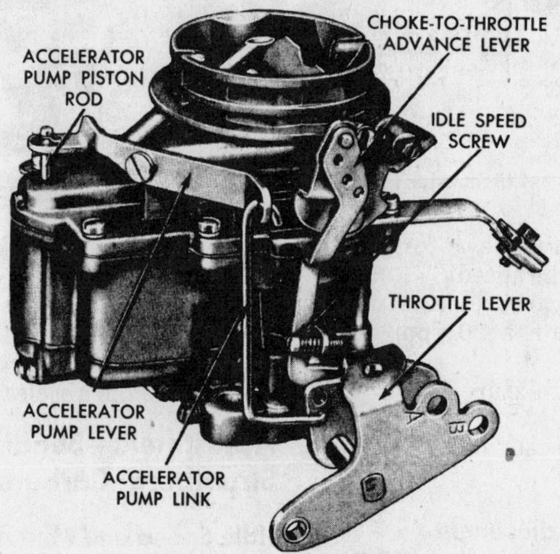

Bendix-Stromberg carburetor
(© G.M.C.)

Fuel Pump

All models covered by this manual utilize single—diaphragm, dual—diaphragm or electric fuel pumps.

Mechanical Fuel Pump

Removal

1. Disconnect all inlet and outlet pipes from fuel pump.
2. Remove fuel pump mounting bolts.
3. Remove fuel pump and gasket. NOTE: On V8 engines, remove fuel pump adapter and gasket if pushrod is to be removed.
4. Transfer fittings if new pump is to be installed.

Installation

1. On V8 engines, install fuel pump pushrod and adapter.
2. Install fuel pump, using new gasket and sealer on mounting bolt threads.
3. Connect fuel lines to pump.
4. Start engine and check for leaks. NOTE: On V8 engines use mechanical fingers or heavy grease to hold push rod up while installing pump.

Electric Fuel Pump

Removal

1. Disconnect battery ground cable.
2. Disconnect pump wiring harness from connector.
3. Disconnect fuel outlet fitting from hose.
4. Remove cap screws and washers.
5. Rotate pump 90° counterclockwise and lift out.

Installing V8 engine fuel pump (© G.M.C.)

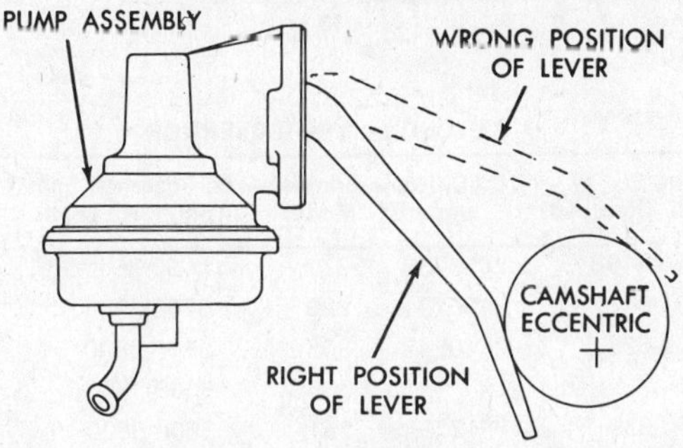

Installing V6 engine fuel pump

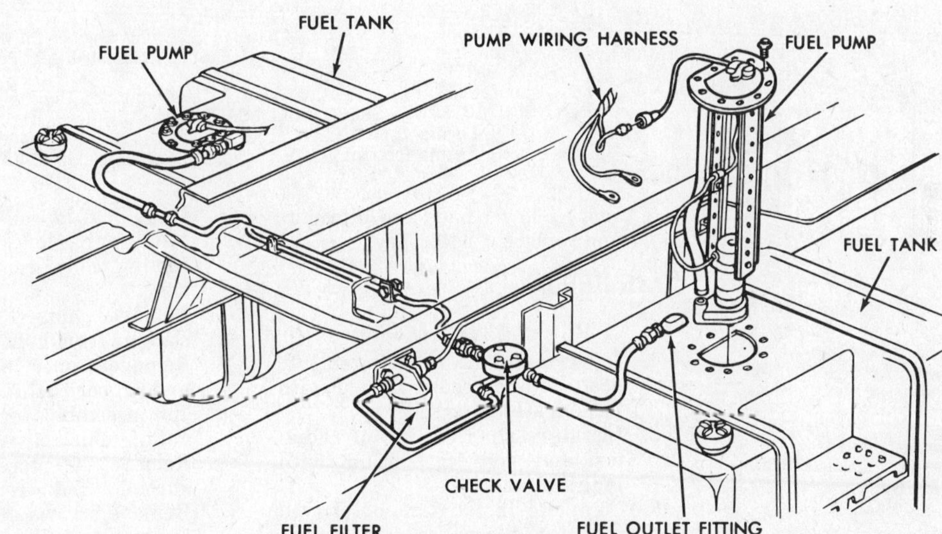

Installing electric fuel pump (© G.M.C.)

Installation

1. Insert pump outlet line into tank and connect to fitting.
2. Carefully install fuel pump and cap screws with washers. Tighten to specifications.
3. Connect pump harness to connector.
4. Connect battery ground cable.

Governor

All models covered by this manual utilize single-throat, dual-throat or hydraulic governors. Governors are adjusted for correct maximum speed and sealed at the factory.

Adjustments

Governor adjustments are pre-set at the factory. However, minor adjustments to satisfy local conditions may be accomplished by turning adjusting cap counterclockwise for higher speed and clockwise for lower speed. One turn on the adjusting cap will vary speed 300-400 rpm or 4-5 mph.

Governor mounting (© G.M.C.)

Cooling System

Radiator

Due to various types of radiator mountings, the following general information applies to all models.

The radiator assembly may include a fan shroud and an oil cooler at the base of radiator core. If equipped

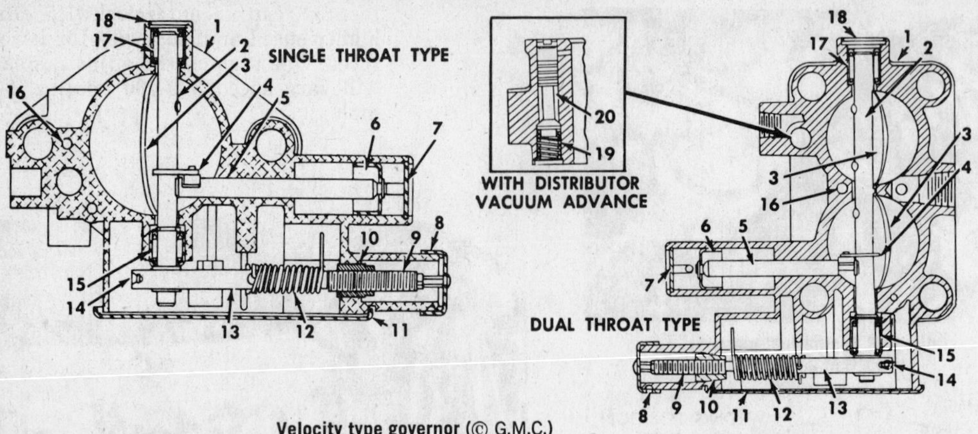

1 Governor body
2 Valve shaft
3 Throttle valve
4 Throttle valve arm
5 Stabilizer piston rod
6 Stabilizer piston
7 Stabilizer piston plug
8 Adjusting screw cap
9 Adjusting screw
10 Adjusting screw bushing
11 Governor cover
12 Operating spring
13 Cam ribbon
14 Cam ribbon clip
15 Roller bearing
16 Vacuum by-pass passage
17 Roller bearing
18 Shaft plug
19 Transfer valve spring
20 Transfer valve

Velocity type governor (© G.M.C.)

with a fan shroud, remove attaching bolts and then lay shroud back over fan blade. When oil lines are removed, make provisions for catching oil drainage from cooler tank and lines. Do not re-use this oil. Replenish transmission to recommended level with fresh fluid after installing radiator.

Some models may be equipped with a separate power steering oil cooler which is attached in front of radiator core by means of cooler support braces. It may be necessary to remove power steering oil cooler in order to replace the radiator core.

Radiator installation—Conventional and cowl models 4500, 5500 (typical) (© G.M.C.)

Radiator Removal

"C" and "S" Models

1. Drain radiator and disconnect water hoses and transmission coolant line (when used).
2. If vehicle is equipped with a fan shroud, remove attaching screws and carefully hang shroud over engine fan assembly to provide clearance for radiator removal.
3. Remove screws securing radiator retainers to radiator support and then remove retainers and front bumper.
4. Lift radiator up out of lower mounts. Lift shroud out of truck.

VELOCITY TYPE GOVERNOR

King-Seeley Model (Stamped)	GMC No. (Stamped)	Engine Model	Max. Governed Speed (rpm) *(No Load)	Spark Advance
651-640B	2456730	230	2400-2600	YES
601-641	2456731	230	3700-3900	YES
901-623	2440843	305E	3600-3800	YES
		305C	3600-3800	YES
900-639	2442733	351	3600-3800	NO
901-685	2472969	351	3600-3800	YES

*With engine broken-in. Full Load RPM is approximately 300 RPM less than No Load RPM and will vary from engine to engine.

HYDRAULIC TYPE GOVERNOR

SPINNER VALVE*
Location .... At Engine Oil Pump
Type .... Centrifugal, Pre-Set
SLAVE UNIT*
Location .... Carburetor Throttle Body
ENGINE GOVERNED SPEED (FULL LOAD)
401 Engine .... 3400 rpm
351 Engine (option) .... 3400 rpm

5. Inspect lower pads and retainers and replace if necessary.

Installation

"C" and "S" Models

1. Lower shroud and radiator into position and secure shroud with bottom attaching screws.
2. Install retainers at top of radiator and connect shroud with four screws.
3. Complete installation of shroud with two screws to radiator retainer.
4. Connect radiator hoses and transmission coolant line, fill cooling system, and check for leaks.
5. Tighten all bolts to specifications.

Radiator Removal

"T" Models

1. Drain radiator.
2. Disconnect throttle linkage at bracket on radiator support.
3. Remove electrical components from radiator support assembly.
4. Disconnect upper and lower coolant hoses at radiator.
5. If vehicle is equipped with air conditioning or power steering cooling coils, remove as necessary.
6. Remove nuts, washers, and springs from U-bolt.
7. Remove upper mounting bolts and rubber bushings.
8. Tilt assembly forward and lift out of vehicle.
9. Remove cap screws from fan shroud and remove shroud. Remove screws attaching radiator core assembly to support and then remove core.

Installation

"T" Models

1. Position radiator core assembly in support and secure with cap screws.
2. Install fan shroud and cap screws.
3. Carefully place radiator and support assembly in truck. Position lower mounts.
4. Assemble radiator upper mounts and complete assembly of lower mounts. When installing lower mount, be sure to position shims and cushions and compress the

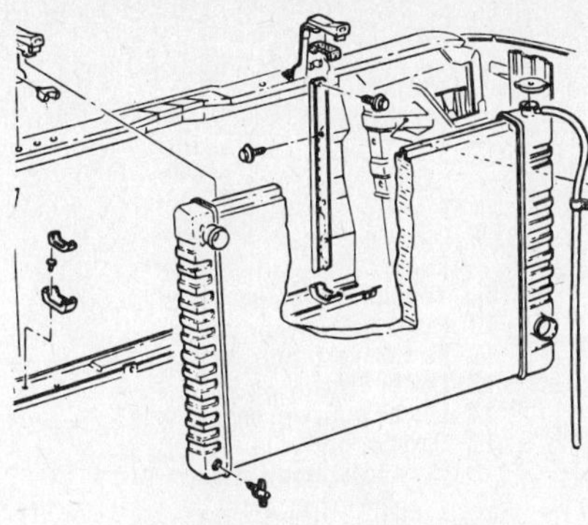

Radiator installation—conventional models 6500 (typical) (© G.M.C.)

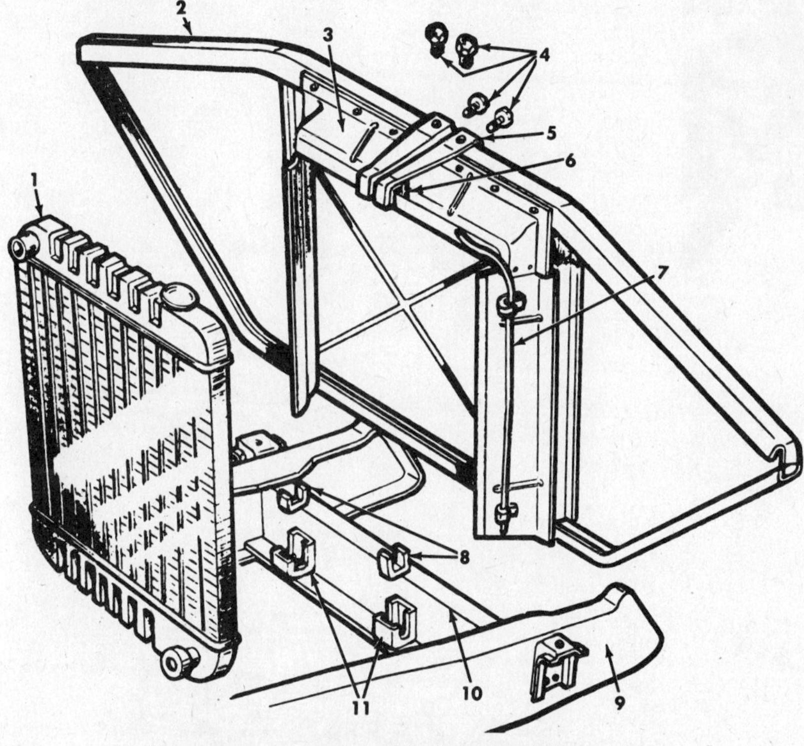

Radiator installation—models 1000-2500 except P/PB (© G.M.C.)

1 Radiator core
2 Sheet metal support assy.
3 Radiator baffle assy.
4 Capscrews
5 Top retainer bracket
6 Rubber pad
7 Overflow hose
8 Rubber pads
9 Frame side rail
10 Frame crossmember
11 Bottom Retainer brackets

mounting springs.

5. Connect upper and lower coolant hoses.
6. Install air conditioning or power steering coolant coils (if removed).
7. Install electrical components on radiator and connect throttle linkage to radiator support.
8. Fill cooling system and inspect for leaks.

Water Pump

Removal

1. Drain cooling system.
2. Remove fan spacers (when used) and pulley(s) from water pump drive hub.
3. Remove all hoses connected to water pump.
4. Remove mounting bolts and washers.
5. Remove pump and gasket.

Installation

Reverse removal procedure, installing new water pump gasket.

Overhaul

Due to various models, overhaul procedures vary considerably. The following basic guide may be used.

1. Support fan hub in an arbor press and press shaft out of hub.
2. Drive seal out of pump body.
3. Clean and inspect water pump components. Check all surfaces for wear and bearings for excessive play. NOTE: Do not clean bearing and shaft assembly in solvent as it will dissolve lubricant.
4. Replace water pump seal and necessary parts.
5. Reassemble and install water pump.

Engine

Exhaust Emission Control

For service and adjustment procedures on various types used, refer to General Repair Section.

Engine Assembly

Three types of gasoline engines are used by models covered in this manual: Inline, V6 and V8. Removal and installation procedures will vary according to engine used and model of truck. Basic guides for various engine and truck models are provided below.

Engine Removal

Inline Engines In Conventional Models

1. Drain radiator.
2. Disconnect battery.
3. Remove hood and attaching parts.
4. Remove grille and radiator support braces.
5. Remove radiator and heater hoses.
6. Remove radiator and grille assembly.
7. Disconnect fuel line at fuel pump.
8. Remove air cleaner and cover carburetor to protect it from dirt.
9. Disconnect choke control and accelerator linkage.
10. Disconnect exhaust pipe from manifold.
11. Disconnect wiring harness and battery cable.
12. Remove hand brake lever and gearshift lever from transmission.
13. Disconnect driveshaft from transmission flange.
14. Attach lifting equipment, remove mounting bolts and rear crossmember.
15. Lift out engine and transmission assembly.

Installation

Inline Engines In Conventional Models

1. Attach lifting equipment and lower assembly into chassis. Install support crossmember and engine mountings.
2. Connect driveshaft.
3. Install handbrake and gearshift levers.
4. Connect exhaust pipe to manifold.
5. Connect wiring harness and carburetor control linkage.
6. Install hood and attaching parts.
7. Install air cleaner, connect fuel line.
8. Fill cooling system.
9. Fill crankcase with oil to the proper level.
10. Install battery.
11. Start engine and check for leaks.

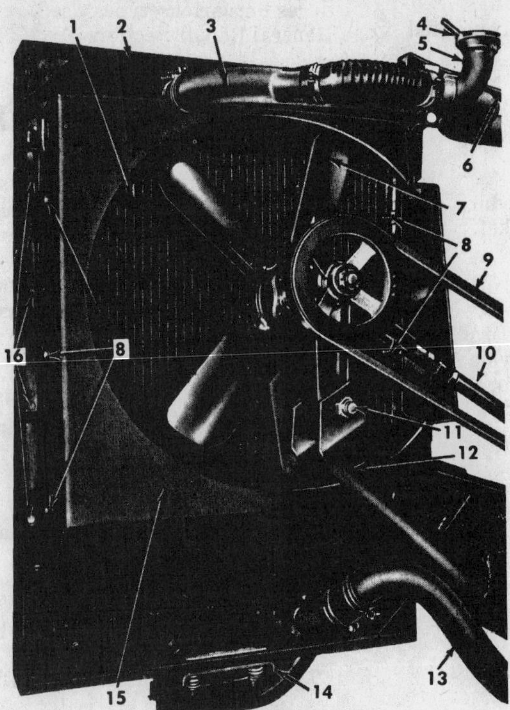

1 Radiator core
2 Support frame
3 Upper hose assy.
4 Filler cap
5 Filler Neck
6 Upper support rod
7 Fan blade
8 Shroud to radiator capscrew
9 Drive belt
10 Tension adjusting rod
11 Pivot bolt and nut
12 Fan drive frame support
13 Lower hose assy.
14 Lower support assy.
15 Fan Shroud
16 Core to support mounting bolt

Radiator installation—SP5000
(© G.M.C.)

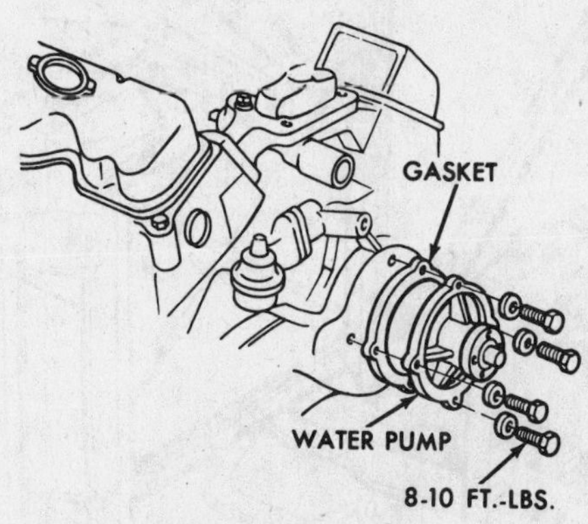

V6 engine water pump
(© G.M.C.)

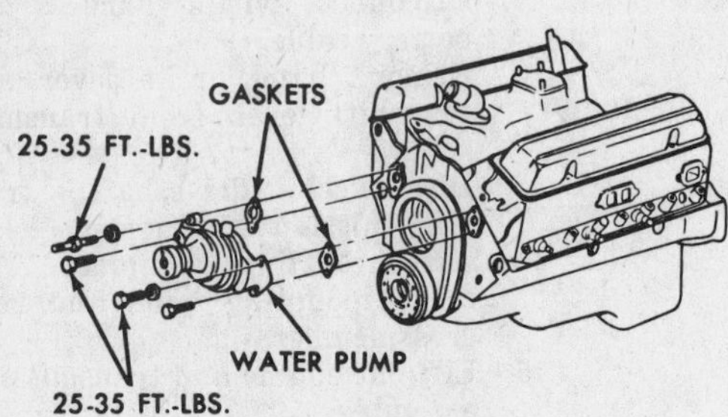

V8 engine water pump
(© G.M.C.)

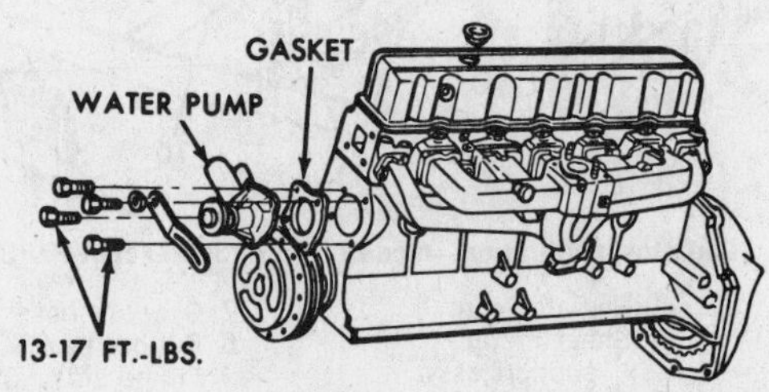

Inline engine water pump
(© G.M.C.)

Pressing bearing and shaft out of water pump
(© G.M.C.)

Water pump components (inline engine)
(© G.M.C.)

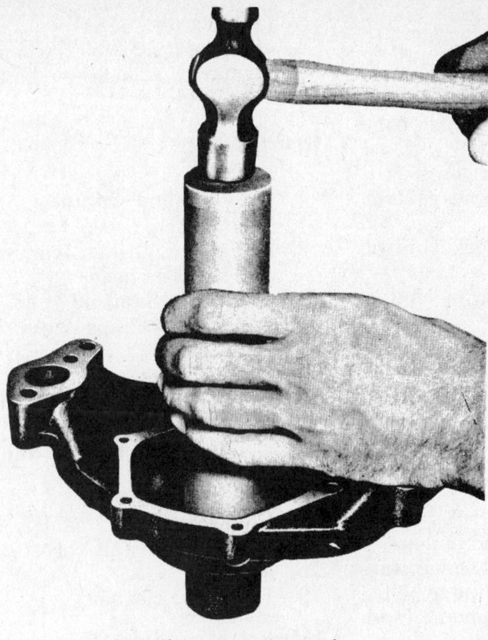

Installing water pump seal
(© G.M.C.)

COAT BORE WITH CEMENT BEFORE ASSEMBLING SEAL

2.880"

1.458"

Water pump (401M and 478M engines)
(© G.M.C.)

1 Pulley hub
2 Shaft and bearing assembly
3 Seal assembly
4 Seal seat
5 Impeller
6 Water pump body

Engine Removal

Inline Engines in Tilt Cab Models

1. Drain cooling system.
2. Disconnect battery cables.
3. Tilt cab forward; remove radiator and shroud.
4. Disconnect shift linkage at control island.
5. Disconnect throttle and choke controls at carburetor.
6. Disconnect parking brake cable and housing.
7. Remove control island mounting bolts; swing control island forward.
8. Disconnect hoses and remove surge tank.
9. Remove right and left island supports.
10. Disconnect cab safety lock, remove cab rear support.
11. Disconnect electrical wiring from engine units.
12. Disconnect all fuel, heater, oil lines from engine.
13. Disconnect exhaust pipe from manifold.
14. Remove engine fan and pulley.
15. Remove rocker arm cover and attach lifting brackets at cylinder head bolts.
16. Attach hoist and take up slack.
17. Remove engine mounting bolts and bolts attaching transmission to engine. Support transmission.
18. Move engine forward until it is disengaged from transmission.
19. Lift engine from the chassis.

Installation

Inline Engines in Tilt Cab Models

Install engine by reversing the removal procedure. Be certain to maintain cleanliness and to avoid damaging the engine parts. After engine is installed, check operation of all control linkages, fill cooling system and check for leaks. Fill crankcase with oil to the proper level.

Engine Removal

V6 Engines in Conventional Models

1. Drain radiator.
2. Disconnect battery.
3. Remove hood and attaching parts.
4. Remove grille and radiator braces.
5. Remove radiator and heater hoses.
6. Disconnect oil cooler lines (when used).
7. Remove grille, radiator, and front bumper.
8. Disconnect fuel line.
9. Disconnect air lines (when used).
10. Disconnect engine ground strap.
11. Disconnect exhaust pipes from manifolds.
12. Disconnect accelerator and choke controls from the carburetor.
13. Disconnect tachometer drive and oil gauge pressure line (when used).
14. Attach lifting equipment and take up slack.
15. Remove clutch housing to flywheel housing bolts.
16. Move engine forward to disengage transmission.
17. Lift engine from the chassis.

Installation

V6 Engines in Conventional Models

Install engine by reversing the removal procedure. Be certain to maintain cleanliness and to avoid damaging the engine parts. After engine is installed, check operation of all control linkages, fill cooling system and check for leaks. Fill crankcase with oil to the proper lever.

Engine Removal

V6 Engines in Tilt Cab Models

1. Drain radiator.
2. Disconnect battery.
3. Disconnect oil cooler lines (when used).
4. Disconnect electrical wiring and cables from the engine units.
5. Disconnect engine ground strap.
6. Disconnect accelerator and choke controls at the carburetor.
7. Disconnect transmission control rods, surge tank hoses, air cleaners and hoses.
8. Remove control island and rear cab support.
9. Disconnect exhaust pipes from manifolds.
10. Disconnect clutch control cylinder, parking brake control and speedometer drive from the rear of the transmission.
11. Disconnect cooling system and heater hoses.
12. Disconnect air lines from compressor (when used).
13. Disconnect driveshaft from transmission.
14. Attach lifting equipment and take up slack.
15. Remove bolts from front and rear mountings.
16. Lift assembly from the chassis.

Installation

V6 Engines in Tilt Cab Models

Install engine by reversing the removal procedure. Be certain to maintain cleanliness and to avoid damaging the engine parts. After engine is installed, check operation of all control linkages, fill cooling system and check for leaks. Fill crankcase with oil to the proper lever.

Engine Removal

V8 Engines in Conventional Models

1. Disconnect battery cables and remove battery.
2. Drain cooling system.
3. Disconnect air intake hose (when used).
4. Disconnect all wiring to engine units and as necessary to remove front end sheet metal.
5. Disconnect radiator and heater hoses.
6. Disconnect fuel line.
7. Remove front end sheet metal, including hood.
8. Remove engine fan and drive belts.
9. Remove power steering pump.
10. Remove air compressor and disconnect air lines (when used).
11. Remove air cleaner and disconnect accelerator and choke cables at the carburetor.
12. Disconnect exhaust pipes from manifolds.
13. Disconnect clutch and transmission controls as necessary.
14. Remove valve covers and attach lifting brackets at cylinder head bolts.
15. Attach lifting equipment and take up slack.
16. Remove bolts from front and rear mountings.
17. Remove bolts attaching transmission to engine.
18. Move engine forward to disengage transmission.
19. Lift engine from the chassis.

NOTE: Engines coupled to an automatic transmission must be removed as a unit. Disconnect all transmission controls accordingly. Transmission may be removed from engine assembly after power plant removal.

Installation

V8 Engines in Conventional Models

Install the engine by reversing the removal procedure. Be certain to maintain cleanliness and to avoid damaging the engine parts. After engine is installed, check operation of all control linkages, fill cooling system and check for leaks. Fill crankcase with oil to the proper evel.

NOTE: Engines coupled to an automatic transmission must be installed as a unit.

1. Remove radiator, support and shroud.
2. Disconnect shift linkage at control island, accelerator and choke cables at carburetor.
3. Disconnect parking brake control.
4. Disconnect surge tank hoses.
5. Remove surge tank and control island rear support.
6. Remove cab safety lock control and cab rear support.
7. Disconnect all wiring to engine units.
8. Disconnect fuel line.
9. Disconnect heater hoses and vacuum/air lines (when used).
10. Disconnect engine ground straps.
11. Disconnect exhaust pipes from manifolds.
12. Disconnect clutch control.
13. Remove engine fan and pulley.
14. Remove valve covers and install lifting brackets at cylinder bolts.
15. Attach lifting equipment and take up slack.
16. Remove bolts attaching transmission to engine.
17. Remove bolts from front and rear mountings.
18. Move engine forward to disengage transmission.
19. Lift engine from the chassis.

Installation

V8 Engines in Tilt Cab Models

Install the engine by reversing the removal procedure. Be certain to maintain cleanliness and to avoid damaging engine parts. After engine is installed, check operation of all control linkages, fill cooling system and check for leaks. Fill crankcase with oil to the proper level.

Manifolds

Removal

Inline Engine

1. Remove air cleaner.
2. Disconnect both throttle rods at bellcrank, remove throttle return spring.
3. Disconnect fuel and vacuum lines, choke cable at carburetor.
4. Disconnect crankcase ventilation hose.
5. Disconnect exhaust pipe at manifold flange.
6. Remove heat stove (when used).
7. Remove attaching bolts and manifold.

Installation

Inline Engine

1. Clean all surfaces.
2. Place new gasket over manifold end studs on head.
3. Position manifold and install bolts and clamps while holding manifold in place.
4. Torque bolts to specifications.
5. Connect exhaust pipe to manifold using new packing.
6. Connect crankcase ventilation hose.
7. Connect fuel and vacuum lines.
8. Connect choke cable, throttle rods, and install throttle return spring.
9. Install air cleaner.

Intake Manifold Removal

V8 Engines

1. Drain radiator and remove air cleaner.
2. Disconnect battery cables, radiator and heater hoses, water pump by-pass, accelerator linkage, choke control, and fuel line at carburetor.
3. Remove attaching bolts and manifold.

Installation

V8 Engines

1. Clean all surfaces.
2. Install manifold seals on block and gaskets on cylinder heads.
3. Install manifold and torque bolts to specifications.
4. To finish installation, reverse removal procedure. Fill cooling system and check for leaks.

Exhaust Manifold Removal

V8 Engines

1. Remove generator and bracket from left manifold. NOTE: On 366 and 427 V8 engines, remove spark plugs.
2. Disconnect exhaust pipe from manifold.

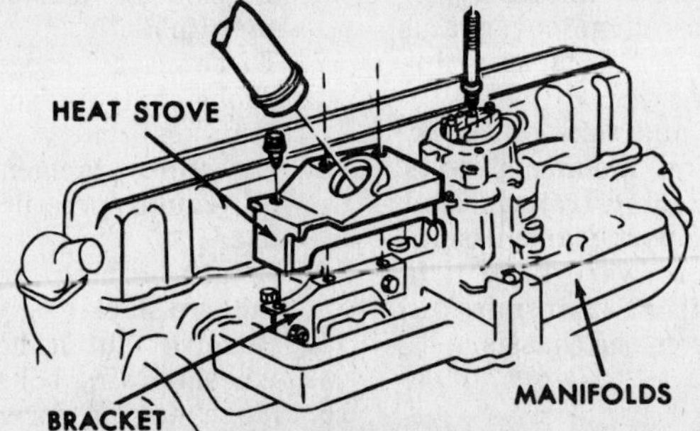

Manifold heat stove (inline engine)
(© G.M.C.)

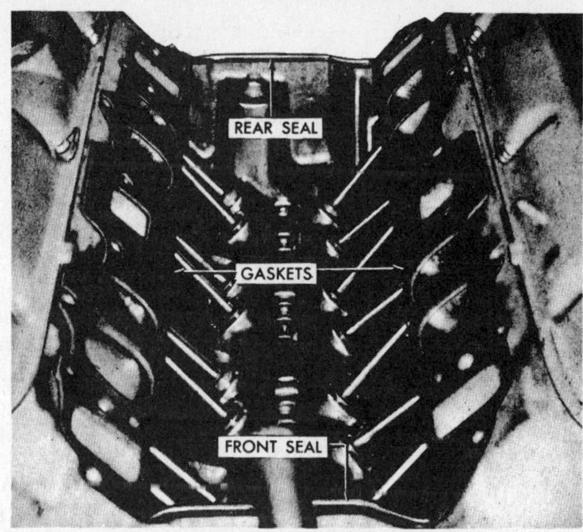

Intake manifold gaskets and seals (V8 engine)
(© G.M.C.)

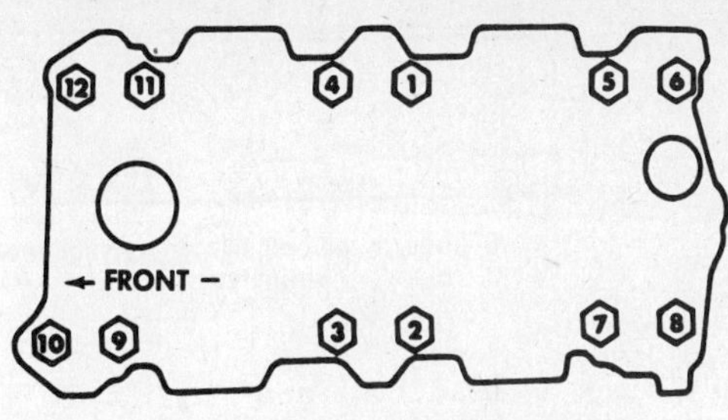

Intake manifold bolt tightening sequence
(350 V8 engine)
(© G.M.C.)

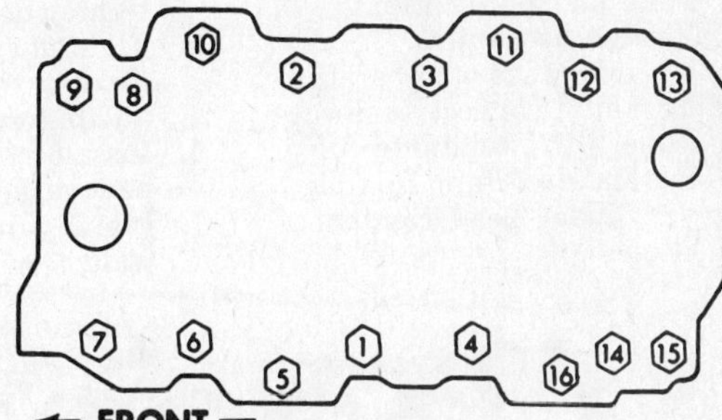

Intake manifold bolt tightening sequence
(366, 427 V8 engines)
(© G.M.C.)

3. Bend back bolt lock tabs and remove manifold bolts.
4. Remove exhaust manifolds.

Installation

V8 Engines

1. Clean all surfaces.

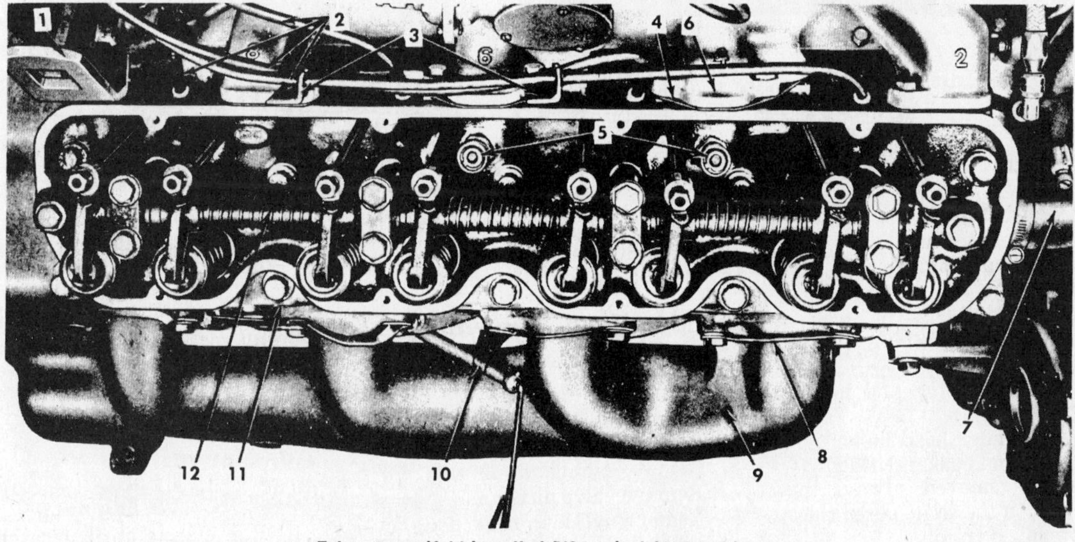

Exhaust manifold installed (V8 engine) (© G.M.C.)

1 Engine lifting bracket
2 Spark plug wires
3 Plug wire supports
4 Intake manifold gasket
5 Crankcase ventilation valves
6 Intake manifold
7 Water outlet hose
8 Exhaust manifold bolt locks
9 Exhaust manifold
10 Dip stick tube clip
11 Exhaust manifold gasket
12 Rocker arms, shaft, and brackets

2. Install bolts with locks and torque in proper sequence to specifications.
3. Connect exhaust pipe to manifold with new packing.
4. Install generator and bracket on left manifold. NOTE: Install spark plugs on 366 and 427 V8 engines.

Cylinder Head

Cylinder Head Removal

Inline Engines

1. Remove manifold assembly.
2. Remove valve mechanism.
3. Drain cooling system (block).
4. Remove fuel and vacuum lines from retaining clip and disconnect wires at temperature sending units.
5. Disconnect radiator hose at water outlet and ground strap at cylinder head.
6. Remove coil.
7. Remove cylinder head bolts, cylinder head and gasket.

Installation

Inline Engines

1. Clean all surfaces and make certain there are no nicks or deep scratches. Cylinder head bolt threads must also be cleaned.
2. Place gasket over dowel pins with the bead up.
3. Place cylinder head over dowel pins carefully.

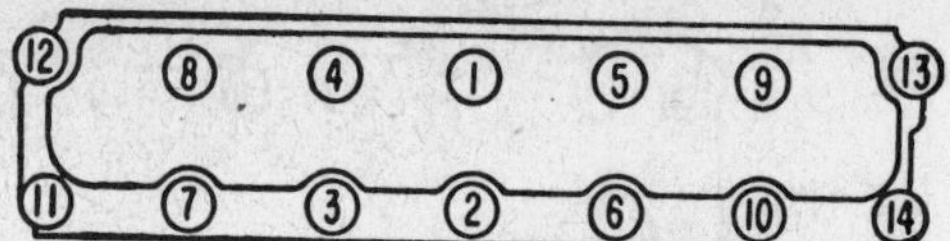

Cylinder Head bolt tightening sequence—inline engines
(© G.M.C.)

4. Apply sealer to head bolts and tighten down finger tight.
5. Tighten cylinder head bolts a little at a time in proper sequence and to torque specifications.
6. Install valve mechanism.
7. Connect wires to temperature sending units, connect fuel vacuum lines to retaining clip. NOTE: Make certain to follow proper cylinder head tightening sequence.

Cylinder head gasket installed (inline engine)
(© G.M.C.)

Cylinder Head Removal

V6 Engines

1. Drain cooling system.
2. Remove exhaust manifold.
3. Remove valve covers and valve mechanism.
4. Disconnect spark plug wires from plugs.
5. Remove water outlet and intake manifolds.
6. Remove cylinder head bolts, cylinder head and gasket. NOTE: If lifters are removed, always install them in the same bores they were removed from.

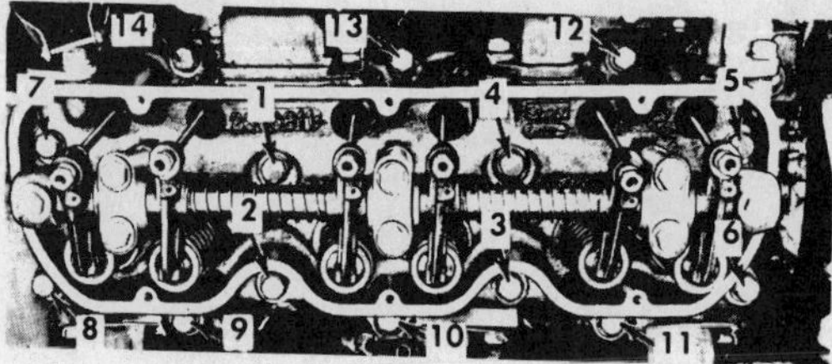

Cylinder head bolt tightening sequence V6 engines
(© G.M.C.)

Installation

V6 Engines

1. Clean all surfaces and make certain there are no nicks or deep scratches. Cylinder head bolt threads must also be cleaned.
2. Place gasket over dowel pins, the word "top" facing up.
3. Place cylinder head over dowel pins carefully.
4. Apply sealer to head bolts and tighten down finger tight.
5. Tighten cylinder head bolts a little at a time in proper sequence and to torque specifications.
6. Install exhaust manifolds, using new gaskets.
7. Install intake manifold and water outlet manifold, using new gaskets.
8. Install valve mechanism and valve cover with new valve cover gasket.

Cylinder Head Removal

V8 Engines

1. Drain cooling system (block).
2. Remove intake manifold.
3. Remove exhaust manifolds.
4. Remove valve mechansim.
5. Remove cylinder head bolts, cylinder head and gasket.

Installation

V8 Engines

1. Clean all surfaces and make certain there are no nicks or deep scratches. Cylinder head bolt threads must also be cleaned.
2. Coat both sides of gasket with a thin coat of sealer. NOTE: Use no sealer on a composition steel-asbestos gasket.
3. Place gasket over dowel pins with bead facing up.
4. Place cylinder head over dowl pins carefully.
5. Apply sealer to head bolts and tighten down finger tight.
6. Tighten cylinder head bolts a little at a time in proper sequence and to torque specifications.
7. Install exhaust manifolds.
8. Install intake manifold.
9. Install valve mechanism and adjust.

Refer to the specifications area for proper head bolt tightening sequences and torques for all Inline, V6 and V8 engines.

Valve Train

Adjustments

Inline and V8 Engines

1. Remove rocker arm cover.
2. With engine running at idle speed, install oil deflector clips to prevent oil splatter.
3. Back off rocker arm stud nut at one rocker arm until it begins to clatter, then tighten it slowly until the clatter just stops. This is zero lash position.
4. Turn nut down ¼ turn and pause for 10 seconds. Repeat this procedure until nut has been turned down for one complete revolution. This allows the hydraulic lifter to adjust itself while the valve completely closes each time.
5. Repeat the above procedure on all rocker arm assemblies.
6. Remove the oil deflector clips and install rocker arm cover using new gasket.

Adjustments

V6 Engines

1. Run engine until it reaches normal operating temperature.
2. Remove rocker arm covers.
3. Using a feeler gauge and a box end wrench, adjust exhaust and intake valve clearance to specifications.
4. Repeat the above procedure for all rocker arms, and check to make certain that all valve rocker arms are receiving sufficient lubrication.

Valve Rocker Arm Removal

Inline and V8 Engines

1. Remove rocker arm cover.
2. Remove rocker arm nuts, rocker arm balls, rocker arms and push rods. NOTE: Place assemblies in a specific order so that they may be installed in their previous positions.

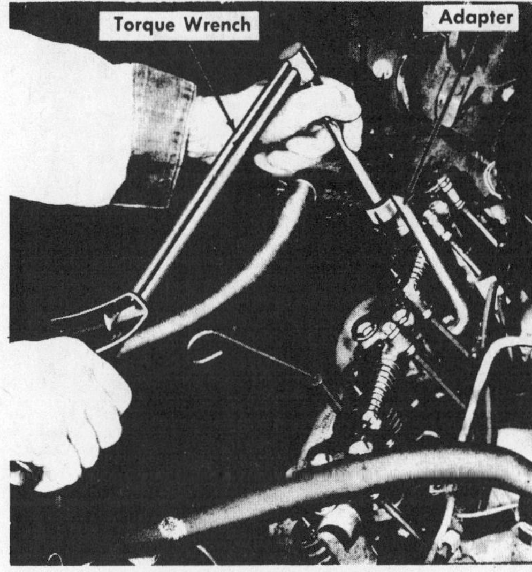

Tightening cylinder head bolts with torque wrench and adapter (© G.M.C.)

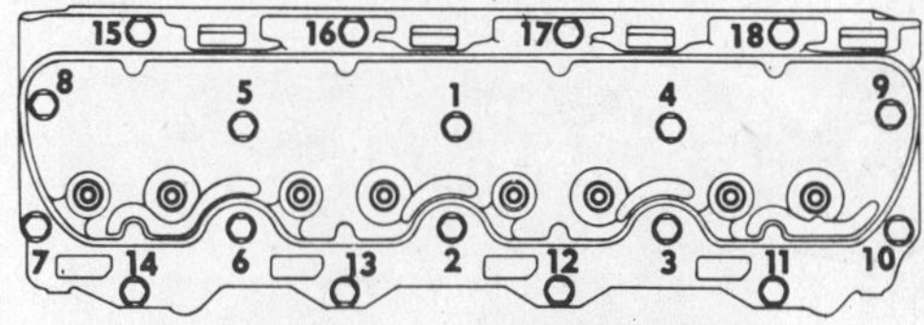

Cylinder head bolt tightening sequence V8 engines (© G.M.C.)

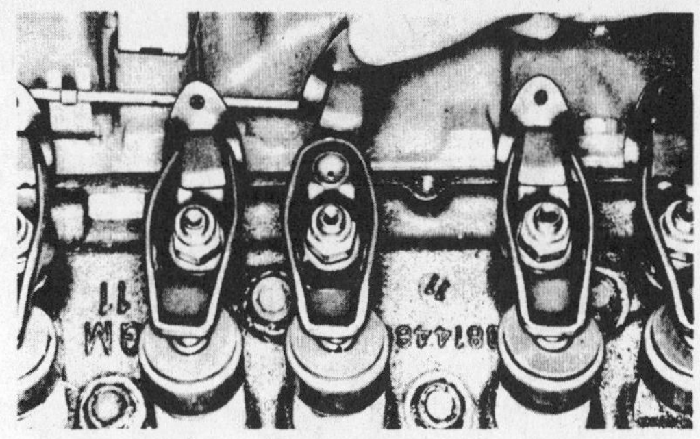
Use of oil deflector clips (© G.M.C.)

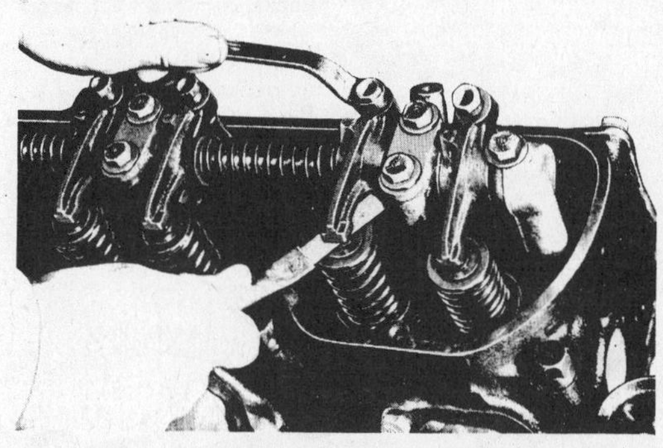
Adjusting rocker arm clearance (V6 engine) (© G.M.C.)

Installation

Inline and V8 Engines

1. Install push rods, making certain they seat in the lifter socket.
2. Install rocker arms, rocker arm balls and rocker arm nuts. Tighten all rocker arm nuts until all lash is eliminated.
3. Adjust valves.

Refer to Engine Rebuilding Section for more details.

Refer to valve specifications for valve spring, stem and seat angle specifications.

NOTE: Whenever installing new rocker arms or rocker arm balls, coat bearing surfaces with Molykote or its equivalent.

Valve Rocker Arm and Shaft Removal

V6 Engines

1. Remove rocker arm covers.
2. Loosen rocker arm shaft bracket bolts until spring pressure is fully relieved from rocker arms.
3. Lift off rocker arm shaft and brackets as an assembly.
4. Remove push rods and place them in a specific order so that they may be installed in their original positions.

Installation

V6 Engines

1. Install push rods in their proper positions.
2. Install rocker arm shaft and bracket assembly.
3. Set clearance between rocker arm shaft end brackets and adjacent rocker arms to specifications. Set initial valve clearance to 0.014″-intake, 0.022″-exhaust.
4. Lubricate rocker arms with engine oil, temporarily install rocker arm covers.
5. Run engine until operating temperature is reached, then stop engine.
6. Adjust valves.

Timing Gears

Crankshaft Gear Removal

Inline Engines

1. Attach gear puller to crankshaft gear (puller screw holes are provided on gear).
2. Turn puller screw and remove gear.
3. Check condition of timing gear key; replace if necessary.

Installation

Inline Engines

1. Install key in crankshaft and coat gear seat with oil.
2. Align key way in gear to key on crankshaft with timing mark toward front of crankshaft.
3. Drive gear into place.

Camshaft Gear Removal

Inline Engines

1. Gear is press fit on camshaft. Place in arbor press and apply pressure to front end of camshaft.
2. Press camshaft out of gear and remove key and spacer.

Installation

Inline Engines

1. Install spacer and key, apply transmission oil on gear seat.
2. Support camshaft at journal, then position gear with timing mark forward and keyway aligned with key in camshaft.
3. Press gear on to camshaft until gear hub stops at spacer.
4. Measure clearance at thrust plate with a feeler gauge. A clearance of 0.001-0.005″ is necessary for proper lubrication.

Idler Gearshaft Removal

V6 and V8 Engines

1. Bend back lock and remove idler gear plate bolts, lock, and plate.

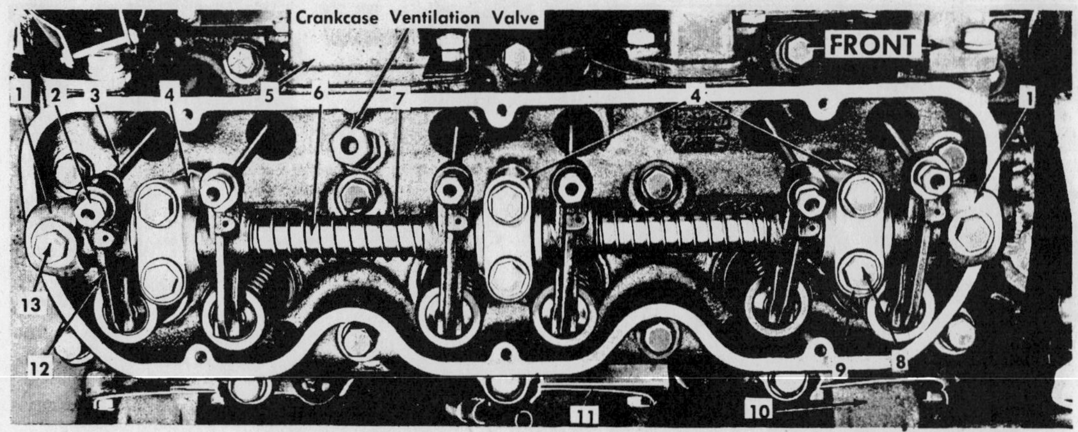

Rocker arm and shaft assembly installed (V6 engine) (© G.M.C)

1 End bracket
2 Adjusting screw
3 Push rod
4 Rocker arm shaft bracket
5 Intake manifold
6 Rocker arm shaft
7 Spring
8 Bracket bolt
9 Flat washer
10 Exhaust manifold
11 Exhaust manifold bolt lock
12 Rocker arm
13 Special bolt

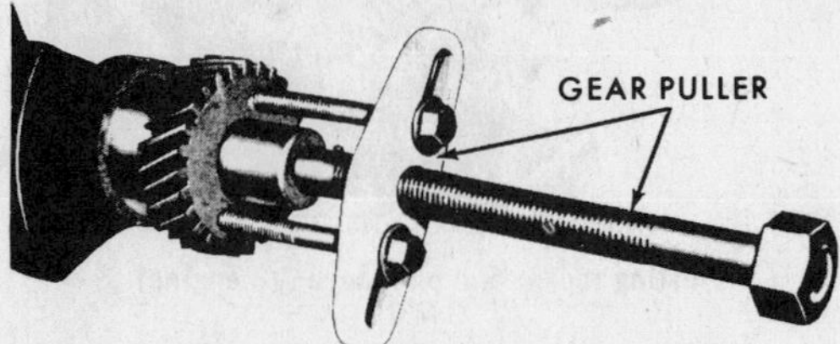

Crankshaft gear removal (inline engine) (© G.M.C.)

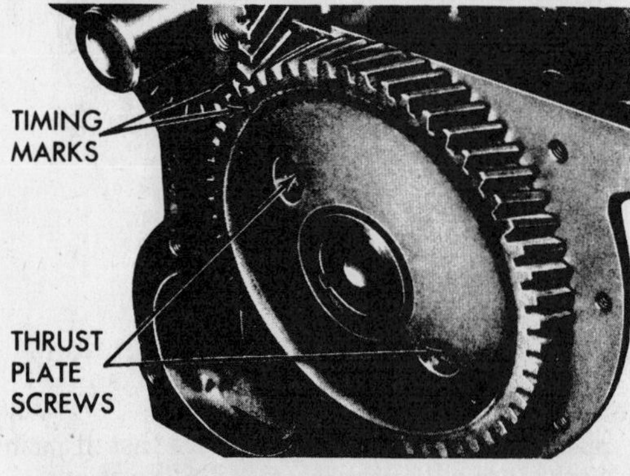

Timing gear marks and thrust plate screws (inline engine) (© G.M.C.)

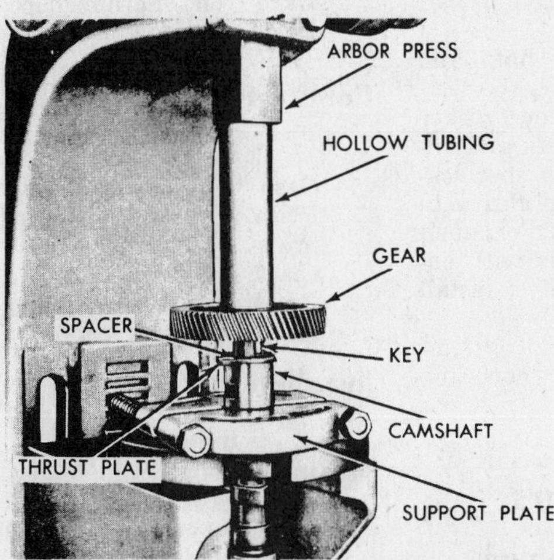

Installing timing gear on camshaft (inline engine) (© G.M.C.)

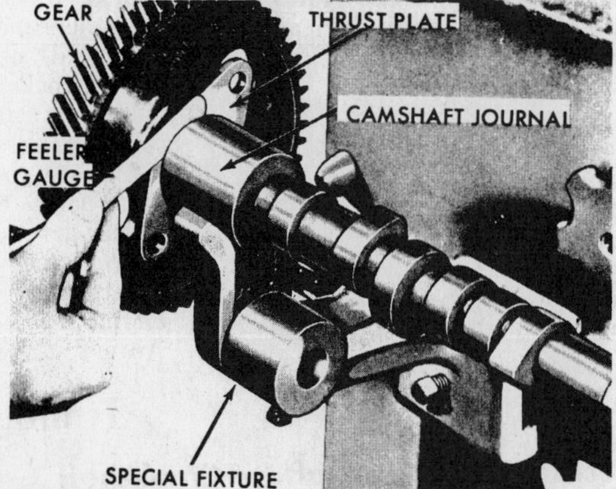

Measuring camshaft thrust plate clearance (inline engine) (© G.M.C.)

2. Remove idler gear assembly from idler gear shaft.
3. Remove bolts holding idler gear shaft to cylinder block and remove shaft.

Installation

V6 and V8 Engines

Due to different configurations of engines, the following procedures are a basic guide. Although the configurations vary, installation steps are similar.

1. Turn crankshaft and camshaft so that the timing marks on gears are towards the idler gear-shaft.
2. Install idler gearshaft, mating marks with those corresponding on other gears in train.
3. Install retainer plates and secure with bolts and lock plates.

Camshaft Removal

Inline Engines

1. Turn crankshaft until alignment mark faces mark on camshaft gear.
2. Remove thrust plate screws and pull out camshaft carefully.

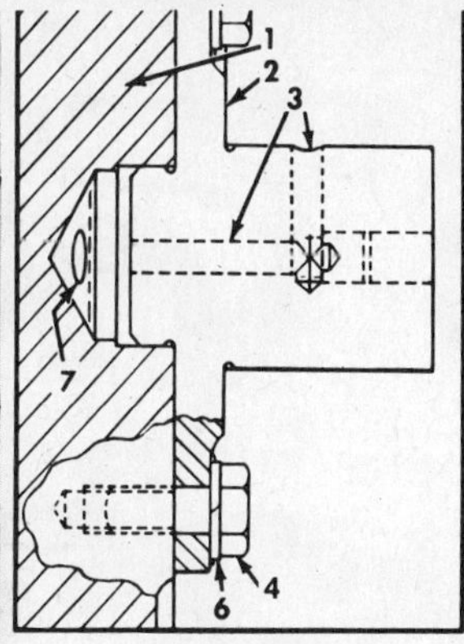

1 Cylinder block
2 Idler gear shaft
3 Oil hole
4 Bolt
5 Crankshaft gear
6 Lock washer
7 Full pressure oil gallery

Timing idler gearshaft (401M and 478M engines) (© G.M.C.)

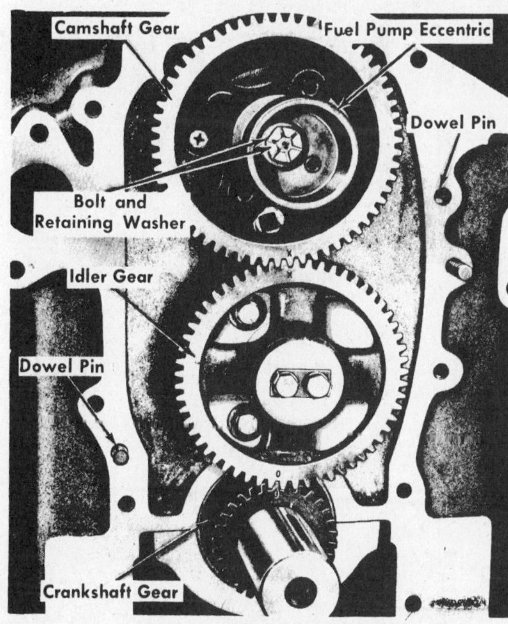

Timing gears and fuel pump eccentric installed (401M and 478M engines (© G.M.C.)

Timing chain and alignment marks (V8 engine) (© G.M.C.)

Installation

Inline Engines

1. Lubricate camshaft bearings and journals with #10W oil.
2. Install camshaft carefully, matching gear alignment marks.
3. Install thrust plate screws and torque to specifications.

Timing Case Cover Removal

1. Remove bolts, washers and cylinder block cap (V6, V8 engines).
2. Carefully remove front cover; discard gasket and oil seal.

Installation

1. Clean all surfaces and glue new gasket to cylinder block.
2. Press new oil seal squarely into bore with seal lip on inner side of cover.
3. Install attaching bolts, washers and cylinder block cap (V6, V8 engines). Torque to specifications.

Piston and Connecting Rod

Removal

1. Ream out top of bore if a piston ring travel ridge is present.
2. Position crankshaft so that a pair of connecting rods can be moved without interference.
3. Remove nuts from connecting

Installing timing case cover oil seal
(© G.M.C.)

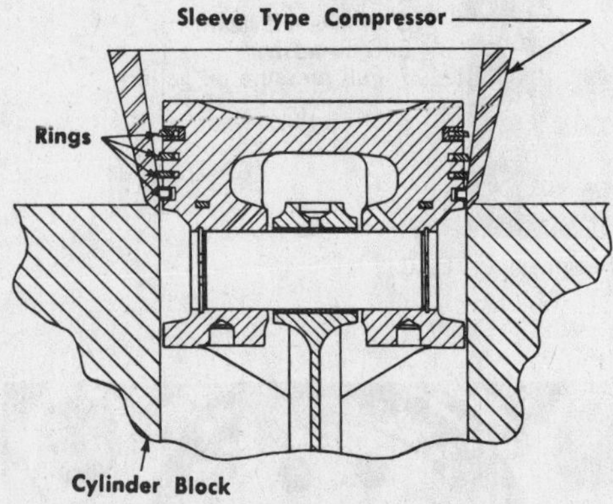

Sleeve type piston ring compressor
(© G.M.C.)

Cylinder numbering and size selection (V6 engine)
(© G.M.C.)

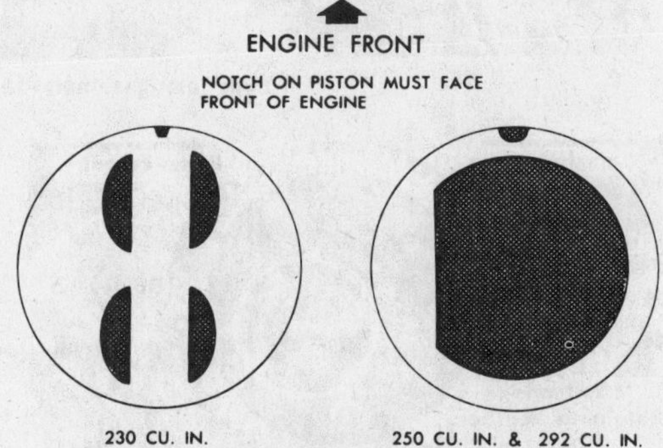

Piston installation (inline engines)
(© G.M.C.)

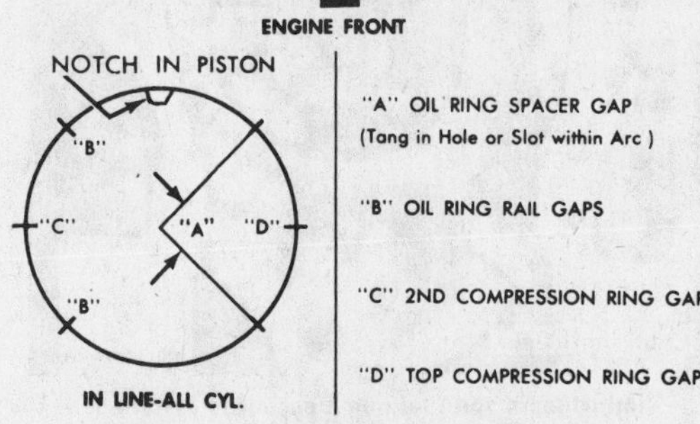

Piston ring gap locations (inline engine)
(© G.M.C.)

rod cap bolts, remove rod cap and lower bearing half.
4. Mark all parts for reassembly.

Installation

1. Clean and coat piston pin, rings, and cylinder bore with engine oil.
2. Stagger piston ring gaps.
3. Place connecting rod bearing halves in rod and cap.
4. Use a ring compressor to install piston and connecting rod assembly in cylinder bore.
5. Install cap and lower bearing half. Lubricate nut threads and torque to specifications.
6. Check bearing clearances.

Refer to General Engine Rebuilding Section for further details on piston and connecting rod assembly and disassembly.

Piston Rings

Piston rings are removed and installed with the use of a spreader tool. Use care not to break the rings.

Crankshaft Bearings

Remove crankshaft bearings very carefully; place in a specific order with corresponding bearing caps and bolts.

Installation

Inline Engines

1. Match service main bearings with crankshaft to be installed, i.e., standard size with new crankshaft and undersize with reconditioned crankshaft.
2. Install bearing upper halves in cylinder block and rear oil seal upper half, seal lip pointing forward.
3. Lubricate inserts and oil seal lip with S.A.E. #10W oil. NOTE: Do not lubricate oil seal ends.
4. Install crankshaft.
5. Install all except rear bearing caps and tighten to specifications.

Piston ring gap specifications
(© G.M.C.)

Ring-Groove Clearance	
Top Ring 230 & 250 Eng.	0.0012"-0.0027"
Top Ring 292 Eng.	0.0020"-0.0040"
2nd Ring 230 & 250 Eng.	0.0012"-0.0032"
2nd Ring 292	0.0020"-0.0040"
Oil Ring 230 & 250 Eng.	0.0000"-0.0050"
Oil 292	0.0005"-0.0055"
Ring Gap	
Compression Rings (All Eng.)	0.0100"-0.0200"
Oil Rings (All Eng.)	0.0150"-0.0550"
Piston Ring Groove Width	
Compression Ring Grooves	
Top Groove	0.0965"-0.0975"
2nd Compression Ring Groove	
All Except 637 Engines	0.0960"-0.0970"
637 Engines	0.0955"-0.0965"
3rd Compression Ring Groove	
305E & 637 Engines	None
Other Engines	0.0955"-0.0965"
Oil (Bottom) Ring Groove	
All Engines	0.1885"-0.1895"
Piston Ring Clearance in Groove	
Top Groove	
305 Series Engines	0.0030"-0.0045"
Other Engines	0.0030"-0.0055"
2nd Compression Ring	
305C, 351C, 351M Engines	0.0030"-0.0055"
401M Engines	0.0030"-0.0045"
478M and 637 Engines	0.0025"-0.0040"
3rd Compression Ring	
305E & 637 Engines	None
Other Engines	0.0025"-0.0040"
Oil (Bottom) Ring	
305C, 351C, 351M & 401M Engines	0.0010"-0.0030"
478M & 637 Engines	0.0020"-0.0035"
478M & 637 Engines	0.0020"-0.0035"
Piston Ring Gap	
Top Ring	
305C & 305E	0.017"-0.027"
351C, 351E & 351M	0.022"-0.032"
401M	0.024"-0.034"
478M & 637	0.026"-0.036"
2nd Ring	
All Except 478 & 637	0.015"-0.025"
478 & 637	0.017"-0.027"
3rd Ring	
All Except 305E, 478M & 637	0.015"-0.025"
478M	0.017"-0.027"
305E & 637	(No. #3 Compression Ring Used)
Oil Control Ring	
Rails on 305E Only	0.015"-0.055"
No Gap on Oil Ring on 305C, 351C, 351M, or 401M, 478M & 637	0.017"-0.032"

(© G.M.C.)

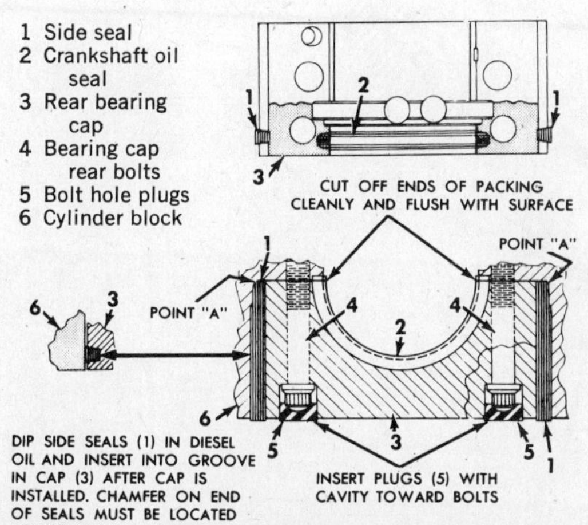

Cross section of rear seals
(© G.M.C.)

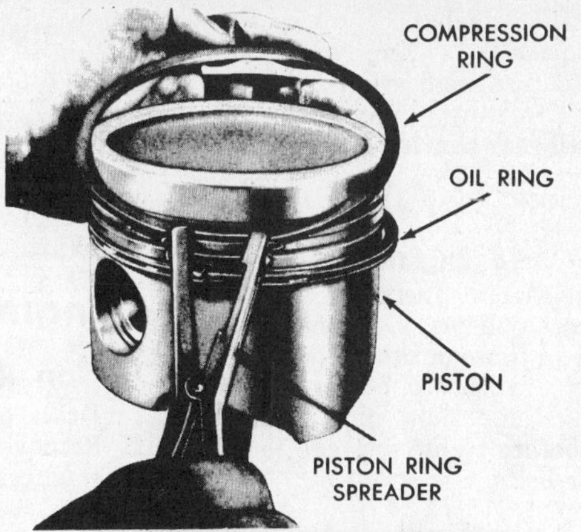

Installing piston rings with spreader tool
(© G.M.C.)

Applying sealer to rear bearing cap area
(© G.M.C.)

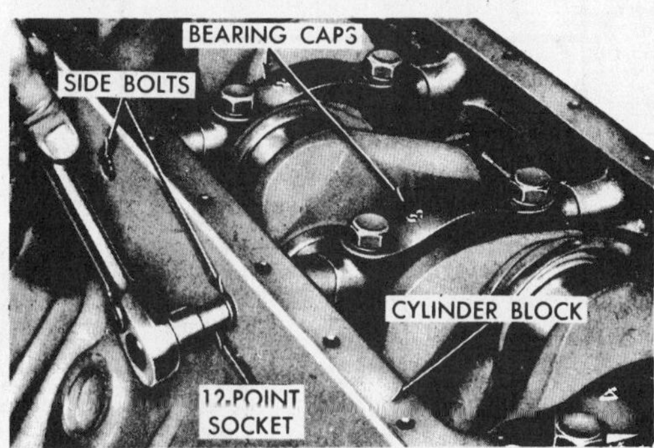

Installing bearing cap side bolts (V8 engine)
(© G.M.C.)

6. Check for any binding bearings, then apply sealer to illustrated area.
7. Initially install rear main bearing cap, then move crankshaft fore and aft to seat the inserts. Tighten to specifications.
8. Check bearing clearances and crankshaft end play.

Installation

V6 Engines

1. Install bearing upper halves in cylinder block.
2. Lubricate bearings with S.A.E. #10W oil and apply sealer to crankshaft rear bearing cap where it joins the crankcase.

3. Install crankshaft.
4. Install all bearing caps and tighten to specifications.
5. Check for any binding bearings.
6. Install rear bearing bolt caps.

Installation

V8 Engines

1. Main bearing installation on V8 engines follows the same procedure as those outlined for V6 engines, with one exception; thread side bolts into bearing cap before tightening cap to cylinder bolts.

Oil Pump Removal

V8 Engines

1. Remove oil pan.
2. Remove pump to rear main bearing cap bolt.
3. Remove pump and extension shaft.

Engine Lubrication

Oil Pan Removal

1. Drain oil.
2. Remove attaching bolts and washers.
3. Remove oil pan, being careful not to damage dip stick.
4. Discard gasket.

Installation

1. Place new gasket on crankcase.
2. Install oil pan with attaching bolts and washers, tighten firmly.
3. Install drain plug and fill with engine oil to the proper level.

Oil Cooler Service

Should foreign matter be suspected of contaminating oil system, back flush oil cooler and lines, using cleaning solvent and compressed air. Do not exceed 100 psi.

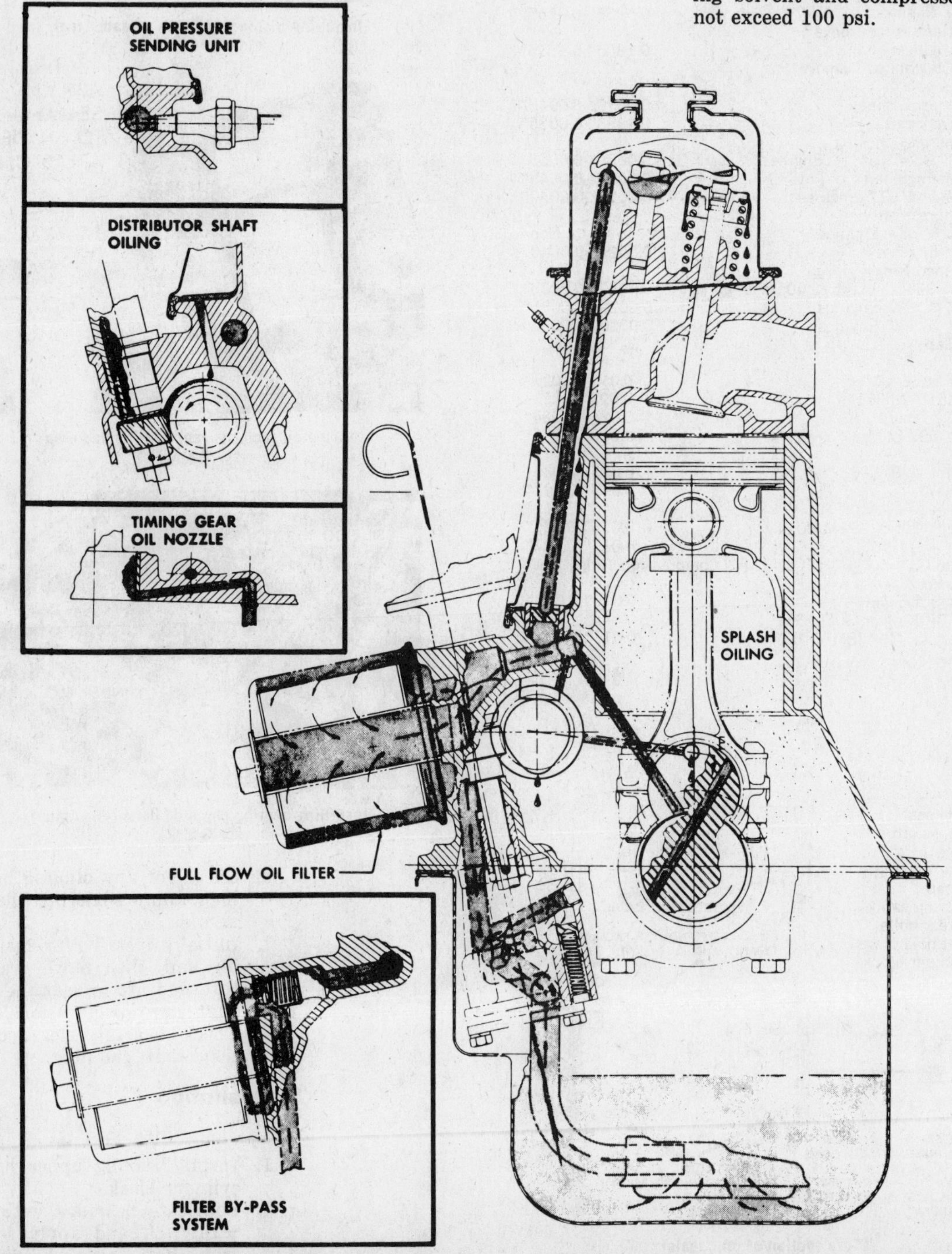

Engine lubrication system (inline engine) (© G.M.C.)

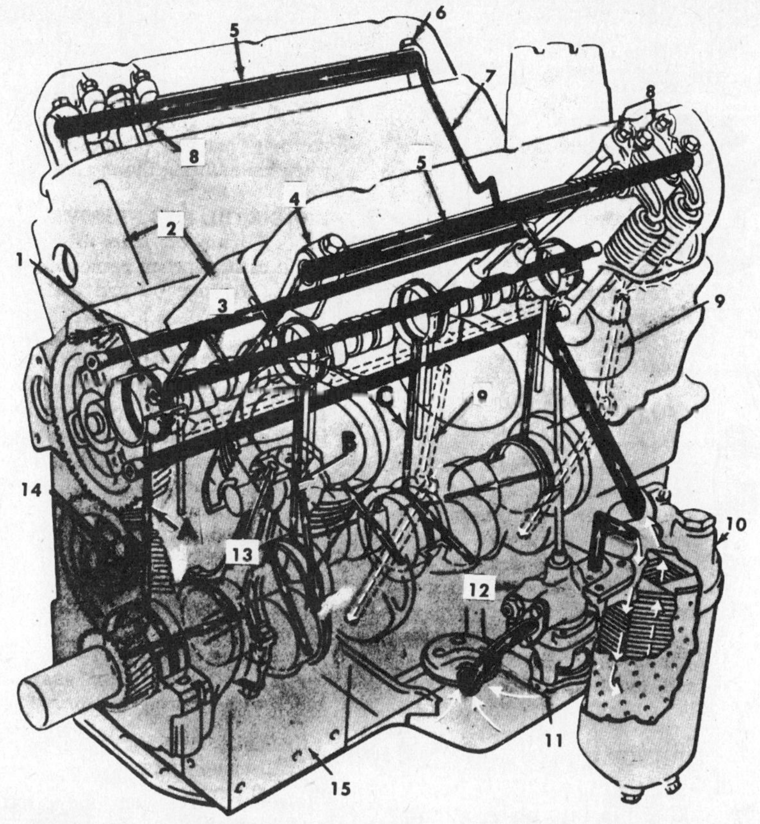

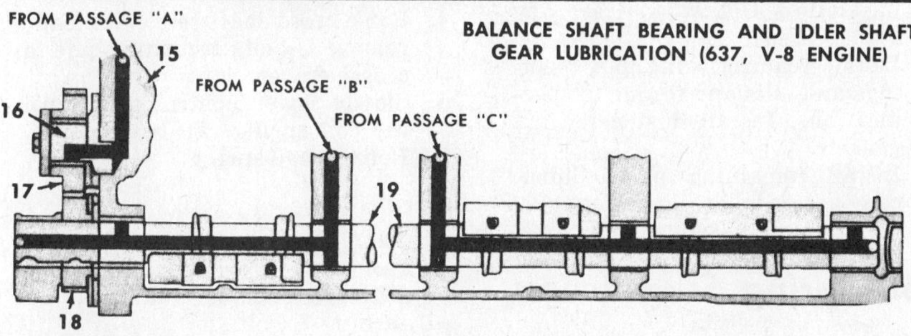

BALANCE SHAFT BEARING AND IDLER SHAFT GEAR LUBRICATION (637, V-8 ENGINE)

1 To timing gears
2 Cylinder heads
3 Oil from camshaft front bearing
4 Rocker arm shaft front bracket
5 Rocker arm shafts
6 Rocker arm shaft rear bracket
7 Oil from camshaft rear bearing
8 Rocker arms
9 Oil drain back holes
10 Oil filter
11 Oil pump inlet screen
12 Oil pump
13 Piston pin splash lubricated
14 Timing idler gear shaft
15 Cylinder block
16 Balance shaft idler gear shaft
17 Balance shaft idler gear
18 Balance shaft gear
19 Balance shaft

Engine lubrication system (V6, V8 engines with gear driven cam) (© G.M.C.)

Oil Pump Removal

Inline Engines

1. Remove oil pan.
2. Remove oil suction pipe bolt and two bolts attaching the pump flange to engine.
3. Remove oil pump and screen.

Installation

Inline Engines

1. Install oil pump, aligning drive shaft with distributor tang. Install suction pipe support bolt.
2. Install oil pan.

Oil Pump Removal

V6 Engines

1. Remove oil pan.
2. Remove two mounting bolts and oil pump.

Installation

V6 Engines

1. Place new gasket on pump flange and install pump, turning shaft as necessary to engage gears.
2. Install mounting bolts and torque to specifications.
3. Install oil pan.

Installation

V8 Engines

1. Install pump and extension shaft, aligning slot with tang on lower end of distributor drive shaft.
2. Install attaching bolt and torque to specifications.
3. Install oil pan.

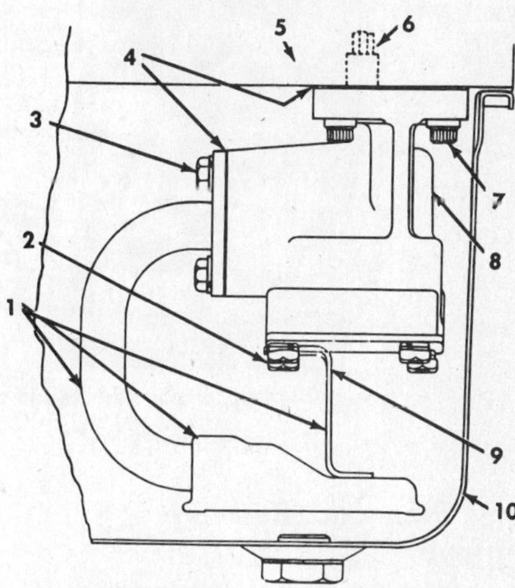

1 Suction tube and screen assy.
2 Bracket bolt (20-25 ft.-lbs.)
3 Flange bolts and lock washers
4 Gaskets
5 Cylinder block
6 Pump drive shaft
7 Pump to block bolts (30-35 ft.-lbs.)
8 Oil Pump
9 Bracket
10 Oil pan

Engine oil pump installation (© G.M.C.)

Front Axles, Suspension

Solid Axle

Front Spring Removal

1. Raise truck frame and support front axle with a floor jack.
2. Remove spring shackle U-bolts and lower the axle.
3. Remove all attaching retainer pins, bolts and nuts from rear hanger.
4. Remove U-bolts, spacers, tow eyes and dowel pins as necessary, then remove spring.

Installation

1. Install rear end of spring with all attaching parts.
2. Raise front end of spring and install attaching parts.
3. Raise front axle to spring and install attaching U-bolts, nuts and washers.
4. Torque all bolts and nuts to specifications.
5. Lower vehicle.

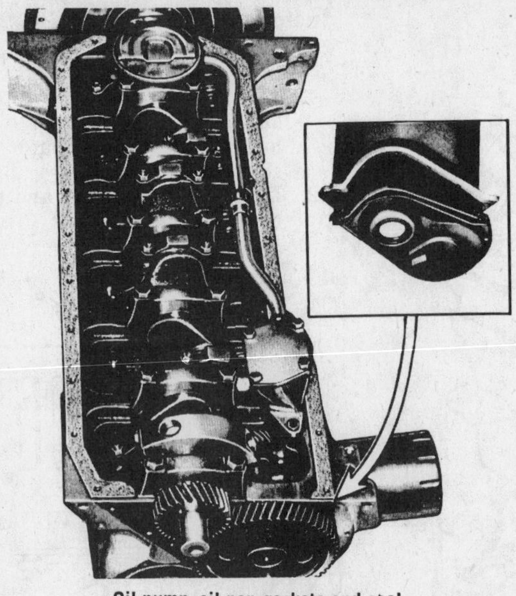

Oil pump, oil pan gaskets and seal (inline engine) (© G.M.C.)

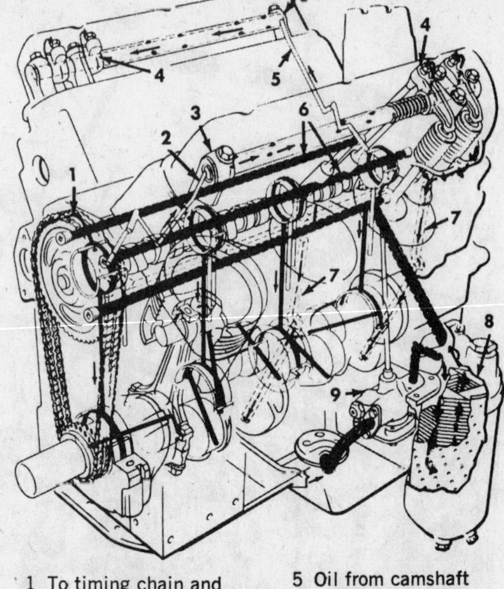

1 To timing chain and sprocket
2 Oil from camshaft front bearing
3 Rocker arm shaft bracket
4 Rocker arms
5 Oil from camshaft rear bearing
6 Oil galleries
7 Oil drain-back holes
8 Oil filter
9 Engine oil pump

Engine lubrication system (V6, V8 engine with chain driven cam) (© G.M.C.)

King Pins and Bushings

Removal

1. Jack up axle and remove hubs and bearings.
2. Remove steering arm from knuckle.
3. Remove king pin draw key by using a brass drift and hammer.
4. Remove king pin cap screws, caps and gaskets.
5. Drive out king pin using a brass drift and hammer.
6. Remove bearings, shims and O-ring.

Installation

1. Clean all parts and coat king pin with S.A.E. #10W oil.
2. Install thrust bearing and knuckle, then raise to take up all clearance.
3. Check thrust bearing minimum clearance with specifications and correct with shims, if necessary.
4. Align king pin holes and partially install king pin.
5. Drive king pin into place, aligning milled slot with draw key (when used).
6. Install required king pin bushings and nuts and torque to specifications. Install dust caps and gaskets.
7. Install remaining parts, lubricate according to specifications, then install bearings and hubs.

Coil Spring Suspension

Coil Spring Removal

1. Raise vehicle and place jack stands under frame, allowing control arms to hang free.
2. Disconnect lower end of shock absorber.
3. Install chain through spring and lower control arm as a safety precaution.
4. Raise cross-shaft to relieve load; remove U-bolts securing shaft to crossmember.
5. Slowly lower control arm until the coil spring can be removed.
6. Remove coil spring.

Installation

1. Install spring and then lift control arm. Position cross-shaft with crossmember and install attaching U-bolts.
2. Connect lower end of shock absorber.
3. Torque all nuts to specifications.
4. Lower vehicle.

Lower Control Arm Removal

1. Remove coil spring.
2. Remove cotter pin from lower ball stud and loosen stud nut.
3. Loosen lower ball stud in steering knuckle, then remove nut.
4. Remove control arm.

Installation

1. Install lower ball stud through steering knuckle and tighten nut.
2. Install spring and control arm.
3. Torque stud to specifications and install cotter pin.

Upper Control Arm Removal

1. Raise vehicle and support lower control arm.
2. Remove wheel assembly.
3. Remove cotter pin from upper ball stud and loosen stud nut.
4. Loosen upper ball stud in steer-

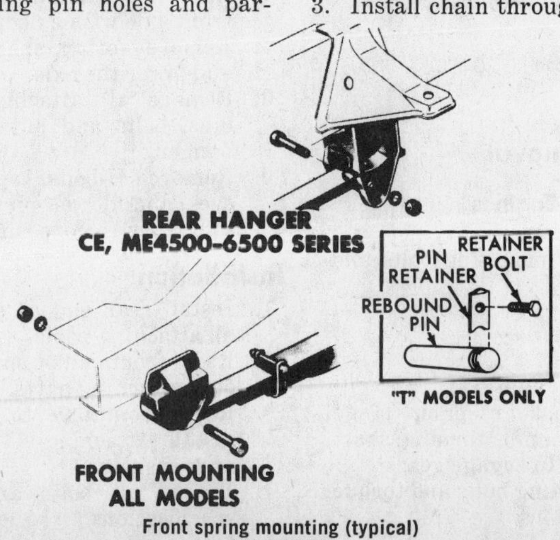

Front spring mounting (typical) (© G.M.C.)

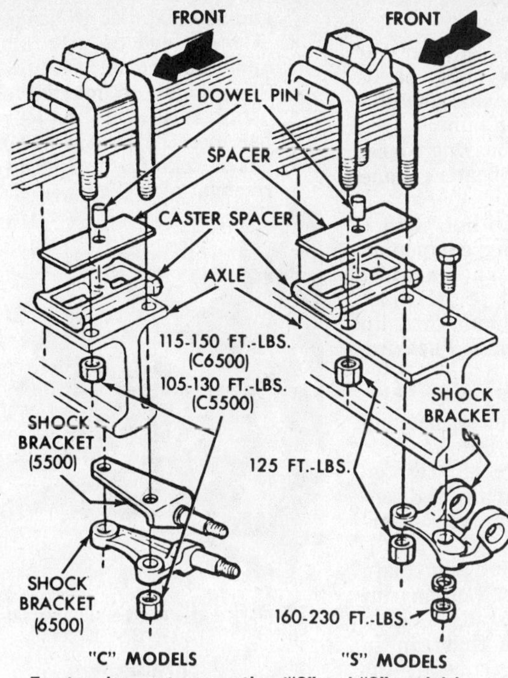

Front spring center mounting ("C" and "S" models)
(© G.M.C.)

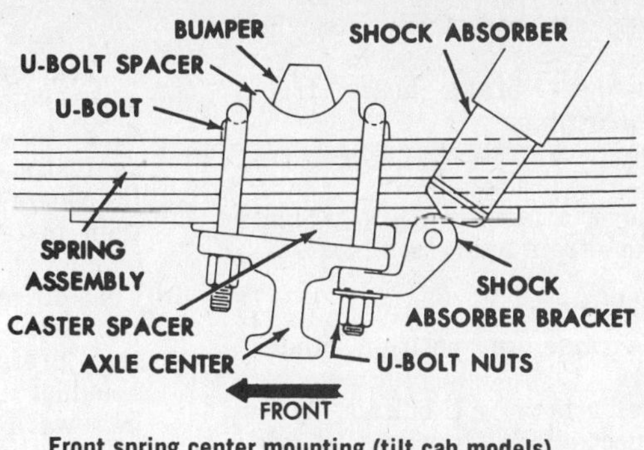

Front spring center mounting (tilt cab models)
(© G.M.C.)

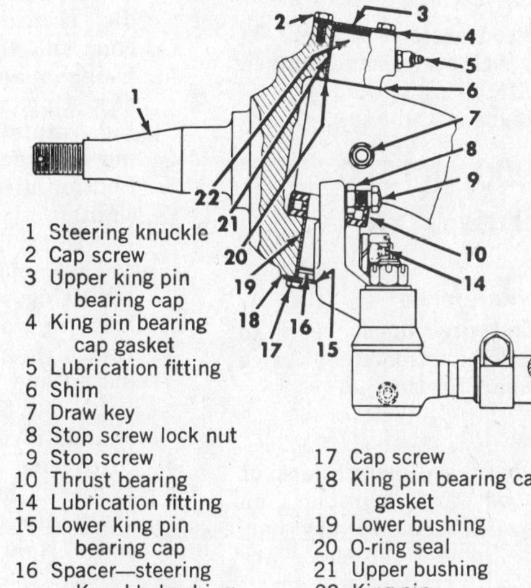

Steering knuckle construction (typical)
(© G.M.C.)

ing knuckle, then remove nut.

5. Remove nuts attaching control arm to crossmember bracket. Remove control arm.

Installation

1. Install control arm in position on bracket. Make certain camber and caster shims are in proper order.
2. Install ball joint stud, nut and cotter pin.
3. Remove lower control arm support and lower vehicle.

Adjustments

Refer to wheel alignment specifications area for necessary information.

Four Wheel Drive Axle

For service on transfer case, see general repair section.

Description

GMC uses two different types of front driving axles. The type used on K1000, K1500 series is a hypoid, single reduction type, consisting of a housing, differential and carrier assembly, axle shaft and universal joint assemblies, steering tie rod assembly and steering knuckle support at outer ends of housing.

The second type KV400 is a single speed spiral bevel type consisting of a housing with removable stub ends that are piloted and bolted to the flange ends of the housing. The outer ends of the hollow stubs are designed to accept upper and lower pivot bearings, which allow the front wheels to steer as well as help drive the vehicle when all wheel drive is necessary.

Removal

1. Disconnect driveshaft from front differential.
2. Raise front end and support with jack stands behind the front springs.

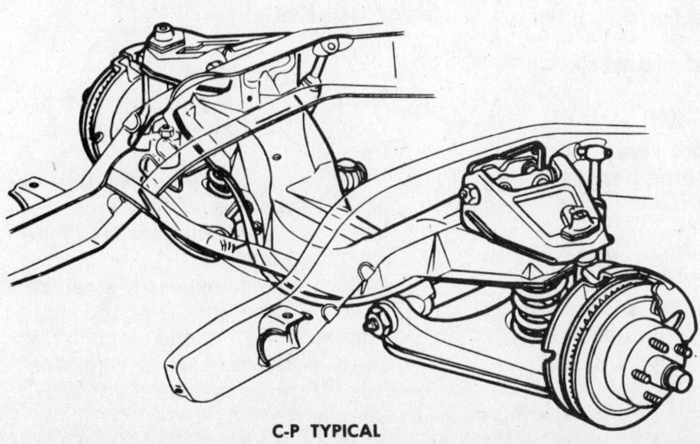

Front suspension—"C" and "P" models (typical)
(© G.M.C.)

Removing coil spring with special tool
(© G.M.C.)

3. Disconnect rod from steering arm.
4. Disconnect brake hoses from frame fittings.
5. Disconnect shock absorbers from axle brackets.
6. Remove attaching U-bolts and remove front axle assembly.

Installation

1. Place axle in position under truck.
2. Install attaching U-bolts.
3. Connect shock absorbers to axle brackets.
4. Connect brake hoses to frame fittings.
5. Connect rod to steering arm.
6. Remove jack stands and connect driveshaft.
7. Lower truck.

K1000, K1500 Series Axle

Reference

For overhaul procedures refer to Spicer, Single, Reduction Rear Axles in General Repair Section.

Hub Removal

1. Remove hub cap, using block of hard wood and hammer on K1000; on K1500 use pry bar. NOTE: Some vehicles are equipped with free-wheeling unit as front hub which must first be removed.
2. On 1500 series vehicles, remove six nuts and lock washers attaching drive flange to hub.
3. Using snap-ring pliers, remove snap-ring attaching drive flange (K1500) or drive gear (K1000) to axle shaft, then remove flange or gear.
4. Using spanner wrench, remove outer lock nut, then remove retainer plate and bearing adjusting nut.
5. Remove hub and brake drum assembly with bearings and oil seal. Use caution that outer bearing cone is not damaged, due to being dropped.

Removing snap-ring at axle shaft (© G.M.C.)

Hub Installation

1. If bearing cups have been removed, install new cups, being sure they are seated solidly against shoulders in hub.
2. Lubricate hub and bearing cones, then install inner bearing cone in hub.
3. Coat oil seal bore in hub with a thin layer of sealing compound, then press seal in until against shoulder in hub. Lip of seal must be toward inside of hub. Coat lip of seal with wheel bearing grease.
4. Install hub assembly over spindle, then install outer bearing cone and adjusting nut.
5. Using spanner wrench, tighten adjusting nut. During tightening, rotate hub to prevent bearing damage.
6. Loosen adjusting nut and again tighten until snug. Loosen nut ⅛ turn and install locking washer, being sure that pin in adjusting nut is in one of the holes in washer.
7. Again using spanner wrench, install and tighten outer locking nut. Tighten nut to 40 foot-pounds torque minimum.
8. On Series 1000 vehicles, install spacer in hub, then install drive gear into end of hub and one end of axle shaft. During installation, rotate gear as necessary to mate hub and shaft splines.
9. On Series 1500 vehicles, install drive flange and gasket at end of hub, with drive shaft and flange mating flange over hub studs. Install and tighten stud nuts and lock washers.
10. Install bolt in threaded end of drive shaft, then pull drive shaft outward to facilitate installation of snap-ring.
11. Install snap-ring at end of drive shaft, using pliers. Remove bolt from threaded end of drive shaft, then install hub cap at end of hub.
12. Apply recommended lubricant in steering knuckle through pipe plug provided for this purpose.

Axle Shaft and Joint

Removal

1. Remove six cap screws and lock washers attaching brake backing plate and spindle to steering knuckle.
2. Remove backing plate from steering knuckle spindle.
3. Grasp outer shaft and pull shaft and universal joint assembly straight out of housing.
4. Remove snap-ring retainer bearing in yoke. NOTE: Snap-rings retaining bearings in yoke are installed in yoke at outer end of bearing on heavy duty K1500, and are installed in bearing cage at inner end of yoke on K1000 and standard K1500.
5. Strike end of journal sharply, using a rawhide mallet or soft hammer. This will force bearing out of yoke far enough to permit removal of trunnion.

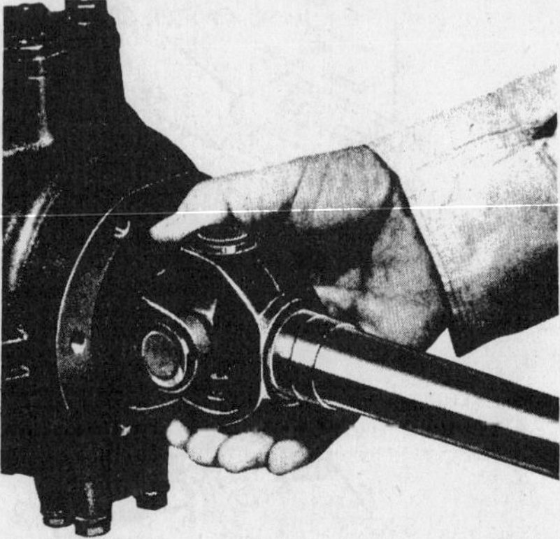

Removing axle shaft and universal joint (© G.M.C.)

Installation

1. Lubricate bearings with high melting point grease, working grease into space around rollers.
2. On K1000 and standard K1500, position trunnion in yoke, then press bearings into yoke over trunnion far enough to install lock rings. Hold journal and lightly tap yoke to seat bearings out against snap-rings. On heavy duty K1500, press bearings into yoke far enough to clear snap-ring grooves, then install snap-rings.
3. Slide axle shaft and universal joint assembly into housing, engaging splines with differential side gear.
4. Install spindle and bushing assembly over axle shaft and against steering knuckle. Install brake backing plate over spindle. Align holes in backing plate and spindle with steering knuckle then install six cap screws and lock washers. Tighten bolts to torque given in "Specifications."

Steering Knuckle

Removal

1. Remove cotter pin and nut attaching tie rod end to steering knuckle.
2. Remove cap screws attaching oil seal retainers, seal felt, and rubber seal and ring assembly to steering knuckle.
3. Using spring scale at steering knuckle arm check pound pull required to rotate steering knuckle. Record this information for reference at time of reassembly.
4. At bottom of steering knuckle, remove four cap screws and lock washers attaching steering

Removing steering knuckle bearing cap
(© G.M.C.)

knuckle bearing cap to knuckle. Remove bearing cap from knuckle.

5. At top of steering knuckle remove cap screws and lock washers or stud nuts. At left side remove tapered dowels from four studs by striking arm sharply with hammer to loosen dowels.
6. Remove bearing cap at right or steering arm at left. Remove and tag shims for reassembly reference.
7. Remove steering knuckle, also upper and lower bearing cones on K1000 and standard K1500. On heavy duty K1500, remove Woodruff key, then remove bushing from upper steering knuckle.

Installation

1. In the order named, install new felt seal and rubber seal and ring assembly, also metal seal ring over end of axle housing.
2. Install steering knuckle bearing cones (or bushing on heavy duty K1500—make sure that Woodruff key is installed properly when installing bushing) in cups at end of axle housing, while steering knuckle is being placed in position.
3. Install lower bearing cap, and secure with cap screws and lock washers tightened to recommended torque.
4. Install upper bearing cap at right side or steering arm at left side, using same shims removed and tagged at time of disassembly. Tighten cap screws or stud nuts to recommended torque. Observe that clearance exists between nut and arm. If no clearance exists, this indicates excessive wear at studs, dowels, or arm holes. Replace worn parts.
5. Check bearing preload, using spring scale in manner illustrated. Add shims to decrease preload or remove shims to increase preload, whenever scale reading is not within limits given in

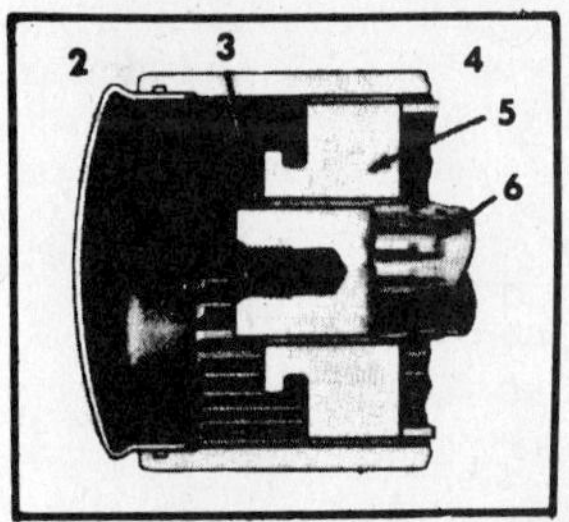

MODEL K1000

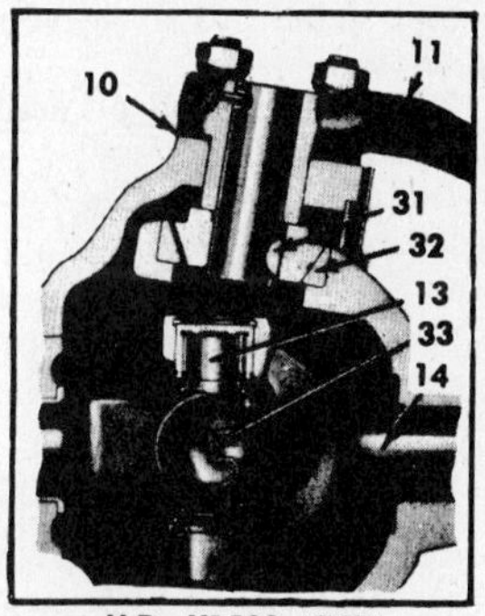

H.D. K1500 (OPT.)

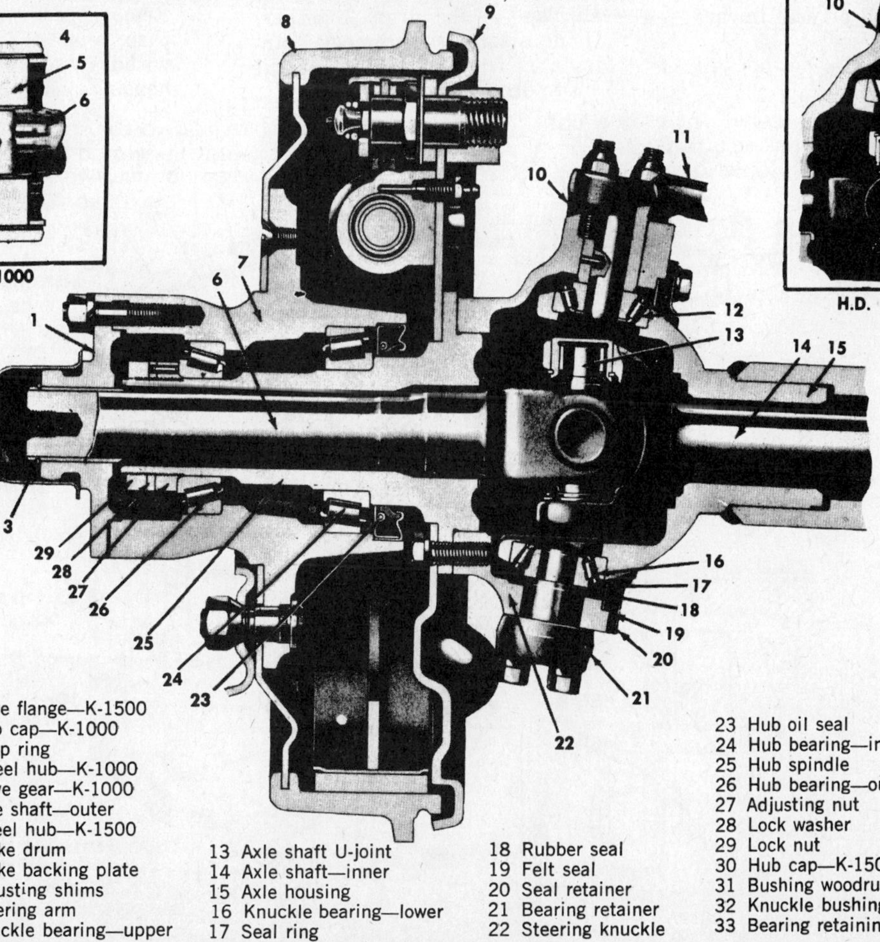

1 Drive flange—K-1500
2 Hub cap—K-1000
3 Snap ring
4 Wheel hub—K-1000
5 Drive gear—K-1000
6 Axle shaft—outer
7 Wheel hub—K-1500
8 Brake drum
9 Brake backing plate
10 Adjusting shims
11 Steering arm
12 Knuckle bearing—upper
13 Axle shaft U-joint
14 Axle shaft—inner
15 Axle housing
16 Knuckle bearing—lower
17 Seal ring
18 Rubber seal
19 Felt seal
20 Seal retainer
21 Bearing retainer
22 Steering knuckle
23 Hub oil seal
24 Hub bearing—inner
25 Hub spindle
26 Hub bearing—outer
27 Adjusting nut
28 Lock washer
29 Lock nut
30 Hub cap—K-1500
31 Bushing woodruff key
32 Knuckle bushing
33 Bearing retaining snap ring

Sectional view of front axle at steering knuckle and wheel hub (© G.M.C.)

"Specifications."

6. Position rubber seal and ring assembly around housing bell and inside opening in steering knuckle, followed by felt seal. Two retainer plates with cap screws and lock washers are used to hole seals in their proper location. NOTE: A film of grease can be used to hole seals in place during installation, which also provides initial lubrication.
7. Install tie rod end to steering knuckle arm. Tighten nut securely and install cotter pin.

Axle Shaft Guide and Oil Seal

Axle shaft guides and oil seals, are located at inner ends of axle housing tube, just outside of the differential bearings. Purpose of guides is to permit installation of axle shaft without damaging oil seal. Seals effectively prevent differential lubricant losses along axle shaft.

Replacement

1. Remove axle shaft and universal joint assembly as instructed in this section.
2. Remove differential assembly as instructed in respective rear axle section.
3. Drive guide and oil seal inward and out of housing.
4. Install new guides in housing tube.
5. Apply axle lubricant to lip of oil seal, then install seal in housing tube with lip of seal inward or toward differential.

Model KV4000 Axle

Reference

For overhaul procedures refer to Rockwell Single Reduction Rear Axle in General Repair section.

Hub and Drum

Removal

1. Bend tangs on lock plate, then remove lock plate bolts, bearing adjusting plate and adjusting shims from spindle. NOTE: Wire adjusting shims together so that same number of shims will be installed that were removed.
2. Remove seal from bearing adjusting plate.
3. Using suitable hoist or chainfall, pull hub and brake drum assembly from spindle. CAUTION: As hub and drum are removed from spindle, outside wheel bearing cone will be removed. Use care not to drop or damage bearing cone.
4. Remove cap screws attaching hub and brake drum together. Using a soft drift, remove bearing cups from hub, being careful not to drop or damage cups.

Installation

1. Press bearing cups into hub.
2. Install brake drum on hub and attach with new cap screws. Tighten cap screws to torque listed in "Specifications" at end of this section.
3. Using suitable hoist or chainfall, place hub and drum over spindle, rotating back and forth to ease hub and drum over the spindle seal. Place outer bearing cone on end of spindle and press into place.
4. Install seal in groove in bearing adjusting plate. Install wheel bearing shims, adjusting plate, lock plates and lock plate bolts. NOTE: Refer to "Radial (Wheel) Bearing Adjustment for number of shims to use. After proper adjustment, secure lock bolts by bending.

Axle Shaft Removal

1. Remove demountable rim or disc wheel cover by removing nuts and washers (when used) from studs and lifting off cover. The wheel cover for demountable rim (spoke type wheels) comes off when the rim is removed. Remove inspection cover from the disc wheel cover.
2. Remove lock wire from bolts, then remove bolts and dowels, withdraw axle shafts from housing, using care not to dam-

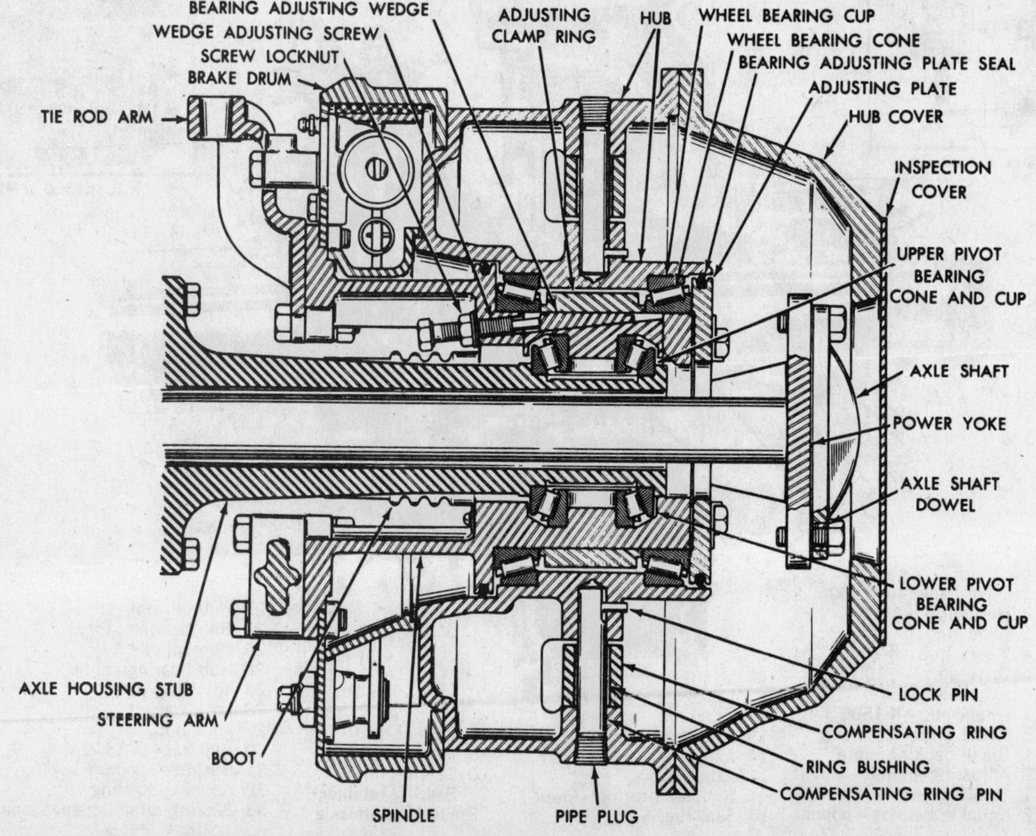

Sectional view of axle outer end (© G.M.C.)

age oil seal in housing.

Installation

1. Install axle shafts into housing, using care not to damage oil seals in housing.
2. Install dowels and bolts attaching axle shaft to power yoke. Tighten bolts firmly, then secure bolts with lock wire.
3. On disc wheel type, install hub cover, then install inspection cover on studs.
4. Hub cover for demountable rim type is installed when the rim is installed.
5. Adjust pivot bearings and check wheel bearing adjustment as directed below.

Spindle Removal

1. At inner side of spindle, loosen lock nut and remove wedge adjusting screw and washer.
2. Using a long thin punch, tap adjusting wedge. This operation will relieve pressure on pivot bearing cones and pivot bearing adjusting wedge clamp ring.
3. Using suitable puller, remove wedge clamp from spindle.
4. Remove 12 screws and lock washers attaching spindle boot and retainers to spindle. Loosen clamp and attaching other end of boot to axle housing stub.
5. Using a long thin punch through knock-out holes in rear of spindle, tap inner wheel bearing cone ½ inch away from spindle flange. Then, using suitable puller, remove bearing cone from spindle. CAUTION: Remove bearing cone evenly or bearing cone may bind and score spindle. Do not drop or damage bearing cone.
6. Spindle and brake backing plate assembly will now drop and rest on stub.
7. Remove pivot bearing cups by driving thin punch through upper and lower knockout holes on inside end of axle housing stub. Lift out top pivot bearing cap, bearing adjusting wedge, and top pivot bearing cone. CAUTION: Do not attempt to remove spindle from housing stub until pivot bearing cups have been driven from housing stub. Also, use extreme caution not to drive punch after cup is loose or punch may slip past cups and damage bearing cage.
8. Tilt back of spindle upward and lift from housing stub. If spindle does not come off readly. DO NOT FORCE, since bearing cup probably is not completely free of housing stub. In this case, repeat preceding step 7.
9. Place spindle on bench and, using a thin punch, drive out lower pivot bearing cone through knock-out holes in bottom of spindle.
10. Remove seal from spindle.
11. Remove cap screws and lock washers attaching tie rod arm, and steering arm (left wheel only) to back of brake backing plate. NOTE: At right wheel, a blank plate is installed in place of steering arm. Separate spindle and brake backing plate by removing bolts and lock washers.

Installation

1. Position brake backing plate assembly on spindle and attach with bolts and lock washers.
2. Position tie rod arm and steering arm (11) (left wheel) or blank plate (right wheel) to brake backing plate; attach with cap screws and lock washers.
3. Lubricate lower pivot bearing cone with clean chassis grease, then press cone into spindle. CAUTION: Make sure that spindle is held firmly during this operation.
4. Place lower pivot bearing cup over lower pivot bearing cone.
5. Position brake backing plate assembly and spindle over end of stub, tilting back upward slightly as the lower pivot cup and cone approach the end of stub.
6. Lubricate upper pivot bearing cup with clean chassis grease, then press cup into spindle.
7. Lubricate and press upper pivot bearing cone into pivot bearing cap. Insert this assembly into pivot bearing hole in top of spindle.
8. Install pivot bearing adjusting wedge into slot on top of pivot bearing cap with rounded surfaced of wedge upward.
9. Using an improvised tool similar to the one illustrated, tighten nuts alernately and evenly until pivot bearing cap is even with surface of spindle. CAUTION: Make sure that hardwood blocks are used between tool and spindle as shown, otherwise damage will occur to spindle and cap.
10. With tool holding pivot bearing cap down, install pivot bearing clamp ring until it is centered over pivot bearing.
11. Using a thin punch through wedge adjusting screw hole in back of spindle, drive pivot bearing adjusting wedge outward in slot until it feels solid. Measure distance from end of wedge to end of spindle as shown. If distance is less than 1⅜ inches, add approximately 0.012 inch shim stock under lower pivot bearing cone for each ⅛ inch it

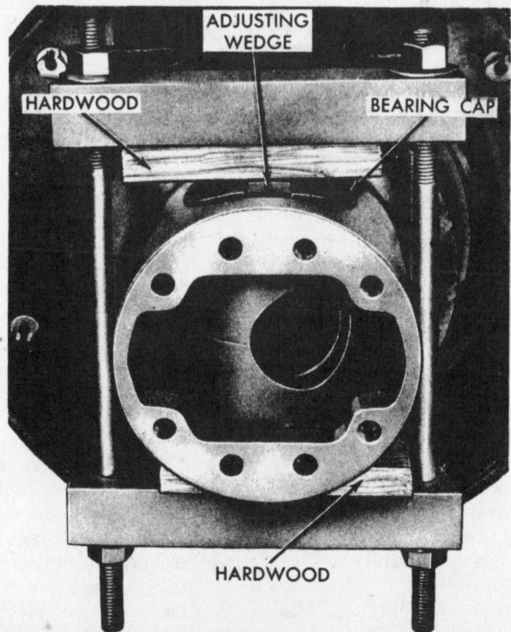

Typical method of installing upper and lower bearing cone, cup and cap
(© G.M.C.)

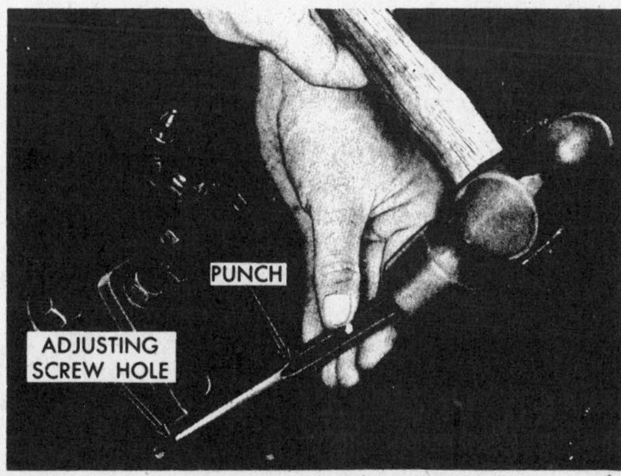

Driving wedge outward on spindle
(© G.M.C.)

is less than the foregoing distance. Release pressure on pivot bearing clamp ring by driving pivot bearing wedge back with punch, then remove clamp ring.

12. Reinstall clamp or through-bolts and bars as shown, then install inner (wheel) bearing cone over spindle. Lubricate wheel bearing cone. Press inner (wheel) bearing cone onto spindle over pivot bearing cap.
13. Remove clamp or though-bolts and bars, then continue pressing bearing cone until it is against flange on spindle.
14. Press pivot bearing clamp ring over spindle. The clamp ring should be pressed as far as it will go but must not contact the cage of the inner bearing cone.
15. Using wedge adjusting screw in inner side of spindle, move pivot bearing wedge outward in pivot bearing cap slot until it feels solid.
16. Install seal in groove in spindle flange. Pack additional bearing grease around bearing clamp ring and inner bearing cone to fill the space between the hub and the spindle when the hub is installed.
17. Position spindle boot to spindle and attach with two retainers and twelve retainer screws and lock washers. Tighten boot clamp at opposite end of housing stub.

Pivot bearing adjustment
(© G.M.C.)

Steering knuckle bearing preload adjusting shims
(© G.M.C.)

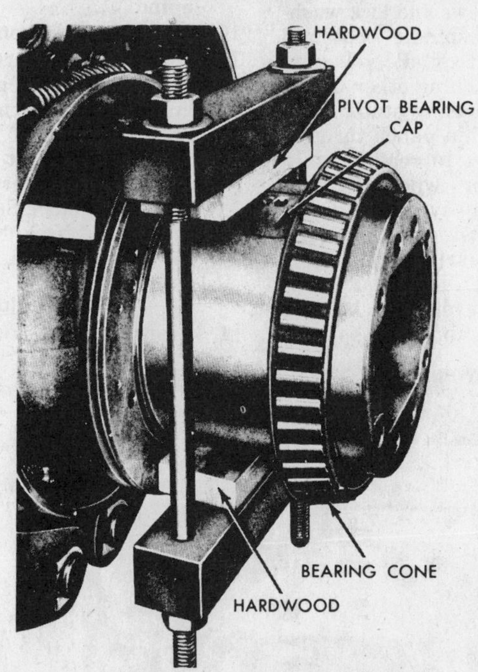

Installing rear bearing cone
(© G.M.C.)

Power Yoke and Compensating Ring

Removal and Disassembly

1. Remove pipe plugs from hub, then remove pins holding power yoke and compensating ring to hub. NOTE: Pins have a 3/8 inch tapped hole to assist in removal of pins.
2. Remove power yoke and compensating ring as an assembly from hub.
3. Remove roll pin, then push out compensating ring to power yoke pin. Power yoke and compensating ring are now separated.

Assembly

1. Position power yoke and compensating ring together, install power yoke pins, and roll pin.
2. Position power yoke and compensating ring assembly (if removed) to hub, then install compensating ring pins and lock pins in hub and compensating ring. Lock pins in hub by installing pipe plugs in hub.

Radial (Wheel) Bearing Adjustment

Radial (wheel) bearing adjustment must be maintained at all times. Adjustment is made each time the bearings are repacked (10,000 miles). However, bearings should be checked for looseness each time the pivot bearings are lubricated and an adjustment made if required. Radial (wheel) bearings are adjusted by means of shims between the bearing adjusting plate spindle end. These shims are in 0.002″, 0.010″, and 0.050″ thicknesses. Sufficient shims should be used to cause only a slight drag when rotating the wheel. Remove tire and rim, disc or case wheel cover, axle shaft, adjusting plate bolts and lock plates, and adjusting plate. Then remove enough shims until a slight drag can be felt when the adjusting plate is attached in place. Bearing adjustment is correct when no play can be felt. After correct adjustment is obtained, secure adjusting plate bolts with lock plates, install axle shaft, wheel cover, and tire and rim.

Free Wheeling Hubs

Free wheeling hubs are available for front wheels on four wheel drive trucks. By disengaging the hubs when four wheel drive is not needed, wear on the front wheel drive train is reduced. The engagement and disengagement of the hubs is a manual operation which must be performed on each front wheel. The hubs must be either fully locked or unlocked and the transfer case control lever must be in two wheel drive position when adjustments are made.

Adjusting wheel bearing
(© G.M.C.)

Hub key positions (typical)
(© G.M.C.)

Steering Gear

Standard Steering Gear

Removal

1. Disconnect steering linkage from pitman arm.
2. Scribe alignment marks on worm shaft and clamp yoke for reassembly.
3. Remove bolts attaching clamp yoke or coupling to steering gear worm shaft.
4. Remove pitman arm nut and washer, then use a puller to remove arm.
5. Remove attaching bolts, nuts and washers, then remove steering gear.

Installation

1. Turn steering wheel to straight-ahead position and center steering gear.
2. Position the steering gear, matching the alignment marks.
3. Install attaching bolts, washers and nuts.
4. Connect clamp yoke or coupling to steering gear worm shaft with attaching parts and torque

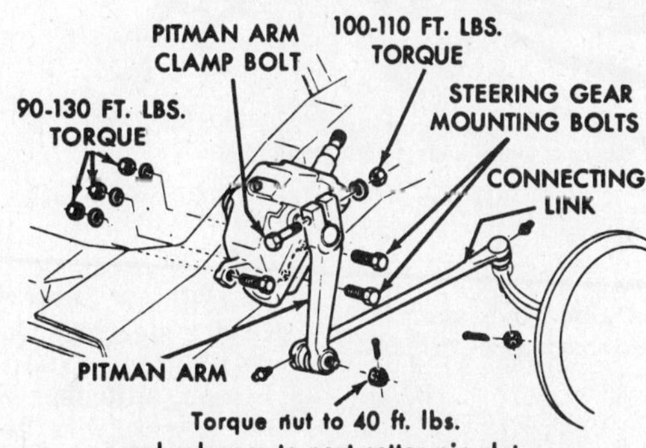

Steering gear and shaft (with flexible coupling)
(© G.M.C.)

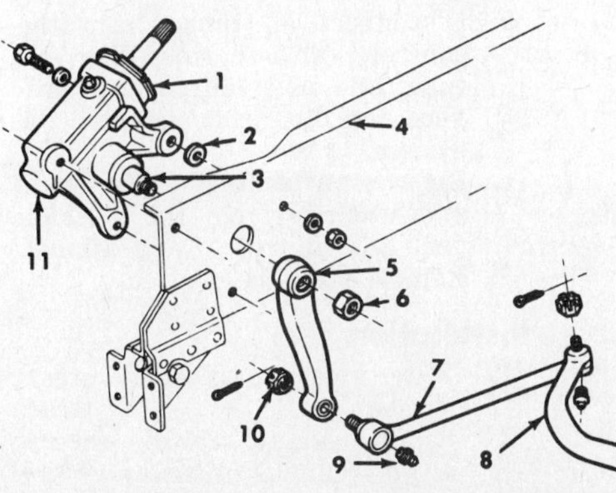

Steering gear and linkage—"T" models (typical)
(© G.M.C.)

1 Worm shaft adjuster lock nut
2 Spacer washer
3 Pitman shaft
4 Frame
5 Pitman arm
6 Pitman shaft nut
7 Drag link
8 Steering arm
9 Lubrication fitting
10 Drag link stud nut
11 Steering gear

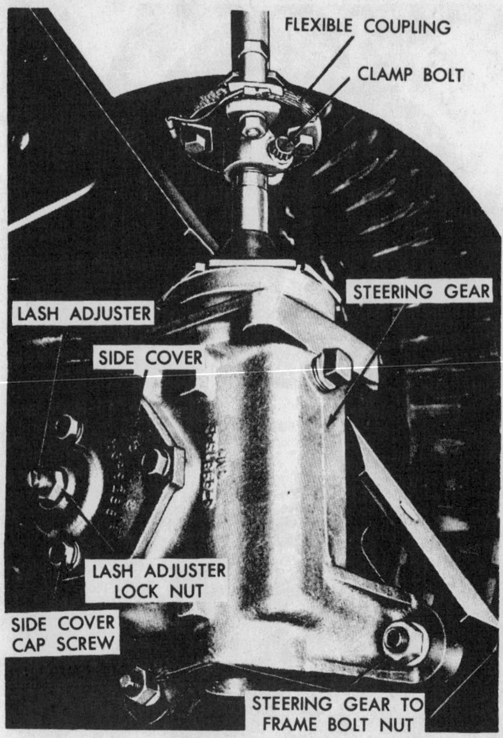

Steering gear and linkage—convential models (typical)
(© G.M.C.)

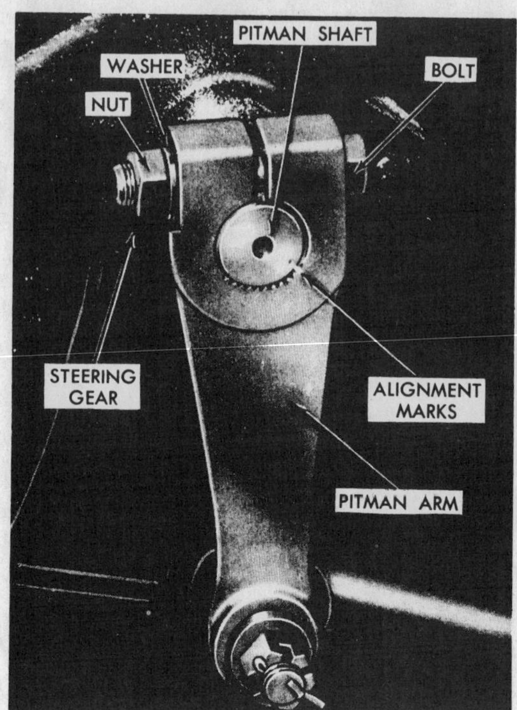

Pitman arm installed (typical)
(© G.M.C.)

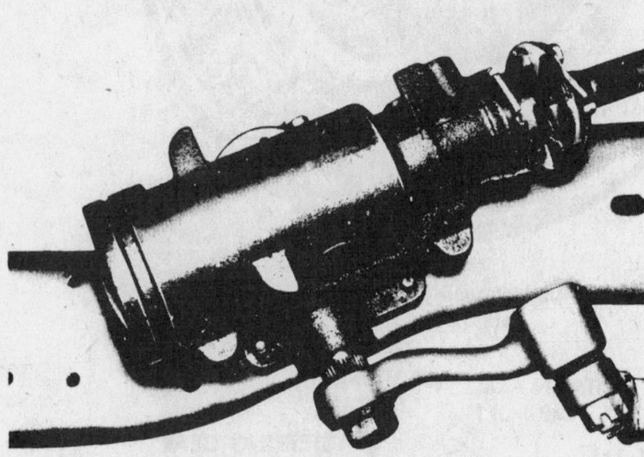

Power steering gear—models 1500-3500 (typical)
(© G.M.C.)

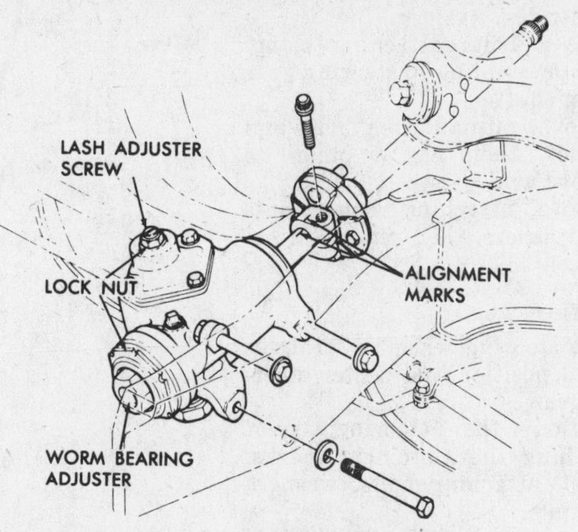

Steering gear adjustment points (typical)
(© G.M.C.)

to specifications.

5. Align pitman arm and shaft; press arm onto shaft and torque to specifications.

Adjustments

Before proceeding to adjust steering gear, check lubricant, front end alignment, tire pressures, shock absorbers, king pins, pitman arm and all mounting bolts for looseness, wear or incorrect adjustment. These are common causes for steering wheel shimmy, clunking or chucking movements.

Worm Bearing

1. Loosen adjuster lock nut and turn screw clockwise until there is no perceptible play.
2. Tighten adjuster lock nut.

Pitman Shaft Lash

1. Center steering wheel and mark its position.
2. Loosen adjuster nut and turn screw clockwise to remove all backlash between gear teeth.
3. Check steering rim pull.

Power Steering Gear

Removal

1. Mark steering gear worm shaft and clamp yoke or coupling for reassembly.
2. Remove connecting rod from pitman arm.
3. Remove attaching pinch bolt, nuts and washers from pitman arm; press pitman arm from shaft.
4. Drain as much fluid as possible from steering gear.
5. Disconnect all tubes from the control valve ports. Plug all tubes and cover all ports to prevent any dirt from entering the system.
6. Remove attaching bolts, nuts and washers from the steering gear and control valve assembly. Remove steering gear.

Installation

1. Center steering wheel and steering gear.
2. Install steering gear by reversing the removal procedure. Make certain to match all alignment marks and to torque all nuts to specifications.

3. Bleed the system and fill reservoir to the proper level.

Adjustments

The only adjustment that can be made on the vehicle is the over-center adjustment.

1. Disconnect pitman arm from shaft, marking the alignment positions.
2. Loosen pitman shaft adjusting screw nut and turn screw out to its limit of travel.
3. Disconnect battery ground cable.
4. Remove horn button.
5. Center steering wheel.
6. Check combined ball and thrust bearing preload by using an in. lbs. torque wrench. Note the highest reading.
7. Tighten pitman shaft adjusting screw and torque steering shaft nut to specifications.
8. Install horn button and connect battery ground cable.
9. Connect pitman arm to shaft, making certain to match alignment marks.

Refer to the General Repair Section for overhaul procedures.

Over center adjustment
(© G.M.C.)

Standard Transmission

The following procedures for removing and installing the transmission are intended as a guide only. Procedures will vary according to optional equipment and individual truck requirements.

Transmission Removal

Except "K" Models

1. Remove floor mat and transmission floor pan cover, then place transmission in neutral and remove gearshift lever and control tower. NOTE: On trucks equipped with SM465 or New Process transmission, remove gearshift only.
2. Place a clean cloth over the transmission opening to prevent the entrance of dirt.
3. Disconnect back-up light switch at transmission.
4. Drain transmission lubricant.
5. Disconnect speedometer cable at transmission and remove parking brake controls.
6. Disconnect driveshaft from transmission.
7. Remove power take-off unit (when used) and cover opening.
8. Position a jack or dolly under the transmission and make certain that all attaching lines and brackets are disconnected.
9. Support rear of engine when mounts are located on the clutch housing.
10. Remove transmission to flywheel housing bolts.
11. Move transmission straight back from the engine, keeping mainshaft in alignment. CAUTION: Do not let the weight of the transmission hang on the clutch disc hub.
12. When transmission is free of the engine, lower jack or dolly and remove transmission.

Installation

Except "K" Models

1. Apply a light coating of high temperature grease to main drive gear bearing retainer and splined portion of driveshaft. CAUTION: Do not apply an excessive amount of grease as it will be thrown onto the clutch facings.
2. To complete transmission installation, place transmission in fourth gear, reverse the removal procedures and torque mounting bolts to specifications. Fill transmission with lubricant to the proper level.

Transmission Removal

"K" Models (3 Speed)

1. Drain transfer case and transmission.
2. Disconnect speedometer cable and TCS connections at transmission.
3. Disconnect driveshaft at U-joint.
4. Remove attaching shift assembly bolt, then push assembly to one side.
5. Supporting transfer case in cradle, remove attaching bolts and case.
6. Disconnect shift control rods from transmission.
7. Support engine rear and remove adapter mount bolts.
8. Remove top 2 transmission to flywheel housing mount bolts and install guide pins.
9. Remove remaining mount bolts and slide transmission straight back on guide pins until it is disengaged from engine.
10. Remove transmission and adapter as an assembly.

Installation

"K" Models (3 Speed)

To install transmission, reverse the removal procedures and fill with lubricant to the proper level.

Transmission Removal

"K" Models (4 Speed)

1. Remove transfer case shift lever retainer.

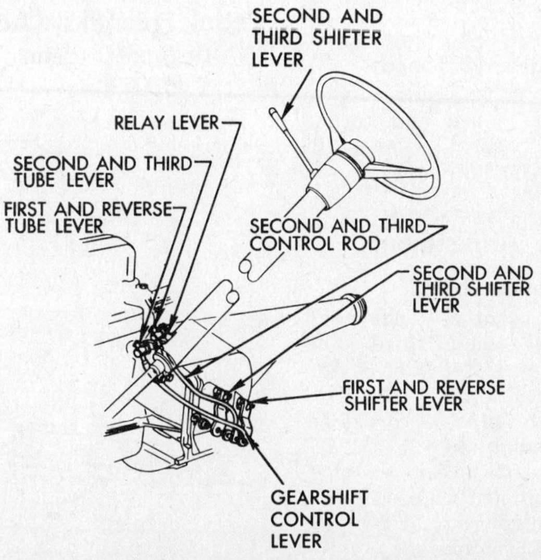

3-speed column shift controls
(© G.M.C.)

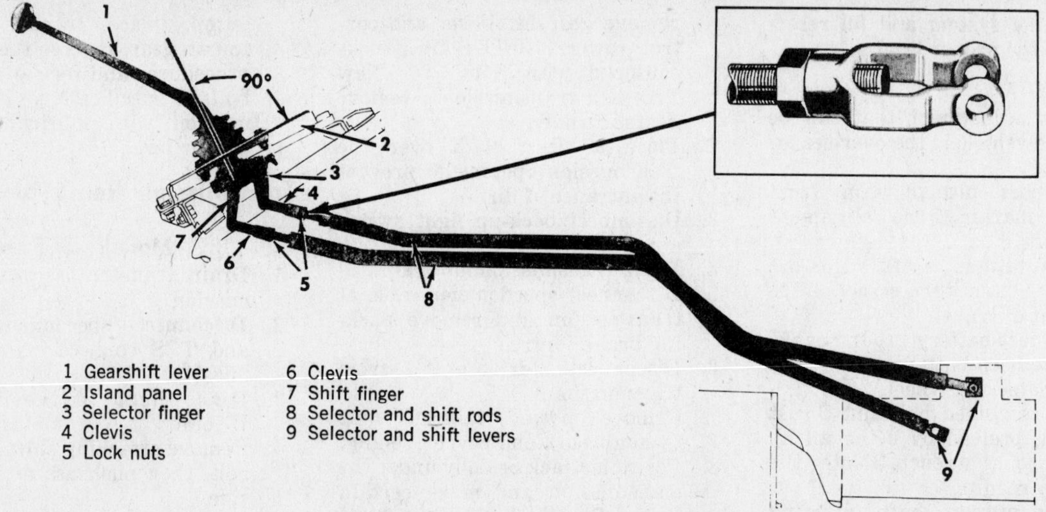

Manual transmission control linkage—tilt cab models (typical) (© G.M.C.)

2. Remove floor mat, shift lever, console and heater duct (when used).
3. Remove transmission floor cover and disconnect shift lever link assembly.
4. Remove all attaching wiring and clamps.
5. Support engine. Drain transmission and transfer case.
6. Disconnect front and rear driveshafts at transfer case.
7. Remove transmission and transfer case to frame bolts and place jack or dolly under transmission assembly.
8. Remove frame crossmember.
9. Remove flywheel housing cover and exhaust crossover pipe (when used).
10. Remove transmission to flywheel housing bolts. Using guide pins, slide assembly back until it disengages the engine.
11. Remove transmission assembly.

Installation

"K" Models (4 Speed)

To install the transmission, reverse the removal procedure and torque mounting bolts to specifications. Fill transmission with lubricant to the proper level.

Shift Linkage Adjustment

Column Shift

1. Disconnect central rods and align both second/third and first/reverse shifter tube levers in neutral position.
2. Install gauge in holes provided to maintain alignment.
3. Position relay levers so that gearshift is in neutral position.
4. Connect control rods to tube levers and then remove gauge.
5. Move gearshift through pattern to check adjustment.

Tilt Cab Models

1. Place transmission selector and shift levers in "neutral" position.
2. Adjust selector and shift rods to provide 90° angularity at the lower end of the gearshift lever to the control island panel by rotating adjustable clevis on each rod to the desired position and then connecting rods and tightening lock nuts.
3. Check adjustment by moving the gearshift through the pattern.
4. Install new cotter pins and lubricate linkage.

Refer to the General Repair Section for complete overhaul procedures, illustrations and out of truck adjustments.

Clutch

Pedal Free Play Adjustment

1. Disconnect return spring and loosen nuts.
2. Apply approximately 5 lbs. force to pushrod in direction of letter "G" in the illustration.
3. Move lever until pedal makes contact with stop.
4. Turn nut as necessary to obtain a clearance of 3/16-1/4" between

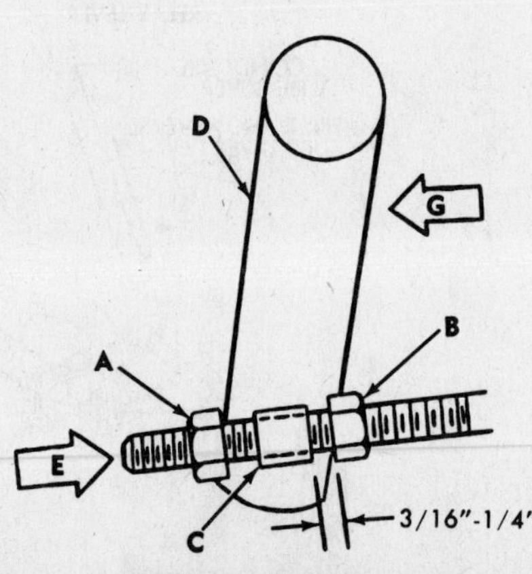

Linkage adjustment (all models, except V6, 427 engines) (© G.M.C.)

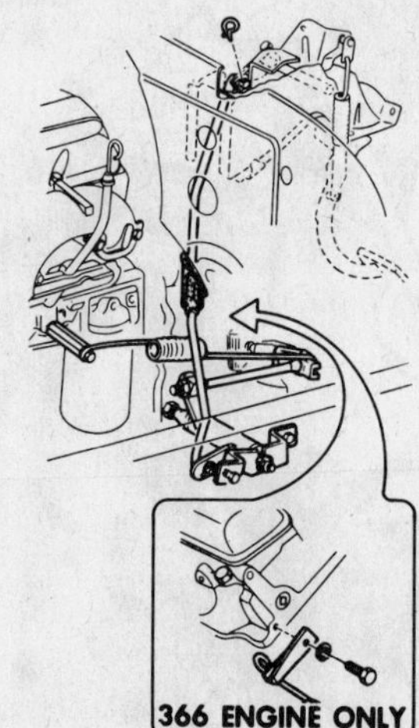

Clutch linkage (CE, SE5500; CE, ME6500) (© G.M.C.)

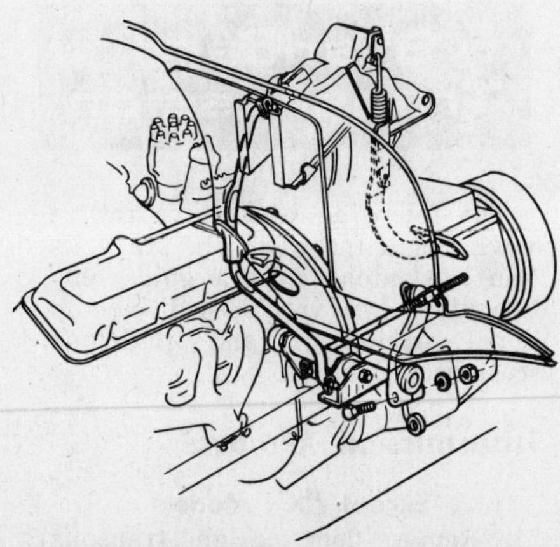

Clutch linkage (CE, ME6500—427 V8 engine) (© G.M.C.)

nut and swivel.
5. Tighten lock nut and connect return spring.
6. Check pedal free play. The clutch pedal free play should be ¾"-1" on all models.

hardwood wedges between release levers and cover.
4. On Lipe- Rollway clutches, install three flat washers and hold down bolts.
5. Make alignment marks on the match.
3. Install cover to flywheel bolts and torque slowly one turn at a time to specifications.
4. Remove aligning tool and wood wedges or hold-down bolts.

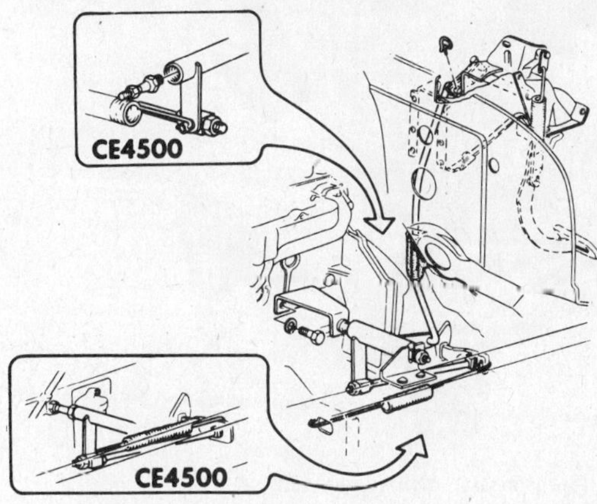

Clutch linkage (CE, CS4500; CS, SS5500)
(© G.M.C.)

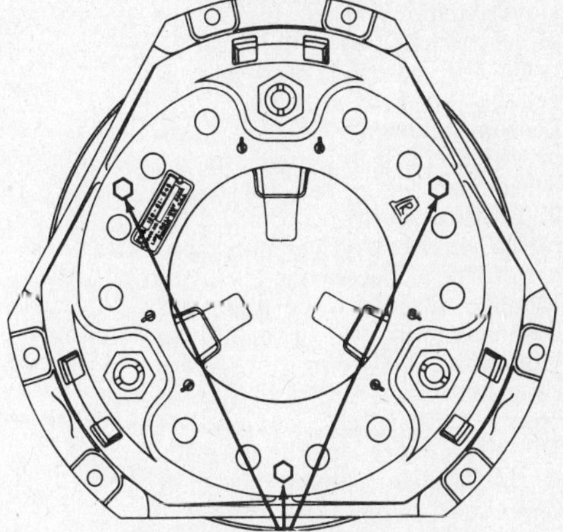

Use of hold-down bolts (Lipe-Rollway)
(© G.M.C.)

Clutch Removal

1. Remove transmission assembly from truck.
2. Remove clutch release fork from ball stud.
3. Install aligning tool or old transmission main drive gear into the clutch hub to support the clutch components during removal. NOTE: To facilitate the removal of Long or Borg and Beck clutch cover assemblies, install clutch cover and engine flywheel for reassembly.
6. Loosen the cover bolts one turn at a time and then remove the clutch assembly.

Installation

1. Install clutch assembly.
2. Install clutch cover assembly using the alignment tool or old transmission main drive gear. Make certain alignment marks
5. Connect clutch release mechanism. Lubricate clutch release bearing sparingly and apply a small amount of high temperature grease to recess in release fork. Tighten ball stud to specifications.
6. Install transmission assembly.

Refer to General Repair Section for clutch overhaul procedures.

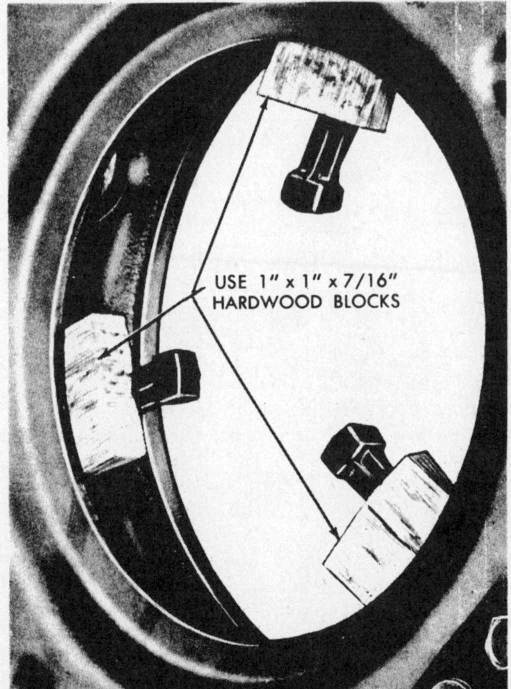

Use of hardwood blocks to remove Long or Borg and Beck clutch assembly
(© G.M.C.)

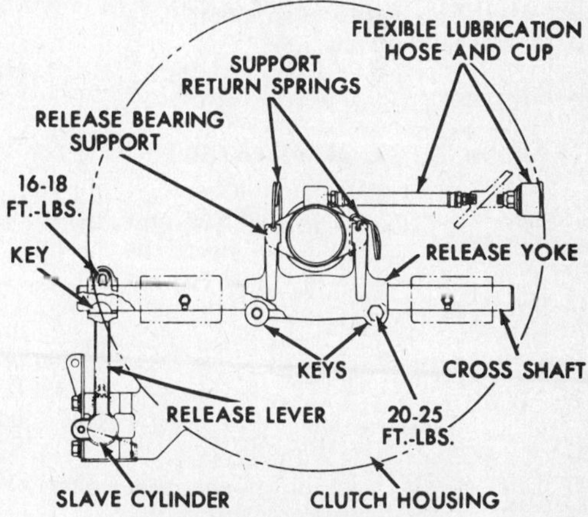

Yoke type clutch release mechanism
(© G.M.C.)

Automatic Transmission

The automatic transmissions covered in this section are Allison, Pow-R-Flo and Turbo-Hydramatic. Removal and installation procedures are covered separately for each. It may be necessary to remove air tanks, fuel tanks, and optional equipment in order to gain access to the transmission.

Transmission Removal

Allison MT40, MT41, AT540

1. Block vehicle so that it cannot move. Remove spark plugs (on diesel engines, turn fuel lever to "shut-off" position) and disconnect battery ground strap.
2. Loosen transmission oil filter cover and allow fluid to drain.
3. Disconnect range selector cable, TV (throttle valve) rod, retarder linkage and vacuum modulator line as necessary.
4. Remove oil filler tube and vent hose assembly. Cover openings.
5. Disconnect oil cooler lines from retarder valve body and wiring from hot oil switch.
6. Disconnect speedometer shaft fitting at transmission.
7. Disconnect driveshaft.
8. Disconnect mechanical parking brake (when used).
9. Through the opening in the flywheel housing, use a pry bar to turn flywheel. Remove the 6 flywheel flex plate retaining nuts while turning.
10. Support transmission with a floor jack, making certain that oil pan does not support the weight of transmission.
11. Support rear of engine and remove converter to frame bolts.
12. Remove attaching flywheel to converter housing bolts.
13. Remove transmission rear mounting bolts and support.
14. Remove transmission.

Installation

Allison MT40, MT41, AT540

To install transmission assembly, reverse the removal procedures and torque mounting bolts to specifications. Fill transmission with oil to the proper level.

Automatic transmission mounted on dolly
(© G.M.C.)

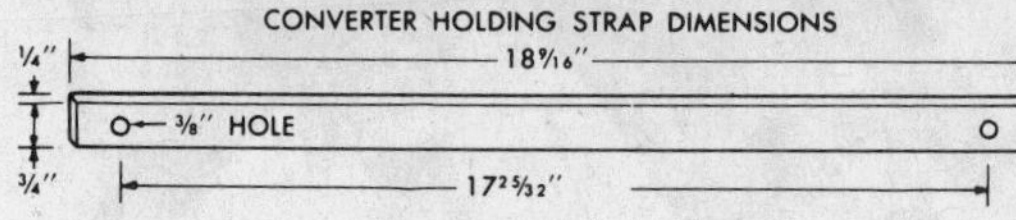

Converter holding strap
(© G.M.C.)

Transmission Removal

Pow-R-Flo

1. Raise truck and drain oil.
2. Disconnect vacuum modulator line, speedometer drive cable and TV control rods from transmission.
3. Disconnect driveshaft.
4. Support transmission with jack or dolly.
5. Disconnect engine rear mount on transmission and remove support crossmember.
6. Remove converter underpan, scribe flywheel—converter alignment marks, then remove attaching bolts.
7. 'support engine at oil pan rail.
8. Lower rear end of transmission slightly and remove upper transmission to engine mounting bolts.
9. Remove remaining mounting bolts.
10. Remove transmission, making certain to keep front end up so that converter does not fall out.
11. Install a converter holding strap as illustrated.

Installation

To install transmission, reverse the removal procedures and torque mounting bolts to specifications. Fill transmission with oil to the proper level.

Transmission Removal

Turbo Hydra-Matic 350, 400 (Except "K" Models)

1. Raise truck and drain oil.
2. Disconnect vacuum modulator line, speedometer drive cable, manual control lever rod and detent cable from transmission.
3. Disconnect driveshaft.
4. Support transmission with jack or dolly.
5. Disconnect engine rear mount on transmission and remove support crossmember.
6. Remove converter underpan, scribe flywheel—converter alignment marks. then remove attaching bolts.
7. Support engine at oil pan rail.
8. Lower rear end of transmission slightly and remove upper transmission to engine mounting bolts.
9. Remove remaining mounting bolts.
10. Remove transmission, making

certain to keep front end up so that converter does not fall out.

Installation

NOTE: Do not permit converter to move forward after removing holding tool or strap.

To install transmission, reverse the removal procedures and torque mounting bolts to specifications. Fill transmission with oil to the proper level.

Transmission Removal

Turbo Hydra-Matic 350, 400 ("K" Models)

1. Raise truck and drain oil.
2. Remove transfer case shift lever and rod.
3. Disconnect vacuum modulator line, speedometer drive cable, manual control lever rod and detent cable from transmission.
4. Disconnect front and rear axle driveshafts at transfer case.
5. Remove attaching transmission to adapter case bolts and support transfer case.
6. Support transmission with jack or dolly.
7. Remove attaching bolts and transfer case.
8. Remove exhaust crossover pipe (when used).
9. Remove support rear crossmember.
10. Remove converter underpan, scribe flywheel—converter alignment marks, then remove flywheel to converter bolts.
11. Support engine at oil pan rail.
12. Lower rear end of transmission slightly and remove upper transmission to engine mounting bolts.
13. Remove remaining mounting bolts.
14. Remove transmission, making certain to keep front end up so that converter does not fall out.

Installation

To install transmission, reverse the removal procedures and torque mounting bolts to specifications. Fill transmission with oil to the proper level.

Refer to the General Repair Section for overhaul procedures.

Adjustments

Before making any checks or adjustments on automatic transmission linkage, test the engine performance. It is important that performance meets specifications. Many times the cause for poor shifting can be traced to the engine, and unnecessary linkage adjustments need not be made.

The following procedures are intended as a guide only. Different models utilize various linkage arrangements, and the adjustment steps followed will vary accordingly.

TV Linkage Adjustment

Allison

1. Start engine and adjust idle speed. Stop engine. NOTE: Letters A through K refer to illustrations.
2. Disconnect clevis (G) from TV lever (F) and position lever (A) 0.060" from stop (B).
3. Set throttle lever (C) at idle and adjust swivels on rod (I) for free entry into levers (A, B).
4. Shorten clevis (G) 2 full turns. Install clevis pin, tighten nut and secure (G) to (F) with cotter pin.
5. With accelerator pedal (D) just touching detent button (E), the throttle lever should be in full open position. Shorten or lengthen rods to achieve correct relationship.
6. Road test truck. Upshift should occur at 50 rpm below top governed engine speed. To raise the shift point, shorten rod (H); to lower shift point, lengthen rod (H).

Manual Linkage Adjustment

Allison

1. Locate selector lever in the illustrated position.
2. Adjust cable as shown in illustration.
3. Disconnect clevis from manual shift lever.
4. Adjust clevis for free entry of pin, then lengthen clevis by 1½ turns, install pin, tighten lock nut, and secure with cotter pin.

TV Linkage Adjustment

Pow-R-Flo With Inline Engines

With pedal depressed, bell crank must be at wide open throttle position. Rod must be 1/64"-1/16" off stop and transmission lever must be against internal stop.

Pow-R-Flo with V8 Engines

1. Remove air cleaner and disconnect accelerator linkage at carburetor.
2. Disconnect accelerator and TV rod return springs.
3. Pull TV upper rod forward until transmission is through detent; adjust swivel on rod so that carburetor is wide open as ball stud contacts end of slot in rod.
4. Connect and adjust accelerator linkage.

Manual Selector Linkage Adjustment

Pow-R-Flo

1. Locate selector lever in "Drive" position.
2. Loosen adjustment swivel at mast jacket lever and rotate transmission lever to the stop in steering column.
3. Tighten swivel. A properly adjusted linkage will prevent selector lever from passing over neutral or drive detents without lifting the lever over the mechanical stop. Re-adjust if necessary.

Manual Selector Linkage Adjustment

Turbo Hydra Matic

To adjust manual selector linkage on Hydra-Matic transmissions, follow same procedure as for the Pow-R-Flo transmission, then adjust the indicator needle as necessary to correspond with transmission detent po-

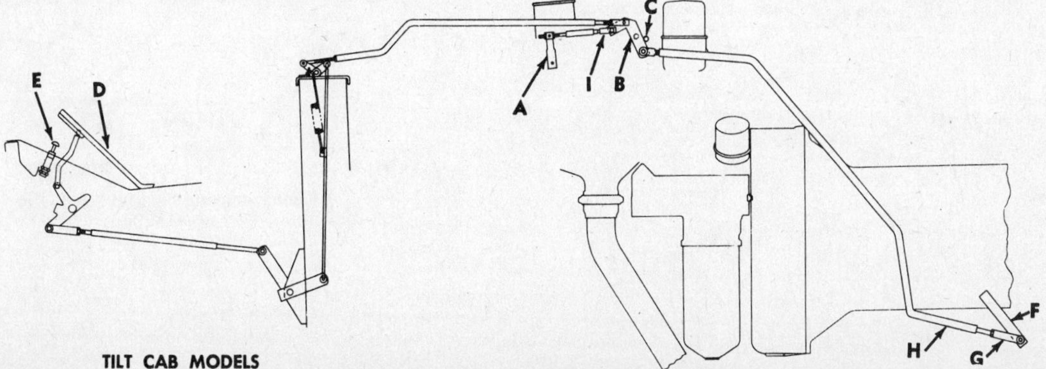

Accelerator and TV linkage (Allison) (© G.M.C.)

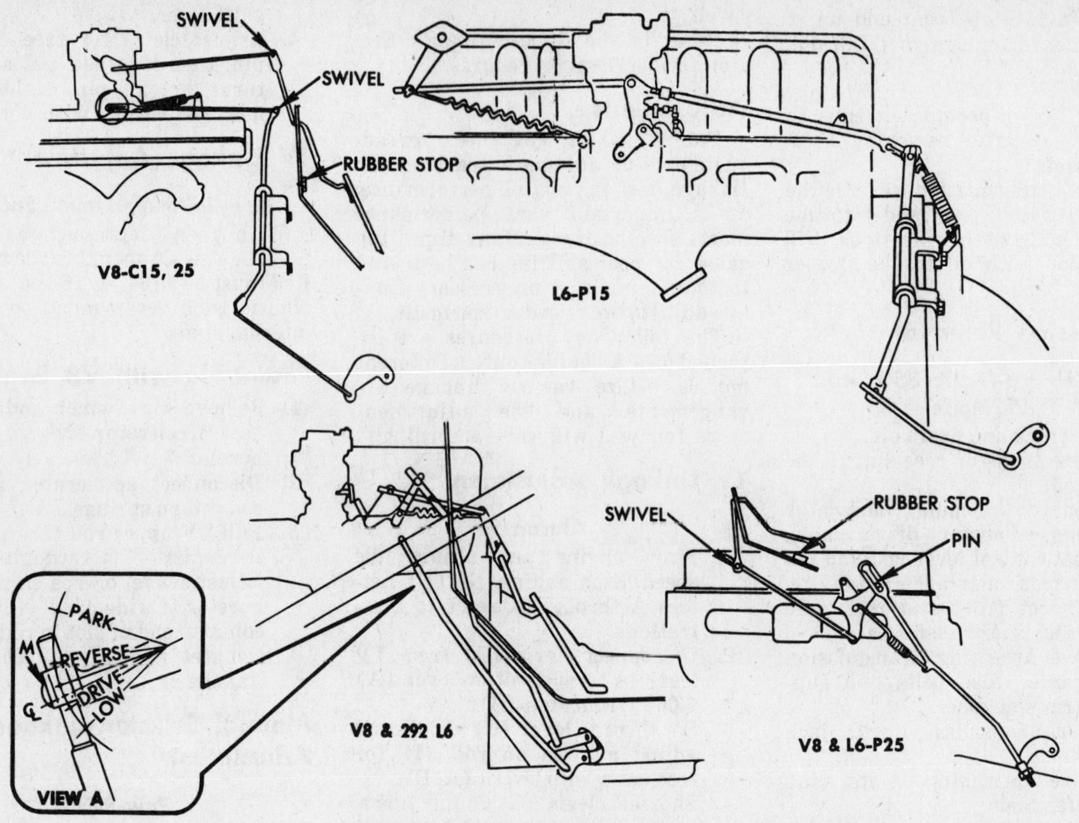

TV linkage adjustment (Pow-R-Flo) (© G.M.C.)

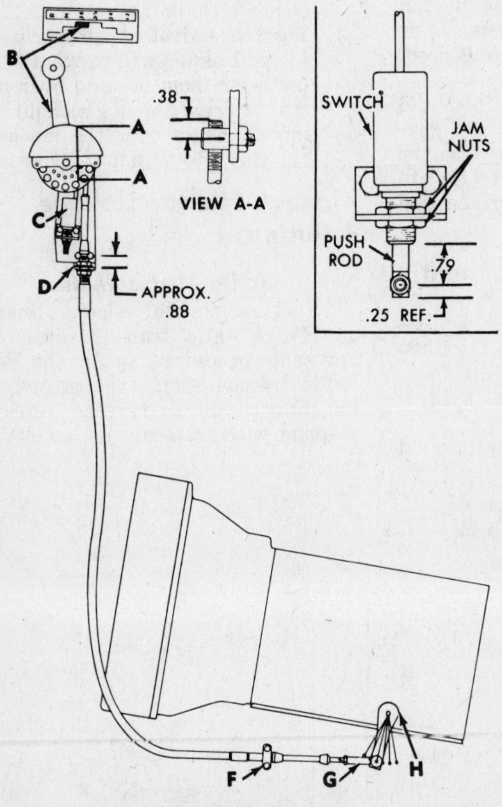

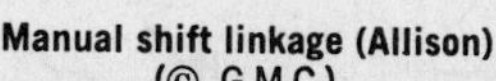

Manual shift linkage (Allison)
(© G.M.C.)

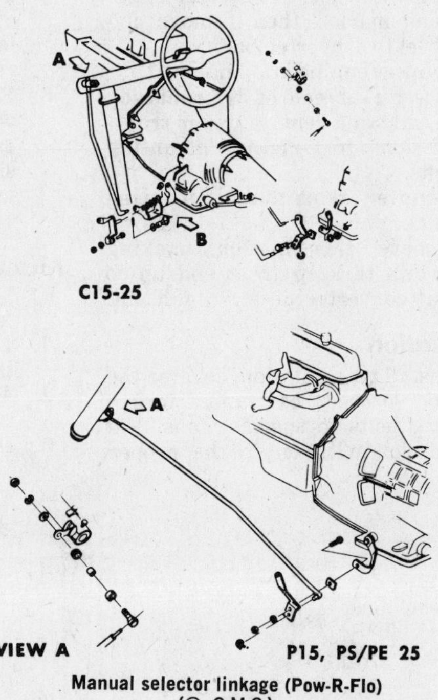

Manual selector linkage (Pow-R-Flo)
(© G.M.C.)

sitions.

Detent Cable Adjustment

Turbo Hydra Matic 350

1. Remove air cleaner and loosen detent cable screw.
2. With choke off and accelerator correctly adjusted, set carburetor lever at wide open position.
3. Pull cable rearward through detent until transmission reaches internal wide open throttle stop.
4. Tighten detent cable screw.

Detent Switch Adjustment

(Turbo Hydra Matic 400)

Adjust detent switch as illustrated.

Refer to the General Repair Section for complete overhaul procedures and wear tolerances.

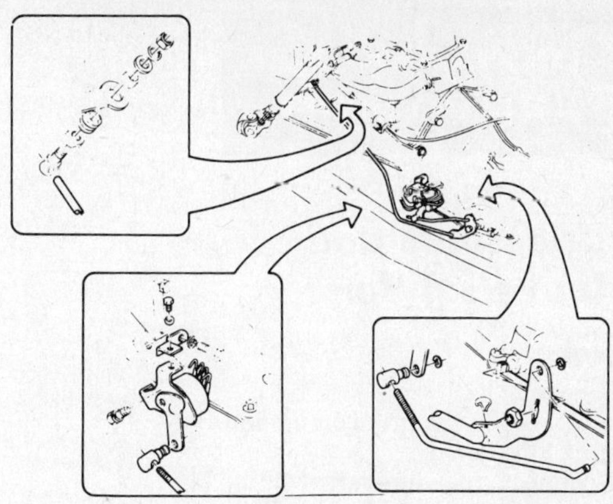

Manual selector linkage—"P" models (Turbo Hydra-Matic) (© G.M.C.)

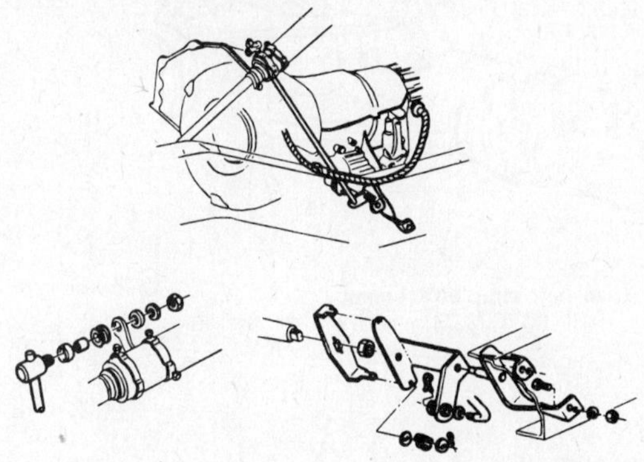

Manual selector linkage—"C" models (Turbo Hydra-Matic) (© G.M.C.)

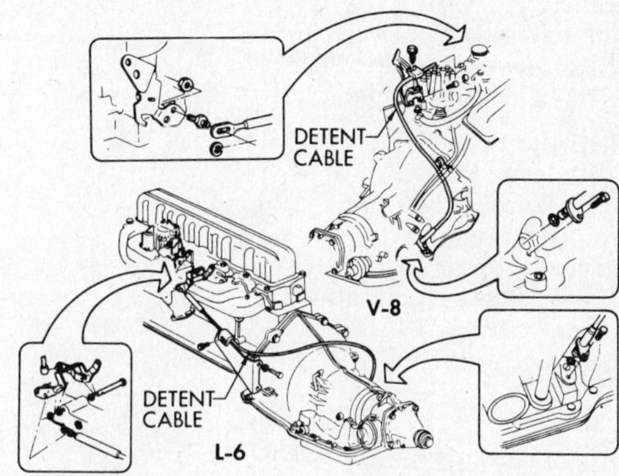

Detent cable adjustment (Turbo Hydra-Matic 350) (© G.M.C)

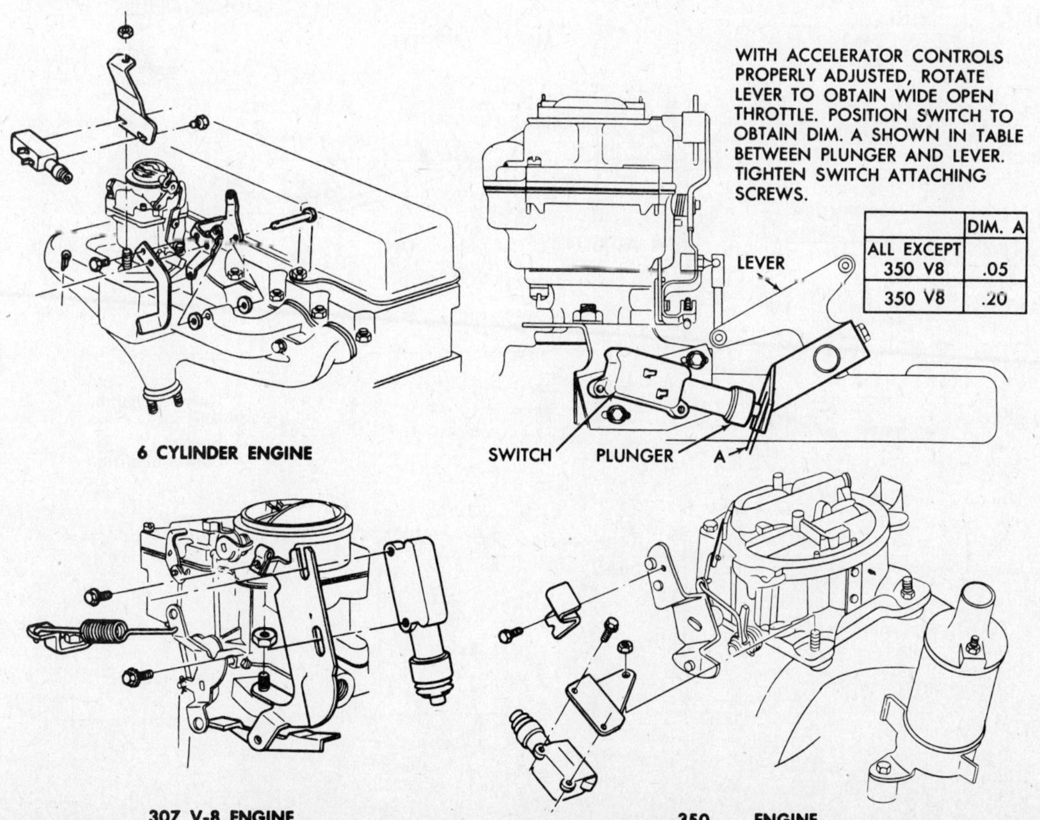

	DIM. A
ALL EXCEPT 350 V8	.05
350 V8	.20

Detent switch adjustment (Turbo Hydra-Matic 400) (© G.M.C.)

Drive Axle, Suspension

Driveshaft and Universal Joint

Removal

1. Raise vehicle.
2. Mark shaft and companion flange alignment.
3. Disconnect rear universal joint by removing attaching U-bolt or strap.
4. Remove bearing support bolts as necessary.
5. Slide driveshaft forward to disengage trunnion, then back to disengage transmission.

Installation

1 Piece Driveshaft

1. Slide shaft into transmission and connect rear U-joint.
2. Torque bolts to specifications.

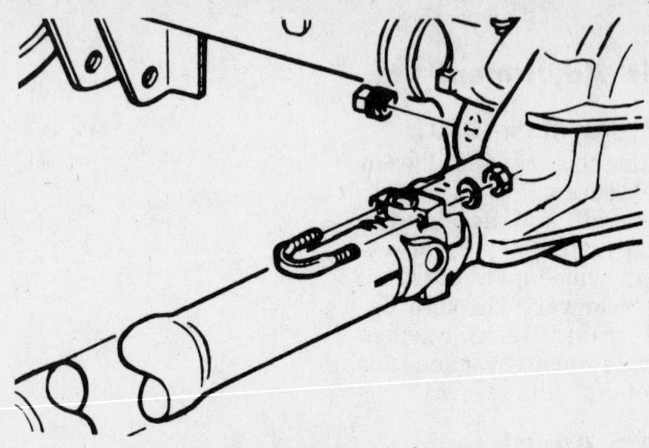

Driveshaft U-bolt attachment
(© G.M.C.)

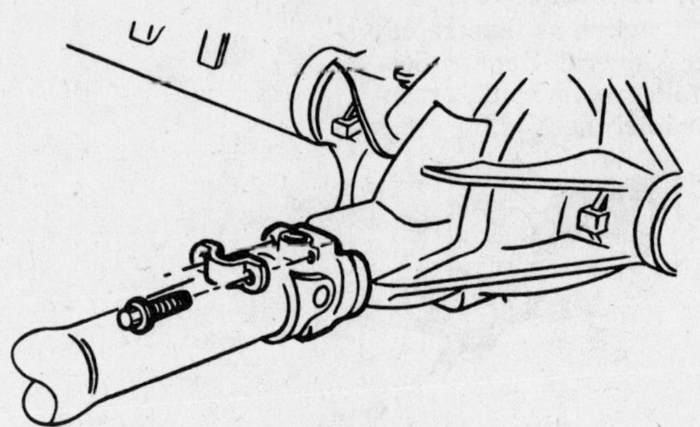

Driveshaft strap attachment
(© G.M.C.)

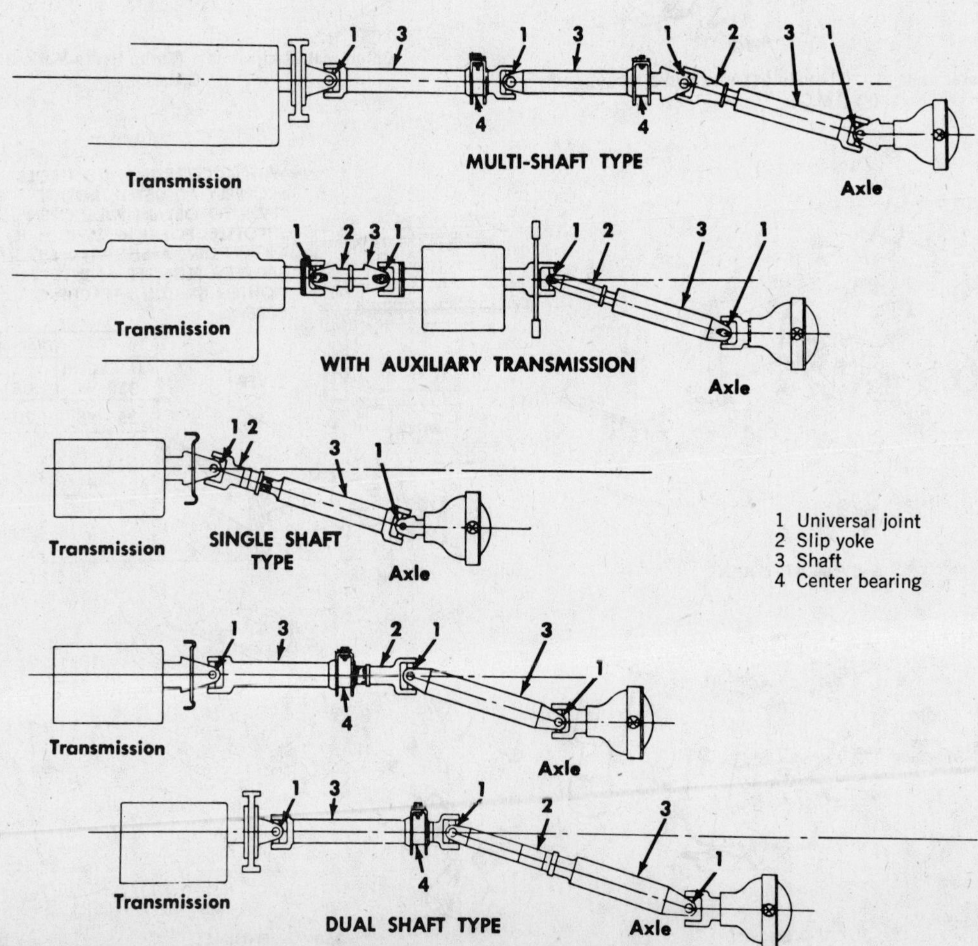

Driveshaft combinations (typical) (© G.M.C.)

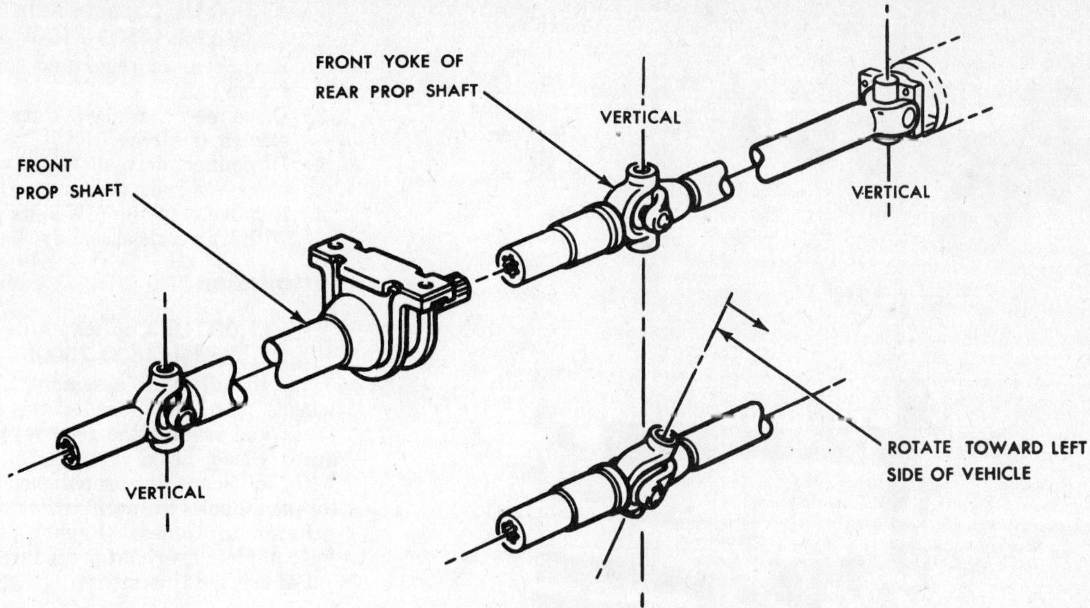

Aligning U-joints (© G.M.C.)

Installation

2 Piece Driveshaft

1. Insert front shaft into transmission and bolt support to crossmember.
2. Install grease cap and gasket on rear splines.
3. Align all U-joint trunnions in the same vertical position, then install rear shaft.
4. Connect rear U-joint to axle.
5. Torque all bolts to specifications and tighten grease cap.

Bearing cap removal (© G.M.C.)

Universal Joint Overhaul

1000-3500 Models

1. Remove bearing lock rings.
2. Support yoke in an arbor press and apply pressure on trunnion until bearing cup is almost out. NOTE: Bearing cup cannot be fully pressed out.
3. Grasp cup with vise and work out of yoke.
4. Repeat procedure on the opposite side.
5. Clean and inspect all parts; replace as necessary. Pack bearings and make certain to fill lubricant reservoirs at end of each trunnion. Place dust seals on trunnions and press into position.
6. Position trunnion into yoke and partially install one bearing cup.
7. Partially install opposite cup and then press them both into place.
8. Install lock rings.

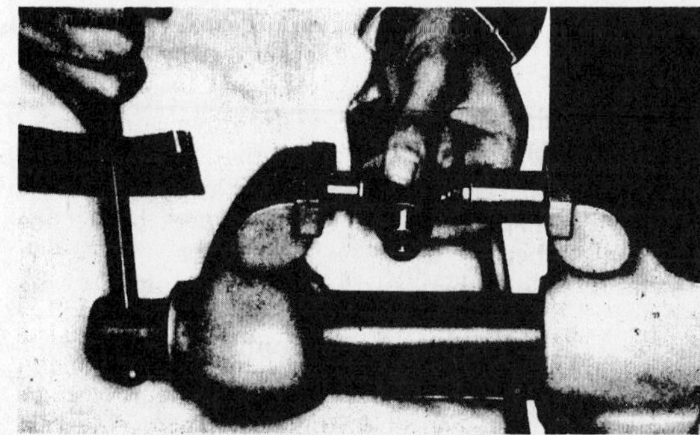

Installing U-joint trunnion (© G.M.C.)

Universal Joint Overhaul

4500-7500 Models

1. Remove bearing retaining snap rings or U-bolts.
2. Strike one side of yoke with hammer to remove bearing. Repeat on opposite side.
3. Tilt journal and remove yoke.
4. Remove remaining bearings in the same manner as step (2).
5. Clean all parts with cleaning fluid. Make certain lubricating passages in journal cross are clear, and all old lubricant has been removed. Check for wear and any missing bearing rollers. If any excessive wear is noted,

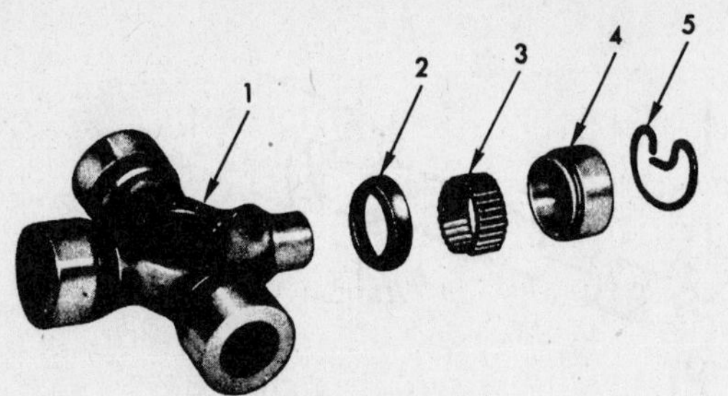

Universal joint repair kit
(© G.M.C.)

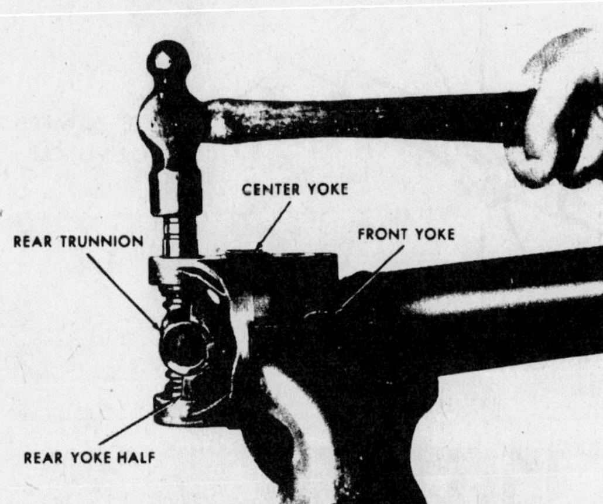

Driving out bearing caps
(© G.M.C.)

discard bearings and journal; replace with new parts. Lubricate as recommended in specifications.
6. Install lubrication fitting in journal.
7. Install journal in yoke, then install bearings using a mallet to tap them in place.
8. Install bearing retaining snap rings or U-bolts and torque nuts (when used) to specifications.

Rear Axle Assembly

Removal

3500 and 5500 Lbs Capacity Axle (Models 1500-3500)

1. Raise truck and support rear axle to relieve load from springs, tie-rod, and shock absorbers.
2. Disconnect tie-rod at axle (when used).
3. Disconnect driveshaft. NOTE: Secure bearing caps to trunnion with tape.
4. Disconnect shock absorbers.
5. Disconnect vent hose.
6. Disconnect brake hose on axle housing. Remove brake drum and disconnect parking brake cable.
7. Make certain coil springs (when used) are compressed, then remove U-bolts, spacers and clamp plates.
8. Withdraw axle assembly.

Installation

3500 and 5500 Lb. Capacity Axle (Models 1500-3500)

To install axle assembly, reverse the removal procedure, bleed brake system, adjust parking brake and torque all bolts to specifications.

Removal

11,000 Lb. Capacity Axle (Models 1500-3500)

1. Raise truck, support frame side rails and remove rear wheels.
2. Disconnect driveshaft. NOTE: Secure bearing caps to trunnion with tape.
3. Disconnect brake hose and shock absorbers.
4. Remove drum and disconnect parking brake.
5. Support axle, remove spring U-bolts and then withdraw assembly.

Installation

11,000 Lb. Capacity Axle (Models 1500-3500)

To install axle assembly, reverse the removal procedure, bleed brake system, adjust parking brake and torque all bolts to specifications.

Removal

11,000 Lb. Capacity Axle (Models 4500-7500)

1. Raise rear of truck and support frame rails.
2. Disconnect brake lines and electrical wiring.
3. Disconnect driveshaft and torque or radius rods (when used).
4. Remove spring U-bolts and withdraw axle assembly.

Installation

11,000 Lb. Capacity Axle (Models 4500-7500)

To install axle assembly, mount wheels and tires, roll axle under truck and reverse the removal procedure. Bleed brake system, fill axle with lubricant to proper level and torque all bolts to specifications.

Refer to General Repair Section for complete overhaul procedures and out of truck adjustments.

Reference

For Service on Eaton and Timken (Rockwell) axles see General Repair Section.

GMC Single Speed Axle Service

H052, H072, H110, H130, H135, H150

Disassembly of Subassemblies

Differential Disassembly

1. Remove lock nut, adjusting screw, and thrust block.
2. Remove two adjuster lock cap screws and locks.
3. Punch-mark bearing caps and carrier to help in locating caps for assembly. Remove bearing adjusters and bearing caps. NOTE: Do not pry caps free with a screwdriver or distort locating dowels.
4. Carefully remove differential assembly from carrier.
5. Use differential side bearing remover to pull bearing cones off each side of case.
6. Make sure that differential case halves are punch-marked so that they can be reassembled in same position.
7. Remove drive gear, and separate case halves.
8. Remove two side gears; differential spider, and four differential pinions.
9. On H110, H135, and H150 models remove pinion and side gear thrust washers to complete differential disassembly.

Drive Pinion Disassembly

1. Remove seal retainer and gasket from carrier.

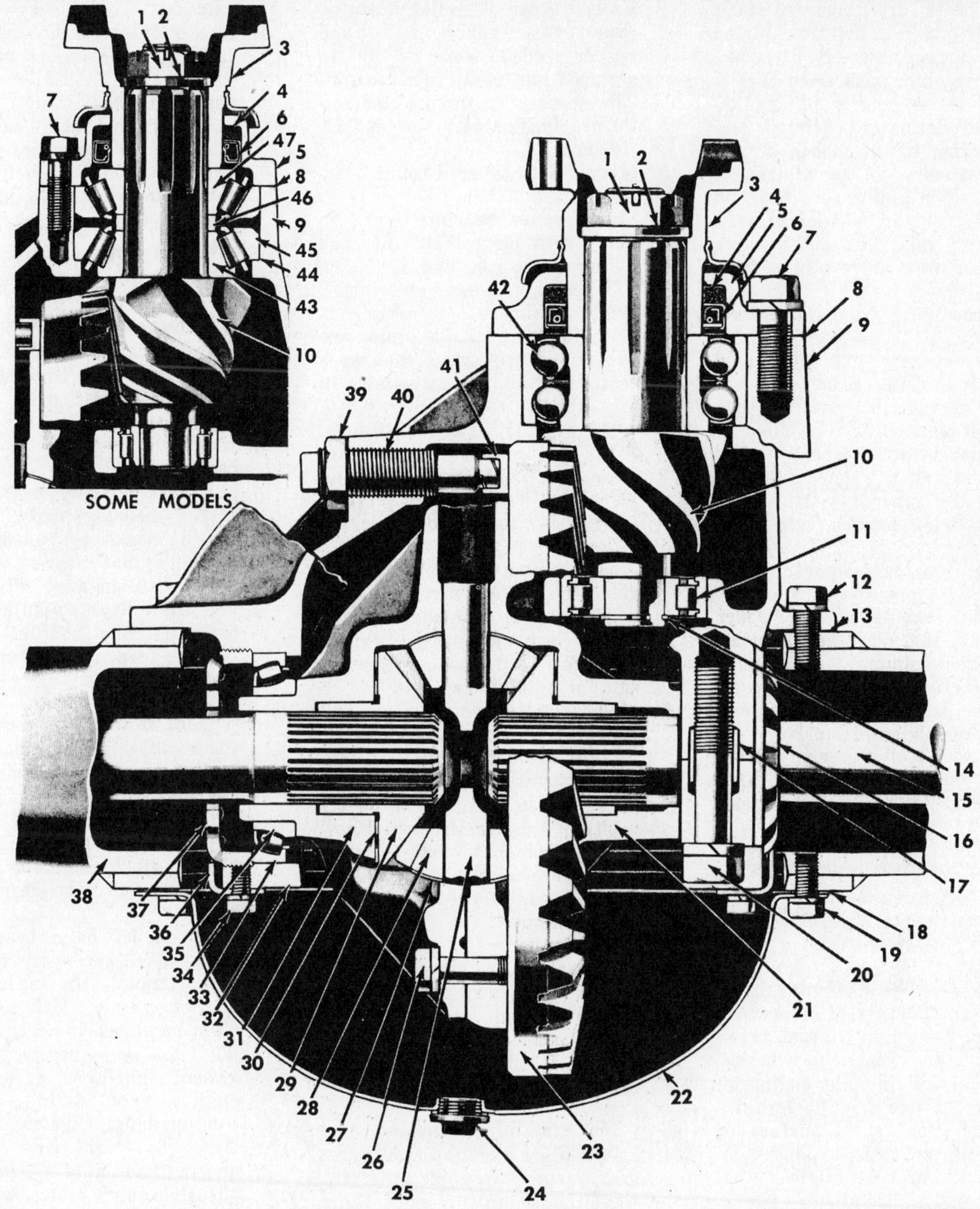

Sectional view of the G.M.C. Corporation single speed differential (© G.M.C.)

1 Yoke nut
2 Yoke washer
3 Propeller shaft yoke
4 Oil seal—felt
5 Seal retainer
6 Oil seal
7 Cap screw
8 Gasket
9 Differential carrier
10 Drive pinion
11 Bearing
12 Cap screw and lock washer
13 Gasket
14 Bearing lock ring (H110, H135)
15 Axle shaft
16 Bearing adjuster—R.H.
17 Locating dowel
18 Gasket
19 Cap screw and lock washer
20 Cap screw and lock washer
21 Differential case—R.H.
22 Housing cover
23 Drive gear
24 Filler plug and gasket
25 Differential spider
26 Cap screw and lock washer
27 Pinion thrust washer (H110, H135, H150)
28 Differential pinion
29 Side gear
30 Side gear thrust washer (H110, H 135, H 150)
31 Differential case—L.H.
32 Bearing cap
33 Bearing cup
34 Cap screw
35 Bearing cone
36 Adjuster lock
37 Bearing adjuster
38 Axle housing
39 Lock nut
40 Adjusting screw
41 Thrust block
42 Ball bearing
43 Bearing cone
44 Adjusting shims
45 Bearing cup
46 Bearing spacer
47 Bearing cone

2. Use brass drift against inner end of pinion to drive out pinion and bearings assembly.
3. Remove shim pack from carrier from those models having tapered roller outer bearings.
4. According to the model, it may be necessary to use a drift to remove the pinion rear bearing.
5. Clamp yoke in soft-jawed vise. Remove yoke nut and washer and separate drive pinion from yoke.
6. Separate yoke from oil seal retainer.
7. Place retainer in a soft-jawed vise and, using a hammer and chisel, remove oil seal and then the felt oil seal.
8. On models with tapered roller outer bearing, remove bearing cup, outer tapered bearing cone, and bearing spacer from drive pinion.
9. Using bearing remover press plate with press, separate bearing cone (some models) or roller bearing (on all other models) from drive pinion.
10. On H110 and H135 models remove bearing lock ring, and use press plates with arbor press to remove roller bearing from inner end of drive pinion. This completes drive pinion disassembly.

Assembly of Subassemblies

NOTE: Thoroughly clean and lubricate all components with axle lubricant before reassembling.

Drive Pinion Assembly

1. Clean counterbore of oil seal retainer. Saturate felt seal in oil and install evenly in retainer. Soak oil seal in light engine oil for about one hour before installing. Coat outer surface of seal lightly with sealing compound to prevent oil leaks between seal and retainer.
2. Install oil seal into retainer with lip of seal toward inner side of retainer. Using a seal installer, press oil seal into retainer with face of seal flush with retainer face.
3. Retainer surface must be clean and smooth to prevent oil leaks between retainer and carrier.
4. On H052, H072, and H150 models, press bearing into place into carrier bore.
5. On H110 and H135 models, press roller bearing into position on drive pinion with chamfered side of inner race facing toward pinion shoulder. Position bearing lock ring to secure bearing on drive pinion. NOTE: Opposed tapered roller bearing cones, two bearing cups, and spacer used on some models are serviced and replaced as a unit. The spacer is a preselected one to provide proper bearing adjustment.
6. Models with tapered roller bearings:
   a. Press inner bearing cone into place with largest side of cone facing pinion gear end.
   b. Thoroughly grease and install original shim pack in carrier. If original ring gear and pinion are reinstalled, use shims that were removed. Shims are available in five thicknesses -0.012, 0.015, 0.018, 0.021, and 0.024 inch. When using new gears, start with one 0.021 inch shim and refer to "General Axle Service" section for details on checking pinion depth.
   c. Insert pinion assembly into carrier (on H150 model), align roller bearing with carrier boss. Install bearing spacer, bearing cup and bearing cone with wide side facing pinion splines.
7. Models with double-row ball bearing: Using a 2-inch pipe or tubing, drive bearing unit into proper seating position.
8. With pinion assembly properly positioned in carrier, install new gasket. Install seal retainer onto yoke, and assemble yoke and retainer assembly onto splined end of drive pinion.
9. Secure retainer to carrier with lock washers and cap screws and torque to specifications.
10. Secure pinion assembly with yoke washer and nut and torque to 220 ft. lbs. This completes drive pinion assembly.

Differential Assembly

1. To facilitate installation of drive gear, install two guide pins (cut ½"-20x2" bolts) in gear. Start guide pins through case flange holes and tap drive gear onto case. If one differential gear is bad, the complete set should be replaced.
2. Lubricate differential case inner walls and all component parts with axle lubricant. Place differential pinions and thrust washers (thrust washers are used only on H110, H135, and H150 axles) on spider.
3. Assemble side gears, pinions and side gear and pinion thrust washers to left half of differential.
4. Assemble drive gear half (right half) of differential, being sure to line up marks on the two halves.
5. Install differential-to-drive gear cap screw and lock washers and tighten evenly until drive gear is flush with case flange. Remove guide pins and install cap screws and torque to specifications.
6. Differential side bearing cones can be installed with special installer tool.

Installation and Subassemblies

Differential Installation

1. Install bearing cap locating dowels in caps. Lubricate side bearings and place bearing cups on bearings.
2. Install differential assembly into carrier. Carefully install bearing adjusters into carrier.
3. Install bearing caps, aligning punch marks previously made. Be sure that bearing adjuster threads are engaged with carrier and caps. Tighten adjusters alternately and evenly. Tighten bearing cap screws until lock washers are flat.

Drive Gear and Pinion Adjustment

1. Loosen bearing cap screws just enough to loosen right-hand bearing adjuster (pinion side) and tighten left-hand bearing adjuster (opposite pinion side.) Using adjuster, remove all backlash between drive gear and pinion.
2. Back off left-hand bearing adjuster about two notches to point where notch in adjuster is aligned with lock. Tighten right-hand bearing adjuster solidly to seat bearing. Again loosen right-hand adjuster enough to free bearing; then retighten snugly against bearing. Draw up right-hand adjuster one or two more notches until adjuster notch aligns with lock.
3. With dial indicator on carrier adjuster, slowly oscillate drive gear and take backlash reading. Backlash should be 0.005 to 0.008-inch.
4. If backlash exceeds 0.008-inch, loosen right-hand adjuster one notch; then tighten left-hand adjuster one notch. If less than 0.005 inch, loosen left-hand adjuster one notch and tighten right-hand adjuster one notch.
5. After backlash has been adjusted, again tighten bearing cap screws until their respective lock washers flatten out.
6. Check drive gear run-out.
7. Install side bearing adjusting nut lock and secure with cap

Determining gear backlash with dial indicator
(© G.M.C.)

screws and lock washers.

Checking Pinion Depth (Models with Tapered Roller Bearings Only)

NOTE: Refer to tooth contact chart in the "General Axle Service" section.

1. Coat drive gear with red lead. Turn pinion shaft several revolutions in both directions while applying considerable drag on drive gear.
2. Pinion depth is determined by shim pack selection. Shim packs are available in thicknesses of: 0.012, 0.015, 0.018, 0.021, and 0.024- inch.
3. Changing pinion depth will again require adjusting backlash. After pinion depth and backlash have been adjusted, torque bearing caps to specifications.

Thrust Block Installation

1. Install thrust block and lock nut to adjusting screw. Thread screw and block into carrier until block contacts drive gear. Rotate gear and note change of drag. Adjust these parts until point of greatest drag is reached. Back screw off about a 30 degree turn to provide 0.005 to 0.007-inch clearance between block and gear. Make certain screw does not turn at all when tightening lock nut to 135 foot-pounds torque.

Adjusting differential bearings
(© G.M.C.)

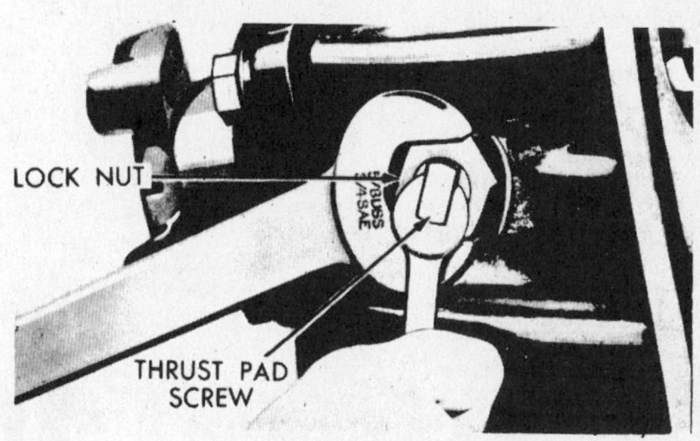

Adjusting drive gear thrust block
(© G.M.C.)

Specifications

GMC H-052, H-072, H-110, H-135, H-150

Make	GMC
Type	Hypoid
Adjustment and Clearances	
Backlash—gear to pinion	0.005"-0.008"
Adjustment method	See text
Pinion backlash adjustment	
Models with tapered bearings	Shims
Models with ball bearing	None
Shim pack thickness	0.021" Initial
Shims available	0.012"-0.015"-0.018"-0.021"-0.024"
Differential bearing adjustment method	Threaded rings
Drive Gear	
Backlast—gear to pinion	0.005"-0.008"
Adjustment method	See text
Runout (mounted to case)	0.006"
Drive Pinion	
Backlash—pinion to drive gear	0.005"-0.008"
Adjustment method	See text
Pinion gear	0.058"-0.062"
Spider	
Diameter of arms—H-052, H-072	0.808".0.809"
Diameter of arms—H-110, H-135	0.874"-0.875"
Diameter of arms—H-150	0.9365"-0.9375"
Thrust Block	
Thickness	0.1845"-0.1885"
Clearance—block to gear	0.005"-0.007"
Axle Shafts	
Diameter of splines—H-052, H-072	1.5275"-1.5325"
Number of splines—H-052, H-072	17
Diameter of splines—H-110, H-135	1.724"-1.732"
Number of splines—H-110, H-135	27
Diameter of Splines—H-150	1.848"-1.856"
Number of Splines—H-150	29
Torque Specifications (Ft. Lbs.)	
Drive gear bolts	
H-052, H-072	85-95
H-110, H-135	100-110

Differential Case	
Runout at flange (max.)	0.002″
Diameter at side gear	
H-052, H-072	1.927″-1.929″
H-110, H-135	2.193″-2.195″
H-150	2.409″-2.411″
Side Gear	
Backlash—side gear to pinion gear	0.004″-0.007″
Hub diameter—H-052, H-072	1.923″-1.925″
Hub diameter—H-110, H-135	2.189″-2.191″
Hub diameter—H-150	2.405″-2.407″
Pinion Gear	
Inside diameter—H-052 H-072	0.814″-0.815″
Inside diameter—H-110, H-135	0.880″-0.881″
Inside diameter—H-150	0.9435″-0.9445″
Thrust Washer Thickness (H-110, H-135, H-150)	
Side gear	0.058″-0.062″

H-150	150-170
Differential side bearing cap bolts	
H-052, H-072	95-105
H-110, H-135, H-150	190-220
Pinion bearing retainer bolts	
H-052, H-072	90-100
H-110, H-135, H-150	160-170
Pinion flange nut	160-280
Diff. bearing adj. nut lock	10-20
Axle shaft flange to hub	
H-052, H-072	85-95
H-110, H-135, H-150	10-20
Carrier to housing	
H-052, H-072	40-50
H-110, H-1.5, H-150	75-90
Axle shaft nuts	
All models	80-100

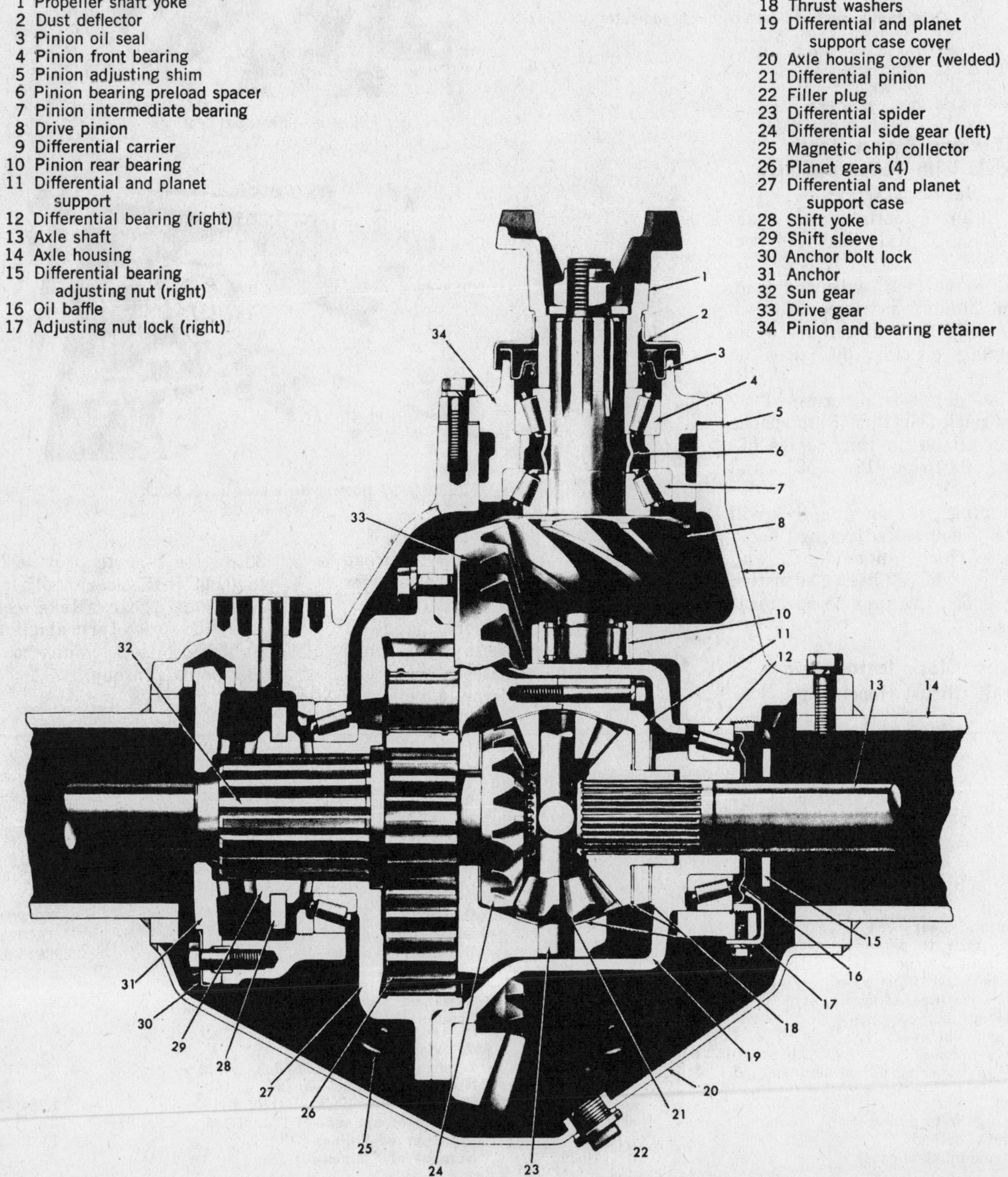

Sectional view of the G.M.C. Corporation 2-speed axle (© G.M.C.)

Model T150

Description and Operation

The Corporation T150 is a 2-speed axle (planetary type) which can be shifted by the driver when desired. Operating the shift control button activates an electric or vacuum shift unit (attached to differential carrier) which, in turn, changes axle speed from low to high or vice-versa.

CAUTION: There is no "Neutral" position. There are just "High" and "Low" ratios. To attempt to coast with axle in a supposedly "Neutral" position could cause serious axle damage.

Differential Carrier Removal

1. Remove all but two cap screws holding carrier to axle housing. Loosen the two remaining cap screws and, with a soft hammer, break carrier loose from housing. CAUTION: Do not use pinch bar. This might cause damage to carrier or housing.
2. Place a roller jack under carrier, remove the two cap screws and remove carrier and differential assembly from housing.
3. Place carrier and differential assembly in a suitable repair stand.
4. Remove shift unit.

Differential and Planetary Removal

1. Remove anchor from end of sun gear.
2. Drive shift lever out of carrier.
3. Remove shift yoke and sleeve assembly. Separate yoke from sleeve.
4. Remove adjusting nut lock.
5. Remove oil trough.
6. Tap bearing caps from carrier.
7. Remove differential and planetary assembly from carrier as-

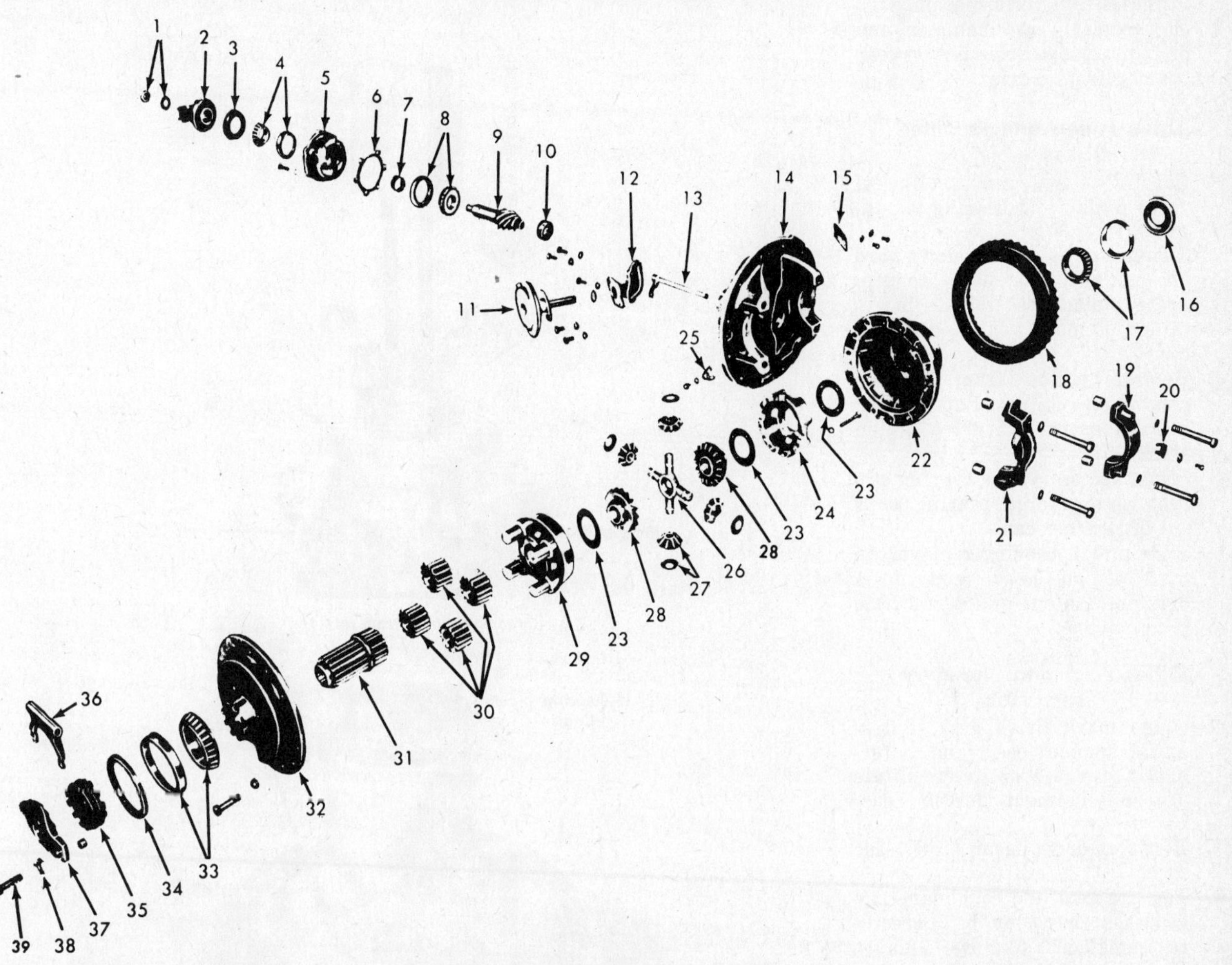

Exploded view of the G.M.C. Corporation 2-speed axle (© G.M.C.)

1 Pinion retaining nut and washer
2 Propeller shaft yoke
3 Pinion oil seal
4 Pinion front bearing cone and cup
5 Pinion and bearing retainer
6 Pinion adjusting shim
7 Pinion bearing preload spacer
8 Pinion Intermediate bearing cone and cup
9 Drive pinion
10 Pinion rear bearing
11 Shift unit (vacuum)
12 Shift unit mounting bracket
13 Shift yoke lever
14 Differential carrier
15 Oil trough
16 Differential bearing adjusting nut (right)
17 Differential bearing cone (right) and cup
18 Drive gear
19 Differential bearing cap (right)
20 Adjusting nut lock (right)
21 Differential bearing cap (left)
22 Differential and planet support case cover
23 Thrust washers
24 Differential and planet support cover
25 Adjusting nut lock (left)
26 Differential spider
27 Differential pinion and thrust washer (4)
28 Differential side gears
29 Differential and planet support
30 Planet gears (4)
31 Sun gear
32 Differential and planet support case
33 Differential bearing cone and cup (left)
34 Differential bearing adjusting nut (left)
35 Shift sleeve
36 Shift yoke
37 Shift anchor
38 Anchor bolt lock washer
39 Anchor bolt

sembly.

CAUTION: DO NOT drop bearing cones and cups.

Drive Pinion and Retainer Removal

1. With carrier still in repair stand, use holding bar to hold propeller shaft yoke while removing nut and washer.
2. Using a soft faced hammer or a blunt chisel, work retainer cap and pinion assembly from carrier.
3. Remove pinion adjusting shim pack and record or tag thickness for reassembly information.
4. If necessary, use hammer and drift to remove drive pinion rear bearing from carrier.

Drive Pinion and Retainer Disassembly

1. Carefully pry pinion oil seal from pinion and bearing retainer.
2. Using a press, press downward on end of pinion shaft to separate pinion assembly from retainer. Remove yoke and deflector.
3. Remove pinion front bearing cone from retainer. Pull bearing preload spacer off drive pinion shaft.
4. When necessary, use bearing cup remover to force bearing cups out of retainer cap.
5. Slide pinion bearing remover up over pinion head, and press drive pinion out of intermediate bearing cone.

Differential and Planetary Disassembly

1. Punch-mark drive gear, differential support case, and differential case cover to facilitate proper alignment during reassembly.
2. Remove drive gear and case cover.
3. Tag sun gear and four planetary gears so they may be correctly reassembled. Remove planet gears.
4. Lift differential and planet support assembly away from support case.
5. Punch-mark planet support cover and support and separate.
6. Again mark or tag all pinion and side gears for reassembly to same positions, and remove them along with their respective thrust washers. Slide four pinion gears off differential spider.
7. Remove differential side bearing cups. Insert brass drift through holes in case and cover and drive left and right side bearing cones off hubs.

Shifter shaft lever removal
(© G.M.C.)

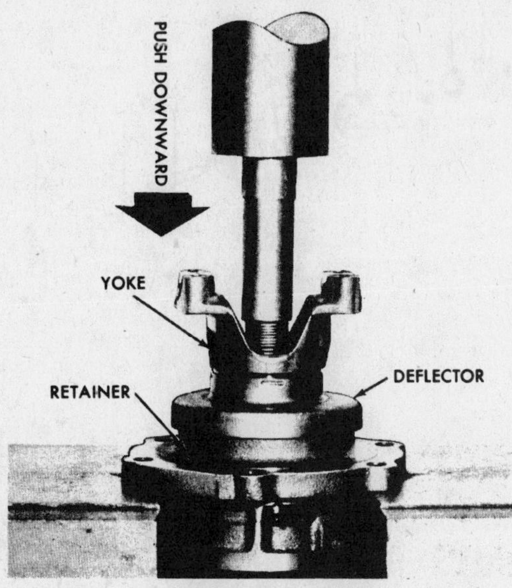

Removing pinion from retainer
(© G.M.C.)

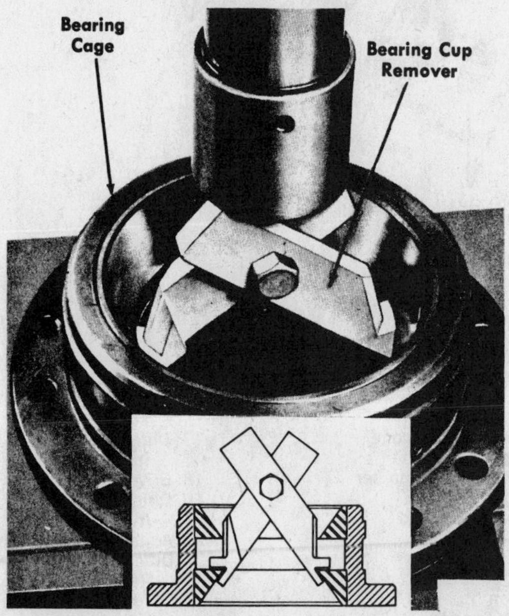

Pinion bearing cup removal
(© G.M.C.)

NOTE: Alternately tap drift from hole on one side to hole on other side to prevent race from binding on hub.

Axle Assembly

Before axle is assembled, make sure that all parts have been thoroughly cleaned, especially oil passages. Lightly lubricate all parts while assembling.

When assembling axle unit, it is recommended that new lock washers and gaskets be installed wherever possible. See "General Axle Service" section for details on cleaning and inspection.

Drive Pinion and Retainer Assembly

Drive pinion and drive gear must be replaced as a matching set.

1. If it was necessary to remove pinion rear bearing, use a driver handle with bearing installer to bottom bearing into position in carrier.
2. Position pinion intermediate bearing cone and cup in pinion bearing retainer with thicker end of cup facing inward. Use driver handle with bearing cup installer to firmly seat cup in place.
3. Follow step 1 procedure to install pinion front bearing and cup to pinion bearing retainer. Seat cup with handle and cup installer.
4. Use arbor press with a 2 inch inner diameter pipe of suitable length to position pinion intermediate bearing cone with thicker end up against shoulder of drive pinion.
5. Place new pinion bearing spacer on pinion up against bearing cone.
6. Position dive pinion assembly in retainer cap assembly, and install pinion front bearing cone in place. Thicker end of cone should face outward.
7. Again use arbor press with a 2 inch inner diameter pipe of suitable length to press inner race of cone up tightly against spacer.
8. Install pinion oil seal in retainer. See "oil seal replacement" in the "General Axle Service" section.

Differential and Planetary Assembly

1. Lubricate thrust washers, pinion gears, spider, and side gears. Assemble pinion gears to arms of differential spider and install all above components into planetary support (match up punch-marks made earlier).
2. Align and secure support cover with new lock washers and cap screws. Tighten cap screws to

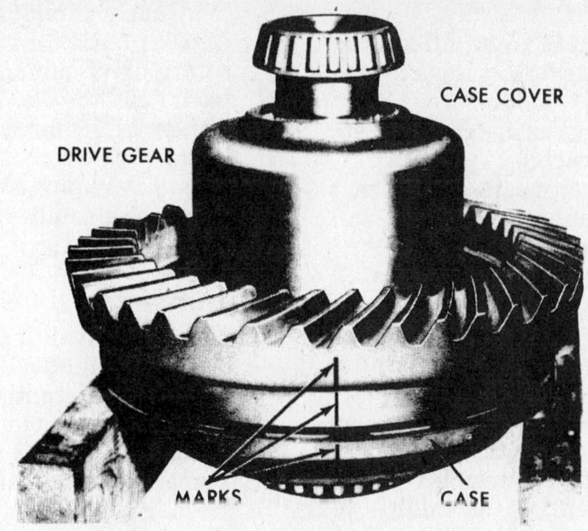

Alignment marks on drive gear, case, and cover
(© G.M.C.)

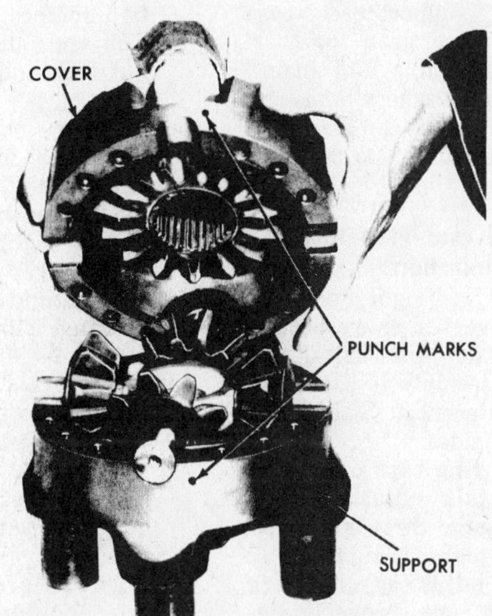

Separating support from cover
(© G.M.C.)

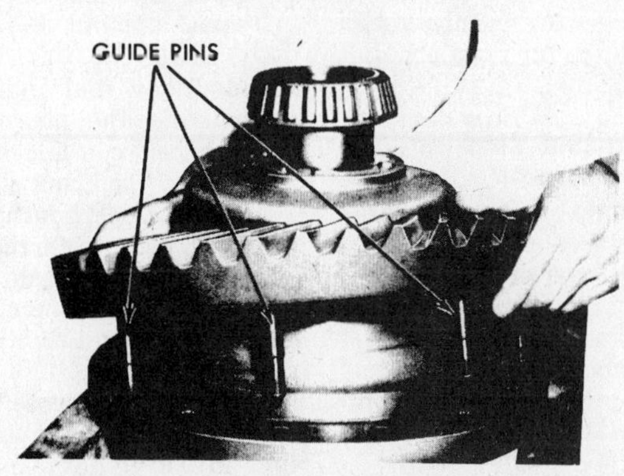

Using improvised guide pins when installing drive gear
(© G.M.C.)

specifications.

3. Install left and right differential bearing cones to support case and support case cover hubs. Use bearing installer for left and right bearings.
4. Install planet gears on journal arms of support. Position sun gear in the planet gears.
5. Align punch-marks and install drive gear to support case cover. Improvised guide pins can be made from drive gear retaining cap screws.
6. Turn differential assembly over so drive gear teeth face downward. Position assembled planet and differential assembly in cover, making sure thrust washer at case bottom is properly positioned.
7. Using lock washers and cap screws, join support case, case cover and drive gear together. Remove guide pins and install rest of lock washers and cap screws. Tighten all cap screws in a cross-wise pattern to specified torque.

Differential and Planetary Installation

1. Position left and right side bearing cups over their respective cones. Position differential and planetary assembly into carrier.
2. Install differential adjusting nuts at both sides.
3. Position bearing caps on carrier making certain adjusting nuts properly engage threads in caps. If bearing caps seat flush in place while adjusting nuts turn freely, caps are properly installed. Use soft hammer to seat caps properly. Tap lightly. CAUTION: Do not force bearing caps on nuts.
4. Tighten cap screws evenly until adjusting nuts turn freely in threads.

Drive Pinion and Retainer Installation

1. Install original shim pack to carrier, making sure shim holes are aligned with carrier cap screw holes.
2. Properly install pinion and retainer assembly to carrier bore. Make sure pilot end of pinion properly seats in pinion rear bearing.
3. Assemble retainer to carrier with new lock washers and cap screws and torque to specifications.
4. Tap yoke onto pinion shaft splined end, making sure proper spline engagement is made.
5. Install and torque pinion washer and nut to end of drive pinion.
6. Continue tightening nut in small degrees until torque required to rotate drive pinion in carrier is from 25 to 35 inch- pounds (when new pinion bearings are installed). Only 5 to 15 in. lbs. torque is required if same bearings are reinstalled.

Drive Gear and Pinion Adjustment

1. Loosen right differential adjusting nut. Tighten left adjusting nut. Use differential nut wrench on right side nut and a drift hammer to the left side nut.
2. Tighten left adjusting nut until drive gear contacts pinion and zero lash is obtained; however, do not force gears into contact so as to bind them.
3. Back off left adjusting nut about two notches to a point where nut lock and nut are aligned. Install nut lock and torque to specifications.
4. Tighten right adjusting nut firmly to force the differential and planet assembly into solid contact with left adjusting nut. Loosen right adjusting nut until it no longer contacts its bearing, then retighten until nut contacts bearing. Tighten right adjusting nut from one to two notches more if old bearings are used, and two to three notches if new bearings are used, to a position where nut and nut lock are aligned. Install nut lock and torque to specifications. NOTE: At this point the differential bearings are properly preloaded. If any additional adjustments are required, make sure that this proper preload remains. If one adjusting nut is loosened, the other nut must be tightened an equal amount to maintain this preload.
5. Mount a dial indicator on the housing and measure the backlash between the drive gear and pinion. Backlash should be from 0.003 to 0.012 inch with 0.005 to 0.008 inch preferred.

NOTE: If backlash is more than 0.012 inch, loosen the right adjusting nut one notch and tighten left adjusting nut one notch. If backlash is less than 0.003 inch, loosen the left adjusting nut one notch and tighten the right adjusting nut one notch.

Checking Pinion Depth

1. Thoroughly clean drive and pinion gear teeth.
2. Paint drive gear teeth light! and evenly with a mixture of powdered red lead and oil.
3. Rotate pinion through several revolutions in both directions until a definite contact pattern is developed on drive gear. Apply pressure to drive gear while turning pinion. This will create load on gears to simulate a driving pattern.
4. Examine the pattern on drive gear teeth. If the pinion depth is correct, the tooth pattern will be centered on the pitch line and toward the toe of drive gear.
5. If the pattern is below the pitch line on drive gear teeth, the pinion is too deep and it will be necessary to remove the pinion assembly and increase the shim thickness between the pinion bearing retainer and the carrier.
6. If the pattern is above the pitch line on drive gear teeth, the pinion is too shallow and it will be necessary to remove the pinion assembly and decrease the shim thickness between the pinion bearing retainer and the carrier
7. Changing the pinion depth will cause some change in backlash. Therefore adjust backlash to maintain correct specifications.
8. Torque bearing cap screws to specifications and recheck drive gear to pinion backlash. Install adjusting nut locks and torque to specifications.
9. Install oil trough to differential carrier, adjust trough to drive gear so that clearance is 0.03 to 0.09-inch. Torque retaining cap screws.

Shifter Components Installation

1. Position shift yoke in shift sleeve groove.
2. Slide yoke and sleeve assembly over sun gear. Splines of sleeve and sun gear should properly mesh.
3. Install shift lever through carrier housing into yoke mating splines together. Tap end of lever lightly to seat it in yoke.
4. Position the shifter unit and gasket over mounting pad, aligning lever in carrier with shift rod in shift unit. NOTE: On axles equipped with electrical shift units, shift electrical leads must be connected to shift unit before installing unit to carrier See section on "electric shift system".
5. Install and torque bolts.
6. Install differential assembly into axle housing.

Specifications

Make	G. M. Corp.
Type	2-Speed planetary
Ratios	5.83:1-7.95:1
Adjustments and Clearances	
Backlash—gear to pinion	0.005"-0.008"
Backlash adjustment method	See text
Pinion backlash adjustment	Shims
Shim pack thickness (starting)	0.021"
Shims Available	0.006"-0.009"-0.012"-0.015"-0.018"-0.021"-0.024"
Pinion bearing adjustment method	Pre-selected spacer
Differential bearing adjustment method	Threaded adjusters
Drive Gear	
Backlash—gear to pinion	0.005"-0.008"
Adjustment method	See text
Gear teeth	
5.83:1-7.95:1	35
Run out-max.	0.005"
Drive Pinion	
Backlash—gear to pinion	0.005"-0.008"
Adjustment method	See text
Bearing pre-load (max. in. lbs.)	
New bearing	15-25
Used bearing	5-15
Gear teeth	
5.83:1-7.95:1	6
Differential Spider	
Diameter of arms	0.9365"-0.9375"
Differential Side Gear	
Backlash	0.007"-0.009"
Hub diameter	2.405"-2.407"
Differential Pinion	
Backlash	0.007"-0.009"
Inside diameter	0.9435"-0.9445"
Differential Case	
Diameter of planet gear studs	1,3122"-1.3132"
Distance across studs	6.583"-6.593"
Run-out at flange (max.)	0.002"
Thrust Washer Thickness	
Side gear	0.058"-0.062"
Pinion gear	0.058"-0.062"
Differential case to case cover	0.058"-0.062"
Planet Gear	
Bushing inside diameter	1.3158"-1.3164"
Sun Gear	
Diameter over retainer	3.339"-3.400"
Backlash	0.004"-0.008"
Shifter Yoke	
Yoke width	0.395"-0.400"
Shifter sleeve	
Backlash	0.004"-0.008"
Width at yoke groove	0.445"-0.457"
Axle Shaft	
Diameter at splines	1.848"-1.856"
Number of splines	29
Torque Specifications (Ft. Lbs.)	
Differential case cap screws	100-110
Planetary support case & cover to bevel gear cap screws	100-110
Differential bearing cap screws	190-220
Differential carrier to housing cap screws	75-90
Universal joint yoke nut	160-280
Anchor plate to differential bearing cap screws	40-45
Differential bearing lock cap screws	10-15
Shift housing to carrier cap screws	25-30
Axle shaft cover cap screws	10-20

GMC Single Reduction, Integral Housing Axles

Models H024, H029, H033, H035, H036

IMPORTANT: Before disassembling unit, perform the following:

1. Inspect axle housing for lubricant leaks before cleaning; then clean thoroughly.
2. Check and record drive gear and pinion backlash.

Differential Case and Drive Pinion Removal

Differential Case Removal

1. Remove wheels and brake drums.
2. Drain lubricant and remove cover.
3. Remove pinion shaft from differential.
4. Remove "C" locks from axle shafts and pull shafts from housing.
5. Extract the differential pinions, side gears and thrust washers and tag them for reassembly.
6. Punch-mark differential bearing caps and housing for proper reassembly and remove caps. NOTE: Do not attempt to pry caps free as this may damage machined face of caps. CAUTION: When prying out differential case do not damage gasket surface on carrier housing.
7. Using a pry bar, pry differential case and ring gear assembly out of carrier. If the differential bearings are under preload, the case will fall free at a certain point; therefore, prevent case from falling.
8. Place both the left and right bearing cups and shims with their respective bearing caps so

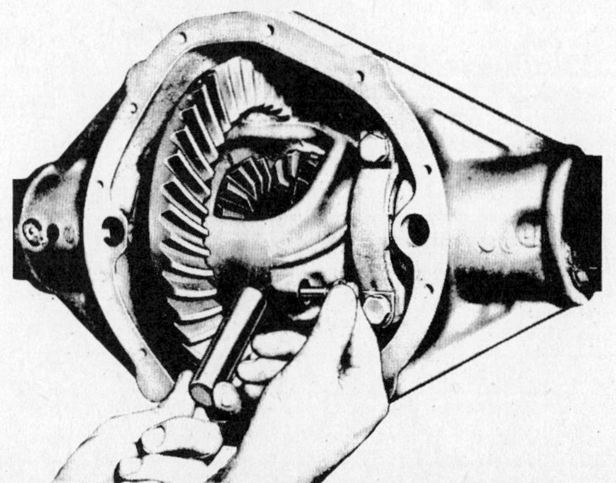

Removing or installing pinion shaft
(© G.M.C.)

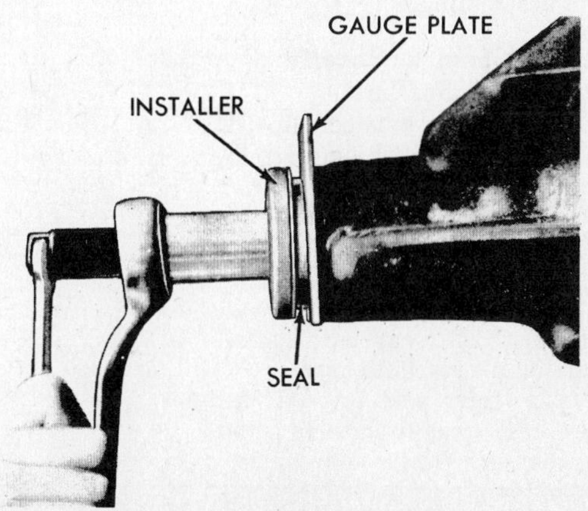

Installing pinion flange oil seal (H024)
(© G.M.C.)

1 Companion flange
2 Deflector
3 Pinion oil seal
4 Pinion front bearing
5 Pinion bearing spacer
6 Drive pinion
7 Pinion rear bearing
8 Shim
9 Differential carrier
10 Thrust washer
11 Shim
12 Gasket
13 Differential bearing
14 "C" lock
15 Differential pinion shaft lock bolt
16 Differential pinion thrust washer
17 Differential pinion shaft
18 Cover
19 Ring gear
20 Ring gear to differential case bolt
21 Differential case
22 Bearing cap
23 Axle shaft
24 Differential side gear
25 Differential pinion
26 Washer
27 Nut

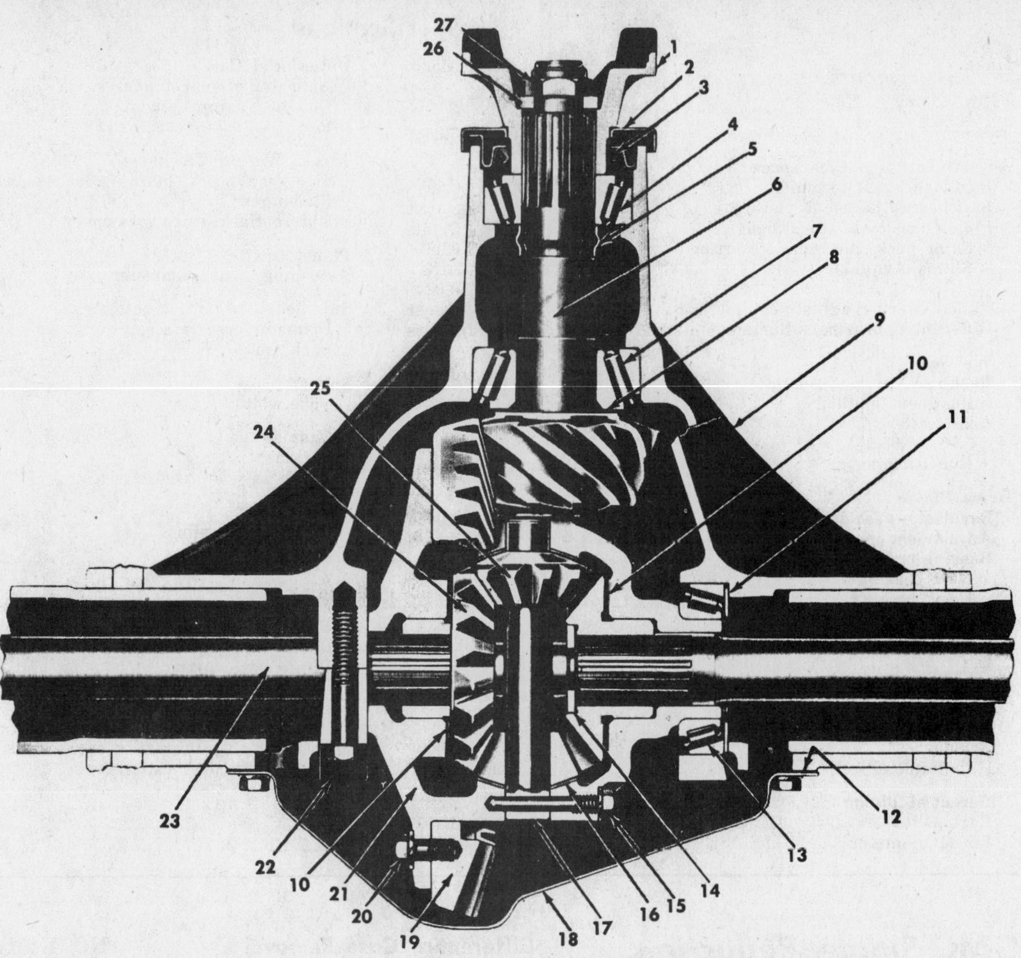

Sectional view of the G.M.C. Corporation single reduction axle (© G.M.C.)

they will be re-installed in their original positions.

Drive Pinion Removal

1. Using a suitable tool, remove and discard flange nut and washer and pull off flange.
2. Using a soft hammer, remove drive pinion. Remove pinion front bearing cone and pinion bearing spacer. Replace spacer when assembling.

Pinion Oil Seal Replacement

1. Pry oil seal out of carrier.
2. Pack the cavity between lips of new oil seal with lithium base lubricant. Place seal in carrier bore and place gauge plate over seal between seal flange and carrier.
3. On H024 axle, use installers and press seal into carrier. On all others, drive seal into carrier.
4. Press or drive seal into carrier bore until gauge plate is snug between seal flange and carrier. Rotate gauge plate 180 degrees from original position; seal must be square in carrier bore.

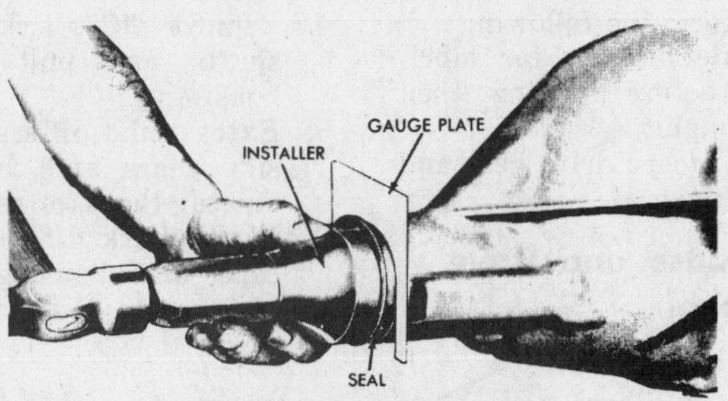

Installing pinion flange oil seal (H029, H033, H035, H036) (© G.M.C.)

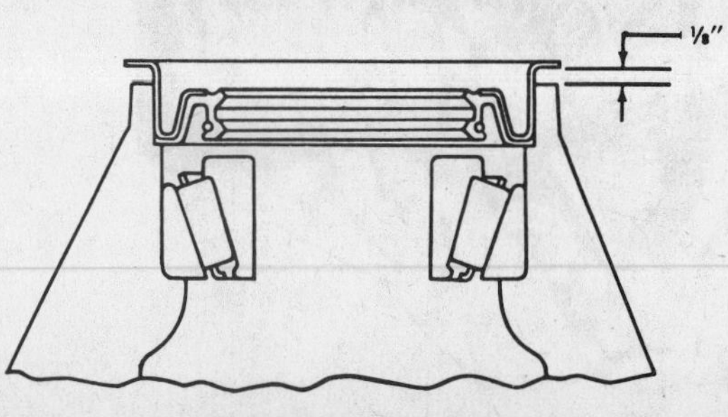

Location of pinion oil seal (© G.M.C.)

5. Using gauge plates will create 1/8" gap between the carrier and seal flange. Applying unnecessary pressure after seal installation may distort the seal.
6. If necessary to replace oil deflector on companion flange, clean up stake points on flange, then install the deflector. Stake in place at three new equally spaced positions.

Pinion and/or Bearing Replacement

1. Tap out front and rear pinion bearing cups from carrier. Remove carefully to avoid cocking the cups in carrier.
2. Use installers to install front and rear bearing cups against carrier shoulders. Do not cock the cups.
3. Remove pinion rear bearing cone and roller assembly, using suitable tools:
   H024 Axle - use press plate holder with remover plates.
   All Other Axles - use a discarded ring gear as a press plate holder for remover plates. Remove shim and record thickness.
4. If the original ring gear and drive pinion and the rear bearing assembly are re-used, then the original shim can also be used.
5. If any one of the three components; the ring gear, pinion, or rear bearing assembly require replacement, attain correct shim thickness by the following methods:

a. Lubricate pinion bearing cone and roller assemblies and place them in proper cups.
b. Position pinion depth setting gauge plate in pinion rear bearing.
   (1) H024 Axle - position gauge plate with lower surface of gauge (X stamped near low side) toward top of carrier.
   (2) All Other Axles - position gauge plate with higher surface toward top of carrier.
c. Insert clamp screw through gauge plate and both of the pinion bearings.
d. Position plug on threaded end of clamp screw and index it in front bearing. Install hex nut and rotate bearings several times to seat them.
e. Tighten hex nut until 20 inch-pounds of torque is required to rotate bearings.
f. After establishing torque, check position of gauge plate in carrier (see step b).
g. Position dial indicator on gauge post of barrel adapter so that indicator button rests on top of tool plunger.
h. Position tool in carrier. Swing tool body so that plunger does not touch gauge plate, and set indicator dial at zero. NOTE: Pinion setting gauge sleeves must be used when gauging all except H024 axles. Adapter must be seated in bearing bores of carrier before measuring depth.
i. Slowly swing inner end of tool plunger across gauge plate until highest indicator reading is obtained. Record and recheck this measurement.
j. All service pinion gears are stamped with a code number on the threaded end of the pinion. The numerical difference between the code number and the gauge reading obtained in step i determines the required thickness of the pinion locating shim.

Example:

Pinion code number	45
Dial indicator reading	16
Difference	29
Proper shim thickness	0.029-in.

NOTE: Shims are available in thicknesses from 0.021 to 0.037-inch. Each shim is etched with its thickness.

6. Remove pinion setting gauge and pinion bearing cone and roller assemblies from carrier.
7. Position the selected shim against pinion head on shaft.
8. Install new cone and roller assembly, using a suitable installer. Press cone tight against shim.

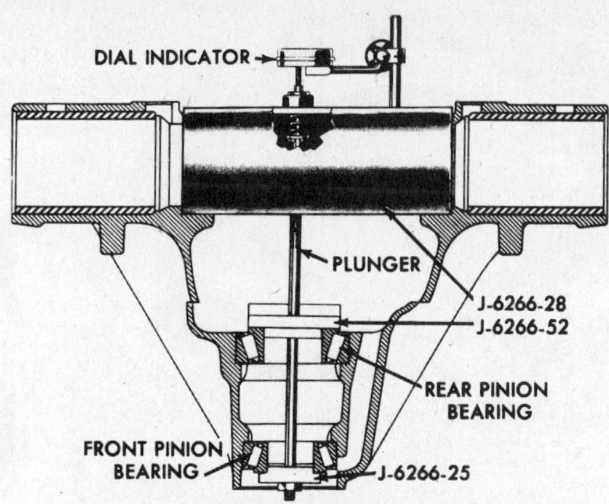

Installation of pinion depth gauge (© G.M.C.)

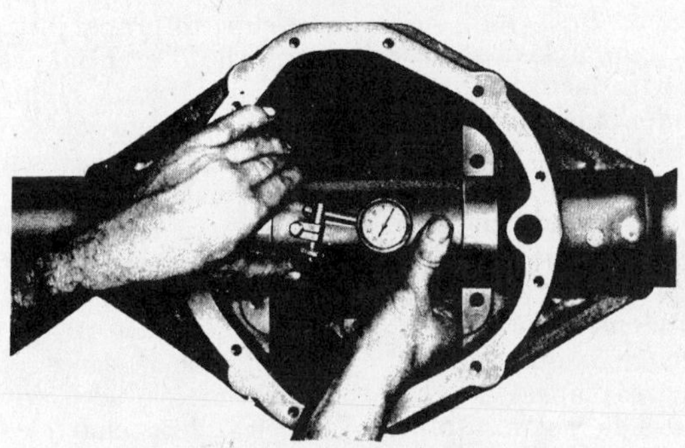
Measuring pinion shim requirement (© G.M.C.)

Differential Bearing Replacement

1. Install the differential bearing remover making sure puller legs are fitted securely in notches of case and against bearing cone.
2. Tighten puller screw to remove bearing.
3. Place new bearing on one hub with thick side of inner race against case and drive into place using suitable tool.
4. Before installing bearing on opposite hub, support differential case on adapter plug to allow case to rest on adapter instead of bearing cage. Install remaining bearing as instructed in step 3.

Ring Gear or Differential Case Replacement

1. Remove ring gear. NOTE: Do not attempt to pry ring gear from case; to do so may cause damage.
2. Install guide pins, made from 3/8"-24 x 1 1/2" long cap screws

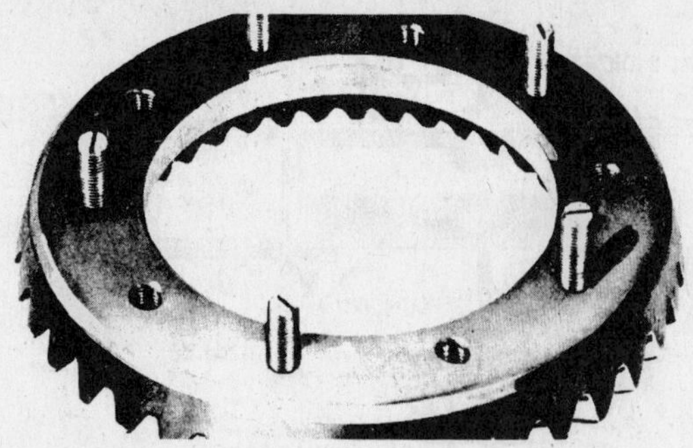

Installation of ring gear guide pins
(© G.M.C.)

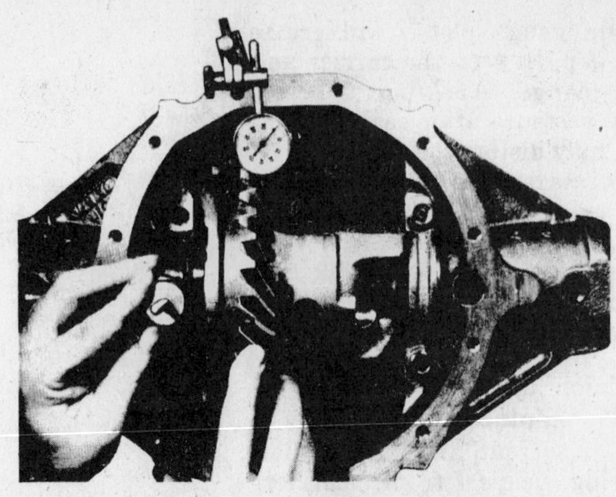

Measuring differential bearing shim requirement
(© G.M.C.)

to ring gear.

3. Position ring gear over pilot diameter of the case. Install every other ring gear bolt and lock washer and tighten so that gear face is flush with face of case.
4. Remove guide pins and install remaining bolts and torque to 40-60 ft.lbs.
5. Install thrust washers and side gears in case; if same parts are used, replace in original sides. Position pinions and thrust washers through loading holes in case 180 degrees apart so that they engage side gears. Rotate gears until pinion shaft holes are aligned and install shaft and lock screw.

Axle Assembly

Drive Pinion and Bearing

1. Position pinion and rear bearing cone and roller assembly in carrier, install a new pinion bearing spacer on shaft, and install pinion front bearing cone and roller assembly.
2. Install flange on pinion shaft using companion flange installer and tool.
3. Pack the cavity between end of pinion splines and pinion flange with a non-hardening sealer before installing washer and nut on pinion.
4. Install washer and a new self-locking nut on pinion shaft. Tighten nut to remove end play. Continue tightening, in small increments, and checking preload with torque wrench and adapter until torque required to rotate pinion is 20 to 30 inch-pounds for new bearings and seal or 5 to 15 inch-pounds when used parts are reinstalled.

Differential Bearing Preload and Ring Gear Adjustment

1. Check bearing cups and cup seat for nicks and burrs and replace if necessary.
2. Lubricate bearings, position cups to proper bearings then install differential assembly in carrier. Install right bearing cap and torque to 55 foot-pounds. Check to be sure cup is seated in carrier bore.
3. Service spacers are available in one thickness only for each axle: 0.170 ± .001-inch for model H024 and 0.160 ± .001-inch for all other axles. Steel service shims are used with the spacer. See shim chart below for shim availability and identification.

Differential Bearing Shim Identification

	Identification Notches			
	I.D.		*O.D.*	
*Thickness**	*H024*	*All Others*	*H024*	*All Others*
.064	0	0	0	2
.066	0	0	1	3
.068	0	0	2	4
.070	0	1	3	0
.072	1	1	0	1
.074	1	1	1	2
.076	1	1	2	3
.078	1	1	3	4
.080	2	2	0	0
.082	2	2	1	1
.084	2	2	2	2
.086	2	2	3	3
.088	3	2	0	4
.090	3	3	1	0
.092	3	3	2	1
.094	3	3	3	2
.096		3		3
.098		3		4
.100		4		0

*Additional shims are available for the H-024 axle.

These shims, with a thickness of 0.052-inch through 0.062-inch, have the shim thickness stamped on the shim. NOTE: Do not reuse original bearing preload shims. They are made of cast iron and may be broken easily.

4. With ring gear tight against the pinion gear (0.000 to 0.001-inch backlash) and with gauging tool inserted between left bearing cup and carrier housing, turn tool adjusting nut clockwise until a noticeable drag is produced. NOTE: Do not apply pressure on bearing so as to cause preload.
5. Tighten locking bolt on the side of the gauge and remove gauge. Using a micrometer, measure the thickness of the two gauging plates. By subtracting the thickness of the service spacer to be used from the thickness of the plates, the thickness of the service shim may be determined.

Example:

Gauge thickness	0.254″
Service spacer to be used	0.070″
Service shim size	0.084″

6. Install the selected shim between the service spacer and bearing. Install the left bearing cap and check backlash for a 0.000 to 0.001-inch reading.
7. Remove right bearing cap and insert tool between right bearing cap and carrier housing. Turn tool adjusting nut clockwise until a noticeable drag is produced. Tighten locking bolt on the side of the tool and remove gauge.
8. Using a micrometer, measure the thickness of the gauge plate. Subtract the service spacer thickness from the total thickness and add 0.008-inch to this figure. This total will be the size of the service shim to be used on the right side.

Example:

Gauge thickness	0.224″
Service spacer	0.170″
	0.054″
Preload	0.008″
Total shim thickness (right side)	0.062″

NOTE: Service shims are available in 0.002-inch graduations. If the shim measurement falls between the available shims, select the shim that is 0.001 inch thinner.

9. Using a soft hammer, tap the selected shim between the service spacer and bearing.
10. Install right bearing cap and torque both caps to 55 foot-pounds.
11. Mount a dial indicator on the carrier and check backlash between ring gear and pinion. Backlash should range within 0.003 to 0.010-inch with a reading of 0.005 to 0.008-inch preferred. Check reading at four equally spaced positions around the ring gear. Variation in reading should not exceed 0.002-inch. NOTE: The dial indicator button should be perpendicular to tooth angle and in line with gear rotation.
12. If variation in backlash exceeds 0.002-inch, measure ring gear and case runout. Gear runout should be a maximum of 0.002-inch; should it be more, check ring gear and case for deformation and/or foreign matter between case and gear.
13. If gear lash is not within limits, correct by decreasing shim thickness on one side and increasing thickness of the other shim the same amount. Total shim thickness must be maintained to maintain the proper preload. (By decreasing shim on right side 0.002-inch and increasing shim thickness on left side by 0.002-inch backlash will decrease by 0.001-inch.

Locking Differentials

Refer to General Repair Section for complete overhaul procedures.

Leaf Spring Removal

(1500-3500 Models)

1. Raise truck.
2. Loosen, but do not remove, spring to shackle retaining nut.
3. Remove shackle to spring hanger attaching bolt.
4. Remove attaching spring to front hanger bolt.
5. Remove U-bolts and then remove spring.

Installation

(1500-3500 Models)

To install leaf spring assembly, reverse the removal procedure and torque nuts and bolts to specifications. NOTE: Torque nuts and bolts *after* lowering the truck.

Coil Spring Removal

1500-3500 Models

1. Raise truck on hoist and support rear axle.
2. Disconnect shock absorber at control arm bracket.
3. Remove upper and lower spring clamps.
4. Lower control arm enough to remove spring.

Installation

1500-3500 Models

1. Position clamp in spring.
2. Install spring and clamp loosely; torque upper clamp nut to specifications.
3. Connect shock absorber and torque to specifications.
4. Torque lower clamp nut to specifications.
5. Remove axle support and lower truck.

Leaf Spring Removal

4500-7500 Models

1. Remove rebound pin locks or retainers, then remove rebound pins.
2. Install a C-clamp on radius leaf, remove eye bolts or radius lead pin clamp bolts, then remove

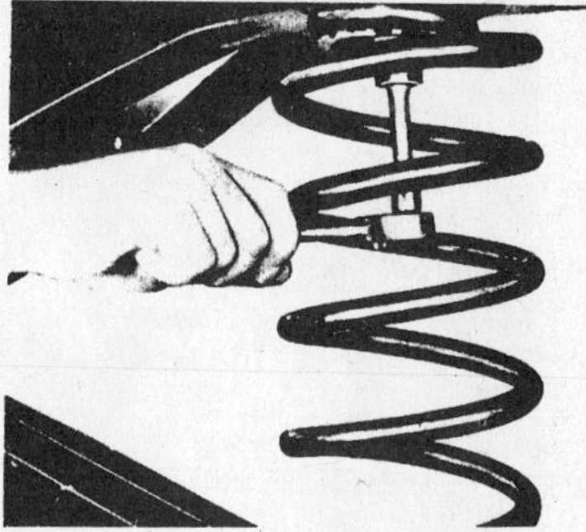

Coil spring removal
(© G.M.C.)

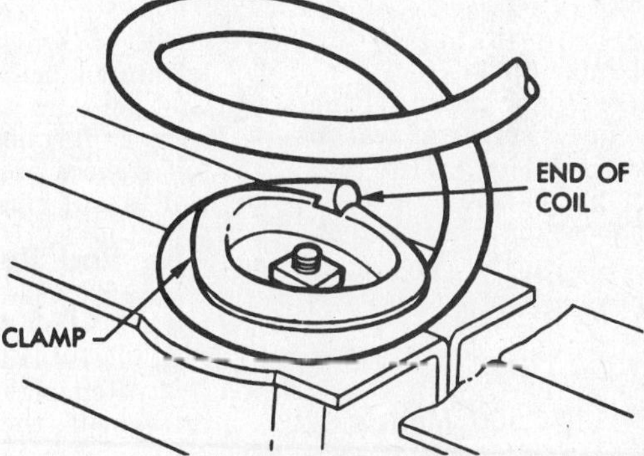

Coil spring clamp installation
(© G.M.C.)

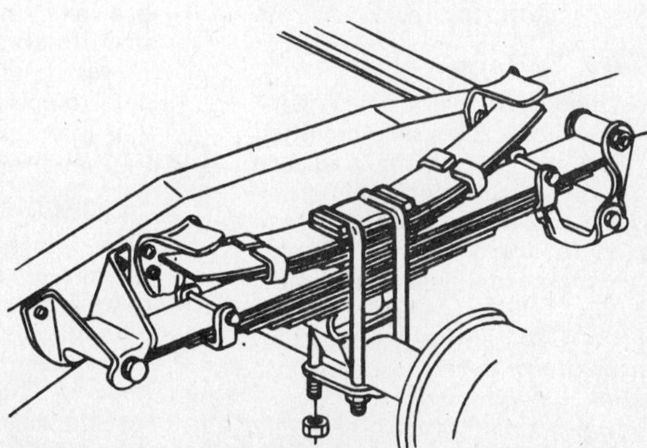

Leaf spring (11,000 lb. axle)
(© G.M.C.)

Specifications

Make	GMC
Type	Hypoid
Models	H-024, H-029, H-033, H-035, and H-036
Adjustment & Clearances	
Backlash—gear to pinion	0.005"-0.008"
Adjustment method	See text
Pinion bearing pre-load (in.-lbs.)	20-35
Pinion backlash adjustment shims Available (0.001" increments)	0.021" to 0.037"
Differential bearing and backlash adjustment method	Selective spacer
Thrust Washer Thickness	
Pinion gear	0.028"-0.032"
Side gear	0.029"-0.031"
Differential pinion shaft Diameter	0.808"-0.809"
Differential pinion gear Inside diameter	0.813"-0.816"
Torque Specifications (Ft. Lbs.)	

Torque Specifications Foot-Pounds

Carrier cover bolts	
H-024, H-029	15-25
H-033, H-035, H-036	20-25
Differential bearing cap bolts	55
Differential pinion lock bolt	15-25
Filler plug	20
Ring gear to case bolts	50

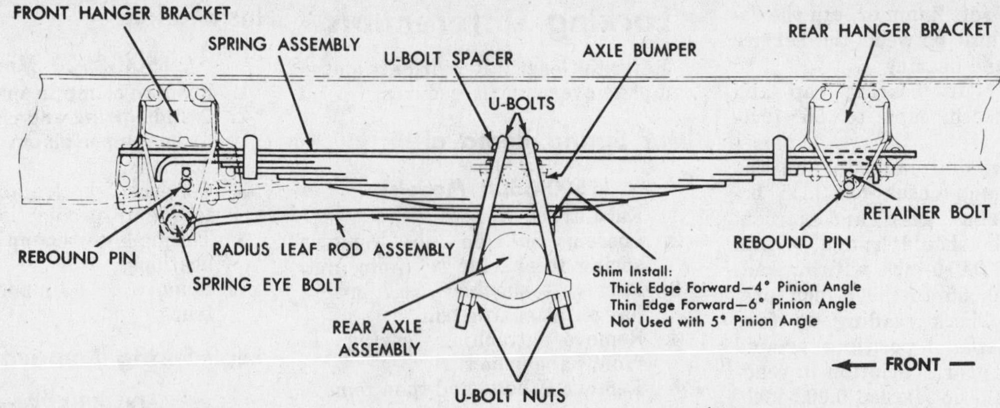

Rear leaf spring suspension (© G.M.C.)

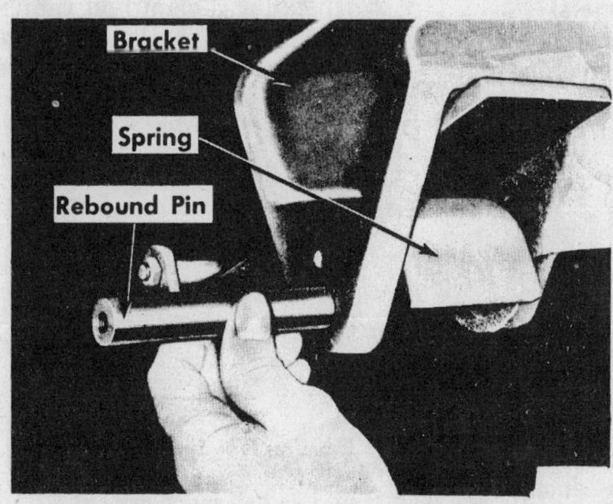

Installing rebound pin (typical)
(© G.M.C.)

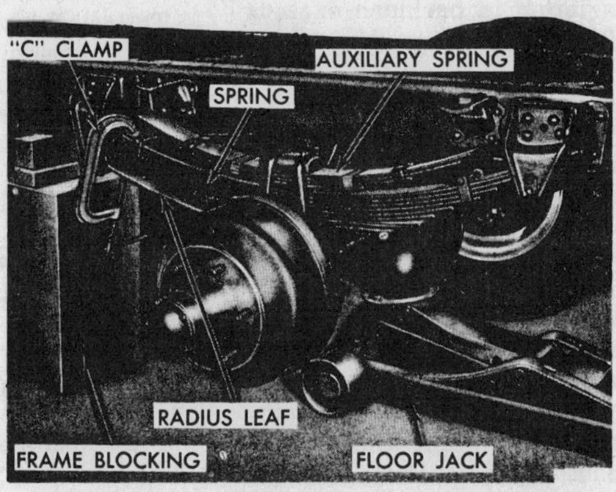

Using C-clamp at radius leaf
(© G.M.C.)

C-clamp.

3. Remove lubrication fitting and disconnect spring at rear mounting.
4. Remove U-bolts, spacer plate and shock absorber bracket.
5. Remove spring and spacer or shim.

Installation

4500-7500 Models

To install leaf spring, reverse the removal procedure and torque all bolts to specifications. NOTE: Torque U-bolts *after* lowering truck.

Auxiliary Springs

Some models are equipped with auxiliary springs. They are mounted to brackets on the frame and are usually held to the main spring by long U-bolts. The purpose of these springs is to provide additional stability under unusual operating conditions.

NOTE: Coil spring suspension uses an auxiliary spring as shown in illustration.

Shock Absorbers

Shock absorbers used are non-adjustable and non-repairable. Maintenance operations are limited to periodic tightening and replacement of rubber mounting grommets. If a shock absorber is worn, the complete unit must be replaced.

Tie Rod Removal

CP1500-C2500 Models

1. Raise truck.
2. Remove attaching nuts and bolts, then remove rod.

Installation

1. Position rod ends in mounting brackets, insert pivot bolts and install nuts finger tight.
2. Lower truck and torque pivot nuts to specifications.

Control Arm Removal

CP1500-C2500 Models

1. Raise truck and relieve load on springs by supporting axle.
2. Place jack under control arm.
3. Remove spring clamp bolt from underside of arm.
4. Remove U-bolt nuts; disconnect shock absorber bracket, and lower end of control arm.
5. Disconnect parking brake lever, then remove pivot bolt and control arm.

Installation

To install control arm, reverse the removal procedure. Torque spring clamp and shock absorber BEFORE lowering truck, torque pivot bolts AFTER.

Stabilizer Shaft

P3500 Model

1. Raise truck and support axle to

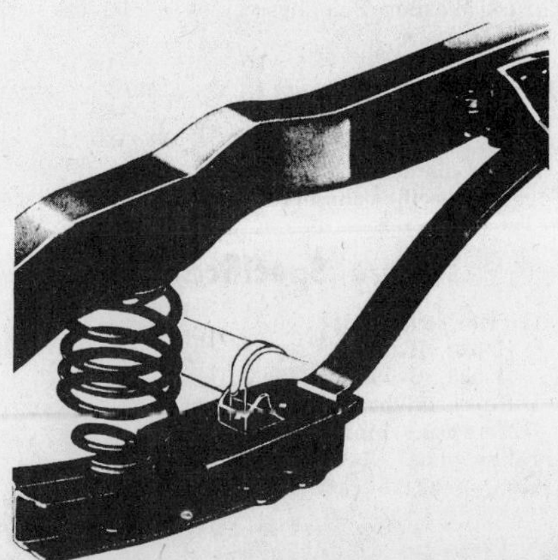

Auxiliary rear spring—models C1500-2500
(© G.M.C.)

relieve load on U-bolts.

2. Remove the forward U-bolt retaining nuts, and remove shaft anchors.
3. Remove shaft retaining brackets and then remove shaft.

Installation

To install stabilizer shaft, reverse the removal procedure. Alternately torque all nuts and bolts to specifications.

NOTE: Make certain that both ends of shaft protrude equally from the anchors.

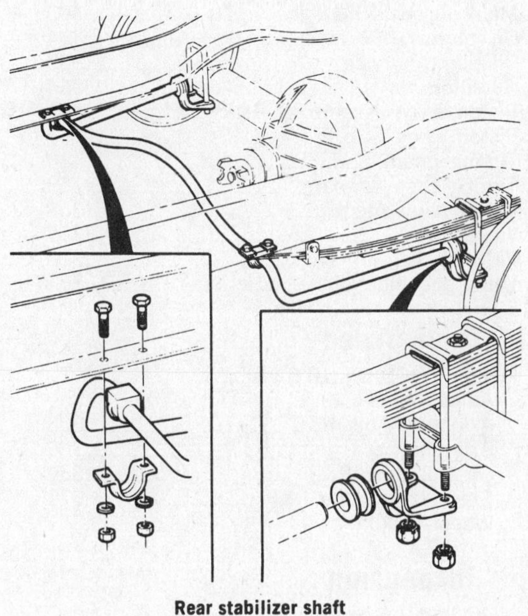

Rear stabilizer shaft
(© G.M.C.)

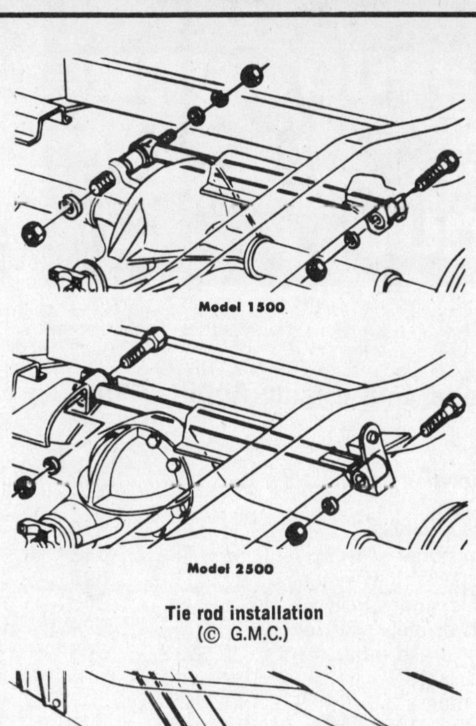

Tie rod installation
(© G.M.C.)

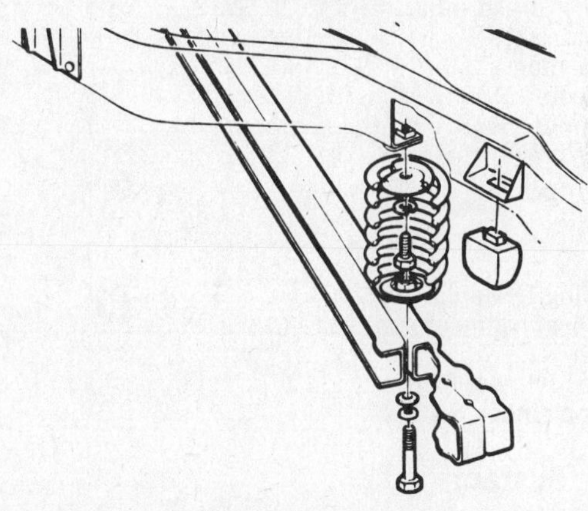

Control arm and spring
(© G.M.C.)

International and Scout

Index

TUNE-UP SPECIFICATIONS

CU. IN. DISPLACEMENT	YEAR	SPARK PLUG GAP	DISTRIBUTOR POINT DWELL	DISTRIBUTOR POINT GAP	IGNITION TIMING DEGREES	CRANKING COMP. PRESSURE	VALVE CLEARANCE IN.	VALVE CLEARANCE EXH.	GOV. R.P.M. NO LOAD	FUEL PUMP PRESS.	IDLE SPEED STD.	IDLE SPEED AUTO.
FOUR CYLINDER												
152	1961-68	.028	75	.016	5B	140	Zero	Zero	—	4-5½	475	—
	1969-71	.030	75	.016	5B	140	Zero	Zero	—	4-5½	475	—
196	1961-71	.030	45	.017	5B	140	Zero	Zero	—	4-5½	475	—
SIX CYLINDER												
BD-220	1961-62	.030	32	.019	4B	130	.025H	.025H	—	3-4½	375	—
BG-220	1963-68	.030	32	.019	4B	130	.025H	.025H	—	3-4½	375	—
BD-240	1961-62	.030	32	.019	4B	130	.025H	.025H	—	3-4½	375	—
BG-241	1963-67	.030	32	.019	4B	130	.025H	.025H	—	3-4½	375	—
	1968-71	.030	32	.018	TDC	—	.025H	.025H	—	3-4½	700	600N
BD-264	1961-62	.030	32	.019	2B	130	.025H	.025H	—	3-4½	375	—
BG-265	1963-67	.030	32	.019	2B	130	.025H	.025H	—	3-4½	375	—
	1968	.030	32	.018	TDC	130	.025H	.025H	—	3-4½	700	600N
BD-282	1961-67	.030	32	.019	6B	115	.018H	.019H	—	3-4½	475	—
BD-308	1961-68	.030	32	.019	3B	110	.019H	.019H	3200	4-5	475	—
RD-372	1961-71	.030	32	.019	5B	120	.025H	.025H	—	3½-5½	475	—
RD-406	1961-68	.030	32	.019	5B	120	.025H	.025H	2750	3½-5½	475	—
RD-450	1961-71	.030	32	.019	5B	120	.025H	.025H	2600	3½-5½	475	—
RD-501	1961-71	.030	32	.019	5B	120	.025H	.025H	2600	3½-5½	475	—
EIGHT CYLINDER												
266	1961-67	.030	30	.016	4B	150	Zero	Zero	—	4½-5¾	475	—
	1968-71	.027	30	.018	2A	150	Zero	Zero	—	4½-5¾	700	600N
	1969	.027	30	.017	4B	150	Zero	Zero	—	4½-5¾	700	600N
304	1961-67	.030	30	.016	TDC	145	Zero	Zero	—	4½-5¾	475	—
	1968-71	.027	30	.018	TDC	145	Zero	Zero	—	4½-5¾	700	600N
345	1961-67	.030	30	.016	TDC	140	Zero	Zero	3800	4½-5¾	475	—
	1968-71	.027	30	.018	TDC	140	Zero	Zero	3800	4½-5¾	700	600N
392	1966-71	.030	30	.019	TDC	140	Zero	Zero	3600	4½-5¾	700	600D
401	1961-71	.027	30	.016	7B	140	Zero	Zero	3400	4-5¼	475	—
461	1961-64	.030	32	.016	7B	125	Zero	Zero	3200	—	475	—
478	1965-71	.027	32	.016	10B	135	Zero	Zero	—	4-5	—	—
549	1961-71	.027	32	.016	7B	135	Zero	Zero	3200	4-5	475	—

GENERAL ENGINE SPECIFICATIONS

CU. IN. DISPLACEMENT	YEAR	BORE AND STROKE	FIRING ORDER	DEVELOPED HORSE POWER @ R.P.M.	DEVELOPED TORQUE @ R.P.M.	COMPRESSION RATIO	CARBURETOR	VALVE LIFTER TYPE	NORMAL OIL PRESSURE
FOUR CYLINDER									
152	1961-63	3.875x3.218	1342	87@4000	135@2400	8.1	1V	Hyd.	50
	1964-71	3.875x3.218	1342	93@4400	143@2400	8.19	1V	Hyd.	50
	1965-67	3.875x3.218	1342	111@4000	166@3200	8.19	1V	Hyd.	50
196	1966-71	4.125x3.656	1342	111@4000	180@2000	8.10	1V	Hyd.	50
SIX CYLINDER									
BD-220	1961-63	3.562x3.687	153624	112@3800	194@1600	7.5	1V	Mech.	35-45
BG-220	1963-68	3.562x3.687	153624	113@3800	194@2000	7.5	1V	Mech.	35-45
BD-240	1961-62	3.562x4.015	153624	141@3800	224@2000	7.5	1V	Mech.	35-45
BG-241	1963-69	3.562x4.015	153624	141@3800	224@2000	7.5	1V	Mech.	35-45
BD-264	1961-62	3.687x4.125	153624	154@3800	248@2400	7.5	1V	Mech.	35-45
BG-265	1963-68	3.687x4.125	153624	154@3800	248@2400	7.5	2V	Mech.	35-45
BD-282	1961-68	3.812x4.125	153624	137@3600	251@1800	6.5	1V	Mech.	35-45
BD-308	1961-71	3.812x4.500	153624	150@3600	280@2000	6.5	2V	Mech.	35-45
RD-372	1961-69	4.375x4.125	153624	165@3200	308@1600	6.7	2V	Mech.	35-45
RD-406	1961-63	4.375x4.500	153624	175@3200	338@1700	6.7	2V	Mech.	35-45

GENERAL ENGINE SPECIFICATIONS

CU. IN. DISPLACE-MENT	YEAR	BORE AND STROKE	FIRING ORDER	DEVELOPED HORSE POWER @ R.P.M.	DEVELOPED TORQUE @ R.P.M.	COM-PRESSION RATIO	CARBUR-ETOR	VALVE LIFTER TYPE	NORMAL OIL PRESSURE
SIX CYLINDER									
RD-406	1964-71	4.375x4.500	153624	193@3200	373@1600	7.1	2V	Mech.	35-45
RD-450	1961-63	4.375x5.000	153624	182@3000	388@1600	6.75	2V	Mech.	35-45
	1964-68	4.375x5.000	153624	199@3000	418@1600	7.06	2V	Mech.	35-45
	1969-71	4.375x5.000	153624	202@3000	422@1600	7.06	2V	Mech.	35-45
RD-501	1961-63	4.500x5.250	153624	212@3000	444@1600	6.5	4V	Mech.	35-45
	1964-71	4.500x5.250	153624	215@3000	451@4160	6.78	4V	Mech.	35-45
EIGHT CYLINDER									
266	1961-69	3.625x3.218	18436572	155@4400	227@2800	8.4	2V	Hyd.	40-50
304	1961-71	3.875x3.218	18436572	193@4400	273@2800	8.19	2V	Hyd.	40-50
345	1961-71	3.875x3.656	18436572	197@4000	309@2200	8.05	2V	Hyd.	40-50
392	1966-67	4.125x3.656	18436572	236@4000	354@2600	8.02	4V	Hyd.	50
	1968-71	4.125x3.656	18436572	236@4000	357@2800	8.02	4V	Hyd.	50
401	1961-68	4.125x3.750	18736542	206@3600	355@2000	7.69	2V	Hyd.	50-60
	1964-70	4.125x3.750	18736542	206@3600	355@1800	7.69	2V	Hyd.	50-60
461	1961-64	4.125x4.312	18736542	226@3600	420@1600	7.21	2V	Hyd.	50-60
478	1965-71	4.500x3.750	18736542	234@3600	431@1800	7.64	2V	Hyd.	50-60
549	1961-71	4.500x4.312	18736542	257@3400	505@2000	7.57	4V	Hyd.	50-60

CRANKSHAFT BEARING JOURNAL SPECIFICATIONS

CU. IN. DISPLACE-MENT	YEAR	MAIN BEARING JOURNALS: JOURNAL DIAMETER	OIL CLEARANCE	SHAFT END PLAY	THRUST ON NO.	BEARING JOURNALS CONNECTING ROD: JOURNAL DIAMETER	OIL CLEARANCE	END PLAY
FOUR CYLINDER								
152	1961-71	2.7484-2.7494	.001-.004	.001-.005	3	2.373-2.374	.0011-.0032	.008-.014
196	1961-71	2.7484-2.7494	.0015-.0035	.003-.008	3	2.373-2.374	.0011-.0036	.008-.014
SIX CYLINDER								
BD-220	1961-63	2.748-2.749	.0012-.0042	.005-.010	3	2.373-2.374	.0011-.0032	.006-.011
BG-220	1963-68	2.748-2.749	.0012-.0042	.005-.010	3	2.373-2.374	.0011-.0032	—
BD-240	1961-62	2.748-2.749	.0012-.0042	.005-.010	3	2.373-2.374	.0011-.0032	.006-.011
BG-241	1963-69	2.748-2.749	.0012-.0042	.005-.010	3	2.373-2.374	.0011-.0032	.005-.011
BD-264	1961-62	2.748-2.749	.0012-.0042	.005-.010	3	2.373-2.374	.0011-.0032	—
BG-265	1963-68	2.748-2.749	.0012-.0042	.005-.010	3	2.373-2.374	.0011-.0032	—
BD-282	1961-68	2.7005-2.7015	.0013-.0043	.006-.014	4	2.122-2.123	.0007-.0032	.006-.012
BD-308	1961-71	2.7005-2.7015	.0013-.0043	.006-.014	4	2.122-2.123	.0007-.0032	.006-.012
RD-372	1961-69	3.2495-3.2505	.0013-.0043	.006-.015	7	2.751-2.752	.0012-.0037	.006-.011
RD-406	1961-71	3.2495-3.2505	.0013-.0043	.006-.015	7	2.751-2.752	.0012-.0037	—
RD-450	1961-71	3.2495-3.2505	.0013-.0043	.006-.015	7	2.751-2.752	.0012-.0037	.006-.013
RD-501	1961-71	3.2495-3.2505	.0013-.0043	.006-.015	7	2.751-2.752	.0012-.0037	.006-.013
EIGHT CYLINDER								
266	1961-69	2.7484-2.7494	.001-.004	.001-.005	3	2.373-2.374	.0011-.0033	.006-.014
304	1961-71	2.7484-2.7494	.001-.004	.001-.005	3	2.373-2.374	.0011-.0033	.006-.014
345	1961-71	2.7484-2.7494	.001-.004	.001-.005	3	2.373-2.374	.0011-.0033	.006-.014
392	1966-71	2.7484-2.7494	.001-.004	.001-.005	3	2.373-2.374	.0011-.0033	—
401	1961-71	3.123-3.124	.0014-.0044	.004-.009	3	2.623-2.624	.0017-.0042	—
461	1961-64	3.123-3.124	.0014-.0044	.004-.009	3	2.623-2.624	.0017-.0042	—
478	1965-71	3.123-3.124	.0014-.0044	.004-.009	3	2.623-2.624	.0017-.0042	.010-.018
549	1961-71	3.123-3.124	.0014-.0044	.004-.009	3	2.623-2.624	.0017-.0042	.010-.018

VALVE SPECIFICATIONS

CU. IN. DISPLACE-MENT	YEAR	LASH (HOT) INCHES INT.	EXH.	ANGLE DEGREES FACE	SEAT	STEM DIA. INCHES INT.	EXH.	STEM CLEARANCE INT.	EXH.	VALVE LIFT INCHES	VALVE SPRING LBS. @ INCHES OPEN	CLOSED	FREE LENGTH INCH
FOUR CYLINDER													
152	1961-71	Zero	Zero	45	46	.372	.371	.001-.0035	.0015-.004	1		188@1.429	2.065
196	1961-71	Zero	Zero	45	45	.372	.371	.001-.0035	.0015-.004	—		188@1.429	2.065

VALVE SPECIFICATIONS

CU. IN. DISPLACE-MENT	YEAR	LASH (HOT) INCHES INT.	EXH.	ANGLE DEGREES FACE	SEAT	STEM DIA. INCHES INT.	EXH.	STEM CLEARANCE INT.	EXH.	VALVE LIFT INCHES	VALVE SPRING LBS. @ INCHES OPEN	CLOSED	FREE LENGTH INCH
SIX CYLINDER													
BD220	1961-62	.025	.025	30	30	.372	.371	.0015-.004	.002-.0045	.398	156@1.683	95@2.081	2.69
BG220	1963-68	.025	.025	30	30	.372	.371	.0015-.004	.002-.0045	.398	156@1.613	95@2.081	2.69
BD240	1961-62	.025	.025	30	30	.372	.371	.0015-.004	.002-.0045	.398	156@1.683	95@2.081	2.69
BG241	1963-71	.025	.025	30	30	.372	.371	.0015-.004	.002-.0045	.398	156@1.683	95@2.081	2.69
BD264	1961-62	.025	.025	30	30	.372	.371	.0015-.004	.002-.0045	.398	156@1.683	95@2.081	2.69
BG265	1963-71	.025	.025	30	30	.372	.371	.0015-.004	.002-.0045	.398	156@1.683	95@2.081	2.69
BD282	1961-68	.019	.019	[2]	[2]	.372	.371	.0015-.004	.002-.0045	.407		182-190@ 1.468	2.187
BD308	1961-68	.019	.019	[2]	[2]	.372	.371	.0015-.004	.002-.0045	.407		182-190@ 1.468	2.187
RD372	1961-71	.025	.025	[2]	[2]	.435	.434	.0015-.004	.002-.0045	.449		133-141@ 1.703[3]	2.562[4]
RD406	1961-69	.025	.025	[2]	[2]	.435	.434	.0015-.004	.002-.0045	.449		133-141@ 1.703[3]	2.562[4]
RD450	1961-71	.025	.025	[2]	[2]	.435	.434	.0015-.004	.002-.0045	.449		133-141@ 1.703[3]	2.562[4]
RD501	1961-71	.025	.025	[2]	[2]	.435	.434	.0015-.004	.002-.0045	.449		133-141@ 1.703[3]	2.562[4]
EIGHT CYLINDER													
266	1961-69	Zero	Zero	45	45	.372	.371	.001-.0038	.0015-.004	[1]		180-195@ 1.429	2.065
304	1961-71	Zero	Zero	45	45	.372	.371	.001-.0035	.0015-.004	[1]		180-195@ 1.429	2.065
345	1961-71	Zero	Zero	45	45	.372	.371	.001-.0035	.0015-.004	[1]		180-195@ 1.429	2.065
392	1966-71	Zero	Zero	[6]	[6]	.372	.414	.001-.0035	.0015-.004	[1]		180-195@ 1.429	2.065
401	1961-71	Zero	Zero	[5]	[5]	.435	.434	.001-.0035	.0015-.004	.426		113-121@ 1.656	2.562[7]
461	1961-64	Zero	Zero	[5]	[5]	.435	.434	.001-.0035	.0015-.004	.426		113-121@ 1.656	2.562[7]
478	1965-71	Zero	Zero	[5]	[5]	.435	.434	.001-.0035	.0015-.004	.426		113-121@ 1.656	2.562[7]
549	1961-71	Zero	Zero	[5]	[5]	.435	.434	.001-.0035	.0015-.004	.426		113-121@ 1.656	2.562[7]

1—Intake .440, Exhaust .395.
2—Intake 15, Exhaust 45.
3—Outer, Inner 83-88 @ 1.50.
4—Outer, Inner 2.343.
5—Intake 15, Exhaust 45.
6—Intake 30, Exhaust 45.
7—Outer, Inner 2.281.

TORQUE SPECIFICATIONS

CU. IN. DISPLACE-MENT	YEAR	CYLINDER HEAD BOLTS FT. LBS.	ROD BEARING BOLTS FT. LBS.	MAIN BEARING BOLTS FT. LBS.	CRANKSHAFT BALANCER BOLTS FT. LBS.	FLYWHEEL TO CRANKSHAFT BOLTS FT. LBS.	MANIFOLDS FT. LBS. INTAKE	EXHAUST
FOUR CYLINDER								
152	1961-71	90-100	45-55	75-80	100-110	45-55	40-45	40-45
196		90-100	45-55	75-80	100-110	45-55	40-45	40-45
SIX CYLINDER								
BD-220	1961-63	85-95	45-55	75-85	Pressed on	70-80	25-30	25-30
BG-220	1963-68	85-95	45-55	75-85	Pressed on	70-80	25-30	25-30
BD-240	1961-62	85-95	45-55	75-85	Pressed on	70-80	25-30	25-30
BG-241	1963-69	85-95	45-55	75-85	Pressed on	70-80	25-30	25-30
BD-264	1961-62	85-95	45-55	75-85	Pressed on	70-80	25-30	25-30
BG-265	1963-68	85-95	45-55	75-85	Pressed on	70-80	25-30	25-30
BD-282, 308	1961-71	100-110	65-75	100-110	Pressed on	90-100	25-30	25-30
RD-372	1961-69	100-110	65-75	100-110	Pressed on	150-160	25-30	25-30
RD-406, 450	1961-71	100-110	65-75	100-110	Pressed on	150-160	25-30	25-30
RD-501	1961-71	100-110	65-75	100-110	Pressed on	150-160	25-30	25-30
EIGHT CYLINDER								
266	1961-69	90-100	45-55	75-85	100-110	45-55	40-45	40-45
304, 345, 392	1961-71	90-100	45-55	75-85	100-110	45-55	40-45	40-45
401, 461, 478	1961-71	80-90	60-70	100-110	Pressed on	90-100	—	—
549	1961-71	80-90	60-70	100-110	Pressed on	90-100	—	—

TRUCK MODELS AND ENGINE APPLICATION

ENGINE IDENTIFICATION—The prefix to the engine serial number designates the engine model. Engine numbers are located on machined boss on cylinder block.

SCOUT MODELS

STANDARD ENGINES	YEAR	MODELS	ENGINE MAKE
4-152-196	1961-70	Scout	Own
V-266	1967-68	Scout	Own
V-304	1969-70	Scout	Own
PT-6-232	1969-70	Scout	Own

LIGHT DUTY MODELS

STANDARD ENGINES	YEAR	MODELS	ENGINE MAKE
4-152	1965	D-900	Own
	1966	900A	Own
	1964	C-900	Own
V6-266	1967	908B	Own
	1968	908C	Own
	1969	1200D	Own
	1969	1300D	Own
	1969	1500D	Own
BG-241	1965	D-1000	Own
	1966	1000A	Own
	1967	1000B	Own
	1968	1000C	Own
	1965	D-1100	Own
	1966	1100A	Own
	1967	1100B	Own
	1968	1100C	Own
	1965	D-1200	Own
	1966	1200A	Own
	1967	1200B	Own
	1968	1200C	Own
	1965	D-1300	Own
	1966	1300A	Own
	1967	1300B	Own
	1968	1300C	Own
	1965	D-1500	Own
	1966	1500A	Own
	1967	1500B	Own
	1968	1500C	Own
	1964	C-1000	Own
	1964	C-1100	Own
	1964	C-1200	Own
	1964	C-1300	Own
	1964	C-1500	Own
PT-6-232	1969-70	1000D	Own
	1969-70	1100D	Own
	1970	1200D	Own
	1970	1300D	Own
	1970	1500D	Own

ACO, CO, VCO, DC, DCO SERIES

STANDARD ENGINES	YEAR	MODELS	ENGINE MAKE
RD-372	1961-68	CO-190	Own
V-401	1961-64	ACOF-190	Own
	1961-64	ACO-195	Own
	1961-64	ACO-200	Own
	1965-70	VCO-190	Own
	1961-70	VCOF-190	Own
	1961-64	VCO-195	Own
	1966-68	VCOT-195	Own
	1961-70	VCO-200	Own
RD-406	1969-70	CO-190	Own
	1961-70	COF-190	Own
	1964-68	COT-195	Own
	1961-70	CO-200	Own
	1961-62	COF-200	Own
V-461	1961-62	ACOF-200	Own
	1961-64	ACO-220	Own
	1961-64	VCO-220	Own
DV-462	1966-68	CO-1950	Own
	1966-68	COF-1950	Own
V-478	1966-67	CO-8190	Own
	1965-70	VCO-220	Own
RD-501	1961-70	CO-220	Own
DV-550	1969-70	CO-1950	Own
	1969-70	COF-1950	Own
C-160	1964-68	DCO-200	Cummins
NH-180	1964-68	DCOF-195H	Cummins
	1969-70	DCO-200	Cummins
	1964-68	DCO-205H	Cummins
NH-230	1969-70	DCO-205H	Cummins

LOADSTAR MODELS

STANDARD ENGINES	YEAR	MODELS	ENGINE MAKE
V-304	1964-70	1600-1700	Own
	1964-70	CO-1600	Own
	1964-70	CO-1700	Own
V-345	1964-70	1800	Own
	1964-70	1890	Own
	1964-70	F-1800	Own
	1964-70	CO-1800	Own
DV-462	1966-70	1750	Own
	1966-68	1850	Own
	1966-68	F-1850	Own
	1969-70	CO-1750	Own
6V-53N	1964-70	1890-D	Detroit
	1964-70	F-1800-D	Detroit
DV-550	1969-70	CO-1850	Own

FLEETSTAR MODELS

STANDARD ENGINES	YEAR	MODELS	ENGINE MAKE
RD-406	1964-67	1900	Own
	1969-70	1910A	Own
	1969-70	F-1910A	Own
	1964-68	F-1900	Own
	1968-70	F-2010A	Own
	1964-68	T-1900	Own
	1968	2010A	Own
RD-450	1964-70	2000	Own
	1969-70	2010A	Own
	1968-70	2110A	Own
DV-462	1966-67	1950	Own
	1966-68	F-1950	Own
	1968	F-2050A	Own
	1968	2050A	Own
DV-550	1969-70	F-2050A	Own
	1969-70	2050A	Own
	1968	2150A	Own
NHE-195	1964-70	2000D	Cummins
	1964-70	F-2000-D	Cummins
	1964-68	T-2000-D	Cummins

R-MODELS

STANDARD ENGINES	YEARS	MODELS	ENGINE MAKE
C-160	1964-68	RD-190	Cummins
	1965-68	RDF-190	Cummins
	1965-68	RD-200	Cummins
RD-372	1961-68	R-185	Own
RD-406	1961-68	R-190	Own
	1961-68	RF-190	Own
	1964-68	RT-195	Own
	1961-68	R-200	Own
	1961-62	RF-200	Own
RD-501	1961-68	R-220	Own

V-MODELS

STANDARD ENGINES	YEARS	MODELS	ENGINE MAKE
V-401	1964-68	V-190	Own
	1961-68	VF-190	Own
	1961-63	V-195	Own
	1964-68	VT-195	Own
	1961-64	V-196	Own
	1961-68	V-200	Own
V-461	1961-62	VF-200	Own
	1961-63	V-210	Own
	1961-63	VF-210	Own
	1961-64	V-220	Own
V-478	1965-68	V-220	Own

4 WHEEL DRIVE MODELS

STANDARD ENGINES	YEAR	MODELS	ENGINE MAKE
PT-6-232	1969-70	1100D	Own
BG-241	1964	G-1100	Own
	1965	D-1100	Own
	1966	1100A	Own
	1967	1100B	Own
	1968	1100C	Own

TRUCK MODELS AND ENGINE APPLICATION continued

STANDARD ENGINE	YEARS	MODELS	ENGINE MAKE
	1965	D-1200	Own
	1966	1200A	Own
	1967	1200B	Own
	1968	1200C	Own
	1965	D-1300	Own
	1966	1300A	Own
	1967	1300B	Own
	1968	1300C	Own
V-266	1969	1200D	Own
	1969	1300D	Own
V-304	1970	1200D	Own
	1970	1300D	Own
	1964-70	1600	Own
	1964-70	1700	Own
RD-372	1961-68	R-190	Own
RD-406	1961-68	RF-190	Own

100, 110, 120 & 130 SERIES

STANDARD ENGINE	YEARS	MODELS	ENGINE MAKE
BD-220	1961-62	G100	Own
	1961-62	C-120	Own
BD-240	1961-62	C-110	Own
	1961-62	C-130	Own
V-266	1963	C-100	Own
	1963	C-110	Own
	1963	C-120	Own
	1963	C-130	Own

140, 150 & 160 SERIES

STANDARD ENGINE	YEARS	MODELS	ENGINE MAKE
BD-240	1961-62	B-140	Own
	1961-62	B-150	Own
	1961-62	BC-150	Own
V 266	1963	B-140	Own
	1963	B-150	Own
	1963	BC-150	Own
BD-264	1961-62	B-160	Own
	1961-62	BC-160	Own
V-304	1963	B-160	Own
	1963	BC-160	Own

170 & 180 SERIES

STANDARD ENGINES	YEAR	MODELS	ENGINE MAKE
BD-282	1961-62	B-170	Own
	1961-62	BC-170	Own
	1961-62	BCF-170	Own
V-304	1963	B-170	Own
	1963	BC-170	Own
	1963	BCF-170	Own
BD-308	1961-62	B-180	Own
	1961-62	BC-180	Own
	1961-62	BCF-180	Own
V-345	1963	B-180	Own
	1963	BC-180	Own
	1963	BCF-180	Own

210 & 230 SERIES

STANDARD ENGINE	YEAR	MODELS	ENGINE MAKE
NH-180	1964-70	210-D	Cummins
	1964-70	F-210-D	Cummins
	1964-70	R-230-D	Cummins
RD-450	1964-70	210	Own
	1964-70	F-210	Own
	1961-63	R-210	Own
	1961-63	RF-210	Own
RD-501	1961-70	F-230	Own
	1961-62	230	Own
V-549	1961-62	230V	Own
	1961-62	F-23-V	Own

400 & 405 SERIES

STANDARD ENGINE	YEAR	MODELS	ENGINE MAKE
6V-71N	1963-67	DC-400	Detroit
	1963-67	DCF-400	Detroit
NH-180	1963-65	DCO-400	Cummins
	1963-65	DCOF-400	Cummins
	1963-65	DCOT-400	Cummins
NHE-195	1963-68	D-400	Cummins
	1963-69	DF-400	Cummins
NH-230	1969-70	D-400	Cummins
	1969-70	DF-400	Cummins
DVT-573	1968-70	DC-400	Own
	1968-70	DCF-400	Own

4000 CAB-OVER ENGINE SERIES

STANDARD ENGINES	YEAR	MODELS	ENGINE MAKE
NHE-195	1965-66	CO-4000-D	Cummins
	1965-66	COF-4000-D	Cummins
	1965-66	COT-4000-D	Cummins
VS-478	1965-67	CO-4000	Own
	1965-67	COF-4000	Own
	1965-67	COT-4000	Own
DVT-573	1967-68	CO-4000-D	Own
	1967-68	COF-4000-D	Own
	1967-68	COT-4000-D	Own
	1968-70	CO-4070-A	Own
	1968-70	COF-4070-A	Own

METRO SERIES

STANDARD ENGINE	YEAR	MODELS	ENGINE MAKE
4-152	1965-66	M-700	Own
	1965-68	M-800	Own
	1965-68	M-1100	Own
	1963-64	CM-75	Own
	1961-64	CM-80	Own
	1963-64	CM-110	Own
4-196	1969-70	M-1100	Own
	1969-70	M-1200	Own
	1969-70	MA-1200	Own
BG-220	1965-68	M-1200	Own
	1967-68	MA-1200	Own
	1965-68	M-1400	Own
	1965-68	M-1500	Own
	1967-68	MA-1500	Own
	1965	AB-1200	Own
	1965	AB-1400	Own
	1964	AM-120	Own
	1964	AM-130	Own
	1964	AB-140	Own
	1964	AM-150	Own
BD-220	1961-62	CM-110	Own
	1961-64	AB-120	Own
	1961-63	AM-120	Own
	1961-63	AM-130	Own
	1961-63	AB-140	Own
	1961-63	AM-150	Own
	1961-62	AMC-150	Own
BD-240	1961-63	AM-160	Own
	1961-62	AMC-160	Own
BG-241	1964	AM-160	Own
	1965-66	M-1600	Own
	1965	MC-1600	Own
BG-265	1965	M-1700	Own
	1965	MC-1700	Own
	1964-65	AM-170	Own
V-266	1969	M-1500	Own
	1969	MA-1500	Own
V-304	1970	M-1500	Own
	1970	MA-1500	Own

WHEEL ALIGNMENT SPECIFICATIONS

YEAR	MODEL	CASTER (Deg.)	CAMBER (Deg.)	TOE-IN (In.)	KING PIN INCLINATION (Deg.)
	4 WHEEL DRIVE				
	FA-15, 16	½	1½	⅛-3/16	7½
	FA-18, 19	½	1½	⅛-3/16	88
	FA-50	2-3	1	1/16-⅛	4
	FA-51	1-2	1½	1/32-3/32	8
	FA-52	1½	1½	1/32-1/16	8
	FA-55, 56	5-7	¾	1/16-3/16	8
	FA-57	3	0	1/16-⅛	0
	FA-58	3	1½	1/32-1/16	8
	FA-59	3	0	1/16-⅛	0
	FA-75, 76	5-7	¾	1/16-3/16	8
	FA-77	5-7	¾	1/16-3/16	8
	FA-140	2-3	0	1/10-⅛	—
	I BEAM AXLE				
	FA-1, 10	2-3	2	⅛-3/16	4
	FA-20	2-3	1	1/16-⅛	4
	FA-28	1-2	1	⅛-3/16	4
	FA-30, 40, 41, 48	2-3	1	1/16-⅛	4
	FA-60, 65, 68	2-3	1	1/16-⅛	4
	FA-69, 70	2-3	1	1/16-⅛	4
	FA-72, 80	2-3	1	1/16-⅛	4
	FA-90	2-3	1	1/16-⅛	4
	FA-91	2-3	1	⅛-3/16	4
	FA-98, 99	2-3	1	⅛-3/16	4
	FA-100, 102	2-3	1	1/16-⅛	5½
	FA-105	2-3	1	3/16-¼	5½
	FA-110	2-3	1	1/16-⅛	5½
	FA-111[1]	2-3	1	3/16-¼	5½
	FA-112, 113	½-2N	1	1/16-⅛	0
	FA-115[1]	2-3	1	3/16-¼	5½
	FA-130	2-3	1	1/16-⅛	4
	FA-132, 133	½-1½	1	1/16-⅛	8
	FA-136, 182	2-3	1	1/16-⅛	5½
	FA-201, 208	2-3	1	3/16-¼	5½
	FA-204, 211	2-3	1	3/16-¼	5½
	FA-212, 215	2-3	1	3/16-¼	5½
	FA-218, 219	2-3	1	3/16-¼	5½
	TORSION BAR SUSPENSION				
	FA-8	1½-2½N	½-1½P	⅛-3/16	8
	FA-9	1½-2½N	½-1½P	⅛-3/16	8

Distributor

Distributor Removal

1. Remove distributor cap.
2. Mark position of rotor by scribing a mark on the distributor body.
3. Mark position of distributor body on the engine block or mounting bracket.
4. If so equipped, remove vacuum advance line, governor lines, and tachometer cable.
5. Loosen clamp screw or hold-down bolt and remove distributor from engine.
6. To install, reverse the above procedure, making sure to align marks which position rotor and distributor body.
7. If the engine has been disturbed (crankshaft position unknown), rotate engine until engine is in No. 1 firing position (No. 8 on V-266, 304, 345, and 392 engines). Compression stroke may be felt by placing finger tightly over spark plug hole as engine is rotating. Holding distributor shaft so that rotor is in No. 1 (or No. 8 on V-266, 304, 345, 392) firing position, insert distributor, rotating slightly until it drops into keyed position.
8. Adjust ignition timing before tightening clamp screw or hold-down bolt.

Reference

For ignition tune-up settings see tune-up specifications at the beginning of this section.

Breaker Points Replacement

1. Unsnap and remove distributor cap.
2. Remove rotor and dust cover if so equipped.
3. Loosen nut retaining primary and condenser leads and remove leads.
4. Remove breaker assembly mounting screws.
5. Remove breaker assembly, carefully freeing conductor spring. Do not lose eccentric screw which may fall out.
6. To install, follow the above procedure in reverse order, being sure to include eccentric screw.
7. Lightly lubricate cam with distributor cam grease.
8. Set breaker gap and ignition timing.

Breaker Point Setting

Internal Adjustment Type

1. Remove distributor cap.
2. Loosen distributor housing clamp screw or hold-down bolt.

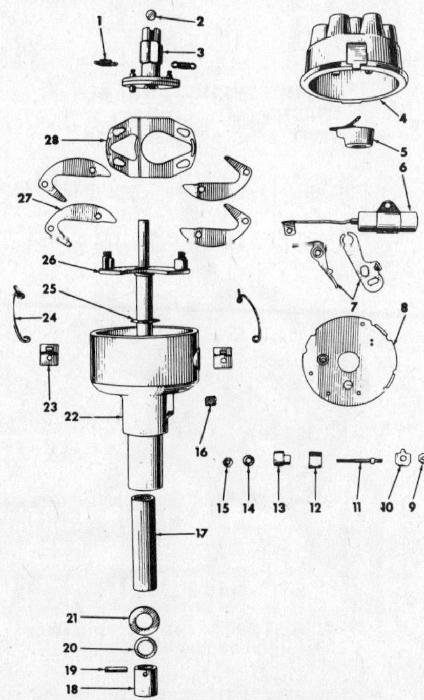

Typical distributor
(© International Harvester Co.)

1 Spring, weight
2 Wick, oil
3 Cam, asm.
4 Cap
5 Rotor
6 Condenser
7 Contact points
8 Plate, breaker
9 Nut
10 Clip
11 Stud, terminal
12 Bushing, outside
13 Bushing, inside
14 Washer
15 Nut
16 Plug, pipe
17 Bushing, shaft
18 Coupling
19 Pin
20 Washer, spacer
21 Washer
22 Housing (body)
23 Support, spring
24 Spring, cap
25 Washer
26 Shaft, asm.
27 Weight
28 Plate, hold down

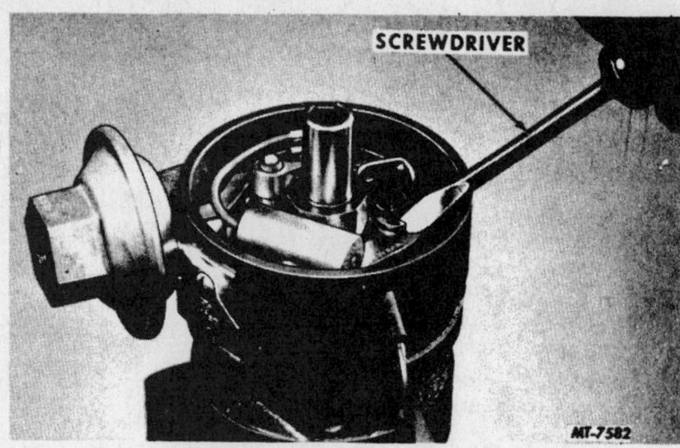

Adjusting point gap—slots
(© International Harvester Co.)

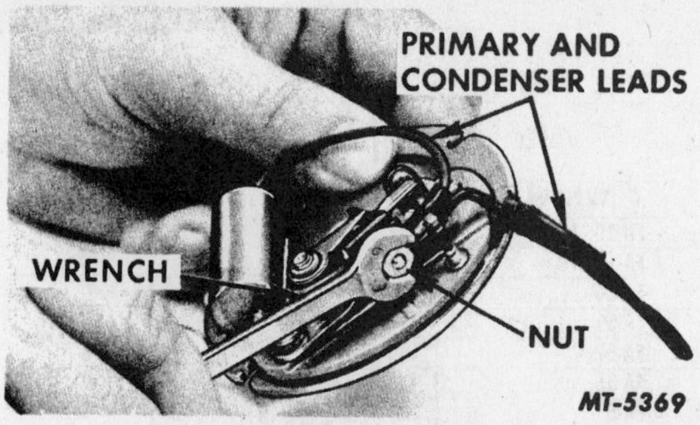

Removing primary condenser
(© International Harvester Co.)

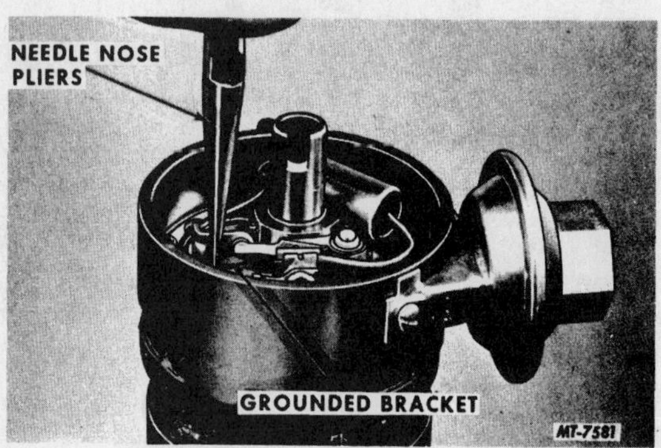

Aligning breaker points
(© International Harvester Co.)

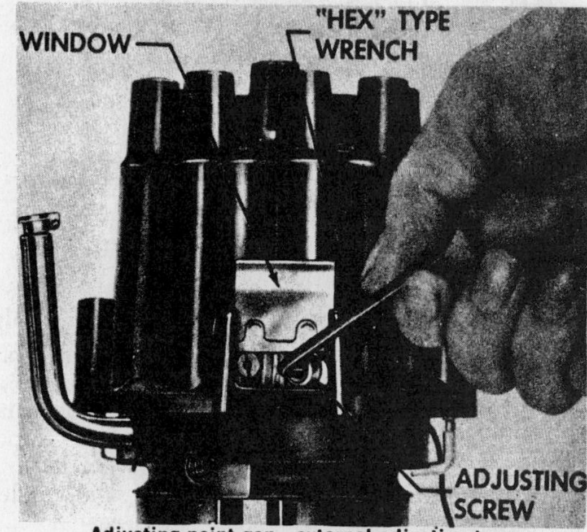

Adjusting point gap—external adjusting type
(© International Harvester Co.)

3. Rotate distributor until cam positions breaker points at maximum gap.
4. Inspect alignment of breaker points and, if necessary, gently bend the stationary contact support (never bend arm) with needle-nose pliers.
5. Loosen lock screws which mount breaker assembly and adjust gap using a small screwdriver in slots of contact bracket and upper plate. On models without slots and with eccentric adjusting screw instead, rotate adjusting screw until proper gap is obtained.
6. Replace cap and set ignition timing.

External Adjustment Type

1. With engine idling, raise window in distributor cap and insert proper "hex" wrench into adjustment screw.
2. Turn wrench clockwise until engine begins to miss, then back off ½ turn, or until dwell meter reads specified dwell angle. NOTE: To remove distributor cap, press down in slot of latch head with a screwdriver and twist.

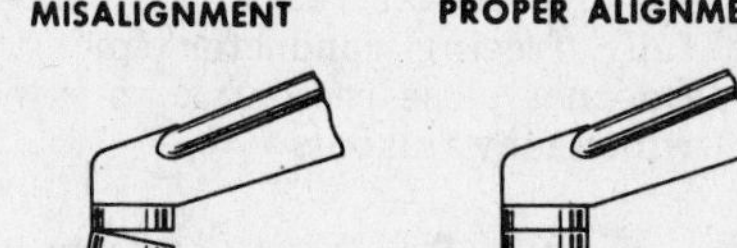

Adjusting point gap—eccentric screw
(© International Harvester Co.)

Magnetic Pulse Distributor

The Delco-Remy transistor ignition system differs from the conventional breaker point/condenser/coil system in that the control of primary coil currents results from magnetic induction. The rotating timer core has vanes which, when lined up with the vanes of the stationary pole piece, establish a magnetic path, whereby inducing a small voltage in a pickup coil. The small current surge is then amplified by a transisterized pulse amplifier which passes a current pulse to the primary windings of the coil.

In the event of engine misfire or surging, other possible sources of misfunction should be checked first, such as carburetion and fuel supply. Then check for breaks in the wiring and for corroded or loose connections.

The timing may be set in the conventional way: rotate the distributor housing while the timing marks are viewed with a timing strobe light.

If the engine will not run at all, remove a lead from one of the spark plugs and hold ½″ from the engine block while cranking engine. If there is no spark, check wiring and connections.

Actual repairs to either the distributor or the amplifier should only be performed by technicians skilled in the handling of electronic equipment.

CAUTION: Never disconnect the high voltage lead between the coil and distributor and never disconnect more than three spark plugs at a time unless the ignition switch is off. To make compression checks, disconnect the harness plug at the amplifier or disconnect the lead at the negative terminal of the coil.

Since the ignition pulse amplifier is completely static and the distributor shaft and bushings have permanent-type lubrication, no periodic maintenance of these components is required.

Ignition Timing

See tune-up specification table at the beginning of this section for timing settings. Timing light is connected to the No. 1 spark plug lead (No. 8 on V-266, 304, 345, 392).

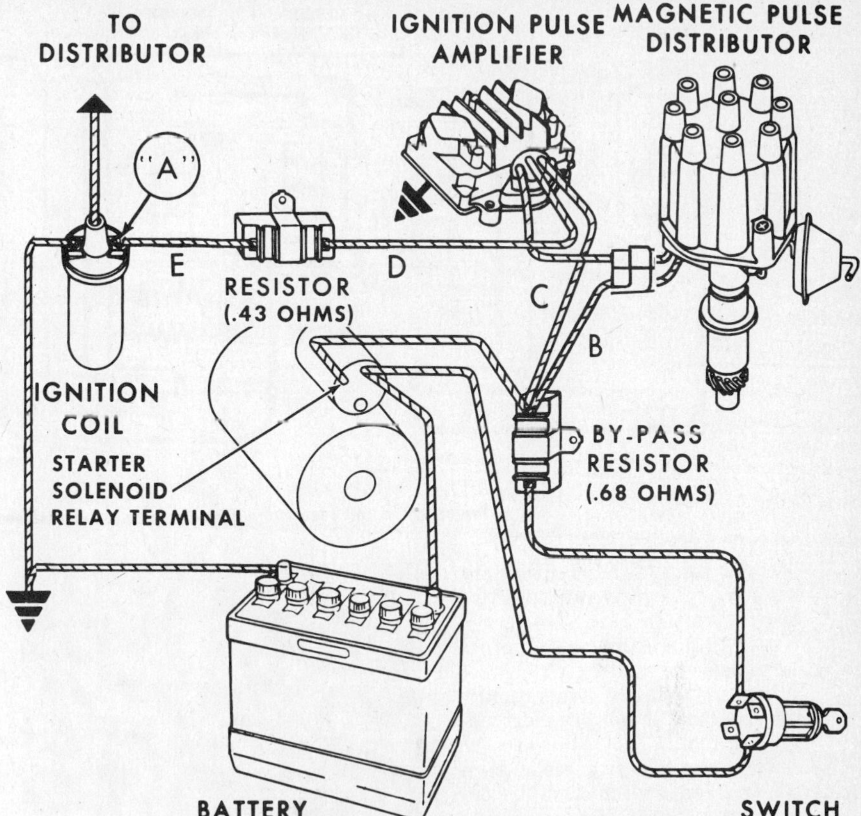

Typical transistor ignition wiring (© International Harvester Co.)

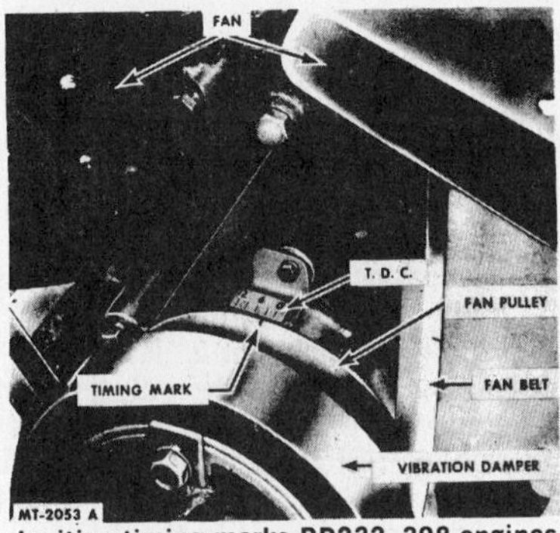

Ignition timing marks BD232, 308 engines
(© International Harvester Co.)

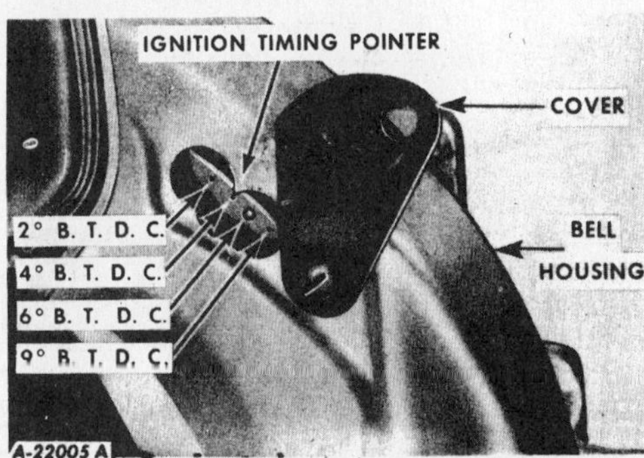

Ignition timing marks BG engine
(© International Harvester Co.)

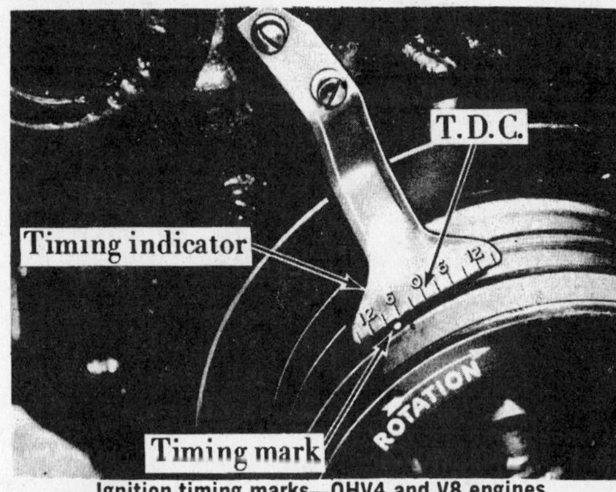

Ignition timing marks—OHV4 and V8 engines
(© International Harvester Co.)

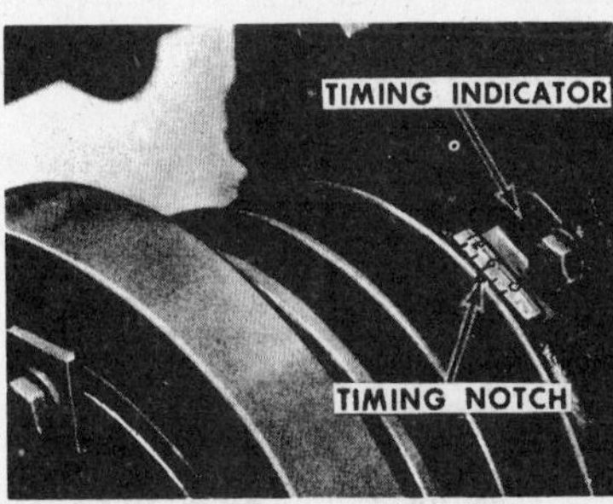

Ignition timing marks RD engine
(© International Harvester Co.)

Generator, Regulator

Generator Removal

1. Remove leads from generator and tag for identification.
2. Loosen generator mounting bolts and adjusting bracket bolt.
3. Push generator towards engine block to remove fan belt. On some models, a tension idler pulley must be loosened.
4. Remove mounting and adjusting bracket bolts, then remove generator.
5. To install, reverse the above procedure. Be sure to pull generator away from engine block while tightening adjusting bracket bolt so that there will be sufficient tension on the fan belt to avoid slippage. Tighten mounting bolts.

Precautions—Alternators

Rectifiers and regulators in alter- incorrect polarity. Observe the fol- nator systems are easily damaged by lowing precautions when wiring and testing circuits:

1. Always be certain of battery polarity.

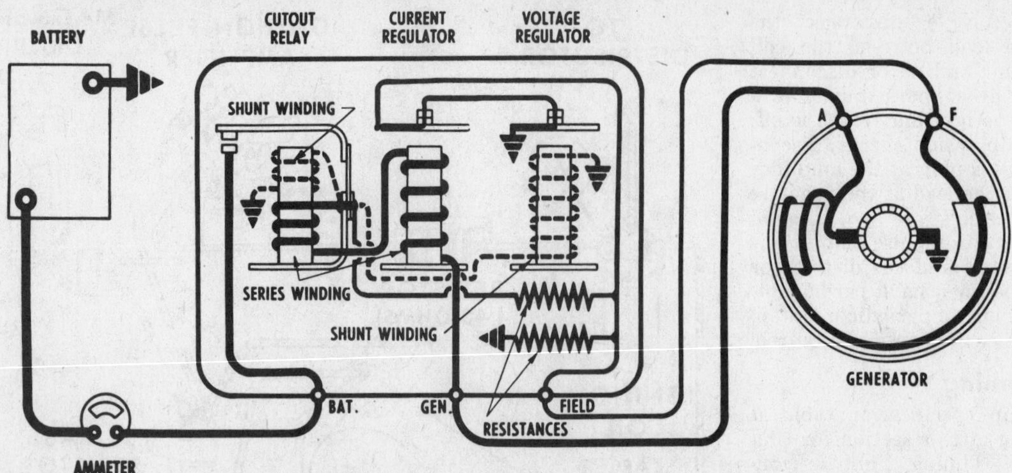

Typical three unit regulator wiring (© International Harvester Co.)

2. Always connect booster battery negative to negative and positive to positive.
3. Never ground alternator output terminal.
4. When adjusting voltage regulator, be careful not to short adjusting tool.
5. Before making any tests, turn off ignition switch and disconnect battery ground.
6. Never use a fast charge with the battery connected unless charging unit is equipped with a special alternator protector.

Polarizing DC Generator

After service or testing, the generator must be polarized with respect to the battery. Check wiring connections and start engine. Momentarily short the "GEN" and "BAT" terminals of the voltage regulator with a screwdriver. Generator will be polarized by the surge of current from the battery.

Voltage Regulators

Reference

For adjustment procedures for AC and DC generator regulators see Electrical Diagnosis Section of General Section.

Voltage Regulator Removal

Three Unit Type

1. Disconnect clamp lead at the hot terminal of battery.
2. Disconnect leads from the "GEN", "BAT", and "F" (field) terminals of voltage regulator. Tag leads for identification.
3. Remove mounting screws and regulator unit from vehicle.
4. To install, reverse the above procedure.
5. Field and Armature ("F" and "GEN") wires may be identified by tracing wires to the generator and looking for the "F" and "A" stamped near the terminals.

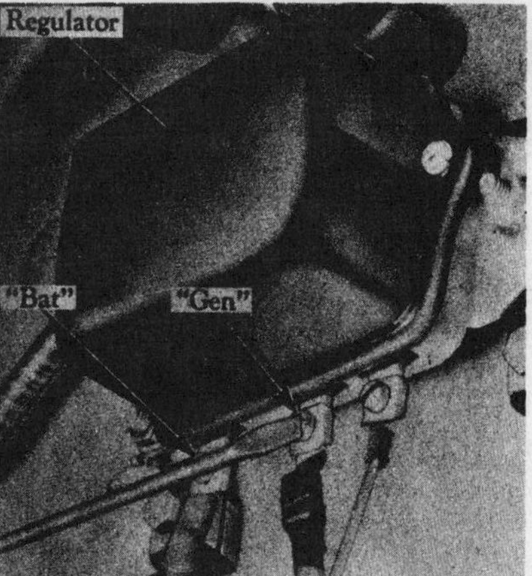

Polarizing D.C. generator (© International Harvester Co.)

6. Connect lead to hot terminal of battery.

Two Unit Type (Used with Alternator)

1. Disconnect clamp lead at the hot terminal of battery.
2. Lift latch and pull off wiring harness connector at regulator terminals.
3. Remove mounting screws and regulator unit from vehicle.
4. To install, reverse the above procedure.
5. Reconnect cable clamp to battery terminal, checking polarity first.

Starter

Reference

For servicing and overhauling starter motors, see Electrical Diagnosis Section of General Section.

Starter Motor—Removal

1. Disconnect cable clamp from hot terminal of battery.
2. Disconnect cable and wire leads from terminals of solenoid assembly, identifying leads with tags. If the solenoid is not mounted directly on the starter motor, disconnect the cable from the solenoid to the motor at the motor terminal.
3. Remove starter motor mounting bolts or stud nuts.
4. Pull starter assembly forward to clear housing and remove starter.
5. To install, reverse the above procedure, installing new tang lockwashers where removed.

Brakes

Hydraulic Brakes

Late model trucks are equipped with a dual hydraulic brake system in which there are separate hydraulic systems for the front and rear brakes. In this dual system a warning light switch operates a warning light on the dashboard when there is a pressure failure in either the front or rear system. A power system may be employed to reduce the effort applied to the brake pedal. See General Repair Section for hydraulic brake service and overhaul.

Master Cylinder—R & R

1. Disconnect hydraulic lines from master cylinder.
2. Disconnect master cylinder pushrod at brake pedal and

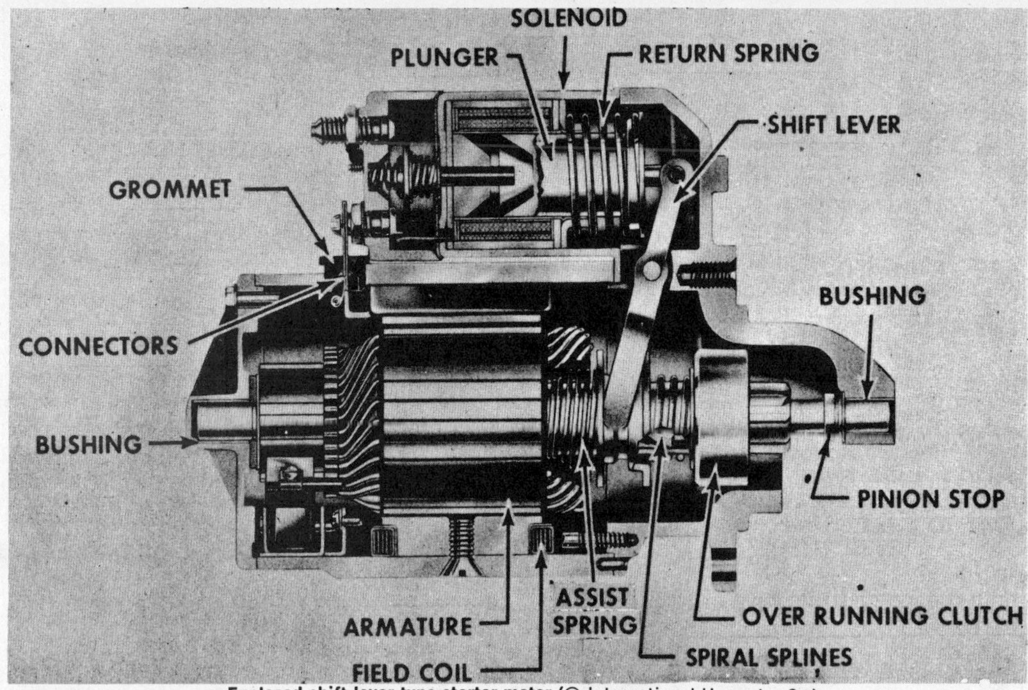

Enclosed shift lever type starter motor (© International Harvester Co.)

remove nuts securing cylinder to dash panel.

3. If master cylinder is mounted on power unit, remove nuts securing master cylinder to power unit and remove cylinder from vehicle.
4. Installation is the reverse of the above procedure.
5. Bleed system.

Resetting the Warning Light Switch

Once a difference of 85-150 psi pressure between the front and rear systems has activated the warning light switch, it will not go off by itself and must be manually reset.

1. Clean switch and disconnect wire from terminal.
2. Unscrew and completely remove switch from body. This will allow the pistons to center and hold the switch in "off" position.
3. Screw switch back into body and reconnect wire to terminal.
4. NOTE: If fluid is in the switch cavity, press brake pedal to see if piston O-ring seals are leaking. If there is leakage, the

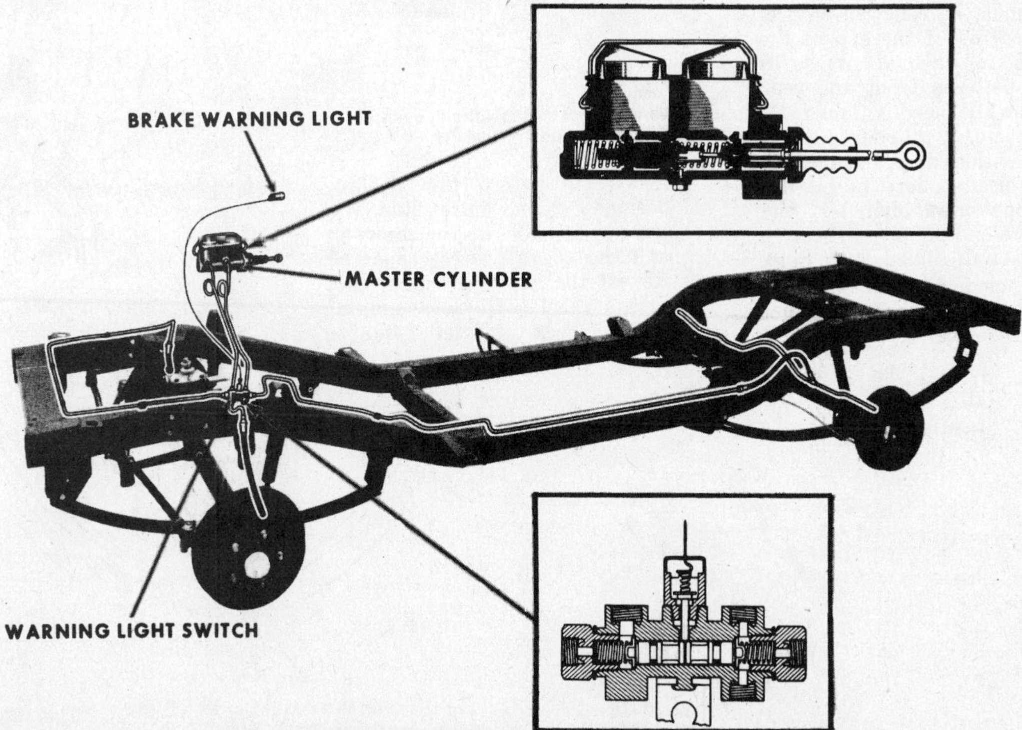

Typical standard dual brake system (© International Harvester Co.)

Tandem master cylinder disconnect points
(© International Harvester Co.)

O-rings must be replaced.

5. Warning light switch should be checked periodically for proper function and the presence of foreign matter and dirt.

Adjusting Brake Shoes

1. Remove rubber dust cover from access hole.
2. Using an adjusting tool or screwdriver, turn star screw until shoes drag on the drum.
3. Rotate star screw back from drag position until drag is completely eliminated.
4. On brakes equipped with automatic adjusters it will be necessary to hold the adjusting lever away from the star wheel with a screwdriver while the adjustment is made.

Bleeding Hydraulic Brakes

1. Before bleeding the brake system, disconnect electrical wire from warning light switch and remove any foreign material or dirt accumulation around warning light switch. Then remove the switch from body. The switch must be removed to prevent shearing of the end of the pin due to unequal pressures created between front and rear systems while bleeding.
2. Fill master cylinder reservoir (s) with clean brake fluid.
3. Attach bleeder hose to bleeder valve on wheel cylinder and place free end of bleeder hose in a jar partially filled with fluid. On some models it may be necessary to take the wheel off to get at the bleeder valve.

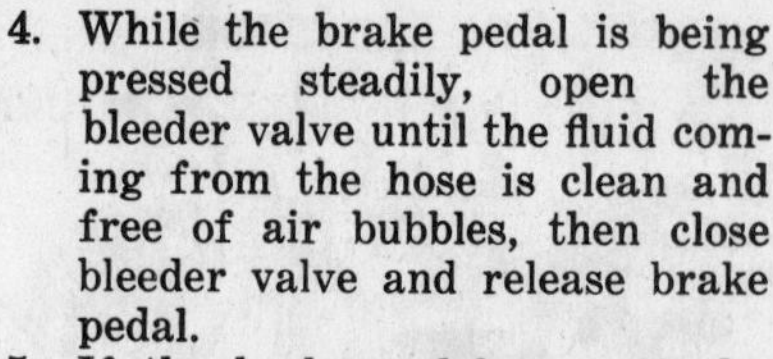

4. While the brake pedal is being pressed steadily, open the bleeder valve until the fluid coming from the hose is clean and free of air bubbles, then close bleeder valve and release brake pedal.
5. If the brake pedal goes to the

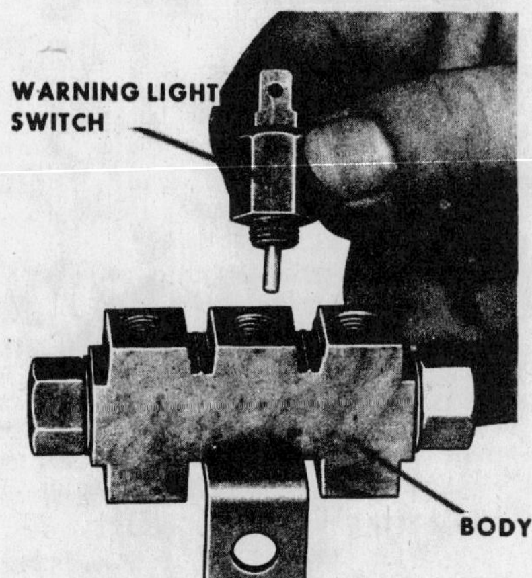

Resetting warning light switch
(© International Harvester Co.)

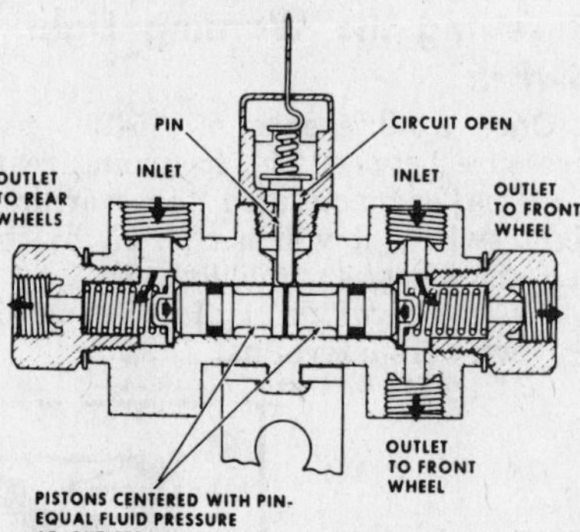

Warning light switch—circuit open
(© International Harvester Co.)

floorboard before the bleeding becomes clean, more fluid will have to be added to the reservoir and the above process repeated.

6. Repeat the above procedure for each wheel cylinder, making sure to check the level of fluid in

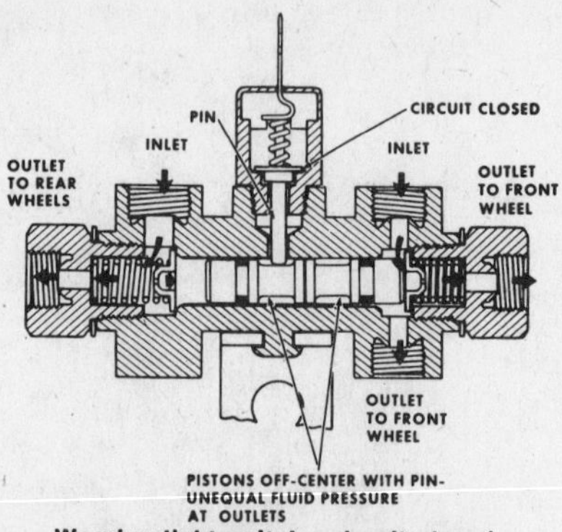

Warning light switch—circuit closed
(© International Harvester Co.)

the reservoir frequently. NOTE: On models equipped with power boosters, the booster must be bled first.

Vacuum Power Brakes

The vacuum power cylinder used with the single and dual hydraulic brake systems assists braking differently than a power booster in that its activation results directly from the foot pedal and not from the master cylinder. There are single and tandem dual types. Both types are mounted on the engine side of the firewall.

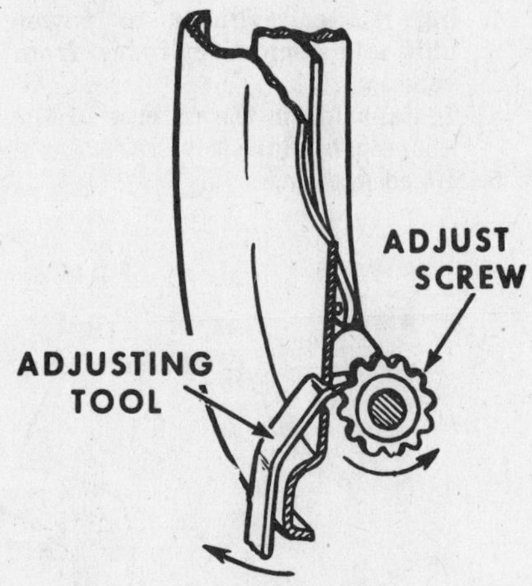

Adjusting brakes
(© International Harvester Co.)

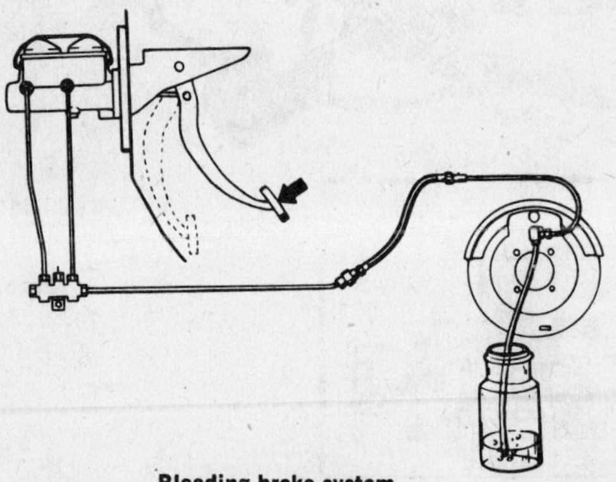
Bleeding brake system
(© International Harvester Co.)

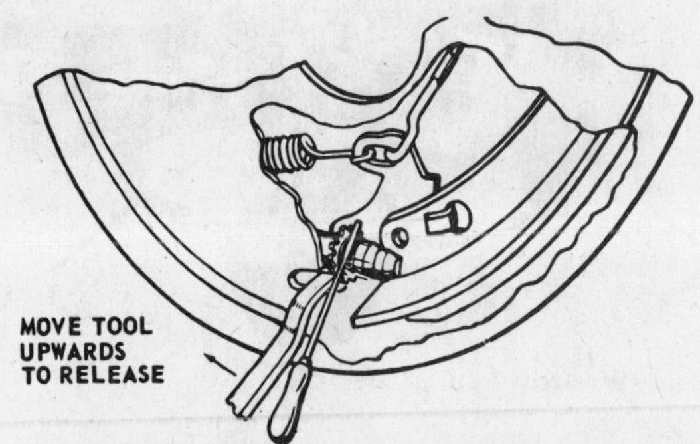

Backing off adjusting screw—self adjusting brakes
(© International Harvester Co.)

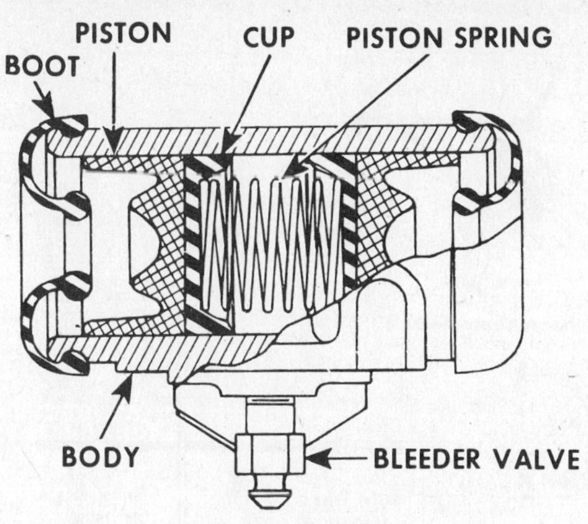

Typical wheel cylinder
(© International Harvester Co.)

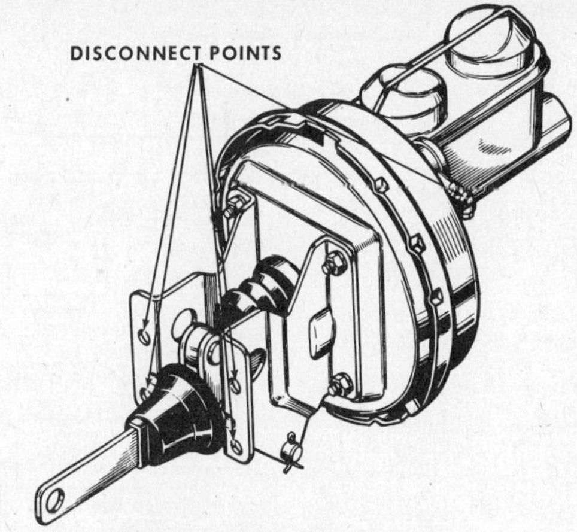

Power cylinder disconnect points
(© International Harvester Co.)

Vacuum Power Brake Cylinder—R & R

1. Disconnect vacuum hose from check valve.
2. Disconnect hydraulic lines from master cylinder.
3. Disconnect pedal link from pedal from inside the cab.
4. Remove bolts which mount the bracket to the firewall.
5. To install reverse the above procedure.
6. Bleed master cylinder output ports while connecting tube nuts which secure lines to ports.
7. Bleed hydraulic brake system.

Vacuum Brake Boosters

Vacuum boosters add pressure to the hydraulic brake system. The activation and amount of pressure is controlled by a hydraulic line from the master cylinder. Disassembly and service procedures for vacuum boosters may be found in the General Repair Section.

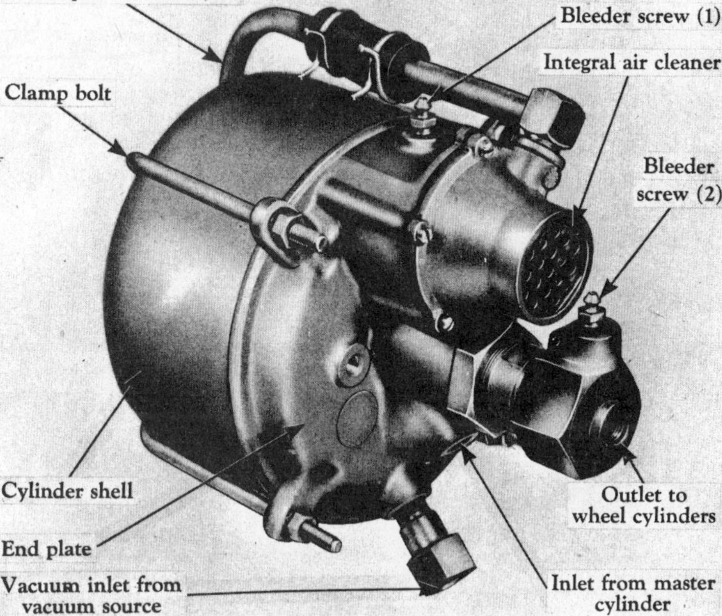

Power cylinder with integral air cleaner (© International Harvester Co.)

Booster—R & R

1. On units lacking integral air filter, remove air inlet hose (from engine air cleaner).
2. Disconnect vacuum inlet tube (coming from engine manifold).

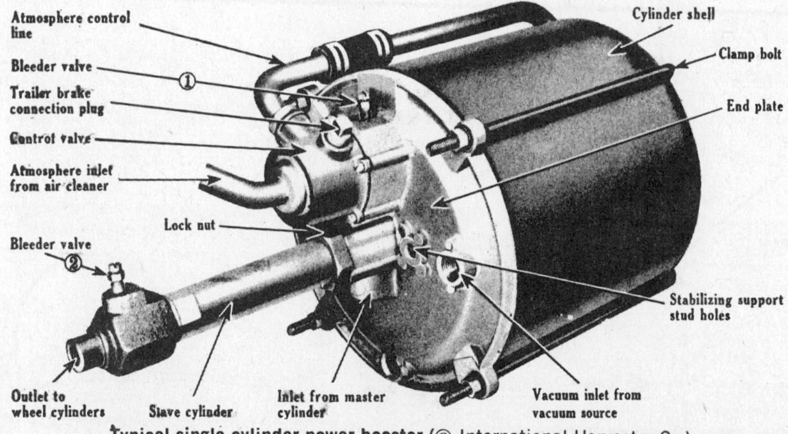

Typical single cylinder power booster (© International Harvester Co.)

3. Disconnect hydraulic line from master cylinder and hydraulic line going to wheel cylinders.
4. Remove mounting bolts and lift out vacuum unit.
5. To install, reverse the above procedure.
6. Bleed complete hydraulic system, starting with cylinder on vacuum unit as described below.

Bleeding Vacuum Booster Systems

1. The booster must be bled before proceeding to wheel cylinders.
2. All vacuum boosters have a bleed valve on the control valve as indicated in the figures by the number "1". This valve must always be bled first.
3. On boosters having an additional bleeder valve on the hydraulic cylinder indicated by the number

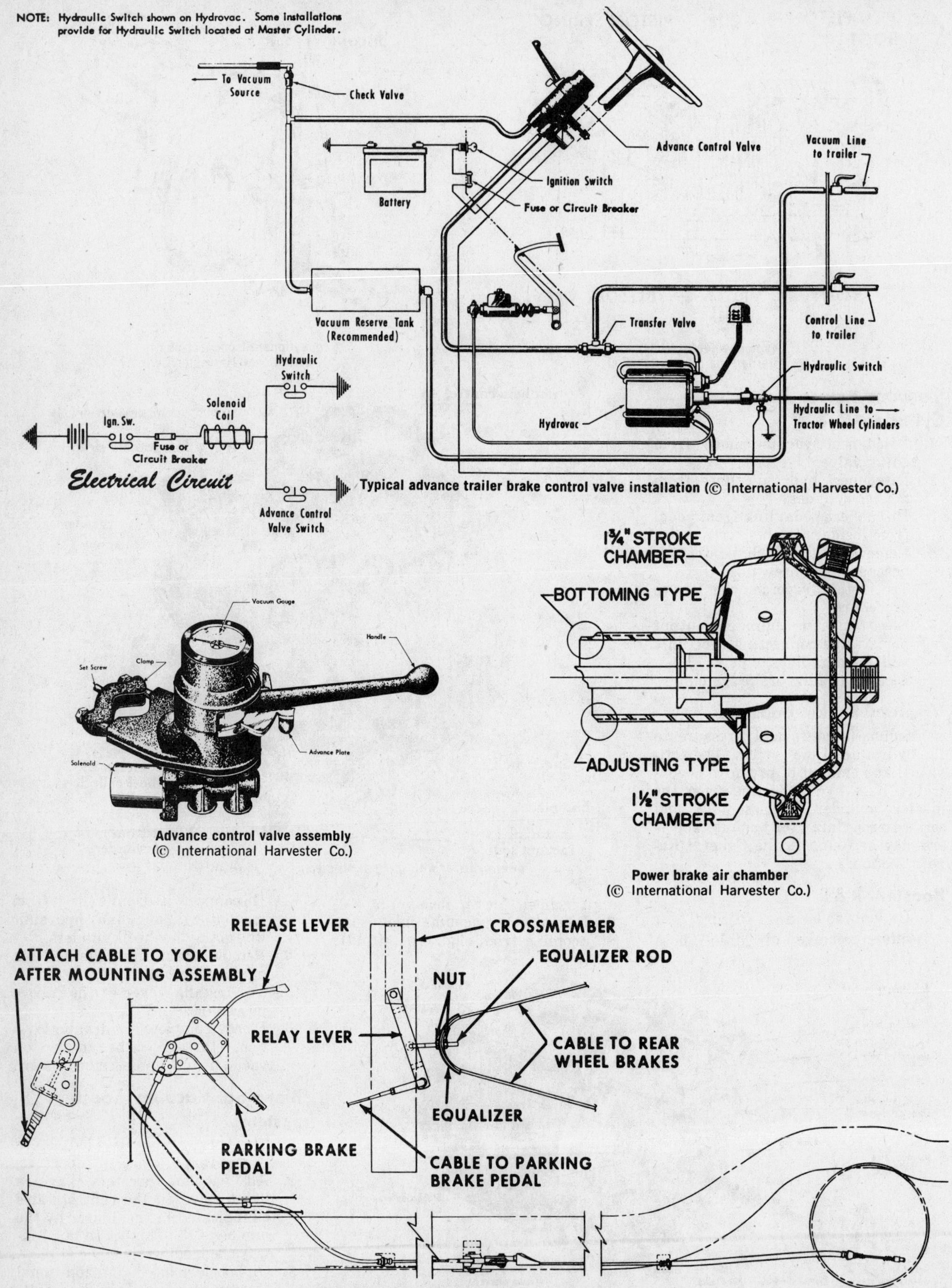

Typical advance trailer brake control valve installation (© International Harvester Co.)

Advance control valve assembly
(© International Harvester Co.)

Power brake air chamber
(© International Harvester Co.)

Parking brake cable adjustment (© International Harvester Co.)

"2", bleed this cylinder after control valve.

4. Bleed wheel cylinders as described in preceding section.

Trailer Brake Hand Control—Adjustment

The advance control valve is used in conjunction with the Hydrovac and trailer brake system to vary the initial braking of the trailer.

1. Place advance plate in full released position (rotate counterclockwise).
2. While coasting on smooth road at 20 mph, apply valve by rotating clockwise until a slight drag is felt from the trailer brakes.
3. Rotate advance plate to where it just touches the valve operating handle. This releases the brakes on the trailer but sets the advance effect.
4. Leaving advance valve controls as set above, gently apply tractor brakes to check the "advance" of the trailer brakes.

Parking Break Adjustment

Rear Brake Type

1. Loosen locknut on the equalizer rod and turn front nut forward several turns.
2. Turn the locknut (rear) forward just enough to remove any slack but not so much that the brake shoes lift of their anchors.
3. Tighten both nuts against the equalizer.

Drive Shaft Band Type

1. Leaving parking brake lever in the extreme release position, check that the cam lever is resting squarely on upper brake band bracket. This is adjusted by removing the clevis pin and readjusting yoke.
2. Adjust screw nut (1) until a clearance of .020-.030" is reached.
3. Adjusting nuts (4) on bolt (5), obtain .020-.030" clearance on lower half of lining and drum.
4. Adjust nuts (2) on bolt (3) for a clearance of .020-.030" clearance on top half of lining.
5. Lock all adjustment with lock nuts.

Air Brake System

Air brake systems are composed of a compressor, a reservoir, brake actuating chambers and a network of lines and valves which control operation. The piston-type air compressor is belt driven directly from the engine and is dependent upon the engine for its lubrication. Pressure in the system is regulated by a governor which starts loading the compressor when the system pressure drop below 95 psi and unloads the compressor when the system pressure reaches 110 psi. See General Section for overhaul of air brake components.

Air Compressor Governor Adjustment

Early Models

1. Check governor filter and supply line for any restriction.
2. Loosen adjusting screw locknut (13) and exhaust valve housing (9).
3. Remove exhaust valve housing (9) with adjusting screw (12), locknut (13), and shims (8) as a complete unit.
4. Replace exhaust valve housing, adjusting screw, locknut and three shims into governor body and tighten.
5. Turn adjusting screw (12) until it sticks out 3/8" from exhaust valve housing.
6. Start truck engine and build up pressure in air brake system until it reaches 115 psi then shut off engine. If governor cuts out before 115 psi then turn adjusting screw out one complete turn and repeat this step.
7. With pressure holding at 115 psi slowly turn adjusting screw out until governor cuts out (dull pop).
8. Start truck engine and slowly bleed pressure until governor cuts in. Cut-in should be between 93-98 psi.
9. If cut-in is below 93 psi, remove exhaust valve housing unit and add shims (one shim equals 4 psi) to adjust cut-in and install as in step 4.
10. If cut-in is above 98 psi, remove exhaust valve housing unit and remove shims to lower cut-in pressure.
11. Check cut-in and cut-out pressure after each adjustment and repeat appropriate steps if nec-

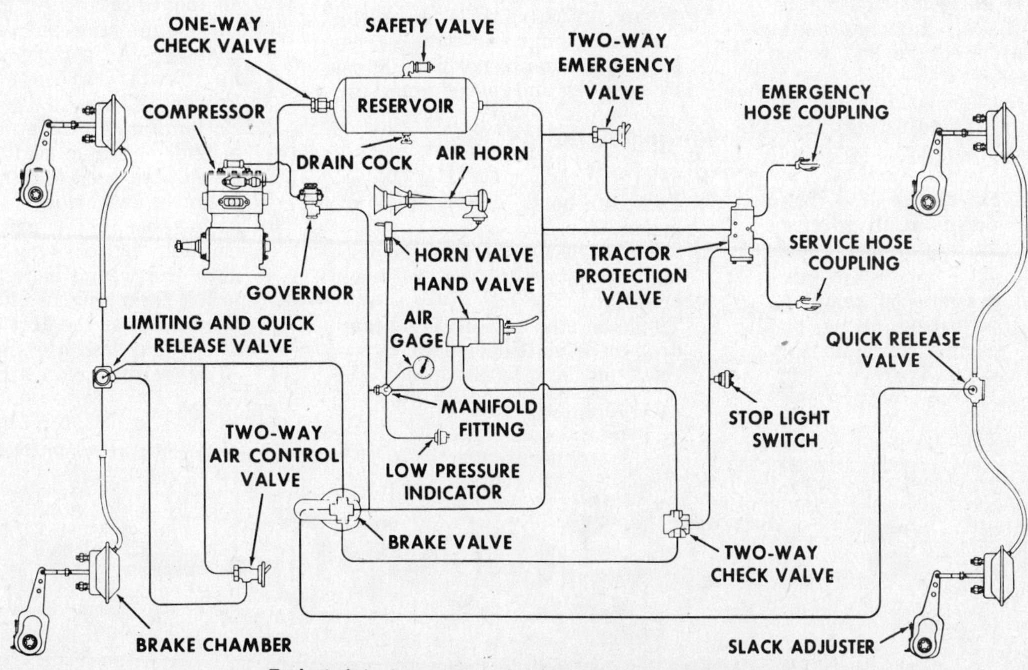

Typical air brake system (© International Harvester Co.)

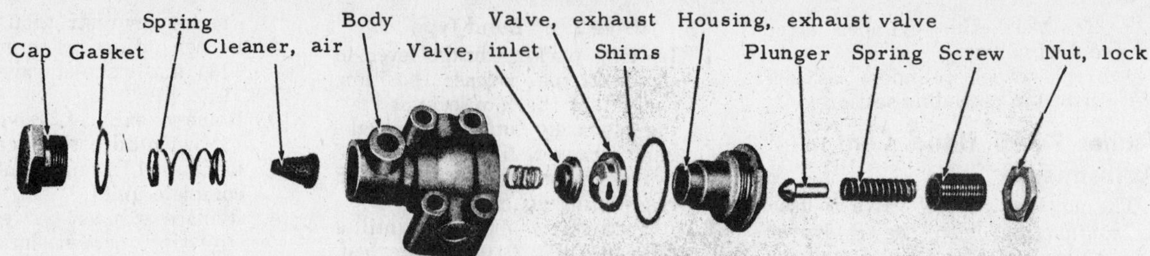

Air compressor governor—early models (© International Harvester Co.)

essary.

12. When adjustments are completed, tighten locknut (13).

Air Compressor Governor Adjustment

Late Models

1. Check governor filter and supply line for any restriction.
2. Loosen adjusting screw locknut (13) and exhaust valve housing locknut (9).
3. Unscrew adjusting screw (12) four turns.
4. Screw in exhaust valve housing (8) until it bottoms (do not tighten—seats are easily ruined).
5. Back off exhaust valve housing (8) ¾ turn.
6. While holding exhaust valve housing, turn in adjusting screw (12) three turns after it has made contact with the spring. A slight resistance should be felt when contact is made. If this contact cannot be felt, turn adjusting screw until it sticks out ⅜" from exhaust valve housing.
7. Start engine and build up air pressure to 115 psi and shut off engine. If governor cuts out before 115 psi, turn adjusting screw out one turn and repeat this step.
8. With pressure holding at 115 psi, turn in adjusting screw until governor cuts out (dull pop).
9. Start truck engine and bleed pressure down until governor cuts in. Cut-in pressure should be 93-98 psi.
10. If cut-in pressure is below 93 psi, hold adjusting screw and turn out exhaust valve housing (1/6 turn equals 5 psi).
11. If cut-in pressure is above 98 psi, hold adjusting screw and turn in exhaust valve housing.
12. Repeat steps until proper cut-in pressure is reached.
13. Check cut-out pressure and adjust if necessary.
14. Tighten adjusting screw locknut and exhaust valve housing locknut.

Air Reservoir Safety Valve Adjustment

1. Connect an accurate air pressure gauge to the emergency line at the rear of the truck and open emergency line valve. With truck engine running, turn air supply valve to the air supply position to bypass governor. Let pressure rise in reservoir until 150 psi is reached then quickly shut off air supply valve.
2. If the safety valve did not blow off at 150 psi or blew off before that pressure, loosen locknut (A) and turn adjusting screw (B) either in for higher pressure setting or out for lower pressure setting.
3. When adjustment is complete, tighten locknut and reduce pressure in system to normal 100 psi by applying and releasing brakes.

Plunger Actuated Brake—Adjustment

1. Jack or hoist wheels free of ground.
2. Remove dust cover from adjusting slot—two places on each brake.
3. Turn the star wheel until heavy drag on drum is developed.
4. Back off bolt barely past light drag.

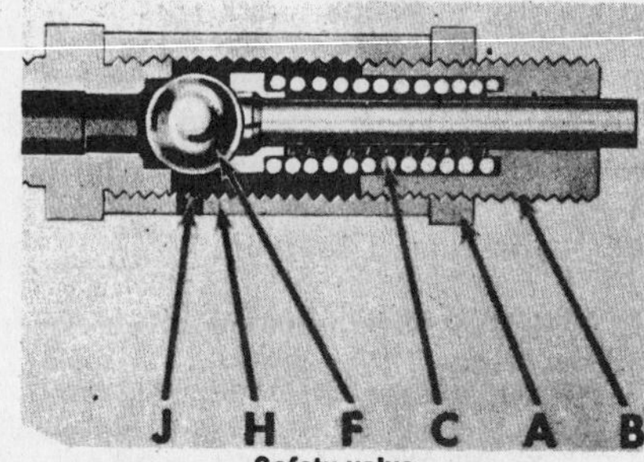

Safety valve
(© International Harvester Co.)

5. Replace dust covers in adjusting slots.
6. Repeat for other brakes.
7. If brakes are equipped with automatic adjusters, check drum to lining clearance. If it is more than .060", adjust brakes manually until they can be serviced. See Unit Repair section for servicing air brakes.

Air Power Unit—Adjustment

1. Determine whether the power unit is the adjustable or bottoming type. Bottoming units have an identification tag fastened to the clamp ring bolt of the air chamber. Adjustable units have no identification markings. Loosen collet nut.
2. Bottoming units automatically provide optimum useful chamber stroke and need only be screwed in until they bottom.
3. Adjustable units are adjusted manually by screwing the unit in until the wedge is just starting to lift the plungers off the abutment seats at the first movement of the diaphragm.
4. After screwing in air chamber

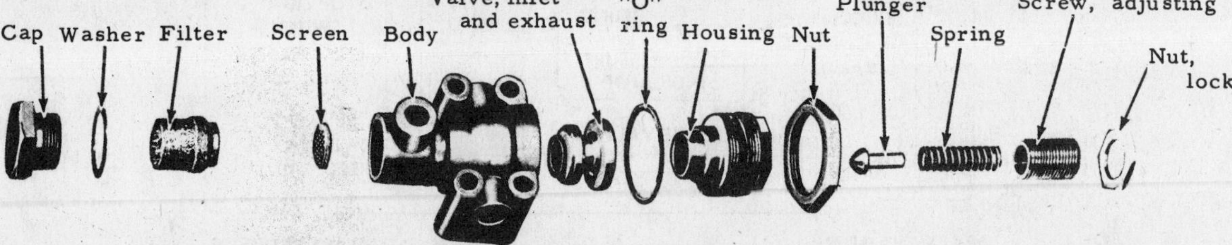

Air compressor governor—late models (© International Harvester Co.)

Adjusting brakes
(© International Harvester Co.)

unit to proper depth, tighten collet nut to lock position.

Air Brake Slack Adjusters—Adjustment

Cam actuated air brakes should be adjusted for lining wear every 2000 miles. Adjustment is made by turning a worm screw on a gear which positions stack adjuster angle.

1. With wheel free to rotate, disconnect pushrod from the slack adjuster to determine whether or not it is in fully released position.
2. Reinsert clevis pin through bottomed pushrod and slack adjuster arm, adjusting worm gear if necessary.
3. Holding the locking sleeve in, adjust worm screw until shoes drag against drum, then back off enough to eliminate drag.
4. Angle that slack adjuster makes when brake is fully applied should not "go over" 90° point.
5. If the slack adjuster goes over the 90° point the maximum force will not be exerted and the pushrod must be adjusted as follows:
6. Carefully disconnect slack adjuster from pushrod—it may snap into the air chamber with considerable force.
7. Loosen locknut on pushrod clevis and thread clevis onto pushrod towards air chamber several turns.
8. Connect pushrod and clevis with pin.

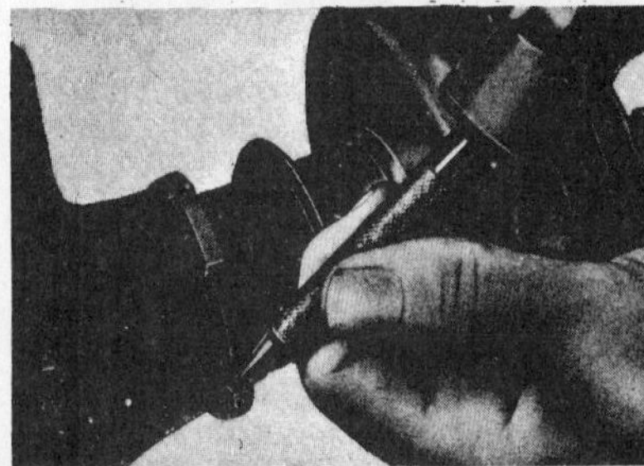
Loosening collect nut—air brake power unit
(© International Harvester Co.)

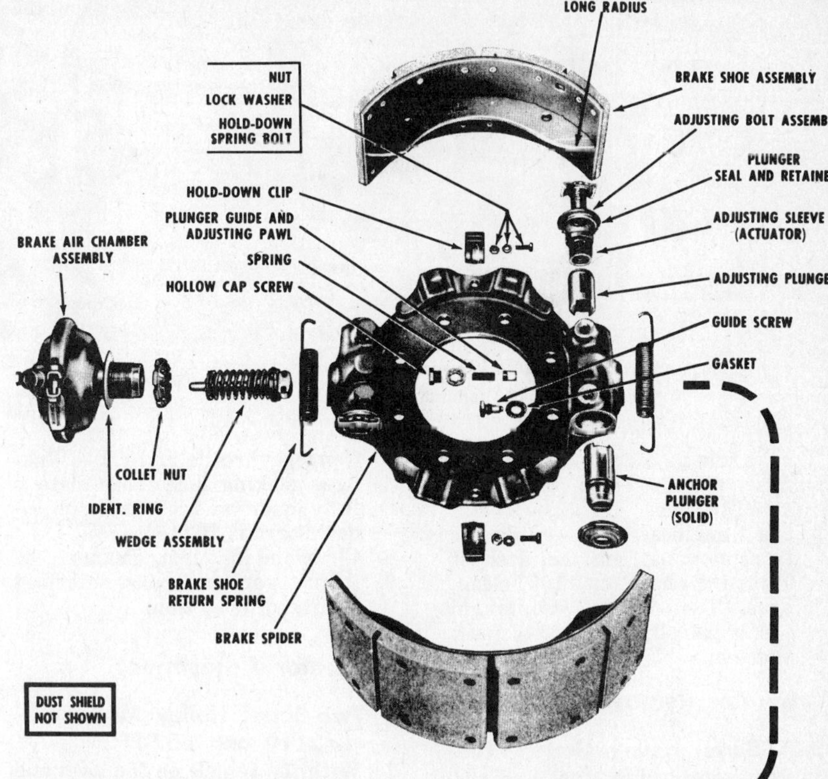

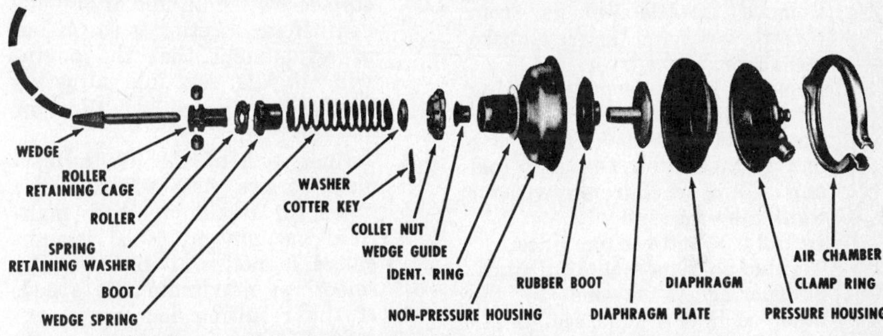

RDA brake with integral plunger housings (© International Harvester Co.)

9. Check pushrod-to-slack adjuster angle again as the brake is applied to make sure that it is not still going over the 90° point.
10. Readjust if necessary.
11. When adjustment is correct tighten locknut on pushrod clevis and install cotter pin which secures clevis pin.

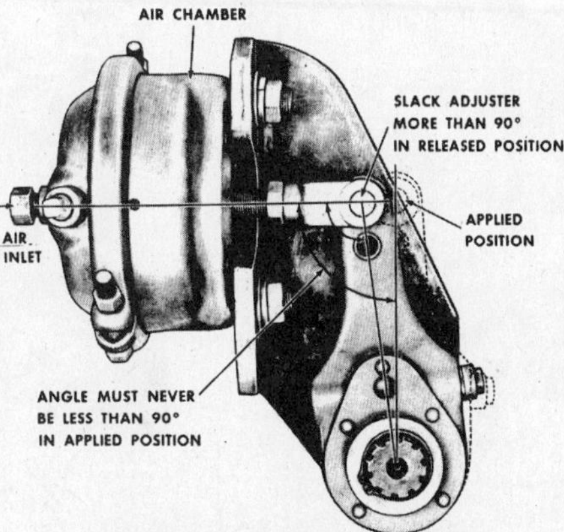

Foundation air brake slack adjuster
(© International Harvester Co.)

Fuel System

Carburetor Adjustment

Single-Barrel Holley Model 1904

1. With choke fully off and engine warm, adjust throttle stop screw for 450 rpm (700 rpm for standard transmission and exhaust emission, 600 rpm for automatic transmission and exhaust emission).
2. Set idle adjusting screw to give highest steady manifold vacuum or, if no vacuum gauge is available, for the smoothest maxi-

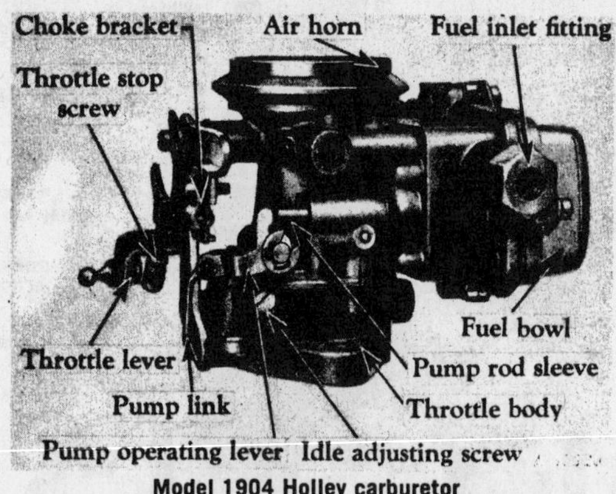

Model 1904 Holley carburetor
(© International Harvester Co.)

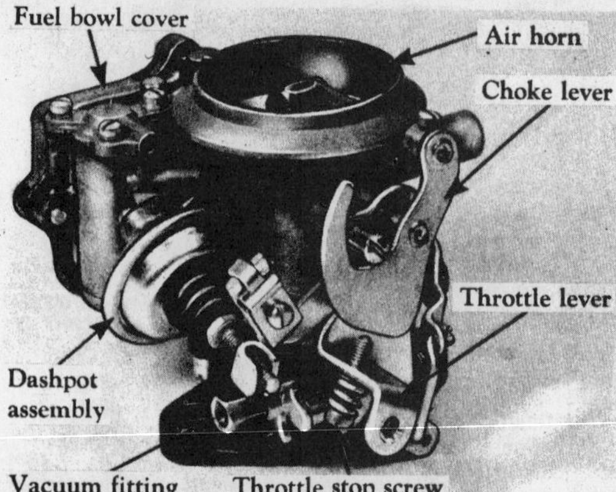

Model 1904 Holley carburetor with dashpot
(© International Harvester Co.)

mum idle speed.
3. Reset throttle stop screw for rpm as above.
4. For engines with automatic transmissions, set the dashpot adjusting screw for 0.100" clearance. The dashpot diaphragm rod is in fully compressed position while this clearance is set.

Carburetor Removal

Single-Barrel Holley Model 1904

1. Remove air filter, fuel line and vacuum line, if fitted.
2. Remove throttle linkage from throttle lever and unscrew choke cable from choke lever.
3. Remove bolts from mounting studs and lift off carburetor.
4. To install, fit a new carburetor flange gasket on the manifold and mount carburetor without tightening the stud nuts.
5. Install fuel and vacuum lines.
6. Tighten bolts on mounting studs, alternating from one to the other so that a good seal is obtained.
7. Connect throttle and choke linkages, making sure choke plate is fully open and choke knob on dashboard is all the way in.
8. Clean and install air cleaner.
9. Adjust carburetor as described in preceding section.

Carburetor Adjustment

Two-Barrel Holley Models 2110 and 852-FFG

1. With the vehicle on the level and engine warm, adjust throttle stop screw for an idle of 350-400 rpm. If carburetion is so far out of adjustment that the engine will not idle, seat idle adjusting needles lightly and back them off one full turn.
2. Adjust each of the idle adjustment screws, first one then the other, for maximum steady manifold vacuum or, if a vacuum gauge is not available, for the smoothest maximum idle speed.
3. If the resulting idle speed exceeds 350-400 rpm, reset throttle stop screw.
4. If equipped with a dashpot (automatic transmission), set the adjusting screw for a clearance of .045-.065" with the dashpot diaphragm fully depressed.

Governor Adjustment

Two-Barrel Holley Models 2100 and 852-FFG

1. Connect tachometer to engine.
2. After engine has warmed up, briefly hold throttle at wide open to determine governor cut-out speed. See specifications table at the beginning of this section for correct governor cut-out speeds.
3. If adjustment is required, stop engine and remove the adjusting hole cover or cover band from the governor valve housing on the distributor.
4. With the ignition off, crank engine until governor valve adjusting screw at the end of the governor valve body appears at the opening.

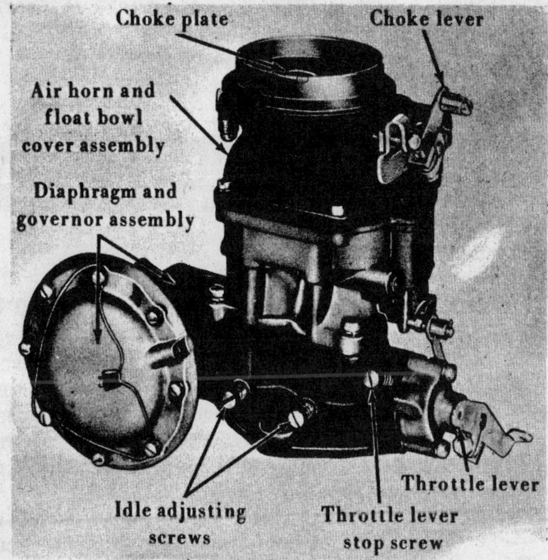

Model 2110G Holley 2 BBL carburetor
(© International Harvester Co.)

Model 4150G carburetor with automatic transmission operating cam
(© International Harvester Co.)

5. Insert screwdriver and turn the adjusting screw: clockwise to increase cut-out speed and counterclockwise to decrease cut-out speed. One full turn of the adjusting screw equals about 150 rpm.
6. When correct cut-out speed is obtained, replace adjusting hole cover or cover band and tighten securely.

Carburetor Removal

Two-Barrel Holley Models 2100 and 852-FFG

1. Remove air cleaner, throttle linkage and choke cable.
2. Disconnect fuel line and distributor and governor vacuum lines.
3. Remove bolts from mounting studs and lift off carburetor.
4. To install, clean manifold mating surface and install a new flange gasket.
5. Install carburetor but do not tighten down stud nuts.
6. Connect fuel line and vacuum lines.
7. Tighten nuts on mounting studs in an alternating fashion so that flange gasket compresses evenly for a good seal.
8. Connect throttle linkage and choke cable, making sure that choke plates are fully open when the choke knob is pushed in.
9. Check throttle for complete travel.
10. Install air cleaner.
11. Adjust carburetor as described in preceding section.

Carburetor Adjustment

Two-Barrel Holley Models 2300 and 23006

1. First set fast idle by adjusting fast idle stud so as to have .018-.020″ clearance between stud and fast idle cam when throttle plates are set for curb idle and choke plate is fully open (2300G). On model without governor (2300), set throttle lever stop screw so that screw just touches fast idle cam at curb idle.
2. With the truck on the level, gently seat idle adjusting screws, then back each off one turn.
3. With warm engine idling, adjust throttle stop screw for an idle of 450-500 rpm.
4. Set one idle adjusting screw to obtain highest steady manifold vacuum reading or, if a vacuum gauge is not available, the smoothest running maximum speed. There should be no more than a ½-turn difference between the two screws at final setting.

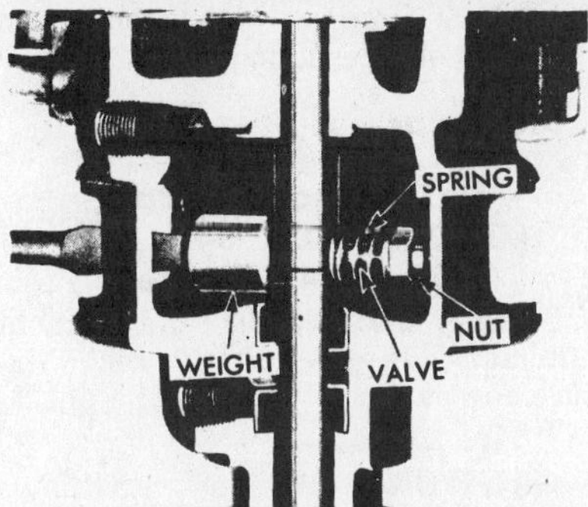

Adjusting spinner governor—distributor
(© International Harvester Co.)

5. If the above adjustment has resulted in increased idle speed, reset idle speed as described in Step 3.
6. On vehicles equipped with automatic transmissions, loosen dashpot jam nut and rotate complete dashpot assembly to obtain .095-.105″ clearance between dashpot pushrod and throttle lever.

Fuel Level Adjustment

Two-Barrel Holley Models 2300 and 2300G

1. Before changing fuel level, check fuel pump output for proper functioning. See Tune-Up Specifications at the beginning of this section for correct fuel pump output rate.
2. With ignition off and air cleaner removed, drain fuel bowl by loosening bottom left bowl mounting screw.
3. Tighten bowl screw.
4. With engine running, remove the sight plug from the bowl. Fuel level should be on line with the threads at bottom of sight plug hole.
5. To adjust fuel level, loosen and hold locknut with a ½″ wrench and turn the adjusting nut with a screwdriver or ⅝″ wrench. Turning clockwise lowers fuel level and turning counterclockwise raises fuel level.
6. Tighten locknut.
7. Check fuel level after engine has run enough to stabilize fuel level and repeat above procedure if necessary.

Pump Discharge Adjustment

Two-Barrel Holley 2300 and 2300G

1. With choke wide open and throttle set for curb idle, lengthen or shorten adjusting bolt (located at override spring on the accelerator pump lever) until bolt touches diaphragm lever and takes up linkage slack.
2. Then lengthen adjusting bolt ½ turn.
3. Tighten nut.

Governor Adjustment

Two-Barrel Holley Model 2300G

Governor adjustment is the same as that described for the Holley model 2110 above. For correct speed setting see table.

Governor Speed RPM

Engine Model	RPM
BD-308	3200
RD-372	2850
RD-406	2750
RD-450	2600
RD-501	2600
V-345	3800
V-392	3600
V-401	3400
V-461	3200
V-478	3400
VS-478	3400
V-549	3200
VS-549	3200

Carburetor Removal

Two-Barrel Holley Models 2300 and 2300G

1. Remove air filter and disconnect fuel line, distributor and governor vacuum lines and throttle and choke linkages.
2. Remove mounting stud nuts and lift off carburetor.
3. Remove flange gasket and discard.
4. To install, clean manifold mating surface and install a new flange gasket.
5. Operate choke and throttle levers to be sure they are functioning properly.
6. Install carburetor and mounting stud nuts, but do not tighten nuts.
7. Connect fuel line, vacuum lines and throttle and choke linkage.
8. Tighten down mounting stud nuts in an alternating criss-cross pattern to make sure that flange gasket is compressed evenly.
9. Check to see that choke plate is fully open and dashboard knob is in when connecting choke.
10. Make all adjustments described in preceding text.
11. Install air cleaner.

Carburetor Removal

Four-Barrel Holley Model 4150

All adjustments and installation procedures are the same for the four-barrel carburetor as for the model 2300 described above except that the four-barrel has two float bowls and the fuel level adjustment is made for each. On trucks equipped with automatic transmissions, make idle adjustments with transmission selector lever in 1-2 drive range while parking brake is on.

Mechanical Spark Advance

Holley Model 2140

On Holley models 4150 and 885 the throttle lever is provided with three (885) or two (4150) pump link hole positions for seasonal requirements. The longer stroke positions are for cold weather conditions and the medium and short stroke positions are for normal and warm weather respectively.

Mechanical Spark Advance

Holley Model 2140

1. Place cable wire in hole of pin in the spark advance lever, but do not tighten.
2. Place cable sleeve in clamp, but do not tighten.
3. Holding a .105" feeler gauge between spark advance lever and spark advance lever stop, set a 15-degree reading on the dampener (use timing light) by adjusting the spark advance cable sleeve in relation to the cable clamp.
4. Tighten clamps and check the 15-degree timing advance reading.
5. Remove feeler gauge and recheck timing which should now be 3 degrees advance.

Carburetor Adjustment

LPG (propane-butane) RD-501, V-304, 345, 401, 461 & 549 Engines

Setting the idle fuel adjustment automatically gives the correct mixture for part and full throttle operation.

CAUTION: Liquified petroleum gas is extremely flammable. Observe all safety precautions regardless of the nature of work being performed. No work is to be done on fuel tanks except by qualified concerns who normally service such containers.

1. Set throttle for fast idle by turning throttle stop screw in from closed position 3 or 4 turns.
2. Start engine and adjust idle adjusting screw in drag link (either end) until engine runs smoothly. Turning screw in (clockwise) enriches mixture.
3. Adjust throttle stop screw for idle of 600 rpm.
4. Readjust idle adjusting screw in drag link for maximum engine speed. If engine speed starts to go above 900 rpm, set back speed with throttle stop screw to 600 rpm and continue adjusting drag link screw for maximum engine speed.
5. Adjust idle to 400 rpm and replace cotter pin in drag link adjusting screw to lock adjustment.

Carburetor Adjustment

LPG (Propane-Butane) Carburetor Adjustment

All OHV 6 Engines Except PT 6 & RD 501

1. Loosen locknut on starting adjusting screw and turn screw clockwise until it bottoms, then back it out the required number of turns (see table). Tighten locknut.
2. Turn idle adjusting screw on the regulating unit clockwise until it bottoms gently, then back it out the required number of turns (see table).
3. On BD engines, loosen the large lock nut on the economizer unit and turn load adjusting screw clockwise to extreme position, then turn counterclockwise the required number of turns (see table). Tighten locknut. On BD engines (engine not running), disconnect vacuum line from economizer before setting load adjustment. Then loosen locknut and turn entire economizer assembly clockwise until it bottoms in carburetor, then counterclockwise the specified number of turns (see table). Temporarily plug the vacuum line and start engine. After the engine is warmed up, set hand throttle at about ⅔ governed speed. Screw economizer body in until engine speed starts to drop and then out until the engine speed starts to

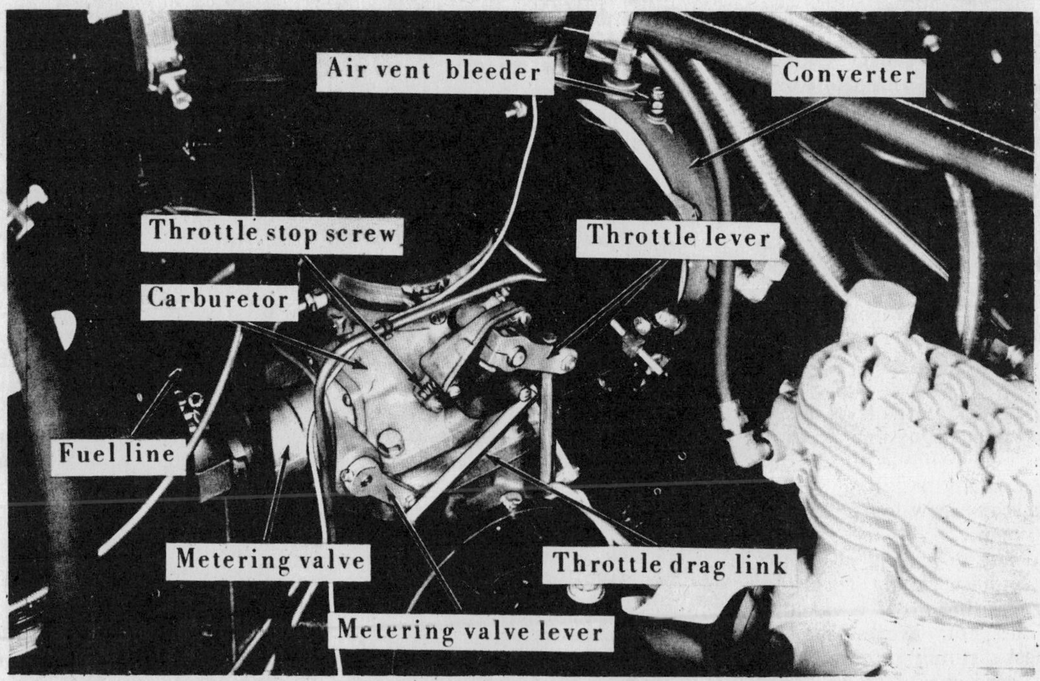

LPG carburetion—V401, 461 & 549 engines (© International Harvester Co.)

LPG Carburetor Adjustment Specifications

Engine	*BD-240 BG-241*	*BD-264 BG-265*	*BD-282*	*BD-308*	*RD-372*	*RD-406*	*RD-450*
Starting Adjusting Screw (number turns off seat)	5/8	7/8	3	2	2	1	2
Economizer (load adjustment) (number turns off seat)	5	7	4-3/4	9-1/2	4-3/8 4-1/2	5 4-11/16	4-3/4 3-3/4
Economizer (part throttle adjustment) (number of clockwise turns after screw has been turned counterclockwise to extreme position)							

drop, then set in between the two extremes and tighten locknut. For part throttle adjustment, loosen small locknut on economizer cover and turn economizer adjusting screw clockwise the required number of turns from bottom position (see table) and tighten locknut.

Fuel Pumps

Reference

Fuel pumps are of conventional design and instructions for servicing may be found in the Unit Repair Section.

Fuel Pump Pressure Test

1. Disconnect fuel line at carburetor inlet and attach pressure gauge between the inlet and disconnected line.
2. Start engine and take reading. Consult Tune-up Specifications at the beginning of this section for correct fuel pump pressure.
3. When engine is stopped, the pressure should remain constant or very slowly return to zero.

Fuel Pump Capacity Test

1. Disconnect fuel line from the fuel pump.
2. Connect a piece of hose to the line so that fuel can be directed into a measuring container.
3. Start engine and note time it takes to fill a pint container. Pump should fill one pint within 20-30 seconds.

Fuel Pump Removal

1. Disconnect inlet and outlet fuel lines from pump.
2. Disconnect windshield wiper vacuum hose if so equipped.
3. Remove mounting stud nuts or bolts and remove pump from engine.
4. To install, reverse the above procedure.

Cooling System

Radiator Removal

1. Drain radiator and block.
2. Remove inlet and outlet water hoses.
3. Remove radiator mounting bolts. On some models it may be necessary to remove radiator shell and support rods or, if the radiator assembly is bolted to the fenders, unbolted at those points.
4. Lift radiator straight up and remove.
5. To install, reverse the above procedure, being sure to check for leaks when filling the cooling system.

Water Pump Removal

1. Drain cooling system.
2. If radiator shrouds hinder access they must be removed before proceding (large V-8's and cab-forward models).
3. Loosen generator pivot bolts and adjusting bolt on bracket to relieve tension on the fan belt and remove belt from water pump pulley. On V(S)-401, 461, 478, 549 engines all accessories are driven by belts from the water pump pulley and are removed by loosening the generator and power steering pump adjusting brackets and pivots. The idler pulley on the belts between the crankshaft and water pump pulleys is then loosened so that these belts may be removed.
4. On V(S)-401, 461, 478, 549 engines the fan blades and pulley are removed.
5. Remove all pipes and hoses connected to the water pump.
6. Remove mounting bolts or stud nuts and water pump. On all models except 4-152, 4-196 and V-266, 304, 345, 392, only the front half of the pump housing is removed for water pump servicing.
7. Installation is the reverse of the above procedure. Be sure to install new gaskets and, if applica-

Hood and radiator disconnect points 401, 461, 478 & 549 engines
(© International Harvester Co.)

LPG carburetor
(© International Harvester Co.)

1 Fuelock-strainer, assembly
2 Fuelock, connection to ignition switch
3 Governor, diaphragm housing
4 Governor, spinner box air line
5 Drag, link idle adjusting screw
6 Spacer (insulator)
7 Throttle, control rod
8 Metering, valve lever
9 Throttle, lever

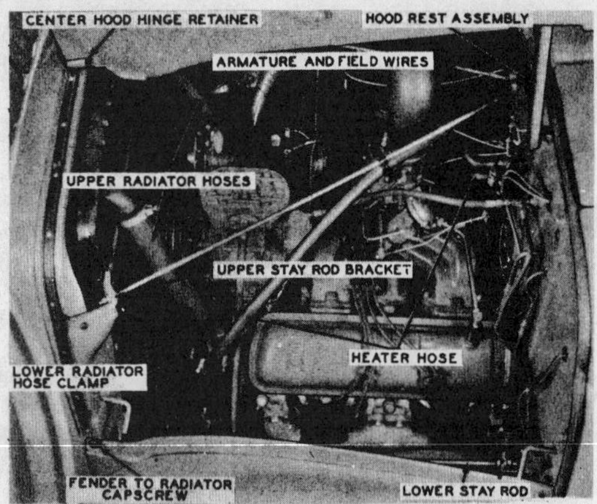

Hood and radiator disconnect points 401, 461, 478 & 549 engines
(© International Harvester Co.)

Alternator drive belt 401, 461, 478 & 549 engines
(© International Harvester Co.)

ble, new O-rings on pipe end fittings.

Water Pump Service

PT-6 Engines

This water pump is nonadjustable, has a packless seal and must be serviced as a complete unit: in the event of malfunction the whole assembly is replaced.

1. Remove pump as described in the preceding section.
2. Clean impeller cavity before installing new pump.
3. Spin shaft on new pump to be sure it rotates freely.
4. Install as described in preceding section, using a new gasket.

Water Pump Disassembly

All Models

1. Drain cooling and remove water pump as described previously.
2. If applicable, remove fan pulley nut and washer.
3. Remove pulley from shaft by pressing or by using a puller.
4. On BD and BG series engines, remove screws and cover plate from impeller end of housing.
5. Remove clip retaining ring from pulley end of shaft.
6. Supporting housing assembly on arbor press, push shaft forward, removing impeller, bearing(s), shaft slinger and seal.
7. If bearing is of smooth type, it

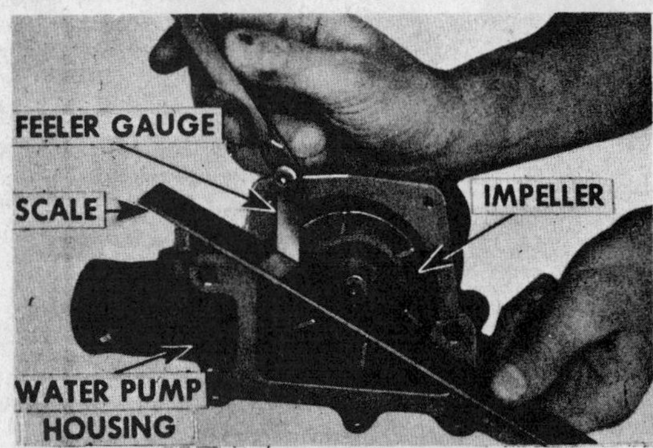

Checking water pump cover to impeller clearance
(© International Harvester Co.)

Water pump impeller parts BD282 & 308 engines
(© International Harvester Co.)

Water pump mounting OHV4 engines
(© International Harvester Co.)

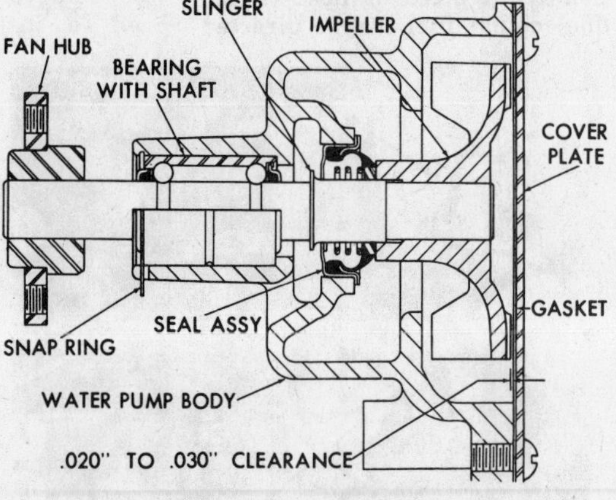

Water pump cross section —typical BD & BG engines
(© International Harvester Co.)

Water pump removal—RD engines
(© International Harvester Co.)

INTERNAL
BY-PASS PORT
ENGINE BLOCK
WATER PUMP
Water pump removal—PT6 engines
(© International Harvester Co.)

cannot be removed from shaft and whole shaft assembly must be replaced if they are damaged. If roller bearings are worn, remove them with a press or puller.

8. On pumps from BD-282, 308 engines, remove snap ring from impeller assembly and take out washer, seal, spring guide, spring and clamp ring.
9. Clean and examine all parts for damage and wear to determine which need replacement.

Water Pump Assembly

Water pump assembly is the reverse of the above procedure except for the following variations.

1. For engine models BD-220, 240, 264 and BG-220, 241, 265, after pressing new seal in body and fan hub (small end out) onto shaft, install shaft, slinger, bearing and fan hub from front end as a unit. Install clip ring in fan end of body and press on impeller. Measure clearance of impeller-to-cover (.020-.030″) and correct if necessary. Install new cover gasket and cover.
2. Model BD-282, 308: Assemble bearings, slinger and lock rings on shaft end, after filling bearing cavity with grease, press shaft assembly into body as a unit. Assemble seal components into impeller and press impeller assembly onto shaft. Press on pulley and install cover with new gasket.

Engine

Positive Crankcase Ventilation Valve

The same PCV valve is used on all engines except the PT-6 and RD series. On V-8 engines it is located in the ventilation line which runs from the intake manifold to the top rear of the crankcase. On RD engines a different PCV valve is mounted on the intake manifold. Another different PCV valve is mounted on the valve cover of the PT-6 engine. These valves should be replaced every 10,000 miles. The direction of ventilation flow is always towards the manifold or carburetor.

Engine Removal

The following is an outline of general engine removal. Removal procedure will vary from truck to truck due to the variety of body models and accessory equipment. Before lifting out engine be certain that everything has been disconnected. Remove anything that might be in the way of the actual lifting.

1. Drain water from radiator and engine block.
2. Drain crankcase oil.
3. Disconnect battery ground cable and remove cable clamp from

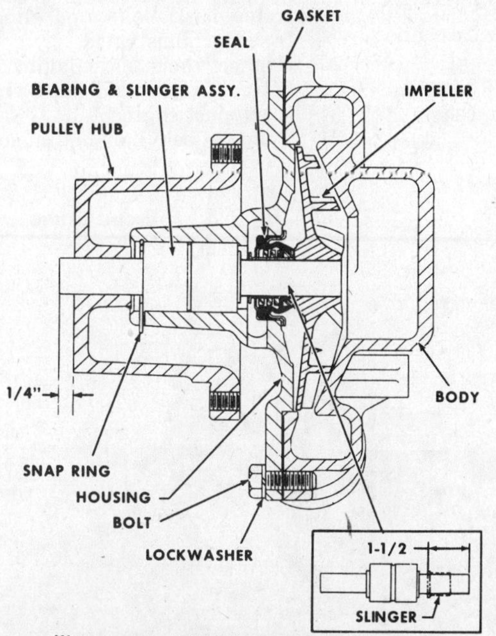

Water pump—V-266, 304, 345 & 392 engines
(© International Harvester Co.)

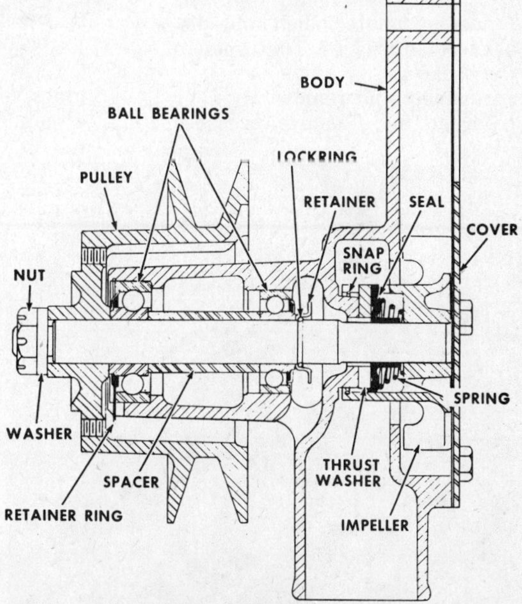

Water pump cover to impeller clearance —BG engines
(© International Harvester Co.)

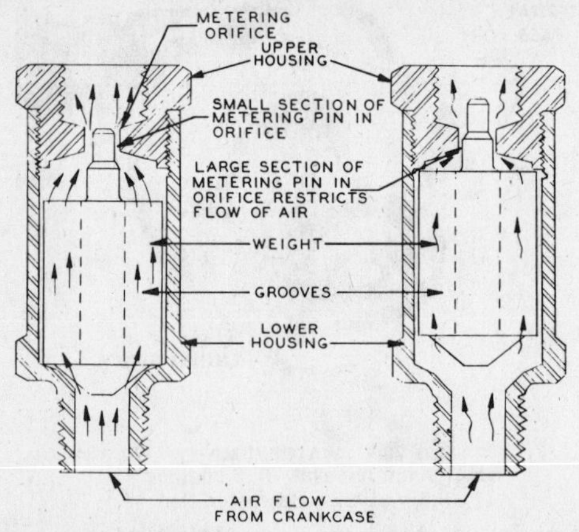

PCV valve RD engines
(© International Harvester Co.)

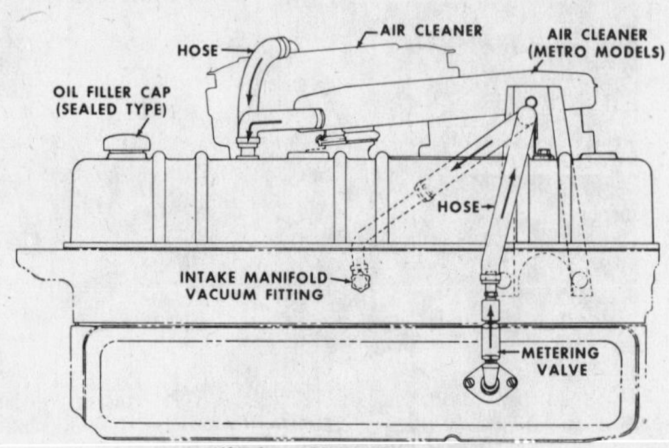

PCV system—BD & BG engines
(© International Harvester Co.)

hot terminal of battery.
4. Remove all water hoses to radiator and heater.
5. Remove fan blades and fan shroud.
6. Remove any radiator cross-brace rods or brackets.
7. Remove radiator mounting bolts and lift out radiator. WARNING: On vehicles with LPG fuel systems observe all safety precautions. Be sure shop procedures are in compliance with local fire regulations. Close all tank valves and exhaust fuel from lines before working on fuel system.
8. On conventional chassis, remove hood hinge bracket mounting bolts and remove hood assembly. On CO models, tilt cab forward and prop securely. On cab-forward models, remove all front end sheet metal: bumper, fenders, radiator shell and disconnect any wiring that goes to these parts.
9. Disconnect and remove air filter from engine. Remove breather hose from air cleaner, if applicable.
10. Disconnect fuel pump inlet line.
11. Remove vacuum lines from manifold and lines from air compressor, if applicable.
12. Disconnect throttle linkage, choke control wire and hand throttle control wire, if applicable. On V-266, 304, 345, 392 engines the carburetor must be removed for the fitting of the lifting fixture.
13. If so equipped, disconnect wire from heater control valve.
14. Disconnect all wiring from engine:
    a. Water temperature gauge sender.
    b. Oil pressure gauge sender.
    c. Generator wires.
    d. Primary ignition wire to resistor.
    e. Starter solenoid wires and battery cable.
15. On V(S)-401, 461, 478, 549 engines, loosen alternator belts and disconnect alternator strap bracket to swing alternator away from thermostat housing. Then remove thermostats and housing.
16. If so equipped, remove tachometer drive at the distributor on the small V-8—or at the rear of the block on the big V-8.
17. Disconnect exhaust pipes at manifolds.
18. If so equipped, remove automatic transmission filler tube, freon compressor lines and disconnect power steering pump line and hose.
19. Install lifting fixtures and suitable sling. On the V(S)-401, 461, 478, 549 engines an eye bolt is installed at rear of intake manifold and a plate where the thermostat was mounted. On V-266, 304, 345, 392 models the lifting fixture is mounted on the intake manifold where the carburetor was removed. On six cylinder engines two brackets are secured by the two extreme head bolts and sling attached as illustrated.
20. Connect hoisting equipment to lifting fixture and hoist enough to support engine.
21. Remove bell housing mounting

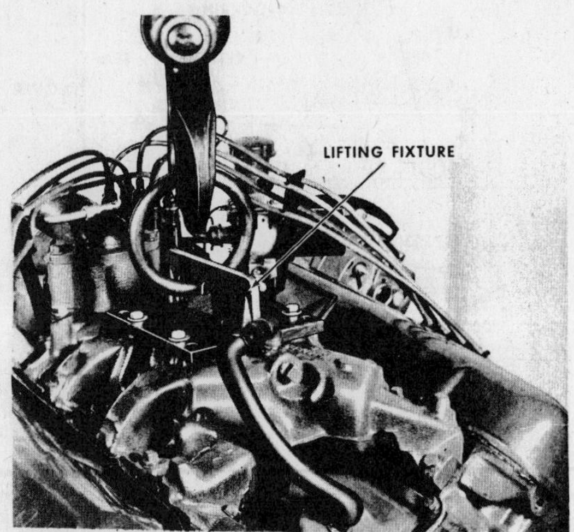

Engine lifting sling—V8 engines
(© International Harvester Co.)

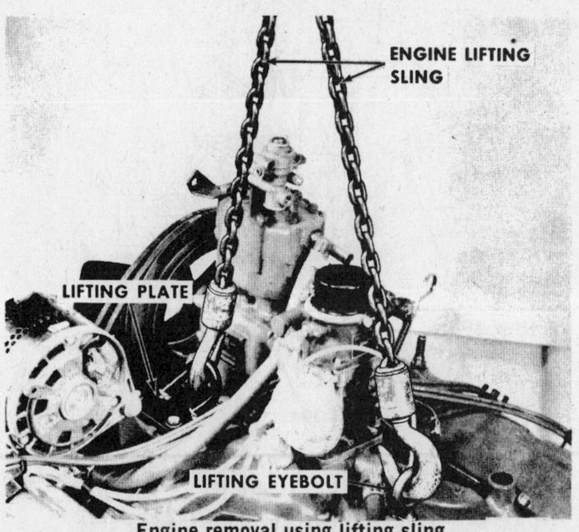

Engine removal using lifting sling
(© International Harvester Co.)

bolts. On the PT-6 and V-8 engines the flywheel housing front cover is removed before the flywheel housing is removed from crankcase. On the BD-282, 308 engines the transmission is unbolted from the bell housing. On vehicles with RD engines the floor panel is removed to provide access to the bolts securing bell housing.

22. Disconnect clutch linkage.
23. Remove front engine mounting bolts. On some models it is easier to unbolt the mount from the frame crossmember.
24. Remove side engine mount bolts.
25. In hoisting out engine, first pull engine forward to clear clutch assembly from transmission, then tilt front up and carefully out of the chassis. CAUTION: Avoid damaging clutch driven disc.
26. Installation of the engine is in general the reverse of the above described procedure. Be careful when installing that wires are not pinched between engine and frame. Lower the engine until transmission main drive gear spline can be aligned with the clutch driven disc. The weight of the engine must remain supported until the bell housing is secured to flywheel housing. After engine has been secured to chassis, remove hoisting equipment and lifting fixtures.

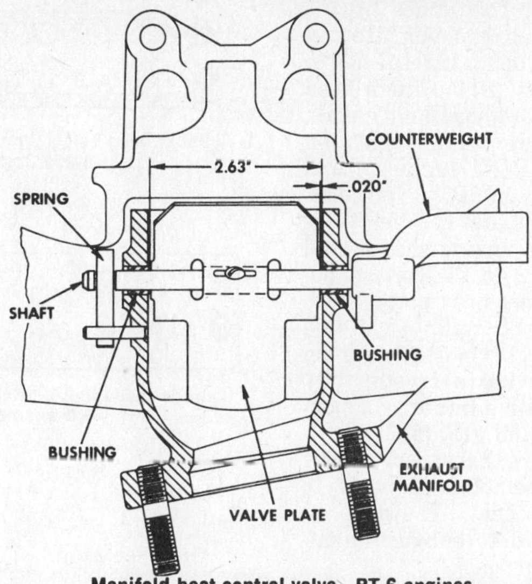

Manifold heat control valve—PT-6 engines
(© International Harvester Co.)

Manifolds

Intake Manifold Removal

4 Cylinder and V8 Engines

1. If engine is in vehicle, remove air cleaner and, if applicable, governor vacuum line.
2. Disconnect throttle linkage, choke cable and fuel line.
3. Remove carburetor.
4. On V-266, 304, 345, 392 engines, disconnect hose from thermostat housing and bracket for spark plug wires.
5. On 4 cylinder models, remove coil, coil mounting bracket and ignition resistor from intake manifold.
6. Remove positive crankcase ventilation pipe and vacuum line.
7. Remove mounting bolts, manifold and gasket.
8. Installation is the reverse of the above procedure. Install new gaskets and tighten the mounting bolts from the center out, torquing to 40-45 ft. lbs.

Exhaust Manifold Removal

4 Cylinder and V8 Engines

1. Disconnect exhaust pipe from manifold.
2. Unbolt exhaust manifold from head.
3. Remove manifold.
4. Installation is the reverse of the above procedure. Install new manifold-to-head gasket and new manifold-to-pipe gasket.
5. Torque manifold-to-head bolts to 40-45 ft. lbs.

Manifolds Removal

6 Cylinder Engines

1. Remove exhaust pipe from manifold.
2. Disconnect PCV line and vacuum lines from intake manifold.
3. Disconnect throttle linkage, fuel line and choke cable from carburetor.
4. Remove air filter and carburetor.
5. Remove exhaust/intake manifold unit and gaskets.
6. Separate intake from exhaust manifold.
7. The PT-6, BD-220, 240, 264, and BG-220, 241, 265 engines are equipped with a manifold heat control valve in the exhaust manifold. To remove this valve, first note position of counterweight in relation to valve plate. Remove thermostatic spring from end of shaft. With a hack saw blade or cutting torch, cut

Intake manifold removal OHV4 & V8 engines
(© International Harvester Co.)

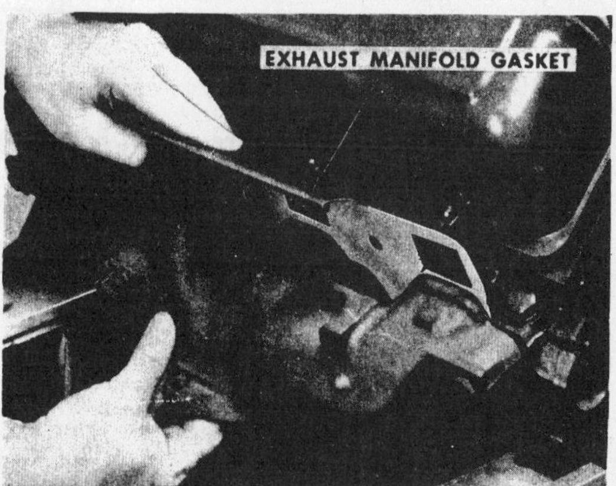

Exhaust manifold removal OHV4 & V8 engines
(© International Harvester Co.)

the shaft on both sides of the valve plate and remove plate and shaft pieces, being careful not to ruin bushings. If bushings need replacement, remove and install, spacing them .3175-.3185″ on BD and BG engines and .3120-.3130″ on PT-6 engines. With valve plate in the "heat on" position, insert shaft, hold counterweight in the correct position and secure plate with screw or tack weld (BD and BG). Install thermostatic spring and hook spring over stop pin. Lubricate with a mixture of penetrating oil and graphite.

8. Intake and exhaust manifolds must be assembled properly to insure alignment. Position intake manifold to exhaust manifold using new gasket.
9. Install nuts and bolts holding the two manifolds together but do not tighten.
10. Position manifolds to cylinder head with intake manifold pilot rings in place and install mounting bolts, but do not tighten.
11. Tighten nuts and bolts which hold manifolds together, torquing to 25-28 ft. lbs.
12. Tighten manifold mounting bolts, torquing to 25-28 ft. lbs.

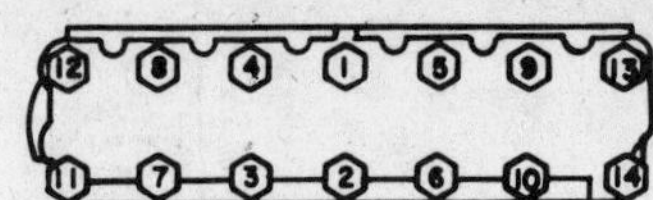

Cylinder head bolt tightening sequence—PT-6-232 engines

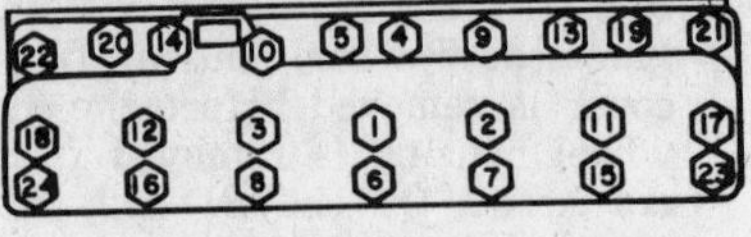

Cylinder head bolt tightening sequence—BD269, 282 & 308 engines

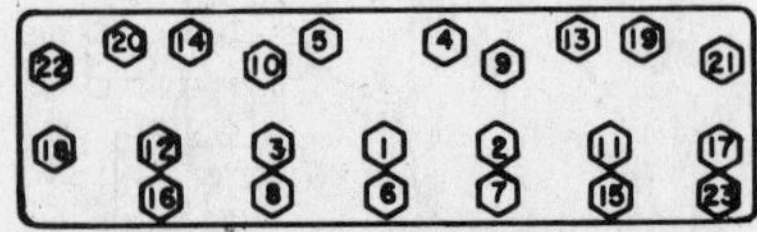

Cylinder head bolt tightening sequence—RD engines

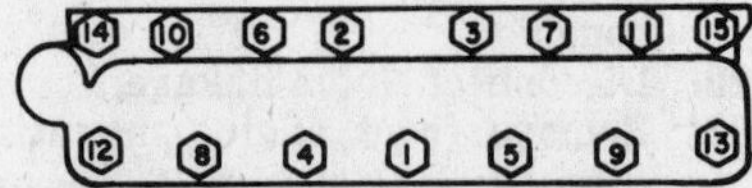

Cylinder head bolt tightening sequence—220, 240, 264, BG220, 241 & 265 engines

Cylinder Head

Cylinder Head Removal

6 Cylinder Engines

1. If the engine is to remain in the vehicle, first do the following: Drain cooling system, disconnect water hose(s) and disconnect the fuel line from the carburetor. On the PT-6 engine, positive crankcase ventilation and vacuum advance lines must also be removed. In some cases, depending on the model, various accessory or other equipment may have to be removed.
2. Disconnect spark plug wires and, if applicable, remove wires from bracket on cylinder head. Identify cylinder number of each wire with tags or marks.
3. Disconnect ignition coil wires and remove coil from cylinder head.
4. Remove manifolds as described in preceding section.
5. On BD and BG engines, disconnect water by-pass hose at cylinder head and remove water pump as described in preceding section.
6. Remove rocker arm cover bolts and remove rocker arm cover and gasket. If there are any dowel sleeves in brackets, note their location.
7. Remove push rods and keep them in order so that they may be replaced in the same locations.
8. Remove cylinder head bolts, marking any odd length or oil feed bolts for proper reinstallation.
9. Remove cylinder head and gasket.
10. Installation is the reverse order of the above instructions. Be sure to note the following steps where applicable.
11. Align new head gasket with bolt holes and carefully place cylinder head into position without damaging or shifting gasket.
12. Install all short head bolts and flat washers, but do not tighten.
13. On the PT-6 engine, apply No. 2 Permatex or equivalent sealant to the threads of the long (4¼″) bolt at position "11". On this engine, proceed to tighten the head bolts to 80-85 ft. lbs. torque in the sequence illustrated. Tighten in approximately 20 ft. lb. steps until proper torque readings are obtained.
14. Install push rods into original positions.
15. Install rocker arm assembly, installing any dowel sleeves which were removed. On BD and BG engines, rocker arm bolts serve as head bolts and all should be tightened in the sequence illustrated at this point. Tighten to 85-95 ft. lbs. torque, except on BD-282 and 308 engines (100-110 ft. lbs.).
16. On RD engines, leave the long oil bolt out and tighten only the short head bolts to 100-110 ft. lbs. torque.
17. On the PT-6 engine, the long rocker arm assembly mounting bolt is placed in the fifth (next to rear) position. Tighten rocker arm assembly mounting bolts to 20-23 ft. lbs. torque, inner first, then outer.
18. On RD engines, insert drilled oil bolt in special oil connector and tighten rocker arm shaft mounting bolts to 25-30 ft. lbs. torque. Be sure to install those bolts with the cover mounting studs in the correct position. Note lock washers which key into end brackets.
19. Adjust rocker to valve clearance. See the following section, "Valve Clearance Adjustment," for correct procedure. The PT-6 engine has hydraulic lifters and cannot be adjusted. See Unit Repair

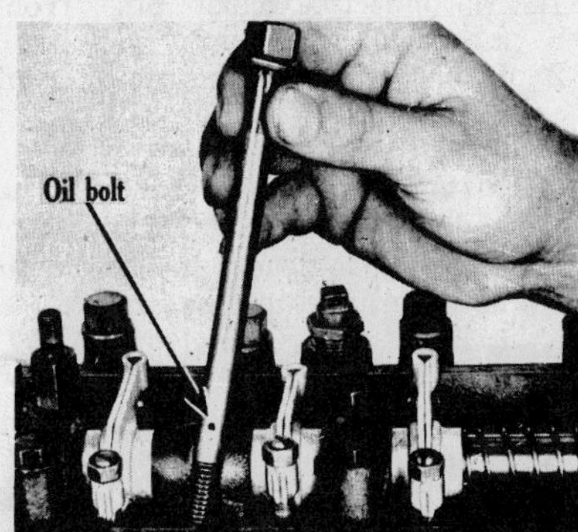

Rocker arm shaft oil feed bolt—RD engines
(© International Harvester Co.)

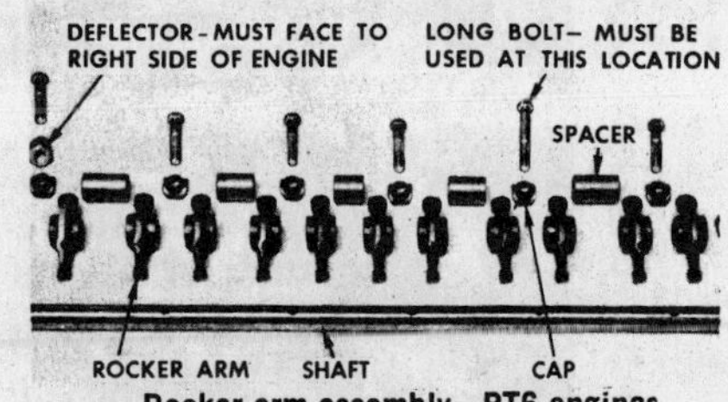

Rocker arm assembly—PT6 engines
(© International Harvester Co.)

Section for hydraulic lifter service operations.

20. Reinstall any components which were removed and have not yet been put back. Replace rocker cover gasket if necessary.

Cylinder Head Removal

V-8 and 4 Cylinder Engines

1. Remove intake and exhaust manifolds as described in preceding section. On V-8's, this may entail removal of the air compressor and air compressor mounting bracket.
2. Head removal is facilitated by the use of a lifting sling which is attached with bolts in the intake manifold mounting bolt holes.
3. Remove cylinder head covers and gaskets.
4. Loosen rocker arm shaft bracket bolts and remove the rocker arm assembly. NOTE: Be sure to remove and keep track of the two dowel sleeves on the end brackets of the rocker arm assembly.
5. Remove pushrods, marking them so that they may be installed in their same locations.
6. Remove spark plug wires.
7. Remove cylinder head bolts.
8. When lifting off cylinder, do not lose the two locating dowel sleeves.
9. Installation is basically the reverse of the above procedure, with the exception of the following additional steps.
10. Be sure to use a new head gasket and to reinstall dowel sleeves when positioning the head and mounting the rocker assembly. Reinstall pushrods in their original locations.
11. On 4-152, 196 and V-266, 304, 345, 392, turn engine crankshaft until leading edge of balance weight on crankshaft pulley is aligned with the zero degree mark on the timing indicator before installing rocker arm assembly.

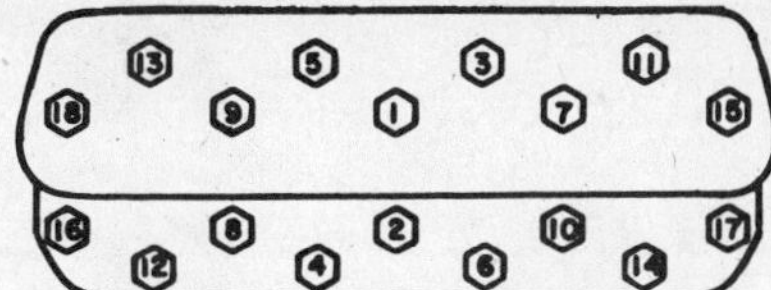

Cylinder head bolt tightening sequence—401, 561 & 549 engines

12. On 4-152, 196 engines, be sure to install rocker assembly so that the oil feed shaft bracket is third from the rear.
13. On V-266, 304, 345, 392 engines, install rocker arm assembly so that the notches at the end of the shaft are facing upward. Oil feed brackets are third from the rear on the right (even numbers) bank and third from the front on the left (odd numbers) bank.
14. On the V(S)-401, 478, 549 engines, rocker arm assembly mounting bolts serve as head bolts and are tightened in the head bolt torque sequence. Torque head bolts in the sequence pattern illustrated to 80-90 ft. lbs. torque. CAUTION: Do not use a power wrench on heads of engines with hydraulic lifters. Torque head bolts slowly so that

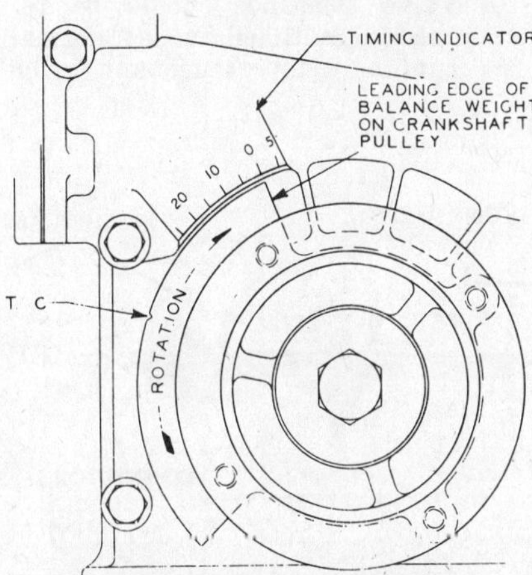

Correct pulley location for installing pushrods—OHV-4 & small V8 engines
(© International Harvester Co.)

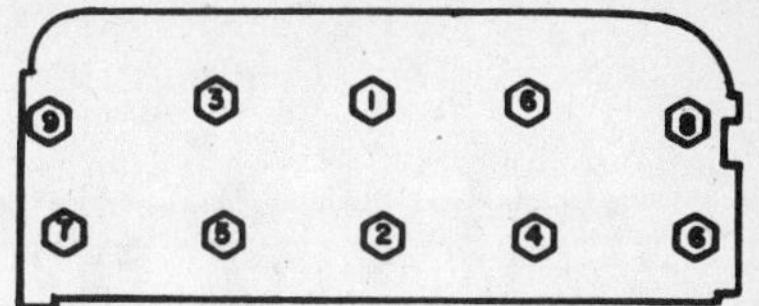

Cylinder head bolt tightening sequence—4-152, 196, V-266, 304, 345 & 392 engines

the leakdown of the lifters may relieve strain from the valve train.

15. On 4-152, 196 and V-266, 304, 345, 392 engines, tighten the head bolts in the sequence illustrated to 90-100 ft. lbs. torque.
16. Retorque head bolts to the specified torque after 1000 miles of operation.
17. Install rocker covers and any other equipment removed for head work. Replace rocker cover gasket if necessary.

Valves

Valve Rotators

RD Engines

Exhaust valves on RD engines have a special stem and valve cap which permit the valve to rotate for an instant during each cycle. The clearance between the valve cap and the valve stem is critical for service life of the valve. The clearance is measured with a special gauge as illustrated. Grind bottom of valve cap to decrease clearance. To increase clearance, grind top of valve stem. If valve keys are removed they must be reinstalled with the wear on the top side.

Valve Train Service

Reference

The PT-6, 4-152, 4-196 and V-8 engines utilized hydraulic lifters for which there is no lash adjustment. Excess noise in the valve train of these engines indicates that service is required. Instructions for servicing

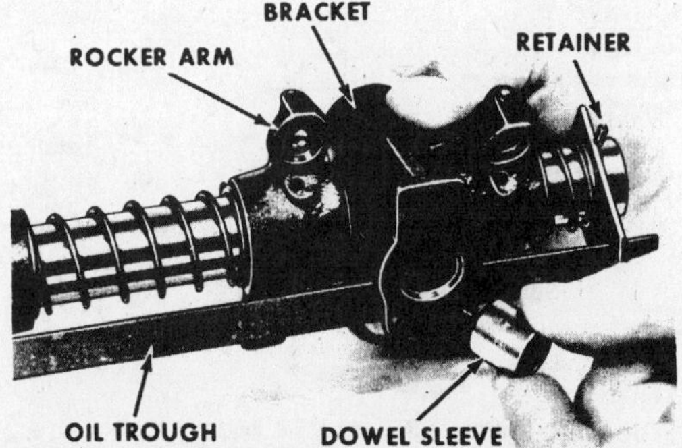

Rocker arm shaft dowel sleeve—OHV-4 and V8 engines
(© International Harvester Co.)

Cylinder head dowel sleeve location—OHV-4 and V8 engines
(© International Harvester Co.)

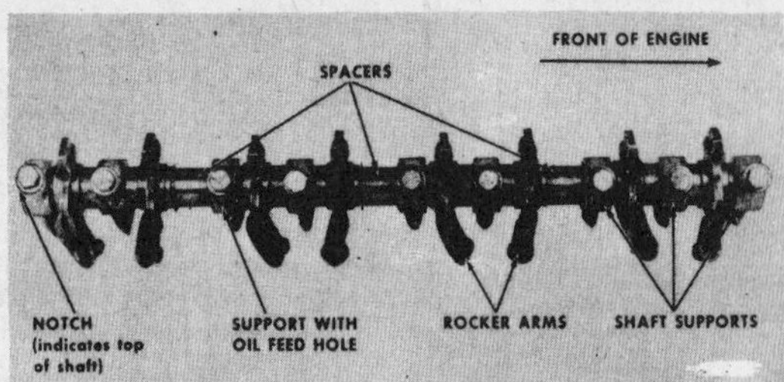

Rocker arm assembly—and V8 engines
(© International Harvester Co.)

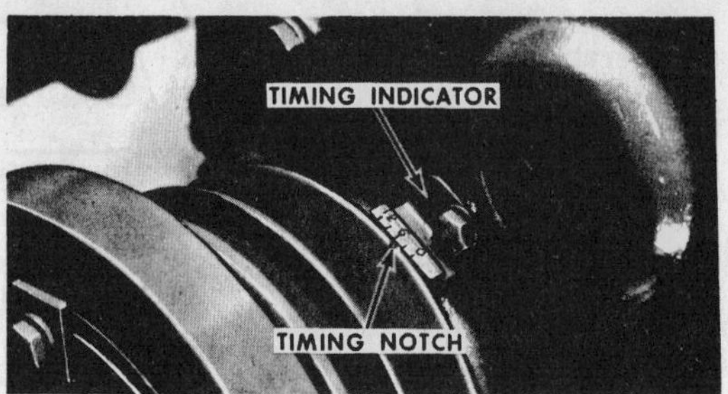

Timing mark alignment for valve adjustment
(© International Harvester Co.)

hydraulic lifters may be found in the General Repair Section.

Valve removal, service, and installation procedures may be found in the Engine Rebuilding Section. See Specifications table at the beginning of this section for valve spring and valve seat angle specifications.

Valve Adjustment

BD, BG and RD Engines

1. Remove valve rocker cover and gasket.
2. Rotate crankshaft until No. 1 cylinder is at top dead center of the compression stroke (both valves closed). Timing marks on the crankshaft pulley of RD and BD-282, 308 engines should be aligned for zero degrees (TDC). On all other 6 cylinder engines the timing marks are located on the flywheel.
3. Clearance is adjusted on both valves. Loosen lock nut.
4. Holding the proper feeler gauge between adjusting screw on the end of the rocker arm and the valve stem, turn adjusting screw until specified clearance is obtained (feeler gauge just held snugly).
5. While holding adjusting screw, tighten lock nut.
6. Recheck clearance.
7. Rotate crankshaft ⅓ turn so that No. 5 cylinder is at top dead center of compression stroke and repeat Steps 3 to 6.
8. Repeat for each cylinder following the sequence of the firing order.
9. Replace rocker cover, using a new gasket if necessary.
10. Valve clearance should be rechecked with engine at normal running temperature and after 500 miles when new or reground valves have been installed.

Rocker Arm Removal

1. Remove rocker cover and gasket.
2. Remove rocker arm assembly mounting bolts and flat washers.
3. Remove rocker assembly.
4. If applicable, remove clip-ring and retainer to disassemble rocker components. On BD-220, 240, 264 and BG-220, 241, 264 engines, drive roll pin from end brackets to remove components. Be sure to keep all parts in order so that they may be replaced in their original positions.
5. Clean all parts thoroughly, making sure that oil passages are clear. If necessary to remove plugs from ends of shaft, drill a hole in one plug, knock out the other with a steel rod, then knock out the drilled plug.

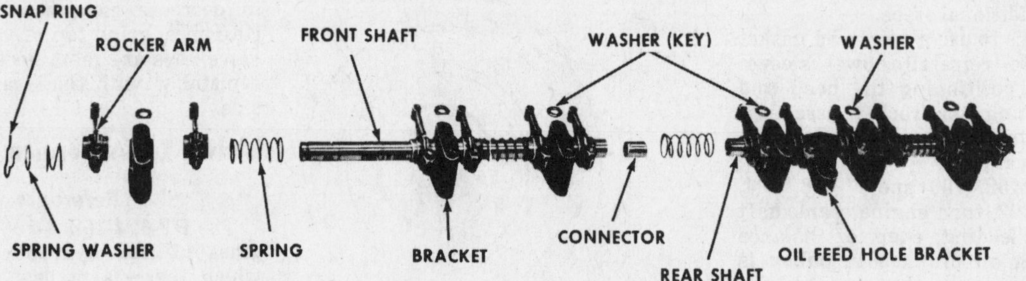

Rocker arm assembly—RD engines (© International Harvester Co.)

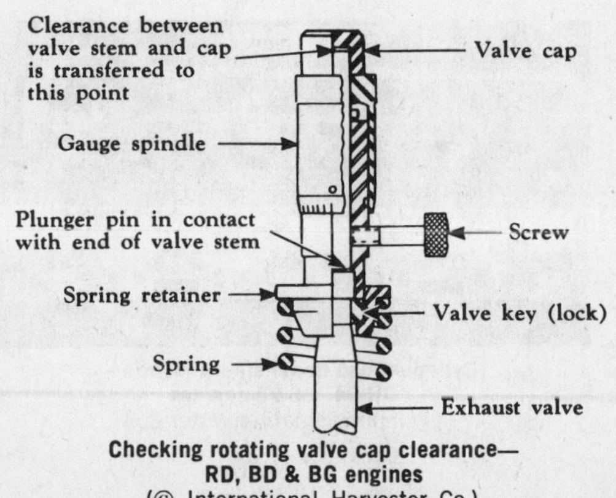

Checking rotating valve cap clearance—RD, BD & BG engines
(© International Harvester Co.)

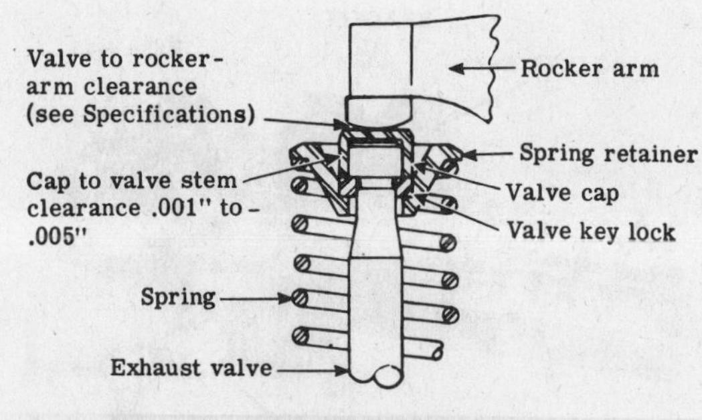

Valve rotators RD, BD & BG engines
(© International Harvester Co.)

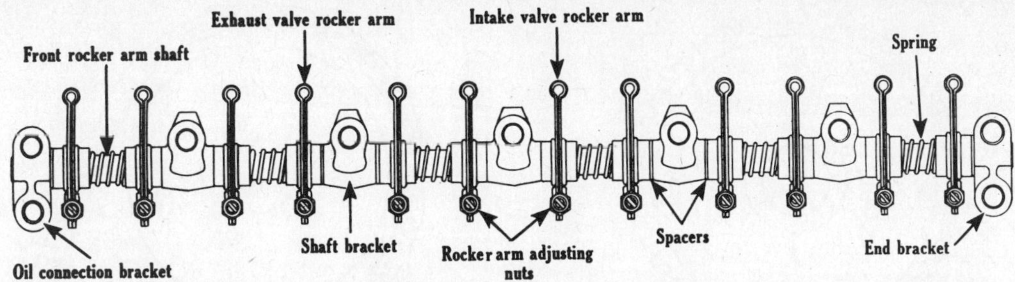

Rocker arm assembly—BD-282 & 308 engines (© International Harvester Co.)

6. Inspect shaft for wear and warpage. Replace bent or worn shaft.
7. On engines without hydraulic lifters (all 6 cyclinder except the PT-6), inspect rocker arm adjusting screws for wear at the contact surface and for damaged threads. Replace any that are defective.
8. Inspect rocker arm shaft bushings for wear. On V(S)-401, 461, 478, 549 and early V-266, 304, 345 engines the rocker arm bushings may be pressed out and new bushings pressed in. On all other engines the bushing is integral with the rocker arm, and if the bushing is worn, the whole rocker arm must be replaced.
9. Inspect valve stem contact pad surfaces of rocker arm and resurface if wear is excessive. Do not remove more than .010″ of material when resurfacing.
10. If applicable, replace any defective tension springs.
11. Remove and inspect push rods one by one (to insure original position). Roll them on a flat surface to check for straightness. Replace any pushrods that are bent, have loose ends or are worn.
12. Reassemble all rocker arm assembly components in their original order. On RD engines, note that lock washers key into shaft and the end brackets.
13. Install rocker arm assembly, making sure that the oil feed bracket is in the proper position and that dowel sleeves are in place. On 4-152, 196 and V-266, 304, 345, 392 engines turn the crankshaft until leading edge of balance weight on crankshaft pulley is aligned with the zero degree mark on the timing indicator before installing rocker arm assembly.
14. Tighten mounting bolts.
15. Adjust rocker arm to valve stem clearance as described above.
16. Install rocker cover, replacing gasket if necessary.

Timing Case & Gears

Crankshaft Pulley Removal

Accessibility of the crankcase pulley and front (timing) cover will vary according to the model. On some vehicles the timing case will be accessible only if the engine is completely removed. The following instructions are general and apply to most front cover repairs and service.

1. Drain cooling system.
2. Disconnect radiator hoses and remove radiator. In some cases the radiator shroud and truck hood must be removed.
3. Loosen front engine mounts and jack up engine enough to provide access to the crankshaft pulley with a puller.
4. Loosen and remove fan belts and remove fan blades.
5. Remove crankshaft pulley retaining bolt. On V(S)-401, 461, 478, 549 engines, scribe a line alongside the timing indicator and remove the indicator from front cover. The line is for reassembly purposes.
6. Using a suitable puller, remove the pulley from the crankshaft. On some models the pulley is in two pieces and the pulley must be unbolted from its hub before the hub is removed with a puller.

Front Oil Seal Removal

1. Remove crankshaft pulley as described in Steps 1 through 6 above.
2. Remove seal. It is preferable to use an appropriate seal puller. On BD-220, 240, 264 and BG-220, 241, 265 engines it will be necessary to remove the tim-

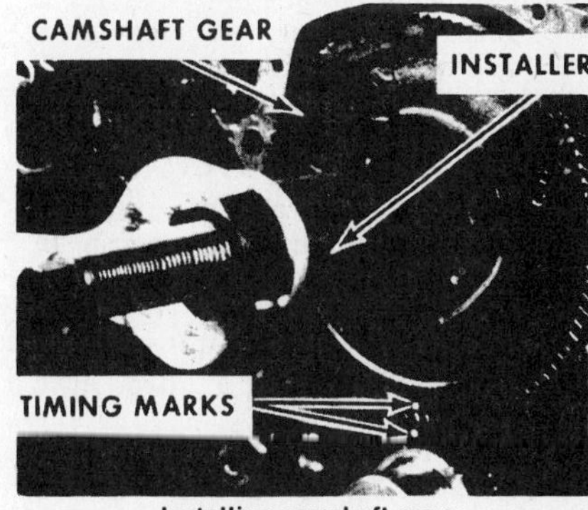

Installing camshaft gear
(© International Harvester Co.)

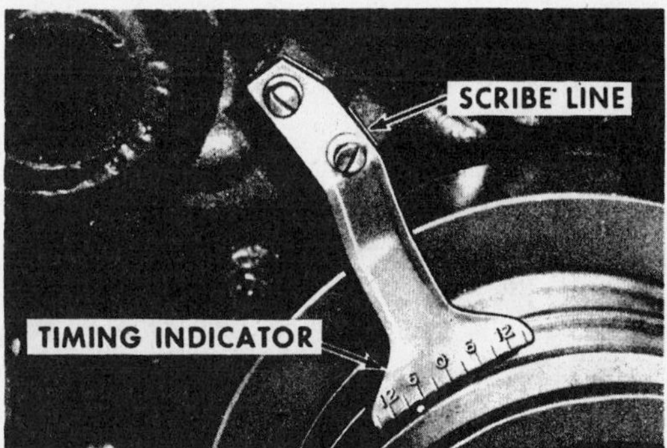

Marking exact position of timing indicator—V8 engines
(© International Harvester Co.)

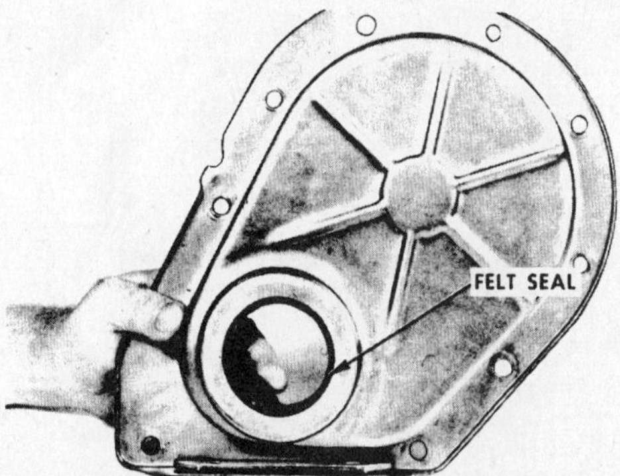

Installing front cover oil seal—BD & BG engines
(© International Harvester Co.)

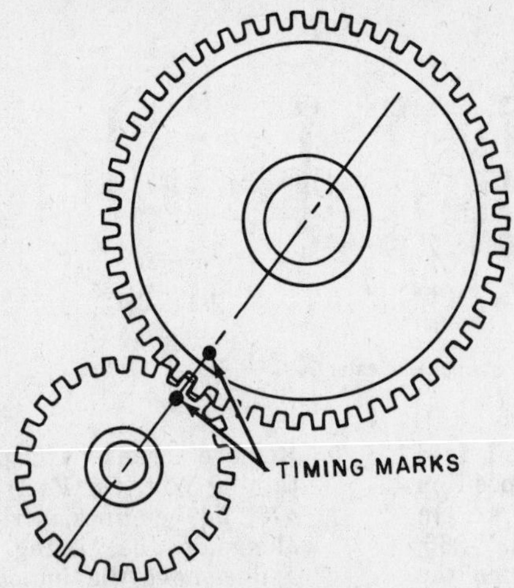

Timing gear alignment marks except PT6 engines

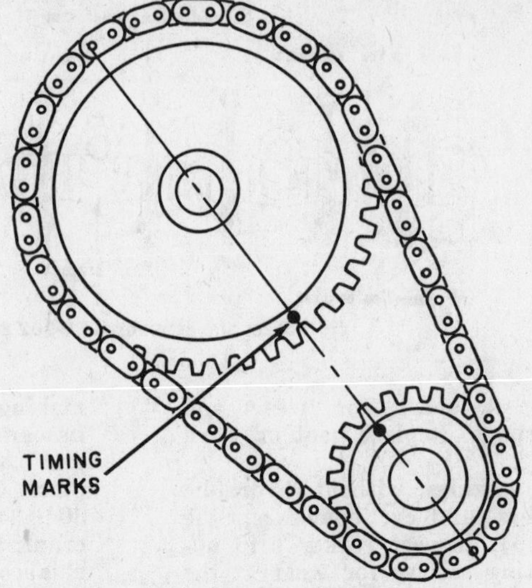

Timing gear alignment marks PT6 engines

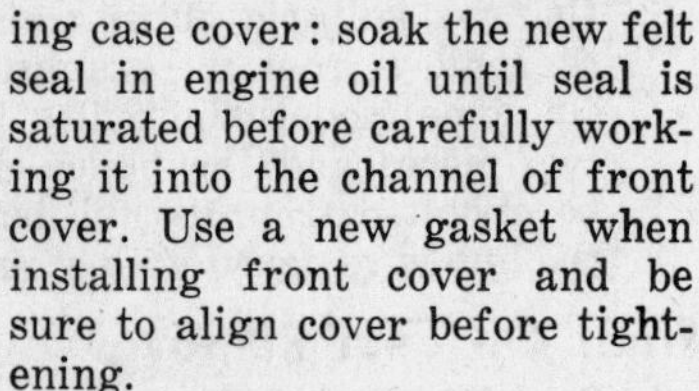

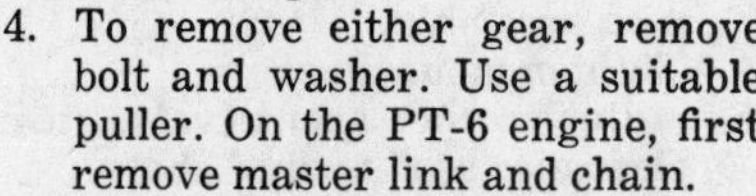

ing case cover: soak the new felt seal in engine oil until seal is saturated before carefully working it into the channel of front cover. Use a new gasket when installing front cover and be sure to align cover before tightening.

3. Install a new seal using a suitable seal installing tool if possible. Lubricate first and be careful not to damage seal or seating surface of cover.
4. Install crankshaft pulley, fan belt and fan blades.
5. Lower engine and tighten mounting bolts.
6. Install radiator, shroud, hoses and whatever else was removed.
7. Fill cooling system.

Timing Gear Removal

Timing gears can be removed without disassembling the engine. In some cases, however, the engine must be removed.

1. Remove crankcase pulley as described in Steps 1 through 6 above.
2. Remove engine front cover.
3. Rotate engine to align timing marks on crankshaft gear and camshaft gear.
4. To remove either gear, remove bolt and washer. Use a suitable puller. On the PT-6 engine, first remove master link and chain.
5. Use a suitable installing tool to install gears. Lubricate with engine oil and insert key in shaft to align gear. Align timing marks as illustrated. Be careful not to damage threads on shaft. Install and tighten retaining bolt.
6. Rotate engine to check that gears are not binding.
7. Check gear backlash with a dial indicator. It should be within .004-.007″ on OHV6 engines and .0005-.0045″ on OHV4 and V8 engines.
8. Use a new gasket when installing front cover and be sure to align cover before tightening. On some models there is an oil slinger on the crankshaft.
9. Install crankshaft pulley, belt and fan blades. Tighten retaining bolt.
10. Lower engine and tighten engine mounting bolts.
11. Install radiator and hoses.
12. Fill cooling system.

Camshaft Removal

1. Remove cylinder head as described previously in "Cylinder Head R&R."
2. Remove pushrods and tappets. On RD engines the tappets are of the mushroom type and must be removed from the bottom. In order that they be out of the way for removing camshaft, either the engine must be turned upside down or they must be pushed up until the spring loaded retainers snap into a groove in the tappet.
3. Remove crankshaft pulley as described above.
4. Remove distributor and fuel pump.
5. Remove oil pan and oil pump.
6. Remove front (timing) cover.
7. Remove two screws which secure the camshaft thrust flange to the crankcase.
8. Remove camshaft and gear. To prevent nicking and damaging camshaft it is best to use a cam-

Timing gear installation—BD282 & 308 engines
(© International Harvester Co.)

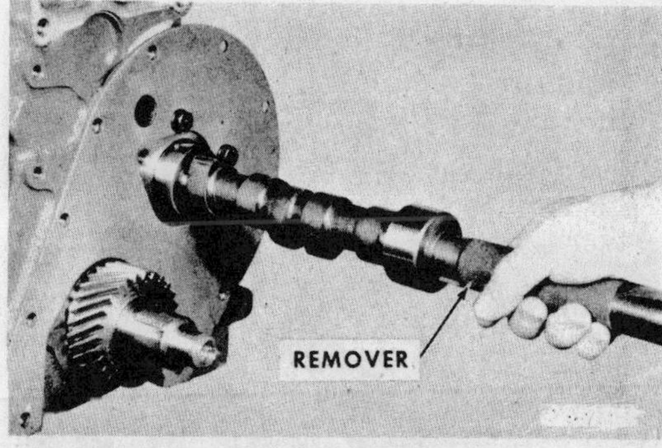

Removing camshaft
(© International Harvester Co.)

shaft removing tool.

9. When installing camshaft and gear coat the bearing surfaces and lobes with lubricant and use an installing tool if possible. Make sure the timing marks are aligned.
10. Working through the two large holes in the gear, insert the two thrust flange screws and tighten them to the specified torque.
11. Check timing gear backlash. If the end play exceeds the limits listed in Specifications, replace thrust flange.
12. Place oil slinger over end of crankshaft.
13. Install front cover using a new gasket. Be sure to align cover before tightening cover bolts to specified torque.
14. Install crankshaft pulley, tightening pulley retaining bolt to specified torque.
15. Install cylinder head (see "Cylinder Head R&R").
16. Install fan belt, fan blades, fuel pump and distributor.
17. Install oil pump and oil pan.
18. If engine was raised, lower engine and tighten engine mounts to specified torque.

Pistons and Connecting Rods

Reference

For piston and connecting rod overhaul procedures see Engine Rebuilding General Section. Bearings are fitted and their clearances checked in the usual manner.

Piston Removal

1. Remove oil pan and oil pump. On some models this may require loosening the engine mounts and jacking up the engine until spacer blocks can be installed. When removing oil pump on big V8's turn crank until counter weight is out of the way.

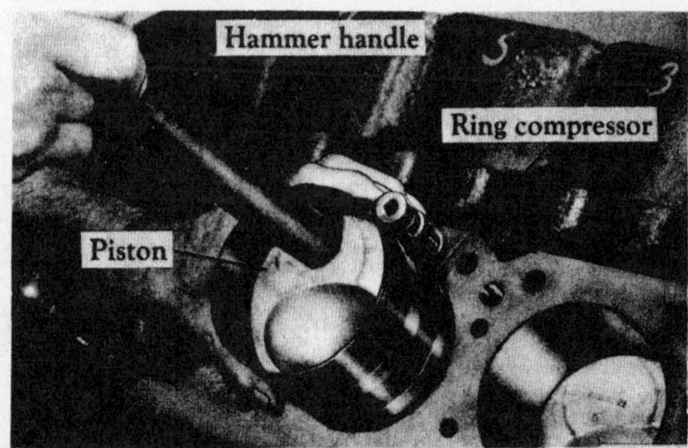

Piston installation
(© International Harvester Co.)

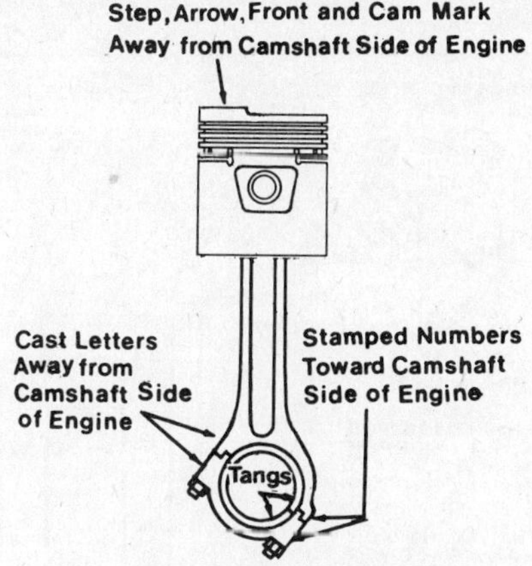

Piston & rod assembly—RD engines
(© International Harvester Co.)

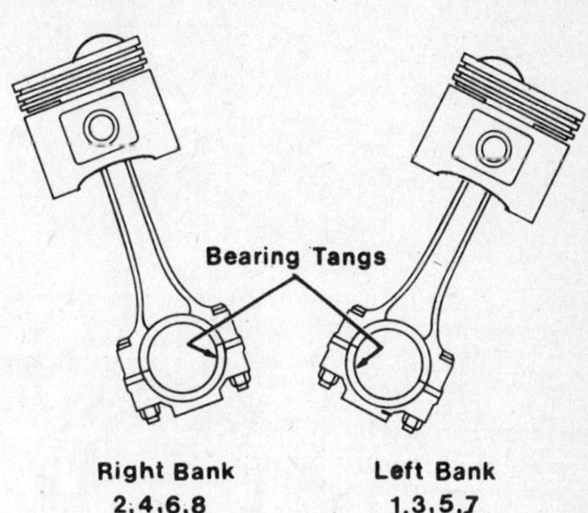

Correct assembly of piston & rods—V8 engines
(© International Harvester Co.)

2. Remove cylinder head. See "Cylinder Head R&R" above.
3. Using a ridge reamer, remove the ridge from the top of the cylinders.
4. Rotate the crankshaft until journal is in lowermost position for removal of connecting rod assemblies. Remove the cap and push the connecting rod and piston up through the cylinder bore. Replace the cap and bearing inserts on the rods so the numbered sides match. The numbers indicate position.
5. To install pistons and connecting rods, rotate crankshaft until No. 1 crankpin is at the bottom of its stroke. Correctly seat rod bearing insert in rod then dip piston assembly in clean oil to lubricate rings. Using a ring compressor, install piston and rod in cylinder. Push piston in, do no strike. On the PT-6 engines, the notch on the top of piston perimeter faces toward the front of the engine (number on connecting rod toward the camshaft). On 4-152, 196 and all V8 engines the piston assembly is installed with the word "UP" toward the top (camshaft) side of the engine block. On all OVH 6 except the PT-6, install piston assembly with the arrow stamped on piston crown toward camshaft.
6. Place lower half of bearing insert in rod cap and lubricate with oil. Assemble bearing cap to connecting rod with the number side of cap on the same side as the number on the connecting rod. Lubricate threads of bolts with engine oil and install bolts, tightening to the correct torque (see Specifications at the beginning of this section).
7. Rotate crankshaft and repeat installation procedure with the rest of the pistons and connecting rods.
8. Install oil pump and oil pan, using a new pan gasket if necessary.
9. Install cylinder head as described in "Cylinder Head R&R" above.
10. If engine was raised, remove spacers and lower engine. Tighten engine mount bolts.

Piston Rings Replacement

1. Remove pistons as described above.
2. Remove both compression rings

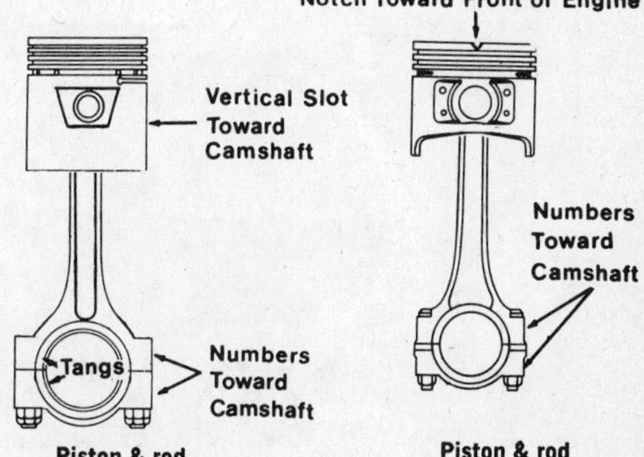

Piston & rod assembly—BD & BG engines

Piston & rod assembly PT-6—232 engines

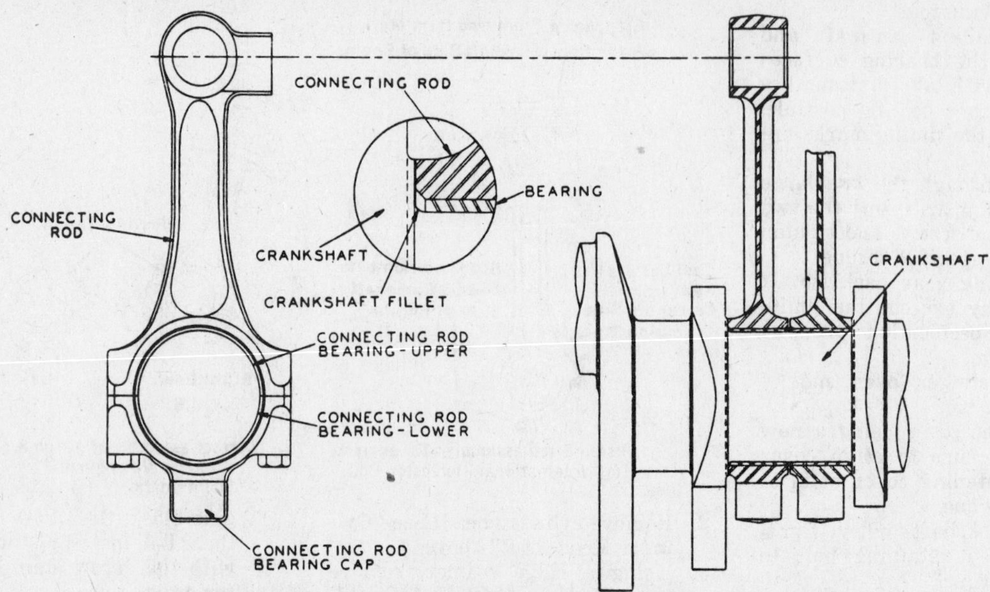

Proper installation of connecting rods to crankshaft (© International Harvester Co.)

and three-piece oil ring.

3. Using rings which correspond to the piston size (standard or oversize), check rings for gap clearance and ring-to-groove side clearance.
4. Install rings on piston with a suitable ring expander tool.
5. Install piston assembly as described above.

Main Bearing Replacement

On most models it is possible to replace main bearings without removing the engine from the vehicle. However, it is easier to do a better job with the engine removed and, if facilities are available for pulling the engine, this is the preferable method. See "Engine R&R" above. For detailed procedures on main bearing, rod bearing and crankshaft servicing see General Repair Section.

1. Remove crankshaft pulley and front (timing) cover.
2. Remove cylinder head(s) and piston assemblies.
3. If the bell housing and transmission were not removed during engine removal, remove them now.
4. On many engines the clutch plate may be compressed by installing three cap screws (3/8"-16x2½" for RD and V(S)-401, 461, 478, 549 engines or 3/8"-16x2" for V-266, 304, 345, 392 engines). If the clutch plate cannot be compressed in this way, cut three ½"x1"x3" wood blocks and insert them between the clutch fingers and back plate. Loosen backing plate mounting bolts slightly if it is difficult to insert wood blocks. A third alternative procedure for compressing the clutch plate is to insert three retaining clips as illustrated. The clutch plate is compressed during removal and installation of the clutch to prevent warpage.
5. Remove the backing plate mounting bolts and clutch assembly.
6. Remove flywheel bolts and pull off flywheel.
7. On BD-282, 308 and RD engines remove the upper and lower rear main bearing oil seal retainers.
8. Remove main bearing caps. On OHV4, V-266, 304, 345, 392, BD-220, 240, 264 and BG-220, 241, 265 engines use a rear main bearing cap puller to remove rear main bearing cap. On RD engines the lower oil seal retainer must be removed before the cap can be unbolted. Note that the caps are numbered and should be reinstalled in their original positions.
9. When installing new main bearings make sure that the oil holes are properly aligned and that bearing tangs are fitted into tang recesses. Thoroughly clean all surfaces and coat lightly with

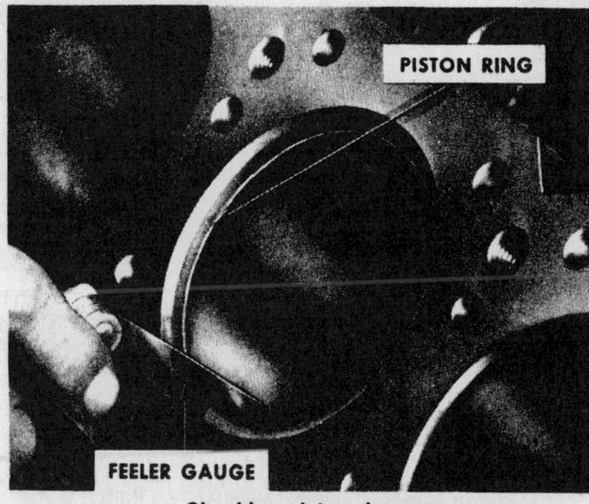

Checking piston ring gap
(© International Harvester Co.)

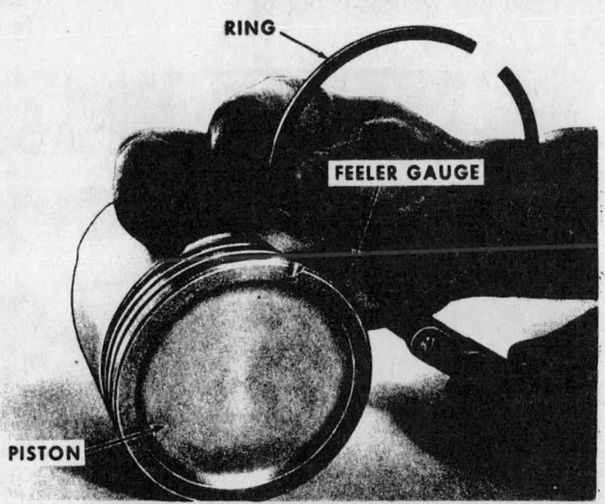

Checking ring groove clearance
(© International Harvester Co.)

Installing rear main bearing cap side oil seals
(© International Harvester Co.)

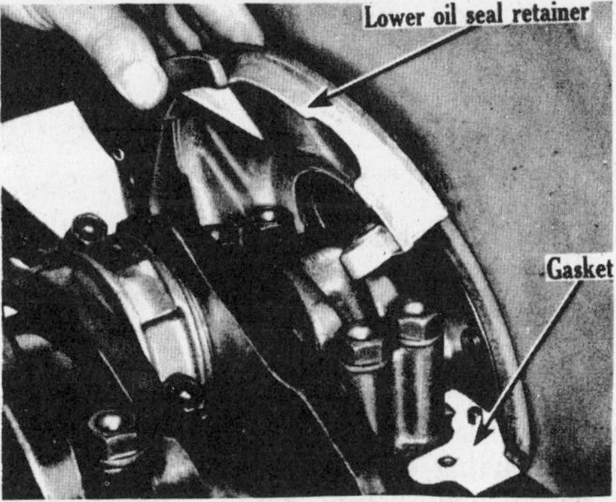

Rear main bearing oil seals—BD-282, 308 & RD engines
(© International Harvester Co.)

oil. Be sure to align timing marks when positioning crankshaft. On the PT-6 engine main bearing caps have an arrow which indicates front of engine. On the OHV4 and V-266, 304, 345, 392 engines the numbered sides of the main bearing caps face the left side of the engine. On the BD, BG and RD engines the numbered side of the bearing caps face the camshaft side of the engine. On V(S)-401, 461, 478, 549 engines the bearing caps are installed with the numbered side facing to the right side of the engine. When tightening main bearing caps, first tap them lightly into place, then tighten bolts in an alternating manner until the specified torque is reached. See Specifications for correct torque.

10. Install a new rear main bearing oil seal. On OHV4 and V-266, 304, 345, 392 engines the round seal is pressed in after the rear main bearing cap is installed. Rear main bearing cap side oil seals are installed on these engines with an installer tool made from a piece of 1/8" welding rod. Puddle a ball on the end of the rod and file the ball to approximately 5.32" diameter. On BG-220, 241, 265 and BD-220, 240, 264 engines, rear main bearing cap side oil seals are installed in the same way. On BD-282, 308 and RD engines the rear upper seal and retainer are installed before the crankshaft and the lower main bearing lower oil seal is installed after the rear main bearing cap, using new gaskets on each side of the lower seal retainer. On V(S)-401, 461, 478, 549 engines the rear main bearing cap side seals are marked for right and left side. On PT-6, BD-220, 240, 264, BG-220, 241, 265 and V(S)-401, 461, 478, 549 engines, the top and bottom rear main bearing oil seals are made of felt material which fits into slots in the block and bearing cap. These must be cut to the correct length while the seal is being held in place with a seal compressing tool as illustrated.
11. Check main bearing clearance and crankshaft endplay and compare to clearance limits listed in Specifications at the beginning of this section. See Engine Rebuilding General Section for clearance measurement and service procedures.
12. Reassemble engine following Steps 1 through 7 in reverse order. Be sure to align clutch driven disc with transmission shaft or clutch aligning tool before tightening clutch plate mounting bolts.

Rear Main Bearing Seal Replacement

OHV 4 and V-226, 304, 345 & 392 Engines

1. Remove transmission, clutch and flywheel.
2. Using remover tool and protector plate, insert remover between seal retainer and crankshaft flange at long notch of protector plate and pry outward. Repeat prying at various locations around the seal. Use short notch of protector plate to pry seal out of position. If the seal retainer is too tight to fit in removing tool, it will be necessary to use a hammer to pierce the retainer in several places first.
3. Using pilot and installing tool, drive new seal into bore until it is flush with the rear face of the crankcase.
4. Install flywheel, clutch and transmission.

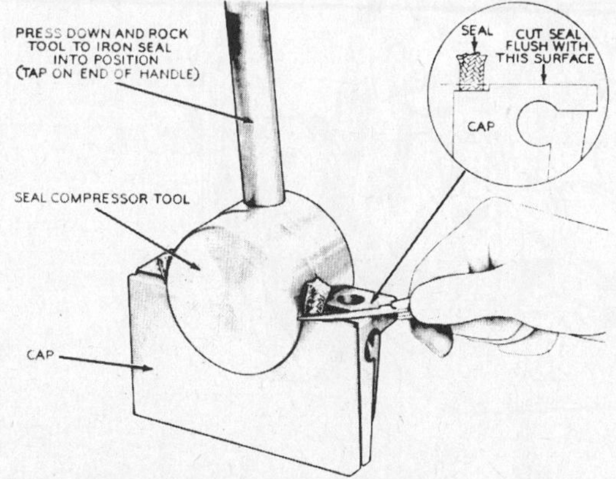

Installation of oil seal in rear main bearing cap
(© International Harvester Co.)

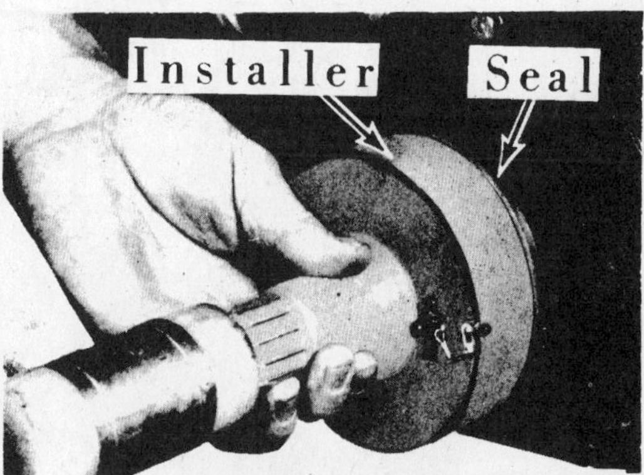

Installing rear main oil seal
(© International Harvester Co.)

Rear Main Bearing Oil Seal Replacement

PT 6

1. PT-6 Drain crankcase and remove oil pan.
2. Remove rear main bearing cap.
3. Remove oil seal from bearing cap and clean cap thoroughly.
4. Loosen all remaining main bearing cap mounting bolts.
5. Using a brass drift and hammer, tap the upper seal until sufficient seal is protruding on the other side to permit pulling it out with pliers.
6. Wipe crankshaft seal surface clean and coat lightly with oil.
7. Coat crankcase surface of upper seal with soap and the lip of seal with No. 40 engine oil.
8. Install upper seal with lip toward front of engine.
9. Coat mating surfaces of crankcase and cap with No. 2 Permatex or equivalent, back surface of seal with soap and lip of seal with No. 40 engine oil.
10. Seat seal firmly into seal recess of cap and apply No. 2 Permatex or equivalent to both chamfered edges of the rear main bearing cap.
11. Install main bearing halves and cap
12. Tighten all main bearing cap mounting bolts to specified torque.
13. Install oil pan.

Engine Lubrication

Oil Filter Replacement

On all models except the PT-6 the oil filter unit is on the left side of the engine block. On the PT-6 it is on the right side and the whole filter is replaced using a strap wrench.

1. Remove drain plug from bottom of filter body, drain oil and replace drain plug.
2. Loosen filter body retaining bolt and remove filter body and element. Check condition of body to base gasket and replace if necessary.
3. Wash filter body with cleaning solvent, being sure to remove all sediment.
4. Install new filter element onto filter base with seal end away from base. Be sure element is fully seated onto base.
5. Install oil filter body and bolt with spring, making sure body seats evenly on gasket. Tighten filter body retaining bolt to 30-35 ft. lbs. torque on all engines except BD-220, 240, 264 and BG-220, 241, 265 where filter body retaining bolt is tightened to 14-16 ft. lbs. torque.
6. Start engine and run for at least 5 minutes until oil is warm and check for leaks.
7. Check crankcase oil level. Lubricant capacity of oil filter is about one quart.

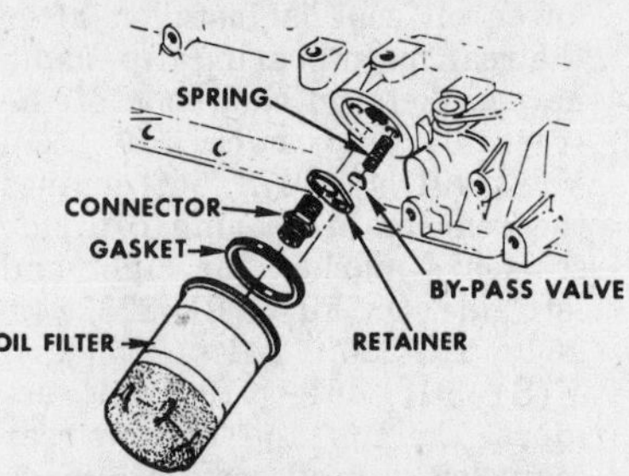

Oil filter bypass valve & spring—PT-6 engines
(© International Harvester Co.)

Oil Pump Removal

1. Drain crankcase and remove oil pan.
2. Remove oil pump mounting bolts and pull straight down on pump to remove.
3. When installing oil pump, guide pump shaft into position and rotate shaft until tang of drive gear is engaged. On PT-6 and V(S)-401, 461, 478, 549 engines install a new oil pump gasket when installing. On BD, BG and RD engines the oil pump shaft drives the distributor shaft and must be installed so that it is correctly timed to the crankshaft. Rotate the crankshaft

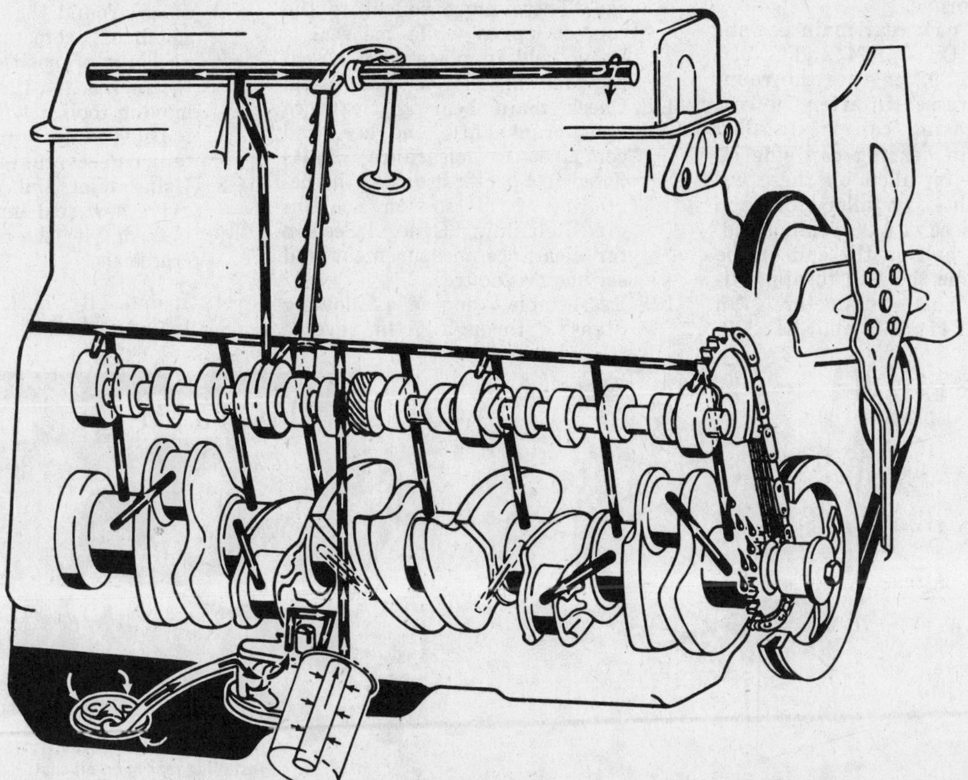
Engine lubrication system PT-6 engines (© International Harvester Co.)

position. On Bd-282, 308 engines the slot on the top of the oil pump shaft must be at right ongles to the side of the engine (transverse to the vehicle). On BD-220, 240, 264 and BG-220, 221, 265 engines the oil pump is installed so that the tang on the top of the pump shaft is at a 30-degree angle to the centerline of the engine. On RD engines the oil pump is installed so that the slot in the top of the shaft is at a 60-degree angle to the side of the engine.

4. Tighten oil pump mounting bolts.
5. Install oil pan and fill crankcase.

Oil Pump Service

1. Thoroughly clean oil pump. Do not disturb or remove pickup tube unless absolutely necessary.
2. Remove pump cover bolts and pump cover.
3. Check gear to body clearance. If it is not within .0025-.0055" on the OHV6 engines or .0007-.0027" on the OHV4 and V8 engines, obtain new parts.
4. Check gear backlash. If it exceeds .011" on OHV4 and V8 engines or .006" on OHV6 engines, replace gears.
5. Check pump shaft clearance in bore. If it exceeds .004" on OHV6 engines or .003" on V8 and OHV4 engines, replace the whole pump assembly.
6. Remove relief valve and spring. Remove any burrs and clean. Be sure to install with bevelled or pointed end in seat. Check that volve moves freely in bore.

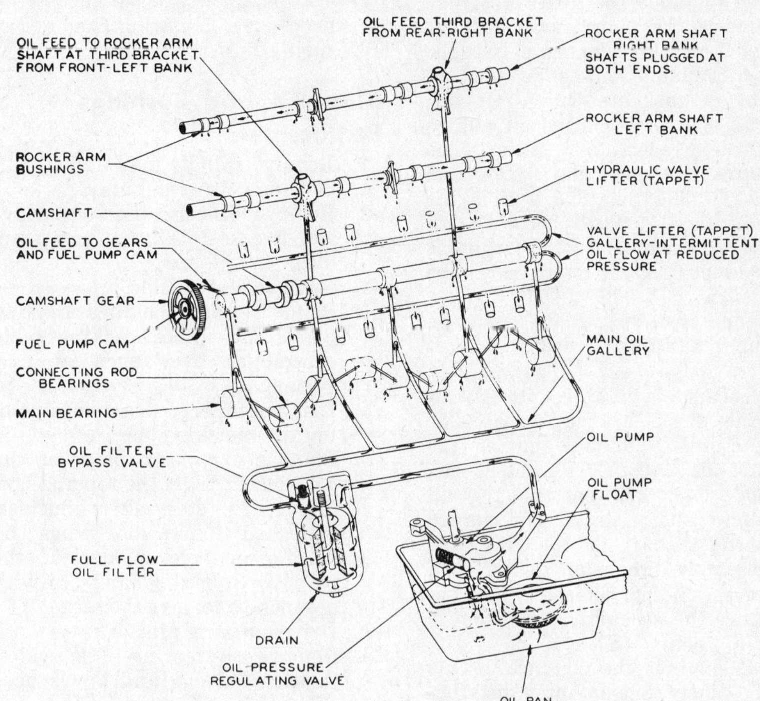

Engine lubrication system V8—engines (© International Harvester Co.)

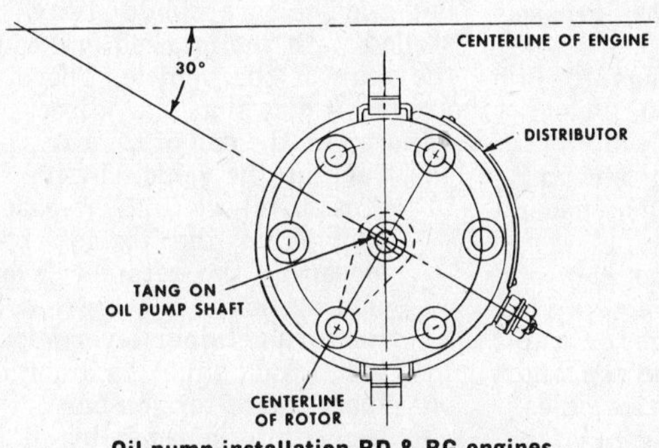

Oil pump installation BD & BG engines
(© International Harvester Co.)

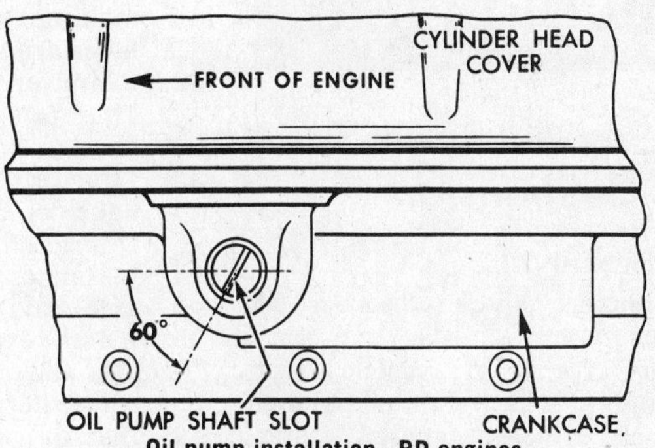

Oil pump installation—RD engines
(© International Harvester Co.)

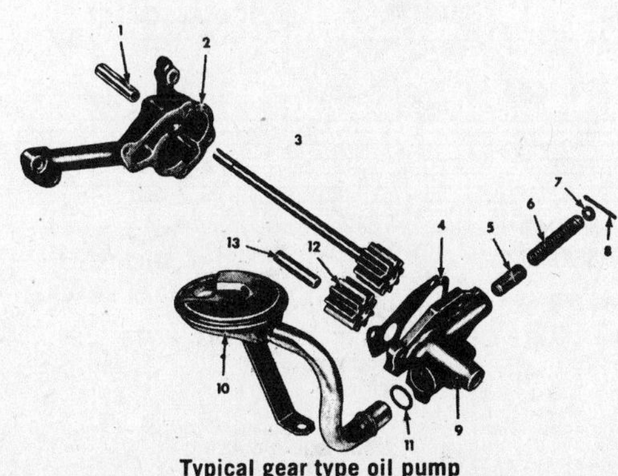

Typical gear type oil pump
(© International Harvester Co.)

Oil pump shaft sleeve installation—OHV4, V266, 304, 345 & 392 engines
(© International Harvester Co.)

7. Check body and gear clearance. This is the distance between the pump gears and the pump cover, except on the PT-6 where it is the distance the gears protrude beyond the pump body. Adjustment of this clearance is made by the addition or removal of cover gaskets. On V(S)-401, 461, 478, 549 engine oil pumps the clearance must be .0015-.009″. On the OHV4 and V-266, 304, 345, 393 engines the clearance is .0015-.006″. On all OHV6 except the PT-6 (which is .000-.004″ *above* pump body) the clearance is .0025-.0055″.
8. When installing drive gears on pump shaft be sure that the correct drive gear to pump body clearance is obtained. On RD engines the clearance is .025-.035″ and on BD-282, 308 engines it is .015-.020″. On OHV4 and V-266, 304, 345, 392 engines the oil pump shaft sleeve is crimped onto the shaft. On the OHV4 the assembly dimension is .200″ and on the V-266, 304, 345, 392 engines the assembly dimension is 375″. On V(S)-401, 461, 478, 549 engines the distance "A" is 2⅞″ for front-mounted distributors, 1-15/16″ for rear-mounted distributors and 2-1/6″ on BG and small BG engines.

Front Suspension

Front I-Beam Suspension

Spring Removal

1. Disconnect shock absorber at lower mount.
2. Raise front of vehicle just enough to take weight off spring.
3. Unbolt U-bolts, tapered caster wedge and U-bolt.
4. Remove lube fittings from spring mountings.
5. Remove spring pins and spring.
6. To install, reverse the above procedure, mounting fixed end of spring first.

King Pin and Bushings Replacement

1. Remove spindle nuts and spindle bearing retaining nuts.
2. Remove wheels, inner bearings and grease retainers from spindles.
3. Remove dirt shields.
4. Remove bolts holding backing plates and place backing plate assemblies over ends of axle I-beam.
5. Remove tapered draw keys holding the knuckle pins.
6. Remove expansion plugs or cap and gasket from the top and bottom of steering knuckles. (Remove expansion plugs by drilling a hole in one of the plugs and driving king pin with a punch to remove the other).
7. Drive out king pin.
8. Remove steering knuckles, thrust bearings and any spacer shims present.
9. Clean all parts thoroughly and inspect for wear and damage.
10. Remove old bushings with an arbor or drift.
11. Install new bushings with an arbor or bushing installing tool, making sure that the grease holes are aligned.
12. Ream or hone bushings to fit king pin with .001-.002″ clearance.
13. Lubricate and install steering knuckle, thrust bearings, spacer shims and king pins.
14. Install draw key (front side of axle) and tighten securely.
15. Insert expansion plugs or cap and gasket seals in the top and bottom of the steering knuckles.
16. Install brake backing plates, tightening bolts securely.
17. Install dirt shields, their retaining screws, cleaned and repacked wheel bearings and new grease seals.
18. Install wheel and spindle nuts, rotating wheel while tightening nut until slight drag is felt. Back off to the first castellation and install new cotter pin. Install
19. Lubricate and check and align front wheels if necessary.

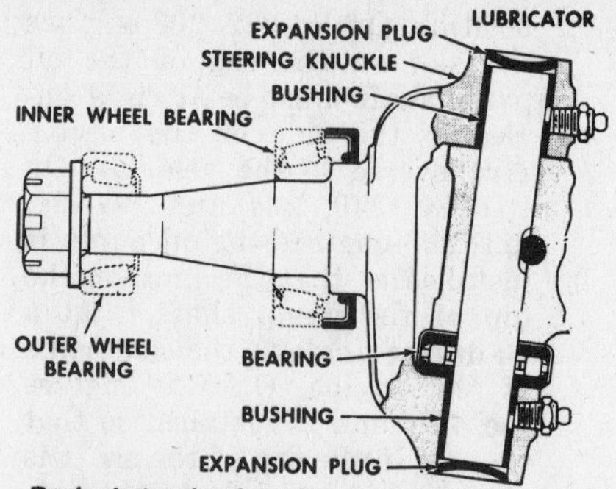

Typical steering knuckle—expansion type seal plugs
(© International Harvester Co.)

Torsion Bar Front Suspension

Torsion Bar Removal

Right and left torsion bars are not interchangeable. The bars are marked with an "L" or "R" on one end and the bars should always be installed with the marked end towards the rear of the vehicle. There is an arrow indicating the direction of wind-up on the end of the bar.

1. Jack up the vehicle by the frame crossmember and release the load from the torsion bar by loosening the retainer lever adjusting bolt.
2. Remove retainer lever adjusting bolt and slide retainer lever from end of torsion bar.
3. Remove torsion bar by sliding it

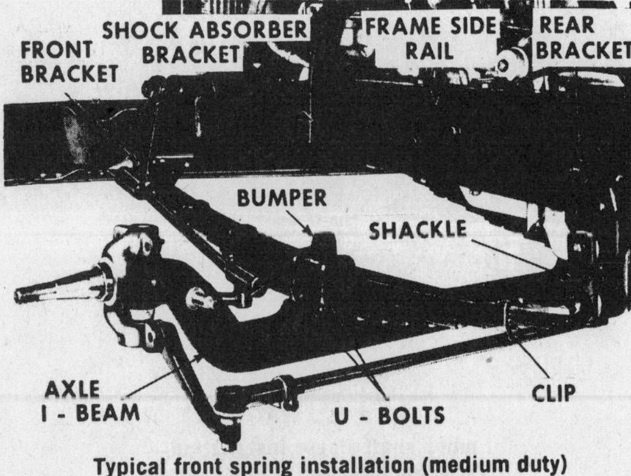

Typical front spring installation (medium duty)
(© International Harvester Co.)

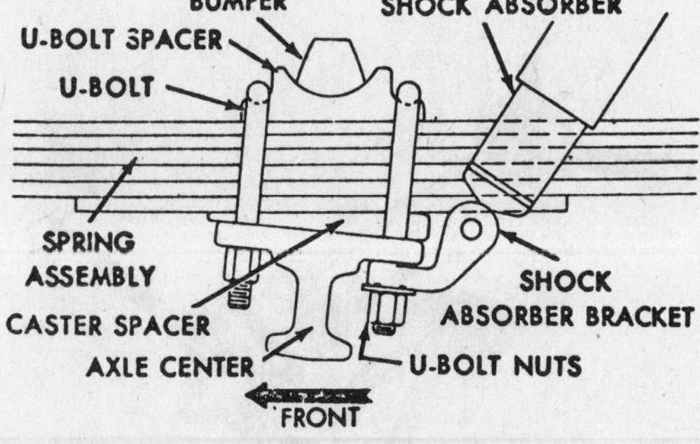

Typical front axle mounting
(© International Harvester Co.)

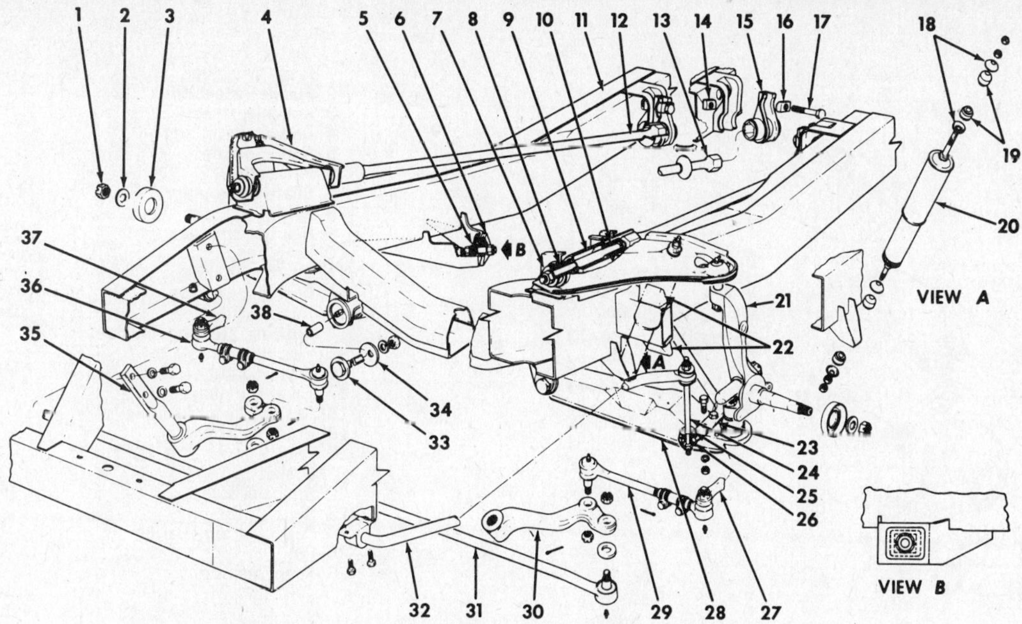

Torsion bar front wheel suspension (© International Harvester Co.)

1 Nut, hex., slotted
2 Washer
3 Seal, oil, front wheel
4 Arm, upper, asm.
5 Cushion, rubber, strut
6 Washer, lower arm strut
7 Washer
8 Bushing, upper control arm, front
9 Spindle, upper control arm
10 Bushing, upper control arm, rear
11 Frame
12 Bar, torsion
13 Seal, torsion bar
14 Nut, adjusting, torsion bar
15 Lever, retainer, torsion bar
16 Washer, adjusting, torsion bar
17 Bolt, hex.-hd.
18 Washer, retaining
19 Cushion, rubber
20 Shock absorber, front
21 Knuckle, steering
22 Bumper, control arm
23 Strut, lower control arm
24 Link, sway bar
25 Retainer, sway bar link cushion
26 Cushion, rubber, sway bar link
27 Arm, steering, left
28 Arm, lower, asm.
29 Link, vertical, left (or tie rod)
30 Arm, pitman
31 Rod, tie, asm.
32 Bar, sway
33 Bolt, hex.-hd.
34 Cam, lower control arm
35 Arm, idler, asm.
36 Link, vertical, right (or tie rod)
37 Arm, steering, right
38 Spacer, lower control arm

rearward. CAUTION: Do not nick or scratch torsion bars—this may create a fracture.

4. To install torsion bar, position torsion bar in upper control arm, observing right and left side and rearward direction as indicated above.
5. Install retainer lever on end of torsion bar and position bar nut in bracket on frame so that torsion bar adjusting bolt may be installed.
6. Insert bolt in bar washer, then through retainer lever and bracket and thread into bar nut.
7. Adjust height by lowering vehicle to ground (check for correct tire pressure), bouncing front end up and down, then turning bolt on torsion bar adjusting lever until correct height is achieved. Measure height between top of lower control arm and lower edge of rubber bumper frame bracket (vehicle unloaded).

Upper Control Arm Removal

1. Jack up vehicle by front frame crossmember until front wheels are off the ground.
2. Remove wheel and torsion bar (see preceding section).
3. Disconnect top mount of shock absorber.
4. Remove cotter pin, nut and dust seal (cut away seal) from lower ball joint.
5. Drive out lower ball joint stud (do not damage threads) or use tightening to 81-135 ft. lbs. torque.
11. Mount strut to lower control arm tightening bolts securely.
12. Connect tie rod end.
13. Position cushion and retainer on sway bar link and place sway bar link into strut with cushion, retainer and nut. Tighten nut until cushion is slightly squished. Insert cotter pin.
14. Mount front wheel.
15. Check alignment (see General Repair Section) and tighten nut on strut to 120-150 ft. lbs. torque and camber adjusting bolt nut to 81-135 ft. lbs. torque.

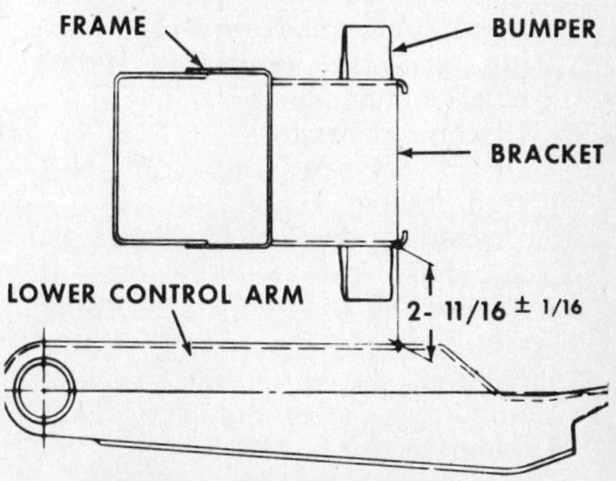

Checking front suspension height
(© International Harvester Co.)

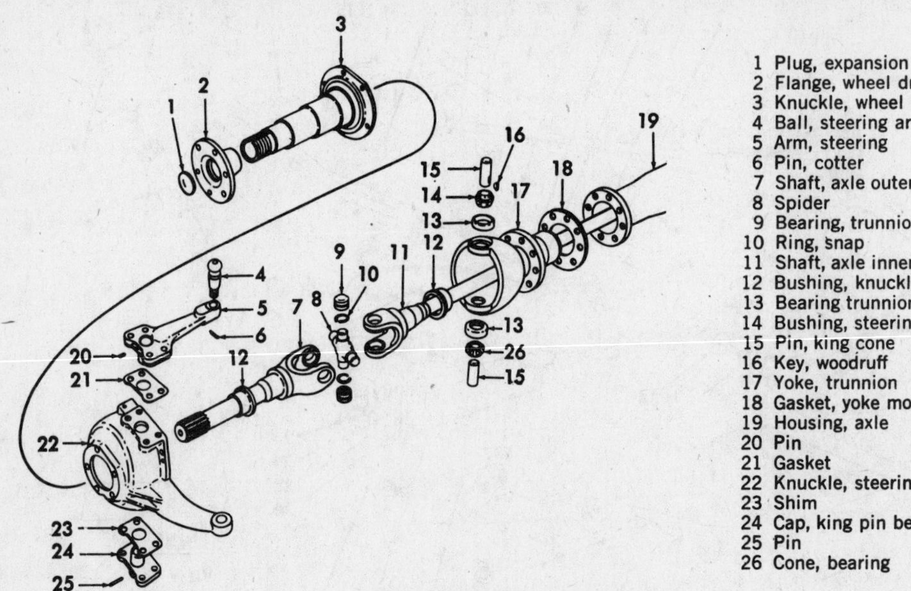

Front drive axle (© International Harvester Co.)

Front Drive Axle

For Service on Transfer Case—see General Repair Section.

Description

The front drive axles are units incorporating hypoid gears and spherical steering knuckles. The axle shaft assemblies are full-floating and may be removed without disassembling the steering knuckles.

Two different means of transmitting driving torque from the axle shaft to the wheel are employed. One type uses a drive flange having a splined ID to mate with the axle shaft splines. The second type has a drive gear splined both internally and externally. The internal splines mate with the axle shaft splines and the external splines index with the splines of the inside of the wheel hub.

Front Drive Axle Removal

1. Jack up truck until load is removed from springs and block up frame to safely hold weight.
2. Drain lubricant from main housing and, if applicable, from wheel end housings.
3. Disconnect brakes.
4. Disconnect drag link from ball stud bracket.
5. Disconnect drive shaft from pinion shaft yoke.
6. Supporting axle with a portable floor jack, remove spring U-bolts.
7. Roll axle assembly out from under truck.
8. To install, reverse the above procedure.

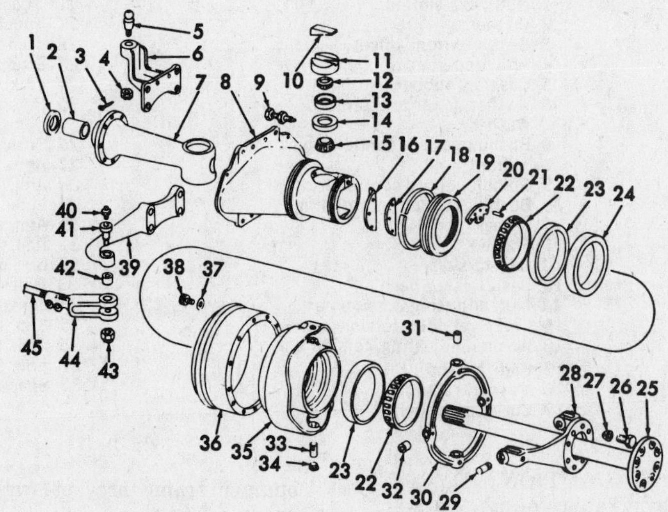

Front drive axle (drive gear type) (© International Harvester Co.)

Front Drive Axle Adjustments

FA-57, 59, 140 Models

Preload on the knuckle bearings of

special ball stud remover and nut.

6. Remove fender splash panel front shield.
7. Remove nut and washers from front end of upper control arm spindle and carefully drive out spindle with hammer.
8. Remove upper control arm.
9. To install, position upper control arm and install spindle through arm and bracket from rear.
10. Install flat washer, lock washer and nut. Tighten securely.
11. Install fender splash panel front shield.
12. Install new dust seal on ball stud, then line up shock absorber with hole in control arm and position ball stud into steering knuckle. Use jack to raise lower control arm until ball stud is well into steering knuckle.
13. Install nut on ball stud. Tighten securely.
14. Install top mounting of shock absorber, tightening just enough to squash rubber cushion slightly.
15. Install torsion bar on upper control arm as described in preceding section.
16. Mount front wheel.
17. Check alignment (see General Repair Section) of steering.

Lower Control Arm Removal

1. Raise vehicle by jacking frame crossmember. Remove wheel.
2. Disconnect sway bar link from strut and remove two bolts which secure strut to lower control arm.
3. Cut away dust seal from lower ball stud and remove cotter pin and nut from lower ball stud.
4. Either drive out ball stud with a soft hammer while supporting control arm or use special ball stud remover and nut.
5. Disconnect tie rod end from either side of vehicle.
6. Remove nut, lockwasher, cam and bolt from lower control arm and frame bracket.
7. Remove control arm and spacer in bushing.
8. To install, place new dust seal on ball stud and position ball stud into steering knuckle.
9. Tighten nut on ball stud and install cotter pin.
10. Position spacer in bushing and, while holding control arm in position, install bolt from front. Install cam, lockwasher, and nut,

these front axles must be maintained at all times. Check for looseness each time knuckle is lubricated.

1. Jack up front end of truck until off-center weight of the wheel is relieved (wheel just barely touching ground).
2. Remove wheel and wheel adapter from hub.
3. Disconnect tie rod and drag link.
4. Remove axle shaft.
5. To remove play (check for play by pushing and pulling on top and bottom of knuckle) and increase preload drag, turn adjusting bolt into back of knuckle. Preload should read (spring scale hooked into end of steering arm) 12 lbs. on FA-57, 59 and 14 lbs. on FA-140.

Models FA 15, 16, 18 and FA 52

Reference for overhaul procedures see International Single Reduction Rear Axle in General Repair Section.

Axle Shaft and Universal Joint

(Axles having drive flange)

Removal

1. Raise vehicle, support with floor stands and remove wheel from vehicle.
2. Remove grease cap and snap ring from end of axle shaft.

1 Cap, grease
2 Ring, snap
3 Bolt, drive flange
4 Washer
5 Flange, drive
6 Gasket, drive flange
7 Bolt, spindle
8 Washer
9 Spindle, wheel
10 Bushing, wheel spindle
11 Shaft, joint
12 Ring, snap
13 Joint, universal assembly
14 Shaft, axle
15 Bolt, king pin bearing cap
16 Knuckle, steering
17 Washer
18 Cap, king pin bearing
19 Shim
20 Plug, filler
21 Ring, oil seal
22 Seal, oil (rubber)
23 Seal, oil (felt)
24 Plate, knuckle retainer
25 Cone, bronze bearing
26 Cup, bronze bearing
27 Housing, axle w/ball yoke
28 Bolt, metal plate retainer
29 Rod, tie

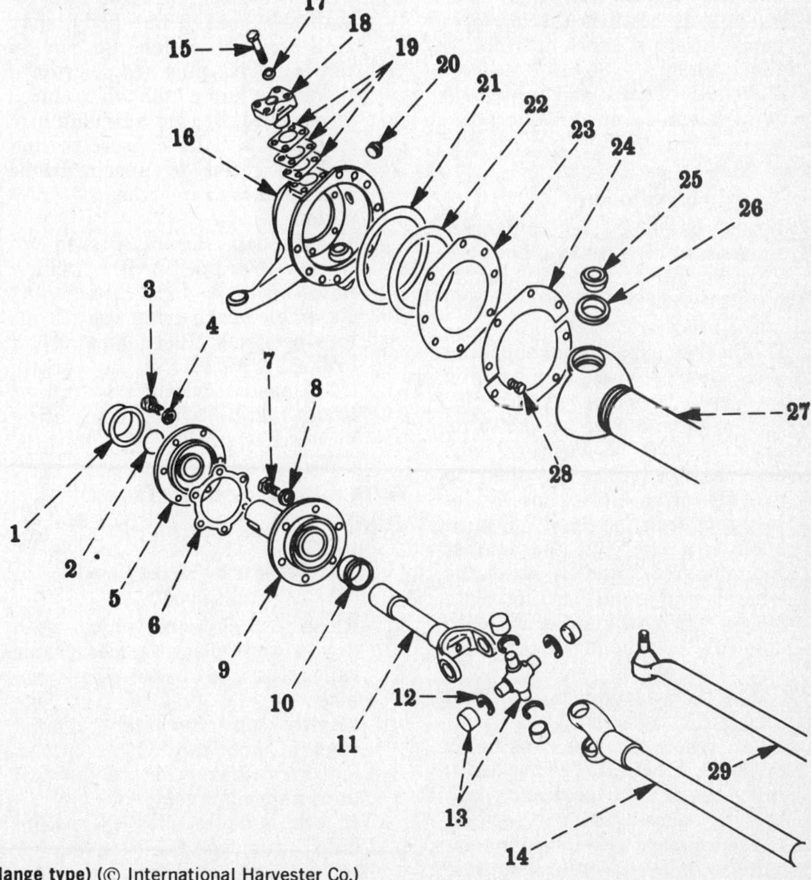

Front drive axle (drive flange type) (© International Harvester Co.)

3. Remove drive flange cap screws, lock-washer, flange and gasket. If equipped with locking hubs, bend up locking tab, take out capscrews and remove clutch body. NOTE: Lift off clutch body holding it errect so as not to let drive pins fall out of body. If they do fall out, be certain to install them during reassembly. Remove hub body. Loosen setscrew and unscrew drag shoe from spindle.
4. Remove brake drum countersunk setscrews, where applicable and remove drum.
5. Bend the lip on the wheel bearing lockwasher away from the outer wheel bearing nut and remove the nut and lockwasher. Remove wheel bearing adjusting nut (inner) and bearing lockwasher.
6. Remove the wheel hub with wheel bearing.
7. Remove backing plate and wheel spindle retaining bolts and lockwashers. Support backing plate to prevent damage to brake hose if hose is not disconnected.
8. Remove wheel bearing spindle with bushing. If spindle bushing requires replacing, press out bushing using an adapter of correct size. An alternate method of bushing removal is the use of a cape chisel or punch to collapse the bushing.
9. Pull axle shaft and universal joint assembly out of axle housing.

Installation

1. Insert axle shaft and universal joint assembly into axle housing. Position splined end of axle shaft into differential pinion gear and push into place.
2. If wheel bearing spindle bushing was removed, press new bushing into spindle using an installer tool or adapter of proper size. Lubricate ID of bushing with chassis lube when installed to provide initial lubrication. Bushing should be pressed in until bushing flange is seated against shoulder in spindle. Assemble wheel spindle and backing plate to steering knuckle. Secure with six (6) bolts and lockwashers and tighten to specifications. Connect hydraulic brake fluid line if disconnected.
3. Pack wheel bearings using a pressure lubricator or by carefully working lubricant into bearing cones by hand. Slide lubricated inner wheel bearing on spindle until it stops against spindle shoulder.
4. Apply thin coating of lubricant specified for wheel bearings to seal lip and install seal into wheel hub using an adapter of correct diameter. Lip of seal should extend towards wheel (away from backing plate assembly).
5. Assemble wheel hub on spindle. Install lubricated outer wheel bearing cone on spindle. Push cone on spindle until it rests against bearing cup.
6. Install wheel bearing lockwasher and adjusting (inner) nut. Tighten adjusting nut until there is a slight drag on the bearings when the hub is turned; then back-off approximately one-sixth turn.
7. Install tang-type lockwasher and lock nut (outer). Tighten nut and bend lockwasher tang over lock nut. If axle is equipped with locking hubs, install drag shoe on spindle and tighten setscrew.
8. Align splines of drive flange with those of axle shaft and secure drive flange and new gasket to wheel hub with capscrews and lockwashers. Tighten capscrews securely. If equipped with locking hubs, lightly lubricate hub body and clutch using a light grade chassis lubricant and install new gasket, hub body, snap ring and hub clutch. Be certain that all drive pins are positioned in locking hub clutch when clutch is installed. Secure hub clutch to wheel hub with capscrews and lock. Tighten to specifications and bend tang over head of capscrew.
9. Install snap ring and grease cup if not equipped with locking hubs.
10. Assemble brake drum and wheels to wheel hub. Bleed and adjust brakes. CAUTION: Be certain that master cylinder is full of brake fluid after completing bleeding operation.

Axle Shaft and Universal Joint

(Axles having drive gear) Removal

1. Raise and support vehicle with floor stands placed under frame rails. Remove wheel from vehicle.
2. Lightly tap alternately around edge of hub cap with hammer and screwdriver or similar tool until hub cap is removed.
3. If axle is equipped with locking hubs, remove the eight (8) socket-head setscrews securing hub clutch assembly to wheel hub assembly. NOTE: Drive pins may fall out of hub clutch when separated from wheel hub assembly. Be certain to replace them during installation.
4. Remove retaining ring from wheel hub if equipped with locking hubs.
5. Remove snap ring from axle shaft.
6. Pull drive gear out of wheel hub. If difficulty is encountered in removing drive gear, obtain a screwdriver or similar tool having the end bent approximately 90° with the handle. Insert end of tool into groove in drive gear and withdraw gear. If necessary, move wheel alternately backward and forward to aid removal of gear.
7. Remove retaining ring and locking hub body, if so equipped.
8. Using Wheel Bearing Adjusting Nut Wrench, remove wheel bearing outer nut and slide lock ring off of axle shaft. Again using wrench, remove wheel bearing inner nut.
9. Pull drive gear spacer out of wheel hub.
10. Remove brake drum from wheel hub and slide wheel hub assembly off of spindle. NOTE: Do not allow tapered roller bearings to drop on floor as bearings may be damaged.
11. Remove screws retaining grease guard to backing plate. Take off grease guard and gasket.
12. Remove the six (6) bolts securing wheel spindle and backing plate to steering knuckle. Pull spindle with bushing off of axle shaft. If spindle bushing requires replacing, press or drive out bushing using an adapter of correct size. An alternate method of bushing removal is the use of a cape chisel or punch to collapse the bushing.
13. Pull axle shaft and universal joint assembly out of axle housing.

Installation

1. Proceed with steps 1 through 5 *of Axle Shaft and Universal Joint Installation* (Axles having drive flange).
2. Insert drive gear spacer over spindle and against outer wheel bearing cup.
3. Position wheel bearing inner adjusting nut Wheel Bearing Adjusting Nut wrench with pin in nut extending toward handle end of wrench. Install nut on spindle and tighten until it is snug against outer wheel bearing; then loosen adjusting nut 1/4 turn.

Align tang on adjusting nut lock ring with groove in wheel spindle. Slide ring on spindle and index pin on adjusting nut with hole in lock ring. If pin will not index with hole in lock ring, turn adjusting nut to the left (Loosen) until it will index. NOTE: When attempting to index pin with hole in lock ring, turn nut very slightly since adjusting nut should be locked with first hole in lock ring past ¼ turn loose. Position wheel bearing outer nut in adjusting nut wrench and install on spindle. Tighten nut securely.

4. Align splines on axle shaft and splines in wheel hub with those of drive gear. Insert drive gear on axle shaft. Push gear into hub until it rests against drive gear spacer. NOTE: Groove on side of gear must be toward hub cap.
5. If axle is equipped with locking hubs, lightly lubricate locking hub body using a light grade chassis lubricant. Align splines and insert hub body into wheel hub.
6. Install snap ring on end of axle shaft.
7. Place retaining ring in groove in wheel hub, if equipped with locking hub.
8. If applicable, lightly grease hub clutch assembly using a light grade chassis lubricant. Be sure that all eight (8) drive pins are positioned in the locking hub clutch. Assemble hub clutch to hub body and secure with eight (8) socket head setscrews.
9. Position hub cap on wheel hub and lightly tap alternately around cap until flange is against edge of hub.
10. Assemble brake drum and wheel to wheel hub. Bleed and adjust brakes. CAUTION: Be certain that master cylinder is full of brake fluid after bleeding operation.

Steering Knuckle

Removal

1. Remove drag link at steering arm and tie-rod at steering knuckle.
2. Remove oil seal retaining bolts from inner flange of steering knuckle and remove oil seals.
3. Remove bolts and lockwashers securing king pin lower bearing cap. Remove bearing cap and shim pack. Retain shim pack for use during reassembly.
4. Remove capscrews or self-locking nuts, which ever is applicable, securing steering arm or upper bearing cap to steering knuckle.
5. Lift steering arm assembly and knuckle until bronze bearing cone will clear ball yoke. Separate steering knuckle from ball yoke. NOTE: Do not allow lower tapered roller bearing cone to drop on floor during removal of steering knuckle.
6. Support steering knuckle and with a long brass drift, drive or press king pin out of bronze bearing cone. NOTE: Be careful not to damage end of king pin during removal of cone.

Installation

1. Assemble steering arm to knuckle using original shim pack. Install self-locking nuts or capscrews and tighten securely.
2. Coat king pin and bronze bearing cone ID and OD with chassis lubricant to prevent galling. Align serrations of new bronze bearing cone with serrations of king pin and press cone on king pin. NOTE: Make sure the cone is pressed all the way on or against the shoulder.
3. With bronze cone and tapered roller bearing pre-lubricated, place tapered roller bearing cone into cup at lower end of ball yoke. While retaining lower bearing cone in position, assemble steering knuckle to ball yoke. Seat bronze cone into cup at upper end of ball yoke.
4. Lubricate lower king pin with chassis lubricant and using original shim pack, install lower bearing cap to knuckle securing with bolts and lockwasher. Tighten bearing cap bolts securely.
5. Assemble opposite knuckle proceeding with instructions similar to those outlined above.
6. Individually check knuckle bearing preload by placing a torque wrench on any one (1) of the steering arm or bearing cap bolts or nuts. Read the starting torque (not rotating torque). Remove or add shims at the lower bearing cap until the specified preload is obtained. Knuckle bearing preload should be checked without ball joint oil seal, drag link or tie-rod installed.
7. Assemble the knuckle oil seals with the split on top. Knuckle retainer plate must be adjacent to ball yoke; followed by rubber seal, felt seal and metal retainer. Install seal retainer bolts and tighten securely.
8. Connect tie-rod to steering knuckle and tighten nut. Connect drag link to steering arm ball. Install cotter keys.

Cleaning, Inspection

All parts of the wheel end assembly should be thoroughly cleaned and dried with compressed air or a lint-free clean cloth.

Inspect all parts for wear, cracks or other damage. Replace all oil seals, felts and gaskets to prevent lubricant leakage.

Front Drive Locking Hubs

Two types of locking hubs are used: manual and Lock-O-Matic. Manual locking hubs are either engaged or disengaged, depending on how they are set. Lock-O-Matic hubs,

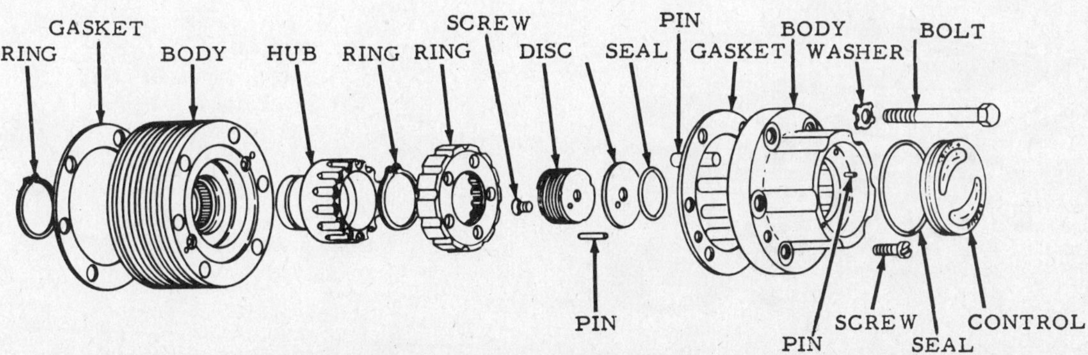

Manual type locking hub (© International Harvester Co.)

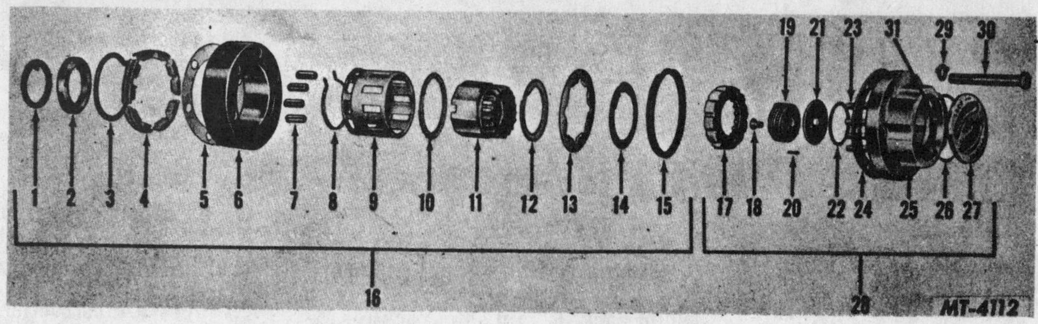

1 Washer, spindle lock
2 Shoe, drag
3 Spring, friction shoe
4 Shoe, friction
5 Gasket
6 Body, hub
7 Roller
8 Spring, centering
9 Cage, roller
10 Ring, lock
11 Hub, axle shaft
12 Ring, lock
13 Washer, trhust
14 Ring, lock
15 Ring, lock
16 Body, hub assembly
17 Ring, clutch
18 Screw, flat-head
19 Screw, clutch
20 Pin, dowel
21 Disc
22 "O"-ring, oil seal
23 Pin, drive
24 Gasket, clutch
25 Body, clutch
26 "O"-ring, oil seal
27 Control, assembly
28 Body, clutch assembly
29 Washer, lock
30 Bolt
31 Pin, stop

Lock-O-Matic locking hub (© International Harvester Co.)

when in "free" position, automatically engage axle and wheel when forward torque is applied by the axle shaft. Thus, whenever front wheel drive is disengaged at the transmission, the wheels free wheel. "Lock" position is required only when engine braking control on the front wheel is desired.

Front Locking Hubs Removal

1. Bend up tabs on mounting bolt lock washers.
2. Remove six (eight) mounting bolts using a thin-walled socket or appropriate hex wrench (externally splined type).
3. When clutch body is lifted off, immediately tilt it up so that the drive pins do not fall out.
4. Remove lock ring holding hub body onto axle shaft and pull off hub body.
5. Remove drag shoe (Lock-O-Matic only) from axle spindle by loosening hex-head set screw and unscrew drag shoe.
6. To install, reverse the above procedure.

Steering Linkage

See General Repair Section for steering alignment procedures. See specifications at the beginning of this section for steering alignment specifications.

Tie Rods

Tie rods are of three-piece construction: rod and two end assemblies. The end assemblies are threaded into the end of the tie rod and adjustment is made by turning them either in or out to shorten or lengthen the tie rod. When tightening the clamp it is important to make sure that the end assembly is threaded in far enough so that the clamping action of the clamp is right over the end pieces. Ball studs are integral in the end assemblies.

When disconnecting ball studs, loosen ball stud nut, then strike the nut with one hammer while another larger hammer is backing up the nut.

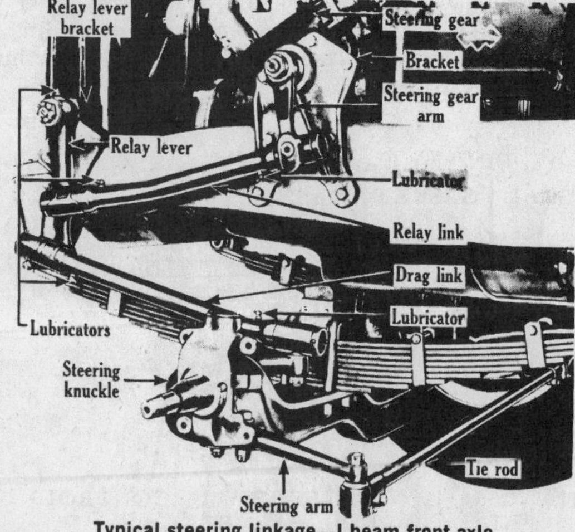

Typical steering linkage—I beam front axle
(© International Harvester Co.)

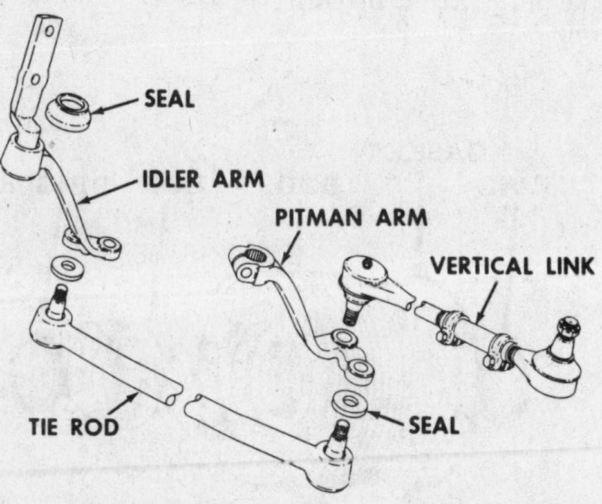

Typical steering linkage—except I beam axle
(© International Harvester Co.)

Steering Gear

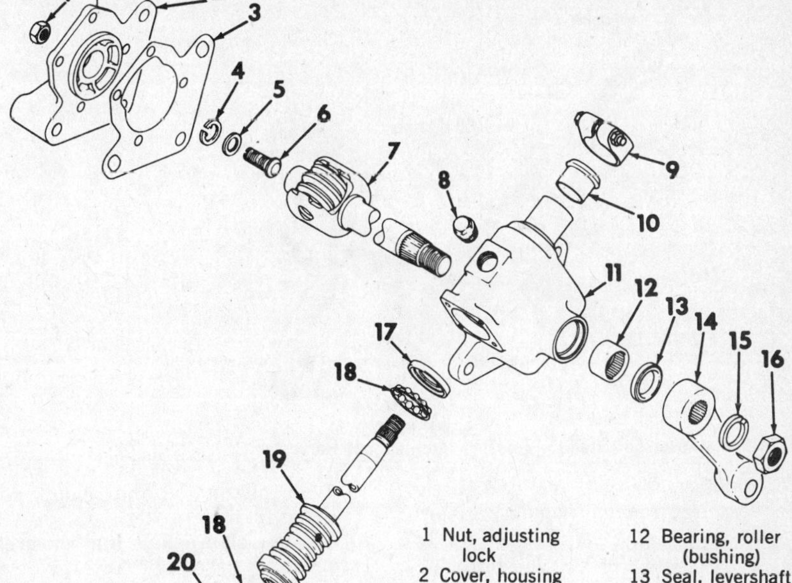

1 Nut, adjusting lock
2 Cover, housing side
3 Gasket, side cover
4 Ring, snap
5 Washer, trhust
6 Screw, adjusting
7 Levershaft, w/roll-assembly
8 Plug, vent
9 Clamp, w/bolt jacket tube
10 Seal, housing oil, upper
11 Housing, steering gear
12 Bearing, roller (bushing)
13 Seal, levershaft
14 Arm, steering
15 Washer, lock
16 Nut, steering arm
17 Cup, bearing upper (small)
18 Bearing, w/retainer
19 Tube, w/worm
20 Cup, bearing lower (large)
21 Shim housing cover .002", .005", .010"
22 Cover, housing

Cam (worm) and roller type steering gear
(© International Harvester Co.)

Steering Gear Removal

1. Loosen collar clamp at bottom of steering wheel column.
2. Remove nut or loosen clamp bolt which secures steering arm to lever shaft, removing steering arm from lever shaft using a suitable puller if necessary.
3. Remove mounting bolts and steering gear assembly.
4. To install, reverse the above procedure, taking special care not to bind steering column if there is no universal joint.

Steering Gear Adjustment

Twin Stud Levershaft Type

1. Free steering gear of all load by disconnecting drag link from steering arm and loosening bracket clamp on steering gear jacket tube.
2. To adjust end play on cam (ball thrust bearings), loosen lock nut and adjusting screw, then unscrew four upper cover (steering column) bolts.
3. Remove (cut) or add shims, replacing and tightening down upper cover to test drag. Drag should be just slight enough so that steering wheel can be moved from lock to lock with one finger.
4. To adjust lever shaft cams for backlash, place steering wheel in middle (straight-forward) position and turn adjusting screw until very slight drag is felt through mid-position range.
5. Tighten lock nut and give final test for drag.
6. Install drag link onto levershaft and tighten clamp on steering gear jacket tube.

Triple Roller Steering Gear

1. To check cam preload, disconnect linkage from steering arm and turn steering wheel through entire range, noting lash area.
2. Check the preload in lash area. It should be 7-13 inch-pounds.
3. If adjustment is necessary, drain lubricant and remove four lower cover bolts.
4. Remove top shim with a knife, being careful not to mutilate remaining shims.
5. Replace lower cover and tighten bolts to 13-22 ft. lbs. torque.
6. Recheck preload and repeat above procedure if necessary.
7. Refill with SAE multi-purpose type gear lubricant.

Cam (Worm) and Roller Type

1. Disconnect linkage from pitman arm and drain lubricant.
2. Loosen locknut (1) at housing side cover, then turn adjusting screw (6) counterclockwise one turn to assure release of levershaft preload.
3. Turn steering wheel tube to

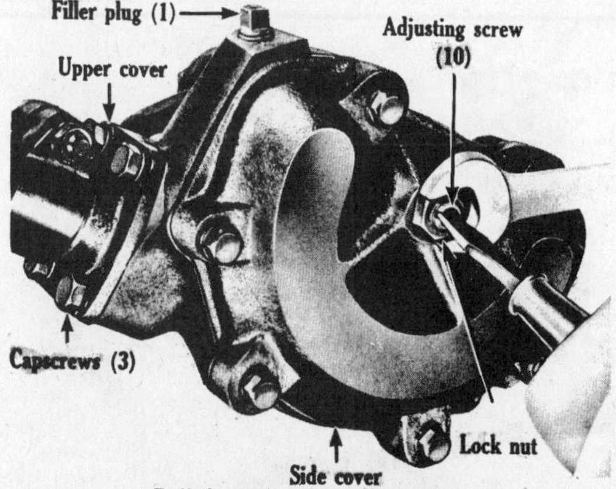

Ball thrust bearing adjustment—
Twin stud levershaft steering gear
(© International Harvester Co.)

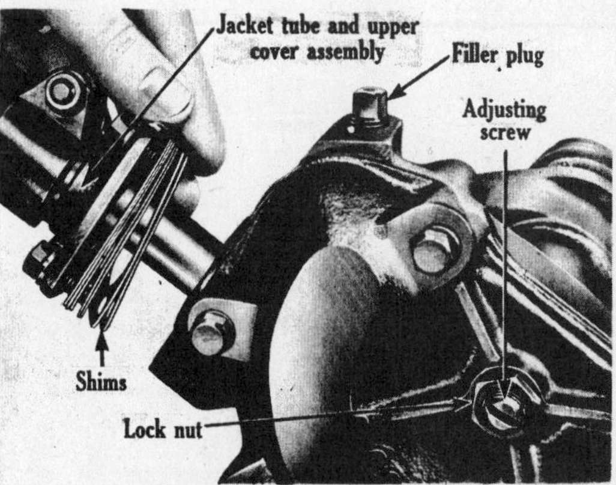

Adjusting cam end play with shims—
Twin stud levershaft steering gear
(© International Harvester Co.)

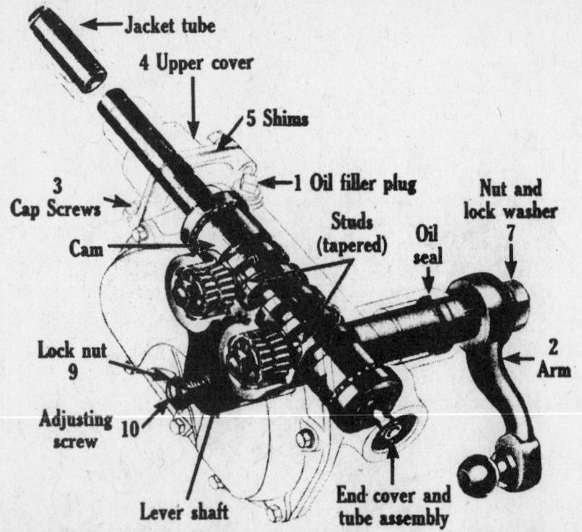

Twin stud levershaft steering gear (© International Harvester Co.)

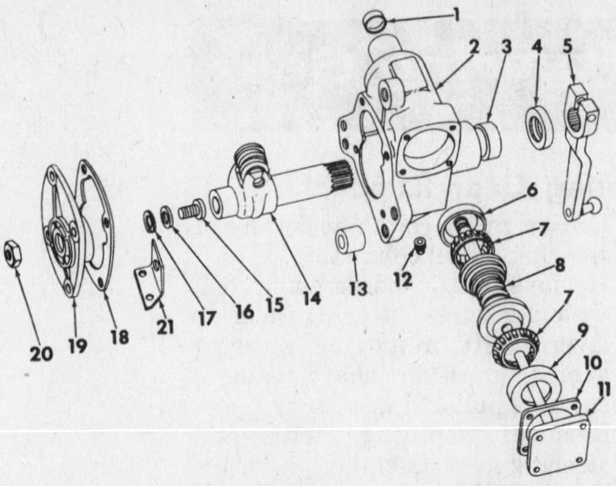

1 Seal, housing upper oil
2 Housing
3 Bushing, housing
4 Seal, housing side oil
5 Arm, steering
6 Bearing, upper cup
7 Bearing, cone
8 Tube, with cam
9 Bearing, lower cup
10 Shim, housing lower cover
11 Cover, housing lower
12 Plug, housing filler
13 Spacer, steering gear mounting
14 Levershaft
15 Screw, levershaft adjusting
16 Washer, thrust
17 Ring, snap
18 Gasket, housing side cover
19 Cover, housing side
20 Nut, hex. jam
21 Bracket, steering gear mounting

Triple roller steering gear
(© International Harvester Co.)

about center of travel and check bearing preload (should register 9/16 to 1⅛ ft. lbs. @ 9″ radius).
4. If preload needs adjustment, drain lubricant and remove four housing cover bolts and housing.
5. Remove one shim.
6. Replace housing cover and bolts, torquing bolts to 18-22 ft. lbs.
7. Check preload and repeat the above procedure if necessary.
8. Adjust levershaft preload by turning adjusting screw (6). Correct levershaft preload is ¾ to 1¼ ft. lbs. @ 9″ radius (over cam preload).
9. Refill with SAE-90 SP type lubricant.

Power Steering Gear

Reference

For overhaul of power steering systems, see General Section.

In-Line Booster Removal

1. Disconnect and plug hydraulic lines from valve and cylinder unit.
2. Loosen clamp bolts and disconnect cylinder link from cylinder.
3. Remove nut and lockwasher from piston rod and remove rod from frame bracket.
4. Loosen clamp bolt and unscrew cylinder assembly from pivot on relay.
5. Installation is the reverse of the above procedure. Be sure to center steering wheel and wheels before tightening clamp bolts of cylinder link. Bleed hydraulic system.

Hydraulic Cylinder Removal

1. Disconnect hydraulic lines from cylinder and plug lines.
2. Unbolt piston rod from frame bracket, noting approximate position of clamp.
3. Disconnect cylinder assembly from steering linkage.
4. Installation is the reverse of the above procedure. Approximate original position of clamp on piston rod, center adjusting steering wheel if necessary.

Separate Control Valve Removal

1. Disconnect and plug hydraulic lines from control valve.
2. Loosen clamp bolts at each end of control valve and remove valve.
3. Installation is the reverse of removal. Since the control valve in this type of power steering system serves, in a sense, as a relay arm, it must be adjusted to center the steering wheel for straight-forward running. Tighten clamp bolts after adjustment is made.

Hydraulic Pump Removal

1. Disconnect hydraulic lines at pump. When hoses are disconnected, secure them in a raised position to prevent leakage. Plug fittings of pump.
2. Remove drive pulley attaching nut.

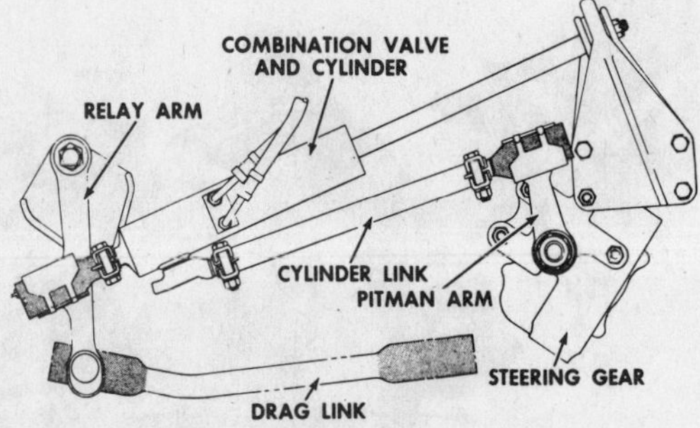

In-line type power steering booster
(© International Harvester Co.)

Separate control valve type power steering installation
(© International Harvester Co.)

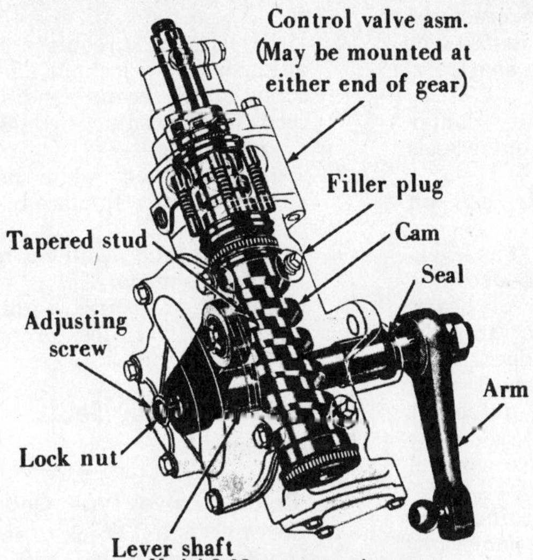

Model S-36 power steering gear with integral concentric valve (© International Harvester Co.)

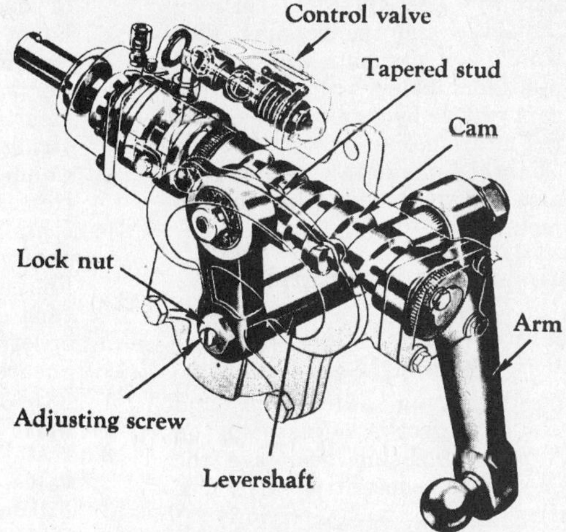

Power steering gear with toggle type integral valve (© International Harvester Co.)

3. Loosen bracket-to-pump mounting bolts, and remove pump belt.
4. Slide pulley from shaft. CAUTION: Do not hammer pulley off shaft as this will damage the pump.
5. Remove bracket-to-pump bolts and take off pump assembly.
6. Installation is the reverse of the above removal procedure. Do not tighten mounting bolts or pulley nut until installation is complete. Move pump until belt is tight, then tighten mounting bolts. Tighten pulley attaching nut last, torquing to 35-45 ft. lbs.

Thrust Bearing Adjustment

Semi-Integral Steering Gear

1. Disconnect steering gear arm and loosen steering column mounting to free steering gear of all load.
2. Free the stud in cam groove by turning gear off center position.
3. Remove three bolts which hold upper cover and remove cover.
4. Remove nut, lockwasher and tongued spacer washer from end of camshaft.
5. Run the nut back up the shaft until it is finger tight to make sure the threads are clean. If the nut does not turn smoothly, clean the threads.
6. Reinstall tongued spacer washer, lockwasher and nut.
7. Tighten nut to 10 ft. lbs. torque, then back off 10-20° (width of one lug on lockwasher) and bend up a lug of lockwasher.
8. Install upper cover.
9. With steering wheel and front wheels centered, connect steering gear arm to linkage and tighten steering column mounting.

Stud in Cam Groove Adjustment

Semi-Integral Steering Gear

The groove of the cam is cut shallower and narrower in the mid-range to provide close adjustment where straight-ahead driving action takes place. Adjust through mid-range and not in an end position.

1. Disconnect steering gear arm and loosen steering column mounting to free steering gear of all load.
2. Tighten side cover and loosen locknut on adjusting screw.
3. Turn adjusting screw until a slight drag is felt when turning the gear through mid-range. No drag is actually necessary and should only be enough to feel the adjustment.
4. Tighten locknut while holding screw.

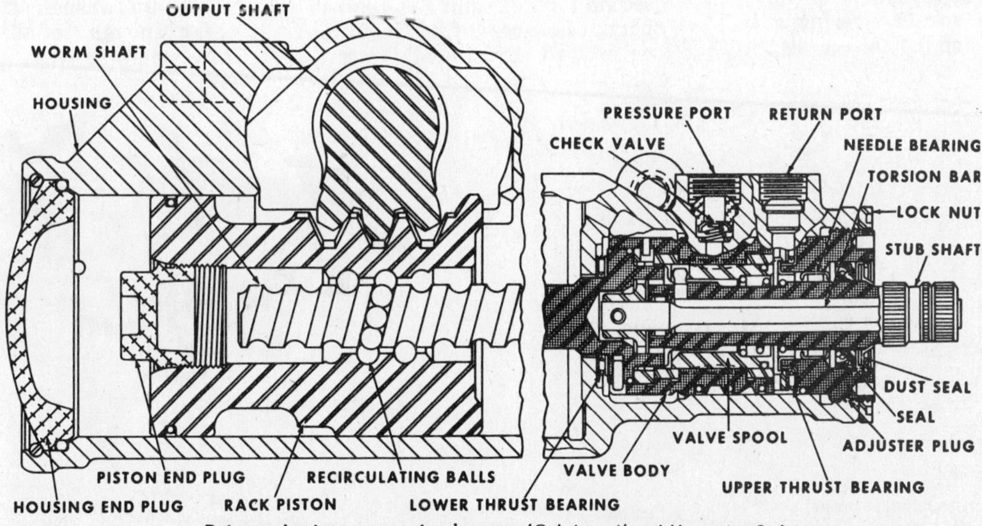

Rotary valve type power steering gear (© International Harvester Co.)

5. Further adjustment is made with the use of shims between the lever and the housing. The shim pack prevents the tapered pin from being pulled into the cam groove by external forces on the levershaft.
6. Connect linkage to steering gear arm and tighten steering column mounting.

Steering Gear Adjustments

Semi-Integral Toggle Type Steering Gear

Thrust bearing adjustment and stud in cam groove adjustment on this type of steering gear are the same as for the concentric valve type described above.

Steering Gear Removal

Concentric and Toggle Valve Steering Gear

1. Remove horn button from steering wheel. Unscrew retaining screws and remove base plate assembly. Remove steering wheel nut.
2. Using a suitable puller, remove steering wheel. NOTE: Where the steering column is the jointed type, the steering column and wheel need not be removed. Loosen nut on steering column shaft collar and remove steering column shaft from gear. Retain woodruff key.
3. Using suitable puller, remove pitman arm from levershaft.
4. Identify hydraulic connecting lines by tagging and marking the valve ports to which they are connected. Disconnect hydraulic lines from valve. Plug all openings.
5. Remove mounting flange bolts and remove gear from chassis.
6. To install, mount steering gear in chassis and fasten securely.
7. Place woodruff key in stud end of steering gear and install collar of steering column shaft. Secure with bolt and nut.
8. Center steering gear. Center steering wheel. Set front wheels straight ahead.
9. Connect drag link to ball on steering arm.
10. Install steering arm on levershaft of gear. If arm does not line up with splines of shaft, turn steering wheel to the right or left 1/4 turn until it does.
11. Secure arm to levershaft with lockwasher and nut. Tighten nut to 250 ft. lbs.
12. Install hydraulic lines to control valve.
13. Fill steering gear housing with SAE-90 multi-purpose lubricant.
14. Fill hydraulic power system reservoir to indicated level with SAE-10 engine oil.

Output Shaft Preload Adjustment

Rotary Valve Type Gear

1. Position steering in the straight-ahead position. Check for lash by moving steering wheel. If there is steering wheel movement without moving the steering arm, over-center adjustment must be made.
2. Disconnect steering arm and remove horn ring.
3. Position steering wheel at center of travel, then turn 1/2 turn off center.
4. Using an inch pound torque wrench and socket on the steering wheel retaining nut, determine the torque required to rotate the shaft slowly through a 20-degree arc. Turn gear to center and take a second reading. If second torque reading is 4-8 inch pounds in excess of first reading, no preload adjustment is necessary.
5. If adjustment is required, loosen adjuster screw locknut and turn screw until second reading exceeds first reading by 4-8 inch pounds.
6. Tighten locknut while holding adjusting screw in place to 27-37 ft. lbs. torque.
7. Recheck torque reading after adjustment is made.
8. Install steering arm, tightening nut to 120-125 ft. lbs. torque.
9. Install horn ring.

Output Shaft Oil Seal Replacement

Rotary Valve Type Gear

1. Clean gear and check to see that leak is at output shaft seal.
2. Remove steering arm nut and lockwasher.
3. Using suitable puller, remove steering arm from output shaft.
4. Place an oil receptacle under the steering gear.
5. Remove seal retaining ring and outer seal back-up washer.
6. With engine running, momentarily hold the steering wheel in the extreme left turn position. This will build up pressure in the upper side and force out seals and back-up washers.
7. Turn off engine and remove seals and back-up washers from shaft.
8. Clean shaft and seal area thoroughly. Cover shaft splines with plastic tape.
9. Install single lip seal and back-up washer first with seal installing tool. Drive in far enough to allow for second seal and washer. Seal must not bottom against bearing.
10. Install double lip seal and second back-up washer. Drive in only far enough to allow clearance for retaining ring.

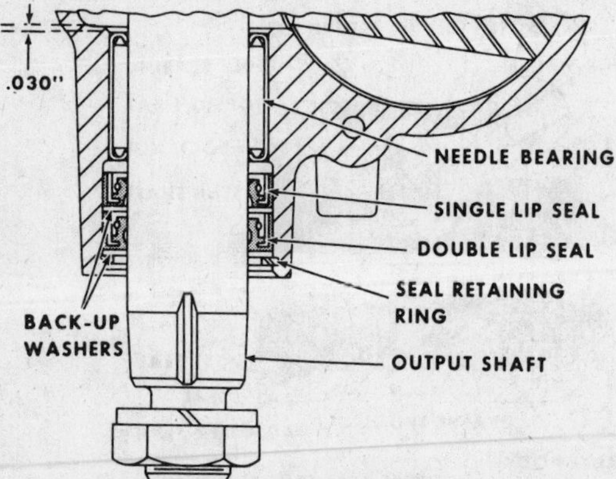

Correct installation of output shaft seals and bearing
S-281, 282
(© International Harvester Co.)

Rotary valve power steering gear with horizontal output shaft
(© International Harvester Co.)

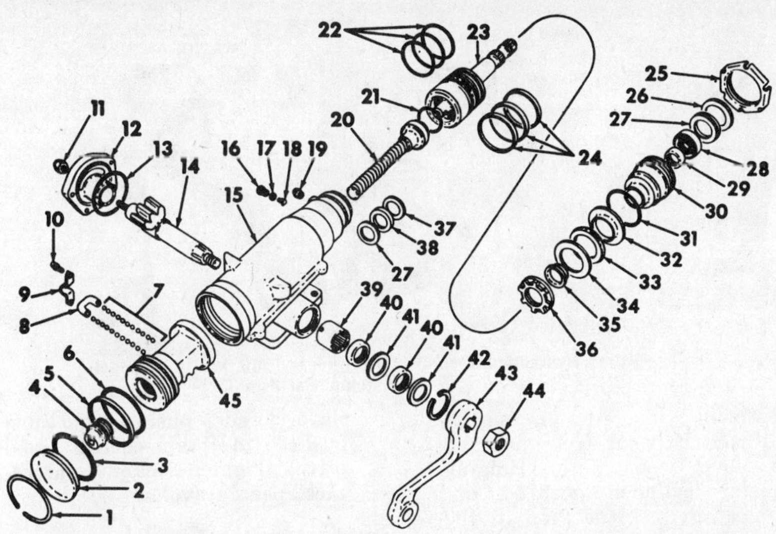

Integral rotary valve type power steering gear (© International Harvester Co.)

1 Ring, retaining
2 Plug, housing end
3 Seal, O-ring
4 Plug, rack piston end
5 Ring, rack piston
6 O-Ring, rack piston backu-up
7 Ball, recirculating
8 Guide, ball return
9 Clamp, ball return guide
10 Screw, clamp
11 Nut, lock output shaft adjuster
12 Cover, housing side
13 Seal, O-ring side cover
14 Shaft, output
15 Housing, gear
16 Seat, pressure connector
17 Valve, poppet check
18 Spring, poppet check valve
19 Seat, return connector
20 Shaft, worm
21 Seal, O-ring
22 O-Ring, valve body back-up
23 Valve, control
24 Ring, valve body
25 Nut, lock adjuster plug
26 Ring, retainer
27 Seal, dust
28 Seal, oil
29 Bearing, Needle
30 Plug, adjuster
31 Seal, O-ring
32 Race, thrust bearing, upper
33 Bearing, thrust upper
34 Race, thrust bearing, upper
35 Retainer, thrust bearing
36 Spacer, thrust bearing
37 Race, thrust bearing, lower
38 Bearing, thrust lower
39 Bearing, needle
40 Seal, output shaft
41 Washer, back-up
42 Ring, seal retaining
43 Arm, steering
44 Nut, steering arm retaining
45 Rack piston

11. Install retaining ring with snap ring pliers. Be certain that ring is seated in groove.
12. Fill pump reservoir to correct level and start engine. After engine has run for five minutes, turn steering wheel to extreme left and release. Check for fluid leakage from new seals. If seals leak they must be replaced with new seals.
13. Remove plastic tape from shaft and install steering arm, lockwasher and nut. Tighten nut to 120-125 ft. lbs. torque.

Steering Gear Removal

Horizontal Output Shaft Type

1. Apply parking brake and raise front of vehicle. Place drip pan under steering gear.
2. Position front wheels straight-ahead and tie steering wheel in centered position.
3. Disconnect and plug hydraulic lines from gear. Tag the lines for identification.
4. Remove nut and lockwasher securing steering arm to output shaft and remove arm from shaft with a suitable puller.
5. Remove lower flexible coupling clamp bolt.
6. Remove steering gear mounting bolts and remove gear from chassis.
7. To install, set gear assembly on center and position gear in chassis.
8. Insert gear stub shaft into lower flexible coupling and install and tighten gear mounting bolts to 55-60 ft. lbs. torque.
9. Install and tighten lower flexible coupling bolt clamp to 30-35 ft. lbs. torque.
10. With steering wheel centered and front wheels straight ahead, place steering arm on output shaft by matching master serrations of arm with shaft. Secure arm to shaft with lockwasher and nut, tightening nut to 120-125 ft. lbs. torque. Untie steering wheel.
11. Remove plugs and connect hydraulic lines to proper ports, tightening connections to 20-30 ft. lbs. torque.
12. Fill power steering system with fluid and start engine. Bleed system.
13. Check system for operation and leaks.
14. Remove drip pan and lower vehicle.

Steering Gear Removal

Vertical Output Shaft Type

1. Follow Steps 1 through 6 of the horizontal shaft gear removal above, leaving out Step 2 (centering and tying steering wheel). Disconnect battery cables, remove battery and battery box from chassis to permit gear removal.
2. To install, follow Steps 7 through 11 of horizontal output shaft gear installation described above.
3. Install battery box, battery and cables.
4. Follow Steps 12 through 14 of horizontal output shaft installation described above.

Power System Bleeding

Rotary Valve Type Gear

1. Fill pump reservoir to correct level with fluid.
2. Start engine and turn steering wheel through entire travel two or three times. This will permit air to escape and be replaced with fluid.
3. Check fluid level and refill if necessary.

Clutch

Hydraulic Clutch Adjustment

10", 11" and 12" Clutches

1. Check clutch pedal height. If it is not approximately 7¾" from the floorboard (measured at right angles from floorboard), loosen two bolts on the clutch pedal stop bracket and move bracket either way until proper pedal height is achieved. Tighten bracket mounting bolts.
2. Clutch pedal push rod to master cylinder piston clearance is adjusted by loosening the locknut on the pushrod and turning the rod either in or out until 3/16" pedal stroke is obtained before clutch pedal push rod contacts

Clutch and brake master cylinder installation
(© International Harvester Co.)

Hydraulic clutch master cylinder—1600 thru 1890 models
(© International Harvester Co.)

master cylinder. Tighten locknut on pushrod and recheck pedal stroke.

3. Release bearing to clutch lever (finger) clearance is adjusted at the slave cylinder pushrod. Measure stroke of clutch pedal required to produce contact of clutch release bearing to clutch release levers. If it is not 1⅞" ± ⅛", loosen locknut on slave cylinder pushrod and rotate pushrod either in or out until proper pedal travel is obtained. Tighten locknut on pushrod and recheck pedal free travel.

Hydraulic Clutch Adjustment

1600 thru 1890 Models

1. Clutch pedal push rod stroke is adjusted by loosening the locknut on the master cylinder pushrod and turning the pushrod in either direction until a pedal height of 5⅝" is achieved. Tighten locknut and recheck pedal height.
2. After adjusting pedal height (step 1), clutch release bearing clearance adjustment is made at the slave cylinder pushrod. Loosen locknut on slave cylinder pushrod and remove cotter pin and yoke pin. Holding clutch release lever forward so that release bearing is in contact with the release fingers and holding slave cylinder pushrod in released (bottomed) position, turn yoke until yoke indexes with clutch release lever hole. Install yoke pin. Check that release bearing is in contact with fingers while slave cylinder push rod is fully bottomed, then remove yoke pin and shorten linkage by turning yoke four (4) complete turns. Connect yoke and clutch release lever with yoke pin and insert cotter pin. Tighten locknut on push rod assembly.

Hydraulic Clutch Adjustment

GM-80, 1100 Models

1. Clutch pedal pushrod stroke adjustment is made by disconnecting clutch pedal from pushrod (remove yoke pin). Holding master cylinder pushrod out snugly against the stop in the end of the cylinder and making sure that the spring is holding the clutch pedal against its stop, adjust yoke on pushrod until yoke can be connected to pedal. Install yoke pin and cotter pin. Tighten locknut on yoke. A clutch pedal free travel of 5-1/6" should result.
2. Clutch finger to bearing clearance is adjusted at the slave cylinder pushrod. Clutch pedal should travel 1½" before clutch bearing makes contact with release fingers. Loosen locknut on slave cylinder pushrod and turn pushrod to obtain correct pedal travel. Tighten locknut and recheck pedal travel.

Clutch Master Cylinder Removal

1. Remove hydraulic line from master cylinder and remove yoke pins connecting pedal to master cylinder pushrod. On models with dual cylinders (brake-/clutch integral unit), disconnect brake hydraulic line, stoplight switch wire and brake pedal. If the fluid reservoir is separate from the cylinder unit, disconnect reservoir fluid line.
2. Remove cylinder assembly mounting bolts and remove cyl-

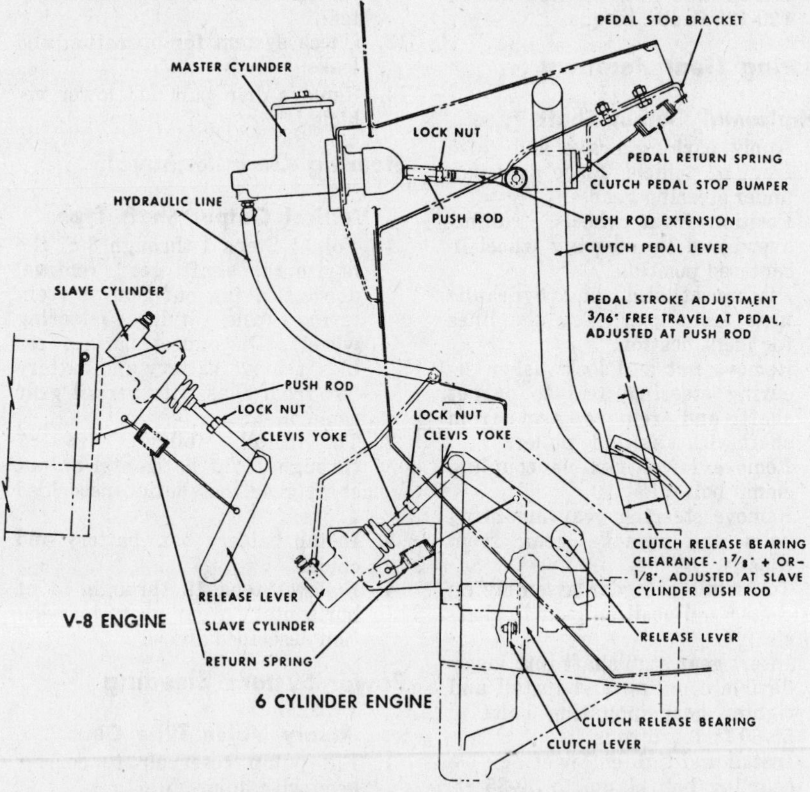

Hydraulic clutch control system (© International Harvester Co.)

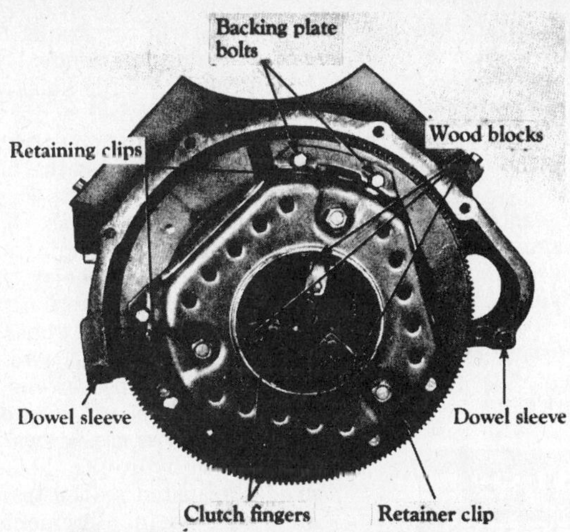

Using wood blocks to compress clutch fingers
(© International Harvester Co.)

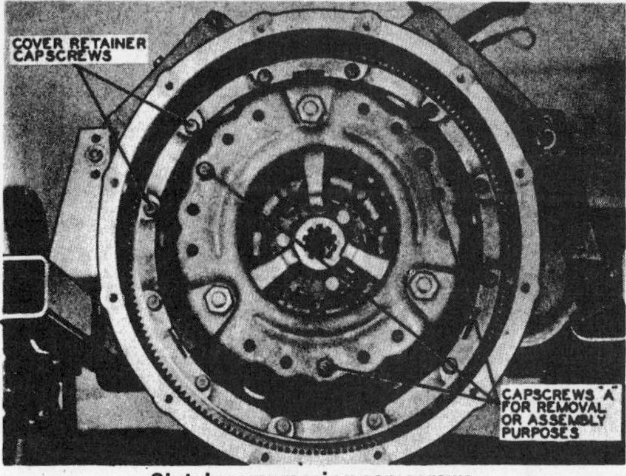

Clutch compressing cap screws
(© International Harvester Co.)

inder.

3. To install, first mount the cylinder unit, then connect hydraulic lines.
4. Adjust clutch pedal as described above.
5. Bleed hydraulic clutch system.

Slave Cylinder Removal

1. Disconnect slave cylinder pushrod from clutch release lever.
2. Disconnect hydraulic line.
3. Unbolt and remove slave cylinder unit.
4. To install, reverse Steps 1 through 3.
5. Adjust clutch pedal as described above.
6. Bleed hydraulic clutch system.

Bleeding Hydraulic Clutch System

1. Fill fluid reservoir with hydraulic brake fluid.
2. Remove dust cover from bleeder screw on slave cylinder and open bleeder screw approximately 3/4 turn.
3. Attach a short bleeder tube to bleeder screw and place the other end in clear container filled with brake fluid.
4. Pump clutch pedal slowly through full stroke repeatedly until only clear (no air bubbles) fluid flows from bleeder hose.
5. Tighten bleeder screw on down stroke of clutch pedal and remove bleeder tube. Replace rubber bleeder screw dust cover.
6. Refill fluid reservoir if necessary.

Clutch Removal

1. Remove transmission. Extreme care should be taken to support the transmission until it is completely removed so that the main shaft splines will clear the driven member. For transmission removal procedures see "Transmission—R&R" immediately following this section.
2. Remove flywheel housing cover.
3. Disconnect clevis yoke from clutch release lever.
4. Compress clutch assembly. On the 13", 14", 15" and 10" (9 spring) clutches, the pressure plate is drilled and tapped so that three retaining cap screws and flat washers may be installed. Tighten the cap screws until flat washers and cap screw heads are seated on the back plate. On the 11", 12" and 10" (6 spring, open back plate type) clutches, three retaining spacers are used to hold the clutch assembly compressed during removal. Slightly loosen the back plate to flywheel mounting screws to wedge the retaining spacers into place. On the 10" six spring (full back plate type) clutch, three 5/8"x3"x1/4" hardwood blocks are used to compress the clutch during removal. Loosen back plate to flywheel retaining screws enough to wedge the blocks between the back plate inner flange and release fingers.
5. Remove back plate to flywheel screws and remove back plate assembly and driven disc.
6. When removing the clutch assembly, observe that the balance mark (spot of white paint) on the back plate flange is located as near as possible to the balance mark ("L") stamped on the flywheel face. These balance marks should be located in the same relative position at clutch installation. If there are no marks, scribe a line to indicate correct position.
7. To install clutch, position the clutch driven member so that the long portion of the hub is toward the rear (all except the 10" 6 spring open back plate type, which may be fitted either way). Clutch must be compressed for correct installation.
8. Place clutch assembly over the driven member on the flywheel so that the balance mark (spot of white paint) is as near as possible to the flywheel balance mark ("L"). Loosely install two or three back plate to flywheel mounting screws.
9. Using a clutch aligning arbor or transmission main drive gear shaft to hold the driven member in place, complete installation of the remaining back plate to flywheel mounting screws and lockwashers. Tighten capscrews alternately and evenly.
10. Remove retaining capscrews, wood blocks or retaining spacers which were used to hold the clutch compressed.
11. Install transmission as described in "Transmission—R&R".
12. Connect linkage to clutch release lever.
13. Install flywheel housing cover.
14. Bleed hydraulic clutch system.
15. Adjust hydraulic clutch actuating system.

Standard Transmission

Reference

For manual transmission overhaul procedures see the Manual Transmission General Section.

Manual Transmission Removal

Removal and installation of manual transmissions will vary in detail, depending on which vehicle is being serviced. The following general procedure includes the basic steps common to all models.

1. Access to the transmission may be improved by removing cab floor panels.
2. Raise vehicle on a hoist or jack up and support with jack stands.
3. Drain the transmission lubricant.
4. Disconnect drive shaft at the transmission. If the vehicle is equipped with a transfer case which is not mounted directly to the transmission, disconnect the shaft between the transfer case and transmission at the yoke. If the vehicle is equipped with a transfer case which is mounted directly to the transmission, it must be removed with the transmission as a unit and the forward and rear drive shafts must be disconnected. Secure shaft out of the way with wire.
5. Disconnect shift linkage from transmission shift levers. If the vehicle is equipped with a transfer case which is mounted directly to the transmission, disconnect the shift linkage from the transfer case shift levers.
6. If the vehicle is equipped with a transmission mounted handbrake, disconnect the handbrake cable at the relay lever.
7. Disconnect speedometer cable from the transmission.
8. Remove the clutch slave cylinder from its mount. Do not disconnect the hydraulic line from the slave cylinder. Secure the push rod to the slave cylinder to avoid ejection of the internal components. Keeping the hydraulic system sealed eliminates the necessity of bleeding.
9. On some models it may be necessary to remove the starter motor.
10. Support the rear of engine by means of a hydraulic jack.
11. Remove the transmission mounting bolts and insulators at the engine rear crossmember. If possible, remove the rear engine crossmember. Remove gear shift lever and housing from top of transmission if applicable.
12. Attach suitable hoisting equipment or jack to transmission and raise enough to support the transmission assembly.
13. Remove top transmission to clutch housing bolts and install transmission guide pins.
14. Remove remaining transmission to clutch housing bolts.
15. Carefully pull transmission rearward, keeping it in line until the main drive gear shaft is clear of the clutch. CAUTION: Extreme care must be exercised to insure that the weight of the transmission does not rest on the hub of the clutch driven disc.
16. Depending on vehicle model, either lift the transmission up through the floorboard and out the right door or lower it with a jack.
17. Installation is the reverse of the above procedure.
18. Fill transmission with fluid.

Automatic Transmission

For automatic transmission overhaul procedures see Automatic Transmission General Section.

Dual Range Automatic

Removal

1. Raise the vehicle with a hoist.
2. Disconnect the fluid filler tube at the oil pan, and drain the fluid. Loosening the tube clip capscrew at the extension on the starting motor will permit rotating filler tube for transmission removal.
3. Disconnect the vacuum line at vacuum unit located at rear of transmission.
4. Disconnect the speedometer cable at speedometer adapter on transmission.
5. Disconnect the hand brake cable at drive shaft brake if chassis is so equipped.
6. Disconnect the shift linkage at manual shift lever on transmission.
7. Disconnect the two oil cooler lines on right side of transmission if chassis is so equipped.
8. Disconnect the drive shaft at transmission companion flange. NOTE: Wire the end of the drive shaft to the frame to permit transmission removal.
9. Place the hydraulic hoist with a suitable transmission lift cradle in position under the transmission oil pan. Adjust the hoist to align the cradle to the transmission oil pan flange so that the weight of the transmission case is supported by the hoist.
10. Remove the transmission case to converter housing upper capscrews and install two pilot studs into the capscrew holes.
11. Remove the transmission case to converter lower capscrews.
12. With the hydraulic hoist and cradle adjusted so the transmission case is in alignment with the converter housing, pull the transmission rearward with the hydraulic hoist to disengage the transmission from the converter housing and converter assembly. Lower transmission and remove from the vehicle.
13. To install, place two transmission pilot studs in the upper transmission to converter housing mounting screw holes.
14. Mount the transmission on a jack and position it under vehicle.
15. Rotate engine until the front pump drive lugs on the converter are in a vertical position.
16. Rotate the front pump until the slots in the pump drive gear are in a vertical position.
17. Apply lubricant similar to lubriplate to seal the surface of converter impeller cover hub.
18. Being extremely careful to align the turbine shaft splines with the turbine hub splines and the converter impeller lugs with the slots in the front pump drive gear, raise transmission and move it forward into the converter housing and converter.
19. Install the transmission to converter housing lower mounting screws. Remove two pilot studs and install upper mounting screws. Tighten all mounting screws securely.
20. Install oil cooler lines on the right side of the transmission if so equipped.
21. Connect the shift linkage at the manual shift lever on the transmission.
22. Connect the hand brake cable to the drive shaft brake if so equipped.
23. Connect the speedometer cable to the transmission.
24. Connect the vacuum line to the vacuum unit located at the rear of transmission.
25. Connect the fluid filler tube to

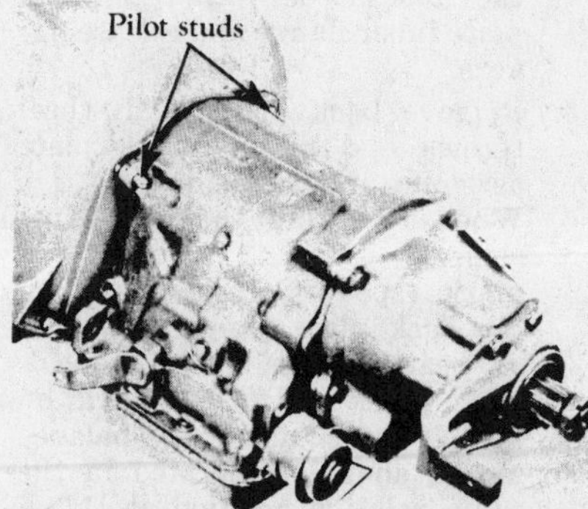

Pilot stud location—automatic transmission
(© International Harvester Co.)

the oil pan, tightening securely. Also tighten tube clip capscrews at the extension on the starter motor.

26. Connect the drive shaft to the transmission companion flange. Tighten mounting screws securely and lock with lock plates.
27. Lower vehicle to floor and fill transmission with type "A" automatic transmission fluid.
28. Road test vehicle to check performance and shift points.

Torque Converter Removal

1. Remove transmission as described above.
2. Disconnect and remove starter motor.
3. If vehicle has conventional chassis, remove floormat and transmission floor opening cover.
4. Install a rear engine support or support the rear weight of the engine with a jack.
5. Remove converter housing to crossmember mounting bolts, lower insulators and retainers.
6. Unbolt and remove rear engine crossmember.
7. Remove eight capscrews and lockwashers which attach converter housing to crankcase adapter and remove converter housing. On some models it may be necessary to lower the engine to provide clearance for converter removal.
8. Remove six nuts which attach the converter assembly to the flywheel assembly and remove converter.
9. To install, carefully place converter into position (do not damage bolt mounting threads) and install six nuts which attach converter to converter drive plate, but do not tighten nuts at this time.
10. After thoroughly cleaning crankcase converter housing adapter, install converter housing and engage the dowels being careful not to damage the dowels or the converter housing.
11. Install eight converter housing mounting capscrews and lockwashers.
12. Install rear engine crossmember.
13. Install upper and lower insulators and retainers, the converter to crossmember mounting bolts and lockwashers. Lower converter housing and engine. With insulators and retainers firmly seated, hand tighten bolts, then give bolts one-half additional turn and lock.
14. Remove rear engine support or jack.
15. If vehicle has conventional chassis, install floormat and transmission floor opening cover.
16. Install starter motor and wiring.
17. Install transmission as described above.
18. Rotate engine and converter assembly through two complete revolutions to center converter (to rotate, remove spark plugs and pry on drive plate ring gear).
19. Tighten converter to the converter drive plate attaching nuts.
20. Install converter housing adapter cover.

Transmission Fluid

1. Transmission fluid should be changed and band adjusted every 15,000 miles.
2. Remove converter housing front plate.
3. Remove one of the converter drain plugs, then rotate converter 180 degrees and remove other converter drain plug.
4. Disconnect fluid filler tube at the transmission oil pan.
5. Drain fluid and remove oil pan. Clean oil pan.
6. Connect filler tube to oil pan and tighten securely.
7. Install drain plugs in converter cover and tighten them to 7-10 ft. lbs. torque.
8. Install converter housing front plate.
9. Add five quarts of type "A" automatic transmission fluid through filler tube.
10. Run engine at idle (do not race) for about two minutes, then add five more quarts of fluid. Let engine idle until it reaches normal operating temperature.
11. Move selector lever through all positions, then place it in "P" (park). Check fluid level and add enough fluid to bring level up to the "F" (full) mark on indicator.

Front Band Adjustment

1. Drain fluid from transmission and remove oil pan (disconnect filler tube from oil pan).
2. Loosen front servo adjusting screw locknut two full turns and check the adjusting screw for free rotation.
3. Pull back on the actuating rod and insert gauge block of the front band adjusting tool (SE-1910) between the servo piston stem and adjusting screw. Tighten adjusting screw until adjusting tool handle overruns. Holding adjusting screw stationary, tighten locknut to 20-25 ft. lbs. torque. Remove gauge block.
4. Install fluid screen and pan, using a new gasket. Connect filler tube to pan.
5. Refill transmission as described above, adding new fluid if necessary.

Rear Band Adjustment

1. If vehicle is conventional model, remove floor mat and transmission cover plate from floor board.
2. Clean adjusting screw threads thoroughly and oil threads.
3. Loosen rear band adjusting locknut.
4. Using tool SE-1909, tighten adjusting screw until wrench overruns, at 10 ft. lbs. torque. NOTE: If adjusting screw is tighter than overrun of wrench,

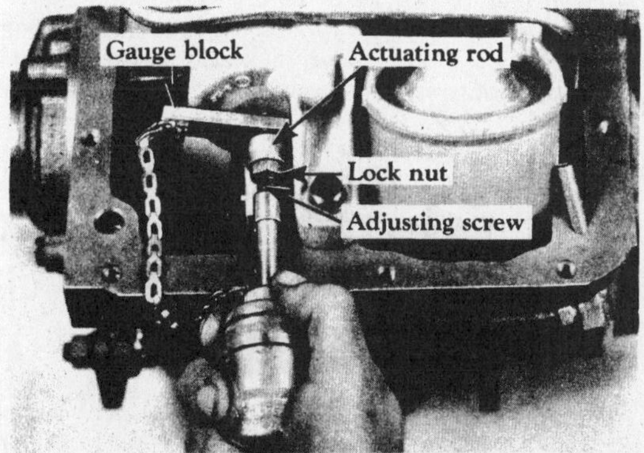

Adjusting front band
(© International Harvester Co.)

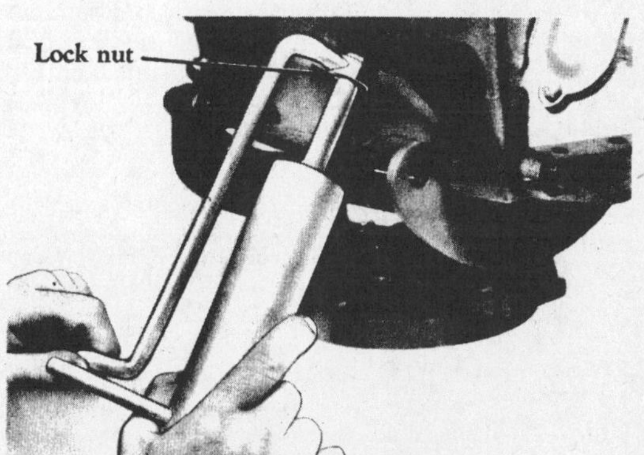

Adjusting rear band
(© International Harvester Co.)

loosen screw and retighten.

5. Back off adjusting screw one and one-half turns, then hold adjusting screw stationary and tighten locknut to 25-40 ft. lbs. torque. CAUTION: Severe damage may result if the adjusting screw is not backed off exactly one and one-half turns.
6. Install transmission cover plate and floor mat to floor board.

Manual Linkage Adjustment

1. With engine off, disconnect the manual shift rod from the selector lever on the steering column and the transmission lever on the conventional chassis, or bellcrank on the Metro chassis.
2. Position selector lever in "D" and place transmission manual lever in the "D" detent (second from the top of the transmission).
3. Position the manual shift rod into the ball joint on the steering column. The opposite end of the rod should be installed in the transmission shift lever on the conventional chassis and secured with a washer and cotter pin. On the Metro chassis, the rod yoke should be positioned on the bellcrank and secured with the clevis pin, washer and cotter pin.
4. Tighten ball joint nut at the steering column lever.
5. Move the selector lever through all positions, checking the alignment of the pointer in all positions.

Kickdown Switch Adjustment

1. On the conventional chassis the kickdown switch is located in the toeboard under the throttle pedal. On the Metro chassis it is mounted on a bracket under the toeboard and operated by a pad welded to one of the throttle linkage rods.
2. Loosen two mounting nuts and turn them either direction until a clearance of 1/4" is obtained between switch and throttle pedal on the conventional chassis and between switch and throttle linkage pad on the Metro chassis.

Vacuum Control Adjustment

1. Connect a tachometer to the engine.
2. Remove the 1/8 inch pipe plug located on the left front of the transmission case. Install a pressure gauge line connection at this point, then connect a pressure gauge to the line and place gauge in cab.
3. Start engine and move selector lever to "D" (drive) position. Apply hand brake and accelerate engine until 1000 rpm is reached. Pressure reading on gauge should be 82-88 psi.
4. If correct pressure is not obtained, loosen locknut on vacuum control unit (located at rear of transmission) and turn vacuum unit clockwise to increase pressure or counterclockwise to decrease pressure. Adjust for proper pressure, then tighten locknut. CAUTION: Do not operate engine over 10 seconds at any one time while performing the above.

U Joints, Drive Lines

Drive Shaft Assembly

It is imperative that all components of the drive train be tight to insure balance. Check companion flanges at the axles and transmission, center bearing mounts and engine mounts.

When assembling drive train, lubricate slip joint (splined) assemblies and universal joint bearings. Make sure that universal joints are kept on parallel planes by observing the arrows stamped on the shaft end and slip yoke.

Universal Joints

To remove universal joints, bend down tabs on bearing bolt lock plate and remove four bolts at each universal joint. Joint and shaft assembly must be removed as a unit to service "R" type trunnion bearings. Do not disassemble drive shaft from slip yoke unless these parts are to be replaced. On vehicles equipped with "CL" type trunnion bearings, the universal joint may be unbolted from both the drive shaft and the companion flange and the whole shaft assembly does not have to be removed to service one joint.

When replacing trunnion bearings, remove retaining clips then carefully drive out one, then the other, bearing. Use new packing washers (seals) when reassembling.

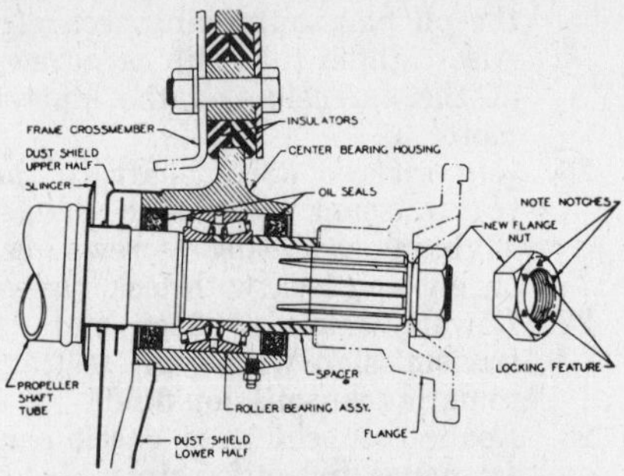

Silent spin type center driveshaft bearing
(© International Harvester Co.)

Rear Axles, Suspension

Reference

For overhaul procedures and out of truck adjustments see Rear Axle General Section.

Rear Axle Assembly Removal

1. Jack and block up truck until load is removed from springs and rear wheels are clear of the ground.
2. Drain differential housing.
3. Disconnect brake lines and parking brake cables (where used).
4. On two speed differentials, disconnect control wires or air hoses from the shift mechanism.
5. Disconnect driveshaft at rear axle companion flange.
6. Support differential on portable floor jack and take off U-bolts at springs.

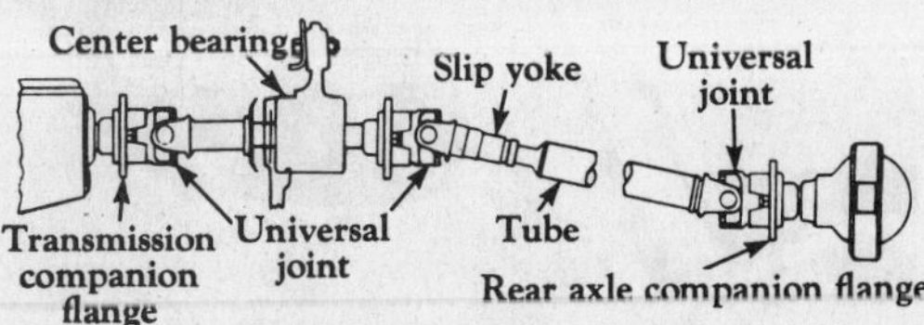

Typical drive shaft assembly
(© International Harvester Co.)

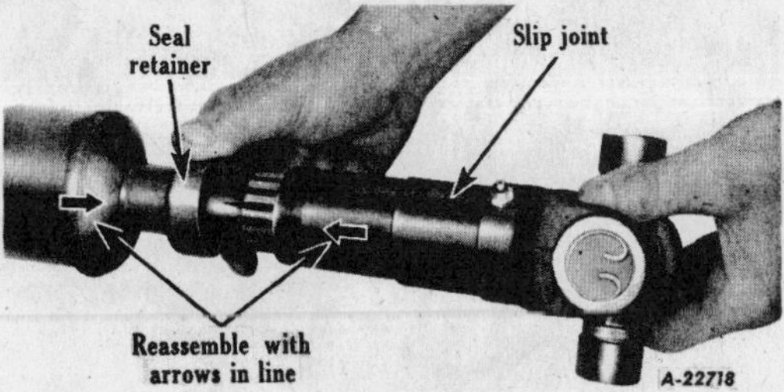

Correct slip joint assembly
(© International Harvester Co.)

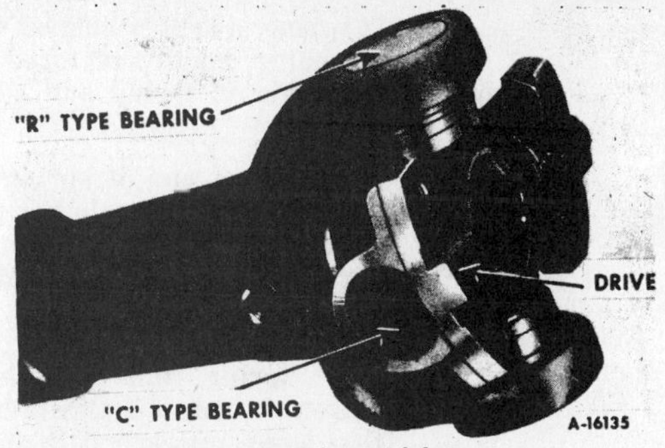

CR type universal joint
(© International Harvester Co.)

"CL" Type trunnion bearing
"CSL" Type trunnion bearing
Lock plate
Drive lug
Trunnion bearing strap
Brake flange threaded

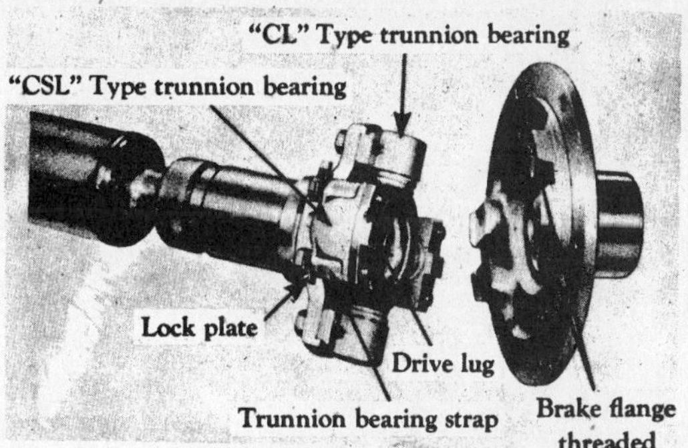

CL type universal joint
(© International Harvester Co.)

7. Roll out axle from under truck.
8. Installation is the reverse of the above procedure. Be sure to bleed hydraulic brake systems. Remove axle housing breather valve and clean thoroughly with solvent.

Rear Axle Shaft Removal

Semi-Floating Type

1. Remove wheel and nut from axle shaft end.
2. Remove hub and drum assembly with a suitable puller.
3. Unbolt and remove brake backing plate and bearing retainer.
4. Pull axle shaft and bearing using suitable puller. Bearings are pressed on.
5. When installing axle shaft assembly, use new oil seals and be careful not to damage seals.
6. Lightly tap bearing cap into axle housing.
7. Install shims on end of axle housing flange and insert backing plate bolts to retain shims.
8. Install backing plate, bearing retainer and seal retainer. Tighten nuts to specified torque.
9. Install wheel hub. Grasp wheel hub and pull outward to be sure that axle shaft is withdrawn as far as possible.
10. Check axle shaft end play as follows: Mount dial indicator on stationary location at right-hand side of axle assembly. Position indicator against end of axle shaft and check shaft end play. If end play is not within .006", shims must be added or removed between backing plate and axle housing flange.
11. Place key in axle shaft and install hub and drum assembly on shaft, securing with washer and nut. Tighten nut and install cotter pin.

Rear Axle Shaft Removal

Full-Floating Type

1. Axle shaft is removed without taking off wheels. Remove axle shaft nuts from studs in the wheel hub.
2. Install puller screws in the two tapped holes provided in the axle shaft flange.
3. Turn in puller screws until axle shaft is loose, then pull axle.
4. Installation is the reverse of the above procedure. Be sure puller screws are removed.

Rear Axle Shaft Removal

Full-Floating Type With Tapered Dowel Mounting

1. Remove flange nuts from studs of wheel hub.
2. Using a heavy hammer, strike sharply on the center of the flange of the axle shaft. This will unseat and loosen tapered dowels.
3. Remove tapered dowels.
4. Push axle flange back into position against wheel hub and strike again with a hammer to spring axle shaft away from the wheel hub. Do not pry on flange.
5. When installing axle shaft, make sure there is between the axle shaft driving flange and lockwasher. Dowel must not be "sunken in."

Locking Differentials

Reference

For overhaul procedures of differentials with "NoSPIN" and "Powr-Lok" locking units see Rear Axle portion of General Section.

Single reduction type axle final drive
(© International Harvester Co.)

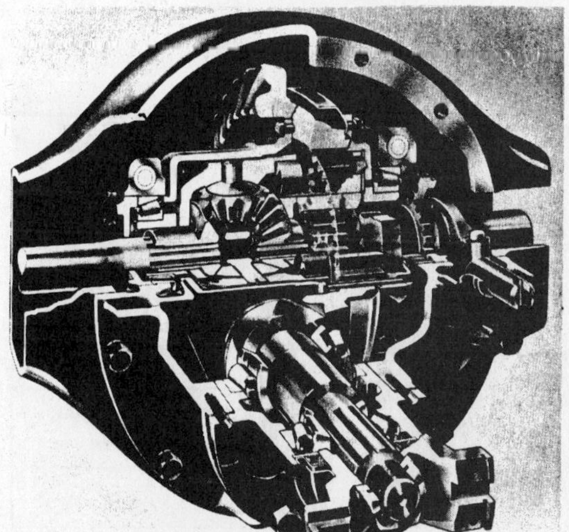

Two speed planetary gear type axle final drive
(© International Harvester Co.)

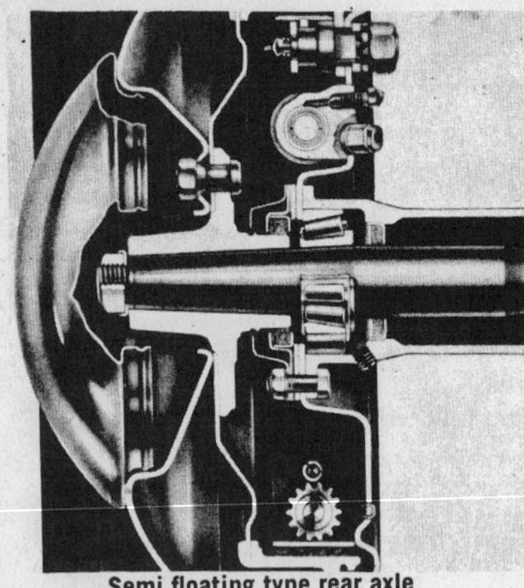
Semi floating type rear axle
(© International Harvester Co.)

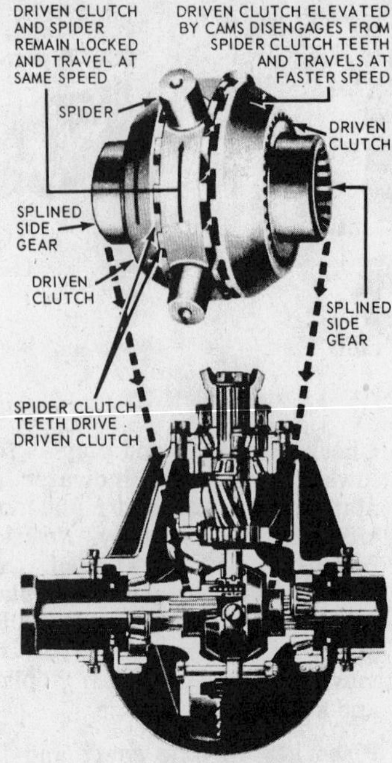

No Spin locking type differential
(© International Harvester Co.)

Rear Spring Removal

1. Place floor jack under truck frame and raise truck sufficiently to relieve weight from spring to be removed.
2. Remove shock absorbers where used.
3. Remove U-bolts, spring bumper and retainer or U-bolt seat.
4. Remove lubricators (not used where springs are equipped with rubber bushings).
5. Remove nuts from spring shackle pins or bracket pins.
6. Slide spring off bracket pin and shackle pin.
7. If spring is rubber bushed, bushing halves may be removed from each side of spring and shackle eye.
8. Install pivot end of spring first. Align shackle end to other frame bracket. When installing nuts on spring pins which are welded or pressed in, be sure that washer is tightened against shoulder of pin. Spring pins which are driven in must be installed so that slot for lock bolt is aligned. Spring pins which are threaded in must be installed so that the lubrication hole is facing up.

   Tighten pin into bracket, then back off one-half turn. Install locknut tightly and install cotter pin. Turn pin out to permit installation of cotter pin.
9. Install lubricators.
10. Install U-bolt seat or retainer and U-bolts. Install U-bolt nuts, but do not tighten.
11. Install shock absorber where used.
12. Lower vehicle.
13. Tighten U-bolt nuts, torquing them according to the following:

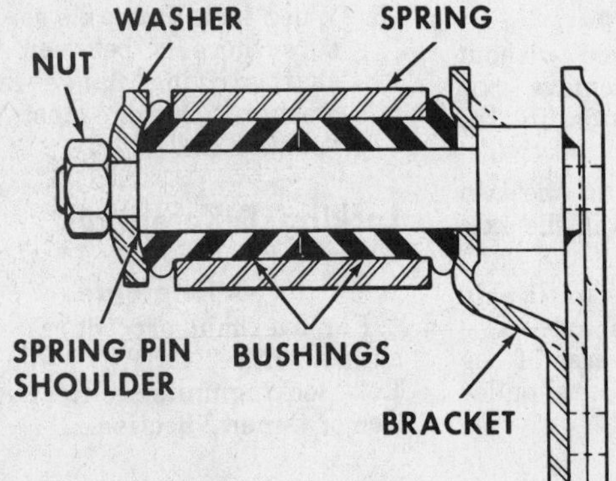

Welded type spring pin
(© International Harvester Co.)

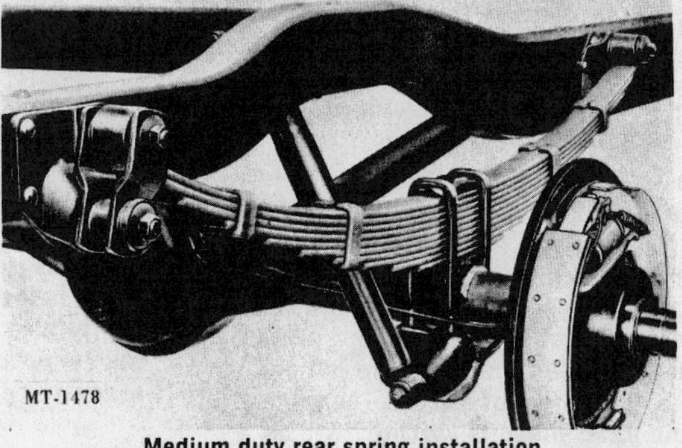

Medium duty rear spring installation
(© International Harvester Co.)

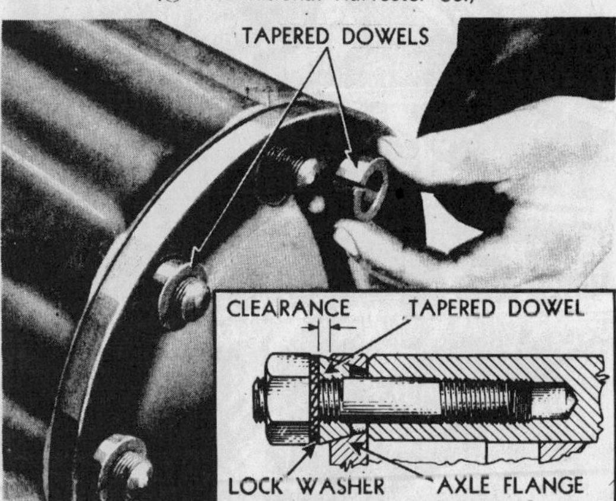

Full floating rear axle shaft tapered dowels
(© International Harvester Co.)

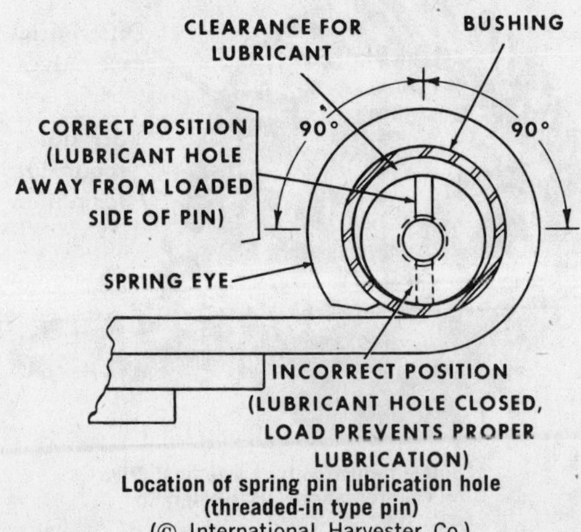

Location of spring pin lubrication hole
(threaded-in type pin)
(© International Harvester Co.)

Index

Jeep Trucks

TUNE-UP SPECIFICATIONS

CU. IN. DISPLACEMENT	YEAR	SPARK PLUG GAP	DISTRIBUTOR POINT DWELL	DISTRIBUTOR POINT GAP	IGNITION TIMING DEGREES	CRANKCASE COMP. PRESSURE	VALVE CLEARANCE	GOV. RPM NO LOAD	FUEL PUMP PRESS	IDLE SPEED* STD.	IDLE SPEED* AUTO.
FOUR CYLINDER											
134[a]	1964	.030	40	.020	5B	90-110	.016	2600	3	600	—
134[b]	1964-71	.030	40	.020	5B	120-130	.016	2600	3	600	—
SIX CYLINDER											
230[1]	1964-65	.030	38	.020	5B	150	.008	—	4½	550	—
232	1966-71	.035	32	.016	[3]	145	Zero	—	5	650-700[6]	—
225[2]	1965-71	.035	30	.016	5B	165	Zero	—	5	550	—
258	1971	.035	31-34	.016	5B	185	Zero	—	4-5½	600	650-700
EIGHT CYLINDER											
327	1966-69	.035	30	.016	[4]	145	Zero	—	4½	650-700	[7]
350	1969-71	.030	30	.016	[5]	165	Zero	—	5	550[8]	600
304	1971	.035	29-31	.016	2½B	185	Zero	—	4-5½	650	650-700
360	1971	.035	29-31	.016	2½B	185	Zero	—	4-5½	650	700-750

1—OHC
2—V6
3—5B w/o emission control, 0 on dist. model 111044 and w/emission control.
4—5B w/o emission control, 0 w/emission control.
5—5B on dist. model 11116964, 0 on 1111330, 1111474 and 1111938 models.
6—550 rpm w/emission control.
7—550 std. 500 auto. w/emission control.
8—650-700 w/emission control.
* With manual transmission in N and automatic in D.
a—L-Head
b—F-Head

FIRING ORDER AND ROTATION

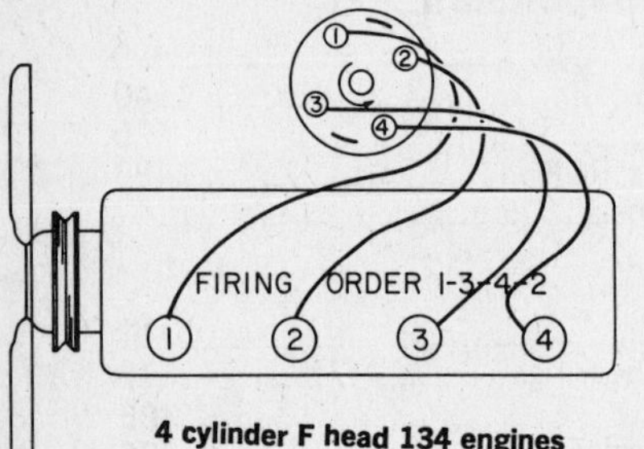

4 cylinder F head 134 engines

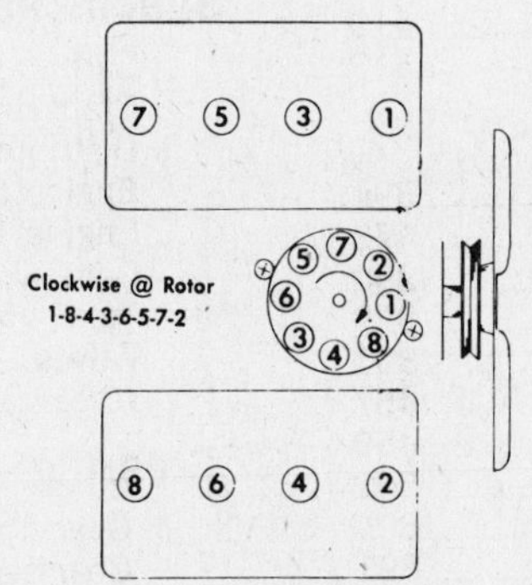

V8 304, 360 engines

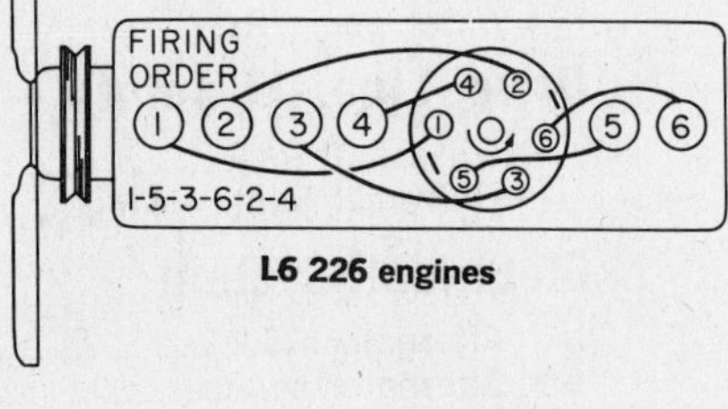

L6 226 engines

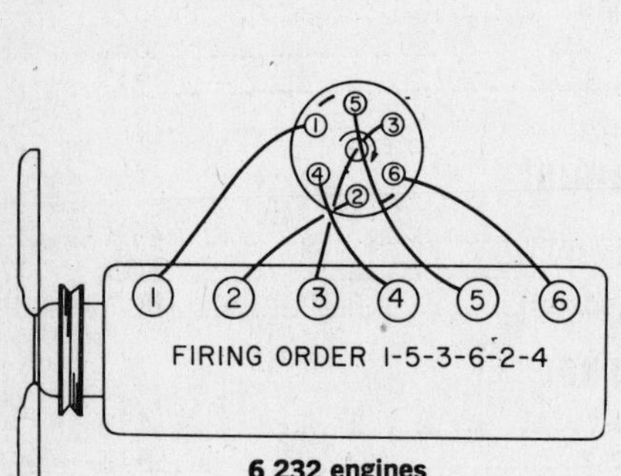

6 232 engines

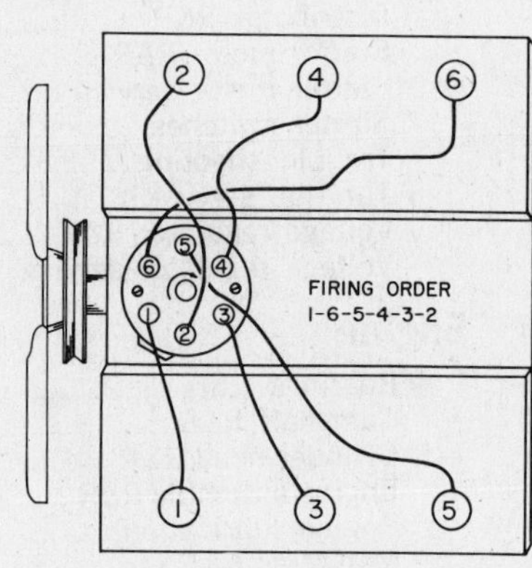

V6 225 engines

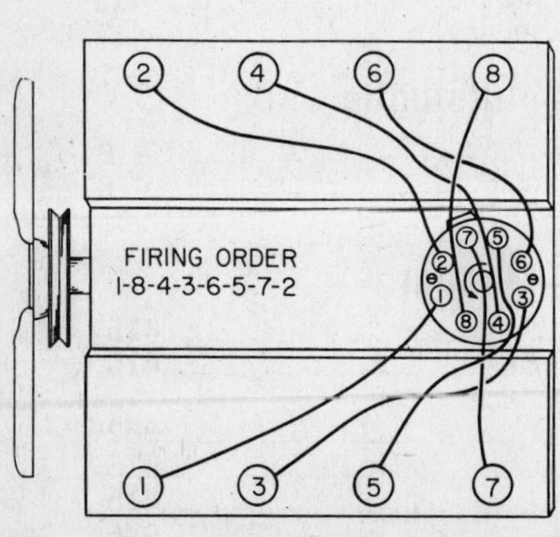

V8 327 engines

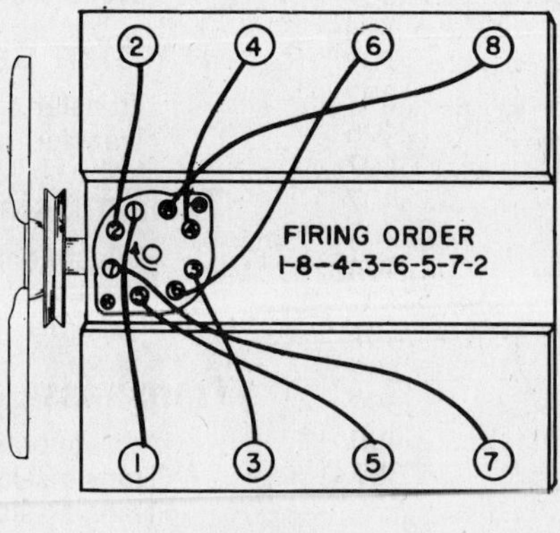

V8 350 engines

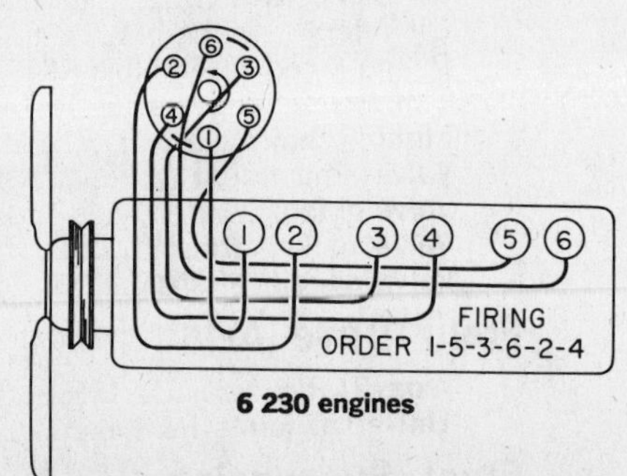

6 230 engines

GENERAL ENGINE SPECIFICATIONS

CU. IN. DISPLACE-MENT	YEAR	BORE AND STROKE	FIRING ORDER	DEVELOPED HORSEPOWER @ R.P.M.	DEVELOPED TORQUE @ R.P.M.	COM-PRESSION RATIO	CARBU-RETOR	VALVE LIFTER TYPE	NORMAL OIL PRESSURE
FOUR CYLINDER									
134[1]	1964	3.125 x 4.375	1-3-4-2	60 @ 4000	105 @ 2000	7.0	1V	Mech.	37[7]
134[2]	1964-71	3.125 x 4.375	1-3-4-2	75 @ 4000	114 @ 2000	[5]	1V	Mech.	35[7]
SIX CYLINDER									
230[3]	1964-65	3.344 x 4.315	1-5-3-6-2-4	140 @ 4000	210 @ 1750	8.5	1V	Mech.	50[7]
232	1966-71	3.750 x 3.500	1-5-3-6-2-4	145 @ 4300	215 @ 1600	8.5	1V	Hyd.	50
225[4]	1965-71	3.750 x 3.400	1-6-5-4-3-2	160 @ 4200	235 @ 2400	9.0	2V	Hyd.	33[8]
258	1971	3.750 x 3.895	1-5-3-6-2-4	150 @ 3800	240 @ 1800	8.0[6]	1V	Hyd.	37[9]
EIGHT CYLINDER									
327	1966-69	4.000 x 3.250	1-8-4-3-6-5-7-2	250 @ 4700	340 @ 2600	8.7	2V	Hyd.	55
350	1969-70	3.800 x 3.850	1-8-4-3-6-5-7-2	230 @ 4400	350 @ 2400	9.0	2V	Hyd.	37[8]
304	1971	3.750 x 3.440	1-8-4-3-6-5-7-2	210 @ 4400	300 @ 2600	8.4	2V	Hyd.	37[9]
360	1971	4.080 x 3.440	1-8-4-3-6-5-7-2	245 @ 4400	365 @ 2600	8.5	2V	Hyd.	37[9]

1—L-Head
2—F-Head.
3—OHC.
4—V-6.
5—7.4, 6.9 or 7.8 to one.
6—Optional 7.6 to one.
7—@ 2000 rpm.
8—@ 2400 rpm.
9—Minimum pressure at 1600 rpm or above.

CRANKSHAFT BEARING JOURNAL SPECIFICATIONS

CU. IN. DISPLACE-MENT	YEAR	MAIN BEARING JOURNALS: JOURNAL DIAMETER	OIL CLEARANCE	SHAFT END PLAY	THRUST ON NO.	CONNECTING ROD BEARING JOURNALS: JOURNAL DIAMETER	OIL CLEARANCE	END PLAY
FOUR CYLINDER								
134[1]	1964	2.3330	.0016	.005	1	1.9375	.0010	.007
134[2]	1964-71	2.3330	.0019	.005	1	1.9375	.0014	.007
SIX CYLINDER								
230[3]	1964-65	2.3750	.0015	.005	Rear	2.0623	.0015	.009
232	1966-71	2.4988	.0012	.005	3	2.0952	.0008	.009
225[4]	1965-71	2.4995	.0009	.006	2	2.0000	.0021	.010
258	1971	2.4986-2.5001	.001-.002	.002-.007	3	2.0934-2.0955	.001-.002	.008-.010
EIGHT CYLINDER								
327	1966-69	2.4991	.0018	.005	1	2.2486	.0015	.010
350	1969-71	2.9995	.0010	.006	3	2.000	.0012	.010
304	1971	[5]	.001-.002[6]	.003-.008	3	2.7464-2.7479	.001-.002	.009-.015
360	1971	[5]	.001-.002[6]	.003-.008	3	2.7464-2.7479	.001-.002	.009-.015

1—L-Head.
2—F-Head.
3—OHC.
4—V-6.
5—Nos. 1—4, 2.7474-2.7489; No. 5, 2.7464-2.7479.
6—Rear main, .002-.003.

VALVE SPECIFICATIONS

CU. IN. DISPLACE-MENT	YEAR	LASH INCHES (HOT)	ANGLE DEGREE: FACE	ANGLE DEGREE: SEAT	STEM DIAMETER: INT.	STEM DIAMETER: EXH.	STEM CLEARANCE: INTAKE	STEM CLEARANCE: EXHAUST	VALVE LIFT INCHES	VALVE SPRING LBS. @ INCHES
FOUR CYLINDER										
134[1]	1964	.016	NA	45	.373	.371	.0015	.0035	.351	53 @ 2 7/64
134[2]	1964-71	.016	NA	46	.373	.371	.0014	.0035	.260	73 @ 1 21/32

VALVE SPECIFICATIONS

CU. IN. DISPLACEMENT	YEAR	LASH INCHES (HOT)	ANGLE DEGREE FACE	SEAT	STEM DIAMETER INT.	EXH.	STEM CLEARANCE INTAKE	EXHAUST	VALVE LIFT INCHES	VALVE SPRING LBS. @ INCHES
SIX CYLINDER										
230[3]	1964-65	.008	NA	45	.340	.339	.0070	.0035	.375	57 @ 1¼
232	1966-71	Zero	—5—		.373	.373	.0020	.0020	.375	100 @ 1 13/16
225[4]	1965-71	Zero	45	45	.3407	.3407	.0020	.0025	.401	10
258	1971	Zero	6	5	—8—		—9—		.254	195 @ 1 7/16
EIGHT CYLINDER										
327	1966-69	Zero	—5—		.372	.372	.0020	.0020	.375	88 @ 1 13/16
350	1969-71	Zero	45	45	.372	.372	.0025	.0025	.371	75 @ 1 11/16
304	1971	Zero	7	5	—8—		—9—		.265	195 @ 1 7/16
360	1971	Zero	7	5	—8—		—9—		.265	195 @ 1 7/16

1—L-Head.
2—F-Head.
3—OHC.
4—V-6.
5—Intake 30°, exhaust 45°.
6—Intake 29°, exhaust 44°.
7—Intake 29°, exhaust 44½°.
8—.3715-.3725, intake and exhaust.
9—.001-.003, intake and exhaust.
10—Intake 64 @ 1 11/16, exhaust 64 @ 1 5/8.

TORQUE SPECIFICATIONS

CU. IN. DISPLACEMENT	YEAR	CYLINDER HEAD BOLTS FT. LBS.	ROD BEARING BOLTS FT. LBS.	MAIN BEARING BOLTS FT. LBS.	CRANKSHAFT BALANCER BOLT FT. LBS.	FLYWHEEL TO CRANKSHAFT BOLTS FT. LBS.	MANIFOLDS FT. LBS. INTAKE	EXHAUST
FOUR CYLINDER								
134[1]	1964	60-70	35-45	65-75	60-70	35-41	29-35	29-35
134[2]	1964-71	60-70	35-45	65-75	60-70	35-41	29-35	29-35
SIX CYLINDER								
230[3]	1964-65	80-95	40-45	85-95	100-130	35-40	15-20	35-40
232	1966-71	80-85	27-30	75-85	70-80	100-110	20-25	20-25
225[4]	1965-71	65-80	30-40	95-120	140-160	50-65	25-35	15-20
258	1971	80 85	26-30	75-85	75-85	100-110	40-45	20-25
EIGHT CYLINDER								
327	1966-69	58-62	46-50	5	70-80	100-110	20-25	20-25
350	1969-71	6	35	110	140-180	60	50	18
304	1971	105-115	26-30	95-105	50-60	100-110	40-45	30-35
360	1971	105-115	26-30	95-105	50-60	100-110	40-45	30-35

1—L-Head.
2—F-Head.
3—OHC.
4—V-6.
5—All but rear 80-85, rear 50-55.
6—Metal gasket 75, composition gasket 80.

WHEEL ALIGNMENT SPECIFICATIONS

MODEL	CASTER (DEGREES)	CAMBER (DEGREES)	TOE-IN (INCHES)	KING-PIN INCLINATION (DEGREES)
CJ (Early)	+3	+1	3/64-3/32	7½
DJ-3A	+3	+1	3/64-3/32	7½
CJ-3B, CJ-5, CJ-6	+3	+1½	3/64-3/32	7½
DJ-5, DJ-6, CJ-5A	+3	+1½	3/64-3/32	7½
CJ-6A	+3	+1½	3/64-3/32	7½
Jeepster	+3[1]	+1½[1]	3/64-3/32	7½
Wagoneer	+3	+1½	3/64-3/32	7½
Gladiator	+3	+1½	3/64-3/32	7½

1—Preset—non-adjustable.

ENGINE MODEL APPLICATION

Model	Year	Engine Make	Engine Model	Crankcase Refill Capacity Qts. ☆	Cooling System Capacity Qts. □
MD	1963-67	Own	F4-134[1]	4	12
CJ3B	1963-64	Own	F4-134[1]	4	12
CJ5	1963-71	Own	F4-134[1]	4	12
CJ6	1963-71	Own	F4-134[1]	4	12
CJ6	1965-71	Buick	V6-225[3]	4	13
C101	1967-71	Own	F4-134[1]	4	12
C101	1967-71	Buick	V6-225[3]	4	13
DJ3A	1963-64	Own	F4-134[1]	4	12
DJ5	1966-71	Own	F4-134[1]	4	12
DJ6	1966-71	Own	F4-134[1]	4	12
DJ6	1966-71	Buick	V6-225[3]	4	13
J162	1963-65	Own	OHC6-230[2]	5	12
J162	1966-71	AM	6-232[4]	5	19
J162	1966-71	AM	V8-327[5]	4	19
J162	1971 (late)	AM	6-258[4]	4	19
J162	1971 (late)	AM	V8-304[7]	4	19
J164	1963-65	Own	OHC6-230[2]	5	12
J164	1966-71	AM	6-232[4]	5	19
J164	1966-71	AM	V8-327[5]	4	19
J164	1968-71	Buick	V8-350[6]	4	15
J164	1971 (late)	AM	6-258[4]	4	19
J164	1971 (late)	AM	V8-304[7]	4	19
J164	1971 (late)	AM	V8-360[7]	4	19

☆ Add 1 qt. with new filter.
□ With heater.
Location of engine number is as follows—
1. Front of block above water pump.
2. Lower right front corner of block behind coil.
3. Front face of block below left head gasket.
5. Stamped on boss above oil filter.
5. On alternator bracket.
6. Left cylinder head between front 2 spark plugs.
7. Right rocker arm cover.

Letters stamped after engine number indicate engine deviations in bore and crankshaft sizes.

Distributor

Distributor Removal

Inline Engines

The distributor assembly on all Jeep 4 and 6 cylinder in-line engines is located on the right side of the engines.

To remove it, take off the distributor cap and wire assembly and bend out of the way. Remove the ignition primary wire from side of the distributor and take off the vacuum lines to the carburetor. Mark the distributor housing and the engine crankcase to insure correct reinstallation. Note the position of the rotor. Remove bolt that holds the distributor down into the block and lift assembly off the engine.

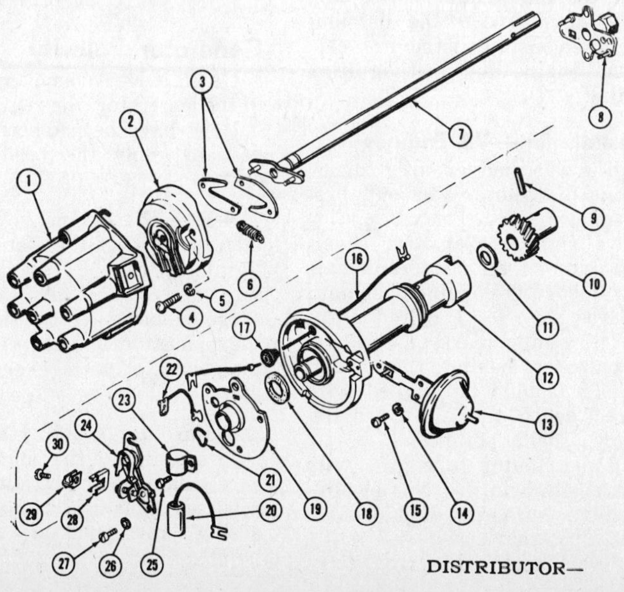

DAUNTLESS V-6 ENGINE

1—Cap Assembly
2—Rotor
3—Governor Weight
4—Rotor Mounting Screw
5—Lock Washer
6—Weight Spring (Governor)
7—Shaft
8—Cam Assembly
9—Gear Pin
10—Drive Gear
11—Spacer Washer
12—Housing
13—Vacuum Control
14—Lock Washer
15—Control Mounting Screw
16—Primary Lead
17—Lead Grommet
18—Washer
19—Breaker Plate
20—Condenser
21—Retaining Spring
22—Ground Lead
23—Condenser Clamp
24—Contact Set
25—Clamp Screw
26—Lock Washer
27—Contact Screw
28—Insulator
29—Spring Clip
30—Screw

DISTRIBUTOR—

Installation—Inline Engines

If the crankshaft has not been rotated, simply match the marks made on removal and reinstall the rotor.

If the crankshaft has been rotated, turn the crankshaft until No. 1 cylinder is at the top of the compression stroke as indicated by air being forced out from No. 1 spark plug opening. Install distributor with rotor pointing toward No. 1 spark plug wire on the distributor cap and the points just opening. Start the engine and set ignition timing.

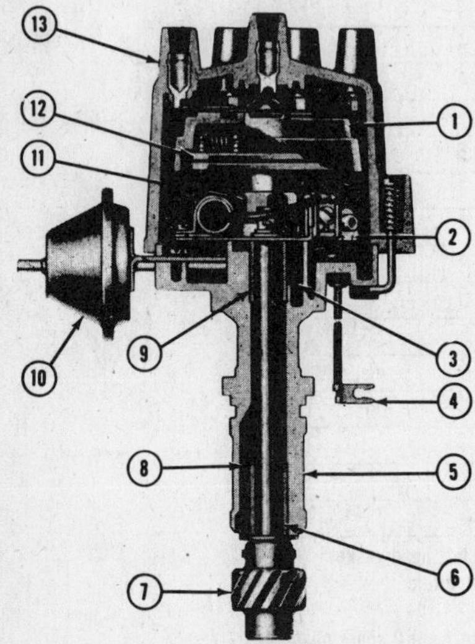

Delco distributor—typical
(© Willys Corp.)

1 Rotor
2 Breaker plate assembly
3 Lubrication reservoir
4 Primary terminal
5 Distributor housing
6 Shaft bushing
7 Gear
8 Access passage
9 Shaft bushing
10 Vacuum assembly
11 Cam
12 Weight assembly
13 Cap

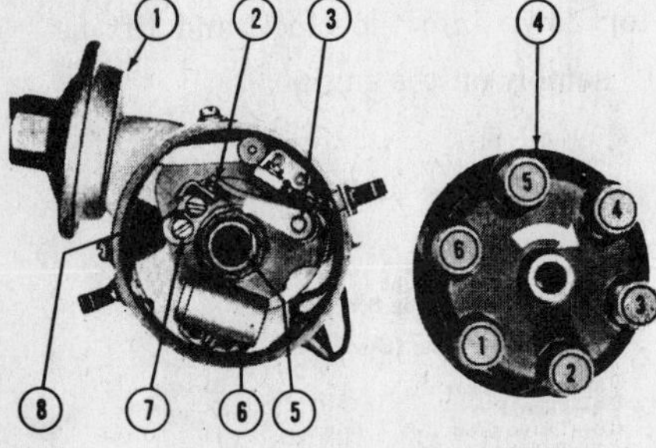

Prestolite distributor—typical
(© Willys Corp.)

1 Vacuum advance unit
2 Distributor points
3 Breaker arm pivot
4 Distributor cap (rotation & firing order)
5 Lubricating wick
6 Condenser
7 Adjusting eccentric screw
8 Adjustment lock screw

Distributor Removal

V6, V8 Engines

Disconnect the distributor primary wire from the coil and the tube from the vacuum unit. Remove distributor cap by inserting a screwdriver into upper slotted end of cap latches, pressing down and turning 90° counterclockwise.

Make a mark on the distributor body in line with the rotor. Matchmark position of vacuum unit to the engine.

Remove clamp to release distributor and remove assembly from crankcase.

CAUTION: Design of the V6-90° engine requires a special form of distributor cam. The distributor may be serviced in the normal manner and should cause no more problem than any other distributor, if the firing plan is thoroughly understood.

The distributor cam is not ground to standard six cylinder indexing intervals. This particular form requires that the original pattern of spark plug wiring be used. The engine will not run in balance if No. 1 spark plug wire is inserted into No. 6 distributor cap tower, even though each wire in firing sequence is advanced to the next distributor tower. There is a difference between the firing intervals of each succeeding cylinder through the 720° engine cycle.

Installation—V6 Engine

1. If engine has been disturbed, rotate the crankshaft to bring the piston of No. 1 cylinder to the top of its compression stroke.
2. Position the distributor in the block with the rotor at No. 1 firing position. Make sure the oil pump intermediate drive shaft is properly seated in the oil pump.
3. Install the distributor lock but do not tighten.
4. Rotate the distributor body clockwise until the breaker points are just starting to open. Tighten the retaining screw.
5. Connect the primary wire and the vacuum line to the distributor, then install distributor cap.
6. Start engine and set ignition timing.

Installation—V8 Engines

If engine was inadvertently turned over while distributor was out, proceed as follows:

Remove right rocker arm cover. Using a wrench on the crankshaft pulley bolt, turn the engine over until both valves for No. 1 cylinder are closed. The timing mark on the harmonic balancer behind the crankshaft pulley should be aligned with the correct degree mark. No. 1 cylinder is now at firing point.

Install distributor in engine with rotor in position to fire No. 1 cylinder. The vacuum unit should align with the matchmark made when distributor was removed. Press down lightly on distributor if it does not seat correctly. Use starter to turn engine until the tang on the distributor shaft slips into the slot in the oil pump shaft. This will not disturb the relationship between the distributor and the camshaft because the drive gear engages before the tang. However, it will be necessary to return the engine to the No. 1 firing point and check that rotor is also at No. 1 firing point. Reconnect vacuum tube and primary wire. Rotate the distributor body slightly until contacts just start to open. Install and tighten distributor clamp. Install distributor cap. Start engine and adjust point dwell.

If the engine has not been disturbed since the distributor was removed proceed as follows:

Insert distributor into the block so that the rotor is pointing to the mark made on distributor housing and the vacuum advance unit is aligned with the match-mark made on the engine. Connect the vacuum tube, primary wire, and install the distributor cap. Install distributor clamp. Check that spark plug wires are correctly routed. Start engine and adjust point dwell and then adjust ignition timing. Rotate distributor body counter-clockwise to advance the timing.

Breaker Points

Breaker point gap and dwell are listed for all engines in the Tune-Up Specifications table in this section. Timing marks and firing order for various models are also illustrated. Refer to the Troubleshooting Section for diagnosis of ignition problems.

Generator, Regulator

Generator Polarity

CAUTION: Whenever the circuits to the generator, the regulator, or the battery have been disconnected it is best to apply the following procedure:

Before the engine is started, momentarily short the Bat. to the Gen. terminals of the regulator with a screwdriver. This gives a momentary surge of current from the battery to the generator, and correctly polarizes the generator with regard to the battery.

Failure to polarize the generator before starting the engine may severely damage the regulator, because reversed polarity causes vibration, arcing, and burning of the relay points.

Alternator R&R

V8 350 Engine

Unfasten bolt holding tension bar to alternator. Push alternator in toward engine to release drive belt. Unfasten mounting bolt to release alternator from engine.

When reinstalling, adjust drive belt to allow ½" play on the longest run between pulleys.

Regulator R&R

L6 232, 258 Engines
V8 302, 327, 360 Engines

Disconnect plug from the regulator. Remove attaching sheet metal screws and lift off regulator. Install in the reverse of removal.

AC Generator

The purpose of this unit is to satisfy the increase in electrical loads that have been imposed upon the car battery by modern conditions of traffic and driving patterns.

The AC generator is explained in the general repair section.

CAUTION: Since the AC generator and regulator are designed for use on only one polarity system, the following precautions must be observed:

a. The polarity of the battery, generator and regulator must be matched and considered before making any electrical connections in the system.

b. When connecting a booster battery, be sure to connect the negative battery terminals together and the positive battery terminals together.

c. When connecting a charger to the battery, connect the charger positive lead to the battery positive terminal. Connect the charger negative lead to the battery negative terminal.

d. Never operate the AC generator on open circuit. Be sure that all connections in the circuit are clean and tight.

e. Do not short across or ground any of the terminals on the AC generator.

f. Do not attempt to polarize the AC generator.

g. Do not use test lamps of more than 12 volts for checking diode continuity.

h. Avoid long soldering times when replacing diodes or transistors. Prolonged heat is damaging to these units.

i. Disconnect the battery ground terminal when servicing any AC system. This will prevent the possibility of accidentally reversing polarity.

Starter Removal

L6, 232, 258 Engines

Remove the oil filler pipe and disconnect the battery and solenoid leads from the starter. From underneath the vehicle, remove the bolts that attach the starter to bell housing and lift out starter.

Install in the reverse of removal. 327V8, 304V8, 360V8 Disconnect bat-

Generator installed (© Willys Corp.)

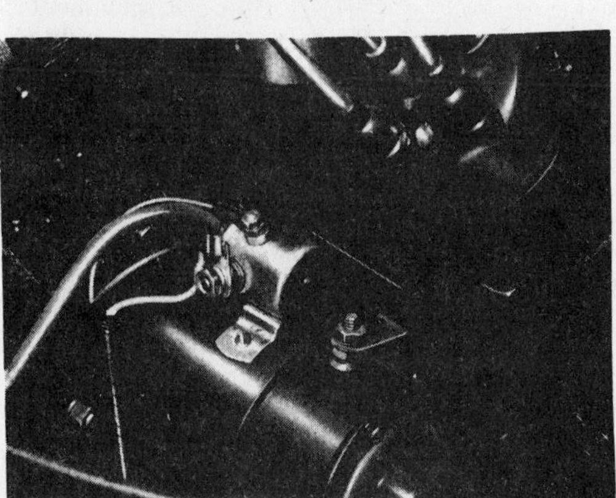

Starter and solenoid (© Willys Corp.)

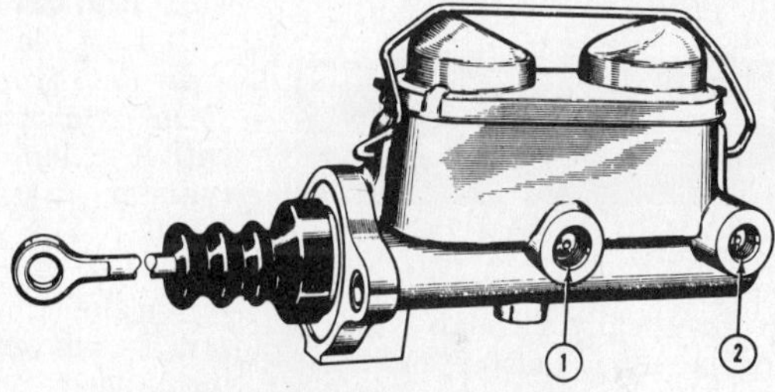

Master cylinder brake line outlets
(© Willys Corp.)

1 Primary outlet—to front wheel brakes
2 Secondary outlet—to rear wheel brakes

Wire locations for alternator hook-up
(© Willys Corp.)

1 Auxiliary terminal
2 Output terminal
3 Auxiliary terminal
4 Field terminal
5 Ground terminal
6 Ground terminal

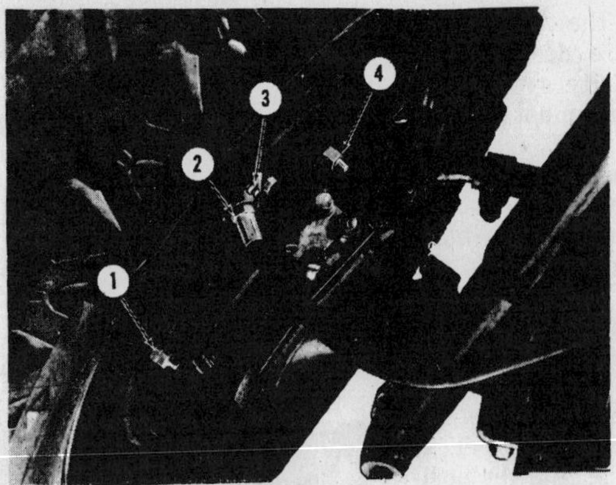

Bleeding brakes (© Willys Corp.)

1 Eccentric locknut
2 Brake hose
3 Bleeder screw
4 Eccentric adjusting screw

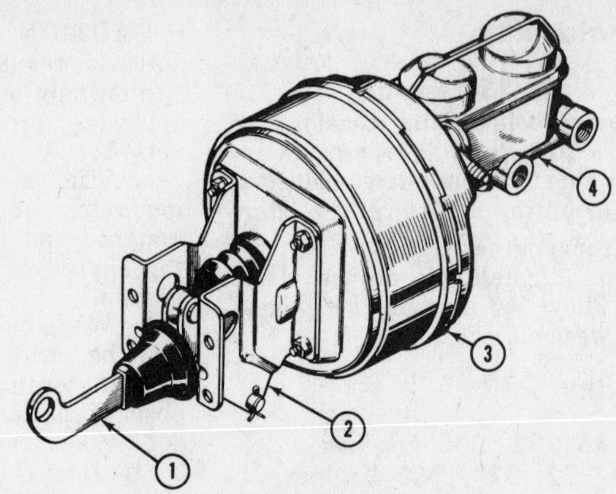

Brake booster unit and master cylinder (© Willys Corp.)

1 Pedal link
2 Mounting bracket
3 Power section
4 Master cylinder

tery lead and solenoid lead from the starter. From underneath the vehicle, remove attaching bolts and lift out the starter. Install in the reverse of removal.

Refer to General Repair Section for overhaul procedures.

Brakes

Master Cylinder

All Jeep brake systems are actuated hydraulically through either a single or a dual master cylinder. Some models are equipped with a power booster that is integral with the master cylinder and mounted on the engine firewall.

To remove the master cylinder, disconnect and plug brake lines, disconnect wires from stoplight switch, remove attaching nuts and lift out the assembly.

Installation is the reverse of the removal procedure. Make certain that all parts are clean. Bleed brakes.

Bleeding Brakes

The hydraulic brake system must be bled whenever a fluid line is disconnected or there is air in the system. A leak is usually indicated by a soft or spongy brake pedal.

1. Clean all dirt from around the master cylinder and the bleeder valves.
2. Fill brake fluid reservoir.
3. Attach bleeder hose to valve on right rear wheel cylinder. Submerge end of hose in jar filled with enough brake fluid to cover hose end.
4. Open bleeder valve ½ to ¾ turn, then have an assistant pump the brake pedal slowly. Observe the air bubbles in the jar and when they cease to appear, close the bleeder valve during a pedal downstroke.
5. The proper brake bleeding sequence on early models is:
   a. Right rear wheel.
   b. Right front wheel.
   c. Left rear wheel.
   d. Left front wheel.

On late models bleed the wheel with the longest line to the master cylinder first, next longest socond, etc.

NOTE: Keep a constant check on the brake fluid reservoir. Make certain it is never so low that air may be introduced into the system. Upon completion of bleeding all wheel cylinders, fill reservoir to bottom of filler neck. Always use fresh brake fluid.

Power Booster

Power assisted brakes are optional on some Jeep models. A Bendix single-diaphragm unit is used and it operates by utilizing manifold vacuum and atmospheric pressure to reduce pedal travel and effort. Freeplay is factory set and not adjustable.

Removal

1. Clean master cylinder and booster unit.
2. Remove cotter and clevis pins securing booster pushrod to pedal linkage.
3. Disconnect vacuum hose from booster check valve.
4. Disconnect fluid lines from master cylinder. Plug line ends and catch any escaping fluid. *Do not re-use brake fluid.*
5. Disconnect stoplight wires from switch.
6. Remove attaching nuts, booster unit assembly and block spacers.
7. Remove attaching nuts and separate master cylinder from booster.

Installation

To install the booster unit, reverse the removal procedure and bleed the brakes.

CAUTION: Do not pressure-bleed power assisted brake systems.

Parking Brakes

The parking brake is operated by a foot pedal and a hand release lever. When the pedal is depressed, the rear brakes are actuated via an adjustable cable.

Some J-Series vehicles may be equipped with a transmission brake mounted at the rear output bearing housing on the transfer case.

Parking Brake Adjustment

1. Make certain service brakes are in adjustment.
2. Raise rear wheels.
3. Disengage parking brake pedal.
4. Loosen locknut on brake cable adjusting rod, located behind from center crossmember.
5. Spin wheels and tighten rod until brakes drag slightly.
6. Back off adjustment until wheels spin freely.
7. Tighten locknut.

Transmission Brake Adjustment

1. Release transmission brake pedal.
2. Rotate transmission brake drum until holes line up with adjusting screws.
3. Turn adjusting screws until shoes are snug in the drum.
4. Back off adjustment screws 7 notches.
5. Make certain there is 3/32″ clearance between drum backing

Transmission brake adjustment
(© Willys Corp.)

1 Ball nut
2 3/32" clearance [2,38 mm.]
3 Adjusting screw

plate and operating lever.

NOTE: If the clearance is incorrect, remove the drum and adjust ball nut on the operating link until correct clearance is obtained.

Refer to General Repair Section for brake overhaul procedures.

Fuel System

Carburetor R&R

Jeep engines use various models of Carter, Rochester and Holley carburetors. To remove the unit, disconnect all hoses, remove retaining wing nut and lift off the air cleaner. Disconnect fuel and vacuum lines, throttle cable and choke rod, then remove attaching nuts and lift off carburetor with gasket.

Install carburetor by reversing the removal procedure.

Governor Adjustment

Four and six cylinder Jeep engines have used three types of governor: Monarch and King-Seeley on early models, Novi on both early and late models. The governor operating unit is mounted on the carburetor and is controlled via cable and dash mounted knob. The governor may be disengaged by pushing the control knob all the way IN on Novi unit, disengaging governor clutch at pulley hub on King-Seeley unit, or latching spring loaded lever at top of carburetor on Monarch unit.

CAUTION: Do not engage or disengage governor on King-Seeley or Monarch models with the engine running.

These governors are all of the centrifugal type and utilize the same mounting bracket and dash control. Adjustments are made by shortening the cable or linkage to obtain an engine speed of 1000 rpm with the dash knob all the way IN on Monarch and King-Seeley types, at the first notch OUT on NOVI type. Each notch OUT increases engine speed by 200 rpm until, at the ninth notch, the engine has a maximum controlled speed of 2600 rpm.

Governor Maintenance

The governor drive belt tension should be maintained at a 1" depression between pulleys with thumb pressure. This can be adjusted by raising or lowering the governor in the mounting bracket.

Check oil level at each lubrication and renew at engine oil change intervals, using the same grade oil. Most units are provided with level indicating plugs.

NOTE: Some Novi units are not equipped with level plugs. The capacity of these units is 2 fluid oz.

CAUTION: Do not fill governor housing above specified level. Overfilling may prevent governor operation and cause damage to the unit.

Cooling System

Radiator R & R

1. Drain radiator by opening drain cock and removing pressure cap.
2. Remove all attaching clamps and radiator hoses.
3. On vehicles equipped with automatic transmission, disconnect and plug oil cooler lines.
4. Remove attaching cap screws and washers. Lift out the radiator core.

Install the radiator by reversing the removal procedure.

CAUTION: Do not run cold water over the outside of pressurized radiators without first removing the radiator cap. When the cap is left on and cold water hits the hot radiator, steam in the radiator condenses very rapidly and may collapse the top radiator tank. This is most likely to happen if the coolant level is below normal.

Water Pump Removal

1. Drain radiator.
2. Remove fan blades and pulley.
3. Disconnect any attaching hoses.
4. Remove mounting screws.
5. Lift out pump. To install water pump, reverse the removal procedure.

NOTE: It is not necessary to remove the radiator.

Water Pump Overhaul

Only the Hurricane F4 engine water pump is serviceable. Pumps on all other models are sealed and must be replaced as a unit.

1. Remove bearing retainer spring.
2. Remove pump impeller and pulley using a suitable puller.
3. Remove the pump seal, shaft with bearing and bearing slinger.

Examine all parts for wear and replace as necessary. To assemble the unit, insert shaft with bearing into the pump body, install seals; press impeller and pulley onto the shaft and make certain shaft end is flush with pulley surface. Move the shaft in the body to align the bearing retainer grooves. Install bearing retainer.

Engine

Jeep vehicles use various inline four, inline six, V6 and V8 engines. Clearance information required for overhauling engines is covered in the Specifications area of this section. The following procedures are general in scope and are intended as a guide only.

Refer to General Repair Section for service procedures on exhaust emission controls.

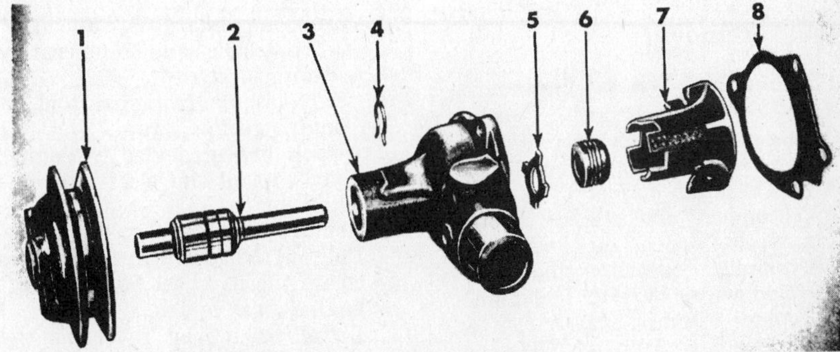

Water pump—F4 engine (© Willys Corp.)

1 Fan and water pump pulley
2 Bearing and shaft
3 Pump body
4 Bearing retaining wire
5 Seal washer
6 Seal assembly
7 Impeller
8 Gasket

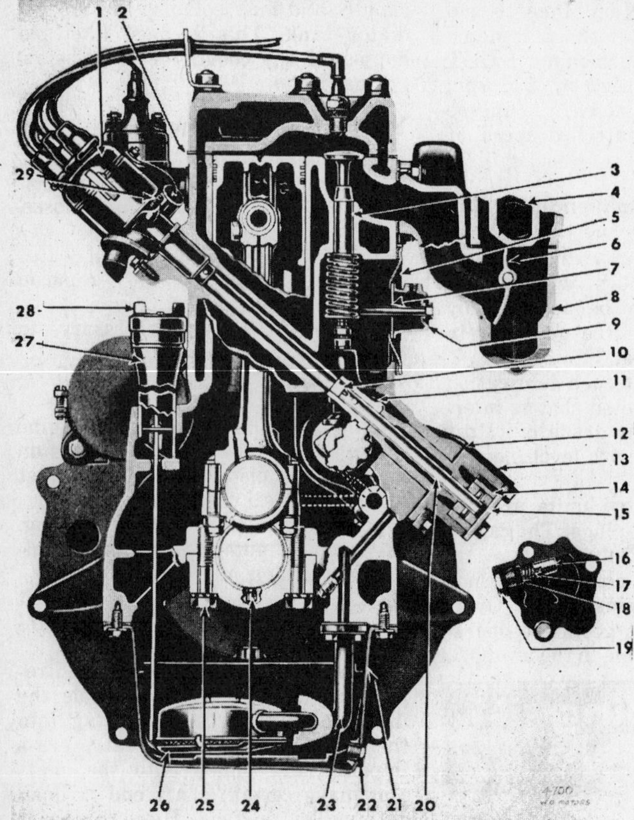

4 cylinder L-head (© Willys Corp.)

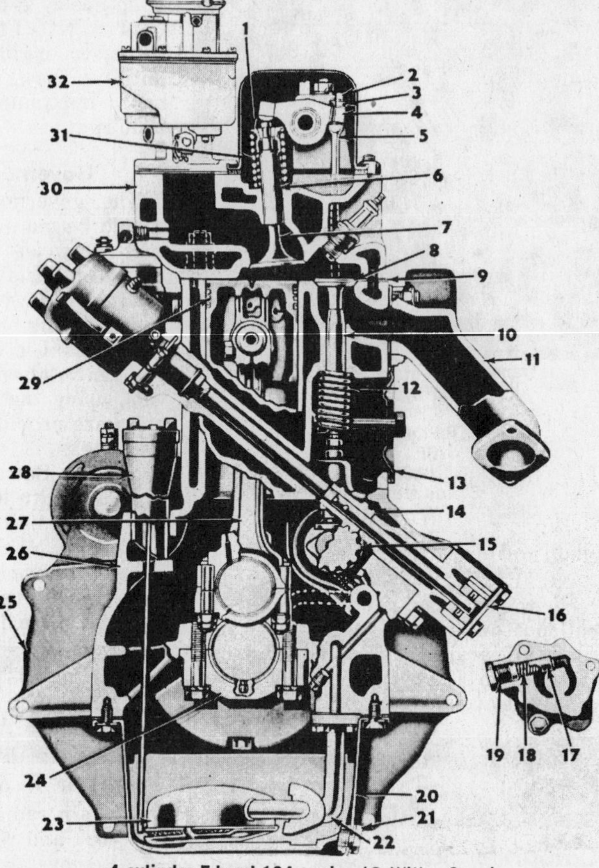

4 cylinder F-head 134 engine (© Willys Corp.)

1 Ignition distributor
2 Cylinder head gasket
3 Exhaust valve guide
4 Intake manifold
5 Valve spring cover
6 Heat control valve
7 Crankcase ventilator gasket
8 Exhaust manifold
9 Crankcase ventilator
10 Distributor shaft friction spring
11 Oil pump driven gear
12 Oil pump gasket
13 Oil pump
14 Oil pump rotor
15 Oil pump coyer
16 Oil relief plunger
17 Relief plunger spring
18 Relief valve shim
19 Relief plunger spring retainer
20 Oil pump shaft
21 Oil pan
22 Drain plug
23 Oil float support
24 Crankshaft bearing dowel
25 Bearing screw
26 Oil float
27 Oil filler tube
28 Oil filler cap & level indicator
29 Distributor oiler

1 Intake valve spring retainer
2 Adjusting screw
3 Nut
4 Rocker arm
5 Push rod
6 Intake valve guide
7 Intake valve
8 Exhaust valve
9 Cylinder head gasket
10 Exhaust valve guide
11 Exhaust Manifold
12 Exhaust valve spring
13 Valve spring cover
14 Oil pump gear
15 Camshaft
16 Oil pump
17 Relief plunger
18 Relief plunger spring
19 Relief spring retainer
20 Oil pan
21 Drain plug
22 Oil Float support
23 Oil float
24 Crankshaft
25 Engine rear plate
26 Cylinder block
27 Connecting rod
28 Oil filler tube
29 Piston
30 Cylinder head
31 Intake valve spring
32 Carburetor

Engine Removal

F-Head and L-Head Engines

1. Drain cooling system.
2. Disconnect battery ground cable.
3. Remove air cleaner and disconnect breather hose at oil filter.
4. Disconnect choke and throttle controls.
5. Disconnect fuel line and windshield wiper hose at fuel pump.
6. Remove radiator stay bar, if so equipped.
7. Remove radiator and heater hoses.
8. Remove fan blades, fan hub, radiator, and shroud.
9. Remove starter motor.
10. Disconnect:
    a. Alternator or generator.
    b. Ignition primary wire at coil.
    c. Oil pressure and temperature sending units.
    d. Exhaust pipe from manifold.
    e. Engine ground strap.
11. Attach litfing device to engine. Unbolt and remove front engine supports.
12. Remove flywheel housing bolts.
13. Pull engine forward until clutch clears the flywheel housing. Lift engine from vehicle.
14. Install engine by reversing the removal procedure.

OHC Tornado 230 Engine

1. Drain engine oil.
2. Remove oil filter.
3. Drain cooling system.
4. Using clean pan under clutch slave, disconnect line at cylinder.
5. Remove hood.
6. Remove radiator and heater hoses.
7. Disconnect transmission oil cooler lines, if equipped with automatic transmission.
8. Remove radiator.
9. Disconnect wires from engine sending units, starter, generator and coil.
10. Remove generator, fan belt, fan and spacer.
11. Remove battery and supports.
12. Disconnect ground cable and engine ground strap at right front engine support.
13. Disconnect exhaust pipe at manifold and bracket at flywheel housing.
14. Remove carburetor.
15. Disconnect flexible line from

6 cylinder—230 cu. in. OHC (© Willys Corp.)

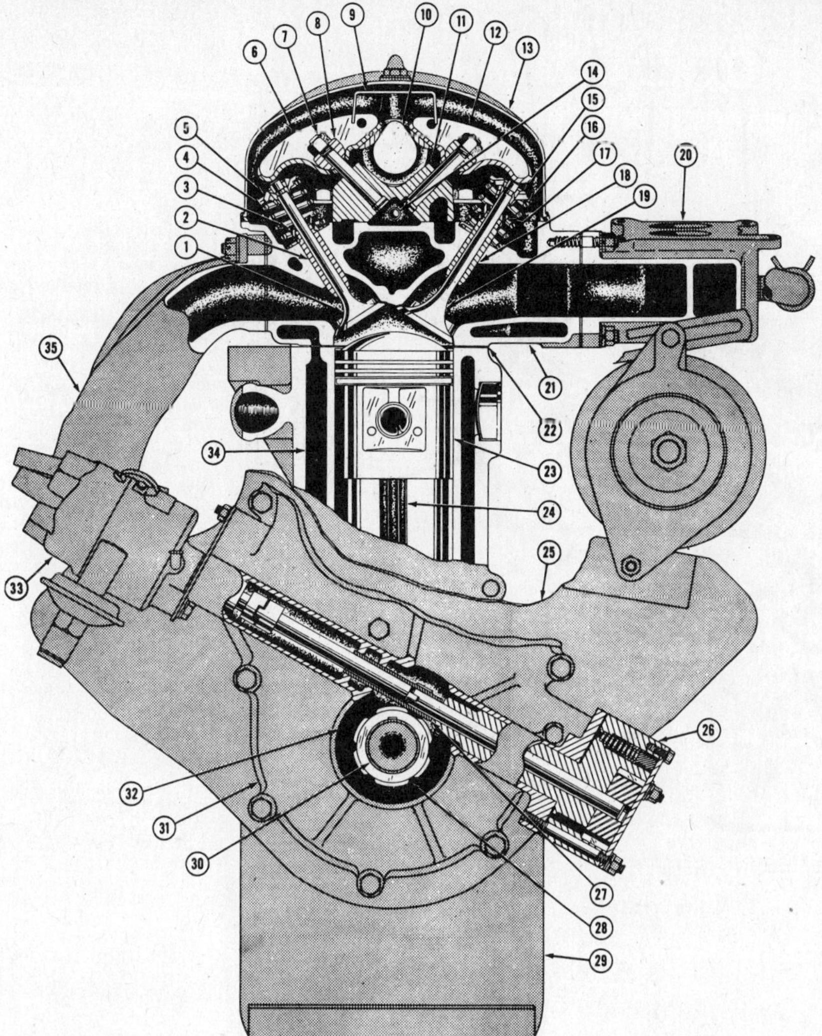

1 Exhaust valve
2 Exhaust valve guide
3 Valve guide seal
4 Valve spring
5 Exhaust valve spring guide
6 Rocker arm
7 Rocker arm stud
8 Rocker arm ball
9 Rocker arm guide
10 Camshaft
11 Cam bearing support deck
12 Intake rocker arm
13 Rocker arm cover
14 Lubrication pipe
15 Valve spring guide
16 Valve spring
17 Valve guide seal
18 Intake valve guide
19 Intake valve
20 Intake manifold
21 Cylinder head
22 Cylinder head gasket
23 Piston
24 Connecting rod
25 Front engine plate
26 Oil pump
27 Oil pump helical gear
28 Oil pump drive gear
29 Oil pan
30 Crankshaft
31 Timing chain cover
32 Timing chain cover oil seal
33 Distributor
34 Cylinder block
35 Exhaust manifold

6 cylinder—232 cu. in. OHV (© Willys Corp.)

1 Cylinder head
2 Spark plug
3 Valve
4 Push rod
5 Rocker arm
6 Rocker arm shaft
7 Rocker arm cover
8 Air cleaner
9 Carburetor
10 Crankcase ventilation hose
11 Intake manifold
12 Manifold heat control valve
13 Exhaust manifold
14 Piston
15 Starting motor
16 Crankshaft
17 Oil pan
18 Connecting rod
19 Cylinder block
20 Camshaft
21 Oil filter
22 Fuel pump
23 Hydraulic valve lifter

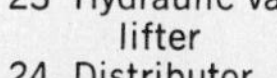

24 Distributor

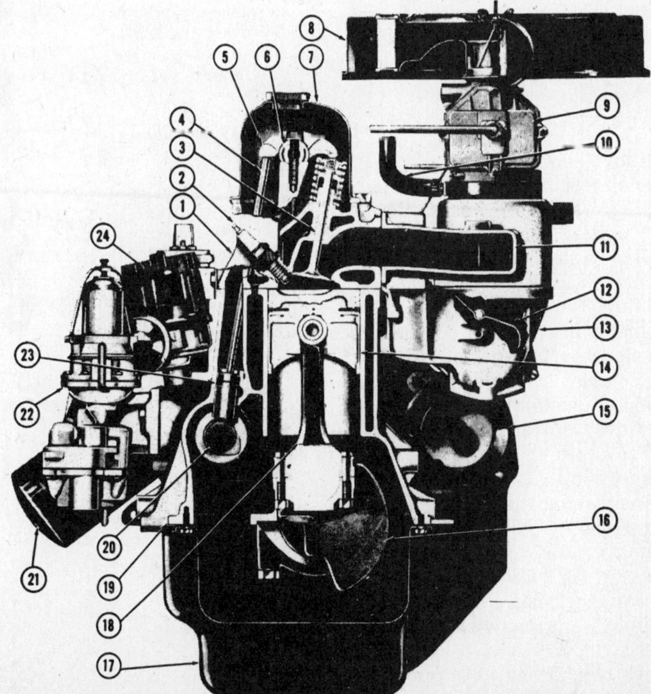

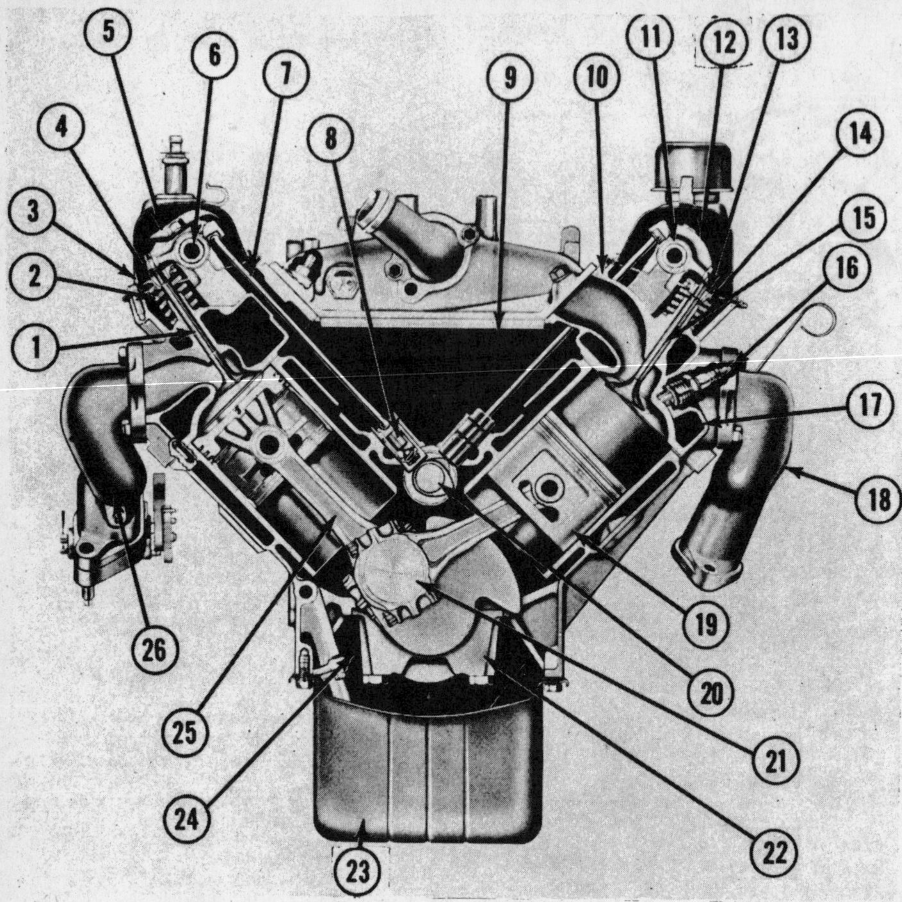

V6 engine—225 cu. in. (© Willys Corp.)

frame-to-engine.
16. Remove front support bolts.
17. Install suitable lifting fixture on engine, preferably at upper left rear and upper right front.
18. Remove transmission.
19. Raise engine slowly and pull forward to clear. Continue to raise until clear and lift from vehicle.
20. Install by reversing the removal procedure.

OHV 6 Engine

1. Remove hood.
2. Disconnect battery ground cable.
3. Remove radiator hoses. Remove automatic transmission oil cooler lines (if so equipped). Remove radiator.
4. Remove fan and pulley.
5. Remove air cleaner. Disconnect accelerator linkage.
6. Disconnect all electrical leads, fuel and vacuum lines.
7. Remove power steering pump (if so equipped).
8. Remove oil filter. On automatic transmission models, remove the transmission filler tube bracket.
9. Remove air conditioning compressor (if so equipped). Do not disconnect hoses.
10. Support engine with lifting device.
11. Unbolt front engine support.
12. Raise and support front of vehi-

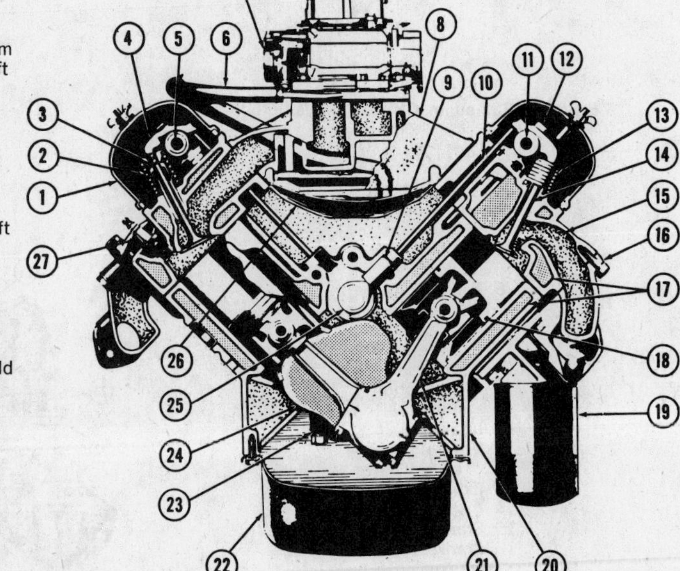

V8—327 cu. in.—typical (© Willys Corp.)

cle.

13. Disconnect exhaust pipe from manifold.
14. Remove oil cooler lines from oil pan (if so equipped).
15. Remove floor mat and cover from cab floorplate.
16. Remove supports and lower vehicle.
17. Support transmission.
18. Remove transmission to engine adapter plate bolts on automatic transmission models. On manual transmission models, remove clutch housing to engine bolts. Remove engine.
19. Install by reversing the removal procedure.

V6 Engines

1. Remove hood if necessary.
2. Disconnect battery ground cable.
3. Remove air cleaner.
4. Drain coolant.
5. Disconnect radiator hoses.
6. Remove radiator support bars.
7. On Universal Series, remove radiator. On Jeepster Series, disconnect headlamp wiring from block on left fender, disconnect horn wiring from horn, disconnect oil cooler lines if equipped with automatic transmission, remove front fenders, radiator, and grille as a unit.
8. Disconnect engine wiring from connectors on firewall.
9. Remove starter motor.
10. Disconnect fuel hoses at right frame rail. Plug hoses.
11. Disconnect throttle and choke.
12. Disconnect exhaust pipes.
13. Place jack under transmission and support weight.
14. Remove front motor mount bolts.
15. Support engine with lifting device.
16. Remove flywheel housing bolts.
17. Raise engine slightly and slide engine forward until engine is free of transmission shaft. Remove engine.
18. Install in reverse of above procedure.

V8 Engines

1. Remove hood.
2. Remove air cleaner.
3. Drain radiator and cylinder block.
4. Disconnect radiator and heater hoses.
5. If equipped with automatic transmission, disconnect oil cooler lines at radiator. Remove radiator.
6. Remove fan, belt and hub.
7. Drain engine oil and remove filter.
8. Disconnect temperature-sender lead, pressure-sender lead; coil, starter solenoid, alternator and distributor leads.
9. Disconnect accelerator cable at carburetor throttle shaft lever and at cable support bracket.
10. Disconnect heater system vacuum valve hose at intake manifold.
11. Disconnect flexible fuel line from frame-to-crankcase at frame end. Plug end of hose.
12. Disconnect exhaust pipes at both manifolds.
13. Remove air conditioning compressor (if so equipped). Do not disconnect hoses.
14. If equipped with manual transmission, disconnect linkage at clutch. Disconnect clutch crossshaft support brackets at flywheel housing and frame.
15. Install suitable lifting fixture on engine.
16. Support transmission on jack.
17. Remove nuts from engine-to-front-support brackets.
18. With manual transmission, remove cap screws from transmission-to-clutch housing. With automatic transmission, remove cap screws attaching transmission housing-to-flywheel housing adapter.
19. Pull engine forward and upward until free from transmission or clutch.
20. Install by reversing the removal procedure.

Manifolds

Due to the variety of engines used in JEEP vehicles, there are many operations involved in the removal or installation of intake/exhaust manifolds. However, steps become apparent when working on a specific model, and it is left up to the mechanic to determine what accessories, hoses and clamps must be removed for access. The following are points that should be observed:

a. When removing compressor on air conditioned models, *do not disconnect hoses.*

b. F4-134 engines have the intake manifold cast in one unit with the cylinder head.

c. Always replace manifold gaskets with the same type as original.

d. Exhaust manifolds can be removed from a V8 engine installed, but not without difficulty.

e. There must be no binding between manifold and mounting bolts or studs. If necessary, enlarge holes just enough to relieve the binding.

f. Torque mounting nuts or bolts to specifications.

g. On inline engines, tighten bolts beginning in the center and alternately moving to each side.

h. On V8 engines, tighten bolts in the order shown in illustrations.

i. Special care must be taken when working on emission controlled engines. Make certain there are no leaks.

Cylinder Head Removal

L-head Engines

1. Drain coolant. Remove radiator hose and disconnect all lines to the carburetor and fuel pump, and all lines and fittings to the carburetor. Take off the carburetor.
2. If the valves are to be worked on, the maniofld should be removed. However, if the head is being taken off simply to replace a gasket, then leave the manifold on.
3. Remove the bolts that hold the cylinder head to the block. Remove the temperature sending unit. Lift off the head.
4. Reverse procedure for installation.

F-head Engines

1. Drain coolant.
2. Remove upper radiator hose. Remove carburetor.

Removing F-head rocker arm assembly (© Willys Corp.)

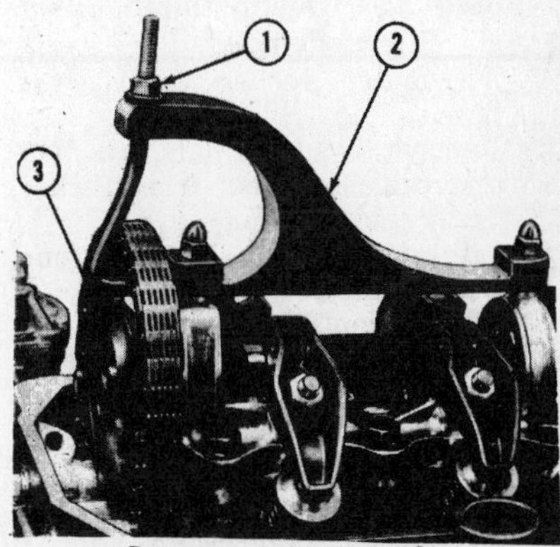

Removing camshaft sprocket (© Willys Corp.)

1 Nut
2 Camshaft sprocket removal and installation tool W-268
3 Camshaft sprocket

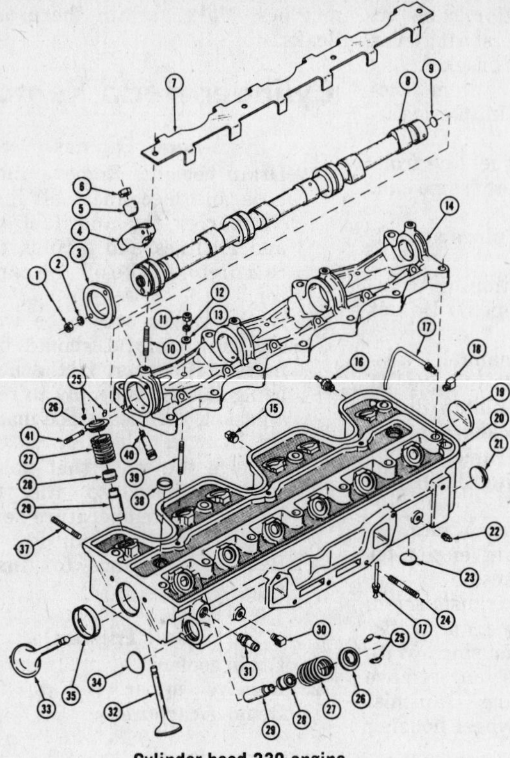
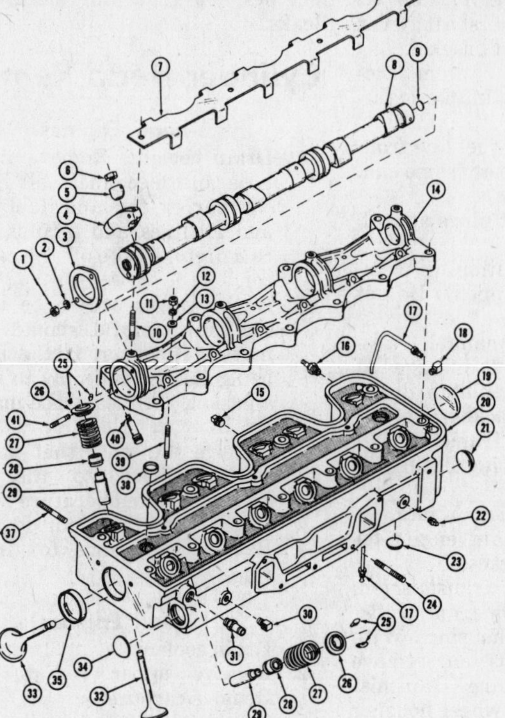

Cylinder head 230 engine
(© Willys Corp.)

1 Nut
2 Lock washer
3 Camshaft retainer
4 Rocker arm
5 Rocker arm ball
6 Rocker arm nut
7 Rocker arm guide
8 Camshaft
9 Plug
10 Stud
11 Nut
12 Lock washer
13 Flat Washer
14 Cam bearing support deck
15 Plug
16 Temperature sending unit
17 Oil tube
18 Elbow
19 Expansion plug
20 Cylinder head
21 Plug
22 Plug
23 Expansion plug
24 Stud
25 Valve lock
26 Valve spring retainer
27 Valve spring
28 Valve guide seal
29 Valve guide
30 Elbow
31 Hose adapter
32 Exhaust valve
33 Intake valve
34 Expansion plug
35 Expansion plug
37 Stud
38 Plug
39 Stud
40 Rocker arm stud
41 Stud

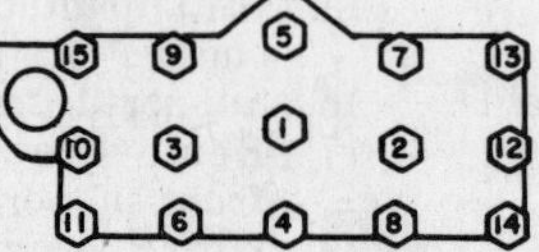

Cylinder head bolt tightening sequence—four-cylinder F-head engines

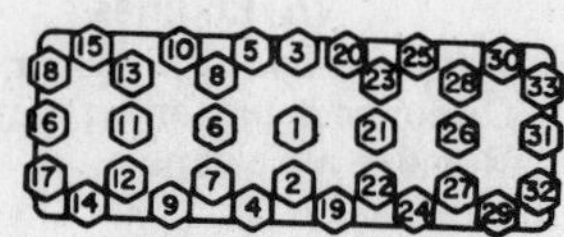

Cylinder head bolt tightening sequence—six-cylinder 226 engines

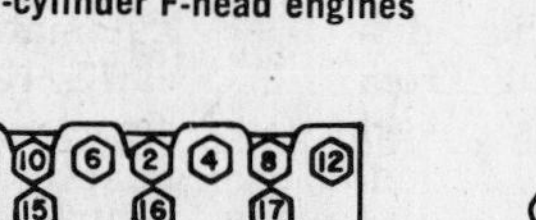

Cylinder head bolt tightening sequence—OHC 6—230 engines

Cylinder head bolt tightening sequence—6—232 engines

3. On early engines, remove bypass hose from front of cylinder head.
4. Remove rocker arm cover.
5. Disconnect oil line.
6. Remove rocker arm attaching stud nuts and rocker arm shaft assembly.
7. Remove cylinder head bolts. One head bolt is located below the carburetor mounting, inside the intake manifold.
8. Lift off cylinder head.
9. Remove pushrods and valve lifters.
10. Reverse procedure for installation.

Tornado 230 (Timing Chain Cover Not Removed)

1. Disconnect rocker cover vent hose.
2. Remove cover cap nuts, washers and cable brackets from rocker cover studs.
3. Lift off cover, gasket and four seal washers.
4. Install camshaft sprocket tool W-268 on cover studs. Insert hook in sprocket and tighten nut to relieve tension on camshaft.
5. Remove capscrew, lock and flat washers and fuel pump eccentric from camshaft sprocket.
6. Pull sprocket forward from pilot on camshaft. With sprocket still in timing chain, release tension on tool W-268 and allow sprocket to rest on bosses in timing chain cover. CAUTION: Do not turn engine while sprocket is removed from camshaft and resting on bosses. This will damage the cover badly. Do not remove sprocket from chain, because this will upset camshaft timing. The chain could also be damaged.
7. Disconnect the lubrication line from rear of head and block.
8. Remove three short and eleven long head-bolts with washers and then lift off head.

To reinstall: be sure all carbon and foreign matter is removed from surfaces and bolt holes.

1. Place head gasket in position. Use no sealer.
2. Carefully place cylinder head on gasket and reverse procedure in preceding steps. Torque head bolts to 65-70 ft. lbs.

OHV 6 Engines

1. Disconnect throttle linkage, fuel lines, water hoses, spark plug wires and vacuum line. Remove valve cover.
2. Remove head mounting nuts: note position of battery strap.
3. Slide a heavy scraper around the head-to-block joint to free gasket. If necessary, reconnect battery ground and crank engine (coil wire out) to allow compression to free head. CAUTION: Do not hammer on head.
4. Before installing head, wire brush studs and make sure they are tight. Clean top surface of block and lower head surface; check head for straightness. If head is out of true 0.006″ over its length (or 0.001″ every 1″) it must be resurfaced on a milling machine. NOTE: When installing, use sealer on both sides of gasket.
5. Install by reversing the removal procedure.

V8 327 Engine

1. Remove oil filler tube, rocker covers, power steering pump, alternator, exhaust manifolds and air conditioner (as equipped). NOTE: Swing air conditioner out of the way without disconnecting hoses.
2. Remove rockers and pushrods.
3. Disconnect water hoses, fuel lines, wiring, vacuum lines; remove distributor and intake manifold.
4. Remove cylinder head bolts and lift off heads carefully, making sure all ground straps, etc. have been disconnected.
5. To install, reverse the procedure.

The cylinder heads have two holes to assist head location. Maximum out of true is 0.006″ for the entire length

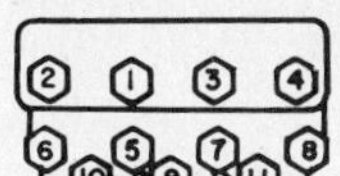

Cylinder head bolt tightening sequence—V6—225 engines

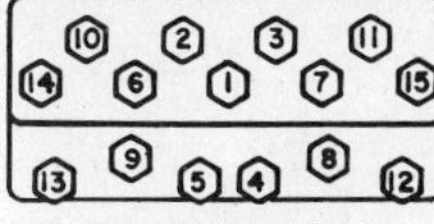

Cylinder head bolt tightening sequence—V8—327 engines

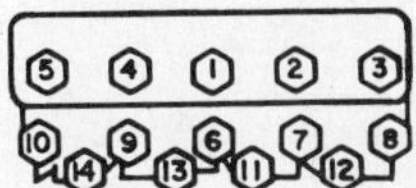

Cylinder head bolt tightening sequence—V8—350 engines

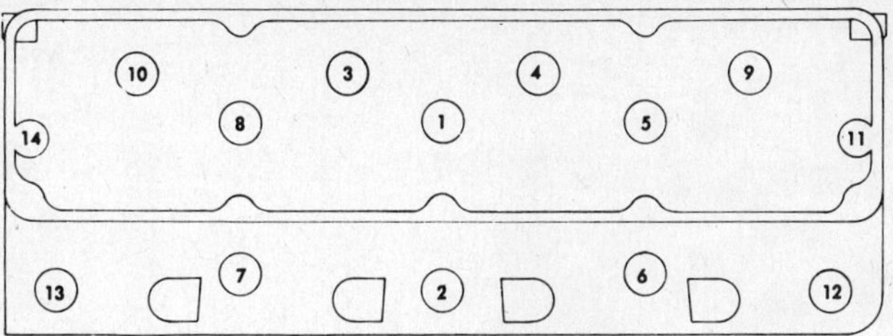

Cylinder head bolt tightening sequence—V8—304 & 360 engines

of head; 0.001″ every 1″. Make sure the rear rocker arm bolts are properly installed, otherwise no oil will get to the rockers.

V8 304, 360 Engines

Procedure is similar to the 327V8, except that rocker lubrication is accomplished through the pushrods and the distributor does not have to be removed. Cylinder head out of true is 0.006″ for the full head length, 0.002″ every 6″ and 0.001″ every 1″. Torque sequence is different as well; see illustrations under Torque Specifications table.

NOTE: Second bolt from front, bottom row, *must* have threads coated with sealer to prevent coolant leakage.

V6 & V8 350 Engines

1. Remove the intake manifold.
2. Remove the rocker cover, then detach the exhaust manifold at the flange connection. NOTE: The exhaust manifold can be disconnected from the head but this procedure takes somewhat longer than detaching it at the exhaust flange connection.
3. Remove the Delcotron and the air conditioning compressor (if so equipped) to remove the right head.
4. Remove the dipstick and power steering pumps (if so equipped) to remove the left head.
5. Remove the rocker cover and the rocker assemblies. Mark them carefully for reassembly. NOTE: There are no oil line connections to the rocker assemblies, since oil is fed through the rocker front bracket.
6. Detach the front water manifold, if applicable, from both cylinder heads, then unbolt and lift off the head. It is important to prevent dirt from entering the engine. The hydraulic lifters, in particular, are very susceptible.

CAUTION: It is important to note that each engine has its own headbolt tightening sequence and torque. Incorrect tightening procedure may cause head warpage and compression loss. Correct sequence and torque for each engine model is shown in illustrations.

Valve Train

Valve Adjustment

Adjustment of valve clearance on most Jeep engines is accomplished in the conventional manner. Necessary information can be found in Tune-Up Specifications. An exception, however, is the 230 inline 6 which utilizes an overhead camshaft. The specific procedure for this engine follows:

If rocker arms are off, install in reverse of removal, as described in cylinder head removal. Or, if arms have not been removed, proceed as follows:

1. Turn down rocker arm nut but do not tighten.
2. Align each arm on stud and install guide to hold it in place.
3. Adjust the nut to .006″ clearance on intake valves and .008″ on exhaust. Always be sure arm is completely off cam when making the adjustment.

NOTE: On some models, Jeep recommends that the manifold be removed to adjust valves.

Valve Removal

L-head Engines

1. Remove the cylinder head and the valve cover.
2. Selecting valves in the down position, compress the valve spring, using a spring compressor, and remove the retainer locks and retainer.
3. Release the pressure from the valve spring and pull the valve up to the top of the cylinder block. Remove the spring.
4. If the valve tends to bind on its way through the guide, push it back in again and dissolve the gum and tar on the bottom of the valve stem which prevents it from coming up through the guide.
5. Reverse procedure to install.

F-head Engines

On F-head engines, the exhaust valves are removed as described above. However, the inlet valve is in the cylinder head and is removed on the bench.

Tornado 230 OHC Engines

1. Place head on blocks to provide hand clearance under it.
2. Remove valve locks and springs. (Discard the valve guide seal.)

To reinstall: always use new guide seals.

1. With head on blocks insert the valves. Apply engine oil to stems.
2. Install seals on stems and push down to seat squarely on guide.
3. Compress spring and insert retainers and valve locks.

Valve Guide Replacement

L-Head Engines

The old guides are removed by driving them through the block into the valve compartment. The valve guides can also be removed by using a puller. When replacing the guides, the top of the exhaust guide must be positioned 1″ below the top face of the cylinder block. The intake guide must be 1-5/16″ below the top face of the cylinder block. A reamer should be run through the new guides after they have been correctly positioned. This is done to remove any distortion caused by the driving operation.

F-Head Engines

The old guides can be driven or pulled out. The top end of the exhaust valve guide must be exactly 1″ below the top face of the cylinder block. The intake guide should be driven, tapered end first, into position from the bottom of the cylinder head. When properly positioned, the end of the guide is flush with the guide bore in the cylinder head. A reamer should be run through the new guides after installation, to repair distortion caused by the driving operation.

V6 OHV, V8 304, 360 Engines

These engines do not have replaceable valve guides.

Check the stem to guide clearance in one of two ways: the valve stem can be measured with a micrometer and the guide with calibrated pilots, then the difference computed; or install the valve into the guide, without spring, and measure the lateral

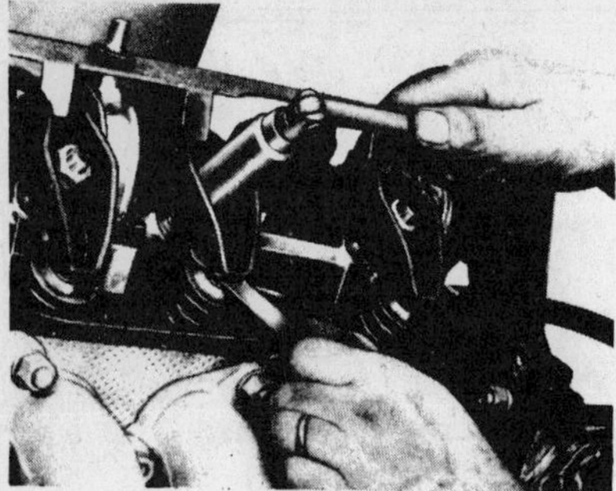

Adjusting valve clearance—Tornado 230
(© Willys Corp.)

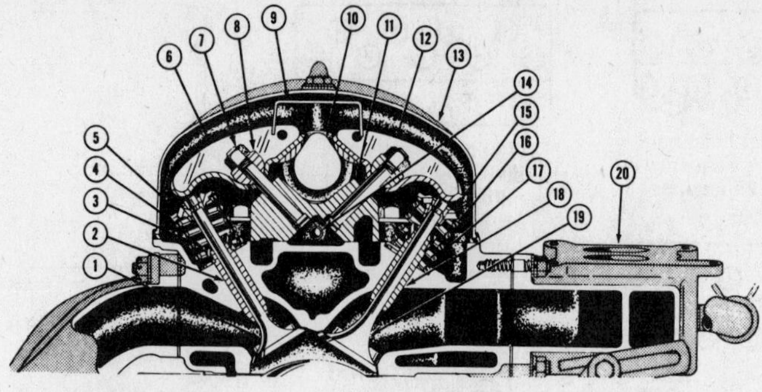

1 Exhaust valve	11 Cam bearing support deck
2 Valve guide	12 Rocker arm
3 Valve guide seal	13 Rocker arm cover
4 Valve spring	14 Oil tube
5 Valve spring retainer	15 Valve spring retainer
6 Rocker arm	16 Valve spring
7 Rocker arm stud	17 Valve guide seal
8 Rocker arm ball	18 Valve guide
9 Rocker arm guide	19 Intake valve
10 Camshaft	20 Intake manifold

Cutaway view—valve section—230 engine
(© Willys Corp.)

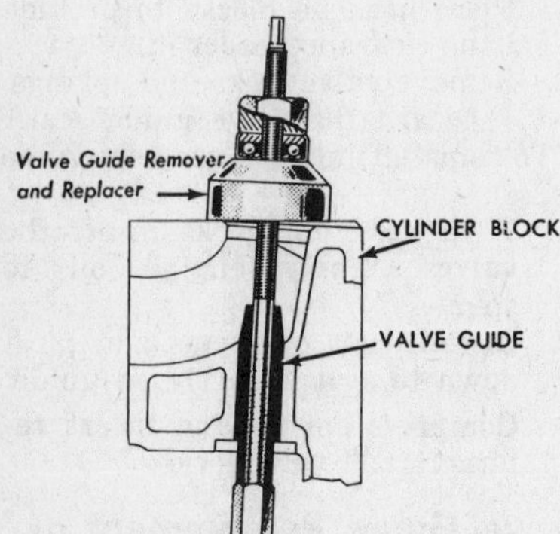

Removing valve guide from cylinder block
(© Willys Corp.)

Valve guide installation demensions—F-head
(© Willys Corp.)

movement using a dial indicator. If stem to guide clearance is excessive, guides must be reamed to the proper oversize. Three valves are available with stems 0.003, 0.015 and 0.030″ larger than standard diameter.

NOTE: The exhaust valve stem is tapered 0.0005-0.001″, smaller diameter toward valve head.

Proper stem to guide clearance is 0.001-0.003″ for both intake and exhaust valves.

No provision is made for adjustment of hydraulic tappet travel. Tappets having various thicknesses of push rod seats are available and can be installed to get a standard center travel position under normal operating conditions.

V8 327 Engines

The valve stem to guide clearance is corrected through replacement of valve guides. The guides are an interference fit in their bores in the cylinder head, and can be replaced by driving out the old guides and driving in the new. The new guides are driven to a depth to permit ¾″ + or — 1/64″ to remain exposed above the cylinder head.

Tool J-21753, when driven until bottomed, establishes the required ¾″ guide height.

Valve stem to guide clearance is .001-.003″ for intake and exhaust.

V6 & V8 350 Engines

Remove the cylinder head, valves and valve spring assemblies. On engines equipped with removable guides, carefully measure the amount the valve guide protrudes from the cylinder head before driving it out so that the new guide can be driven down exactly that amount. Make a stack of washers equivalent to the protrusion of the guide before removing it from the head.

When driving out the valve guides, support the cylinder head as near to the guide as is practical.

A pilot type driver should be used and the guide driven out from the bottom, or, it may be pressed out if an arbor press is available.

Place the new guide in the top of the head and tap it gently to insure that it is starting straight. Once straight, it can be driven into position.

When the new valve guide has been driven in the correct distance, insert a new valve into the guide to make sure that the valve will operate freely up and down. The slightest sign of binding in the new valve guide indicates that the guide itself has become riveted over or slightly warped in the driving process and will have to be reamed.

Removable valve guides should be finish-reamed to size after installation. Use a reamer that will give the valve stem to guide clearance listed in the Valve Specifications table.

NOTE: Since 1967, all guides are integral with the cylinder head.

In cases of excessive guide-to-valve stem clearance, the guides can be reamed and oversize valves installed.

Always reface the valve seat when new guides have been installed to be absolutely certain that the valve seat is in alignment with the new guide.

Refer to the Valve Specifications table for valve spring, seat and stem dimensions.

Rocker Arm Assembly Removal

V6 OHV Engine

The rocker shaft assembly is secured to the cylinder head with six cap bolts. Oil pressure for rocker lubrication is supplied from the main oil gallery to No. 5 rocker support via No. 3 camshaft bearing. Rocker shaft is 0.8575-0.8585″ diameter; oil clearance is 0.003-0.005″.

1. Remove valve cover.
2. Unbolt cap bolts and remove rockers and shaft. NOTE: Hold rockers in place using large rubber bands.
3. Reverse preceding to install.

V8 304 & 360 Engines

Individually mounted, pressed steel rocker arms operate the valves.

These rockers are mounted on threaded studs and are held by a pivot ball and locknut. The hollow pushrods conduct oil from each hydraulic tappet to the rockers. There is a metering system in each tappet, consisting of a stepped lower pushrods cap surface and a flat plate. Any loss of lubrication to the rockers usually can be traced to failure of this part, or to a blocked pushrod oil passage. The pushrods rub against the cylinder head during operation and serve to maintain the correct rocker to valve stem angle.

1. Remove valve covers, after first removing any accessories and the air cleaner preheat tube.
2. Loosen and remove the retaining locknuts, ball pivots and rocker arms. It is a good idea to lay them out in order, along with their respective pushrods.

NOTE: When installing new threaded studs, make sure hex nut is fully seated and tightened to 65-70 ft. lbs. Retaining locknuts are tightened to 20-25 ft. lbs.

V8 327 Engine

The rocker shaft assembly is secured to the head with four cap bolts. The hollow rocker shafts serve as oil galleries for the rocker arms, push rod ends and valve stems. Oil pressure is supplied by the valve tappet main oil gallery and enters the rocker shafts via passages in the block and heads through a special drilled bolt at the rear of each shaft. Although the shaft assemblies are interchangeable between banks, two different rocker arms are used to actuate intake and exhaust valves. Rocker shafts are 0.8580-0.8585″ diameter; oil clearance is 0.002″.

V6 & V8 350 Engines

1. Disconnect plug wires at the spark plugs and tie back out of the way.
2. Remove screws holding the rocker arm cover to the cylinder head. Remove rocker arm cover and gasket.
3. Remove rocker arm shaft bracket-to-cylinder head attaching bolts. Remove rocker arm and shaft assembly.
4. Remove the pushrods. These should be reinstalled in their original locations.
5. If lifters are to be serviced, remove them. If not, protect them with clean cloth. It is extremely important to protect the hydraulic lifters from dirt.
6. Reverse the removal procedures to install.

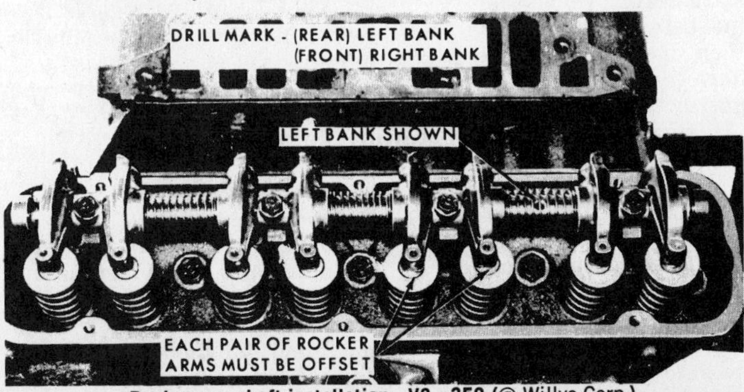

Rocker arm shaft installation—V8—350 (© Willys Corp.)

Timing Gears

Timing Case Cover and Oil Seal Replacement

L-Head and F-Head Engines

To remove the timing case cover, it is necessary to take off the radiator, the fan, and the pulleys. Remove bolts, nuts, and lockwashers from timing gear cover. Remove the cover, timing pointer and cover gasket; discard gasket. Remove and discard the crankshaft oil seal. Remove the oil slinger and spacer from the crankshaft. The timing gears may now be removed with a puller. Reverse above procedure for installation. Replace seals and gasket.

Timing Case Cover and Chain Removal

Tornado 230 OHC Engine

1. Remove hose from water port on cover. Then remove eight bolts, lock and flat washers, and three nuts holding cover to front engine plate.

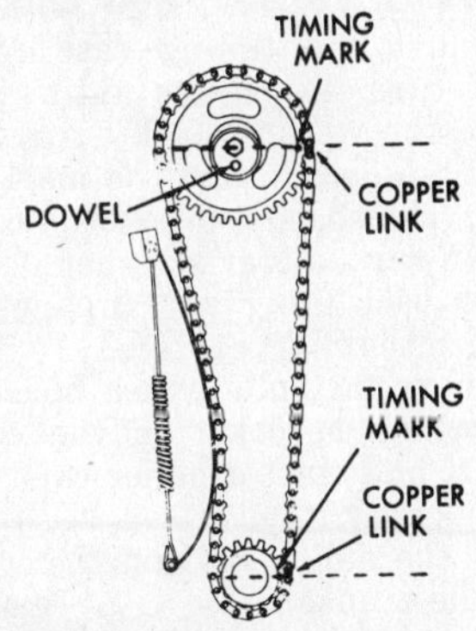

Aligning timing marks—230—6 cylinder OHC (© Willys Corp.)

2. Remove the chain cover, lifting eye and gaskets.
3. To check for excess chain wear with chain and tensioner in position, measure distance between chain sides at narrowest point. If less than 3.38″, chain should be replaced.
4. Slide oil slinger and oil pump drive gear off the crankshaft.
5. Install camshaft sprocket tool W-268 on the cover studs. Insert hook in camshaft sprocket and tighten nut to relieve tension on camshaft.
6. Remove capscrew, lock and flat washers and fuel pump eccentric from sprocket. Pull sprocket forward from pilot on camshaft. Release hook and sprocket off crankshaft.
7. Remove pin from top of tensioner, and remove the tensioner blade and spring from the lower mounting stud.
8. Remove chain guide bracket from front engine plate.

To reinstall: Reverse the above. Proper camshaft timing is accomplished by turning No. 1 piston to top of stroke with crankshaft sprocket key up, at twelve o'clock position, and camshaft sprocket dowel down at six o'clock position. Both No. 1 intake and exhaust valves should be closed.

Front Crankshaft Oil Seal Replacement

230 OHC Engine

1. Remove vibration damper.
2. Thread housing of tool into crankshaft oil seal. Turn screw clockwise to force out seal.

To install: be sure there are no burrs to damage new seal.

1. Coat outer edge of seal with a good sealing compound and place the seal on shaft with lip toward inside. Drive seal into place with tool.

Timing Case Cover and Oil Seal Replacement

V6 OHV Engine

The timing chain cover has a seal and oil slinger to prevent oil leakage past the crankshaft pulley hub.

1. Remove all V-belts, fan blades and pulley.
2. Remove vibration damper.
3. Remove oil pan to cover bolts and cover to block bolts.
4. Raise cover and pull oil pan front seal up far enough to extract the tabs from the holes in the cover.
5. Remove cover gasket from block; cut off seal tab flush with front face of block.
6. Clean all mating surfaces and remove oil seal.

Removing oil seal—V8—327
(© Willys Corp.)

7. Install new front oil seal, using proper size arbor.
8. Install new neoprene front oil pan seal, cutting off protruding tab to match original.
9. Position cover on block and install bolts. Tighten cover bolts to 4-6 ft. lbs.; four lower bolts to 10-12 ft. lbs.
10. Install vibration damper, tightening bolt to 50-60 ft. lbs.

NOTE: Front oil seal can be installed with cover in place only if proper tool or duplicate is available.

V8 304 & 360 Engines

The die-cast timing cover incorporates an oil seal at the vibration damper hub. This seal must be installed from the rear; therefore, the cover must be removed from the engine in every case to replace the front seal.

1. Drain coolant and remove hoses from cover.
2. Remove distributor, fuel pump, alternator drive belt, accessory drive belts, fan and hub assembly.
3. Remove the vibration damper bolt, then pull off the damper.
4. Remove air conditioner compressor and power steering pump, if so equipped, and swing them out of the way *without* disconnecting hoses.
5. Remove the two front oil pan bolts from beneath the car, then remove the eight 9/16″ hex head cover bolts.
6. Remove cover from block, then clean all parts and mating surfaces and remove oil seal.
7. Coat new seal lips with Vaseline and surface with sealer, then drive seal into cover bore until it seats against the outer cover face. Use a proper size arbor for this job.
8. Remove lower dowel pin from cylinder block; this must be replaced when cover is in position, but before bolts are installed.
9. Cut the oil pan gasket flush with the block on both sides of the pan.
10. Cut corresponding pieces of gasket from another oil pan gasket and cement them to the cover. Install neoprene oil pan front seal into cover and align cork gasket tabs with pan seal.
11. Apply Permatex No. 2 to gaskets, then position cover. Install oil pan bolts and tighten evenly until cover lines up with upper dowel pin.
12. Install lower dowel pin, then cover to block bolts; tighten to 20-30 ft. lbs.
13. Install all removed parts and adjust ignition timing.

Timing Chain Replacement

V6 OHV & V8 304, 360 Engines

1. Remove the timing case cover and turn the engine until mark on the crankshaft sprocket points upward, and the mark on the camshaft sprocket points downward. Marks should be near each other and in line between the shaft centers.
2. Remove the bolts which hold the camshaft sprocket to the camshaft and start a puller over the crank gear.
3. Pull the timing gear off the front of the crankshaft.
4. On the bench, arrange the new chain over the sprockets so that the marks are nearest each other and in line between their own centers, then carry this to the engine. Start the crank gear on its key and arrange the camshaft to that when the three bolts line up, the marks are between shaft centers.

NOTE: On 6 cylinder engines, locate the marked cam tooth at one o'clock position; mark on crank should be at mesh point. There should be 15 pins or 7½ links of chain between the two marks.

On V8 engines, locate the marked cam tooth on a horizontal line at three or nine o'clock position; mark on crank at point of mesh. Count the number of links between marks; should be 20 pins or 10 links.

5. Secure the cam gear to the camshaft and force the crankshaft gear all the way on the shaft.
6. Reassemble the front of the engine.

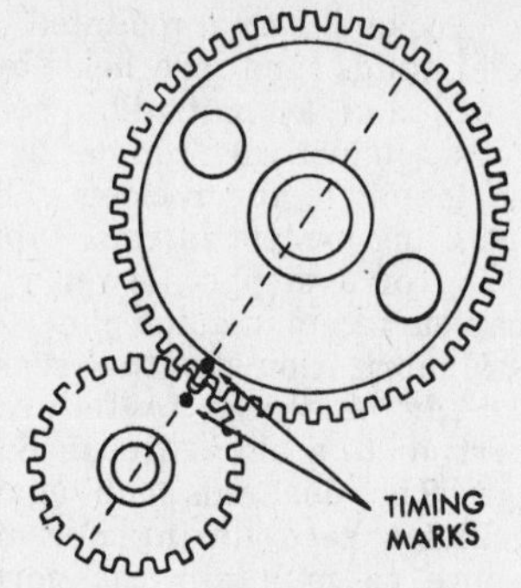

Aligning timing marks—4 cylinder
(© Willys Corp.)

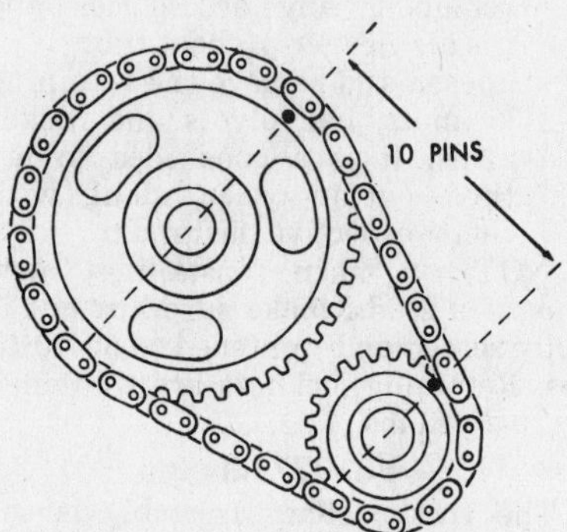

Aligning timing marks—6 cylinder—226
(© Willys Corp.)

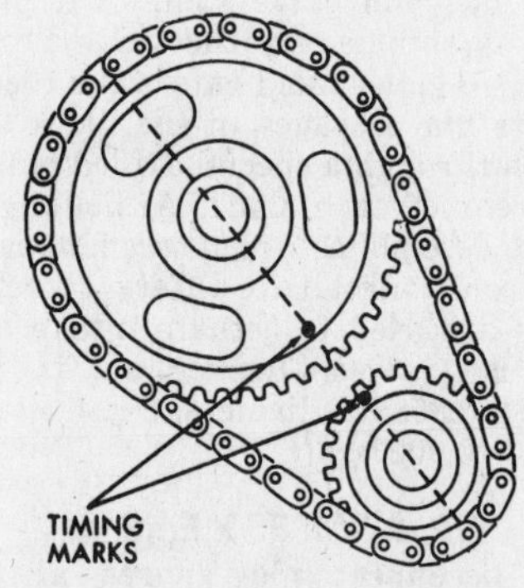

Aligning timing marks—6 cylinder—232
(© Willys Corp.)

Timing Case Cover and Chain Removal

V6 Engines

1. Drain cooling system.
2. Disconnect radiator and heater hoses at water pump and disconnect lower radiator hose at radiator. Remove attaching bolts and brackets. Remove radiator.
3. Remove fan, pulleys and belt(s).
4. Remove crankshaft pulley.

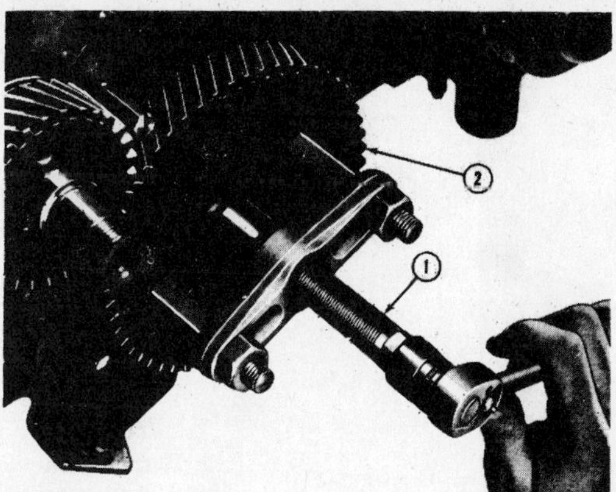

1 Puller W-172
2 Camshaft gear

Pulling timing gears (© Willys Corp.)

TIMING MARKS

Aligning timing marks—V6, V8—typical (© Willys Corp.)

5. Remove harmonic balancer from crankshaft.
6. If truck has power steering, remove the pump bracket bolts and move the steering pump out of the way.
7. Disconnect lines and remove the fuel pump.
8. Remove generator.
9. Remove distributor cap and spark plug wire retainers from brackets on rocker arm cover. Swing distributor cap, with wires, out of the way. Disconnect distributor primary wire.
10. Remove distributor.
11. Loosen and slide front clamp on thermostat by-pass hose rearward.
12. Remove bolts attaching timing cover to cylinder block. Remove two oil pan-to-timing cover bolts.
13. Lift off the timing case cover.
14. Temporarily install harmonic balancer bolt and washer to the end of crankshaft. Rotate crankshaft so that sprockets are positioned as for timing (shafts and sprocket O-marks on a centerline). Now remove harmonic balancer bolt with a sharp rap on the wrench handle to prevent changing the position of the sprockets.
15. Remove crankshaft front oil slinger.
16. Remove bolt and special washer holding the camshaft distributor drive gear and fuel pump eccentric to the camshaft. Slide gear and eccentric off the shaft.
17. Use two large screwdrivers to alternately pry the camshaft sprocket then the crankshaft sprocket forward and off their respective shafts.
18. Thoroughly clean the sprockets, distributor drive gear, fuel pump eccentric and crankshaft oil slinger.

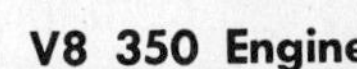

V8 350 Engine

1. Drain cooling system.
2. Remove radiator, fan, fan pulley and belt, crankshaft pulley and pulley reinforcement.
3. Remove fuel pump and Delcotron.
4. Remove distributor.
5. Loosen clamp on thermostat bypass hose.
6. Remove harmonic balancer.
7. Remove timing chain cover to crankcase bolts. Remove oil pan to timing chain cover bolts. Thoroughly clean cover and crankcase surface.
8. Align timing marks on sprockets.
9. Remove bolt, special washer, camshaft distributor drive gear, and fuel pump eccentric from camshaft. Remove crankshaft oil slinger.
10. Use two large screwdrivers to alternately pry the camshaft sprocket, then the crankshaft sprocket, forward and off their respective shafts.

Timing Case Cover and Chain Installation

V6 & V8 350 Engines

1. Make sure, with sprockets temporarily installed, that No. 1 piston is at top dead center and the camshaft sprocket O-mark is straight down and on a centerline with both shafts.
2. Remove the camshaft sprocket and assemble the timing chain on both sprockets. Then slide the sprockets-and-chain assembly on the shafts with the O-marks in their closed together position and on a centerline with the sprocket hubs.
3. Assemble slinger on crankshaft with I.D. against the sprocket, (concave side toward front of engine).
4. Slide fuel pump eccentric on camshaft and Woodruff key with oil groove forwrd.
5. Install distributor drive gear.
6. Install eccentric bolt and retaining washer. Torque to 40-55 ft. lbs.
7. Install timing case cover by reversing removal procedure, paying particular attention to the following points.

a. Remove oil pump cover and pack space around the oil pump gears completely full of petroleum jelly. There must be no air space left inside the pump. Reinstall the pump cover using new gasket.
b. The gasket surface of the block and timing chain cover must be clean and smooth. Use a new gasket correctly positioned.
c. Install chain cover, making certain the dowel pins engage the holes before starting the attaching bolts.
d. Lube the bolt threads and then install them.
e. If the truck has power steering, the front pump bracket should be installed at this time.
f. Lube the O.D. of the harmonic balancer hub before installation to prevent damage to the seal when starting the engine.

Camshaft Removal

F-HEAD and L-HEAD ENGINES

1. Remove timing case cover.
2. Remove fuel pump, oil pump, camshaft timing gear and thrust plate.
3. Carefully withdraw camshaft and valve lifters.
4. Reverse the preceding to install.

CAUTION: Make certain oil pump and drive gears are properly aligned. ligned.

Toronado 230 OHC Engine Removal (Head Removed)

1. Lift off rocker arm guide.
2. Turn rocker arms that have no tension, parallel to camshaft. Then rotate shaft until more

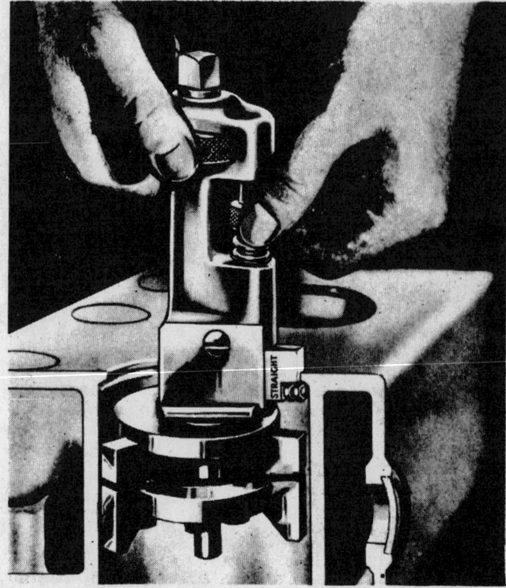

Removing ridge with reamer (© Willys Corp.)

arms are free and turn them parallel. Continue untill all arms are off cams.
3. Remove retainer from front of camshaft bearing deck and pull shaft forward.
4. By removing three nuts with washers, bearing deck can now be lifted free.

Inspection

1. Clean camshaft thoroughly with solvent. See that all oil passages are clear. Runout of shaft must not exceed .0005". Check diameter of journals.
   Front ....1.9965—1.9975"
   No. 2 ....1.8715—1.8725"
   No. 3 ....1.7465—1.7475"
   No. 4 ....1.3715—1.3725"
2. Check deck for cracks and distortions.
3. Check diameter of bearing bores.
   Front ....1.9995—2.0005"
   No. 2 ....1.8745—1.8755"
   No. 3 ....1.7495—1.7505"
   No. 4 ....1.3745—1.3755"
   Maximum running clearance .004"

Installation

1. Place camshaft bearing deck on cylinder head and install nuts and washers. Tighten evenly.
2. Lubricate the bearings with engine oil and slide shaft into the bearings from the front.
3. Secure shaft in place with the retainer plate, nuts and washers.

V6 & V8 Engines

1. Remove fuel pump and distributor.
2. Remove distributor/oil pump drive gear.
3. Remove valve lifters.
4. Remove timing chain and sprockets.
5. Carefully withdraw camshaft.
6. Reverse the preceding to install.

Pistons, Connecting Rods and Main Bearings

Piston Assembly

Removal
F-Head, L-Head, OHC 6

1. Remove cylinder head and oil pan.
2. Remove ridge from tops of cylinder bores, using a ridge reamer.
3. One at a time, remove connecting rod caps and push piston assemblies out of the top of the block. Number all pistons, connecting rods, and caps on removal.
4. Remove old rings with ring expander.
5: Release piston pin lock screws and force out pins.
6. Check cylinder bores for distortion, taper, and other evidence of excessive wear. Bore and hone as necessary.

Installation

1. Assemble piston to rod by pushing in and locking the pin.
2. Using a ring expander, install piston rings. Install bottom (oil) ring first, center ring second, and top ring last.
3. Coat all bearing surfaces, rings, and piston skirt with engine oil.
4. Turn down the crankpin of the cylinder being worked on.
5. Make sure that the gaps in the rings are not in line.
6. Using a ring compressor, install the piston and rod assembly into the cylinder and carefully tap down until the rod bearing is solidly seated on the crankpin.
7. Install cap and lower bearing shell. Torque to the specified figure.
8. Install all piston assemblies in the same manner.
9. Install cylinder head and oil pan.

Removal
V6 OHV V8 304, 327, 360

Remove the cylinder head and oil pan, and crank the engine so that one pair of pistons are in the down position. Use a cylinder ring ridge remover to cut the ridge off the top of the cylinders. Now, working from underneath the truck, remove the two bolts which hold the rod-bearing cap. Remove the cap and push the rod and piston assembly up out of the block. Immediately replace the cap and run the nuts up finger-tight so that the cap will not get turned, or the bearing will not be lost.

NOTE: Use rubber hose on rod bolts to protect journals.

Installation

On engines using split-skirt pistons, the slit in the skirt must be installed opposite the oil squirt hole in the connecting rod. Solid skirt pistons are assembled so that the boss, or dimple, (and, in some instances, the letter F) at the top of the piston is on the same side of the connecting rod as the boss, which will be found on the connecting rod channel about halfway up the rod.

The piston and rod assemblies are united to the engine from the top and the dimple, or dot, on the top of the piston goes toward the front. On those engines having split-skirt pistons, the slit in the skirt of the piston goes toward the left side of the engine.

Piston Assembly

Removal
V6 & V8 350 Engines

1. Remove cylinder heads.
2. Remove oil pan.
3. Examine cylinder bores for top ridge. If ridge exists, remove it before taking pistons out.
4. Number all the pistons, connecting rods and caps. On the V6 engine the right bank is numbered 2-4-6; the left bank, 1-3-5, from the front. V8 engines are numbered 1-3-5-7, left; and 2-4-6-8, right.
5. With No. 1 crankpin straight down, remove cap and bearing shell from No. 1 connecting rod. Install connecting rod bolt guides to hold upper half of the bearing

shell in place.

6. Push piston and rod assembly up out of the cylinder. Then remove bolt guides and reinstall cap and bearing shell on the rod.
7. Remove the remaining rod and piston assemblies in the same manner.
8. Carefully remove old rings with piston ring expander.
9. Carefully press out the old pin.

NOTE: Check the cylinder bores for distortion, taper or other damage. Any cylinders requiring attention may be bored or honed the same as any other conventional cast iron cylinder block.

Installation

1. Carefully assemble the piston to the connecting rod (press in the pin).
2. Remove piston and rod from the press. Rock the piston on the pin to be sure pin or piston boss was not damaged during the pressing operation.
3. Install ring expander in lower ring groove. Position the ends of the expander above the piston pin where groove is not slotted. The ends of the expander must butt together.
4. Install oil ring rails over expander with gaps up on same side of piston as oil spurt hole in connecting rod.
5. Install compression rings, (with a ring expander) in top and center groove.
6. Coat all bearing surfaces, rings and piston skirt with engine oil.
7. Position the crankpin of the cylinder being worked on down.
8. Remove connecting rod bearing cap and with upper bearing shell correctly seated in the rod, install connecting rod bolt guides. Make sure the gaps in the two oil rings rails are up toward the center of the engine. Make sure the gaps of the compressing rings are not in line with each other or the oil ring rails. Be sure the ends of the oil ring spacer-expander are butted and not overlapped.
9. With a ring compressor, install the piston and rod assembly into the cylinder bore and carefully tap down until the rod bearing is solidly seated on the crankpin.
10. Remove the connecting rod bolt guides and install cap and lower bearing shell. Torque to the specified figure.
11. Install other piston and rod assemblies in the same manner.
12. When the assemblies are all installed, the oil spurt holes will be up and the rib on the edge of the rod cap will be on the same side as the conical boss on the connecting rod web. These marks will be toward the other connecting rod on the same crankpin.
13. Accumulated end clearance between rod bearings on any crankpin should be .005 to .012".
14. Install oil screen and oil pan.
15. Install cylinder heads.

NOTE: Before starting a new or reconditioned engine it is advisable to pack the oil pump with petroleum jelly to insure pump priming for immediate lubrication.

Fitting Rings and Pins

F-Head, L-Head, OHC 6

When new rings are installed without reboring the cylinders, the cylinder wall glaze should be broken by honing.

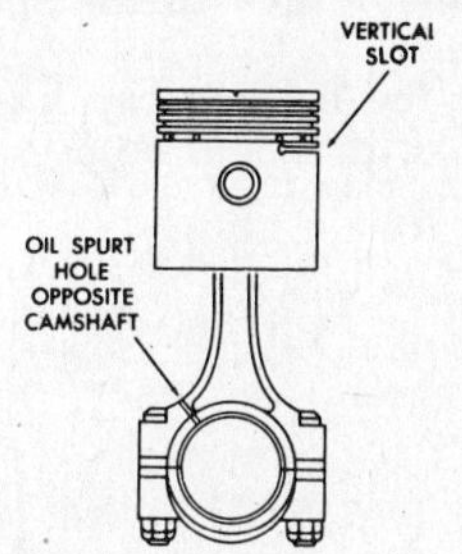

Piston to rod assembly—L4 and F4
(© Willys Corp.)

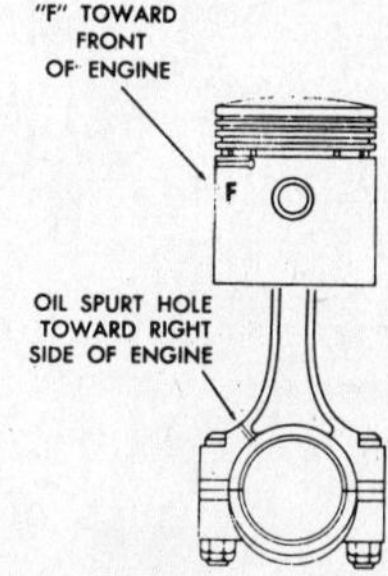

Piston to rod assembly—OHC 6—230
(© Willys Corp.)

New piston rings should be checked for end gap and clearance in cylinder bores and ring grooves. When fitting new rings, compression ring side clearance should be no more than .006" for four-cylinder engines. Any clearance greater than this indicates a need for a new piston. End gap of compression rings is checked by pushing the ring to the bottom of the bore in which it will operate. Compression ring end gap should be at least .007" for four-cylinder engines.

Piston pins should be a push-fit. If they are excessively loose, the piston must be replaced.

When assembling the rod and piston assemblies to the four-cylinder engine, the T-slot in the piston should be on the left side. The oil spurt hole should face to the right, away from the camshaft and the T-slot. On the 226 six-cylinder engine, the oil spray hole should face the camshaft. On the 230 OHC engine, the "F" marking on the piston should be to the front and the oil spurt hole to the right.

Piston to cylinder wall clearance should be checked with a ribbon gauge and a spring scale. The scale should register 5-10 lbs. to pull a .003" ribbon gauge between the piston and the cylinder wall on four-cylinder engines.

OHV 6 232 Engines

232 pistons have a concave head with one notch. Specified piston to cylinder bore clearance is 0.0005-0.0013".

Ring side clearance on No. 1 and No. 2 ring should be 0.0015-0.0035"; 0.0000-0.020"; 0.015-0.055" on oil control rail.

V8 327 Engines

Piston pins are a press fit in connecting rod, hand fit in piston at 68°F. Before assembly, clean ring grooves using broken ring or commercial groove cleaner. Piston to cylinder bore clearance at top land should be 0.028-0.032"; at skirt top 0.0009-0.0025"; at skirt bottom 0.0009-0.0015".

Piston ring groove clearance should be 0.002-0.006" for compression rings, 0.0001-0.004" for oil ring. Ring end gap, with ring near bottom of cylinder, should be 0.010-0.020" for compression rings, 0.015-0.055" for ring rail.

Piston rings should be arranged with the end gaps 120° apart, with no gap being placed over the pin boss.

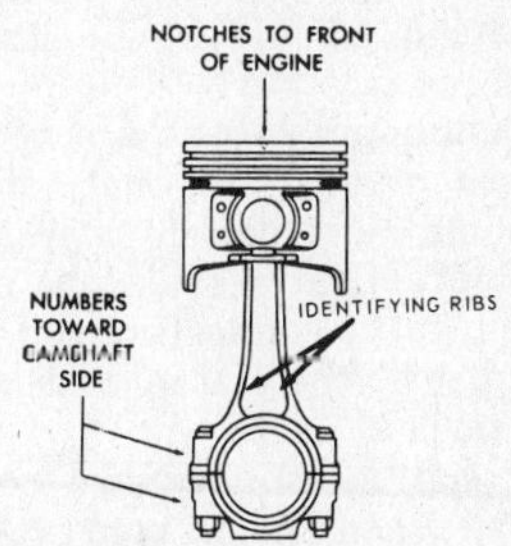

Piston to rod assembly—OHV 6—232
(© Willys Corp.)

V6, V8 350 Engines

When new rings are installed without reboring the cylinders, cylinder wall glaze should be broken. This can be done by using the finest grade stones in a cylinder hone.

New piston rings must be checked for end gap and clearance in cylinder and ring grooves.

When fitting new rings to new pistons the side clearance for compres-

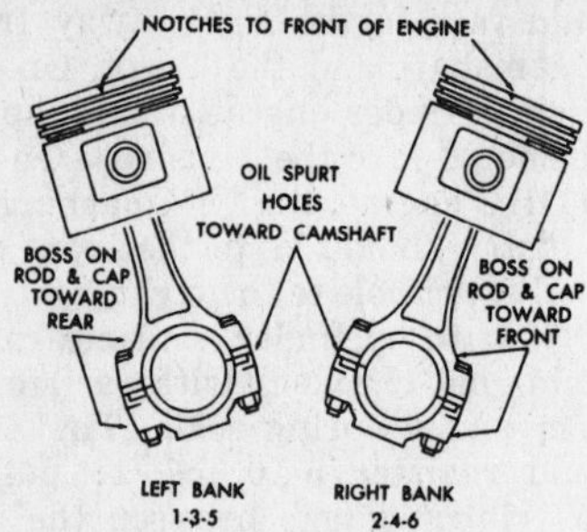

Piston to rod assembly—V6
(© Willys Corp.)

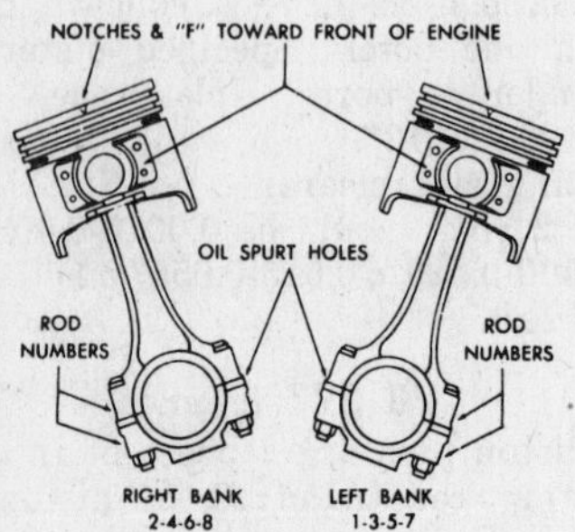

Piston to rod assembly—V8
(© Willys Corp.)

sion rings should be .003 to .005″. Side clearance of the oil ring should be .0035 to .0095″.

Check end gap of compression rings by placing them in the bore in which they will operate. Then push them to the bottom of the bore with a piston. Now measure the end gap in each ring. The end gap should be no less than .010″ for 350 V8 engines (1968-70), and .015 for all 1964-67 engines. For all 1968-70 V8 engines, oil end gap should be no less than .015 in.

If piston pin bosses are worn out of round or oversize, the piston and pin should be replaced. Oversize pins are not practical because the pin is a press fit in the connecting rod. Piston pins must fit the piston with an easy finger push at 70°F.

The rod assemblies are correctly installed when the oil spurt holes are toward the camshaft, the boss on the rod is on the same side as the boss on the rod cap, and these bosses are toward the other connecting rod on the same crankpin.

Connecting Rod Bearings

1. Remove connecting rod cap with bearing shell. Wipe all oil from the bearing area.
2. Place a piece of Plastigage lengthwise along the bottom center of the lower bearing shell. Then install cap with bearing shell and torque the bolt nuts to the specified figure from the Torque Specifications table. NOTE: Do not turn crankshaft.
3. Remove the cap and shell. The gauge material will be found flattend and adhering to either the bearing shell or the crankpin. Do not remove it.
4. Using the scale that comes with the gauge, measure the flattened gauge material at its widest point. The number within the graduation which comes closest to the width of the gauging material indicates the bearing to crankpin clearance in thousandths of an inch.
5. If a new bearing is required, try a standard, then each undersize bearing in turn until one is found that is within specifications.
6. With the proper bearing selected, clean off the gauging material, reinstall the bearing cap and torque to the specified figure.
7. After the bearing cap has been torqued, it should be possible to move the connecting rod back and forth on the crankpin, the extent of end clearance.

Main Bearings

To determine the amount of bearing clearance, place a piece of Plastigage in the cap (on the dry bearing) and install the cap. Tighten cap bolts to proper torque specification, without turning crankshaft, then remove cap and Plastigage. Measure the width of the crushed Plastigage strip, using the scale on the package. If clearance is too great, install bearing inserts with thicker backing. Do not, under any circumstances, place shim stock under the bearing or file the caps to reduce clearance. If oil clearance is too small, bearing inserts with thinner backing are available.

NOTE: When fitting main bearings, keep all caps tight except the one being checked. Support weight of

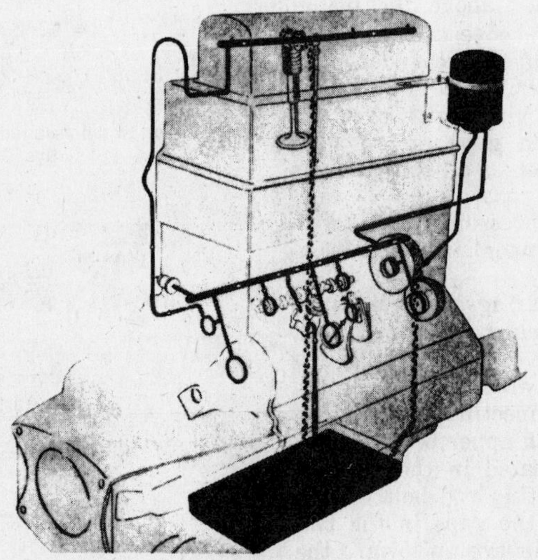

Engine lubrication system—F4
(© Willys Corp.)

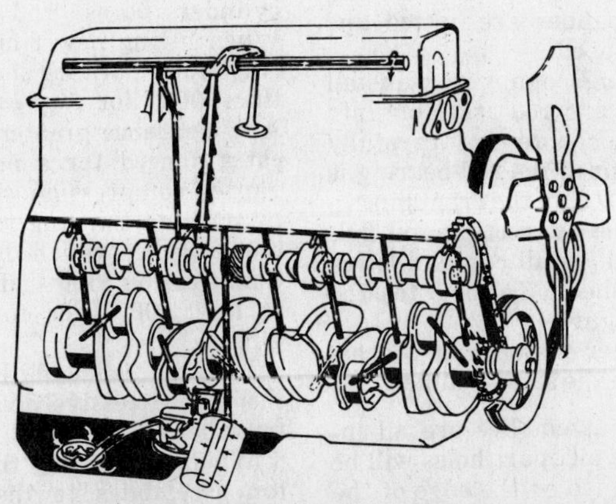

Engine lubrication system—6—232
(© Willys Corp.)

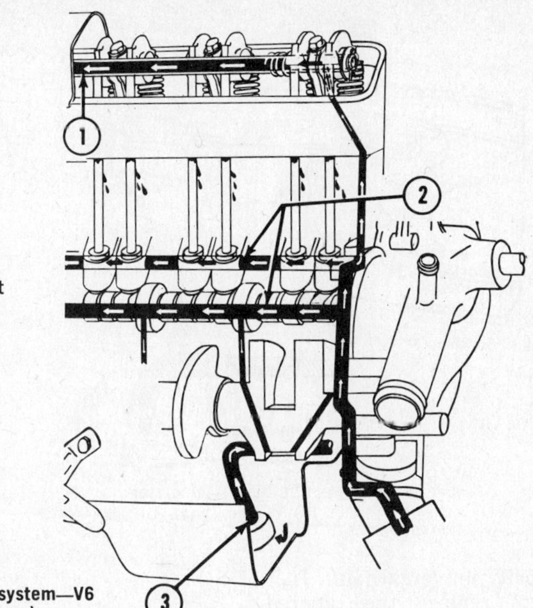

1 Rocker arm shaft
2 Main oil line
3 Oil inlet

Engine lubrication system—V6
(© Willys Corp.)

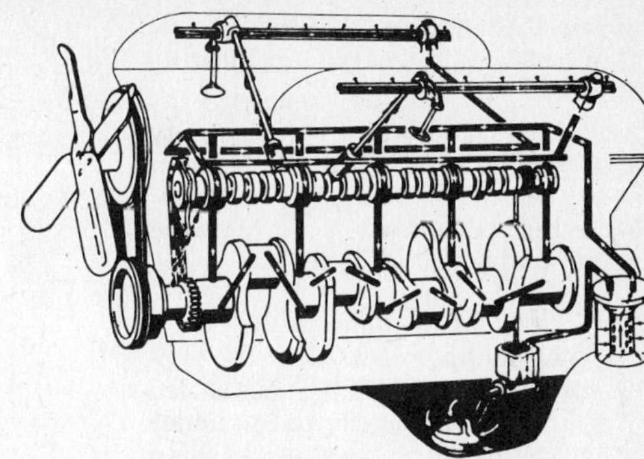

Engine lubrication system—V8—327
(© Willys Corp.)

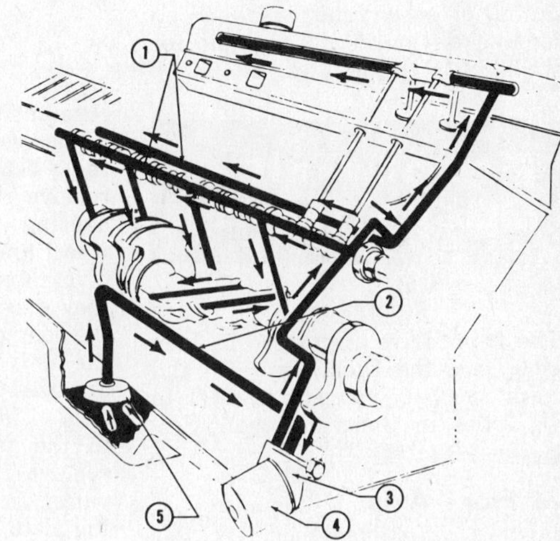

Engine lubrication system—V8—350
(© Willys Corp.)

1 Valve lifter oil galleries
2 Main oil gallery
3 Oil pump
4 Oil filter
5 Oil pickup screen

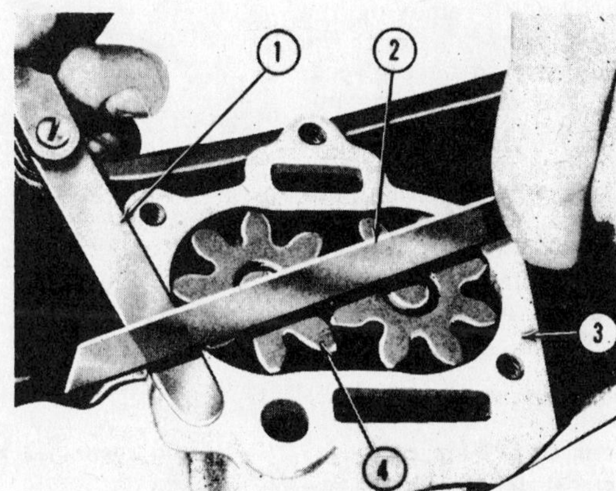

1 Feeler gauge
2 Straight edge
3 Pump body
4 Pump gears

Checking oil pump gear end clearance
(© Willys Corp.)

crank with a screw jack for best results.

Lacking a micrometer, Plastigage can be used to check journal taper. Place strip of Plastigage lengthwise along the bearing insert (aligned with long axis of engine) and tighten cap to proper torque. If the journal is tapered, the Plastigage will be wider at one end.

Main bearing journal and connecting rod journal specifications can be found in the Specifications area of this section.

Refer to the Engine Rebuilding Section for general information on engine overhaul procedures.

Engine Lubrication

Oil Pan

Due to the variety of engines used in Jeep vehicles, oil pan R & R procedures range from simply removing the attaching bolts to removing the front end components for access. The steps required, however, become obvious when ascertained from a certain model equipped with a specific engine.

Oil Filter

The oil filter used on most Jeep vehicles is a disposable element, and should changed as recommended in the owners manual. When installing a new filter, follow this procedure:

1. Coat the gasket on the new filter with oil.
2. Place the new filter in position on the block.
3. Hand tighten until contact is made between the filter gasket and the adapter face.
4. Tighten by further turning the filter two-thirds turn.
5. Run the engine at fast idle and check for oil leaks.
6. Check the oil and fill crankcase to level if necessary.

Oil Pump

OHV, 327 V8 Engines

The oil pump is driven by the distributor drive shaft. Oil pump R&R does not, however, affect distributor timing because the drive gear remains in mesh with the camshaft gear.

With a straightedge across the pump body and gears, clearance should be 0.000-0.004" (gears should project above body). Do not disturb location of tube in pump body if possible. Measure clearance between gears and wall of gear cavity opposite point of gear mesh; gap should be 0.0005"-0.0025" for 232, 0.008" for 327 V8. The oil pressure relief valve is set at the factory to 60 psi and is not adjustable.

V8 304, 360 Engines

The oil pump is located in, and as part of, the timeing cover. The pump is driven by the distributor drive shaft. Oil pump R&R does not affect distributor timing.

Remove pump cover and place a straightedge across pump body and gears. Clearance should be .0025-0.0065" (gears projecting above body). Measure clearance between gears and wall of gear cavity opposite point of gear mesh; gap should be 0.002-0.004". The oil pressure relief valve is set to 75 psi at the factory and is not adjustable.

V6, V8 350 Engines

The oil pump is located in the timing chain cover, where it is connected by a drilled passage in the cylinder crankcase to an oil screen housing and standpipe assembly.

Oil is drawn into the pump through the screen and pipe and is discharged to the oil pump cover assembly. The cover assembly consists of an oil presusre relief valve, an oil filter by-pass valve and a nipple for installation of the oil filter.

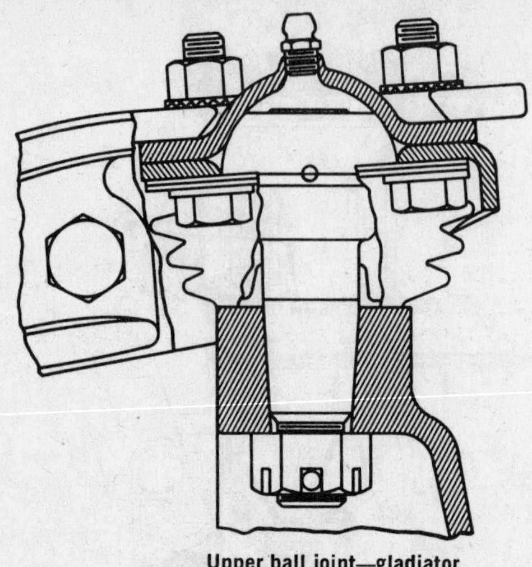

Upper ball joint—gladiator
(© Willys Corp.)

Reference

The front drive axles used in Jeep vehicles are the Dana Type 27 and 44. For overhaul procedures refer to Rear Axles in General Repair Section.

Live Front Axle

On four-wheel-drive models, caster is adjusted by placing shims between the spring pads on the front axle housing and the top of the spring.

This method should only be used where it is necessary to adjust both sides of the vehicle the same amount. In the event the caster angle is incorrect because of sag of the front leaf springs, it is advisable to replace the springs rather than use caster wedges. Camber can not be adjusted.

Solid Front Axle

Universal models with two wheel drive have a solid front axle. The axle may be either of tubular construction or a forged I-beam. Springs may be slung either under or over the axle. Standard caster and camber are built into the front axle. Camber cannot be changed, but caster can be adjusted by placing tapered shims between the springs and spring seats.

King-Pin Replacement

Four Wheel Drive

An upper and lower pivot pin is used in the four-wheel drive models. Both upper and lower pins are held to the universal joint housing by four cap screws. There are two tapered roller bearings, one top and one bottom, in the axle housing, exactly centered across the neutral point of the constant velocity universal joint. If it is desired to replace the tapered roller bearings, it will be necessary to remove the universal joint outer housing. This involves removing the wheel and the stationary axle. If the pivot pins, only, are to be replaced, they can be removed by taking out the four capscrews that hold them to the universal joint housing. Shims are used under the head of the pivot pins to insure zero up and down play in the tapered roller bearings. To remove the pivot pins, take off the wheel, brake drum, and brake backing plate.

Independent Suspension

Wagoneer and Gladiator

Some two-wheel drive vehicles are equipped with an independent front suspension system with torsion bars, an upper support assembly and a tubular front axle. The axle is in two sections, hinged at the center. Knuckle supports are mounted between the axle ends and the upper supports by means of lower and upper ball joints.

The independent front suspension is also available on four-wheel drive vehicles. The general difference is that the lower support axle is hinged at the differential.

Independent Suspension Alignment

To check caster and camber, it is necessary that both sections of the front axle be on the exact level. With vehicle on level floor, check each section with a level or other accurate method. An uneven or unlevel condition is corrected by adjusting the bolt at frame end of torsion bar. Tightening this bolt lowers the wheel end. Be sure to tighten locknut any time these adjusting bolts are disturbed.

To adjust caster, loosen jam nuts at each end of strut tube and turn

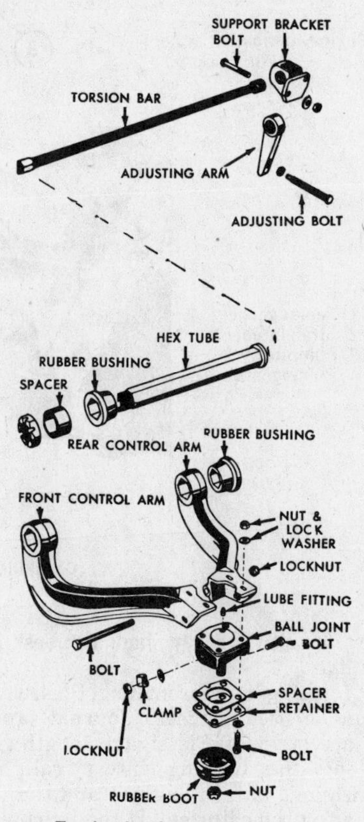

Torsion bar installation
(© Willys Corp.)

tube until specified caster is obtained, then tighten locknuts and recheck caster.

To adjust camber, loosen the control-arm-to-ball-joint bolts that are mounted in slotted holes. Move all joints until specified camber is obtained and retighten the bolts.

Ball Joint Replacement—Wagoneer and Gladiator

Ball joints are bolted to the support arms and mounted in the knuckle support by the conventional taper with castellated nut.

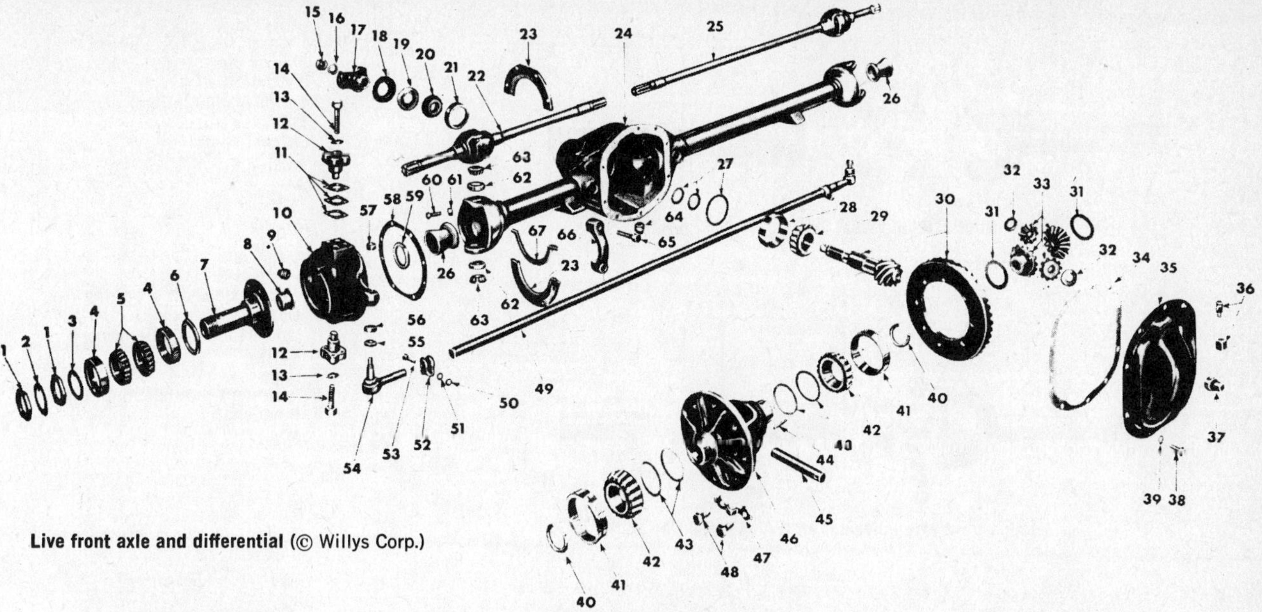

Live front axle and differential (© Willys Corp.)

1 Wheel bearing nut
2 Locking washer
3 Wheel bearing washer
4 Wheel bearing cup
5 Wheel bearing cone and rollers
6 Wheel bearing oil seal
7 Wheel spindle
8 Wheel spindle bushing
9 Knuckle housing filler plug
10 Knuckle and arm—left
11 Adjusting shims
12 Bearing cap
13 Lockwasher
14 Bearing cap bolt
15 Pinion huglock nut
16 Pinion washer
17 Universal joint yoke
18 Pinion shaft oil seal
19 Bearing oil slinger
20 Bearing cone and rollers
21 Bearing cup
22 Right universal joint and shaft
23 Knuckle oil seal retainer
24 Front axle housing
25 Left Universal joint and shaft
26 Axle shaft guide
27 Pinion bearing adjusting shims
28 Pinion shaft bearing cup
29 Pinion shaft bearing cone and rollers
30 Drive gear and pinion
31 Side gear thrust washer
32 Pinion case thrust washer
33 Differential gears
34 Housing cover gasket
35 Housing cover
36 Housing breather
37 Filler plug
38 Housing cover bolt
39 Lockwasher
40 Retaining ring
41 Differential bearing cup
42 Differential bearing cone and rollers
43 Differential bearing adjusting shims
44 Pinion shaft lock pin
45 Pinion shaft
46 Differential case
47 Drive gear lock strap
48 Drive gear bolts
49 Steering tie rod
50 Tie rod clamp nut
51 Lockwasher
52 Tie rod socket clamp
53 Tie rod clamp screw
54 Tie rod socket
55 Dust cover
56 Washer
57 Tie rod stud nut
58 Steering knuckle gasket
59 Universal joint thrust washer
60 Knuckle stop bolt
61 Stop bolt nut
62 King pin bearing cup
63 King pin bearing cone and rollers
64 Housing drain plug
65 Bearing Cap bolt
66 Differential bearing cap
67 Knuckle oil seal

Torsion Bar Replacement—Wagoneer and Gladiator

The torsion bars are marked on the front (hex) end with either L or R to indicate the side. Never alter this location.

The adjusting arm at the rear of the bar has two adjusting bolt indentations. When installing the arm on the bar, place it on the bar with the upper indentation next to frame on J-100 vehicles. On J-200 and J-300 vehicles, install the arm on the bar with the lower indentation next to frame.

Front Axle Assembly Removal

Exc. Four Wheel Drive

1. With front of truck raised and at lower end.
2. Keep the bar parallel to frame, wheel and axle hanging free.
3. Back off adjusting screw at rear of bar until inner end of screw is flush with frame at inside of side rail.
4. Remove the two bolts attaching the rear bar anchor support to the frame side rail.
5. Slide torsion bar, with adjusting arm and bracket, to the rear to remove from vehicle. The split grommet or seal at front will come out with bar.

Installation

1. With front of car raised and supported under frame with wheels and axles hanging free, insert the hex end of bar in the hex tube of upper support.
2. Keeping the bar parallel to frame, slide adjusting arm on bar, holding lower end of arm against frame.
3. Mark the relative position of the arm to the bar on the serrations for further reference. Then remove the arm.
4. Install the sealing grommet between bar and hex tube by sliding the bar back about 1″. Place the grommet on bar and slide into position in tube. Be sure a good seal is obtained.
5. Use a wooden wedge and pry the rear of bar away from rail so that adjusting arm and support bracket can be installed with lower end against frame and two serrations separated from the make made in step 3, above.
6. Remove wedge, then bolt bracket to frame. Torque nuts to 45-50 ft. lb.
7. Lower vehicle to floor and reconnect shock absorber.
8. Level axle with adjusting screw, as described in the paragraphs covering front alignment.
9. Tighten adjusting screw jam nut.

NOTE: If adjusting screw travel is not sufficient to level axle, change position of arm on bar one serration at a time. (See 5 above.)

Front Axle Assembly Removal

Four Wheel Drive

1. Raise the front end of the vehicle

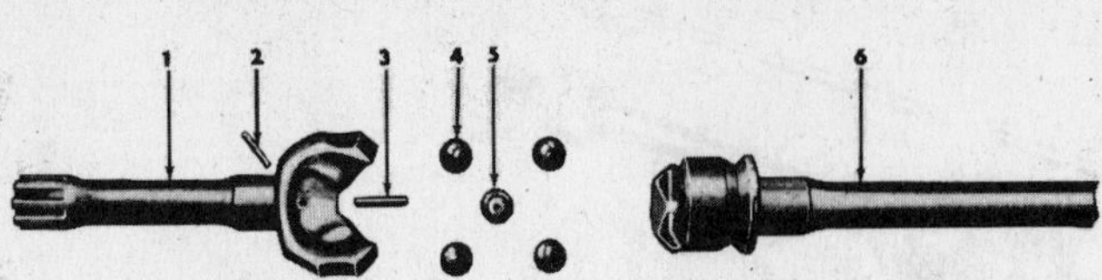

1 Outer shaft
2 Lock pin
3 Center ball pin
4 Universal joint ball
5 Center ball
6 Inner shaft

Bendix front axle universal joint (© Willys Corp.)

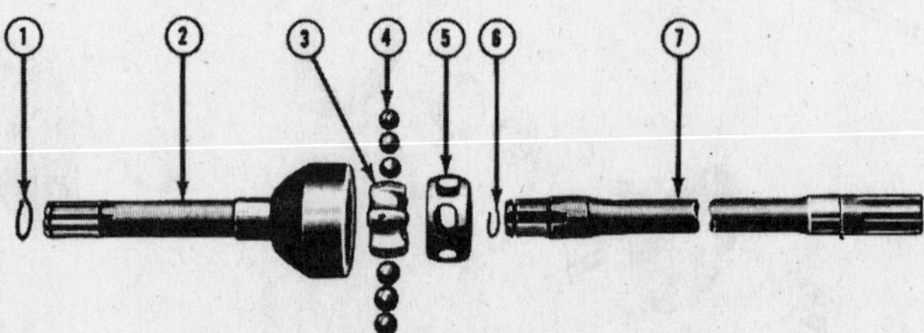

1 Outer axle shaft snap ring
2 Outer shaft
3 Universal joint inner race
4 Ball
5 Cage
6 Axle shaft retainer snap ring
7 Inner shaft

Rzeppa front axle universal joint (© Willys Corp.)

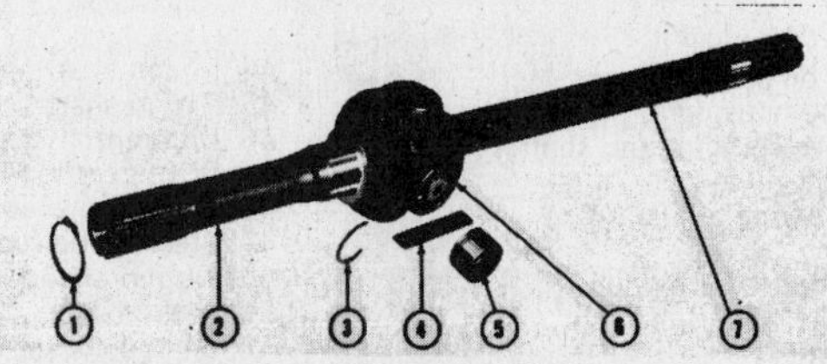

1 Outer axle shaft snap ring
2 Outer shaft
3 Bearing retainer snap ring
4 Bearing rollers
5 Bearing retainer
6 Universal joint journal assembly
7 Inner shaft

Spicer front axle universal joint (© Willys Corp.)

and safely support the frame behind the springs.

2. Remove the wheels by removing the wheel discs and lug nuts.
3. Disconnect the propeller shaft at the front universal companion flange.
4. Disconnect the steering connecting rod at the ball and socket connection on the steering knuckle.
5. Disconnect the shock absorbers at the axle mounting pads.
6. Disconnect the brake hydraulic hoses at the connections between front brake lines and flexible hoses.
7. Support the axle assembly on a jack, ready for removal.
8. On vehicles with the springs slung over the axle, remove the nuts from the spring to axle U-bolt clips, remove the spring clip plates, and slide the axle assembly from underneath the vehicle. On vehicles with the springs under the axle, remove the nuts from the spring clips and remove the spring clip plates. Then disconnect the spring from the spring shackles by removing the lower spring shackle bolts. Lower the front springs to the floor and slide the axle assembly from underneath the vehicle.

Installation

The procedure for installing the solid front axle varies slightly, depending on whether the springs are slung over or under the axle. These variations are noted in the following procedure.

1. Support the axle assembly on a jack and slide into position under the vehicle.
2. On vehicles with the springs slung under the axle, swing the spring into position and reassemble the spring shackle.
3. Replace the spring clip plates and spring clips.
4. Connect the brake hydraulic hoses at the connections between the front brake lines and the flexible hoses.
5. Connect the shock absorbers at the axle mounting pads.
6. Connect the propeller shaft.
7. Connect the steering connecting rod at the ball and socket connection on the steering knuckle.
8. Adjust and bleed the brakes.
9. Remove supports and lower the front end of the vehicle.
10. Check front end wheel alignment.
11. Check turning angle.

Front Axle Universal Joints

Three types of constant velocity universal joints are used on Jeep four wheel drives. The first is the Bendix type universal joint, the second the Rzeppa type, and the third the Spicer type.

Removal

1. Remove the wheel.
2. Remove hub dust cap.
3. Remove axle shaft driving flange bolts.
4. Apply and hold foot brakes. Remove axle shaft flange with a puller.
5. Release lip on lockwasher, remove outer nut, lockwasher, adjusting nut, and bearing lockwasher. Use a special wrench for these nuts.
6. Remove wheel hub and drum assembly with the bearings.
7. Remove hydraulic brake tube, backing plate screws, spindle, axle shaft and universal joint assembly.
8. Install in reverse order of removal.

Bendix Joint

The factory no longer supplies replacement component parts for the Bendix universal joint. Rebuilding these universals requires complex shop equipment and is economically unfeasible. However, the complete universal joint assembly may be replaced.

If the assembly falls apart upon removal from the vehicle, reassemble as follows:

1. Place the differential half of the axle shaft in a vise, with the ground portion above the jaws.
2. Install the center ball in the socket in the shaft, with the hole

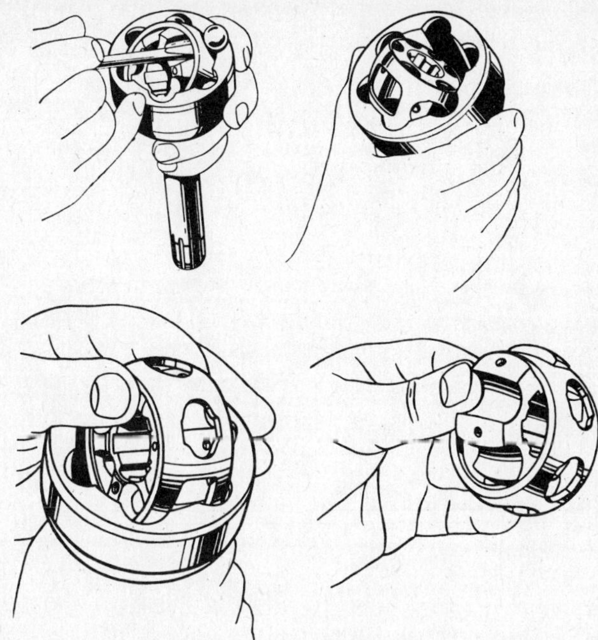

Disassembly of Rzeppa joint (© Willys Corp.)

and groove toward you.
3. Drop the center ball pin into the drilled passage in the wheel half of the shaft.
4. Place the wheel half of the shaft on the center ball. Then slip three balls into the raceways.
5. Turn the center ball until the groove lines up with the raceway for the remaining ball. Slip the ball into the raceway and straighten up the wheel end of the shaft.
6. Turn the center ball until the center ball pin drops into the hole in the ball.
7. Install the retainer pin and prick punch both ends to lock it in place.
8 After reassembly, grasp both ends of the shaft and twist the ends back and forth. Should excessive wear be indicated by back lash or lost motion, the assembly should be replaced.

Rzeppa Joint

1. To dismantle the Rzeppa joint, remove the three screws (some axles have no screws) that hold the front axle shaft to the joint itself, and pull the shaft out of the splined inner race. To take out the axle shaft retainer, remove the retainer ring on the shaft. Push down on the various points of the inner race and cage until the balls can be removed with the help of a small screwdriver.
2. There are two large elongated holes in the cage. Turn the cage so that the two bosses in the spindle shaft will drop into the elongated holes in the cage. Then, the cage can be lifted out.
3. To remove the inner race, turn it so that one of the bosses will drop into an elongated hole in this cage, then shift the race to one side and lift it out.
4. Reverse procedure to reassemble.

Spicer Joint

The Spicer universal joint is a cross and roller unit with needle bearings. It is quite similar in design to the Spicer driveshaft universal joint. Disassembly is as follows:

1. Remove snap-rings.
2. Press on end of one bearing until opposite bearing is pushed from yoke arm.
3. Turn joint over. Press first bearing back out of arm by pressing on exposed end of journal shaft. Repeat this operation for the other two bearings, then lift out journal assembly by sliding to one side.
4. Wash all parts in solvent and inspect for wear. Replace all worn parts.
5. Install new gaskets on the journal assembly. Make certain that the grease channel in each journal trunnion is open.
6. Pack bearing cones one-third full of grease and install the rollers.
7. Assemble in reverse order of disassembly. If the joint binds when assembled, tap the arms lightly to relieve any pressure on the bearings at the end of the journal.

Steering Linkage

Steering Connecting Rod

The steering connecting rod is of the ball and socket type. All ball seat springs are identical except for their location. The ball joints must be loose enough to allow free movement, yet tight enough to prevent end play.

Removal

1. Remove cotter pins and nuts from both ends.
2. Remove rod.
3. Inspect all parts and replace as necessary. NOTE: Ball joints on late model vehicles cannnot be disassembled for service or inspection.
4. Locate wheels in the straight—ahead position.
5. Locate the steering arm parallel to the centerline of the vehicle.
6. Align steering arm and gearshaft at high point and then install the steering connecting rod with nuts and new cotter pins.

Tie Rods

The tie rods are a three piece construction consisting of the rod and two ball and socket assemblies. Right-hand and left-hand threads on the rods provide toe-in adjustment without removing the rod.

NOTE: Early production F4-134 4x2 vehicles are equipped with a divided-type tie rod connecting the steering knuckles. On these vehicles, each wheel must be adjusted independently.

Tie Rod Removal

1. Remove cotter pins and nuts at both ends.
2. Using a puller or expansion fork, remove tie rods from steering knuckle arms.
3. Separate the joint seals and remove the socket assembly by loosening the clamp bolt nuts and unscrewing the unit.
4. Inspect all parts and replace as necessary.
5. Install by reversing the removal procedure. Use new seals and cotter pins, then torque nuts to 38-42 ft. lbs. If steering arm was removed, torque nut to 70-90 ft. lbs.

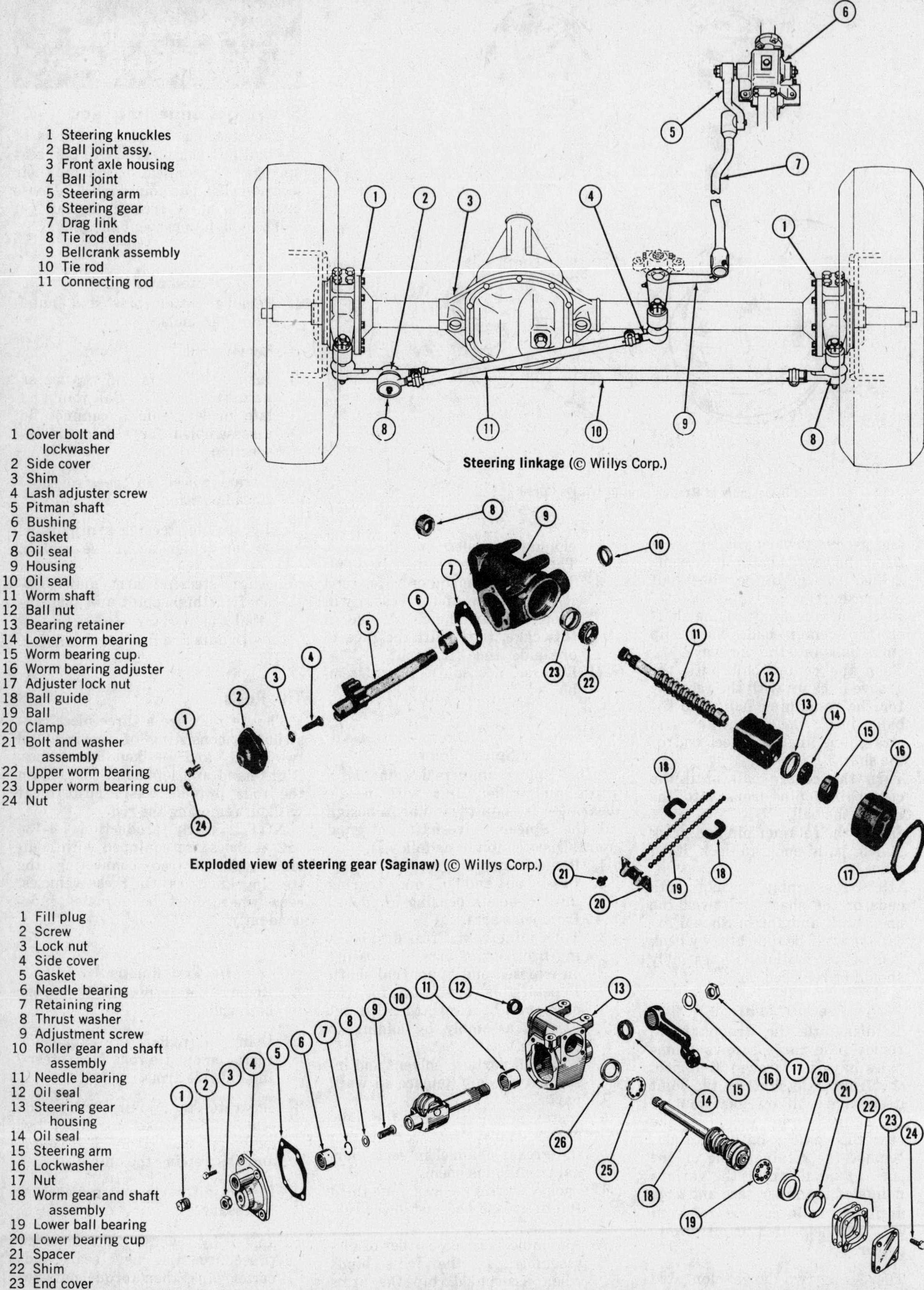

Steering linkage (© Willys Corp.)

Exploded view of steering gear (Saginaw) (© Willys Corp.)

Exploded view of steering gear—Ross worm and roller (© Willys Corp.)

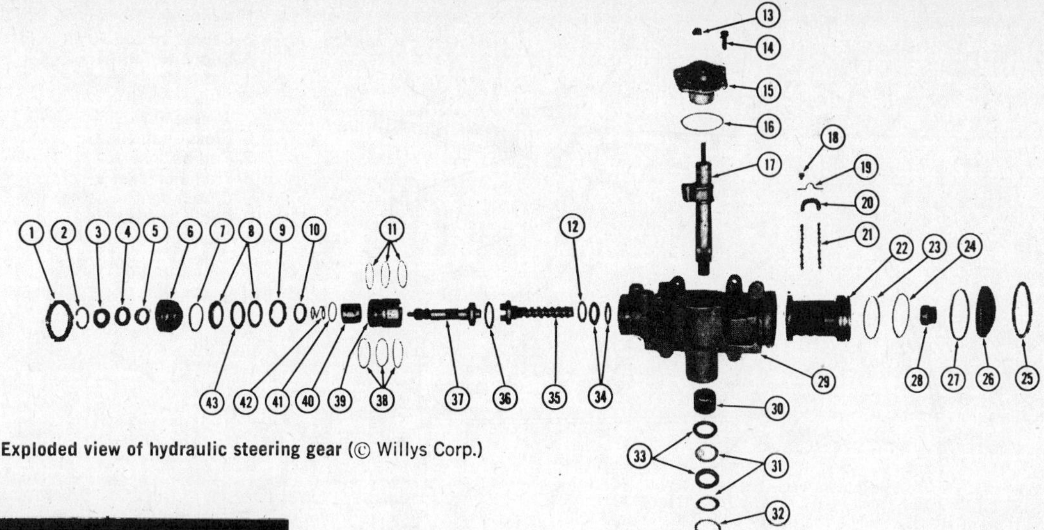

Exploded view of hydraulic steering gear (© Willys Corp.)

1 Locknut
2 Retaining ring
3 Dust seal
4 Oil seal
5 Bearing
6 Adjuster plug
7 O-ring seal
8 Thrust bearing races
9 Spacer
10 Bearing retainer
11 O-ring back-up seals
12 Thrust bearing
13 Nut
14 Bolt and lockwasher
15 Side cover
16 O-ring seal
17 Pitman shaft assembly
18 Screw and lockwasher
19 Clamp
20 Ball return guide
21 Balls
22 Rack-piston nut
23 O-ring back-up seal
24 Piston ring
25 Retaining ring
26 Housing end plug
27 O-ring seal
28 Rack-piston end
29 Housing
30 Bearing
31 Washer
32 Retaining ring
33 Oil seals
34 Thrust bearing races
35 Worm
36 O-ring seal
37 Stub shaft torsion bar assembly
38 Valve body rings
39 Valve body
40 Valve spool
41 O-ring spool dampener seal
42 Spool spring
43 Thrust bearing

Steering Gear

Standard Steering Gear Removal

Universal Series

1. Remove directional signal unit from steering column.
2. Remove steering column bracket from instrument panel.
3. Remove upper section of the floor pan.
4. Disconnect shift rods from lower end of steering column.
5. Disconnect horn wire at lower end of steering assembly.
6. Remove steering gear arm.
7. Unbolt steering gear housing from frame. Remove assembly by bringing it up through the floor pan opening.
8. Install in reverse of above.

Jeepster, Gladiator, and Wagoneer

1. Disconnect the steering gear from the steering column by removing the flexible coupling clamp screw.
2. Disconnect the drag link from the steering gear arm.
3. Remove housing bolts from frame. Remove steering gear from engine compartment.
4. Reverse procedure to install.

Power Steering Gear Removal

1. Disconnect hoses from pressure and return ports. Raise hoses above pump to prevent oil loss.
2. Remove flexible coupling clamp screw.
3. Remove steering gear arm.
4. Remove steering gear mounting bolts. Remove steering gear from vehicle.
5. Reverse procedure to install.

Refer to the General Reapir Section for details on overhauling standard and power steering gears.

Clutch

Pedal Adjustment

Universal Series, Jeepster

Adjust the linkage at the turnbuckle on the cable from the clutch fork control lever so that the clutch pedal can be depressed 1" before clutch disengagement starts.

Gladiator, Wagoneer

1. Disconnect adjustable rod from clutch pedal.
2. Adjust clutch pedal stop bolt for a positive over-center action. This is done by turning the stop bolt in or out to obtain clutch pedal travel of ¼-½" before the over-center spring assists the pedal to the floorboard. The pedal need not be the same height as the brake pedal.
3. Adjust rod from brake pedal to cross-shaft so that proper angle is obtained between arm of cross-shaft and top of left rfame rail. For the 350 V8, the correct angle is thirty degrees. For the 327 V8 and the 232 OHV 6, the correct angle is forty-nine degrees. This angle may be measured with a protractor.
4. Adjust the cross-shaft to throw-out lever link so that the clutch pedal can be depressed 1" before clutch engagement starts.

NOTE: All J-Series left hand drive vehicles equipped with OHV6-258, 304V8 and 360V8 engines are utilizing a new cable actuated linkage. To adjust cable follow this procedure:

1. Lift clutch pedal up against the support bracket stop.
2. Disconnect clutch fork return spring.
3. Loosen the ball adjusting nut for some cable slack.
4. Turn the ball adjusting nut until slack is taken up and the clutch throw-out bearing contacts the pressure plate fingers.
5. Back off adjusting nut ¾ turn to provide proper free-play and then tighten jam nut.
6. Connect clutch fork return spring.

If the clutch cable adjustment does not provide satisfactory disengagement, the pedal height may be adjusted by following these steps:

1. Lift pedal up against the support bracket stop.
2. Adjust the stop to provide 6½" clearance between pedal and floorpan by turning stop screw located on top of the support

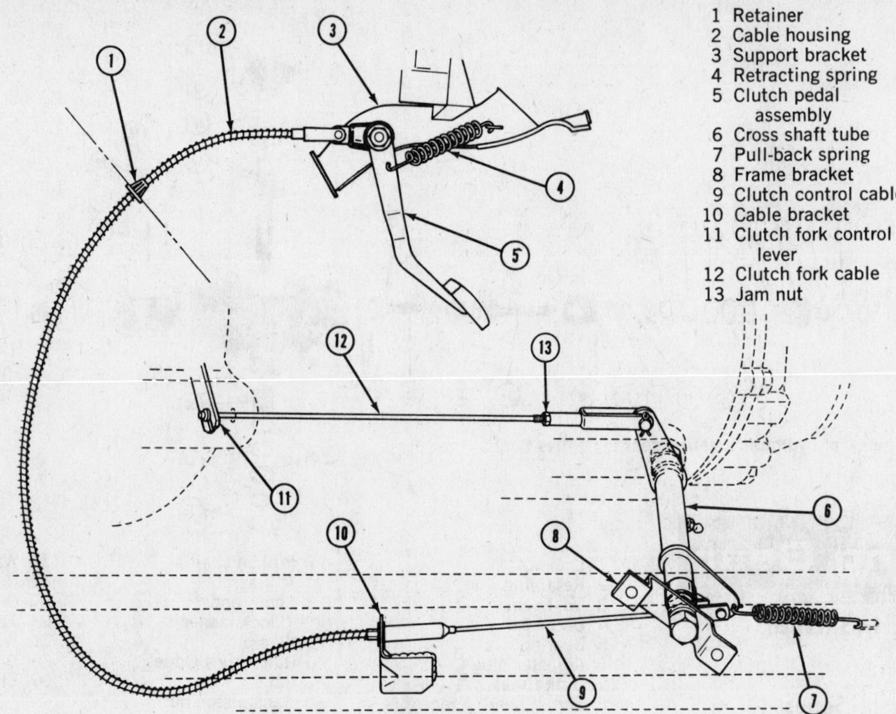

Clutch linkage—Jeepster (© Willys Corp.)

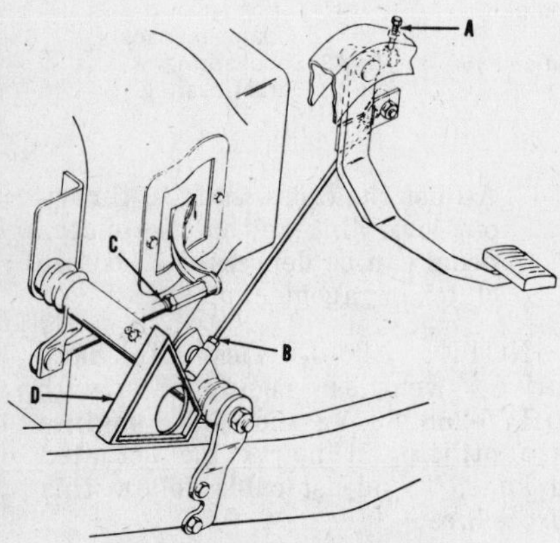

Clutch linkage—Gladiator (© Willys Corp.)

A Pedal height adjustment point
B Cross shaft arm position adjustment
C Clutch pedal free play adjustment
D Tool W-341 or W-317

bracket directly behind the instrument cluster.

3. Readjust clutch control cable.

Clutch Removal

All Models Except 350 V8 and 225 V6

1. Remove transmission.
2. Disconnect clutch linkage.
3. Mark the clutch pressure plate and engine flywheel so the clutch will be reassembled in the same position.
4. Remove the clutch pressure plate bracket bolts alternately, a little at a time, to prevent distortion.
5. Remove the pressure plate assembly and driven plate from the flywheel.

Installation

NOTE: The clutch release bearing is lubricated during assembly and need not be lubricated at any other time.

1. Put a very small amount of light grease in the flywheel pilot bushing. Install the driven plate with short end of hub toward flywheel. Place the pressure plate assembly in position.
2. Using a clutch plate aligning arbor or a spare transmission main shaft, align the driven plate splines. Tighten the pressure plate screws evenly. Remove aligning arbor.
3. Assemble flywheel housing to engine. Make sure that the clutch release bearing carrier return spring is hooked in place. Reverse order of clutch assembly removal procedure to complete installation.

Clutch Removal

V6 225 & V8 350 Engines

1. Mark universal joint and transmission shaft companion flange for proper indexing at time of installation. Remove two U-bolts and disconnect driveshaft at the front joint. Slide the driveshaft rearward as far as possible and tie to one side.
2. Disconnect shift linkage from transmission.
3. Disconnect speedometer cable at transmission.
4. Loosen all three exhaust pipe ball joints to permit transmission and rear of engine to be lowered.
5. Remove two bolts holding transmission mounting pad to transmission support. Leave mounting pad bolted to transmission.
6. With a padded jack under the engine, raise the unit until the transmission mounting pad just clears the transmission support.
7. Remove four bolts holding transmission support to body members. Remove support, then lower the jack to allow transmission to clear the underbody.
8. Remove upper left transmission to flywheel housing bolt and install a guide pin. Remove lower right bolt and install a guide pin.
9. Remove the other two transmission attaching bolts. Slide the transmission back until the drive gear shaft disengages the clutch disc and clears the flywheel housing. Lower the transmission.
10. Remove pedal return spring from clutch fork.
11. Remove flywheel housing.
12. Remove throw-out bearing from
13. Disconnect clutch fork from ball stud.
14. Mark clutch cover and flywheel to assure proper balance on reassembly.
15. Loosen clutch cover to flywheel bolts one turn at a time until spring pressure is released.
16. Support pressure plate and cover assembly while removing last bolts, then remove cover assembly and driven plate.

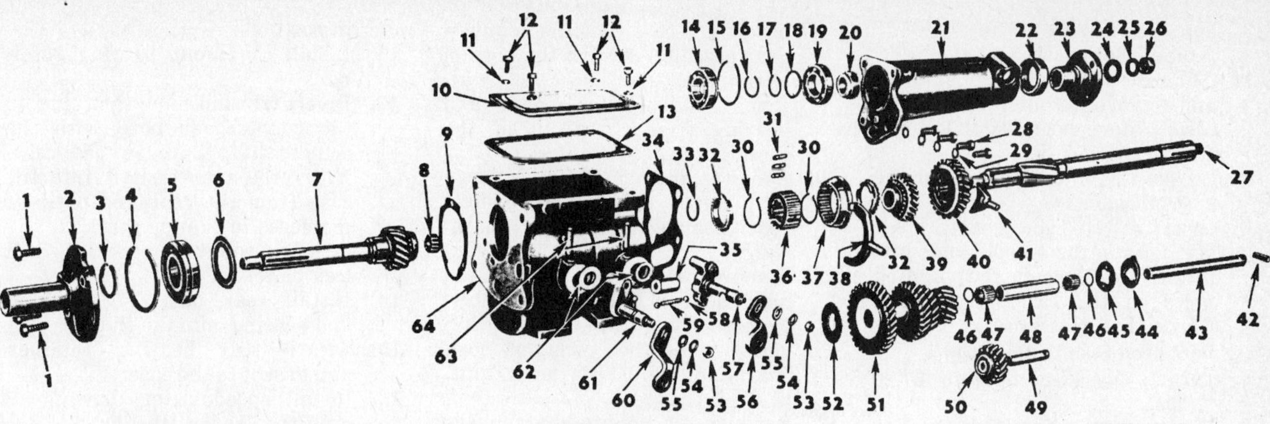

1 Main bearing retainer bolt
2 Main bearing retainer
3 Main drive gear snap ring
4 Bearing snap ring
5 Main drive gear bearing
6 Oil baffle
7 Main drive gear
8 Pilot bearing rollers
9 Bearing retainer gasket
10 Case cover
11 Case cover bolt gasket
12 Case cover bolt
13 Case cover gasket
14 Rear main shaft bearing
15 Rear bearing snap ring
16 Mainshaft snap ring
17 Rear bearing snap ring
18 Rear bearing washer
19 Rear mainshaft bearing
20 Speedometer drive gear
21 Rear bearing retainer
22 Mainshaft oil seal
23 Coupling flange
24 Mainshaft washer
25 Mainshaft nut lockwasher
26 Mainshaft nut
27 Mainshaft
28 Rear bearing retainer bolt
29 Retainer bolt lockwasher
30 Synchronizer spring
31 Synchronizer shifting plate
32 Blocking ring
33 Clutch hub snap ring
34 Rear bearing retainer gasket
35 Interlock sleeve
36 Clutch hub
37 Clutch sleeve
38 High and intermediate shift fork
39 Second speed gear
40 Low and reverse gear
41 Low and reverse shift fork
42 Idler and countershaft lock plate
43 Countershaft
44 Thrust washer
45 Thrust Washer
46 Countershaft bearing shift spacer
47 Countershaft bearing rollers
48 Countershaft bearing long spacer
49 Reverse idler gear shaft
50 Reverse idler gear
51 Countershaft gear
52 Thrust washer
53 Control lever to shaft nut
54 Lever to shaft lockwasher
55 Lever to shaft washer
56 Low and reverse control lever
57 Low and reverse shift lever
58 Poppet ball
59 Poppet spring
60 High and intermediate control lever
61 High and intermediate shift lever
62 Shift shaft oil seal
63 Shift lever shaft pin
64 Transmission case

Warner T-96 three-speed transmission—two-wheel drive (© Willys Corp.)

INSTALLATION

Install clutch by reversing removal procedure. Use a clutch aligning pilot or a spare main drive gear through the hub of driven plate and into the pilot bushing. Be sure to align the clutch cover-to-flywheel index marks.

Manual Transmission

Transmission Removal

The transmission and transfer case can be removed as a unit. These instructions apply to both three and four-speed transmissions, and also generally to two-wheel drive models which have no transfer case.

Universal Series

1. Drain transmission and transfer case.
2. Remove floor pan inspection plate.
3. Remove shift lever and housing, or disconnect remote control rods, depending on the models.
4. If vehicle has power take off, remove shift lever.
5. Disconnect front and rear driveshafts from transfer case. Disconnect power take off drive shaft.
6. Disconnect speedometer cable.
7. Disconnect hand brake cable.
8. Disconnect clutch release cable or rod.
9. Place jacks under engine and transmission, protecting the oil pan with a wooden block.
10. Remove rear crossmember.
11. Unbolt transmission from flywheel housing.
12. Force transmission to the right to disengage clutch control lever tube ball joint.
13. Lower jacks. Slide transmission and transfer case rearward until clutch shaft clears the flywheel housing.
14. Lower transmission jack. Remove assembly from under vehicle.
15. To install, reverse procedure.

Jeepster

The procedure for these models is the same as that for the Universal series, with the substitution of the following steps:

2. Remove right front seat, floor mat, and floorboard center section. Disconnect backup switch wires.
10. Remove rear crossmember. Remove transmission and transfer case stabilizer brackets.

Wagoneer and Gladiator

The procedure for these models is the same as that for the Universal series, with the substitution of the following step:

2. Remove the transmission access cover.

Shift Linkage Adjustment

Universal Series—Column Shift

1. Disconnect shift rods at transmission.
2. Put transmission levers in neutral positions. NOTE: Lock gearshift levers in neutral positions by putting a 1/4" dia. rod through the gearshift levers and housing at the bottom of the steering column.
3. Adjust length of shift rods and reconnect.
4. If shifting from first to second is difficult or transmission hangs in first gear, shorten the first-reverse rod one turn at a time until the condition is corrected.

Jeepster—Console Shift

1. Remove plug from hole in left side of console. If there is no

hole, cut a 1⅛" dia. hole or remove the console.
2. Lift the shift tower rubber cover and remove the plug in the shift tower. Move the selector lever to the neutral position.
3. Loosen the adjusting nuts at the transmission.
4. Insert a 3/16" dia. rod through the holes in the console and shift tower, and through the aligning holes in the two shift levers. Check that transmission shift levers are in neutral positions.
5. Torque adjusting nuts to 15-20 ft. lbs.
6. Remove adjusting rod, replace plugs, check shifting action. If selector lever interferes with console, relocate console.

Wagoneer and Gladiator—Column Shift

1. Put selector lever in neutral position.
2. Loosen shift rod adjusting nuts at transmission. Place shift levers in neutral position.
3. Insert a 3/16" dia. rod through remote control shift levers and housing at bottom of steering column.
4. Torque adjusting nuts to 15-20 ft. lbs. Remove adjusting rod.

Warner T-96 3 Speed

3-Speed Transmission

The Warner T-96 is a three-speed column-mounted synchronized transmission used for two-wheel drive Jeeps only. The four-wheel drive vehicles use the flood-mounted Warner T-90 three-speed.

Disassembly of Transmission

1. Drain the transmission, remove the top cover and gasket.
2. Remove clutch shaft bearing retainer and the shaft and bearing snap-rings.
3. Loop a piece of wire around the mainshaft, to the rear of first-speed sliding gear, and fasten the ends of the wire to two front transmission screws. This will support the mainshaft during the following operations.
4. Remove companion flange, rear bearing retainer and gasket.
5. Remove oil seal, speedometer drive gear, and mainshaft rear bearing from the rear bearing retainer.
6. Remove the shifting fork and shoe by sliding the mainshaft slightly to the rear and cocking the shaft away from the fork.
7. Remove the countershaft and idler shaft lock plate.
8. With a dummy shaft and soft hammer, drive the countershaft out of the case. Let the countergear assembly rest in the bottom of the case.
9. Remove the clutch shaft and bearing from the front of the case.
10. Remove the small and large snap-rings and the mainshaft rear bearing from the mainshaft.
11. Remove the blocker ring, clutch hub and synchronizer assembly.
12. Remove low and reverse sliding gears and the constant-mesh gear and mainshaft as a unit, through the top.
13. Remove the countershaft gears from the top.
14. Drive the reverse idler shaft out through the rear, then remove the idler gear.

Assembly of Transmission

1. With reverse idler gear in place, tap the idler shaft into place.
2. Assemble the countershaft gear by inserting a dummy shaft and the tubular bearing spacer into the countergear. Grease both ends of the gear bore and insert 20 bearing rollers into each end. Add a roller bearing spacer washer to each end of the gear and place the assembly in the bottom of the case, large end of gear forward.
3. Install the mainshaft rear bearing onto the mainshaft with the closed side of the bearing facing the front. Replace the bearing snap-ring and mainshaft snap-ring.
4. Start the shaft through the rear of the case and assemble the low and reverse sliding gear on the shaft, fork groove toward the rear.
5. Assemble second-speed gear on the shaft, synchronizer teeth toward the front.
6. To assemble the synchronizer unit, install the two springs in the high and intermediate clutch hub. These springs must be installed with the spring tension opposed. Install the three synchronizer shifting plates into the three slots in the hub, with the smooth side of the plates out. With the plates in position, slip the second and third-speed clutch sleeve over the hub. Install the two blocking rings, one on each side of the hub.
7. Install shifting fork and shoe.
8. Grease the clutch shaft pilot bore and install 13 bearing rollers.
9. Install the clutch shaft main drive gear and bearing assembly (closed side of bearing toward inside of case).
10. Enter the mainshaft bearing in the case and assemble the shaft in position.
11. Install the front bearing retainer.
12. Invert transmission, then line up the countergear bore with the countershaft bore in the case. Enter the countershaft into the case from the rear and entirely displace the dummy shaft.
13. Install countershaft-idler-shaft lock plate.
14. Install rear bearing snap-ring and bearing onto the shaft.
15. Attach rear bearing retainer and gasket to the case.
16. Install speedometer drive gear onto the shaft with the shoulder of the gear front. Replace rear oil seal if necessary.
17. Install companion flange and check operation of transmission.
18. Fill with lubricant to level, then install transmission case cover.

Transfer Case Removal

The transfer case can also be removed as a separate unit.

Jeepster

1. Drain transmission and transfer case.
2. Remove transfer case shift lever.
3. Disconnect driveshafts.
4. Disconnect speedometer cable.
5. Disconnect brake cable (directly under transfer case).
6. Disconnect clutch cables from cross-shaft.
7. Disconnect clutch control cross-shaft ball joint at frame.
8. Remove transfer case stabilizer bracket.
9. Remove bolts securing transfer case to transmission. Slide transfer case rearward to remove.
10. Reinstall in reverse order of above steps.

Gladiator and Wagoneer

This procedure is the same as that detailed above for removal of the Jeepster transfer case with the substitution of the following steps:

5. Disconnect parking brake spring from fuel tank flange. Remove clevis pin from brake cable connecting bracket.
6. Remove exhaust pipe bracket bolts.

Delete Step 7.
Delete Step 8.

Universal Series

1. Drain transmission and transfer case.
2. Disconnect brake cable.
3. Disconnect driveshafts.
4. Disconnect speedometer cable.
5. Disconnect transfer case shift levers.
6. Remove cover plate on rear of transfer case. Remove cotter key, nut, and washer from trans-

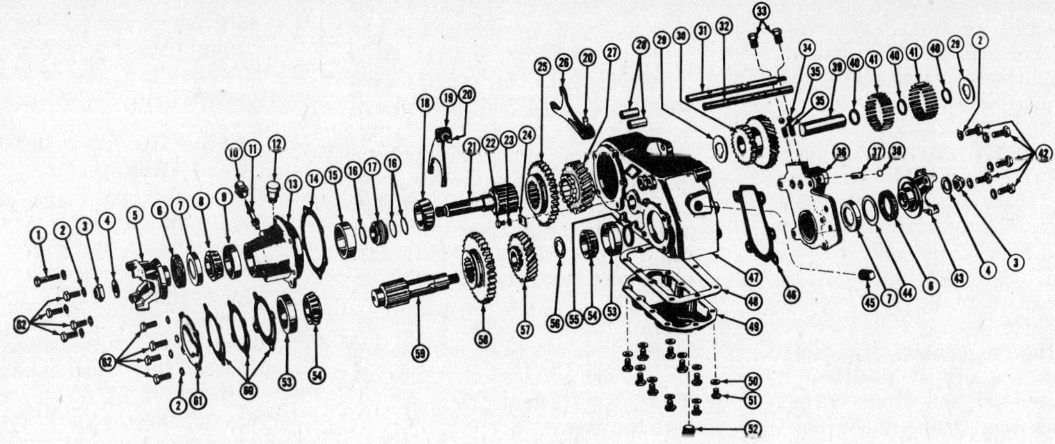

Transfer case (© Willys Corp.)

1 Long bolt
2 Lock washer
3 Nut
4 Flat washer
5 Rear propeller shaft yoke
6 Felt seal
7 Yoke oil seal
8 Cone and roller
9 Bearing cup
10 Speedometer driven gear sleeve
11 Speedometer driven gear
12 Breather
13 Rear bearing cap
14 Rear bearing cap gasket
15 Bearing cup
16 Shims
17 Speedometer drive gear
18 Cone and roller
19 Outer shift fork
20 Shift fork bolt
21 Rear output shaft
22 Bolt
23 Lock washer
24 Lock plate
25 Mainshaft sliding gear
26 Inner shift fork
27 Mainshaft gear
28 Shift rod caps
29 Thrust washer
30 Intermediate gear
31 Inner shift rail
32 Outer shift rail
33 Poppet plug
34 Poppet ball
35 Poppet spring
36 Shift rail housing
37 Shift rail interlock
38 Plug
39 Intermediate shaft
40 Bearing spacer
41 Needle bearings
42 Bolt
43 Front propeller shaft yoke
44 Oil seal gasket
45 Oil fill plug
46 Shift rail housing gasket
47 Case
48 Bottom cover gasket
49 Bottom cover
50 Lock washer
51 Bolt
52 Oil drain plug
53 Bearing cup
54 Cone and roller
55 Thrust washer
56 Thrust washer
57 Front output shaft gear
58 Front output shaft sliding gear
59 Front output shaft
60 Shims
61 Cover plate
62 Bolt

mission main shaft.

7. If possible, remove transfer case main drive gear from transmission mainshaft.
8. Remove transfer case mounting bracket bolts and nuts.
9. Unbolt transmission from transfer case.
10. Remove transfer case. If main drive gear has not been removed in Step 7, proceed as follows: Brace the end of the transmission mainshaft so that it cannot move in the transmission, pull the transfer case to the rear to remove. Be careful that the transmission mainshaft bearing, which bears in both housings, remains in the transmission case.
11. Installation is the reverse of removal procedure.

Transfer Case Disassembly

The transfer case can be disassembled as follows:

1. Remove the rear bearing cap assembly.
2. Remove bottom cover.
3. Remove lock plate bolt, lock washer and lock plate.
4. Drive the intermediate shaft out to rear of case using special tool. This tool allows the two sets of needle bearings and three spacers to remain in position as the shaft is withdrawn. The aligner should be centered in the intermediate gear assembly to avoid interference from the thrust washers.
5. Remove the intermediate gear through the bottom of the case.
6. Remove front output shaft yoke. Remove the felt oil seal, the oil seal gasket and front oil seal.
7. Remove rear cover. CAUTION: When removing rear cover, care should be exercised to avoid damaging gasket and shim separating cover plate from transfer case.
8. Using a soft face hammer, drive the rear bearing cup from the case.
9. Loosen and remove the inner shift fork bolt. Tap the underdrive and direct shift rail to the rear of the case to remove shift rail cap. Then tap inner rail out the front of the case. The main gear and inner shift fork can then be removed. NOTE: Front refers to the transmission side of the transfer case.
10. Remove shift rail housing assembly from the case and outer shift rail.
11. Wedge the front bearing cone and roller assembly from its seat on the output shaft. Drive the front bearing cone out of the case. Loosen the snap-ring and slide the shaft through the rear of the case. NOTE: A snap-ring is used on early models only. Current models use a thrust washer on each side of the bearing.
12. With the shaft removed, the output shaft sliding gear can be lifted from the outer fork. The fork can then be turned and the shift rail fork bolt removed.

Transfer Case Assembly

NOTE: Design changes have been incorporated in the mainshaft, intermediate and output shaft gears on silent-type transfer cases. These late design gears are not interchangeable with early type gears. Should replacement be required, individual gears should be replaced with the identifying numbers on each.

1. Slide the front-wheel-drive shift rail partially into case. Place front-wheel-drive shift fork on the rail with the shift rod fork bolt hole aligned with the countersunk hole on the rail. Replace the shift rail fork bolt and torque to 12-15 ft. lbs. and replace safety wire.
2. Place the front-wheel-drive shift fork in the proper position in the case. Set the front output shaft sliding gear in the shift fork with the gear facing the front of the transfer case.
3. Install the rear cone and roller on the front output shaft.
4. Hold the output shaft gear in place and insert the output shaft.
5. Install the thrust washer and snap-ring. NOTE: A snap-ring is used on early models only. Current models use a thrust washer on each side of the bearing.
6. Install front cone and roller on the front output shaft.
7. Install the front and rear bearing cup.
8. Install the shift rail housing gasket, shift rail housing, lock washers, and bolts and torque to 28 to 30 lb-tf.
9. Replace rear cover shim set, rear cover plate, lock washers, and bolts (28-32 ft. lbs.).
10. Check the output shaft bearing adjustment using a dial indicator. Position the shaft in the extreme rear position, set the dial indicator on zero, and pry the output shaft forward. A reading of .001″ to .003″ should be obtained. This clearance can be altered by changing the rear cover shims. Shims for this adjustment are available as follows:
    .003″
    .010″
    .031″
11. Position the outer shift rail so it will allow the shift rail interlocks to enter the detents in the rod as the inner shit rail is inserted in the shift rod housing.
12. Start the inner drive shift rail into the case along with its shift fork. Place the mainshaft gear on the fork with the gear facing the front of the transfer case. Push the shift rail into the case and through the fork until the countersunk hole on the rod aligns with the shift fork bolt hole. Replace the bolt and torque to 12-15 ft. lbs.
13. Place the thrust washers with the tang aligned to the groove in the case. The rear thrust washer can be held in place by just starting the intermediate shaft into the case. The front thrust washer can be held with heavy grease
14. Position the intermediate gear in the case. Using a soft-faced hammer drive the intermediate shaft into the intermediate gear Install intermediate shaft lock plate, lock washer, and bolt. Torque to 12-15 ft.lbs.
15. Install the rear bearing cap assembly. Torque the long bolt and four short bolts 28 to 32 lbs. ft.
16. Tap the shift rail cups about 3/8″ into the case.
17. Install the lower cover gasket, the lower cover, lock washers, and bolts (12-15 ft. lbs.).
18. Replace the oil seal gasket and felt oil seal.
19. Install the front and rear propeller shaft yokes (225-250 ft. lbs.).

Automatic Transmission

When automatic transmission trouble is reported, a road test and careful diagnosis are in order. Transmission Removal, Replacement and Linkage Adjustments are covered in the following paragraphs. The automatic transmission currently used in Jeep vehicles is the General Motors Turbo Hydra-Matic. For test procedures, transmission overhaul and other detailed information, see the General Repair Section.

Transmission Removal

1. Disconnect battery ground strap. Release parking brake. Raise and support vehicle.
2. Drain and remove transfer case.
3. Disconnect:
   a. Electrical lead case connector.
   b. Vacuum line at modulator.
   c. Oil cooler lines.
   d. Shift linkage.
4. Remove exhaust pipe assembly from muffler and exhaust manifolds.
5. Remove hand brake cable plate from crossmember.
6. Support transmission with a jack.
7. Remove crossmember.
8. Remove converter dust shield from transmission case.
9. Remove bolts attaching torque converter to flex plate.
10. Lower transmission until jack is barely supporting it.
11. Remove transmission mounting bolts.
12. Raise transmission to its normal position, slide rearward, and lower away from vehicle. CAUTION: Keep rear of transmission lower than front to avoid dropping the converter.
13. Installation is the reverse of removal.

Cable Operated Linkage Adjustment

1. Disconnect control cable at transmission lever and place transmission shift lever in neutral.
2. Place control lever in neutral position.
3. Loosen two nuts at upper end of control cable housing and move housing up or down until cable exactly matches position of lever on transmission.
4. Lock nuts on housing and connect cable to lever.

Rod Operated Linkage Adjustment

1. Remove adjusting block from transmission shift lever.
2. Make sure that transmission lever is in neutral position.
3. Place selector lever in Neutral position and hold firmly against the stop.
4. Loosen locknuts on adjusting block. Install block on transmission lever. Tighten locknuts to 6-12 ft. lbs.
5. Check shifting operation. If console interferes with shift selector lever, reposition console.

Dashpot Adjustment

A dashpot is provided on automatic transmission Jeep vehicles to prevent the throttle from closing too rapidly and causing the engine to stall. The dashpot is located on the throttle linkage at the carburetor. Adjustments are made with the engine at normal idling speed. There should be a clearance of approximately 3/32″ between the dashpot stem and the throttle lever. If stalling persists, this clearance may be lessened as necessary.

Neutral Safety Switch Adjustment

1. Make certain the shift linkage is correctly adjusted.
2. Set the handbrake and the footbrake. Put the handlever on the steering column in drive position. Hold thc ignition key (or starter button) on and slowly move the handlever toward neutral until the starter cranks and the engine runs.
3. Without moving the lever further, press the accelerator to determine whether or not the transmission is really in neutral.
4. If all is correct, the engine will have started when the handlever got to the neutral position, and the transmission will not be in gear.
5. Adjust the neutral safety switch

by turning it and its mounting bracket until the above conditions have been met.

U Joints, Drive Lines

Driveshaft and U-Joints

The drive of four wheel drive Universal and Jeepster models from the transfer case to the front and rear axles is through two tubular driveshafts. Each driveshaft has two cross and roller universal joints. Two wheel drive models drive through a single driveshaft with two universal joints. Each driveshaft has a splined slip joint at one end to allow for variations in length.

Jeepster V6 models have a front driveshaft made up of two shafts with three universal joints and one slip joint. The shorter of the two shafts, directly ahead of the transfer case, has a shaft support bearing.

Gladiator and Wagoneer models use several types and sizes of driveshafts, depending upon various transmission and equipment options. These are divided into two basic types. The first is that with two cross and roller joints and a slip joint. The second has a cross and roller joint at one end, and a ball and trunnion universal joint at the other end. Automatic transmission Gladiator and Wagoneer models have the slip joint end of the front driveshaft at the axle rather than at the transfer case, as on all other models.

Cross and Roller Universal Joint

Snap Ring Type Disassembly and Repair

1. Remove snap-rings.
2. Press on end of one bearing until opposite bearing is pushed from yoke arm.
3. Turn joint over. Press first bearing back out of arm by pressing on exposed end of journal shaft Repeat this operation for the other two bearings, then lift out journal assembly by sliding to one side.
4. Wash all parts in solvent and inspect for wear. Replace all worn parts.
5. Install new gaskets on the journal assembly. Make certain that the grease channel in each journal trunnion is open.
6. Pack bearing cones one-third full of grease and install the rollers.
7. Assemble in reverse order of disassembly. If the joint binds when assembled, tap the arms lightly to relieve any pressure on the bearings at the end of the journal.

U-Bolt Type Disassembly and Repair

Remove the attaching U-bolts to release one set of bearing races. Slide the driveshaft into the yoke flange to remove the races. The rest of the disassembly and repair procedure is the same as that given above for the snap ring type of cross and roller joint. The correct U-bolt torque is 15-20 ft. lbs.

Ball and Trunnion Universal Joint

Disassembly and Repair

1. Clamp shaft firmly in vise.
2. Bend grease cover lugs away from universal joint body. Remove cover and gasket.
3. Remove two clamps from dust cover. Push joint body toward driveshaft tube. Remove two each, centering buttons, spring washers, ball and roller bearings, and thrust washers, from trunnion pin.

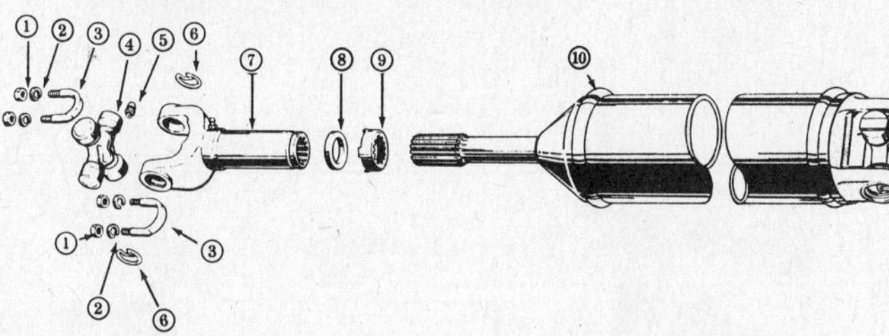

1 U-bolt nut
2 U-bolt washer
3 U-bolt
4 U-joint journal
5 Lubrication fitting
6 Snap ring
7 U-joint sleeve yoke
8 Rubber washer
9 Dust cap
10 Propeller shaft tube

Rear propeller shaft—Gladiator truck and camper (© Willys Corp.)

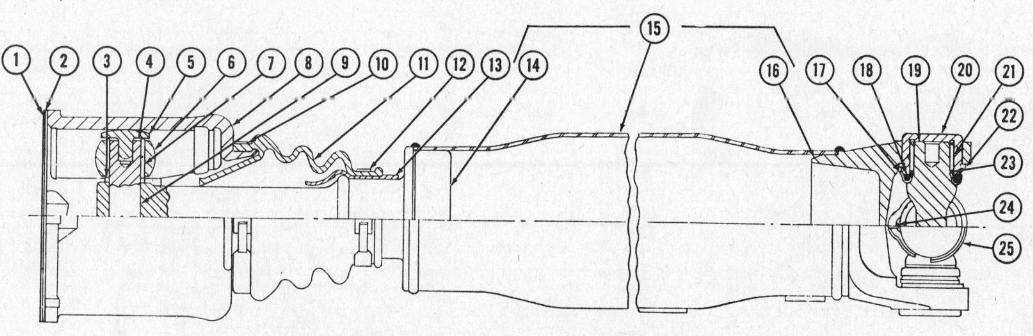

Rear propeller shaft—ball and trunion type (© Willys Corp.)

1 Grease cover
2 Gasket
3 Thrust washer
4 Spring washer
5 Centering button
6 Bearing ball
7 Bearing roller
8 Universal joint body
9 Trunnion pin
10 Clamp
11 Dust cover
12 Clamp
13 Breather
14 Ballhead
15 Tube
16 Tube yoke
17 Seal retainer
18 Bearing seal
19 Cross
20 Bearing cup
21 Bearing roller
22 Cup retainer ring
23 Roller retainer
24 Tie link
25 Bearing block retainer

4. Press trunnion pin from ballhead.
5. If ballhead is bent out of alignment or if trunnion pin bore is worn or damaged, replace driveshaft.

To reassemble:

6. Secure larger end of dust cover to joint body with larger of two clamps. Install smaller clamp. Fit cover over ballhead shaft.
7. Push universal joint cover toward driveshaft tube. Press trunnion pin into centered position. If trunnion pin is not centered, imbalance will result.
8. Install thrust washers, ball and roller bearings, spring washer, and centering buttons on trunnion pin. Compress centering buttons. Move joint body to hold buttons in place.
9. Insert breather between dust cover and ballhead shaft, along length of shaft. Breather must extend no more than 1/2" beyond dust cover. Tighten clamp screw to secure cover to shaft. Cut away any portion of dust cover protruding under clamps.
10. Pack raceways around ball and roller bearings with about two ounces of universal joint grease.
11. Position gasket and grease cover on body. Bend lugs of cover into notches of body. Move body back and forth to distribute grease in raceways.

Rear Axles, Suspension

The rear axle assembly on all Jeep trucks is of the shim adjusted type. The front driving axle on four-wheel drive models is serviced in exactly the same way as the rear driving axle and many of the parts are interchangeable.

Rear Axle Removal

Support the back end of the vehicle on stands at the frame in front of the rear springs. Disconnect the driveshaft at the rear universal joint companion flange. Disconnect the brake hoses, cables and shock absorbers.

Take off the U-Bolt nuts that hold the rear spring to the rear axle housing tubes. Lower the springs to the floor and pull the rear axle assembly out from under the vehicle. To install, reverse the removal procedure.

Refer to General Repair Section for rear axle overhaul.

Rear Spring Removal

Support the weight of the vehicle on jacks at the frame in front of the rear spring and take the bolts and threaded bushings out of the rear spring shackle.

Remove the nut and bolt from the front eye of the spring where it attaches to the frame bracet. Remove the U-bolts that hold the spring to the axle and lower the spring from under the vehicle. To install, reverse the removal procedure.

Rear Shock Absorber Removal

The bottoms of rear shock absorbers are mounted to a single bolt on the U-bolt plate of the rear spring.

The tops of shock absorbers are mounted to a bracket on the frame.

Remove the locknuts and washers from the top and bottom, then the shock absorber can be pulled off together with its rubber bushings. If the shock absorber is defective, it should be replaced with either a new or rebuilt one. To install, reverse the removal procedure.

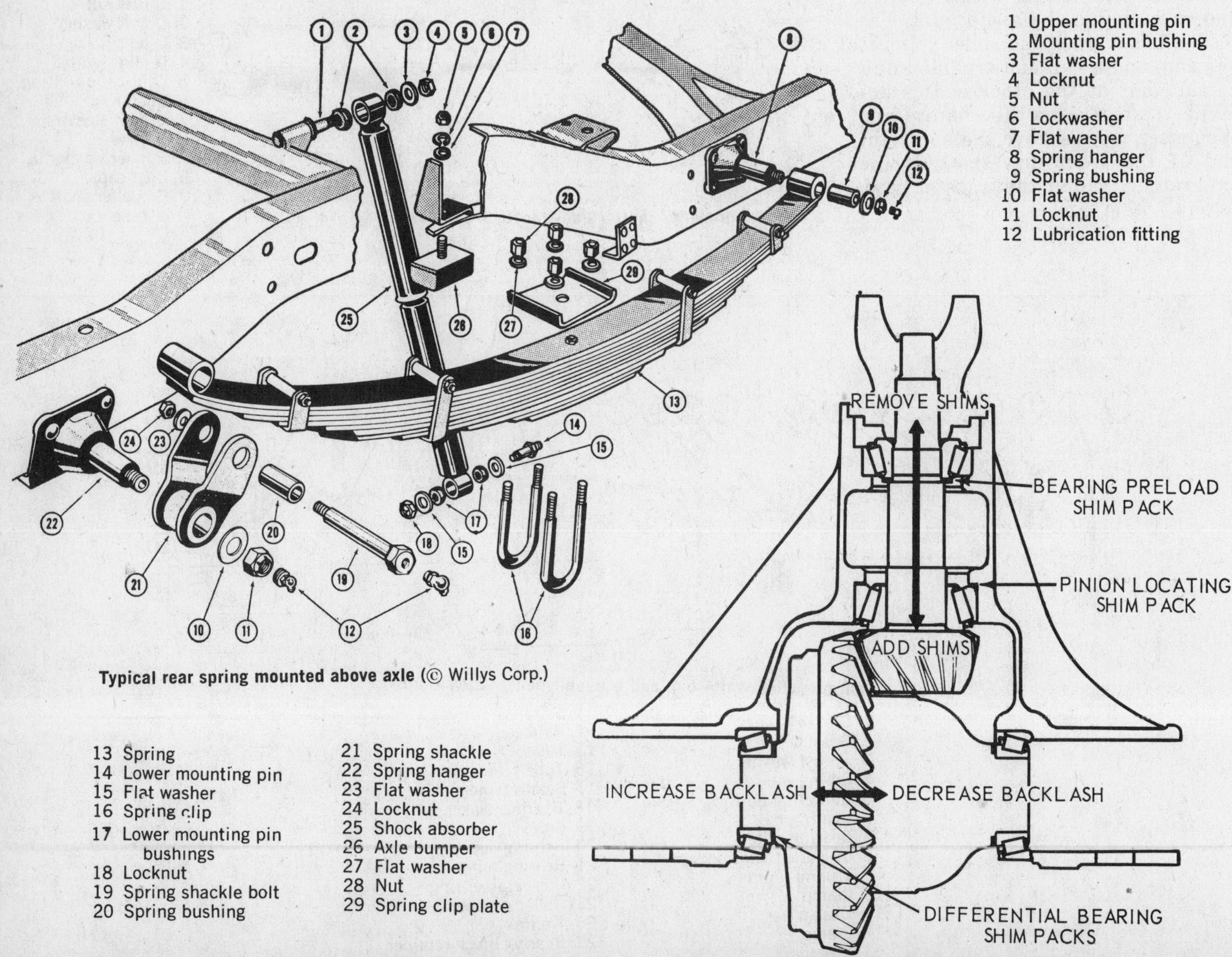

1 Upper mounting pin
2 Mounting pin bushing
3 Flat washer
4 Locknut
5 Nut
6 Lockwasher
7 Flat washer
8 Spring hanger
9 Spring bushing
10 Flat washer
11 Locknut
12 Lubrication fitting

Typical rear spring mounted above axle (© Willys Corp.)

13 Spring
14 Lower mounting pin
15 Flat washer
16 Spring clip
17 Lower mounting pin bushings
18 Locknut
19 Spring shackle bolt
20 Spring bushing
21 Spring shackle
22 Spring hanger
23 Flat washer
24 Locknut
25 Shock absorber
26 Axle bumper
27 Flat washer
28 Nut
29 Spring clip plate

Differential shim pack locations (© Willys Corp.)

Volkswagen Trucks

Index

TUNE-UP SPECIFICATIONS

ENGINE MODEL	YEAR	SPARK PLUG GAP (IN.)	DISTRIBUTOR POINT DWELL (DEG.)	POINT GAP (IN.)	IGNITION TIMING (DEG.) ■	CRANKING COMPRESSION (PSI)	VALVE CLEARANCE ▲ (IN.)	GOVERNED RPM	FUEL PUMP PRESS. (PSI)	IDLE SPEED COLD	IDLE SPEED HOT
1200 (36 HP)	up to 5/60	.026	50	.016	7½B	100-120	.004	3900	1.3-1.8	800-900	550
1200 (41.5 HP)	up to 9/64	.026	50	.016	*	100-128	.008 int. .012 ext.	4200	2.5	800-900	550
1500 (51 HP)	up to 7/65	.026	50	.016	10B	121-142	.008 int. .012 ext.	—	3.5	800-900	550
1500 (53 HP)	up to 7/67	.026	50	.016	*** 7.5B	114-142	.004	—	3.5	800-900	550
1600 (57, 60 HP)	from 8/67	.026	50	.016	0	114-142	**	—	3.5	800-900	550

* 7½B up to 8/66, 10B from engine #D0 095 049
** .008—intake, .012—exhaust up to #710799.
.004—intake and exhaust from #710800.
*** 0° for exhaust emission controlled engines.
▲ If any conflict occurs between chart and decal on engine fan housing, use specifications on decal.
■ These settings are approximate. Altitude, fuel octane rating and condition of individual engines are all factors which will cause the settings to vary.
B—before top dead center.

GENERAL ENGINE SPECIFICATIONS

DISPLACEMENT (CU. IN./CC.)	YEAR	BORE AND STROKE (IN.)	FIRING ORDER	DEVELOPED HORSEPOWER @ RPM (SAE)	DEVELOPED TORQUE @ RPM (FT. LBS.)	COMPRESSION RATIO	CARBURETOR	VALVE LIFTER TYPE	NORMAL OIL PRESSURE @ 2500 RPM (PSI)
1200 72.74/ 1192	up to 5/60	3.03 x 2.52	1-4-3-2	36 @ 3700	60 @ 2400	6.6:1	Solex 28 PCI	Mech.	28.0
1200 72.74/ 1192	up to 9/64	3.03 x 2.52	1-4-3-2	41.5 @ 3900	65 @ 2400	7.0:1	Solex 28 PICT or 28 PICT-1	Mech.	28.0
1500 91.10/ 1493	up to 7/65	3.27 x 2.72	1-4-3-2	51 @ 4000	74 @ 2600	7.8:1	Solex 28 PICT or 28 PICT-1	Mech.	28.0
1500 91.10/ 1493	up to 7/67	3.27 x 2.72	1-4-3-2	53 @ 4200	78 @ 2600	7.5:1	Solex 30 PICT-1 or 30 PICT-2**	Mech.	28.0
1600 96.66/ 1584	from 8/67	3.36 x 2.72	1-4-3-2	57 @ 4400	82 @ 3000	*	Solex 30 PICT-2 or 34 PICT-3	Mech.	28.0

* 7.7:1 from engine #B 0091 149;
exhaust emission controlled engines,
7.5:1 from #B 5039 390.
** 30 PICT-2 is used on exhaust emission controlled vehicles.

CRANKSHAFT BEARING JOURNAL SPECIFICATIONS

		MAIN BEARING JOURNALS				CONN. ROD BEARING JOURNALS		
ENGINE MODEL	YEAR	JOURNAL DIAMETER (IN.) 1-3	4	AXIAL CLEARANCE (IN.)	RADIAL CLEARANCE (IN.)	JOURNAL DIAMETER (IN.)	RADIAL CLEARANCE (IN.)	AXIAL CLEARANCE (IN.)
1200 (36 HP)	up to 5/60	1.9685	1.5748	.0027-.005	.002-.004	1.9685	.0008-.0024	.0067-.016
1200 (41.5 HP)	up to 9/64	2.1653	1.5748	.0027-.005**	*	2.1654	.0008-.003	.004-.016
1500 (51 HP)	up to 7/65	2.1653	1.5748	.0027-.005**	*	2.1653	.0008-.0027	.004-.016
1500 (53 HP)	up to 7/67	2.1653	1.5748	.0027-.005**	*	2.1653	.0008-.0027	.004-.016
1600 (57, 60 HP)	from 8/67	2.1653	1.5748	.0027-.005**	*	2.1653	.0008-.0027	.004-.016

* Bearings No. 1-3 (from 8/65: bearings 1 and 3)
up to #3 472 699—.001-.0035
up to #3 520 332—.0016-.0035
from #3 520 333—.0016-.004
Bearing No. 4—.002-.004
Bearing No. 2 (from 8/65)—.001-.0035.
** Figures given are for main journal No. 1 up to #3 491 699.
Main journal No. 2 requires a clearance of .0024-.005.

TORQUE SPECIFICATIONS
Transmission and Rear Axle (Fully Synchronized)

Description	Class, Thread	Torque ft. lbs.
Double ball bearing:	C 35N M 35 x 1.5	87
Double taper roller bearing:	C 35N M 35 x 1.5	144
Retaining screws, pinion bearing:	10K M 10 x 1.5	36
Pinion nut	CK 45K M 22 x 1.5	43*
Drive shaft nut:	CK 45K/C 35 M 22 x 1.5	43*
Reverse lever guide screw:	8G M 7 x 1	14
Selector fork screws:	C45 KN M 8 x 1.25	14
Ring gear screws:	10K M 10 x 1.5	43
Final drive cover nuts:	8G M 8 x 1.25	22
Axle tube retainer nuts:	6G M 8 x 1.25	14
Oil drain plug and oil filler plug:	Muk 7 M 24 x 1.5	14
Nut on driven shaft (type 2 from 8/63):	6S M 30 x 1.5	108
Nut on rear axle driven shaft (type 2 from chassis number 1144303):	C45KN M 30 x 1.5	217 (250 max.)
Transmission carrier on frame:	8G M 18 x 1.5	166
Spring plate/ reduction gear screws	10K M 12 x 1.5	72-87

*—Tighten first to 86 ft. lbs. and then back off, and finally tighten to 43 ft. lbs.

SPECIFICATIONS
Rear Axle and Transmission (Full Synchromesh)

	Tolerance (new)	Wear Limit
1st and 4th speed gearwheels, axial clearance: all	.10-.25 (.004-.010) (Keep to lower limit, .004)	
Synchronizer rings/ gear wheels, clearance between end faces of toothed rings: all	1.10 (.043)	.60 (.024)

mm. (in.)	Tolerance (new)	Wear Limit
Shift fork/operating sleeve axial clearance for 1st/2nd, 3rd/4th speeds: all	.10-.30 (.004-.012)	
Drive shaft, front (surface for 3rd gear needle bearing, run-out): all	maximum .02 (.0008)	

Rear axle shaft; flange/ fulcrum plates/ differential side gears (4 parts) clearance		
all	.04-.24 (.0015-.009)	.25 (.010)
Rear axle shaft; flange/differential side gear clearance, measured across the convex faces:		
all	.03-.10 (.001-.004)	.20 (.008)
Rear axle shafts; measured between centers, measured at bearing seat, run-out:		
all	maximum .05 (.002)	
Preload of transmission case halves and final drive covers on differential ball bearings:	.14 (.005)	
Plastic packing/ transmission case/ axle tube/final drive cover clearance:		
all	.25-.35 (.010-.014)	.40 (.016)
Run-out of reduction gear shaft (Type 2):	maximum .01 (.0004)	
Inside diameter, gearshift housing bushes:		
all	15.05-15.03 (.592-.591)	15.25 (.600)
Inner shift lever, diameter:		
all	15.00-14.96 (.590-.588)	14.75 (.580)
Starter bush,, inside diameter:		
all	12.55-12.57 (.493-.494)	12.65 (.497)
Starter shaft/bush radial clearance:		
all	.09-.14 (.0035-.005)	.25 (.010)

MODEL IDENTIFICATION

Model Designation

221-225	Micro Bus
231-237	Kombi
241	Deluxe Micro Bus (9-seater)
251	Deluxe Micro Bus (7-seater)
261-267	Pick-up
271-273	Ambulance
281-285	Micro Bus (7-seater)

Serial No. Location

Engine: located at one or both of the following:

1. Stamped on generator support below firing order.
2. Stamped on crankcase flange at generator support.

Chassis:

1. Identification plate on fresh air duct—right hand side in cab.
2. Engine cover plate at battery.

TORQUE SPECIFICATIONS

ENGINE MODEL	YEAR	CYLINDER HEAD NUTS	CONN. ROD BOLTS AND NUTS	CRANK-CASE NUTS	FLY-WHEEL GLAND NUT	CLUTCH TO FLY-WHEEL	CRANK-SHAFT PULLEY	ENGINE MOUNT BOLTS	OIL DRAIN PLUG	OIL PUMP NUTS	GENERATOR PULLEY
1200 (36 HP)	up to 5/60	26-27	22-25	22	217	18	29-36	22	22-29	14	40-47
1200 (41.5 HP)	up to 9/64	23	22-25	25	217	18	29-36	22	25	14	40-47
1500 (51 HP)	up to 7/65	23	22-25	25	217	18	29-36	22	25	14	40-47
1500 (53 HP)	up to 7/67	23	22-25	25	217	18	29-36	22	25	14	40-47
1600 (57, 60 HP)	from 8/67	23	22-25	25	217	18	29-36	22	25	14	40-47

Note: All torque specifications are given in ft., lbs.

WHEEL ALIGNMENT SPECIFICATIONS

(UNLOADED)

MODEL	CASTER (DEG.)	CAMBER (DEG.)	TOE-IN (IN.)	WHEEL PIVOT RATIO INNER	OUTER
up to chassis **#217 148 459**	max. 1°	max. 40′	.0215 ± .043*	34	28
from chassis **#218 000 001**	3° ± 40′	2° ± 25′	0.0-.086	—	—

* On vehicles with 15″ wheels: .0235± .047

VALVE SPECIFICATIONS

ENGINE MODEL	YEAR	LASH (HOT) (IN.)** INT.	EXT.	SEAT ANGLE (DEG.)	STEM DIAMETER (IN.) INT.	EXT.	STEM CLEARANCE (IN.) INT.	EXT.	VALVE SPRING PRESSURE (LBS.)	LOADED LENGTH (IN.)
1200 (36 HP)	up to 5/60	.004	.004	45	.2740	.2736	.0019	.0023	74	1.10
1200 (41.5 HP)	up to 9/64	.008	.012	45	.3128	.3116	.0022	.0032	74	1.10
1500 (51 HP)	up to 7/65	.008	.012	45	.3126	.3114	—	—	74	1.10
1500 (53 HP)	up to 7/67	.004	.004	45	.3126	.3114	—	—	74	1.10
1600 (57, 60 HP)	from 8/67	*	*	45	.3130	.3118	—	—	74	1.10

* .008—intake, .012—exhaust up to engine #710799.
.004—intake and exha.st from #710800.

** If any conflict occurs between chart and decal on fan housing, use specifications on decal.

Distributor

Distributor Removal

1. Remove distributor cap, primary wire and vacuum line at distributor.
2. Turn engine until contact end of distributor rotor is aligned with notch in distributor rim, denoting No. 1 firing position. Scribe a mark on the distributor body and engine block, showing the position of the body in the block.
3. Remove the distributor hold-down screw and lift the distributor up and out of the engine.

Installation

1. If the crankshaft has been rotated, turn the engine until the piston of No. 1 cylinder is at the top of its compression stroke.
2. Position the distributer to the block so that the vacuum control unit is in its normal position.
3. Position the rotor to point toward notch in rim at five o'clock position. Place distributor in the engine and push down to engage distributor drive.
4. While holding the distributor down in place, operate the starter a few times to make certain the distributor driveshaft is engaged. Install hold-down clamp and bolt, then tighten snugly. Once again, rotate the crankshaft pulley until No. 1 cylinder is at the compression stroke and the mark is on 0°.
5. Turn distributor body slightly until points just open. Tighten distributor clamp bolt.
6. Place distributor cap in position and see that the rotor lines up with the notch and the terminal lead for No. 1 spark plug.
7. Install cap, distributor primary wire and check plug wires.
8. Reconnect vacuum hose to control assembly, then set timing to specifications.

Relation of rotor to timing marks at No. 1 cylinder firing position
(© Volkswagen)

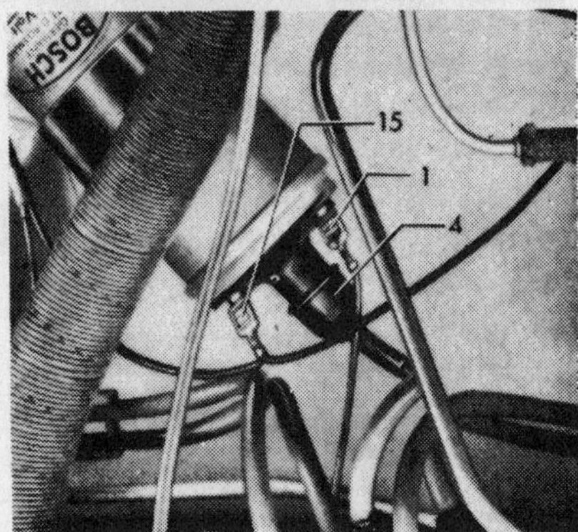

1 To distributor breaker points
4 High-voltage lead to distributor cap
15 To ignition/starter switch

Connections at the coil
(© Volkswagen)

Position of distributor driveshaft offset before insertion. Dotted line indicates position of offset when installed.
(© Volkswagen)

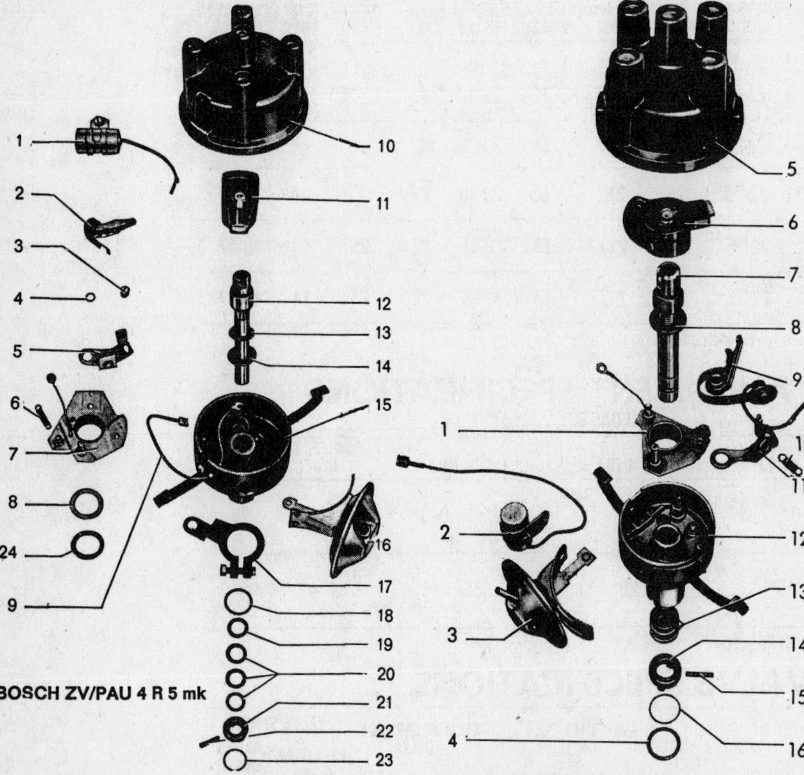

1 Condenser
2 Contact breaker arm
3 Securing screw with flat and spring washers
4 Insulating washer
5 Contact breaker point
7 Breaker plate with ground cable
8 Plastic washer
9 Low tension cable
10 Distributor cap
11 Rotor
12 Distributor shaft
13 Steel washer
14 Fiber washer
15 Distributor housing
16 Vacuum advance
17 Clip
18 Sealing ring
19 Fiber washer
20 Shim
21 Driving dog
22 Pin
23 Locking spring
24 Shim

Exploded view—Bosch distributor
(© Volkswagen)

1 Breaker plate with ground cable
2 Condenser
3 Vacuum advance unit
4 Sealing ring
5 Distributor cap
6 Rotor
7 Distributor shaft
8 Fiber washer
9 Contact breaker arm with spring
10 Return spring
11 Contact breaker point
12 Distributor housing
13 Steel washers
14 Driving dog
15 Pin
16 Locking ring

Exploded view—VW distributor
(© Volkswagen)

Breaker Points Replacement

When the contact points become worn and/or badly burnt, replace them. Remove distributor cap and rotor. Take off the electrical lead to the breaker arm. Remove the retaining screw at the fixed point. Loosen and lift the circlip from the breaker arm shaft and remove the breaker arm. Make certain that the circlip does not fall into the distributor body.

Installation of the new points is the reverse of the preceding, except that care should be taken to ensure that the washers on the breaker arm shaft are correctly positioned. Do not omit the circlip. Adjust the breaker point gap to specifications and set the ignition timing with the engine cold.

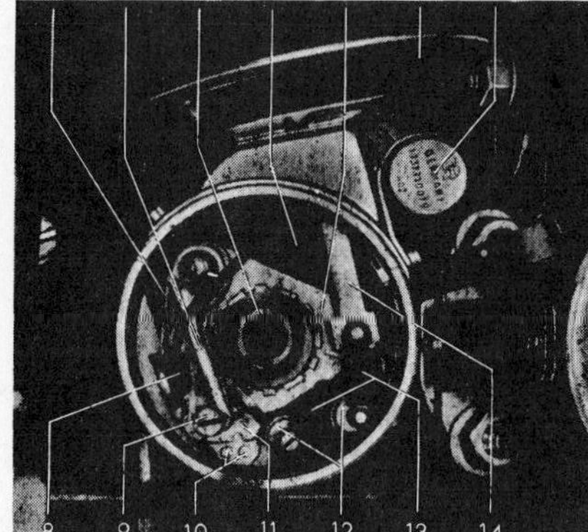

Interior of a typical VW distributor
(© Volkswagen)

1 Spring for breaker arm
2 Breaker arm
3 Distributor with cam
4 Connection for contact
5 Breaker plate
6 Vacuum unit
7 Condenser
8 Insultaor
9 Securing screw
10 Pins on breaker plate
11 Breaker point
12 Eccentrics for return springs
13 Return springs
14 Pull rod

Ignition Timing

Always set point gap to the proper specification before setting ignition timing. Depending on the model year, there may be one, two, or three timing notches in the crankshaft pulley. These correspond, from left to right, to 0° B.T.D.C., 7.5° B.T.D.C. and 10° B.T.D.C. Exhaust emission controlled engines generally have only the 0° mark.

1. Crank the engine until the timing mark on the crankshaft pulley lines up approximately with the vertical crankcase joint or timing pointer, and the distributor rotor arm is in the position for firing No. 1 cylinder. CAUTION: Do not set timing on No. 3 cylinder firing position or timing will be retarded.
2. Loosen clamp screw of the distributor retainer.
3. Connect one lead of a 12-volt test lamp to terminal No. 1 of ignition coil and the other lead to ground.
4. Switch on ignition.
5. Rotate the distributor body clockwise until the contact points are closed, then slowly turn counter-clockwise until the breaker points begin to open and the test lamp lights.
6. Tighten clamp screw retainer.
7. Reinstall rotor and distributor cap.

The ignition is correctly timed for all four cylinders if the lamp lights when the right-hand mark on the pulley is exactly in its highest, or lowest, position (in line with the crankcase joint) while slowly cranking the engine.

NOTE: The adjustment of the ignition firing point on a cold engine must always be done with a test lamp. A stroboscopic lamp should not be used, as it will alter the entire setting range. However, it is recommended that exhaust emission controlled engines using the fully vacuum advanced distributor be timed with the stroboscopic light.

Timing emission controlled engine with a strobe light
(© Volkswagen)

Generator, Regulator

Through 1966 the generator was of the 6-volt, DC-type. A 12-volt unit has been used since that date. It is equipped with ball bearings that are factory packed with a high melting point grease. Lubrication, in general, is necessary only during overhaul. Never use ordinary grease. Brush wear should be checked if trouble is experienced or when doing repairs on the generator. Service operations in no way differ from conventional procedures as covered in the General Repair Section. A voltmeter should be used to test the generator as follows:

1. With a fully charged battery in the car, disconnect lead cable from the right-hand (outside) terminal of the regulator. Connect the positive lead of a voltmeter to the same terminal of the regulator, then ground the negative voltmeter lead.
2. Start the engine and increase rpm until voltage is at a maximum. Voltage should gradually increase to 7.4-8.1 volts.
3. Switch off engine. Needle should jump back to Zero just before the engine stops.

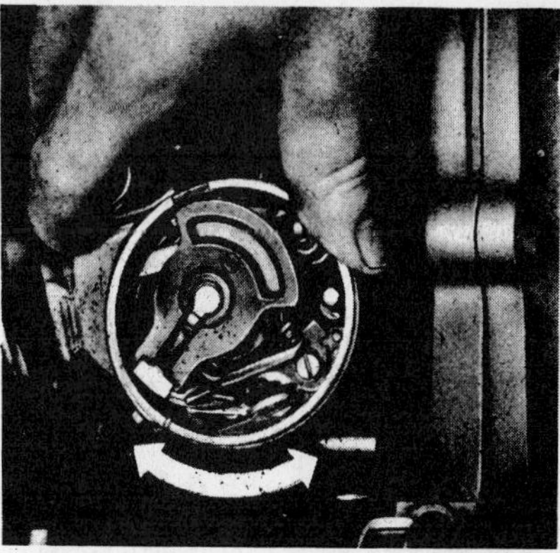

Turning distributor body clockwise advances ignition, counter-clockwise retards ignition
(© Volkswagen)

Generator Removal

1. Disconnect battery ground cable.
2. Disconnect cables from voltage regulator.
3. Remove air cleaner and carburetor.
5. Remove generator hold-down strap.
6. Remove cooling air thermostat. NOTE: The screws can be removed with a socket inserted through the holes in the lower air deflector plate.
7. Detach warm air hoses from fan housing.
8. Remove the two attaching screws and lift out fan housing.
9. Remove four screws in fan housing cover and take off generator with fan.

Installation

Install generator by reversing the removal procedure.

Voltage Regulator Removal

1. Take off the connections from terminals B + (51) and (61) at the regulator.
2. Remove the attaching screws and the regulator.
3. Disconnect the electrical cables from the bottom of the regulator. These are marked + (D+) and F (DF).

Installation

Installation of the regulator is the

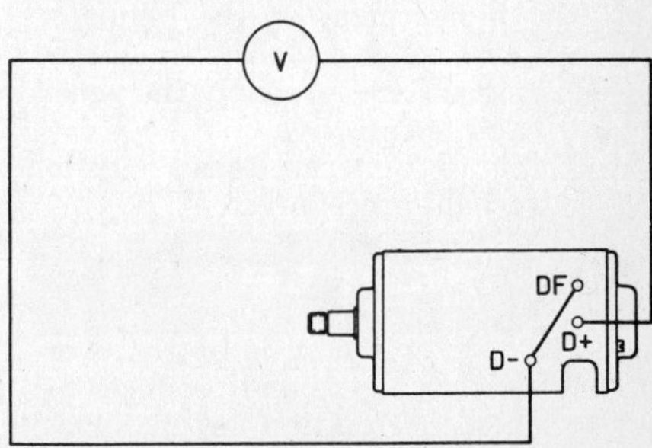

Schematic for making quick check for generator without regulator. Test must only take a few seconds, otherwise the generator will be damaged.

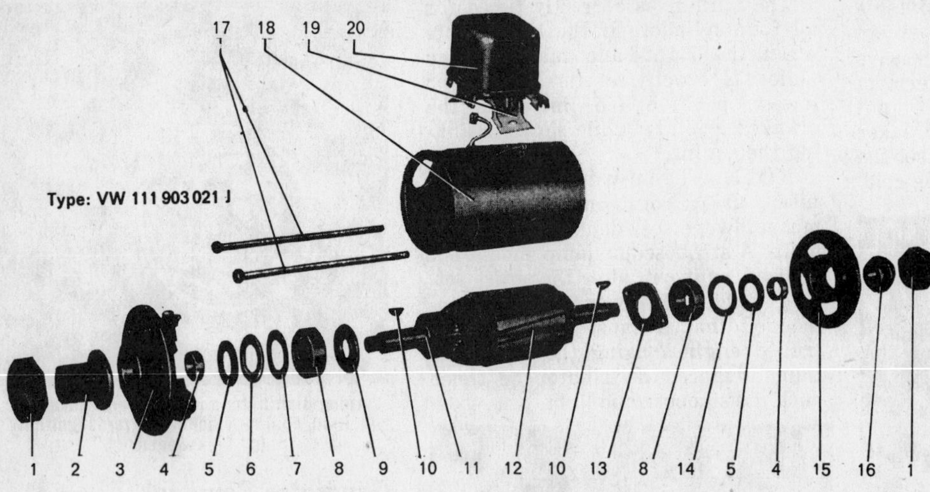

1 Nut
2 Pulley hub
3 Brush holder end plate
4 Spacer ring
5 Felt washer
6 Retainer
7 Thrust ring
8 Ball bearing
9 Washer
10 Key
11 Spacer
12 Armature
13 Bearing retainer
14 Thrust ring
15 End plate
16 Fan hub
17 Housing screws
18 Housing and field assembly
19 Slotted screw
20 Regulator

VW generator (© Volkswagen)

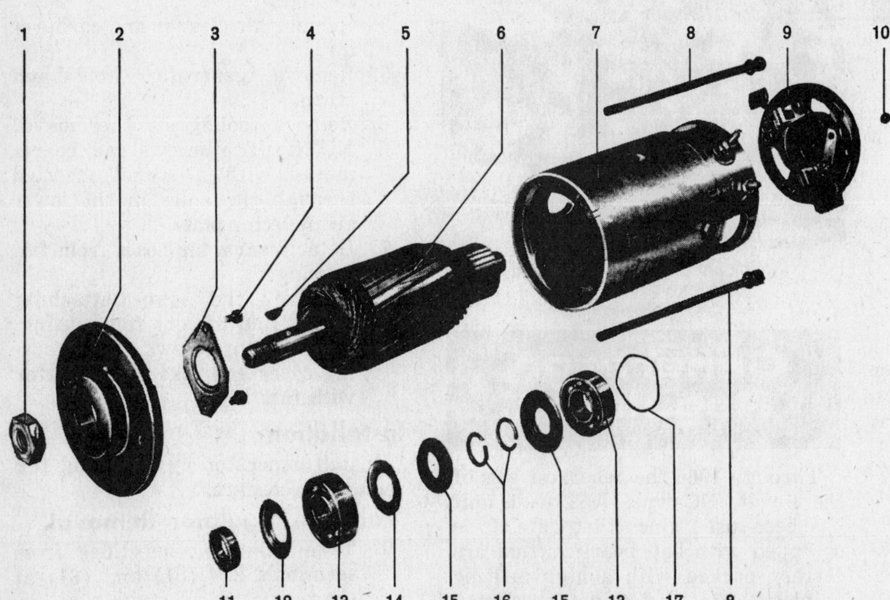

1 Nut
2 End plate
3 Retaining plate
4 Screw
5 Woodruff key
6 Armature
7 Pole housing
8 Housing screw
9 End plate with brush holders
10 Screw
11 Spacer
12 Washer
13 Bearing
14 Washer
15 Washer
16 Circlip
17 Spring ring

Bosch generator (© Volkswagen)

reverse of the preceding, but it should be noted that the thicker cable (coming from the positive brush of the generator) must be attached at the regulator bottom to terminal + (D+). The thin cable coming from the generator field windings should be attached to the F (DF) terminal. If the replacement of the regulator does not correct a deficiency in the charging system, probably the generator itself is defective.

Refer to General Repair Section for overhaul procedures.

Starter

The starter motor is of the overrunning clutch type and produces 0.5 hp. When the ignition key is turned it actuates a solenoid switch, which in turn engages the motor.

If the starter will not operate when the switch is closed, first check the starter solenoid. This can be done

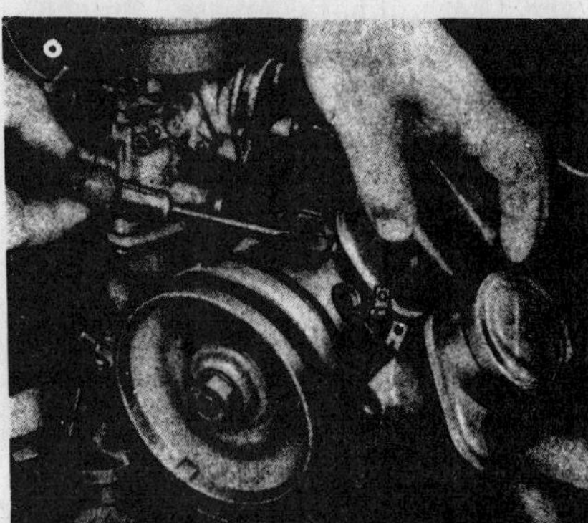

Removing voltage regulator (early models). All recent models have the regulator mounted on the right sidewall of the engine compartment.
(© Volkswagen)

by bridging the two heavy solenoid terminals with a heavy wire. This will eliminate the solenoid from the starting circuit and close a line directly to the starter. If the starter motor rotates, the trouble is probably in the solenoid. If the starter motor fails to rotate, the trouble is likely to be in the motor. The solenoid cannot be replaced without removing the starter.

Removal

1. Disconnect negative battery lead.
2. Disconnect wiring from solenoid.
3. Remove two retaining nuts which attach starter to transmission case.

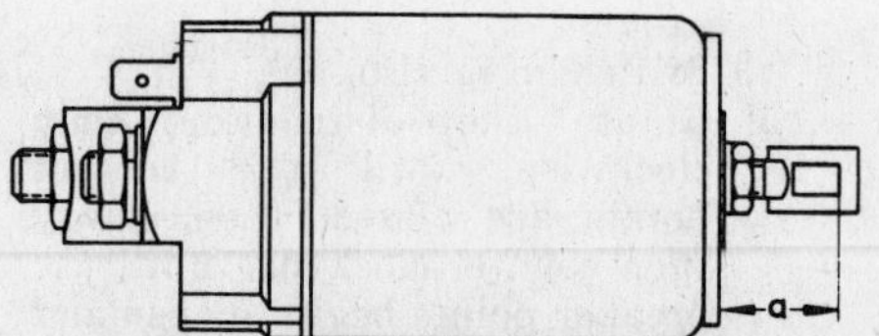

When a new solenoid is installed, distance "a" should be 19 mm. from the switch flange to the pull rod eye with the magnet pulled in
(© Volkswagen)

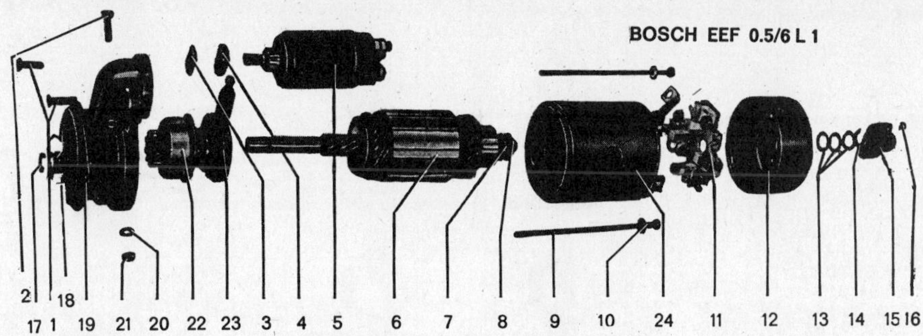

1 Securing screws
2 Bearing bolt
3 Support washer
4 Rubber seal
5 Solenoid
6 Armature
7 Steel washer
8 Synthetic washer
9 Housing screws
10 Washer
11 Brush holder
12 End plate
13 Shims
14 Lockwasher
15 End cap
16 Screws
17 Circlip
18 Stop ring
19 Intermediate bracket
20 Spring washer
21 Nut
22 Drive pinion
23 Shift lever
24 Housing

Bosch starter motor (© Volkswagen)

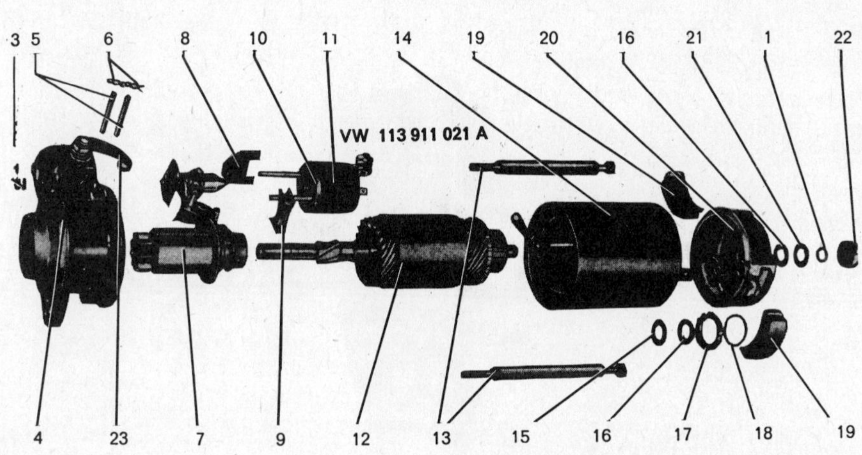

1 Circlip
2 Cup washer
3 Nuts and lockwashers
4 Intermediate bracket
5 Pivot pins
6 Spring clips
7 Drive pinion with linkage and solenoid core
8 Insulating plate
9 Moulded rubber seal
10 Insulating disc
11 Solenoid housing
12 Armature
13 Housing screws
14 Housing and field assembly
15 Steel washer
16 Bronze washer
17 Friction washer
18 Thrust ring
19 Brush inspection cover
20 Commutator end plate
21 Steel washer
22 Cap
23 Connecting strip

VW starter motor (© Volkswagen)

4. Withdraw the starter motor assembly.

Installation

Install starter motor by reversing the removal procedure.

Refer to General Repair Section for overhaul procedures.

Brakes

Master Cylinder Removal

All Except 1971 Models

NOTE: On recent models, the brake fluid reservoir is located inside the cab. Procedures will vary accordingly.

1. Remove access pan.
2. Disconnect brake fluid reservoir from master cylinder and catch escaping fluid.
3. Disconnect brake lines from master cylinder.
4. Cover openings to prevent contamination.

1 Cover
2 Fluid reservoir
3 Bracket
4 Line
5 Stop light switch
6 Master cylinder body
7 Check valve
8 Piston return spring
9 Rubber plug
10 By-pass port
11 Main cup
12 Piston washer
13 Intake port
14 Piston
15 Secondary cup
16 Piston stop plate
17 Lock ring
18 Piston push rod
19 Boot

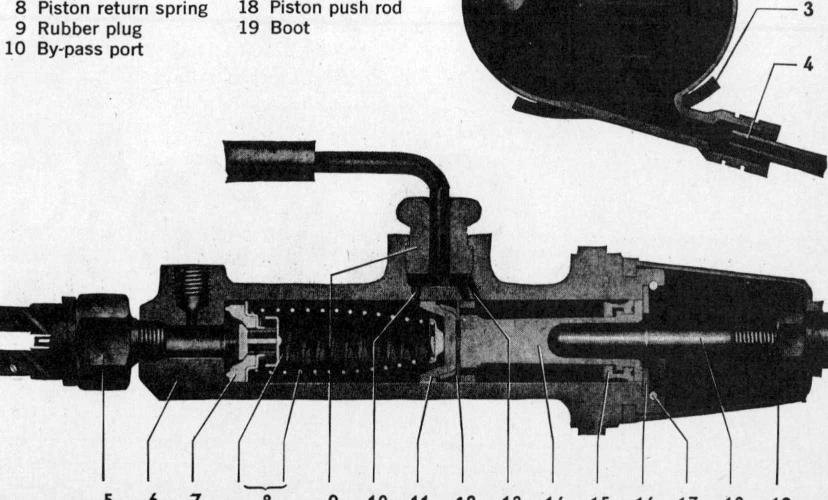

Single circuit master cylinder (© Volkswagen)

5. Remove attaching nuts and master cylinder.

Installation

To install master cylinder, reverse the removal procedure and make certain that vent hole in pushrod boot faces downward. Bleed brake system.

Master Cylinder Removal

1971 Models

1. Press brake fluid reservoir out of rear sealing plug and catch fluid; pull reservoir out of second sealing plug.
2. Disconnect brake lines and tag for identification. NOTE: On 1971 models, the front brake line is connected to the rear brakes and the rear line to the front brakes.
3. Remove two attaching nuts and withdraw master cylinder from brake servo unit.

Installation

To install the master cylinder, reverse the removal procedure and bleed the brake system.

Bleeding Brakes

1. When bleeding brakes, always begin with wheel farthest away from the master cylinder. The sequence is:
   a. Right rear wheel
   b. Left rear wheel
   c. Right front wheel
   d. Left front wheel.
2. Remove rubber cap from bleeder valve and attach hose.
3. Submerge the free end of the hose in a container partially filled with brake fluid. The end of the drain hose should, if possible, be

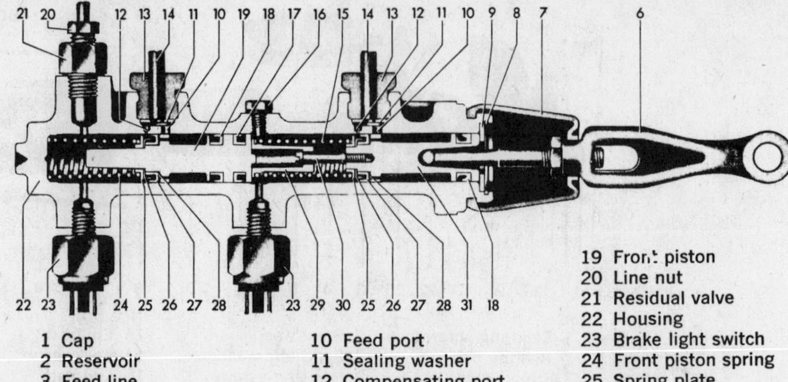

1 Cap
2 Reservoir
3 Feed line
4 Line seal
5 Line nut
6 Push rod
7 Boot
8 Spring ring
9 Stop ring
10 Feed port
11 Sealing washer
12 Compensating port
13 Sealing plug
14 Feed line
15 Rear piston spring
16 Stop screw
17 Seal
18 Cup-secondary
19 Front piston
20 Line nut
21 Residual valve
22 Housing
23 Brake light switch
24 Front piston spring
25 Spring plate
26 Support ring
27 Cup-primary
28 Cup washer
29 Stop sleeve
30 Limiting screw
31 Rear piston

Dual circuit master cylinder (© Volkswagen)

Master cylinder and power booster (1971 models) (© Volkswagen)

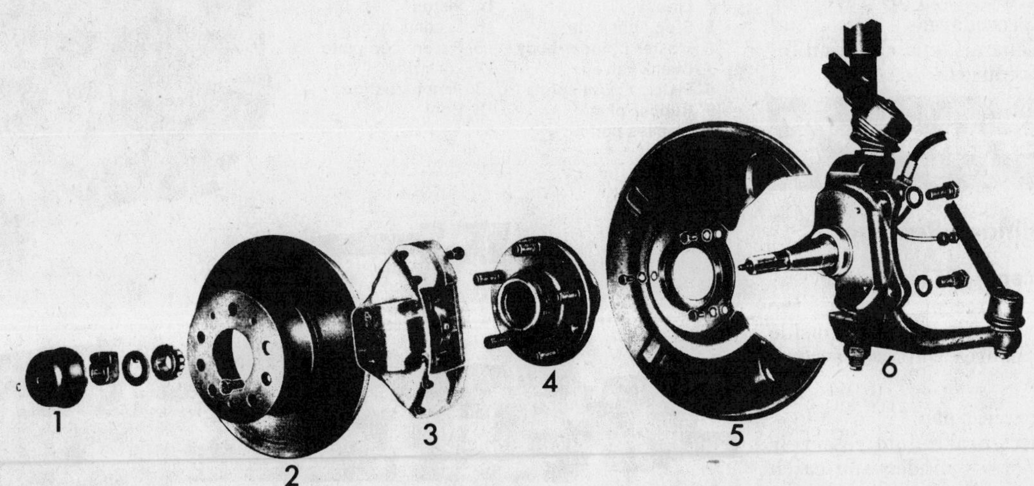

Front disc brake assembly (1971 models): (1) dust cap, (2) brake disc, (3) caliper, (4) front wheel hub, (5) splash shield, (6) steering knuckle (© Volkswagen)

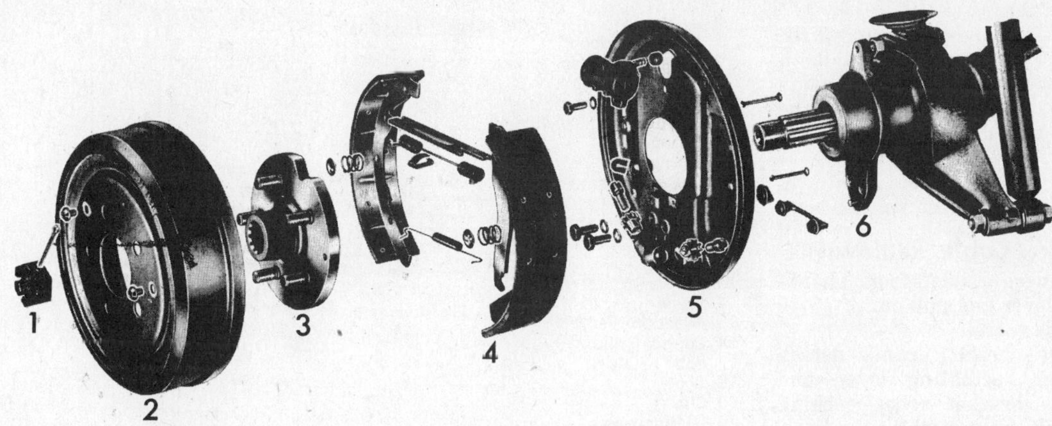

Rear brake assembly (1971 models): (1) slotted nut, (2) brake drum, (3) rear wheel hub, (4) brake shoes, (5) backing plate, (6) bearing housing and wheel shaft (© Volkswagen)

above the level of the bleeder valve.

4. Open the bleeder valve between ½ and 1 turn.
5. Pump the brake pedal several times until air bubbles cease to appear in container.
6. Keep the brake pedal in the fully depressed position on the last stroke and close the bleeder valve.
7. Disconnect the bleeder hose and install protective cap.

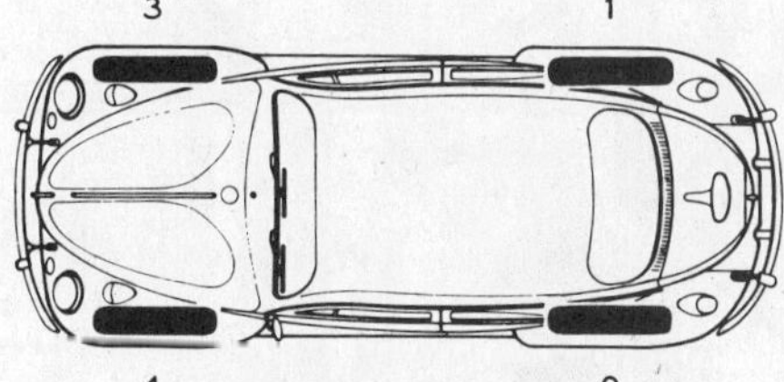

Brake bleeding sequence (all VW types and models) (© Volkswagen)

8. Repeat the preceding operations on the other wheels. Make certain the brake fluid level in the reservoir is sufficient to ensure that air is not drawn in. After bleeding the complete system, check the brake fluid level and fill as necessary.

Power Booster

1971 VW truck models are equipped with a power assisted brake system of which the main unit is a vacuum servo attached to the master cylinder. The servo is mechanically actuated by the brake pedal and is operated by the pressure differential between intake manifold vacuum and atomospheric pressure.

Pressure Regulator

1971 VW trucks are equipped with a brake pressure regulator mounted on the inside of the left side member near the front. The unit regulates hydraulic pressure in the rear brake circuit to ensure safe and optimal braking operation.

Parking Brakes

Adjustment

Unless adjustments are of major proportions, or parts replacement needed, the parking brake may be adjusted inside the vehicle.

1. Adjust rear brakes.
2. Raise both rear wheels.
3. Lift up rubber boot on handbrake lever until cable adjusting nuts are accessible.
4. Back off locknuts, then tighten

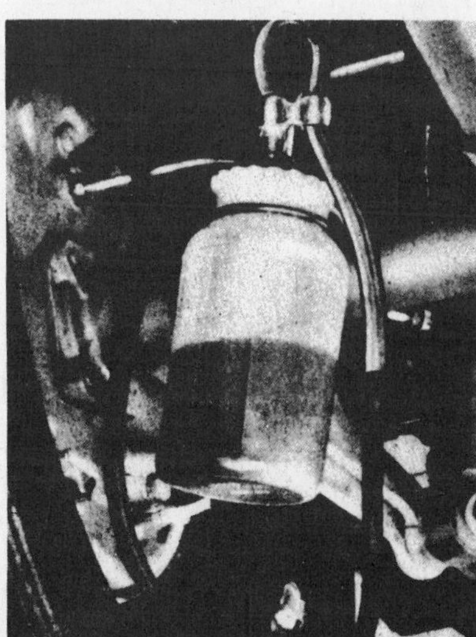

Brake bleeder hose and container (© Volkswagen)

Checking brake fluid reservoir (© Volkswagen)

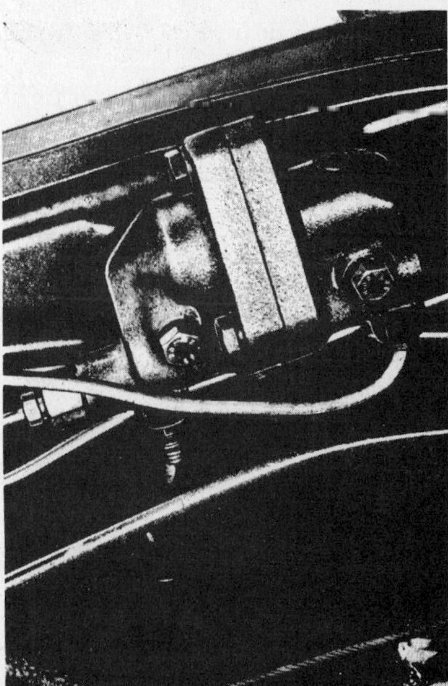

Brake pressure regulator (1971 models) (© Volkswagen)

adjusting nuts to a point where the rear wheels will still turn freely when the hand-brake is in off position.

5. Pull the hand-lever up three notches, then check that both rear wheels have the same value of brake hold. Application to the sixth notch should lock the wheels.
6. Secure the locknuts and re-position hand-lever rubber boot.

Handbrake Cable Removal

1. Disconnect cable from hand-brake lever and pull out of guide towards rear.
2. Remove brake drum, detach cable at actuating lever and remove bracket from backing plate. Withdraw cable.

Installation

1. Fasten brake cable and bracket to backing plate. The curved guide must point upward.
2. Connect brake cable to actuating lever and install drum.
3. Route brake cable around curvature on handbrake lever and install adjusting screw.
4. Adjust parking brake.

Fuel System

Carburetor

Solex carburetors are used on all models. Prior to 1961, a model 28PCI with manual choke was used. Since 1961 the 28 PICT, 30 PICT, or 34 PICT, with automatic choke, is used.

Carburetor Removal

1. Remove pre-heater pipe from air cleaner intake.
2. Pull crankcase breather pipe from air cleaner. Disconnect thermostatic control wire from air cleaner.
3. Loosen clamp on cleaner and remove.
4. Remove fuel and vacuum hoses from carburetor.
5. Pull automatic choke and electromagnetic pilot jet cables off.
6. Detach accelerator cable from throttle valve lever and remove spring, spring plate and cable pin.
7. Remove two attaching nuts and take off carburetor.

Installation

1. Fit a new gasket on intake manifold flange.
2. Install carburetor and tighten nuts evenly.
3. Secure accelerator cable so that there is about 0.040″ play between throttle valve lever and the stop on the carburetor body when the accelerator pedal is fully depressed.

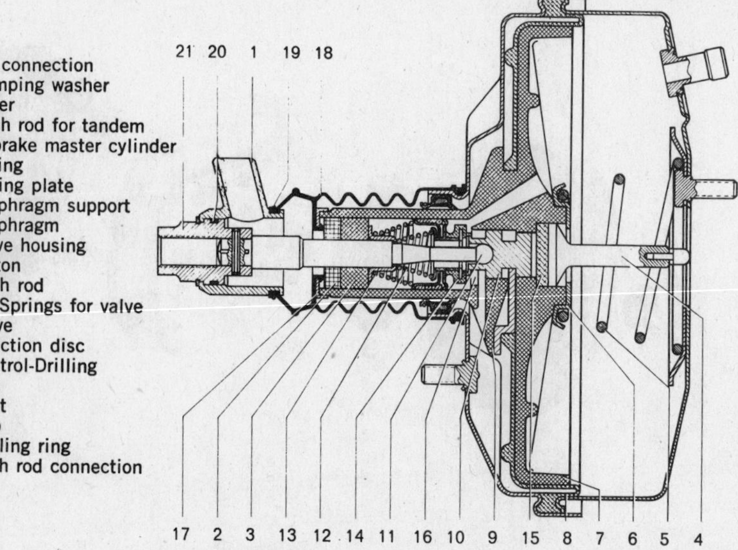

1 Air connection
2 Damping washer
3 Filter
4 Push rod for tandem brake master cylinder
5 Spring
6 Spring plate
7 Diaphragm support
8 Diaphragm
9 Valve housing
10 Piston
11 Push rod
12/13 Springs for valve
14 Valve
15 Reaction disc
16 Control-Drilling
17 Cap
18 Boot
19 Clip
20 Sealing ring
21 Push rod connection

Brake power booster (1971 models) (© Volkswagen)

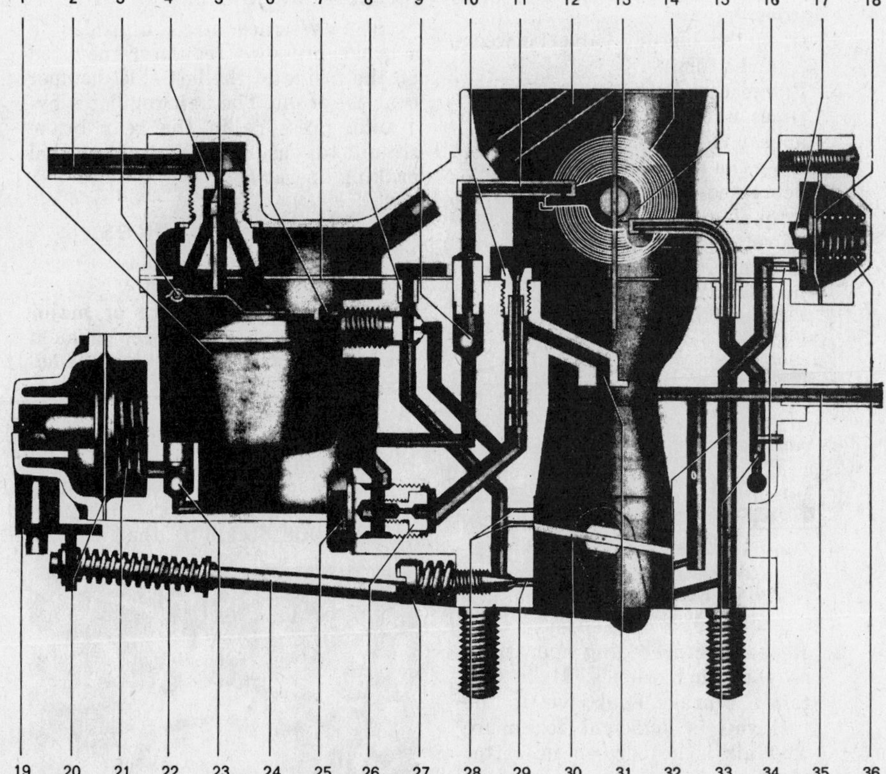

1 Float
2 Fuel line
3 Float lever
4 Float needle valve
5 Float needle
6 Pilot jet
7 Gasket
8 Pilot air drilling
9 Ball check valve in power fuel system
10 Air correction jet with emulsion tube
11 Power fuel tube
12 Float bowl vent tube
13 Choke valve
14 Bi-metal spring
15 Operating lever
16 Accelerator pump discharge tube
17 Diaphragm rod
18 Vacuum diaphragm
19 Pump lever
20 Pump diaphragm
21 Spring
22 Push rod spring
23 Ball check valve for accelerator pump
24 Pump connector rod
25 Main jet carrier
26 Main jet
27 Volume control screw
28 By-pass port
29 Idle port
30 Throttle valve
31 Discharge arm
32 Vacuum drilling
33 Ball check valve in accelerator pump drilling
34 Jet in vacuum drilling
35 Vacuum connection
36 Diaphragm spring

Solex 28 PICT-1 carburetor (© Volkswagen)

4. Start engine, warm up, then adjust idle.

Check—Electromagnetic Cut-off Jet

1. Pull cable from terminal.
2. Turn ignition on and touch terminal with cable end. The needle should move in and out with a clicking noise as the cable makes and breaks contact.
3. If cut-off valve does not work when checked, or if the engine still tends to run on, the valve must be replaced.

NOTE: In the open position, the electromagnetic cut-off valve is switched off and the fuel flow to the pilot jet is open continuously.

Adjustment—Idle Speed

This should only be done when the engine is warm. Make certain that the idle adjusting screw is not resting on one of the steps of the fast idle cam.

1. Set hot idling speed to specified rpm with idle adjusting screw.
2. Turn volume control screw (air bypass screw on 30PICT-3 and 34PICT-3 carburetor) in slowly until the engine speed begins to drop, then turn the screw out until the engine runs smoothly. Next, turn the volume control screw about ¼ turn clockwise.
3. Engine should not stall when throttle is snapped shut from wide open to idle.

Accelerator Cable Removal

1. Disconnect accelerator cable from throttle valve lever.
2. Compress the spring at carburetor and remove spring seat, sleeve and spring.
3. Detach bolt from accelerator pedal and disconnect cable.
4. Pull accelerator cable out from its guide tube in the fan housing.
5. Pull plastic hose from cable.
6. Remove rubber boot at end of cable guide tubes.
7. Pull the cable forward, out of the tube.

Automatic choke terminal (© Volkswagen)

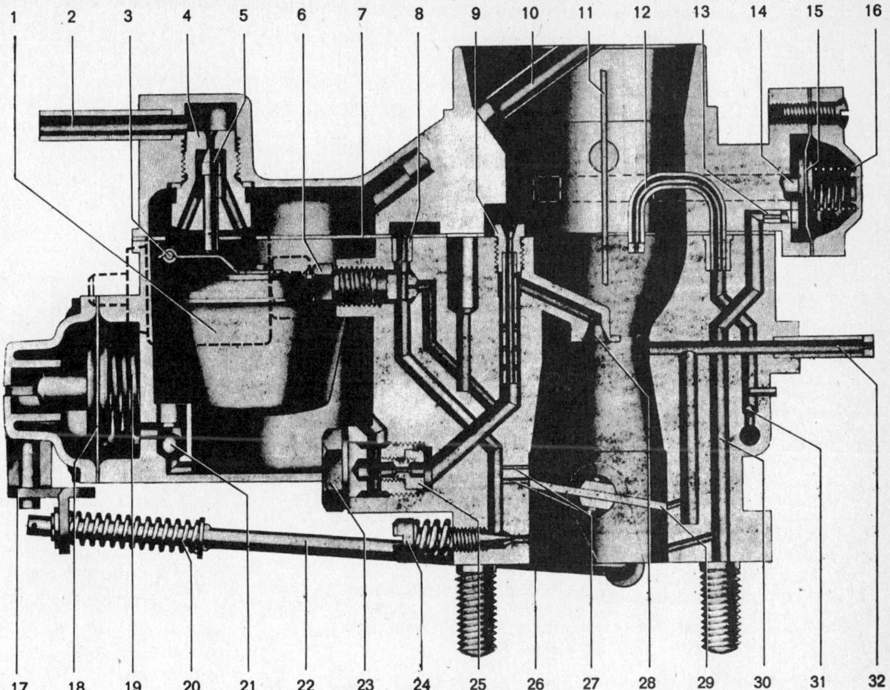

1 Float
2 Fuel line
3 Float lever
4 Float needle valve
5 Float needle
6 Electro-magnetic pilot jet
7 Gasket
8 Pilot air drilling
9 Air correction jet with emulsion tube
10 Float bowl vent tube
11 Choke valve
12 Accelerator pump discharge tube
13 Jet in vacuum drilling
14 Diaphragm rod
15 Vacuum diaphragm
16 Spring for vacuum diaphragm
17 Pump lever
18 Pump diaphragm
19 Pump spring
20 Spring
21 Ball check valve for accelerator pump
22 Pull rod for accelerator pump
23 Main jet carrier
24 Volume control screw
25 Main jet
26 Idle port
27 By-pass port
28 Discharge arm
29 Throttle valve
30 Vacuum drilling
31 Ball check valve in accelerator pump drilling
32 Vacuum connection

The carburetors on the Karmann Ghia models are fitted with a power fuel system

Solex 30 PICT-1 carburetor (© Volkswagen)

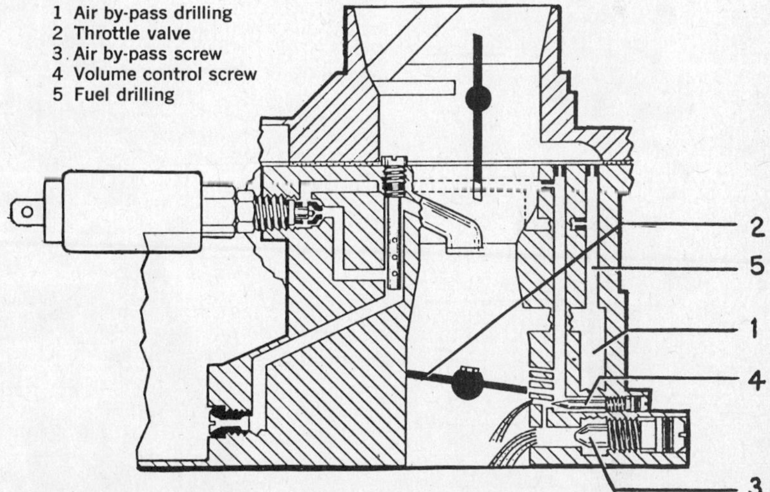

Solex 30 PICT-3 carburetor. The volume control screw is factory set. Idling adjustments are made with the air bypass screw. (© Volkswagen)

Installation

1. Lubricate accelerator cable with universal grease, then install by reversing the removal procedure.
2. Make certain that the rubber boot and the plastic hose are correctly seated to keep water from entering the guide tubes.
3. Special care must be taken when attaching the accelerator cable to the throttle valve lever to avoid breakage of the cable at full throttle. Open the throttle

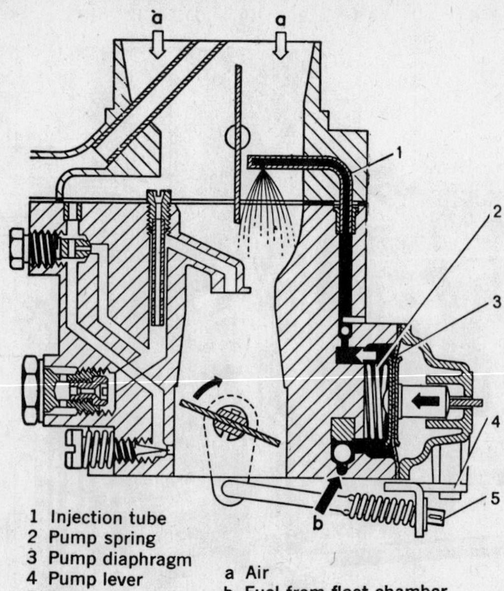

1 Injection tube
2 Pump spring
3 Pump diaphragm
4 Pump lever
5 Connecting rod

a Air
b Fuel from float chamber

Typical Solex carburetor, showing internal parts
(© Volkswagen)

1 2 3 4 5 6

1 Accelerator cable guide tube
2 Accelerator cable
3 Accelerator cable spring
4 Spring sleeve
5 Spring seat
6 Accelerator cable swivel pin

Accelerator linkage
(© Volkswagen)

valve so that there is a clearance of about 0.040″ between the throttle lever and the stop at the carburetor body.

4. Fully depress accelerator pedal and connect cable to throttle valve.

Fuel Pump Removal

1. Disconnect fuel line and hose from pump.
2. Remove mounting nuts from flange.
4. Remove pump pushrod, intermediate flange and gaskets.

Installation

Fit intermediate flange onto the crankcase with two new gaskets and insert pushrod (rounded end down). The complete stroke, from high lobe of cam to low radius should be about 0.160″. This can be obtained by selecting the proper number of flange gaskets.

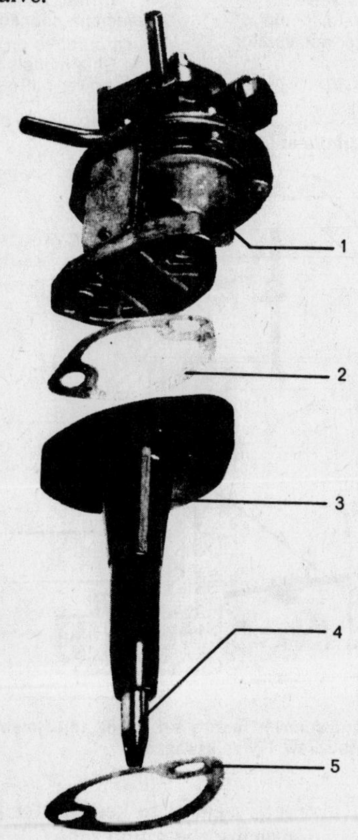

1 Fuel pump
2 Gasket
3 Plastic intermediate flange
4 Push rod
5 Gasket

Cross-sectional view, mechanical fuel pump
(© Volkswagen)

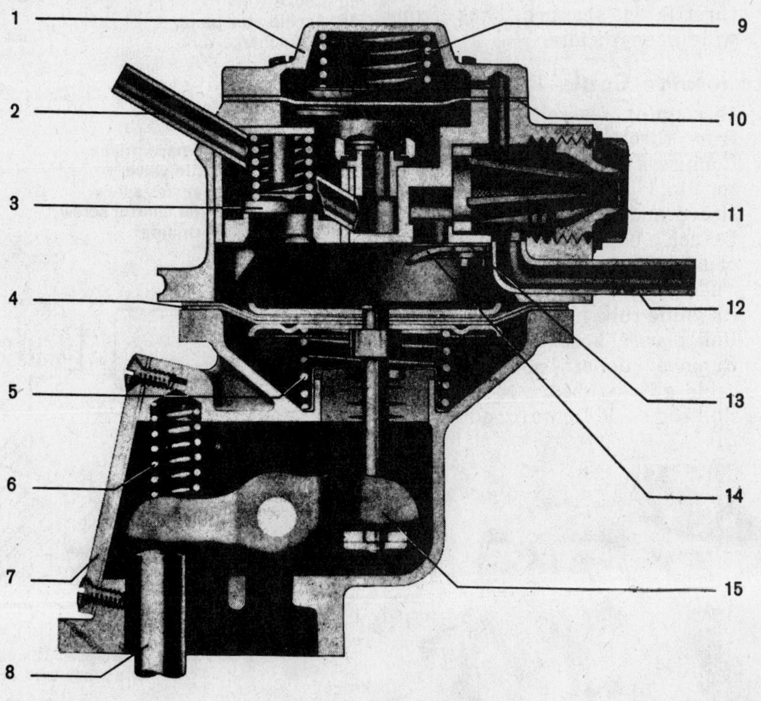

1 Cover
2 Fuel outlet
3 Pressure valve
4 Diaphragm
5 Diaphragm spring
6 Pump lever spring
7 Sealing plate
8 Push rod
9 Spring for cut-off diaphragm
10 Cut-off diaphragm
11 Strainer
12 Suction pipe
13 Suction valve
14 Suction valve retainer
15 Pump lever

Lower fuel pump parts

Governors

VW trucks used a speed limiting governor through 1967. The unit is pre-adjusted and factory sealed. If governor failure is diagnosed, replace the unit.

Cooling System

The engine is cooled by a fan attached to the extended generator shaft. It is driven by the crankshaft pulley through an adjustable V-belt at about twice the engine rpm. The fan draws air through an opening in the housing. The air then passes through the fins of cylinders and cylinder heads. Air flow is directed by deflector plates, some in the fan housing and others covering the cylinders. The throttle ring at the air intake opening of the fan housing is thermostatically controlled, which insures quickly attained and steadily maintained operating temperatures.

Fan Housing Removal

1. Disconnect battery.
2. Remove engine.
3. Disconnect cables from generator, carburetor, ignition coil, and oil pressure switch.

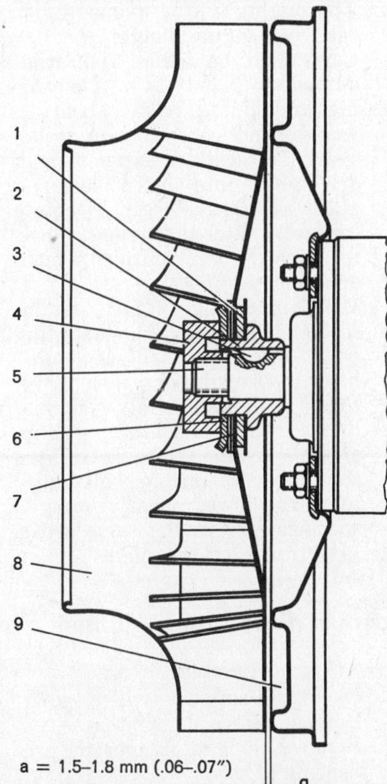

Cooling fan (© Volkswagen)

Location of speed limiting governor (© Volkswagen)

4. Disconnect vacuum line from distributor and fuel hose from carburetor.
5. Remove accelerator cable and conduit tube.
6. Remove carburetor.
7. Remove fan belt.
8. Remove generator strap and disconnect cable from ignition coil.
9. Remove ignition cable clamps.
10. Remove slotted screws from both sides of fan housing.
11. Detach spring from automatic cooling air control and remove throttle-ring screws.
12. Lift off fan housing and generator as a unit.

Fan housing attaching screws (© Volkswagen)

Removing fan housing (© Volkswagen)

Installation

Install the fan housing by reversing the removal procedure.

Engine

Exhaust Emission Control System

The device used on exhaust emission controlled VW trucks 1968-71, is a throttle valve regulator. This device holds the throttle open slightly on deceleration to prevent an excessively rich mixture.

Removal

1. Disconnect vacuum hose.
2. Remove three attaching screws.
3. Remove retainer ring and regulator. On 1970-71 models, the throttle regulator consists of two parts, connected by a hose. The operating unit is mounted at the carburetor, and the control unit is located on the left sidewall of the engine compartment.
4. Unhook control rod at lever.

Installation

Install throttle regulator by reversing the removal procedure.

Adjustment

1. Engine must be at operating temperature, with automatic choke fully open.
2. With engine running, turn regulator adjusting screw clockwise until control rod just starts to move throttle valve lever. The stop collar on the control rod will be against the regulator body. Engine speed should be 1700-1800 rpm.
3. If speed is too high, shorten control rod.
4. After adjustment, tighten lock nuts on rod.
5. Turn regulator adjusting screw counterclockwise until an idle speed of 850 rpm is obtained.
6. Increase engine speed to 3000 rpm, then release throttle valve lever. Engine should take 3-4 seconds to return to idle.

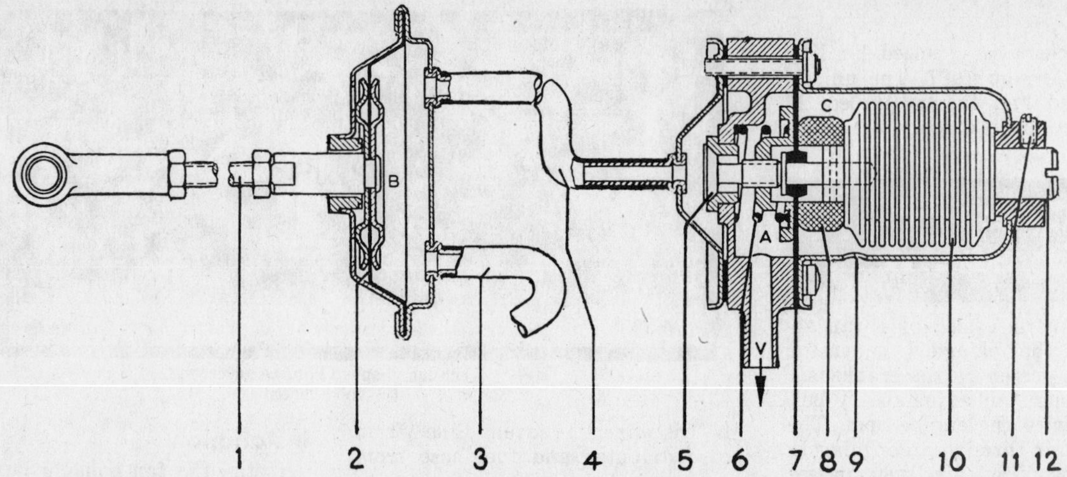

1 Pull rod
2 Operating diaphragm
3 Hose to the vacuum drilling in the carburetor
4 Hose between operating and control part
5 Valve
6 Spring
7 Control diaphragm
8 Plastic foam filter
9 Drilling
10 Altitude corrector
11 Lock screw
12 Adjusting screw

Two-piece throttle regulator (© Volkswagen)

1 Diaphragm
2 Spring
3 Valve
4 Diaphragm
5 Spring
6 Control rod
7 Stop collar
8 Passage in valve
9 Filter
10 Vent passage
11 Altitude compensator
12 Adjustment screw
13 Lock screw

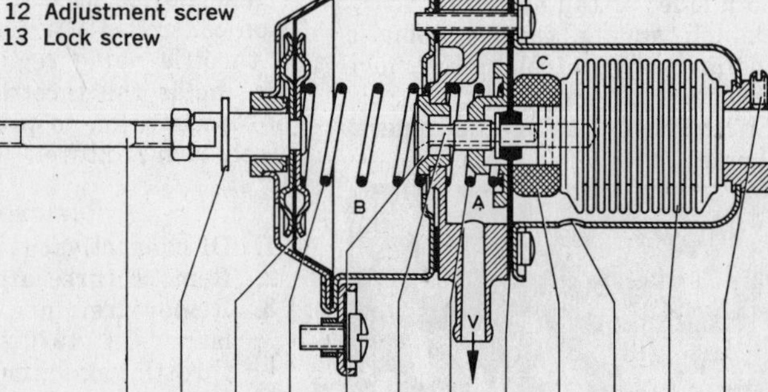

One-piece throttle regulator (© Volkswagen)

NOTE: Incorrect throttle regulator adjustment may cause erratic idle, excessively high idle speed, and backfiring on deceleration.

Engine Assembly Removal

1. Disconnect battery ground strap, generator cables, and voltage regulator wires.
2. Remove air cleaner.
3. Disconnect throttle cable from carburetor. Disconnect wires from automatic choke, coil, electromagnetic cut-off jet, and oil pressure sending unit.
4. Disconnect and plug fuel hose.
5. Raise truck about three feet.
6. Remove hoses between engine and heat exchangers. Disconnect heater flap cables. Remove rear cover plate, rear crossmember and engine carrier bolts. Unscrew two lower engine mounting nuts. NOTE: Cover plate may remain with engine on pre-1967 models.
7. Place a suitable jack under engine, and support transmission.
8. Raise jack to support engine. Have an assistant hold two upper engine mounting bolts. Remove nuts.
9. Roll engine and jack backwards slightly so that clutch clears transmission main driveshaft.
10. Lower engine.

Installation

Installation is a reversal of the removal operations, but the following points should be observed:

a. Install engine only with engine rear cover plate removed.
b. Loosen mounting screw on the distributor. Turn distributor for clearance.
c. Check central position of clutch plate.
d. Check clutch release bearing and clutch release plate for wear and cracks. Replace, if necessary.
e. Examine needle bearing in flywheel gland nut for wear and pack it with (0.35 oz.) universal grease.
f. Lubricate starter, shaft bushing, starter drive pinion, and flywheel gear ring with multipurpose grease.
g. Lubricate main drive shaft splines and pilot with transmission oil. Apply with a clean dry cloth.
h. Thoroughly clean transmission case and engine flange.
i. Care must be taken to prevent damage to gland nut needle bearing and clutch release bearing. Avoid bending the main driveshaft. To facilitate entry of main drive shaft into clutch plate and gland nut needle bearing, rotate engine at V-belt (engage a gear to steady transmission main driveshaft).
j. When installing engine, first insert the lower engine mounting bolts into their corresponding holes in transmission case flange. Press engine firmly against flange until it is contacting properly all around. Initially tighten the upper mounting bolt nuts; then, the lower ones. Torque to specifications in the same order.
k. Adjust accelerator cable.
l. Adjust ignition timing.

Exhaust Pipes and Muffler

Removal

1. Raise and support truck at rear.
2. Remove rear cover plate.
3. Remove nuts at flanges of preheating pipe.
4. Loosen clamps and remove tail pipes.
5. Loosen clamps at front of exhaust pipes and heater boxes.
6. Remove nuts from muffler flanges.
7. Draw muffler back and remove

from below. Remove gasket from cylinder head flanges, muffler and pre-heating pipe.

Installation

Install in reverse order of removal, and check the following:

a. Check muffler and exhaust pipes for cracks and damage. If necessary, the pipes can be straightened. The welded joint of the muffler and tail pipe is particularly susceptible to damage by impacts. Leaks may result in exhaust fumes entering the engine compartment and interior of the car when the heater is turned on. Always replace all bent or out-of-round tail pipes. If the cartridges are no longer serviceable, the pipes have to be replaced.
b. There should be a perfect seal at connection to front exhaust pipes.

Heat Exchangers

Removal

1. Remove exhaust pipe clamps, the clamps between heat exchanger and exhaust pipe, and the rear engine cover plate.
2. Remove nuts on cylinder head and warm air pipe connecting clips.
3. Remove heat exchanger. Check outer shell and exhaust pipes for damage and leakage. If the heat exchangers leak, there could be a possibility of poisonous gases entering the heating system. Sealing surfaces must be clean and smooth, and flanges that are distorted or bent through excessive tightening should be straightened or machined.

Installation

To install heat exchangers, reverse the removal procedure. Use new gaskets and ensure that all connections are gastight. Heat exchangers must be attached at the cylinder heads with self-locking M8 hexagon nuts. It is not permissible for any other type

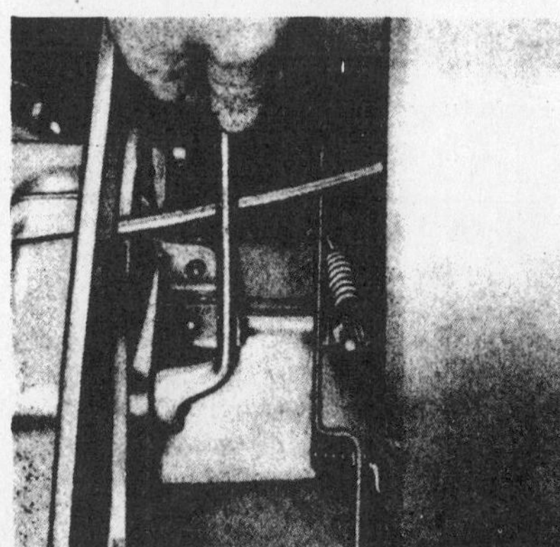

Removing upper engine mounting bolts (© Volkswagen)

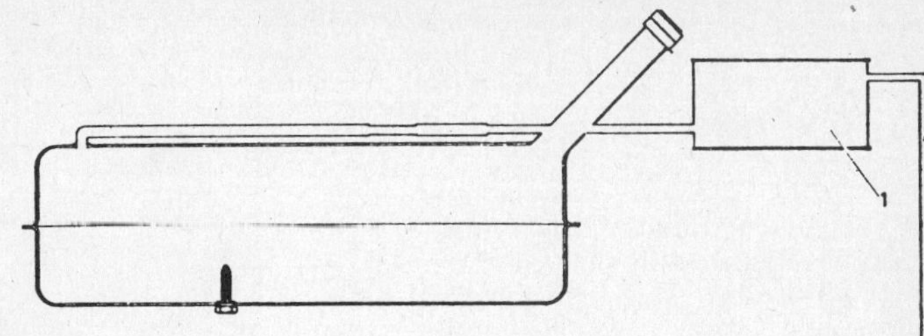

1 Expansion tank
2 Fuel vapor line
3 Pressure hose (from cooling air blower to filter container)
4 Suction hose (from filter container to oil bath air cleaner)
5 Crankcase ventilation

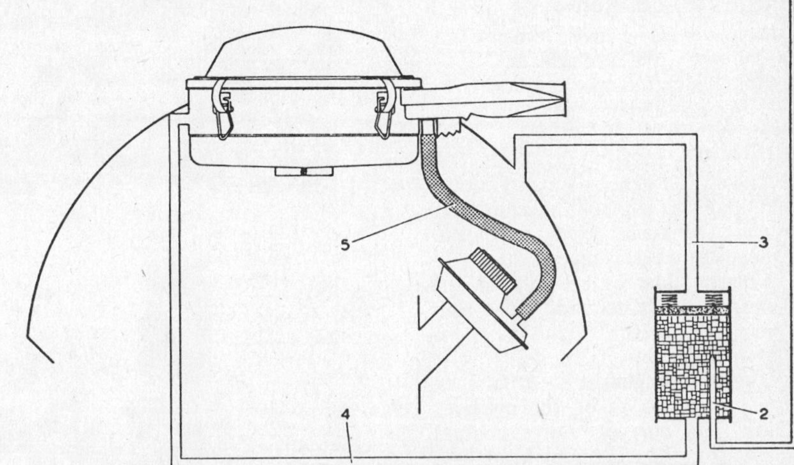

Activated charcoal filter system used on all VW vehicles sold in California, 1970 (© Volkswagen)

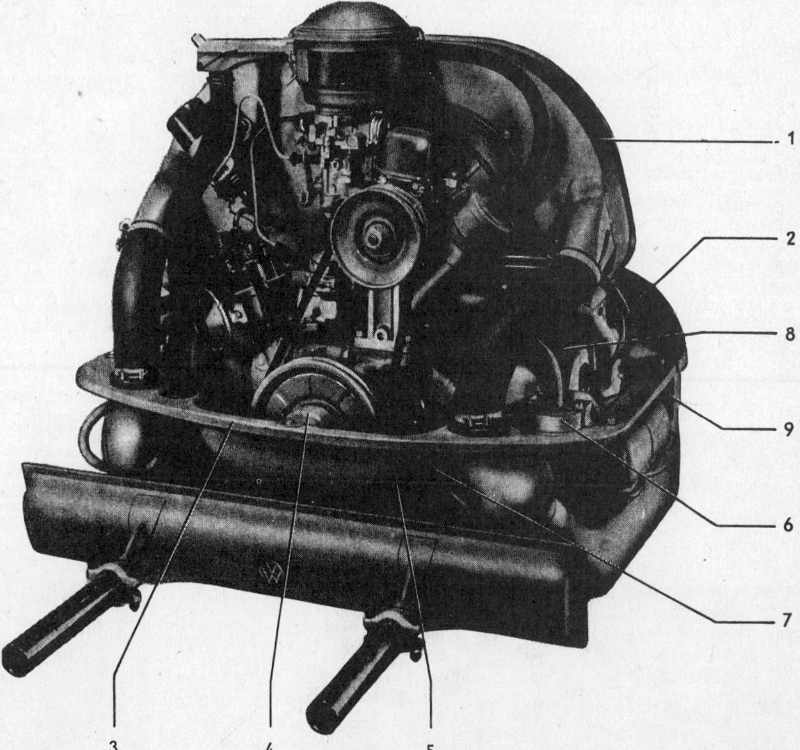

1 Fan housing
2 Front engine cover plate
3 Rear engine cover plate
4 Fan pulley cover
5 Fan pulley lower plate
6 Pre-heater pipe sealing plate
7 Air deflector plate
8 Cylinder cover plate
9 Screening plate

Engine external parts (© Volkswagen)

of nut to be used, even with lockwashers.

Cylinder Head

Each pair of cylinders has one mutual detachable cylinder head, made of a light-alloy casting. The cylinder heads are also provided with fins for cooling and they have shrunk-in valve seat inserts and valve guides. No gasket is used between cylinder and cylinder head. However, copper-asbestos gaskets between the flanges of cylinder and cylinder head, prevent leakage of combustion gases.

Cylinder Head Removal

1. Remove valve cover and gasket.
2. Remove valve mechanism.
3. Remove cylinder head nuts.
4. Lift off cylinder head.

Installation

1. Check for cracks or any other damage to combustion chambers and exhaust ports. Cracked heads must be replaced.
2. Check studs for security in the crankcase. If necessary, use Helicoil, or its equivalent, as a repair method.
3. There is no gasket used between the upper edge of the cylinder and the corresponding contact surface of the cylinder head.
4. Replace gasket between shoulder of cylinder and cylinder head. The slotted side of gasket must be toward the cylinder head.
5. Make sure that the oil seals at the ends of the pushrod tubes are correctly seated.
6. Install cylinder head nut washers.
7. Coat cylinder head nuts with graphite paste, then screw them down finger tight. Tighten initially, in correct sequence, to 7 ft. lbs. torque.
8. Then torque to specifications.
9. Install valve mechanism.
10. Install valve cover and new gasket.

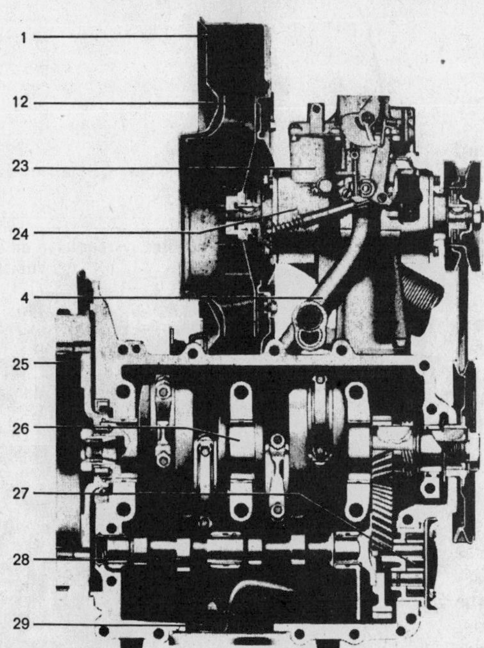

1 Fan housing
2 Ignition coil
3 Oil cooler
4 Intake manifold
5 Fuel pump
6 Ignition distributor
7 Oil pressure switch
8 Valve
9 Cylinder
10 Piston
11 Oil pressure relief valve
12 Fan
13 Oil filter and breather
14 Pre-heating pipe
15 Connecting rod
16 Spark plug
17 Cylinder head
18 Thermostat
19 Rocker arm
20 Push rod
21 Heat exchanger
22 Cam follower
23 Carburetor
24 Generator
25 Flywheel
26 Crankshaft
27 Oil pump
28 Camshaft
29 Oil strainer

Cross-sectional view, 1500 engine (© Volkswagen)

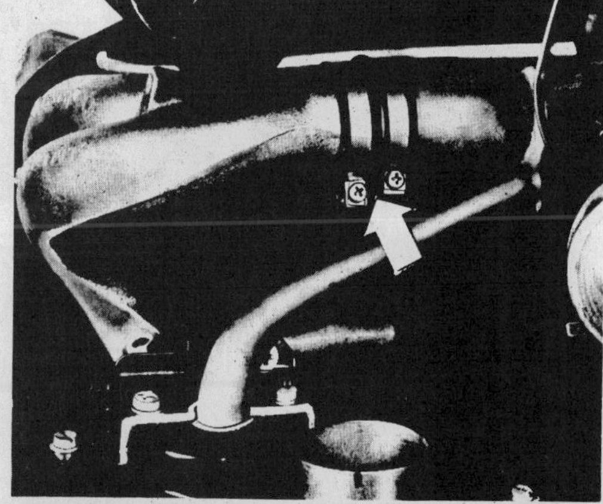

New intake manifold and attaching clamps 1971 models (© Volkswagen)

New dual port cylinder head 1971 models (© Volkswagen)

CYLINDER-HEAD BOLT TIGHTENING SEQUENCE

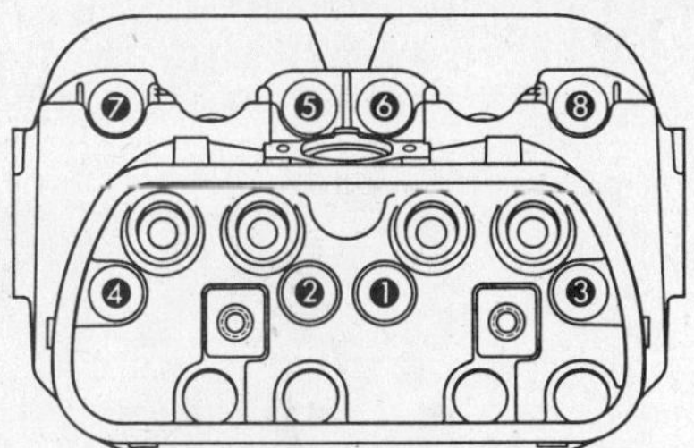

Tighten nuts to 1 mkg (7 ft. lbs.) first in the order shown

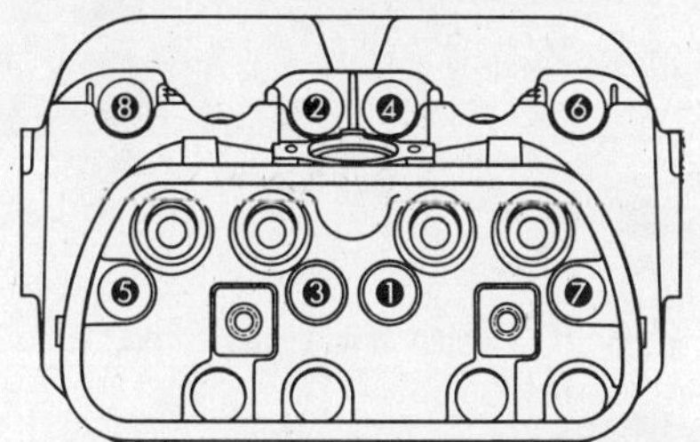

Fully tighten nuts to specified torque in this order

Refer to Specifications for cylinder head bolt tightening sequences and torques.

Valve Train

The camshaft is supported by three bearings in the crankcase. It is driven, through helical gears, by the crankshaft. Valves are operated by cam lobes via cam followers, pushrods and rocker arms. Each cam operates, in turn, one of the valves of two opposed cylinders. Exhaust valves are plated with chrome-nickel steel.

Valve Adjustment

Remove valve covers and proceed as follows:

1. Rotate crankshaft until No. 1 cylinder is up on compression stroke and the distributor rotor points to No. 1 plug wire pick-up. Both intake and exhaust valves in No. 1 cylinder are now closed. The valve tappets are on the low point of No. 1 cylinder camshaft lobe.

Valve adjustment
(© Volkswagen)

2. Check and adjust valve lash with a feeler gauge. (See specifications chart for clearance). Since 1964, a sticker on the fan housing has specified clearances.
3. Lock adjusting screw and recheck clearance.
4. Rotate engine ½ turn counterclockwise (reverse of running rotation), using a spark plug wrench on the generator pulley nut. Set valves on No. 2 cylinder.
5. Rotate another ½ turn counterclockwise; set valves on No. 3 cylinder on the other side of the truck.
6. Rotate ½ turn counterclockwise once more; set valves on No. 4 cylinder.
7. Install valve covers with new gaskets. Re-position distributor cap.

It is also possible to adjust valves in normal firing order sequence, 1-4-3-2, rotating the engine clockwise. It is helpful to mark the fan pulley directly opposite the 0° mark in order to determine precisely when the engine is turned ½ revolution.

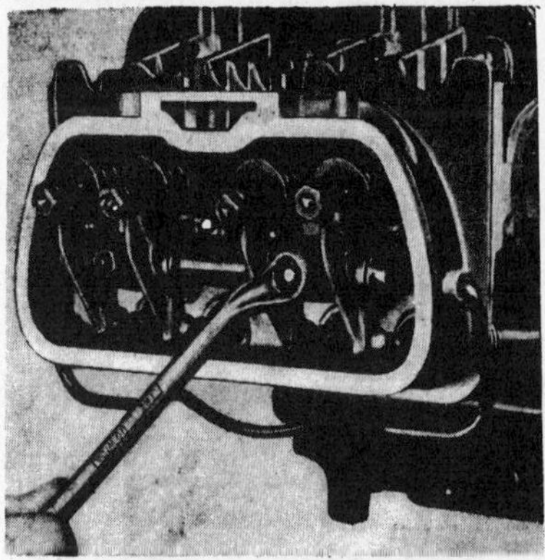

Removing rocker arm shaft
(© Volkswagen)

Valve Rocker Arm and Shaft Removal

1. Remove the valve cover and gasket. NOTE: If valve covers are dirty, clean thoroughly before removing. Any dirt falling on the rockers or valve springs can cause considerable damage and eventual engine failure.
2. Remove rocker arm shaft retaining nuts.
3. Remove rocker arm shaft and rocker arms.
4. Remove the stud seals.

Installation

Install by reversing the removal procedure, in addition to the following:

a. Install new stud seals. Ball ends of pushrods must be centered in sockets of rocker arms. Torque nuts to 14 ft. lbs.
b. To help valves rotate during operation, rocker arm adjusting screws should contact the tip of the valve stem slightly off center. (To the right.)
c. Adjust valves.
d. Reinstall valve cover with new gasket.

Disassembly and Assembly

1. Remove spring clips from rocker arm shaft.
2. Remove washers, rocker arms, and bearing supports.

Recently, the sealing between cylinder head and valve cover was modified. The sealing surface on the cylinder head, below the intake manifold, is now straight, and the valve cover has been modified to suit. The older valve cover and cork gasket must not be used for engines with modified cylinder heads. If these parts are used, sealing near the intake port will be defective.

Note the following points:

1. Check rocker arm shaft for wear.
2. Examine seats, ball sockets of rocker arms and valve adjusting screws for wear.
3. Loosen adjusting screws prior to installing rocker arms.

Servicing Valves

The valves are removed from their respective locations, serviced and reinstalled in the same way as their counterparts in American manufacture. However, the following items will bear attention.

Replacement of valve guides is not possible without tools and other facilities capable of chilling and shrinking the guides into place. Deposits and other buildup may be removed by reaming or broaching.

Damaged valve seat inserts may be reconditioned with a 45° seat cutter. Do not chamfer the 15° outer edge to exceed the outer diameter of the insert. Inserts cannot be replaced without special facilities.

Rocker arm mechanism (© Volkswagen)

Rocker arm support location (© Volkswagen)

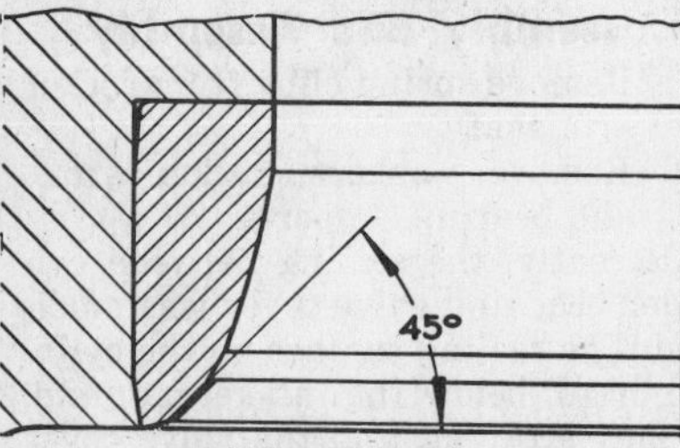

Valve seat angle (© Volkswagen)

To rework the valve seat, cut the seat to 45°. Stop cutting as soon as an even and concentric seat has been achieved. Then, slightly chamfer the lower valve seat with a 75° cutter. Next, cut the 15° seat chamfer on the upper seat edge until the correct seat width is obtained.

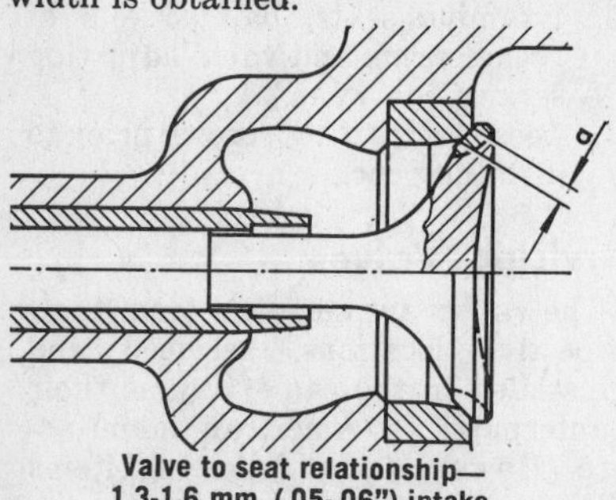

Valve to seat relationship—1.3-1.6 mm. (.05-.06") intake, 1.7-2.0 mm. (.06-.08") exhaust (© Volkswagen)

After grinding the valve, or lapping the valve face and seat, blue test the sealing surface as a precaution against gas leaks.

Camshaft and Timing Gears

Removal of the camshaft requires that the crankcase be split. The camshaft and camshaft bearing shells are then easily removed. Before reinstalling the camshaft, it should be checked for wear of the lobe faces and bearing points. In addition, the riveted joint between the camshaft timing gear and the camshaft should be examined for security. If there is slight damage to the camshaft, it may be smoothed with a silicon carbide oilstone.

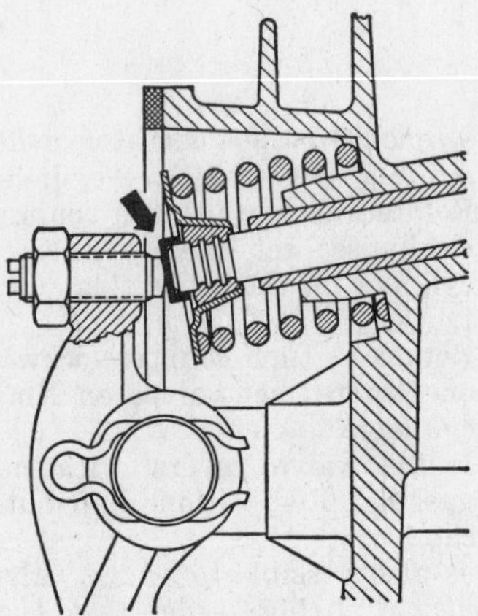

Valves with a damaged stem end are still usable by installing a small cap on stem (© Volkswagen)

Camshaft in recent engines runs in three shell-type bearings. End thrust of camshaft is measured at the bearing nearest the timing gear. (© Volkswagen)

A 100-120 grit stone is first used to smooth the damaged area, and then a 280-320 stone may be used for final polishing. The camshaft should be checked for runout, which should not exceed .0008". The timing gear should be checked for correct tooth contact and for wear, and the edges of the camshaft bearing bores lightly chamfered to avoid seizure. If the camshaft shells removed are either worn or damaged, new shells should be fitted.

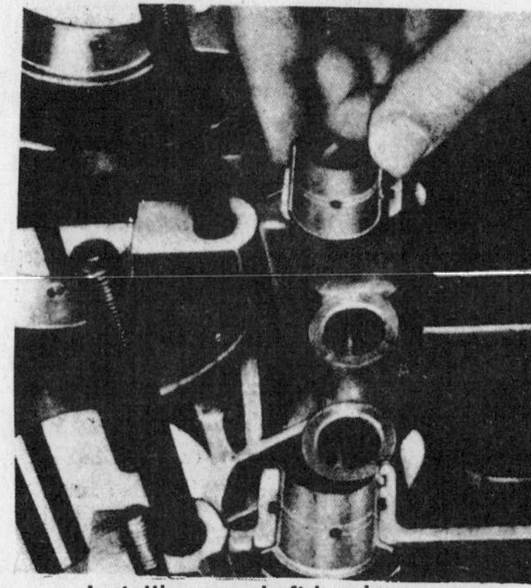

Installing camshaft bearings (© Volkswagen)

The camshaft bearing shells should be installed with the tabs engaging the notches in the crankcase. Before installing camshaft, the bearing journals and cams should be generously coated with oil. When the camshaft is installed, care should be taken to ensure that the timing gear tooth marked "0" is located between the two teeth of the crankshaft timing gear marked by a center punch.

Checking cam face for wear (© Volkswagen)

Location of timing marks (© Volkswagen)

Cylinders

The four cylinders are cast of special alloys, and are interchangeable. Cylinders are provided with integral cooling fins.

Removing cylinder
(© Volkswagen)

Cylinder Removal

1. Remove valve pushrods and pushrod tubes.
2. Remove deflector plate below cylinders.
3. Take off cylinders.

Piston installation
(© Volkswagen)

Installation

When installing, note the following:

a. Check cylinder wear. If necessary, replace with another matched cylinder and piston assembly of the same size.
b. Check cylinder seating surface on crankcase. Cylinder shoulder and gasket must be clean. Foreign matter at this point may cause distortion.
c. Use a new cylinder to crankcase gasket.
d. Liberally oil piston rings, and piston pin.
e. Compress rings with compressing tool. Be sure ring gaps are adequate and staggered on the piston. The oil ring must be inserted into the cylinder so that its gap is positioned up when the pistons are in their horizontal position in the engine.
f. Lubricate cylinder wall. Crankcase studs must not contact cylinder cooling fins.
g. Install deflector plates. Make sure they are correctly seated.
h. Install pushrod tubes with new seals and pushrods. Insert the tubes so that the seat is facing upward. Before installing used tubes, they should be stretched to assure a proper length for sealing.

Use a feeler gauge to measure ring gap
(© Volkswagen)

Pistons

Pistons are of light-metal alloy and are equipped with three rings, the bottom one being an oil ring.

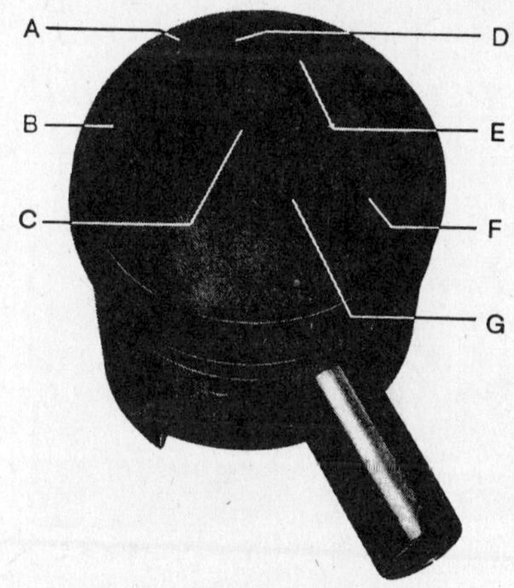

Piston markings
a. Arrow must point towards flywheel
b. Piston pin bore size
c. Paint spot indicating matching sizes
d. Letter corresponds to index of part number
e. Weight grading (+ or —)
f. Paint spot indicating weight grading (—) brown (+) grey
g. Piston size in mm.
(© Volkswagen)

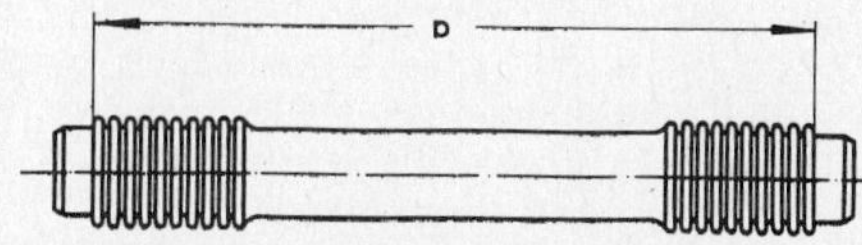

Pushrod tube length (a) should be 180.5-181.5 mm. for 1200 engine, 190-191 mm. for 1500, 1600 engines
(© Volkswagen)

Piston Removal

1. Remove cylinder.
2. Mark the piston and its position.
3. Remove piston pin circlip.
4. Heat piston to 175°F.
5. Remove piston pin with a pilot drift.
6. If piston rings are to be removed, use a piston ring removing tool.

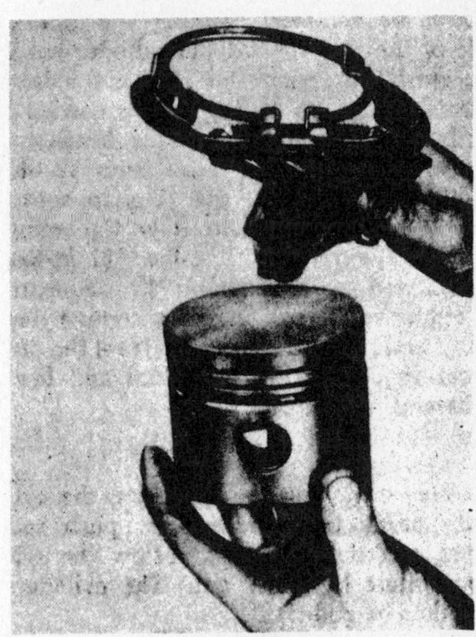

Removing piston rings
(© Volkswagen)

Installation

Assembling of piston and rod components is not unlike most engines of American manufacture. However, note the following:

a. Carefully clean the piston and ring grooves (don't scratch or otherwise damage grooves.)
b. Check for piston wear. If replacement is necessary, install one of a corresponding size. Difference in weight of pistons in any one engine must not exceed 10 grams.
c. Use piston rings of correct size. Compression ring gaps should be 0.012″-0.018″ with a maximum of 0.035″. Oil scraper ring gap should be 0.010″-0.016″ with a maximum of 0.035″.

When reinstalling the cylinder, make sure the ring gap is at the top and that each gap is offset by 120°. Check piston ring side clearance with a feeler gauge. Side clearance should be as follows:

No. 1 ring (compression) 0.0026-0.0036″ (1200). .0031-.0043″ (1500, 1600).

No. 2 ring (compression) 0.0018-0.0028″. (All)

No. 3 ring (oil scraper) 0.0010-0.0020″. (All)

Make sure that the compression rings are installed right-side up. (The marking "top" or "oben" toward the top of the piston.)

Insert the piston pin circlip, facing

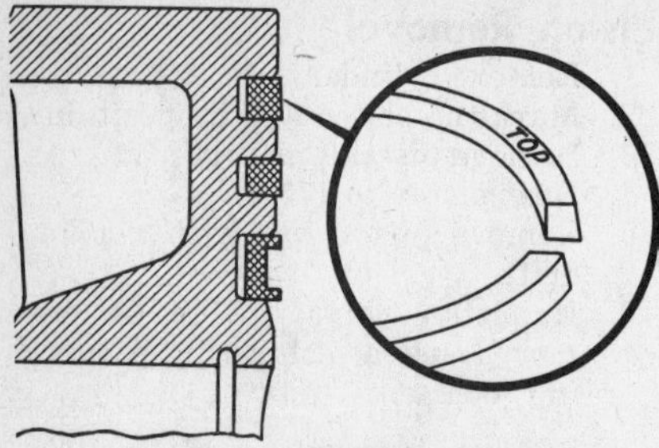

Piston ring installation
(© Volkswagen)

toward the flywheel. Because piston pin holes are offset, make sure that the arrow (or word "vorn") points toward the flywheel. This offset is to help accommodate thrust loads that amplify, and lead to, objectionable piston slap.

Check and fit piston pin. The pin may be found to be a light finger-push fit in the piston, even when the piston is cold. This condition is quite normal, even to the extent of the pin sliding out of the piston of its own weight. For pistons with a hole diameter in excess of 0.7874", oversize pins are available.

Measuring piston—cylinder clearance
(© Volkswagen)

Checking piston ring side clearance
(© Volkswagen)

Clearance between piston pin and connecting rod bushing should be .0004-0008". If clearance is near the wear limit of 0.0016", replace the piston pin and the rod bushing. It is not advisable to install an oversize pin in this case.

Heat the piston, in oil, to about 177°F in all cases where the pin is not a light finger-push fit in the cold piston.

Insert the other circlip. It is important that the circlips fit in their grooves perfectly.

Piston to Cylinder Clearance

The fitting clearance between piston and cylinder should be 0.0014-0.0021", with a wear limit of 0.008". Maximum out-of-round limit is 0.0004".

Besides wear, oil consumption is a good indication of whether or not a new cylinder and piston should be installed. If oil consumption is more than 1 qt./600 miles, the engine probably needs reconditioning.

Crankcase, Crankshaft and Connecting Rods

Crankcase

The crankcase is a light metal alloy die casting. The crankcase halves are machined in pairs to very close tolerances. Consequently, replacements must be made in pairs.

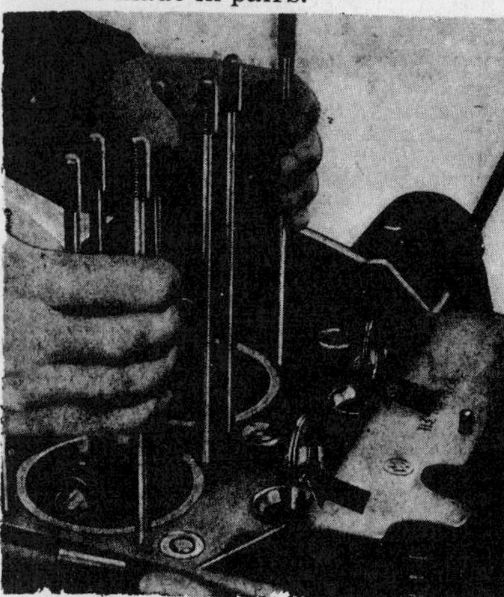
Removal and installation of crankcase sections
(© Volkswagen)

Crankshaft

The crankshaft is heat-treated at all bearing points. The shaft is supported by four special light-metal bearings. No. 2 bearing (as seen from the clutch) is of the split type. No. 1 bearing is lead-coated and takes crankshaft thrust. The flywheel, with starter gear, is held by a gland nut and additionally held to the crankshaft by four dowel pins. The timing gear and distributor drive gear are held in place by Woodruff keys. The fan drive pulley is bolted to the crankshaft. An oil seal is fitted to the clutch side of the crankshaft and an oil slinger and oil return thread on the other side.

Connecting Rods

The crankshaft ends of the four connecting rods contain replaceable lead-bronze bearings. Piston pin ends are provided with bronze bushings. Piston pins are full-floating.

Note connecting rod marks pointing upward
(© Volkswagen)

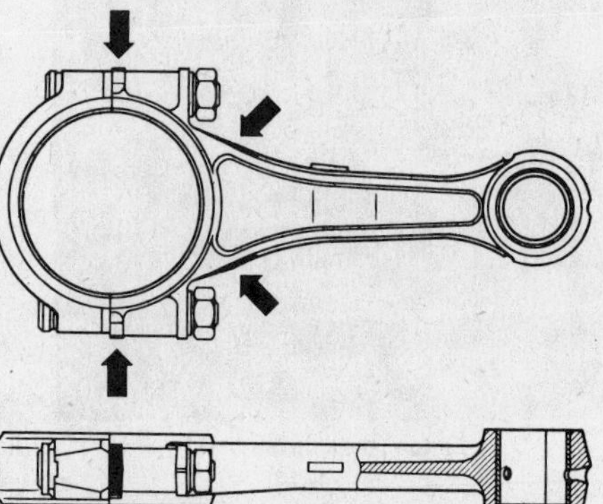
Maximum weight difference between connecting rods in one engine is 10 grams. Metal can be removed from the arrowed portions of the connecting rod.
(© Volkswagen)

Disassembly of Crankcase

1. Remove oil pressure switch.
2. Remove crankcase nuts.
3. Keep cam followers of right crankcase half in position with retaining springs.
4. Remove right crankcase half (use a rubber hammer). Do not try to pry apart with a screwdriver or wedge.
5. Remove crankshaft oil seal.
6. Remove camshaft end-plug.
7. Take out crankshaft and camshaft.
8. Remove cam followers.
9. Remove bearing shells and oil pressure relief valve.
10. Remove connecting rod clamping bolts, rods and caps.

Installation—Crankshaft

1. The crankcase must not have sharp edges at points of junction.

2. Check dowel pins for tightness.
3. Place one half of No. 2 crankshaft bearing in the crankcase.
4. Slide on crankshaft bearing No. 1 so that the dowel pin hole is toward the flywheel.
5. Install crankshaft. Make sure that the dowel pins are correctly seated in the crankshaft bearings.

Installation—Connecting Rods

1. Check weight of connecting rods. The difference in weight of the rods in one engine must not be in excess of 10 grams to maintain proper engine balance. If necessary, metal should be removed from the heavier connecting rods at the points indicated in the drawing.

Measuring connecting rod axial play with a feeler gauge
(© Volkswagen)

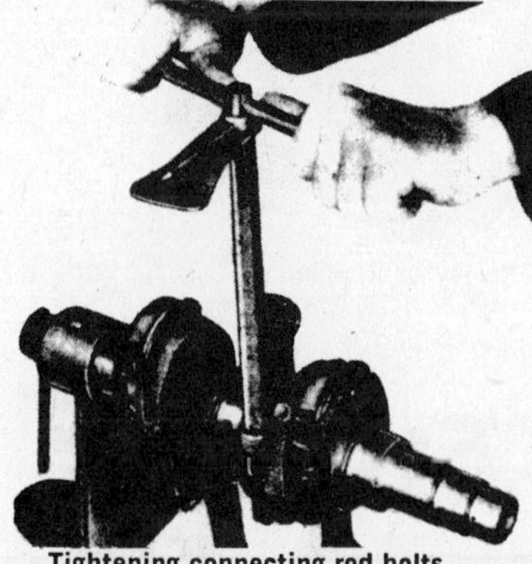

Tightening connecting rod bolts
(© Volkswagen)

2. Inspect piston pin bushing. With a new bushing, the correct clearance is indicated by a light finger-push fit of the pin at room temperature.
3. Check and, if necessary, correct connecting rod alignment.
4. Reinsert connecting rod bearing shells after all parts have been thoroughly cleaned, then assemble connecting rods on crankshaft. The identification numbers stamped on connecting rods and bearing caps must be on the same side.
5. Tighten connecting rod bolts. A slight pretension between the bearing halves, which is likely to occur when tightening connecting rod bolts, can be eliminated by light hammer taps. The connecting rods, lubricated with engine oil prior to assembly, must slide onto the crank pin by their own weight. The connecting rod bushings must not be scraped, reamed or filed during assembly.
6. Secure connecting rod bolts in place.

Assembly of Crankcase

In addition to reversing disassembly procedure, check the following:

1. Check crankcase for damage and cracks.
2. Clean crankcase thoroughly, especially mating and sealing surfaces. Flush and blow out all ducts and passages.
3. Check oil suction pipe for leaks.
4. Install cam followers.
5. Check and install oil pressure switch.
6. Check timing marks on the gears, and be sure crankshaft oil slinger is correctly installed.
7. Install camshaft.
8. Install camshaft end plug, using sealing compound. Install thrust washers and crankshaft oil seal. The oil seal must rest squarely on the bottom of its recess in the crankcase.
9. Spread a thin film of sealing compound on the crankcase joining faces. Use care so that no sealing compound enters the oil passages of crankshaft or camshaft bearings.
10. Keep cam followers of right crankcase half in place by using retaining springs.
11. Join crankcase halves and evenly torque to specifications. NOTE: First tighten the 8mm nut which is beside the 12mm stud of crankshaft bearing No. 1. Only then should the 12mm nuts be tightened fully.

Crankshaft End-Play

Crankshaft end-play should be read with a dial indicator and should be 0.0028-0.0047″, the wear limit being 0.006″. With engine installed in the vehicle, the indicator may be mounted to read shaft end-play at the pulley. If convenient, an indicator may be mounted on the flywheel end and end-play read directly from the flywheel.

Before the M12 nuts are fully tightened the M8 nut near the No. 1 crankshaft bearing must be tightened to 14 ft. lbs.
(© Volkswagen)

Measuring crankshaft end-play
(© Volkswagen)

Adjustment

1. Force the installed crankshaft towards the flywheel side of the engine (with flywheel removed) so that it contacts the inner

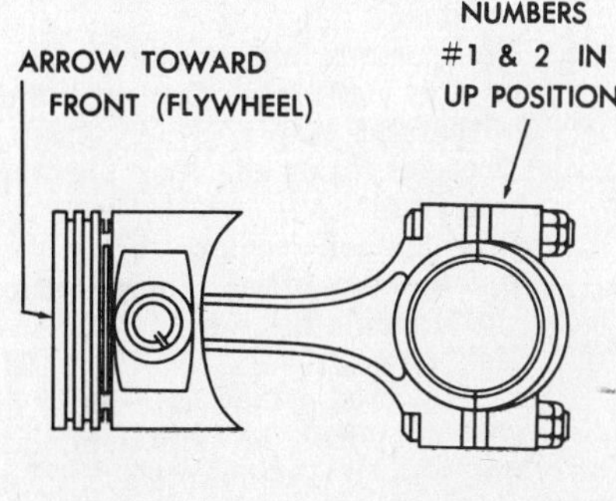

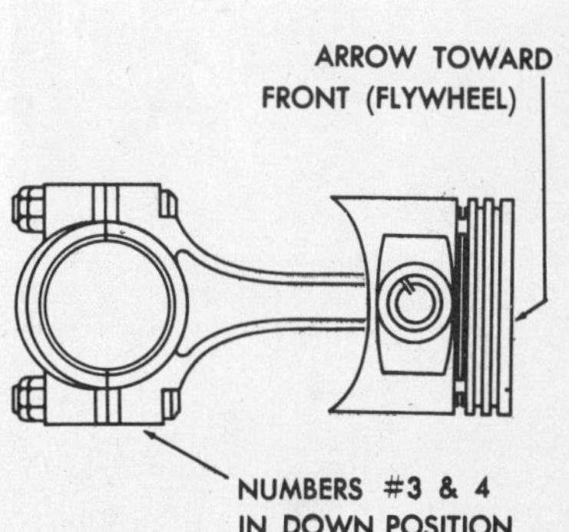

WHILE ASSEMBLING RODS TO CRANKSHAFT, (RODS IN VERTICAL POSITION) ALL ROD NUMBERS ARE ON RIGHT SIDE, VIEWED FROM FLYWHEEL END.

Piston and rod installation (© Volkswagen)

thrust surface of No. 1 bearing.
2. Insert dial gauge in flywheel seat so that it contacts the crankshaft, and measure distance from crankshaft face to outer face of main bearing No. 1.
3. Place a gauge on the flywheel flange and measure depth of crankshaft seat.
4. The thickness of the shims to be used is decided by the difference in both readings (taking into account the gasket). Shims for this purpose are available in various thicknesses. Desirable end-play is obtained by adding or subtracting shims at the outer end of the main bearing. Never use more than one gasket.

Engine Lubrication

A gear-type oil pump is located on the distributor side of the engine and is driven by the camshaft. Oil is drawn from the lowest point of the crankcase and forced into passages via an oil cooler. Part of the oil is fed through the crankshaft to the main and rod bearings, and some routed to lubricate the camshaft bearings. The remainder is fed through hollow pushrods to the rocker arms and valve stems. Cylinder walls, pistons and piston pins are lubricated by splash. Oil then returns to the crankcase, to be filtered by a gauze strainer before again entering circulation.

The oil cooler is positioned in the ducted air flow. It is located so that oil forced by the pump must pass through it before reaching lubrication points. In cold weather, an oil pressure relief valve makes possible direct engine lubrication without the colder, thicker oil passing through the cooler.

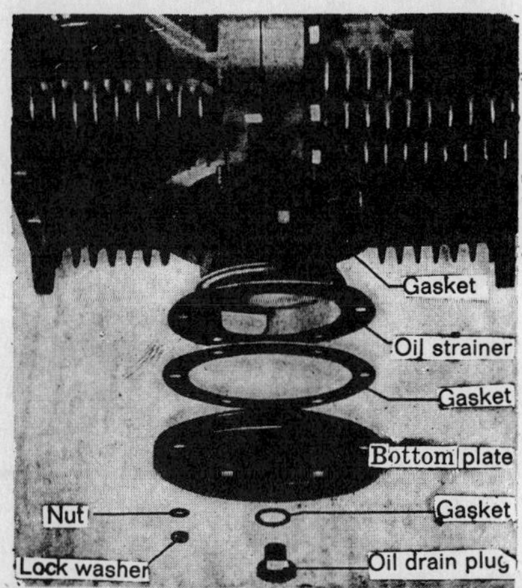

Oil strainer
(© Volkswagen)

Oil Strainer Removal

1. Remove retaining nuts from strainer bottom plate.
2. Remove the bottom plate.
3. Remove strainer and gaskets.

Installation

Install by reversing the removal procedure and noting the following precautions:

a. Make certain the suction pipe is correctly seated in the strainer.
b. Check that all of the sealing surfaces are straight and clean. NOTE: To avoid distorting the bottom plate, especially if using thicker gaskets, do not overtorque.
c. Always check the oil pressure relief valve when any discrepancies are found in oil circulation or pressure, or when the oil cooler is leaky. Should the plunger stick in closed position, there is a possibility of causing a leak in the cooler. Should the plunger stick in open position, oil will flow directly back to the sump.

Oil Cooler Removal

1. Remove fan housing.
2. Remove oil cooler retaining nuts.
3. Remove oil cooler and gaskets.

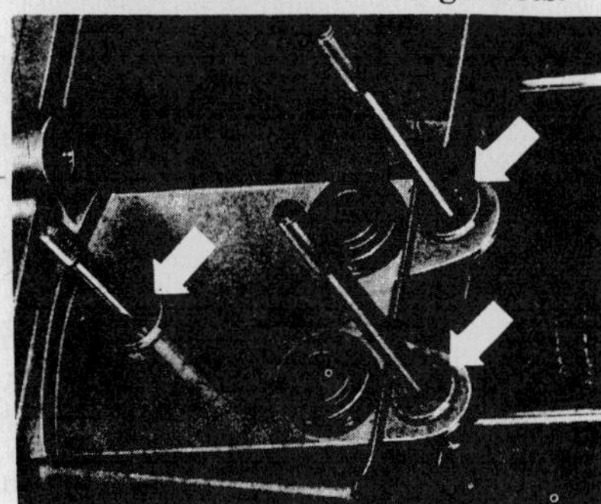

Arrows indicate spacer rings used to prevent oil cooler seals from being overly compressed and stopping the flow of oil
(© Volkswagen)

Installation

Install by reversing the removal procedure and noting the following precautions:

a. Check studs and bracket on cooler for tightness. Cooler should withstand 85 psi.
b. If cooler leaks, check oil pressure relief valve.
c. Ribs on oil cooler should not touch one another. The partition sheet should be tight.
d. Use new gaskets. NOTE: 1971 trucks have a new aluminum oil cooler with an intermediate flange and is mounted further forward. A separate cooling air supply is provided.

Oil Pump Removal

1. Remove nuts on oil pump cover, then remove cover and gasket.

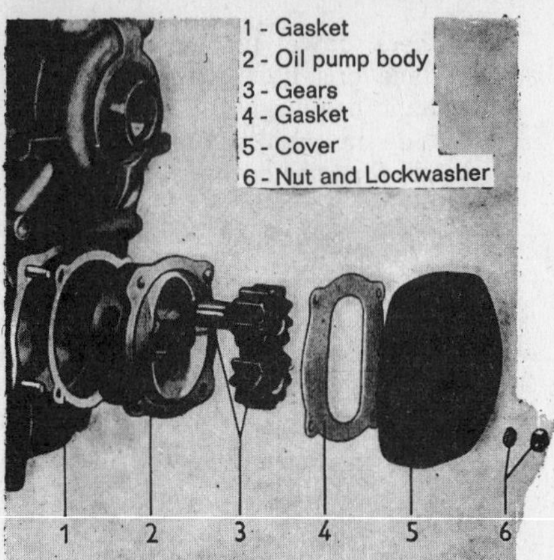

Oil pump
(© Volkswagen)

2. Remove gears.
3. Pull out the oil pump body with extractor.
4. Check all pump parts for wear. Excessive wear will cause low oil pressure. Gear backlash should be 0.0012-0.0032".
5. Check idler gear pin for tightness. If necessary, peen it securely in position, or replace the pump body.

Removing oil pump with special extractor
(© Volkswagen)

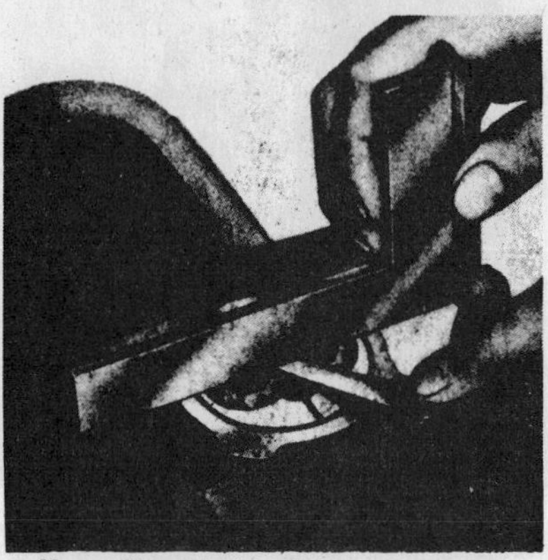

Measuring end-play of oil pump gears
(© Volkswagen)

Installation

1. Install pump body with new gasket.
2. Insert oil pump pilot shaft into body.
3. Turn camshaft 360°. This should

center the oil pump drive shaft position with the slot in the camshaft.

4. Remove oil pump pilot. Install gears.
5. Place a straight edge across pump body, then insert a fcclcr gauge between straight edge and gears. Clearance should not exceed 0.004″ with gasket removed.
6. Use new gasket without sealant, and install pump cover.

Front Axle, Suspension

VW trucks utilize a two tube axle beam with trailing arm torsion bar suspension and a stabilizer bar. Prior to 1966, king and link pins were used; since then, VW trucks come equipped with ball joints.

Torsion Bars

Upper and lower torsion bars consisting of six narrow and three wide leaves are contained in their respective axle beam tubes.

Removal

1. Remove wheels and both steering knuckles complete with brake drums and backing plates. Attach assemblies to axle with wire.
2. Remove shock absorber. Remove torsion arms on one side.
3. Disconnect front gearshift rod at coupling.
4. Loosen set screw lock nuts and remove screws.
5. Remove torsion bars.

Installation

1. Coat torsion bars with lithium grease.
2. Tape end of torsion bar leaves and insert, noting positions of countersinks for set screws.
3. Install remaining parts and lubricate torsion arm bearings with general purpose grease.

Link Pin Removal

1. Raise front end of truck.
2. Remove front wheels, drums, backing plate. Disconnect speed-

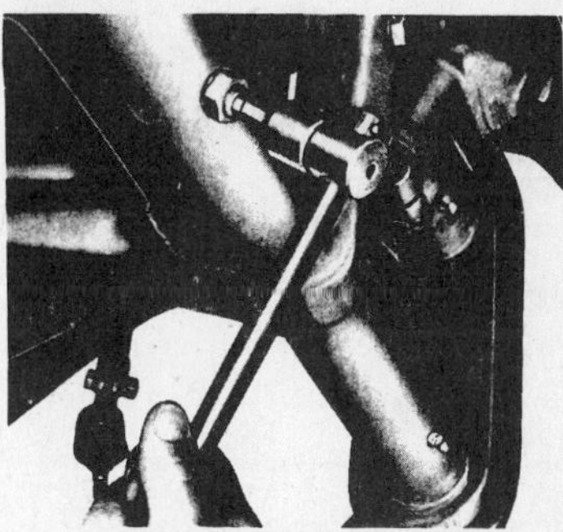

Loosening torsion bar set screws (© Volkswagen)

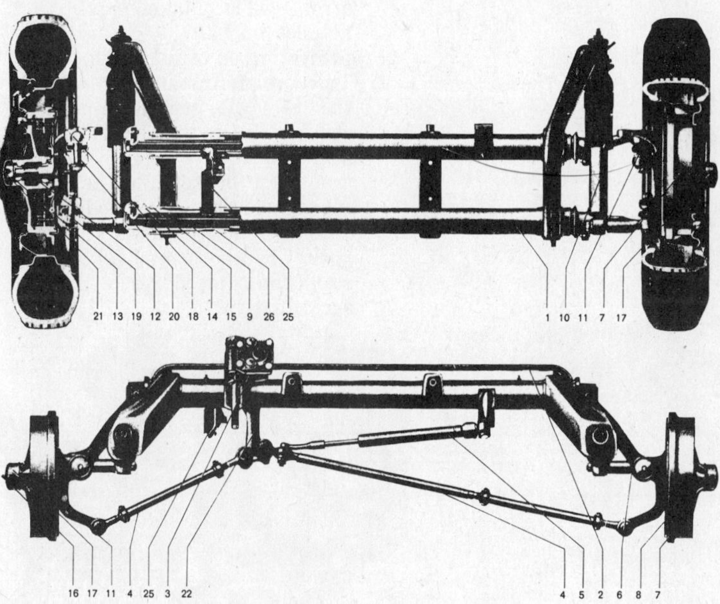

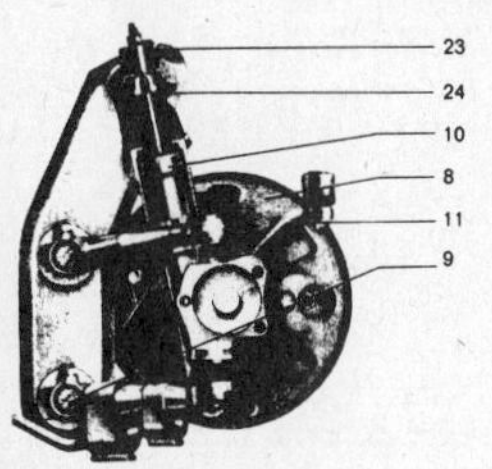

1 Suspension cross tube
2 Stabilizer bar
3 Steering gearbox
4 Tierods
5 Steering damper
6 Control arm
7 Brake drum
8 Brake back plate
9 Torsion bar
10 Shock absorber
11 Steering arm
12 Inner wheel bearing
13 Outer wheel bearing
14 Control arm seal
15 Control arm needle bearing
16 Speedometer drive cable
17 Inner hub cap
18 Upper ball joint
19 Lower ball joint
20 Eccentric bushing for camber adjustment
21 Clamp nut for wheel bearing adjustment
22 Pitman arm
23 Damper ring
24 Rubber stop
25 Steering lock limit stop
26 Plastic control arm bushing

Front axle and suspension assembly (© Volkswagen)

Late model front axle and suspension (© Volkswagen)

ometer cable and outer tie rod.
3. Remove torsion arm pinch bolts.
4. Remove torsion arm link and stub axle by driving out both link pins. Examine all parts carefully and replace as necessary.

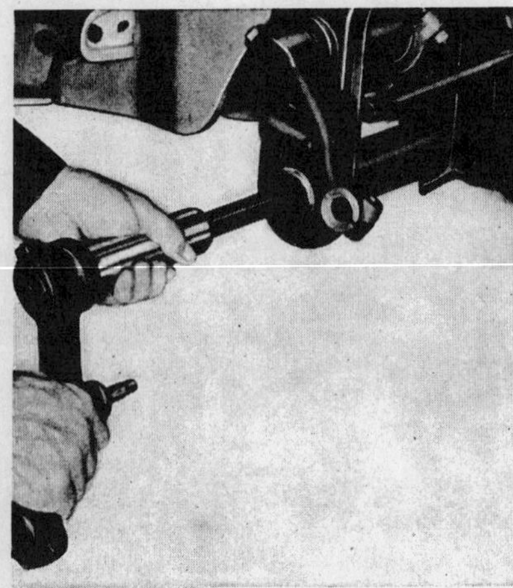

Removing torsion arm and bar
(© Volkswagen)

Installation

1. Measure offset of torsion arm eye faces. By using .5mm shims, set the offset to 7 mm. NOTE: There must always be 8 shims and one retainer with dust excluder fitted to one torsion arm link pin.
2. Install link pins and shims with universal grease.
3. Reassemble remaining parts.
4. Adjust torsion arm pins, front wheel bearings and front end alignment. Bleed and adjust brakes.

Ball Joint Removal

1. Remove wheel and brake drum. Disconnect stabilizer bar and speedometer cable.
2. Remove torsion arms.
3. Remove hexagon nuts and press out ball joints.
4. Check ball joint free play (0.3mm-2mm) and dust seals.

1 Torsion arm link pin
2 Shims
3 Torsion arm link
4 Dust-excluder
5 Retainer for dust excluder

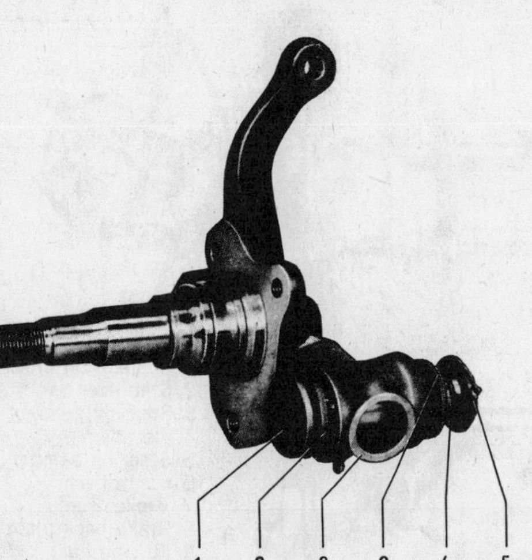

Steering knuckle with link pin assembly
(© Volkswagen)

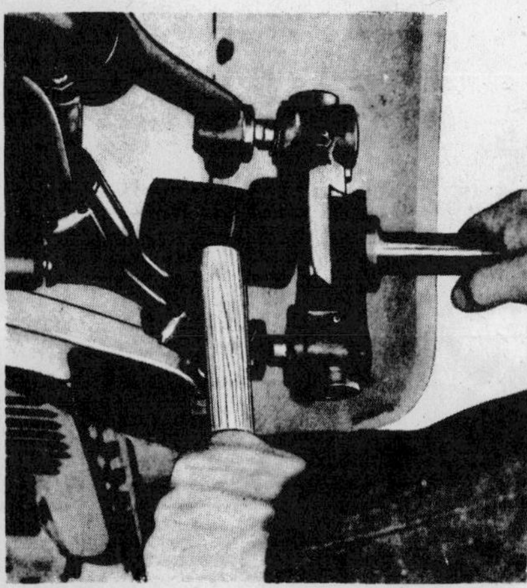

Removing stub axle and link pins
(© Volkswagen)

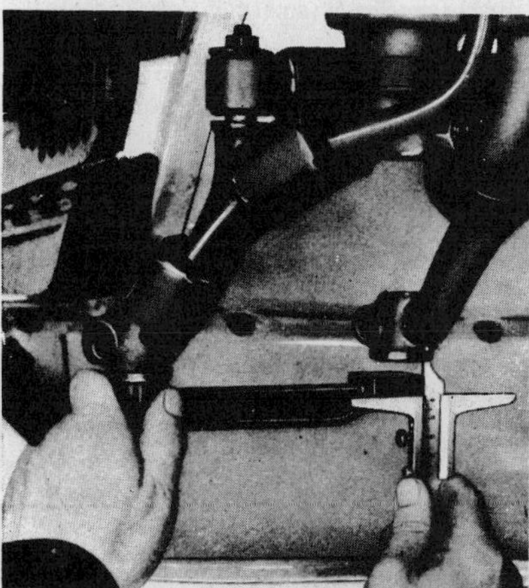

Measuring torsion arm offset
(© Volkswagen)

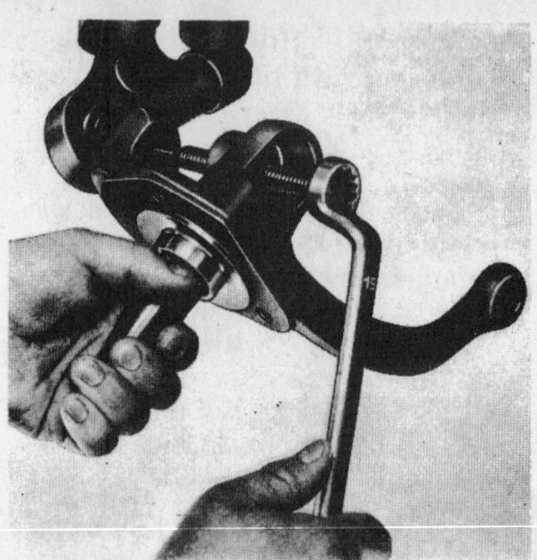

Pressing out ball joints
(© Volkswagen)

Installation

NOTE: Ball joints are available standard size (2 grooves 180° apart) and oversize (2 notches 45° from grooves). Oversize torsion arms are also available ("B" stamped on arm).

1. Press new ball joint into torsion arm. NOTE: Make certain that notches on ball joint align with projection on torsion arm.
2. To complete installation, reverse the removal procedures, check camber and toe-in. NOTE: 1971 VW trucks are equipped with front disc brakes and the steering knuckle has been modified to accommodate the discs and calipers. The above removal and installation procedures will vary accordingly.

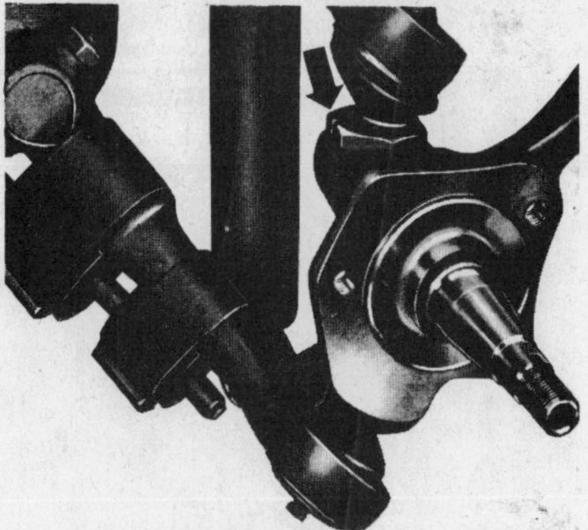

Make certain notch in eccentric bush is pointing forward
(© Volkswagen)

Stabilizer

1. Remove clamp retaining clip.
2. Bend up clamps and remove plates.
3. Remove nut from securing bolt on lower torsion arm.
4. Remove stabilizer, check for damaged parts and replace as necessary.

Installation

To install stabilizer, reverse the removal procedure and torque securing bolt on lower torsion arm to specifications.

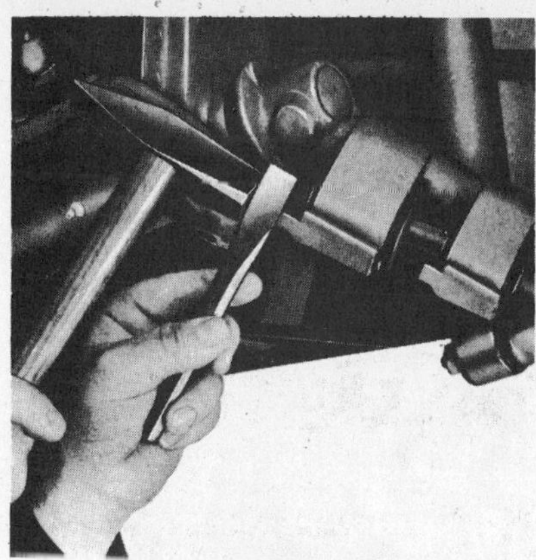
Removing stabilizer bar
(© Volkswagen)

Refer to Wheel Alignment Specifications Table.

Steering Linkage

On VW trucks, the drop arm transmits steering wheel movements through the steering gear, an adjustable draglink, then through a swing lever and 2 tie rods. One tie rod is adjustable and the other has a fixed length. A hydraulic steering damper is connected to the axle beam and the swing lever.

Installing stabilizer bar
(© Volkswagen)

Tie Rod Removal

1. Disconnect steering damper from swing lever.
2. Remove cotter pins and nuts from tie rod ends.
3. Press out tie rod ends.

CAUTION: Do not damage rubber seals on tie rod ends. Bent tie rods must be replaced, not straightened.

Installation

1. Install adjustable tie rod on the right side with right-hand thread at steering knuckle end. Install other tie rod.
2. Install end nuts and torque to specifications. Install cotter pins.
3. Turn both adjustment nuts on adjustable tie rod to stop in either directoin. Tighten nuts on clamp bolts.

Pressing tie rod ends out with special tool
(© Volkswagen)

4. Connect steering damper.
5. Adjust toe-in.

Swing Lever and Shaft Removal

1. Remove cover plate.
2. Remove cotter pins and nuts from inner tie rod ends and press drag link out of swing lever.
3. Disconnect steering damper from swing lever.
4. Put tension on lever with a clamp, release lockplate and remove bolt.

Using clamp to remove swing lever
(© Volkswagen)

5. Remove clamp and swing lever.
6. Pry off end cap for swing lever shaft and pull shaft out.

Installation

Install swing lever and shaft by reversing the removal procedure.

Steering Damper Replacement

Remove the steering damper by releasing the lock plate and removing the bolt at the axle beam bracket. Then disconnect damper at swing lever.

Reverse procedure to install.

Steering Gear

VW trucks are equipped with a worm and peg type steering gear. Steering gear and column are two separate parts joined by a rubber-/fabric disc coupling. The gear housing is mounted at the side member of the frame.

Steering wheel movements are transmitted via the column and coupling to the worm spindle, which runs in ball bearings. The peg is mounted in taper rollers on an arm on the sector shaft and contacts the flanks of the sector shaft arm.

Steering Gear Removal

1. Remove turn signal switch.
2. Remove cover plate under foot pedals.
3. Press drag link off drop arm.
4. Press drop arm off shaft.
5. Loosen steering coupling flange securing bolt.

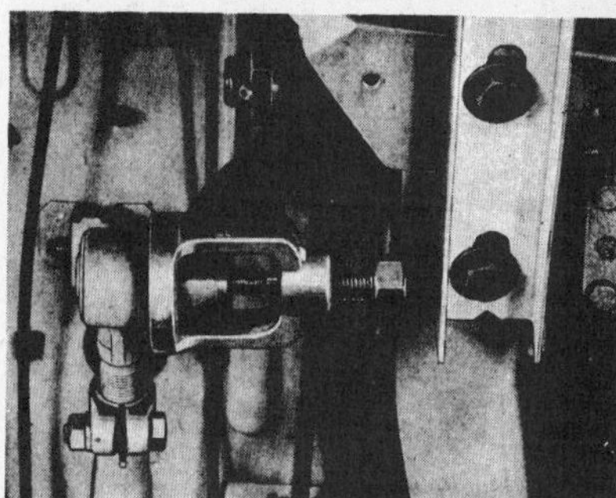
Pressing drag link off drop arm
(© Volkswagen)

6. Remove gear housing mounting bolts.
7. Push steering column and coupling upward and remove steering gear.

Loosening steering coupling securing bolt
(© Volkswagen)

Installation

To install the steering gear, reverse the removal procedure, but first note the following:

a. Press drop arm onto shaft. *Do not drive it on.*

Arrow indicates steering gear housing mounting bolts late models
(© Volkswagen)

b. Make certain that alignment marks on drop arm and shaft coincide.
c. Set steering wheel in straight ahead position before connecting coupling. The tongue of the turn signal cancelling ring must point to the left.

Drop arm alignment mark
(© Volkswagen)

Adjustment

In general, steering gear adjustments should be performed by an authorized VW dealer. However, steering "tightness" should be 8-10 cmkg. through the steering wheel center position. This can be adjusted by turning the steering wheel while an assistant turns the adjusting screw In (stiff) and then Out (loose) to the specified "tightness."

Clutch

Pedal movement is transmitted through a cable to the release mechanism. As pressure is applied to the pedal, the release levers are moved inward by the release bearing. The pressure plate is moved away from the driven plate, disengaging the clutch.

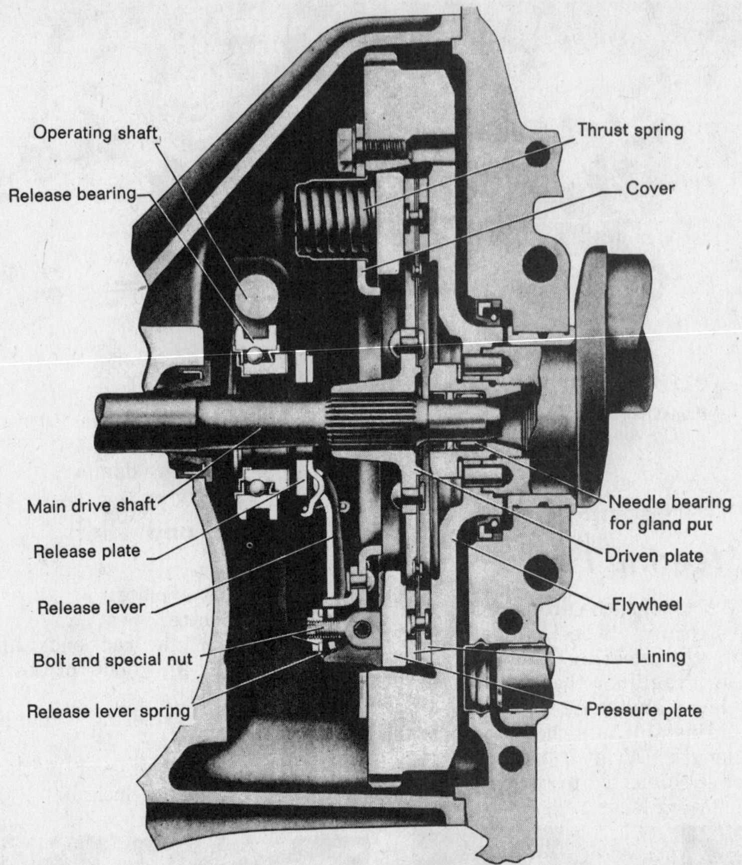

Cross-section of clutch assembly
(© Volkswagen)

Adjustment

Adjustment is limited to clutch pedal free-play. An adjustment of the pressure plate is only necessary when the clutch is disassembled for parts replacement. The clutch release bearing is a carbon thrust ring or ball type bearing and requires no maintenance.

Measured at the clutch pedal, the free play should be 0.4-0.8". Clearance may be set at the adjusting nut on the cable end.

1. Release locknut on the threaded cable end.
2. Adjust clutch clearance by turning the adjusting nut until proper pedal clearance is obtained.
3. Secure the adjustment with the locknut.

NOTE: Late models have a self locking wing nut for adjustment.

Clutch Removal

1. Remove engine.
2. Remove clutch to flywheel attaching bolts by gradually, and alternately, backing the bolts out of the flywheel.
3. Take off clutch cover.
4. Lift out clutch-driven (lined) plate.

Installation

Upon installation, reverse above

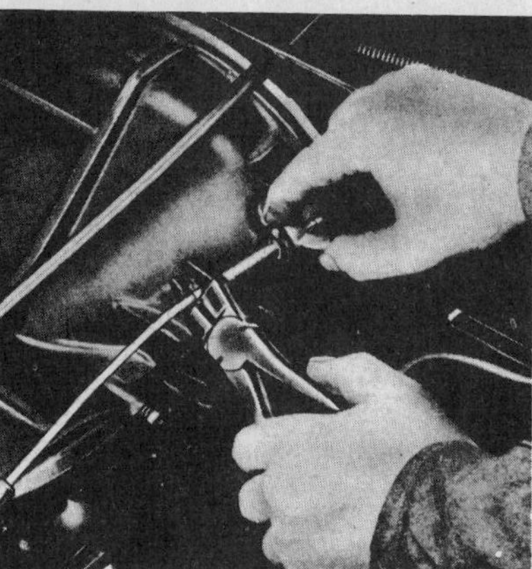

Adjusting clutch pedal free-play
(© Volkswagen)

procedure, and observe the following:

a. Inspect and resurface pressure plate if worn in excess of 0.008". The friction surface should be polished.
b. Inspect driven plate and replace it if any doubt of reliability exists.
c. Examine release levers and springs.
d. Inspect release plate for damage or heat discoloration.
e. Check release bearing or carbon thrust ring. Replace com-

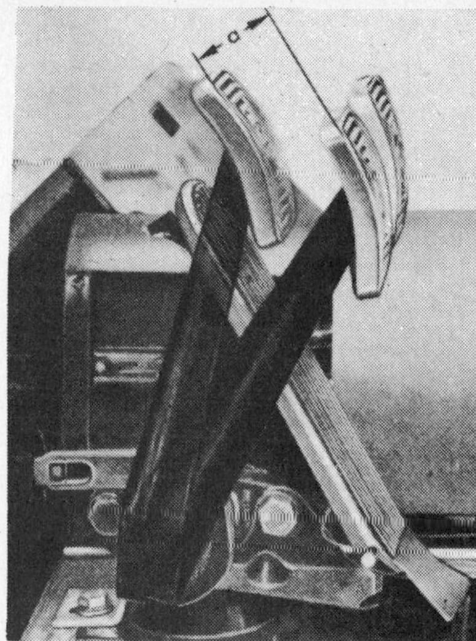

Pedal free-play (a) should be 10-20 mm. (.4-.8")
(© Volkswagen)

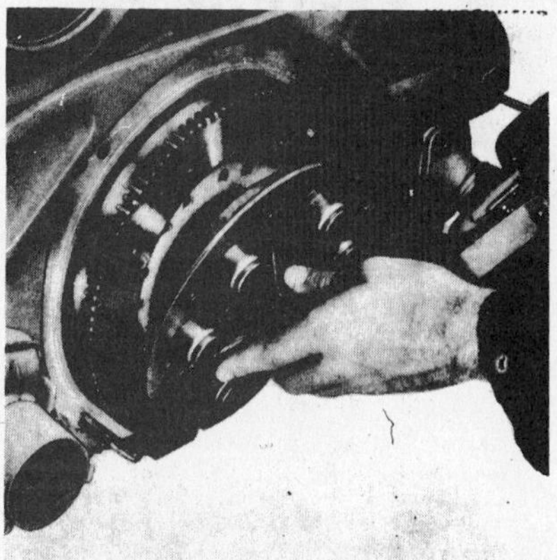

Removing clutch pressure plate
(© Volkswagen)

Remove pressure plate bolts by slowly and alternately loosening bolts to prevent plate distortion
(© Volkswagen)

plete release bearing, if necessary.

f. Inspect bearing points of clutch operating shaft in transmission case for wear.

NOTE: A ball-type release bearing of different construction is available. Because of greater durability, it should be used as a replacement part instead of the carbon type.

g. Lubricate needle bearing in flywheel gland nut with about 10gr. of universal grease.

h. Reinstall driven (lined) plate, using a pilot mandrel to insure correct centering alignment.

i. Evenly, and alternately, tighten clutch-to-flywheel attaching bolts.

j. Check proper distance and parallelism between clutch cover contact face at flywheel and the clutch release plate. Use a clutch adjustment gauge.

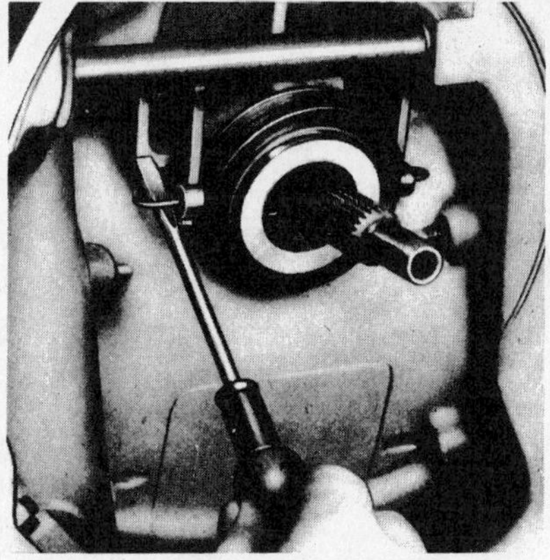

Removing release bearing retaining clips
(© Volkswagen)

Clutch Cable Removal

1. Remove left rear wheel.
2. Disconnect cable from operating lever on transmission.
3. Pull rubber boot off guide tube and cable.
4. Remove cover plate.
5. Disconnect master cylinder piston pushrod and unbolt pedal assembly (except 1971 models).
6. Disconnect cable from pedal cluster.
7. Pull cable forward through hole uncovered when pedal cluster was removed.

Installation

Install in reverse of the above. Lubricate thoroughly with chassis lubricant. Insert enough washers between case bracket and cable guide to cause guide to sag slightly at transmission.

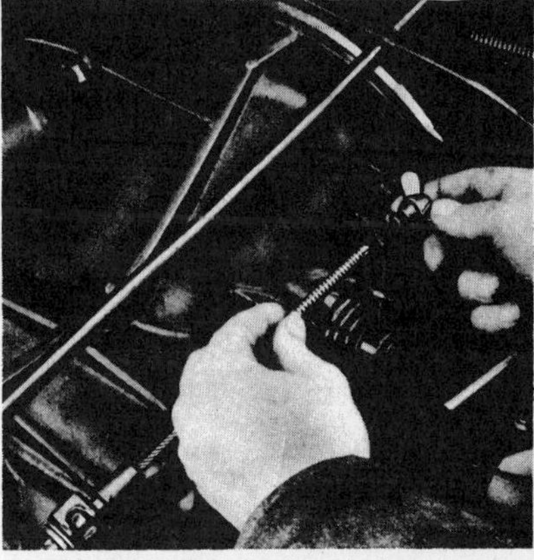

Disconnecting clutch cable from operating lever
(© Volkswagen)

Transmission, Rear Axle

The wheels were driven from the transmission via swing axles and reduction gearboxes until 1968 when double-jointed axles were incorporated, eliminating the need for the reduction units.

Transaxle Removal

1. Remove engine.
2. Remove rear wheels (swing axle type).
3. Disconnect brake lines at rear wheels, plug the lines.
4. Disconnect parking brake cables from push bar at the frame and withdraw cables from conduit tubes.
5. Remove bolts at rear axle shaft bearing (swing axle type).
6. On models with double-jointed rear axles, disconnect inner

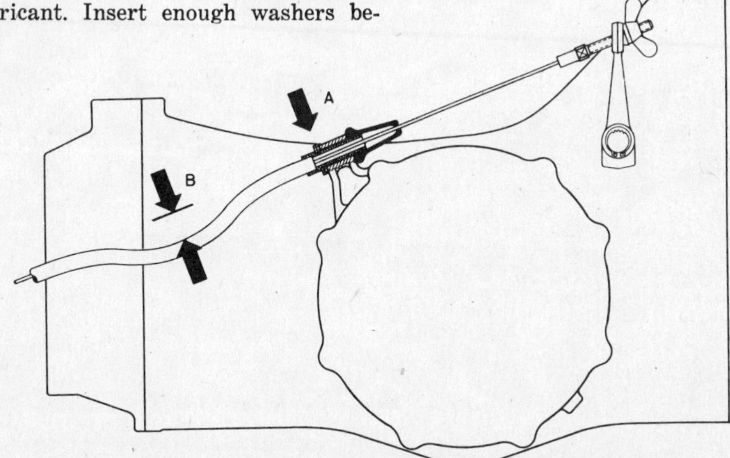

Smooth clutch action requires a slight sag in the cable. (B) should be 20-30 mm. Shorten tube or add washers at (A) to achieve proper dimension.
(© Volkswagen)

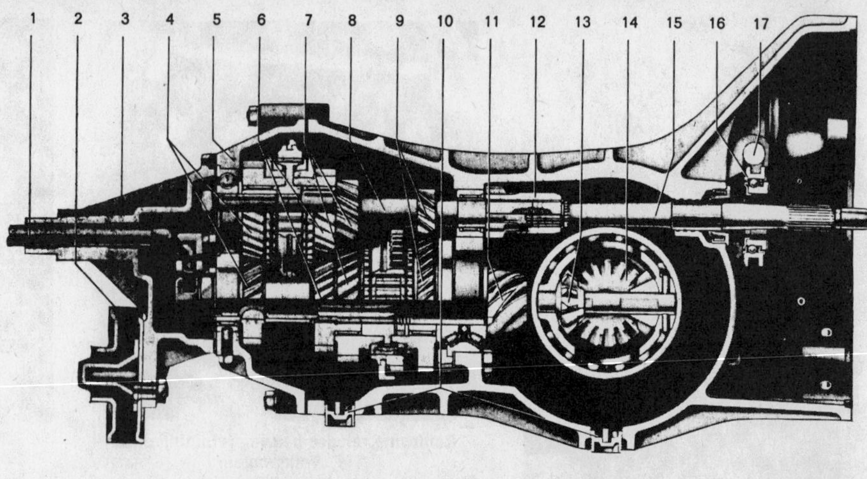

1 Transmission shift lever
2 Bonded rubber mounting
3 Gearshift housing
4 4th speed
5 Gear carrier
6 3rd speed
7 2nd speed
8 Main drive shaft, front
9 1st speed
10 Oil drain plugs
11 Drive pinion
12 Reverse gear
13 Differential pinion
14 Differential side gear
15 Main drive shaft, rear
16 Clutch release bearing
17 Clutch operating shaft
18 Reverse sliding gear
19 Reverse shaft
20 Oil filler plug
21 Reverse drive gear
22 Ring gear
23 Rear axle shaft
24 Fulcrum plate
25 Differential housing

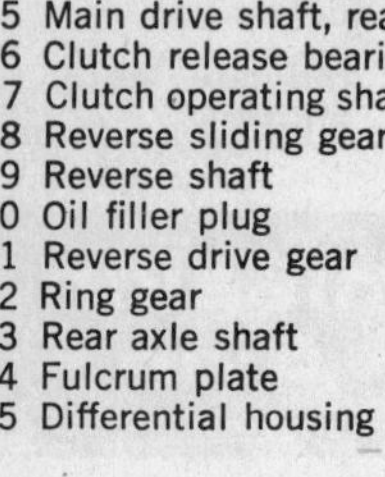

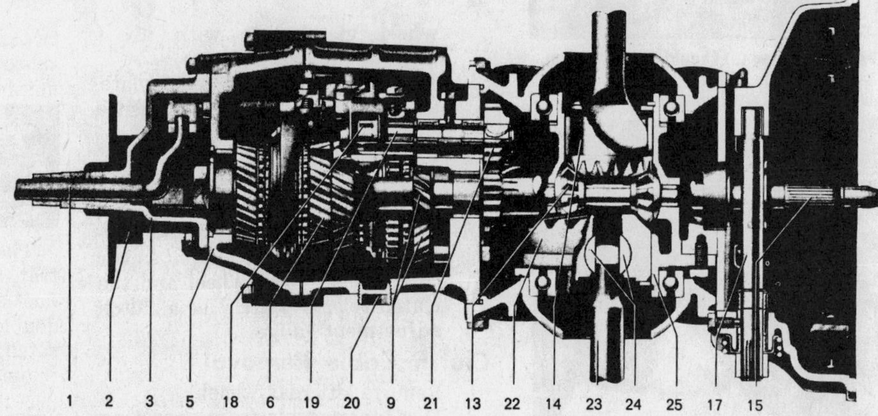

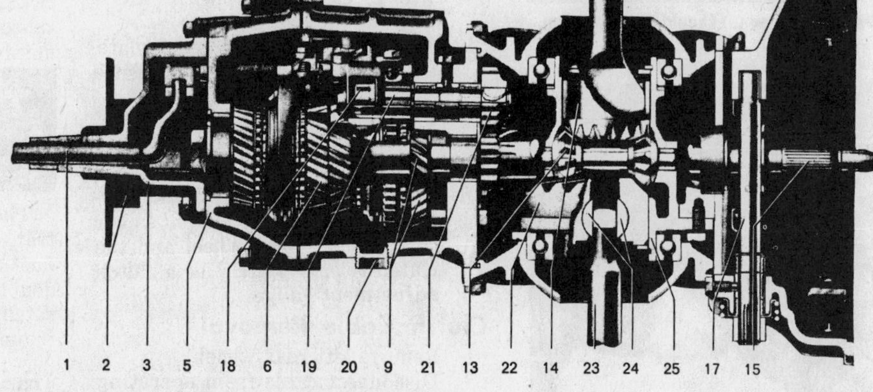

Cross-section of transaxle (© Volkswagen)

Double-jointed rear axles are used beginning 1968 (© Volkswagen)

joints and wire shafts to the frame. Disconnect outer joints if the truck must be moved after transmission assembly removal.

7. Disconnect clutch release cable from operating shaft lever and pull it from the guide plate.
8. Disconnect wires from the starter motor.
9. Disconnect shift rod in back of the coupling.
10. Remove nuts from mounting studs at front of transmission.
11. Remove lower shock absorber mounting bolts. Mark positions of rear torsion bar radius arms with relation to rear axle bearing housings.
12. Disconnect ground strap. Remove nuts from compensator spring (when used).
13. Support unit with jack. Remove two attaching bolts.
14. Withdraw transaxle to the rear. Be careful not to damage the main driveshaft.

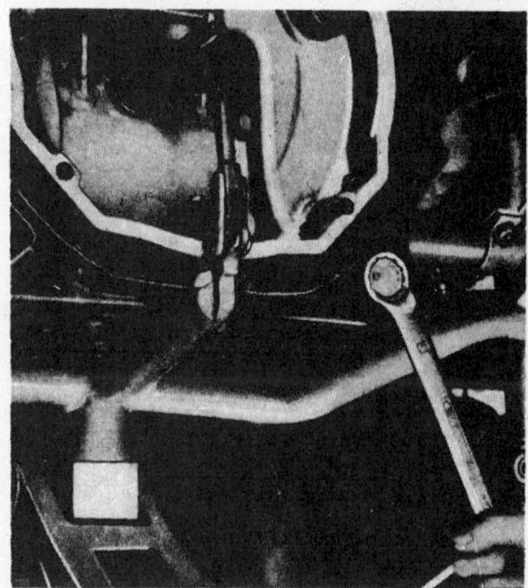

Removing transmission carrier bolts
(© Volkswagen)

Installation

To install the transmission assembly, reverse the removal procedure, torque all mounting bolts to specifications, adjust clutch, then bleed and adjust brakes.

Shift Linkage

The shift linkage on VW trucks is comprised of the gearshift assembly and a straight shift rod with two couplings. The only adjustment possible is a slight movement of the gearshift assembly stop plate in cases where the shift lever "pops" out of gear.

The gearshift lever can be removed after the front floor mat has been lifted and the screws removed that attach the gearshift lever ball housing to the central frame. After the two retaining screws have been removed, the gearshift lever, ball housing, rubber boot, and spring are removed as a unit. The spring will have to be turned in order to clear the pin.

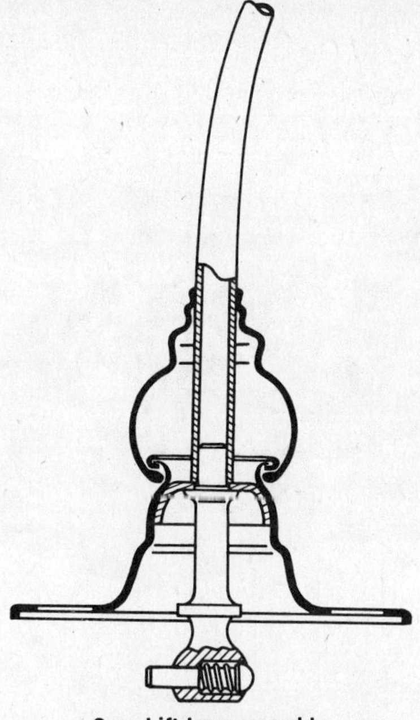

Gearshift lever assembly
(© Volkswagen)

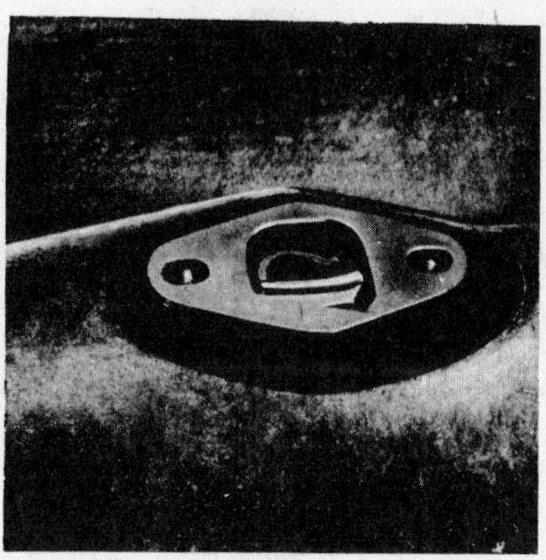

Installing gearshift lever stop plate
(© Volkswagen)

Remove the stop plate, clean all components and check for wear.

Installation of the gearshift lever is the reverse of the preceding. Replace any worn parts. Make certain that the locating pin is a firm fit, but not overly tight. The spring in the steel ball should be checked for tension and replaced if necessary. When installing the stop plate, make certain that the turned-up ramp is on the right-hand side. Lubricate all parts generously with universal grease. After installation is completed, operate the various gears in order to check ease of movement.

Axle Boot Replacement

The original rear axle boot (dust sleeves) are of a one-piece design and must be cut open in order to be removed for replacement. A split-type axle boot is available for replacement which can be installed and then tightened down. To remove the axle boot, take off the retaining clip at each end, and cut off the damaged boot.

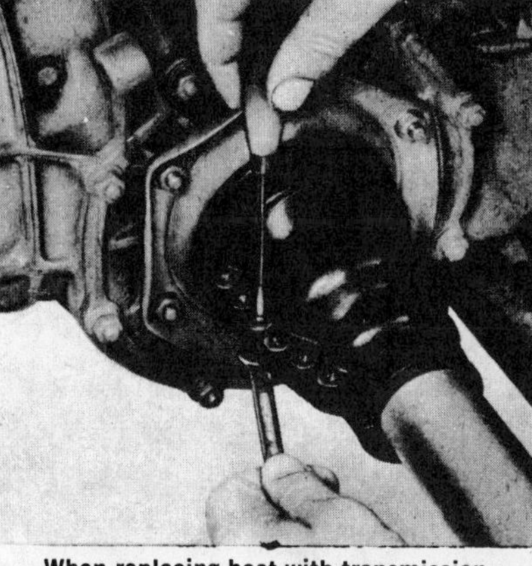

When replacing boot with transmission installed, insert screws from the bottom and hold nuts on the top
(© Volkswagen)

Clean thoroughly both the axle tube and the axle tube retainer so that the new boot will fit securely.

Upon installation, put a light coating of sealing compound on the joining faces of the boot and ensure that the smaller diameter of the boot is equal to 89 mm. When positioning the new boot, keep the joining faces in a horizontal plane and toward the rear of the axle. Tighten the joining screws and the retaining clips (do not overtighten) only after the rear axle is in a loaded condition, and be sure that the boot is not twisted.

Double-jointed rear axles are equipped with one-piece boots at either end of each shaft. Replacement requires dissassembly of couplings.

Reconditioning Transaxle

Disassembly

1. Remove gear selector housing.
2. Pry off lock plates which secure drive pinion and driveshaft nuts.
3. Lock transmission by engaging both reverse and high gears.
4. Remove drive pinion and main driveshaft nuts. Then remove and discard lock plates.
5. Remove gear carrier stud nuts.
6. Position the assembly so that the left-hand final drive cover faces up.
7. Remove stud nuts from left-hand final drive cover, then remove the cover.
8. Attach tool VW 297 to the right-hand final drive cover studs, then press out the differential. NOTE: When removing the differential, make note of the thicknesses and positioning of the differential shims to simplify reassembly.
9. Loosen retaining ring that secures reverse gear on the main driveshaft. Then, slide reverse gear toward the rear and screw main driveshaft apart.
10. Remove reverse gear and retaining ring and withdraw the rear

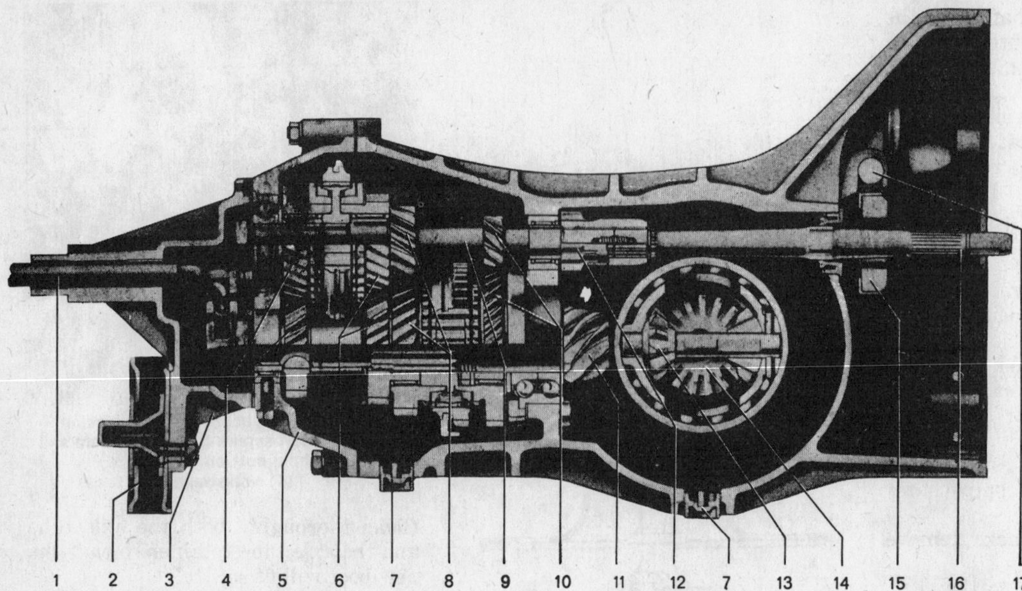

Cross-section of VW transaxle (© Volkswagen)

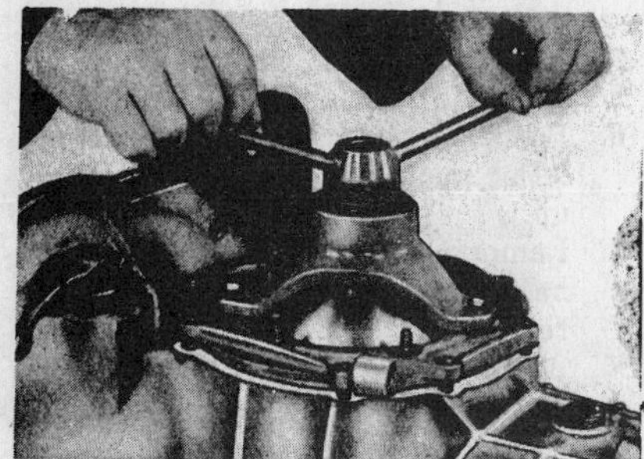

Pressing out differential with VW tool 297 (© Volkswagen)

main shaft toward the rear. CAUTION: Don't damage the oil seal.

11. Remove tool VW 297 and right-hand final drive cover.
12. Release lock tabs and remove attaching screws, then remove drive pinion ball bearing retainer.

Removing transmission from case (tool VW 296) (© Volkswagen)

13. Press transmission out of case with tool VW 296 or suitable alternate. Note thickness of pinion shims to simplify reassembly.
14. Spread and remove snap-ring, then pull off reverse drive gear.
15. Remove Woodruff key and withdraw reverse gear shaft and thrust washer from transmission case.
16. Remove security screw from reverse gear shaft needle bearing spacer sleeve.
17. With a suitable drift, drive out the reverse gear shaft needle bearings and spacer sleeve.
18. Remove security screw from the needle bearing of the main driveshaft.
19. With a suitable drift, drive out the main driveshaft needle bearing.
20. Press out ball bearings from both final drive covers.
21. Remove clutch release bearing and operating shaft.

Assembly

NOTE: clean and inspect the case and all components for wear, damage or any indication of malfunction, and replace as necessary. The starting motor armature, brushes and bushings should be inspected and dealt with, accordingly. Check clutch operating shaft and bushings for wear, replace if necessary.

1. Press ball bearings into both, final drive covers.
2. Insert needle bearings for reverse gear shaft and spacer sleeve, then secure.
3. Install main driveshaft needle bearing with a suitable drift, then secure.
4. Install reverse shaft, Woodruff key thrust washer and gear, then secure with snap-ring.
5. Locate drive pinion shims over bearing, then turn two 4″ guide studs into bearing retainer to assure retainer and shim alignment during transmission-to-case assembly.
6. Push reverse selector and sliding gear onto reverse lever and engage reverse gear.
7. With a new carrier gasket in place, carefully insert the transmission into the case (the 4″ guide screws will help at this time).

Tightening bearing retaining bolts to 36 ft. lbs.
(© Volkswagen)

8. Remove guide screws, then install transmission-to-case attaching screws and lock plates. Torque to 36 ft. lbs.
9. Lubricate lip of oil seal, then install rear half of main driveshaft. Screw both halves of the driveshaft together. Back them off until the splines of the reverse gear are in line, then install reverse gear snap-ring.
10. With new gasket in place, install right-hand, final drive cover. Torque to 18 ft. lbs.
11. With shims properly inserted, install differential in case.
12. Now, install gear carrier nuts and torque to 14 ft. lbs.
13. Lock transmission by engaging both reverse and high gears at the same time.

Tightening main driveshaft and pinion nuts
(© Volkswagen)

14. Torque the main driveshaft nut to 87 ft. lbs. Loosen the nut, then retighten to a final 43 ft. lbs. torque. Secure with lock plate.
15. Torque the drive pinion nut to 43 ft. lbs. and secure with lock plate.

CAUTION: When installing gearshift housing, make sure that the three selector shafts are in neutral.

Gear Carrier Disassembly

1. Remove reverse selector fork, including reverse sliding gear, from reverse lever.
2. Remove and note thickness of drive pinion ball bearing shims.
3. Clamp gear carrier in vise equipped with soft jaws.

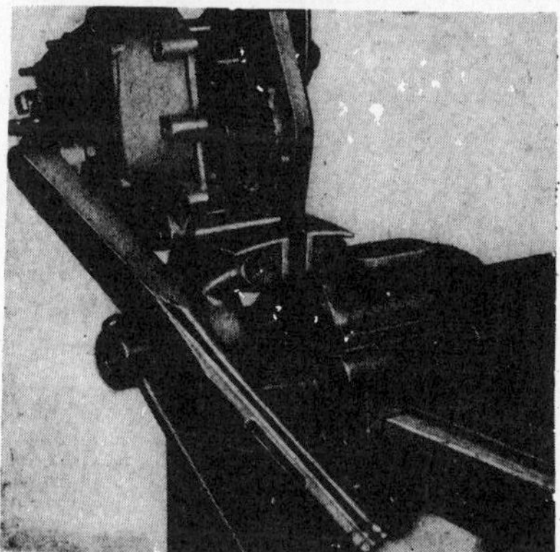

Gear carrier mounted on vise
(© Volkswagen)

4. Loosen shifting fork lock screws, then remove first-second shifting fork.
5. Withdraw the shifting fork shaft from third-fourth shifting fork.
6. For security, place a strong rubber band around first-second operating sleeve and main shaft.
7. Mount the assembly in a press, case end up, and press on the main shaft, to remove transmission from gear carrier.
8. Remove screw which holds drive pinion needle bearing, then press out bearing.
9. Press out main driveshaft bearing.
10. Clamp gear carrier in vise with soft jaws, then remove reverse lever guide screw.
11. Withdraw reverse gear selector shaft and remove reverse lever guide.
12. Withdraw first-second selector shaft and remove reverse lever from support.
13. Withdraw third-fourth selector shaft.
14. Remove plungers and detent balls. Then, hook out detent springs with a small screwdriver.

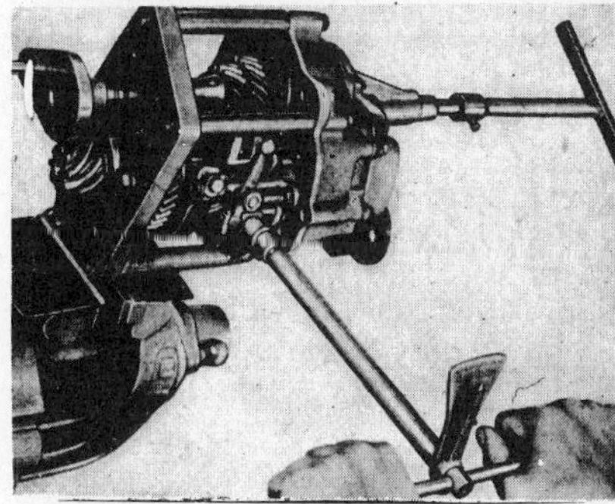

Gearshift housing mounted on vise
(© Volkswagen)

Gear Carrier Assembly

NOTE: Check all components for damage and wear. Replace parts, if necessary. Free length of detent springs should be 1.0″. The wear, or fatigue, limit is 0.9″. A force of 33-44 ft. lbs. applied to the ends of the selector shafts should be required to unseat the detent balls when shifting.

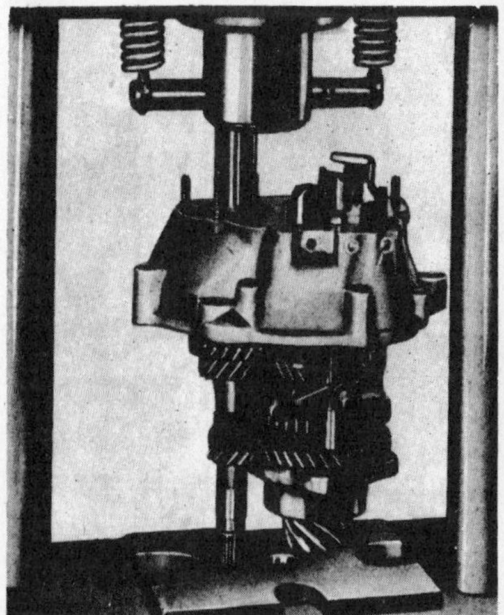

Pressing gear assembly out of gear carrier. Note location of heavy rubber band.
(© Volkswagen)

1. Insert detent springs through the selector shaft holes. NOTE: due to design, the springs for first-second and reverse gear detents can be more easily installed by inserting them into the top halves first.
2. Install reverse selector shaft including reverse lever and reverse lever guide.
3. Install selector shafts for first-second and for third-fourth

gears. Don't forget the two interlocking plungers. This is a safety feature guarding against shifting into two gears at one time.

4. Check drive needle bearing, and main driveshaft ball bearing for condition. Replace, if necessary. Secure drive pinion needle bearing in the gear carrier.
5. Position gear carrier on a suitable support and press main driveshaft ball bearing into position.
6. Check selector forks for wear. Fork-to-operating sleeve clearance should be 0.004-0.012". Clearance greater than this warrants parts replacement.
7. Position the selector fork for third-fourth gears. Then, press transmission into the gear carrier. While pressing, take care that the third-fourth selector fork does not become jammed. Also with a heavy rubber band, secure first-second gears to the main driveshaft.
8. Install first-second selector fork.
9. Attach reverse gear fork with reverse sliding gear onto selector lever.
10. Adjust gear selector forks.

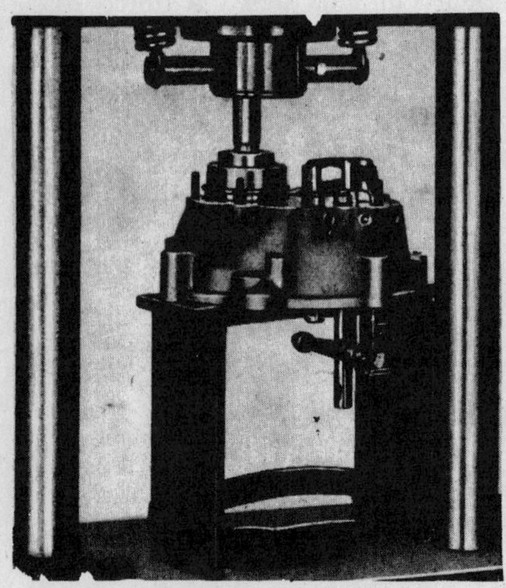

Pressing main driveshaft ball bearing into position in gear carrier (© Volkswagen)

Selector Fork Adjustment

NOTE: At this point, special tools are required to make the adjustments.

1. Place transmission, drive pinion shims and gasket for gear carrier on test tool VW 294 and secure gear carrier with four screws.
2. Tighten drive-pinion bearing-retainer, with two screws located diagonally, to 36 ft. lbs. torque.
3. Push crank of the test tool onto splines of main driveshaft so that the main shaft is locked by the crank. Engage first and second gears.
4. With a torque wrench, tighten the main driveshaft nut to 87 ft. lbs. Then, loosen the nut and retighten to 43 ft. lbs. and lock it.
5. Tighten drive pinion nut to 43 ft. lbs. and lock it.
6. Attach gearshift housing and shifting handle. By attaching the gearshift housing, correct seating of the main drive shaft bearing in its recess in the gear carrier is guaranteed.
7. Position first-second and third-fourth selector forks so that they move freely in the operating sleeve while in neutral, and when various gears are engaged.
8. Position reverse gear selector fork so that reverse sliding gear is centered between the operating sleeve and second gear of the main driveshaft with second gear engaged. The fork must also engage properly in reverse gear of the drive pinion when reverse gear is engaged.
9. Using a T-handle, torque wrench and socket, tighten the selector fork locking screws to 18 ft. lbs. Tighten the reverse lever guide screw to 14 ft. lbs. torque.
10. Remove gearshift housing and transmission from tool VW 294.

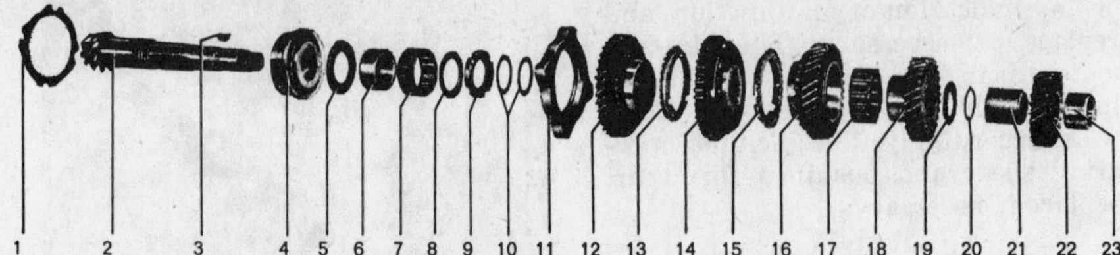

Exploded view, drive pinion and components (© Volkswagen)

1 Shim
2 Drive pinion
3 Woodruff key for 4th gear
4 Roller bearing
5 Thrust washer for 1st gear
6 Needle bearing inner race (1st gear)
7 Needle cage (1st gear)
8 Thrust washer for needle bearing (1st gear)
9 Round nut
10 Shims, end play 1st gear
11 Roller bearing retainer
12 1st gear
13 Synchronizer stop ring (1st gear)
14 Clutch gear 1st and 2nd gears, and reverse gear
15 Synchronizer stop ring (2nd gear)
16 2nd gear
17 Needle cage (2nd gear)
18 3rd gear
19 Concave washer
20 Shims for concave washer
21 Spacer sleeve
22 4th gear
23 Inner race, needle bearing in gear carrier

Drive Pinion Reconditioning

Disassembly

1. Press out inner race of needle bearing and fourth gear, then remove Woodruff key from the shaft.
2. Remove spacer sleeve, concave washer shims and the concave washer.
3. Remove second and third gears with needle cage and second gear synchronizer stop ring.
4. Remove clutch gear for first and second gears, including springs, shifting plates and operating sleeve. Disassemble parts.

Inspection

1. Inspect all components for wear or other damage; replace as necessary. If pinion and ring gear require replacement, a matched set is in order (note matching number on both gears).
2. If drive pinion or ball bearing is replaced, the drive pinion and ring gear must be adjusted.
3. Whenever a damaged gear is replaced, the mating gear should also be replaced. Worn or otherwise damaged first and second speed gears require a replacement of the front main driveshaft.
4. Clean and check all synchronizer components for wear. Clearance between the synchronizer stop ring face and the clutch teeth of the corresponding gear should be about 0.043". If the wear limit of 0.024" has been reached, the stop ring should be replaced.
5. If a gear will not engage, even though the clutch is fully released, the probable cause is wear in the slots of the stop ring. Replace worn parts.

Assembly

1. In preparation, the inner races of the ball bearing and the needle bearing inner race for first gear should be heated in an oil bath to about 194°F.
2. Slide one inner ball bearing race onto the drive pinion.
3. Slide the ball bearing onto the drive pinion. Then, slide the second inner race on so that the bearing parts numbers are exactly opposite each other.

4. Slide first gear thrust washer and needle bearing inner race onto the drive pinion.
5. With components mounted in a press, push all parts into correct position.
6. Tighten round nut to 90 ft. lbs. torque.
7. Install shims for first gear. After the clutch gear for first and second gears has been installed, end-play of 0.004-0.010″ should be checked between thrust washer and first gear. Correct, if necessary. Shims of various thicknesses are available.
8. Position first gear stop ring on the cone surface of the gear. (First and second synchronizer stop rings are not interchangeable.)
9. Assemble the synchronizer unit for first and second gears. Slide operating sleeve on the clutch gear so that its shifting plate slots are in line with the slots in the clutch gear. With the shifting plates in position, install the two snap-rings, offset to each other.
10. Slide the synchronizer assembly onto the drive pinion. The longer hub should be toward the face of the drive pinion splines. Turn first gear stop ring until shifting plates engage with the slots.
11. Adjust the concave washer to produce the prescribed spring travel of 0.007 ± 0.0004″.
12. The fourth speed gear and needle bearing inner race should be heated in an oil bath of 194°F. before being pressed into position.
13. Insert Woodruff key for fourth gear into drive pinion.
14. Slide fourth gear onto the drive pinion, wide shoulder facing the spacer sleeve.
15. Press fourth speed gear and needle bearing inner race fully into position.

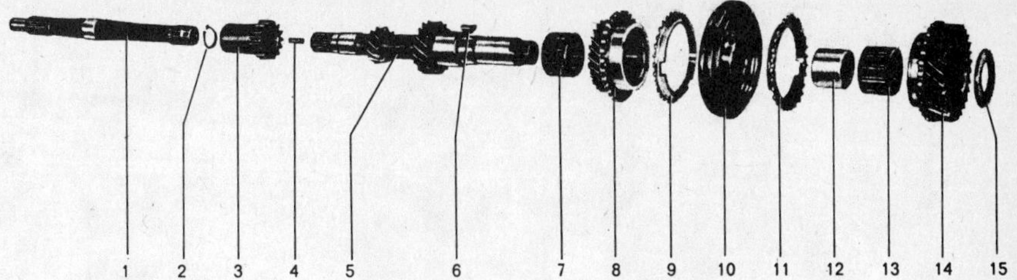

Exploded view, main driveshaft, and components (© Volkswagen)

1 Main drive shaft rear half
2 Circlip for reverse gear
3 Reverse gear on drive shaft
4 Stud
5 Main drive shaft front half
6 Woodruff key for clutch gear
7 Needle cage (3rd gear)
8 3rd gear
9 Synchronizer stop ring (3rd gear)
10 Clutch gear (3rd and 4th speeds)
11 Synchronizer stop ring (4th gear)
12 Needle bearing inner race (4th gear)
13 Needle cage (4th gear)
14 4th gear
15 Thrust washer (4th gear)

Main Driveshaft Reconditioning

Disassembly

1. Remove thrust washer, fourth gear, needle bearing cage and stop ring.
2. Remove fourth speed needle bearing inner race, clutch gear for third and fourth speed and third gear.
3. Remove needle bearing cage for third gear.
4. Strip down synchronizing unit for third and fourth gears.

Inspection

1. Clean and inspect all parts for wear or other damage.
2. Place front main driveshaft between two centers and, with a dial indicator, check for runout at the contact surface of third gear needle bearing. Runout must not exceed 0.0006″.
NOTE: If excessive runout warrants replacement of the front main driveshaft, the gear wheels for first and second speeds on the drive pinion must also be replaced at the same time.
3. Check clearance between the stop ring face and the clutch teeth of the corresponding gear with a feeler gauge. Normal clearance is 0.043″. If a wear limit of 0.024″ has been reached, stop rings need replacement.
4. If a gear resists engagement, even though the clutch is fully released, it may be due to misalignment of the teeth of the stop ring with the splines of the operating sleeve. This is caused by wear in the slots of the stop ring.
5. Check fourth gear thrust washer for wear. Replace, if necessary.

Assembly

1. Assemble synchronizing unit for third and fourth gears. To hold lash between the clutch gear and operating sleeve to a minimum, the sleeve and clutch gear are matched and etched for identification. Position the shifting plates and install the two snap-rings, offset to each other. Be sure that the ring ends engage behind the shifting plates.
2. Insert clutch gear Woodruff key into the main driveshaft. Then, place third gear synchronizer stop ring on the cone of the gear.
3. Press clutch gear for third and fourth gears into position. The identifying figure "4" on the clutch gear must be towards fourth gear. Third gear is lifted slightly and turned until the stop ring engages in the shifting plates.
4. Press fourth gear needle bearing inner race into position.

Differential Reconditioning

Disassembly

1. Put differential in holding fixture.
2. Cut and remove safety lock wire and ring gear attaching screws.
3. Lift off ring gear.
4. After driving out the lock pin, push out the differential pinion shaft, then remove differential pinions.

Assembly

1. Check differential pinion concave thrust surfaces in the differential housing. If scored or worn, replace differential housing.
2. Install differential pinion gears and shaft, then install the pinion shaft lock pin and peen it into place.
3. Examine ring gear for wear or damage. If necessary to replace, ring and drive pinion must be replaced as a matched pair.

Details of tensioning ring for pinion (1969-71 models). The flats on the outer race of the double tapered roller bearing rest against mating flats in the transmission housing and prevent turning of the race when the tensioning ring is adjusted. (© Volkswagen)

Threaded bearing rings are used on 1969-71 models. These permit easier adjustment of the rear axle drive and are secured by a lock plate as shown. (© Volkswagen)

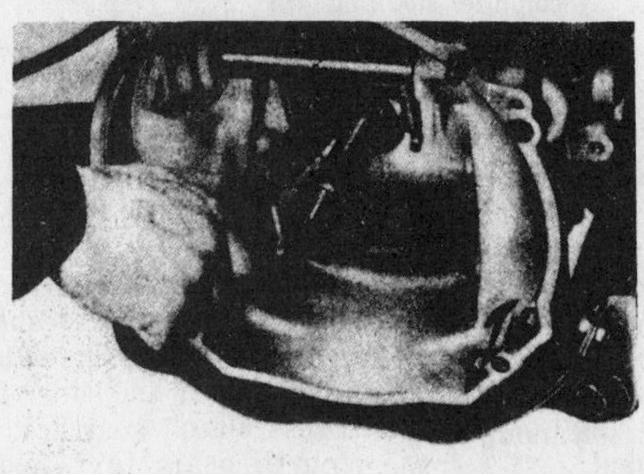

Removing main driveshaft oil seal (© Volkswagen)

Installing main driveshaft oil seal (© Volkswagen)

NOTE: Replacement of drive pinion and ring gear, or the differential housing, requires readjustment of the transmission.

4. Install and tighten ring gear attaching screws to 43 ft. lbs.
5. Insert ring gear attaching screw safety wire, to place a clockwise force on the attaching screws. Twist ends of safety wire and cut off.

Pinion and Ring Gear Adjustment

Quiet operation with minimum wear of final drive is directly dependent upon pinion and ring gear relationship. For this reason, drive pinion and ring gears are produced in matched pairs and are so identified. Silent operation is obtained by adjusting the drive pinion endwise, with the ring gear lifted enough out of the fully engaged position (without backlash) to insure backlash being within the prescribed tolerance of 0.0067—0.0098″. Any tolerance difference from standard is measured and marked on the pinion face.

Normally, it is necessary to readjust the ring gear and drive pinion only if parts which directly affect the adjustments have had to be replaced. It is desirable to readjust the ring gear if the differential housing, final drive cover or a differential bearing has been replaced. The pinion and ring gear *must* be readjusted if the transmission case, the gear itself, or the drive pinion ball bearing has been replaced.

To be sure of silent operation, the pinion must first be adjusted by installing shims between the ball bearing and the contact surface at the transmission case. This is to establish the factory setting of distance from the center line of the ring gear to the drive pinion face.

Both final drive covers must be installed with a preload of 0.0055″. After determining the thickness of the shims, a preload of 0.0028″ must be established on both sides.

Main Driveshaft Oil Seal Removal

1. Remove the engine.
2. Remove clutch release bearing.
3. Carefully remove the faulty oil seal from the transmission case.

Installation

1. Lightly coat the outer edge of the new seal with sealing compound. Lubricate the main driveshaft and the seal lip.
2. Slide oil seal onto the main driveshaft, then drive it into position with a suitable driving sleeve or pipe.

Electrical Section

Index

Electrical Diagnosis

To satisfy the growing trend toward organized engine diagnosis and tune-up, the following gauge and meter hook-ups, as well as diagnosis procedures are covered. The most sophisticated tune-up and diagnostic facilities are no more than a complex of the basic gauges and meters in common, everyday use. Therefore, to understand gauge and meter hookups, their applications and procedures, it is to be equipped with the know-how to perform the most exacting diagnosis.

Testing the Battery

Specific Gravity Test—Hydrometer

Before attempting any electrical checks, it is important that the condition of the battery be known.

The battery is an electrochemical warehouse for the energy and current requirements of the various electrical components of the vehicle. This all-important unit serves three different purposes. It supplies current for the starting motor, ignition system, lights, accessories, etc. It helps control voltage in the entire electrical system, and it furnishes current to the system when electrical demands are greater than the output of the generator.

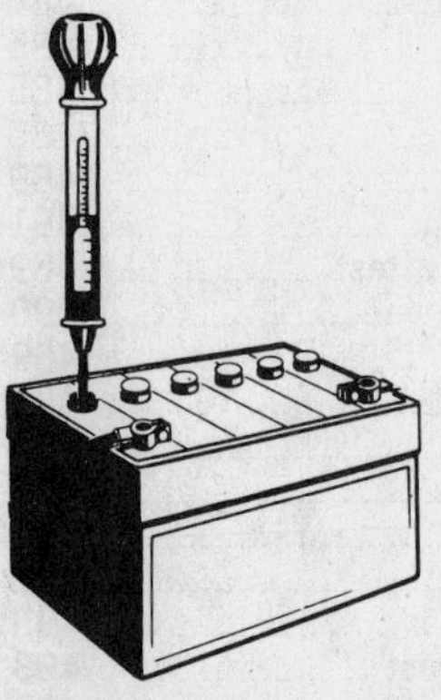

While not technically exact, a practical measurement of the chemical condition of the battery is indicated by measuring the specific gravity of the acid (electrolyte) contained in each cell. The electrolyte in a fully charged battery is usually between 1.260 and 1.280 times as heavy as pure water at the same temperature. Variations in the specific gravity readings for a fully charged battery may differ. Therefore, it is most important that all battery cells produce an equal reading.

As a battery discharges, a chemical change takes place within each cell. The sulphate factor of the electrolyte combines chemically with the battery plates, reducing the weight of the electrolyte. A reading of the specific gravity of the acid, or electrolyte, of any partially charged battery, will therefore be less than that taken in a fully charged one.

The hydrometer is the instrument in general use for determining the specific gravity of liquids. The battery hydrometer is readily available from many sources, including your local auto replacement parts house. The following chart gives an indication of specific gravity value, related to battery charge condition.

Specific Gravity Reading	*Charged Condition*
1.260-1.280	Fully charged
1.230-1.250	Three-quarter charged
1.200-1.220	One-half charged
1.170-1.190	One-quarter charged
1.140-1.160	Just about flat
1.110-1.130	All the way down

Testing Battery Polarity

Battery polarity is very important, especially since the introduction of AC generators. Permanent damage to the diodes of alternators (AC generators) will result from reversing polarity.

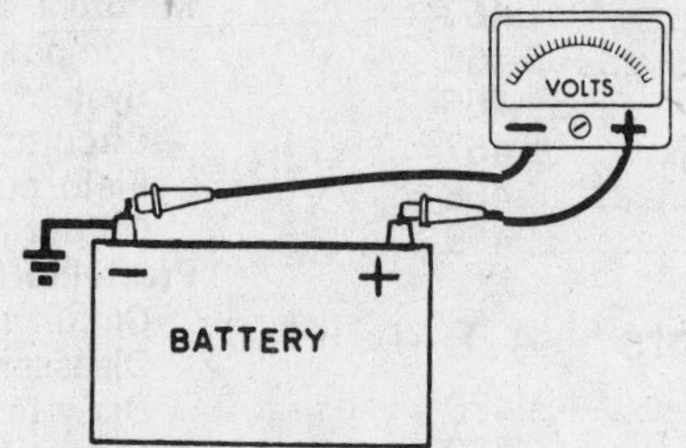

To determine battery polarity, turn the voltmeter selector to the high reading scale. Connect voltmeter leads to the battery posts. If the gauge needle moves in the correct direction, the positive lead of the meter is on the positive (+) post of the battery. If the gauge needle moves in the wrong direction, polarity is reversed.

Know Your Instruments

Ohmmeter

An ohmmeter is used to measure electrical resistance in a unit or circuit. The ohmmeter has a self-contained power supply. In use, it is connected across (or in parallel with) the terminals of the unit being tested.

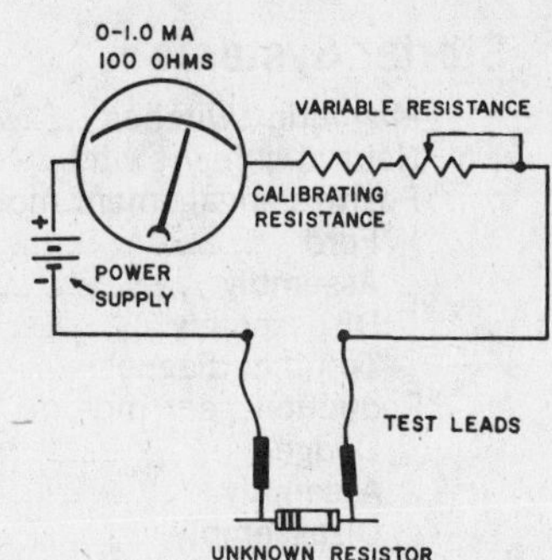

Ammeter

An ammeter is used to measure current (amount of electricity) flowing through a unit, or circuit. Ammeters are always connected in the line (in series) with the unit or circuit being tested.

Voltmeter

A voltmeter is used to measure voltage (electrical pressure) pushing the current through a unit, or circuit. The meter is connected across the terminals of the unit being tested. The meter reading will be the difference in pressure (voltage drop) between the two sides of the unit.

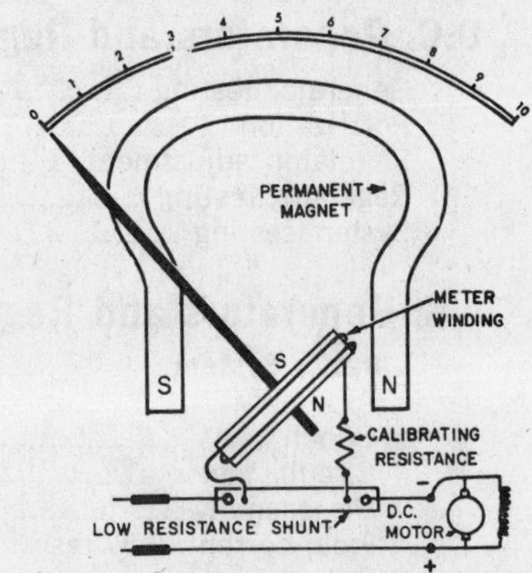

Testing Battery Capacity

It is not conclusive enough that a specific gravity test be made of the chemical condition of the battery by hydrometer. The electrical aspects must also be known. The battery must have capacity. It must be capable of maintaining a useful voltage, even while delivering the heavy load required in cranking the engine.

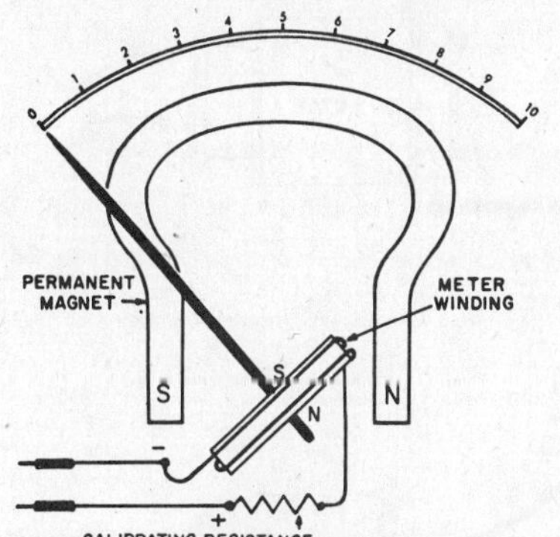

Capacity Test

While there are many very good testers available for the specific purpose of testing batteries, a satisfactory battery capacity test can be made with a simple voltmeter.

With engine at operating temperature, proceed as follows:

With prods (two ice picks will do) forced into the center of each battery post, and the voltmeter set to the high voltage scale (16-20 volts), connect voltmeter test leads to the battery post prods. Turn on the lights, heater, and accessories. Remove the center (high tension) wire from the distributor cap and ground it. Crank the engine for 20 second periods, three or four times. Wait about one-half minute between cranking sessions to prevent

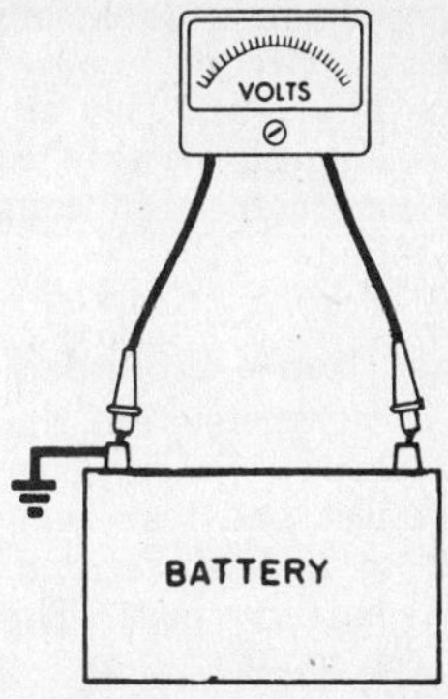

overheating the starter. During these cranking tests, the voltage should not drop below 5 volts for a 6-volt battery or 10 volts for a 12-volt battery. Even at temperatures below freezing, the voltmeter should not register below 9.4 volts on a 12-volt system.

Testing the Starting Motor

Extreme load conditions of the starter motor and its circuit require that the battery be kept in a fully charged condition and that starter circuit resistance be kept at a maximum.

Testing the Starter Circuit

The starter circuit should be divided and tested in four separate phases:

1. Cranking voltage check.
2. Amperage draw.
3. Voltage drop—grounded side.
4. Voltage drop—battery side.

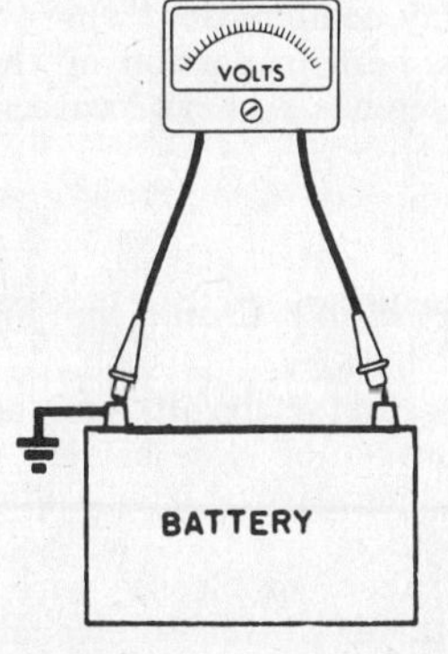

Cranking Voltage

Turn voltmeter selector to 8-10 volt scale for cars equipped with 6-volt systems, and to the 16-20 volt scale for cars equipped with 12-volt systems.

Connect voltmeter leads to prods tapped into the battery posts (observe polarity and reverse meter leads if necessary). Remove the high tension wire from the distributor cap and ground it to prevent starting. Now, close the starting switch. Observe both voltmeter reading and cranking speed. The cranking speed should be even, and at a satisfactory rate of speed, with a voltmeter reading of 4.8 volts or more for 6-volt systems, and at least 9.6 volts for 12-volt systems.

Compare this voltage reading with the reading obtained in the battery capacity test. There should be no more than a difference of 0.3 volt for 6-volt systems or 0.6 volt for 12-volt systems between the two readings. If this reading is satisfactory and the starting motor cranks the engine with sufficient speed, the starting motor circuit is in good condition.

Amperage Draw

The amount of current the starter motor draws is usually (but not always) associated with the physical or mechanical aspects of cranking the engine. (Mechanical trouble in the engine, frozen or worn starter parts, misaligned starter or starter components, etc.) Because starter motor amperage draw is directly influenced by anything restricting the free turning of the motor, or starter, it is important that the engine and all components be at operating temperatures.

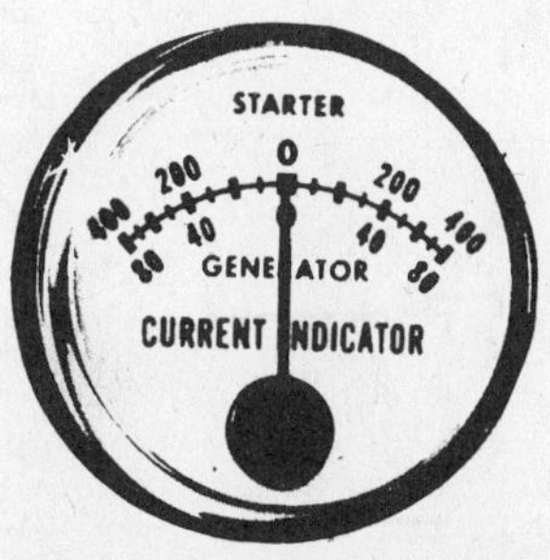

To measure starter current draw, remove the high tension wire from the center of the distributor cap and ground it. A very simple and inexpensive starter current indicator is available from your instrument and test equipment supplier or from the larger tool houses. This indicator is an induction type gauge and shows, without disconnecting any wires, starter current draw.

Place the yoke of the meter directly over the insulated starter supply cable (cable must be straight for a minimum of 2 in.). Close the starter switch for about 20 seconds. Watch the meter dial and record the average reading. If the indicator swings in the wrong direction, reverse the position of the meter. On 6-volt systems, normal draw for small to medium size engines is 150 to 225 amperes. Larger and high compression engines may draw as much as 400 amperes. On 12-volt systems, the current draw should be about one half the amount registered for the 6-volt system.

More exacting, but complex equipment is available from many name brand manufacturers. This equipment consists of a combination voltmeter, ammeter, and carbon pile rheostat. When using this equipment, follow the equipment manufacturer's procedures and recommendations.

High amperage and lazy performance would suggest, an excessively stiff engine, friction in the starter or starter drive, grounded starter field or armature.

Normal amperage and lazy performance suggest, high resistance, possibly poor connections somewhere in the starter circuit.

Low amperage and lazy or no performance suggest, battery condition poor or bad cables or connections along the line.

Voltage Drop—Grounded Side

With a voltmeter on the 3-volt scale, without disconnecting any wires, connect one test lead of the voltmeter to a prod secured in the grounded battery post. The other test lead is connected to a cleaned, bare metal portion of the starter motor housing. Close the starter switch and note the voltmeter reading. If the reading is the same as battery reading, the ground circuit is open somewhere between the battery and the starter. In many cases the reading will be very small. The reading shown will indicate voltage drop (loss) between battery ground post and starter housing. The drop should not exceed 0.2 volt for a 6-volt system or 0.4 volt for a 12-volt system. If the voltage drop is above the specified amount, the next step is to isolate and correct the cause. It can be a bad cable or connection anywhere in the battery-to-starter ground circuit. A check of this type should progress along the various points of possible trouble, between the battery ground post and the starter motor housing, until the trouble spot has been located.

NOTE: due to the design of the Chrysler reduction gear starter, testing is limited to measuring voltage drop to starter cable connection.

Voltage Drop—Battery Side

Bad starter cranking may result from poor connections or faulty components of the battery or hot phase of the starter motor circuit. To check this phase of the circuit, without disconnecting any wires, connect one lead of a voltmeter to a prod secured in the hot post of the battery and the other voltmeter lead to the terminal of the starting motor. The meter should be set to the 16-20 volt scale. Before closing the starter switch, the voltmeter reading will be that of the battery. After closing the starter switch, change the selector on the voltmeter to the 3-volt scale. With a jumper wire between the relay battery terminal and the relay starter switch terminal, crank the engine. If the starting motor cranks the engine, the relay (solenoid) is operating.

While the engine is being cranked, watch the voltmeter. It should not register more than 0.5 volt. If more than this, check each part of the circuit for voltage drop to isolate the trouble, (high resistance).

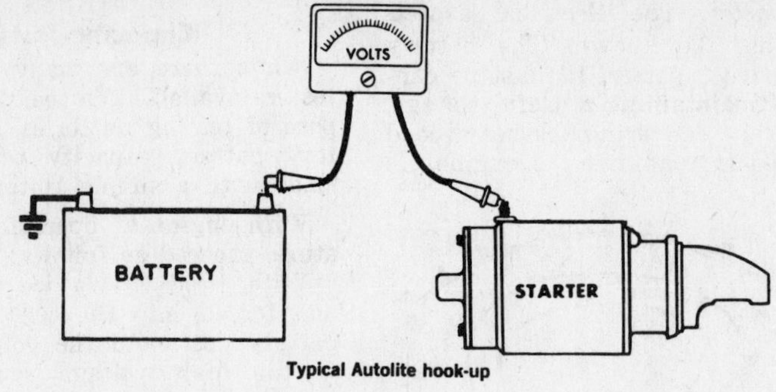

Typical Autolite hook-up

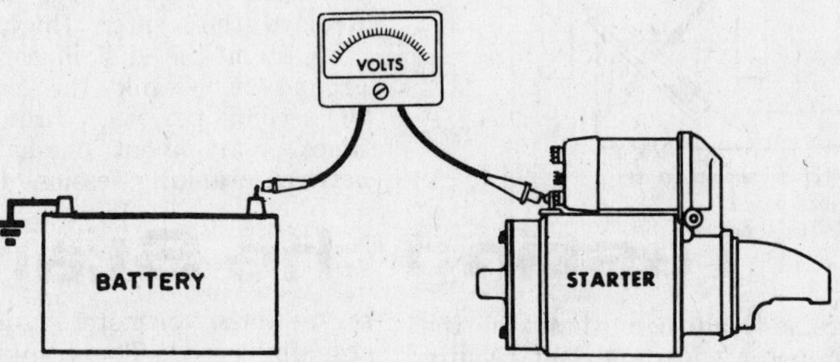

Typical Delco-Remy hook-up

Without disturbing the voltmeter-to-battery hook-up, move the free voltmeter lead to the battery terminal of the relay (solenoid), and crank the engine. The voltmeter should show no more than 0.1 volt.

If this reading is correct, move the same voltmeter lead to the starting motor terminal of the relay (solenoid). While the engine is being cranked, the voltmeter should show no more than 0.3 volt. If it does, the trouble lies in the relay.

If the reading is correct, the trouble is in the cable or connections between the relay and the starting motor.

Terms Used

MAGNETIC Switch. An electrically operated switch whose only function is to make contact for the starter. May be located on the starter, on the engine side of the firewall or on the fender apron.

SOL. (Solenoid). An electrically operated switch whose function is to make electrical contact for the starter, and in addition shift the starter clutch into mesh with the flywheel. No relay is used. Always located on the starter.

SOL AND REL (Solenoid and Relay). A solenoid having a separate relay, the relay being located some distance from the solenoid, usually on the fender apron or the engine side of the firewall. The solenoid is always located on the starter.

SOL-REL (Solenoid-Relay). A solenoid-relay combination, where the relay is a built-in portion of the solenoid assembly. Always located on the starter.

Starter

Starter Won't Crank the Engine

1. Dead battery.
2. Open starter circuit, such as:
   A. Broken or loose battery cables.
   B. Inoperative starter motor solenoid.
   C. Broken or loose wire from starter switch to solenoid.
   D. Poor solenoid or starter ground.
   E. Bad starter switch, (ignition,

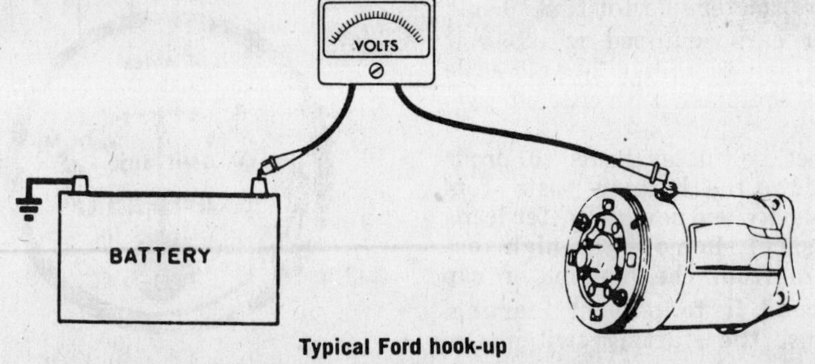

Typical Ford hook-up

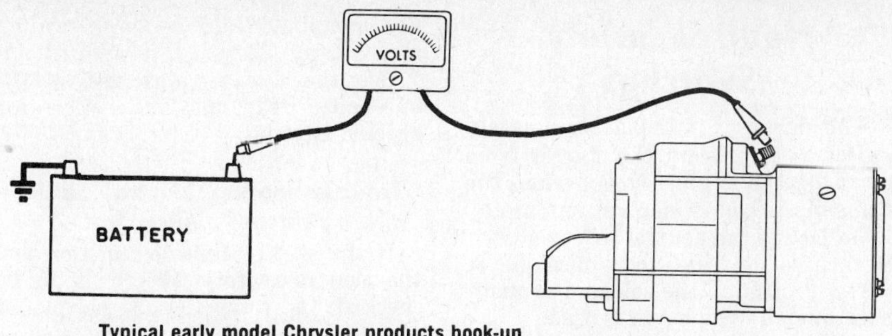

Typical early model Chrysler products hook-up

dash button or carburetor).

3. Defective starter internal circuit, such as:
   A. Dirty or burnt commutator.
   B. Stuck, worn or broken brushes.
   C. Open or shorted armature.
   D. Open or grounded fields.
4. Starter motor mechanical faults, such as:
   A. Jammed armature end bearings.
   B. Bad bearing, allowing armature to rub fields.
   C. Bent shaft.
   D. Broken starter housing.
   E. Bad starter worm or drive mechanism.
   F. Bad starter drive or flywheel driven gear.
5. Engine hard or impossible to crank, such as:
   A. Hydrostatic lock, water in combustion chamber.
   B. Crankshaft seizing in bearings.
   C. Piston or ring seizing.
   D. Bent or broken connecting rod.
   E. Seizing of connecting rod bearing.
   F. Flywheel jammed or broken.
   G. In some remote cases, an incandescent particle in the combustion chamber of a hot engine will prevent starting.

   This condition acts like a low battery or ignition timing so far advanced that the engine kicks back. The piston refuses to pass over top center. A two or three minute wait is generally enough to cool the troubled spot and temporarily clear the fault.

Starter Spins Free, Won't Engage

1. Sticking or broken drive mechanism.

Switches and Solenoids

Magnetic Switches

Magnetic Switches with Two Control Terminals

On this type of magnetic switch current is supplied from the ignition switch or transmission neutral button to one of the magnetic switch control terminals. The other control terminal is connected to the transmission neutral safety switch (on the transmission) where it is grounded.

Magnetic Switches with Ignition Resistor By-Pass Terminals

Used with 12-volt systems. All normally use a magnetic switch with a single control terminal. The second terminal is an ignition resistor by-pass terminal. To trouble-shoot this type of switch, ignore the ignition terminal and check according to the instructions given for magnetic switches with internal grounds.

Solenoids Without Relays

This type of starter solenoid is always mounted on the starter. Makes electrical contact for the starter and pulls the starter and drive clutch into mesh with the flywheel. The Chrysler reduction gear starter has this solenoid embodied in the starter housing.

There is only one control terminal on the solenoid. Except for Chevrolet, all of the 12-volt models are fitted with an ignition resistor by-pass terminal on the solenoid.

The ignition by-pass terminal is usually marked IGN.

Solenoids With Separate Relays

The solenoid itself is always mounted on the starter. In addition to making contact for the starter, it also pulls the starter drive clutch gear into mesh with the flywheel. A single control terminal is used on the solenoid itself.

Solenoids With Built-In Relays

These units are always mounted on

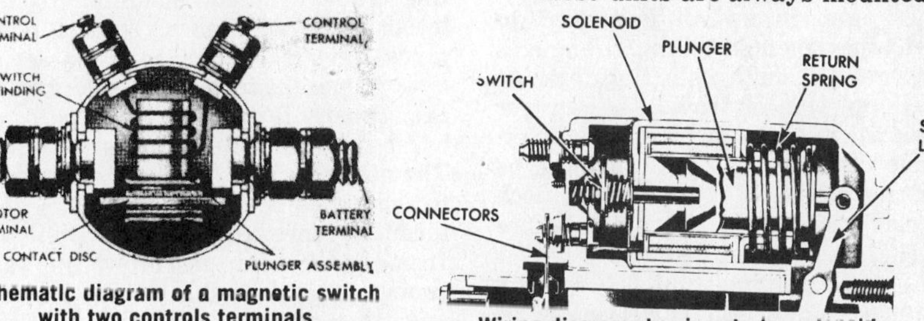

Schematic diagram of a magnetic switch with two controls terminals

Wiring diagram showing starter solenoid mounted on cranking motor

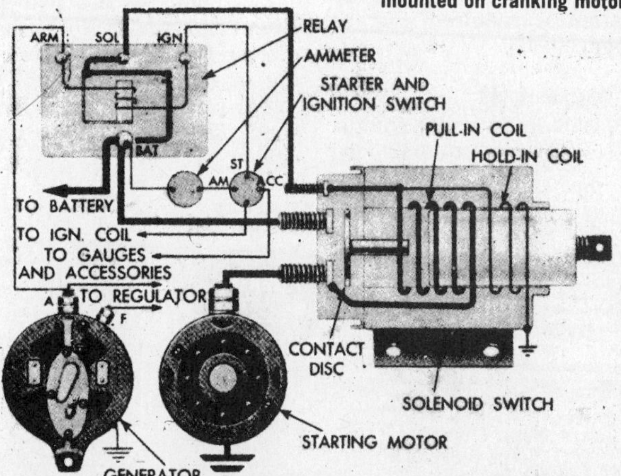

Pictorial drawing of solenoid with a separate relay

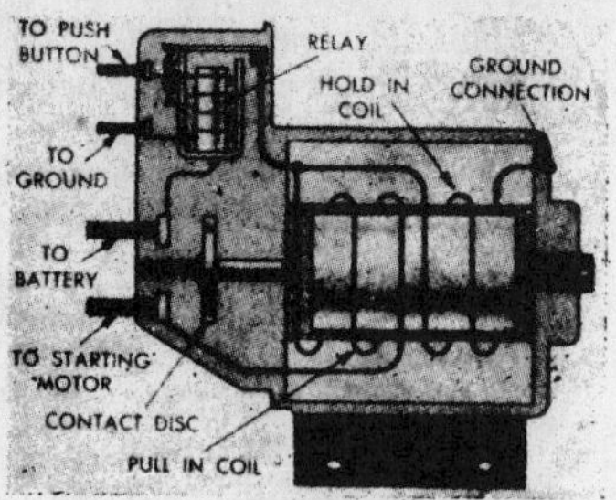

Pictorial drawing of solenoid with a built-in relay

the starter and are connected, through linkage, to the starter drive clutch. The relay portion is a square box built into and integral with the front end of the solenoid assembly.

Neutral Safety Switches

The purpose of the neutral safety switch is to prevent the starter from cranking the engine except when the transmission is in neutral or park.

On Dodge the neutral safety switch is located on the transmission. It serves to ground the solenoid or magnetic switch, whichever is used.

On all other trucks the neutral safety switch is located either at the bottom of the steering column, where it contacts the shift mechanism, or on the steering column, underneath the dash.

On most cars, the neutral safety switch and the back-up light switch are combined into a single switch mechanism.

See the car sections and/or the automatic transmission section for specific details.

Troubleshooting Neutral Safety Switches Quick Test

If the starter fails to function and the neutral safety switch is to be checked, a jumper can be placed across its terminals. If the starter then functions the safety switch is defective.

In the case of Dodge the neutral safety switch has one wire. This wire must be grounded for testing purposes. If the starter works with the wire grounded, the switch is defective.

Reduction-Gear Starting Motor

Dodge Trucks

This starter weighs 15 pounds and has 15% fewer parts. The housing is die-cast aluminum.

A 3.5 to 1 reduction, combined with the starter to ring gear ratio, results in a total gear reduction of about 45 to 1.

NOTE: the high-pitched sound is caused by the higher starter speed.

The positive shift solenoid is enclosed in the starter housing and is energized through the ignition switch. When ignition switch is turned to start, the solenoid plunger engages drive gear through a shifting fork. At the completion of travel, the plunger closes a switch to revolve the starter.

The tension of the spring-type shifting prevents a butt-tooth lock up and motor will not start before total shift.

An overrunning clutch prevents motor damage if key is held on after engine starts.

No lubrication is required due to Oilite bearings.

Disassembly

1. Support assembly in a vise equipped with soft jaws. Do not clamp. Care must be used not to distort or damage the die cast aluminum.
2. Remove the thru-bolts and the end housing.
3. Carefully pull the armature up and out of the gear housing, and the starter frame and field assembly. Remove the steel and fiber thrust washer.

NOTE: on eight cylinder engines the starting motors have the wire of the shunt field coil soldered to the brush terminal. The six cylinder engines have the four coils in series and do not have a wire soldered to the brush terminal. One pair of brushes is connected to this terminal. The other pair of brushes is attached to the series field coils by means of a terminal screw. Carefully pull the frame and field assembly up just enough to expose the terminal screw and the solder connection of the shunt field at the brush terminal. Place two wood blocks between the starter frame and starter gear housing to facilitate removal of the terminal screw and unsoldering of the shunt field wire at the brush terminal.

4. Support the brush terminal with a finger behind terminal and remove screw.
5. On eight cylinder engine starters unsolder the shunt field coil lead from the brush terminal and housing.
6. The brush holder plate with terminal, contact and brushes is serviced as an assembly.
7. Clean all old sealer from around plate and housing.
8. Remove the brush holder attaching screw.
9. On the shunt type, unsolder the solenoid winding from the brush terminal.
10. Remove nut, washer and insulator from solenoid terminal.
11. Remove brush holder plate with brushes as an assembly.
12. Remove gear housing ground screw.
13. The solenoid assembly can be removed from the well.
14. Remove nut, washer and seal from starter battery terminal and remove terminal from plate.
15. Remove solenoid contact and plunger from solenoid and remove the coil sleeve.

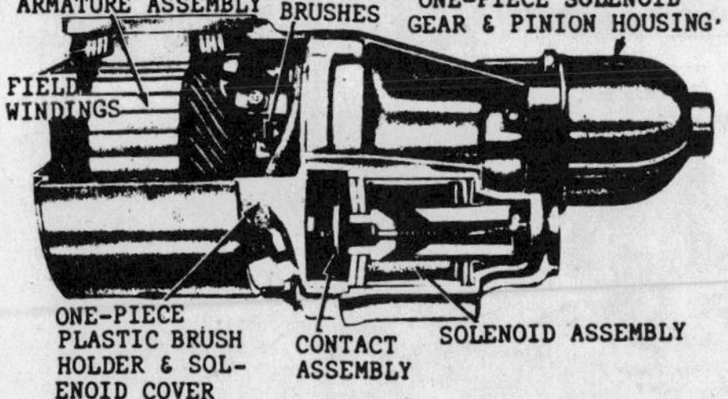

Reduction gear starting motor (solenoid side)

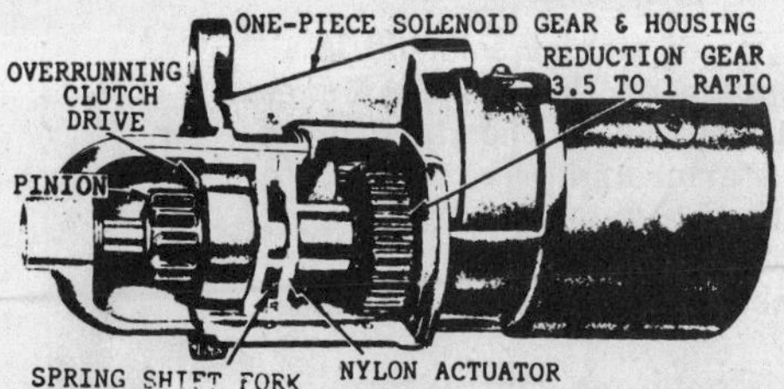

Reduction gear starting motor (reduction gear side)

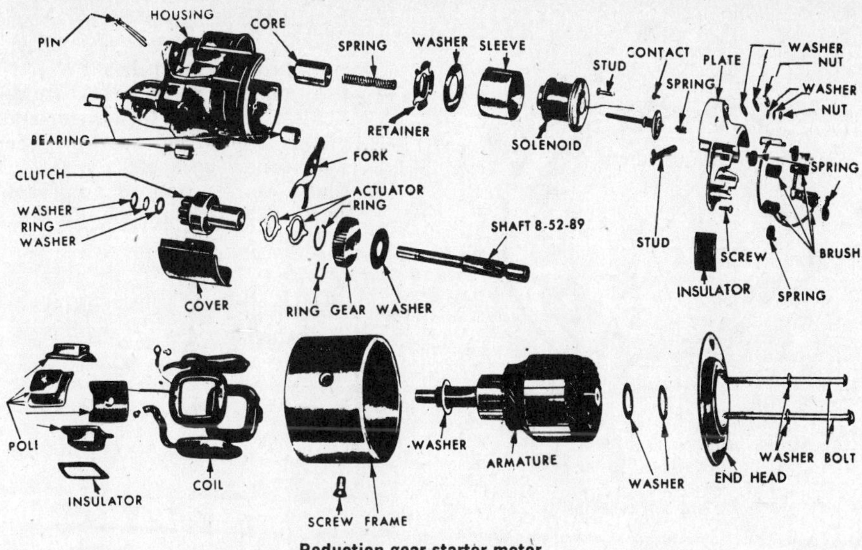

Reduction gear starter motor

16. Remove the solenoid return spring, coil retaining washer, retainer and the dust cover from the gear housing.
17. Release the snap-ring that locates the driven gear on pinion shaft.
18. Release front retaining ring.
19. Push pinion shaft toward the rear and remove snap-ring, thrust washers, clutch and pinion, and two shift fork nylon actuators.
20. Remove driven gear and friction washer.
21. Pull shifting fork forward and remove moving core.
22. Remove fork retainer pin and shifting fork assembly. The gear housing with bushings is servinced as an essembly.

To Reassemble: reverse the above procedures. At last portion of assembly, after gear housing ground screw has been securely tightened, clean area at joint between brush holder plate to field frame and housing mating joint. Apply a bead of brush plate sealer around four sides of joint. Be sure the joints are thoroughly sealed.

Ford Positive Engagement Starter

This starting motor is a series-parallel wound, four pole, four brush unit. It is equipped with an over-running clutch drive pinion, which is engaged with the flywheel ring gear by an actuating lever, operated by a movable pole piece. This pole piece is hinged to the starter frame and can drop into position through an opening in the frame.

Three conventional field coils are located at three pole piece positions. The fourth field coil is designed to serve also as an engaging coil and a hold-in coil for the operation of the drive pinion.

When the ignition switch is turned to the start position, the starter relay is energized and current flows from the battery to the starter motor terminal. This prime surge of current first flows through the starter engaging coil, creating a very strong magnetic field. This magnetism draws the movable pole piece down toward the starter frame, which then causes the lever attached to it to move the starter pinion into engagement with the flywheel ring gear.

When the movable pole shoe is fully seated, it opens the field coil, grounding contacts, and the starter is then in normal operation. A holding coil is used to hold the movable pole shoe in the fully seated position during the engine cranking operation.

Trucks equipped with automatic transmissions have a starter neutral switch circuit control. This is to prevent operation of the starter if the selector lever is not in neutral or park.

Reconditioning Procedure

Disassembly

1. Remove brush cover band and starter drive gear actuating lever cover. Observe the brush lead locations for reassembly, then remove the brushes from their holders.
2. Remove the thru-bolts, starter drive gear housing and the drive gear actuating lever return spring.
3. Remove the pivot pin retaining the starter gear actuating lever and remove the lever and the armature.
4. Remove the stop ring retainer. Remove and discard the stop ring holding the drive gear to the armature shaft; then remove the drive gear assembly.
5. Remove the brush end plate.
6. Remove the two screws holding the ground brushes to the frame.
7. On the field coil that operates the starter drive gear actuating lever, bend the tab up on the field retainer and remove the field coil retainer.
8. Remove the three coil retaining screws. Unsolder the field coil leads from the terminal screw, then remove the pole shoes and coils from the frame (use a 300 watt iron)
9. Remove the starter terminal nut, washer, insulator and terminal

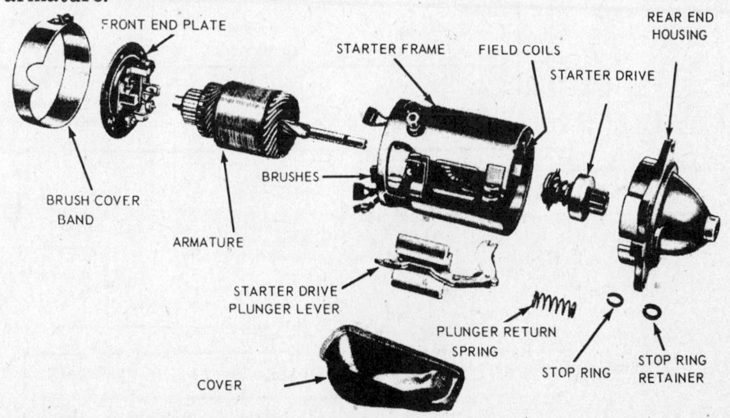

Starter motor

from the starter frame.

Assembly

1. Install starter terminal, insulator, washers and retaining nut in the frame. (Be sure to position the slot in the screw perpendicular to the frame end surface.)
2. Position coils and pole pieces, with the coil leads in the terminal screw slot, then install the retaining screws. As the pole screws are tightened, strike the frame several sharp hammer blows to align the pole shoes. Tighten, then stake the screws.
3. Install solenoid coil and retainer and bend the tabs to hold the coils to the frame.
4. Solder the field coils and solenoid wire to the starter terminal, using rosin-core solder and a 300 watt iron.
5. Check for continuity and ground connections in the assembled coils.
6. Position the solenoid coil ground terminal over the nearest ground screw hole.
7. Position the ground brushes to the starter frame and install retaining screws.
8. Position the brush end plate to the frame, with the end plate boss in the frame slot.
9. Lightly Lubriplate the armature shaft splines and install the starter drive gear assembly on the shaft. Install a new retaining stop ring and stop ring retainer.

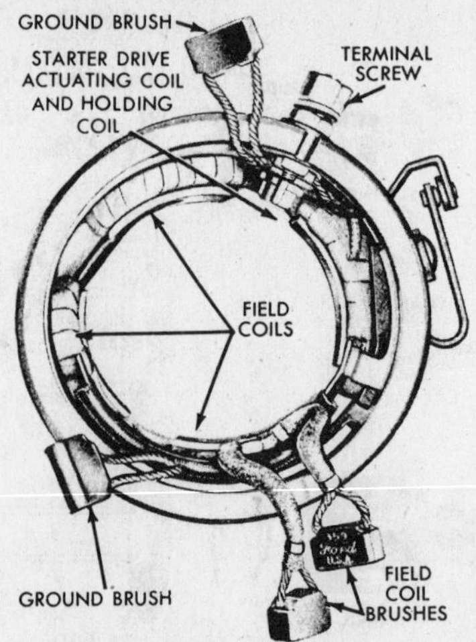

Field coil assembly

10. Position the fiber thrust washer on the commutator end of the armature shaft, then position the armature in the starter frame.
11. Position the starter drive gear actuating lever to the frame and starter drive assembly, and install the pivot pin.
12. Position the drive actuating lever return spring and the drive gear housing to the frame, then install and tighten the through bolts. Do not pinch brush leads between brush plate and frame. Be sure that the stop ring retainer is properly seated in the drive housing.
13. Install the brushes in the brush holders, and center the brush springs on the brushes.
14. Position the drive gear actuating lever cover on the starter and install the brush cover band with a new gasket.
15. Check starter no-load amperage draw. This should be 70 amperes.

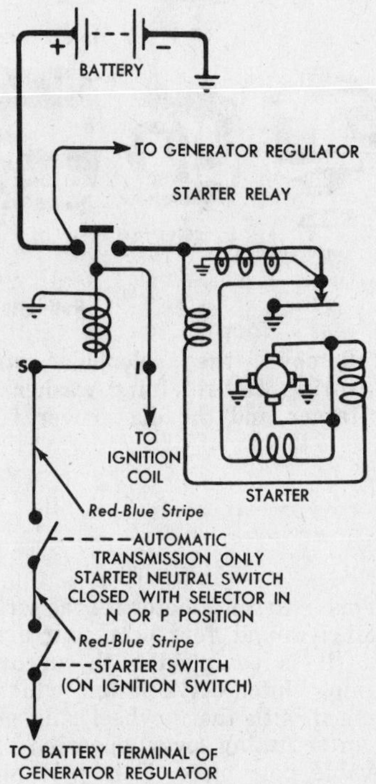

Starting circuit

Starter Cranks Engine Slowly—Road Map

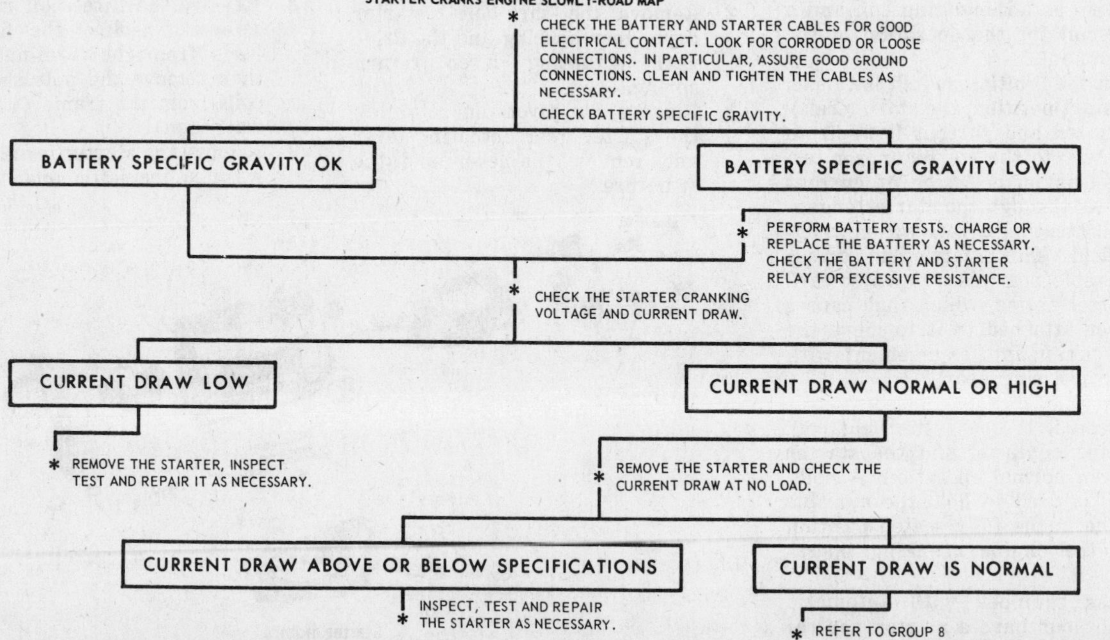

Ignition System

The Ignition System is divided into two circuits; a low voltage or primary circuit, and a high voltage or secondary circuit.

The primary circuit carries current, (usually modified for ignition by a resistor, on 12-volt systems) at battery voltage. It includes the battery, ignition-starter switch, starter relay, ignition ballast resistor, primary winding of the coil, condenser, contact points, and ground.

The secondary circuit begins with the ignition coil. Secondary voltage is a product of the coil and emerges from the secondary terminal and flows through a cable to the distributor cap. It is distributed by the rotor, through the distributor cap and cables, to the spark plugs, and to ground.

Caution: Secondary circuit pressure could reach as high as 30,000 volts.

Coil Polarity

Coil polarity is predetermined and must match the circuit polarity of the system being tested. It is an established fact that the electron flow through the spark plug is better from the hotter center plug electrode-to-ground than by the opposite route, from ground-to-center electrode. Therefore, negative ground polarity has been established as standard. There is about a 14% difference in required voltage of the two polarity designs at idling speed. This differential increases with engine speed.

Correct coil polarity can be checked on the truck by connecting a voltmeter negative lead to the ignition coil secondary wire, and the positive voltmeter lead to engine ground. If the voltmeter reading is up-scale, polarity is correct; if voltmeter reading is down-scale, polarity is reversed.

Lately, automotive batteries are designed with the battery posts on the same side of the battery, opposed to the earlier diagonal post design. Therefore, terminal size and cable length will discourage improper battery installation. This results in the battery and distributor terminals of the coil being the most likely points of possible reversal of polarity.

Another tentative, but less precise, method is to hold a regular carbon-cored wooden lead pencil in the gap between a disconnected spark plug wire and ground. It is possible to observe the direction of spark flow, from wire-to-pencil-to-ground when polarity is correct.

Primary Circuit Test

A quick, tentative check of the 12 volt ignition primary circuit (including ballast resistor) can be made with a simple voltmeter, as follows:

1. With engine at operating temperature, but stopped, and the distributor side of the ignition coil grounded with a jumper wire, hook up a voltmeter between the ignition coil (switch side) and a good ground.
2. Jiggle the ignition switch (switch on) and watch the meter. An unstable needle will indicate a defective ignition switch.
3. With ignition switch on (engine stopped) the voltmeter should read 5.5 to 7 volts for 12-volt systems.
4. Crank the engine. Voltmeter should read at least 9 volts during cranking period.
5. Now remove the jumper wire from the coil. Start the engine. Voltmeter should read from 9.0 volts to 11.5 volts (depending upon generator output) while running.

Coil Resistance, with Ohmmeter —Primary Circuit

To check ignition coil resistance, primary side, switch ohmmeter to low scale. Connect the ohmmeter leads across the primary terminals of the coil and read the low ohms scale.

Coils requiring ballast resistors should read about 1.0 ohm resistance. 12-volt coils, not requiring external ballast resistors, should read about 4.0 ohms resistance.

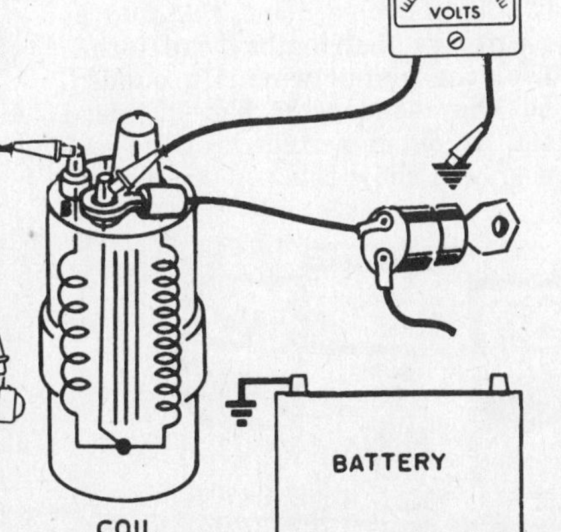

Coil Resistance, with Ohmmeter —Secondary Circuit

To check ignition coil resistance, secondary side, switch ohmmeter to high scale. Connect one test lead to the distributor cap end of the coil secondary cable. Connect the other test lead to the distributor terminal of the coil. A coil in satisfactory condition should show between 4 K and 8 K on the scale. Some special coils (Mallory, etc.) may show a resistance as high as 13 K. If the reading is much lower than 4 K, the coil probably has shorted secondary turns. If the reading is extremely high (40 K or more) the secondary winding is either open, there is a bad connection at the coil terminal, or resistance is high in the cable.

If both primary and secondary windings of the coil test good, but the ignition system is still unsatisfactory, check the system further.

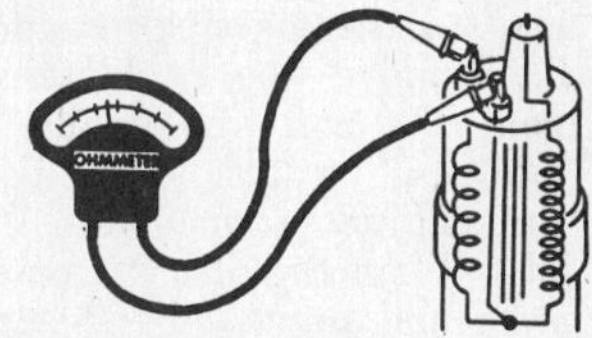

Ballast Resistor

Some sort of ballast resistor is used with most trucks equipped with 12-volt ignition systems. This resistance may be built into the ignition coil, or it may be a special wire of specific resistance, comprising the primary ignition circuit.

To provide a greater safety margin of sufficient voltage for high speed operation, a special ignition coil is used with whatever type of ballast resistance is used. Other reasons for ballast resistance are to limit to a safe maximum the primary current flow through the coil and through the distributor contact points. This helps protect the contact points at slow engine speed when they are closed for a longer period of time. The resistor also protects against excessive build-up of primary current when the ignition switch is on with the engine stopped and ignition points closed.

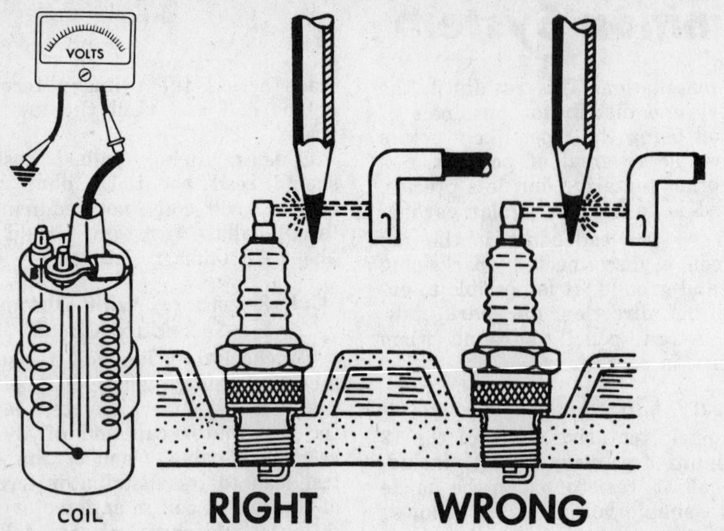

On some systems, the resistor is removed from the ignition circuit during engine cranking, then with the ignition connected directly to battery voltage. This keeps ignition voltage as high as possible while cranking. The by-pass type system can have the by-pass factor built into the ignition switch, or it may be part of the starter solenoid.

Primary Circuit—Distributor Side

With the voltmeter on the 16-20 volt scale, connect one voltmeter lead to ground. Connect the other voltmeter lead to the distributor side of the coil. Remove the high tension wire from the coil and ground it. Close ignition switch and slowly bump the engine to open and close the points. When the distributor contacts make and break during cranking, the voltmeter reading should be from one-third to one-half battery voltage. Normally, with engine stopped and with points open, the reading will be the same as battery voltage. Furthermore, with the engine stopped and the points closed and in good condition, the reading will be close to zero.

If while cranking, the voltmeter reading remains zero or close to it, the trouble may be one or more of the following:

A. No current at distributor. Disconnect the distributor primary wire from the top of the coil. Now, take a voltmeter reading from the distributor terminal of the coil to make sure that the current is going through the circuit.

B. Points are not opening because of mechanical (points or cam) failure or maladjustment. Dual points in parallel, one set not opening.

C. The movable point, the stud at the primary distributor wire terminal, or the pigtail wire is grounded.

D. The condenser has a dead short. An ohmmeter check of the condenser will show this condition. Connect one test lead of an ohmmeter to the body of the condenser and the other test lead to the pigtail. If the meter shows the slightest reading, the condenser is shorted. With a few exceptions, a visual inspection of the distributor contact points will generally indicate the condition of the condenser. An open, or shorted condenser will not function. A condenser of too great capacity will cause metal to transfer from the movable distributor point to the stationary point. This will cause a pit on the movable point. An under-capacity condenser, causes metal to leave the stationary point and build up on the movable point.

Any excessive resistance in either the primary or secondary circuits will upset the sensitive balance of the ignition system and cause the ignition points to pit.

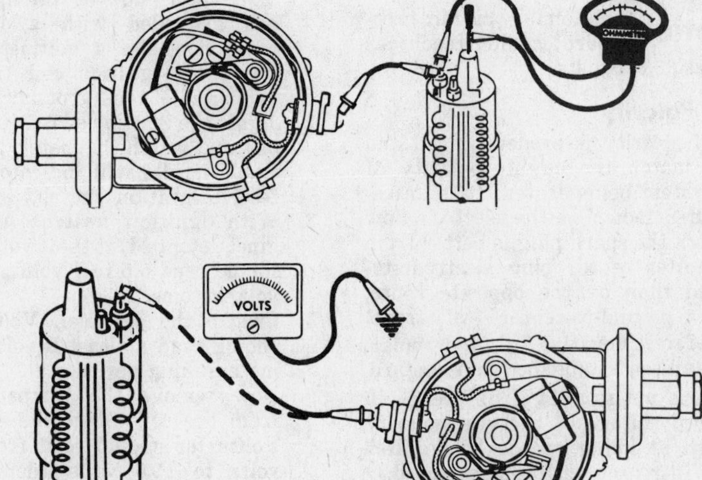

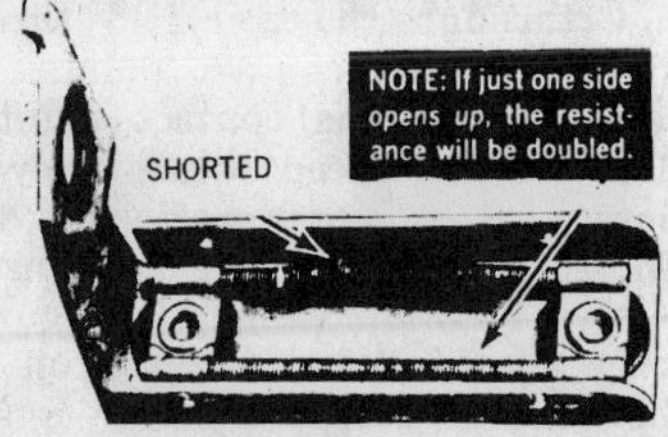

Ballast resistor

Ignition Point Dwell

It is very important that point dwell be adjusted to exact specifications before any attempt is made to time the engine.

Point dwell (cam angle) is the degree value for the closed attitude of ignition points for each make-and-break period of a distributor cycle. It is that phase of ignition system functioning during which the coil becomes saturated (builds up to voltage capacity) for its next discharge at the moment of point opening.

Some current production truck engines demand in excess of 23,000 spark plug firings per minute to fire their cylinders. This places a tremendous demand upon the ignition system, particularly the aspect of coil

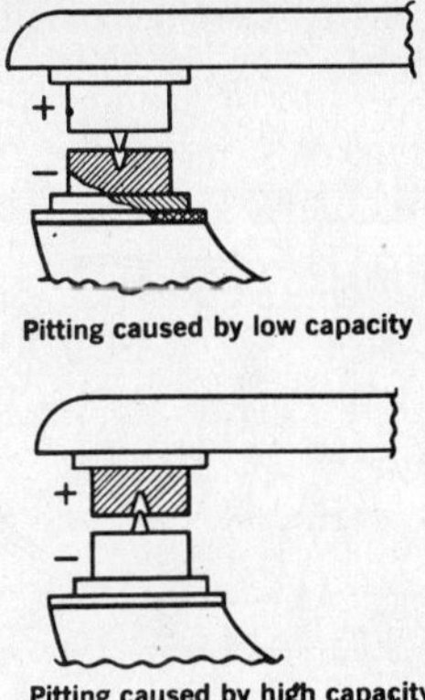

build up (saturation) and discharge time.

While it is true that ignition points can be adjusted by using a thickness gauge, the results, even when using new points, are sometimes inconclusive. Point gap is incidental to particular distributor cam shape and could be misleading. This is one reason for the use of a dwell meter.

Another point in favor of the dwell meter is its ability to detect high resistance, (oxidized points, poor connections, etc.). The dwell meter, a modified voltmeter, often includes a band on the extreme high end of the scale to indicate excessive point resistance. Follow instrument manufacturer's instructions to get the most out of your particular equipment.

The most informative procedure is to use both methods (dwell meter and point gap) then compare the two. Many times the comparison is surprising, and leads to the location of previously unnoticed distributor troubles.

Using the Dwell Meter

1. With distributor vacuum control line disconnected and plugged, turn the meter selector switch to the eight lobe position (eight cylinder engines) or the six lobe position (six cylinder engines). On four cylinder engines, follow instrument makers' instructions, or select the eight lobe position and double the reading for eight cylinder engines.
2. Connect one tach-dwell meter lead to the coil terminal of the distributor and the other meter lead to ground.
3. Start the engine and operate it at idle speed. Note reading on dwell meter. On eight cylinder engines, (single contacts) dwell should read 26°-32°. Double contacts should read 26°-32° (each set), or 34°-40° combined. Six cylinder engines should show a dwell of 36°-45° and four cylinder engines, a dwell in the area of 40°. These are tentative figures and cover a wide latitude. It is therefore, urgent that manufacturers' specifications be followed without exception.

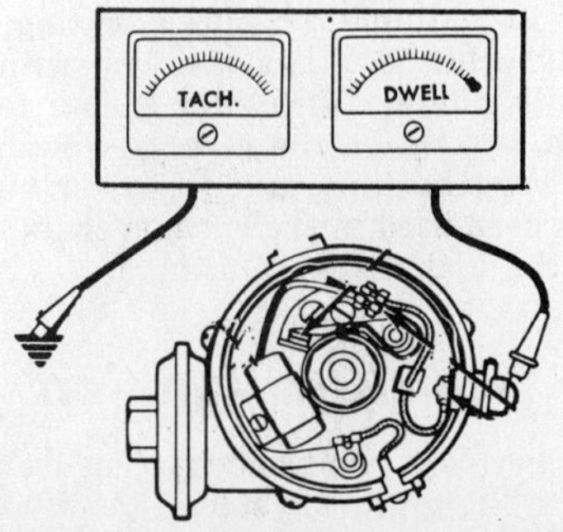

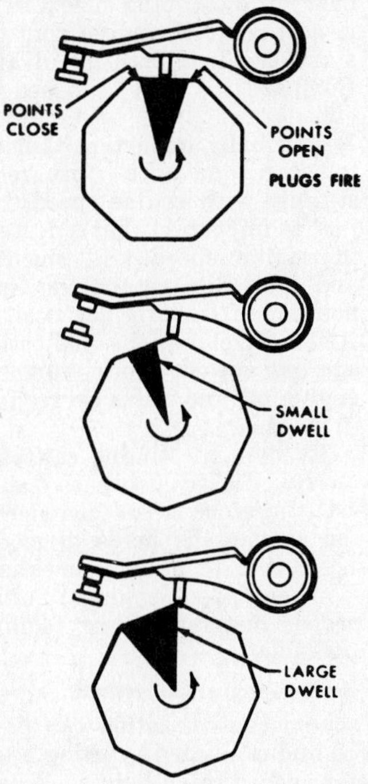

An excessive variation in dwell, (over 3°) as engine speed is increased usually indicates a worn distributor shaft, bushing, breaker plate or high resistance in either primary or secondary circuits.

NOTE: on some Auto-Lite or Ford distributors, a pivoted, movable type breaker plate is used. This pivoted plate, operated by the vacuum control unit, carries the contacts and rotates on its own center, independent of the distributor cam center. This design affects a running dwell variation of as much as 12°. To check this type distributor, hook up the distributor vacuum control line. Increase engine rpm and observe dwell changes at various engine rpm and throttle attitudes.

NOTE: experience dictates that all distributor adjustments are best performed with the use of a good off-car distributor tester.

Dwell information at idle speed is given for each engine in Tune-up Specifications Table of all of the cars in the Car Section of this manual.

Ignition Timing

Ignition timing is a term applied to the relationship of piston travel and moment of spark in a gas engine.

Due to the many variables involved, such as compression ratio, temperature, humidity, elevation, fuel octane value, engine condition, work load, etc. published timing data must be considered approximate; some tolerance permitted.

Ignition timing consists of basic (prime) timing and dynamic (variable) timing.

It is very important that point dwell be correct before setting timing.

Basic Timing

Basic timing can be checked quite accurately by using one of the many timing lights, (strobe-flashers) available. A timing light, when properly connected to No. 1 spark wire, (or the exact opposite cylinder in firing sequence of any multiple cylinder, four stroke cycle automotive engine) will indicate the moment of ignition for that cylinder. Index markings may be on either the rotating member of the crankshaft, (vibration damper or flywheel) with the pointer stationary, or the index may be on an engine stationary member, with the pointer or scribe mark rotating.

NOTE: because ignition timing is directly affected by distributor contact spacing, points should be adjusted to specifications before timing is attempted.

1. Unless otherwise stated by the manufacturer, the distributor control vacuum line should be disconnected, and plugged, to prevent fuel induction disturbance.

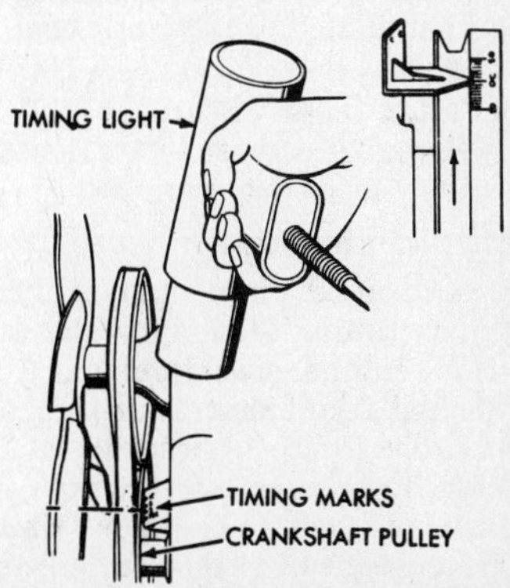

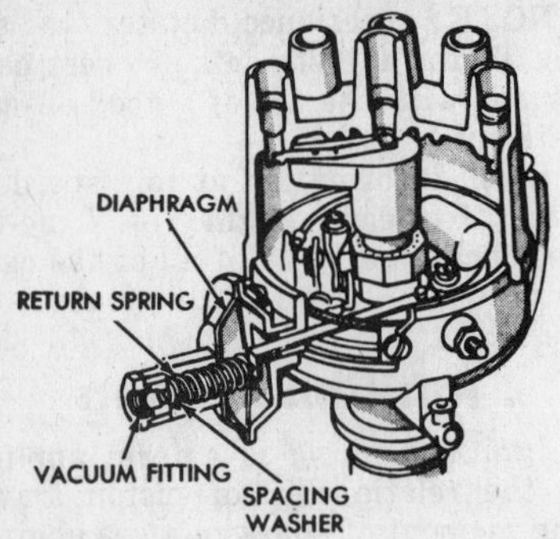

2. Hook up the timing light, (power or otherwise) according to the equipment instructions.
3. With engine at operating temperature and adjusted to function smoothly, run engine at low idle. Use a tachometer and be sure the rpm is below the speed of governor advance influence.
4. Shine the timing light on the indexing area (balancer or flywheel) and note the degree value indicated by the pointer.
5. Rotate the distributor body one way or the other until the pointer appears to correspond with the index value published.

Caution Power timing (on the road adjusting for ping) cannot be tolerated, especially on engines equipped with exhaust emission (air pollution) control devices.

Possible Indications and Causes

If The Flash Is Intermittent:

A. The test light is defective.
B. The test light has a bad connection.
C. Distributor points are bad or badly out of adjustment.
D. Distributor grounding is poor.
E. Distributor cap is cracked or tracking.
F. Spark plug gaps too small.
G. Broken or badly worn rotor.

If Pointer Appears To Move On The Index Scale (Unfixed At Constant Engine Speed):

A. Distributor governor weights loose or with broken springs.
B. Distributor shaft or bushing worn.
C. Rotor loose or broken.
D. Distributor base plate loose.
E. Cam lobes worn.

Dynamic Timing

To accurately check and calibrate dynamic timing through all attitudes of engine operation, more sophisticated equipment than the common strobe-light is needed. A distributor tester, an oscillograph, or one of the more complex timing lights equipped with an advance value index is needed.

It is possible, however, to determine to some degree, the action of both governor advance and vacuum control mechanisms with a tachometer and a timing light.

NOTE: before checking dynamic timing with a timing light, extend the index graduations on the timing member involved, by about 30°. This should be done with chalk or white paint, in increments of 5°, on the rotating member, whether that member carries the index or the pointer. Some measurements and extreme care will be necessary in making this extension.

Governor Control

1. Repeat Steps 1 through 4 of basic timing procedures.
2. By watching the timing light flash on the timing index, determine the exact engine rpm that starts the distributor to advance. Compare this with published specifications.
3. It is equally important that distributor advance progresses steadily with engine speed. It is just as important that a decrease in engine speed will smoothly and gradually return the index pointer to its original position.
4. After checking the indications against specifications, turn the engine off and make corrections, if necessary.

NOTE: dynamic timing cannot be *accurately* checked using the above method; therefore it is recommended that no attempt be made to modify advance curves (especially on exhaust emission equipped engines) unless the proper distributor test facilities are available.

Vacuum Control

Vacuum control action can be observed and evaluated by using a tachometer and a timing light.

This type of spark control, whether used as the only means of control or used in conjunction with a governor type mechanism, operates through a spring loaded vacuum chamber. This chamber is attached to the side of the distributor, then, through linkage, to the breaker plate (or pick-up assembly of transistorized magnetic pulse distributors).

Carefully metered vacuum is piped to one side of the spring loaded diaphragm of the vacuum unit. Vacuum controlled timing is then the result of differential (vacuum-spring) pressures.

In the case of vacuum-only controls, (Ford Loadmatic, etc.) metering is more critical; therefore, a manometer or a very accurately calibrated vacuum gauge is required, in conjunction with the tachometer and timing light.

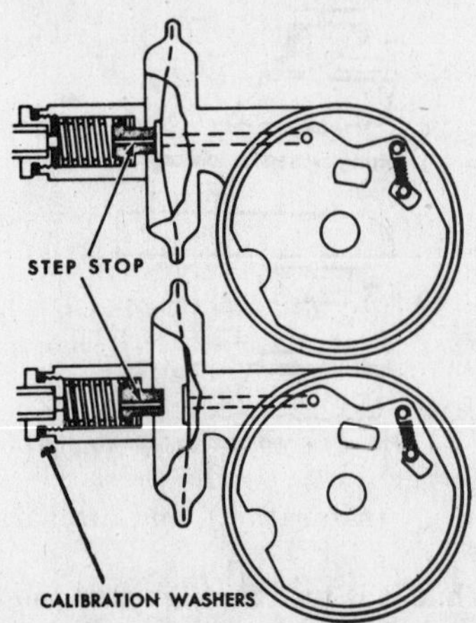

To Check Vacuum Control:

1. Hook up a tachometer and the timing light in the conventional manner.
2. Connect a good vacuum gauge or a manometer into the vacuum line between the carburetor and distributor.
3. With engine at operating temperature and adjusted to function smoothly, run engine at low idle.
4. Shine timing light on the indexing area and observe the vacuum reading and timing light index relationship.
5. Compare these readings with published vacuum advance data.

Indications and Causes

If timing is not within degree range at specified vacuum reading, a faulty vacuum or mechanical control mechanism, or Loadmatic control mechanism is defective.

If all parts are good, adjustments in control valve can be made by changing the calibration washers between the vacuum chamber spring and the spring retaining nut. Adding washers will decrease the amount of advance. Removing washers will increase the advance. After one vacuum setting has been adjusted, the others should be checked. Do not change original rpm setting when going to a different vacuum setting.

If other settings are not within limits, there is incorrect spring tension, leakage in the vacuum chamber and/or the line, or the wrong stop has been used in the vacuum chamber of the diaphragm housing.

Transistor Ignition

There are two basic types of transistorized ignition systems; those with breaker points, and those without. Both types furnish more uniform electrical performance throughout the speed range of the engine than does the conventional system, and they operate with a negligible amount of maintenance.

Because we are dealing with transistors and diodes, it is advisable to discontinue some of the previous methods of ignition circuit testing. Heat, shock, or reverse polarity may cause extensive damage to the components of the system.

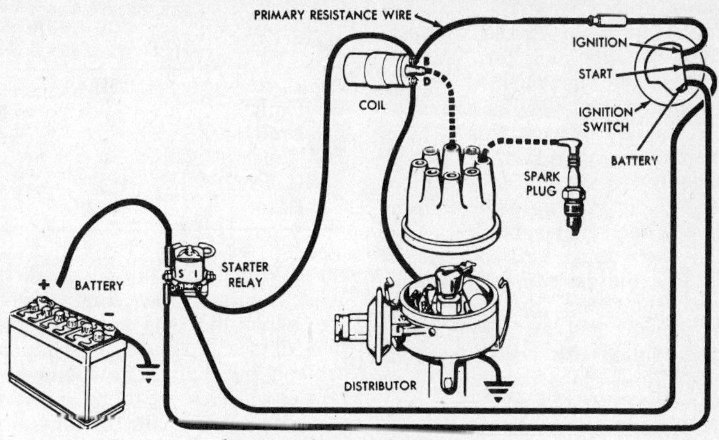

Breaker point type distributor circuit

Breaker Point Type

Trouble Checks

1. Check for the existence and approximate quality of spark by pulling the high-tension wire out of the distributor cap. With ignition switch on and the loose end of this wire held about ¼ in. from the engine block, crank the engine. This should produce a good, strong spark.
2. Reconnect the high-tension coil wire to the distributor cap and make a similar test at the spark plugs. A good spark at the plugs indicates the trouble to be other than ignition output failure.
3. If the spark is weak or non-existent, remove the cover from the mounting plate and connect a dwell meter to the tachometer block. Hook up the red lead to the terminal in the red area and the black lead to black.
4. With ignition on, crank engine and note meter reading. A dwell angle of less than 45° (for an eight lobe cam) indicates that the transistor is working properly.
5. A dwell meter reading of zero indicates that the breaker points are dirty or not closing and should be replaced or adjusted.
   A dwell meter reading of 45° (8 lobe cam) indicates the following:
   A. Ignition system is not being supplied with current.
   B. Breaker points are not opening.
   C. Transistor is defective.
6. Disconnect the bullet connector from the distributor lead and again crank the engine. A meter reading of zero indicates trouble in the breaker points. A meter reading of 45° (eight lobe cam) indicates power source or transistor trouble. To determine which, connect a voltmeter, or test light to the red/green lead terminal of the ballast resistor and crank the engine. A reading of 45° or steady light indicates transistor failure. Replace the transistor amplifier assembly. Absence of any indication shows an open circuit between the battery and the transistor.
7. A weak spark in Steps 1 or 2 indicates a weak ignition coil. Turn ignition off, replace coil, then repeat Step 1. Do not attempt to test coil, because its low impedance will cause inaccurate readings.
8. To jump the ignition switch from under the hood, disconnect the ballast resistor-to-ignition switch wire (red with green chaser) at the ballast resistor. Then, con-

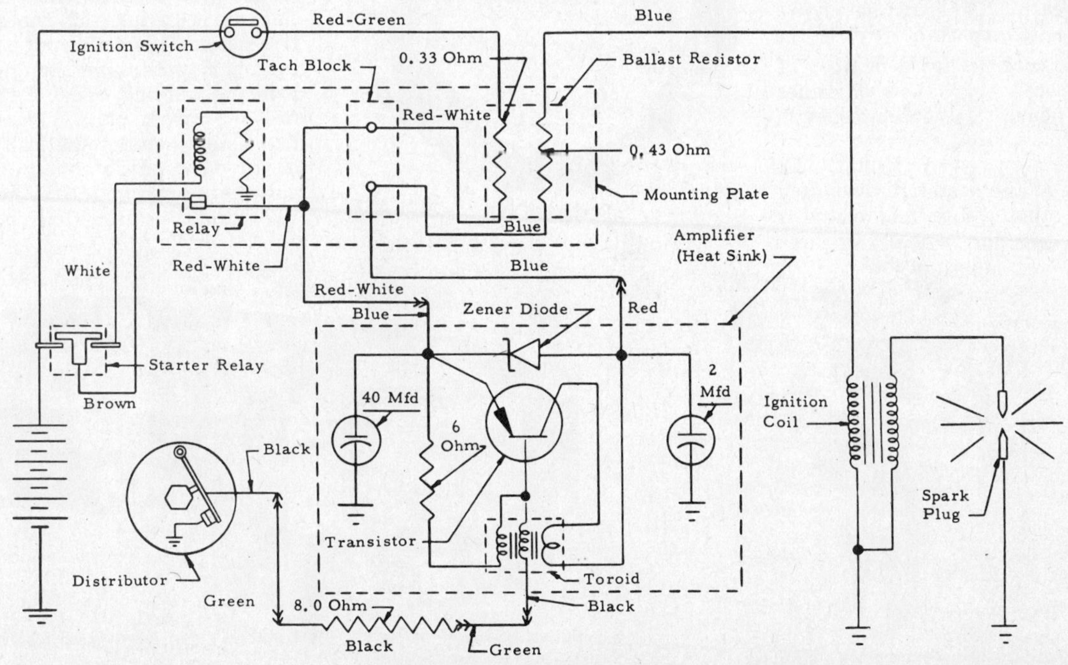

Breaker point type schematic circuit

nect a jumper from the positive battery terminal to the vacated ballast resistor blade terminal. If the resistor is not open, the ignition system will now be supplied with current. Check this provision before going further.

9. The only locations from which to get troubleshooting information are the tachometer block terminals, the ballast resistor terminals and the distributor primary bullet connector. By connecting a voltmeter and an ammeter at these points, with a well charged battery and the brown wire disconnected from the cold start relay, cranking amperages and voltages may be obtained that should correspond with the following chart.

Reference	Cranking rpm Volts	Cranking rpm Amps	Idle (700 rpm) Volts	Idle (700 rpm) Amps	Normal (1500 rpm) Volts	Normal (1500 rpm) Amps
A—Battery	10.4	—	13.2	—	14.7	—
B—Emitter	9.5	4.6	13.0	5.6	14.0	12.5
C—Emitter	8.0	4.6	11.2	5.6	10.0	12.5
D—Collector	4.0	4.2	4.6	5.0	9.5	12.0
E—Collector	2.0	4.2	2.2	5.0	4.5	12.0
F—Base	4.0	0.4	5.8	0.6	3.5	0.5

Caution Do not pierce insulation material to obtain meter readings.

Magnetic Pulse Type

The Delco-Remy, magnetic pulse, fully transistorized ignition system uses a magnetic pulse distributor—no breaker points. This system switches power electronically rather than with ignition contact points. Instead of the familiar cam and breaker plate assembly, this distributor uses a rotating iron timer core and a magnetic pickup assembly. The magnetic pick-up assembly consists of a bearing plate on which are sandwiched a ceramic ring-type permanent magnet, two pole pieces and a pick-up coil. The pole pieces are doughnut shaped steel plates with accurately spaced internal teeth, one tooth for each cylinder of the engine.

A critically important part is the iron timer core. It has a number of equally spaced projections or vanes and is attached to, and rotates with, the distributor shaft.

The transistor control unit, the switchbox of the system, is mounted in an aluminum case and contains three transistors, a zener diode, a condenser and five small resistors. The zener diode is a circuit protection device. Remaining components control and switch ignition-coil current electronically; there are no moving parts in the control unit.

The ignition coil is of standard design except for a special winding. The external primary resistor is a ceramic type, similar to those used on various conventional systems.

The magnetic pulse distributor provides a triggering pulse or signal for the transistor control unit. Within the distributor, a magnetic field is produced through the internal teeth of the upper and lower pole pieces by the permanent magnet between them. As the vanes of the iron timer core on the distributor shaft pass near the pole teeth as the shaft rotates, the magnetic field alternately builds up and collapses. Thus, a voltage pulse is induced in the pick-up coil each time a vane of the iron core passes a tooth on the pole pieces.

Each voltage pulse is conducted to the transistor control unit where it turns on the triggering transistor, causing it to turn off the switching transistor. This action interrupts the current flow through the ignition coil primary winding, causing the coil to fire the spark plug. The switching transistor then automatically returns to an on condition, permitting coil current to build up for the next firing.

The rotating iron timer core is de-

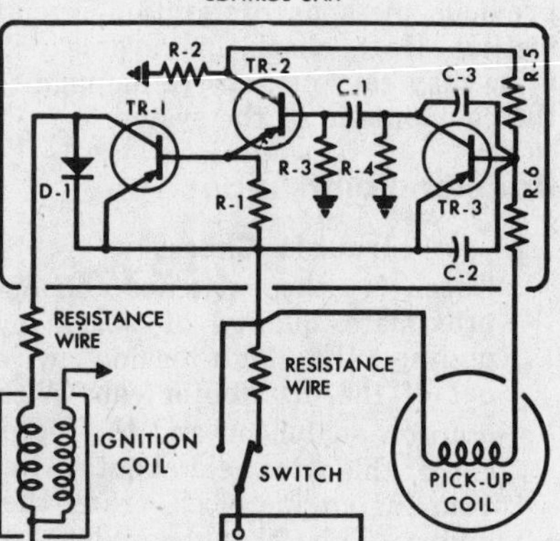

Pulse distributor schematic circuit

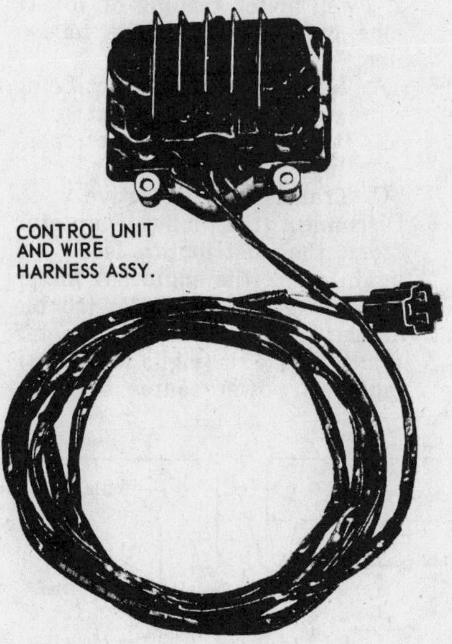

Control unit

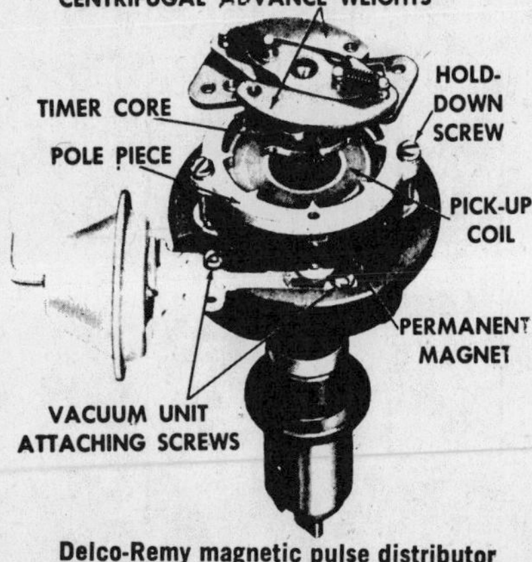

Delco-Remy magnetic pulse distributor

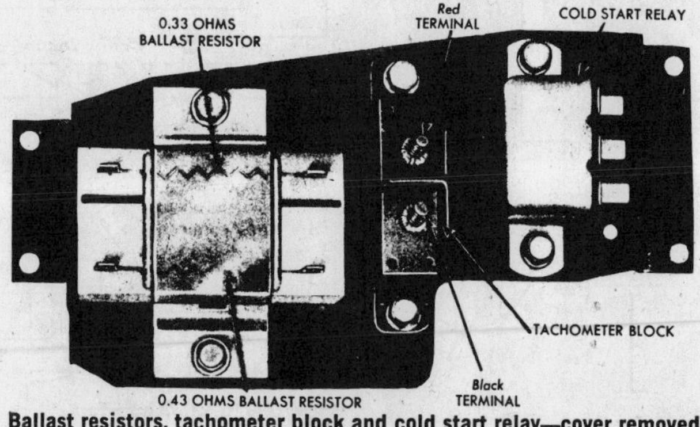

Ballast resistors, tachometer block and cold start relay—cover removed

signed with multiple vanes, four in the case of eight cylinder engines, and three in the case of six cylinders.

Diagnosis

This diagnosis guide has been taken from material furnished General Motors Corporation. It can be applied, however, to other transistorized ignition systems of the same basic type.

Cautions

1. Don't use 18 volts or 24 volts for emergency starting.
2. Never crank engine with coil high-tension lead or more than three spark plug leads disconnected.
3. Don't short circuit between coil positive terminal and ground.
4. On any repair that necessitates replacement of control unit or ignition resistor, perform complete charging system check before releasing the unit. Basic cause of trouble may be high or uncontrolled charging rate.

Intermittent Miss

1. Check pick-up coil connector to make sure that wire harness leads and pick-up coil leads are tight in connector bodies.
2. Check for loose connections throughout the system.
3. Engine roughness or miss indicates a short or open in the distributor pick-up coil. Connect an ohmmeter between two distributor pick-up coil terminals in connector body. Resistance should read 300-400 ohms. If resistance is infinite, coil is open; if resistance is low, coil is shorted. In either case, the pick-up coil must be replaced.
4. Connect an ohmmeter from either of the terminals to the distributor housing. The reading should be infinite. If not, the wiring is grounded.

Diagnosis

Hard or No Start

Disconnect any one spark plug lead and crank the engine while holding the lead about 1/4 in. from ground. Caution: Do not perform this test by using the coil or distributor secondary wire—damage to the system will result.

If Spark Occurs

Reconnect spark plug. Problem is not in ignition system.

If No Spark Occurs

1. Reconnect spark plug.
2. Check ignition coil primary by connecting an ohmmeter between the two terminals. An infinite reading indicates an open primary.
3. Check ignition coil secondary by connecting an ohmmeter between high-voltage center tower and either primary terminal. If the reading is infinite, the secondary is open.
4. Check ground resistor with a low-range ohmmeter. Turn ignition switch off and connect leads across resistor terminals. The reading should be .43 ohms.
5. Check by-pass resistor with a low-range ohmmeter. Reading should be .68 ohms with ignition switch off.
6. Check continuity of system as a whole, using a low-range (0-20 volt) voltmeter, in the following manner:

STEP 1

A. Connect the voltmeter between ignition coil positive terminal and ground.

B. Turn on ignition switch and observe reading. Voltage should be 7-9 volts.

C. If reading is 11-12 volts, there is an open circuit between this point and ground. The circuit includes the coil primary winding, ballast resistor and connecting wiring.

D. If reading is zero, there is an open circuit between this point and battery. Go on to Step 2.

STEP 2

A. Connect voltmeter between other ballast resistor and ground. Observe reading with ignition switch on.

B. If the reading is 11-12 volts, there is an open circuit between this ballast resistor and the ignition coil. The circuit consists of the control unit and associated wiring. If wiring is OK, the control unit must be replaced.

Spark Plug Inspection

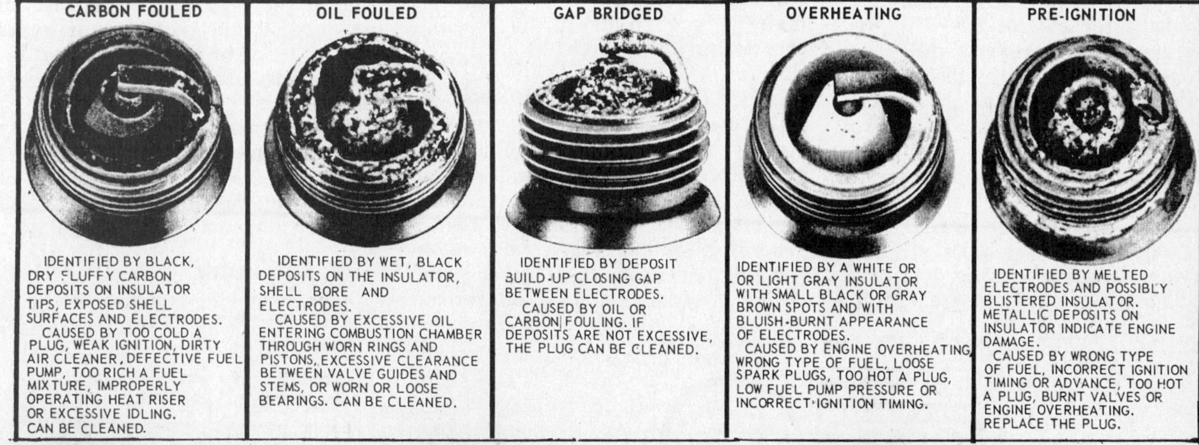

CARBON FOULED — IDENTIFIED BY BLACK, DRY FLUFFY CARBON DEPOSITS ON INSULATOR TIPS, EXPOSED SHELL SURFACES AND ELECTRODES. CAUSED BY TOO COLD A PLUG, WEAK IGNITION, DIRTY AIR CLEANER, DEFECTIVE FUEL PUMP, TOO RICH A FUEL MIXTURE, IMPROPERLY OPERATING HEAT RISER OR EXCESSIVE IDLING. CAN BE CLEANED.

OIL FOULED — IDENTIFIED BY WET, BLACK DEPOSITS ON THE INSULATOR, SHELL BORE AND ELECTRODES. CAUSED BY EXCESSIVE OIL ENTERING COMBUSTION CHAMBER THROUGH WORN RINGS AND PISTONS, EXCESSIVE CLEARANCE BETWEEN VALVE GUIDES AND STEMS, OR WORN OR LOOSE BEARINGS. CAN BE CLEANED.

GAP BRIDGED — IDENTIFIED BY DEPOSIT BUILD-UP CLOSING GAP BETWEEN ELECTRODES. CAUSED BY OIL OR CARBON FOULING. IF DEPOSITS ARE NOT EXCESSIVE, THE PLUG CAN BE CLEANED.

OVERHEATING — IDENTIFIED BY A WHITE OR OR LIGHT GRAY INSULATOR WITH SMALL BLACK OR GRAY BROWN SPOTS AND WITH BLUISH-BURNT APPEARANCE OF ELECTRODES. CAUSED BY ENGINE OVERHEATING, WRONG TYPE OF FUEL, LOOSE SPARK PLUGS, TOO HOT A PLUG, LOW FUEL PUMP PRESSURE OR INCORRECT IGNITION TIMING.

PRE-IGNITION — IDENTIFIED BY MELTED ELECTRODES AND POSSIBLY BLISTERED INSULATOR. METALLIC DEPOSITS ON INSULATOR INDICATE ENGINE DAMAGE. CAUSED BY WRONG TYPE OF FUEL, INCORRECT IGNITION TIMING OR ADVANCE, TOO HOT A PLUG, BURNT VALVES OR ENGINE OVERHEATING. REPLACE THE PLUG.

LEAD FOULED — IDENTIFIED BY DARK GRAY, BLACK, YELLOW OR TAN DEPOSITS OR A FUSED GLAZED COATING ON THE INSULATOR TIP. CAUSED BY HIGHLY LEADED GASOLINE. CAN BE CLEANED.

FUSED SPOT DEPOSIT — IDENTIFIED BY MELTED OR SPOTTY DEPOSITS RESEMBLING BUBBLES OR BLISTERS. CAUSED BY SUDDEN ACCELERATION. CAN BE CLEANED.

WORN — IDENTIFIED BY SEVERELY ERODED OR WORN ELECTRODES. CAUSED BY NORMAL WEAR. SHOULD BE REPLACED.

Testing DC Generator Systems

The generator system consists of the generator, generator regulator (voltage relay, current relay, and cut out relay) battery, charge indicator, and all the wires and other parts involved in the charging circuit.

Basically there are two types of DC charging systems in current use. These are different only in the way in which the field circuit of the generator is connected and grounded.

In the A type circuit, generally associated with General Motors and Chrysler products, the field circuit is externally grounded. The field circuit is connected to the armature terminal in the generator, and is grounded outside the generator through the regulator contacts.

The B type circuit, generally associated with Ford products, has an internally grounded field. The field circuit is connected to the armature circuit in the regulator, and is grounded inside the generator.

Generator Trouble-Shooting

NOTE: all DC generators with regulators used on Ford products are regulated at the main brush connection to the field coil rather than at the grounded end of the field.

Most generator electrical troubles fall into one of three categories: (a) intermittent or low output. (b) output too high. (c) no output.

Generator Output Too High

If the generator is delivering too much output there is one of two things wrong, either the field coils are grounded internally, or the regulator is not functioning properly.

Make a quick check by disconnecting the field lead at the generator. This will be the smaller of the two wires attached to the side of the generator. If this causes the output to drop to a very low value, then the regulator is at fault or the field wire is grounded somewhere in its harness. If, after disconnecting the field, the generator output remains too high, there is a ground in the field circuit inside of the generator, and the field coil should be replaced.

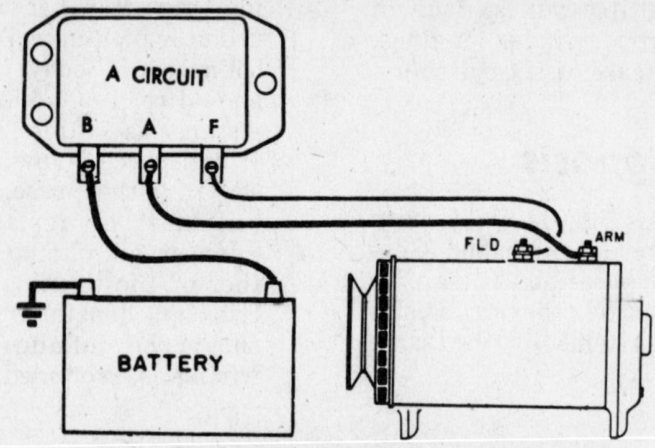

Connect jumper wire to battery (B) terminal of regulator. Momentarily, touch the other end of jumper to the armature terminal of the generator or regulator.

Generator Output Too Low

To check the voltage; if no generator output is indicated proceed as follows:

1. Hook up voltmeter between the two battery posts (use prods).
2. Run the engine at 1500-1800 rpm and observe voltmeter reading. An increase in reading, beyond battery voltage indicates that the charging system is working.
3. Compare this reading with specifications. If voltage output is less than specifications, trouble may be in the generator or regulator.

Caution When DC generators are used with Delco-Remy regulators having double contact voltage control, do not ground the field lead, as this may cause the high voltage points in the regulators to burn.

Test Instruments Required

Commercial test sets are made especially for testing regulators and generators conveniently and easily; however, if a test set is not available, the instruments necessary to test a generator, cutout relay, voltage or current regulator are: a voltmeter with a full scale reading from zero to 10 volts (for 6-volt systems) or zero to 20 volts (for 12-volt systems), an ammeter with a full scale reading from minus 5 amp. to 40 amp. positive, a 3/4 ohm variable resistance capable of carrying 50 amp. (for 6-volt systems) or a 1½ ohm variable resistance (for 12-volt systems). It is well to have also a 1½ ohm 1000 watt variable resistor to test batteries.

Polarizing the Generator

Because the DC generator will build up voltage that will cause current to flow in either direction, depending upon the polarity of residual magnetism of the pole shoes, the DC generator must be polarized. Any time a DC generator has been repaired or replaced on a car, the generator must be polarized before starting the engine.

Generators of the A circuitry type are polarized by connecting a jumper lead from the battery terminal of the regulator to the armature terminal of the regulator or generator. A touch of the jumper lead is all that is necessary to polarize the generator.

Generators of the B circuitry type are polarized by disconnecting the field lead at the regulator and momentarily flashing this lead to the battery terminal of the regulator.

The Regulator

The generator regulator is the next

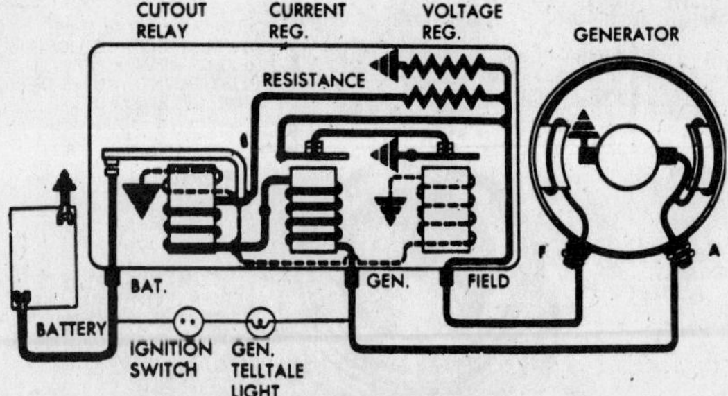

Typical A-type circuit used with early model Autolite and Delco-Remy charging systems

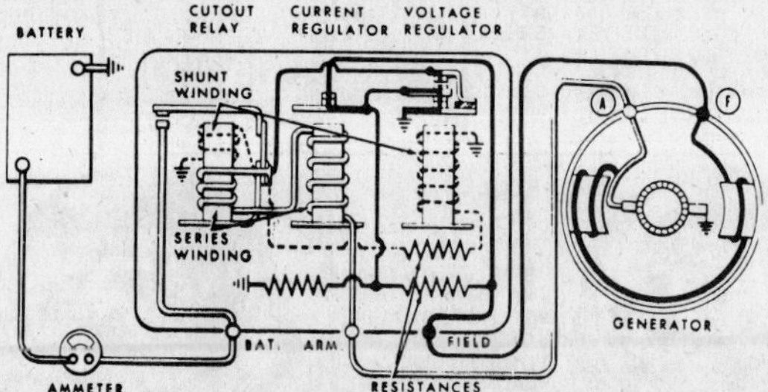

Typical B-type circuit used with Ford products charging systems

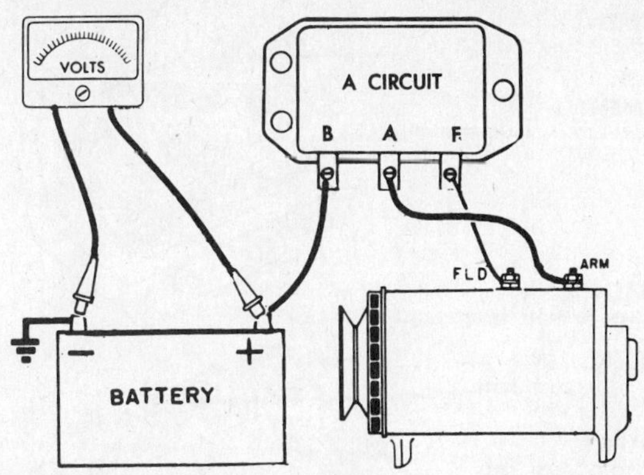

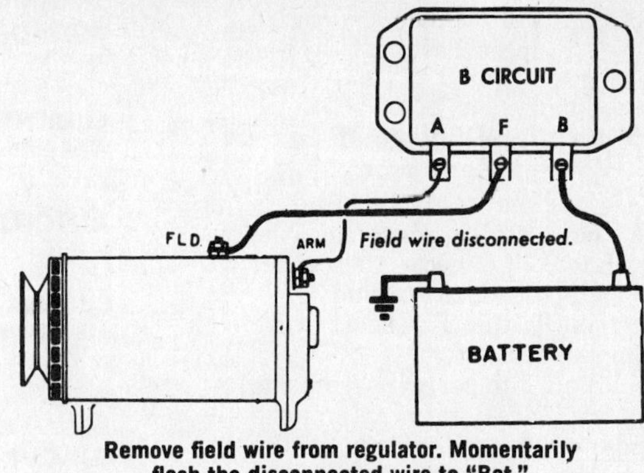

Remove field wire from regulator. Momentarily flash the disconnected wire to "Bat." terminal of regulator.

step in diagnosing a faulty charging system. Manufacturers' recommendations are that, when making any of the following tests, all units to be tested be kept at normal operating temperatures. This usually takes about 15 minutes of engine running. Readings should all be taken with the regulator cover in place. It does make a difference, due to magnetic influence.

A Circuit—Single Point Voltage Regulator

1. Hook up one voltmeter lead to the battery terminal of the regulator. Connect the other voltmeter lead to ground.
2. Connect a jumper wire from the F terminal of the regulator (or the generator) to ground.

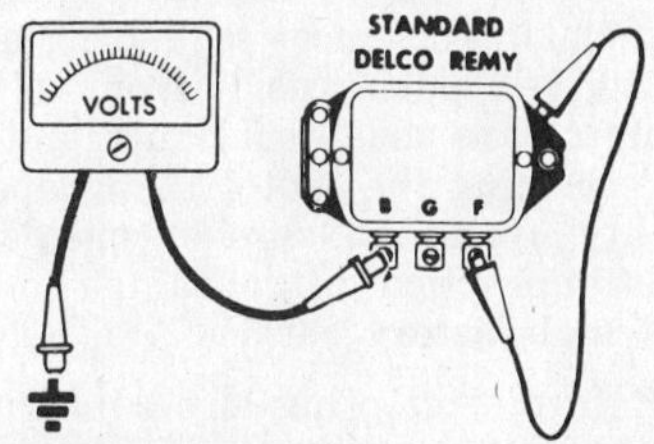

3. Start the engine, then slowly increase engine speed until the voltage just exceeds specifications. Hold this speed only long enough to determine that the generator is capable of producing 7.8 volts (6-volt system), or at least 15.4 volts (12-volt system).

Caution Do not increase engine speed beyond 1 volt of specifications.

If generator voltage output is adequate, repair or replace regulator.

If generator voltage output is under specifications, repair or replace the generator.

A Circuit—Dual Point Voltage Regulator

1. Hook up one voltmeter lead to the battery terminal of the regulator. Connect the other voltmeter lead to ground.
2. With this type regulator, the F (field) wire must be disconnected from the generator or regulator.

Caution Even a momentary grounding of the field terminal of the regulator will burn the upper contacts of the voltage regulator.

3. Connect a jumper wire from the F (field) terminal of the generator (not the regulator) to ground.
4. Start engine, then slowly increase engine speed until the voltage just exceeds specifications. Hold this speed only long enough to determine that the generator is capable of producing 15.4 volts (12-volt system).

Caution Do not increase engine speed beyond 1 volt of specifications.

B Circuit—Single Point Voltage Regulator

1. Hook up one voltmeter lead to the battery terminal of the regulator. Connect the other voltmeter lead to ground.
2. Run a jumper wire between the A (armature) and F (field) terminals of either the regulator or generator.

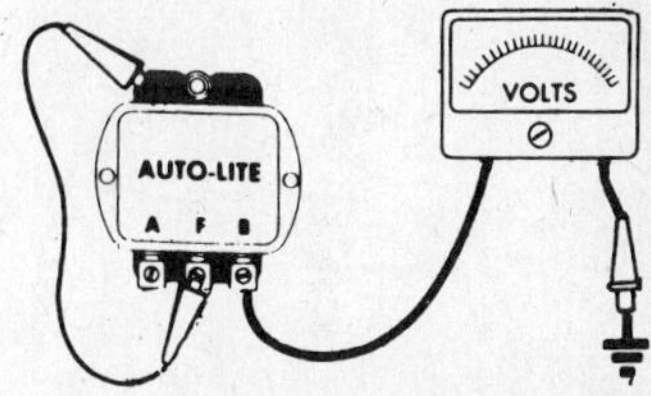

3. Start engine and slowly increase engine speed until the voltage just exceeds specifications. Hold this speed only long enough to determine that the generator is capable of producing 7.8 volts (6-volt system), or at least 15.4 volts (12-volt system).

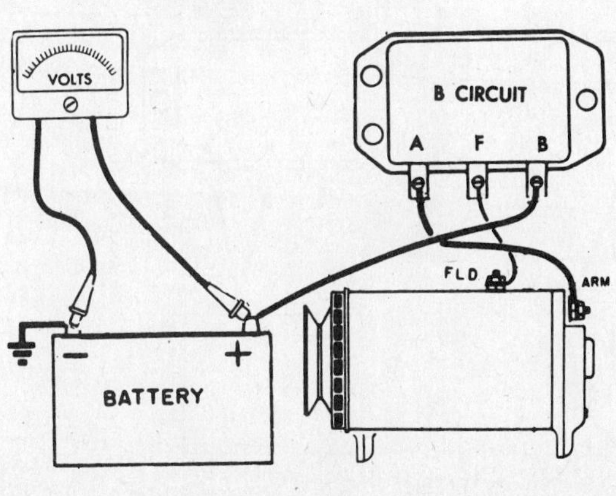

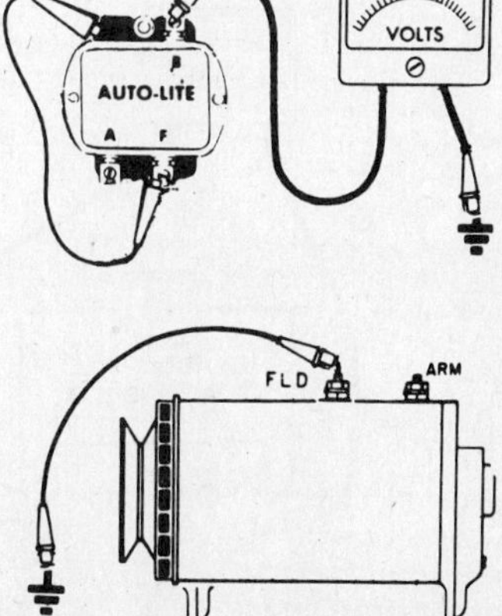

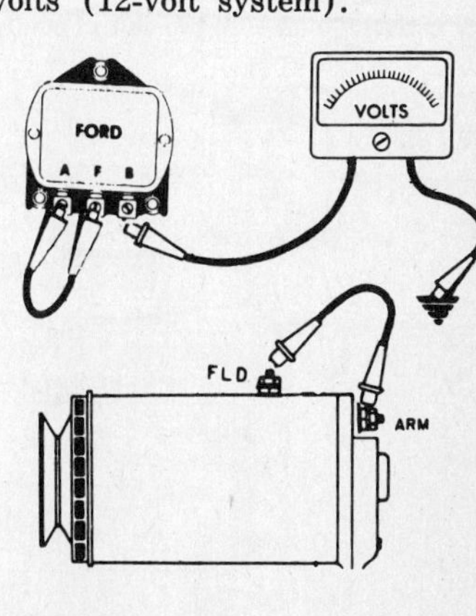

Caution Do not increase engine speed beyond 1 volt of specifications.

B Circuit—Dual Point Voltage Regulator

1. Hook up one voltmeter lead to the battery terminal of the regulator. Connect the other voltmeter lead to ground.
2. Disconnect the F (field) wire from the regulator.
3. Hook up a jumper wire from the A (armature) terminal of the regulator or generator to the wire just disconnected from the regulator.

Caution Even a momentary energizing of the regulator field terminal will cause burning and permanent damage to the voltage regulator upper points. As a precautionary measure, because it is sometimes difficult to identify single point from dual point regulators, follow the procedure for the dual set unit.

4. Start engine, then slowly increase engine speed until voltage just exceeds specifications. Hold this speed only long enough to determine that the generator is capable of producing 15.4 volts (12-volt system.)

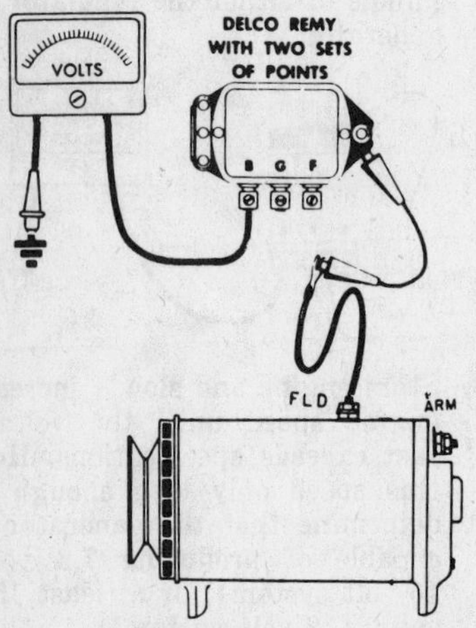

Delco-Remy with two sets of points

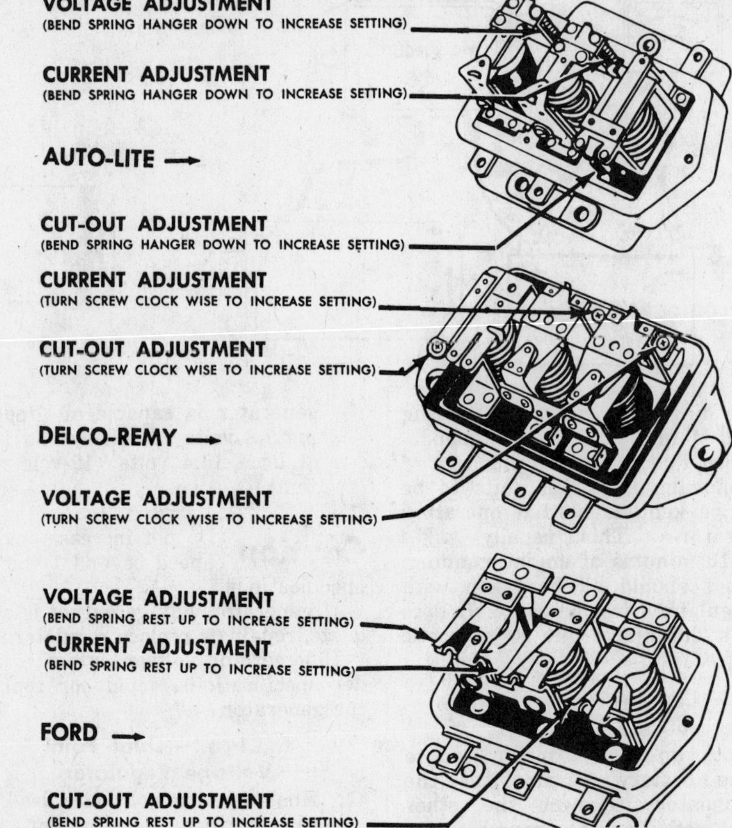

Caution Do not increase engine speed beyond 1 volt of specifications.

Adjusting the Voltage Regulator

Most regulator troubles are caused by oxidized or burned regulating, or current limiting points. These points, like distributor breaker points, have a limited life span. Average point oscillating frequency of the voltage regulating unit may be as much as 70,000-75,000 cycles per hour.

Experience dictates that both customer and mechanic are best served by the following practice. Aside from simple voltage regulator adjustment, any malfunctions of the regulator (voltage regulator, current regulator, or cut-out) are best handled by renewing the entire regulating unit. Remember that most regulating units that give trouble (aside from voltage control) are usually fatigued and are approaching the end of their dependability span. All things considered, it is impractical to guarantee continued satisfactory service.

Before attempting any adjustment of the regulator, two tests should be made; both at generator and regulator operating temperatures. These tests are to establish the voltage and amperage output of the system under practical conditions—a partially charged battery, and a battery

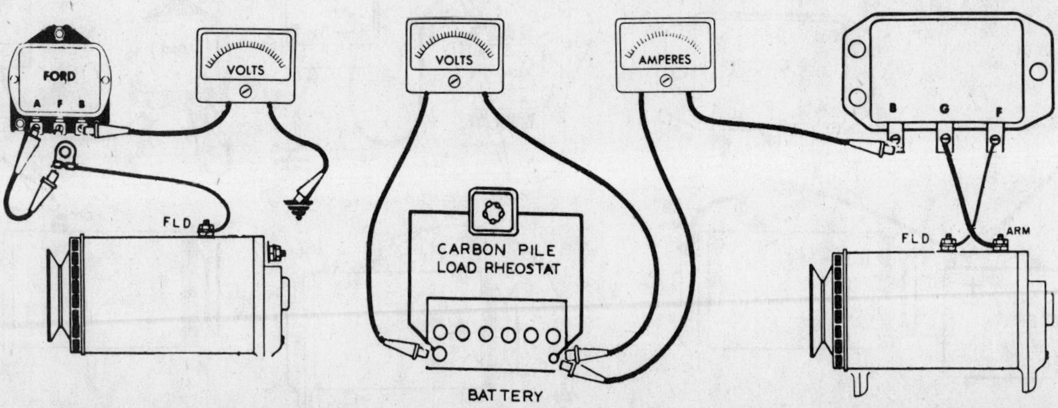

which is fully charged.

Bear in mind that the voltage output should remain constant. The amperage reading, however, will be influenced by the charge condition of the battery. A low battery requiring greater generator output (higher amp. reading) than a battery of full charge.

Connect the voltmeter and ammeter as illustrated.

Test 1

Discharge the battery (if it is fully charged) by using a carbon pile, or turn on headlights, heater, radio, etc. Disconnect the distributor cap center wire and ground it. Operate the starter to partially discharge the battery.

Reconnect the distributor cap center wire, then start the engine. Slowly accelerate and watch the meters. Note highest reading on both voltmeter and ammeter.

This is the maximum charging potential of this generator-regulator setting.

Test 2

With the same meter hook-up as in Test 1, run the engine at about 1500-2000 rpm, long enough to be reasonably sure that the battery is fully charged; or, place a 1/4 ohm resistor in series with the voltage regulator battery wire. This will influence the charging system to the same degree as that of a fully charged battery.

NOTE: the 1/4 ohm resistor is the accepted standard used to electrically simulate a fully charged battery.

Most generator testers have a built-in resistor for this specific purpose.

NOTE: a current limiter (when operating properly) will cut back to practically zero amps. charge, when the 1/4 ohm resistance is in series with the battery.

AC Generators and Regulators

Is It the Alternator or the Voltage Regulator?

The first step in diagnosing troubles of the charging system, is to identify the source of failure. Does the fault lie in the alternator or the regulator? The next move depends upon preference or necessity; either repair or replace the offending unit.

It is just as easy to separate an alternator, electrically, from the AC regulator as it is to separate its counterpart, the DC generator from its regulator.

AC generator output is controlled by the amount of current supplied to the field circuit of the system.

Unlike the DC generator, an AC generator is capable of producing substantial current at idle speed. Higher maximum output is also a possibility. This presents a potential danger when testing. As a precaution, a field rheostat should be used in the field circuit when making the following isolation test. The field rheostat permits positive control of the amount of current allowed to pass through the field circuit during the isolation test. Unregulated alternator capacity could ruin the unit.

NOTE: most manufacturers of precision gauges offer special test connectors, in sets, that will adapt to the leads and connections of any AC charging system.

Caution Before attempting the isolation test, disconnect the field wire from the regulator. Failure to take this precaution can cause instant burning and permanent damage to the regulator.

Isolation Test

(By-passing the Regulator)

1. Connect voltmeter leads to two prods driven into the battery posts.
2. Disconnect field wire from the FLD terminal of the voltage regulator.
3. Connect one lead of a field rheostat to the undisturbed IGN terminal of the regulator, and the other field rheostat lead to the wire that was removed from the FLD terminal of the regulator.
4. With field rheostat turned to the low side of the scale, (high resistance) start the engine and adjust throttle to about 2,000 rpm.
5. Slowly move field rheostat control knob to decrease resistance, (allowing more current to flow through the field circuit) until voltmeter reading slightly exceeds manufacturers' specifications.

NOTE: under load conditions, observe the alternator for arcing or any other evidence of malfunction.

6. If alternator performs satisfactorily, repair or replace the regulator. Conversely, if the voltmeter reading is zero, or below specifications, repair or replace the alternator.

Alternator Test Plans

The following is a procedure pattern for testing the various alternators and their control systems.

There are certain precautionary measures that apply to alternator tests in general. These items are listed in detail to avoid repetition when testing each make of alternator, and to encourage a habit of good test procedure.

1. Check alternator drive belt for condition and tension.
2. Disconnect battery cables, check physical, chemical, and electrical condition of battery.
3. Be absolutely sure of polarity before connecting any battery in the circuit. Reversed polarity will ruin the diodes.
4. Never use a battery charger to start the engine.

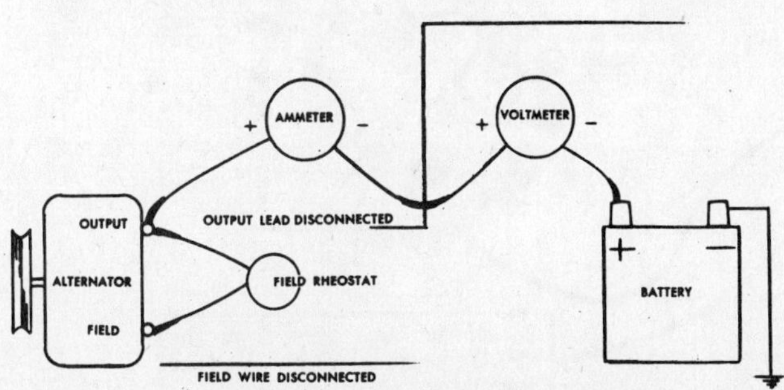

Plan to check charging circuit resistance

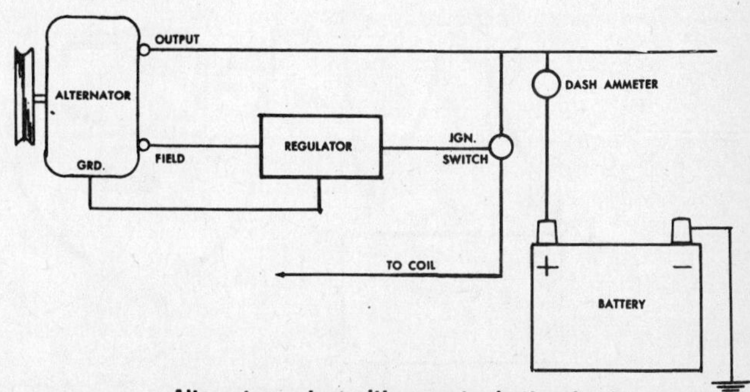

Alternator system with ammeter in the circuit

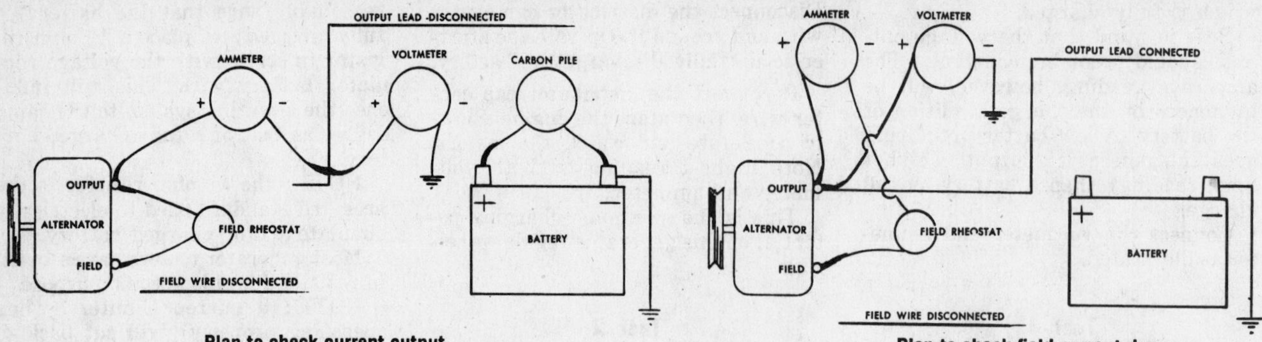

Plan to check current output

Plan to check field current draw

5. Disconnect both battery cables when making a battery recharge hook-up.
6. Be sure of polarity hook-up when using a booster battery for starting.
7. Never ground the alternator output or battery terminal.
8. Never ground the field circuit between alternator and regulator.
9. Never run any alternator on an open circuit with the field energized.
10. Never try to polarize an alternator.
11. Do not attempt to motor an alternator.
12. The regulator cover must be in place when taking voltage limiter readings.
13. The ignition switch must be in off position when removing or installing the regulator cover.
14. Use insulated tools only to make adjustments to the regulator.
15. When making engine idle speed adjustments, always consider potential load factors that influence engine rpm. To compensate for electrical load, switch on the lights, radio, heater, air conditioner, etc.

Diagnosis

Low or No Charging

1. Blown fuse.
2. Broken or loose fan belt.
3. Voltage regulator not working.
4. Brushes sticking.
5. Slip ring dirty.
6. Open circuit.
7. Bad wiring connections.
8. Bad diode rectifier.
9. High resistance in charging circuit.
10. Voltage regulator needs adjusting.
11. Grounded stator.
12. May be open rectifiers (check all three phases).
13. If rectifiers are found blown or open, check capacitor.

Noisy Unit

1. Damaged rotor bearings.
2. Poor alignment of unit.
3. Broken or loose belt.
4. Open diode rectifiers.

Regulator Points Burnt or Stuck

1. Regulator set too high.
2. Poor ground connections.
3. Shorted generator field.
4. Regulator air gap incorrect.

The Chrysler Alternator

Circuit Resistance Test

1. Disconnect battery ground cable.
2. Disconnect the lead from the alternator output terminal.
3. Hook up an ammeter as follows:
   A. Connect the positive lead to the alternator output terminal.
   B. Connect the negative lead to the lead just disconnected from the alternator output terminal.
4. Hook up voltmeter as follows:
   A. Connect the positive voltmeter lead to the lead just disconnected from the alternator output terminal.
   B. Connect the negative voltmeter lead to the positive battery post.

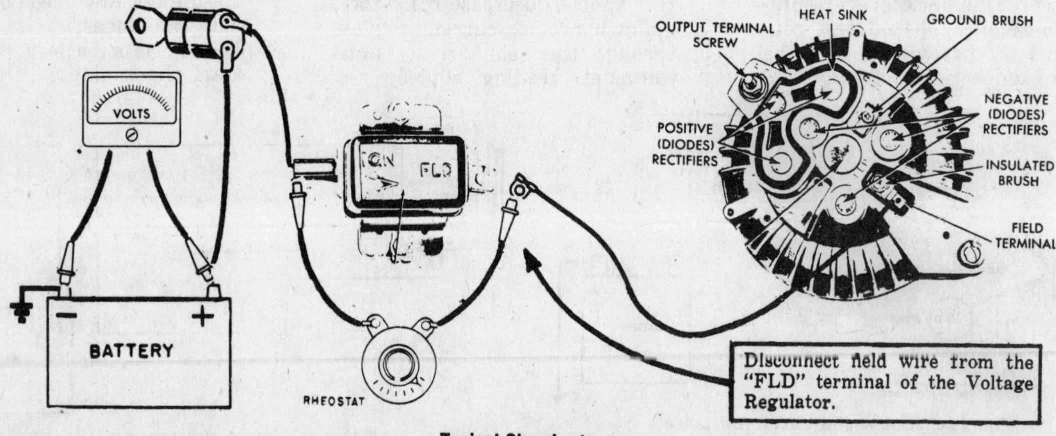

Typical Chrysler type

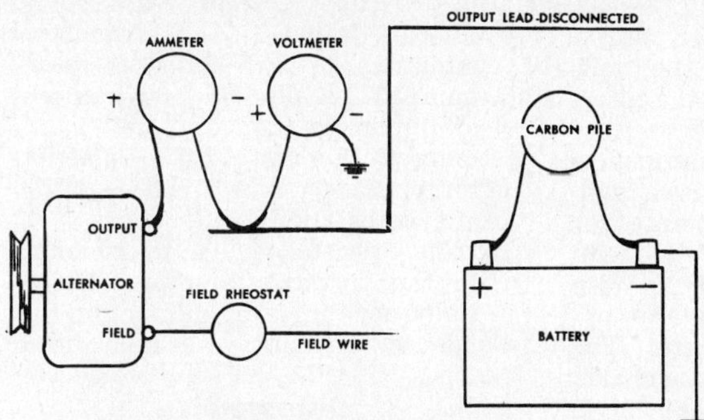

Plan to check voltage regulator setting

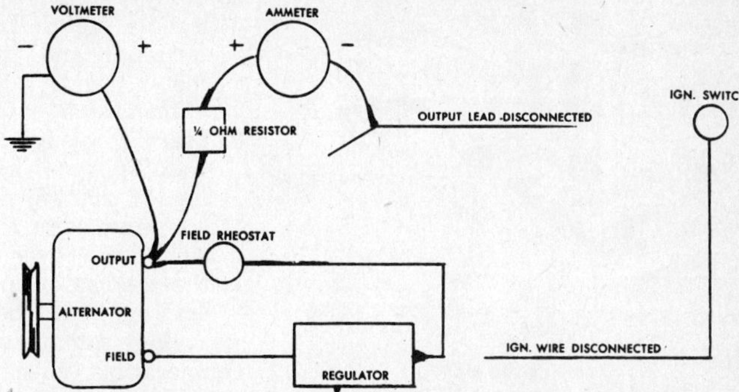

Plan to check voltage regulator with a ¼ ohm resistor in the circuit

5. Disconnect the lead from the alternator field terminal.
6. With field rheostat set to the open position, connect rheostat leads to the alternator field terminal and the alternator output terminal.
7. Hook up a tachometer to the engine.
8. Connect the battery ground cable.
9. Start the engine and set speed to recommended rpm.
10. Slowly adjust the field rheostat toward the closed position until the ammeter registers 10 amps.
11. The voltmeter reading will now show the voltage drop in the charging circuit. There should not be more than 0.2 volt drop.
12. Adjust field rheostat to the open position.
13. If the voltage drop exceeds 0.2 volt, stop the engine, clean and tighten all circuit connections, then repeat the test.

Current Output Test

1. The ammeter and field rheostat hook up should remain the same as for the circuit resistance check.
2. Connect the voltmeter negative lead to the battery negative post.
3. With carbon pile load control set in the off position, connect one lead to each battery post.
4. Start the engine and adjust speed to recommended rpm.
5. Slowly move the field rheostat control toward the closed position. Note voltmeter and ammeter readings. Maintain a 15 volt reading by adjusting the carbon pile control. With field rheostat closed, note ammeter reading.
6. Now, open the field rheostat and turn the carbon pile control to off position.
7. Compare ammeter reading with manufacturer's specifications. The reading should be no less than specified.
8. If below specifications:
   A. Check drive belt tension, adjust if necessary, then repeat the test.
   B. If results are still below specifications, internal trouble is indicated. Make a field current draw test.
9. If the readings are satisfactory, the next test, field current draw will be unnecessary.

Field Current Draw Test

Caution Disconnect battery ground at the battery, then:

1. With the output lead connected to the alternator output terminal, connect an ammeter positive lead to the alternator output terminal.
2. Connect the ammeter negative lead to a field rheostat lead.
3. Turn the field rheostat control to the open position.
4. Now, connect the remaining field rheostat lead to the alternator field terminal.
5. Hook up the voltmeter leads by connecting the positive lead to the alternator output terminal and the negative lead to ground.
6. The ground cable may now be reconnected to the battery negative post.
7. Turn the field rheostat control to the closed position, then check the ammeter and voltmeter readings.
8. Turn the field rheostat control to the open position, then compare the ammeter and voltmeter readings with manufacturers' specifications.
9. If readings are below specifications, the trouble probably lies in the brushes or slip rings.
10. If readings are above specifications, look for trouble in the rotor field windings.
11. If readings are as specified, but the alternator did not deliver its rated output, look for trouble in the stator or diodes.
12. Replace the alternator.

Voltage Regulator Setting

1. With the battery ground cable disconnected at the battery and the lead disconnected from the alternator output terminal, hook up an ammeter as follows:
   A. Connect the ammeter positive lead to the alternator output terminal.
   B. Connect the ammeter negative lead to the lead just disconnected from the alternator output terminal.
2. Hook up a voltmeter as follows:
   A. Connect the voltmeter positive lead to the lead just disconnected from the alternator output terminal.
   B. Connect the negative lead to ground.
3. Disconnect lead from alternator field terminal.
4. Hook up a field rheostat (with control in open position) to the alternator field terminal and to the lead which was just disconnected from this field terminal.
5. Connect a tachometer to the engine.
6. Hook up the ground cable to the battery.
7. Hook up a carbon pile (load control turned to the off position) between the battery posts.
8. With engine operating at 1500 rpm, adjust field rheostat control to the closed position and watch the voltmeter and ammeter.

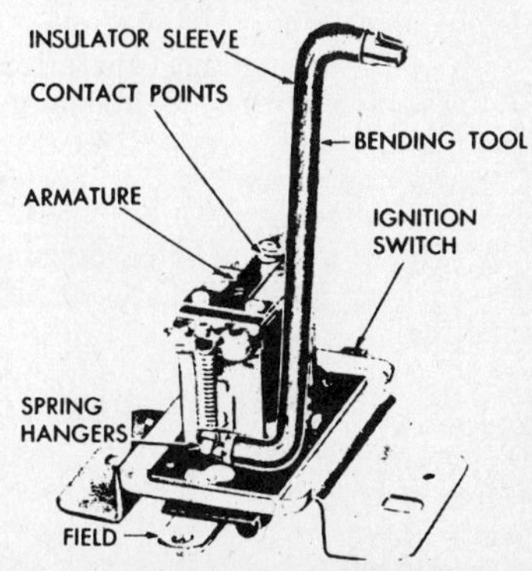

Adjusting spring tension

Checking the air gap

Caution Voltmeter reading must not exceed 15 volts. Continue to run the engine at this setting until the regulator has reached operating temperature.

9. With field rheostat in fully closed position, drop engine speed to recommended rpm for testing.
10. If the charging rate is above recommendations, the battery is probably in an undercharged condition. Either recharge the battery or replace it with a battery in fully charged condition.
11. If the charging rate is below 15 amps, regulate the carbon pile load to obtain a 15 amp rate.
12. With the voltage regulator temperature at running specifications, turn the carbon pile load control off and increase engine rpm to manufacturer's specifications. The ammeter should read 5 amps. or less and voltage should increase 0.2 volt to 0.7 volt. This indicates that both sets of points are working, within specified limits.
13. If the regulator fails to produce the above results, replace the regulator.

Voltage Regulator Specifications and Setting Test

Volts 12
Ground Polarity ....Negative
Point Gap ...... .015 ± .001 in.
Air gap .... .048 to .052 in.
(Measure gap with gauge touching nylon stops. Points closed with .052 in. gauge installed. Points open with .048 in. gauge installed.)

1. Connect an ammeter in series with the alternator output terminal (Bat.) and the wire disconnected from alternator DC output terminal.
2. Connect a DC voltmeter positive lead to the alternator DC output terminal and ground the voltmeter negative lead to the alternator frame or regulator base.
3. Start the engine and adjust to 1400 rpm and an ammeter reading of 10 amperes. Operate for 15 minutes to stabilize the temperature (cover in place). With the alternator and regulator operating, read the voltmeter. The voltage should be as in the chart:

Temperature checked about 2 in. from the cover. There will be a slightly higher voltage at higher engine speeds. However, this must not exceed 0.7 volts at any temperature range.

Caution Do not short circuit between the spring hanger and base or spring. Use an insulated bending tool. Grounding the spring hanger will damage the regulator (burn the contact spring).

Adjust the voltage if required by bending the lower spring hanger of the regulator down to increase voltage, up to decrease voltage.

Adjusting Voltage Regulator Air Gap

Set upper contact gap to get .048 in.-.052 in. air gap. Check air gap with a test lamp connected between the ignition and field terminals on the regulator. Insert the .048 in. wire gauge between the armature and the magnet core at the hanger side of the nylon stops. Press the armature plate down. Contacts should open and test light should go out. Insert the .052 in. gauge in the same position and depress the armature. Upper contacts should be closed and test lamp should remain lighted. Bend upper contact support as necessary to maintain the air gap adjustment.

Adjusting Lower Contact Clearance

Set lower contact gap to .015 in. (± .001 in.) by bending the lower contact arm. Press the armature down so that the armature rests on the nylon stop and recheck the contact gap.

Note: press down on the armature and not on the contact spring.

Specifications

Rotation ....clockwise at drive end
Voltage 12
Standard output (Amperes) 35
Heavy duty output 40
Brushes (number) 2
Field coil draw ......2.38 amperes minimum to 2.75 amperes maximum at 12-volts or 2.97 amperes minimum to 3.43 amperes maximum at 15 volts at 70° F alternator operating temperature at 750 alternator rpm.
Rectifier resistance ..4 to 10 ohms in the forward direction. Essentially none in reverse direction
Condenser capacity .. .5 microfarad

Disassembly

To prevent damage to the brush assemblies they should be removed before proceeding with the disassembly of the alternator. The insulated brush is mounted in a plastic holder that positions the brush vertically against one of the slip rings.

1. Remove the retaining screw, flat washer, nylon washer and field terminal and carefully lift the plastic holder containing the spring and brush assembly from the end housing.
2. The ground brush is positioned horizontally against the remaining slip ring and is retained in the holder that is integral with the end housing. Remove the retaining screw and lift the clip, spring and brush assembly from the end housing.

Caution The stator is laminated, don't burr the stator or end housings.

3. Remove the through bolts and pry between the stator and drive end housing with a thin blade screwdriver. Carefully separate the drive end housing, pulley and rotor assembly from the stator and rectifier housing assembly.
4. The pulley is an interference fit on the rotor shaft. Remove with puller, tool C-3615 and special adapters, tool SP-3002.
5. Remove the three nuts and washers and, while supporting the end frame, tap the rotor shaft with a plastic hammer and separate the rotor and end housing.
6. The drive end ball bearing is an interference fit with the rotor shaft. Remove the bearing with puller, tool C-3615 and adapters as follows:
   A. Position the center screw of puller on rotor shaft.
   B. Place the thin lower end of the adapters SP-3375 under the bearing equally spaced and the upper end of the adapters around the center screw.
   C. Hold adapters and center screw in position with the sleeve.

Operating Voltage (°F)—Surrounding Temperature

Temp. in degrees	20°	40°	60°	80°	100°	120°	140°
Minimum setting	13.9	13.82	13.74	13.65	13.56	13.48	13.40
	to	to	to	to	to	to	to
Maximum setting	14.5	14.42	14.34	14.25	14.16	14.08	14.0

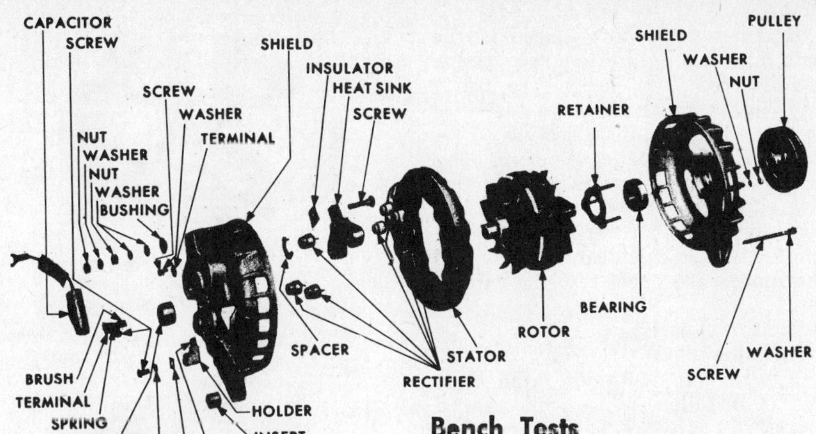

Alternator

Insulator brush

Caution Tool sleeve must bottom on bearings, otherwise adapters may be damaged.

D. Turning center screw clockwise while holding the body of the tool will draw the bearing from the shaft.

NOTE: further dismantling of the rotor is not advisable, as the remainder of the rotor assembly is not serviced separately.

7. Remove the DC output terminal nuts and washers and remove terminal screw and inside capacitor (on units so equipped).

NOTE: the heat sink is also held in place by the terminal screw.

8. Remove the insulator.

NOTE: three positive rectifiers are pressed into the heat sink and three negative rectifiers in the end housing. When removing the rectifiers, it is necessary to support the end housing and/or heat sink to prevent damage to these castings. Another caution is in order relative to the diode rectifiers. Don't subject them to unnecessary jolting. Heavy vibration or shock may ruin them.

A. Cut rectifier wire at point of crimp.
B. Support rectifier housing on tool C-3771.

NOTE: this tool is cut away and slotted to fit over the wires and around the bosses in the housing. Be sure that the bore of the tool completely surrounds the rectifier, then press the rectifier out of the housing with tool SP-3380.

NOTE: the roller bearing in the rectifier end frame is a press fit. To protect the end housing it is necessary to support the housing with tool SP-3383 when pressing the bearing out with tool C-3770.

Bench Tests

Field Circuit Open

1. Disconnect field terminal at the alternator and the voltage regulator.
2. Connect a DC ammeter positive lead to the alternator DC output terminal.
3. Connect the ammeter negative lead to the alternator field terminal.

Field Current Draw

12 volts ....2.38-2.75 amps.
15 volts ....2.97-3.43 amps.
(70°F, alternator rpm 750)

Testing Silicon Diode Rectifiers With Ohmmeter

Preferred method—rectifiers open in all three phases.

Disassemble the alternator and separate the wires at the Y-connection of the stator.

There are six diode rectifiers mounted in the back of the alternator. Three of them are marked with a plus (+), and three are marked with a minus (—). These marks indicate diode case polarity.

To test, set ohmmeter to its lowest range. If case is marked positive (+), place positive meter probe to case and negative probe to the diode lead. Meter should read between 4 and 10 ohms. Now, reverse leads of ohmmeter, connecting negative meter probe to positive case and positive meter probe to wire of rectifier. Set meter on a high range. Meter needle should move very little, if any (infinite reading). Do this to all three positive diode rectifiers.

The three with minus (—) marks on their cases are checked the same way as above. Only now the negative ohmmeter probe is connected to the case for a reading of 4 to 10 ohms. Reverse leads as above for the other part to test.

If a reading of 4 to 10 ohms is obtained in one direction and no reading (infinity) is read on the ohmmeter in the other direction, diode rectifiers are good. If either infinity or a low resistance is obtained in both directions on a rectifier, it must be replaced.

If meter reads more than 10 ohms when ohmmeter positive probe is

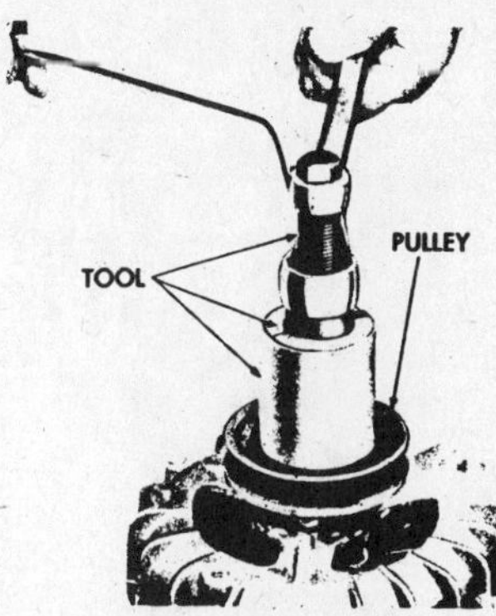

Removing the pulley

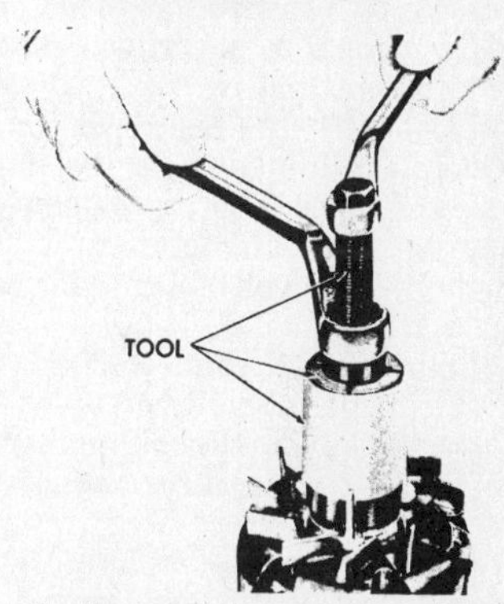

Pulling bearing from rotor shaft

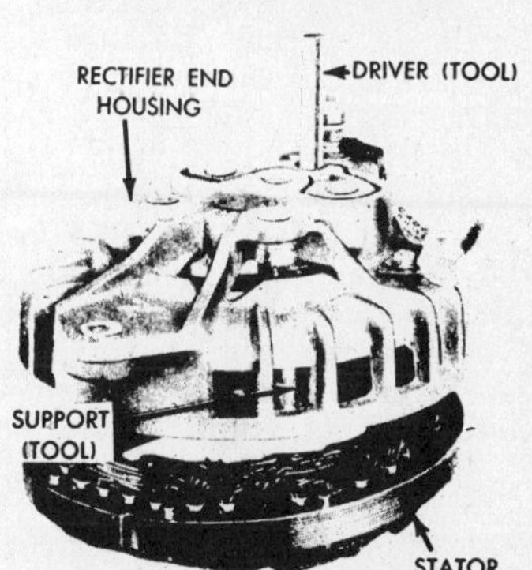

Removing a rectifier

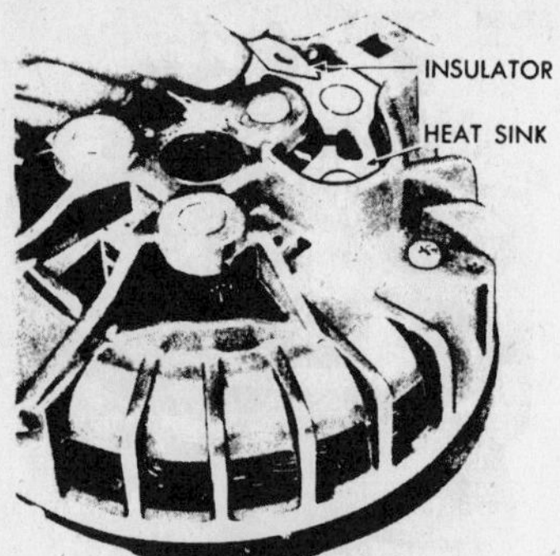

Heat sink and insulator

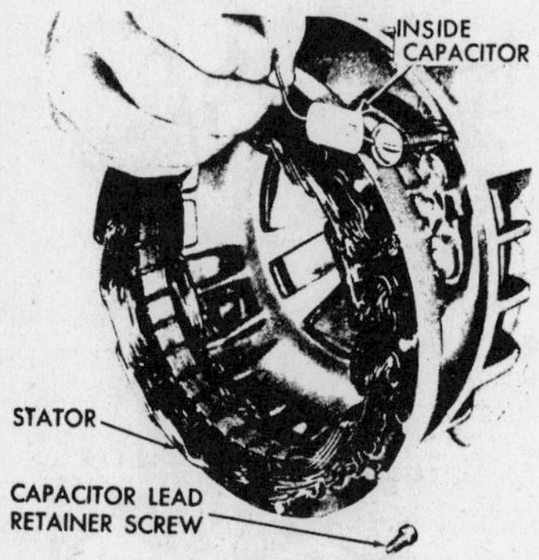

Inside capacitor

connected to positive on diode, and negative probe to negative, replace diode rectifier.

NOTE: with this test, it is necessary to determine the polarity of the ohmmeter probes. This can be done by connecting the ohmmeter to a DC voltmeter. The voltmeter will read up-scale when the positive probe of the ohmmeter is connected to the positive side of the voltmeter and the negative probe of the ohmmeter is connected to the negative side of the voltmeter.

Alternate method—test light.

Make-up a tester as shown in sketch. Refer to first paragraph of the preferred method. Be sure lead from center of the diode rectifiers is disconnected.

To test rectifiers with plus (+) case, touch positive probe of tester to case and minus (—) probe to lead wire of rectifier. Bulb should light if rectifier is good. If bulb does not light, replace rectifier.

Now reverse tester probe connections to rectifier. Bulb should not light. If bulb does light, replace rectifier.

For testing minus (—) marked cases, follow above procedure, except that now bulb should light with negative probe of tester touching rectifier case and positive probe touching lead wire.

Rectifier is good if the bulb lights when tester probes are connected one way, and does not light when tester connections are reversed.

Rectifier must be replaced if the bulb does not light either way tester is connected. Also, replace rectifier if bulb lights for both ways tester is connected to the diode rectifier.

NOTE: the usual cause of an open or blown diode or rectifier is a defective capacitor or a battery that has been installed in reverse polarity. If the battery is installed properly and the diodes are open, test the capacitor.

Capacitor capacity:
(int. installed)
............158 microfarad, min.
(ext. installed) .... .5 microfarad

Ground Stator

1. Disconnect the diode rectifiers from the stator leads.
2. Test from stator leads to stator core, using a 110-volt test lamp. Replace stator assembly if grounded.

Low Output

(About 50% output accompanied with a growl-hum caused by a shorted phase or a shorted rectifier.)

Perform Steps 1, 2 and 3 (rectifier open in all three phases). If the rectifiers are found to be within specifications, replace the stator assembly.

Current Output Too High (No Control) Caused by Open Rectifier or Open Phase

Perform Steps 1, 2 and 3 (rectifier open in all three phases). If the rectifier tests satisfactorily, inspect the stator connections before replacing the stator.

Assembly

1. Support the heat sink or rectifier end housing on circular plate, tool SP-3377.
2. Check rectifier identification to be sure the correct rectifier is being used. The part numbers are stamped on the case of the rectifier. They are also marked, red for positive and black for negative.
3. Start the new rectifier into the casting and press it in with tool C-3772.
4. Crimp attach the new rectifier wire to the wires disconnected at removal.
5. Support the end housing on tool SP-3383 so that the notch in the support tool will clear the raised section of the heat sink and press the bearing into position with tool SP-3381.

NOTE: new bearings are pre-lubricated, additional lubrication is not required.

6. Insert the drive end bearing in the drive end housing and install the bearing plate, washers and nuts to hold the bearing in place.
7. Position the bearing and drive end housing on the rotor shaft and while supporting the base of the rotor shaft, press the bearing and housing in position on the

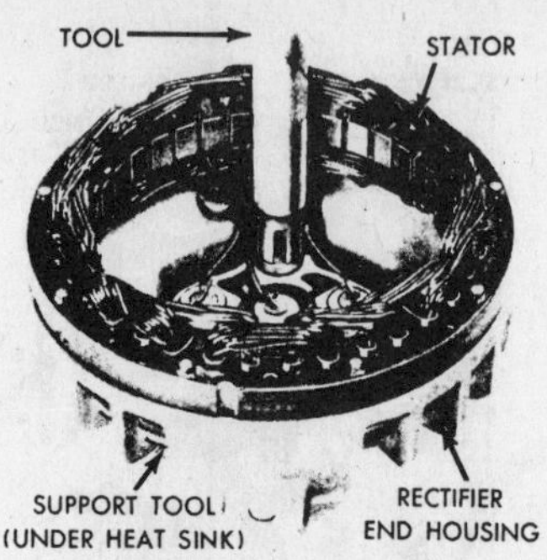

Installing diode rectifier

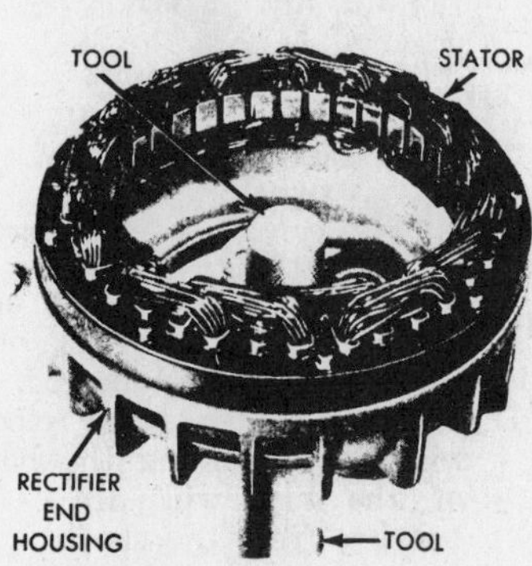

Installing end frame bearing

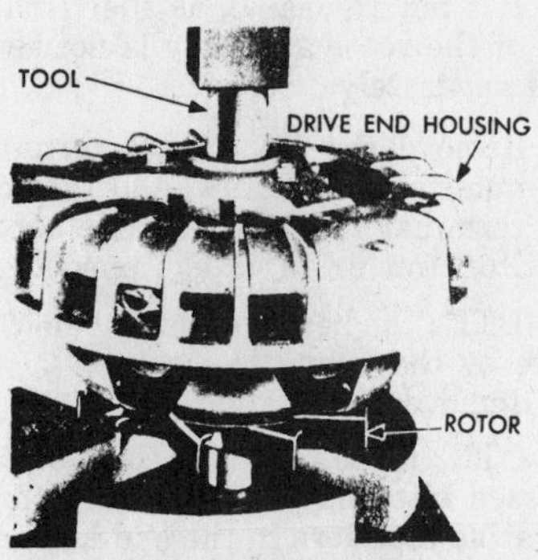

Installing drive end frame and bearing on rotor shaft

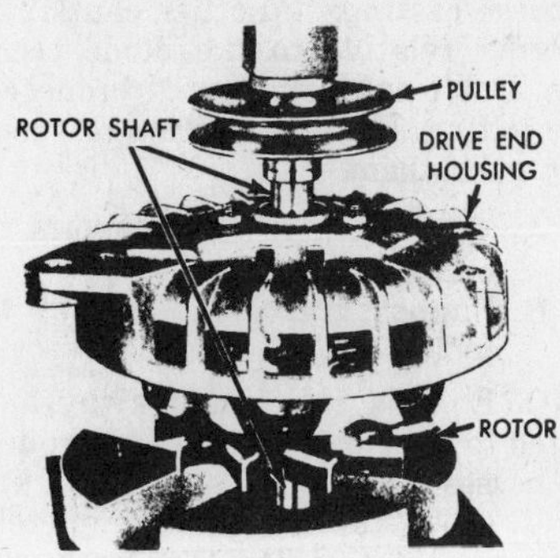

Installing the pulley

rotor shaft with an arbor press and tool C-3769.

Caution Be careful that there is no cocking of the bearing at installation; or damage will result. Press the bearing on the rotor shaft until the bearing contacts the shoulder on the rotor shaft.

8. Install pulley on rotor shaft. Shaft of rotor must be supported so that all pressing force is on the pulley hub and rotor shaft.

NOTE: Do not exceed 6,800 lbs. pressure. Pulley hub should just contact bearing inner race.

9. Some alternators will be found to have the capacitor mounted internally. Be sure the heat sink insulator is in place.
10. Install the output terminal screw with the capacitor attached through the heat sink and end housing.
11. Install insulating washers, lockwashers and locknuts.
12. Make sure the heat sink and insulator are in place and tighten the locknut.
13. Position the stator on the rectifier end housing. Be sure that all of the rectifier connectors and phase leads are free of interference with the rotor fan blades and that the capacitor (internally mounted) lead has clearance.
14. Position the rotor assembly in the rectifier end housing. Align the through bolt holes in the stator with both end housings.
15. Enter stator shaft in the rectifier end housing bearing, compress stator and both end housings manually and install through bolts, washers and nuts.
16. Install the insulated brush and terminal attaching screw.
17. Install the ground screw and attaching screw (see illustration).
18. Rotate pulley slowly to be sure the rotor fan blades do not hit the rectifier and stator connectors.

Testing the Alternator System (In the Truck)

With the battery fully charged and in good condition and the engine at normal operating temperature, proceed with tests as follows:

Caution Never ground the field circuit between the alternator and the regulator as this will result in damage to the voltage regulator.

Charging Circuit Resistance Test

1. Connect a DC ammeter which will read a minimum of 40 amperes in series with the alternator DC output terminal and the DC output lead which was disconnected from the alternator.
2. Connect a DC voltmeter positive lead to the DC output lead that was disconnected from the alternator, and the voltmeter negative lead to the battery positive post.

NOTE: A voltage drop test across each connection will locate any bad connections.

3. Start the engine and adjust the speed to produce 10 amperes from the alternator. The voltage reading should not exceed .2 volt. If there is higher voltage drop, clean and tighten all connections in the charging circuit and recheck charging circuit resistance.

Delcotron By Delco-Remy

Although the unit is built to give long periods of trouble-free service, a regular inspection procedure should be followed to enjoy the maximum life that is built into each generator.

Inspection

Frequency of inspection is determined by exposure to adverse operating conditions. High speed operation, high temperatures, dust and dirt all increase wear on brushes, slip rings and bearings.

At regular periods, inspect terminals for corrosion and loose connections, and the wiring for frayed insulation. Check mounting bolts for tightness, and the belt for alignment, proper tension and wear. Because of higher load capacity and the higher inertia of the heavy rotor used in AC generators, belt tension is more critical. Tension should be adjusted according to the vehicle manufacturer's recommendations. In most cases this will be slightly greater than for DC generators.

Noisy Generator

Noise in a Delcotron may be caused by worn or dirty bearings, loose mounting or a loose drive pulley. In the self-rectifying generator, noise may come from a shorted or open diode.

Indicator or Ammeter

There are two types of regulators used with this system.

A. A three-unit regulator, containing a voltage regulator, a field relay, and an indicator lamp relay.
B. A two-unit regulator, containing a voltage regulator, and a field relay. In this instance, the indicator lamp relay is omitted. The two unit regulator is used in circuits equipped with an ammeter. There is no L terminal on the regulator.

Except for the indicator lamp relay test, all other tests are conducted in the same way.

Indicator Lamp Relay Test

1. Turn ignition switch on; do not start the engine. If indicator does not burn, check for burned out bulb.
2. If light does burn, but stays on after the engine is started and

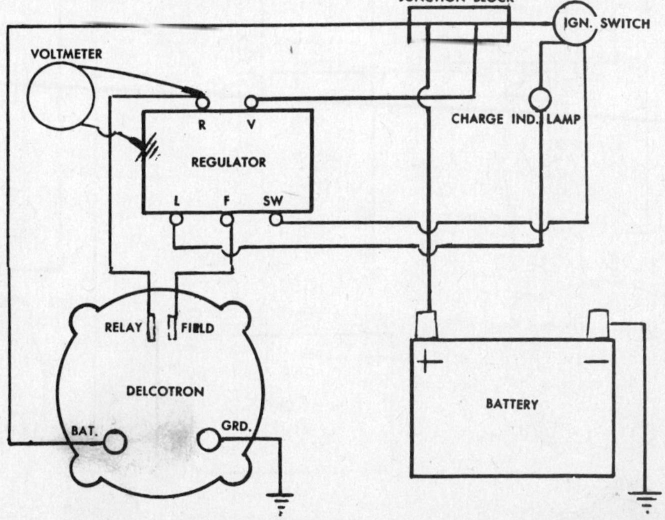

Plan to check indicator lamp relay

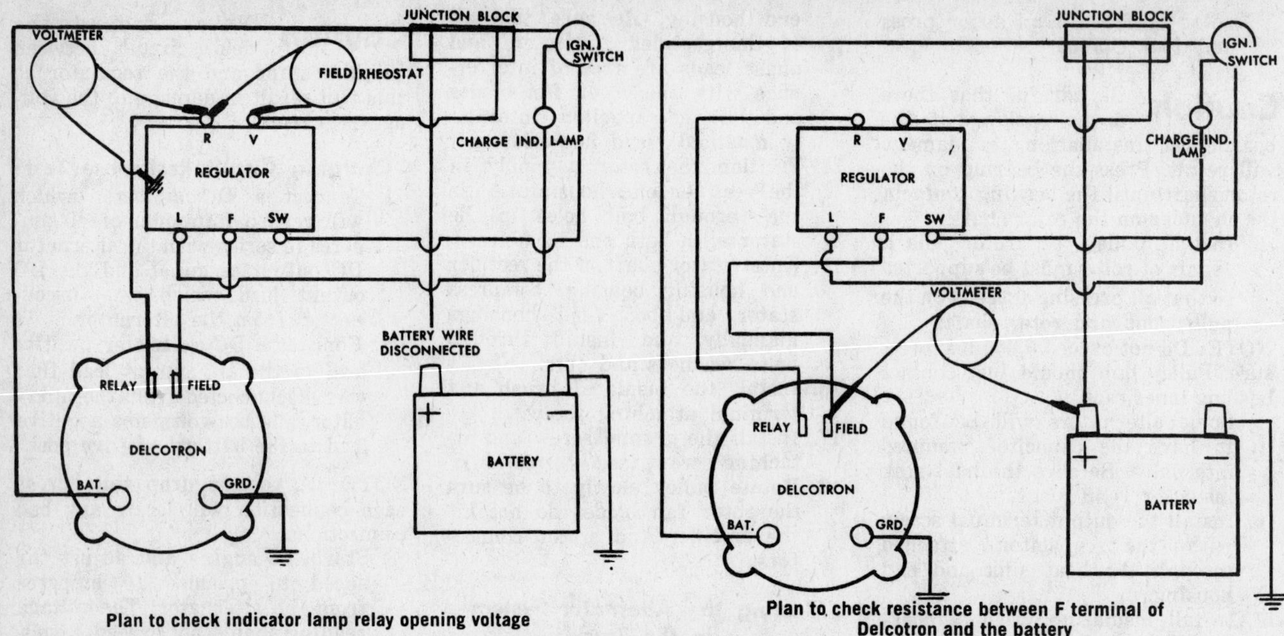

Plan to check indicator lamp relay opening voltage

Plan to check resistance between F terminal of Delcotron and the battery

the generator is in operation:

A. Connect voltmeter leads to the R terminal and a ground on the regulator.

B. If voltmeter reading is more than 5 volts, the indicator lamp relay is defective.

C. If voltmeter reading is 5 volts or less, trouble lies elsewhere in the system.

Indicator Lamp Relay Opening Voltage Test

1. With a 50-75 ohm field rheostat connected to the R and V terminals of the regulator, turn rheostat control to the open position.
2. Connect a voltmeter to the R and ground terminal on the regulator.
3. Turn the field rheostat control slowly, to reduce resistance, then note voltage the instant the relay opens.
4. Compare this reading with truck manufacturers', or Delcotron, specifications.

Field Relay Test

1. Connect a voltmeter to the F terminal and the ground on the regulator.
2. Turn ignition switch on; do not start the engine. Voltmeter should read battery voltage.
3. If voltmeter reads zero, check field relay closing voltage.

Field Relay Closing Voltage Test

1. Disconnect lead at SW terminal of regulator.
2. Connect a 50-75 ohm field rheostat to the SW terminal. Connect the other rheostat lead to the lead which was disconnected from the SW terminal. Then, turn the field rheostat control to the open position.

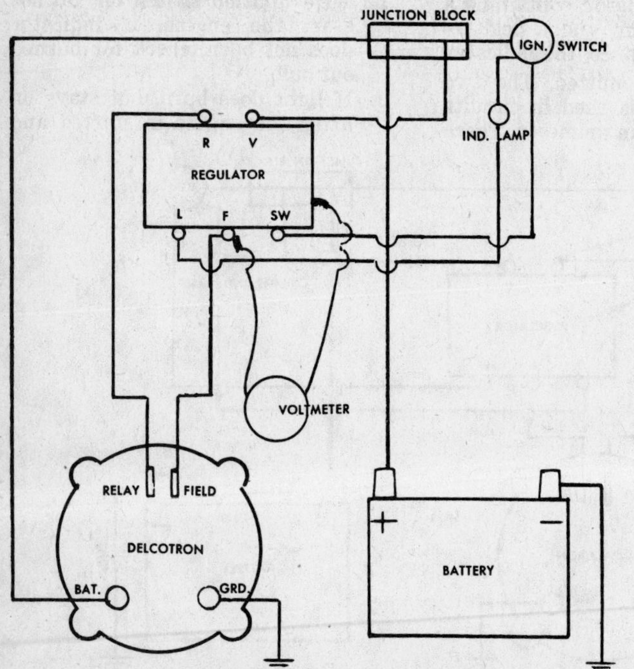

Plan to check Delcotron field relay

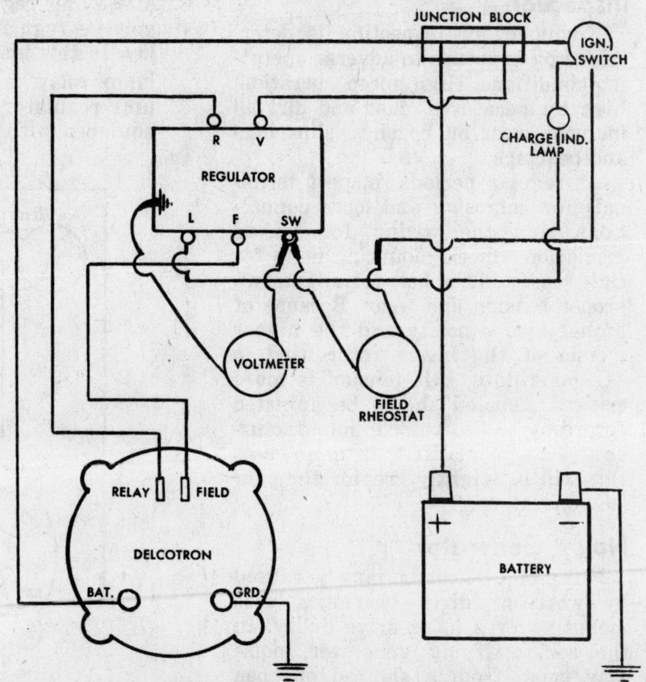

Plan for checking field relay closing voltage

3. Connect voltmeter leads to SW terminal and ground of the regulator.
4. Turn field rheostat control slowly, to reduce resistance, then note the voltage the instant the relay closes.
5. Compare this voltmeter reading with car manufacturers', or Delcotron, specifications.

Resistance Test—Delcotron F Terminal to Battery Positive Post

Caution Serious damage to the regulator will result by accidentally grounding the field terminal.

1. Hook up a voltmeter to the field terminal of the Delcotron and the battery, positive post.
2. Turn on ignition switch but do not start the engine.
3. If voltmeter reading is more than 0.3 volt, clean and tighten:
   A. All connections between the V terminal on the regulator and the battery positive post.
   B. All connections between the F terminal on the regulator and the Delcotron field terminal.
   C. Connections at Bat. terminal of the Delcotron.
4. If voltmeter reading is still more than 0.3 volt, the trouble lies in the field relay or the voltage regulator contacts, or a shorted or grounded field. This can be determined by the next test.

Field Current Draw Test

1. Disconnect the lead from the F terminal of the regulator.
2. Hook an ammeter to the lead just disconnected and to the F terminal of the regulator.
3. Turn ignition switch on and note the ammeter reading.
4. Compare this reading with truck manufacturers', or Delcotron, specifications.

Delcotron Output Test

1. Disconnect lead from Bat. terminal of Delcotron.
2. Hook an ammeter to the lead just disconnected, and to the Bat. terminal of the Delcotron.
3. Hook up the voltmeter leads to the Bat. terminal and ground terminal of the Delcotron.
4. Disconnect the lead from the F terminal of the regulator.
5. Hook up a field rheostat to the V terminal of the regulator and to the lead that was disconnected from the F terminal of the regulator. Rotate the field rheostat control knob to the open position.

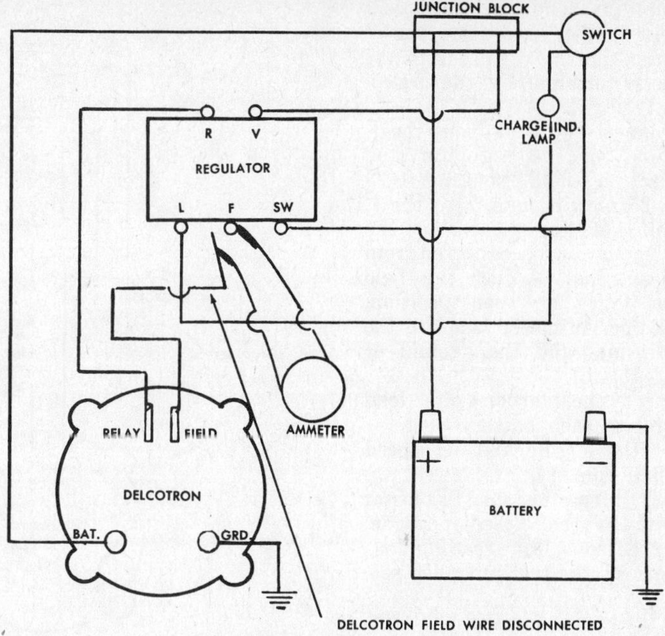

Plan to check field current draw

6. With a carbon pile load control hooked up to the battery posts, start the engine and set engine rpm to manufacturers' specifications.
7. Slowly turn field rheostat control knob toward closed position. Note ammeter and voltmeter readings.

Caution Be careful not to exceed the recommended regulator voltage setting. This is controlled by the carbon pile load.

8. Compare ammeter and voltmeter readings with specifications.

Voltage Regulator Setting Test

1. Disconnect the lead from Bat. terminal of regulator.
2. Connect ammeter leads and a ¼ ohm resistor (25 watts or more) in series with the Bat. terminal of the Relcotron and the lead which was disconnected from this terminal.
3. Disconnect lead from the V term-

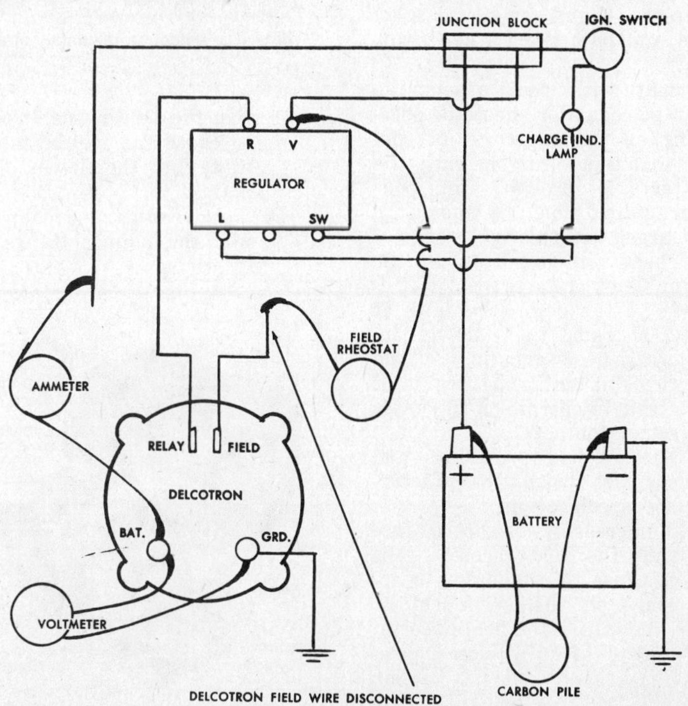

Plan to check Delcotron output

inal of the regulator, then connect a jumper lead from the V terminal on the regulator to the battery terminal on the Delcotron.

4. Disconnect the lead from the F terminal of the regulator and connect a field rheostat (25 watt-25 ohm or more) to the F terminal of the regulator and the lead which was disconnected from this terminal. Adjust the field rheostat to the open position.
5. Hook the voltmeter leads to the V terminal and the ground of the regulator.
6. Connect the carbon pile load control to each battery post.
7. Start the engine and set speed to 1500 rpm.
8. Slowly turn the field rheostat control to the closed position. Be sure that voltage reading does not exceed the recommended setting.
9. Run the engine for about 15 minutes at this speed with the regulator cover in place.
10. Now, cycle the Delcotron.
    A. Turn field rheostat control to full open position.
    B. Alternately disconnect and reconnect the jumper lead at the V terminal of the regulator.
    C. Return field rheostat control to fully closed position.

Caution Do not disconnect the field rheostat while the engine is running or the control is in closed position.

11. Increase engine speed to 2500 rpm and note the voltage reading.
12. Compare with specifications. The voltage regulator should be operating on the upper set of contacts. If this is not the case, the battery is probably in poor charge condition and should be recharged or replaced.
13. To check voltage setting on the lower set of contacts:
    A. Have the engine running at 2500 rpm, then slowly increase resistance in the field rheostat until the regulator starts to operate on the lower set of contacts.
    B. Note voltage reading and compare with manufacturers' specifications.
    C. If increasing the resistance with the field rheostat fails to cause the regulator to operate on the lower set of points, turn the field rheostat control to fully closed position, then turn the carbon pile load control to lightly load the battery. Now, adjust the field rheostat control to cause the regulator to operate on the lower set of points.
    D. Note reading and compare it with the manufacturers' specifications.

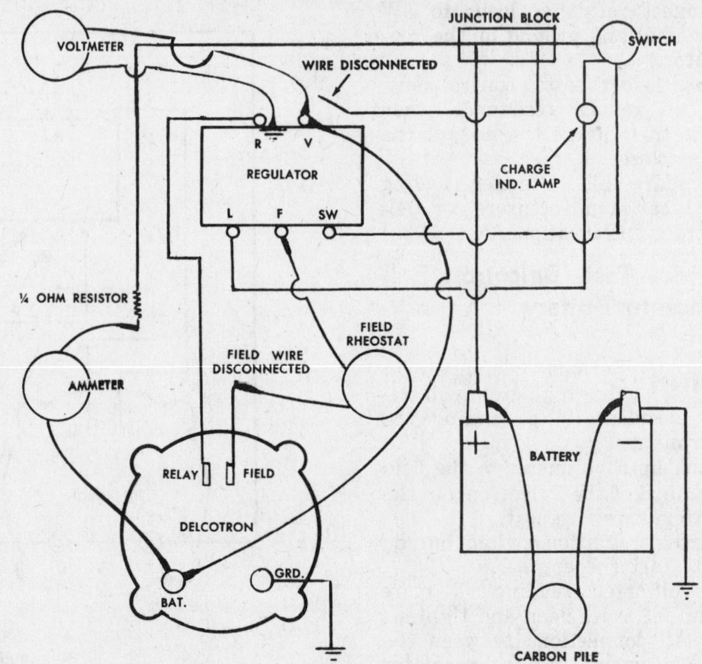

Plan to check voltage regulator setting

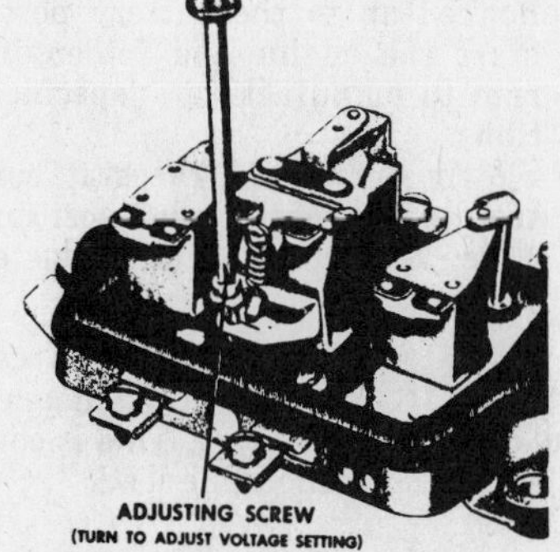

Adjusting Delcotron regulator voltage

Disassembly

After long periods of operation, or at engine overhaul, the generator should be removed, disassembled and cleaned. The unit consists of four main components—the two end frames, the stator and the rotor.

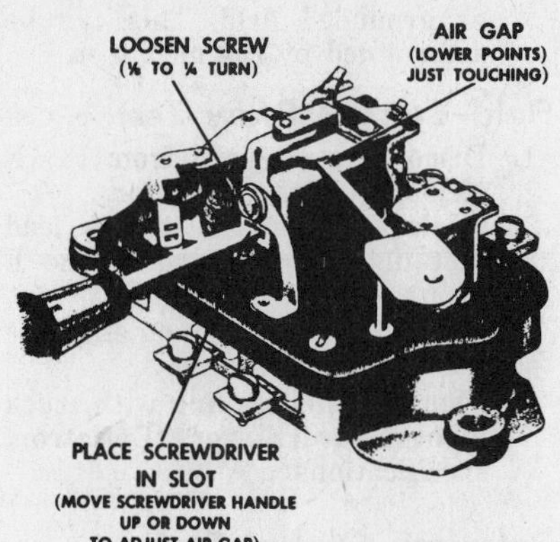

Adjusting Delcotron regulator air gap

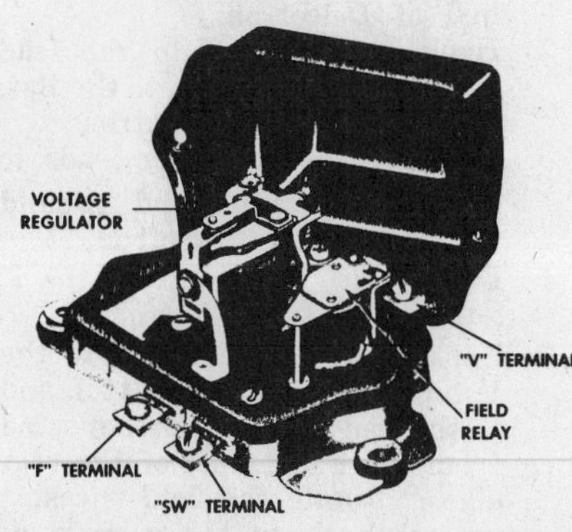

Three-unit and two-unit Delcotron regulators

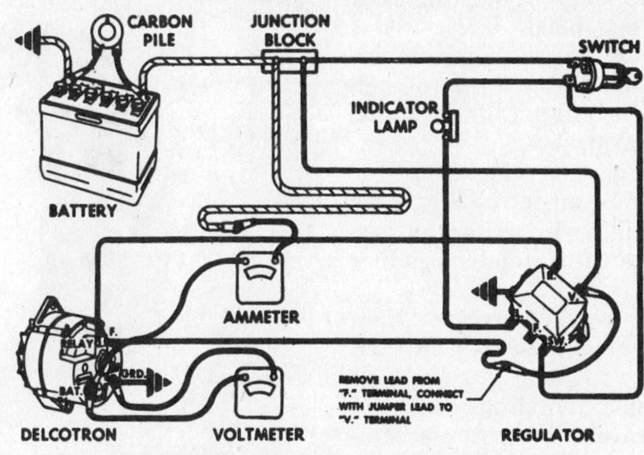

Checking Delcotron regulator output

1. Remove four thru-bolts.
2. Separate drive end frame and rotor from stator assembly by prying with screwdriver. Note that separation is between stator frame and drive end frame.
3. Place tape over slip ring end frame bearing to seal dirt.
4. Lightly clamp rotor in vise to remove shaft nut.

Caution Do not distort rotor by tightening vise too much.

5. After nut removal, take off washer, pulley, fan and collar.
6. Separate drive end frame from rotor shaft.

Diode Tests

There are six silicon diodes mounted on the slip ring end frame assembly. Three of these diodes are mounted in the end frame, and three are mounted into a bracket, or heat sink, which is attached to, but insulated from, the slip ring end frame. The Bat. terminal on the generator is attached to the insulated heat sink.

All diodes are marked with either a + or — on the hexagonal head, to identify the polarity of the case. On a generator to be used with a negative ground system, the negative case diodes are mounted into the slip ring end frame and the positive case diodes are mounted into the insulated heat sink. Diodes with a negative case have positive polarity leads, whereas positive case diodes have negative polarity leads. To further identify these diodes, the negative case diodes have right-hand threads and the positive case diodes left-hand threads.

Diodes can be checked for shorts or opens with an ohmmeter. To check for shorts, connect the negative lead of the ohmmeter to the negative case of the diode. Connect the positive lead of the ohmmeter to the positive lead of the diode. Reverse the connections for positive case

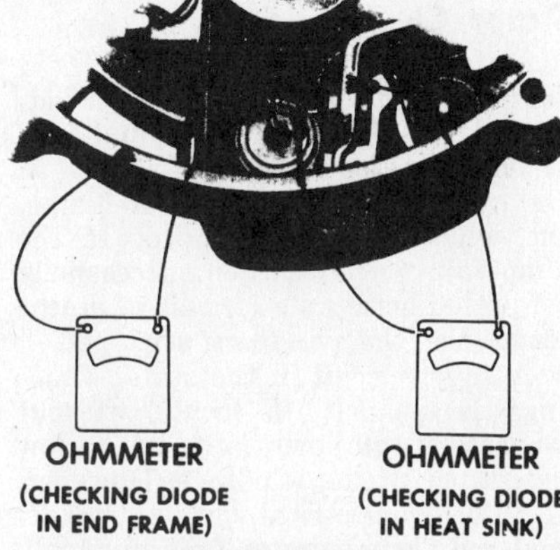

Checking diodes

diodes. Ohmmeter readings may vary considerably when checking diodes, but if the reading is below 300 ohms, the diode most likely is faulty and should be replaced. Push and pull on the lead to show up loose connections. Use an ohmmeter scale on which the 300 ohm value can be accurately read.

NOTE: the polarity of the ohmmeter leads must be determined. This can be done by connecting the ohmmeter to a DC voltmeter. The voltmeter will read up scale when the positive lead of the ohmmeter is connected to the positive side of the voltmeter and the ohmmeter negative lead is connected to the negative side of the voltmeter.

To check for an open circuit, connect the negative lead of the ohmmeter to the positive lead of the diode and the positive lead of the ohmmeter to the negative case of the diode. Reverse the connections for positive case diodes. If the ohmmeter reads an infinite resistance (all the way), the diode is open and must be replaced.

Diode Replacement

To replace a diode that is mounted in the outside frame, use diagonal cutters to clip the leads on each side of the diode lead. Leave about ½ in. of lead length on each side of the diode lead to match the replacement diode. Remove the defective diode.

Before installing the new diode, lightly coat the threads with silicon grease or light engine oil. Install the diode and torque to 200 in. lbs. Strip about ½ in. of insulation from the long lead which is connected to the nylon terminal holder, and place over the long lead the insulating sleeve which is supplied with the new diode. Join the ends of the leads of the new diode to the respective leads in the end frame, using the special connectors provided with the new diode. Crimp the connectors tightly over the ends of the wires and solder securely. Then push the sleeve over the soldered connector.

Caution Use only 60% tin, 40% lead solder, or other solder with melting point of 360° F or above.

To replace a diode mounted in the heat sink, it is necessary to remove the heat sink from the end frame. This is done by clipping the lead midway between each pair of negative and positive case diodes, removing the nylon terminal holder from the frame and the leads from the holder, and then removing the Bat. terminal and the heat sink attaching screws. It is not necessary to clip

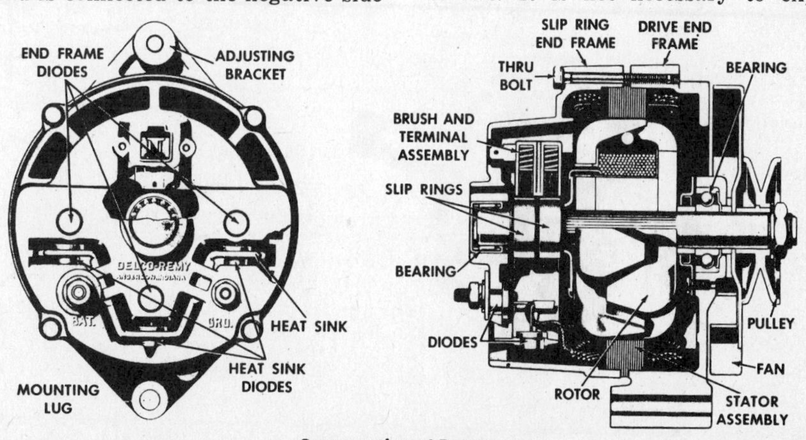

Cross-section of Delcotron

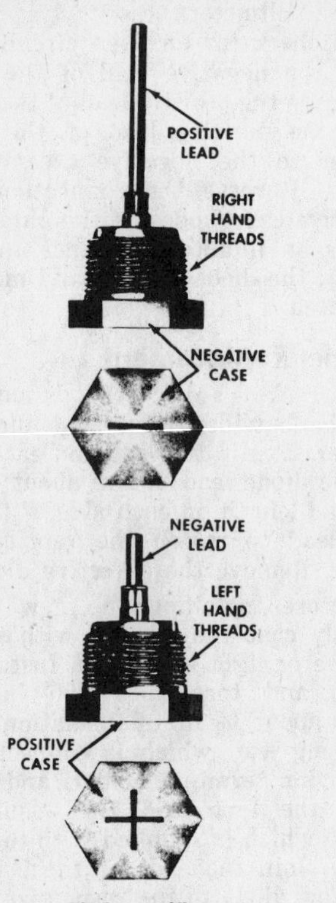

Diode rectifiers

the long insulated leads attached to the diodes mounted in the outside end frame.

Caution Negative case diodes have right-hand threads, and positive case diodes have left-hand threads.

After removing the defective diode, lightly coat the threads of the new diode with lubricant, install, torque and solder.

Rotor Checks

The rotor may be checked electrically for grounded, open, or shorted field coils.

To check for grounds, connect a 100-volt test light from either slip ring to the rotor shaft or to the laminations. If the lamp lights, the field windings are grounded.

To check for opens, connect the leads of a 110-volt test light to each slip ring. If the lamp fails to light, the windings are open.

The windings are checked for short-circuits by connecting a battery and ammeter in series with the two slip rings. Note the ammeter reading and refer to the chart.

An ammeter reading greater than the specified value indicates shorted windings.

Since the field windings are not serviced separately, the rotor assembly must be replaced if the windings are defective.

Stator Checks

Stator windings may be checked for grounded, open, or shorted windings. If a 110-volt test lamp lights when connected from any terminal in the nylon holder to the stator frame, the windings are grounded. If the lamp fails to light when successively connected between each pair of stator terminals, the windings are open.

A short circuit in the stator windings is difficult to locate without laboratory equipment, due to the low resistance of the windings. However, if all other electrical checks are normal and the generator fails to supply the rated output, shorted stator windings are indicated.

Slip Ring Servicing and Replacement

Slip rings which are rough or out of round should be trued in a lathe to

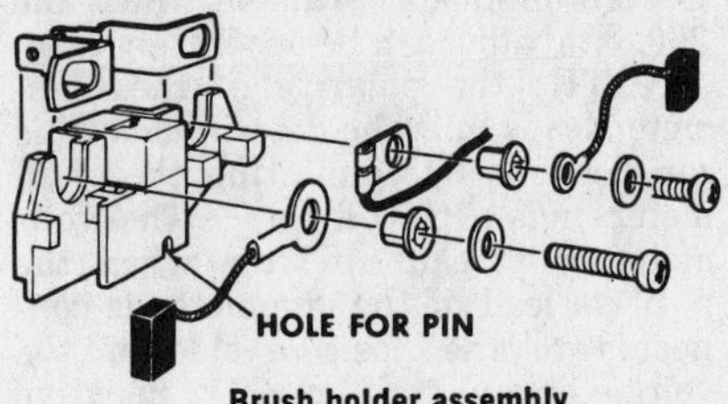

Brush holder assembly

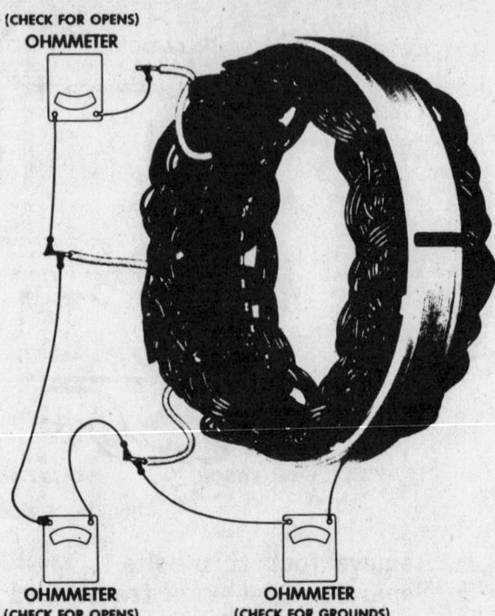

Checking Delcotron stator

.001 in. maximum indicator reading. Remove only enough material to make the rings smooth and round. Finish with 400 grit or finer polishing cloth and blow away all dust.

Slip rings which must be replaced can be removed from the shaft with a gear puller, after the leads have been unsoldered. The new assembly should be pressed on with a sleeve which just fits over the shaft; this will apply all the pressure to the inner slip ring collar and prevent damage to the outer slip ring. Only pure tin solder should be used when reconnecting field leads.

Brush Replacement

The extent of brush wear can be determined by comparison with a new brush. If brushes are one-half worn, they should be replaced.

1. Remove brush holder assembly from end frame by removing two holder assembly screws.
2. Place springs and brushes in the holder and insert straight wire or pin into holes at bottom of holder to retain brushes.
3. Attach holder assembly onto end frame.

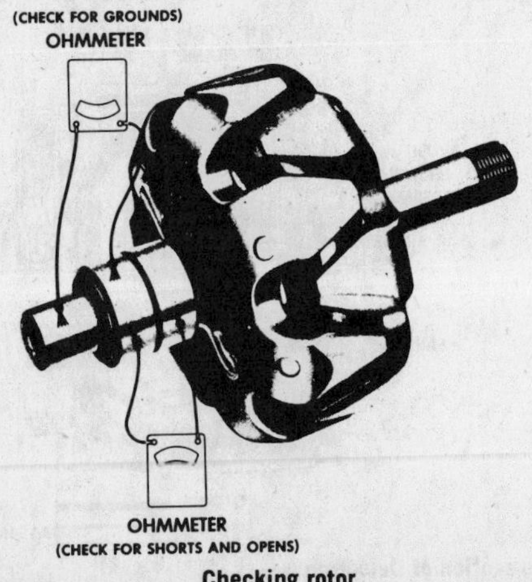

Checking rotor

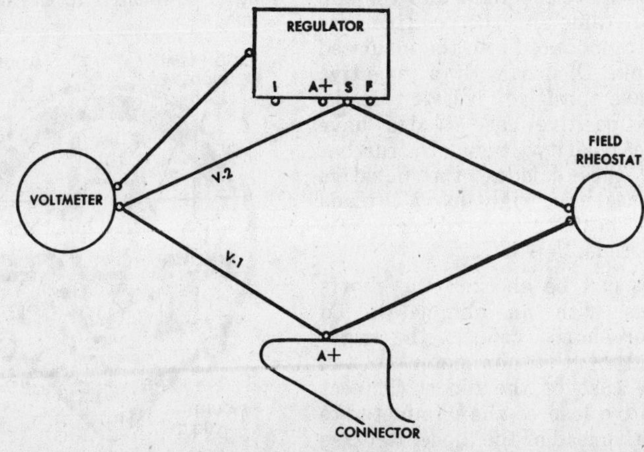

Plan to make field relay checks

The Ford System

To Make All Following Tests

In addition to the regular precautionary measures:

1. Disconnect both battery cables, clean the terminal posts and clamps, then reconnect the ground cable only.
2. Install a special battery make-and-break adapter switch between battery, positive (+) post, and battery cable. Close the adapter switch.

Field Relay Test

1. Withdraw regulator main connector and remove regulator cover.
2. Connect field rheostat leads to the S terminal of the regulator and the A+ terminal of the regulator. Place rheostat control in open position.
3. Connect one voltmeter lead to the regulator body (ground). Run the other voltmeter lead to the A+ regulator terminal.
4. Turn ignition switch on. The reading should be the same as existing battery voltage.
5. Remove the voltmeter connection from the regulator A+ terminal and connect it to the S terminal.
6. Now, slowly turn the rheostat control knob until field relay contacts close. Note voltage reading at this instant. This is relay closing voltage.
7. Repeat Step 6 several times. If closing voltage is not as specified by the manufacturer, or the contacts are not operating properly, replace the regulator.

Alternator Output on the Car

1. Connect test ammeter leads to the battery adapter switch. Open and close switch, and check polarity.

NOTE: when the battery adapter switch is opened, current will flow through the test ammeter. Never operate the alternator with an open circuit.

2. Withdraw main connector from the regulator. Connect the field rheostat leads to the A+ and F terminals of the main connector. Set field rheostat to open position.
3. Connect carbon pile load control leads to the battery posts.
4. Connect voltmeter lads to their polar respective battery posts.
5. Throw the battery adapter switch to the closed position, then start the engine.
6. Open the battery adapter switch. Current being generated will now flow through the test ammeter.

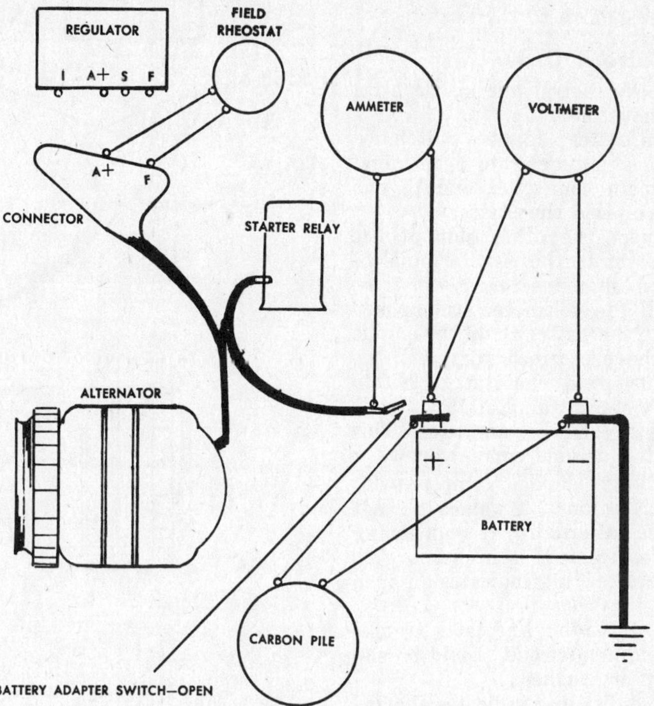

Plan to make output checks

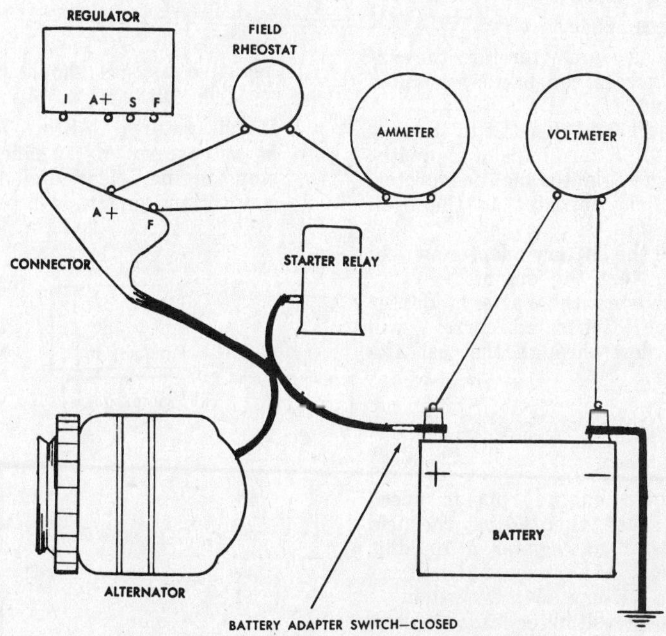

Plan to make field current draw check

7. Increase engine speed to specified rpm, then adjust the field rheostat until the voltmeter registers exactly 15 volts.
8. Read the ammeter, then add 5 amps. to this reading, to determine the total alternator output. The addition of 5 amps. to the meter reading is to compensate for the current used by the ignition, and the alternator field circuits.

NOTE: maximum current output may not be possible if the battery is fully charged. When this situation exists, turn the field rheostat toward the resistance out position, holding the voltage at 15 volts by applying a load with the carbon pile load control.

If the rated output is not produced, go on to the next test.

Field Current Draw Test

1. Remove carbon pile load control from last hook-up.
2. Close battery adapter switch.
3. Connect ammeter to F terminal of main connector, and to one side of field rheostat.
4. Connect the other side of the rheostat to the A+ terminal of the main connector.
5. With the voltmeter still hooked up to the battery, run the engine at the prescribed rpm.
6. Adjust field rheostat to obtain voltmeter reading of 15 volts.
7. Now, read the ammeter. This reading is field current draw.
8. Reading should comply with specifications. If values do not agree, alternator reconditioning or replacement is in order.
   A zero reading indicates an open circuit.
   A low reading indicates trouble in the field circuit; could be slip rings or brushes.
   A high reading indicates shorted or grounded turns in the fields.

Charging Circuit Resistance Test

1. Hook the ammeter into the circuit across the battery adapter switch.
2. Connect field rheostat to the A+ and the F terminals of the withdrawn regulator main connector. Set field rheostat to the open position.
3. Close the battery adapter switch, then start the engine.
4. Now, open the battery adapter switch. Generated current will now flow through the test ammeter.

Caution Never operate the alternator on an open circuit.

5. Increase engine rpm to specified speed, then adjust the field rheostat to register a 10 amp. charge. Do not exceed 15 volts.
6. Close battery adapter switch.
7. Connect voltmeter leads to alternator output terminal and positive post of the battery. The voltmeter will indicate voltage drop in the circuit between alternator and battery. It should not exceed 0.3 volt.
8. Now, change voltmeter leads to the alternator frame and the battery negative post. This voltmeter reading will show voltage drop in the circuit between alternator frame and the battery, negative post. It should not exceed .05 volt.

If voltage drop in Steps 7 and 8 is in excess of specifications, stop engine, clear and tighten connections and repeat the test.

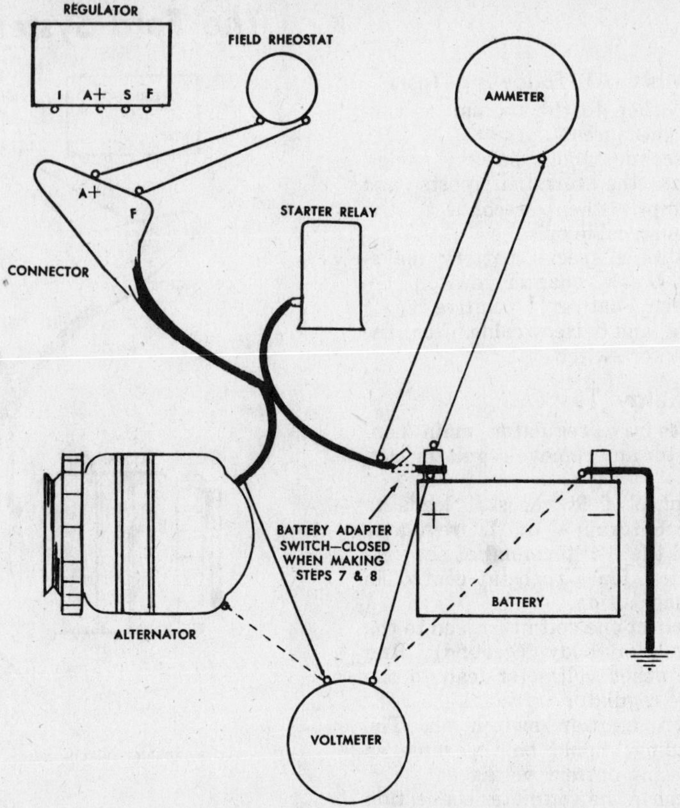

Plan to make charging circuit resistance check

Voltage Limiter Test

NOTE: all limiter (regulator) tests and calibrations must be made at operating temperature, with the regulator cover in place.

1. With the regulator main connec-

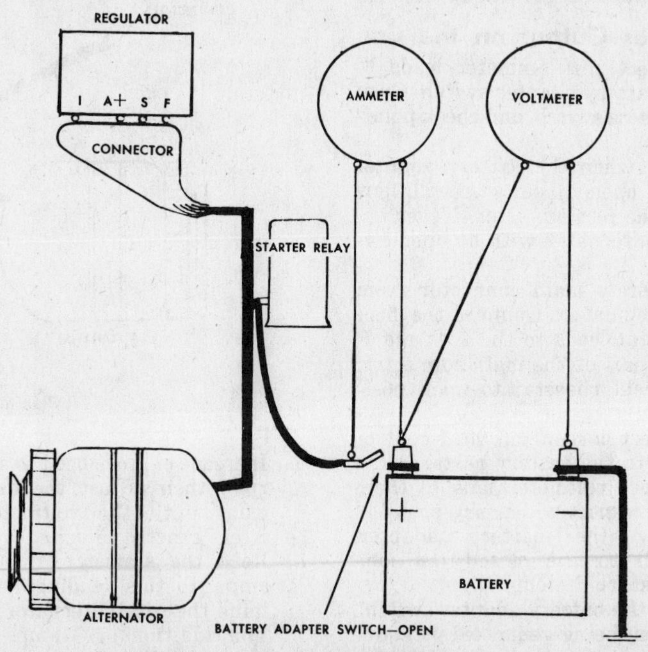

Plan to make voltage limiter check

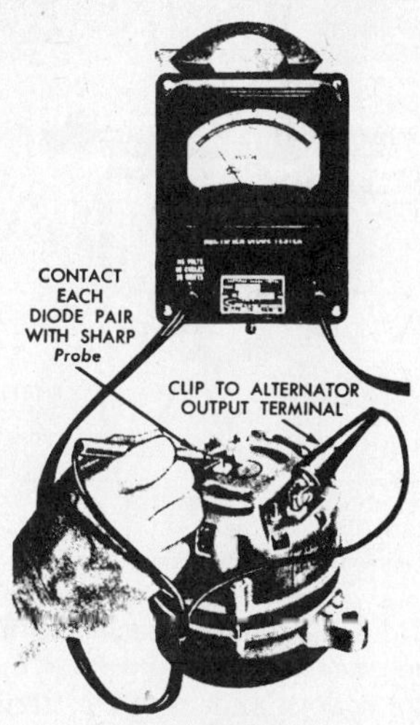

Positive diode test

CONTACT EACH DIODE PAIR WITH SHARP Probe

CLIP TO ALTERNATOR FRAME

Negative diode test

tor plugged into the regulator, hook the test ammeter to the battery positive terminal and to the battery adapter switch (switch open).

2. Connect voltmeter to both positive and negative posts of battery.
3. Close the battery adapter switch then start the engine.
4. Open the battery adapter switch. Now, start the engine and run it at specified rpm for about five minutes.
5. If test ammeter registers more than 10 amps. stop the engine, disconnect battery cables and replace, or charge, the battery.
6. Then, reconnect cables to fully charged battery, and run the engine at specified rpm for about five minutes.
7. Check voltmeter reading against specifications. With battery charged and voltage setting as specified, the ammeter should read less than 2 amps.
8. If results do not agree with specifications, replace the regulator.

Diode Tests

To test positive diodes, make connections as shown. Contact the probe to each diode lead.

To test negative diodes, make connections as shown. Follow the same procedure as for positive diodes.

Good diodes will be indicated as 2 amps. or more and readings alike within two graduations.

Field Circuit Test

Current draw should show within specifications. If there is little or no current flow, the field or brushes have a high resistance or are open. A current flow much higher than specifications indicates shorted or grounded turns or brush leads touching. If the test indicates the field to be shorted or open and the field brush assembly or slip rings are not at fault, the entire rotor must be replaced.

Regulator Bench Adjustments

Erratic operation of the regulator, indicated by erratic movement of the voltmeter during a voltage limiter test, may be caused by dirty or pitted regulator contact points. To clean them, use a fine abrasive paper, then wipe with carbon tetrachloride. Use a chemically clean thickness gauge to space the point gap.

The difference between the upper stage and lower stage regulation (0.3 volt), is determined by the voltage limiter point and core gaps.

Adjust the point gap first. (See illustration) Loosen the left-side lock screw one-quarter turn. Use a screwdriver in the adjusting slot above the lock screw. Adjust upper contacts to 0.010-0.015 in.

Adjust the core gap (See illustration) with upper contacts closed. Loosen center lock screw one-quarter turn. With a screwdriver inserted in the adjusting slot, below the lock screw, adjust core gap to 0.045-0.052 in. Measure gap clearance between the armature and the core.

Tighten lock screw and recheck both point gap and core gap adjustments.

Regulator voltage adjustments

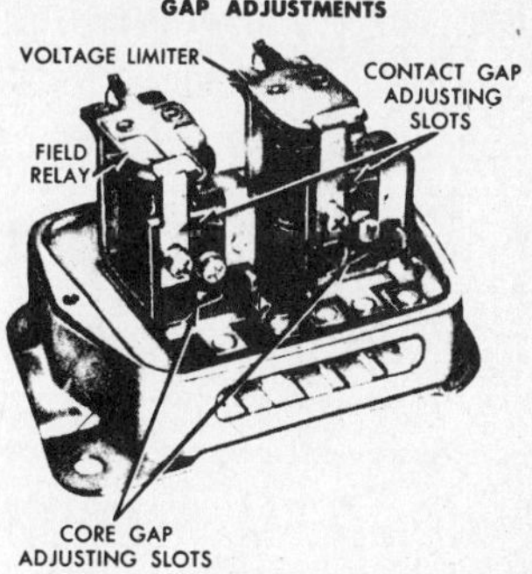

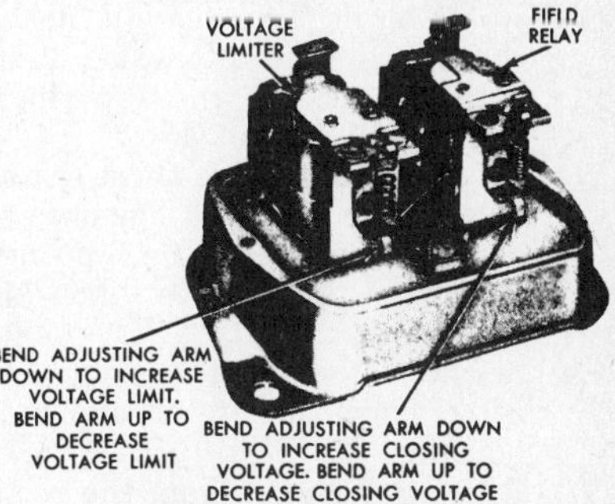

Regulator adjustments

(See illustration) must be made with the regulator at normal operating temperature.

The field relay closing voltage is adjusted by bending the spring arm. To increase the closing voltage, bend the spring arm down. To decrease the closing voltage, bend the spring arm up.

The voltage limit adjustment (See illustration) is set by bending the voltage limiting spring arm. To increase the voltage setting, bend adjusting arm down. To decrease the voltage setting, bend adjusting arm up.

Before setting the voltage and before making a final voltage test, the alternator speed must be reduced to zero and the ignition switch opened momentarily, to cycle the regulator.

Overhaul

Disassembly

1. Mark both end housings with a

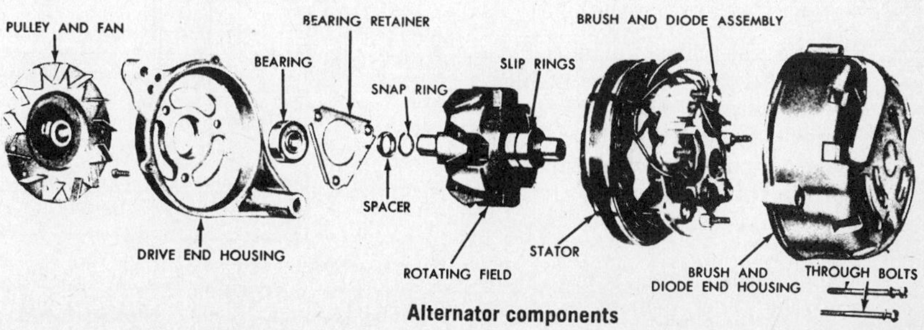

Alternator components

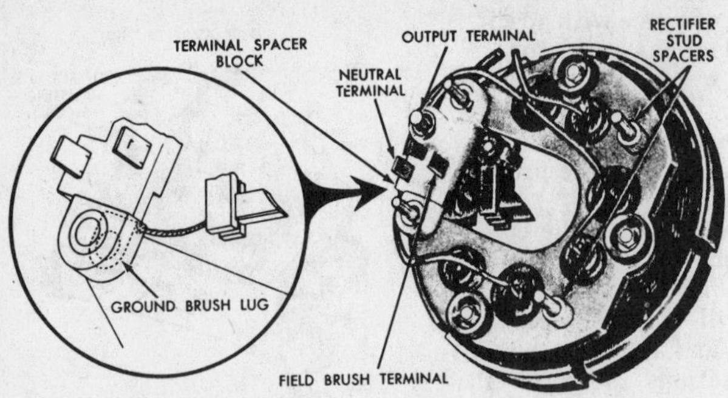

Stator, heat sink and terminal spacer assembly

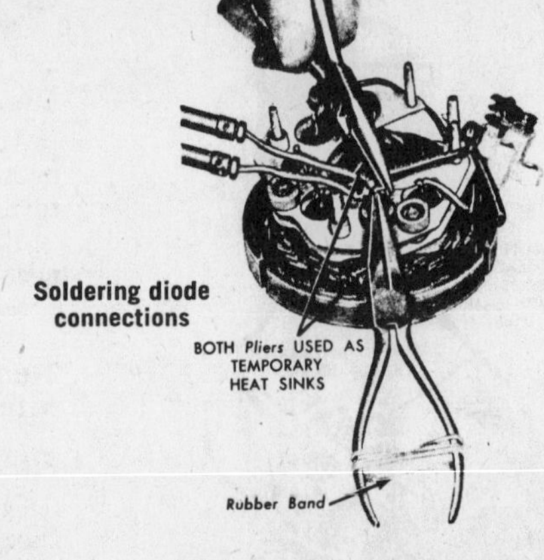

Soldering diode connections

scribe mark for assembly. Reach through a ventilation slot, raise both brushes off the slip rings, and install a short length of 1/8 in. rod or stiff wire through the hole in the rear end housing, to hold the brushes off the slip rings

2. Remove the three housing thru bolts.
3. Separate the front housing and rotor from the stator and rear housing.
4. Remove the nuts from the rectifier to rear housing mounting studs, and remove the rear housing. Remove the two spacer sleeves from the rectifier plate studs.
5. If replacement is necessary, press the bearing from the rear end housing.
6. Remove the terminal spacer block assembly from the stud and unsolder the neutral wire from the spacer block neutral terminal.
7. If the brushes are being replaced, straighten the field brush terminal blade locking tabs and remove the terminal blade from the terminal spacer block. Remove the brushes and holders from the assembly.
8. If either diode plate is being replaced, carefully unsolder the leads from the diodes.

Caution Use only a 100-watt soldering iron. Leave the soldering iron in contact with the diode terminals only long enough to remove the wires. Use pliers as temporary heat sinks in order to protect the diodes.

9. Remove the three insulated diode plate screws and the insulators, and separate the diode plates.
10. Remove the drive pulley. On alternator pulleys with threaded holes in the outer end of the pulley, use a standard puller for removal.
11. Remove the three screws that hold the front bearing retainer, and remove the front housing.
12. If the bearing is being replaced, pull, using a bearing puller. Remove the bearing retainer and spacer. It will not be necessary to remove the stop ring, unless it has been damaged.

Cleaning and Inspection

1. The rotor, stator, diode rectifier assemblies, and bearings are not to be cleaned with solvent. These parts are to be wiped off with a clean cloth. Cleaning solvent may cause damage to the electrical parts or contaminate the bearing internal lubricant. Wash all other parts in solvent and dry them.
2. Rotate the front bearing on the driveshaft. Check for any scraping noise, looseness or roughness that will indicate that the bearing is excessively worn. As the bearing is being rotated, look for excessive lubricant leakage. If any of these conditions exist, replace the bearing.
3. Place the rear end housing on the slip ring end of the shaft and rotate the bearing on the shaft. Make a similar check for noise, looseness or roughness. Inspect the rollers and cage for damage. Replace the bearing if these conditions exist, or if the lubricant is missing or contaminated.
4. Check both the front and rear housings for cracks. Check the front housing for stripped threads in the mounting holes. Replace defective housings.
5. Pulleys that have been removed and installed several times may have to be replaced because of increased bore diameter. A pulley is not suitable for reuse if more than one-quarter of the shaft length will enter the pulley bore with light pressure. Replace any pulley that is bent.
6. Check all wire leads on both the stator and rotor assemblies for loose soldered connections, and for burned insulation. Solder all poor connections. Replace parts that show burned insulation.
7. Check the slip rings for damaged insulation and runout. If the slip rings are more than 0.0005 in. out of round, take a light cut (minimum diameter limit 1.2

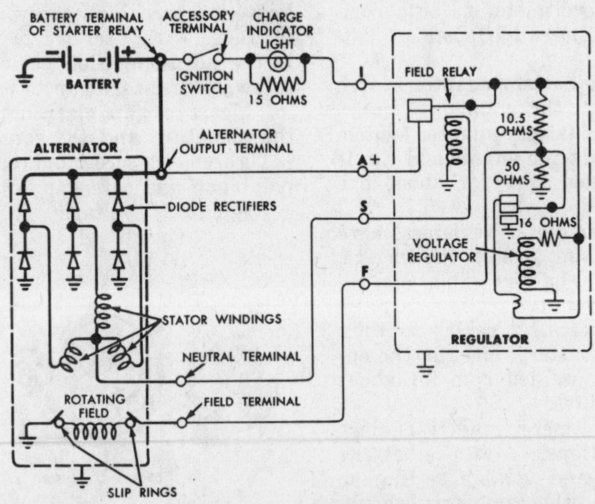

Ford alternator schematic (© Ford Motor Co.)

in.) from the face of the rings to true them. If the slip rings are badly damaged, the entire rotor will have to be replaced, as they are serviced as a complete assembly.

8. Replace any parts that are burned or cracked. Replace brushes that are worn to less than 0.350 in. in length. Replace the brush spring if it has less than 7-12 oz. tension.

Assembly

1. If the stop ring on the driveshaft was damaged, install a new stop ring. Push the new ring onto the shaft and into the groove.
2. Position the front bearing spacer on the driveshaft against the stop-ring, and position the bearing retainer on the shaft with the flat surface of the retainer outward.
3. Putting pressure on the inner race only, press the new bearing onto the shaft until it contacts the spacer.
4. Place the front housing over the shaft, with the bearing positioned in the front housing cavity. Install the bearing retainer mounting screws.
5. Press the pulley onto the shaft until the hub just touches the inner race of the front bearing.
6. If a new diode plate is being installed, mount the two plates together so that they are insulated from each other (insulating spacer between the plates are cupped insulator under the screw head). Do not tighten the screws at this time. Solder the wire leads to the diodes in as short a time as possible to avoid heat damage. Use only a 100-watt iron.
7. Insert the new field brush terminal blade into the slot in the terminal spacer block, with the brush pig-tail extended toward the brush holder pivots.
8. Install the brush holders and brush spring onto the terminal spacer block, then position the brushes in the brush holders.
9. Solder the neutral wire to the neutral terminal. Position the terminal spacer block assembly on the rectifier plate mounting studs, with the ground brush lug over the mounting stud farthest from the output terminal. Tighten the diode plate assembly screws.
10. Place the spacers on the rectifier mounting studs farthest from the terminal block.
11. Install the rear bearing so that the open end of the bearing is flush with the inner surface of the housing boss. Allow space under the outer end of the bearing during installation.
12. Place the rectifier plate and stator assembly in the rear end housing and mount the rectifier plates to the housing.
13. Retract the brushes and insert a short length of ⅛ in. rod or stiff wire through the hole in the rear end housing to hold the brushes in the retracted position.
14. Wipe clean the rear bearing surface of the rotor shaft.
15. Position the rear housing and stator assembly over the rotor and align the scribe marks made during disassembly, install the housing through bolts. Remove the brush retracting rod.

The Leece-Neville System

Field and Lamp Relay Test

1. Disconnect the battery wire from B terminal of the regulator.
2. Disconnect the N wire from the regulator.
3. With the field rheostat in the open position, connect its leads to the disconnected battery wire and the N terminal of the regulator.
4. Hook up a voltmeter to the regulator N terminal and to a good ground.
5. Slowly adjust the field rheostat toward the closed position. The field relay contacts should close somewhere between 1.9 and 2.4 volts.

Load Relay Test

1. Disconnect the battery wire from B terminal of the regulator.
2. With field rheostat in the open position, connect its leads to the disconnected battery wire and the regulator Ign. terminal.
3. Hook up a voltmeter to the regulator Ign. terminal and to a good ground.
4. Slowly adjust field rheostat toward the closed position while watching the voltmeter. The load

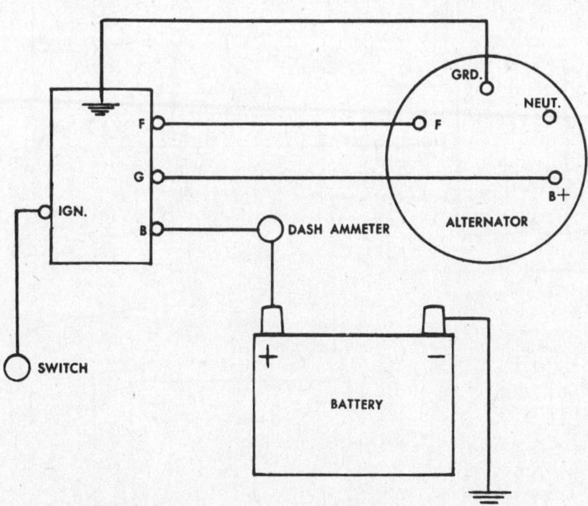

Wiring plan of Leece-Neville 6000 negative ground system, ammeter equipped

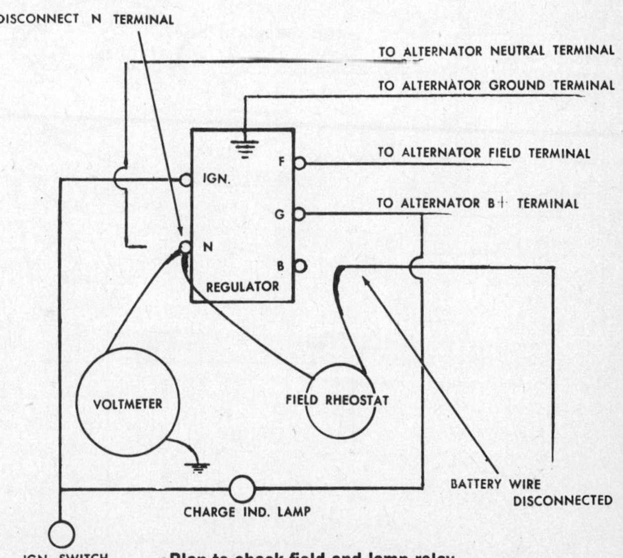

Plan to check field and lamp relay

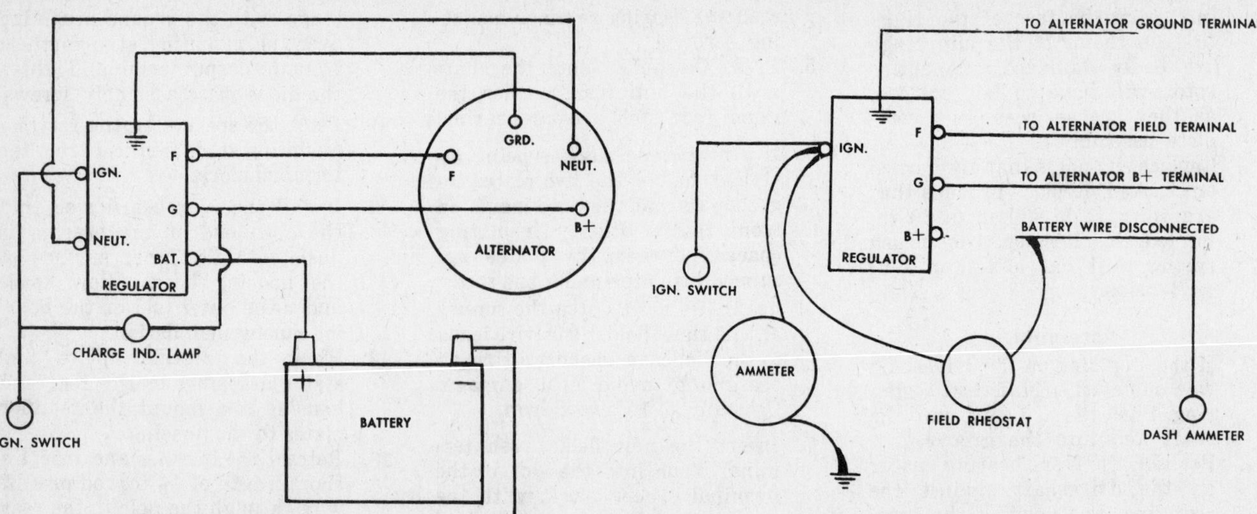

Wiring plan of Leece-Neville 6000 negative ground system, charge indicator light equipped

Plan to check load relay

relay contacts should close somewhere between 5.8 and 6.2 volts.

Rated Output Test

1. With battery disconnected, ignition switch in off position, and the wire disconnected at the alternator B+ terminal, hook an ammeter between the alternator B+ terminal and the wire that was just disconnected from this terminal.
2. Disconnect wire from the alternator F terminal.
3. With the field rheostat adjusted to open position, connect its leads to the alternator F terminal and the alternator B+ terminal.
4. Hook up a voltmeter between the alternator B+ terminal and ground.
5. Reconnect battery cables.
6. Connect a carbon pile load control between the battery posts.
7. With a tachometer connected to the engine, start the engine and set its speed at the recommended rpm.
8. While watching both ammeter and voltmeter, adjust the carbon pile load control to maintain 15 volts. When field rheostat control is fully closed, note voltmeter and ammeter readings.
9. Adjust field rheostat to open position and carbon pile control to off.
10. Compare readings with specifications. Readings should be at least equal to rated output specified by the manufacturer. If output complies with specifications, proceed to the voltage regulator test. If readings are below rated output, it indicates possible internal troubles.

Field Current Draw Test

1. Disconnect battery ground cable.
2. Disconnect carbon pile, voltmeter, ammeter and field rheostat from the previous check.
3. Reconnect the regular circuit wire to the alternator B+ terminal.
4. With the field rheostat adjusted to the open position, connect one of its leads to the alternator B+ terminal and the other lead to a test ammeter lead.
5. Connect the remaining ammeter lead to the alternator F terminal.
6. Connect one voltmeter lead to the alternator F terminal and the remaining voltmeter lead to ground.

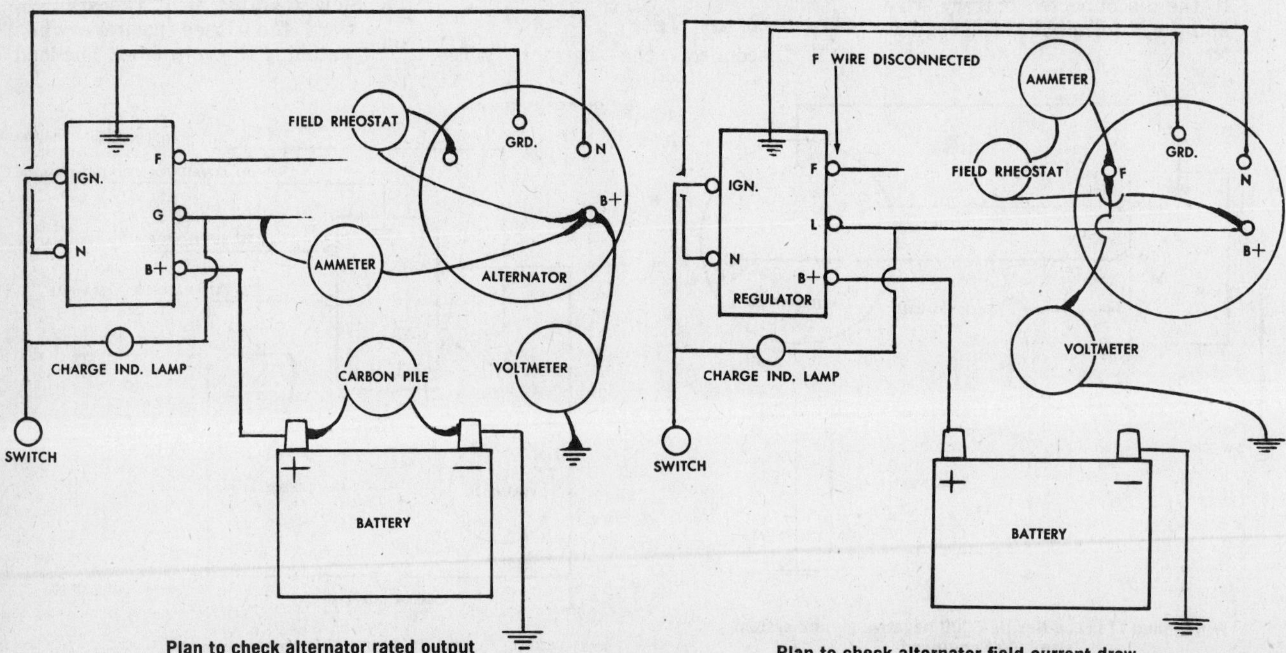

Plan to check alternator rated output

Plan to check alternator field current draw

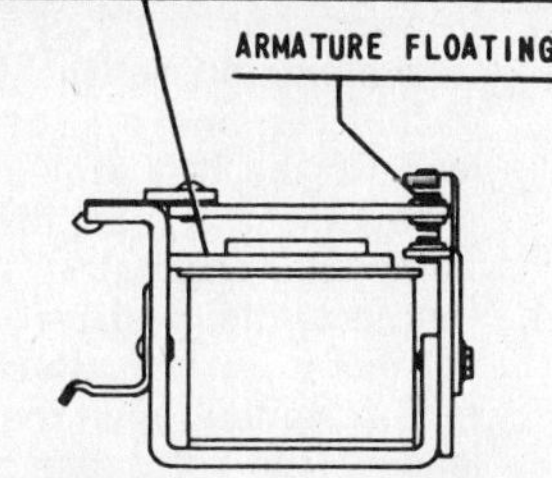

REGULATOR ARMATURE ADJUSTMENT

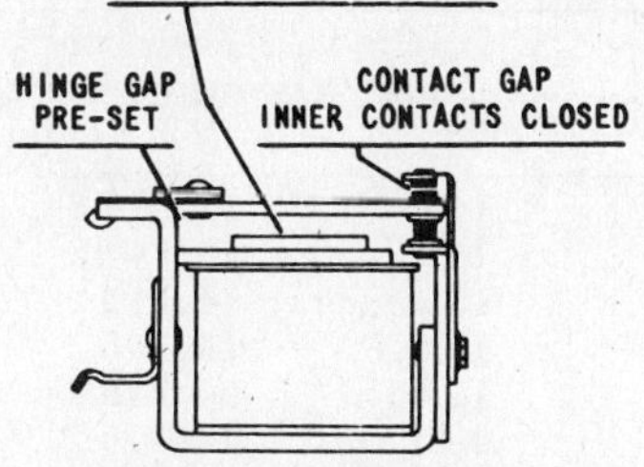

REGULATOR GAP SETTINGS

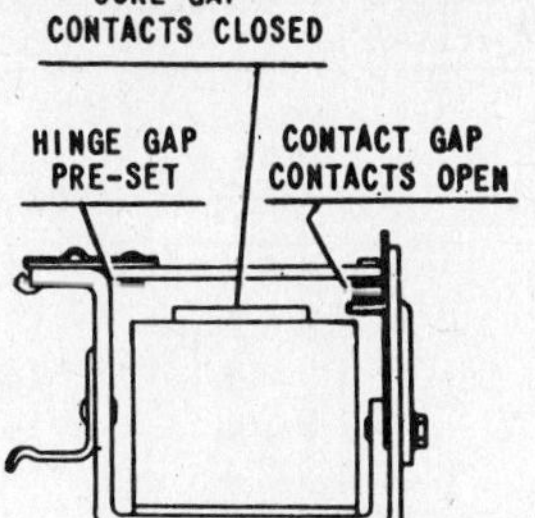

RELAY GAP SETTINGS

Adjusting Leece-Neville regulator

7. Reconnect battery ground cable, start the engine, and run it at about 1,000 rpm.
8. With field rheostat in closed position, read the ammeter and voltmeter for a very brief period.
9. Compare these readings with specifications.
10. If readings are low, it indicates trouble in slip rings or brushes.
11. If readings are too high, it indicates trouble in the rotor field windings.
12. If readings are as specified on an alternator which did not deliver its rated output, look for trouble in the stator or diodes.

Voltage Regulator Test

NOTE: manufacturers' recommended settings are established with the regulator cover off. Generally, a decrease of 0.2 to 0.3 volt will result when the cover is installed and the regulator brought to normal operating temperature.

1. Disconnect battery, be sure the ignition switch is off, and disconnect the alternator B+ terminal.
2. Hook up an ammeter to the alternator B+ terminal and to the wire just disconnected from this terminal.
3. Disconnect the wire from the alternator F terminal.
4. With the field rheostat turned to the open position, connect one rheostat lead to the alternator F terminal and the other rheostat lead to the wire just disconnected from the F terminal.
5. Connect voltmeter leads to the B terminal of the regulator and to a good ground.
6. Reconnect battery cables.
7. Hook up a carbon pile across the battery posts.
8. Connect a pair of 1,000 ohm + earphones to the regulator F terminal and the L (gen.) regulator terminal.
9. Start the engine and gradually increase its speed while listening for a vibrating sound in the earphones. This indicates the operation of the regulator top contacts. Note voltmeter reading, compared with manufacturers' specifications.
10. Continue to increase engine rpm until earphones cease to pick up vibration. Voltage should read maximum just before vibrating sound stops. Compare with manufacturers' specifications. The silencing of the vibration indicates transfer of action to the lower contacts.
11. Resume a gradual increase in engine rpm until the vibrating sound starts again. This sound is produced by the lower contacts. Compare voltmeter reading with specifications.

Final Regulator Setting

This is a final setting, to be made at operating temperature through all variations of speed and vibration.

1. Run the engine about 15 minutes, or enough to develop normal operating temperature at the regulator.
2. Set engine speed at 1,750 rpm.
3. Adjust carbon pile load to produce a 25 amp. charging rate.
4. Open and close the field rheostat four or five times.
5. Turn carbon pile load to full off.
6. With field rheostat fully closed, note the voltmeter reading and compare it with regulator operating specifications.
7. If regulator does not operate within specified limits, replace it.

Disassembly

1. Remove two brush-holder assembly screws and remove holder with brushes.
2. Remove shaft nut, preventing pulley from slipping by gripping a fan belt around pulley and in vise. Remove pulley.
3. Remove four thru-bolts and carefully pry two end housings apart.
4. Place tape over slip ring end housing bearing to keep out dirt.
5. Remove fan, key and spacer and with puller remove drive end housing.
6. Bearings from both housings can be removed after taking off retainer at drive end or tape from slip ring end.
7. To remove individual rectifier, loosen solder around cell while pressing it out. A piece of asbestos or fiber will help concentrate heat.

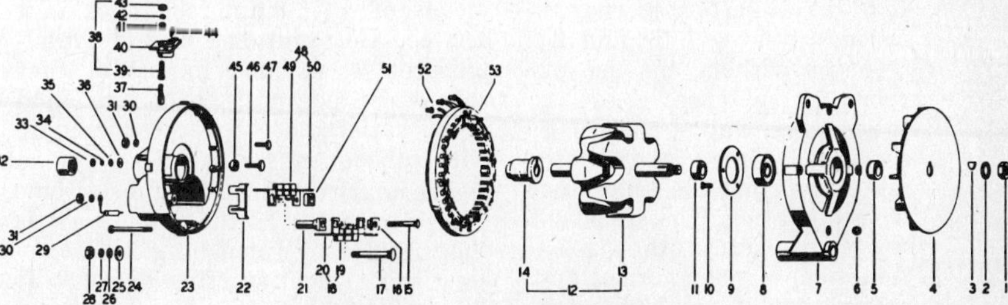

Exploded view Leece-Neville alternator

1 Rotor shaft nut
2 Shaft nut washer
3 Woodruff key
4 Fan assembly
5 Fan spacer
6 Bolt nut
7 Drive end frame
8 Ball bearing
9 Ball bearing retainer plate
10 Bearing retainer plate screws
11 Spacer
12 Rotor and slip ring assembly
13 Rotor
14 Slip ring
15 Screw terminal
16 Bushing insulator
17 Terminal screw
18 Rectifier assembly
19 Rectifier
20 Rectifier
21 Insulator bushing
22 Support-rectifier
23 Slip ring end housing
24 Thru bolt
25 Guard washer
26 Washer
27 Washer
28 Hex nut
29 Capacitor assembly
30 Washer
31 Hex nut
32 Roller bearing
33 Nut
34 Lockwasher
35 Guard washer
36 Insulation washer
37 Brush and spring assembly
38 Brush holder assembly
39 Screw
40 Brush holder only
41 Guard washer
42 Lockwasher
43 Nut
44 Screw
45 Insulator bushing
46 Terminal screw
47 Terminal screw
48 Rectifier assembly
49 Rectifier
50 Rectifier mount
51 Spacer insulator
52 Eyelet
53 Stator assembly

Voltage Setting (Cover off)

Regulator Number	*Relay Closing*	*Starts to Regulate*	*Transfer Voltage (max.)*	*Regulator Operating Voltage, Bottom Contact*
3532 RA	5.8-6.2	13.9-14.3	14.7	13.9-14.3
3533 RA	5.8-6.2	13.9-14.3	14.7	13.9-14.3
3628 RA	1.9-2.4	14.6-15.2	15.4	14.6-15.2
3629 RA	1.9-2.4	14.6-15.2	15.4	14.6-15.2
3630 RA	1.9-2.4	14.6-15.2	15.4	14.6-15.2
3631 RA	1.9-2.4	14.6-15.2	15.4	14.6-15.2
3687 RA	2.0-2.1	14.2-14.4	14.8	14.2-14.4*

* 3000 rpm Alternator Speed

NOTE: voltage regulator settings will be approximately ½ volt lower with the cover on. When regulator cover is securely fastened in place, and at maximum operating temperature, voltage will decrease approximately 0.2-0.3. Gaps may be varied above or below to meet settings desired.

Air Gap and Point Settings (in.)

	Voltage Regulator		*Relay Element*	
Regulator Number	*Contact Gap Outer Contacts Open*	*Core Gap Inner Contacts Closed*	*Contact Gap Contacts Open*	*Core Gap Contacts Closed**
3532 RA	.018-.020	.031-.039	.018-.020	.011-.013
3533 RA	.018-.020	.031-.039	.018-.020	.011-.013
3628 RA	.018-.020	.030-.035	.018-.020	.005-.007
3629 RA	.018-.020	.030-.035	.018-.020	.005-.007
3630 RA	.018-.020	.030-.035	.018-.020	.005-.007
3631 RA	.018-.020	.030-.035	.018-.020	.005-.007
3687 RA	.018-.020	.035-.043	.018-.020	.009-.011

* Settings are made with contacts closed and armature held to core.

CAUTION: when checking these regulators for maximum output do not use a jumper from F terminal to ground, or F terminal to G terminal. Doing so will result in burned jumpers, or fused contacts.

The Motorola System

The Motorola alternator is designed to pass all the DC current through an isolation diode. This has two advantages.

A. It prevents battery discharge through the regulator and alternator without the use of relays or switches.

B. It renders a way of operating a signal lamp to indicate whether or not the generator is in operation. The signal is connected across the isolation diode. Under normal operating conditions, alternator voltage output is nearly the same as battery voltage. This creates a low voltage flow across the isolation diode. The voltage value is not enough to cause the signal light to burn, indicating the alternator is in operation.

Due to the nature of the alternator, residual magnetism is at near zero when the unit is at rest. It is, therefore, necessary to provide some small current to excite the field prior to generating current. With Motorola, this priming current is supplied by means of a 75 ohm resistance unit between the ignition coil and the alternator. It is quite important that this resistance unit be checked and found satisfactory before proceeding with subsequent tests.

The charge indicator light on some trucks operates in the same way as this resistor by furnishing the necessary initial field starting current. If this resistor circuit is open (a burned out indicator lamp) the alternator will not function.

The regulator is a sealed unit and should require no adjustment. It is therefore, recommended that non-functioning regulators be replaced.

Alternator System Test

1. Be sure that the battery is disconnected and the ignition switch is off.
2. Disconnect the wire from the alternator output terminal.
3. Connect the positive lead of a test ammeter to the alternator output terminal and the negative lead of the test ammeter to the wire that was just disconnected from this terminal.
4. Connect the positive lead of a voltmeter to the alternator output terminal and the negative lead of the voltmeter to ground.
5. Reconnect the battery.
6. Connect a carbon pile load control unit (control in off position) to both battery posts.
7. Start engine and run at fast idle for as long as is required to bring it to normal operating temperature.
8. Gradually increase rpm and adjust carbon pile control until current output is reached.
9. Operation is normal if the system develops within 5 amps. of the rated output and voltage registers 14 ± 1 volts.
10. If voltmeter registers over 15 volts, at rated output, replace the regulator.
11. If system is satisfactory at low engine rpm but output is not enough at higher rpm, check for slipping of the drive belt.
12. If current output is low and the output terminal voltage is more than 13 volts, check the isolation diode.
13. If the current output and the output terminal voltage are both low, check the alternator rated output.
14. If current output at specified terminal voltage is produced, check resistance of the charging circuit.

Alternator Output Test

This check is of the alternator only.

1. The ammeter, voltmeter and carbon pile test instruments remain connected into the circuit as with the last check.
2. Disconnect the battery, also the wire from the alternator field terminal.
3. With a field rheostat, adjusted to open position, connect its leads to the alternator field terminal and to the alternator output terminal.
4. Reconnect the battery.
5. Start and run the engine at 1750 rpm.
6. Gradually adjust field rheostat toward the closed position while watching the voltmeter and ammeter (do not exceed 15 volts). Control this voltage with the carbon pile load adjustment. When field rheostat has reached the closed position, note ammeter reading.

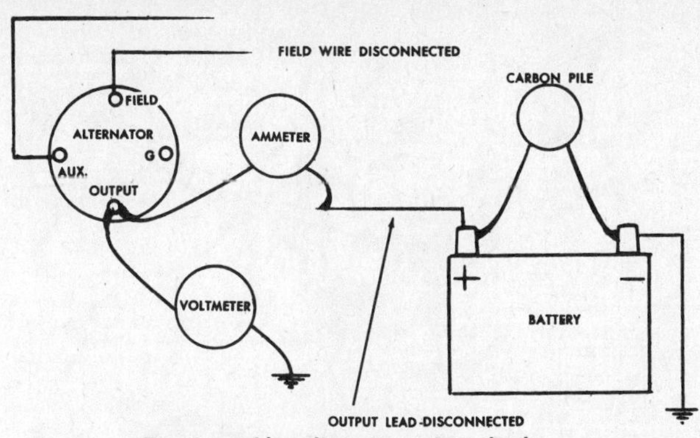

Plan for making alternator system checks

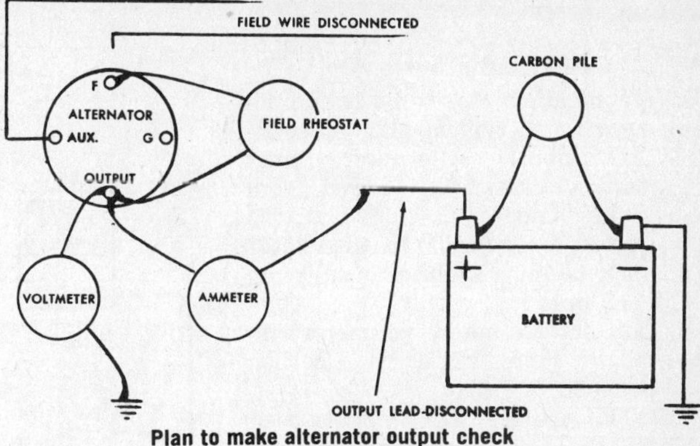

Plan to make alternator output check

7. Adjust field rheostat to the open position and the carbon pile load control off.
8. Compare notes taken in Step 6 with manufacturers' specifications.
9. If readings are low, check drive belt for proper tension.

Field Current Draw Test

1. With battery disconnected, disconnect the wires from the alternator output terminal and the alternator field terminal.
2. With a field rheostat in the open position, connect its leads to the disconnected alternator output wire and to the positive lead of the test ammeter.
3. Connect the negative ammeter lead to the alternator field terminal.
4. Connect the positive voltmeter lead to the alternator field terminal.
5. Connect the negative voltmeter lead to the alternator ground terminal.
6. Reconnect the battery.
7. Start and run the engine at fast idle.
8. Adjust field rheostat to closed position, then note the voltmeter and ammeter readings.
9. Adjust field rheostat control to the open position.
10. Compare the readings obtained in Step 8 with manufacturers' specifications.
11. If readings are zero, there is an indication of trouble in the field coil, or the connections between field coil and slip ring.
12. If readings are low, there is probable trouble in the slip rings or brushes.
13. If readings are high, the field coil is probably shorted.
14. If readings are normal, on an alternator which failed to produce its rated output, the probable cause lies in the stator or diodes. Replace the alternator in this case.

Charging Circuit Resistance Test

1. With battery disconnected and the ignition switch off, disconnect the wire from the alternator output terminal.
2. Connect the positive lead of a test ammeter to the alternator output terminal.
3. Connect the negative lead of the ammeter to the wire just disconnected from the alternator output terminal.
4. Disconnect the wire from the alternator field terminal.
5. With a field rheostat in open position, connect one of its leads to the alternator field terminal.
6. Connect the other field rheostat lead to the alternator output terminal.
7. Reconnect the battery.
8. With a carbon pile load control in the off position, hook it to both battery posts.
9. Start and set to 1500-1700 rpm.
10. Adjust field rheostat control toward the closed position enough to get a charging rate of 10 amps. Use the carbon pile load control to prevent exceeding 15 volts. Hold at 15 volts.
11. Disconnect voltmeter from the alternator output terminal and the ground.
12. Reconnect voltmeter positive lead to the disconnected alternator output wire.
13. Connect voltmeter negative lead to the battery positive post.
14. Note reading on voltmeter. This is the voltage drop in the hot circuit. It should not exceed 0.3 volt.
15. Disconnect voltmeter from alternator output wire and the battery post.
16. Reconnect voltmeter positive lead to the battery negative post.
17. Connect voltmeter negative lead to the alternator ground terminal.
18. Note voltmeter reading. This is the voltage drop in the ground circuit. This reading should not exceed 0.15 volt.

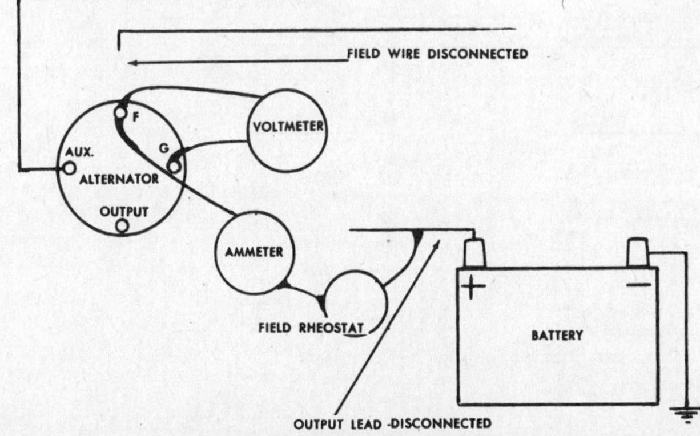

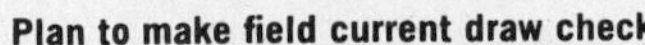
Plan to make field current draw check

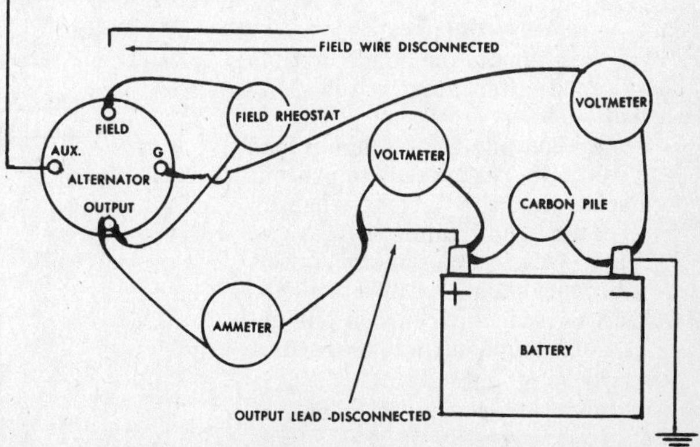

Plan to make charging circuit resistance check

Bench Tests

Alternator System

1. Mount alternator to be tested according to typical plan. (See illustration.) Alternator must turn clockwise as viewed from pulley end.
2. Connect regulator to alternator and mount regulator solidly on heat sink.
3. Connect ammeter, voltmeter, indicator lamp, battery and carbon pile load.

NOTE: the No. 57X lamp is used to excite field of alternator to develop an output. The resistor wire, or any 75 ohm, 3 watt resistor may be used.

Optional Alternator Test

This test excludes the regulator from the circuit and can be conducted if the regulator is suspected and a known good regulator is not available.

1. Use the same procedure as described in previous paragraph with the exception of the next two steps.
2. Disconnect voltage regulator plug and the field terminal wire.
3. Connect a 40 ohm (3 amp.) rheostat from alternator field terminal to output terminal. Set rheostat to maximum resistance.
4. Start electric drive motor. Increase load with carbon pile and at the same time increase field current by reduction of rheostat resistance.

Caution Do not allow output terminal voltage to exceed 15 volts.

5. Continue to increase the load and decrease rheostat resistance while holding output voltage below 15 volts until rheostat resistance is zero. At this point, maximum field current is being applied.

Alternator is working if the rated output is available. If rated current output is not available, check alternator.

Regulator Test

This test should be made with a known good alternator and a fully charged battery.

1. Set carbon pile for minimum load (maximum resistance) to prevent discharging the battery when alternator is not running.
2. Start electric drive motor (alternator rpm should be 3000 to 4000).
3. Increase load with carbon pile until a 10 amp. output is reached. Allow a 15 minute temperature stabilization period. Regulator is working properly if the voltage at output terminal is according to specifications and the alternator is supplying a 10 amp. load.

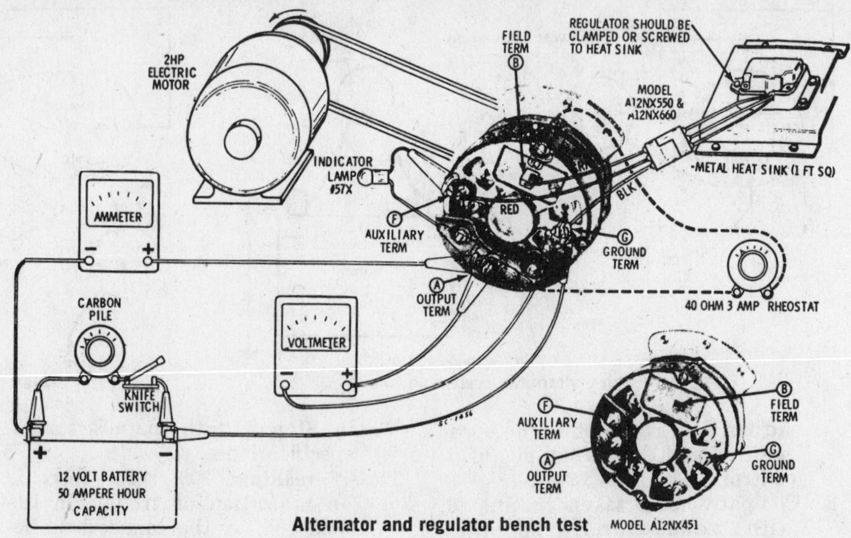

Alternator and regulator bench test

Isolation Diode Circuit Test

Excessive leakage through the isolation diode will discharge the battery. The rate of discharge depends upon the degree of leakage. Normal and tolerable leakage is less than .001 amperes.

1. To check isolation diode leakage, connect the regulator to the battery. (See illustration.) Do not operate the alternator.
2. Measure the voltage from auxiliary terminal F to ground terminal G. The voltage appearing at the auxiliary terminal should not exceed 0.1 volt. Voltage greater than this indicates leakage through the isolation diode. Check the isolation diode with a commercial diode tester, or with a 12-volt DC test lamp.

Alternator Components Test

Rotor (Field Coil) Test

This test checks the condition of the field coil for open or shorted field coil turns, badly worn or sticky brushes and open connections.

1. Construct a field current test circuit. (See illustration).
2. Connect test circuit to field terminal and ground terminal (test point B and G).

NOTE: set rheostat to maximum resistance (40 ohms) before making connections.

3. Slowly reduce resistance of rheostat to zero. With full battery voltage applied to field coil (battery must be fully charged), the field current should be 1.2 to 1.7 amps. Turn rotor by hand while taking reading to indicate value of brush contact. However, a slight fluctuation of current (.2 amps.) is normal.
4. If current is not within limits, inspect brushes and slip rings for dirt, bad brushes and connections. Check brush assemblies for shorts and continuity.

Reinstall repaired or known good brush assembly and repeat

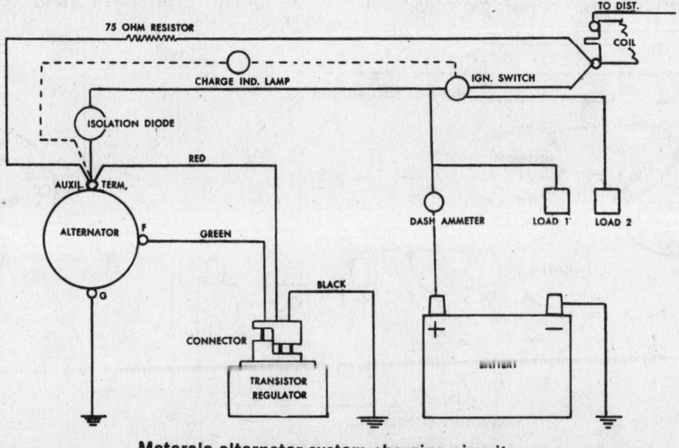

Motorola alternator system charging circuit

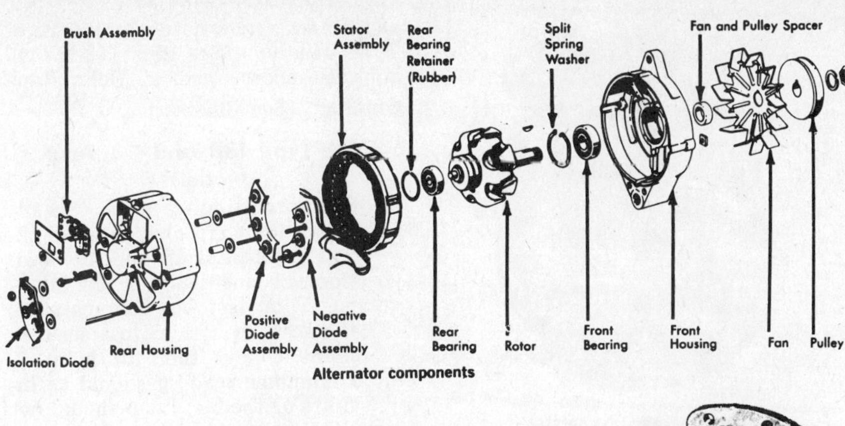

Alternator components

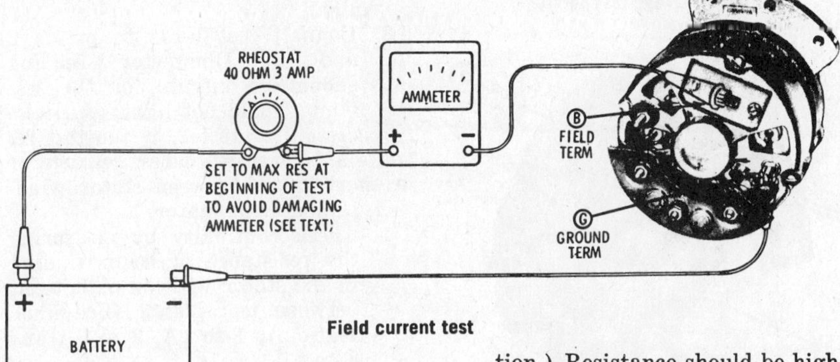

Field current test

the test. If field current is above the maximum value, it indicates that the field coil is shorted or rotor-to-field coil has shorted turns.

If field current is zero, it indicates that the field coil or coil-to-slip ring connection is open. If the field current is much less than the value specified, it indicates a poor coil-to-slip ring connection or poor brush-to-slip ring connection.

Repeat field current test on rotor by connecting the test circuit to rotor slip rings to ascertain findings after rotor has been removed from alternator. Field current will be about 0.2 amperes higher than the maximum value, due to normal brush slip ring contact resistance.

Rotor Open Circuit Test

An ohmmeter may be used to check continuity of the rotor. Connect ohmmeter probes to field terminal and ground terminal (test points B and G. See illustration). Resistance should be about 6 ohms. If resistance is high, field coil is open.

Brush Assembly Test

Insulation

1. Connect ohmmeter or a test lamp to field terminal and bracket (test points A and D). (See illustration.) Resistance should be high, or the test lamp should not light. If results are contrary, brush assembly is shorted.

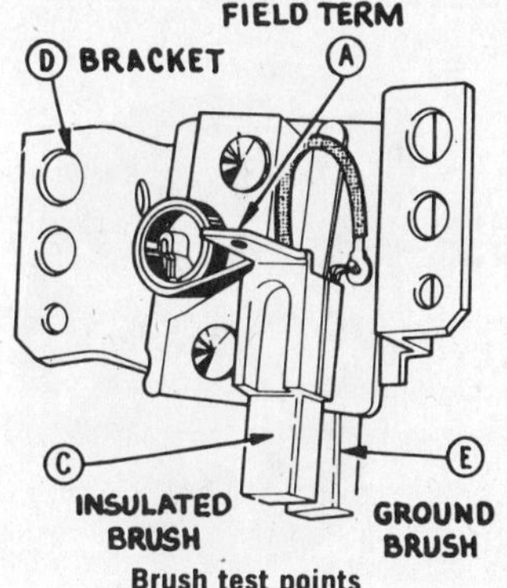

Brush test points

Continuity

2. Connect an ohmmeter to field terminal and brush (points A and C). Resistance should be zero. Move brush and brush lead wire to make sure that the brush lead wire connections are not intermittent. Resistance should not vary when brush and lead wire are being moved around.
3. Connect ohmmeter to bracket and grounded brush, points E and D. Resistance should be zero. Repeat same test on brush lead wire as in Step 2.

Isolation Diode Test

If a commercial diode tester is not available, use a 12-volt DC test lamp only, otherwise diodes can be damaged.

1. Connect the test lamp to output terminal and auxiliary terminal. Then reverse the test probes. Test lamp should light in one direction only. If test light lights in both directions, the isolation diode is shorted. If lamp won't light in either direction, the diode is open.

In-Circuit Rectifier Diode Test

Any commercial in-circuit diode tester will suffice to make the check. If the test indicates the diodes to be bad, recheck diodes individually after the diode assemblies have been disconnected from the stator assembly. Shorted stator coil or shorted insulating washers or sleeves on positive diode assembly would make diodes appear to be shorted.

1. To check negative diode assembly, connect tester to test points G and H. (See illustration.) Then, successively check between test points G and J and G and K.
2. To check positive diode assembly, connect tester to test points F and L. Then successively check between test points F and M and F and N.

Rectifier Diode Test, With Lamp

When an in-circuit diode tester is not available, a 12-volt DC test lamp may be used to indicate a shorted diode. The lamp, however, will not show an open condition unless all three diodes of either assembly are open.

1. Connect test light probes to points G and H, then reverse test probes. The lamp should light in one direction but not in the other. If the test lamp lights in both directions, one or more of the rectifier diodes is shorted. If the test lamp does not light in ei-

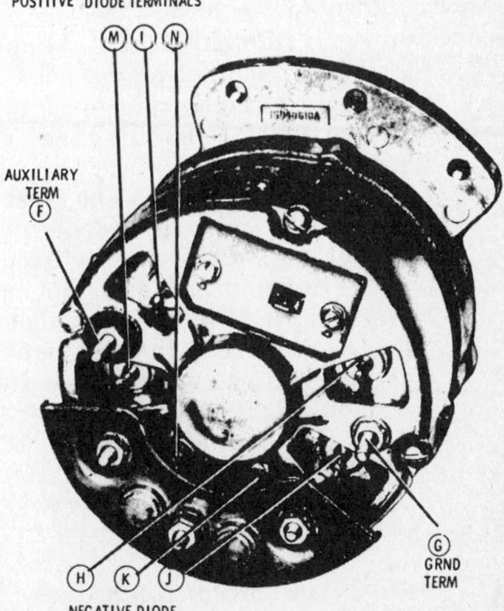

In-circuit diode test points

ther direction, all three diodes in the assembly are open. Recheck diodes individually after disassembly to pinpoint results.

NOTE: a shorted stator coil to core would appear as a shorted negative rectifier diode assembly. Also check stator for shorts after disassembly.

2. To check positive diode assembly, connect test probes to points F and L. Then reverse test probes. The same procedure and results apply as in Step 1.

Rotor Leakage Test

This is a check of the field coil for leakage or shorts to rotor poles. An ohmmeter or test lamp (12V or 120V) may be used.

1. Remove the brush assembly to gain access to rotor slip rings.
2. Connect ohmmeter or test lamp probes to one of the slip rings and the ground terminal, points G and P. (See illustration.)

Ohmmeter resistance should be infinite or test lamp should not light. If condition is contrary, leakage or a short exists between field coil and rotor.

Repeat test after rotor has been removed from the alternator to pinpoint findings.

In-Circuit Stator Leak Test

When making this test, consideration must be given to the rectifier diodes that are connected to the stator winding. The negative diode assembly will conduct in one direction when properly polarized. A shorted diode in the negative rectifier-diode assembly will make the stator appear to be shorted. Therefore, the rectifier-diode plate assembly and stator must be checked individually after the alternator has been disassembled if the problem has been narrowed down to the stator.

1. Connect a 12-volt DC test lamp to a diode terminal of the negative diode assembly and ground terminal, points G and H. (See illustration.)
2. Reverse test probes. The test lamp should light in one direction but not in the other direction. If lamp does not light in either direction, it indicates that all three rectifiers in the negative diode assembly are open. If the lamp lights in both directions, the stator winding is shorted to stator or one of the negative rectifier diodes is shorted.

Out-of-Circuit Stator Leak Test

Disassemble alternator and remove the rectifier-diode plates and stator as an assembly. (See illustration.)

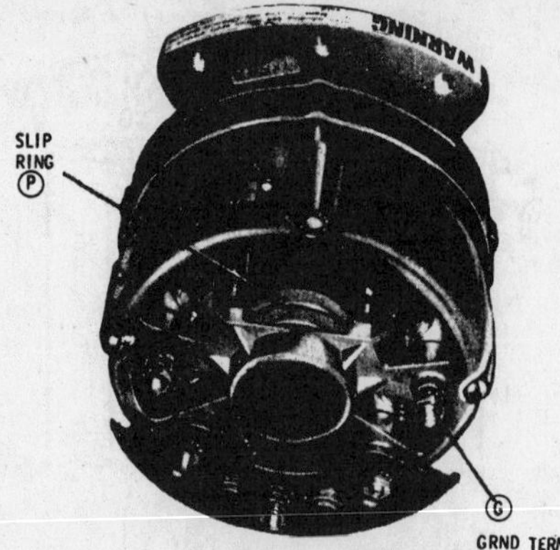

Rotor leakage test points

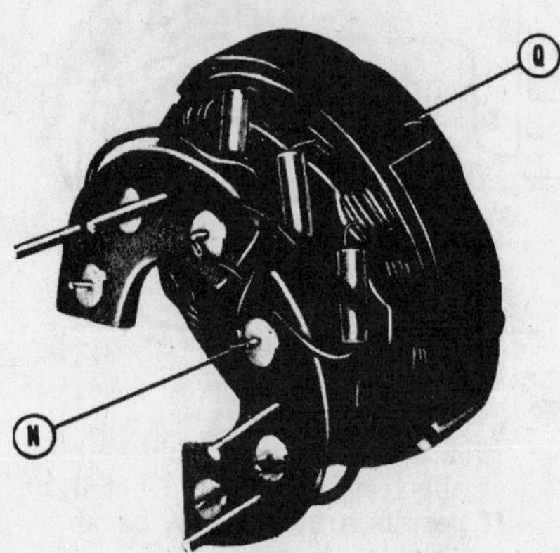

Stator leakage test points

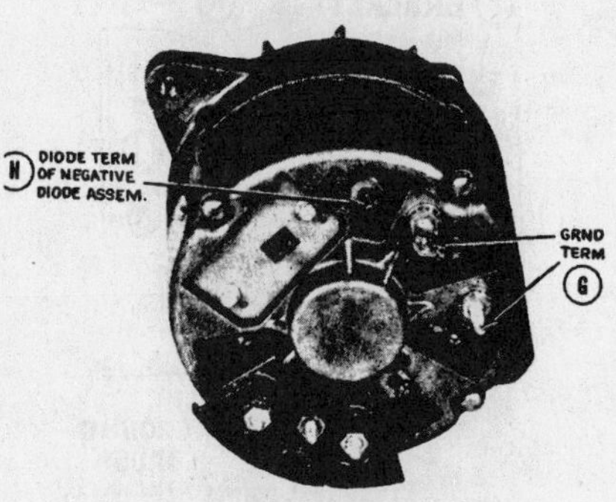

In-circuit stator leakage test points

An ohmmeter or 12-volt DC test lamp may be used.

1. Connect ohmmeter or test lamp probes to one of the rectifier diode terminals and to the stator test points N and Q.

   Resistance reading should be infinite (or the test light should not light). If result is contrary, high leakage or a short exists between stator winding and stator. In either case, stator should be replaced.

Stator Coil Leak and Continuity Test

This check is for shorts or leakage between stator coil windings. The 30 and 40 amp. alternators use a Wye-Type winding. (See illustration.) 45 ampere models use a Delta type winding. (See illustration.)

Wye Type (30 and 40 Amp. Models)

1. Separate winding ends (See illustration.) An ohmmeter or 12-volt DC test lamp may be used.
2. Connect one lead of the ohmmeter or test lamp to point 1. Connect the other test lead to point 2 and then to point 3. Ohmmeter reading should be infinite or the test lamp should not light.
3. Connect test leads to points 2 and 3. Ohmmeter reading should be infinite, or the test lamp should not light.

In test 2 or test 3, if the test results are contrary, excess leakage or a short exists between stator windings; replace the stator.

4. Check continuity by measuring the resistance of each winding in the stator with an ohmmeter, between test points (See illustration.), 1 to 1A, 2 to 2A and 3 to 3A.

   Resistance should be very low (about 0.1 ohm).

Never replace stator until all other components have been checked and proven satisfactory.

Delta Type (45 Amp. Models)

1. Separate stator winding ends. (See illustration.) An ohmmeter or 12-volt DC test lamp may be used.
2. Connect one lead of the ohmmeter or test lamp to point 4. Connect the other test lead to point 5 and then to point 6. Ohmmeter reading should be infinite or the test lamp should not light.
3. Connect test leads to test points 5 and 6. Ohmmeter reading should be infinite, or the test lamp should not light.

In test 2 or test 3, if the test results are contrary, excess leakage or a short exists between stator windings; replace the stator.

4. Check continuity by measuring the resistance of each winding in the stator with an ohmmeter placed between test points 4 to 4A, 5 to 5A and 6 to 6A. (See illustration.)

   Resistance should be very low (about 0.1 ohm).

Never replace stator until all other components have been checked and proven satisfactory.

Voltage Regulator Test

If previous checks did not prove the regulator bad, but some question still

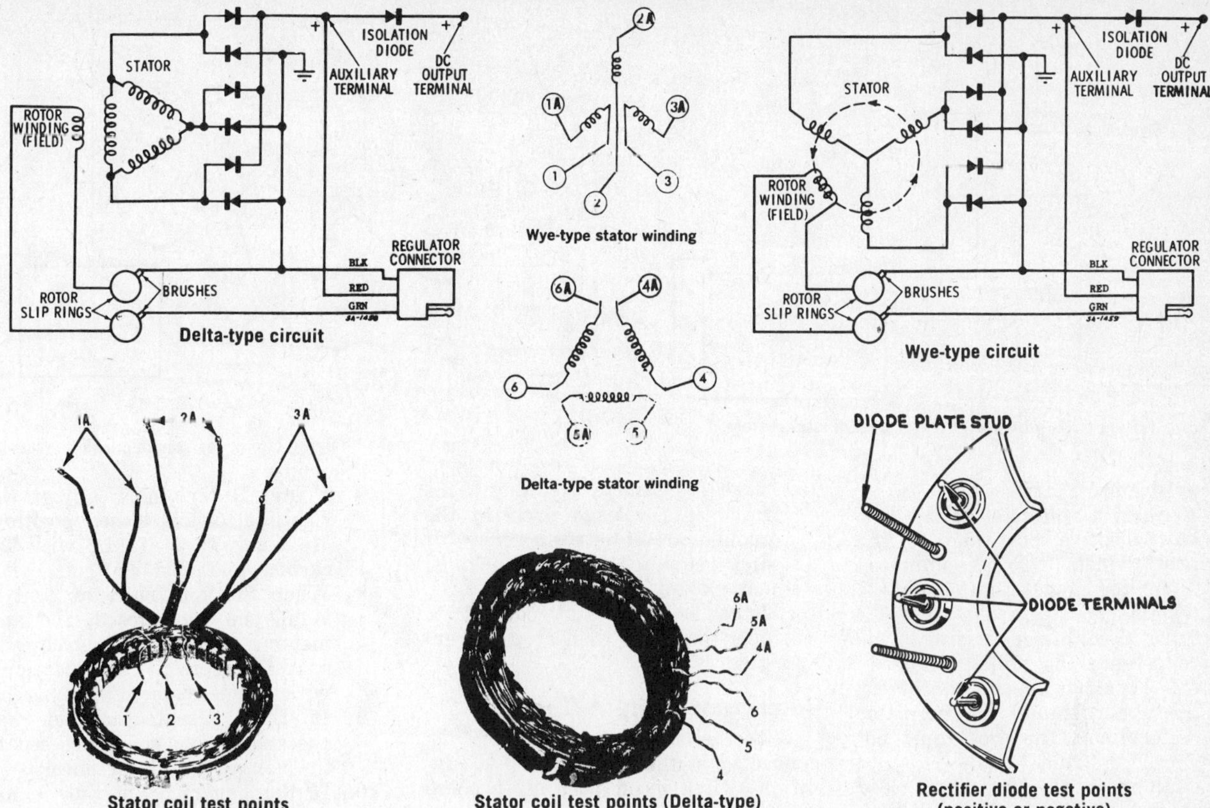

Delta-type circuit

Wye-type stator winding

Wye-type circuit

Delta-type stator winding

Stator coil test points (Wye-type)

Stator coil test points (Delta-type)

Rectifier diode test points (positive or negative)

exists as to reliability, the system can be checked while installed and operating in the car. A volt-ampere tester can be used. The system should be first tested by taking a reading of output current and the voltage at the output terminal. With a carbon pile rheostat connected across the output terminal or battery, rated current of the alternator should be available with at least 13 volts.

If this is not obtainable, shut down the engine and disconnect the regulator from the system. Insert a variable resistance in series between the output terminal and the field terminal of the alternator. Start the engine, with maximum resistance in the circuit. Then slowly decrease field resistance while increasing the load on the output of the alternator.

Caution Observe voltage at output terminal and be sure to decrease the field resistance and increase the output load without exceeding 15 volts at the output terminal.

Continue to decrease field resistance and increase output load until there is no resistance in the field circuit. If rated current output is now obtained with 13 volts at the output terminal, the voltage regulator is bad. If rated current is not available under these conditions, the alternator is bad and must be removed for repairs or replacement.

Out-of-Circuit Rectifier Diode Test

If a commercial diode tester is not available, check the diodes with a 12-volt DC test lamp only.

Caution When unsoldering the stator wires from the rectifier diode assembly, provide a heat sink to the diode terminal with a pair of longnosed pliers.

1. Connect test lamp probes to diode terminal and diode plate stud (see illustration), then reverse test lamp probes. The test light should light in one direction but not in the other.

   If the test lamp lights in both directions, the diode is shorted. If test lamp does not light in either direction, the diode is open.

   Test the remaining diodes of the assembly in the same manner. Replace entire assembly if one of the diodes is found to be bad.

The Prestolite System

The Prestolite AC generator regulator with a circuit breaker incorporates a polarity sensing feature for the purpose of isolating generator output from battery potential when the system is out of operation. This feature prevents damage to the components of the charging system in the event of battery polarity reversal.

Circuit Resistance Test

1. With the battery ground cable disconnected at the battery, and the lead disconnected from the generator output A terminal, hook up an ammeter as follows:
   A. Connect an ammeter, positive lead to the generator output A terminal.
   B. Connect the ammeter, negative lead to the lead that was just removed from the generator A terminal.
2. Disconnect the lead from the generator, field F terminal.
3. With a field rheostat control turned to open position, connect one lead of this rheostat to the generator F terminal and the other lead to the lead which was just disconnected from this F terminal.
4. Hook up an engine tachometer.
5. Connect battery ground cable.
6. Start engine and set speed to 850 rpm.
7. Adjust field rheostat toward closed position enough to effect

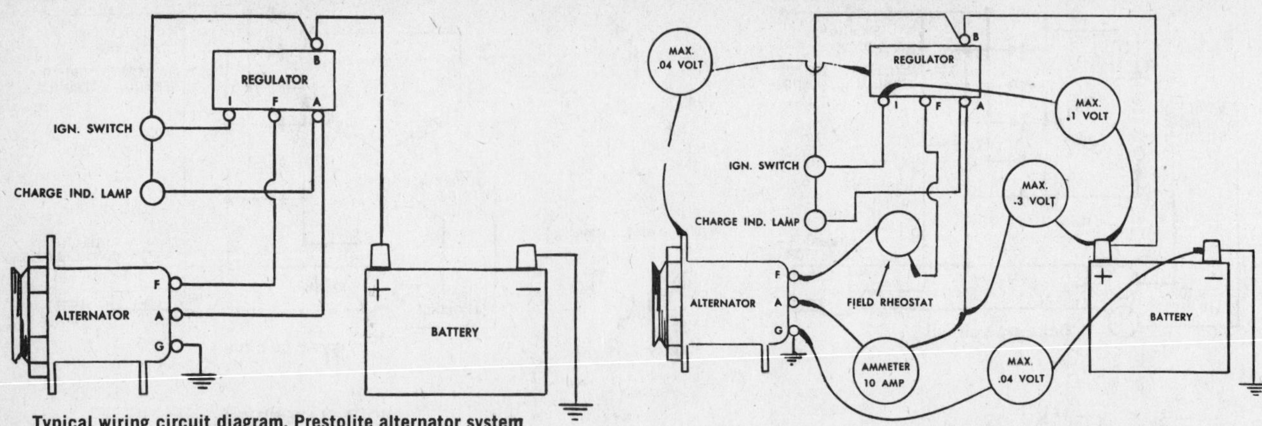

Typical wiring circuit diagram, Prestolite alternator system

Plan to make charging circuit resistance check

a 10 amp. charging rate.

8. Connect a voltmeter to the battery positive post and to the lead which was disconnected from the generator output A terminal.
9. Take a voltmeter reading. This represents the voltage drop in the circuit between the battery positive post and the regulator A terminal. The drop must not exceed 0.3 volt.
10. Disconnect the voltmeter lead from the regulator A lead, then connect this voltmeter lead to the regulator I terminal.
11. Take a voltmeter reading. This represents the voltage drop in the circuit between the battery, positive post and the regulator, I terminal. The drop must not exceed 0.1 volt.
12. Disconnect both voltmeter leads, then connect one voltmeter lead to the battery negative post. Connect the other voltmeter lead to the housing of the generator.
13. Take a voltmeter reading. This represents voltage drop in the ground circuit between the battery, negative post and the generator. The drop must not exceed 0.04 volt.
14. Disconnect the voltmeter lead from the battery negative post and connect this same voltmeter lead to a good ground on the regulator.
15. Take a voltmeter reading. This represents voltage drop in the ground circuit between generator and regulator. The drop must not exceed 0.04 volt.
16. Turn field rheostat control to open position, then stop the engine.

Alternator Output Test

With the battery ground cable disconnected at the battery, and the ignition switch in off position, proceed as follows:

1. Disconnect the leads from regulator terminals A, F and B. Then connect the leads all together and temporarily insulate them.
2. Hook up a voltmeter to the generator output A terminal and the generator frame.
3. Connect an ammeter between the generator output A terminal and spliced connection of the leads removed from the regulator A, F and B terminals.
4. Reconnect the battery ground cable.
5. With a carbon pile adjusted to the open position, connect it to both battery posts. Then start the engine and adjust the speed to 1750 rpm.
6. With a field rheostat connected to the generator F terminal and spliced connection of the leads removed from the regulator A, F and B terminals, adjust the rheostat toward closed position.
7. Hold a voltage of 14.2 with the carbon pile load control.
8. When the field rheostat control is all the way closed, the ammeter reading should agree with manufacturers' specifications, with a tolerance of ± 2 amps.
9. If the generator output has checked out as good, proceed to the voltage regulator check.
10. If the generator output is not OK, make a field current draw check.
11. Adjust field rheostat to open, turn carbon pile to off position, then stop the engine.
12. Disconnect the battery ground cable at the battery.
13. Break the splice, then reconnect all of the leads to their original locations on the regulator and generator.
14. Disconnect the test instruments.

Field Current Draw Test

1. Disconnect the generator F terminal and insulate the lead to prevent accidental grounding.
2. Connect an ammeter and a field rheostat in series, between the generator F terminal and the generator A terminal in the following manner:
   A. With a field rheostat set in the open position, connect one of its leads to the generator A terminal and the other lead to the test ammeter.
   B. Connect the other test ammeter lead to the generator F terminal.
3. Hook up a voltmeter by connecting one voltmeter lead to the generator F terminal and the other lead to the generator frame.
4. Reconnect the battery ground cable.
5. Turn ignition switch on.
6. Adjust the field rheostat to ob-

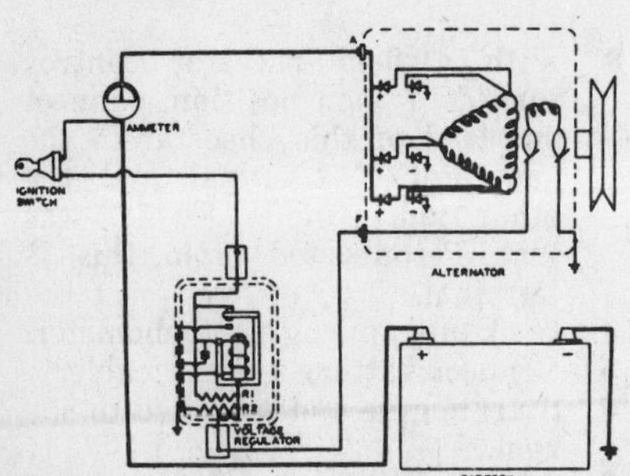

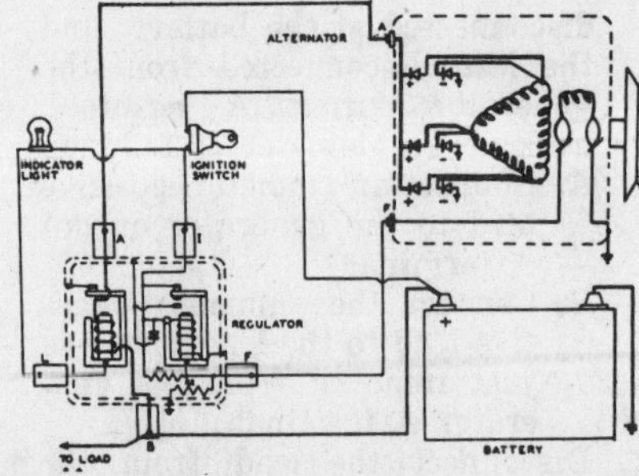

Single and two-unit Prestolite circuits

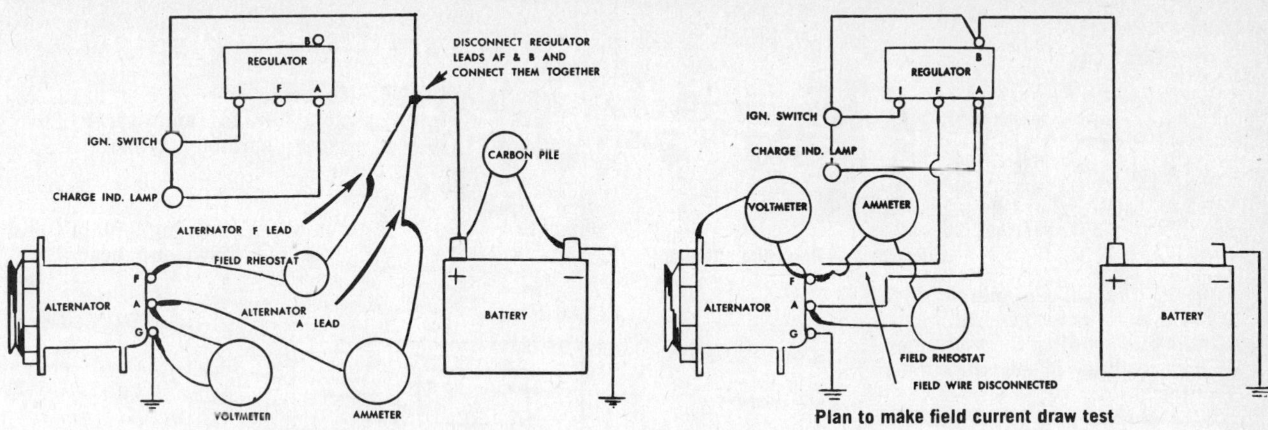

Plan to make alternator output test

Plan to make field current draw test

tain recommended voltage.

7. Now, read the ammeter. This represents the rotor field current draw.
8. Adjust field rheostat to open position, and turn ignition switch off.
9. Compare the reading with manufacturers' specifications.
   A. If the reading is too low, it indicates trouble, probably slip rings or brushes.
   B. If the reading is too high, it indicates a short in the field winding.
   C. If the reading is as specified on a generator which did not deliver its rated output, look for trouble in the diodes.

Voltage Regulator Setting

1. With the battery ground cable disconnected at the battery and the ignition switch in off position, hook up an ammeter to the generator A terminal and to the lead just disconnected from this A terminal.
2. Connect a field rheostat to the generator F terminal and to the lead just disconnected from this F terminal. Adjust rheostat to open position.
3. Connect a voltmeter to the regulator B terminal and a good ground on the frame of the regulator.
4. Connect the battery ground cable.
5. Hook up a carbon pile (load control turned to the off position) between the battery posts.
6. Start the engine and while operating at 850 rpm, adjust the field rheostat to obtain a 10 amp. charge. Be careful not to exceed factory voltage recommendation. Run engine long enough to develop normal regulator operating temperature.
7. Open, then fully close the field rheostat to cycle the system.

Alternator

	Model No. ALC 5001	*Model No. ALD 5001*	*Model No. ALD 5005*
Rotation—Clockwise, Drive End	Yes	Yes	Yes
Voltage	12	12	12
Rated Output (Amps.)	45	40	40
Brushes (No.)	2	2	2
Rotor Field Coil Draw (At 70°F) At 10 Volts	2.34—2.43 Amps.	2.32—2.42 Amps.	2.32—2.42 Amps.
Current Output—4200 rpm (Engine speed 1750 rpm)	42 Amps. 14.2 Volts	38 Amps. 14.2 Volts	38 Amps. 14.2 Volts
Ground Polarity	Negative	Negative	Negative
Control	VR	VR	VR

Voltage Regulator

	Model No. VBS 6201A	*Model No. VBT 6201A*	*Model No. VBS 6201A-1*
Volts	12	12	12
Ground Polarity	Negative	Negative	Negative
Point Gap (in.)	.010	.010	.010
Air Gap (in.)	.034-.038	.034-.038	.034-.038
Relay Air Gap (in.)	.015-.020	——	.015-.020
Relay Opening (Amps.)	2.0-2.5	——	2.0-2.5
Relay Closing (Amps.)	1.5 Max.	——	1.5 Max.
Operating Voltage (Upper (Contact) 50°F 80°F 110°F 140°F 14.3 14.1 13.0 13.7	Tolerance ±.2	—All Models—	
Voltage Spread (Between upper and lower contact operation)	.1-.3 Volts	.1-.3 Volts	.1-.3 Volts
Capacitor (Color band indicates ground end)	.1 MFD	.1 MFD	.1 MFD
Resistance			
R^1	10 Ohms.	10 Ohms.	10 Ohms.
R^2	20 Ohms.	20 Ohms.	20 Ohms.
VR Winding	52-58 Ohms.	52-58 Ohms.	52-58 Ohms.
1600-1800 rpm Alternator Speed, 15 minute warm-up, 10 Amp. load		—All Models—	
3400-3600 rpm Alternator Speed, 15 Amp. load Upper contacts—2-7 Amp. Charge rate—lower grounding contacts		—All Models—	
All tests to be made with a fully charged battery		—All Models—	

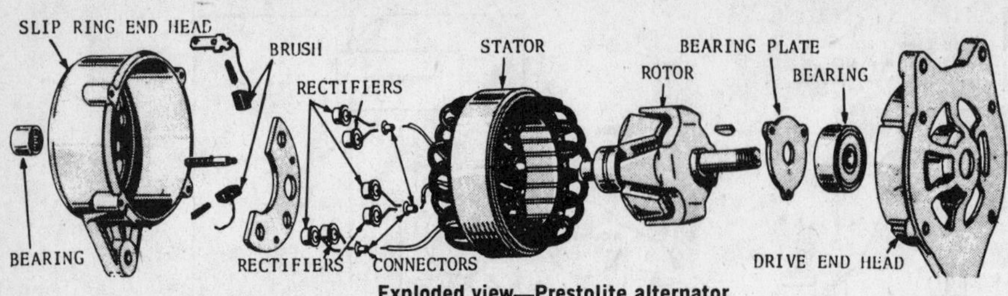

Exploded view—Prestolite alternator

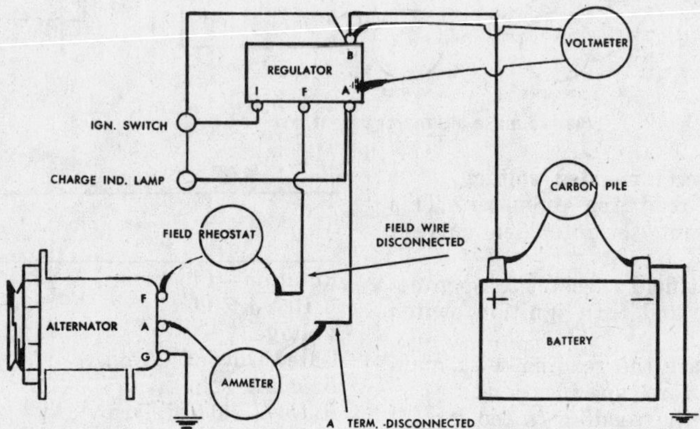

Plan to make voltage regulator check

8. Adjust the carbon pile load to obtain a 10 amp. generator output while reading the voltmeter. This reading is on the upper contacts.
9. Turn carbon pile to off position and increase engine rpm to 1750, then read the voltmeter. This voltage should increase and the amperage decrease if the regulator lower point set is working. This is known as spread.
10. If the battery is in fully charged condition, the spread may be checked in the following manner.
    A. Adjust load control to produce 15 amps. of charge, then read the voltmeter. This reading is on the upper set of points.
    B. Adjust load control to off position, wait about one-half minute, then read the voltmeter. This reading is on the lower set of points. The difference between the two readings is spread.
    C. Spread should be 0.2 to 0.5 volts higher when operating on lower grounding contact. Operation on lower contacts must not exceed 14.7 volts. If necessary, adjust regulator so as not to exceed 14.7 volts.
11. If regulator does not operate within specifications, renew the regulator.

Disassembly

1. Remove thru bolts and tap ends lightly with plastic hammer to separate ends from rotor.
2. Remove nuts and washers from negative rectifier brackets, and the nuts, washers and insulator bushings from the positive rectifier brackets, and separate the slip ring end head.
3. Remove insulated brush, gripping brass terminal on brush head with pliers and pulling from field terminal insulator.
4. Remove screw that attaches ground brush. Do not lose brush springs.
5. To remove pulley nut, grip pulley with fan belt and vise to hold while breaking nut loose. Then remove pulley with suitable puller.
6. To remove drive end head, remove key, fan and spacer. Then, using suitable puller remove head.
7. Remove retaining plate and press out drive end head bearing.
8. The slip end head bearing can be removed with a puller.
9. The rectifiers can now be pressed out and in. In cutting and crimping leads keep as close to the sleeve as possible.

Regulators

The voltage regulator is a dual contact type. Field F terminal and ignition I terminal are insulated from base. A regulating resistor is connected between these terminals.

To adjust, remove the cover, loosen stationary contact support screw and move support up or down. Use following specification tables for settings.

C.S.I. AC Generator

The C.S.I. system is an integrated AC generating system containing a built-in voltage regulator. Removal and displacement is essentially the same as for the standard AC generator. Specialized service procedures are as follows:

Diode Trio Initial Testing

1. Before removing this unit, easily identified in the illustration, connect an ohmmeter between the brush lead clip and the end frame. The lowest reading scale should be used for this test.
2. After taking a reading, reverse the lead connections. If the meter reads zero, the brush lead clip is probably grounded, due to omission of the insulating sleeve or insulating washer.

Diode Trio Removal

1. Remove the three nuts which secure the stator.
2. Remove stator.
3. Remove the screw which secures the diode trio lead clip, then remove diode trio.

NOTE: The position of the insulating washer on the screw is critical; make sure it is returned to the same position on reassembly.

Diode Trio Testing

1. Connect an ohmmeter, on lowest range, between the single brush connector and one stator lead connector (see illustration).
2. Observe the reading, then reverse the meter leads. Repeat this test with each of the other two stator lead connectors. The readings on each of these tests should NOT be identical, there

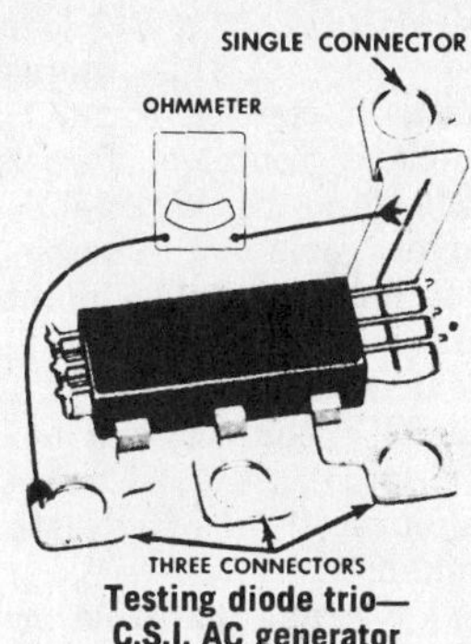

Testing diode trio—C.S.I. AC generator

should be one low and one high reading for each test. If this is not the case, replace the diode trio.

CAUTION: Do not use high voltage on the diode trio.

Rectifier Bridge Testing

1. Connect an ohmmeter between the heat sink (ground) and the base of one of the three terminals (see illustration). Then, reverse the meter leads and take a reading. If both readings are identical, the bridge is defective and must be replaced.
2. Repeat this test with the remaining two terminals, then between the INSULATED heat sink (as opposed to the GROUNDED heat sink in previous test) and each of the three terminals. As before, if any two readings are identical, on reversing the meter leads, the rectifier bridge must be replaced.

Rectifier Bridge Removal

1. Remove the attaching screw and the BAT. terminal screw.
2. Disconnect the condenser lead.
3. Remove the rectifier bridge.

NOTE: The insulator between the insulated heat sink and the end frame is extremely important to the operation of the unit. It must be replaced in exactly the same position on reassembly.

Brush and/or Voltage Regulator R & R

1. Remove two brush holder screws and stator lead to strap nut and washer, brush holder screws and one of the diode trio lead strap attaching screws.

NOTE: The insulating washers must be replaced in the same position on reassembly.

2. Remove brush holder and brushes. The voltage regulator may also be removed at this time, if desired.

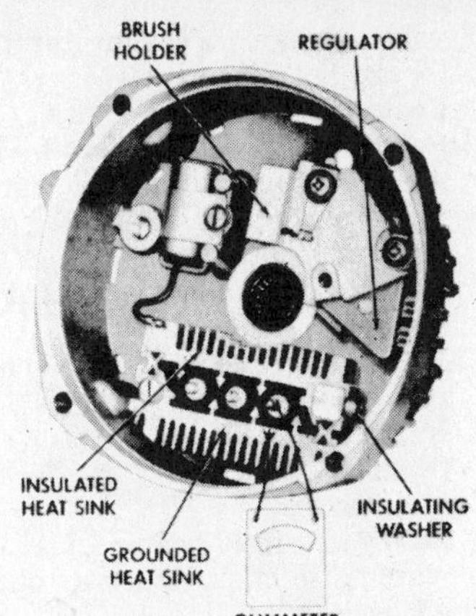

Testing rectifier bridge diodes—C.S.I. AC generator

Grounding tab for voltage regulator test—C.S.I. AC generator

3. Brushes and brush springs must be free of corrosion and must be undamaged and completely free of oil or grease.
4. Insert spring and brushes into holder, noting whether they slide freely without binding. Insert wooden or plastic toothpick into bottom hole in holder to retain brushes.

NOTE: The brush holder is serviced as a unit; individual parts are not available.

5. Reassemble in reverse order of disassembly.

Voltage Regulator Testing

NOTE: The voltage regulator must be tested with the C.S.I. unit still in place.

1. Disconnect battery ground strap.
2. Connect an ammeter in series with the BAT. terminal of the generator and the lead removed from that terminal.
3. Reconnect battery ground strap, then turn on all accessories to place a load on the system.
4. Connect a carbon pile across the battery terminals.

Brush holder—C.S.I. generator

5. Ground the field winding by inserting an insulated screwdriver into the test hole in the alternator frame and depressing the tab. Do not push the tab into the generator more than 1 in. (See illustration.)
6. Run the engine at moderate rpm, equivalent to 30-40 mph in high gear, and adjust the carbon pile to obtain maximum current output.
7. If the output is within 10% of the rated output of the alternator and the system does not charge properly, the voltage regulator is defective and must be replaced.

Generator—C.S.I.
- Amps.—cold rating 55
- Output @ rpm ....30 @ 2000
- Output @ rpm ....55 @ 5000
- Field current draw 4.0-4.5

Regulator—C.S.I.
- Model ....1116368 (Pontiac parts no.)
- Normal range .....13.5-16.0 volts

Slip Ring End Frame Bearing and Seal R & R

1. With stator removed, press out bearing and seal, using a socket or similar tool that fits inside the end frame housing. Press from outside to inside, supporting the frame inside with a hollow cylinder (large, deep socket) to allow the seal and bearing to pass.
2. The bearings are sealed for life and permanently lubricated. If a bearing is dry, do not attempt to repack it, as it will throw off the grease and contaminate the inside of the generator.
3. Using a flat plate, press the new bearing from the outside toward the inside. A large vise is a handy press, but care must be exercised so that end frame is not distorted or cracked. Again, use a deep socket to support the inside of the end frame.
4. From inside the end frame, insert seal and press flush with housing.
5. Install stator and reconnect leads.

Diagnosis

Diagnosing engine problems requires a combination of knowledge, mechanical skill and good test equipment. However, testing equipment is only as good as the skill of the person operating it.

Engine trouble can be separated into four general groups:

1. Won't start
2. Performs poorly
3. Improper lubrication
4. Noise

Won't Start

Assuming the engine will crank, there are four reasons why an engine won't start:

1. The combustion chamber is not receiving adequate spark.
2. The proper fuel-air mixture is not reaching the cylinders.
3. Poor compression.
4. Timing is incorrect.

Some of the above reasons overlap in scope. However, a thorough probe into all four factors should uncover the scientific fault.

Weak or No Spark To Combustion Chambers

1. Burnt or poorly gapped distributor points.
2. Short or open condenser.
3. Short or open coil.
4. Poor primary circuit from ignition switch to points in distributor.
5. Neutral safety switch bad or out of adjustment.
6. Low or dead battery.
7. On overdrive equipped cars, bad kickdown switch.
8. High starter draw.
9. Defective ignition switch.
10. High resistance anywhere in primary or secondary ignition circuit.
11. Moisture and dirt on distributor cap, ignition wires, and plug porcelains.
12. Cracked distributor cap.
13. Broken rotor.
14. Reversed coil polarity.

Improper Fuel—Air Mixture To Cylinders

1. Fuel tank empty or line to fuel pump blocked or open. Many car fuel pumps are now equipped with a replaceable filter in the tank.
2. Fuel tank not vented to atmosphere.
3. Weak or completely bad fuel pump. (Make fuel pump volume and pressure test.)
4. Fuel stoppage at carburetor filter or float level valve.
5. Leaking carburetor float.
6. Poorly adjusted float level.
7. Air, (vacuum) leak at carburetor or intake manifold, (beware of faulty double action fuel pumps and vacuum operated accessories).
8. Poor compression, (low vacuum reading).
9. Inferior fuel.
10. Obstructed or dirty carburetor air cleaner.
11. Leaky manifold heat riser.
12. Automatic choke stuck or out of adjustment.

NOTE: a choke thermostat spring that has fatigued needs replacement, not mere adjustment.

13. Engine valves not seating properly, burnt, sticky or out of adjustment.
14. Hydraulic valve lifter trouble (improper oil pressure, worn or stuck tappets).
15. Camshaft wear or breakage.
16. Valve timing incorrect.
17. Manifold heat control valve not working.
18. Vaporlock, under certain conditions.
19. Low engine operating temperature (below 170° F).
20. High engine operating temperature (above 190° F).

Poor Compression

1. Poorly seating exhaust or intake valves.
2. Worn or sludged-up rings.
3. Blown head gasket.
4. Valve timing incorrect.
5. Cracked or broken piston.
6. Beware of short connecting rods in cars equipped with dual engine options. It is mechanically possible to install the connecting rods of the shorter stroked engine into the bores and onto the crankshaft of the higher displacement engine. This error will shorten the piston stroke and result in low compression.

Timing Incorrect

1. Poorly gapped distributor points.
2. Distributor static timing incorrect.
3. Distributor governor advance, faulty.
4. Distributor, vacuum control, defective.
5. Distribution of secondary current to spark plugs, out of firing sequence.
6. Ignition timing not coincident with cylinder timing.
7. Valve timing incorrect.

Performs Poorly

The purpose of this manual is to point out, in concise form, the best and quickest route to factory performance standards. Special performance coverage is not possible here.

1. Distributor trouble, points, condenser, timing, etc.
2. Weak coil.
3. Bad or incorrect spark plugs or wiring.
4. Carburetor out of adjustment or broken.
5. Leaky intake manifold or carburetor gasket.
6. Leaky vacuum operated units or accessories.
7. Poor fuel—compression ratio—timing balance.
8. Faulty fuel supply.
9. Poor compression, valves, rings, gasket, etc.
10. Exhaust back pressure—clogged muffler or tail pipe.
11. Clogged air filter or inlet.
12. Cooling system failure.
13. Leaky heat riser or stuck heat control valve.

Improper Lubrication

1. Low oil level.
2. Very high oil level (causing foaming).
3. Clogged oil pump screen.
4. Oil pump sucking air, loose pump mount inside crankcase.
5. Dirty oil.
6. Clogged or saturated oil filter.
7. Oil contamination, (such as water, acid, gum, abrasives, antifreeze, etc.)
8. Improper viscosity or quality of oil.
9. By-pass valve stuck.

NOTE: all name-brand oils are good, and engine manufacturers' recommendations should be followed. However, extreme service exposure may alter engine requirements necessitating more frequent oil changes, heavy duty oil, use of detergents, etc.

Noise

As long as combustion and reciprocating engines are used to furnish power, a certain degree of noise will be present. The best we can do is to keep the noise level as low as possible.

To catalogue all of the causes of noise would require coverage larger than one volume will permit. We therefore will limit our list to mechanical causes most common to the automotive gasoline engine.

1. Valve Noise.
   - A. Sticky valves.
   - B. Stuck hydraulic tappets.
   - C. Dry hydraulic tappets.
   - D. Bent valve stem.

E. Warped valve head.
F. Broken valve spring.
G. Tappet out of adjustment.
H. Rocker arm loose.
I. Pushrod bent or worn.
J. Rocker shaft worn or loose.
K. Valve or tappet guide worn.

2. Piston Noise.
A. Collapsed or broken piston.
B. Scored piston or cylinder wall.
C. Broken piston rings.
D. Carbon on piston and cylinder head making physical contact.
E. Top cylinder ridge striking top piston ring.
F. Loose or broken piston pin.

3. Crankshaft Bearing Noise.
A. Loose connecting rod bearing.
B. Loose main bearing.
C. Bent connecting rod, (sounds like bearing).
D. Loose flywheel or converter, (sounds like bearing).
E. Loose crankshaft damper or pulley, (sounds like bearing).
F. Crankshaft end-play, (noticeable when actuating clutch).
G. Crankshaft misalignment.

4. Detonation.

Detonation is spontaneous combustion within the cylinder. It is caused by an imbalance of compression ratio, heat, fuel value, and timing. Detonation can be annoying, wasteful and very destructive to engine parts.

The following factors or combinations should be checked as contributing elements.

A. Cooling system temperature.
B. Spark plug appearance.
C. Ignition timing index.
D. Fuel octane rating.
E. Incandescence within the combustion area caused by carbon particles, sharp edges, burnt spark plugs, etc.
F. Lean carburetor mixture.
G. Stuck manifold heat-control valve.

Professional Approach

The Oscilloscope

It is a time consuming job even to remove spark plugs from some of the V8 engines. Therefore, it is good logic to test engine components while performing their normal duties under various conditions. The oscilloscope will do this.

While this tool is no cure-all, it does produce a television screen picture of the situation as it exists within the running engine.

This picture can be translated into functions of the engine that are familiar to the mechanic.

A good oscilloscope can determine:

1. Compression balance.
2. Condition of spark plugs.
3. Condition of distributor points.
4. Ignition coil or condenser problems.
5. Bad ignition wiring.
6. Distributor point dwell.
7. Cracked distributor cap.
8. Worn or broken rotor.
9. Worn distributor points.
10. Bad secondary wires and terminals.
11. Reversed polarity.

It is not possible here to outline the various oscilloscope hook-ups. Follow the manufacturer's instructions.

The following operations depend largely upon the results of the oscilloscope picture.

Compression Check

Due to the added torque of modern engine starting systems, plus changes in engine camshaft design, it is no longer practical to determine cylinder compression balance by listening to the starter while cranking the engine. For positive cranking pressure readings, use a cylinder compression gauge.

Because engine design and other factors influence compression, a pressure test of all of the cylinders in any one engine will furnish a yardstick of comparison for that particular engine only. Therefore there can be no table established for compression pressure standards.

1. Run the engine until normal temperature has been reached.
2. Carefully remove spark plug wires.
3. Blow foreign matter from spark plug wells. Then loosen plugs one turn.
4. Replace plug wires, start engine and snap throttle open once or twice (this should clear the engine cylinders of dislodged carbon particles).
5. Stop engine and remove plug wires and spark plugs.
6. Remove carburetor air cleaner or cleaners and (depending upon intake manifold design) block throttle valve or valves wide open.
7. Hook up starter remote control cable and switch. Then, using a compression gauge in the cylinder, crank the engine through about four compression strokes. Record the highest gauge pressure for that cylinder.
8. Proceed with remaining cylinders in the same manner.
9. Some variation in cylinders is to be expected; however, the difference should not exceed 15 lbs.

Poor Compression

In the event of poor compression in two adjacent cylinders of a multicylinder engine, the probable cause is a blown head gasket between them. This condition can generally be identified by an identical pressure reading for the two cylinders. The condition can also be spotted by a popping back through the carburetor.

Low compression may also be the result of a leaky head gasket at a point between the compression chamber and a coolant passage of the water jacket. This will usually affect individual cylinders and will probably manifest itself as excess water in the crankcase. A rusty dipstick or water droplets in the oil filler cap is also a good indication of coolant entering the crankcase. A bad coolant leak into the combustion chamber may stop the crankshaft from turning. The coolant hydraulically prevents completion of the compression stroke in the bad cylinder. Any further attempt at cranking the engine, under these conditions, can cause severe damage.

To locate a compression leak, if the cooling system is not involved, pour a tablespoon full of SAE 30 oil into the combustion chamber. Crank the engine to spread the oil. If the gauge reading is 10 psi. or more higher than the original reading, bad rings are a probability. If the compression pressure has not been improved, the trouble could be valves. However, one other remote possibility would be a crack or hole in the piston that has been temporarily sealed by oil.

Compression Troubles—Causes

Generally, compression troubles show up in the form of hard starting, oil consumption, or poor engine performance, (especially at idle). There is also the possibility of backfiring at the carburetor and afterburning in the muffler.

The best way to check compression pressures is with a compression gauge inserted into the combustion chamber at the spark plug hole. Crank the engine at least four revolutions, then record the reading. All cylinders should read within 20 lbs.

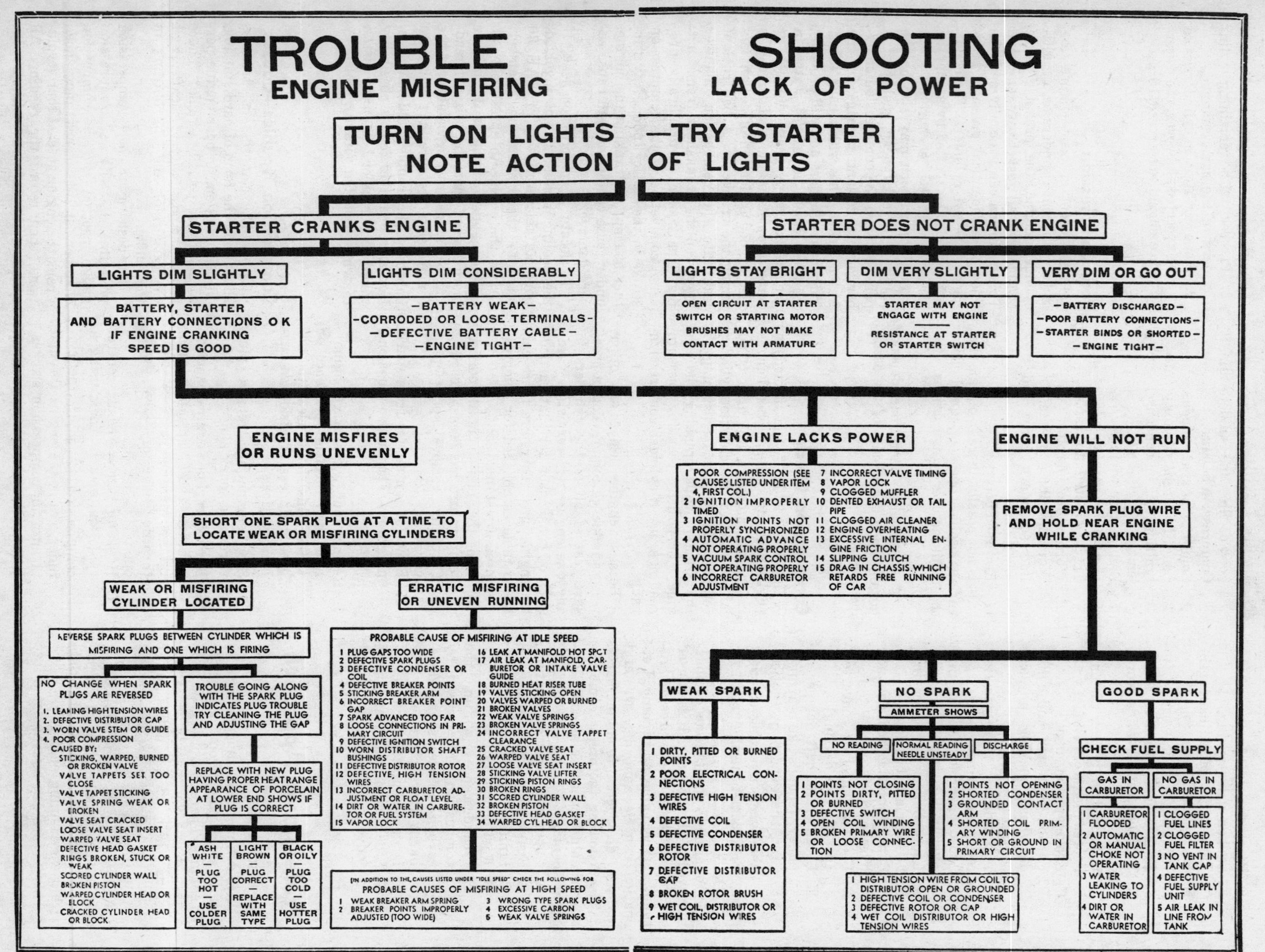
TROUBLE SHOOTING
ENGINE MISFIRING
LACK OF POWER
TURN ON LIGHTS —TRY STARTER NOTE ACTION OF LIGHTS
STARTER CRANKS ENGINE
STARTER DOES NOT CRANK ENGINE
LIGHTS DIM SLIGHTLY
BATTERY, STARTER AND BATTERY CONNECTIONS O K IF ENGINE CRANKING SPEED IS GOOD
LIGHTS DIM CONSIDERABLY
—BATTERY WEAK—
—CORRODED OR LOOSE TERMINALS—
—DEFECTIVE BATTERY CABLE—
—ENGINE TIGHT—
LIGHTS STAY BRIGHT
OPEN CIRCUIT AT STARTER SWITCH OR STARTING MOTOR BRUSHES MAY NOT MAKE CONTACT WITH ARMATURE
DIM VERY SLIGHTLY
STARTER MAY NOT ENGAGE WITH ENGINE
RESISTANCE AT STARTER OR STARTER SWITCH
VERY DIM OR GO OUT
—BATTERY DISCHARGED—
—POOR BATTERY CONNECTIONS—
—STARTER BINDS OR SHORTED—
—ENGINE TIGHT—
ENGINE MISFIRES OR RUNS UNEVENLY
SHORT ONE SPARK PLUG AT A TIME TO LOCATE WEAK OR MISFIRING CYLINDERS
WEAK OR MISFIRING CYLINDER LOCATED
REVERSE SPARK PLUGS BETWEEN CYLINDER WHICH IS MISFIRING AND ONE WHICH IS FIRING
NO CHANGE WHEN SPARK PLUGS ARE REVERSED
1. LEAKING HIGH TENSION WIRES
2. DEFECTIVE DISTRIBUTOR CAP
3. WORN VALVE STEM OR GUIDE
4. POOR COMPRESSION
CAUSED BY:
STICKING, WARPED, BURNED OR BROKEN VALVE
VALVE TAPPETS SET TOO CLOSE
VALVE TAPPET STICKING
VALVE SPRING WEAK OR BROKEN
VALVE SEAT CRACKED
LOOSE VALVE SEAT INSERT
WARPED VALVE SEAT
DEFECTIVE HEAD GASKET
RINGS BROKEN, STUCK OR WEAK
SCORED CYLINDER WALL
BROKEN PISTON
WARPED CYLINDER HEAD OR BLOCK
CRACKED CYLINDER HEAD OR BLOCK
TROUBLE GOING ALONG WITH THE SPARK PLUG INDICATES PLUG TROUBLE TRY CLEANING THE PLUG AND ADJUSTING THE GAP
REPLACE WITH NEW PLUG HAVING PROPER HEAT RANGE APPEARANCE OF PORCELAIN AT LOWER END SHOWS IF PLUG IS CORRECT
ASH WHITE — PLUG TOO HOT — USE COLDER PLUG
LIGHT BROWN — PLUG CORRECT — REPLACE WITH SAME TYPE
BLACK OR OILY — PLUG TOO COLD — USE HOTTER PLUG
ERRATIC MISFIRING OR UNEVEN RUNNING
PROBABLE CAUSE OF MISFIRING AT IDLE SPEED
1 PLUG GAPS TOO WIDE
2 DEFECTIVE SPARK PLUGS
3 DEFECTIVE CONDENSER OR COIL
4 DEFECTIVE BREAKER POINTS
5 STICKING BREAKER ARM
6 INCORRECT BREAKER POINT GAP
7 SPARK ADVANCED TOO FAR
8 LOOSE CONNECTIONS IN PRIMARY CIRCUIT
9 DEFECTIVE IGNITION SWITCH
10 WORN DISTRIBUTOR SHAFT BUSHINGS
11 DEFECTIVE DISTRIBUTOR ROTOR
12 DEFECTIVE, HIGH TENSION WIRES
13 INCORRECT CARBURETOR ADJUSTMENT OR FLOAT LEVEL
14 DIRT OR WATER IN CARBURETOR OR FUEL SYSTEM
15 VAPOR LOCK
16 LEAK AT MANIFOLD HOT SPOT
17 AIR LEAK AT MANIFOLD, CARBURETOR OR INTAKE VALVE GUIDE
18 BURNED HEAT RISER TUBE
19 VALVES STICKING OPEN
20 VALVES WARPED OR BURNED
21 BROKEN VALVES
22 WEAK VALVE SPRINGS
23 BROKEN VALVE SPRINGS
24 INCORRECT VALVE TAPPET CLEARANCE
25 CRACKED VALVE SEAT
26 WARPED VALVE SEAT
27 LOOSE VALVE SEAT INSERT
28 STICKING VALVE LIFTER
29 STICKING PISTON RINGS
30 BROKEN RINGS
31 SCORED CYLINDER WALL
32 BROKEN PISTON
33 DEFECTIVE HEAD GASKET
34 WARPED CYL HEAD OR BLOCK
(IN ADDITION TO THE CAUSES LISTED UNDER "IDLE SPEED" CHECK THE FOLLOWING FOR
PROBABLE CAUSES OF MISFIRING AT HIGH SPEED
1 WEAK BREAKER ARM SPRING
2 BREAKER POINTS IMPROPERLY ADJUSTED (TOO WIDE)
3 WRONG TYPE SPARK PLUGS
4 EXCESSIVE CARBON
6 WEAK VALVE SPRINGS
ENGINE LACKS POWER
1 POOR COMPRESSION (SEE CAUSES LISTED UNDER ITEM 4, FIRST COL.)
2 IGNITION IMPROPERLY TIMED
3 IGNITION POINTS NOT PROPERLY SYNCHRONIZED
4 AUTOMATIC ADVANCE NOT OPERATING PROPERLY
5 VACUUM SPARK CONTROL NOT OPERATING PROPERLY
6 INCORRECT CARBURETOR ADJUSTMENT
7 INCORRECT VALVE TIMING
8 VAPOR LOCK
9 CLOGGED MUFFLER
10 DENTED EXHAUST OR TAIL PIPE
11 CLOGGED AIR CLEANER
12 ENGINE OVERHEATING
13 EXCESSIVE INTERNAL ENGINE FRICTION
14 SLIPPING CLUTCH
15 DRAG IN CHASSIS WHICH RETARDS FREE RUNNING OF CAR
ENGINE WILL NOT RUN
REMOVE SPARK PLUG WIRE AND HOLD NEAR ENGINE WHILE CRANKING
WEAK SPARK
1 DIRTY, PITTED OR BURNED POINTS
2 POOR ELECTRICAL CONNECTIONS
3 DEFECTIVE HIGH TENSION WIRES
4 DEFECTIVE COIL
5 DEFECTIVE CONDENSER
6 DEFECTIVE DISTRIBUTOR ROTOR
7 DEFECTIVE DISTRIBUTOR CAP
8 BROKEN ROTOR BRUSH
9 WET COIL, DISTRIBUTOR OR HIGH TENSION WIRES
NO SPARK
AMMETER SHOWS
NO READING
1 POINTS NOT CLOSING
2 POINTS DIRTY, PITTED OR BURNED
3 DEFECTIVE SWITCH
4 OPEN COIL WINDING
5 BROKEN PRIMARY WIRE OR LOOSE CONNECTION
NORMAL READING NEEDLE UNSTEADY
1 HIGH TENSION WIRE FROM COIL TO DISTRIBUTOR OPEN OR GROUNDED
2 DEFECTIVE COIL OR CONDENSER
3 DEFECTIVE ROTOR OR CAP
4 WET COIL DISTRIBUTOR OR HIGH TENSION WIRES
DISCHARGE
1 POINTS NOT OPENING
2 SHORTED CONDENSER
3 GROUNDED CONTACT ARM
4 SHORTED COIL PRIMARY WINDING
5 SHORT OR GROUND IN PRIMARY CIRCUIT
GOOD SPARK
CHECK FUEL SUPPLY
GAS IN CARBURETOR
1 CARBURETOR FLOODED
2 AUTOMATIC OR MANUAL CHOKE NOT OPERATING
3 WATER LEAKING TO CYLINDERS
4 DIRT OR WATER IN CARBURETOR
NO GAS IN CARBURETOR
1 CLOGGED FUEL LINES
2 CLOGGED FUEL FILTER
3 NO VENT IN TANK CAP
4 DEFECTIVE FUEL SUPPLY UNIT
5 AIR LEAK IN LINE FROM TANK

of specified cranking pressures and be within 20 lbs. of each other.

1. Worn or sludge choked rings.
2. Broken rings or pistons.
3. Bent or wrong connecting rod or piston.
4. Blown or leaking head gasket.
5. Hydro-locked engine.
6. Leaky cylinder block, or heads.
7. Poorly seated valves.
8. Incorrect valve timing.
9. Broken timing chain or gears.
10. Worn or broken camshaft.
11. Insufficient valve train lash.

Vacuum Reading	*Possible Reasons*	*Next Test*
Steady gauge reading 18–20" at all speeds. Throttle is released and engine speed quickly cuts from over 2000 rpm to idle. Needle jumps 2–5" above normal and then quickly drops to normal without pause or hesitation.	Normal engine performance.	Vacuum okay. Go to compression tests.
Steady low reading. Figure A. (less than 2" drop)	Retarded ignition timing.	Loosen clamp, rotate distributor to reset timing. Check gauge improvement.
Steady, very low reading. Figure B.	Late valve timing.	Check valve timing. Make compression tests.
Steady, extremely low reading. (up to 15" drop) Figure C.	Severely warped or cracked intake manifold. Bad carburetor-to-manifold gasket.	Inspect manifold. Squirt oil around seal to detect leak.
Pointer does not jump much above normal when throttle is quickly closed and engine speed is cut from above 2000 rpm to idle. Figure A.	Piston rings may be worn or defective and are blowing into crankcase.	Take compression test of cylinders to pinpoint trouble.
Pointer jumps 2–5" above normal upon quick deceleration but hesitates at higher pressure before returning to normal. Figure B.	Restricted exhaust system is causing backpressure on engine.	Check exhaust for dents, restrictions, clogged muffler.
Pointer (rhythmically drops 1–7" below normal vacuum at regular intervals.	Leaking combustion chamber or valve; (ignition or plug failure involving one cylinder).	Make compression tests; (make ignition check).
Pointer drops rapidly but intermittently (not every time) and then recovers.	Valve sticking at times won't close tight.	Note which valve sticks. Apply penetrating oil to one valve guide at a time. Problem will correct itself temporarily.

Compression Troubles—Corrections

1. Worn or sludge choked rings do, in extreme cases, leak compression so badly that starting is impossible. This is a condition of gradual development, however, and not likely to happen overnight. When ring condition has deteriorated to this degree, oil consumption, smoky exhaust, plug fouling and general poor performance is evident. To isolate a ring condition from other causes of poor compression, take a compression reading in the regular manner and record the results. Then, squirt about a tablespoon full of SAE 30 oil into all the cylinders and take a second compression test and record these readings. An appreciable increase in pressure reading will indicate probable ring failure or sludging. In either case, this evidence warrants removal of at least one piston assembly for visual inspection.

If, upon examination, rings or piston ring grooves are worn, renew the necessary parts. If rings and grooves are merely choked with carbon and sludge, carefully clean out the piston grooves and drainback holes, then install new, correctly sized rings. Never reinstall the old rings.

2. Broken rings or pistons cause poor compression in varying degrees, proportional to the amount of breakage. It is possible, but not likely, to have breakage in all of the cylinders of a multi-cylinder engine. Breakage in all, or most, of the cylinders could result in hard starting and poor performance in addition to oil consumption and other difficulties. However, if the breakage is confined to one or two cylinders of a six or eight cylinder engine, poor idle, stalling and an uneven flow of power will be the result. To isolate the trouble, check for the miss (electrically). Remove the spark plugs from suspicious cylinders and check for fouling, then take a compression reading on all of the cylinders. All cylinders should read within 20 psi of each other. The piston will have to be removed from the low compression cylinder to make any kind of correction. At this time, (piston removed) a visual inspection should pinpoint the trouble—whether it is rings or piston. Renew the offending part.

3. A bent rod is a short rod, but a wrong rod or piston can be either too short or too long.

A bent connecting rod will reduce (proportional to the degree of the bend) the total compression potential of that cylinder. A bent rod, unless it is severe enough to interfere with crankshaft rotation, may cause a noise, but should not result in hard starting. It may, however, due to low compression pressure, cause rough idling and poor performance.

The presence of wrong parts, (piston or connecting rod) in an engine that is in service is rather remote but entirely possible.

If the wrong piston or rod results in the piston extending too far above normal travel, interference would occur and something would surely lock up or break.

In the case of a short rod, a piston designed for lower compression ratio, or a piston built with less than proper length above the piston pin, lower compression pressures will result in that cylinder than in other normal cylinders of the same engine.

If a compression gauge reading indicates this condition, remove the cylinder head/heads and compare the piston top position with that of its opposing cylinder. With the exception of the 90°, V6, the comparison cylinder is the one directly opposed in firing sequence to the one in question. If the piston in the bad cylinder is at a lower point of stroke than its comparison piston, remove the piston and rod assembly for visual inspection. Also determine the cause. Coolant in the combustion area at the time of cranking is the usual cause of a bent rod.

4. A blown or leaky head gasket may manifest itself in more than one

Vacuum Reading	*Possible Reasons*	*Next Test*
Pointer wavers rapidly between 10–20" at idle becoming worse with higher rpm.	Weak or broken spring causing valve to close slowly.	Remove valve covers; check condition of springs.
Wavers irregularly at idle; fluctuates rapidly in smaller range at higher rpm.	Manifold leak at intake port—upsets and reduces cylinder draft.	Squirt oil around manifold; check vacuum increase when oil fills leak. Replace faulty gasket.
Drifts at idle; stabilizes at higher engine rpm.	Burnt valve; combustion chamber leak.	Make compression tests.
Wavers irregularly in one range despite engine speed.	Unbalanced carburetion; improper spark plug gap, ignition timing; poor valve seating.	Adjust carburetors; check plug gap; check distributor and advance spark; make compression tests.
Vacuum averages lower than normal at idle, needle fluctuates almost 3" on both sides of normal.	Worn valve guides admitting air—upsetting carburetion.	Squirt oil on guide seals. Check vacuum improvement.

way. It may or may not result in extensive engine damage. At the first sign of an engine exhaust or coolant leak, locate and correct the trouble.

An engine cylinder exhaust leak, except in the case of severe piston and ring damage (where the exhaust leak is into the crankcase) is usually at the cylinder head gasket. This leak may be an external one, and it is generally audible and fairly easy to locate with an oil can or by listening. The more difficult ones are those which connect adjacent cylinders, or those which leak exhaust gases into the cooling system, and coolant into the cylinders.

When a cylinder head gasket is open between adjacent cylinders, there are symptoms of crossfiring and loss of power with poor idle and bad low speed engine performance. There is also a possibility of backfiring at the carburetor. Do not operate a car, while in this condition, without the carburetor air cleaner. The air cleaner is a pretty good flame-trap in preventing fire. Proof of this type cylinder head leak is indicated by identical low compression readings in adjacent cylinders.

When the cylinder head gasket is open from the cylinder compression chamber to the cooling system, one or more symptoms may be present. There may or may not (depending upon the extent of leak) be an engine miss due to a wet spark plug tip. There may be indication of water in the oil pan. This should cause droplets of condensation to form on the oil dipstick and the underside of the oil fill tube cap. This sort of leak can cause extensive engine damage, especially to connecting rods and pistons. There is also the threat of antifreeze damage to other internal engine parts.

If the leak is very small, (a temporary condition) there may be a tendency of the coolant to show foam or bubbles in the expansion tank of the radiator. This is usually the first indication of leak between the combustion area and the cooling system and should be corrected immediately.

The most acute stage of head gasket coolant leak is hydraulic lock. This is an advanced condition brought on by coolant leaking into the cylinder while the engine is stopped (usually overnight). Due to the incompressibility of water, the piston is locked in the cylinder on its compression stroke. Result, a bent rod or worse.

To identify cylinder head leak and isolate it requires some simple deduction.

First, identify the leak as an exhaust leak (external or between cylinders). If it is this type leak, the compression gauge, plus some common sense, will localize it. Remove the head, plane or otherwise resurface it, and reinstall it with a new head gasket. Torque head to manufacturer's specifications.

Second, if the leak is into the cooling system, a cooling system (radiator) pressure gauge should reveal the trouble. This gauge, installed in place of the radiator pressure cap and pumped up to about 20 psi., should retain this pressure for about 5 minutes.

NOTE: leaving the gauge on for extended periods may be misleading, because the engine cools and pressures drop due to natural contraction.

An appreciable drop in cooling system pressure indicates a leak somewhere in the cooling system. A visual inspection of spark plugs is a good barometer of presence of water in a cylinder.

Remove the cylinder head, and depending upon the degree of leak and how long the leak has existed, do operations necessary to restore the engine to normal.

NOTE: if permanent antifreeze has circulated through the lubrication system of the engine for any length of time, damage to internal engine parts could be extensive.

While the following procedure is no panacea, it will remove the residue resulting from ethylene glycol leaking into the engine. Pour a solution of 60% engine oil and 40% butyl cellusolve in the crankcase. Run the engine at idle for ½ hour. Drain the oil pan, then, flush by running the engine at idle with a mixture of 60% engine oil and 40% kerosene. Drain and refill crankcase with appropriate viscosity engine oil.

5. A hydro-locked engine mistakenly diagnosed as a bad starter, or a weak battery, is likely to produce a bent connecting rod or worse. The cause of engine lock-up should be thoroughly investigated before further efforts to crank the engine are attempted.

6. Leaky cylinder block or heads is a rather rare condition, but one that does occur now and then. It may be due to porosity, a crack, or the result of overboring a cylinder. There is also the possibility of steel sleeve-to-cylinder head chafing of the head gasket on aluminum engines. This action is slow in developing, but may cause a leak at the head gasket. A combustion chamber containing very little, or no carbon, is a pretty good indication of water having been present in the cylinder.

7. Poorly seated valves may be the result of insufficient valve lash, weak or broken valve springs, loose or cracked valve seat inserts, sticking valves, worn valve stems or guides, and warped or burned valve heads. Excessively high oil pressure has occasionally prevented valves from seating in hydraulic tappet-equipped engines.

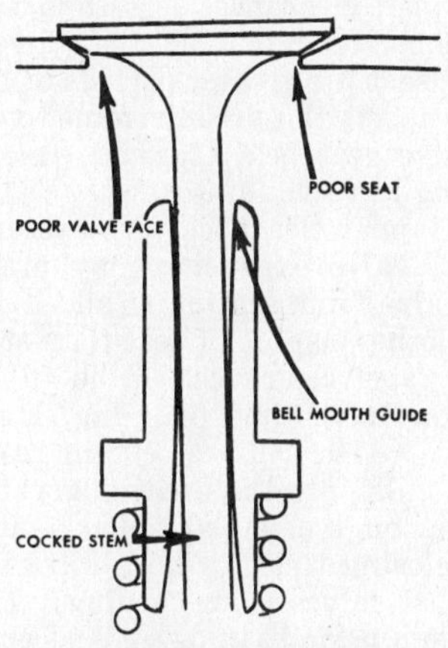

Valve stem and seat wear

Aside from noise, malfunctioning of any part of the valve train will influence intake manifold pressure, and engine performance. This is readily detectable through the use of a vacuum gauge.

A compression gauge test on the engine should isolate the troublesome cylinder, or cylinders.

Insufficient valve lash is a contributing factor in causing burned valves because it reduces the dwell time of the valve face contact with the valve seat. Heat transfer of the hot valve head to the comparatively cool valve seat is reduced, causing valve temperatures to mount beyond their heat tolerances. This results in valve head warping and burning. In addition, reduced valve lash changes the intended valve timing pattern of opening, closing, and duration. See section on vacuum gauge for correct method of valve lash adjustment.

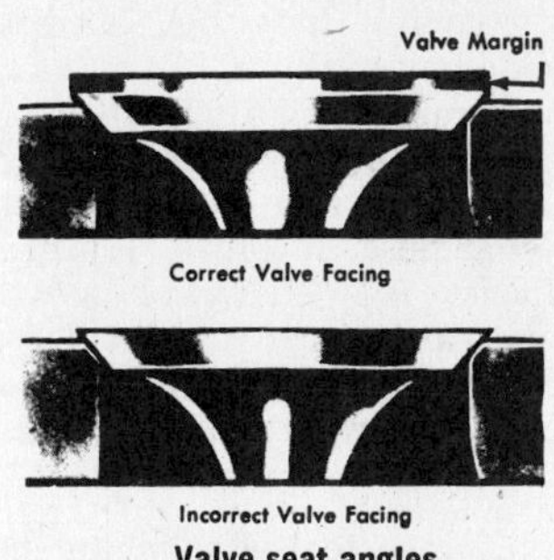

Valve seat angles

Weak or broken valve springs may, or may not, cause noise. The condition and degree of valve spring failure controls the amount of influence this situation has on engine performance. To detect some cases of weak or broken springs, a visual inspection of the valve springs may be required.

Loose or cracked valve seat inserts act the same as poorly seated valves from any other cause. They can be detected with a vacuum gauge and located with a compression gauge; then identified by visual inspection.

A loose or damaged valve seat insert may be replaced by removing the old seat with a special valve seat insert remover or, by drilling two holes in the old insert (on opposite sides). Be very careful to use a drill of smaller diameter than the width of the seat insert, and not to drill all the way through the insert. Split the seat into two halves with a sharp chisel. Loose seats, in many cases, may be lifted out without drilling or chiseling.

After the old seat has been removed, thoroughly clean the seat counterbore of head or block (depending upon engine design). The new insert should measure from .002 to .004 in. larger O.D. than the I.D. of the counterbore, both measurements taken at room temperature. It may be necessary to enlarge the counterbore to accommodate an oversize valve seat insert. Special equipment is necessary for this operation.

When satisfied that the counterbore is clean and the correct size for the replacement insert, (.002 to .004 in. less than the O.D. of the insert) pack the insert in dry ice. Permit insert to remain in dry ice for 10 minutes. It will now drive into the counterbore with an adequate flat-surfaced driver.

These inserts are exceptionally hard and require a high speed reseating grinder to obtain a satisfactory contact angle for the valve face.

Sticking valves manifest themselves by clicking (valve tap), engine miss, or both. Valve stem-to-guide clearance has been reduced by build-up of varnish and hard carbon to the extent of preventing the valve spring from returning the valve to its seat. As varnish and carbon (both good insulators) start to form on the valve stem and in the guide, heat transfer is reduced and valve operating temperatures rise. As temperatures go up, valve seats burn and temperatures rise even higher. This is a vicious cycle, repairable only by grinding valves and cleaning carbon, and replacing necessary parts.

Advanced engine design, better temperature control, and improved lubricating oils have greatly reduced the sticking valve problem. However close observance to manufacturers' valve specifications, plus careful workmanship and the renewal of valve stem seats, should prevent any recurrence of the sticking valve problem.

Worn valve stems or guides, are very closely related to sticking valves and require the same corrective measures.

Worn stems or guides permit misalignment of the valve face with its seat. This, in addition to affecting compression, permits hot exhaust gases and carbon to reach and insulate the bearing surfaces of the valve stem from the guide. The transfer of heat from valve head-to-stem-to-guide is the most vital area of valve cooling in the system. Poor heat transfer results in a ruined exhaust valve.

In the case of worn intake valve stems, or guides, loosely fitting valve guides permit poor seat alignment, plus the passage of excess oil into the combustion chambers. This condition contributes to oil consumption, carbon and varnish formation and early oil control ring failure due to gum and carbon. If valve stem-to-guide clearance is greater than specifications, renew the guides; the valves too, if the stems are worn.

Cylinder heads with guides cast integrally with the head, can be reamed to accommodate valves with oversize stems. In either case, fit to factory recommendations.

Warped or burned valve heads require replacement, as do valves with stretched stems or separated heads.

In any event, the cause of such condition should be investigated and corrected to prevent repetition of the same failure.

Valve heads that have pulled off their stems, or stems which have stretched, are both good proof of excessive valve spring stiffness.

8. Seriously incorrect valve timing is unusual except in instances of careless installation of gears or chain at the time of replacement.

There is, however, a possibility of chain jumping when there is extreme wear in chain and sprockets. Very old engines of three point chain suspension are also subject to this fault if proper chain tension is neglected. There is also the possibility of timing drive belt jumping on the overhead cam engine, if the drive belt is out of adjustment.

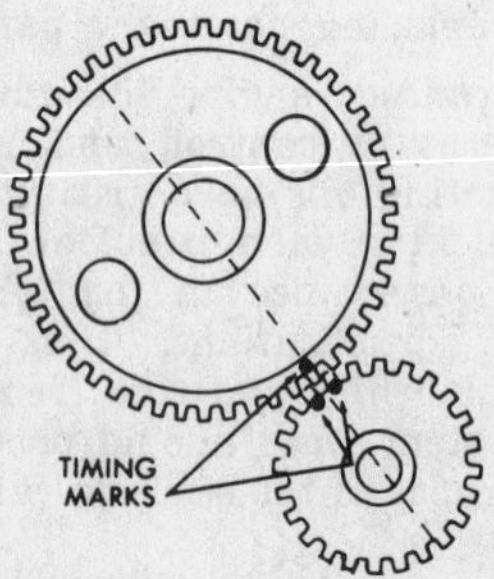

Timing mark alignment—gear

This ingenious design of belt drive for the camshaft and the distributor-fuel pump-oil pump assembly is three point suspended and critical to tension adjustment. An engine which is out of valve timing, to any great degree will not run. Any attempt to crank it may damage valves and/or pistons due to interference (overhead valve engines). An engine which is out of time by 180° will not only fail to start, but may catch fire if an attempt is made to start it.

A jumped chain, depending upon the number of links and sprocket teeth involved, will affect engine performance in varying degrees from sluggish response to complete failure and possible damage.

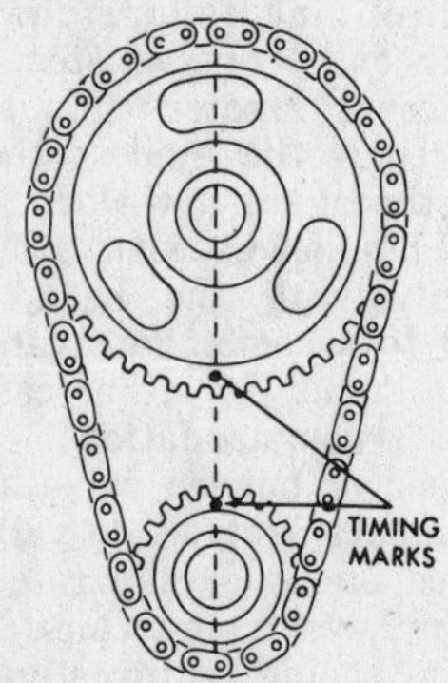

Timing mark alignment—chain

Because the distributor is usually driven by the camshaft, valve timing is relative to distributor timing. A camshaft or crankshaft out of time by only one tooth, or link, will influence distributor timing. In fact, a quick check for a jumped chain is to match spark timing with the crankshaft timing index. A compression check should reflect any change in valve timing by an overall low reading. A vacuum gauge reading will also show lows in inches of mercury.

Regardless of cause, (careless installation of chain or gears, or jumped and out of register valve timing) the timing case cover must be removed to re-establish correct timing.

NOTE: after establishing correct valve timing, take a compression reading to affirm, or rule out, the possibility of valve or other valve-to-piston interference damage.

9. A broken timing chair, or gears, provide obvious evidence. With few exceptions the distributor rotor will not rotate when cranking the engine.

A positive check for broken timing chain or gears involves removal of rocker covers and watching for valve train response to crankshaft rotation. No reaction indicates a broken drive chain, broken sprocket, broken gear, or a broken camshaft. In any case, it requires removal of the timing case cover for visual inspection. Replace necessary parts, then take a compression test to check the possibility of valve-to-piston interference damage.

10. A worn camshaft and a broken camshaft are worlds apart in symptoms. A worn camshaft presents a problem in diagnosis, depending upon the degree of wear. It produces varying results on a compression gauge and hard to recognize values on a vacuum gauge.

The simplest and most positive check is to measure intake and exhaust valve lift of all of the cylinders with a dial indicator. Then, compare these readings with each other, and with the specifications given in the Valve Specifications Charts of the truck involved. These charts are near the beginning of each truck coverage, in the Truck Section.

A worn camshaft can usually be attributed to one of two things, poor lubrication or excessively heavy valve springs. In either case, renew the camshaft, (and possibly the tappets) weigh valve springs, and, if necessary, replace them with springs of standard pressure and length. And finally, clean the oil supply area and use high quality oil of correct viscosity.

A broken camshaft will prevent the engine from running. It will react according to the location of fracture. It is most likely to break at or just behind the gear or sprocket. In this case it will produce symptoms of a broken chain or gears.

If the shaft is broken anywhere else along its length, the valve train servicing cylinders beyond the break will be dead. Valve action beyond the break will stop, while action ahead of the break will respond to crankshaft rotation (assuming there is no valve head-to-piston interference to prevent the crank from turning). At any rate, a new camshaft is in order.

NOTE: it is very likely that valve head or piston damage has resulted from engine out-of-time crankshaft rotation. Take a compression test of all of the cylinders.

11. Insufficient valve train lash, or not enough tappet clearance, is a very common and costly condition that goes undetected for long periods. It goes unnoticed because there are no accompanying noises as there are with excess tappet clearance.

The prime damage resulting from too little tappet clearance is valve burning.

Tappet clearances less than specifications, tend to hold the valve off of its seat for greater periods of time. This upsets the predetermined valve-to-valve seat heat transfer time, resulting in valve failure.

If tappet clearances are extremely small, valve expansion may prevent the valve from seating at all.

Another aspect of less-than-standard tappet clearances is the effect it has on valve time planning. Engine designers, to achieve certain results, have built into the breathing pattern of the engine, a particular opening and closing time for both intake and exhaust valves (valve timing). There is also a period (in degrees of crankshaft rotation) during which both intake and exhaust valves are open (valve overlap). This timing design is planned with specific tappet clearances in mind. Any deviation from established tappet clearances (valve lash) upsets the entire timing pattern and reduces engine performance.

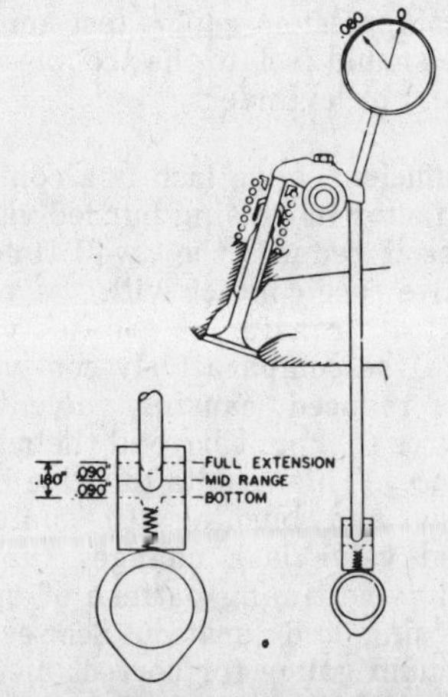

Measuring hydraulic tappet clearances

Adjust mechanical tappets to factory specifications according to hot or cold recommendations. If specifications call for a hot adjustment, run the engine long enough to stabilize engine temperatures. Also, if components of the valve train have been disturbed in any way, it is good practice to run the engine long enough to settle mechanical clearances to normal running fit before final adjustment. Adjust hydraulic tappet systems at that point of the valve train designed for this purpose.

Hydraulic tappet systems are designed to operate at zero lash. All valve train lash is taken up hydraulically by tappet design, and the valve functions with no clearance.

All hydraulic tappets have a built-in plunger travel-limit, through which extremes in valve train variables are compensated. An ideal adjustment of a tappet is, therefore, midway in its plunger dry travel limit. This allows (depending upon design) about .060-.080 in. above or below the center of plunger travel for automatic hydraulic positioning of the plunger. While these are typical tolerances, they are safe and illustrate the latitude of hydraulic plunger limits.

There are factory recommended procedures for adjusting hydraulic tappet clearances. See Valve System in each truck coverage, in the Truck Section.

However, the following is a typical and safe procedure to consider regardless of the provisions made for adjustment:

With No. 1 cylinder on compression stroke (piston on top and distributor rotor pointing to No. 1 distributor cap tower) apply pressure, through leverage, to the tappet plunger. On rocker arm equipped engines, this is accomplished by applying pressure to the pushrod or tappet end of the rocker. Apply pressure until all of the residual oil bleeds out of the tappet body. When empty, measure the extreme tappet plunger travel. Then, adjust the member of the valve train, provided for this purpose, to achieve a half-way position of plunger travel limit. Go through the same procedure on the other valve of the same cylinder. When adjustment of both valves is complete for No. 1 cylinder, proceed to the next cylinder in firing order, and repeat the operation just completed.

This method is more time consuming than some factory recommended practices, but it is a safe and typical procedure that works.

Vacuum Gauge

The vacuum gauge can be a very useful instrument in the hands of an experienced mechanic. It does, however, have its limitations. To know these limits and to use the vacuum gauge as intended is a vital part of engine diagnosis.

Due to atmospheric variables, engine design (even with engines of the same basic series) and many other factors, it is impractical to establish a fixed vacuum gauge reading for any make or model engine. Still, a vacuum reading, in inches of mercury (in. Hg.), is a very reliable index of performance value for comparison purposes.

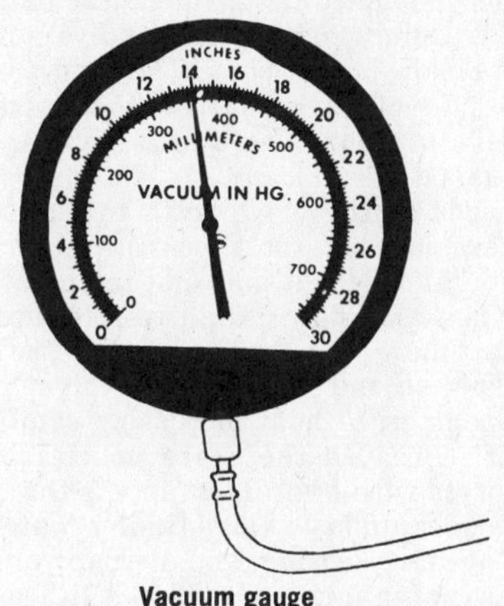

Vacuum gauge

Primary Engine Analysis

Most engines are equipped with some sort of plug or connection in the intake manifold. Remove the plug or fitting and replace it with a suitable vacuum gauge adapter. This connection must be at some point on the intake manifold, on the engine side of the carburetor throttle plate, (the underside of a downdraft carburetor). Connect a tachometer to the engine, and set the idle speed to specifications, in neutral. While running the engine, observe the following:

1. If the reading is low but steady, it indicates a condition that affects all the cylinders, such as late valve timing, late ignition timing, or an intake manifold leak. Any of the above conditions can result in a reduction of up to 2 in. Hg. A more severe condition, (cracked intake manifold, warped intake manifold or very bad carburetor to manifold gasket) can result in an intake manifold vacuum reading drop of up to 15 in. Hg.
2. If the reading fluctuates, with rhythm, (needle continues to waver with a regular pattern) it indicates trouble in one area. A spark plug may be fouled, a valve seat burned, a head gasket blown, a distributor cap cracked or tracking, or any number of things that would upset normal combustion in one cylinder.
3. A wavering and irregular gauge needle may be caused by any of the conditions listed in the above paragraph, but with the conditions existing in more than one cylinder. Other items that may cause an irregular gauge needle are poorly adjusted carburetor, high carburetor float level, wear in distributor shaft or bushing, faulty distributor advance control mechanism, excessively advanced or retarded spark timing, dual ignition points unsynchronized, wide spark plug gaps or poorly seated intake valves.
4. If the pointer wavers with irregularity, and the range of the pointer becomes greater with an increase in engine speed, the symptoms would indicate weak or broken valve springs. If the range of the pointer decreases, but wavers more rapidly with increased engine speed, the difficulty probably lies in an intake manifold leak. If the pointer becomes more stable with an increase in engine speed, indication would be toward trouble in the carburetor or ignition.
5. Normal response to sudden throttle opening and closing is a wide sweep of the gauge needle. If this does not occur, there must be leakage in the intake system. If failure of manifold gaskets or valve seats has been explored, poorly sealing piston rings are a possibility.
6. If the distributor timing is advanced to record the highest steady vacuum gauge reading, then retarded to reduce the gauge reading ½ in. Hg., and if the gauge reading is holding steady within the normal range for this engine, read the spark setting with a timing light. Ignition timing should index to specifications, plus or minus 2°.

Specific Conditions

Low Vacuum Gauge Reading

If the gauge needle registers a low reading, a correction may be effected by an ignition timing adjustment. In the event that this does not correct the situation, explore the possibilities of a leak in the intake system by the following procedure:

1. Remove the carburetor air cleaner.
2. Disconnect the primary lead from the ignition switch side of the ignition coil and, if using an auxiliary starter switch, have the ignition switch in the on position before bumping the starter. On some cars, failure to observe this precaution can cause damage to the grounding circuit in the ignition switch.
3. Crank the engine for about ten revolutions, while the hand is held tightly over the carburetor air horn. A vacuum gauge reading during the cranking period should register 13 in. Hg. or better. Individual engine design characteristics prevent the establishment of exact values for this test. If the reading is low, the next step should narrow down the source of the leak.
4. Remove the carburetor and very thoroughly seal off the carburetor opening in the intake manifold. Repeat the same cranking procedure as in the previous step and watch the gauge reading. If the reading is higher than in the previous test, the leak is in the carburetor, or at the carburetor to manifold mounting-flange. Some of the carburetor vacuum leaks could be in the distributor vacuum control line, the throttle shaft, a cracked or broken carburetor body or mounting flange, or a bad mounting gasket.
5. Another means of detecting vacuum leaks is by squirting oil at the suspected point and watching the vacuum gauge needle. The gauge needle should rise when oil is applied to the spot.
6. Exhaust restrictions (back pressure) can also cause a low vacuum gauge reading. The engine must breathe freely through both intake and exhaust systems to produce maximum power. Restriction anywhere in the exhaust system (tailpipe, muffler, resonator, exhaust pipe, exhaust manifold, manifold heat control valve or in the exhaust valve ports) can cause back pressure, especially at high engine speed. This will show as lower than normal vacuum gauge reading, at sustained, higher, engine rpm.

Unsteady Gauge Reading

If the gauge needle wavers throughout a wide range, the trouble could be a blown head gasket between adjacent cylinders, ignition cross-fire, caused by poor plug wire insulation or induction firing of cylinders, or a cracked distributor cap. The trouble could be one or more weak or broken valve springs, spark plugs that are old or fouled from oil or a rich mixture or poorly gapped. Sticky valves, worn valve guides and poorly seating valves can also cause an unsteady needle. To isolate the trouble and make the diagnosis more conclusive it is suggested that precise and related gauges and instruments be used.

Vacuum Meter Route To Hydraulic Tappet Adjustment

The hydraulic valve lifter automatically adjusts to valve train clearances throughout the entire range of engine temperatures.

Unlike the solid tappet, hydraulic lifters compensate for valve lash and operate at zero lift clearance. This is accomplished by using engine oil held by a plunger and check valve within a hollow tappet body. The tappet body is directly responsive to camshaft lobe contour. The tappet plunger adjusts hydraulically to the clearance needs of the valve train to maintain zero lash at all times; through all operating conditions and temperature changes. There is a two-fold advantage here. The first is quiet operation. The second is greater valve port openings without increasing cam lobe lift. Because there are no clearance losses with hydraulic tappets through valve train lash, valve timing controls, (opening, closing, and overlap valves) are not influenced by tappet clearance, as with solid lifters.

Hydraulic tappets, however, all have one thing in common; they must be adjusted or their components selected to maintain certain mechanical limits. Zero tappet clearance is then adjusted hydraulically within the confines of these plunger travel extremes.

If valve train linkage is, in effect, too long, the tappet plunger will be forced against the bottom of its tappet body. This condition will prevent the engine valve from seating, causing engine miss, valve burning, extended valve overlap, and valve or piston damage.

The opposite of this condition, is pushrods or other valve train components which are, in effect, too short. This situation, if beyond the mechanical limits of tappet plunger travel, demands more automatic take-up than plunger travel allows, defeating the purpose of the system. This causes excessive valve train noise, poor engine performance due to late valve opening and early valve closing (diminishing overlap) and reduced engine breathing.

Because of tappet plunger travel limits, and the fact that the length of the tappet assembly is in a state of constant change, valve train components must be held within close dimensions, or some provision made for adjustment, so that an attitude of the plunger can be established somewhere near mid-way of its possible travel limits. This is a safety precaution to insure the greatest latitude of automatic lash adjustment. Some engine designs use selective length pushrods to establish this safety factor. These rods are of various lengths, graduated in increments of .060 in. Other designs control initial valve train length right in the tappet assembly by using selective tappet components. Still others have adjustments provided for in either the rocker arm, (pushrod end) or at the rocker arm pedestal mount. In both of the later designs, (adjustable types) primary adjustment specifications are supplied by the car manufacturer. Due to difference in thread sizes of the adjusting elements and rocker-to-valve lift ratios, it is impractical to generalize and assume a fixed number of adjusting screw or pedestal nut turns needed to locate a safe mid-way position for plunger travel within the tappet body.

In the event that specifications are not available for hydraulic valve tappet adjustments on any specific engine, the following vacuum meter method can be safely employed.

1. Hook up a vacuum gauge to the intake manifold in the usual way, so that it is in plain view while adjusting the valves.
2. Remove the rocker cover. On V8 engines, select the rocker cover on the most accessible bank of cylinders.
3. With a strip of aluminum foil, (heavy cardboard will do) fashion an oil splash deflector to protect the engine and everything in the immediate vicinity against oil drench.
4. With en ine running at normal operating temperature, reduce valve lash at the adjusting point, (in quarter turn stages) while watching the vacuum meter.
5. Continue with these quarter turn stages until the tappet plunger travel limit has been reached. The limit will have been reached when the hydraulic compensating factor of the tappet can no longer accommodate the adjustment. This will show on the vacuum meter as a cylinder miss.
6. From this point, turn the adjustment counterclockwise, in quarter turn increments, until the opposite extreme is reached in tappet plunger travel. This end of

travel limit is indicated by tappet noise that persists after 15 seconds of engine operation.

7. Carefully count the turns of adjustment needed to adjust from one plunger travel limit to the other. Halfway between these two limits is the ideal position of preliminary adjustment.
8. Conduct the same adjustment procedure on the other valve of the same cylinder.

NOTE: intake and exhaust valve adjustments may or may not be identical.

9. After establishing the amount of turns required to obtain a midway plunger position for one cylinder, proceed with the other engine cylinders. Use the vacuum meter to find the plunger bottom limit, then back off the adjustment the predetermined amount to obtain a half-way plunger travel position. This is a safe margin of travel to allow for hydraulic tappet action.

Battery, Cranking

Whenever electrical trouble develops it is wise to make a quick check of battery and cables to be sure that the source of current is adequate. This check will also shed some light on the engine cranking system.

1. Switch on the headlights.
2. With lights shining on a wall or other reflective surface, close the starter switch.

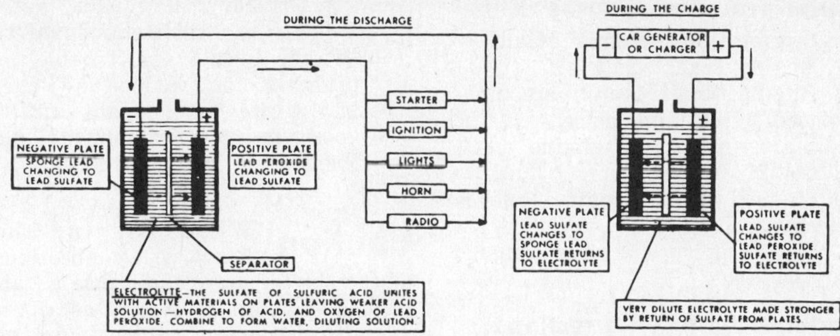

Schematic diagram of battery electro-chemical action

3. When the starter switch is closed, one of three things will normally happen: (A.) lights will remain bright and the engine will crank at normal speed; (B.) lights will dim considerably; or go out; (C.) lights will not be influenced, and no cranking will take place.

(A.) The first situation indicates a normal electrical condition of the battery, cables and connections, and the cranking system.

(B.) The second condition indicates a poor connection in the cranking circuit between battery and starter motor, or, the battery is only partially charged. Or, there is a condition in the starting motor, or in the engine itself which causes an excessive draw on battery current. A low battery will manifest itself in a clattering sound at the starter solenoid (when the solenoid is energized). Test battery with a hydrometer and give it a high rate discharge test to isolate the trouble. If battery is found to be OK, check the cranking motor.

(C.) The third condition indicates an open circuit somewhere in the cranking motor, starter switch, solenoid or wiring.

Cranking Troubles—Causes

Caution Trucks equipped with manual shift transmissions can be push-started. However, some automatic transmission-equipped trucks (due to no-rear-pump-design) cannot be push-started. In these cases a fully charged battery must be installed or jumper cables used for cranking current. Be very careful not to reverse polarity especially on systems using alternating current generators. Permanent damage may be done to the diodes of the alternator.

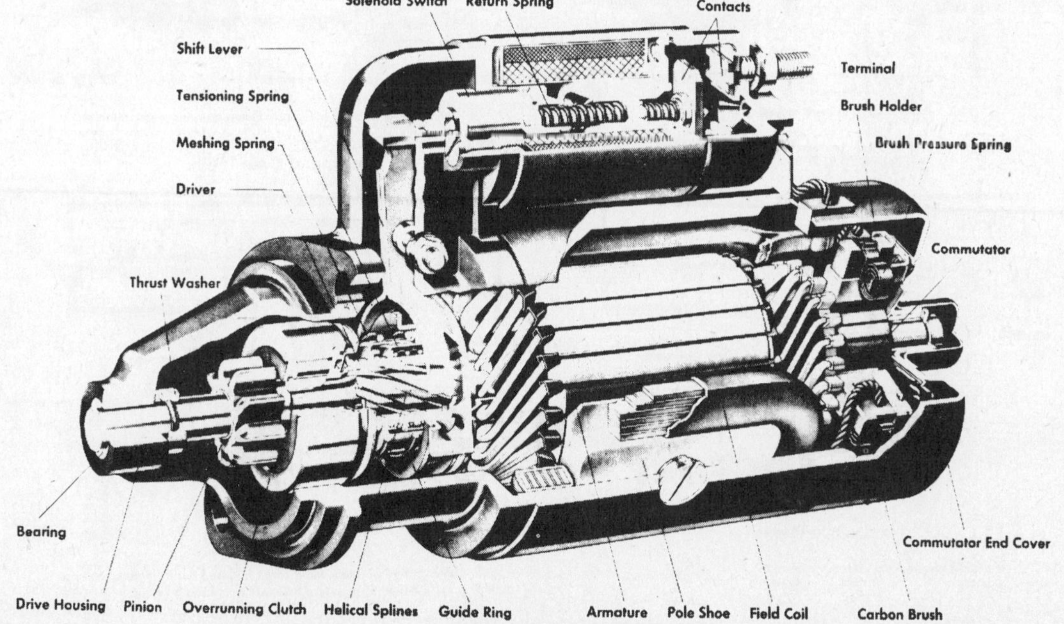

Typical starter motor

Starter Troubles—Causes

1. Starter won't respond at all.
2. Engine cranks slowly.
3. Engine won't crank, accompanied by clacking noise.
4. Starter turns but engine won't crank.
5. Starter cranks engine but is noisy.
6. Starter drive will not disengage flywheel.

Starter Troubles—Corrections

1. Starter won't respond, may be caused by any one or more of the items listed under Battery Troubles—Causes. In addition, there may be an open circuit in the cranking system. This can be in the ignition-starter switch, the starter solenoid, any of the cranking circuit wires, or in the starter motor proper. To correct the situation, turn on headlamps and close the starter switch. If lights dim or go off, check electrical supply and battery connections; charge battery, or tighten connections. If lights are not affected, the trouble may lie in an open circuit. It may just be a faulty, or maladjusted, automatic transmission starter safety switch. Locate the trouble by bridging the various switches and wiring components until a good circuit is established and the starter motor turns.

Caution When bridging the heavy wire connections at the starter or solenoid, use a battery cable, or its equivalent as a preventative measure against burning the hands.

By process of elimination, the trouble spot can be isolated and the component repaired or replaced.

2. Slow cranking may be the result of mechanical resistance of the engine (heavy oil, seized engine parts, low temperatures, bent parts, etc.). There is also a possibility of high friction or mechanical interference within the starter motor or drive unit. A third possibility is electrical resistance in the starter.

   If slow cranking is the result of mechanical resistance in the engine, check engine oil for viscosity. Drain heavy oil and refill crank case to level with oil appropriate to temperature conditions.

   If slow cranking is caused by seizing of engine parts, or bent parts causing unusual friction, undue engine resistance may be felt by removing all of the spark plugs which eliminates the effects of compression. Then, try to turn the crankshaft by the fan belt, or a socket and L-handle applied to the vibration damper attaching bolt, or, by prying on the starter driven gear (flywheel gear) teeth. If undue resistance is experienced in turning the crankshaft, explore engine for damage.

   If electrical resistance in the starter is to blame, the cause may be dirty or corroded connections in armature circuit, field coils damaged, bad brushes, or brush holders, damaged armature. Locate the trouble, repair or replace the unit.

3. If the engine won't crank and closing the starting circuit causes a clacking sound at the

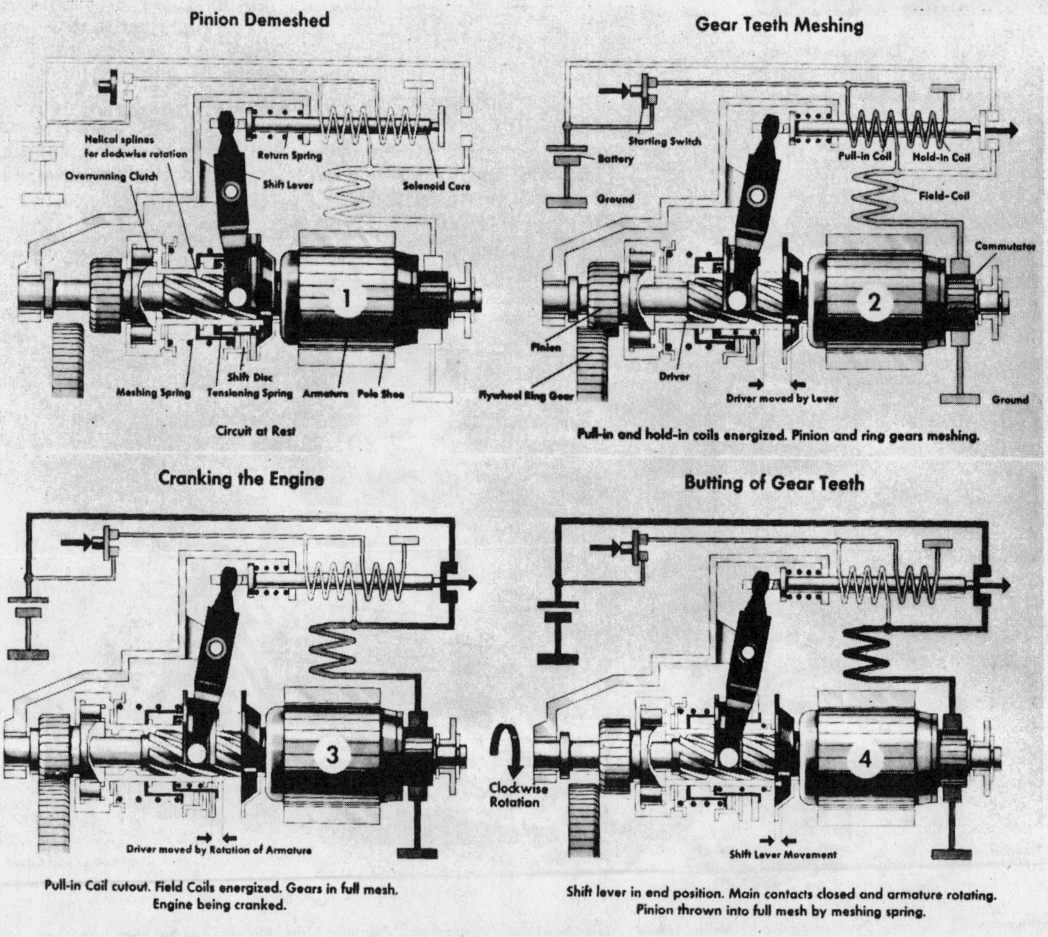
Pinion Demeshed
Helical splines for clockwise rotation
Overrunning Clutch
Return Spring
Shift Lever
Solenoid Core
Meshing Spring
Shift Disc
Tensioning Spring
Armature
Pole Shoe
1
Circuit at Rest
Gear Teeth Meshing
Starting Switch
Battery
Ground
Pull-in Coil
Hold-in Coil
Field-Coil
Commutator
Pinion
Driver
Flywheel Ring Gear
Driver moved by Lever
Ground
2
Pull-in and hold-in coils energized. Pinion and ring gears meshing.
Cranking the Engine
3
Driver moved by Rotation of Armature
Pull-in Coil cutout. Field Coils energized. Gears in full mesh. Engine being cranked.
Butting of Gear Teeth
Clockwise Rotation
4
Shift Lever Movement
Shift lever in end position. Main contacts closed and armature rotating. Pinion thrown into full mesh by meshing spring.

Typical starter motor operation

starter solenoid, the trouble probably lies in battery voltage being below that required to overcome starter solenoid switch spring tension.

4. If the starter turns but the engine won't crank, the trouble can lie in either of two areas.

   The engine is seized or locked, or the starter drive mechanism is damaged.

   In the first instance, check for a water locked cylinder (head gasket leak) damaged piston, connecting rod, or any other condition that could seize the engine.

   In the other instance, the starter drive mechanism is not working. The Bendix spring or bolt may be broken, pinion inertia shaft gummy or bent, drive housing broken, pinion broken, starter driven gear missing teeth, armature shaft broken.

   In the overrunning clutch type of drive, the overrunning clutch may be worn.

5. Where the starter cranks the engine, accompanied by noise, the engine itself may be damaged. In addition, there may be damage to the starter drive, or driven gear. This may even cause jamming between the starter drive and the driven gear of the engine. In case of jamming, remove the starter and make the necessary repairs to drive or driven gears.

   Misalignment of armature or pole pieces may cause interference and resulting noise. Remove starter and make necessary repairs.

6. If the starter drive gear will not disengage the driven gear, either the solenoid switch is energized, the solenoid switch is sticking closed, or there is mechanical interference with the releasing mechanism. Correct the trouble by making electrical checks of the ignition-starter switch and the solenoid. If this check does not reveal the trouble, remove the starter and correct the mechanical difficulty.

Ignition System

1. Select the most accessible spark plug and remove its distributor wire.
2. Hold this exposed distributor wire top ¼ in. from the spark plug terminal.

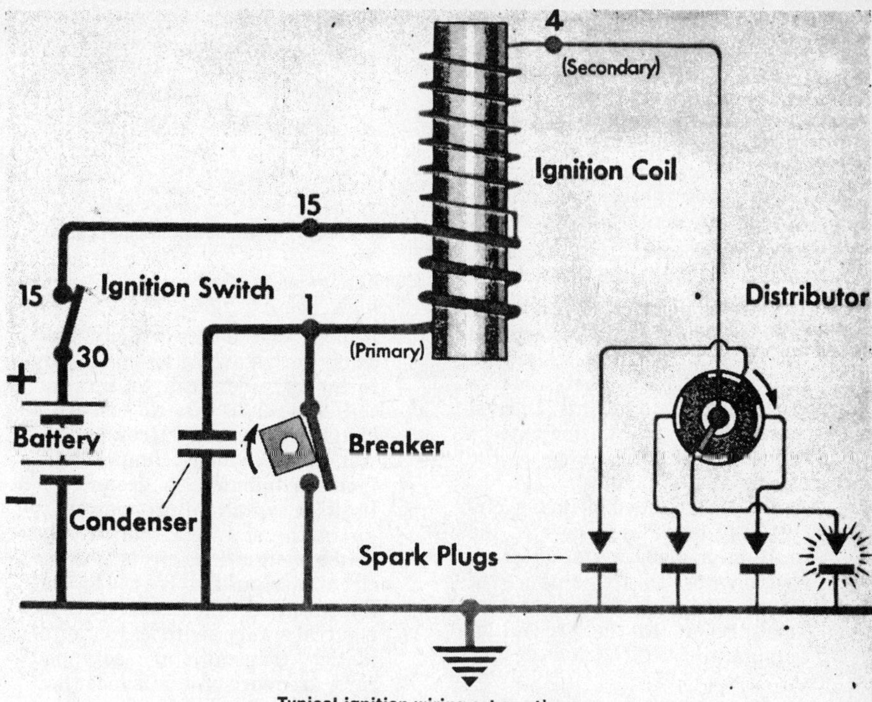

Typical ignition wiring schematic

3. Have someone crank the engine, (ignition switch on). A good, fat spark should bridge the ¼ in. gap, once every two revolutions of the crankshaft, (four-stroke-cycle engines, or once every revolution for two-stroke-cycle engines). If current is reaching this point, read Fuel System Troubles.

Ignition System Troubles —Causes

In general, hard starting and engine failure problems can be traced to some phase of the electrical system (battery, points, distributor, coil, etc.).

If the electrical supply and cranking systems have been checked out and approved or corrected, the following electrical causes for hard starting and engine failure should be checked.

1. Burned or damaged distributor points.
2. Points out of adjustment.
3. Defective condenser.
4. Shorted or open primary circuit.
5. Faulty ballast resistor (12 volt systems).
6. Ignition coil failure.
7. Poor distributor ground.
8. Ignition switch failure.
9. Neutral safety switch out of adjustment.
10. Bad kickdown switch on overdrive equipped cars.
11. Moisture on distributor cap (inside or out).
12. Cracked or carbon tracked distributor cap.
13. Failure of spark plugs.
14. Failure of plug or distributor wires.
15. Induction firing of cylinders.
16. Distributor rotor damage.
17. Incorrect distributor firing sequence.

Ignition System Troubles —Corrections

1. A visual inspection of the points will reveal their physical condition and give a fair indication of their electrical value in the primary circuit. Appearance of the points will also furnish a fair index to the condition of the condenser. Burned or otherwise damaged ignition points may cause hard starting and very poor engine performance. Do not file or otherwise recondition points. It is poor economy. Renew the set. If points show burning, renew the condenser also.

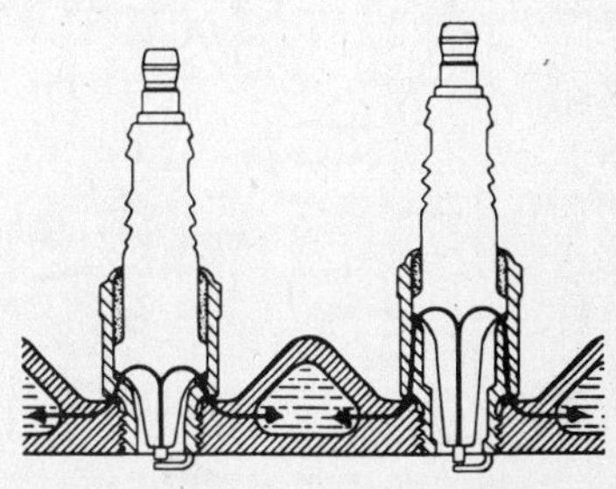

Heat travel in hot and cold spark plugs

NOTE: always reset ignition timing after replacing ignition points. Point gap, or dwell time, is directly related to ignition timing.

2. A visual inspection of point gap will indicate (within the scope of starting or normal engine performance) whether or not trouble lies in points out of adjustment. If necessary, adjust points, then set distributor timing.
3. The best indication of condenser failure (short of an electrical test with a condenser tester), is to examine the contact surfaces of the distributor points. Burned or cindered points indicate a faulty condenser. Renew the condenser and points.
4. A shorted or open primary circuit may occur anywhere in the ignition primary wiring or other components. In the absence of meters or other testing equipment, resort to the process of elimination.
5. A faulty ballast resistor will usually result in burned distributor points, or in some instances, where the resistor is by-passed by the starter switch, the engine will start and run only while the starter switch is engaged. Replace ballast resistor.
6. Ignition coil failure is possible, but improbable, due to quality control and product improvement. However, an open or a shorted coil is a possibility. Coil deterioration is usually a gradual process and occurs over a period of time. This dying process manifests itself by hard starting, cylinder miss under heavy load, and engine miss at high rpm.
7. A poor distributor ground may cause hard starting and poor performance, identical to ignition coil failure. In case of suspected distributor ground trouble, install a permanent jumper wire from distributor to ground.
8. Ignition switch failure may show up in the starter circuit or the primary ignition circuit. Some circuit designs involve the ballast resistor. See Unit Repair Section.
9. Neutral safety switches, on automatic transmission equipped cars, are more of a nuisance than a threat in hard starting or poor performance cases. If the starter motor fails to respond to normal starting procedures, (lights and other electrical units function normally) try all transmission selector positions. If the starter motor still fails to respond, use a jumper wire on the safety switch (transmission in park, or neutral position). If the jumper wire closes the starter circuit, renew the safety switch. If the jumper has no effect upon the starter, the trouble is elsewhere. If movement of the safety switch corrects the trouble, adjust the switch so that starting may be accomplished in park or neutral only.
10. The purpose of a kickdown switch on overdrive equipped cars is to interrupt the primary ignition circuit, momentarily cutting the engine and transmission torque long enough to permit a gear change. Due to the nature of this switch, the ignition primary circuit could remain open if the switch is defective. Make a circuit continuity check on this switch and, if necessary, replace.
11. Moisture is a detriment to the ignition system in many ways, especially when the parts involved are dirty.

    Under certain atmospheric and heat conditions, moisture will form on various surfaces of the ignition system. The coil, high tension wires, spark plug porcelains, and distributor cap are all parts subject to short circuits due to moisture, especially when dirty. An effective approach to correcting moisture troubles of the ignition system is to thoroughly clean all of the ignition circuit wires (primary and secondary), plus coil surfaces and the inside and outside surfaces of the distributor cap.
12. Carbon tracking and cracks inside the distributor cap may be a cause of hard starting. This condition is quite common to some materials, but it is aggravated by moisture. If cracks or tracking are present, renew the distributor cap.
13. Spark plug failure may be the result of many things, from breakage to plain fatigue. However, hard starting problems resulting from plug failure are usually caused by a short in the secondary circuit. This short may be the result of high resistance at the spark plug electrodes (plug gap too wide) or badly fouled plug tip. Or, it may be a cracked or dirt-shorted porcelain.

Spark Plug Torque

Thread size	*Cast-Iron Heads*	*Aluminum Heads*
10 mm.	14	11
14 mm.	30	27
18 mm.	34*	32
7/8 in.—18	37	35

* 17 ft. lbs. for tapered plugs using no gaskets.

A spark plug causing poor engine performance usually manifests itself by causing the cylinder to misfire under heavy engine load (open throttle at low speed). While an oscilloscope will quickly identify spark plug difficulties, a visual check of the plugs is generally enough to reveal any existing trouble. If at all in doubt, replace with a correctly gapped new plug of the proper heat range.

14. Spark plug and distributor wires, like other components of the secondary ignition circuit (coil, heavy coil wire, distributor cap, rotor, plug wires, and spark plugs) carry very high voltage. This high pressure (voltage) must be contained by good dielectric insulation (or adequate dry air space). This means that the wire insulation must not be cracked, contaminated or damaged.

    Especially subject to damage due to rough handling is the nonmetallic type of secondary voltage distributor and plug cables.

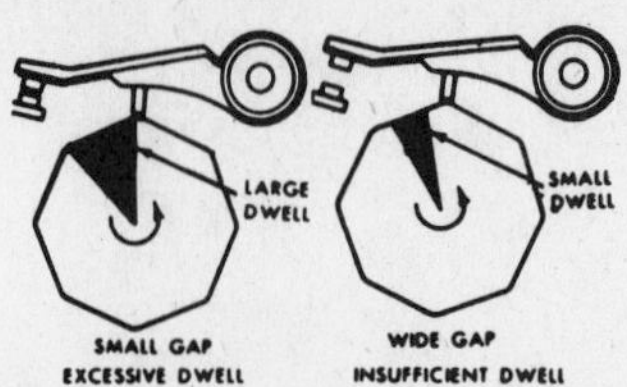

Dwell angle as a function of point gap

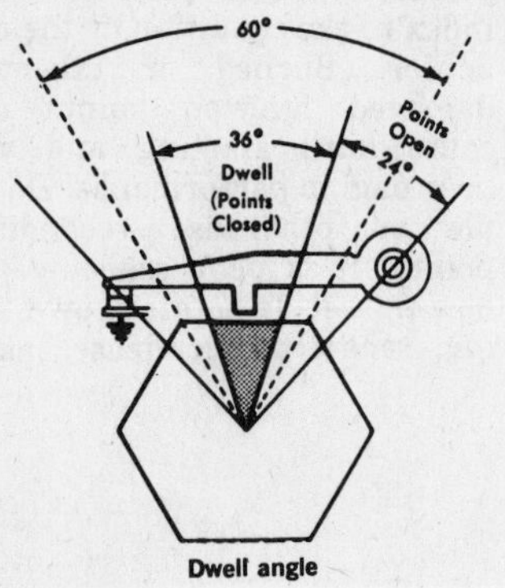

Dwell angle

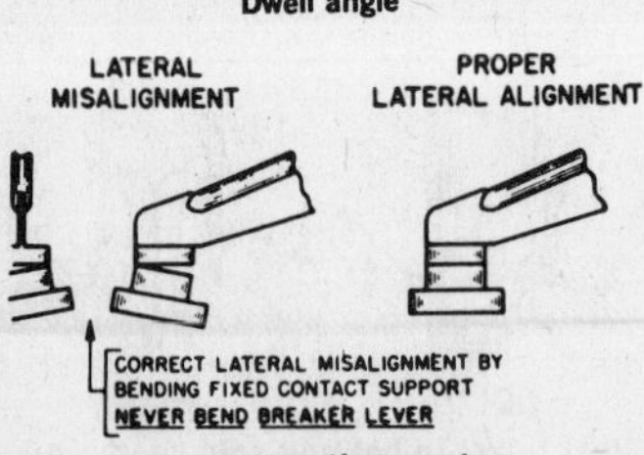

Point alignment

Primary Winding without Current
No Magnetic Field

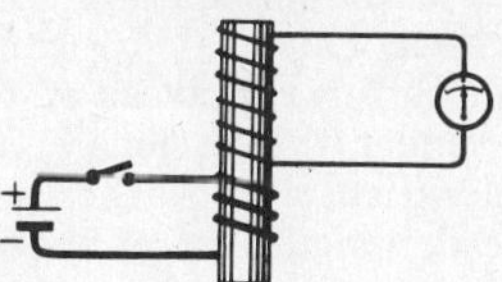

Cutting-in Process
Development of Magnetic Field

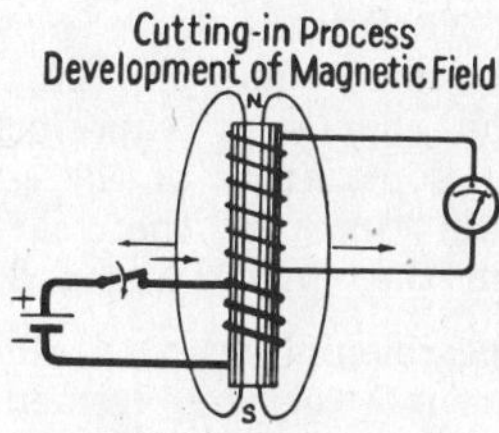

DC Current in Primary Winding
Constant Magnetic Field

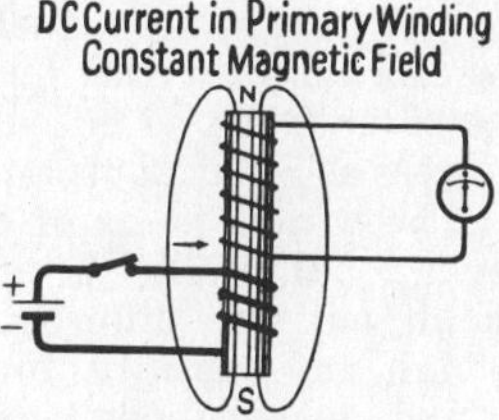

Interrupting Process
Collapse of Magnetic Field

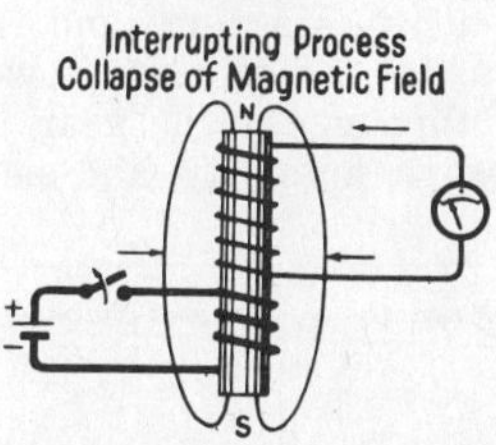

Ignition coil operation

Instead of a wire core, these cables have a core of carbon-impregnated string calibrated to a predetermined resistance.

Bending or other rough handling of this cable fractures the carbon core and increases resistance to the point of hard starting and engine miss.

15. Induction firing is a crossfiring of cylinders of consecutive firing order. Spark plugs are fired out of time by induced voltage. This condition may cause backfiring, engine roughness, detonation and possible engine damage.

Any time high voltage is being conducted by cable, a magnetic field is present around that cable. If another plug cable is sufficiently close, and parallel, to the first cable, enough induced voltage may be absorbed by the second to fire both cylinders at the same time. If the induction-fired plug is the next in firing order, timing is extremely overadvanced in that one cylinder.

To ensure against induction firing of consecutively firing cylinders, separate the two critical cables as much as possible. Cross the cables if you must, but don't run them parallel.

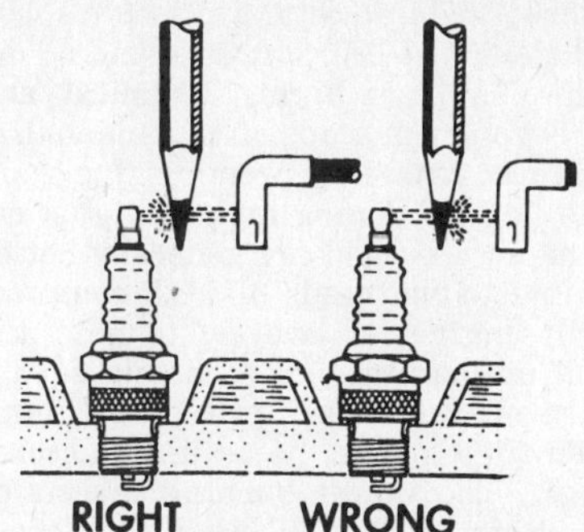

Coil polarity determined by watching spark. Spark jumps from wire to pencil to plug if correct.

16. Distributor rotor failure is a possibility. Any physical damage should be obvious upon inspection; the center, or collector brush, may be worn or broken; or the distributor rotor finger broken or burned to the extent of causing high secondary voltage resistance. Rotor fit on the distributor shaft should be snug and positive.

A quick check for a grounded rotor is to remove the center wire from the distributor cap and hold it about ¼ in. from the distributor rotor, while someone cranks the engine ignition on. If a spark occurs across this gap, the rotor is grounded. If at all in doubt about the rotor, replace it.

Cap

Rotor

Spring Clips

Vacuum Advance Unit

Distributor Housing

Typical distributor

17. Incorrect distributor firing sequence is probably caused by disturbance of the original cylinder timing. This is most likely to occur as the outcome of some maintenance operation involving the distributor cap or spark plugs. The effect could be, engine miss, backfiring (with a possibility of fire) and failure of the engine to run. While it is technically possible to time the ignition to any engine cylinder that happens to be at the top of its compression stroke, it is wise to stick to the original wiring plan. The spark plug cable length, predetermined cable resistance, distributor vacuum control line postion, etc., are all reasons why the original design should be followed. See Firing Order illustrations near the beginning of each truck in the Truck Section.

Fuel System

Fuel Value

Any material used to produce heat or power by combustion may be called fuel. However, for our purpose, and to satisfy the demands of the popular American made automobile, all fuels except those familiar to the general public will be excluded from this treatment. Diesel oil and the exotic fuels of competition do not apply here. They belong, and serve their purpose in an entirely different field. Commercial fuel is known to all of us as gasoline.

Automotive fuel is referred to as gasoline. However, weight for weight, air is about 15 times as necessary as gasoline in supplying a useful combustible mixture for the average American truck engine.

Gasoline, as we buy it, is especially compounded and blended to satisfy many requirements. The finished product is as carefully planned as the engine in which it is to be used. However, both engine and fuel must be somewhat of a compromise. There must be a flexibility of application in matching the fuel to the engine and to its work load.

Among the many fuel qualities essential to good performance and long engine life, and the one which is most optional, is the octane rating (speed of burning).

Speed of burning is controlled by many things, some of which are inherent in the crude from which the gasoline is made, some controlled by refining (cracking, mixing, etc.) and some, by the addition of varying quantities of antiknock compounds.

Tetraethyl lead, benzol, alcohol, etc. are some of the substances used to control speed of burning and establish octane values. The burning characteristics of the fuel must be compatible with engine design, torque requirements, and the compression ratio of the engine used.

Uncontrolled burning (detonation) can be defined as an explosion of the last parts of the burning mixture and is usually, but not always, audible as a ping or knock. Detonation is not always the result of a poor selection of fuels; other factors contribute. They may be combustion chamber deposits, cooling system inadequacies, lean fuel mixtures, ignition timing and controls, etc. Regardless of cause, detonation can produce extensive and permanent engine damage in short order. When most high compression engines are adjusted to factory specifications, and to develop their maximum power and fuel economy, they require a fuel of 90 to 100+ octane value. Also, if the chosen fuel satisfies a properly tuned engine, nothing can be gained by using a fuel of higher octane number.

The octane number of a fuel is established, with some variations in the laboratory, by using a reference fuel and a test engine. Usual test procedure has been to run a fuel of unknown antiknock value in a specific single-cylinder test engine, and to record the intensity of knock. Then, run a fuel in the same test engine, consisting of known amounts of iso-octane and normal heptane that will produce the same resistance to detonation as the fuel being tested. The percentage of iso-octane comprising the reference fuel now assumes a meaning. It represents an octane number; one that can be used to identify the burning characteristics of the fuel being tested.

For fuels with antiknock qualities above 100, the reference fuel used is 100% iso-octane, plus a known amount of antiknock additive. As an example: the antiknock value of a certain premium fuel, using tetraethyl lead as a knock deterrent, might be expressed as 100 + 1.5. This would indicate that the gasoline has the same antiknock characteristics as pure iso-octane to which 1.5 milliliters of tetraethyl lead had been added to each gallon of iso-octane. Above 100 octane, values also employ a formula by which the milliliters of antiknock additive are computed and transposed into octane numbers above 100, such as 105, 110, 115, and so on. This becomes highly technical and is beyond the scope of this manual.

To summarize: premium fuels are the slower burning fuels of higher octane number and are generally better suited to the needs of high compression engines. However, to gain the full mechanical and economic advantage of this higher priced fuel, ignition timing must be adjusted accordingly. The slower burning aspects of premium fuel will usually tolerate earlier ignition timing, other things being equal.

Vaporlock

A most difficult problem of fuel and the automobile fuel system is vaporlock. This has been greatly reduced as our knowledge of refining and fuel technology in general has increased.

The function of an ideal fuel system is that of delivering a continuous and uninterrupted supply of reliable fuel to the engine at the pressure required and in whatever quantity needed to satisfy the various engine and driver demands.

One aim in fuel system design is to avoid any route or trapping of the fuel that may contribute to the retention of heat. This could cause bubbles or vapor to form in areas of the fuel system under the various conditions of acceleration, hot weather and high altitude driving. Most of these problems have been solved by a combination of engine fuel induction design and by fuel technology, plus geographic and seasonal planning. However, the chance of vaporlock still exists in some areas of the country, at certain times of the year—generally in the spring and fall.

The petroleum industry, anticipating seasonal fuel requirements, attempts to satisfy these atmospheric needs by adjusting their fuel compounding formula to the humidity and heat of summer as encountered in such places as Saint Louis and New Orleans. The winter needs of Duluth or International Falls, Minnesota, call for an entirely different compound—high in volatility for easy starting and efficient burning during cold weather starting and engine warm-up. If the same fuel were to be used throughout the year for all the pressure, humidity, and elevation

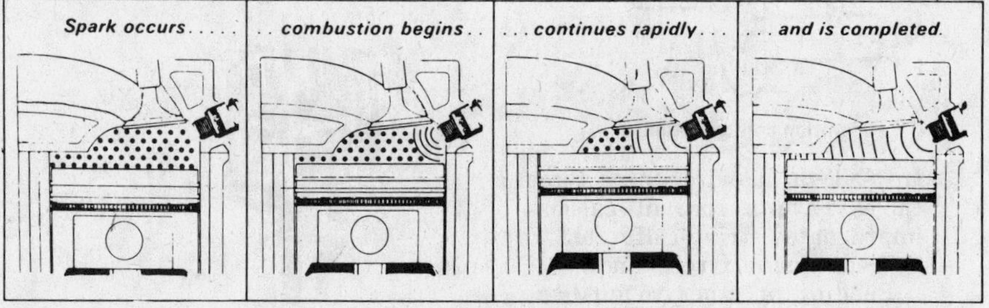

Normal combustion

Preignition

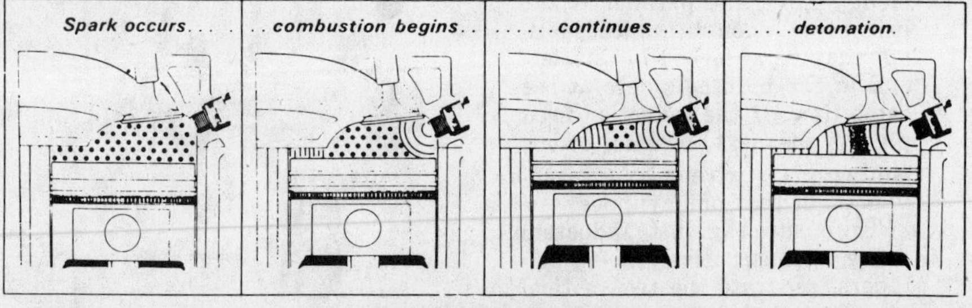

Detonation ("knock-ping")

differences in the United States, there would be constant combustion trouble.

Because of the pressure drop in the fuel line, on the suction side of the fuel pump, there is a tendency for fuel to boil or bubble under sub-normal boiling temperatures. Also, the volume of the fuel in the vapor state is over 1,000 times its volume in the liquid state. This aggravates the matter still more by reducing the weight of the fuel being delivered. When occupied by vapor instead of liquid fuel, the pump is in a state of vaporlock.

When this condition exists, the pump is incapable of delivering a continuous flow of fuel to the carburetor. This, of course, interrupts engine performance and in extreme cases stops the engine completely. The carburetor cannot successfully meter a mixture of vapor and fuel. Therefore, lean mixtures, rough operation, and engine stalling result.

Fuel System Troubles—Causes

If the electrical supply system, the cranking system, and the ignition systems have been eliminated as cause for hard starting or poor engine performance, fuel is the next area to explore.

Following are some of the difficulties encountered with the fuel system, including induction.

1. No fuel at the fuel tank standpipe.
2. No fuel discharging into the carburetor throat.
3. Flooding of fuel at the carburetor.
4. No fuel at the carburetor inlet.
5. No fuel at the fuel pump inlet.
6. Poor mixture due to induction leak.
7. Poor performance due to heat riser.
8. Poor performance due to vaporlock.
9. The carburetor choke.
10. Carburetor icing.

Fuel System Troubles —Corrections

1. The first thing to determine is whether or not there is fuel in the fuel tank. The gas gauge could be inoperative; there may be an obstruction in the gas line at the fuel pick-up, (standpipe) or at the fuel tank filter. There is a past history of obstruction and leakage failure of the flex-line that connects the gas tank line to the fuel pump. The gas tank bottom may be bent from striking a road obstruction, or the tank may be air locked due to the substitution of a radiator cap for the ventilated gas tank cap. On cars not equipped with gas tank vent tubes, an unvented tank cap may cause the tank to collapse and the engine to stop.

   A bent tank or a collapsed tank may influence the gas gauge reading and prevent normal standpipe functions, even with plenty of fuel still remaining in the tank. Aside from visual inspection, blow a reverse flow of air into the tank from the disconnected fuel line and listen at the open end of the fill-pipe for escaping air. No sound of escaping air indicates obstruction some place in the line or tank. Clear sound of escaping air indicates no fuel at the standpipe opening in the tank. A gurgling sound indicates the presence of fuel, (or other liquid) in the tank.

2. The next step, after being sure of a supply of fuel in the tank, is to check for fuel discharge into the intake manifold, at the carburetor throat.

   To do this, remove the carburetor air cleaner (downdraft carburetors) and while looking down the carburetor throat snap the throttle open once or twice. A spurt of fuel into the throat area will indicate the presence of fuel in the carburetor. No fuel at this point could suggest failure of the accelerator pump to discharge fuel. The more likely cause, however, is an empty carburetor bowl; failure of fuel to enter the carburetor. If fuel is present at the carburetor inlet, but not in the carburetor bowl, trouble probably lies in the inlet filter, the needle valve, or the float being poorly adjusted or binding. A more detailed examination at this point should isolate the trouble.

3. Flooding of fuel at the carburetor may be misleading and, likely as not, caused by poor ignition, bad timing or some other malfunction, aside from the fuel system.

   Carburetor-induced flooding is generally caused by a loaded float, a cracked carburetor body, a loose carburetor plug or jet, or a faulty needle valve or seat. In any event (aside from needle and seat trouble), carburetor work is required.

4. If, by disconnecting the feed line at the carburetor inlet, there is no fuel flow while cranking the engine, the fuel line filter is clogged, or the fuel pump is not working.

   To check the filter, disconnect the fuel line on the inlet side of the filter and look for fuel flow from the pump while cranking the engine.

   If fuel flows at this point, but not from the carburetor side of the filter, there must be an obstruction in the filter. Renew the filter. If there is still no discharge from the pump through this line, the pump is inoperative. Replace the pump, and, in the case of pumps operated by pushrods, renew the rods.

   NOTE: an increasing number of fuel pumps are sealed at manufacture and are not to be serviced. Check pump construction before attempting to rebuild the unit.

5. The only other reason for lack of fuel supply should lie in the fuel tank or lines which were covered at the beginning of this treatment under Fuel System —Troubles.

6. An induction system leak at the intake manifold may cause hard starting, poor performance, burned valves, detonation, and, in some engine designs, oil consumption.

   Unless supercharged, the intake manifold is subject to negative air pressure (vacuum); directly related to, and influenced, by design, atmospheric conditions, and attitude of operation. These variables prevent establishing any fixed set of values for vacuum meter readings covering all engines. However, all of the induction system, from carburetor throttle plate to intake valve ports, is subject to air leaks and the resulting fuel-to-air imbalance.

   Air leaks in the induction system are most common in the area of crankcase emission control valves, automatic transmission modulator valves, intake manifold gaskets, carburetor mounting flange gaskets, distributor vacuum control lines or diaphragm, double acting fuel pumps, vacuum operated windshield wipers, power brakes, or cracked intake manifolds.

   In the event of a crankcase emission control valve not seating, (a very common fault), a double acting fuel pump diaphragm leaking, or an intake manifold gasket leak, (352, 390 Ford, and some others), engine oil fumes may be inducted into the combustion chambers. This situation may result in engine oil consumption in addition to a vacuum leak.

The same is true in the case of an automatic transmission modulator valve that is leaking, except that instead of engine oil being inducted, transmission oil and air may enter the combustion area and be burned.

Hard starting or rough idling due to an induction system leak depends upon the degree of the leak. If the leak is bad enough, the engine will refuse to start due to a lean mixture. If the leak is small, engine idle will be affected to the extent of fuel-to-air ratio imbalance.

A pretty good barometer of an air leak is the carburetor idle mixture adjustment necessary to obtain a smooth running engine. An air leak anywhere in the induction system will require a reduction of air at the fuel-to-air mixture adjusting screw to produce good idle. If a smooth idle can only be had by closing, or nearly closing off the idle air adjustment, it is logical to assume that there is an air leak somewhere in the induction system.

If it has been established that there is an induction system leak, the next step is to locate it.

A rule-of-thumb process of elimination is to check out each possibility of leak, one at a time, while watching for a change in engine idle speed. When the source of trouble has been temporarily disconnected from the induction system (as an example: a bad power brake supply line) and the manifold connection capped, there should be a noticeable change in engine rpm.

If all of the potential troublemakers associated with the intake manifold check out OK, the leak is probably in the intake manifold itself, or at the intake manifold or carburetor flange gaskets. If the suspected leak is at an accessible spot, a squirt of oil in that area will be drawn into the induction system through the opening. This action will affect manifold pressure and fuel mixture, resulting in a change in engine idle speed. Subsequent applications of oil to the intake manifold and carburetor flange gasket areas should help locate the troubled spot if it does exist at these attaching points. The same method of squirt-and-observe may be used to explore suspicious looking cracks in the intake manifold. When the leak is located, repair or replace the troublesome unit.

7. Poor performance due to heat riser failure is rather remote except in the area of the heat control valve.

   The purpose of the heat riser is to assist in vaporizing the atomized fuel-air mixture from the carburetor.

   The heat riser is a portion of the exhaust system separate from, but immediately adjacent to, the intake manifold; it is generally a part of the exhaust manifold. This heat riser is equipped with a spring and counterweight loaded exhaust flow control valve. The purpose of this valve is to direct exhaust gases around the walls of the intake manifold to help vaporize fuel while the engine is below optimum combustion temperatures; then, as the engine warms up, to divert the excessive heat of exhaust gases away from the intake manifold.

   There is a remote possibility of exhaust gases being admitted into the intake manifold at this spot through a cracked housing or (in some cases) a bad gasket.

   The most common failure in the heat riser area is with the manifold heat control valve. The valve may remain open (counterweight in the down position) reducing exhaust influence on the induction gas temperatures. This situation would tend to reduce engine efficiency and build up crankcase dilution and sludge. Free the control valve and, if necessary, renew the control valve spring.

8. Vaporlock is a partial or complete stoppage of fuel flow caused by fuel vaporizing in the liquid fuel area of the system.

   Partial vaporlock affects performance by restricting the flow of liquid gas at, or to, the carburetor. This condition is first noticeable at idle speeds (rough idle and stalling). An engine operating with vaporlock may respond to acceleration with the same degree of hesitation as that resulting from a carburetor with a bad accelerator pump, or it may tend to ping due to lean mixture.

   Complete vaporlock will stop the engine and make it very difficult to restart until the engine and the fuel system have cooled sufficiently to reduce the vapor in the system.

   To correct vaporlock, be sure to use a premium fuel. Check the antipercolator passages in the carburetor. Check fuel pump pressure (low pump pressure will aggravate vaporlock). Be sure fuel lines are insulated from the exhaust system and that a generous amount of air flow is routed to cool the lines. An insulator block may be necessary between carburetor and intake manifold.

   Vaporlock may occur more frequently at high altitudes or in the event of a sudden warm spell in early spring, before the refineries have changed to summer type fuels.

   Percolation is another condition caused by boiling, this time in the carburetor. In this case, usually at idle or after a hard run. Due to expansion, liquid gasoline is dribbled from the carburetor jets into the intake manifold, causing a flooded engine. An engine which has stalled due to flooding will usually respond to about ten seconds of wide open throttle cranking.

9. The carburetor choke is designed to change the ratio of gasoline-to-air through the progression of heat changes in the engine. Its prime purpose is to aid in starting a cold engine by supplying a rich fuel mixture.

   The simple choke uses a flue-type plate, mounted slightly off-center in the carburetor throat, above the throttle plate. It is controlled manually by the operator. However, the automatic choke has been almost entirely accepted by the motoring public, because a properly functioning automatic choke does a better job of constantly adjusting the air-to-fuel ratio from one temperature extreme of the engine to the other.

   A sensing device is designed and calibrated to react, by expansion or contraction, to the slightest warmup temperature change, and to compensate for the change in choke setting. The same degree of surveillance and manual adjustment by using a hand operated choke is impossible. To check for hard starting due to malfunctioning of the choke, (manual or automatic) make sure that the choke plate is entirely closing off the carburetor throat when choke is applied (cold engine).

   To check closing of the automatic choke, remove the air cleaner, then open throttle once, all the way. The unloader tang in the automatic choke mechanism should now permit the choke plate to close. If it does not, linkage is binding or out of adjustment. Choke adjustment should very closely comply with manufacturers' specifications. Index marks (usually scribed on the choke thermostat housing) are for this purpose.

However, adjustment of the thermostat housing will usually satisfy minor requirements, but only renewal of the thermostat spring can entirely replace the calibration originally built into the part.

In the absence of marks or specifications, a rule-of-thumb automatic choke adjustment is:

First, make sure that the engine is cold and that choke plate and linkage are free.

Second, adjust the tension on the thermostat spring to just close the choke plate in the carburetor throat.

Third, rotate thermostat cover in the direction of choke closing, (rich) about 10°. On Chrysler and some General Motors products, using the well-type choke thermostat, loosen the mounting post locknut and adjust index marks to specifications, or bend choke connecting link to effect the same choke attitude as previously stated (about two scribe marks on the calibration plate).

10. Carburetor icing is a phenomenon familiar to temperate and frigid climates. It can, however, happen under certain atmospheric conditions, almost anywhere.

Air at 40°F may support almost 1/2 lb. of water per 1000 cu. ft. This is not much water, but it is enough to cause icing.

The moisture laden air enters the carburetor throat and becomes part of the atomized mixture. As the fuel and water laden air emerge from the carburetor venturi, gas expansion and consequent refrigeration (heat absorption from surrounding area) take place.

If the air is humid, is moderately low in temperature, and the fuel is high in volatility, ice may form on the throttle plate. As fuel evaporates, it adds to the cooling effect of expansion and the throttle plate temperature is quickly lowered to below freezing. Air-borne water particles are promptly frozen and accumulate on the throttle plate. Any formation of ice at this point will interfere with normal air flow and the mechanical movement of the throttle valve itself. This may cause stalling and erratic idle, with poor low speed performance.

Recently, the larger oil companies are treating their products with ice-retarding additives to prevent this condition. If confronted with carburetor icing, be sure that your fuel supply is winter blended for this purpose. Anhydrous compounds (under various trade names) are available from most gas stations for the absorption of water from fuel tanks. This additive should also help in a case of suspected icing.

To Increase the Freezing Protection of Anti-Freeze Solutions Already Installed

Cooling System Capacity Quarts	Number of Quarts of **ALCOHOL** Anti-Freeze Required to Increase Protection													
	From +20°F. to					From +10°F. to					From 0°F. to			
	0°	−10°	−20°	−30°	−40°	0°	−10°	−20°	−30°	−40°	−10°	−20°	−30°	−40°
10	2	2 3/4	3 1/2	4	4 1/2	1	2	2 1/3	3 1/4	3 3/4	1	1 3/4	2 1/2	3
12	2 1/2	3 1/4	4	4 3/4	5 1/4	1 1/4	2 1/4	3	3 3/4	4 1/2	1 1/4	2	2 3/4	3 1/2
14	3	4	4 3/4	5 1/2	6	1 1/2	2 1/2	3 1/2	4 1/2	5	1 1/4	2 1/2	3 1/4	4
16	3 1/4	4 1/2	5 1/2	6 1/4	7	1 3/4	3	4	5	5 3/4	1 1/2	2 3/4	3 3/4	4 3/4
18	3 3/4	5	6	7	7 3/4	2	3 1/4	4 1/2	5 3/4	6 1/2	1 3/4	3	4 1/4	5 1/4
20	4	5 1/2	6 3/4	7 3/4	8 3/4	2	3 1/4	5	6 1/4	7 1/4	1 3/4	3 1/2	4 3/4	5 3/4
22	4 1/2	6	7 1/2	8 1/2	9 1/2	2 1/4	4	5 1/2	6 3/4	8	2	3 3/4	5 1/4	6 1/2
24	5	6 3/4	8	9 1/4	10 1/2	2 1/2	4 1/2	6	7 1/2	8 3/4	2 1/4	4	5 1/2	7
26	5 1/4	7 1/4	8 3/4	10	11 1/4	2 3/4	4 3/4	6 1/2	8	9 1/2	2 1/2	4 1/2	6	7 1/2
28	5 3/4	7 3/4	9 1/2	11	12	3	5 1/4	7	8 3/4	10 1/4	2 1/2	4 3/4	6 1/2	8
30	6	8 1/4	10	11 3/4	13	3	5 1/2	7 1/2	9 1/4	10 3/4	2 3/4	5	7	8 3/4

Test radiator solution with proper tester. Determine from the table the number of quarts of solution to be drawn off from a full cooling system and replace with concentrated anti-freeze, to give the desired increased protection. For example, to increase protection of a 22-quart cooling system containing Alcohol anti-freeze, from +10°F. to −20°F. will require the replacement of 5 1/2 quarts of solution with concentrated anti-freeze.

Cooling System Capacity Quarts	Number of Quarts of **ETHYLENE GLYCOL** Anti-Freeze Required to Increase Protection													
	From +20°F. to					From +10°F. to					From 0°F. to			
	0°	−10°	−20°	−30°	−40°	0°	−10°	−20°	−30°	−40°	−10°	−20°	−30°	−40°
10	1 3/4	2 1/4	3	3 1/2	3 3/4	3/4	1 1/2	2 1/4	2 3/4	3 1/4	3/4	1 1/2	2	2 1/2
12	2	2 3/4	3 1/2	4	4 1/2	1	1 3/4	2 1/2	3 1/4	3 3/4	1	1 3/4	2 1/2	3 1/4
14	2 1/4	3 1/4	4	4 3/4	5 1/2	1 1/4	2	3	3 3/4	4 1/2	1	2	3	3 1/2
16	2 1/2	3 1/2	4 1/2	5 1/4	6	1 1/4	2 1/2	3 1/2	4 1/4	5 1/4	1 1/4	2 1/4	3 1/4	4
18	3	4	5	6	7	1 1/2	2 3/4	4	5	5 3/4	1 1/2	2 1/2	3 3/4	4 3/4
20	3 1/4	4 1/2	5 3/4	6 3/4	7 1/2	1 3/4	3	4 1/4	5 1/2	6 1/2	1 1/2	2 3/4	4 1/4	5 1/4
22	3 1/2	5	6 1/4	7 1/4	8 1/4	1 3/4	3 1/4	4 3/4	6	7 1/4	1 3/4	3 1/4	4 1/2	5 1/2
24	4	5 1/2	7	8	9	2	3 1/2	5	6 1/2	7 1/2	1 3/4	3 1/2	5	6
26	4 1/4	6	7 1/2	8 3/4	10	2	4	5 1/2	7	8 1/4	2	3 3/4	5 1/2	6 3/4
28	4 1/2	6 1/4	8	9 1/2	10 1/2	2 1/4	4 1/4	6	7 1/2	9	2	4	5 3/4	7 1/4
30	5	6 3/4	8 1/2	10	11 1/2	2 1/2	4 1/2	6 1/2	8	9 1/2	2 1/4	4 1/4	6 1/4	7 3/4

Test radiator solution with proper hydrometer. Determine from the table the number of quarts of solution to be drawn off from a full cooling system and replace with undiluted anti-freeze, to give the desired increased protection. For example, to increase protection of a 22-quart cooling system containing Ethylene Glycol (permanent type) anti-freeze, from +20°F. to −20°F. will require the replacement of 6 1/4 quarts of solution with undiluted anti-freeze.

ANTI-FREEZE INFORMATION

Freezing and Boiling Points of Solutions According to Percentage of Alcohol or Ethylene Glycol

Freezing Point of Solation	Alcohol Volume %	Alcohol Solution Boils at	Ethylene Glycol Volume %	Ethylene Glycol Solution Boils at
20°F.	12	196°F.	16	216°F.
10°F.	20	189°F.	25	218°F.
0°F.	27	184°F.	33	220°F.
−10°F.	32	181°F.	39	222°F.
−20°F.	38	178°F.	44	224°F.
−30°F.	42	176°F.	48	225°F.

Note: above boiling points are at sea level. For every 1,000 feet of altitude, boiling points are approximately 2°F. lower than those shown. For every pound of pressure exerted by the pressure cap, the boiling points are approximately 3°F. higher than those shown.

ANTI-FREEZE CHART

Temperatures Shown in Degrees Fahrenheit +32 is Freezing

Cooling System Capacity Quarts	Quarts of ALCOHOL Needed for Protection to Temperatures Shown Below												
	1	2	3	4	5	6	7	8	9	10	11	12	13
10	+23°	+11°	− 5°	−27°									
11	+25	+13	0	−18	−40°								
12		+15	+ 3	−12	−31								
13		+17	+ 7	− 7	−23								
14		+19	+ 9	− 3	−17	−34°							
15		+20	+11	+ 1	−12	−27							
16		+21	+13	+ 3	− 8	−21	−36°						
17		+22	+16	+ 6	− 4	−16	−29						
18		+23	+17	+ 8	− 1	−12	−25	−38°					
19		+24	+17	+ 9	+ 2	− 8	−21	−32					
20			+18	+11	+ 4	− 5	−16	−27	−39°				
21			+19	+12	+ 5	− 3	−12	−22	−34				
22			+20	+14	+ 7	0	− 9	−18	−29	−40°			
23			+21	+15	+ 8	+ 2	− 7	−15	−25	−36°			
24			+21	+16	+10	+ 4	− 4	−12	−21	−31			
25			+22	+17	+11	+ 6	− 2	− 9	−18	−27	−37°		
26			+22	+17	+12	+ 7	+ 1	− 7	−14	−23	−32		
27			+23	+18	+13	+ 8	+ 3	− 5	−12	−20	−28	−39°	
28			+23	+19	+14	+ 9	+ 4	− 3	− 9	−17	−25	−34	
29			+24	+19	+15	+10	+ 6	− 1	− 7	−15	−22	−30	−39°
30			+24	+20	+16	+11	+ 7	+ 1	− 5	−12	−19	−27	−35

+ Figures are above Zero, but below Freezing.

− Figures are below Zero. Also below Freezing.

Cooling System Capacity Quarts	Quarts of ETHYLENE GLYCOL Needed for Protection to Temperatures Shown Below													
	1	2	3	4	5	6	7	8	9	10	11	12	13	14
10	+24°	+16°	+ 4°	−12°	−34°	−62°								
11	+25	+18	+ 8	− 6	−23	−47								
12	+26	+19	+10	0	−15	−34	−57°							
13	+27	+21	+13	+ 3	− 9	−25	−45							
14			+15	+ 6	− 5	−18	−34							
15			+16	+ 8	0	−12	−26							
16			+17	+10	+ 2	− 8	−19	−34	−52°					
17			+18	+12	+ 5	− 4	−14	−27	−42					
18			+19	+14	+ 7	0	−10	−21	−34	−50°				
19			+20	+15	+ 9	+ 2	− 7	−16	−28	−42				
20				+16	+10	+ 4	− 3	−12	−22	−34	−48°			
21				+17	+12	+ 6	0	− 9	−17	−28	−41			
22				+18	+13	+ 8	+ 2	− 6	−14	−23	−34	−47°		
23				+19	+14	+ 9	+ 4	− 3	−10	−19	−29	−40		
24				+19	+15	+10	+ 5	0	− 8	−15	−23	−34	−46°	
25				+20	+16	+12	+ 7	+ 1	− 5	−12	−20	−29	−40	−50°
26				+17	+13	+ 8	+ 3	3	9	−16	−25	−34	−44	
27				+18	+14	+ 9	+ 5	− 1	− 7	−13	−21	−29	−39	
28				+18	+15	+10	+ 6	+ 1	− 5	−11	−18	−25	−34	
29				+19	+16	+12	+ 7	+ 2	− 3	− 8	−15	−22	−29	
30				+20	+17	+13	+ 8	+ 4	− 1	− 6	−12	−18	−25	

For capacities over 30 quarts divide true capacity by 3. Find quarts Anti-Freeze for the 1/3 and multiply by 3 for quarts to add.

TROUBLE DIAGNOSIS

Condition	*Possible Cause*	*Correction*
Insufficient brakes	1. Improper brake adjustment. 2. Worn lining. 3. Sticking brakes. 4. Brake valve pressure low. 5. Slack adjuster to diaphragm rod not adjusted properly. 6. Master cylinder low on brake fluid.	1. Adjust brakes. 2. Replace brake lining and adjust brakes. 3. Lubricate brake pivots and support platforms. 4. Inspect for leaks and obstructed brake lines. 5. Adjust slack adjuster. 6. Fill master cylinder and inspect for leaks.
Brakes apply slowly	1. Improper brake adjustment or lack of lubrication. 2. Low air pressure. 3. Brake valve delivery pressure low. 4. Excessive leakage with brakes applied. 5. Restriction in brake line or hose.	1. Adjust brakes and lubricate linkage. 2. Check belt tension and compressor for output. Adjust as necessary. 3. Check valve pressure and clean or replace as necessary. 4. Inspect all fittings and lines for leaks and repair as necessary. 5. Clean or replace brake line or hose.
Spongy pedal	1. Air in hydraulic system. 2. Swollen rubber parts due to contaminated brake fluid. 3. Improper brake shoe adjustment. 4. Brake fluid with low boiling point. 5. Brake drums ground excessively.	1. Fill and bleed hydraulic system. 2. Clean hydraulic system and recondition wheel cylinders and master cylinder. 3. Adjust brakes. 4. Flush hydraulic system and refill with proper brake fluid. 5. Replace brake drums.
Erratic brakes	1. Linings soaked with grease or brake fluid. 2. Primary and secondary shoes mounted in wrong position.	1. Correct the leak and replace brake lining. 2. Match the primary and secondary shoes and mount in proper position.
Chattering brakes	1. Improper adjustment of brake shoes. 2. Loose front wheel bearings. 3. Hard spots in brake drum. 4. Out-of-round brake drums. 5. Grease or brake fluid on lining.	1. Adjust brakes. 2. Clean, pack and adjust wheel bearings. 3. Grind or replace brake drums. 4. Grind or replace brake drums. 5. Correct leak and replace brake lining.
Squealing brakes	1. Incorrect lining. 2. Distorted brakedrum. 3. Bent brake support plate. 4. Bent brake shoes. 5. Foreign material embedded in brake lining. 6. Dust or dirt in brake drum. 7. Shoes dragging on support plate. 8. Loose support plate. 9. Loose anchor bolts. 10. Loose lining on brake shoes or improperly ground lining.	1. Install correct lining. 2. Grind or replace brake drum. 3. Replace brake support plate. 4. Replace brake shoes. 5. Replace brake shoes. 6. Use compressed air and blow out drums and support plate and shoes. 7. Sand support plate platforms and lubricate. 8. Tighten support plate attaching nuts. 9. Tighten anchor bolts. 10. Replace brake shoes and cam-grind lining.
Brakes fading	1. Improper brake adjustment. 2. Improper brake lining. 3. Improper type of brake fluid. 4. Brake drums ground excessively.	1. Adjust brakes correctly. 2. Replace brake lining. 3. Drain, flush and refill hydraulic system. 4. Replace brake drums.
Dragging brakes	1. Improper brake adjustment. 2. Distorted cylinder cups. 3. Brake shoe seized on anchor bolt. 4. Broken brake shoe return spring. 5. Loose anchor bolt. 6. Distorted brake shoe. 7. Loose wheel bearings. 8. Obstruction in brake line. 9. Swollen cups in wheel cylinder or master cylinder. 10. Master cylinder linkage improperly adjusted.	1. Correct adjust brakes. 2. Recondition or replace cylinder. 3. Clean and lubricate anchor bolt. 4. Replace brake shoe return spring. 5. Adjust and tighten anchor bolt. 6. Replace defective brake shoes. 7. Lubricate and adjust wheel bearings. 8. Clean or replace brake line. 9. Recondition wheel or master cylinder. 10. Correctly adjust master cylinder linkage.
Hard pedal	1. Incorrect brake lining. 2. Incorrect brake adjustment. 3. Frozen brake pedal linkage. 4. Restricted brake line or hose.	1. Install matched brake lining. 2. Adjust brakes and check fluid. 3. Free up and lubricate brake linkage. 4. Clean out or replace brake line hose.
Wheel locks	1. Loose or torn brake lining. 2. Incorrect wheel bearing adjustment. 3. Wheel cylinder cups sticking. 4. Saturated brake lining.	1. Replace brake lining. 2. Clean, pack and adjust wheel bearings. 3. Recondition or replace the wheel cylinder. 4. Reline both front or rears or all four brakes.

Brakes fade (high speed)	1. Improper brake adjustment. 2. Distorted or out of round brake drums. 3. Overheated brake drums. 4. Incorrect brake fluid (low boiling temperature). 5. Saturated brake lining.	1. Adjust brakes and check fluid. 2. Grind or replace the drums. 3. Inspect for dragging brakes. 4. Drain flush and refill and bleed the hydraulic brake system. 5. Reline brakes as necessary.

HYDRAULIC BRAKES

Servicing the hydraulic system is chiefly a matter of adjustments, replacement of worn or damaged parts and correcting the damage caused by grit, dirt or contaminated brake fluid. It is highly important to make sure the brake system is clean and tightly sealed when a brake job is completed and that only approved heavy duty brake fluid is used.

The approved heavy duty type brake fluid retains the correct consistency throughout the widest range of temperature variation, will not affect rubber cups, helps protect the metal parts of the brake system against failure and assures long trouble-free brake operation.

Never use brake fluid from a container that has been used for any other liquid. Mineral oil, alcohol, anti-freeze, or cleaning solvents, even in very small quantities, will contaminate brake fluid. Contaminated brake fluid will cause piston cups and the valve in the master cylinder to swell or deteriorate.

Brake adjustment is required after installation of new or relined brake shoes. Adjustment is also necessary whenever excessive travel of pedal is needed to start braking action.

Low Pedal

Normal brake lining wear reduces pedal reserve. Low pedal reserve may also be caused by the lack of brake fluid in the master cylinder. The wear condition may be compensated for by a minor brake adjustment. Check fluid level in master cylinder and add as required.

Fluid Loss

If the master cylinder requires constant addition of hydraulic fluid, fluid may be leaking past the piston cups in the master cylinder or brake cylinders, the hydraulic lines; hoses or connections may be loose or broken. Loose connections should be tightened, or other necessary repairs or parts replacement made and the hydraulic brake system bled.

Fluid Contamination

To determine if contamination exists in the brake fluid, as indicated by swollen, deteriorated rubber cups, the following tests can be made.

Place a small amount of the drained brake fluid into a small clear glass bottle. Separation of the fluid into distinct layers will indicate mineral oil content. Be safe and discard old brake fluid that has been bled from the system. Fluid drained from the bleeding operation may contain dirt particles or other contamination and should not be reused.

Brake Adjustment

Normally self adjusting brakes will not require manual adjustment but in the event of a brake reline it may be advisable to make the initial adjustment manually to speed up adjusting time.

Automatic Adjuster Check

Place vehicle on a hoist, with a helper in the driver's seat to apply brakes. Remove plug from rear adjustment slot in each brake support plate to observe adjuster star wheel. Then, to exclude possibility of maximum adjustment; that is, the adjuster refuses to operate because the closest possible adjustment has been reached; the star wheel should be backed off approximately 30 notches. It will be necessary to hold adjuster lever away from star wheel to allow backing off of the adjustment.

Spin the wheel and brake drum in reverse direction and apply brakes vigorously. This will provide the necessary inertia to cause the secondary brake shoe to leave the anchor. The wrap up effect will move the secondary shoe, and cable will pull the adjuster lever up. Upon release of brake pedal, the lever should snap downward, turning star wheel. Thus, a definite rotation of adjuster star wheel can be observed if automatic adjuster is working properly. If by the described procedure one or more automatic adjusters do not function properly, the respective drum must be removed for adjuster servicing.

Hydraulic Line Repair

Steel tubing is used in the hydraulic lines between the master cylinder and the front brake tube connector, and between the rear brake tube connector and the rear brake cylinders. Flexible hoses connect the brake tube to the front brake cylinders and to the rear brake tube connector.

When replacing hydraulic brake tubing, hoses, or connectors, tighten all connections securely. After replacement, bleed the brake system at the wheel cylinders and at the booster, if so equipped.

Brake Tube

If a section of the brake tube becomes damaged,the entire section should be replaced with tubing of the same type, size, shape, and length. *Copper tubing should not be used in the hydraulic system.* When bending brake tubing to fit the frame or rear-axle contours, be careful not to kink or crack the tube.

All breake tubing should be double flared to provide good leak-proof connections. Always clean the inside of a new brake tube with clean isopropyl alcohol.

Brake Hose

A flexible brake hose should be replaced if it shows signs of softening, cracking, or other damage.

When installing a new brake hose, position the hose to avoid contact with other truck parts.

Pressure Differential Switch

The hydraulic system safety switch is used to warn vehicle operator that one of the hydraulic systems has failed. A failure in one part of the brake system does not result in failure of the entire hydraulic brake system.

As pressure falls in one system the other system's normal pressure forces piston to inoperative side contacting switch terminal, causing a red warning light to come on in instrument panel, thus, warning operator of vehicle that one of the systems has failed and should be repaired.

The safety switch body is mounted in a vertical position, with the brake tubes connected to opposite sides.

The component parts of the switch body are not serviced. However, terminal unit can be removed if a malfunction occurs and a new terminal unit installed.

Centralizing the Pressure Differential Valve

1. Turn the ignition switch to the ACC or ON position. Loosen the pressure differential valve inlet tube nut of the system that remained operative, or the side op-

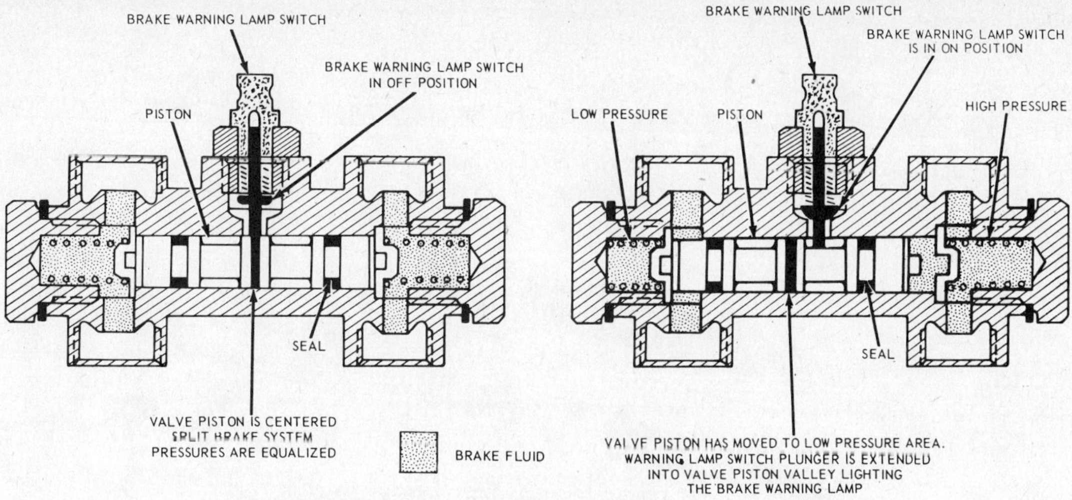

Differential valve system—with split hydraulic brakes (© Ford Motor Co.)

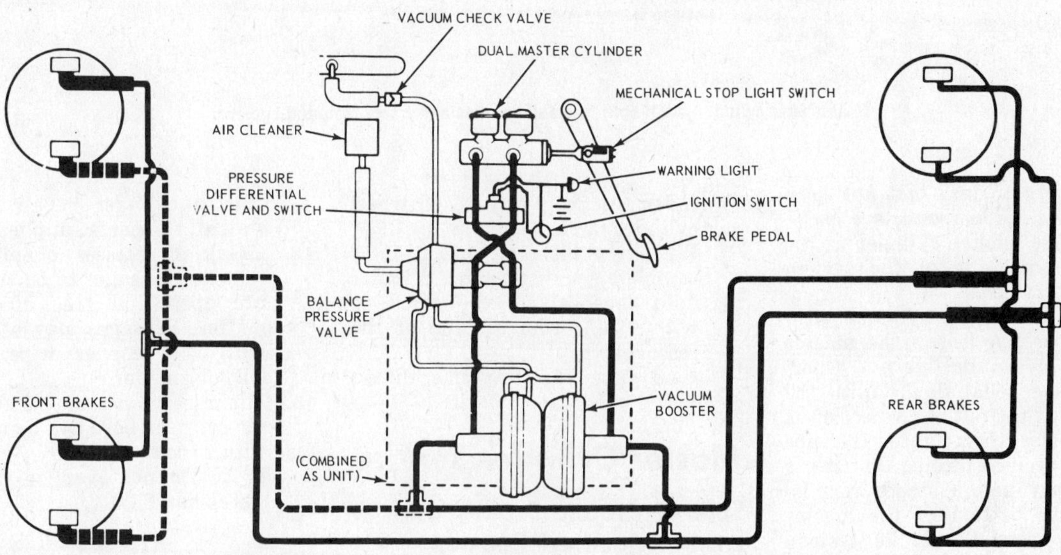

Split hydraulic brake system—with frame mounted booster (© Ford Motor Co.)

posite the system that was bled last. Operate the brake pedal carefully and gradually until the pressure differential valve is returned to a centralized position and the brake warning light goes out. Tighten the tube nut.

2. Check the fluid level in the master cylinder reservoirs and fill them to within 1/4" of the top with the specified brake fluid.
3. Turn the ignition switch to the OFF position.

With Split Hydraulic Brakes

The pressure differential valve used with the split hydraulic brake system has a self-centering spring. Use the following procedure to reset the valve:

1. Remove the switch connector wire.
2. Remove the threaded hex-shaped electrical switch body from the center of the valve. This allows the valve centering springs to re-position the valve.
3. Install the electrical switch and connect the wire.
4. Apply the brakes a few times and check the operation of the warning light. The light should go on with the ignition switch in the START position only.

Bleeding Brakes

Manual Bleeding

Conventional, Single-Hydraulic Master Cylinder

1. Attach a rubber drain tube to the bleeder screw of the brake wheel cylinder. The end of the tube should fit snugly around the bleeder screw.
2. Submerge the free end of the tube in a container partially filled with clean brake fluid. Loosen the bleeder screw.
3. Push the brake pedal down slowly by hand, allowing it to return slowly to the fully-released position. Repeat this operation until air bubbles cease to appear at the submerged end of the tube.
4. When the fluid is completely free of air bubbles, close the bleeder screw and remove the drain tube.
5. Repeat this procedure at each brake cylinder. Refill the master cylinder reservoir after each brake cylinder is bled and when the bleeding operation is completed.

Manual Bleeding

Dual Hydraulic Master Cylinder

The primary and secondary hydraulic brake systems are individual systems and are bled separately. Bleed the longest line first on the individual system being serviced. *During the complete bleeding operation, do not allow the reservoir to run dry.* Keep the master cylinder reservoirs filled with the specified brake fluid.

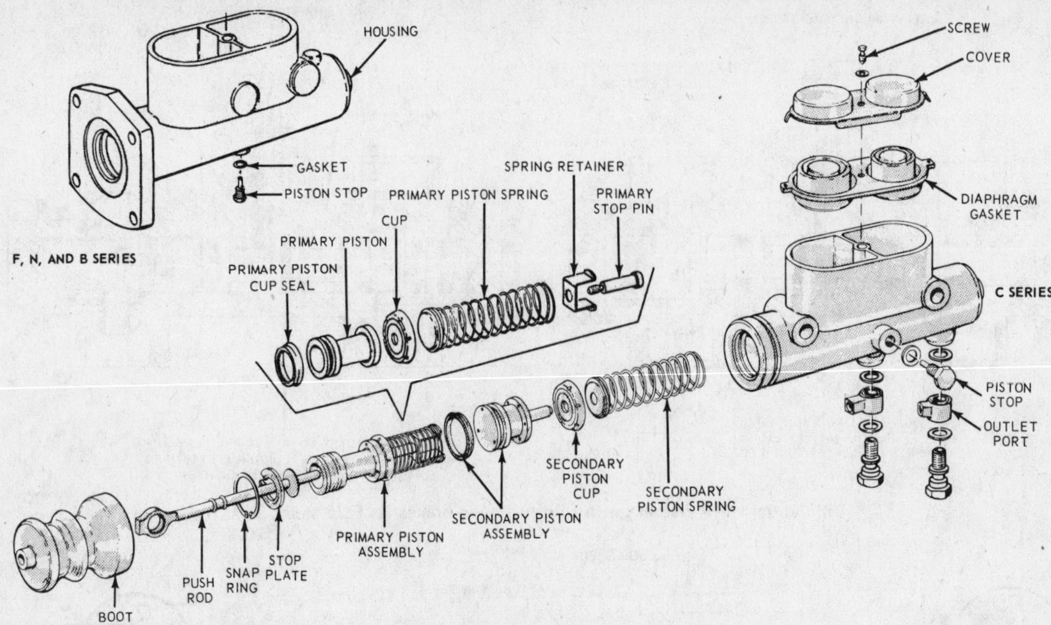

Dual master cylinder—with split hydraulic brakes and frame mounted booster
(© Ford Motor Co.)

Never use brake fluid that has been drained from the hydraulic system.

1. Bleed the master cylinder at the outlet port side of the system being serviced.

NOTE: On a master cylinder without bleed screws, loosen the master cylinder to hydraulic line nut. Operate the brake pedal slowly until the brake fluid at the outlet connection is free of bubbles, then tighten the tube nut to the specified torque. Do not use the secondary piston stop screw located on the bottom of the master cylinder to bleed the brake system. Loosening or removing this screw could result in damage to the secondary piston or stop screw.

1. Position a suitable 3/8" box wrench on the bleeder fitting on the brake wheel cylinder. Attach a rubber drain tube to the bleeder fitting. The end of the tube should fit snugly around the bleeder fitting.
3. Submerge the free end of the tube in a container partially filled with clean brake fluid, and loosen the bleeder fitting approximately 3/4 turn.
4. Push the brake pedal down slowly thru its full travel. Close the bleeder fitting, then return the pedal to the fully-released position. Repeat this operation until air bubbles cease to appear at the submerged end of the bleeder tube.
5. When the fluid is completely free of air bubbles, close the bleeder fitting and remove the bleeder tube.
6. Repeat this procedure at the brake wheel cylinder on the opposite side. Refill the master cylinder reservoir after each wheel cylinder is bled.
   When the bleeding operation is complete, the master cylinder fluid level should be filled to within 1/4" from the top of the reservoirs.
7. Centralize the pressure differential valve.

Master Cylinder Service

Split Hydraulic Brakes and Frame Mounted Booster

Disassembly

1. Clean the outside of the master cylinder. Remove the cylinder cover screw. Lift off the cover and the diaphragm gasket and pour off excess brake fluid. Use the push rod to stroke the cylinder forcing fluid from the cylinder through the outlet ports.
2. Loosen and remove the piston stop screw and gasket from the right hand side of the cylinder.
3. Pull back the push rod boot and remove the snap ring from the groove in the end of the cylinder bore.
4. Remove the push rod and stop plate from the master cylinder.
5. Remove the internal parts from the master cylinder. If the parts will not slide out apply air pressure at the secondary outlet port.

Inspection and Repair

1. Clean all parts in alcohol. Inspect the parts for chipping, excessive wear or damage. Replace them as required. When using a master cylinder repair kit, install all the parts supplied.
2. Check all recesses, openings and internal passages to be sure they are open and free of foreign matter. Passages may be probed with soft copper wire, 0.020" OD, or smaller.
3. Minor scratches or blemishes in the cylinder bore can be removed with crocus cloth or a clean up hone. Do not oversize the bore more than 0.007".

Assembly

1. Dip all parts except the master cylinder in clean hydraulic brake fluid of the specified type.
2. Install the rear rubber cup on the secondary piston with the cup lip facing the rear. All other cups face the front or closed end of the cylinder.
3. Assemble and install the secondary piston spring, front cup, and the secondary piston.
4. Install the piston stop screw and gasket, making sure the screw enters the cylinder behind the rear of the secondary piston.
5. Assemble and install the primary piston and push rod parts.
6. Locate the stop plate in the seat in the bore and engage the snap ring into the groove at the rear of the cylinder.
7. Install the push rod boot onto the push rod and the groove of the cylinder housing.
8. Bleed the master cylinder.

Bleeding the Master Cylinder

Before the master cylinder is installed on the vehicle, the unit should be bled.

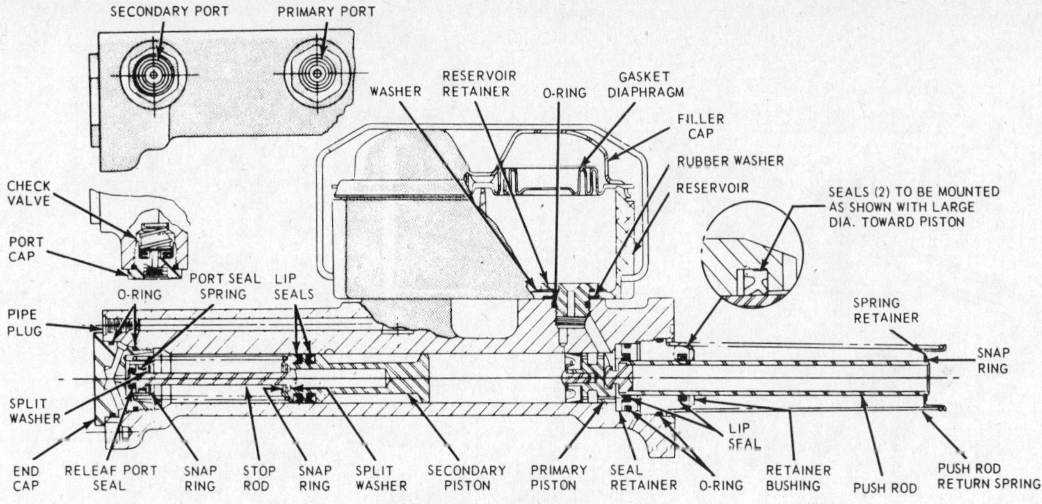

Dual master cylinder—with midland ross dash mounted booster (© Ford Motor Co.)

1. Support the master cylinder body in a vise, and fill both fluid reservoirs with the specified brake fluid.
2. Loosely intall plugs in the front and rear brake outlet bores. Depress the primary piston several times until air bubbles cease to appear in the brake fluid.
3. Tighten the plugs and attempt to depress the piston. The piston travel should be restricted after all air is expelled.
4. Remove the plugs. Install the cover and diaphragm gasket assembly, and make sure the cover screw is tightened securely.

Split Brake System and Dash Mounted Booster

Disassembly

1. Clean the outside of the cylinder and remove the filler cap and gasket (diaphragm). Pour out any brake fluid that may remain in the reservoir. Stroke the push rod three times to remove fluid from the dylinder bore.
2. Remove the reservoir retainers, washers, and reservoir from the master cylinder body.
3. Remove the two rubber washers from the reservoir and the two O-rings from the reservoir retainers.
4. Remove the snap ring, spring retainer and push rod spring.
5. Unscrew the retainer bushing counterclockwise and remove the push rod, retainer bushing, seal retainer and primary piston from the master cylinder.
6. Remove the primary piston from the push rod and discard it.
7. Remove the seal retainer, and retainer bushing from the push rod. Remove the two lip seals and the two Orings from the retainer bushing.
8. Unscrew the end cap counterclockwise and remove the end cap and secondary piston assembly from the master cylinder.
9. Remove the snap ring from the secondary piston and remove the piston and return spring from the end cap and stop rod assembly.
10. Remove the two lip seals from the piston.
11. Remove the snap ring from the end cap and remove the secondary piston stop rod, relief port seal spring, the two snap rings and the two split washers from the end cap.
12. Remove the relief port seal from the secondary piston stop rod.
13. Remove the O-rings from the end cap.
14. Remove the primary and secondary port caps and discard.
15. Remove the check valves and springs from the ports.
16. Remove the pipe plug from the end of the master cylinder.

Assembly

1. Wash all metal parts in alcohol before assembly. Dip all parts except the master cylinder body in clean hydraulic brake fluid of the specified type. When using a master cylinder repair kit, install all of the parts supplied.
2. Install the pipe plug in the end of the master cylinder.
3. Install a new primary piston into the front end of the master cylinder bore. Push the piston through the bore until it is flush with the retainer bushing recess. Use a non-metallic object which will not scratch the bore.
4. Assemble the O-rings and the two lip seals on the retainer bushing. Be sure the lip seals fit into the undercuts in the center of the bushing with their large diameters toward the piston end.
5. Install the retainer bushing onto the closed end of the push rod and push it onto the push rod approximately half way. Be sure the lip seal at the piston end of the retainer bushing remains in the undercut portion of the retainer bushing.
6. Install the seal retainer onto the closed end of the push rod with the raised lip toward the retainer bushing.
7. Insert the push rod into the master cylinder bore and hook the push rod onto the primary piston.
8. Slide the seal retainer into the recess in the master cylinder bore.
9. Screw the retainer bushing into the master cylinder body and tighten to 15-20 ft-lbs torque.
10. Install the push spring with the large end toward the master cylinder and install the spring retainer and snap ring.
11. Install the O-rings on the end cap.
12. Install the relief port seal on the secondary piston stop rod.
13. Place the port seal spring, split washer (largest of two), and snap ring (largest of two) on the piston stop rod.
14. Slide the assembly into the end cap and engage the snap ring into its groove.
15. Install the lip seals on the secondary piston with the large diameters facing outward.
16. Place the secondary piston return spring on the end cap assembly.

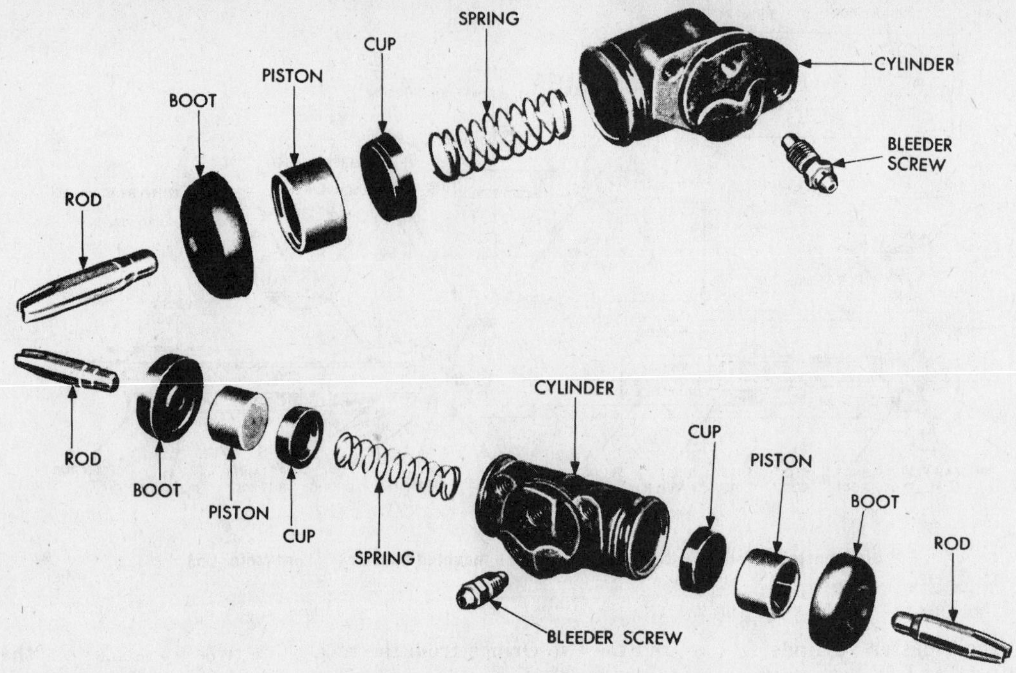

Wheel cylinder (typical) (© Chrysler Corp.)

17. Compress the spring and place the remaining snap ring and split washer on the piston stop rod.
18. Slide the piston stop rod into the secondary piston and engage the snap ring in its groove.
19. Slide the end cap and piston assembly into the master cylinder bore and screw the end cap into the master cylinder body. Tighten the cap to 15-20 ft-lbs torque.
20. Install washers on the reservoir retainer and place the retainers in the mounting holes of the reservoir.
21. Place the rubber washers and O-rings on the retainers.
22. Place the reservoir and retainer assembly on the master cylinder body and tighten the retainers to 15-20 ft-lbs torque.
23. Replace the springs and check valves in the output ports of the cylinder.
24. Replace the primary and secondary port caps. Tighten to 15-20 ft-lbs torque.
25. Install the mounting seal on the flange of the master cylinder. Install the filler cap and gasket (diaphragm).

Wheel Cylinders

1. In case of a leak, remove brake shoes (replace if soaked with grease or brake fluid), boots, piston wheel cylinder cups and wheel cylinder cup expansion spring. NOTE: A slight amount of fluid on boot may not be a leak, but may be preservative oil used on assembly.
2. Wash wheel cylinder bore with clean brake fluid and inspect for scoring or pitting.

Use extreme care in cleaning the wheel cylinder after reconditioning. Remove all dust or grit by flushing the cylinder with alcohol; wipe dry with a clean lintless cloth and clean a second time with alcohol. Dry the wheel cylinder with air pressure, then flush with clean brake fluid. (Be sure the bleeder screw port and the bleeder screw are clean and open.)

Wheel cylinder bores or pistons that are badly scored or coroded should be replaced. The old piston cups should be discarded when reconditioning wheel cylinders.

Cylinder walls that have light scratches, or show signs of corrosion, can usually be cleaned with crocus cloth, using a circular motion. However, cylinders that have deep scratches or scoring may be honed, providing the diameter of the cylinder bore is not increased more than .002". *A cylinder that does not clean up at .002" should be discarded and a new cylinder installed. (Black stains on the cylinder walls are caused by the piston cups and will do no harm.)*

Should inspection reveal the necessity of installing a new wheel cylinder proceed as follows:

1. Disconnect brake hose from brake tube at frame bracket (front wheels) or disconnect the brake tube from wheel cylinder (rear wheels).
2. Disconnect brake hose from wheel cylinder (front wheels only) and remove wheel cylinder attaching bolts, then slide wheel cylinder out of support.

Disassembly (Front or Rear)

1. Remove boots and push rods.
2. Press in on one end of cylinder and force out piston, cup, piston spring, cup and piston.

Assembly (Front or Rear)

Before assembling pistons and new cups in wheel cylinder, dip them in brake fluid. If boots are deteriorated, cracked or do not fit tightly on brake shoe push rod, as well as wheel cylinder casting, new boots should be installed.

1. Wash wheel cylinder with alcohol and blow dry with air.
2. Install expansion spring in cylinder. Install wheel cylinder cups in each end of cylinder with open end of cups facing each other.
3. Install wheel cylinder pistons in each end of cylinder with recessed end of pistons facing open ends of cylinder.
4. Install boots over ends of cylinder. Keep assembly compressed with aid of a brake cylinder clamp until brake shoes are assembled.

Brake Service

Non-Servo Type

This brake is a non-servo, floating

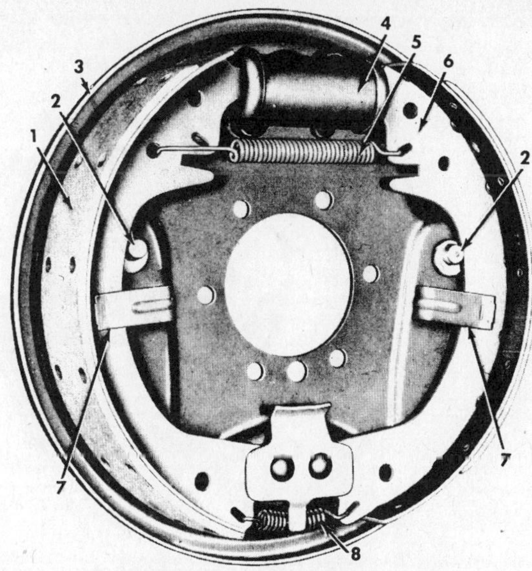

Non servo type brake installed (© G.M.C.)

1 Secondary shoe
2 Adjusting cam
3 Backing plate
4 Wheel cylinder
5 Shoe return spring
6 Primary shoe
7 Shoe hold-down spring
8 Shoe anchor spring

shoe type brake. Upper ends of shoes extend through wheel cylinder boots and contact inserts in wheel cylinder pistons. Shoe ends are held firmly against pistons by the brake shoe return spring. Lower ends of shoes are held against a fixed anchor plate by the anchor spring. Hold-down spring at center of each shoe holds shoes in alignment. Lining-to-drum clearance adjustment is made through eccentric cam type adjusting studs.

Brake Shoe Removal

1. Back off brake adjustment, then remove brake drum.
2. Remove brake shoe return spring. Spread upper end of shoes until they are clear of wheel cylinders and hold-down springs, then disengage shoes from anchor plate at bottom. Remove anchor spring from shoes.
3. Do not depress brake pedal while shoes are removed.

Cleaning and Inspection

1. Clean all dirt out of breake drum. Inspect drum for roughness, scoring, or out-of-round. Replace or recondition drum as necessary.
2. Carefully pull lower edge of each wheel cylinder boot away from cylinder and note whether interior is excessively wet with brake fluid. Excessive fluid indicates leakage past piston cups, requiring overhaul of wheel cylinder. NOTE: A slight amount of fluid is nearly always present and acts as a lubricant for pistons.
3. Check backing plate attaching bolts to make sure they are tight. Clean all rust and dirt from ledges on backing plate where shoe rims make contact using fine emery cloth.
4. Inspect the shoe return and anchor springs and hold-down springs. If broken, cracked, or weakened by rust or corrosion, replace springs.
5. If brake linings are worn to the extent that replacement is necessary, replace linings.

Brake Shoe Installation

1. Inspect brake shoe lining assemblies and make sure there are no nicks or burrs on edges of shoes which contact backing plate.
2. Apply a light film of grease at the following points: where shoe webs contact hold-down springs, where anchor ends of shoe webs contact anchor plate, and at six places where shoe rims contact ledges on backing plate.
3. Install hold-down springs on backing plate. Hook anchor spring into slot at bottom of each shoe. Swing upper ends of shoes apart and position at backing plate, with lower ends of shoe webs engaging anchor plate and with anchor spring behind extension on anchor plate. NOTE: The shoe with the shorter lining must be to the rear of the vehicle.
4. Swing shoes up into position with center of shoe webs engaging hold-down springs, and with upper ends inserted through wheel cylinder boots.
5. Install brake shoe return spring, being sure short end is hooked into slotted hole in rear shoe and long end in round hole in front shoe.
6. Install brake drum and wheel. Adjust brakes.

Wagner

Twin Action Type

Twin-action brake is a four-anchor type. Brake shoes are self-centering in operation, and both shoes are self-energizing in both forward and reverse.

Two wheel cylinders are mounted on opposite sides of the backing plate. One brake shoe is mounted above wheel cylinders and one below. Sliding pivot type anchor is used at front end of upper shoe and at rear end of lower shoe. Adjustable anchor is used at front end of lower shoe and at rear end of upper shoe. Four shoe return springs hold shoe ends firmly against anchors when brakes are released.

Anchor brackets are steel forgings, attached to flange on axle housing in conjunction with the backing plate. At adjustable anchor end of each shoe, shoe web bears against flat head of adjusting screw which threads into anchor bracket. The adjusting screw heads are notched and are rotated for brake adjustment through access holes in backing plate. A lock spring which fits over anchor bracket holds adjusting screw in position.

The brake backing plate has six machined bearing surfaces, three for each shoe, against which the inner edge of each shoe bears. Two brake shoe guide bolts are riveted to backing plate and extend through holes in center of brake shoe web. Shoes are retained on guide bolts by flat washers, nuts, and cotter pins.

Wheel cylinder push rods make contact between wheel cylinder pistons and brake shoes.

Inner edge of brake drum has a groove which fits over a flange on the edge of backing plate, forming a seal against the entrance of dirt and mud.

Twin-Action Type Rear Brake

Brake Shoe Removal

1. Remove brake drums. NOTE: If brake drums are worn severely, it may be necessary to retract the adjusting screws.
2. Remove the brake shoe pull back springs. NOTE: Since wheel cylinder piston stops are incorporated in the anchor brackets, it

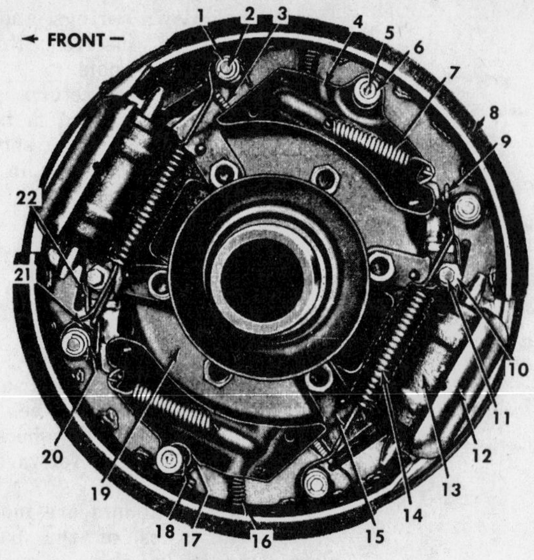

Twin action self adjusting brakes (© G.M.C.)

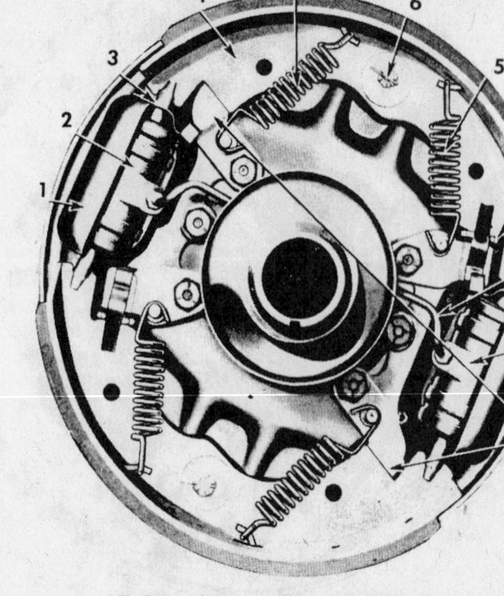

Twin action type brake installed (© G.M.C.)

1 Hold-down pin spring lock
2 Hold-down pin
3 Adjusting screw
4 Adjusting lever
5 Adjusting lever pin spring
6 Hold-down spring cup
7 Lever override spring
8 Brake shoe and lining
9 Adjusting lever pivot
10 Adjusting lever cam
11 Adjusting lever bolt
12 Wheel cylinder sheild
13 Wheel cylinder
14 Brake shoe return spring
15 Brake shoe anchor
16 Lever return spring
17 Adjusting lever pin sleeve
18 Hold-down spring
19 Brake backing plate
20 Hold-down pin retainer
21 Hold-down pin spring
22 Adjusting lever link

1 Heat shield
2 Front wheel cylinder
3 Dust shield
4 Brake shoe
5 Brake shoe return spring
6 Brake shoe guide bolt
7 Adjusting screw
8 Hydraulic line
9 Rear wheel cylinder
10 Brake shoe anchor

is not necessary to install whee cylinder clamps when the brake shoes are removed.

3. Loosen the adjusting lever cam cap screw, and while holding the star wheel end of the adjusting lever past the star wheel, remove the cap screw and cam.
4. Remove the brake shoe hold down springs and pins by compressing the spring and, at the same time, pushing the pin back through the flange plate toward the tool. Then, keeping the spring compressed, remove the lock ("C"-washer) from the pin with a magnet.
5. Lift off the brake shoe and self-adjuster lever as an assembly.
6. The self-adjuster lever can now be removed from the brake shoe by removing the hold-down spring and pin. Remove lever return spring also. NOTE: The adjusting lever, override spring and pivot are an assembly. It is not recommended that they be disassembled for service purposes unless they are broken. It is much easier to assemble and disassemble the brake leaving them intact.
7. Thread the adjusting screw out of the brake shoe anchor and remove and discard the friction spring.
8. Clean all dirt out of brake drum. Inspect drums for roughness, scoring or out-of-round. Replace or recondition drums as necessary.
9. Carefully pull lower edges of wheel cylinder boots away from cylinders. If brake fluid flows out, overhaul of the wheel cylinders is necessary. NOTE: A slight amount of fluid is nearly always present and acts as a lubricant for the piston.
10. Inspect flange plate for oil leakage past axle shaft oil seals. Install seals if necessary.

Brake Shoe Installation

1. Put a light film of lubricant on shoe bearing surfaces of brake flange plate and on threads of adjusting screw.
2. Thread adjusting screw completely into anchor without friction spring to be sure threads are clean and screw turns easily. Then remove screws, position a new friction spring on screw and reinstall in anchor.
3. Assemble self-adjuster assembly and lever return spring to brake shoe and position adjusting lever link on adjusting lever pivot.
4. Position hold-down pins in flange plate.
5. Install brake shoe and self-adjuster assemblies onto hold down pins. Insert ends of shoes in wheel cylinder push rods and legs of friction springs. NOTE: Make sure the toe of the shoe is against the adjusting screw.
6. Install cup, spring and retainer on end of hold-down pin. With spring compressed, push the hold-down pin back through the flange plate toward the tool and install the lock on the pin.
7. Install brake shoe return springs.
8. Holding the star wheel end of the adjusting lever as far as possible past the star wheel, position the adjusting lever cam into the adjusting lever link and assemble with cap screw.
9. Check the brake shoes for being centered by measuring the distance from the lining surface to the edge of the flange plate at several points. To center the shoes, tap the upper or lower end of the shoes with a plastic mallet until the distances at each end become equal.
10. Locate the adjusting lever .020″ to .039″ above the outside diameter of the adjusting screw thread by loosening the cap screw and turning the adjusting cam. NOTE: To determine .020″ to .039″, turn the adjusting screw 2 full turns out from the fully retracted position. Hold a .060″ wire gauge at a 90° angle with the star wheel edge of the adjusting lever. Turn the adjusting cam until the adjusting lever and threaded area on the adjusting screw just touch the wire.

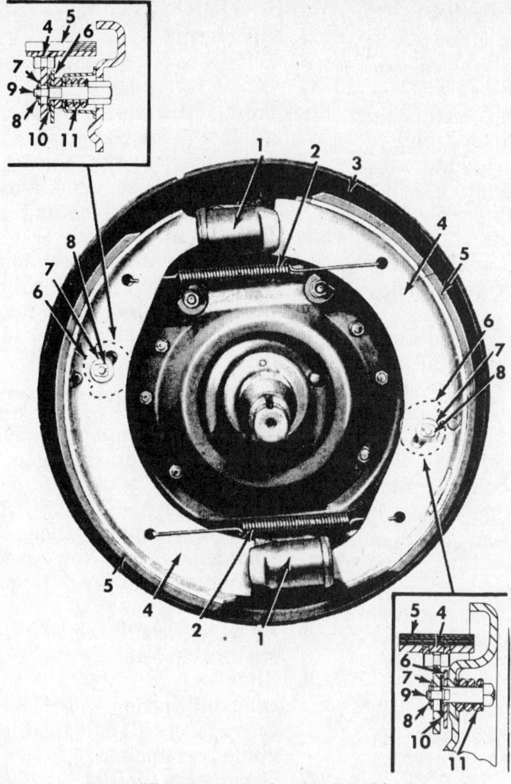

Type "F" brake assembly (© G.M.C.)

1 Wheel cylinder
2 Brake shoe return spring
3 Backing plate
4 Brake shoe
5 Brake lining
6 Brake shoe adjusting cam
7 Brake shoe guide washer
8 Brake shoe guide C-washer
9 Adjusting cam and shoe guide stud
10 Shoe guide anti-rattle washer
11 Adjusting cam spring

Type "FR3" brake assembly (© G.M.C.)

1 Wheel cylinder heat sheild
2 Upper wheel cylinder
3 Anchor pin
4 Return spring (short)
5 Guide washer
6 Guide bolt
7 Guide bolt nut lock wire
8 Brake shoe and lining assembly
9 Return spring (long)
10 Adjusting wheel lock spring
11 Adjusting wheel
12 Lower wheel cylinder
13 Backing plate

11. Secure the adjusting cam cap screw and retract the adjusting screw.
12. Install brake drums and wheels.
13. Adjust the brakes by making several forward and reverse stops until a satisfactory brake pedal height results.

Wagner

Type "F"

Two identical brake shoes are arranged on backing plate so that their toes are diagonally opposite. Two single-end wheel cylinders are arranged so that each cylinder is mounted between the toe of one shoe and the heel of the other. The two wheel cylinder pistons apply an equal amount of force to the toe of each shoe. Each cylinder casting is shaped to provide an anchor block for the brake shoe heel.

Each shoe is adjusted by means of an eccentric cam which contacts a pin pressed into brake shoe web. Each cam is attached to the backing plate by a cam and shoe guide stud which protrudes through a slot in the shoe web and, in conjunction with flat washers and C-washers, also serves as a shoe hold-down. Two return springs are connected between the shoes, one at each toe and heel.

With vehicle moving forward, both shoes are forward acting (primary shoes), self-energizing in forward direction of drum rotation. With vehicle in reverse, both shoes are reverse acting since neither is self-energized in the reverse direction of drum rotation.

Brake Shoe Removal

1. Remove both brake shoe return springs, using brake spring pliers.
2. Remove C-washer and flat washer from each adjusting cam and hold-down stud. Lift shoes off backing plate.

Cleaning and Inspection

1. Clean all dirt out of brake drum. Inspect drum for roughness, scoring, or out-of-round. Replace or recondition brake drum as necessary.
2. Inspect wheel bearings and oil seals.
3. Check backing plate attaching bolts to make sure they are tight. Clean all dirt off backing plate.
4. Inspect brake shoe return springs. If broken, cracked, or weakened, replace with new springs.
5. Check cam and shoe guide stud and friction spring on backing plate for corrosion or binding. Cam stud should turn easily with a wrench but should not be loose. If frozen, lubricate with kerosene or penetrating oil and work free.
6. Examine brake shoe linings for wear. Lining should be replaced if worn down close to rivet heads.

Brake Shoe Installation

1. Install anti-rattle spring washer on each cam and shoe guide stud, pronged side facing adjusting cam.
2. Place shoe assembly on backing plate with cam and shoe guide stud inserted through hole in shoe web; locate shoe toe in wheel cylinder piston shoe guide and position shoe heel in slot in anchor block.
3. Install flat washer and C-washer on cam and shoe guide stud. Crimp ends of C-washer together.
4. After installing both shoes, install brake shoe return springs.

To install each spring, place spring end with short hook in toe of shoe, then using brake spring pliers, stretch spring and secure long hook end in heel of opposite shoe.

5. install hub and brake drum assembly.
6. Adjust brake.
7. After checking pedal operation, road test vehicle.

Wagner

Type "FR-3"

Each brake is equipped with two double-end wheel cylinders which apply hydraulic pressure to both the toe and the heel of two identical, self-centering shoes. The shoes anchor at either toe or heel, depending upon the direction of rotation. Each adjusting screw is threaded into or out of its support by means of an adjusting wheel. Adjusting wheels are accessible through adjusting slots in the backing plate.

Brake Shoe Removal

1. Remove hub and brake drum assembly.
2. Install wheel cylinder clamps to hold pistons in cylinders.
3. Remove brake shoe return springs.
4. Remove lock wires, nuts, and washers from brake shoe guide bolts, then remove brake shoe assemblies.
5. Remove screws attaching adjusting wheel lock springs to anchor supports. Thread each adjusting screw from the shoe side of its anchor support by turning adjusting wheels, then lift adjusting wheels out of slots in anchor supports.

Brake Shoe Installation

1. *Install adjusting screws and wheels in anchor supports dry; use no lubricant.* Insert each adjusting wheel in slot in anchor support, insert threaded end of adjusting screw in anchor support, then turn adjusting wheel to thread adjusting screw into anchor support. Insert anchor pins into holes in anchor supports, with slots in pins facing slots in supports.
2. Install brake shoes with cutaway end of shoe web next to adjusting screw and with ends of shoes engaging slots in wheel cylinder push rods and anchor pins. Install flat washer and nut on each brake shoe guide bolt. Tighten nuts finger-tight, then back off nuts only far enough to allow movement of shoes without binding.
3. Install brake shoe return springs, hooking one end of each spring in brake shoe web, then hook other end over anchor pins.
4. Remove wheel cylinder clamps.
5. Install hub and brake drum assembly.
6. Adjust brakes.
7. After checking pedal operation, road test vehicle.

Bendix

Duo Servo Type

Removing Front Brake Shoes

With the vehicle elevated on a hoist, jack or suitable stands remove front wheel and drums.

1. Remove brake shoe return springs. (Note how secondary spring overlaps primary spring.)
2. Remove brake shoe retainer, spring and nails.
3. Slide eye of automatic adjuster cable off anchor and unhook from lever. Remove cable, cable guide and anchor plate.
4. Disconnect lever spring from lever and disengage from shoe web. Remove spring and lever.
5. Remove the primary and secondary brake shoe assemblies and adjusting star wheel from support. Install wheel cylinder clamps to hold pistons in cylinders.

Removing Rear Brake Shoes

1. With the vehicle elevated on a hoist, jack or suitable stand, remove rear wheel, and drum retaining clips. Remove drum.
2. Remove brake shoe return springs. (Note how secondary spring overlaps primary spring.)
3. Remove brake shoe retainers, springs and nails.
4. Slide eye of automatic adjuster cable off anchor and then unhook from lever. Remove cable, cable guide and anchor plate.
5. Disconnect lever spring from lever and disengage from shoe web. Remove spring and lever.
6. Spread anchor ends of the primary and secondary shoes and remove parking brake strut and spring.
7. Disengage parking brake cable from parking brake lever and remove brake assembly.
8. Remove the primary and secondary brake shoe assemblies and adjusting star wheel from support. Install wheel cylinder to hold pistons in cylinders.

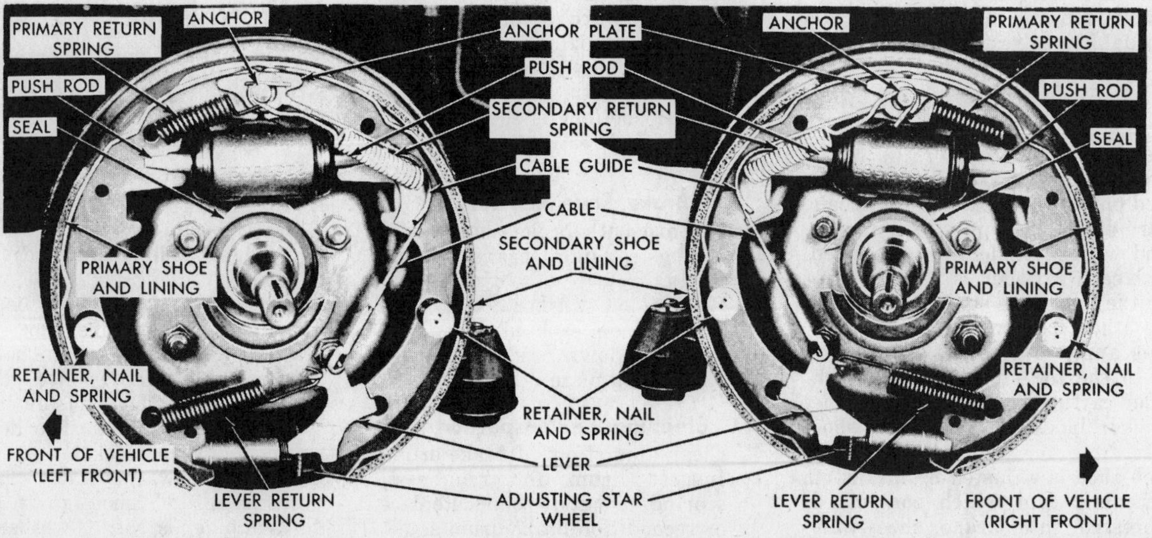

Brake assemblies front (© Chrysler Corp.)

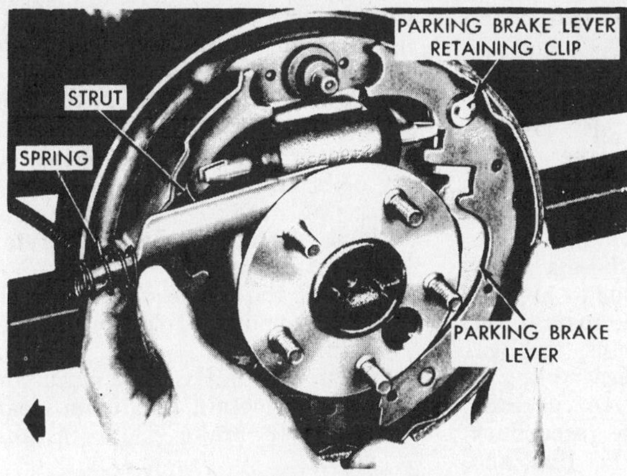

Removing or installing parking brake strut and spring—rear (© Chrysler Corp.)

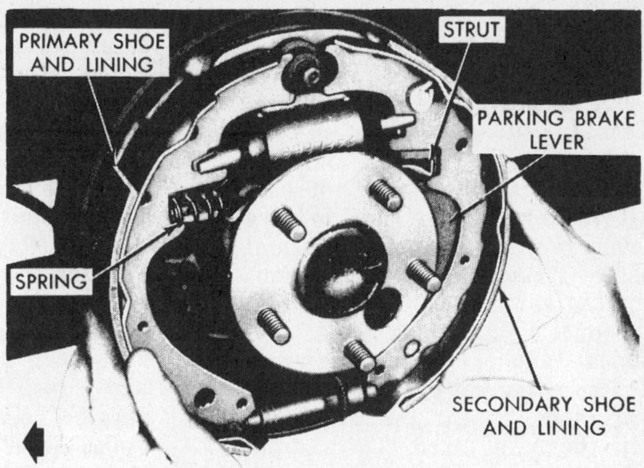

Installing brake shoes (© Chrysler Corp.)

Installing Front Brake Shoes

1. Match a primary with a secondary brake shoe and place them in their relative position on a work bench.
2. Lubricate threads of adjusting screw and install it between the primary and secondary shoes with star wheel next to secondary shoe. The star adjusting wheels are stamped "R" (right side) and "L" (left side), and indicate their location on vehicle.
3. Overlap anchor ends of primary and secondary brake shoes and install adjusting spring lever.
4. Spread anchor ends of brake shoes to maintain adjusting lever and spring in position.
5. Holding brake shoes in their relative position, place brake shoe assembly on support and over the anchor pin.
6. Install nails, cups, springs and retainers.
7. Install anchor pin plate.
8. Install cable guide in the secondary shoe and place the "eye" of adjusting cable over anchor pin.
9. Install return spring in primary shoe. Slide spring over anchor.
10. Install return spring in secondary shoe and slide over anchor. (Be sure the secondary spring overlaps primary).
11. Place adjusting cable cover guide and engage hook of cable into adjusting lever.
12. Install brake drum.
13. Adjust brakes.
14. After checking brake pedal operation, road test vehicle.

Installing Rear Brake Shoes

1. Inspect the platforms of support for nicks or burrs. Apply a thin coat of lubricant to support platforms.
2. Attach parking brake lever to the back side of the secondary shoe.
3. Place the secondary and primary shoe in their relative position on a work bench.
4. Lubricate threads of adjusting screw and install it between the primary and secondary shoes with star wheel next to secondary shoe. The star adjusting wheels are stamped "R" (right side) and "L" (left side), and indicate their location on vehicle.
5. Overlap anchor ends of the primary and secondary brake shoes and install adjusting spring and lever.
6. Hold the brake shoes in their relative position and engage parking brake cable into parking brake lever.
7. Install parking brake strut and spring between the parking brake lever and primary shoe.
8. Place brake shoes on the support and install retainer nails, springs and retainers.
9. Install anchor pin plate.
10. Install "eye" of adjusting cable over anchor pin and install return spring between primary shoe and anchor pin.
11. Install cable guide in secondary shoe then install secondary return spring. (Be sure secondary spring overlaps primary.)
12. Place adjusting cable in groove of cable guide and engage hook of cable into adjusting lever.
13. Install brake drum and retaining clips.
14. Adjust brakes.

Bendix

Two-Piston Single Cylinder Hydraulically Actuated Type

Description

Both shoes pivot on anchor pins at the bottom of the support plate. The shoes are actuated by one wheel cylinder which is of the double piston type. Specification for heel and toe clearance of shoes should be strictly followed to obtain efficient brake operation.

Brake Shoe Removal

1. Back off the adjusting cam and remove wheel and drum assembly.
2. Remove brake shoe return spring.
3. Install wheel cylinder brake clamp to prevent pistons from being forced out of cylinder.
4. Remove "C" washer, oil washer and retainer, guide spring retainer and guide spring from anchor bolts to remove brake shoes.

Brake Shoe Installation

1. Install brake shoes, oil washers and retainers on anchor bolts and secure with "C" washers.
2. Install brake return spring.
3. Install wheel and drum assembly.

Adjustments

Since tapered brake lining is thicker at the center than at the ends, the adjustment procedures outlined in the paragraphs that follow must be performed in order to assure maximum braking efficiency.

Minor Adjustment

1. Jack up truck so that one wheel can be rotated freely.
2. Then, while rotating that wheel forward and backward, bring the shoe out to the drum with the adjusting cam until a light drag is obtained.
3. Back off the adjustment until the wheel is free to turn.
4. Repeat this procedure on the other shoe.

Major Adjustment

1. Inspect the fluid level in the master cylinder and add fluid if the

level is 3/8" to 1/2" from the top of the reservoir or lower.

2. Loosen lock nuts and turn brake shoe anchor bolts to the fully released position.
3. Adjust the anchor bolt and cam and the minor adjustment cam at the top of the shoe to give equal clearance at the toe and heel. Make sure that sufficient center contact is maintained to produce a slight drag.
4. Lock anchor adjusting nut. After adjusting the clearance on one shoe, repeat the procedure on the other shoe. Then apply the brakes a couple of times to make sure adjustment is up to specifications.

NOTE: Whenever cams are adjusted, check brakes by applying pressure on the brake pedal a couple of times so as to make sure wheel drag has not increased, since the spring loaded cams may cause shoe adjustment to change by shifting position. Wheel should only have a slight drag at room temperature.

Bendix

Single Anchor Brake Shoe Replacement

Brake Shoe Removal

1. Remove the wheel and drum. *Do not push down the brake pedal after the brake drum has been removed.* On a truck equipped with a vacuum or air booster, be sure the engine is stopped and there is no vacuum or air pressure in the system before disconnecting the hydraulic lines.
2. Clamp the brake cylinder boots against the ends of the cylinder, and remove the brake shoe retracting springs from both shoes.
3. Remove the anchor pin plate.
4. Remove the hold-down spring cups and springs from the shoes, and remove the shoes and the adjusting screw parts from the carrier plate. *Do not let oil or grease touch the brake linings.* If the shoes on a rear brake assembly are being removed, remove the parking brake lever, link, and spring with the shoes. Unhook the parking brake cable from the lever as the shoes are being removed.
5. If the shoes are from a rear brake assembly, remove the parking brake lever from the secondary shoe.

Brake Shoe Installation

1. Coat all points of contact between the brake shoes and the other brake assembly parts with Lubri-plate or a similar lubricant. Lubricate the adjusting screw threads.
2. Place the adjusting screw, socket and nut on the brake shoes so that the star wheel on the screw is opposite the adjusting hole in the carrier plate. Then install the adjusting screw spring.
3. Position the brake shoes and the adjusting screw parts on the carrier plate, and install the hold-down spring pins, springs, and cups. When assembling a rear brake, connect the parking brake lever to the secondary shoe, and install the link and spring with the shoes. Be sure to hook the parking brake cable to the lever.
4. Install the anchor pin plate on the pin.
5. Install the brake shoe retracting springs on both shoes. *The primary shoe spring must be installed first.*
6. Remove the clamp from the brake cylinder boots.
7. Install the wheel and drum.
8. Bleed the system and adjust the brakes. Check the brake pedal operation after bleeding the system.

Bendix

Double Anchor Brake Shoe Replacement

1. Remove the wheel and drum. *Do not push down the brake pedal after the brake drum has been removed.* On trucks equipped with vacuum boosters, be sure the engine is stopped and there is no vacuum in the system before disconnecting the hydraulic lines.
2. Clamp the brake cylinder boots against the ends of the cylinder, and remove the brake shoe retracting springs from both shoes.
3. At each shoe, remove the 2 brake shoe retainers and washers from the hold-down pins and remove the spring and pin from the carrier plate. Remove the anchor pin retainers and remove the shoes from the anchor pins. *Do not allow grease or oil to touch the linings.*
4. Clean all brake assembly parts. If the adjusting cams do not operate freely apply a small quantity of lubricating oil to points where the shaft of the cam enters the carrier plate. Wipe dirt and corrosion off the plate.
5. Clean the ledges on the carrier plate with sandpaper. Coat all points of contact between the brake shoes and the other brake assembly parts with high temperature grease.
6. Position the brake shoes on the carrier plate with the heel (lower) end of the shoes over the anchor pins and the toe (upper) end of the shoes engaged in the brake cylinder link. Install the hold-down spring pins, spring, washers and retainers.
7. Install the anchor pin retainers and then install the brake shoe return spring.
8. Turn the brake shoe adjusting cams to obtain maximum clearance for brake drum installation.
9. Install the wheel and drum assembly.
10. Bleed the brake system and adjust the brakes.
11. Check brake pedal operation and road test.

Bendix

Two-Cylinder Brake Shoe Replacement

Removal

1. Remove the wheel, and then remove the drum or the hub and drum assembly. *Mark the hub and drum to aid assembly in the same position.* On trucks equipped with vacuum or air boosters, be sure the engine is stopped and there is no vacuum or air pressure in the system before disconnecting the hydraulic lines.
2. Clamp the brake cylinder boots against the ends of the cylinder and remove the four brake shoe retracting springs.
3. Remove the brake shoe guide bolt cotter pin, nut, washer, and bolt from both shoes, and remove the shoes from the carrier plate.
4. Remove the clamp-type adjusting wheel lock from the anchor pin support, and unthread the adjusting screw and wheel assembly from the anchor pin support.

Installation

1. Clean the carrier plate ledges with sandpaper. Coat all points of contact between the brake shoes and other brake assembly parts with high temperature grease.
2. Thread the adjusting screw and wheel assembly into the anchor pin support and install the clamp-type adjusting wheel lock.

   Thread the adjusting wheel into the support so that the brake shoe will rest against the adjusting wheel end.
3. Place the brake shoe over the

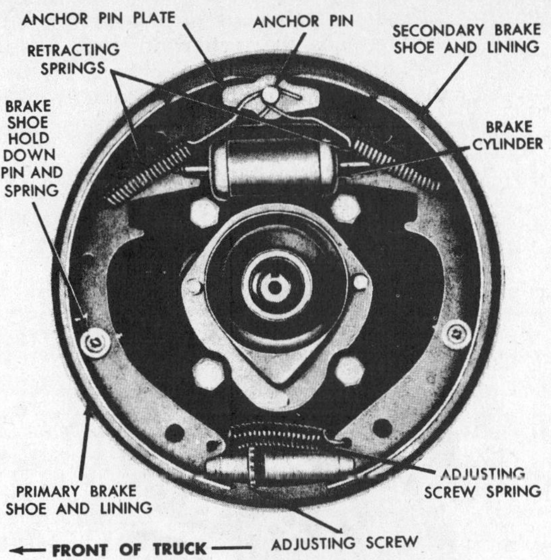

Duo-servo single anchor brake assembly
(© Ford Motor Co.)

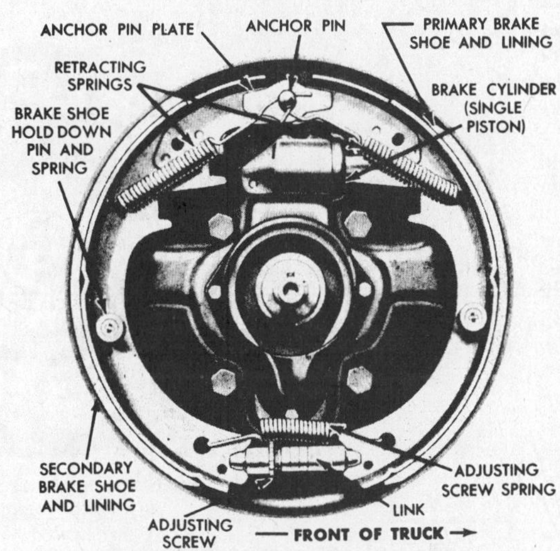

Uni-servo single anchor brake assembly
(© Ford Motor Co.)

two brake shoe anchor pins, insert the ends in the brake cylinder links, and install the shoe guide bolt, washer, and nut. Finger tighten the nut, then back off one full turn, and install the cotter pin.

4. Install the four retracting springs.
5. Remove the cylinder clamps, install the drum or the hub and drum assembly, then install the wheel assembly. Align the marks on the hub and drum during installation.
6. Bleed and adjust the brakes.
7. Check pedal operation and road test.

Bendix

Brake Shoe Adjustment

The brake drums should be at normal room temperature, when the brake shoes are adjusted. If the shoes are adjusted when the shoes are hot and expanded, the shoes may drag as the drums cool and contract.

A minor brake adjustment reestablishes the brake lining-to-drum clearance and compensates for normal lining wear.

A major brake adjustment includes the adjustment of the brake shoe anchor pins as well as the brake shoes. Adjustment of the anchor pin permits the centering of the brake shoes in the drum.

A major brake adjustment should be performed when dragging brakes are not corrected by a minor adjustment, when brake shoes are relined or replaced, or when brake drums are machined.

Adjustment procedures for each type of brake assembly are given under the applicable heading.

The brake shoe adjustment procedures for the uniservo single anchor brake assmebly are the same as those for the duo-servo single anchor type.

Duo-Servo Single Anchor Brake

The duo-servo single-anchor brake is adjusted by turning an adjusting screw located between the lower ends of the shoes.

1. Raise the truck until the wheels clear the floor.
2. Remove the cover from the adjusting hole at the bottom of the brake carrier plate, and turn the adjusting screw inside the hole to expand the brake shoes until they drag against the brake drum.
3. When the shoes are against the drum, back off the adjusting screw 10 or 12 notches so that

Duo-servo brake shoe adjustment
(© Ford Motor Co.)

the drum rotates freely without drag.

4. Install the adjusting hole cover on the brake carrier plate.
5. Check and adjust the other three brake assemblies. When adjusting the rear brake shoes, check the parking brake cables for proper adjustment. Make sure that there is clearance between the ends of the parking brake link and the shoes.
6. Apply the brakes. If the pedal travels more than halfway down between the released position and the floor, too much clearance exists between the brake shoes and the drums. Repeat steps 2 and 3 above. Internal inspection and/or bleeding may be necessary.
7. When all brake shoes have been properly adjusted, road test the truck and check the operation of the brakes. *Perform the road test only when the brakes will apply and the truck can be safely stopped.*

Single Anchor Pin Adjustment

1. Raise the truck until the wheel clears the floor.
2. Rotate the drum until the feeler slot is opposite the lower end of the secondary (rear) brake shoe.
3. Insert a 0.010-inch feeler gauge through the slot in the drum. Move the feeler up along the secondary shoe unit it is wedged between the sedondary shoe and the drum.
4. Turn the adjusting screw (star wheel) to expand the brake shoes until a heavy drag is felt against the drum. Back off the adjusting screw just enough to establish a clearance of 0.010″, between the shoe and the drum at a point 1½″ from each end of the secondary shoe. This adjustment will provide correct operating clearance for both the primary and secondary shoes. If the 0.010″ clearance cannot be obtained at both ends of the secondary shoe, the anchor pin must be adjusted.
5. To adjust the anchor pin setting, loosen the anchor pin nut just enough to permit moving the pin up or down by tapping the nut with a soft hammer. *Do not back the nut off too far or the shoes will move out of position when the nut is tightened.* Tap the anchor pin in a direction that will allow the shoes to center in the drum and provide an operating clearance of 0.010″. Torque the anchor pin nut to 80-100 ft-lbs. Recheck the secondary shoe clearance at both the heel and toe ends of the shoe.
6. When all brake shoes and anchor pins have been properly adjusted, road test the truck and check the operation of the brakes. *Perform the road test only when the brakes will apply and the truck can be safely stopped.*

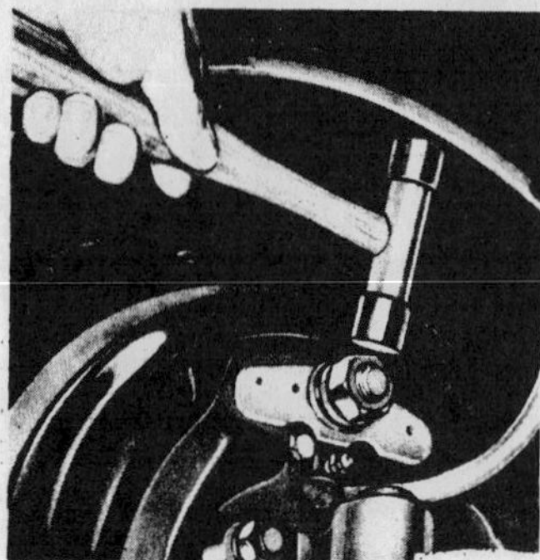
Anchor adjustment
(© Ford Motor Co.)

Double Anchor Pin Adjustment

1. Raise the truck until the wheels clear the floor.
2. Rotate the drum until the feeler slot is opposite the lower (heel) end of the secondary (rear) brake shoe.
3. Insert a 0.007″ feeler gauge through the slot in the drum. Move the feeler up along the secondary shoe until it is wedged between the shoe and the drum.
4. Loosen the secondary shoe anchor pin nut. Turn the secondary shoe anchor pin until the brake shoe-to-drum clearance at a point 1½″ from the heel end of the shoe is 0.007″, Remove the feeler gauge.
5. Rotate the drum until the feeler slot is opposite the upper (toe) end of the secondary brake shoe.
6. Insert a 0.010″ feeler gauge through the slot in the drum. Move the feeler gauge down along the secondary shoe until it is wedged between the shoe and the drum. Turn the adjusting cam, to expand the brake shoe, until a heavy drag is felt against the drum.
7. Turn the anchor pin until the brake shoe-to-drum clearance at a point 1½″ from the toe end of the shoe is 0.010″. Remove the feeler gauge.
8. Torque the anchor pin nut to 80-100 ft-lbs. Recheck the heel and toe clearances.
9. Using the preceding secondary brake shoe adjustment procedure as a guide, adjust the primary brake shoe-to-drum clearance.
10. Road test the truck and check the operation of the brakes. *Perform the road test only when the brakes will apply and the truck can be safely stopped.*

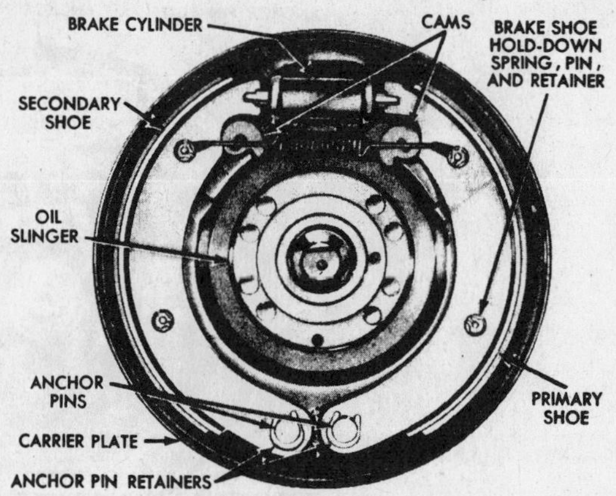

Double anchor brake assembly
(© Ford Motor Co.)

Kelsey Hayes

Front Brake Shoes

Removal

1. Raise the vehicle until the wheel clears the floor. Remove the wheel, drum and hub assembly.
2. Clamp the wheel cylinder boots

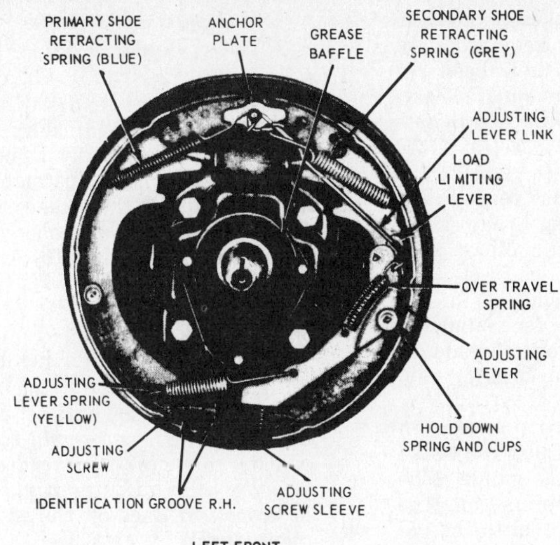

Kelsey hayes hydraulic brake assembly
(© Ford Motor Co.)

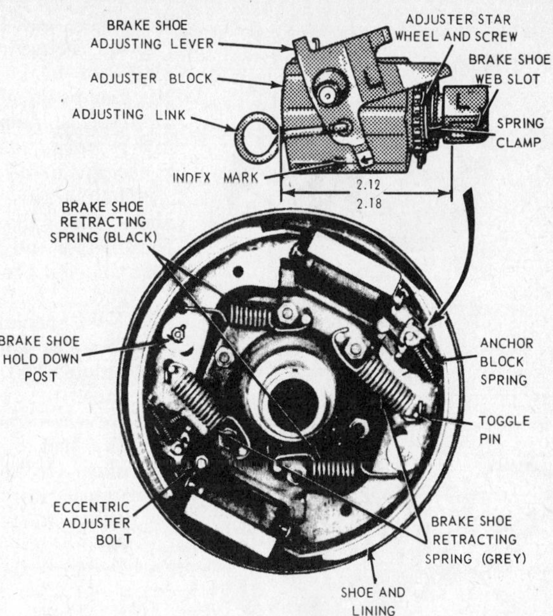

Kelsey hayes rear brake assembly
(© Ford Motor Co.)

against the ends of the cylinder.

3. Remove the brake shoe retracting springs from both shoes.
4. Remove the adjusting lever link, anchor plate and the adjusting lever spring.
5. Remove the hold down spring cups, springs and the adjusting lever.
6. Remove the brake shoes and adjuster screw assembly from the backing plate.

Installation

1. Clean all brake dust from the brake assembly parts with a *clean dry* rag.
2. Coat all points of contact between the shoes and other brake parts with high temperature grease.
3. Coat the adjuster screw with high temperature grease before assembly. Thread the adjuster screw into the adjuster screw sleeve.
4. Position the brake shoes on the backing plate and install the adjusting lever, hold down pins, springs and cups.
5. Position the adjuster screw assembly on the brake shoes so that the star wheel is opposite the adjusting slot in the backing plate. Install the adjusting lever spring.
6. Install the anchor plate and adjusting lever link.
7. Install the secondary brake shoe retracting spring.
8. Install the primary brake shoe retracting spring.
9. Remove the clamp from the wheel cylinder boots.
10. Install the wheel, drum and hub assembly.
11. Adjust the brakes. Subsequent adjustment will be automatic.

Rear Brake Shoes

Removal

1. Raise the truck until the wheel clears the floor.
2. Remove the wheel, hub and drum assembly.
3. Clamp the brake cylinder boots against the ends of the cylinder with brake piston clamps.
4. Note the two different types of brake shoe retracting springs and remove the springs.
5. Remove the brake shoe hold down post cotter key, nut, and shoe hold down washer.
6. Loosen and remove the eccentric adjuster bolt, lock washer, eccentric and adjusting link.
7. Remove the shoe and lining assembly from the backing plate.
8. Remove the anchor block spring and slide the adjuster assembly from the shoe web.
9. Remove the adjuster star wheel and screw from the adjuster block. Unthread the star wheel from the adjuster screw.

Installation

1. Wipe all brake dust from the brake assembly parts with a *clean dry* rag. Coat all points of contact between brake shoes and other parts with high temperature grease.
2. Coat the adjuster screw and the inside of the adjuster block with high temperature grease.
3. Thread the adjuster screw onto the star wheel and insert the adjuster screw assembly into the adjuster block. Maintain a 2.12-2.18 inch dimension from the end of the adjuster block to the adjuster screw web slot.
4. Install the adjuster assembly onto the shoe web and attach the anchor block spring.
5. Place the brake shoe over the retracting spring toggle pin and insert the ends of the shoe in the wheel cylinder links.
6. Install the shoe hold down washer and nut. Do not install the cotter pin.
7. Install the four brake shoe retracting springs. Make sure the retracting springs are installed. On 15 x 5″ brakes the inner hook ends face the wheel cylinders. On 15 x 4″ brakes the inner hook ends face the center of the axle.
8. Install the adjusting link, eccentric, lockwasher and adjuster bolt. Do not tighten.
9. Remove the brake piston clamps.
10. Tighten the shoe hold down nut until there is 0.015-0.025″ clearance between the shoe and hold down washer with the shoe held against the backing plate. Install the cotter pin.
11. Center the shoes on the backing plate. Using a ½″ wrench, rotate the adjuster eccentric until the adjusting lever is at the index mark. Tighten the eccentric adjuster bolt to specification.
12. Install the wheel, hub and drum assembly.

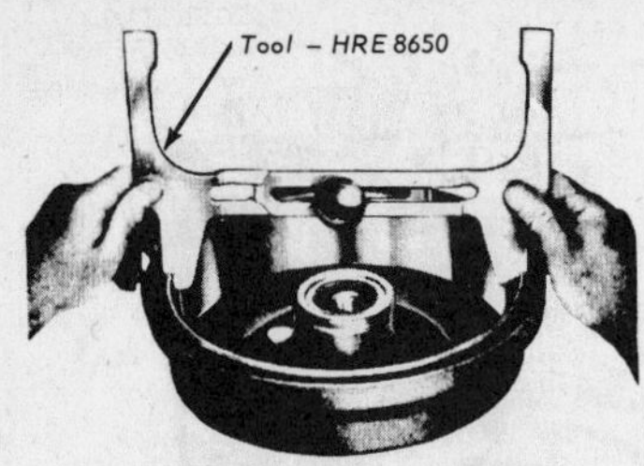

Measuring brake drum
(© Ford Motor Co.)

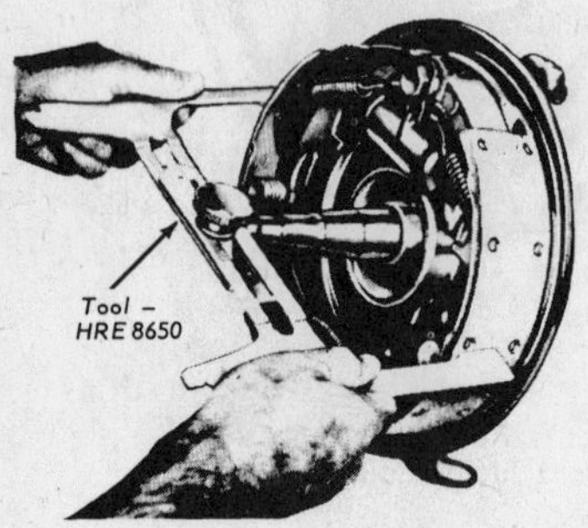

Measuring brake shoes
(© Ford Motor Co.)

13. Adjust the brake to obtain a slight drag. Subsequent adjustments will be automatic.

Brake Shoe Adjustment

The brake drums should be at normal room temperature, when the brake shoes are adjusted. If the shoes are adjusted when the shoes are hot and expanded, the shoes may drag as the drums cool and contract.

The brake shoes are automatically adjusted when the vehicle is driven in reverse and the brakes applied. A manual adjustment is required only after the brake shoes have been relined or replaced. *The manual adjustment is performed while the drums are removed, using the tool and the procedure detailed below.*

When adjusting the rear brake shoes, check the parking brake cables for proper adjustment. Make sure that the equalizer operates freely.

To adjust the brake shoes:

1. Use special tool (see illustration) and adjust to the inside diameter of the drum braking surface.
2. Reverse the tool as shown in illustration and adjust the brake shoes to touch the gauge. The gauge contact points on the shoes must be parallel to the vehicle with the center line through the center of the axle. Hold the automatic adjusting lever out of engagement while rotating the adjusting screw, to prevent burring the screw slots. Make sure the adjusting screw rotates freely.
3. Apply a small quantity of high temperature grease to the points where the shoes contact the carrier plate, being careful not to get the lubricant on the linings.
4. Install the drums. Install the retaining nuts and tighten securely.
5. Install the wheels on the drums and tighten the mounting nuts to specification.
6. Complete the adjustment by applying the brakes several times while backing the vehicle.
7. After the brake shoes have been properly adjusted, check the operation of the brakes by making several stops while operating in a forward direction.

Self Adjusting Brake—Two-Cylinder Front

Two-cylinder front brakes are adjusted by means of exposed, hex-head, self-locking cam adjusters. The brakes are to be manually adjusted initially. Subsequent adjustment is automatic. To adjust this brake:

1. Raise the vehicle and check the front brakes for drag by rotating the wheels.
2. Adjust one shoe by rotating the wheel backward and forward while turning the cam hex-head with a wrench. Bring the shoe out to the drum until a light drag is felt. *Do not apply excessive force on the hex head cam, as automatic adjuster parts can be damaged.* Back off the adjustment until the wheel turns freely. Adjust the other cam on the same wheel in the same manner.
3. Adjust the other front wheel brake using the procedure above.
4. Apply the brakes and recheck the adjustment.

Self Adjusting Brakes—Rear

The brake shoes are automatically adjusted when the vehicle is driven in reverse and the brakes applied. A manual adjustment is required only after the brake shoes have been relined or replaced.

The two-cylinder brake assembly brake shoes are adjusted by turning adjusting wheels reached through slots in the backing plate.

Two types of two-cylinder brake assemblies are used on truck rear wheels. The assemblies differ primarily in the retracting spring hookup, and in the design of the adjusting screws and locks. However, the service procedures are the same for both

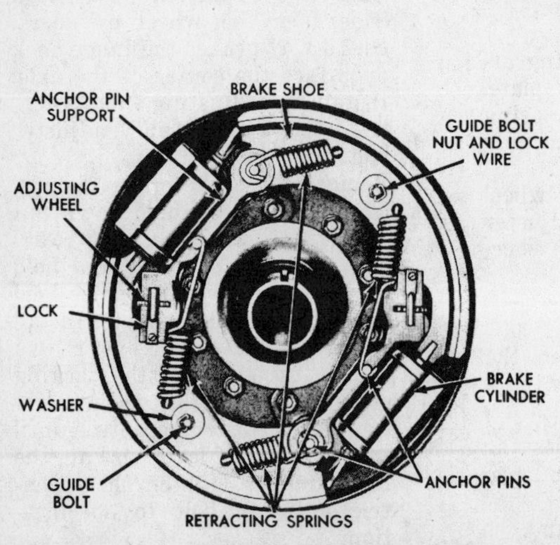

Two cylinder brake—unequal length springs
(© Ford Motor Co.)

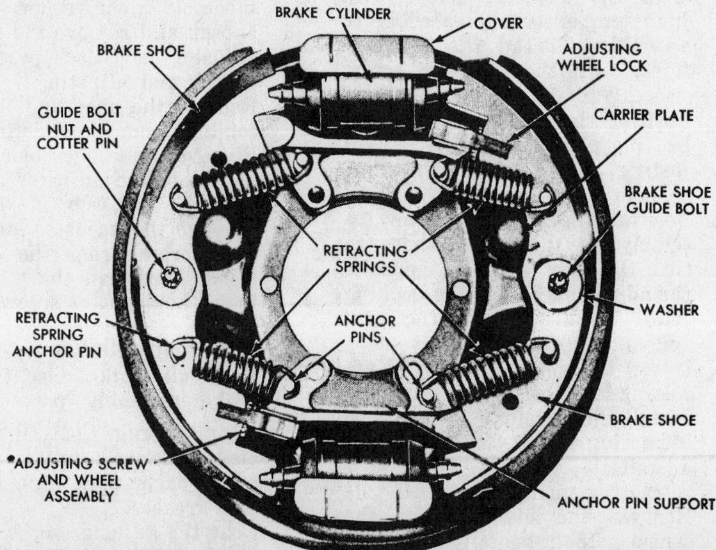

Two cylinder brake—equal length springs (© Ford Motor Co.)

assemblies.

The brake adjustment is made with the vehicle raised. Check the brake drag by rotating the drum in the direction of forward rotation as the adjustment is made.

1. Remove the adjusting slot covers from the backing plate.
2. Turn the rear (secondary shoe) adjusting screw inside the hole to expand the brake shoe until a slight drag is felt against the brake drum.
3. Repeat the above procedure on the front (primary) brake shoe.
4. Replace the adjusting hole covers.
5. Complete the adjustment by applying the brakes several times while backing the vehicle.
6. After the brake shoes have been properly adjusted, check the operation of the brakes by making several stops while operating in a forward direction.

Parking Brakes

Internal Shoe Type

Nine-Inch Diameter Drum

1. Release the parking brake lever in the cab.
2. From under the truck, remove the cotter pin from the parking brake linkage adjusting clevis pin. Remove the clevis pin.
3. Lengthen the parking brake adjusting link by turning the clevis. Continue to lengthen the adjusting link until the shoes seat against the drum when the clevis pin is installed.
4. Remove the clevis pin and shorten the linkage adjustment until there is 0.010″ clearance between the shoes and the drum. The measurement should be taken at all points around the drum with the clevis pin installed.
5. Install a new cotter pin in the clevis retaining pin and check the brake operation.

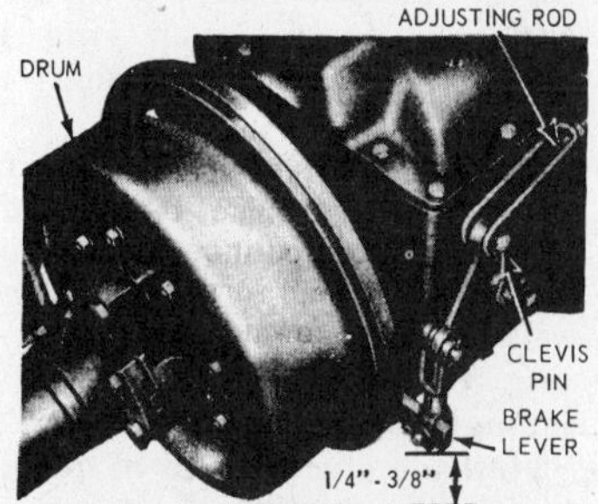

Shoe type parking brake
(© Ford Motor Co.)

Twelve-Inch Diameter Drum

There is no internal adjustment on this brake. Adjustment is made on the linkage. Remove the clevis pin, loosen the nuts on the adjusting rod, and turn the clevis on the rod until a ¼-⅜″ free play is obtained at the brake lever. Tighten the nuts, and connect the clevis to the bellcrank with the clevis pin.

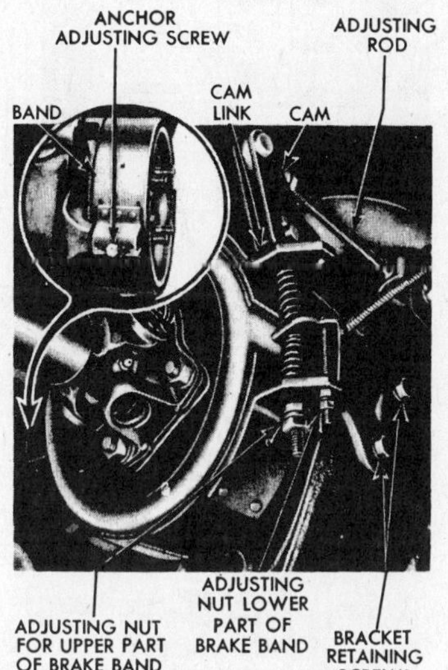

Typical external band type parking brake
(© Ford Motor Co.)

External Band Type

1. On cable-controlled parking brakes, move the parking brake lever to the fully released position. On a vehicle with a rod-type linkage, set the lever at the first notch.
2. Check the position of the cam to make sure the flat portion is resting on the brake band bracket. If the cam is not flat with the bracket, remove the clevis pin from the upper part of the cam, and adjust the clevis rod to allow the flat portion of the cam to rest on the brake band bracket. Install the clevis pin and cotter pin.
3. Remove the lock wire from the anchor adjusing screw, and turn the adjusting screw clockwise until a clearance of 0.010″ is established between the brake lining and the brake drum at the anchor bracket. Install the lock wire in the anchor adjusting screw.
4. Loosen the lock nut on the adjusting screw for the lower half of the brake band, and adjust the screw to establish a 0.010″ clearance between the lining and the brake drum at the lower half of the brake band. Tighten the lock nut.
5. Turn the upper band adjusting rod nut until a 0.010 clearance is established between the upper half of the band and the drum.
6. Apply and release brake several times to insure full release.

Air Spring Type Parking Brake

Description

The spring type parking brake is air actuated and is operated in conjunction with the rear wheel service brake air chamber. The spring is held in the retracted (or off) position by air pressure from a protected third air reservoir. As the air pressure is released from the cylinder housing, the spring is released thereby actuating the service brake push rod and applying the brakes.

Service Procedures

Removal

1. Remove all dirt and grease from exterior of brake chamber, using a suitable type of cleaning solvent and brush. Release slack adjusters.
2. Disconnect brake chamber push rod by removing clevis pin.
3. Disconnect air lines.
4. Remove nuts and washers from mounting bolts, remove brake chamber and spring brake assembly.

Disassembly

1. Remove protective rubber boot.
2. Rotate release handle clockwise so the release bolt acts as a jack screw to draw piston toward spring plate compressing spring between these two units. The release nut must be pulled up sufficiently to completely remove all spring pressure from slack adjuster. The unit will be in position shown in illustration. *In case the manual release requires extremely high toque, or will not move, it may mean that the piston "O" ring is wedged between top of piston and bore, thereby obstructing its movement. It is recommended that air pressure be used to cause piston movement while manual release is attempted.*
3. Remove clamp ring joining spring brake chamber to non-pressure housing. *Mark both non-pressure and pressure plates with relation to clamp ring, so bolts of clamp ring will be at same location when reassembled.*
4. Remove spring brake chamber from non-pressure chamber.
5. Remove piston shaft screw and plunger.
6. Press down on spring plate so that it is recessed in chamber bore sufficiently to clear retainer rings.

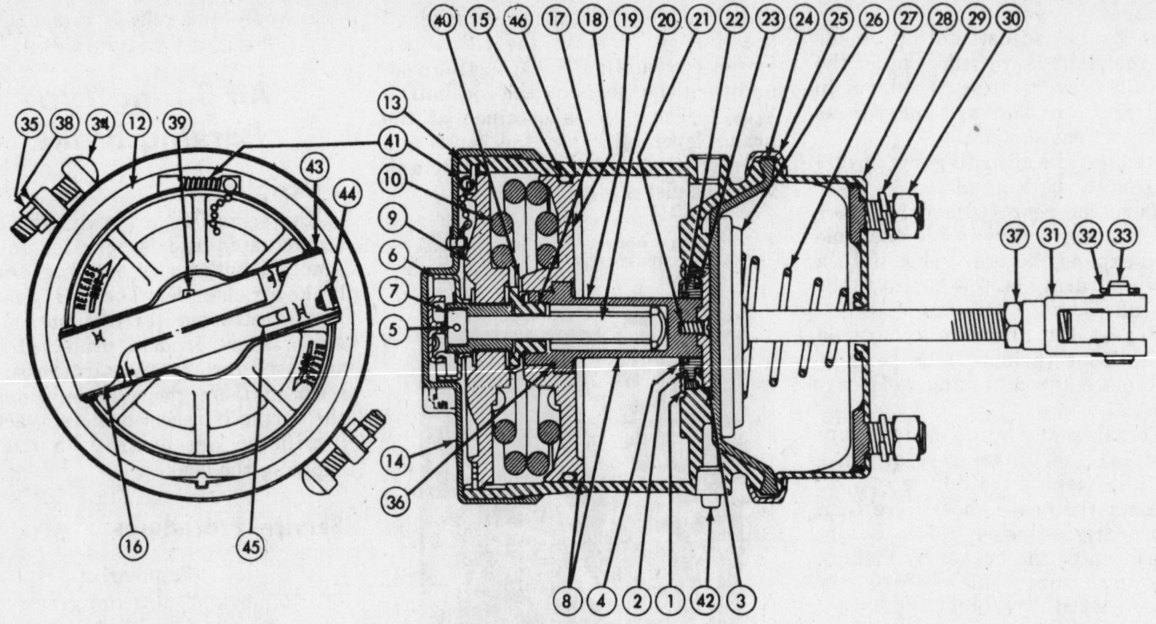

Spring type parking brake (© Chrysler Corp.)

1 Screw
2 Bushing
3 Plunger
4 Cap
5 Pin
6 Cross bar
7 Nut
8 Piston-cover-spring (sub-assy).
9 Cover (sub assy.)
10 Spring
11 Retaining ring (sub assy.)
12 Retaining ring
13 Cylinder housing
14 Protective boot
15 Seal "O" ring
16 Handle W/O stop
17 Piston nut
18 Piston
19 Piston shaft
20 Rlease bolt
21 Screw
22 Seal "O" ring
23 Seal "O" ring
24 Diaphragm
25 Clamp band
26 Push rod
27 Spring
28 Non-pressure housing
29 Lock washer
30 Nut
31 Yoke
32 Cotterpin
33 Clevis pin
34 Bolt
35 Nut
36 Seal "O" ring
37 Jam nut
38 Washer
39 Snap ring
40 Tooth washer
41 Lock spring
42 Pipe plug
43 Rivet
44 Spring
45 Handle with stop
46 Piston-cover-spring

7. Remove retainer ring spring and retainer rings, so that spring plate is free to pass through open end of chamber housing.
8. Remove piston shaft, piston, spring and spring plate assembly out of chamber housing.
9. Remove snap ring retaining the piston shaft so the piston shaft can be withdrawn from its bore in the piston.
10. Remove the "O" rings from piston, piston shaft and inside of nylon bushing in chamber housing.
11. Clean piston, piston shaft, and inside of the chamber thoroughly to remove any old lubricant and foreign matter. Inspect the chamber bore and polish if rough or pitted. If deeply pitted or gouged the chamber should be replaced.

Should it ever be necessary to remove the application spring, place the piston, spring and spring plate assembly on a hydraulic press bed with the spring plate facing up. Block up this assembly between the press bed and the piston to allow space for inserting an open end wrench to hold the head of the release bolt. Place an opensided sleeve on the spring plate and apply sufficient pressure to overcome the spring tension.

CAUTION: Never attempt to remove the release bolt, unless the piston, spring and spring plate assembly is held safely in a hydraulic press.

Using a socket wrench with a ratchet adaptor, inserted through the open-sided sleeve and at the same time holding the head of the release bolt with an open end wrench, rotate the release nut counterclockwise until the release bolt is free. Slowly release the press pressure until the spring tension is completely removed.

To reassemble, place the spring on the spring cover plate and install the piston on top of the spring. Place on press bed in the same manner as outlined for removal with the exception that in this instance, the piston should be up. This will facilitate the positioning of the key washer. Next, install the key washer, making sure it is keyed to the piston. Apply pressure to compress the spring. Thread the release bolt into the release nut until the head of the bolt contacts the key washer. Release pressure and remove the spring assembly.

Assembly

1. Install new "O" rings on piston, piston shaft and in nylon bushing. Coat "O" rings lightly with Lubri-plate prior to installation.
2. Coat cylinder bore, piston edge, piston bore and piston shaft with Lubri-plate.
3. Insert piston shaft in piston bore and install snap ring in groove to retain piston shaft in place.
4. Install piston, piston shaft, spring and spring plate assembly in housing. Care must be exercised to line the piston shaft with nylon bushing so the "O" ring in nylon bushing is not damaged by piston shaft.
5. Install plunger on end of piston shaft with piston shaft screw. Coat piston shaft screw with lok-tite or equivalent to lock screw in place.
6. Install retainer rings in their grooves at open end of chamber housing. Install retainer ring

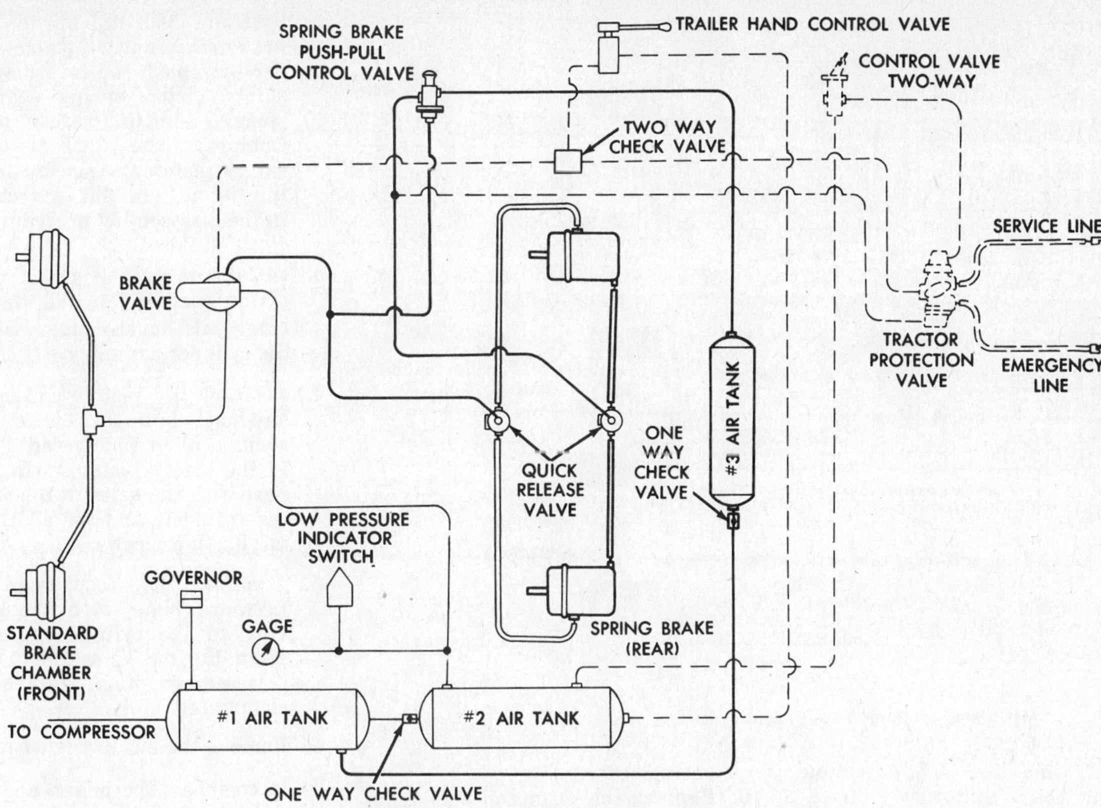

Air spring type parking brake system (© Chrysler Corp.)

spring to keep retainer rings in place back in their grooves. Push on piston shaft plunger so the spring plate is seated in place. Check retainer rings to make sure they are back in their groove and the pilot ring on spring plate fits inside retainer rings.
7. Assemble spring brake assembly to the non-pressure housing of service brake. Be sure the diaphragm and clamp beads on non-pressure housing and spring brake chamber are all concentric.
8. Install clamp ring in proper position aligning marks made previously.
9. Turn release handle until it reaches the positive stop. Do not force past the stop. At this point the two handles should lay flat. Install protective boot.

Installation

1. install unit on vehicle, install nuts and washers.
2. Connect air lines.
3. Connect brake chamber push rod to slack adjuster.
4. Adjust brakes.

Spring Brake Manual Release

MGM Short Stop

If air pressure fails in the Shortstop piston chamber, the power spring applies the brakes, and, unless pressure can be re-established, the service brakes must be released as follows in order to move the truck:

1. Remove the bolt and nut holding the cap and filter to the housing and remove the cap and filter.
2. Using a 9/16″ deep-socket wrench, unscrew the release bolt until it turns freely. The brake shoe pressure is now released. Follow this procedure until all Shortstop units are released.
3. When air pressure has been restored, screw the release bolt in until the lockwasher holds it securely. This MUST be done to regain Shortstop protection.

Maxibrake

Principles of Operation

The Maxibrake chamber (used on the rear axle only) is much like the conventional brake chamber, and differs only in that it contains an independently operated spring loaded piston which, when released due to low air pressure, will set the service brakes.

Normal air pressure applied to the safety chamber and piston keeps the piston spring compressed, while the service brakes continue to operate normally.

A manual control valve located in the cab exhausts the air from the safety chamber, so that the safety piston spring pressure can be used for emergency stops.

The control valve and safety chamber spring and piston are also used to set the service brakes for parking.

Overhaul

Removal and Disassembly

1. Release all the air from the system and then disconnect the air lines from the brake chamber.
2. Disconnect the push rod yoke from the slack adjuster.
3. Remove the mounting nuts and remove the brake chamber.
4. Remove all dirt and grease from the brake chamber using a brush and a cleaning solvent and inspect for broken or damaged parts.
5. Before disassembling the brake chamber, mark both the pressure plate and cylinder assembly with relation to the clamping ring and the air line fittings, so that the unit can be reassembled in the same position.
6. Remove the clevis yoke and the flanged nut from the push rod and install a ¾″ OD x ⅝″ ID flat washer and a ⅝ NF nut on the push rod—tighten the nut until the plate end of the push rod is seated on the safety piston spring support. It is necessary to compress the push rod return

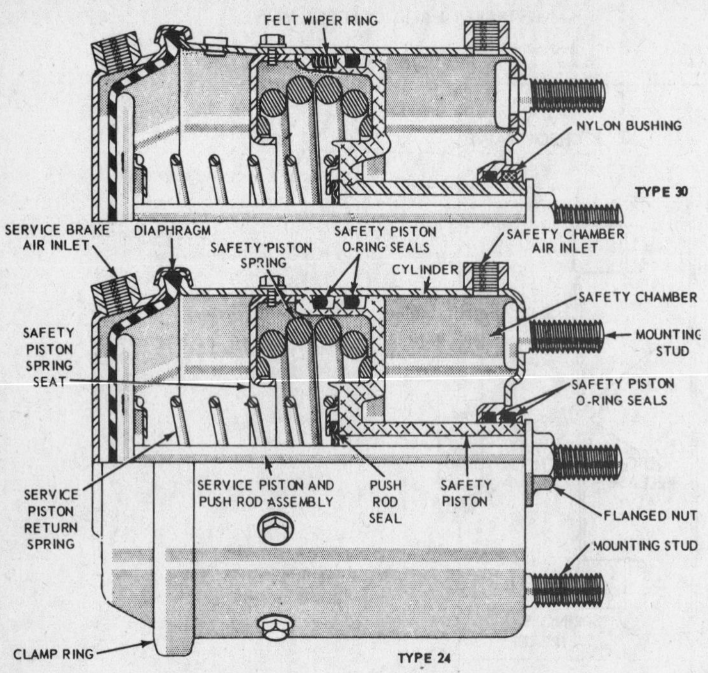

Maxibrake—sectional view (© Ford Motor Co.)

spring and the safety piston spring, so the unit may be disassembled safely without spring pressure on the safety piston spring support, and the diaphragm and pressure plate assembly.

7. Remove the clamp ring, pressure plate, and the service diaphragm from the cylinder assembly.
8. Remove the eight cap screws that secure the safety piston spring support to the cylinder body and remove the complete inner assembly.
9. Set the push rod and piston assembly on a work bench and unthread and remove the nut and washer used to compress the springs. With the spring tension removed, disassemble the push rod, return spring, safety piston, safety piston spring, and the spring seat.
10. Remove the push rod seal from the bore of the piston and remove the "O" ring seals from the piston and the cylinder.

Assembly and Installation

Always be sure that the correct return spring is used in any brake chamber. *Also be sure that the brake chamber on the opposite side of the axle has the same return spring; otherwise uneven braking will result.*

If a new diaphragm is installed in the brake chamber on one side of the axle, a new one should be installed in the corresponding brake chamber on the opposite side also; otherwise uneven braking may result.

1. Coat the safety piston and the inside of the cylinder assembly with a light coating of Lubriplate or other suitable lubricant.
2. Rest the push rod upright on a flat surface and assemble in order—the push rod return spring, safety piston spring seat and spring, and the safety piston. Compress the push rod and safety piston springs by installing the nut and flat washer used in the disassembly procedure.
3. Install the push rod seal in the piston bore and install the "O" ring seals on the piston and in the cylinder assembly.
4. Position the piston and spring assembly into the cylinder assembly, align the threaded holes in the safety piston spring support with the holes in the side of the cylinder, and install the retaining cap screws.
5. Position the diaphragm and pressure plate with the clamp ring to the cylinder assembly, align the marks made prior to disassembly and tighten the clamp ring.
6. Remove the nut and washer used to compress the piston and push rod return spring.
7. Connect the air lines to the brake chamber and build up the air pressure.
8. With the safety chamber under pressure and the safety piston in a retracted position, run the flange nut up snug on the push rod and install the clevis yoke. Maintain a distance of 2 13/16 ± 1/16" between the centerline of the clevis pin holes in the yoke and the mounting flats of the cylinder assembly. Tighten the flange nut against the yoke to lock it in place.
9. Position the brake chamber assembly to the mounting bracket and install the retaining nuts.
10. Connect the push rod yoke to the slack adjuster.

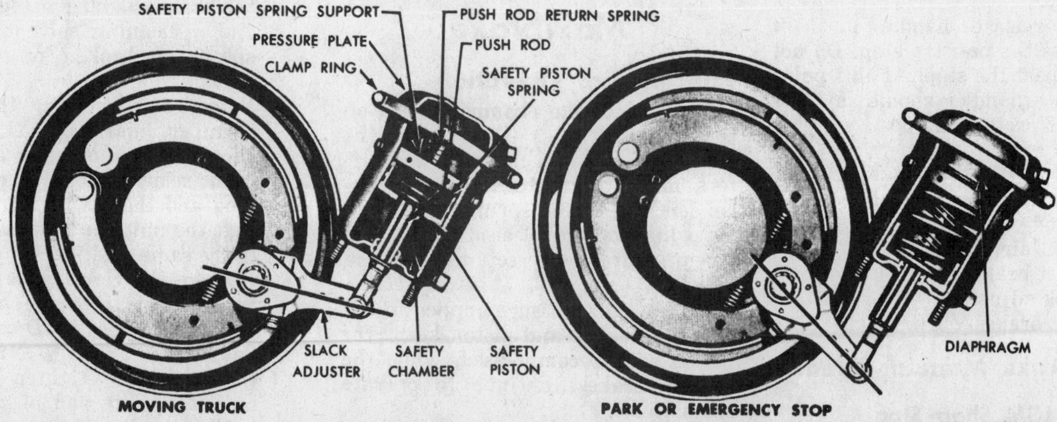

Maxibrake operation (© Ford Motor Co.)

POWER BRAKES TROUBLE DIAGNOSIS

Condition	*Possible Cause*	*Correction*
Vacuum leak (booster in released position)	1. End plate, center plate or control valve body gaskets leak. 2. Distortion of end plate. 3. Misalignment of control valve poppet. 4. Loose vacuum cylinder bolts. 5. Loose control valve body screws. 6. Large control valve poppet spring not centered in spring retainer.	1. Recondition booster unit. 2. Replace end plate. 3. Disassemble, clean and correctly reassemble. 4. Coat vacuum cylinder bolts lightly with a suitable sealing compound and tighten to specified torque. 5. Tighten control valve body screws to specified torque. 6. Disassemble unit and correctly reassemble.
Vacuum leak (booster in applied position)	1. Leak at control valve poppet and seat. 2. Dry or faulty piston leather packing. 3. Faulty control valve diaphragm assembly.	1. Clean and inspect poppet and seat for damage and repair as necessary. 2. Clean and lubricate piston leather or replace. 3. Replace faulty parts.
External hydraulic leaks	1. Gasket ("O" ring) leaking at hydraulic end plate joint. 2. Fluid leaking at copper gasket under hydraulic cylinder end cap.	1. Disassemble clean and replace ("O" ring) gasket and reassemble. 2. Remove end cap and inspect copper gasket and seat install new copper gasket.
Internal hydraulic leak at low pressures	1. Control valve hydraulic piston cup failure. 2. Faulty push rod seal.	1. Recondition control valve unit. 2. Replace push rod seal.
Internal leaks at high pressure	1. Fluid passing copper gasket under hydraulic fitting in control valve. 2. Inspect cups and seals of master cylinder for cuts and scores. 3. Inspect cups of the control valve hydraulic piston.	1. Clean and inspect gasket and fitting, replace if faulty. 2. Hone master cylinder and replace cups and seals. 3. Replace faulty cups.
Hydraulic pressure buildup (without added input)	1. Check hydraulic piston check valve and slot for foreign material under valve.	1. Clean or replace valve and seats as condition indicates.
Failure to release	1. Weak vacuum cylinder piston return spring. 2. Dry vacuum piston leather packing. 3. Swollen rubber cups due to inferior or contaminated brake fluid. 4. Damaged or dented vacuum cylinder shell. 5. Dirty or sticky control valve piston.	1. Replace vacuum cylinder piston return spring. 2. Lubricate vacuum piston leather packing. 3. Flush hydraulic system and recondition or replace all cylinders. 4. Replace vacuum cylinder shell. 5. Recondition control valve assembly.
Failure of booster to operate within specified pressures	1. Rusty, dirty or distorted vacuum cylinder shell. 2. Dry or worn vacuum cylinder leather packing. 3. Swollen rubber cups due to inferior brake fluid. 4. Worn or scored hydraulic cups. 5. Dirt, rust or foreign matter in any component of the system.	1. Clean or replace vacuum cylinder shell. 2. Recondition and lubricate the vacuum booster. 3. Recondition the master cylinder. Replace brake fluid. 4. Recondition the master cylinder. 5. Recondition and lubricate the brake booster assembly.
Loss of fluid	1. Fluid leaking past cup in master cylinder. 2. Brake wheel cylinders leaking. 3. Loose hydraulic hose connectors. 4. Leaking stop light switch.	1. Recondition master cylinder or replace. 2. Recondition or replace wheel cylinders. 3. Inspect and tighten all hydraulic connections. 4. Replace stop light switch.
Presence of brake fluid on hy-power vaccum cylinder	1. Piston cup or push rod seal leaking.	1. Recondition master cylinder.
Pedal kicks back against foot when brakes are applied	1. Vacuum leakage. 2. Dirt under control valve or damaged seat. 3. Weak or broken spring.	1. Inspect and correct vacuum leak. 2. Clean and recondition booster assembly. 3. Replace spring.
Brakes are slow to release Note: First, jack up truck and determine whether or not the wheels are dragging.	1. Incorrect pedal linkage adjustment. 2. Compensating port of master cylinder plugged. 3. Brake shoes sticking. 4. Weak brake shoe return spring. 5. Booster control valve piston sticking. 6. Booster air filter clogged. 7. Control valve diaphragm return spring missing.	1. Adjust and lubricate pedal linkage. 2. Clean master cylinder with compressed air. 3. Free up and lubricate brake shoes. 4. Replace brake shoe return spring. 5. Clean booster control valve piston and lubricate. 6. Clean air filter in mineral spirits. 7. Install new control valve return spring.

	8. Defective check valve in slave cylinder piston.	8. Recondition slave cylinder pistons.
	9. Dirt under atmospheric valve disc.	9. Clean atmospheric valve.
Engine runs unevenly at idle with brakes released	1. Vacuum leakage.	1. Inspect and tighten all vacuum fittings.
	2. Dirt under control valve disc or damaged seat.	2. Clean control valve or replace.
	3. Defective spring.	3. Replace defective spring.
Engine runs evenly and pedal is hard with brakes applied	1. Control valve piston assembly not seating on vacuum disc.	1. Clean or replace control valve piston assembly.
	2. Defective control valve plate and diaphragm.	2. Replace control valve plate and diaphragm.
	3. Defective pressure plate and diaphragm.	3. Replace pressure plate and diaphragm.
Brake pedal is hard at different intervals	1. Defective manifold check valve.	1. Clean or replace manifold check valve.
	2. Slave cylinder piston sticking due to dirt or inferior brake fluid.	2. Clean and recondition slave cylinder.
	3. Brake booster air cleaner clogged.	3. Clean air cleaner in mineral spirits and blow dry with compressed air.

Power Brake Boosters

Brake System Preliminary Checks

Always check the fluid level in the brake master cylinder reservoir(s) before performing the test procedures. If the fluid level is not within ¼″ of the top of the master cylinder reservoirs, add the specified brake fluid.

Push the brake pedal down as far as it will go. If the pedal travels more than halfway between the released position and the floor, adjust the brakes. If the vehicle is equipped with automatic brake adjusters, several sharp brake applications while backing up may be necessary to adjust the brakes.

Road test the vehicle and apply the brakes at a speed of about 20 mph to see if the vehicle stops evenly. If not, the brakes should be adjusted. *Perform the road test only when the brakes will apply and the vehicle can be safely stopped.*

Dual Brake Warning Light System Tests

1. Turn the ignition switch to the ACC or ON position. If the light on the brake warning lamp remains on, the condition may be caused by a shorted or broken switch, grounded switch wires or the differential pressure valve is not centered. Centralize the differential pressure valve. If the warning light remains on, check the switch connector and wire for a grounded condition and repair or replace the wire assembly. If the condition of the wire is good, replace the brake warning lamp switch.
2. Turn the ignition switch to the start position. If the brake warning lamp does not light, check the light and wiring and replace or repair wiring as necessary. When both brake systems are functioning normally, the equal pressure at the pressure differential valve during brake pedal application keeps the valve centered. The brake warning light will be on only when the ignition key is in the start position.
3. If the brake warning lamp does not light when a pressure differential condition exists in the brake system, the warning lamp may be burned out, the warning lamp switch is inoperative or the switch to lamp wiring has an open circuit. Check the bulb and replace it, if required. Check the switch to lamp wires for an open circuit and repair or re place them, if required. If the warning lamp still does not light, replace the switch.

Power Brake Function Test

With the engine stopped, eliminate all vacuum from the system by pumping the brake pedal several times. Then push the pedal down as far as it will go, and note the effort required to hold it in this position. If the pedal gradually moves downward under this pressure, the hydraulic system is leaking and should be checked by a hydraulic pressure test.

With the brake pedal still pushed down, start the engine. If the vacuum system is ooerating properly, the pedal will move downward. If the pedal position does not change, the vacuum system is not operating properly and should be checked by a vacuum test.

Vacuum Booster Check Valve Test

Disconnect the line from the bottom of the vacuum check valve, and connect a vacuum gauge to the valve. Start the engine, run it at idle speed, and check the reading on the vacuum gauge.

The gauge should register 17-19″ with standard transmission and 14-15″ in Drive range if equipped with an automatic transmission. Stop the engine and note the rate of vacuum drop. If the vacuum drops more than one inch in 15 seconds, the check valve is leaking. If the vacuum reading does not reach 18″ or is unsteady, an engine tuneup is needed.

Remove the gauge and reconnect the vacuum line to the check valve.

Vacuum Booster Test—Bendix Piston Type

Disconnect the vacuum line from the booster end plate. Install a tee fitting in the end plate, and connect a vacuum gauge (No. 1) and vacuum line to the fitting. Install a second vacuum gauge (No. 2) in place of the pipe plug in the booster control valve body.

Start the engine, and note the vacuum reading on both gauges. If both gauges do not register manifold vacuum, air is leaking into the vacuum system. If both gauges register manifold vacuum, stop the engine and note the rate of vacuum drop on both gauges. If the drop exceeds one inch in 15 seconds on either gauge, air is leaking into the vacuum system. Tighten all vacuum connections and repeat the test. If leakage still exists, the leak may be localized as follows:

1. Disconnect the vacuum line and gauge No. 1 from the booster.
2. Connect vacuum gauge No. 1 directly to the vacuum line. Start the engine and note the gauge reading. Stop the engine and check the rate of vacuum drop. If gauge No. 1 does not register manifold vacuum, or if the vacuum drop exceeds 1″ in 15 seconds, the leak is in the vacuum line or check valve connections.
3. Reconnect vacuum gauge No. 1 and the vacuum line to the tee fitting. Start the engine, and run it at idle speed for one minute. Depress the brake pedal sufficiently to cause vacuum gauge No. 2 to read from zero to 1 inch of vac uum. Gauge No. 1 should register manifold vacuum of 17-19″ with standard transmission and

14-16" in Drive range if equipped with an automatic transmission. If the drop of vacuum on gauge No. 2 is slow, the air cleaner, or air cleaner line, may be plugged. Inspect and if necessary, clean the air cleaner.

4. Release the brake pedal and observe the action of gauge No. 2. Upon releasing the pedal, the vacuum gauge must register increasing vacuum until manifold vacuum is reached. The rate of increase must be smooth, with no lag or slowness in the return to manifold vacuum. If the gauge readings are not as outlined, the booster is not operating properly and should be removed and overhauled.

Vacuum Booster Test—Diaphragm Type

This procedure can be used to test all diaphragm boosters which are equipped with a pipe thread outlet on the atmosphere portion of the diaphragm chamber.

Remove the pipe plug from the rear half of the booster chamber, and install a vacuum gauge. Start the engine and run it at idle speed. The gauge should register 18-21" of vacuum.

1. With the engine runnig, depress the brake pedal with enough pressure to show a zero reading on the vacuum gauge. Hold the pedal in the applied position for one minute. Any downward movement of the pedal during this time indicates a brake fluid leak. Any kickback (upward movement) of the pedal indicates brake fluid is leaking past the hydraulic piston check valve.
2. With the engine running, push

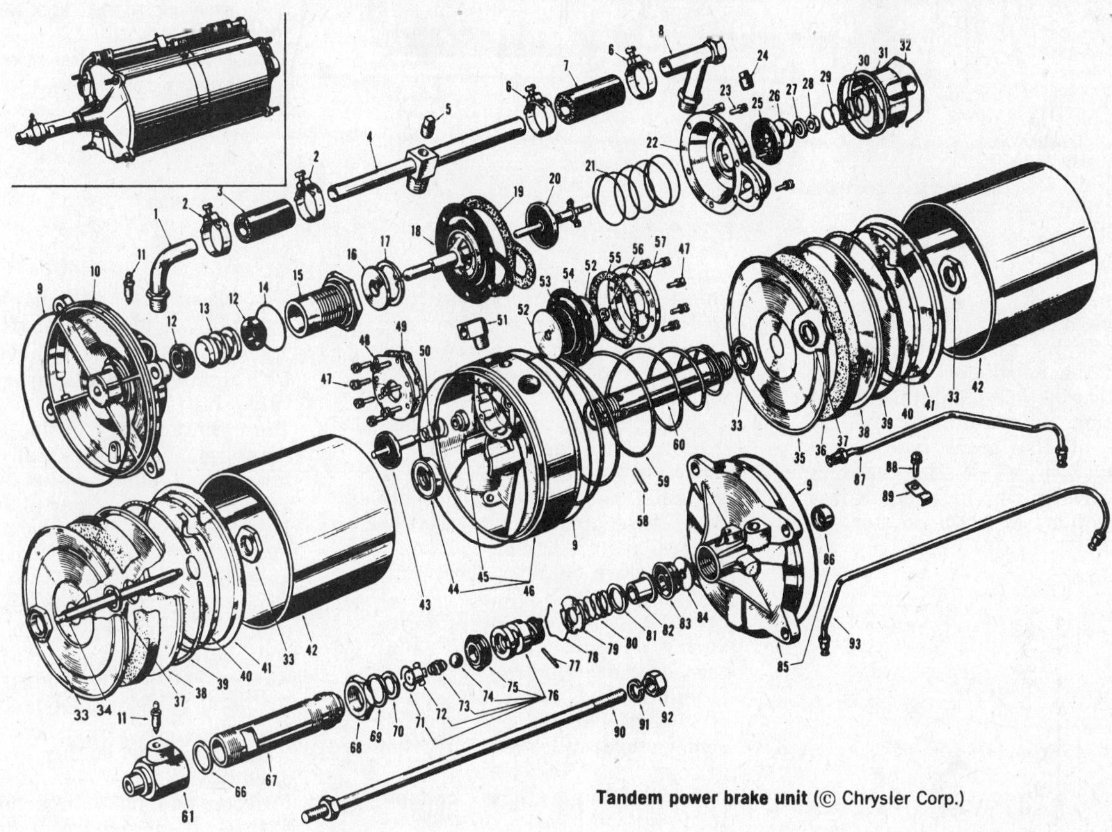

Tandem power brake unit (© Chrysler Corp.)

1 Tube & bushing
2 Clamp—hose
3 Hose—vacuum ¾x2½"
4 Tube # fitting—vacuum
5 Plug—pipe (⅛")
6 Clamp—hose (1")
7 Hose—vacuum 1"x3"
8 Tee—1" hose ¾" pipe, male & female
9 Gasket—center plate & end plate
10 Plate—cylinder end
11 Valve—bleeder
12 Cup—hydraulic valve piston
13 Piston—hydraulic valve
14 Seal—hyd. valve fitting
15 Fitting—hyd. valve piston
16 Washer—stop
17 Ring—retainer
18 Diaphragm & plates—control valve
19 Gasket—poppet (valve body)
20 Shaft & vac. poppet—control valve
21 Spring—poppet valve
22 Body—control valve
23 Screw & lockwasher
24 Plug—(⅜")
25 Seal—poppet valve
26 Valve—poppet
27 Washer—poppet valve
28 Nut—Hex (#6-32)
29 Spring—poppet valve (small)
30 Gasket—A. C. tube & cover
31 Tube & cover—air inlet
32 Snap ring—air inlet tube & cover
33 Nut—piston rod
34 Push rod—piston
35 Plate—piston (outer)
36 Packing—piston
37 Seal—vacuum piston
38 Plate—piston (inner)
39 Wick—piston
40 Ring—piston expander
41 Plate—retainer (piston felt & exp. ring)
42 Shell—vac. cyl.
43 Shaft & seal (fast application valve)
44 Seal—center plate piston rod
45 Seal—Center plate poppet valve
46 Center plate & seals
47 Screw & lockwasher fast application valve
48 Seat—poppet (fast application valve)
49 Gasket—poppet seat
50 Spring—return—valve poppet
51 Elbow—inverted flared tube
52 Plate—diaphragm
53 Gasket—diaphragm plate
54 Diaphragm—F. A. valve
55 Gasket—cover (F. A. valve)
56 Nut—thin hex. check (¼"-28)
57 Cover—fast application valve
58 Pin—retainer (push rod)
59 Spring—return (vac. piston)
60 Piston rod & thrust cup
61 Cap—end—hydraulic cylinder
66 Gasket—end cap
67 Tube—hydraulic cylinder
68 Nut—hyd. cyl. tube
69 Seal—hyd. cyl. tube nut
70 Seal—hyd. cyl.
71 Snap ring—ball retainer
72 Retainer—ball
73 Spring—ball return
74 Ball (hyd. piston check valve)
75 Cup—hyd. piston
76 Piston—hydraulic
77 Pin—retainer, hydraulic piston
78 Snap ring
79 Washer—stop
80 Spring—retainer
81 Sleeve—retainer
82 Retainer—seal
83 Hyd. seal
84 Washer—guide
85 End plate & seal
86 Seal—oil (end plate)
87 Tube—vacuum by-pass
88 Screw & lockwasher—clip attached
89 Clip—tube (¼")
90 Stud—cylinder attaching
91 Lockwasher—cylinder attaching
92 Nut—hex. (½"-20) cylinder attaching
93 Tube—hyd. by-pass

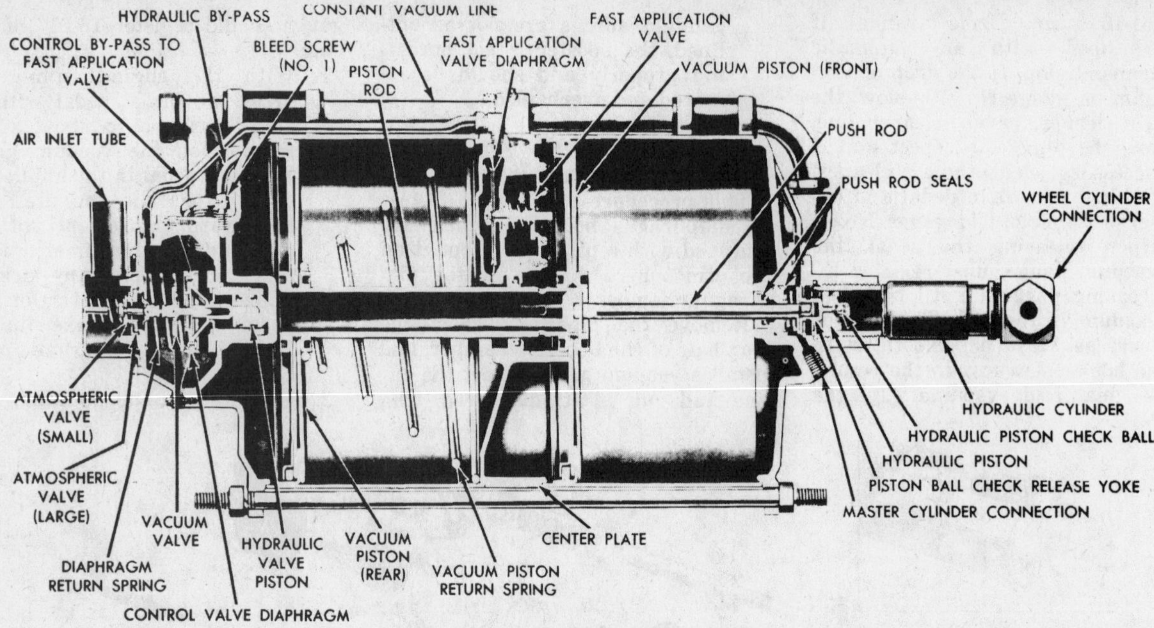

Tandem power brake (sectional view) (© Chrysler Corp.)

down on the brake pedal with sufficient pressure to show a zero reading on the vacuum gauge. Hold the pedal down, and shut the engine off. Maintain pedal position for one minute. A kickback of the pedal indicates a vacuum leak in the vacuum check valve, in the vacuum line connections, or in the booster.

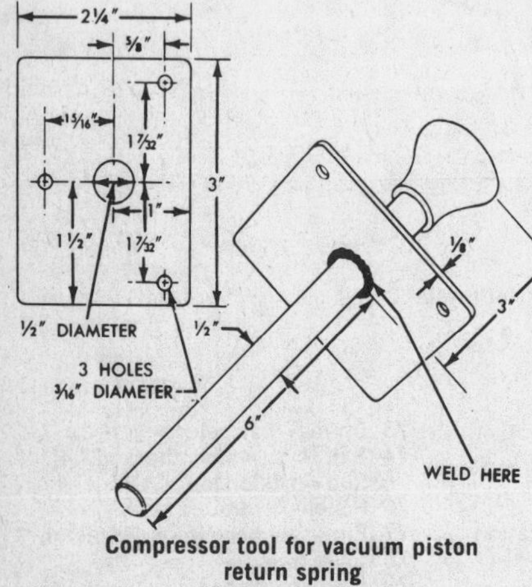

Compressor tool for vacuum piston return spring
(© Chrysler Corp.)

Hydraulic Tandem Brake Unit

Disassembly

1. Disconnect hydraulic and vacuum by-pass tube from valve body.
2. Remove control valve air inlet fitting from control valve body.
3. Remove control valve body and valve parts from end plate.
4. Make a special tool. NOTE: If this to be a regular service this tool is recommended. For one time or emergency, a vise, "C" clamps, and a guide tube 10" long may be used.
5. Insert tool through end plate opening, and force vacuum cylinder piston forward.
6. Attach flange of tool to end plate with three valve body cover screws.
7. Loosen slave cylinder check nut, and remove slave cylinder.
8. Compress push rod pin retaining spring, remove retainer pin, then remove hydraulic piston from push rod.
9. Hold end cap in a vise, and remove hydraulic cylinder from cap.
10. Loosen vacuum hose clamps, then slide both hoses on the vacuum tube toward center plate.
11. Remove hydraulic by-pass tube from rear end plate, then remove return spring compression tool from end plate.
12. Remove the nuts and studs from power cylinder, then disassemble end plates, cylinder shells and center plate assembly.
13. Force center plate and vacuum piston together, and insert a rod through hole in piston rod to hold piston return spring in the compressed position.
14. Place assembly ring over piston, then remove piston assembly, but keep piston parts assembled in assembly ring. After vacuum tubes and tee fittings have been removed from center plate, position plate on a flat surface.
15. Remove fast application valve cover.
16. To disassemble the diaphragm assembly, hold valve shaft with a screw driver, and remove nut.
17. Lift retainer and diaphragm off valve shaft.
18. Turn center plate upside down, then remove valve seat plate screws and plate, gasket, valve and spring from center plate.
19. Position front end plate assembly on a flat surface with flat side down.
20. Remove the "O" ring seal, snap ring and retainer washer, push rod seal spring and flange washer, push rod rubber cup seal, and guide washer from end plate.
21. Drive push rod leather seal out of end plate.
22. Position end plate in a holding fixture, then remove hydraulic valve fitting with a 1-⅞" socket wrench.
23. Push hydraulic piston out of valve fitting, and remove gasket from fittings.

Clean all metal parts in a suitable cleaning fluid. After cleaning, wash all the hydraulic system parts in alcohol.

Examine the bore of the cylinder shells for rust and corrosion and polish with fine steel wool or crocus cloth if necessary.

If the cylinders are badly pitted or scored, install new cylinders.

If felt type wicks are worn, replace them with cotton type wicks.

Use overhaul kit and install ALL parts contained. Do not gamble on ANY old parts that the kit replaces.

Assembly

1. Install nut on piston rod with

flat side of nut upward.

2. Position larger diameter piston plate on piston rod with chamfered side of hole at top. Guide rubber seal ring over threads of piston rod.
3. Place assembly ring on a flat surface, then install leather packing with lip side upward and smaller diameter piston plate with chamfered side of hole downward in the ring.
4. Cut a new piece of wick to the required length, then place it against inner face of leather packing lip.
5. Assemble expander ring against wick with gripper points upward, and hook notched end of spring under the clip near opposite end of spring. Position cut of retainer plate over loop of the spring.
6. Hold piston parts in the assembly ring, assemble them on end of piston rod, then install nut on tip of piston assembly. Tighten nut until it is flush with end of rod. Stake nuts securely at two places.
7. Clamp staked nut firmly in a vise, and tighten nut on opposite side of piston plate solidly against piston plate.
8. Press the fast application valve stem and push rod seals into center plate. The application valve seal must be flush with bottom of hole. The push rod seal should rest against the shoulder of center plate. Position center plate. Then place valve spring on top of seal with the small end at top.
9. Install the bullet-nosed tool at threaded end of valve shaft, and insert valve shaft through seal. Position gasket on center plate.
10. Place valve seat plate, with seat side downward, on gasket, and install screws and lockwashers.
11. Turn center plate over. Place lower diaphragm plate on valve shaft with rounded edge at top, then place diaphragm gasket at top of plate. Position diaphragm on top of gasket so screw holes and the bypass hole index with the identical holes in center plate.
12. Install the other diaphragm plate with rounded edge facing diaphragm.
13. Install valve shaft nut on valve shaft. Use a screw driver to prevent shaft from turning, and tighten nut. Stake nut securely at opposite points.
14. Position cover gasket and cover plate, then install screw and lockwashers.
15. Place piston return spring over piston rod with small end of spring at bottom.
16. Carefully guide piston rod through leather seal in center plate, with piston stop flanges of center plate facing upward. Press center plate down against spring, and insert a rod in piston rod. Thread piston rod nut on piston rod, with flat side of nut upward to limit of threads.
17. If forward piston was disassembled to replace leather piston packing, cotton wicking, or other parts, assemble the piston parts in the ring and turn assembly ring over.
18. Remove larger piston plate and "O" ring seal.
19. With assembly ring still in place, guide the remaining piston parts over end of push rod and against piston nut. Carefully install "O" ring seal over threads of piston rod.
20. Place the larger diameter piston plate on piston rod with chamfered side of hole toward "O" ring seal.
21. Assemble large end of push rod in end of piston rod and install retainer pin. Install piston rod nut on end of piston rod with flat side downward. Tighten nut until it is flush with face of piston rod, then stake nut securely at opposite points.
22. Hold piston rod nut in a vise or with a wrench, and tighten inner nut securely against piston. Care must be exercised when tightening inner nut to prevent expander spring retainer plate from shifting.
23. Remove assembly ring, then remove rod holding return spring compressed. Install a new copper gasket in end cap.
24. The hydraulic cylinder must be assembled with milled flats next to end cap. Tighten hydraulic cylinder solidly in end cap, then thread check nut on hydraulic cylinder up to the limit of the threads.
25. Install check nut seal (if used) in groove of cylinder tube. Install bleeder screw in cap.
26. Press push rod leather seal into hydraulic cylinder bore of front end plate from inner side of plate with lip of seal toward outer end of the plate. Install push rod seal parts.
27. The chamfered side of stop washer is down, lip of cup is up, flat side of washer is next to cup, and small end of spring is down. Place washer against spring. Install snap ring in inner groove of end plate.
28. Install stop washer with flat side in control valve hydraulic fitting. Install stop washer retaining ring.
29. Dip hydraulic piston cups in brake fluid, and assemble them on the hydraulic piston with lips of cups positioned away from each other. Insert piston into the fitting with open end of piston toward stop washer.
30. Install a new gasket on the hydraulic fitting (copper gasket on fitting without the groove, and a rubber seal gasket on fitting with the groove). Install the hydraulic fitting in end plate with a 1-7/8" socket wrench. Tighten fitting equipped with a rubber gasket firmly, and fitting equipped with a copper gasket to 324-330 foot-pounds.
31. Assemble vacuum control parts in control body. Install a new lead washer.
32. Hold slave cylinder end cap in a vise, and thread cylinder into end plate. Install T-fitting and tubes on center plate.
33. Position an end plate gasket on the plate, place cylinder shell on end plate, and coat interior of cylinder with vacuum cylinder oil.
34. Dip cylinder piston on packing in vacuum cylinder oil and allow the excess oil to drain off the wickings.
35. Position a gasket on ledge of center plate, then carefully guide push rod through seal in front end plate. At the same time, align the vacuum tube in end plate with vacuum tube on center plate. Slide hose in place to contact the two vacuum tubes.
36. Position a new gasket at center plate ledge.
37. Coat the interior of cylinder shell with vacuum cylinder oil, then tip cylinder at a 45 degree angle to prevent damage to the piston leather packing.
38. Carefully push the cylinder over piston and onto center plate.
39. Place a new gasket on ledge of end plate, then install end plate on cylinder, aligning end plate vacuum tube and center plate tube. Install cylinder studs and tighten nuts evenly.
40. To assemble the hydraulic piston parts, place large end of spring in retainer cup, then install check ball in piston body behind spring.
41. Dip piston cup in brake fluid, then install it on piston with lip of cup toward check ball.
42. Position the vacuum hoses on tubes, and tighten hose clamps firmly.
43. Connect hydraulic by-pass tube to front and rear end plate.
44. Remove slave cylinder from end plates, then insert and attach return spring compressing tool.
45. Assemble hydraulic piston on push rod.

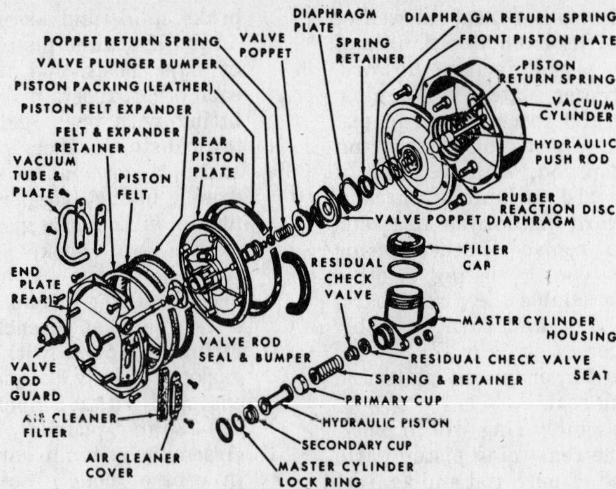

Bendix master vac unit (© Ford Motor Co.)

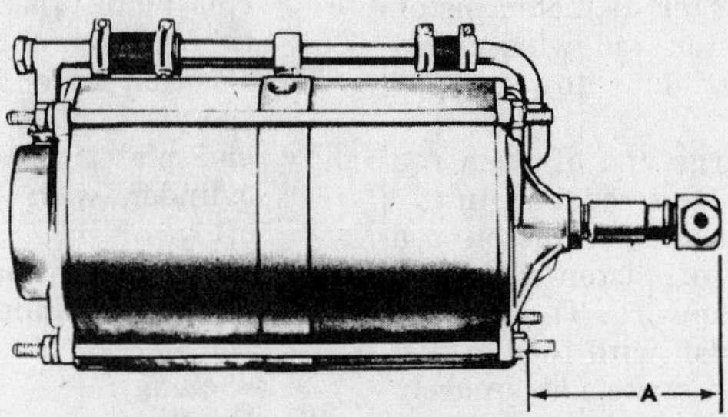

Adjusting hydraulic cylinder length
(© Chrysler Corp.)

46. Make certain lock ring is positioned over the retainer pin. Install hydraulic gasket in the plate. Carefully guide the hydraulic cylinder over piston cup, and thread cylinder into end plate.
47. Adjust cylinder 7¾", measuring between points shown in illustration.
48. Align bleeder screw in end cap with bleeder screw in control valve.
49. Remove spring compressing tool. After cylinder length adjustment is completed, tighten cylinder check nut solidly.
50. Install guide pins, made from 8-32 x 2½" machine screws with the heads cut off, in end plate.
51. Install diaphragm with diaphragm stem inserted into hydraulic control piston hole. Place diaphragm return spring and control valve body on top of diaphragm.
52. Remove guide pins, one at a time, and replace each guide pin with an attaching screw and a new lock washer. Tighten screws progressively and firmly.
53. Install air inlet fitting in control body, then install retainer.
54. Install vacuum by-pass tube.
55. Inspect assembly to see that all bolts, nuts, screws, washers, and plugs are in place, and that all tubes, clamps, and fittings are firmly tightened.

Installation

1. Position assembly on mounting brackets, and install attaching bolts.
2. Tighten bolts firmly.
3. Connect stop light wires and hydraulic lines to stop light switch.
4. Attach vacuum hose to booster.
5. Connect master cylinder hydraulic line to booster control valve.
6. Connect wheel cylinder hydraulic line to booster end cap.
7. Attach air inlet hose to control valve air inlet fitting, then check and tighten connections.
8. Remove lubricating plugs from end and center plates.
9. Add vacuum cylinder oil to level of filler holes, install plugs, then bleed hydraulic system.

Bendix Master Vac

Removal

1. Disconnect clevis at brake pedal to push rod.
2. Remove vacuum hoses from power cylinder.
3. Disconnect hydraulic line from master cylinder.
4. Remove the four attaching nuts and lock washers that hold the unit to the firewall. Remove the power brake unit.

Disassembly

2. Remove four master cylinder to vacuum cylinder attaching nuts and washers.
2. Separate master cylinder from vacuum cylinder, then remove the rubber seal from the outer groove at end of master cylinder.
3. Remove the push rod from the power section. (Do not disturb adjusting screw.)
4. Remove push rod boot and valve operating rod.
5. Scribe alignment marks across the rear shell and vacuum cylinder. Remove all but two of the end plate attaching screws (opposite each other). Hold down on the rear shell while removing the two remaining screws to prevent the piston return spring from expanding.
6. Scribe a mark across the face of the piston, to index the mark on the rear shell, and remove rear shell with vacuum piston and piston return spring.
7. Remove vacuum hose from vacuum piston and from vacuum tube on inside of rear shell. Separate rear shell from vacuum piston.
8. Remove air cleaner and vacuum tube assembly, and air filter from the rear shell.
9. Spring the felt retaining ring enough to disengage ring from grooves in bosses on rear piston plate.
10. Remove piston felt and expander ring from piston assembly.
11. Remove six piston plate attaching screws and separate front piston plate and piston packing from piston plate.
12. Remove valve return spring, floating control valve and diaphragm assembly, valve spring and diaphragm plate. Separate floating control valve spring-retainer and control valve diaphragm from control valve.
13. Remove rubber reaction disc and shim (if present) from front piston plate. NOTE: Do not remove the valve operating rod and valve plunger from the rear piston plate unless it is necessary to replace defective parts. Normally, the next two steps can be omitted.
14. When it is necessary to replace the valve operating rod or valve plunger, remove valve rod seal from groove in piston plate and pull seal over end of rod.
15. Hold piston with valve plunger

side down and inject alcohol into valve plunger through opening around valve rod. This will wet the rubber lock in the plunger. Then drive or pry valve plunger off the valve rod. NOTE: If master cylinder is not to be rebuilt, omit Steps 16-19.

16. Remove snap-ring from groove in base at end of master cylinder.
17. Remove piston assembly, primary cup, retainer spring, and check-valve from master cylinder.
18. Remove filler cap and gasket from master cylinder body.
19. Remove secondary cup from master cylinder piston.

Cleaning Note

After disassembly, cleaning of all metal parts in satisfactory commercial cleaner solvent is recommended. Use only alcohol or Declene on rubber parts or parts containing rubber. After cleaning and drying, metal parts should be rewashed in clean alcohol or Declene before assembly.

Assembly

Steps 1-5 apply to a completely disassembled master cylinder. Otherwise, omit these steps.

1. Coat bore of master cylinder with brake fluid.
2. Dip secondary cup in brake fluid and install on master cylinder piston.
3. Dip other piston parts in brake fluid and assemble the piston. Install piston.
4. Install snap-ring into groove of cylinder.
5. Use new gasket and install filler cap.
6. Assemble valve rod seal on rod and insert valve rod through the piston. Dip valve plunger in alcohol and assemble to ball end of valve rod. Be sure ball end of rod is locked in place in plunger.
7. Assemble floating control valve diaphragm over end of floating control valve. Be sure diaphragm is in recess of floating control valve. Press control valve spring retainer over end of control valve and diaphragm.
8. Clamp valve operating rod in a vise with rear piston plate up. Lay leather piston packing on rear piston plate with lip of leather over edge of piston plate.
9. Install floating control valve return spring over end of valve plunger.
10. Assemble diaphragm plate to diaphragm and assemble floating control valve with diaphragm in recess of rear piston plate.
11. Install floating control valve spring over retainer. Align and assemble front piston plate with rear piston plate. Center the floating control valve spring on front piston plate and center valve plunger stem in hole of piston.
12. Holding front and rear piston plates together, loosely install six piston plate cap screws.
13. Install shim and rubber reaction disc in recess at center of front piston plate. NOTE: A piston assembling ring is handy in assembling the piston.
14. Place the assembling tool over piston packing, turn piston assembly upside down and assemble the expander ring against inside lip of leather packing. Saturate felt with Vacuum Cylinder Oil or shock absorber fluid—type A, then assemble in expander ring. Assemble retainer ring over bosses on rear piston plate. Be sure retainer is anchored in grooves of piston plate.
15. Assemble air cleaner filter over vacuum tube of air cleaner and attach air cleaner shell in position with screws.
16. Slide vacuum hose onto vacuum inlet tube of piston and align hose to lay flat against piston.
17. Wipe a coat of vacuum cylinder oil on bore of cylinder. Remove assembling ring from vacuum piston and coat leather piston packing with vacuum cylinder oil.
18. Install rear shell over end of valve operating rod and attach vacuum hose to tube end on each side of end plate.
19. Center small diameter end of piston return spring in vacuum cylinder. Center large diameter of spring on piston. Check alignment mark on piston with marks on vacuum cylinder and rear shell, compress spring and install two attaching screws at opposite sides to hold rear shell and cylinder together. Now, install balance of screws and tighten evenly.
20. Dip small end of pushrod boot in alcohol and assemble guard over end of valve operating rod and over flange of shell.
21. Insert large end of pushrod through hole in end of vacuum cylinder and guide into hole of front piston plate. NOTE: Before going on with assembly, check the distance from the outer end of the pushrod to the master cylinder mounting surface on the vacuum cylinder. This measurement should be 1.195-1.200".
22. After pushrod adjustment is correct, replace rubber seal in groove on master cylinder body.
23. Assemble master cylinder to the vacuum cylinder at four studs. Replace lock washers and nut and securely tighten.

Bendix Dual Diaphragm Type

This unit features a direct pedal connection to a vacuum unit mounted on the firewall, with the master cylinder directly mounted to booster. diaphragms and is under constant engine vacuum. When brakes are applied, the control valve is opened to allow atmospheric pressure behind both diaphragms. This provides the power boost to the master cylinder.

This vacuum-suspended system provides reserve against fade. Pedal linkages are eliminated, no additional vacuum storage tanks are needed.

NOTE—do not attempt to disassemble the booster. It is serviced only by the dealer.

Midland Ross Diaphragm Type

The self-contained booster assembly is mounted on the engine side of the firewall. It is connected directly to the brake pedal. This booster is not equipped with a separate vacuum tank.

The master cylinder is attached to the forward side of the booster. The balance of the hydraulic brake sys-

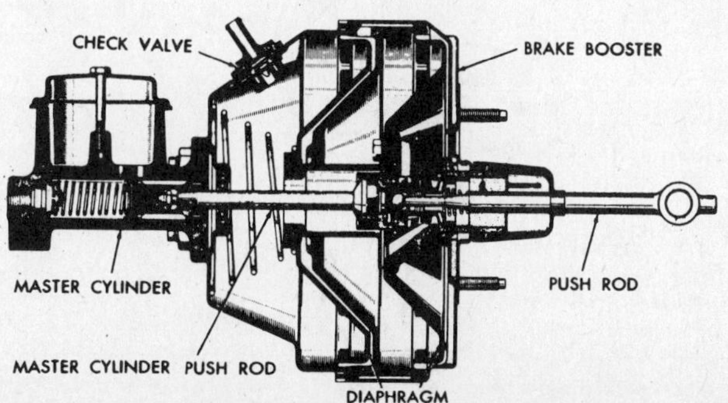

Cutaway view of brake booster and master cylinder
(© Chrysler Corp.)

tem is identical to other standard service brakes.

Booster Disassembly

1. Separate master cylinder from booster body.
2. Remove air filter cover and hub and the filter from the booster body.
3. Remove the vacuum manifold mounting bolt, manifold, gaskets and vacuum check valve from the booster body.
4. Disconnect the valve operating rod from the lever by removing its retaining clip, washers, and pivot pin.
5. Disconnect the lever from the booster end plate brackets by removing its retaining clip, washers, and pivot pin.
6. Remove two brackets from the end plate.
7. Remove the rubber boot from the valve operating rod.
8. To remove the bellows, control valve, and diaphragm assemblies, remove large C-ring that holds the rear seal adapter assembly to the booster end plate.
9. Scribe matching lines on the booster body and the end plate. Then remove the ten retaining screws. Tap the outside of the plate with a soft hammer and separate the plate from the booster body.
10. Push the bellows assembly into the vacuum chamber and remove the bellows, control valve, and diaphragm as an assembly from the booster body.
11. Remove the outer O-ring from the control valve hub.
12. To disassemble the bellows, pushrod, and control valve assemblies, remove the large bellows retaining ring, bellows, bellows retainer, and support ring from the diaphragm and valve assembly.
13. Remove the retainer and support ring from the bellows.
14. Remove pushrod assembly, the reaction lever and ring assembly, and the rubber reaction ring from the control valve hub.
15. Remove the reaction cone and cushion ring from the pushrod assembly. Then disassemble the reaction levers from the ring.
16. Remove the two plastic plunger guides from the control valve plunger. Then remove the retainer that holds the reaction load ring and atmospheric valve on the control valve hub.
17. Slide the reaction load ring and atmospheric valve from the control valve hub.
18. Separate the control valve hub and the plunger assembly from the diaphragm by sliding the plunger and rear seal adapter from the rear of the hub. Then remove the hub outer O-ring from the front side of the diaphragm.
19. To disassemble the control valve plunger, remove the hub rear seal adapter from the valve plunger assembly, and remove the seal from the adapter.
20. Remove the O-rings, the seal, and the fiber gaskets from the

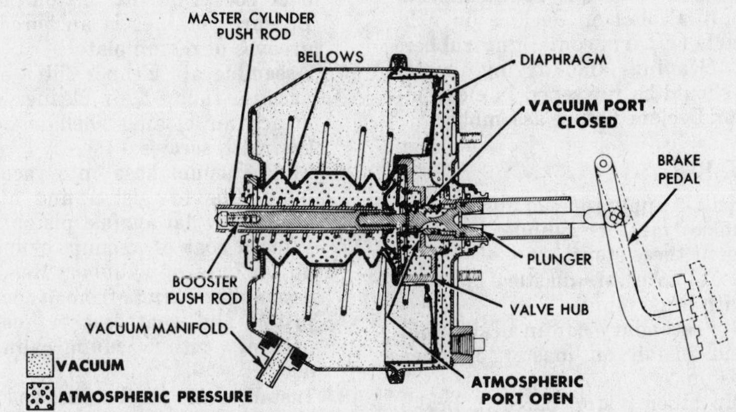

Midland Diaphragm-Type Booster in Applied Position

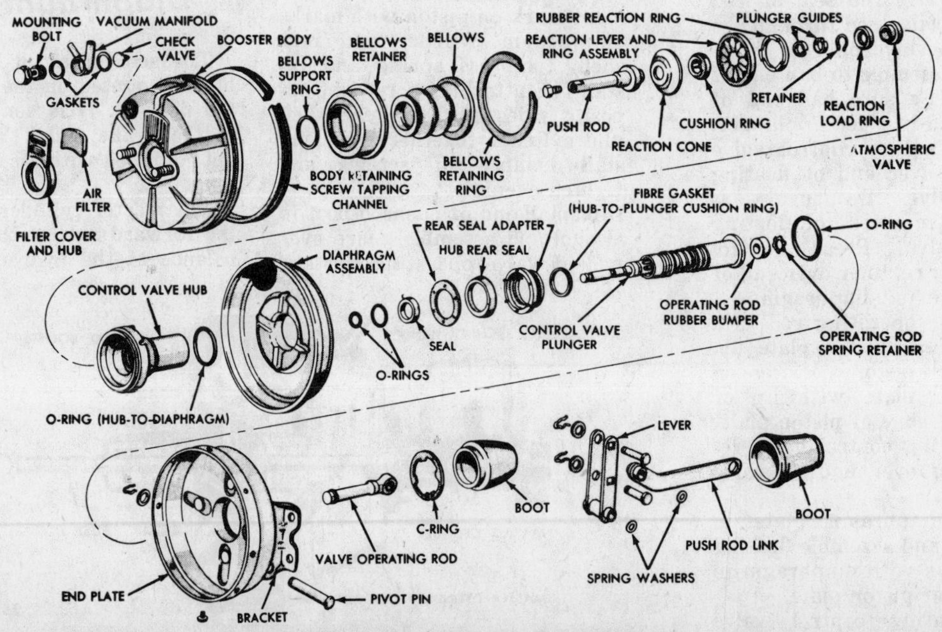

Disassembled view of booster (© Ford Motor Co.)

plunger.

21. If the plunger assembly needs to be replaced, hold the plunger and pull out the valve operating rod with pliers. Do not separate the operating rod and plunger unless the plunger is to be replaced.

Assembly

1. If valve operating rod was removed for replacement of plunger, install a new rubber bumper and spring retainer on the rod before installing it on the replacement plunger. Then push the rod firmly until it bottoms in the plunger.
2. Install fiber gaskets, plunger seal, and the two O-rings on the plunger assembly.
3. Install the valve hub rear seal in the adapter assembly with the sealing lip toward the rear. Then slide the adapter assembly onto the plunger with the small diameter end of the hub toward the rear.
4. To assemble the control valve, pushrod, and bellows assemblies, install the hub outer O-ring. Then install the plunger with the seal adapter and the hub on the diaphragm. To do this, hol the hub on the front side of the diaphragm and insert the plunger assembly in the hub from the rear side of the diaphragm.
5. Install atmospheric valve and then the reaction load ring onto the plunger and hub. Compress the valve spring, and install the load ring retainer into the groove of the plunger.
6. Install two plastic plunger guides into their grooves on the plunger.
7. Install rubber reaction ring into the valve hub so that the ring locating knob indexes in the notch in the hub, with the ring tips toward the front.
8. Assemble the reaction lever and ring assembly, and install the assembly into the valve hub.
9. Install the reaction cone and cushion ring on the pushrod. Then install the pushrod assembly on the valve hub so that the plunger indexes in the rod.
10. Assemble the bellows, retainer, and support ring. The ring should be positioned on the middle fold of the bellows.
11. Position the bellows assembly on the diaphragm, and secure it with the retaining ring. Make sure the retaining ring is fully seated.
12. Install the bellows, control valve, and diaphragm assemblies with a screwdriver, moving the booster body retaining screw tapping channel just enough to provide a new surface for the self-tapping attaching screws.
13. Install the diaphragm, the control valve components, and the bellows as an assembly into the booster body. (Be sure the lip of the diaphragm is evenly positioned on the retaining radius of the booster body.) Pull the front lip of the bellows through the booster body, and position it around the outer groove of the body.
14. Install O-ring in the front side of the end plate, and locate the plate on the booster body. Align the scribed lines, compress the two assemblies together with a clamp. Then install all ten self-tapping attaching screws.
15. Install the large C-ring onto the rear seal adapter at the rear side of the end plate.

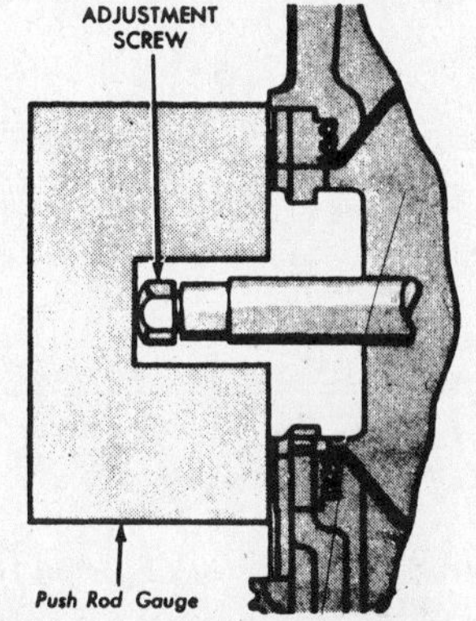

Checking pushrod screw with gauge
(© Ford Motor Co.)

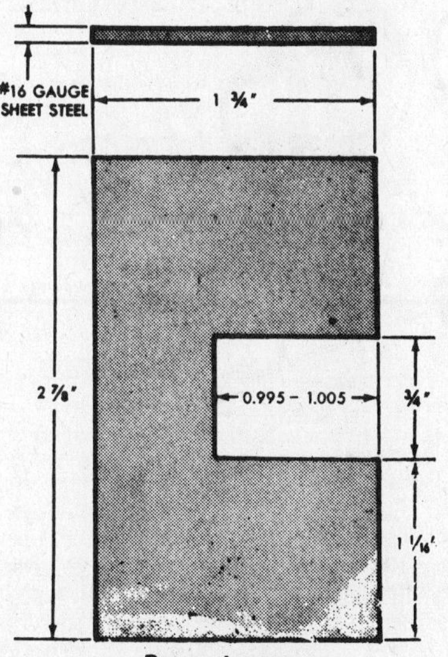

Pusnrod gauge
(© Ford Motor Co.)

Pushrod Adjustment

The pushrod has an adjusting screw to maintain the correct relationship between the control valve plunger and the master cylinder piston after the booster is completely assembled. If this screw is not properly adjusted, the brakes may drag.

To check adjustment of the screw, make a gauge to the dimensions shown. Place this gauge against the master cylinder mounting surface of the booster body. The pushrod screw should be adjusted so that the end of the screw just touches the inner edge of the slot in the gauge.

Booster Installation

1. Install rubber boot on the valve operating rod.
2. Position the two mounting brackets on the end plate, and install retaining nuts.
3. Connect the lever assembly to the lower end of the mounting brackets with its pivot pin. Then install the spring washer and retaining clip.
4. Connect the valve operating rod to the upper end of the lever with its pivot pin, washer, and retaining clip.
5. Install the vacuum check valve, the vacuum manifold, the two gaskets, and the mounting bolt. Torque the mounting bolt to 8-10 ft. lbs.

Midland Slave Cylinder Type

The Midland Slave cylinder is a remote type, without mechanical operation, utilizing vacuum to boost the hydraulic pressure between master and wheel cylinder.

Booster and Slave Cylinder Removal

1. Disconnect master cylinder and wheel cylinder hydraulic lines from unit.
2. Disconnect vacuum hose from check valve.
3. Remove mounting bracket attaching screws and remove from vehicle.

Booster and Slave Cylinder Disassembly

1. Scribe match marks on both sections of chamber for proper reassembly alignment.
2. Punch mark the flanges of control valve housing and slave cylinder housing. Mark opposite each other for proper reassembly position.
3. Remove slave cylinder and cap, with copper gasket, from end of slave cylinder.
4. Remove slave cylinder spring and retainer.
5. Remove by-pass tube.
6. Separate halves of vacuum chamber by removing clamp.
7. Remove control valve from slave

1 Tube
2 Clamp
3 Nut
4 Diaphragm and pressure plate
5 Push rod
6 Diaphragm return spring
7 Seat retainer snap ring
8 Seal retainer washer
9 Block vee seal
10 Bushing guide
11 Lockwasher
12 O-ring
13 Front chamber
14 O-ring air seal
15 Snap ring
16 Check valve
17 Spring
18 Slave cylinder piston
19 Gasket
20 Control valve piston
21 Control valve diaphragm
22 Control valve plate
23 Tinnerman nut
24 Control diaphragm spring
25 Control valve disc
26 Control valve spring
27 Capscrew
28 Screen
29 Felt filter
30 Screen
31 Snap ring
32 O-ring
33 Control valve housing
34 Valve seat
35 Control valve piston cup
36 Slave cylinder
37 Slave piston cup
38 Slave cylinder spring
39 Slave cylinder end cap
40 Copper gasket
41 Spring retainer
42 Bleeder screw
43 Vacuum valve cap
44 Gasket
45 Spring
46 Disc
47 Valve body
48 Push rod nut
49 Clamp screw
50 Rear chamber
51 Grommet

Midland booster unit and slave unit (© Jeep Corp.)

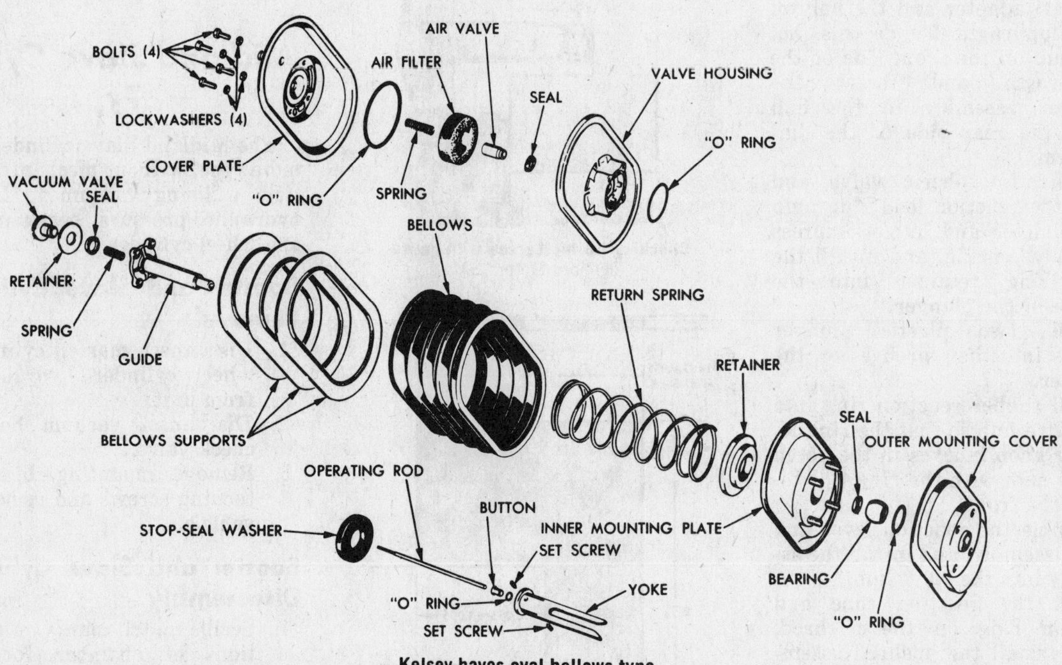

Kelsey-hayes oval bellows type

chamber and remove control valve piston.

8. Remove snap-ring and disassemble control valve by removing screen, felt filter, screen, O-ring, valve disc and spring.
9. Remove control diaphragm spring and control valve piston from slave cylinder body.
10. Disconnect slave cylinder from front chamber be unscrewing pushrod bushing.
11. Push slave cylinder piston and slave piston cup out of slave cylinder. Thoroughly clean and inspect all parts. Any valve leakage, diaphragm leakage, piston cup damage, or bore roughness can prevent proper operation. Minor metal roughness may be cleaned with crocus cloth.
12. Assemble by reversing above procedures.
13. Reinstall in vehicle and connect hydraulic and vacuum lines.

Kelsey Hayes Bellows Type

Removal

1. Use a pedal depressor. Depress the pedal to prevent trigger arm from extending beyond the bracket limits. If the pedal linkage is permitted to extend

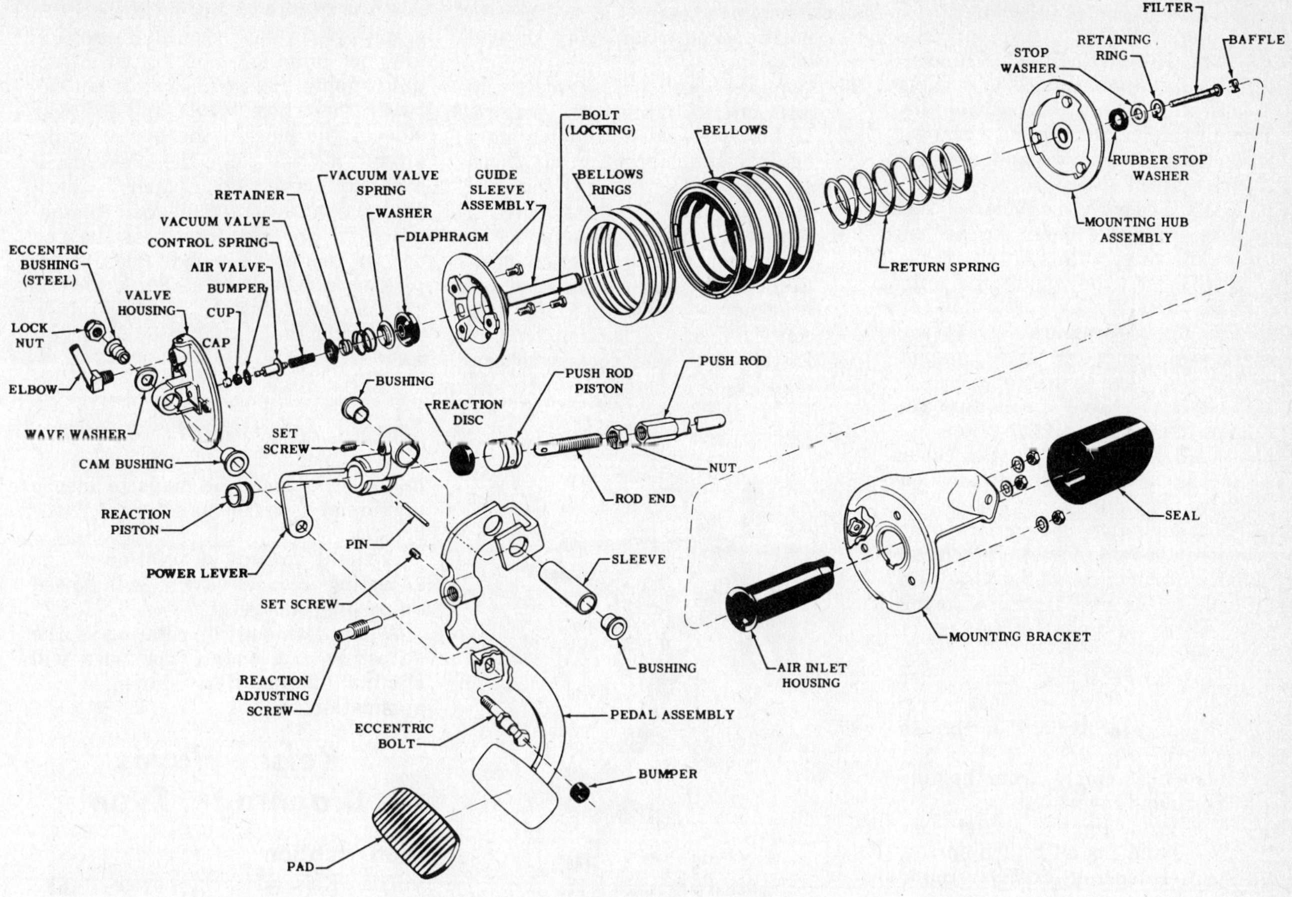

Kelsey-hayes round bellows type (© G.M. Corp.)

through the hole in the firewall, the trigger arm may be damaged.
2. Disconnect the vacuum hose at power vent.
3. Remove master cylinder power unit and bracket assembly, nuts and lock washers.
4. Withdraw the unit from the firewall. Don't lose the nylon bushing at the pedal linkage crosspin.

Disassembly

1. Remove mounting plate to unit attaching nuts.
2. Slide plate off and away from unit.
3. Remove rubber stop seal washer.
4. With an Allen wrench, back out two set screws enough to permit removal of yoke.
5. Slide yoke from end of guide and away from unit.
6. Remove rubber stop seal washer.
7. Lift valve operating rod out of unit; remove, and discard valve operating rod button-seal.
8. Remove nuts that attach outer mounting plate.
9. Gently pry and lift the plate straight up and away from the unit.
10. Compress bellows by hand to expose the guide bearing. Slide bearing off end of guide.
11. Remove and discard bearing seal from outside bearing.
12. Peel outer lip of bellows from around inner mounting plate.
13. Remove plate and lift out return spring and return spring retainer.
14. Remove bolts and lock washers that attach valve cover to valve. Lift off cover.
15. Remove and discard O-ring from valve cover.
16. Remove air valve spring from center of valve.
17. Remove air filter and pull the air valve out of the housing using a small bent wire (paper clip).
18. Place valve housing, end down, on bench. Remove bellows from valve by peeling back outer lip of bellows.
19. Lift bellows up, away from the valve.
20. Remove guide to valve body bolts and lift off guide to expose vacuum valve, valve spring and seals.
21. Remove seals, then lift out vacuum valve and retainer.
22. Remove valve housing to guide seal.
23. Insert valve housing and remove air valve seal from its groove in the valve body.

Assembly

Lubricate all seals and O-rings with silicone grease before installation.

1. Insert new air valve seal into bore of valve housing (with lips of seal facing out).
2. Position new vacuum valve in retainer.
3. Invert valve housing and install vacuum valve and retainer in housing.
4. Press down firmly on retainer to snap it in place.
5. Position new valve housing-to-guide seal in groove provided.
6. Install new vacuum valve seal in bore guide, (lip of seal toward bottom of bore).
7. Install vacuum valve spring in center of valve.
8. Position guide over vacuum valve, lining up bolt in guide with bolt holes in valve body.
9. Lower guide down against valve body. Be certain that the tapered portion of valve enters seal evenly.
10. Press down on guide to seal and install bolts and lock washers. Tighten bolts evenly.
11. If new bellows is being installed,

position supports in bellows.

12. Using holding fixture (made from 3" length of 4" diameter pipe to support guide and valve assembly in upright position, install the bellows. Be sure arrows on edge of bellows and housing are aligned.
13. With assembly in holding fixture, wipe the outer surface of the air valve with silicone grease and insert the small end into bore of housing.
14. Use finger pressure to test for free movement of valve against vacuum valve spring.
15. Install air valve spring into recess in air valve and air filter.
16. Install new valve housing cover O-ring on shoulder provided on valve body hub.
17. Position valve body cover over valve housing, with notch in edge of cover matching arrow on bellows. Be sure air valve spring rests on dimple in center of cover.
18. Press cover down evenly over valve housing to seat over O-ring, install bolts, then tighten securely.
19. Remove assembly from holding fixture and invert unit.
20. Wipe guide lightly with silicone grease and install return spring.
21. Position spring evenly around hub of valve housing and guide.
22. Place spring retainer and inner mounting plate over spring (be sure the arrow marks on the plate are in line with the arrow on the edge of the bellows).
23. Compress return spring and fold bellows lip over edge of plate.
24. Install new guide bearing seal in groove inside bearing bore.
25. Seat the seal snugly in the bearing.
26. Lubricate inside of bearing with silicone grease and slide it over guide, while compressing the bellows. Bearing to be installed with lip of seal facing out.
27. Push bearing down over guide and into pocket of plate.
28. Release bellows and the bearing will ride up guide with plate into position.
29. Install bearing to mounting plate O-ring and lower outer mounting plate down on assembly.
30. Install nuts and draw down finger tight.
31. Slide new valve operating rod seal ring over nylon bumper on end of rod and into groove.
32. Install rod in center of guide.
33. Press on end of rod to test for free operation or movement of air and vacuum vanes. A two-step movement should be felt when rod is depressed and released fully.
34. Place new stop seal washer in position and install yoke on end of guide.
35. Compress bellows slightly and alternately tighten set screws. Hub of yoke must be down snug against shoulder of guide, with set screws aligned with tapered holes in guide.
36. Tighten mounting plate nuts.
37. Place mounting bracket in position, with long centerline of bracket at right angle to long centerline of unit section.
38. Install nuts and lock washers, then tighten securely.

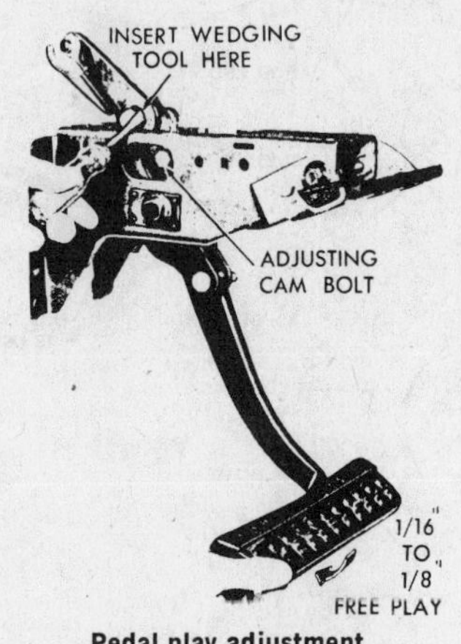

Pedal play adjustment
(© Ford Motor Co.)

Pedal Free-Play

A pedal free-play check should be made with no vacuum in the system. Apply the brakes several times (engine not running) to exhaust the vacuum supply. Insert a screwdriver between the trigger pivot and the rear side of the hole in the power brake lever. This will force the brake pedal and the power lever apart. Check free-play with screwdriver in this position by pressing lightly at the pad end of the brake pedal. Pedal free-play should be 1/16"-1/8". If play is not correct, adjust by lengthening or shortening the master cylinder push-rod.

Trigger Adjustment

After pedal free-play is adjusted, final check should be made to insure maximum performance of the booster.

A slight amount of rotation of the adjusting cam clockwise will speed up a slow pedal return.

A slight amount of rotation of the adjusting cam counterclockwise will eliminate a time delay during a fast application.

Kelsey-Hayes Diaphragm Type

Identification

The Kelsey-Hayes power brake unit can be identified by the twistlock method of locking the housing and cover together, plus the white-colored vacuum check valve assembly.

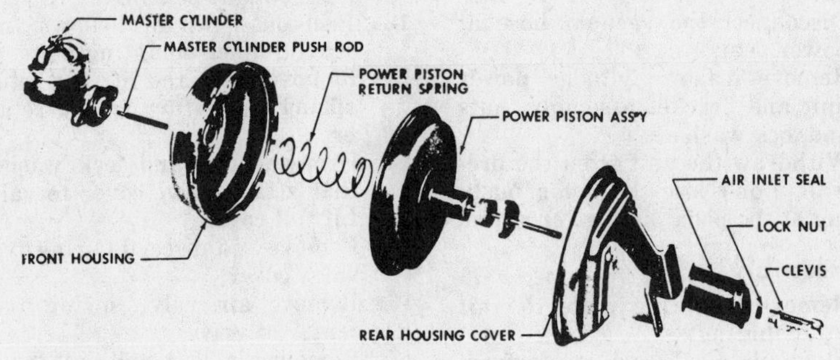

Power brake unit (© G.M. Corp.)

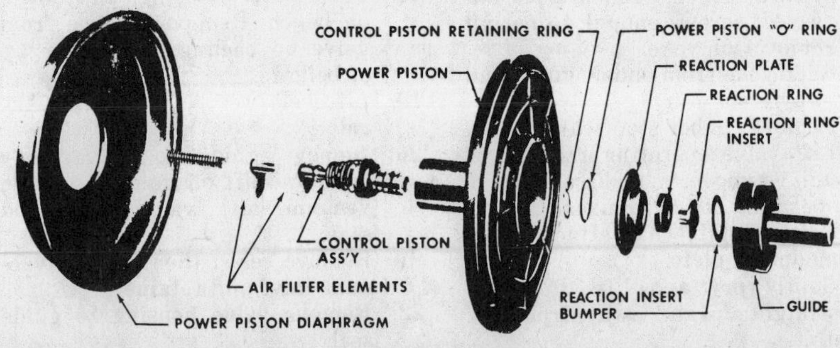

Power piston assembly (© G.M. Corp.)

Removal

1. With engine off, apply brakes several times to equalize internal brake pressure.
2. Disconnect hydraulic line from master cylinder.
3. Disconnect vacuum hose from power brake check valve.
4. Disconnect power brake from brake pedal (under instrument panel).
5. Disconnect power brake unit from dash panel.
6. Remove power brake and master cylinder assembly from the vehicle.

Disassembly

1. Separate master cylinder from power brake unit.
2. Remove master cylinder pushrod and air cleaner plate.
3. Mount the power unit in a vise aith the master cylinder attaching-studs up.
4. Scribe an index line across the housing and cover for reassembly reference.
5. Pry out the housing lock. Do not damage the lock, as it must be used at assembly.
6. Remove check valve from cover by prying out of rubber grommet.
7. Place parking brake flange holding tool over the master cylinder mounting studs.
8. Rotate the tool and cover in a counterclockwise direction. Then, separate the cover from the housing. This will expose the power piston return spring and diaphragm.
9. Lift out the power piston return spring. Remove the brake unit from the vise.
10. Remove power piston by slowly lifting the piston straight up.
11. Remove air cleaner, guide seal and seal retainer from the cover.
12. Remove the block seal from the center hole of the housing, using a blunt drift. (Don't scratch the bore of the housing, it could cause a vacuum leak.)

Power Piston Disassembly

1. Remove power piston diaphragm from the power piston. Keep it clean.
2. Remove screws that attach the plastic guide to the power piston. Remove guide and place to one side.
3. Remove the power piston square seal ring, reaction ring insert, reaction ring and reaction plate.
4. Depress operating rod slightly, then remove the Truarc snap-ring.
5. Remove control piston by pulling the operating rod.
6. Remove the O-ring seal from the end of the control piston.
7. Remove the filter elements and dust felt from the control piston rod.

Cleaning and Inspection

Thoroughly wash all metal parts in a suitable solvent and dry with compressed air. The power diaphragm, plastic power piston and guide should be washed in a mild soap and water solution. Blow dust and all cleaning material out of internal passages. All rubber parts should be replaced, regardless of condition. Install new air filters at assembly. Inspect all parts for scoring, pits, dents or nicks. Small imperfections can be smoothed out with crocus cloth. Replace all badly damaged parts.

Assembly

When assembling, be sure that all rubber parts, except the diaphragm and the reaction ring are lubricated with silicone grease.

1. Install control piston O-ring onto the piston.
2. Lubricate and install the control piston into the power piston. Install the Truarc snap-ring into its groove. Wipe all lubricant off the end of the control piston.
3. Install air filter elements and felt seal over the pushrod and down past the retaining shoulder on the rod. Install the power piston square seal ring into its groove.
4. Install the reaction plate in the power piston. Align the three holes with those in the power piston.
5. Install the rubber reaction ring in the reaction plate. Do not lubricate this ring.
6. Lubricate outer diameter of the reacton insert and install in the reaction ring.
7. Install reaction insert bumper into the guide.
8. Place guide on the power piston, align the holes with the aligning points on the power piston. Install retaining screws and torque to 80-100 in. lbs.
9. Install diaphragm on power piston; be sure that the diaphragm is correctly seated in the power piston groove.
10. With the housing blocked to prevent damage, install the block seal in the housing.
11. Install a new cover seal on the retainer and lubricate thoroughly, inside and out, with silicone grease, then install in the cover bore. Install new air filter.
12. Lubricate check valve grommet and install the vacuum check valve.
13. Mount the power unit in a vise, with master cylinder attaching studs up.
14. Apply a light coating of silicone grease to the bead, *outer edge only*, of the power piston diaphragm.
15. Install the power piston assembly in the housing with the operating rod down.
16. Install the power piston return spring into the flange of the guide.
17. Place the cover over the return spring and press down on the cover. At the same time, pilot the guide through the seal.
18. Rotate the cover to lock it to the housing. Be sure the scribe lines are in correct index and that the diaphragm is not pinched during assembly.
19. Install the housing lock on one of the long tangs of the housing.
20. Remove the power unit from the vise.
21. Install the master cylinder pushrod and air cleaner plate, then install the master cylinder on the studs. Install attaching nuts and washers. Torque to 200 in. lbs.

Installation

1. Install firewall to power brake seal.
2. Install power brake unit onto firewall and torque the attaching nuts to 200 in. lbs.
3. Install pushrod to brake pedal attaching bolt. Torque to 30 ft. lbs.
4. Install vacuum hose onto the power brake unit.
5. Attach the hydraulic tube and fill the master cylinder. Bleed hydraulic system.
6. Adjust stop-light switch if necessary.

AIR BRAKES TROUBLE DIAGNOSIS

Condition	Possible Cause	Correction
Insufficient brakes	1. Brakes need adjusting. 2. Low air pressure (below 80 pounds). 3. Brake valve delivery pressure below normal.	1. Adjust brakes. 2. Inspect air compressor and inspect all fittings and lines for leaks. 3. Inspect air compressor and repair or replace.
Brakes apply too slowly	1. Brakes need adjusting or lubricating. 2. Low air pressure (below 80 pounds). 3. Brake valve delivery pressure below normal. 4. Excessive leakage with brakes applied. 5. Restricted tubing or hose.	1. Adjust brakes and lubricate brake anchors and brake support platforms. 2. Inspect compressor and air lines, repair as necessary. 3. Inspect pressure and air lines, repair as necessary. 4. Inspect all lines and fittings and repair as necessary. 5. Clean or replace tubing or hose.
Brakes no not apply	1. No air pressure in brake system. 2. Restricted or broken tubing or hose. 3. Defective brake valve.	1. Inspect air compressor and drive belt. 2. Clean out air system or replace broken hose. 3. Replace brake valve.
Brakes do not release	1. Brake shoes binding. 2. Brake valve not in fully released position. 3. Defective brake valve. 4. Restriction in air lines or hose.	1. Clean and lubricate all brake shoe anchors. 2. Align and adjust valve. 3. Replace brake valve. 4. Clean out all air lines or hoses.
Air pressure will not raise to normal	1. Defective air gauge (registering incorrectly.) 2. Excessive leakage. 3. Air reservoir drain cock open. 4. Governor out of adjustment. 5. No clearance at compressor. 6. Slipping compressor drive belt. 7. Defective or worn compressor.	1. Replace the air gauge. 2. Inspect all joints with soapy water and correct as necessary. 3. Close reservoir drain cock. 4. Inspect and adjust governor. 5. Check and adjust compressor unloading valves. 6. Adjust compressor drive belt. 7. Replace air compressor.
Air pressure raises slowly to normal	1. Excessive leakage. 2. Clogged compressor air filter. 3. No clearance at compressor unloading valves. 4. Compressor discharge valves caking. 5. Slipping compressor drive belt. 6. Worn compressor. 7. Excessive carbon in compressor cylinder head or discharge line.	1. Inspect all lines and fittings, then repair as necessary. 2. Clean and air dry the compressor air filter. 3. Clean, reseat and adjust the compressor valves. 4. Clean the carbon and reseat the valves. 5. Tighten or replace the compressor drive belt. 6. Replace the air compressor. 7. Clean the carbon and reseat the valves.
Air pressure rises above normal	1. Defective air gauge (registering incorrectly). 2. Governor out of adjustment. 3. Defective governor. 4. Restriction in the line between governor and the compressor. 5. Too much clearance at compressor unloader valves. 6. Excessive carbon in compressor cylinder head. 7. Compressor unloader valves stuck closed.	1. Replace the air gauge. 2. Clean and adjust governor. 3. Replace governor. 4. Clean all air lines and recheck fittings for leaks. 5. Adjust unloader valves. 6. Clean the carbon and reseat the valves. 7. Clean and seat the valves.
Air pressure drops quickly with the engine stopped and brakes released	1. Leaking brake valve. 2. Leaking air brake line or hose. 3. Compressor discharge valves leaking. 4. Governor leaking. 5. Excessive leakage in any part of the air brake system.	1. Clean, reseat or replace the brake valve. 2. Test all air brake joints with soap suds and repair as necessary. 3. Reseat or replace the discharge valve. 4. Reseat or replace the governor. 5. Test the air brake joints with soap suds and repair as necessary.
Air pressure drops quickly with engine stopped and brakes fully applied	1. Brake chamber diaphragm leaking. 2. Brake valve leaking. 3. Leakage elsewhere in the system.	1. Recondition or replace the brake booster. 2. Rebuild or replace the brake valve. 3. Repair as necessary.
Compressor knock	1. Drive pulley loose. 2. Back lash in drive gears or drive coupling. 3. Bearings worn or burned out. 4. Excessive carbon in compressor cylinder head.	1. Tighten pulley nut, or install a new pulley if inner diameter of the hub is worn. 2. If drive gears or coupling show back lash replace as necessary. 3. Replace compressor. 4. Clean carbon from cylinder head.

Safety valve blows off	1. Safety valve out of adjustment.	1. Adjust safety valve. Turn adjusting screw clockwise to raise blow-off pressure and counterclockwise to lower blow-off pressure. Adjust blow-off pressure to 150 pounds.
	2. Pressure in air system above normal.	2. Refer to "Air Pressure Rises Above Normal."
	3. Governor out of adjustment.	3. Adjust governor to maintain pressure at 80-to 85 pounds and compression at 100 to 150 pounds.
Excessive oil or water in air brake system	1. Reservoir too full of oil or water.	1. Drain reservoir more frequently.
	2. Compressor passing excessive amount of oil.	2. If condition exists, compressor is worn. Replace the compressor.
	3. Compressor air strainer is dirty.	3. Wash air cleaner in mineral spirits and dry with compressed air.

AIR BRAKES

Air Supply System

The air supply system is used with the full air brake system. In the full air system, air pressure is applied directly to the shoes through a diaphragm and mechanical linkage.

If the brake system is not operating properly, the air supply system should be checked first.

Operating Tests

Before performing any of the following tests, operate the engine until the air pressure builds up to 90 psi. With the air brake system charged, open the drain cocks in each reservoir. Close the drain cocks after all moisture is drained from the reservoirs. Some models have automatic moisture ejector valves and do not require manual draining.

Low Pressure Indicator

Exhaust the brake system pressure and observe the pressure at which the warning buzzer sounds. The contacts in the indicator should close the circuit to the buzzer, when reservoir pressure is between 58 psi minimum and 65 psi maximum. If the buzzer does not start to sound within this pressure range during discharge, or if a sounding buzzer does not stop within this pressure range during the pressure buildup, the electrical connections are loose or the indicator valve is not operating properly.

Reservoir Safety Valve

To determine if the safety valve is operative, pull the exposed end of the valve stem. If the safety valve does not blow off when the stem is pulled, the valve ball is probably stuck in its seat. In such a case, remove and disassemble the valve for cleaning.

Automatic Moisture Ejector Valve

With the system charged, make several foot valve applications and note each time an application is made if an exhaust of air occurs at the exhaust port of drain valve. If no air comes out, push the wire stem. If no air comes out, the filter is plugged and the valve should be removed and cleaned.

NOTE: Because the automatic moisture ejector valve functions as reservoir pressure is reduced, excessive leakage in the system will cause constant exhausting of the valve.

Governor

With the engine running, build up air pressure in the system, and observe at what pressure reading on the dash gauge the pressure stops climbing. This is the point of governor cutout which should be between 118 and 125 lbs.

With the engine still running, slowly reduce the air pressure in the sytem by applying and releasing the brakes. Observe the pressure reading on the dash gauge at the point where the pressure starts to build up again. This is the point of governor cut-in which should be between 98 and 104 lbs.

If the governor does not cut the compressor in and out according to these specifications, adjust the governor pressure settings. Before adjusting the governor, check the accuracy of the dash gauge with a test gauge.

Check Pressure Build-Up

With the engine running at fast idle speed, observe the time required to raise system pressure from 50 to 90 lbs. If more than five minutes is required, perform the leak tests as outlined in the following paragraphs.

Also check for low engine idle speed, a slipping comperssor drive belt, excessive carbon in the compressor cylinder head, or a worn out air compressor.

Leak Tests

Compressor

With the engine stopped, discharge valve leakage can be detected by carefully listening at the compressor for the sound of escaping air. With air pressure applied to the unloader cavity (with governor cut-off), remove the air filter or the air pick up tube and check for air leaks by squirting oil around the unloader plunger and stem. If excessive air leaks are found, replace the unloader mechanism.

Governor

With the governor in the cutout position, test for leakage at the exhaust valve by applying soap suds to the exhaust vent in the body.

With the governor in the cut-in position, test for leakage of the inlet valve by applying soap suds to the exhaust vent in the body.

In either of the foregoing tests, leakage in excess of 1" soap bubble in three seconds indicates the governor should be replaced.

Reservoir Safety Valve

Coat the end of the safety valve with soap suds. Leaks causing not more than a 3" soap bubble in three seconds are permissable.

Automatic Moisture Ejector Valve

With the system charged and pressure stabilized in the system, there should be no leaks at the drain valve exhaust. A constant slight exhaust of air at the drain valve exhaust could be caused by excessive leakage in the air brake system.

Air Brakes

Some of the air brake system components vary slightly from one vehicle model to another in design or location. However, all components are essentially the same in principle and service procedure.

Operating Tests

Check Stop Light Switch

With all air pressure exhausted from the air brake system, start the engine and move the brake valve to the applied position. Stop lights should light before the dash gauge registers 5 psi. Release the brakes.

Quick Release Valve and Relay Valve

With the air brake system fully charged, apply the brakes. Inspect the brake action on the wheels controlled by the quick release valve or relay valve in question. The brakes should apply promptly. Release the brakes and inspect to be sure that the air pressure is exhausted rapidly from the exhaust port. Be sure the exhaust port is not restricted.

Leak Tests

With the engine stopped and the brakes fully applied, watch the rate of drop in air pressure as registered by the dash gauge. With the engine stopped and the reservoirs charged to the governor cutout pressure (118-125 psi), the rate of drop should not exceed 2 psi per minute. The rate of drop should also not exceed 3 psi per minute after the initial drop with brakes fully applied. If the pressure drops faster than specified, check the items outlined in the following paragraphs.

Brake Control Valve

With the pedal fully released, coat the exhaust port with soap suds to check for leaks. With the pedal fully applied, coat the exhaust port with soap suds and check for leaks. Leaks causing not more than a three" soap bubble in three seconds are permissable.

Brake Chambers

With the brakes fully applied, coat the clamp ring and bolt flanges holding the diaphragm in place with soap suds. No leaks are permissable.

Quick Release Valve

With brakes applied, coat the exhaust port with soap suds to detect leakage. Leakage in excess of a 3" soap bubble in three seconds is not permissable.

Relay Valve

With the brakes *released,* coat the exhaust port with soap suds and ob-

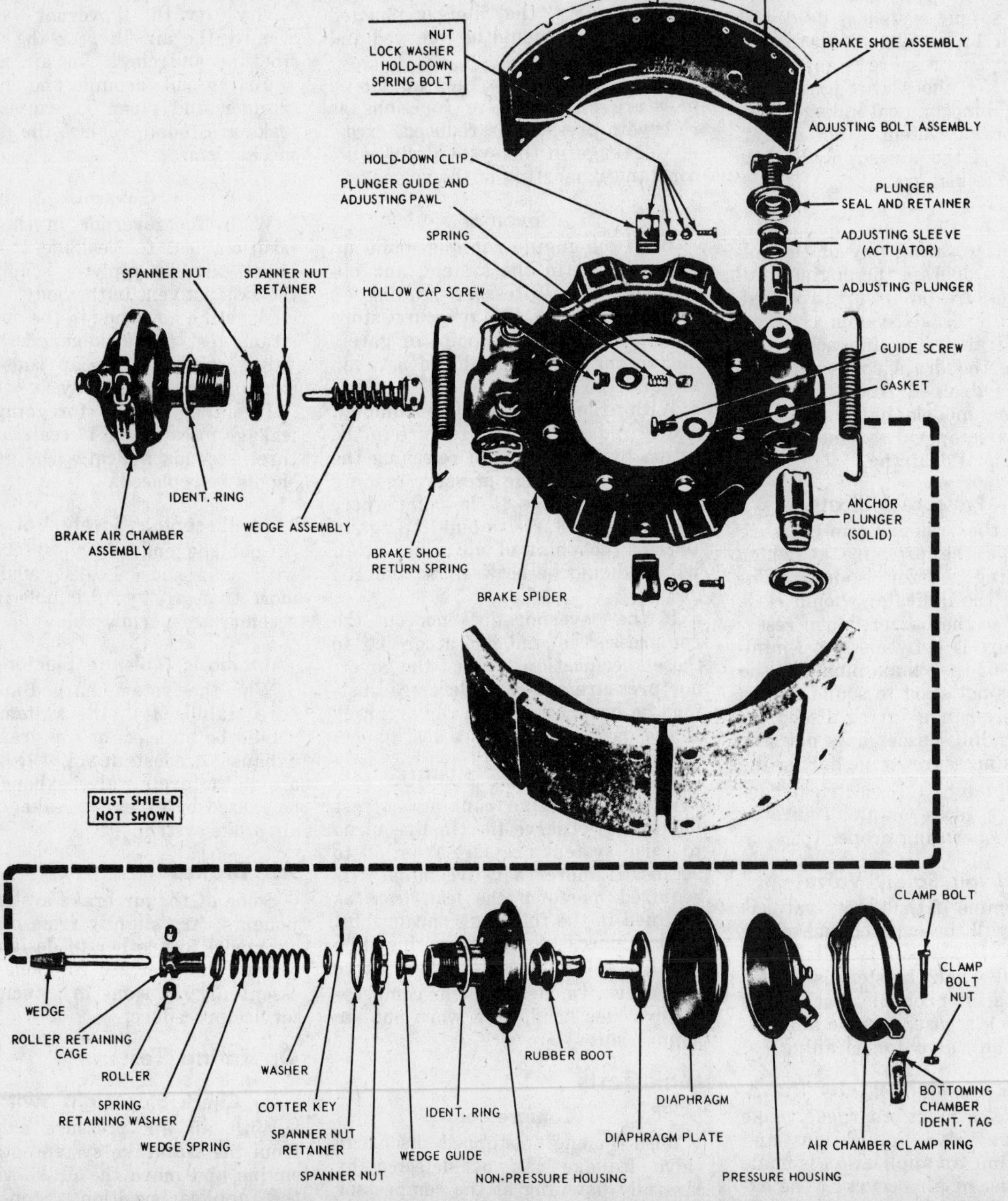

Rockwell double wedge brake—disassembled view—typical (© Ford Motor Co.)

serve the leakage.

With the brakes fully *applied*, coat the exhaust port with soap suds and observe the leakage.

Leakage in either of the foregoing tests should not exceed a 3" soap bubble in three seconds.

Air Brakes Rockwell Wedge Type

Service Air Chamber Removal

NOTE: Exhaust all air pressure from the system before attempting repair work.

1. Disconnect the air inlet line.
2. Using a drift and a light hammer, loosen the spanner nut.
3. Unscrew the service chamber assembly from the wedge housing.

Installation

1. Check position of the wedge in plunger housing to make certain wedge assembly is properly

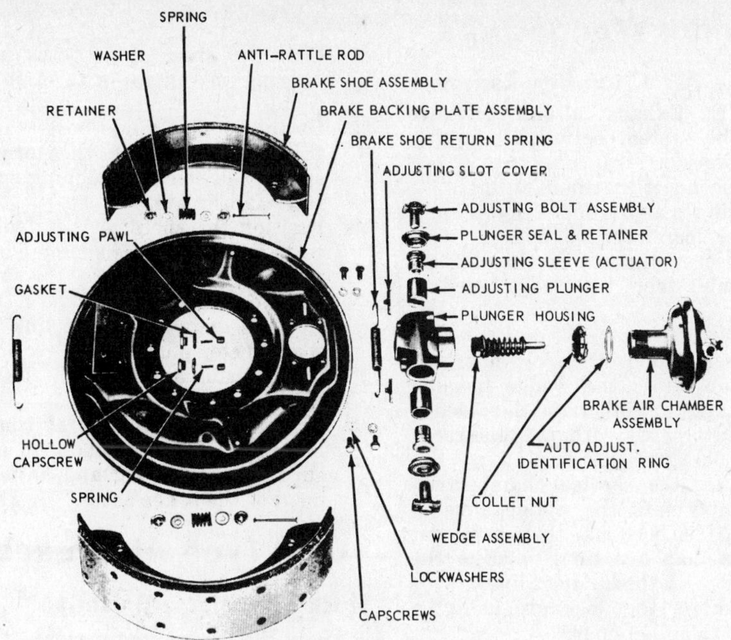

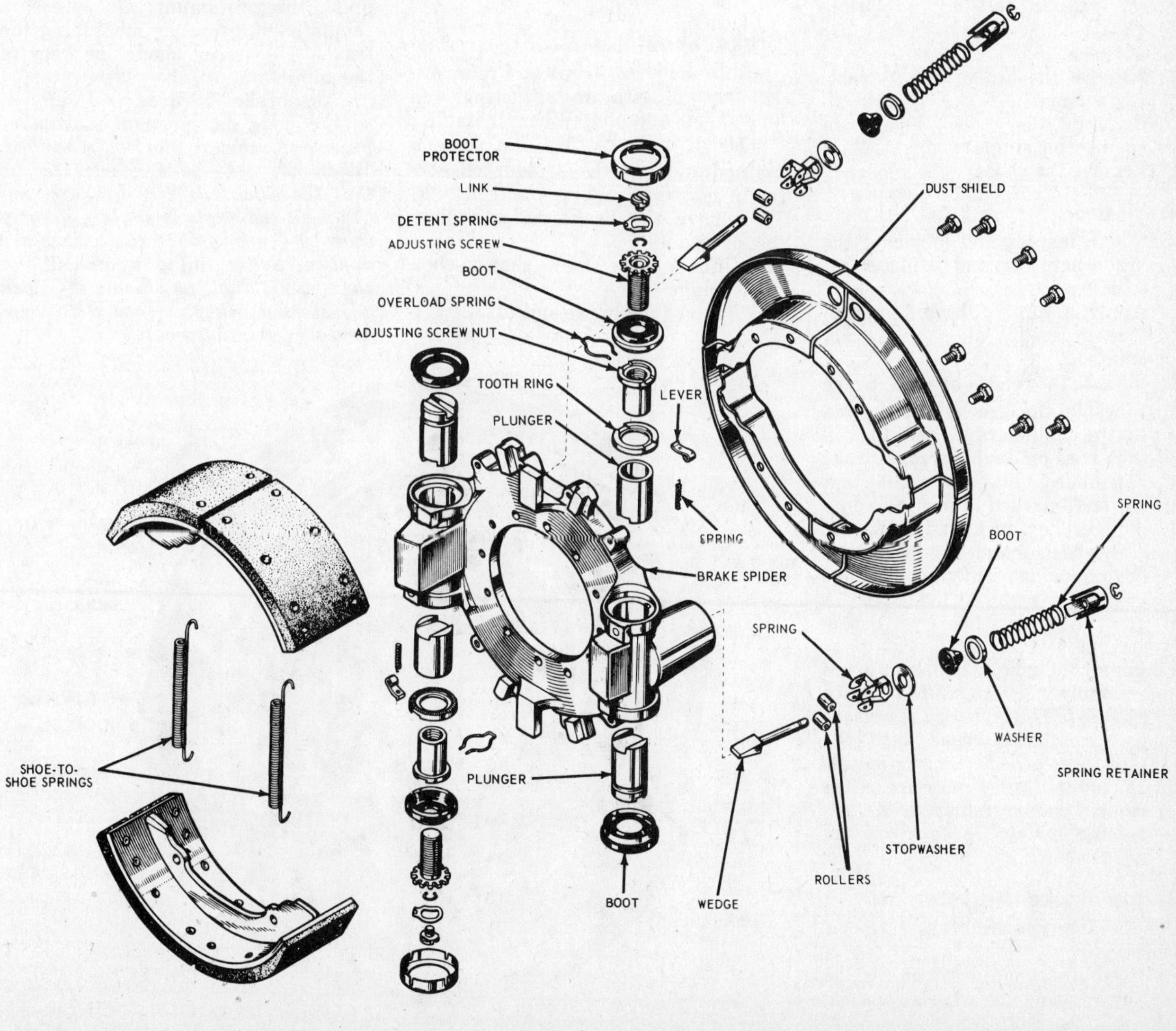

Rockwell single wedge brake—disassembled (© Ford Motor Co.)

Bendix wedge brake—disassembled view (© Ford Motor Co.)

seated. Be sure to replace automatic adjusting identification ring on service chamber tube. Thread spanner nut onto power unit tube.
2. Screw the service chamber into the plunger housing until it bottoms (spanner nut loose).
3. Align connection ports with brake lines, if necessary, by unscrewing service chamber not more than one full turn.
4. Connect brake lines.
5. Make the hold a full pressure brake application. Drive spanner nut with a drift and hammer until it is tight against the plunger housing. Release the brake pressure.
6. Check for leaks at all connections.

Brake Shoe Removal

1. Remove the wheel, hub, and drum assembly. *If equipped with Fail-Safe units, be sure that the brakes are released (actuating spring compressed by turning the release bolt approximately 18 to 21 turns clockwise.) Do not force.*
2. Remove the brake shoe retracting springs.
3. Remove the shoe hold-down springs on single wedge brakes.
4. Remove the shoes.

Installation

1. Clean, inspect and lubricate the brake actuator and adjuster assemblies.
2. Apply a film of high temperature grease at all shoe contact points.
3. Mount the ends of the brake shoes in the grooves in the actuating plungers. When installing shoes on double wedge brake assemblies, make certain that the end, marked is mounted on a plunger having an adjusting or star wheel. Install the shoe hold-down springs on single wedge brakes.
4. Install new shoe retracting springs.
5. Install the wheel, hub, and drum assembly. *If equipped with Fail-Safe Units, turn the release bolt counterclockwise until the stop is reached (approximately 18 to 21 turns) to release the manual compression of the actuating spring. Do not force the release bolt.*

Wedge Brake Adjustment

The wedge type air brakes are self adjusting.

A preliminary adjustment can be made by rotating the wheels forward and applying air to the brake chambers 25 or 30 times.

Bendix Wedge Type

Service Air Chamber Removal

NOTE: Exhaust all air pressure from the system before attempting repair work.

1. Disconnect the air inlet line.
2. Using a drift and a light hammer, loosen the locknut.
3. Unscrew the service chamber assembly from the wedge housing.

Installation

1. Insert the service chamber assembly into the wedge housing making sure that the wedge shaft mates with the piston or diaphragm shaft seat.
2. Screw the service chamber assembly into the wedge housing until it bottoms, then back out less than one turn to align the unit with the air inlet line.
3. Tighten the locknut, using a drift and hammer.
4. Connect the air inlet line and restore system air pressure. Check for operation.

Brake Shoe Removal

All brake shoes front and rear, are constructed with an adjusting end and an anchor end. When installing the shoes, make certain that the end marked ADJ. END is mounted correctly in the adjusting plunger link. To remove the brake shoes, follow this procedure:

1. Unhook the two shoe-to-shoe springs.
2. Remove the brake shoes.

Installation

1. Coat the shoe slots in the anchoring plungers with Lubriplate.
2. Clean the shoe guide bosses and the steady rests on the torque spider and coat the rubbing surfaces Lubriplate.
3. Position the shoes in the steady rests and install the shoe-to-shoe springs. On rear brakes, be sure the end of the shoe marked ADJ. END is engaged in the link at the adjuster plunger.
4. Install drum and hub, wheel and tire.
5. Apply the brakes several times before moving the truck, to assure proper seating and adjustment of the brake shoes.

Cam Type Air Brakes

Slack Adjuster Adjustment

Apply the brakes and measure the travel of the brake chamber push rod. If equipped with a Maxi-brake unit, the minimum air pressure should be 90 psi while measuring the travel. The travel should be kept to the minimum possible without causing the brakes to drag. *Adjustment of the yoke on the brake chamber push rod should not be changed. When new, the yoke is adjusted so that the slack adjuster brake chamber push rod angle is slightly greater than 90 degrees when the brakes are applied. Brake lining wear will not change this angle as long as the slack adjusters are kept adjusted to compensate for lining wear.*

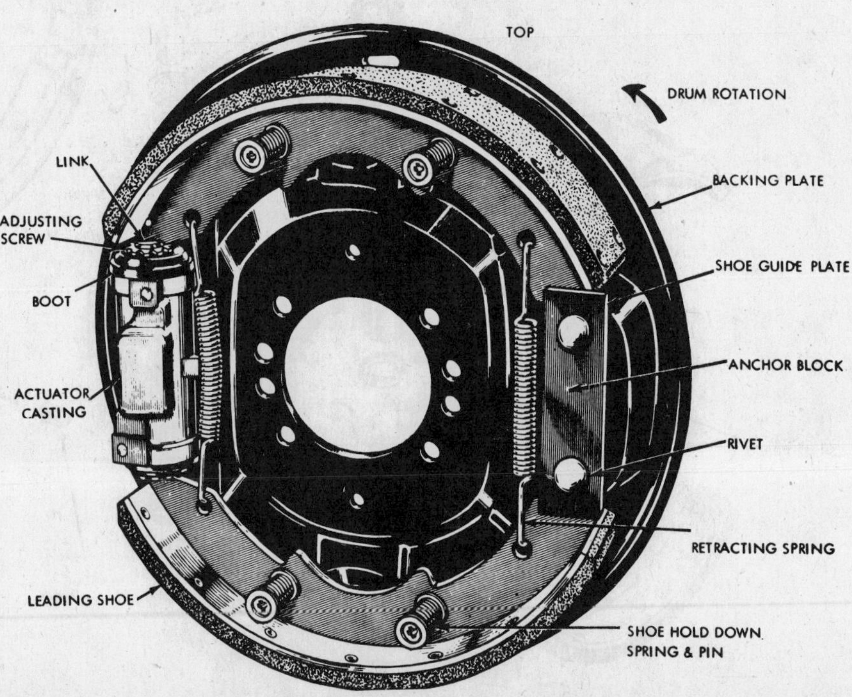

Front non-servo Bendix wedge brake (© Ford Motor Co.)

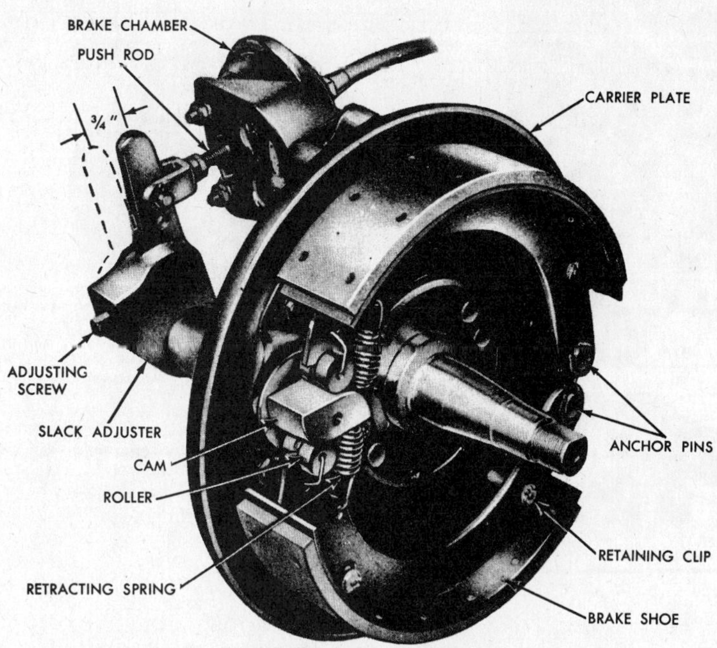

Typical front brake assembly–S-Cam Type © Ford Motor Co.)

HYDRAULIC BRAKE PEDAL FREE TRAVEL

All Trucks ①	3/16–3/8 Inch

① Free travel is not adjustable on vehicles with a dash mounted booster or dual hydraulic brake system.

BRAKE CHAMBER PUSH ROD ADJUSTMENT TABLE – S CAM BRAKES ONLY

Brake Chamber Type		Max. Travel	Adj. Travel
Front-Type R.P.O.	#9	1-3/8 Inch	3/4 Inch
	#12	1-3/8 Inch	3/4 Inch
	#16	1-3/4 Inch	3/4 Inch
Rear-Type R.P.O.	#24	1-3/4 Inch	1 Inch
	#30	2 Inch	1 Inch

ROTOR DIMENSIONS (Inches)

Minimum Rotor Thickness	0.940
Rotor Thickness Maximum Variation	0.001
Surface Flatness (Maximum)	0.0007
Lateral Runout (Maximum)	0.002
Rotor Surface Finish	15–80 R.M.S.

AIR BRAKE SYSTEM PRESSURE SETTINGS

Safety Valve Setting (Air Reservoir)	150 psi
Warning Buzzer Operating Pressure	58-65 psi
Cut-out Pressure (Governor)	118-125 psi
Cut-in Pressure (Governor)	98-104 psi

BRAKE DRUM REPAIR LIMITS (BRAKE LATHE)

Maximum allowable stock removal or drum inside diameter oversize: Brake drums up to and including 14 1/8 inches nominal diameter –0.060 inch beyond original diameter.
Brake drums larger than 14 1/8 inches nominal diameter – .080 inch beyond original diameter. Refer to Truck Master Parts Catalog for original drum inside diameter.

Front

This procedure applies only to trucks equipped with S-cam operated brakes.

A push rod travel, that reaches or exceeds the maximum indicates need of adjustment. Turn the adjusting screw clockwise until the push rod travels 3/4" in going from released to fully applied position. When making the adjustment, turn the screw in quarter turns.

Rear

This procedure applies to vehicles equipped with either standard or Maxi-brake S-cam type slack adjusters.

A push rod travel, that reaches or exceeds the maximum indicates need of adjustment. Depress the lock sleeve and turn the hexagon head of the wormshaft clockwise until the push rod travels one inch in going from released to fully applied position. Be sure that the lock sleeve comes back out and engages the hexagon head of the wormshaft sa as to lock the adjustment.

When adjusting either front or rear slack adjusters, raise the wheels and make certain that there is no brake drag.

Service Air Chamber Removal

1. Release all air from the system, then disconnect the air line at the brake chamber.
2. Disconnect the push rod clevis from the slack adjuster.
3. Remove the attaching nuts and the brake chamber assembly.

Installation

1. Position the brake chamber assembly on the mounting bracket and install the attaching nuts.
2. Install the clevis and cotter pin.
3. Connect the air line to the brake chamber and build up air pressure.
4. Adjust the brakes.

Slack Adjuster Removal

1. Remove the clevis pin attaching the slack adjuster to the brake chamber push rod.
2. Remove the lock ring (front) or cotter pin (rear) attaching the slack adjuster to the camshaft.
3. Mark the position of the slack adjuster on the camshaft, then slide the slack adjuster off the shaft.

Installation

1. Place the slack adjuster on the camshaft, aligning the locating marks. Excessive front camshaft end play may be remedied by installing an additional spacer at the cam end of the camshaft. Install the lock ring or the cotter pin.
2. Connect the brake chamber push rod to the slack adjuster by installing the clevis pin in the upper hole, and install the cotter pin.
3. Lubricate the slack adjuster, and adjust the brakes.

Front Brake Shoe and Camshaft

Removal

1. Remove the brake shoe retracting spring from the brake shoes and the C-washer from each anchor pin.
2. Remove the four brake shoe retaining clips, then slide the brake shoes off the anchor pin.
3. Mark the position of the slack adjuster on the camshaft housing.
4. Disconnect the brake chamber clevis, and remove the slack adjuster from the camshaft.
5. Pull the camshaft out of the camshaft housing.

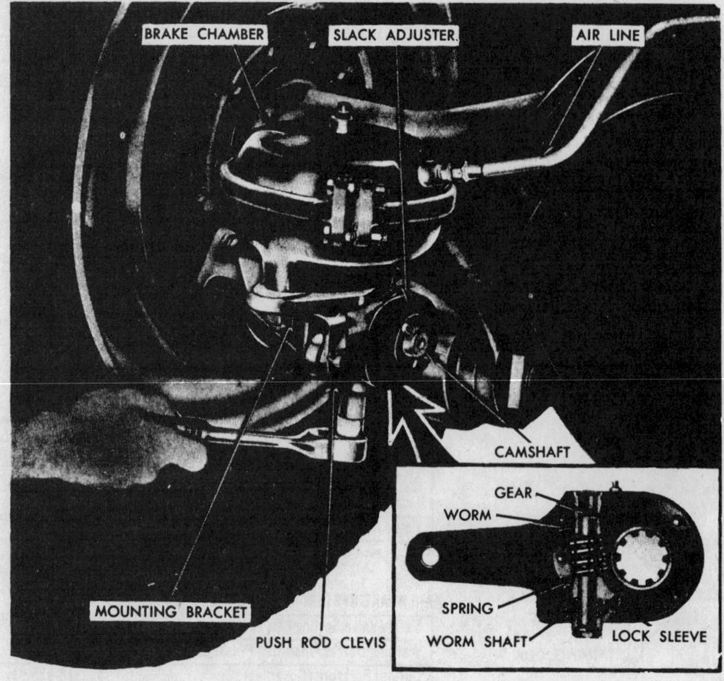

Rear brake adjustment (© Ford Motor Co.)

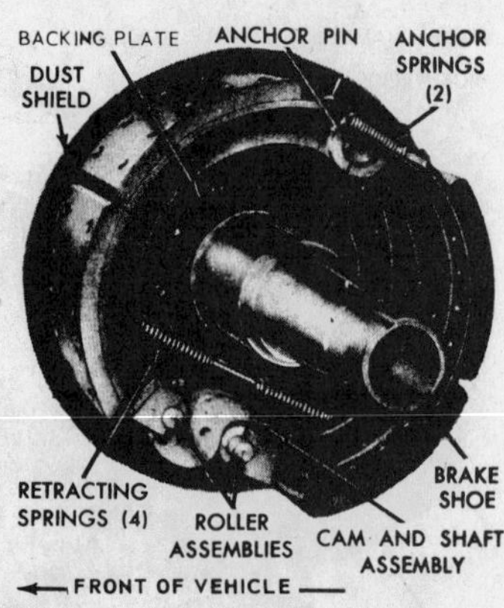

Rear brake assembly—5—cam type (© Ford Motor Co.)

Installation

1. Install the camshaft in the camshaft housing.
2. Slide the brake shoes on the anchor pins, and install a new C-washer on each anchor pin. Tighten the anchor pin lock nuts. Install the brake shoe hold down clips.
3. Install the brake shoe retracting spring.
4. Install the slack adjuster on the camshaft, lining up the marks. Install the camshaft snap ring.
5. Connect the brake chamber push rod clevis to the slack adjuster by installing the pin in the upper hole of the slack adjuster.
6. Install the hub and drum and wheel.

Rear Brake Shoe and Camshaft—Eaton Type

Removal

1. Remove the axel shaft, wheels, and hub and drum assembly.
2. Remove the retracting springs and anchor springs, then remove the brake shoes and cam roller assemblies.
3. Mark the position of the slack adjuster on the camshaft, then remove the slack adjuster.
4. Remove the camshaft from the backing plate.

Installation

1. Insert the camshaft through the backing plate and into the camshaft housing.
2. Install the brake chamber and bracket assembly.
3. Install the slack adjuster on the camshaft, aligning the locating marks, and install the cotter pin.
4. Lubricate the camshaft, rollers, and pins with Lubriplate. Do not lubricate the cam face.
5. Position the cam rollers and pins in the brake shoes, then place the brake shoes in position on the anchor pin and cam.
6. Install the retracting springs and anchor springs.
7. Install the hub, wheels, and axle shaft.
8. Adjust the brakes and slack adjuster.

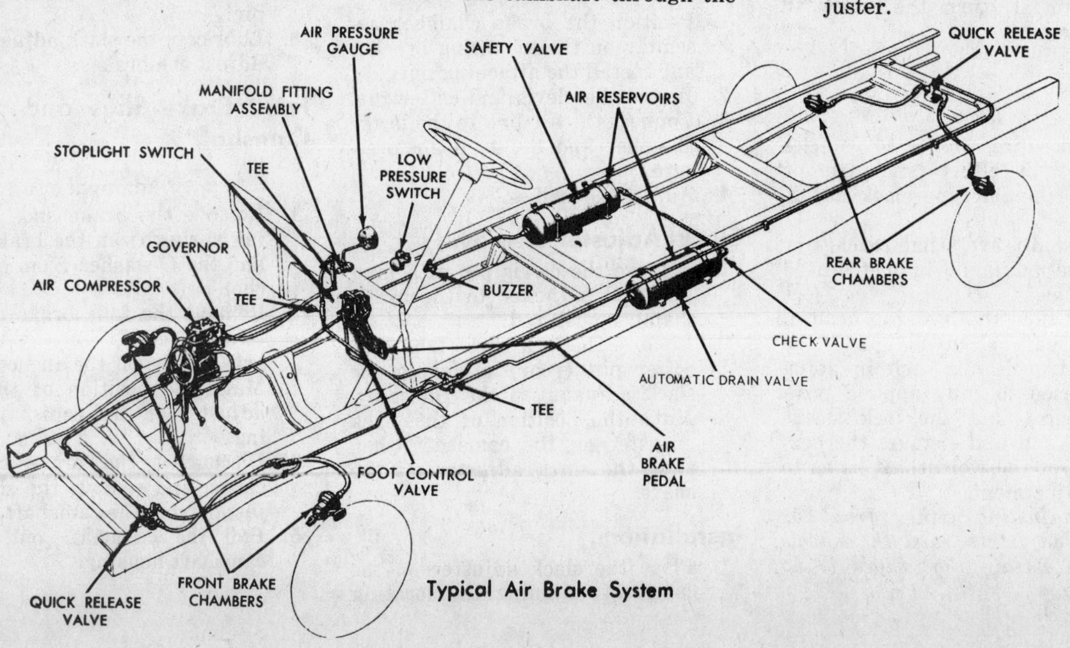

Typical Air Brake System

Floating Caliper Disc Brakes

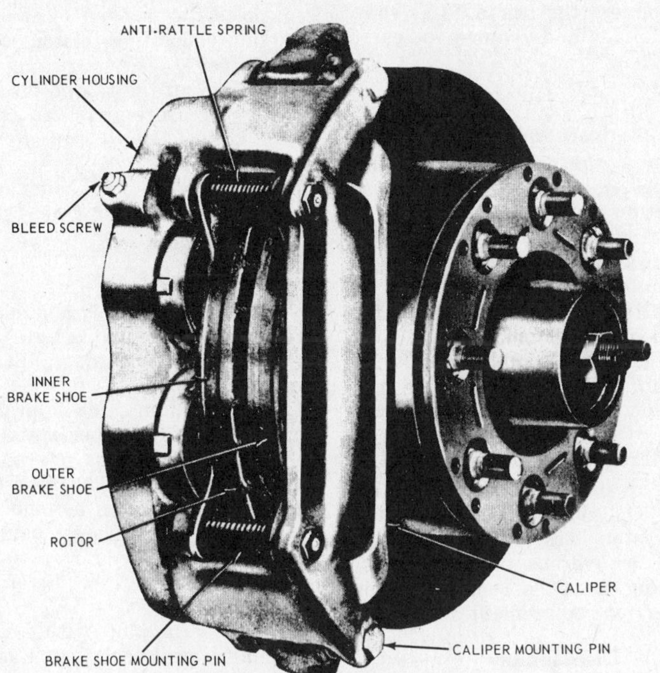

Floating caliper disc brake (© Ford Motor Co.)

The cylinder housing contains the two pistons. The pistons are fitted with an insulator on thc front and a seal on the back lip. A friction ring is attached to the back of the piston with a shouldered cap screw. The pistons and cylinder bores are protected by boot seals which are fitted to a groove in the piston and attached to the cylinder housing with retainers. The cylinder assembly is attached to the caliper with two cap screws and washers.

The anchor plate is bolted directly to the spindle. It positions the caliper assembly over the rotor forward of the spindle.

Disc Brake Adjustment

The front disc brake assembly is designed so that it is inherently self-adjusting and requires no manual adjustment.

Automatic adjustment for lining wear is achieved by the piston and friction ring sliding outward in the cylinder bore. The piston assumes a new position in the cylinder and maintains the correct adjustment.

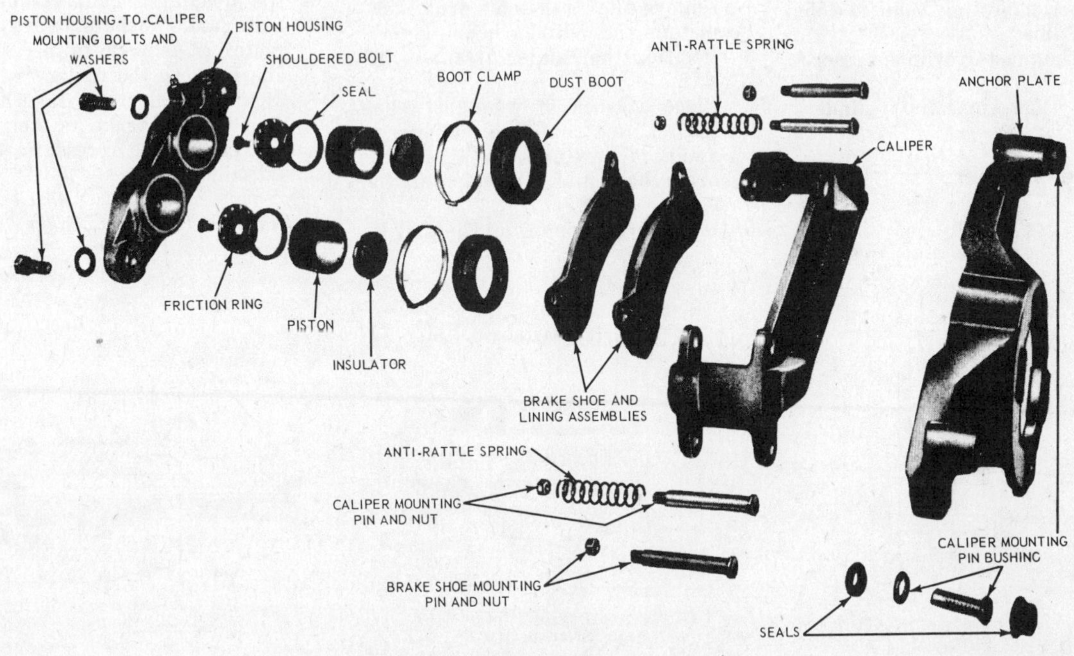

Front disc brake disassembled (© Ford Motor Co.)

The disc brake is a floating caliper design with two pistons on one side of the rotor. It is a two piece unit consisting of the caliper and cylinder housing. The caliper is mounted to the anchor plate on two mounting pins which travel in bushings in the anchor plate. The bushings and pins are protected by boot type seals.

Two brake shoe and lining assemblies are used in each caliper, one on each side of the rotor. The shoes are identical and are attached to the caliper with two mounting pins.

Front Disc Brake Shoe and Lining

Replace shoe and lining assemblies when lining is worn to a minimum of 1/16″ in thickness (combined thickness of shoe and lining ¼″ minimum).

Removal

1. Remove the shoe and lining mounting pins, anti-rattle springs and old shoe and lining assemblies.

Installation

1. Remove the master cylinder cover.
2. Loosen the piston housing-to-caliper mounting bolts sufficiently to permit the installation of new shoe and lining assemblies. *Do not move pistons.*
3. Install new shoe and lining assemblies. Install the brake shoe mounting pins and anti-rattle springs. *Be sure that the spring tangs are located in the holes provided in the shoe plates.*
4. Torque the brake shoe mounting pins to 17-23 ft-lbs.
5. Reset the pistons to the correct location in the cylinders by placing shims or feeler gauges of .023 to .035″ thickness between the shoe plate of the outboard shoe and lining assembly and the caliper; then, retighten the piston housing-to-caliper mounting bolts. *Keep the cylinder housing square with the caliper.*
6. Loosen the piston housing-to-caliper mounting bolts and remove the shims.
7. Torque the piston housing-to-caliper mounting bolts to 155 to 185 ft-lbs.
8. Check the master cylinder reservoirs.
9. Install the master cylinder cover.

Disc Brake Caliper

Removal

1. Remove the wheel and tire assembly.
2. Remove the pins and nuts retaining the caliper assembly to the anchor plate.
3. Disconnect the brake hose from the caliper and remove the caliper.

Installation

1. Connect the brake hose to the caliper.
2. Pssotion the caliper assembly to the anchor plate and install the retaining pins and nuts. Torque the nuts to specifications.
3. Install drum and wheel and bleed brake system.

If the caliper assembly is leaking the piston assemblies must be removed from the piston housing and replaced. If the cylinder bores are scored, corroded or excessive wear is evident, the piston housing must be replaced. *Do not hone the cylinder bores.* Piston assemblies are not available for oversize bores. The piston housing must be removed from the caliper for replacement.

Disassembly

1. Remove the two pins and nuts retaining the caliper to the support. Disconnect the flexible brake hose and plug the end to prevent brake fluid leakage.
2. Remove the boot retainers and remove the dust boots from the pistons and cylinder housing.
3. Position the caliper assembly in a vise.
4. Place a block of wood between the caliper and the cylinders, and apply low pressure air to the brake hose inlet. One piston will be forced out.
5. Reverse the piston and install it by hand pressure back into the cylinder bore far enough to form a seal. Block the reversed piston from moving out of the bore and place the wooden block between the remaining piston and the caliper.
6. Force out the second piston with low pressure air. *Care should be taken as the piston is forced out of the bore.*
7. Remove the two bolts and separate the caliper from the cylinder housing.

Assembly

The piston assembly and dust boots are not to be reused. A new set is to be used each time the caliper is assembled.

1. Apply a film of clean brake fluid in the cylinder bores and on the piston assemblies. *Do not apply brake fluid on the insulators.*
2. Start the piston assemblies into the cylinder bores using firm hand pressure. *Exercise care to avoid cocking the piston in the bore.*
3. Lightly tapping with a rawhide mallet, seat each piston assembly until the friction ring bottoms out in the cylinder bore.
4. Install the piston dust boots and retainers.
5. Position the piston housing on the caliper and install the piston housing-to-caliper mounting bolts and washers. Torque the piston housing-to-caliper mounting bolts to 155 to 185 ft-lbs.
6. Install the flexible brake hose.
7. Bleed the brake system and centralize the pressure differential valve.

Do not move the vehicle after working on the disc brakes until a firm brake pedal is obtained.

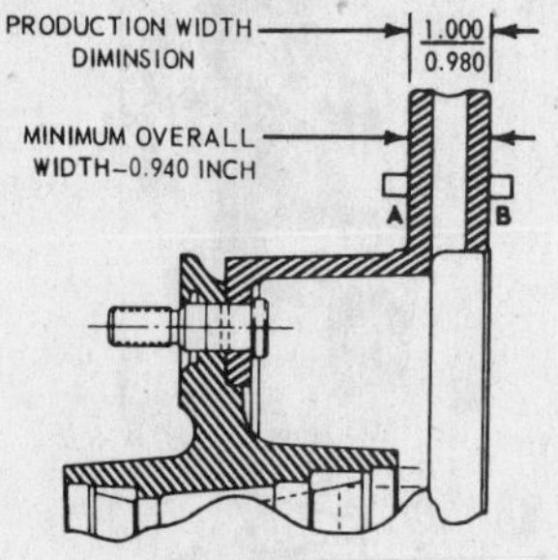

Disc Brake Rotor Service Limits

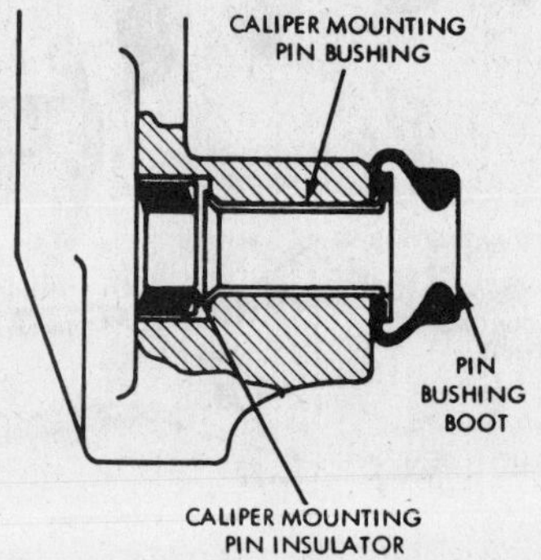

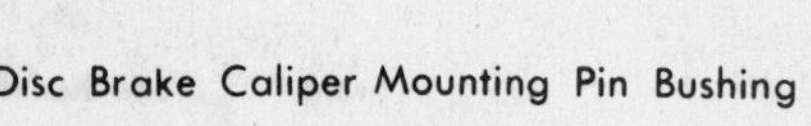

Disc Brake Caliper Mounting Pin Bushing

DISC BRAKE SHOE AND LINING DIMENSIONS (Inches)

Lining Length	7.42
Lining Area (Per Brake)	25.88 Sq. In
Lining Thickness	0.333 nominal
Shoe and Lining Maximum Wear Limit	1/4
Lining Maximum Wear Limit (from front surface of shoe)	1/16

TORQUE LIMITS—FRONT BRAKES—DISC TYPE (FT-LBS)

Description	Ft-Lbs
Brake Shoe Mounting Pins	17–23
Piston Housing-to-Caliper Mounting Bolts	155–185

ENGINE SECTION

Gasoline Engines Rebuilding

Diesel Engines

Cylinder Head

Cleaning

1. Clean all carbon from combustion chambers and valve ports.
2. Thoroughly clean the valve guides.
3. Clean all carbon and sludge from pushrods and rocker arms.
4. Remove carbon deposits from head gasket mating surfaces.

Inspection

Carefully inspect the cylinder head for any cracks in the exhaust ports, combustion chambers, or external cracks in the water cooling jacket.

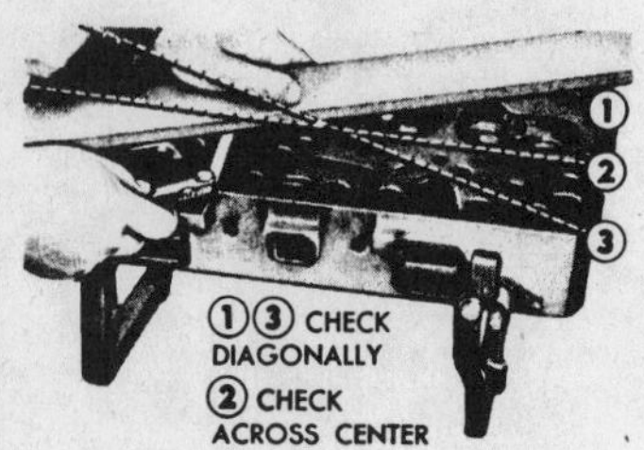

Using straight edge to check for cylinder head warpage
(© Ford Motor Co.)

Feeler gauge
Straight edge
CYLINDER BLOCK

Checking cylinder block for distortion
(© Willys Corp.)

Checking Valve Stem Clearance

Too much valve stem to bore clearance will cause excessive oil consumption and may cause valve breakage. Insufficient clearance will result in noisy and sticky valve operation.

Measure valve stem clearance as follows: Clamp a dial indicator on one side of the rocker arm cover gasket rail, locating the indicator so that movement of the valve from side to side will cause a direct movement of the indicator stem. Position the indicator stem to contact the side of the valve stem just above the valve guide.

With the valve head dropped about 1/16″ off the valve seat, move the stem of the valve from side to side with light pressure to obtain a clearance reading. If clearance exceeds specifications, it will be necessary to ream or replace the valve guides.

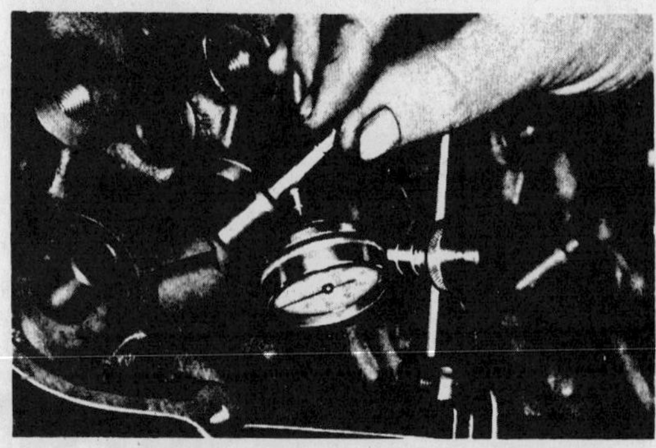

Measuring valve stem clearance
(© G.M. Corp.)

Reconditioning Valve Seats

Reconditioning the valve seats is very important because the seating must be perfect for the engine to deliver the specified power and performance.

Another important factor is the cooling of the valve heads. Good con tact between each valve and its seat in the cylinder head is imperative to insure that the heat in the valve head will be properly dissipated.

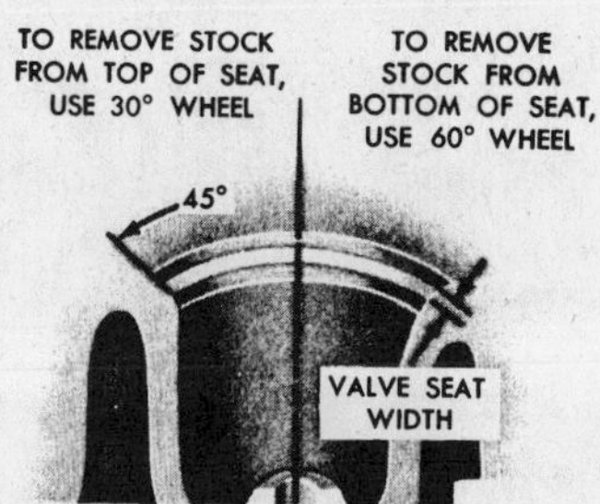

Valve seat reconditioning angles
(© Ford Motor Co.)

Several different types of equipment are available for reconditioning valve seats. The recommendations of the manufacturer of the equipment being used should be carefully followed to attain proper results. Regardless of equipment used, however, it is essential that valve guide bores be free from carbon or dirt to insure proper centering of the pilot in the guide.

1. Install and expand pilot in the valve guide bore.
2. Place a roughing or forming stone over the pilot and just clean up the seat. NOTE: Use a stone that is cut to specifications.
3. Remove roughing or forming stone and install a finishing stone, cut to specifications, over the pilot and cut just enough metal to provide a smooth finish.
4. Narrow down the valve seats to the specified width. NOTE: This operation is done by using grinding stones of the recommended angle value to raise or lower the seat.
5. Remove expanding pilot and clean cylinder head carefully to remove all chips and grindings from the preceeding operations.
6. Measure valve concentricity.

Rocker Arm Stud Replacement

Rocker arm studs that have damaged threads or are loose in the cylinder head should be replaced.

Some engines have press-fit studs that are available in oversizes. The

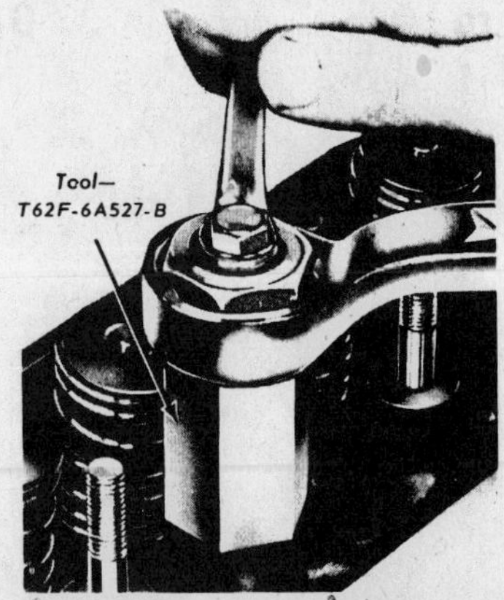

Removing the rocker arm stud
(© Ford Motor Co.)

old stud must be removed with a puller and then the hole reamed to the proper oversize. When installing a new stud, coat the press-fit area with hypoid axle lubricant.

Other engines have screw-in studs. The threads in the cylinder head must be retapped using Heli-Coil, or in some cases, tapped to fit an oversized stud. When installing a new stud, coat the cylinder head end with sealer.

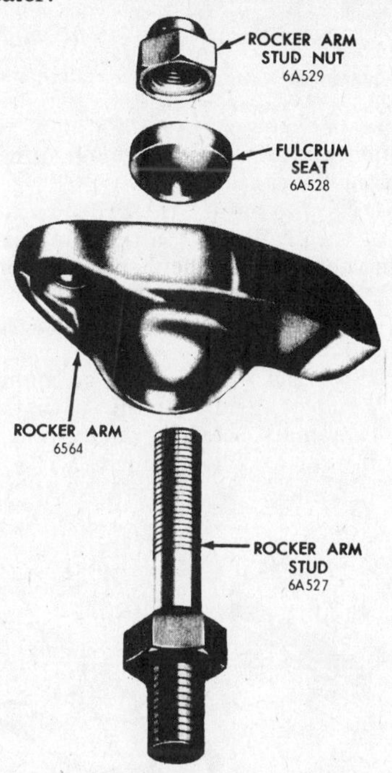

Volve rocker arm and stud assembly
(© Ford Motor Co.)

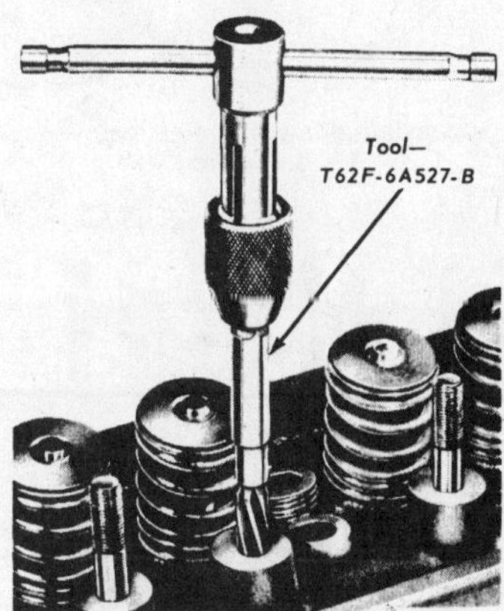

Reaming rocker arm stud bore
(© Ford Motor Co.)

Valves

Cleaning and Inspection

Clean valves on a buffing wheel and inspect for burned heads, cracked faces or damaged stems. Discard any burned, warped or cracked valves.

Valve Refacing

Valves that are pitted can be refaced to the proper angle. Valve stems which show excessive wear, or valves that are warped should be replaced.

NOTE: When an excessively

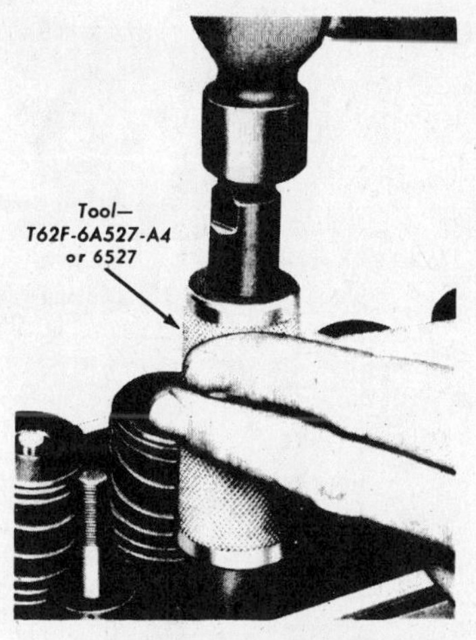

Installing rocker arm stud
(© Ford Motor Co.)

warped valve head is refaced, a knife edge will be ground on all or part of the head due to the amount of metal that must be removed. Knife edges lead to breakage, burning or pre-ignition due to heat localization and improper dissipation. If the edge of the valve head is less than 1/32" (3/64" ext.) thick after grinding, replace the valve.

Several types of equipment are available for valve refacing. The manufacturer recommendations of the equipment being used should be followed carefully to attain proper results.

1. If necessary, dress the grinding wheel to make sure it is smooth and true. Set chuck at angle specified for valve.
2. Clamp the valve stem in the chuck.
3. Start the refacing machine and move the valve head in line with the grinder wheel.
4. Turn the feed screw until the valve head just contacts the wheel. Move valve back and forth across the wheel and regulate the feed screw to provide light contact.
5. Continue grinding until the entire valve face is true and smooth. NOTE: Make sure the valve head edge thickness is greater than 1/32" (3/64" ext.).
6. Remove valve from chuck and place the stem in the "V" block. Feed valve stem squarely against grinding wheel to remove any pit from rocker arm

1 Valve refacer 2 Valve

Refacing valves (© Willys Corp.)

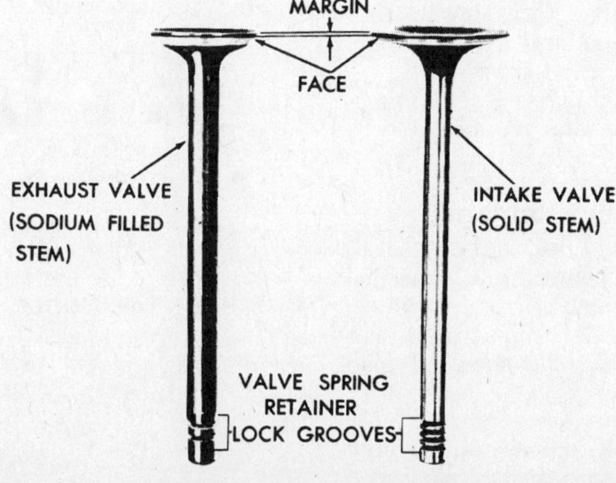

Intake and exhaust valves—typical
(© Chrysler Corp.)

end. CAUTION: Only the extreme end of the valve stem is hardened to resist wear. Do not grind excessively.

1 Valve seat refacer
2 Cylinder bock
3 Valve seats.

Refacing valve seats (© Willys Corp.)

7. After cleaning valve face and cylinder head valve seat, make pencil marks about ¼″ apart across the valve face; place the valve in the cylinder head and give it ½ turn in each direction while exerting firm pressure on valve head.
8. Remove valve and check face carefully. If all pencil marks have not been removed at the point of contact with the valve seat, it will be necessary to repeat the refacing operation and again check for proper seating. NOTE: A more accurate method of checking valve seating is by applying Prussian Blue to the valve seat, then installing valve and rotating it with light pressure. If the blue is transferred to the center of the valve face, seating is satisfactory. If the blue is transferred to the top edge of valve face, lower the seat; if transferred to bottom edge of face, raise the seat.
9. Grind and check the remaining valves in the same manner.

Checking Valve Springs

Springs should be compressed to the specified height and checked against the given pressure valve. Springs should be replaced if not within 10 lbs. of the specified load (without dampers).

Inspect each valve spring for squareness with a steel square and surface plate. Test spring from both ends and if it is more than 1/16″ out-of-square, replace it.

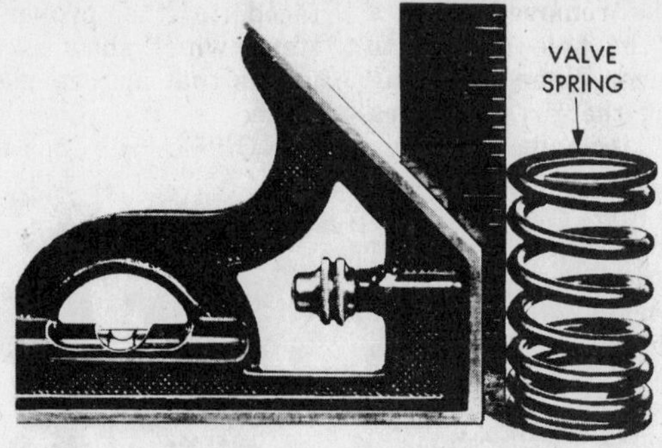

Inspecting valve spring squareness
(© Chrysler Corp.)

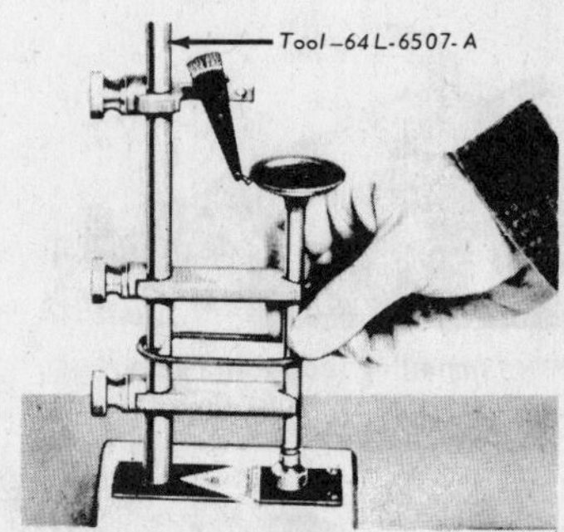

Valve face runout
(© Ford Motor Co.)

Main Bearings

Inspection

In general (except thrust bearing), the lower half of the bearing shows a greater wear and the most distress from fatigue. If upon inspection the lower half is suitable for use, it can be assumed that the upper half is also satisfactory. If the lower half shows evidence of wear or damage, both upper and lower bearing halves should be replaced. Always replace bearing halves in pairs.

Checking Clearance

To obtain the most accurate results with Plastigage (or its equivalent), make certain the crankshaft rests on the upper bearings so that the total clearance can be measured between the lower bearing and journal.

NOTE: If checking with engine in vehicle, support the crankshaft at the damper and flywheel to remove upper bearing clearance.

NOTE: To assure the proper seating of the crankshaft, all bearing cap bolts should be at their specified torque. Wipe oil from journal and bearing surfaces before making measurement.

1. With the oil pan and oil pump removed, and starting with the rear main bearing, remove bearing cap and clean journal.

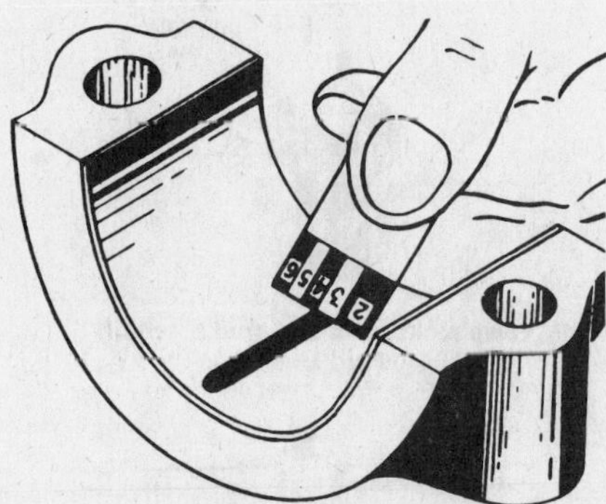

Measuring flattened plastigauge
(© G.M. Corp.)

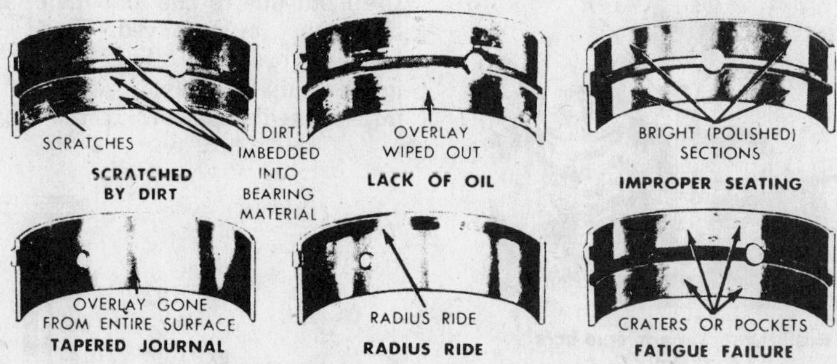

Typical bearing failures (© Ford Motor Co.)

2. Place a piece of gauging plastic, the full width of the bearing (parallel to crankshaft), on the journal. CAUTION: Do not rotate the crankshaft with the gauging plastic installed.
3. Install the bearing cap and torque the retaining bolts to specifications.

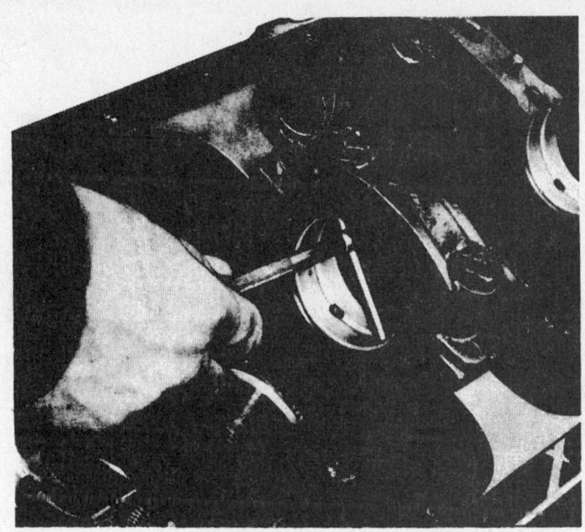

Measuring main bearing bores
(© Willys Corp.)

4. Remove bearing cap. Without removing the gauging plastic, measure its compressed width (at widest point) with the graduations on the gauging plastic envelope. NOTE: Should the gauge indicate journal taper or out-of-round, measure the journal diameter with a micrometer to make certain it falls within specifications.

5. If the bearing clearance is within limits, the insert is satisfactory. If not, replace the inserts (upper and lower).

6. Try undersize bearing inserts until specifications are met. If necessary, regrind the crankshaft journal to fit the next undersize: NOTE: If a new bearing cap is being installed and clearance is below specifications, check for any nicks or burrs and add shims if necessary.

7. Proceed to the next bearing. After all bearings have been checked, rotate the crankshaft to make certain there is no binding.

Connecting Rod Bearings

Checking Clearance

Use the same method as outlined in Main Bearings to check clearance. Undersize bearings are available for standard and reground crankshafts.

When fitting inserts for an out-of-round crankpin, make certain that the bearing is fitted to the *maximum* diameter; otherwise rapid bearing failure will occur.

Also, measure all connecting rod side clearances and compare to specifications.

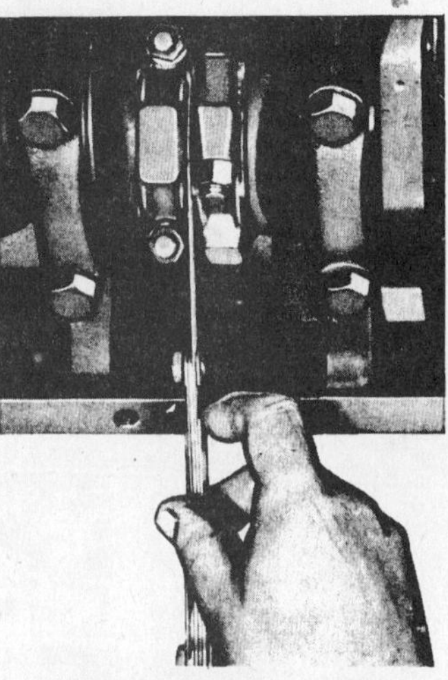

Connecting rod side clearance
(© Ford Motor Co.)

Pistons and Connecting Rods

Cleaning and Inspection

Pistons

Remove varnish from piston skirts and pins with a cleaning solvent. Clean the ring grooves with a groove cleaner and make sure oil ring holes and slots are free from obstruction.

CAUTION: Do not use a wire brush to clean any part of the piston.

Inspect the piston for cracked or wavy, worn ring lands, cracked, scuffed or damaged skirts and pitted or eroded crown. Check ring grooves for any nicks or burrs.

Connecting Rods

Wash connecting rods in cleaning solvent and dry with compressed air. Check for twisted or bent rods and inspect for nicks or cracks.

Checking Piston Pin Clearance

The piston is designed to maintain adequate clearance under all engine operating conditions. On some engines the piston pins are available in oversizes, requiring the pin bore to be reamed for proper fitting. Other engines have piston pins that can only be replaced as an assembly with the piston.

Piston pins and bores must be free of varnish or scuffing when being measured. The pin should be measured with a micrometer and the bore with a dial gauge or inside micrometer. Clearance beyond specifications requires replacement.

Fitting Piston Rings

1. Insert piston rings into the cylinder in which they are to be installed. Use an inverted piston to push the rings about 2" from the bottom of the bore.
2. Measure ring gap with feeler stock and compare to specifications for individual rings.
3. Measure side clearance between piston ring and ring land.
4. Position rings on the piston with installation tool.

Piston Selection

Check used piston to cylinder bore clearance as follows:

1. Measure the cylinder bore diameter with a telescope gauge. NOTE: Make measurement 2½" from top of cylinder bore.
2. Measure the piston diameter at skirt across center line of piston pin.
3. Subtract measurements to obtain

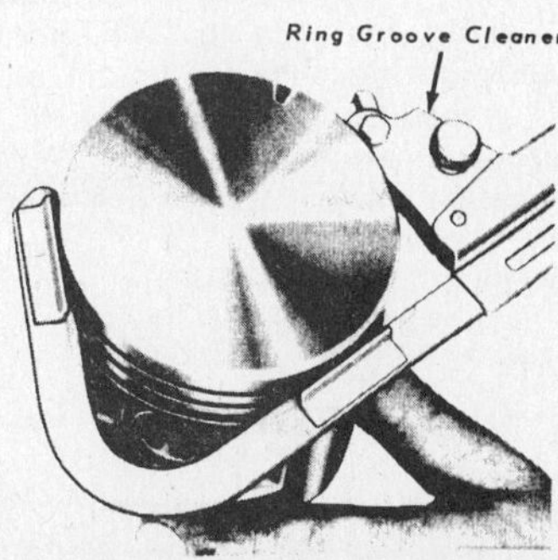

Cleaning ring grooves—typical
(© Ford Motor Co.)

Measuring ring side clearance
(© Ford Motor Co.)

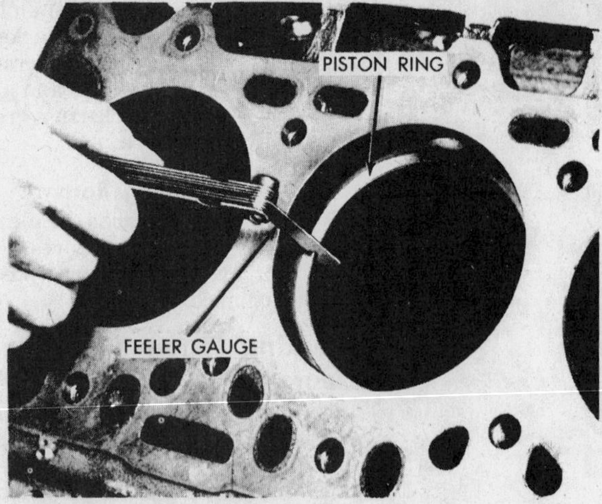

Measuring ring gap with feeler gauge (© Chrysler Corp.)

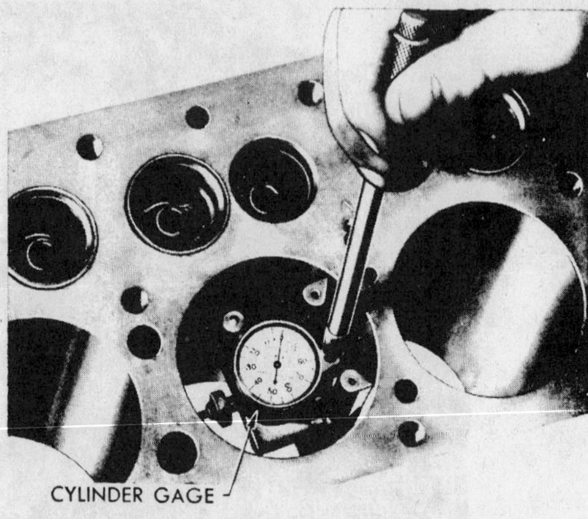

Measuring cylinder bore (© Chrysler Corp.)

Installing piston rings (© Chrysler Corp.)

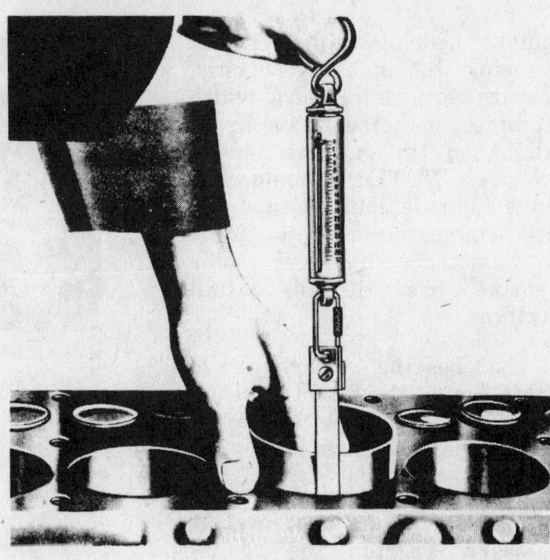

Fitting piston in inverted position (© Chrysler Corp.)

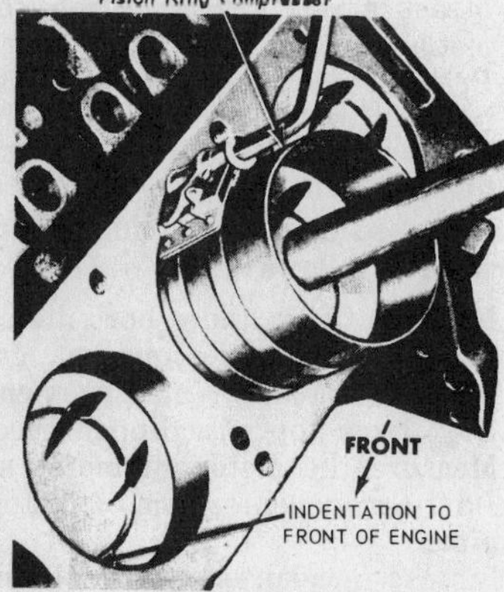

Installing piston (© Ford Motor Co.)

piston to bore clearance.

If used piston clearance is excessive, determine if a new piston can be obtained to fit the bore diameter within specifications.

If the cylinder bore must be reconditioned, measure the new piston diameter, then hone the cylinder to obtain the proper clearance. Mark the piston to identify which cylinder it is fitted for. If installing used pistons, be sure to match them to their original bores.

Crankshaft

Cleaning and Inspection

1. Wash crankshaft in cleaning solvent and dry with compressed air.
2. Using a micrometer, measure main bearing journals and crankpins for out-of-round, taper or undersize.
3. Measure crankshaft run-out by supporting front and rear main bearing journals in "V" blocks and checking the front and rear intermediate journals with a dial indicator.
4. Check measurements with specifications.
5. Replace or recondition crankshaft if beyond given limits.

Camshaft

Cleaning and Inspection

1. Wash camshaft in cleaning solvent and dry with compressed air.
2. Measure bearing journals with a micrometer. If out-of-round exceeds .001", replace the camshaft.
3. Check alignment by placing the camshaft in "V" blocks and measuring out-of-true with a dial indicator. If it is out more than .002" indicator reading, replace the camshaft.
4. Inspect camshaft timing gear and thrust plate (if so equipped) for any signs of wear or damage.
5. Inspect bearings for excessive wear or damage and replace as necessary.

CAUTION: When installing camshaft bearings, make certain oil holes in bearings and block are properly aligned.

Cylinder Block

Cleaning and Inspection

1. Wash cylinder block thoroughly in solvent and clean all gasket surfaces.
2. Remove gallery plugs and clean

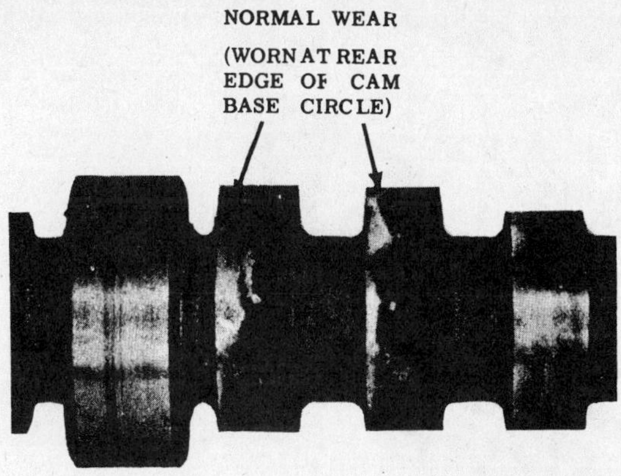

Inspect for camshaft wear (© G.M. Corp.)

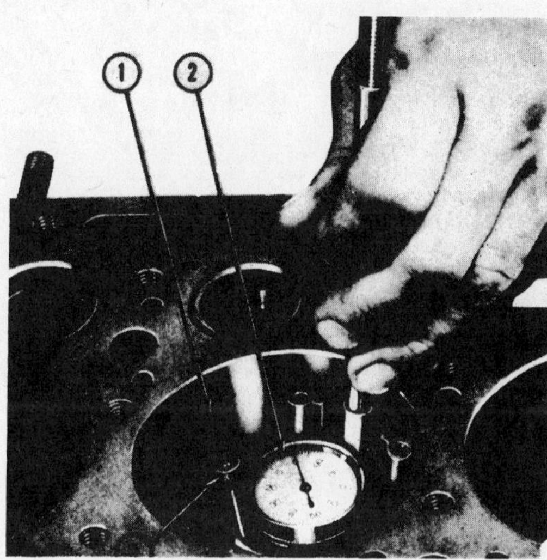

1 Cylinder bore
2 Cylinder bore checking gauge
3 Lock screw

Checking cylinder bore (© Willys Corp.)

Honing cylinder bore (© Willys Corp.)

all oil passages. NOTE: These plugs may be removed with a sharp punch, or they may be drilled and pried out.

3. Clean and inspect water passages.
4. Check for cracks in the cylinder walls, water jacket, valve lifter bores and main bearing webs.

Checking Cylinder Bore

Measure the cylinder walls for taper, out-of-round or excessive ridge at top of ring travel. This should be done with a dial indicator. Set the gauge so that the thrust pin must be forced in about ¼″ in order to insert gauge into the cylinder bore. Center gauge in cylinder and turn dial to "0". Carefully work gauge up and down in the bore to determine taper; turn to different points around cylinder wall to determine out-of-round condition.

If cylinders were found to exceed specifications, honing or boring will be necessary.

Cylinder Conditioning

If the cylinder block inspection indicated that the block was suitable for continued use except for out-of-round or tapered cylinders, recondition bores to fit high limit or oversize pistons. If the cylinders have less than .005″ taper or wear, they can be conditioned with a hone and fitted with high limit standard size pistons. If more than .005″ taper or wear, they should be bored and then honed to the smallest oversize that will permit complete resurfacing of all the cylinders.

When pistons are being fitted, cylinder bores should be cleaned with a bristle brush and a hot water-/detergent wash. After cleaning, the bores should be swabbed several times with light engine oil on a clean cloth and then wiped dry. It is essential that a good cleaning operation be performed.

CAUTION: If any abrasive material remains in the cylinder bore, it will cause rapid wear of the rings, bore and piston as well as bearings lubricated by the contaminated oil.

NOTE: Do not clean cylinders with gasoline or kerosene.

Cylinder Bore

1. Before using any type of boring bar, the top of the cylinder block should be filed off to remove any carbon build-up or burrs. This is very important. Should burrs or

Removing ridge from cylinder bore
(© Chrysler Corp.)

Cross hatch pattern (© Chrysler Corp.)

build-up be present, the boring bar may be tilted, which would result in the rebored cylinder wall not being perpendicular to the crankshaft centerline.

2. The piston to be fitted should be measured with a micrometer at the center of the piston skirt and at right angles to the piston pin. The cylinder should be bored to the same diameter as the piston and then honed to give the specified clearance.
3. Carefully follow instructions provided by manufacturer of equipment being used.

Cylinder Honing

1. Follow the manufacturers recommendations for use of the hone and for cleaning and lubrication during the honing operation.
2. Clean cylinder bore and check piston fit occasionally during the honing operation. CAUTION: Handle the piston with care and do not attempt to force it into the cylinder before the bore has been honed to the correct size. The piston may become distorted through careless handling.
3. When finish honing a cylinder bore, move the hone up and down at a sufficient speed to obtain very fine, uniform surface finish marks in a cross-hatch pattern of approximately 45 to 65 degrees. The marks should be clean but not sharp and free from imbedded particles and torn or folded metal.
4. Permanently mark the piston for the cylinder to which it has been fitted and proceed to hone the remaining cylinders and fit their respective pistons.

Cummins Diesel Engines

Index

Specifications

Trouble Diagnosis

Cooling System

Electrical

Engine Service

Fuel System

GENERAL SPECIFICATIONS

ENGINE MODEL	NO. OF CYLINDERS	BORE & STROKE	PISTON DISP. CU. IN.	MAXIMUM HORSEPOWER @ R.P.M.	FIRING ORDER RIGHT HAND ROTATION	FIRING ORDER LEFT HAND ROTATION	LUBE OIL PRESSURE @ GOVERNED SPEED
C-90	4	4 7/16 x 5	310	90 @ 2000	1-2-4-3	1-3-4-2	50 @ 2000
C-105	4	4 7/16 x 5	310	105 @ 2500	1-2-4-3	1-3-4-2	50 @ 2500
C-140	4	4 7/16 x 5	310	140 @ 2500	1-2-4-3	1-3-4-2	50 @ 2500
C-160	6	4 7/16 x 5	464	160 @ 2500	1-5-3-6-2-4	1-4-2-6-3-5	50 @ 2500
CF-160	6	4 7/16 x 5	464	160 @ 2800	1-5-3-6-2-4	1-4-2-6-3-5	50 @ 2800
CR-160	6	4 7/16 x 5	464	160 @ 2200	1-5-3-6-2-4	1-4-2-6-3-5	50 @ 2200
C-175	6	4 7/16 x 5	464	175 @ 2500	1-5-3-6-2-4	1-4-2-6-3-5	50 @ 2500
C-180	6	4 7/16 x 5	464	180 @ 2500	1-5-3-6-2-4	1-4-2-6-3-5	50 @ 2500
C-190	6	4 7/16 x 5	464	190 @ 2500	1-5-3-6-2-4	1-4-2-6-3-5	50 @ 2500
C-200	6	4 7/16 x 5	464	200 @ 2500	1-5-3-6-2-4	1-4-2-6-3-5	50 @ 2500
J-70	4	4⅛ x 5	267	70 @ 2000	1-2-4-3	1-3-4-2	50 @ 2000
J-80	4	4⅛ x 5	267	80 @ 2000	1-2-4-3	1-3-4-2	50 @ 2500
J-120	4	4⅛ x 5	267	120 @ 2500	1-2-4-3	1-3-4-2	50 @ 2500
J-6	6	4⅛ x 5	401	100 @ 1800	1-5-3-6-2-4	1-4-2-6-3-5	50 @ 1800
JNR-100	6	4⅛ x 5	401	100 @ 1800	1-5-3-6-2-4	1-4-2-6-3-5	50 @ 1800
JF-6	6	4⅛ x 5	401	110 @ 2200	1-5-3-6-2-4	1-4-2-6-3-5	50 @ 2200
JN-130	6	4⅛ x 5	401	130 @ 2500	1-5-3-6-2-4	1-4-2-6-3-5	50 @ 2500
JN-6	6	4⅛ x 5	401	130 @ 2500	1-5-3-6-2-4	1-4-2-6-3-5	50 @ 2500
JNF-130	6	4⅛ x 5	401	130 @ 2800	1-5-3-6-2-4	1-4-2-6-3-5	50 @ 2800
JS-6	6	4⅛ x 5	401	160 @ 2500	1-5-3-6-2-4	1-4-2-6-3-5	50 @ 2500
JNS-6	6	4⅛ x 5	401	175 @ 2500	1-5-3-6-2-4	1-4-2-6-3-5	50 @ 2500
JT-6	6	4⅛ x 5	401	175 @ 2500	1-5-3-6-2-4	1-4-2-6-3-5	50 @ 2500
HRC-4	4	5⅛ x 6	495	115 @ 1800	1-2-4-3	1-3-4-2	50 @ 1800
H-135	6	4⅞ x 6	672	135 @ 1800	1-5-3-6-2-4	1-4-2-6-3-5	50 @ 1800
H-6	6	4⅞ x 6	672	160 @ 1800	1-5-3-6-2-4	1-4-2-6-3-5	50 @ 1800
HR-6	6	5⅛ x 6	743	175 @ 1800	1-5-3-6-2-4	1-4-2-6-3-5	50 @ 1800
HS-6	6	4⅞ x 6	672	210 @ 1800	1-5-3-6-2-4	1-4-2-6-3-5	50 @ 1800
HRS-6	6	5⅛ x 6	743	240 @ 1800	1-5-3-6-2-4	1-4-2-6-3-5	50 @ 1800
HRF-6	6	5⅛ x 6	743	190 @ 2000	1-5-3-6-2-4	1-4-2-6-3-5	50 @ 2000
HU-170	6	4⅞ x 6	672	170 @ 1800	1-5-3-6-2-4	1-4-2-6-3-5	50 @ 1800
NHC-4	4	5⅛ x 6	495	130 @ 2000	1-2-4-3	1-3-4-2	50 @ 2000
NH-135	4	5½ x 6	570	135 @ 2100	1-2-4-3	1-3-4-2	50 @ 2100
NH-160	4	5½ x 6	570	160 @ 2100	1-2-4-3	1-3-4-2	50 @ 2100
NH-180	6	4⅞ x 6	672	180 @ 2100	1-5-3-6-2-4	1-4-2-6-3-5	50 @ 2100
NHS-180	6	5⅛ x 6	743	180 @ 1950	1-5-3-6-2-4	1-4-2-6-3-5	50 @ 2000
NHE-195	6	5⅛ x 6	743	195 @ 1950	1-5-3-6-2-4	1-4-2-6-3-5	50 @ 1950
NH-200	6	5⅛ x 6	743	200 @ 1950	1-5-3-6-2-4	1-4-2-6-3-5	50 @ 1950
NH-220	6	5⅛ x 6	743	220 @ 2100	1-5-3-6-2-4	1-4-2-6-3-5	50 @ 2100
NHE-220	6	5½ x 6	855	220 @ 2100	1-5-3-6-2-4	1-4-2-6-3-5	50 @ 2100
NHE-225	6	5½ x 6	855	225 @ 1950	1-5-3-6-2-4	1-4-2-6-3-5	50 @ 1950
NH-230	6	5½ x 6	855	230 @ 2100	1-5-3-6-2-4	1-4-2-6-3-5	50 @ 2100
NHD-230	6	5½ x 6	855	220 @ 2100	1-5-3-6-2-4	1-4-2-6-3-5	50 @ 2100
NH-250	6	5½ x 6	855	250 @ 2100	1-5-3-6-2-4	1-4-2-6-3-5	50 @ 2100
NHCT-270	6	5½ x 6	855	—	1-5-3-6-2-4	1-4-2-6-3-5	50 @ 2100
NTC-335	6	5½ x 6	855	—	1-5-3-6-2-4	1-4-2-6-3-5	50 @ 2100
NHS-6	6	5⅛ x 6	743	290 @ 2100	1-5-3-6-2-4	1-4-2-6-3-5	50 @ 2100
NHRS-6	6	5⅛ x 6	743	320 @ 2100	1-5-3-6-2-4	1-4-2-6-3-5	50 @ 2100
NT-165	4	5⅛ x 6	495	165 @ 2000	1-2-4-3	1-3-4-2	50 @ 2000
NT-180	4	5⅛ x 6	495	180 @ 2100	1-2-4-3	1-3-4-2	50 @ 2100
NT-200	4	5⅛ x 6	459	200 @ 2100	1-2-4-3	1-3-4-2	50 @ 2100
NTE-235	6	5⅛ x 6	743	235 @ 2100	1-5-3-6-2-4	1-4-2-6-3-5	50 @ 2100
NT-6	6	5⅛ x 6	743	250 @ 2100	1-5-3-6-2-4	1-4-2-6-3-5	50 @ 2100
NTO-6	6	5⅛ x 6	743	262 @ 2100	1-5-3-6-2-4	1-4-2-6-3-5	50 @ 2100
NT-280	6	5½ x 6	855	280 @ 2100	1-5-3-6-2-4	1-4-2-6-3-5	50 @ 2100

GENERAL SPECIFICATIONS - Cont'd.

ENGINE MODEL	NO. OF CYLINDERS	BORE & STROKE	PISTON DISP. CU. IN.	MAXIMUM HORSEPOWER @ R.P.M.	FIRING ORDER RIGHT HAND ROTATION	FIRING ORDER LEFT HAND ROTATION	LUBE OIL PRESSURE @ GOVERNED SPEED
NRT-6	6	5⅛ x 6	743	300 @ 2100	1-5-3-6-2-4	1-4-2-6-3-5	50 @ 2100
NT-310	6	5½ x 6	855	310 @ 2100	1-5-3-6-2-4	1-4-2-6-3-5	50 @ 2100
NRTO-6	6	5⅛ x 6	743	335 @ 2100	1-5-3-6-2-4	1-4-2-6-3-5	50 @ 2100
NT-335	6	5½ x 6	855	335 @ 2100	1-5-3-6-2-4	1-4-2-6-3-5	50 @ 2100
NT-350	6	5½ x 6	855	350 @ 2100	1-5-3-6-2-4	1-4-2-6-3-5	50 @ 2100
NT-380	6	5½ x 6	855	380 @ 2300	1-5-3-6-2-4	1-4-2-6-3-5	50 @ 2300
V6-140	6	4⅝ x 3½	352	140 @ 3300	1-4-2-5-3-6	—	55 @ 3300
V6R-180	6	5½ x 4⅛	588	180 @ 2300	1-4-2-5-3-6	1-6-3-5-2-4	40 @ 2300
V6E-195	6	5½ x 4⅛	588	195 @ 2500	1-4-2-5-3-6	1-6-3-5-2-4	40 @ 2500
V6-200	6	5½ x 4⅛	588	200 @ 2600	1-4-2-5-3-6	1-6-3-5-2-4	40 @ 2600
V6-215M	6	5½ x 4⅛	588	215 @ 3000	1-4-2-5-3-6	1-6-3-5-2-4	40 @ 3000
V6N-215M	6	5½ x 4⅛	588	215 @ 3000	1-4-2-5-3-6	1-6-3-5-2-4	40 @ 3000
VT6N-280M	6	5½ x 4⅛	588	280 @ 3000	1-4-2-5-3-6	1-6-3-5-2-4	40 @ 3000
V8E-170	8	4⅝ x 3½	470	170 @ 3300	1-5-4-8-6-3-7-2	—	55 @ 3300
V8-185	8	4⅝ x 3½	470	185 @ 3300	1-5-4-8-6-3-7-2	—	55 @ 3300
V8E-235	8	5½ x 4⅛	785	235 @ 2400	1-5-4-8-6-3-7-2	1-2-7-3-6-8-4-5	40 @ 2400
V8R-240	8	5½ x 4⅛	785	240 @ 2300	1-5-4-8-6-3-7-2	1-2-7-3-6-8-4-5	40 @ 2300
V8-265	8	5½ x 4⅛	785	265 @ 2600	1-5-4-8-6-3-7-2	1-2-7-3-6-8-4-5	40 @ 2600
V8-300M	8	5½ x 4⅛	785	300 @ 3000	1-5-4-8-6-3-7-2	1-2-7-3-6-8-4-5	40 @ 3000
V8N-300M	8	5½ x 4⅛	785	300 @ 3000	1-5-4-8-6-3-7-2	1-2-7-3-6-8-4-5	40 @ 3000
VT8-370M	8	5½ x 4⅛	785	370 @ 3000	1-5-4-8-6-3-7-2	1-2-7-3-6-8-4-5	40 @ 3000
VT8N-370M	8	5½ x 4⅛	785	370 @ 3000	1-5-4-8-6-3-7-2	1-2-7-3-6-8-4-5	40 @ 3000
V8-350	8	5½ x 5	950	350 @ 2500	1-5-4-8-6-3-7-2	1-2-7-3-6-8-4-5	50 @ 2500
VT8-430	8	5½ x 5	950	350 @ 2500	1-5-4-8-6-3-7-2	1-2-7-3-6-8-4-5	50 @ 2500
V8-903	8	5½ x 4¾	903	—	1-5-4-8-6-3-7-2	1-2-7-3-6-8-4-5	30-55 @ 2600

CRANKSHAFT AND BEARING SPECIFICATIONS

ENGINE MODEL	MAIN BEARING JOURNAL DIAMETER	MAIN BEARING CLEARANCE	ROD BEARING JOURNAL DIAMETER	ROD BEARING CLEARANCE	CRANKSHAFT END PLAY
J, C	3.874-3.875	.0018-.0048	2.624-2.625	.002-.0045	.005-.0015
N, NH	4.499-4.500	.0015-.0050	3.124-3.125	.0015-.0045	.007-.0017
V6-Vim	3.499-3.500	.0015-.0045	3.124-3.125	.0015-.0045	.005-.0015
V6-140	3.499-3.500	.0015-.0045	2.499-2.500	.0015-.0045	.004-.0014
V6-140	3.249-3.250	.0015-.0045	2.499-2.500	.0015-.0045	.004-.0014
V8-185	3.499-3.500	.0015-.0045	2.499-2.500	.0015-.0045	.004-.0014
V8-185	3.249-3.250	.0015-.0045	2.499-2.500	.0015-.0045	.004-.0014
V8-Vine	3.499-3.500	.0015-.0045	3.124-3.125	.0015-.0045	.005-.015
V8-903	3.749-3.750	.0015-.005	3.124-3.125	.0015-.0045	.005-.015
V8 All others	4.249-4.250	.0015-.005	3.124-3.125	.0015-.0045	.006-.012

PISTONS, PINS, RINGS SPECIFICATIONS

ENGINE SERIES	PISTON CLEARANCE IN LINER	PISTON PIN DIAMETER	RING END GAP MINIMUM COMP.	RING END GAP MINIMUM OIL	LINER INSIDE DIAMETER
C	.010	1.4988-1.4990	.013	.013	4.437-4.438
J	.006-.0065	1.4988-1.4990	.013	.013	4.125-4.126
H & NH 4⅞″ Bore	.007-.0075	1.9988-1.9990	*	*	4.876-4.8775
H & NH 5⅛″ Bore	.012-.0125	1.9988-1.9990	*	*	5.1245-5.1260
NH 5½″ Bore	.0125-.013	1.9988-1.9990	*	*	5.4995-5.5010
V6-Vim—V8-Vine	.001-.0014	1.7488-1.7490	*	*	5.4995-5.5010

PISTONS, PINS, RINGS SPECIFICATIONS - Cont'd.

ENGINE SERIES	PISTON CLEARANCE IN LINER	PISTON PIN DIAMETER	RING END GAP MINIMUM COMP.	RING END GAP MINIMUM OIL	LINER INSIDE DIAMETER
V6-140, V8-185	.0085-.0110	1.3738-1.3740	.013	.015	5.3990-5.4010
V8-350, VT8-430	.001-.014	1.9988-1.9990	*	*	5.4995-5.5010
V8-903	.0095-.0120	1.7488-1.7490	*	*	5.4995-5.5010

* Types of rings used determines gap clearance.

Trouble Diagnosis

The satisfactory performance of a Diesel engine depends on two items of foremost importance, (1) Sufficiently high compression pressure, and (2) The injection of the proper amount of fuel at the right time.

The first one of these items depends entirely on pistons, piston rings, valves and valve operating mechanism; the second item depends on injectors and their operating mechanism, and fuel system.

Lack of engine power, uneven running, excessive vibration, and tendency to stall when idling may be caused by either a compression loss or faulty injector operation.

The causes of trouble symptoms may be varied; therefore a hit-and-miss search should be avoided. A proper diagnosis of symptoms is an orderly process of diagnosing the symptoms. An "orderly process" means to check the most probable common cause first; then proceed with the next probable cause.

Hard Starting or Failure To Start

1. Fuel shut off valve closed or fuel tank empty.
2. Inferior quality fuel.
3. Restricted fuel lines.
4. Fuel pump pressure regulation faulty.
5. Plugged injector spray holes.
6. Broken fuel pump drive shaft.
7. Gear pump gears scored or worn.
8. Injector inlet or drain connections loose.
9. Water in fuel.
10. Air leaks in fuel suction line.
11. Incorrect injector timing.
12. Valve leakage.
13. Restricted air intake.
14. Engine in need of overhaul.
15. Incorrect valve timing.

Engine Runs but Misses

1. Restricted fuel lines.
2. Water in fuel or poor quality fuel.
3. Air leaks in fuel suction line.
4. Injectors improperly adjusted or plugged.
5. Low compression, intake or exhaust valves leaking.

Excessive Smoke

1. Restricted fuel lines.
2. Plugged injector spray holes.
3. Inferior quality fuel.
4. Incorrect injector timing.
5. Injectors improperly adjusted.
6. Intake manifold or cylinder head gasket leak.
7. Restricted air intake.
8. High exhaust back pressure.
9. Broken or worn piston rings.
10. Engine in need of overhaul.
11. Incorrect valve timing.
12. Worn or scored cylinder liners or pistons.
13. Engine overloaded.

Low Power or Loss of Power

1. Inferior quality fuel.
2. Water in fuel.
3. Fuel suction line leaking.
4. Restricted fuel lines.
5. Fuel pump inoperative.
6. Plugged injector spray holes.
7. Dirty fuel filters or screens.
8. Gear pump gears scored or worn.
9. Improperly adjusted throttle linkage.
10. Incorrect injection timing.
11. Air in system.
12. Sticking stop control (fuel shut off).
13. Restricted air intake.
14. High exhaust back pressure.
15. Intake manifold or cylinder head gasket leakage.
16. Low compression—intake or exhaust valve leakage.
17. Broken or worn piston rings.
18. Incorrect bearing clearances.
19. Worn or scored cylinder liners or pistons.
20. Engine in need of overhaul.
21. Incorrect valve timing.
22. Dirty air cleaner.
23. Overheating engine.

Excessive Fuel Consumption

1. Inferior quality fuel.
2. Restricted fuel lines.
3. Fuel pump pressure regulator broken or improperly adjusted.
4. Fuel leaks—external or internal.
5. Plugged injector spray holes.
6. Injectors not adjusted properly.
7. Cracked injector body or cup.
8. Restricted air intake.
9. High exhaust back pressure.
10. Engine overloaded.
11. Incorrect bearing clearances.
12. Engine in need of overhaul.

Excessive Oil Consumption

1. External or internal oil leaks.
2. Cylinder oil control not working.
3. Wrong grade oil for climatic conditions.
4. Broken or worn piston rings.
5. Engine in need of overhaul.
6. Worn or scored cylinder liners or pistons.

Low Lubrication Oil Pressure

1. Oil suction line restricted.
2. Oil pressure regulator valve not working.
3. Crankcase oil level too low.
4. Wrong grade of oil for conditions.
5. Insufficient coolant.
6. Worn water pump.
7. Coolant thermostat not working.
8. Loose fan belts.
9. Clogged coolant passages.
10. Clogged oil cooler.
11. Radiator core openings restricted.
12. Air in cooling system.
13. Insufficient radiator capacity.
14. Leaking coolant hoses, connections or gaskets.
15. Incorrect bearing clearances.
16. Engine in need of overhaul.
17. Engine overloaded.

Coolant Temperature Too High

1. Low coolant level.
2. Air leaks in suction line.
3. Low coolant level.
4. Engine overloaded.
5. Injectors not properly adjusted.
6. Injector pipe partially clogged.
7. Faulty injectors.
8. Injector timing too early.
9. Worn or scored cylinder liners or pistons.
10. Broken valve springs.
11. Crankshaft vibration damper faulty.
12. Excessive crankshaft end clearance.
13. Flywheel loose or unbalanced.
14. Broken or worn piston rings.
15. Incorrect bearing clearances.
16. Engine in need of overhaul.
17. Broken tooth in engine gear train.
18. Loose mounting bolts.

Description and Operation

The four-stroke-cycle, NH-Series diesel engines have a compression ratio of 15.5:1. The V-6 diesel engine has a piston displacement of 588 cubic inches and a compression ratio of 16.1:1. The rating plate identification symbol for the engine is "2". Overhead valves are push rod actuated by cam followers operated off the camshaft.

The four-stroke cycle naturally-aspirated, C-Series diesel engines have a compression ratio of 15.8:1. The supercharged C-180 engine has a gear-driven air pump that rotates at 1.8 times engine speed to force additional air into the engine cylinders. This enables the engine to burn more fuel and develop more horsepower than the naturally-aspirated C-160 and CF-160 engines. The compression ratio of the C-180 engine is 14.5:1. Overhead valves are push rod actuated by roller type tappets off the camshaft. Four valves (two intake and two exhaust) are used in each cylinder to provide maximum induction and exhaust air flow.

The PT (pressure-time) fuel pump is driven by the air compressor at engine speed. The engine speed governor is incorporated in the fuel pump. The tachometer is coupled to the fuel pump main shaft. The fuel pump supplies fuel under high pressure to the injectors; one for each cylinder.

The fuel injectors meter and inject fuel into the cylinders. The injectors are operated and timed by push rods actuated by the camshaft and cam followers. Engine timing can be varied by changing the angular relationship of the cam followers to the camshaft.

The variable-speed, mechanical governor has two purposes: it maintains sufficient fuel delivery to the injectors for idling with the throttle control in idling position, and it cuts off fuel to the injectors above maximum rated rpm.

The engines are pressure lubricated by a gear-type pump driven off the camshaft. The oil pump is externally mounted just below the air compressor. Oil is drawn into the pump by an external oil line connected to the oil pan sump. The oil flows through a full-flow oil filter to the engine gallery (header) for distribution to the engine moving parts. An optional, by-pass oil filter (Luber-Finer) is available to supplement the full-flow filter.

A replaceable-element (dry-type) crankcase breather is mounted on the front rocker housing cover.

A belt-driven, centrifugal-type water pump circulates coolant around the cylinder liners, through the cylinder head, and around the injector sleeves.

Cummins V6 diesel engine
(© Cummins Engine Co.)

C-160 naturally aspirated diesel engine
(© Cummins Engine Co.)

C-180 supercharged diesel
(© Cummins Engine Co.)

Fuel System

Description and Operation

The Cummins PT fuel system delivers fuel to each cylinder of the engine in equal, pre-determined amounts; thus PT is an abbreviation for pressure-time. The fuel system consists of the supply tank(s), fuel filter, fuel pump, governor, injectors, fuel shut-off valve, and the fuel supply and drain lines.

The fuel pump is coupled to the air compressor which is driven from the engine gear train. The fuel pump main shaft turns at engine crankshaft speed, and drives the gear pump, governor and tachometer shaft.

The fuel pump consists of a gear pump to draw fuel from the supply tank and deliver it to the injectors under pressure, and a governor and throttle to control fuel pressure to the injectors. A pulsation damper prolongs gear pump life, as it smoothes the flow of fuel through the pump.

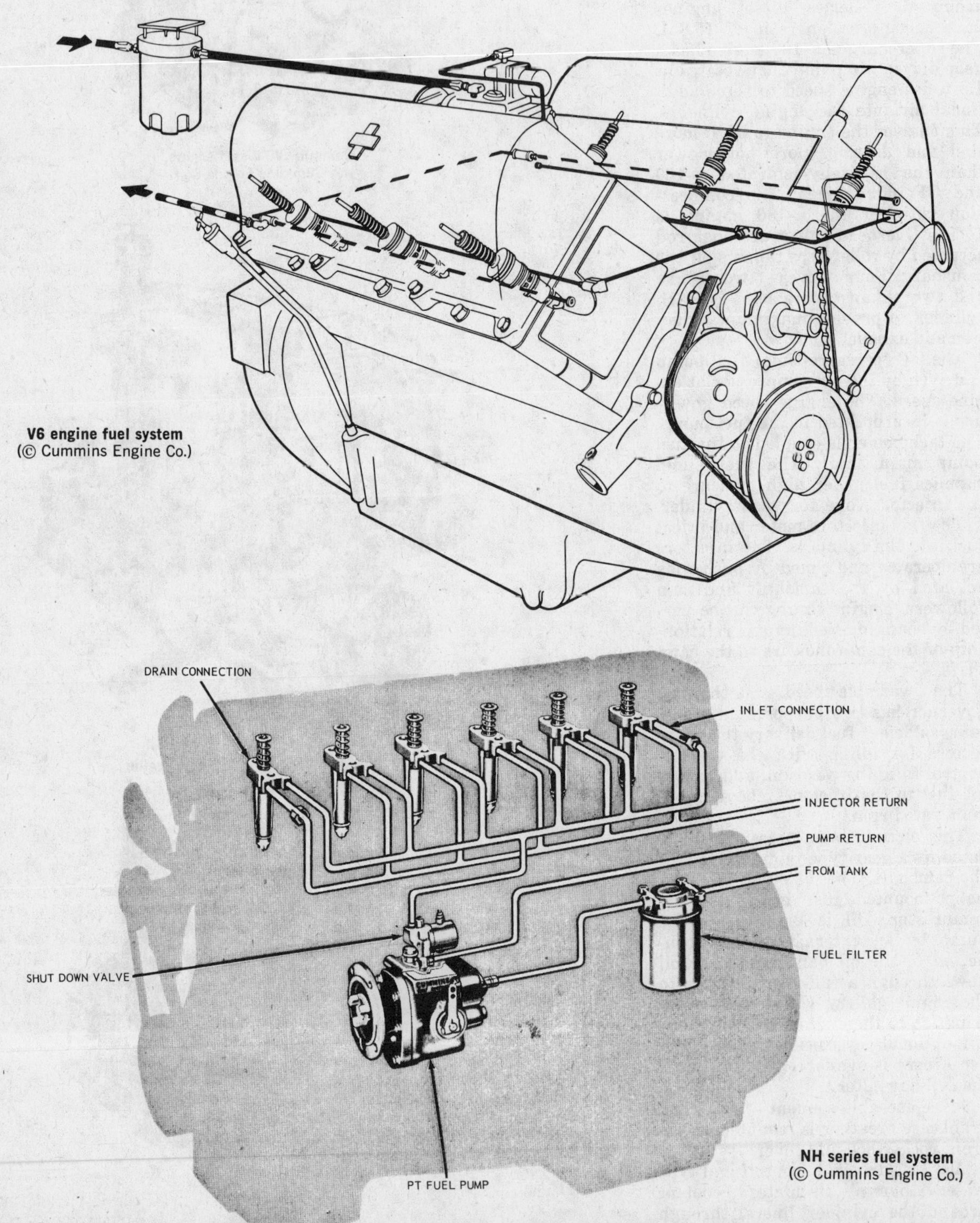

V6 engine fuel system
(© Cummins Engine Co.)

NH series fuel system
(© Cummins Engine Co.)

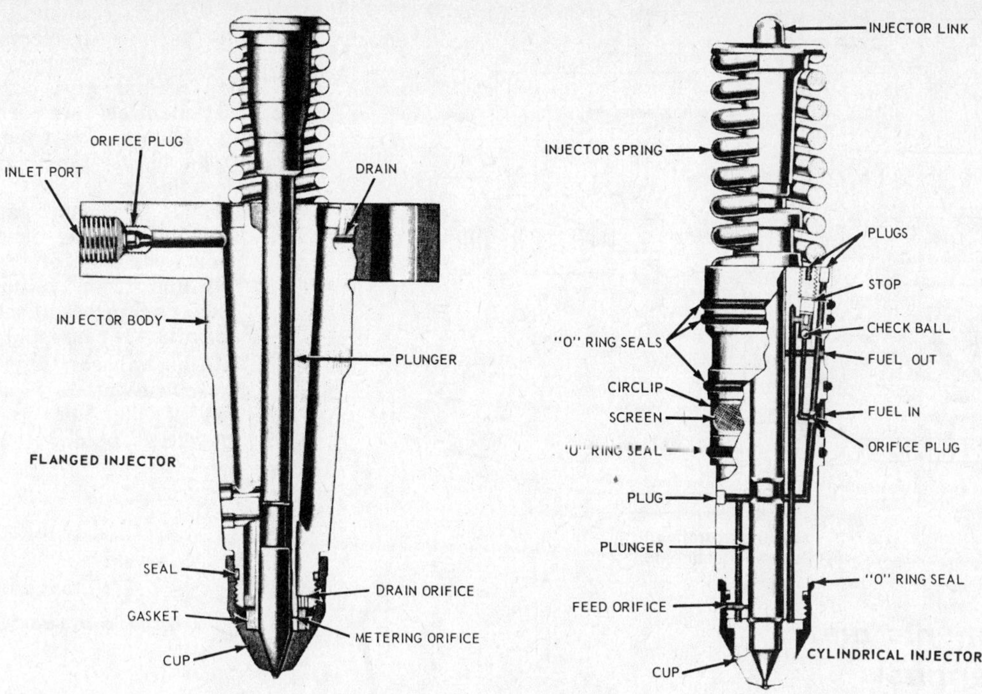

Flanged and cylindrical injectors
(© Cummins Engine Co.)

The gear pump receives fuel from the supply tank and pumps the fuel under pressure, varying with engine speed, through the filter screen and governor to the throttle and to the injectors. The filter screen, mounted in the top of the fuel pump, prevents damage to the fuel pump and injectors by filtering from the fuel any foreign particles that may be present. To provide fuel pump cooling a small amount of fuel is bled from the fuel pump and returned to the fuel tank. Thus, a circulation of cooling fuel is provided.

At idle speed, the main throttle shaft passage is closed, allowing fuel to flow around the throttle shaft to the idle port in the governor barrel. At engine speeds above idle, the fuel flows through the main throttle shaft hole and enters the main fuel port in the governor barrel.

When the throttle lever is moved to the idle position and the vehicle is moving in excess of idle speed, a small amount of throttle leakage is provided to purge the injectors of air. The PT fuel pump governor controls both idle and high speed. On the C- and NH-Series engines except the NH-250, the fuel manifold is a tube mounted externally on the engine, with equal length branches (tubing) to the injectors. On the V-6, V-8, and NH-250 engines the manifolds are drilled passages, one in each cylinder head, that are aligned wtih a passageway in the injector body. These fuel manifolds are connected to the pressure side of the fuel pump by a common fuel line.

Fuel circulates through the injector at all times, except during a short period following injection into the cylinder. From the inlet fuel flows down the inlet passage of the injector, around the injector plunger, between the body end and cup, up the drain passage to the drain connections and manifold and back to the supply tank.

As the plunger comes up the injector feed passage is opened and fuel flows through the metering orifice into the cup. At the same time, fuel flows past the cup and out the drain orifice. The amount of fuel which enters the cup is controlled by the fuel pressure against the metering orifice. Fuel pressure is controlled by the fuel pump.

The plunger, during injection, comes down until the metering orifice is closed and the fuel in the cup is injected into the cylinder. While the plunger is seated in the cup, all fuel flow in the injector is stopped.

On the C- and NH-Series engines, except the NH-250, a flanged injector is used. The fuel manifold is connected to the inlet port of the injector flange. A removable inlet screen is installed in each inlet port for final fuel filtration. The drain port is located adjacent to the inlet port. The drain ports are connected by a drain manifold to return surplus fuel to the supply tank.

The V-6, V-8 and NH-250 engines utilize a cylindrical injector. Two radial grooves (annuli) on the injector body index with two drilled passages in each cylinder head, which serve as fuel inlet and drain manifolds. The inlet annulus contains a fine mesh screen for final fuel filtration. A fuel crossover drain tube, at the flywheel end of the engine, connects the two cylinder head drain passages and a common line returns the unused fuel to the fuel tank.

The fuel grooves around the cylindrical injectors are separated by O-rings which seal against the cylinder head injector bore. This forms a leak-proof passage between the injectors and the cylinder head injector bore surface. The injectors contain an orifice plug which can be varied in inside diameter to achieve identical fuel delivery through all injectors.

Cold Starting Systems

To assist in cold weather starting various systems are available. The preheater consists of a glow plug which is electrically heated by the battery and a hand priming pump to spray fuel into the intake manifold. The fuel burning in the manifold heats the intake air. *Never use ether when using the preheater.*

Another cold weather starting aid is the ether quick-start, measured-shot system. This system consists of an ether tank and a manually controlled metering valve or quick start choke to inject shots of ether into the intake manifold.

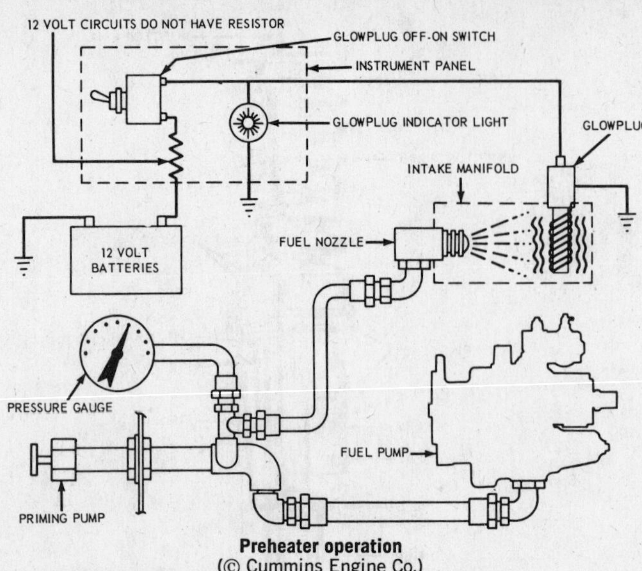

Preheater operation
(© Cummins Engine Co.)

Adjustments and Repairs

Adjustments

Fuel Pump

Only those fuel pump adjustments described herein should be performed in the truck. Make the adjustments in the order given.

In-chassis adjustments of the fuel pump are based on fuel manifold pressure and fuel supply vacuum. To determine these pressures follow the procedures below.

The following adjustment procedures refer to forward throttle screw and rear throttle screw. The forward throttle screw is closer to the drive end of the fuel pump.

Before Making Adjustments

1. Operate the engine until the oil temperature reaches 140° to 160° F. Make all fuel pump or injector settings on a hot engine.

In-vehicle adjustments of the full pump are based on fuel manifold pressure and fuel supply vacuum. Determine these pressures by snap reading which provides a method of finding maximum full manifold pressure and fuel supply vacuum without a dynamometer. Obtain manifold pressure and fuel supply vacuum readings when the engine is at full load and rated speed. *When the engine is accelerated to full throttle, full engine load is momentarily attained when the engine reaches rated speed.* Fuel pressure and vacuum gauge readings increase with engine speed until rated speed is reached. At this point the gauge hand hesitates and falls off due to governor action at speeds above rated speed. It is necessary to read the maximum swing of the pressure gauge hand quickly. The snap reading technique is not as accurate as measurements obtained with a dynamometer.

Snap reading gives an indication of fuel manifold pressure and fuel supply vacuum. *For a more dependable reading, use the average of five snap readings.*

2. Install a vacuum gauge in the fuel supply line. Check the suction restriction of the fuel supply line. If the vacuum reading exceeds 8 inches of mercury, determine the cause and correct.
3. Adjust valve and injector lash to specifications.
4. Check high-idle or maximum governed speed.

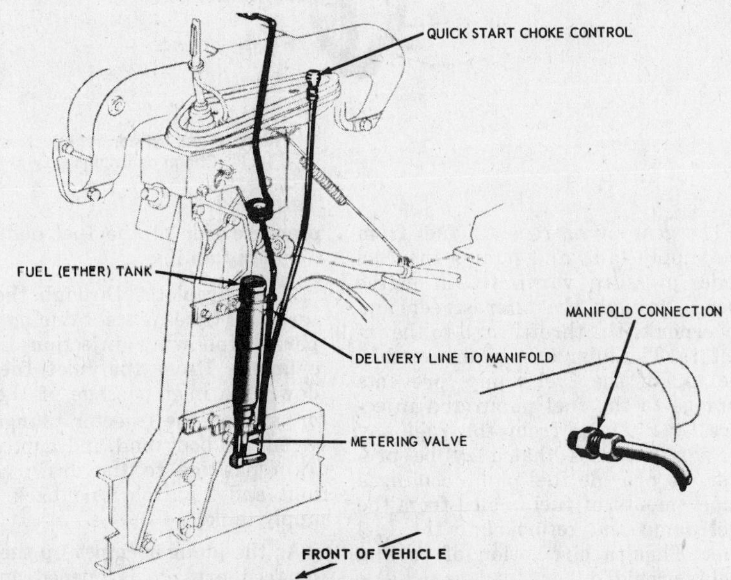

Ether quick start unit
(© Cummins Engine Co.)

Fuel pump adjustments
(© Cummins Engine Co.)

Rear Throttle Screw Adjustment

1. Connect a manifold pressure gauge at the manifold pressure gauge connection. Check the full manifold pressure at rated speed and full load.
2. Turn the rear throttle screw out until the highest fuel manifold pressure reading is obtained.
3. Turn the rear throttle screw in to reduce the fuel manifold pressure 5 psi. Do not increase the rear throttle adjustment more than 5 psi or the engine speed at which peak torque occurs will change. Throttle restriction over 5 psi allows unauthorized adjustment to raise fuel manifold pressure, thereby overfueling the engine.

Forward Throttle Screw or Throttle Leakage Adjustment

1. With the engine operating at idle speed, turn in the forward throttle screw until the engine gains speed. Back the screw out two full turns.
2. Stop the engine and remove the spring pack cover plug and adjust the idle governor screw to idle the engine at specified rpm (see specifications).
3. Operate the engine until it is purged of the air let in.
4. Check the idle speed.
5. Check deceleration; if it is too slow, the throttle leakage is excessive. If the engine falters or dies when idle speed is reached, the throttle leakage is too low. Adjust the screw to obtain permissible deceleration time.
6. Any change in the desired idle speed is made with the governor idle screw. Follow the sequence under Idle Speed Adjustments.

Idle Speed Adjustments

With the engine stopped remove the pipe plug from the spring pack cover.

The idle adjustment screw is held in position with a spring clip. Turn the screw in to increase, or out to decrease the speed.

Replace the pipe plug. With the engine running, air which collected in the spring pack housing will cause a rough idle temporarily. This will stabilize when the housing fills with fuel.

Fuel Filter Element Replacement

The fuel filter has a disposable-type element. Replace it at the specified interval, even though it may appear serviceable. Unscrew the combination filter case and element and discard it. Insall the new filter case and element assembly and tighten it by hand until the O-ring seal touches the filter head. Then tighten it an additonal ¼ to ½ turn by hand. *If the replacement filter doesn't have an integral O-ring seal, use a new O-ring for installation.*

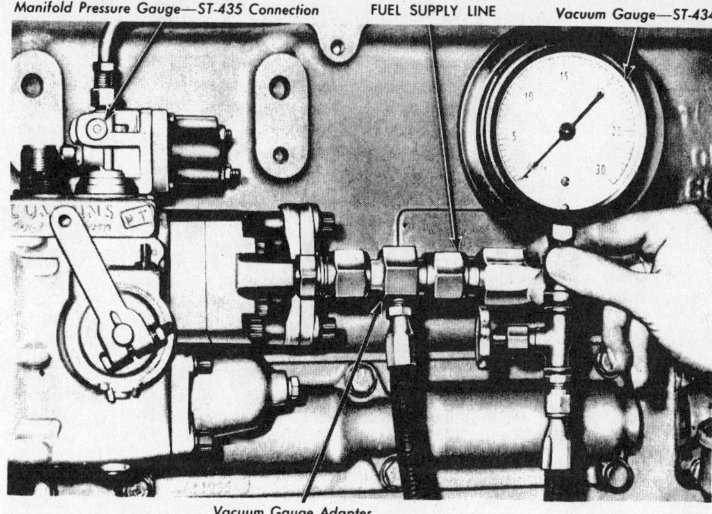

Fuel pump gauge connections
(© Cummins Engine Co.)

Typical chassis mooted fuel filter V6 engine
(© Cummins Engine Co.)

Engine mounted fuel filter NH series
(© Cummins Engine Co.)

Fuel Pump Screen

Remove the retainer cap from the fuel pump. Remove the spring and lift out the filter screen assembly.

Remove the top screen retainer from the filter screen assembly. Wash the screen and magnet in cleaning solvent and dry with compressed air. Install the top screen retainer.

Install the filter screen, *with the hole down,* in the fuel pump.

Install the spring and retainer cap. Torque the retainer cap to specifications.

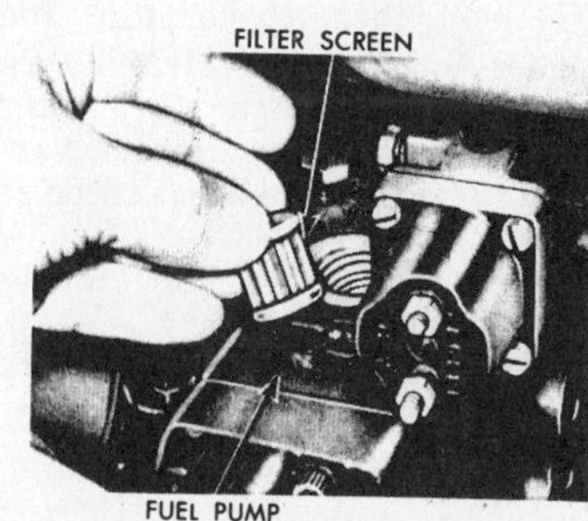

Fuel filter screen removal
(© Cummins Engine Co.)

Fuel Pump Removal

NH-Series Engines

1. Disconnect the accelerator return spring. Disconnect the hand throttle control, tachometer cable and accelerator rod at the fuel pump. Disconnect the lead to the fuel shut-off valve.
2. Disconnect the primer fuel pump line and fuel supply line at the full pump. Remove the fuel outlet line from the shut-off valve and full manifold. Disconnect the fuel bleed line.
3. Remove the full pump mounting bolts. Remove the fuel pump, gasket and pump drive rubber buffer.

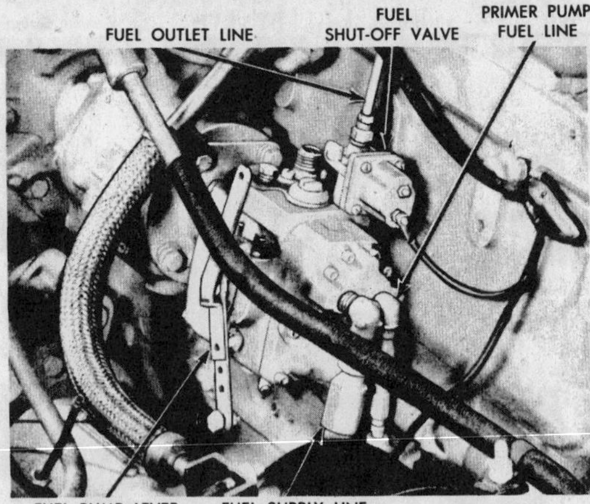

Typical fuel pump installation NH series (© Cummins Engine Co.)

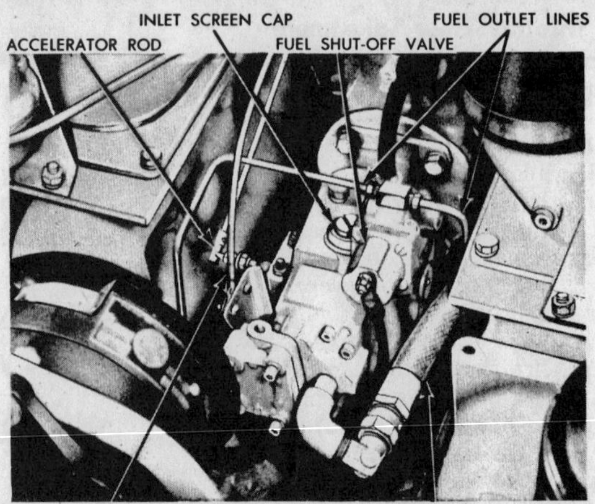

Typical fuel pump installation V6 engines (© Cummins Engine Co.)

Installation

1. Clean the gasket surfaces of the fuel pump and air compressor.
2. Install the pump, drive rubber buffer. Position a new fuel pump gasket on the air compressor and install the fuel pump. Torque the mounting bolts to specifications.
3. Connect the primer fuel pump line and fuel supply line to the fuel pump. Connect the fuel outlet line to the fuel manifold and fuel shut-off valve. Connect the fuel bleed line.
4. Connct the accelerator rod, hand throttle control and tachometer cable to the fuel pump. Connect the fuel shut-off valve lead. Connect the accelerator return spring.
5. Check the accelerator linkage and adjust if necessary.
6. Start the engine and check for leaks.

Fuel Pump Removal

V-6 and V-8 Engines

1. Disconnect the air cleaner inlet air tube from the air intake connection on the right intake manifold. Remove the air intake connection and air cross-over connection from the intake manifolds.
2. Disconnect the fuel shut-off valve lead. Disconnect the hand throttle control, accelerator rod and tachometer cable from the fuel pump.
3. Disconnect the fuel supply line and the fuel outlet line(s) from the fuel pump and shut-off valve. Disconnect the fuel bleed line.
4. Remove the fuel pump to air compressor mounting bolts, and remove the fuel pump. Remove the gasket and the pump drive rubber buffer.

Installation

1. Clean the gasket surfaces of the fuel pump and air compressor.
2. Install the pump drive rubber buffer. Use a new gasket and install the fuel pump on the air compressor. Torque the mounting bolts to specifications.
3. Connect the fuel outlet line(s) to the fuel shut-off valve. Connect the fuel supply line to the fuel pump. Connect the fuel bleed line.
4. Connect the accelerator rod, hand throttle control and tachometer cable to the fuel pump. Connect the fuel shut-off valve lead. Check the accelerator linkage and adjust if necessary.
5. Install the air cross-over connection and air intake connection on the intake manifolds. Torque the retaining bolts to specifications. Connect the air cleaner inlet air tube to the air intake connection.
6. Start the engine and check for air and fuel leaks.

Fuel Pump Hydraulic Governor Drive

The fuel pump/hydraulic governor drive is used whenever a hydraulic governor is needed for a particular engine application. The governor mounts atop the housing and the fuel pump is coupled behind the housing.

Disassembly

1. Remove governor drive assembly from governor reservoir. Remove and discard gasket.
2. On governors with 2:1 gear ratio, press out governor drive shaft from gear end. Remove snap ring, ball key and collar.
3. On governors with 3:1 gear ratio, press on shaft from gear end to separate all units from housing.
4. Remove snap ring and ball key; then press out shaft.
5. Remove capscrews and lockwashers and separate drive gear and support assmbly from reservoir.
6. Remove drain plug, dipstick, vent plug and elbow.
7. Remove shaft locknut and washer from drive shaft.
8. Use puller to remove coupling, spacer and governor drive gear.
9. Press on small end of shaft to remove shaft from support.
10. Press on large end of shaft to remove drive gear. Remove keys from shaft key way.
11. Remove snap ring from support. Invert housing and press out rear bearing and oil seal. Discard oil seal.

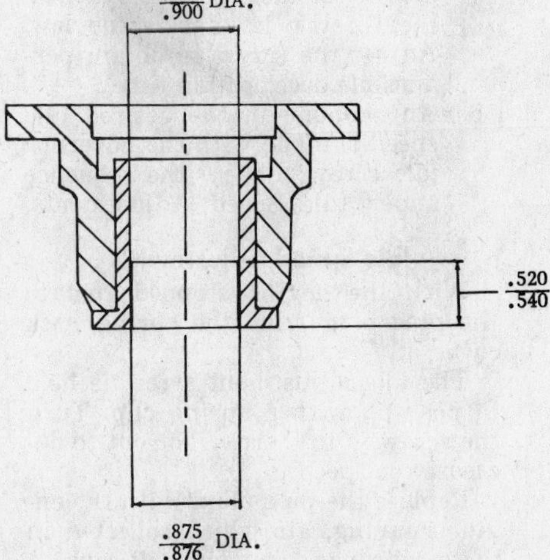

Bearing and retainer assembly (© Cummins Engine Co.)

Cleaning and Inspection

1. Clean all parts in approved cleaning solvent and dry thoroughly with clean cloth or air jet.
2. Check bearing for worn race or rough action.
3. Check gears for chipped or broken teeth or uneven wear.
4. Check governor shaft housing oil holes. Make certain they are open.

5. Inspect support and reservoir for cracks, breaks, or rough mating surfaces.

Assembly

1. Lubricate outside of oil seal and press into housing from large end. Open end of seal must be down. Check to see that oil holes in housing are open.
2. Invert housing. Coat outside of rear bearing with lubricant and press bearing into housing to shoulder. Insert snap ring, flat side down.
3. Lubricate large end of shaft. Place key in shaft and press shaft into gear against shoulder. Place flat side, not beveled side, of gear hub against shoulder.
4. Press small end of shaft assembly into large end of housing. Coat shaft first with lubricant so that oil seal will not be damaged.
5. Lubricate shaft and press governor drive gear on small end against bearing in housing.
6. Insert key; then press on coupling. Shoulder of coupling goes against gear.
7. Install flat washer and shaft lock nut.
8. Place reservoir in vise with governor drive studs up. Install dipstick, vent plug, weatherhead fitting, and drain plug.
9. Place gaskets and install drive gear and housing assembly to serial number side of reservoir with four capscrews and lockwashers. Large oil hole in housing must be at top.
10. On governors with 2:1 gear ratio:
    a. Drop thrust washer into housing.
    b. Lubricate ball key and insert in drive shaft; install snap ring.
    c. Line up ball key with thrust washer, invert assembly, and press on gear. Allow .003/.006 inch end play. Check with feeler gauge.
11. On governor with 3:1 gear ratio:
    a. Press governor drive shaft into washer flush with bottom side. Note relief in washer to start shaft.
    b. Press shaft assembly into cylinder until shoulder on shaft is flush with end of cylinder.
    c. Slide this assembly into governor drive housing so that flatwasher rests on bronze bushing.
    d. Invert assembly and install ball key, collared washer and snap ring.
    e. Press on end of cylinder until flat washer is against bronze bushing.
    f. Press gear into position allowing .003/.006 inch end play. Check with feeler gauge.

Fuel Injectors

Removal

NH-Series Engines (except NH-250)

1. Remove the rocker housing cover(s).
2. Disconnect the fuel manifold and fuel return line from the injector inlet and drain connections. Remove the fuel inlet screen . Remove the fuel inlet and drain connections from the injector.

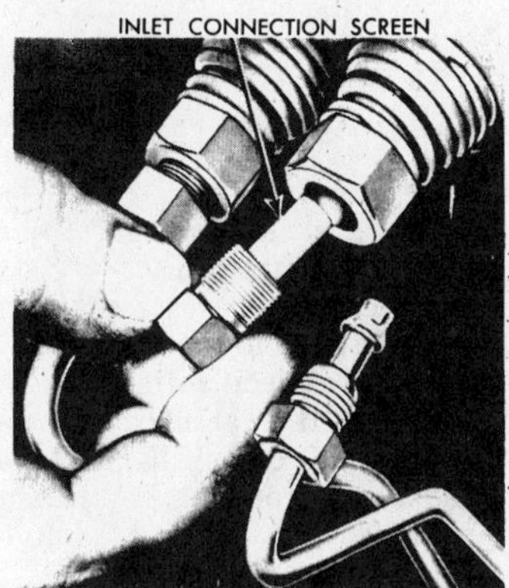

Removing injector inlet screen
(© Cummins Engine Co.)

3. Loosen the injector rocker lever lock nut and unscrew the adjusting screw until the push rod can be disengaged. Disengage the push rod and tip the rocker lever away from the injector.

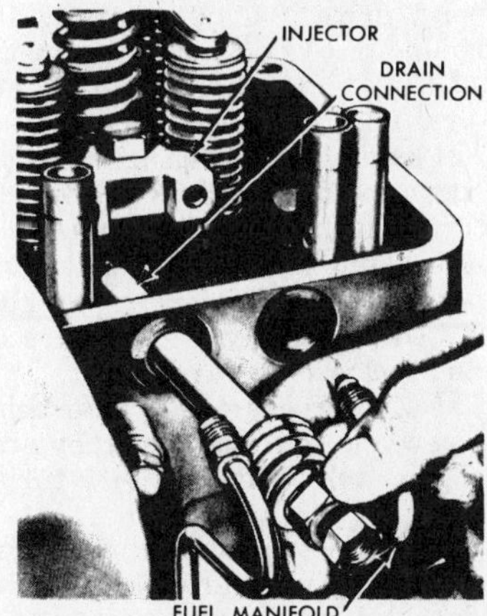

Injector fuel inlet and drain connections
(© Cummins Engine Co.)

4. Remove the injector retaining screws and lift the injector from the cylinder head. *Do not bruise the injector tip. Do not turn the injector bottom side up or the plunger will fall out. Leave the plunger in the injector as the plungers are not interchangeable.*

Installation

1. Insert the injector in the cylinder head. *Be sure the plunger is positioned with the plunger class mark centered between the inlet and drain connections.*
2. Lubricate the retaining screw threads. Start, *but do not tighten*, the retaining screws. Align the injector by installing the inlet and drain connections 2 turns in the injector. Torque the retaining screws alternately to specifications.

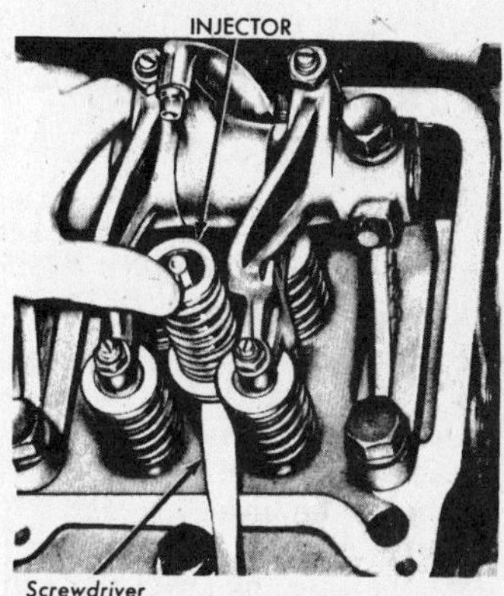

Typical cylindrical injector removal
(© Cummins Engine Co.)

3. Torque the inlet and drain connections to specifications. Install the fuel inlet screen and connect the fuel manifold and fuel return line.
4. Position the push rod under the rocker lever and adjust the injector rocker lever lash to specifications.
5. Install the rocker housing cover(s). Partially tighten the cover screws.
6. Operate the engine until the oil temperature is 140°F, and adjust the injector lash to specifications.

Fuel Injectors Removal

V-6, V-8, and NH-250 Engines

1. On some model trucks, it will be necessary to remove the right side air cleaner for right cylinder bank operations.
2. On some model trucks, it will be necessary to disconnect the brace rod from the left side of the transmission remote control mounting support and position it aside. Disconnect the accelerator pedal rod at the cross-shaft on the engine.
3. Remove the valve covers.
4. Remove the power steering pump and drive bolts from the engine. Leave the hoses attached and position the power steering pump out of the way.
5. Loosen the lock nut and back-off the injector rocker lever adjusting screw until the push rod can

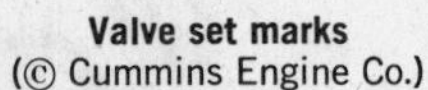

Valve set marks
(© Cummins Engine Co.)

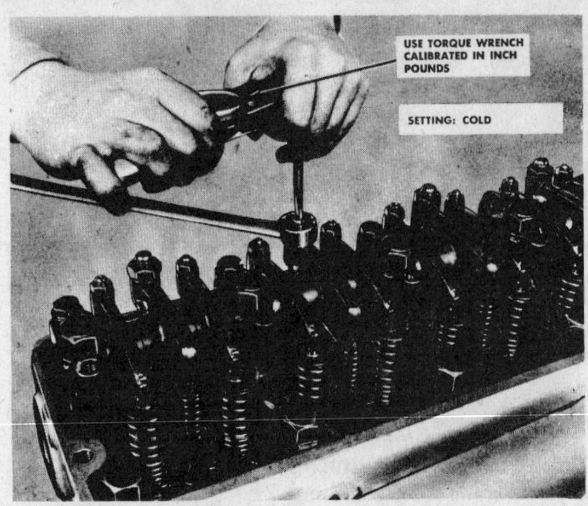

Adjusting injector plunger
(© Cummins Engine Co.)

be disengaged. Hold the push rod aside and tip the rocker lever away from the injector to clear the injector link.

6. Remove the injector clamp retaining screws and the clamps. Pry the injector from the cylinder head. Remove the O-rings.

Avoid bruising the injector tip. Do not turn the injector upside down as the plunger might fall out. Injector plungers are not inter-changeable.

Installation

1. Clean the injector sleeve with a cloth-wrapped stick.
2. Install new O-rings on the injector, and coat the O-rings with lubricant.
3. Install the injector in the cylinder head. *Be sure the fuel inlet hole is toward the camshaft.* Seat the injector in the sleeve by giving it a quick, hard push with a wooden hammer handle. A snap should be heard as the injector cup seats in the sleeve.
4. Install the hold-down clamp and torque the retaining screws to specifications.
5. Depress the injector springs with a screwdriver (use as a lever with blade under rocker lever shaft), and engage the injector plunger link with the rocker lever. At the same time engage the push rod with the rocker lever adjusting screw.
6. Adjust the injector lash to specifications. Tighten the lock nut. Install the cylinder head cover valve cover if removed and partially tighten the cover screws.
7. Install the right air cleaner, if removed.
8. Operate the engine until the oil temperature is 140°F. Remove the valve cover or cylinder head cover and adjust the injector lash to specifications.
9. Install the power steering pump and drive belts. Adjust the belt tension to specifications.
10. Connect the accelerator pedal rod to the cross shaft. Connect the brace rod to the transmission remote control mounting support.

Injector Adjustment

1. Turn engine, in direction of rotation, to No. 1 top-center firing position. In this position, intake and exhaust valves for No. 1 cylinder are closed.
2. Continue rotating crankshaft until valve set mark on accessory drive pulley aligns with timing marks on gear case cover. (1-6 VS on 6 cylinder, 1-4 VS on 4-cylinder engines.) When these marks align, the engine is in position to adjust valves and injector plunger for No. 1 cylinder.
3. Check intake and exhaust valve position of cylinder to be adjusted. See that valves are closed and rocker levers free.
4. Check threads on adjusting screw and nut. See that they are clean, well-oiled and free-turning.
5. Turn injector adjusting screw down until plunger contacts cup. Turn adjusting screw an additional 15° to squeeze oil from cup.
6. Slack off adjusting screw one turn.
7. Tighten adjusting screw to 70°F. setting. Use a torque wrench equipped wtih a screwdriver adaptor, graduated in inch-pound divisions, and having a maximum capacity of 150 inch-pounds.

   Setting at 70°F. 48 inch-pounds.

   Setting at 140°F. 60 inch-pounds.
8. Lock screw in place with jam nut.
9. Make final adjustment when engine is at operating (140°F.) temperature.

Crosshead Adjustment

It is necessary to adjust the crossheads before making valve adjustments. Some crossheads pilot over a solid guide while others pilot within a tubular guide.

1. Loosen valve crosshead adjusting screw locknut and back off screw one turn.

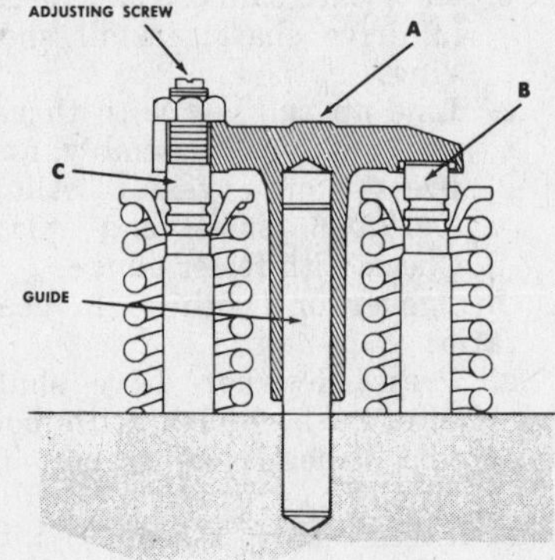

Alignment of crosshead-stem and guide
(© Cummins Engine Co.)

2. Use light finger pressure at the rocker lever contact surface to hold crosshead in contact with valve stem nearest the push rod.
3. Turn adjusting screw down until it contacts its mating valve stem.
4. For new crossheads and guides, advance adjusting screw one-

third of one hex (20 degrees) to straighten the stem in its guide and to compensate for slack in threads. With worn crossheads and guides, it may be necessary to advance the screw as much as 30 degrees in order to straighten the stem in its guide.

5. Hold the adjusting screw in this position and tighten locknut to 25/30 foot-pounds torque.
6. Check clearance between crosshead and valve spring retainer with wire gauge. There must be a minimum of .020 inch clearance at this point.

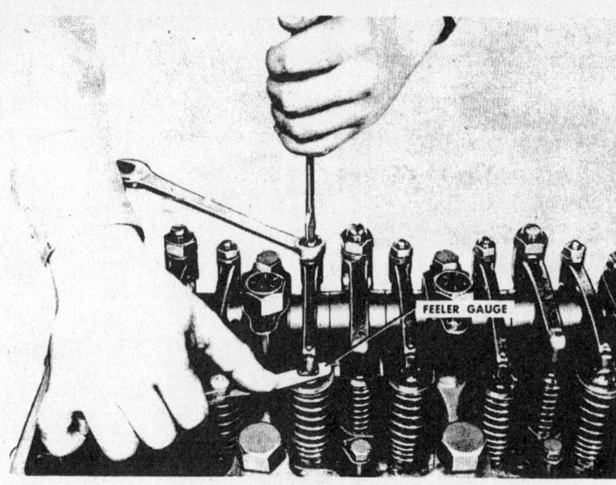

Adjusting valves
(© Cummins Engine Co.)

Supercharger

Preliminary Inspection

Before disassembling the supercharger the following inspection procedures must be observed.

1. Check for excessive oil at the air outlet port indicating broken piston ring oil seals.
2. Check radial clearance in bearings:
   a. Remove pump-end cover and force fuel oil through the oil inlet to flush *all* lubricating oil from bearings.
   b. Install an indicator gauge on the rotor timing gear outer diameter.
   c. Check total radial movement by moving gear from side to side. If movement exceeds .003 inch, disassemble unit for a complete bearing inspection.
3. Check rotor shaft end play.
   a. Install a dial indicator at end of rotor shaft.
   b. Push shaft back and forth: note indicator reading.
   c. If total end play exceeds .005 inch, disassemble supercharger and inspect thrust faces.
   d. Perform this operation on both rotor shafts.
4. Check timing gear backlash.
   a. Install an indicator gauge to supercharger housing and check rotor timing gear backlash.
   b. If backlash exceeds .004 inch, a new set of gears must be installed.

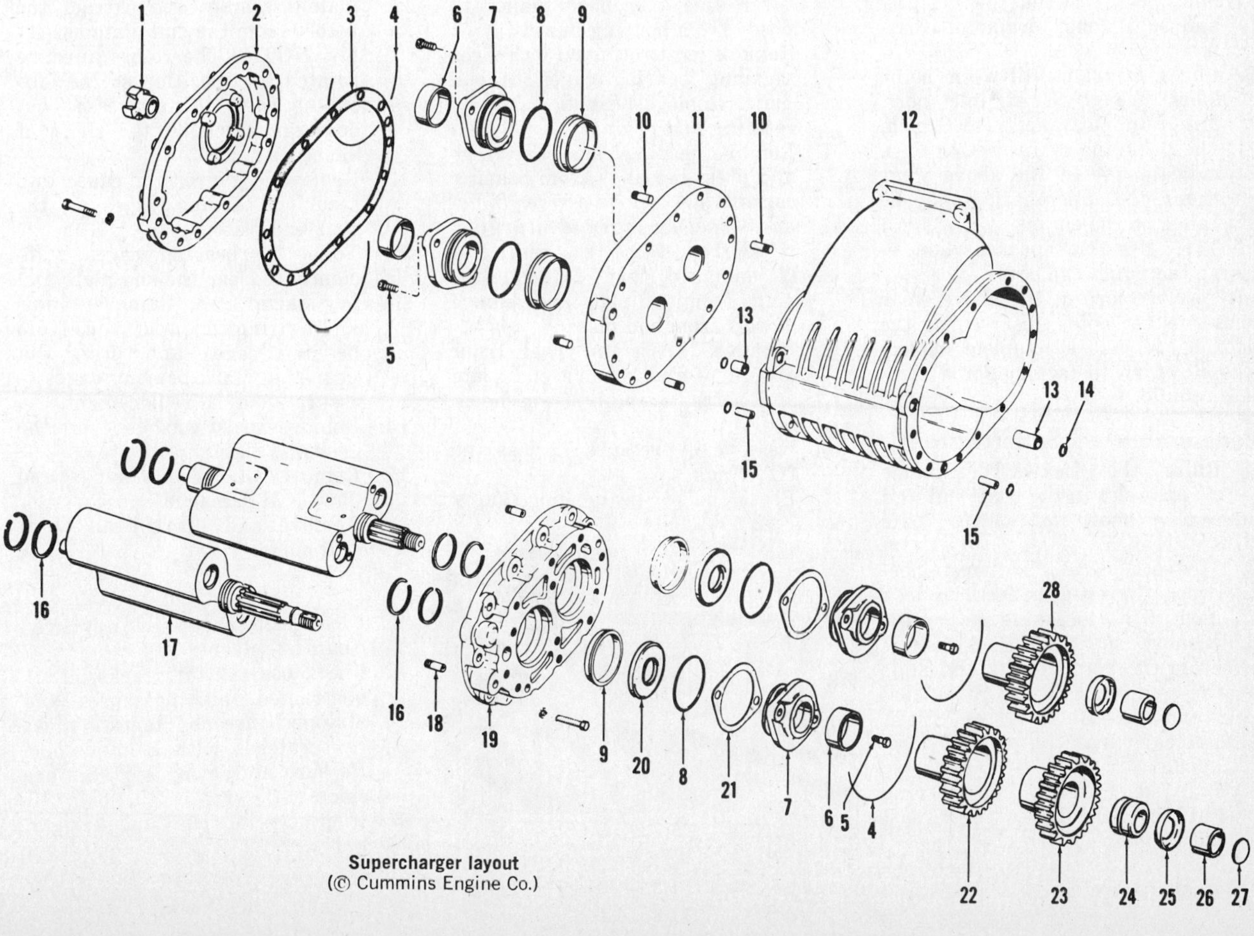

Supercharger layout
(© Cummins Engine Co.)

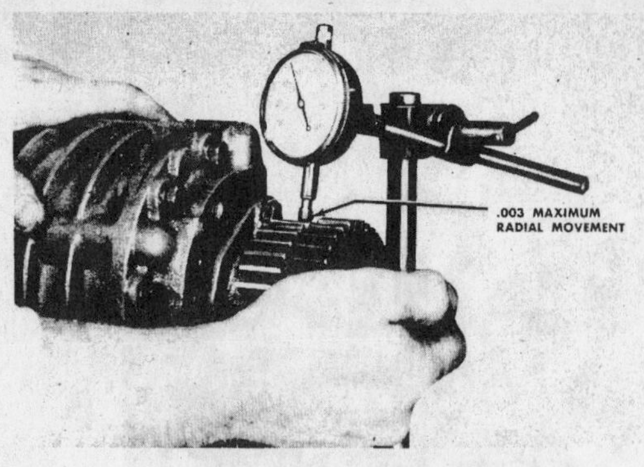

Checking radial bearing clearance
(© Cummins Engine Co.)

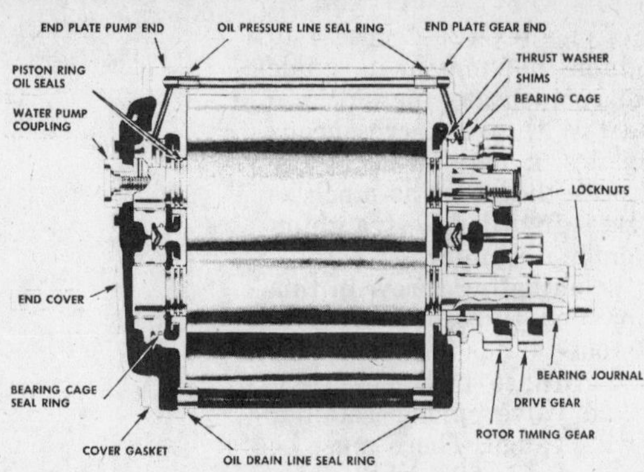

Supercharger—cross section
(© Cummins Engine Co.)

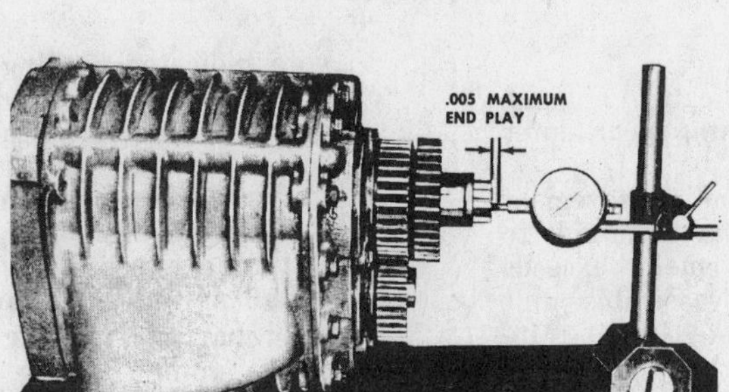

Checking end play
(© Cummins Engine Co.)

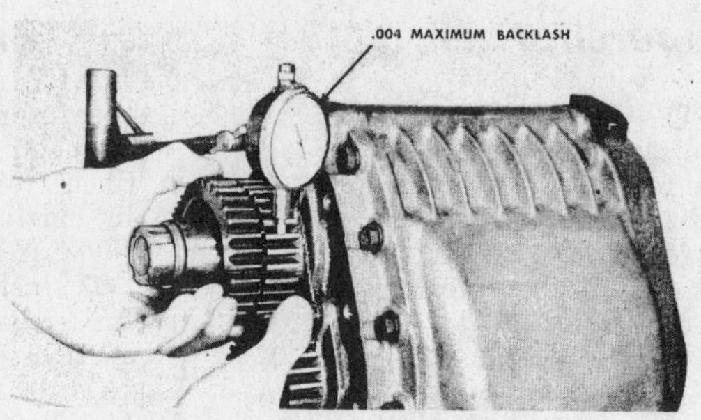

Checking gear backlash
(© Cummins Engine Co.)

5. Insert a feeler gauge into the inlet port between the housing and rotor lobe. Minimum clearance is .005 inch.
6. Check clearance between rotor lobes through the air inlet port. Minimum clearance is .006 inch.

If the preliminary inspection does not indicate any of the above wear conditions, the supercharger may be reinstalled on the engine.

NOTE: Use a new gasket when replacing the pump-end cover.

If one or more of the above wear conditions are noted, disassemble the supercharger for a complete inspection or return to factory for a complete rebuild.

Disassembly of Supercharger

1. Raise the lockwasher flange clear of slot in the shaft nut and remove shaft nut with a shaft nut wrench.
2. Wedge a piece of soft metal between timing gear teeth to lock gears while loosening shaft nuts.
3. Remove shaft nut lockwashers from the rotor shafts and slide the outboard bearing journal from the drive rotor shaft. Remove expansion plugs if damaged.
4. Pull the water pump coupling half from the driven rotor shaft with a gear puller.
5. Remove capscrews and lock washers securing end cover and gasket. Discard gasket. Tap cover with a rubber mallet to loosen from housing dowels.
6. Remove capscrews and lockwires securing bearing cages to end plate. Remove bearing cages by rotating and prying.
7. Remove bearing cage seal rings and press bearings from bearing cages. *Mark bearing cages to assure replacement in identical position from which removed.*
8. If damaged, pry oil collector rings from end plate and remove dowels from end plate.
9. Remove capscrews from front end plate and remove end plate and rotor assembly from housing.
10. Remove oil pressure ferrules and "O" rings.
11. Press drive gear and timing gears from the rotors and end plate assembly and extract the rotors from the end plate assembly. NOTE: The rotors must be rotated into position so the lobe of the rotor being pressed out does not catch on the shaft of the other rotor.
12. Remove lockwires and capscrews securing bearing cages to the gear end plate.
13. Turn the bearing cages sufficiently to clear the end plate and pry them free. Remove shims and bearing cage seal rings from bearing cages and press out bearings. Mark bearing cages to assure identical replacement.
14. Remove thrust washers from the gear end plate.
15. Remove oil collector rings and dowels, if damaged.
16. Remove and discard all shaft seal rings.

Removing rotor shaft locknuts
(© Cummins Engine Co.)

Inspection

1. Clean all parts in approved cleaning solvent.
2. Check housing for cracks, nicks, obstructed oil passages and stripped threads. Remove nicks or scratches with a handstone. Be sure all mating surfaces are smooth.
3. Inspect rotors for undue wear, burrs, pits, scratches, or other damage. Check threaded ends, shoulders, spline bearing sur-

faces, and seal ring grooves for wear. Small burrs and imperfections on the roto lobes can be dressed down with a handstone. If the lobe surfaces or rotor shafts are badly scored or damaged, discard rotor set.

4. Inspect timing gears, drive gear and all gear hubs for cracks and broken or worn teeth, damaged splines and excessive wear. CAUTION: Rotors, timing gears and the driven gear are not interchangeable. If one of these components is worn or damaged, it must be replaced as part of a complete set of rotors and gears. Do not attempt to replace a single component that is not a part of the original or a completely new set.
5. Examine end plates for cracks or damaged seal ring bores. Check for snug dowel fits. Excessive wear and roughness in the seal ring bores will not allow the seal rings to seat properly, thus the end plates must be discarded and replaced with new parts.
6. Check end cover for cracks. End cover *must* have a smooth mating surface.
7. Inspect bearing cages for cracks or excessive wear. Discard defective bearing cages. Bearing cage assemblies are also available in .010 and .020 inch *undersize.*
8. Inspect bearings for scratches or scoring. Check bearing bores with inside micrometers. If bore exceeds 1.3765 inch, discard bearings.
9. Examine thrust washers for burrs, cracks and wear. Discard damaged or worn thrust washers.
10. Check outboard bearing journal for nicks, scoring or excessive wear.
11. Inspect water pump drive coupling half for excessive wear.
12. Check end thrust by measuring bearing cage width and distance from thrust face of gear to end of gear hub. Bearing cage width must be .002/.005 inch less than length of gear hub. If difference between these dimensions is greater than .005 inch, install new gears, thrust washers, and bearing cages.

Assembly of Supercharger

1. Use new shaft nut lockwashers, expansion plugs, seal rings, oil collector rings and gaskets during reassembly.
2. Install shaft seal rings on new rotors.
3. Install new bearing cage seal rings on bearing cages.
4. Press bearings into bearing cages and oil collector rings into end plates. Press in new end plate dowels, if removed.
5. Install oil pressure ferrules, drain ferrules and ferrule seal rings in housing.
6. Position thrust washers, shims, and bearing cages into gear end plate; secure with capscrews and lockwires. NOTE: If old bearing cages are reused, replace in same hole from which removed. Use same shims as originally removed from respective cages. Use .005 inch total shim thickness under each bearing cage. Shim thickness may have to be adjusted when rotor end clearance is checked.
7. Press water pump coupling on the driven rotor shaft extension so that the shaft end is flush with the water pump coupling counterbore.
8. Lubricate the gear end plate seal ring seats and bearings with clean, light engine oil and insert splined shaft end of driven rotor in the bottom hole in the gear end plate. NOTE: Do not damage seal rings while pressing into gear end plate.
9. Position timing gear on drive rotor shaft and press into position.
10. Insert driven rotor shaft through the second hole in the gear end plate and press on timing gear making sure rotors are positioned *exactly* 90° apart as the timing gears mesh.
11. Press drive gear on drive rotor shaft snugly against timing gear and install outboard bearing journal on drive rotor shaft.
12. Install shaft nut lockwashers and shaft nuts on the rotor shaft and tighten securely. Wedge a piece of soft metal or rag between the gear teeth to lock gears while tighting locknuts.
13. Position the expansion plugs on locknuts and tap into place.
14. Push rotors towards gear end plate and check end clearance. End clearance should be .003/.004 inch. Add or remove shims under bearing cage mounting flange to obtain correct end clearance. If shims must be changed, remove locknuts and gears as described in disassembly instructions.
15. Position housing over rotors against end plate and secure with lockwashers and capscrews.
16. Lubricate bearings and seal rings in end plate and position end plate to housing. *Do not damage shaft seal rings.* Tap into place.
17. Position end cover and new gasket to end plate; secure with lockwashers and capscrews.

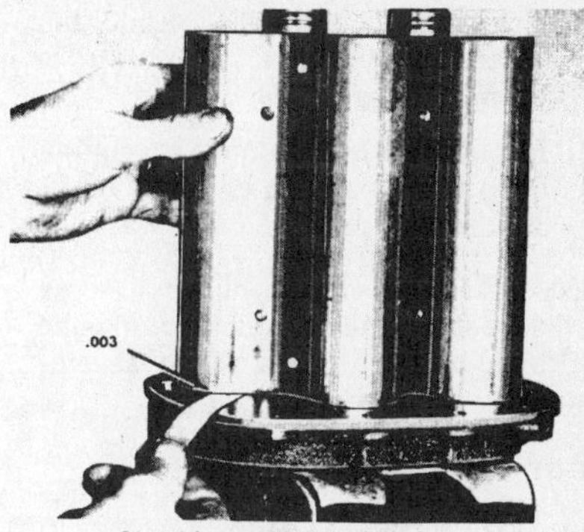

Checking rotor end clearance
(© Cummins Engine Co.)

18. Turn drive gear by hand to check for smooth, free operation.

Supercharger Idler Gear Assembly

It should not be necessary to rebuild this unit unless it has become noisy or loose, thus indicating broken leaf springs or worn bushins.

If disassembly is necessary, proceed as follows:

1. Remove capscrews and idler drive hub, blower gear, thrust washer, and spring retaining cover from assembly.
2. Carefully pry and remove idler leaf springs, 4 spring retaining rings, and separate idler driven gear from spring retainer.

Repair

1. Replace all broken or damaged idler leaf springs.
2. Check two supercharger idler gear bushings and three idler hub bushings.
   a. New idler gear bushings are 1.501/1.500 inside diameter, bushings pressed in place.
   b. New idler hub bushings are 1.501/1.500 inside diameter, idler bushings pressed in place.
   c. Idler gear shaft is 1.4985/1.4975 outside diameter.
3. Check thrust washer for wear. Replace as needed.

Assembly

1. Place spring retainer over idler driven gear cam and drive idler leaf springs and four pins in place. CAUTION: Idler leaf springs are made from spring steel and will cause a serious injury if allowed to fly loose as they are forced between gear cam and spring retainer.
2. Assemble thrust washer to idler gear hub.
3. Mount retainer plate, blower gear and idler gear hub and fasten with six capscrews.
4. Peen capscrews in place.

Gear Train

1. Check all drive and driven gears, crankshaft, camshaft, and idler gears for cracks, chipping or signs of wear.
2. Replace all gears showing visible deep wear pattern or other tooth damage.

NOTE: The extent of gear wear can be determined by checking gear backlash after all gears are assembled.

Gear Case Cover

Disassembly

1. Remove crankshaft oil seal and fuel pump and compressor drive oil seal.
2. Remove bearing race at fuel pump drive, if used.

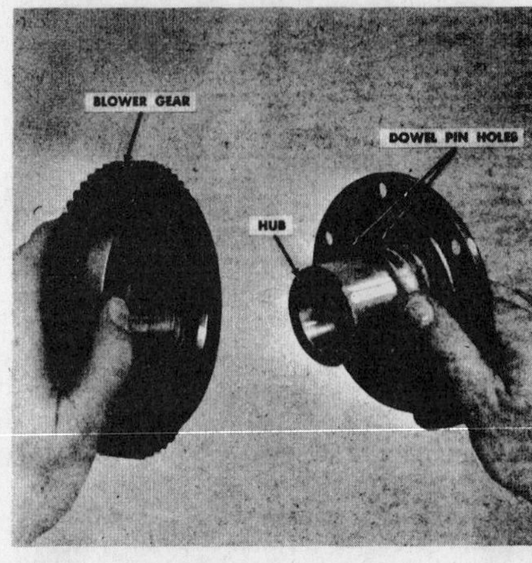

Assembling supercharger idler gears
(© Cummins Engine Co.)

Inspection and Repair

1. Check bearings, if used; replace if rough or worn. This is a two piece bearing, one-half remains on drive shaft with outer race only in gear cover.
2. Check fuel pump and compressor drive shaft bushing in cover. If replacement is necessary knock out old bushing and press in new one with suitable driver.
3. A replaceable steel trunnion bushing, may be used to repair worn trunnions. To use bushing:
   a. Machine gear case trunnion to 4.747/4.750 inches outer diameter.
   b. Press bushing over machined trunnion with chamfered side of bushing toward gear case cover.

Assembly

Do not install oil seals until gear case cover is ready to be installed on engine.

Turbocharger

The information listed below covers procedures for cleaning turbocharger compressor wheels and checking bearing clearances.

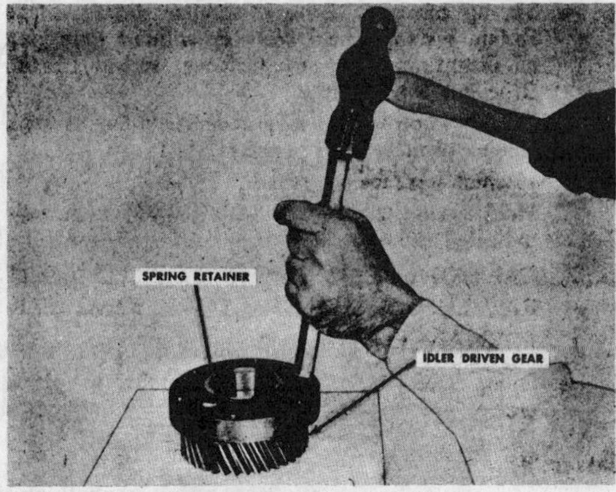

Installing idler leaf springs
(© Cummins Engine Co.)

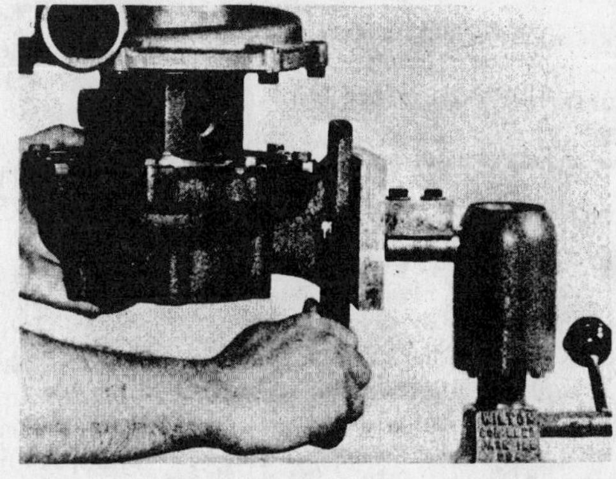
Supercharger mounting fixture
(© Cummins Engine Co.)

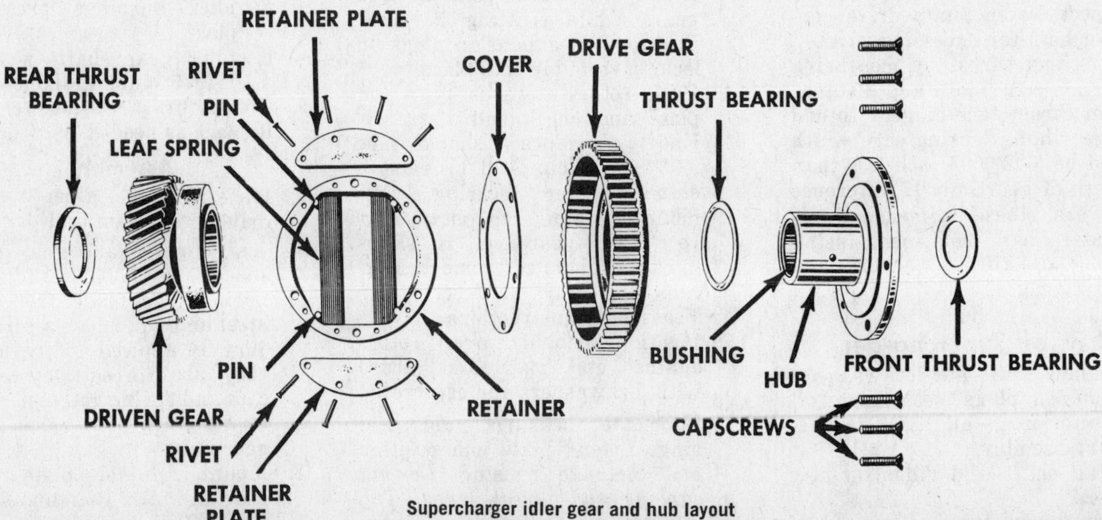

Supercharger idler gear and hub layout
(© Cummins Engine Co.)

T-506 Turbocharger

Currently, T-506 turbochargers utilize a universal main casing which can be rotated 360° to simplify mounting arrangement and facilitate positioning oil drain.

Formerly, a stationary front cover was used.

Disassembly of Turbocharger

1. Clean exterior of turbocharger.
2. Attach turbocharger to Assembly Stand.

Cleaning and Inspection

1. Clean compressor wheel.
   a. Use Bendix cleaner or equivalent; NEVER use a caustic solution which will attack aluminum.
   b. Use nylon or hog bristle brush; NEVER use wire brush.
   c. Immerse compressor wheel end in cleaning solution.
   d. Dry thoroughly with compressed air.
2. Check bearing clearances.
   Use a dial indicator to indicate side and end-play of rotor shaft. Check as follows:
   a. Fasten a dial indicator to turbine casing.
   b. Place indicator point against hub of turbine wheel.
   c. Force turbine wheel up and down, or sideways; note total indicator reading.
   d. Remove one capscrew from front plate (compressor wheel end) and replace with a long stud bolt.

Removing front cover plate
(© Cummins Engine Co.)

3. Remove capscrews and lockplates from exhaust casing on turbine end; remove universal main casing or front cover plate.
   e. Attach an indicator to long stud bolt and register indicator point against flat on end of rotor shaft.
   f. Push shaft sideways, noting total indicator reading.
   g. Move indicator point to end of shaft.
   h. Check end-play of rotor assembly.

Checking bearing clearance
(© Cummins Engine Co.)

   i. Compare readings with limits shown in following table.

Type	*Min. Radial Clearance*	*Rotor End Play*
T-506	.008	.003/.011
T-350	.0135	.003/.008

If radial or end clearance exceeds the maximum limits, send turbocharger to a factory approved rebuild station for bearing replacement.

T-350 Turbocharger

Disassembly of Turbocharger

Before disassembling, clean exterior thoroughly. Mark housing position with a scribe mark.

1. Attach turbocharger to Assembly Stand.
2. Remove capscrews and lockplates from the exhaust outlet connection. Remove connection and gasket.
3. Remove capscrews, lockwashers and flatwashers from bearing housing to compressor casing. Lift off compressor casing.
4. Remove capscrews and lockplates from the bearing or main housing to turbine casing. Lift bearing housing assembly from turbine casing.

Cleaning

1. Immerse parts in Turco Super-Carb or similar solvent. CAUTION: Never use a caustic solution or solvent that may attack aluminum, stellite or ni-resist alloys.
2. Allow parts to soak to remove carbon. A soft bristle brush may be used to remove heavy deposits. *Never use wire or stiff bristle brush.*
3. Steam clean thoroughly to remove all carbon and grease. Apply steam liberally to oil passages in the bearing housing.
4. Blow off excess water and dry with compressed air.

Inspection and Assembly of Turbocharger

1. Place a new "O" ring on compressor end of bearing housing and coat with oil.
2. Install compressor casing aligning scribe marks made at disassembly.
3. Check impeller radial clearance between impeller vans and compressor casing. Impeller wheel must be pushed to side and minimum clearance checked. See Table for clearance.
4. Check turbine wheel radial clearance between turbin wheel vans and turbine casing. Turbine wheel must be pushed to side and minimum clearance checked. It should be .0135.
5. Use a dial indicator and check rotor end play. See Table for end play.
6. Turn rotor by hand to be sure no internal interference is present.
7. Install pipe fittings in bearing housing as required.
8. Install exhaust connection using Never-Seez anti-gall compound on the capscrew threads.
9. Cover all inlets and outlets to prevent dirt entry.

Aneroid Control

Aneroid controls used with turbochargers have the bellows spring travel preset and cover sealed in place at the factory. The only adjustment required is fuel rate adjustment. *Do not attempt to repair aneroid control. If malfunctioning, replace with new assembly.*

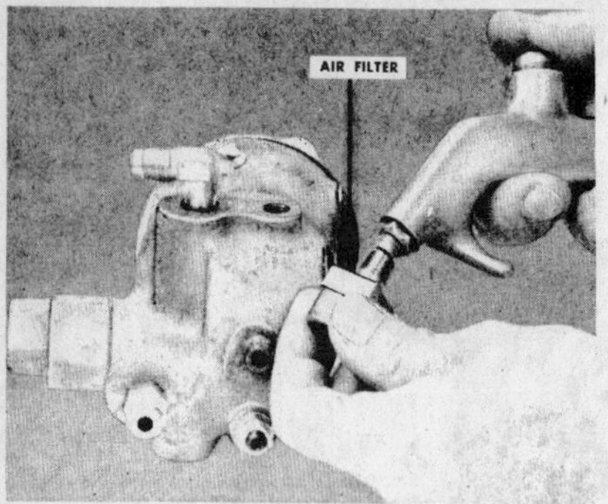

Cleaning aneroid control air filter
(© Cummins Engine Co.)

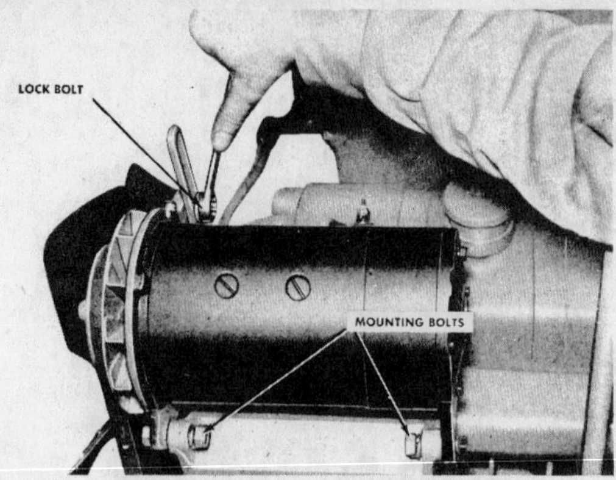

Removing belt driven generator
(© Cummins Engine Co.)

Cleaning and Lubrication

1. Clean air filter assembly by reverse flushing with compressed air.
2. Fill aneroid control cavity with clean lubricating oil.

Alternator

Self-rectifying A.C. generators are designed and constructed to give long periods of trouble-free service with a minimum amount of maintenance. The rotor is mounted on ball bearings, and each bearing has a grease reservoir which eliminates the need of periodic lubrication. Only two brushes are required to carry current through the two slip rings to the field coils which are wound on the four pole rotor. The brushes are extra long and under normal operating conditions will provide long periods of service.

The stator windings are assembled on the inside of a laminated core that forms the generator frame. Six rectifier diodes are mounted in the slip ring end frame, and are connected to the stator windings through connectors mounted internally in two nylon holders, or a separately mounted rectifier, and they act to change the generator A.C. voltages to a D.C. voltage which appears at the "BAT" terminal on the generator.

Even though the generator is constructed to give long periods of trouble-free service, a regular inspection procedure should be followed to obtain the maximum life from the generator.

Generator

The shunt generator converts mechanical energy to electrical energy, supply current for electrical equipment by replacing electricity consumed from the battery.

The shunt generator requires external current regulation in the form of a current regulator, voltage regulator, and cut-off relay, which control generator output under all operating conditions.

Removal

1. Disconnect wiring leads from generator.
2. On belt driven models, remove drive belt. On some C and J models it may be necessary to disconnect No. 1 cylinder injector inlet and drain manifolds to remove generator.
3. Remove belts from genrator bracket and lift off generator and bracket.
4. Remove bracket from generator.

Installation

1. Mount bracket to generator, be sure the bracket is mounted to generator so that oil cup and passages are in proper position.
2. On gear driven generators, install rubber buffer between generator coupling and drive coupling and connect the two units.
3. Mount generator and bracket to block.
4. On belt driven models, install drive belt.
5. Connect generator wiring leads to proper terminals.

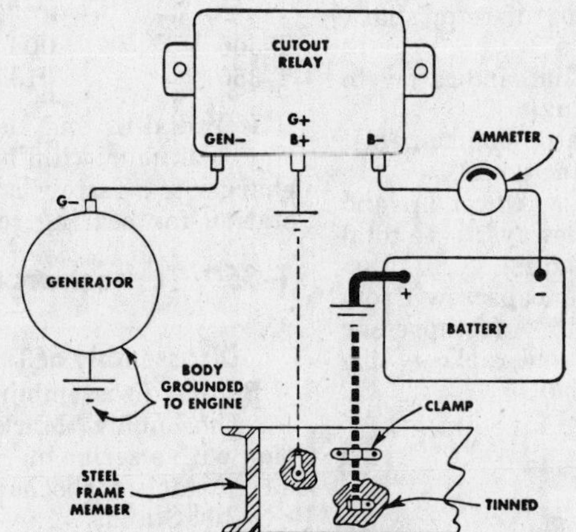

Basic generator wiring cut-out relay
(© Cummins Engine Co.)

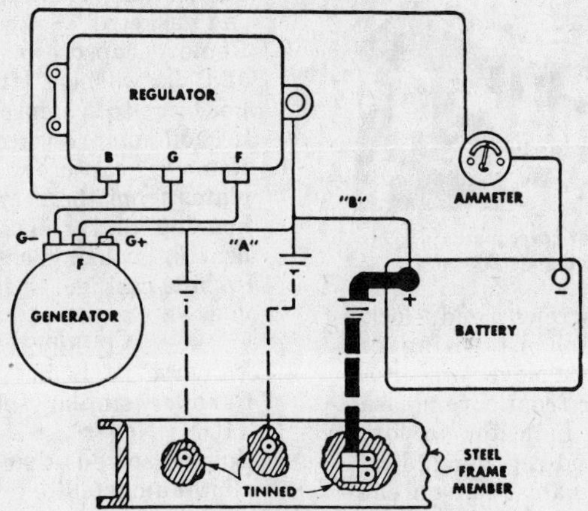

Basic generator wiring-leece-neville
(© Cummins Engine Co.)

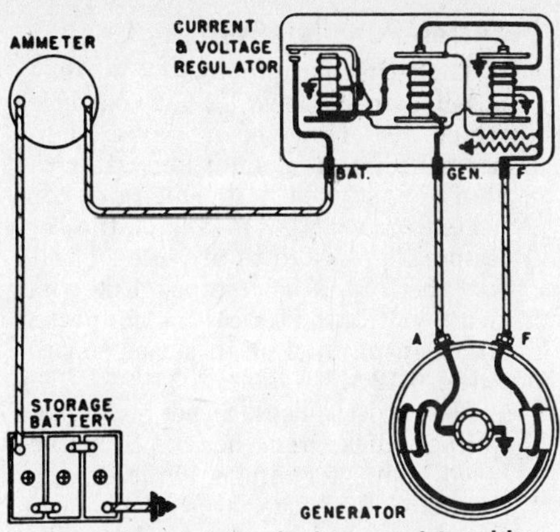

Leece neville current and voltage regulator wiring
(© Cumminc Engino Co.)

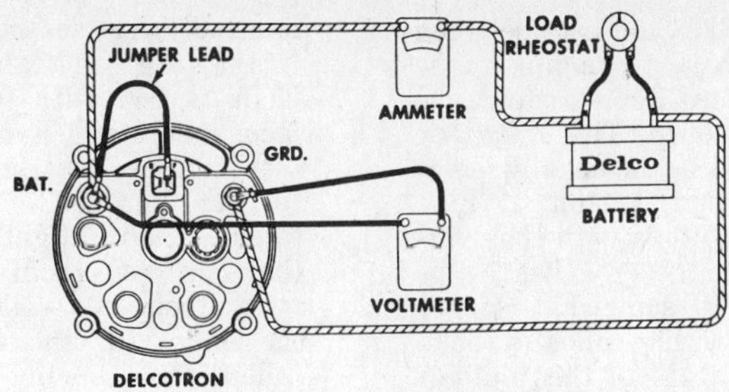

Alternator output—bench test
(© Cummins Engine Co.)

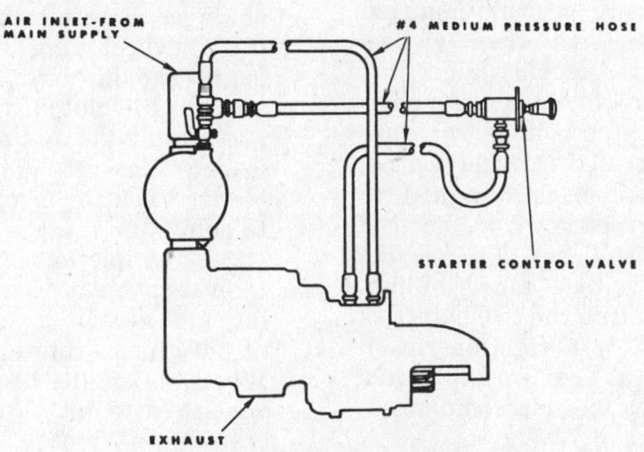

Ingersoll rand air starter piping
(© Cummins Engine Co.)

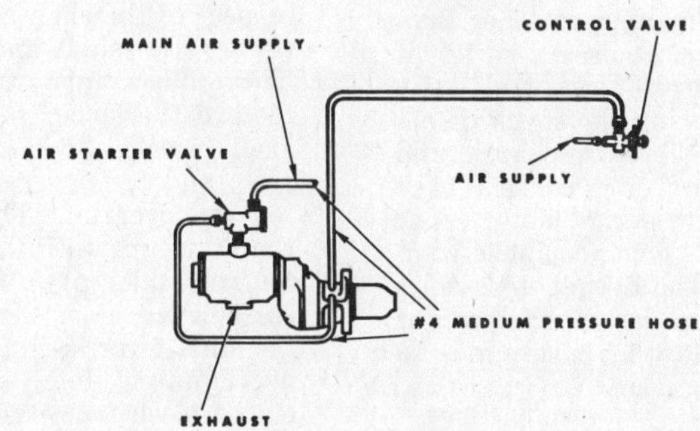

Bendix westinghouse air starter piping
(© Cummins Engine Co.)

Starter Motors

Air Starter

An improved air starting system with increased starting motor torque is now used on current production engines without increasing required air pressure above 120 psi. The air piping system reduces the drive torque engagement of starter drives and flywheel ring gears, therefore, improving service life.

A specially hardened flywheel ring gear is now used and is available for service. On all new installations make sure the letter "W" appears on the ring gear near the part number. This indicates the ring gear is special hardened.

Air Starter Removal

1. Relieve air system before disconnecting air supply to starter.
2. Depress starter handle to bleed off air in starter.
3. Disconnect main union between starter handle and motor.
4. Unbolt starter from flywheel housing.
5. Support starter and slide it back to disengage starter drive from flywheel ring gear.

Installation

1. Start one capscrew in mounting flange to hold starter during installation.
2. Some applications use a spacer between mounting flange and flywheel housing. Be certain spacer is in place.
3. Slide starter into flywheel housing opening, engaging the drive with flywheel ring gear.
4. Install remaining mounting bolts and tighten securely.
5. Connect air supply line to starter.

Electric Starter

The starter motor used on Cummins engines is a special overload motor capable of delivering high horsepower. In order to obtain this power, it is necessary to build the cranking motor with a minimum of resistance so a large current will be taken through it. The starter motor should be used for short periods only—30 seconds maximum to avoid the possibility of burning out.

Removal

1. Disconnect battery cable and all electrical leads from starter.
2. Unbolt and remove starter motor and spacer (if used).

Installation

1. Before installation starter should be checked for type used. There are several different type drives used that must be matched with flywheel ring gears.
2. Place the spacer (if used) on starter.
3. Install starter to flywheel mounting bolts and tighten securely.
4. Connect wires and cables to starter and battery.

Starter Motor Controls

1. Because of extremely high current flow during cranking, a positive means of connecting and disconnecting the battery and cranking motor must be used. The switch used must have contacts heavy enough to carry the current without burning. A manually operated switch mounted on the floor board or cranking motor frame is the simplest type.
2. Some applications with Bendix drive use a magnetic switch which when energized draws in a plunger and causes a contact

disc to make contact between two terminals to complete the circuit from the battery to cranking motor. The magnetic switch winding is usually energized by a push button.

3. Some applications with the overrunnig clutch, or Dyer type drive, use a somewhat larger magnetic switch called a solenoid switch. Here, the plunger not only thrusts against a contact disc to close the battery-to-cranking motor circuit, but is also linked to the shift lever so that the drive pinion is shifted into mesh with the flywheel teeth by the solenoid action.
4. Cummins engines require a comparatively high voltage to assure adequate cranking. The series-parallel system is designed to provide a means of connecting two batteries in series to provide increased voltage for cranking, and reconecting the two batteries in parallel for normal operation of electrical equipment after starting has been accomplished.

Friction Clutch Type Bendix Drive

This type of drive performs in much the same manner as other Bendix drives except it uses a series of spring-loaded clutch plates which slip momentarily during the shock of engagement to relieve the shock and prevent it from being carried back through the cranking motor. The slipping stops as engagement is completed so that cranking torque is transmitted from the cranking motor armature through the drive pinion to the flywheel ring gear.

Overrunning Clutch Drive

1. The overrunning clutch is designed to provide positive meshing and disengagement of the drive pinion and flywheel ring gear. It uses a shift lever which slides the clutch and drive pinion assembly along the armature shaft so it can be meshed and disengaged as required. The clutch transmits cranking torque from cranking motor to the engine flywheel but permits the drive pinion to overrun, or run faster than, the armature after the engine is started. This protects the armature from excessive speed during the brief interval that the drive pinion remains in mesh.
2. The overrunning clutch consists of a shell and sleeve assembly which is splined internally to match splines on the armature shaft. Thus, both the shell and sleeve assembly and armature shaft must turn together. A pinion and collar assembly fit loosely into the shell, and the collar is in contact with four matched steel rollers which are assembled into notches cut in the inner face of the shell. These notches taper inward lightlsy so that there is less room in the end away from the rollers than in the end with the rollers. The rollers are spring loaded by small plungers.
3. When the shift lever is operated, the clutch assembly is moved endways along the armature shaft so the pinion meshes with the flywheel ring gear. If the teeth should butt instead of mesh, the clutch spring compresses so the pinion is spring loaded against the ring-gear teeth. When the armature begins to rotate, meshing takes place at once. Completion of the shift lever movement closes the cranking motor switch so the armature begins to rotate.
4. When the engine begins to operate, it attempts to drive the cranking motor armature through the pinion, faster than the armature is rotating. This causes the pinion to rotate with respect to the shell so that it overruns the shell and armature. The rollers are turned back toward the larger section of the shell notches where they are free, and thus, permit, the pinion to overrun. This protects the armature until the automatic controls take over so that the shift lever is released, causing the shift lever spring to pull the overrunning clutch drive pinion out of mesh from the engine flywheel ring gear. This shift lever movement also opens the cranking motor switch so that the armature stops rotating.
5. The overrunning clutch pinion requires the same ring gear as the Bendix pinion.

Series-Parallel Switch

The series-parallel switch makes it possible to use two 12-volt batteries which are connected in parrallel for normal operating conditions after the engine is started, but which are connected in series by means of the series-parallel switch to provide 24 volts for the cranking motor. Likewise, two 6-volt batteries can be connected either in parallel or in series to provide a 6-12 volt system.

The switch uses a heavy copper contact disk and heavy tungsten-faced main terminals, which resist the effects of the arcs that occur when the circuits are broken. The main cranking current is carried through these contacts and terminals. In addition, there are contacts in the terminal plate assembly which complete the parallel connections between the batteries for normal operation and also complete the connections that energize the cranking motor solenoid in the cranking position.

After cranking has been accomplished and the series-parallel switch is released, the two batteries again become connected in parallel to provide 12-volt operation of the equipment. In the mechanically operated switch a quick-break mechanism, consisting of a pair of triggers and a cam, causes the contact disk to be snapped away from the stationary contacts very quickly so that there is a very small amount of arcing.

Due to the high voltage of the starting circuit and the great amount of power available from the two batteries, it is essential that every precaution be taken to avoid short circuits or grounds. All wires should be of sufficient size to carry the electrical load to which they are subjected without overheating. Stranded wire and cable should be used throughout to reduce the possibility of breakage because of vibration. All connections should be clean and tight and all terminal clips should be soldered to the

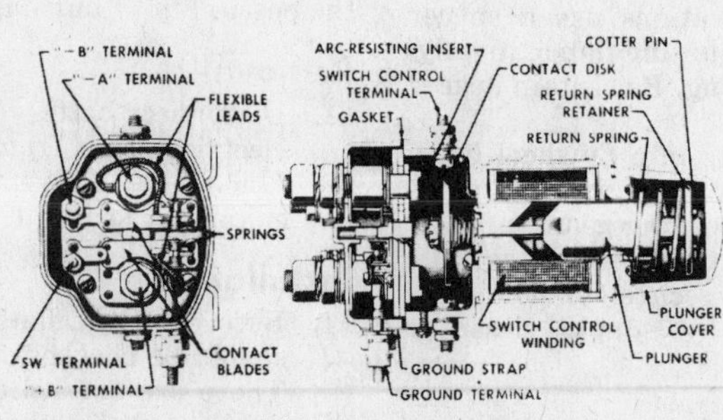

Series parallel switch cross section
(© Cummins Engine Co.)

wires or cables. Only rosin flux should be used to solder electrical connections. All wires should be adequately insulated and supported at enough points to prevent movement and consequent chafing through of the insulation. Rubber boots, rubber tape or friction tape and shellac should be applied to cover all exposed terminals and clips. This will prevent accidental grounding of an exposed terminal which could cause serious damage to the system.

Cooling System

Water Pump Removal

NH Engines

1. Drain the cooling system.
2. Remove the fan. Remove the alternator drive belt.
3. Remove the water pump retaining ring capscrews, and disengage the water pump drive belts. Remove the retaining ring and water pump body. Remove and discard the gasket. *On some engines, the fan hub bracket is an integrale part of the water pump retaining ring.*

Installation

NH Engines

1. Clean the gasket surfaces on the engine and the water pump.
2. Position the retaining ring and a new copper gasket on the pump. Position the pump in the engine block, and install, but do not tighten, the pump retaining ring bolts.
3. Install the alternator and water pump drive belts on the water pump pulley. Tighten the water pump drive belt and tighten the pump retaining ring bolts alternately starting on side away from belts.
4. Place the alternator drive belt on the alternator pulley and adjust. Tighten the alternator adjusting arm and mounting bolts.
5. Install the fan.
6. Fill and bleed the cooling system. Operate the engine and check for coolant leaks.

Water Pump Removal

V-6 & V-8 Engines

1. Drain the cooling system.
2. Remove the alternator drive belt. Loosen the fan drive belt adjusting screw, and remove the drive belts from the fan and water pump pulleys.
3. Loosen the radiator lower hose at the water pump. Loosen the hose clamps on the by-pass hose connecting the water pump to the thermostat housing. Disconnect the heater and corrosion resistor hoses at the water pump.
4. Disconnect the temperature and warning light sending unit leads at the sending units on the thermostat housing. Disconnect the radiator upper hose and the radiator supply tank vent line at the thermostat housing. *Leave the heater hose and shutterstat air hoses connected.*
5. Remove the thermostat housing from the cylinder head and position it out of the way.
6. Remove the water pump from the engine and radiator lower hose. Discard the pump gasket.

Installation

V-6 & V-8 Engines

1. Clean the gasket surfaces of the thermostat housing, water pump, cylinder head and cylinder block.
2. Apply water-resistant sealer to a new water pump gasket and position it on the water pump housing. Insert the water pump lower elbow in the radiator lower hose, and install the water pump on the engine block. Torque the pump attaching screws to specifications.
3. Use water-resistant sealer and position a new thermostat housing gasket on the cylinder head. Install the thermostat housing; be sure the thermostat housing to water pump by-pass hose and clamps are in place. Tighten the by-pass hose clamps and the mounting bolts.
4. Connect the radiator upper hose and the radiator supply tank vent line to the thermostat housing. Connect the temperature and warning light sending unit leads.
5. Connect the heater and corrosion resistor hoses to the water pump. Tighten the radiator lower hose clamp.
6. Install the fan and water pump drive belts and the alternator drive belt.
7. Fill and bleed the cooling system. Operate the engine and check for coolant leaks.

Water Pump—Overhaul

Supercharger Driven

Disassembly

1. Remove mounting capscrews, lockwashers, gasket and cover from water pump body.
2. Pull drive coupling from shaft.
3. Remove outer snap-ring from coupling end of pump body.
4. Support pump body on its mounting flange in an arbor press and press out bearing and shaft assembly from impeller and pump housing.
5. Press shaft seal out of pump body.
6. Remove inner snap-ring from housing.

Inspection

1. Inspect water pump bearing(s). Replace bearing(s) with rough or worn races.
2. Inspect water pump impeller. Replace if cracked or corroded to extent that it will interfere with circulation.
3. Measure impeller bore and shaft outer diameter. There must be a minimum of .0015 inch press-fit between shaft and impeller; replace if necessary.
4. Inspect water pump body seal face.
5. Inspect water pump mounting parts for cracks. Replace as necessary.
6. Examine carbon seal carefully to make sure it is not cracked or chipped.
7. Inspect ceramic seat.

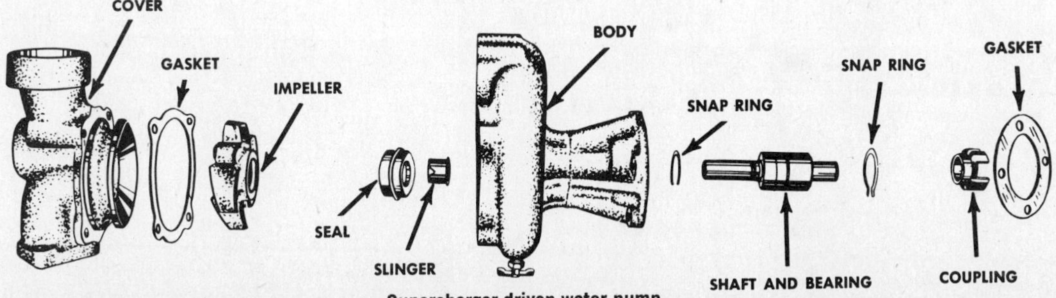

Supercharger driven water pump
(© Cummins Engine Co.)

Replacing Ceramic Seat

1. Strike damaged seat with a sharp tool perpendicular to axis of impeller.
2. Scrape adhesive from counterbore, be careful not to damage counterbore surface.
3. Check counterbore of impeller. It must be 1.042/1.046 in diameter and square to the axis of .624/.625 inch bore and within .002 inch total indicator runout.
4. Wash and de-grease impeller in an approved cleaning solvent and air dry. *The bore must be chemically clean to insure a good strong water tight bond.*
5. Apply Bonding Film in counterbore. Care must be used to prevent contamination of film by dust, dirt, oil, moisture or fingerprints or use of film more than six months old.
6. Remove bonding film liner, it may be necessary to pick liner to start separation.
7. Place ceramic seat in counterbore with identification mark (dimple) against adhesive. Rotate seat to insure a continuous bond.
8. Apply a 15 pound weight on ceramic seat and place assembly in temperature controlled oven at 345°/355°F. for 55 to 65 minutes. NOTE: The temperature and time must be closely controlled to obtain proper bond.
9. Check ceramic seat after curing for squareness to the axis of the .625/.625 inch bore. It must be within .004 inch total indicator reading. Check for scratches, holes, chips or cracks. All unusuable parts must be discarded and usable assemblies protected against further damage.

Assembly

1. Install inner snap-ring.
2. Support pump body on its cover mounting face and press bearing and shaft assembly in place against inner snap-ring. When pressing bearings onto shaft, apply load on bearing inner race only.
3. Install outer snap-ring. NOTE: Current production water pump bodies are machined for beveled snap-rings. Older models use flat snap-rings. Use correct body and snap-ring combination. Flat and beveled snap-rings are not interchangeable.
4. Press drive coupling onto shaft and flush with end of shaft.
5. Support pump on shaft and install slinger over shaft until flange is 1.805/1.825 from end of shaft.
6. Apply crane sealer to the bottom side or seat of seal driving flange.
7. Press seal in place, apply force on driving lip only. Check carbon for damage before going further.
8. Clean seal with lint free cloth to remove dirt, oil or grease.
9. Press impeller on shaft. Face of impeller hub should be .872/.878 inch below cover mounting face on body. CAUTION: Use extreme care when pressing impeller to prevent damaging ceramic seal.
10. Assemble lockwashers, capscrews and new gasket to water pump cover.
11. Mount cover to pump body and turn shaft to be sure that it is free.

Water Pump Overhaul

Belt Driven

Disassembly

1. Remove mounting capscrews and lockwashers; lift cover and gasket from pump body.
2. Remove lock capscrew from pulley and of shaft.
3. Pull belt pulley from shaft.
4. Remove outer snap-ring from pump housing.
5. Support pump on its pulley face; press shaft and bearings from pump housing and impeller.
6. Press seal assembly from housing.
7. Press two bearings and spacer from shaft.
8. Clean all parts in approved cleaning solvent. Remove all rust, scale and corrosion from cover, body and impeller.

Inspection

1. Check shaft, impeller and pulley sheaves for excessive wear or damage.
2. Check shaft outside diameter in impeller area. Shaft must be .0015 inches or more larger than impeller bore diameter. *If interference fit between shaft and impeller is less than* 0015 *inch, discard impeller.*
3. Check ball bearings for rough or binding operation, excessive looseness and worn or damaged races.
4. Discard all defective parts.

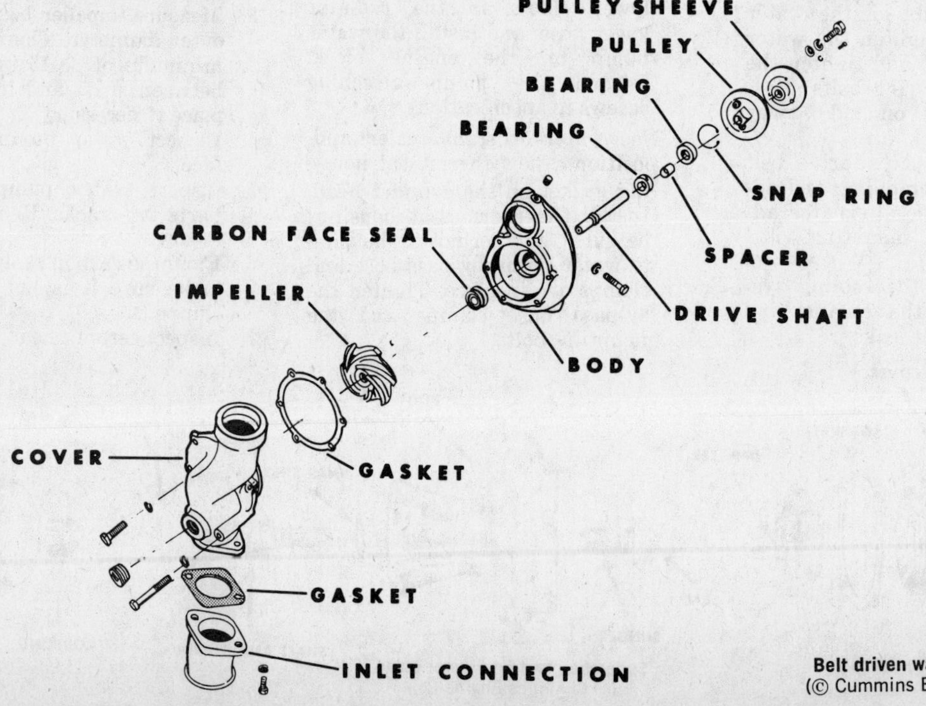

Belt driven water pump
(© Cummins Engine Co.)

Assembly

1. Assemble oil slinger to shaft over pulley end of shaft, if used.
2. Press small roller bearing, spacer and larger roller bearing on shaft.
3. Support housing on cover face; press in shaft and bearings.
4. Insert outer snap-ring. NOTE: Current production water pump bodies are machined for beveled snap-rings. Older models use flat snap-rings. Replace same type snap-ring as removed. Flat and beveled snap-rings are not interchangeable.
5. Support housing on pulley face.
6. Examine carbon seal carefully to see that it is not cracked or chipped.
7. Locate housing so seal will press square into its bore.
8. Apply sealer to nose of seal housing which seats at bottom of seal bore.
9. Press seal into pump body with force applied on driving lip (flange on seal housing) of seal. *Apply only enough force to seat nose of seal in housing seal bore.* CAUTION: Seal does not seat on driving lip.
10. Check to make sure carbon washer has not cracked during assembly.
11. Lubricate carbon seal face with a light coat of petroleum jelly. *Do not use grease.*
12. Press impeller on shaft. Ceramic face of impeller hub should be .623/.625 inch below cover face of housing. Press impeller straight on pump shaft to prevent cracking ceramic seat, rendering seat useless. NOTE: Do not use old-style seal seats and rubber seat rings with carbon seals and ceramic face impellers. This combination will result in seal failure from excessive compression.
13. Assemble lockwashers, capscrews and new gasket to cover.
14. Mount cover to housing.
15. Press pulley on shaft.
16. Assemble lockwasher and capscrew to shaft.

Thermostats

1. Using new gasket, install new or tested thermostat in thermostat housing. NOTE: If thermostat with "V" notch is used, plug vent hole in thermostat housing.
2. If water-cooled turbocharger is used, install new "O" ring on water by-pass coupling.
3. Install thermostat with vent hole *at top*. Failure to do so may result in air lock and incomplete coolant circulation.
4. Install thermostat housing with washers and capscrews.

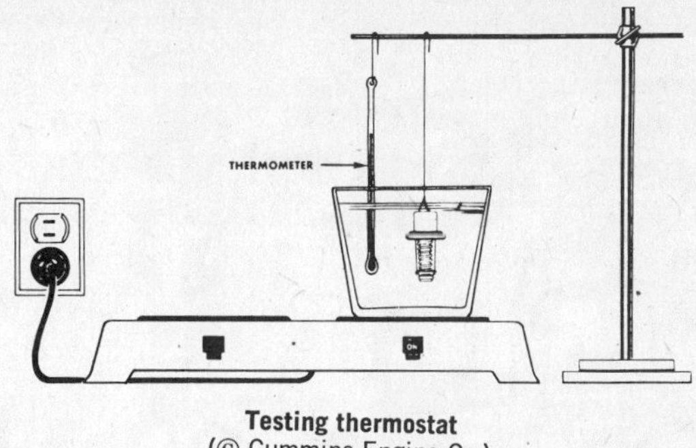

Testing thermostat
(© Cummins Engine Co.)

5. Connect air compressor and turbocharger water outlet lines, if used.
6. Connect water outlet hose. NOTE: The by-pass to water pump hose connection on supercharged engines must be assembled with a shield to protect it from exhaust manifold heat. Four cylinder engines use a small thermostat. Always replace same type thermostat as removed.

Coolant Manifold

Coolant Manifold—Removal

In-line Engines

Remove engine compartment covers or tilt cab whichever be the case.

1. Drain the engine cooling system.
2. Disconnect the high temperature warning light and the coolant temperature sending unit leads at the coolant manifold.

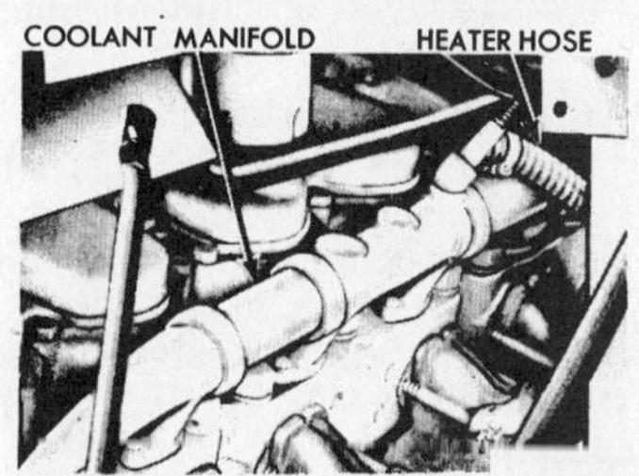

Typical coolant manifold
(© Cummins Engine Co.)

3. Close the shut-off valve at the shutterstat, and disconnect the air hoses at the shutterstat.
4. Disconnect the heater hose from the coolant manifold. Disconnect the radiator upper hose and the air compressor coolant line from the thermostat housing. Loosen the hose clamps on the cooler coolant elbow.
5. Remove the retaining bolts; then, remove the coolant manifold as an assembly, or in sections if necessary. Discard the gaskets.
6. If the coolant manifold was removed as an asembly, separate the sections. Remove the coupling O-ring seals.

Installation

1. Clean the gasket surfaces of the coolant manifold and cylinder heads. Clean the O-ring seal surfaces on the coolant manifold and couplings.
2. Apply lubricant to new coupling O-ring seals, and assemble the coolant manifold sections, couplings and seals.

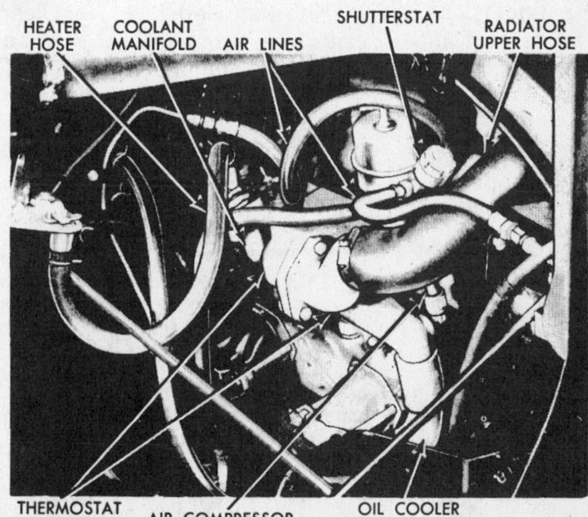

Shutterstat and thermostat housing connections N series
(© Cummins Engine Co.)

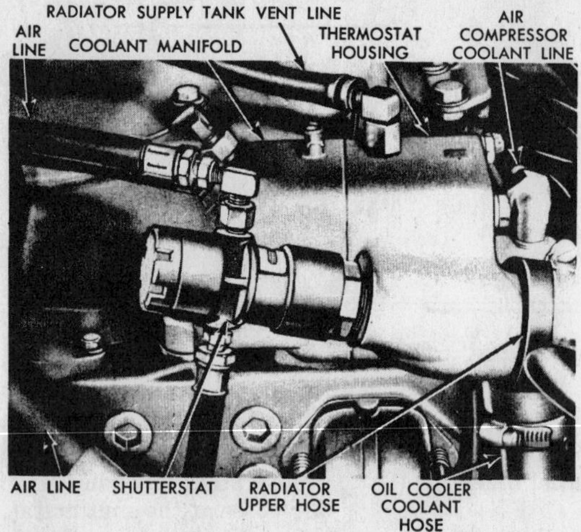

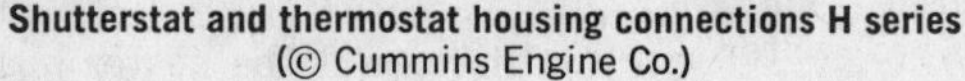

Shutterstat and thermostat housing connections H series
(© Cummins Engine Co.)

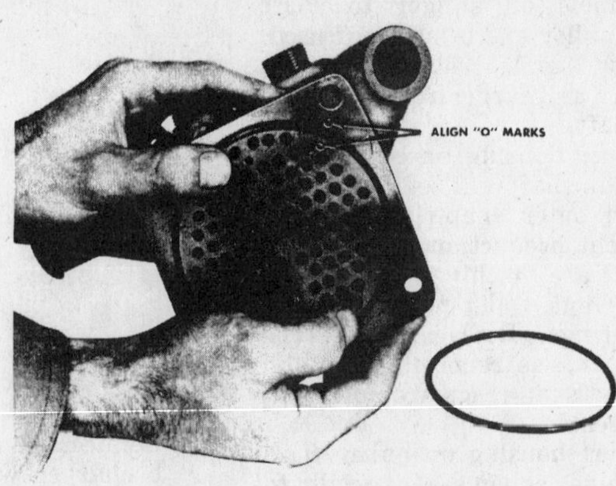

Installing oil cooler element
(© Cummins Engine Co.)

3. Position new gaskets coated with water-resistant sealer on the coolant manifold. Position the manifold on the cylinder heads, and install and tighten the retaining bolts.
4. Position the hose on the oil cooler coolant elbow and the thermostat housing, and tighten the hose clamps. Connect the radiator upper hose and the air compressor coolant line to the thermostat housing. Connect the heater hose to the coolant manifold.
5. Connect the air hoses to the shutterstat.
6. Connect the high temperature warning light and the coolant temperature sending unit leads at the coolant manifold.
7. Fill and bleed the cooling system. Operate the engine and check for coolant and air leaks.

Lubricating Oil Cooler

Disassembly

1. Remove top exposed "O" ring under the brass retainer being careful not to scratch or mar the sealing surface on the element.
2. Clean out lube oil and contaminates trapped in housing by forcing cleaner through the oil ports.
3. Remove the element from housing, by inserting two 7/32 inch rods 8 inches long into the outside row of tubes opposite each other. NOTE: The rods should not drag bottom of housing.
4. Place a flat bar on top of housing and bundle faces between rods and rotate element in housing to unseal lower "O" ring. NOTE: While turning element lift up gradually on rods to free "O" rings. When up about 5/32 inch, element should be free to lift out of housing.
5. Discard "O" rings and retainer.

Cleaning and Inspection

1. Clean cooler core immediately after removal with approved cleaning solvent that will not harm non-ferrous metal.
2. Inspect element for corrosion or cracks where tubes are welded to end plates.
3. Clean housing in approved cleaning solvent and inspect for cracks or damage.

Repair

1. To repair damaged tubes insert a smaller outside diameter tube inside damaged tube. Cut and flare ends, then solder securely. CAUTION: Do not damage adjacent tubes with heat while soldering.
2. Do not restrict more than 5% of total number of tubes in this manner. If more than 5% of tubes are defective, discard element.

Assembly

1. Lubricate rubber "O" ring and place in groove at bottom of housing.
2. Push element into housing, aligning index marks on housing and element.
3. Press second "O" ring around top of element with a wooden block to assure equal pressure around ring circumference.
4. Place new retainer ring over rubber "O" ring.
5. Assemble new gasket and front cover to housing.
6. Check for oil leaks.

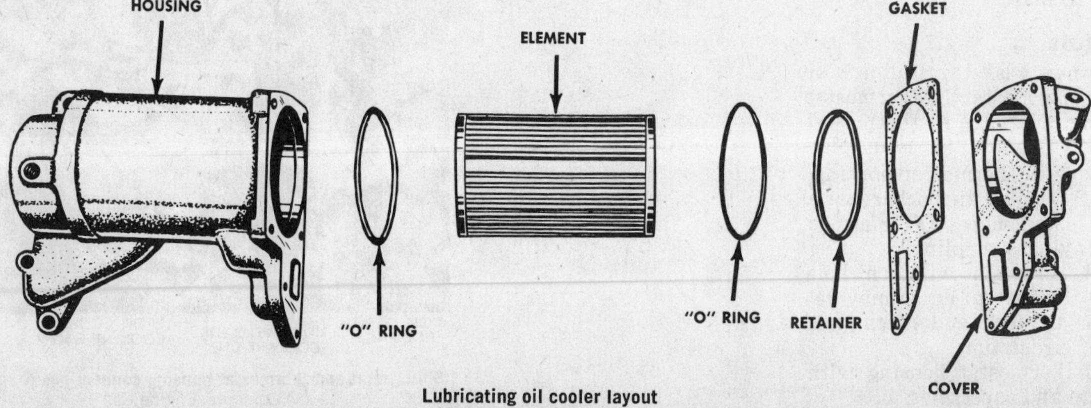

Lubricating oil cooler layout
(© Cummins Engine Co.)

Suction Tube

1. Remove the mounting capscrews from flange mounted suction tube to lube pump body.
2. Remove retaining clip and screen from suction bell.
3. Clean screen and tube; soak in solvent, dry with compressed air.
4. Inspect parts for damage and replace as needed.
5. Reassemble screen.
6. When "O" rings are used on the suction tubes, install new ones.

Heat Exchanger

Disassembly

1. Remove all flanges, hose and connections from heat exchanger.
2. Remove cover plates from oil cooler and water cooler sections of heat exchanger.
3. Remove both oil and water cooling units, or core, from housing.

Assembly

1. Install oil cooler and water cooler units in heat exchanger housing.
2. Replace all old gaskets with new ones. Dip new gasket in light machine oil for 2 minutes before installing.
3. Assemble covers and mounting brackets with lockwashers and capscrews.
4. Replace disintegrated zincs with new zincs.
5. Seal core outlet and fill core with oil or water depending upon type of core.
6. Seal inlet with fitting designed for application of an air hose and gauge.
7. Subject core to specified pressure allowing only atmospheric pressure in the casing.
8. Permit unit to stand for 15 to 20 minutes; then check pressure gauge for pressure drop which will denote a tube or header leak.
9. To test case, seal coolant outlet and fill casing with water, then follow same procedure as in the core test. A pressure drop on gauge will denote a casing leak.
10. If core is not intended for immediate use after repair and test, it should be prepared for storage.
    a. Allow unit to drain thoroughly and blow out remaining liquid with air.
    b. Flush light machine oil or soluble oil through tubes and drain off excess.
    c. Seal all inlets and outlets to prevent entrance of dirt or foreign matter.

Corrosion Resistor

Disassembly

1. Remove capscrews and washers from resistor cover. Remove cover, gaskets, and upper plate.
2. Lift element from resistor body.
3. Lift out lower plate (sacrificial metal plate), and spring.
4. Remove drain plug from body.

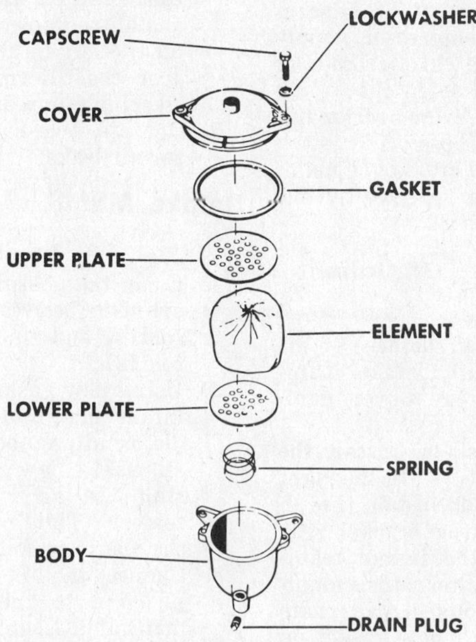

Corrosion resistor—layout
(© Cummins Engine Co.)

Inspection and Repair

1. Buff or polish sacrificial plate to remove scale and expose metal. Discard plate if less than 50% of metal surface can be exposed by polishing.
2. Inspect resistor body and cover for cracks or leaks.
3. Inspect spring, drain plug and capscrews for wear. Replace as necessary.

Assembly

1. Install spring in resistor housing.
2. Install lower plate, new element and upper plate.
3. Install new gasket to resistor cover. Secure cover to housing with capscrews and washers.
4. Install pipe plug.

Manifolds

Intake Manifold Removal

V-6 Engines Type 1

1. Remove the power steering pump mounting bolts and position the pump out of the way where necessary.
2. Loosen the clamp and remove the inlet air flex tube from the air cross-over manifold. Disconnect the air compressor supply line at the air-cross-over manifold. Loosen the hose clamps on the cross-over manifold connection hose and remove air manifold.
3. On the right intake manifold, remove the alternator bracket rear bolt and loosen the 2 front bolts.
   On the left intake manifold, remove the alternator adjusting arm to left intake manifold bolt.
4. Remove the intake manifold(s).

Intake Manifold Removal

Type 2

1. Open the air reservoir drain cock and exhaust the system. Disconnect the inlet and outlet lines from the shutterstat.
2. On a right intake manifold, remove the corrosion resistor from the air cleaners support frame, and attach it to the cowl with wire. Disconnect the air compressor supply line from the right air cleaner. For one intake manifold, remove the support frame braces from the air cleaner support. For both intake manifolds, remove the air cleaners and support frame as an assembly. Remove the air cleaner(s), support frame and inlet air tube(s) assembly from the intake manifold.
3. Remove the power steering pump mounting bolts and tie the pump out of the way where necessary.
4. On the right intake manifold, remove the alternator bracket rear bolt and loosen the 2 front bolts. On the left intake manifold, remove the alternator ad-

justing arm to left intake manifold bolt.
5. Remove the intake manifold (s).

Intake Manifold Removal

Type 3

1. Release the cab locks, tilt the cab forward and lock it in place.
2. Remove the inlet air tube and hoses from the air cleaner and air cross-over manifold. Disconnect the air compressor supply line from the air cross-over manifold. Loosen the hose clamps on the cross-over manifold connection hose.
3. Remove the air cross-over manifold(s) and gasket(s). Remove the intake manifold (s).

Intake Manifold Installation

Type 1

1. Clean the gasket surfaces of the cylinder head(s), intake manifold (s) and air cross-over manifold.
2. Using new gaskets, install the intake manifold (s). On the right intake manifold, install the alternator mounting bracket rear bolt. Tighten the intake manifold bolts and alternator mounting bracket bolts in alternate steps. Position a new gasket on the inlet port flange of the intake manifold (s), and install the air cross-over manifold. On the left intake manifold, attach the alternator adjusting arm.
3. Connect the air compressor supply line to the air cross-over manifold. Connect the inlet air flex tube to the air cross-over manifold and tighten the hose clamp.
4. Install the power steering pump. Adjust the alternator and power steering pump drive belt.
5. Operate the engine and check for air leaks.

Intake Manifold Installation

Type 2

1. Clean the gasket surfaces of the cylinder head(s), intake manifold(s), inlet air tube adapter(s) and air cleaners support frame.
2. Using new gaskets, install the intake manifold (s). On the right intake manifold, install the alternator mounting bracket rear bolt. Tighten the intake manifold bolts and alternator mounting bolts in alternate steps. On the left intake manifold, attach the alternator adjusting arm.
3. Position new gasket(s) on the inlet port flange of the intake manifold(s). Place new gasket(s) between the inlet air tube adapter(s) and the base of the air cleaner support(s). Install the air cleaner(s) and support frame assembly (ies) on the intake manifold(s).
4. Connect the air compressor supply line to the right air cleaner. Install the corrosion resistor on the air cleaners support frame. Connect the inlet and outlet lines to the shutterstat.
5. Install the power steering pump on the left intake manifold. Adjust the alternator and power steering pump drive belt.
6. Operate the engine and check for air leaks.

Intake Manifold Installation

Type 3

1. Clean the gasket surfaces of the cylinder head(s), intake manifold(s) and air cross-over manifold(s).
2. Using new gasket(s), install the intake manifold(s) and tighten the retaining bolts in alternate steps. Use new gasket(s) and install the air cross-over manifold(s). Tighten the clamps on the manifold connection hose.
3. Connect the air compressor supply line to the air cross-over manifold. Install the inlet air tube and hoses on the air cleaner and air cross-over manifold.
4. Operate the engine and check for air leaks.
5. Lower the cab and lock it in position.

Intake Manifold Removal

In-line Engines

1. Drain the cooling system.
2. Disconnect both coolant hoses from the radiator supply tank. Remove the radiator overflow tube from the retaining clamps. Disconnect the windshield washer hose at the "Y" connection.
3. In most cases it is necessary to remove the engine hood to cowl retaining screws. Remove the engine hood to grille retaining bolts. Use a hoist to remove the engine hood assembly.
4. Loosen the hose clamps, and remove the air inlet tube from the air cleaner to the intake manifold.
5. Disconnect the glow plug lead and the primer fuel line from the intake manifold preheater, if so equipped.
6. Disconnect the compressor air inlet line from the compressor, and remove it from the intake manifold. Disconnect the air compressor coolant line from the compressor and the engine coolant manifold. Remove the retaining clip from the rocker cover; then remove the compressor coolant line.
7. Remove the engine compartment covers from the cab floor.
8. Remove the retaining bolts; then remove the intake manifold.

Intake Manifold Removal

Tilt Cab Models

1. Release the cab locks and tilt the cab forward.
2. Loosen the hose clamps, and remove the air inlet tube from the intake manifold and air cleaner. Remove the air cleaner assembly.
3. Disconnect the glow plug lead and the primer fuel line from the intake manifold preheater, if so equipped.
4. Remove the air compressor air inlet line from the intake manifold and air compressor. Remove the parking brake retaining clip from the intake manifold.
5. Remove the retaining bolts; then remove the intake manifold.

Intake Manifold Installation

In-line Engines

1. Clean the gasket surfaces on the intake manifold and cylinder heads.
2. Using new gaskets, install the intake manifold and tighten the manifold bolts in sequence.
3. Install the compressor coolant line on the air compressor and the engine coolant manifold. Attach the retaining clip to the front rocker cover. Install the compressor air inlet line on the compressor and intake manifold.
4. Connect the primer fuel line and glow plug lead to the intake manifold preheater, if so equipped.
5. Install the air inlet tube on the intake manifold and air cleaner, and tighten the hose clamps.
6. If removed, use a hoist to position the engine hood assembly on the cowl and grille. Install and tighten the hood to cowl screws and hood to grille bolts.
7. Position the radiator overflow tube in the retaining clamps, and tighten the clamps. Connect the coolant hoses to the radiator supply tank. Connect the windshield washer hose.
8. Install the engine compartment covers on the cab floor.
9. Fill and bleed the cooling system.
10. Start the engine and check for coolant and air leaks.

Intake Manifold Installation

Tilt Cab Models

1. Clean the gasket surfaces on the intake manifold and cylinder heads.
2. Using new gaskets, install the intake manifold. Tighten the manifold bolts in sequence.
3. Install the parking brake retaining clip on the intake manifold. Install the air compressor air inlet line on the compressor and the intake manifold.
4. Connect the primer fuel line and glow plug lead to the intake manifold preheater, if so equipped.
5. Install the air cleaner assembly. Install the air inlet tube on the intake manifold and air cleaner, and tighten the hose clamps.
6. Lower the cab and lock it in position.

Cylinder Head

Cylinder Head Removal

NH Engines

1. Remove the fuel manifold, coolant manifold, exhaust manifold, intake manifold, and rocker housing(s).
2. Remove the injector and valve push rods in order, and place them in a rack for installation in the same position from which they were removed.
3. Remove the compression release lever return spring and retaining bolt.
4. Remove the injector inlet and drain connections.

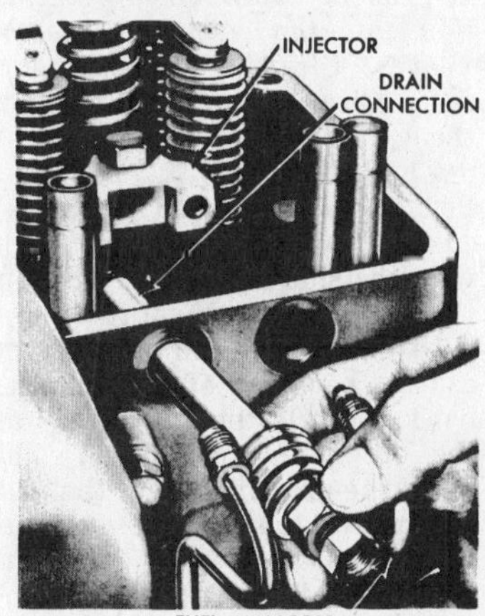

Removing injector drain connection
(© Cummins Engine Co.)

5. Remove the injector hold-down bolts and lift or pry the injectors from the cylinder heads. *Do not turn the injectors upside down, thus avoiding dropping the plungers.*
6. Loosen and remove the cylinder head bolts. Using a lifting eye and a hoist, remove the cylinder head(s), and place them on a bench, with the valves horizontal. Remove the grommet retainers. Remove and discard the grommets, O-rings and gaskets.

Installation

NH Engines

1. Carefully remove excess carbon deposits from the cylinder head(s). *Do not use a scraper or wire brush in the injector sleeve area, to prevent distortion or mutilation of the copper injector sleeves.* Clean the O-ring, grommet and gasket surfaces of the cylinder head(s) and cylinder block. Clean the gasket surfaces of the intake and exhaust manifolds.
2. Check the cylinder liner protrusion of all liners.

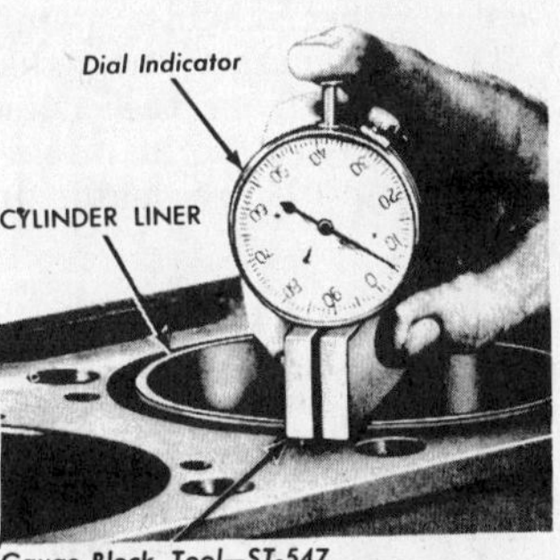

Checking cylinder liner protrusion
(© Cummins Engine Co.)

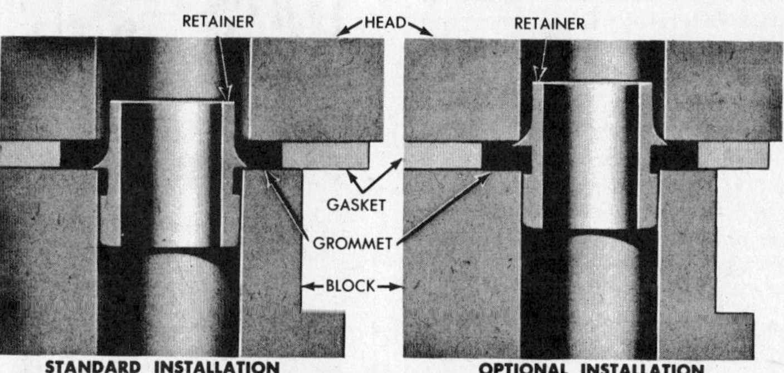

Installing grommets and retainers
(© Cummins Engine Co.)

3. Press new grommet retainers, with the small end up, in the coolant passages of the cylinder block. Position a new cylinder head gasket on the engine block and cylinder head dowels so that the gasket side marked "TOP" is facing up. Install the grommets on the grommet retainers, and press the grommets into the gasket holes. *Avoid all contact between grommets and fuel or lubricating oil to prevent damage due to swelling.* The optional installation of the grommet retainer above the grommet may become necessary when the cylinder head has 15/32 inch coolant holes or when the holes are eroded.
4. Using lifting eye and a hoist, install the cylider head(s).
5. Lubricate the cylinder head bolt threads and washers with engine oil. Install the bolts and torque them in sequence in 100 ft-lb increments to the specifications.
6. Install the injectors, following the procedures described in this section. *Screw the inlet and drain connections into the injectors about 3 turns to align the injectors before tightening the injector hold-down bolts.*

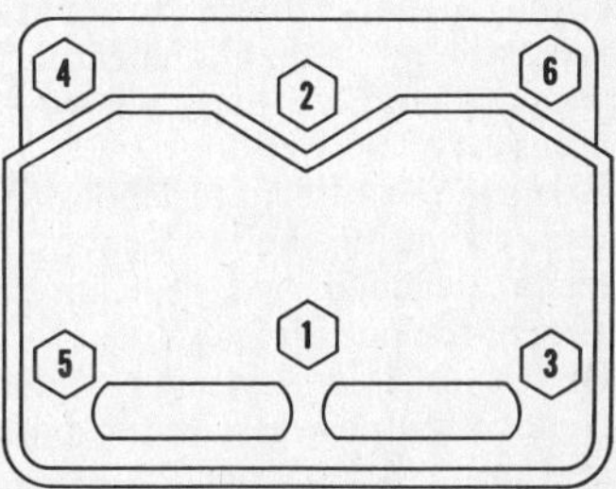

Cylinder head bolt torque sequence
(© Cummins Engine Co.)

7. Install the compression release lever return spring and retaining bolt.
8. Install the injector and valve push rods in the same position from which they were removed.
9. Install the rocker housing(s), intake manifold, exhaust manifold, coolant manifold and fuel manifold, and adjust the valve cross-heads and injector and valve lash.
10. Fill and bleed the cooling system. Operate the engine and check for fuel, oil and coolant leaks. When the engine reaches normal operating temperature (140°F oil temperature), remove the rocker housing cover(s), and adjust the injector and valve lash to specifications. Install the rocker housing cover(s).

Cylinder Head Removal

V-6 & V-8 Engines

1. Drain the cooling system and exhaust the air reservoir. Disconnect the battery cables.
2. Remove the engine hood assembly where necessary.
3. Disconnect the headlamp wiring harness and remove the grille and headlamp assembly(ies). Remove the front fender(s) where necessary.
4. Loosen the clamps and remove the steering gear shaft to steering wheel shaft universal joint. Position the steering gear shaft out of the way where necessary.
5. Remove the radiator brace rod from the left side of the radiator support and frame rail where necessary.
6. Remove the alternator mounting and adjusting bolts. Leave the leads attached and position the alternator out of the way.
7. On the left cylinder head, remove the power steering pump and drive belts from the engine. Leave the hoses attached and position the power steering pump out of the way. On the right cylinder head, remove only the steering pump drive belts.
8. Loosen the fan drive belts. Remove the cooling fan and hub assembly, spacers and drive belts from the engine.
9. On a right cylinder head, disconnect the shutterstat air hoses at the shutterstat. Disconnect the heater hoses at the thermostat housing and the water pump. Disconnect the coolant temperature and warning light sending unit leads. Loosen the water pump to thermostat housing by-pass hose clamp. Remove the thermostat housing and shutterstat assembly.
10. On the right cylinder head, remove the dipstick tube assembly. Remove the air inlet duct from the air cleaner and air cross-over manifold.
11. Disconnect the accelerator rod and the tachometer cable at the fuel pump. Disconnect the service brake air hose at the brake treadle valve. Remove the air hose from the brake treadle valve to the air reservoir line.
12. On some models it may be necessary to disconnect the grille to cab brace rods at the cab. Remove the cab front support to chassis bolts and nuts. Attach a sling and hoist to the cab supports and raise the cab approximately 4 inches.
13. On the left cylinder head, disconnect the air compressor, supply line at the left air cross-over manifold. Loosen the hose clamps and remove the air cross-over manifold(s) and gasket(s).
14. Remove the valve cover(s) and gasket(s) and cylinder head cover(s) and gasket(s.
15. On the right cylinder head, remove the alternator mounting bracket. Remove the intake manifold(s) and gasket(s).
16. Disconnect the fuel supply line at the front of the cylinder head(s). Disconnect the fuel return line at the rear of the cylinder head(s).
17. On the right cylinder head, disconnect the air compressor coolant line at the coolant cross-over tube. Remove the coolant cross-over tube(s) from the cylinder head(s).
18. Remove the push rod cover(s) and gasket(s).
19. Remove the exhaust manifold bolts and separate the exhaust manifold(s) from the cylinder head(s). Leave the manifold(s) attached to the resonator inlet pipe(s).

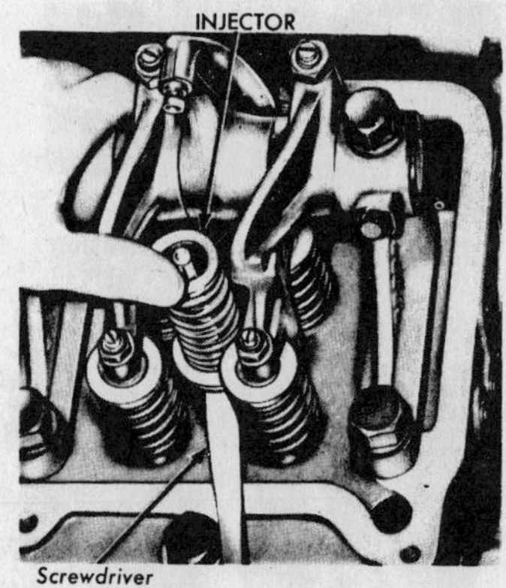

Typical cylindrical injector removal
(© Cummins Engine Co.)

20. Loosen the lock nuts and back off all of the injector and valve rocker lever adjusting screws. Remove the rocker lever support screws. Remove the injector and valve push rods and place them in a rack for installation in the same position from which they were removed. Remove the rocker lever assembly(ies) with the cylinder head(s).
21. Remove the injector hold-down clamp screws and clamps. Pry the injectors loose from the cylinder head. *It may be necessary to use a tool such as shown for removal of the rear injectors.* Remove the injectors and O-rings. *Do not remove the injector plunger, since they are not interchangeable between injectors.*

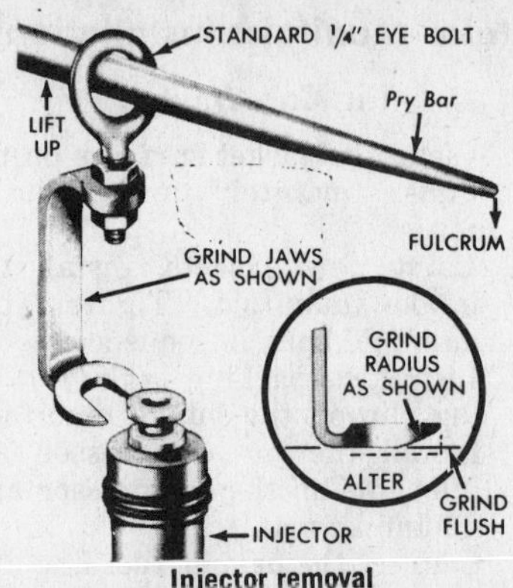

Injector removal
(© Cummins Engine Co.)

22. Remove the remaining cylinder head bolts. If the rear bolts cannot be removed due to interference with the cab supports, split a 1½-inch length of rubber hose and install it around the bolt. This will hold the bolt above the bottom of the cylinder head.
23. Install a lifting bracket on the cylinder head, and use a hoist to remove the cylinder head(s). Remove the crossheads and place them in a rack for installation in the same position.
24. Remove the cylinder head gaskets, grommets, grommet retainers and O-rings. Remove the exhaust manifold gasket(s).

Cylinder Head Installation

V-6 & V-8 Engines

1. Carefully remove excess carbon deposits from the cylinder head. *Do not use a scraper or wire brush in the injector sleeve area, to prevent distortion or mutilation of the copper injector sleeves.* Clean all gasket surfaces. Clean the injector bores of the cylinder head with a clean rag and stick.
2. Position a new head gasket(s) on the cylinder block and dowels with the side marked "TOP" up. Press new grommet retainers, with the small end up, in the coolant passages of the cylinder block. Install the grommets on the grommet retainers, and press the grommets into the gasket holes. *Avoid all contact between grommets and fuel or lubricating oil to prevent damage due to swelling.* The optional installation of the grommet retainer above the grommet may be necessary when the cylinder head has 15/32-inch coolant holes or when the holes are eroded.
3. Install the crossheads on the cylinder head(s). Position the rocker lever assembly on the cylinder head. Lubricate the bolt threads and position the rear cylinder head(s) with a 1½-inch bolt.

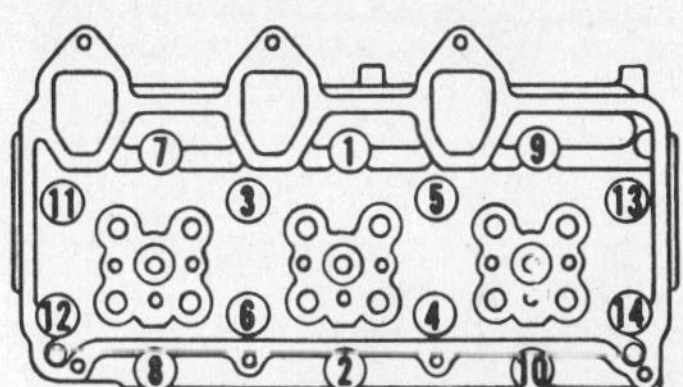
Cylinder head bolt torque sequence
(© Cummins Engine Co.)

4. Install the injectors and hold-down clamps. Torque the clamp screws to specifications.
5. Install the push rods in the same position from which they were removed. Lubricate the cylinder head bolt threads and washers with engine oil. Install the bolts and torque them to specifications in 30 ft-lb increments, following the sequence.
6. Adjust the crossheads and the injector and valve lash.
7. Using new gaskets, install the exhaust manifold(s). Torque the bolts in 15 ft-lb increments to specifications.
8. Use new gasket(s) and install the push rod cover(s).
9. Install the coolant cross-over tube(s) on the cylinder head(s). On the right cylinder head, connect the air compressor coolant line to the coolant cross-over tube.
10. Connect the fuel return line at the rear of the cylinder head(s). Connect the fuel supply line at the front of the cylinder head(s).
11. Using new gasket(s), install the intake manifold(s). On the right cylinder head, install the alternator mounting bracket.
12. Coat the upper surface of new gaskets and position the gaskets on the cylinder head cover(s) and valve cover(s). Install the cylinder head cover(s) and valve cover(s). *Partially tighten the valve cover screws.*
13. Install the air cross-over manifold(s) with new gasket(s). Tighten the screws and hose clamps. On the left cylinder head, connect the air compressor supply line to the left air cross-over manifold.
14. Install the inlet air duct on the air cross-over manifold, and tighten the hose clamp. On the right cylinder head, install the dipstick tube assembly.
15. Install the thermostat housing and shutterstat assembly. Tighten the hose clamps. Connect the coolant temperature and warning light sending unit leads. Connect the radiator upper hose and heater hoses to the thermostat housing and water pump. Connect the shutterstat air hoses to the shutterstat.

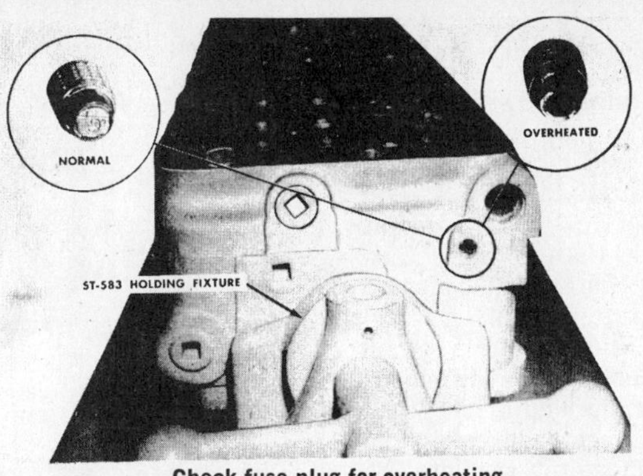

Check fuse plug for overheating
(© Cummins Engine Co.)

16. Install the cooling fan and hub assembly, spacers and drive belts.
17. Install the alternator, but do not install the drive belt at this time.
18. Connect the battery cables. Fill and bleed the cooling system. Operate the engine until the oil temperature is 140°F. Remove the valve cover(s) and adjust the injector and valve lash to specifications. Install the valve cover(s) and tighten the screws in alternate steps.
19. Install the alternator drive belt.
20. Lower the cab. Install and tighten the cab front support to chassis bolts, insulators and nuts. Connect the grille to cab brace rods to the cab.
21. Install the air hose to the brake treadle valve and the air reservoir line. Connect the service brake air hose to the brake treadle valve. Connect the tachometer cable and accelerator rod to the fuel pump. Adjust the accelerator linkage.
22. On the left cylinder head, install the power steering pump. Install the drive belts and adjust the belt deflection to specifications.
23. Install the radiator left brace rod.
24. Connect the steering gear shaft to the steering wheel shaft.
25. Install the front fender(s). Install the headlamp and grille assembly(ies). Connect the headlamp wiring harness.
26. Install the engine hood assembly.
27. Operate the engine and check for air, oil and coolant leaks.

Rebuilding Cylinder Head

Valve Guides

1. Where replacement is required, drive out valve guides from underside of cylinder head.
2. Install new valve guides with Valve Guide Driver.
3. If reaming of valve guide is necessary to install valves ream valve guide from bottom side of cylinder head, using a drill press and floating tool holder. Use lubricating oil or soluble oil and water solution for a good finish. CAUTION: Special care must be used to avoid breaking carbide tips. Sharpen carbide tipped tools on a diamond impregnated wheel.

Valve Crosshead Guides

1. Remove guides to be replaced, using Puller which contains different size collets to fit the various guides. NOTE: After Engine Serial No. 298655, engines are equipped with "solid" pin-type crosshead guides and crossheads with hollow stems. Old and new-style crossheads and guides may be used in the same cylinder head.
2. Press in new guides. NOTE: *A special solid guide has been released to permit the new hollow crossheads in cylinder heads machined for the larger diameter hollow guide.*

Replace Injector Sleeves

1. Remove worn sleeves by cutting them from cylinder head with a ⅜ inch gouge chisel (sometimes called a muffler sleeve cutting tool) and driving out from lower end. NOTE: Remove all foreign material from injector sleeve sealing area.

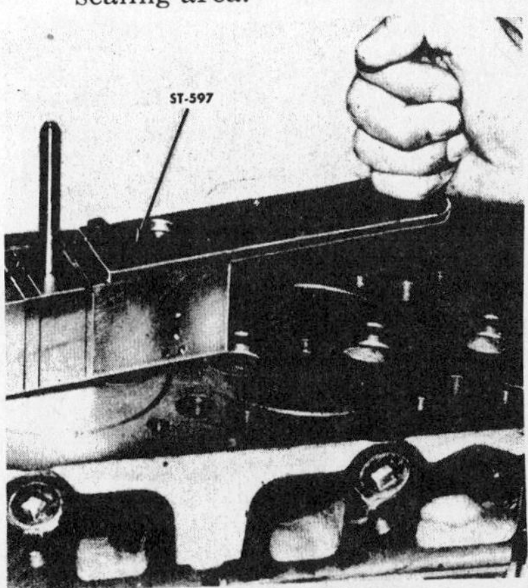

Regrooving cylinder head with special tool
(© Cummins Engine Co.)

2. Bead sleeve seat area of heads not previously beaded. This will provide an improved seal.
   a. Install the bead cutter in seat cutter holder and position with Cutter Pilot in a drill press. Set drill press speed at not more than 75 rpm. Cutter may be turned by hand using a tap wrench.
   b. Set cylinder head on drill press table, allowing clearance for the end of the bead cutter to protrude below the head surface into a pilot. The pilot can be made by recessing a ½ inch drill bushing in a plate which is centered below the drill spindle and secured in place.
   c. Before starting drill press motor, insert cutter, adapter and pilot into injector bore to insure proper alignment.
   d. Remove cutter, adapter and pilot, lubricate cutter with cutting oil and start cutting operation, applying a steady moderate pressure. CAUTION: Do not cut more than .010 deep.
   e. When the proper depth has been obtained, allow the cutter to dwell for approximately 10 seconds to insure a good seat and clean grooves.
   f. A special cutter is used to cut a 30° angle chamfer at the lower edge of the 60° seat. Stop when the upper end of the 30° angle chamfer is approximately 9/64 inch from the bottom bead.
   g. Remove bluing from 60° seat.
3. Drive in injector sleeve with proper injector sleeve driver.
4. Remove driver from injector sleeve.
5. Seal upper portion of sleeves with expanding roller. Apply force to expand rollers.
6. Remove the injector hold down tool.
7. Seal injector sleeve in lower seating (tapered) area, with special tool.
8. Cut injector seat to provide proper injector seat and injector tip protrusion, of .040 to .055 inch.

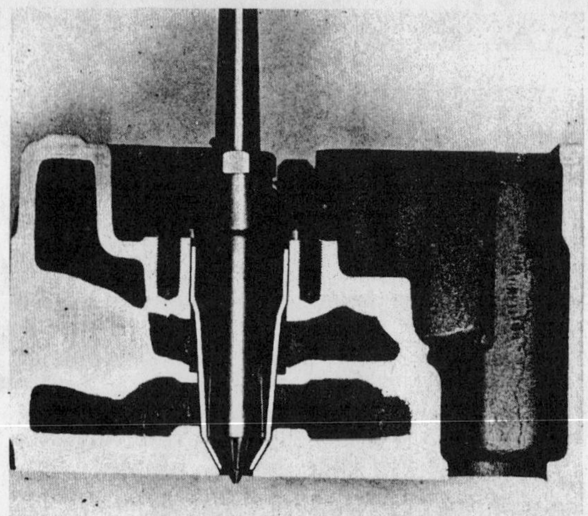

Sealing lower end of injector sleeve
(© Cummins Engine Co.)

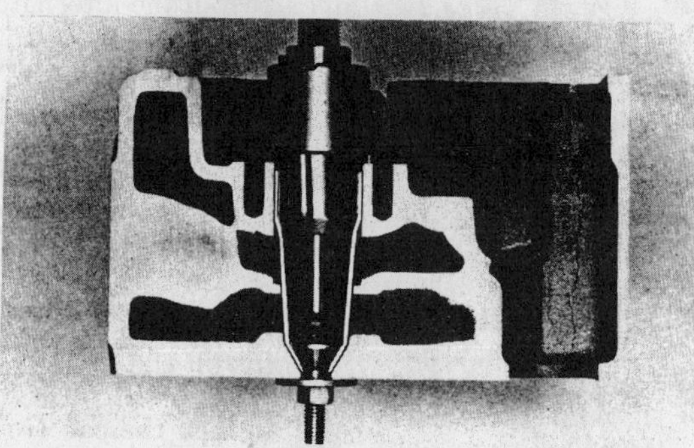

Sealing upper end of injector sleeve
(© Cummins Engine Co.)

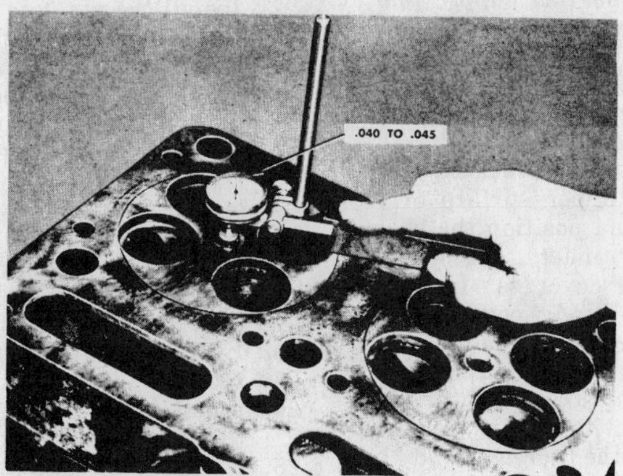

Measuring injector tip protrusion
(© Cummins Engine Co.)

Replace Valve Seat Inserts

1. Remove loose or excessively worn valve seat inserts.
2. Enlarge counterbore to next oversize. Inserts are available in standard .010, .020, .030, and .040 inch oversizes.
3. Use Valve Seat Insert Tool to hold and drive cutters which come in sets. This tool must be driven by an electric motor.

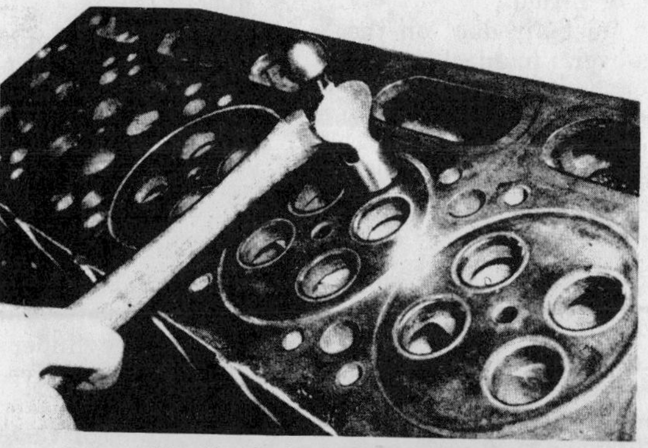

Checking for loose valve seat inserts
(© Cummins Engine Co.)

4. Machine counterbore .006/.010 inch deeper than insert height to permit peening of head to hold insert.
5. Install valve seat insert.
6. Peen insert in head with peening tool. A ¼-inch diameter round-end punch may be used.

Grind Valve Seats

1. Check condition of grinding equipment.
   a. Mandrels must be straight and of proper size to fit in reamed valve guides.
   b. Bushings in the grinder must be clean and must fit properly on guide mandrel.
   c. Bearings of drive unit must be in good condition.
2. Dress stone to 30° from horizontal.

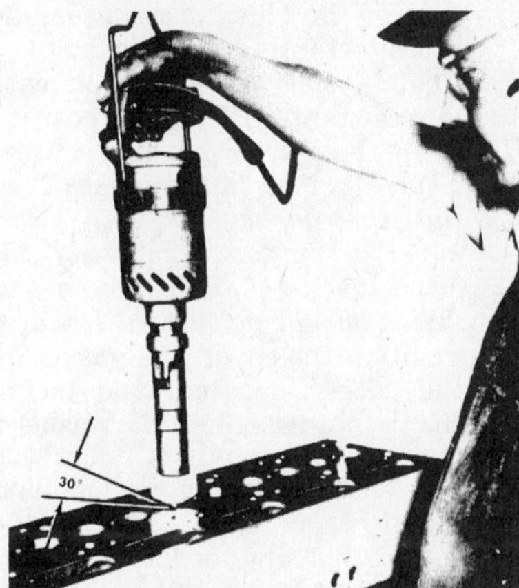

Refacing valve seats
(© Cummins Engine Co.)

3. Grind valve seats, holding seating motor as nearly vertical as possible. A severe angle will cause the seat to be out-of-true depending upon the amount of wear in the grinder bearings, mandrel bushines, etc., even though the grinder has a universal joint.

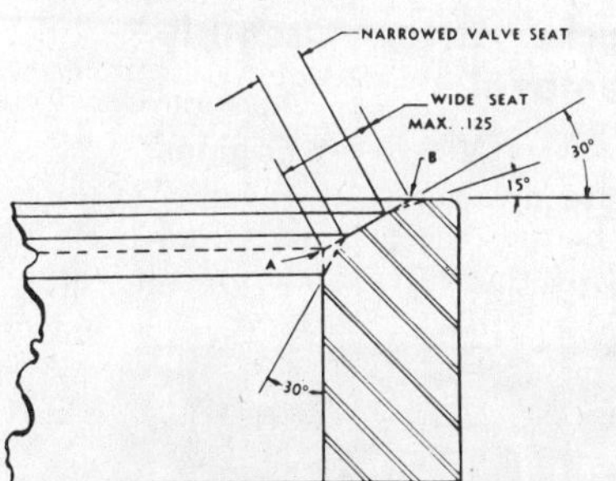

Valve seat insert—cross section
(© Cummins Engine Co.)

4. Check valve seat width which should be 1/16 to ⅛ inch.
   a. If ground seat is wider than the maximum ⅛ inch, stock can be removed from points "A" and "B" with specially dressed valve seat grinder stones.
   b. Narrowing should not extend beyond chamfer on seat insert. Chamfer provides for peen metal.
5. Dress wheel for final finish.
6. Finish grind with light touches of stone against face.
7. Check guide alignment with eccentrimeter.
   a. Run-out should not exceed .001 inch.
   b. The gauge must be a perfect fit on pilot mandrel.

Grind Valves

1. Check valve grinder setting by using a new valve and an indicator gauge.
   a. Chuck valve on guide area of stem. Reliever portions on both ends of guide area are not necessarily concentric to guide area of stem.
   b. Indicate on ground face of valve.
   c. Turn valve and mark high spot on head of valve.
   d. Rechuck and valve 180° from first position.
   e. Repeat "b" and "c". If the high spots are same for both "a" and "d" positions, the valve is warped. If high spots occur in different positions, chuck is out of alignment. Runout should not exceed .001 inch.
2. Check bearings of machine.
3. The grinding wheel must be the proper grade and properly dressed to avoid chatter and grind marks.
4. Wet grind valves to an exact 30° angle from horizontal.
5. Valves and seats properly ground with precision equipment should not require lapping to effect an airtight seal; however, a small amount of lapping is permissible if necessary in order to pass vacuum test.

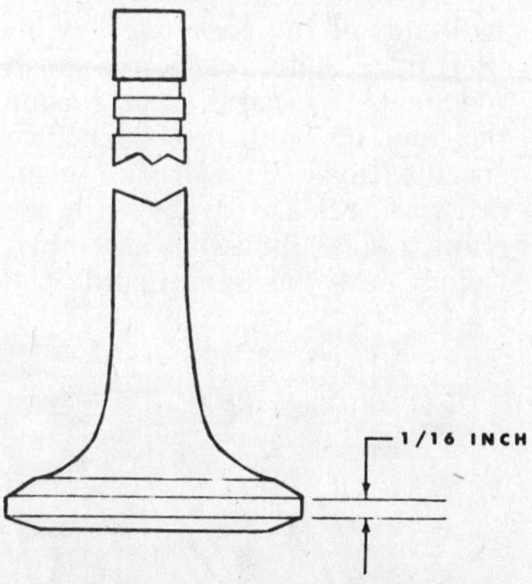

Minimum valve head rim thickness
(© Cummins Engine Co.)

6. Check rim thickness. If rim is thinner than 1/16 inch, valve is not suitable for use because of the danger of burning and cupping.
7. Check valve in a finish reamed guide and against a newly ground valve seat face. Pencil mark valve as shown in illustration, drop into position and rotate 10 degrees.
8. A true seat will be indicated if all pencil marks are broken. If pencil marks are not broken, the valve seat tools need dressing or the machine has not been properly adjusted.

Assemble Valves and Springs

1. Insert valves.
2. Place cylinder head face down on a wooden bench to prevent marring milled surface.
3. Assemble lower valve spring guides on valve guides.
4. Assemble springs. NOTE: *Reground valve heads seat deeper in cylinder head causing valve stem to protrude further above the guide. This allows valve spring to extend beyond length limits and causes weak spring action. Therefore, up to two spacers may be used to reduce valve spring length.* CAUTION: Too many spacers will cause the compressed spring to become a solid sleeve.
5. Assemble upper valve spring guide. Insert half-collets.
6. Use Valve Spring Compressor to compress valve spring. Use new half-collets.

Test Valves and Seats for Leakage

A vacuum tester to check valves and seats for leakage is available. It consists of a vacuum pump, vacuum gauge and suction cup. Use with any 6-volt battery source or 110-volt electrical outlet as required. Follow manufacturers procedures for operation.

CAUTION Never vacuum test cylinder head with injectors installed. Installation of injectors while head is removed from block could cause misalignment of valves in valve seat and result in leakage during the vacuum test which would not necessarily occur during actual engine operation.

Valves and seats must be dry and clean.

NOTE: It is possible to mistake leakage around the valve seat insert for valve seat leakage. If this type of leakage, is suspected, apply grease around the outside edge of the insert to make a grease seal. Perform the vacuum test and inspect the grease seal for a break indicating air leakage between the wall of counterbore and valve seat insert. If a leak around valve seat insert is found, correction is required before continuing with the test.

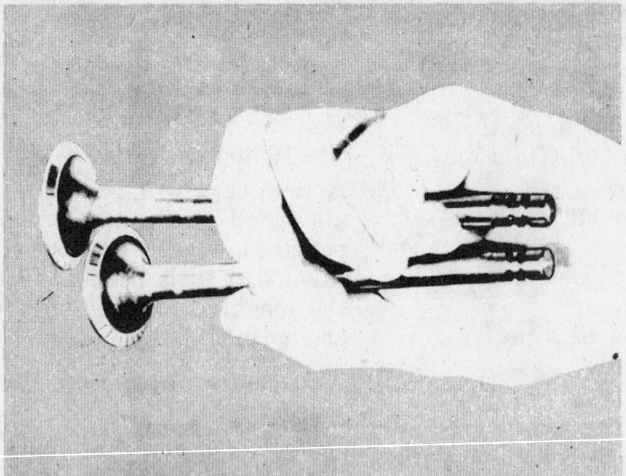

Pencil marks on valves
(© Cummins Engine Co.)

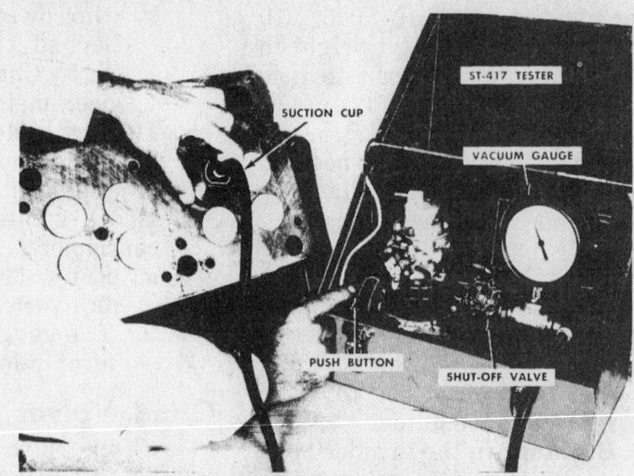

Vacuum testing valves for leaks
(© Cummins Engine Co.)

Install Crossheads

1. Insert valve crossheads in crosshead guides, or assemble valve crossheads over crosshead guides, depending upon design.
2. Install crosshead retainer to keep crosshead in position and insure correct valve-to-crosshead and rocker lever contact.

Check Vent Holes

Check the vent hole at the top of the cylinder head and at the front of every other rocker shaft bearing. *On all supercharged and turbocharged engines the vent holes must be plugged with a 1/8 inch pipe plug.* On naturally aspirated engines, a vented plug must be installed.

Compression Release

Disassembly

1. Remove mounting stud nuts and lockwashers.
2. Lift compression release housing, shaft, lever and spring from cylinder head.
3. Inspect and install a new packing gland, if necessary.

Assembly

1. Reassemble compression release to cylinder head, being careful to let one end of spring ride against housing with other end held against upper stud bolt.
2. Clamp lever in place so that open position will lift valves 1/16 inch maximum.

Rocker Assembly and Housing

Rocker Housing Removal

N & NH In-line Engines

1. Remove the rocker housing covers. Remove the lubricating oil pipe caps and gaskets.
2. Loosen the locknuts and back off the adjusting screws two or three turns on all rocker levers.
3. Remove the rocker housing retaining bolts and lift the rocker housing assemblies from the engine by grasping the ends of the injector rocker. Leave the compression lever attached to the linkage on No. 1 cylinder.

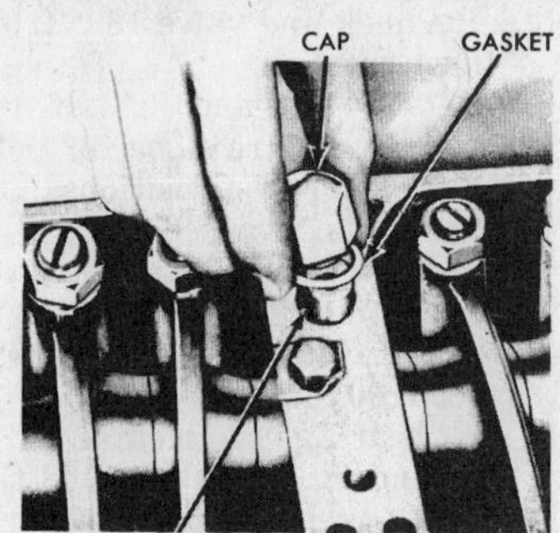

Removing oil pipe cap
(© Cummins Engine Co.)

Installation

N & NH Engines

1. Clean the gasket surfaces of the cylinder heads, rocker housings and covers.
2. Using a new housing gasket, position the rocker housing(s) on the cylinder heads with the ball-ends of the rocker levers fitting into their respective push rod sockets. Install and torque the housing bolts in sequence to specifications. Install the compression release arm with the front rocker housing assembly.
3. Using new gaskets, install the lubricating oil pipe caps and torque to specifications.
4. Adjust the valve crossheads and the injector and valve lash.
5. Coat a new cove gasket with oil-resistant sealer and position it on the rocker housing covers. *Care must be taken in positioning the gasket to the rocker cover to prevent covering the crankcase vent or leaving a gap which would permit oil leakage.* Position the cover and gasket on the rocker housing, and install the retaining bolts and washers.
6. Operate the engine and check for leaks. When engine oil temperature is 140°F. remove the rocker housing covers and adjust the injector and valve lash.

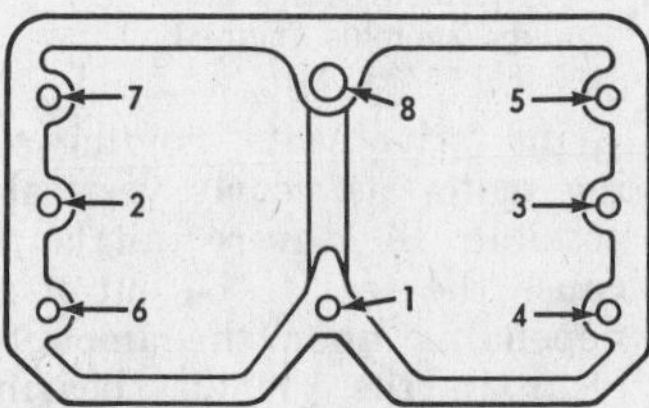

Rocker housing torque sequence
(© Cummins Engine Co.)

Rocker Lever Assembly Removal

V-6 & V-8 Engines

Remove the valve cover.

Loosen the lock nuts and back off all of the valve and injector rocker

Rocker lever removal
(© Cummins Engine Co.)

lever adjusting screws. Hold the rocker levers together with rubber bands. Remove the rocker lever support screws and remove the rocker lever assembly (ies).

Installation

V-6 & V-8 Engines

Clean all parts before reassembly.

1. Back off the rocker lever adjusting screws. Lubricate the valve and injector rocker lever pads and adjusting screws with engine oil. Install the rocker lever assembly (ies) and torque the mounting screws to specifications (cylinder head bolt torque).
2. Adjust the crossheads and injector and valve rocker lash.
3. Install the valve cover (s), *and partially tighten the cover screws.*
4. Connect the accelerator rod to the fuel pump. Operate the engine until the oil temperature is 140°F. *Be sure the air reservoir drain cock is open.* Remove the valve cover (s) and adjust the injector and valve rocker lash. Install the valve cover (s) and cover screws. Tighten the cover screws in alternate steps.

Cam Follower Housing Assembly Removal

In-line Engines

Remove the rocker housing assembly (ies).

1. Remove the valve and injector push rods, and place them in a rack for installation in the proper sequence.
2. Remove the cam follower housing assembly for cylinders Nos. 5 and 6. Discard the gasket.
3. Remove the fuel pump. Remove the cam follower housing assembly for cylinders Nos. 3 and 4. Discard the gasket.
4. Remove the air compressor.
5. Remove the cam follower housing assembly for Cylinders Nos. 1 and 2. Discard the gasket.

Inspect and clean all parts before assembly.

Installation

In-line Engines

1. Clean the gasket surfaces of the cam follower housings and cylinder block. Using new gaskets, install the cam follower housing assembly (ies), and tighten the retaining screws.
2. Install the valve and injector push rods in the same sequence that they were removed.
3. Remove the fuel injectors from Nos. 1, 3 and 5 cylinders and time the engine.

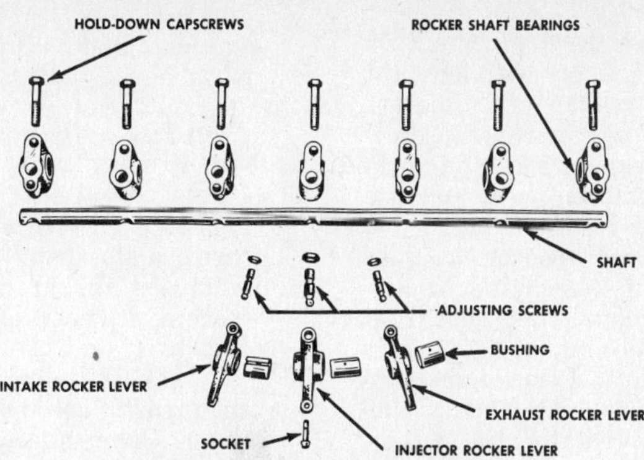

Rocker levers, shafts and bearings
(© Cummins Engine Co.)

Valve Adjustment

The same crankshaft position used in setting the injectors is used for setting the intake and exhaust valves. Set valves after injectors are adjusted.

1. Loosen the locknut and adjusting screw. Insert a feeler gauge between the rocker lever and top of the valve stem or crosshead and turn screw down until the lever just touches the feeler gauge.

Install the rocker housing(s) and adjust the injector and valve lash. Install the rocker housing covers.

Install air compressor and fuel pump.

Operate the engine and check for leaks. When the engine reaches normal operating temperature (140°F oil temperature), adjust the valve and injector lash to specifications.

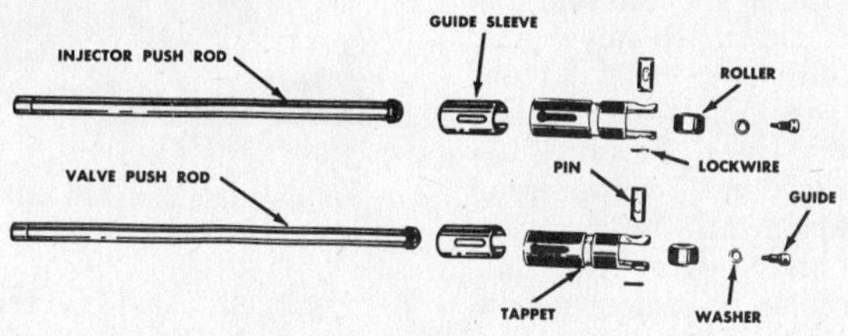

Tappets and push rods
(© Cummins Engine Co.)

Valve clearances are:

Valve	70°F.	140°F.
Intake	.017	.015
Exhaust	.027	.025

2. Lock adjusting screw in position with jam nut. Recheck valve clearance after tightening jam nut.
3. Continue turning crankshaft in direction of rotation, performing adjustments, until all valves are adjusted correctly.
4. Make final adjustment when engine is at operating (140°F.) temperature.
5. Continue adjustments, each cylinder in firing order, until all cylinders are adjusted. This will require two complete revolutions of the crankshaft.

Time the Engine

Clean the injector seats with a rag wrapped around a stick. *Do not use a metal tool for cleaning; scratched seats may result in compression leaks.*

Gear Case Cover and Seal

Gear Case Cover Removal

In-line Engines

1. Drain the cooling system and the crankcase.
2. When necessary release the cab locks and tilt the cab forward.
3. Remove the radiator and shutter assembly. Remove the front crossmember (radiator support) from the frame where necessary.
4. Remove the oil pan.
5. Remove the cooling fan. Remove all drive belts. Remove the fan hub and bracket assembly. Rmove the fan drive pulley from the compressor crankshaft.
6. Remove the power steering pump bracket to engine bolts and position the pump and bracket assembly out of the way.
7. Remove the crankshaft damper capscrews, and pull the damper off the crankshaft. It may be nec-

essary to tap the damper with a soft hammer in order to loosen it from the crankshaft. Remove the crankshaft flange capscrew and retainer, or nut and lockplate on some engines, and use puller to remove the flange.

8. Use a jack and wood block under the front of the engine to support it. Remove the engine front support retaining bolts, spacers and insulators. Remove the support bracket cap bolts and bracket cap. Raise the engine and remove the support bracket and insulators as an assembly.
9. Remove the compressor crankshaft pulley nut. Remove the compressor crankshaft pulley. Remove the crankshaft key.
10. Remove the gear case retaining bolts. Using a soft hammer, loosen the gear case cover from the cylinder block, and remove the cover. Remove the seals from the cover. Remove the camshaft thrust-plate, O-ring seal and spacers, if so equipped.

Installation

1. Clean the oil pan and gear case cover with solvent. Be sure all gasket surfaces and oil seal recesses are clean. Remove and clean the oil pump inlet screen.
2. Apply oil-resistant sealer to the OD of the new cover seals (crankshaft and compressor shaft) and install the seals in the gear case cover. Use oil-resistant sealer to cement a new gasket to the gear case cover.
3. Apply lubricant to the oil seal lips and the seal surface of the compressor shaft. Install the gear case cover and tighten the retaining bolts.
4. Position the engine front support and insulator assembly on the frame crossmember, and lower the engine onto the support bracket. Install the support bracket cap, lower insulators, spacers, and retaining bolts. Torque the bracket to frame bolts, and then the bracket cap bolts to specifications.
5. If equipped with a camshaft thrust plate, install it as follows: Hold the thrust plate, without spacers, in position against the camshaft, and use feeler gauges to check the clearance between the thrust plate and the gear case cover. Using micrometers, select enough spacers to bring the camshaft end clearance within specifications. Place the spacers on the thrust plate. Apply Lubriplate to a new O-ring and install it on the thrust plate. Install the thrust plate on the gear case cover and tighten the screws.

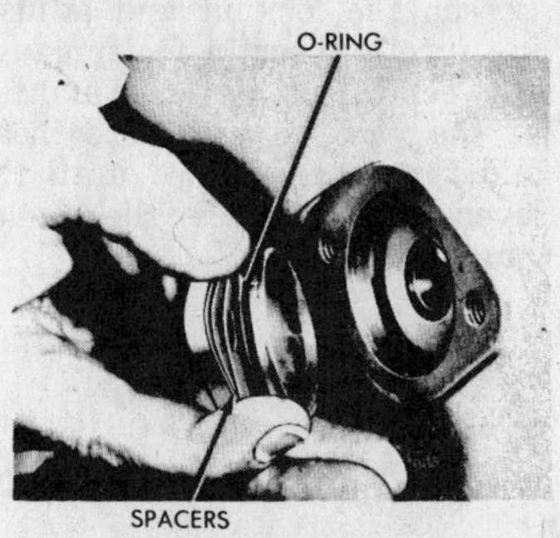

Installing camshaft thrust plate
(© Cummins Engine Co.)

6. Coat the seal surfaces of the crankshaft flange wtih lubricant and install the flange on the crankshaft. Install the flange lockplate and lock nut and torque to specifications. Bend the lockplate to secure the nut. Install the crankshaft damper on the crankshaft flange and tighten the retaining screws.
7. Install the fan drive pulley on the compressor crankshaft.
8. Install the power steering pump and bracket assembly on the engine.
9. Install the fan hub and bracket assembly. Torque the screws to specifications. Position the cooling fan, alternator and power steering pump drive belts in the proper pulleys. Install the cooling fan.
10. Install the oil pan.
11. Install the front crossmember, and install the radiator and shutter assembly if removed.
12. Fill and bleed the cooling system. Fill the crankcase. Operate the engine and check for oil and coolant leaks.

Cylinder Front Cover Oil Seal Removal

V-6 & V-8 Engines

1. Drain the cooling system. Disconnect the battery cables.
2. Remove the shutter and radiator.
3. Remove the alternator, cooling fan and power steering pump drive belts.
4. Remove the cooling fan. Remove the crankshaft damper and the crankcase pulley.
5. Punch two holes in the cylinder front cover oil seal. Install a self-tapping screw in each punched hole, and pry against the screws to remove the oil seal.

Installation

Apply oil-resistant sealer to the OD of a new oil seal. Lubricate the oil seal lips and the crankshaft with engine oil. Install the seal.

Reverse the removal procedure.

Camshaft

For best operation we do not recommend camshaft lobe regrinding.

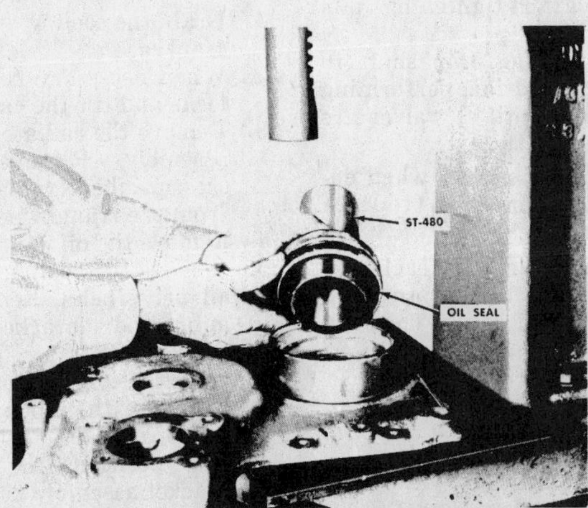

Installing crankshaft seal in gear case cover
(© Cummins Engine Co.)

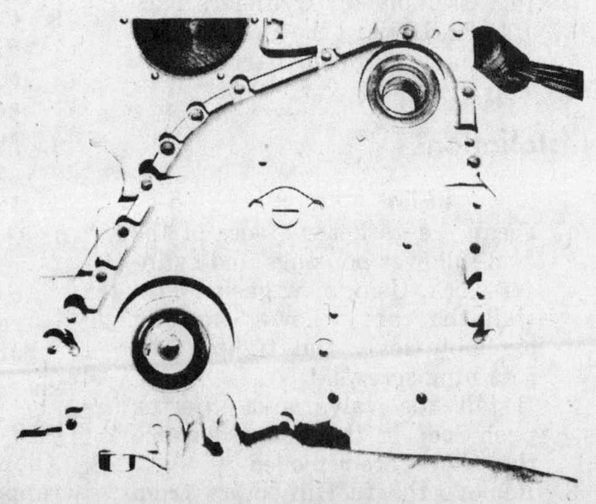
Installing gear case cover
(© Cummins Engine Co.)

Journal Wear

New camshaft journal diameter is 1.872/1,873 inches. This allows for .0015/.0045 inch oil clearances between the journal and bushing.

1. Replace camshaft if journals are smaller than 1.871 inches.
2. Replace any camshaft with scuffed, scored or cracked injector or valve lobes. Check by magnetic inspection for possible cracks.

Camshaft Gear and Thrust Bearing

The interference fit camshaft gear is keyed to the camshaft. The type of keys used are shown in illustration. The key controls engine timing limits, it may be straight or offset as shown.

The current camshaft thrust bearing is mounted with two instead of three capscrews; interchangeable with older bearing mounted with three capscrews.

Do not remove camshaft gear unless absolutely necessary. If inspection shows it is necessary to remove gear, do so by one of two following methods:

Camshafts with three capscrews mounted thrust bearing.

Removal

1. Slide two steel bars, 4 inches by 1 inch by one-half inch, behind gear and thrust bearing.
2. Insert gear puller jaws through access holes in gear and install piston pin through piston and rod bores.
3. Tighten puller bolt until gear is free of camshaft.
4. Camshafts with two capscrew mounted thrust bearing.
   a. Place camshaft and gear in press. Support gear as near hub as possible by using short bars laying parallel with thrust bearing.
   b. Press camshaft from gear.

NOTE: Care must be taken to prevent gear breakage due to improper use of press and support bars.

After gear is free of camshaft:

Removing camshaft
(© Cummins Engine Co.)

Installation

1. Note type of Key used. Replace key.
2. Coat gear hub area of camshaft with Lubriplate.
3. Install camshaft thrust bushing on camshaft with grooves in bushing toward gear.
4. Heat gear evenly to 400°/500°F. with heating torch (not a cutting torch).
5. Press on new camshaft gear, aligning gear keyway with camshaft key.
6. Check between thrust bearing and camshaft gear for .007 to .011 inch clearance for new thrust bearing.

Pistons and Connecting Rods

Pistons and Connecting Rods Removal

Typical of All Engines

1. Drain the cooling system and the crankcase and remove the exhaust manifold(s), intake manifold(s), cylinder head or valve cover(s), cylinder Head(s), oil pan, and oil pump.
2. Scrape all of the carbon from the top of the cylinder liners.
3. Remove the connecting rod cap.
4. Push the connecting rod and piston assembly out of the top of the cylinder. *Avoid damage to the crankshaft journal or the cylinder liner when removing the piston and connecting rod.*
5. Remove the bearings and identify them with the cylinder numbers. Assemble the connecting rod, cap, bolts and nuts as each rod and piston assembly is removed.

Disassembly

1. Using piston ring expander, remove the piston rings.

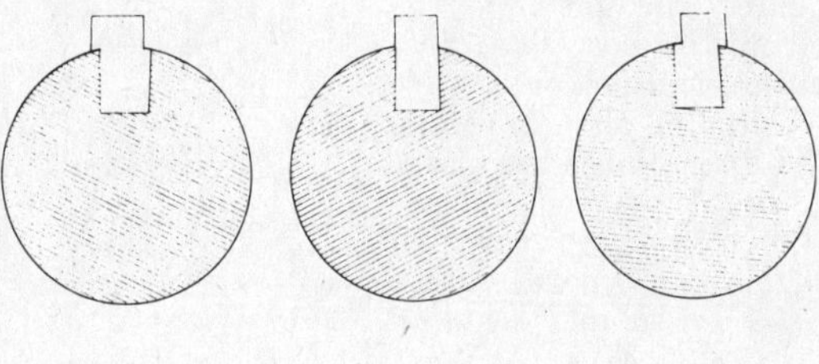

Camshaft gear keys from gear case end
(© Cummins Engine Co.)

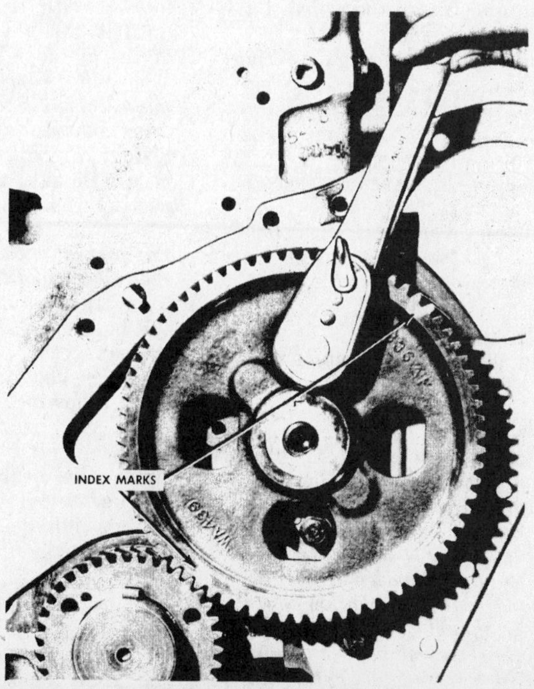

Tightening camshaft retaining bolts
(© Cummins Engine Co.)

Checking clearance between thrust washer
(© Cummins Engine Co.)

Checking piston ring gap
(© Cummins Engine Co.)

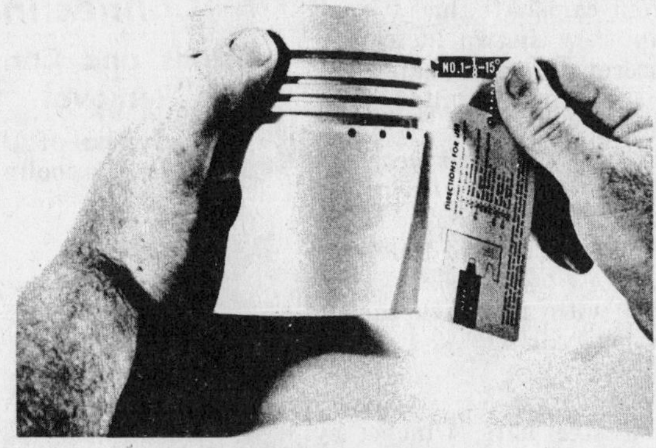
Checking ring groove wear
(© Cummins Engine Co.)

2. Remove the piston pin retaining rings. *Heat the pistons in hot water; then remove the piston pins.*
3. Remove carbon deposits from the piston surfaces. Clean gum or varnish from the piston pins, piston skirt and piston rings with solvent. *Do not use* a caustic cleaning solution or a wire brush to clean pistons. Make sure the oil ring holes are clean. *Do not use a ring groove cleaning tool or a broken piston ring to clean the ring grooves. Use a soft bristle brush and cleaning solvent.*
4. Inspect the pistons, piston pins and piston rings.

Assembly

1. Install one piston pin retaining ring in the piston. Heat the piston in hot water and install the piston pin. Install the remaining piston pin retainer.
2. Install the piston rings on the piston, using a piston ring, expander. The side of the piston ring marked "TOP" must be toward the top of the piston. If new piston rings are installed, fit them to the piston and the cylinder bore. *Never use chrome-plated piston rings in a chrome-plated cylinder liner.*

Installation

1. Oil the piston rings, pistons and cylinder walls with clean engine oil. *Be sure to install the pistons in the same cylinders from which they were fitted. The numbers on the connecting rod and bearing cap must be on the same side when installed in the cylinder bore. If a connecting rod is ever transposed from one block or cylinder to another, new bearings should be fitted and the connecting rod should be numbered to correspond with the new cylinder number.*
2. Make sure the ring gaps are properly spaced around the circumference of the piston but not in line with the piston pin. Install the piston ring compressor on the piston and push the piston in with a hammer handle until it is slightly below the top of the cylinder liner. *If a band-type ring compressor is used, make certain the inner band does not slip down and bind the piston, or ring breakage will occur.* Be sure to guide the connecting rods to avoid damaging the crankshaft journals. *Install the piston with the number on the rod toward the camshaft.*
3. Turn the crankshaft throw to the bottom of its stroke. Install the connecting rod bearings, and check the clearance of each bearing following the procedure under "Connecting Rod Bearing Replacement."
4. After the bearings have been checked and found satisfactory, apply a light coat of engine oil to the journals and bearings. Install the connecting rod cap. Torque the bolts to specifications. Lock the tab washers.
5. After the piston and connecting rod assemblies have been installed, check the connecting rod bearing side clearance.
6. Install the oil pump, oil pan, cylinder head(s), cylinder head cover(s), intake manifold(s), and exhaust manifold(s).
7. Adjust the valve crossheads; then adjust the injector and valve lash. Torque the rocker lever lock nuts to specifications.
8. Fill the cooling system and crankcase. Operate the engine until the oil temperature is 140°F. Remove the cylinder head covers and adjust the injector and valve lash. Check for oil, air, fuel and collant leaks. Install the cylinder head covers.

Cylinder Liners

Cylinder Liner Removal

Typical—All Engines

1. Drain the cooling system and the crankcase.
2. Remove the following: coolant manifold, exhaust manifold, fuel manifold, intake manifold, rocker housing assembly(ies), cylinder head(s), oil pan and piston(s) and connecting rod(s).
3. Remove the cylinder liner, using liner puller (or equivalent). If more than one liner is removed, identify them for installation in the same position as removed.

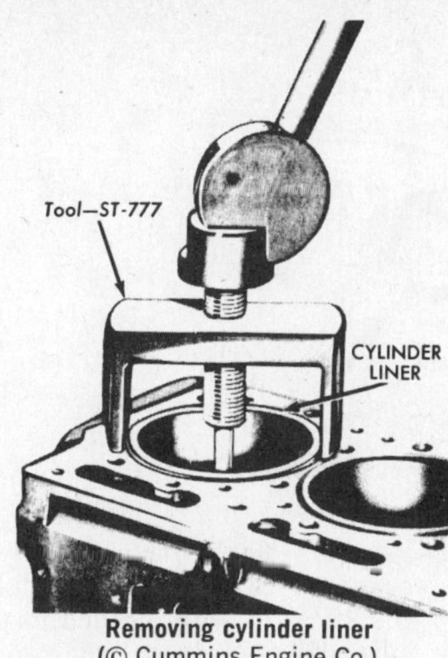

Removing cylinder liner
(© Cummins Engine Co.)

Inspection and Repair

Inspect the cylinder liners and cylinder liner counterbore (crankcase) and repair as necessary. *Before discarding a cylinder liner worn beyond the maximum wear limit, determine if it can be ground oversize for use with the next oversize piston. If it is necessary to grind the ID of one liner, inspect all liners for conformance to wear limits.*

Check the diametrical clearance of the cylinder liner to cylinder bore in the liner O-ring seal area. *It must be within specifications.*

Installation

1. Check the cylinder liner protrusion by measuring the liner flange and liner counterbore. If necessary, install shims around the liner to provide the specified protrusion.
2. Lubricate new cylinder liner O-rings with clean engine oil, and install them in the liner seal grooves. Be sure the O-rings are not twisted in the grooves.

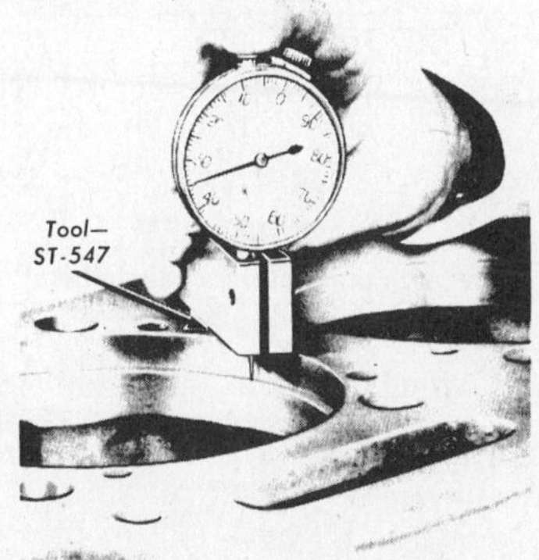

Measuring cylinder liner counterbore depth
(© Cummins Engine Co.)

3. Use engine oil to lubricate the machined portions of the liner bore in the cylinder block.
4. Carefully position the cylinder liner in the same cylinder bore from which it was removed. *Do*

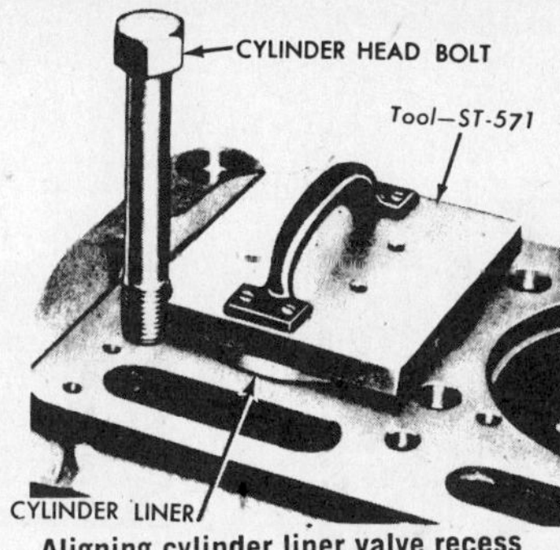

Aligning cylinder liner valve recess
(© Cummins Engine Co.)

not use beaded liners with steel-asbestos type head gasket. On NH-195 engines, align the cylinder head capscrew. Align valves as follows: Install one cylinder head capscrew. Align tool locators with the liner valve recesses and index the notch in tool with the capscrew. Push the liner in place. *Be sure O-rings are not displaced as the cylinder liner passes the top counterbore.*

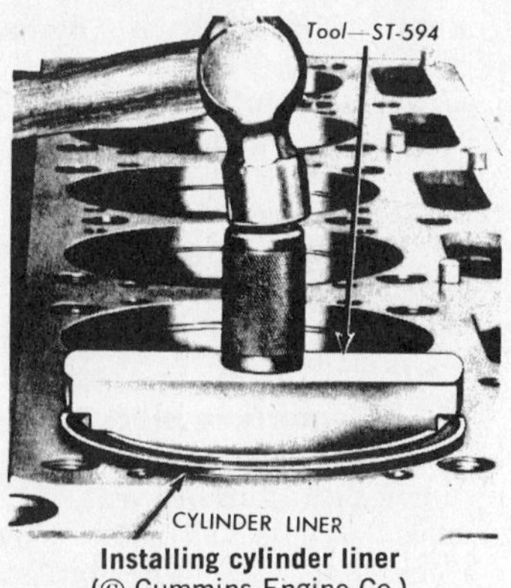

Installing cylinder liner
(© Cummins Engine Co.)

5. Drive the press-fit liner into the cylinder block bore with liner driver and a hammer.
6. Check the liner protrusion at 4 equidistant points; it must be within specifications. Use a dial bore gauge to check the cylinder liner bore for roundness at several points within range of the piston travel. If the liner bore is more than 0.001 inch out-of-round, remove the liner and check for possible binding condition which would cause distortion of the liner.

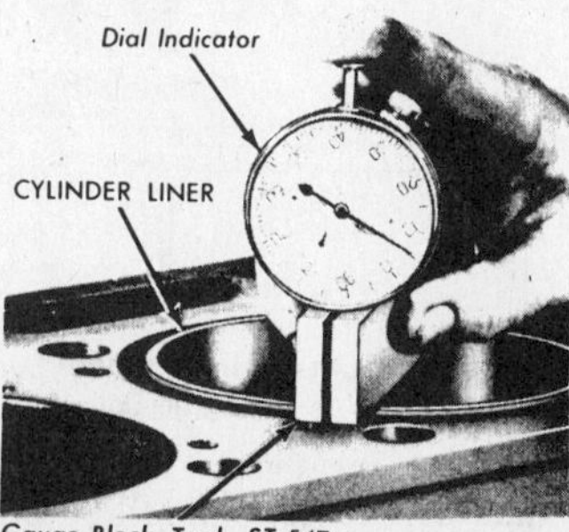

Checking cylinder liner protrusion
(© Cummins Engine Co.)

7. Using news gaskets, install the piston(s) and connecting rod(s), cylinder head(s), oil pan and rocker housing assembly(ies), and perform the necessary adjustments for the valve crossheads and injector and valve lash. Install the intake manifold, exhaust manifold, coolant manifold and fuel manifold.
8. Fill the cooling system and crankcase. Operate the engine and check for full, oil, coolant and air leaks. When the engine reaches normal operating temperature, check and adjust the injector and valve lash. Use the following specifics for liner counterbore.

Check Cylinder Liner Counterbore

1. Remove all corrosion and carbon deposits. These would affect readings obtained from block gauge.
2. Set gauge on block and depress indicator stem until indicator point touches block. Set dial to "0".
3. Position indicator in gauge block so stem moves about .10 inch to reach "0" on gauge. This leaves maximum amount of indicator travel available.
4. With indicator at "0", position gauge on deck so that indicator stem is over liner ledge.
5. Depress indicator stem till its point contacts liner ledge.
6. Read depth of counterbore shown on indicator.
7. Check each liner edge at four or more equi-distant locations. NOTE: The liner ledge must not be "cupped" more than .00075 inch. ("Cupped" refers to the condition where that part of the cylinder liner ledge next to the liner is the highest point of the ledge surface). The depth must not vary more than .001 inch.
8. The counterbore at top of a new block is .30925/.31050 inch deep and a minimum of 5.187/5.189 inches in diameter on C Series and 4.874/4.876 on J Series engines. If counterbore exceeds these limits oversize liners are available. *Only top 1/8 inch of counterbore provides press-fit.*
9. An installed cylinder liner must protrude .0045/.00675 inch above milled surface of block. To check protrusion *without* pressing liner into block:
   a. Measure liner flange outside bead with micrometer. *Do not include bead on top of liner flange in measurement.*
   b. Measure counterbore depth with dial indicator depth gauge.

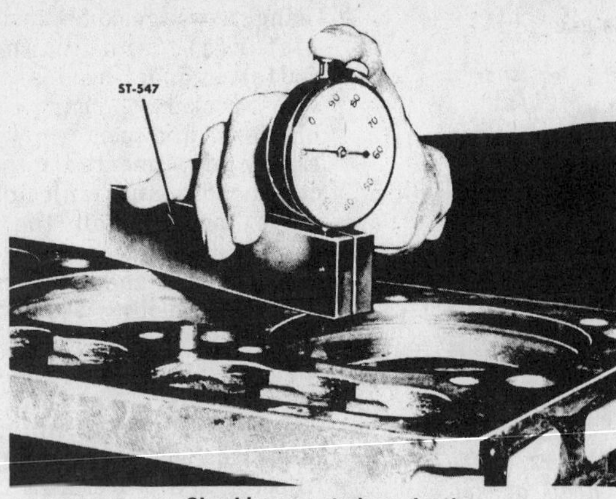

Checking counterbore depth
(© Cummins Engine Co.)

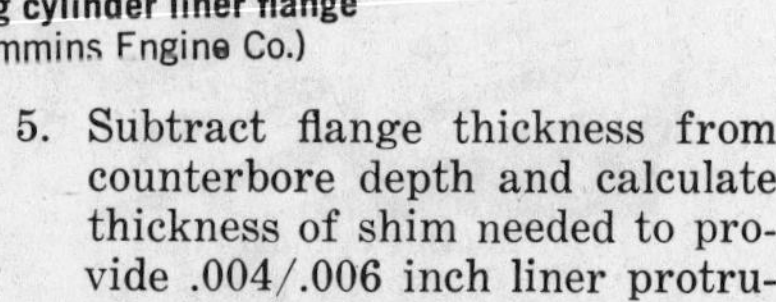

Measuring cylinder liner flange
(© Cummins Engine Co.)

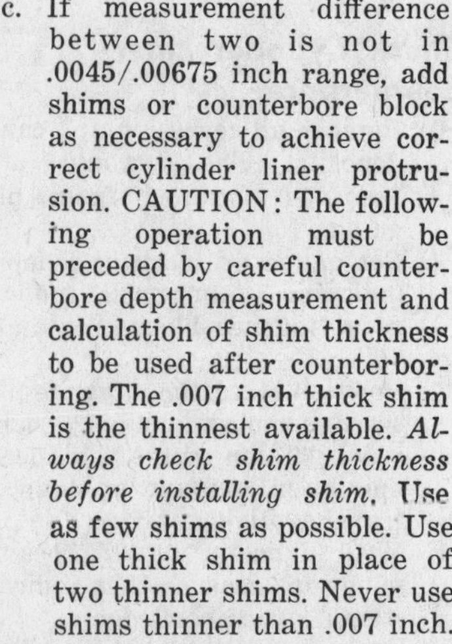

c. If measurement difference between two is not in .0045/.00675 inch range, add shims or counterbore block as necessary to achieve correct cylinder liner protrusion. CAUTION: The following operation must be preceded by careful counterbore depth measurement and calculation of shim thickness to be used after counterboring. The .007 inch thick shim is the thinnest available. *Always check shim thickness before installing shim.* Use as few shims as possible. Use one thick shim in place of two thinner shims. Never use shims thinner than .007 inch.

Counterbore Cylinder Liner Ledge

(A special tool for this is available from Cummins)

1. Loosen adjustable tool head lock collar and remove tool holder.
2. Place upper adapter in position and fasten with capscrews.
3. Reposition tool holder, tightening adjustable tool head lock collar finger tight.
4. Install lower adaptor plate on tool with capscrews.

Installing Tool in Block

1. Raise tool bit until tip is flush with tool holder. *Tool bit set screws are not to be loosened to raise or lower tool bits.*
2. Make sure top and bottom adjustable locating pins are retracted and flush with housing before inserting tool in bore. The socket head screws on upper adaptor plate, above pins control this movement.
3. Insert tool into block bore so locating surfaces are on water jacket side of block. Position top of upper adaptor plate 1/32 inch below counterbore.
4. Tighten adjustable locating pins against bore with socket head wrench and extension.
5. Insert wooden block between capscrews inserted in block to prevent tool head from rotating counter-clockwise.
6. Insert handle in socket and rotate counterclockwise to loosen adjustable tool head lock collar.
7. Move tool head out until tool bit contacts counterbore edge.
8. Rotate collar clockwise, by hand, to lock.
9. Lower tool bit until it engages counterbore and remove wooden block. Rotate head clockwise to see if it binds.
10. Replace wooden block between capscrews. Check tool head position then lock in place by turning handle clockwise.

Counterbore block

1. Screw tool bit down until it touches counterbore seat.
2. Insert handle and rotate slowly, clockwise, until tool bit stops cutting.
3. If necessary, continue cutting by feeding tool bit down. Feed dial graduations are approximately .002 inch. Cut only ½ graduation at a time. Remove only enough metal to clean up counterbore.

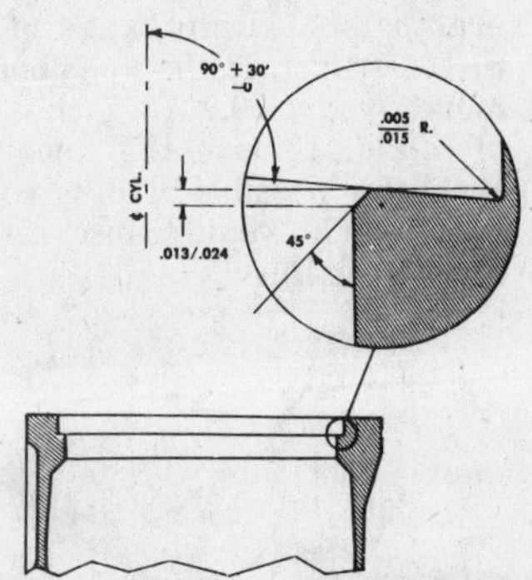

Cross section of new block counterbore
(© Cummins Engine Co.)

4. Check counterbore depth with dial indicator depth gauge. Measure cylinder liner flange. Do not include head on liner.
5. Subtract flange thickness from counterbore depth and calculate thickness of shim needed to provide .004/.006 inch liner protrusion above block.

Oversize Press-fit Liners for J Series

1. Recheck counterbore diameter to assure it is not over 4.876 inch on J Series blocks.
2. If diameter is within standard limits, standard press-fit liners can be installed. If diameter is over 4.876 inches, it will be necessary to counterbore to 4.894/4.896 to accommodate .020 inch oversized press-fit liners. CAUTION: This operation must be performed with a vertical boring bar or cylinder boring machine. Required accuracy cannot be held by counterboring tool.

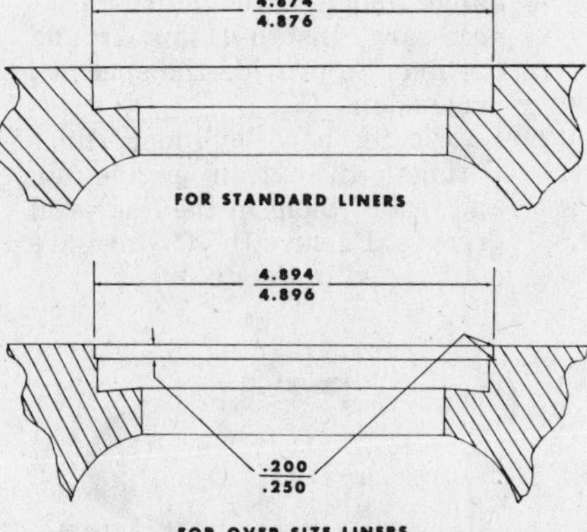

Oversize press-fit liner counterbore
(© Cummins Engine Co.)

3. Extend cut to .200/.250 inch below block surface. CAUTION: Do not extend cut full depth of counterbore or liner shims will not locate correctly.
4. Remove sharp corners and burrs.

Lapping Counterbore in Block

(Non-Press-fit liners only)

If the cylinder liner flanges and counterbore are not perfectly smooth, the counterbore may be lapped.

1. Place Grade A grit lapping compound on counterbore ledge.

2. Insert cylinder liner.
3. Apply light and even pressure while lapping. Rotate liner one complete revolution, then lap in 30° strokes. Add a few drops of lube oil each 2 or 3 revolutions to keep lapping compound moist.
4. *Remove all lapping compound from counterbore and liner flange.*
5. Apply light coat of prussian blue and check seat. *A full seat must be indicated on both counterbore and liner flange.*
6. Repeat lapping operation as necessary.

Crankshaft

Journals

Main bearing journals of a new crankshaft are 3.874/3.875 inches outside diameter. Regrind if worn below 3.872 outside diameter. If crankpin journals are worn more than .002 inches below low limit or are out-of-round in excess of .0015 inches, regrind crankshaft.

Crankshafts should be reground to standard undersizer to fit available standard main bearings and connecting rob bearings. Main bearings are available in .010, .020, .030, and .040 inch undersize. Undersize connecting rod bearings are available in corresponding undersizes.

Oil Passages

1. Use a rod and rag, just as you would to clean a rifle barrel, to check and completely clean oil passages in crankshaft.
2. Replace pipe plugs.
   a. Coat threads with John Crane sealer or equivalent.
   b. Tighten to 5 ft. lbs.
   c. Stake to prevent loosening.

Thrust Flange

If crankshaft thrust flange is worn as much as .015 inch or grooved as deep as .005 inch, build up by welding and regrind to size.

Crankshaft Gear

If it is necessary to remove crankshaft gear:

1. Attach puller to gear.
2. Apply 75/100 ft. lbs. on puller screw.
3. Heat gear with a heating torch—not a cutting torch—to 300°/400°F. The gear will expand, making it easier to pull.

To assemble gear:

1. Heat gear evenly to 400°/500°F with a heating torch (not a cutting torch).
2. Drive onto crankshaft with tubing.

Crankshaft End Play

C and J Series Engines

The rear main bearing consists of two shells and four thrust half-rings. The thrust half-rings, like the shells, are interchangeable.

The thrust half-rings are held in place by dowels in the cap—two for each half-ring—and by counterbored recesses in the block and cap. The grooved babbitt faces fit next to the crankshaft flanges. Crankshaft end clearances for new bearings and a new shaft will be .004-.009″. Worn shafts and thrust rings should not be reused if end clearance is in excess of .022″. Check end clearance as follows:

1. Attach a dial indicator securely to the cylinder block with the contact point of the gauge resting on the crankshaft flange end face.
2. With a small bar, pry the crankshaft toward the front of the engine and set the gauge at zero. Then pry the crankshaft toward the rear of the engine.
3. If the clearance is less than .004″, loosen the nuts slightly and shift the crankshaft first toward the front end of the engine and then toward the rear.
4. Retighten the nuts by the template method outlined previously and recheck the end clearance.

H and NH Engines

Procedure for checking crankshaft end play is similar to that outlined above except that the limits are .007″ to .013″.

V-6 & V-8 Engines

Crankshaft end clearance for a new shaft and thrust rings should be .005-.015″. Check end clearance as follows:

1. Attach a dial indicator securely to the block with the contact point of the gauge resting on crankshaft flange face.
2. With a pry bar, pry crankshaft toward front of engine and set the gauge at zero.
3. Pry crankshaft toward rear of engine. If the end clearance is less than .005″ loosen capscrews slightly and shift crankshaft

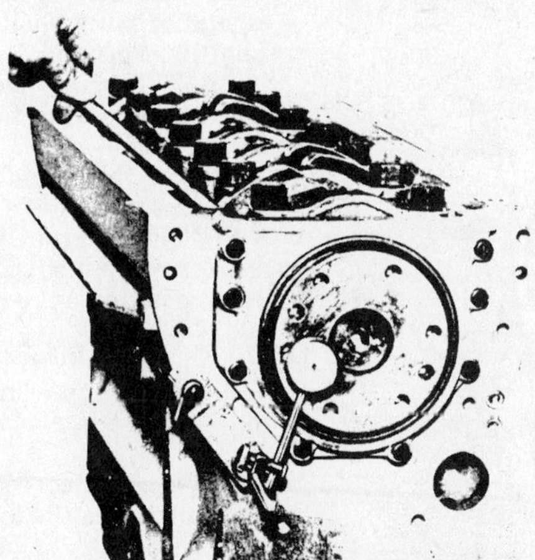

Checking crankshaft end clearance
(© Cummins Engine Co.)

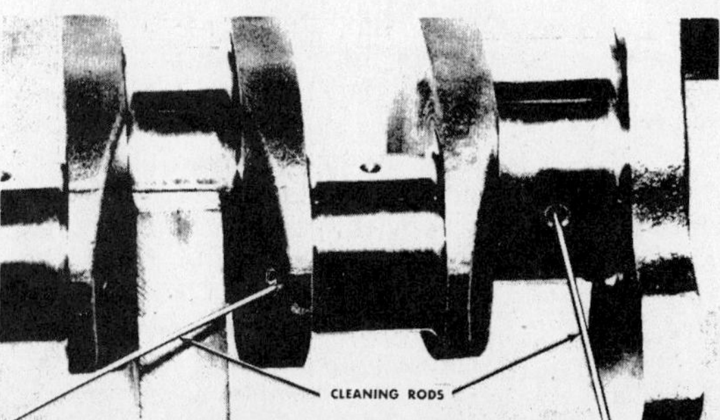

Cleaning oil passages
(© Cummins Engine Co.)

Checking thrust flange wear
(© Cummins Engine Co.)

toward front of engine, then toward rear of engine.

4. Retighten the capscrews by the template method outlined previously and recheck end clearance.

Crankshaft Rear Oil Seal

All Engines—The rear cover has a braided asbestos seal around the crankshaft. When the rear cover is assembled to the cylinder block its bore must be in line with the main bearing bore. Cement a new gasket over the dowel pins on the rear of the cylinder block. Assemble the upper cover plate over the dowel pins and tighten the four cup screws. With crankshaft pushed toward the cover plate, check the clearance between the crankshaft flange and the opposing face of the cover place.

Clearance should be a minimum of .004″. The clearance of .004″ to .006″ can be obtained by using gaskets between the cover plate and the cylinder block.

The clearance between the crankshaft and bore of the cover plate should be .009 to .011″ (.006″ on H and NH) around the entire circumference. This clearance is provided when the original rear cover is installed at the factory and maintained by locating dowels. This can be checked after the old asbestos seal has been removed by using a .009″ feeler gauge between the shaft and upper cover.

Removing rear cover
(© Cummins Engine Co.)

Remove the cover plate and install new asbestos seals into the recess of both upper and lower cover plates. New seals must be beveled on three sides of each end 13/20″ by 45°, leaving the inside edge square. The ends of the seals should extend 1/32″ above the joining surfaces of the cover plates. Seals should be soaked in lubricating oil an hour or more before installing. Make sure they are well seated in their grooves.

Cement new connecting gaskets to the lower cover plate. Assemble the lower plate to the upper plate and bolt together tightly. Install capscrews to cover plates and pull up evenly to the cylinder block over the dowel pins.

Main and Connecting Rod Bearings

All Cummins main and connecting rod bearings are precision parts with shell thickness, bearing material and bearing crash accurately calculated and held to close tolerances. Both standard and undersized bearings are provided with recommended clearance for the oil film. *Under no circumstances should any attempt be made to scrape or ream these bearings nor should they be lapped or filed to increase oil clearances.*

A properly fitted bearing, after a reasonable period of service, will appear dull gray; indicating it is running on an oil film. Bright spots indicate metal-to-metal contact; black spots excessive clearance.

CAUTION: Never use shims with main or connecting rod bearing shells.

Main Bearings

All current engines have grooveless lower main bearing shells and grooved upper shells. Grooveless lower main bearing shells can be installed in engines with serial numbers previous to Serial No. 113353 provided the crankshaft journals do not have prominent ridges formed from wear with the grooved type lower shells. If the ridge is higher than .001 inch, it will be necessary to install grooved shells until the crankshaft is reground.

Main bearing shells are held in place by a locking tang or lip on each shell which mates with milled recesses in the block and cap opposite the camshaft side of the engine.

NOTE: If grooved shells are to be reused, they must be installed in the same position as removed.

Inspection

Inspect connecting rod and main bearing shells for the following defects:

1. Fatigue, corrosive damage, or pitting in the loaded area.
2. Evidence of overheating, i.e., badly discolored or burnished surface.
3. Excessive lead wiping.
4. High spot due to dirt behind bearing.
5. Cracks on the bearing surface or on back of shell.
6. Excessive edge loading or fretting.

Check scratches on the bearing surface. Scratches deep enough to result in ridges on either side of scratch will cause contact during operation and lead to engine failure.

It is not necessary to discard shells due to *minor* discoloration, eroded lead plate, slight scratches or imperfection outside the load area.

Connecting Rod Bearing Replacement

Typical—All Engines

Bearing clearance can be checked by using micrometers or by using Plastigage as outlined in the following procedure. If the Plastigage method is employed, use new standard-size bearings.

1. Drain the crankcase. Remove the oil pan, if necessary, remove the oil pump.
2. Remove the cap from the connecting rod to which new bearings are to be fitted. Push the piston part way up the cylinder.
3. Remove the bearings from the connecting rod and cap. Clean the crankshaft journal, connecting rod and bearing cap.

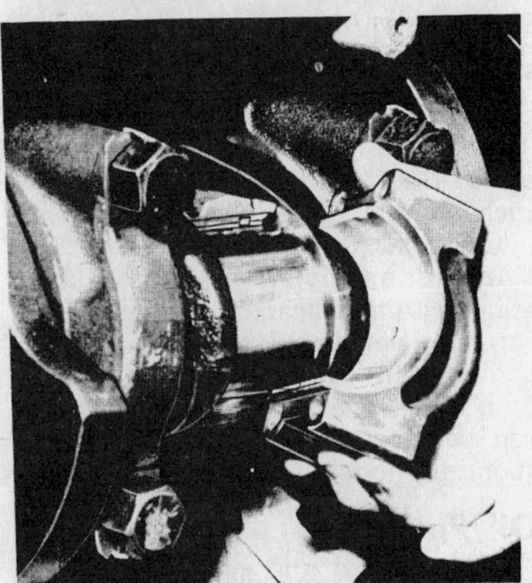

Installing connecting rod gap
(© Cummins Engine Co.)

4. Install new bearings in the connecting rod and cap. Pull the connecting rod assembly down firmly on the crankshaft journal.
5. Place a piece of Plastigage on the lower bearing surface, the full width of the cap and about ¼ inch off-center.
6. Install the cap and torque the connecting rod nuts to 140 ft-lbs. *Do not turn the crankshaft while the Plastigage is in place.*
7. Remove the cap. then using the Plastigage scale, check the width of the Plastigage. When checking the width of the Plastigage, check at the widest point in order to get the minimum clearance. The difference between the two readings is the taper.
8. Check the bearing side clearance; it must be to specifications. After the bearing clearance has been checked and found to be within the specified limits, clean the Plastigage from the crankshaft journal. *If standard-size bearings or the next undersize bearing does not provide the specified clearance, then crankshaft grinding or replacement is indicated.*

9. Apply Lubriplate to the journal and bearings, then install the connecting rod cap. Install new lock plates and torque the rod nuts to specifications. Bend the tabs on the lock plates to secure the nuts.
10. Repeat the procedure for the remaining connecting rods that require new bearings.
11. Install the oil pump. Install the oil pan.
12. Fill the crankcase. Operate the engine at fast idle and check for oil leaks.

Main Bearing Replacement

In-line Engines

Bearing clearance can be checked by using micrometers or by using Plastigage as outlined in the following procedure. If the Plastigage method is employed, use new standard-size bearings.

1. Drain the crankcase. Remove the oil pan.
2. Remove the main bearing cap to which new bearings are to be installed. *Replace one bearing at a time, leaving the other bearings securely fastened.*
3. Remove the thrust washers. Rotate the crankshaft with barring tool, and force the upper bearing out of the block.
4. Remove the bearing from the cap. Clean the crankshaft journal and bearing inserts.
5. All upper main bearings are grooved and drilled for lubrication. Numbers 1, 3 and 5 are alike and Nos. 2, 4 and 6 are alike. Number 7 has the oil groove off center, and it must not be interchanged with the other bearings. The wide portion of the bearing is installed toward the flywheel end.
6. Apply lubricant to the upper main bearing, and insert it between the crankshaft journal and crankcase web. Rotate the crankshaft until the bearing seats itself. *The groove on each bearing for the dowel ring must match with the counterbore at the capscrew hole on the exhaust manifold side of the block.*
7. Install the upper thrust rings with the babbit sides *next to the crankshaft flanges.* The upper thrust rings are not doweled to the block. The doweled lower halves prevent them from turning.
8. Replace the cap bearing. The lower main bearings are plain with no grooves or drillings.
9. Support the crankshaft so that its weight will not compress the Plastigage and provide a false reading. Position the support so that it will bear against the counterweight adjoining the bearing which is being checked.
10. Place a piece of Plastigage on the bearing surface the full width of the bearing cap and ¼ inch off-center.
11. On the No. 7 (rear) main bearing, install the lower thrust rings. *The lower thrust rings must be held by the dowels in the main bearing cap.*
12. Install the cap and torque the bolts to 150 ft-lbs. *Do not turn the crankshaft while the Plastigage is in place.*
13. Remove the cap, then using the Plastigage scale, check the width of the Plastigage. When checking the width of the Plastigage, check at the widest point in order to get the minimum clearance. Check at the narrowest point in order to get the maximum clearance. The difference between the two readings is the taper.
14. After the bearing clearance has been checked and found to be within the specified limits, clean off the Plastigage. *If standard-size bearings or the next undersize bearing does not provide the specified clearance, then crankshaft grinding or replacement is indicated.*

Checking rod to crankshaft clearance
(© Cummins Engine Co.)

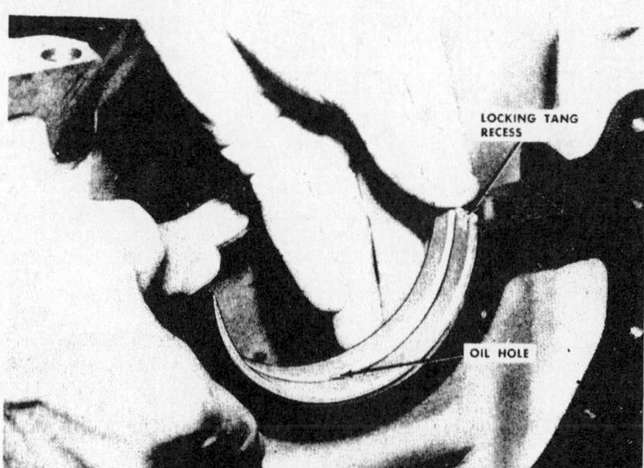

Laying upper main bearing shells
(© Cummins Engine Co.)

Measuring main bearing shells
(© Cummins Engine Co.)

Installing thrust rings
(© Cummins Engine Co.)

Tightening main bearing capscrews
(© Cummins Engine Co.)

15. Apply lubricant to the bearing and journal. Install the bearing cap, using new lock plates.
16. Torque the bolts to specifications. Bend the tabs on the lock plates to secure the bolts.

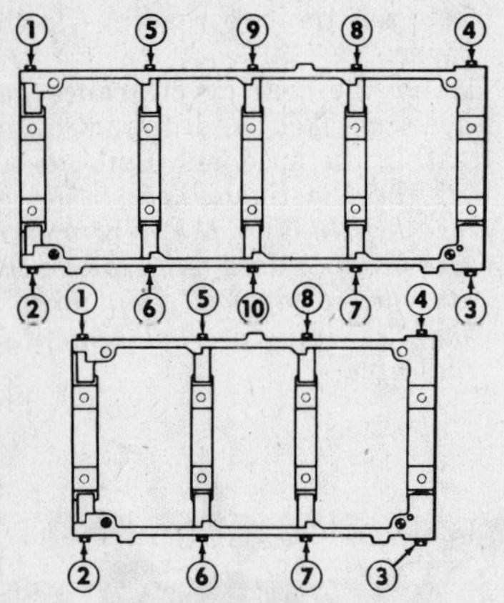

Main bearing side cap screw torque sequence
(© Cummins Engine Co.)

17. Repeat the procedure for the remaining bearings that require replacement.
18. Install the oil pan.
19. Fill the crankcase. Operate the engine at fast idle and check for oil leaks.

Main Bearing Replacement

V-6 & V-8 Engines

Bearing clearance can be checked by using micrometers or by using Plastigage as outlined in the following procedure. If the Plastigage method is employed, use new standard-size bearings.

1. Drain the crankcase. Remove the oil pan and oil pump.
2. Remove the main bearing cap side bolts from both sides of the engine block.
3. Remove the cap bolts from the main bearing to which new bearings are to be installed. Use a small pry-bar to loosen the bearing cap. Remove the bearing cap. *Replace one bearing at a time, leaving the other bearings securely fastened.*
4. Rotate the crankshaft with the barring tool and force the upper bearing out of the block. On the rear main bearing, remove the upper thrust half-rings from the block.
5. Remove the bearing from the from the bearing cap dowels. Clean the crankshaft journal and bearing inserts.
6. Only the upper main bearings are grooved and drilled for lubrication. Numbers 1 and 4 are alike and Nos. 2 and 3 are alike.
7. Apply Lubriplate to the upper main bearing, and insert it between the crankshaft journal and crankcase web. Rotate the crankshaft until the bearing seats itself. *The groove on each bearing for the dowel ring must match with the counterbore at the capscrew hole on the exhaust manifold side of the block.*
8. Install the upper thrust rings with the *grooved side next to the crankshaft flange.* The upper thrust rings are not doweled to the block; the doweled lower halves prevent them from turning.
9. The lower main bearings are plain with no grooves or drillings. Numbers 1 and 4 are alike and Nos. 2 and 3 are alike.
10. Support the crankshaft so that its weight will not compress the Plastigage and provide an erroneous reading. Position the support so that it will bear against the counterweight adjoining the bearing which is being checked.
11. Place a piece of Plastigage on the bearing surface the full width of the bearing cap and 1/4 inch off-center.
12. On the rear main bearing, install the lower thrust rings on the dowels in the main bearing cap.
13. Install the cap and torque the bolts to 180 ft-lbs. *Do not turn the crankshaft while the Plastigage is in place.*

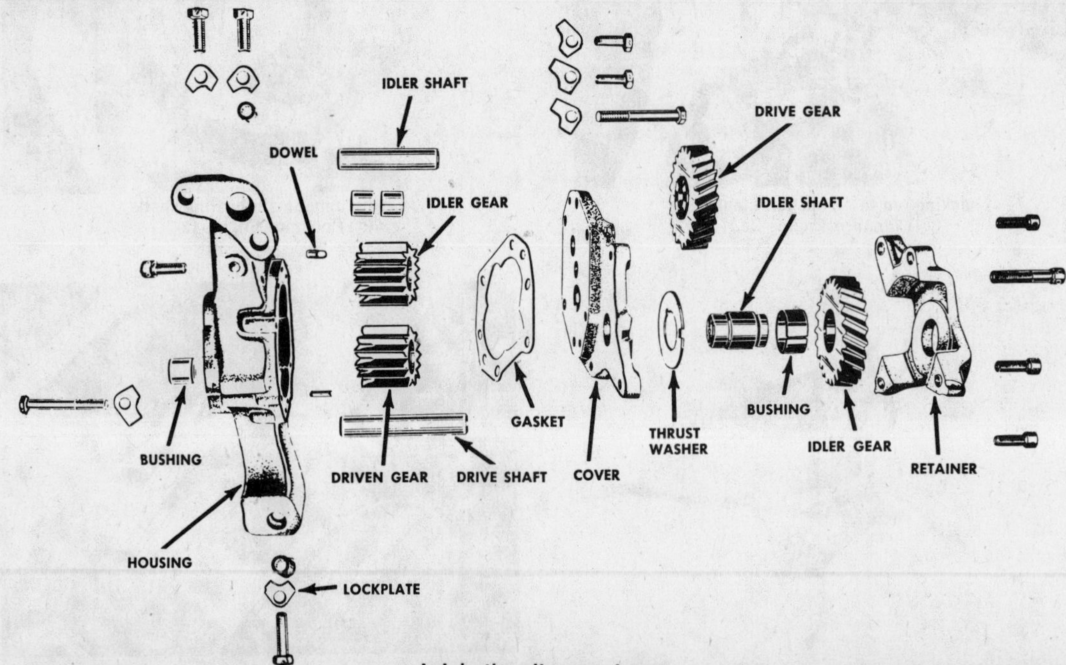

Lubricating oil pump—layout
(© Cummins Engine Co.)

14. Remove the cap, then using the Plastigage scale, check the width of the Plastigage. When checking the width of the Plastigage, check at the widest point in order to get the minimum clearance. Check at the narrowest point in order to get the maximum clearance. The difference between the two readings is the taper.
15. After the bearing clearance has been checked and found to be within the specified limits, clean off the Plastigage. *If standard-size bearings or the next undersize bearing does not provide the specified clearance, then crankshaft grinding or replacement is indicated.*
16. Apply Lubriplate to the bearing and journal. Install the bearing cap, using new lock plates.
17. Torque the bolts to specifications. Bend the tabs on the lock plates to secure the bolts.
18. Repeat the procedure for the remaining bearings that require replacement.
19. Torque the main bearing side capscrews to specifications, following the sequence.
20. Install the oil pump and oil pan.
21. Fill the crankcase. Operate the engine at fast idle and check for oil leaks.

Engine Oil Pump

C and J Series Engines

The lubricating oil pump is the gear type located in the crankcase below the crankshaft. It is driven by an idler gear off the pinion gear.

Excessively worn parts or assemblies must be replaced. Bushings and bodies should be replaced as assemblies because bushings must be properly located and line-bored.

When new, the pump parts have the following dimensions: Idler and driver shaft bushings .6165-.6175″. Idler and driver shaft outside diameter .6150-.6155″. Idler gear bushing .9925-.9935″. Idler gear spindle .990-.991″.

1. To assemble the pump, place the driver gear over the shaft with the marked end to the oil inlet side of the body.
2. Assemble the driver gear and shaft to the cover. Then press the drive gear to the shaft, leaving .002″ clearance between gear and cover.
3. Assemble gasket and cover to pump.
4. Assemble spindle to idler gear.
5. Assemble thrust washer with its locking lip matching the milled recess in the pump cover.
6. Assemble the idler gear and spindle to the cover. The spindle is dowelled to the cover with two dowels. These dowels are a press fit in the cover and should protrude approximately 5/16″ into the spindle.
7. Assemble the by-pass valve plunger, spring, spring retainer to the body with the clamp provided.

H and NH Engines

The standard oil pump in these engines is of the two-gear type. In servicing these pumps, note the following:

1. The ball bearing outer race must not turn in the ball bearing cage.
2. The gears must show no excessive wear, or be scored or otherwise damaged.
3. The drive shaft must be replaced if it has been turning in the inner race of the ball bearing; if it is worn smaller than .8735″ where it bears against the bracket bushing, or if it is worn smaller than .8705″ on the body end.
4. The bracket bushing should not be used if its inside diameter is worn larger than .887″.
5. Idler pins should be replaced if worn smaller than .873″.
6. Replace bracket or cover if finished surfaces are scored or visibly worn larger than 2.301″ inside diameter. Maximum gear to pocket clearance should never exceed .008″ or .004″ on a side.
7. The by-pass valve in the body should not open below 75 lbs.
8. When assembling the pump, the pump gear should be pressed on the shaft so there is a clearance of .0015″ between the gear and bracket.

Oil Filter Replacement

The standard full-flow oil filter is remote-mounted. The optional by-pass oil filter (Luber-Finer) is also remote-mounted.

Full-Flow Oil Filter

To change the standard oil filter element, remove the element from the case and wipe it with clean cloths. *Do not wash the filter bag.*

Reverse the bag and inspect it. If bearing metal or grit is found,

Typical oil filter and luber-finer installation
(© Cummins Engine Co.)

immediately inspect the connecting rod and main bearings. Thoroughly wash all parts, except the bag. Install new gaskets and filter bag. If the filter bag is incorrectly installed, the studs may pierce the filter bag.

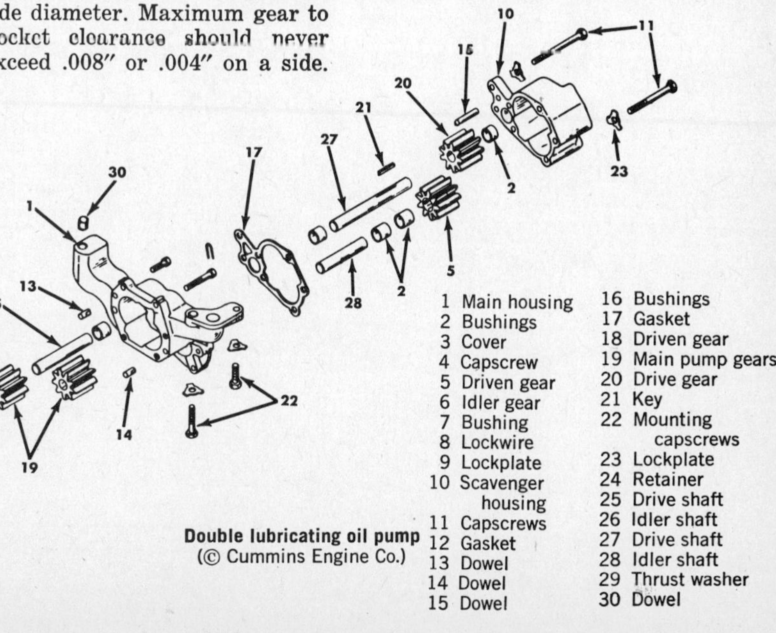

Double lubricating oil pump
(© Cummins Engine Co.)

1 Main housing
2 Bushings
3 Cover
4 Capscrew
5 Driven gear
6 Idler gear
7 Bushing
8 Lockwire
9 Lockplate
10 Scavenger housing
11 Capscrews
12 Gasket
13 Dowel
14 Dowel
15 Dowel
16 Bushings
17 Gasket
18 Driven gear
19 Main pump gears
20 Drive gear
21 Key
22 Mounting capscrews
23 Lockplate
24 Retainer
25 Drive shaft
26 Idler shaft
27 Drive shaft
28 Idler shaft
29 Thrust washer
30 Dowel

Ford Diesel Engines

Index

GENERAL SPECIFICATIONS

ENGINE MODEL	BORE AND STROKE	HORSEPOWER @ R.P.M.	COMPRESSION PRESSUE CRANKING SPEED	FIRING ORDER	GOVERNOR SPEED NO LOAD	IDLE SPEED
4-220	3.9375 x 4.526	70 @ 2500	365	1-2-4-3	2700	500-550
4-242	4.1250 x 4.516	83 @ 2800	365	1-2-4-3	3090	500-550
6-330	3.9375 x 4.526	112 @ 2500	365	1-5-3-6-2-4	2700	500-550
6-363	4.1250 x 4.516	128 @ 2800	365	1-5-3-6-2-4	3090	500-550

PISTONS, PINS, RINGS, CRANKSHAFT AND BEARINGS

ENGINE MODEL	PISTON CLEARANCE	PISTON RING GAP MINIMUM COMP.	PISTON RING GAP MINIMUM OIL	PISTON PIN DIAMETER	ROD BEARINGS SHAFT DIAMETER	ROD BEARINGS BEARING CLEARANCE	MAIN BEARINGS SHAFT DIAMETER	MAIN BEARINGS BEARING CLEARANCE	SHAFT END PLAY	THRUST ON BEARING NO.
4-220	.004-.005	.011	.011	1.374	2.4997-2.5005	.001-.0028	3.002-3.0010	.001-.0028	.002-.010	Center
4-242	.007-.008	.013	.013	1.375	2.6242-2.6250	.002-.0041	3.002-3.0010	.002-.0041	.002-.010	Center
6-330	.004-.005	.011	.011	1.374	2.4997-2.5005	.001-.0028	3.002-3.0010	.001-.0028	.002-.010	Center
6-363	.007-.008	.013	.013	1.375	2.6242-2.6250	.002-.0041	3.002-3.0010	.002-.0041	.002-.010	Center

VALVE SPECIFICATIONS

ENGINE MODEL	VALVE LASH (HOT) IN.	VALVE LASH (HOT) EX.	VALVE FACE ANGLE	VALVE STEM CLEARANCE INTAKE	VALVE STEM CLEARANCE EXHAUST	VALVE GUIDE BORE	VALVE STEM DIAMETER INTAKE	VALVE STEM DIAMETER EXHAUST	VALVE SPRINGS FREE LENGTH	VALVE SPRINGS COMPRESSED LENGTH AND LOAD LBS.
4-220	.015	.012	29	.001-.003	.002-.004	.375-.376	.3735	.3728	2½	1.98 @ 65
4-242	.015	.012	29	.001-.003	.002-.004	.375-.376	.3735	.3728	2.31	1.98 @ 65
6-330	.015	.012	29	.001-.003	.002-.004	.375-.376	.3735	.3728	2½	1.98 @ 65
6-363	.015	.012	29	.001-.003	.002-.004	.375-.376	.3735	.3728	2.31	1.98 @ 65

ENGINE TORQUE SPECIFICATIONS

ENGINE MODEL	CYLINDER HEAD FT. LBS.	MANIFOLD TO HEAD FT. LBS.	CONN. ROD FT. LBS.	MAIN BEARING CAP FT. LBS.	FLYWHEEL TO CRANKSHAFT FT. LBS.	CAMSHAFT GEAR BOLT FT. LBS.	INJECTOR BOLTS FT. LBS.	OIL PAN BOLTS FT. LBS.
4-220	85-90	17-22	55-60	115-120	80-90	95-100	15	15-17
4-242	85-90	17-22	85-90	115-120	80-90	95-100	15	22-24
6-330	85-90	17-22	55-60	115-120	80-90	95-100	15	15-17
6-363	85-90	17-22	85-90	115-120	80-90	95-100	15	22-24

Trouble Diagnosis

The satisfactory performance of a Diesel engine depends on two items of foremost importance (1), Sufficiently high compression pressure, and (2) The injection of the proper amount of fuel at the right time.

The first one of these items depends entirely on pistons, piston rings, valves and valve operating mechanism; the second item depends on injectors and their operating mechanism, and fuel system.

Lack of engine power, uneven running, excessive vibration, and tendency to stall when idling may be caused by either a compression loss or faulty injector operation.

The causes of trouble symptoms may be varied; therefore a hit-and-miss search should be avoided. A proper diagnosis of symptoms is an orderly process of diagnosing the symptoms. An "orderly process" means to check the most probable common cause first; then proceed with the next probable cause.

Starter Will Not Crank Engine

1. Transmission or power take-off auxiliary engaged.
2. Battery terminals loose or broken.
3. Battery discharged.
4. Starter switch damaged, or wires loose or broken.
5. Starter clutch or solenoid malfunction.
6. Starter drive locked.
7. Hydraulic lock, water or oil in combustion chamber.

Hard Starting or Failure To Start

1. Correct starting procedures not being followed.
2. Cold start aid inoperative.
3. Battery low, slow cranking speed.
4. Starter equipment malfunctioning.
5. Engine oil too heavy.
6. Blocked exhaust system.
7. Air filter dirty.
8. Low engine compression due to defective valves or piston rings.
9. Insufficient fuel in tank.
10. Water or ice in fuel tank.
11. Excessive fuel device inoperative.
12. Fuel injection parts scored, poor delivery.
13. Advance mechanism, in advance position should be in retarded position when engine is to be started.
14. Fuel injection pump not timed properly.
15. Air in the fuel system.
16. Fuel oil filter plugged or restricted.
17. Fuel lift pump not operating.
18. Leak in high pressure delivery lines.

Excessive Vibration

1. Engine bearings worn.
2. Engine supports broken or loose.

3. Difference in compression pressures between cylinders.
4. Injector setting pressures unequal.
5. Unequal fuel delivery, line resistance.
6. Air in fuel system.

Low Engine Torque

1. Excessive exhaust back pressure.
2. Engine valve timing not correct.
3. Fuel filters dirty.
4. High pressure fuel line leaks.
5. Poor atomization of fuel.
6. Dirty or cracked injectors
7. Fuel injection pump to engine timing wrong.
8. Throttle stop set too low.
9. Inferior quality fuel.
10. Advance device not working.
11. Brakes binding.

Engine Knocks

1. Low coolant level.
2. Engine overloaded.
3. Crankshaft vibration damper malfunction.
4. Excessive crankshaft end clearance.
5. Flywheel loose or unbalanced.
6. Broken or worn piston rings.
7. Incorrect bearing clearances.
8. Damaged or worn main or connecting rod bearings.
9. Broken tooth in engine gear train.
10. Worn or scored cylinder liners or pistons.
11. Broken valve springs.
12. Fuel injection pump timing too early.
13. Poor atomization of fuel.
14. Octane value of fuel low.

Excessive Smoke

BLACK SMOKE consists of a large number of particles of carbon; this carbon forms when the fuel is heated in oxygen-lean regions in the combustion chamber.

BLUE SMOKE consists of a large number of particles of fuel oil of about 0.5 microns diameter or less; there particles are recondensed droplets of unburned fuel or incompletely burned fuel. These small particles cause blue light to be scattered. When an engine is running fast but under light load, regions of the combustion chamber may be at too low a temperature to permit ignition and blue smoke would appear. When viewed in transmitted light, the blue smoke appears brown.

WHITE SMOKE consists of a large number of particles of fuel oil larger than about 1.0 micron diameter. To produce white smoke, the fuel must have time to condense into larger droplets than for blue smoke. A cold engine running at light load and low speed could produce white smoke.

1. Restricted air intake.
2. High exhaust back pressure.
3. Intake manifold or cylinder head gasket leakage.
4. Cracked cylinder head or block.
5. Broken or worn piston rings.
6. Engine in need of overhaul.
7. Incorrect valve timing.
8. Worn or scored cylinder liners or pistons.
9. Engine overload.
10. Low compression.
11. Inferior quality fuel.
12. Restricted fuel lines.
13. Plugged injector spray holes.
14. Incorrect injector timing.
15. Injectors improperly adjusted.
16. Fuel injection pump to engine timing retarded.
17. Injector pump improperly adjusted.
18. Broken fuel delivery valve or valve sticking.

Engine Gradually Loses Power Then Stops

1. Low compression.
2. Engine valve clearance too small.
3. Air leak at suction side of fuel lines.
4. Choked fuel filter.
5. Damaged control linkage.
6. Fuel tank vent clogged.
7. Leak off line blocked.
8. Nozzle and delivery valve stuck open.

Engine Cannot Reach Maximum Speed

1. Poor condition of engine.
2. Throttle stop improperly adjusted.
3. Maximum speed setting too low.
4. Broken or wrong type governor springs.
5. Dirty air filter.

Excessive Fuel Comsumption

1. Restricted air intake.
2. High exhaust back pressure.
3. Engine overloaded.
4. Engine in need of overhaul.
5. Inferior quality fuel.
6. Restricted fuel lines or filter.
7. Fuel leaks external or internal.
8. Plugged injector spray holes.
9. Injectors not adjusted properly.
10. Cracked injector body or cap.

Excessive Oil Consumption

1. Broken or worn piston rings.
2. Worn or scored cylinder liners or pistons.
3. External or internal oil leaks.
4. Faulty cylinder oil control.
5. Wrong grade oil for conditions.
6. Engine in need of overhaul.
7. Loose crankcase breather vent.

Low Lubrication Oil Pressure

1. Incorrect bearing clearances.
2. Engine overloaded.
3. Insufficient coolant.
4. Worn water pump.
5. Coolant thermostat not working.
6. Loose fan belts.
7. Clogged coolant passages.
8. Clogged oil cooler.
9. Radiator core openings restricted.
10. Air in cooling system.
11. Leaking coolant hoses, connections or gaskets.
12. Insufficient radiator capacity.
13. Oil suction line restricted or cracked.
14. Oil pickup screen blocked.
15. Crankcase oil level too low.
16. Wrong grade of oil for conditions.
17. Engine in need of overhaul.

General Information

The 363 six-cylinder Ford diesel engine has a piston displacement of 363 cubic inches and a compression ratio of 16.5:1.

The warranty plate identification symbol for the engine is W. The 363 engine is available in the B-, C-, F- and N-6000-7000 Truck Series.

For C-Series installation, the cooling fan is mounted on the crankshaft vibration damper and the oil bath air cleaner is attached to the intake manifold at the rear of the engine.

For B-, F- and N-Series installations, the cooling fan is mounted on the water pump hub and the oil bath air cleaner is attached to the cylinder head with the lifting bracket bolts at the front of the engine.

The engine is a four-stroke-cycle-diesel with overhead valves that are push rod operated from a camshaft in the right side of the cylinder block.

The exhaust valves and intake valves are the free turning type.

A diaphragm-type fuel lift pump,

mounted on the lower right side of the engine block, provides a continuous supply of fuel to the injection pump. The lift pump is driven by an eccentric on the engine camshaft.

The distributor-type fuel injection pump incorporates a mechanical governor. The accelerator linkage is connected to the throttle lever; a governor spring and idling spring connect the throttle lever to the governor control arm to regulate engine speeds from idle to full throttle. The injection pump also incorporated an excess fuel device for cold starting, an automatic advance and start retard mechanism, and a fuel shut-off solenoid for stopping the engine.

The pump is driven at one half engine speed by the timing gear in mesh with the camshaft gear.

From the fuel lift pump, the fuel passes through a replaceable element-type filter to the injection pump. The injection pump distributes high pressure charges of fuel to the injectors; one for each engine cylinder.

An optional air compressor for air brake systems is mounted beneath the fuel injection pump and bolted to the rear of the timing gear housing. It is gear driven directly off the timing gears and runs at engine speed.

The pressure lubrication system is fed by a gear type oil pump incorporating a spring-loaded relief valve to limit the maximum oil pressure. A full-flow oil filter with a replaceable element filters the entire output of the oil pump before the oil enters the engine.

Fresh air enters the engine through a filter in the oil filler cap. This filter may be either a gauze type or an oil bath type, depending on engine application. Air passes down the breather tube to the crankcase, then up through the push rod drillings and oil drain holes to the rocker cover. Crankcase vapors, mixed with air, leave the rocker cover through a breather pipe connected to the air cleaner for return to the engine induction system. Engine internal pressure variations are compensated for by a vent assembly, open to the atmosphere, mounted on the oil pan.

In—Vehicle Adjustments

Idle Speed Adjustment

Check the engine high (governed no-load) rpm and low idle rpm. Use of a direct-reading tachometer is recommended.

If the high idle or low idle rpm is not to specifications, free up or adjust the throttle linkage before making any adjustment of the governor settings. The idle settings, both high and low, are adjusted at the factory and any deviation from specifications should be due to the throttle linkage assembly or operation.

If throttle linkage adjustment will not correct the idle speeds to specifications, follow the procedure given below to adjust both high and low idle. *Only qualified personnel should perform this operation.*

High and Low RPM Adjustment

Check the engine rpm with an accurate tachometer. Install the tachometer on the adapter located on the front cover. The reading taken at this point, with a 1:1 tachometer, will be one-half engine rpm.

Remove the high idle adjustment screw cover from the rear of the governor. Turn the high idle adjusting screw clockwise to increase or counterclockwise to decrease high idle speed.

If the adjusting screw requires alignment to install the cover, turn the screw in a clockwise direction the minimum distance required for installation.

Adjust low idle speed by loosening locknut and turning the adjustable stop. Turning the stop IN decreases and OUT increases the low idle speed. Tighten the locknut and recheck the adjustment.

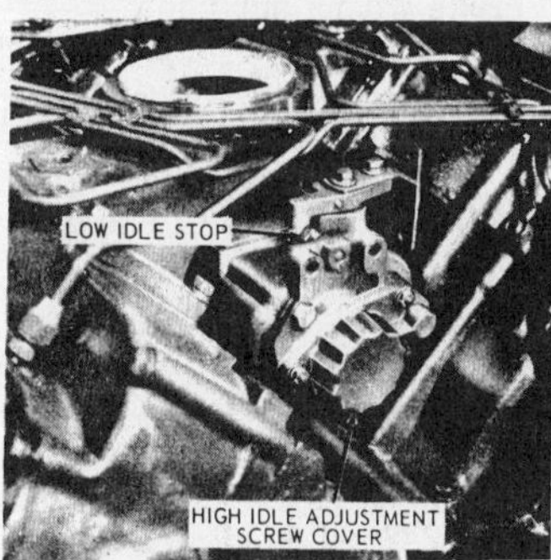

Idle adjustment locations
(© Ford Motor Co.)

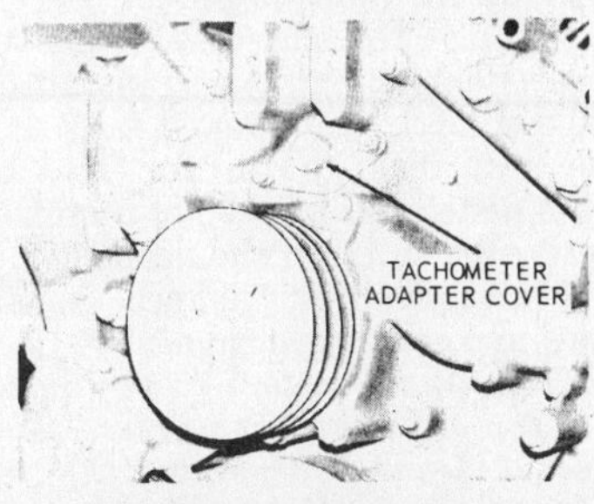

Tachometer adapter location
(© Ford Motor Co.)

Fuel Pump and Injector Testing

Diagnosis

Diesel engine performance complaints usually are attributed to the basic engine or to the fuel system. If the trouble is isolated to the fuel system, it should fall under one of the basic headings in the Trouble Shooting Chart. When a particular trouble cannot be traced to a definite cause, check out each possible cause and make the necessary correction before proceeding to the next probable cause. Always check the most easily corrected cause first.

Fuel Lift Pump

Efficiency Test

Providing there are no leaks or obstructions in the fuel system, a quick check on the pump efficiency can be made as follows:

1. Remove the air bleed screw from the inlet side of the secondary fuel filter.
2. Operate the hand-priming lever in the normal manner. There should be a well-defined surge of fuel for each working stroke of the pump. If there is no resistance of the diaphragm spring, it is likely that the diaphragm is held down. This is due to the operating lever being on the high point of the eccentric. It will be necessary to rotate the engine approximately one turn.

   If the pump does not operate correctly, check the vacuum and delivery pressure with a suitable vacuum and pressure gauge.

Inlet Vacuum Test

1. Operate the lift pump hand primer to fill the injection pump gallery.
2. Disconnect the fuel inlet pipe from the pump, and connect the vacuum gauge to the pump inlet union.
3. Start the engine, and allow it to operate at idle speed. The vacuum reading should be at least 8-½ inches of mercury.
4. Stop the engine. The reading should take at least a minute to drop to zero. Should the reading drop more quickly than this, an air leak or faulty outlet valve is indicated.
5. Bleed the fuel system after connecting the fuel lines. This test can be carried out at any point between the lift pump and fuel tank to check for the air leaks in the fuel system as a whole. By starting the tests at the fuel lift pump and working towards the fuel tank, it will be possible to determine the faulty component.

Delivery Pressure Test

1. Operate the lift pump hand primer to fill the injection pump gallery.
2. Disconnect the fuel outlet pipe from the pump, and connect the

pressure gauge to the pump outlet.
3. Start the engine, and observe the pressure at idle speed. Increase the speed, and check throughout the speed range that the pressure is between 6 to 10 psi. Low fuel pump pressure may affect engine performance due to a lack of fuel.
4. Bleed the system after connecting the fuel line.

Injector Testing

For testing of the injectors, use Tool and adhere to the tool manufacturers instructions.

Complete injectors received for servicing should be briefly tested in the condition received before any cleaning or ajdustment is carried out, to determine the approximate condition.

1. Check injection pressure.
2. Examine quality of spray, which should atomize.
3. Examine for blocked spray holes or cracked tips.
4. Examine for leakage from nozzle nut, indicating faulty joint face between nozzle and holder.

Having obtained an idea of condition, remove nozzle from holder and withdraw needle. If the tip of needle is blued from overheating, or if the seat is seriously scored or damaged, the nozzle and needle are unfit for further service and must be replaced.

Care should be taken when testing injectors that the fuel spray does not contact the hands, as it will penetrate the skin due to the high pressure and atomization of the fuel.

Before disassembling an injector, clean it externally with fuel oil.

The pressure gauge of the injector test stand should be checked at regular intervals if accuracy of testing is to be maintained.

The injector should be tested to determine whether after adjustment the nozzle is fit for further service. A satisfactory injector must pass four tests:

1. Nozzle opening pressure.
2. Needle valve stem back leakage.
3. Atomization.
4. Needle seat leakage.

Nozzle Opening Pressure

Connect the injector to the nozzle test stand and loosen the injector cap nut. Adjust the nozzle opening pressure to 262 psi by rotating the spring adjusting nut through the leak-off pipe drilling in the cap nut. Tighten the cap nut securely, taking care that the spring adjusting nut does not turn.

To obtain a more accurate reading of the pressure, open the valve on the test stand not more than one-half turn from the closed position which will effectively reduce needle fluctuation.

Needle Valve Stem Back Leakage

Fully open the valve on the nozzle test stand, bring the test pressure up to 218 psi and check the time for it to fall to 145 psi. The time taken should be between 6 and 45 seconds for a serviced injector. The time taken for a new injector from stock should be between 15 and 45 seconds.

If the time taken is less than 6 seconds the lapped faces on the nozzle and injector body may be damaged or distorted, or there may be dirt between the nozzle and injector body faces.

If the time taken is more than 45 seconds it is possible that the needle valve is seized in the nozzle body or the spray holes are completely blocked.

Atomization

Close the valve on the nozzle tester, operate the machine at 60-85 strokes per minute, using the handle, or flywheel where provided, and examine the four sprays.

Each spray should atomize well with no visible streaks or distortion, spreading out about 2 in. at a point 4 in. from the nozzle tip. The injector should break with a hard note.

When checking the atomization the valve on the nozzle test stand must be kept closed to prevent damage to the gauge and give a true indication of the condition of the nozzle.

Needle Seat Leakage

Wipe the nozzle tip dry. Operate the tester three or four times and the nozzle tip should remain dry.

In doubtful cases hold the injection pressure at 247 psi, holding a piece of blotting paper against the nozzle tip. The fuel stain should not exceed ½ in. in diameter in one minute.

If the injector passes the above tests satisfactorily, it can be installed on the engine. If, however, it fails the needle seat leakage test or if the spray is distorted or does not atomize properly, the injector should be completely disassembled, cleaned, reassembled and tested once again.

When testing injectors from an engine, if the nozzle opening pressure is between 245 and 268 psi and the injector passes all other tests, do not adjust the opening pressure as these limits are acceptable.

In addition, the nozzle holder should be examined as follows:

1. Examine the joint face on which the nozzle is secured for scratches or trapped foreign particles.
2. Remove the spring from the holder and check that it is not broken or corroded and that the ends are perfectly square. Renew if defective, nozzles which pass the above tests for atomization, seat dryness and back leakage are satisfactory for further service.

Fuel System

Description

The Ford Dorset 363 Diesel fuel system consists of fuel tank(s), primary fuel filter, fuel lift pump, secondary fuel filter, injection pump, fuel injectors and fuel lines.

The fuel flow is shown in illustration.

The purpose of the injection pump is to deliver varying quantities of fuel according to engine load and speed. The fuel is delivered under high pressure and at a predetermined point in the engine cycle.

Fuel Lift Pump

The fuel lift pump is mounted at the rear of the engine block on the same side as the injection pump. It is driven from an eccentric on the engine camshaft.

On rotation of the camshaft, the eccentric actuates the fuel pump rocker arm and link, which pulls the diaphragm inwards against the pressure of the return spring. This creates a partial vacuum in the pump chamber, causing the inlet valve to open and draw fuel through the fuel inlet line to the diaphragm chamber.

Further movement of the camshaft eccentric allows the rocker arm to return, and the diaphragm is pushed outwards by the return spring, causing the inlet valve to close and the outlet valve to open. The fuel is then forced through the replaceable element filter to the injection pump. The pulsator diaphragm between the pump outer body and the cover helps reduce fuel delivery surge.

When the injection pump is full of fuel, pressure created in the diaphragm chamber holds the diaphragm in against the action of the return spring until fuel is delivered by the injection pump.

During the time the diaphragm is held in by the fuel pressure, the rocker arm idles on the camshaft eccentric without operating the link.

Fuel Filters

There are two fuel filters on all vehicles equipped with a Ford Dorset 363 Diesel engine; a primary fuel filter, made up of a sediment bowl and a gauze screen or water separator, and a secondary fuel filter with a replaceable paper element. Both filters are in-line types. The primary

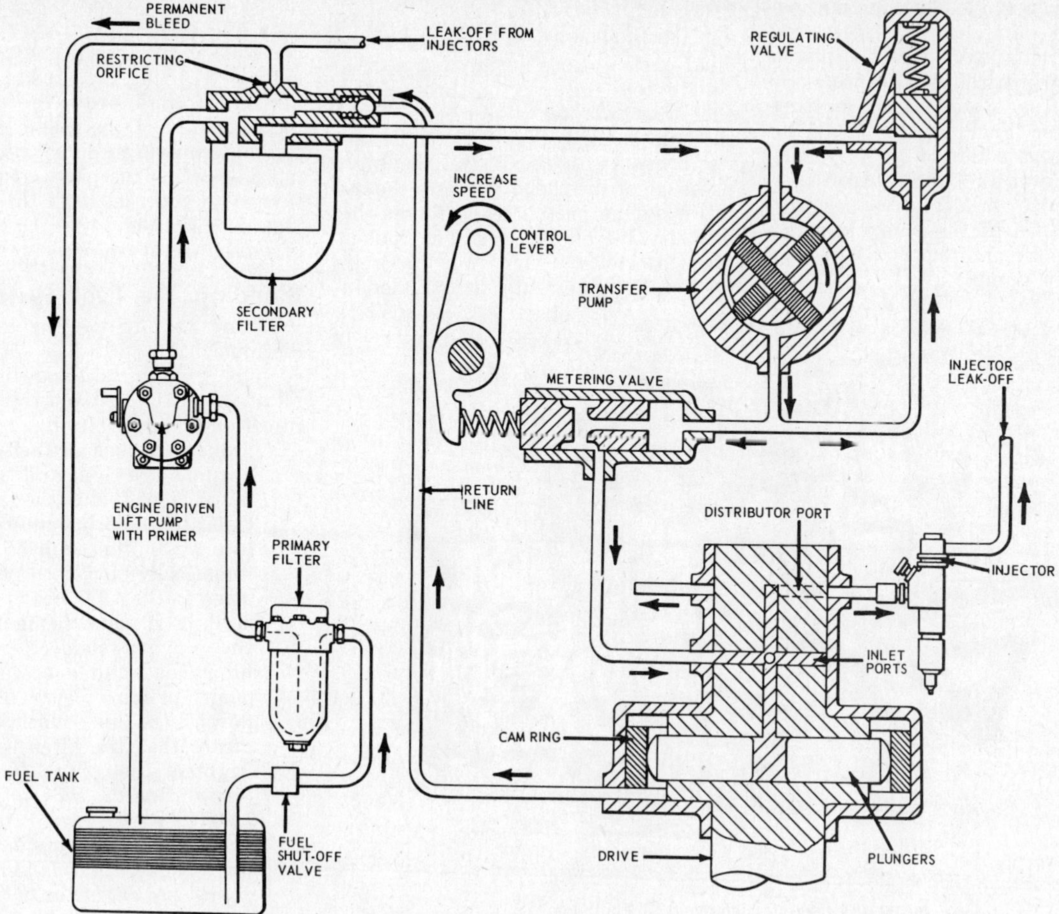

Ford dorset 363 Diesel fuel system (© Ford Motor Co.)

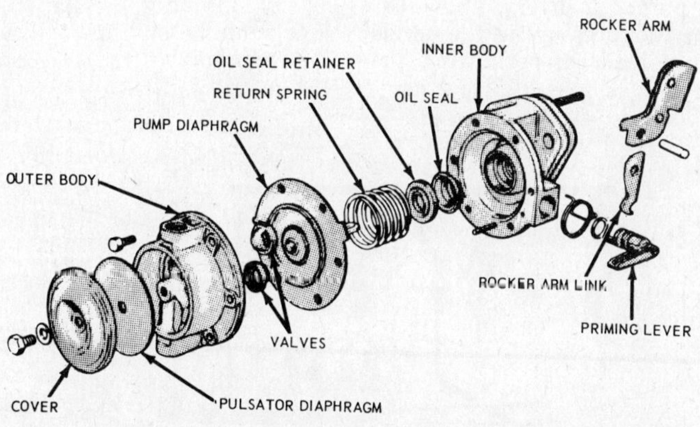

Ford dorset 363 fuel lift pump assembly (© Ford Motor Co.)

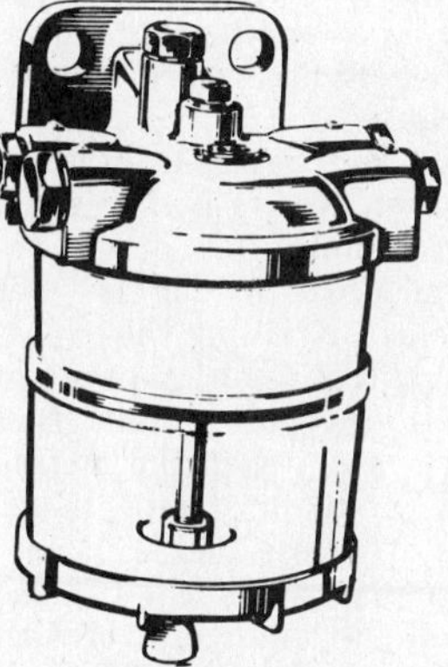

Primary fuel filter
(© Ford Motor Co.)

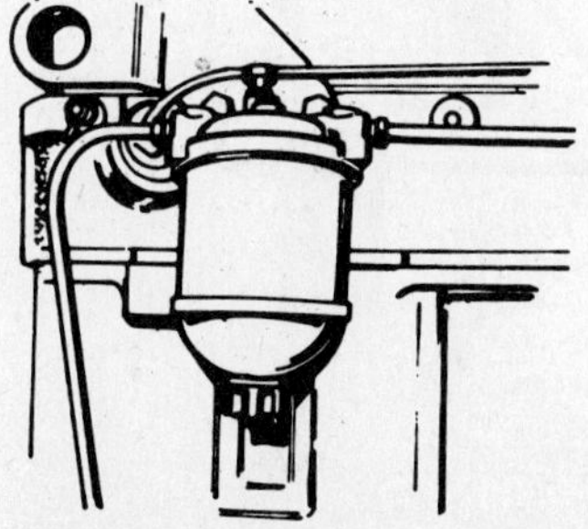

Secondary fuel filter
(© Ford Motor Co.)

fuel filter is located on the vehicle frame, whereas the secondary fuel-filter is mounted on the engine.

Injection Pump

The CAV fuel injection pump Model DPA (Distributor Pump, Type A), is used on the Ford Dorset 363 Diesel engines.

Fuel is supplied to the injection pump from the fuel tank, through a primary fuel filter, to the fuel lift pump, through the secondary fuel filter to the vane-type transfer pump within the injection pump assembly. The transfer pump supplies the pressure requirements of the injection pump. Regulated transfer pump pressure is then routed through a governor-controlled metering valve and then through a shuttle valve to the high pressure pumping element.

A centrifugal governor regulates engine speed through pump fuel metering control. An excess fuel device allows additional fuel metering for starting.

Injection timing advance is accomplished by moving the cam ring in which the pumping element works. Transfer pump pressure, a piston and springs control the advance.

The engine is stopped by shutting off metered fuel at the metering valve through action of a rotary solenoid acting on the stop control lever of the pump.

Lubrication of the pump is satisfied by the diesel oil normally flowing through the pump.

Fuel Injectors

Each injector consists of two principal parts: nozzle holder and nozzle. Fuel enters the injector through the fuel inlet adapter and passes down the hole in the nozzle body to the annular groove in the body. The high pressure of the fuel overcomes the injector spring pressure and forces the needle valve off its seat. The fuel is then injected through four holes in the nozzle tip and into the cylinder in a highly atomized state. When the injection pump delivery valve(s) closes, the fuel pressure in the nozzle is suddenly reduced, permitting the nozzle spring to overcome fuel pressure and seat the needle valve, thus completing the injection cycle to the cylinder. During the injection period a part of high pressure fuel leaks past the stem of the needle valve and its guide providing lubrication to the nozzle parts. This excess fuel is returned to the fuel tank through the leak-off manifold connected to the top of each injector cap nut.

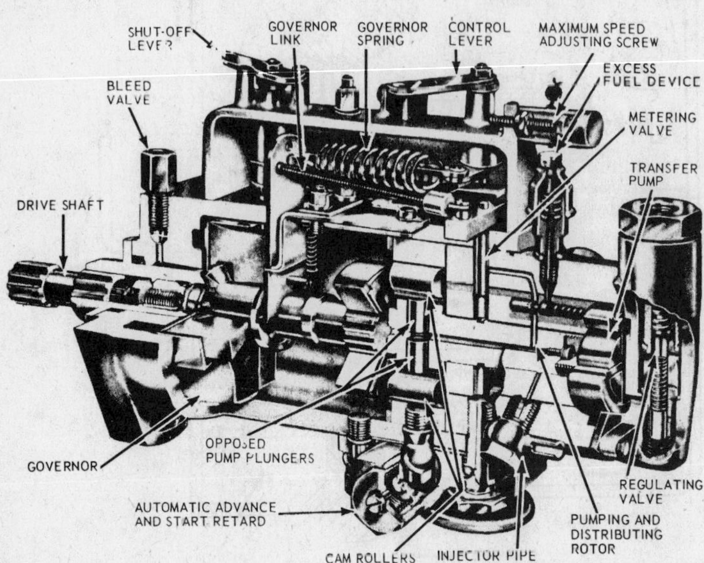

C.A.V. model DPA fuel injection pump (© Ford Motor Co.)

Bleeding the Fuel System

If any part of the fuel system is disconnected or air has entered the system, it will be necessary to remove all air from the fuel and to prime the injection pump by bleeding.

1. Make sure that all fuel pipe connections are tight and that there is sufficient fuel in the tank.
2. Operate the lift pump priming lever. The filter will be bled automatically by the permanent bleed in the filter head. After installing a new element, loosen the plugged connection on the filter head and operate the lift pump priming lever until fuel flows from this connection to indicate that the filter is primed. Tighten the plug. *If the lift pump cam on the engine camshaft is on maximum lift, it will render the fuel pump priming lever inoperative. If this occurs, rotate the engine until the priming lever can be operated.*
3. Repeat the procedure at the injection pump inlet connection.

On initial installation, or after running out of fuel, additional priming of the injection pump

Excess Fuel Device

An excess fuel device is provided for starting the engine on initial starts or when it has cooled to ambient temperature.

The excess fuel device control is situated between Nos. 1 and 4 injector pipe banjo connections on the injection pump. Move the toggle lever fully to one side by pulling the excess fuel remote control knob and return immediately to provide excess fuel for initial starts or when the engine has reached ambient temperature. The quantity of excess fuel is pre-set by fixed stop plates which limit the pumping element plungers stroke. The excess fuel valve, when released, also closes the fuel line to the advance mechanism. The cam ring is thus held in the fully retarded position, to assist starting, until the excess fuel valve is returned automatically to the normal running position by transfer pressure acting on the valve end at 1200 rpm or more.

Injection Lines

The injection lines are of heat treated steel to withstand the high pressure of the pump discharge. Compression-type fittings are used to connect the lines at the banjo-type fittings at the pump and fuel inlet adapters at the injectors.

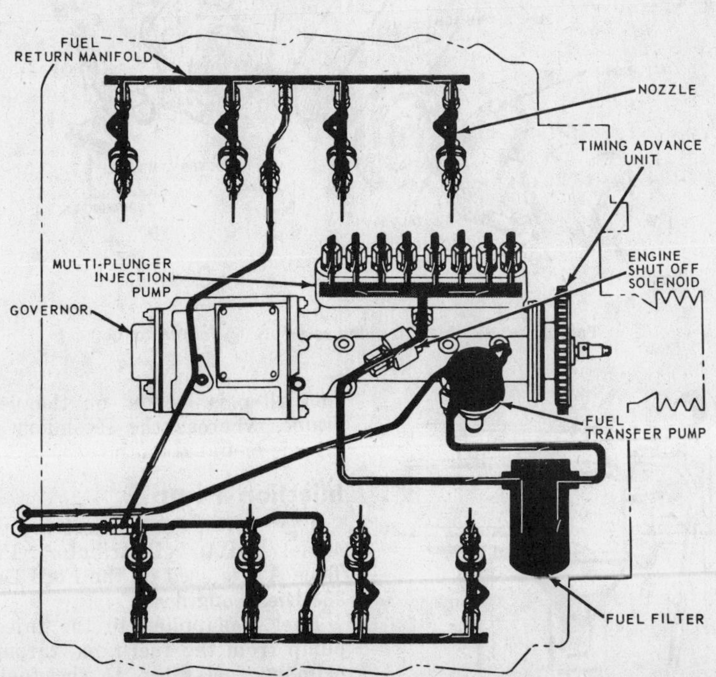

Ford V8 series Diesel engine fuel system

Fuel line arrangement (© Ford Motor Co.)

and injector pipes will also be necessary.

4. Loosen the bleed valve on the governor housing and operate toe lift pump priming lever until the fuel flow is free of air. Tighten the governor housing bleed valve.
5. Unscrew any two injector inlet adapter seal nuts and loosen the corresponding inlet adapters. With the throttle lever in the fully open position, operate the starter motor until the engine fires on the remaining cylinders. Tighten the injector inlet adapters and then the seal nuts.

Wipe all surplus fuel from the injection pump and filter body.

Be sure to expel all air from the system, or misfiring and erratic operation will result.

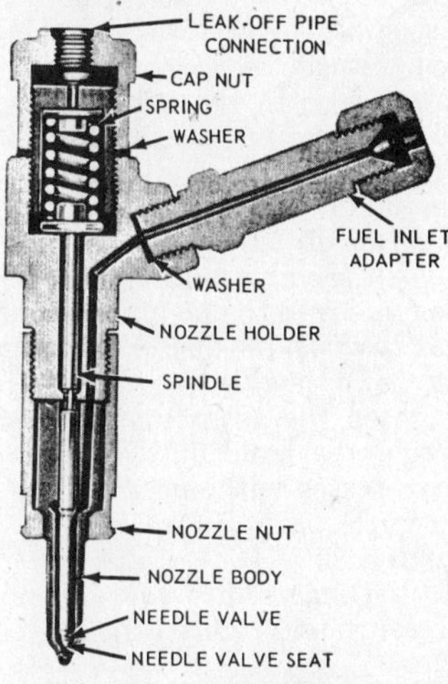

Fuel injector-sectional view (© Ford Motor Co.)

Fuel Injector—Cleaning Inspection & Overhaul

Injector Disassembly

Do not disassemble the nozzle unless testing indicates that servicing is necessary.

Use extreme care in keeping the work area and tools clean. Handle all parts with care to avoid any damage.

1. Place the nozzle in the holding tool and secure the tool in a vise. Do not clamp any part of the nozzle body directly in the vise.
2. Loosen pressure adjusting screw locknut.
3. Holding the nozzle in one hand, invert it and back out the pressure adjusting screw, allowing the spring, spring seats and ball washer to fall into your hand. The valve may slide out, by its own weight, and should be handled carefully by its stem.
4. If the valve does not fall out, remove it with the retractor. To prevent bending the valve, bottom it in the body with the retractor. Push down on the retractor body to mount the collet. Turn the knurled nut counterclockwise to secure the collet and withdraw the valve.
5. Place the parts in solvent to loosen carbon and deposits of foreign material. Do not soak the body assembly in solvent for over 1-2 hours. The solvent can damage the epoxy bond used to secure the body assembly components together.

Cleaning and Inspection

A Nozzle Cleaning Kit is available and contains all the special tools required for servicing the injection nozzle.

1. Use the brush to clean the tip and body exterior.
2. Secure the cleaning wire (0.008—0.009 in. dia.) in pin vise with 1/32 in. to 1/16 in. of wire protruding. A longer length of wire can bottom in the sac hole and break off in the orifice. Remove any burrs from the wire tip with the stone. Stoning a flat surface on one side of the wire helps in reaming carbon from a clogged orifice. Insert the wire into each orifice and rotate it slowly until it turns freely.

Do not use a punching action to remove deposits from the orifices. Select the wire (0.011 in. maximum diameter) and repeat the cleaning procedure. Flush the body thoroughly and inspect the tip. If any orifices are chipped at the edges or eroded to an extent that the spray pattern is affected, replace the nozzle.

Cleaning valve (© Ford Motor Co.)

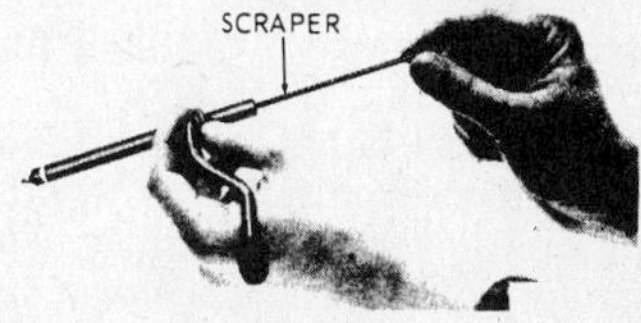

Cleaning nozzle orifice (© Ford Motor Co.)

3. Use scraper to remove any deposits from the seat area.
4. Insert drill into the nozzle body and rotate it to remove any accumulations from the sac hole area.
5. After cleaning the sac hole area, repeat the orifice cleaning procedure.
6. Use brass wire brush to remove deposits from the seating area on the tip of valve. Inspect the valve seat for any pitting or erosion which will cause leakage. *Never use a steel wire brush on nozzle parts.*
7. Use solvent and cleaning pad to remove varnish deposits from the valve.
8. Inspect the guide area of the valve for scratches which might cause sticking. This area will generally be polished on one side during operation and visible vertical marks are normal.

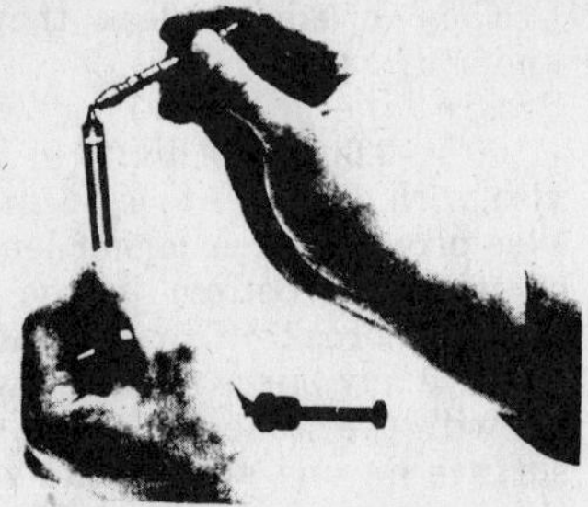
Cleaning nozzle valve seat
(© Ford Motor Co.)

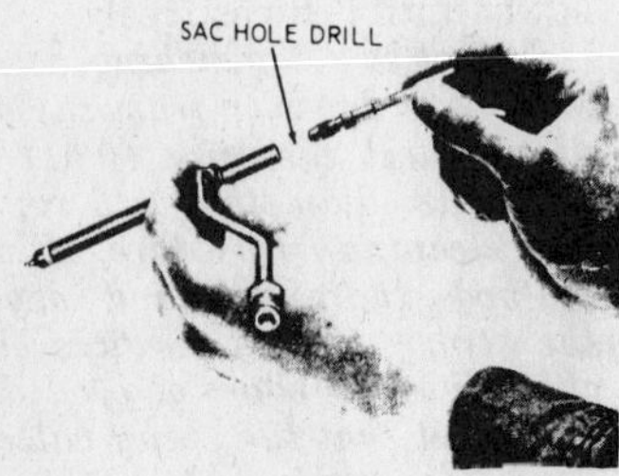

Cleaning sac hole
(© Ford Motor Co.)

Reconditioning

If cleaning does not restore the nozzle to its proper operating condition, the valve seat or guide can be reconditioned.

Lap the guide as follows:

1. Place a small amount of Lapping Compound on the valve in the guide area.
2. Slide valve into body.
3. Bottom the valve in the body and grasp it with retractor.
4. Rotate the valve in the guide about ten revolutions while raising and lowering it slightly. *The amount of material removal required is normally only a few millionths of an inch. Never use motor driven chucks for this operation.*
5. Flush thoroughly and wash the compound from the valve and nozzle before assembling.
6. Check the return leakage. If it is still low, repeat the lapping procedure until the correct leakage is obtained.

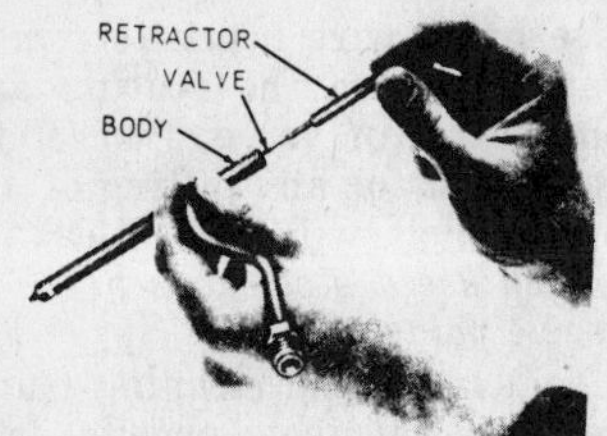

Lapping valve and seat
(© Ford Motor Co.)

Lap the valve to the tip seat as follows:

1. Place a small amount of Lapping Compound on the valve seat.
2. Slide the valve into the body.
3. Bottom the valve in the body and grasp it with the Valve Retractor.
4. Return the valve by hand, first clockwise then counterclockwise for a total or 3-5 revolutions. *Never attempt to use motor driven chucks for this purpose. Excessive lapping will destroy the interference angle between the seat and valve.*
5. Flush body thoroughly, wash the valve and reassemble.
6. Check seat condition and chatter on the tester. If it is not satisfactory discard the nozzle.

Injector Assembly

Before assembly, wash all parts thoroughly. Flush the body to remove any debris or lapping compound. Assemble while all parts are wet with clean fuel.

1. Handle valve by its shank and slide it partially into the body.
2. Assemble the ball washer, spring upper seat, spring and spring lower seat to the lift and pressure adjusting screw assembly.
3. Tilt the nozzle body and with spring lower seat in contact with the top of valve, as illustrated, push the valve and spring components into the body. *Be careful not to dislodge spring lower seat during assembly.*
4. Tighten the adjusting screw assembly by hand until the spring compresses with enough force to hold all parts in place (8—10 turns).
5. Adjust valve lift and opening pressure and tighten the locknut.

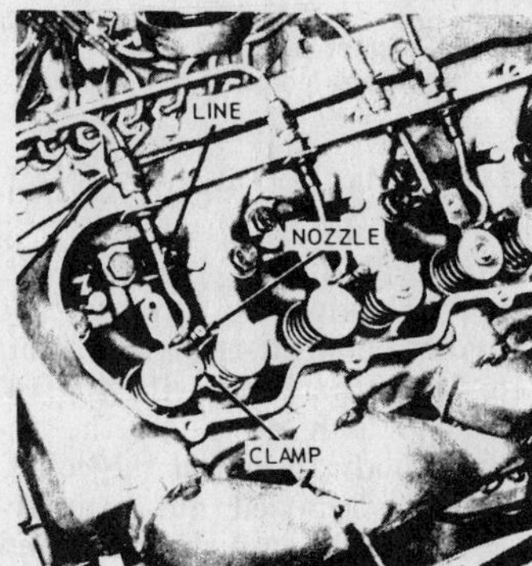

Injector and clamp arrangement
(© Ford Motor Co.)

Fuel Lift Pump

Removal

1. Disconnect the fuel inlet flexible line at the lift pump.
2. Disconnect both ends of the fuel line between the lift pump and secondary fuel filter.
3. Remove the two nuts and lockwashers, and remove the lift pump and gasket.

Installation

1. Clean the gasket surfaces on the lift pump and engine block.
2. Use a new gasket and install the lift pump on the block. Torque the mounting nuts to specification.
3. Install the fuel line between the lift pump and secondary fuel filter and tighten the coupling nuts.
4. Connect the fuel inlet flexible line to the lift pump. Tighten the coupling nut; then bleed the fuel system.

Injectors

Removal

1. Remove the rocker cover and gasket.
2. Disconnect the injector leak-off manifold at each injector and at the return line. Remove the leak-off manifold.
3. Disconnect the fuel lines at the injectors. Cover the openings (connections) in the injectors with plastic caps or plugs to prevent the entrance of dirt, engine oil, etc.
4. Remove the injector mounting bolts and remove the injectors. If the injector is tight in the cylinder head, use the injector lifting bar to prevent damaging the injector. Remove the copper washers from the injector recesses in the cylinder head.

Cleaning and Inspection

Refer to injector cleaning and inspection instructions.

Before installing an injector, check the injector recess in the cylinder head; it must be clean and free of any carbon deposits. Inspect the ferrules on the fuel lines to be sure they are in good condition, thus ensuring a leak-proof connection.

Flush the fuel lines with clean diesel fuel and blow out with compressed air.

Installation

1. Install a new oil seal on the injector inlet adapter.
2. Place a new copper washer on the injector and position the injector in the cylinder head. Install the retaining bolts and torque to specifications, *but do not exceed specifications.*
3. Install the fuel lines and tighten the injector and injection pump connections securely.
4. Install the injector leak-off tube and tighten all connections; then bleed the system.
5. Start the engine and check for

fuel line connections for leaks. Be sure the injectors do not leak combustion gases at the cylinder head.

6. Position a new gasket in the rocker cover and install the cover. Torque the cover bolts to specifications.

Fuel injection pump installation
(© Ford Motor Co.)

Injection Pump

The distributor-type injection pump is mounted horizontally on the right side of the engine and is driven at half engine speed by a timing gear in mesh with the camshaft gear.

Removal

1. Disconnect the fuel shut-off solenoid; then remove the solenoid and bracket from the pump.
2. Disconnect the injector pipes. Install caps or plugs on the injector pipes and injection pump openings.
3. Disconnect and install caps or plugs on the feed and return pipes from the inlet and outlet connections on the injection pump.
4. Disconnect the accelerator linkage and return spring. Disconnect the cable and the return assist spring from the excess fuel device.
5. Remove the injection pump, mounting plate and gear assembly from the engine.
6. Remove the pump drive gear and pull the gear off the drive hub.
7. Remove the injection pump mounting plate.

Injection Pump Timing

Timing marks are machined on the pump drive plate and cam ring and, as these are fixed, no timing adjustment is necessary. However, the injection pump should be set in the timed position to facilitate assembly on the engine.

1. Remove the inspection cover from the injection pump body.
2. Turn the injection pump until the timing marks on the drive plate and cam rings are in alignment.
3. Remove the sealing bolt from the pump flange.
4. Substitute the timing locking bolt for the sealing bolt and tighten to 25 in. lb. Lock the pump in the timed position. The bracket attached to the locking bolt covers the two upper holes in the pump mounting flange to make sure of removal of the locking bolt when installing the pump on the engine.
5. Install the inspection cover. Tighten the bolts and seal with a wire and lead seal.

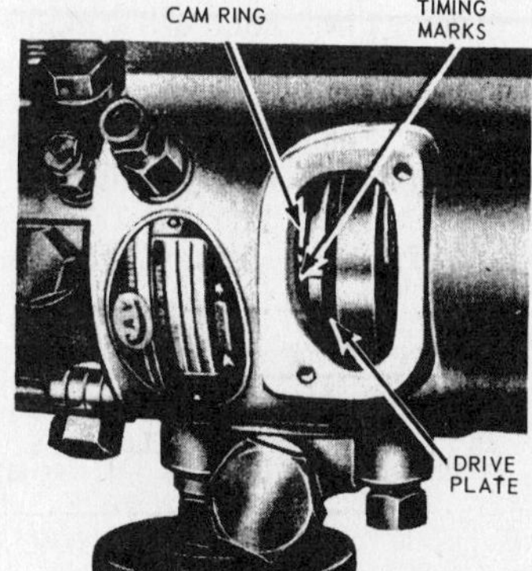

Injection pump timing marks
(© Ford Motor Co.)

Installation

1. Locate the injection pump on the mounting plate and retain with the lower bolt, lock and flat washers, but do not tighten. *The timing locking bolt and bracket should not be removed until the injection pump is on the engine.*
2. Install the drive gear on the drive hub. Locate the dowel in the slot in the drive hub and retain the gear with three bolts and internally-toothed lockwashers.
3. Rotate the crankshaft until the timing mark is in line with the 9-degree mark in the flywheel timing scale with No. 1 piston approaching the top of the compression stroke. *When the engine is on the correct stroke a timing mark on the rear face of the camshaft gear will be visible in the injection pump mounting opening.*
4. Install the injection pump on the mounting plate. Tighten one bolt finger tight to hold the pump in the timed position and remove the timing locking bolt and bracket. Install the two remaining bolts, spring and plain washers and tighten. Install a sealing bolt with a copper washer in the pump body flange. *If the injection pump is not locked in the timed position, it will be necessary to remove the inspection cover on the pump body and assemble the pump to the engine so that the timing marks on the drive plate and cam ring are in alignment.*
5. Install the injection pump, mounting plate and gear assembly on the engine. Turn the injection pump clockwise on the mounting plate, so that the single retaining bolt is at the end of the slotted hole in the flange to allow for the gear teeth helix. Locate a new O-ring on the mounting plate and install the assembly on the engine, secure the mounting plate with four bolts, one nut and a lock washer.
6. Connect the accelerator linkage and return spring. Connect the control cable and the return assist spring to the excess fuel device. Make certain the excess fuel device returns to the vertical position when the control button is pushed inward.
7. Install the fuel shut-off solenoid bracket. Connect the solenoid feed wire and energize the solenoid; then, *with the fuel shut-off lever in the full (on) position,* install the solenoid.
8. Remove the protective caps or plugs; then connect the inlet and return pipes to the inlet and outlet connections on the injection pump. Connect the injector pipes to the banjo connectors on the

injection pump and the corresponding injectors.

9. Bleed the fuel system.

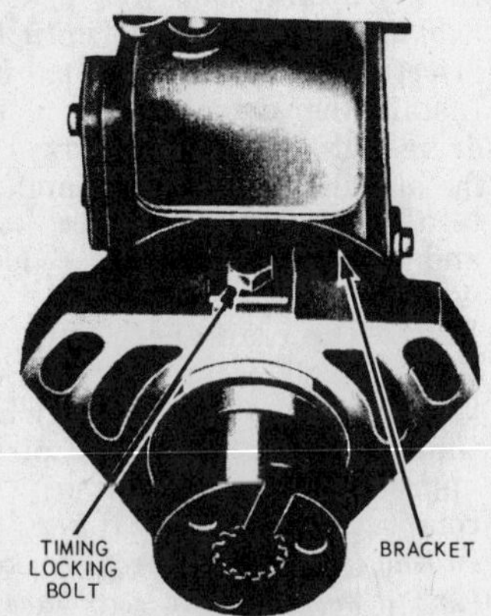

Timing lock bolt
(© Ford Motor Co.)

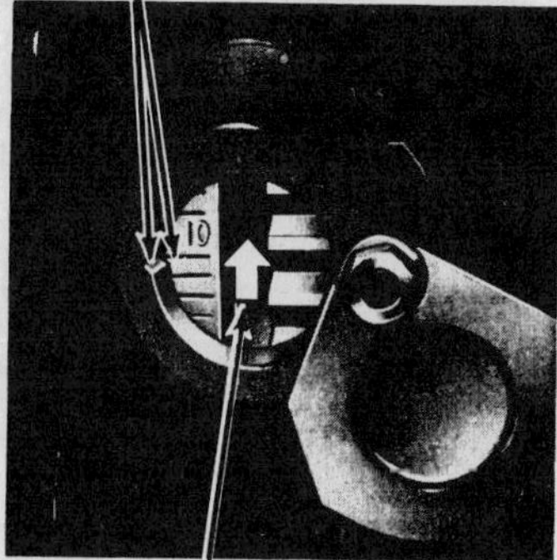

Engine timing marks
(© Ford Motor Co.)

Water Pump

Removal

B, C, F and N Series

1. Drain the cooling system.
2. Remove the bolts and lock washers securing the fan and spacer to the water pump hub and remove the fan and spacer.
3. Loosen the alternator adjusting arm bolt and the alternator mounting bolt; push the alternator in toward the engine to relieve the belt tension. Remove the fan drive belt and the water pump drive pulley.
4. Disconnect the radiator lower hose at the radiator. Remove the hose from the gear-case cover retainer and position it out of the way. Loosen the radiator lower hose clamp at the water pump.
5. Remove the bolts and lock washers securing the water pump and alternator adjusting arm and remove the pump and arm.

Installation

1. Clean the gasket surfaces of the water pump and cylinder block.
2. Apply water-resistant sealer to both sides of a new gasket and position the gasket on the water pump.
3. Position the water pump and alternator adjusting arm on the cylinder block, and install lock washers and bolts. Torque the bolts to specifications.
4. Connect the hose to the water pump.
5. Connect the radiator lower hose at the radiator, and secure the hose at the rear case cover retainer.
6. Install the fan drive belt and water pump pulley. Install the fan and spacer on the water pump hub and tighten the bolts to specifications.
7. Adjust the drive belt tension to specifications. Tighten the alternator adjusting arm and mounting bolts.
8. Fill the cooling system. Start the engine and idle for a short time. Check for coolant leaks and proper coolant level.

Governor and Stop Control

Governor and Stop Control Operation

The mechanical governor is of the flyweight type, and gives sensitive control throughout the complete speed range and at all loads. The weights are held in a carrier clamped between the driving hub and a step on the driving shaft. The weight assembly, drive shaft and hub rotate as a single unit. The weights are a sliding fit in the carrier pockets, and are shaped so that in operation they pivot on one edge. As the weights move in or out under varying centrifugal force, according to the pump speed, they operate a thrust sleeve which is a sliding fit on the drive shaft, moving it axially to control the governor linkage.

The governor control linkage, which transmits movement of the thrust sleeve to the metering valve, is enclosed by the governor control cover mounted on the upper face of the pump housing. The throttle and shutoff shafts project through this cover and the control levers are mounted externally.

Model	ENGINE SPEED—RPM		
	High Idle	Full Load	Low Idle (+0,-10 RPM)
150 HP	3380	3200	525
175 HP	3450	3200	525
200 HP	3320	3000	525
225 HP	3080	2800	525

Movement of the governor weights causes the thrust sleeve to move axially along the drive shaft. The governor control arm is free to pivot about a fulcrum provided on the control bracket and is held in contact with the end face of the thrust sleeve by spring tension. A spring-loaded hook lever connects the upper end of the governor control arm with the lever which is secured to the metering valve. Any movement of the governor weights in response to fluctuations of engine speed results in movement of the metering valve and a corresponding change of fuel metering. The eccentric shut-off shaft is operated by movement of a lever. Movement of the shaft is transmitted to the control lever on the metering valve by the shut-off bar and rotates the metering valve to a position where the metering port is completely closed. The hook lever is spring-loaded so that this movement can be achieved without need for overcoming the resistance of the governor weights. When the shut-off control is operated, the light spring is compressed and the end of the hook lever passes through the governor control arm.

Speed selection is made by moving the throttle lever which is mounted on the throttle shaft. A swivel link is connected to a lever which is integral with the throttle shaft. The governor spring connects the swivel link with the idling spring guide which passes through a hole in the governor control arm. When the lever is moved to obtain increased engine speed, the light idling spring is compressed as the guide is drawn through the conrol arm and tension is then applied to the main spring. Tension of the main spring acting on the control arm is transmitted to the thrust sleeve, and provides resistance to movement of the governor weights. Adjustment of the governor characteristics to suit a particular engine application is made at the time of assembly.

The metering valve consists of a small shaft, slotted at one end. The valve is situated in the metering valve bore in the hydraulic head through which the fuel passes from the transfer pump to the inlet ports of the rotor. Rotation of the valve controls the area of the metering orifice, and regulates the fuel supply to the element by controlling the metering pressure in the fuel passage.

Variations in the speed of the engine, and therefore of the pump, cause movement of the flyweights which is transmitted to the thrust sleeve, and then to the governor control arm. This is spring-loaded during idling by the light idling spring, and at higher speeds by the main control spring.

Movement of the throttle lever adjusts the load on the governor control spring, bringing about a change in the position of the control arm, and of the metering valve, admitting more or less fuel to the pump as required. When the selected speed has been reached, it will be maintained within close limits by governor action. An increase in engine speed, resulting from decreased engine load, will cause the weights to move outward. Such movement turns the metering valve toward the closed position, and engine speed falls in response to reduced fueling.

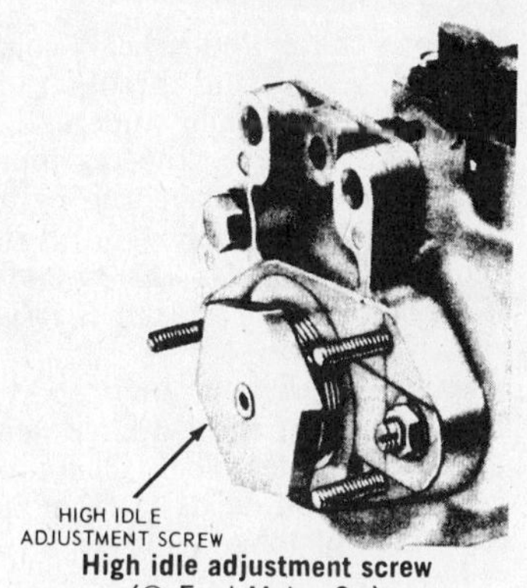

High idle adjustment screw
(© Ford Motor Co.)

If engine speed falls, the weights move inward, causing an increase of fueling which restores selected engine speed.

Tensioning of the governor spring provides increased resistance to movement of the governor control arm under the influence of the governor weights, so that with greater tension resulting from increased throttle opening, governor control will be at higher rpm.

Within the idling speed range, tension is removed from the governor spring and the light idling spring gives sensitive control at low rpm.

The engine can be shut down by means of the fuel shut-off lever. The solenoid-actuated shut-off lever overrides the governor to rotate the metering valve to the no-fuel position; regardless of the position of the throttle lever.

Manifolds

Manifold Removal

B, C, F and N Series

1. On B-, F- and N-Series trucks remove the air cleaner to intake manifold duct, but do not remove the air cleaner.
2. On C-Series trucks, loosen the air cleaner duct to intake manifold clamp screw. Disconnect the vent hose at the valve rocker cover. Remove the air cleaner support bracket bolts, and remove the bracket, air cleaner and hoses as an assembly.
3. Disconnect the hand throttle control cable.
4. Remove the bolt, lock washer and nut securing starter motor heat shield clamp to exhaust manifold or muffler inlet pipe. Remove the heat shield.
5. Remove the nuts and bolts and separate the exhaust inlet pipe. Remove the heat shield.
6. Remove the nuts and bolts and separate the exhaust inlet pipe from the exhaust inlet pipe from the exhaust manifold.
7. Remove all the manifold nuts, bolts and washers except one bolt at each end of the exhaust manifold and the exhaust manifold center bolt. Remove the intake manifold and gaskets. Remove the remaining three bolts and washers, and remove the exhaust manifold and gaskets. Some production engines are being built without exhaust manifold gaskets. Do not separate the exhaust manifold sections unless replacement of a section is necessary.

Installation

1. Clean the gasket surfaces of the manifolds and cylinder head. Install exhaust manifold gaskets on all engines during installation.
2. Using new gaskets, position the exhaust manifold on the cylinder head, and secure it in place with one bolt and washer in the center, and one bolt and washer in each end of the manifold.
3. Use new gaskets and install the intake manifold. Install the remaining bolts and washers. Torque all bolts in sequence to specifications.
4. Use a new gasket and attach the exhaust inlet pipe to the exhaust manifold. Install the remaining bolts, washers and nuts, and torque to specification.
5. Place the starter motor heat shield in position with the bracket around the exhaust manifold or muffler inlet pipe. Secure the bracket with a nut, lock washer and bolt.
6. Install the hand throttle control cable.
7. On C-Series trucks, install the air cleaner and bracket assembly on the intake manifold. Connect the vent hose to the valve rocker cover. Connect the air cleaner duct to the intake manifold.
8. On B-, F- and N-Series trucks, install the air cleaner duct on the intake manifold and air cleaner, and tighten the duct clamps.

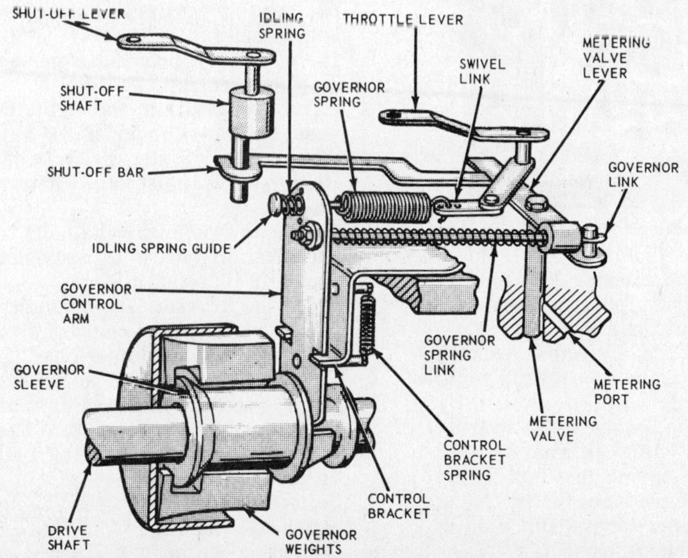

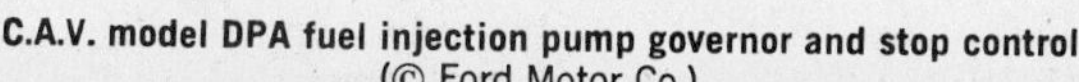
C.A.V. model DPA fuel injection pump governor and stop control
(© Ford Motor Co.)

"C" series engine (© Ford Motor Co.)

"N" series engine (© Ford Motor Co.)

Engine Service

Cylinder Head Removal

C-Series

1. Release the cab locks and tilt the cab forward.
2. Drain the cooling system.
3. Disconnect the vent hose at the valve rocker cover. Loosen the air intake duct clamp at the intake manifold. Remove the air cleaner cover wing bolt, and remove the air cleaner duct and vent hose assembly. Leave the air cleaner support attached to the intake manifold.
4. Disconnect the hand throttle control cable. Disconnect the throttle control rod at the cross shaft assembly, and remove the cross shaft assembly from the cylinder head.
5. Remove the bolts and nuts and disconnect the exhaust inlet pipe at the exhaust manifold.
6. Disconnect the auxiliary coolant tank lines at the coolant outlet elbow.
7. Loosen the lower hose clamp on the radiator upper hose. Unscrew the attaching bolts, and remove the coolant outlet elbow and thermostat.
8. Disconnect the heater hose at the cylinder head.
9. Disconnect the temperature sending unit wire.
10. Remove the valve rocker cover.
11. Remove two bolts that attach the secondary fuel filter and engine rear lifting bracket to the cylinder head. Remove the lifting bracket, but leave the fuel filter attached to the fuel lines.

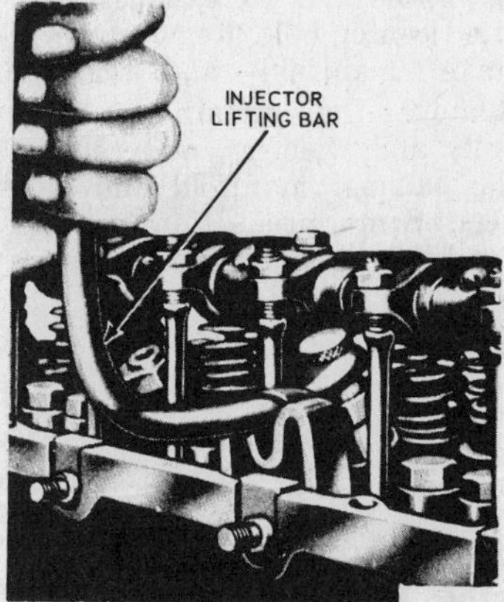

Removing an injector (© Ford Motor Co.)

12. Loosen the injector fuel lines at the injection pump; disconnect the lines at the injectors.
13. Remove the injector leak-off manifold from the injectors and the cylinder head.
14. Loosen the rocker shaft support bolts evenly and alternately until the valve spring pressure is relieved. Remove the bolts. Tie a cord around the end supports to prevent the rocker arm shaft assembly from becoming disassembled during removal. Lift the rocker arm shaft assembly from the cylinder head.
15. Remove the push rods in the sequence and place them in a rack for installation in the same sequence.
16. Remove the valve stem caps and position them in sequence in a container to facilitate installation on the same valves from which they were removed.
17. Remove the injector leak-off line from the injector and cylinder head.
18. Remove the cylinder head bolts. Attach the lifting brackets to the cylinder head, and use a hoist to remove the cylinder head. Carefully place the cylinder head assembly on wood blocks. *Do not let the cylinder head rest on any part of the fuel injectors.*
19. Clean all carbon and gasket material from the cylinder head and the cylinder block. Clean excessive carbon deposits from the top of the pistons.

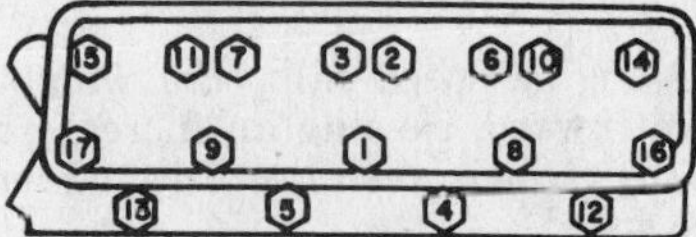

Cylinder head tightening sequence 4 cylinder engines (© Ford Motor Co.)

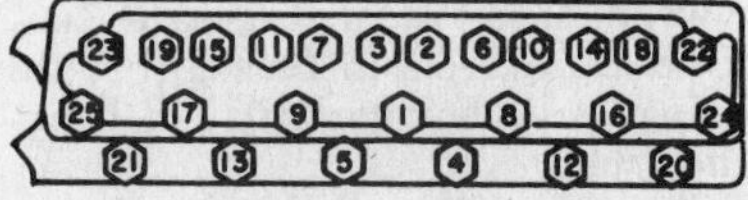

Cylinder head tightening sequence 6 cylinder engines (© Ford Motor Co.)

Installation

1. Check the flatness of the cylinder head and cylinder block gasket surfaces.
2. Install the cylinder head gasket (without sealer).
3. Carefully position the cylinder head on the cylinder block and install the cylinder head bolts. Remove the hoist and lifting brackets.
4. Torque the cylinder head bolts to specification in the sequence shown in illustration.
5. Place the injector leak-off manifold in position and connect it to the injector and cylinder head.
6. Connect the fuel lines to the injectors; tighten the lines only at the injection pump. Bleed the full system and tighten the fuel lines at the injectors.
7. Connect the injector leak-off line at the cylinder head.
8. Lubricate the push rod seats in the valve tappets with engine oil. Install the push rod in the same

cylinder head bores from which they were removed, making sure each push rod is seated in the tappet.

9. Install the valve stem caps on the same valves from which they were removed. Position the rocker arm assembly on the cylinder head. Install the rocker arm shaft support bolts; torque them evenly and alternately to specifications.
10. Make an initial valve lash adjustment with the engine cold.
11. Place a new gasket in the valve rocker cover and install it on the cylinder head. Do not secure tight.
12. Attach the engine rear lifting bracket and secondary fuel filter bracket to the cylinder head.
13. Connect the radiator upper hose to the coolant outlet elbow.
14. Connect the heater hose at the cylinder head.
15. Connect the wire to the temperature sending unit.
16. Connect the auxiliary coolant tank line at the coolant outlet elbow.
17. Attach the exhaust inlet pipe to the exhaust manifold. Use a new gasket.
18. Install the cross shaft assembly on the front of the cylinder head. Connect the throttle control rod to the cross shaft. Connect the hand throttle control cable.
19. Install the air cleaner and connect the air duct to the intake manifold. Connect the vent hose to the valve rocker cover. Tighten the hose clamps.
20. Fill and bleed the cooling system. Check oil level and replenish if necessary.
21. Start the engine and allow to idle for a short time. Check coolant level and replenish, if necessary. Continue to operate engine until engine reaches normal operating temperature. Check for coolant and fuel leaks. Stop the engine.
22. Remove the valve rocker cover. Torque the cylinder head bolts in sequence to specifications while the engine is at normal operating temperature.
23. Adjust the valve lash to specifications while the engine is operating at normal operating temperature.
24. Install the valve rocker cover and torque the attaching screws to specifications. Connect the vent hose to the rocker cover.
25. Return the cab to its normal position and secure it with the cab locks.

Cylinder Head Removal

B- and F-Series

1. Disconnect the battery cables.
2. Disconnect the vent hose from the valve rocker arm cover and remove the air cleaner assembly.
3. Drain the cooling system.
4. Disconnect the radiator upper hose at the radiator.
5. Disconnect the heater hose at the cylinder head.
6. Disconnect the power brake vacuum line, if so equipped, and position it out of the way.
7. Remove the starter motor heat shield from the muffler inlet pipe and loosen the heat shield clamp at the exhaust manifold.
8. Disconnect the muffler inlet pipe at the exhaust manifold, and remove the starter motor heat shield.
9. Disconnect the engine wiring harness at the fuel shut-off solenoid, temperature sending unit and oil pressure sending unit. Position the harness out of the way.
10. Disconnect and remove two fuel lines from the fuel filter to the injection pump.
11. Disconnect the fuel return lines from the cylinder head to the fuel filter, and from the cylinder block to the chassis line.
12. Disconnect the fuel line from the lift pump to the fuel filter at the lift pump end.
13. Remove the fuel filter and line from the cylinder head.
14. Remove six fuel lines from the injection pump to the injectors.
15. Remove the valve rocker cover. Loosen the rocker shaft support bolts evenly and in sequence until the valve spring pressure is relieved. Tie a cord around the end supports to prevent the rocker arm shaft assembly from becoming disassembled during removal. Remove the retaining bolts and remove the rocker arm shaft assembly.
16. Remove the valve stem caps and position them in a container to facilitate installation on the same valves from which they were removed.
17. Remove the push rods in sequence and place them in a rack for installation in the same sequence.
18. Remove the injector leak-off manifold from the injectors and the cylinder head.
19. Remove the cylinder head bolts. Remove the cylinder head with a hoist. Carefully place the cylinder head assembly on wood blocks. *Do not let the cylinder head rest on any part of the fuel injectors.*
20. Clean all carbon and gasket material from the cylinder head and the cylinder block. Clean excess carbon deposits from the top of the pistons.

Installation

1. Check the flatness of the cylinder head and cylinder block gasket surfaces.
2. Position a new cylinder head gasket on the cylinder block.
3. Carefully place the cylinder head on the cylinder block, and install the cylinder head retaining bolts.
4. Torque the cylinder head bolts to specification in the sequence shown in illustration.
5. Place the injector leak-off manifold in position and connect it at the injectors and cylinder head.
6. Lubricate the push rod sets in the valve tappets with engine oil. Install the push rods in the same cylinder head bores from which they were removed, making sure each push rod is seated in its tappet. Install the valve stem caps on the same valves from which they were removed.
7. Position the rocker arm assembly on the cylinder head and install the retaining bolts. Torque the bolts evenly and alternately to specifications.
8. Position the fuel lines between the injector pump and the injectors, replace the seals, and connect the lines at both ends.
9. Position the fuel filter and lifting adapter to the cylinder head, install the retaining bolts, and connect the return line to the cylinder head.
10. Position the fuel line between the lift pump and fuel filter, and connect it at the fuel filter end.
11. Position and connect the two fuel lines at the fuel injector pump and the fuel filter.
12. Install the fuel return line from the cylinder head to the chassis line.
13. Connect the radiator upper hose.
14. Connect the heater hose at the cylinder head.
15. Position the vacuum line on the brackets and install the retaining bolts.
16. Position the engine wiring harness and connect it to the sending units and to the fuel shut-off solenoid.
17. Connect the power brake vacuum line, if so equipped, at the side of the intake manifold.
18. Connect the muffler inlet pipe at the exhaust manifold.
19. Place the starter motor heat shield in position and secure it at the exhaust manifold and exhaust pipe.

20. Check and adjust the valve lash (cold) to specifications.
21. Fill the cooling system.
22. Connect the battery cables.
23. Start the engine and allow it to reach normal operating temperature. Check for coolant and fuel leaks. Turn off the engine.
24. While engine is still hot, retorque the cylinder head retaining bolts to specifications.
25. With engine at normal operating temperature, check and adjust the valve lash to specifications.
26. Clean the rocker arm cover and the cover gasket surface at the cylinder head. Position a new gasket on the valve rocker arm rocker cover, and install the rocker arm cover on the cylinder head. Install the retaining screws.
27. Install the air cleaner assembly.
28. Connect the vent hose at the valve rocker cover.

Cylinder Head Removal

N-Series

1. Remove the engine hood assembly.
2. Drain the cooling system.
3. Remove the air cleaner assembly, hoses, mounting bracket and engine lifting bracket.
4. Disconnect the radiator upper hose at the engine.
5. Disconnect the two heater hoses at the cylinder head.
6. Disconnect two wires at the rotary fuel solenoid. Disconnect one wire at the temperature sending unit, and position the wiring harness out of the way.
7. Remove the accelerator pedal. Position the floor mat to one side and remove the shift lever boot retainer and floor pan. Push the boot down through the opening and remove the two-speed axle switch from the shift lever, if so equipped.
8. Remove the starter motor heat shield from the exhaust manifold.
9. Disconnect the muffler inlet pipe at the exhaust manifold.
10. Disconnect the throttle linkage and hand throttle cable, and position them out of the way.
11. Remove the accelerator bell crank from the cylinder head. Disconnect linkage and position it out of the way as necessary.
12. Disconnect the fuel return line at the cylinder head.
13. Disconnect three fuel lines from the fuel filter. Remove the fuel filter and lifting eye from the cylinder head.
14. Remove two fuel lines between the fuel filter and the fuel injection pump.
15. Remove six fuel lines between the injection pump and the fuel injectors.
16. Remove the valve rocker cover.
17. Loosen the rocker shaft support bolts evenly and in sequence until the valve spring pressure is relieved. Tie a cord around the end supports to prevent the rockers from becoming disassembled during removal. Remove the retaining bolts and remove the rocker arm shaft assembly.
18. Remove the push rods in sequence and place them in a rack for installation in the same sequence.
19. Remove the injector leak-off manifold from the injectors and cylinder head.
20. Remove the valve stem caps and position them in sequence in a container to facilitate installation in the same valves from which they were removed.
21. Loosen the cylinder head bolts in the reverse sequence of that shown in illustration. Remove the bolts.
22. Attach lifting brackets to the cylinder head and use a hoist to remove the cylinder head.

    Carefully place the cylinder head assembly on wood blocks. *Do not let the cylinder head rest on any part of the fuel injectors.*
23. Clean all carbon and gasket material from the cylinder head and the cylinder block. Clean excessive carbon deposits from the top of the pistons.

Installation

1. Check the flatness of the cylinder head and cylinder block gasket surfaces.
2. Position a new cylinder head gasket on the cylinder block.
3. Place the cylinder head on the cylinder block and loosely install the cylinder head retaining bolts.
4. Torque the cylinder head bolts to specifications in the sequence shown in illustration.
5. Place the injector leak-off manifold in position and connect it at the injectors and cylinder head.
6. Position the fuel lines between the injection pump and the injectors, replace the seals, and connect the lines.
7. Position and connect two fuel lines at the fuel filter and injection pump.
8. Install the fuel filter and lifting bracket on the cylinder head.
9. Install the fuel return line to the cylinder head and chassis line.
10. Connect three lines at the fuel filter and one line at the bypass fuel return line.
11. Lubricate the push rod seats in the valve tappets with engine oil. Install the push rods in the same cylinder head bores from which they were removed, making sure each push rod is seated in its tappet. Install the valve stem caps on the same valves from which they were removed.
12. Position the rocker arm assembly on the cylinder head and install the retaining bolts. Torque the bolts evenly and alternately to specifications.
13. Check and adjust the valve lash (cold) to specifications.
14. Install the air cleaner support and lifting bracket on the cylinder head.
15. Connect the two heater hoses to the cylinder head.
16. Connect the radiator upper hose.
17. Install the bell crank to the cylinder head and connect the throttle linkage.
18. Connect the hand throttle cable.
19. Position the wiring harness and connect it to the temperature sending unit and the fuel shut-off solenoid.
20. Connect the muffler inlet pipe to the exhaust manifold.
21. Place the starter motor heat shield in position and secure it at the exhaust manifold and exhaust pipe.
22. Install the hood assembly.
23. Fill the cooling system.
24. Start the engine and allow it to reach normal operating temperature. Check for coolant and fuel leaks. Turn off the engine.
25. While the engine is still hot, retorque the cylinder head retaining bolts to specifications.
26. With the engine at normal operating temperature, check and adjust the valve lash to specifications.
27. Clean the rocker arm cover and the cover gasket surface at the cylinder head. Position a new gasket on the valve rocker arm cover and position the rocker arm cover on the cylinder head. Install the retaining screws.
28. Install the two-speed axle switch on the shift lever, if so equipped. Install the shift lever boot, retainer, floor pan, floor mat and accelerator pedal.
29. Install the air cleaner assembly.
30. Connect the vent hose at the valve rocker cover.

Valve Rocker Cover, Rocker Arms & Shaft

Valve Rocker Cover—Removal

B-, C-, F- and N-Series

1. Disconnect the vent hose at the valve rocker cover.
2. On B-, F- and N-Series trucks, remove the air cleaner assembly.

3. On N-Series trucks, remove the accelerator pedal. Position the floor mat to one side and remove the shift lever boot retainer and floor pan. Push the boot down through the opening and remove the two-speed axle switch from the shift lever if so equipped.
4. Remove the valve rocker cover screws and lift it off the cylinder head.

Installation

1. Clean the gasket surfaces of the cylinder head and valve rocker cover. Clean the inside of the rocker cover with solvent and dry with compressed air.
2. Place a new gasket on the rocker cover and position both on the cylinder head. Install and tighten the cover screws.
3. On N-Series trucks, install the two-speed axle switch on the shift lever (if so equipped). Install the shift lever boot, retainer, floor pan, floor mat and accelerator pedal.
4. On B-, F- and N-Series trucks, install the air cleaner assembly.
5. Connect the vent hose to the valve rocker cover.

Rocker Arm Shaft Assembly Removal

B, C, F and N Series

1. Disconnect the vent hose at the valve rocker cover.
2. On B-, F- and N-Series trucks, remove the air cleaner assembly.
3. On N-Series trucks, remove the accelerator pedal. Position the floor mat to one side and remove the shift lever boot retainer and floor pan. Push the boot down through the opening and remove the two-speed axle switch from the shift lever, if so equipped.
4. Remove the valve rocker cover.
5. Loosen the rocker shaft support bolts evenly and in sequence until the valve spring pressure is relieved. Tie a cord around the end supports to prevent the rocker arms and shaft assembly from becoming disassembled during removal. Remove the retaining bolts and remove the rocker arm shaft assembly.

Installation

1. Lubricate the valve rockers and the push rod sockets in the valve lifters with engine oil.
2. Position the rocker arm shaft assembly on the cylinder head. Be sure all valve rocker arms are aligned with their respective valves and push rods.
3. Install the rocker shaft support spring washers and bolts, and tighten them two turns at a time in sequence. Finally, torque the bolts to specifications.
4. Operate the engine until normal operating temperature is attained; check and adjust the valve lash to specifications.
5. Using new gasket, install rocker cover.
6. On N-Series trucks, install the two-speed axle switch on the shift lever, if so equipped. Install the shift lever boot, retainer, floor pan, floor mat and accelerator pedal.
7. On B-, F- and N-Series trucks, install the air cleaner assembly.
8. Connect the vent hose at the valve rocker cover.

Push Rod Replacement

B-, C-, F- and N-Series

1. Disconnect the vent hose at the valve rocker cover.
2. On B-, F- and N-Series vehicles, remove the air cleaner assembly.
3. On N-Series vehicles remove the accelerator pedal. Position the floor mat to one side and remove the shift lever boot retainer and floor pan. Push the boot down through the opening and remove the two speed axle switch from the shift lever, if so equipped.
4. Remove the rocker arm cover.
5. Crank the engine until the piston for the push rod to be replaced is on top dead center.
6. Back off the adjusting screw, slide the rocker arm to one side, and lift the push rod from the cylinder head.
7. Lubricate the push rod socket of the valve lifter with engine oil. Position the new push rod in the cylinder head bore, ball end first. The rod should automatically engage the tappet.
8. Engage the cup end of the push rod with the ball end of the adjusting screw and slide the rocker arm into position on the valve stem.
9. Operate the engine until normal operating temperature is attained; check and adjust the valve lash to specifications.
10. Using new gasket, install rocker cover.
11. On N-Series trucks, install the two-speed axle switch on the shift lever, if so equipped. Install the shift lever boot, retainer, floor pan, floor mat and accelerator pedal.
12. On B-, F- and N-Series trucks, install the air cleaner assembly. Connect the vent hose at the valve rocker cover.

Timing Gear Cover & Seals

Timing Gear Cover Removal

C-Series

1. Release the cab locks and tilt the cab forward.
2. Drain the cooling system.
3. Disconnect the battery ground cable from the battery.
4. Disconnect the throttle control rod from the cross shaft assembly.
5. Disconnect the shutterstat air line at the shutterstat on air compressor equipped engines. Disconnect the shutterstat vacuum line at the shutterstat on vacuum pump equipped engines.
6. Remove the radiator upper hose and shutterstat assembly.
7. Disconnect the heater hose from the radiator return manifold.
8. If equipped with an air compressor, disconnect the air compressor coolant return hose from the radiator return manifold.
9. Loosen the hose clamps, and remove the radiator return manifold and hoses from the engine and radiator.
10. Remove the radiator mounting bolts; then lift the radiator out of the radiator support.
11. Remove the cooling fan and fan hub from the crankshaft vibration damper.
12. If equipped with an air compressor and power steering, remove the drive belts.
13. Loosen the alternator mounting bolts. Loosen the alternator adjusting arm bolt and remove the drive belt.
14. If equipped with power steering and air compressor, remove the belt drive pulleys from the crankshaft vibration damper.
15. Remove the crankshaft pulley (vibration damper) nut and washer. Install the crankshaft pulley remover on the pulley and remove it from the crankshaft.
16. Remove the timing gear cover bolts. Remove the timing gear cover and gasket.

Front Oil Seal Replacement

Use a remover and replacer tool to press the oil seal out of the timing gear cover, and press a new seal into the cover.

1. Clean the timing gear cover and the gasket surfaces of the timing gear housing.
2. Position a new gasket on the timing gear housing with contact cement. Install the timing gear cover.
3. Install the mounting bolts and lock washers in the timing gear cover. Torque the bolts to specifications in sequence.
4. Align the keyway in the crankshaft pulley with the key in the crankshaft and carefully install the pulley to avoid damaging the front oil seal.

5. Install the crankshaft pulley nut and washer and torque to specifications.
6. If equipped with power steering and air compressor, install the belt drive pulleys on the crankshaft vibration damper.
7. Install the alternator drive belt. Adjust the belt tension to specification, and tighten the alternator adjusting arm bolt and alternator mounting bolts.
8. If equipped with power steering and air compressor, install the drive belts, and adjust the tension of each belt to specifications.
9. Install the cooling fan hub and cooling fan on the crankshaft vibration damper.
10. Position the radiator in the radiator support and install the mounting bolts.
11. Install the radiator return manifold and hoses on the engine and radiator. Tighten the hose clamps.
12. If equipped with an air compressor, connect the compressor coolant return hose to the radiator return manifold.
13. Connect the heater hose to the radiator return manifold.
14. Install the radiator upper hose and shutterstat assembly on the radiator neck and coolant outlet elbow.
15. On vacuum pump equipped engines, connect the vacuum line to the shutterstat.

    On air compressor equipped engines, connect the air supply line to the shutterstat.
16. Connect the throttle control rod to the cross shaft assembly.
17. Connect the battery ground cable to the battery.
18. Fill and bleed the cooling system.
19. Start the engine and idle for a short time. Check for coolant leaks and proper coolant level.
20. Tilt the cab back to its normal position and secure it with the cab locks.

Timing Gear Cover Removal

B- and F- Series

1. Drain the cooling system.
2. Disconnect the battery ground cable from the battery.
3. Disconnect the upper and lower coolant hoses from the radiator.
4. Remove the cooling fan and spacer from the water pump.
5. Remove the bolts securing the radiator to the radiator support and remove the radiator.
6. Loosen the alternator adjusting arm bracket, and remove the water pump pulley and alternator drive belt.
7. Remove the crankshaft pulley (vibration damper) retaining bolt. Install the crankshaft pulley remover on the pulley and remove it from the crankshaft.
8. Remove the water line bracket and throttle return spring from the gear case cover.
9. Remove the retaining bolts and remove the timing gear cover.

Front Oil Seal Replacement

Use a remover and replacer tool to press the oil seal out of the timing gear cover and press a new seal into the cover.

Installation

1. Clean the timing gear cover and the gasket surface of the gear case.
2. Apply contact cement on the gear case gasket surface and install a new gasket.
3. Install the cover. Install the cover bolts and torque them to specifications in sequence.
4. Install the crankshaft pulley on the crankshaft. Torque the bolt to specifications.
5. Install the water pump pulley and alternator drive belt on the water pump. Adjust the belt tension to specifications.
6. Install the water line bracket to the gear case cover, and connect the throttle return spring.
7. Place the radiator assembly in position and secure it to the radiator support.
8. Connect the upper and lower hoses to the radiator.
9. Install the fan and spacer assembly on the water pump.
10. Fill the cooling system. Start the engine and idle for a short time. Check for coolant leaks and proper coolant.
11. Connect the battery gound cable.

Timing Gear Cover Removal

N-Series

1. Drain the cooling system.
2. Remove the hood from the vehicle.
3. Disconnect the upper and lower coolant hoses from the radiator.
4. Remove the fan and spacer assembly.
5. Remove the shutterstat line from the radiator shroud.
6. Disconnect the shutterstat linkage at the air cylinder.
7. Remove the bolts attaching the air cylinder to the radiator support and remove the air cylinder.
8. Remove bolts attaching the radiator, shroud and shutters to the radiator support and remove the radiator and shutter assembly.
9. Loosen the power steering pump retaining bolts and remove the drive belt.
10. Loosen the alternator retaining bolts and remove the drive belt.
11. Remove the crankshaft pulley (vibration damper).
12. Remove the water hose bracket from the timing gear cover.
13. Remove the timing gear cover retaining bolts and remove the cover.

Front Oil Seal Replacement

Use a remover and replacer tool to press the oil seal out of the timing gear cover. Use the same tool to press a new seal into the cover.

Installation

1. Clean the timing gear cover and the gasket surface of the timing gear housing.
2. Clean the crankshaft pulley seal surface.
3. Apply contact cement on the gear case gasket surface and install a new gasket.
4. Install the timing gear cover. Install the cover bolts and torque them to specifications in sequence.
5. Install the water hose and bracket on the timing gear cover.
6. Install the crankshaft pulley (vibration damper) on the crankshaft. Torque the bolts to specifications.
7. Install the water pump pulley, the fan drive belt and the power steering pump belt.
8. Install the radiator and shutter assemblies.
9. Install the shutter air cylinder on the radiator support.
10. Connect the shutter linkage to the air cylinder.
11. Install the fan and spacer assembly.
12. Adjust the tension on the fan and power steering pump drive belts to specifications.
13. Connect the upper and lower hoses to the radiator.
14. Fill the cooling system. Start the engine and idle for a short time. Check for coolant leaks and proper coolant level.
15. Install the hood assembly.

Timing Gear Replacement

B, C, F and N Series

1. Remove the timing gear cover, following the appropriate procedures under Timing Gear Cover Removal.
2. Hold the camshaft with special tool and unscrew the camshaft gear retaining bolt. Remove the camshaft gear from the camshaft.
3. Use a gear puller to remove the crankshaft gear.

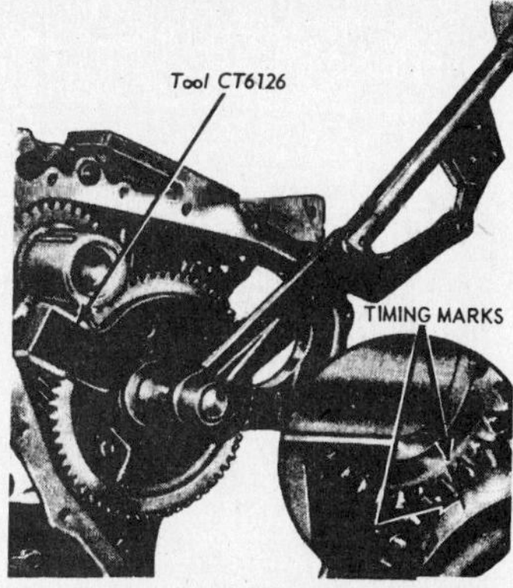

Removing or installing camshaft gear
(© Ford Motor Co.)

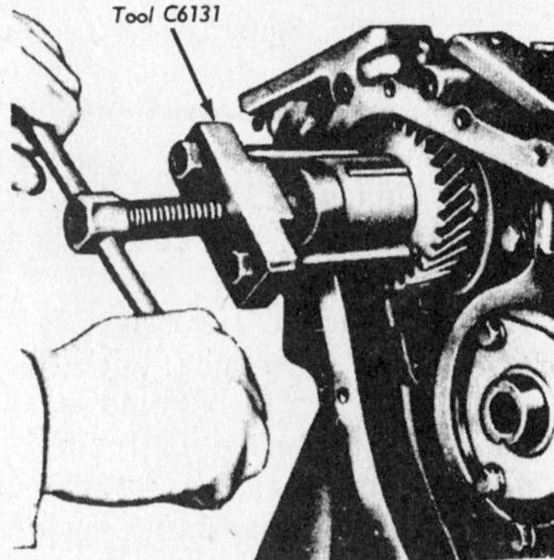

Removing crankshaft gear
(© Ford Motor Co.)

Installation

1. Install the crankshaft gear on the crankshaft.
2. Install the camshaft gear on the camshaft with the key and keyway aligned and the gear timing marks aligned with the auxiliary drive shaft gear and crankshaft gear timing marks.
3. Install the bolt, plain washer and a new lock washer in the camshaft and torque to specifications, while holding the camshaft. *Do not drive the gear on the camshaft; pull it on with the retaining bolts.*
4. Install the timing gear cover, following the procedures for B-, C-, F- or N-Series trucks under Timing Gear Cover Installation.

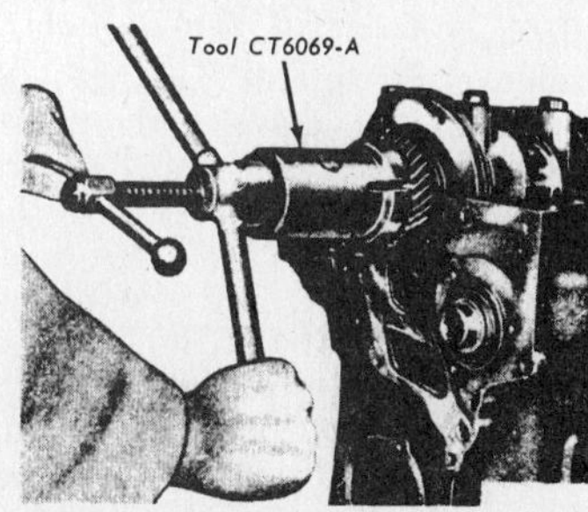

Installing crankshaft gear
(© Ford Motor Co.)

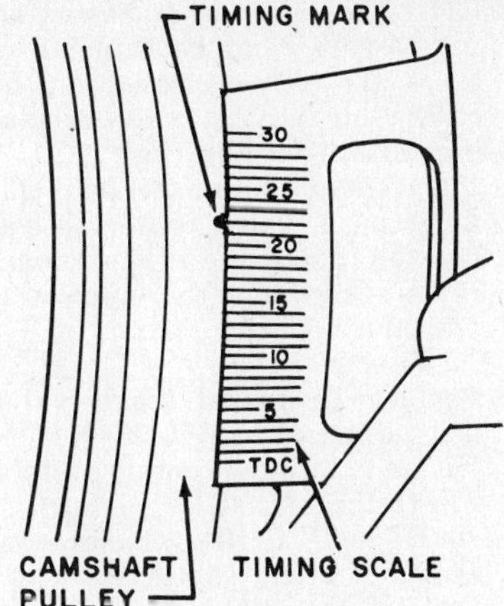

Timing marks 4-242 and 6-330 engines
(© Ford Motor Co.)

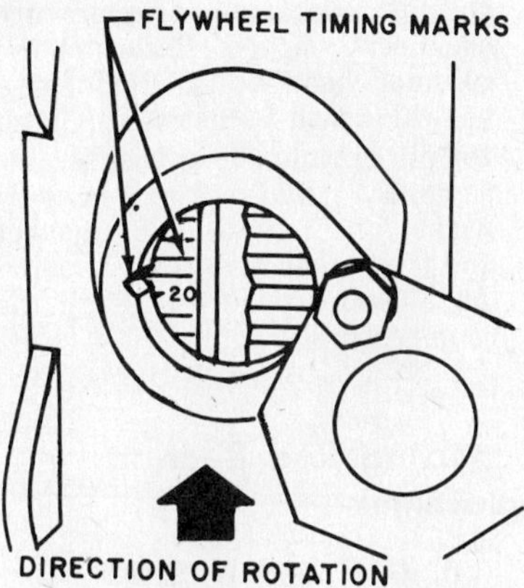

Timing marks 4-220 and 6-363 engines
(© Ford Motor Co.)

Pistons and Connecting Rods

Piston Removal

B-, C-, F- and N-Series

1. Drain the cooling system and the crankcase.
2. On B- and F-Series vehicles, disconnect the batteries.
3. On N-Series vehicles, remove the hood assembly.
4. Remove the air cleaner, exhaust and intake manifolds, valve rocker cover, valve rocker assembly, cylinder head, oil pan and oil pump following the procedures in this section for the pertinent B-, C-, F- or N-Series.
5. Remove any ridge and/or deposits from the upper portion of the cylinder liners as follows: Turn the crankshaft until the piston to be removed is at the bottom of its travel. Place a cloth on the piston head to collect the cuttings. Remove the ridge with a ridge cutter. Follow the instructions furnished by the tool manufacturer. *Never cut into the ring travel area in excess of specifications.*
6. Make sure all of the connecting rods and caps are marked so that they can be installed in their original locations. Remove the connecting rod cap.
7. Push the connecting rod and piston assembly out of the top of the cylinder with the handle end of a hammer. *Avoid damage to the crankshaft journal or the cylinder liner when removing the piston and connecting rod.*

Cleaning and Inspection

Remove the bearings from the rod and cap. Identify the bearings if they are to be used again. Clean the connecting rod in solvent, including the rod bore and the back of the inserts. *Do not use a caustic cleaning solution. Blow out all passages with compressed air.*

Remove deposits from the piston surfaces. Clean gum or varnish from the piston skirt, piston pins and rings with solvent. *Do not use a caustic cleaning solution or a wire brush to clean pistons.* Clean the ring grooves with a ring groove cleaner. Make sure the oil ring slots (or holes) are clean.

The connecting rods, pistons and related parts should be carefully inspected and checked for conformance to specifications.

Disassembly

1. Remove the bearing inserts from the connecting rod and cap.
2. Mark the pistons and pins to assure assembly with the same rod and installation in the same cylinder from which they were removed.
3. Remove the piston rings with a ring remover tool.
4. Remove the piston pin retainers and push out the pins. Immersing the piston in hot water will aid in removing the pins.
5. Clean the deposits and gum or varnish from the piston surfaces. Clean the ring grooves with a ring groove cleaner. Make sure the oil ring holes are clean.
6. Inspect the pistons for excessive wear, scoring, cracks, and erosion or detonation damage.

Assembly

1. Lubricate all parts with light engine oil.
2. Assemble the piston and connecting rod so the arrow on the piston and the word front on the connecting rod face the front of the engine. Position the rod between the piston pin bosses and press the piston pin into place. Install the piston pin retainer.
3. Install the piston rings on the piston. Check the ring side clearance.

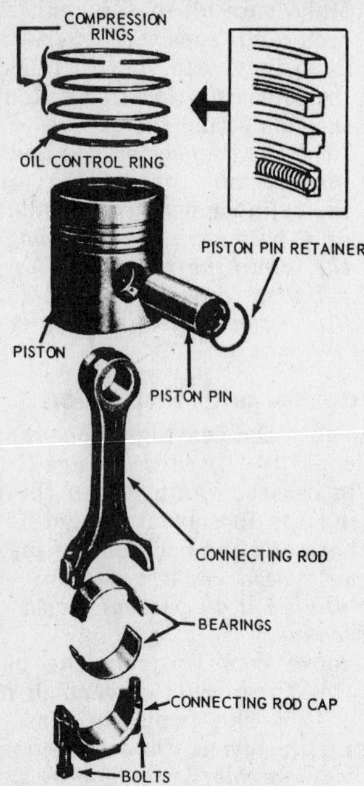

Piston and connecting rod assembly
(© Ford Motor Co.)

Installation

1. Install the lower rod bearing inserts.
2. Oil the piston rings, pistons and cylinder walls with light engine oil.
3. Be sure to install the pistons in the same cylinders from which they were removed, or to which they were fitted. The connecting rod and piston are correctly positioned when the arrow on the piston and the word *Front* on the connecting rod are toward the front of the engine.
4. Position the piston ring gaps equally around the piston, but not directly above the piston pin ends. Install the piston ring compressor on the piston.
5. Turn the crankshaft throw to the bottom of its stroke; then install the piston from the top of the block. Push the piston in with a hammer handle; then install the upper bearing insert. Push the piston and connecting rod downward until the connecting rod bearing insert seats on the crankshaft journal. Be sure to guide the connecting rod to avoid damaging the crankshaft journal.
6. Check the clearance of each bearing following the procedure under Connecting Rod Bearing Replacement.
7. After the bearings have been checked and found satisfactory, apply engine oil to the journals and bearings. Install the connecting rod cap. Torque the bolts to specifications.
8. After the piston and connecting rod assembly has been installed, check the side clearance of the connecting rod to make certain it is within specification.
9. Install the oil pump, oil pan, cylinder head, valve rocker assembly and intake and exhaust manifolds following the applicable procedures in this section for B-, C-, F- or N-Series.
10. Perform an initial (cold) valve lash adjustment.
11. Fill and bleed the cooling system. Fill the crankcase.
12. On B- and F-Series vehicles, connect the battery cables.
13. Operate the engine at idle for a short time. Check the coolant level and replenish if required. Continue to operate engine until normal operating temperature has been reached. Retorque the cylinder head bolts. Perform a hot valve lash adjustment. Check for oil, air and coolant leaks.
14. Clean the valve rocker arm cover gasket and install a new gasket and the rocker arm cover.
15. On N-Series vehicles, install the hood assembly.

Connecting Rod Bearing Replacement

B, C, F and N Series

When installing new bearings, check the clearance by using Plastigage as outlined in the following procedure.

1. Drain the crankcase. Remove the oil pan.
2. Turn the crankshaft until the connecting rod journal for the connecting rod to which new bearings are to be fitted is at BDC. Remove the connecting rod cap and push the piston and rod part way up the cylinder.
3. Remove the bearings from the connecting rod and cap. Clean the crankshaft journal and the connecting rod and cap.
4. Install the new standard size bearings in the connecting rod and cap. Pull the connecting rod assembly down firmly on the crankshaft journal.
5. Place a piece of Plastigage on the lower bearing surface, the full width of the cap and about ¼ inch off center.
6. Install the cap and torque the connecting rod nuts to specification. *Do not turn the crankshaft while the Plastigage is in place.*
7. Remove the cap; then using the Plastigage scale, check the width of the Plastigage. When checking the width of the Plastigage, check at the widest point in order to get the minimum clearance. Check at the narrowest point, in order to get the maximum clearance. The difference between the two readings is the taper.

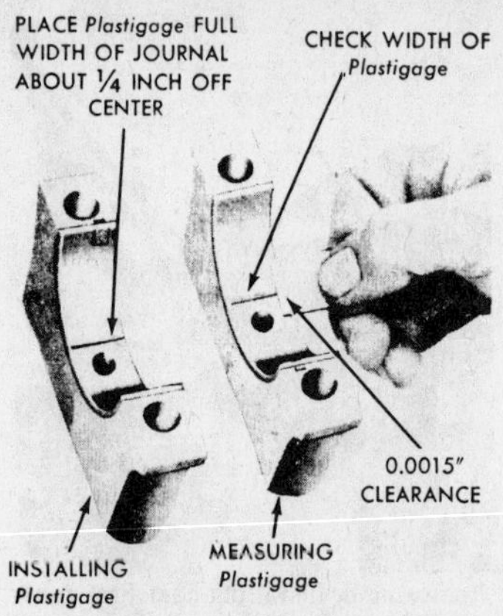

Installing and measuring plastigage in typical bearing cap
(© Ford Motor Co.)

8. If the standard bearings do not bring the clearance within the specified limits, remove the crankshaft, and refinish the connecting rod journal. Then install an undersize bearing. Check the side clearance of the connecting rod to make certain it is within specification.
9. After the bearing has been fitted, clean the Plastigage from the crankshaft journal and bearing. Apply engine oil to the journal and bearings; then install the connecting rod cap. Torque the rod nuts to specifications.
10. Repeat the procedure for the remaining connecting rods that require new bearings.
11. Install the oil pan following the procedure outlined under Oil Pan Installation, B-, C-, F- or N-Series.
12. Fill the crankcase with the proper grade of lubricant. Operate the engine at fast idle and check for oil leaks.

Main Bearing Replacement

B, C, F and N Series

1. Remove the oil pan.
2. Remove the oil pump, spacer and pickup tube.
3. Remove the main bearing cap. Remove and discard the seals from the rear cap. *Replace one bearing at a time, leaving the other bearings securely fastened.*
4. Insert an upper main bearing removal tool in the oil hole in the crankcase. Rotate the crankshaft in the direction of engine rotation to force the bearing out of the block. Remove the bearing insert from the cap.
5. Clean the crankshaft journal and bearing cap.

6. Check the crankshaft thrust face for excessive wear or nicked or pitted surface.
7. *Install new, standard size main bearings for a Plastigage check.* To install the upper main bearing, place the plain end of the bearing over the shaft on the locking tang side of the block. Using tool in the oil hole in the crankshaft, rotate the crankshaft in the opposite direction of engine rotation until the bearing seats itself. Remove the tool.
8. Support the crankshaft so that its weight will not compress the Plastigage and provide an erroneous reading. Position the support so that it will bear against the counterweight adjoining the bearing which is being checked.
9. Position a bearing in the bearing cap. Place a piece of Plastigage on the bearing surface the full width of the bearing cap and 1/4 inch off center.
10. Install the cap and torque the bolts to specification. *Do not turn the crankshaft while the Plastigage is in place.*
11. Remove the cap; then, using the Plastigage scale, check the width of the Plastigage. When checking the width of the Plastigage, check at the widest point in order to get the minimum clearance. Check at the narrowest point in order to get the maximum clearance. The difference between the two readings is the taper.
12. If the standard bearings do not bring the clearance within specified limits, remove the crankshaft, and refinish the crankshaft journal; then install an undersize bearing.
13. After the bearing has been fitted, clean off the Plastigage and apply engine oil to the bearing and journal. Install a new rear oil seal in the rear cap and trim the ends of the seal. Install the bearing cap, using new lock plates.
14. Torque the bolts to specifications. Bend the tabs on the lock plates to secure the bolts.
15. Repeat the procedure for the remaining bearings that require replacement.
16. Check crankshaft end play by installing a dial indicator so that the contact point rests against a crankshaft flange and the indicator axis is parallel to the crankshaft axis.
17. Force the crankshaft toward the rear of the engine. Set the dial on zero. Push the crankshaft forward and note the reading on the dial.
18. If the end play exceeds specifications, replace the thrust washers with oversize washers which are available to obtain correct end play.
19. Install the oil pump and pick-up tube.
20. Install the oil pan.
21. Fill the crankcase with the proper grade of lubricant. Start the engine and check for oil leaks.

Crankshaft Rear Oil Seal Replacement

To replace the crankshaft rear oil seal, it is necessary to remove the engine from the vehicle and install it on a work stand.

Oil Pan Removal

1. Drain the engine crankcase.
2. Loosen the retaining bracket and remove the dipstick and dipstick tube.
3. On N-Series vehicles, remove the hood assembly. On C-Series, tilt the cab forward. On B- and F-Series vehicles, remove the clutch equalizer arm bracket at the cylinder block.
4. Disconnect the air compressor return line at the crankcase. Remove the alternator bracket from the cylinder block and position it out of the way.
5. Remove the engine front support bracket, bolts, washers and nuts. Using an overhead hoist attached to the engine front lifting bracket, lift the engine just enough to remove the engine front support bracket. Remove the bolts and nuts retaining the front support insulator bracket to the frame crossmember, and remove the insulator bracket.
6. Remove the oil pan retaining bolts and remove the oil pan.

Installation

1. Clean the oil pan, oil pump pickup tube screen, and all gasket and seal surfaces on the underside of the engine crankcase.

Check the crankcase vent assembly for looseness. If it is loose, remove it and clean all oil and dirt from the contact areas. Apply Loctite sealer to the contact areas and install the vent assembly. If the vent assembly is excessively loose, install an oversize vent assembly.

2. Apply a coating of contact cement and position new gaskets on the oil pan. Install new oil pan gaskets on the cylinder block so the end of the pan gasket laps *over* the lip of the rear main bearing seal and the front end of the pan gasket will lay *under* the lip of the pan front seal.
3. If a new oil pan is being installed, remove the crankcase vent assembly from the old oil pan. Clean all dirt and oil from the contact areas. Apply Loctite sealer and install the vent tube in the new oil pan. If the vent tube assembly fits too loosely, install an oversize vent assembly.
4. Carefully position the oil pan on the engine crankcase and install the oil pan bolts. Torque the bolts in sequence to specifications.
5. Install the front support insulator bracket on the frame cross-member. Install the insulators and engine front support bracket. Lower the engine, and torque all bolts and nuts to specifications. Remove the hoist from the engine. On N-Series vehicles with air brakes, connect the air line on the support, and connect the compressor return line at the crankcase. On B- and F- Series vehicles, install the clutch equalizer arm bracket at the cylinder block.
6. Install the alternator and alternator bracket on the cylinder block. Adjust the drive belt tension to specifications.
7. Install the oil level dipstick tube and dipstick.
8. Fill the crankcase with the recommended engine oil.
9. On N-Series vehicles, install the hood assembly. On C-Series vehicles, lower the cab and secure the cab locks.
10. Start the engine and check for oil leaks.

Oil Pump Removal

1. Remove the oil pan.
2. Remove the oil pump pickup tube and screen assembly from the oil pump.

Installation

1. Clean the oil pump and cylinder block mounting surfaces. Clean the oil pump pickup tube and screen assembly.
2. Position the oil pump and spacer to the cylinder block, and install and tighten the mounting bolts.
3. Install the oil pump pickup tube and screen assembly on the oil pump.
4. Install the oil pan.

GMC (Detroit) 2-Cycle Diesel Engines

Index

GENERAL SPECIFICATIONS

ENGINE MODEL	BORE & STROKE	PISTON DISP. CU. IN.	HORSEPOWER @ R.P.M.	TORQUE @ R.P.M.	FIRING ORDER* RIGHT HAND ROTATION	FIRING ORDER* LEFT HAND ROTATION	GOVERNOR SPEED NO LOAD	IDLE SPEED R.P.M.
3-53	3.875 x 4.50	159	81 @ 2500	200 @ 1500	1-3-2	1-2-3	**	450
4-53	3.875 x 4.50	212	122 @ 2500	271 @ 1500	1-3-4-2	1-2-4-3	**	450
6V-53	3.875 x 4.50	319	171 @ 2500	423 @ 1500	△	△	**	450
3-71	4.250 x 5.00	213	102 @ 2500	277 @ 1400	1-3-2	1-2-3	2100	385-400
4-71	4.250 x 5.00	284	143 @ 2100	375 @ 1600	1-3-4-2	1-2-4-3	2150	385-400
4-71E	4.250 x 5.00	284	140 @ 2100	375 @ 1600	1-3-4-2	1-2-4-3	2150	385-400
4-71SE	4.250 x 5.00	284	140 @ 2100	375 @ 1600	1-3-4-2	1-2-4-3	2150	385-400
4-71T	4.250 x 5.00	284	171 @ 2300	411 @ 1600	1-3-4-2	1-2-4-3	2450	385-400
6-71E	4.250 x 5.00	426	219 @ 2100	574 @ 1600	1-5-3-6-2-4	1-4-2-6-3-5	2150	385-400
6-71N	4.250 x 5.00	426	218 @ 2100	605 @ 1200	1-5-3-6-2-4	1-4-2-6-3-5	2340	400
6-71SE	4.250 x 5.00	426	210 @ 2100	575 @ 1600	1-5-3-6-2-4	1-4-2-6-3-5	2150	385-400
6-71T	4.250 x 5.00	426	235 @ 2100	630 @ 1600	1-5-3-6-2-4	1-4-2-6-3-5	2150	385-400
6V-71	4.250 x 5.00	426	210 @ 2100	565 @ 1200	△	△	2340	550
6V-71N	4.250 x 5.00	426	218 @ 2100	605 @ 1200	△	△	2340	550
8V-71	4.250 x 5.00	567	280 @ 2100	750 @ 1200	△	△	2340	550
8V-71N	4.250 x 5.00	567	270 @ 2100	760 @ 1200	△	△	2340	550

* Rotation is determined by standing at front of engine, if crankshaft rotates clockwise engine is right hand rotation, and specified as "R" model. If rotation is counterclockwise engine is left hand rotation, and specified as "L" model.

** Designated on unit name plate.

△ Firing order designated on engine decal.

CRANKSHAFT AND BEARING SPECIFICATIONS

ENGINE SERIES	MAIN BEARING JOURNAL DIAMETER	MAIN BEARING CLEARANCE	SHAFT END THRUST ON BEARING NO.	SHAFT END PLAY	ROD BEARING JOURNAL DIAMETER	ROD BEARING CLEARANCE
53	2.999-3.000	.0013-.0042	Rear	.004-.011	2.449-2.500	.0015-.0045
V-53	3.499-3.000	.0025-.0057	Rear	.004-.011	2.749-2.750	.0017-.0046
71	3.499-3.000	.0014-.0044	Rear	.004-.011	2.749-2.750	.0014-.0044
V-71	4.499-4.500	.0012-.0046	Rear	.004-.011	2.999-3.000	.0014-.0044

PISTONS, PINS, RINGS SPECIFICATIONS

ENGINE SERIES	PISTON CLEARANCE TOP OF SKIRT	PISTON CLEARANCE BOTTOM OF SKIRT	PISTON PIN DIAMETER	PISTON TO PIN BUSHING CLEARANCE	RING END GAP COMP.	RING END GAP OIL	CYLINDER LINER INSIDE DIAMETER
53, V53	.0052-.0083	.0052-.0083	1.3746-1.3750	.0025-.0034	.020-.046	.010-.025	3.8752-3.8767
71, V71	.004-.0078	.004-.0078	1.4996-1.5000	.0025-.0034	.018-.043	.008-.023	4.2495-4.2511
V-711 & 71T	.006-.0098	.006-.0098	1.4996-1.5000	.0025-.0034	.018-.043	.008-.023	4.2495-4.2511

ENGINE TORQUE SPECIFICATIONS

ENGINE SERIES	CYLINDER HEAD FT. LBS. CAST IRON BLOCK NUTS	CYLINDER HEAD FT. LBS. CAST IRON BLOCK BOLTS	MAIN BEARING BOLTS FT. LBS.	CONN. ROD BOLTS FT. LBS.	ROCKER SHAFT FT. LBS.	VALVE BRIDGE GUIDE FT. LBS.	CRANKSHAFT END BOLT FT. LBS.
53	170-180	——	120-130	40-45	50-55	——	——
V-53	170-180	——	120-130	25-30	50-55	——	——
71	165-175*	180-190	180-190▲	65-75	90-100	46-50	180-200
V-71	165-175	180-190	180-190	65-75	90-100	46-50	180-200

* Aluminum block nuts 140-160.

▲ Aluminum block 120-140.

FIRING ORDER AND ROTATION

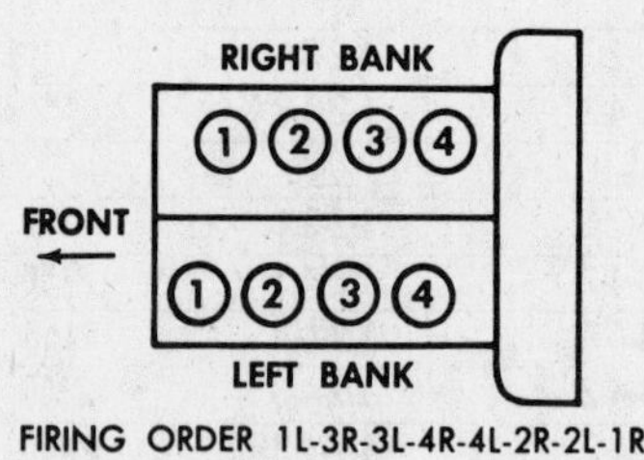

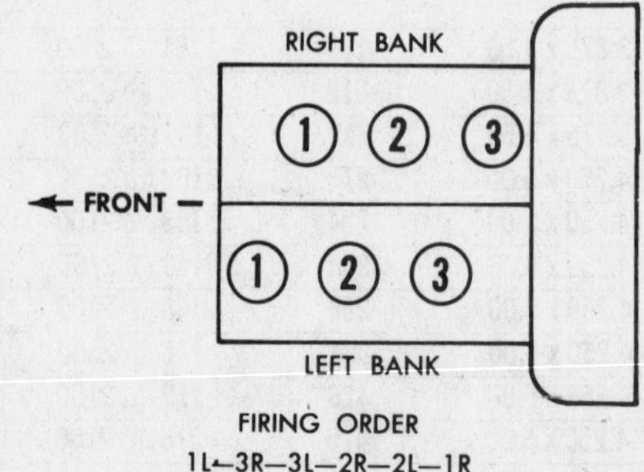

Trouble Diagnosis

The satisfactory performance of a Diesel engine depends on two items of foremost importance, (1) Sufficiently high compression pressure, and (2) The injection of the proper amount of fuel at the right time.

The first one of these items depends entirely on pistons, piston rings, valves and valve operating mechanism; the second item depends on injectors and their operating mechanism, and fuel system.

Lack of engine power, uneven running, excessive vibration, and tendency to stall when idling may be caused by either a compression loss or faulty injector operation.

The causes of trouble symptoms may be varied; therefore a hit-and-miss search should be avoided. A proper diagnosis of symptoms is an orderly process of diagnosing the symptoms. An "orderly process" means to check the most probable common cause first; then proceed with the next probable cause.

Hard Starting R.M.P.

1. Poor or shorted electrical connections.
2. Undercharged or defective battery.
3. Low ambient temperature—use starting aid.
4. Faulty starter or loose starter connections.
5. Infrequent oil changes—change oil.

Low Compression

1. Exhaust valves sticking or burned.
2. Compression rings worn or broken.
3. Cylinder head gasket leaking.
4. Improper valve clearance adjustment.
5. Blower not functioning.
6. Emergency shutoff valve partially clogged or completely closed.

Fuel Problems

1. Injector racks not in full position.
2. Fuel tank or fuel filter empty.
3. Improper grade and type fuel.
4. Diluted fuel.
5. Improperly filtered or restricted fuel flow.
6. Air in fuel system.
7. Faulty fuel pump.

Uneven Running or Frequent Stalling

1. Cylinders cutting out due to incorrect valve adjustment.
2. Insufficient fuel supply.
3. Faulty injectors.
4. Improper injector timing.
5. Incorrect rack setting.
6. Injector tip spray leaks.
7. Cylinder pressures low.
8. Governor instability.
9. Binding injector rack.
10. Faulty adjustments—perform tune up.
11. Improper grade and type of fuel.
12. Diluted fuel.
13. Improperly filtered or restricted fuel flow.

Detonation

1. Oil picked up by air stream.
2. Clogged fuel filter.
3. Accumulation in air box.
4. Defective blower to cylinder block gasket.
5. Leaking blower oil seals.
6. Low coolant temperature.
7. Faulty injectors.
8. Improper injector timing.
9. Injector check valve leaking.
10. Injector spray tip holes enlarged.
11. Broken injector spray tip.

Lack of Power

1. Governor gap setting incorrect.
2. Rack setting incorrect.
3. Injector timing incorrect.
4. Valve clearance incorrect.
5. Insufficient fuel.
6. Air cleaners damaged or clogged.
7. Cylinder liner air inlet ports clogged.
8. Low engine compression.
9. Blower air intake obstructed.
10. Excessive exhaust rack pressure.

General Information

The Diesel engine is an internal combustion power unit, in which the heat of fuel is converted into work in the cylinder of the engine.

Diesel engines differ from gasoline engines principally in the method used to introduce and ignite the fuel. Gasoline engines draw a mixture of fuel and air through the carburetor into the combustion chamber, where it is compressed, then ignited by an electric spark. In the Diesel engines, air alone is compressed in the cylinder; then, a charge of fuel is sprayed into the cylinder, after the air has been compressed, and ignition is accomplished by the heat of compression.

The 2-Cycle Engine

In the two-cycle engine, intake and exhaust take place during part of the compression and power strokes as shown in illustrations. A two-cycle engine, therefore, does not function as an air pump, so an external means of supplying the air is provided. A specially designed blower, on the top of the engine, forces cleaned air into

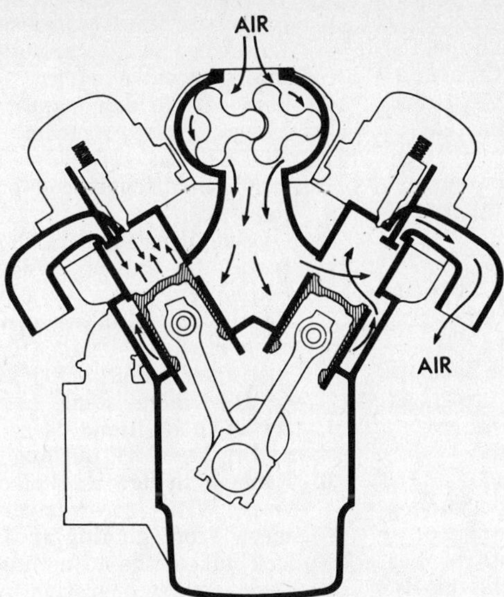

AIR ENTERING COMBUSTION CHAMBER THROUGH CYLINDER LINER PORTS

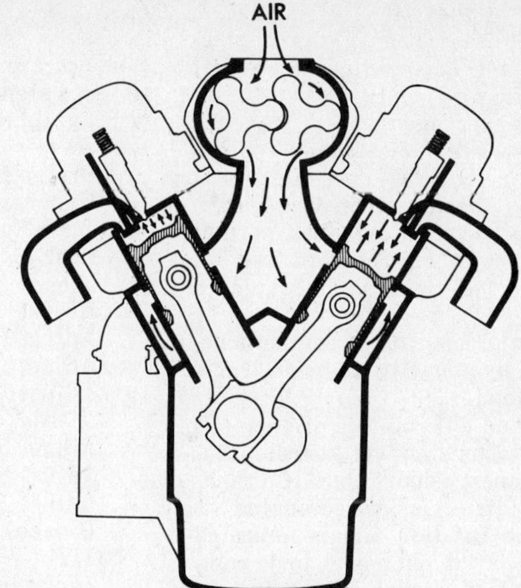

AIR BEING COMPRESSED WITH THE EXHAUST VALVE CLOSED

Operation of GM Detroit two cycle diesel engine (© G.M.C.)

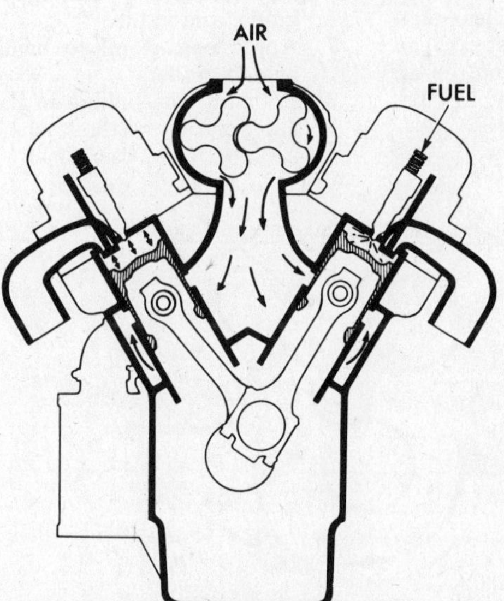

CHARGE OF FUEL BEING INJECTED INTO COMBUSTION CHAMBER

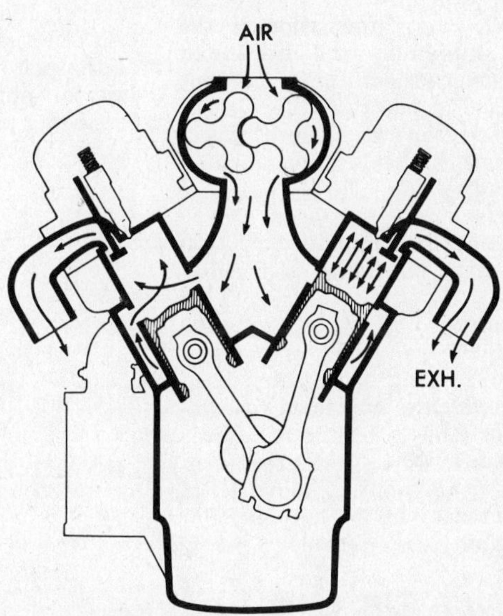

EXHAUST TAKING PLACE AND CYLINDER ABOUT TO BE SWEPT WITH CLEAN SCAVENGING AIR

Operation of GM Detroit two cycle diesel engine (© G.M.C.)

the cylinders to expel the exhaust gases and fill the cylinders with fresh air for combustion.

A series of ports cut into the circumference of the cylinder wall (liner), above the piston, in its lowest position, admits air from the blower into the cylinder when top face of piston uncovers the ports. The swirling flow of air toward the exhaust valve produces a scavenging effect, leaving the cylinders full of clean air when the piston rises and covers the inlet ports.

As piston continues on upward stroke, exhaust valve close and the charge of fresh air is subjected to the final compression. Air in cylinder is heated to approximately 1000°F. while being compressed.

Shortly before the piston reaches its highest position, the required amount of fuel is sprayed into the combustion space by the unit fuel injector. The intense heat generated during the high compression of the air ignites the fine fuel spray immediately, and the combustion continues as long as the fuel spray lasts. The resulting pressure forces the piston downward to provide a power stroke.

As piston nears the bottom of the downward stroke, exhaust valves are opened and burnt gases are released. Still further downward movements of piston uncovers liner ports and cycle is repeated.

This entire combustion cycle is completed in each cylinder for each revolution of the crankshaft, or, in other words, two strokes; hence, the "two stroke cycle."

Diesel Engine Data

Engine model and serial number are stamped on cylinder block at right side near rear end plate.

When ordering engine parts, order by part number and description, and refer to engine model and serial numbers.

Right and left rotation of engine is

indicated by the letters "R" or "L" in the model designation. Truck engines are "R" and coach engines are left "L" rotation.

Certain arrangement of standard accessories are indicated by the letters "A," "B," "C" or "D." Both truck and coach engines are identified by the letter "C," indicating that the starter is on the left and oil cooler on the right as indicated in figure.

Right and left side of engine is determined by standing at rear (transmission) end.

Right and left rotation of engine is determined by standing at front (opposite transmission) end. If crankshaft rotates clockwise engine is right-hand rotation and is indicated by the letter "R" in model, or if rotation is anti-clockwise engine is left-hand rotation and is indicated by the letter "L" in model.

Minimum and Maximum Engine RPM

The following information is the approved minimum and maximum full-load governor setting for current engines used in truck models. Do not permit engine operation with governor settings higher than indicated for full load setting.

Trucks

Maximum (Full Range) 2100
Maximum (Dual Range Reduced Speed) 1900
Minimum 400

NOTE: Above RPM are taken from blower using tachometer head -1549207 which is corrected to compensate for 2.05 to 1 ratio of blower to crankshaft. When corrected tachometer is not available, above RPM can be increased by 5%, or 50 RPM per thousand.

Tune Up and Adjustments

Engine Tune-Up

NOTE: Before tune-up procedure is started it is important that air cleaners and fuel filters are serviced as described in applicable maintenance manuals. Crankcase breather tube and air box drains must be clean and unobstructed. Air box drains may be cleaned with compressed air.

CAUTION: Remove or at least loosen air box hand hole cover, otherwise blower or end plate gaskets may be damaged by excessive air pressure.

Tune-Up Procedures

To completely tune-up an engine, all adjustments except bridge balancing adjustment and exhaust valve cold setting must be performed only after engine has reached its normal operating temperature.

Results obtained from an engine tune-up are usually unsatisfactory, unless a step-by-step, systematic, and orderly approach is used. Proceed in the following sequence:

1. Bridge Balancing Adjustment
2. Exhaust Valve Lash Adjustment
3. Time Fuel Injectors
4. Back-out Buffer Screw
5. Loosen Throttle Delay Cylinder
6. Adjust Idle Speed-Preliminary
7. Adjust Low Speed Gap
8. Adjust Injector Control Racks
9. Adjust Maximum No-Load Speeds
10. Adjust Idle Speed—Final
11. Adjust Buffer Screw
12. Adjust Throttle Delay Cylinder (Coach)

NOTE: Whenever a push rod has been disconnected from the clevis, the push rod must be screwed back into place until end of push rod appears through the clevis. If this is not done, the piston may hit the head of the valve when the engine is being turned, due to the small clearance, between the valves and piston head at the piston's upper position, or an injector plunger may "Bottom" before being properly adjusted.

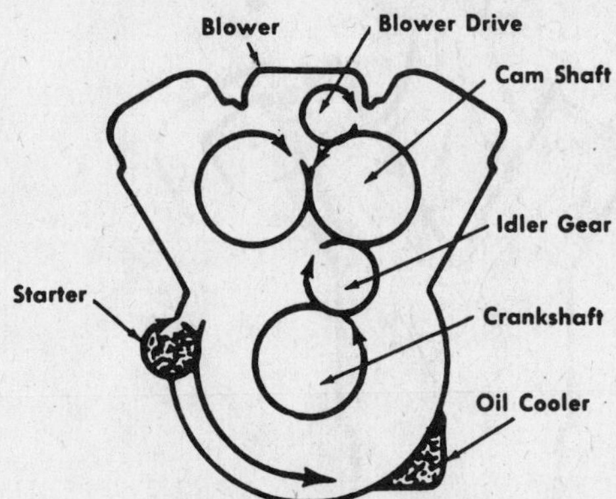

MODEL RC (TRUCK)
Engine rotation and accessory location
(© G.M.C.)

Clearance between exhaust valve stem and bridge with engine at operating temperature is important and should be maintained. Too little clearance causes a loss of compression, misfiring of cylinders and eventual burning of valves and valve seats. Too much clearance results in noisy operation of the engine, especially in the low speed range.

Bridge Balancing Adjustment

The exhaust valve bridge assembly is adjusted and the adjustment screw locked securely at the time the cylinder head is installed on the engine. Until wear occurs with the operation of the engine, no further adjustment is required on the exhaust valve bridge.

1. Remove injector fuel jumper lines, then remove rocker arm shaft brackets. Lift rocker arms and swing back to provide accessibility to valve bridge.
2. Remove bridge and spring (when used) from guide. NOTE: Use of bridge springs has been discontinued on latest engines.
3. Loosen adjusting screw lock nut.
4. Install bridge on bridge guide without spring.
5. Press straight down on the pallet surface of bridge. Turn adjusting screw until it just touches the valve stem, then turn screw an additional 1/8 to 1/4 turn and tighten lock nut finger.
6. Remove bridge and place in a vise. With screwdriver, hold screw from turning and tighten lock nut on the adjusting screw. Complete the operation by tightening the lock nut to 25 ft. lbs. torque, being sure that screw does not turn. IMPORTANT: Do not tighten while on engine, as binding may damage bridge, guide, and valve.
7. Apply engine oil to bridge and bridge guide.
8. Reinstall the bridge in its original position without the bridge spring.
9. Place a .0015" feeler under each end of the bridge. NOTE: Feeler used at inner end of bridge must be narrow enough to fit in bridge locating groove. Pressing down on the pallet surface of the bridge, both feelers must be tight. If both feelers are not tight, readjust the screw as previously instructed.
10. Remove the bridge and reinstall in its original position with the bridge spring (when used) in place.
11. Adjust remaining bridges as instructed in previous paragraphs.
12. If cylinder head has been removed, reinstall on the engine. Tighten cylinder head stud nuts to their specified torque before assembling the rocker shaft

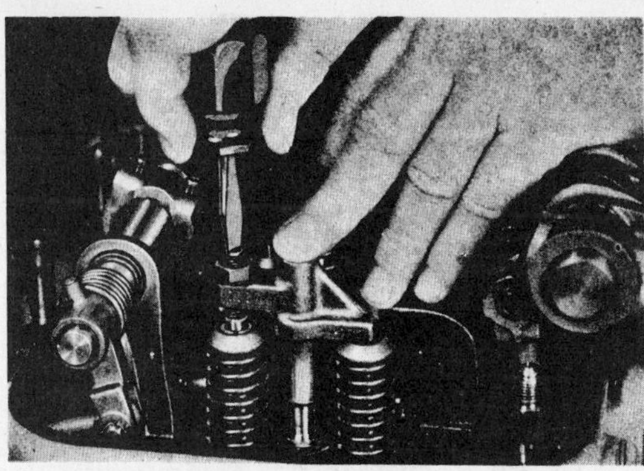

Adjusting valve bridge
(© G.M.C.)

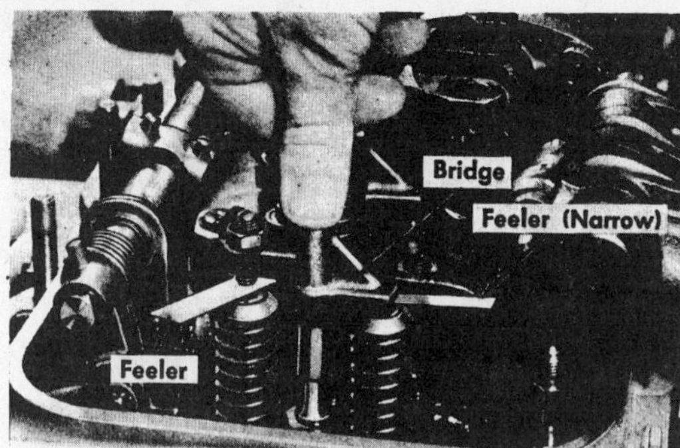

Valve bridge adjustment check
(© G.M.C.)

brackets to the head.

13. Install the rocker arm assemblies, *being sure valve bridges are properly positioned on the inner valve stems.*
14. Tighten rocker shaft bracket bolts to their recommended torque.
15. Reconnect fuel jumper lines to injectors and connectors.

Valve Lash Adjustment

Valve lash adjustment must always be made with the engine COLD. Cold setting is .015″ GO—.017″ NO GO; hot setting is .013″ GO—.015″ NO GO.

All valves may be lashed in firing order sequence during one full revolution of the crankshaft.

Valve lash must always be adjusted at the push rod. Do not disturb bridge adjusting screw.

1. Place governor throttle control lever in the NO FUEL position.
2. Rotate crankshaft until the injector follower is fully depressed on the cylinder being adjusted.
3. Loosen valve push rod lock nut.
4. Place .017″ feeler gauge between valve stem and valve bridge adjusting screw on engines with bridge spring, or between bridge and rocker arm on engines not using bridge spring. Adjust push rod to obtain a smooth "pull" on the feeler gauge.
5. Remove feeler gauge. Hold push rod with wrench and tighten push rod lock nut.
6. Check and adjust remaining valves in manner described in previous paragraphs.
7. With engine at operating temperature (160°F. to 180°F.), recheck clearances. At this time, a .013″ feeler gauge should pass between the end of the valve stem and the adjusting screw on the bridge (or between rocker arm and the bridge), and a .015" feeler gauge should not pass through. Readjust push rod if necessary.

Injector Timing

To properly time the injector, the injector follower-guide must be adjusted to a definite height.

1. Set governor control lever in the NO FUEL (off) position.
2. Turn engine crankshaft manually or by means of the starter, until the exhaust valve rocker arms are fully depressed, for that particular cylinder.
3. The injector is identified by a colored tab stamped onto the injector body. Injector is timed with 1.460″ gauge.
4. Place the injector timing gauge in the hole provided on top of the injector body with one of the "flats" toward the injector.
5. Adjust the injector rocker arm by loosening lock nut and turning the push rod with an end wrench, until the bottom of the timing guage head will just pass over (drag lightly) the top of the injector follower guide.
6. Hold push rod from turning and tighten lock nut. Recheck adjustment with injector timing gauge and readjust if necessary.

Governor Adjustments

Governor used on these engines is a limiting speed double weight type, which controls the right and left injector control racks.

Following adjustments must be performed in the sequence given, but not until valves and injectors are in proper adjustment as previously described.

IMPORTANT: Tachometer drive ratio at blower is 2.05 times engine speed and rotation is counterclockwise. Make allowances accordingly or use corrected tachometer head when performing engine tune-up procedures.

Idle Speed Adjustment

1. Remove governor high speed spring cover to governor housing.
2. Start engine and operate at idle speed while observing RPM at tachometer.
3. To adjust, loosen lock nut and turn idle adjusting screw IN to increase or OUT to decrease speed. Lock adjusting screw with lock nut when idling speed is approximately 15 RPM below desired setting.

Low Speed Spring Gap Adjustment

When necessary to adjust, proceed as follows:

1. Remove governor control housing cover.
2. Start engine and run engine at 800-1000 RPM by manual operation of the differential lever. WARNING: Do not overspeed engine.
3. Measure gap between low speed spring cap and plunger. If gap is not between .001″ to .002″, loosen lock nut and turn adjusting screw as necessary to obtain desired gap. Tighten lock nut, then recheck gap.
4. Stop engine, then reinstall governor control housing cover and lever assembly to governor housing.

Positioning Injector Racks

The position of the injector control racks must be properly adjusted in relation to the governor.

The letters R or L indicate injector location in right or left cylinder bank when viewed from rear of engine.

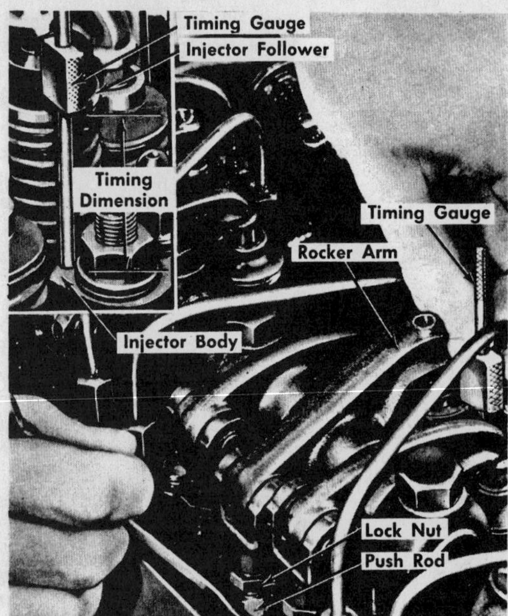

Timing fuel injector
(© G.M.C.)

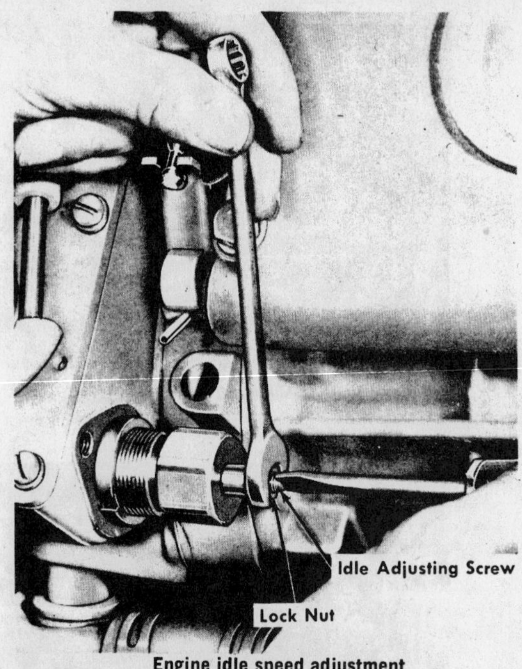

Engine idle speed adjustment
(© G.M.C.)

Cylinders are numbered starting at front of the engine.

1. Disconnect any linkage attached to the governor throttle contol lever.
2. Loosen idle speed adjusting screw until ½″ of threads project from lock nut.
3. Remove rocker covers from cylinder heads.
4. Loosen all inner and outer injector control rack adjusting screws in right and left cylinder bank. Be sure all injector rack control levers are free on the injector control tubes. NOTE: On coaches equipped with Hydraulic transmission, loosen two nuts attaching throttle delay clamp to injector control tube.
5. Move governor throttle control lever to FULL FUEL position and hold in that position with light finger pressure. Turn *inner* adjusting screw of #1L injector rack control lever until clevis pin binds, then tighten *outer* adjustinf screw. NOTE: When the setting is correct, the injector rack will be snug on the pin of the rack control lever and still maintain a snug (not loose or tight) fit at clevis pin, while throttle is in FULL FUEL position and inner and outer adjusting screws are tight.
6. At right bank, repeat procedure previously described in paragraph 5 for left bank.
7. Set #2 and #3 injector racks to #1 rack for their respective heads.
8. Turn idle speed adjusting screw in until it projects 3/16″ from the lock nut, so to permit starting the engine.

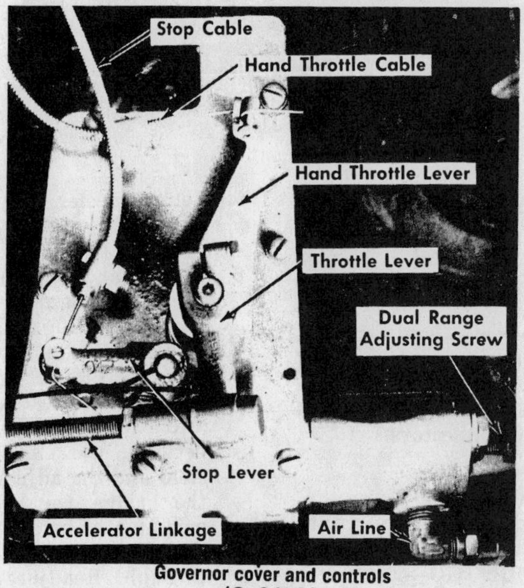

Stop Cable
Hand Throttle Cable
Hand Throttle Lever
Throttle Lever
Dual Range Adjusting Screw
Stop Lever
Accelerator Linkage
Air Line

Governor cover and controls
(© G.M.C.)

High Speed No-Load Adjustment

Some governors are equipped with a device for reducing the engine RPM when in transmission or rear axle high speeds. These governors are referred to as "Dual Range Type" and are used on some truck engines.

Except Dual Range

1. Loosen the high speed spring retainer lock nut using a spanner wrench.
2. Start engine and operate at maximum speed, while observing engine RPM at tachometer.
3. Turn high speed adjuster IN to increase or OUT to decrease speed until desired no-load setting is obtained.
4. Hold adjuster, then tighten lock nut, using spanner wrench.
5. Recheck and if necessary readjust after tightening lock nut.

Dual Range

Two types of pistons have been used on Dual Range governors. Early type incorporated a piston with a threaded sleeve, while latest type sleeve is positioned in piston by a shim pack.

Maximum High Speed Adjustment

(Early Type)

1. Start engine and operate at full speed. Be sure air is supplied to

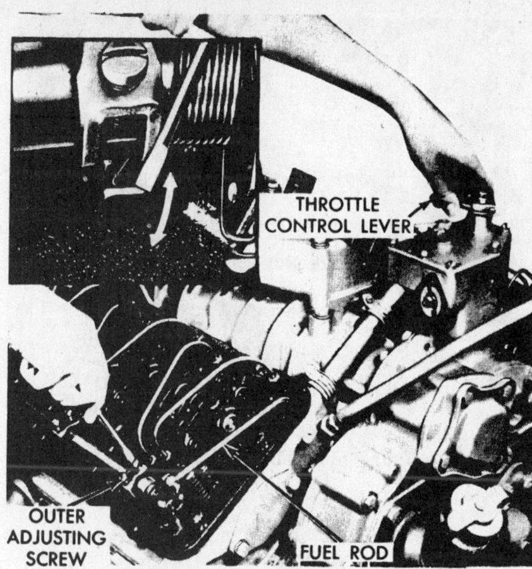

Adjusting No. 3L injector rack control lever
(© G.M.C.)

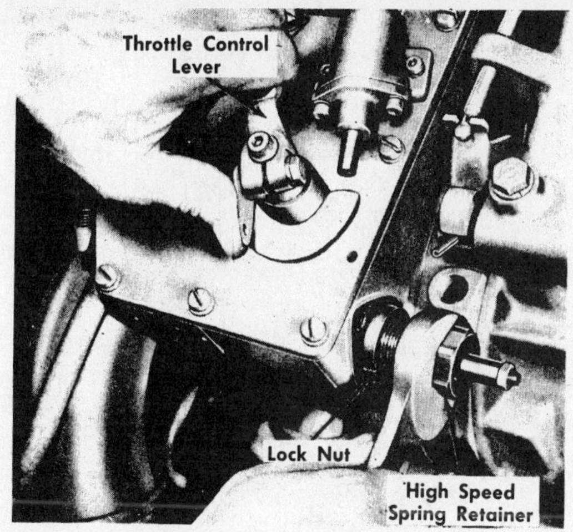

Engine high speed no-load adjustment
(except dual range)
(© G.M.C.)

governor. No load speed is 125-150 RPM above full load speed.

2. Remove two bolts attaching piston housing to governor control housing. Then remove housing and piston assembly.
3. Remove piston and sleeve assembly with seal ring from piston housing.
4. Measure distance from end of piston to end of sleeve. This dimension should be approximately 25/32″.
5. Should it be necessary to increase engine RPM the dimension should be increased. Also, when necessary to decrease engine RPM the dimension should be decreased. NOTE: Each full turn of piston and sleeve will change engine approximately 100 RPM.
6. Install piston and sleeve assembly in piston housing, then install piston housing to governor control housing.
7. Check for proper setting and readjust as necessary.

Reduced High Speed Adjustment

(Early Type)

1. Disconnect wire at governor air supply solenoid so as to prevent air reaching governor.
2. Start engine and operate at full speed while observing RPM at tachometer. Proper adjustment is approximately 200 RPM below maximum no-load speed.
3. Loosen lock nut and turn adjusting screw as necessary to obtain proper reduced high speed RPM. Lock screw with nut when proper adjustment is obtained.
4. Should it be necessary to increase engine RPM turn adjusting bolt in to increase, or out to decrease engine RPM.
5. Reconnect wire at solenoid when adjustment is completed.

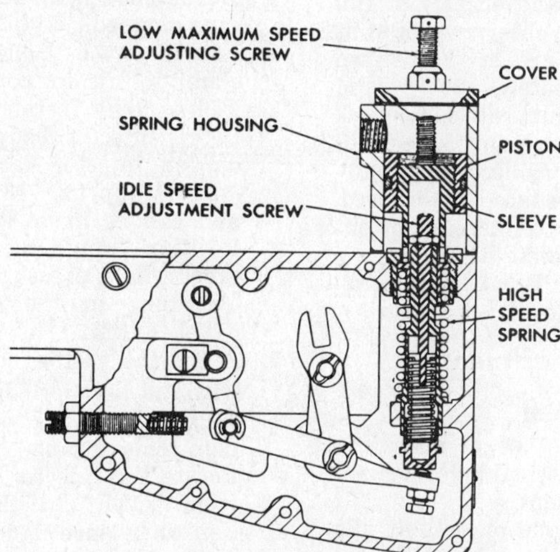

Dual range governor (early type)
(© G.M.C.)

Maximum High Speed Adjustment

(Late Type)

1. Start with a pack of four .100″ and then .010″ shims. Turn low maximum speed screw out until it extends 1¼″.
2. Disconnect air line so as to prevent air reaching governor piston.
3. Start engine and operate at full speed. No load speed is 125-150 RPM above full load speed.
4. Turn the low maximum speed adjusting screw inward until the desired high maximum no-load speed is obtained.
5. Stop engine, then remove spring housing and piston assembly.
6. Measure distance from inner edge of piston to inner edge of housing, when piston is against adjusting screw.
7. Remove sleeve from piston, then remove shims equal to the distance the piston is from the edge of housing.
8. Install sleeve in the piston, then install piston assembly in spring housing. Install spring housing assembly onto the governor.
9. Start engine and operate at full throttle with air applied at governor. Observe tachometer.
10. Remove air pressure from governor and stop engine. Remove or install shims as required to obtain desired high maximum no-load speed. Remove shims to decrease or add shims to increase engine speed. Each .010″ of shims removed or added will change engine speed approximately 10 RPM.

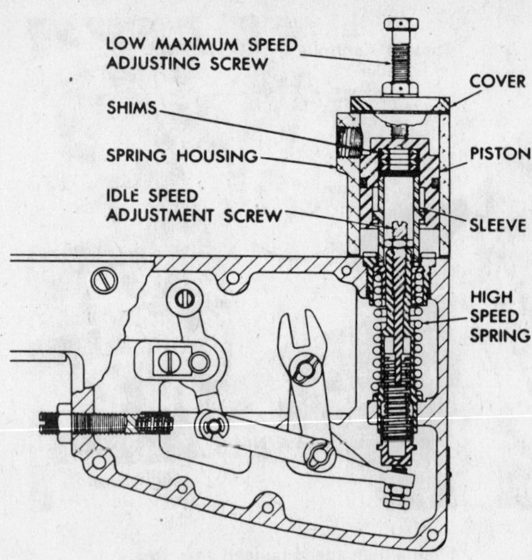

Governor springs—dual range
(© G.M.C.)

Buffer spring screw adjustment
(© G.M.C.)

Reduced High Speed Adjustment

(Late Type)

1. Disconnect air line so to prevent air reaching governor piston.
2. Start engine and operate at full throttle while observing RPM at tachometer. Proper adjustmen is approximately 200 RPM below maximum no-load speed.
3. Turn low maximum speed adjusting screw as necessary to obtain proper reduced high speed. Turn screw in to increase, or out to decrease engine RPM.
4. Reconnect air line when adjustment is completed.

Idle Speed Adjustment

Final

The engine must be at operating temperature when making the final idle speed adjustment.

1. Start engine and operate at idle speed while observing RPM at tachometer.
2. If necessary to adjust, loosen lock nut and turn idle adjusting screw IN to increase or OUT to decrease. Lock adjusting screw with lock nut when idle speed is approximately 15 RPM below desired setting.
3. Install governor spring housing assembly to governor housing.

Buffer Spring Adjustment

With the idle speed adjusted, and engine at operating temperature adjust buffer spring screw as follows:

1. Turn buffer screw IN until "surge" or "roll" is eliminated and engine idles evenly. NOTE: Do not increase engine idle speed more than 15 RPM with the buffer screw.
2. Hold buffer screw and tighten lock nut.

Throttle Delay Adjustment

The following instructions outline a procedure to follow when adjusting the throttle delay cylinder, used on coaches having hydraulic transmission.

1. Adjustment is made with the engine stopped.
2. Loosen two bolts attaching clamp to injector control tube.
3. Temporarily install a gauge between injector body and shoulder on injector rack. Gauge is .404" (approx. 13/32") thick and can be made locally.
4. Position gauge as shown and exert a light pressure on the control tube in the direction of FULL FUEL.
5. Align the piston so it is flush with the cylinder edge.
6. Tighten the two clamps bolts, then remove gauge.
7. Rotate the injector control rack from "OFF" to "FULL" position to be sure it does not bind.

NOTE: Each time the injector racks are set the throttle delay must be first taken out of adjustment; injector racks are then set and the throttle delay readjusted.

Blower

Description And Operation

In the scavenging process employed in GM 71 Series two cycle engines, air is forced into cylinders by blower which thoroughly sweeps out all of the burnt gases through the exhaust valve ports, and also helps to cool internal engine parts, particularly exhaust valves. At the beginning of compression stroke, therefore, each cylinder is filled with fresh, clean air, which permits highly efficient combustion.

The blower designed especially for efficient diesel operation, supplies the fresh air needed for combustion and scavenging. Its operation is similar to that of a gear-type pump. Two hollow three-lobe rotors revolve with very close clearances in a housing bolted to the top deck of the cylinder block, between the two banks of cylinders. To provide continuous and uniform displacement of air, the rotor lobes are made with a helical (spiral) form.

Two timing gears, located on the drive end of the rotor shafts, space the rotor lobes with a close tolerance; therefore, as the lobes of the two rotors do not touch at any time, no lubrication is required. However, build-up of oil and carbon deposits on the rotor lobes improves the sealing clearance and tends to increase the air flow.

Oil seals located in the blower end plates prevent air leakage and also keep the oil, used for lubricating the timing gears and rotor shaft bearings from entering the rotor compartment.

Blower Removal

The engine governor components are assembled in a combination governor housing and blower front end plate cover. The fuel pump is also attached to the front end of the blower. Therefore, when removing the blower assembly from the engine, the governor and fuel pump will also be removed at the same time.

1. Remove the manifold and blower screen.
2. Loosen oil pressure line fitting from rear of blower to blower drive support and slide fitting back on tube.
3. Loosen hose clamp on blower drive support-to-blower seal.
4. Remove flywheel housing cover at blower drive support.
5. Remove snap ring and withdraw blower drive shaft from blower.
6. Remove by-pass tube between thermostat housings.
7. Remove fuel inlet and outlet lines to fuel pump. Also, remove

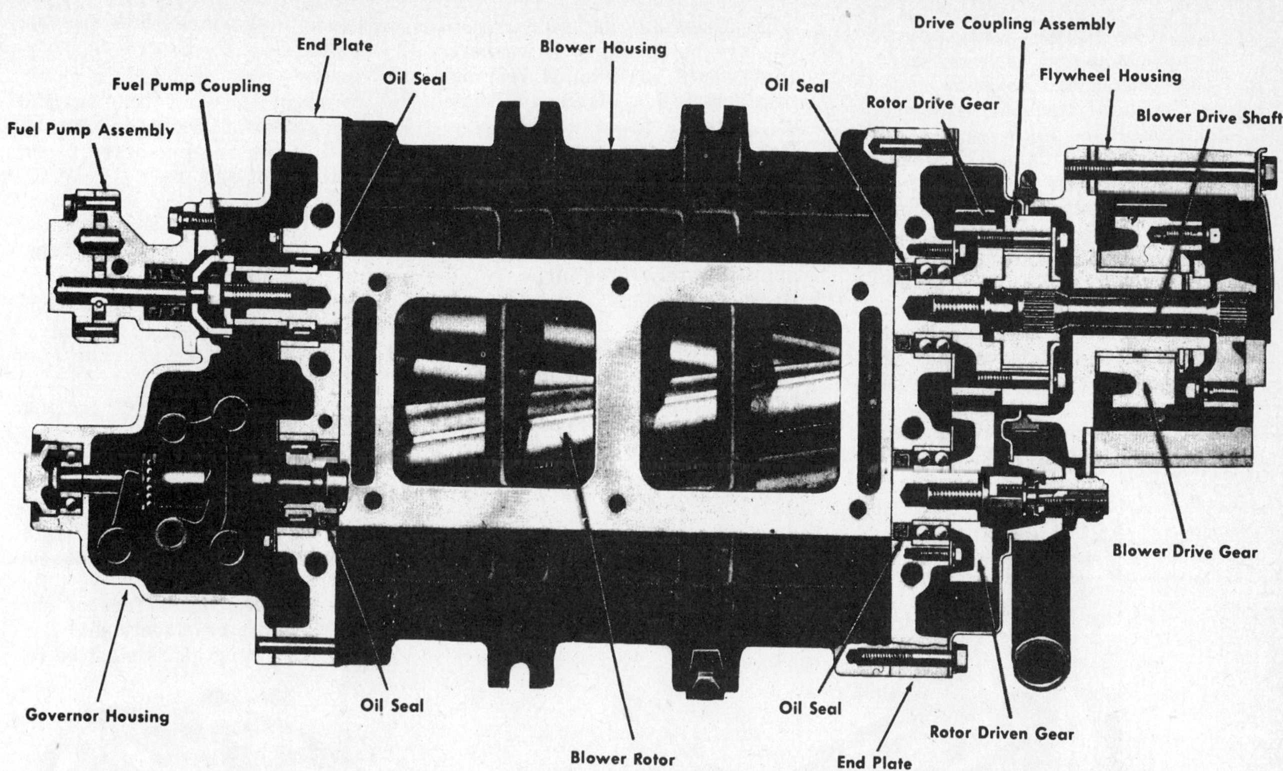

Blower assembly—showing drive mechanism, fuel pump and governor mounting (© G.M.C.)

the fuel return cross-over tube between cylinder heads.

8. Remove rocker covers.
9. Remove governor cover.
10. Disconnect and remove fuel rods.
11. Loosen hose clamps and slide governor fuel rod cover hose back on each side of governer.
12. Remove bolt and washer through top of each end plate which secures blower to cylinder block.
13. Remove two blower-to-block bolts, retaining lugs and washers on each side of blower.
14. Check to make sure any other tubing or accessories are disconnected which may interfere with removal of blower.
15. Thread eyebolts in diagonally opposite air inlet manifold-to-blower tapped holes and attach lifting sling.
16. Lift blower up slightly and move forward to detach blower from seal at drive end. Then lift blower up and away from engine. Remove blower gasket.

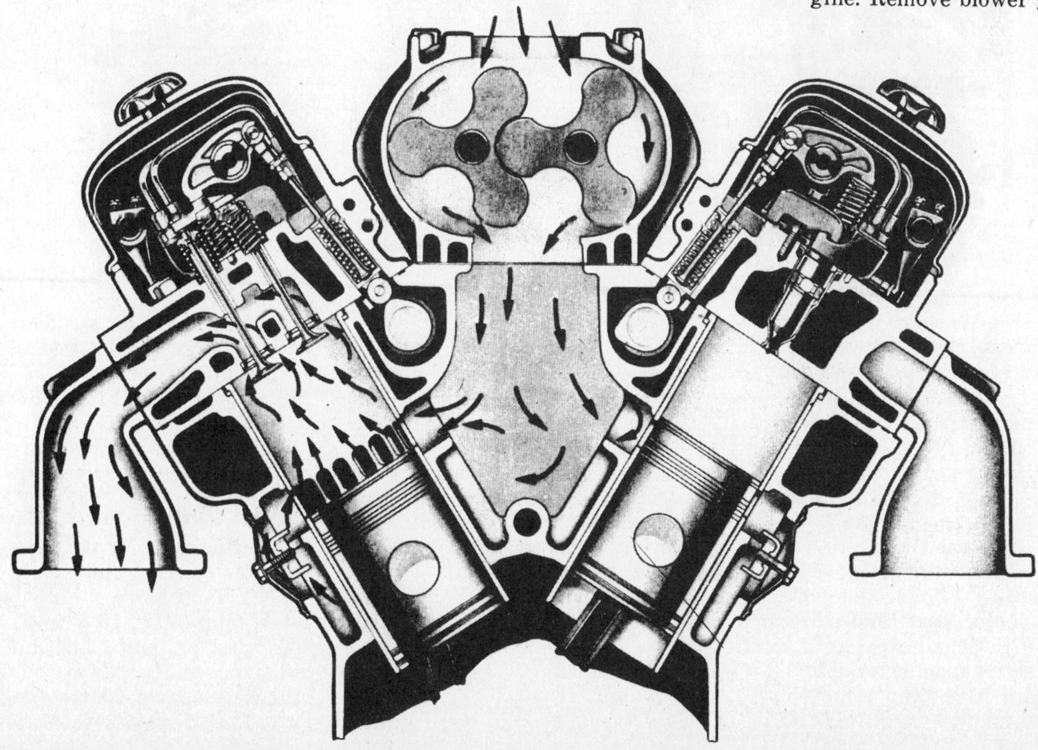

Air intake system through blower and engine (© G.M.C.)

Blower Disassembly

1. Remove bolts and washers securing rear end plate cover to blower, including tachometer drive adaptor. Remove gasket.
2. Remove six bolts and lock washers which secure flexible blower drive coupling to right-hand helix blower timing gear. Remove retainer and coupling.
3. Remove bolts and washers which secure the combination front end plate cover and governor housing to blower. Remove housing and gasket. Fuel pump may be removed with governor housing. Remove fuel pump driving disc, spacer and driving fork.

Removing blower gears
(© G.M.C.)

Removing or installing bearing retainers
(© G.M.C.)

4. Place a clean cloth between rotors, then remove the Allen head bolts and spacers which secure the timing gears to the blower rotor shafts.
5. Remove timing gears, using pullers installed as shown in illustration. Both gears must be pulled at the same time.
6. Secure pullers to gears with 5/16″-24 x 1½″ bolts (two bolts on L.H. helix gear and three bolts on R.H. helix gear).
7. Remove shims from rotor shafts, after gears have been removed. Note the number and thicknss of shims on each rotor shaft to ensure identical replacement when assembling blower.
8. Remove bolts and lock washers that secure rotor shaft bearing retainers to both front and rear end plates. Remove retainers.
9. Remove the two special screws that secure the rear end plate to the blower housing, and loosen the two special screws securing the front end plate to housing approximately three turns.
10. Install two pullers on blower end plate as shown in illustration. Align holes in each puller flange with tapped holes in end plate and secure pullers to the end plate with six ¼″-20 x 1¼″ or longer bolts. NOTE: Be sure that the ¼″-20 bolts are threaded all the way into the tapped holes in the end plate to provide maximum anchorage for the pullers and to eliminate possible damage to the end plate.
11. Turn the two puller screws uniformly clockwise to withdraw end plate and bearings from blower housing and rotors as shown in illustration.
12. Remove blower front end plate in the same manner as described above for rear plate.
13. Remove rotors from blower housing.
14. New seals should be installed. The seals may be removed from the end plates at the same time the individual bearings are removed.
15. Insert long end of remover through seal and bearing and bring ram of press down on opposite end, forcing bearing and seal out of end plate.

Blower Inspection

After the blower has been disassembled, wash all parts thoroughly in clean fuel oil, blow dry with compressed air, and inspect as follows:

1. Races and balls or rollers of bearings.
2. Lip type oil seals for scoring, charring, or hardening.
3. Blower rotor lobes and sealing rib for burrs or scoring.
4. Rotor shaft serrations and bearing surfaces for wear or burrs.
5. Inside of blower housing for burrs and scoring.
6. The finished inside face of end plates must be smooth and flat.
7. Blower timing gears must be replaced as a set when worn or damaged to the point where the backlash exceeds .004″.

Removing blower end plate
(© G.M.C.)

8. Replace blower drive shaft if bent or serrations are worn badly.
9. Make sure blower drive coupling springs (pack) and cam are intact and not worn.
10. Clean out all oil holes and cavities.
11. If blower timing gear serrations are worn, replace gears.

Rotor Timing and Clearances

At this stage of the blower assembly, the blower rotors must be timed.

NOTE: Before timing blower, install four 5/16″-18 x 2½″ bolts and ⅜″ spacers temporarily at each end to secure end plates to housing. After timing, remove spacers and bolts.

1. The blower rotors, when properly positioned in the housing, run with a slight clearance be-

Removing oil seal and bearing
(© G.M.C.)

Installing oil seal in end plate
(© G.M.C.)

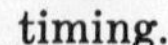

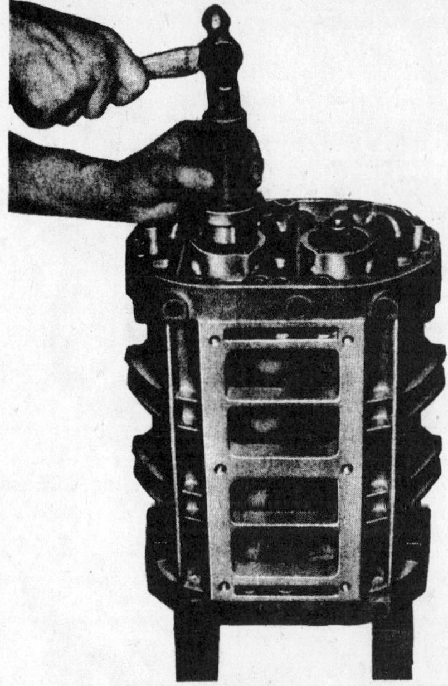

Installing roller bearings in rear end plate
(© G.M.C.)

tween the lobes. This clearance may be varied by moving one of the helical gears in or out on the shaft relative to the other gear.

2. If the right-hand helix gear is moved out, the right-hand helix rotor will turn counterclockwise when viewed from the gear end. If the left-hand helix gear is moved out, the left-hand helix rotor will turn clockwise when viewed from the gear end. This positioning of the gear, to obtain the proper clearance between the rotor lobes, is known as blower timing.
3. Moving the gears OUT or IN on the rotors is accomplished by adding or removing shims between the gear hub and the bearing.
4. The clearance between rotor lobes may be checked with various thickness feeler ribbons ½″ wide. When measuring clearances of more than .005″, laminated feelers that are made up of .002″, .003″ or .005″ feeler stock are more practical and suitable than one single thick feeler gauge. Clearances should be measured from both the inlet and outlet sides of the blower.
5. Time rotors to have from .002″ to .006″ clearance between the TRAILING edge of the right-hand helix rotor and the LEADING edge of the left-hand helix rotor ("CC" clearance) measured from both the inlet and outlet sides as shown in illustrations. If possible, keep this clearance to the minimum (.002″). Then check clearance between LEADING edge of right-hand helix rotor and TRAILING edge of left-hand helix rotor ("C" clearance) for the minimum clearance of .012″. Rotor-to-rotor measurements should be taken 1″ from each end and at center of blower.

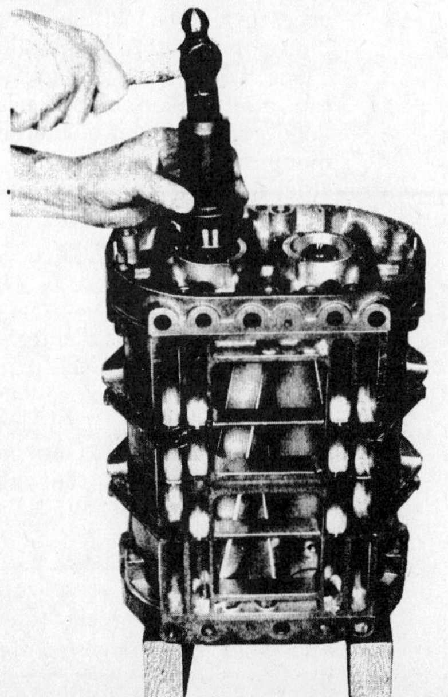

Installing roller bearings in front end plate
(© G.M.C.)

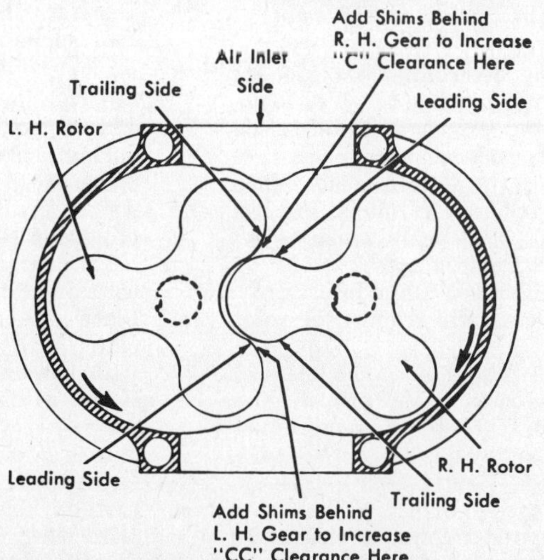

Proper location of shims for correct rotor clearances
(© G.M.C.)

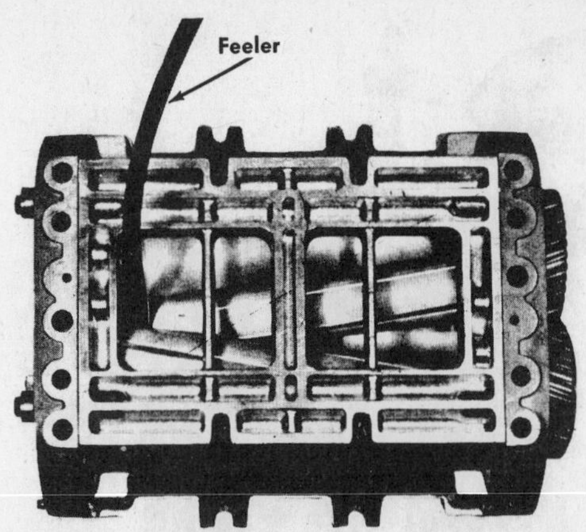

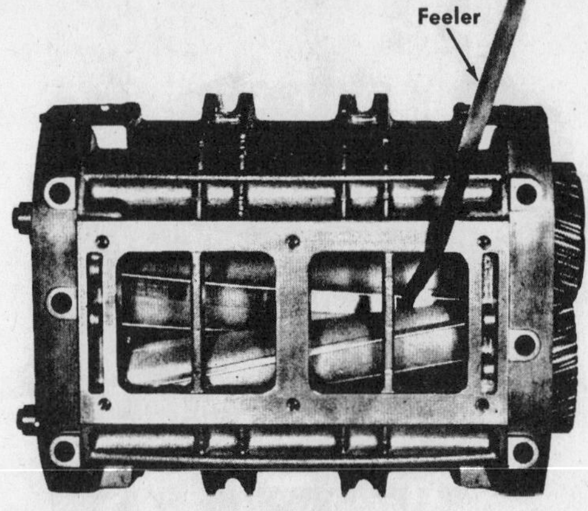

Measuring "CC" and "C" clearances (© G.M.C.)

Installing blower timing gears (© G.M.C.)

Measuring end clearance between rotor and end plate (© G.M.C.)

Using pilot tools to install rotors (© G.M.C.)

6. Having determined the amount one rotor must be revolved to obtain the proper clearance, add shims back of proper gear to produce the desired result. When more or fewer shims are required, both gears must be removed from the rotors.
7. Placing a .003" shim in back of a rotor gear will revolve the rotor .001".
8. Install the required thickness of shims back of the proper gear and next to the bearing inner race and reinstall both gears. Recheck clearances between rotor lobes.
9. Determine minimum clearances at points "A" and "B" shown in illustration. Insert feelers, between end plates and ends of rotors. This operation must be performed at both ends of each lobe, making 12 measurements in all.

Blower Assembly

1. After blower rotors are timed, complete assembly of blower as follows:
   a. Set drive coupling support on two wood blocks as shown in illustration.
   b. Install spring seats in grooves of coupling support.
   c. Apply grease to springs to hold the leaves together and slide the two spring packs, consisting of 21 leaves per pack, into support.
   d. Place blower drive cam over end of tool, insert tool between spring packs and press cam into place.
2. Attach flexible blower drive coupling and retainer to right-hand helix gear and secure with six bolts and lock washers.
3. Place gasket on blower rear end plate.
4. Attach rear end plate cover and secure with bolts and lock washers.
5. Attach tachometer drive adaptor, if used.
6. Install fuel pump driving disc and spacer.
7. Place gasket on blower front end plate.
8. Install governor assembly (combination governor and front end plate cover) on front end plate and secure with bolts and washers.

NOTE: Make certain that fuel pump driving fork is in registration with fuel pump driving disc. Governor weight shaft is splined to front left-hand helix rotor shaft.

Blower Installation

1. After blower is assembled and timed, and end plate cover and accessories are installed in place, blower is ready to be installed.
2. Place a new blower gasket on top of cylinder block, using a good grade of non-hardening cement to prevent gasket from shifting.

Fuel Pump

Tests

If engine operation indicates insufficient supply of fuel to the injectors and the fuel level is not low in the supply tank, check the fuel flow between the restricted fitting in the fuel return passage in the cylinder head and the fuel supply tank.

Fuel Flow Check

1. Disconnect the fuel return line from the fitting at the fuel tank and hold the open end of the pipe in a convenient receptacle.
2. Start and run the engine at 1200 r.p.m. and measure the fuel flow

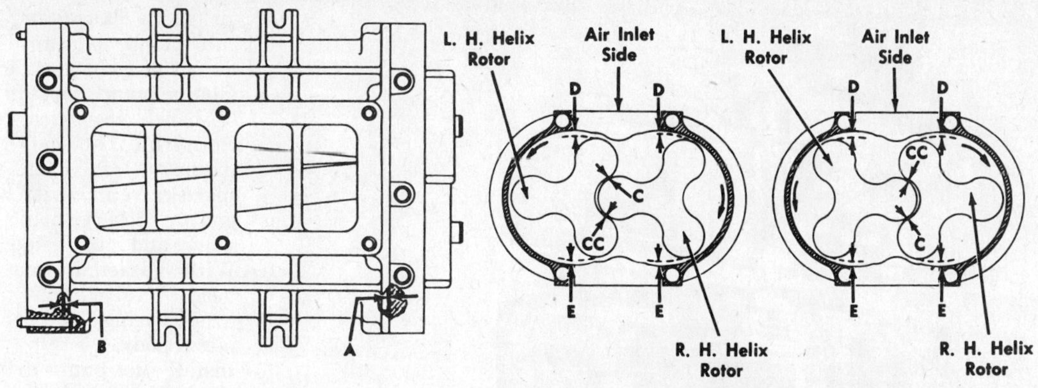

VIEWS FROM GEAR END OF BLOWER

NOTE: Time rotors to dimensions on above chart for clearance between trailing side of R.H. Helix Rotor and leading side of L.H. Helix Rotor (cc) from both inlet and outlet side of blower.

	A	B	C	CC	D	E
MIN.	.007"	.014"	.012"	.002"	.016"	.004"
MAX.				.006"		

Chart of minimum blower clearances (© G.M.C.)

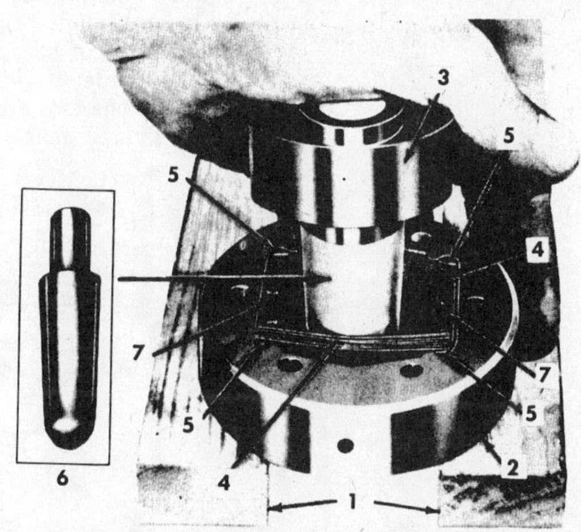

Inserting blower drive cam between springs—using spreader tool (© G.M.C.)

1 Wood blocks
2 Drive spring support
3 Blower drive cam
4 Blower drive spring
5 Spring seat
6 Spring spreader tool
7 Spring seat

return for a period of one minute. Approximately one half gallon of fuel should flow from the return tube per minute.

3. Be sure all connections are tight so that no air will be drawn into the fuel system; then immerse the end of the fuel line in the fuel container. Air bubbles rising to the surface of the liquid will indicate a leak on the suction side of the pump.
4. Whenever the fuel flow check indicates there is insufficient flow for satisfactory engine performance, proceed as follows:
   a. Renew the element in the strainer as outlined in respective applicable vehicle manual.
   b. Start the engine and run it at 1200 r.p.m. to check the fuel flow. If the fuel flow is still unsatisfactory continue as follows.
   c. Renew the element in the fuel filter. If the fuel flow is still unsatisfactory continue as follows.
   d. Substitute another fuel pump that is known to be in good condition and again check the flow. When changing a fuel pump, clean all fuel lines with compressed air and be sure all fuel line connections are tight.

Check Fuel Pump

If the fuel pump fails to function satisfactorily, check for broken pump shaft, or dirt in relief valve.

1. Insert the end of a wire through one of the pump body drain holes, then crank the engine momentarily and see if wire vibrates. Vibration will be felt if pump shaft rotates.
2. Without removing the pump from the engine, remove relief valve screw, then remove spring, pin, and valve. Wash parts and blow out valve cavity with compressed air. Install valve parts.

Fuel Pump Removal

1. Disconnect fuel lines from inlet and outlet openings of the fuel pump.
2. Disconnect drain line from fuel pump, if used.
3. Unscrew three pump attaching bolt and washer assemblies and withdraw pump.
4. Check drive coupling and if broken, replace.

Fuel Pump Disassembly

With the fuel pump removed from the engine, disassemble the pump as follows:

1. Remove eight cover bolts, then withdraw the pump cover away from the pump body and off the two cover dowels.
2. Withdraw drive shaft, drive gear and gear retaining ball as an assembly from the pump body.
3. Remove drive gear, if necessary from shaft being careful not to misplace the locking ball.
4. Remove driven gear and shaft as an assembly from pump body.
5. Remove valve screw, holding hand on screw to relieve valve spring tension.
6. Remove spring, pin, and valve from valve cavity in pump body.
7. If inspection indicates oil seals require replacing, remove in manner illustrated, by clamping pump body in a bench vise and screwing threaded end of tool shaft into outer oil seal (seal nearest to bolting flange). Then tap pilot end of shaft with hammer thus removing seal. Repeat this operation to remove the inner seal.

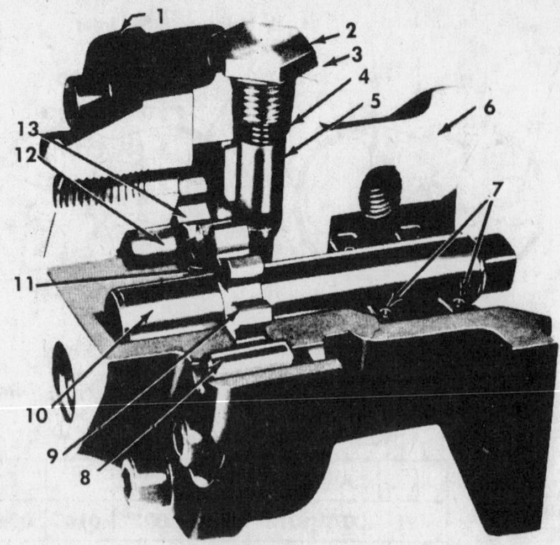

Fuel pump assembly
(© G.M.C.)

1 Pump cover
2 Valve plug
3 Gasket
4 Valve spring
5 Relief valve
6 Pump body
7 Oil seals
8 Dowel pin
9 Drive gear
10 Drive shaft
11 Retaining ball
12 Driven shaft
13 Driven gear

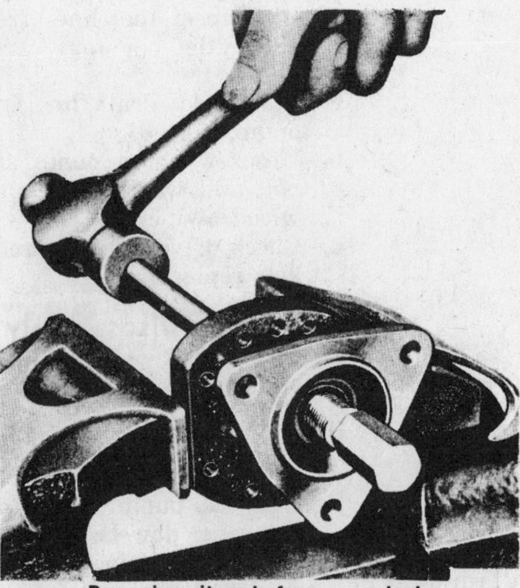

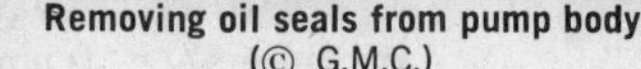
Removing oil seals from pump body
(© G.M.C.)

Inspection

1. When the fuel pump has been disassembled, all parts should be washed in clean fuel oil, blown dry with compressed air and inspected.
2. Oil seals once removed from the pump body should be discarded and replaced with new seals. Lips of oil seals must fit snug around the pump shaft.
3. Pump gear teeth should be checked for scoring or chipping. If gear teeth are scored or chipped, they should be replaced.
4. Mating faces of the pump body and cover must be flat and smooth and fit tightly together.
5. The relief valve must be free from score marks and must fit its seat in the pump body. If the relief valve is scored and cannot be cleaned up with crocus cloth, the valve must be replaced.

Fuel Pump Assembly

1. Place inner oil seal on pilot of installer with lip of seal facing shoulder on handle.
2. With pump supported on wood blocks, insert pilot of installer into pump body so seal starts straight into pump flange, then drive seal into place in counterbore of flange until it bottoms.
3. Place adaptor on pilot end of installer with shorter end of adaptor against shoulder on installer. Position outer oil seal on adaptor with lip of seal facing adaptor, then insert pilot of installer into pump so seal starts straight in pump flange and drive seal into pump body until the shoulder of adaptor contracts body.
4. Clamp pump body in soft jaws of bench vise with relief valve cavity up. Lubricate the outside diameter of relief valve and place valve in cavity with hollow end up. Insert spring inside the valve and pin inside of spring. With gasket in place next to head of valve screw place screw over spring and thread into pump body.
5. Install fuel pump drive gear, if removed, over plain end of drive shaft with slot in gear facing plain end of shaft. This operation is very important. Press gear beyond locking ball retaining hole. Then place ball in hole and press gear back until end of slot contacts ball.
square end of shaft into opening
6. Lubricate pump shaft and insert square end of shaft into opening at gear side of pump body and through the two oil seals.
7. Place driven gear shaft and gear assembly in pump body with chamfered end of gear teeth facing pump body.

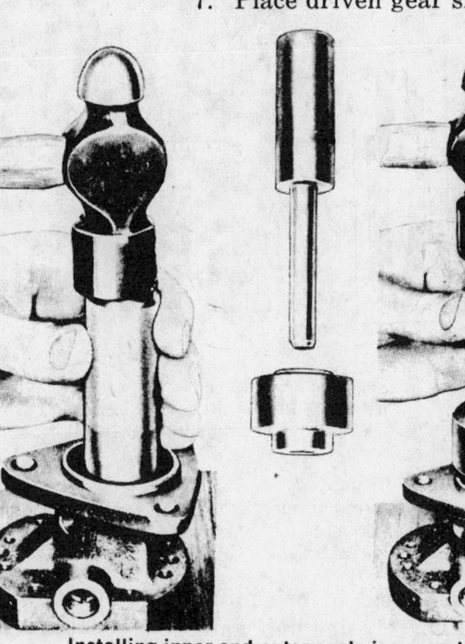

Installing inner and outer seals in pump body
(© G.M.C.)

8. Lubricate gears and shafts with clean engine oil.
9. Apply a thin coat of reputable sealer on face of pump cover outside of gear pocket area, then place cover against pump body with two dowel pins in cover entering holes in pump body. The cover can be installed in only one position over the two shafts.
10. Secure cover in place.
11. After assembly, rotate pump shaft by hand to make certain that parts rotate freely. If binding exists, it may be necessary to tap corner of pump cover with a hammer to relieve binding.

Fuel Pump Installation

1. Affix a new gasket to pump body and locate pump drive coupling over square end of fuel pump drive shaft.
2. Install fuel pump on engine and secure.
3. Connect inlet and outlet fuel lines to the fuel pump.
4. Connect drain tube, if used, to pump body.

Fuel Injectors

Description and Operation

The cross section of the injector illustrated, shows the various fuel injector parts. Fuel oil supplied to injector enters the dropforged steel body at the top through the filter cap. After passing through the filter element inlet passage, the fuel oil fills the supply chamber between bushing and spill deflector. The plunger operates up an ddown in this bushing, the bore of which is connected to fuel supply by two funnel-shaped ports.

Motion of injector rocker arm is transmitted to plunger by follower which bears against plunger spring. Follower is positioned in body by a follower stop pin. In addition to up and down motion, the plunger can be rotated, in operation, around its axis by gear, which is in mesh with the control rack. The fuel is metered by an upper helix and lower helix which are machined into lower end of plunger. The relation of these helixes to the two ports changes with the rotation of the plunger. As plunger moves downward, fuel oil in high-pressure cylinder or bushing is first displaced through the ports back into supply chamber until lower edge of plunger closes the lower port. Remaining oil is then forced upward through center passage in plunger into recess between upper helix and the lower cut-off from which it can still flow back into supply chamber until helix closes upper port. Rotation of plunger, by changing position of helix, retards or advances the closing of the ports and beginning and ending of injection period, at the same time increasing or decreasing desired amount of fuel which remains under plunger for injection into the cylinder.

Illustration shows the various plunger positions from NO INJECTION to FULL INJECTION.

Illustration shows four positions for downward travel of plunger, rack fixed. On downward travel of plunger, the metered amount of fuel is forced through center passage of the valve assembly, through check valve, and against spray tip valve. When sufficient fuel pressure is built up, valve is forced off its seat and fuel is forced through small orifices in spray tip and atomized into the combustion chamber.

Constant circulation of fresh, cool fuel through the injectors, which renews the fuel supply in the chamber, helps to maintain even operating temperatures of injectors, and also effectively removes all traces of air which might otherwise accumulate in system and interfere with accurate metering of fuel.

The fuel injector outlet opening, which returns the excess fuel oil supplied by fuel pump, is directly adjacent to inlet opening.

Refer to illustration for injector identifying marks. The correct injector must be used and type can be determined by checking injector in engine for number which appears on color tag pressed into body.

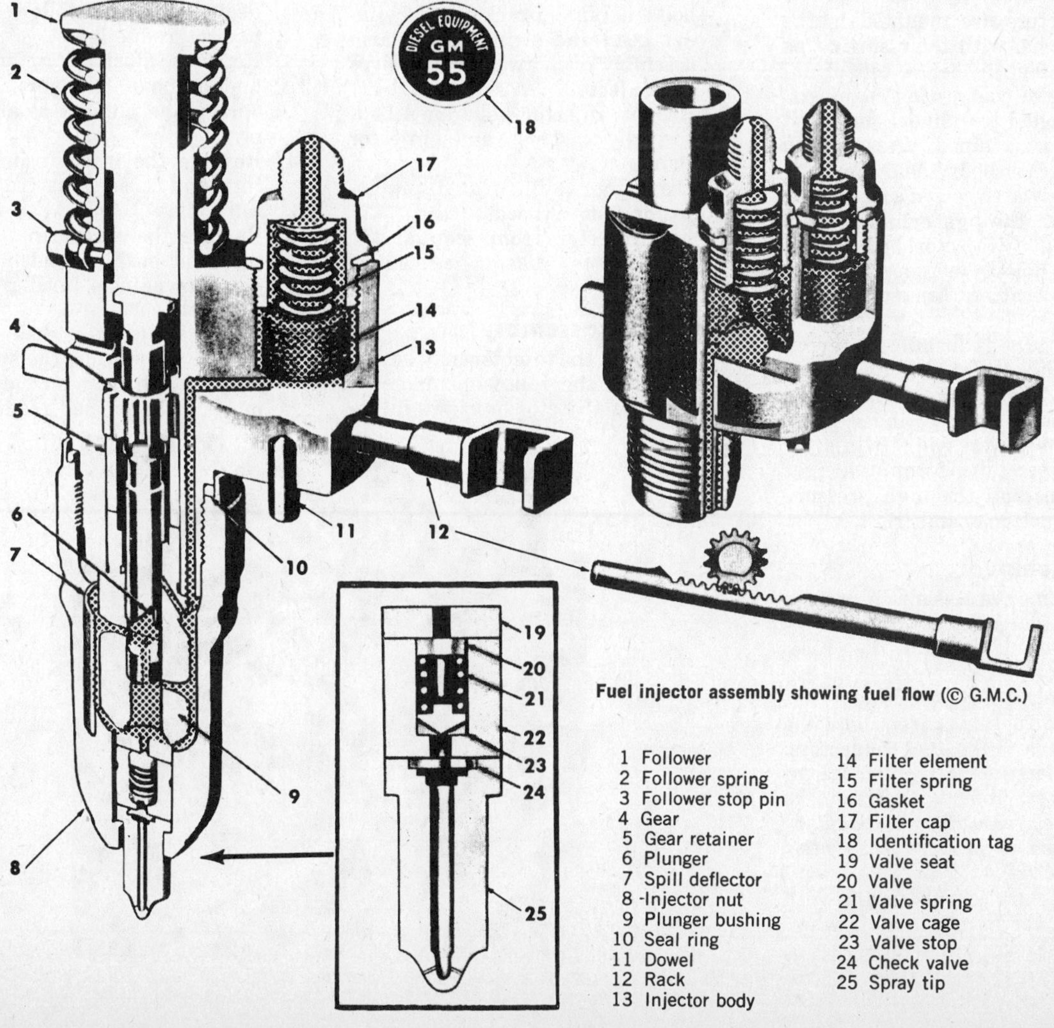

Fuel injector assembly showing fuel flow (© G.M.C.)

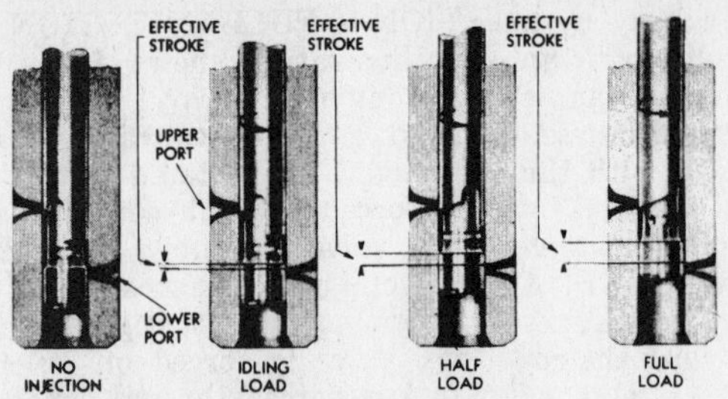

Fuel Metering From No Injection To Full Injection, Produced By Rotating Plunger with Control Rack

Fuel metering produced by rotating plunger
(© G.M.C.)

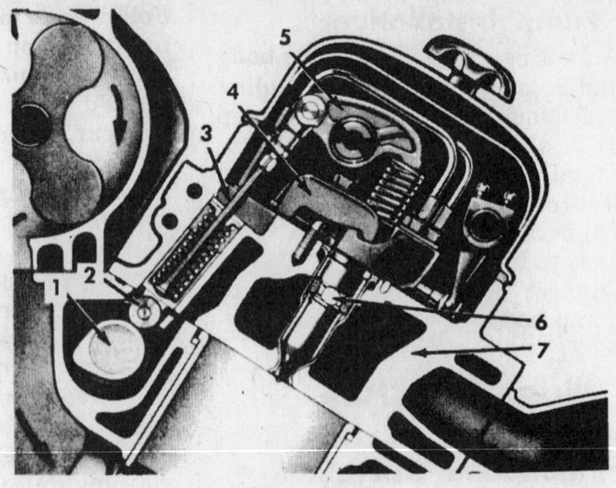

Injector installed
(© G.M.C.)

1 Camshaft
2 Cam follower assy.
3 Push rod
4 Hold-down clamp

5 Rocker arm
6 Injector assy.
7 Cylinder head

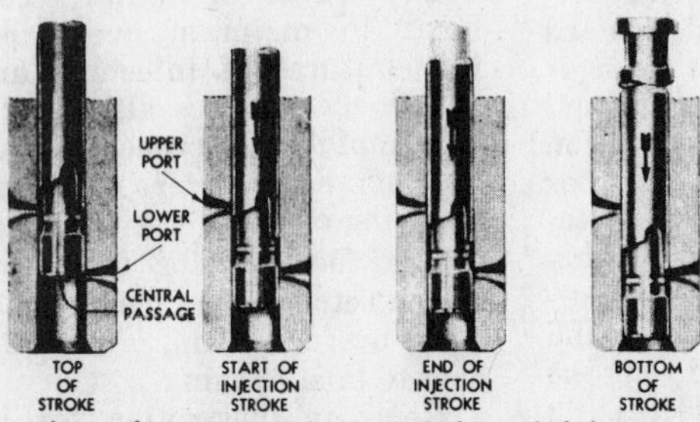

Phases of Injector Operation By Vertical Travel of Plunger

Injector operation by vertical travel of plunger
(© G.M.C.)

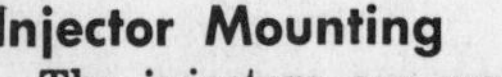

Injector Mounting

The injectors are mounted in the cylinder heads, with their spray tips projecting slightly below top of inside surface of combustion chambers. A clamp, bolted to cylinder head and fitting into a machined recess in each side of injector body, holds injector in place in a water-cooled copper tube which passes through cylinder head. A dowel pin in injector body registers with a hole in cylinder head for accurately locating injector assembly.

A copper tube is installed in cylinder head with a seal ring at flanged upper end. The lower end is peened into a recess of the cylinder head. The tapered lower end of injector seats in copper tube, forming a tight seal to withstand the high pressure inside combustion chamber.

Injector Removal

If it becomes necessary to remove one of the fuel injectors for inspection or replacement, follow the procedure given below:

1. Remove valve rocker cover.
2. Remove fuel lines from both the injector and the fuel connectors. *Immediately after removal of fuel lines from an injector, the two fuel feed fittings should be protected to prevent dirt entering injector.*
3. If necessary, crank engine with the starter or a bar at flywheel ring gear until the three rocker arm clevis pins, at outer end of arms, are in line.
4. Loosen two rocker arm bracket bolts holding brackets to cylinder head and swing rocker arm assembly over away from valves and injector.
5. Remove injector hold-down bolt, special washer, and injector clamp.
6. Using tool as illustrated, pry injector from its seat.
7. Lift injector from seat, at the same time disengage control rack linkage.

Injector Disassembly

If required, the injector may be disassembled in the following manner:

1. Support injector upright in injector assembly fixture, and remove filter caps, springs, filter elements and gaskets. NOTE: Whenever injector is disassembled, filter elements and gaskets should be discarded and replaced with new filters and gaskets.
2. Compress follower spring. Then, using a screwdriver, raise spring above stop pin and withdraw pin. Allow follower spring to rise gradually.
3. Refer to illustration for details and remove plunger follower, spring and plunger as an assembly.
4. Reverse the injector in the fixture and loosen nut from injector body.
5. Remove the spray tip and valve parts off bushing and place in a clean receptacle until ready for assembly.
6. When an injector has been in use for some time, the spray tip, even though clean on the outside, may not be pushed readily from

Injector removal
(© G.M.C.)

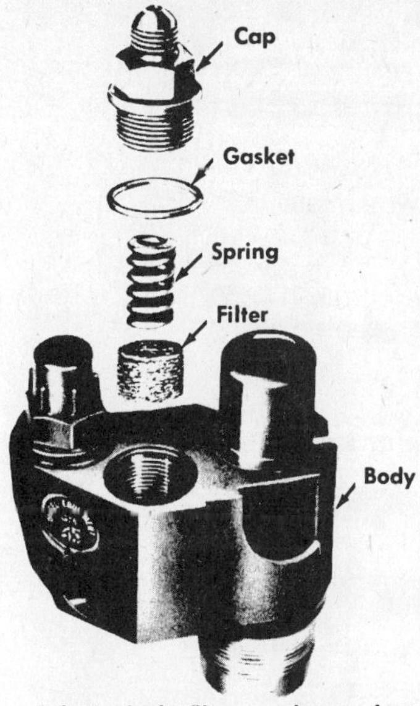

Injector body, filters, springs and cap
(© G.M.C.)

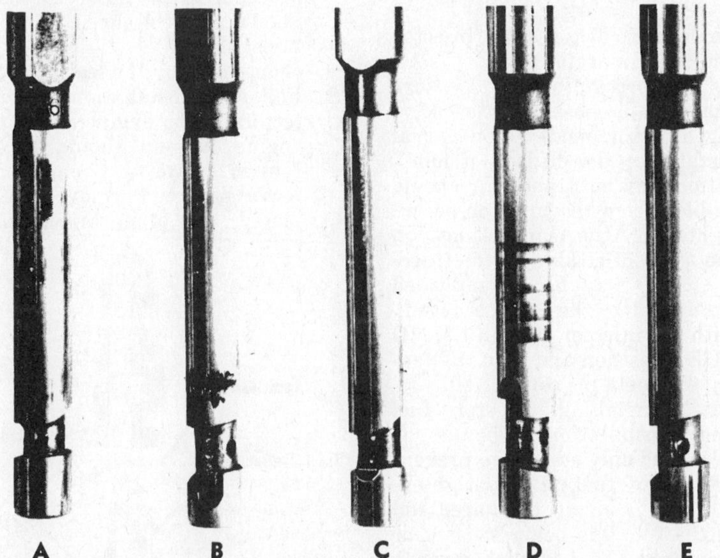

Damaged and unusable plungers (© G.M.C.)

A. Tight rack causing binding in up and down movement.
B. Dirt in fuel. This shows advanced stages of abrasive matter in fuel.
C. Chipped at lower helix.
D. High pressure scoring caused by a plugged tip or wrong size tip being installed.
E. The condition shown can be caused by either lack of fuel at high speeds or water in fuel.

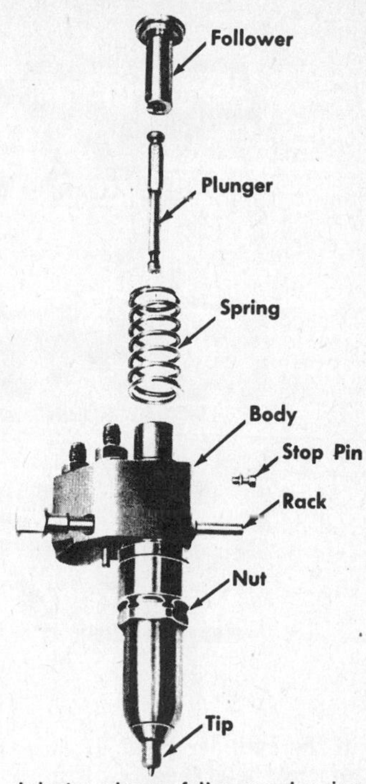

Injector, plunger follower and spring
(© G.M.C.)

the nut with the fingers. In this event, support the nut on a wood block and drive the tip down through the nut, as shown in illustration.

7. Remove spill deflector, and seal ring from injector nut.
8. Remove plunger bushing, gear retainer, and gear from injector body.
9. Withdraw injector control rack from injector body.

Injector Assembly

Before starting to assemble an injector, it is necessary to have an extremely clean bench on which to work and place the parts. Refer to illustrations for proper relative positions of the injector parts and the methods for their assembly prior to proceeding with assembly. Since the plunger and bushing are matched parts, they must be considered as one piece and, if one is replaced, both must be replaced.

Assemble Injector Filters

New filters and gaskets should always be used when reassembling injectors.

1. Holding the injector body right side up, place a filter in each of the fuel cavities in the top of the injector body. Note that the fuel filters have a dimple in one end. When assembling the filters, always have the dimple at the bottom.
2. Place a spring above each filter, a new gasket up against the shoulder of each filter cap, lubricate the threads, and tighten the filter cap in place in the injector body to a torque of 65 to 75 ft.-lbs., using a 9/16″ deep socket wrench. It is important that the filter caps be tightened securely so as to compress the gaskets and effect a good seal with the injector body. Also, when the caps are tightened, they compress the filter springs which hold the filters securely in place so all fuel entering the injector is properly filtered.
3. Install covers on injector filter caps to prevent any dirt particles from entering injector. Be sure covers are clean.

Injector Testing

Before placing a reconditioned injector in service, all of the tests (except the visual inspection of the plunger) previously outlined in this section under "Injector Tests" must be performed again.

If an injector is not to be used immediately, caps should be installed on the injector caps. The injector test oil remaining in the injector after the fuel output test will serve as a rust preventive while the injector is in storage.

Injector Installation

Before installing a new or reconditioned injector in an engine, the carbon deposits must be removed from the beveled seat of the injector hole

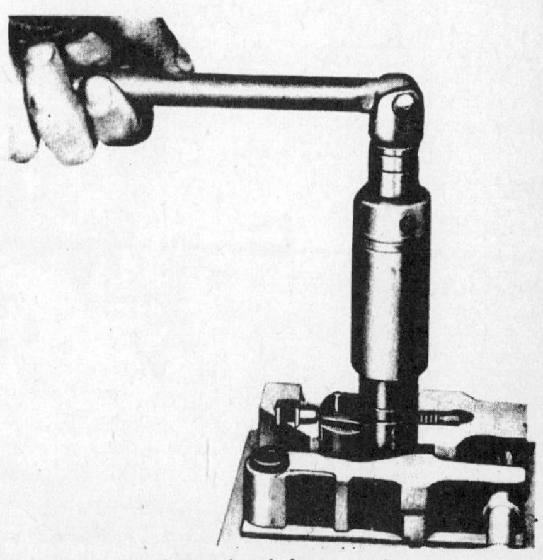

Removing injector nut
(© G.M.C.)

CLEANING BUSHING

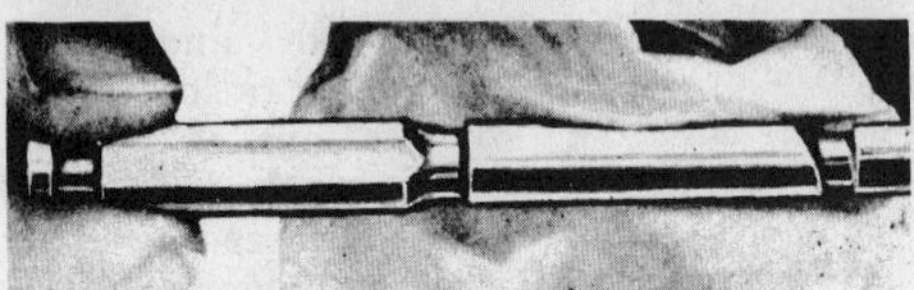
POLISHING PLUNGER WITH TISSUE

DRYING BUSHING WITH FILTERED AIR

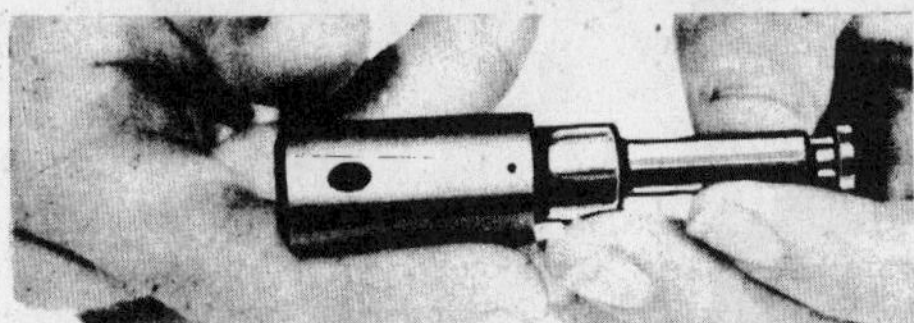
TESTING FIT OF PLUNGER IN BUSHING

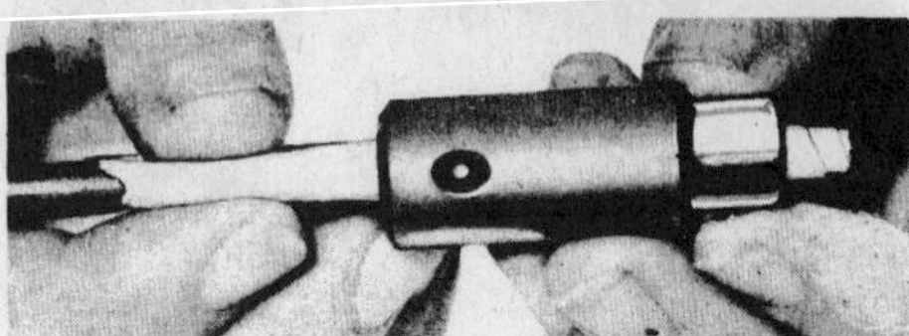
CLEANING BUSHING WITH TISSUE AND TOOL

CLEANING VALVE NUT

Cleaning plunger, bushing and nut
(© G.M.C.)

tube in the cylinder head. If not, the injector may be cocked resulting in a fractured spray tip.

Injector tube bevel seat reamer should be used to clean the carbon out of the tube before installing the injector. Refer to "Reaming" in "CYLINDER HEAD" section. Care must be exercised to remove ONLY the carbon so that the proper clearance between the injector body and cylinder head is maintained.

1. Insert the injector into the injector tube with the locating dowel registering with the locating hole in the cylinder head and with the pin on the injector control tube lever registering with the injector control rack lever.
2. Place injector clamp in position, then install washer and bolt. Tighten bolt to 20-25 ft.-lbs. NOTE: Check injector rack for free movement. Excess torque will cause the injector control rack to stick or bind.
3. Move rocker arm assembly into position and secure rocker arm bracket bolts to torque of 90 to 100 ft.-lbs.
4. Connect fuel pipes to injector and fuel connectors.
5. As a precautionary measure against any possibility of scoring injector parts upon initial installation due to lack of lubrication, any entrapped air should be bled from the injector before tightening the connections on the fuel outlet side of the injector. This may be accomplished by cranking the engine briefly with the injector rack in the NO FUEL position and then tightening the fuel pipe connection.
6. When installing injector fuel lines, connections should be tightened only enough to prevent leakage of fuel. Excess tightening may result in the flared end of the fuel line being twisted or fractured. A torque wrench adapter is essential to properly tighten fuel line connector nut to 12-15 ft. lbs. torque. Use of this adapter and torque wrench is highly recommended.
7. When all injector lines are installed, the engine should be run long enough (during tune-up procedure) to check for leaks. Should leaks occur, the connections should be tightened only enough to stop the leak.
8. Following installation of the injectors in the engine, a complete engine tune-up should be performed. However, if only one injector has been removed and replaced, and other injectors and

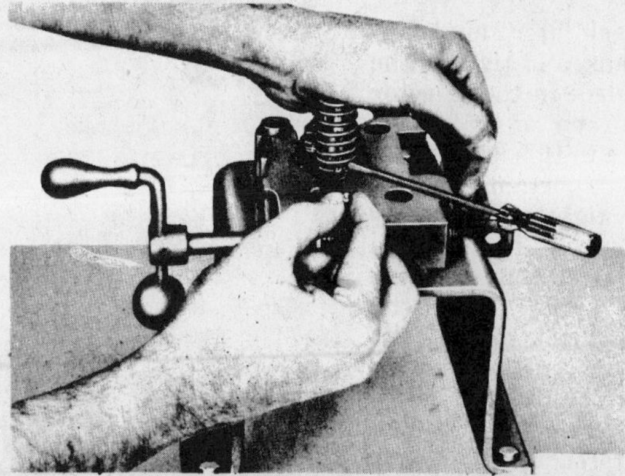
Removing injector follower stop pin
(© G.M.C.)

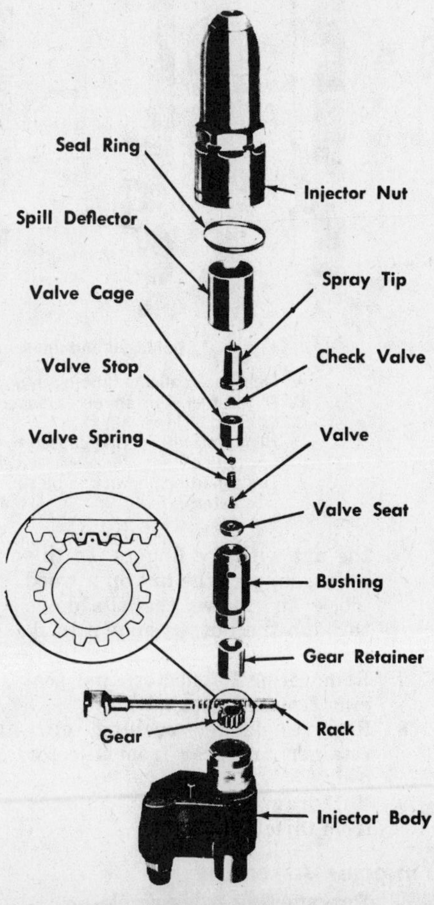

Injector body, nut, rack, bushing and spray tip details
(© G.M.C.)

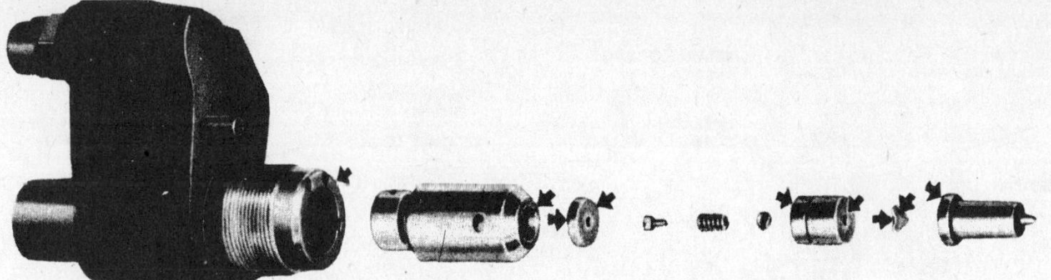

Sealing surfaces of injector parts requiring lapping (© G.M.C.)

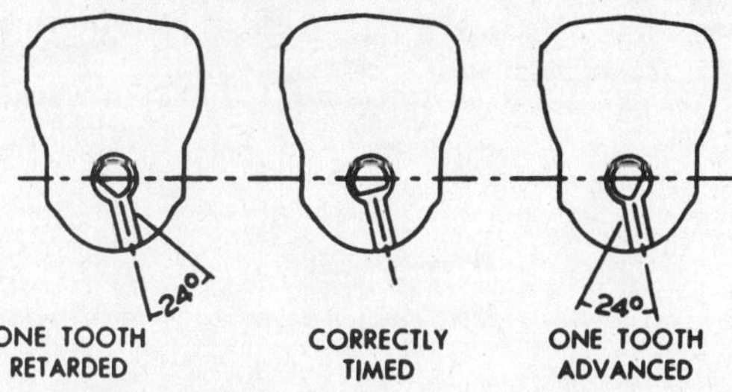

Injector rack to gear giming (© G.M.C.)

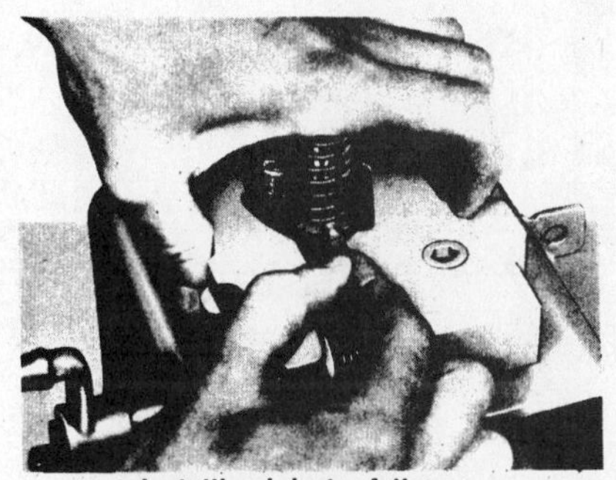

Installing injector follower (© G.M.C.)

the governor adjustment have not been disturbed, it will only be necessary to adjust the clearance of the valves, valve bridge, and time the injector for the one cylinder, and position the control rack on the cylinder involved to correspond with that of the other racks.

Assemble Rack and Gear

When rack and gear are assembled, the marked tooth of the gear must be engaged between the two marked teeth on the rack.

1. Hold the injector body bottom nd up and slide the rack through the proper hole in the body. The two marked teeth can then be observed when looking into the bore for the gear from the bottom of the injector body. The injector rack can be placed in the injector body in only one position and have the tooth marks show in the opening for the gear.
2. Holding the rack in position so the tooth marks show, slide the gear into proper engagement with the rack.
3. Slide gear retainer down on top of gear; then place plunger bushing down onto retainer with locating pin in bushing guided into slot of injector body.

Governors

Description

The limiting speed governor uses two high speed and two low speed weights; each set of weights having a fixed stop for the inner and outer positions. A high and low speed spring is also used in this governor; the former works with the high speed weights to limit the maximum engine speed, the latter works with both the low and high speed weights to control the engine idling speed.

The travel of the governor weights, between their inner and outer positions, is transferred to the injector racks by a system of cams and levers over which a manual control can be used.

The governor, which is mounted at front of blower is divided into two main assemblies in separate housings. These assemblies are: Governor control housing and governor weight and lower housing, and the cover.

The two sets of weights are carried on a horizontal weight shaft inside the governor weight housing. The weight carrier shaft is mounted on an annular ball bearing at one end and opposite end is supported inside and driven by hollow blower rotor shaft. The blower end of governor shaft is serrated and engages with corresponding serrations inside blower shaft, which drives the governor shaft and weights.

Control mechanism transfers motion of governor weights to the injector racks. This mechanism consists of a vertical shaft mounted inside a housing, with a fork or yoke fixed at lower end, an operating lever fixed at upper end, and a high and low speed governing spring with suitable adjustments. The vertical shaft is mounted on annular ball bearings at upper and lower ends.

The motion of the governor weights is transferred to the vertical shaft through a movable riser on the weight carrier shaft and the fork on the lower end of the vertical shaft. This motion is, in turn, transferred to the injector control tube by means of the operating and differential levers on the upper end of the vertical shaft.

The cover assembly serves as a carrier for the throttle control lever, stop lever, and covers the top of the control housing.

The lower portion of governor is lubricated by means of a slinger attached to front end of blower lower rotor shaft. This slinger dips into a well of oil dammed up in blower housing cover and throws the oil onto all parts within governor weight housing. The upper portion of the governor, including the vertical shaft bearings and the control mechanism, is lubricated partly by splash from oil slinger on weight carrier shaft and partly by return oil through the vertical housing from cylinder head.

Governor Removal

1. Remove injector and rocker arm covers.
2. Remove cover and gasket from governor housing.
3. Remove the right bank fuel rod by removing the screw type pin, in the control link operating lever, and the clevis pin at the control tube lever and withdraw the fuel rod across cylinder head while rotating rod.
4. Remove the left bank fuel rod by removing the governor operating lever link connecting pin from the control link operating lever after removing the spring retainer that holds the governor operating lever to the differ-

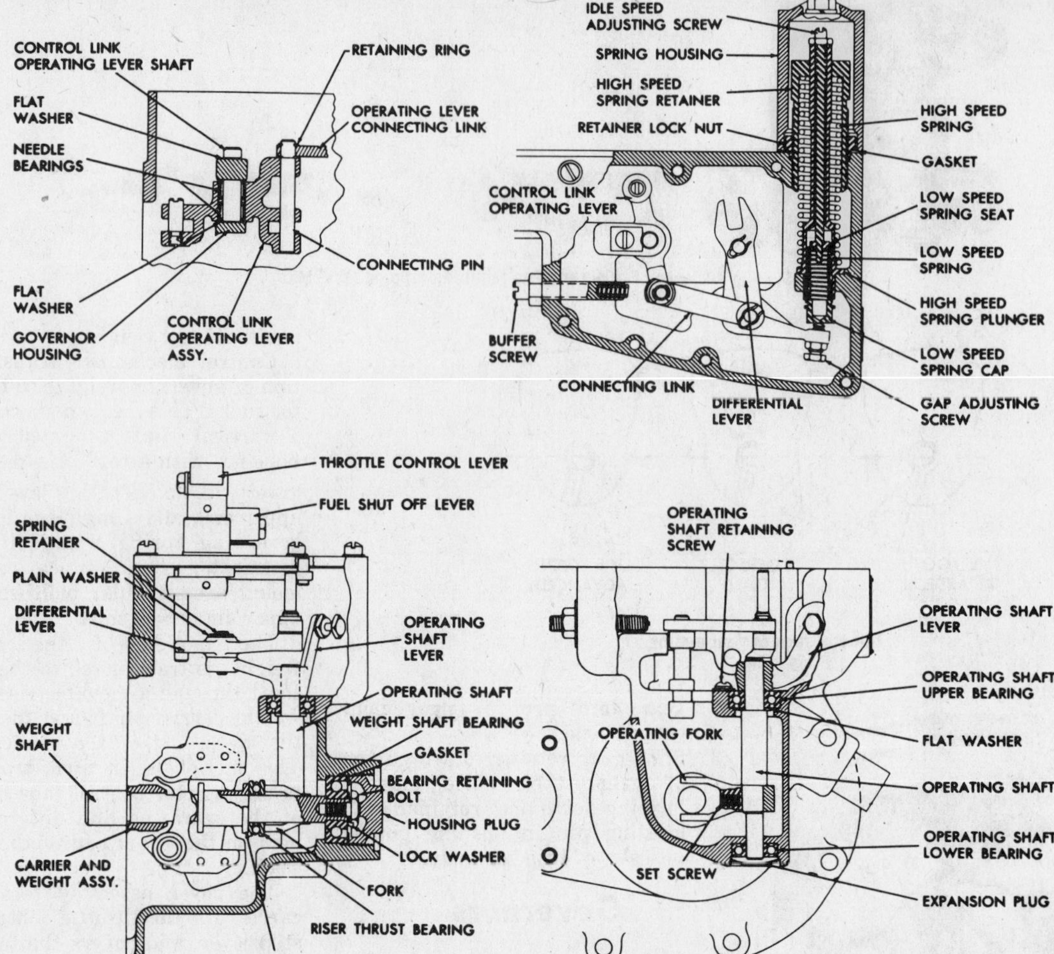

Limiting speed governor (© G.M.C.)

ential lever, then lift upwards on the governor operating link. Remove the clevis pin at the control tube lever and withdraw fuel rod across cylinder head while rotating rod.

5. Loosen the hose clamps on the fuel rod covers and slide each hose and clamp toward the governor.
6. Loosen hose clamps on water by-pass tube. Slide hoses and clamps onto by-pass tube and remove tube from engine.
7. Disconnect and remove the fuel lines from the fuel pump.
8. Remove retaining bolts and slide the governor and fuel pump assembly straight forward, from the blower dowels. Remove governor-to-blower gasket. NOTE: The fuel pump drive coupling may stay with either the fuel pump or the blower rotor shaft. Remove the drive coupling.
9. Remove three bolts and remove the fuel pump and gasket from the governor housing.

Governor Disassembly

Cover

With cover removed from the control housing, disassemble the governor as follows:

1. Loosen governor throttle control lever retaining bolt, and lift control lever from throttle shaft.
2. Remove tapered pin from spacer. Lift lever spacer and seal ring retainer from throttle shaft. Withdraw shaft from cover.
3. Remove seal ring from governor cover.
4. Remove fuel shut-off lever.
5. Remove lock ring from shaft and seal ring retainer (two flat washers).
6. Slide shaft from cover and remove seal ring.
7. At this stage of disassembly, wash cover assembly (containing needle bearings) thoroughly in clean fuel oil and inspect needle bearings for wear or damage. If bearings are satisfactory for further use, removal is unnecessary.
8. Inspect fuel shut-off shaft bushing. If bushing is damaged, replace governor cover.
9. If needle bearing removal is necessary, then press both bearings out of cover.

Spring (Except Dual Range)

1. Place control housing in soft jaws of vise.
2. Remove two bolts attaching high speed spring retainer cover to housing, then remove cover.
3. Loosen lock nut. Remove high speed spring retainer, idle adjusting screw, high speed spring, spring plunger, low speed spring, spring seat, and spring cap as an assembly.

Spring (Dual Range)

1. Remove two bolts and withdraw spring housing, cover, piston, sleeve, and low maximum speed adjustment screws as an assembly.
2. Remove high speed spring retainer, and withdraw high and low speed springs and related parts as an assembly.

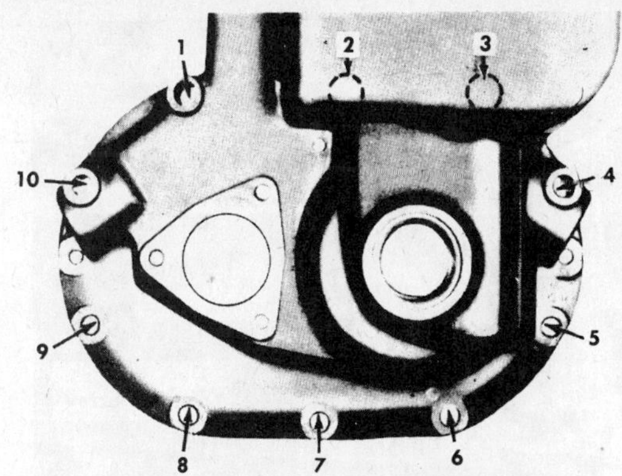

Location and size of governor housing retaining bolts
(© G.M.C.)

Location	Washer	Bolt
4	Copper	5/16″-18 x 5-¼″
10	Copper	5/16″-18 x 4″
1	Lock	5/16″-18 x 3-¾″
2-3-5-6-7-8-9	Lock	5/16″-18 x 2-¼″

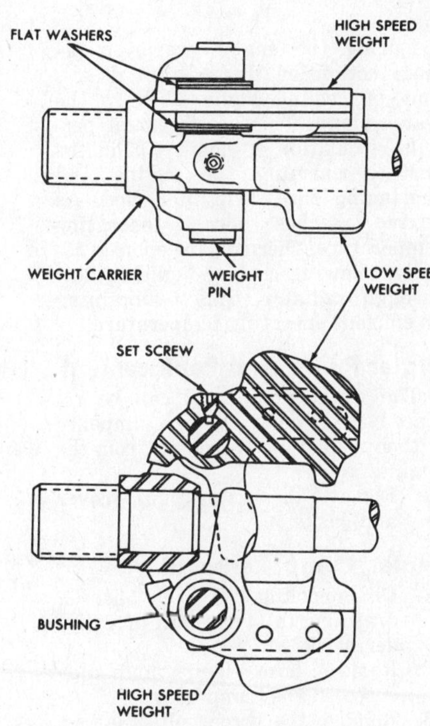

View of governor weights
(© G.M.C.)

Weights

1. Remove the governor weight housing cap, and gasket.
2. Remove bearing retaining bolt.
3. Thread a 5/16″-24 x 3″ bolt into tapped end of weight shaft, and press shaft from bearing.
4. Slide riser thrust bearing and governor riser from shaft. This bearing is specially designed to absorb thrust load; therefore, looseness between the mating parts does not indicate excessive wear.
5. Remove weight shaft bearing from governor housing.
6. Mark low and high speed weights and carrier with a center punch for identification, also note position of flat washers so that the parts can be replaced in original position.
7. Using a 3/32″ Allen wrench remove Allen set screw from low speed weights. Withdraw pins and governor weights. NOTE: If necessary the bushings in the high speed weights may be removed at this time.
8. If required, the weight carrier may be pressed from governor weight shaft and a new carrier installed.

Operating Shaft

1. Lift differential lever off of pin of operating shaft lever after removing retainer clip and washer.
2. Remove bearing retaining screw, flat washer, and lock washer.
3. Remove expansion plug from bottom of control housing.
4. Loosen operating fork set screw.
5. Support control housing bottom side up on bed of press and insert a 9/16″ open end wrench between operating fork and governor housing. Using a brass rod, press operating shaft from operating fork. Withdraw operating shaft, operating lever, and upper bearing as an assembly from control housing.
6. Support operating shaft lever and upper bearing on bed of arbor press. Using a brass rod, press operating shaft from operating lever and upper bearing.

Link Operating Lever

1. Remove retaining screw from governor housing and withdraw governor control lever shaft lock clip.
2. Slide governor control link operating lever shaft from governor housing. Remove governor control link operating lever assembly and two flat washers.
3. Remove the needle bearings, if necessary.

Governor Inspection

Inspect all bearings to be sure that they are satisfactory for further use.

Inspect spring seats, plungers, adjusting screws, lock nuts, and other parts of control housing for defects that might affect governor operation.

Inspect operating shaft and shaft bearing for excessive wear. If excessive wear is noted, a new bearing or shaft must be installed.

Examine riser thrust bearing for excessive wear, flat spots or corrosion. If any of these conditions exist, a new thrust bearing assembly must be installed.

Inspect roller bearings and throttle shaft for excessive wear or flat spots. If one or both conditions exist, new bearings and throttle shaft must be installed.

If new bearings are installed in the governor cover, the lower bearing should be flush with the lower end of the bearing boss. The upper bearing must be pressed in approximately ⅛″ below the top surface of the upper bearing boss.

Examine weight carrier pins and bushings for excessive wear and flat spots. If either of these conditions exist, new parts must be installed.

Weights should be assembled and checked for free movement.

Governor Assembly

Cover

1. Start upper needle bearing straight into bearing bore of cover with number on bearing up. Then press bearing into cover.
2. Reverse cover on bed of press (inner face of cover up). Start second bearing straight into bearing bore of cover with number on bearing up. Place a flat washer over pilot of remover tool, insert pilot of tool into bearing and under ram of press, then press bearing down into cover until washer contacts cover.
3. Lubricate throttle shaft needle bearings with multi-purpose grease. Then insert throttle shaft through bearings.
4. Insert seal ring over shaft and into counterbore against upper bearing. Place retainer over shaft and against seal ring.
5. Start spacer over throttle shaft with holes in lever and shaft for tapered pin in alignment.
6. Press spacer down on shaft until holes in spacer are in line with

hole in shaft.
7. Insert tapered pin in hole of spacer, then drive pin into place.
8. Position throttle control lever on throttle shaft and tighten retaining bolt.
9. Slide fuel shut-off lever shaft through bushing and place lever, under governor cover, on right side of pin (viewed from blower end of governor.)
10. Place seal ring on fuel shut off lever shaft and seal ring retainer (two flat washers) and retain with lock ring.
11. Install fuel shut-off lever on shaft and secure with clamping bolt.

Installation

1. Place gasket on fuel pump and mount fuel pump on governor housing.
2. Place fuel pump drive fork on fuel pump shaft. Rotate pump shaft until fork aligns with drive on blower rotor.
3. Slide governor and fuel pump assembly straight on dowels of blower housing. Align splines of weight shaft with splines in blower rotor and fuel pump coupling with drive while assembling governor to blower.
4. Insert bolts and washers at locations as indicated and tighten alternately and evenly.
5. Reconnect fuel lines at fuel pump.
6. Install water by-pass tube between thermostat housing with the use of hoses and hose clamps.
7. Slide each hose on the fuel rod covers and tighten hose clamps.
8. Assemble the governor operating lever link connecting pin to the govrnor operating lever connecting link as follows:
   a. Insert one control link operating lever retaining ring on inner groove of pin.
   b. Insert connecting link over end of pin and against retaining ring.
   c. Insert one control link operating lever retaining ring on outer groove of pin.
9. Insert fuel rods between cylinder heads and governor as follows:
10. Install right fuel rod:
   a. Insert fuel rod through fuel rod cover and into control link operating lever.
   b. Align rod end with opening in the control link operating lever and insert pin. Screw pin into postion and tighten securely.
11. Install left fuel rod:
   a. Place on shim on differential lever.
   b. Slide the operating lever link connecting pin into the control link operating lever and at the same time slide the connecting link over the pin of the differential lever.
   c. Secure the assembly by placing shim over pin of differential lever and retain with the spring retainer.
12. Place governor housing cover-gasket on housing and install governor cover. Be sure governor control lever assembly enters slot of differential lever and shut down lever, on under side of cover, is between the stop pin and the differential pin. Tighten screws securely.
13. Reconnect control linkage to throttle and stop control levers at top of cover.
14. Perform tune-up.

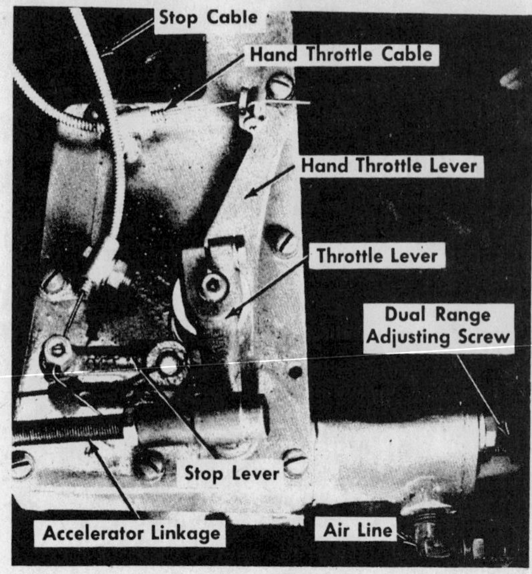

Governor installed
(© G.M.C.)

Cooling System

Description

Control of engine temperature is accomplished by means of two thermostats controlling the flow of cooling liquid within a sealed cooling system. A sealed system utilizes a pressure value which maintains a slight pressure within the system when engine is running at normal operating temperature, thus raising the efficiency of the system.

Coolant is drawn from the lower portion of the radiator by the water pump and is forced through the oil cooler housing and into the cylinder block. From the cylinder block the coolant passes up through the cylinder head and, when the engine is at normal operating temperature, through the thermostat housing and into the upper portion of the radiator. Then the coolant passes down a series of tubes, where the coolant temperature is lowered by the air stream created by the revolving fan.

During the engine warm-up period, action of thermostats directs flow of cooling liquid back to the water pump. This arrangement permits circulation of liquid within the engine, warming the engine and shortening the warm-up period. As engine reaches normal operating temperature, thermostats open gradually, allowing cooling liquid to flow through radiator, thus maintaining an efficient operating temperature.

Water Pump Seal Replacement

The water pump seal can be replaced by removing the impeller without removing the pump from the engine.

1. Remove the water pump cover and gasket.

Water Pump Removal

1. Drain cooling system by opening drain cocks at corners of cylinder block.
2. Remove hose clamps and slide hoses off the pump body.
3. Remove the three bolts that secure the pump to the balance weight cover, then lift the pump away from the engine being careful not to damage teeth of water pump drive gear.

Disassembly

1. Remove the cover and impeller.
2. Remove bearing retaining snap ring by placing pliers through one of the holes in the water pump drive gear.
3. Push the pump shaft, bearings and gear from housing.
4. Press gear from shaft.
5. Inspect the pump seals and remove only if cracked or worn. New seals should be used for replacement.

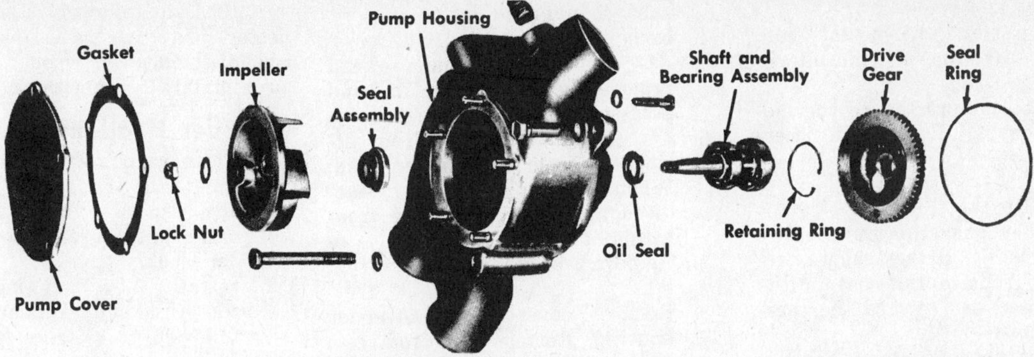

Water pump components (© G.M.C.)

Removing retaining ring (© G.M.C.)

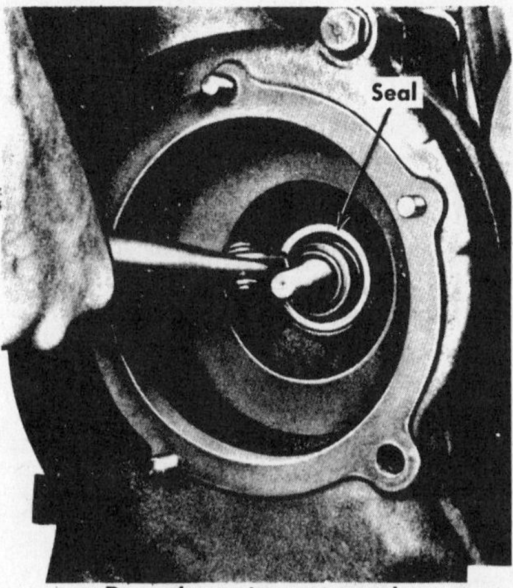

Removing water pump seal (© G.M.C.)

Pressing drive gear from shaft (© G.M.C.)

Inspection

1. Wash all the pump parts thoroughly in clean fuel oil and blow dry with compressed air, then inspect.
2. Ball bearings and races should be examined for indications of corrosion or pitting.

Assembly

1. Apply a film of lube oil to the outside diameter of the seal and place it so the lip is facing the bearings. Tap the seal into the pump housing.
2. Mount pump body in an arbor press with impeller side upward. Using a suitable hollow tool (to slide over seal face and spring) place on outer casing and press water seal into pump housing.
3. Apply film of lube oil to shaft, then slide shaft and bearings in pump housing. Install bearing retaining ring. NOTE: Early engines have pump gear and camshaft gear with 59 and 42 teeth respectively. Latest pump gear and camshaft gear have 92 and 66 teeth respectively. Early and latest type gears are not interchangeable.
4. Place water pump in arbor press. Support shaft on impeller end and press the drive gea onto shaft, against the inner race of bearing. CAUTION: Support should be placed directly between shaft and base of press. Pump housing or studs should not be allowed to touch press while gear is being installed.
5. Apply a thin film of oil to the ceramic seat of impeller and place on tapered shaft. Place the washer and lock nut on shaf and tighten to 30-35 ft-lbs. torque.
6. Measure the clearance betweer the impeller and pump housing. There should be a minimum clearance of .015″. This can be checked by placing a feeler gauge in the water outlet opening.
7. Using a new gasket between cover and body tighten nuts securely.

Water Pump Installation

1. Mount the pump on the engine and tighten the three bolts.
2. Slide the hose into position on the pump and tighten the clamps.
3. Fill the cooling system with clean fresh water.

Thermostat

Description

The temperature of the coolant is controlled by two thermostats, one for each cylinder head. On truck engines, thermostats are installed in separate housing attached directly to cylinder head. On coach engines both thermostats are installed in a single housing attached to right cylinder head.

Removal

1. Drain cooling system to necessary level.
2. Remove the hose connections from the thermostat housing cover.
3. Remove the bolts which secure the cover to the thermostat hous-

ing.

4. Remove the thermostat and clean seat for thermostat in housing.
5. Inspect seal pressed in thermostat housing. Remove if necessary.

Installation

1. Place new gasket on the thermostat housing. If the seal was removed, replace the seal in the the closed end toward the thermostat.
2. Set the thermostat in housing and replace the cover and hoses.
3. Fill cooling system and check for leaks.

Engine Repair Section

Cylinder Head

The cylinder head and/or gasket at either right-hand or left-hand cylinder bank may be replaced in manner described below:

Cylinder Head Removal

1. Drain cooling system. Remove engine access cover from inside cab.
2. Disconnect battery.
3. Disconnect exhaust pipe from exhaust manifold.
4. Remove exhaust manifold.
5. At front of cylinder head remove thermostat housing and accessory brackets (when used).
6. Disconnect fuel lines from fittings at front of cylinder head. When removing left-hand head, disconnect fuel return line from fitting at rear of head.
7. Remove rocker arm cover from head.
8. Remove cover from governor housing. Remove nut from fuel rod, then remove pin attaching link to tube lever and remove link.
9. Inside governor housing, remove fuel rod.
10. Loosen hose clamps, then move hoses as necessary to permit removal of rod cover (tube).
11. Remove injector rack control tube and bracket assembly.
12. Remove cylinder head bolts in gradual stages to relieve spring pressure. When bolts have been removed, lift cylinder head assembly off cylinder block. Remove seals and gaskets from cylinder liners and from recesses in block.

CAUTION: When resting the cylinder head assembly on a bench protect the cam follower rollers and injector spray tips by testing the valve side of the head on wooden blocks approximately 2 inches thick.

Cylinder Head Installation

1. Clean carbon from tops of pistons and, if necessary, remove any deposits found in groove and counterbores in top of cylinder block.
2. Install new cylinder head compression gaskets and seals as follows:
   a. Install a new compression gasket on each cylinder liner.
   b. Place new seal rings in the counterbores of water and oil holes in cylinder block.
   c. Install a new oil seal in milled groove near the outer edge of area covered by cylinder head. NOTE: Oil seals, and compression gaskets should never be re-used.
3. Install guide studs in head bolt holes in cylinder block to insure positive location of head without disturbing seals and gasket. CAUTION: Compression gaskets and/or seals which are jarred out of their proper location will allow leaks and "blow-by" which will result in poor performance and damage to engine.
4. Wipe bottom of cylinder head clean, then lower cylinder head onto guide studs and down into contact with block. Lubricate threads and pressure area of bolt heads with S.A.E. #30 engine oil, then start all cylinder head bolts. Beginning at camshaft side of cylinder head

Governor cover housing removed showing fuel rod connecting screws
(© G.M.C.)

1 Fuel rod to R.H. cylinder head
2 Governor springs
3 Fuel rod-to-lever screws
4 Governor housing
5 Fuel rod to L.H. cylinder head
6 Fuel rod operating lever

V6-engine with rocker arm cover removed
(© G.M.C.)

Fuel rod and link installation
(© G.M.C.)

1 Governor housing
2 Hose and clamp
3 Control rod cover
4 Fuel control rod
5 Rod Nut
6 Lower link
7 Link pin
8 Injector control tube lever
9 Control tube spring
10 Control tube
11 Cylinder head (L.H.)

Installing cylinder head on engine
(© G.M.C.)

tighten head bolts lightly to overcome tension of cam follower springs.

5. Tighten cylinder head bolts about one-half turn in sequence. Use torque wrench for final tightening of cylinder head bolts. Correct torque is 170 to 180 foot-pounds: Do not tighten bolts beyond specified torque.
6. Cover oil drain holes in head to prevent foreign objects from falling into holes. Install injectors (if removed). Check push rods to see that each one is threaded completely through clevis, then tip rocker arms into position with valve bridges squarely positioned at valve stems. Install rocker arm shaft bracket bolts and tighten to 50 foot-pounds torque.
7. Set injector control tube and lever assembly in place and install attaching bolts finger tight. Check injector control tube levers for engagement with slots in injector control racks. Also, be sure ends of rack control tube return spring are properly hooked; i.e., one end hooked around adjacent control tube bracket. Tighten bracket to head bolts and torque to 10 to 12 foot-pounds.
8. Try operating the injector control tube to determine if return spring rotates tube back to "No-Fuel" position after tube is manually moved to "Full-Fuel" position. If there is binding present, strike the control tube brackets lightly with soft hammer to correct any misalignment of tube bearings.
9. Install fuel rod through opening in top of governor housing; pass rod through hoses, clamps, and tubular cover (used at left-hand head). Attach fuel rod to governor lever with screw inside governor housing. Install governor housing cover with new gasket. Assemble hose and clamps to secure fuel rod cover.
10. Install fuel link between fuel rod and lever on control tube.
11. Connect fuel line at fitting at rear of left-hand cylinder head.
12. Mount thermostat housing on front of cylinder head.
13. Install exhaust manifold. Tighten manifold stud nuts to 25 to 40 foot-pounds.
14. Connect exhaust pipe. Fill cooling system and check for leaks.
15. Adjust exhaust valve clearance. Set injector timing.
16. Start engine and operate until normal operating temperature is reached, then recheck cylinder head bolt torque and make final check of exhaust valve clearance.
17. Install rocker arm cover on cylinder head.

Valve Seats

Inspect valve seat to determine if they are fit for further use. Inspection should include cleanliness, concentricity, flatness, and presence of cracks. If exhaust valve seat inserts are loose in cylinder head, or if for any reason due to wear pitting, etc., replacement of valve seat is necessary, oversize (.010") exhaust valve seat inserts are available.

The valve seat inserts are shrunk into the cylinder head and, therefore, must be replaced as outlined in the following procedure to avoid damage to the cylinder head:

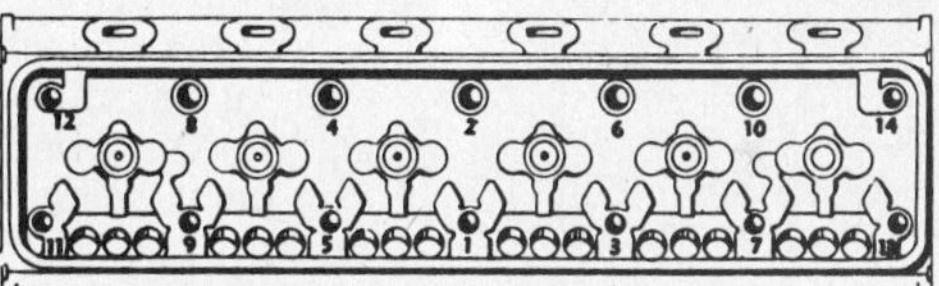

Cylinder head tightening sequence in-line 6 cyl. engine
(© G.M.C.)

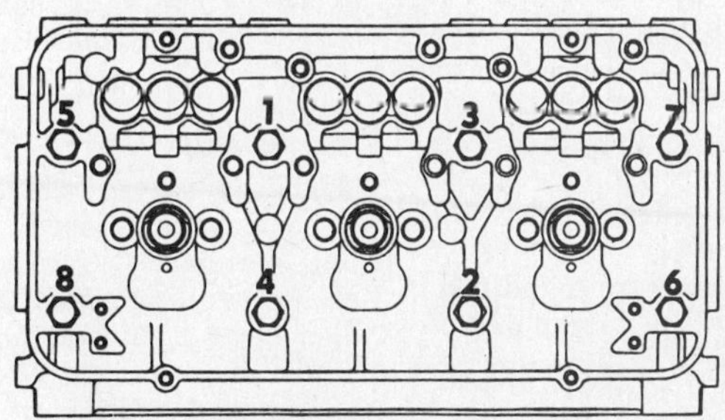

Cylinder head tightening sequence V6-engine
(© G.M.C.)

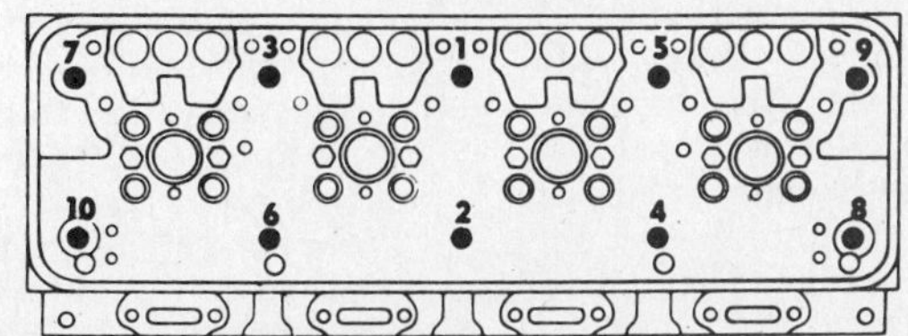

Cylinder head tightening sequence in-line 4 cyl. and V8 engines
(© G.M.C.)

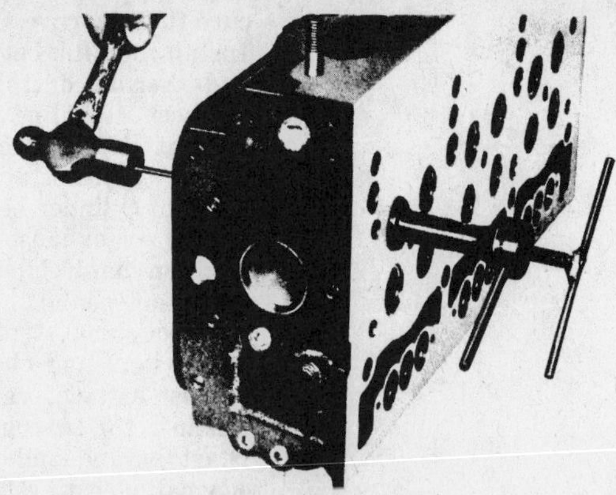
Removing valve seat insert
(© G.M.C.)

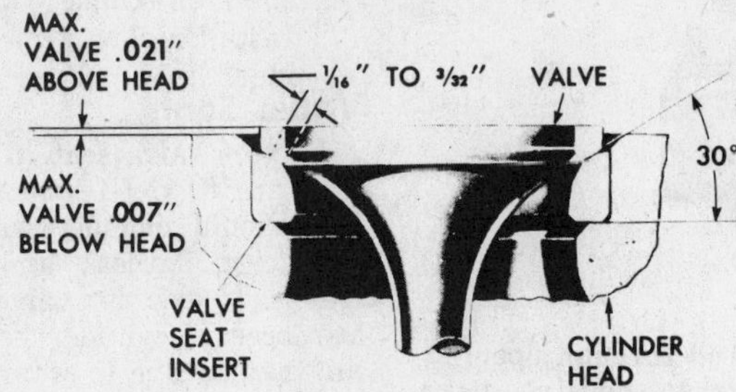

Installation of valve and valve seat insert
(© G.M.C.)

Checking valve seat concentricity
(© G.M.C.)

Valve Seat Removal

1. Place cylinder head on its side on workbench.
2. Place collet of tool inside valve insert so that bottom of collet is flush with bottom of insert.
3. Hold the collet handle and turn the T handle to expand collet cone and insert is held securely by the tool.
4. Insert drive bar of tool through valve guide.
5. Tap the drive bar once or twice to move the insert about 1/16″ away from its seat in the cylinder head.
6. Loosen the collet cone and move the tool into the insert slightly so that the narrow flange at the bottom of the collet is below the valve seat insert.
7. Tighten the collet cone and continue to drive the insert out of the cylinder head.

Valve Seat Installation

1. Wash the counterbores in the cylinder head for the valve seat inserts with trichloroethylene or other good solvent. Also, wash the valve inserts with the same solvent. Dry the counterbores and inserts with compressed air.
2. Inspect the counterbores for cleanliness, concentricity, flatness and cracks.
3. Immerse the cylinder head for at least 30 minutes in water heated to 180°F. to 200°F. At the same time, cool the valve seat insert as much as possible (dry ice may be used for this purpose).
4. Rest the cylinder head, bottom side up, on bench and lay an insert in counterbore—valve seat up. If the temperature of the two parts are allowed to become nearly the same, installation may become difficult and damage to the parts may result.
5. Using tool, drive insert down tight into counterbore.
6. Grind the valve seat insert and check it for concentricity in relation to the valve guide.

Recondition Valve Seat

Exhaust valves which are to be reused may be refaced, if necessary, using standard refacing procedure. Before installing either a new or used valve, examine the valve insert in the cylinder head for proper valve seating. The proper angle for the seating face of both the valve and valve insert is 30°. The angle of the valve seat insert must be exactly the same as the angle of the valve face so as to provide proper seating of the valve.

Grind the inserts as follows:

1. First apply a 30° grinding wheel on valve seat insert.
2. Use a 60° grinding wheel to open the throat of the insert.
3. Then grind top surface with a 15° wheel to narrow width of the seat from 1/16″ to 3/32″ The 30° face of the in-sert may be adjusted relative to the center of the valve face with the 15° and 60° grinding wheels.

CAUTION: Do not permit grinding wheels to contact the cylinder head when grinding the inserts.

4. After valve inserts have been ground, the cylinder head should be thoroughly cleaned. Then check the concentricity of the valve seats relative to the valve guides. Total runout for a good valve seat should not exceed .002″. If total runout exceeds .002″ check for bent valve guide before regrinding insert.
5. After valve seats have been ground, the position of the contact area between the valve and valve insert should be determined in the following manner:
   a. Apply a light coat of Prussian Blue or similar paste to the valve seat insert.
   b. Lower stem of valve in the valve guide and "bounce" valve on seat. *Do not rotate valve.* This procedure will show (on the valve face) the area of contact. The most desirable area of contact is at the center of the valve face.

Injector Tube

Whenever inspection indicates that injector copper tube in cylinder head requires replacement, the operation must be performed with the greatest of care and with special tools in the manner following:

Injector Tube Removal

1. Attach cylinder head holding plates to the cylinder head or support the cylinder head on its side with exhaust ports down. Place the injector tube installer into injector tube.
2. Insert pilot through the small opening in injector tube and thread pilot into hole in end of installer.
3. Tap end of pilot with hammer to loosen injector tube. Lift tube, pilot, and installer from cylinder head.

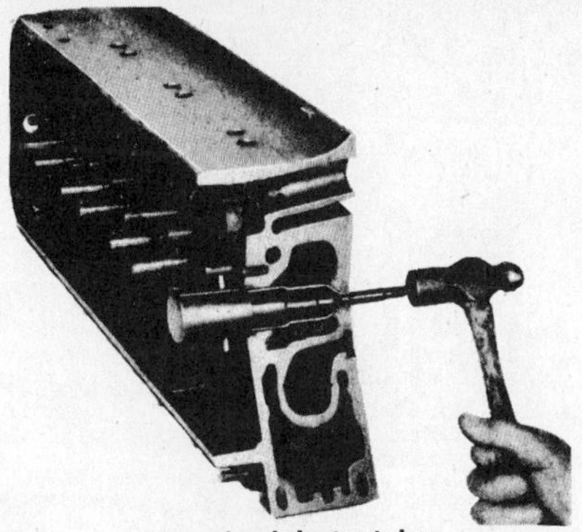
Removing injector tube
(© G.M.C.)

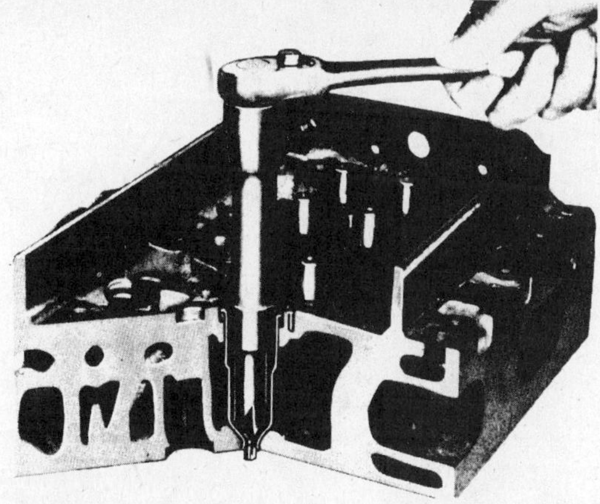
Reaming injector tube beuel seat for injector body nut
(© G.M.C.)

Inspection

Installation of the injector tube requires careful preparation and inspection to make sure that the area of the cylinder head is clean so that when tube contacts the cast iron cylinder head, foreign material will not prevent tube seating at bottom or sealing at top.

Injector Tube Installation

1. Place injector tube sealing ring in cylinder head injector tube counterbore.
2. Place driver in injector tube, insert pilot through the small opening of injector tube and thread pilot tapped end of driver.
3. Slip the injector tube into injector bore and drive into place. The flange at upper end of tube will seat on the seal ring and into the counterbore of cylinder head when the injector tube is properly positioned.
4. With the injector tube properly positioned in cylinder head. flare lower end of injector tube, as follows:
   a. Turn cylinder head bottom side up, remove pilot and thread flaring tool into tapped end of driver.
   b. Then, using a socket and torque wrench, apply approximately 30 ft.-lb. torque on flaring tool.
   c. Remove injector tube installing tools and proceed to ream the injector tube.

Valve Guides

Cleaning And Inspection

After cleaning, inspect the valve guides for fractures, scoring or excessive wear and replace if necessary. The inside diameter of a new valve guide is .3125″ to .3135″ which will produce a valve stem-to-guide clearance, with a new valve, of .002″ to .004″. If the clearance exceeds .005″, install a new guide and/or valve.

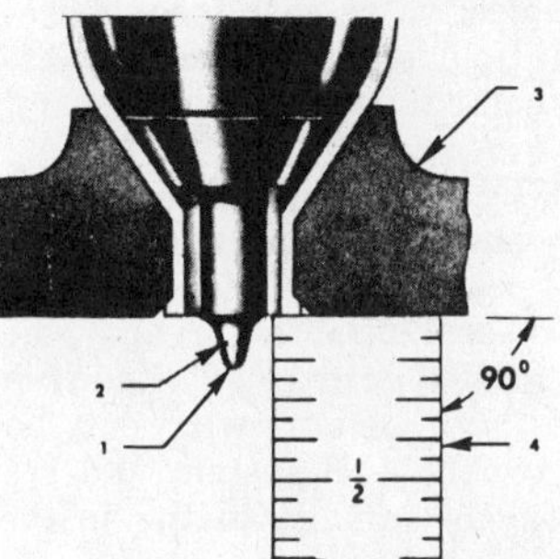

Checking location of injector spray tip in relation to surface of cylinder head
(© G.M.C.)

1 Spray tip
2 Orifice—injector spray tip
3 Cylinder head
4 Straight edge-steel

Valve Guide Removal

1. Support the cylinder head (bottom side up) on wood blocks 2″ above the workbench.
2. Drive valve guide out of cylinder head.

Valve Guide Installation

Rest the bottom of the cylinder head on a workbench, and install guide as follows:

1. Remove exhaust valve bridge guides.
2. Insert the threaded end of the valve guide into installer. Valve guides must be installed with internal threads toward top to provide for lubrication of valve stems.
3. Locate the valve guide squarely in the top of cylinder head and tap gently to start it into place.
4. With the guide properly started, drive in until its upper end projects .88″ above the top of the cylinder head. This dimension is automatically provided by the valve guide installer tool. NOTE: Service valve guides are "pre-finished" and, therefore, do not require reaming.
5. Install threaded valve bridge guides. Tighten to 45-50 ft. lbs. Latest type guides are pressed into cylinder head.

Valve Bridge and Guide

Early engines used an exhaust valve bridge guide which was threaded into cylinder head. Threaded bridge guides were superseded by a straight guide which is pressed into cylinder head. Valve bridge springs have now been eliminated on latest engines.

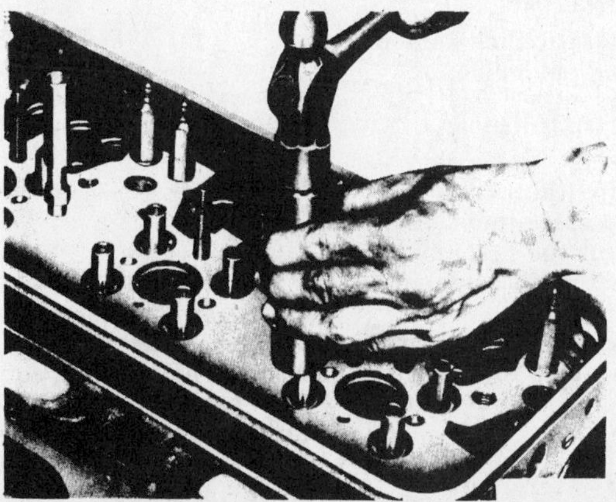
Installing exhaust valve guide
(© G.M.C.)

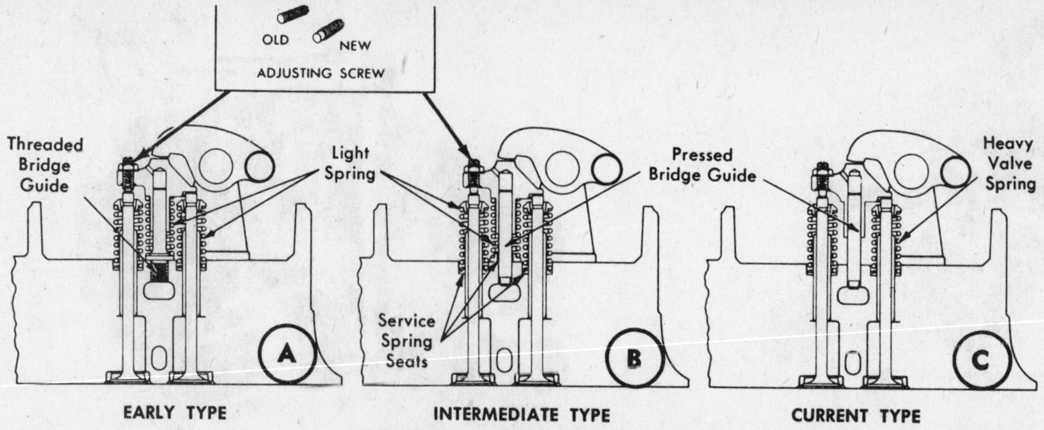

Exhaust valve bridge and guide (© G.M.C.)

A combination of soft steel guide and a soft steel bridge must be avoided, otherwise premature wear will occur.

Valve bridge springs can be removed and discharged on any engine whenever desirable; however, it is suggested that they be removed at time of overhaul. On engines used in trucks and parlor coaches heavier exhaust valve springs must be used when bridge springs are removed.

Bridge Guide Removal

1. Threaded guide can be identified by the hexagon section at the base of the guide and can be removed by using a thin wall socket.
2. On pressed guides, file or grind two notches 1/16″ deep on opposite sides of the guide and about ¾″ from upper end.
3. Place tool spacer over end of guide, then place remover tool over guide with two screws in alignment with two notches. Tighten set screws securely.
4. Thread nut onto remover tool and turn to pull guide from cylinder head.
5. Should guide be broken, drill a hole about ½″ deep in end of guide with #3 (.2130″) drill. Tap the guide with ¼″-28 bottoming tap. Thread adapter into guide, then attach slide hammer to adapter and pull guide.

Bridge Guide Installation

1. Threaded bridge guide may be installed, using thin wall socket.
2. Start pressed guide into cylinder head (undercut end first).
3. Use installer tool to drive guide into place.
4. Use of installer tool will properly position guide to its proper height of 2.04″ above cylinder head.

Cylinder Head Assembly

New service replacement cylinder heads are equipped with valve guides, bridge guides, valve seat inserts, exhaust manifold studs, water nozzles, injector hole tubes and necessary plugs.

CAUTION: When installing plugs in fuel manifolds, apply a small amount of sealant to threads of plugs only. Work sealant into threads and wipe off excess with clean, lint-free cloth so that sealant will not be washed into the fuel system and result in serious damage to the injectors.

When a new cylinder head is to be used, the parts listed above should be removed from the old head and installed in the new head. If the old cylinder head is to be reused, the parts listed below should be installed in the old head prior to installation of the head to the cylinder block.

1. Exhaust valves and springs, cam followers and springs, valve and injector rocker arms and shafts should be assembled to cylinder head.
2. Using new steel washers, install fuel connectors and tighten to 35-40 ft.-lbs. torque.

Valve and Injector Mechanism

Description

Rocker Arms

Valve and injector rocker arms for each cylinder operate on a separate shaft supported by two cast iron brackets. A single bolt fastens each bracket securely to top of cylinder head.

Cam Followers

Contact between cam followers and cam is made by a hardened steel roller. The roller is equipped with a steel-backed bronze bushing running directly on a pin in lower end of cam follower. A separate coil spring, located inside of the hollow cam follower, is held in place in cylinder head by a spring seat retainer. A dropforged steel guide is provided for each set of three cam followers. This guide, located on bottom of cylinder head, keeps the rollers in line with cams and also serves as a retainer during assembly and disassembly.

Maintenance

Some service operations may be accomplished on cylinder head, valves, and injectors assembly without removing the cylinder head assembly from the block. These operations are:

1. Valve Lash.
2. Valve Spring Replacement.
3. Valve Bridge Adjustment.
4. Rocker Arm, Shaft, or Shaft Bracket Replacement.
5. Injector Replacement.
6. Cam Follower Spring Replacement.
7. Cam Follower Replacement.
8. Push Rod Replacemet.

Valve Lash and Bridge Adjustment

CAUTION: Whenever a push rod has been disconnected from the push rod clevis, the rod must be screwed back into the clevis, flush with the top of the threaded portion of the clevis before valve lash is checked. *If this is not done, before engine is turned, the pistom may hit head of valve due to the small clearance between valves and piston head at the piston upper position.*

Correct valve lash is important due to high compression pressures. Too little clearance causes a loss of compression, missing cylinder, and eventual burning of valves and valve seats. Too much clearance between valve stem and valve rocker arm results in noisy operation of engine, especially in idling range.

NOTE: It is recommended when lashing valves to set them first cold; then start engine and warm up to normal operating temperature. Reset valve lash after engine has warmed up to operating temperature.

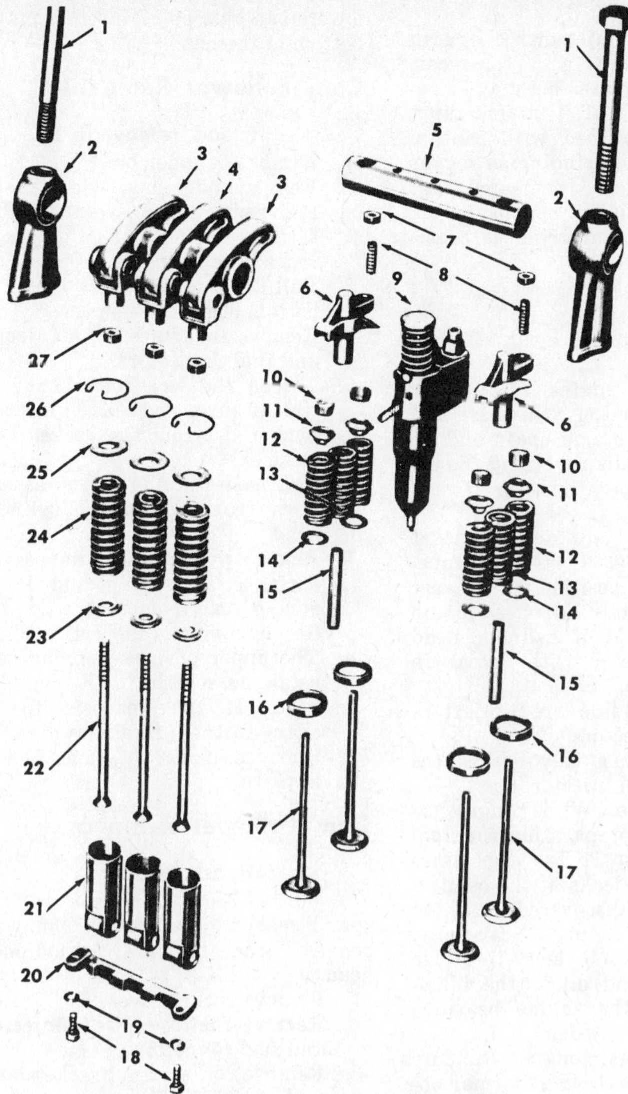

Valves, injector and operating mechanism
(© G.M.C.)

1 Bracket bolt
2 Rocker shaft bracket
3 Valve rocker arm
4 Injector rocker arm
5 Rocker shaft
6 Valve bridge
7 Screw nut
8 Adjusting screw
9 Injector assembly
10 Valve spring lock
11 Valve spring cap
12 Valve spring
13 Bridge spring (Early models)
14 Valve spring seat
15 Bridge guide (Pressed Type)
16 Valve seat insert
17 Exhaust valve
18 Guide bolt
19 Lock washer
20 Cam follower guide
21 Cam follower
22 Push rod
23 Spring seat—Lower
24 Push rod spring
25 Spring seat—Upper
26 Spring seat retainer
27 Lock nut

Valve Spring

It is possible, if occasion requires, to remove or replace the exhaust valve springs without removing cylinder head. The springs, however, are normally removed when the head is off the engine. Both methods are covered in paragraph following.

Valve Spring Removal

(Head installed)

Procedure for removing exhaust valve springs while cylinder head is installed is as follows:

1. Remove rocker cover.
2. Bring valve and injector rocker arms in line horizontally.
3. Remove fuel lines from injectors and fuel connectors.
4. Remove the two bolts holding rocker arm shaft brackets to cylinder head then remove brackets and shaft. Lift rocker arms up and away from the valves.
5. Remove exhaust valve bridges and bridge springs.
6. Remove cylinder block air box cover so that piston travel may be observed, then turn crankshaft until piston is at top of stroke.
7. Thread valve spring compressor adaptor into rocker shaft bolt hole in cylinder head. Apply pressure to end of valve spring compressor handle to compress valve spring. Remove the two-piece tapered spring lock.
8. Release tool and remove valve spring cap, valve spring and spring seat.

Compressing valve spring
(© G.M.C.)

Valve Spring Removal

(Head removed)

To remove the exhaust valve spring with the cylinder head removed from the engine, use the following procedure:

1. Support the cylinder head on wood blocks 2" above the workbench so as to keep the cam followers clear of workbench.
2. Remove fuel lines from injector and fuel connectors.
3. Remove the two bolts holding rocker arm shaft brackets to cylinder head. Lift rocker arms and brackets up and away from injector.
4. Remove fuel injector.
5. Remove exhaust valve bridges and bridge springs.
6. Remove exhaust valve spring from cylinder head as previously outlined. In addition, use a block of wood under cylinder head to support exhaust valve.

Inspection

After removing valve spring, clean with fuel oil and dry with compressed air. Check spring for pitted or fractured coils. Then, using spring tester, test spring load.

Valve Removal

With the cylinder head removed from the engine and valve springs removed, number each valve and adjacent area prior to removal to facilitate later assembly to the same seat. Then withdraw valves from cylinder head.

Inspection

1. Scrape the carbon from the valve stem, wash with clean fuel oil, and check for scratches or scuff marks.

2. Valve faces should be smooth, and free from ridges and pits. Carbon on the face of the valve indicates a faulty seat and a resultant leak or "blow-by." If any of these conditions exist, a new valve should be installed or the valve refaced to an angle of 30°. NOTE: The valve face angle must be identical to the valve seat angle.
3. Valve heads should be square with the valve stem and should not be warped.

Valve Installation

With the cylinder head thoroughly cleaned, the valve guides checked or replaced and the valves and valve inserts ground, install the valves as follows:

1. Apply a light coat of engine oil to the valve stems and install them in the cylinder head.
2. Secure the valves in place temporarily with masking tape. Then turn head over, resting valve heads on wood block or board and install spring seats, valve springs, valve spring caps and locks by reversing the procedure for removal.

NOTE: After valves have been installed, check to make sure the heads of the valves do not project more than .021" beyond surface of cylinder head.

Rocker Arms and Shaft Removal

1. Remove valve rocker cover.
2. Remove fuel lines from injector and fuel connectors.
3. Bring push rod ends—outer ends—or injector and valve rocker arms in line horizontally.
4. Remove the two bolts which hold the rocker arm shaft brackets to the cylinder head. Remove brackets and shaft.
5. Loosen the lock nut at upper end of push rod, next to clevis, and unscrew the rocker arm from the push rod.

Inspection

1. Make certain that oil passages in rocker arm shaft and bracket bolts are open and clean.
2. Inspect rocker arm shaft and bushings inside the rocker arms for excessive wear. Clearance should be .001" to .0025" with new parts. A maximum clearance of .004" is allowable with worn parts.
3. Check push rod clevis to rocker arm bushings and pins for excessive wear. The clearance bebetween the steel clevis pin bushing and the bronze rocker arm bushing is .0015" to .003". The side clearance between the clevis and rocker arm should be from .008" to .017".
4. Examine the injector rocker arm pallet (contact face) for wear. The rocker arm pallet may be refaced up to .010" by grinding. However, proceed with caution when surface grinding so rocker arms are not overheated. All radii and finish should be as close to original grind as possible.

Installation

1. Install cylinder head, if removed.
2. Apply clean engine oil to outer surface of rocker arm shaft and install rocker arm shaft and/or rocker arms by reversing the sequence of operations for removal.
3. Tighten rocker arm bracket bolts to 90-100 ft.-lb. torque. Then check position of exhaust valve bridges. Valve stem on camshaft side of cylinder head should register with recess in bridge guide.
4. Connect fuel lines from injectors to fuel connectors.
5. Adjust exhaust valve clearances and time fuel injectors.
6. Start engine. While engine is running in preparation for final tune-up, inspect the fuel lines for leaks. If leaks at the connections are discovered, tighten connecting nuts carefully. Should fuel oil leak into the crankcase and dilute the lubricating oil, the engine bearings will be seriously damaged.
7. Perform final engine tune-up after engine reaches normal operating temperature.

Cam Follower

Cam followers may be removed from either the top or bottom of the cylinder head. When followers are removed from the bottom, removal of the cylinder head will be necessary; when they are removed from the top, cylinder head removal is unnecessary. If the cylinder head is off the engine for any reason, the cam followers can best be removed from the bottom of the head.

Cam Follower Removal

(Head removed)

1. Remove cylinder head.
2. Rest cylinder head on its side and remove the two bolts that secure cam follower guide to cylinder head. Remove guide.
3. Pull the cam followers from the bottom of the cylinder head.
4. Remove fuel lines from injector and fuel connectors.
5. Loosen the lock nuts at upper end of push rods, and unscrew push rods from the rocker arm clevises.
6. Pull push rod and spring assemblies from bottom of cylinder head.
7. Remove push rod lock nut, upper spring seat, spring and lower spring seat from each push rod for cleaning and inspection.
8. The upper push rod spring seat retainers remain in the cylinder head. If the head is to be changed, these retainers must be removed, if not, they may be left in place.

Cam Follower Removal

(Head installed)

A push rod, push rod spring, spring seats and cam follower may be removed from the top of the cylinder head.

1. Remove rocker cover.
2. Remove fuel lines from injector and fuel connectors.
3. Remove rocker arm brackets and rocker arm shaft.
4. Loosen lock nut at upper end of push rod, next to clevis, and unscrew rocker arm from push rod to be removed.
5. Run nut out on push rod so that tool may be inserted between the nut and the upper spring seat, with lower end of tool resting on upper spring seat.
6. Screw nut down on upper end of push rod, thus compressing push rod spring, relieving spring seat

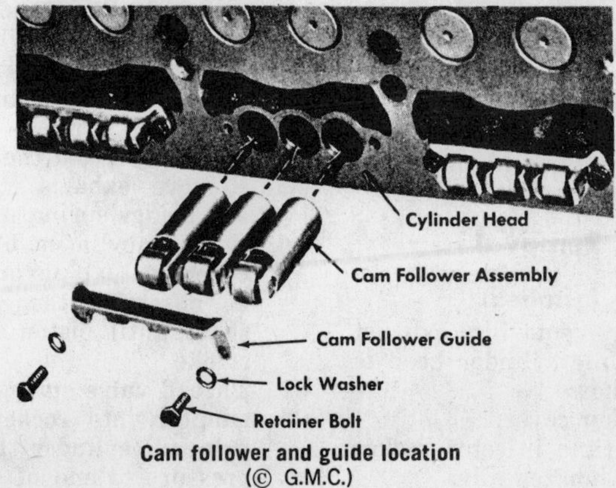

Cam follower and guide location
(© G.M.C.)

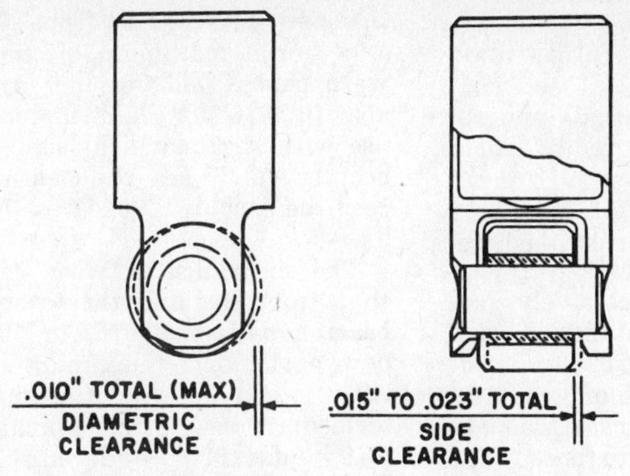

Cam roller wear clearance
(© G.M.C.)

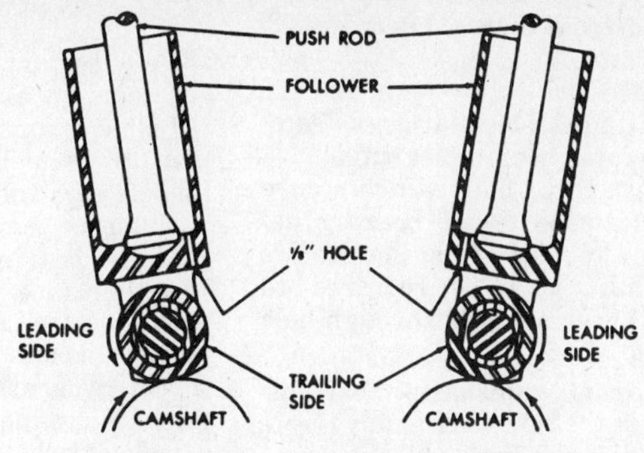

Installation of cam followers
(© G.M.C.)

retainer.

7. Remove retainer from cylinder head with a screwdriver or similar tool.
8. Unscrew nut at outer end of push rod, thus releasing spring.
9. Pull push rod, spring, spring seats and cam followers out through top of cylinder head.

Replace Roller And Pin

1. Lock holding tool securely in vise and place cam follower in the groove in top of tool with follower pin resting on top of corresponding size plunger.
2. With suitable drift, drive pin from follower. Exercise caution in removing cam follower body and roller from holder, as follower pin is seated on top of spring loaded plunger.
3. Position follower body in groove of holding tool with the proper size tool plunger extending through roller pin hole in one of the legs of the follower body.
4. Coat new roller bushing and pin with engine oil.
5. With roller assembly placed properly on tool, align pin with hole in follower and carefully drive pin into the assembly until end of pin is centered in legs of follower.
6. Check side clearance between roller and follower body. This clearance should be .015″ to .023″.

Cam Follower Installation

(Head removed)

To assemble the cam follower and push rod assembly through the bottom of the cylinder head proceed as follows:

1. Assemble over the push rod, in order listed, lower spring seat, push rod spring, upper spring seat, and push rod lock nut.
2. With the upper spring seat retainer in place in the cylinder head, slide the push rod assemblies into position from bottom of cylinder head.
3. Screw push rod lock nut down on upper end of push rod as far as possible, and screw push rod into clevis until end of rod is flush with or above inner side of clevis.
4. Note the oil hole in the bottom of the follower. With this oil hole pointing away from the valves, so that the hole is not covered by the follower guide, slide the followers into position from bottom of head. NOTE: To insure initial lubrication of the follower roller pin, immerse cam follower assemblies in clean lubricating oil for at least five minutes before installing them in cylinder head.
5. Secure follower guide to bottom of cylinder head to hold group of cam followers in place. Then check to be sure there is clearance between the cam follower legs and the cam follower guide.

Cam Follower Installation

(Head installed)

1. With the oil hole in the bottom of the follower over the trailing side of roller (cam follower oil hole toward outside of cylinder head), insert follower into bore in head. NOTE: To insure initial lubrication of the follower roller pin, immerse cam follower assemblies in clean lubricating oil for at least five minutes before installing them in cyclinder head.
2. Install lower spring seat, push rod spring and upper spring seat on push rod in the order listed, and set the assembly down into the cam follower.
3. Start nut on outer end of push rod, and install tool beneath nut on push rod and against upper spring seat. Then screw nut down on push rod until spring is compressed sufficiently to permit retainer to be inserted in cylinder head. Partially collapse retainer and install in groove in the cylinder head.
4. Unscrew nut at outer end of push rod and remove tool.
5. Screw lock nut as far as possible down on push rod, then screw rocker arm clevis down on push rod until the end of the push rod is flush with or above inner side of clevis.
6. Observe that the injector rocker arm (the center arm of the group) is slightly different from the exhaust valve rocker arms; the boss for the shaft on the valve rocker arms is longer on one side of the arm than on the other. The extended boss of valve rocker arms must face the injector rocker arm.

Camshaft

Camshaft Removal

Whenever an engine is being completely reconditioned or the camshafts, camshaft gears, bearings or thrust washers need replacing, the camshafts must be removed from the engine in the following manner:

1. Remove all accessories and assemblies with their attaching parts necessary to mount engine on overhaul stand.
2. Remove cylinder head.
3. Remove flywheel and flywheel housing.
4. Remove water pump.
5. Remove balance weight cover.
6. Remove bolts securing retainer plates to camshaft timing gears. Then remove retainer plates.
7. Wedge a clean rag between gears. Using a socket wrench, remove nuts from both ends of each camshaft.
8. Attach puller to camshaft pulley. Use adaptor between end of camshaft and puller screw to protect end of camshaft.
9. Remove water pump drive gear from front end of right bank camshaft.
10. Remove Woodruff key and

spacer from forward end of both camshafts.

11. Remove lock screw from the top of cylinder block at each camshaft intermediate bearing.
12. Remove three bolts which secure each camshaft end bearing assembly to rear of engine. Rotate camshaft gear as required to reveal bearing bolts through hole in web of gear.
13. Withdraw camshaft, bearings and gear as an assembly from rear end of cylinder block.
14. Remove three bolts from each camshaft front end bearing. Then, withdraw bearings from cylinder block and front end plate. If the bearings cannot be withdrawn readily by hand, remove by prying under bearing flange.

Disassembly

1. Remove gear from camshaft.
2. Slide camshaft rear end bearing and thrust washers off camshaft
3. Remove lock rings from camshaft intermediate bearings then separate and remove two halves of each bearing.

Inspection

Be sure that oil holes in camshaft end bearings are clean.

Inspect cams and journals and replace the camshaft if scored or worn. Inspect cam followers.

Examine both faces of camshaft rear end bearing and thrust washers. If either face is scored or if thrust washers are worn excessively, replace washers. New standard size thrust washers are .120″ to .122″ thick. Examine surfaces of gear and camshaft which the thrust washers contact; if these surfaces are scratched but not severely scored, they may be smoothed down with an oil stone. However, if score marks are too deep to be removed or parts are badly worn, new parts must be used.

Clearance between the thrust washer and thrust shoulder of the camshaft, using new parts, is from .004″ to .012″, or a maximum of .018″ with used parts. Thrust washers are available in .005″ and .010″ oversize and may be used to reduce excessive clearance within the specified limits of .004″ to .012″.

The clearance between new camshaft end journals and their respective new bearings is from .0025″ to .004″, or a maximum of .006″ with worn parts. End bearings are available in .010″ or 020″ undersize for use with shafts which have worn or been reground and the clearances exceed the specified .0025″ to .004″ limits.

The clearance between the camshaft journals and the intermediate bearings is from .0025″ to .005″ with new parts, or a maximum of .009″ with worn parts. Camshaft intermediate bearings are available in .010″ and .020″ undersize for use with worn or reground shafts in which the clearances exceed the .0025″ to .005″ limits.

Bushings must be finished bored to a 20 R.M.S. finish after installation. Also inside diameter of bushing must be square with rear face of bearing within .0015″ total indicator reading. Camshaft rear end bearing bushings must project .045″ to .055″ from each end of bearing. Bushings in camshaft front end bearing do not project from bearing. End of inner bushing in front end bearing should be installed flush with end of bearing; end of outer bushing should be flush with counterbore in bearing.

Removing camshaft gear retaining nut (© G.M.C.)

Removing camshaft bearing bolts (© G.M.C.)

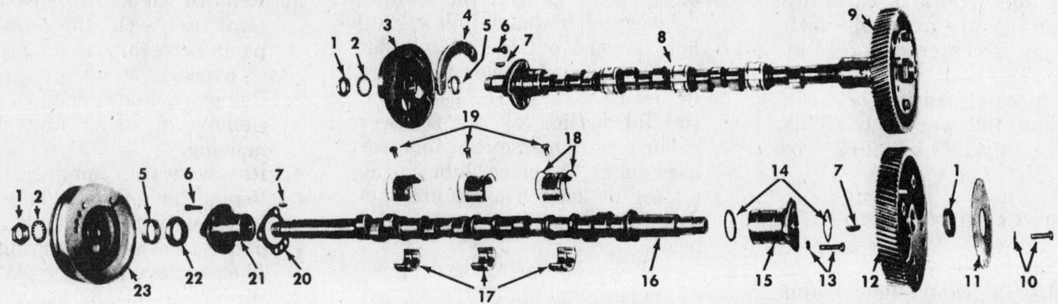

Camshaft components (© G.M.C.)

1 Gear retaining nut
2 Lock washer
3 Water pump drive gear
4 Balance weight
5 Spacer
6 Weight bolt
7 Woodruff key
8 Camshaft—right
9 Timing gear-right
10 Retainer bolt and lock washer
11 Nut retainer
12 Timing gear-left
13 Retainer bolt and lock washer
14 Thrust washer
15 Rear bearing
16 Camshaft—left
17 Intermediate bearing
18 Lock ring
19 Set screw
20 Gasket
21 Front bearing
22 Oil seal
23 Camshaft pulley

If necessary, replace oil seal in left bank camshaft front end bearing.

Examine teeth of water pump drive gear and camshaft gears for evidence of scoring, pitting and wear. Replace gears if necessary.

Camshaft Assembly

Assemble parts on camshaft as follows:

1. Apply heavy cup grease to the steel face of camshaft thrust washers and install thrust washers against each end of camshaft rear bearing. Be sure steel face of washer is next to bearing.
2. Lubricate the camshaft rear bearing journal and slide rear bearing onto camshaft journal with bolting flange of bearing toward outer (gear) end of shaft.
3. Install timing gear on camshaft.
4. Lubricate the camshaft intermediate bearing journals, then place the two halves of each intermediate bearing on camshaft journal and lock halves together with two lock rings. Assemble lock rings with gap in upper bearing and ends equal distance (approximately ½ inch) above split line of bearing.

Camshaft Installation

1. Insert forward end of assembled camshaft through opening in rear end plate until the first intermediate bearing enters bore. Continue to work the camshaft and bearings into the cylinder block until gear teeth are about to engage the teeth of mating gear. Use care not to damage cam lobes when installing shaft.
2. Then, with the timing marks on the mating gears in alignment, slide camshaft gear into mesh.
3. Secure camshaft rear bearing to cylinder block. Rotate camshaft gear as required to install bearing bolts through hole in web of gear. Tighten bolts to 35-40 ft.-lb. torque.
4. Turn camshaft intermediate bearings so that locking holes in bearings align with holes in top of cylinder block and secure in place with lock screws.
5. Install opposite camshaft as outlined in preceding paragraphs.
6. Using a new bearing to end plate gasket, install left bank camshaft front end bearing—the one with the oil seal—in the cylinder block. Secure bearing in place. Tighten bolts to 35-40 ft.-lbs. torque.
7. Install right bank camshaft front end bearing—the one without the oil seal—in the cylinder block. Tighten bearing retaining bolts to 35-40 ft.-lb. torque.
8. Lubricate outside diameter of camshaft front spacer and slide spacer onto front end of left bank camshaft.
9. Install camshaft front spacer on right bank camshaft.
10. Install Woodruff keys in keyways in front end of each camshaft.
11. Install pulley on front end of left bank camshaft and water pump drive gear on right bank camshaft.
12. Slip an internal tooth lock washer over front end of each camshaft. Star nuts on forward end of both camshafts. NOTE: Early engines have water pump gear, and camshaft gear with 59 and 42 teeth respectively. Latest pump gear and camshaft gear have 92 and 66 teeth respectively. Early and latest type gears are not interchangeable.

Removing or installing camshaft assembly (© G.M.C.)

13. Start nuts on rear end of each camshaft.
14. Wedge a clean rag between the camshaft gears to prevent their rotation; then, using a 1½" socket wrench, tighten nut on each end of both camshafts to 300-325 ft.-lb. torque.
15. Secure camshaft timing gear nuts with gear nut retainers, bolts and lock washers. Tighten gear nut retainer bolts to 35-39 ft.-lb. torque.
16. Check clearance between thrust washer and thrust shoulder of camshaft. Clearance should be .004" to .012", or a maximum of .018" with used parts.
17. Check backlash between mating gears. Backlash should be .003" to .008", and should not exceed .010" between worn gears.
18. Install flywheel housing and other parts or assemblies, that were removed from the engine.

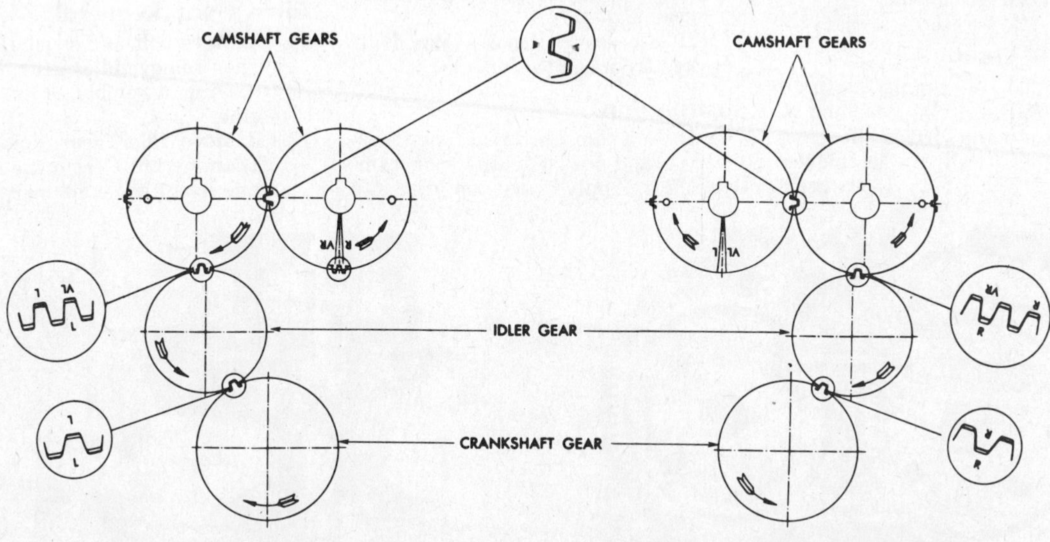

Gear train and timing marks (© G.M.C.)

Gear Train

Description

The gear train consists of a crankshaft gear, an idler gear, two camshaft gears and a blower drive gear.

The crankshaft gear is bolted to a flange at the rear end of the crankshaft. The idler gear is mounted on a stationary hub on either the right or left side of the engine depending upon the engine rotation. The camshaft gears are pressed on and keyed to their respective shafts and each is secured by a nut and gear nut retainer.

The two camshaft gears mesh with each other and run at the same speed as the crankshaft gear. Since the former two gears must be in time with each other, and the two as a unit, in time with the crankshaft gear, timing marks have been stamped in the face of the gears to facilitate correct gear train timing. When assembling the engine, it is important to remember engine rotation. Then line up the appropriate timing marks on the gears as each gear is installed on the engine.

Camshaft gear installed
(© G.M.C.)

Crankshaft Gear

The crankshaft timing gear is bolted to a flange at the rear end of the crankshaft and drives the camshaft gears, as well as the blower drive gear, through an idler gear. One gear attaching bolt hole is offset so that the gear can be attached in only one position.

Crankshaft Gear Removal

1. Remove six bolts retaining gear to crankshaft.
2. Remove gear using a suitable gear puller.

Installation

1. Position gear on rear end of crankshaft with all six bolt holes in gear aligned with tapped holes in the crankshaft flange. Since one bolt hole is offset, the gear can be attached in only one position on the crankshaft.
2. Align timing mark on crankshaft gear with corresponding mark on the idler gear.
3. Install gear to crankshaft bolts, then tighten bolts to specified torque (35-39 ft.-lb.)
4. Check backlash between mating gears. Backlash should be .003″ to .008″, and should not exceed .010″ between worn gears.

Camshaft Gears

Since the two camshaft gears must be in time with each other, timing marks are stamped on the rim of both gears. Also, since these two gears as a unit must be in time with the crankshaft, timing marks are located on the idler and crankshaft gears.

Camshaft Gear Removal

1. Remove camshafts from engine.
2. Place one of the camshaft and gear assemblies in arbor press with gear suitably supported.
3. Then, using a short piece of one inch O.D. brass rod between end of camshaft and ram of press, force camshaft out of camshaft gear.
4. If necessary, remove Woodruff key from camshaft.

Installation

1. Install camshaft rear end bearing and thrust washers on camshaft. Apply heavy cup grease to the steel face of camshaft thrust washers and place a washer on each end of camshaft rear bearing. Steel face of washer is next to bearing.
2. Lubricate the camshaft rear bearing journal and slide rear bearing onto camshaft journal with bolting flange of bearing toward outer (gear) end of shaft.
3. Start camshaft gear over end of camshaft with key in shaft registering with keyway in gear.
4. Press gear tight against shoulder on shaft in manner illustrated in Fig. 5. If available, camshaft gear installer may be used for this purpose.
5. Start camshaft gear retaining nut on camshaft. Tighten nut after shaft is installed in cylinder block.
6. Install camshaft in cylinder block.

Idler Gear

The idler gear is mounted on a double row, tapered roller bearing, which in turn is supported on a stationary hub. A bolt passes through the hub and rear end plate. A dowel in the hub correctly positions the hub and prevents the hub from rotating.

The idler gear bearing cup has a light press fit in the gear and is held in place by a retainer. The idler gear bearing cones are pressed onto the gear hub and do not rotate. A spacer separates the two bearing cones.

A left-hand helix gear is provided for right-hand rotation engines, and a right-hand helix gear is provided for left-hand rotation engines.

An idler gear hole spacer (dummy hub) is used on the side opposite the idler gear.

Idler Gear Removal

1. Remove bolt and special washer. Then remove idler gear, hub and bearing assembly from the engine.
2. Remove idler gear hold spacer (dummy hub) from the opposite side in the same manner.

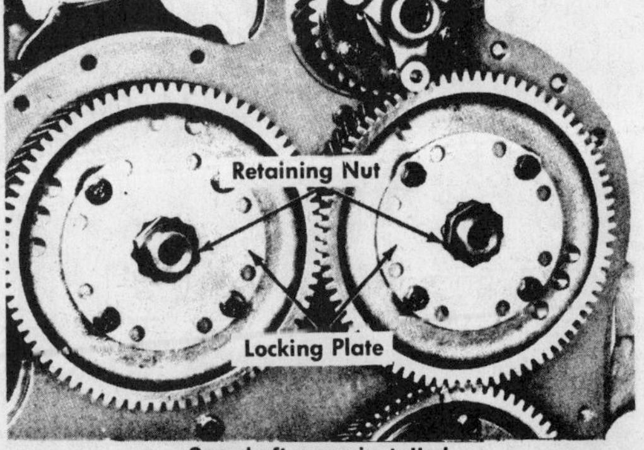

Camshaft gears installed
(© G.M.C.)

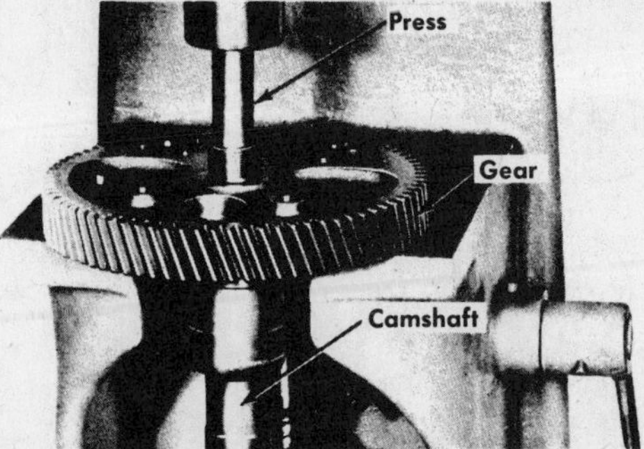

Pressing gear off camshaft
(© G.M.C.)

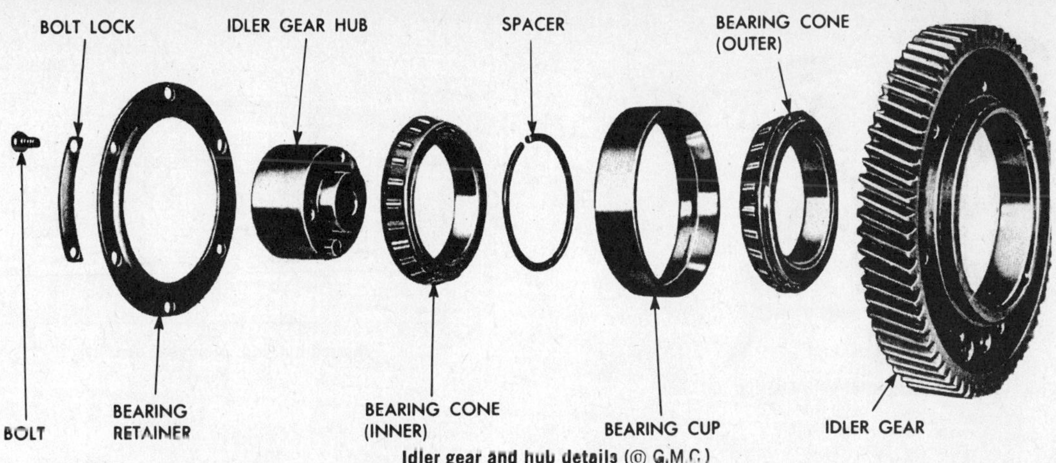

Idler gear and hub details (© G.M.C.)

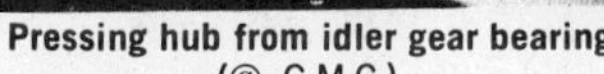
Pressing hub from idler gear bearing (© G.M.C.)

Idler gear installed (© G.M.C.)

3. Remove bearing retainer. NOTE: Component parts of idler gear bearing are mated; therefore, match-mark the parts during disassembly to assure they will be reassembled in their original positions.
4. Place idler gear and bearing assembly in arbor press. While rotating the idler gear to prevent brinelling of bearing, press the hub out of the bearing.
5. Tap bearing cup (outer race) from idler gear by using a brass drift alternately at four notches provided in shoulder of gear.

Assembly

Pay attention to matching marks previously made on parts to assure their reassembly in same positions from which they were removed and proceed as follows:

1. Support idler gear, with shoulder down, on bed of arbor press, locate bearing cup (outer race) at bearing bore of gear, and press cup into place tight against shoulder in gear.
2. Support one bearing cone, numbered side down, on bed of arbor press and lower idler gear and bearing cup assembly down over the bearing cone.
3. Lay spacer ring on face of bearing cone.
4. Place second bearing cone, numbered side up, in idler gear and bearing cup assembly and against spacer ring.
5. Position the idler gear hub over the bearing cones so that the oil hole in hub is 180° from gap in spacer ring.
6. Press hub into idler gear bearing cones, while rotating the gear to seat rollers properly between cones, until face or hub which will be adjacent to cylinder block end plate is flush with the corresponding face of bearing cone. Bearing cones should be supported so as not to load the bearing rollers during this operation.
7. Prior to installing and securing the bearing retainer, check the pre-load of the bearing assembly as outlined below.

Then, when the torque required to rotate the idler gear is within specified limits, secure bearing retainer to the idler gear with three bolt locks.

Pre-Load Check

If the mating crankshaft and camshaft gears are not already mounted on the engine, the torque required to rotate the idler gear may be check by mounting the idler gear in position on the engine, using a steel plate 4″ square and 3/8″ thick against the hub and cone as follows under heading "Engine Mounted Method."

However, if the crankshaft and camshaft gears are on the engine, a suitable fixture, which may be held in a vise, can be made locally to accomplish a "Bench Test Method" of determining torque. Three plates, a 1/2″-13 x 1-3/4″ bolt and a plain washer are used with a 1/2″-13 nut and plain washer for mounting. One of the plates is used to take the place of a flywheel housing, and the other two plates, the cylinder block. "Engine-mounted" conditions are simulated by tightening the nut to 80-90 ft.-lb. torque and tightening the three plate-to-hub attaching bolts to 25-40 ft.-lb. torque. The components of the fixture may be made from steel stock.

The idler gear bearing should be cleaned and lubricated with clean light engine oil prior to the pre-load test. Idler gear assemblies which include new bearings should be "worked in" by grasping the gear firmly by hand and rotating the gear back and forth several times.

Checking idler gear bearing pre-load
(© G.M.C.)

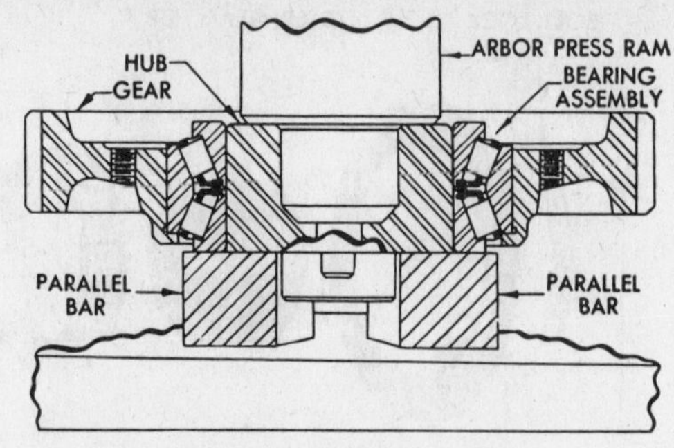

Pressing hub into idler gear bearing
(© G.M.C.)

Idler Gear Installation

1. Position the crankshaft gear and camshaft gear so that the match marks will align with those on the idler gear.
2. With these marks in alignment, start the idler gear into mesh with the crankshaft gear and the camshaft gear, and simultaneously rotate the gear hub so that the hollow pin at the inner face of the hub nearly registers with the hole in the end plate.
3. Then simultaneously roll the idler gear into position, and align the hollow dowel with the hole in the end plate. Gently tap the hub until the hub seats against the end plate.
4. After making sure that the hub is tight against the end plate, secure the idler gear assembly in place with a ½″-13 bolt and special washer. Tighten bolt to 80-90 ft.-lb. torque.
5. Lubricate the idler gear and bearing liberally with clean engine oil.
6. Check backlash between mating gears. Backlash should be .003″ to .008″, and should not exceed .010″ between worn gears.

Installing idler gear assembly
(© G.M.C.)

Blower Drive Gear and Support Assembly

The blower drive gear, is mounted on the blower drive gear support, which is attached to the cylinder block rear end plate. This gear is driven by the right cylinder bank camshaft gear.

Removal

1. Remove blower.
2. Remove two blower drive support-to-cylinder block rear end plate attaching bolts with copper washers and tap the assembly away from the end plate, using care not to damage the gear teeth.

Disassembly

1. Clamp blower drive gear support in soft jaws of bench vise.
2. Remove three spring plate gear bolts and lock washers.
3. Remove spring plates and blower drive gear hub as an assembly from gear. If necessary, spring plates may be removed from hub.
4. Straighten lugs on blower drive gear support nut lock plate, then remove nut.
5. Remove lock plate, blower drive gear thrust washer, thrust bearing and gear from support.

Inspection

Examine faces of thrust bearings and thrust washer and, if scored or worn excessively replace.

Check inside diameter of blower drive gear bearings for wear; also check outside diameter of support hub on which gear bearings ride. The inside diameter of new bearings in 1.6260″ to 1.6265″. The clearance between bearings and support should be .001″ to .0025″ with new parts and a maximum of .005″ with used parts. Install new parts, whenever clearance exceeds the maximum.

If new bearings are installed in blower drive gear, outer end of bearings must be pressed in flush with sides of gear and bore of bearings should be square with bolt boss faces and pitch diameter of teeth of gear within .003″ total indicator reading, after reaming bushings to twenty micro-inches.

Assembly

1. With blower drive support clamped in soft jaws of bench vise, position one of the blower drive gear thrust bearings on support so that tangs on bearing register with holes in support.
2. Lubricate hub of support, bearings in gear, both thrust bearings and the blower drive gear, support thrust washer with clean engine oil.
3. Slide gear on hub with flat side of gear down.
4. Install second thrust bearing on support with tangs on bearing facing up.
5. Position blower drive support thrust washer on support so that slots in thrust washer register with tangs on bearing.
6. Install gear on support with lock washer and nut. Tighten nut to 50-60 ft.-lb torque and bend lugs

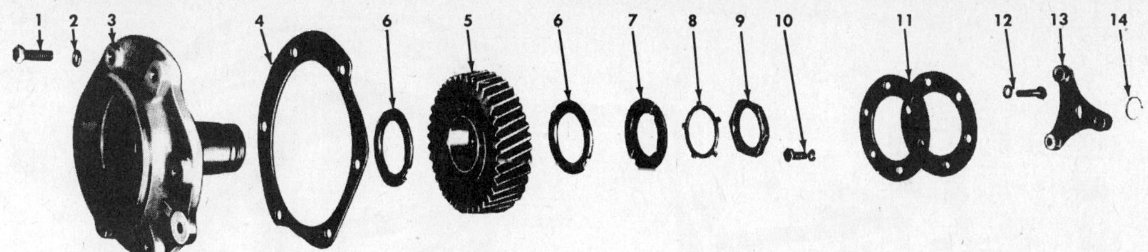

Blower drive gear and support components (© G.M.C.)

1 Support to plate bolt
2 Copper washer
3 Blower drive gear support
4 Gasket
5 Blower drive gear
6 Thrust bearing
7 Thrust washer
8 Lock plate
9 Drive gear support nut
10 Plate to hub bolt and lockwasher
11 Spring plate
12 Plate to gear bolt and lockwasher
13 Gear hub
14 Snap ring

Blower drive gear assembly installed (© G.M.C.)

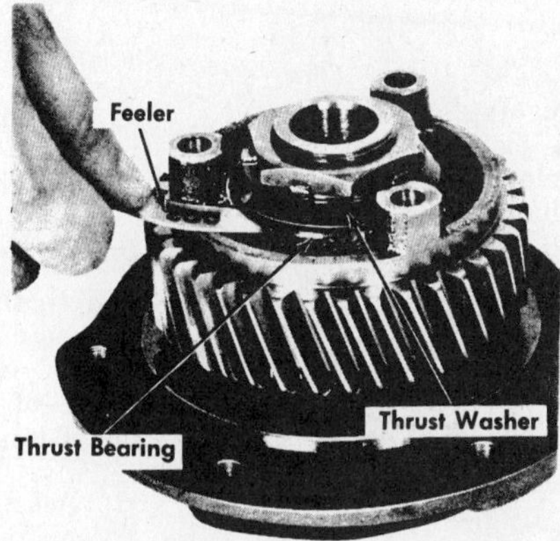

Checking clearance between thrust washer and thrust bearing (© G.M.C.)

on lock washer against flats on nut to secure nut.

7. Check clearance between blower drive gear support thrust washer and blower drive gear thrust bearing. Clearance should be .005" to .010", and should not exceed .012" between worn parts.
8. If spring plates were removed from blower drive gear hub, attach spring plates to hub with three bolts and lock washers. Tighten bolts to 35-39 ft.-lb. torque.
9. Assemble spring plates and hub to gear with three bolts and lock washers. Tighten bolts to 35-39 ft.-lb. torque.

Blower Drive Gear and Support Assembly Installation

1. Using a new gasket, attach gear and support assembly to cylinder block rear end plate with two bolts and copper washers. Tighten bolts to 25-30 ft.-lb. torque.
2. Check backlash between blower drive gear and camshaft gear. Backlash should be .003" to .008" with worn parts.
3. Remove four fly-wheel housing-to-blower drive support bolts. Then install blower.

Piston and Piston Rings

Inspection

Excessively worn or scored pistons, rings and cylinder liners indicate improper maintenance or operating conditions which should be corrected as quickly as possible.

Piston

1. A careful examination of the piston should be made for scoring, cracks, worn or damaged ring grooves, plugged oil drain holes, or indications of excessive heat such as may melt the tin coating on the pistons. Pistons which are heavily scored, overheated, cracked or excessively widened ring grooves should be discarded. Pistons which are only slightly scored may be cleaned up and reused.
2. Examine the inside of the piston closely for cracks across the struts and discard piston if such cracks are present. The pistons may be checked for cracks for use of the various methods of magnetic particle inspection.
3. Inspect the top of the piston crown for burned spots or other indications of overheating such as carbon formation in the underside of the piston crown. Such spots or carbon coating on underside of piston may indicate a lack of sufficient oil spray on the underside of piston via the drilled passage in the connecting rod.

Piston Pin Bushing

1. Inspect and measure the inside diameter of the piston pin bushings in each piston and, also inspect and measure the piston pin. With new parts, the piston pin-to-bushing clearance should be from .0025" to .0034". However, with worn parts, a maximum clearance of .010" is allowable.

A .010" oversize piston pin is available to aid in obtaining the proper clearance with worn bushings.

Piston Pin Bushing Removal

1. Place piston in holding fixture.

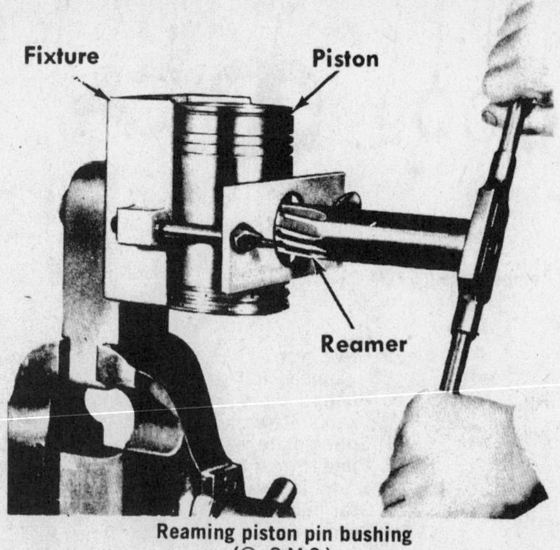

Reaming piston pin bushing
(© G.M.C.)

Removing or installing piston rings
(© G.M.C.)

2. Drive bushing out of piston.
3. Revolve piston 180° in fixture and remove the second piston pin bushing in the same manner.

Installation

1. When installing bushings in a piston, locate the split or joint at the bottom, that is away from the piston head.
2. Insert spacer in hole in fixture and place piston on fixture so that spacer protrudes into bushing bore.
3. Insert installer in a bushing; then slide the bushing and installer inside piston and position over inside edge of lower bushing bore.
4. Insert handle through upper bushing bore and into installer.
5. Using hammer on upper end of handle, drive bushing into piston bushing bore until bushing bottoms on spacer.
6. Turn piston over in fixture and install second bushing in a similar manner.

Reaming

The bushing must be reamed after pressing into place.

1. Clamp piston bushing reaming fixture in vise, then insert guide bushing in fixture and secure with set screw.
2. Place piston assembly in fixture and insert pilot end of reamer, through clamping bar, piston pin bushings, and into guide bushing.
3. With piston, fixture and reamer in alignment, tighten wing nuts securely.
4. Turning reamer in a clockwise direction only, with uniform motion, both when reaming and withdrawing reamer, ream the piston pin bushings.
5. Remove piston from fixture. Blow out chips resulting from reaming and check bushings.

Piston Ring Installation

With the connecting rod assembly inspected and assembled to the piston, be certain to check proper location of piston rings assembled on the piston.

1. Assemble compression rings on piston, and stagger ring gaps around piston. When installing compression or oil control rings, do not spread the rings more than is necessary to slip them on piston to avoid overstressing rings. CAUTION: The top compression ring is a tapered face ring. Therefore, this ring must be installed with the side marked "T or "TOP" facing up.

Piston and ring assembly
(© G.M.C.)

1 Compression rings
2 Piston
3 Bushing
4 Piston pin
5 Retainer
6 Expander
7 Oil ring

2. Install oil control rings by hand with the scraping edge down. First install expander being careful not to overlap ends of expander. Second, install top oil ring with gap 180° from gap in expander. Third install bottom oil ring with gap 45° from gap of top oil ring. Recheck to be sure ends of expander are not overlapped. NOTE: Upper oil control ring, used on "N" series truck and all coach engines, has chrome plated wiping edge, and must be installed on top of other rings.
3. New rings should always be used.

Fitting Pistons

1. Measurements of pistons and bore for pistons in cylinder liners should be taken at room temperature (70°F.).
2. Measurements should be taken on the piston skirt lengthwise and crosswise of the piston pin. The piston taper should not exceed .0005" from bottom compression ring groove to bottom of piston.
3. Piston-to-liner clearance should be from .004" to .0078". With used parts, a maximum clearance of .012" is allowable. This clearance should be checked at four places, 90° apart, around the circumference of the piston.
4. Cylinder liner bores should be round within .002" and straight within .001". when fitted into the cylinder block. Measure cylinder liner bores with a suitable gauge, both lengthwise and crosswise of the piston pin throughout the entire length of the cylinder liner.

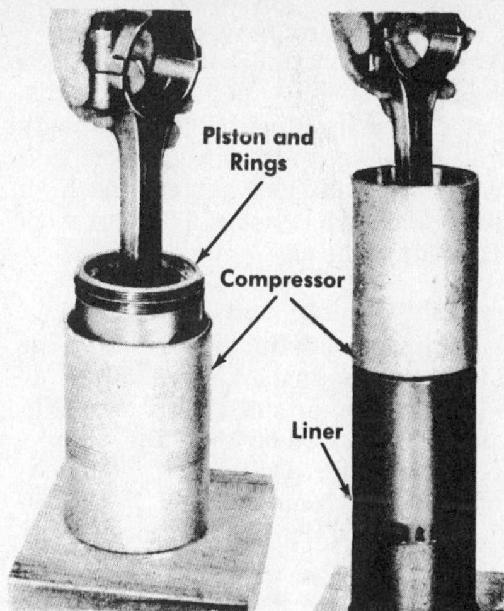

Installing piston assembly in ring compressor and cylinder assembly
(© G.M.C.)

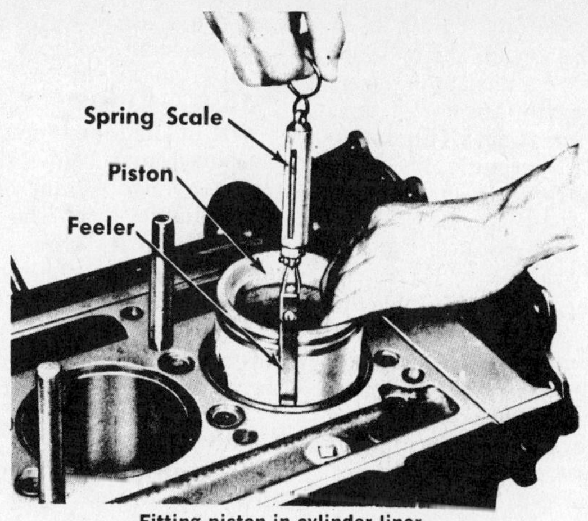

Fitting piston in cylinder liner
(© G.M.C.)

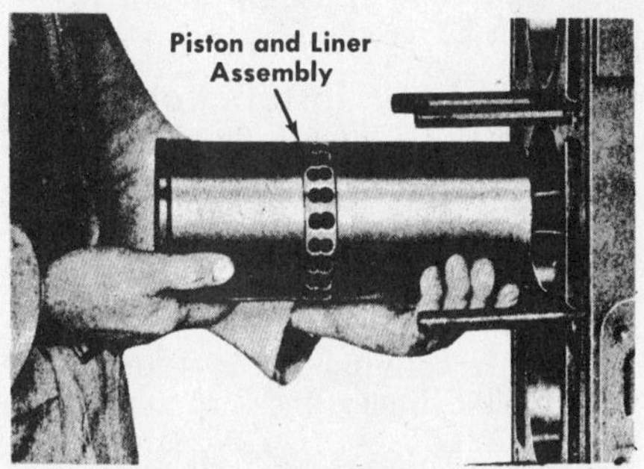

Installing piston assembly and liner in cylinder block
(© G.M.C.)

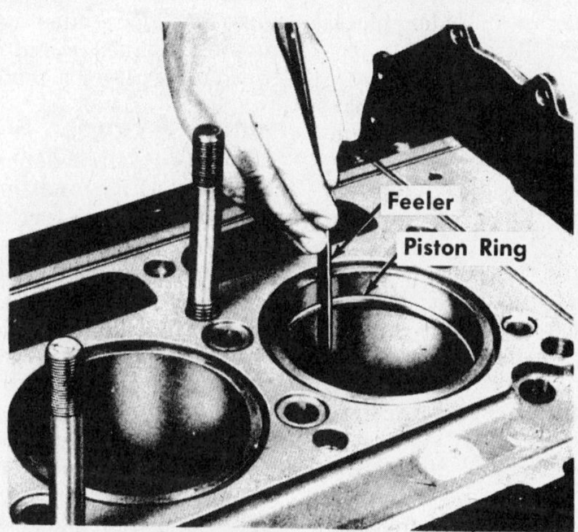

Measuring piston ring gap
(© G.M.C.)

5. Check the piston-to-liner clearance while the piston is held upside down in the liner. The liner should be in place in the cylinder block, otherwise inaccurate readings will be obtained. Ths clearance should always be checked when installing either new or used pistons and liners.
6. A feeler gauge set may be used for this purpose. The set consists of a feeler gauge pack, spring scale, and swivel connection. The spring scale, attached to the feeler gauge pack by means of the swivel connection, is used to measure the force in pounds required to withdraw the feeler from between the piston and liner.
7. Select the feeler ribbon with a thickness that will require approximately six pounds pull to remove. The clearance will be .001″ greater than the thickness of the feeler used, i.e., a feeler .004″ thick indicate a clearance of .005″ when withdrawn at a pull of six pounds. Feeler ribbon used for checking this clearance must be perfectly flat and free of nicks and scratches.
8. If any bind between the piston and liner is detected, remove the piston and liner and inspect them for burrs.
9. Service pistons are available in standard size, and in .010″, .020″, and .030″ oversize. These pistons all weigh the same within very close limits. Therefore, one or more oversize pistons may be installed in an engine without causing damage to the engine. Since cylinder liners are furnished in standard inside diameter only, the installation of oversize pistons becomes necessary only when cylinder liners have been rehoned.

Fitting Piston Rings

1. Insert one ring at a time inside the liner and far enough down in the bore to be on the wiping area of the rings when piston is installed. To assure that the ring is parallel with top of liner, use a piston to crowd the ring into liner bore; then measure gap with a feeler gauge.
2. If the piston ring gap is below the specified limits, it may be increased by stoning the ends of the ring. Stone both ends of the piston ring in such a direction that the stone will cut from the outside (chrome plated) surface of ring toward the inside surface. This will prevent any chipping or peeling of the chrome plate. The ends of the ring must remain square and chamfer must be approximately .015″ on outer edge.
3. Check ring clearances in the piston grooves. Nominal ring groove widths, which may vary ± .001″, and ring clearances in grooves are given in "SPECIFICATIONS" section.

When an oversize piston is installed, piston rings of the same oversize must also be installed.

Cylinder Liners

Description

The cylinder liners used in V-71 engines are of the replaceable dry type, made of hardened alloy cast iron and are a slip fit in the cylinder block.

A flange at the top of each liner fits into a counterbore in the cylinder block and rests on a cast iron insert to provide accurate alignment and positioning of the liners. Compression is sealed with an individual laminated compression gasket for each cylinder.

Honing Liner

Cylinder liners are available in standard size inside diameter only, therefore installation of oversize pistons becomes necessary when liners are honed oversize. Also, liners are available in oversize outside dimensions which must be used whenever cylinder block bores are honed.

1. Liners should not be honed in the cylinder block, but should be removed and placed in a honing fixture (a scrap cylinder block makes an excellent honing fixture). If it is necessary to hone liners in the cylinder block that is to be used in building up the engine, the engine must be dismantled, and then, after honing, the block must be thoroughly cleaned.
2. Honing should be done, with a 120 grit stone, in such a manner as to produce a crisscross pattern with hone marks on a 45° axis. This operation may be performed using emery cloth if a hone is unavailable.
3. When cylinder liner has been honed, inspect to be sure liner is free of burrs over its entire area.
4. After honing, the liners must conform to the same limits on taper and out-of-round as a standard size liner, and the piston-to-liner clearance must be the same as that specified for standard parts.

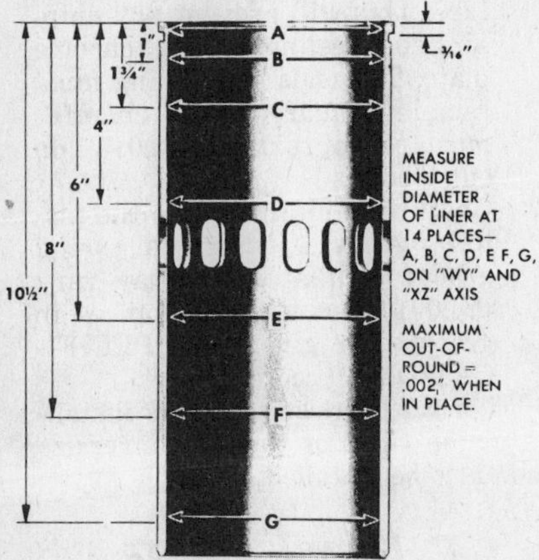

Cylinder liner measurement diagram
(© G.M.C.)

Taper and Out-of-Round

If a liner is worn to such an extent that the taper or out-of-round limits have been exceeded, the liner must be honed out for oversize pistons or the liner must be replaced.

Remove Ridge

The inside diameter of a used liner measured just below the top of the ring travel must not exceed the unworn diameter at the top by more than .004". A large step than this may cause interference with new compression rings. In order to prevent ring breakage caused by this difference in diameter, hone the liner just enough to remove this ridge.

Break Glaze

Never install new piston rings in a used liner unless the glaze in the liner is broken.

Even though the liner taper and out-of-round are within specifications, the glaze must be removed by working a hone up and down the full length of the liner a few times.

Honing Cylinder Block

The fit of a liner depends to a great extent upon the condition of the bore before honing. Distortion may cause low spots that will clean up. A low spot is not objectionable above the ports if it does not exceed 1¼" or the size of a half dollar. Below the ports, larger spots are permissible.

Roughing and finishing stones should be fairly coarse. A No. 80 grit stone may be used for roughing, and a No. 120 grit stone is satisfactory for finishing.

The following inspection should be made before honing cylinder block:

1. Clean bore and inlet port opening.
2. Measure the bore for high spots and the most narrow section.
3. Liners are fitted from .0005" to .0025" loose. A clearance of .0005" produces a slip fit and .0024" clearance allows the liner to slide freely into place. Refer to chart for standard and oversize cylinder liner bore in cylinder block.

Rough Honing

Insert hone in bore and adjust stones snugly to the most narrow section.

Start hone and "feel out" bore for high spots. These will cause an increased drag on the stone. Move hone up and down bore with short overlapping strokes about 1" long: Concentrate on the high spots in the first cut. Do not hone as long at the ports as in the rest of the bore—this area, as a rule, cuts away more rapidly.

When bore is fairly clean, remove hone to inspect the stones and measure bore. Decide carefully which spots must be honed most. To move the hone from top to bottom of bore will not correct an out-of-round condition. To remain in one spot too long may cause bore to become tapered. Where and how much to hone can be judged by feel. A heavy cut in distorted bore produces a more steady drag on the hone than a light cut and so makes it difficult to feel the high spots. Therefore, use a light cut with frequent stone adjustment.

Finish Honing and Fitting Liner

Rough hone cylinder bore until the liner can be pushed from 3" to 4" into the bore, or until bore is within approximately .005" of the diameter of the liner. Do not expect finishing stones to remove more than .001" of stock, or to true up the bore to any extent.

Work the finish hone with short, rapid strokes up and down the bore. Use light tension on the stones and hone only enough to allow the liner to enter the bore either with a light push fit or a free slip fit.

Cylinder Liner Installation

Install the cylinder liner in the block and measure the distance from top of liner flange to top of block to assure proper sealing of the cylinder head compression gaskets as follows:

1. Clean liner and be sure bore and counterbore in block is clean.
2. Check cylinder liner counterbore depth.
3. Place a cylinder liner insert in counterbore in cylinder block. NOTE: Cylinder liner inserts are available in .004" and .008" thinner sizes as well as standard size for both standard to .005" oversize and .010", .020" and 030" oversize outside diameter cylinder liners. Matching oversize inserts should be installed whenever oversize (O.D.) liners are used.
4. Push liner into cylinder block by hand, until liner flange rests on insert. If the liner does not slide freely into place, withdraw, turn 90° and insert liner again. Each liner should slide freely into place to assure there will be no distortion.

Honing bore of cylinder block
(© G.M.C.)

Cylinder liner removal
(© G.M.C.)

Checking bore at cylinder block
(© G.M.C.)

5. Clamp liner in place with cylinder liner hold-down clamps.
6. Measure the distance from the top of liner flange to top of block, using a dial indicator. When in place, top of liner flange should be from .045" to .050" below top of cylinder block, and there must not be over .001" difference in height below top of block between any two adjacent liners when gauged on longitudinal cylinder centerline.

Connecting Rod and Bearings

Bearing Removal

(Connecting Rod Installed)

When removal of connecting rod bearing shells becomes necessary, they may be removed as follows:

1. Remove the oil pan.
2. Disconnect and remove the lubricating oil pump suction pipe and screen assembly from main bearing cap.
3. Remove one connecting rod bearing cap. Push connecting rod and piston assembly up into cylinder liner far enough to permit removal of upper bearing shell.
4. Install bearing shells before another cap is removed.

Bearing Installation

1. Rotate crankshaft until connecting rod journal is at the bottom of its travel, wipe the journal clean and lubricate with clean engine oil.
2. Install upper bearing shell—the one without an oil groove.
3. With tang of upper bearing shell in groove of connecting rod, pull piston and rod assembly down until upper rod bearing seats firmly on crankshaft journal.
4. Place lower bearing shell—the one with the oil groove—in bearing cap, with tang of shell in groove of cap, and lubricate with clean engine oil.
5. Note identifying marks on cap and rod and assemble cap to rod. Tighten connecting rod bolt nuts to 65-75 ft.-lbs. torque.
6. Install lubricating oil pump suction pipe and screen assembly.
7. Install oil pan and fill crankcase with recommended lubricating oil to "FULL" mark on dipstick.
8. If new bearings were installed, operate engine on run-in schedule.

Assembly of Rod and Piston

(Conecting Rod to Piston)

Apply clean engine oil to the piston pin and bushings and proceed with assembly of the rod to piston in the following manner:

1. Rest piston in holding fixture. Place a new piston pin retainer in either side of piston. Position installer tool over retainer and strike tool just hard enough to cause a deflection in the piston pin retainer and even seating of retainer. Driving too hard against the tool may force the piston bushing inward, thus reducing the piston pin end clearance.
2. Place upper end of connecting rod between piston pin bosses in line with piston pin holes and slide pin into position. The piston pin should slip readily into position without forcing if clearances are correct.
3. Install second piston pin retainer as outlined above. After piston pin retainers have been installed, it is advisable to visually check for piston pin end clearance by cocking rod on pin and shifting pin in its bushings.

Piston and Rod Installation

1. With piston assembled to connecting rod and piston ring in place, apply clean engine oil to piston, rings, and inside of piston ring compressor.
2. Place compressor on wood bench or table with tapered side of compressor up.
3. Stagger the piston ring gaps properly on the piston, being careful that oil ring expanders are not overlapped.

Installing cylinder liner in block
(© G.M.C.)

Cylinder Liner and Cylinder Bore Dimension Chart

Size	Liner Diameter	Block Diameter	Use Next Oversize Liner when Bore Measures
Std.	4.6250″ 4.6260″	4.6265″ 4.6275″	4.6280″
0.005″	4.6300″ 4.6310″	4.6315″ 4.6325″	4.633″
0.010″	4.6350″ 4.6360″	4.6365″ 4.6375″	4.638″
0.020″	4.6450″ 4.6460″	4.6465″ 4.6475″	4.648″
0.030″	4.6550″ 4.6560″	4.6565″ 4.6575″	4.658″

4. Start the top of the piston straight into compressor, then push piston down until it contacts wood block.
5. Place the ring compressor, piston, and connecting rod assembly on the liner. Carefully push the piston and rod assembly down into the liner until piston is free of the ring compressor, using care to avoid ring breakage. Remove the compressor.
6. Rotate the crankshaft until connecting rod journal is at bottom of its travel, wipe the journal clean and lubricate journal with clean engine oil.
7. Lubricate and install upper bearing shell—the one without an oil groove—in the connecting rod.
8. Note that each connecting rod and its cap are stamped on one side—1L, 1R, 2L, 2R, etc. These numbers and letters are for identification purposes and indicate the particular cylinder in which each is used. These positions should always be maintained when rebuilding an engine.
9. Position the piston, rod and liner assembly in its proper location according to marks on liner and with connecting rod numbers and letters toward outside of the cylinder block. Slide the liner, pistons, and rod assembly straight into the block bore until the flange of liner seats on the insert in cylinder block counterbore. CAUTION: The centerline of the connecting rod is slightly offset. Therefore, when installing to crankshaft, be sure that the narrow side of the two connecting rods on the crankshaft journal are together to avoid cocking the rod.
10. Lubricate and place lower bearing shell—the one with the oil groove—in connecting rod cap with tang of shell in groove of cap.
11. Assemble cap to rod with identifying marks on cap and rod adjacent to each other. Tighten connecting rod bolt nuts to 65-75 ft.-lbs. torque.
12. Check connecting rod side clearance. The clearance between each pair of connecting rods should be .008″ to .016″ with new parts.
13. Remove cylinder liner hold-down clamps.

Crankshaft and Main Bearings

Crankshaft Removal

When necessary to remove crankshaft the operation may be performed as follows:

1. Drain oil, then remove the oil pan.
2. Remove the lubricating oil pump screen and suction pipe assembly.
3. Remove hydraulic fan assembly.
4. Remove flywheel and flywheel housing.
5. Remove crankshaft front cover.
6. Remove connecting rod bearing caps. Note that each cap and rod is stamped with a number corresponding with the cylinder number.
7. Remove main bearing caps. Note that each cap is stamped with a number which corresponds with number stamped on cylinder block.
8. Lift crankshaft, timing gear, oil pump drive spline as an assembly from crankshaft.
9. Remove main bearing inserts from cankcase and bearing caps, also thrust washers at rear main bearing. Carefully identify each bearing so that it can be replaced in its original location.

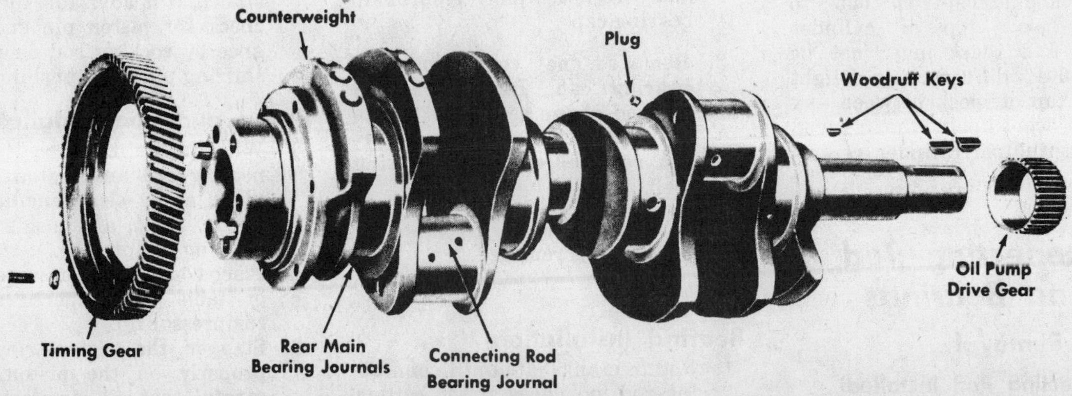

Crankshaft and gears (© G.M.C.)

Main Bearings Removal

(Crankshaft Installed)

When removal of main bearing shells becomes necessary, and the removal of the crankshaft is not required or undesirable, this operation may be performed by using the following procedure.

NOTE: Remove bearing shells one at a time, inspect, and reinstall or replace, replacing all shells if only one or more need replacing.

All crankshaft main bearing journals except the rear are drilled for an oil passage.

1. Remove the oil pan to expose the main bearing caps.
2. Remove the lubricating oil pump intake pipe assembly. NOTE: In text following, main bearing stabilizers are mentioned in several instances. Early model engines used these parts which have since been discontinued and any reference made to stabilizers should be disregarded on latest engines.
3. Remove only one main bearing cap stabilizer at a time, then place washers on main bearing bolts just removed, equal to thickness of stabilizer and reinstall bolts. Remove remaining stabilizer(s) in a like manner.
4. Remove main bearing caps using temporarily installed cap screws and pinch bars.
5. To remove all except rear main bearing shell, insert a 5/16" x 1" bolt with a ½" diameter and a 1/16" thick head (made from a standard bolt) into the crankshaft journal oil hole, then revolve the shaft to the right (clockwise) and roll the bearing shell out of position. The head of the bolt should not extend beyond the outside diameter of the shell.
6. Two-piece thrust washers are used each side of the rear main bearing. The lower half of these washers will be removed when removing the rear main bearing cap; upper half can be removed upon removal of bearing cap by pushing on end of washer with a small rod, thus forcing washer around and out on opposite side of bearing.
7. Remove rear main bearing upper shell by driving on the edge of the bearing shell with a small curved rod, at the same time revolving the crankshaft, thus rolling the shell from its position.

Main Bearings Installation

(Crankshaft Installed)

Make sure parts are clean. Apply clean engine oil to each crankshaft journal and install main bearing shells by reversing the sequence of operations given for removal.

Upper and lower main bearing shells are not alike; the upper shell is grooved and drilled for lubrication—the lower shell is not. Be sure to install the grooved and drilled shells in the bearing caps, otherwise the oil the cylinder block and plain shells in feed to the upper end of the connecting rods will be blocked off.

1. When installing the upper main bearing shells with crankshaft in place, start the end of the shell having no tang around the crankshaft journal, so that when shell is in place the tang will fit into groove in the shell support.
2. Assemble crankshaft thrust washer before installing rear main bearing cap. Clean both halves of thrust washer carefully, removing any burrs from the seats—*the slightest particle between washers and crankshaft of dirt may decrease clearance beyond limits.*

Slide upper halves of thrust washers into place in their grooves; then assemble lower halves over dowel pins in bearing cap. NOTE: Main bearing caps are bored in position and marked 1, 2, 3, etc. They must be replaced in their original positions.

3. With lower bearing shell installed in bearing cap, install cap and draw bolts up snug. Then rap cap sharply with soft hammer to seat cap properly and draw cap bolts uniformly tight, to 180-190 ft.-lbs. torque. NOTE: If the bearings have been installed properly, the crankshaft will turn freely with all main bearing caps bolted tight.
4. Install main bearing cap stabilizers by reversing their removal procedure. Tighten main bearing bolts to 180-190 ft.-lbs. torque and 7/16"-14 x 1-1/8" stabilizer cylinder block bolts, if used, to 70-75 ft.-lbs. torque.
5. Check crankshaft end play at thrust washers. This clearance should be from .004" to .011" with new parts or a maximum of .018" with used parts. Insufficient clearance will usually denote misalignment of the rear main bearing. In such case, loosen and retighten the rear main bearing cap. If lack of clearance is still present, dirt or a burr on inner face of one or

Removing main bearing cap
(© G.M.C.)

Removing rear main bearing upper shell
(© G.M.C.)

Checking crankshaft end play
(© G.M.C.)

more of the thrust washers may be the cause.
6. Install lubricating oil pump intake pipe assembly.
7. Install oil pan with new gasket. Fill crankcase to proper level.

Crankshaft Installation

If shells previously used are to be used again, install them in the same locations from which they were removed.

When a new crankshaft is installed, all new main and connecting rod (upper and lower) bearing shells should also be installed.

With oil pump drive gear, and crankshaft timing gear, assembled on the front and rear ends respectively of the crankshaft, the crankshaft may be installed as follows:

1. Install upper grooved bearing shells in the cylinder block.
2. Apply clean engine oil to all crankshaft journals and set crankshaft in place so that timing marks on the crankshaft timing gear and the gear train idler gear match.
3. Install the upper halves of the rear main bearing thrust washers on each side of the bearing, and the doweled lower halves on each side of the rear main bearing cap.
4. With lower main bearing shells installed in bearing caps, install caps and stabilizers in their original position and draw bolts up snug. Then rap caps sharply with a soft hammer to seat them properly, and draw bearing cap bolts uniformly tight, starting with center cap and working alternately towards both ends of block, to 180-190 ft.-lbs. torque. Tighten 7/16"-14 x 1-1/8" stabilizer to cylined block bolts, if used, to 70-75 ft.-lbs. torque. NOTE: If bearings have been installed properly, the crankshaft will turn freely with all main bearing cap bolts drawn to specified torque.

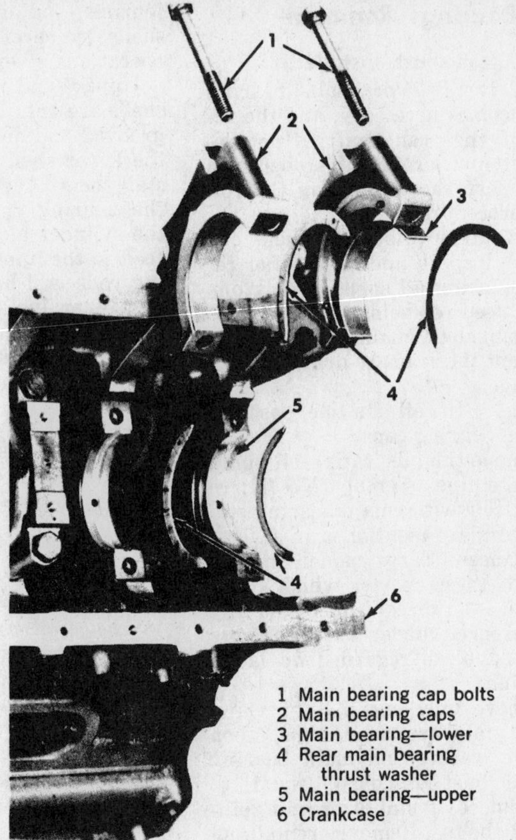

Upper and lower main bearings, thrust washers and seals
(© G.M.C.)

5. Check crankshaft end play at thrust washers. This clearance should be .004" to .011" with new parts or a maximum of .018" with used parts. Insufficient clearance will usually denote misalignment of the rear main bearing. In such case, loosen the bearing cap, then retighten as described above. If lack of clearance is still present, either dirt or a burr on the inner face of one or more of the thrust washers may be the cause.
6. Lubricate and install connecting rod bearings.
7. Install flywheel housing and flywheel.
8. Install crankshaft front cover and oil pump assembly.
9. Affix new gaskct to bolting flange and secure oil pan in place with bolts and lock washers.
10. Fill crankcase to the proper level with recommended oil.

Oil Seal Removal

If inspection reveals a worn or damaged oil seal, it must be replaced. Remove the oil seal as follows:

1. Remove flywheel housing as directed in respective section of this manual.
2. Support crankshaft flywheel housing on wood blocks. Then drive out old oil seal.

Oil Seal Sleeve Installation

When the oil seal spacer can no longer be used, an oil seal sleeve may be pressed on the crankshaft to provide a replaceable wear surface at the point of contact with the rear oil seal. The oil seal sleeve may be used with either the single lip or double lip type oil seal, and can also be used in conjunction with the seal spacer. However, oversize oil seals must be used with the oil seal sleeve. Installation of the oil seal sleeve is performed as follows:

1. Stone all high spots off the circumference of the crankshaft.
2. Coat the area of the shaft where the seal will be positioned with shellac or equivalent sealer.
3. Press the sleeve onto the shaft. The sleeve must be *pressed squarely on the shaft.*
4. Wipe off all excess sealer.

Rear Oil Seal Installation

1. Support inner face of flywheel housing on a flat surface.
2. Install rear oil seal spacer, if used, against shoulder in oil seal counterbore in housing.
3. Apply a non-hardening sealant to the outer edge of the oil seal and position the seal with the lip pointing toward the inner face (toward shoulder in counterbore) of the housing.

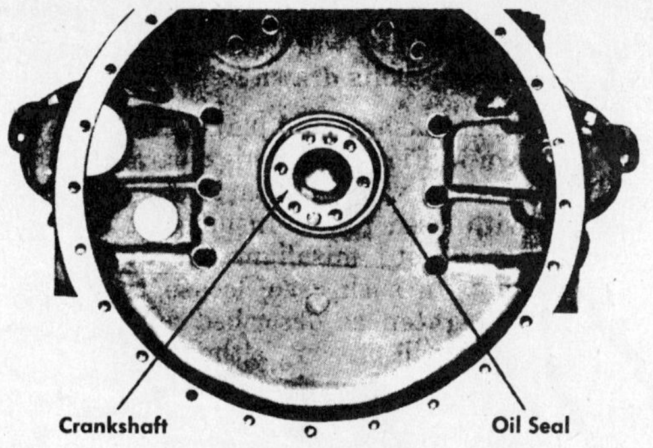
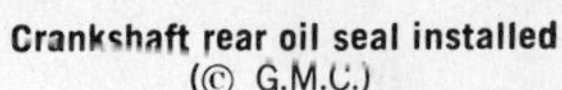

Crankshaft rear oil seal installed
(© G.M.C.)

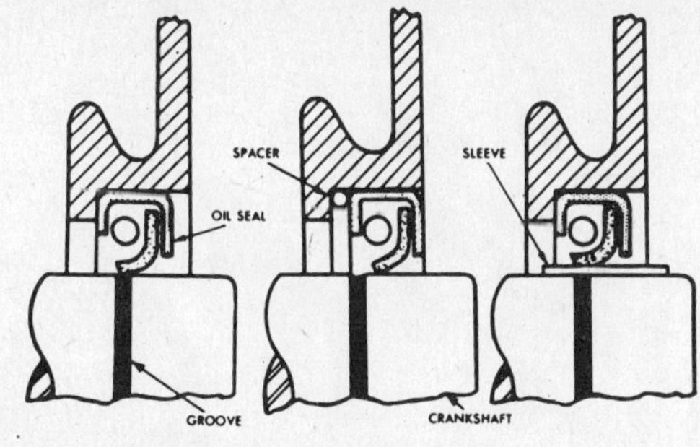

Use of oil seal spacer and sleeve on grooved crankshaft
(© G.M.C.)

4. Drive oil seal against seal spacer or shoulder in oil seal counterbore of housing.
5. If flywheel housing has not been removed from engine, lubricate lip of seal with Lubriplate or equivalent. Slip seal over crankshaft and start squarely into counterbore of housing. Using a hardwood block and hammer, tap seal alternately around edge of casing until seal is in place.
6. Remove all excess sealant from housing and oil seal.
7. Coat lip of oil seal lightly with Lubriplate or equivalent.
8. When installing flywheel housing on engine, use oil seal expander to avoid damage to lip of seal.

Engine Lubrication System

Illustrations show the flow of oil through engine lubricating system including the various components such as the oil pump, full flow oil filter, oil cooler, pressure regulator, and by-pass valve.

The oil pump is placed in the crankshaft front cover and consists of a pair of spur gears, one large and one small, which mesh together and ride in a cavity inside the crankshaft front cover. The large gear is concentric with and splined to a pump drive hub on the front end of the crankshaft. The pump idler gear is much smaller and runs on a bushing and hardened steel shaft pressed into the crankshaft cover.

Oil is drawn by suction from the oil pan through the intake screen and pipe to the oil pump where it is pressurized. The oil then passes from the pump into a short gallery in the cylinder block to the oil cooler adaptor plate. At the same time, oil from the pump is directed to a spring-loaded pressure relief valve mounted on the cylinder block. This valve discharges excess oil directly to the oil sump when the pump pressure exceeds 100 p.s.i.

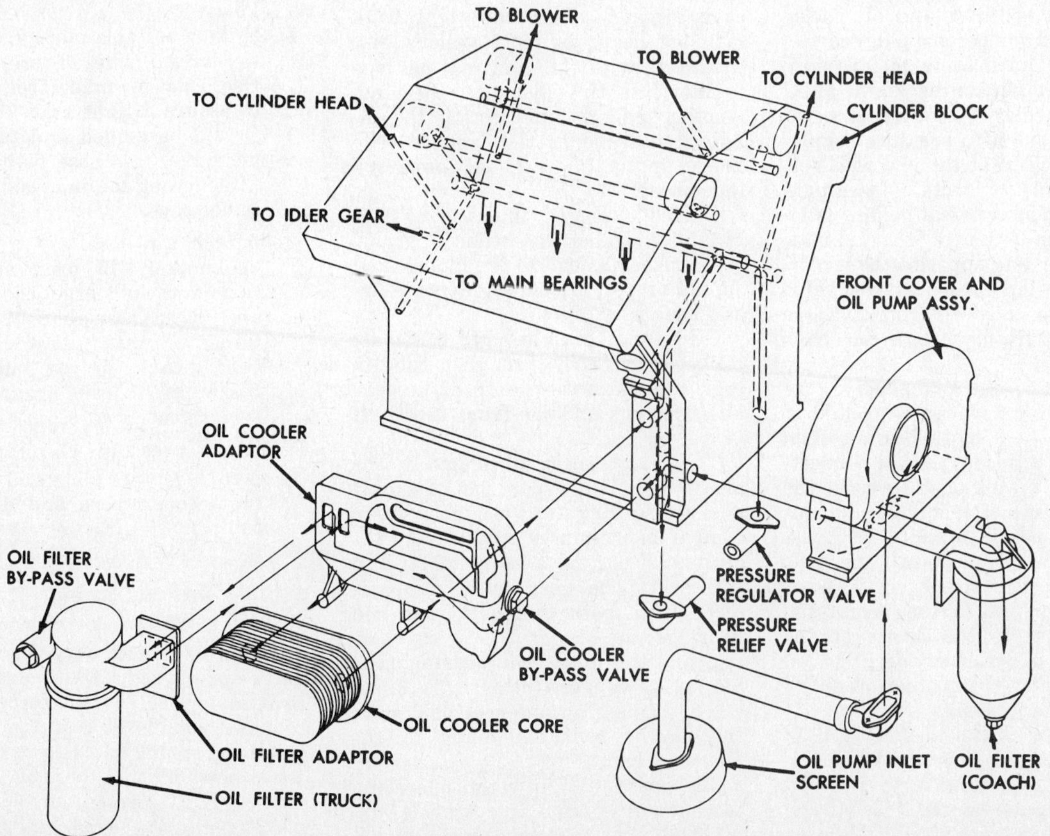

Diagram of engine lubrication system (© G.M.C.)

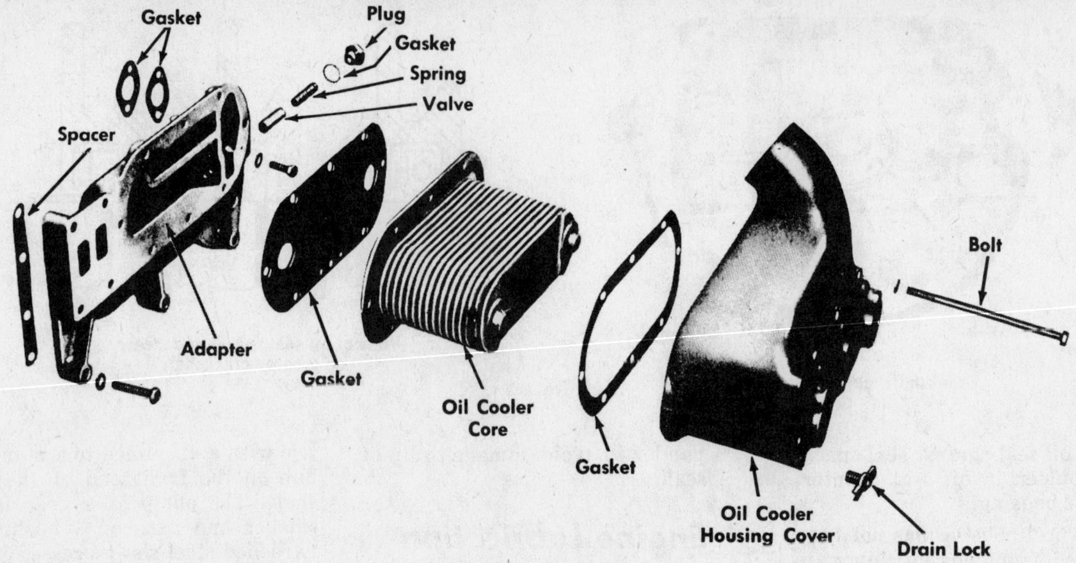

Oil cooler components (typical) (© G.M.C.)

From the oil cooler adaptor plate, the oil passed into the full flow filter through the oil cooler (truck engines only) and then back into the cylinder block where a short vertical oil gallery and a short diagonal oil gallery carry the oil to the main longitudinal oil gallery through the middle of the block. On engines used in coaches, oil filter is mounted at crankcase front cover and oil from pump goes directly to filter and returns to cylinder block. Valves are also provided to by-pass the oil filter and oil cooler should either one become plugged.

Stabilized lubricating oil pressure is maintained within the engine at all speeds, regardless of the oil temperature, by means of a pressure regulator valve located at the end of a vertical oil gallery connected to the main oil gallery. This vertical gallery is located at the front of the cylinder block on the side opposite the cooler. When the oil pressure at the valve exceeds 50 p.s.i., the regulator valve opens, discharging excess oil back into the sump.

From the main oil gallery, the pressurized oil flows through drilled passages to each main bearing then passes to an adjacent pair of connecting rods by means of grooves in the unloaded halves of the main and connecting rod bearings and drilled passages in the crankshaft. The rifle drilled connecting rods carry oil from the rod bearings to the piston pin bushings and to the nozzle at the upper end of each connecting rod which provides the cooling oil spray for the piston crowns.

At the rear of the block, two diagonally drilled oil passages which intersect the main oil gallery, carry oil to the two rear camshaft end bearings. Oil is then conducted through the rifle drilled camshaft to the intermediate and front end bearings. Oil from the camshaft intermediate bearings is directed against the camshaft lobes and cam rollers which run in an oil bath. This oil from the intermediate bearings provides lubrication of the cam lobes immediately after starting the engine when the oil is cold and before camshaft bearing oil flow and oil drainage from the cylinder head have had time to build up.

The diagonally drilled oil passage on the right side at the rear of the block intersects with a vertical passage to carry oil to the right bank cylinder head. A short gallery also intersects with this diagonal passage to lubricate the idler gear bearing. Another gallery intersecting the diagonal passage at the front of the block supplies oil to the left bank cylinder head.

Drilled passages, intersecting longitudinal galleries which parallel the camshafts, lead to the blower and supply oil for the blower drive gears and bearings.

Oil from the right-hand camshaft pocket is directed through a tube to lubricate the water pump drive gear and bearings and the front camshaft gear.

The gear train is lubricated by the overflow of oil from the camshaft pockets spilling into the gear train compartment and by splash from the oil pan. A certain amount of oil also spills into the gear train compartment from both camshaft rear end bearings, the blower drive gear bearing, and the idler gear bearing. The blower drive gear bearing is lubricated through an external pipe from the blower rear end plate to the blower drive support.

The valve and injector operating mechanism is lubricated from a longitudinal oil passage, on the camshaft side of each cylinder head, which connects to the main oil gallery in the cylinder block. Oil from this passage enters the drilled rocker arm shafts through the lower end of the rocker shaft bolts and rocker shaft brackets. Excess oil from the rocker arms lubricates the exhaust valves and cam followers.

Oil Cooler Testing

Pressure Check Core

After the oil cooler core has been cleaned, it may be checked for leaks as follows:

1. Make a suitable plate and attach to flanged side of cooler core. Use a gasket made from rubber to assure a tight seal. The plate should be drilled and tapped to permit an air hose fitting to be attached at the inlet side of the cooler core.
2. Attach air hose and apply approximately 75 p.s.i. air pressure and submerge cooler core and plate assembly in a container of water. Any leaks will be indicated by air bubbles in the water. If leaks are indicated, replace cooler core.
3. After pressure check is completed, remove plate and air hose from cooler core and dry with compressed air.

By-Pass Spring

Inspect valve and spring for wear and replace if necessary. The by-pass valve spring has a free length of approximately 2-1/64″. A force of 13⅜ to 14⅝ pounds is required to compress the spring to a length of 1.793″ when new. When a force of 12 lbs. or less will compress the spring to 1.793″, replace the spring. The spring may be checked in spring tester.

GMC Toro-Flow Diesel Engines

Index

GENERAL SPECIFICATIONS

ENGINE MODEL	BORE AND STROKE	HORSEPOWER @ R.P.M.	TORQUE FT. LBS. @ R.P.M.	COMPRESSION PRESSURE @ 600 R.P.M.	FIRING ORDER	GOVERNED SPEED R.P.M.	IDLE SPEED
D-351-V6	4.56 x 3.58	130 @ 3200	234 @ 2000	500	1-6-5-4-3-2	3200	625-650
D-478-V6	5.125 x 3.86	150 @ 3200	275 @ 2000	500	1-6-5-4-3-2	3200	625-650
DH-478-V6	5.125 x 3.86	170 @ 3200	310 @ 2000	500	1-6-5-4-3-2	3200	625-650
D-637-V8	5.125 x 3.86	195 @ 2600	—	500	1-8-4-3-6-5-7-2	2600	625-650
DH-637-V8	5.125 x 3.86	220 @ 2600	—	500	1-8-4-3-6-5-7-2	2800	625-650

PISTONS, PINS, RINGS, CRANKSHAFT AND BEARINGS

ENGINE MODEL	PISTON CLEARANCE	PISTON RING END GAP MINIMUM		PISTON PIN DIAMETER	ROD BEARINGS		MAIN BEARING		SHAFT END PLAY	THRUST ON BEARING NO.
		COMP.	OIL		SHAFT DIAMETER	BEARING CLEARANCE	SHAFT DIAMETER	BEARING CLEARANCE		
D-351-VP	.0062-.0068	.015	.013	1.6148-1.6150	2.8112-2.8122	.001-.0031	3.1237-3.1247	.0013-.0039	.003-.008	3
478-V6	.0067-.0073	.017	.017	1.6148-1.6150	2.8112-2.8122	.001-.0031	3.1237-3.1247	.0013-.0039	.003-.008	3
637-V8	.0067-.0073	.017	.017	1.6148-1.6150	2.8112-2.8122	.001-.0031	3.1237-3.1247	.0013-.0039	.003-.008	4

VALVE SPECIFICATIONS

ENGINE MODEL	VALVE LASH (HOT)		VALVE FACE ANGLE (DEG.)	VALVE STEM CLEARANCE		VALVE STEM DIAMETER		VALVE SPRINGS FREE LENGTH	
	IN.	EXH.		INTAKE	EXHAUST	INTAKE	EXHAUST	INNER	OUTER
D351-V6	.010	.018	45	.0015-.003	.002-.0035	.3407-34.12	.3402-.3407	2.46	2.67
478-V6	.010	.018	45	.0015-.003	.0025-.004	.3725-.3730	.4340-.4345	2.46	2.67
637-V8	.010	.018	45	.0015-.003	.0025-.004	.3725-.3730	.4340-.4345	2.46	2.67

ENGINE TORQUE SPECIFICATIONS

ENGINE MODEL	CYLINDER HEAD FT. LBS.	INTAKE MANIFOLD FT. LBS.	EXHAUST MANIFOLD FT. LBS.	CONN. ROD FT. LBS.	MAIN BEARING CAPS FT. LBS.	DAMPER TO CRANKSHAFT BOLT FT. LBS.	FLYWHEEL TO CRANKSHAFT FT. LBS.	CAMSHAFT GEAR BOLT FT. LBS.	OIL PUMP TO BLOCK BOLTS FT. LBS.	OIL PAN BOLTS FT. LBS.
D351-V6	130-135	20-25	15-20	55-65	—	200-210	100-110	50-60	30-35	10-15
478-V6	130-135	20-25	15-20	55-65	—	240-260	100-110	50-60	30-35	10-15
637-V8	130-135	20-25	15-20	55-65	—	240-260	100-110	50-60	30-35	10-15

Trouble Diagnosis

The satisfactory performance of a Diesel engine depends on two items of foremost importance, (1) Sufficiently high compression pressure, and (2) The injection of the proper amount of fuel at the right time.

The first one of these items depends entirely on pistons, piston rings, valves and valve operating mechanism; the second item depends on injectors and their operating mechanism, and fuel system.

Lack of engine power, uneven running, excessive vibration, and tendency to stall when idling may be caused by either a compression loss or faulty injector operation.

The causes of trouble symptoms may be varied; therefore a hit-and-miss search should be avoided. A proper diagnosis of symptoms is an orderly process of diagnosing the symptoms. An "orderly process" means to check the most probable common cause first; then proceed with the next probable cause.

Hard Starting

1. Improper oil viscosity.
2. Low battery output.
3. Defective starter or solenoid.
4. Low temperature.
5. Burned or warped valves.
6. Improper valve lash.
7. Worn or broken piston rings.
8. Defective cylinder head gasket.
9. Fuel line shut off valve closed.
10. Engine stop mechanism not released.
11. Low fuel supply.
12. Clogged vent in fuel tank cap.
13. Clogged fuel filters.
14. Broken fuel line allowing air leak into system.
15. Air trapped in system.
16. Water or ice in fuel system.
17. Defective fuel supply pump.
18. Overflow valve stuck or leaking.
19. Low fuel delivery.
20. Improper grade or type fuel.

Abnormal Engine Operation

1. Idle speed set too low.
2. Cylinder misfiring.
3. Burned or sticking valves.
4. Engine temperature too hot or too cold.
5. Fuel system deficiencies.
6. Detonation due to improper injector timing.
7. Defective injection nozzles.
8. Lack of power due to improper valve adjustment.
9. Insufficient fuel.
10. Insufficient air.
11. Excessive exhaust back pressure.
12. Low cylinder compression.

Excessive Black or Gray Smoke

1. Insufficient combustion air.
2. Exhaust pipe or muffler clogged.
3. Injection pump improperly timed to engine.
4. Incorrect engine valve timing.
5. Injector nozzles leaky, worn or improper opening pressure.
6. Wrong grade and type of fuel.
7. Engine overheating.
8. Poor cylinder compression.
9. Damaged or worn piston rings and/or pistons.
10. Cylinders overfueled.

High Lubricating Oil Consumption

1. Oil lines or connections leaking.
2. Leaking gaskets.
3. Crankcase oil level too high.
4. Pistons and/or rings worn or damaged.

Excessive White or Blue Smoke

1. Oil level in air cleaner too high.
2. Injection pump improperly timed to engine.
3. Engine crankcase oil level too high.
4. Engine running too cool.
5. Poor cylinder compression.
6. Damaged or worn pistons and/ or rings.
7. Wrong grade or type of fuel.

Low Engine Oil Pressure

1. Defective oil gauge or sending unit.
2. Oil viscosity too low.
3. Oil diluted with fuel oil.
4. Suction loss.
5. Weak or broken relief valve spring in oil pump.
6. Worn oil pump.
7. Excessive clearance at crankshaft, camshaft or balance shaft bearings.

NOTE: In case of no oil pressure the oil pump drive shaft or drive gear teeth could be worn to point where oil pump is not driven. Inspection can be made by removing the oil pump and tachometer drive housing and gear at rear of engine.

Engine Overheats

1. Scale deposits in cooling system.
2. Air flow thru radiator restricted or clogged.
3. Loose fan drive belt.
4. Low coolant level.
5. Hoses collapsed.
6. Defective thermostats.
7. Combustion gases in coolant water.
8. Incorrect injection pump to engine timing.

Engine Tune-Up

Description

GMC Toro-Flow Diesel truck engines are four stroke cycle type of 60-degree, V-6 and V-8 design. Fuel for combustion is injected directly into combustion area through hole-type nozzles—one nozzle for each cylinder. Fuel injection pump has a single plunger with distributor type hydraulic head. Pump is mounted between cylinder heads and is driven from drive gear bolted to engine camshaft gear.

Illustrations show D478 engine with typical accessories installed, and typical V-8 engine, model D637. Cross section view of Toro-Flow engine shown.

The descriptions of the various components are applicable to all of the engines in the Toro-Flow Diesel series: namely, D351, D and DH478, and D and DH637 unless otherwise indicated.

Before performing other tune-up procedure, check battery electrolyte specific gravity at each cell to be sure battery is fully charged.

Check Cylinder Compression

1. Start engine and run until normal operation temperature is reached.
2. Stop engine and remove high pressure line clamps. Remove the high pressure line between injection pump and nozzle holder at cylinder to be checked.

   Remove the nut at each end from the threads at pump and nozzle holder and lift the line away from both units without bending.
3. Disconnect leak-off hoses from tee or elbow on injection nozzle holder. Remove nozzle holder retaining bolts and pull the holder assembly out of well in cylinder head. Clean nozzle holder cavity

Typical D478 Toro flow diesel engine

'iews of D637 Toro flow diesel engine (© G.M.C.)

Gauge and adapter for checking compression (© G.M.C.)

1 Fuel leak-off hose
2 Injection nozzle bolts and lock washers
3 Compression gauge and hose
4 Leak-off hose connector
5 Adapter
6 Fuel injection pump assembly
7 Adapter and fuel hose assembly
8 Overflow valve
9 Fuel receptacle
10 Fuel return line (hose)
11 Fuel supply pump assembly
12 Fuel secondary filter

and gasket seat in cylinder head, then turn engine over with starter to blow loose carbon out of combustion chamber and nozzle holder cavity. Use a nozzle holder copper gasket at bottom of well and install the compression gauge adapter in place of nozzle holder as shown, using the nozzle holder bolts to hold the adapter in place. Connect gauge to the adapter. Be sure all connections are tight.

4. If a rear cylinder is being checked, insert plug in the disconnected leak-off hose. When other cylinders are being checked, join the disconnected leak-off hoses with a two-way or three-way connector, as required.
5. Install adapter and hose in outlet port in hydraulic head on injection pump and place hose in receptacle to catch fuel oil while running the engine. CAUTION: Under no condition should the high pressure outlet port on the injection pump be plugged to prevent the escape of fuel.
6. Start the engine and allow engine to idle at 625 rpm. Observe and record the compression pressure shown on compression gauge. NOTE: Do not attempt to obtain compression pressure by cranking engine with starter.
7. Perform this operation on each cylinder. The compression pressure in any one cylinder should be not less than 500 psi at 625 rpm. Also, there should not be more than a 30 psi difference between cylinders.

Cylinder Head Bolts

Check cylinder head bolts for proper torque. Normally head bolts should not need tightening at tune-up intervals.

Manifold Bolts

Check manifold bolts for proper torque and be sure end bolts have been securely locked.

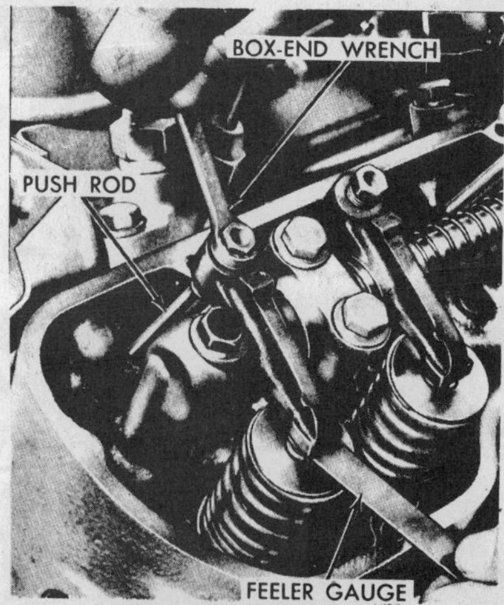

Adjusting valves
(© G.M.C.)

Valve Clearance

Engine must be at normal operating temperature. Check and set exhaust valves to .018 and intake to .010 inch clearance.

Inspect Fuel System

1. Check all fuel lines for evidence or leaking.
2. Check and service fuel and air filters as directed in "owner's and driver's manual."
3. Check accelerator controls and

Adjusting engine idle speed
(© G.M.C.)

linkage for binding. Check proper operation of stop control. (manual or solonoid type)

4. Check engine idle speed which should be 625 RPM. To adjust, remove lower acord nut at rear of injection pump. With engine running, loosen lock nut and turn adjusting screw. Retighten lock nut and install acord nut.

NOTE: In instances where engine still does not perform properly, it may be necessary to remove the fuel injection nozzles and check the nozzle opening pressure and spray pattern.

Fuel System

Description

The fuel system used with Toro-Flow Diesel engines includes the various components schematically (illustrated).

Fuel Injection Pump Assembly

The fuel injection pump assembly is of the PSJ series manufactured by American Bosch Arma Corporation.

Injection pump assembly is mounted on machined rear face of engine front cover assembly. Pump assembly is held in place by three studs and nuts.

The high pressure pump is the single plunger type, which distributes equal amounts of fuel to the fuel injection nozzles, at the cylinders, in the proper firing sequence.

Injection pump is gear driven from a pump drive gear bolted to front face of engine camshaft gear. Pump input shaft, on which the pump driven gear is mounted, rotates at engine crankshaft speed. The cam lobes on input shaft actuate the pump plunger to inject fuel to cylinders for each revolution of the engine crankshaft.

Included in the fuel injection pump assembly are the following units or devices:

1. Fuel supply pump.
2. Hydraulic head assembly
3. Timing advance mechanism.
4. Governor and fuel control unit.
5. Excess fuel device for starting.

An overflow valve assembly is installed on the hydraulic head housing and incorporates a valve assembly which maintains proper fuel pressure within the fuel chamber to assure an adequate supply of fuel to the pump plunger at all times.

Seal wires are installed by the manufacturer and in no case are the seals to be removed or the pump disassembled except by authorized personnel.

Complete replacement pumps are available through G.M.C. Truck dealers.

Fuel Injection Nozzle

Holder Assemblies

The fuel injection nozzle and holder assemblies are utilized to carry the high pressure fuel through the cylinder head to nozzle tip and deliver it to the combustion chamber.

The nozzle holder consists of a forged body which houses the spindle and spring, and has a high pressure fuel duct. The spindle bore and spring chamber are utilized as a passage for leak-off fuel which seeps past and lubricates the nozzle valve.

The nozzle valve and body are a closely matched pair which must always be used together as a unit. *Valves and valve bodies are not interchangable*; however, matched nozzle and valve assemblies are available. Nozzle and valve assembly is located on nozzle holder by dowel pins and the assembly is firmly seated at lapped mating surfaces on body and nozzle holder by the nozzle cap nut. A high pressure duct in nozzle valve body aligns with duct in nozzle holder to carry high pressure fuel to the valve seat area. Pressure spring at upper part of holder seats at a flange on spindle, and spring is retained by the pressure adjusting nut. Spring pressure is transferred through the spindle to the nozzle valve. Spring holds the valve on its seat in nozzle body.

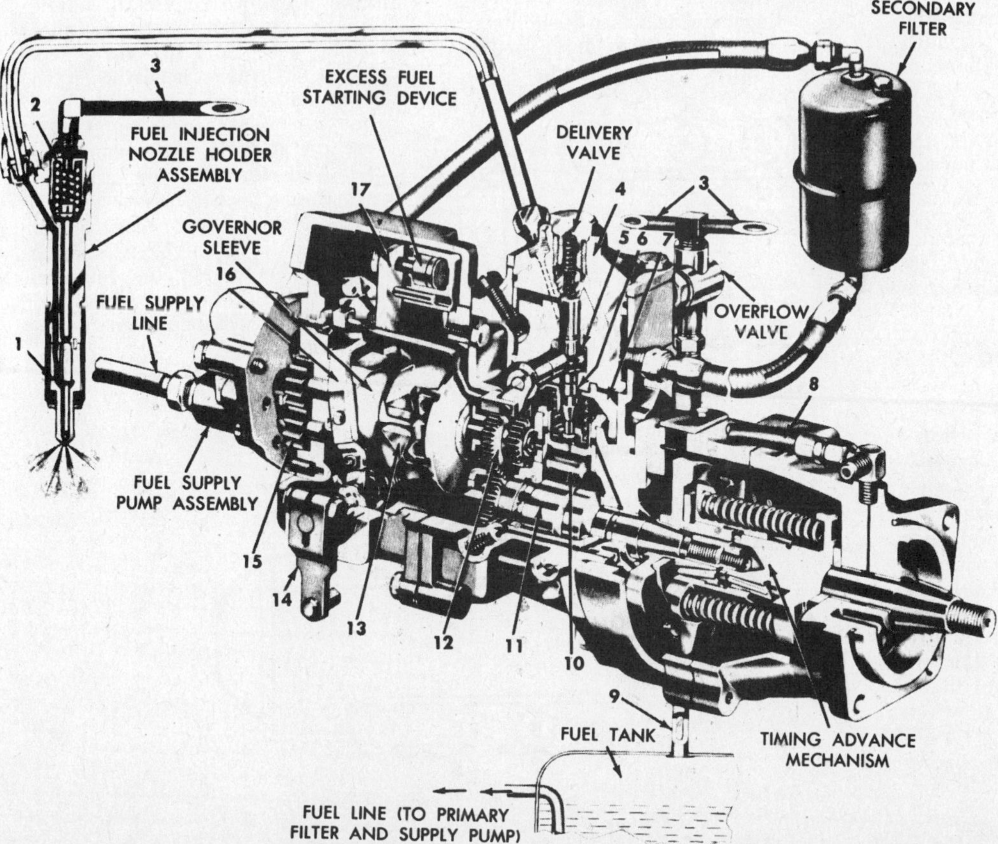

Arrangement of fuel system units (8 cyl. engines) (© G.M.C.)

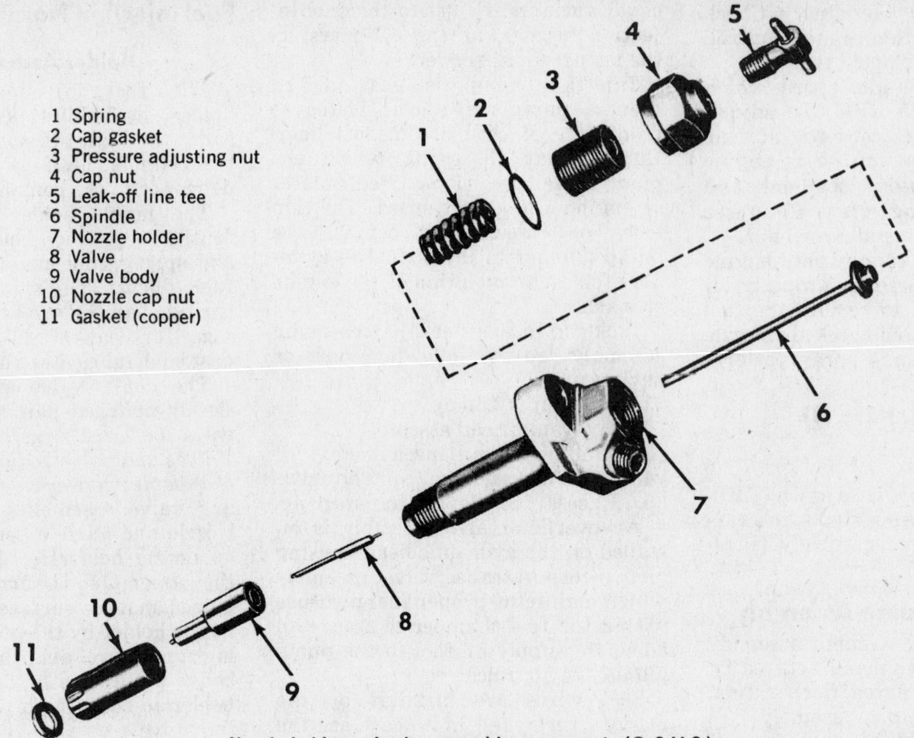

Nozzle holder and valve assembly components (© G.M.C.)

A perfect seal is necessary at valve seat to prevent fuel dribble as well as to prevent any of the combustion gases in cylinder from entering the spray nozzle interior chamber.

The cap nut at upper end of nozzle holder assembly serves to lock the spring adjusting nut and is threaded to accept a leak-off tee of elbow to which is attached the leak-off hose.

A high pressure fuel line from outlet port in injection pump hydraulic head is connected to threaded portion on nozzle body forging.

The fuel injection nozzle holder assemblies are held in place in cylinder heads by two bolts; and a copper gasket is used at bottom of each nozzle well in head.

Fuel Injection Nozzles and High Pressure Lines

Fuel Injection Nozzle Operation

Fuel under pressure is fed from the rotary single plunger injection pump to the appropriate nozzle via the high pressure pipe line and finds its way through the ducts in the nozzle holder and valve body to the lower end of valve. When the pressure reaches 3000 psi, the valve will lift, and fuel is injected through holes in nozzle tip and into combustion chamber. Nozzle valve closes again when the line pressure drops. Any leak-back through the leak-off line fitting is passed back to the junction fitting on injection pump overflow valve.

Locating a Misfiring Cylinder

This procedure will not serve to detect a nozzle with incorrect popping pressure within a moderate range. Such a malfunction can only be determined by removal of nozzle assembly from engine and checking on test stand.

1. Connect an accurate tachometer at the tachometer drive fitting on engine.

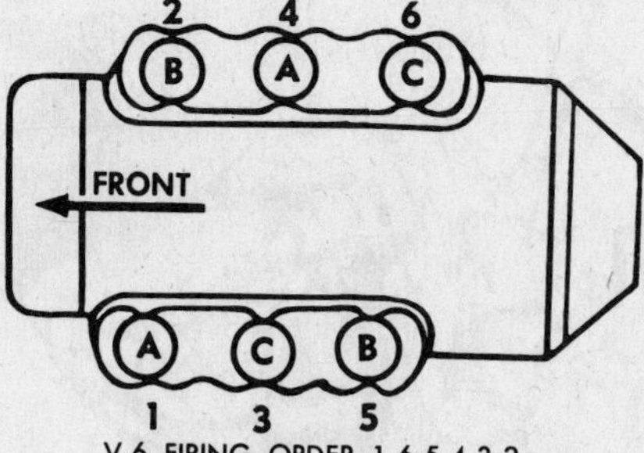

Firing order and mated cylinders 6 cyl. Toro flow engines (© G.M.C.)

2. With engine idling, loosen a high pressure line nut at injection nozzle holder. When a high pressure line nut is loosened, the pressure build-up will not be great enough to cause the nozzle to deliver fuel to the cylinder being tested and no power will result. If there is little or no drop in engine rpm when the line nut is loosened, the nozzle may be at fault and it should be removed for cleaning and inspection.

NOTE: Nut at high pressure line must remain loose only long enough to observe the tachometer reading, since fuel will spill from the loosened nut with each discharge from the injection pump port.

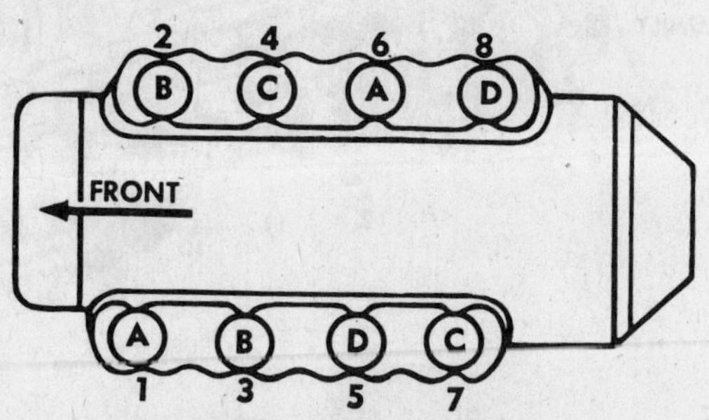

Firing order and mated cylinders 8 cyl. Toro flow engines (© G.M.C.)

Nozzle and Holder Assembly Maintenance

Normally, unless engine performance, or other trouble diagnosis symptoms indicate a malfunction of fuel injection nozzles, the nozzle and holder assemblies should not be removed from engine.

When it becomes necessary to remove nozzle and holder assemblies, follow the procedures given to remove, clean, and test the units.

Removing Nozzle and Holder Assemblies

1. Disconnect the high pressure line nut at the fuel injection nozzle holder and at fuel injection pump hydraulic head.
2. Remove the clamp assembly from line being removed then remove the high pressure line. IMPORTANT: High pressure line must be disconnected at both ends and clamp must be removed so line can be removed without bending. Install dust caps at injection pump outlet port and at nozzle holder when line is removed.
3. Force leak-off hose off fitting in top of nozzle holder. Remove the two nozzle holder bolts and lock washers, then pull nozzle holder assembly out of cylinder head, meanwhile using air hose to blow away any dirt particles which may be loosened as the nozzle holder is lifted out.
4. Remove copper gasket then plug the opening in cylinder head to prevent objects from being accidentally dropped into nozzle well.

Inspection Before Disassembly

NOTE: It is recommended that each nozzle assembly be tested for leakage and valve opening pressure as well as for spray pattern before disassembly. If nozzle assembly is found to be in good condition, it should not be disassembled, but should only be cleaned externally. If the holes in nozzle tip are clogged as indicated by unsatisfactory spray pattern, the components should be disassembled before attempting to clean the holes.

Disassembly

1. With nozzle holder mounted on fixture or held in vise, loosen cap nut and remove nut and gasket from spring pressure adjusting nut.
2. With Allen wrench, remove spring pressure adjusting nut from nozzle holder. Remove spring and spindle. IMPORTANT: Do not proceed with step 3 unless pressure adjusting nut has been loosened to relieve spring pressure.
3. Invert nozzle holder and remove the nozzle cap nut from nozzle holder, then separate valve body from the nozzle holder.

Cleaning and Inspection

The nozzle tip should be cleaned with a brass wire brush before disassembling the valve body from nozzle holder. The nozzle tip orifices should be cleaned using orifice needle and holder. Care must be used when cleaning orifices to avoid breaking orifice cleaning needle in hole. After disassembly, all parts should be carefully cleaned. If lapped surfaces on holder and mating surface on valve body are scratched, remove dowel pins from nozzle holder and polish the surface on lapping block using special fine lapping compound. Also polish the mating surface on valve body. Install new dowel pins after nozzle holder surface has been lapped.

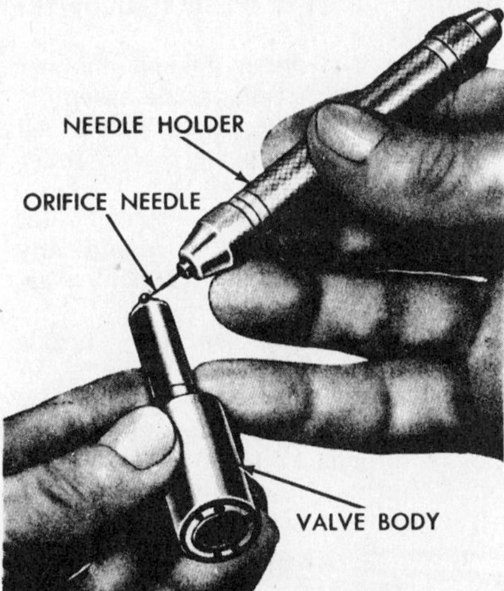

Using special needle to clean spray holes in nozzle valve body (© G.M.C.)

Assembling Injection Nozzle Parts

1. Dip valve and body in clean fuel and insert valve in body. NOTE: The valve must be free in the body. By lifting the valve about one-third of its length out of the body, the valve should slide back to its seat without aid when the assembly is held at a 45 degree angle.
2. Mount nozzle holder in holding fixture, then set valve body in place on nozzle holder dowel pins and screw nozzle cap nut onto nozzle holder. Before tightening cap nut, use centering sleeve over nozzle tip to locate the nozzle valve body in center of opening in cap nut. After nut has been tightened sufficiently to seat parts, remove centering sleeve and tighten cap nut (10) to 50 to 55 foot-pounds.
3. Set nozzle holder upright in holding fixture or vise and insert spindle into holder. Place spring on spindle, then thread spring pressure adjusting nut into threads in nozzle holder. Place cap nut gasket over nut, then install cap nut on threads on adjusting nut.

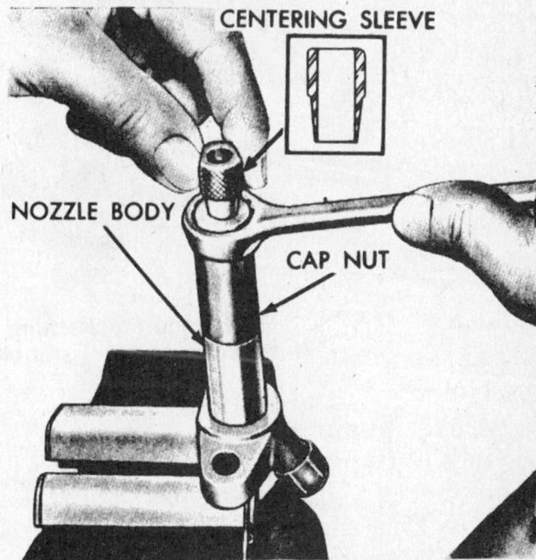

Using centering sleeve to locate valve body while tightening cap nut (© G.M.C.)

4. Check nozzle on test fixture for spray pattern and valve opening pressure.
5. Setting Injection Nozzle Valve Opening Pressure. Using test pump, proceed as instructed below to set the valve opening pressure and test for leaks.

With nozzle holder assembly connected to tester, actuate the test stand handle rapidly (about 25 strokes per minute) to expel air from nozzle and holder and to "settle" the spring and nozzle loading column.

Depress operating handle slowly to raise pressure. Continue to depress handle and note the gauge pressure at which the nozzle valve opens. If opening pressure is not as specified, remove the leak-off tee and loosen cap nut so Allen wrench can be used to adjust spring pressure.

Use Allen wrench to turn pressure adjusting nut and change spring pressure. Turning nut clockwise increases pressure. Repeat valve opening pressure test each time adjusting nut is changed until correct opening pressure is obtained.

NOTE: When new pressure adjusting spring is installed, adjust the opening pressure 10% higher than specification to allow for spring set.

After correct valve opening pressure is obtained, tighten cap nut firmly to lock the adjustment. Recheck for valve-opening pressure after cap nut is tightened.

Operate test pump handle with several fast sharp strokes, meanwhile observing spray pattern. Spray should be in the nature of finely atomized sprays indicating that all holes are open. D351 engines have five orifices in each nozzle tip. Nozzle tips on other engines have only four orifices.

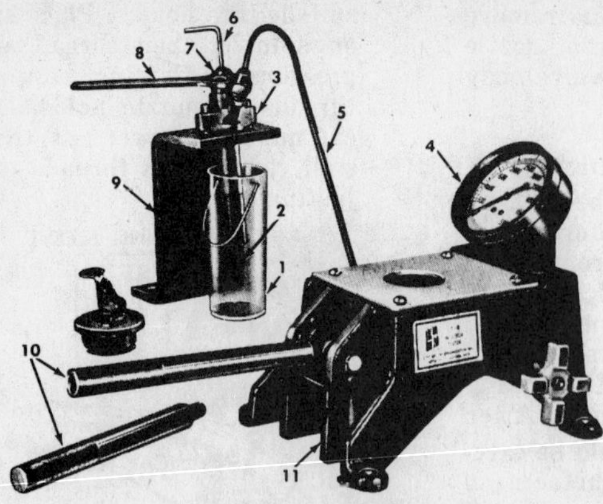

Test stand for checking injection nozzle operation (© G.M.C.)

Stroke pump slowly (approx. 3 seconds). Some degree of "chatter" should occur, indicating that nozzle valve is free and component parts are correctly assembled.

Depress the pump handle slowly with a 10-second stroke and hold the pressure slightly (approx. 100 lbs.) below nozzle valve opening pressure to check for valve seat leakage. No fuel droplets should appear. Occasionally a slight wetting of the tip (2) may be noticed. This is permissible since it is caused from hydraulically balancing the spring and nozzle valve.

Remove the nozzle holder assembly from test stand and if nozzle holder is not to be installed immediately, it should be wrapped in clean paper.

If nozzle does not operate properly, replace valve and body or install rebuilt nozzle holder assembly.

Nozzle Holder Assembly Installation

Use seat cleaner and wrench handle first to clean seat, and the bore in cylinder head through which the injection nozzle valve body extends, then use brush to finish cleaning the well cavity.

1. Use new copper gasket at lower end of injection nozzle assembly and insert the nozzle holder assembly into place in cylinder head.
2. Gradually tighten nozzle holder bolts alternately to avoid any tendency to bend the holder assembly.
3. Final tension on two nozzle holder bolts should be equal to seat the assembly squarely on copper gasket. Correct torque reading is 17 to 20 foot-pounds.
4. Connect leak-off lines at tee or elbow on nozzle holder. Place the high pressure line in place so that fittings on both ends line up squarely with respective threads at both the injection pump and the nozzle holder. Use torque wrench and adapter to tighten nut a hydraulic head to 16 to 19 ft.-lbs. Tighten nuts at injector nozzle holders to 22 to 26 foot-pounds.

Injection Timing

The fuel injection pump assembly is timed to the engine when pump assembly is installed, and should not require any subsequent alteration if the installation is done properly.

In the even there is reason to suspect that fuel injection is not properly timed, the following procedure is necessary to check the timing.

Same procedure is used both on the 6-cylinder and 8-cylinder engines except as indicated in text.

Checking Injection Timing (With All Fuel Units Installed)

1. Remove the cover and gasket from right side of fuel injection pump to expose the alignment mark in the opening below the control unit lever.
2. On 6-cylinder engines, remove the access cover from top of engine front cover assembly to expose pointer and mark on injection pump hub. On 8-cylinder engines, remove the inspection plate from top of advance mechanism housing to expose the pointer and timing mark.
3. Remove left hand rocker arm cover, then crank engine to place

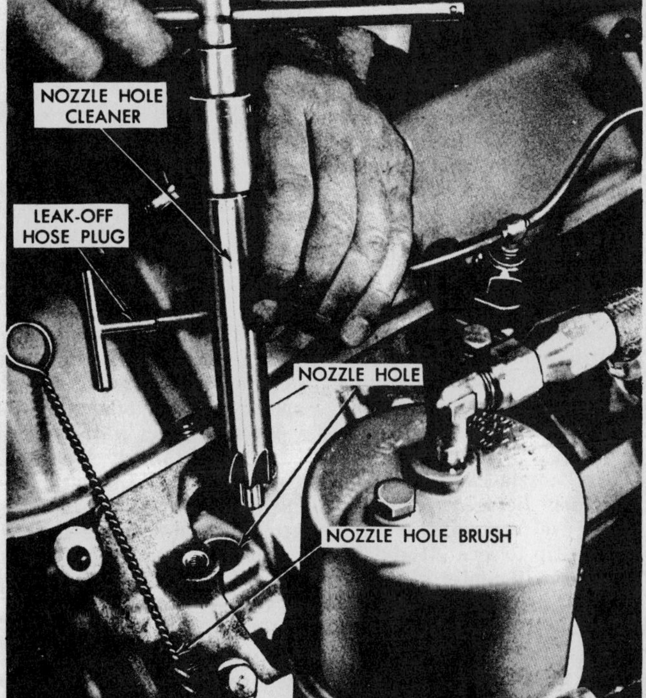

Cylinder head nozzle well cleaning equipment (© G.M.C.)

No. 1 piston on compression stroke—(both valves will then be closed and push rods can be turned with fingers). Slowly crank the engine until the "INJ" mark on crankshaft damper is aligned with pointer in engine front cover. At this point pump should be injecting fuel into No. 1 cylinder.

4. If 6-cylinder engine is correctly timed, the mark and pointer will be indexed and mark on face gear viewed through cover opening in pump housing will be in the position shown in the illustration. If 8-cylinder engine is correctly timed, the mark and pointer will be indered and mark on pump face gear viewed through cover opening in pump housing will be in the position shown in the illustration.
5. If the mark on pump drive hub is not indexed with pointer, or if the mark on face gear is not visible in opening, the injection timing is not correct. However, before proceeding to reset the injection timing, recheck to make sure No. 1 piston is on compression stroke and "INJ" mark on damper is aligned with pointer.

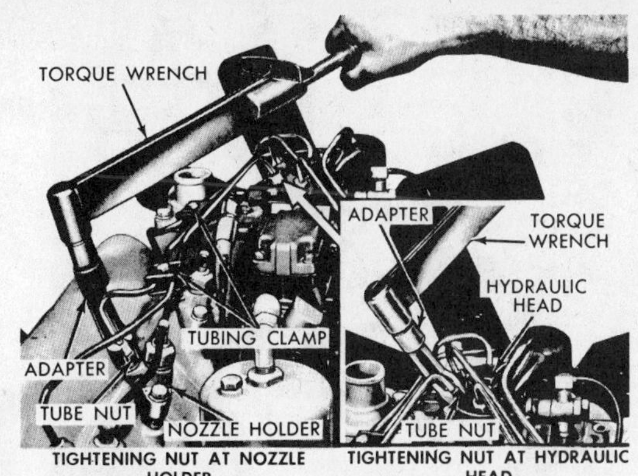

Tightening nuts on high pressure lines (© G.M.C.)

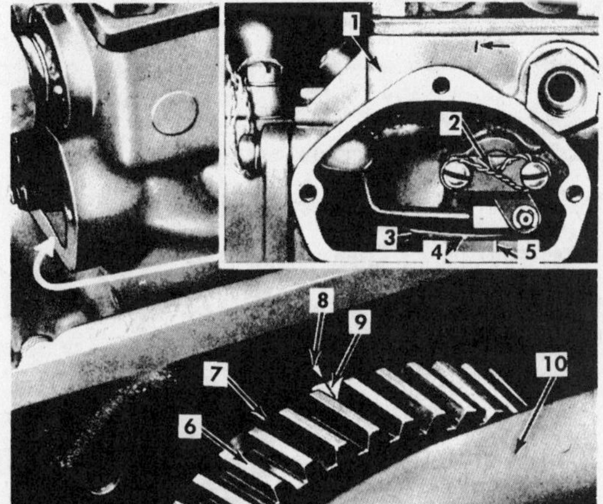

Timing marks at face gear and at injection pump gear flange (6 cyl. engines) (© G.M.C.)

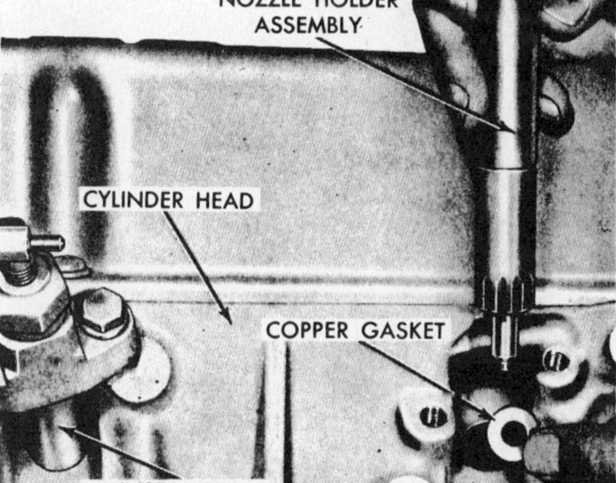

Installing fuel injection nozzle assembly (© G.M.C.)

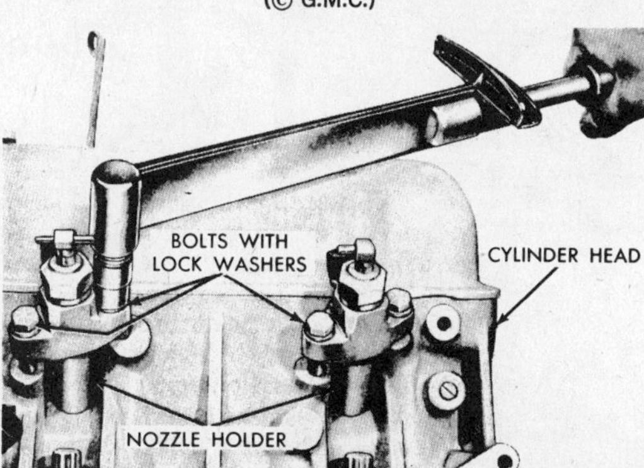

Tightening nozzle holder bolts with torque wrench (© G.M.C.)

Setting Injection Timing

The elongated holes in injection pump driven gear make possible the setting of injection timing when installing the fuel injection pump assembly as well as for making correction of timing when necessary.

With engine crankshaft positioned for firing on No. 1 cylinder use special wrench and box end wrench to loosen the driven gear mounting bolts.

Bring engine back to firing position on No. 1 cylinder before loosening the last bolt.

With bolts loose, use special wrench to turn injection pump shaft and hub as necessary to align mark on hub with pointer for 6-cylinder engines or to index and mark pointer when viewed through opening on 8-cylinder engines. Hold the shaft with wrench and tighten driven gear mounting bolts.

Recheck to make sure of exact indexing of marks.

Fuel Injection System

Illustrations show cut-away views of fuel injection pump for 6-cylinder engines. Same construction is used on pumps for 8-cylinder engines.

1 "INJ" mark on hub
2 Advance mechanism housing
3 Pointer
4 Fuel injection pump assembly
5 Pointer in front cover
6 Crankshaft damper assembly

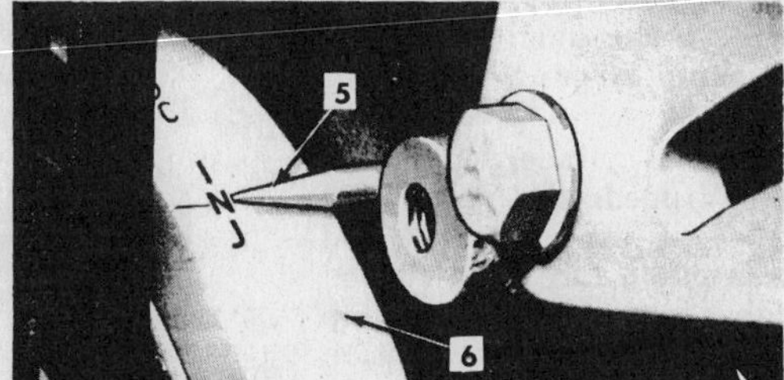

POINTER AND MARK AT PUMP ADVANCE COVER OPENING

POINTER AND MARKS AT CRANKSHAFT PULLEY

Timing marks at advance mechanism and crankshaft damper (8 cylinder engines) (© G.M.C.)

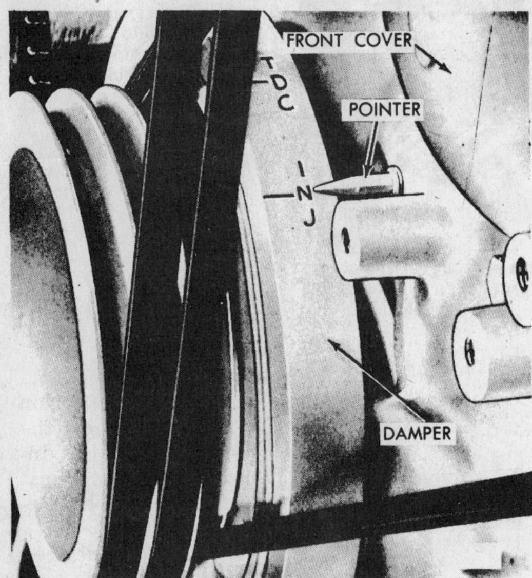

Timing marks (6 cylinder engine) (© G.M.C.)

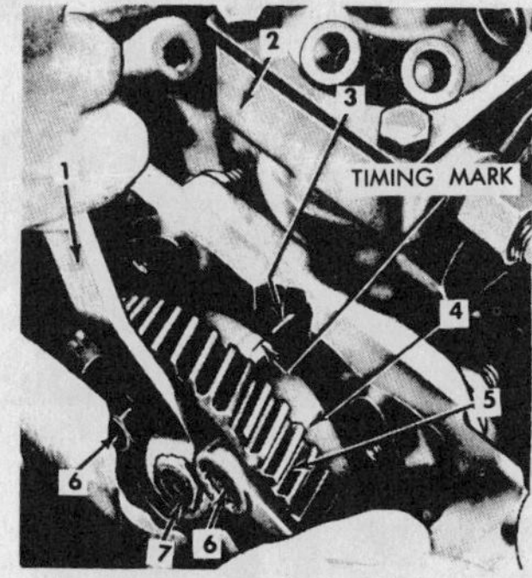

1 Pump shaft holding wrench (special tool)
2 Fuel injection pump assembly
3 Pointer
4 Driven gear mounting hub
5 Injection pump driven gear
6 Driven gear mounting bolts
7 Hub retaining nut

Using special wrench to hold pump shaft while tightening driven gear bolts (© G.M.C.)

DELIVERY VALVE SPRING
CAP
VALVE RETAINER
HEAD LOCATING SCREW
DELIVERY VALVE
SOCKET HEAD SCREW
PLUNGER
RETAINER
FUEL CONTROL UNIT
SPACER
PIN
LOCKWIRE
CONTROL UNIT AND ROD RETAINER PLATE
FACE GEAR
METERING SLEEVE
CONTROL ROD

View of hydraulic head showing internal components (© G.M.C.)

Service Operations

The service operations contained herein can be accomplished without removing the fuel injection pump assembly from the engine. WARNING: Do not attempt to work on the fuel injection pump, nozzles, or high pressure lines in a dusty area. Extreme precautions must be taken to prevent any dust particles from entering the fuel passages in lines and nozzles. Any dirt or abrasive material permitted to enter the fuel supply port on fuel injection pump could quickly cause extensive damage to, or possible ruin of the pump hydraulic head mechanism.

Fuel Delivery Valve

Removal

Wash off top of the head assembly and blow dry with air hose.

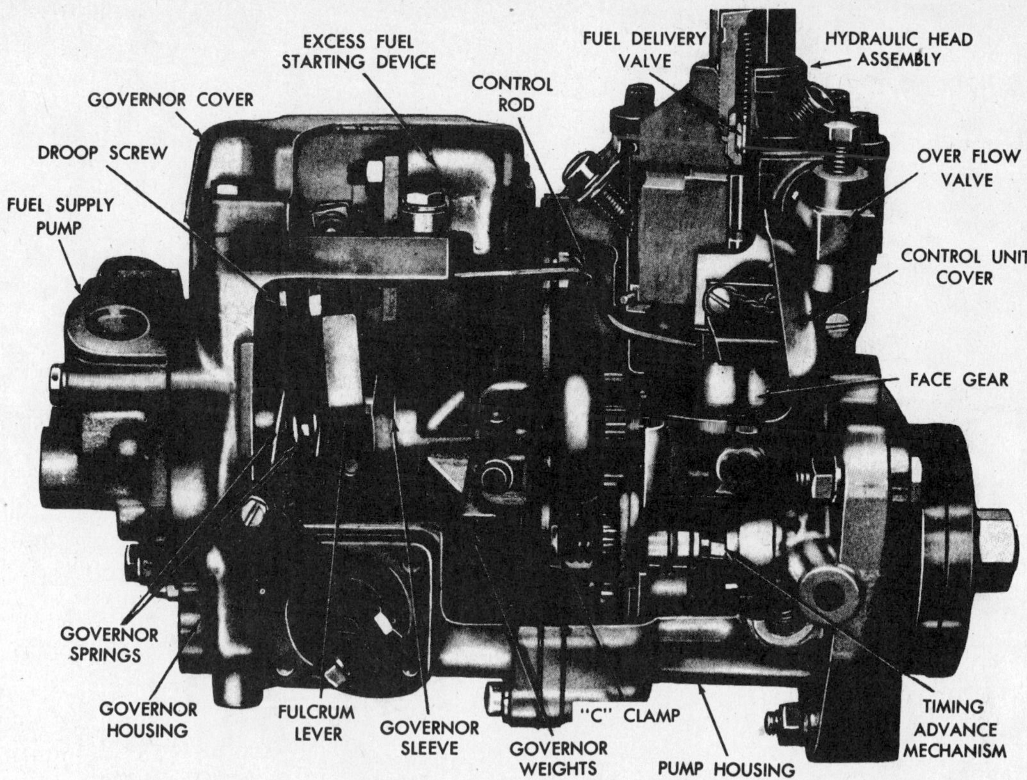

Cut away view of fuel injection pump (6 cyl. engines) (© G.M.C.)

Remove delivery valve cap, then remove spring from cavity remove the valve from its seat.

Using special wrench adapter, remove the delivery valve retainer from head assembly.

Use needle-nose pliers or tweezers to reach into cavity and remove the delivery valve seat.

Installation

CAUTION: Use utmost care to keep delivery valve and retaining parts absolutely clean during installation.

Place fuel delivery valve and seat assembly in position in hydraulic head cavity, then install the retainer. Use adapter and torque wrench to tighten valve retainer to 65 to 70 foot-pounds torque; then loosen the retainer and retorque to 65-70 foot-pounds. Tightening the retainer twice positively seats the parts to prevent any fuel leakage.

Place delivery valve spring over pilot on delivery valve and install cap using torque wrench to tighten cap once to 55 to 60 foot-pounds.

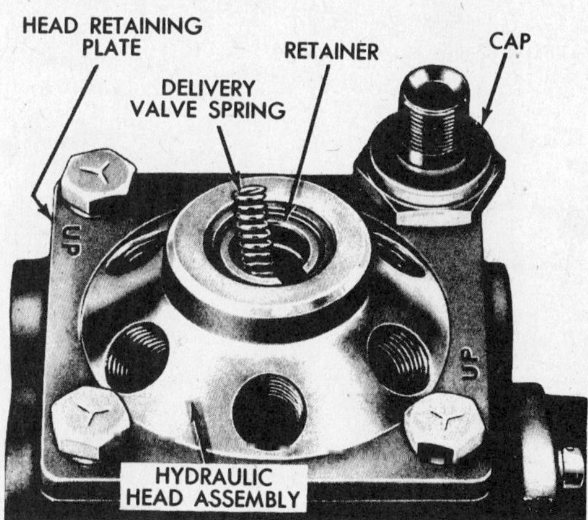

Injection pump cap, spring and valve retainer (© G.M.C.)

Control Unit Assembly

Removal

Remove the four control unit cover attaching screws, then remove cover and gasket.

Place a clean lint-free cloth in opening so parts cannot fall into pump interior as they are removed.

On early type pumps, remove the retainer ring which secures control rod to lever on control unit. Late production pumps have a different design at control rod and the retainer plate prevents disengagement of rod from lever.

Remove lock wire from plate screws. Remove screws, plate, and the spacers which retain the control unit, then disengage the control rod from lever.

Marking the parts is necessary so the control unit can be installed in original location and avoid changing the pump calibration.

Carefully withdraw the control unit assembly from bore in housing, using two thin screwdrivers diagonally across from each other to start the unit out of bore.

Remove O-ring seal from control unit. Hold the control unit level so the pin will not fall out of place.

Installation

Using a clean screwdriver, carefully insert it through the control unit opening in the pump housing and carefully move the metering sleeve downward to its lowest-position on plunger.

Lubricate the control unit O-ring and assemble it to the control unit.

Holding the control unit, pin, and O-ring assembly, with the control

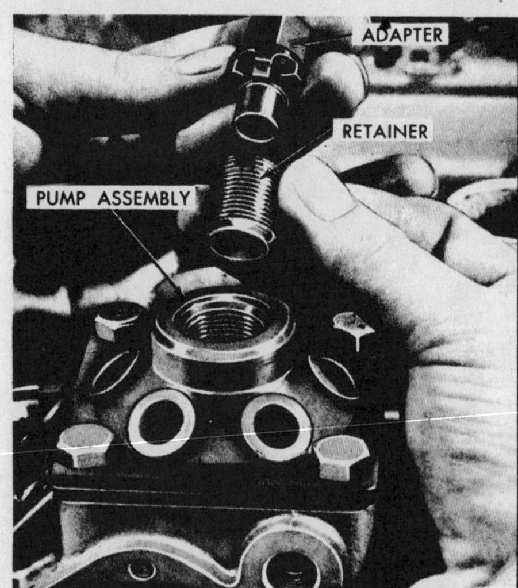

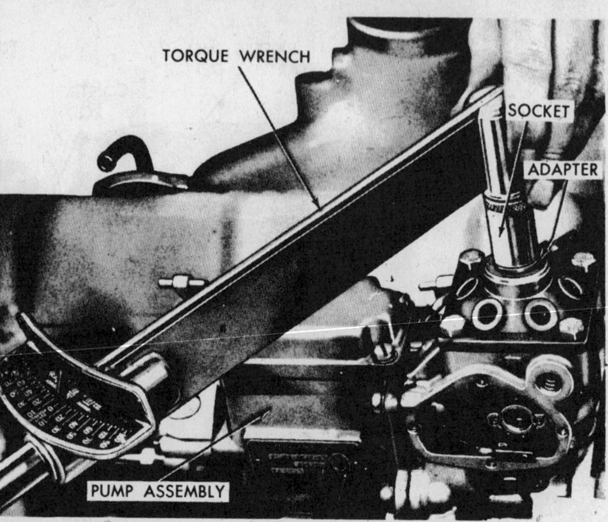

Installing fuel delivery valve retainer with adapter and torque wrench (© G.M.C.)

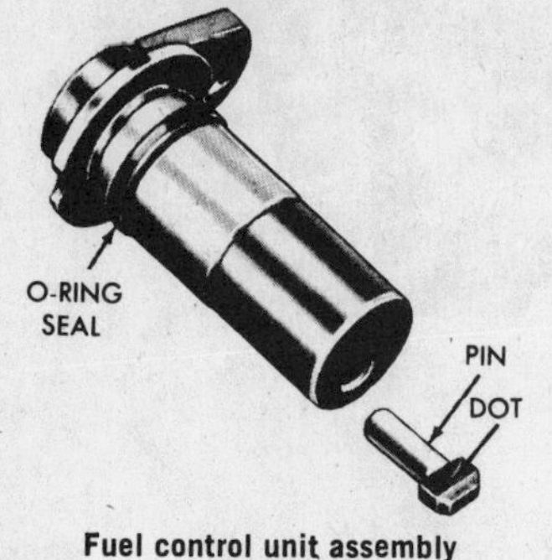

Fuel control unit assembly (© G.M.C.)

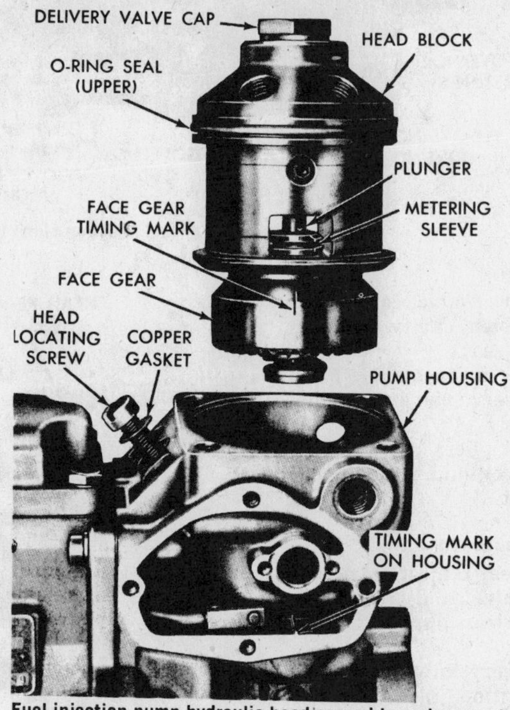

Fuel injection pump hydraulic head assembly replacement (© G.M.C.)

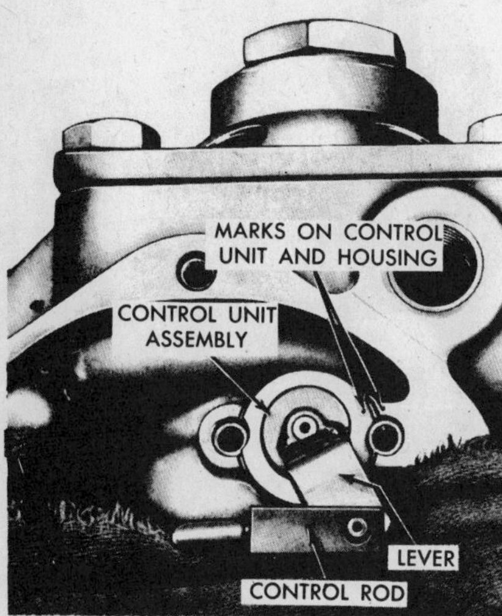

Control unit retaining parts and alignment marks (© G.M.C.)

unit arm horizontal and pointing toward the rear of the pump and with the pin horizontal and the identification dot up, insert the assembly into the pump housing.

If the pin is not properly positioned, the control unit arm can not be rotated 360 degrees.

Rotate the control unit bushing, which was marked so the screw scallops in the control unit bushing are aligned with the holes for the retainer plate attaching screws and the control unit bushing flange in the same position as before removal.

On early pump, engage the control rod with hole in control unit lever, then install new retainer ring which secures rod to lever.

Assemble control unit retaining plate, screws (with lock washers), and spacers then install parts to retain the control unit. Tighten screws to 18 to 33 inch-pounds. Install lock wire through screw heads. On late production pumps, the retaining plate retains the control unit and also prevents control rod from becoming disengaged from lever.

Using new gasket, install control unit cover and secure with screws and lock washers.

Overflow Valve

NOTE: Parts of latest type injection pump overflow valve assembly are shown in illustration. The complete valve assembly may be installed or the valve and/or spring shown may be installed.

Overflow Valve Removal

1. Disconnect leak-off lines from fitting at valve and disconnect fuel return line.
2. Using wrench on hex-shaped portion of valve assembly remove the assembly from injection pump body.

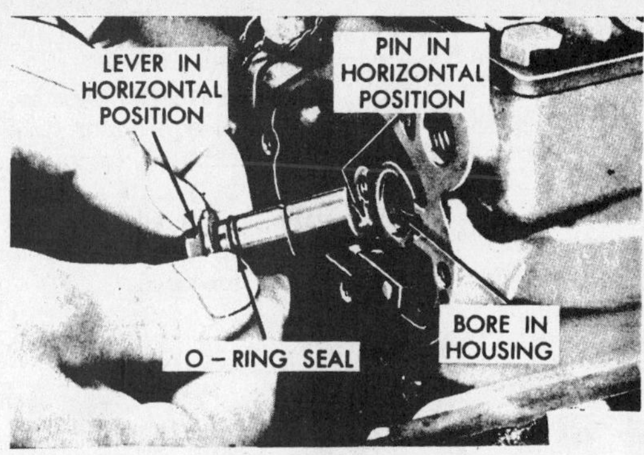

Control unit installation
(© G.M.C.)

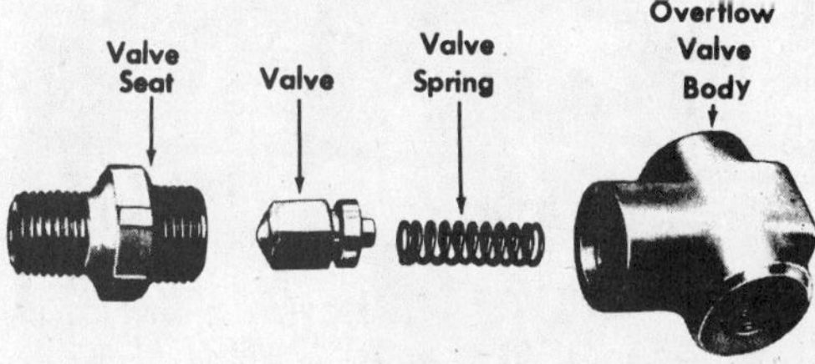

Overflow valve (typical)
(© G.M.C.)

Disassembly

Grip the overflow valve body in vise fitted with soft jaws, then screw the valve seat out of valve body. Remove valve and spring. Some assemblies may have spacer washers which are used in manufacture to provide correct setting.

Assembly

Place spring, (spacers, if removed), and valve in valve body; then after positioning the valve seat over valve, thread the valve seat into body. Tighten the valve seat securely. NOTE: Overflow valve spring may be shimmed if necessary, to provide 40 psi at governed speed.

Overflow Valve Installation

Screw the overflow valve assembly into threaded port in injection pump body, using wrench on the hex-shaped portion of valve.

Install fittings and connect return line and leak-off lines to overflow valve body.

Fuel Supply Pump

Fuel Supply Pump Removal

Disconnect the fuel lines and remove fittings from supply pump.

Remove the three supply vump attaching bolts and lock washers, then remove the supply pump and gasket. CAUTION: As supply pump is removed the governor inner spring guide and spring spacers are free to fall out of place. Exercise necessary care to prevent loss of these parts. Plug the fuel inlet and outlet line openings to prevent dirt from entering.

Fuel Supply Pump Disassembly

Remove governor outer spring guide from pump assembly.

Remove the five screws and lock washers which attach cover to insert. Tap the insert lightly with plastic hammer to separate insert from cover. Remove gears from insert.

Remove relief valve retainer screw and remove spring and relief valve assembly.

Supply Pump Component Inspection

Inspect for wear in gear cavities in pump insert. Also look for evidence of worn surface or scoring on cover area at which contact is made with gears.

Note condition of the oil seal in pump insert.

Examine relief valve parts. Use new parts when assembling pump if any of the components are defective relief valve should pass fuel through center in only one direction.

Inspect idler gear shaft which is a press fit in bore in insert. If pin is worn, scored, or loose in bore, obtain a new insert and pin assembly.

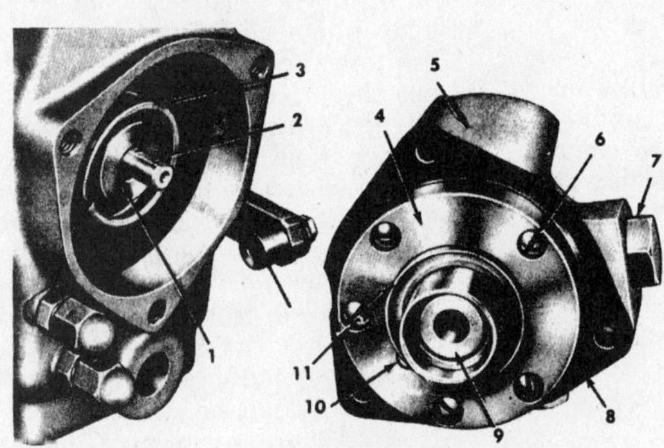

1 Governor inner (high speed) spring guide
2 Flat on pump drive shaft
3 Governor outer (low speed) spring
4 Pump insert
5 Pump cover
6 Insert to cover screws and lock washers
7 Relief valve retainer screw
8 Gasket
9 Oil Seal
10 Pump idler gear pin
11 Outer (low speed) spring guide

Fuel supply pump and injection pump assembly
(© G.M.C.)

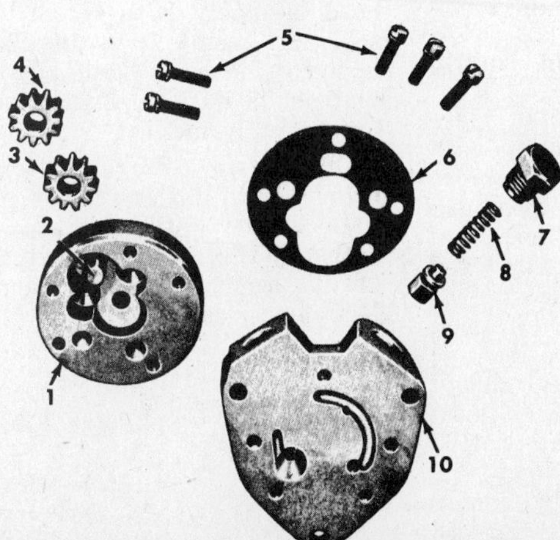

1 Insert assembly
2 Pin (pressed into Item 1)
3 Drive gear
4 Idler gear
5 Screws with lock washers
6 Gasket
7 Valve spring retainer cap
8 Valve spring
9 Relief valve assembly
10 Pump cover

Fuel supply pump components
(© G.M.C.)

Assembling Fuel Supply Pump

Dip each of the gears in clean fuel oil and place gears in cavity in insert assembly.

Using new gasket. Screws with lock washers must be tightened evenly and firmly.

Dip relief valve and spring in fuel oil, then install valve with the spring pilot engaged with spring. Install spring retainer cap and tighten firmly.

Fuel Supply Pump Installation

Check governor, inner and outer springs to make certain the inner spring guide and original spacers are in place. Outer spring guide must be in place at pump insert.

Place gasket on cover flange with bolt holes aligned.

Observe through opening in oil seal the position of flat in pump gear bore. A clean screwdriver may be used to turn the gear so as to align the gear with flat on shaft.

Move supply pump assembly into position at injection pump housing using care to engage drive gear with flat on shaft. Install and tighten supply pump attaching bolts.

Connect fuel lines to fittings at supply pump, remove vent plug from top of secondary fuel filter and bleed air from pump and lines.

Replacing Hydraulic Head Assembly

In cases where the hydraulic head is in satisfactory operating condition, but it becomes necessary to remove the head assembly to replace the O-ring seals or other parts of the pump, it is possible to remove and install the hydraulic head without removing the pump assembly from the engine; and recalibrating is not required.

Hydraulic Head Removal

Disconnect and remove fuel high pressure lines, then plug or cap the openings in the hydraulic head and nozzles.

Remove injection pump control unit assembly.

Turn engine crankshaft to place No. 1 piston in firing position with the marking on crankshaft damper aligned with pointer, and the mark on face gear (visible in inspection window in pump housing) indexed with mark on housing. Make sure the No. 1 piston is on compression stroke.

NOTE: Mark on face gear should be indexed with housing mark, even though the damper mark may not be exactly registered with pointer.

Remove the head assembly locating screw and gasket. Remove retaining plate. Tap the hydraulic head assembly lightly with plastic or lead hammer or slightly rotate the assembly with a wrench on the delivery valve cap to loosen it in housing bore. Raise the hydraulic head assembly up out of the pump housing. Remove upper seal ring from groove in head assembly. Remove the head lower seal ring from bottom of bore in pump housing. *Do not turn engine crankshaft while hydraulic head is removed from pump.*

Prime the fuel system.

Install equipment which may have been removed to gain access to the injection pump assembly. After engine is started, inspect for fuel leakage at hydraulic head, and high pressure fuel lines.

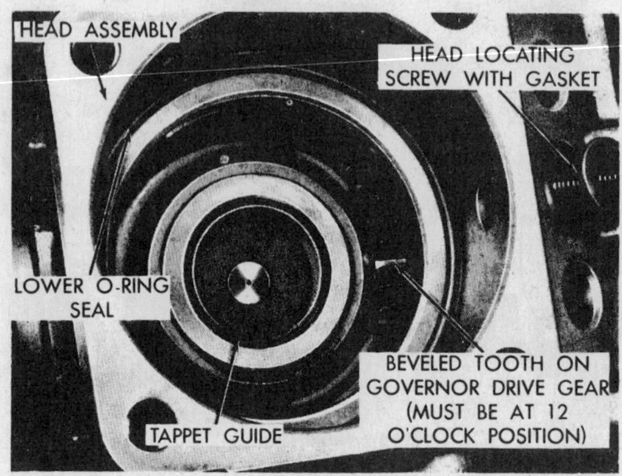

Fuel injection pump with hydraulic head removed
(© G.M.C.)

Hydraulic Head Installation

Lubricate the hydraulic head O-ring seals, then place lower ring in position at bottom of bore in pump body.

Place upper O-ring seal in groove in hydraulic head.

Position the hydraulic head assembly so the locating slot in head block is aligned with head locating screw; and turn face gear so that timing mark on gear is aligned with mark on housing. Insert head assembly into housing bore. Teeth on face gear must mesh with drive gear teeth.

Install head locating screw with copper washer (gasket) and if necessary, rotate head assembly so the locating screw can be turned freely—indicating no interference. Tighten locating screw to 10 to 11 foot-pounds torque.

Place head retaining plate over the head assembly with word "UP" on top, and install bolts in diagonally opposite corners. Gradually tighten plate bolts until sure the gear teeth are properly meshed, then install remaining two bolts and tighten all bolts to 13 to 15 foot-pounds.

Install the control unit assembly.

Install the fuel lines between hydraulic head oulet ports and fuel injection nozzles.

Internal Governor Spring Pack Adjustment

(Without Special Tool)

Break the fuel injection pump seal (if used), back out idle adjusting screw, and remove three bolts attaching the fuel supply pump to the governor housing.

Remove the governor cover and gasket.

Remove fuel supply pump. Remove inner and outer governor springs and adjusting spacers (noting the position of spacers and spring guides. The inner spring is the high speed spring and must have a gap. The outer spring is the low speed spring and must be precompressed. Determine the proper shim pack behind the governor springs with supply pump gasket in place as follows: NOTE: The flat on the fuel pump drive shaft must engage with the gear in the supply pump.

Inner Spring. Position governor sleeve assembly in forward position as shown in illustration. Then, place adjusting spacers between inner spring and the spring guide so that when supply pump with gasket is held in installed position (flush with governor housing), inner spring can be turned but has no end play. This

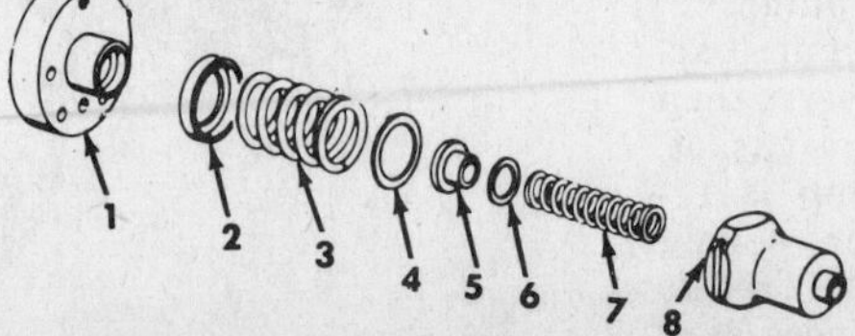

1 Supply pump
2 Outer spring guide
3 Outer spring
4 Outer spring spacer
5 Inner spring guide
6 Inner spring spacer
7 Inner spring
8 Governor sleeve

Governor spring and spacer arrangement
(© G.M.C.)

can be checked with a finger through governor cover opening. Remove supply pump and remove adjusting spacers to obtain proper gap of 0.089 to 0.108 inch on both the 6-cylinder engines and the 8-cylinder engines.

Outer Spring. Place adjusting spacers between governor sleeve and outer spring so that when supply pump with gasket is held in installed position, the outer spring can be turned but has no end play. Then, remove supply pump and add adjusting spacers with total thickness of 0.059 to 0.079 inch to give proper precompression on outer spring.

NOTE: Do not install outer spring when checking spacer pack for inner spring or install inner spring when checking spacer pack for outer spring.

Reinstall the inner and outer governor springs with their respective spacers as previously determined.

Reinstall the fuel supply pump and new gasket, taking care that the inner and outer spring guides do not fall off the supply pump insert. The flat on the fuel pump drive shaft must engage with the gear in the supply pump. Exercise care so that seal is not damaged.

Reinstall governor cover. Turn the idle speed adjustment screw to seven or eight threads are visible, then install screw lock nut.

Start engine and adjust idle speed to 625-675 spm with full accessory load. Set high speed at 3440 spm no-load on 6-cylinder engine, or to 3250 rpm on 8-cylinder engines.

NOTE: Range of idle screw adjustment after setting by above method is approximately one turn. More adjustment than this may allow droop screw, to rest against excess fuel piston stop plate and give erratic idle.

Connect the accelerator linkage and stop linkage, making sure that full travel of the accelerator lever can be obtained.

Internal Governor Spring Pack Adjustment

(Using Special Tool)

A special tool is available for use to accurately select injection pump governor spring spacers. The tool serves in determining the required spacers, both for the inner (high speed) and the outer (low speed) spring. Refer to illustration for location of spacers. Whenever occasion arises for checking either of the governor springs, the other spring should also be checked. Tool may be used without removing the injection pump assembly from engine.

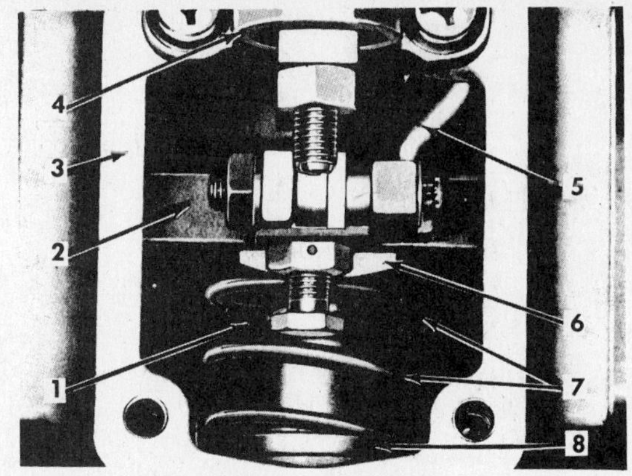

1 Inner (high speed) spring
2 Fulcrum lever assy.
3 Governor housing
4 Excess fuel starting device
5 Control rod
6 Governor sleeve
7 Outer (low speed) spring
8 Outer spring guide

Governor mechanism
(© G.M.C.)

Assembly and Adjustment After Governor Spring Spacer Selection

Place inner and outer governor springs and their respective spacers in position in governor housing, then install fuel supply pump. The flat on governor shaft must engage drive gear in supply pump. Tighten supply pump mounting bolts to 5 to 6 foot-pounds torque.

Connect fuel lines at fittings in supply pump cover. Install cover on top of governor housing. Connect controls if they have been disconnected; and adjust controls for full travel in both directions.

Check and, if necessary, adjust high speed with no-load. Tighten the adjusting screw lock nuts immediately after making the adjustment.

NOTE: The normal idle and maximum speeds depend almost entirely on the characteristics of the governor springs, hence the speeds can only be varied to a limited degree by the adjusting screws at rear of governor housing.

Checking for Air Leaks in Fuel Supply (Suction) Line

CAUTION: Exercise necessary care to prevent any dirt from entering the fuel system when fuel lines are disconnected in making following tests.

Disconnect outlet line from fuel supply pump and install sight glass, or plastic line so that fuel may be observed while engine is running.

Start engine, then look for air bubbles in the pump discharge line.

If a leak is apparent in the suction lines, filter or fittings, a sight glass or section of plastic line may be installed at inlet fitting on supply pump to determine if air is reaching pump through suction side of system. If no bubbles are observed at inlet connection, but continue to be present at outlet line, a defective supply pump is indicated.

NOTE: Be sure the fuel filter between fuel tank and pump is not clogged, and that filter gaskets are in good condition.

Checking for Inadequate Fuel Pump Delivery and/or Overflow Valve Malfunction

Make necessary inspection to determine that fuel filters are not clogged.

Remove, clean, and inspect the supply pump relief valve assembly and spring. Also, disconnect lines from overflow valve and remove the valve assembly from the fuel injection pump. Disassemble the overflow valve, inspect parts. Replace overflow valve or parts as required.

Check supply pump pressure as follows:

Install pressure gauge in line between supply pump outlet and secondary filter.

Remove overflow valve and install a fuel shut-off valve, connecting the fuel return line to the valve discharge opening.

Open the valve slightly and then start the engine. While running the engine a 2400 rpm momentarily close the fuel shut-off valve. The pressure gauge should show between 55 and 65 psi.

CAUTION: Keeping the shut-off valve closed for any period of time can cause the injection pump plunger to overheat and seize.

If pressures are appreciably lower than specified the supply pump should be overhauled or the unit should be replaced with a new supply pump assembly.

Remove shut-off valve and pressure gauge, and reinstall overflow valve assembly.

Fuel Injection Pump Assembly

NOTE: The fuel injection pump assembly is available for service replacement as a complete assembly. In most instances the required repairs may be made without removing the injection pump assembly from the engine.

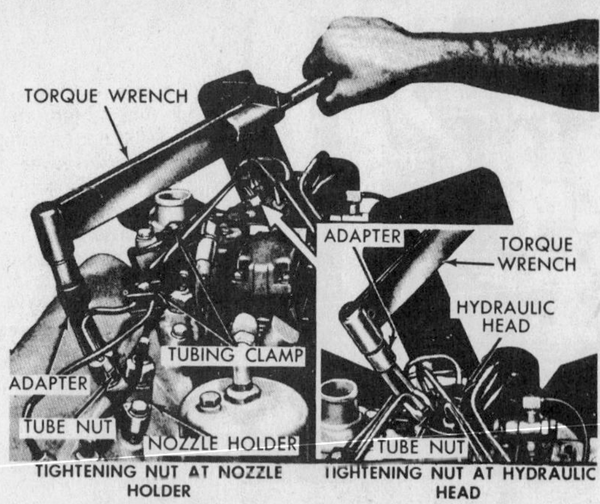

Torque wrench adapter for tightening nuts on high pressure lines (© G.M.C.)

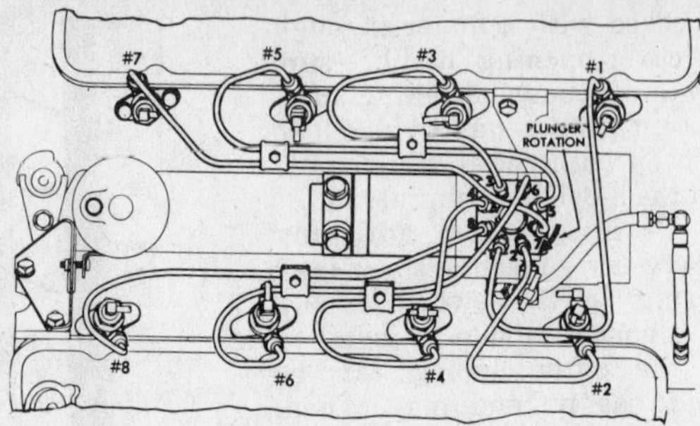

Fuel high pressure line installation (8 cyl. engines) (© G.M.C.)

Fuel Injection Pump Replacement

Replacement should only be made if it definitely indicated that the fuel injection pump assembly is at fault and is not repairable without removing the unit from the engine.

Fuel Injection Pump Removal

CAUTION: Do not attempt to work on the fuel injection pump, nozzles, or high pressure lines in a dusty area. Extreme precautions must be taken to prevent any dust particles from entering the fuel passages in lines and nozzles. Any dirt or abrasive material permitted to enter the fuel supply port on fuel injection pump could quickly cause extensive damage to, or possible ruin of the pump hydraulic head mechanism.

Preliminary Operations (All Engines)

Depending on type of vehicle and accessory equipment, remove the necessary equipment to provide access to fuel injection pump assembly, high pressure fuel lines and engine controls. Carefully observe the arrangement of accelerator control linkage, and the engine stop mechanism. A stop solenoid or an engine stop air cylinder is mounted on the injection pump assembly. Disconnect wire from stop solenoid terminal (when used)/ Disconnect stop control cable and disconnect accelerator linkage from lever at left side of injection pump assembly.

Remove tubing clamps which are shown in illustration. Use the adapters shown and loosen high pressure tubing nuts at fuel injection nozzles and at pump hydraulic head. Use air hose to blow away any loose dirt particles at hydraulic head and at nozzles. Remove the high pressure tubing using care not to bend tubing.

NOTE: To facilitate installation, each line may be tagged with identification number corresponding with cylinder numbers.

Insert plugs in pump ports and cap the fittings at injection nozzles as soon as lines are removed. The importance of cleanliness cannot be over-emphasized.

Illustrations show caps at injection nozzles and plugs in hydraulic head ports.

Disconnect fuel leak-off lines from overflow valve.

Replacing Fuel Injection Pump on 6-Cylinder Engine

Disconnect fuel lines from fittings on supply pump at rear end of injection pump assembly. Also disconnect the fuel line at left side of injection pump housing. Cap or plug all openings to prevent entrance of dust.

At right side of pump assembly, disconnect lubricating oil line and the fuel return line at the overflow valve assembly.

Remove the gear access cover from top of engine front cover to provide access to injection pump driven gear and attaching bolts. The driven gear must be removed from hub on pump shaft before the injection pump assembly can be removed from engine.

CAUTION: To prevent accidental dropping of bolt washers into engine front cover and out of reach, pack clean shop rags into cavity below the gear attaching bolts. Do not crank engine until the rags have been removed.

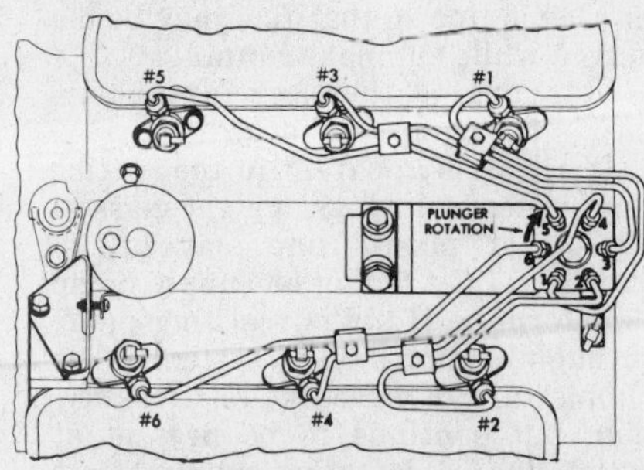

Fuel high pressure line installation (6 cyl. models) (© G.M.C.)

When removing the last of the three pump driven gear bolts, hold the pump shaft from turning with special wrench.

Remove the stud nuts and washers which secure the fuel injection pump assembly to engine front cover, then remove the pump assembly. Remove the sealing ring from pump mounting flange.

Remove pump driven gear from opening in front cover.

Installation

Preliminary Operations

If a new fuel injection pump assembly is being installed, it will be necessary to transfer the fuel line and oil line fittings from the removed pump assembly to the new pump. Observe the position of each fitting as it is removed, and install it in same position on new pump assembly.

CAUTION: Carefully clean any accumulated dirt from fittings before installing in replacement pump assembly and install dust caps to exclude any foreign material when the fittings are installed.

Inspect gear teeth on injection pump drive gear and driven gear before installing pump. Be sure the mounting surface on pump flange and the mating surface at engine front cover are clean.

Remove the cover from rigth-hand side of injection pump so alignment marks on face gear and ledge can be seen.

Fuel Injection Pump Installation

Set fuel injection pump driven gear in place through access opening in top of engine front cover. Driven gear teeth must engage teeth on pump drive gear and flat side of gear must be toward rear.

Check position of rocker arms at No. 1 cylinder to be sure No. 1 piston is on compression stroke. Observe "INJ" mark on crankshaft damper assembly which must be indexed with the pointer on front cover.

Through opening in right-hand side of fuel injection pump assembly, look for mark on edge of face gear. If mark is not visible, turn the pump shaft until mark comes into view, then set the mark on hub in alignment with pointer in pump housing.

Install seal ring on pilot at forward side of pump mounting flange, then lift the injection pump assembly into position on mounting studs.

Install plain washer and nut on each of the three pump mounting studs and tighten the nuts evenly to seat pump flange firmly on cover.

Check the position of threaded hole in pump hub in relation to elongated slot in driven gear. If necessary, change the position of gear so threaded hole in hub is approximately centered in slot in gear. The gear teeth can be lifted out of mesh with drive gear to change gear position.

Start one of the driven gear mounting bolts with plain washer through driven gear slot and into mounting hub, then using special wrench hold pump hub timing mark in alignment with pointer and tighten gear mounting bolt firmly.

Crank the engine as necessary to bring other driven gear bolt holes into position for installing remaining two bolts; install bolts and plain washers, then tighten bolts to 35 to 40 foot-pounds.

Install pump side cover and gear access cover connect oil supply line, and fuel return to overflow valve.

Mount a new secondary filter on filter bracket and connect fuel lines.

Connect accelerator control linkage and engine stop mechanism.

CAUTION: The fuel injection nozzles should be inspected and repaired as necessary, or replaced with new nozzles whenever a new or rebuilt fuel injection pump is installed on engine. Attempting to start an engine having defective injection nozzles can damage or ruin a fuel injection pump assembly.

Install high pressure fuel lines.

Prime the fuel system, before attempting to start engine. During priming procedure, the supply line should remain disconnected from fitting on left side of pump assembly until all air has been purged from filters, supply pump, and lines; then continue to flush fuel through open end of line to avoid the possibility of any loose particles entering the fuel chamber surrounding the hydraulic head assembly.

Start engine and inspect all fuel line and lubricating oil line connections for leakage.

Check and adjust engine idle speed if required.

Replacing Fuel Injection Pump on 8-Cylinder Engine

Removal

Disconnect fuel lines from fittings on supply pump at rear end of injection pump assembly. Also disconnect the fuel supply line at left side of injection pump housing. Cap or plug all openings to prevent entrance of dust.

Disconnect and remove lubricating oil lines.

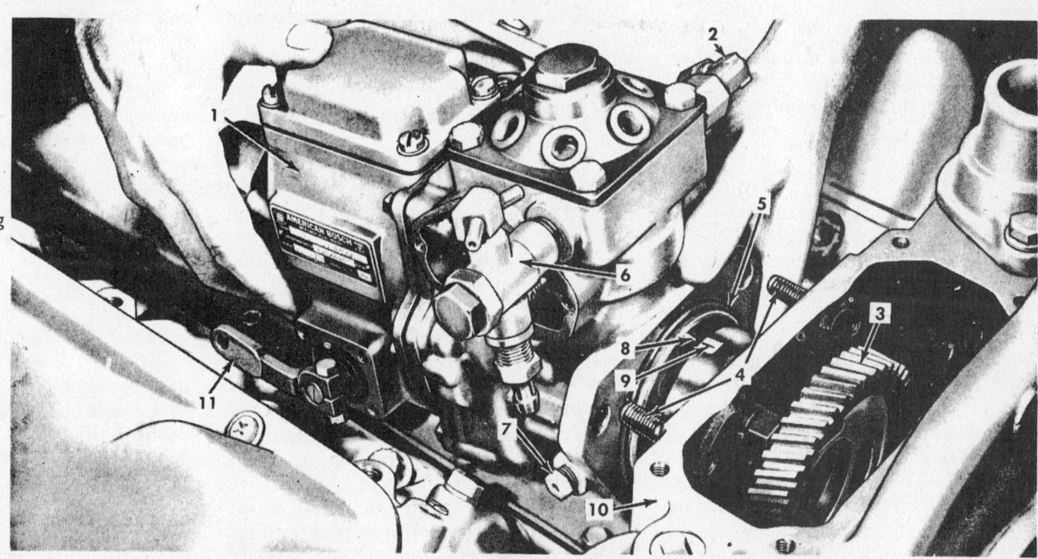

Installing fuel injection pump assembly (6 cyl. engines) (© G.M.C.)

Installing fuel injection pump assembly (8 cyl. engines) (© G.M.C.)

At rear end of injection pump loosen clamps on oil drain hose. Pull hose connector elbow out of grommet in valve lifter cover; then remove connector and hose.

Remove two bolts and washers which hold pump support and bracket together; then remove the two bolts and washers at lifter compartment cover. Remove the pump support bracket.

Remove the gear access cover from top of engine front cover to provide access to injection pump driven gear and attaching bolts. The driven gear must be removed from hub on pump shaft before the injection pump assembly can be removed from engine.

When removing the last of the three pump driven gear bolts hold the pump shaft from turning with special wrench.

Remove the two lower mounting bolts and washers, first, then place a suitable wood block under rear of injection pump to support the assembly while two upper bolts and washers are removed from mounting studs.

Remove the fuel injection pump from engine; then remove driven gear from front cover. Remove sealing ring from pilot at pump mounting flange.

1 Bolt with lock washer and plain washer
2 Bolt with lock washer and plain washer
3 Injection pump support
4 Fuel injection pump assembly
5 Nipple
6 Oil drain hose
7 Hose clamp
8 Pump support bracket
9 Hose connector elbow
10 Grommet
11 Lifter compartment cover

Injection pump rear support and lubricating oil drain (8 cyl. engines) (© G.M.C.)

Installation

Preliminary Operations

If a new fuel injection pump assembly is being installed, it will be necessary to transfer the fuel line and oil line fittings from the removed pump assembly to the new pump. Observe the position of each fitting as it is removed, and install it in same position on new pump assembly.

CAUTION: Carefully clean any accumulated dirt from fittings before installing in replacement pump assembly and install dust caps to exclude any foreign material when the fittings are installed.

Inspect gear teeth on injection pump drive gear and driven gear before installing pump. Be sure the mounting surface on pump flange and the mating surface at engine front cover are clean.

Remove the cover from right-hand side of injection pump so alignment marks on face gear and ledge can be seen.

Fuel Injection Pump Installation

Set fuel injection pump driven gear in place through access opening in top of engine front cover. Driven gear teeth must engage teeth on pump drive gear and flat side of gear must be toward rear.

Check position of rocker arms at No. 1 cylinder to be sure No. 1 piston is on compression stroke. Observe "INJ" mark on crankshaft damper assembly which must be indexed with the pointer on front cover.

Through opening in right-hand side of fuel injection pump assembly, look for mark on edge of face gear. If mark is not visible turn the pump shaft until mark comes into view. Through inspection plate opening in top of advance mechanism housing check the position of mark in relation to pointer. If necessary turn pump shaft to index mark with pointer.

Install injection pump support on bottom of pump housing using two bolts with lock washers.

Install seal ring on pilot at forward side of pump mounting flange, then lift the injection pump assembly into position on mounting studs.

Install plain washer and nut on each of the four pump mounting studs and tighten the nuts evenly to seat pump flange firmly on cover.

NOTE: A suitable block may be inserted between rear of pump and lifter compartment cover to support pump while installing nuts and washers at mounting flange.

Place injection pump support bracket in place on valve lifter cover with holes for bolts aligned with threaded holes in cylinder block and weld nuts on injection pump support.

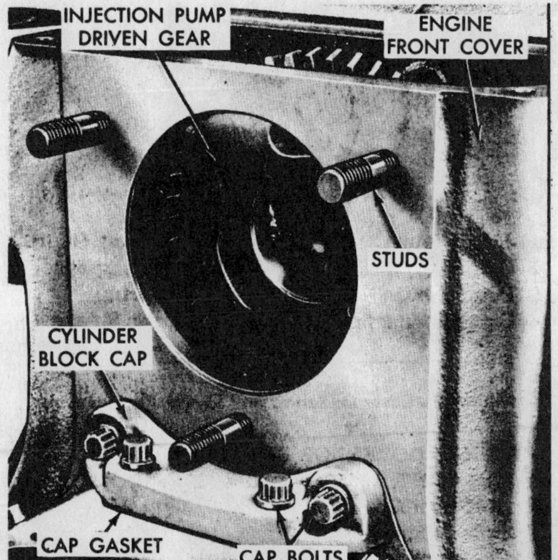

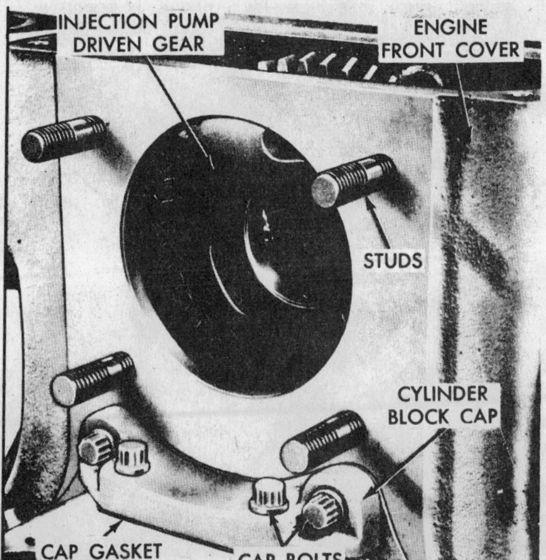

Injection pump driven gear and pump mounting studs (© G.M.C.)

Install two bolts with lock washers and plain washers but tighten these bolts only enough to bring support and bracket into contact with each other. Install two bolts with lock washers and plain washers to secure the pump support bracket, then tighten the bolts which clamp the bracket to the pump support. Install nipple in threaded hole in pump housing, insert grommet in hole in lifter cover; then assemble oil drain hose and elbow. Hose must be clamped at nipple and end of elbow must be inserted into grommet.

Check the position of threaded hole in pump hub in relation to elongated slot in driven gear. If necessary, change the position of gear so threaded hole in hub is approximately centered in slow gear. The gear teeth can be lifted out of mesh with drive gear to change gear position.

Start one of the driven gear mounting bolts with plain washer through slot in driven gear and into drive hub on pump shaft. Use special wrench to hold pump shaft so timing mark is indexed with pointer while tightening gear mounting bolt firmly.

Crank the engine as necessary to bring other driven gear bolt holes into position for installing remaining two bolts, then install bolts and plain washers and tighten bolts to 35 to 40 foot-pounds.

Install cover on pump housing. Install inspection plate and gasket on top of advance mechanism housing. Install gear access cover on engine front cover assembly.

Connect lubrication oil supply lines at fittings on housings. Connect the fuel return line to overflow valve assembly.

Thoroughly clean and inspect the fuel lines to be used in connecting the secondary filter. Mount a new secondary fuel filter on filter bracket with the fuel lines connected.

Connect accelerator control linkage and engine stop mechanism.

CAUTION: The fuel injection nozzles should be inspected and/or repaired as necessary, or replaced with new nozzles, whenever a new or rebuilt fuel injection pump is installed on engine. Attempting to start an engine having defective injection nozzles can damage or ruin a fuel injection pump assembly.

Install high pressure fuel lines.

Prime the fuel system before attempting to start engine. During priming procedure the supply line should remain disconnected from fitting in left side of pump assembly until all air has been purged from filters, supply pump, and lines; then continue to flush fuel through open end of line to avoid the possibility of any loose particles entering the chamber surrounding the hydraulic head assembly.

Start engine and inspect all fuel line and lubricating oil line connections for leakage.

Check engine idle speed and, if necessary, adjust to proper setting.

Water Pump

General

The engines covered are equipped with either of two water pumps shown in illustrations.

Type 1 pump is used on all 6-cylinder engines except DH478, unless engine is in vehicle equipped with air conditioning, in which case type 2 pump is used.

Type 2 is the standard water pump used on all 8-cylinder engines and DH478, 6-cylinder engines. Overhaul procedure for each type of pump is given separately under appropriate headings below.

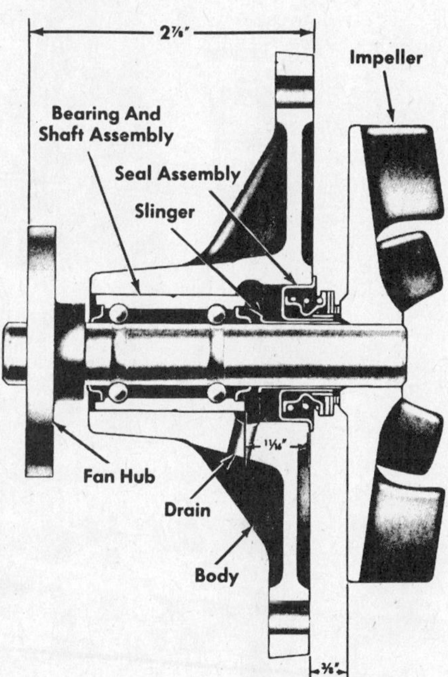

Water pump (6 cyl. engines exc. DH 478) (© G.M.C.)

Type 1 Water Pump Overhaul

Disassembly

1. Support the hub and press shaft out.
2. Support pump body on press and press on front end of shaft to force shaft bearing, and impeller assembly out of body toward rear.
3. Support impeller as near as possible as near as possible to hub at forward side, then press on rear end of shaft to remove impeller from shaft. With impeller removed from shaft, remove seal assembly.
4. Shaft and bearing assembly and seal must be replaced whenever pump is disassembled. Surface contracted by seal on impeller hub must be smooth and flat. Late pumps do not have slinger.

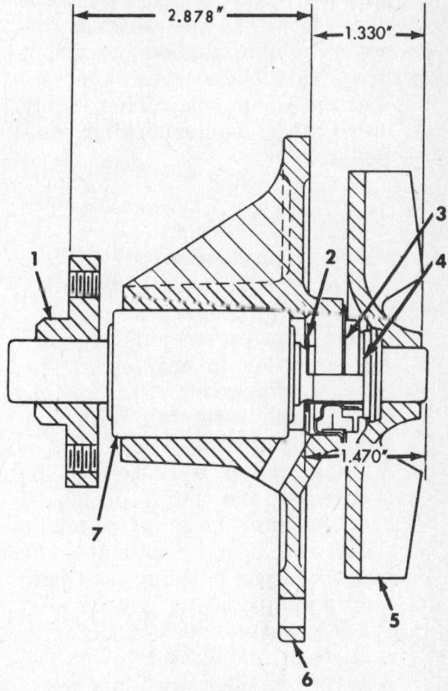

Water pump (6 cyl. DH 478 and all 8 cyl. engines) (© G.M.C.)

1 Pulley hub
2 Slinger
3 Seal assembly
4 Seal seat
5 Impeller
6 Pump body
7 Shaft and bearing assembly

Assembly

1. Be sure bore through pump body is clean and free from burrs.
2. Install shaft and bearing assembly in pump body, pressing on bearing outer race. Proper location of bearing and shaft assembly is shown in illustration. Measure from rear face of body to bearing as shown.
3. Coat outer surface of seal which fits into pump body with sealing compound, then press seal assembly into body.
4. Press fan hub on front end of pump shaft to dimension shown in illustration. Hub front face must be located 2-⅞ inches from near surface of pump body.
5. Install impeller on rear end of pump shaft, using pressure at rear face of impeller hub while supporting front end of shaft. Locate impeller so a space of ⅜ inches exists between impeller and pump body.

Type 2 Water Pump Overhaul

Disassembly

1. Support water pump pulley hub at rear surface and press shaft out of hub.

2. Insert spacers between pump body and impeller, then while supporting pump body with shaft in vertical position, press the pump shaft out of impeller and force bearing out of body.
3. Remove seal assembly from pump body. If seal seat in impeller is not in good condition, use a thin blade to pry the seal seat out of impeller. Thoroughly clean the counterbore in impeller.

Assembly

1. On early production pumps, the slinger should be 1.470 inches from end of shaft as shown. Late pumps do not have slinger.
2. Apply sealer in seal cavity in body, then press new seal assembly squarely into place with seal flange seated against body.
3. Support pump body solidly on press bed and press on shaft bearing outer housing to install shaft and bearing assembly in body. Bearing housing must bottom in pump body.
4. Place neoprene seal on ceramic seat, then install seat in the recess in impeller with neoprene seal bottomed in counterbore.
5. Support front end of pump shaft and press impeller onto rear end of shaft until rear face of impeller hub is 1.330 inches from body mounting flange as shown in illustration.
6. While supporting rear end of pump shaft, press pulley hub on front end of shaft to dimension shown.

Manifolds

Manifold Removal

NOTE: With engine in vehicle, the exhaust pipes must be disconnected from exhaust manifold flanges before removing exhaust manifolds. Air intake hoses and any brackets bolted to intake manifolds must also be removed. On V-8 engines, the balance tube and connecting hoses must be removed.

Bend lock away from each of the exhaust manifold end bolts, then remove the short bolt attaching intake manifold to cylinder head.

Remove the bolts and clamps holding manifolds to cylinder head, then remove the intake manifold.

Remove the short bolt attaching exhaust manifold to cylinder head, and remove the exhaust manifold and gaskets.

Manifold Installation

Manifolds are attached in similar manner at both cylinder heads. In some instances accessory support brackets must be removed to gain access to manifold bolts, if engine is installed in vehicle.

Place bolt lock on exhaust manifold short end bolt, then insert bolt through hole in end of exhaust manifold. Place clamp on clamp bolt exhaust manifold. Place clamp on clamp bolt and insert clamp bolt through hole in exhaust manifold flange. Place manifold gasket at exhaust manifold so it is held in proper position by bolts.

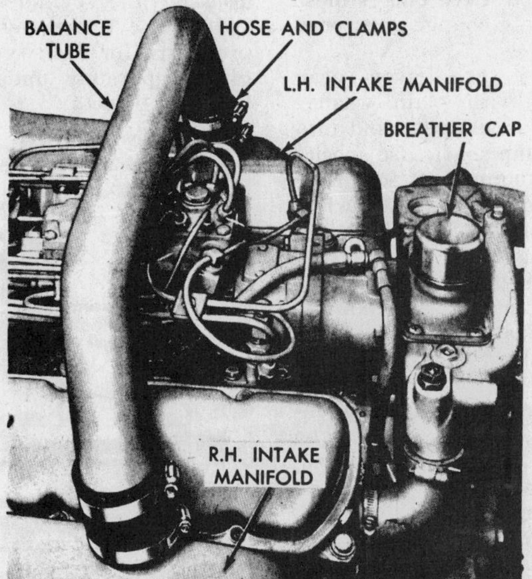

Manifold balance tube installation (8 cyl. engines) (© G.M.C.)

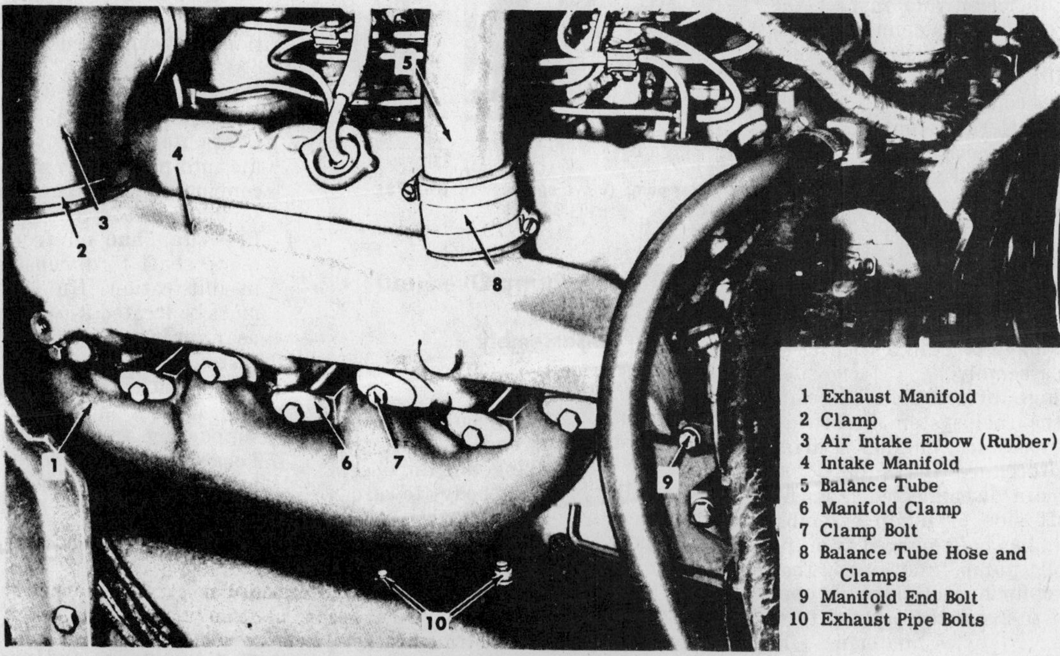

Manifolds and attaching parts on 8 cyl. engines (right side) (© G.M.C.)

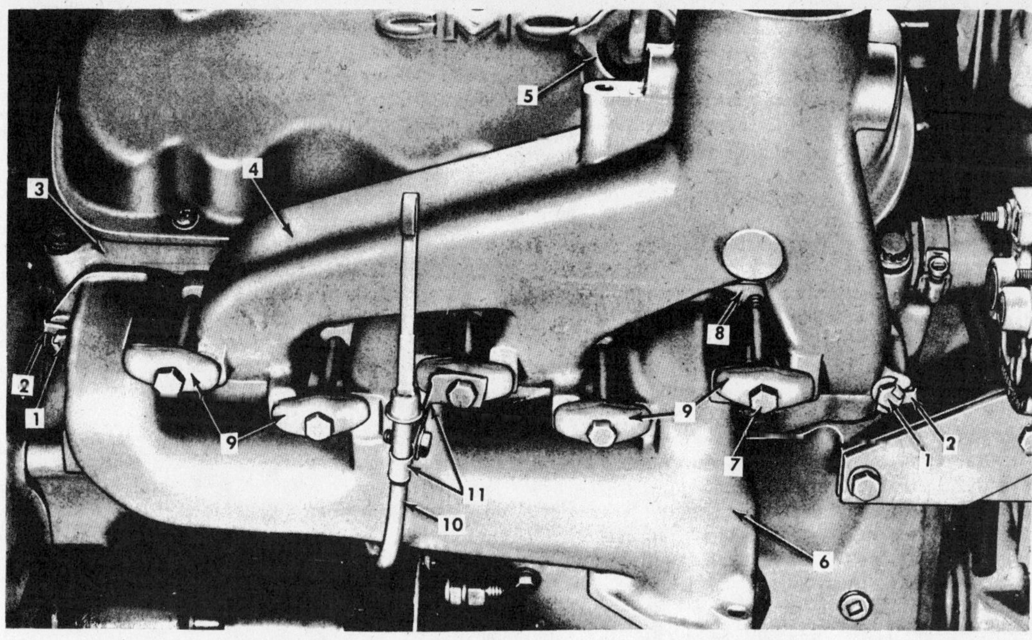

Manifolds and attaching parts on 6 cyl. engines (right side) (© G.M.C.)

1 End bolt
2 Bolt lock
3 Cylinder head
4 Intake manifold
5 Crankcase ventilation cap
6 Exhaust manifold
7 Clamp bolts
8 Gasket
9 Manifold clamps
10 Dip stick tube
11 Tube clamp and bracket

Hold exhaust manifold and gasket against cylinder head and start the two bolts into tapped holes.

Place lock on long end bolt and insert bolt through hole in intake manifold. Position intake manifold at cylinder head and start end bolt into tapped hole in head. Install a clamp bolt with clamp through hole in intake manifold flange and thread bolt into cylinder head to properly locate intake manifold. Tighten clamp bolts with the respective clamps bridging bosses at intake and exhaust, manifolds sufficiently to hold intake and exhaust manifolds in place.

Install remaining clamps and clamp bolts and position the clamps to contact manifold bosses squarely.

Tighten exhaust manifold end bolt to 15 to 20 foot-pounds torque. Tighten intake manifold end bolt to 20 to 25 foot-pounds, and tighten intake and exhaust manifold clamp bolts to 20 to 25 foot-pounds. Bend locks to secure the exhaust manifold end bolts.

Install balance tube between intake manifolds.

Engine Repairs

Cylinder Head Overhaul

General

The two cylinder heads on each engine are identical except for position of water outlet sleeve and core hole plug, and procedure is same to repair either cylinder.

Cylinder heads for D/DH478 and D/DH637 engines are constructed as shown in sectional view of engines. D351 engine cylinder heads are similar to heads on D/DH478 and D/DH637 except that they do not have exhaust valve seat inserts.

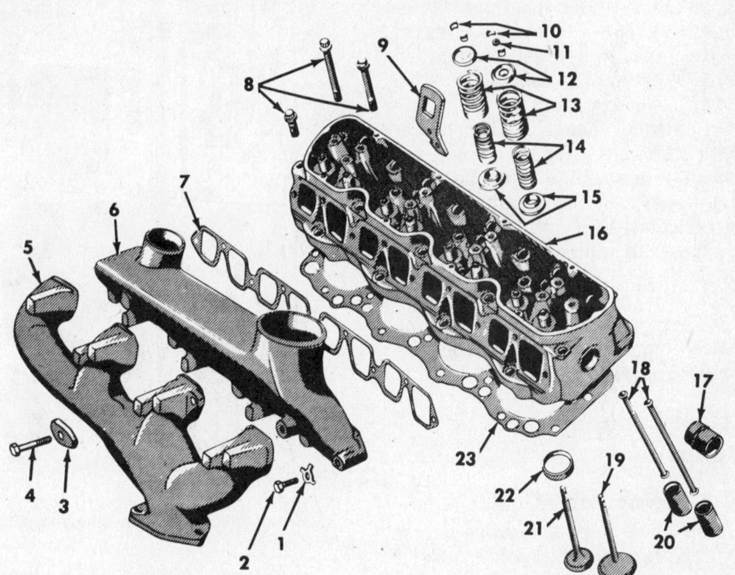

Cylinder head components and associated parts (8 cyl. engine) (© G.M.C.)

1 Bolt lock
2 End bolt
3 Clamp
4 Clamp bolt
5 Exhaust manifold
6 Intake manifold
7 Manifold gasket
8 Cylinder head bolts
9 Lifting bracket
10 Valve keys
11 Intake valve seal
12 Spring cap
13 Valve outer springs
14 Valve inner springs
15 Valve rotators
16 Cylinder head
17 Water tube
18 Push rods
19 Intake valve
20 Valve lifters
22 Exhaust valve seat insert
23 Cylinder head gasket

Unless otherwise noted, the cylinder head repair procedures apply to all Toro-Flow Diesel engines. Illustration shows cylinder head components and associated parts for 8-cylinder engines.

Cleaning

Flush out water passages, and clean oil drain-back holes and hole at bottom of end rocker arm shaft bracket which supplies oil to valve overhead mechanism.

Disassembling Cylinder Head

1. Using valve spring compressor, relieve pressure of valve springs against retaining parts.
2. Remove valve keys, release the spring compressor, then at intake valve, remove springs and

spring cap. After springs and retaining parts are removed from intake valve stem. Remove intake valve from cylinder head.
3. After releasing spring compressor at exhaust valves, remove springs and spring cap, then remove exhaust valve from cylinder head.
4. Remove valve rotators from cylinder head.

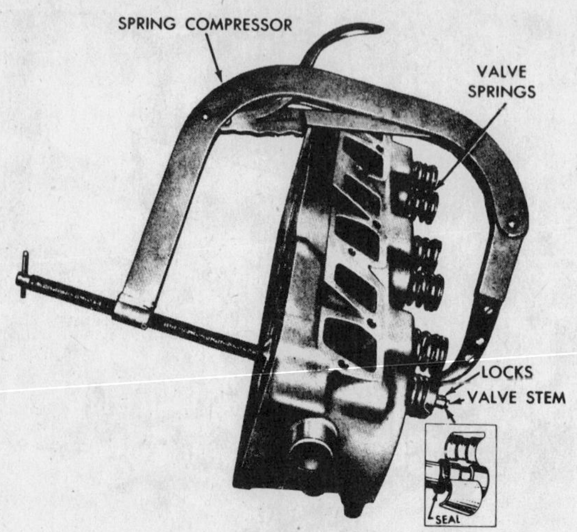

Use of valve spring compressor
(© G.M.C.)

Cleaning and Inspection of Cylinder Head Components

1. Clean deposits from valve stems, and ports in cylinder head.
2. Use injection nozzle well cleaning tools to remove any carbon deposits from nozzle wells.
3. Test valve springs for tension with valve spring tester.
4. Check valves for burned or pitted faces and for wear or corrosion at valve stems. NOTE: Valves with oversize stems are available for use when guide bores in cylinder head are excessively worn. Guides are integral with head and must be reamed out to provide proper fit with oversize valve stem.
5. On cylinder heads with replaceable exhaust valve seat rings, inspect rings which must be tight in head and seats must be in good condition.
6. Inspect all plugs for evidence of leakage.
7. Visually inspect valve spring retaining parts. Also examine valve rotators for evidence of wear and damage.

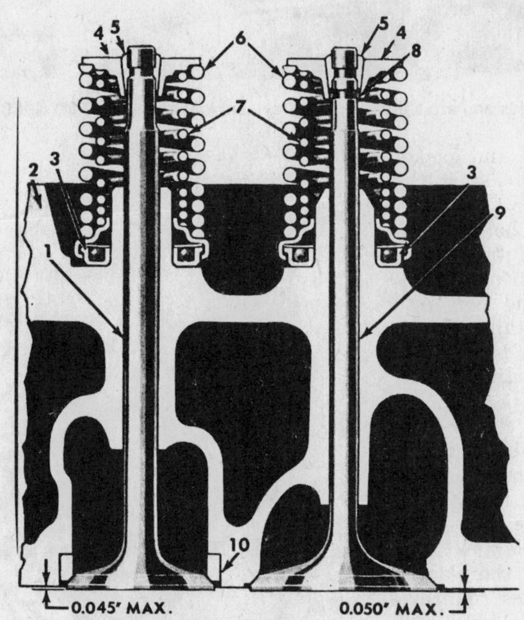

Sectional view through cylinder head and valves
(© G.M.C.)

Repair of Cylinder Head Components

Reaming Valve Guides

If clearance between valve stems and guides is excessive, select service valve with oversize stem for use in rebuilding cylinder head. Intake and exhaust valves are available with 0.020, 0.030, and 0.040 inch oversize stems.

Reamers are of proper dimensions to provide correct clearance for valve stem with corresponding oversize.

Replacing Exhaust Valve Seat Rings (All Except D351 Engines)

In cases where exhaust valve seat ring is damaged, the ring may be replaced as follows:

Assemble special exhaust valve seat insert remover in cylinder head as shown. Press tool firmly against ring, then while holding tool with handle, tighten screw to expand tool which will engage inner edge of ring.

Attach slide hammer to threaded end of tool screw, then slide weight sharply to end of rod to remove seat ring.

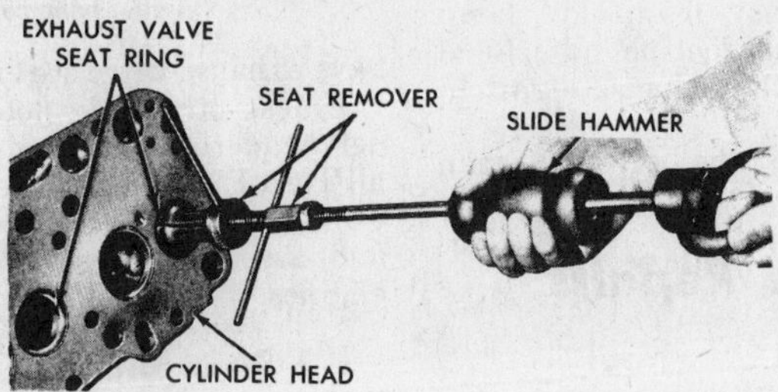

Removing exhaust valve seat ring with special tool
(© G.M.C.)

Clean cylinder head.

Pack new inserts in dry ice for minimum of 15 minutes.

Preheat cylinder head by immersion in water at a temperature of 180°F., to 200°F. Place cylinder head on bench, blow out each insert counterbore with air, then lay chilled insert in counterbore with valve side toward installer.

Using valve seat installer, insert pilot end of tool into guide, then drive insert down tight into counterbore. This operation must be done quickly while the valve seat inserts are cold. Due to extreme hardness of material, exhaust valve seats must be finished with special grinding equipment.

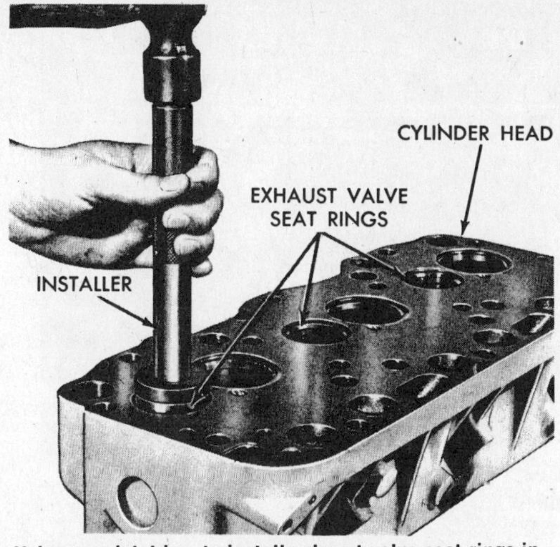

Using special driver to install exhaust valve seat rings in head
(© G.M.C.)

Cylinder head tightening sequence (6 cylinder engine)
(© G.M.C.)

Reconditioning Valve Seats

Reconditioning of valve seats on high compression engines is very important because seating of valves must be as near perfect as possible in order to obtain the maximum power and performance built into the engine.

IMPORTANT: Before attempting to grind any seat, valve port and valve seat must be free from any foreign deposits such as carbon, grease, etc. Valve guide must be thoroughly cleaned of carbon or dirt with a wire brush.

Use a valve seat grinder pilot which fits snugly in valve guide.

Seat-grinding stone must be accurately dressed to 45-degree angle for grinding intake and exhaust valve seats. After grinding, use dial indicator to check concentricity of valve seat with pilot hole. Seat should be concentric with pilot within 0.002 inch (Total Indicator Reading).

NOTE: When installing new valve seat inserts and/or new valves in cylinder head, measure distance from cylinder head surface to top of valve head with valve contacting seat. Intake valves must not project more than 0.050 inch above head; and exhaust valves must not project more than 0.045 inch. Grind necessary amount of stock from valve face to obtain proper dimension.

Test valve for perfect contact with seat in cylinder head.

Refacing Valves

Valves that are slightly pitted or burned can be refaced to the proper angle.

Set chuck at a 45 degree angle for both the intake and the exhaust valves.

Take light cut from face of valve by passing grinding wheel across valve until valve face is true and smooth.

NOTE: Care must be taken while grinding not to remove too much stock from valve face. If it should be necessary to reduce thickness of intake valve head to 0.055 inch or less at outer edge of valve head to obtain smooth face, discard valve. Exhaust valves should not be used if head at outer edge is less than 1/16 inch after refacing.

Test valves for contact with seats in cylinder head.

Assembling Cylinder Head Components

Lubricate valve rotators with engine oil before assembling to cylinder head. Keep all components clean and apply SAE 90 hypoid gear lubricant for at least 1½ inches at tip of all valve stems prior to installation.

Set valve rotator in place at cylinder head and insert valve through guide.

Set inner and outer springs in place on rotator with close-wound coils toward cylinder head and place spring cap (4) on springs.

Use spring compressor to hold valve in place and at same time compress springs. On intake valves install oil seal in lower groove in intake valve stem. Place two valve keys in valve stem groove, then release the spring compressor.

Valve Operating Mechanism

General

Mechanism for operating the intake and exhaust valves consists of mechanical lifters at camshaft, tubular push rods, and rocker arms mounted on hardened steel shaft. Each rocker arm is equipped with a self-locking screw for adjusting valve lash.

On 6-cylinder engines, the rocker arm shaft are each supported on five cast aluminum brackets. Construction on 8-cylinder engines is similar to that on 6-cylinder models but there are two more rocker arms and six brackets support the rocker arm shafts.

Inspection of Rocker Arms and Shafts

1. Wash rocker arms, shaft, and bracket assemblies in solvent. Oil holes in rocker arms must not be clogged.
2. Check torque required to turn adjusting screw in rocker arm. If screw turns with less than 5 foot-pounds, or if screw threads are not in good condition, replace screw.
3. Examine shaft for evidence of wear. Replace worn parts when assembling.

IMPORTANT: When installing new adjusting screws in rocker arms, lubricate screw threads and threads in rocker arm with engine oil prior to assembly.

Damper and Crankshaft Pulley

General

Latest engines have a counterbore in damper hub to accomodate a seal ring which seals against oil leakage. When installing crankshaft damper look for counterbore at rear edge of hub bore and install new seal ring on crankshaft as instructed below. The special installer may not be required on some (late) engines on which the oil seal ring is used but must be used on all other engines. Whenever a new damper assembly is being installed, the late type with counterbore and seal ring should be used.

1. Place the seal ring over end of crankshaft and position the ring squarely on crankshaft at inner end of damper key. *Do not place seal ring against slinger.* The seal must roll into hub counterbore when damper is installed.

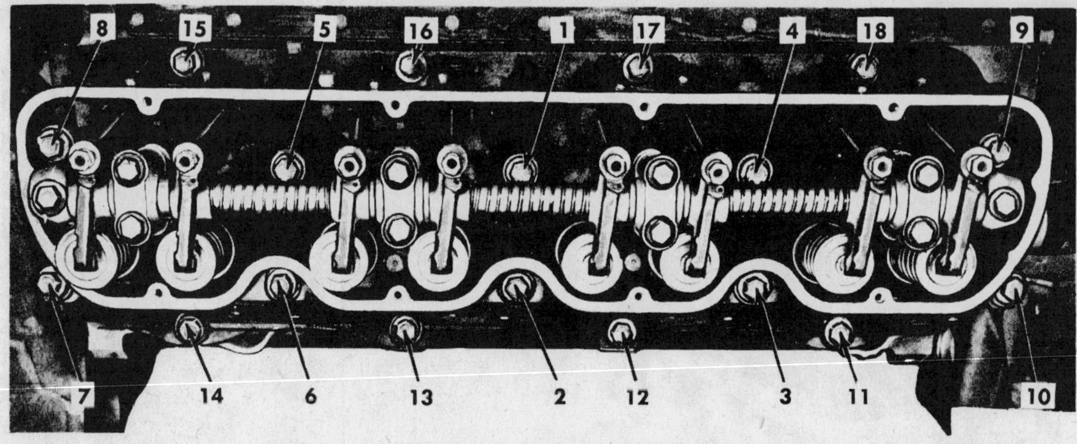

Cylinder head tightening sequence (8 cylinder engine) (© G.M.C.)

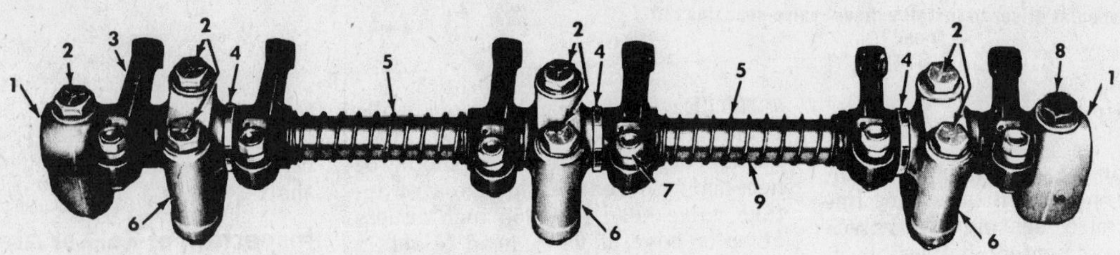

Valve rocker arm layout (6 cyl. engines) (© G.M.C.)

1 End bracket
2 Bracket bolt and plain washer
3 Rocker arm
4 Spacer
5 Spring
6 Rocker arm shaft bracket
7 Adjusting screw
8 Special bolt
9 Shaft

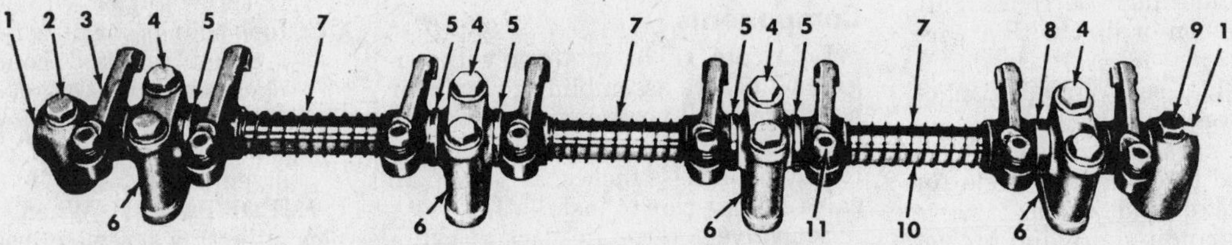

Valve rocker arm layout (8 cyl. engines) (© G.M.C.)

1 End bracket
2 End bracket bolt and plain washer
3 Rocker arm
4 Bracket bolt and plain washer
5 Rocker arm spacer
6 Shaft bracket
7 Spring
8 Thick spacer
9 Special bolt and plain washer
10 Rocker arm shaft
11 Adjusting screw

Valve rocker arm assembly (© G.M.C.)

Installing damper on crankshaft (using special tools) (© G.M.C.)

1 Seal "O" ring
2 Slinger
3 Key
4 Installer
5 Installer screw
6 Thrust bearing
7 Crankshaft damper
8 Crankshaft
9 Engine front cover

2. Apply engine oil on damper hub at seal surface, then start damper onto crankshaft with keyway aligned with key. Assemble installer, screw, and thrust bearing and tighten screw firmly into threaded hole in crankshaft. Turn the nut on screw to force damper into place on crankshaft. Installer is not required on late engines.
3. Assemble cone, retainer and damper retainer bolt. Tighten bolt to 200 to 210 foot-pounds with torque wrench.

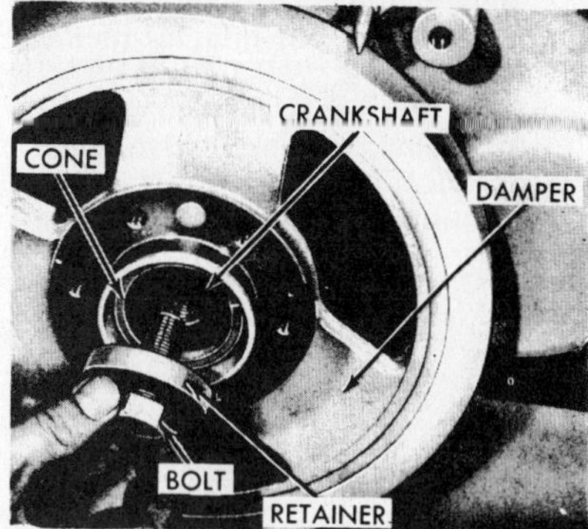

Crankshaft damper retaining parts
(© G.M.C.)

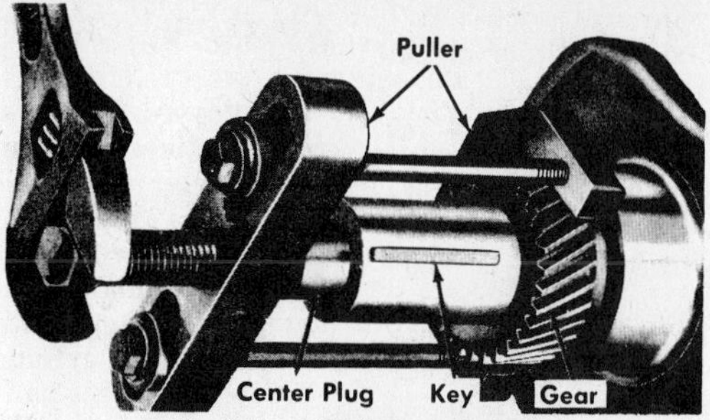

Removing gear from camshaft
(© G.M.C.)

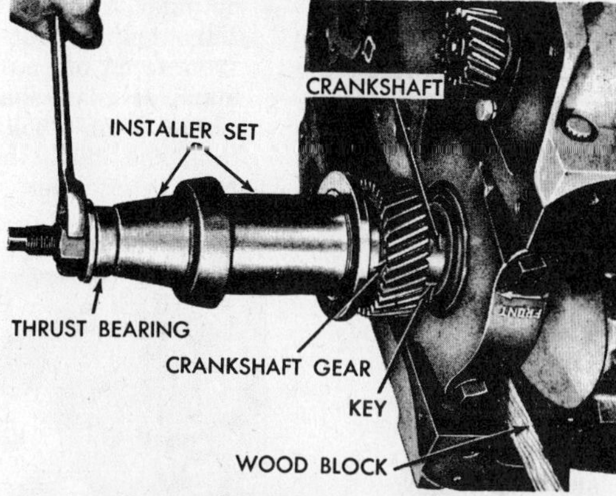

Installing crankshaft gear (using special tools)
(© G.M.C.)

Checking timing gear backlash
(© G.M.C.)

Engine Front Cover Removal

NOTE: The thermostat housing and engine water pump assembly may remain on front cover during cover removal.

1. At rear side of engine front cover, remove bolts which attach cap to cylinder block and front cover, then remove cap and gasket.
2. At front side of front cover assembly, remove the bolts and washers which attach cover to cylinder block.
3. Jar the cover loose with a lead hammer, and remove the cover. Cover assembly must be lifted upward sufficiently to clear the injection pump drive gear before it can be moved forward.

Gear Train Removal

1. Remove four bolts attaching injection pump drive gear to camshaft gear, then remove drive gear.
2. Bend lock plates away from plate retaining bolts. Remove bolts and gear retainer plates from idler gear shafts. Remove idler gears.
3. Gears are keyed to respective shafts and may remain on shafts until shafts are removed from cylinder block. Crankshaft gear can be removed from crankshaft with special puller, with crankshaft either installed or removed. An arbor press should be used to replace camshaft gear or balance shaft gear. Before the gear can be removed from V-8 engine balance shaft, the balance weight must be removed.

Gear Train Installation

1. Turn crankshaft so "O" mark on gear is at 12 o'clock position. Turn camshaft gear so "X" mark is at 6 o'clock position.
2. Lubricate bushing in camshaft idler gear, then install idler gear on idler gear shaft so "X" marks are indexed and "O" marks are indexed.
3. Using two bolts and lock plate, install gear retaining plate at idler gear shaft. Tighten bolts to 15 to 20 foot-pounds, then bend corners of lock plate to secure bolts.
4. Lubricate bushing in balance shaft idler gear then position gear so alignment marks are indexed with marks on gears.
5. Retain idler gear with retainer plate and bolts in same manner as described in step 3 above.
6. Using narrow feeler gauge, check gear back lash between gear sets. Make backlash check

at several points at each gear; there must be no tight spots in any position.

7. Install injection pump drive gear on camshaft gear with self-locking bolts. Tighten bolts with torque wrench to 35 to 40 foot-pounds with bolt threads oiled.
8. Check torque on camshaft gear retainer bolt. With bolt threads oiled the proper torque is 50 to 60 foot-pounds.

Engine Front Cover Installation

1. Locate front cover gasket at front of cylinder block with bolt holes in gasket aligned with holes in cylinder block.
2. Carefully guide front cover over injection pump drive gear and over end of crankshaft. Oil seal in cover and gear teeth may be damaged if care is not used in positioning cover assembly.
3. Install four short bolts with lock washers, then install long bolts with lock washers on all except the one bolt which passes through water passage which requires a copper washer. Copper washer serves as a gasket to prevent water leakage. Tighten front cover to cylinder block bolts to 22 to 27 foot-pounds torque.
4. At top of cylinder block, behind front cover, install cylinder block cap using new cap gasket.

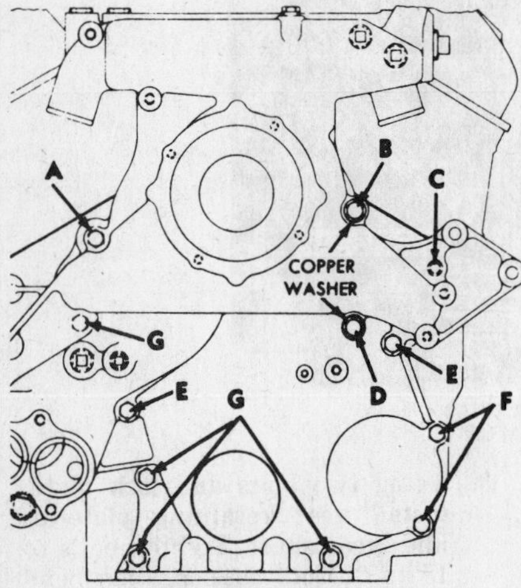

Front cover bolt arrangement and torquing instructions (© G.M.C.)

Bolt Location	Length (Inches)	Ft. Lb. Torque
A	4-¼	25-30
B	4-½	10-15
C	2	35-45
D	2-⅞	10-15
E	2-⅞	25-30
F	3-¾	25-30
G	1	25-30

Checking Engine Valve Timing

Valves must open and close in correct relationship to upper and lower dead center of crankshaft. When a check of valve timing is necessary, following procedure may be used referring to markings at crankshaft damper for determining top dead center on No. 1 cylinder.

1. Remove left-hand rocker cover from cylinder head to provide access to rocker arms at No. 1 cylinder.
2. Turn engine clockwise (viewed from front of engine) to "UDC" mark at crankshaft damper on compression stroke. Both the intake and the exhaust valve on No. 1 cylinder will then be closed.
3. Adjust valve lash on No. 1 exhaust valve (front valve) to exactly 0.054 inch on 6-cylinder engines; or to 0.057 inch on 8-cylinder engines.
4. Turn engine clockwise until No. 1 exhaust valve opens and begins to close, then with fingers try turning push rod of No. 1 exhaust valve as engine is cranked slowly. When push rod rotates with finger pressure, the "UDC" mark on damper should be at pointer. This will be about 1 revolution from starting point. If push rod starts to rotae at any point within one-quarter inch either side of "UDC" mark, the valve timing is correct. Be sure to adjust exhaust valve clearance to 0.018 inch after performing the foregoing check.

1 Camshaft gear
2 Injection pump drive gear
3 Drive gear bolts
4 Self locking bolt
5 Camshaft gear retainer
6 Lock plates
7 Balance shaft idler gear
8 Balance shaft thrust plate
9 Balance shaft gear
10 Gear retainer plate
11 Plate retaining bolts
12 Crankshaft balancer key
13 Cylinder block
14 Camshaft idler gear

Gear train and timing marks (V6 engine) (© G.M.C.)

1 Drive gear bolts
2 Camshaft gear
3 Injection pump drive gear
4 Camshaft idler gear
5 Lock plates
6 Plate retaining bolts
7 Gear retainer plate
8 Crankshaft gear
9 Crankshaft
10 Balance shaft gear
11 Balance shaft
12 Hole plug (ball)
13 Balance shaft front weight
14 Thrust plate
15 Balance shaft idler gear

Gear train and timing marks (V8 engine) (© G.M.C.)

5. If when checking valve timing, the push rod starts to rotate at a point more than three-quarters inch either side of the "UDC" mark, the camshaft can be considered "out of time." NOTE: When valve timing has been corrected, it will be necessary to retime the fuel injection pump.

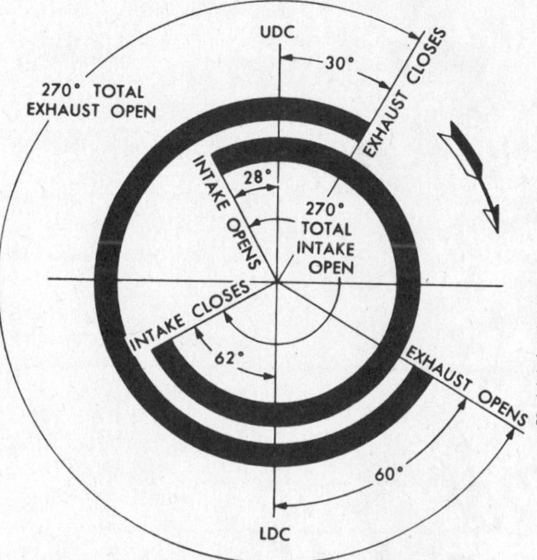

Valve timing diagram (all Toro flow diesel engines) (© G.M.C.)

Balance Shaft, Gear and Thrust Plate

Balance Shaft Removal

NOTE: Balance shaft cannot be removed from cylinder block until bolts which secure weights to the balance shaft have been removed. Self-locking bolts secure the weights on V-8 engines. Locks under weight bolt heads are used on V-6 engines. Special wedges are required to expand weights and relieve clamping action so balance shaft can be removed.

1. Remove balance shaft weight bolts from all weights.
2. Insert wedges in slots in balance shaft weights and tap each wedge lightly to just relieve clamping pressure of weights on shaft.
3. At front of cylinder block, remove the two bolts and washers which secure balance shaft thrust plate to block, then remove balance shaft, by pulling shaft forward through bearings and removing weights from crankcase as each one drops off shaft.
4. On V-8 engine remove spacer plate from balance shaft and gear assembly.

The balance shaft, gear, and thrust plate may be inspected without removing gear from shaft. Clean all parts thoroughly before beginning inspection. Be sure oil passages in shaft are unobstructed and clean.

Inspection

1. Check balance shaft bearing surfaces for evidence of scoring and for wear. Use micrometer to measure shaft diameter at bearing areas. There are four bearing areas on V-6 balance shafts, and five bearing areas on V-8 balance shafts. Diameter of new balance shaft is 1.4705 to 1.4695 inches at bearing areas.
2. On 6-cylinder engines, measure clearance between thrust plate and balance shaft gear hub using feeler gauge. Clearance (endplay) should be 0.003 to 0.005 inch.
3. On 8-Cylinder engines use feeler gauge in manner similar to that shown in figure 45 to measure clearance between thrust plate and gear. Correct clearance between these parts if 0.002 to 0.006 inch.

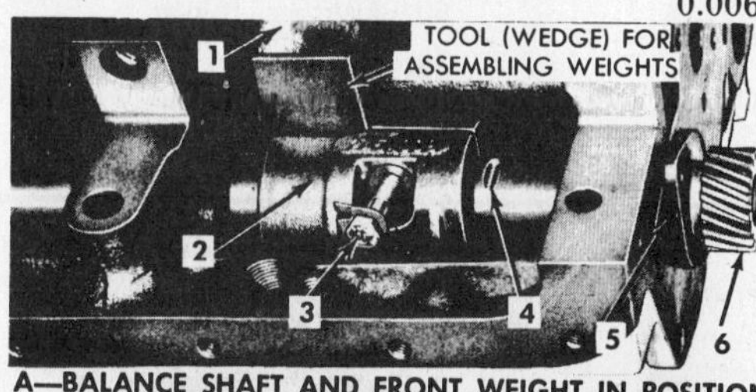

1 Cylinder block
2 Balance weight
3 Bolt with lock
4 Notch in balance shaft
5 Thrust plate
6 Balance shaft gear
7 Thrust plate bolt with lock washer

Balance shaft and weight installation (© G.M.C.)

4. Mount balance shaft in Vee blocks and use dial indicator to measure shaft runout. With shaft supported at ends, runout should no exceed 0.002 inch for 6-cylinder engines or 0.003 inch for 8-cylinder engines (total indicator reading).

Balance Shaft Gear and Thrust Plate Replacement (D351 and D, DH478 Engines)

Removal

Using suitable press plates, support the balance shaft gear while applying pressure on front end of shaft with arbor press. Press shaft out of gear, then remove gear key from slot in shaft and remove thrust plate.

Installation

1. Place thrust plate on balance shaft with the trade mark and part number facing forward.
2. Drive key into place in slot.
3. While supporting rear end of balance shaft, start gear squarely onto shaft with keyway in gear aligned with key in shaft. Extended hub on gear must be toward thrust plate. Timing mark on gear is at front side of gear.
4. Complete the gear installation by using a hollow driver between press and gear hub. Slowly press gear into position while using feeler gauge to measure the space between gear hub and thrust plate.

Balance Shaft Weight, Gear, and Thrust Plate Replacement (D, DH637 Engines)

General

In the event it should be necessary to replace balance shaft on 8-cylinder engines the balance weight pin hole must be drilled and taper reamed at assembly.

Balance Shaft Weight and Gear Removal

1. Use a suitable punch and hammer to drive tapered pin out of weight and shaft.
2. Support rear side of thrust washer on arbor press plate, then press on front end of balance shaft and force the shaft out of gear and weight. CAUTION: When pressing balance shaft out of gear and weight, press plate used to support the thrust washer, must be positioned so as to allow gear and weight keys to clear the plate without interference. Support the thrust washer close to shaft to avoid bending the thrust washer.

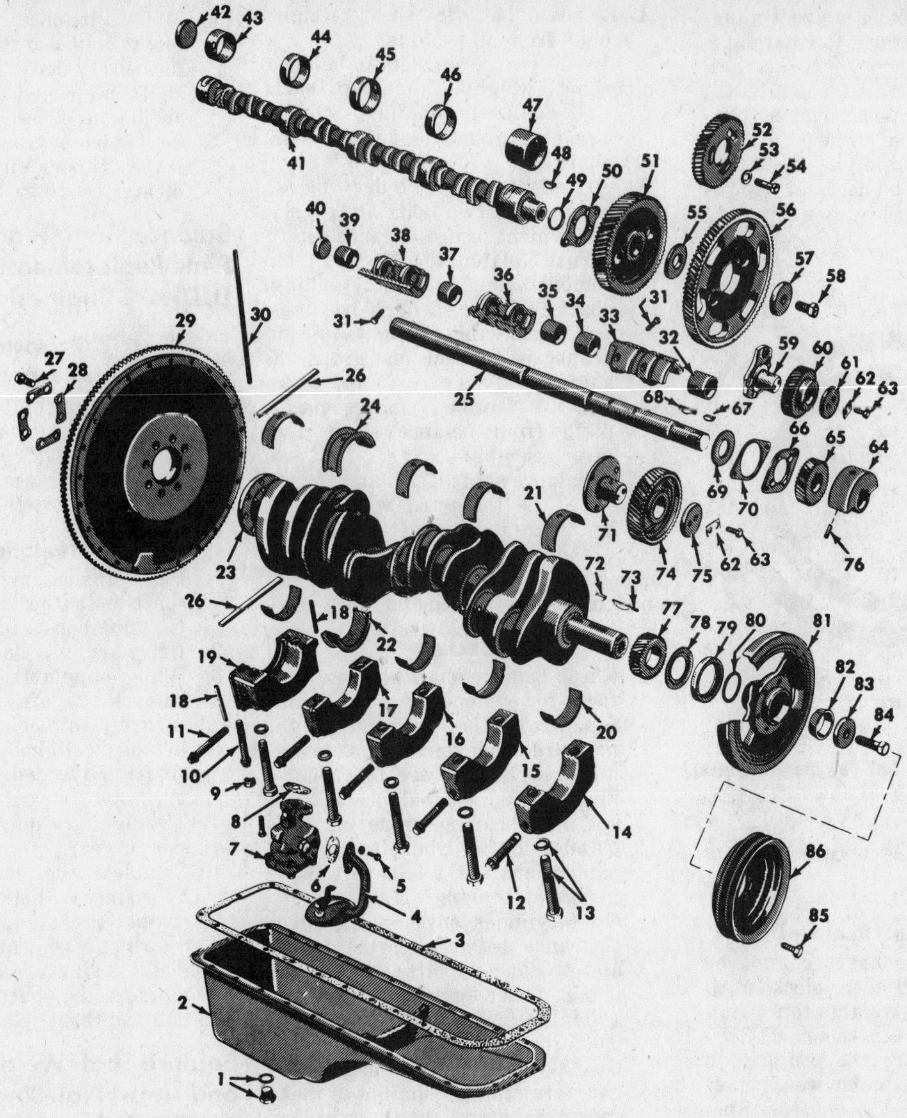

Crankshaft, camshaft, balance shaft and associated parts (8 cyl. engine) (© G.M.C.)

1 Drain plug and gasket
2 Oil pan
3 Pan gasket
4 Oil inlet screen and pipe assembly
5 Pipe flange bolt
6 Gasket
7 Engine oil pump
8 Pump to block gasket
9 Plug
10 Bearing cap rear bolt
11 Rear bearing cap side bolt
12 Cap side bolts (except rear)
13 Bearing cap bolt and washer
14 No. 1 bearing cap
15 No. 2 bearing cap
16 No. 3 bearing cap
17 No. 4 bearing cap
18 Rear bearing cap side seal
19 Rear bearing cap
20 Crankshaft no. 1, 2, 3, and 5 lower bearing
21 Crankshaft no. 1, 2, 3, and 5 upper bearing
22 No. 4 lower bearing
23 Crankshaft
24 No. 4 upper bearing
25 Balance shaft
26 Crankshaft rear bearing seal
27 Flywheel bolts
28 Bolt lock plates
29 Flywheel assembly
30 Oil pump drive shaft
31 Balance shaft weight bolt
32 Balance shaft front (No. 1) bearing
33 Balance shaft no. 2 weight
34 Balance shaft no. 2 bearing
35 Balance shaft no. 3 bearing
36 Balance shaft no. 3 weight
37 Balance shaft no. 4 bearing
38 Balance shaft no. 4 weight
39 Balance shaft rear (no. 5) bearing
40 Hole plug
41 Camshaft
42 Camshaft bearing hole plug
43 Camshaft rear (no. 5) bearing
44 Camshaft no. 4 bearing
45 Camshaft no. 3 bearing
46 Camshaft no. 2 bearing
47 Camshaft no. 1 bearing
48 Camshaft gear key
49 Spacer
50 Camshaft thrust plate
51 Camshaft gear
52 Fuel injection pump gear
53 Washer
54 Pump gear bolt
55 Spacing washer
56 Fuel injection pump drive gear
57 Gear retainer washer
58 Self-locking bolt
59 Idler gear shaft
60 Balance shaft idler gear
61 Gear retainer plate
62 Lock plates
63 Plate retaining bolts
64 Balance shaft front (no. 1) weight
65 Balance shaft gear
66 Thrust plate
67 Weight key
68 Gear key
69 Thrust washer
70 Spacer
71 Camshaft idler gear shaft
72 Crankshaft gear key
73 Crankshaft damper key
74 Camshaft idler gear
75 Gear retainer plate
76 Balance shaft weight pin
77 Crankshaft gear
78 Oil slinger
79 Oil seal assembly
80 Oil seal ring
81 Damper
82 Damper cone
83 Damper retainer
84 Retainer bolt
85 Pulley bolt
86 Crankshaft pulley

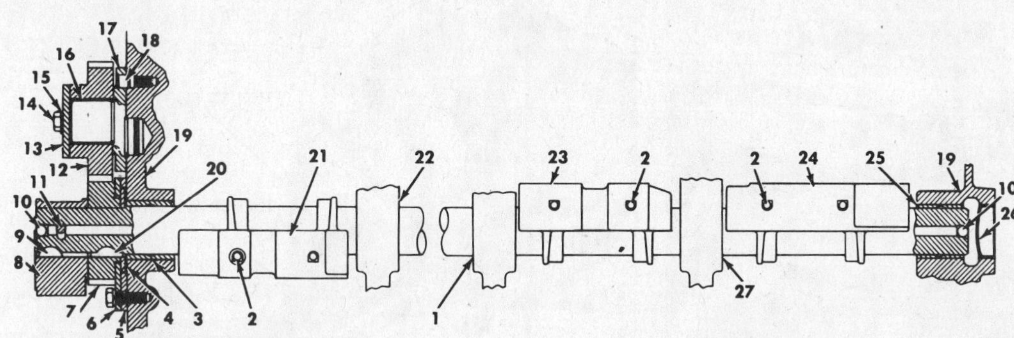

Balance shaft, weight and idler gear installed (V8 engines) (© G.M.C.)

1 No. 3 bearing
2 Balance weight bolt
3 No. 1 (front) bearing
4 Thrust washer
5 Spacer plate
6 Thrust plate
7 Balance shaft gear
8 No. 1 (front) weight
9 Weight key
10 Steel ball (plug)
11 Weight pin
12 Idler gear
13 Gear retainer plate
14 Plate retaining bolts
15 Lock plate
16 Gear bushing
17 Idler gear shaft
18 Dowel pin
19 Cylinder block assembly
20 Gear key
21 No. 2 weight
22 No. 2 bearing
23 No. 3 weight
24 No. 4 (rear) weight
25 No. 5 bearing
26 Balance shaft hole plug
27 No. 4 bearing

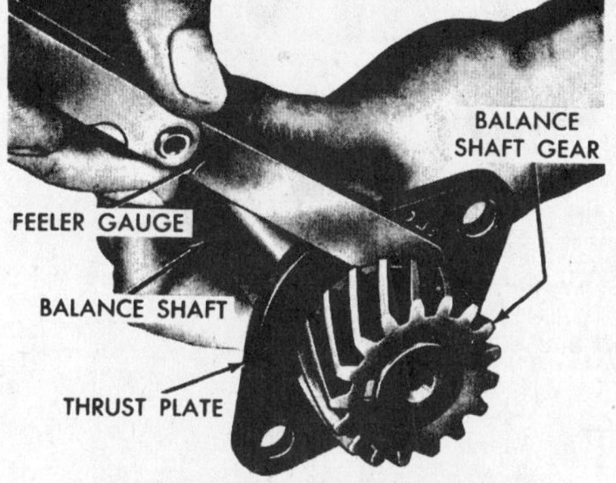

Checking clearance between thrust plate and balance shaft gear (V6 engine) (© G.M.C.)

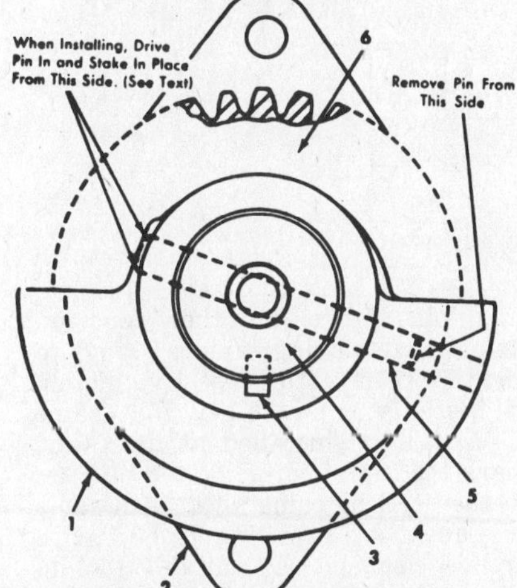

Balance weight shaft weight pin installation (8 cyl. engines) (© G.M.C.)

1 No. 1 (front) balance weight
2 Thrust plate
3 Weight key
4 Balance shaft
5 Tapered pin
6 Balance shaft gear

Balance Shaft, Weight, and Gear Assembly Procedure

General Information

1. The procedure for installing gear and weight on a new balance shaft differs from procedure required when the original balance shaft is used. Each procedure is covered separately under 2. and 3. following:
2. Assembling Parts Using Original Balance Shaft
   a. With keys installed in respective keyways, place thrust washer over keys and into place against shoulder on balance shaft.
   b. Lubricate the front area on balance shaft and the bore through gear and weight with engine then start balance shaft gear onto front end of shaft with keyway aligned with keys and gear extended hub toward thrust washer. Support rear end of balance shaft and press the gear into place. Hold the thrust plate so it does not catch between gear hub and thrust washer as gear is pressed into place.
   c. Press balance shaft weight onto balance shaft until solidly seated against gear.
   d. Use No. 5 tapered reamer to clean up tapered hole in weight and shaft, then use air hose to blow into drilled oil passage and blow out any cuttings which may be in oil holes. Also flush out oil passages with clean solvent.
   e. Drive in new tapered pin to secure balance shaft front weight to balance shaft referring to illustration for pin installation views. Stake the pin hole in weight to secure tapered pin.
3. Assembling Parts Using New Balance Shaft and Weight
   a. Accomplish the procedure as instructed under steps 2. a., b., and c. to assemble thrust plate gear and weight on balance shaft.
   b. Using drill press and 0.25 inch, long shank drill piloted in pin hole in balance weight, drill squarely through balance shaft. NOTE: If a previously-used balance weight is used, pilot the drill from the thick side of weight. If a new weight is used a straight pilot hole is provided for use in drilling pin hole in shaft.
   c. After pin hole has been drilled in balance weight shaft, use No. 5 tapered reamer to ream the pin hole in weight and shaft. Ream the pin hole sufficiently to allow new pin to enter freely until only 3/32-inch of pin is above weight surface. When reaming is completed and before pin is driven into place, use air hose and blow all cuttings out of oil hole at center of balance shaft. Also flush out the oil passages with clean solvent.
   d. Using punch and hammer, drive tapered pin into place until large end of pin is just below surface of weight, then use staking tool and stake edge of pin hole to secure the pin.
   e. Plug oil hole in each end of balance weight shaft with 11/32-inch diameter steel ball. Drive each ball in 0.030 inch below surface of shaft.

Balance Shaft Bearings

Inspect balance shaft bearings for scoring. Also use inside micrometer to determine inside diameter at each bearing. If damage to bearings is apparent, or if extensive wear is indicated, the balance shaft bearings should be replaced.

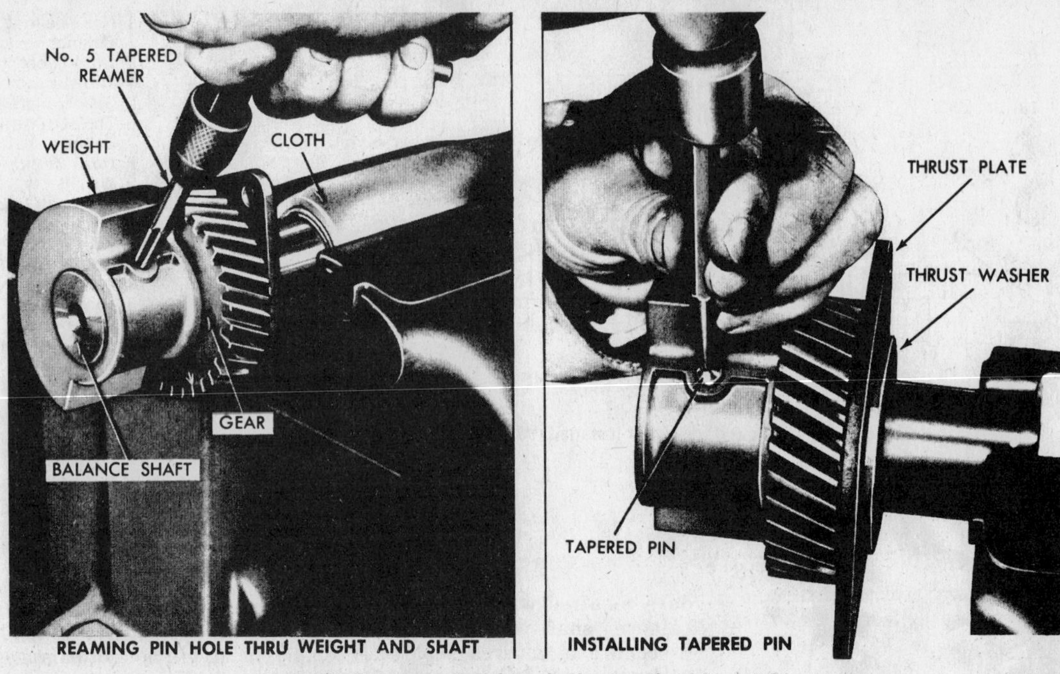

Installing balance shaft weight pin (8 cyl. engines) (© G.M.C.)

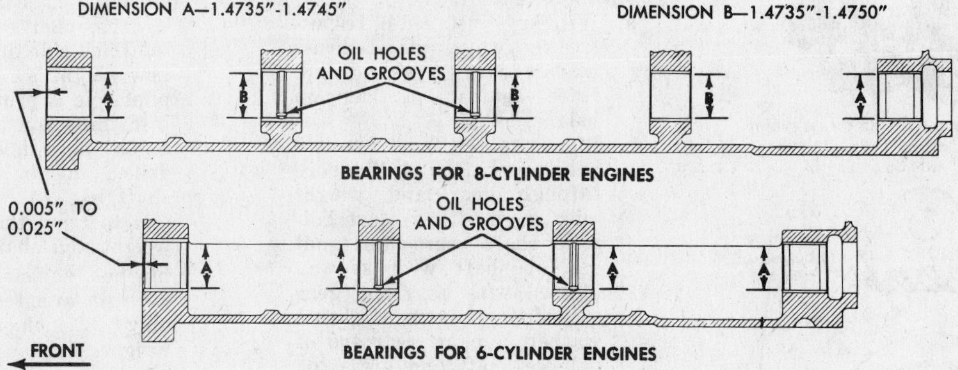

Balance shaft bearing installation (© G.M.C.)

Balance Shaft Bearing Replacement

Pre-sized balance shaft bearings are available for service replacement for both the 6-cylinder and 8-cylinder engines. The bearings provide proper fit without reaming. Four bearings are used on 6-cylinder engines and five are used on 8-cylinder engines.

Cylinder block must be stripped and flywheel housing removed to permit use of special tools in replacing balance shaft bearings. Crankshaft should also be removed for easy access to balance shaft bearing area.

Since the outside dimension of each bearing is different than other bearings, the balance shaft bearings will fit only their respective bores. Smallest diameter bore is at rear and bore sizes increase progressively toward front. Bearings have a chamfer at outer edge to facilitate installation.

Be sure all oil supply passages in cylinder block are clean before installing new balance shaft bearings. Use suitable tool to provide smooth chamfer at forward edge of each balance shaft bearing bore. Dip bearing assemblies in light engine oil prior to installation.

Notice that two of the bearings have oil holes and oil grooves. When installing these bearings, *an oil hole must be aligned with hole in block.*

IMPORTANT: Be sure to remove from cylinder block any shavings or metal particles which have resulted from the bearing installation procedure. Also recheck each bearing position to see that split in bearing is at top of bore and that oil hole in intermediate bearings registers with oil hole in cylinder block. Plug should be driven in slightly below surface of block.

Piston, Rod, and Bearing Cleaning and Inspection

Cleaning

Immerse all parts in dry-cleaning solvent to loosen and remove accumulated oil, sludge, or other deposits. Remove piston rings and tag rings to identify them with respective piston. If there is a possibility that same rings will be installed at assembly, mark the top of top ring and oil ring so they can be reinstalled with same side upward. Clean ring grooves with groove cleaner. Use suitable tool to clean oil drain holes in oil ring groove.

Checking Piston Ring Fit

After thoroughly cleaning piston rings and ring grooves in pistons, try fit of piston rings in respective cylinder bore.

1. Place piston rings in cylinder one at a time and push ring at least half-way down cylinder bore, using head of piston to position ring squarely in bore. Measure ring gap with feeler gauge. If gap is too small, remove ring and dress off ends of ring with fine cut file or other tool designed for this purpose.

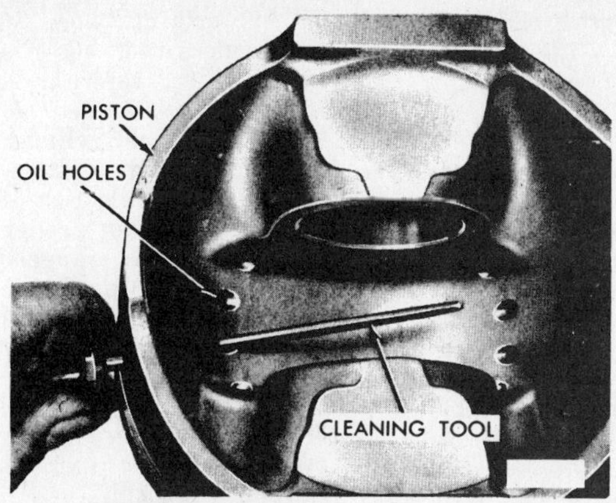

Cleaning oil holes in oil ring groove in piston
(© G.M.C.)

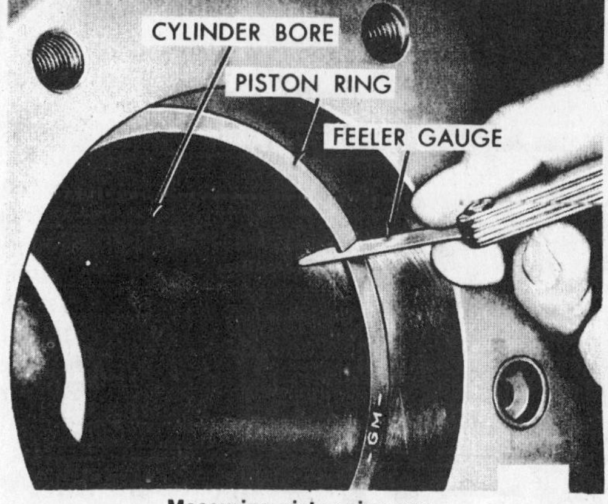

Measuring piston ring gap
(© G.M.C.)

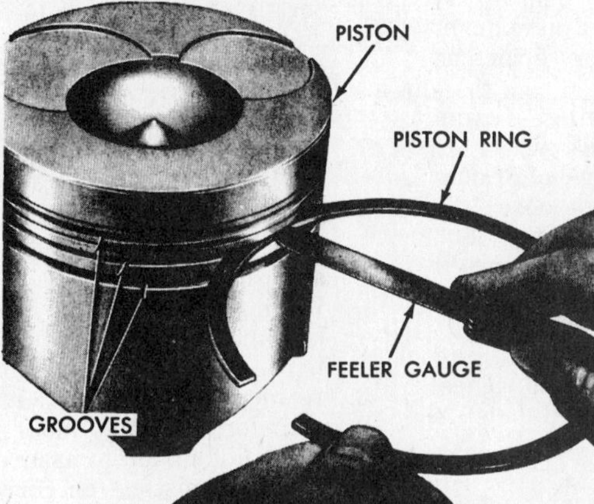

Measuring piston ring clearance in groove
(© G.M.C.)

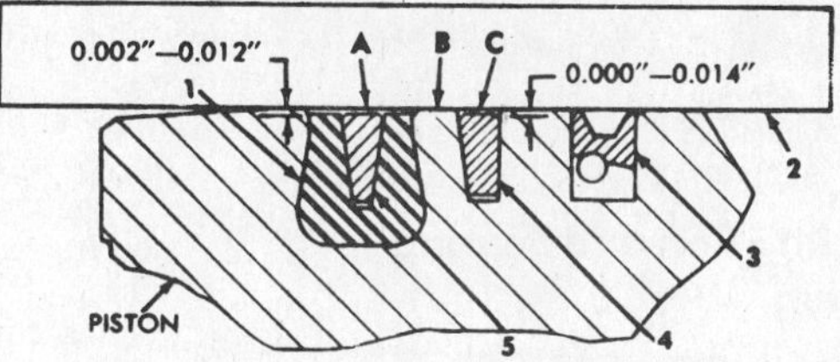

Checking for wear at piston and rings
(© G.M.C.)

1 Top piston ring insert (integral with piston)
2 Straightedge
3 Oil control ring
4 2nd compression ring (½ keystone type, see text)
5 Top compression ring (keystone type)

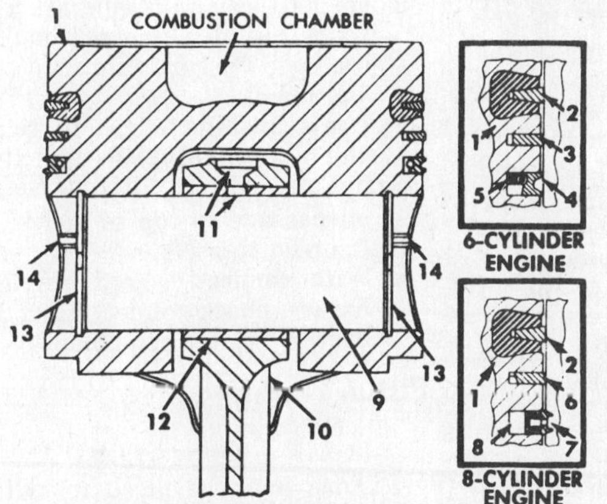

Cross section view of piston and connecting rod
(© G.M.C.)

1 Piston
2 Top compression ring (keystone type)
3 2nd compression ring (tapered face)
4 Oil control ring
5 Expander spring
6 2nd compression ring (taper face, reverse twist)
7 Oil control ring
8 Expander
9 Piston pin
10 Connecting rod
11 Oil hole in rod and bushing
12 Bushing
13 Piston pin retainer
14 Oil groove

2. If piston ring gap is within specified dimensions, as determined in step 1. above, the rings should be checked for fit in grooves in piston.
   a. Using piston ring spreader tool install rings in respective grooves.
   b. On all except turbo-charged engines, use feeler gauge to measure clearance between 2nd compression ring and piston ring land.
   c. On all engines, use feeler gauge to measure clearance between oil control ring and ring land.
   d. At top compression ring and 2nd compresssion ring on turbo-charged engines check fit of each compression ring in groove. Because of normal taper to the keystone and one-half keystone rings, feeler gauges cannot be used to check ring fit.

Clamp piston firmly in horizontal position so piston rings will hang downward with tapered surfaces seated in tapered groove.

Using dial indicator, check position of top ring surface "A" and 2nd compression ring surface "C" in relation to surface on piston ring land "B".

Surface "A" on top compression ring should normally be 0.002 to 0.012 inch below ring land surface, while surface "C" on 2nd compression ring used with turbo-charged engines should normally be 0.000 to 0.014 inch below ring land.

IMPORTANT: When checking position of piston rings, do not use for reference any area on piston other than the surface and do not indicate from surface of steel insert since this is below the surface of piston.

Piston and Pin Inspection

Remove piston pin retainers and push out piston pin.

Measure each piston at 7/8 inch above bottom of skirt at right angle to pin bore and compare dimension with diameter at bottom of cylinder bore in which piston was installed.

Inspect piston ring lands and grooves for wear and other damage. Measure piston pin bores in piston bosses, and compare with diameter of pins. Piston pins should have clearance of 0.005 to 0.007 inch in respective pistons (oversize pins are available).

NOTE: New service pistons are fitted with piston pins.

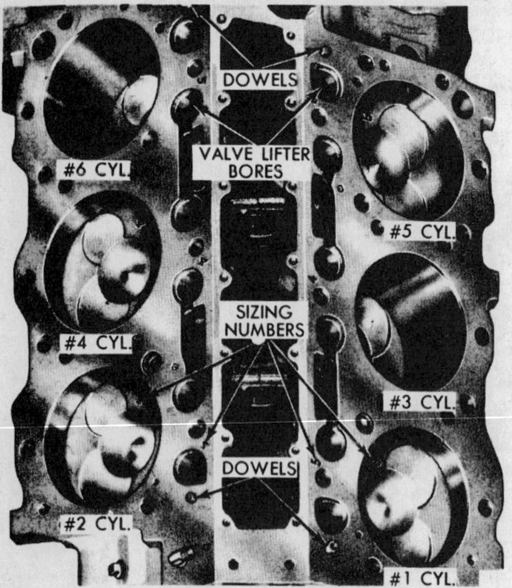

Cylinder numbering arrangement and size selection numbers (6 cylinder engine) (© G.M.C.)

Connecting Rod and Bearing Inspection

Connecting Rod Inspection

1. With bearing halves removed from rod and cap, install cap and tighten rod bolt nuts to 60 foot-pounds torque. Check bore at lower end for elongation. If bore is out-of-round, the rod should be replaced or reconditioned. Examine surfaces in rod and cap which are contacted by bearing halves. If there is evidence of fretting of metal at these surfaces, the surfaces must be polished to provide a smooth surface for bearing halves to seat against. If bore is round and within specifications, make careful visual inspection of piston pin bushing for evidence of wear. Test fit of piston pin in bushing by measuring pin O.D. and bushing I.D. At 70°F., there should be a clearance of 0.008 to 0.0014 inch.

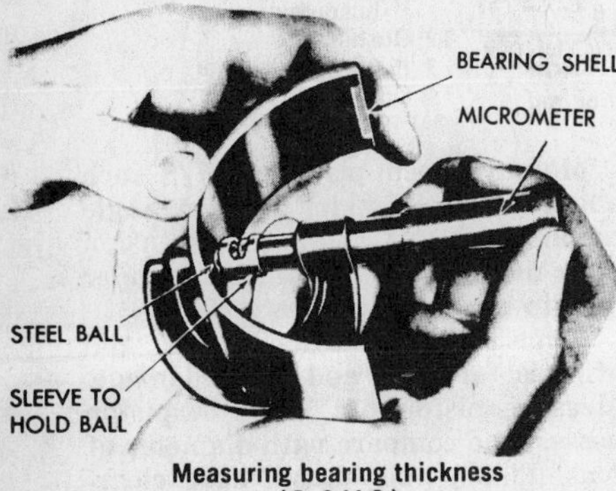

Measuring bearing thickness (© G.M.C.)

Connecting Rod Alignment

2. Connecting rod assembly should be placed in suitable aligning fixture to determine if rod is twisted or bent. Piston pin hole must be parallel with axis of crankpin hole in all planes within .002 inch in 7 inches.

Bearings

3. Carefully inspect connecting rod bearing halves for evidence of scores, chipping, or flaking out of bearing metal. If a visual inspection reveals any of these defects, replace with new parts. Measure each bearing half with accurate reading tube micrometer. Take measurement at right angle to split line.

Connecting Rod Repair

If inspection indicates that connecting rod piston pin bushing requires replacement, install new bushing which is furnished for service as follows:

1. Remove old bushing, using driver and arbor press.
2. Inspect bore in upper end of connecting rod. Measure bore I.D. which must be 1.802 to 1.803 inches to assure satisfactory fit of new bushing. Clean oil hole at top of rod.
3. Support connecting rod and press new bushing into place, using care to align oil hole in bushing with hole in top of connecting rod.
4. Diamond bore and hone bushing to provide 0.008 to 0.0014 inch clearance of pin in bushing at normal room temperature of 70°F. Suitable fixture should be used to assure finished hole alignment.
5. Dress bushing edges to remove any portion of bushing extending beyond edge of rod. Be sure oil passage in top of rod is free from cuttings.
6. With connecting rod alignment fixture, check connecting rod for bent or twisted condition.

Piston Fitting

General

Pistons must be fitted to cylinder bores by measuring to assure correct clearance between piston skirt and cylinder wall. Pistons and piston rings are available in oversize dimensions. The pistons must be assembled on respective connecting rods and installed in original positions in block. Pistons should be stamped with corresponding cylinder number. Number 1 cylinder is at front of left bank and cylinder Number 2 is at front of right bank, thus left bank cylinders are numbered from front to rear as shown for 6-cylinder engine.

Fitting Pistons in New or Reconditioned Cylinder Block

1. When necessary to select replacement pistons for new block or for original bore in block which does not have a ring-travel ridge, refer to selection size number stamped on top of block adjacent cylinder bore. number is used to indicate bore size to permit selection of standard size piston for proper fit. Selection numbers range from 1 through 7 for production. For service use, three standard size pistons are available: Size 1 for use in cylinders marked either 1 or 2; size 3 for cylinders marked 3 or 4; and size 5 for cylinders marked 5 or 6; and size 7 for cylinders marked 7.
2. Oversize pistons are available and do not have selection numbers. Cylinders must be rebored and honed to proper dimensions to provide correct fit when installing oversize pistions. CAUTION: Whenever possible, remove crankshaft when reboring or honing cylinder bores. If crankshaft is not removed, it must be covered to keep abrasive away from crankshaft bearings. Wash cylinder bores after honing and wipe dry before checking piston fit.
3. As new piston is fitted to each cylinder, stamp cylinder number on top of piston to assure installation of pistons on corresponding connecting rod and in proper cylinder. Refer to figure 41 for cylinder numbering arrangement.

Preparing Cylinder Bores When Re-Ringing Pistons

Ridge must be removed completely. Use polishing hone to break glaze. At end of honing operation allow hone to work free in bore. Do not remove while hone is still cutting. Clean cylinder walls with soap and water and stiff scrub brush, then wipe with clean cloth or absorbent paper. Apply engine oil to cylinder walls to prevent rusting.

Assembly of Connecting Rod and Piston

1. If original pistons and connecting rods are to be installed, refer to marks (numbers) on connecting rods and assemble rods to pistons from which they were removed. When new pistons are installed, assemble pistons on rods bearing the numbers of cylinders for which pistons were fitted.
2. Apply engine oil on piston pin, rod bushing and pin bosses; then hold rod between pin bosses in piston and push piston pin through piston and connecting rod. Always use a new retainer ring in groove at each end of piston.

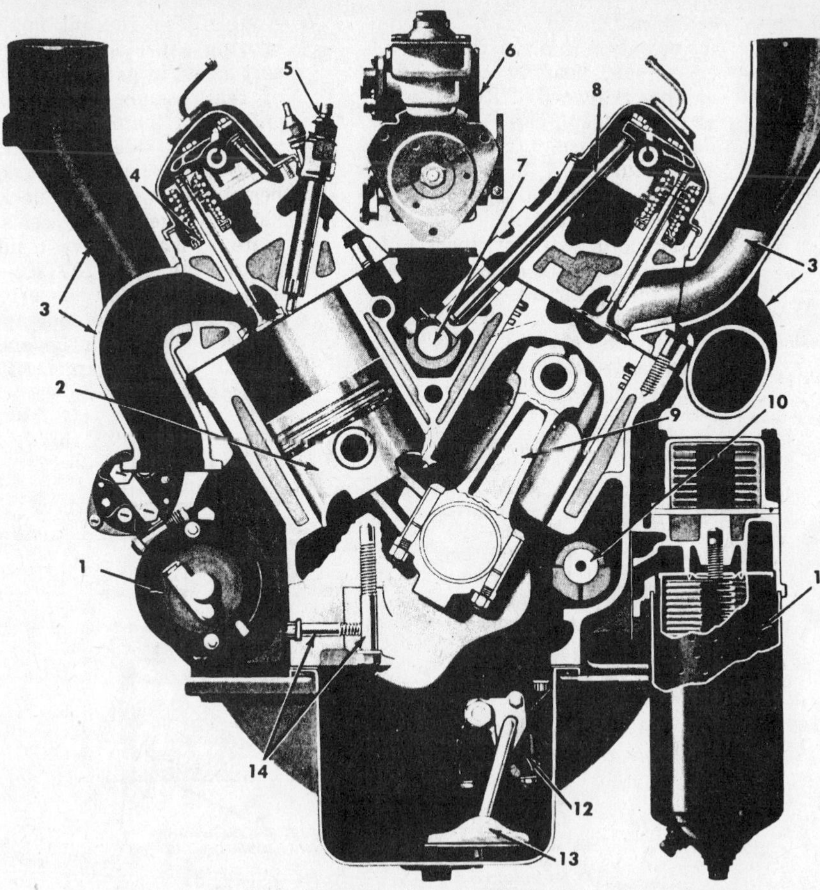

Sectional view of Toro flow diesel engine (© G.M.C.)

3. Check alignment of piston and connecting rod on alignment fixture.

Removing Crankshaft and Bearings

1. Remove plugs which seal rear bolt holes in rear bearing cap.
2. Remove the bearing cap side bolts, the heads of which are located at outer sides of cylinder block.
3. Remove balance of bearing cap bolts and washers. Then at thrust bearing cap, use bearing cap remover tool and slide hammer to remove the bearing cap. This must be pulled straight out of block to avoid bending or loosening dowel pins as well as to prevent damage to thrust faces on main bearing halves.
4. At other bearing caps, if necessary, use a round bar in bolt hole to work cap out of block; or the tool and slide hammer may be employed at all except rear bearing cap.
5. Lift crankshaft straight out of cylinder block assembly to prevent any binding which could damage thrust faces on thrust bearing.
6. Remove bearing upper halves from cylinder block and lower halves from bearing caps. Tag each pair of bearing halves, so they may be reinstalled in original positions.

Crankcase ready for Oil pan installation (© G.M.C.)

Crankshaft Rear Bearing Oil Seal

Crankshaft rear bearing oil seal consists of two pieces of special packing. One piece is installed in groove in rear bearing cap and the other piece is installed in similar groove in cylinder block. Crankshaft is knurled and polished at area used to prevent oil leakage at sides of crankshaft rear bearing cap and plugs are used to seal rear bolt holes.

Seal Installation

1. Apply cement in seal groove in cylinder block and in crankshaft rear bearing cap.
2. Position seal in groove in block and pack seal firmly into place in groove.
3. In similar manner, install seal in bearing cap.
4. Using a sharp knife; cut off both ends of each seal which project out of grooves.

Installing Crankshaft and Bearings

Thoroughly clean to remove all cuttings and abrasive material.

1. Place crankshaft bearing upper halves in respective bearing bores in crankcase, then apply engine oil on each bearing. Apply sealer on cylinder block area contacted by crankshaft rear bearing cap.
2. Lower crankshaft into place in

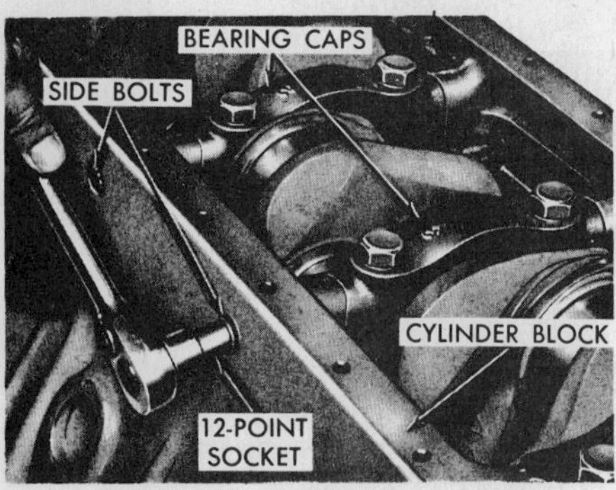

Removing or installing crankshaft rear main bearing side bolts (© G.M.C.)

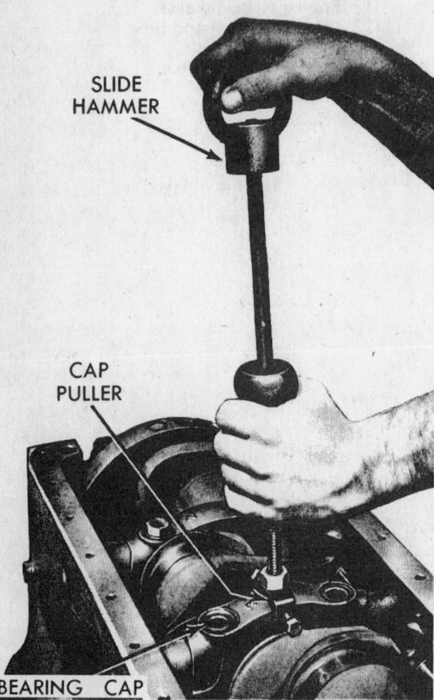

Removing crankshaft No. 3 bearing cap with special tool (© G.M.C.)

Dowel pins in crankcase at crankshaft No. 3 bearing (© G.M.C.)

crankcase, and with bearing lower halves in place, position all crankshaft bearing caps. Each cap has the word "FRONT" cast at front edge of cap and caps are numbered from front to rear with numerals 1, 2, 3, etc.

3. Lubricate all bearing cap bolts and bolt washers. Insert the 5/8-11 bolts with washers i nto holes in bearing caps and start bolts into threads in cylinder block, but do not tighten bolts until side (1/2-13) bolts have been started into threads in bearing caps.

7. Apply Diesel fuel oil on the two bearing cap side seals, then insert a seal in groove at each side of rear bearing cap chamfered end first. Chamfer must be toword outer side of crankcase to mate with radius at broached bearing cap seat in block. The narrow edge of side seals must mate with narrow side of grooves in cap. NOTE: When side seals are fully inserted, exposed end will protrude approximately 0.045 inch beyond surface of bearing cap. *Do not cut off side seals.*

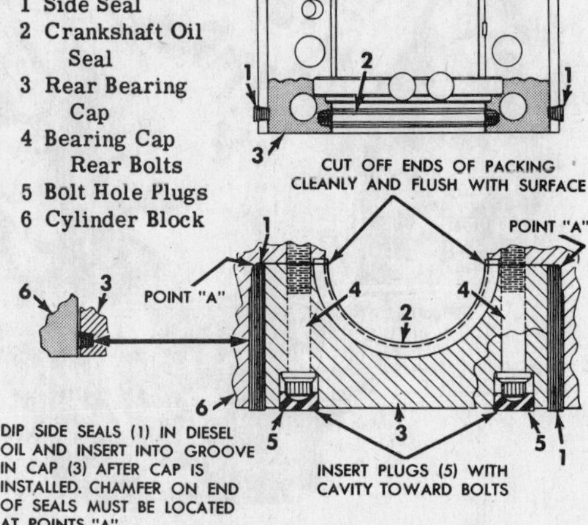

Cross section at seals and bearing cap bolts (© G.M.C.)

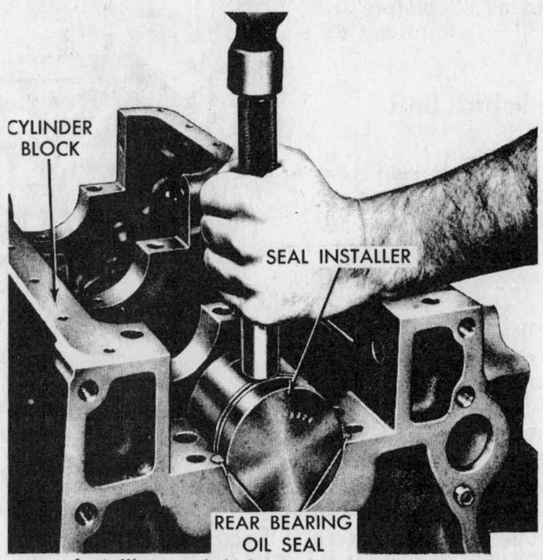

Installing crankshaft rear bearing oil seal with special tool (© G.M.C.)

4. Insert the side bolts from outer sides of crankcase and start each bolt into threads in bearing caps. Insert two 1/2-13 rear bearing cap (vertical) bolts and start threads into block.
5. Tighten the 5/8-11 bearing cap-to-cylinder block bolts to 170 to 180 foot-pounds.
6. Tighten all 1/2-13 bolts to 90 to 100 foot-pounds.
8. Install two bolt hole plugs in bearing cap to seal the holes and prevent oil leakage.
9. Crankshaft must turn freely with all cap bolts tightened.

Camshaft, Gear and Thrust Plate

Camshaft Removal

Remove thrust plate attaching bolts and lock washers at front end

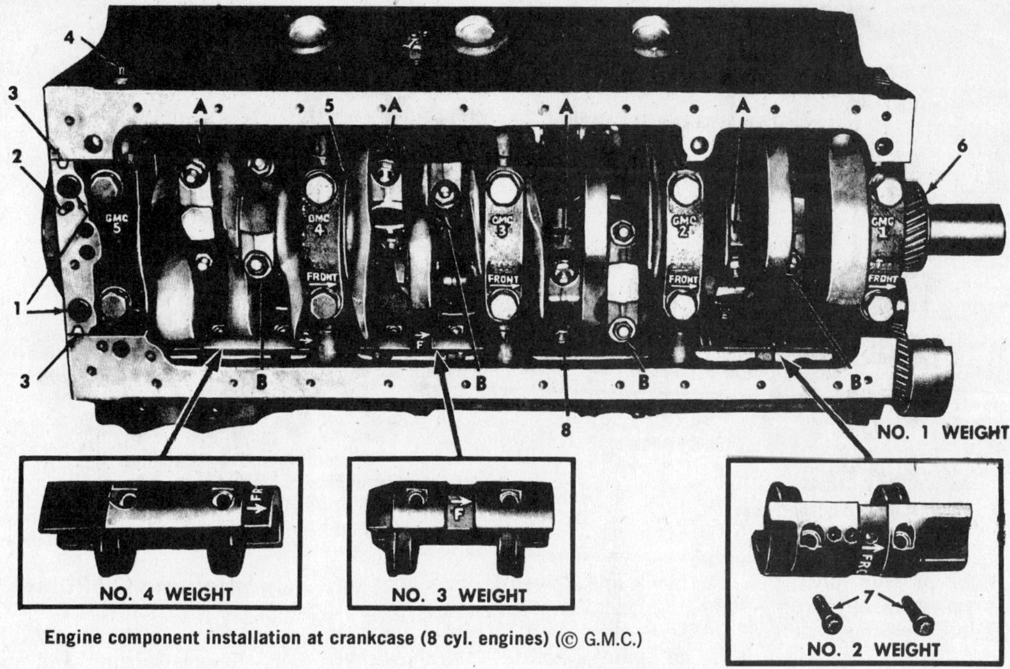

Engine component installation at crankcase (8 cyl. engines) (© G.M.C.)

A - Rod identification numbers (2, 4, 6, 8)
B - Rod identification numbers (1, 3, 5, 7)
1 Hole plug
2 Oil pan stud
3 Rear bearing cap side seal
4 Bearing cap side bolts
5 Crankshaft thrust bearing
6 Oil slinger
7 Weight clamp bolts
8 Balance shaft

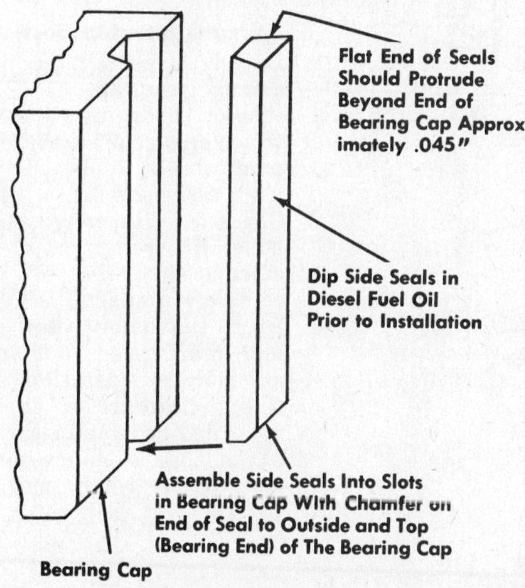

Bearing cap side seal installation (© G.M.C.)

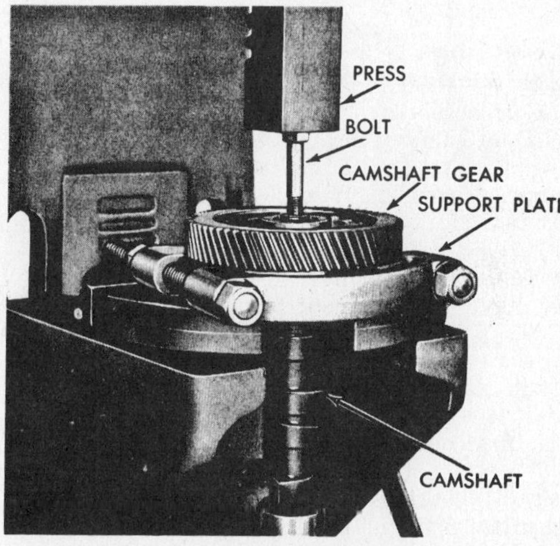

PRESS
BOLT
CAMSHAFT GEAR
SUPPORT PLATE
CAMSHAFT

Removing camshaft gear (© G.M.C.)

of camshaft. Turn gear as necessary to align holes in gear with bolts.

Carefully pull camshaft assembly forward to remove from cylinder block. Do not damage bearings.

1. Check camshaft for general condition. Bearing journals should not be scored or burred.
2. Support camshaft at end journals, then with dial indicator, check camshaft for straightness.
3. Inspect thrust plate for wear at thrust surfaces. Replace plate and spacer if worn. NOTE: If the camshaft gear has not been removed from camshaft, the extent of wear on thrust plate may be determined with feeler gauge by measuring space between thrust plate and shoulder on camshaft. Correct clearance is 0.0045 to 0.0085 inch.
4. Inspect camshaft gear for wear and damage at teeth. If gear teeth are not in good condition: gear must be replaced.

Camshaft Gear Replacement

1. Remove bolt, retainer, and spacer washer from camshaft.
2. Position camshaft and gear assembly in arbor press, and press the camshaft out of gear. A bolt tightened ino tapped hole in camshaft may be used to apply pressure to camshaft.
3. Remove key from slot in camshaft, then remove spacer and thrust plate.
4. Position spacer on camshaft with chamfered side toward camshaft shoulder. Place thrust plate over spacer and install key in keyway.
5. Position camshaft in arbor press with support plate clamped below front journal. Place gear at camshaft with the keyway in gear aligned with key in camshaft. Use hollow tubing as

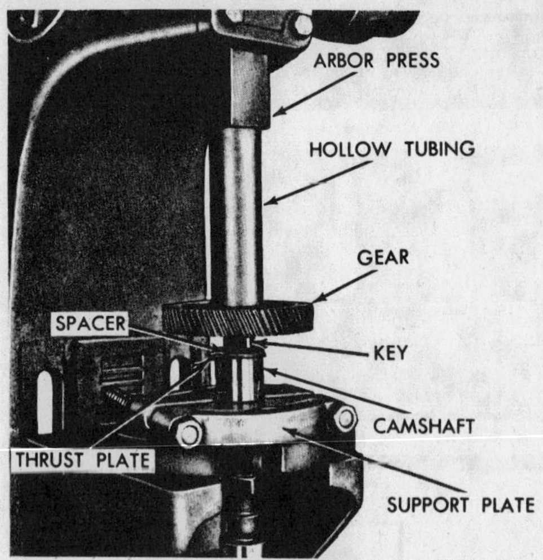

Installing camshaft gear
(© G.M.C.)

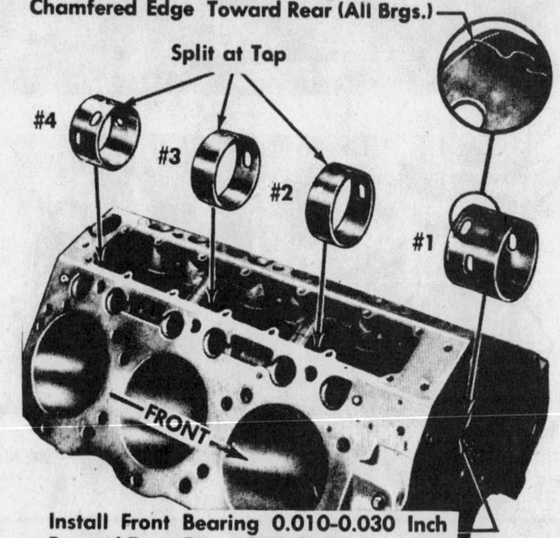

Camshaft bearing installation (V6 engine)
(© G.M.C.)

shown to apply pressure on gear hub, and press gear onto camshaft until hub bottoms solidly at spacer.

6. Install the spacer washer at camshaft gear hub, then install thick retaining washer and self-blocking bolt. Final tightening of bolt may be deferred until camshaft and gear train are installed.

Camshaft Bearings

Inspect each camshaft bearing for scoring, wear, or looseness.

Measure I.D. of camshaft bearings and compare with O.D. of corresponding camshaft journal. If excessive wear is indicated, replace camshaft bearings.

Pre-sized camshaft bearings are available for service replacement for all engines.

Although these bearings provide proper fit without reaming no attempt should be made to replace them without first obtaining the required special tool set.

All camshaft bearings can be pulled forward through the block. It is recommended that all bearings be removed before installing any new camshaft bearings. Replacement procedures vary to some degree between the 6 and 8 cylinder engines.

NOTE: That when installing bearings, split must be on top and chamfered end must be toward the rear. This will properly position oil holes.

IMPORTANT: Make sure all shavings and metal particles which may have resulted from bearing installation, are removed from block. Also recheck each bearing position to insure the split is properly located at top.

Engine Oil Pump and Drive

The engine oil pump assembly is located in the engine crankcase. The pump assembly is bolted to the cylinder block and driven from a gear on the rear portion of the camshaft. Oil intake is through a screen at bottom of oil pan. Illustrations show installed view of oil pump and inlet screen assembly.

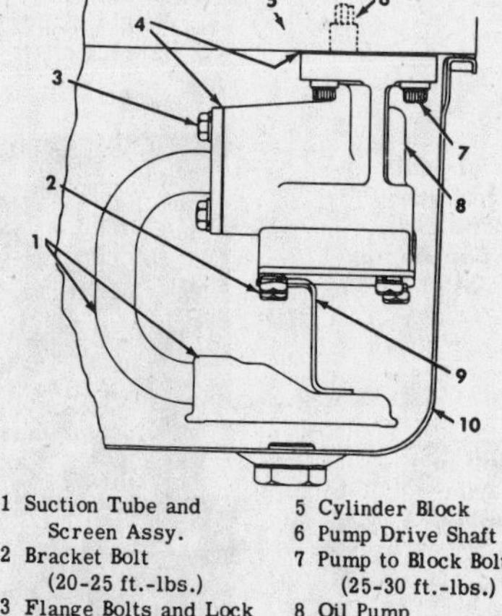

1 Suspension Tube and Screen Assy.
2 Bracket Bolt (20-25 ft.-lbs.)
3 Flange Bolts and Lock Washers
4 Gaskets
5 Cylinder Block
6 Pump Drive Shaft
7 Pump to Block Bolts (25-30 ft.-lbs.)
8 Oil Pump
9 Bracket
10 Oil Pan

Oil pump suction screen (late type engines)
(© G.M.C.)

Overhauling Oil Pump

Disassembly

1. Remove spring and valve from pump body.
2. Remove pump cover from body.
3. Remove inner rotor and shaft assembly, then remove outer rotor from cavity in body.

Cleaning and Inspection

1. Be sure screen and suction pipe assembly is clean.
2. Inspect ends of drive shaft which engage drive sockets in oil pump shafts. Replace drive shaft if excessively worn or damaged.
3. Check fit of inner rotor shaft in body. If excessive wear is indicated at either the shaft or body, replace worn parts.
4. Place the outer rotor in body and insert inner rotor and shaft assembly in operating position. Check clearance between outer rotor and body and clearance between edge of inner rotor lobe and outer rotor with feeler

1 Damper (In Screen Support)
2 Oil Inlet Screen and Pipe Assy.
3 Rod Identification Numbers (2, 4 and 6)
4 Rod Identification Numbers (1, 3 and 5)
5 Gaskets
6 Engine Oil Pump Assy.
7 Bearing Cap Side Seal (2 used)
8 Oil Pan Stud (1 used)
9 Hole Plug (2 used)

Crankcase ready for oil pan installation (early 6 cyl. engines)
(© G.M.C.)

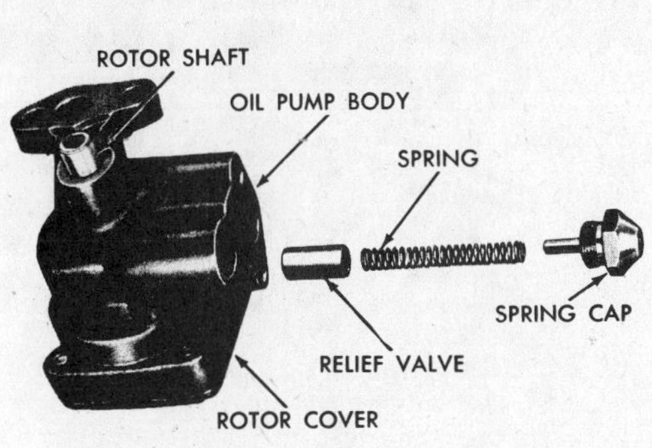

Oil pump and relief valve parts (typical)
(© G.M.C.)

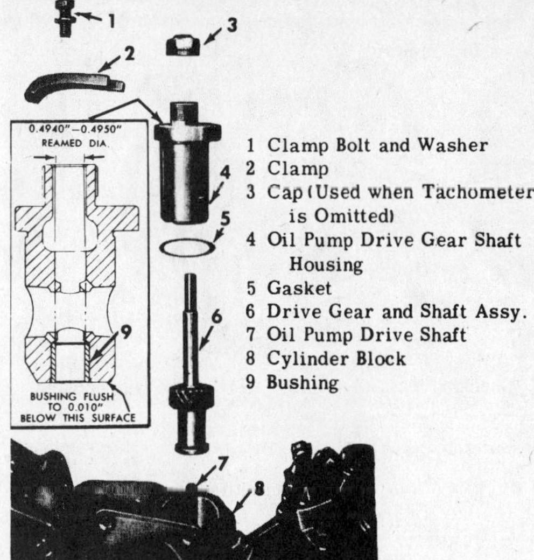

Oil pump and tachometer drive parts
(© G.M.C.)

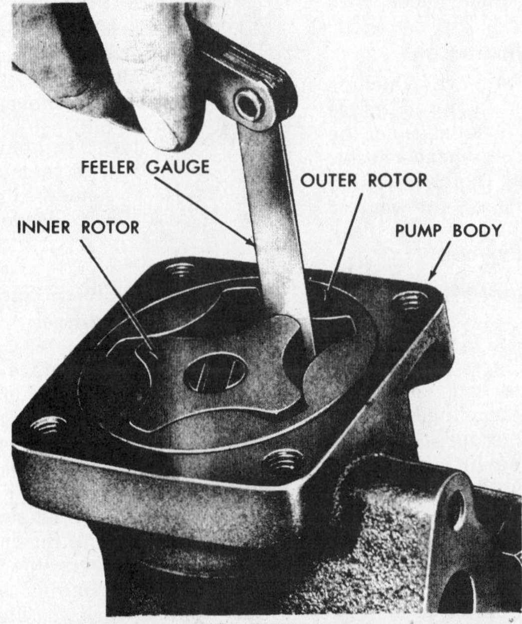

CHECKING INNER-TO-OUTER ROTOR CLEARANCE

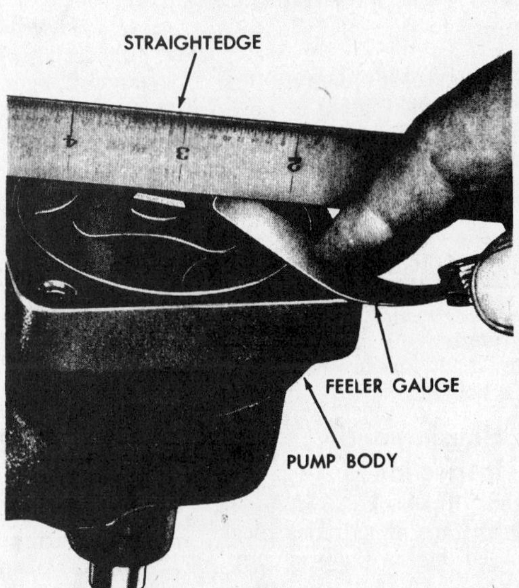

MEASURING ROTOR END CLEARANCE

Checking oil pump for wear (© G.M.C.)

gauge. If clearances are greater than specified in "Specifications," replace parts as necessary. Inner rotor and shaft are furnished for service as an assembly. With rotors in pump body, place straightedge across rotors and body, then with feeler gauge, measure clearance between rotors and straightedge. Clearance should be 0.0011 to 0.0039 inch.

5. Use straightedge to check rotor side of pump cover for flatness. Also look for grooves and other evidence of wear on pump cover. Replace cover if not in good condition.
6. Inspect relief valve and valve spring. On 6-cylinder engines without turbo-charger spring should have 14.7 to 16.3 pounds pressure when compressed to 1.69 inches. Spring free length should be 2.72 inches.

On turbo-charged 6-cylinder engines and 8-cylinder engines, free length of relief valve spring is 2.72 inches; and spring pressure is 17.8 to 19.4 pounds when compressed to 1.69 inches.

Assembling Oil Pump

1. Coat all oil pump parts with engine oil, then place outer rotor in pump body. Insert inner rotor shaft through bore in oil pump body and move inner rotor into mesh with outer rotor.
2. Install cover on pump body and retain with four cover screws. Try turning pump shaft which should turn freely without drag through six or more revolutions. If shaft cannot be turned or if binding occurs when shaft is turned, disassemble pump and make necessary corrections.
3. Insert relief valve and spring into body, then install spring cap.

Oil Pump Drive Shaft and Housing

The shaft and housing which drives the engine oil pump are installed at rear of cylinder block. The shaft has an attached gear which meshes with spiral gear teeth on camshaft. When tachometer is used, the cap is omitted and tachometer drive shaft housing is connected to threaded housing.

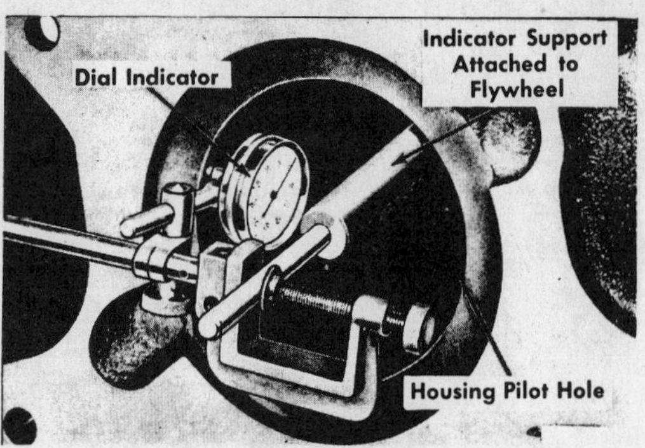

Checking location of pilot hole in apron type housing
(© G.M.C.)

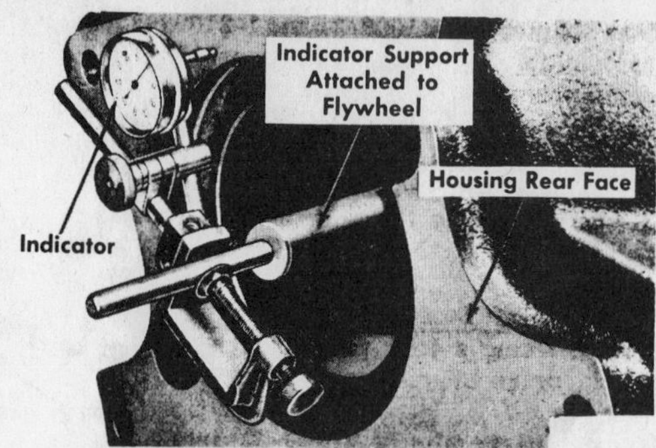

Checking flywheel housing for squareness (apron type)
(© G.M.C.)

Inspection

Check oil passages in housing and check clearance between shaft and bushing in housing. If bushing is worn, a new bushing may be installed.

If drive gear or shaft is worn or otherwise damaged, a new shaft and gear assembly must be installed at assembly.

Housing Bushing Replacement

1. Drive worn bushing out of housing and discard bushing.
2. Inspect edge of bore in housing and remove any sharp edges.
3. Press new bushing into housing to dimension shown.
4. If necessary to provide free fit of drive gear and shaft assembly in bushing, ream the bushing. Apply engine oil on shaft and bushing and insert shaft into place in housing.

Flywheel Housing and Flywheel Inspection

Cast iron flywheel housing is bolted to rear face of cylinder block and is located by two dowel pins. Some D351 engines have an apron type housing with pressed metal under pan. These housings have a small pilot opening in which the transmission drive gear retainer fits. Bosses are provided on these housings for attaching engine rear mounting brackets.

Other housings have a large SAE type opening to which the transmission bell housing is attached; inspection to determine squareness of housing rear face and concentricity of pilot opening should be made with housings bolted to cylinder block.

Flywheel Inspection

Inspect flywheel surface which is contacted by clutch facing. Surface must be smooth and should not be grooved or show deep heat checks. On flywheels having notches which drive clutch plate, inspect for wear at notches. Inspect starter ring gear which is shrunk on flywheel.

Correcting Flywheel Housing Misalignment

If flywheel housing is misaligned as indicated by check, cause of misalignment must be determined if possible and necessary measures must be taken to remedy the condition.

1. Remove housing from cylinder block and look for dirt or burrs on mating surfaces which may prevent housing from seating against cylinder block.
2. If misalignment is due to distortion, or combination of tolerances, try installing another housing from service stock.
3. When a selection of housings is not available, housing bore may be aligned by removing dowel pins from cylinder block, then align housing by shifting housing while held loosely in place by mounting bolts. If necessary, enlarge the mounting bolt holes to permit additional movement.
4. When aligned, tighten housing bolts firmly, then ream dowel pin holes to a convenient oversize and install overside dowel pins.

Machining Clutch Surface on Flywheel

When flywheel surface contacted by clutch facing is found to be scored, burned or worn, the flywheel can be restored to serviceable condition by machining to provide a smooth, flat surface. Do not remove more than 1/32-inch of stock in machining. After machining friction surface on recessed type flywheel, remove a corresponding amount of stock from surface to which clutch cover is bolted.

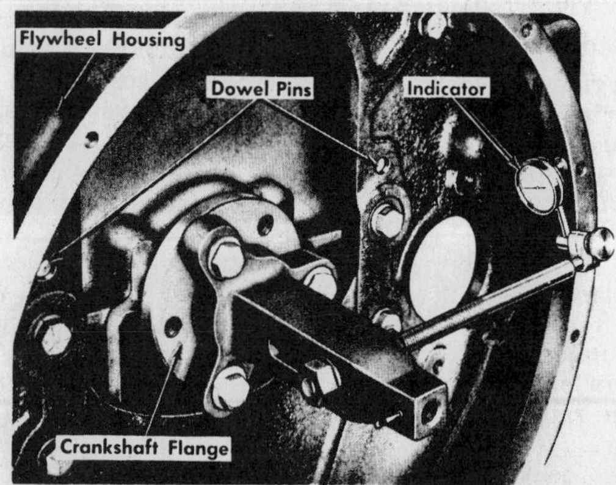

Checking for concentricity of flywheel housing pilot bore
(© G.M.C.)

Checking for squareness of bolting flange on flywheel housing
(© G.M.C.)

Perkins Diesel Engines

Index

Specifications

Trouble Diagnosis

Cooling System

Engine Service

Fuel System

GENERAL SPECIFICATIONS

ENGINE MODEL	BORE AND STROKE	HORSEPOWER @ R.P.M.	TORQUE FT. LBS. @ R.P.M.	COMPRESSION PRESSURE CRANKING SPEED	FIRING ORDER	GOVERNED SPEED NO LOAD R.P.M.	GOVERNED SPEED FULL LOAD R.P.M.	GOVERNED SPEED IDLE SPEED
354D	3.875 x 5	120 @ 2800	260 @ 1450	430	153624	3000	2800	525

PISTONS, PINS, RINGS, CRANKSHAFT AND BEARINGS

ENGINE MODEL	PISTON CLEARANCE	PISTON RING END GAP MINIMUM COMP.	PISTON RING END GAP MINIMUM OIL	PISTON PIN DIAMETER	ROD BEARING SHAFT DIAMETER	ROD BEARING BEARING CLEARANCE	MAIN BEARING SHAFT DIAMETER	MAIN BEARING BEARING CLEARANCE	SHAFT END PLAY	THRUST ON BEARING NO.
354D	.0059	.015	.011	1.375	2.499-2.4995	.002-.004	2.9985-2.999	.0025-.0045	.006-.014	4

VALVE SPECIFICATIONS

ENGINE MODEL	VALVE LASH (HOT)	VALVE FACE ANGLE	VALVE STEM CLEARANCE INTAKE	VALVE STEM CLEARANCE EXHAUST	VALVE GUIDE BORE	VALVE STEM DIAMETER INTAKE	VALVE STEM DIAMETER EXHAUST	VALVE SPRINGS TEST LENGTH INNER	VALVE SPRINGS TEST LENGTH OUTER	VALVE SPRINGS TEST PRESS. LBS. INNER	VALVE SPRINGS TEST PRESS. LBS. OUTER
354D	.010	45°	.0015-.0035	.002-.004	.3750-.3760	.3725-.3735	.3720-.3730	1 9/16" @ 15 lbs.	1 25/32" @ 40 lb.	1 9/61" @ 15 lb.	1 25/32" @ 40 lb

ENGINE TORQUE SPECIFICATIONS

ENGINE MODEL	CYLINDER HEAD FT. LBS.	INTAKE MANIFOLD FT. LBS.	EXHAUST MANIFOLD FT. LBS.	CONN. ROD FT. LBS.	MAIN BEARING CAPS FT. LBS.	CHANKSHAFT END NUT FT. LBS.	FLYWHEEL CRANKSHAFT TO FT. LBS.	CAMSHAFT GEAR BOLT FT. LBS.	FUEL INJECTOR NUTS FT. LBS.	OIL PAN BOLTS FT. LBS.
354D	1	31-36	41-45	65-70	145-150	250-275	75-80	45-50	23-26	10-15

1—7/16" studs 55-60 lbs. ½" studs 80 lbs.

Trouble Diagnosis

The satisfactory performance of a Diesel engine depends on two items of foremost importance, (1) Sufficiently high compression pressure, and (2) The injection of the proper amount of fuel at the right time.

The first one of these items depends entirely on pistons, piston rings, valves and valve operating mechanism; the second item depends on injectors and their operating mechanism, and fuel system.

Lack of engine power, uneven running, excessive vibration, and tendency to stall when idling may be caused by either a compression loss or faulty injector operation.

The causes of trouble symptoms may be varied; therefore a hit-and-miss search should be avoided. A proper diagnosis of symptoms is an orderly process of diagnosing the symptoms. An "orderly process" means to check the most probable common cause first; then proceed with the next probable cause.

Hard Starting

1. No fuel at injectors.
   a. No fuel in tank.
   b. Stop control in "stop" position.
   c. Air in fuel system.
2. Oil in crankcase too heavy.
3. Wrong type fuel oil.
4. Injection pump timing wrong.
5. Injectors in need of service.
6. Cold starting aid inoperative.
7. Poor compression in one or more cylinders.

No Power (Exhaust Clean)

1. Restricted fuel supply.
   a. Restriction on suction side of fuel pump.
   b. Air leak on suction side of fuel pump.
   c. Block fuel filter.
   d. Faulty low pressure fuel pump.
2. Incorrect fuel injection pump delivery.

Low Power Max R.P.M. Low (Clean Exhaust)

1. Throttle lever not reaching wide open position.
2. Air in fuel system.

Low Power, Engine Misfires (Clean Exhaust)

1. One or more broken or cracked fuel lines.

Low Power Engine Smooth (Smoky Exhaust)

1. Blocked air cleaner.
2. Wrong injector settings.
3. Incorrect valve lash.
4. Wrong grade fuel oil.
5. Injection pump timing late.

Low Power (Engine and Exhaust Overheat)

1. Injection timing late.

Low Power Engine Misfires (Dirty Exhaust)

1. One or more injectors faulty.
2. Injection pump timing late.
3. Broken parts in fuel injection pump.
4. Valves bad in one or more cylinders.

Low Power Engine Misfires Engine Has Metallic Knock (Dirty Exhaust)

1. Exhaust valves badly carboned.
2. Needle stuck in injector.
3. One or more rocker levers broken.
4. One or more push rods bent.

Blow By From Breather Tube

1. One or more pistions and/or liners scored.

Power Good Poor Fuel Mileage (Exhaust Smoky and Black)

1. Fuel pump delivery too high due to unauthorized adjustment.

Fuel Oil in Oil Pan

1. Diaphragm on low pressure pump leaking.
2. "O" ring on fuel injection pump leaking.
3. Bad injectors.

Water in Oil Pan or Oil in Radiator

1. Cracked head or block.
2. Blown head gasket.

General Description

The Perkins-6-354 Diesel engine is a vertical four stroke cycle power unit. It is entirely of British Design and Manufacture and embodies the results of experience gained in production of Diesel Engines over a period of many years.

The Perkins-6-354 Diesel engine is a six-cylinder direct injection unit having a 3⅞" bore and 5" stroke.

Fuel System

The efficient operation of a diesel engine depends on the correct amount of fuel being injected into the cylinder at exactly the right time in the operating cycle. It also depends upon each cylinder being fully charged with air that has been compressed to the correct pressure and temperature in order to provide the necessary oxygen for complete and efficient combustion of the injected fuel oil.

Trouble shooting the fuel system becomes basically a process of elimination of the various components to ascertain which one is not functioning as it should. From this it follows that any malfunction in the combustion cycle will result in inefficient and/or incomplete burning of the fuel and air mixture, therefore, the most common complaint is likely to be "No Power."

The causes of "No Power" fall into two major categories which are fairly easy to diagnose, the Key being the condition of the exhaust gas.

If the *correct* amount of fuel is being injected but power is low, the exhaust gasses will be heavy and generally black, brown or whitish brown in color due to incomplete combustion in the cylinders.

If too much fuel is being injected the exhaust will be black in color but the power will be good.

If sufficient fuel is being injected and power is low, the exhaust gasses will be hardly visible due to complete burning of the mixture in the cylinders.

Other associated complaints will be in the nature of:

1. Hard starting.
2. Flames in exhaust pipe.
3. Rough idle and missing at light loads.
4. Noisy and vibrating.
5. Overheating (especially the exhaust).
6. Low governed speed.

Fuel Filters

Always be careful to keep dirt of any kind from the fuel system. Within the system itself much has been done to be sure that only clean fuel oil reaches the fuel injection pump and nozzles. Fuel oil filters are provided as follows:

The *primary filter* is a screen unit located in the upper half of the fuel supply pump.

It should be removed for cleaning, every 12,000 miles or oftener as conditions warrant. The primary filter may be removed by unscrewing the bolt which secures the domed cover to the top of the fuel supply pump.

When reassembling after cleaning, make sure that a good joint is made between cover and fuel supply pump body. Any leakage of air here may cause air locks in the fuel system.

The *secondary* or *final filter* contains a paper element, this element being located between top and bottom covers the filter. Do not attempt to clean the paper element, it should be *replaced* every 20,000 miles.

Fuel Filter Replacement

1. Unscrew bolt in center of top cover.
2. Remove filter bottom cover.
3. Remove paper element and discard.
4. Clean filter top and bottom covers.
5. Make sure that rubber joints are in good condition or replace.
6. After reassembling, prime fuel system.

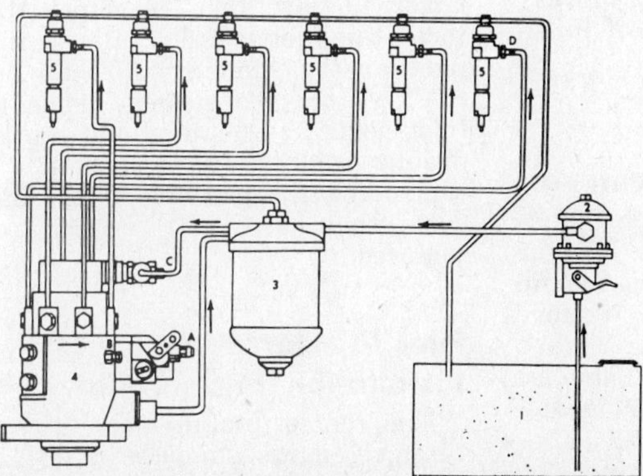

1 Tank
2 Supply pump
3 Filter
4 Injection pump
5 Injection nozzles
A Vent screw—governor housing
B Vent screw—head locking screw
C Fitting—pump fuel inlet
D Unions—Nozzle fuel inlet

Fuel system with C.A.V. hydraulic governed injection pump
(© Chrysler Corp.)

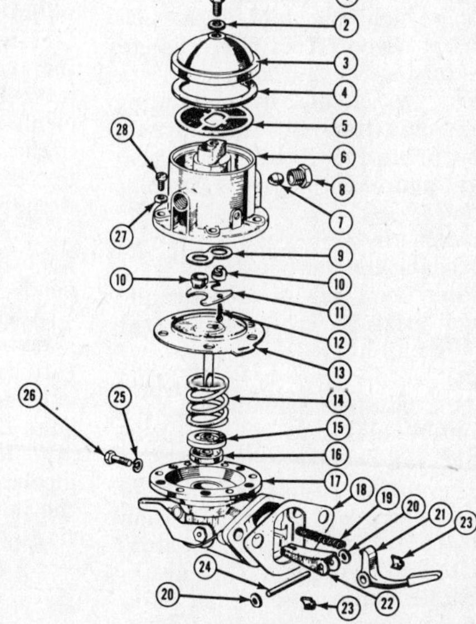

Fuel pump
(© Chrysler Corp.)

1 Bolt, fuel pump cover
2 Washer
3 Cover, fuel pump
4 Gasket, cover
5 Screen, fuel filter
6 Body, pump, upper half
7 Sleeve
8 Nut
9 Gasket, inlet & outlet valve
10 Valve, inlet & outlet
11 Retainer, valve
12 Screw, retainer
13 Diaphragm
14 Spring, diaphragm
15 Retainer, oil seal
16 Seal, oil
17 Body, pump lower half
18 Gasket, pump mounting
19 Spring, lever
20 Washer, rocker arm pin
21 Arm, rocker
22 Lever
23 Retainer
24 Pin, rocker arm
25. Washer, lock
26 Bolt
27 Washer
28 Screw

Removing fuel pump from engine
(© Chrysler Corp.)

Installing fuel filter
(© Chrysler Corp.)

Fuel Supply Pump

The fuel supply pump is of the diaphragm type similar to the type used on gasoline engines. It is located on the right side of the engine and driven by an eccentric cam on the camshaft. A hand primer is an integral part of the fuel supply pump. Use the hand primer to pump fuel from tank until supply pump, filters, pipes, and injection pump are filled with fuel.

Priming System

Whenever an attempt is made to start a new or rebuilt engine, an engine on which the fuel lines have been disconnected (fuel filter change, service of injection pump, etc.), or an engine which has been standing idle for some time, the fuel system must be primed or bled. The procedure for priming the fuel system is as follows:

1. Loosen air vent screw on top of governor control housing.
2. Loosen vent screw in hydraulic head locking screw on side of fuel pump body.
3. Operate priming lever of fuel supply pump and when fuel, free from bubbles, flows from around from air bubbles, flows from each venting point, tighten head locking screw vent first and then vent screw on governor housing.
4. Loosen pipe union fitting at injection pump fuel inlet and supply pump. When fuel, free threads, retighten fitting.
5. Loosen unions at nozzle ends of two of high pressure fuel injection pipes.
6. Set accelerator at full open position and make sure "stop" control is in "run" position.
7. Crank engine until fuel oil, free from air bubbles, flows from both fuel pipes.
8. Retighten unions on fuel injection pipes. The engine is now ready for starting.

Fuel Injection Pump

The C.A.V. Model DPA fuel injection pump is a distributor type pump incorporating an all speed governor and an automatic advance.

Pumping is effected by a single pumping element, having twin opposed plungers, situated transversely in a central rotating member which also acts as a distributor. The rotor revolves in a stationary member, known as the hydraulic head. The pump plungers are operated by contact with cam lobes on a stationary internal cam ring. The fuel is metered before entering the pumping element, and the accurately metered high pressure charges are distributed to the engine cylinders in correct firing order and at the required timing intervals through a system of ports in the rotor and the hydraulic head.

A simple hydraulic type governor is embodied in the pump to give accurate control of engine speed throughout the complete speed range of the engine and under all conditions of engine loading. An automatic advance mechanism is also provided to vary the point of commencement of injection.

Fuel Injection Pump Removal

Disconnect the fuel injector lines at the injectors and at the injector pump. Unbolt the mounting clamp from the cylinder head and remove the six injector lines as an assembly.

Injector lines must be handled carefully to avoid bending or damaging. Dirt or chips should not be allowed to enter fuel lines. Do not disassemble injector line assembly unless one or more of the lines are to be replaced. Cover or tape fuel openings on the injection pump to prevent dirt from entering the pump.

Disconnect the accelerator and stop cable, remove the three injection pump attaching stud nuts and lift out the injection pump.

Fuel Injection Pump Repairs

Disassembly or repair of the fuel injection pump should never be attempted by anyone other than an authorized C.A.V. dealer, since special equipment is needed to properly service and repair this assembly. Satisfactory repair and adjustment are impossible without proper test equipment and procedures.

Fuel Metering

Apart from small losses which occur during the injection stroke, the total volume of fuel introduced into the element is passed on to the nozzle. Metering is effected, therefore, by regulating the volume of fuel which enters the element at each charging stroke. The volume of the charge is governed by two principal factors—the fuel pressure at the inlet port, and the time available for fuel to flow into the element while the inlet ports in the rotor and the hydraulic head are in register. It is by controlling the pressure at the inlet port that accurate metering is achieved.

Fuel Injector Pump Installation and Timing

The correct static injection pump timing (engine stopped) is 24° before top dead center. If the procedure we are covering here is followed carefully, the correct specified timing will result.

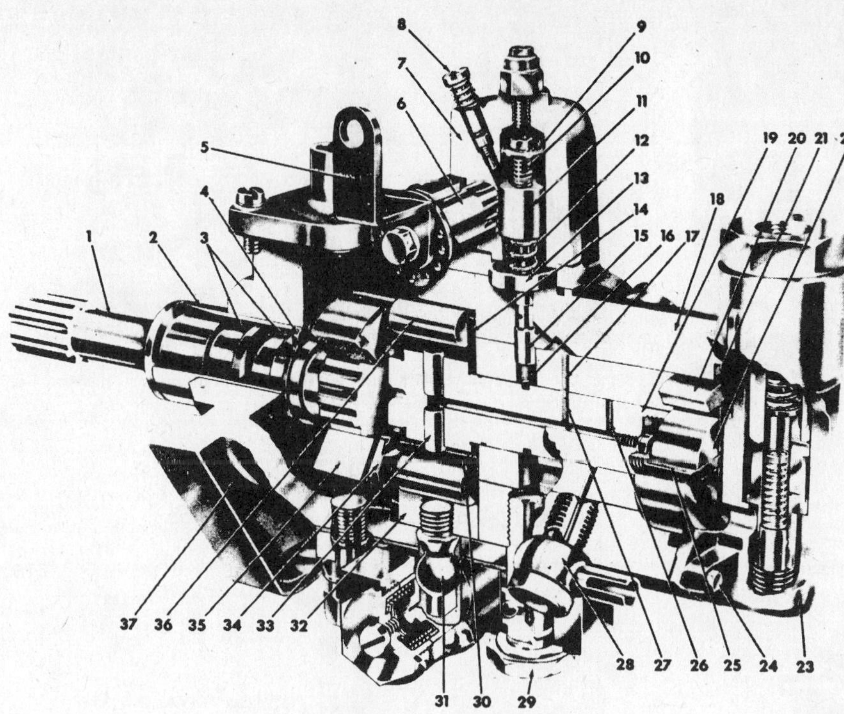

C.A.V. fuel injection pump (© Chrysler Corp.)

1 Shaft, splined
2 Tube, pilot
3 Seals, oil
4 Ring, snap
5 Lever, control
6 Shaft, pinion
7 Housing, governor
8 Screw, idle
9 Washer
10 Spring, idle
11 Rack
12 Spring, governor
13 Plate, dished (dashpot)
14 Plate, roller to roller adjusting
15 Valve, metering
16 Chamber, metering
17 Port, charging
18 Head, hydraulic
19 Rotor, distributing
20 Liner, transfer pump
21 Seal, "O" ring
22 Rotor, transfer pump
23 Plate, end
24 Bolt, end plate
25 Vane, sliding
26 Port, distributor
27 Hole, radial
28 Connector, nozzle pipe
29 Fitting, head locating with damper
30 Shoe, roller
31 Screw, cam advance
32 Ring, cam
33 Plunger
34 Plate, roller to roller adjusting
35 Plate, drive
36 Roller, cam
37 Housing, pump

The fuel injection pump adapter plate has a slot, approximatley 1/8" wide in its inside diameter. Also, on the edge of the adapter plate flange, adjacent to one of the bolt holes a scribed line will be found.

Set the adapter plate in position on the three mounting studs with the scribe line next to the stud which is farthest from the center of the engine.

The timing mark for top dead center is located on the front face of flywheel. A pointer is located on flywheel housing.

To check timing, make certain the number one piston is at exact top dead center, and is on the compression stroke as follows: With valve cover removed rotate the crankshaft with the flywheel. When the number six exhaust valve is just seating, align the mark on the flywheel with the pointer. Number one cylinder will be at T.D.C.

A slot approximately 1/8" wide can be seen on the top edge of the fuel injection pump drive hub on the vertical shaft.

Rotate the auxiliary shaft and fuel injection pump drive shaft in the direction of engine rotation, to where the 1/8" slot in injector pump drive hub exactly aligns with the 1/8" slot in inside diameter of adapter plate.

Place the auxiliary drive shaft gear on front of the shaft with chamfered side in, and so when it is against the mounting flange on shaft, the bolt holes in the flange are at center of slotted holes in the gear. If the bolt holes will not center in the slot-

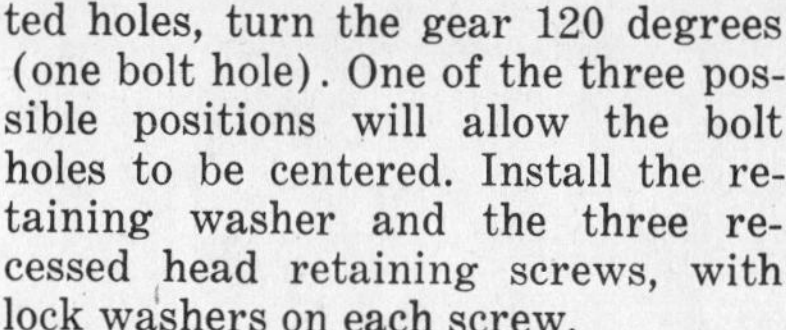
ted holes, turn the gear 120 degrees (one bolt hole). One of the three possible positions will allow the bolt holes to be centered. Install the retaining washer and the three recessed head retaining screws, with lock washers on each screw.

Check to make sure that the 1/8" slot in fuel injection pump drive hub is exactly aligned with corresponding slot in adapter plate. If some slight correction is necessary, bring the slots into alignment by turning injection pump vertical drive shaft. Then tighten the three gear retaining screws securely.

With the gasket positioned on the studs, align the master spline on the fuel injection pump shaft with the master spline in the vertical shaft, and set injection pump on adapter plate.

Align scribed line on injection pump mounting flange with scribed line on adapter plate, and tighten the three retaining nuts securely.

With Gasket Sealer on each side of gaskets, install camshaft gear cover and auxiliary drive shaft gear cover and tighten the bolts.

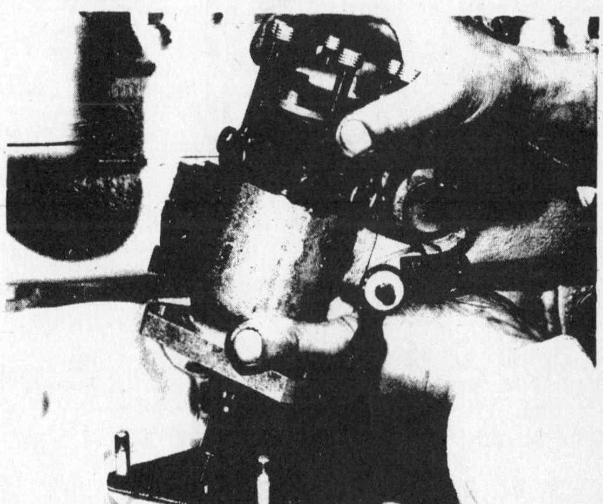

Removing injection pump
(© Chrysler Corp.)

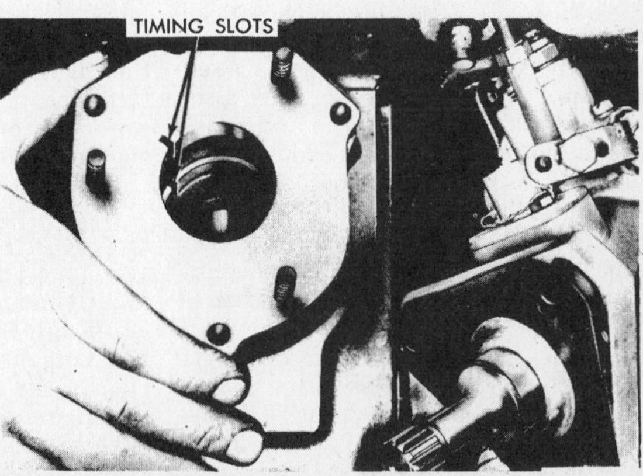

Alignment of timing slots
(© Chrysler Corp.)

Alignment of scribed line on injector pump and adapter plate
(© Chrysler Corp.)

Timing mark on flywheel and pointer
(© Chrysler Corp.)

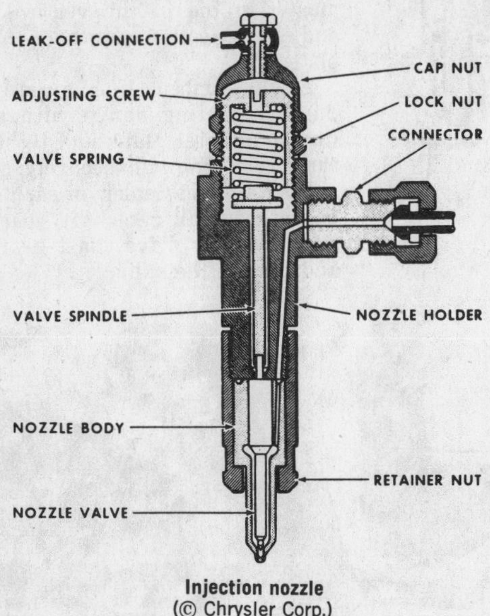

Injection nozzle
(© Chrysler Corp.)

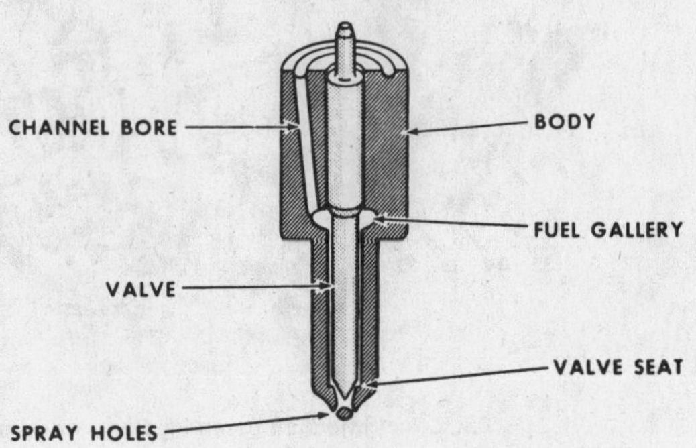

Nozzle valve and body (removed from holder)
(© Chrysler Corp.)

Removing nozzle assembly
(© Chrysler Corp.)

Install the vibration damper and pulley assembly, retaining washer and nut, tightening the nut to 250 foot-pounds.

Injector Nozzles

General Information

The performance of the high speed diesel engine depends largely on the proper function of its fuel injection system. For maximum efficiency it is essential the engine be not only provided with metered amounts of fuel at exactly timed intervals, but also that it receives each charge of fuel in the proper condition so it can be completely consumed without causing smoke in the exhaust. This briefly is the function of the injection nozzle assembly. The complete assembly consists of a nozzle and a nozzle holder.

Nozzle Maintenance

All nozzles should be removed from the engine at regular intervals. Just how long these intervals should be, depends on the different conditions under which the engine will operate. Where ideal conditions of good combustion, adequate cooling, and absolutely clean fuel are realized, the nozzles will need little attention. Since the efficiency of the nozzles vitally affects the performance and economical operation of the diesel engine, no engine should be allowed to run with nozzles that are defective.

Nozzle trouble is usually indicated by one or more of the following symptoms:

1. Cylinder knock.
2. Engine overheating
3. Loss of power
4. Smoky exhaust (black)
5. Increased fuel consumption.

While the above faults may be caused by defective nozzles, it should also be determined that they are not caused by other engine troubles such as wrong fuel, water in fuel, dirty or damaged filters, incorrect maximum fuel setting, defective engine lubrication, incorrect pump timing, incorrect engine valve timing, or faulty valves.

If everything else is in order and the nozzles are still suspected, the nozzle causing the trouble can often be found by releasing the pipe union nut on each nozzle in turn, with engine running and listening to the idling performance of each of the cylinders.

Nozzle Testing

To test a doubtful nozzle, loosen injection pipe at both ends and remove nozzle holder from cylinder head. *A blast of compressed air around each nozzle before loosening the holder*

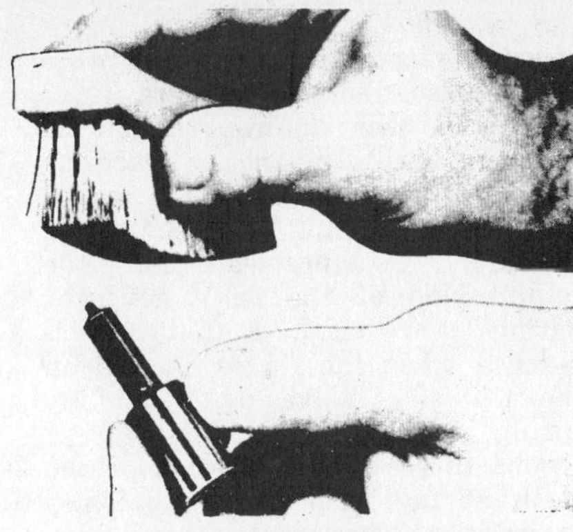
Cleaning nozzle with brass wire brush
(© Chrysler Corp.)

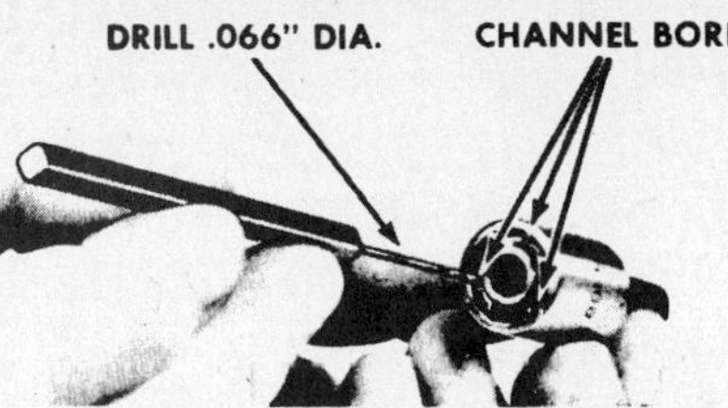

Cleaning nozzle body channel bores
(© Chrysler Corp.)

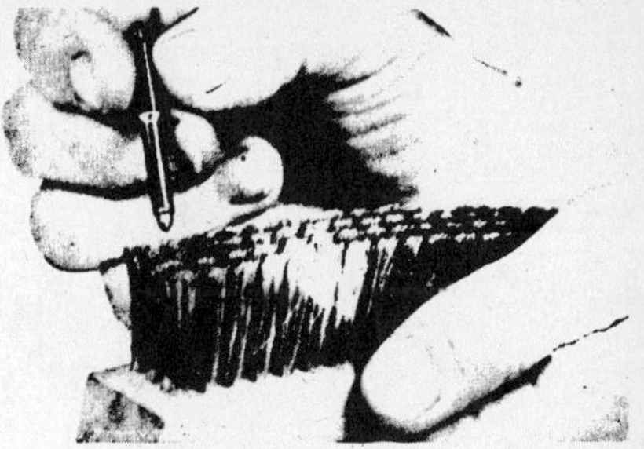
Cleaning valve tip with brass wire brush
(© Chrysler Corp.)

will help prevent dirt or moisture from entering the combustion chamber when nozzle is removed. Turn the nozzle and holder around the injection pipe so that nozzle points away from engine. Retighten both ends of injection line. Next, loosen pipe unions at the other nozzles to prevent fuel oil from being sprayed into cylinders. Turn engine with starter until the removed nozzle sprays fuel into the air. If spray is "wet," or "streaky," or to one side, or if the nozzle "dribbles," remove and install a complete new or reconditioned unit.

WARNING: Keep hands away from spray. The working pressure will cause oil to penetrate the skin.

After making a nozzle replacement, the faulty unit should be sent to a test bench for cleaning and testing.

Nozzle Cleaning, Inspection

Nozzle maintenance like injection pump maintenance should be performed in a clean dust-free place where no other work is performed. A work bench with a holding fixture or small vise with soft jaws is essential for making the disassembly. A hand test pump with a good supply of clean diesel fuel or test oil should also be provided.

1. Attach injecton nozzle to hand test pump and check completely for spray pattern nozzle opening pressure setting, and back leakage.
2. If nozzle is faulty secure nozzle assembly in holding fixture or vise. Release pressure on nozzle valve spring by loosening lock nut and adjusting screw. Remove nozzle retainer nut and nozzle.
3. Inspect nozzle for carbon and note whether valve lifts out freely. Brush all carbon from outside with a brass wire brush. Place body and valve in clean fuel oil or cleaning solvent to soak and soften carbon. *The nozzle should be free from all damage and not "blued" from overheating. All polished surfaces should be relatively bright without scratches or dull patches. All pressure surfaces must be clean since these must mate to form a high pressure joint between nozzle holder and nozzle.*
4. Clean small feed channel bores with drill or wire of .066 inch diameter. These bores are rarely choked and insertion of drill or wire by hand will be sufficient.
5. Insert probe or groove scraper in fuel gallery and press against side of cavity to clear all carbon deposits from this area.
6. Clean all carbon from valve seat area by rotating and pressing probe on to seat.
7. Clear spray holes with appropriate size cleaning wire. Do not break wire in holes since such particles are almost impossible to remove (Hole Dia-.0126 in.).
8. Install nozzle in a flushing tool that can be coupled to a nozzle hand test pump and wash out all carbon particles. Force fuel or test oil through nozzle vigorously since this is best way to remove loosened particles that may still be present both in body cavities and spray holes.
9. Clean nozzle valve tip by brushing away carbon with a brass wire brush. To assemble valve into nozzle, immerse both items in clean fuel oil and fit them together under surface so as to prevent closely fitting lapped surfaces from being touched by hand. *If nozzle is blued or seat has a dull ring indicating wear or pitting, complete unit should be set aside. No attempt should be made to lap nozzle valve and body unless special training and equipment are available.*
10. Make sure lapped pressure faces on both nozzle and holder are clean and free from metalic particles. If holder has been disassembled, all parts should be thoroughly washed in fuel oil or cleaning solvent.

Injector Installation

Before installing injectors, make certain that all of the old copper sealing washers have been removed from the recesses in the cylinder head and have been discarded. Use only new copper sealing washers of the correct replacement part number. Old copper sealing washers can be removed with a piece of bent wire.

The recess in cylinder head, the faces of the copper washer, and corresponding face on injector must be thoroughly clean to avoid possible combustion leakage.

Place copper washer in position, and then injector. Make sure injector is an easy fit in the recess and on attaching studs, and that it can be placed down on copper washer without any force of any kind.

The nuts on attaching studs should then be tightened down evenly in order to prevent the injector nozzle from becoming cocked and bound in cylinder head.

This is very important, since any unevenness in tightening down may cause distortion and eventual failure of the injector nozzle, and will most certainly result in faulty sealing at copper washer.

Governor

The hydraulic governor is of simple design, the working parts being contained in a small housing. The control lever is carried on a pinion shaft, the pinion meshing with a rack which is free to slide on the metering valve stem.

The metering valve slides in a chamber in the hydraulic head, into which bore the diagonally drilled metering port opens.

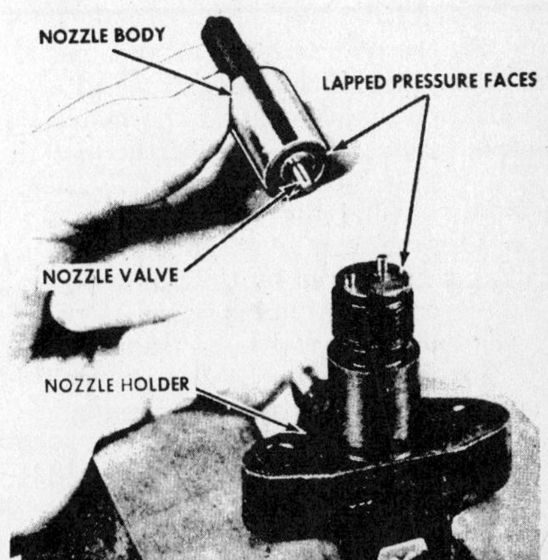

Pressure faces of nozzle and holder
(© Chrysler Corp.)

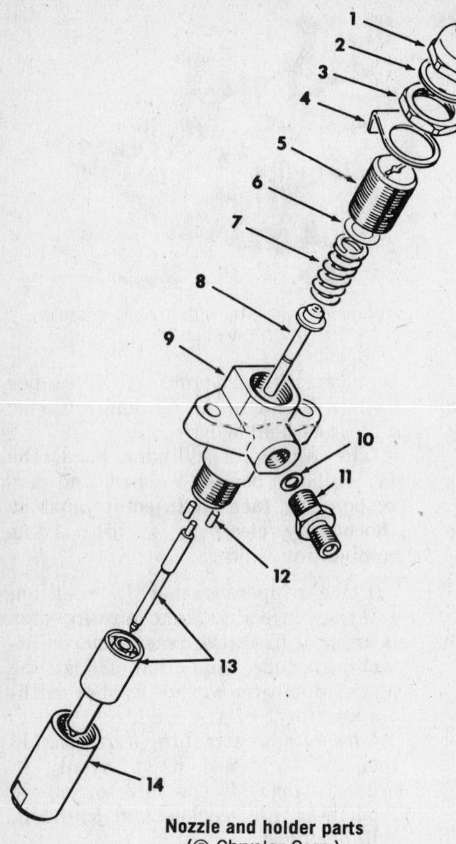

1 Nut, cap
2 Gasket, cap nut
3 Nut, lock
4 Washer, locknut tab
5 Screw, valve spring adjusting
6 Washer, adjusting screw
7 Spring, valve
8 Spindle, valve
9 Holder, nozzle
10 Gasket, connector
11 Connector, inlet
12 Pin, dowel
13 Nozzle, body and valve assy.
14 Nut, nozzle retainer

Nozzle and holder parts
(© Chrysler Corp.)

A self-centering damping washer is carried on the valve stem against a shoulder, the governor spring being held between the plate and the rack. The plate slides in a cylindrical bore filled with fuel, and acts as a dashpot to damp out any violent movement of the metering valve.

An idling spring is located between the rack and the washer fitted at the top of the valve spindle and known as the shut-off washer. A screw is placed so as to form an idling stop.

The governor is operated by fuel at transfer pressure which is fed from the annular groove surrounding the pump rotor. The fuel passes through the metering valve, which is hollow, and via transverse holes to an annular space around the valve.

End wise movement of the metering valve varies the area of the metering port which registers with the annulus around the valve; the effective area of the port is that part which is uncovered by the inner edge of the groove or annulus.

The metering valve is loaded by the governor spring and this load may be manually adjusted by moving the control lever.

As the engine control is operated to give increased speed, the valve is pushed to the full open position by the governor spring. When engine speed increases, transfer pressure increases also, and this pressure forces the valve back against the spring pressure until a balance is reached.

When the engine control is moved towards the idling stop, the idling spring is compressed, and the compression of the main governor spring is reduced. Equilibrium is reached when the forces exerted on the metering valve by the idling spring and fuel at transfer pressure are balanced by compression of the main spring. The latter becomes progressively less as the engine control is moved towards the idling stop, thus enabling the reduced transfer pressure at low speeds to operate the metering valve and perform the governing function throughout the idling range.

Details of the valve and the shut-off mechanism are shown in illustration. The shut-off spindle is carried in the governor housing, and carries a half-round end or "cam," which contacts the underside of the shut-off washer. Rotation of the spindle by the shut-off lever lifts the metering valve to a position where the metering port is blanked off, and thus stops the engine.

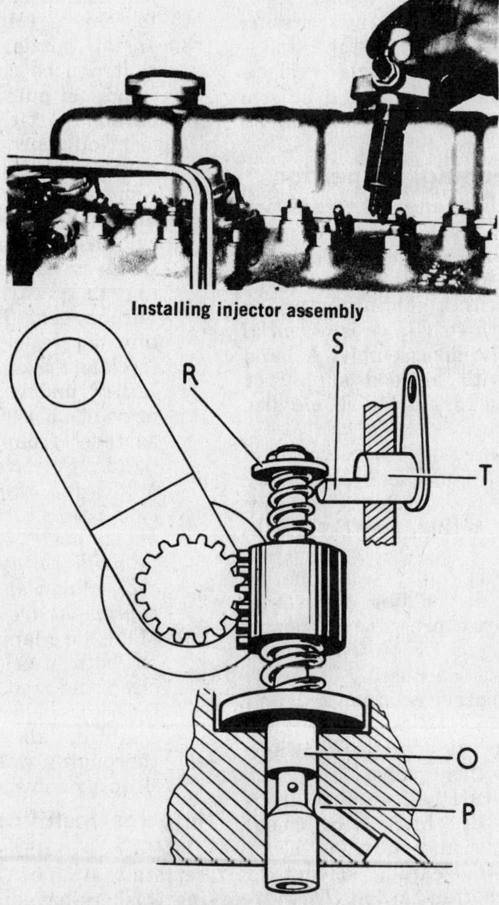

Installing injector assembly

Details of motoring valve and shut-off spindle of hydraulic governor
(© Chrysler Corp.)

Automatic Advance

Under full load conditions, the max imum amount of fuel is introduced into the element, and the plungers and actuating rollers are forced outwards to the limit of their travel. As the rotor turns, the rollers are brought into contact with cam lobes on the cam ring. The point of contact is near the base of the cams.

Under lightly loaded conditions, fueling is decreased and the plunger travel is proportionally reduced. Contact between roller and cam is now made at a point near the cam peak.

The advance device corrects the tendency of the pump to retard timing under varying load conditions at constant speed.

The device illustrated provides progressive advancement of injection timing as engine speed is increased.

The piston is free to slide in a cylinder machined in the body of the device. Movement of this piston is transmitted to the cam ring by the ball-ended lever, causing the cam ring to rotate within the pump housing.

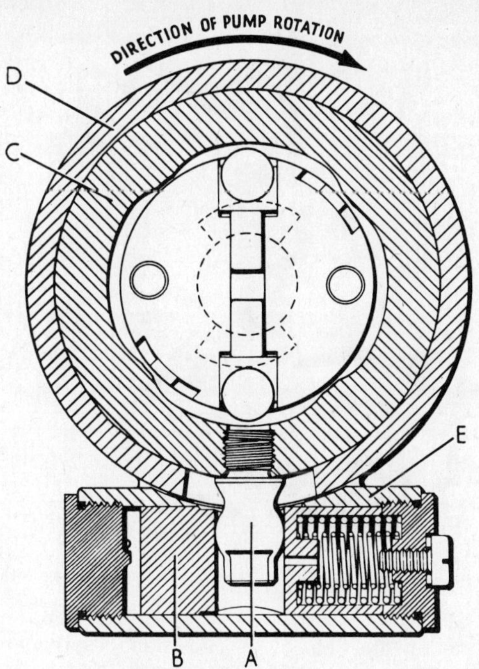

Automatic advance mechanism
(© Chrysler Corp.)

Pressure exerted on the piston by the springs, tends to hold the piston and the cam ring in the fully retarded position.

Fuel oil at transfer pressure enters the device through a fuel passage in the screw which secures the device to the pump housing. Transfer prssur acts upon the piston and tends to move the cam ring towards the fully advanced position.

Transfer pressure increases progressively as the engine speed is raised, and the piston is moved along the cylinder to compress the springs and move the cam ring towards the fully advanced position. When engine speed is decreased, transfer pressure falls, and the piston and cam ring are moved towards the retarded position by spring pressure.

The impact of the actuating rollers on the cam lobes at commencement of injection tends to move the cam ring towards the retarded position. Such movement is prevented by a non-return valve situated in the fuel passage in the screw securing the device to the pump housing. Normal leakage between the piston and the cylinder permits the device to return to the retarded position when the engine speed falls.

Any desired timing advance up to a maximum of 9° (pump) is obtainable, and the engine speed at which this is attained can be varied by fitting stronger or weaker springs. The stronger the spring the higher will be the engine speed at which maximum timing advance is attained. Fine adjustment is made by shims fitted between the springs and the spring cap.

Governor No-Load Speed Setting

1. Warm engine to normal operating temperature.
2. Use accurate tachometer for checking engine speed.
3. Increase engine speed until governor control is apparent; this should be 3600-3700 rpm. If necessary, break seal and readjust by changing tension on governor spring. Increasing tension increases speed 50 rpm per turn of nut.

Water Pump

Removal and Installation

1. Drain cooling system and remove fan belt and fan.
2. Use a suitable puller and remove pump pulley.

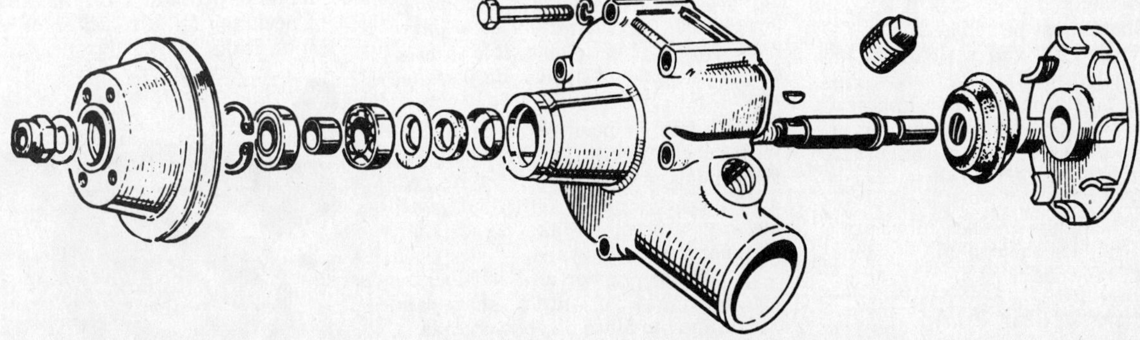

Water pump (disassembled view) (© Chrysler Corp.)

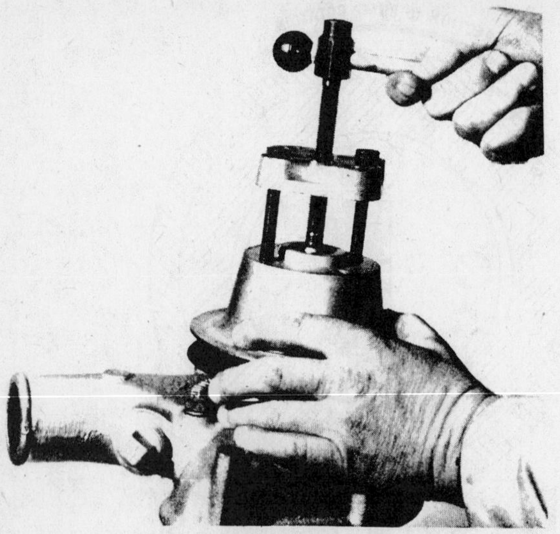

Removing water pump pulley
(© Chrysler Corp.)

Installing bearing retainer snap ring
(© Chrysler Corp.)

3. Remove the pump to block mounting bolts and remove the pump.
4. Install by reversing the removal procedures.

Servicing Water Pump

Remove the self-locking nut and flat washer which secure water pump pulley to pump shaft.

Using remover, pull the pulley from pump shaft. Remove key.

Press water pump shaft, complete with impeller, out through the rear of pump body. Press impeller off shaft.

Using snap ring pliers, remove bearing retaining snap ring from front of pump body.

With a suitable tool, press the two bearings and spacer out through front of pump body.

To complete disassembly of water pump, remove front seal, retainer, and flange.

Inspection of Water Pump Parts

Examine pump body for cracks, damage or corrosion.

Examine pump shaft for wear. If pump bearing inner races rotate on shaft, shaft must be replaced.

Clean all rust and scale from impeller, and inspect it for cracks and damage. Examine impeller hub sealing surface for wear or scoring. If impeller shows any damage, cracks or wear at seal surface, it should be replaced.

Wash bearings in thin lubricating oil, and replace them if any evidence of wear is found.

Assemble Water Pump

Press rear bearing onto front of shaft, and against shoulder, with sealed end of bearing toward rear of shaft.

Position bearing spacer on shaft, and press front bearing against spacer with sealed end of bearing toward front end of shaft.

Place front seal retaining flange in position against rear face of rear bearing. This dished flange must be positioned so the center of flange is not in contact with bearing.

Position first the front seal, and then seal retainer against retainer flange.

Half fill the space between the two bearings with short fibre water pump grease, or multi-purpose chassis grease and press the complete assembly into pump body through front end. Then position bearing snap ring firmly in groove, using snap ring pliers.

Place a new rear seal in pump on rear end of pump shaft with carbon face to rear so it will contact the impeller hub. Make sure seal is resting squarely, and is not cocked in any way.

At this point, the shaft should be rotated by hand to be sure it turns without binding.

Some of the attaching bolts must be entered in the holes in the pump body before pressing on the pump pulley, since it is not possible to position them after the pulley is installed

With key in position in shaft and with necessary attaching bolts in their holes, support shaft at its rear end, and press pulley onto shaft, with keyway aligned. Make sure shaft does not move rearward.

Install flat washer and self-locking nut on front of pump shaft and tighten nut to 50 to 55 foot-pounds.

Press impeller onto shaft to where clearance between pump body and inner edge of impeller vanes is between .012″ and .019″.

Engine Section

Engine Removal and Installation

1. Disconnect battery.
2. Drain cooling system and engine oil.
3. Disconnect fuel in-line and return line, and exhaust pipe. Remove air cleaner.
4. Disconnect wiring for alternator, gauges, switches, etc.
5. Bleed air booster brake and disconnect line.
6. Disconnect hydraulic clutch line, stop control cable accelerator and hand throttle, coolant and heater hoses.
7. Remove radiator.
8. Remove driveshaft and transmission.
9. Install engine lifting sling.
10. Remove front engine support bolts, rear engine support nuts and lift the engine assembly from the chassis. *When removing Perkins Diesel Engines it may be necessary to shift lifting hook from one notch to another to lift engine at required angle for clearance.*
11. Reverse procedure for installing.
12. Check for oil, air, water or vacuum leaks.

Checking impeller to pump body clearance

Cylinder Head

Removal

1. Disconnect battery cables, drain radiator and block.
2. Remove air cleaner, and disconnect breather pipe.
3. Remove cylinder head cover from head.
4. Remove rocker arm support stud nuts. The rocker arm assembly complete with lubrication tube and "O" ring can now be removed as an assembly.
5. Carefully lift valve push rods out of engine. CAUTION: It is possible to drop No. 2, 3, 10 and 11 push rods down into oil pan and if this occurs, they cannot be retrieved without removing oil pan.
6. Disconnect fuel injector lines. Unbolt mounting clamp from cylinder head and remove six injectors lines as an assembly. *Injector lines must be handled carefully to avoid bending or damaging, and dirt or chips should not be allowed to enter fuel lines.*
7. Remove cylinder head to water pump by-pass tube.
8. Remove fuel lines.
9. Remove six injectors and copper sealing washers. *If injectors stick, tap them sideways carefully with a soft hammer to loosen them. Place injectors where tips will not be damaged, do not use a wire brush or other abrasive on injectors.*
10. Remove upper radiator hose and heater hoses.
11. Disconnect exhaust pipe at manifold flange and fuel return line bracket.
12. Remove 32 cylinder head stud nuts.
13. Remove voltage regulator to prevent possible damage. *Avoid damage to cylinder head and block surfaces by careless prying under cylinder block.*
14. Remove No. 4 and 5 rocker shaft studs, install lifting fixture on cylinder head and remove.

Installation

1. Install intake and exhaust manifolds, using new gaskets. Use the short bolts for the third manifold bolt from each end to avoid bolt interference with the push rods.
2. The mating surfaces of cylinder head and cylinder block must be clean. A cracked head, must, of course, be renewed.
3. If the longitudinal bow in the head is more than 0.006", or the transverse boy exceeds 0.003", then machining of the head joint face is necessary. Machining is also necessary if the head has deep scratches, scores, nicks, or fret marks, in particular, across the areas where the gasket bore eyelets seal, or, where they run into water or oil apertures. *No more than 0.001" should ever be removed from the gasket face of the head* and if the head cannot be cleaned by removing 0.010" then it must be renewed. The surface finish of the head should be of a medium ground finish of 60/100 micro inches, or equivalent to the top face of the cylinder block. *Only the minimum amount of metal should ever be removed from the head face* and the amount removed should be stamped on the head face in case further resurfacing becomes necessary. Care should be taken in selecting the area for stamping.
4. If the head bottom face has been machined, check that the valve heads are recessed below the head face by not less than 0.029". If the valve heads are recessed less than 0.029" then the valve seats must be ground until the valve heads are recessed at least 0.029" and not more than 0.049". After machining of the head the atomizer nozzle protrusion must not be greater than 0.2165" and this figure *must not* be achieved by the use of additional atomizer seating washers as these may be inadvertently removed at a later date and result in a loss of power.
5. The cylinder head studs and nuts must be examined for damaged threads or other signs of wear. Studs must fit snugly into the cylinder block. With a light smear of oil on the threads screw the studs into the block tightening to 10 ft/lbs, when they should not be slack or wobble. Any suspect studs should be renewed as should any loose fitting nuts.
6. IMPORTANT: The relief counter-bore between the block and the top of the sleeve *must* be free of carbon deposits. The gasket cannot seal properly unless the counter-bore is perfectly clean.
7. Place gasket on block face, using gasket as supplied, *dry, with no jointing compound*
8. Fit cylinder head carefully so as not to damage threads on studs, or, gasket. Lightly oil threads and working face of cylinder head nuts and fit nuts.
9. The head must be tightened as follows: Using an accurate torque wrench, with the engine cold and rocker assembly removed from engine:
   a. Pull down to 80 ft/lbs (½" studs) following the sequence shown.
   b. Pull down to 85 ft/lbs (½" studs) following same sequence.
   c. Pull down to 85 ft/lbs (½" studs) *again*, following same sequence. This final tightening of the nuts should be carried out to ensure that no loss of tension has occurred on studs earlier in the tightening sequence.
10. Install all push rods, being careful not to drop any of them into the crankcase.
11. Replace rocker assembly. The oil feed pipe to the rockers locates in a hole in the cylinder head and a rubber "O" ring should fit around the stem of the pipe when the rockers have been fitted. In order to ensure the new

Cylinder head tightening sequence
(© Chrysler Corp.)

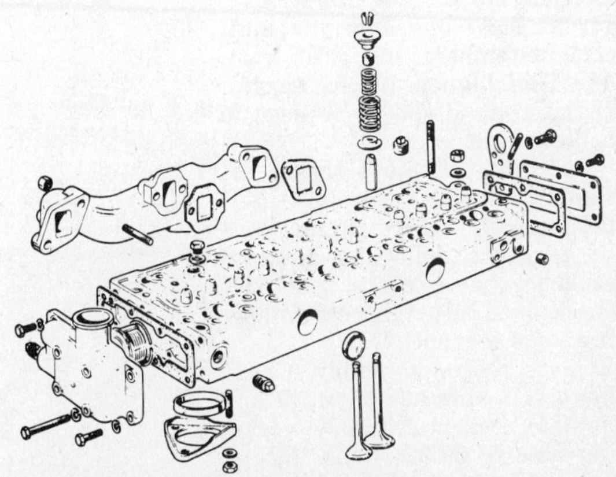

Cylinder head assembly (typical)
(© Chrysler Corp.)

HELI-COIL INSERT CHART

Heli-Coil Insert			Drill	Tap	Inserting Tool	Extract-ing Tool
Thread Size	Part No.	Insert Length	Size	Part No.	Part No.	Part No.
1/2-20	1185-4	3/8″	17/64(.266)	4 CPB	528-4N	1227-6
5/16-18	1185-5	15/32″	Q(.332)	5 CPB	528-5N	1227-6
3/8-16	1185-6	9/16″	X(.397)	6 CPB	528-6N	1227-6
7/16-14	1185-7	21/32″	29/64(.453)	7 CPB	528-7N	1227-16
1/2-13	1185-8	3/4″	33/64(.516)	8 CPB	528-8N	1227-16

seal locates correctly, fit it immediately below the lower convolution and as the pipe is inserted into the cylinder head the "O" ring will roll up and over the lower convolution and locate itself correctly between the two convolutions. If, before inserting the pipe in the cylinder head, the "O" ring is fitted *between* the convolutions then it will roll up and over the upper convolution when inserting the pipe and fail to make an effective seal. Always fit a new "O" ring.

12. Rocker assembly shaft pillar securing nuts should be tightened to 29-32 ft/lbs.
13. Adjust valve lash (clearance)—Inlet and Exhaust to 0.012″—engine cold.
14. Using new copper gaskets, install the fuel injectors in cylinder head.
15. Install fuel lines.
16. Install six injector lines as an assembly.
17. Install cylinder head to water pump by-pass tube, upper radiator hose, heater hoses and voltage regulator.
18. Connect exhaust pipe to manifold flange. Install fuel return line bracket.
19. Fill cooling system. Connect battery cables.
20. Start engine and idle (550 r.p.m.) for a few minutes, checking that the valve action is satisfactory and lubricating oil is reaching the rockers.
21. Run engine at 1200/1500 r.p.m. for at least *one hour*, or until coolant temperature is, at least, 180°F or higher. If necessary, a radiator blind should be used to achieve this.
22. Stop engine. Remove rocker assembly. Check head nut tightness quickly before engine loses temperature, following diagram sequence as before. AGAIN check head nut tightness following same sequence.
23. Replace rocker assembly. Check fit of "O" ring as at item 9 and tighten rocker assembly securing nuts to 29-32 ft/lbs. Adjust valve lash (clearance) to 0.010″—engine hot.
24. Restart engine and idle at 550 r.p.m. Check the oil feed to the rockers and check for leak at the "O" ring around the rocker feed pipe. Check that the valve lash (clearance) is correct and that no valve is sticking. IMPORTANT: A retightening of cylinder head nuts must be made at approximately 250milesor at the end of two weeks of the gasket change.
25. Use special adapter wrench to tighten nuts underneath the rocker arms. Readjust tappets to .010″ clearance "hot."

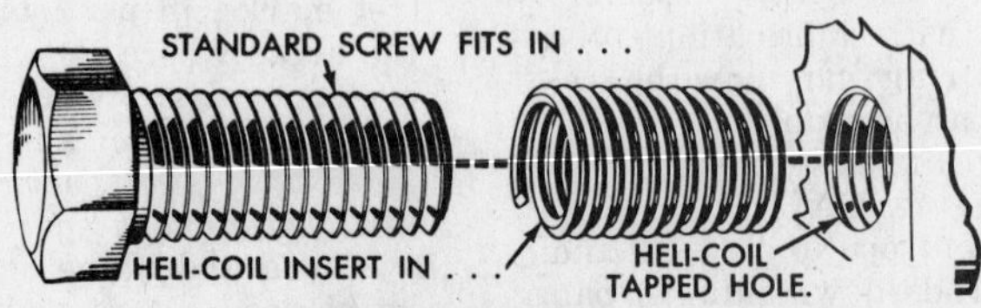

Heli-coil installation
(© Chrysler Corp.)

Repair of Damaged or Worn Threads

Damaged or worn threads can be repaired by the use of Heli-Coils. Essentially, this repair consists of drilling out worn or damaged threads, tapping the hole with a special Heli-Coil Tap, and installing a Heli-Coil Insert into the tapped hole. This brings the hole back to its original thread size

The following chart lists the threaded hole sizes which are used in the engine block and the necessary tools and inserts for the repair of damaged or worn thread. Heli-Coil tools and inserts are readily available from automotive parts jobbers.

Servicing Cylinder Head

In the Perkins 354 Diesel Engine, carbon rarely, if ever, forms in the combustion chambers in sufficient quantity to require periodic decarbonizing of the engine. Valve ports require cleaning at every head service.

Due to high thermal efficiency and other characteriestics, the valves in this engine are relatively free from trouble due to overheating.

As noted in the maintenance schedule for this engine, it is recommended that tappet clearances be checked at 18,000 mile intervals. Both intake and exhaust should be adjusted to .010″ hot.

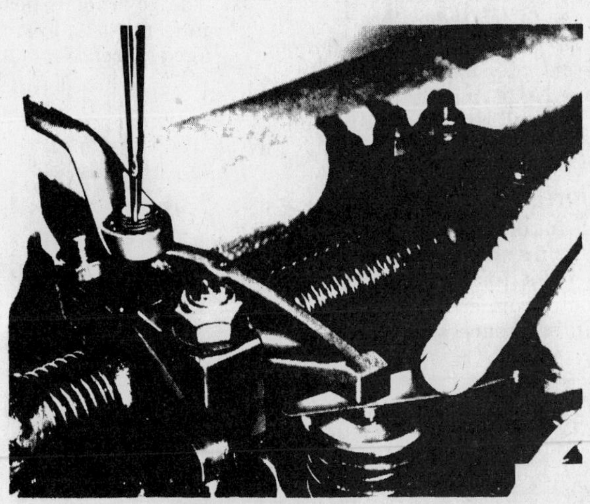
Adjusting tappet clearance
(© Chrysler Corp.)

Disassembly of Cylinder Head

Remove manifolds.

Note that on this diesel engine no heat riser connection is required between intake and exhaust manifolds.

Clean gasket material from manifolds or cylinder head.

Remove thermostat and housing assembly.

Pry out retaining snap ring, and remove thermostat from housing.

All intake and exhaust valves are numbered consecutively from one to six, commencing at the front of the engine.

The cylinder head is marked with corresponding numbers opposite the valve seats.

Using a valve spring compressor, remove the valve locks, spring retainers, inner and outer springs, and the intake valve stem seals.

Remove valves from cylinder head, and remove spring seats from top end of valve guides.

A complete new set of valve springs should be installed whenever the engine undergoes a major overhaul.

Valve stem to guide clearance (new): Intake—.0015″ to .0035″. Exhaust—.002″ to .004″.

If valve stem to guide clearance is excessive, the worn parts should be replaced. Valve guide bore diameter (new) for intake and exhaust valve guides is .375″ to .376″.

Stem diameters for new valves are .3725″ to .3735″ for intake valves and .372″ to .373″ for exhaust valves.

With a new head and valves, the top surface of all valves should be recessed not less than .029″ and not more than .039″ below the surface of the cylinder head.

Clean the valves thoroughly, and examine them carefully.

Any new valves used should be stamped with the same number as the discarded valve, which they replaced.

Remove any carbon deposits from the cylinder head combustion chambers and valve ports.

Thoroughly clean water passages in cylinder head. If excessive scale is present, a proper cleaning solution should be used.

Grind Valves

Valves and valve seats should be reconditioned in the conventional way, either using grinding compound or accepted valve and seat refacing equipment. Valve seat and valve face angle are both 45 degrees.

After valves and seats have been reconditioned, the valve head depth must be checked. Use a straight edge and feeler gauge to check this dimension. It must be between the limits of .029″ and .060″.

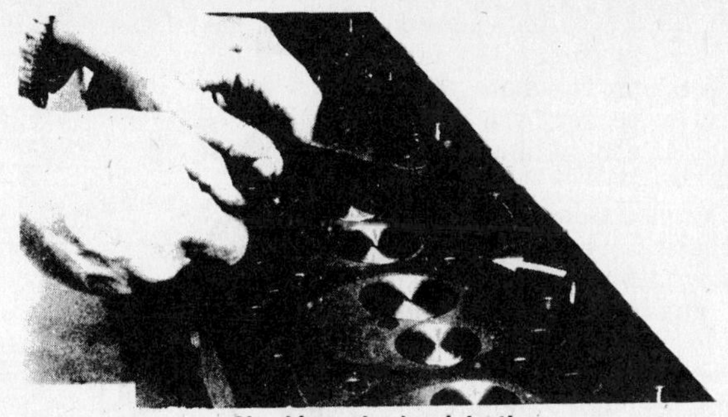

Checking valve head depth
(© Chrysler Corp.)

It is essential that valve heights be held within these limits to provide clearance between valve and piston, and to maintain correct combustion chamber volume.

Valve seat inserts are not installed in these engines in production. However, if a seat is worn or damaged to such an extent that reconditioning places the valve depth beyond the limits of .029″ to .060″, a counterbore can be machined into the cylinder head and a valve seat insert can be installed.

Before you can install a valve seat insert, a new valve guide must be installed.

Valve Guides

Press out old valve guide, and thoroughly clean bore in cylinder head.

Press in a new valve guide, to where the top of the guide protrudes ⅝″ above the spring seat machined surface on the cylinder head. Coat valve guides with engine oil to reduce friction during installation.

Using valve guide bore as a pilot, machine a counterbore in the cylinder head to the required dimensions.

Remove all chips and thoroughly clean insert counterbore, removing any burrs which may be present.

Again using valve guide bore as a pilot, press insert home with an installing tool.

Use a steady pressure with either a hand or hydraulic press. The tool will insure squareness. Under no circumstances should the insert be hammered in. Also, do not use lubrication when pressing in the insert. Chill seats with dry ice to reduce interference while installing them.

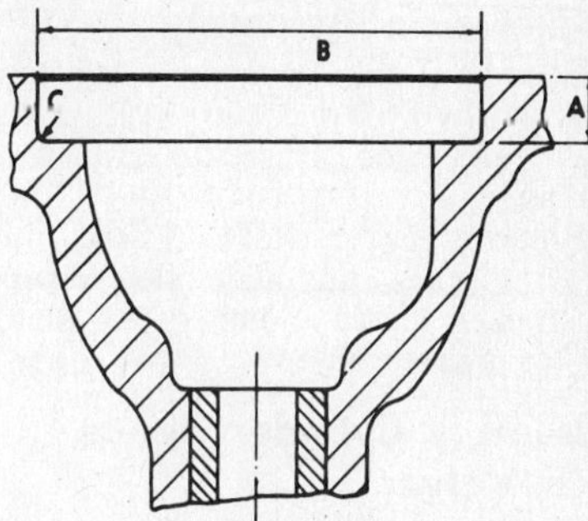

Valve seat counterbore dimensions
(© Chrysler Corp.)

Intake
A .283 to .288 in.
B 2.0165 to 2.0175 in.
C Radius .015 in. (max.)

Exhaust
A .375 to .380 in.
B 1.678 to 1.679 in.
C Radius .015 in. (max.)

Visually inspect to make sure that insert has been pressed in squarely, and that it is flush with bottom of counterbore.

Using valve guide bore as a pilot, machine "flare" in insert to dimensions shown. Remove any chips or burrs from seat.

Grind insert seat to a 45° angle (90° included angle), and to where valve head depth below cylinder head face is within limits of .029″ to .039″.

It is advisable to work as closely as possible to the minimum figure in order to allow for reseating at a later date if required.

An existing insert may also be replaced in the same manner, except that it will not be necessary to machine a counterbore.

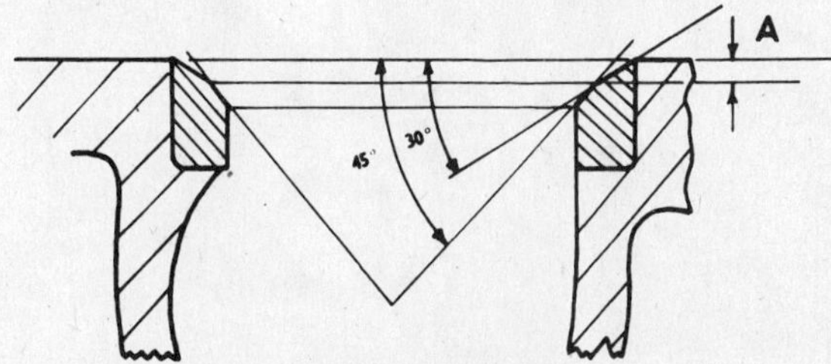

Relieve seat at 30 degrees to dimension A .094 to .099 inch
(© Chrysler Corp.)

The gasket face of cylinder head may be resurfaced to eliminate score marks, warpage, etc. No more than .010" should ever be removed from the gasket face of the cylinder head however.

To replace valve guides, press out old guides. Clean bores in cylinder head, and remove all burrs.

Coat new guides with oil, and press them into where they protrude ⅝" above the cylinder head. Care should be exercised, since the guides are made of cast iron and are, therefore, very brittle.

Rocker Arm Assembly

Remove retaining snap rings and end washers from ends of rocker shaft, and slide off rocker arms and springs.

Remove rocker shaft oil feed pipe locating screw, and slide oil feed pipe off rocker shaft. Remove the small "O" ring from pipe.

Assemble Cylinder Heads and Valves

Install valves in their proper positions as numbered, place valve seat washers in position, and install new valve stem seals (open end to valve guides) on the intake valves.

Position inner and outer valve springs so close coils are next to the cylinder head, and install valve retainers and locks.

All valve springs on this engine incorporate a damper coil (close coil). Care must be taken to assure that this damper coil is replaced nearest to the cylinder head.

Install gasket, thermostat and tapered snap ring in the thermostat housing, and using a new gasket, install the assembly on the cylinder head.

Using a new gasket, install rear cover on cylinder head.

Install intake and exhaust manifolds using new gaskets. Use short bolts for third manifold bolt from each end to avoid bolt interference with push rods.

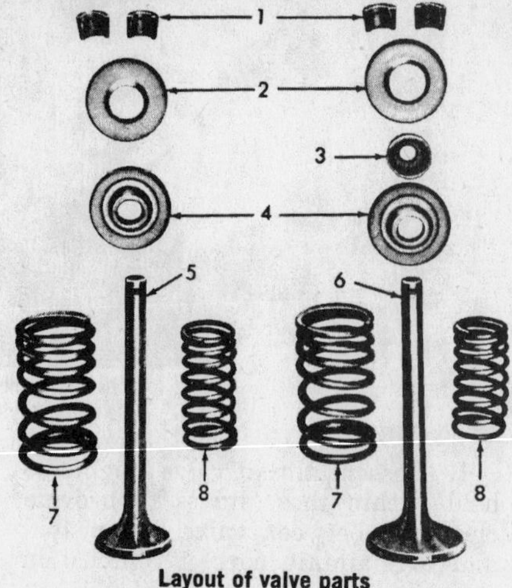

1 Valve locks
2 Valve spring seats
3 Intake valve stem seals
4 Valve spring retainers
5 Exhaust valve
6 Intake valve
7 Outer valve spring
8 Inner valve spring

Layout of valve parts (© Chrysler Corp.)

Timing Gears and Camshaft

Removal

1. Remove vibration damper retaining screw and lock.
2. Slide the vibration damper assembly off the splined end of the crankshaft.
3. Remove camshaft gear cover and auxiliary drive gear cover or tachometer drive adapter from timing gear case.
4. Remove auxiliary shaft drive gear by unscrewing three recessed head retaining screws and the retaining plate.
5. Remove camshaft retaining screw, washer and lock plate.
6. Pull camshaft gear. *Avoid driving the camshaft back against the plug in the rear wall of the cylinder block, since an oil leak could develop if this plug is disturbed.*
7. Remove bolts and remove the timing gear case.
8. Remove two self-locking nuts and remove camshaft idler gear and auxiliary shaft idle gear.

Note that the camshaft idler gear can be identified as having a timing mark (punch mark), while the auxiliary shaft idler gear has no timing mark.

The two idler gear hubs are doweled, and can be readily removed from the hub mounting studs by gripping the end of the rolled pin and tapping hub with a soft hammer.

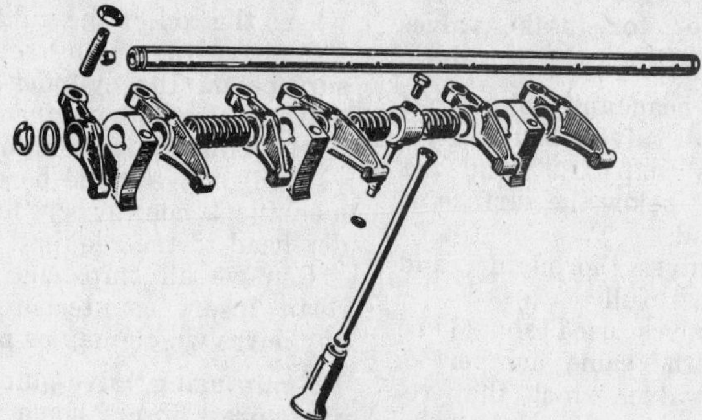

Rocker shaft assembly (© Chrysler Corp.)

Removing auxiliary drive gear (© Chrysler Corp.)

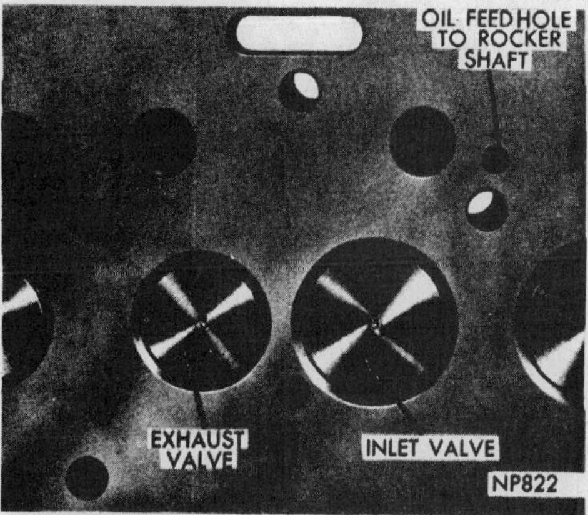

Valve numbering (© Chrysler Corp.)

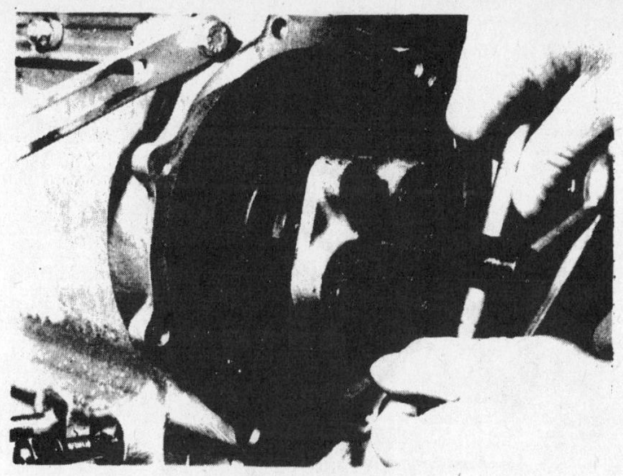
Removing camshaft gear (© Chrysler Corp.)

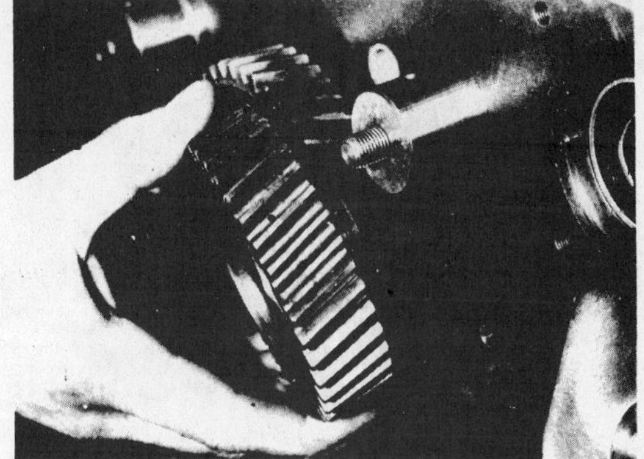
Removing idler gear (© Chrysler Corp.)

Camshaft and Auxiliary Drive Shaft

The camshaft is supported by four pressure fed bearings and is driven by helical type gears. The thrust washers used to control end thrust of both the camshaft and auxiliary drive shaft are fitted in machined recesses in the front of the cylinder block and are located by dowel pins. Before the thrust washers, camshaft or auxiliary drive shaft can be removed, the timing gear case must be removed.

Camshaft Removal (with Gear Case and Gears Removed)

1. Remove the rocker arm cover.
2. Remove the six rocker arm support stud nuts and flat washers. The rocker arm assembly complete with lubrication tube and "O" ring can now be removed as an assembly.
3. Lift the push rods out of the engine. Do this carefully since it is possible to drop No. 2, 3, 10 and 11 push rods down into the crankcase.
4. Disconnect the fuel lines, remove the pump attaching screws and remove the fuel pump from the engine.
5. Remove the alternator.
6. Remove push rod inspection covers.
7. Lift tappets to full travel and hold in full position with clothes pins, carefully remove camshaft and thrust washer.

Auxiliary Drive Shaft Removal (Gear Case and Gears Removed)

Disconnect the fuel injector lines at the injectors and at the injector pump. Unbolt the mounting clamp from the cylinder head and remove the six injector lines as an assembly.

Injector lines must be handled carefully to avoid bending or damaging. Cover or tape fuel openings on the injection pump to prevent dirt from entering the pump.

1. Disconnect the accelerator and stop cable, remove the three injection pump attaching stud nuts and lift out the injection pump.
2. Remove the three attaching stud nuts and lift the injection pump adapter from the engine.
3. Disconnect the coupling and lines and remove the vacuum pump or air compressor.
4. Loosen the coupling clamp bolt, and remove the coupling from rear end of auxiliary drive shaft.
5. Remove the woodruff key from the rear end of the auxiliary shaft.
6. Pull out the auxiliary drive shaft and the two half moon shaped thrust washers.

If a suitable puller is available the injector and engine oil pump vertical drive shaft assembly can be removed from the top. If tool is not available the following steps are necessary:

Remove the dipstick and dipstick tube.

Remove the attaching screws and remove the oil pump assembly.

Disconnect the oil delivery housing from the crankcase by removing the two attaching bolts.

Loosen the locknut, and unscrew the oil pump locating set screw. This screw is located outside the cylinder block. Now remove the oil pump and oil delivery housing assembly.

The two parts of this assembly are connected by a short pipe which is a push fit in each component.

Inspect the short pipe for wear.

Tap out the injector pump and engine oil pump vertical drive shaft assembly from inside the crankcase.

Remove the seal from the rear end of the auxiliary drive shaft bore in the crankcase. This can be done by prying behind the lip extension of the seal retainer.

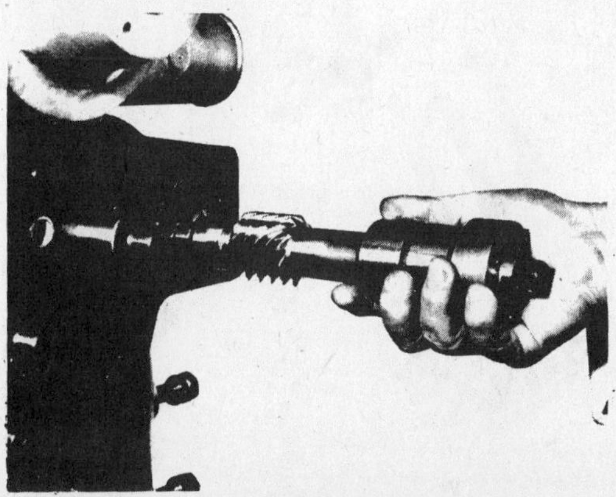
Removing auxiliary drive shaft (© Chrysler Corp.)

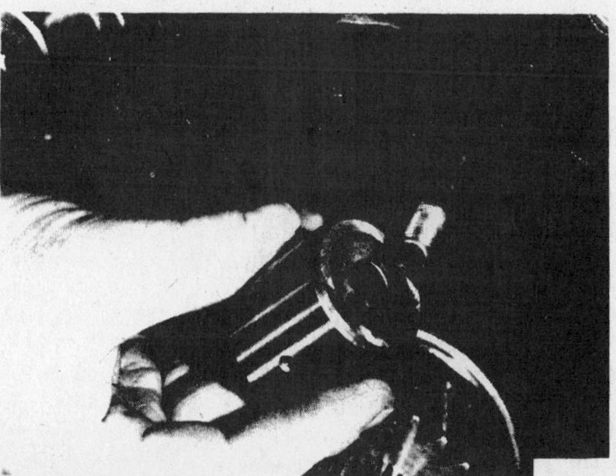
Removing idler gear hub (© Chrysler Corp.)

Removing auxiliary drive gear (© Chrysler Corp.)

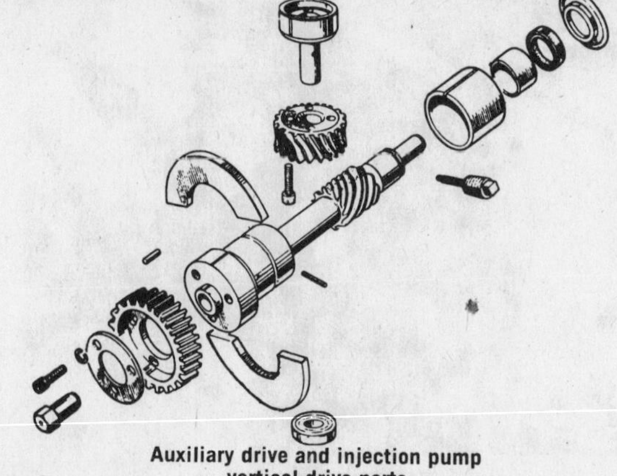

Auxiliary drive and injection pump vertical drive parts
(© Chrysler Corp.)

The engine oil pump and injector pump vertical drive shaft can be removed with a suitable puller, if the engine oil pan and oil pump are not to be removed.

Injector Pump Vertical Drive Removal

Use a suitable puller with fine jaws to remove the bearing, being careful not to damage the bronze gear.

Remove the four recessed screws, support the gear carefully, and press the shaft out of the gear.

To reassemble, press the bronze gear onto the injection pump vertical drive shaft with holes in gear and flange aligned, and with counter-bored side away from flange and secure it with the retaining screws. Then press a new bearing on the shaft. Use a new gear if necessary.

Insert the vertical shaft, gear and bearing assembly in the cylinder block, and push it down into position.

On a few engines, one or more steel shim .002″ thick is fitted beneath the bearing. Fit the shim (shims) into the block first and then slide complete vertical drive assembly into block on top of shim (shims). Always replace shim (or shims) into block from which they came. *Do not* fit shims into a block which did not have them in the first place.

The vertical shaft and gear must be installed before installing the horizontal positioned auxiliary drive shaft.

Auxiliary Drive Shaft Removal

Place the two thrust washer halves in the groove on the auxiliary drive shaft immediately behind the timing gear mounting flange on the auxiliary drive shaft, and with the chamfer to the rear. Then enter the shaft into the cylinder block bore so the two thrust washer halves straddle the small locating dowel in the recess at the front of the cylinder block. Do this carefully so as not to damage the bronze gear or the worm gear on the auxiliary shaft.

With the key in place in front end of crankshaft, place crankshaft gear on shaft with timing mark on gear toward front of engine, and using a suitable driver, drive gear into place on shaft.

Turn crankshaft until number one and number six pistons are at top dead center. The timing mark on flywheel can be used to accurately determine this position. Also, the line on front face of crankshaft is vertical in respect to engine when number one and number six are at top dead center.

Install Camshaft and Tappets

Examine camshaft for wear or pitting on cam lobes. If condition is not satisfactory, a new camshaft must be installed.

Oil camshaft lightly, and carefully slide it into place in cylinder block.

Do not drive on front end of camshaft for any reason, since this will dislodge the camshaft plug in the rear of the cylinder block, and an oil leak will result.

Do not install camshaft gear until timing gear case has been installed. The timing case must be installed first.

Place camshaft thrust washer in place, chamfered side in, and so small dowel in cylinder block is entered in hole provided in thrust washer.

Idler Gears

Place the two idler gear hubs on their mounting studs at front of cylinder block, so ends with largest chamfer are toward cylinder block and their hollow dowels are aligned with holes provided. Tap hubs into place with a soft hammer.

The hollow dowels in idler gear hubs also serve as oil feed passages for idler gears.

The two idler gears are different. The timing marks are on camshaft idler gear. The auxiliary drive idler gear is plain.

Vertical drive parts
(© Chrysler Corp.)

Place camshaft idler gear on its hub, engaging it with crankshaft gear so the two adjacent teeth with timing marks on idler gear straddle the one tooth on crankshaft gear which has a timing mark.

Secure camshaft idler gear with retaining washer and self-locking nut. Tighten nut to 45 to 50 foot-pounds.

Install auxiliary drive idler gear in exactly the same way, except that there are no timing marks to be concerned with on the auxiliary drive idler gear.

Pistons and Rings

Piston and Rod Removal

1. Remove cylinder head assembly as outlined earlier in the engine section.
2. Remove oil dipstick and tube.
3. Remove oil pan attaching bolts and remove oil pan and sump assembly.
4. Disconnect oil delivery housing from crankcase.
5. Loosen the locknut and unscrew the oil pump locating screw.
6. Remove oil pump and oil delivery housing assembly.
7. Remove top ridge of cylinder bores with a ridge reamer before removing pistons from cylinder block.
8. Turn crankshaft so that two connecting rod journals are at bottom center.
9. Remove connecting rod caps and inserts, and remove rod and piston assemblies from cylinder bores.
10. Keep related parts of each assembly together for convenience when matching for reassembly.

Dissassemble Piston and Rod Assemblies

Remove five piston rings.

Remove the piston pin retaining rings from both ends of pin bore in piston.

Make sure the ends of the pin bores are clean, and remove any burrs around the retainer grooves.

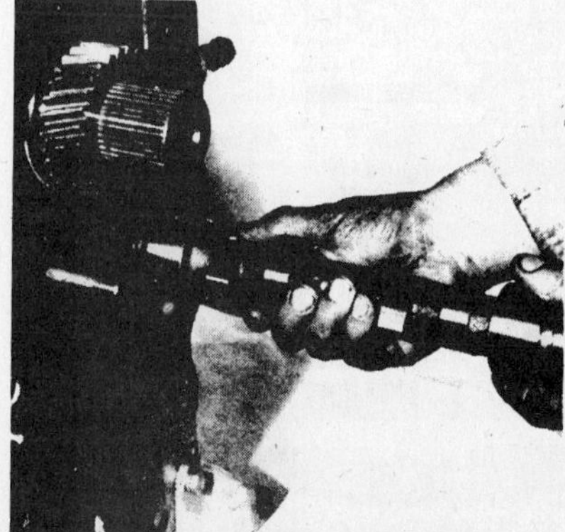

Installing camshaft (© Chrysler Corp.)

Warm the piston up to about 120°F. This can be done by immersing the pistons in clean liquid of that temperature for a short period of time. Do not use a torch.

After warming the piston to 120°F., it should be possible to remove pin by pushing it out of bore.

If the piston pin bushings are worn, they can be replaced.

Replacing Piston Pin Bushings

Using a suitable pressing tool, press the pin bushing out of the connecting rod.

Piston pins and bushings are supplied in standard size only. Standard pin diameter is 1.375″.

Position a new bushing so the oil hole will align with the oil hole at the top of the connecting rod, and press the bushing into the connecting rod bore.

Ream the bushing to provide pin clearance of .0007″ to .0017″.

Connecting rod alignment should be checked on a reliable fixture. The piston pin should be parallel and in the same plane with the bearing bore centerline within .001″.

Alignment of timing marks on drive gears (© Chrysler Corp.)

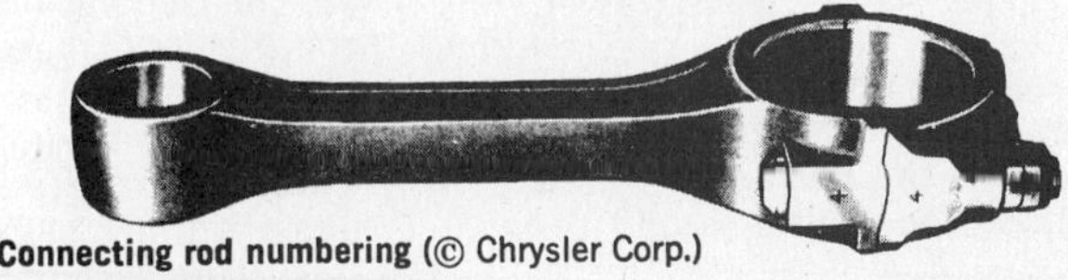

Connecting rod numbering (© Chrysler Corp.)

Cleaning and Inspecting Pistons

Use a ring groove cleaning tool to clean the ring grooves, being careful not to gouge or damage the groove surfaces.

A power wire brush should never be used to clean pistons.

Examine the piston carefully for cracks or other defects.

If a piston ring groove has been damaged by a broken ring, or if ring grooves have been worn excessively wide, due to high mileage, or if piston skirt is scored, the piston should be replaced.

When a new piston is being installed, stamp it for the cylinder position number in which it is to be installed.

All pistons in any one engine must be of same size.

Installing camshaft thrust washer (© Chrysler Corp.)

Fitting New Piston Rings

New rings should be checked in the

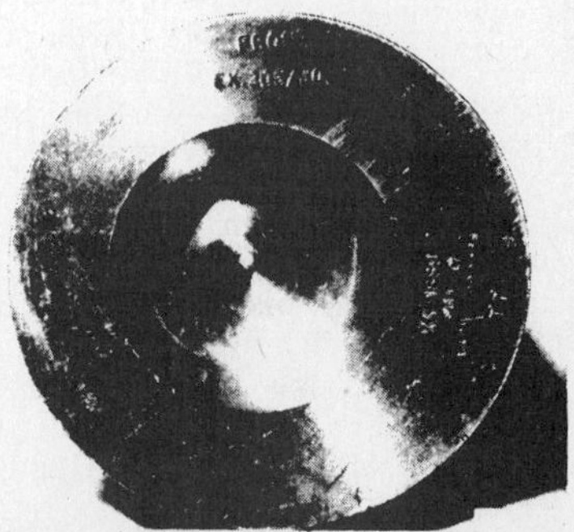

Toroidal cavity in piston note markings (© Chrysler Corp.)

cylinder bore for correct ring gap.

To check ring gap in worn cylinder liners the ring should be positioned at the bottom of the bore, below the ring travel area, where minimum wear has occurred.

With the ring positioned squarely in the cylinder, check the gap with a feeler gauge.

The ring can be positioned squarely in the cylinder bore by using a piston to push it down into the bore.

Ring gap at the top compression ring should be .015″ to .019″. The second and third compression rings, and also the upper and lower oil rings should have a gap of .011″ to .016″.

New rings are available in standard size for installation in new liners and worn liners which have not been rebored. They are also available in .030″ oversize for use *only* in rebored liners.

New rings must be thoroughly washed before installation.

Assembling Piston and Connecting Rod Assembly

Heat piston to 120°F. before installing piston pin.

Coat the pin with light engine oil.

Position the piston and connecting rod so the word front on the piston will be toward the front of the engine when the stamped numbers on the connecting rod are toward the side of the engine opposite the camshaft.

Push the piston pin through the piston pin hole and rod bushing, and center the pin between the two retainer ring grooves in the piston.

Make sure the piston is centered between the grooves, and install both retaining rings.

Assure that both pin retaining rings are perfectly seated in their grooves.

When installing the piston pin, *do not* have one of the retaining rings in place, and drive the pin against it to permit installation of the second retaining ring.

This practice can result in damage to the groove or ring, and result in the ring eventually coming out of the groove, permitting the pin to seriously damage the cylinder liner.

Install the two oil rings.

Note that the 2nd and 3rd compression rings are tapered, and are marked "T" for top side.

In current production, the second and third compression rings are internally stepped. These rings must be assembled to the piston so that the step faces the crown of the piston.

The number one (top) compression ring is chrome plated, and can be installed either side up. Install this ring last.

Space the piston ring gaps equally around the piston, and so they are not in line with one another.

Connecting rod bearing upper and lower inserts are both alike. Also note that the parting faces of the rod and cap are serrated to ensure accurate positioning of the cap, and under no circumstances should they be filed.

Connecting rod bolts should be carefully inspected for possible damage, and should be replaced if they are not in excellent condition.

The original self-locking nuts must be replaced with new ones, since they will have lost some of their prevailing torque.

When replacing connecting rod bolts or nuts, use only the correct factory supplied replacement parts.

Connecting rod bearings are available in standard size, and in .010″, .020″, and .030″ undersizes.

Place upper and lower connecting rod bearing inserts in position in the rod bore.

Make sure the piston and rod assembly and the cylinder bore are perfectly clean, and oil them with engine oil.

Piston and Rod Installation

1. Position the crankshaft so the throw for the rod and piston being installed is at bottom center.
2. Install the piston and rod assembly in the cylinder.
3. Make sure the assembly is in the cylinder for which it is marked and that the word *front* on the piston is toward the front of the engine, and that the numbered side of the connecting rod is opposite from the camshaft side of the engine.
4. Pull the rod into position at the crankshaft journal, and making sure the bearing inserts are both properly positioned, install the conncting rod cap and bearing in place.
5. Install the two connecting rod bolts with new self-locking nuts. Connecting rod bolt heads have two flats. The largest flat must be positioned toward the connecting rod. Tighten to 65 to 70 foot-pounds.

With a properly fitted piston and rod assembly, the piston should protrude above the top of the cylinder block no less than .003, and no more than .0095″ when at top dead center. This can be checked by placing a straightedge across the top of the liner and with a feeler gauge, measure the liner protrusion above the top surface of the cylinder block and the gap between the piston top and the straight edge (the smallest height must be to the piston).

The difference between the two dimensions is the height of the piston

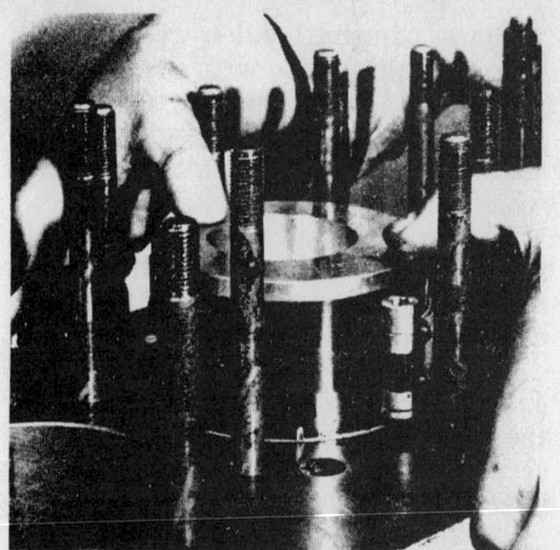

Installing piston (© Chrysler Corp.)

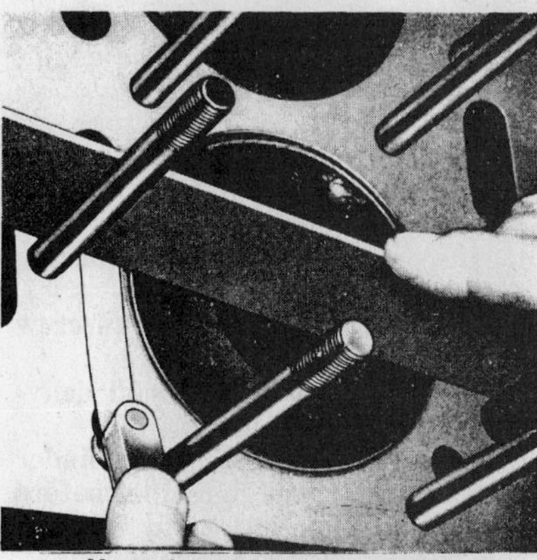

Measuring cylinder liner height (© Chrysler Corp.)

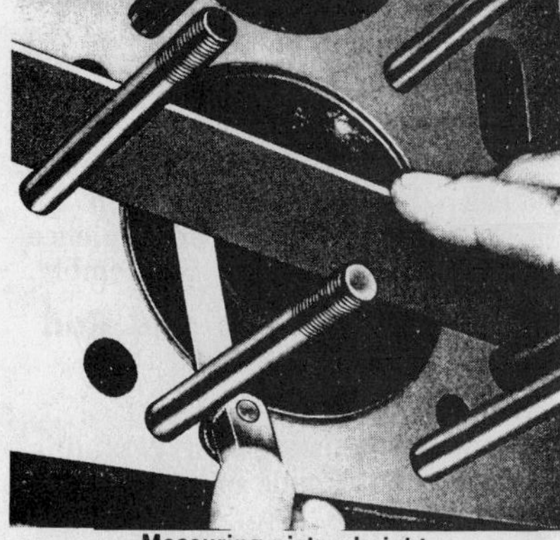

Measuring piston height (© Chrysler Corp.)

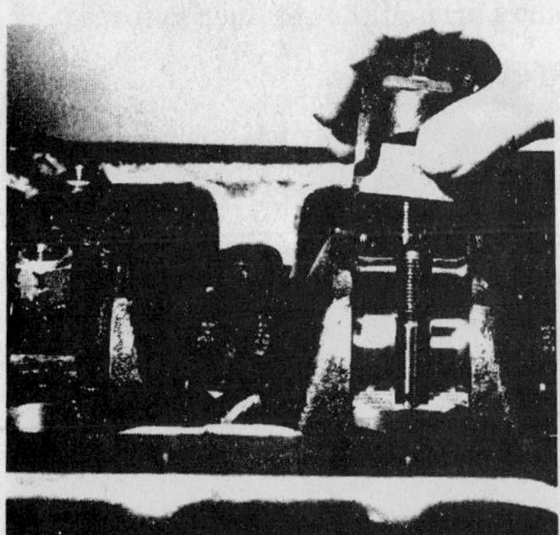

Installing connecting rod cap (© Chrysler Corp.)

above the block. If the piston height is excessive, the piston must be removed from the engine and the top machined to bring the height within the specified limits. Should the piston height be too low at top dead center, it must be replaced.

Piston protrusion above the top of the block is most important and should always be checked at TDC. Service pistons should not require machining if they are stamped with the letter "L" on the crown.

Cylinder Liners

Servicing Cylinder Liners

The Dry type cylinder liners are pressed into cylinder block with a .003″ to .005″ interference fit. Pressing force required is approximately ten tons.

Liners must be bored and honed after they have been pressed into the cylinder block. For a standard piston, the finished honed inside diameter of the liner must be between 3.877″ and 3.8785″.

If liners are worn or scored, they can be rebored to .030″ oversize. Finished inside diameter must be between 3.907″ and 3.9085″.

All pistons in any one engine must be of the same size. *Liners should be carefully inspected for cracks or other damage before making a decision whether to rebore or replace a liner.*

During reboring, it is most important that true alignment of the bores relative to the crankshaft centerline be maintained.

If cylinder liners are not acceptable for reboring to .030″ oversize, they must be pressed out, and new liners pressed into the cylinder block.

The first step when installing new liners is to remove all cylinder head attaching studs from the top of the cylinder block.

With cylinder block placed in a suitable press, cylinder liners must be pressed out through top of cylinder block, using the proper tool to adapt the press ram to the bottom of the cylinder liner.

Make sure the outside of liners are clean and well oiled before pressing them into the cylinder block.

When pressing in liners, the press load should be released several times during the first inch to allow the liner to centralize itself in the cylinder block parent bore. *Cylinder liners can be removed and installed with engine in truck. Also chilling liners with dry ice may reduce pressing effort required.*

The latest type of cylinder liner protrudes .030″ to .035″ above the block face. This liner should be bored and honed to size in the same manner as the earlier recessed-block type liner. *The earlier-type liner must not be pulled up above the top surface of the block.*

After they are pressed in, the liners should be finish bored to 3.877″ to 3.878″.

When work on the cylinder liners has been completed, reinstall cylinder head attaching studs, replacing any which have been weakened by corrosion, or damaged.

Crankshaft and Bearings

Crankshaft Removal

1. Remove oil dipstick and tube.
2. Remove oil pan attaching bolts and remove oil pan and sump assembly.
3. Disconnect oil delivery housing from crankcase.
4. Loosen the locknut and unscrew the oil pump locating screw.
5. Remove oil pump and oil delivery housing assembly.
6. Remove two vertical bolts which attach lower half of rear main bearing oil seal retainer to cylinder block.
7. Remove upper and lower halves of seal retainer.
8. Remove attaching screws from front and rear main bearing bridge pieces and lift both bridge pieces out of cylinder block.
9. Bend down tabs on main bearing bolt locks and remove main bearing bolts.
10. Remove center (no. 4) main bearing cap along with the two lower half crankshaft thrust washers.
11. Remove six remaining main bearing caps and lift out the crankshaft. NOTE: Identification marks on main bearing caps are positioned away from camshaft side.

Servicing Crankshaft and Bearings

Bearing clearance at the seven main bearings is .0025″ to .0045″. Specified clearance at connecting rod bearings is .0015″ to .003″.

Main and connecting rod bearings are both available in standard, .010″, .020″, and .030″ undersize.

Crankshaft end clearance is specified .002″ to .014″, and is controlled by four semi-circular thrust washers, two on each side of the center (No. 4) main bearing. These thrust washers are available in .0075″ oversize to overcome end thrust wear. Lower thrust washers have locating tabs, while upper thrust washers do not.

.0075″ oversize thrust washers, can be used on both sides of No. 4 main bearing to reduce end play by .015″ when required. If two standard thickness thrust washers are used on one side of No. 4 main bearing, and two oversize washers are used on the other side, crankshaft end play will be reduced by .0075″.

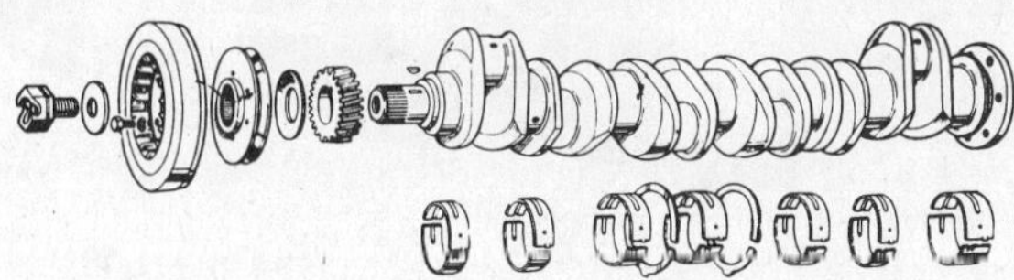

View of crankshaft and bearings
(© Chrysler Corp.)

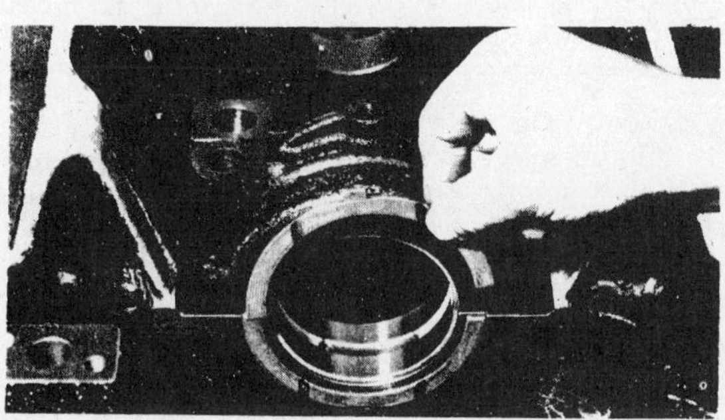

Location of crankshaft thrust washers
(© Chrysler Corp.)

Care must be taken to avoid placing one standard and one oversize thrust washer on the same side of No. 4 main bearing.

Specified end play at connecting rod bearings is .0095″ to .0135″.

Under normal circumstances, by the time the main bearings and thrust washers require replacing, the crankshaft will need to be removed for regrinding. However, if for any reason, one or more of bearings or thrust washers have to be removed for inspection or replacement, this can be done without removing crankshaft from engine.

Main Bearings

To remove a main bearing without removing the crankshaft, take off the cap of the bearing involved, and loosen the remaining main bearing bolts one or two turns.

Before No. 1 or No. 7 main bearing caps can be removed, it is necessary to remove the main bearing bridge piece at the end involved.

To remove front main bearing bridge piece, it is necessary to remove two recessed screws attaching it to cylinder block, as well as the two lower timing case attaching screws.

Crankshaft Thrust Washers

To replace crankshaft thrust washers with the crankshaft in place, remove the center (No. 4) main bearing cap, and remove the two bottom half thrust washers from the recesses in the cap.

The two top half thrust washers can now be removed by sliding them around from one side, using a piece of wood or similar tool, and rotating them until they can be removed.

After replacing individual main bearings or thrust washers, make sure all main bearing bolts which have been loosened are tightened to 145 to 150 foot-pounds and secured with new lock tabs.

Main bearing cap bolts now have a steel shim between cap and lock tab to prevent the bolt head from biting into the lock tab.

Crankshaft Installation

Before the crankshaft and bearings are installed, all oil passages in the cylinder block and crankshaft must be thoroughly clean.

CAUTION: In no case should bolts other than the specified main bearing bolts be used, since they are of special heat treated high grade steel.

Removing main bearing upper half
(© Chrysler Corp.)

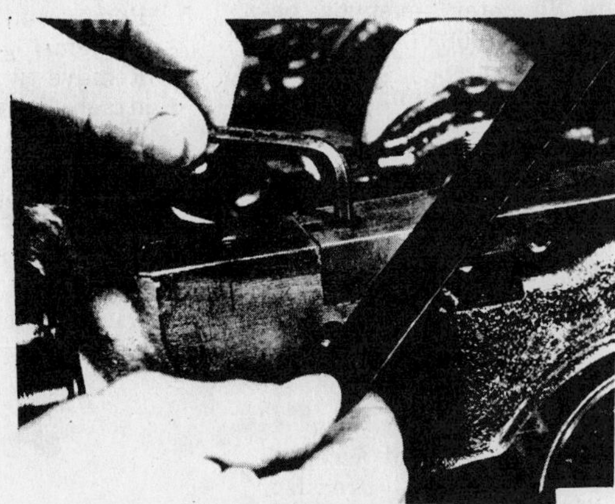

Aligning bridge piece
(© Chrysler Corp.)

When removing the rear main bearing bridge, it is necessary to remove the two recessed screws attaching it to the cylinder block, and the two lower rear main bearing oil seal housing attaching screws.

To remove the top half of a main bearing, using a suitable piece of wood or tool, apply pressure to the end of the bearing opposite from the locating tab, and rotate bearing around crankshaft.

Locating tabs are on camshaft side of engine.

When installing a new bearing shell start the upper half, plain end first, and rotate the shell around the crankshaft and into position.

Make sure the bearing shells and the main bearing bores in the block and caps are free of all foreign matter, and place the main bearing upper halves in position in the cylinder block.

No. 4 main bearing is wider than the others. Also, upper main bearings have large slotted oil holes, which are not found in the lower halves.

1. Oil the upper bearings lightly, and place the crankshaft in position.
2. Lightly lubricate the two upper thrust washers (no locating tabs) and slide them into places in the recesses provided on each side of No. 4 main bearing in the cylinder block.
3. Place lower main bearings in bearing caps. Place the two lower thrust washers on the No. 4 main bearing cap so their locating tabs are positioned in the slots provided in the cap.
4. The main bearing caps are numbered as to their positions, No. 1 being at the front of the engine, and must be installed accordingly.
5. Install caps with bearings so bearing locating tabs are on the same side of the engine as tabs on upper halves.
6. When caps are properly installed, their stamped serial numbers will be in line on the same side of the engine. Check main bearing clearances, using shim stock or plasti-gage. Clearance at all seven main bearings should be .0025″ to .0045″.

   When using plasti-gage to measure main bearing clearances with engine in truck, support the crankshaft to take up clearance between the upper bearing and the crankshaft journal. This can be done by snugging bearing caps of the adjacent bearings with a strip of .005″ to .015″ cardboard between lower bearing and journal. When doing this, avoid unnecessary strain on crankshaft and bearing, or false reading may be obtained. Do not rotate crankshaft while plasti-gage is installed. Be sure to remove cardboard before installing oil pan.

7. Use new tab locks on the main bearing bolts, and tighten evenly to 145 to 150 foot-pounds.
8. Check crankshaft end play.
9. Bend lock tabs to secure the main bearing bolts. Check crankshaft for free rotation.

Removing rear main bearing oil seal
(© Chrysler Corp.)

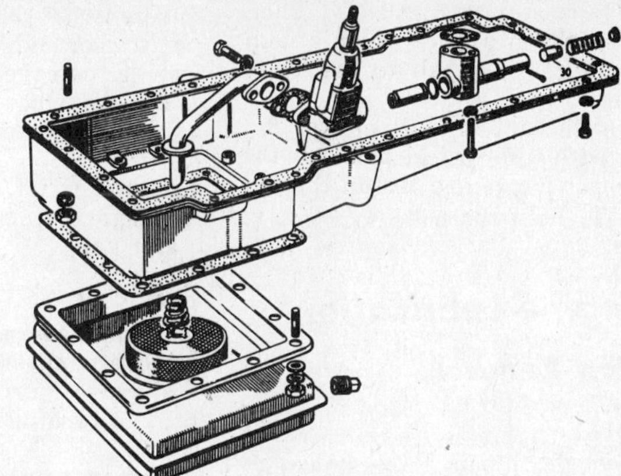
Engine oil pan and sump assembly
(© Chrysler Corp.)

Removing engine oil pump
(© Chrysler Corp.)

Installing Main Bearing Bridge Pieces

Make sure front and rear main bearing bridge pieces are clean, coat attaching surfaces with Gasket Sealer, and place them in position. Place new end seals in grooves provided.

Start recessed attaching screws, and using a straight-edge to align the bridge pieces so they are flush with front and rear faces of cylinder block, tighten screws securely.

Crankshaft Rear Oil Seal

The crankshaft rear oil seal is composed of two rubber cored woven asbestos strips which are inserted in the upper and lower halves of the seal retainer.

The seal surface around the rear of the crankshaft has a shallow spiral oil return groove recessed to a depth of .004″ to .008″.

The seal strips come cut to length, and they must never be shortened.

Place one half of seal retainer in a smooth jawed vise with seal groove facing upward.

Imbed about one inch of each end of a seal strip into ends of groove so each end projects .010″ to .020″ beyond retainer parting face. Allowing middle portion of seal strip to bulge out of groove will enable you to do this.

With thumb or fingers, press the remainder of strip into groove, working from center. Then use any convenient smooth round bar to further imbed the seal strip by rolling and pressing its inner diameter.

This procedure results in compression of the seal material near each end, to prevent the seal ends from pulling away and leaving a gap when the assembly is tightened around the crankshaft.

Install the remaining seal strip in the other half of the seal retainer, using the same methods to position and seat the seal material.

Make sure gasket faces are clean and apply Gasket Sealer, to both sides of new upper and lower retainer gaskets. Also, apply a light coat of sealer to the parting faces between upper and lower seal retainers.

Spread a film of graphited grease over the inside diameter of the upper and lower seals.

Assemble seal retainer halves around crankshaft, drawing the halves together squarely with two bolts.

Make certain upper and lower halves pull completely together, with no ragged edges of the seal ends caught between the parting faces.

Rotate the seal and retainer assembly around crankshaft to make sure it turns freely on the shaft. (This can be done if clutch housing has been removed).

With upper and lower gaskets in place, bolt the seal and retainer assembly to the rear of the engine.

With the retainer to cylinder block attaching bolts pulled up snugly, loosen the two bolts which hold the upper and lower retainer halves together. Make sure the retainer to cylinder block attaching bolts are all tight (Do not back them off). Then retighten the two bolts which attach the upper retainer half to the lower retainer bolt.

Align the index hole in the flywheel with the index hole in the crankshaft flange and install the flywheel. Tighten the bolts to 75 foot-pounds.

Engine Lubrication

Oil Pan Removal

1. Remove dipstick and dipstick tube.
2. Remove oil pan attaching screws and remove oil pan and sump assembly.

Oil Pump Removal

Disconnect oil delivery housing from crankcase by removing two attaching bolts. Loosen the locknut and unscrew the oil pump locating screw. This screw is located outside cylinder block below fuel injection pump.

Remove oil pump and oil delivery housing assembly. The oil pump and oil delivery housing are connected by a short pipe which is a push fit in each component.

Oil Pump and Oil Delivery Housing

The oil pump and oil delivery housing are both a push fit on the connecting pipe. Pull them both loose from the pipe and remove the two "O" rings from their internal grooves in the two assemblies and discard them. Whenever these seals are disturbed, they must be replaced. Inspect the connecting pipe for wear at "O" ring seal surfaces.

Servicing Relief Valve

Remove cotter key, spring retainer, spring and plunger from relief valve bore in oil delivery housing. *Do not* stretch or distort spring.

Wash housing and relief valve parts thoroughly, and replace any worn or damaged parts.

Lubricate bore in delivery housing, and install plunger with small end outward.

Install relief valve spring and retainer, and secure them in place with cotter key.

Servicing Oil Pump

Remove two attaching screws, and remove pump intake tube.

Remove four pump cover to pump body attaching screws and remove cover.

Remove pump shaft and inner rotor and outer rotor.

Thoroughly clean all parts and inspect rotors for cracks and scores.

Install inner and outer rotor in pump body, making sure chamfered edge of outer rotor enters pump body first.

Check clearance between maximum diameter of inner rotor and minimum diameter of outer rotor at all points, using a feeler gauge. This clearance between inner and outer rotor should be between .004" and .008".

The clearance between outer rotor and body must fall between .005" and .010". A clearance of .002" to .005" must be maintained between top of rotor and end plate.

If pump rotors or body show excessive scoring or other damage, or if the above mentioned clearances are exceeded, the oil pump assembly must be replaced.

The oil pump parts are not available individually. The pump must be replaced as an assembly.

Thoroughly lubricate interior surfaces of pump and rotors. Make sure outer rotor is positioned in pump body chamfered end first, and install pump cover, securing it with four attaching screws.

Clean pump intake tube, and attach it to oil pump, using a new gasket. Tighten the two bolts firmly.

Install new "O" rings in the recesses in the pipe bores in the oil pump and oil delivery housing. Lubricate the "O" rings and connector pipe with engine oil, and place one end of the pipe in the oil pump body and the other end in the oil delivery housing. Be careful not to dislodge the "O" rings from their grooves.

Place oil pump and delivery housing assembly in position in the engine crankcase, while engaging the splines of oil pump shaft with splines in the pump vertical drive shaft.

Install oil pump retaining screw through side of the engine so it engages the oil pump to hold it in position. *Do not* tighten screw at this time.

Place a new gasket between the oil delivery housing and engine, and attach housing with two bolts.

Tighten oil pump retaining screw and lock it in place with locknut.

Oil Pan, Sump Well and Screen

Place a new gasket on the oil pan, with Gasket Sealer, on both sides and install the pan on the engine, tightening the bolts firmly. Avoid tightening the bolts too tightly, since this can distort the oil pan sealing surface.

Clean the pump well and screen thoroughly, and using a new gasket and Sealer, attach the sump well to engine pan. Make sure oil pickup tube is properly positioned in the screen as sump well and screen assembly are placed in position.

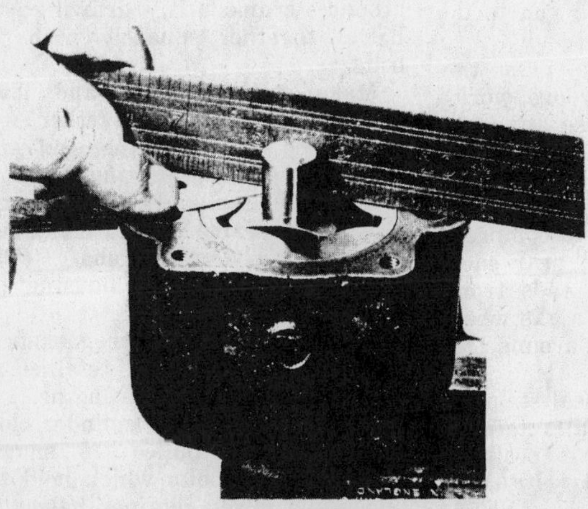

Checking end clearance of rotors
(© Chrysler Corp.)

Checking clearance between rotors
(© Chrysler Corp.)

Chevrolet Truck

YEAR	MODEL OR TYPE	FLOAT LEVEL (IN.)	FLOAT DROP (IN.)	Pump Travel Setting (IN.)	CHOKE SETTING Unloader (IN.)	CHOKE SETTING Housing	ON THE TRUCK ADJUSTMENTS Idle Screw Turns Open	Idle Speed (RPM)	Fast Idle Speed (RPM)	Dashpot Plunger Clearance (IN.)
1961-62	Updraft (C.O.E.)	1/32	None	—	—	—	½–1½	—	—	—
1963-65	YF-3402S	⅜	—	—	—	—	½–2	—	—	—
1963-66	YF-3379S	⅜	1 3/16	—	—	—	½–2	—	—	—
1964-65	YF-3821S	½	1¼	—	—	—	¾–2¼	—	—	—
1964	YF-3821SA	7/16	1¼	—	—	—	¼–2¼	—	—	—
1964	YF-3821SB	7/16	1¼	—	—	—	¼–2¼	—	—	—
1964-66	CF-3379SA	7/16	1¼	—	—	—	¾–2½	—	—	—
1964-66	YF-3379SB	7/16	1¼	—	—	—	¾–2½	—	—	—
1964-66	YF-3402SA	7/16	1¼	—	—	—	¾–2½	—	—	—
1965-66	YF-3975S	7/16	1¼	—	—	—	¼–2¼	—	—	—
1965-66	YF-3976S	7/16	1¼	—	—	—	¼–2¼	—	—	—
1965-66	YF-4043S	7/16	1¼	—	—	—	¼–2¼	—	—	—
1965-66	YF-4044S	7/16	1¼	—	—	—	¼–2¼	—	—	—
1965-66	YF-4044SA	7/16	1¼	—	—	—	¼–2¼	—	—	—
1965-66	YF-4145S	7/16	1¼	—	—	—	¼–2¼	—	—	—
1965-66	YF-4145SA	7/16	1¼	—	—	—	¼–2¼	—	—	—
1966	YF-4072S	½	1¼	—	—	—	¼–1½	—	—	—
1966	YF-4073S	½	1¼	—	—	—	¼–1½	—	—	—
1966	YF-4085S	½	1¼	—	—	—	¼–1½	—	—	—
1966	YF-4086S	½	1¼	—	—	—	¼–1½	—	—	—
1967	YF-4369S	7/32	1¼	—	—	—	¼–1¾	—	—	—
1967	YF-4370S	7/32	1¼	—	—	—	½–2	—	—	—
1967	YF-4371S	7/32	1¼	—	—	—	¼–1¾	—	—	—
1967	YF-4372S	7/32	1¼	—	—	—	¼–1¾	—	—	—
1967	YF-4373S	7/32	1¼	—	—	—	¾–2½	—	—	—
1967	YF-4374S	7/32	1¼	—	—	—	¾–2½	—	—	—
1967	YF-4375S	7/32	1¼	—	—	—	¼–2¼	—	—	—
1967	YF-4376S	7/32	1¼	—	—	—	¼–2¼	—	—	—

Dodge Truck

MODELS—BBS

YEAR	MODEL OR TYPE	FLOAT LEVEL (IN.)	FLOAT DROP (IN.)	Pump Travel Setting (IN.)	CHOKE SETTING Unloader (IN.)	CHOKE SETTING Housing	Idle Screw Turns Open	Idle Speed (RPM)	Fast Idle Speed (RPM)	Dashpot Plunger Clearance (IN.)
1961	3000S	7/32	23/32	Note 1	—	—	¼–2	—	—	—
	3001S	7/32	23/32	Note 1	—	—	¼–1¾	—	—	—
	3110S	7/32	23/32	Note 1	—	—	¼–2	—	—	—
	3111S	7/32	23/32	Note 1	3/16	—	¼–2	—	1300	—
	3112S	7/32	23/32	Note 1	3/16	—	¼–1¾	—	1400	—
	3121S	7/32	23/32	Note 1	—	—	¼–2	—	—	—
	3135S	7/32	23/32	Note 1	—	—	¼–2	—	—	—
	3136S	7/32	23/32	Note 1	—	—	¼–1¾	—	—	—
	3138S	7/32	23/32	Note 1	3/16	—	¼–2	—	1300	—
	3139S	7/32	23/32	Note 1	3/16	—	¼–1¾	—	1400	—
1962	3272S	7/32	23/32	Note 1	—	—	¼–2	—	—	—
	3273S	7/32	23/32	Note 1	—	—	¼–1¾	—	—	—
	3274S	7/32	23/32	Note 1	—	—	¼–2	—	—	—
	3275S	7/32	23/32	Note 1	3/16	2 Rich	¼–2	—	1300	—
	3278S	7/32	23/32	Note 1	—	—	¼–2	—	—	—
	3279S	7/32	23/32	Note 1	—	—	¼–1¾	—	—	—
1962-63	3280S	7/32	23/32	Note 1	3/16	2 Rich	¼–2	—	1300	—
	3181S	7/32	23/32	Note 1	3/16	2 Rich	¼–1¾	—	1400	—
	3401S	7/32	23/32	Note 1	—	—	¼–2	—	—	—
1962-68	3277S	7/32	23/32	Note 1	—	—	¼–2	—	—	—
1963	3492S	7/32	23/32	Note 1	—	—	¼–2	—	—	—
1963-65	3491S	7/32	23/32	Note 1	—	—	¼–1¾	—	—	—
1964	3812S	¼	23/32	Note 1	3/16	2 Rich	¼–3	—	700	—
	3813S	¼	23/32	Note 1	3/16	2 Rich	¼–3	—	700	—

YEAR	MODEL OR TYPE	FLOAT LEVEL (IN.)	FLOAT DROP (IN.)	Pump Travel Setting (IN.)	CHOKE SETTING Unloader (IN.)	CHOKE SETTING Housing	ON THE TRUCK ADJUSTMENTS Idle Screw Turns Open	ON THE TRUCK ADJUSTMENTS Idle Speed (RPM)	ON THE TRUCK ADJUSTMENTS Fast Idle Speed (RPM)	ON THE TRUCK ADJUSTMENTS Dashpot Plunger Clearance (IN.)
Dodge Truck, Continued										
1964-65	3699S	¼	23/32	Note 1	3/16	2 Rich	¼–3	—	700	—
1966	4175S	¼	23/32	Note 1	—	—	2–3	—	—	—
	4176S	¼	23/32	Note 1	3/16	2 Rich	1½–2½	—	1550	—
	4178S	¼	23/32	Note 1	3/16	2 Rich	1½–2½	—	700	—
1966-67	4177S	¼	23/32	Note 1	—	—	¾–1¾	—	—	—
1967-68	4334S	¼	23/32	Note 1	—	—	¾–1¾	—	—	—
	4340S	7/32	23/32	Note 1	—	—	2–3	—	—	—
	4341S	¼	23/32	Note 1	—	—	1½–2½	—	—	—
	4342S	¼	23/32	Note 1	—	—	1½–2½	—	700	—
1968	4478S	¼	23/32	Note 1	—	—	1–2	—	2800	—
1969	4658S	¼	23/32	Note 1	—	—	1–2	—	2600	—
	4659S	¼	23/32	Note 1	3/16	2 Rich	1–2	—	700	—
	4629S	¼	23/32	Note 1	—	—	1–2	—	2800	—
	4630S	¼	23/32	Note 1	3/16	2 Rich	1–2	—	1550	—
	4703S	¼	23/32	Note 1	—	—	1–2	—	—	—
MODELS—BBD										
1961-68	2905S	17/64	23/32	1 1/32	—	—	¼–1½	—	—	—
	2905SA	17/64	23/32	1 1/32	—	—	¼–1½	—	—	—
1966-67	4113S	¼	23/32	Note 1	¼	2 Rich	½–2¾	—	700	—
	4113SA	¼	23/32	Note 1	¼	2 Rich	½–2¾	—	700	—
	4114S	¼	23/32	Note 1	¼	2 Rich	½–2¾	—	700	—
	4114SA	¼	23/32	Note 1	¼	2 Rich	½–2¾	—	700	—
	4115S	¼	23/32	1 1/64	¼	Index	2½–3¼	—	1400	—
	4115SA	¼	23/32	1 1/64	¼	Index	2½–3¼	—	1400	—
	4116S	¼	23/32	1 1/64	¼	2 Rich	2½–3	—	1500	—
	4116SA	¼	23/32	1 1/64	¼	2 Rich	2½–3	—	1500	—
1967	4296S	11/32	23/32	1	¼	2 Rich	¼–1½	—	700	—
	4297S	11/32	23/32	1	¼	2 Rich	¼–1½	—	700	—
	4306S	11/32	23/32	29/32	¼	2 Rich	¼–1½	—	Note 2	—
	4307S	11/32	23/32	29/32	¼	2 Rich	¼–1½	—	Note 2	—
1968	4422S	5/16	23/32	1	¼	2 Rich	1½	—	1600	—
	4423S	5/16	23/32	1	¼	2 Rich	1½	—	1600	—
	4420S	¼	23/32	Note 1	¼	2 Rich	1	—	1300	—
	4421S	¼	23/32	Note 1	¼	2 Rich	1	—	1500	—
1969	4613S	5/16	23/32	1	¼	2 Rich	1½	—	1600	—
	4614S	5/16	23/32	1	¼	2 Rich	1½	—	1600	—
	4748S	5/16	23/32	1	¼	2 Rich	1½	—	1600	—
MODELS—AFB										
1961-62	2906S	7/32	33/64	—	—	—	⅛–1½	—	—	—
1963-66	3452S	7/32	33/64	—	—	—	⅛–1½	—	—	—
1967-68	4393S	7/32	33/64	—	—	—	⅛–1½	—	—	—

Note 1—When bowel vent is properly adjusted pump is automatically adjusted.
Note 2—Standard Transmission 1700 rpm. Automatic Transmission 1400 rpm.

YEAR	MODEL OR TYPE	FLOAT LEVEL (IN.)	FLOAT DROP (IN.)	Pump Travel Setting (IN.)	CHOKE SETTING Unloader (IN.)	CHOKE SETTING Housing	Idle Screw Turns Open	Idle Speed (RPM)	Fast Idle Speed (RPM)	Dashpot Plunger Clearance (IN.)
Ford Truck										
1968	C8UF9510-G (1 BBL)	7/32[1]	—	—	—	—	1½	—	—	.100
1969	C8UF9510-M (1 BBL)	7/32[1]	—	—	—	—	—	775-500	—	—
	C8TF9510-BE (1 BBL)	7/32[1]	—	—	—	—	—	750	—	.100
	C9TF9510-E (1 BBL)	7/32[1]	—	—	—	—	—	[2]	—	.100
	C9TF9510-M (1 BBL)	7/32[1]	—	—	—	—	—	775-500	—	—
	C9TF9510-F (1 BBL)	7/32[1]	—	—	—	—	—	[2]	—	.100
1970 & Up	D0TF9510-F (1 BBL)	7/32[1]	—	—	Lean	—	—	775-500	—	—
	C9TF9510-F (1 BBL)	7/32[1]	—	—	—	—	—	[2]	—	7/64

YEAR	MODEL OR TYPE	FLOAT LEVEL (IN.)	FLOAT DROP (IN.)	Pump Travel Setting	CHOKE SETTING Unloader (IN.)	CHOKE SETTING Housing	ON THE TRUCK ADJUSTMENTS Idle Screw Turns Open	ON THE TRUCK ADJUSTMENTS Idle Speed (RPM)	ON THE TRUCK ADJUSTMENTS Fast Idle Speed (RPM)	ON THE TRUCK ADJUSTMENTS Dashpot Plunger Clearance (IN.)
Ford Truck Continued										
	DOTF9510-G (1 BBL	7/32 [1]	—	—	—	—	—	550 500	—	—
	DOTF9510-K (1 BBL)	7/32 [1]	—	—	Lean	—	—	[2]	—	7/64

Note 1—From bead of upper body to lowest surface of float when inverted.
Note 2—Standard Transmission—600 RPM. Automatic Transmission—550 RPM.

GMC Trucks

YEAR	MODEL OR TYPE	FLOAT LEVEL (IN.)	FLOAT DROP (IN.)	Pump Travel Setting	Unloader (IN.)	Housing	Idle Screw Turns Open	Idle Speed (RPM)	Fast Idle Speed (RPM)	Dashpot Plunger Clearance (IN.)
1963-64	YF	3/8	1 3/16	—	—	—	1/2–2	—	—	—
1964-66	YF-3402	7/16	1 3/16	—	—	—	1/2–2	500	—	—
	YF-3379	7/16	1 1/4	—	—	—	3/4–2 1/2	500	—	—
	YF-4373S	7/32	1 1/4	—	—	—	3/4–2 1/2	500	—	—
	YF-4374S	7/32	1 1/4	—	—	—	3/4–2 1/2	500	—	—
1964	YF-3821	7/16	1 1/4	—	—	—	1/4–2 1/4	500	—	—
	YF-3975S	7/16	1 1/4	—	—	—	1/4–2 1/4	500	—	—
1965	YF-3976S	7/16	1 1/4	—	—	—	1/4–2 1/4	500	—	—
	YF-4043S	7/16	1 1/4	—	—	—	1/4–2 1/4	500	—	—
	YF-4044	7/16	1 1/4	—	—	—	1/4–2 1/4	500	—	—
1966	YF-4072S	1/2	1 1/4	—	—	—	1/4–1 1/2	700	—	—
	YF-4073S	1/2	1 1/4	—	—	—	1/4–1 1/2	700	—	—
	YF-4085S	1/2	1 1/4	—	—	—	1/4–1 1/2	700	—	—
	YF-4086S	1/2	1 1/4	—	—	—	1/4–1 1/2	700	—	—
1967	YF-4369S	7/32	1 3/16	—	—	—	1/4–1 3/4	650	—	—
	YF-4370S	7/32	1 3/16	—	—	—	1/2–2	650	—	—
	YF-4371S	7/32	1 3/16	—	—	—	1/4–1 3/4	650	—	—
	YF-4372S	7/32	1 3/16	—	—	—	1/2–2	650	—	—
	YF-4375S	7/32	1 3/16	—	—	—	1/4–2 1/4	500	—	—
	YF-4376S	7/32	1 3/16	—	—	—	1/4–2 1/4	500	—	—

Note: For further information shown below see illustration.
1. Fast idle adjustment.
2. Unloader adjustment.
3. Metering rod adjustment.
4. Float drop adjustment.

Jeep Truck

YEAR	MODEL OR TYPE	FLOAT LEVEL (IN.)	FLOAT DROP (IN.)	Pump Travel Setting	Unloader (IN.)	Housing	Idle Screw Turns Open	Idle Speed (RPM)	Fast Idle Speed (RPM)	Dashpot Plunger Clearance (IN.)
1961-62	WCD-2204S	3/16	None	11/32	1/8	—	1–2	—	—	—
	WGD-2052SA	—	None	1/2	9/64	—	1/2–1 1/2	—	—	—
	YF-951S	5/16	None	None	None	None	3/4–1 3/4	—	—	—
	YF-951SA	5/16	None	None	None	None	3/4–1 3/4	—	—	—
1961-63	YF-2467S	9/32	1 1/4	—	None	None	1–2 1/2	—	—	—

Note: For further information on settings see illustration.

CARTER UPDRAFT TYPE

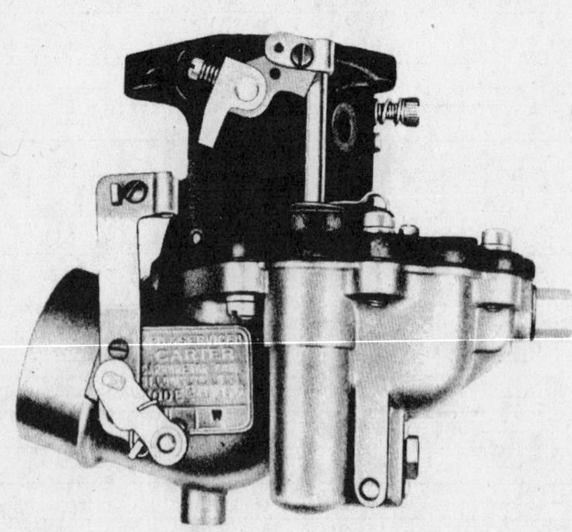

1961-72 updraft type

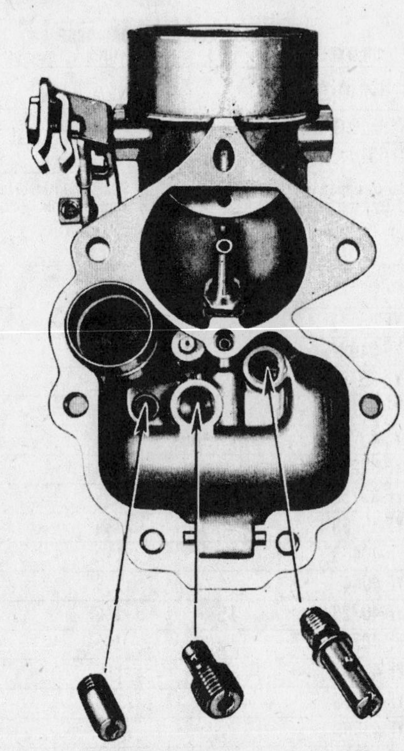

Carburetor jet installation

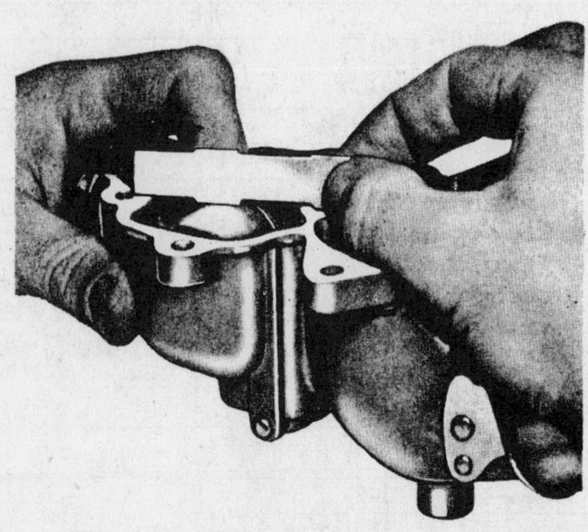

Checking float level

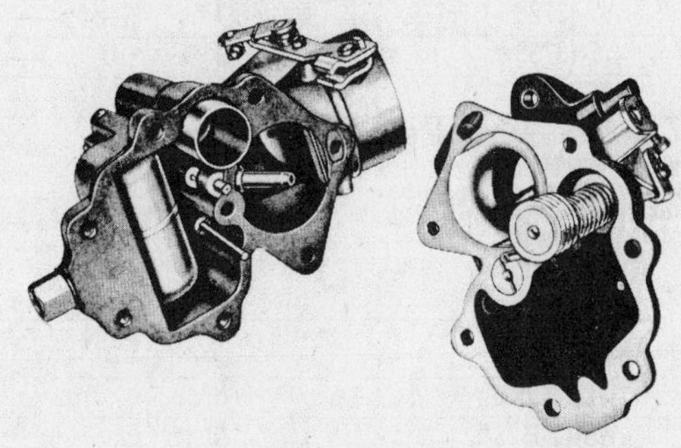

Bowl cover assembly

SINGLE BARREL—YF TYPE

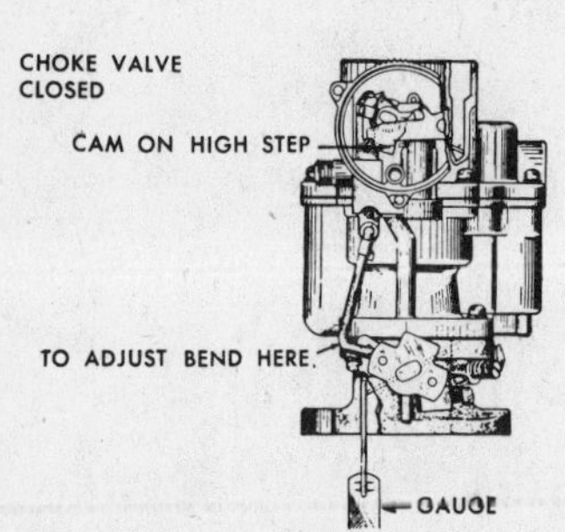

YF fast idle adjustment

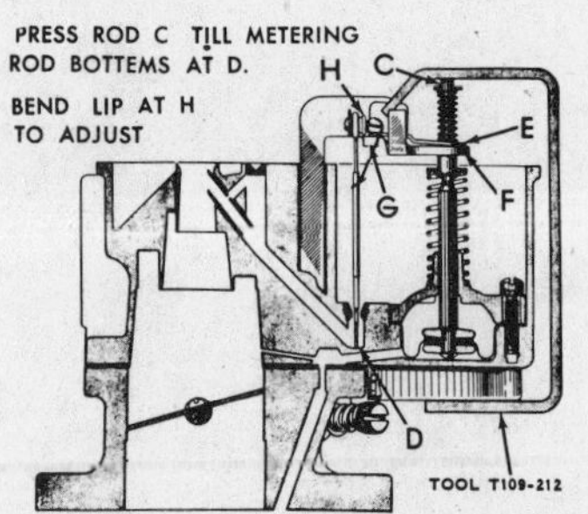

YF metering rod adjustment

SINGLE BARREL—YF TYPE

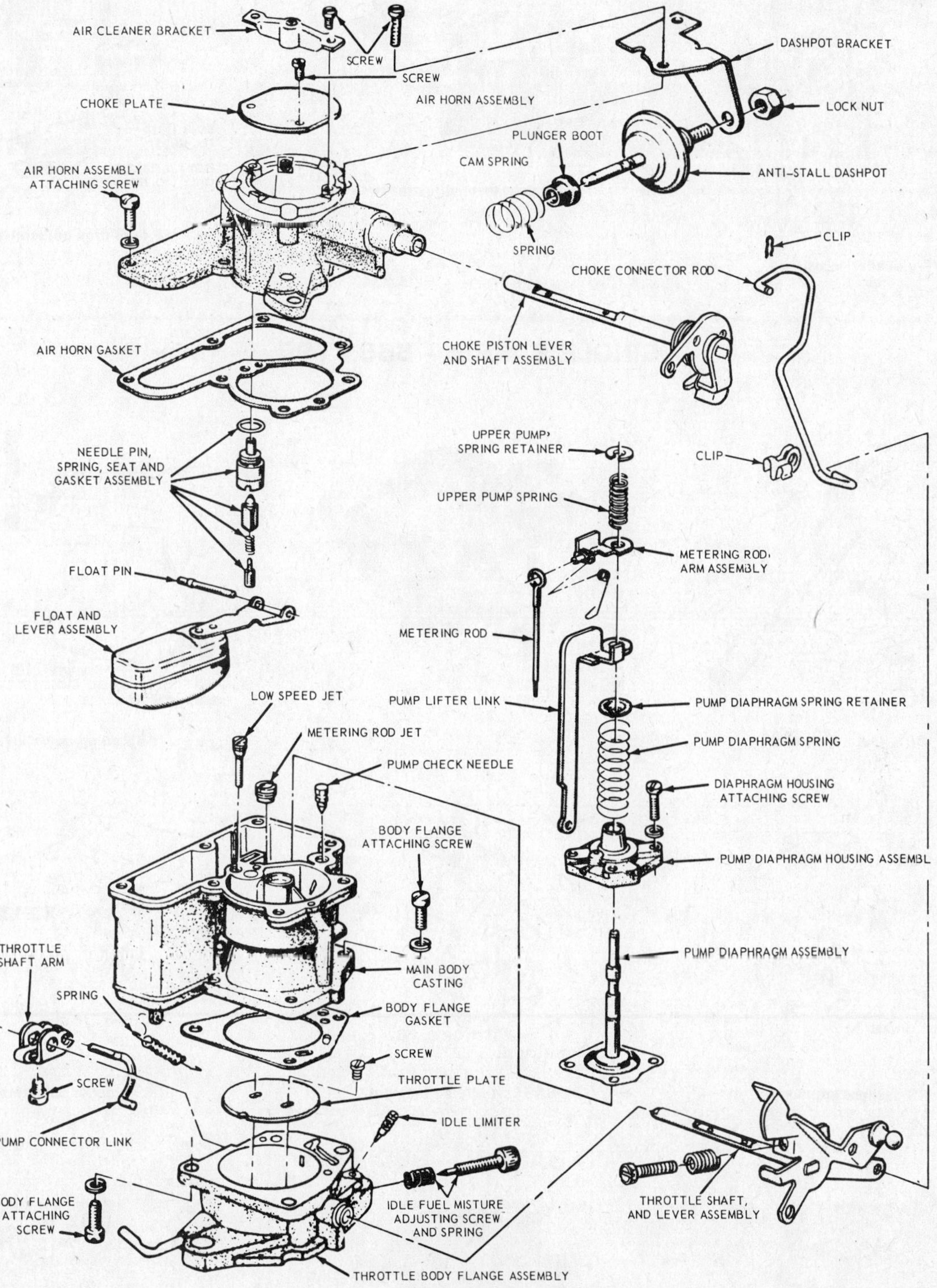

Single barrel YF carburetor—exploded view

SINGLE BARREL—YF TYPE continued

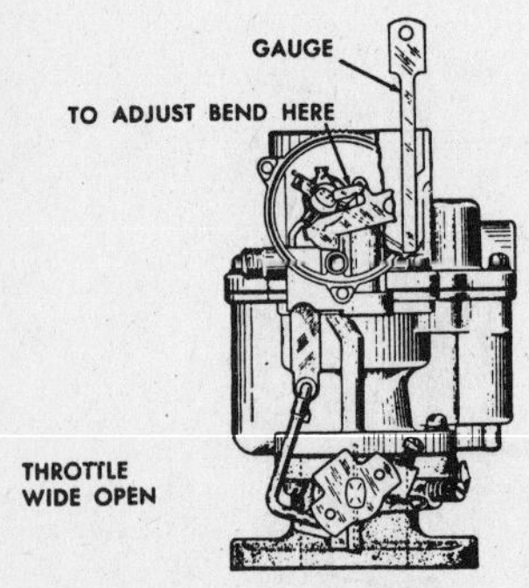

YF unloader adjustment

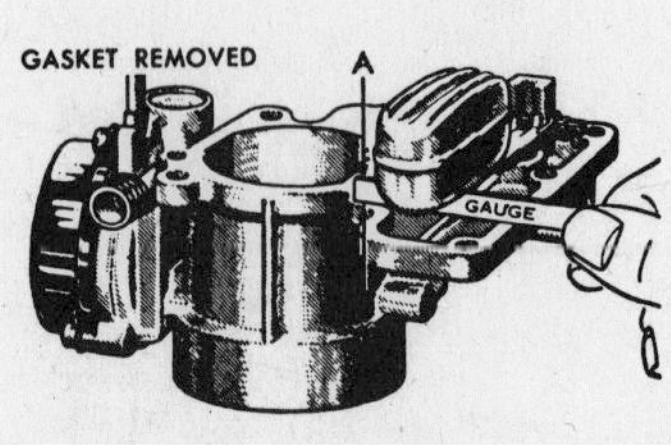

YF float level adjustment

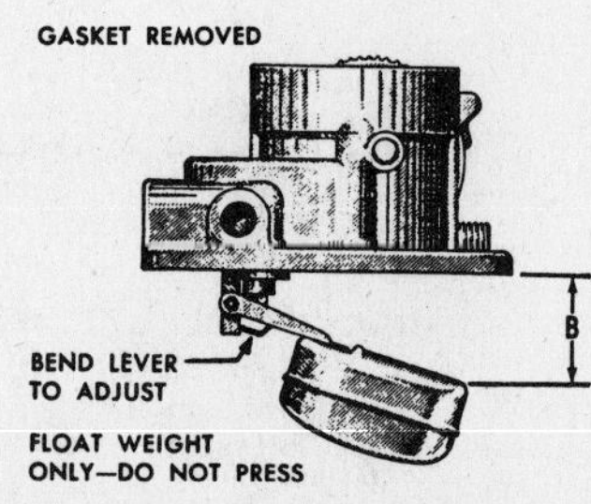

YF float drop adjustment

SINGLE BARREL—BBS TYPE

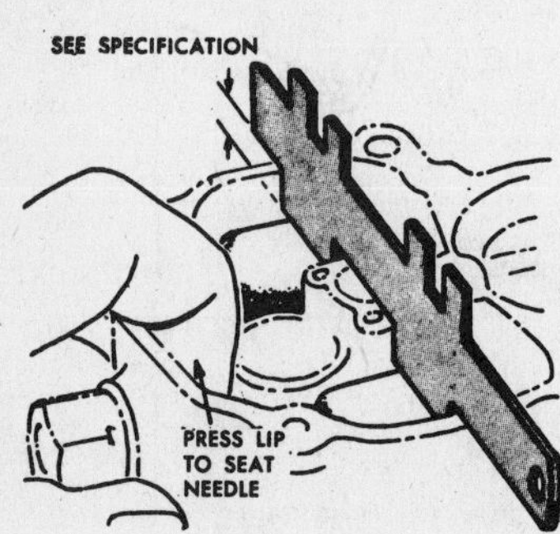

BBS float adjustment

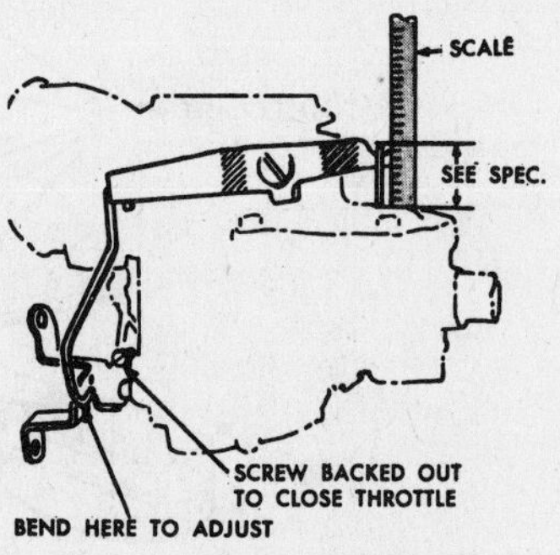

BBS pump adjustment

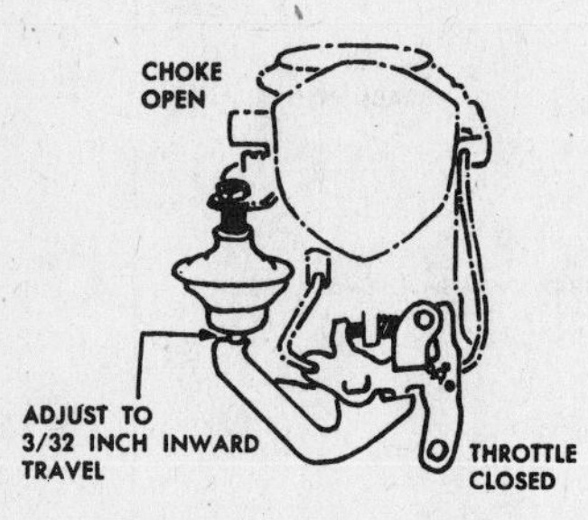

BBS dashpot adjustment

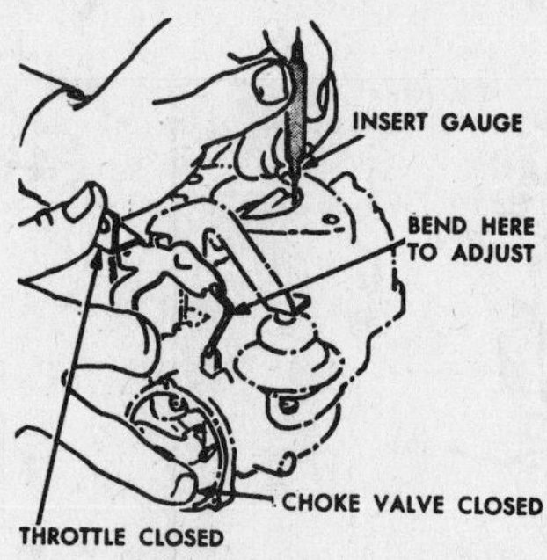

BBS fast idle adjustment

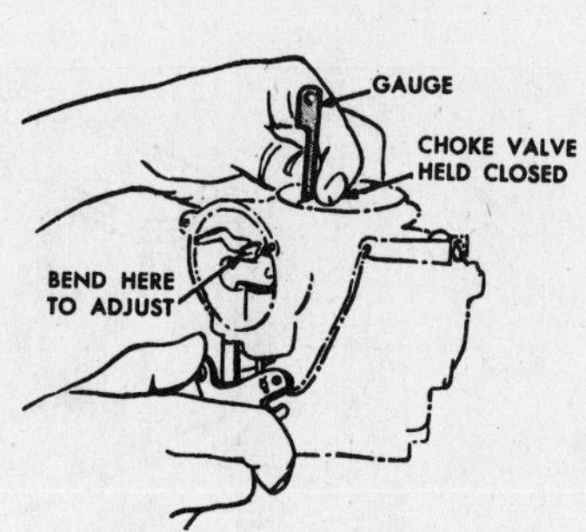

BBS unloader adjustment

TWO BARREL—BBD TYPE

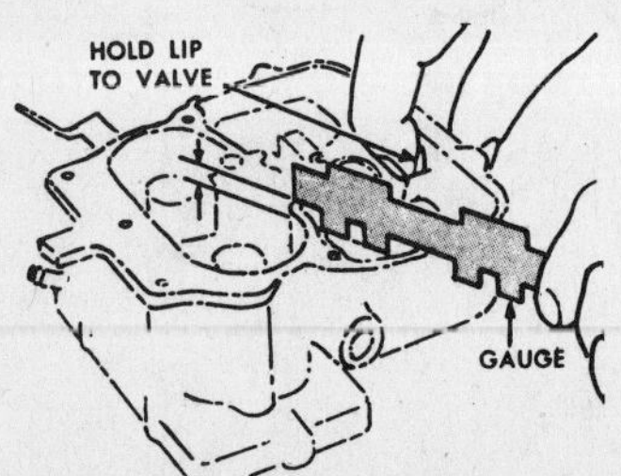

BBD float adjustment

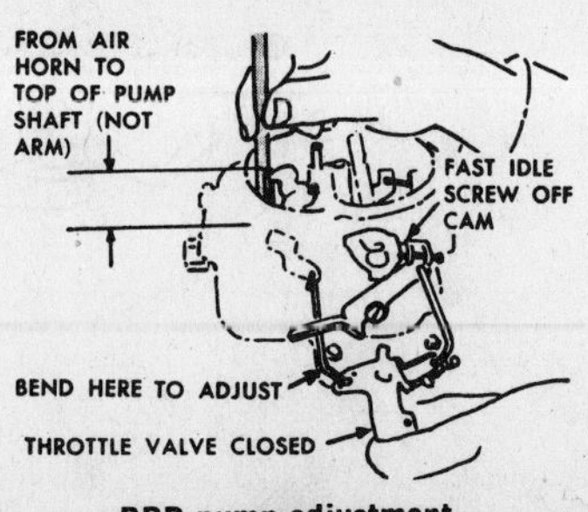

BBD pump adjustment

SINGLE BARREL—BBS TYPE

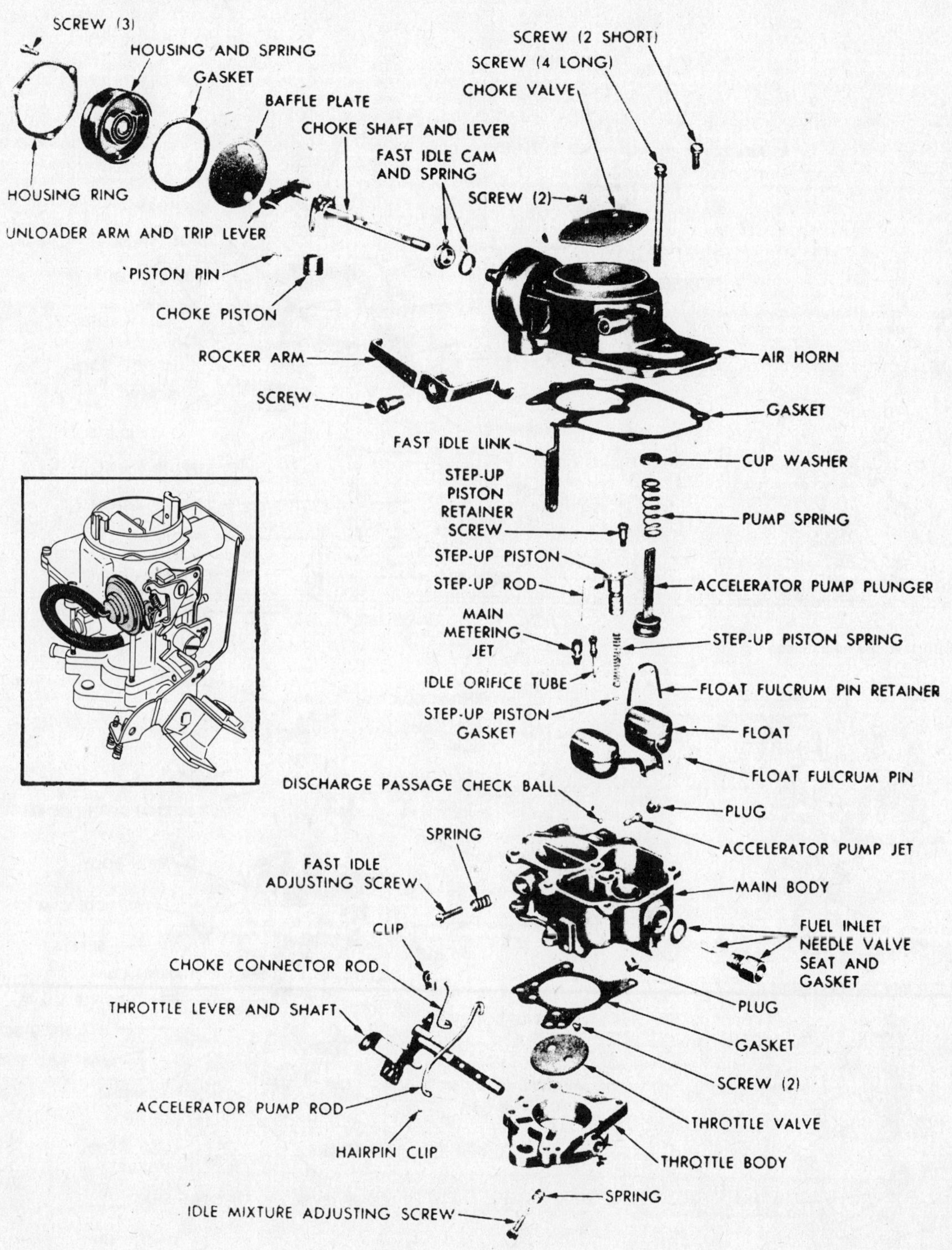

Carter BBS single barrel—typical

TWO BARREL—BBD TYPE continued

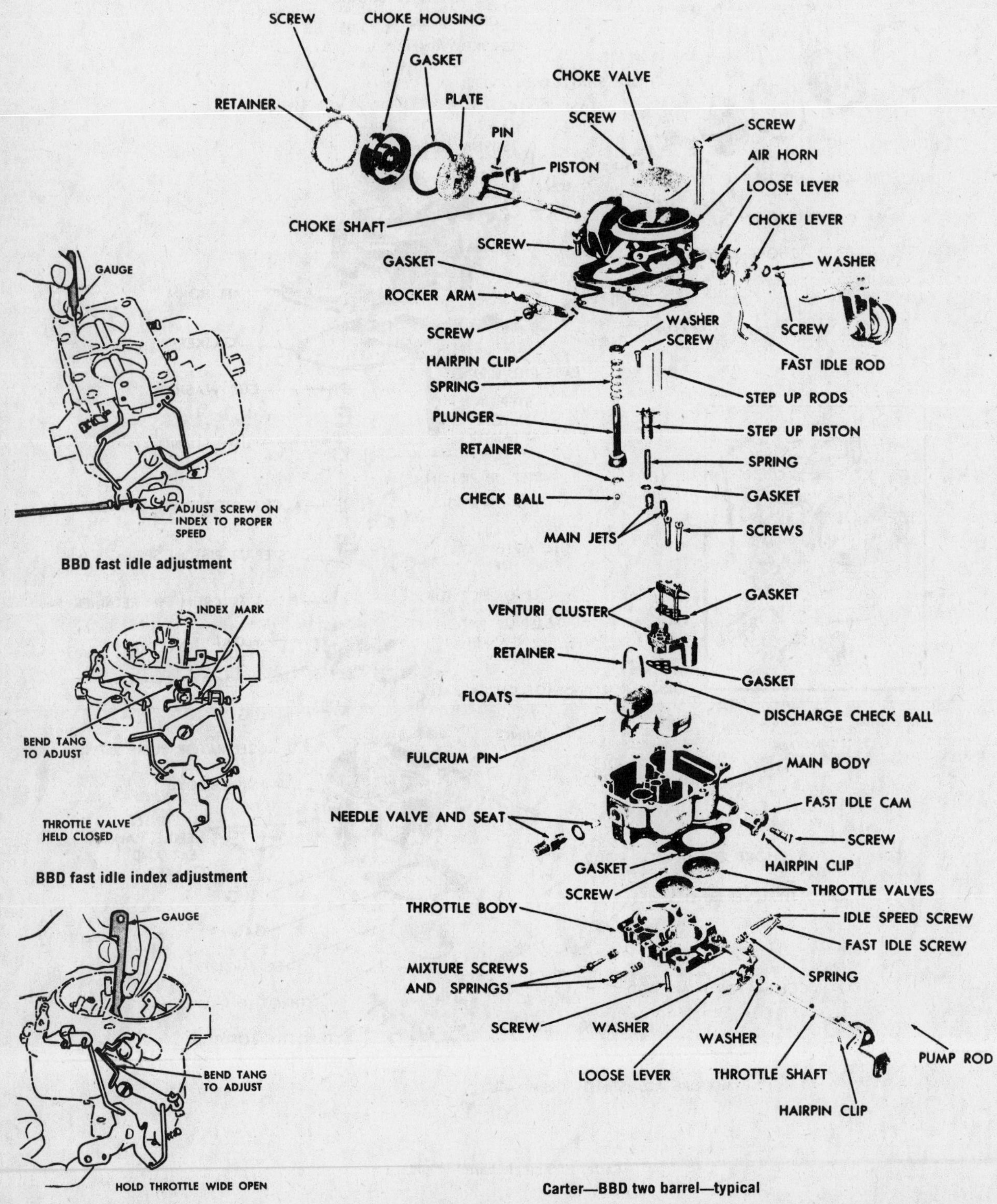

BBD fast idle adjustment

BBD fast idle index adjustment

Carter—BBD two barrel—typical

BBD unloader adjustment

TWO BARREL—WCD TYPE

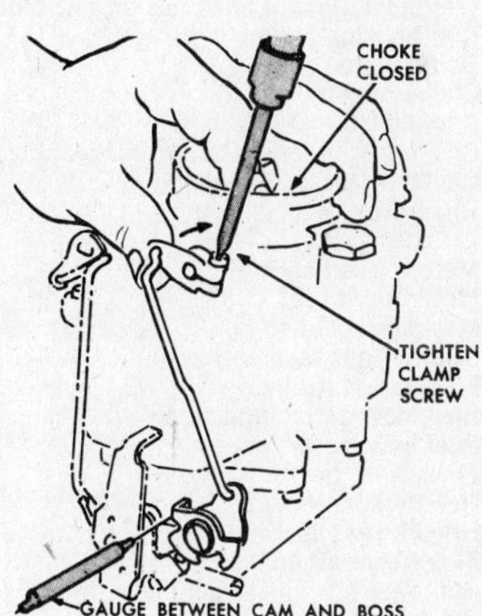

WCD fast idle adjustment (step 1)

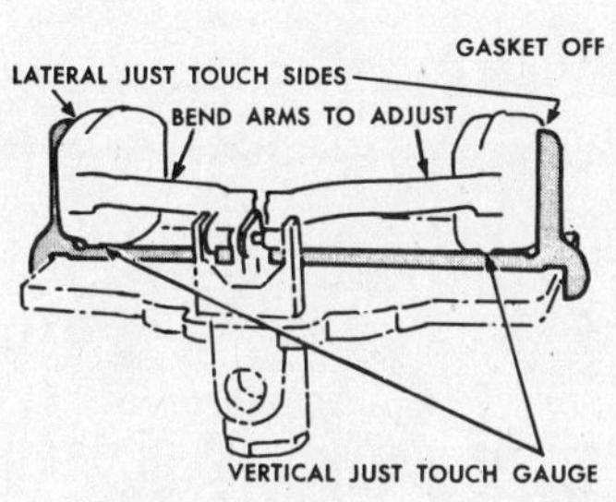

WCD float adjustment

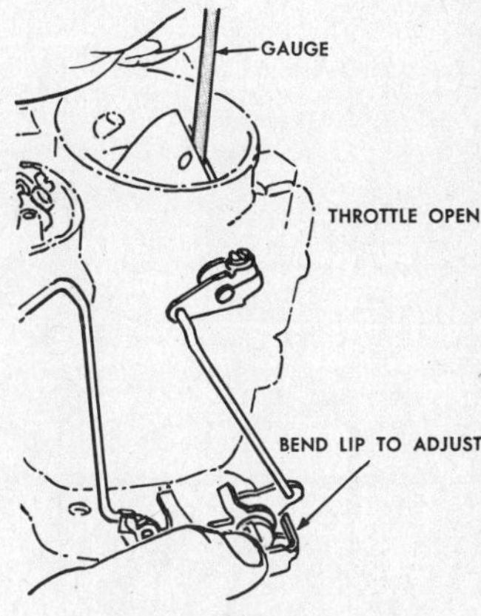

WCD unloader adjustment

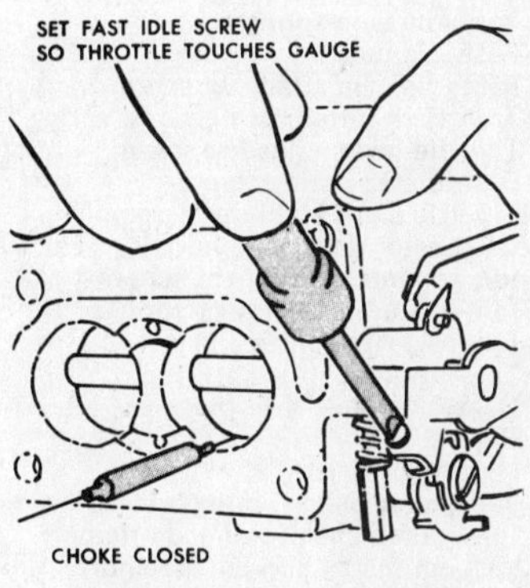

WCD fast idle adjustment (step 2)

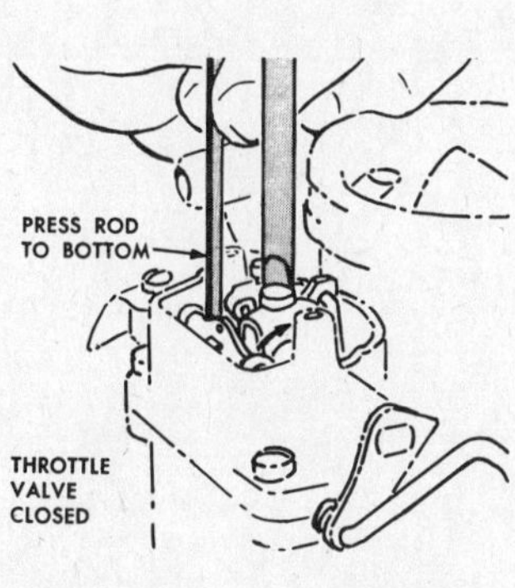

WCD metering rod adjustment

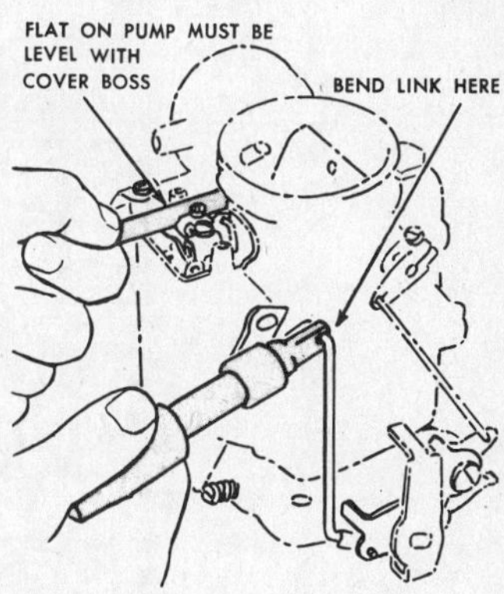

WCD pump adjustment

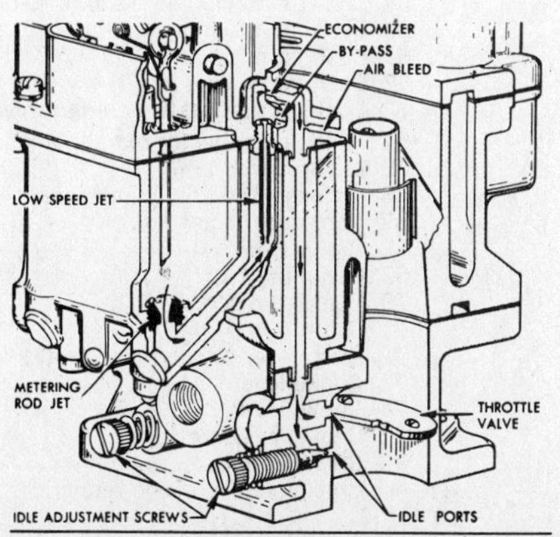

WCD low speed system

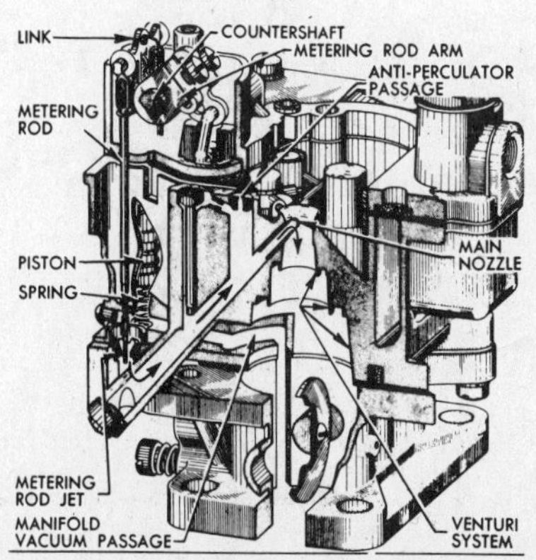

WCD high speed and power systems

TWO BARREL—WCD TYPE continued

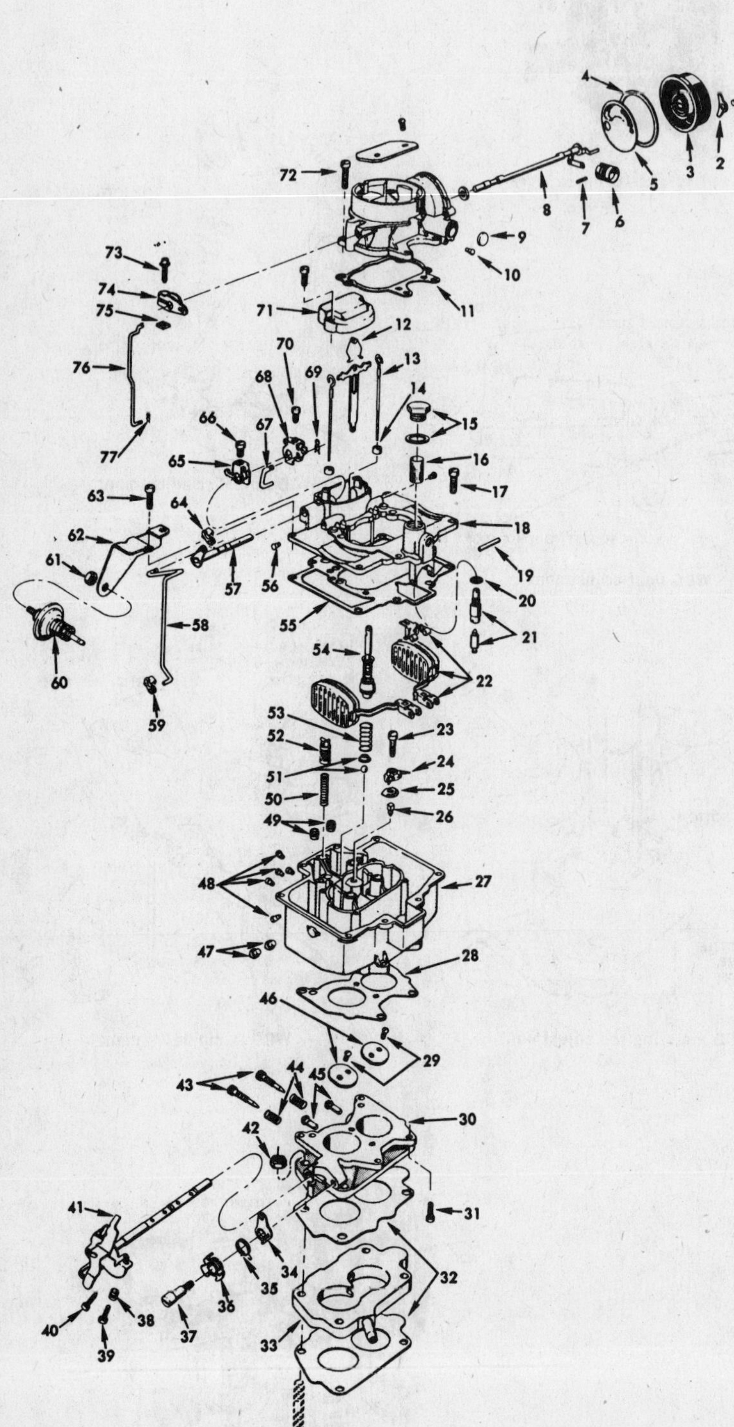

Assembly sequence—model WCD carburetor

1 Coil housing attaching screws (3)
2 Coil housing retainer (3)
3 Thermostatic coil and housing assembly
4 Coil housing gasket
5 Baffle plate
6 Choke piston
7 Choke piston pin
8 Choke piston lever and shaft assembly
9 Choke piston passage plug
10 Rivet plug
11 Air horn gasket
12 Metering rod spring
13 Metering rod (2)
14 Metering rod disc (2)
15 Strainer nut assembly
16 Bowl cover strainer
17 Bowl cover attaching screw (4)
18 Fuel bowl cover
19 Float lever pin
20 Needle seat gasket
21 Needle seat assembly
22 Float lever assembly
23 Pump jet housing attaching screw
24 Pump jet and housing assembly
25 Pump jet housing gasket
26 Pump check needle
27 Fuel bowl
28 Throttle body gasket
29 Throttle valve attaching screw (4)
30 Throttle body
31 Throttle body attaching screws (4)
32 Flange gasket (2)
33 Flange adaptor
34 Cam trip lever
35 Fast idle cam spring
36 Fast idle cam
37 Fast idle cam attaching screw
38 Throttle lever adjusting screw spring
39 Throttle lever adjusting screw
40 Fast idle adjusting screw
41 Throttle shaft and lever assembly
42 Carburetor hold-down nut
43 Idle mixture adjustment screws
44 Idle mixture adjustment springs
45 Idle port rivet plugs
46 Throttle valves
47 Nozzle passage rivet plugs
48 Rivet plugs
49 Metering rod jets
50 Vacumeter piston spring
51 Inlet pump check ball and retainer
52 Vacuum piston and pin assembly
53 Lower pump spring
54 Pump plunger assembly
55 Bowl cover gasket
56 Rivet plug
57 Pump operating lever and countershaft assembly
58 Throttle connector rod
59 Throttle connector rod lower retainer
60 Dashpot assembly
61 Dashpot nut
62 Dashpot bracket
63 Dashpot bracket attaching screw (2)
64 Throttle connector rod upper retainer
65 Metering rod arm
66 Metering rod arm clamp screw
67 Pump connector link
68 Pump arm
69 Retaining clip
70 Pump arm screw
71 Dust cover
72 Dust cover attaching screw (2)
73 Choke lever screw
74 Choke lever
75 Choke lever nut
76 Choke connector rod
77 Choke connector rod retainer

TWO BARREL—WGD TYPE

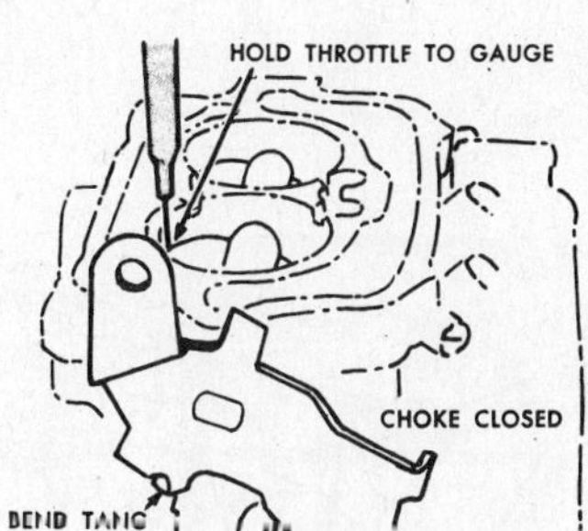

WGD fast idle adjustment

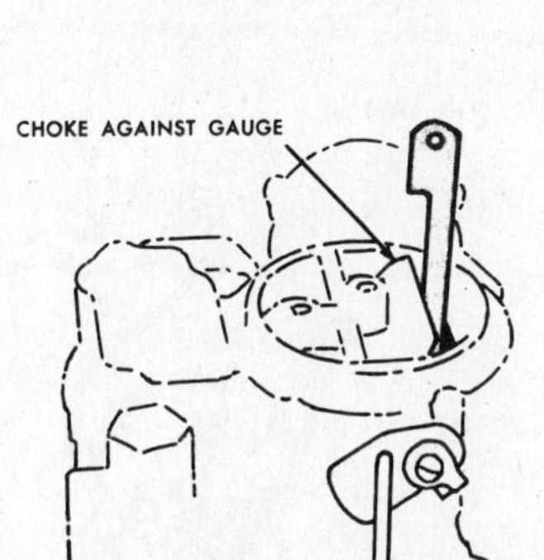

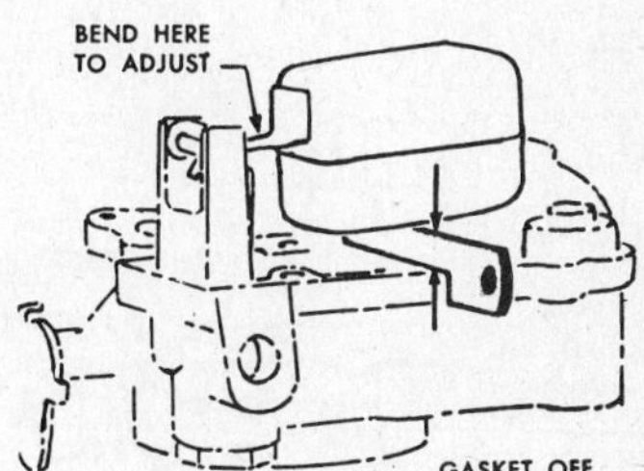

WGD float adjustment

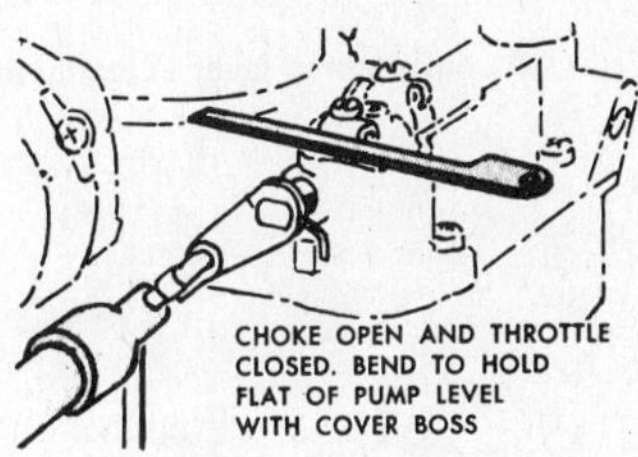

WGD pump adjustment

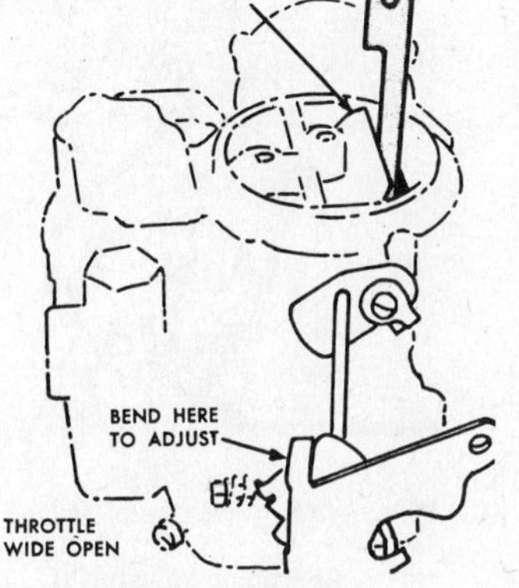

WGD unloader adjustment

TIGHTEN
REVOLVE ARM TO TOUCH LINK
HOLD RODS ON SEAT

WGD metering rod adjustment

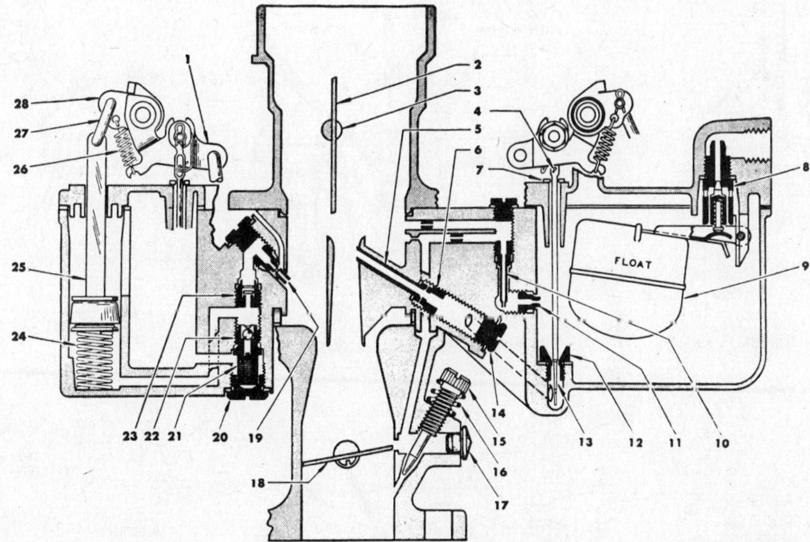

WGD two barrel carburetor

1 Pump operating lever assembly
2 Choke valve assembly
3 Choke shaft and lever assembly
4 Metering rod spring
5 Nozzle
6 Nozzle retaining plug
7 Metering rod disc
8 Needle, pin, spring and seat assembly
9 Float and lever assembly
10 Low speed jet assembly
11 Idle well jet
12 Metering rod jet and gasket assembly
13 Metering rod
14 Nozzle passage plug and gasket assembly
15 Idle adjustment screw
16 Idle adjustment screw spring
17 Idle port rivet plug
18 Throttle valve
19 Pump jet
20 Pump jet strainer nut
21 Pump jet strainer
22 Intake ball check assembly
23 Discharge disc check assembly
24 Pump plunger spring
25 Pump plunger and rod assembly
26 Pump arm spring
27 Pump connecting link
28 Pump arm and collar assembly

FOUR BARREL—AFB TYPE

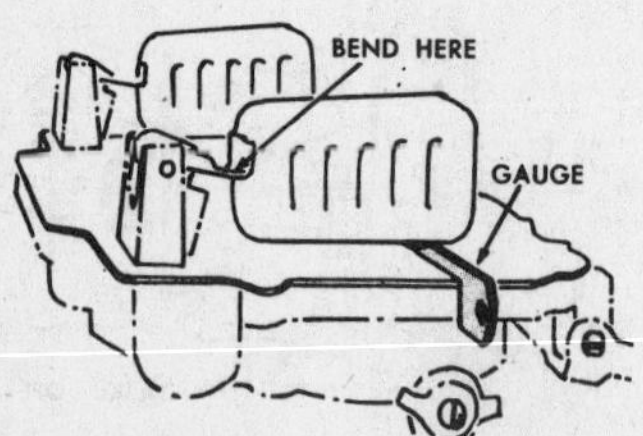

AFB float level adjustment

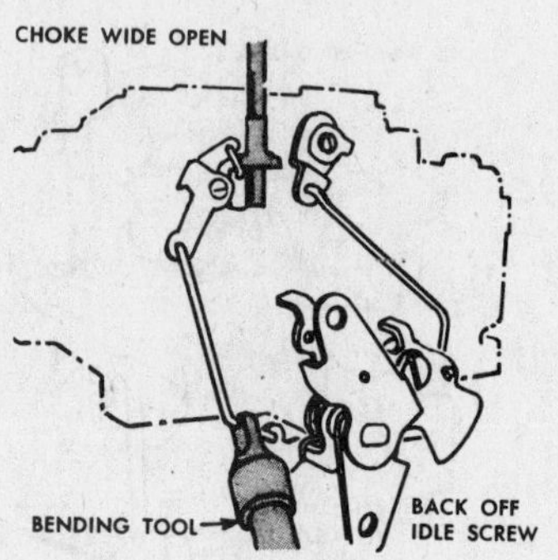

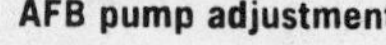

AFB pump adjustment

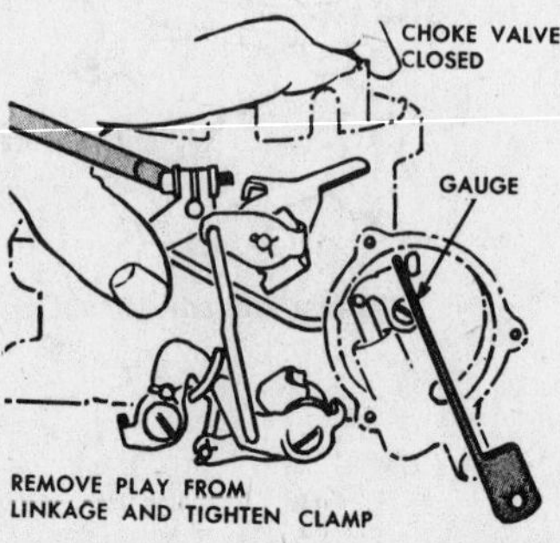

AFB choke piston lever adjustment

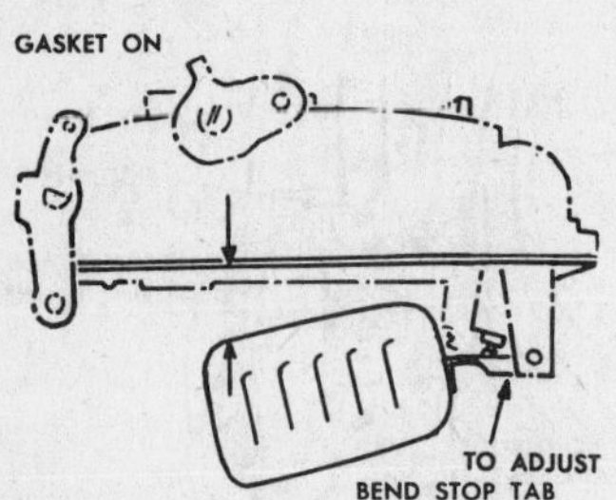

AFB float drop adjustment

AFB dashpot adjustment

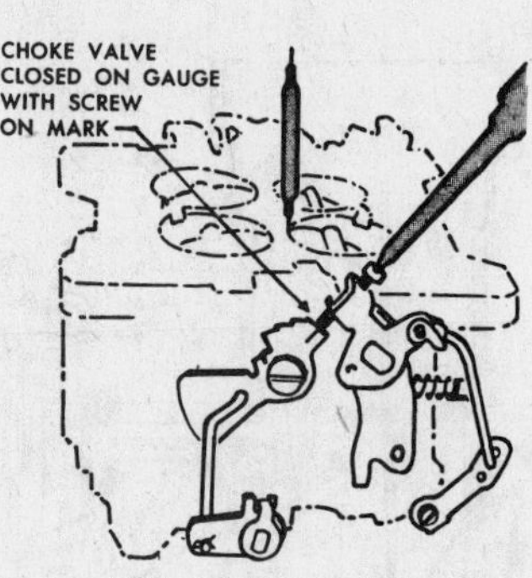
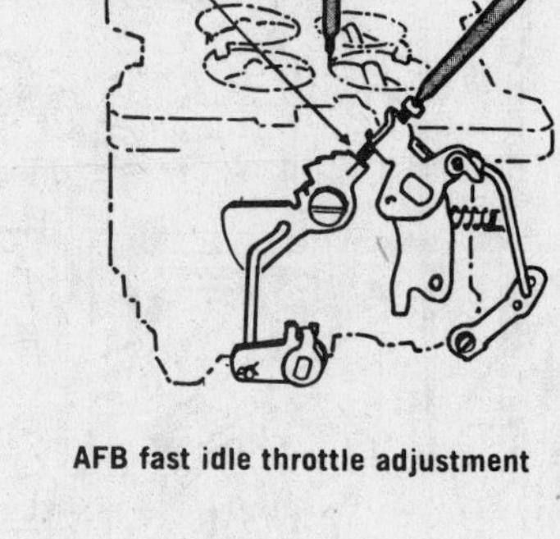

AFB fast idle throttle adjustment

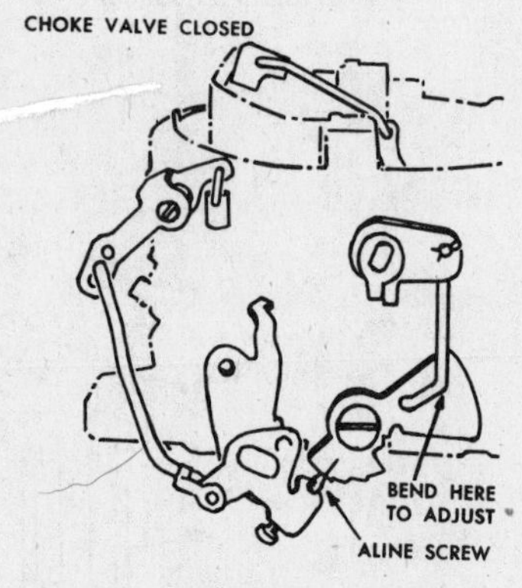

AFB fast idle linkage adjustment

PRIMARY OPEN TO SPECIFICATION

SECONDARY STARTS TO OPEN

BEND HERE

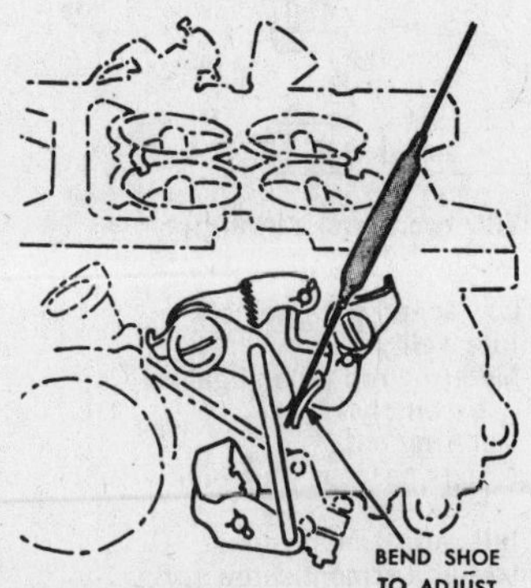

AFB secondary throttle adjustment

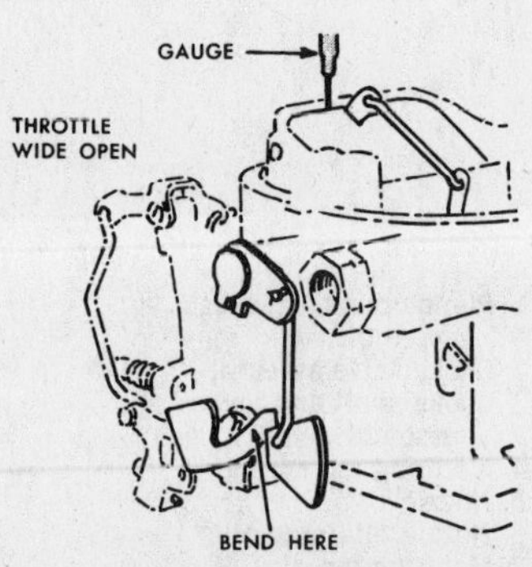

AFB unloader adjustment

FOUR BARREL—AFB TYPE

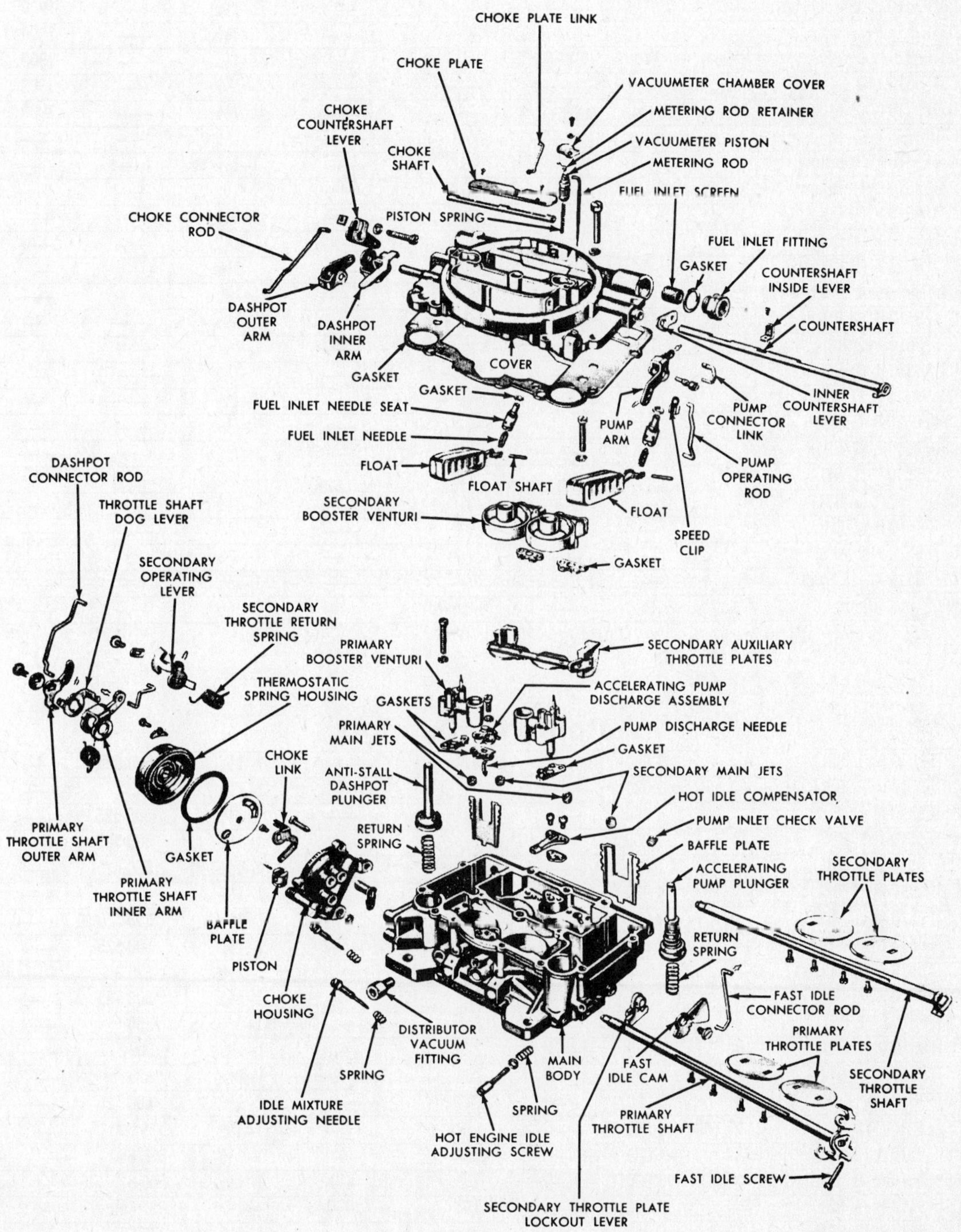

Carter AFB four barrel—typical

YEAR	MODEL OR TYPE	Float Level (IN.)	Fuel Level (IN.)	Fast Idle Cam (IN.)	Pump Travel Setting	Choke Setting	Idle Screw Turns Open	ON THE TRUCK ADJUSTMENTS Idle Speed (RPM)	Fast Idle Speed (RPM)	Dashpot Plunger Clearance (IN.)
Ford Truck										
1962	C2TE9510L	13/64	3/4	—	—	—	1–1½	—	—	—
	Other 1 BBL Carbs.	13/64	11/16	—	—	—	1–1½	—	—	—
1963	All 1 BBL Carbs.	1	—	—	—	—	4–5	—	—	1½-2
	C3TF9510-E (2 BBL)	—	[1]	—	—	—	1–1½	—	1900	5/64
	C3TF9510-B (2 BBL)	—	[1]	—	—	—	1–1½	—	1900	5/64
	C3TF9510-H (2 BBL)	21/32	—	—	—	—	1–1½	—	1900	5/64
	C3TF9510-J (2 BBL)	21/32	—	—	—	—	1–1½	—	1900	—
	C3TF9510-K (2 BBL)	21/32	—	—	—	—	1–1½	—	1900	5/64
1964	C3UF9510-F (1 BBL)	1	—	—	3/16[2]	—	1–1½	—	—	3½[3]
	C3TF9510-T (1 BBL)	1	—	—	3/16[2]	—	1–1½	—	—	3½[3]
	C3TF9510-U (1 BBL)	1	—	—	3/16[2]	—	1–1½	—	—	3½[3]
	C3TF9510-V (1 BBL)	1	—	—	3/16[2]	—	1–1½	—	—	3½[3]
	C3TF9510-Y (1 BBL)	1	—	—	3/16[2]	—	1–1½	—	—	3½[3]
	C3TF9510-Z (1 BBL)	1	—	—	3/16[2]	—	1–1½	—	—	3½[3]
	C4TF9510-E (1 BBL)	1	—	—	3/16[2]	—	1–1½	—	—	3½[3]
	CT3F9510-H (2 BBL)	21/32	29/32	—	Inboard	—	1–1½	—	—	—
	CT3F9510-J (2 BBL)	21/32	29/32	—	Inboard	—	1–1½	—	—	5/16
	C3TF9510-K (2 BBL)	21/32	29/32	—	Inboard	—	1–1½	—	—	—
1965	C5UF9510-A (1 BBL)	[4]	—	—	3/16[2]	—	1–1½	—	—	3½[3]
	C5UF9510-B (1 BBL)	[4]	—	—	3/16[2]	—	1–1½	—	—	3½[3]
	C5UF9510-E (1 BBL)	[4]	—	—	3/16[2]	—	1–1½	—	—	3½[3]
	C5UF9510-F (1 BBL)	[4]	—	—	3/16[2]	—	1–1½	—	—	3½[3]
	C5TF9510-G (1 BBL)	[4]	—	—	7/32[2]	—	1–1½	—	—	3½[3]
	C5TF9510-H (1 BBL)	[4]	—	—	7/32[2]	—	1–1½	—	—	3½[3]
	C5TF9510-J (1 BBL)	[4]	—	—	7/32[2]	—	1–1½	—	—	3½[3]
	C5TF9510-AC (1 BBL)	[4]	—	—	7/32[2]	—	1–1½	—	—	3½[3]
	All 2 BBL Carbs.	29/64	29/32	—	Inboard	—	1–1½	—	—	—

Autolite Carburetors

YEAR	MODEL OR TYPE	Float Level (IN.)	Fuel Level (IN.)	Fast Idle Cam (IN.)	Pump Travel Setting	Choke Setting	Idle Screw Turns Open	Idle Speed (RPM)	Fast Idle Speed (RPM)	Dashpot Plunger Clearance (IN.)
1966	C5TF9510-G (1 BBL)	—	1.090	—	.23[2]	—	1–1½	500-525	—	3½[3]
	C6TF9510-H (1 BBL)	—	1.020	—	.21[2]	—	1–1½	600	—	3½[3]
	C5TF9510-M (1 BBL)	—	1.090	—	.23[2]	—	1–1½	500-525	—	3½[3]
	C6TF9510-J (1 BBL)	—	1.200	—	.21[2]	—	1–1½	500-525	—	3½[3]
	C6TF9510-E (1 BBL)	—	1.020	—	.22[2]	—	1–1½	500-525	—	3½[3]
	C6TF9510-M (1 BBL)	—	1.020	—	.22[2]	—	1–1½	600	—	—
	C5TF9510-AC (1 BBL)	—	1.090	—	.22[2]	—	1–1½	500-525	—	—
	C5TF9510-N (1 BBL)	—	1.090	—	.23[2]	—	1–1½	500-525	—	—
	C6TF9510-K (1 BBL)	—	1.020	—	.21[2]	—	1–1½	625	—	—
	C5TF9510-R (1 BBL)	—	1.090	—	.23[2]	—	1–1½	500-525	—	3½[3]
	C6TF9510-L (1 BBL)	—	1.020	—	.21[2]	—	1–1½	550	—	3½[3]
	C6TF9510-D (1 BBL)	—	1.020	—	.22[2]	—	1–1½	500-575	—	—
	C6TF9510-N (1 BBL)	—	1.020	—	.22[2]	—	1–1½	625	—	—
	C5TF9510-AH (1 BBL)	—	1.090	—	.21[2]	—	1–1½	500-525	—	—
	C5UF9510-L (1 BBL)	—	1.090	—	.19[2]	—	1–1½	575-600	—	—
	C6UF9510-A (1 BBL)	—	1.090	—	.19[2]	—	1–1½	625-650	—	—
	C5UF9510-M (1 BBL)	—	1.090	—	.19[2]	—	1–1½	500-525	—	3½[3]
	C6UF9510-B (1 BBL)	—	1.090	—	.19[2]	—	1–1½	625-650	—	3½[3]
	C6TF9510-B (2 BBL)	.875	0.470	—	Inboard	—	1–1½	575-600	—	—
	C6TF9510-R (2 BBL)	.910	0.450	—	Inboard	—	1–1½	625	—	—
	C6TF9510-C (2 BBL)	.875	0.470	—	Inboard	—	1–1½	475-500	—	0.060-0.090
	C6TF9510-S (2 BBL)	.910	0.450	—	Inboard	—	1–1½	550	—	0.060-0.090
	C6TF9510-T (2 BBL)	.910	0.531	—	Inboard	—	1–1½	575-600	—	0.060-0.090
	C6TF9510-A (2 BBL)	.875	0.470	—	Inboard	—	1–1½	575-600	—	—

YEAR	MODEL OR TYPE	Float Level (IN.)	Fuel Level (IN.)	Fast Idle Cam (IN.)	Pump Travel Setting	Choke Setting	Idle Screw Turns Open	Idle Speed (RPM)	Fast Idle Speed (RPM)	Dashpot Plunger Clearance (IN.)
							ON THE TRUCK ADJUSTMENTS			
Ford Truck, Continued										
	Autolite Carburetors									
1967	C5UF9510-A (1 BBL)	1 3/32	—	—	.19[2]	—	1–1½	575	—	3½[3]
	C5UF9510-L (1 BBL)	1 3/32	—	—	.19[2]	—	1–1½	575	—	3½[3]
	C5TF9510-G (1 BBL)	1 3/32	—	—	.21[2]	—	1–1½	500	—	—
	C5TF9510-H (1 BBL)	1 3/32	—	—	.21[2]	—	1–1½	500	—	3½[3]
	C7TF9510-R (1 BBL)	1 3/32	—	—	.21[2]	—	1–1½	600	—	2[3]
	C7TF9510-T (1 BBL)	1 3/32	—	—	.21[2]	—	1–1½	600	—	2[3]
	C5TF9510-N (1 BBL)	1 3/32	—	—	.21[2]	—	1–1½	500	—	—
	C5TF9510-R (1 BBL)	1 3/32	—	—	.21[2]	—	1–1½	500	—	3½[3]
	C5TF9510-AC (1 BBL)	1 3/32	—	—	.22[2]	—	1–1½	500	—	—
	C5TF9510-AH (1 BBL)	1 3/32	—	—	.22[2]	—	1–1½	500	—	—
	C6TF9510-D (1 BBL)	1 3/32	—	—	.22[2]	—	1–1½	500	—	—
	C6TF9510-E (1 BBL)	1 3/32	—	—	.22[2]	—	1–1½	500	—	—
	C7TF9510-S (1 BBL)	1 3/32	—	—	.21[2]	—	1–1½	600	—	2[3]
	C7TF9510-L (1 BBL)	1 3/32	—	—	.21[2]	—	1–1½	600	—	2[3]
	C7TF9510-M (1 BBL)	1 3/32	—	—	.21[2]	—	1–1½	500	—	2[3]
	C7TF9510-N (1 BBL)	1 3/32	—	—	.21[2]	—	1–1½	600	—	2[3]
	C7TF9510-J (2 BBL)	17/32	29/32	—	Inboard	—	1–1½	550	—	—
	C7TF9510-E (2 BBL)	17/32	29/32	—	Inboard	—	1–1½	550	—	⅛[3]
	C7TF9510-F (2 BBL)	31/64	7/8	—	Inboard	—	1–1½	475	—	⅛[3]
	C7TF9510-G (2 BBL)	17/32	29/32	—	Inboard	—	1–1½	625	—	⅛[3]
	C7TF9510-H (2 BBL)	17/32	29/32	—	Inboard	—	1–1½	550	—	⅛[3]
	C7TF9510-J (2 BBL)	31/64	7/8	—	Inboard	—	1–1½	550	—	⅛[3]
1968	C8TF9510-J (1 BBL)	1 3/32	—	—	.21	—	1–1½	—	—	—
	C8TF9510-K (1 BBL)	1 3/32	—	—	.21	—	1–1½	—	—	3½[3]
	C8TF9510-C (1 BBL)	1 3/32	—	—	.21	—	1–1½	—	—	.100
	C8TF9510-M (1 BBL)	1 3/32	—	—	.21	—	1–1½	—	—	—
	C8TF9510-L (1 BBL)	1 1/64	—	—	.21	—	1–1½	—	—	—
	C8TF9510-R (1 BBL)	1 3/32	—	—	.21	—	1–1½	—	—	—
	C8TF9510-S (1 BBL)	1 3/32	—	—	.21	—	1–1½	—	—	3½[3]
	C8TF9510-E (1 BBL)	1 3/32	—	—	.22	—	1–1½	—	—	.100
	C8TF9510-F (1 BBL)	1 3/32	—	—	.22	—	1–1½	—	—	.100
	C8TF9510-T (1 BBL)	1 1/64	—	—	.22	—	1–1½	—	—	—
	C8TF9510-U (1 BBL)	1 3/32	—	—	.22	—	1–1½	—	—	—
	C8TF9510-G (1 BBL)	1 1/64	—	—	.22	—	1–1½	—	—	.100
	C7TF9510-J (2 BBL)	31/64	—	—	w/A.T.	—	1–1½	—	—	—
	C8TF9510-Y (2 BBL)	31/64	—	—	[5]	—	1–1½	—	—	—
	C8TF9510-Z (2 BBL)	31/64	—	—	[5]	—	1–1½	—	—	⅛
	C8TF9510-AB (2 BBL)	31/64	—	—	[5]	—	1–1½	—	—	⅛
	C8TF9510-AE (2 BBL)	31/64	—	—	[5]	—	1–1½	—	—	⅛
	C8TF9510-AD (2 BBL)	31/64	—	—	[5]	—	1–1½	—	—	⅛
1969	C8TF9510-C (1 BBL)	1 3/32	—	—	.22	—	1–1½	500	2700	.100
	C8TF9510-L (1 BBL)	1 3/32	—	—	.22	—	1–1½	600	—	—
	C8TF9510-M (1 BBL)	1 3/32	—	—	.22	—	1–1½	600	—	—
	C8UF9510-R (1 BBL)	1 3/32	—	—	.21	—	1–1½	525	—	3[3]
	C8UF9510-S (1 BBL)	1 3/32	—	—	.21	—	1–1½	600	—	—
	C8TF9510-AK (1 BBL)	1 3/32	—	—	.22	—	1–1½	600	—	—
	C8TF9510-F (1 BBL)	1 3/32	—	—	.22	—	Limiter Cap	500	2700	.100
	C8TF9510-S (1 BBL)	1 3/32	—	—	.21	—	1–1½	525	—	3½[3]
	C8TF9510-T (1 BBL)	1 1/32	—	—	.22	—	1–1½	600	—	—
	C8TF9510-U (1 BBL)	1 3/32	—	—	.22	—	1–1½	600	—	—
	C9TF9510-G (1 BBL)	1 3/32	—	—	.19	—	Limiter Cap	600	2700	.080
	C9TF9510-H (1 BBL)	1 3/32	—	—	.19	—	Limiter Cap	600	2700	.080
	C9UF9510-A (2 BBL)	17/32	29/32	—	Inboard	—	Limiter Cap	650	1000	⅛

YEAR	MODEL OR TYPE	Float Level	Fuel Level	Fast Idle Cam	Pump Travel Setting	Choke Setting	Idle Screw Turns Dpen	ON THE TRUCK ADJUSTMENTS Idle Speed	Fast Idle Speed	Dashpot Plunger Clearance
Ford Truck, Continued										

Autolite Carburetors

YEAR	MODEL OR TYPE	Float Level	Fuel Level	Fast Idle Cam	Pump Travel Setting	Choke Setting	Idle Screw Turns Dpen	Idle Speed	Fast Idle Speed	Dashpot Plunger Clearance
	C9UF9510-B (2 BBL)	17/32	29/32	—	Inboard	—	Limiter Cap	550	1000	1/8
	C9TF9510-A (2 BBL)	31/64	7/8	—	Inboard	—	Limiter Cap	600	1200	—
	C9TF9510-J (2 BBL)	31/64	7/8	—	Inboard	—	Limiter Cap	650	1200	1/8
	C9TF9510-K (2 BBL)	31/64	7/8	—	Inboard	—	Limiter Cap	550	1400	1/8
	C8TF9510-Z (2 BBL)	31/64	7/8	—	Inboard	—	1–1½	650	1400	1/8
	C8TF9510-AZ (2 BBL)	31/64	7/8	—	Inboard	—	1–1½	550	1200	—
1970	DOBF9510-C (2 BBL)	17/32	29/32	—	Inboard	1-Rich	—	675	1400	5/64
	DOUF9510-B (2 BBL)	7/16	13/16	—	Inboard	2-Rich	—	500-800	1400	—
	DOUF9501-C (2 BBL)	7/16	13/16	—	Inboard	—	—	600	1600	5/64
	DOUF9510-E (2 BBL)	7/16	13/16	—	Inboard	—	—	500-600	1600	—
	DOUF9510-F (2 BBL)	7/16	13/16	—	Inboard	—	—	600	1600	5/64
	DOUF9510-G (2 BBL)	7/16	13/16	—	Inboard	2-Rich	—	650	1400	5/64
	DOTF9510-A (2 BBL)	7/16	13/16	—	Inboard	—	—	550	1500	—
	DOTF9510-B (2 BBL)	31/64	7/8	—	Inboard	—	—	650	1500	1/8
1970 & Up	DOTF9510-N (2 BBL)	31/64	7/8	—	Inboard	—	—	500-650	1500	—
	DOTF9510-C (2 BBL)	7/16	13/16	—	Inboard	—	—	550	1500	1/8
	DOTF9510-M (2 BBL)	7/16	13/16	—	Inboard	—	—	550-500	1500	—
	DOTF9510-R (2 BBL)	7/16	13/16	—	Inboard	—	—	650	1500	1/8
	DOTF9510-S (2 BBL)	31/64	7/8	—	Inboard	—	—	550	1500	1/8

Note 1—Fuel Level Setting: (Wet) Lower Edge of Sight Plug.
(Dry) Top of Float Parallel with Top of Fuel Bowl (Bowl Inverted).
Note 2—Clearance from Pump Cover to Pin with Throttle Plate Closed.
Note 3—Secondary Throttle Plate Setting Turns After Screw Contacts Lever.
Note 4—Metal Float—1 3/32", Rubber Float—1".
Note 5—Pump Setting: Primary—7/8". Secondary—3/4".

SINGLE BARREL AUTOLITE

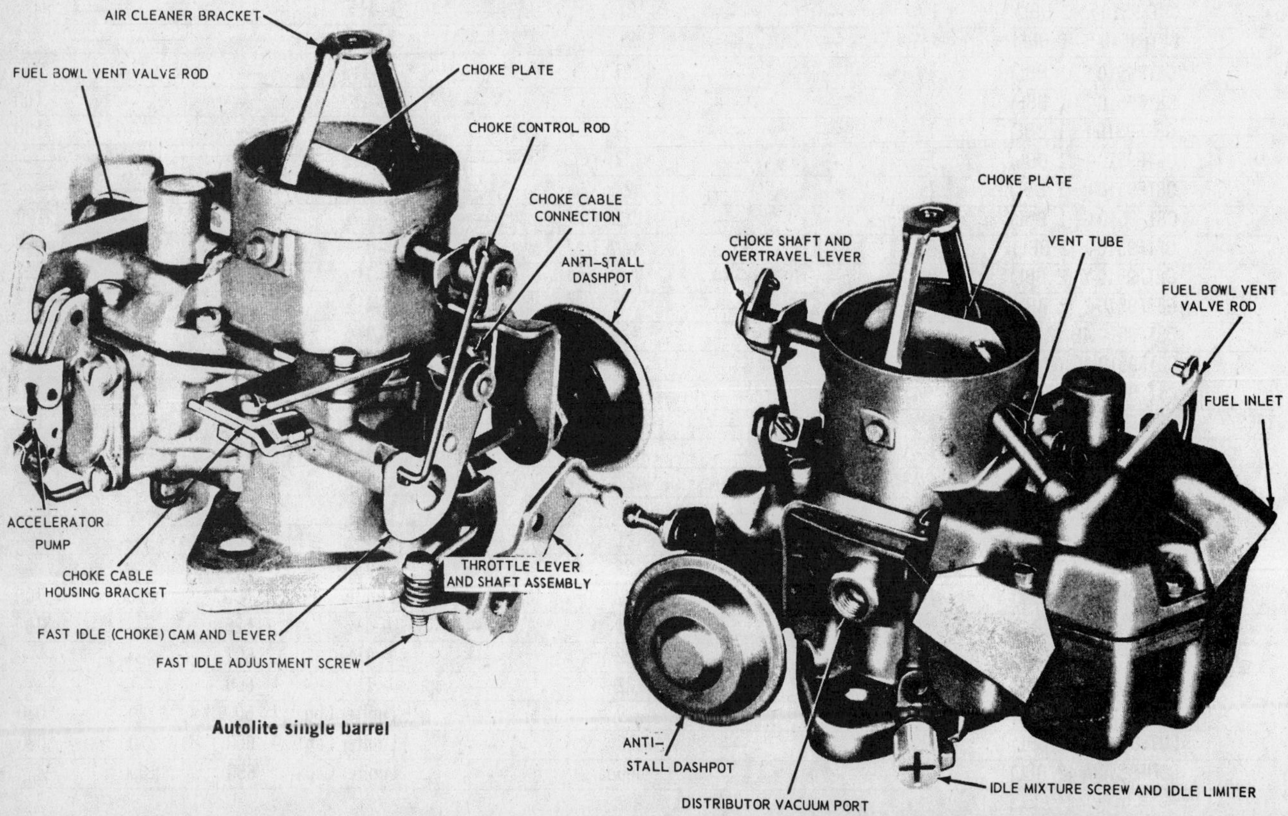

Autolite single barrel

Autolite single barrel with external dashpot

SINGLE BARREL AUTOLITE

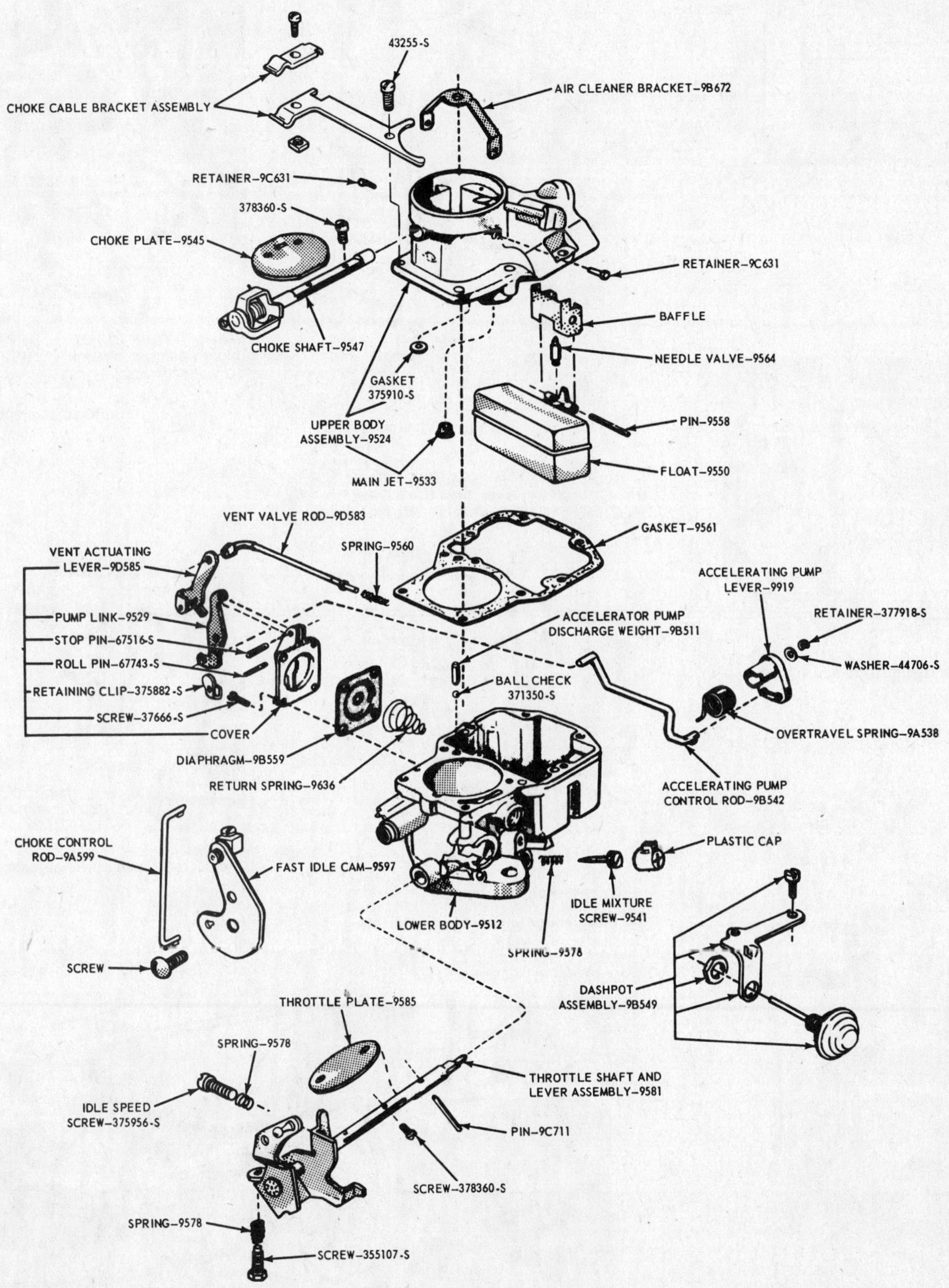

Single barrel autolite—exploded view

SINGLE BARREL FORD

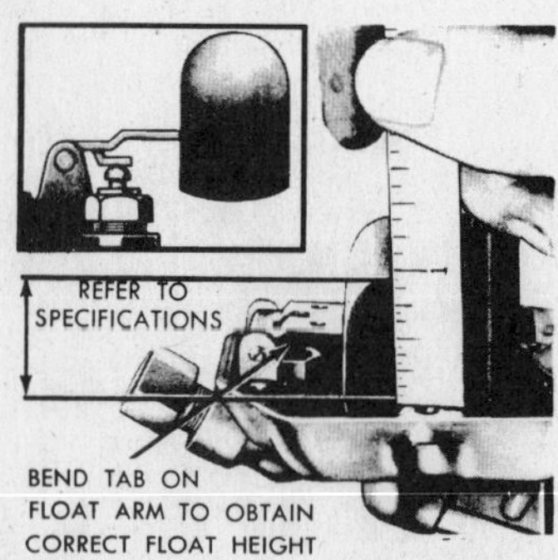

Float adjustment

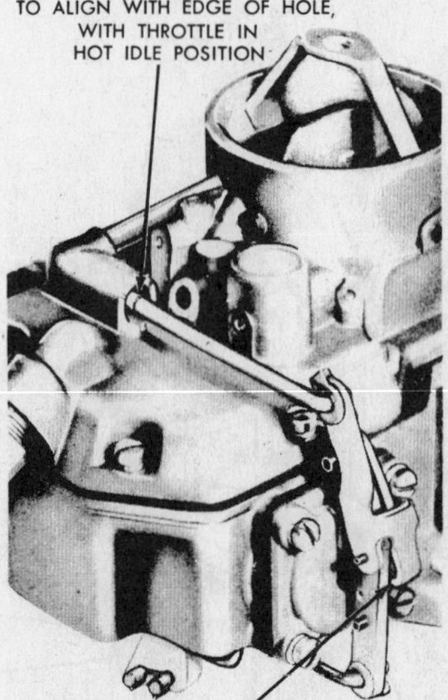

Float bowl vent valve adjustment

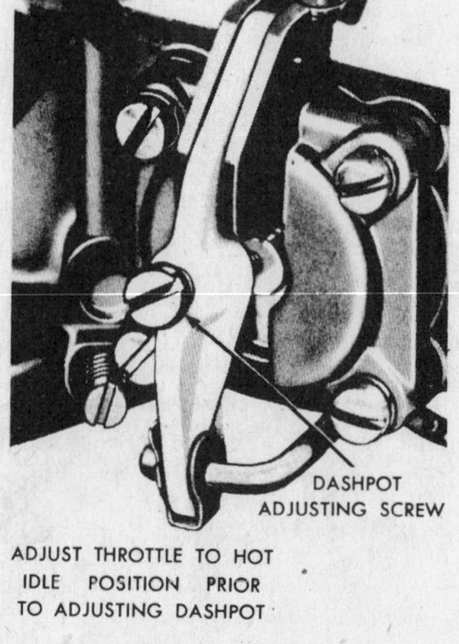

Anti stall dashpot adjustment

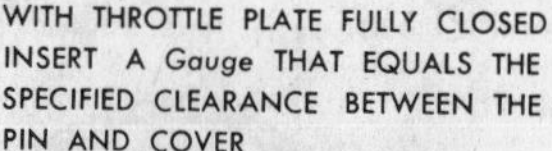

Idle fuel mixture adjustment

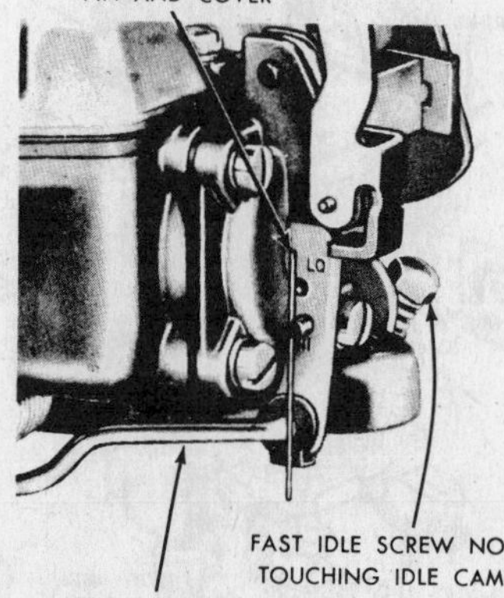

Accelerator pump rod adjustment

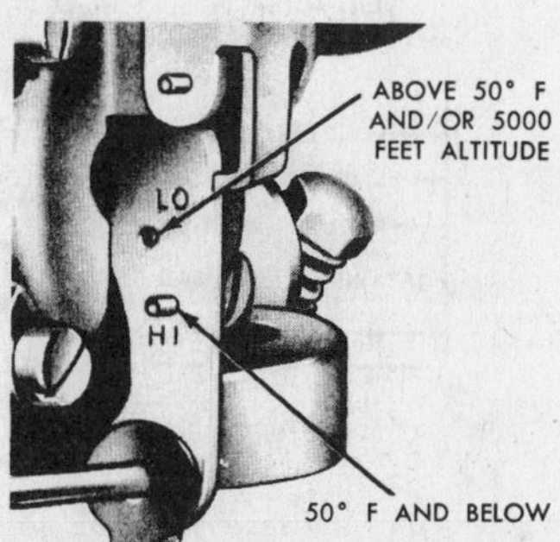

Accelerator pump lever adjustment

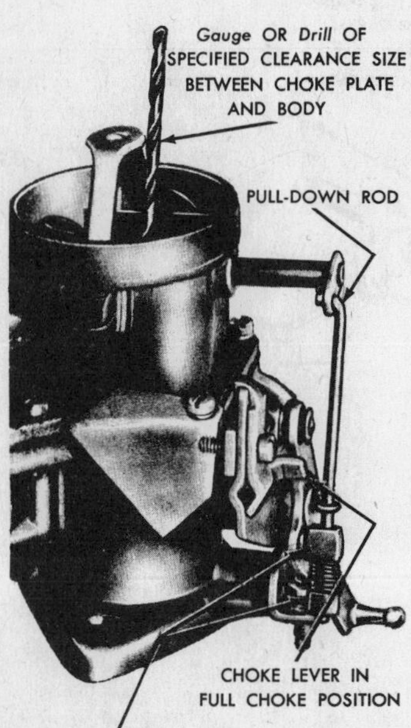

Choke adjustment

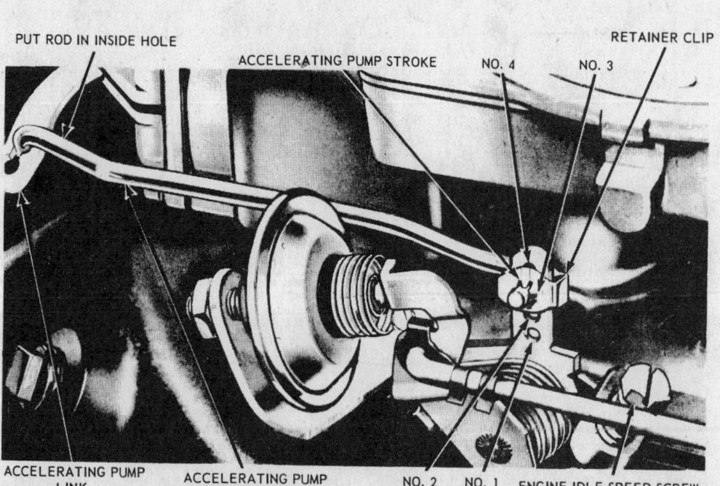

Accelerator pump adjustment

IDLE MIXTURE SCREW
(NEEDLE)

SINGLE BARREL FORD

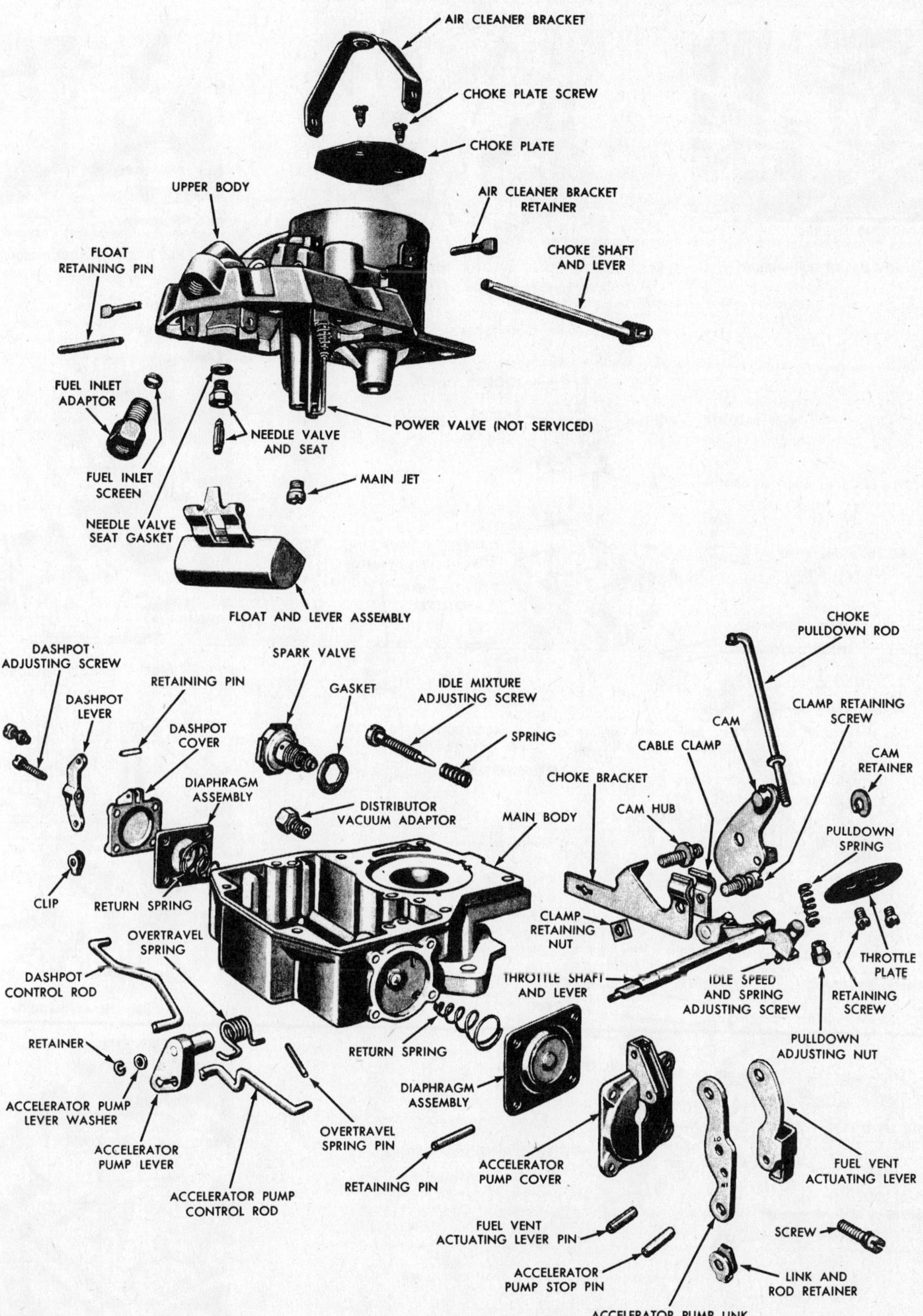

Ford single barrel—exploded view

TWO BARREL—FORD

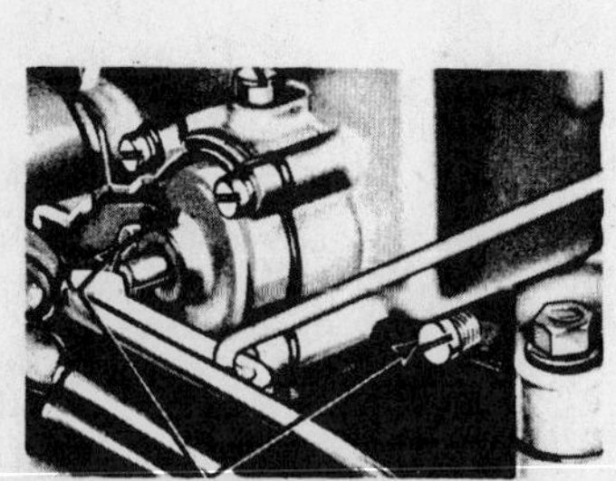

Idle speed adjustment

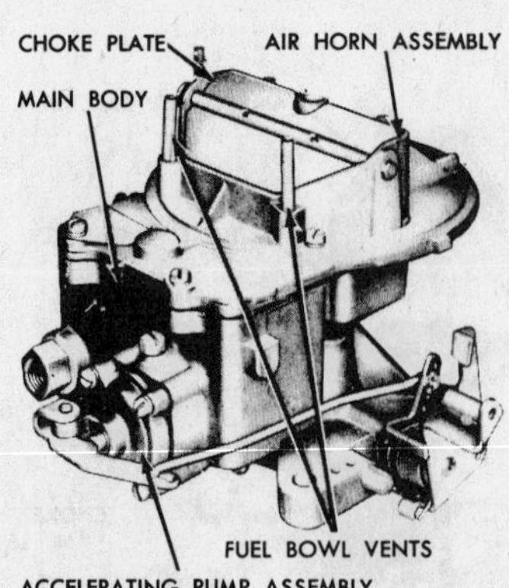

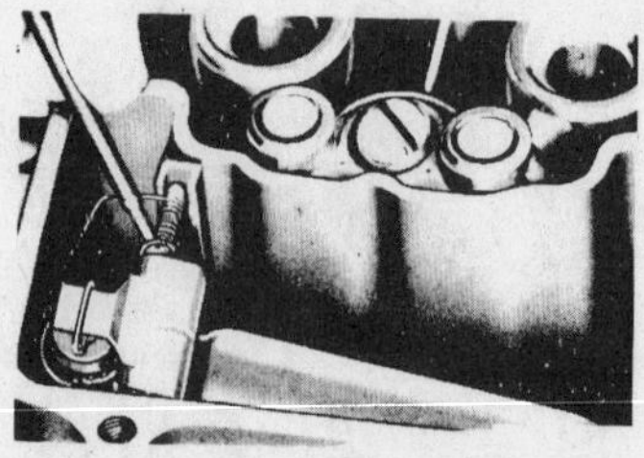

Float shaft retainer removal

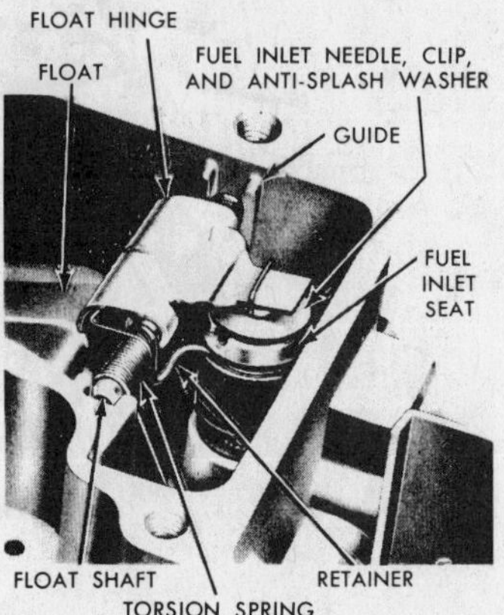

Float assembly installed

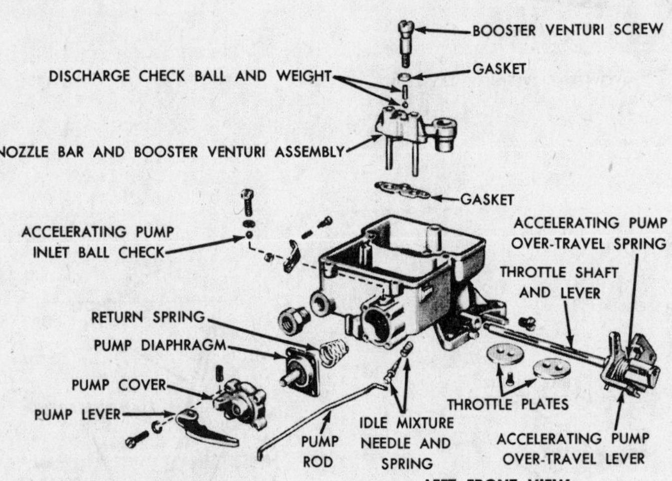

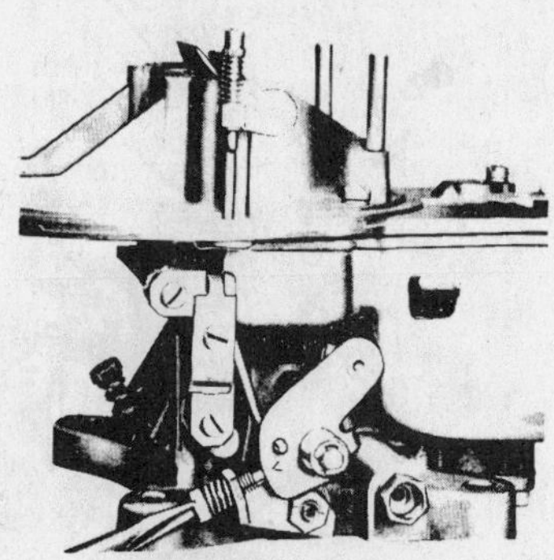

Fast idle adjustment

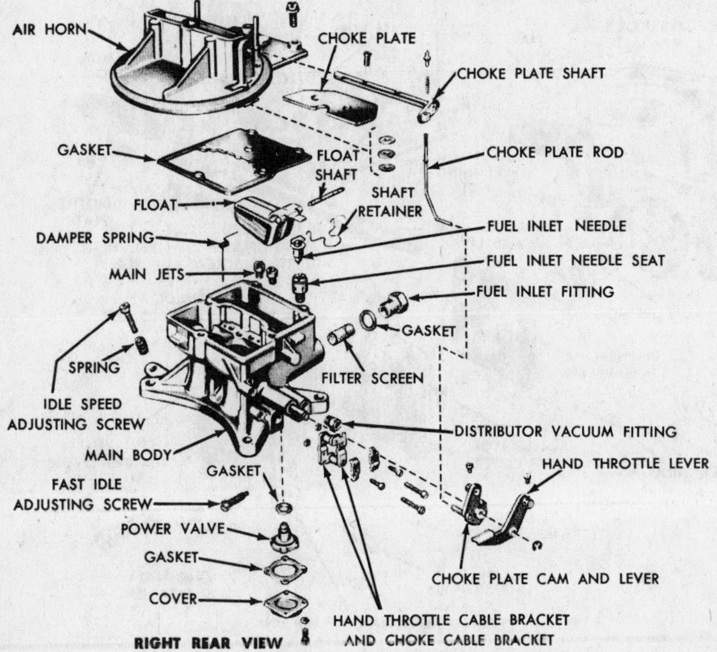

Ford two barrel—disassembled view

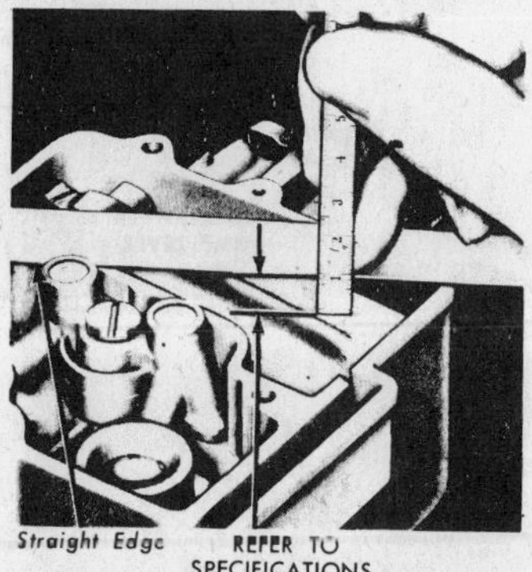

Fuel level adjustment

YEAR	MODEL OR TYPE	Float Level (IN.)	Fuel Level (IN.)	Bowl Vent Valve (IN.)	Pump Travel Setting (IN.)	CHOKE SETTING Unloader (IN.)	CHOKE SETTING Housing	Idle Screw Turns Out	ON THE TRUCK ADJUSTMENTS Air Bypass Turns Open	ON THE TRUCK ADJUSTMENTS Idle Speed (RPM)	ON THE TRUCK ADJUSTMENTS Fast Idle Speed (RPM)	ON THE TRUCK ADJUSTMENTS Dashpot Plunger Clearance (IN.)
Chevrolet Truck												
1968	R3887A	1	2	.060	.015	—	—	3	—	—	2000	—
	R4098A	1	2	.060	.015	—	—	3	—	—	2000	—
1969-70	R4199A	1	2	.060	.015	—	—	3	—	—	2000	—
	R4200A	1	2	.060	.015	—	—	3	—	—	2000	—

Note 1—Float Level. Primary—.195". Secondary—.250".
Note 2—Float adjustment: Fuel level should be plus or minus 1/32 in. with threads at bottom of sight holes. To adjust turn adjusting nut on top of bowl clockwise, to lower, counterclockwise to raise.

YEAR	MODEL OR TYPE	Float Level (IN.)	Fuel Level (IN.)	Bowl Vent Valve (IN.)	Pump Travel Setting (IN.)	CHOKE SETTING Unloader (IN.)	CHOKE SETTING Housing	Idle Screw Turns Out	Air Bypass Turns Open	Idle Speed (RPM)	Fast Idle Speed (RPM)	Dashpot Plunger Clearance (IN.)
Dodge Truck												
1966-67	R-3226A (1 BBL)	1	27/32	3/32	—	2	2-Rich	2	—	700*	1500[3]	—
	R-3227A (1 BBL)	1	27/32	3/32	—	2	2-Rich	2	—	650*	1550[3]	—
	R-3228A (1 BBL)	1	27/32	3/32	—	2	2-Rich	2	—	650*	1550[3]	—
	R-3229A (1 BBL)	1	27/32	3/32	—	2	2-Rich	2	—	650*	1550[3]	—
	R-3397A (1 BBL)	1	27/32	3/32	—	2	2-Rich	2	—	550*	700[4]	—
	R-3398A (1 BBL)	1	27/32	3/32	—	2	2-Rich	2	—	550*	700[4]	—
	R-3399A (1 BBL)	1	27/32	3/32	—	2	2-Rich	2	—	550*	700[4]	—
1968	R-3982A (1 BBL)	1	27/32	3/32	—	2	2-Rich	2	—	—	1400[4]	—
	R-3983A (1 BBL)	1	27/32	3/32	—	2	2-Rich	2	—	—	1600[4]	—
	R-3984A (1 BBL)	1	27/32	3/32	—	2	2-Rich	2	—	—	1400[4]	—
	R-3985A (1 BBL)	1	27/32	3/32	—	2	2-Rich	2	—	—	1600[4]	—
1969	R-3653A (2 BBL)	5	—	—	—	—	None	1	—	500	‘.035	—
	R-3652A (2 BBL)	5	—	—	—	—	None	1	—	500	‘.035	—
	R-3270A (4 BBL)	5	—	—	—	—	None	1	—	500	‘.066	—

* With headlights on.
Note 1—Use gauge C-3903.
Note 2—See fast idle cam position then adjust.
Note 3—Fast idle speed. Engine hot and screw on second highest step of cam.
Note 4—Fast idle speed. Engine hot and screw on lowest step of cam.
Note 5—Float setting. (Dry) Float parting line parallel with floor of bowl. (Wet) Fuel level with bottom of sight plug hole.

YEAR	CARB. PART NO.	MODEL OR TYPE	Float Level	Fuel Level	Bowl Vent Valve	Pump Travel Setting	CHOKE SETTING Unloader	CHOKE SETTING Housing	ON THE TRUCK ADJUSTMENTS Idle Screw Turns Out	ON THE TRUCK ADJUSTMENTS Air Bypass Turns Open	ON THE TRUCK ADJUSTMENTS Idle Speed	ON THE TRUCK ADJUSTMENTS Fast Idle Speed	ON THE TRUCK ADJUSTMENTS Dashpot Plunger Clearance
Jeep Truck													
1962	R-2415A	2300	—	1	1/16	.015	—	—	1	—	—	—	—
1962-64	R-2640A	2300	—	1	1/16	.015	—	Index	1	—	—	—	.070
1964	R-2647A	1920	—	3/4	—	2	—	—	1	—	—	—	1/16
1964	R-2647AS	1920	—	3/4	—	2	—	—	1	—	—	—	1/16
1965-67	R-2647-1A	1920	—	3/4	—	2	—	—	1	—	—	—	1/16
1964	R-2651A	1920	—	3/4	—	2	—	Index	1	—	—	2100[3]	1/16
1964	R-2651AS	1920	—	3/4	—	2	—	Index	1	—	—	2100[3]	1/16
1965-67	R-2651-1A	1920	—	3/4	—	2	—	Index	1	—	—	2100[3]	1/16
1964	R-2934A	2300	—	1	1/16	.015	—	Index	1	—	—	—	.070
1965-67	R-3234A	2209	9/16	5/8	5/64	2	3/16	Index	1	—	—	1800[3]	5/32
1965-67	R-3262A	2209	9/16	5/8	5/64	2	3/16	Index	1	—	—	1800[3]	—

Note 1—Bottom Edge of Sight Plug hole.
Note 2—With link in inboard hole in pump lever, place over travel lever in longest stroke hole. For extremely cold weather, intermediate for moderate, and short stroke for warm weather.
Note 3—With engine hot and your adjustment screw on highest step of cam.

YEAR	MODEL OR TYPE	Float Level (IN.)	Fuel Level (IN.)	Bowl Vent Valve (IN.)	Pump Travel Setting (IN.)	CHOKE SETTING Unloader (IN.)	Housing	Idle Screw Turns Out	ON THE TRUCK ADJUSTMENTS Air Bypass Turns Open	Idle Speed (RPM)	Fast Idle Speed (RPM)	Dashpot Plunger Clearance (IN.)
Ford Trucks												
1961	CIUE9510-A (1 BBL)	11/64	23/32	—	—	—	—	1–1½	—	—	—	—
	CIUE9510-B (1 BBL)	11/64	23/32	—	—	—	—	1–1½	—	—	—	—
	Other (1 BBL)	13/64	11/16	—	—	—	—	1–1½	—	—	—	5/64
1961-62	All (2 BBL)	7/8	[1]	—	—	—	—	1–1½	—	—	—	—
	All (4 BBL)	[2]	[1]	—	—	—	—	1–1½	—	—	[3]	—
1963	All (4 BBL)	[2]	[1]	—	—	—	—	1–1½	—	—	[3]	—
1964	C3TE9510-G (2 BBL)	[2]	[1]	—	.015	—	—	1–1½	—	500-550	2600	—
	C3TE9510-J (2 BBL)	[2]	[1]	—	.015	—	—	1–1½	—	500-550	2600	—
	C4TF9510-A (2 BBL)	[2]	[1]	—	—	—	—	1–1½	—	—	[3]	—
	C4TF9510-C (2 BBL)	[2]	[1]	—	—	—	—	1–1½	—	—	[3]	—
	C3TE9510-F (4 BBL)	[2]	[1]	—	—	—	—	1–1½	—	—	[3]	—
	C4TF9510-F (4 BBL)	[2]	[1]	—	—	—	—	1–1½	—	—	[3]	—
	C3TE9510-C (4 BBL)	[2]	[1]	—	—	—	—	1–1½	—	500-550	[3]	—
	C3TE9510-D (4 BBL)	[2]	[1]	—	—	—	—	1–1½	—	500-550	[3]	—
	C3TE9510-H (4 BBL)	[2]	[1]	—	—	—	—	1–1½	—	500-550	[3]	—
1985	All (2 BBL)	[2]	[1]	—	.015	—	—	1–1½	—	—	2600	—
	All (4 BBL)	[2]	[1]	—	.015	—	—	1–1½	—	—	2600	—
1966	All (2 BBL)	[2]	[1]	—	—	—	—	1–1½	—	—	[3]	—
	All (4 BBL)	[2]	[1]	—	—	—	—	1–1½	—	—	[3]	—
1967	C5TF9510-AS (2 BBL)	[2]	[1]	—	"Hi"	—	—	1–1½	—	[4]	2600	—
	C5TF9510-AU (2 BBL)	[2]	[1]	—	"Hi"	—	—	1–1½	—	[4]	2600	—
	C3TF9510-C (4 BBL)	[2]	[1]	—	#2	—	—	1–1½	—	[4]	[3]	—
	C3TF9510-D (4 BBL)	[2]	[1]	—	#2	—	—	1–1½	—	[4]	[3]	—
	C3TF9510-H (4 BBL)	[2]	[1]	—	#2	—	—	1–1½	—	[4]	[3]	—
	C5TF9510-AT (4 BBL)	[2]	[1]	—	#2	—	—	1–1½	—	[4]	2600	—
1968	C7TF9510-A (2 BBL)	[2]	[1]	—	#2	—	—	1–1½	—	—	—	—
	C8TF9510-AT (2 BBL)	[2]	[1]	—	#2	—	—	1–1½	—	—	—	—
	C7TF9510-AD (2 BBL)	[2]	[1]	—	#2	—	—	1–1½	—	—	—	—
	C8TF9510-AR (2 BBL)	[2]	[1]	—	#2	—	—	1–1½	—	—	—	—
	C7TF9510-AE (4 BBL)	[2]	[1]	—	#1	—	—	1–1½	—	—	—	—
	C8TF9510-AS (4 BBL)	[2]	[1]	—	#1	—	—	1–1½	—	—	—	—
	C3TF9510-H (4 BBL)	[2]	[1]	—	#2	—	—	1–1½	—	—	—	—
	C3TF9510-C (4 BBL)	[2]	[1]	—	#2	—	—	1–1½	—	—	—	—
	C3TF9510-D (4 BBL)	[2]	[1]	—	#2	—	—	1–1½	—	—	—	—
1969	C8TF9510-AR (2 BBL)	[2]	[1]	—	#2	—	—	—	—	550	2300	—
	C8TF9510-AS (2 BBL)	[2]	[1]	—	#1	—	—	—	—	550	2300	—
	C8TF9510-AT (2 BBL)	[2]	[1]	—	#2	—	—	—	—	550	2300	—
	C9HF9510-A (2 BBL)	[2]	[1]	—	#2	—	—	—	—	550	2300	—
	C9HF9510-B (2 BBL)	[2]	[1]	—	#2	—	—	—	—	550	2300	—
	C9HF9510-C (2 BBL)	[2]	[1]	—	#2	—	—	—	—	550	2300	—
	C3TE9510-C (4 BBL)	[2]	[1]	—	#2	—	—	—	—	550	2300	—
	C3TE9510-D (4 BBL)	[2]	[1]	—	#2	—	—	—	—	550	2300	—
	C3TE9510-H (4 BBL)	[2]	[1]	—	#2	—	—	—	—	550	2300	—
	C9HF9510-D (4 BBL)	[2]	[1]	—	#2	—	—	—	—	550	2300	—
	C9HF9510-E (4 BBL)	[2]	[1]	—	#2	—	—	—	—	550	2300	—
	C9HF9510-F (4 BBL)	[2]	[1]	—	#2	—	—	—	—	550	2300	—
1970	C9HF9510-A (2 BBL)	[2]	[1]	—	#2	—	—	—	—	575-550	2300	—
	C9HF9510-B (2 BBL)	[2]	[1]	—	#2	—	—	—	—	575-550	2300	—
	C9HF9510-C (4 BBL)	[2]	[1]	—	#2	—	—	—	—	575-550	2300	—
	DOHF9510-A (4 BBL)	[2]	[1]	—	#2	—	—	—	—	575-550	2300	—
	DOHF9510-B (4 BBL)	[2]	[1]	—	#2	—	—	—	—	575-550	2300	—
	DOHF9510-C (4 BBL)	[2]	[1]	—	#2	—	—	—	—	575-550	2300	—

Note 1 Bottom edge of sight plug hole.
Note 2—Top of float parallel with top of fuel bowl (bowl inverted).
Note 3—Clearance between fast idle cam and fast idle screw of .010-.015.
Note 4—Idle speed setting. A—Standard Transmission—525 RPM. B—Automatic Transmission—500 RPM.

YEAR	MODEL OR TYPE	Float Level	Fuel Level	Bowl Vent Valve	Pump Travel Setting	CHOKE SETTING Unloader	CHOKE SETTING Housing	ON THE TRUCK ADJUSTMENTS Idle Screw Turns Out	Air Bypass Turns Open	Idle Speed	Fast Idle Speed	Dashpot Plunger Clearance
GMC Truck												
1961-62	R-1388-1A (6)	—	¾	—	—	—	—	1–1½	—	500	—	—
1969	R-4098A (V-8)	[1]	[2]	—	.015	—	—	1½	—	500	—	—
	R-3887A (V-8)	[1]	[2]	—	.015	—	—	1½	—	500	—	—
	R-4200A (V-8)	[1]	[2]	—	.015	—	—	1½	—	500	—	—
	R-4199A (V-8)	[1]	[2]	—	.015	—	—	1½	—	500	—	—

Note 1—Float level. A—Primary—.195. B—Secondary—.250.
Note 2—Lower edge of sight plug hole.

CARB. MODEL	CARB. PART NO.	Float Level	Pump Link Position	Fuel Level	Idlo Mix. Screw Turn Out	Fast Idle Setting	Dashpot Clearance	Choke Setting
International Truck								
852-FFG	2691-1A	1¼	Center	—	½	—	—	—
852-FFG	2410-1	1¼	Center	—	½-¾	—	—	—
852-FFG	2409-2	1¼	Center	—	⅞-1⅛	—	—	—
852-FFG	3086	1¼	Center	—	½-¾	—	—	—
2140-G	864-1	¼	—	—	⅜-⅝	—	—	—
2140-G	977	¼	—	—	⅜-⅝	—	—	—
2140-G	987-2	¼	—	—	1⅞-2⅛	—	—	—
2140-G	1348-1	¼	—	—	1⅞-2⅛	—	—	—
2140-G	2407	¼	—	—	1⅞-2⅛	—	—	—
2140-G	2408	¼	—	—	1⅞-2⅛	—	—	—
2140-G	2461	¼	—	—	1⅞-2⅛	—	—	—
2140-G	2486	¼	—	—	1⅞-2⅛	—	—	—
885-FFG	126582	7/32	Center	—	1¼-1¾	—	—	—
885-FFG	126583	7/32	Center	—	1-1½	—	—	—
885-FFG	260612	7/32	Center	—	1-1½	—	—	—
1904	2494	—	—	—	1	—	—	—
1904	3117	23/32 [1]	—	—	1	—	—	—
1904	3479	—	—	—	[2]	—	—	—
1904	3862	—	—	—	[2]	—	—	—
1904	3716	—	—	—	1	—	—	—
1904	3842	—	—	—	1	—	—	—
1904	1418	—	—	—	¾-1¼	—	—	—
1904	1419	—	—	—	¾-1¼	—	.095-.105	—
1904	3478	—	—	—	[2]	—	—	—
1904	3499	—	—	—	[2]	—	—	—
1904	1420	—	—	—	1	—	—	—
1904	1421	—	—	—	1	—	—	—
1904	3443	—	—	—	[2]	—	—	—
1904	3496	—	—	—	[2]	—	.095-.105	—
1904	1485	—	—	—	1	—	—	—
1904	1650	—	—	—	1	—	—	—
2110	1389	1 11/32	Center	—	¼-1¾	—	—	—
2110	1565	1 11/32	Center	—	¼-1¾	—	—	—
2110	1812	1 11/32	Center	—	¼-1¾	—	—	—
2110	1433	1 11/32	Center	—	¼-1¾	—	.045-.065	—
2110G	1487-1-2	1 11/32	Center	—	1-1½	—	—	—
2110G	1488-1	1 11/32	Center	—	1-1½	—	—	—
2300	1710	—	#1 Hole	⅜ [3]	¾	—	1/16	—
2300G	1706-2	—	#2 Hole	⅜ [3]	⅞	.018-.020	—	—
2300G	1707-2	—	#2 Hole	⅜ [3]	1½	.018-.020	—	—
4150G	1708	—	.015	[4]	¾	.025	—	—

Note 1—With carbuertor held upside down measure from flat on float to inner edge of bowl.
Note 2—Using vacuum gauge adjust to maximum vacuum.
Note 3—Fuel pump pressure at 5½ PSI.
Note 4—Primary float ⅜". Secondary float ⅝".

HOLLEY MODEL 1920

Checking float setting

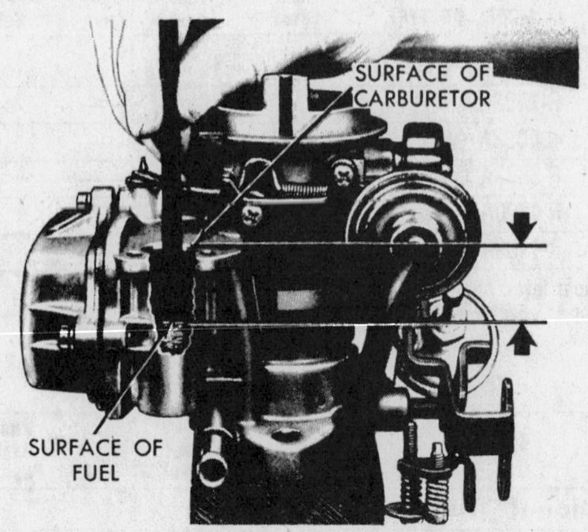

Measuring wet fuel level

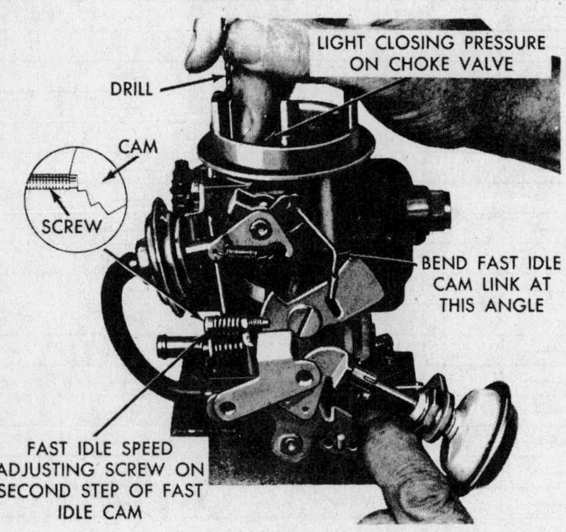

Fast idle cam adjustment

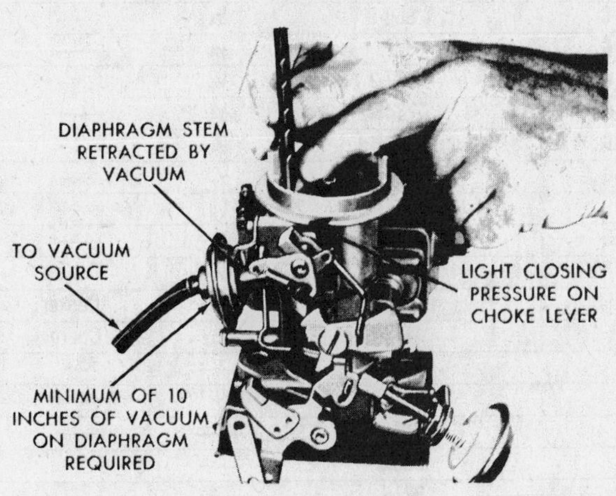

Choke vacuum kick setting

HOLLEY MODEL 2300G

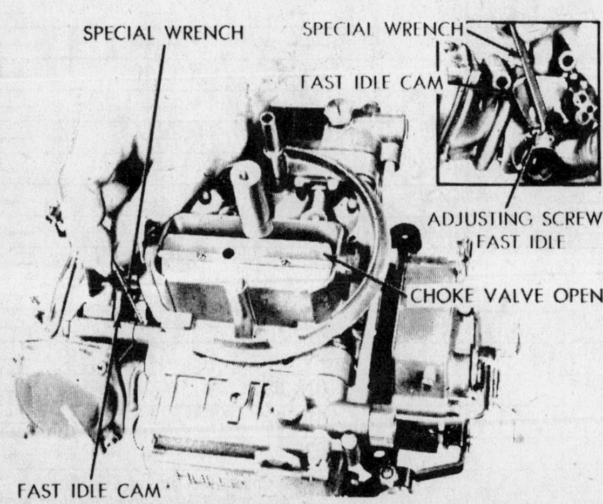

Fast idle speed adjustment

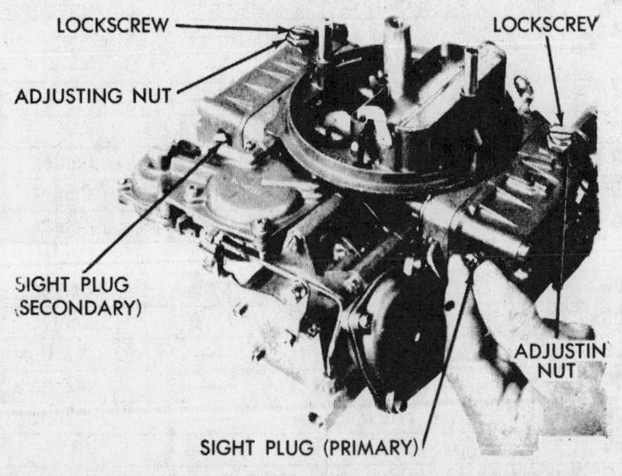

Fuel level sight plug location

HOLLEY MODEL 2300G continued

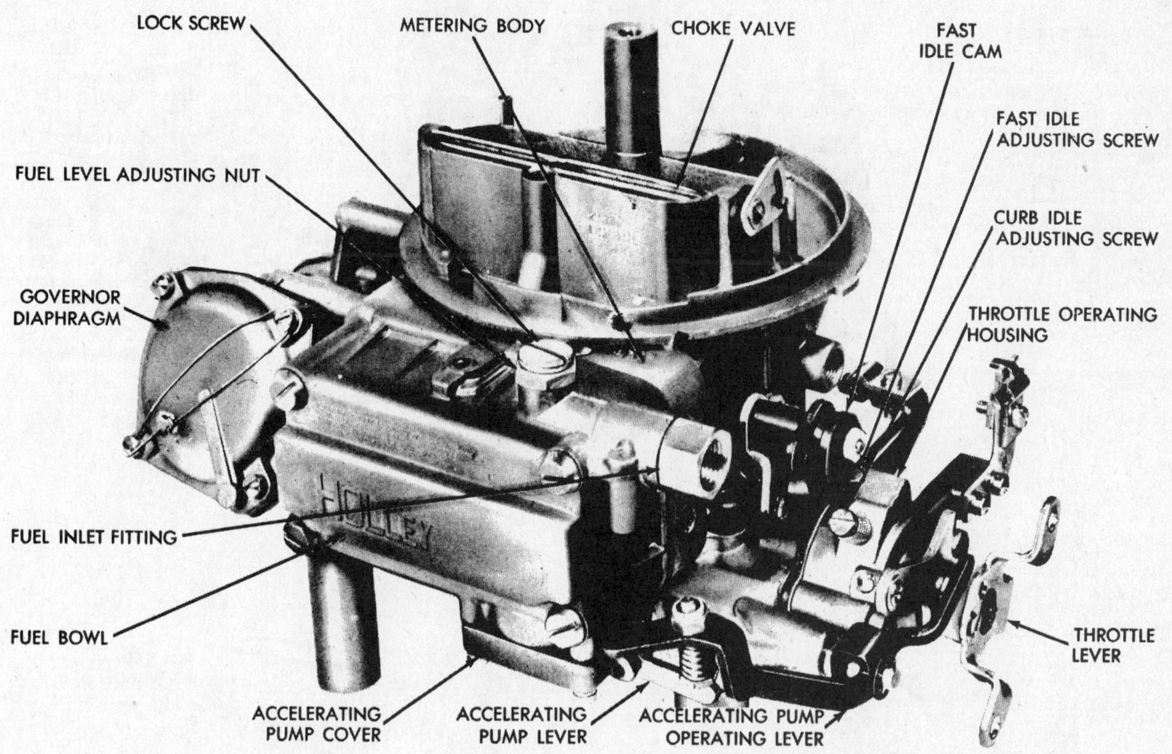

Holley model 2300G carburetor

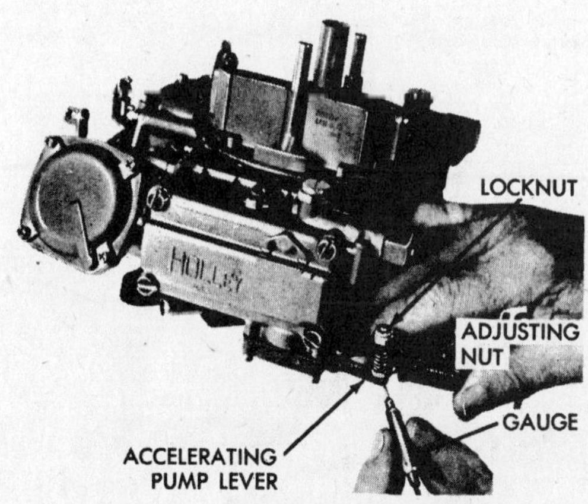

Checking accelerating pump lever clearance

Adjusting fuel level

HOLLEY MODEL 4150G

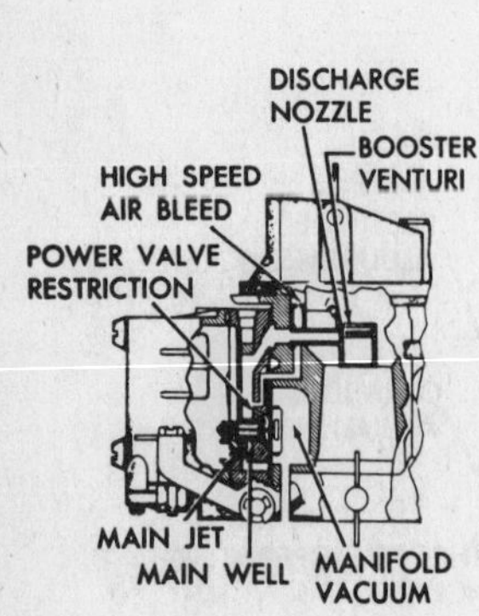

Power system

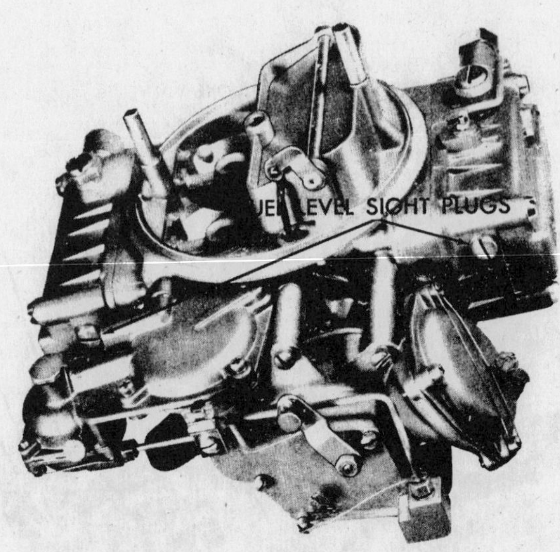

Model 4150G four barrel

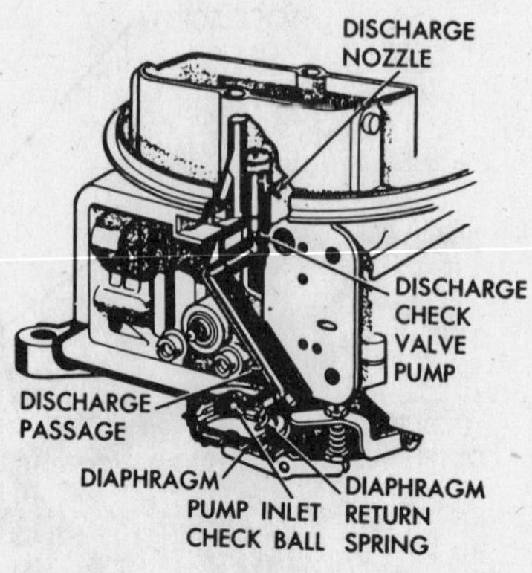

Pump system

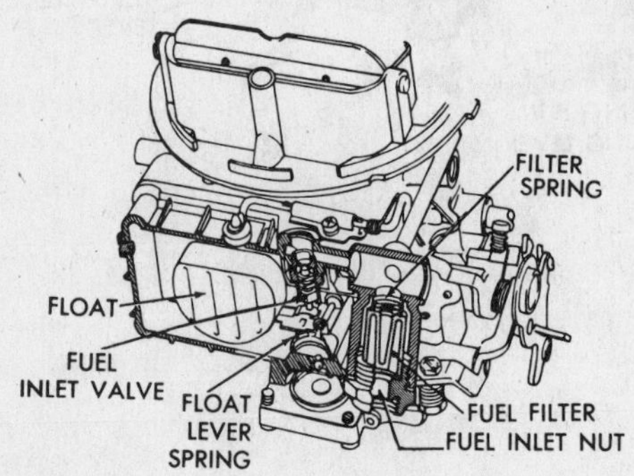

Fuel inlet system

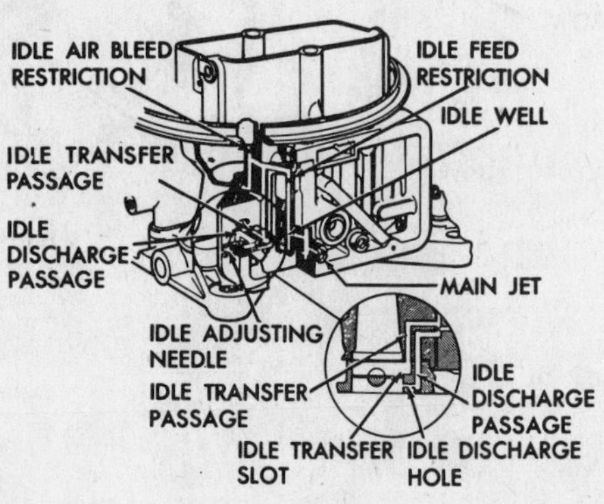

Idle system

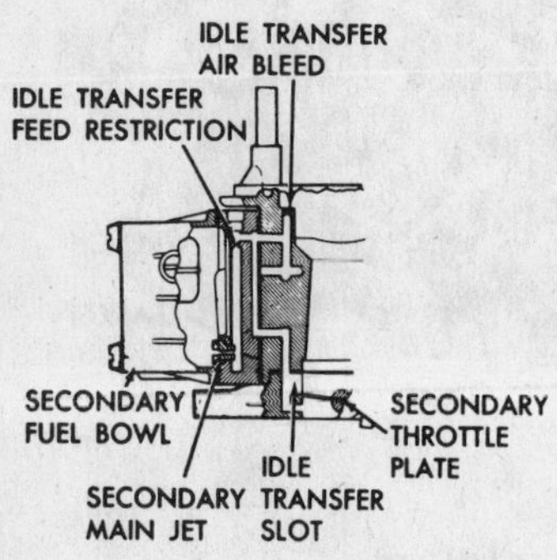

Secondary idle system (idle and low speed)

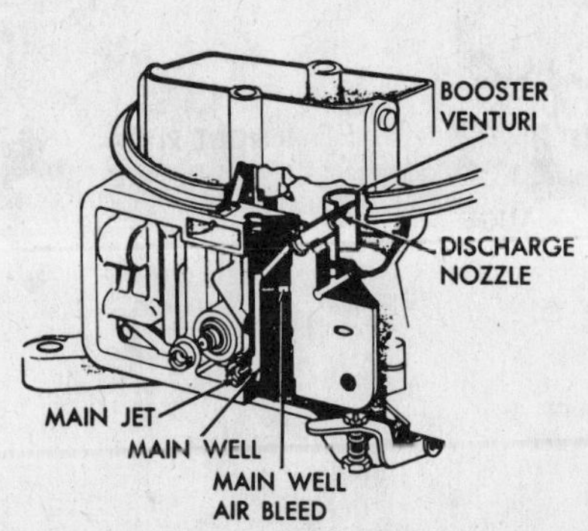

Main metering system

DIAPHRAGM
CHAMBER
PRIMARY
VENTURI
PICK-UP
DIAPHRAGM
DIAPHRAGM
ROD
SECONDARY
THROTTLE
PLATE

Secondary throttle operating system

HOLLEY TWO BARREL

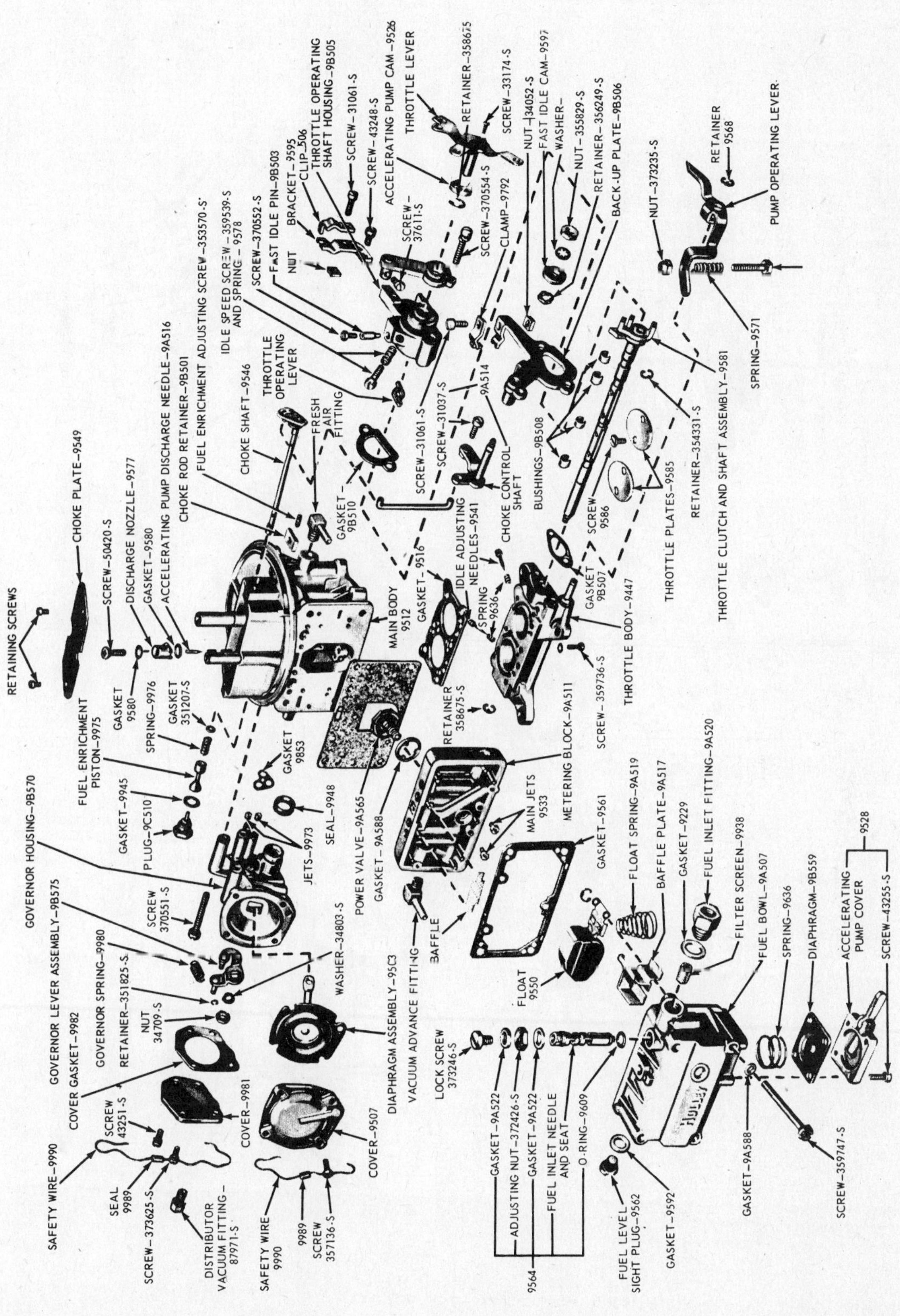

Holley two barrel—typical

HOLLEY FOUR BARREL

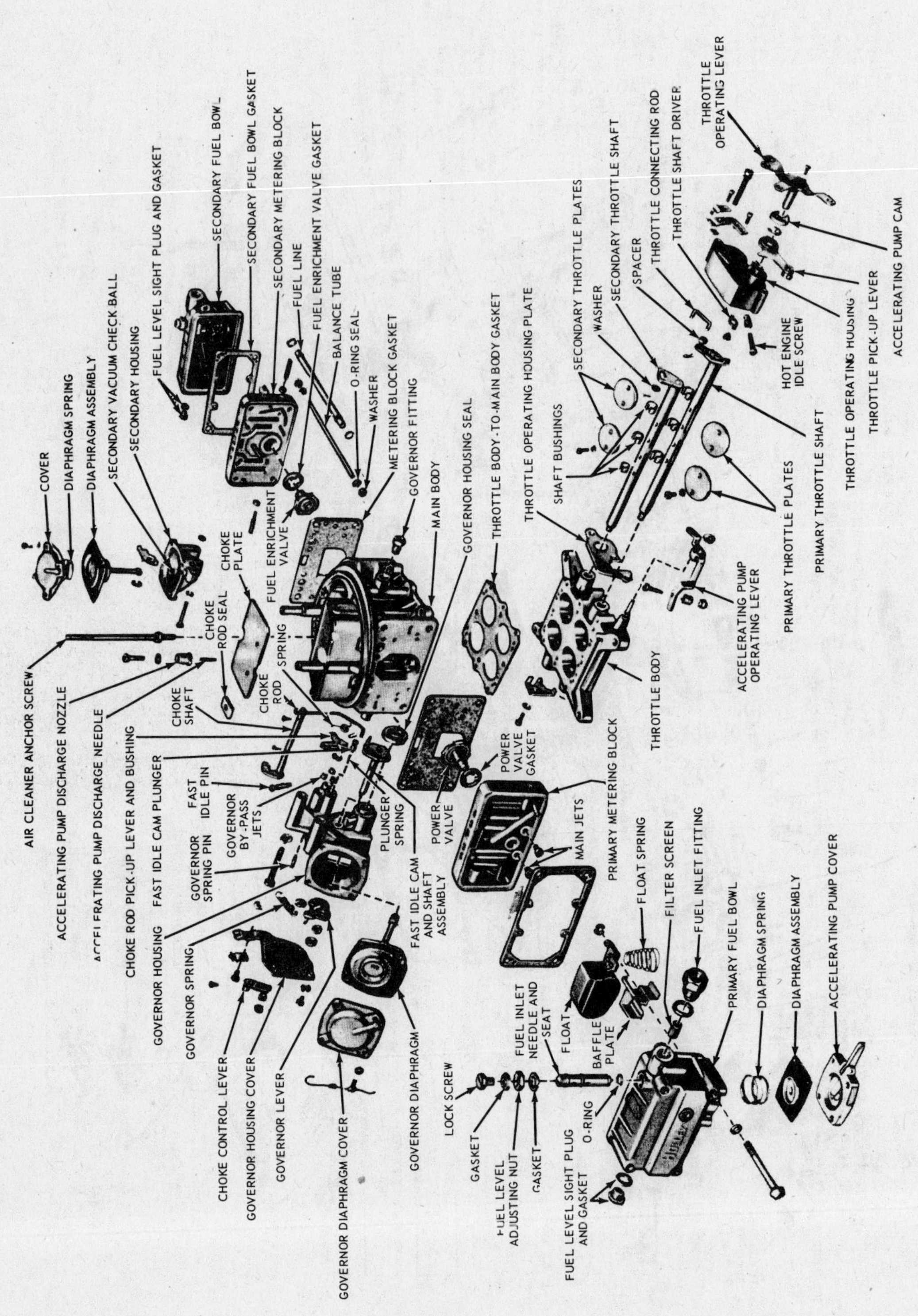

Holley four barrel—typical

HOLLEY MODEL 2110 AND 2110G

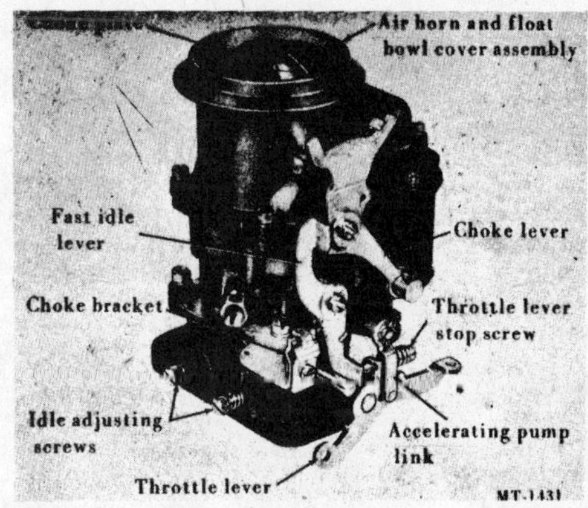

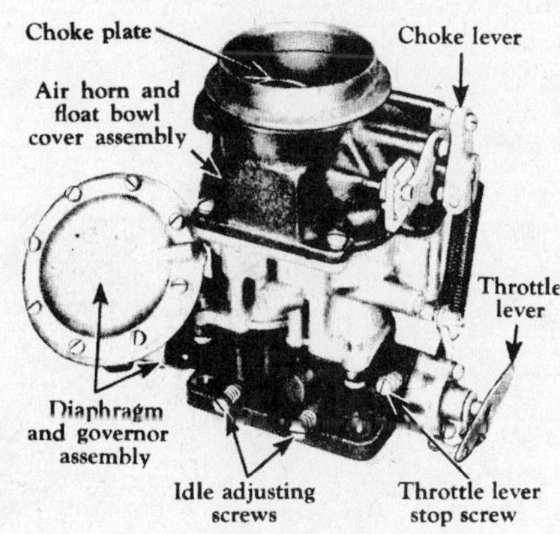

HOLLEY MODEL 2300

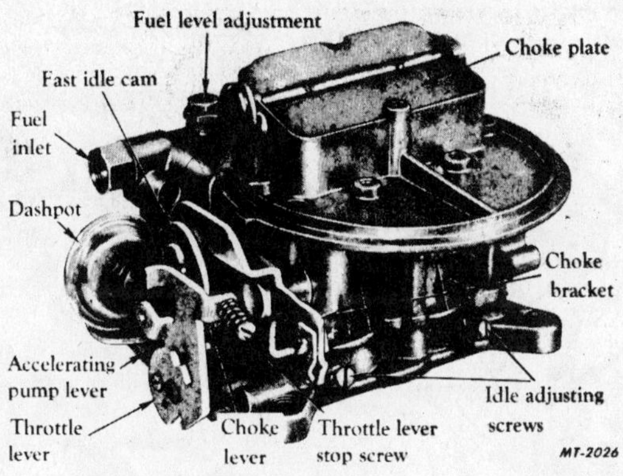

HOLLEY MODEL 885 FFG

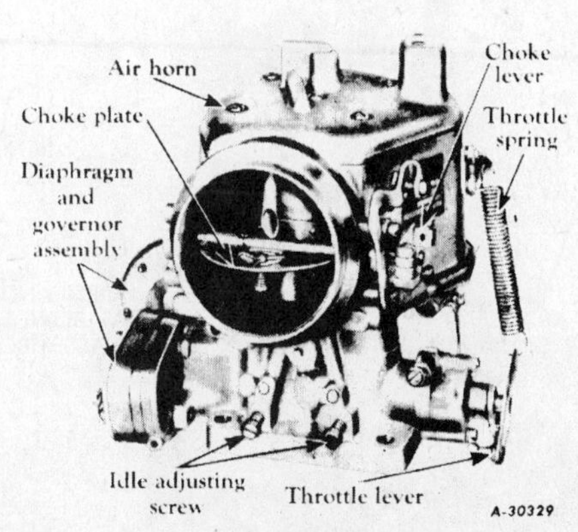

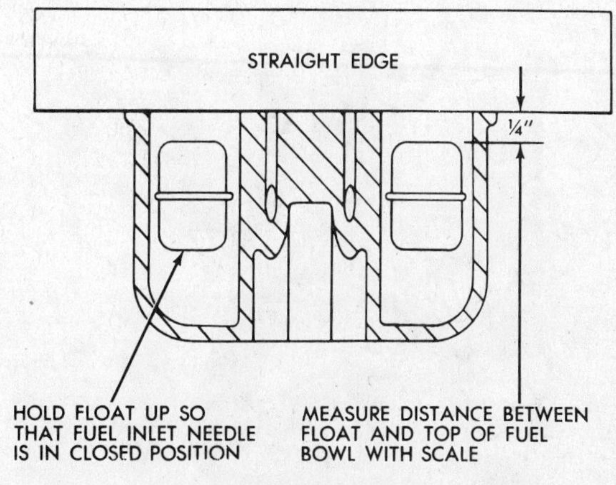

Measuring float level

HOLLEY MODEL 852 FFG

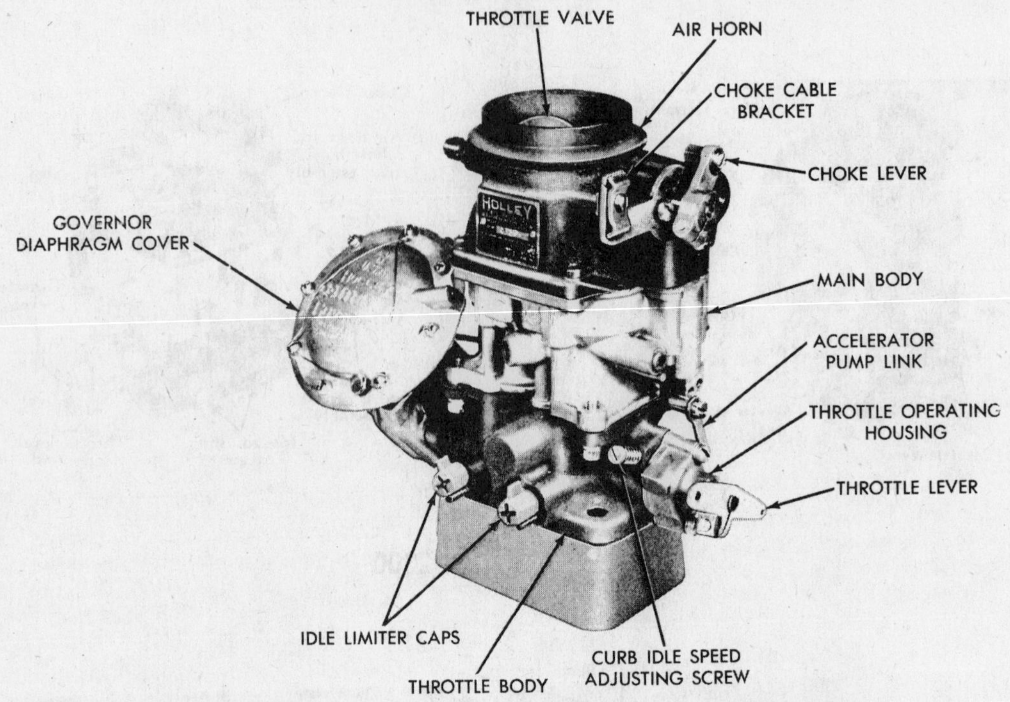

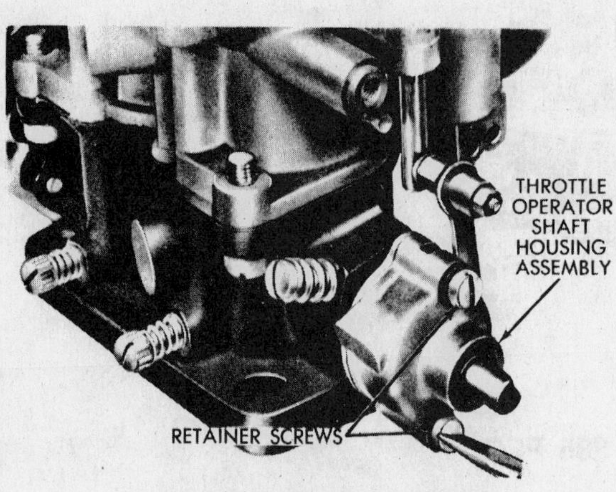

Throttle operating housing—removal

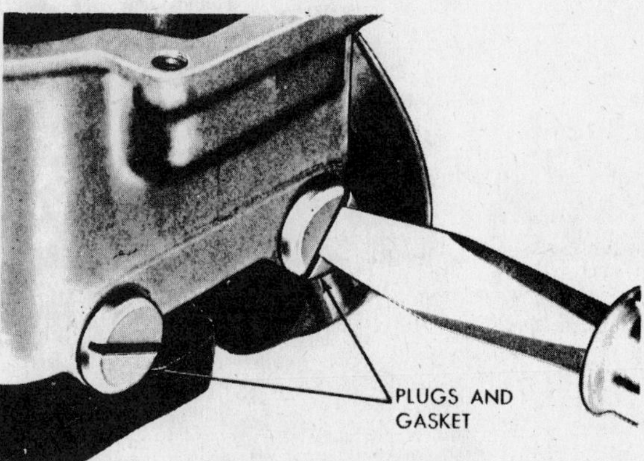

Main jet passage plugs

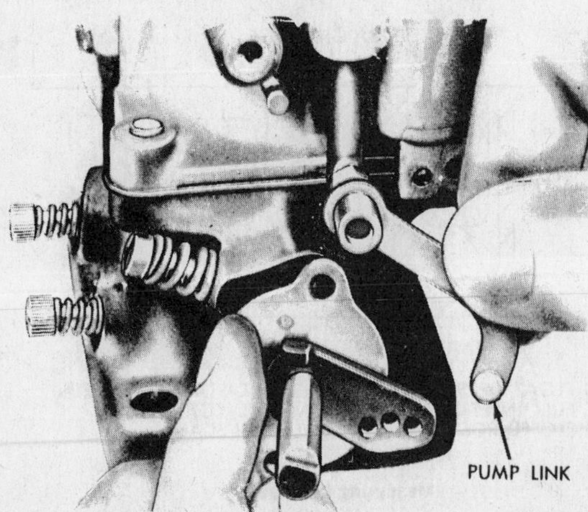

Accelerator pump link

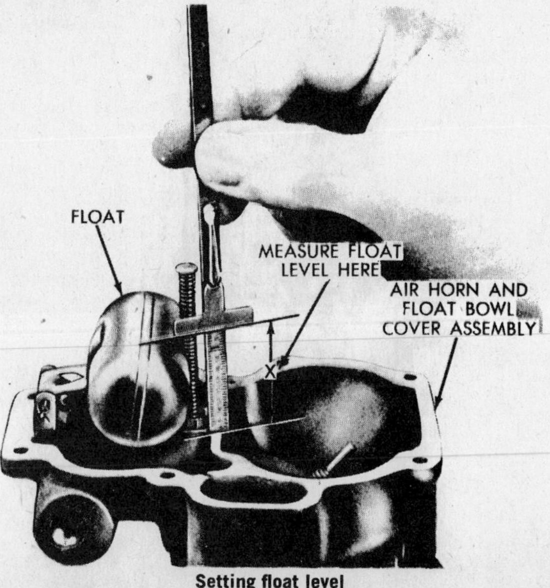

Setting float level

HOLLEY MODEL 2140G

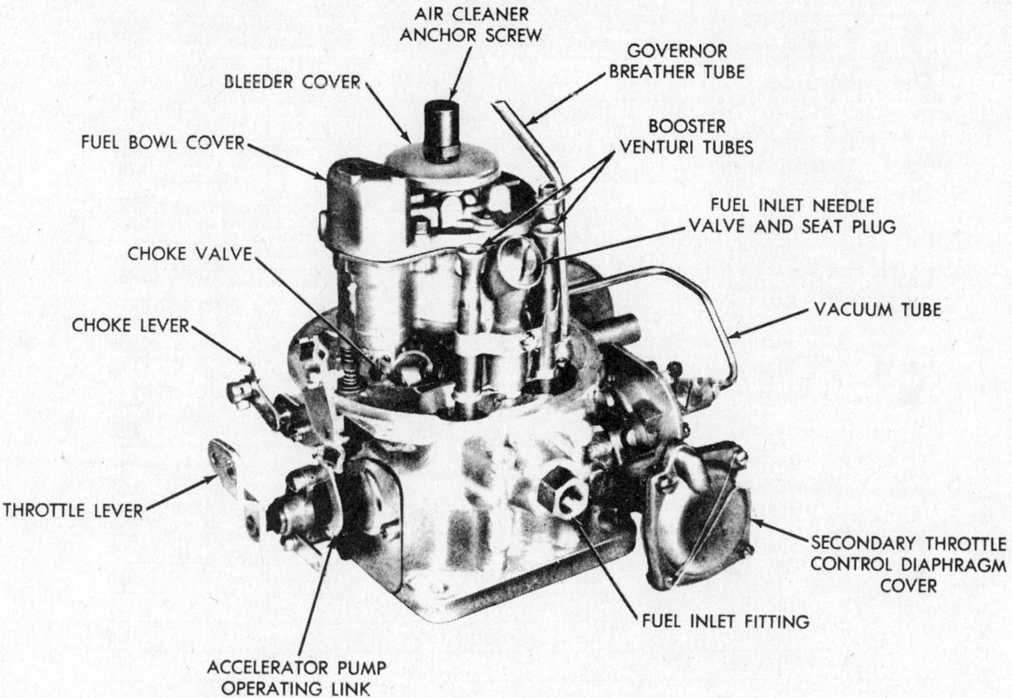

Holley model 2140G four barrel

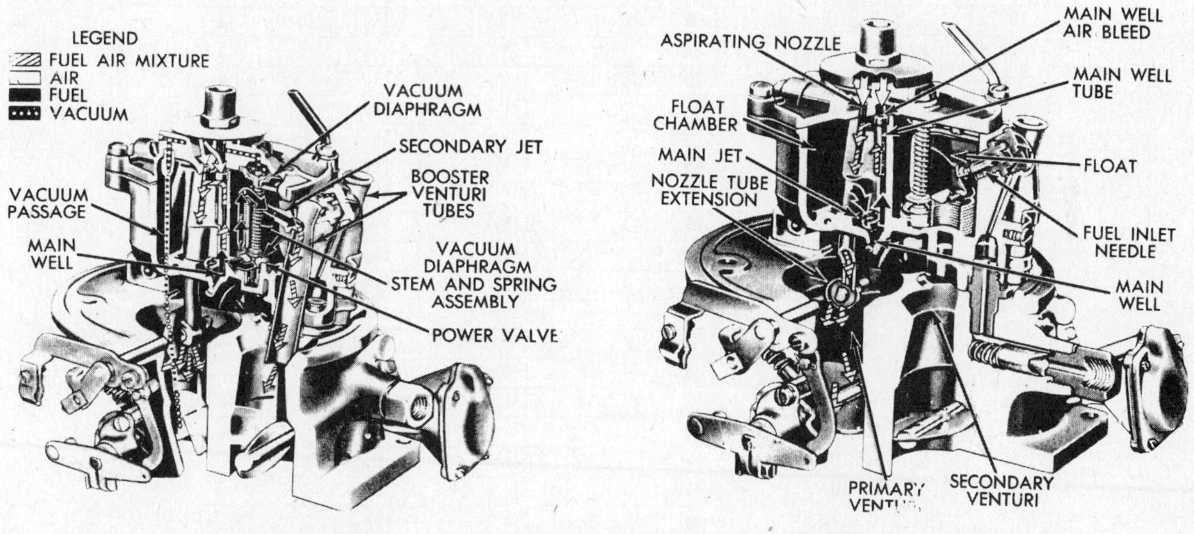

Power valve system

Main metering system

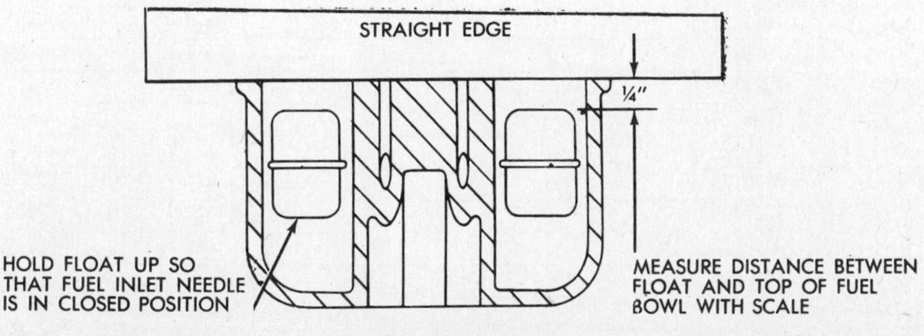

Measuring float drop

YEAR	MODEL OR TYPE	FLOAT LEVEL (IN.)	FLOAT DROP (IN.)	PUMP ROD	IDLE VENT

Chevrolet Truck

MODEL—B

YEAR	MODEL OR TYPE	FLOAT LEVEL (IN.)	FLOAT DROP (IN.)	PUMP ROD	IDLE VENT
1961-62	7015011	$1\frac{9}{32}$	$1\frac{3}{4}$	—	—
	7015013	$1\frac{9}{32}$	$1\frac{3}{4}$	—	—
	7015021	$1\frac{9}{32}$	$1\frac{3}{4}$	—	—
1963	7023013	$1\frac{9}{32}$	$1\frac{3}{4}$	—	.055
1963-65	7023011	$1\frac{9}{32}$	$1\frac{3}{4}$	—	.055
	7023017	$1\frac{9}{32}$	$1\frac{3}{4}$	—	.055
1964-66	7024009	$1\frac{9}{32}$	$1\frac{3}{4}$	—	.055
1966	7023021	$1\frac{9}{32}$	$1\frac{3}{4}$	—	.055
	7026011	$1\frac{9}{32}$	$1\frac{3}{4}$	—	.055
	7026019	$1\frac{9}{32}$	$1\frac{3}{4}$	—	.055
	7026029	$1\frac{9}{32}$	$1\frac{3}{4}$	—	.055
	7036009	$1\frac{9}{32}$	$1\frac{3}{4}$	—	.055
1966-67	7026017	$1\frac{9}{32}$	$1\frac{3}{4}$	—	.055
1967	7027009	$1\frac{9}{32}$	$1\frac{3}{4}$	—	.055
	7027011	$1\frac{9}{32}$	$1\frac{3}{4}$	—	.055
	7027029	$1\frac{9}{32}$	$1\frac{3}{4}$	—	.055
	7037009	$1\frac{9}{32}$	$1\frac{3}{4}$	—	.055

MODEL—2G

YEAR	MODEL OR TYPE	FLOAT LEVEL (IN.)	FLOAT DROP (IN.)	PUMP ROD	IDLE VENT
1961	7015017	$\frac{3}{4}$	$1\frac{29}{32}$	$1\frac{1}{8}$	1
1961-62	7015019	$\frac{3}{4}$	$1\frac{29}{32}$	$1\frac{1}{8}$	1
1962-68	7020109	$\frac{3}{4}$	$1\frac{29}{32}$	$1\frac{1}{8}$	1
1963-66	7023009	$\frac{3}{4}$	$1\frac{29}{32}$	$1\frac{1}{8}$	—
	7023010	$\frac{3}{4}$	$1\frac{29}{32}$	$1\frac{1}{8}$	—
	7023022	$\frac{3}{4}$	$1\frac{29}{32}$	$1\frac{1}{8}$	—
1966	7036100	$\frac{3}{4}$	$1\frac{29}{32}$	$1\frac{1}{8}$	—
	7036105	$\frac{3}{4}$	$1\frac{29}{32}$	$1\frac{1}{8}$	—
1966-67	7026113	$\frac{5}{8}$	$1\frac{29}{32}$	$1\frac{3}{16}$	—
1967	7027100	$\frac{3}{4}$	$1\frac{29}{32}$	$1\frac{1}{8}$	—
	7027105	$\frac{3}{4}$	$1\frac{29}{32}$	$1\frac{1}{8}$	—
	7027106	$\frac{3}{4}$	$1\frac{29}{32}$	$1\frac{1}{8}$	—
	7037100	$\frac{3}{4}$	$1\frac{29}{32}$	$1\frac{1}{8}$	—
	7037105	$\frac{3}{4}$	$1\frac{29}{32}$	$1\frac{1}{8}$	—
1968	7028015	$\frac{3}{4}$	$1\frac{3}{4}$	$1\frac{1}{8}$	—
	7028100	$\frac{3}{4}$	$1\frac{3}{4}$	$1\frac{1}{8}$	—
	7028106	$\frac{3}{4}$	$1\frac{3}{4}$	$1\frac{1}{8}$	—
	7028107	$\frac{3}{4}$	$1\frac{3}{4}$	$1\frac{1}{8}$	1
	7028111	$\frac{3}{4}$	$1\frac{3}{4}$	$1\frac{1}{8}$	—
	7028125	$\frac{3}{4}$	$1\frac{3}{4}$	$1\frac{1}{8}$	1
	7028127	$\frac{3}{4}$	$1\frac{3}{4}$	$1\frac{1}{8}$	—
1969	7029105	$\frac{27}{32}$	$1\frac{3}{4}$	$1\frac{1}{8}$	.020
	7029107	$\frac{27}{32}$	$1\frac{3}{4}$	$1\frac{1}{8}$	—
	7029111	$\frac{27}{32}$	$1\frac{3}{4}$	$1\frac{1}{8}$	—
	7029123	$\frac{3}{4}$	$1\frac{3}{4}$	$1\frac{7}{16}$	—
	7029124	$\frac{3}{4}$	$1\frac{3}{4}$	$1\frac{7}{16}$	—
	7029125	$\frac{27}{32}$	$1\frac{3}{4}$	$1\frac{1}{8}$	—
1970	7040125	$\frac{23}{32}$	$1\frac{3}{4}$	$1\frac{3}{8}$	.027
	7040405	$\frac{23}{32}$	$1\frac{3}{4}$	$1\frac{3}{8}$	.027
	7040108	$\frac{27}{32}$	$1\frac{3}{4}$	$1\frac{3}{8}$	.027
	7040123	$\frac{23}{32}$	$1\frac{3}{4}$	$1\frac{17}{32}$	.020
	7040124	$\frac{23}{32}$	$1\frac{3}{4}$	$1\frac{17}{32}$	.020

YEAR	MODEL OR TYPE	FLOAT LEVEL (IN.)	FLOAT DROP (IN.)	PUMP ROD	IDLE VENT
Chevrolet Truck, Continued					
		MODEL—4G			
1961	7015025	[1]	2 1/4	1 1/16	31/32
1962-65	7020025	[1]	2 1/4	1 1/16	31/32
	7020029	[1]	2 1/4	1 1/16	31/32
1965-66	7025125	[2]	2 1/4	1 1/16[3]	31/32
	7036125	[2]	2 1/4	1 1/16[3]	31/32
1967	7027125	[2]	2 1/4	1 1/16[3]	31/32
	7037125	[2]	2 1/4	1 1/16[3]	31/32

Note 1—Primary 1 5/8". Secondary 1 11/16".
Note 2—Primary 1 11/16". Secondary 1 3/4".
Note 3—Pump rod in outer hole.

MODEL—M & MV

YEAR	MODEL OR TYPE	Float Level (IN.)	Idle Speed Screw Setting	Metering Rod	Choke Rod	Fast Idle (Running)	Idle Vent
1968	7028006	9/32	[1]	.150	.150	2400	.050
	7028007	9/32	[1]	.170	.150	2400	.050
	7028010	9/32	[1]	.150	.150	2400	.050
	7028011	9/32	[1]	.170	.150	2400	.050
	7028012	9/32	[1]	.090	.150	2400	.050
	7028013	9/32	[1]	.090	.150	2400	.050
1969	7029007	1/4	[1]	.070	.150	2400	.050
	7029011	1/4	[1]	.070	.150	2400	.050
	7029012	1/4	[1]	.070	.150	2400	.050
	7029021	1/4	[1]	.070	.150	2400	.050
	7029022	1/4	[1]	.070	.245	2400	—
1970	7040011	1/4	[1]	.070	.150	2400	—
	7040012	1/4	[1]	.070	.150	2400	—
	7040021	1/4	[1]	.070	.190	2400	—
	7040025	1/4	[1]	.070	.180	2400	—
	7040022	1/4	[1]	.070	.275	2400	—
	7040026	1/4	[1]	.070	.275	2400	—

Note 1—Adjust idle speed screw until it just contacts the lever tang. For automatic transmission add another 1 1/4 turns and 2 turns for standard transmission.

MODEL—4 MV

YEAR	MODEL OR TYPE	Float Level (IN.)	Air Valve Dashpot	Secondary Metering Rod	PUMP ROD Adj.	PUMP ROD Hole	Idle Vent	Fast Idle (Bench)	Choke Rod	Vacuum Break	Choke Unloader	Air Valve Spring Wind-up
1968	7028211	3/16	.015	27/32	9/32	Inner	3/8	2 Turns	.100	.245	.300	7/8
	7028213	1/4	.015	27/32	9/32	Inner	3/8	2 Turns	.100	.245	.300	3/8
1969	7029214	1/4	.015	—	5/16	Inner	3/8	2 Turns	.100	.245	.450	13/16
	7029223	7/32	.015	—	5/16	Inner	3/8	2 Turns	.100	.245	.450	7/16
1970	7040511	1/4	.020	—	5/16	Inner	—	2 Turns	.100	.245	.450	7/16
	7040513	1/4	.020	—	5/16	Inner	—	2 Turns	.100	.245	.450	7/16
	7040208	1/4	.020	—	5/16	Inner	—	2 Turns	.100	.245	.450	7/16
	7040509	1/4	.020	—	5/16	Inner	—	2 Turns	.100	[1]	.450	13/16
	7040206	1/4	.020	—	5/16	Inner	—	2 Turns	.100	.245	.450	13/16

Note 1—Vacuum Break. A—Auto. Trans.—.245. Stand. Trans.—.275.

YEAR	Carb. Model	Fuel Level (Wet)	Float Level (Dry)	Float Drop	Pump Setting	Idle Vent Setting	Hot Idle Speed (RPM)	Idle Mix Screw Setting	Choke Setting
Jeep Truck									
				MODEL—2GV					
1969-70	7028088	—	1 1/64	1 7/8	13/16	—	650	2	[1]

Note 1—Standard hole.

YEAR	Carb. Model	Fuel Level (Wet)	Float Level (Dry)	Float Drop	Pump Setting	Idle Vent Setting	Hot Idle Speed (RPM)	Idle Mix Screw Setting	Choke Setting
GMC Truck									
				MODEL—B					
1963-66	7023011	—	1 9/32	1¾	—	.050	500	1	—
	7023017	—	1 9/32	1¾	—	.050	500	1	—
1967	7024009	—	1 9/32	1¾	—	.050	500[1]	1	—
	7026011	—	1 9/32	1¾	—	.050	500[1]	1	—
	7026017	—	1 9/32	1¾	—	.066	500[1]	1	—
	7026029	—	1 9/32	1¾	—	.050	500[1]	1	—
	7027009	—	1 9/32	1¾	—	.066	500[1]	1	—
	7027011	—	1 9/32	1¾	—	.066	500[1]	1	—
	7027029	—	1 9/32	1¾	—	.066	500[1]	1	—
	7037009	—	1 9/32	1¾	—	.050	500[1]	1	—
				MODEL—2G					
1967	7027100	—	¾	1 29/32	1⅛	—	525[2]	1	—
	7027105	—	¾	1 29/32	1⅛	—	525[2]	1	—
	7027106	—	¾	1 29/32	1⅛	—	525[2]	1	—
	7027109	—	¾	1 29/32	1⅛	—	525[2]	1	—
	7037100	—	¾	1 29/32	1⅛	—	525[2]	1	—
	7037105	—	¾	1 29/32	1⅛	—	525[2]	1	—
1968	7027105	—	¾	1¾	1⅛	—	525[1]	1	—
	7028105	—	¾	1¾	1⅛	—	550[3]	1	—
	7028107	—	¾	1¾	1⅛	—	550[3]	1	—
1969	7029107	—	27/32	1¾	1⅛	—	550[3]	1	—
	7029108	—	27/32	1¾	1⅛	—	550[3]	1	—
	7029125	—	27/32	1¾	1⅛	—	550[3]	1	—
				MODEL—2GV					
1969	7029105	—	27/32	1¾	1⅛	—	550[3]	1	—
	7029121	—	1 9/32	1⅜	1 13/32	—	500	1	—
				MODEL—4G					
1967	7027125	—	[4]	2¼	1 1/16	.030	525[2]	1	—
	7037125	—	[4]	2¼	1 1/16	.030	525[2]	1	—
				MODEL—M & MV					
1968	7028010	—	11/32	—	—	—	525[1]	1	—
Type	7028011	—	11/32	—	—	—	525[1]	1	—
(M)	7028012	—	11/32	—	—	—	525[1]	1	—
	7028013	—	11/32	—	—	—	525[1]	1	—
1969	7029007	—	9/32	—	Inboard	—	525[1]	1	.150
Type	7029011	—	9/32	—	Inboard	—	525[1]	1	.150
(M)	7029012	—	9/32	—	Inboard	—	525[1]	1	.150
1969	7029007	—	¼	—	[5]	—	525[1]	1	.150
Type	7029021	—	¼	—	[5]	—	525[1]	1	.180
(MV)	7029022	—	¼	—	[5]	—	525[1]	1	.245
				MODEL—4M & 4MV					
1968	7028213	—	9/32	—	9/32	—	500	1	[5]
Type (4M)	7028217	—	3/16	—	9/32	—	500	1	[5]
1969	7029233	—	7/32	—	5/16	⅜	500	1	[5]
Type (4MV)	7029214	—	¼	—	5/16	⅜	700[1]	1	[5]

Note 1—With air condition and manual transmission: 700 RPM.
With air condition and automatic transmission with 292 engine: 600 RPM.

Note 2—With manual transmission and air condition: 650 RPM.
With automatic transmission: 550 RPM.

Note 3—With emission control. A—Manual transmission: 700 RPM. B—Automatic transmission: 600 RPM.

Note 4—Primary: 1 17/32″. Secondary: 1 19/32″.

Note 5—One rod diameter interference.

ROCHESTER—MODEL B

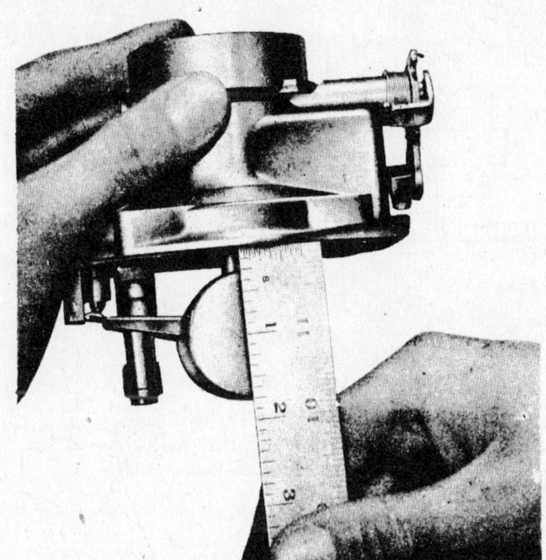

Checking float drop

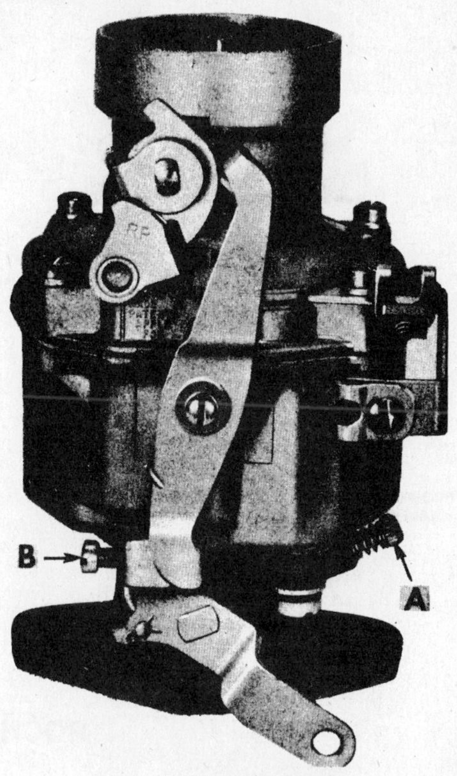

Idle and mixture adjustments

Checking float level

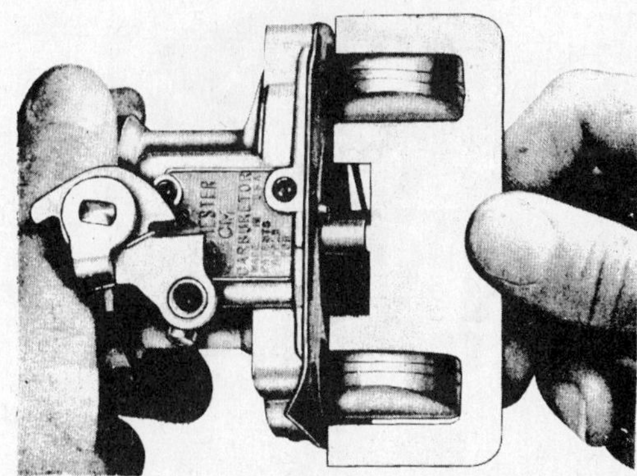

Checking float clearance

ROCHESTER MODEL 2G

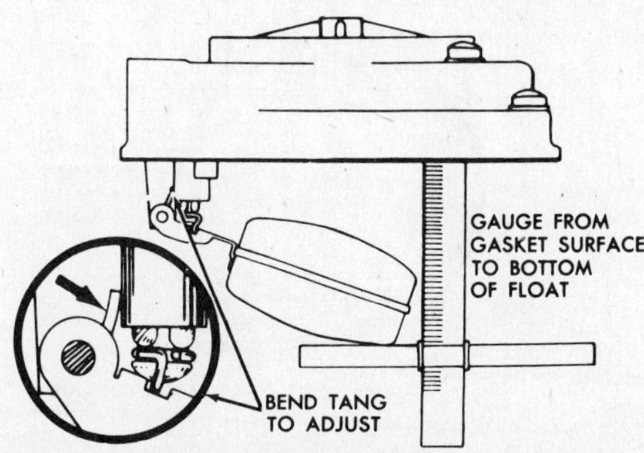

Float drop adjustment

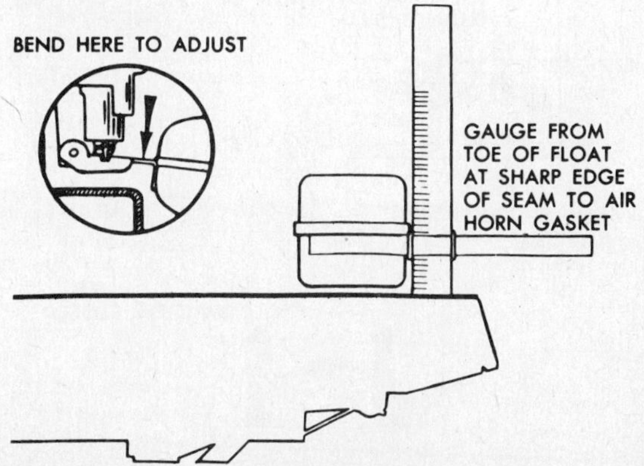

Float level adjustment

ROCHESTER MODEL 2G continued

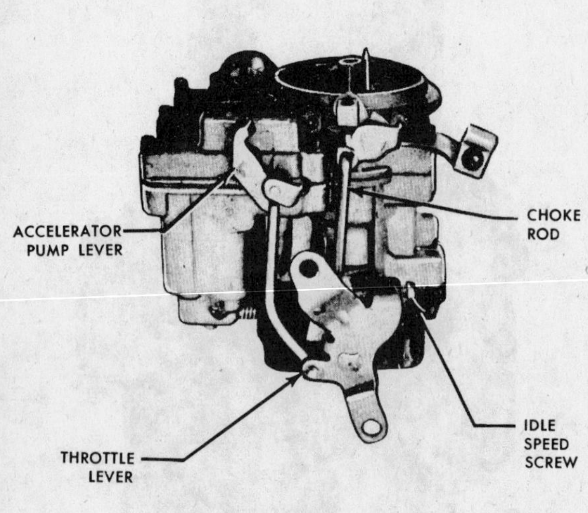

Rochester model 2G carburetor

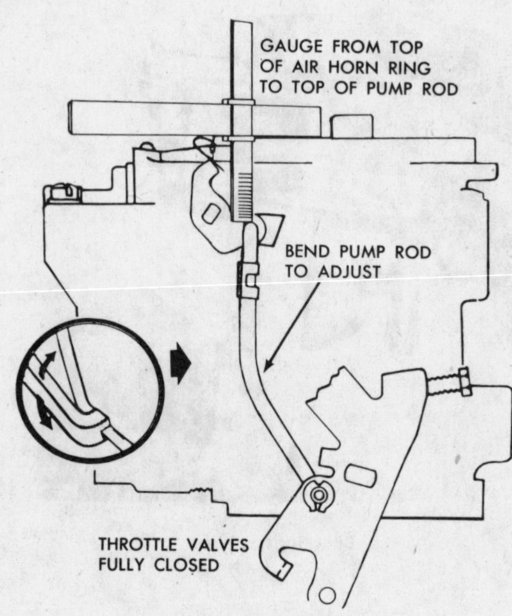

Accelerator pump rod adjustment

ROCHESTER MODEL 4G

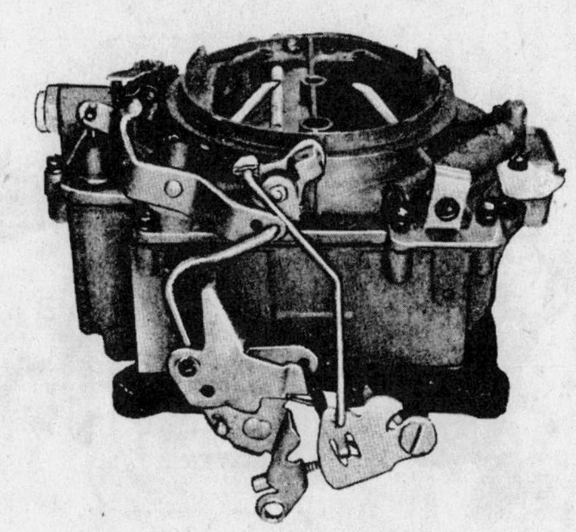

Rochester 4G carburetor

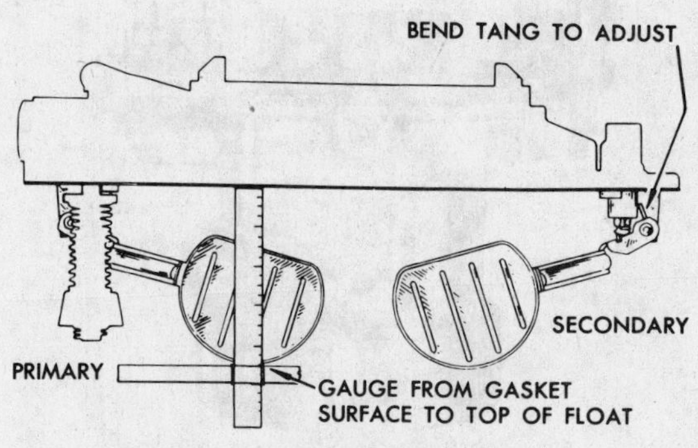

Float drop adjustment

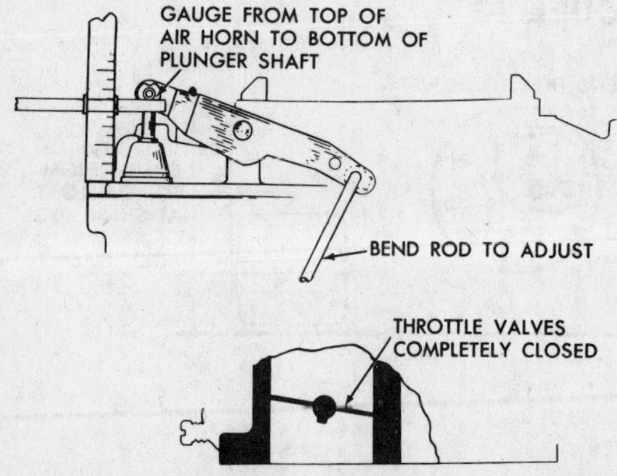

Accelerator pump rod adjustment

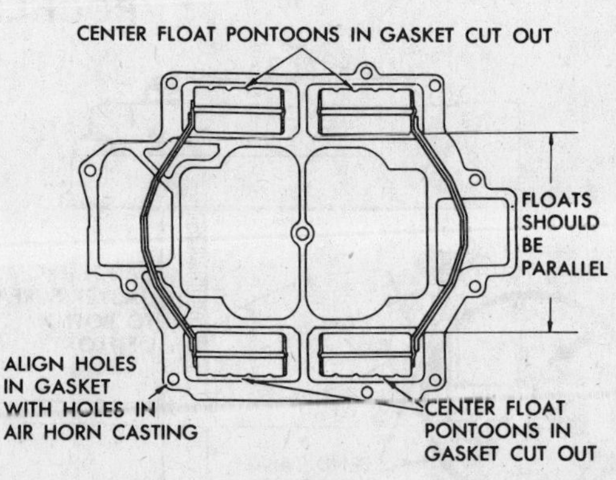

Float alignment

ROCHESTER MODEL 4G continued

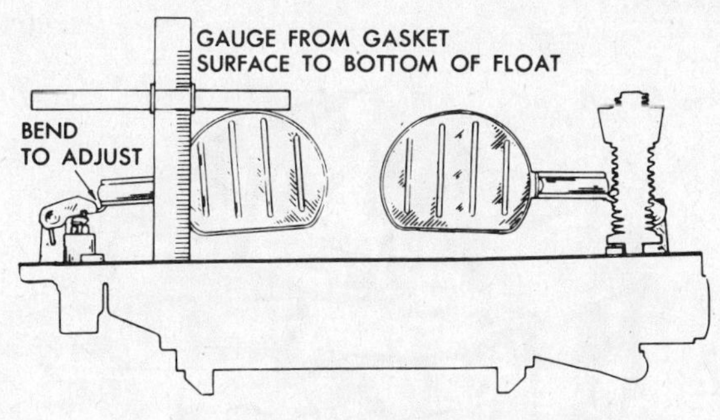

Float level adjustment

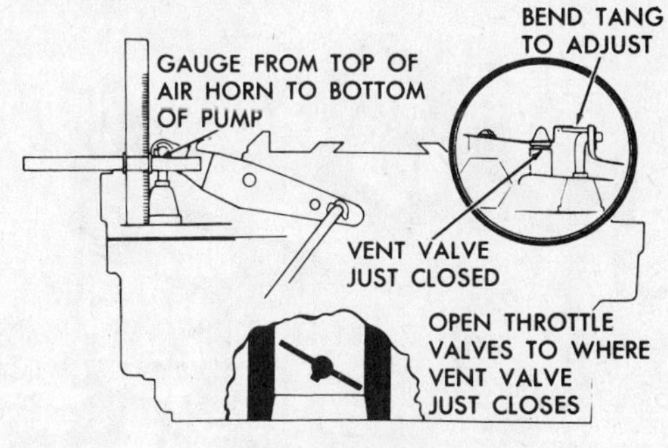

Idle vent adjustment

ROCHESTER MODELS M AND MV

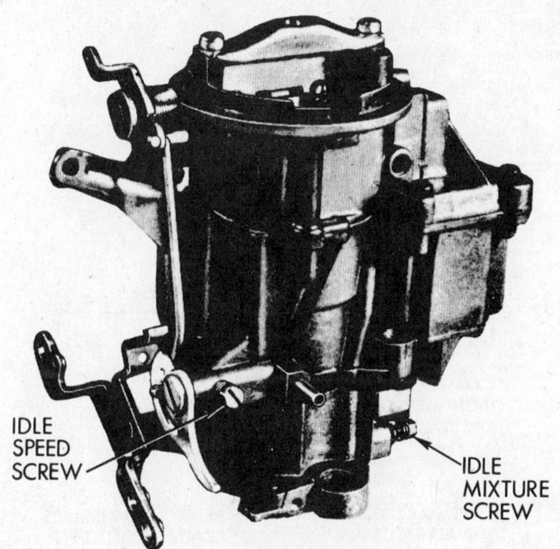

Rochester monojet carburetor

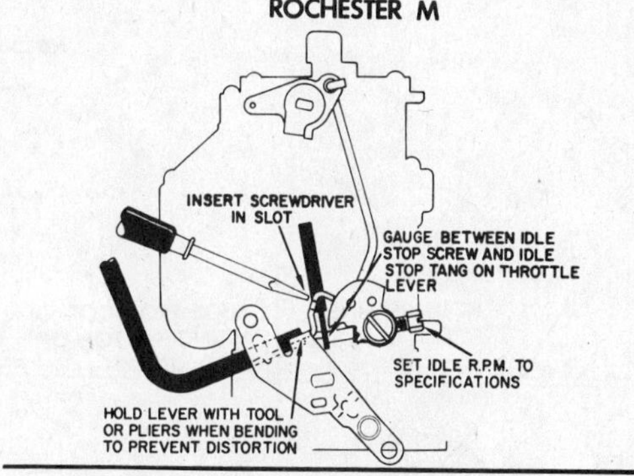

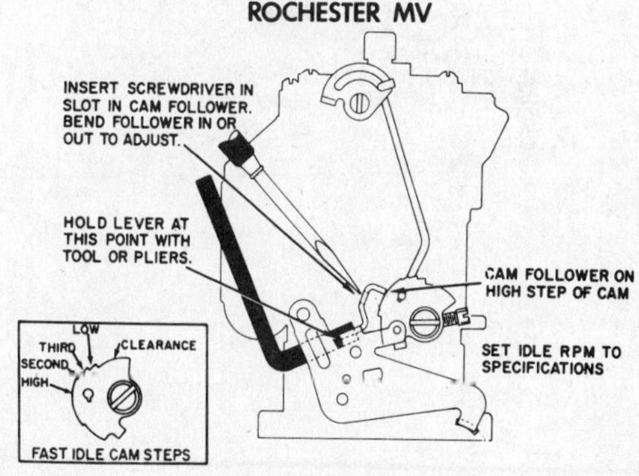

Fast idle adjustment

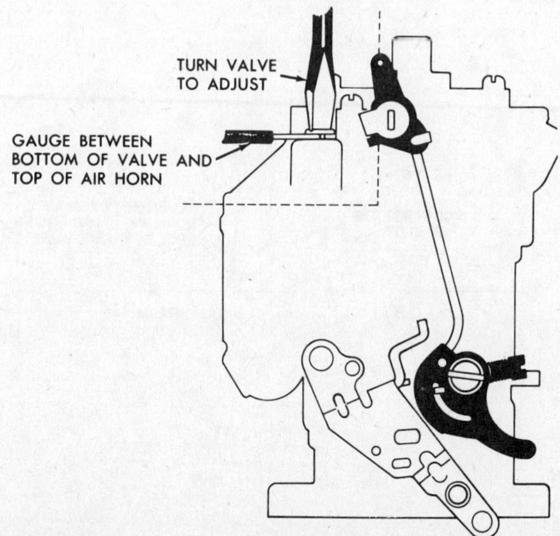

Idle vent adjustment

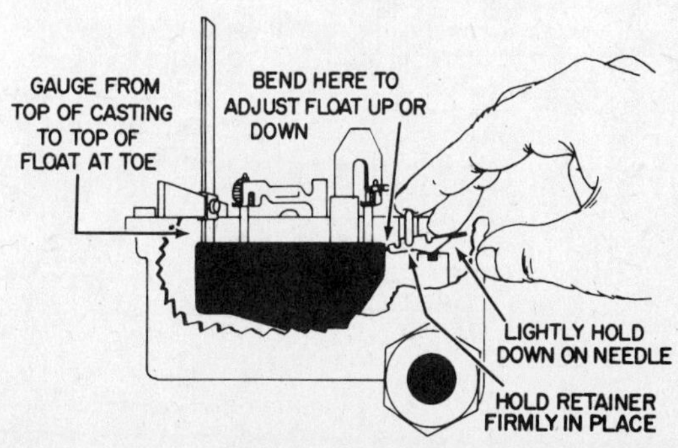

Float level adjustment

ROCHESTER MODEL 4MV

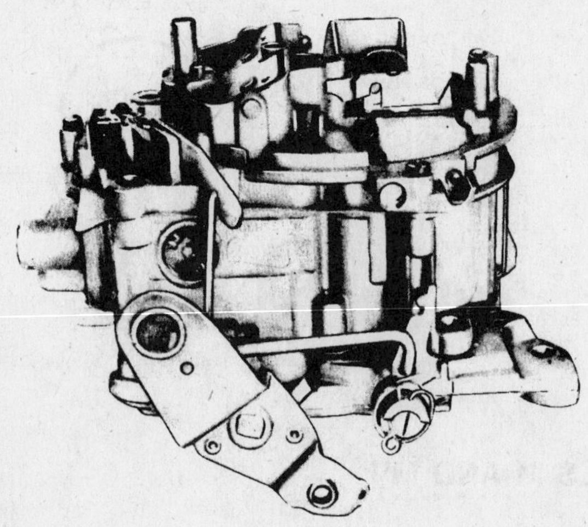

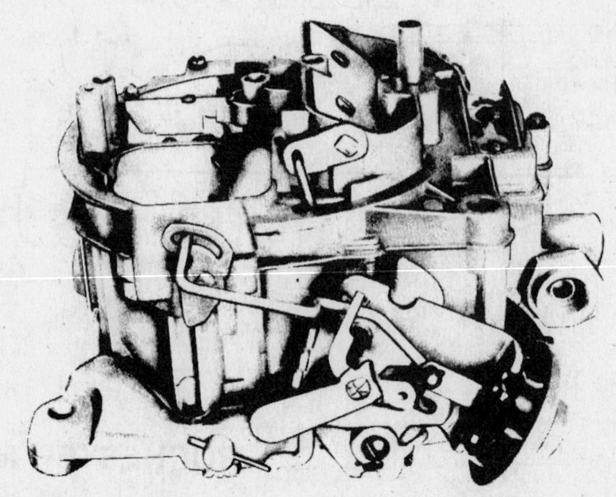

Rochester 4MV carburetor

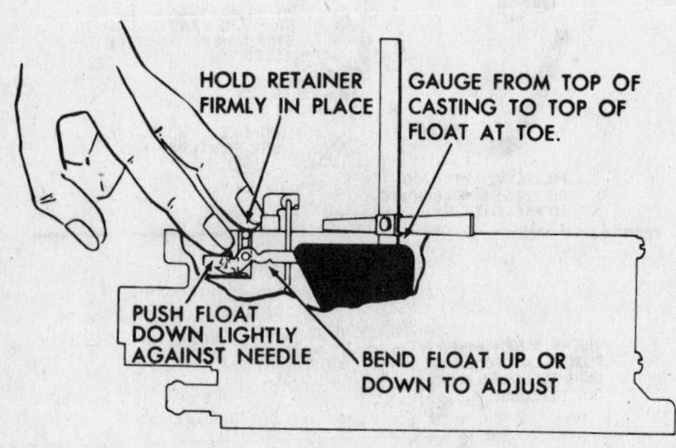

Float level adjustment

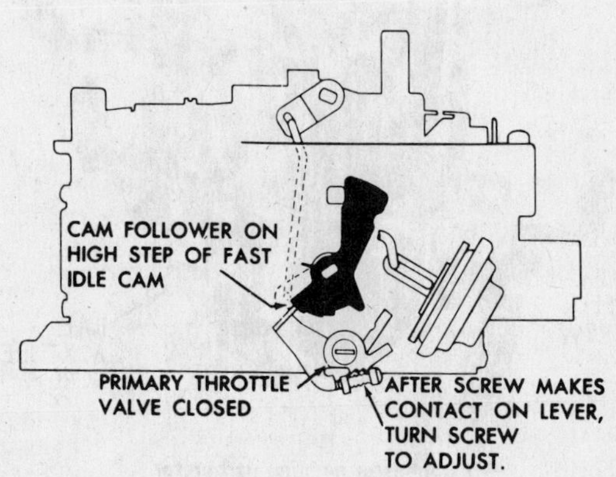

Fast idle adjustment

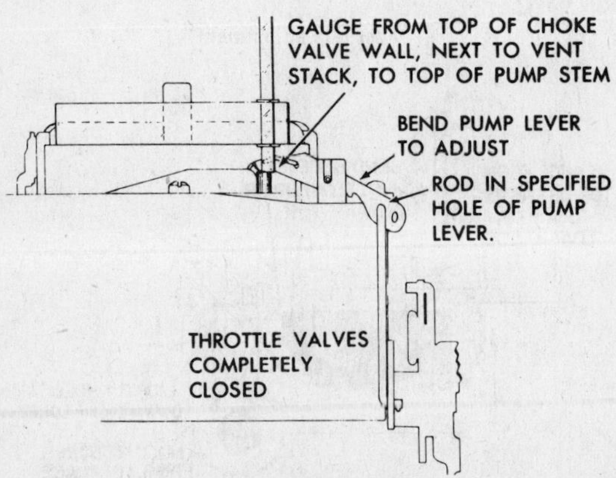

Pump rod adjustment

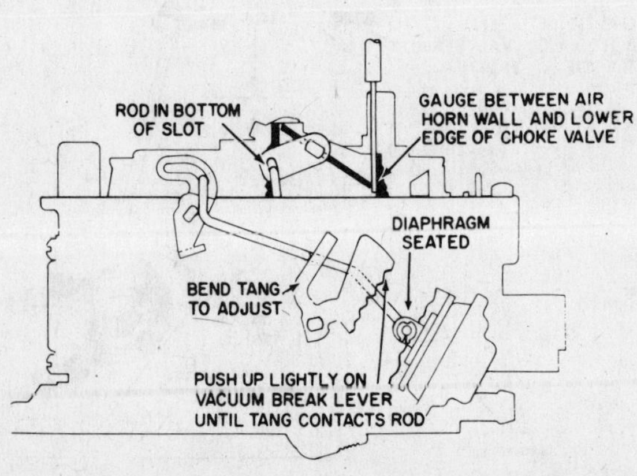

Vacuum break adjustment

ROCHESTER MODEL 4MV continued

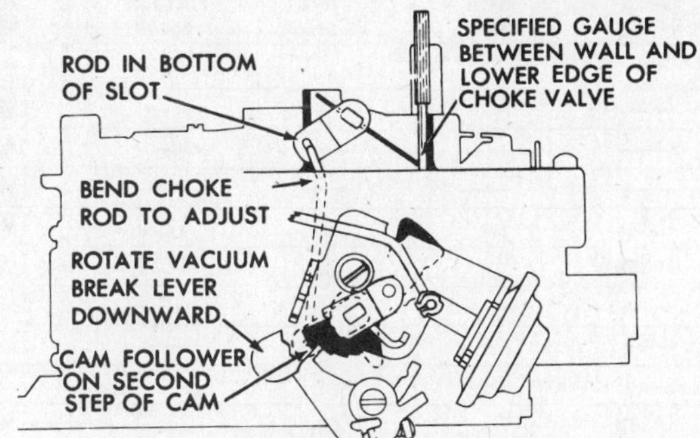

Choke rod adjustment

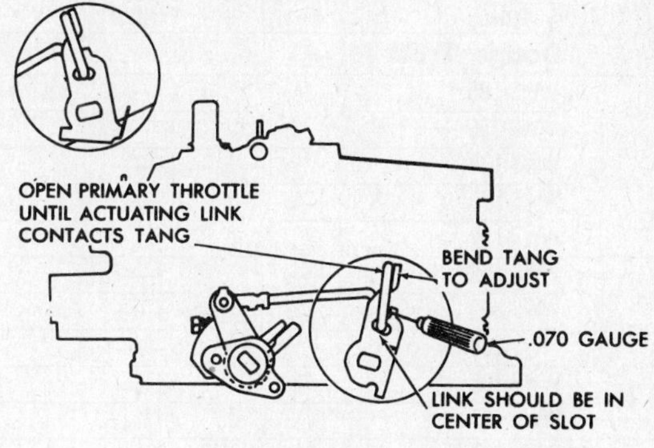

Secondary opening adjustment

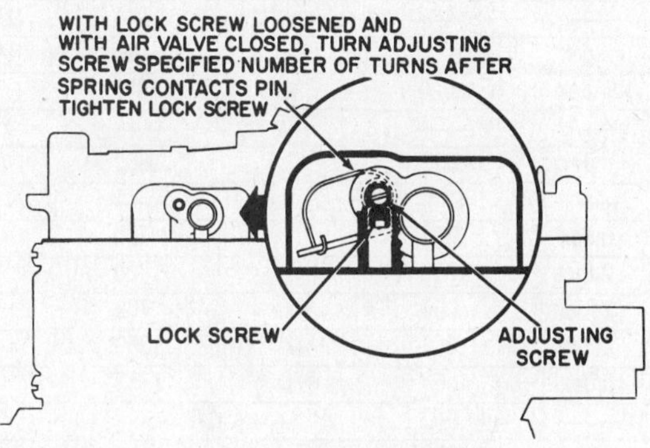

Air valve spring adjustment

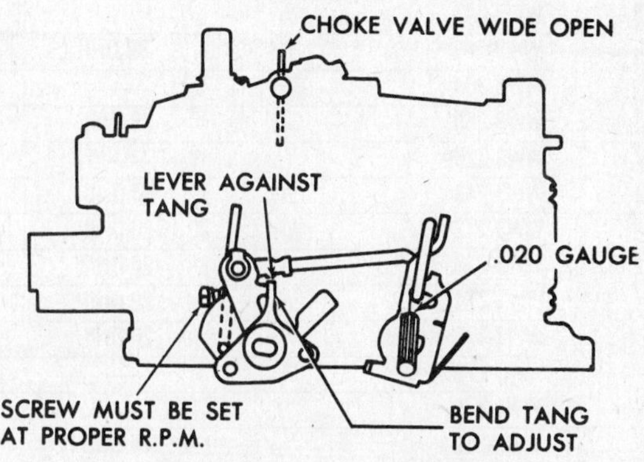

Secondary closing adjustment

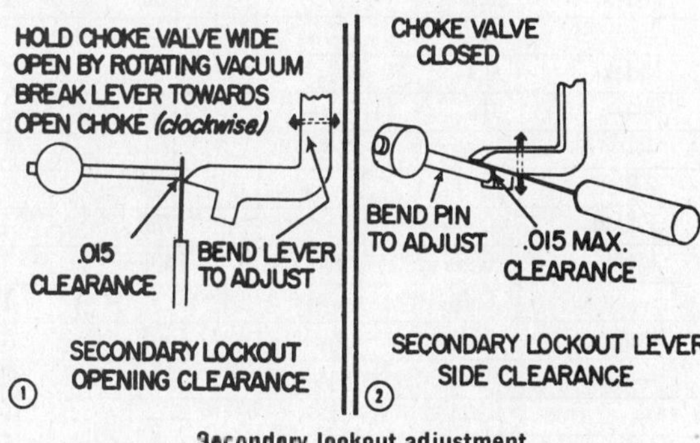

Secondary lookout adjustment

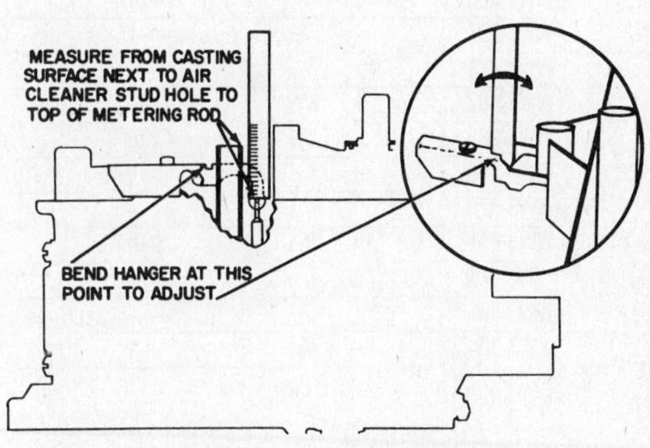

Secondary metering adjustment

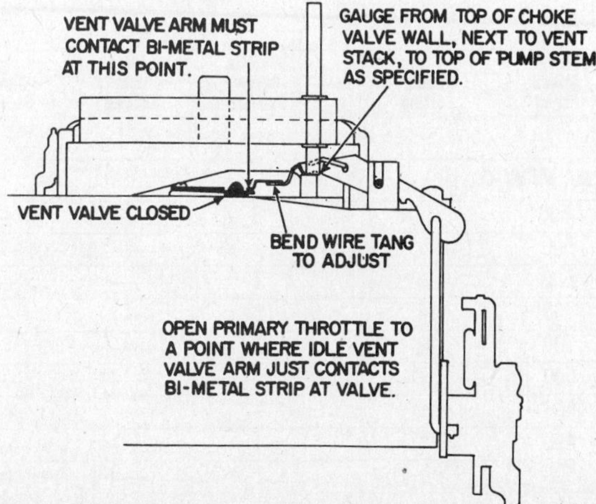

Idle vent adjustment

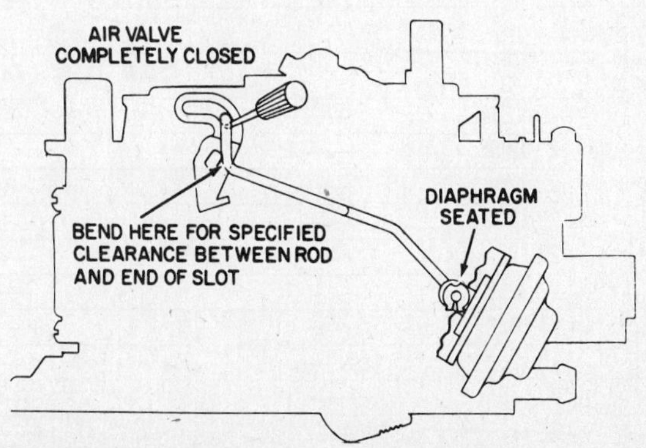

Air valve dashpot adjustment

YEAR	Model or Type	Float Level	Fast Idle Cam Position	Vacuum Kick	Choke Setting	Bowl Vent	Choke Unloader	Fast Idle Speed	Idle Mix. Screw Adjust
	Dodge Truck								
1961	WW3-185	7/32	—	—	—	—	—	—	1¼-1⅜
	WW3-190	7/32	—	—	—	—	—	—	1¼-1⅜
	WW3-194	7/32	—	—	—	—	—	—	1¼-1⅜
	WW3-195	7/32	13/64	⅜	Index	5/64	15/64	1250	1¼-1⅜
	WW3-197	7/32	13/64	⅜	Index	5/64	15/64	1250	1¼-1⅜
1962	WW3-202	7/32	—	—	—	—	—	—	1¼-1⅜
	WW3-203	7/32	—	—	—	—	—	—	1¼-1⅜
	WW3-204	7/32	—	—	—	—	—	—	1¼-1⅜
	WW3-205	7/32	13/64	⅜	Index	5/64	15/64	1250	1¼-1⅜
	WW3-207	7/32	13/64	⅜	Index	5/64	15/64	1250	1¼-1⅜
1963	WW3-227	7/32	13/64	19/64	Index	5/64	15/64	1250	1¼-1⅜
1963-65	WW3-226	7/32	—	—	—	—	—	—	1¼-1⅜
1963-68	WW3-225	7/32	—	—	—	—	—	—	1¼-1⅜
1964-65	WW3-243	7/32	17/64	13/64	Index	5/64	15/64	700	1¼-1⅜
1966	WW3-263	5/32	38 Drill	22 Drill	Index	.020	15/64	1300	1½
	WW3-264	7/32	—	—	—	—	—	—	1½
	WW3-265	7/32	28 Drill	D-Drill	Index	.050	5/16	1600	1½
1966-67	WW3-226A	7/32	—	—	—	—	—	—	1¼
	WW3-243	7/32	44 Drill	4 Drill	Index	.060	5/16	700	1¼
1967	WW3-272	7/32	20 Drill	A Drill	2 Rich	.060	5/16	700	1¼
	WW3-273	7/32	20 Drill	4 Drill	2 Rich	.060	5/16	700	1¼
	WW3-274	7/32	20 Drill	A Drill	Index	.050	5/16	1350	1½
	WW3-275	7/32	20 Drill	4 Drill	Index	.050	5/16	1350	1½
	WW3-278	7/32	—	—	—	.060	—	—	1¼
	WW3-279	7/32	—	—	—	.050	—	—	1½
	WW3-280	7/32	44 Drill	4 Drill	2 Rich	.060	5/16	700	1¼
	WW3-281	7/32	20 Drill	4 Drill	Index	.050	5/16	1400	1½
1968	WW3-284	7/32	—	—	—	.050	—	—	1½
	WW3-286	7/32	20 Drill	A Drill	Index	.050	5/16	1400	1½
	WW3-291	7/32	—	—	—	.060	—	—	1¼
1968-69	WW3-283	7/32	—	—	—	—	—	—	1⅞
	WW3-287	7/32	43 Drill	2 Drill	2 Rich	.060	15/64	700	1¼
1969	WW3-289	7/32	43 Drill	42 Drill	2 Rich	.060	15/64	700	1¼
	WW3-299	7/32	20 Drill	A Drill	Index	.050	5/16	1400	1½
	WW3-300	7/32	—	—	—	.050	—	—	1½
	WW3-301	7/32	20 Drill	A Drill	Index	.050	5/16	1400	1½
	WW3-302	7/32	—	—	—	.050	—	—	1½
	WW3-303	7/32	—	—	—	—	—	—	1¼-1⅜
	WW3-304	7/32	—	—	—	—	—	—	1¼-1⅜

YEAR	Carb. Model	Fuel Level (Wet)	Float Level (Dry)	Float Drop	Hot Idle Speed (RPM)	Pump Setting	Idle Mix. Screw Setting	Idle Vent Setting	Choke Setting
GMC Trucks									
			CARBURETOR TYPE WW-2						
1961	23-123A	—	3/16	—	500	¼	1	—	—
	23-124A	—	3/16	—	500	¼	1	—	—
	23-120A	—	3/16	—	500	¼	1	—	—
	23-121A	—	3/16	—	500	¼	1	—	—
	23-122A	—	3/16	—	500	¼	1	—	—
	23-126B	—	3/16	—	500	15/16	1	—	—
1962	23-133A	—	⅛[1]	—	500	15/16	1	—	—
	23-125A	—	3/16	—	500	15/16	1	—	—
1962-63	23-138	—	⅛[1]	—	500	15/16	1	—	—
1962-64	23-142	—	⅛[1]	—	500	15/16	1	—	—
	23-143	—	⅛[1]	—	500	15/16	1	—	—

YEAR	Carb. Model	Fuel Level (Wet)	Float Level (Dry)	Float Drop	Hot Idle Speed (RPM)	Pump Setting	Idle Mix. Screw Setting	Idle Vent Setting	Choke Setting
GMC Truck, Continued									
1962-65	23-139	—	1/8[1]	—	500	15/16	1	—	—
1963	23-151	—	1/8[1]	—	500	15/16	1	—	—
	23-152	—	1/8[1]	—	500	15/16	1	—	—
	23-137	—	1/8[1]	—	500	15/16	1	—	—
1964	23-158	—	1/8[1]	—	500	15/16	1	—	—
1964-65	23-153A	—	1/8[1]	—	500	15/16	1	—	—
	23-138A	—	1/8[1]	—	500	15/16	1	—	—
1965	23-158A	—	1/8[1]	—	500	15/16	1	—	—
	23-168	—	3/16	—	500	15/16	1	—	—
1966-67	23-181	—	1/0	—	500[2]	.160	1	—	—
	23-182	—	3/16	—	500[2]	.160	1	—	—
	23-164	—	3/16	—	500[2]	.160	1	—	—
1967	23-161	—	3/16	—	500[2]	.160	1	—	—
	381186	—	3/16	—	500[2]	.160	1	—	—
1968	23-207	—	[3]	—	550	.420-.450	1	—	—
	23-195A	—	[3]	—	550	.420-.450	1	—	—
	23-182A	—	[3]	—	550	.420-.450	1	—	—
	23-200A	—	[3]	—	550	.420-.450	1	—	—
1969	23-203	—	.190	—	550	.420-.450	1	—	—
	23-195A	—	.190	—	550	.420-.450	1	—	—
	23-221	—	.190	—	550	.420-.450	1	—	—
	23-204	—	.190	—	550	.420-.450	1	—	—
	23-200	—	.190	—	550	.420-.450	1	—	—
	23-221	—	.190	—	550	.420-.450	1	—	—

CARBURETOR TYPE WWC3

YEAR	Carb. Model	Fuel Level (Wet)	Float Level (Dry)	Float Drop	Hot Idle Speed (RPM)	Pump Setting	Idle Mix. Screw Setting	Idle Vent Setting	Choke Setting
1961	23-125	—	3/16	—	500	1/16	1	—	—
1962	23-144	—	1/8[1]	—	500	1/16	1	—	—
1962-64	23-147	—	1/8[1]	—	500	1/16	1	—	—
	23-146	—	1/8[1]	—	500	1/16	1	—	—
1963-64	23-148	—	1/8[1]	—	500	1/16	1	—	—
1964	23-149	—	1/8[1]	—	500	1/16	1	—	—
1964-65	23-137A	—	1/8[1]	—	500	.190	1	—	—
1965	23-171	—	5/32	—	500	.190	1	—	—
	23-173	—	5/32	—	500	.190	1	—	—

TYPE WWC3 SERIES M

YEAR	Carb. Model	Fuel Level (Wet)	Float Level (Dry)	Float Drop	Hot Idle Speed (RPM)	Pump Setting	Idle Mix. Screw Setting	Idle Vent Setting	Choke Setting
1966-67	23-185	—	5/32	—	500	.280	1	—	—
	23-184	—	5/32	—	500	.280	1	—	—
	23-185B	—	5/32	—	500	.280	1	—	—
1967	381187	—	5/32	—	500	.280	1	—	—
	381188	—	5/32	—	500	.280	1	—	—
1968	23-184C	—	[3]	—	550	.420-.450	1	—	—
1969	23-217	—	.160	—	550	.420-.450	1	—	—
	23-184C	—	.160	—	550	.420-.450	1	—	—

Note 1—5/32" with viton-tipped valve.
Note 2—With Manual Trans. and A.C.—650 RPM. Automatic Trans.—550 RPM.
Note 3—Firmly hold tab on float against needle valve, then measure distance from top of fuel bowl to top of float.

STROMBERG TYPE—WW2

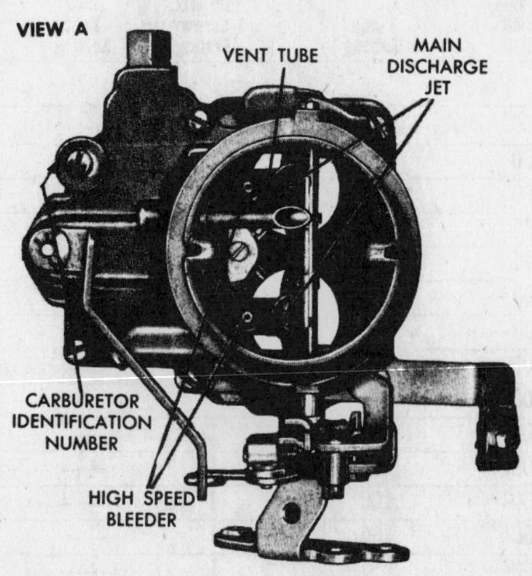

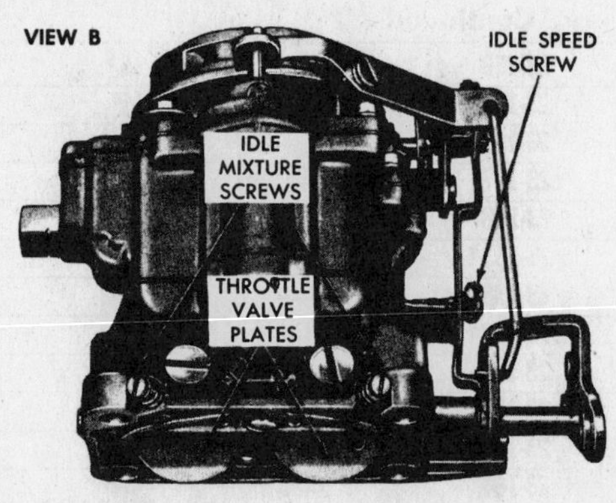

Type WW-2 carburetor

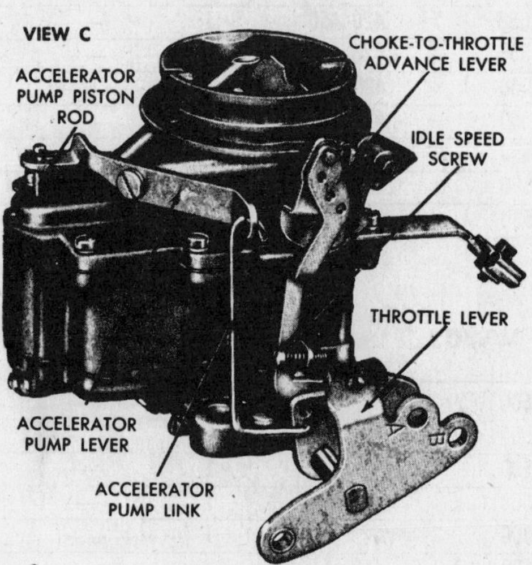

Type WW-2 carburetor

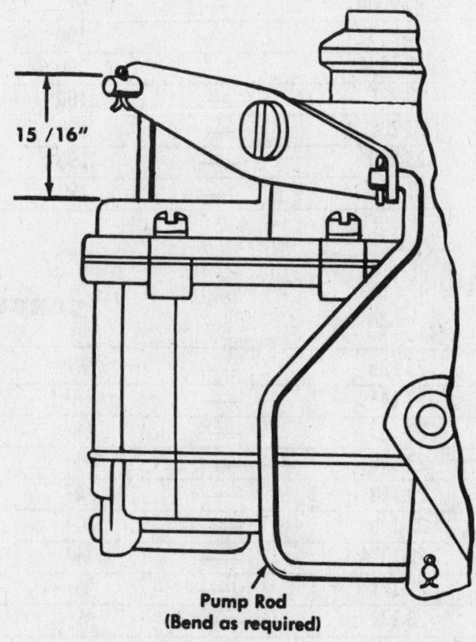

Accelerator pump rod adjustment (early type)

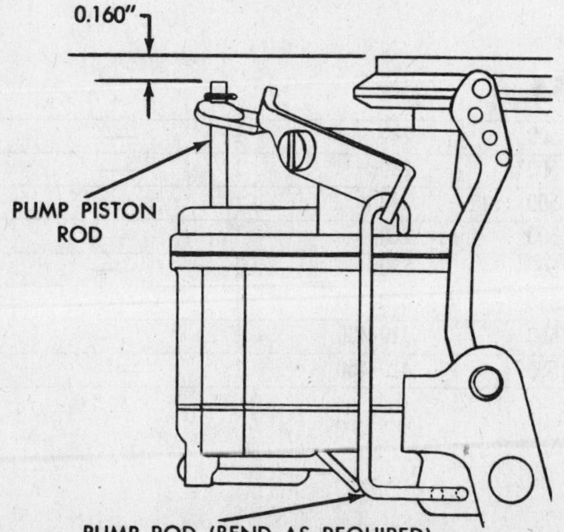

Accelerator pump rod adjustment (late type)

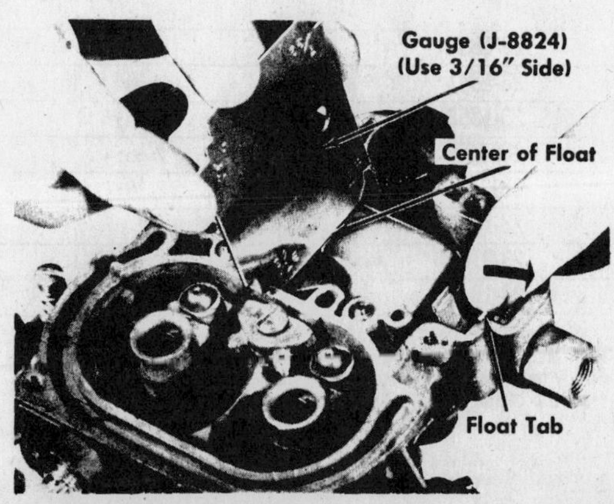

Float level adjustment

STROMBERG TYPE—WW3

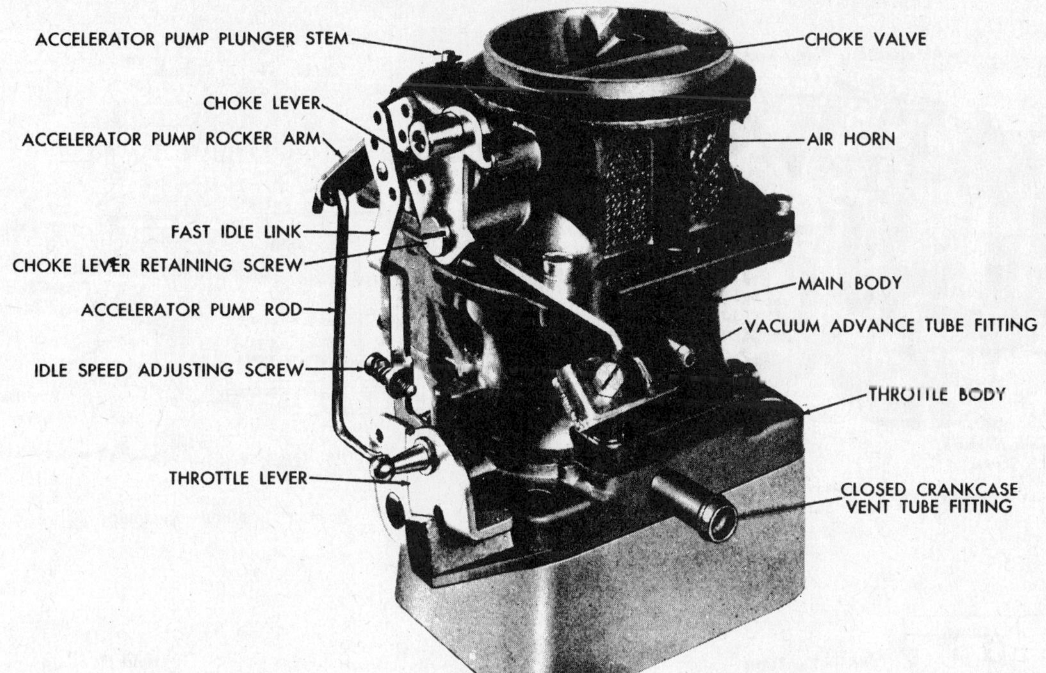

Type WW-3 carburetor

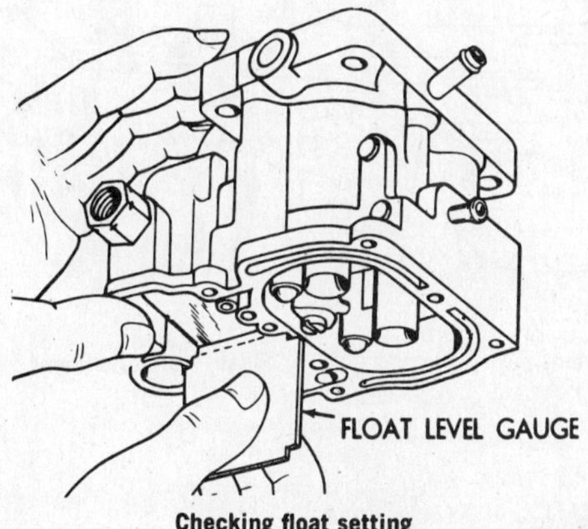

Checking float setting

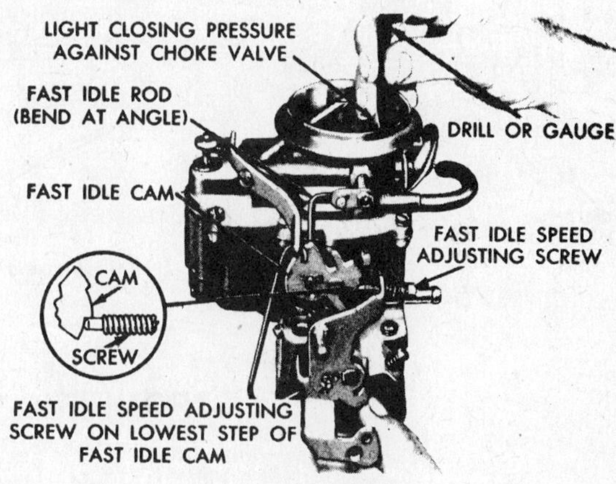

Fast idle cam adjustment

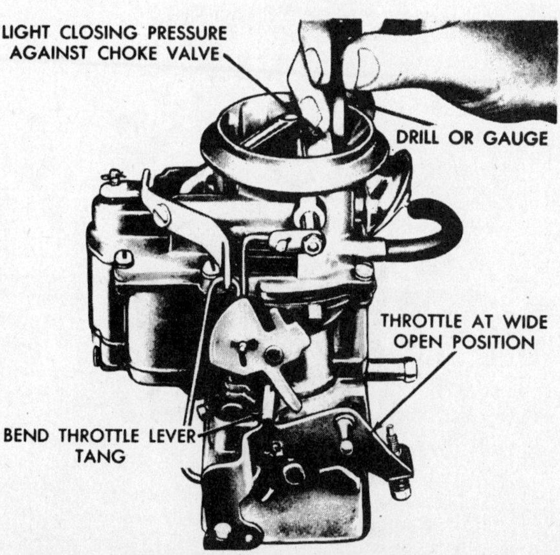

Unloader adjustment (wide open kick)

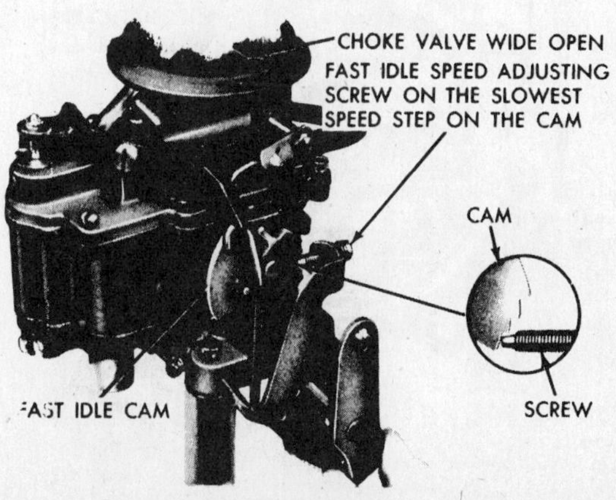

Fast idle speed adjustment (on vehicle)

STROMBERG TYPE—WWC-3

Type WWC-3 carburetor

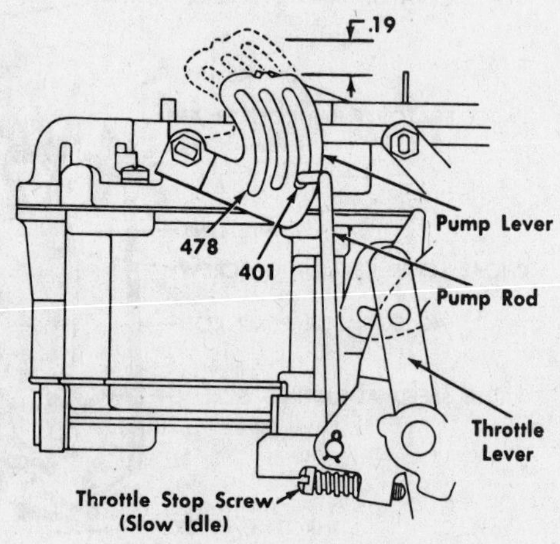

Accelerator pump adjustment

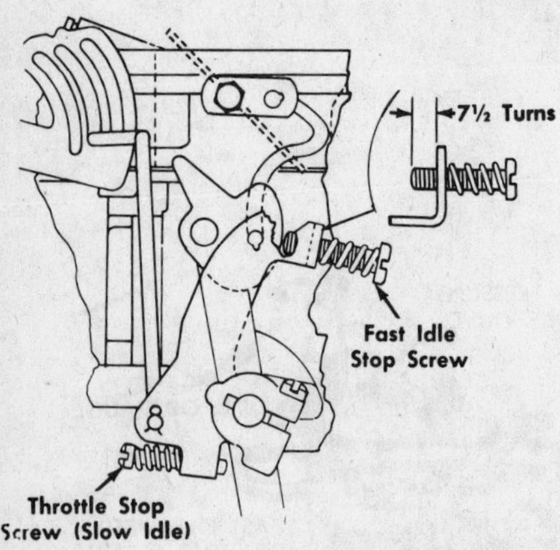

Fast idle adjustment

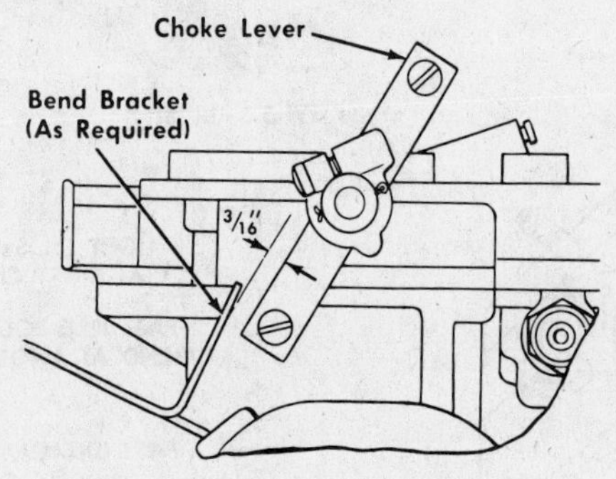

Choke over travel adjustment

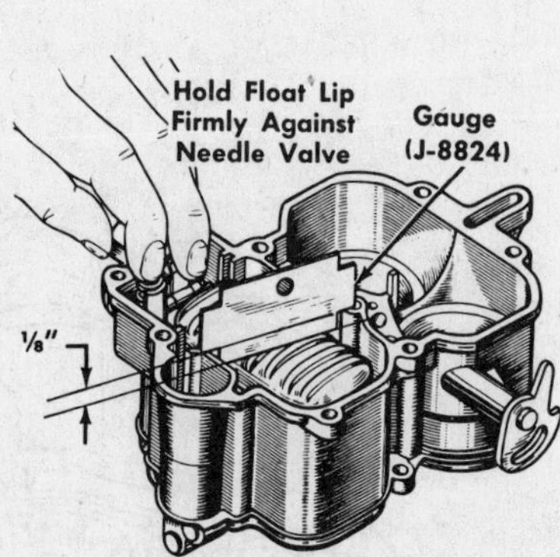

Float level adjustment

STROMBERG TYPE—WWC-3M

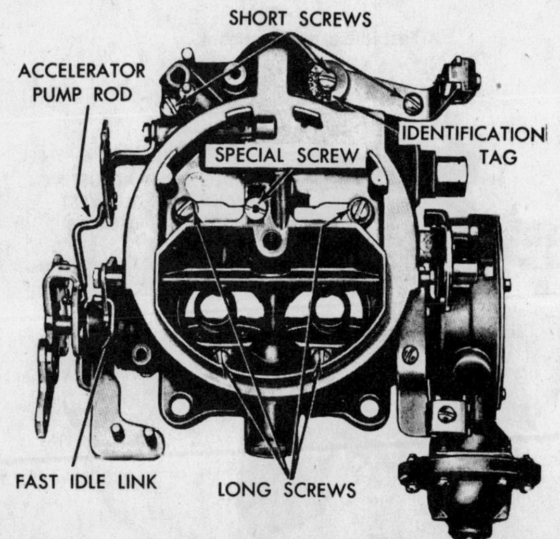

Type WWC-3M carburetor

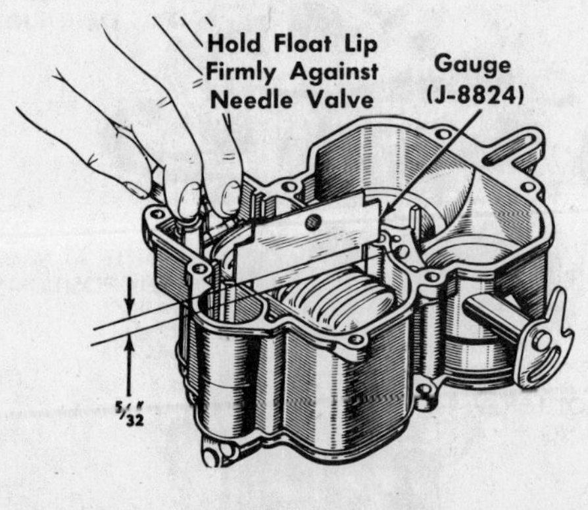

Float level adjustment

Exhaust Emission Systems

In the past few years, development of exhaust emission controls has been stimulated by a growing federal and public concern about air pollution. Regulations are currently in effect prescribing the maximum allowable emission of unburned hydrocarbons (HC) and poisonous carbon monoxide (CO) in engine exhaust. Emissions from engine crankcase and fuel supply are also restricted. In future years, further regulations will be enforced concerning emission of oxides of nitrogen (NO_x).

To comply with government regulations concerning vehicle exhaust, many engine alterations had to be made. All of these changes are intended to effect more complete burning of the fuel. The result should be a substantial reduction in unburned hydrocarbons and other noxious fumes in terminal exhaust. This is the prime reason for modification.

The highly complex nature of the subject matter prevents any simple solution to the case. Rather, it requires that more sophisticated devices be incorporated into the system to achieve tighter controls over terminal exhaust levels.

To provide best vehicle operation with lowest emission of harmful by-products, the car manufacturer's specifications and maintenance recommendations must be followed to the letter.

To ensure the high state of control needed to minimize terminal exhaust problems and still preserve safe and satisfactory performance levels, the following engine adjustment and control factors must be maintained:

A. Engine idle speed.
B. Ignition timing.
C. Engine idle air-fuel ratio.
D. Vacuum advance control valve (where used).
E. Air injector pump and circuit (where that type system is used).

Because this information is both vital and relative to engine and engine application rather than to engine alone, pertinent tune up data will be found posted in a conspicuous place in the engine compartment of all American built trucks beginning with 1968.

Many service procedures, tests, and adjustments have to be changed from those of previous years, particularly in the areas of fuel induction and ignition. To maintain the required results, the fuel-air ratio must not be overly rich and the engine must be kept in good operating condition.

Emission Systems Diagnosis Guide

Symptoms—Rough Idle
Fuel System

1. Leak in vacuum system (lines, connections, diaphragms, etc.).
2. Engine idle too low.
3. Idle fuel mixture incorrect.
4. Air leaks at manifold, carburetor, etc.
5. Power valve leaking fuel.
6. Idle fuel system air bleeds or fuel passages restricted.
7. Secondary throttle not closing (4-V carburetor).
8. Float setting incorrect.
9. Hot and cold air intake system stuck in Heat On position.

Ignition System

1. Defective or poorly adjusted points.
2. Poorly functioning spark plugs.
3. Incorrect ignition timing.
4. Insufficient secondary voltage at plug wires.

Exhaust System

1. Exhaust control valve inoperative (if so equipped).

Engine

1. Leak in vacuum system (lines, connections, diaphragms, etc.).
2. Air leaks at manifold, carburetor, etc.
3. Poor compression (head gasket, exhaust or intake valve leaks, failure of rings, cracked or broken piston, etc.).
4. Inoperative crankcase ventilator (PCV) valve, or restricted tubing.
5. Improperly adjusted valve tappets.
6. Worn camshaft lobes.
7. Incorrect valve timing.

Overheating at Idle

With engine operating, check warning light, or temperature gauge. Trouble could develop in the distributor vacuum control valve (temperature sensing valve).

Engine Stalls
Fuel System

1. Idle speed too low.
2. Idle mixture out of adjustment.
3. Carburetor fast idle too low.
4. Choke out of calibration or adjustment.
5. Choke mechanism binding.
6. Float level too high.
7. Interference with fuel flow.
8. Bad fuel pump.
9. Obstructed fuel lines or tank vent.
10. Carburetor icing.
11. Vapor lock.
12. Inoperative carburetor dashpot.

Engine Noises
Thermactor Pump

The thermactor pump, like any air pump, may produce a detectable sound. This noise should not, however, be of a level audible to anyone within the passenger compartment.

A new air pump, until broken in, may produce a slight squealing or chirping sound.

If pump noise is objectionable, check the following:

1. Drive belt alignment and tension.
2. Loose mounting.
3. Hoses disconnected or leaking.
4. Interference of hoses and body.
5. Defective centrifugal filter fan.
6. Defective relief valve.
7. Improper pressure-setting plug, broken spring, or plug missing. If, after checking the above noise factors, the trouble still persists, replace or repair the pump.

Ignition

1. Ignition, initial timing, too far advanced.
2. Poor engine mounting.
3. Leaking cylinder head gasket.
4. Crankcase ventilator circuit inoperative (stuck open or closed).
5. Poor compression, valves, tappet clearance, or piston and ring assemblies.
6. Worn camshaft lobes.
7. Incorrect valve timing.

Exhaust System

1. Air by-pass valve vacuum line collapsed, plugged, disconnected or leaking, causing backfire.
2. Malfunctioning air by-pass valve, causing backfire.
3. Malfunctioning distributor vacuum advance control valve, causing backfire.
4. Exhaust system leak.

General

The following systems, or variations thereof, are used to ventilate the crankcase of four cycle engines. The many designs range from a simple road draft tube, to multiple and complicated gas emission types, some of which include special ignition and induction systems. These breathing devices tend to reduce crankcase oil contamination which may result in engine sludging and wear. The prime purpose of the more complex designs is to reduce the discharge of poisonous unburned hydrocarbons into the air we breathe.

No matter what the name, how simple or involved the ventilating system, they all need attention to a varying degree, depending upon design and the amount of work they perform.

Type 1 Road Draft Tube

The only service required for this system is a periodic cleaning of crankcase air intake filters and road draft tubes.

The breathing filter should be thoroughly cleaned with a solvent, then saturated with light oil and blown clean at 6,000 mile intervals (or less, if conditions warrant it).

The road draft tube requires less frequent attention. Driving and engine conditions determine the service intervals to prevent sludge formations in the tube or oil separator.

If there is any evidence of crankcase pressure, (leaking seals, engine sludging, etc.) the tube should be checked as a possible source of trouble. This is always a good precaution on all engine reconditioning jobs.

Type 1 Tests

Symptoms

Symptoms of crankcase ventilation failure of the Type 1 system is heavy engine sludging, excessive oil filter tube smoking, poor rocker arm and tappet lubrication, fouled spark plugs, main bearing and engine seals leaking, etc.

Test

A simple and tentative test of the ventilating system may be made by the following checks:

1. Make sure that the oil filter cap and filter (if so equipped) is clean and clear of obstruction.
2. Admit small quantities of compressed air into the oil filler tube, while noting the ability of the draft tube to exhaust this air. The engine should be at operating temperature for this test.

Type 2 Air Cleaner Type

Air cleaner type crankcase ventilating systems do not use a control valve. Air entering the carburetor, through the air cleaner, picks up crankcase gases by way of an emission tube. Emission flow is controlled by the amount of air allowed to enter the crankcase via the crankcase breather and cap. The breather cap usually contains a filter.

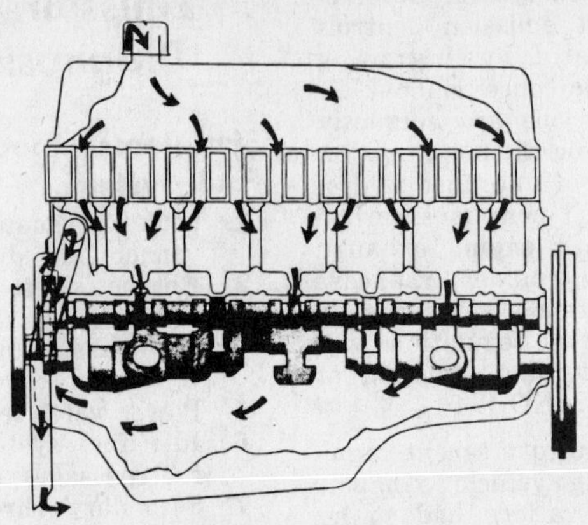
Road draft type of crankcase ventilation

Service to this type emission system should focus upon the two points of filtration: the crankcase air inlet, and the carburetor air cleaner.

Service intervals should not exceed 4,000 miles.

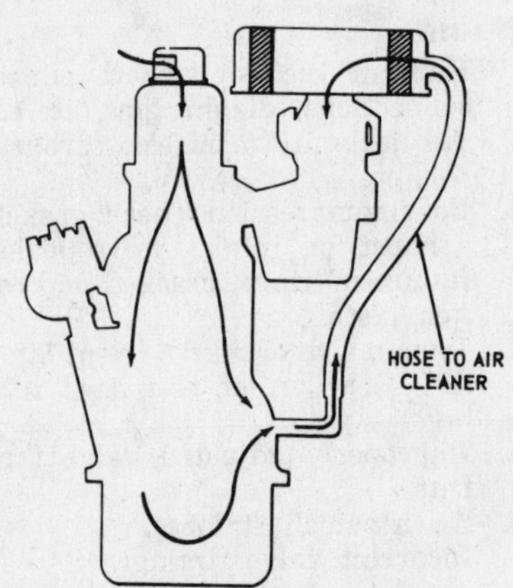

Air cleaner type system

Type 2 Tests

Symptoms

Symptoms of crankcase ventilating failure of the Type 2 system are the same as with Type 1.

Test

1. Make sure that the oil filler cap and cap filter (if so equipped) are clean.
2. Clean or replace the carburetor air cleaner.
3. Bring engine to operating temperature.
4. With the engine not running, blow small quantities of compressed air into the oil filler Note the ability of the crankcase-to-carburetor air cleaner tube to exhaust these oil fumes and air. A clean system will permit free flow of air.

Type 3 Flow Control (PCV) Valve

Outside air entering the engine via the breather cap passes through the crankcase and is admitted, along with poisonous and otherwise harmful by-pass gases, to the intake manifold for combustion in the engine. Because these gases (air and unburned hydrocarbons) are admitted to the induction system on the engine side of the carburetor throttle plate, this flow must be controlled. A valve (many are spring loaded) regulates the flow. During idle (low manifold pressure) intake manifold vacuum is high. The high vacuum overcomes plunger weight (or valve spring tension) and seats the plunger in the valve. With the plunger seated, all of the ventilating air passes through a calibrated orifice in the valve plunger. This results in minimum crankcase ventilation.

As engine speed increases, and manifold vacuum decreases, the plunger weight (or valve spring) un-

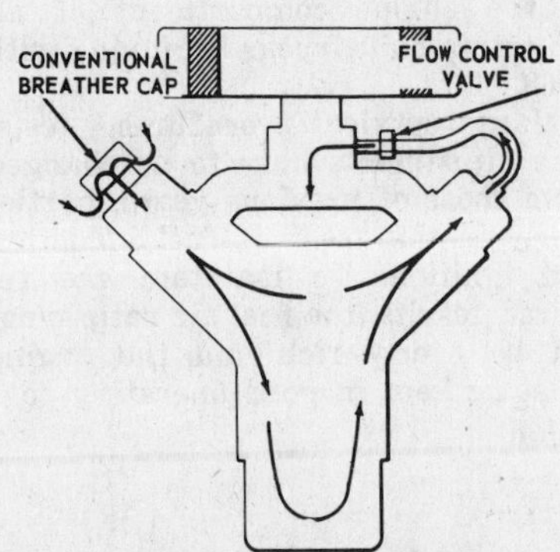

Flow control valve type system

seats the control valve plunger. This increases crankcase air flow and results in maximum ventilation.

Service to this unit is confined to the air breather inlet and the regulator valve. In some cases the valve assembly does not come apart. A faulty valve must be repaired or replaced. Service periods on this type of system depend mainly upon driving and engine conditions; however, service intervals should not exceed 6,000 miles.

Type 3 Tests

Symptoms

Because Type 3 enters the induction system on the engine side of the carburetor throttle plate, fuel-air ratio is involved. A plugged or obstructed ventilating system reveals itself in the same manner as Types 1 and 2, sludging, etc.

An open, or poorly seated, regulator valve upsets the carburetor fuel-air mixture. Therefore, excess crankcase fumes entering the intake manifold at idle speed cause an uneven engine and stalling. The degree of imbalance depends upon the amount of crankcase fumes allowed to leak past the poorly seated regulator valve.

Gauge Test

There are various devices available for testing this equipment, mainly by reading positive or negative crankcase pressures.

Alternate Test

Failure of the Type 3 system falls into two general categories: the system is obstructed (reduced, or no crankcase ventilation) or, there is too much ventilation (regulator valve not seated at engine idle).

The first condition, (not enough ventilation) builds up crankcase pressure and results in sludging and other failures peculiar to Types-1 and 2. An obstructed condition may be detected in the system by observing its ability to pass compressed air and crankcase fumes through the system, (including the regulator valve).

The second condition, too much ventilation, (regulator valve not seating at idle) usually manifests itself in the form of rough engine idle and stalling. This situation is quite common. It may be very misleading because the fuel-air ratio is unbalanced, and resembles a case of intake manifold leak, or carburetor trouble.

To test the second condition:

1. Bring engine to operating temperature.
2. Hook up a tachometer to the idling engine and record the rpm.
3. Disconnect the regulator valve from the line to the intake manifold.
4. Make a plug (see note below) with a metered hole of the same value as that of the disconnected regulator valve. Then insert the plug in the end of the disconnected line to the intake manifold.
5. Compare engine rpm with that which was recorded with the regulator valve in place. Any difference (± 20 rpm) indicates a poorly seated regulator valve.

NOTE: make a tapered plug of hard rubber, plastic, hard wood, metal, etc., that will fit into the PCV hose end (or connection) to the intake manifold. Drill a hole, lengthwise, through the tapered plug, the same size as the hole in the end of the regulator valve plunger.

There are various orifice sizes used, depending upon the cubic inch displacement of the engine involved. The following is a general engine size-to-valve plunger orifice chart.

Engine size, cu. in.	*Orifice size,*	*Approximate*
90-140	.056-.075 in.	1/16 in.
141-200	.074-.088 in.	5/64 in.
201-275	.087-.099 in.	3/32 in.
276-350	.098-.112 in.	7/64 in.
351- up	.111-.125 in.	1/8 in.

When properly inserted, this tool will admit the same amount of air into the induction system as the standard equipment regulator valve, in good operating condition. Five test plugs (of various orifice sizes) are enough to test all popular American made truck engines for regulator valve condition at engine idle.

Type 4 Fully Closed Ventilating Systems

This system breathes filtered air through a tube running from the carburetor air cleaner to the crankcase

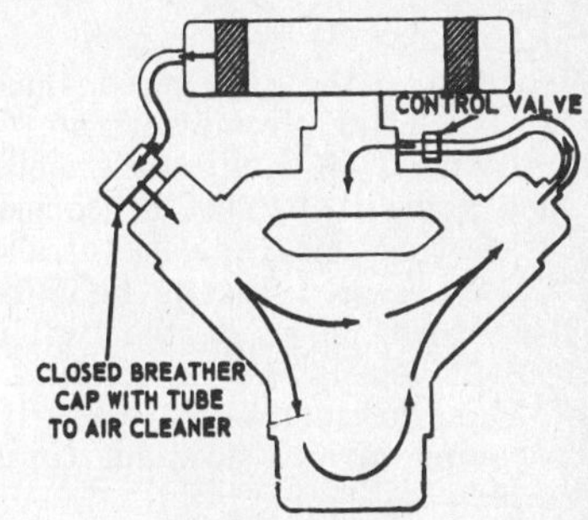

Closed ventilation system

(a closed cap is used on oil filler tube). The emission side of the system is of the flow control valve type or a variation thereof. A flame arrestor may be incorporated into the inlet side of the system. Being a fully closed ventilating system, don't forget, when checking engine oil, to replace the dip stick all the way, tc completely seal the dip stick opening.

Service to the fully closed system should not exceed 6,000 mile intervals.

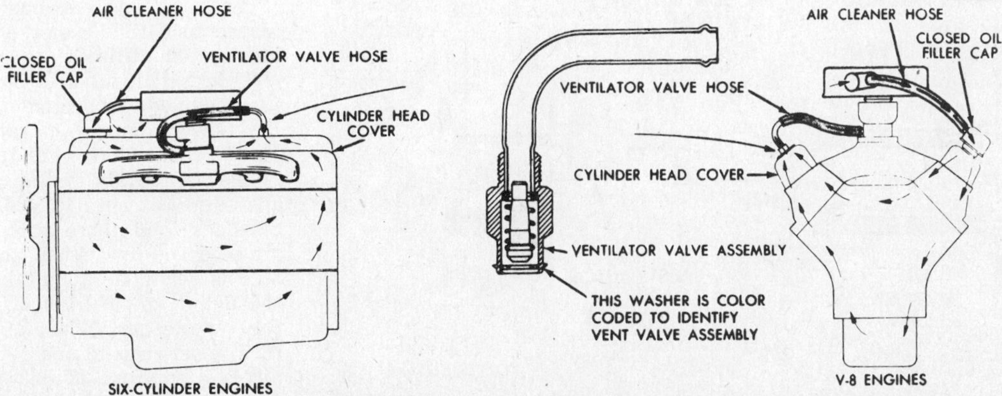

Fully closed ventilation system

Type 4 Tests

Symptoms

This system is fully closed and depends upon the carburetor air cleaner for crankcase inlet breathing. While the engine is idling, or at low throttle operation, system failures are potentially the same as Type 3. However, at part throttle or high speed operation, any restriction of air flow into the system (dirty air cleaner or flame trap) may cause negative crankcase pressures. This condition may tend to cause premature oil failure and sludging.

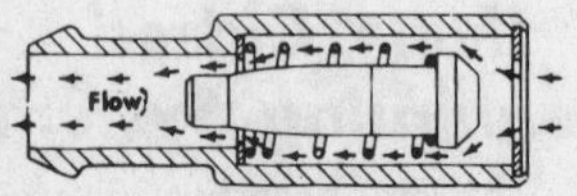

PCV valve (typical)

Test

Make test of the high speed phase of the ventilating circuit with an air hose as with Type 3, alternate method. The flame trap must be considered in testing this system as it also can become clogged. Test of the idling or low speed phase of the system (too much ventilation) is conducted in the same manner as Type 3, with plugs having various sized apertures.

Type 5 Chrysler System

The CAP, Cleaner Air Package, system is designed to constantly control carburetion and ignition timing at the best settings for performance and combustion throughout all driving requirements and conditions. These adjustments, if maintained, will keep the engine at a good performance level and within the exhaust requirements of federal law.

In the past, normal engines have had comparatively low exhaust emissions at cruise and acceleration attitudes. Objections occur in the area of deceleration and low speed operation. Therefore, the CAP system concentrates on reduction of emission in the idle, and deceleration ranges.

The CAP system contains a carburetor and distributor which have been redesigned, and a vacuum advance control valve on cars with manual transmissions.

The carburetor is calibrated to provide leaner mixtures at idle and at low speed. The distributor is designed to give retarded timing at idle. The vacuum advance control valve, in conjunction with the distributor, provides advanced timing during deceleration.

A number of dimensional changes have been made that reshape the intake manifold and combustion chamber for more even mixture distribution and better combustion.

CAP idle timing, for all engines, is retarded. Exhaust emission is reduced at idle by using leaner air-fuel mixtures, increased engine speed, and retarded ignition timing. The increased air flow at this idle condition is similar to the distribution and combustion conditions of cruise.

The whole plan is to operate with late timing during idle, and with conventional spark advance during acceleration and cruise.

The vacuum advance control valve provides additional spark advance during deceleration.

Engine applications involving manual shift transmissions require slightly different handling. They need earlier ignition of the fuel mixture to accomplish efficient combustion and to more completely consume residual fuels.

The vacuum advance control valve is connected by hoses to the carburetor, the intake manifold, and to the distributor vacuum chamber. Carburetor vacuum and manifold vacuum act on the vacuum advance control valve. From these two signals, the vacuum advance control valve senses engine speed and load conditions, and relays a vacuum command to the distributor to modify spark timing when necessary.

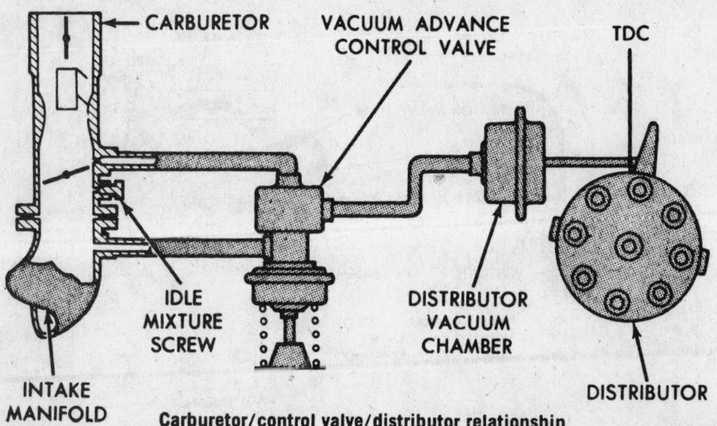

Carburetor/control valve/distributor relationship

Initial, or basic, timing may be retarded as much as 15° from conventional timing. The vacuum advance control valve does not affect timing at idle because the distributor vacuum chamber receives the same vacuum signal as in the conventional system, namely, carburetor vacuum. This is not strong enough to overcome the distributor vacuum diaphragm spring.

Manifold vacuum acts on the vacuum control valve diaphragm. However, it is not strong enough to overcome the vacuum control spring. The spring holds the vacuum control valve closed to manifold vacuum and open to low carburetor vacuum.

Under acceleration and during normal cruise, the throttle is opened up and the increased air flow through the carburetor throat creates carburetor vacuum much greater than under closed throttle conditions.

Manifold vacuum is not enough to overcome the vacuum advance control valve spring. However, the stronger carburetor vacuum overcomes the distributor vacuum diaphragm spring, advancing spark timing through both vacuum circuits.

The conventional system (without exhaust emission control) permits greatest objectionable emissions during deceleration. Carburetor vacuum is too weak to overcome the distributor vacuum advance diaphragm spring.

Manifold vacuum is at its strongest during deceleration. Therefore, the CAP system, when equipped with a vacuum advance control valve, uses manifold vacuum instead of carburetor vacuum to control spark timing. To summarize: during deceleration, manifold vacuum is strong enough to overcome the vacuum advance control valve spring and the distributor vacuum diaphragm spring, moving the spark timing to maximum advance.

1970 Models

The CAP system has been improved to CAS, Cleaner Air System. This system utilizes:

1. Heated air intake system.
2. Modified carburetor.
3. Lower compression ratio.
4. Solenoid retarded distributor.

The heated air system is used on all engines except 340, 426 Hemi, 440 Six-Pack, and those with the fresh air scoop option. When air temperature is below 10° F, intake air flows through a manifold heat stove into the air cleaner. When air temperature is between 10 and 100°F, intake air is a mixture of heated and unheated air. The volume of heated and

Vacuum advance control valve

unheated air is regulated by a thermostat, a vacuum diaphragm, and an air control valve in the air cleaner housing. The thermostat regulates the air control valve opening. Under conditions of greatly reduced vacuum, such as a sudden burst of acceleration, the vacuum diaphragm overrides the thermostat to open the air control valve fully to unheated air.

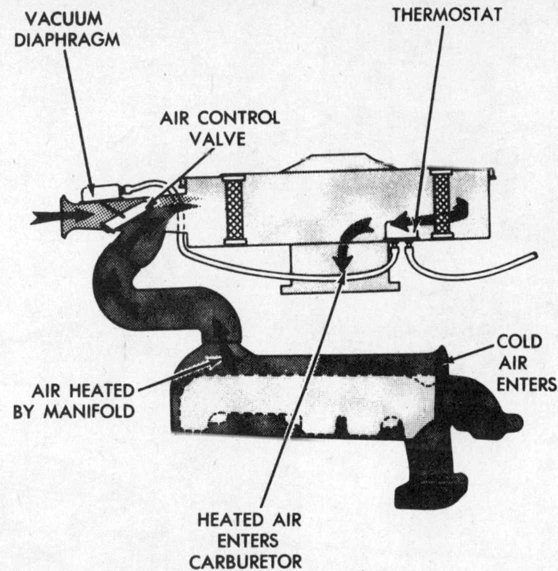

Heated air intake system

Carburetors have leaner mixtures and external idle mixture limiting devices. The automatic choke has been redesigned to release more quickly on engine warmup. An electrical solenoid throttle stop is used on 340, 440, 440 Six-Pack, and 426 Hemi engines. These engines use high idle speeds to achieve acceptable emission levels. The solenoid throttle stop deenergizes when the ignition is switched off, allowing the throttle blades to close more completely. This prevents running on.

318, 383, and 440 (except 440 Six-Pack) engines have lower compression ratios to reduce hydrocarbon emissions.

All 383 and 440 (except 440 Six-Pack) engines have a solenoid in the distributor advance mechanism to retard ignition timing when the throttle is closed. This system is inactivated during cold starting. Timing must be set at closed throttle to give full retard.

All 1970 vehicles sold in California have an Evaporation Control System, ECS, to reduce evaporation losses from the fuel system. The system has an expansion tank in the main fuel tank. This prevents spillage due to expansion of warm fuel. A special filler cap with a two way relief valve is used. An internal pressure differential of .5-1 PSI, caused by thermal expansion, opens the valve, as does an external pressure differential of .25-5 PSI, caused by fuel usage. Fuel vapors from the carburetor and fuel tank are routed to the crankcase ventilation system. A separator is installed to prevent liquid fuel from entering the crankcase ventilation system.

To insure that exhaust emissions are maintained within the limits of legislation without objectionable effects on performance, engine inspection is recommended at intervals not to exceed 12 months.

The following engine checks should be made at these periods:

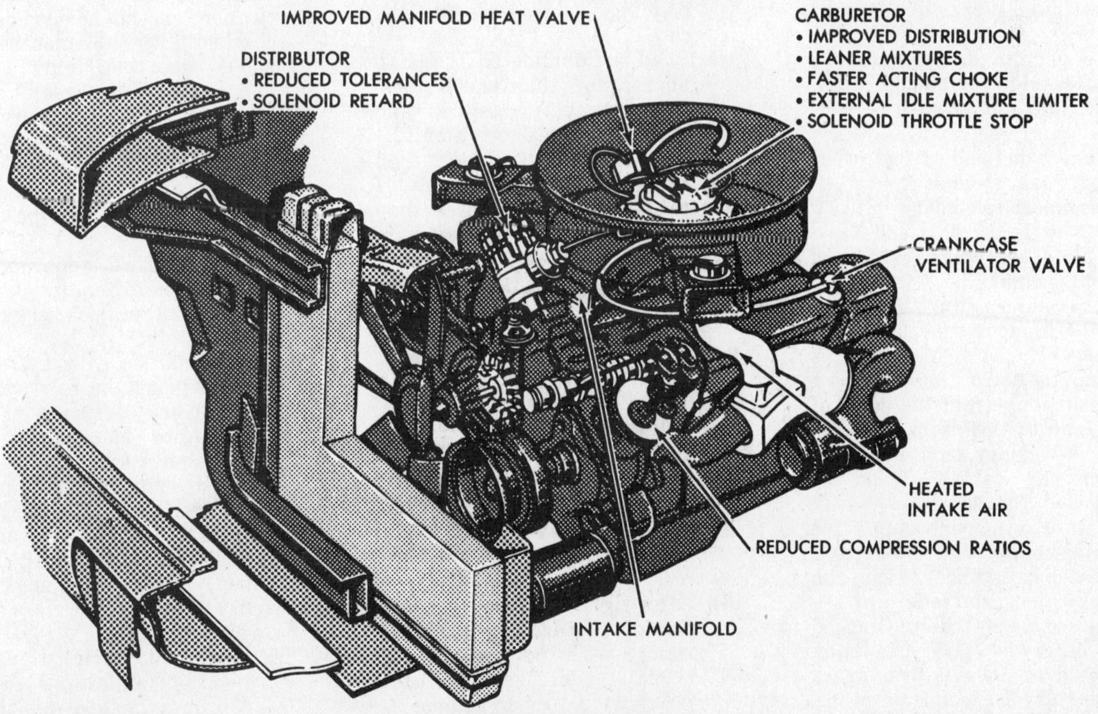

Cleaner air system features

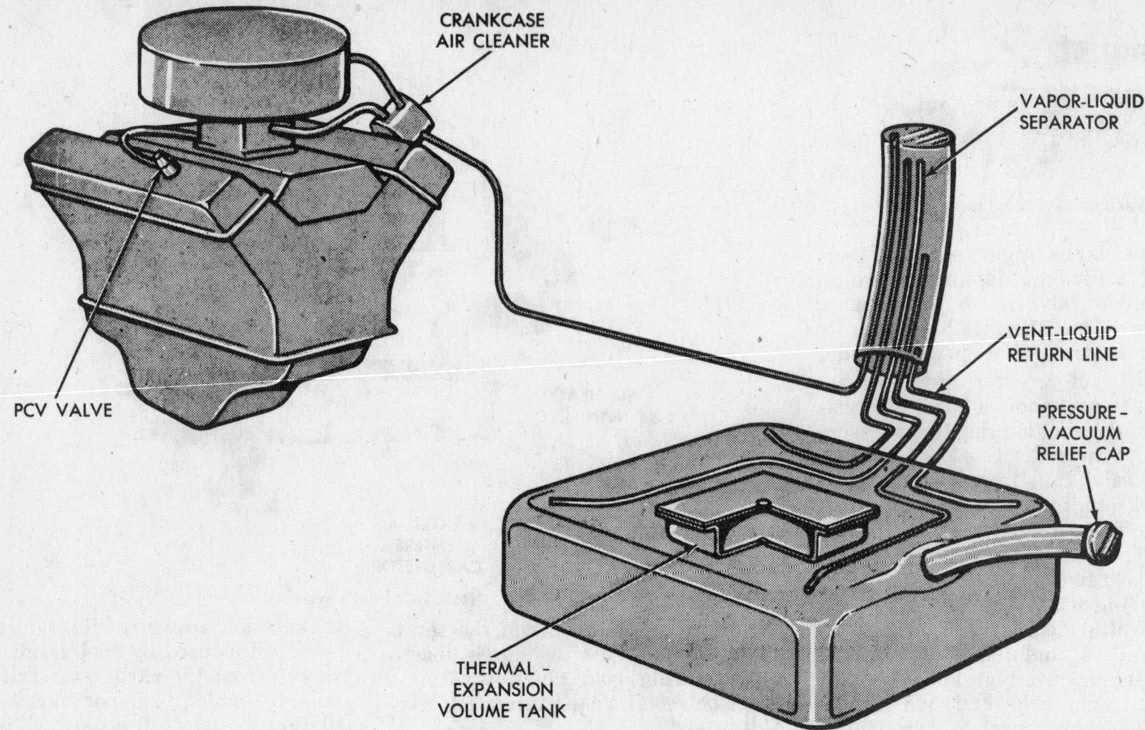

Evaporation control system

1. Check spark plugs.
   A. Clean/renew and gap as necessary.
   B. Be sure they are of the proper heat range.
   C. Torque to 30 ft. lbs.
2. Check distributor breaker points.
   A. Replace if necessary and adjust to recommended dwell or gap.
   B. Clean and lubricate cam and wick.
   C. Apply five to ten drops of light engine oil to the oil cup.
3. Check ignition system operation.
   A. Connect one end of test probe to a good ground.
   B. Disconnect secondary ignition cable at spark plug end.
   C. Insulate secondary cable end from ground.
   D. With engine idling, move test probe along entire length of cable. If cable insulation is breaking down, there will be a spark jump from the point of trouble to the probe.
   E. The secondary (coil to distributor cap cable) should be checked the same way.
   F. Be sure one spark plug cable is disconnected, (to create greater resistance). Then, run probe along the length of the coil secondary cable. Cracked or otherwise poor insulation should be obvious by a spark jump at the point of probe. Bad cables should be replaced.
4. Resistance of secondary cables should also be checked. Use an ohmmeter for this purpose.
   A. Remove cable from spark plug and install proper adapter between cable and spark plug.
   B. Remove cap from distributor, (secondary cables attached).
   C. Connect ohmmeter between plug adapter and the corresponding electrode inside the cap.
   D. Read the ohmmeter. If resistance is more than 30,000 ohms, remove cable from cap and check cable resistance only.
   E. If resistance is still more than 30,000 ohms, replace cable. If resistance is much less than 30,000 ohms, clean cap wire towers or renew the cap.
5. Inspect ignition coil for indications of oil leakage. Any indication of oil leakage justifies replacing the coil.
6. Test battery with a hydrometer. Specific gravity should be 1.220 or more, with temperature corrections. Add mineral-free water if required, to bring fluid up to correct level.
   A. Clean battery posts and cable terminals.
   B. After tightening the cable post clamps, coat battery posts and clamps with light grease.
   C. Reseal any breaks around the posts with rubber cement to retard corrosion.
7. The carburetor choke shaft should be serviced with carburetor cleaner to prevent sticking from gum deposits. Be sure the choke operates freely.
8. To satisfy normal driving conditions, the carburetor air cleaner should be inspected and cleaned every 6 months. Replace it every 2 years.
   If equipped with an oil bath cleaner, the oil level should be checked every 6 months, and should be thoroughly cleaned and refilled once a year.
9. Inspect, and if necessary, free the manifold heat control valve with manifold heat control valve solvent. Apply solvent and work the shaft only when the unit is cold.
10. A very critical and much neglected item of engine performance is the crankcase emission control valve.
    The crankcase emission control valve depends entirely upon the fine balance of spring pressure opposed to manifold vacuum. This balance can very easily be upset by small deposits of varnish or sludge. A closed valve induces crankcase pressure and engine sludge. A poorly seated (open) valve upsets engine idle and results in poor low speed operation.
    Inspect and service the closed crankcase ventilating system every 6 months and replace the control valve every 12 months.

A. A tentative check of PCV valve operation is to idle the engine.
B. Disconnect the ventilator valve assembly from the rocker cover. You should be able to hear the valve plunger, when shaking the valve.
C. If the valve is open, a hissing sound will be heard from the valve opening and vacuum can be felt with the finger.
D. If the valve is closed, or the line is obstructed anywhere between the valve and the intake manifold, crankcase pressure will develop. Check for plugging of the hose, freedom of the connection at the carburetor base or a valve stuck closed. Free vacuum passages. Renew the PCV valve if necessary.
E. Another approach is through the use of a tachometer hookup while pinching the PCV hose. If pinching the hose has no effect on engine idle rpm, the system is plugged or the PCV valve is not opening.
If pinching the hose smooths out the idle, the PCV valve is not seating.

11. To adjust curb idle, have the engine warm and running, with a tachometer hooked up. Adjust idle rpm to factory specifications.
A. The air cleaner must be installed, transmission in neutral, and headlights (six cylinder cars only) on high beam. If car is equipped with air conditioner, turn it off.
On cars equipped with a dash pot, adjust the stem so it does not contact throttle lever.

12. Check ignition timing.
A. Disconnect the distributor vacuum line and plug the opening to prevent vacuum leak.
B. Have air cleaner installed, transmission in neutral and headlights (six cylinder cars only) on high beam.
C. Set ignition basic timing to factory specifications.
D. On 1970 models, check distributor solenoid for proper operation by disconnecting wire at carburetor. Timing should advance 5½ degrees and engine speed should increase.
E. Unplug and reconnect vacuum line. Basic timing should remain at factory recommendations.

13. To adjust air/fuel ratio, use a combustion analyzer and tachometer.
A. Warm up the engine thoroughly.
B. Transmission in Neutral, and headlights, (six cylinder cars only) on high beam and engine running at prescribed rpm.
C. Disconnect hose between distributor vacuum control assembly (manual transmission) and intake manifold, at control valve end. Plug end of hose.
D. Insert probe of combustion analyzer into tail pipe as far as possible (minimum of two feet). If garage exhaust system is used, a plenum chamber or other means must be used to reduce the vacuum of the exhaust system to ½ in. water or less.

14. The air/fuel ratio specified for CAP is 14:1 or higher (air cleaner installed). The ratio for CAS should be 14.2:1.

NOTE: when using the combustion analyzer to adjust air/fuel ratio, do not rotate mixture screws more than 1/16 turn at a time. The ratio must be changed in very small increments. The higher the reading, the leaner the mixture. Idle mixture adjustment limiting caps must not be removed unless idle mixture is being set with a combustion analyzer. Maintain correct idle rpm during mixture adjustments.

A. Adjust mixture screw 1/16 turn richer (counterclockwise) then wait ten seconds for meter to stabilize.
B. Repeat Step A until meter shows a definite increase in richness (less than 14.0).
C. Then adjust mixing screw 1/16 turn leaner (clockwise) until the ratio reads factory recommendations or higher.
D. If idle speed changes as mixture screw is adjusted, readjust independently to obtain smooth idle, providing you stay within the recommended air/fuel ratio range.
F. Unplug and reconnect distributor vacuum control hose. If idle speed changes, adjust control valve setting.

NOTE: if air cleaner was removed to make mixture screw adjustments, recheck air/fuel reading after installing cleaner. Readjust to specified value or higher.

15. To check setting of distributor vacuum control valve:
A. Warm up engine.
B. Connect a tachometer.
C. Connect a vacuum gauge into the distributor vacuum line. Use a t-fitting with the same inside diameter as the line.
D. If the carburetor is equipped with a dashpot, adjust so that it does not contact the throttle lever at idle speed.
E. Disconnect and plug the hose that connects the distributor vacuum control valve to the intake manifold.
F. Remove the distributor vacuum hose at the distributor and plug the hose. Distributor vacuum must be 0-6 in. Hg. with the engine idling. If reading is higher than 6 in. Hg., recheck idle speed, timing, and air/fuel ratio.

16. To check operation of distributor vacuum control valve:
A. Remove vacuum connection plugs and reconnect vacuum hoses.
B. Remove the distributor vacuum valve cover.
C. Run engine speed up to 2000 rpm and hold for about 5 seconds.
D. Release the throttle. Distributor vacuum should increase to about 15 in. Hg. for a minimum of 1 second, distributor vacuum must then fall below 6 inches within 3 seconds after throttle is released.

17. To adjust vacuum control valve. If it requires less than 1 second or more than 3 seconds to obtain the correct vacuum reading:
A. Turn the adjusting screw counterclockwise to increase the time distributor vacuum remains above 6 in. Hg., or clockwise to decrease the time distributor vacuum remains above 6 in. Hg. One turn of the adjusting screw changes the valve setting about ½ in. Hg. If the valve cannot be adjusted to specifications, it must be replaced.
B. Install vacuum control valve cover and reset carburetor dashpot.

18. A carburetor dashpot is a common name given to a device used to slow down the closing of the throttle when the accelerator pedal is suddenly released. The purpose of the dashpot is to prevent engine stalling.
To adjust the dashpot:
A. With engine idling at recommended rpm and air/fuel mixture properly adjusted, connect a tachometer to the engine.
B. Postion throttle lever so that the actuating tab on the lever contacts the stem of the dashpot, but does not depress it.
C. If adjustment is necessary, loosen the locknut that holds

the dashpot to the bracket. Rotate the unit to obtain the desired setting. Tighten the locknut.

D. Recheck distributor vacuum control valve.

E. If distributor vacuum does not fall below 6 in. of Hg. within 4 seconds after throttle has been released, readjust or replace dashpot.

19. Road test the truck, noting performance in all driving ranges. If deficiencies exist, they should be corrected before the car is released to the owner.
All adjustments should be in the interest of better performance and economy. However, any changes must comply with CAP specifications and anti-smog legislation.

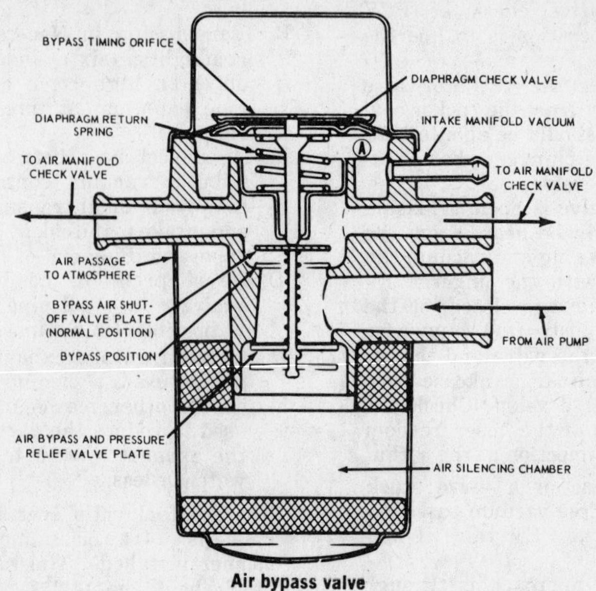

Air bypass valve

Caution If contrary or confusing tune-up data is encountered, refer to the decal containing information pertinent to the specific engine-vehicle application. This decal is posted in a conspicuous location in the engine compartment of each vehicle, beginning with 1968 production.

Type 6 The Ford System

The Ford Motor Company employs two methods of exhaust emission control, the IMCO (improved combustion) and the Thermactor (air injection) types. Both of these types are used extensively throughout their family of engines. The Thermactor type can be readily identified by the belt driven air pump.

The IMCO system produces an acceptable level of emissions by use of carburetor and distributor modifications; no air pump is necessary.

With this system, the exhaust gas emissions are reduced in the combustion system rather than by burning them in the exhaust manifolds.

The Thermactor method of exhaust emission control provides injected fresh air into the hot exhaust stream through the engine exhaust ports. At this point, the fresh air mixes with the hot exhaust gases, extending the burning period of these gases. This induced burning lowers the hydrocarbon and carbon monoxide content of exhaust by converting some of it into harmless carbon dioxide and water.

The Thermactor system consists of the following major parts:

1. Air supply pump.
2. Air by-pass valve.
3. Check valves.
4. Internal or external air manifold/s.
5. Air supply tubes (external air manifolds only).

Air for the Thermactor system is cleaned by a centrifugal filter fan mounted on the air pump driveshaft. An element-type air cleaner is not required. A pressure relief valve is installed in the pump housing to prevent air pump outlet pressure from becoming excessive. The pressure setting of the relief valve is controlled by a replaceable plastic plug. Air pump bearings are sealed and lubricated with a lifetime lubricant. Rotor vane and bearing clearances are established during initial assembly. No adjustments are required.

Air supply from the pump is controlled by the air bypass valve. During engine deceleration, the air bypass valve opens and air delivery to the cylinder head ports is momentarily diverted to the atmosphere.

A check valve is incorporated in the air inlet side of the air manifold/s to prevent exhaust backflow into the air pump and air bypass valve during the air bypass cycle. This valve also is utilized in the case of drive belt or pump failure.

Pertinent tune-up data such as engine idle speed, ignition timing, engine idle air/fuel ratio, etc. will be found posted on a decal, in a conspicuous location in the engine compartment of all cars beginning with 1968.

The truck manufacturer installs the necessary equipment to control vehicle air pollutants; it is the responsibility of the owner to see that this equipment remains effective by maintaining it to the manufacturers' recommendations. Even a clogged air cleaner may not seem important to the unknowing truck owner, but it is most detrimental to proper performance, fuel economy and emission control.

Crankcase Ventilator System

Crankcase ventilator systems are covered earlier in this General Repair Section and must be maintained in good repair to complement either the IMCO or Thermactor systems of exhaust emission control.

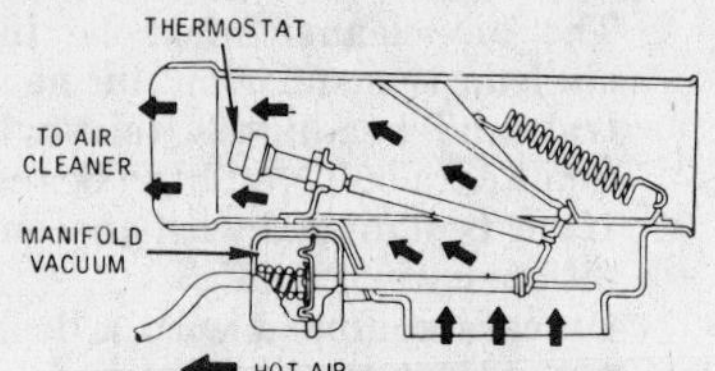

Duct and valve assembly in heat-on position—warm-up

Ventilator System Test

1. Replace the crankcase ventilator regulator valve with a known good valve of identical design.
2. Start the engine and compare idle conditions with the prior idle conditions. If engine idle is satisfactory (with new valve installed) trouble exists in the old valve and it should be replaced.
3. If loping or rough idle still persists with the good regulator valve in place, the trouble is elsewhere. Check crankcase ventilator system for restriction at the intake manifold or carburetor spacer.
4. If the system is not restricted, explore further the aspects of tune-up and the various elements of exhaust emission control.

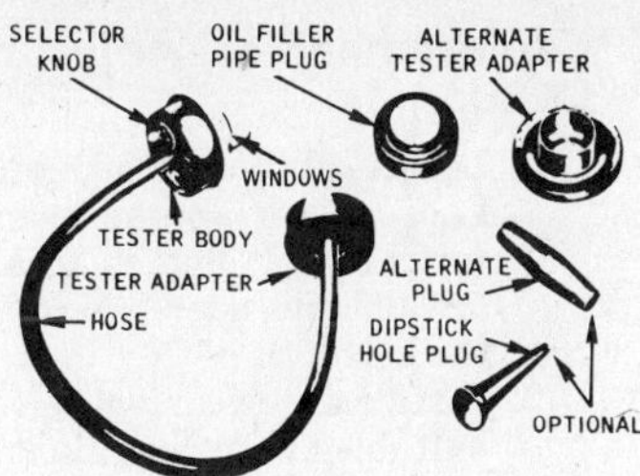

AC crankcase ventilation system tester

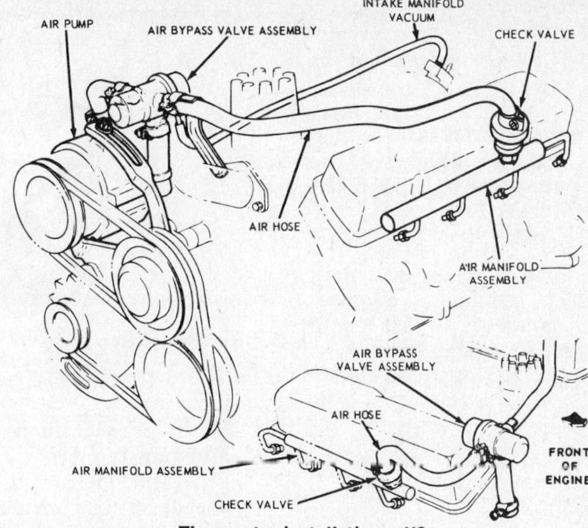

Thermactor installation —V8

AC Ventilator System Test Method

This tester (AC) is operated by engine vacuum through the engine oil filler tube opening.

1. With engine operating at normal temperature, connect one end of hose to tester body, the other end to the tester adapter.
2. Use plug supplied with the tester to close the opening in the dipstick tube.
3. Insert tester adapter into the filler cap opening and turn the selector knob to No. 2 for the six cylinder 240 cu.in. and the V8 engines. Turn the knob to No. 4 for the six cylinder 170 and 200 cu. in. engines.
4. Disconnect the air inlet hose at the oil filler tube or oil filler cap and plug the tube (or cap) and hose openings.
5. With plugs secure, and tester tube free of kinks, hold tester body upright and note color in the tester windows. See chart for probable causes of trouble in the crankcase ventilation system.
6. Clean or replace the troublesome components. Then, repeat tests.

Thermactor Diagnosis and Tests

Prior to performing any extensive tests of the Thermactor system:

1. Be sure that a problem exists.
2. Determine that the engine, as a basic unit, is functioning properly by performing the following:
   disconnect the air bypass valve vacuum sensing line at the intake manifold. Plug the manifold connection to prevent leakage.
3. Normal engine diagnosis procedures can then be performed.

Air Pump Test

1. To test the air supply pump, a test gauge adapter must be made. Make the adapter as follows:
   A. Obtain a ½ in. pipe T.
   B. A 2 in. length of ½ in. galvanized pipe, threaded at one end only.
   C. A ½″ pipe plug.
   D. A ½ in. reducer bushing or suitable gauge adapter.
   E. Apply sealer to the threads of the 2 in. length of pipe and screw it into one end of the T.
   F. Apply sealer to the pipe plug and install it into the other end of the T.
   G. Apply sealer to the threads of the ½ in. reducer bushing or adapter for the pressure gauge and install it in the side opening of the T.
   H. Drill an 11/32 in. (0.3437) diameter hole through the center of the pipe plug. Clean out the chips.
   I. Install a standard fuel pump or other suitable testing gauge into the side opening of the T. The gauge must be graduated in ¼ psi increments.
2. Bring engine to operating temperature.
3. Inspect all hoses and connections for leaks. Correct if necessary.
4. Check air pump belt tension; adjust if necessary.
5. Disconnect air supply hose/s at air manifold check valve/s. If there are two valves, block off one hose with a tapered plug; secure plug with a clamp to prevent blowout.
6. Insert open pipe end of test gauge adapter in other air supply hose. Clamp hose to adapter to prevent blowout.
7. Position adapter and test gauge so that air discharge from the drilled hole in the adapter will cause no trouble.
8. Connect tachometer to engine.

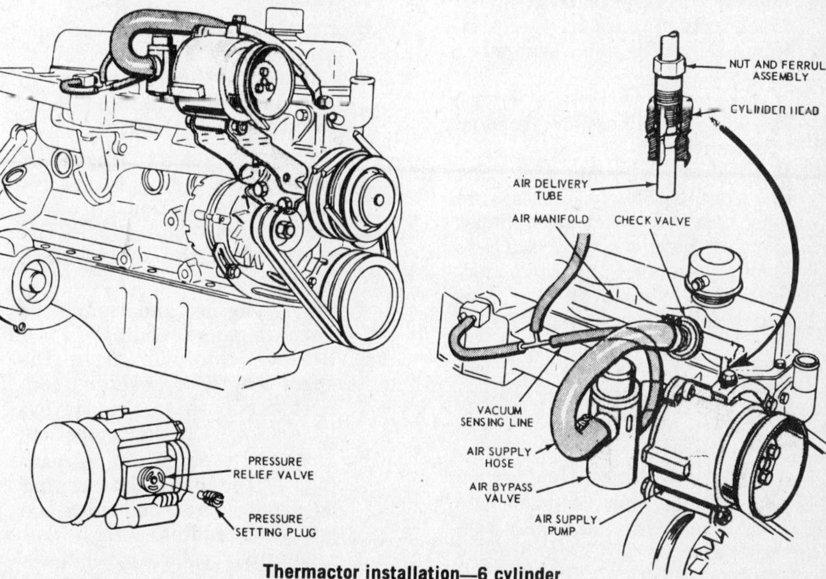

Thermactor installation—6 cylinder

9. Start engine and slowly increase to 1500 rpm. Air pressure registered on the gauge should be greater than 1 psi.
10. If air pressure does not meet or exceed above pressures disconnect and plug air supply hose at the bypass valve. Clamp the plug in place and repeat the pressure test.
11. If air pump pressure still does not meet minimum requirements, install a new air pump and repeat the pump test.
12. Replace the air pump as determined by the result of this test.

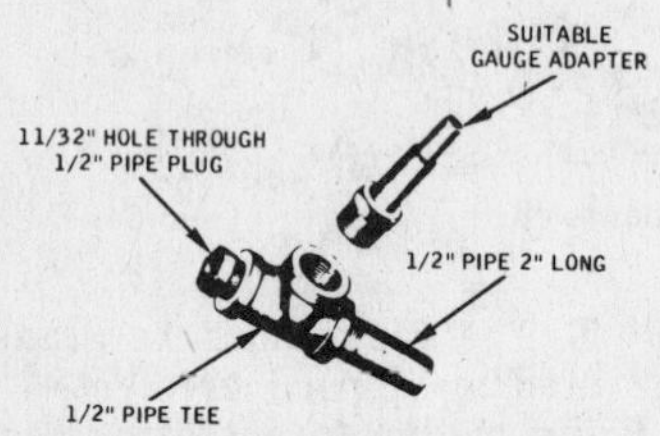

Air supply pump test gauge adapter

Check Valve Test

This test can be performed at the same time as the air pump test.

1. Run engine until it reaches operating temperature.
2. Inspect all hoses and connections. Correct any existing leaks before testing check valve operation.
3. Disconnect air supply hose/s at the check valve/s.
4. Note the position of the valve plate inside the valve body. It should be lightly positioned against the valve seat, away from the air manifold.
5. Insert a probe into the hose connection on the check valve and depress the valve plate. It should freely return to its original position against the valve seat when released.
   If there are two check valves, check both valves for freedom of operation.
6. With hose/s disconnected, start the engine. Slowly increase to 1500 rpm and watch for exhaust leaks at the check valve/s. There should be none. The valve may flutter or vibrate at idle. This is normal, due to exhaust pulsations in the manifold.
7. If check valve/s does not meet recommended conditions (Steps 4, 5, and 6), replace.

Air Bypass Valve Tests

1. Remove hose that connects air bypass valve to air manifold check valve at the bypass valve side.

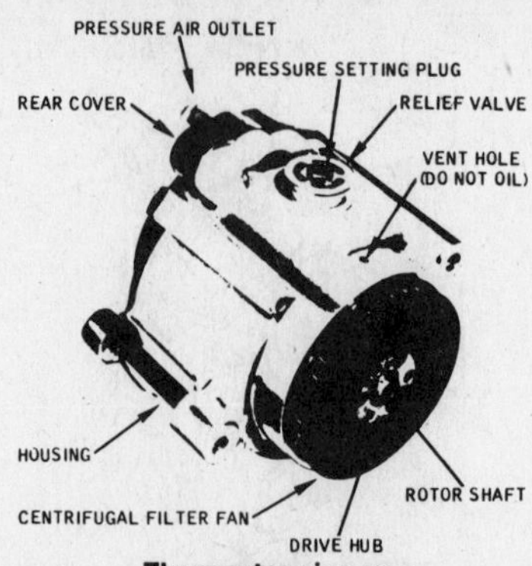

Thermactor air pump

2. With transmission in neutral and parking brake on, start engine and operate at normal idle speed. Be sure air is flowing from the air bypass valve hose connection. Air pressure should be noted, as this is the normal delivery flow to the air manifold/s.
3. Momentarily (for about 5 seconds) pinch the vacuum hose to the bypass valve. This duplicates the air bypass cycle.
4. Release the pinched vacuum hose. Air flow through the air bypass valve should diminish or stop for a short period. The length of time required to resume normal flow cannot be established. Variables in engine vacuum and the length of time the vacuum line is pinched off are determining factors.
5. Check the by-pass valve for diaphragm leakage by performing the following check:
   A. Remove the vacuum supply hose to the air bypass valve at the bypass valve connection.
   B. Insert a T-fitting into the vacuum supply hose.
   C. Connect a vacuum gauge to one of the remaining hose connections on the T.
   D. Connect a short length of hose (about 3 in.) to the remaining connection.
   E. Insert a suitable plug in the open end of the short length of hose.
   F. Start engine and note the vacuum gauge reading.
   G. Remove the plug from the short length of hose and connect the hose to the air bypass valve vacuum connection.
   H. Note the vacuum gauge reading. If the indicated reading does not correspond with the previous reading after about 1 minute, replace air bypass valve.

Replacement or Adjustment of Belt

1. Loosen air pump adjusting bolt. Loosen air pump-to-mounting bracket bolt and push air pump toward cylinder block. Remove the belt.
2. Install a new drive belt. With a suitable bar, pry against the rear cover of the air pump to obtain the specified belt tension.
3. Then, retighten the pump mounting bolts.

NOTE: always use a belt tension gauge (T63L-8620-A) to check belt tension, and follow tool manufacturers' instructions and specifications. Any belt that has operated for 10 minutes can be considered a used belt. Adjust accordingly.

Air Bypass Valve Replacement

1. Disconnect air and vacuum hoses at the air bypass valve body.
2. Position the air by-pass valve, and connect the respective hoses.

Check Valve Replacement

1. Disconnect air supply hose at the valve. (Use a 1¼ in. crowfoot wrench, the valve has a standard, right-hand pipe thread).
2. Clean the threads on the air manifold adapter (air supply tube on 289 or 302 V8 engine) with a wire brush. Do not blow compressed air through the check valve in either direction.
3. Install check valve and tighten.
4. Connect air supply hose.

Air Manifold (Except 289 or 302 V8)

Removal

1. Disconnect air supply hose at check valve, position the hose out of the way and remove the valve.
2. Loosen all of the air manifold-to-cylinder head tube coupling nuts (compression fittings).

Cleaning and Inspection

Inspect air manifold for damaged threads and fittings and for leaking connections. Repair or replace as required.

Clean manifold and associated parts with kerosene. Do not dry with compressed air.

Installation

1. Position the air manifold/s on the cylinder head. Be sure all of the tube coupling nuts are aligned with the cylinder head.
2. Screw each coupling nut into the cylinder head, 1-2 threads. Tighten the tube coupling nuts.

3. Install the check valve and torque it to specifications.
4. Connect air supply hose to the check valve.

Air Supply Tube (289 V8)

Removal

1. Disconnect air supply hose at the check valve and position hose out of the way.
2. Remove check valve.
3. Remove air supply tube bolt and seal washer.
4. Carefully remove air supply tube and seal washer from the cylinder head.

Cleaning and Inspection

Inspect air supply tube for evidence of leaking threads or seal surfaces. Examine the attaching bolt head, seal washers and supply tube surface for leaks. Inspect the attaching bolt and cylinder head threads for damage.

Clean air supply tube, seal washers and bolt with kerosene. Do not dry with compressed air.

Installation

1. Install seal washer and air supply tube on cylinder head. Be sure it is positioned in the same manner as before removal.
2. Install seal washer and mounting bolt. Torque to specifications.
3. Install check valve; torque to specifications.
4. Connect air supply hose to the check valve.

Air Nozzle Replacement (Except 289 or 302 V8)

Normally, air nozzles should be replaced during cylinder head reconditioning. A nozzle may be replaced, however, without removing the cylinder head, by removing the air manifold and using a hooked tool.

Clean nozzles with kerosene and a stiff bristle brush. Inspect air nozzles for eroded tips.

Air Pump Filter Fan Replacement

1. Loosen air pump as described in earlier procedures.
2. Remove drive pulley attaching bolts and pull the pulley off the air pump shaft.
3. Pry the outer disc loose, then remove the centrifugal filter fan. Care must be used to prevent foreign matter from entering the air intake hole, especially if the fan breaks during removal. Do not attempt to remove the metal drive hub.
4. Install the new filter fan by drawing it into position with the pulley bolts.

NOTE: some 1966-67 air pumps have air filters with replaceable non-cleanable elements.

Air Pump

Removal

1. Disconnect air inlet and outlet hoses at the air pump.
2. Loosen pump belt tension adjuster.
3. Disengage drive belt.
4. Remove mounting bolt and air pump.

Installation

1. Position air pump on the mounting bracket and install the mounting bolt.
2. Place drive belt in pulleys and attach the adjusting arm to the air pump.
3. Adjust drive belt tension to specifications and tighten adjusting arm and mounting bolts.
4. Connect air inlet and outlet hoses to the air pump.

Air Pump Relief Valve

Replacement

Do not disassemble the air pump on the car to replace relief valve, but remove the pump from the engine.

1. Position tool T66L-9A486-D on the air pump and remove the relief valve with the aid of a slide hammer (T59L-100-B).
2. Position relief valve on the pump housing and hold tool T66L-9A486-B in position.
3. Use a hammer to lightly tap the tool until the relief valve is seated.

Relief Valve Pressure-Setting Plug Replacement

1. Compress locking tabs inward (together) and remove the plastic pressure setting plug.
2. Before installing the new plug, be sure that the plug is the correct one. The plugs are color-coded.
3. Insert the plug in the relief valve hole and push in until it snaps into place.

Fuel System

Hot and Cold Air Intake

All, except high performance and police interceptor engines use a hot and cold intake system which regulates the temperature of carburetor intake air. This system improves engine performance during warm-up. It reduces the tendency of the carburetor to ice before reaching normal operating temperature.

The heat factor of carburetor intake air is controlled by a valve plate and a vacuum override built into a duct attached to the air cleaner. The exhaust manifold shroud tube is attached to a shroud over the exhaust manifold, which is used as a heat source. The duct has an opening at the outer end to permit entry of cooler air from the engine compartment. A thermostatic bulb within the duct and the vacuum override motor attached to the duct and connected to the thermostat lever provides the means to balance the air temperature for various engine operating conditions.

During warm-up, the thermostat is in the retracted position. The valve plate is held in the heat-on position (up) by the valve plate spring, shutting off the air from the engine compartment. All air is then drawn from the shroud around the exhaust manifold.

During cold acceleration, additional intake air is provided by the vacuum motor control. Decrease in intake manifold vacuum during acceleration permits the vacuum motor to override the thermostat control. This opens the system to both engine compartment air and heated air from the exhaust manifold shroud.

As the temperature of the air passing the thermostatic bulb increases, the thermostat starts to expand and forces the valve plate down. This allows cooler air from the engine compartment to enter the air cleaner. When the air reaches maximum temperature, the valve plate will be in heat-off position (down) so that only engine compartment air is being used.

The 390 GT V8 engine is equipped with a similar duct and valve assembly. It operates in the same manner as on other engines, except that the vacuum override is not used. Instead, a vacuum motor is installed on the outer edge of the air cleaner. When manifold vacuum is low, during engine loading or high-speed operation, a spring in the vacuum motor opens the motor valve plate in the air cleaner. This provides the optimum air supply for greater volumetric efficiency needed for full-power operation.

Carburetor Adjustments

Since 1968 the carburetors on all Ford Motor Company trucks are equipped with idle fuel mixture adjustment limiters. These limiters control the maximum idle fuel richness and help prevent unqualified persons from making overly rich idle adjustments. There are two kinds of idle limiters: external and internal.

The external-type plastic idle limiter cap is installed on the head of the idle fuel mixture adjusting screw/s.

Any adjustment made on carburetors having this type of limiter must be within the range of the idle adjusting limiter.

NOTE: under no circumstances should the idle adjusting limiters or the limiter stops on the carburetor be mutilated or deformed to render the limiter inoperative.

The power valve cover must be installed with the limiter stops on the cover in position to provide a positive stop for the tabs on the idle adjusting limiters. A satisfactory idle should be obtainable within the range of the idle adjusting limiters, if all other engine systems are operating within specifications.

The internal needle-type limiter is located in the idle channel and is not externally visible. It is capped by a lead seal. The limiter is installed and sealed during manufacture.

Following are the normal procedures necessary to properly adjust engine idle and fuel mixture. Specific operations should be followed in the proper sequence whenever the idle speed or idle fuel adjustments are made.

Normal Idle Fuel Settings (Engine Off)

1. Set idle fuel mixture screw/s and limiter cap/s to the full counterclockwise position.
   On carburetors without limiter caps, establish an initial idle mixture screw setting by turning the screw inward until it is lightly seated; then turning it outward one to one and one-half turns. Do not turn the screw/s tightly against their seats. Damage may result which will require renewal of the screw/s.
2. Back off the idle speed adjusting screw until the throttle plate/s seat in the throtle bore/s.
3. Be sure the dashpot or solenoid throttle positioner (if so equipped) is not interfering with the throttle lever. It may be necessary to loosen the dashpot or solenoid to allow the throttle plate to seat.
4. Turn the idle speed adjusting screw inward until it just makes contact with the screw stop on the throttle shaft and lever assembly. Then, turn the screw outward one and one-half turns to establish a preliminary idle speed adjustment.
5. Set parking brake before making the idle mixture and speed adjustments. On a car with a parking brake (vacuum) release, remove the vacuum line from the power unit of the vacuum release parking brake assembly. Plug vacuum line, then set parking brake. The vacuum power unit must be deactivated to keep the parking brake engaged when the engine is operated with transmission in Drive.

Installing idle limiters

Normal Idle Fuel Settings (Engine Running)

1. Engine temperature must be at stable operating level before any attempt is made at idle adjustments.

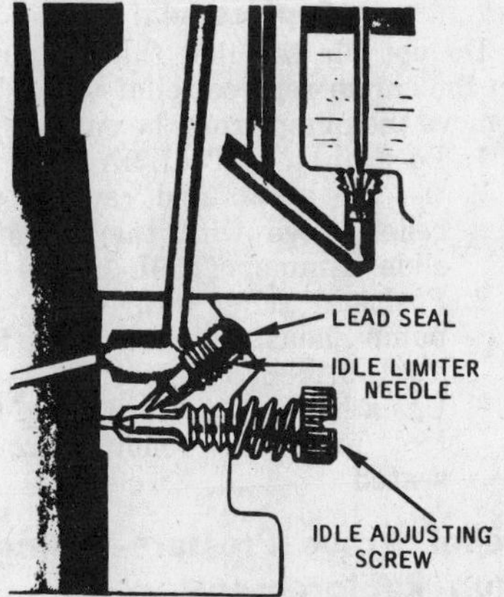

Idler adjusting screw and limiter (Carter 1-V)

2. Check initial ignition timing and distributor advance and retard.

NOTE: use an accurate tachometer when checking initial timing, idle fuel mixture and speed as outlined in a later paragraph (initial ignition timing).

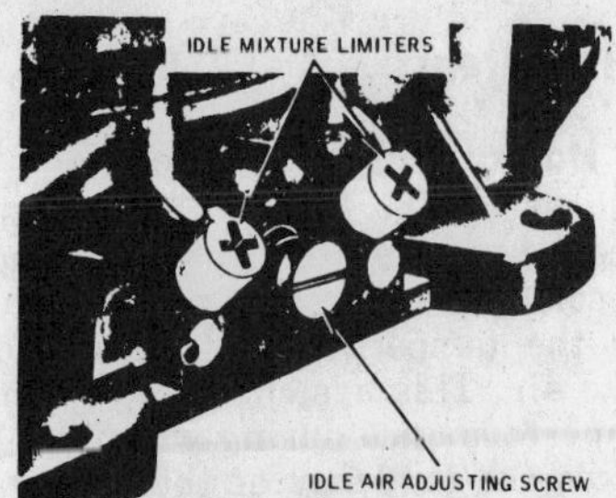

Idle air adjusting screw and mixture limiters (Carter 4-V)

3. On manual shift transmissions, the idle setting must be made only when the transmission is in Neutral. On automatic transmissions, the idle setting is made with the selector lever in Drive, except as noted when using an exhaust analyzer.
4. Be sure the choke plate is in fully open position.
5. On carburetors equipped with a hot idle compensator, or where the idle compensator is in the crankcase ventilation hose, be sure the compensator is seated to allow for proper idle adjustment.
6. Turn headlights on high beam, to place the alternator under load, in order to properly adjust engine idle speed.
7. Final idle speed is adjusted with the air conditioner turned off.
8. Adjust engine curb idle to specifications.
9. Turn idle mixture screw/s inward to obtain the smoothest idle possible within the range of idler limiter/s. Turn idle mixture screws inward an equal amount. Check for idle smoothness only with air cleaner installed.

Additional Idle Speed and Mixture Procedures

If a satisfactory idle is not obtained after following the above procedure, additional checks may be necessary.

1. Check the following items and, if necessary, correct.
   A. Vacuum leaks.
   B. Ignition system wiring.
   C. Spark plugs.
   D. Distributor point condition and dwell.
   E. Initial ignition timing.
2. If idle condition is not satisfactory after above items have been checked, perform the following mechanical checks.
   A. Fuel level and fuel bowl vent.
   B. Crankcase ventilation system.
   C. Valve lash (mechanical tappets) and dry tappet clearance, (hydraulic tappets) using the collapsed tappet method for checking.
   D. Engine compression.
3. After going through the above checks, there may still be unsatisfactory performance. The cause may be a lean idle fuel mixture. If this condition is encountered, check the air-fuel ratio with the aid of an exhaust analyzer. With it, adjust the ratio to specifications.

Exhaust Gas Analyzer

The use of the gas analyzer is recommended only after the Normal Fuel Setting Procedures and Additional Idle Speed and Mixture Procedures have been performed, and engine idle is still unsatisfactory.

Except for laboratory equipment, all brand name gas analyzers in common use depend upon thermal conductivity to register.

A typical procedure is as follows:

1. Connect a gas analyzer to the truck.
2. If the truck is equipped with a Thermactor type exhaust emission system, disconnect the air injector pump supply hose at the pump or check valve/s. Do not adjust for the drop in engine idle speed, which occurs when the air supply hose is disconnected. However, note the amount of rpm drop for use in Step 4.
3. Observe gas analyzer reading.

   The value must be taken with air cleaner installed. Refer to specifications for the proper air-fuel ratio.
4. Turn idle mixture adjusting screw/s as required, within the range of the idle limiter, until the required ratio is obtained. On multi-venturi carburetors, turn screws an equal amount. Correct for any changes in engine idle speed immediately, as soon as the idle screw/s are turned. Refer to the drop in engine rpm obtained when the Thermactor air pump hose/s were disconnected in Step 2, then correct idle speed to the rpm noted. Allow at least 10 seconds following each idle mixture screw adjustment for the analyzer reading to properly respond and stabilize.

NOTE: thermal conductivity exhaust gas analyzers indicate a false, rich reading if the air-fuel mixture is extremely lean. To check for this condition, partially hand choke the carburetor, or quickly open and close the throttle a few times to momentarily enrich the mixture. The meter will reflect the false rich condition, then will deflect in the lean direction as the rich condition subsides. The meter will gradually stabilize to a richer reading as the abnormally lean air-fuel ratio is regained.

Trucks equipped with automatic transmissions must be in Neutral while above is being done.

5. If air-fuel ratio is to specifications, and the various engine systems are functioning properly, no further adjustments should be made.

Exhaust analyzer

If air-fuel ratio is not to specifications, as indicated by the analyzer, it may be corrected by altering the controlled limits of the carburetor idle fuel system. Refer to the following procedures:

Removal and Installation of Idle Limiter Caps

1. Remove the plastic limiter caps by cutting them with side cutters and a knife. After the cut is made, pry the limiter apart.
2. Adjust carburetor air-fuel ratio, using the exhaust analyzer.
3. When air-fuel ratio is within limits, install a colored plastic service limiter cap.

   When installing the cap, use care not to disturb the idle mixture. Position the cap so that it is in the maximum counterclockwise position with the tab of the limiter against the stop on the carburetor. The idle mixture adjusting screw will then be at the maximum allowable outward, or rich, setting.

   Install service cap by pushing with the thumb or with a 3/8 in. socket extension.
4. Recheck the air-fuel ratio with air cleaner installed, using the exhaust gas analyzer.

Removal and Installation of Lead Seal and Readjustment of Idle Limiter

1. Remove the lead seal covering the idle limiting needle in the throttle body. Pick it out with an ice pick.
2. With idle adjusting needle at maximum rich setting, slowly back out the idle limiter, one-sixteenth turn at a time, until the specified air-fuel ratio reading is obtained on the exhaust analyzer.
3. After obtaining the specified air-fuel ratio reading, install a new lead seal over the idle limiter. Drive the seal into the hole with a small punch until the lead contacts the head of the screw. After the idle limiter has been reset, and the air-fuel ratio and idle conditions are found to be satisfactory, stamp or scribe the letter R on the carburetor identification tag, just above the name Autolite, to indicate that the carburetor has been reworked.

Ignition System

Emission control features in the ignition system are:

1. Dual-diaphragm vacuum advance distributor.
2. Distributor vacuum control valve (coolant temperature sensing).
3. Distributor vacuum advance control valve (deceleration).
4. Distributor modulator.

All distributors are equipped with both vacuum and centrifugal advance units. Vacuum advance governs the ignition timing (spark advance) at low engine speeds (rpm) or low engine loading. The centrifugal advance, in combination with the vacuum advance, controls the ignition timing at higher engine speeds or heavy engine loading to provide the correct ignition timing for maximum engine performance. A dual-diaphragm advance is used on some engines to provide additional ignition timing retardation during engine idle operation.

The distributor vacuum control valve advances the spark timing under conditions of prolonged idling, thus preventing overheating. The deceleration valve provides advanced timing on deceleration. The distributor modulator prevents spark advance below a set vehicle speed on either acceleration or deceleration.

Dual Advance Distributor

Single-Diaphragm Vacuum Advance Distributor

The distributor has two independently operated spark advance systems. A centrifugal advance mechanism is influenced by engine rpm.

The vacuum advance has a spring-loaded diaphragm connected to the breaker plate assembly. The diaphragm is activated to work against spring pressure by vacuum. When vacuum increases, diaphragm movement causes the movable breaker plate to pivot on the stationary subplate. The breaker point rubbing block, which is positioned on the opposite side of the cam from the pivot pin, then moves in the opposite direction of distributor rotation and advances the spark timing. As the movable breaker plate is rotated from the retarded position to the full-advance position, the point dwell decreases slightly. This is due to the breaker point rubbing block and the cam rotating on different axes.

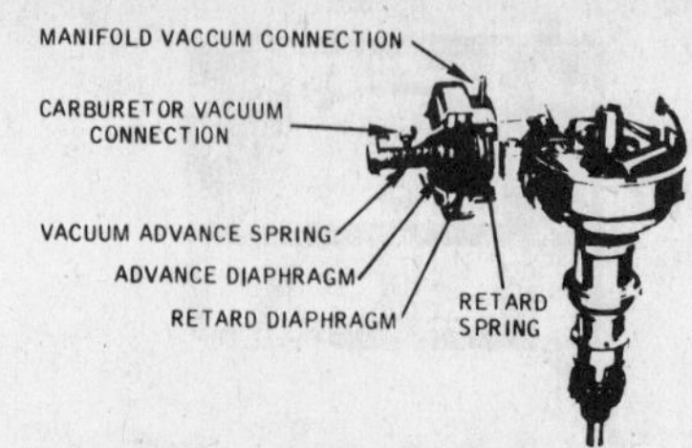

Distributor with dual-diaphragm vacuum advance

Dual-Diaphragm Vacuum Advance Distributor

On dual-diaphragm distributors, the centrifugal advance unit is the same as on single-diaphragm units. The dual-diaphragm unit consists of two independently operating diaphragms. The advance (primary) diaphragm uses carburetor vacuum to advance ignition timing. The retard (secondary) diaphragm is activated by intake manifold vacuum, which provides additional timing retardation during closed throttle deceleration and idle.

The advance diaphragm (outer) is coupled to the movable breaker plate in a manner similar to that in single-diaphragm distributors. An increase in vacuum moves the diaphragm against the advance diaphragm spring. This action causes the movable braker plate to oppose distributor rotation; therefore, ignition timing is advanced. This advance is calibrated to occur during normal road-load operation, but not during deceleration or idle.

When intake manifold vacuum is applied to the retard diaphragm (inner), it moves in toward the distributor. This permits the diaphragm spring to move the breaker plate in the same direction as distributor rotation. This retardation phase of ignition timing occurs during engine idle or deceleration, except when a distributor modulator is installed in the vacuum supply line.

Distributor Modulator

The distributor modulator ensures close control of distributor spark advance during acceleration and deceleration. Modulator components are a speed sensor, a thermal switch, an electronic control amplifier, and a three way solenoid valve. All these units operate together to control vacuum to the distributor. The control amplifier and solenoid valve are a single unit mounted inside the passenger compartment. The speed sensor is connected to the speedometer cable. The thermal switch is mounted near either front door hinge pillar on the outside of the cowl panel. The modulator prevents distributor vacuum spark advance until a speed of 21-31 mph is reached when accelerating, and cuts out vacuum advance when a speed of 25-15 mph is reached on deceleration.

Distributor Vacuum Control Valve

The distributor vacuum control valve (temperature-sensing valve), is incorporated into the distributor vacuum advance supply line in order to provide advanced timing during prolonged idling. This valve is installed in the coolant outlet housing in order to sense engine coolant temperatures. Normally, the valve connects two ports: regular source vacuum at the carburetor and the distributor port. During periods of prolonged idle, if engine temperature rises, the valve closes the regular source (intake manifold vacuum) and connects the distributor port to the alternate source vacuum port. On certain engines, the latter port is capped with a filter. The advanced timing causes an immediate increase in engine speed, which will be maintained until engine temperature returns to normal.

Distributor Vacuum Deceleration Control Valve

On some engines, a distributor vacuum advance control valve (deceleration valve) is incorporated into the distributor vacuum system to provide

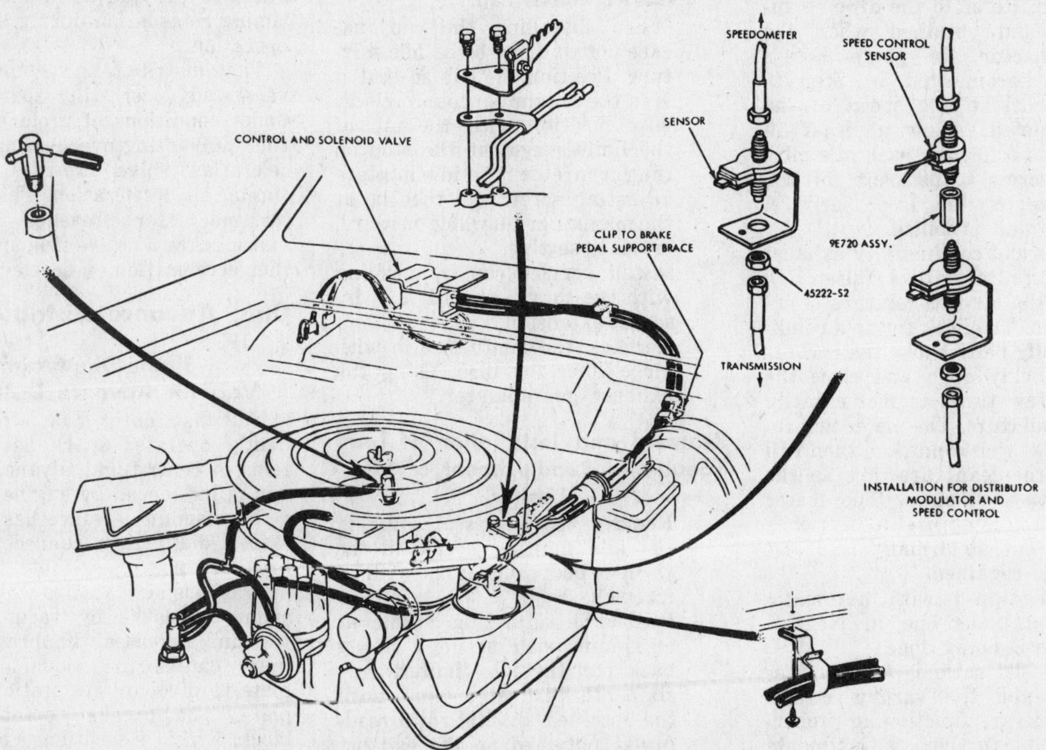

Typical distributor modulator installation (© Ford Motor Company)

additional control of ignition timing. This device is used in conjunction with the dual-diaphragm vacuum advance unit. Normally, the advance diaphragm (outer) is connected to a vacuum port on the carburetor. During deceleration, when intake manifold vacuum rises, the deceleration valve closes off the carburetor vacuum and provides direct intake manifold vacuum to the distributor advance diaphram (outer). This permits maximum ignition advance to prevent after-burning or popping in the engine exhaust system. When the vehicle slows down and the engine is operating at idle, the deceleration valve shuts off intake manifold vacuum and opens the carburetor vacuum to the distributor.

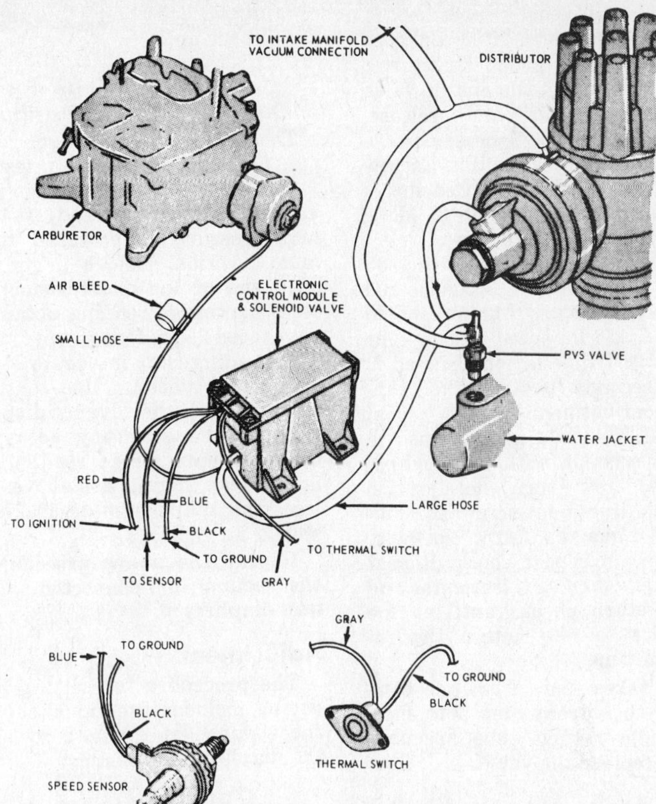

Distributor modulator details (© Ford Motor Company)

Diagnosis and Tests

To pinpoint engine problems caused by the distributor vacuum system, refer to Emission Control Systems Diagnosis Guide.

To test ignition electrical system use an oscilloscope, following recommended procedures. In order to check the distributor advance vacuum system the vacuum lines must be correctly connected. Verify the complaint or symptom; then check the operation of the distributor vacuum control valve, vacuum advance control valve, dual-diaphragm vacuum advance, and distributor modulator.

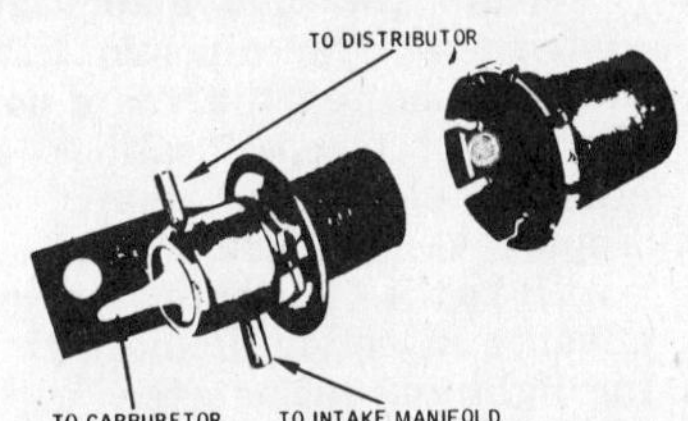

Distributor vacuum advance control valve

Distributor Vacuum Control Valve Test

1. Check routing and connection of all vacuum hoses.
2. Attach a tachometer to the engine.
3. Bring engine up to normal operating temperature. Engine must not be overheated.
4. Note engine rpm, transmission in Neutral and throttle in curb idle position.
5. Disconnect vacuum hose from intake manifold at temperature-sensing valve. Plug or clamp the hose.
6. Note idle rpm with hose disconnected. If there is no change in rpm, the valve is good. If there is a drop of 100 or more rpm, the valve should be replaced.
7. Check that the all-season cooling mixture is to specifications, and that the correct radiator cap is in place and functioning.
8. Block radiator air flow to induce a higher than normal temperature condition.
9. Continue to operate until the engine temperature or heat indicator shows above normal.
   If engine speed by this time has increased 100 or more rpm, the temperature-sensing valve is satisfactory. If not, it should be replaced.

Distributor Vacuum Deceleration Control Valve Test

1. Connect a tachometer to the engine and bring engine to normal operating temperature.
2. Check idle speed and set to specifications with headlights on high beam if necessary.
3. Turn off headlights and note idle rpm.
4. Remove plastic cover from valve. Slowly turn adjusting screw counterclockwise without pressing in. After five and no more than six turns, idle speed

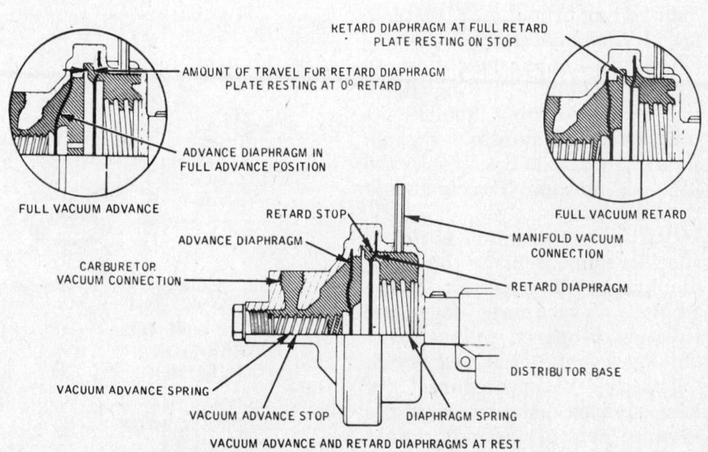

Dual diaphragm vacuum advance mechanism

should suddenly increase to about 1000 rpm. If speed does not increase after six turns, push inward on the end of valve spring retainer and release. Speed should now increase.
5. Slowly turn adjusting screw clockwise until idle speed drops to speed noted in Step 3. Make one more turn clockwise.
6. Increase engine speed to 200 rpm, hold for five seconds, and release throttle. Engine should return to idle speed within four seconds. If idle is not resumed in four seconds, back off the dashpot adjustment and repeat check. If idle is not resumed in three seconds with the dashpot backed off, turn deceleration valve adjustment screw an additional quarter turn clockwise and again repeat check. Repeat quarter turn adjustments and idle return checks until engine returns to idle within the required time.
7. If it takes more than one complete turn from Step 5 to meet the idle return time specification, replace the valve.

Dual-Diaphragm Vacuum Advance and Vacuum Retard Functional Check

1. To check vacuum advance, disconnect the vacuum lines from both the advance (outer) and retard (inner) diaphragms. Plug the line removed from the retard diaphragm.

   Connect a tachometer and timing light to the engine. Increase idle speed by setting the screw on the first step of the fast idle cam. Note ignition timing setting, using a timing light.

   Connect the carburetor vacuum line to the advance diaphragm. If the timing advances immediately, the advance unit is functioning properly. Adjust idle speed to 550-600 rpm.
2. Check vacuum retardation as follows: using a timing light, note ignition timing. Remove the plug from the manifold vacuum line and correct the line to the inner diaphragm. Timing should retard immediately.
3. If vacuum retardation is not to specifications, replace the dual-diaphragm advance unit. If the advance (vacuum) does not function properly, calibrate the unit on a distributor test stand, following the procedures for dual advance distributors. If the advance part of the unit cannot be calibrated, or if either diaphragm is leaking, replace the dual-diaphragm vacuum advance unit.

Diaphragm Leak Test Dual-Diaphragm Distributors

To check the diaphragm for leakage, place distributor on a test stand.

Without connecting the vacuum line to the distributor, adjust the vacuum pressure of the tester to maximum position. Hold a finger on the open end of the tester vacuum hose. Note maximum reading obtained. Do not exceed 25 in. Hg.

If reading is 25 in. Hg. or less, connect tester vacuum line to the vacuum fitting of the advance diaphragm. Without changing any adjustments, the maximum gauge reading should not be less than it was above. If it is less, the diaphragm is leaking and should be replaced.

Repeat the above procedure with the vacuum line connected to the retard diaphragm.

Adjustments

The procedure for setting ignition timing includes functional checks for the advance and retard positions of the diaphragm assembly.

Initial Ignition Timing

1. Clean and mark timing pointer and index marks. Be sure the distributor vacuum lines are properly connected.
2. Disconnect the vacuum line (single-diaphragm distributors) or vacuum lines (dual-diaphragm distributors), and plug the disconnected vacuum line/s.
3. Connect a timing light to No. 1 cylinder plug wire. Hook up a tachometer.
4. Start engine, reduce idle speed to 600 rpm, and adjust initial timing to specifications.
5. Check mechanical (centrifugal) advance for proper operation. Start engine and accelerate to about 2000 rpm. If timing advances, the centrifugal advance is functioning. Note the engine speed when advance begins and how far (in degrees) it advances. Stop the engine.
6. Unplug the carburetor vacuum line and connect it to the distributor vacuum advance unit (outer diaphragm on dual-diaphragm distributors). Start engine and set idle to about 2000 rpm. Note engine speed when advance begins and the degrees of advance. Advance should begin sooner and extend farther than when checking the mechanical advance alone. Stop the engine.
7. Check vacuum retardation on dual-diaphragm distributors. Connect the intake manifold vacuum line to the retard diaphragm side of the vacuum advance. Operate engine at normal idle speed. Initial timing should retard to zero (TDC). On some engines it will go as low as 6° ATDC.
8. If the vacuum advance or vacuum retard phases (dual-diaphragm distributors) are not working properly (refer to Steps 6 and 7 above), remove the distributor and check it on a distributor tester.

   Replace the dual diaphragm unit if the advance portion cannot be calibrated, the retard portion is not to specifications, or either diaphragm is leaking.
9. Unplug vacuum line/s and connect it to the distributor vacuum advance assembly. Remove timing light and tachometer.

Evaporative Emission Control System—1970 Models

Due to regulations regarding gaso-

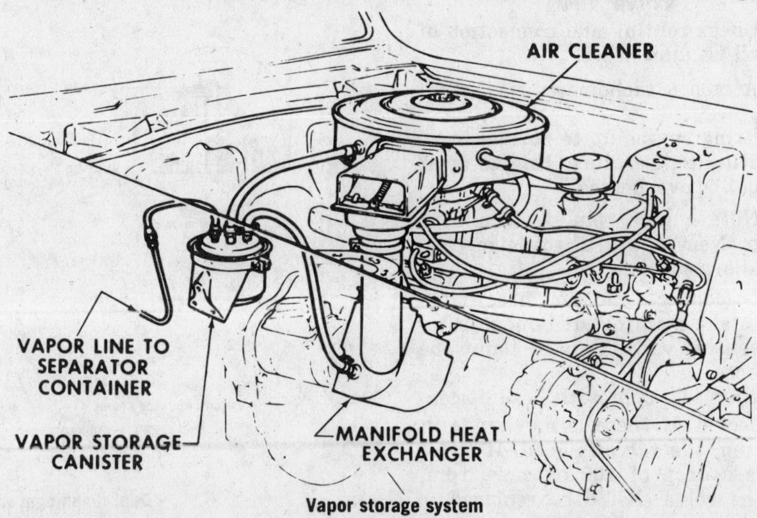

Vapor storage system

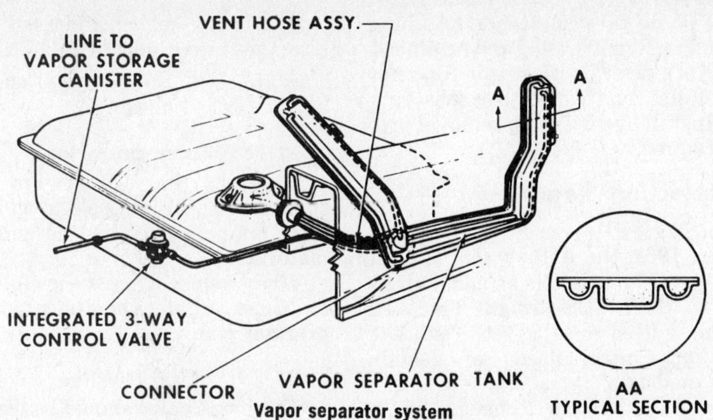

Vapor separator system

line vapor emission in the State of California, all Ford Motor Company trucks shipped into that state are equipped with an evaporative emission control system for 1970.

The system uses:

1. A non-vented filler cap
2. A fill vent and a vapor vent, both located inside the fuel tank.
3. A fuel expansion tank or vapor separator.
4. A three-way control valve.
5. A carbon canister.

The fill vent and the vapor vent both deliver fuel vapors to the vapor separator. The vapor separator returns any liquid fuel to the fuel tank and vapor to the carbon canister through the three-way valve. The three way valve also relieves vacuum within the fuel tank, caused by fuel consumption or thermal contraction, and pressure, caused by thermal expansion or a blocked vapor line. The carbon canister stores fuel vapors until they are drawn into the engine air cleaner and burned. On vehicles not equipped with a carbon canister, fuel vapor is discharged into the crankcase ventilation system through the PCV valve.

Type 7 General Motors Systems

Description

The General Motors Corporation has two basic systems of exhaust emission control to satisfy the needs of their truck requirements. These two systems are the Controlled Combustion System (CCS) and the Air Injection Reaction (AIR) system. These two systems are easily recognized and identifiable by the presence or absence of an air injector pump.

The Controlled Combustion System (CCS) consists of an air cleaner assembly which includes a temperature sensor, vacuum motor, control damper assembly and the necessary connecting vacuum hoses.

The Air Injection Reactor (AIR) system consists of a belt driven air pump which forces air through manifolds or special heads into the area of the exhaust valves.

Caution Never attempt to operate a vehicle equipped with the AIR system with the pump drive disconnected.

Controlled Combustion System (CCS)

The Controlled Combustion System (CCS) functions as follows: During engine warm-up with engine compartment temperatures 85°F or below, the temperature sensor is closed. This allows engine vacuum to be directed to the vacuum motor, closing the damper to outside air. With the damper closed, the cool air will flow through the openings at the ends of the shroud, where it is heated. The heated air then flows up through the hot air pipe and adapter into the air cleaner. As the temperature inside the cleaner reaches about 100°F, the sensor bleeds off vacuum to the vacuum motor, causing the control damper to open, permitting underhood air to be admitted and mixed with the heated air from the heat shroud. This mixture tends to keep the carburetor inlet air temperature at about 100°F.

Under full throttle or below 6-8 in. Hg. the vacuum motor will no longer hold the valve open to hot air. The hot air pipe is closed off, allowing only outside air to enter the air cleaner.

The vacuum motor and control damper assembly in the left snorkel of some special option engines have no sensor and are controlled only by intake manifold vacuum. On these models, the snorkel remains closed until full throttle is obtained. With intake manifold vacuum at 6-8 in. Hg. the control damper assembly will open, allowing maximum air flow into the air cleaner.

Functional Checks

Vacuum Motor and Damper Assy.

1. With engine off, remove air cleaner cover and tape a thermometer (J-5421) to the air cleaner next to the sensor.

NOTE: if temperature is below 80°F, continue to Step 2. If temperature is above 80°F, remove air cleaner and allow to cool to at least 75°F.

2. Install a T into the vacuum line, at vacuum motor, and connect a vacuum gauge into the line.
3. With engine off, control damper will be open.
4. Install the cover on the air cleaner, without wing nut, and start engine. With engine at idle speed, the control damper should close, unless surrounding temperature is above 85°F.

NOTE: if surrounding temperature is above 85°F, make sure control damper is completely open by 128°F.

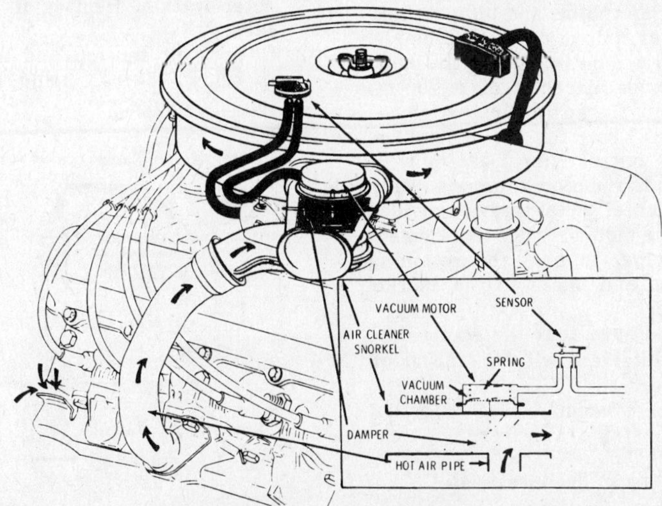

Controlled combustion system

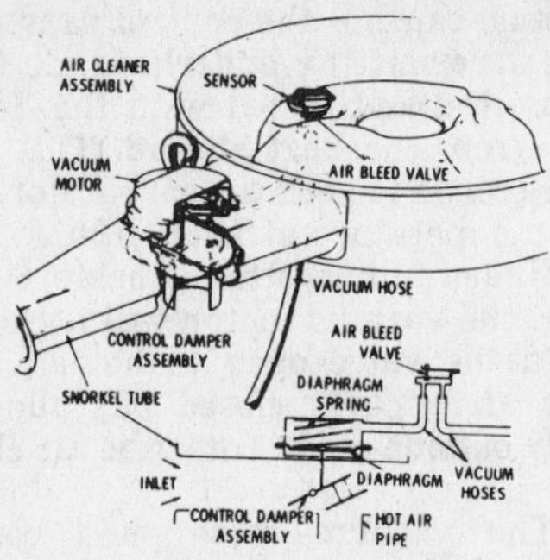

Operation (regulating mode)

5. Watch control damper in snorkel. When it begins to move toward the open position (opening to outside air), quickly remove cover on air cleaner and record the readings on thermometer and vacuum gauge.

Specifications for Damper

Temperature: 85°F—starts to open
128°F—fully open

Vacuum at motor: 5-9 in. Hg. when damper assembly is closed to outside air.

Diagnosis

1. If temperature is within specifications, the CCS is functioning properly.
2. If temperature is not within specifications, but vacuum is correct (5-9 in. Hg.), replace the sensor.
3. If neither temperature nor vacuum are within specifications, replace vacuum motor.

Vacuum Motor Replacement

1. Remove air cleaner.
2. Disconnect vacuum hose from motor.
3. Drill out the two spot welds with a 1/16 in. drill, then, enlarge the holes as necessary.
4. Remove motor retaining strap.
5. Lift up motor, and unhook linkage at control damper assembly.
6. Drill a 7/64 in. hole in the snorkel tube at center of motor retaining strap in illustration.
7. Insert vacuum motor linkage into control damper assembly.
8. Use the motor retaining strap and sheet metal screw, provided in the motor service replacement package, to hold the retaining strap and motor to the snorkel tube.
9. Make sure that the screw does not interfere with operation of damper.
10. Connect vacuum hose to motor and install air cleaner.

Sensor Replacement

1. Remove air cleaner.
2. Detach hoses at sensor.
3. Pry up tabs on sensor retaining clips. Remove clips and retainers. Note position of sensor for reinstallation, then remove sensor.
4. Install by reversing removal procedure.

Air Injection Reactor (AIR) System

Since 1968, the AIR system is used on General Motors trucks as an alternate to their CCS design. The AIR system is used to satisfy the exhaust emission control needs of certain truck models.

The AIR system consists of a belt-driven air injection pump, air injection tubes (or specially designed cylinder heads that contain air passages) to the rear of each exhaust valve. There is a diverter valve and silencer on the air pump to control pressures within the system, and a check valve to protect the hoses and pump from hot gases.

NOTE: do not attempt to operate vehicle with drive belt disconnected.

Air Pump

Intake air is admitted through a centrifugal fan at the front of the pump. There, dirt and other materials are separated from the air by centrifugal force. Air is routed from the pump to the air injection manifold, or the specially cast cylinder head/s, through flexible tubes.

The only serviceable component of the air pump is the centrifugal fan. Do not consider the pump to be defective if it squeaks when turned by hand. Do not lubricate the pump.

NOTE: When steam, or solvent cleaning the engine, mask off the centrifugal filter fan to prevent contamination.

Drive Belt

1. Inspect drive belt for wear or deterioration. Replace if necessary.
2. Check belt tension and adjust, if below 75 lbs., using a belt tension gauge.

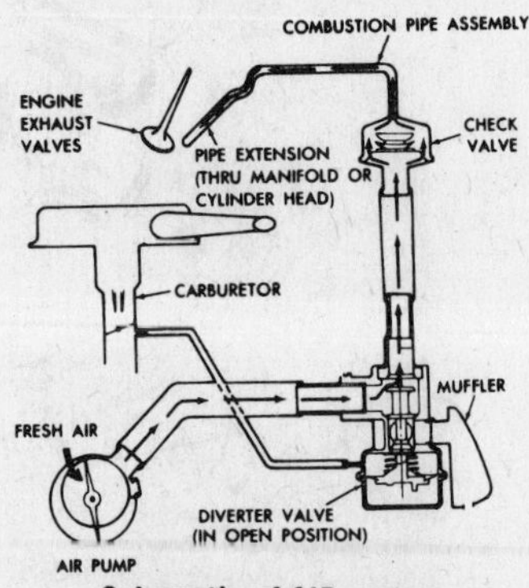

Schematic of AIR system
(© G.M. Corp.)

3. A used belt should read 75 ±5 lbs. and a new belt 125 ±5 lbs.

Do not pry on pump housing.

Tube and Hose

Hoses of the AIR system are of special composition, able to withstand high temperature. Use no substitute material.

When replacing or renewing hoses or tubes, route them according to original plan.

Check Valve

The check valve should be inspected whenever the pump outlet tube is disconnected from the check valve, or whenever check valve failure is suspected.

To test the check valve, blow through the valve, then attempt to suck back through it. Flow should be in only one direction (toward the tube).

Air Injection Tubes or Nozzles

There are different methods of air injection into the exhaust system (ducts and injection nozzles cast into the head/s, nozzles screwed into the head/s, and nozzles screwed into the exhaust manifold/s at each exhaust port).

Regardless of the method used, the air discharge orifice must be clear and show no indication of burning. The orifices or nozzles should be examined whenever the exhaust manifold or head is removed for any purpose. Clean or renew nozzles as necessary.

Air Injection Manifold/s, Where Used

The air injection manifold/s is/are held in place by clamps. These clamps must be installed correctly to insure proper sealing. Each feeder tube of the manifold is sealed by a packing gland which fits on the tube below the flange.

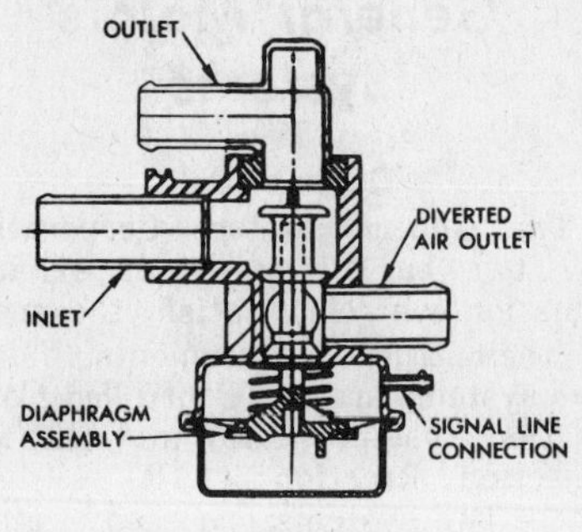

Diverter valve

Diverter Valve and Check Valve

The diverter valve is attached, or adjacent, to the side of the pump. Its

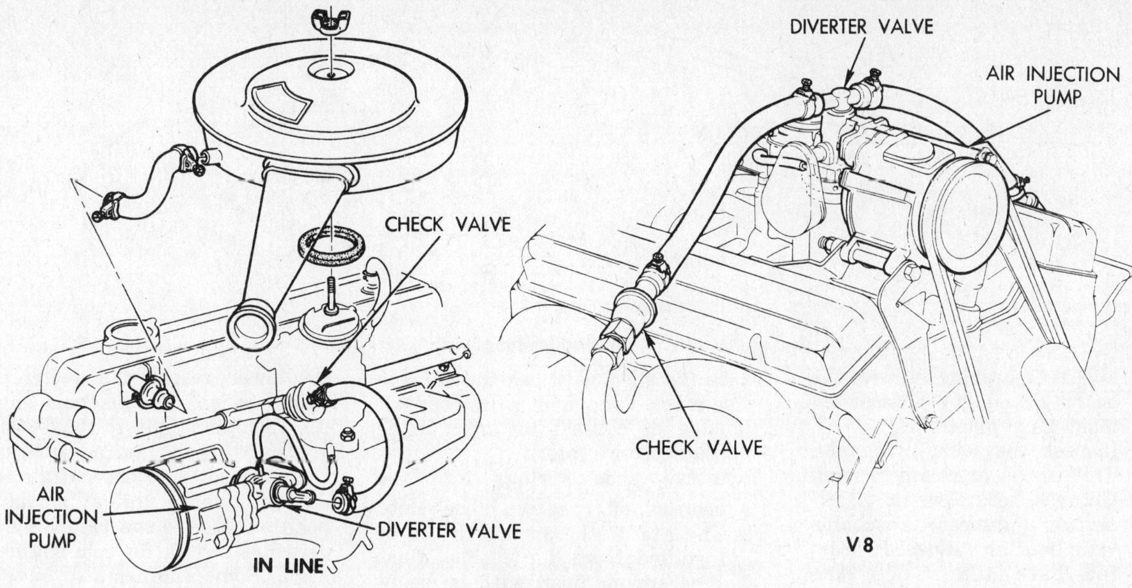

Air injection reactor system

purpose is to sense manifold vacuum through a fitting at the carburetor. During sudden deceleration, vacuum increases, causing the valve to open, allowing air from the injector pump to pass through the valve and silencer to the atmosphere. Approximate duration of the valve opening is 2 seconds. This valve also controls pressure within the system by diverting excessive pump output to the atmosphere, through the silencer.

In most cases, the air injection manifold is fitted with a screw-on check valve near the right cylinder head. This valve has a one-way diaphragm which prevents hot exhaust gases from backing up into the hose and pump, causing damage. This is to protect the system in the event of pump belt failure, abnormally high exhaust system pressure, or air delivery hose breakage.

Air Injection Pump Reconditioning

Caution The following reconditioning procedure is submitted for the convenience of shops having adequate facilities, and is not a General Motors Corporation common practice or recommended policy.

The vane-type air injection pump as used with the AIR system consists of parts as illustrated in the accompanying exploded view.

NOTE: before disassembly, rotate the drive hub quickly, first three-quarter turn counterclockwise, then one-quarter turn clockwise. Roughness may be felt which could indicate vane bearing failure.

1. Place the drive hub in a vise and remove the cover assembly by tapping straight up with a plastic mallet.
2. Remove the rear rotor ring attaching screws, then remove the rear rotor ring and bearing assembly and rear carbon seal. Discard the seal.
3. Remove the vane assemblies.
4. Remove the vane shoes with needle nose pliers, then remove shoe springs. Carbon shoes chip easily; use caution.

Caution When cleaning for inspection, under no circumstances should the rotor or cover assemblies be immersed in cleaning solvent.

Cleaning and Inspection

1. Blow carbon dust from the housing and rotor assembly and cover assembly with compressed air.
2. Wipe stubborn deposits from the components with a cloth saturated with kerosene. Remaining deposits that do not respond to petroleum solvents may be removed with denatured alcohol.
3. Inspect inside of housing for vane or rotor wear. Excessive wear justifies replacement of housing and rotor.
4. Inspect rear cover as follows:
   A. Check rear bearing inner race for grooves or scratches. This damage indicates prob-

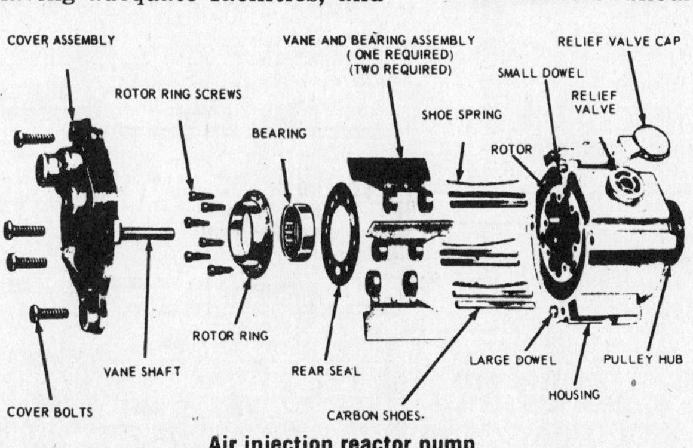

Air injection reactor pump

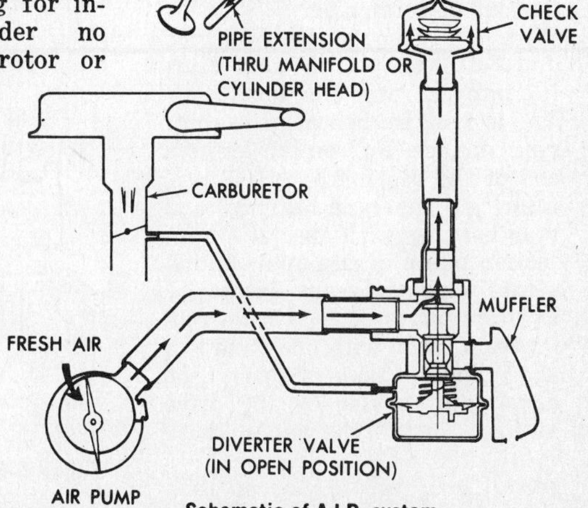

Schematic of A.I.R. system

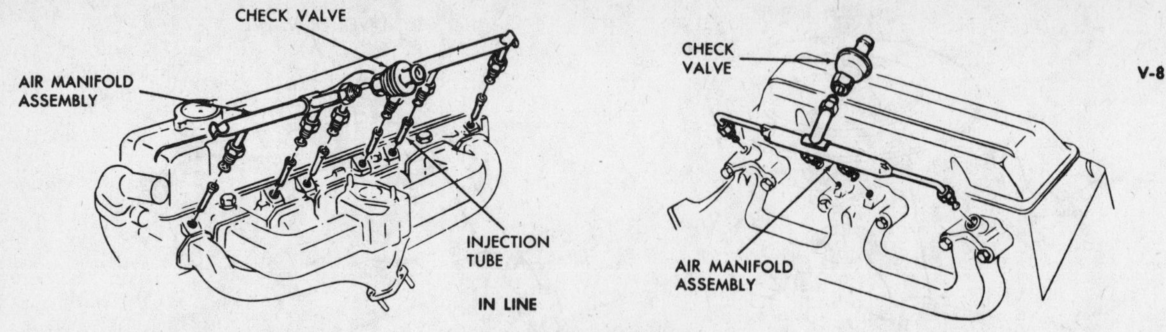

Air injection tubes

able rear bearing failure; the bearing and cover assembly must be replaced.

B. Inspect the vane pivot pin. This pin is precision ground. Grooves, scratches, or discoloration indicate probable vane bearing failure. If bearings have failed, a new vane assembly is required.

5. Clean rear rotor ring and bearing in kerosene, then dry with compressed air. Check rear bearing for failure. The degree of bearing failure may necessitate replacing rotor and housing assembly.
6. Clean vane assemblies in kerosene, then dry with compressed air. Check vanes and bearings for wear or damage. Inspect the pivot pin again for confirmation of bearing failure. All corners of the vanes must be square. Broken edges require vane replacement.
7. Check carbon shoes for excessive wear or chipping. Inspect the surface contacting the vane. The shoes should show small grooves from action. This condition is normal. However, chipped or broken shoes must be replaced.

Rear Bearing Replacement and Pump Assembly

1. With bearing remover J-21058 and J-21844, pull the rear bearing out of rotor ring.
2. With the same tools (J-21085 and J-21844), pull the rear bearing into the rotor ring until bearing is 1/32 in. beneath the rotor ring surface. Pull on the lettered end of the bearing.
3. Lubricate the vane bearings and rear bearing with special air injection pump grease or its equivalent; wipe away any excess.
4. Position vanes on $3/8$ x 4 in. rod.
5. Position rotor with one vane slot at stripper, then support the housing in a vise by the drive hub and install the vanes (with rod).
6. Install one carbon shoe on each side of every vane. Shoes must be installed with bearing surface against vane and with rounded edge of contact toward outside diameter of rotor.
7. Install shoe springs into the deepest of the two shoe slots. The arc of the spring should be installed toward the shoe. Push shoe spring flush with or below rotor surface.
8. Install a new carbon seal, with cupped lip toward rear cover, and the rear rotor ring onto the end of the rotor. Carbon seal and rear rotor ring bolt hole design allows installation in only one position.
9. Apply Loctite or its equivalent to the rear rotor ring attaching screw thread, then install screws and evenly torque to 37 in. lbs.
10. Remove the $3/8$ in. rod from the vanes, then start the cover into position.
11. Install cover attaching bolts and torque to 10 ft. lbs.

NOTE: in some cases a chirping or squeaking noise may be heard coming from the pump for the first 5 or 10 miles after a pump reconditioning. This is a normal condition.

Transmission Control Spark (TCS)

On most 1970 models, distributor vacuum advance has been eliminated in the lower forward gears. A solenoid vacuum switch is energized in the lower gears by a switch at the transmission. The solenoid shuts off the vacuum supply to the distributor, venting the vacuum advance unit to the carburetor to prevent air locking of the advance unit at an advanced position. TCS is overridden by a temperature switch for cold engine operation. Some engines also have a hot override switch. Vacuum advance is provided only in high gear, except for four speed transmissions, which have vacuum advance in third and fourth gears.

TCS Troubleshooting

If full vacuum is found in all gears, the cause may be:

1. Fuse blown.
2. Wire disconnected at solenoid.
3. Wire disconnected at transmission switch.
4. Transmission switch failed.
5. Temperature override switch energized—check by disconnecting electrical lead.
6. Solenoid failed.

If no vacuum is found in high gear, the cause may be:

1. Clean air line and distributor vacuum line reversed at solenoid.
2. Foreign material in solenoid.
3. Plunger return spring broken.
4. Distributor or manifold vacuum hose broken or disconnected.
5. Transmission switch or wire shorted to ground.

TRANSMISSION CONTROLLED VACUUM SPARK ADVANCE SYSTEM

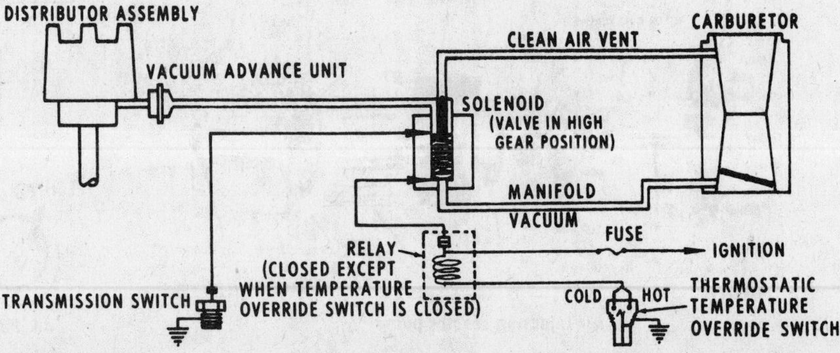

Evaporative Emission Control System (ECS)

ECS is installed on all 1970 models sold in California. The function of this system is to prevent fuel vapors from escaping to the atmosphere. A special non-vented filler cap is used.

This cap is equipped with a two way valve to relieve pressure or vacuum within the fuel tank. A liquid-vapor separator is mounted in front of the gasoline tank. The separator prevents liquid fuel from passing to the vapor storage canister in the engine compartment. The canister contains a filter which must be cleaned every 12,000 miles. From the canister, vapors are vented to the crankcase ventilation system and/or to the carburetor air cleaner intake.

Canister and/or Canister Filter Removal

1. Raise vehicle on hoist.
2. Note installed position of hoses on canister.
3. Disconnect hoses from top of canister.
4. Loosen clamps and remove canister.
5. If replacing filter, remove bottom of canister and pull out filter.

Canister and/or Canister Filter Inspection

1. Check hose connection openings. Assure that they are open.
2. On four barrel carburetor models, check operation of purge valve by applying vacuum to the valve. A good valve will hold vacuum.

Canister and/or Canister Filter Installation

1. Install new filter.
2. Assemble bottom of canister to canister body.
3. Install canister and tighten clamp bolts.
4. Connect hoses to top of canister in same position as in Step 3 above.

Canister Purge Valve Disassembly

1. Disconnect lines at valve.
2. Snap off valve cap (Slowly remove cap as diaphragm is under spring tension). Remove diaphragm, spring retainer and spring.
3. Replace parts as necessary. Check orifice openings.

Canister Purge Valve Assembly

1. Install spring, spring retainer, diaphragm and cap.
2. Connect lines to valve.

Separator Removal

1. Raise vehicle on hoist.
2. Disconnect lines from separator.
3. Remove retaining screw and remove separator.

Separator Installation

1. Install separator and its retaining screw.
2. Connect lines to separator.
3. Lower vehicle and remove from hoist.

COMBINATION EMISSION CONTROL SYSTEM

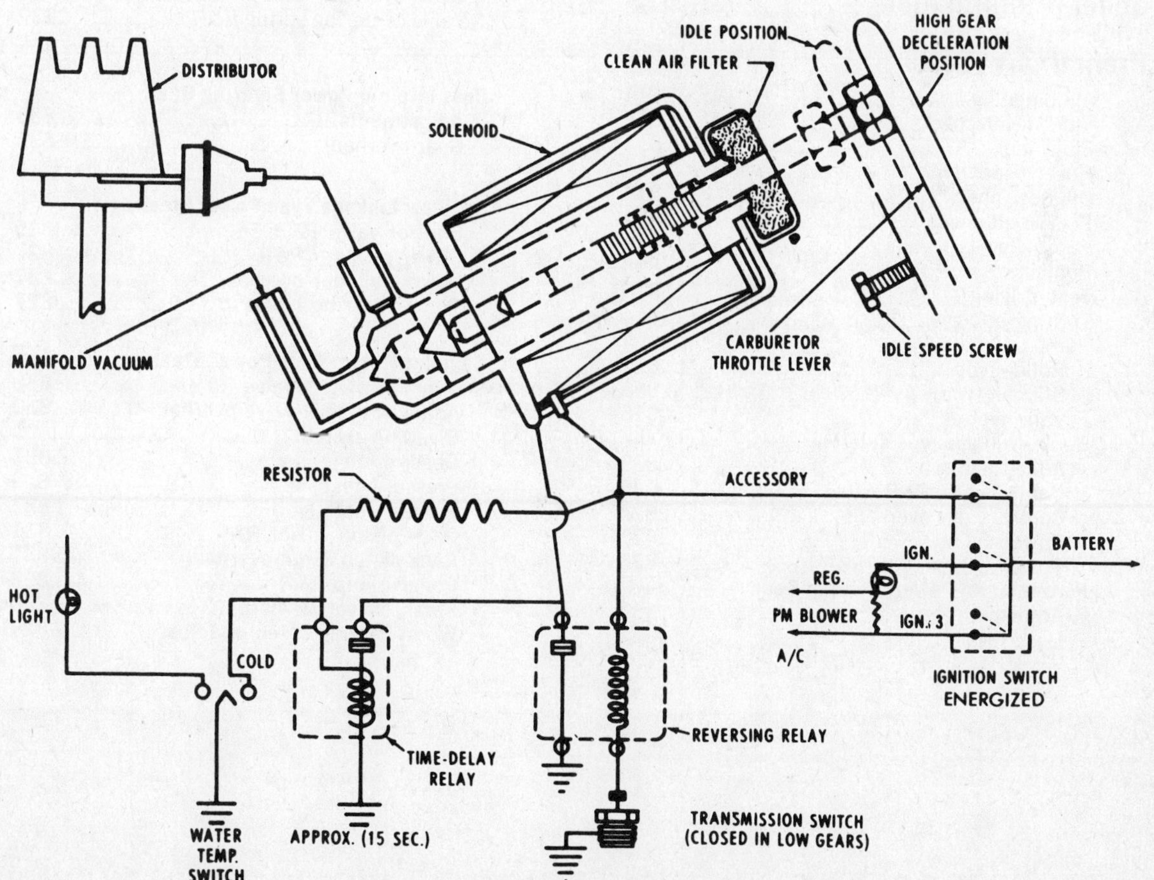

Combination emission control system schematic

Steering Gears

Index

Manual Steering

Power Steering

STEERING TROUBLE DIAGNOSIS

Condition	Possible Cause	Correction
	Steering Gear	
Excessive Play or Looseness in the Steering	(1) Steering gear shaft adjusted too loose or shaft and/or bushing badly worn.	(1) Replace worn parts and adjust according to instructions.
	(2) Excessive steering gear worm end play due to bearing adjustment.	(2) Adjust according to instructions.
	(3) Steering linkage loose or worn.	(3) Replace worn parts.
	(4) Front wheel bearings improperly adjusted.	(4) Adjust wheel bearings.
	(5) Steering arm loose on steering gear shaft.	(5) Inspect for damage to the gear shaft and steering arm, replace parts as necessary.
	(6) Steering gear housing attaching bolts loose.	(6) Tighten the attaching bolts to specifications.
	(7) Steering arms loose at steering knuckles.	(7) Tighten according to specifications.
	(8) Worn king pins or bushings.	(8) Replace king pins and bushings.
	(9) Loose spring shackles.	(9) Adjust or replace parts as necessary.
Hard Steering	(1) Low or uneven tire pressure.	(1) Inflate the tires to recommended pressures.
	(2) Insufficient lubricant in the steering gear housing or in steering linkage.	(2) Lubricate as necessary.
	(3) Steering gear shaft adjusted too tight.	(3) Adjust according to instructions.
	(4) Improper caster or tie-in.	(4) Align the wheels.
	(5) Steering column misaligned.	(5) See "Steering Gear Alignment."
	(6) Loose, worn or broken pump belt.	(6) Adjust or replace belt.
	(7) Air in system.	(7) Bleed air from system.
	(8) Low fluid level in the pump reservoir.	(8) Fill to correct level.
	(9) Pump output pressure low.	(9) See "Pressure Test."
	(10) Leakage at power cylinder piston rings. (Linkage type).	(10) Replace piston rings and repair as required.
	(11) Binding or bent cylinder linkage. (Linkage type).	(11) Replace or repair as required.
	(12) Valve spool and/or sleeve sticking. (Linkage type).	(12) Free-up or replace as required.
Pull to One Side (Tendency of the Vehicle to Veer in one Direction Only)	(1) Incorrect tire pressure or tire sizes not uniform.	(1) Check tire sizes and inflate the tires to recommended pressures.
	(2) Wheel bearings improperly adjusted.	(2) Adjust wheel bearings.
	(3) Dragging brakes.	(3) Inspect for weak, or broken brake shoe spring, binding pedal.
	(4) Improper caster, camber or toe-in.	(4) Adjust to specifications.
	(5) Grease, dirt, oil or brake fluid on brake linings.	(5) Inspect, replace and adjust as necessary.
	(6) Broken or sagging rear springs.	(6) Replace the rear springs.
	(7) Bent front axle, linkage or steering knuckle.	(7) Replace the parts as necessary.
	(8) Worn or tight king pin bushings.	(8) Lubricate or replace as necessary.
Wander or Weave	(1) Improper caster, camber or toe-in.	(1) Adjust to specifications.
	(2) Worn king pin and bushings.	(2) Replace parts as required.
	(3) Worn or improperly adjusted front wheel bearings.	(3) Adjust or replace parts as necessary.
	(4) Loose spring shackles.	(4) Adjust or replace parts as necessary.
	(5) Incorrect tire pressure or tire sizes not uniform.	(5) Check tire sizes and inflate tires to recommended pressure.
	(6) Loose steering gear mounting bolts.	(6) Tighten to specifications.
	(7) Tight king pin bushings.	(7) Lubricate or ream to proper fit.
	(8) Tight king pin thrust bearings.	(8) Adjust to .001 to .005 inch clearance.
Wheel Tramp (Excessive Vertical Motion of Wheels)	(1) Incorrect tire pressure.	(1) Inflate the tires to recommended pressures.
	(2) Improper balance of wheels, tires and brake drums.	(2) Balance as necessary.
	(3) Loose tie rod ends or steering connections.	(3) Inspect and repair as necessary.
	(4) Worn or inoperative shock absorbers.	(4) Replace the shock absorbers.
	(5) Excessive run-out of brake drums, wheels or tires.	(5) Repair or replace as required.
Shimmy	(1) Badly worn and/or unevenly worn tires.	(1) Rotate tires or replace if necessary.
	(2) Wheels and tires out of balance.	(2) Balance wheel and tire assemblies.
	(3) Worn or loose steering linkage parts.	(3) Replace parts as required.
	(4) Worn king pins and bushings.	(4) Replace king pins and bushings.
	(5) Loose steering gear adjustments.	(5) Adjust steering gear as necessary.
	(6) Loose wheel bearings.	(6) Adjust wheel bearings.
	(7) Improper caster setting.	(7) Adjust caster to specifications.
	(8) Weak or broken springs.	(8) Replace as required.
	(9) Incorrect tire pressure or tire sizes not uniform.	(9) Check tire sizes and inflate tires to recommended pressure.
	(10) Faulty shock absorbers.	(10) Replace as necessary.
	(11) Power cylinder loose at bracket.	(11) Tighten or replace bushings as necessary.
	(12) Power cylinder not aligned in same plane as tie rod.	(12) Correct the alignment.
	(13) Improper valve spool nut adjustment allowing control valve end play.	(13) Adjust according to instructions.
	(14) Loose steering gear mounting bolts.	(14) Tighten to specifications.

STEERING TROUBLE DIAGNOSIS

Condition	Possible Cause	Correction
Intermittent or No Power Assist	(1) Belt slipping and/or low fluid level.	(1) Adjust or replace belt. Add fluid as necessary.
	(2) Piston or rod binding in power cylinder. (Linkage type).	(2) Repair or replace piston and rod.
	(3) Sliding sleeve stuck in control valve. (Linkage type).	(3) Free-up or replace sleeve.
	(4) Improper pump operation.	(4) Refer to "Power Steering Pump."
Poor or No Recovery from Turns	(1) Improper caster setting.	(1) Adjust to specifications.
	(2) Steering gear adjustments too tight.	(2) Adjust according to instructions.
	(3) Improper spool nut adjustment. (Linkage type).	(3) Adjust according to instructions.
	(4) Valve spool installed backwards. (Linkage Type).	(4) Install valve spool correctly.
	(5) Low tire pressure.	(5) Inflate tires to recommended pressure.
	(6) Tight steering linkage.	(6) Lubricate as necessary.
	(7) King pins frozen.	(7) Lubricate as necessary.
	POWER STEERING PUMP	
Intermittant Assist	(1) Flow control valve sticking.	(1) Pressure test pump and service as necessary.
	(2) Slipping belt.	(2) Adjust belt.
	(3) Low fluid level.	(3) Inspect and correct fluid level.
	(4) Low pump efficiency.	(4) Pressure test pump and service as necessary.
No Assist	(1) Pump seizure.	(1) Replace pump.
	(2) Broken slipper spring(s).	(2) Recondition pump or replace as necessary.
	(3) Flow control bore plug ring not in place.	(3) Replace snap ring. Inspect groove for depth.
	(4) Flow control valve sticking.	(4) Pressure test pump and service as necessary.
No Assist When Parking Only	(1) Wrong pressure relief valve.	(1) Install proper relief valve.
	(2) Broken "O" ring on flow control bore plug.	(2) Replace "O" ring.
	(3) Loose pressure relief valve.	(3) Tighten valve. DO NOT ADJUST.
	(4) Low pump efficiency.	(4) Pressure test pump and service as necessary.
Noisy Pump	(1) Low fluid level.	(1) Inspect and correct fluid level.
	(2) Belt noise.	(2) Inspect for pulley alignment, paint or grease on pulley and correct. Adjust belt.
	(3) Foreign material blocking pump housing oil inlet hole.	(3) Remove reservoir, visually check inlet oil hole and service as necessary.
Pump Vibration	(1) Pump hose interference with sheet metal or brake lines.	(1) Reroute hoses.
	(2) Belt loose.	(2) Adjust belt.
	(3) Pulley loose or out of round.	(3) Replace pulley.
	(4) Crankshaft pulley loose or damaged.	(4) Replace crankshaft pulley.
	(5) Bracket pivot bolts loose.	(5) If unable to tighten, replace bracket.
Pump Leaks	(1) Cap or filler neck leaks.	(1) Correct fluid level.
	(2) Reservoir solder joints leak.	(2) Resolder or replace reservoir as necessary.
	(3) Reservoir "O" ring leaking.	(3) Inspect sealing area of reservoir. Replace "O" ring or reservoir as necessary.
	(4) Shaft seal leaking.	(4) Replace seal.
	(5) Loose rear bracket bolts.	(5) Tighten bolts.
	(6) Loose or faulty high pressure ferrule.	(6) Tighten fitting to 24 foot-pounds or replace as necessary.
	(7) Rear bolt holes stripped or casting cracked.	(7) Repair, if possible, or replace pump.

Manual Steering Gears

Manual Steering Gear Service

Steering Gear Alignment

Before any steering gear adjustments are made, it is recommended that the front end of the truck be raised and a thorough inspection be made for stiffness or lost motion in the steering gear, steering linkage and front suspension. Worn or damaged parts should be replaced, since a satisfactory adjustment of the steering gear cannot be obtained if bent or badly worn parts exist.

It is also very important that the steering gear be properly aligned in the truck. Misalignment of the gear places a stress on the steering worm shaft, therefore a proper adjustment

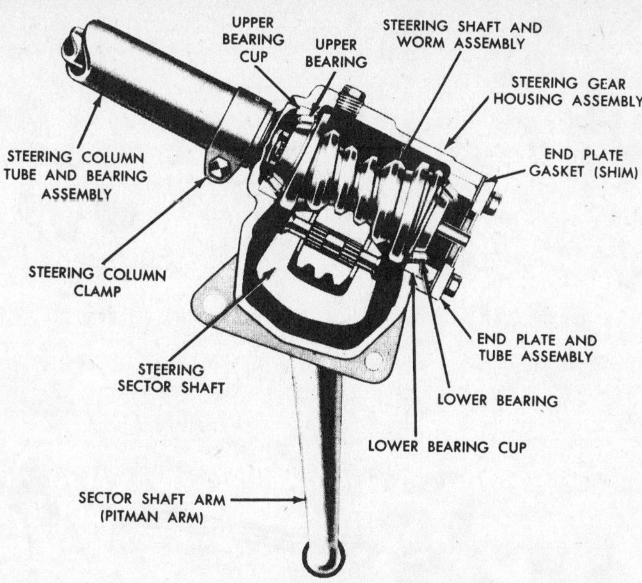

Typical gemmer steering gear
(© Ford Motor Co.)

is impossible. To align the steering gear, loosen the steering gear-to-frame mounting bolts to permit the gear to align itself. Check the steering gear to frame mounting seat, if there is a gap at any of the mounting bolts, proper alignment may be obtained by placing shims where excessive gap appears. Tighten the steering gear-to-frame bolts. Alignment of the gear in the truck is very important and should be done carefully so that a satisfactory, trouble-free gear adjustment may be obtained.

Gemmer Worm and Double Roller Tooth Type

With Screw Adjusted Mesh

The steering gear is of the worm and roller type with a 24 to 1 gear ratio. The cross shaft is straddle mounted with a bearing surface at the top and bottom points of the shaft mounting areas. The three tooth cross shaft roller is mounted in ball bearings. The proper lubricant used in the gear box is S.A.E. 90 Extreme Pressure Lubricant.

The external adjustments given below will remove all play from the steering gear.

Worm Bearing Adjustment

1. Turn the steering wheel about one full turn from straight ahead and secure it so it doesn't move.
2. Determine if there is any worm gear end-play by shaking the front wheel sideways and noting if there is any end movement that may be felt between the steering wheel hub and the steering jacket tube. (Be sure any movement noted is not looseness in the steering jacket tube.)
3. If end play is present, adjust the worm bearings by loosening the four cover cap screws about 1/8". Separate the top shim, using a knife blade, and remove it. Do not damage the remaining shims or gaskets.
4. Replace the cover and recheck the end-play again. If necessary, repeat steps 2 and 3 until the end-play movement is as small as possible without tightening the steering gear too much. NOTE: Adjustment may be done with the Pitman arm disconnected. With the steering wheel turned about one full turn from straight ahead, using a spring scale tool, adjust with the shims as given above until the spring scale pull is between 1/4 and 5/8 ft. lbs.

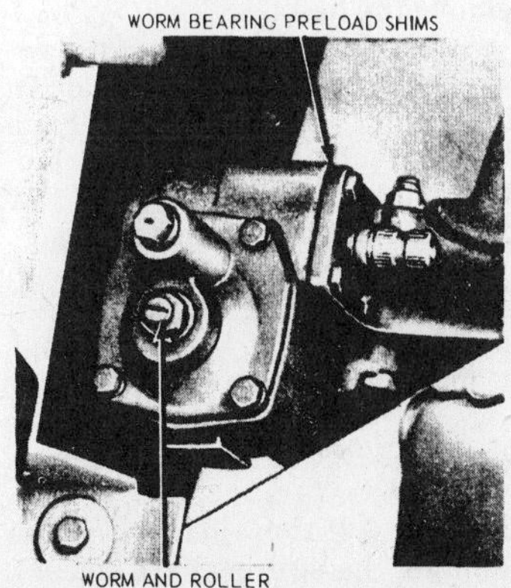

Steering gear adjustments
(© Ford Motor Co.)

Cross Shaft Roller and Worm Mesh Adjustment

1. Turn the steering wheel to the middle of its turning limits with the Pitman arm disconnected. The steering gear roller should be on the worm high spot.
2. Shake the Pitman arm sideways to determine the amount of clearance between the worm cross shaft roller. Movement of more than 1/32" indicates that the roller and worm mesh must be adjusted.
3. Loosen the adjusting screw lock nut and tighten the external cross shaft adjusting screw a small amount. Recheck the clearance by shaking the Pitman arm. Repeat until the clearance is correct. (Do not overtighten.) NOTE: The cross shaft roller and worm mesh adjustment may be done, using a spring scale tool, by measuring the amount of wheel pull as the external cross shaft adjusting screw is tightened. When the spring scale pull is between 7/8 and 1 1/8 ft. lbs., the adjustment is correct.
4. Tighten the Pitman arm attaching nut to 100-125 ft. lbs. The steering wheel nut (if loosened) should be tightened to 15-20 ft. lbs. torque.

Steering Gear Disassembly and Assembly

1. Remove steering gear oil seal, using a suitable puller.
2. Remove crosshaft, using an arbor to prevent bearings from dropping out.
3. Remove cover, shims and cover gasket.
4. Remove worm gear, thrust bearings and bearing cups.
5. Clean and inspect all parts, replace as necessary. NOTE: If either thrust bearing is excessively worn, replace them both.

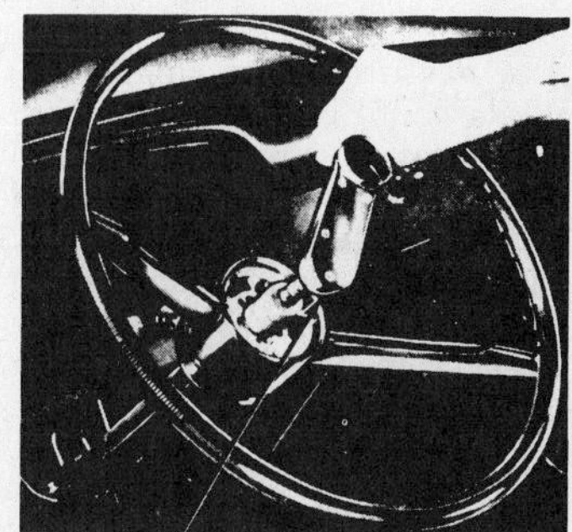

Checking steering gear preload
(© Ford Motor Co.)

6. Reassemble steering gear, using new oil seal.
7. Perform worm bearing and crosshaft roller and worm mesh adjustments.
8. Lubricate to specifications.

Ford Steering Gear—Recirculating Ball Type

Steering Worm and Sector Gear Adjustments

The ball nut assembly and the sector gear must be adjusted properly to maintain a minimum amount of steering shaft end play and a minimum amount of backlash between the sector gear and the ball nut. There are only two adjustments that may be done on this steering gear and they should be done as given below:

1. Disconnect the Pitman arm from the steering Pitman-to-idler arm rod.
2. Loosen the locknut on the sector shaft adjustment screw and turn the adjusting screw counterclockwise.
3. Measure the worm bearing preload by attaching an in. lbs. torque wrench to the steering wheel nut. With the steering wheel off center, note the reading required to rotate input shaft about 1½ turns either side of center. If the torque reading is not about 4-5 in. lbs., adjust the gear as given in the next step.
4. Loosen the steering shaft bearing adjuster lock nut and tighten or back off the bearing adjusting screw until the preload is within the specified limits.
5. Tighten the steering shaft bearing adjuster lock nut, and recheck the preload torque.
6. Turn the steering wheel slowly to either stop. Turn gently against the stop to avoid possible damage to the ball return guides. Then rotate the wheel 2¾ turns to center the ball nut.
7. Turn the sector adjusting screw clockwise until the proper torque (9-10 in. lbs.) is obtained that is necessary to rotate the worm gear past its center (high spot).
8. While holding the sector adjusting screw, tighten the sector screw adjusting locknut to the proper torque (32-40 ft. lbs.) and recheck the backlash adjustment.
9. Connect the Pitman arm to the steering arm-to-idler arm rod.

Steering Gear Disassembly and Assembly

1. Rotate the steering shaft three turns from either stop.
2. Remove the sector shaft adjusting screw locknut and the housing cover bolts and remove the sector shaft with the cover. Remove the cover from the shaft by turning the screw clockwise. Keep the shim with the screw.
3. Loosen the worm bearing adjuster nut and remove the adjuster assembly and the steering shaft upper bearing.
4. Carefully pull the steering shaft and ball nut from the housing, and remove the steering shaft lower bearing. Do not run the ball nut to either end of the worm gear to prevent damaging the ball return guides. Disassemble the ball nut only if there are signs of binding or tightness.
5. To disassemble the ball nut, remove the ball return guide clamp and the ball return guides from the ball nut. Keep ball nut clamp side up until ready to remove the ball bearings.
6. Turn the ball nut over and rotate the worm shaft from side to side until all 50 balls have dropped out into a clean pan. With all balls removed, the nut will slide off the wormshaft.
7. Remove the upper bearing cup from the bearing adjuster and the lower cup from the housing. It may be necessary to tap the housing or the adjuster on a wooden block to jar the bearing cups loose.
8. If the inspection shows bearing damage, the sector shaft bearing and the oil seal should be pressed out.
9. If the sector shaft bearing and oil seal was removed, press a new bearing and oil seal into the housing. Do not clean, wash, or soak seals in cleaning solvent. Apply the recommended steering gear lubricant to the housing and seals.
10. Install the bearing cup in the lower end of the housing and a bearing cup in the adjuster nut.
11. Install a new seal in the bearing adjuster if the old seal was removed.
12. Insert the ball guides into the holes in the ball nut, lightly tapping them, if necessary, to seat them.
13. Insert 25 balls into the hole in the top of each ball guide. If necessary, rotate the shaft slightly to distribute the balls evenly in the circuit.
14. Install the ball guide clamp, tightening the screws to the proper torque. Check that the worm shaft rotates freely.
15. Coat the threads of the steering shaft bearing adjuster, the housing cover bolts, and the sector adjusting screw with a suitable oil-resistant sealing compound. Do not apply sealer to female threads and do not get sealer on the steering shaft bearings.
16. Coat the worm bearings, sector shaft bearings, and gear teeth with steering gear lubricant.
17. Clamp the housing in a vise, with the sector shaft axis horizontal, and place the steering shaft lower bearing in its cup. Place the steering shaft and ball nut assemblies in the housing.

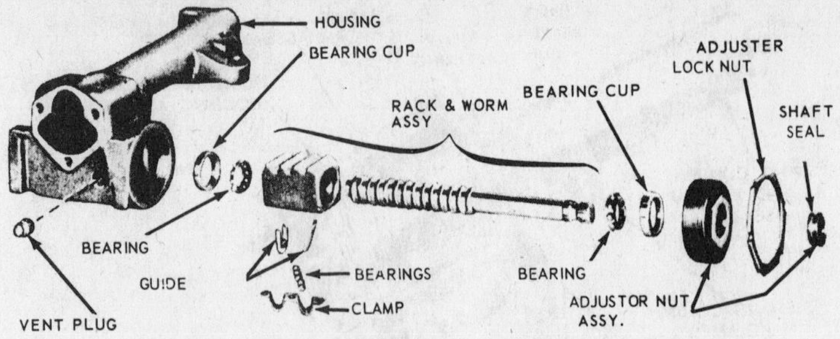

Steering shaft and related parts—Ford recirculating ball gear
(© Ford Motor Co.)

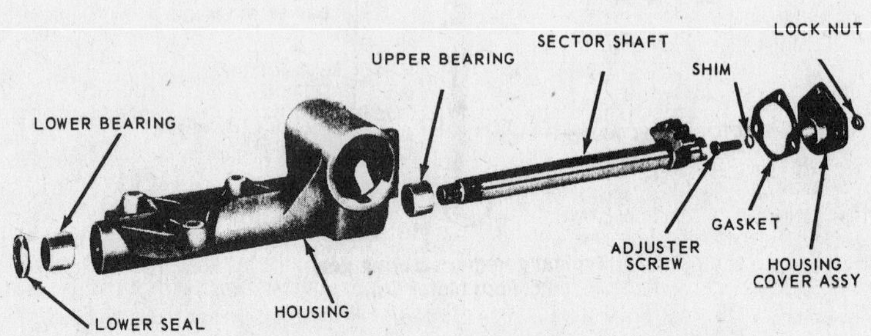

Sector shaft and housing—Ford recirculating ball gear
(© Ford Motor Co.)

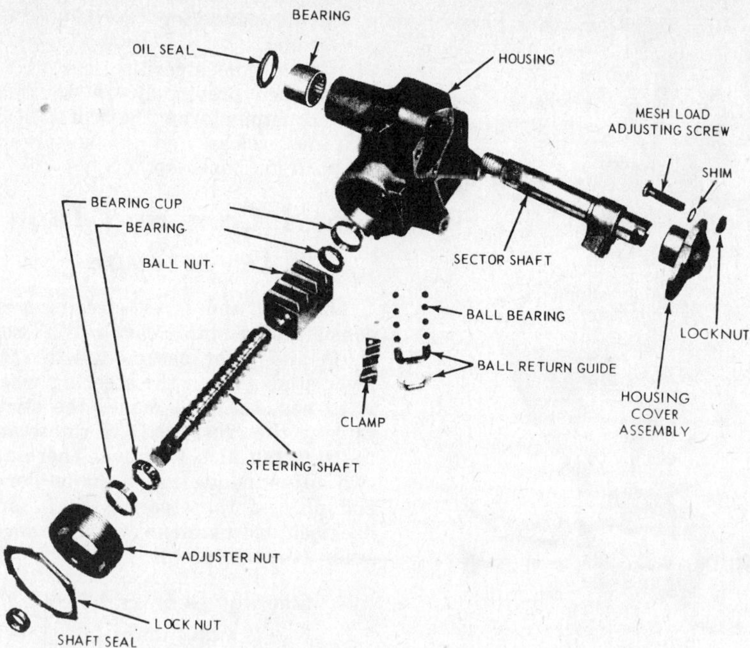

Saginaw recirculating ball type steering gear (© Ford Motor Co.)

18. Position the steering shaft upper bearing on top of the worm gear and install the steering shaft bearing adjuster, adjuster nut, and the bearing cup. Leave the nut loose.
19. Adjust the worm bearing preload according to the instructions given earlier.
20. Position the sector adjusting screw and adjuster shim, and check for a clearance of not more than 0.002″ between the screw head and the end of the sector shaft. If the clearance exceeds 0.002″, add enough shims to reduce the clearance to under 0.002″ clearance.
21. Start the sector shaft adjusting screw into the housing cover. Install a new gasket on the cover.
22. Rotate the steering shaft until the ball nut teeth mesh with the sector gear teeth, tilting the housing so the ball will tip toward the housing cover opening.
23. Lubricate the sector shaft journal and install the sector shaft and cover. With the cover moved to one side, fill the gear with lubricant (about 0.97 lb.). Push the cover and the sector shaft into place, and install the two top housing bolts. Do not tighten the bolts until checking to see that there is some lash between the ball nut and the sector gear teeth. Hold or push the cover away from the ball nut and tighten the bolts to the proper torque (30-40 ft. lbs.).
24. Loosely install the sector shaft adjusting screw lock nut and adjust the sector shaft mesh load as given earlier. Tighten the adjusting screw lock nut.

Saginaw Recirculating Ball Type

The steering gear is of the recirculating ball nut type. The ball nut, mounted on the worm gear, is driven by means of steel balls which circulate in helical grooves in both the worm and nut. Ball return guides attached to the nut serve to recirculate the two sets of balls in the grooves. As the steering wheel is turned to the right, the ball nut moves upward. When the wheel is turned to the left, the ball nut moves downward.

The sector teeth on the pinion shaft and the ball nut are designed so that they fit the tightest when the steering wheel is straight ahead. This mesh action is adjusted by an adjusting screw which moves the pinion shaft endwise until the teeth mesh properly. The worm bearing adjuster provides proper preloading of the upper and lower bearings.

Before doing the adjustment procedures given below, ensure that the steering problem is not caused by faulty suspension components, bad front end alignment, etc. Then, proceed with the following adjustments.

Worm Bearing Preload Adjustment

1. Disconnect the ball stud from the Pitman arm, and retighten the Pitman arm nut.
2. Loosen the Pitman shaft adjusting screw lock nut and back off adjusting screw a few turns.
3. Attach a spring scale to the steering wheel and measure the pull needed to move the steering wheel when off the high point. The pull should be between 1/3 and 3/8 ft. lbs.
4. To adjust the worm bearing, loosen the worm bearing adjuster lock nut with a brass drift and turn the adjuster screw until the proper pull is obtained. When adjustment is correct, tighten the adjuster lock nut, and recheck with the spring scale again.

Sector and Ball Nut Backlash Adjustment

1. After the worm bearing preload has been adjusted correctly, loosen the Pitman shaft adjusting screw lock nut and turn the Pitman shaft adjusting screw clockwise until a pull of 3/4 to 1 1/3 ft. lbs. is shown on the spring scale. When the adjustment is correct, tighten the Pitman shaft adjusting screw lock nut and recheck the adjustment.
2. Turn the steering wheel to the center of its turning limits (pitman arm disconnected). If the steering wheel is removed, the mark on the steering shaft should be at top center.
3. Connect the ball stud to the Pitman arm, tightening the attaching nut to the proper torque (115 ft. lbs.).

Steering Gear Disassembly and Assembly

1. After removing the steering gear from the truck, place the steering gear assembly in a bench vise.
2. Rotate the worm shaft until it is centered with the mark facing upward. Remove three cover attaching screws and the adjusting screw lock nut. Remove the cover and gasket by turning adjusting screw clockwise through the cover.
3. Remove the adjusting screw with its shim from the slot in the end of the pitman shaft. Remove the pitman shaft from the housing being careful not to damage the seal in the housing.
4. Loosen the worm bearing adjuster lock nut with a brass drift and remove the adjuster and bearing. Remove the bearing retainer with a screwdriver.
5. Remove the worm and shaft assembly with the ball nut assembly and bearing. Remove the ball nut return guide clamp by removing screws. Remove the guides, turn ball nut over, and remove the steel balls by rotating the shaft from side to side. After all the steel balls have

been removed, take the ball nut off the worm shaft.

6. Clean all parts in solvent. Inspect all bearings, bearing cups, bushings, seals, worm groove, and gear teeth for signs of wear, scoring, pitting, etc. If the pitman shaft bushings or seal, steering shaft seal, or upper and lower bearing cups need replacement, see the replacement procedures given below.
7. Remove the pitman shaft seal with a screwdriver or punch. If there is leakage around the threads of the bearing adjuster, apply a non-hardening sealer.
8. Remove faulty bushings from the pitman shaft with puller and slide hammer. Install new bushings, seating the inner end of the bushing flush with the inside surface of the housing.
9. Remove the steering shaft seal with a punch or screwdriver. Tap new seal in place, using a section of tubing to seat the seal.
10. Remove the upper or lower bearing cup from the worm bearing adjuster or steering gear housing. Install the new bearing cups.
11. Lubricate all seals, bushings, and bearings before installing into the steering gear assembly.
12. Position the ball nut on the worm shaft. Install the steel balls in the return guides and the ball nut, placing an equal number in each circuit of the ball nut. Install the return guide clamp and screws. CAUTION: Do not rotate the worm shaft while installing the steel balls since the balls may enter the crossover passage between the circuits, causing incorrect operation of the ball nut.
13. Place bearing on shaft above the worm gear, center ball nut on worm gear; then, slide the steering shaft, bearing, and ball nut into the housing. Do not damage the steering shaft seal in the housing.
14. Place the bearing in the worm adjuster, install the bearing retainer, and install the adjuster and lock nut on the housing, tightening it just enough to hold the bearing in place.
15. Install the pitman shaft adjusting screw and selective shim in the pitman shaft. Be sure there is no more than 0.002 in. of end play of the screw in the slot. If the end play is more than 0.002 in., install a new selective shim to get the proper clearance. Shims are available in four thicknesses: 0.063″, 0.064″, 0.067″, and 0.069″.
16. Install the pitman shaft and adjusting screw with the sector and ball nut correctly positioned.
17. Install the cover and gasket on the adjusting screw, turning screw counterclockwise until it extends through the cover from 5/8 to 3/4″. Install the cover attaching screws.
18. Tighten the pitman shaft adjusting screw so that the teeth on the shaft and the ball nut engage but do not bind. Final adjustment must be made later.
19. Install the pitman shaft seal.
20. Fill steering gear with a good quality chassis lubricant. Turn the steering gear from one extreme to the other to make sure it does not bind. Do not allow the ball nut to strike the ends of the ball races on the worm gear to avoid damaging the ball return guides.
21. Install the steering gear as described previously. Do the final adjustments on the worm bearing preload and the sector and ball nut backlash.

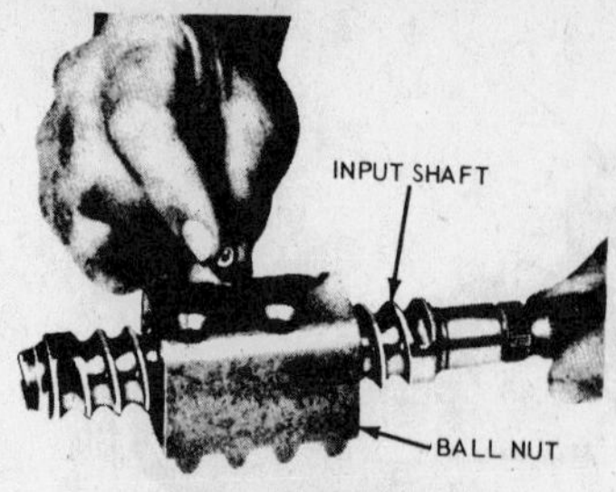

Loading ball nut
(© Ford Motor Co.)

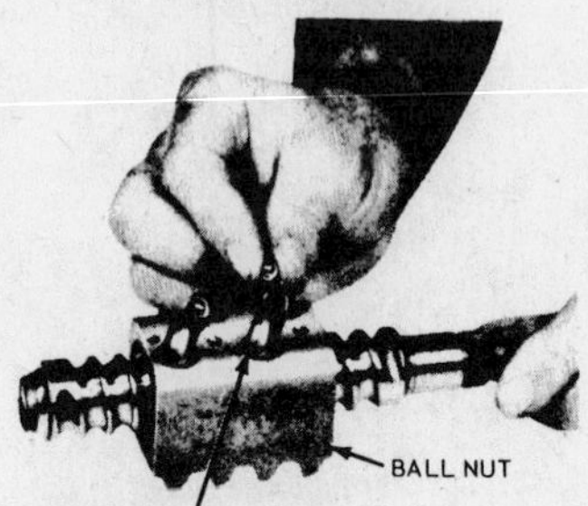

Loading ball return guides
(© Ford Motor Co.)

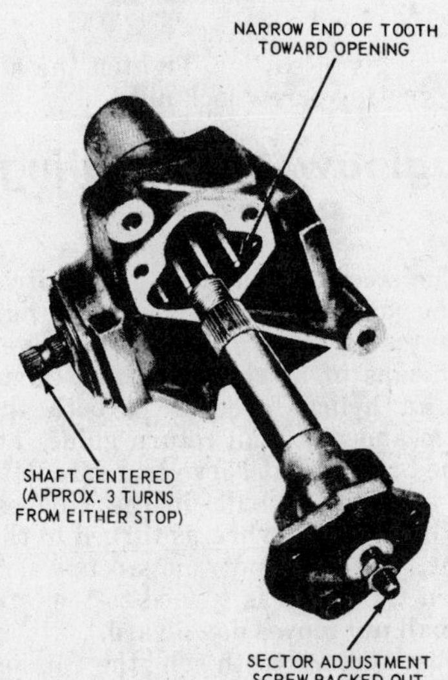

Installing sector shaft
(© Ford Motor Co.)

Ross Cam and Twin Lever Type

The cam and lever steering gear consists of a spiral cam and a cross shaft and lever assembly with two lever studs. When the steering wheel is turned, the cam moves the studs, causing the cross shaft to rotate and the steering arm to move. There are two adjustments that must be done: end play of the steering shaft, and backlash adjustment of the lever studs (tapered pins).

Steering Gear End-Play Adjustment

The steering gear is adjusted for minimum end-play by removing shims which are located between the upper cover and the steering gear housing. Before doing this adjustment, loosen the housing side cover adjusting screw to free the pins in the cam groove. Loosen the cover enough to remove one or more shims as required. As each shim is removed, retighten the cover and check the end-play. Adjustment should leave a slight drag in the steering gear but still allow it to turn easily. Replacement shims are available in three thicknesses: 0.002″, 0.003″, and 0.010″. (0.0508, 0.0762, and 0.254 mm).

Steering Gear Backlash Adjustment

The steering gear lever studs (tapered pins) backlash adjustment is done by turning the adjusting screw in until a slight drag is felt through the mid-position when turning the steering wheel slowly from one stop to the other. This adjustment is done when the steering wheel is centered in the straight ahead driving position. The cam groove is cut shallow in this area to provide a close adjustment of the pins. Do not adjust the screw in any other position of the steering gear.

Steering Gear Disassembly and Assembly

NOTE: When disassembling early production models, the line across the face of the steering arm and the end of the shaft should match. On later production models, blind splines on the lever shaft and in the steering gear arm engage, allowing correct positioning of the arm.

1. Remove the steering gear arm.

1 Nut
2 Lockwasher
3 Steering gear arm
4 Lever shaft oil seal
5 Outer housing bushing
6 Inner housing bushing
7 Filler plug
8 Cover and tube
9 Ball retaining ring
10 Cup
11 Ball (steel)
12 Tube and cam
13 Shims
14 Upper cover
15 Lockwasher
16 Bolt
17 Steering wheel
18 Horn button retainer
19 Horn button
20 Horn button cap
21 Nut
22 Spring
23 Spring seat
24 Bearing
25 Horn cable
26 Horn button spring
27 Spring cup
28 Steering column
29 Oil hole cover
30 Clamp
31 Adjusting screw
32 Nut
33 Bolt
34 Side cover
35 Gasket
36 Shaft and lever
37 Housing

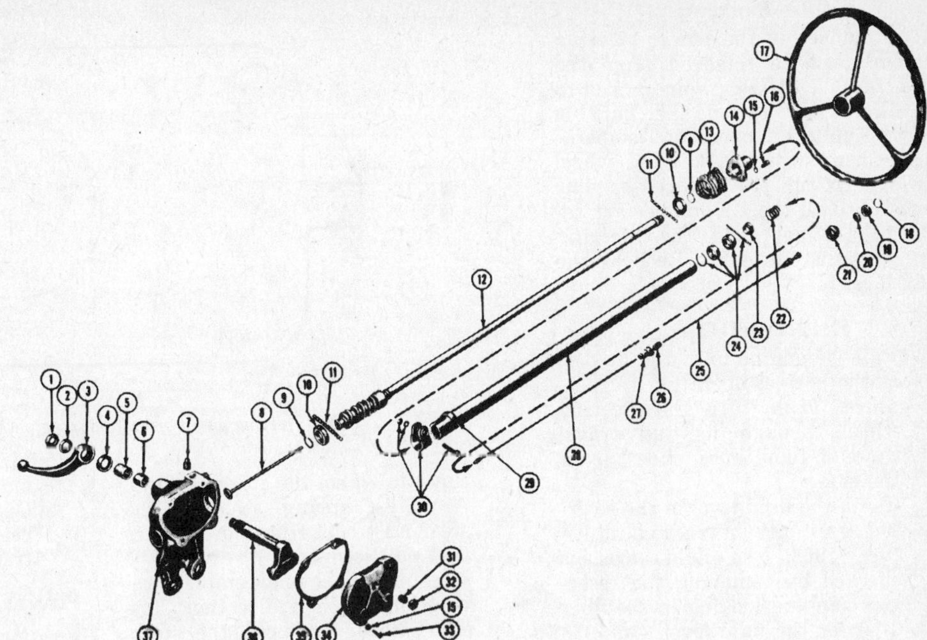

Ross cam and twin lever type steering gear (© American Motors Jeep Corp.)

2. Loosen the adjusting screw lock nut and unscrew the adjusting screw two turns.
3. Remove the side cover screws and washers. Remove the side cover and gasket.
4. Remove the lever shaft.
5. Remove the upper cover plate screws, the upper cover, and gasket.
6. Inspect all bearings, seals, cam grooves, etc. for wear, chipping, scoring and other damage. Replace all worn parts.
7. Assemble all parts to the wheel tube in the reverse order of disassembly. Assemble the cam, wheel tube, and bearing assembly and install in the housing, seating the lower bearing ball cup correctly in the housing. NOTE: New plastic retainer type cam bearings are available for Ross steering gears that replace, and are interchangeable with, the lock ring type cam bearings on gears equipped with early type cams.
8. With the adjusting shims installed in the housing, install the upper cover and adjust the cam bearings.
9. Install the lever shaft, gasket, and side cover on the housing. Set the adjusting screw for a minimum backlash of the studs in the cam groove, with the steering gear at the center point of travel.
10. Assemble the upper bearing spring and spring seat in the jacket tube, being sure the spring seat is positioned correctly. Install it with the long flange down against the bearing and not up inside the spring coil.
11. Install the steering gear assembly in the truck, reversing the removal procedure.
12. After installing the steering gear assembly in the truck, install the steering wheel temporarily and position the steering gear in the midposition (straight ahead). Do this by slowly turning the steering wheel from one stop to the other, then turning it to the middle of its range.
13. With the steering wheel held steady and the front wheels facing straight ahead, install the steering arm on the lever shaft, with the ball end down. If properly installed, the line across the face of the arm and the end of the shaft should match.

Power Steering Gears

General Information

The procedures for maintaining, adjusting, and repairing the power steering systems and components discussed in this chapter are to be done only after determining that the steering linkages and front suspension systems are correctly aligned and in good condition. All worn or damaged parts should be replaced before attempting to align the power steering systems. After correcting any condition that could affect the power steering, do the preliminary tests of the steering system components.

Preliminary Tests

Lubrication

Proper lubrication of the steering linkage and the front suspension components is very important for the proper operation of the steering systems of trucks equipped with power steering. Check the steering gear box for sufficient lubricant by removing the filler plug and checking the level. Add enough fluid gear oil S.A.E. 90 to bring the oil level to the filler plug hole if necessary.

CAUTION: Do not use a pressure gun to add fluid gear oil because the pressure will force the oil out of the steering gear box.

NOTE: The Dodge power steering systems use the same lubricant in the steering gear box and in the power steering pump reservoir.

Air Bleeding

Air bubbles in the power steering system must be removed from the fluid. Be sure the reservoir is filled to the proper level and the fluid is warmed up to the operating temperature. Then, turn the steering wheel through its full travel three or four times until all the air bubbles are removed. Do not hold the steering wheel against its stops. Recheck the fluid level.

Fluid Level Check

1. Run the engine until the fluid is at the normal operating temperature. Then, turn the steering wheel through its full travel three or four times, and shut off the engine.
2. Check the fluid level in the steering reservoir. On trucks built before 1968, the fluid level is checked by removing the reservoir cap and looking in the filler tube for the fluid level. On 1968 and later trucks, a dipstick is provided in the filler tube that shows the proper fluid level. If the fluid level is low, add enough fluid to raise the level to the Full mark on the dipstick or filler tube.

Pump Belt Check

1. Inspect the pump belt for cracks, glazing, or worn places. Using a belt tension gauge, check the belt tension for the proper range of adjustment. The amount of tension varies with the make of truck and the condition of the belt. New belts (those belts used less than 15 minutes) require a higher figure. The belt deflection method of adjustment may be used only if a belt tension gauge is not available. The belt should be adjusted for a deflection of 3 to ½″.

Fluid Leaks

Check all possible leakage points (hoses, power steering pump, or steering gear) for loss of fluid. Turn engine on and rotate the steering wheel from stop to stop several times. Tighten all loose fittings and replace any defective lines or valve seats.

Turning Effort

Check the turning effort required to turn the steering wheel after aligning the front wheels and inflating the tires to the proper pressure.

1. With the vehicle on dry pavement and the front wheel straight ahead, set the parking brake and turn the engine on.
2. After a short warm-up period for the engine, turn the steering wheel back and forth several times to warm the steering fluid.
3. Attach a spring scale to the steering wheel rim and measure the pull required to turn the steering wheel one complete revolution in each direction. The effort needed to turn the steering wheel should not exceed the limits specified.

NOTE: This test may be done with the steering wheel removed and a torque wrench applied on the steering wheel nut.

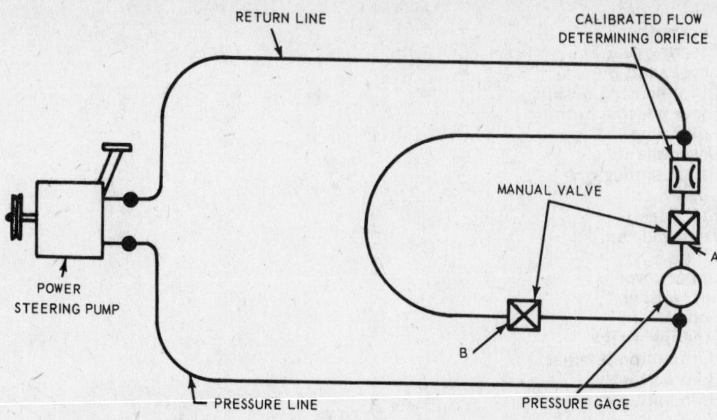

Power steering pump test circuit diagram (© Ford Motor Co.)

Power Steering Pump Flow

Since the power steering pump provides all the power assist in a power steering system, the pump must operate properly at all times for the system to work. After performing all the checks given above, the power steering pump may be tested for proper flow by the following procedure:

1. Disconnect the pressure and return lines at the power steering pump and connect the test pressure and return lines. The test lines are connected to a pressure gauge and two manual valves.
2. Open the two manual valves, connect a tachometer to the engine, and start the engine. Run the engine at idle speed until the reservoir fluid temperature reaches about 165-175 degrees Fahrenheit. This temperature must be maintained during the test. Manual valve B may be partially opened to create a back pressure of no more than 350 psi to aid the temperature rise. Reservoir fluid must be at the proper level.
3. After the engine and the reservoir fluid are sufficiently warmed up, close the manual valve B. Note the pressure gauge reading. It must be a minimum of 620 psi.
4. If the pressure reading is below the minimum acceptable pressure, the pump is defective and must be repaired. If the pressure reading is at or above the minimum value, the pump is normal. Open manual valve B and proceed to the pump fluid pressure test.

Power Steering Pump Fluid Pressure Test

1. Keep the lines and pressure gauge connected as in the Pump Flow Test.
2. With manual valve A and B opened fully, run the engine at the proper idle speed. Then, close manual valve A and manual valve B, in that order. CAUTION: Do not keep both valves closed for more than 5 seconds since the fluid temperature will increase abnormally and cause unnecessary wear to the pump.
3. With both manual valves closed, the pressure reading should be as given in the specifications. If the pressure is below the minimum reading, the pump is defective and must be repaired. If the pressure reading is at or above the minimum reading, the pump is normal and the power steering gear or power assist control valve must be checked.

Checking the Oil Flow and Pressure Relief Valve in the Pump Assembly

When the wheels are turned hard right, or hard left, against the stops, the oil flow and pressure relief valves come into action. If these valves are working and are not stuck there should be a slight buzzing noise.

CAUTION: Do not hold the wheels in the extreme position for over three or four seconds because, if the pressure relief valve is not working, the pressure could get high enough to damage the system.

Power Steering Hose Inspection

1. Inspect both the input and output hoses of the power steering pump for worn spots, cracks, or signs of leakage. Replace hose if defective, being sure to recon-

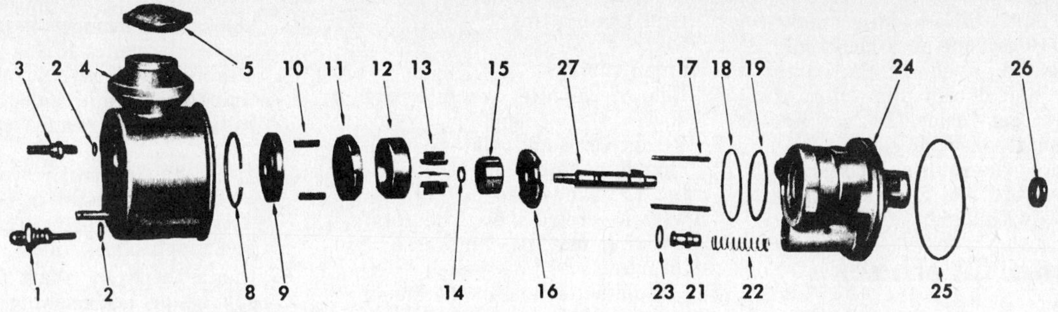

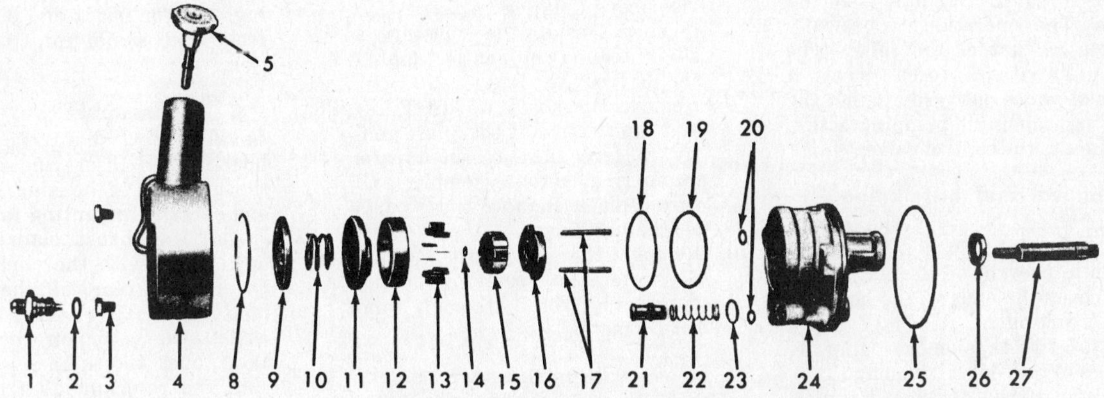

Vane type power steering pumps (© G.M.C.)

1 Union
2 Union "O" ring seal
3 Mounting studs
4 Reservoir
5 Dip stick and cover
8 End plate retaining ring
9 End plate
10 Spring
11 Pressure plate
12 Pump ring
13 Vanes
14 Drive shaft retaining ring
15 Rotor
16 Thrust plate
17 Dowel pins
18 End plate "O" ring
19 Pressure plate "O" ring
20 Mounting stud square ring seals
21 Flow control valve
22 Flow control valve spring
23 Flow control valve square ring seal
24 Pump housing
25 Reservoir "O" ring seal
26 Shaft seal
27 Shaft

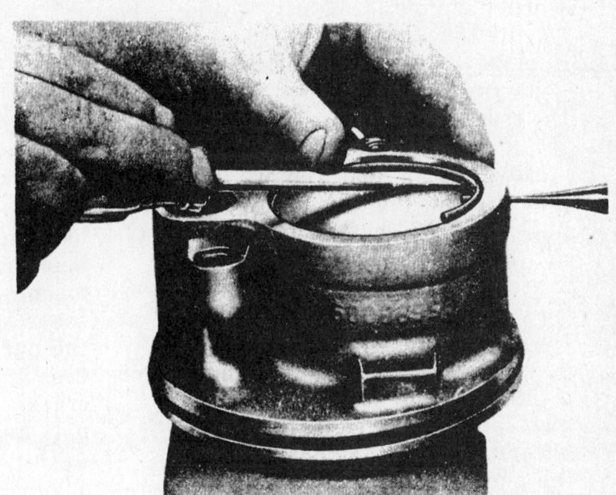

Removing end plate ring (© G.M.C.)

nect the replacement hose properly. Many power steering hoses are identified as to where they are to be connected by special means, such as fittings that will only fit on the correct pump fitting, or hoses of special lengths.

Test Driving Truck to Check the Power Steering

When test driving to check power steering, drive at a speed between 15 and 20 mph. Make several turns in each direction. When a turn is completed, the front wheels should return to the straight ahead position with very little help from the driver.

If the front wheels fail to return as they should and yet the steering linkage is free, well oiled and properly adjusted, the trouble is probably due to misalignment of the power cylinder or improper adjustment of the spool valve.

The power steering oil pump supplies all the power assist used in power steering systems of all designs. There are various designs of oil pumps used by the truck manufacturers but all pumps supply power to operate the steering systems with the least effort. All power steering pumps have a reservoir tank built onto the oil pump. These pumps are driven by belts turned by pulleys on either the engine, the rear of the generator, or the front of the crankshaft.

During operation of the engine at idle speed, there is provision for the power steering pump to supply more fluid pressure. During driving speeds or when the truck is moving straight ahead, less pressure is needed and the excess is relieved through a pressure relief and flow control valve. The pressure relief part of the valve is inside the flow control and is basically the same for all pumps. The flow control valve regulates, or controls, the constant flow of fluid from the pump as it varies with the demands of the steering gear. The pressure relief valve limits the hydraulic pressure built up when the steering gear is turned against its stops.

During pump disassembly, make sure all work is done on a clean surface. Clean the outside of the pump thoroughly and do not allow dirt of any kind to get inside. Do not immerse the shaft oil seal in solvent.

If replacing the rotor shaft seal, be extremely careful not to scratch sealing surfaces with tools.

Pump Overhaul

Vane Type Power Steering Pump

The vane type power steering pump is used in Saginaw steering systems. The operation is basically the same as that of the roller type pumps. Centrifugal force moves a number of vanes outward against the pump ring, causing a pumping action of the fluid to the control valve.

Removal and Installation

1. Disconnect hoses at the pump, securing them in a raised position to prevent oil drainage. Cap or cover the ends of the hoses to keep dirt out.
2. Install two caps on the pump fittings to prevent oil drainage.
3. Loosen the bracket-to-pump mounting nuts, move pump toward engine slightly, and remove the pump drive belt.
4. Remove the bracket-to-pump bolts and remove the pump from the truck.
5. While holding the drive pulley steady, loosen and remove the pulley attaching nut. Slide the pulley off the shaft. NOTE: Do not hammer the pulley off the shaft.
6. To install the pump on the truck, reverse the removal procedure. Always use a new pulley nut, tightening it to 35-45 ft. lbs. torque.
7. After reconnecting the hoses to the pump, fill the reservoir with fluid and bleed the pump of air by turning the drive pulley counterclockwise (as viewed from the front) until air bubbles do not appear.
8. Install the pump drive belt over the pulley, move the pump against the belt until tight enough, then tighten the mounting bolts and nuts.
9. Bleed the air from the system.

Disassembly

1. Clean the outside of the pump in a non-toxic solvent before disassembling.
2. Mount the pump in a vise, being careful not to squeeze the front hub too tight.
3. Remove the union and seal.
4. Remove the reservoir retaining studs and separate the reservoir from the housing.
5. Remove the mounting bolt and union O-rings.
6. Remove the filter and filter cage; discard the element.
7. Remove the end plate retaining ring by compressing the retaining ring and then prying it out with a screwdriver. The retaining ring may be compressed by inserting a small punch in the 1/8" diameter hole in the housing and pushing in until the ring clears the groove.
8. Remove the end plate. The end plate is spring-loaded and should rise above the housing level. If it is stuck inside the housing, a slight rocking or gentle tapping should free the plate.
9. Remove the shaft woodruff key and tap the end of the shaft gently to free the pressure plate, pump ring, rotor assembly, and thrust plate. Remove these parts as one unit.
10. Remove the end plate O-ring. Separate the pressure plate, pump ring, rotor assembly, and thrust plate.

Inspection

Clean all metal parts in a non-toxic solvent and inspect them as given below:

1. Check the flow control valve for free movement in the housing bore. If the valve is sticking, see if there is dirt or rough sport in the bore.
2. Check the cap screw in the end of the flow control valve for looseness. Tighten if necessary being careful not to damage the machined surfaces.
3. Inspect the pressure plate and the pump plate surfaces for flatness and check that there are no cracks or scores in the parts. Do not mistake the normal wear marks for scoring.
4. Check the vanes in the rotor assembly for free movement and that they were installed with the radiused edge toward the pump ring.
5. If the flow control valve plunger is defective, install a new part. The valve is factory calibrated and supplied as a unit.
6. Check the drive shaft for worn splines, breaks, bushing material pick-up, etc.
7. Replace all rubber seals and O-rings removed from the pump.
8. Check the reservoir, studs, casting, etc. for burrs and other defects that would impair operation.

Assembly

1. Install a new shaft seal in the housing and insert the shaft at the hub end of housing, splined end entering mounting face side.
2. Install the thrust plate on the dowel pins with the ported side facing the rear of the pump housing.
3. Install the rotor on the pump shaft over the splined end. Be sure the rotor moves freely on the splines. Countersunk side must be toward the shaft.
4. Install the shaft retaining ring. Install the pump ring on the dowel pins with the rotation arrow toward the rear of the pump housing. Rotation is clockwise as seen from the pulley.
5. Install the vanes in the rotor slots with the radius edge towards the outside.
6. Lubricate the outside diameter and chamfer of the pressure plate with petroleum jelly so as not to damage the O-ring and install the plate on the dowel pins with the ported face toward the pump ring. Seat the pressure

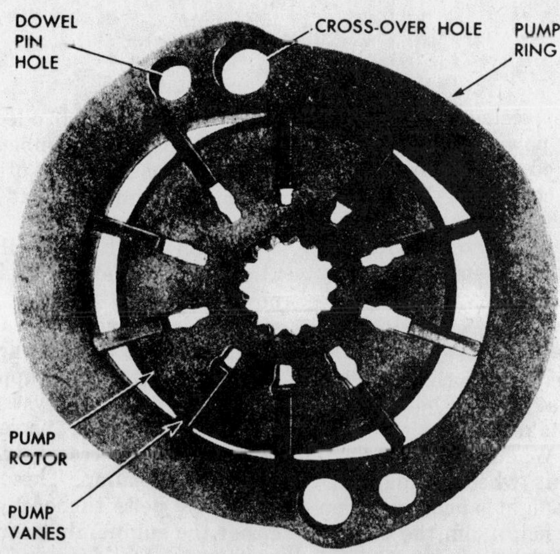

Correct vane assembly (© G.M.C.)

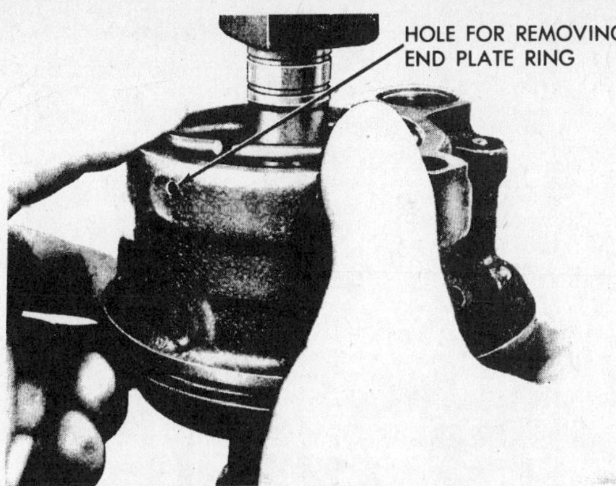

Installing end plate retaining ring (© G.M.C.)

Installing flow control valve (© G.M.C.)

plate by placing a large socket on top of the plate and pushing down with the hand.

7. Install the pressure plate spring in the center groove of the plate.
8. Install the end plate O-ring. Lubricate the outside diameter and chamfer of the end plate with petroleum jelly so as not to damage the O-ring and install the end plate in the housing, using an arbor press. Install the end plate retaining ring while pump is in the arbor press. Be sure the ring is in the groove and the ring gap is positioned properly.
9. Install the flow control spring and plunger, hex head screw end in bore first. Install the filter cage, new filter stud seals and union seal.
10. Place the reservoir in the normal position and press down until the reservoir seats on the housing. Check the position of the stud seals and the union seal.
11. Install the studs, union, and drive shaft woodruff key. Support the shaft on the opposite side of the key when tapping the key into place.

Roller Type Power Steering Pump

The roller type power steering pump is designed similar to other constant flow centrifugal force pumps. A star-shaped rotor forces 12 steel rollers against the inside surface of a cam ring. As the rollers follow the eccentric pattern of the cam ring, oil is drawn into the inlet ports and exhausted through the discharge ports while the rollers are moved into vee shaped cavities of the rotor, forcing oil into the high pressure circuit. A flow control valve permits a regulated amount of oil to return to the intake side of the pump when excess output is produced during high speed operation. This reduces the power needs to drive the pump and minimizes temperature build-up.

The flow control valve used in one make of pump is a two-stage valve. Oil under high pressure passes through two holes into a metering circuit located in a sealed oil passage. At low speed, about 2.7 gpm. passes to the gear. As speed increases and the valve moves, excess oil is bypassed to the inlet and the valve blocks flow through one hole. This drops the oil flow to about 1.6 gpm. at high speeds.

When steering conditions produce excessive pressure needs (such as turning the wheels against the stops), the pressure built up in the steering gear exerts force on the spring end of the flow control valve.

This end of the valve contains the pressure relief valve. High pressure lifts the relief valve ball from its seat, allowing oil to flow through a trigger orifice located in the front land of the flow control valve. This reduces pressure on the spring end of the valve which then opens and allows the oil to return to the intake side of the pump. This action limits the maximum pressure output of the pump to a safe level. Normally, the pressure needs of the pump are below the maximum limits, causing the pressure relief ball and the flow control valve to remain closed.

Removal

1. Loosen the pump mounting and locking bolts and remove the belt.
2. Disconnect both hoses at the pump. Cap and tie the hoses out of the way. Cap the hose fittings on the pump.
3. Remove the mounting and locking bolts, the pump and brackets from the truck.

Installation

1. Position the pump and brackets on the engine and install the mounting and locking bolts.
2. Install the drive belt and adjust for the proper tension.
3. Connect the pressure and return hoses, using a new pressure hose O-ring.
4. Fill the pump reservoir to the top of the filler neck with power steering fluid.
5. Start the engine and turn the steering wheel several times from stop to stop to bleed the pump of air. Check the oil level and add fluid if necessary.

NOTE: When checking the oil level, see that the level is as follows: engine cold-bottom of filler tube; engine hot-half way up filler tube.

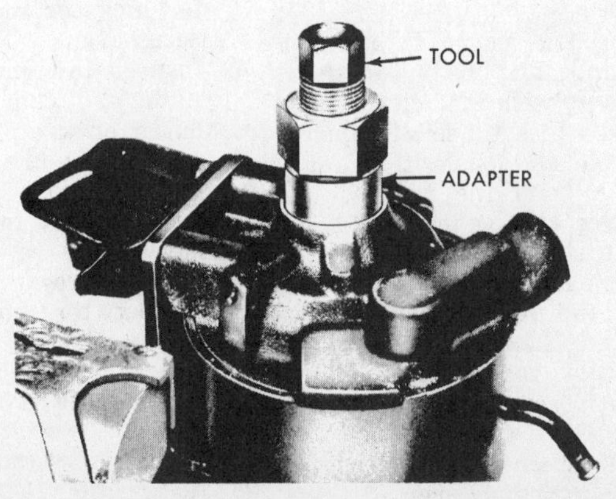

Removing shaft seal (© Chrysler Corp.)

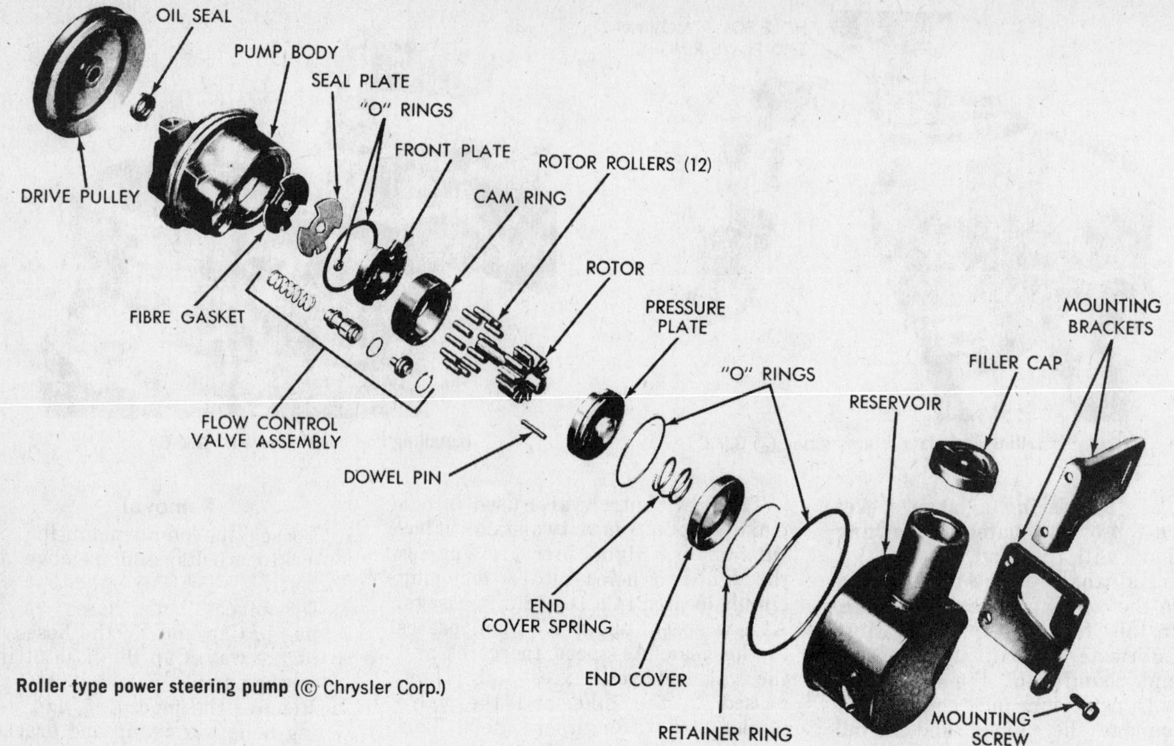

Roller type power steering pump (© Chrysler Corp.)

Disassembly

1. Remove pump from engine, drain reservoir, and clean outside of pump. Clamp the pump in a vise at the mounting bracket.
2. Remove the drive pulley.
3. Remove the shaft seal by installing the seal remover adapter over the end of the drive shaft with the large end toward the pump. Place the seal remover tool over the shaft and through the adapter. Then, screw the tapered thread well into the metal portion of the seal. Tighten the large drive nut and remove the seal.
4. Remove the pump from the vise and remove the bracket mounting bolts. Remove the bracket.
5. Remove the reservoir and place the pump in a soft-faced vise with the shaft down. Discard the mounting bolt and the reservoir O-rings.
6. Move the end cover retaining ring around until one end of the ring lines up with the hole in the pump body. Insert a small punch in the hole and push it in far enough to bend the ring so a screwdriver can be inserted between the ring and the housing. Remove the ring.
7. Remove the end cover and spring from the housing. It may be necessary to tap the cover gently to loosen it in the housing.
8. Remove the pump from the vise and turn the pump over so the rotating group may come out of the housing. Tap the end of the drive shaft to loosen these parts. Lift the pump body off the rotating group. Check that the seal plate is removed from the bottom of the housing bore.
9. Discard the O-rings from the pressure plate and end cover.
10. Remove the snap-ring, bore plug, flow control valve and spring from the housing. Discard the O-ring. If necessary to dismantle the flow control valve for cleaning, see the procedure for disassembly.

Inspection

1. Remove the clean out plug with an Allen wrench.
2. Wash all metal parts in clean, non-toxic solvent. Blow out all passages with compressed air and air dry all cleaned parts.
3. Inspect the drive shaft for excessive wear and the seal area for nicks or scoring. Replace if necessary.
4. Inspect the end plates, rollers, rotor and cam ring for nicks, burrs, or scratches. If any of the components are damaged enough to cause poor operation of the pump, all the interior parts may have to be replaced to prevent later failures.
5. Inspect the pump body drive shaft bushing for excessive wear. Replace the pump body and bushing as one assembly.

Assembly

1. Install the ⅛" pipe clean out plug, tightening it to 80 in. lbs. torque.
2. Place the pump body on a clean flat surface and install a new shaft seal into the bore.
3. Install a new end cover O-ring into the groove in the pump bore. Be sure to lubricate the O-ring with power steering fluid before installing it.
4. Lubricate and install a new O-ring in the groove on the pump body where the reservoir fits snugly.
5. Install the brass seal plate to the bottom of the housing bore. Align the notch in the seal plate with the dowel pin hole in the housing.
6. Carefully install the front plate with the chamfered edge down in the pump bore. Align the index notch in the plate with the dowel pin hole in the housing. CAUTION: Be extremely careful to align the dowel pin hole properly. Pump can be completely assembled with the dowel pin not seated properly in the hole.
7. Place the dowel pin the cam ring and position the cam ring inside the pump bore. Notch in the cam ring must be facing up (away from the pulley end of pump housing). If the cam ring has two notches, one machined and one cast, install the cam ring with the machined notch up. Check the amount of dowel pin extending above the cam ring surface. If more than 3/16" is showing, the dowel pin is not seated in the index hole in the

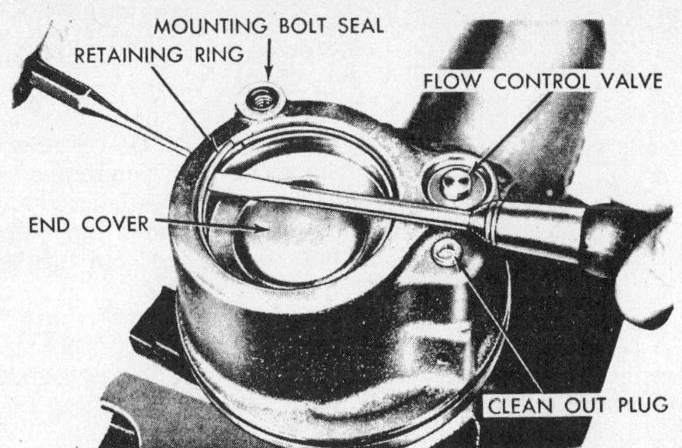

Removing end cover retaining ring (© Chrysler Corp.)

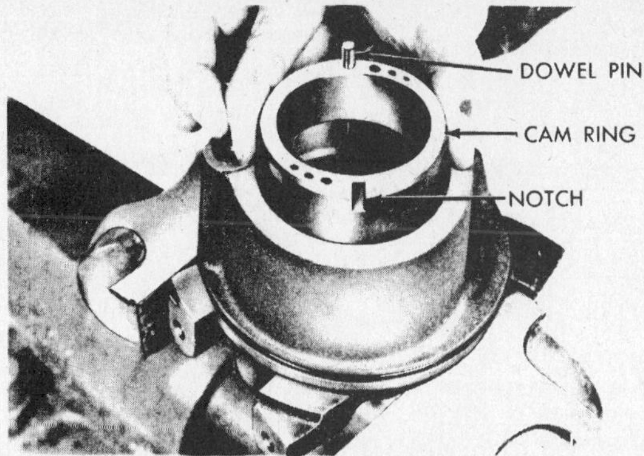

Installing cam ring (© Chrysler Corp.)

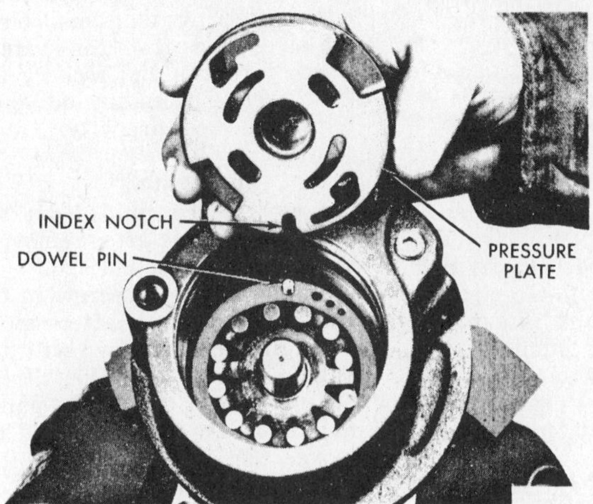

Installing pressure plate (© Chrysler Corp.)

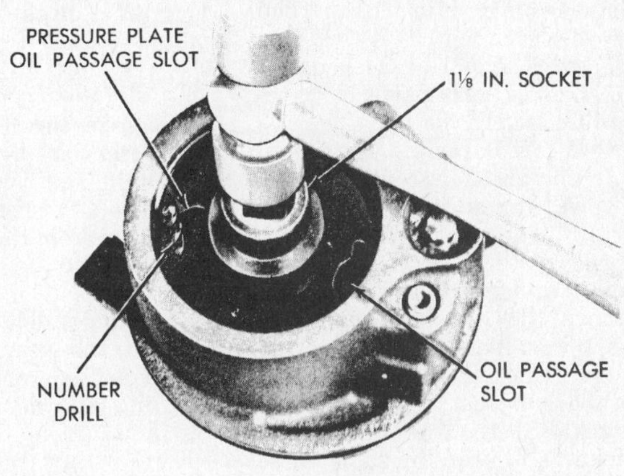

Seating pressure plate (© Chrysler Corp.)

housing.

8. Install the rotor and shaft in the cam ring and carefully install the 12 steel rollers in the cavities of the rotor. Lubricate the rotor, rollers, and the inside surface of the cam ring with power steering fluid. Rotate the shaft by hand to be sure all the rollers are seated parallel with the shaft and are not sticking or binding.
9. Position the pressure plate by carefully aligning the index notch on the plate with the dowel pin and inserting a clean drill (number 13 to 16) in the cam ring oil hole next to the dowel pin notch until it bottoms on the housing floor.
10. Lubricate and install a new O-ring on the pressure plate. Position the pressure plate in the pump bore so that the dowel pin is in the index notch on the plate and the drill extends through the oil passage in the pressure plate. Seat the pressure plate on the cam ring using a clean 1⅛″ socket and a soft-faced hammer to tap it gently. Remove the drill and inspect the plate at both oil passage slots to be sure that the plate is squarely seated on the cam ring.
11. Place the large coil spring over the raised portion of the installed pressure plate.
12. Place the end cover, lip edge facing up, over the spring. Press the end cover down below the retaining ring groove. Install the retaining ring in the groove. Be sure the end cover chamfer is squarely seated against the snap-ring.
13. Replace the reservoir mounting bolt seal.
14. Lubricate the flow control valve assembly with power steering fluid and insert the valve spring and valve in the bore. Install a new O-ring on the bore plug, lubricate with fluid, and carefully install in the bore. Install the snap-ring with the sharp edge up. Do not depress the bore plug more than 1/16″ below the snap-ring groove.
15. Place the reservoir on the pump body and visually align the mounting bolt hole. Tap the reservoir down on the pump with a plastic-faced hammer.
16. Remove the pump from the vise and install the mounting brackets with the mounting bolts on the pump. Tighten the bolts to 18 ft. lbs. torque.
17. Install the drive pulley by using the installer tool as follows: place the pulley on the end of the shaft and thread the installer tool into the ⅜″ threaded hole in the end of the shaft. Put the installer shaft in a vise and tighten the drive nut against the thrust bearing, pressing the pulley on the shaft until it is flush. Do not try to press the pulley on the shaft without the special installer tool since the pump interior will be damaged by any other installation procedure. A small amount of drive shaft end play will be seen when the pulley is installed. This end play is necessary and will be minimized by a thin coat of oil between the rotor and the end plates when the pump is operating.
18. Install the pump assembly on the engine, install the drive belt and hoses (use new O-ring on pressure hose), and check for leaks.

Flow Control Valve Disassembly

1. After removing the pump from the engine and the reservoir from the pump, remove the snap-ring and plug from the flow bore. Discard the O-ring.
2. Depress the control valve against the spring pressure and allow the valve to spring out of

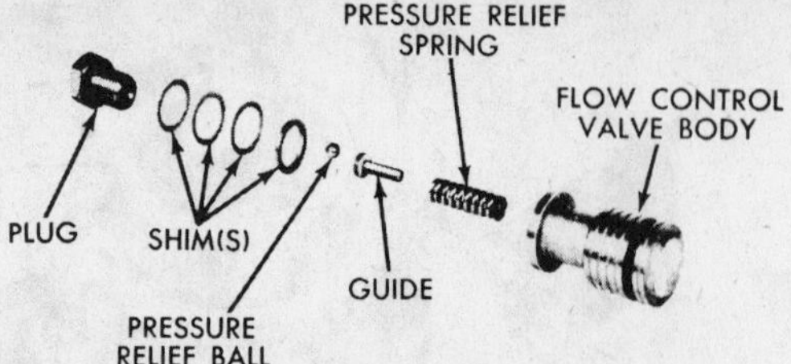

Flow control valve (© Chrysler Corp.)

the bore. If the valve is stuck in the bore or it did not come out of the bore far enough, it may be necessary to tap the housing lightly to remove it.

3. If the valve has dirt or foreign particles on it or in its bore, the rest of the pump needs cleaning. The hoses should be flushed and the steering gear valve body reconditioned. If the valve bore is badly scored, replace the pump body and the flow control valve.
4. Remove any nicks or burrs by gently rubbing the valve with crocus cloth. Clamp the valve land in a vise with soft-jaws and remove the hex head ball seat and shims. Note the number and gauge (thickness) of the shims on the ball seat. They must be re-installed for the same shim thickness to keep the same value of relief pressure.
5. Remove the valve from the vise and remove the pressure relief ball, guide, and spring.

Flow Control Valve Assembly

1. Insert the spring, guide and pressure relief ball in the end of the flow control valve.
2. Install the hex head plug using the exact number and thickness shims that were removed. Tighten the plug to 80 in. lbs. torque.
3. Lubricate the valve with power steering fluid and insert the flow control valve spring and valve in the housing bore. Install a new O-ring on the bore plug, lubricate with fluid and carefully install into the bore. Install the snap-ring. Do not depress the bore plug more than 1/16″ beyond the snap-ring groove.

Slipper Type Power Steering Pump

The slipper type power steering pump is a belt-driven constant displacement assembly that uses a number of spring-loaded slippers in the pump rotor to force oil from the inlet side to the flow control valve. Openings in the metering pin allow a flow of about two gpm. of fluid to the steering gear before the flow control valve directs the excess fluid to the inlet side of the pump again. Maximum pressure in the pump is limited by the pressure relief valve which opens when the oil pressure exceeds the maximum limits.

The slipper type power steering pump discussed in this section is used on Ford trucks and is called the Ford-Thompson power steering pump.

Removal and Installation

1. Drain the fluid from the pump reservoir by disconnecting the fluid return hose at the pump. Then, disconnect the pressure hose from the pump.
2. Remove the mounting bolts from the front of the pump. On eight cylinder engines, there is a nut on the rear of the pump that must be removed. After removing all the mounting bolts and nuts from the pump, move the unit inward to loosen the belt tension and remove the belt from the pulley. Then remove the pump from the truck.
3. To reinstall the pump after maintenance or repair, position the pump on the mounting bracket and loosely install the mounting bolts and nuts. Put the drive belt over the pulley and move the pump outward against the belt until the proper belt tension is obtained. Measure the belt tension with a gauge for the proper adjustment. Only in cases where a belt tension gauge is not available should the belt deflection method be used. If the belt deflection method is used, be sure to check the belt with a tension gauge at the earliest time since the deflection method is not accurate.
4. Tighten the mounting bolts and nuts to the specified torque limits.
5. Tighten the pressure hose fitting hex nut to the proper torque. Then connect the pressure hose to the pump and tighten the hose nut to the proper torque.
6. Connect the fluid return hose to the pump and tighten the clamp.
7. Fill the pump reservoir with power steering fluid and bleed the air bubbles from the system.
8. Check for leaks and recheck the fluid level. If necessary, add fluid to raise the level properly.

Disassembly

1. Drain as much fluid from the pump as possible after removing the pump from the truck.
2. Install a 3/8-16″ capscrew in the end of the pump shaft to avoid damaging the shaft end with the pulley remover tool. Install the pulley remover tool on the pulley hub and place the pump and remover tool in a vise. Hold the pump steady and turn the tool nut counterclockwise to draw the pulley off the shaft. The pulley must be removed without in and out pressure on the pump shaft to avoid damaging the internal thrust washers.
3. Remove the pump reservoir by installing the pump in a holding fixture with an adapter plate in a vise with the reservoir facing up.
4. Remove the outlet fitting hex nut and any other attaching parts from the reservoir case.

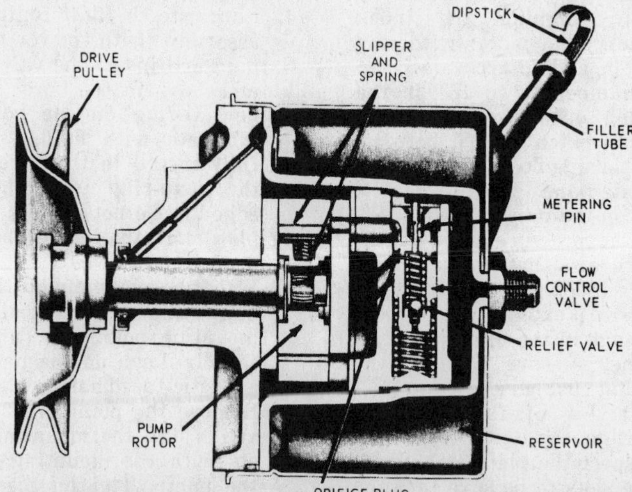

Ford Thompson power steering pump, sectional view (© Ford Motor Co.)

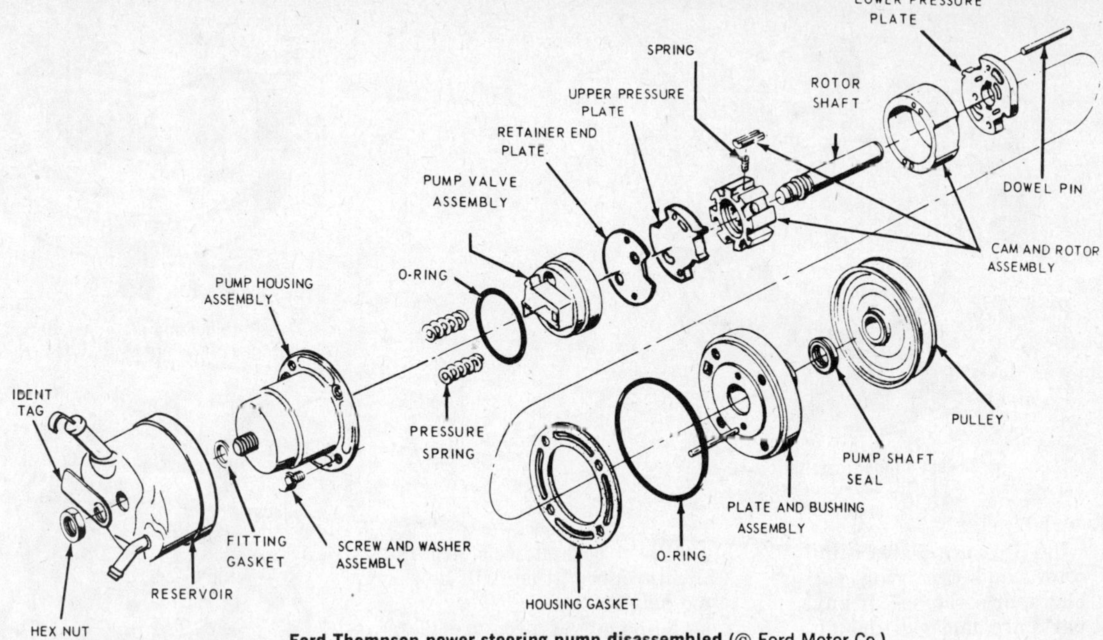

Ford Thompson power steering pump disassembled (© Ford Motor Co.)

5. Invert the pump so the reservoir is now facing down. Using a wooden block, remove the reservoir by tapping around the flange until the reservoir is loose. Remove the reservoir O-ring seal and the outlet fitting gasket from the pump.
6. Again invert the pump assembly in the vise, remove the pump housing holding bolts and the pump housing.

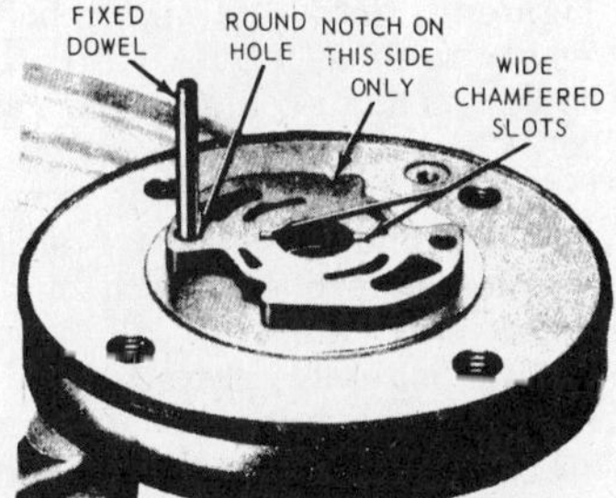

Lower pressure plate installed (© Ford Motor Co.)

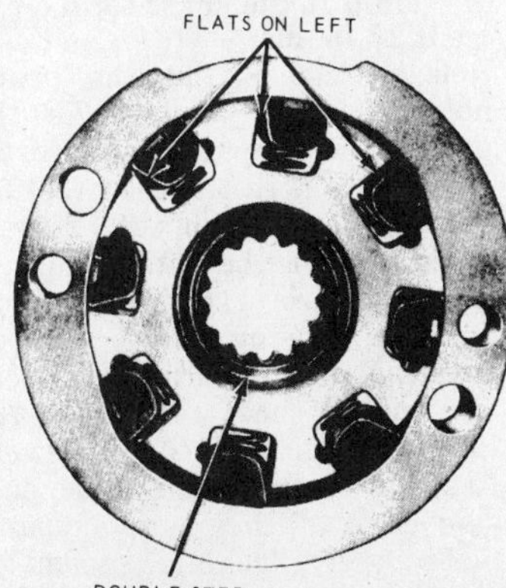

Correct slipper installation—Ford (© Ford Motor Co.)

7. Remove the housing cover, the O-ring seal and the pressure springs from inside the pump housing. Remove the pump cover gasket and discard it.
8. Remove the retainer end plate and upper pressure plate. In some pumps, the end plate and the upper pressure plate are made as one unit.
9. Remove the loose fitting dowel pin. Be careful not to bend the fixed dowel pin which remains in the housing plate assembly.
10. Remove the rotor assembly being careful not to let the slippers and springs fall out of the rotor. It may not be necessary to disassemble the rotor assembly unless the lower pressure plate, housing plate, rotor shaft and/or seal is to be replaced. However, the rotor assembly may be disassembled by removing the slippers and springs from the cam ring.
11. Remove any rust, dirt, burrs, or scoring from the pulley end of the rotor shaft before removing the shaft from the housing plate. The shaft must come out without restrictions to avoid scoring or damaging the bushing. Remove the pump rotor shaft.
12. Remove the lower pressure plate.
13. Remove the rotor shaft seal after first wrapping a piece of 0.005" shim stock around the shaft and pushing it into the inside of the seal until it touches the bushing. With a sharp tool, pierce the seal body and pry the seal out. Do not damage the bushing, housing, or the shaft. Install a new seal using a soft-faced hammer.
14. If the pump has a flow control valve, disassemble according to instructions given in the section on the roller type power steering pump.

Inspection

1. Wash all metal parts in clean, non-toxic solvent. Blow out all oil passages with compressed air and air dry all cleaned parts.
2. Inspect the drive shaft for excessive wear and seal area for nicks or scoring. Replace if necessary.

Cam and rotor installation (© Ford Motor Co.)

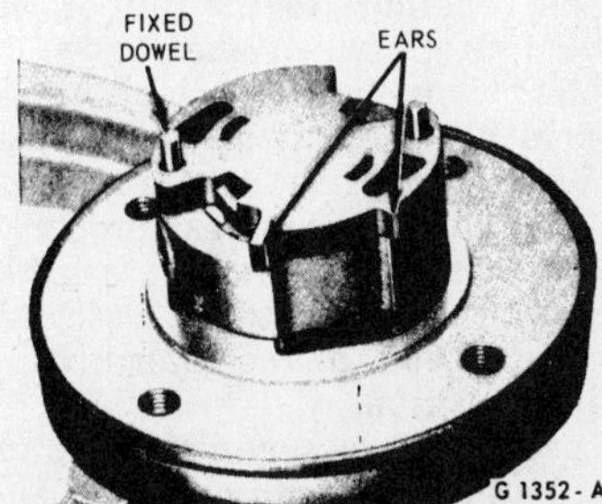

Upper pressure plate installation (© Ford Motor Co.)

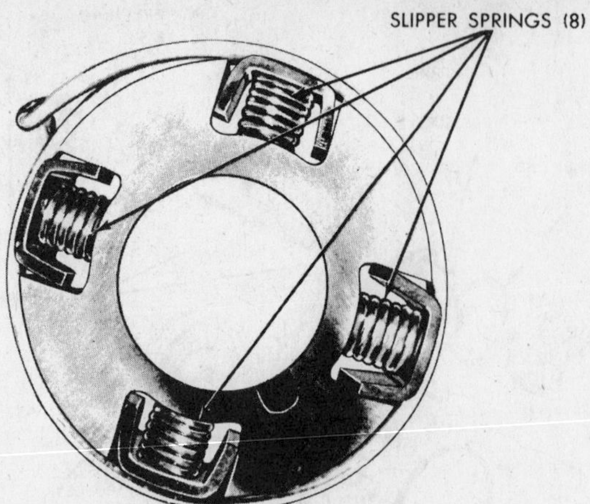

Correct slipper installation—Dodge
(© Chrysler Corp.)

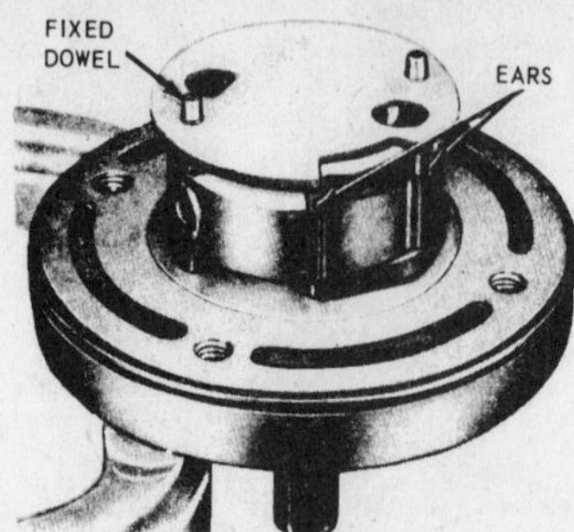

Retainer end plate installation
(© Ford Motor Co.)

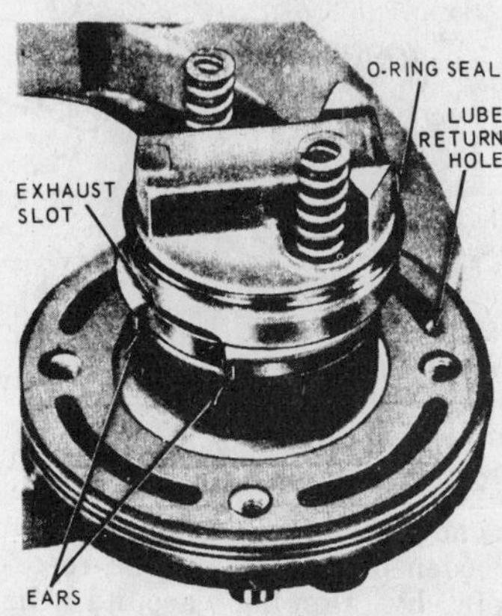

Valve and pressure spring installation
(© Ford Motor Co.)

3. Inspect the pressure plates, slippers, rotor, and cam ring for nicks, burrs, or scratches. If any of the parts are damaged enough to cause poor operation or binding of the pump, replace the defective part.
4. Inspect the pump body drive shaft bushing for excessive wear. Replace if necessary.

Assembly

1. With the pump assembly positioned on the adapter plate in the holding fixture, install the lower pressure plate on the anchor pin with the chamfered slots at the center hole facing up.
2. Lubricate the rotor shaft with power steering fluid and insert the shaft into the lower pressure and housing plates.
3. Assemble the rotor, slippers, and springs by wrapping a piece of wire around the rotor, installing the springs, and sliding a slipper in each groove of the rotor over the springs. Then, insert the assembly into the cam ring. Be sure the flat side of the slippers are toward the left side. Be sure that the springs are installed straight and are not cocked to one side under the slippers.
4. Install the cam ring and rotor assembly on the drive shaft with the fixed dowel passing through the first hole to the left of the cam notch when the arrow on the cam outside diameter is pointing toward the lower pressure plate. If the cam and rotor assembly does not seat properly, turn the rotor shaft slightly until the spline teeth mesh, allowing the cam and rotor to drop into position.
5. Insert the looser fitting dowel through the cam insert and lower pressure plate into the hole in the housing plate assembly. When both dowels are installed properly, they will be the same height.
6. Install the upper pressure plate so the tapered notch is facing down against the cam insert. The fixed dowel should pass through the round dowel hole and the loose dowel through the long hole. The slot between the ears on the outside of the pressure plate should match the notch on the cam insert.
7. Install the retainer end plate so the slot on the end plate matches the notches on the upper pressure plate and the cam insert.
8. Install the pump valve assembly O-ring seal on the pump valve assembly. Do not twist the seal.
9. Place the pump valve assembly on top of the retainer end plate with the large exhaust slot on the pump valve in line with the outside notches of the cam, upper pressure plate, and retainer end plate. All parts must be fully seated. If correctly installed, the relief valve stem will be in line with the lube return hole in the pump housing plate.
10. Put small amounts of vaseline on the pump housing plate to hold the cover gasket in place. Install the cover gasket in place.
11. Insert the pressure plate springs into the pockets in the pump valve assembly.
12. Plug the intake hole in the housing.
13. Lubricate the inside of the housing and the housing cover seal with power steering fluid. Install two studs for use as positioning guides, one in the bolt hole nearest the drain hole and the other in the bolt hole on the opposite side of the housing plate.
14. Align the small lube hole in the housing rim and the lube hole in the housing plate. Install the housing, using a steady, even, downward pressure. Do not jar the pressure spring out of position. Remove the guide studs and loosely install the housing retaining bolts finger tight.
15. Tighten the retaining bolts evenly to 28-32 ft. lbs. until the housing flange contacts the gasket.
16. Install a $^3/_8$-16 hex head screw into the end of the rotor shaft and put a torque wrench on it. Check the amount of torque needed to rotate the rotor shaft. If the torque is more than 15 in. lbs., loosen the retaining bolts slightly and rotate the rotor shaft. Then, retighten the retaining bolts evenly. Do not use the pump if the shaft torque exceeds 15 in. lbs.
17. Release the pin in the bench holding fixture and shake the pump assembly back and forth. If there is a rattle, the pressure springs have fallen out of their seats and must be reinstalled.
18. Install the reservoir O-ring seal on the housing plate without twisting it. Lubricate the seal and install the reservoir, aligning the notch in the reservoir flange with the notch in the outside edge of the pump housing plate and bushing assembly. Using only a soft-faced hammer, tap at the rear outer corners of the reservoir. Inspect the assem-

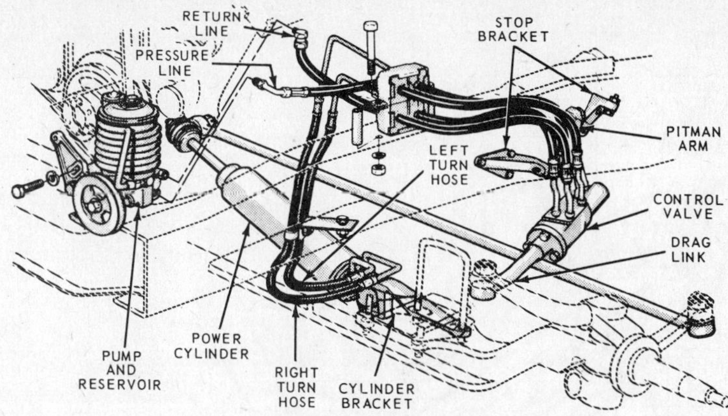

Power steering installation—typical
(© Ford Motor Co.)

bly to be sure the reservoir is fully seated on the housing plate.

19. Install the identification tag (if one was removed) on the outlet valve fitting. Install the outlet valve fitting nut and tighten to 43-45 ft. lbs. torque.
20. Turn the pump assembly over and install the pulley using the tool used to remove the pulley. Turn the tool nut clockwise to draw the pulley on the shaft until it is flush with the shaft end. Do not exert inward and outward pressures on the shaft to avoid damaging the internal thrust areas. Remove the tool.

Bendix Linkage—Type Power Steering System

The Bendix linkage-type power steering is a hydraulically controlled system composed of an integral pump and fluid reservoir, a control valve, a power cylinder, connecting fluid lines, and the steering linkage. The hydraulic pump, which is driven by a belt turned by the engine, draws fluid from the reservoir and provides pressure through hoses to the control valve and the power cylinder. There is a pressure relief valve to limit the pressures within the steering system to a safe level. After the fluid has passed from the pump to the control valve and the power cylinder, it returns to the reservoir.

In-Truck Adjustments

Control Valve Centering Spring Adjustment

1. Raise the truck and remove the spring cap attaching screws and remove the spring cap. CAUTION: Be very careful not to position the hoist adapters of two post hoists under the suspension and/or steering components. Place the hoist adapters under the front suspension lower arms.
2. Tighten the adjusting nut snug (about 90-100 in. lbs.); then, loosen the nut 1/4 turn (90 degrees). Do not turn the adjusting nut too tight.
3. Place the spring cap on the valve housing. Lubricate and install the attaching screws and washers. Tighten the screws to 72-100 in. lbs. torque.
4. Lower the truck and start the engine. Check the steering effort using a spring scale attached to the steering wheel rim for a pull of no more than 12 lbs.

Power Steering Control Valve

Removal and Installation

1. Raise the truck on a hoist. If a two post hoist is used, be sure to place the hoist adapters under the front suspension steering arms. Do not allow the hoist adapters to contact the steering linkage.
2. Disconnect the four fluid line fittings at the control valve and drain the fluid from the lines. Turn the front wheels back and forth to force all the fluid from the system.
3. Loosen the clamping nut and bolt at the right end of the sleeve.
4. Remove the roll pin from the steering arm-to-idler arm rod through the slot in the sleeve.
5. Remove the control valve ball stud nut.
6. Remove the ball stud from the sector shaft arm.
7. After turning the front wheels fully to the left, unthread the control valve from the center link steering arm-to-idler arm rod.
8. To install the control valve, thread the valve on the center link until about four threads are still visible.
9. Position the ball stud in the sector shaft arm.
10. Measure the distance between the grease plug in the sleeve and the stud at the inner end of the left spindle connecting rod. If the distance is not correct, disconnect the ball stud from the sector shaft arm and turn the valve on the center link until the correct distance is obtained.
11. When the distance is correct and the ball stud is positioned in the sector shaft arm, align the hole in the steering arm-to-idler arm rod with the slot near the end of the valve sleeve. Install the roll pin in the rod hole to lock the valve in place on the rod.
12. Tighten the valve sleeve clamp bolt to the proper torque.
13. Install the ball stud nut and tighten to the proper torque. Install a new cotter pin.
14. Connect all fluid lines to the control valve and tighten all fittings securely. Do not over-tighten.
15. Fill the fluid reservoir with power steering fluid to the full mark on the dipstick.
16. Start the engine and run it for a few minutes to warm the fluid in the power steering system. Turn the steering wheel back and forth to the stops and check the system for leaks.
17. Increase the engine idle speed to about 1000 rpm. Turn the steering wheel back and forth several times, then stop the engine. Check the control valve and hose connections for leaks.
18. Recheck the fluid level and add fluid if necessary.
19. Start the engine again, and check the position of the steering wheel when the front wheels are straight ahead. Do not make any adjustments until toe-in is checked.
20. With engine running, check front wheel toe-in.
21. Check steering wheel turning effort which should be equal in both directions.

Power Steering Power Cylinder Removal and Installation

1. Disconnect the two fluid lines from the power cylinder and drain the fluid.
2. Remove the pal nut, attaching nut, washer and the insulator from the end of the power cylinder rod. Remove the cotter pin and castellated nut holding the power cylinder stud to the center link.
3. Disconnect the power cylinder stud from the center link.
4. Remove the insulator sleeve and washer from the end of the power cylinder.

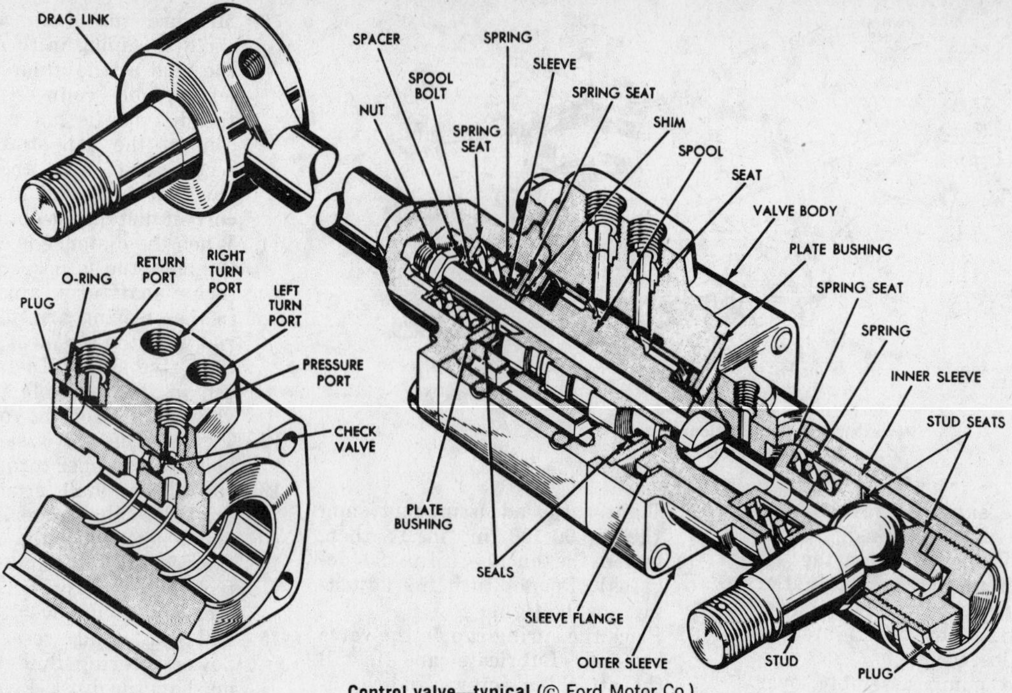

Control valve—typical (© Ford Motor Co.)

5. Inspect the tube fittings and seats in the power cylinder for nicks, burrs, or other damage. Replace the seats or tubes if damaged.
6. Install the washer, sleeve and the insulator on the end of the power cylinder rod.
7. While extending the rod as far as possible, insert the rod in the bracket on the frame and then, compress the rod so the stud may be inserted in the center link. Secure the stud with the castellated nut and a new cotter pin.
8. Install the insulater, washer, nut, and a pal nut on the power cylinder rod.
9. Connect the two fluid lines to their proper ports on the power cylinder.
10. Fill the reservoir with power steering fluid to the full mark on the dipstick. Start the engine and run for a few minutes to warm the fluid. Turn the steering wheel back and forth to the stops to fill the system. Stop the engine.
11. Recheck the fluid level and add fluid if necessary. Check for fluid leaks.
12. Start the engine again, turn the steering wheel back and forth, and check for leaks while the engine is running.

Control Valve Disassembly and Assembly

1. Clean the outside of the control valve of dirt and fluid.
2. Remove the centering spring cap from the valve housing. The control valve should be put in a soft-faced bench vise during disassembly. Clamp the control valve around the sleeve flange only to avoid damaging the valve housing, spool, or sleeve.
3. Remove the nut from the end of the valve spool bolt. Remove the washers, spacer, centering spring, adapter, and the bushing from the bolt and valve housing.
4. Remove the two bolts holding the valve housing and the sleeve together. Separate the valve housing and the sleeve.
5. Remove the plug from the sleeve. Push the valve spool out of the centering spring end of the valve housing, and remove the seal from the spool.
6. Remove the spacer, bushing and valve housing.
7. Drive the pin out of the travel regulator stop with a punch and hammer. Pull the head of the valve spool bolt tightly against the travel regulator stop before driving the pin out of the stop.
8. Turn the travel regulator stop counterclockwise in the valve sleeve to remove the stop from the sleeve.
9. Remove the valve spool bolt, spacer, and rubber washer from the travel regulator stop.
10. Remove the rubber boot and clamp from the valve sleeve. Slide the bumper, spring, and ball stud seat out of the valve sleeve and remove the ball stud socket from the sleeve.
11. Remove the return port hose seat and the return port relief valve.
12. Remove the spring plug and O-ring. Then remove the reaction limiting valve.
13. Replace all worn or damaged hose seats by using an Easy-Out screw extractor or a bolt of proper size as a puller. Tap the existing hole in the hose seat, using a starting tap of the correct size. Remove all metal chips from the hose seat after tapping. Place a nut and washer on a bolt of the same size as the tapped hole. The washer must be large enough to cover the hose seat port. Insert the bolt in the tapped hole and remove the hose seat by turning the nut clockwise and drawing the bolt out. Install a new hose seal in the port, and thread a bolt of the correct size in the port. Tighten the bolt enough to bottom the seal in the port.
14. Coat all parts of the control valve assembly with power steering fluid. Seals should be coated with lubricant before installation.
15. Install the reaction limiting valve, spring and plug. Install the return port relief valve and the hose seat.
16. Insert one of the ball stud seats (flat end first) into the ball stud socket, and insert the threaded end of the ball stud into the socket.
17. Place the socket in the control valve sleeve so that the threaded end of the ball stud can be pulled out through the slot.
18. Place the other ball stud seat, spring, and bumper in the

socket. Install and securely tighten the travel regulator stop.

19. Loosen the stop just enough to align the nearest hole in the stop with the slot in the ball stud socket and install the stop pin in the ball stud socket, travel regulator stop, and valve spool bolt.
20. Install the rubber boot, clamp, and the plug on the control valve sleeve. Be sure the lubrication fitting is turned on tightly and does not bind on the ball stud socket.
21. Insert the valve spool in the valve housing, rotating it while installing it.
22. Move the spool toward the centering spring end of the housing, and place the small seal bushing and spacer in the sleeve end of the housing.
23. Press the valve spool against the inner lip of the seal and, at the same time, guide the lip of the seal over the spool with a small screwdriver. Do not nick or scratch the seal or the spool during installation.
24. Place the sleeve end of the housing on a flat surface so that the seal, bushing and spacer are at the bottom end; then push down the valve spool until it stops.
25. Carefully install the spool seal and bushing in the centering spring end of the housing. Press the seal against the end of the spool, guiding the seal over the spool with a small screwdriver. Do not nick or scratch the seal or the spool during installation.
26. Pick up the housing, and slide the spool back and forth in the housing to check for free movement.
27. Place the valve sleeve on the housing so that the ball stud is on the same side of the housing as the ports for the two power cylinder lines. Install the two bolts in the sleeve, and torque them to the proper torque.
28. Place the adapter on the centering spring end of the housing, and install the bushing, washers, spacers and centering spring on the valve spool bolt.
29. Compress the centering spring and install the nut on the bolt. Tighten the nut snug (about 90-100 in. lbs.); then, loosen it not more than 1/4 turn. Do not over-tighten to avoid breaking the stop pin at the travel regulator stop.
30. Move the ball stud back and forth to check for free movement.
31. Lubricate the two cap attaching bolts. Install the centering spring cap on the valve housing, and tighten the two cap bolts to the proper torque.
32. Install the nut on the ball stud so that the valve can be put in a vise. Then, push forward on the cap end of the valve to check the valve spool for free movement.
33. Turn the valve around in the vise, and push forward on the sleeve end to check for free movement.

Power Cylinder Seal Removal and Installation

1. Clamp the power cylinder in a vise and remove the snap-ring from the end of the cylinder. Do not distort or crack the cylinder in the vise.
2. Pull the piston rod out all the way to remove the scraper, bushing, and seals. If the seals cannot be removed in this manner, remove them by carefully prying them out of the cylinder with a sharp pick. Do not damage the shaft or seal seat.
3. Coat the new seals with power steering fluid and place the parts on the piston rod. Coat with grease or lubricant.
4. Push the rod in all the way, and install the parts in the cylinder with a deep socket slightly smaller than the cylinder opening.

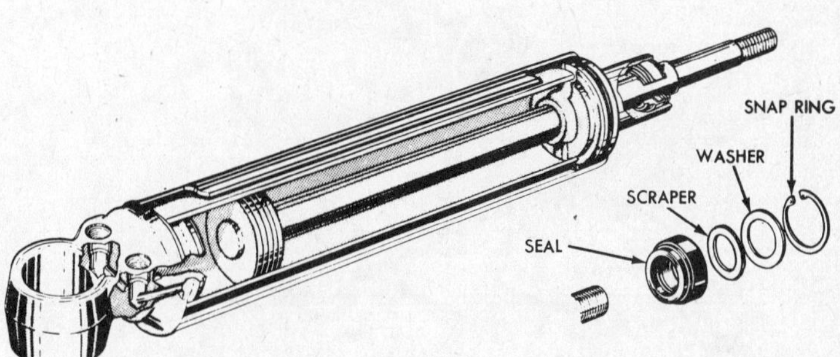

Power cylinder—typical (© Ford Motor Co.)

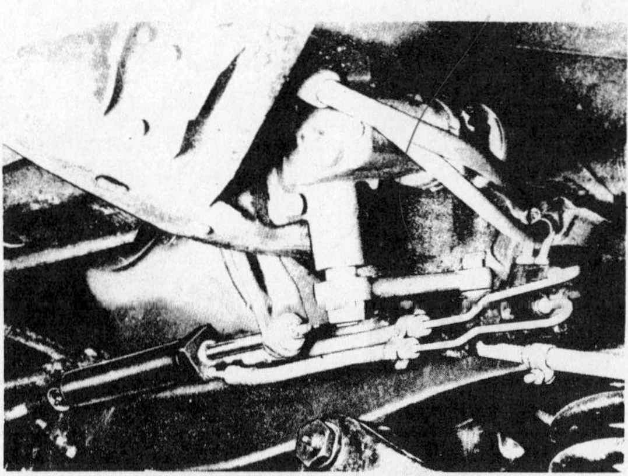
Chevrolet light duty power cylinder
(© G.M.C.)

Removal and Replacement

To remove or install the power steering pump, see the section on the slipper type pump.

Saginaw Linkage—Type Power Steering System

Control Valve

Removal

1. Raise front of vehicle and place on stands.
2. Remove relay rod to control valve clamp bolt.
3. Disconnect two pump to control valve hose connections and allow fluid to drain into a container, then disconnect the valve to power cylinder hoses.
4. Remove ball stud to pitman arm retaining nut and disconnect control valve.
5. Turn steering gear so that pitman arm is away from valve, to allow working room, and unscrew control valve from relay rod.
6. Remove control valve from vehicle.

Disassembly

1. Place valve assembly in vise with dust cap end up, then remove dust cap.

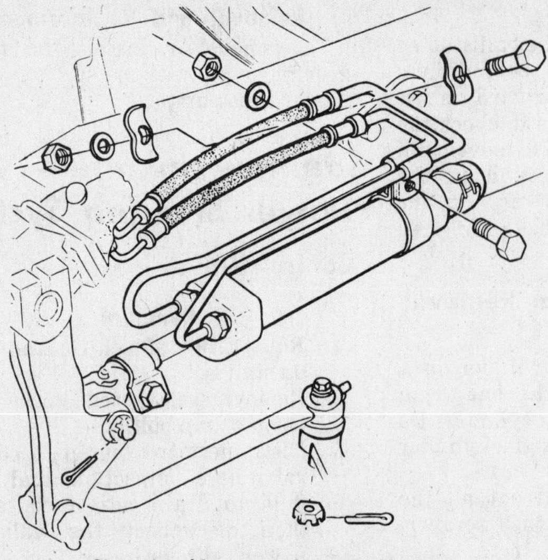
Chevrolet side mounted power cylinder
(© G.M.C.)

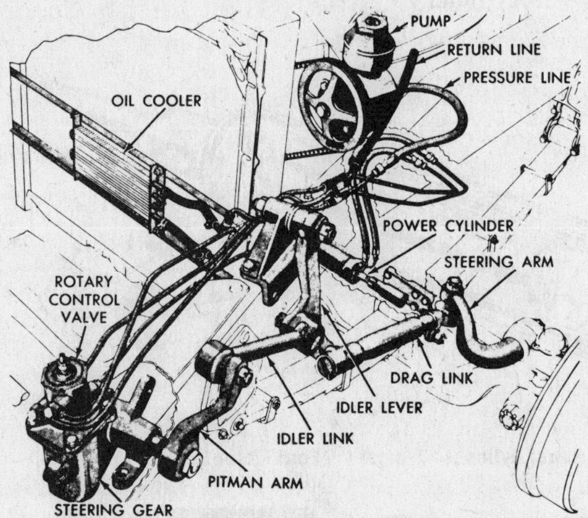

G.M.C. power steering system—tilt cab—typical
(© G.M.C.)

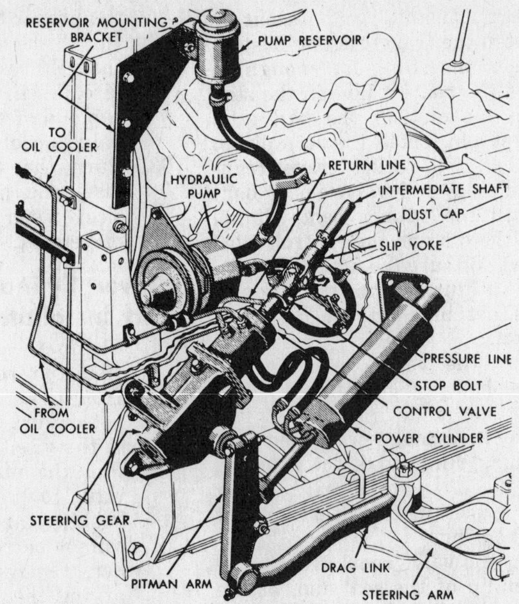

G.M.C. power steering system—conventional cab—typical
(© G.M.C.)

7. Carefully turn adjuster plug out of sleeve. Use care not to nick the top surface.
8. If necessary to replace a connector seat, tap threads in center hole using a 5/16-18 tap. Thread a bolt with a nut and a flat washer into the tapped hole so the washer is against the face of the port boss and the nut is against the washer. Hold the bolt from turning while backing the nut off the bolt. This will force the washer against the port boss face and back out the bolt, drawing the connector seat from the top cover housing. Discard the old connector seat and clean the housing out thoroughly to remove any metal tapping chips. Drive a new connector seat against the housing seat, being careful not to damage ei-

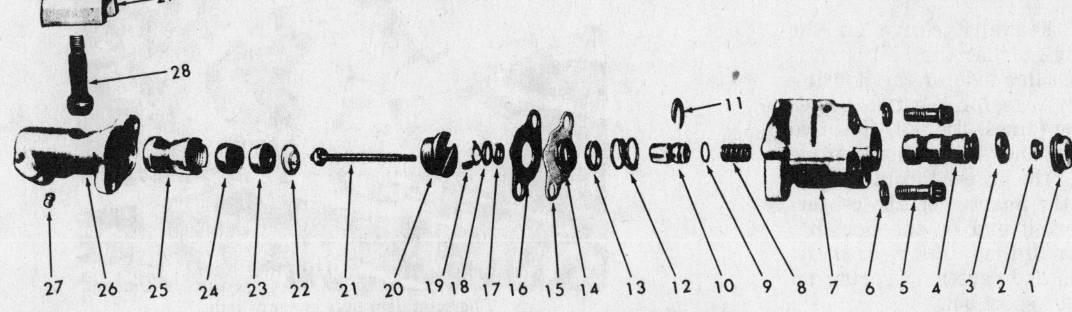

Chevrolet power steering control valve (© G.M.C.)

1 Dust cover
2 Adjusting nut
3 Vee block seal
4 Valve spool
5 Valve mounting bolts
6 Lock washer
7 Valve housing
8 Valve adjustment spring
9 "O" ring seal
10 Valve reaction spool
11 Spring thrust washer
12 Valve spring
13 Spring retainer
14 Annulus seal
15 Annulus spacer
16 Gasket
17 Valve shaft washer
18 "O" ring seal
19 Plug to sleeve key
20 Ball adjuster nut
21 Valve shaft
22 Ball seat spring
23 Ball seat
24 Ball seat
25 Sleeve bearing
26 Adapter housing
27 Lubrication fitting
28 Ball stud
29 Cover

2. Remove adjusting nut.
3. Remove valve to adapter bolts then remove housing and spool from adapter.
4. Remove spool from housing.
5. Remove spring, reaction spool, washer, reaction spring and seal. O-ring may now be removed from reaction spool.
6. Remove annulus spacer, valve shaft washer and plug-to-sleeve key.

ther seat.

9. Remove adapter from vise and turn over to allow spring and one of the two ball seats to drop out.
10. Remove ball stud with other ball seat and allow sleeve to fall free.

Inspection

1. Wash all parts in non-toxic solvent and blow dry with air.
2. Inspect all parts for scratches, burrs, distortion, excessive wear and replace all worn or damaged parts.
3. Replace all seals and gaskets.

Assembly

1. Install sleeve and ball seat in adapter, then the ball stud and then the other ball seat and spring (small end down).
2. Place adapter in vise. Put the shaft through the seat in the adjuster plug and screw adjuster plug into sleeve.
3. Turn plug in until tight, then back off until slot lines up with notches in sleeve.
4. Insert key. Be sure small tangs on end of key fit into notches in sleeve.
5. Install valve shaft washer, annulus spacer, reaction seal (lip up), spring retainer, reaction spring and spool, then washer and adjustment spring. Install O-ring seal on reaction spool before installing spool on shaft. Install washer with chamfer up.
6. Install seal on valve spool with lip down. Then install spool, being careful not to jam spool in housing.
7. Install housing with spool onto adapter. The side ports should be on the same side as the ball stud. Bolt the housing to the adapter.
8. Depress the valve spool and turn the locknut into the shaft about four turns. Use a clean wrench or socket.

NOTE: Always use a new nut.

Installation and Balancing

1. Install the control valve on the relay rod so that control valve bottoms, then back off enough (if necessary) to install the clamp bolt. Do not back off more than two turns. There should be approximately 1/16-1/8" gap.
2. Tighten control valve clamping-bolt and install ball stud to pitman arm.
3. Reconnect the four hoses to the valve.
4. Fill system with type A fluid and bleed air by running engine, then slowly turning wheels from lock to lock with engine idling. Be sure to keep reservoir full during this process. Do not replace dust cover before the following balancing procedure is completed.
5. Disconnect the piston rod from frame bracket if not already separated.
6. If piston rod is retracted, turn adjusting nut clockwise until rod begins to move out. Then turn nut counterclockwise until rod just begins to move in. Now, turn the nut clockwise exactly half the rotation needed to change the direction of piston rod movement. If piston rod is extended before starting, reverse the above to get the midpoint in piston movement. CAUTION. Do not turn the nut back and forth more than is absolutely necessary to balance the valve.

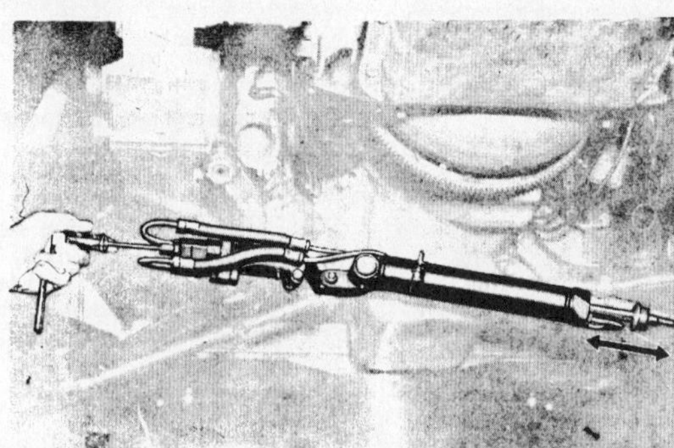

Balancing control valve (© G.M.C.)

7. With valve properly balanced it should be possible to move the rod in and out manually.
8. Shut off engine and connect piston rod to frame bracket.
9. Restart engine with front wheels still off ground. If the wheels do not turn in either direction from center, the valve has been properly balanced. Correct the condition by rebalancing the valve if necessary.
10. After proper adjustment, grease the end of valve and install dust cap.

Power Cylinder

Removal

1. Remove the two hoses which are connected to the cylinder and drain fluid into a container.
2. Remove power cylinder from frame bracket.
3. Remove cotter pin and nut and pull stud out of relay rod.
4. Remove cylinder from vehicle.

Inspection

1. Check seals for leaks around cylinder rod. If leaks are found, replace seals.
2. Check hose connection seats for damage and replace if necessary.
3. For service other than seat or seal replacement, it is necessary to replace the power cylinder.
4. The ball stud may be replaced by removing snap-ring.

Disassembly and Assembly

1. To remove piston rod seal, remove snap-ring and pull out on rod. Remove back-up washer, piston rod scraper and piston rod seal from rod.
2. To remove the ball stud, depress the end plug and remove the snap-ring. Push on the end of the ball stud and the end plug, spring, spring seat, ball stud and seal may be removed. If the ball seat is to be replaced, it must be pressed out.
3. Reverse disassembly procedure. Be sure snap-ring is properly seated.

Installation

1. Install power cylinder on vehicle in reverse of removal procedure.
2. Reconnect the hydraulic lines, fill system and bleed out air as described in the installation and balancing section of control valve servicing.

Power Steering Hoses

Carefully inspect the hoses. When installing, be sure to place in such a position as to avoid all chafing or other abuse when making sharp turns.

Saginaw Rotary Type Power Steering

The rotary type power steering gear is designed with all components in one housing.

The power cylinder is an integral part of the gear housing. A double-acting type piston allows oil pressure to be applied to either side of the piston. The one-piece piston and power rack is meshed to the sector shaft.

The hydraulic control valve is composed of a sleeve and valve spool. The spool is held in the neutral position by the torsion bar and spool actuator. Twisting of the torsion bar moves the valve spool, allowing oil pressure to be directed to either side of the

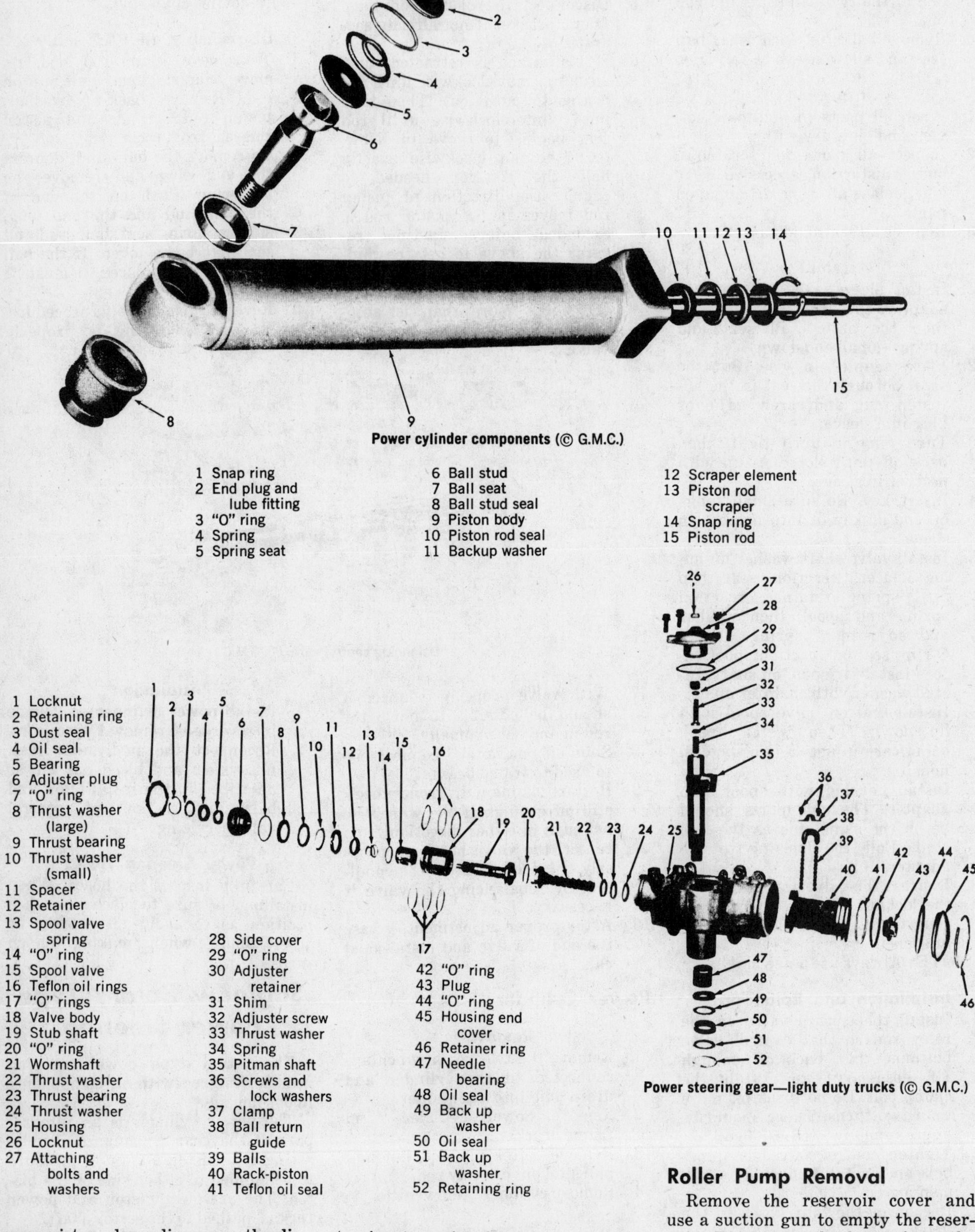

Power cylinder components (© G.M.C.)

1 Snap ring
2 End plug and lube fitting
3 "O" ring
4 Spring
5 Spring seat
6 Ball stud
7 Ball seat
8 Ball stud seal
9 Piston body
10 Piston rod seal
11 Backup washer
12 Scraper element
13 Piston rod scraper
14 Snap ring
15 Piston rod

1 Locknut
2 Retaining ring
3 Dust seal
4 Oil seal
5 Bearing
6 Adjuster plug
7 "O" ring
8 Thrust washer (large)
9 Thrust bearing
10 Thrust washer (small)
11 Spacer
12 Retainer
13 Spool valve spring
14 "O" ring
15 Spool valve
16 Teflon oil rings
17 "O" rings
18 Valve body
19 Stub shaft
20 "O" ring
21 Wormshaft
22 Thrust washer
23 Thrust bearing
24 Thrust washer
25 Housing
26 Locknut
27 Attaching bolts and washers
28 Side cover
29 "O" ring
30 Adjuster retainer
31 Shim
32 Adjuster screw
33 Thrust washer
34 Spring
35 Pitman shaft
36 Screws and lock washers
37 Clamp
38 Ball return guide
39 Balls
40 Rack-piston
41 Teflon oil seal
42 "O" ring
43 Plug
44 "O" ring
45 Housing end cover
46 Retainer ring
47 Needle bearing
48 Oil seal
49 Back up washer
50 Oil seal
51 Back up washer
52 Retaining ring

Power steering gear—light duty trucks (© G.M.C.)

power piston, depending upon the directional rotation of the steering wheel, to give power assist.

On many trucks of the General Motors Corporation, a modified version of the rotary valve power steering system provides variable ratio steering to assist the driver to steer the truck easier and safer. The steering gear ratio will vary from a high ratio of about 16:1 while steering straight ahead to a lower gear ratio of about 12.1:1 while making a full turn to either side.

Roller Pump Removal

Remove the reservoir cover and use a suction gun to empty the reservoir. Disconnect the hoses from the pump and tie them in a raised position to prevent oil drainage. Loosen the pump adjusting screw and remove the pump belt, then take out the retaining bolts and remove the pump and reservoir.

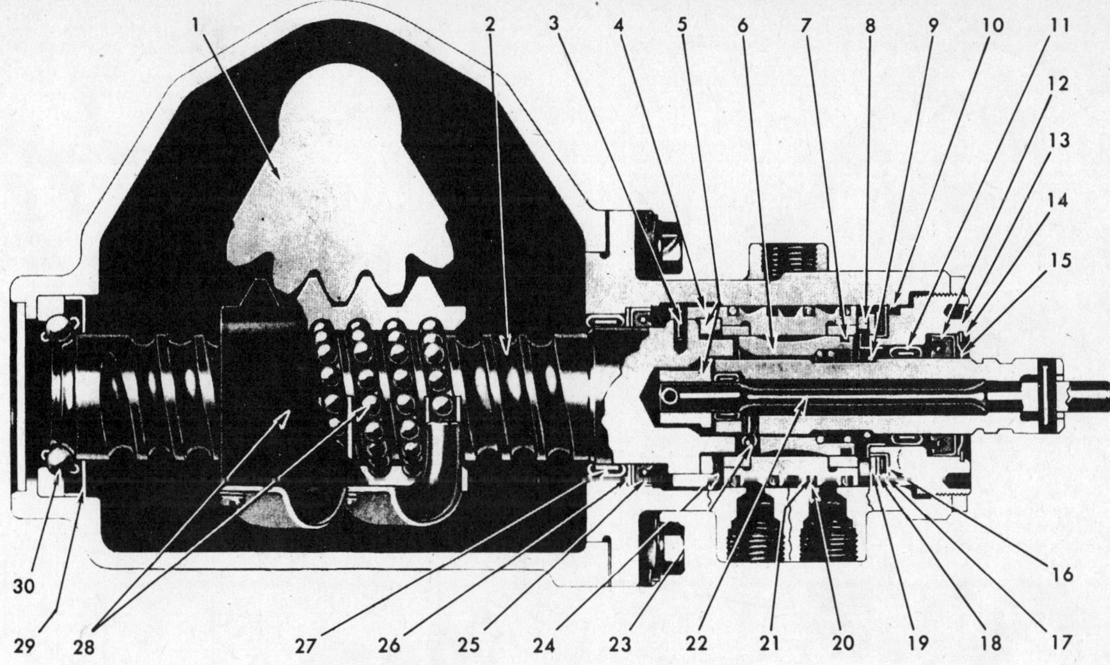

Power steering gear—medium duty trucks (© G.M.C.)

1 Sector
2 Wormshaft
3 Body drive pin
4 Valve body
5 Cap assembly
6 Valve spool
7 Spool dampener "O" ring
8 Thrust bearing spacer
9 Spool spring
10 Adjuster plug "O" ring seal
11 Adjuster plug needle bearing
12 Adjuster plug shaft seal
13 Adjuster plug
14 Adjuster plug snap ring
15 Adjuster plug dust seal
16 Bearing race
17 Upper thrust bearing
18 Bearing race
19 Spacer
20 Valve body ring
21 Ring back-up seal
22 Torsion bar
23 Spool valve pin
24 Valve body pin
25 Top cover (valve) seal
26 Back-up washer
27 Top cover (valve) bearing
28 Ball nut and balls
29 Bearing retainer
30 Lower thrust bearing

Installation

Position the pump assembly and install the retaining bolts. Be sure there is clearance between the pump bracket and the engine front support bracket. Install the hoses and place the pump belt on the pulley. Adjust the belt to ½" deflection, then tighten the adjusting screw.

Connect the hoses to the pump assembly.

Fill the reservoir to within ½" of the top with automatic transmission fluid type A.

Start the engine and rotate the steering wheel several times to the right and left to expel air from the system, then recheck the oil level and install the reservoir cover.

Power Steering Unit

Fluid Used

This unit uses automatic transmission fluid type A. The fluid capacity is 4½ pints.

Bleeding the System

Fill the pump reservoir to within ½" of the top. Start and run the engine to attain normal operating temperatures. Now, turn the steering wheel through its entire travel three or four times to expel air from the system, then recheck the fluid level.

Checking Steering Effort

Run the engine to attain normal operating temperatures. With the wheels on a dry floor, hook a pull scale to the spoke of the steering wheel at the outer edge. The effort required to turn the steering wheel should be 3½-5 lbs. If the pull is not within these limits, check the hydraulic pressure.

Pressure Test

To check the hydraulic pressure, disconnect the pressure hose from the gear. Now connect the pressure gauge between the pressure hose from the pump and the steering gear housing. Run the engine to attain normal operating temperatures, then turn the wheel to a full right and a full left turn to the wheel stops.

Hold the wheel in this position only long enough to obtain an accurate reading.

The pressure gauge reading should be within the limits specified. If the pressure reading is less than the minimum needed for proper operation, close the valve at the gauge and see if the reading increases. If the pressure is still low, the pump is defective and needs repair. If the pressure reading is at or near the minimum reading, the pump is normal and needs only an adjustment of the power steering gear or power assist control valve.

Worm Bearing Preload and Sector Mesh Adjustments

Disconnect the pitman arm from the sector shaft, then back off on the sector shaft adjusting screw on the sector shaft cover.

Center the steering on the high point, then attach a pull scale to the spoke of the steering wheel at the outer edge. The pull required to keep the wheel moving for one complete turn should be ½-⅔ lbs.

If the pull is not within these limits, loosen the thrust bearing locknut and tighten or back off on the valve sleeve adjuster locknut to bring the preload within limits. Tighten the thrust bearing locknut and recheck the preload.

Slowly rotate the steering wheel several times, then center the steering on the high point. Now, turn the sector shaft adjusting screw until a steering wheel pull of 1-1½ lbs. is required to move the worm through the center point. Tighten the sector shaft adjusting screw locknut and recheck the sector mesh adjustment.

Install the pitman arm and draw the arm in position with the nut.

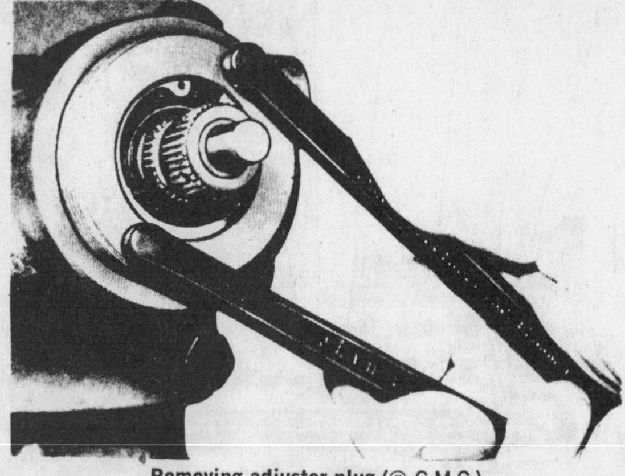
Removing adjuster plug (© G.M.C.)

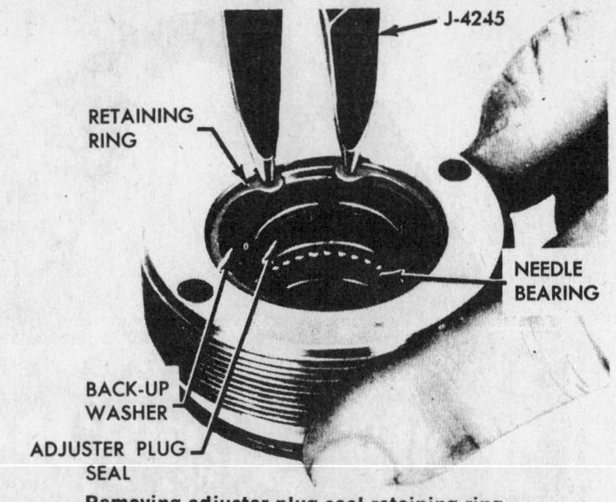

Removing adjuster plug seal retaining ring (© G.M.C.)

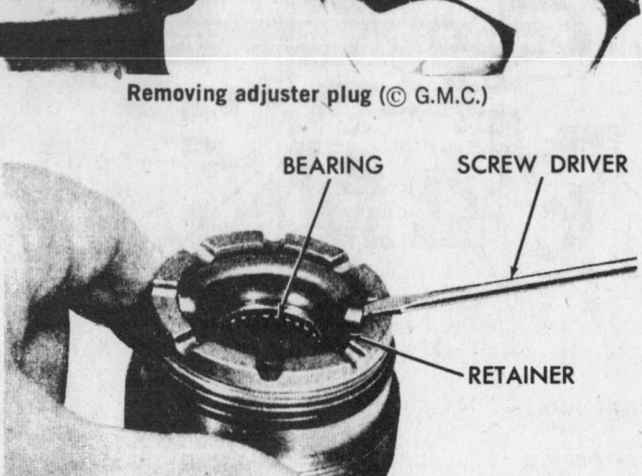

Removing thrust bearing retainer (© G.M.C.)

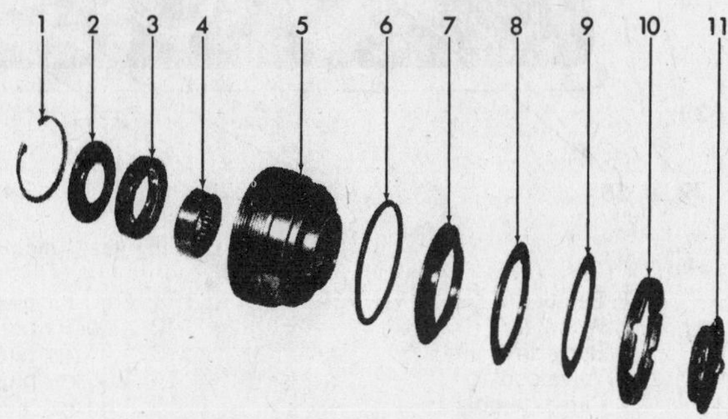

Adjuster plug (© G.M.C.)

1 Retaining ring
2 Dust seal
3 Oil seal
4 Needle bearing
5 Adjuster plug
6 "O" ring
7 Thrust washer (large)
8 Thrust bearing
9 Thrust washer (small)
10 Spacer
11 Retainer

Service Operations

Adjuster Plug and Rotary Valve Removal

1. Thoroughly clean exterior of gear assembly. Drain by holding valve ports down and rotating worm back and forth through entire travel.
2. Place gear in vise.
3. Loosen adjuster plug locknut with punch. Remove adjuster plug with spanner.
4. Remove rotary valve assembly by grasping stub shaft and pulling it out.

Adjuster Plug Disassembly & Assembly

1. Remove upper thrust bearing retainer with screwdriver. Be careful not to damage bearing bore. Discard retainer. Remove spacer, upper bearing and races.
2. Remove and discard adjuster plug O-ring.
3. Remove stub shaft seal retaining ring (Truarc pliers will help) and remove and discard dust seal.
4. Remove stub shaft seal by prying out with screwdriver and discard.
5. Examine needle bearing and, if required, remove same by pressing from thrust bearing end.
6. Inspect thrust bearing spacer, bearing rollers and races.
7. Reassemble in reverse of above.

Rotary Valve Disassembly

Repairs are seldom needed. Do not disassemble unless absolutely necessary. If the O-ring seal on valve spool dampener needs replacement, perform this portion of operation only.

1. Remove cap-to-worm O-ring seal and discard.
2. Remove valve spool spring by prying on small coil with small screwdriver to work spring onto bearing surface of stub shaft. Slide spring off shaft. Be careful not to damage shaft surface.
3. Remove valve spool by holding the valve assembly in one hand with the stub shaft pointing down. Insert the end of pencil or wood rod through opening in valve body cap and push spool until it is out far enough to be removed. In this procedure, rotate to prevent jamming. If spool becomes jammed it may be necessary to remove stub shaft, torsion bar and cap assembly.

Rotary Valve Assembly

CAUTION: All parts must be free and clear of dirt, chips, etc., before assembly and must be protected after.

1. Lubricate three new back-up O-ring seals with automatic transmission oil and reassemble in the ring grooves of valve body. Assemble three new valve body rings in the grooves over the O-ring seals by carefully slipping over the valve body. NOTE: If the valve body rings seem loose or twisted in the grooves, the heat of the oil during operation will cause them to straighten.
2. Lubricate a new dampener O-ring with automatic transmission oil and install in valve spool groove.
3. Assemble stub shaft torsion bar and cap assembly in the valve body, aligning the groove in the valve cap with the pin in the valve body. Tap lightly with soft remainder of assembly. Valve body pin must be in the cap groove. Hold parts together during the remainder of assembly.

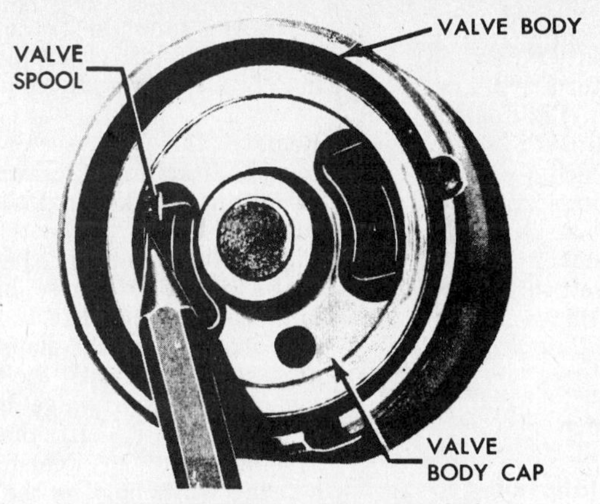

Separating valve spool from valve body (© G.M.C.)

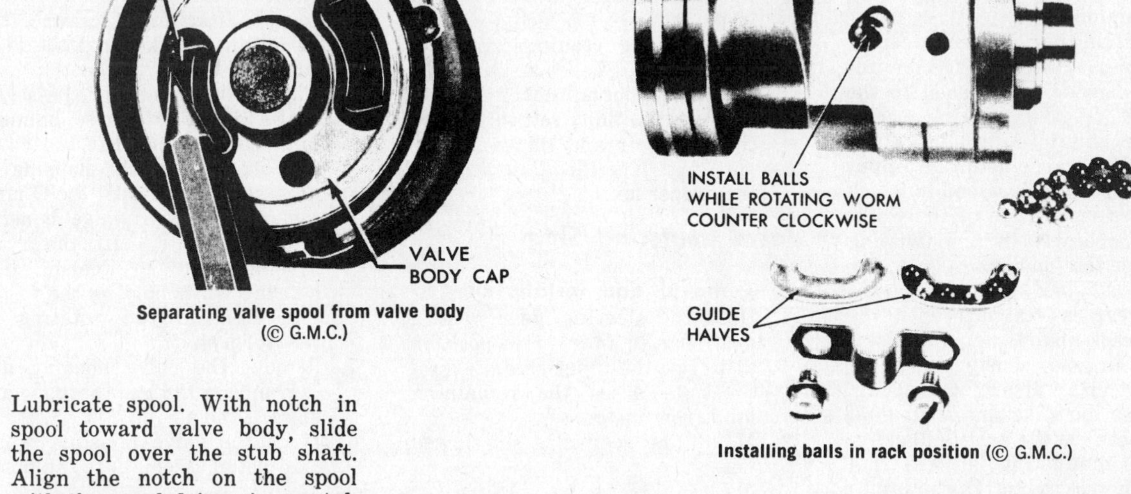

Installing balls in rack position (© G.M.C.)

4. Lubricate spool. With notch in spool toward valve body, slide the spool over the stub shaft. Align the notch on the spool with the spool drive pin on stub shaft and carefully engage spool in valve body bore. Push spool evenly and with slight rotating motion until it reaches the drive pin. Rotate slowly, with some pressure, until notch engages pin. Be sure dampener O-ring seal is evenly distributed in the spool groove. CAUTION: Use extreme care because spool to valve body clearance is very small. Damage is easily caused.
5. With seal protector over stub shaft, slide valve spool spring over shaft, with small diameter of spring going over shaft last. Work spring onto shaft until small coil is located in stub shaft groove.
6. Lubricate a new cap to O-ring seal and install in valve body.

Adjuster Plug and Rotary Valve Installation

1. Align narrow pin slot on valve body with valve body drive pin on the worm. Insert the valve assembly into gear housing by pressing against valve body with finger tips. Do not press on stub shaft or torsion bar. The return hole in the gear housing should be fully visible when properly assembled. CAUTION: Do not press on stub shaft as this may cause shaft and cap to pull out of valve body, allowing the spool dampener O-ring seal to slip into valve body oil grooves.
2. With seal protector over end of stub shaft, install adjuster plug assembly into gear housing snugly with spanner, then back plug off approximately one-eighth turn. Install plug locknut but do not tighten. Adjust preload as described in the adjustment section.
3. After adjustment, tighten locknut.

Pitman Shaft Removal and Installation

1. Completely drain the gear assembly and thoroughly clean the outside.
2. Place gear in vise.
3. Rotate stub shaft until pitman shaft gear is in center position. Remove side cover retaining bolts.
4. Tap end of pitman shaft with soft hammer and slide shaft out of housing.
5. Remove and discard side cover O-ring seal.
6. The seals, washers, retainers and bearings may now be removed and examined.
7. Examine all parts for wear or damage and replace as required.
8. Install in reverse of above. Make proper adjustment as described in adjustment section.

Rack-Piston Nut and Worm Assembly Removal

1. Completely drain the gear assembly and thoroughly clean the outside.
2. Remove pitman shaft assembly as previously described.
3. Rotate housing end plug retaining ring so that one end of ring is over hole in gear housing. Spring one end of ring so screwdriver can be inserted to lift it out.
4. Rotate stub shaft to full left turn position to force end plug out of housing.
5. Remove and discard housing end plug O-ring seal.
6. Remove rack-piston nut end plug with $\frac{1}{2}''$ square drive.
7. Insert special tool in end of worm. Turn stub shaft so that rack-piston nut will go into tool and then remove rack-piston nut from gear housing.
8. Remove adjuster plug and rotary valve assemblies as previously described.
9. Remove worm and lower thrust bearing and races.
10. Remove cap O-ring seal and discard.

Rack-Piston Nut and Worm Disassembly and Assembly

1. Remove and discard piston ring and back-up O-ring on rack piston nut.
2. Remove ball guide clamp and return guide.
3. Place nut on clean cloth and remove ball retaining tool. Make sure all balls are removed.
4. Inspect all parts for wear, nicks, scoring or burrs. If worm or rack-pinion nut need replacing, both must be replaced as a matched pair.
5. In reassembling reverse the above.

NOTE: When assembling, alternate black and white balls, and install guide and clamp. Packing with grease helps in holding during assembly. When new balls are used, various sizes are available and a selection must be made to secure proper torque when making the high point adjustment.

Rack-Piston Nut and Worm Assembly Installation

1. Install in reverse of removal procedure.
2. In all cases use new O-ring seals.
3. Make adjustments as previously described.

Ford Integral Power Steering Gear

The Ford integral power steering unit is a torsion-bar type.

The torsion bar power steering unit includes a worm and one-piece rack piston, which is meshed to the gear teeth on the steering sector shaft. The unit also includes a hydraulic valve, valve actuator, input shaft and torsion bar assembly which are mounted on the end of the worm shaft and operated by the twisting action of the torsion bar.

The torsion-bar type of power steering gear is designed with the one piece rack-piston, worm and sector shaft in one housing and the valve spool in an attaching housing. This makes possible internal fluid passages between the valve and cylinder, thus eliminating all external lines and hoses, except the pressure and return hoses between the pump and gear assembly.

The power cylinder is an integral part of the gear housing. The piston is double acting, in that fluid pressure may be applied to either side of the piston.

A selective metal shim, located in the valve housing of the gear is for the purpose of tailoring steering gear efforts. If efforts are not within specifications they can be changed by increasing or decreasing shim thickness as follows:

Efforts heavy to the left—Increase shim thickness.

Efforts light to the left—Decrease shim thickness.

Steering Gear Adjustments

The only adjustment which can be performed is the total over center position load, to eliminate excessive lash between the sector and rack teeth.

1. Disconnect the Pitman arm from the sector shaft.
2. Disconnect the fluid return line at the reservoir, at the same time cap the reservoir return line pipe.
3. Place the end of the return line in a clean container and cycle the steering wheel in both directions as required, to discharge the fluid from the gear.
4. Turn the steering wheel to 45 degrees from the left stop.
5. Using an in-lb torque wrench on the steering wheel nut, determine the torque required to rotate the shaft slowly through an approximately ⅛ turn from the 45 degree position.
6. Turn the steering gear back to center, then determine the torque required to rotate the shaft back and forth across the center position. Loosen the adjuster nut, and turn the adjuster screw until the reading is 11-12 in-lb greater than the torque 45 degrees from the stop. Tighten the lock nut while holding the screw in place.
7. Recheck the readings and replace the Pitman arm and the steering wheel hub cover.
8. Correct the fluid return line to the reservoir and fill the reservoir with specified lubricant to the proper level.

Valve Centering Shim

Removal and Installation

1. Hold the steering gear over a drain pan in an inverted position and cycle the input shaft several times to drain the remaining fluid from the gear.
2. Mount the gear in a soft-jawed vise.
3. Turn the input shaft to either stop then, turn it back approximately 1¾ turns to center the gear.
4. Remove the two sector shaft cover attaching screws, the brake line bracket and the identification tag.
5. Tap the lower end of the sector shaft with a soft-faced hammer to loosen it, then lift the cover and shaft from the housing as an assembly. Discard the O-ring.
6. Remove the four valve housing attaching bolts. Lift the valve housing from the steering gear housing while holding the piston to prevent it from rotating off the worm shaft.
7. Remove the valve housing and the lube passage O-rings and discard them.
8. Place the valve housing, worm and piston assembly in the bench

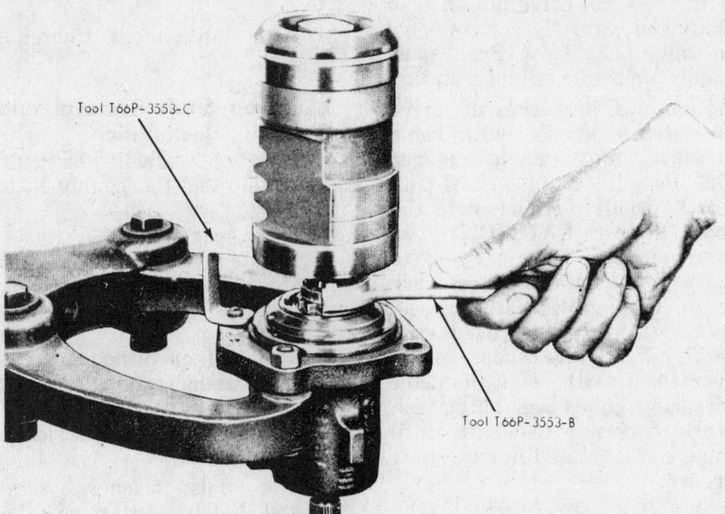

Removing worm bearing race nut (© Ford Motor Co.)

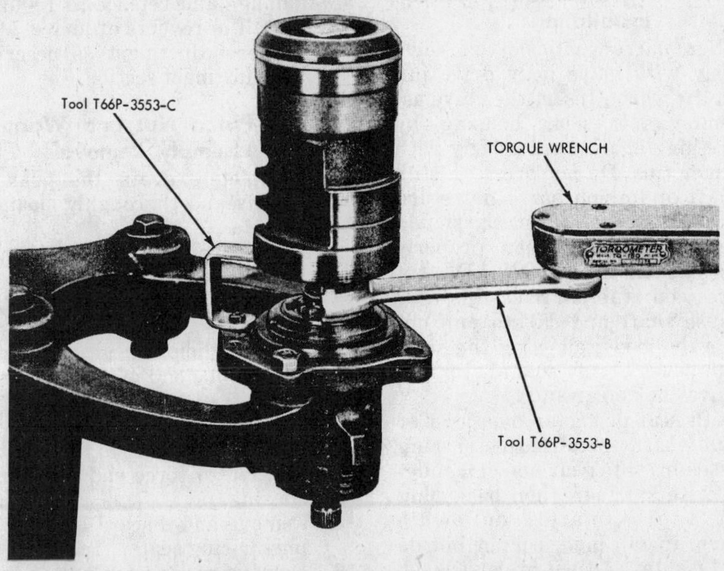

Installing worm bearing race nut (© Ford Motor Co.)

mounted holding fixture with the piston on the top.

9. Rotate the piston upward (back off) 3½ turns.
10. Insert Tool T66P-3553-C (with the arm facing away from the piston) into a bolt hole in the valve housing. Rotate the arm into position under the piston.
11. Loosen the Allen head race nut set screw from the valve housing.
12. Using Tool T66P-3553-B, loosen the worm bearing race nut.
13. Lift the piston-worm assembly from the valve housing. During removal hold the piston to prevent it from spinning off at the shaft.
14. Change the power steering valve centering shim.
15. Install the piston-worm assembly into the valve housing. Hold the piston worm to prevent it from spinning off of the shaft.
16. Install the worm bearing race nut and torque to 2-8 in-lbs using Tool T66P-3553-B.
17. Install the race nut set screw (Allen head) through the valve housing.
18. Rotate the piston upward (back off) ½ turn and remove Tool T66P-3553-C.
19. Remove the valve housing, worm, and piston assembly from the holding fixture.
20. Position a new lube passage O-ring in the counterbore of the gear housing.
21. Apply vaseline to the teflon seal on the piston.
22. Place a new O-ring on the valve housing.
23. Slide the piston and valve into the gear housing being careful not to damage the teflon seal.
24. Align the lube passage in the valve housing with the one in the gear housing, and install but do not tighten the attaching bolts.
25. Rotate the ball nut so that the teeth are in the same place as the sector teeth. Tighten the four valve housing attaching bolts to 35-45 ft-lbs.
26. Position the sector shaft cover O-ring in the steering gear housing. Turn the input shaft as required to center the piston.
27. Apply vaseline to the sector shaft journal; then, position the sector shaft and cover assembly in the gear housing. Install the brake line bracket, steering gear identification tag and the two sector shaft cover attaching studs.
28. Position an in-lb torque wrench on the gear input shaft and adjust the meshload to approximately 4 in-lbs. Then, torque the sector shaft cover attaching studs to 55-70 ft-lbs.
29. After the cover attaching bolts have been tightened to specification, adjust the mesh load to 17 in-lbs with an in-lb torque wrench.

Steering Gear Disassembly

1. Hold the steering gear over a drain pan in an inverted position and cycle the input shaft several times to drain the remaining fluid from the gear.
2. Mount the gear in a soft-jawed vise.
3. Remove the lock nut from the adjusting screw.
4. Turn the input shaft to either stop then, turn it back approximately 1¾ turns to center the gear.
5. Remove the two sector shaft cover attaching studs, the brake line bracket and the identification tag.
6. Tap the lower end of the sector shaft with a soft-hammer to loosen it, then lift the cover and shaft from the housing as an assembly. Discard the O-ring.
7. Turn the sector shaft cover counterclockwise off the adjuster screw.
8. Remove the four valve housing attaching bolts. Lift the valve housing from the steering gear housing while holding the piston to prevent it from rotating off the worm shaft. Remove the valve housing and the lube passage O-rings and discard them.
9. Stand the valve body and piston on end with the piston end down. Rotate the input shaft counterclockwise out of the piston allowing the ball bearings to drop into the piston.
10. Place a cloth over the open end of the piston and turn it upside down to remove the balls.
11. Remove the two screws that attach the ball guide clamp to the ball nut and remove the clamp and the guides.

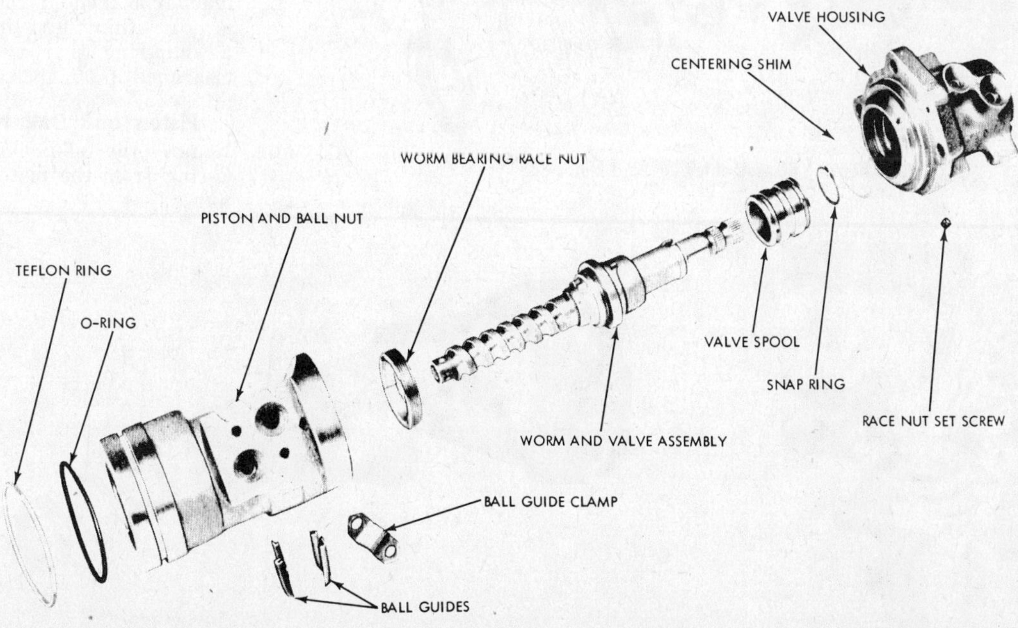

Ball nut and valve housing (© Ford Motor Co.)

12. Install the valve body assembly in the holding fixture (do not clamp in a vise) and loosen the race nut screw (Allen head) from the valve housing and remove the worm bearing race nut.
13. Carefully slide the input shaft, worm and valve assembly out of the valve housing. Due to the close diametrical clearance between the spool and housing, the slightest cocking of the spool may cause it to jam in the housing.
14. Remove the shim from the valve housing bore.

Valve Housing

1. Remove the dust seal from the rear of the valve housing and discard the seal.
2. Remove the snap-ring from the valve housing.
3. Turn the fixture to place the valve housing in an inverted position.
4. Insert special tool in the valve body assembly opposite the seal end and gently tap the bearing and seal out of the housing. Discard the seal. Caution must be exercised when inserting and removing the tool to prevent damage to the valve bore in the housing.
5. Remove the fluid inlet and outlet tube seats with an EZ-out if they are damaged.
6. Coat the fluid inlet and outlet tube seats with vaseline and position them in the housing. Install and tighten the tube nuts to press the seats to the proper location.
7. Coat the bearing and seal surface of the housing with a film of vaseline.
8. Seat the bearing in the valve housing. Make sure that the bearing is free to rotate.
9. Dip the new oil seal in gear lubricant; then, place it in the housing with the metal side of the seal facing outward. Drive the seal into the housing until the outer edge of seal does not quite clear the snap-ring groove.
10. Place the snap-ring in the housing; then, drive on the ring until the snap-ring seats in its groove to properly locate the seal.
11. Place the dust seal in the housing with the dished side (rubber side) facing out. Drive the dust seal into place. The seal must be located behind the undercut in the input shaft when it is installed.

Worm and Valve

1. Remove the snap-ring from the end of the actuator.
2. Slide the control valve spool off the actuator.
3. Install the valve spool evenly and slowly with a slight oscillating motion into the flanged end of valve housing with the valve identification groove between the valve spool lands outward, checking for freedom of valve movement within the housing working area. The valve spool should enter the housing bore freely and fall by its own weight.
4. If the valve spool is not free, check for burrs at the outward edges of the working lands in the housing and remove with a hard stone.
5. Check the valve for burrs and if burrs are found, stone the valve in a radial direction only. Check for freedom of the valve again.
6. Remove the valve spool from the housing.
7. Slide the spool onto the actuator making sure that the groove in the spool annulus is toward the worm.
8. Install the snap-ring to retain the spool. The beveled ID of the snap-ring must be assembled toward the spool.
9. Check the clearance between the spool and the snap-ring. The clearance should be between .0005-.035 inch. If the clearance is not within these limits, select a snap-ring that will allow a clearance of .002 inch.

Piston and Ball Nut

1. Remove the teflon ring and the O-ring from the piston and ball nut.

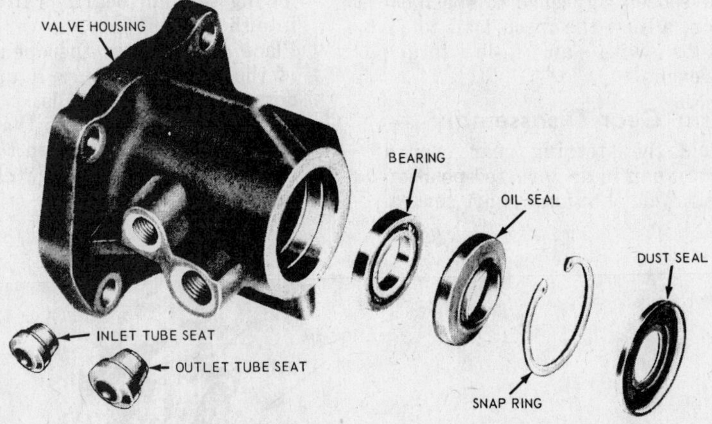

Valve housing disassembled (© Ford Motor Co.)

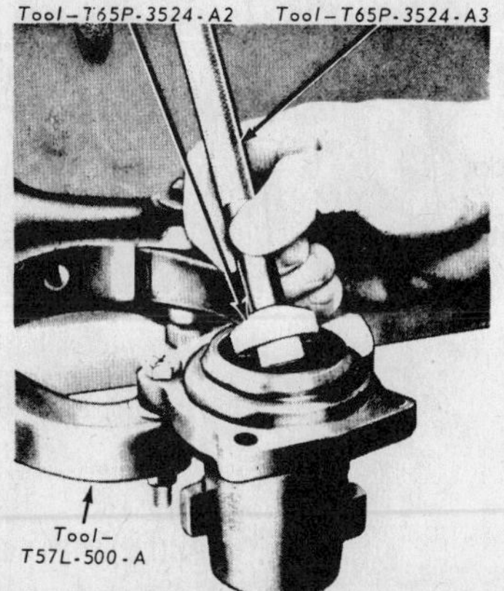

Removing bearing and oil seal (© Ford Motor Co.)

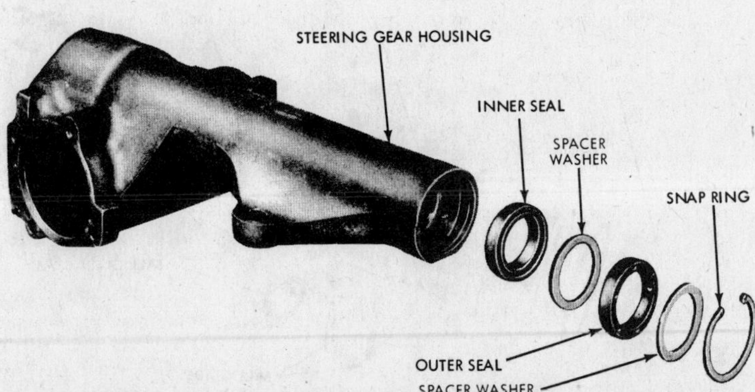

Steering gear housing (© Ford Motor Co.)

2. Dip a new O-ring in gear lubricant and install it on the piston and ball nut.
3. Install a new teflon ring on the piston and ball nut being careful not to stretch it any more than necessary.

Steering Gear Housing

1. Remove the snap-ring and the spacer washer from the lower end of the steering gear housing.
2. Remove the lower seal from the housing. Lift the spacer washer from the housing.
3. Remove the upper seal in the same manner as the lower seal. Some housings require only one seal and one spacer.
4. Dip both sector shaft seals in gear lubricant.
5. Apply lubricant to the sector shaft seal bore of the housing and position the sector shaft inner seal into the housing with the lip facing inward. Press the seal into place. Place a spacer washer (0.090 inch) on top of the seal and apply more lubricant to the housing bore.
6. Place the outer seal in the housing with the lip facing inward and press it into place. Then, place a 0.090 inch spacer washer on top of the seal.
7. Position the snap-ring in the housing. Press the snap-ring into the housing to properly locate the seals and engage the snap-ring in the groove.

Steering Gear Assembly

Do not clean, wash, or soak seals in cleaning solvent.

1. Mount the valve housing in the holding fixture with the flanged end up.
2. Place the required thickness valve spool centering shim in the housing.
3. Carefully install the worm and valve in the housing.
4. Install the race nut in the housing and torque it to 42 ft-lbs.
5. Install the race nut set screw (Allen head) through the valve housing and torque to 20-25 in-lbs.
6. Place the piston on the bench with the ball guide holes facing up. Insert the worm shaft into the piston so that the first groove is in alignment with the hole nearest to the center of the piston.
7. Place the ball guide in the piston. Place the 27 to 29 balls, depending on the piston design, in the ball guide turning the worm in a clockwise direction as viewed from the input end of the shaft. If all of the balls have not been fed into the guide upon reaching the right stop, rotate the input shaft in one direction and then in the other while installing the balls. After the balls have been installed, do not rotate the input shaft or the piston more than 3½ turns off the right stop to prevent the balls from falling out of the circuit.
8. Secure the guides in the ball nut with the clamp.
9. Position a new lube passage O-ring in the counterbore of the gear housing.
10. Apply vaseline to the teflon seal on the piston.
11. Place a new O-ring on the valve housing.
12. Slide the piston and valve into the gear housing being careful not to damage the teflon seal.
13. Align the lube passage in the valve housing with the one in the gear housing and install but do not tighten the attaching bolts.
14. Rotate the ball nut so that the teeth are in the same plane as the sector teeth. Tighten the four valve housing attaching bolts to 35-45 ft-lbs.
15. Position the sector shaft cover O-ring in the steering gear housing. Turn the input shaft as required to center the piston.
16. Apply vaseline to the sector shaft journal then position the sector shaft and cover assembly in the gear housing. Install the brake line bracket, the steering identification tag and two sector shaft cover attaching bolts. Torque the bolts to 55-70 ft-lbs.
17. Attach an in-lb torque wrench to the input shaft. Adjust the mesh load to 17 in-lbs.

Ross HF-54 and HF-64 Integral Power Steering Gear

Adjustments

Unloader Valve Adjustment

This unloader valve adjustment is for right turn only on HF-54 Model gears and for both turns on HF-64 Model gears. Prior to performing the following procedure, obtain the vehicle's straight ahead position by driving the vehicle with hands off the steering wheel thus allowing the unit to find its own center. Now mark the steering column to steering wheel with chalk or masking tape.

1. Check the front wheel turning angles and adjust as required with the wheels off the ground.
2. Position the wheels straight ahead and lower the vehicle.
3. RIGHT TURN—HF-54 OR HF-64 GEARS: With the engine at idle, the vehicle standing still and the fluid at normal operating temperature, rotate the steering wheel to the right the prescribed number of turns.

   H-54 .... 1¾
   H-64 - 2 port 1¼
   H-64 - 4 port 1½

   Hold in this position.
4. Loosen the locknut and turn the unloader valve pressure adjusting screw until an audible hiss is heard. Tighten the locknut.
5. Return the wheel to a straight ahead position while the vehicle is moving. With the vehicle standing still, again rotate the steering wheel the prescribed turns; then, check for the audible hiss. Readjust if necessary as in Step 4 and check once more as in this step. It is important to remember that the HF-64 gear has a pitman arm stop for the right turn cast on the gear housing. The pitman arm must not contact this stop prior to contacting the unloader valve. When the hiss is heard during the adjustment, the clearance between the pitman arm and the cast stop should be 1/16 to ⅛-inch minimum.
6. *Left turn—HF-64 gear only:* Repeat Steps 3, 4, and 5 while rotating the steering wheel to the left 1¾ turns.

Sector Shaft Adjustment

1. Disconnect the drag link from the Pitman arm.
2. Center the steering wheel. Grasp the Pitman arm and check it for free movement (lash) between the sector shaft and the rack piston.
3. If free movement is noted (lash), remove the steering gear from the vehicle.
4. Loosen the sector shaft adjustment screw locknut on the side cover.
5. After rotating the input shaft through its full travel for a minimum of five cycles, adjust the sector shaft adjusting screw to provide 15-20 in-lb torque as the input shaft is rotated 90 degrees each side of center.
6. Back out the adjusting screw one turn and note the torque required to move the input shaft 90 degrees each side of the center position. Move the adjusting screw in to provide an increase in torque of 2-4 in-lb at a point within 45 degrees each side of center after the adjusting screw jam nut is first tightened snug. Now torque to a final 20-25 ft-lb. The input torque of the completely assembled gear, minus hydraulic oil, should not exceed

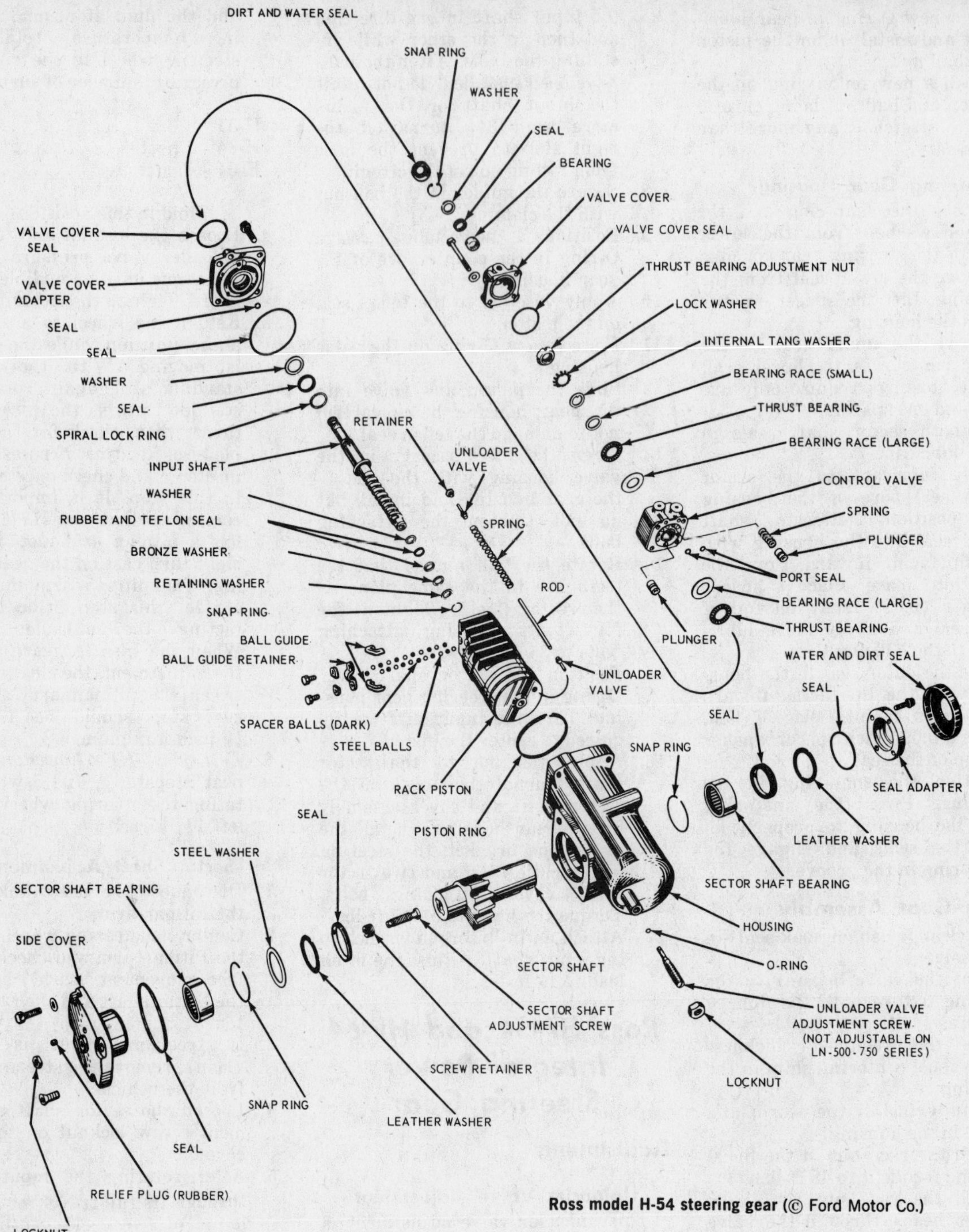

Ross model H-54 steering gear (© Ford Motor Co.)

15 in-lb for the full travel of the output shaft.

7. Install the steering gear in the vehicle.
8. Connect the drag link to the Pitman arm.
9. Connect the pump lines and refill the system with the specified fluid.

Disassembly

1. Rotate the input shaft so the index mark on the end of the sector shaft is perpendicular to the center-line of the gear (straight-ahead position).
2. Remove the side cover attaching screws and washers.
3. Tap lightly on the end of the sector shaft with a soft hammer to disengage the side cover seal and allow the housing to drain.
4. Remove all nicks, burrs, rust and paint before removing the shaft. Lift the side cover and sector shaft from the housing as an assembly.
5. Remove the sector shaft seal adapter attaching screws and remove the adapter from the housing.
6. Remove the four screws that attach the control valve adapter to the housing.
7. Remove the control valve and rack piston from the housing as an assembly.
8. Remove the sector shaft adjustment screw lock nut. Turn the adjustment clockwise until free of the side cover.
9. Remove the unloader valve retainer, unloader valves, rod and the spring from the rack piston.
10. If all parts appear undamaged, do not disassemble the rack piston assembly. If there is evidence of damage, place the rack

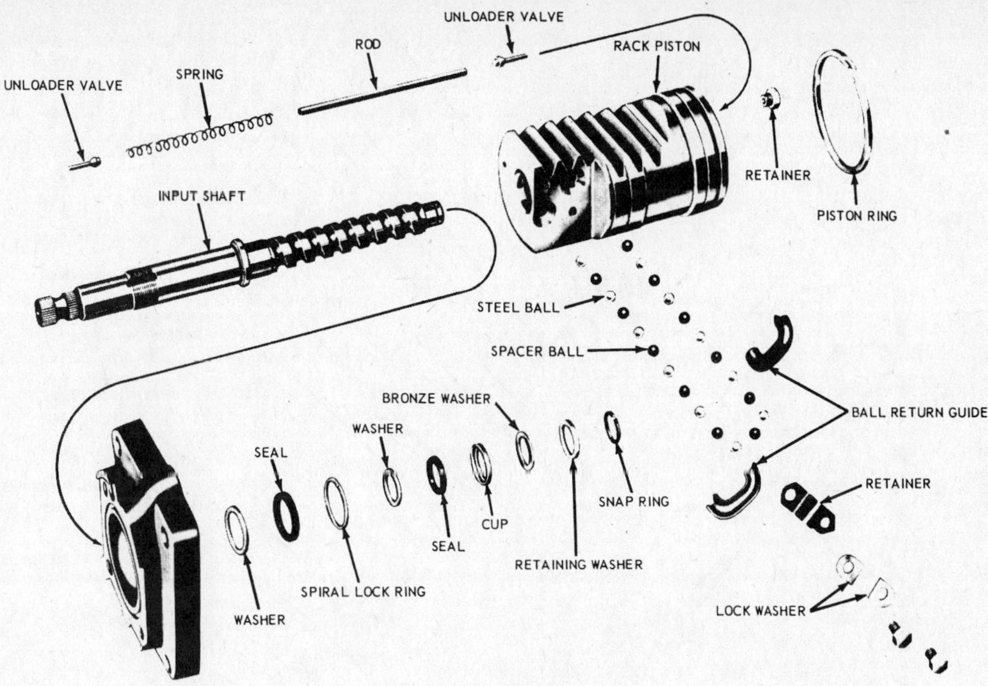

Input shaft seals and retainers (© Ford Motor Co.)

piston on a clean surface with the ball return guides facing upward. Remove the two ball return guide retainer attaching screws, lock washers, guide retainer, guide and balls. It may be necessary to tilt the rack piston over a clean pan and oscillate the worm shaft to empty the rack of all the balls. Lift the worm shaft from the rack after all the balls have been removed.

11. Carefully hold the input shaft in a vise equipped with soft jaws. Remove the snap-ring, washer, bronze washer, cup, seal and washer. It may be necessary to cut the teflon cup off the shaft.
12. Remove the valve cover dirt and water seal.
13. Remove the four valve cover attaching screws. Lift the cover from the control valve.
14. Unstake the thrust bearing adjustment nut lock washer and remove the adjustment nut.
15. Remove the lock washer, internal tang washer, bearing race (small), thrust bearing and the large bearing race.
16. Lift the control valve and the control valve adapter from the input shaft.
17. Remove spiral lock ring, seal and washer from the counterbore of the valve cover adapter. Discard the washer and seal.
18. Do not disassemble the valve unless absolutely necessary. The valve is the control center of the hydraulic system. The major parts, which are the body and spool, are machined to very close tolerances and with precision machined edges. The spool and valve body are selectively fitted at the factory, and therefore these two parts are not separately replaceable. If either is damaged or excessively worn, the complete valve assembly should be replaced. Good performance of power steering is not assured if a mismatched valve spool and body are used. Care should be exercised in the handling of these parts to prevent damage. Sealing edges of the valve bore and the spool should not be broken. This will result in excessive leakage and reduced hydraulic power. If valve parts should drop out during gear disassembly, reassemble the valve as follows:
    a. Clean all parts with a clean petroleum base solvent and blow dry with clean, dry air.
    b. Insert the valve spool in the control valve making certain that the machined identification groove in the ID of one end of the spool is toward the gear housing.
    c. There are 7 sets of plungers, each set having one reaction spring. Insert the 6 solid centering plunger sets first along with one spring per set. The remaining plunger set should be inserted in the valve body with the small hole on each plunger facing outboard.

Cleaning and Inspection

1. All parts should be cleaned in a clean petroleum base solvent and blown dry with clean dry air. Avoid wiping parts with a cloth, since lint may cause binding and sticking of closely fitted components.
2. Inspect the worm grooves in the rack piston and on the input shaft for wear scores. Inspect the OD of the rack piston and the ring or teeth for wear or scores. On the HF-64 gear, the ball nut and input shaft are serviced as a matched assembly. Therefore, both must be replaced if either are worn or damaged. The rack piston is not matched.
3. Inspect the inside ends of the ball return guides for wear or damage.
4. Inspect the housing bore for wear or scores or being cracked and replace as required.
5. Inspect the sector shaft teeth for wear or the bearing surfaces for wear or scores.
6. Replace the sector shaft bearings if worn or damaged. Note the sector shaft bearing in the side cover is replaced as part of the side cover assembly.
7. Replace all seals at time of disassembly.

Assembly

1. Lubricate all rubber parts prior to assembly.
2. If the sector shaft bearing was removed from the steering gear housing, install the snap-ring in the outboard side of the housing (HF-54 gear only).
3. Place the steering gear housing

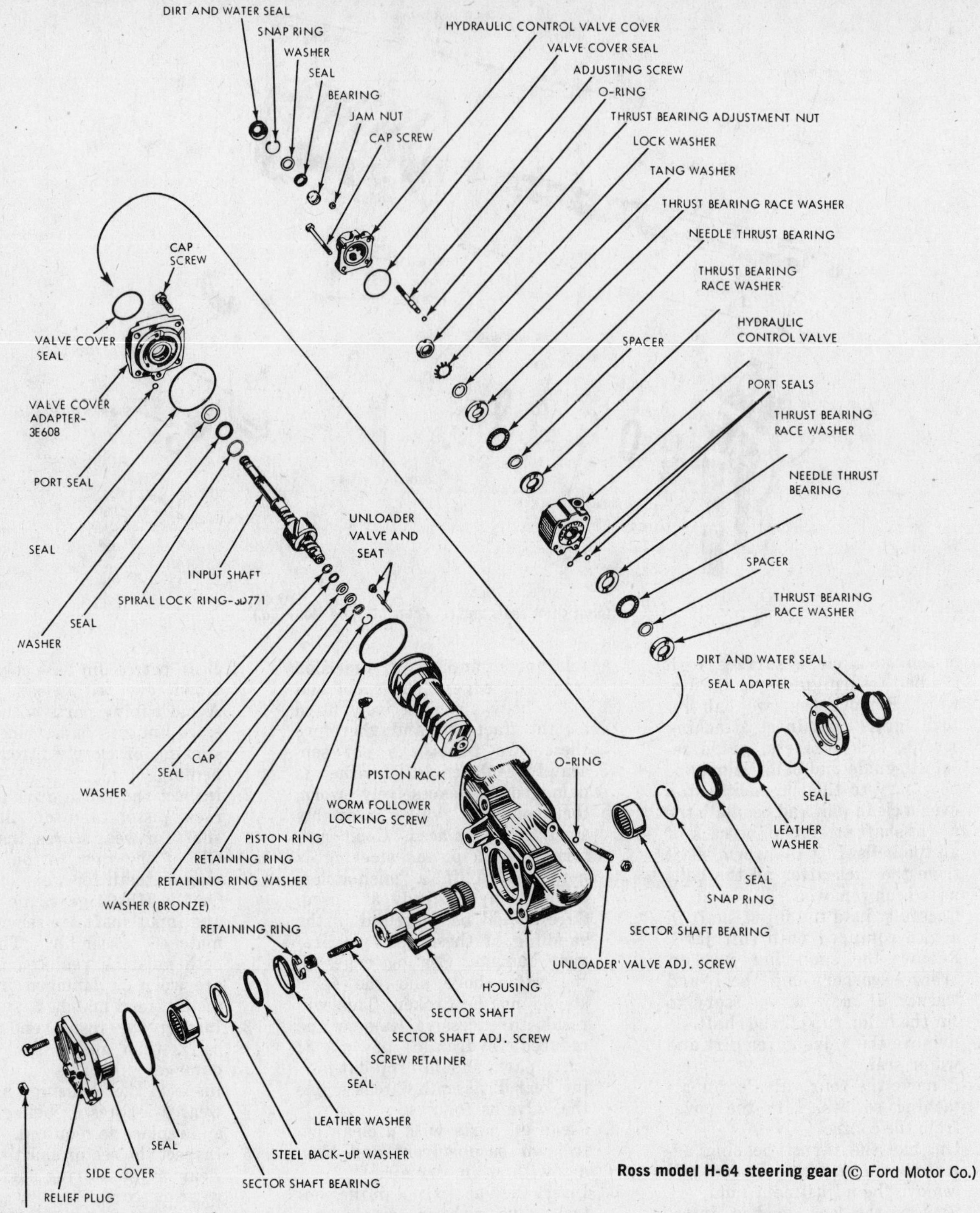

Ross model H-64 steering gear (© Ford Motor Co.)

in a press with the side cover area on a wood block to prevent damage to the machined area.

4. Position the bearing on the housing with the numbered end facing up. Carefully press the bearing into the housing until the outer surface is flush. Use a tool that pilots in the ID of the bearing and contacts the bearing end surface.
5. Coat the unloader valve pressure adjusting screw O-ring liberally with clean grease or oil. Carefully slide it into the groove on the non-threaded end of the adjusting screw.
6. Thread the adjusting screw into the lower end of the housing leaving 7/8 inch of the screw exposed. Install the lock nut on the adjusting screw and tighten it securely.
7. Carefully secure the input shaft in a vise equipped with soft jaws to permit access to both ends of the shaft.
8. On HF-54 gears, slide the bearing race (large) thrust bearing, control valve (with cylinder ports toward the shoulder), bearing race (small), internal tang washer, lock washer and thrust bearing adjustment nut. On HF-64 gears, slide the thrust bearing race washer, spacer, control valve (with cylinder ports toward the shoulder), needle thrust bearing, thrust bearing race washer, tang washer, lock washer and thrust bearing adjustment nut.
9. Tighten the adjustment nut to 20 ft-lbs, then back it off 1/2-1 lock washer tangs. Bend one

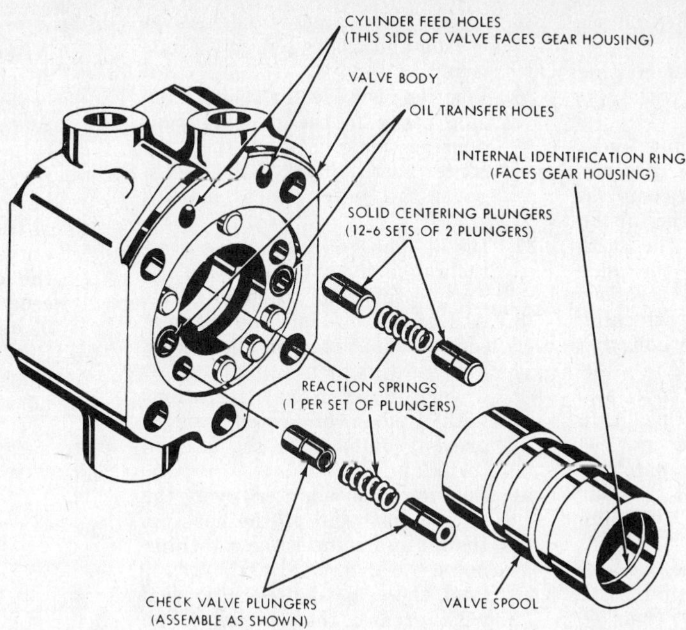

Hydraulic valve control assembly (© Ford Motor Co.)

tang of the lock washer into the slot provided on the adjustment nut. When adjusted in this manner, the control valve should rotate freely on the shaft with a torque of 2-3½ in-lbs and have no perceptible end play.

10. Assemble a new washer seal and the spiral lock ring in the counterbore of the valve cover adapter. Make sure that the lip of seal is facing toward the spiral lock ring.
11. Coat a new valve cover seal and two new cylinder port seals with grease to retain them in place. Position the seals in the recesses provided in the control valve cover adapter on the surface adjacent to the control valve.
12. Reposition the input shaft in the vise securing the serrated end
13. Slip the adapter over the worn groove end of the input shaft. Align the cylinder port seals with the ports in the control valve. Install one of the attaching bolts finger tight to facilitate assembly.
14. Assemble the washer (steel), a new rubber seal, new teflon cup with the lip toward the seal, bronze washer and retaining washer. Compress the washer and seal, then install the snap-ring on the end of the input shaft. Make sure that the snap-ring is fully seated in the groove and the recessed area of the retaining washer.
15. Secure the rack piston in a soft-jawed vise with the ball guide holes facing upward.
16. Carefully expand the piston ring and install it in the piston groove.
17. Place the two unloader valves, spring, and rod in the rack piston. Apply a drop of sealer to the threads of the retainer. Install and torque the retainer to 25 ft-lbs.
18. Coat the input shaft seal at the end of worm with grease and place it in the rack piston bore.
19. Assemble sixteen balls while rotating the input shaft counterclockwise. The black spacer balls and the polished steel balls must be installed alternately. Coat the ball return guides with grease to retain the balls, then install the six remaining balls in the guides making sure that the balls in the guide alternate with the last balls installed in the rack piston. If a ball is lost, no more than three black spacer balls may be used for replacement. Secure the guide retaining clip to the rack piston with two screws and washers. Torque the screws to 30-35 ft-lbs and bend the tab of the locking washer against the flat.
20. Grip the serrated end of the sector shaft in a soft-jawed vise.
21. Coat the head of the sector shaft adjusting screw with grease. Position the head of adjusting screw into the slot in the end of sector shaft.
22. Install a new sector shaft adjustment screw retainer in the end of shaft. Tighten the retainer to permit free rotation of screw without perceptible end play. Stake the retainer in the two slots provided and recheck the rotation effort.
23. If the pressure relief plug has been removed or ruptured, press a new one into the side cover until it is flush with the surface.
24. Assemble the snap-ring, steel washer (with taper toward the snap-ring), leather washer and the two piece seal into the side cover. The seal has Oil Side molded into one side and must be visible after installation.
25. Coat the end of sector shaft with lubricant. Rotate the sector shaft adjusting screw counterclockwise to thread it into the side cover. Rotate the screw until a firm stop is reaced. Make sure that the shaft seal has not fallen out of position.
26. Place the outer seal in the seal adapter. Then install the leather washer and inner seal making sure that the side having the mold. Oil Side is visible after installation.
27. If the input shaft needle bearing has been removed from the control valve cover it must be installed with a tool that will pilot in the bearing and have clearance in the cover bore. The bearing must be pressed from the part number end, and to a depth of 1⅛ inches from the face of the valve cover. After installation of the bearing, make sure that all rollers rotate freely.
28. Install the seal on the control valve cover with the lip facing toward the needle bearing. Coat the washer with grease and install it on the cover. Install the snap-ring to secure the seal and washer.
29. Pack the new dirt and water seal

with grease and install it on the control valve cover.

30. Secure the steering gear housing in a vise equipped with soft jaws.
31. Lubricate the steering gear housing bore. Start the rack piston into the bore, then compress the ring and move the piston into position so that the teeth are visible through the side cover opening. Install the four adapter - to - housing attaching bolts. Remove the one bolt that was previously installed.
32. Lubricate a new valve cover seal with grease and position it in the recess of the valve cover.
33. Slide the valve cover onto the input shaft and install the four cover-to-control valve attaching bolts.
34. Rotate the input shaft as required to align the center tooth of the rack piston (marked tooth) with the side cover opening.
35. Lubricate a new side cover O-ring and position it on the side cover.
36. Position the sector shaft and side cover to the steering gear housing making sure that the center tooth (marked tooth) engages the center space (marked space).
37. Install the four side cover attaching bolts and lock washers. Torque the bolts to 45-55 ft-lbs.
38. Adjust sector shaft adjustment screw as outlined in the Sector Shaft Adjustment.
39. Cover the sector shaft serrations with a layer of scotch tape to prevent damage to the seal in the adapter.
40. Position the adapter over the sector shaft and on the housing. Install and tighten the attaching bolts.
41. Pack the seal adapter outer seal with grease, then install it on the adapter to prevent water entry.

Final Checks

1. After rotating the input shaft through its full travel for a minimum of five cycles, recheck the sector shaft adjustment. No rotational lash or bind of the sector shaft in center position is permissible.
2. If the gear is properly assembled and adjusted, the input torque of the empty gear should not exceed 15 in-lbs over full travel of 95 degrees at the output shaft.
3. Reverse-torque applied to output shaft for full gear travel should not exceed 50 ft-lbs.

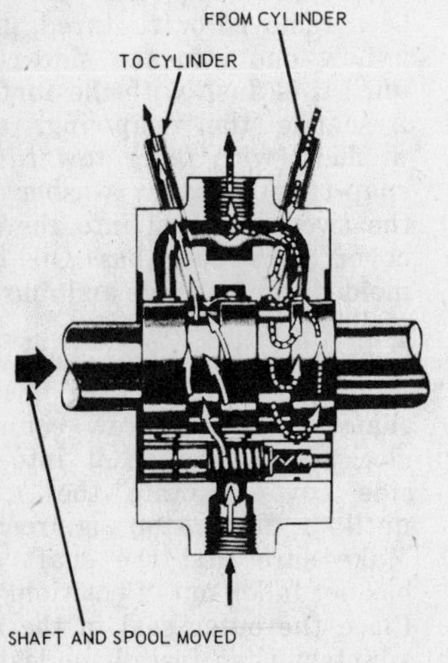

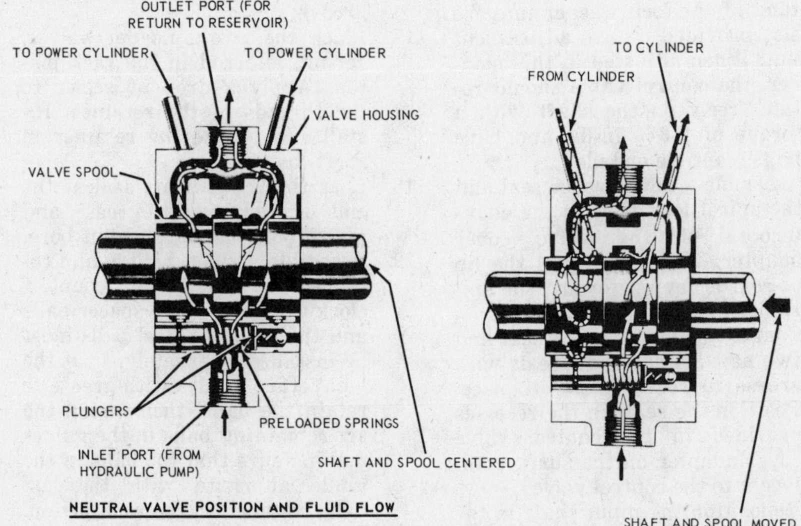

Power Flow

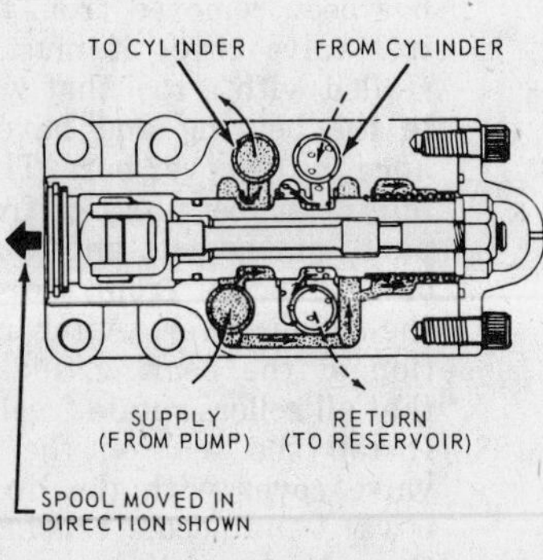

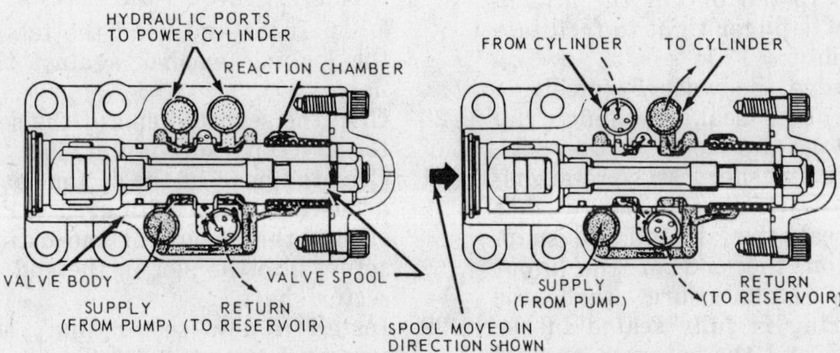

Semi-Integral Power Steering Gear Valve Power Flows

Truck Front End Trouble Diagnosis

Steering Wheel Spoke Position Not Centered

1. Start with steering gear set on high-spot.
2. Check for proper toe-in.
3. Check for proper relation between lengths of each tie rod.

Front End Rides Hard

1. Improper tires.
2. Improper air pressure.
3. Shock absorbers too severe or malfunctioning.

Rides Too Soft

1. Improper tire pressure.
2. Loss of spring load-rate, (weak springs).
3. Weak or leaking shock absorbers.

Truck Steers to One Side At All Times

1. Incorrect caster angle.
2. Incorrect camber angle.
3. Incorrect kingpin inclination or wheel support angle.
4. Unequal air pressure or unequal tread.
5. Unequal or one-side brake drag.
6. Unequal shock absorber control.
7. Bent or damaged steering suspension components.
8. Uneven or weak spring condition, front or rear, causing truck to sit unevenly.
9. Improper tracking.

Truck Steers to One Side Only When Brakes Are Applied

1. Improper brake adjustment, damaged or worn shoes or anchors.
2. Grease or foreign substance on brake lining.
3. Excessive wear or bent condition in suspension components.

Truck Steers Down Off Crowned Road But Normally on Flat Road

1. Excessive positive camber at one or both sides.
2. Weak or uneven shock absorber action.
3. Excessive or unequal wear in suspension components.

Truck Wanders—Steers Erratically

1. Incorrect caster.
2. Improper tire pressure or unequal treads.
3. Excessively worn or damaged suspension components.
4. Power steering gear damaged, causing power assist to function abnormally.

Truck Steers Hard

1. Binding steering or suspension parts.
2. Improper lubrication.
3. Improper (too large) tires.
4. Low tire pressure.

Tires Cup on Outside Edge With Ripple Wear Pattern

1. Generally incorrect camber or toe-in.

Tires Wear Unevenly in Center and Faster Than Outer Edges

1. Generally too much tire pressure.

Tires Wear and Scuff on Both Outer Edges, Not in Center

1. Generally low tire pressure.

Uneven Outer Wear—Center and Inner Edge Wear Normal

1. With adjustments normal this is usually caused by driving into turns at too high speed. Do not confuse with outer edge cupping.

Unequal Tire Wear Between Front Wheels

1. Unequal tire pressure.
2. Unequal tire quality or size.
3. Bent or worn steering suspension components.
4. Improper tracking.

Tire Squeal on Turns

1. Low tire pressure.
2. Driving into turn too fast.
3. Damaged or misaligned parts causing improper front wheel toe-out steering radius.
4. Improper camber adjustment.

Wheel Bounce

1. Unequal tire pressure.
2. Unbalanced wheels or tires.
3. Excessive wheel or tire run-out.
4. Weak or broken front springs.
5. Inoperative shock absorber.
6. Loose or damaged wheel bearings.

Noisy Front End

1. Lack of, or improper, lubrication.
2. Loose tie rod ends.
3. Worn spring shackle.
4. Inoperative shock absorber.
5. Loose U-bolts or clips.
6. Broken spring.
7. Worn universal (FWD).
8. Worn differential (FWD).

Lubricant Leaking Into Drums

1. Too much differential lubricant (FWD).
2. Clogged axle housing vent (FWD).
3. Damaged or worn universal driveshaft oil seal (FWD).
4. Loose steering knuckle flange bearings (FWD).
5. Defective outer oil seal.
6. Rough spindle bearing surface.
7. Wheel bearings over-packed or using wrong type lubricant.
8. Clogged wheel bearing oil slinger drain.
9. Cracked steering knuckle outer flange.

CONDITION	RAPID WEAR AT SHOULDERS	RAPID WEAR AT CENTER	CRACKED TREADS	WEAR ON ONE SIDE	FEATHERED EDGE	BALD SPOTS
CAUSE	UNDER INFLATION	OVER INFLATION	UNDER-INFLATION OR EXCESSIVE SPEED	IMPROPER CAMBER	INCORRECT TOE	WHEEL UNBALANCED
CORRECTION	ADJUST PRESSURE TO SPECIFICATIONS WHEN TIRES ARE COOL			ADJUST CAMBER TO SPECIFICATIONS	ADJUST FOR TOE-IN 1/8 INCH	DYNAMIC OR STATIC BALANCE WHEELS

Wheel Alignment

For a truck to have safe steering control with a minimum of tire wear, certain established rules must be followed. These rules fix the values of planes, angles and radii relative to each other and to truck and tire dimensions. Some factors are built in, with no provision for adjustment; others are adjustable within limits. The entire system, being a relative one, depends upon all value factors, separately and combined. It is therefore difficult to change some of the established settings without influencing others.

This system is called steering geometry or wheel alignment and requires a complete check of all the factors involved. Definitions of these factors and the effect each one has on the truck are given in the following paragraphs.

For adjustment data relative to each separate truck and year, refer to the individual truck sections.

Toe-in, Relative to Steering Wheel Position

Toe-in, or straightaway alignment, is a value given the negative distance between the front extremes of the two front, or rear, wheels relative to a like masurement taken at the rear extremes of the same wheels. This factor of alignment is blamed for more steering and tire wear troubles than any other. The careless or inexperienced mechanic will attempt all sorts of corrective measures with a turn of the tie-rod adjustments.

Always check steering wheel alignment in conjunction with and at the same time as, toe-in. In fact, the steering wheel spoke position, with the truck on a straight section of highway, may be the first indication of front end misalignment. Check the spoke position relative to straight-ahead truck travel. If the wheel is not in a normal straight position, the condition may be corrected during toe-in adjustment.

1. Loosen the tie-rod adjusting clamps.
2. If the steering wheel position is satisfactory, shorten or lengthen both tie-rods (the same amount) to the required toe-in specifications.

If, however, after correcting the toe-in value, the steering wheel position is wrong, shorten the left and lengthen the right tie-rod, or lengthen the left and shorten the right tie-rod (the same amount) to obtain the desired steering wheel position.

If the truck has been wrecked, or indicates any evidence of steering gear or linkage disturbance, the pitman arm should be disconnected from the sector shaft. The steering wheel (or gear) should be disconnected and turned from extreme right to exteme left to determine the halfway point in its turning scope. This will be the spot on the gear that is in action during straight ahead driving and in which position the steering gear should be adjusted. With the steering wheel in the straight-ahead position and the steering gear adjusted to zero lash status, reconnect the pitman arm.

Steering Geometry

Camber Angle

Camber is the amount that the front wheels are inclined outward at the top. Camber is spoken of, and measured, in degrees from the perpendicular.

The purpose of the camber angle is to take some of the load off the spindle outboard bearing.

Caster Angle

Caster is the amount that the king-pin (or in the case of trucks without king-pins, the knuckle support pivots) is tilted towards the back of the truck. Caster is usually spoken of, and measured, in degrees. Positive caster means that the top of the kingpin is tilted toward the back of the truck. Positive caster is indicated by the sign +.

Negative caster is exactly the opposite; the top of the kingpin is tilted toward the front of the truck. This is generally indicated by the sign –.

Negative caster is sometimes re-

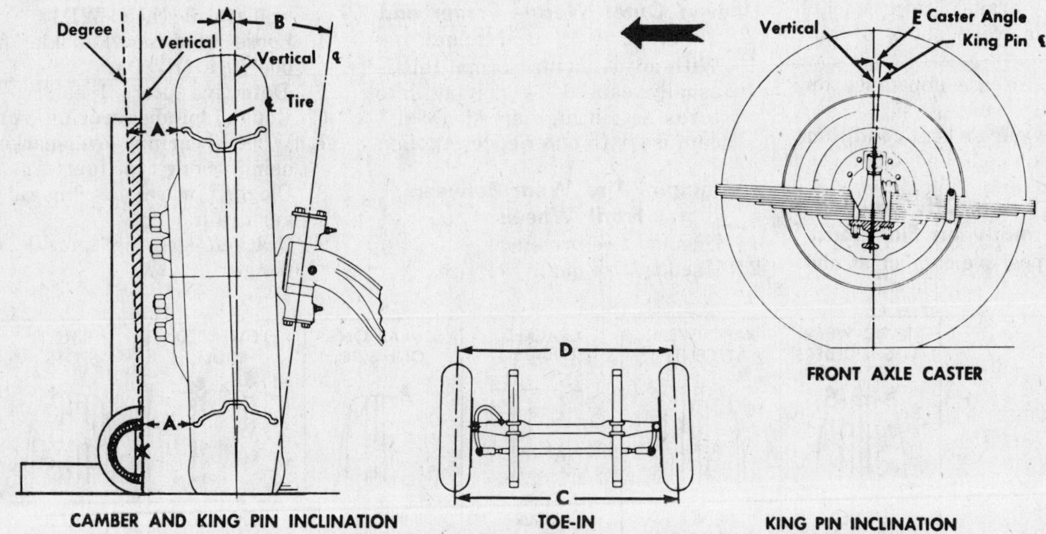

*A Camber (degrees positive)
*B King pin inclination (degrees)
*C Minus D Toe-in (inches)
*E Caster (degrees positive)
*Refer to "Specifications" for correct dimensions

Front end alignment chart (© G.M.C.)

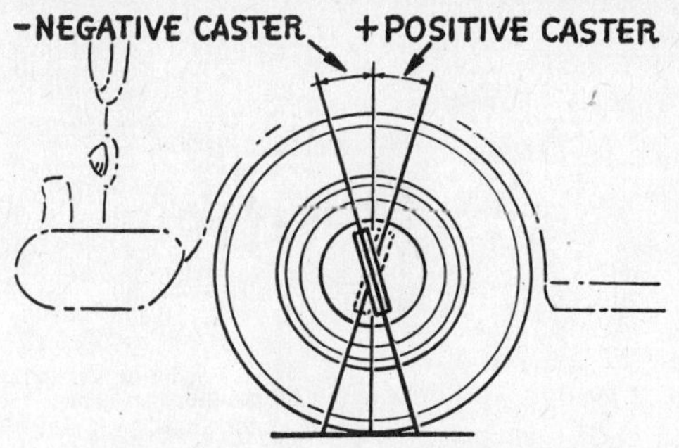

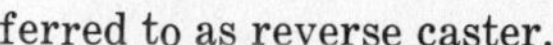
Caster angle, note that if the pivot tilts forward, caster is negative, tilted back, caster is positive

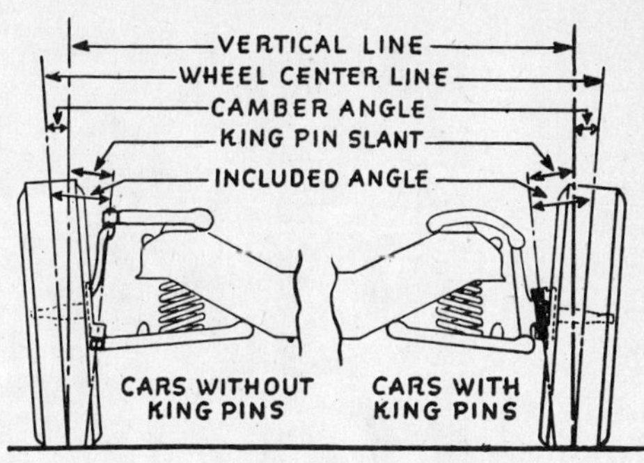

Camber, king pin slant and included angle

ferred to as reverse caster.

The effect of positive caster is to cause the truck to steer in the direction in which it tends to go. This is not necessarily a straight line, since trucks with independently sprung front wheels usually steer easily. Positive caster in the front wheels may cause the truck to steer down off a crowned road or steer in the direction of a cross wind. For this reason, many of our modern trucks are arranged with negative caster so that the opposite is true; the truck tends to steer up a crowned road and into a cross wind.

Angle of Kingpin Inclination

In addition to the caster angle, the kingpins (or knuckle support pivots) are also inclined toward each other at the top. This angle is known as kingpin inclination and is usually spoken of, and measured, in degrees.

The effect of kingpin inclination is to cause the wheels to steer in a straight line, regardless of outside forces such as crowned roads, cross winds, etc., which may tend to make it steer at a tangent. As the spindle is moved from extreme right to extreme left it apparently rises and falls. Notice that it reaches its highest position when the wheels are in the straight-ahead position. In actual operation, the spindle cannot rise and fall because the wheel is in constant contact with the ground.

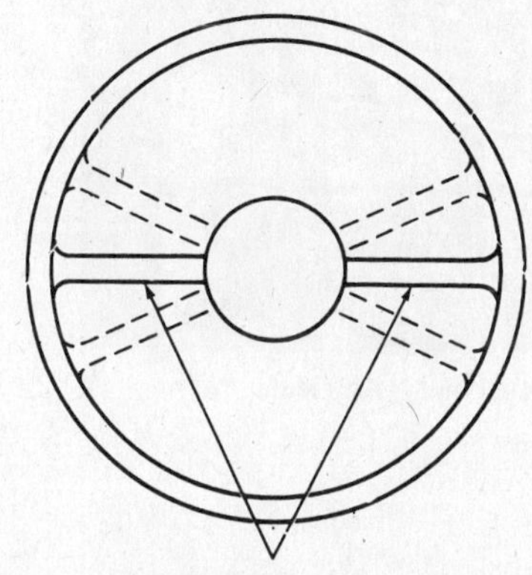
Steering wheel position

Therefore, the truck itself will rise at the extreme right turn and come to its lowest point at the straight-ahead position, and again rise for an extreme left turn. The weight of the truck will tend to cause the wheels to come to the straight-ahead position, which is the lowest position of the truck itself.

Included Angle

Included angle is the name given to that angle which includes kingpin inclination and camber. It is the relationship between the centerline of the wheel and the centerline of the kingpin (or the knuckle support pivots). This angle is built into the knuckle (spindle) forging and will remain constant throughout the life of the truck, unless the spindle itself is damaged.

When checking a truck on the front end stand, always measure kingpin inclination as well as camber unless some provision is made on the stand for checking condition of the spindle. Where no such provision is made, add the kingpin inclination to the camber for each side of the truck. These totals should be exactly the same, regardless of how far from the norm the readings may be.

For example, the left side of the truck checks 5½° kingpin inclination and 1° positive camber—total 6½°.

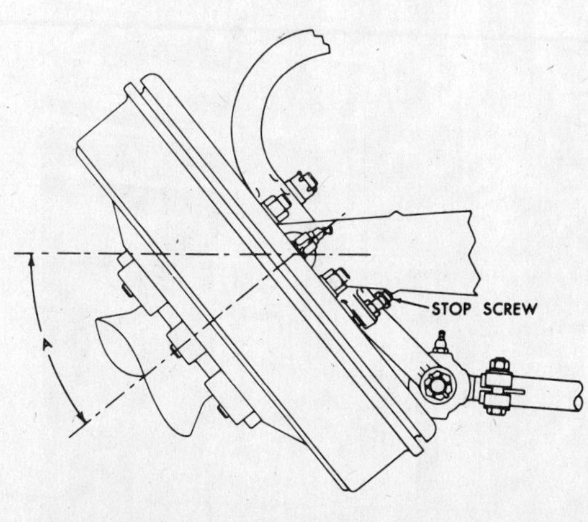

Stop screw adjustment (© G.M. Corp.)

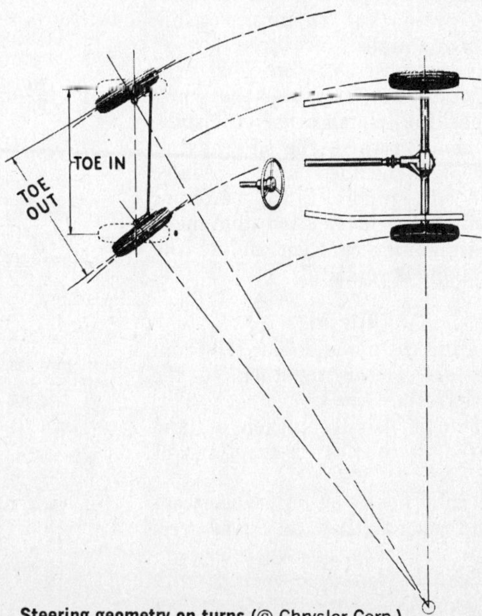

Steering geometry on turns (© Chrysler Corp.)

Twin-I-Beam caster decrease tool installation (© Ford Motor Co.)

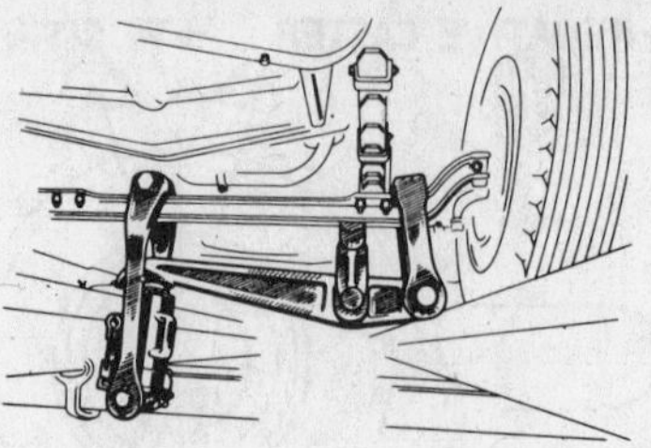

Tool installation for camber increase (© Ford Motor Co.)

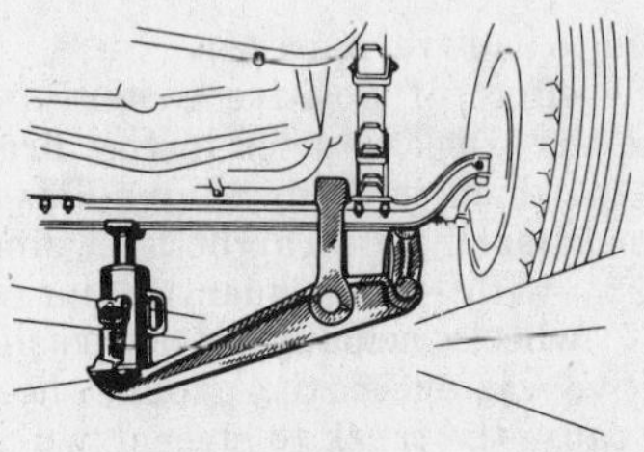

Tool installation for camber decrease (© Ford Motor Co.)

Since both sides check exactly the same for the included angle, it is unlikely that both spindles, in this instance, are bent. Adjusting to correct for camber will automatically set correct kingpin inclination.

A bent spindle would show up like this: left side of the truck has $\frac{3}{4}°$ positive camber, $5\frac{1}{4}°$ kingpin inclination—total 6° included angle. Right side of truck has $1\frac{1}{4}°$ positive camber, 6° kingpin inclination—total $7\frac{1}{4}°$ included angle. One of these spindles is bent and if adjustments are made to correct camber, the kingpin inclination will be incorrect due to the bent spindle.

Since the most common cause of a bent spindle is striking the curb when parking, which causes the spindle to bend upward, the side having the greater included angle usually has the bent spindle. It will be found impossible to achieve good alignment and minimum tire wear unless the bent spindle is replaced.

Toe-in

Toe-in is the amount that the front wheels are closer together at the front than they are at the back. This dimension is usually spoken of, and measured, in inches or fractions of inches.

Generally speaking, the wheels are toed-in because they are cambered. When a truck operates with 0° camber it will be found to operate with zero toe-in. As the required camber increases, so does the toe-in. The reason for this is that the cambered wheel tends to steer in the direction in which it is cambered. Therefore it is necessary to overcome this tendency of the wheel by compensating very slightly in the direction opposite to that in which it tends to roll. Caster and camber both have an effect on toe-in. Therefore toe-in is the last thing on the front end which should be corrected. Always set caster, camber and kingpin inclination (included angle) before setting toe-in.

Toe-out Steering Radius

When a truck is steered into a turn, the outside wheel of the vehicle scribes a much larger circle than the inside wheel. Therefore, the outside wheel must be steered to a somewhat less angle than the inside wheel. This difference in angle is often called toe-out.

Twin-I-Beam caster increase tool installation (© Ford Motor Co.)

The change in angle from toe-in in the straight-ahead position to toe-out in the turn is caused by the relative position of the steering arms to the kingpin and to each other.

If a line were drawn from the center of the kingpin through the center of the steering arm-tie rod attaching hole at each wheel, these lines would be found to cross almost exactly in the center of the rear axle.

If the front end angles, including toe-in, are set correctly, and the toe-out is found to be incorrect, one or both of the steering arms are bent.

Tracking

While tracking is more a function of the rear axle and frame, it is difficult to align the front suspension when the truck does not track straight. Tracking means that the centerline of the rear axle follows exactly the path of the centerline of the front axle when the truck is moving in a straight line.

On trucks that have equal tread, front and rear, the rear tires will follow in exactly the tread of the front tires, when moving in a straight line. However, there are many trucks whose rear tread is wider than the front tread. On such trucks, the rear axle tread will straddle the front axle tread an equal amount on both sides, when moving in a straight line.

Perhaps the easiest way to check a truck for tracking is to stand directly in back of it and watch it move in a straight line down the street. If the observer will stand as near to the center of the truck as possible, he can readily observe, even with the difference in perspective between the front and rear wheels, whether or not they are tracking properly. If the truck is found to track incorrectly, the difficulty will be found in either the frame or in the rear axle alignment.

Another more accurate method to check tracking is to park the truck on a level floor and drop a plumb-line from the extreme outer edge of the front suspension lower A-frame. Use

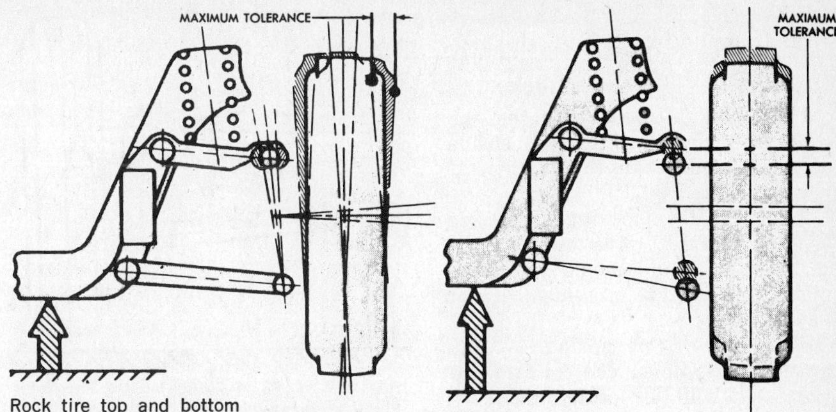

Rock tire top and bottom
Reject if movement at tire sidewall exceeds maximum tolerance, but do not confuse wheel bearing looseness with ball joint wear

Check ball joint radial (side) play

Reject if axial play in ball joint exceeds maximum tolerance

Check ball joint axial (up and down) play

the same drop point on each side of the truck. Make a chalk line where the plumb-line strikes the floor. Do the same with the rear axle, selecting a point on the rear axle housing for the plumb-line.

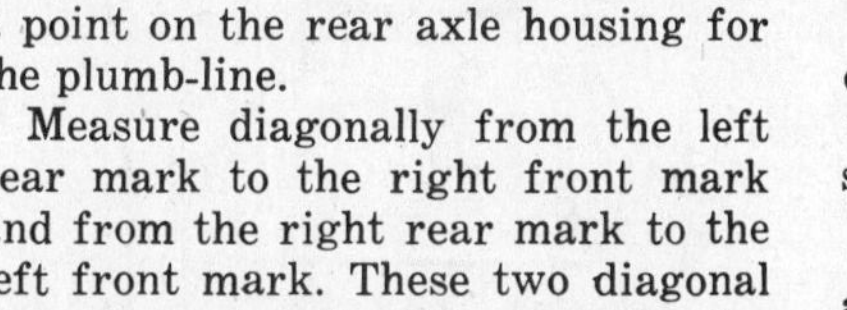

Measure diagonally from the left rear mark to the right front mark and from the right rear mark to the left front mark. These two diagonal measurements should be exactly the same. A 1/4″ variation is acceptable.

If the diagonal measurements taken are different, measure from the right rear mark to the right front mark and from the left rear to the left front. These two measurements should also be the same within 1/4″.

Checking lower ball joint (typical)
(© G.M. Corp.)

If the diagonal measurements are different, but the longitudinal measurements are the same, the frame is swayed (diamond shaped).

However, in the event that the diagonal measurements are unequal and the longitudinal measurements are also unequal, and the truck is tracking incorrectly, the rear axle is misaligned.

If the diagonal and longitudinal measurements are both unequal, but the truck appears to track correctly on the street, a kneeback is indicated.

NOTE: A kneeback means that one complete side of the front suspension is bent back. This is often caused by crimping the front wheels against the curb when parking the vehicle, then starting up without straightening the wheels out.

Suspension and Ball Joint Checks

When checking the suspension and ball joints, it is advisable to follow the manufacturer's recommendations. For all practical purposes,

Removing tie rod end from steering knuckle
(© Chrysler Corp.)

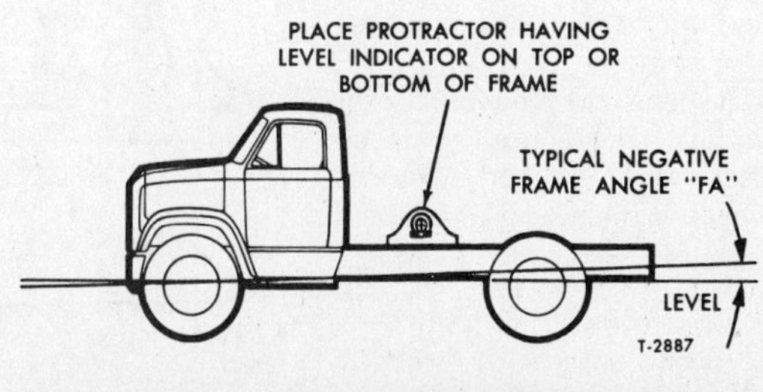

Method of checking frame angle
(© G.M.C.)

however, the following general procedures ae applicable.

Suspension System Check

This check is made with the ball joints fully loaded, so that suspension elements other than the ball joints may be checked.

When the front spring or torsion bar is supported by the lower control arm, the jackstand should be located under the front crossmember or frame.

When the front spring is supported by the upper control arm, the jackstand should be located under the lower control arm.

Vertical or horizontal movement at

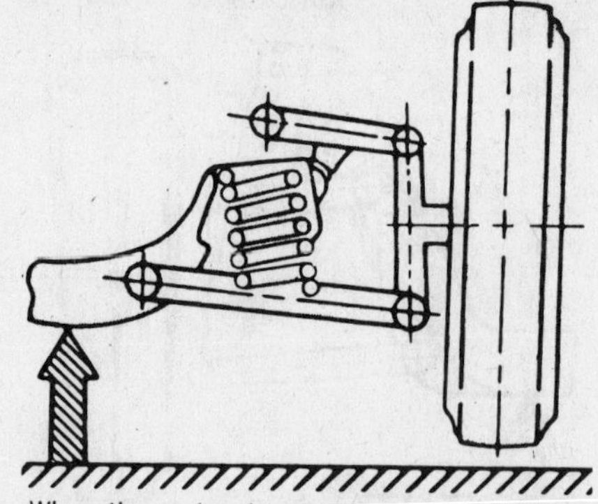

When the spring is supported on the lower control arm, vehicle must be jacked from the frame or cross member

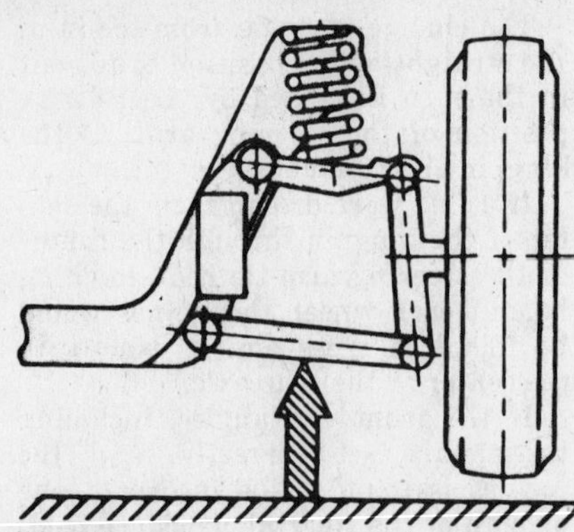

When the spring is supported by the upper control arm, the vehicle must be jacked at the lower control arm

Steering and suspension jacking procedure

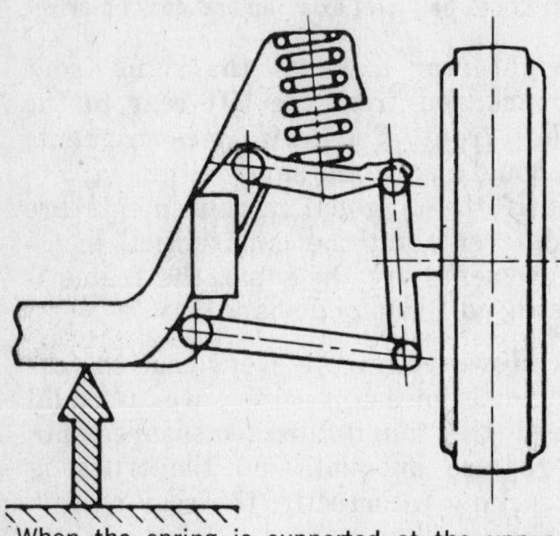

When the spring is supported at the upper control arm, the truck must be hoisted at the frame

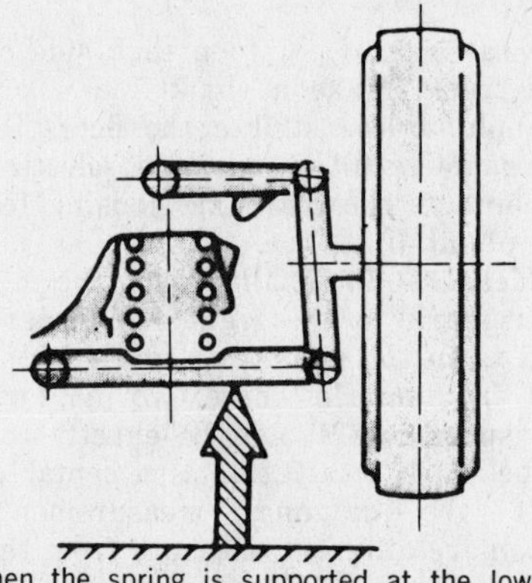

When the spring is supported at the lower control arm, truck must be hoisted at the arm Reject if upper joint is perceptibly loose

Ball joint inspection jacking procedure

the road wheel should not exceed the following:

Up to and including 16 inches	¼″
16 to 18 inches	⅓″
More than 18 inches	½″

Ball Joint Check

When checking the ball joints for any wear, they must be free of any load.

When the front spring or torsion bar is supported by the lower control arm, the jackstand should be positioned under the lower control arm.

When the front spring is supported by the upper control arm, the jackstand should be located under the front crossmember or frame.

Replace the upper ball joint if any noticeable play is present in the joint when the spring is supported by the upper control arm.

Replace the load carying ball joint if the sideplay (horizontal motion) of the wheel, when rocked, exceeds specifications; or if the up and down (vertical motion) exceeds specifications.

Wheel Bearing and Seal Replacement

Place jack under lower suspension arm. Remove hub cover and grease cap. Remove spindle nut, keyed washer and outer bearing. Slide off hub and drum.

NOTE: In some cases, drum removal may require loosening of brake adjustment.

At this point, brakes and drums should be inspected for their condition.

With hub and drum on bench, remove seal and inner bearing. Thoroughly clean all parts. Drive out inner and outer races of roller type. Use care not to mar the bearing surfaces.

Pack bearings with approved lubricant. When replacing cups, use a bearing race driver if possible. If a punch is used, make sure it is blunt and then drive parts in very carefully to avoid cocking the bearings.

Install new grease seal in hub. Assemble hub and drum on spindle and replace the outer bearing, key washer and nut.

A common method of adjustment is to tighten to zero clearance and then back off to first cotter pin castellation. Some manufacturers recommend tightening to approximately 10 to 12 ft. lbs., then backing off nut 1/6 turn. If cotter pin hole does not line up, loosen slightly.

Readjust brake if necessary and install grease cap and hub cover. Remove jack.

Kingpin and Bushing Replacement

Kingpins and bushings can be placed in two general classes; (A) with bushings in knuckle, (B) with bushings in spindle.

Jack up the truck and remove the

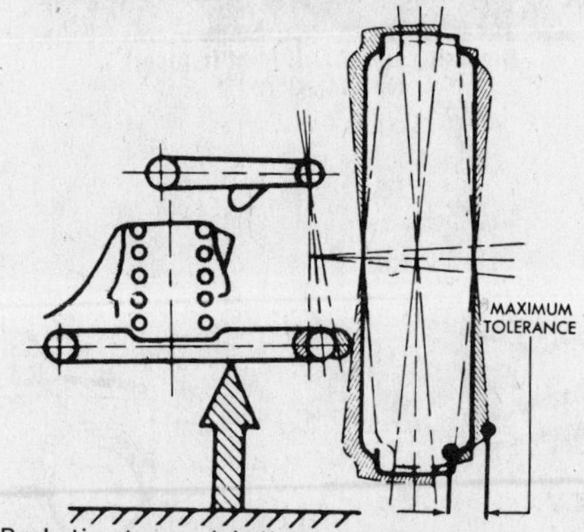

Rock tire top and bottom
Reject if movement at tire sidewall exceeds maximum tolerance, but do not confuse wheel bearing looseness with ball joint wear

Check ball joint radial (side) play

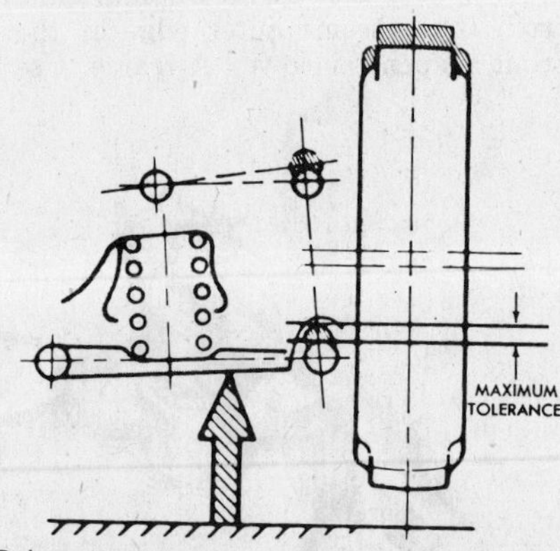

Reject if axial play in ball joint exceeds maximum tolerance

Check ball joint axial (up and down) play

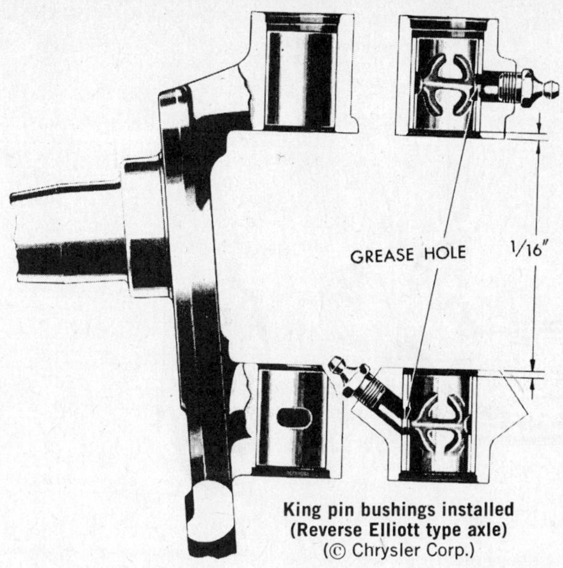

King pin bushings installed
(Reverse Elliott type axle)
(© Chrysler Corp.)

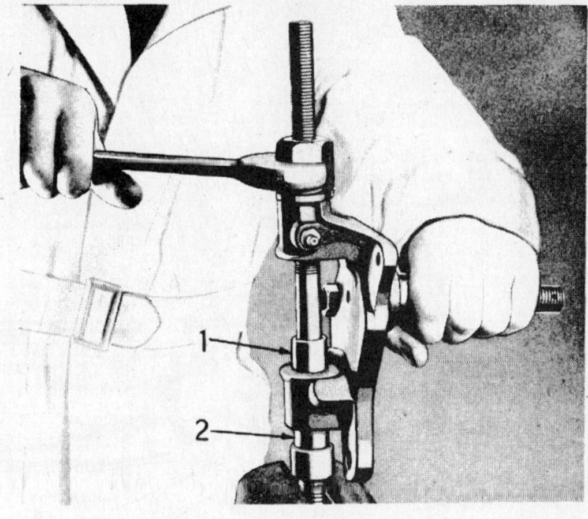

Removing king pin bushings (reverse Elliott type axle)
(© Chrysler Corp.)

hub as described in the wheel bearing section.

1. Remove backing plate to knuckle bolts and lift assembly, with brakes, from the knuckle. Suspend it with a piece of wire to prevent damage to brake hose.
2. Drive out lock pin or bolt. With a sharp punch, remove top welch plug. Now drive pin and lower welch plug down through knuckle and support.
3. Drive bushings from the spindle and replace them. Be sure, when driving new bushing, that grease holes line up with those in knuckle.
4. Align and ream bushings to a snug running fit for the new kingpin.
5. Insert the kingpin through the top of the spindle, support, thrust bearing (with shims to control vertical play) and into the spindle bottom. Keep the kingpin in proper rotation so that the lockpin can be inserted. Install lockpin or bolt. Install upper and lower welch plugs.
6. Install backing plate with steering arms and lubricate properly.
7. Install hubs, drums and wheels, then remove jack.

Ball Joint Replacement

Upper Ball Joint R & R Riveted Type

On some trucks, the upper ball joint is riveted to the control arm. Place jack under lower arm and raise wheel clear of the floor. Remove wheel. Remove nut from ball joint. If joint is being replaced, it may be driven out with a heavy hammer. If threads are to be saved, a

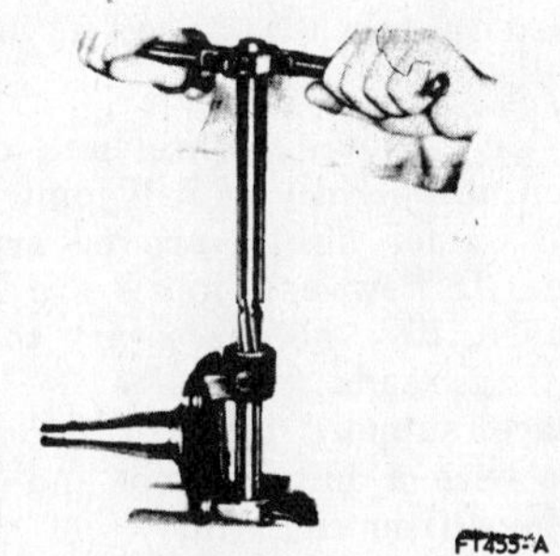

Reaming bushings
(© Ford Motor Co.)

spreader tool should be used.

After removing joint from knuckle support, cut off rivets at upper arm. Drilling rivets eases this job.

To replace the ball joint: install in upper arm, using special bolts supplied with new joint. Do not use ordinary bolts.

Next, set the taper into the upper end of the knuckle support and install nut and cotter pin. Check alignment.

Threaded Type

On some trucks, the upper ball joint is threaded into the control arm.

Place jack under lower control arm and relieve load on torsion bar. Raise wheel clear of floor. Remove wheel. Remove nut from ball joint. If ball joint is being replaced, it may be driven out with a heavy hammer. If

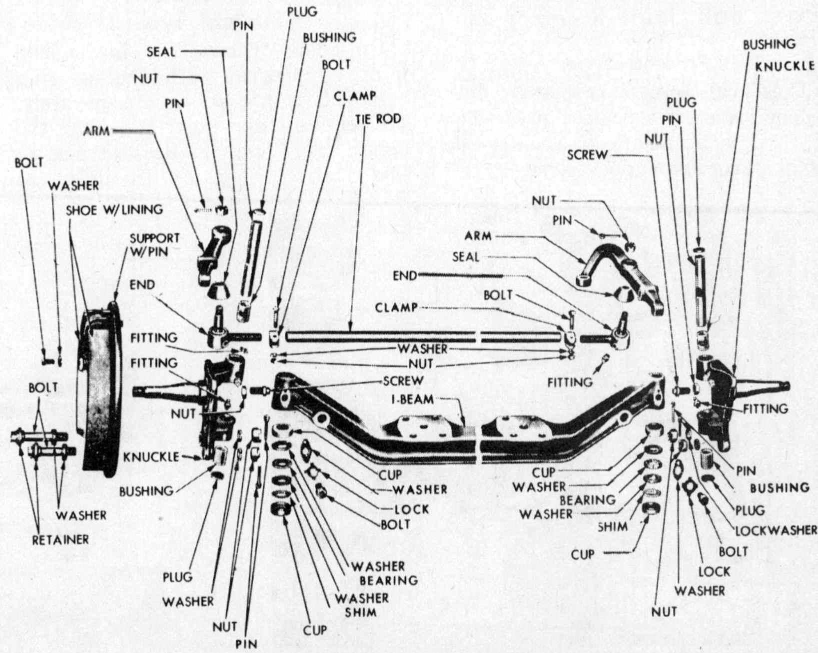

Reverse Elliott type front axle (© Chrysler Corp.)

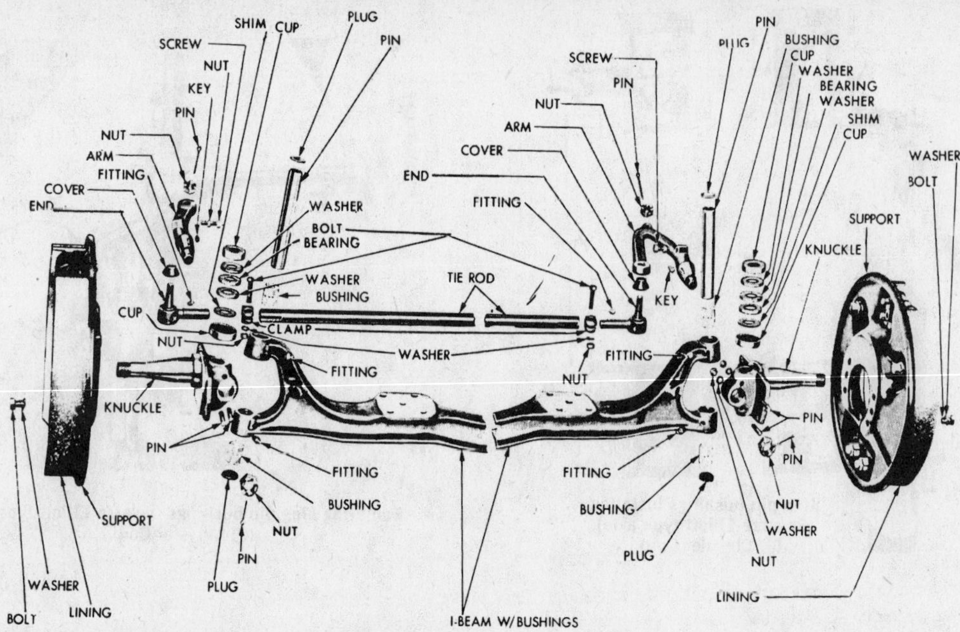

Elliott type front axle (© Chrysler Corp.)

threads are to be saved, use a spreader tool.

After removing from knuckle support, the ball joint can be unscrewed from the support arm. Special tools are recommended for this operation.

When replacing the ball joint, be sure to engage the threads into the control arm squarely. Torque to 125 ft. lbs. If this torque cannot be obtained, check for bad threads in arm or on joint. Install new balloon seal.

Place joint in knuckle and install nut. Reload torsion bar (if so equipped) and reset height.

Lower Ball Joint R & R

Pressed Type

These ball joints are pressed into support arms. To replace pressed-in units, it is necessary to remove the front spring and support arm.

After removing wheel and drum, loosen nut slightly at ball joint taper and hammer lightly around area to loosen. If new ball joints are being installed, it is not necessary to protect the threads.

Place support arm in an arbor press with a suitable tool and press ball joint from the arm.

Install ball joint by reversing the pressing procedure.

NOTE: Special tools of the C-clamp type are available and can be used on some trucks to avoid removal of front spring and support arm.

Integral Type

On some trucks, the lower ball joint is integral with the steering arm and is not serviced separately. To service this unit: Remove the upper arm bumper. Raise truck so that front suspension is under no load. If jacks are used, a support must be placed between the jack and K-member.

1. Remove the wheel and drum assembly. Remove the two lower bolts holding the steering arm to the backing plate.
2. Disconnect tie-rod end from the steering arm. Do not damage seal.
3. Remove the ball joint stud from the lower control arm. A spreading tool will aid in this operation.
4. Install new seal on ball joint. Bolt the steering arm to the backing plate. Insert the ball joint into control arm and torque nut to 100 ft. lbs.
5. Connect the tie-rod end. Install drum and wheel. Reload and adjust torsion bar (if so equipped) and reset height.

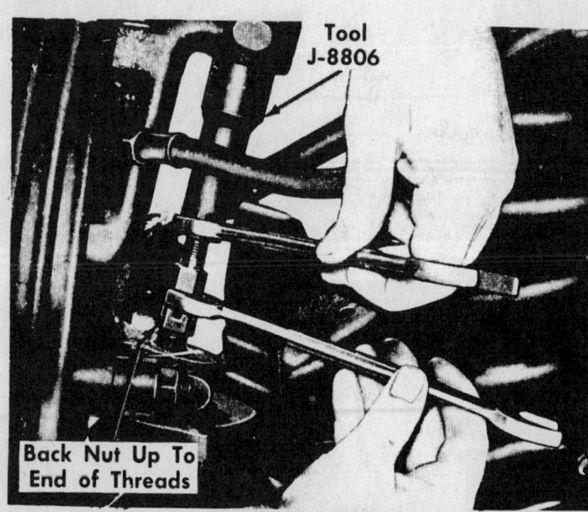

Loosening lower ball joint stud (© G.M. Corp.)

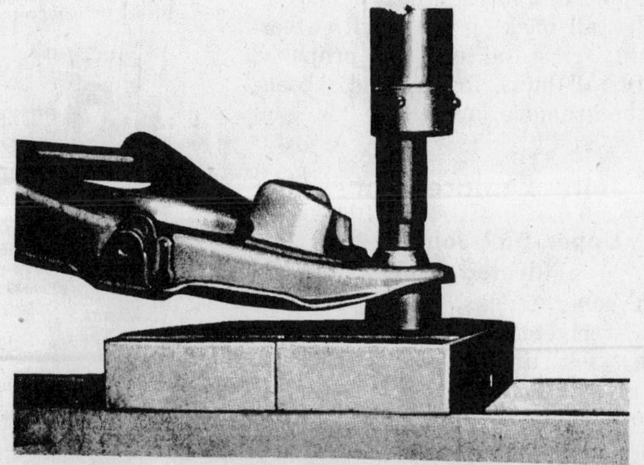
Removing lower ball Joint (© G.M. Corp.)

Transfer Cases

Index

Transfer Case Trouble Analysis

Slips Out of Gear (High-Low)

1. Shifting poppet spring weak.
2. Bearing broken or worn.
3. Shifting fork bent.
4. Improper control rod adjustment.

Slips Out of Front Wheel Drive

1. Shifting poppet spring weak or broken.
2. Bearing worn or broken.
3. Excessive shaft end-play.
4. Shifting fork bent.

Hard Shifting

1. Lack of lubricant.
2. Shift lever binding on shaft.
3. Shifting poppet ball scored.
4. Shifting fork bent.
5. Low tire pressure.

Backlash

1. Companion yoke loose.
2. Transfer case loose on mounts.
3. Internal parts excessively worn.

Noisy

1. Low lubricant level.
2. Bearings improperly adjusted or excessively worn.
3. Gears worn or damaged.
4. Improper alignment of driveshafts or U-joints.

Oil Leakage

1. Excessive amount of lubricant in case.
2. Vent clogged.
3. Gaskets or seals leaking.
4. Bearings loose or damaged.
5. Driveshaft yoke mating surfaces scored.

Overheating

1. Excessive or insufficient amount of lubricant.
2. Bearing adjustment too tight.

Cleaning and Inspection

Cleaning

During overhaul, all components of the transfer case (except bearing assemblies) should be thoroughly cleaned with solvent and dried with air pressure prior to inspection and reassembly.

1. Clean the bearing assemblies as follows. NOTE: Proper cleaning of bearings is of utmost importance. Bearings should always be cleaned separately from other parts.
   a. Soak all bearing assemblies in CLEAN solvent, gasoline, or fuel oil. Bearings should never be cleaned in a hot solution tank.
   b. Slush bearings in solvent until all old lubricant is loosened. Hold races so that bearings will not rotate; then clean bearings with a soft bristled brush until all dirt has been removed. Remove loose particles of dirt by tapping bearing flat against a block of wood.
   c. Rinse bearings in clean solvent; then blow bearings dry with air pressure. CAUTION: Do not spin bearings while drying.
   d. After drying, rotate each bearing slowly while examining balls or rollers for roughness, damage, or excessive wear. Replace all bearings that are not in first class condition. NOTE: After cleaning and inspecting bearings, lubricate generously with recommended lubricant, then wrap each bearing in clean paper until ready for reassembly.
2. Remove all portions of old gaskets from parts, using a stiff brush or scraper.

Inspection

1. Inspect all parts for discoloration or warpage.
2. Examine all gears and splines for chipped, worn, broken or nicked teeth. Small nicks or burrs may be removed with a fine abrasive stone.
3. Inspect the breather assembly to make sure that it is open and not damaged.
4. Check all threaded parts for damaged, stripped, or crossed threads.
5. Replace all gaskets, oil seals and snap-rings.
6. Inspect housings, retainers and covers for cracks or other damage. Replace the damaged parts.
7. Inspect keys and keyways for condition and fit.
8. Inspect shift forks for wear, distortion or any other damage.
9. Check detent ball springs for free length, compressed length, distortion or collapsed coils.
10. Check bearing fit on their respective shafts and in their bores or cups. Inspect bearings, shafts and cups for wear. NOTE: If either bearings or cups are worn or damaged, it is advisable to replace both parts.
11. Inspect all bearing rollers or balls for pitting or galling.
12. Examine detent balls for corrosion or brinneling. If shift bar detents show wear, replace them.
13. Replace all worn or damaged parts. When assembling the transfer case, coat all moving parts with recommended lubricant.

Coleman Models 22 and 42

Description

Both models are 2 speed units and are operated by two shift levers in the cab. Model 22 transmits power to the front drive axle only when necessary, whereas model 42 transmits power at all times and provides full differential action between front and rear axles.

Oil Seal Replacement

1. Drain lubricant from transfer case.
2. Disconnect applicable driveshaft.
3. Remove parking brake.
4. Remove cotter pin (if used) and nut from U-joint yoke.
5. Using a suitable puller, remove U-joint yoke from shaft.
6. Remove bolts attaching bearing cover to case. Remove cover and gasket. Discard gasket.
7. Drive oil seal from bearing cover. Discard oil seal.
8. Coat outer diameter of new oil seal with suitable sealer and press or drive into bearing retainer with lip of seal facing inward.
9. Using a new gasket, install bearing retainer. NOTE: Make sure oil passages are aligned when installing gasket and cover. Tighten bolts securely.
10. Press driveshaft U-joint yoke on shaft and install nut and new cotter pin (if used). Tighten nut securely.
11. Install parking brake.
12. Connect applicable driveshaft.
13. Replace lubricant in transfer case. Refer to manufacturers specifications for type lubricant and amount to be installed.
14. Adjust transfer case control rods.

Shift Rod Adjustment

1. If not previously removed, disconnect transfer case high-low shift rod and declutcher, or differential shift rod, from transfer case shift shafts. Loosen lock nuts on both rod clevises.
2. Shift transfer case into LOCK position and connect declutcher or differential shift rod to shift shaft at transfer case. Adjust clevis on rod to obtain 0.750″ minimum clearance between shift lever and floor pan. Tighten lock nut securely.
3. Shift transfer case into UNLOCK and NEUTRAL position.
4. Connect high-low shift rod to shaft at transfer case, adjusting clevis on rod so that high-low shift lever touches lug on LOCK-UNLOCK lever.

Disassembly

Case

1. Remove drain and filler plugs and drain lubricant from the transfer case.
2. Place transfer case assembly on

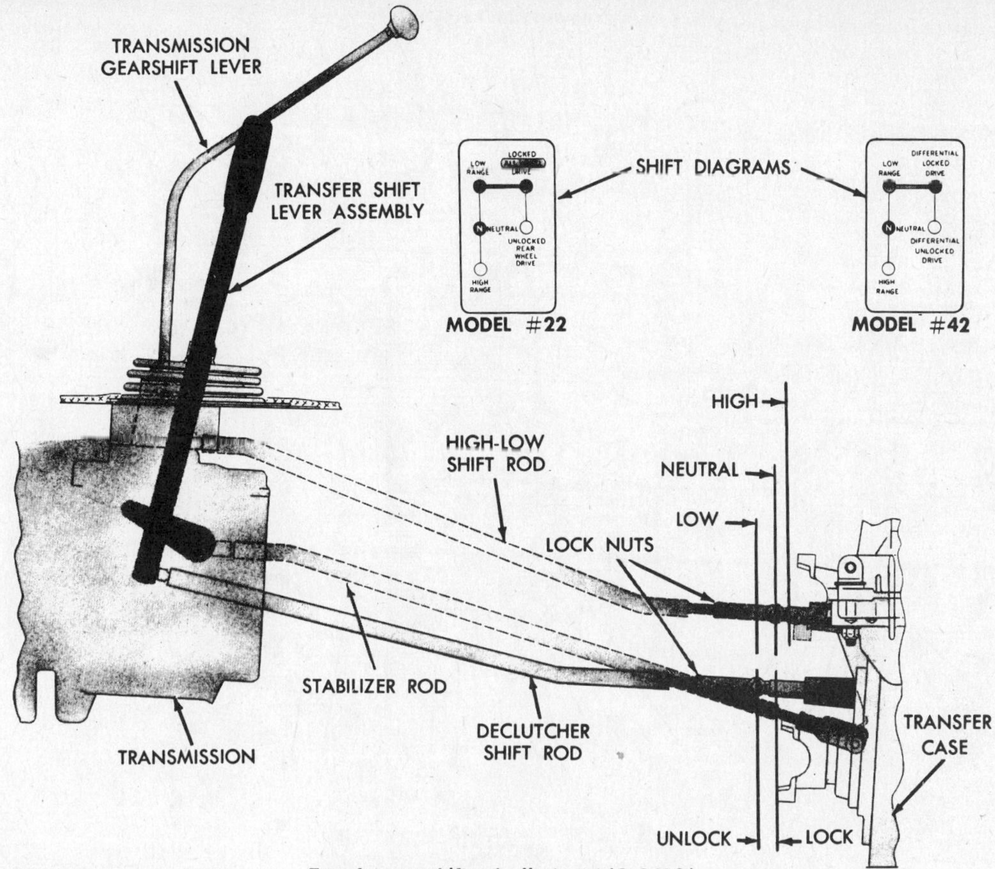

Transfer case shift rod adjustment (© G.M.C.)

work bench with front housing pointing down.

3. Remove parking brake parts.
4. Turn the assembly over and remove nut and lock washer; then remove front output shaft end yoke.
5. Remove nut and lock washer; then remove input shaft end yoke.
6. Remove shift bar eyes from high-low shift bar and declutcher or differential shift bar.
7. Remove two bolts and lock washers; then remove high-low shift bar adapter.
8. Remove spring retainer, spring and poppet ball.
9. Remove two bolts and lock washers; then remove the declutcher or differential shift bar adapter.
10. Remove spring retainer, spring and poppet ball from bore in adapter.
11. Remove four bolts and lock washers; then remove front output shaft bearing cap and gasket. Discard gasket.
12. Remove snap-ring from front output shaft bearing. Using a suitable puller, remove front output shaft assembly.
13. Remove front output shaft sliding lock gear.
14. Remove four bolts and lock washers; then remove center shaft front bearing cap and shim set. Tag shim set for reassembly.
15. Remove four bolts and lock washers; then remove input shaft front bearing cap and shim set. Tag shim set for reassembly.
16. Turn transfer case assembly over and remove six bolts and lock washers attaching rear output shaft bearing cap to housing. Remove bearing cap and shim set. Tag shim set for reassembly. NOTE: On Model 42, rear output shaft, ball bearing assembly and speedometer drive gear will come out with the bearing cap. After removal of bearing cap and shaft, remove differential assembly.
17. On Model 22, pull rear output shaft assembly out of transfer case rear housing. Assembly on Model 22 consists of output shaft, outer bearing assembly, speedometer drive gear, bearing spacer, rear output shaft gear, inner bearing assembly, pilot bushing and two output shaft gear keys.
18. Remove four bolts and lock washers attaching center shaft rear bearing cap. Remove bearing cap and gasket. Discard gasket.
19. Remove six bolts and lock washers; then remove power take-off

1 Transfer case front housing
2 Input shaft front bearing cap oil seal
3 Input shaft
4 High-low shift bar
5 Center shaft front bearing cap
6 Declutcher shift bar
7 Puller screws
8 Front output shaft
9 Puller
10 Magnetic drain plug
11 Speedometer driven gear and sleeve assembly
12 Power take-off adapter
13 Transfer case rear housing

Removing front output shaft assembly (© G.M.C.)

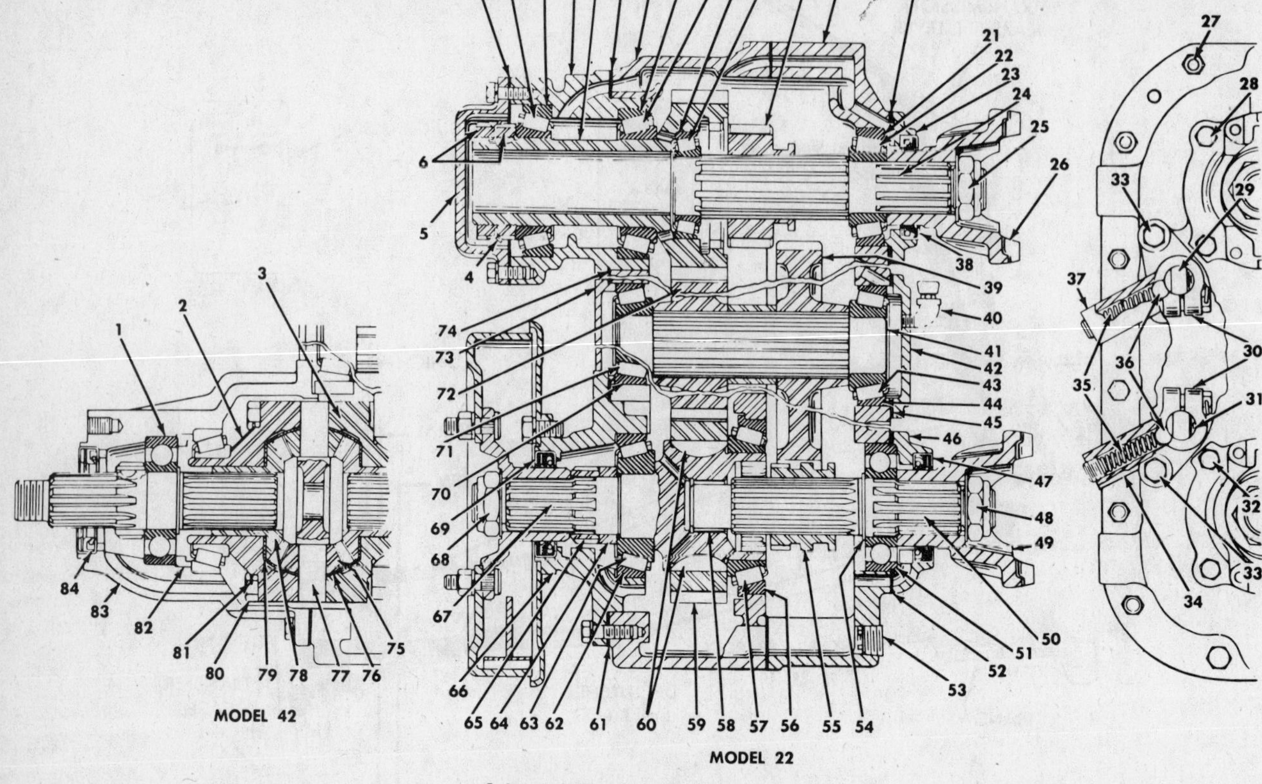

Coleman model 22 and 42 transfer case
(© G.M.C.)

*1 Rear output shaft ball bearing assy.
*2 Differential housing rear half
*3 Differential housing front (lock) half
4 Nut lock
5 Power take-off adapter cover
6 Input shaft high gear bearing nuts
7 Gasket
8 High gear bearing
9 High gear bearing cup
10 Power take-off adpater
11 Input shaft high gear and shaft
12 Gasket
13 Rear housing
14 High gear bearing cup
15 High gear bearing
16 Input shaft rear bearing cup
17 Input shaft rear bearing
18 Input shaft high-low sliding gear
19 Front housing
20 Shim set
21 Input shaft front bearing cup
22 Input shaft front bearing
23 Input shaft front bearing cap
25 Nut
26 Input shaft end yoke
25 Nut
26 Input shaft end yokke
27 Bolt
28 Bolt
29 High-low shift bar
30 Shift forks
31 Declutcher shift bar
32 Bolt
33 Bolts
34 Declutcher shift bar adapter
35 Shifter poppet springs
36 Shifter poppet balls
37 High-low shift bar adapter
38 Input shaft front bearing cap oil seal
39 Center shaft low gear
40 Breather assy.
41 Center shaft
42 Center shaft front bearing cap
43 Center shaft front bearing
44 Center shaft front bearing cup
45 Shim set
46 Front output shaft front bearing cap
47 Oil seal
48 Nut
49 Front output shaft end yoke
50 Front output shaft
51 Front output shaft bearing
52 Gasket
53 Drain plug
54 Snap ring
55 Front output shaft sliding lock gear
56 Rear output shaft inner bearing cup
57 Rear output shaft inner bearing
58 Bushing
59 Rear output shaft gear
60 Rear output shaft gear keys
61 Shim set
62 Rear output shaft outer bearing cup
63 Rear output shaft outer bearing
64 Spacer
65 Speedometer drive gear
66 Rear output shaft bearing cap
67 Rear output shaft
68 Nut
69 Rear output shaft bearing cap oil seal
70 Center shaft bearing cup
71 Center shaft bearing
72 Center shaft high gear
73 Center shaft rear bearing cap
74 Gasket
*75 Differential spider gears
*76 Thrust washers
*77 Differential spider shaft
*78 Differential side gears
*79 Thrust washers
*80 Bolt
*81 Lock wire
82 Spacer
*83 Rear output shaft bearing cap
*84 Oil seal

cover and gasket. Discard gasket.

20. Bend back tangs of nut lock and using a spanner wrench, remove first input shaft high gear rear bearing nut.
21. Remove nut lock; then remove second input shaft high gear rear bearing nut.
22. Remove input shaft high gear bearing.
23. Remove six bolts and lock washers attaching power take-off adapter. Remove adapter and gasket. Discard gasket.
24. Remove twelve bolts, nuts, and lock washers, and three bolts and lock washers attaching transfer case front to rear housing. Separate housings and remove gasket. Discard gasket.
25. Remove declutcher or differential shift bar and fork. Remove high-low shift bar and fork.
26. Remove input shaft assembly from high speed gear. Remove input shaft high speed gear.
27. Remove center shaft assembly.
28. Remove O-ring seal from groove of declutcher or differential shift bar. Remove safety wire

and bolt; then remove shift fork. Discard O-ring seal and safety wire.

29. Remove O-ring seal from groove of high-low shift bar. Remove lock wire and bolt; then remove shift fork. Discard O-ring seal and safety wire.
30. Using a soft-faced hammer, tap rear output shaft inner bearing cup out of rear housing. Tap out center shaft rear bearing cup.
31. Using a soft-faced hammer, tap center shaft front bearing cup and input shaft front bearing cup out of front housing.

Rear Output Shaft Model 22

1. Remove speedometer drive gear and bearing spacer.
2. Using bearing remover plates or other suitable tool, press outer bearing assembly off rear output shaft.
3. Using an arbor press and remover plates or other suitable tool, press off rear output shaft gear and inner bearing.
4. Remove two Woodruff keys from slots in rear output shaft.

Model 42

1. Remove differential side bearing cup from inside cap, using a suitable puller. Remove bearing spacer.
2. Remove snap-ring from output shaft at front side of ball bearing.
3. Support the assembly in an arbor press, using a sleeve over the threaded end of the shaft that will bear against end of speedometer drive gear. Press shaft out of bearing and speedometer drive gear.
4. Remove ball bearing assembly using a suitable puller.

Differential—Model 42

1. Remove lock wire; then remove bolts securing differential housing front and rear halves.
2. Separate front and rear housing halves.
3. Remove side gears, thrust washers, spider shaft, spider gears and thrust washers.
4. If bearings in housing front and rear halves require replacement, remove them with a suitable puller.

NOTE: Rear output shaft gear is installed on differential housing front half on Model 42. Gear can be removed, if necessary, in same manner described in step 3 under Rear Output Shaft Disassembly—Model 22.

Center Shaft

1. Using an arbor press and suitable remover plates, press high speed gear and rear bearing assembly off center shaft.
2. Remove center shaft gear spacer.
3. Using an arbor press and remover plates, press off low speed gear and center shaft front bearing.

Input Shaft

1. Using a press and suitable remover plates, press off input shaft front bearing.
2. Remove input shaft high-low sliding gear.
3. Press input shaft rear bearing off shaft.

Front Output Shaft

1. Using an arbor press and remover plates, press front output shaft bearing assembly off shaft.
2. Using Tru-arc pliers, remove bearing to shaft snap-ring.

Input Shaft and High Speed Gear

Using an arbor press and remover plates, press input shaft high gear bearing off shaft.

Using a hammer and punch (through two holes in input shaft high gear), drive high gear bearing cup out of bore in gear.

Power Take-Off Adapter

Using an arbor press and sleeve, press the two input shaft high gear bearing cups out of bores in power take-off adapter housing.

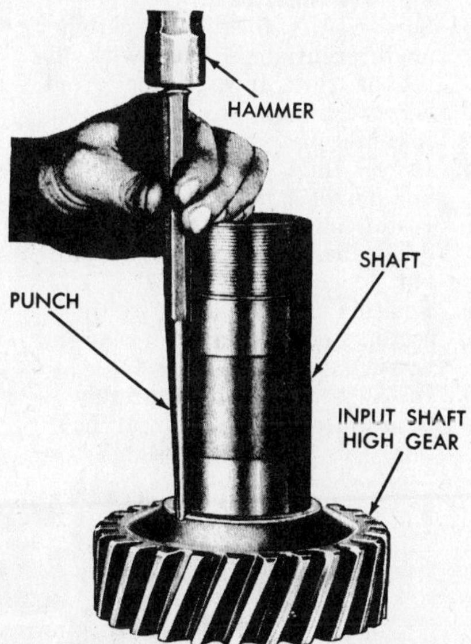

Removing input shaft high gear bearing cup (© G.M.C.)

Rear Output Shaft Bearing Cap Model 22

1. Remove speedometer driven gear and sleeve assembly.
2. Press outer bearing cup out of bore in bearing cap.
3. Press or drive bearing cap oil seal out of cap. Discard oil seal.

Input Shaft Front Bearing Cap

Using a press and suitable sleeve or punch and hammer, remove input shaft front bearing cap oil seal. Discard oil seal.

Front Output Shaft Bearing Cap

Press or drive front output shaft bearing cap oil seal out of cap. Discard oil seal.

Assembly

Rear Output Shaft Model 22

1. Using an arbor press and suitable installer sleeve, press front output shaft pilot bushing into bore of rear output shaft.
2. Press two gear retaining keys in slots of rear output shaft.
3. Using an arbor press and suitable sleeve, press rear output shaft gear on shaft.
4. Press inner bearing assembly onto rear output shaft.
5. Press outer bearing assembly onto rear output shaft.
6. Install spacer and speedometer drive gear by pressing onto shaft against outer bearing race.

Rear Output Shaft and Bearing Cap Model 42

1. Press new oil seal into outer end of bearing cap.
2. Install snap-ring in groove near center of rear output shaft.
3. Install bearing assembly over threaded end of shaft and press until bearing inner race seats against snap-ring.
4. Install speedometer drive gear over threaded end of shaft and press against ball bearing inner race.
5. Insert shaft and bearing assembly into bearing cap; then while supporting outer end of cap, press on bearing outer race to install bearing.
6. Install bearing spacer; then press differential side gear bearing cup into cap.

Differential Assembly Model 42

1. Coat inner walls of differential housing halves and all the internal differential components with recommended lubricant.
2. If removed, install rear output shaft gear on differential housing front half and install bearing on housing front and rear halves, using an arbor press or suitable driver.
3. Place new thrust washer and side gear in differential housing rear half. Install spider shaft, with spider gears, and thrust washers in housing rear half; then install the other side gear and thrust washer.
4. Place housing front half over the assembly, then install attaching bolts and tighten firmly.
5. Check for free rotation of gears; then secure bolts with lock wire.

Center Shaft

1. Using an arbor press and suitable sleeve, press center shaft low gear on center shaft.
2. With a suitable sleeve, press center shaft front bearing on center shaft.
3. Turn the assembly over and position center shaft gear spacer on center shaft.
4. Using an arbor press and suitable sleeve, press high speed gear on center shaft.
5. Press center shaft rear bearing on center shaft. Be sure all parts fit together tightly.

Input Shaft

1. Press input shaft rear bearing assembly on input shaft.
2. Position input shaft high-low sliding gear on input shaft.
3. Using an arbor press and suitable sleeve, press front bearing assembly on input shaft.

Front Output Shaft

1. Using Tru-Arc pliers, install front output shaft bearing-to-output shaft snap-ring in groove of shaft.
2. With arbor press and suitable sleeve, press front output shaft bearing assembly on front output shaft.

Input Shaft and High Gear

1. Press input shaft rear bearing cup into bore of gear.
2. Using an arbor press and suitable sleeve, press input shaft high gear bearing on shaft of input gear.

Power Take-Off Adapter

With an arbor press and suitable sleeve, press two input shaft high gear bearing cups into bores of power take-off adapter.

Rear Output Shaft Bearing Cap Model 22

1. Using an arbor press and suitable sleeve, press new oil seal into bore of bearing cap.
2. Press outer bearing cup into bore of bearing cap.
3. Install speedometer driven gear and sleeve into bore of bearing cap.

Input Shaft Front Bearing Cap

Using an arbor press and suitable sleeve, press new oil seal into bore of input shaft front bearing cap.

Front Output Shaft Bearing Cap

With arbor press and suitable sleeve, press new oil seal into bore of front output shaft bearing cap.

Case

NOTE: When installing shims and bearing caps, be sure oil drain-back holes and passages are not covered.

Much care should be taken in setting tapered roller bearings so they are neither too tight nor too loose. As a general guide, the front input shaft bearing should be set from 0.003″ to 0.005″. The input shaft high gear rear bearing should be set from 0.000″ to 0.002″. Both center shaft bearings should be set from 0.003″ to 0.005″. The lower rear output shaft bearing should be set from 0.003″ to 0.005″.

To adjust bearings, tighten bearing caps to a snug fit; then measure the gap between inside of bearing cap and housing with feeler gauge. Add the foregoing dimensions to the measured gap for total shim thickness. Shims are available in 0.005″, 0.015″ and 0.020″ thicknesses.

1. Press or drive rear output shaft inner bearing cup into bore of transfer case rear housing.
2. Use a soft hammer and tap two front to rear housing dowel pins into bores in rear housing.
3. Screw shift fork on high-low shift bar with offset of fork to the rear. Screw fork on bar approximately to center of threads on shift bar.
4. Install shift fork retaining bolt and secure with new lock wire.
5. Install new O-ring in groove of high-low shift bar.
6. Screw shift fork on declutcher or differential shift bar with offset of fork toward the front. Screw fork on bar approximately to center of threads on bar.
7. Install shift fork retaining bolt and new lock wire.
8. Install new O-ring in groove of declutcher or differential shift bar.
9. Position transfer case rear housing on wood blocks with rear end down.
10. Install center shaft assembly in bore of transfer case rear housing. Position the assembly so that high speed gear is toward the rear of housing.
11. Install input shaft high speed gear assembly in bore of transfer case rear housing, meshing teeth of high speed gear with teeth of center shaft high speed gear.
12. Position input shaft assembly in bore of input shaft high speed gear assembly, meshing splines of shaft with splines of gear.
13. Position shift fork and high-low shift bar assembly in transfer case rear housing, engaging prongs of shift fork with groove of input shaft high-low sliding gear.
14. Place declutcher or differential shift bar and fork assembly in bore of transfer case rear housing.
15. Position new gasket on mating surface of transfer case rear housing.
16. Place transfer case front housing on rear housing, aligning dowel pins in rear housing with holes in front housing.
17. Install twelve bolts, nuts and lock washers, and three bolts and lock washers attaching transfer case front housing to rear housing. Tighten all bolts and nuts securely.
18. Turn transfer case over and position power take-off adapter assembly and gasket over bore in rear housing. Install six adapter-to-housing bolts and lock washers. Tighten bolts securely.
19. Position input shaft high gear bearing assembly on input high gear shaft. Install first high gear bearing nut on input high gear shaft. Using a spanner wrench, tighten nut securely.
20. Install bearing nut lock over bearing nut with inner tab of lock engaging slot in input high speed gear shaft.
21. Install second bearing nut on shaft of input high speed gear.

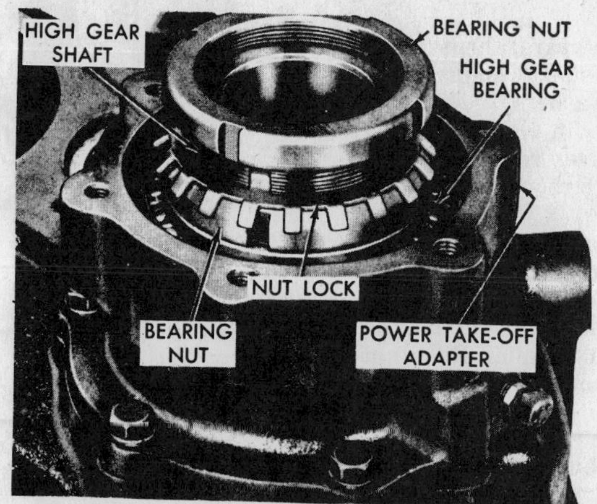

Installing input shaft high gear bearing nuts
(© G.M.C.)

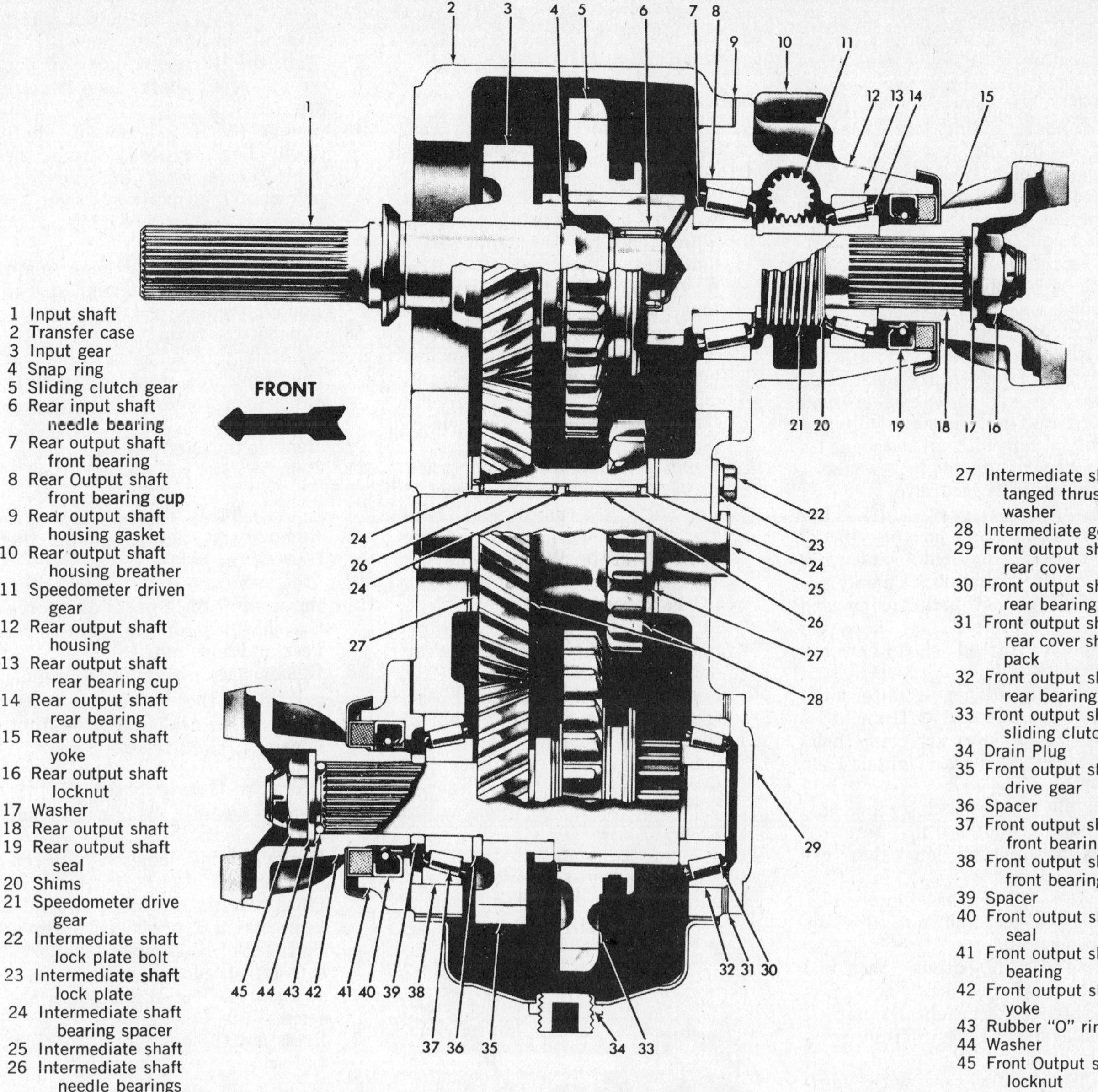

Dana model 20 transfer case (© G.M.C.)

Tighten nut securely. Bend outer tangs of nut lock into grooves of nearest slots in both bearing nuts.

22. Install power take-off adapter cover and new gasket on power take-off adapter. Tighten the six attaching bolts and lock washers firmly.
23. Using a soft-faced hammer, tap center shaft bearing cup into bore of rear housing.
24. Position center shaft rear bearing cap and new gasket over center shaft bore in rear housing. Install four bolts and lock washers attaching cap to housing. Tighten bolts securely.
25. *Model 22 Only*. Install rear output shaft assembly, with teeth of output shaft gear meshing with teeth of center shaft high gear. Position shim set, then install rear output shaft bearing cap on rear housing. Install six attaching bolts and lock washers and tighten firmly.
26. *Model 42 Only*. Install differential assembly, with gear on differential housing front half meshing with center shaft high gear. Position shim set on transfer case rear housing, then install rear output shaft and bearing cap assembly, with output shaft splines engaging splines in differential side gear. Install bearing cap attaching bolts and lock washers and tighten firmly.
27. Turn transfer case over and install input shaft front bearing cup. Use a soft-faced hammer, to tap cup into bore of front housing.
28. Install input shaft front bearing shim set and front bearing cap on transfer case front housing, aligning oil groove in bearing cap with oil passage in front housing.
29. Install four attaching bolts and lock washers. Tighten bolts firmly.
30. Using a soft-faced hammer, tap center shaft bearing cup into bore of front housing.
31. Position shim set and center shaft front bearing cap over bore in front housing. Install four bolts and lock washers. Tighten bolts firmly.
32. Install front output shaft sliding lock gear in front housing, engaging forks of declutcher or differential shift bar and engaging teeth of lock gear with internal teeth of rear output shaft gear on Model 22, or internal teeth of differential hous-

ing front half on Model 42.

33. Position front output shaft assembly in transfer case front housing, meshing splines of shaft with splines of front output shaft sliding lock gear. On Model 22, pilot end of shaft will engage pilot bushing in end of rear output shaft; on Model 42, splined end of shaft will mesh with splines in side gear in differential housing front half. Tap the assembly into position in front housing until snap-ring on front bearing is seated firmly against front housing.
34. Position front output shaft bearing cap and new gasket over bore in front housing, aligning slot in cap with oil passage. Install four bolts and lock washers. Tighten bolts securely.
35. Install high-low shift bar adapter on front housing. Install two attaching bolts and lock washers. Tighten bolts firmly.
36. Install poppet ball, spring and spring retainer in bore of adapter. Install shift bar eye and lock nut.
37. Install declutcher or differential shift bar adapter on front housing. Install two attaching bolts and lock washers. Tighten bolts firmly.
38. Install poppet ball, spring and spring retainer in bore of adapter. Install shift bar eye and lock nut.
39. Install input shaft end yoke, lock washer and nut. Tighten nut securely.
40. Install front output shaft end yoke, lock washer, and nut. Tighten nut securely.
41. Install drain plug in front housing.
42. Refill transfer case with lubricant.
43. Install filler plug elbow and nipple assembly in front housing. Install plug in elbow.
44. Turn transfer case assembly over and install parking brake components.

BEARING CLEARANCE	
Front Input Shaft Bearing	0.003-0.005"
Input Shaft High Gear Rear Bearing	0.000-0.002"
Center Shaft Bearings	0.003-0.005"
Lower Rear Output Shaft Bearing	0.003-0.005"

GEAR BACKLASH	
Center Shaft Low Gear	0.006-0.010"
Center Shaft High Gear	0.006-0.010"

Dana Model 20

Description

The Dana Model 20 is a two-speed gearbox that controls the power from the transmission to the front and rear driving axles. Positions of the transfer case are: four-wheel-drive low (4L), neutral (N), two-wheel-drive high (2H) and four-wheel-drive high (4H).

Disassembly

1. Clean any dirt from the transfer case and remove the bottom cover plate.
2. Remove the retaining plug, flat washer, detent spring and ball which engages the front drive shift rail detent rod. Then, remove plug from front drive detent rod access hole.
3. Remove the retaining plug, detent spring and ball which engages the rear drive shift rail detent rod.
4. Remove the idler shaft lock-plate.
5. Using a hammer and soft drift, drive the idler shaft rearward and out of the case; then lift out the thrust washers and idler gear. NOTE: When removing the idler gear, do not lose any of the rollers.
6. Remove the flange retaining nuts from the front and rear output shafts.
7. Remove the flange from the front and rear output shafts. Discard the O-ring.
8. Remove the bolts securing the adapter housing to the case; then remove the adapter as an assembly.
9. Remove the bolts which attach the rear output shaft bearing retainer to the case; then remove the retainer and output shaft as an assembly.

Removing rear output shaft subassembly (© G.M.C.)

NOTE: Be sure not to lose any of the rollers.

10. Disconnect the shift rail link from the two shift rails.
11. Lift out the rear output shaft sliding gear.
12. Remove the setscrew securing the rear fork to the shift rail; then remove the rear drive shift rail and fork.
13. Remove the front output shaft rear cover and shims. Fasten the shims together.
14. Remove the front output shaft bearing retainer and gasket.
15. Tap the threaded end of the front output shaft; then remove the rear cup.
16. Angle the front output shaft front bearing away from the main drive gear to allow removal of the snap-ring; then tap the shaft and rear bearing out of the case.
17. Lift out the sliding gear, main drive gear, front bearing, spacer and snap-ring.
18. Remove the front cup.
19. Remove the setscrew securing the front shift fork to the shift rail; then remove the rail and fork.
20. Remove the detent rods.
21. Remove shift rail oil seal.

Input Shaft

1. Remove the snap-ring from the front of the shaft.
2. Place the adapter housing and input shaft on a press and force the shaft out of the main drive gear and housing.
3. Remove the bearing retaining snap-ring; then remove bearing.
4. Remove the seal in the adapter housing.

Rear Output Shaft

1. Remove needle bearings from bore of shaft.
2. Remove speedometer driven gear.
3. Place bearing retainer and shaft assembly in a press; then force shaft out of retainer.
4. Lift off speedometer drive gear and shims. Tag shims for reassembly.
5. Press out the outer cup, bearing and seal.
6. Remove the inner cup.
7. Remove the inner bearing.

Front Output Shaft

Using the sliding gear as a base, press rear bearing off shaft.

Removing front output shaft rear (inner) bearing (© G.M.C.)

Assembly

Input Shaft

1. Install a new seal in the adapter housing.
2. Install bearing in the housing and secure with snap-ring.
3. Using the main drive gear as a base, force the input shaft through the housing, seal, bearings and main drive gear. Secure with snap-ring on front of shaft.

Rear Output Shaft

1. Press the shaft into the inner bearing.

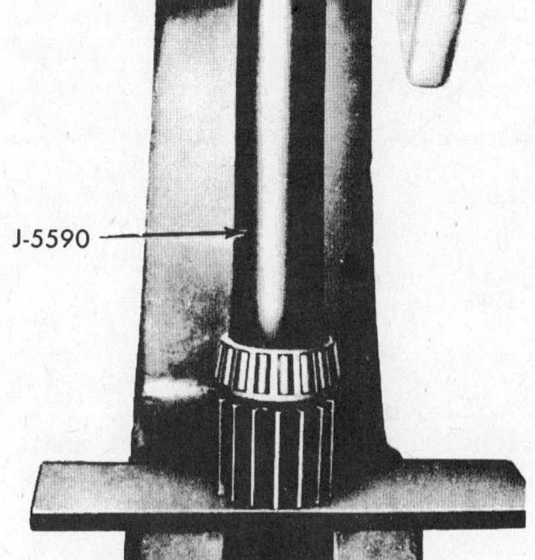

Installing rear output shaft front (inner) bearing (© G.M.C.)

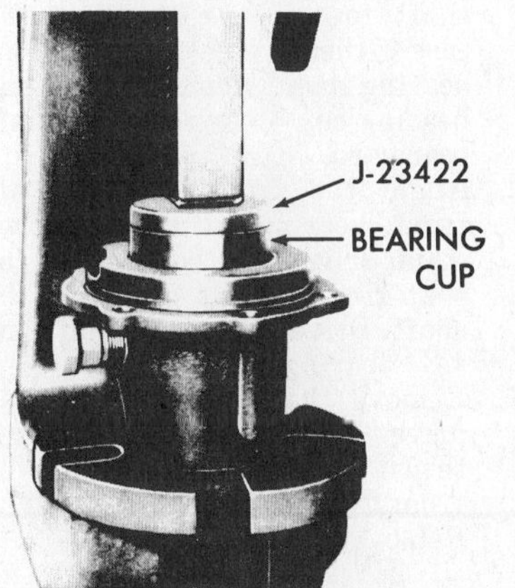

Installing rear output shaft front (inner) bearing cup (© G.M.C.)

2. Install outer cup in the bearing retainer.
3. Install the inner cup.
4. Position the outer bearing in the retainer; then place the shims and speedometer drive gear on the shaft. Install shaft in the bearing retainer housing.
5. Place the bearing retainer and shaft in a vise. Install the output shaft flange and torque the retaining nut to specifications.
6. With a dial indicator on the flange end of the shaft, measure end-play. Adjust shim pack between the speedometer drive gear and outer bearing to achieve correct clearance.
7. After setting correct end-play, remove flange and press bearing retainer seal into housing.
8. Install bearing and secure with the snap-ring.

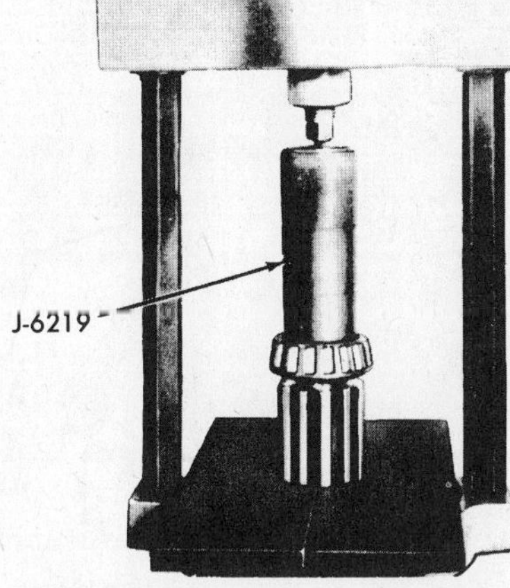

Installing front output shaft rear bearing (© G.M.C.)

9. Install the speedometer driven gear.

Front Output Shaft

Using a press, force front output rear bearing on shaft.

Shift Rail Oil Seals

Using the tool shown in illustration, install the two shift rail oil seals.

Case

1. Install the front detent rod in the case.
2. Slide the front drive shift rail all the way into the case and place the shift fork on the rail as it enters the case. Secure the fork to the rail with the setscrew.
3. Position the front output shaft sliding gear in the shift fork.
4. Install the rear detent rod.
5. Slide the rear drive shift rail into the case and position the shift fork on the rail as the rail enters the case. Secure the fork to the rail with the setscrew. NOTE: The shift rails should be inserted so that the detents are positioned as shown in illustration.
6. While holding the sliding gear and main drive gear in position, install the front output shaft and rear bearing assembly through the two gears.
7. Install the main drive gear spacer and secure with the snap-ring.
8. Install the front output shaft rear bearing cup.
9. Place the front output shaft rear cover and shims on the case and install the attaching bolts.
10. Install the front output shaft front bearing on the shaft. Install the front bearing cup.
11. If the front bearing retainer oil seal was removed, install a new seal. Position the bearing retainer and gasket to the case and install the attaching bolts.
12. Place the rear output shaft rear bearing retainer on a work bench and install 13 needle bearings in the splined hub of the output shaft, using vaseline or grease.
13. Position the rear output shaft rear bearing retainer assembly to the case and install the attaching bolts.
14. Install the rear output shaft sliding gear in the shifting fork and on the splines of the output shaft.
15. Position the adapter housing assembly on the rear output shaft and case. Install the attaching bolts.
16. Install the roller bearings in the bore of the idler shaft gear with vaseline or grease.
17. Position the idler gear and thrust washers in the case; then

Installing front output shaft front bearing (© G.M.C.)

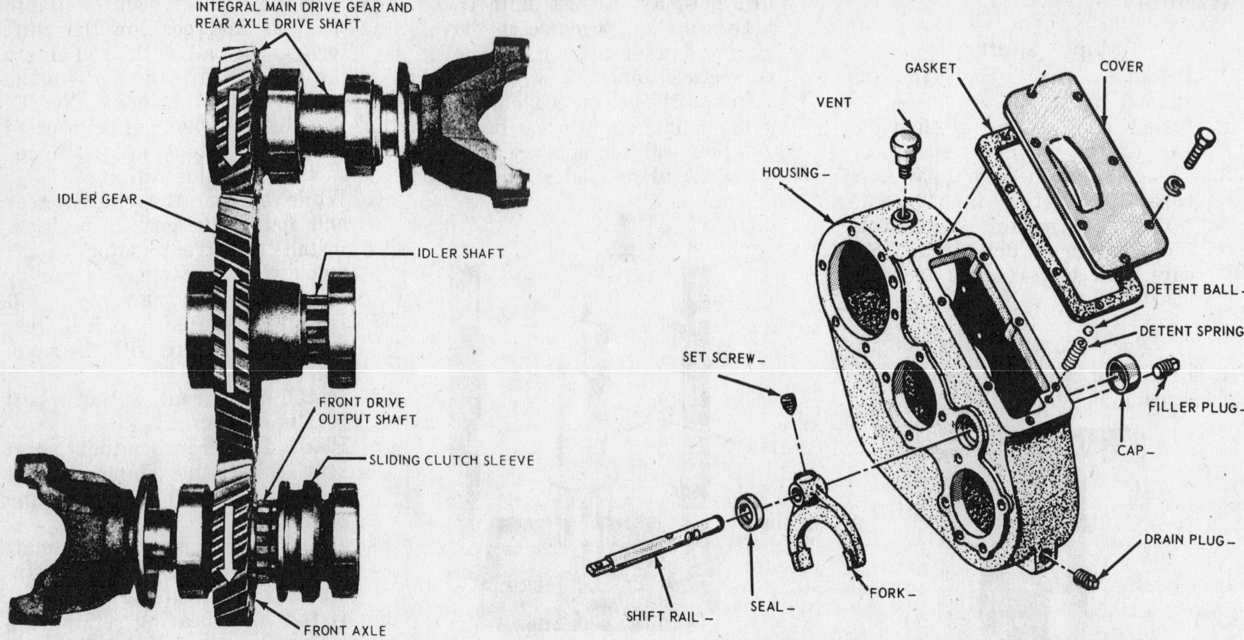

Dana model 21 transfer case gear train
(© Ford Motor Corp.)

Transfer case housing and related parts
(© Ford Motor Corp.)

drive the idler shaft into the rear of the case through the idler gear and thrust washers. NOTE: After installing the idler shaft, tap the sides of the case to relieve any possible binding.

18. Install the idler shaft lock plate.
19. Secure the shift rail link to the two shift rails.
20. Install the front and rear drive shift rail detent balls, springs and retaining plugs. NOTE: Be sure that the heavier loaded spring and flat washer are installed in the front drive shift rail.
21. Install the rod access hole plug.
22. Install the flange, washer and retaining nut on each of the output shafts. Be sure to install a new O-ring in the front output shaft flange. Torque the attaching nuts to specifications.
23. With a dial indicator on the front drive output shaft, check the end-play. If not within specifications, adjust the shim pack at the front output shaft rear cover.
24. Place the cover plate on the case and install the attaching bolts.

Specifications

END PLAY

Front Output Shaft	0.003-0.007″
Rear Output Shaft	0.003-0.007″

TORQUE LIMITS (FT. LBS.)

Transfer Case to Transmission Extension Bolts	20-30
Transfer Case to Transmission Output Shaft Nut	60-80
Front Output Shaft Rear Cover Bolts	25-32
Front Output Shaft Bearing Retainer Bolts	25-32
Idler Shaft Cover Bolts	25-32

Dana Model 21 (Single-Speed)

Description

The Dana Model 21 is a single-speed gearbox that transmits power to the front driving axle. There are two positions of the transfer case; front drive axle engaged and front drive axle disengaged.

Disassembly

1. Clean all dirt from transfer case and drain lubricant.
2. Remove bolts that attach the cover to the top of the case; then remove the cover.
3. Remove the setscrew securing the shift fork to the rail. Tap the shift rail rearward; then remove the rail cap from the rear of the case.
4. Remove the shift rail and fork.
5. Remove the detent spring and ball which engages the front drive shift rail.
6. Remove the flange attaching nuts, flat washer and O-ring from the front and rear output shafts. Discard the O-rings.
7. Remove the flange from the front and rear output shafts.
8. Remove the bolts that attach the rear output shaft bearing retainer to the case; then remove the retainer and output shaft as an assembly.
9. Remove the front and rear idler shaft covers.
10. Using a hammer and soft drift, drive the idler shaft and rear idler bearing rearward out of the case; then lift out the front bearing and idler gear.
11. Remove the front output shaft bearing retainer and gasket. Remove the retainer seal if it is worn or damaged.
12. Remove the front output shaft rear cover and shims. Tie the shims together for reassembly.
13. Tap the end of the front output shaft toward the front of the case; then remove the front bearing cup. Remove the rear bearing cup by tapping the shaft rearward.
14. Angle the front output shaft front bearing away from the main drive gear to remove the snap-ring from its groove in the shaft. Drive the output shaft and rear bearing out of the case.
15. Remove the sliding gear, main drive gear, front bearing, thrust washer and snap-ring from the case.
16. Remove the shift rail seal.

Front Output Shaft

To remove the front output shaft rear bearing, use the sliding gear as a base and press off the bearing.

Idler Shaft

1. Remove the snap-ring from the idler shaft.
2. Using the idler gear as a base, press the idler shaft out of the rear bearing.

Rear Output Shaft

1. To remove the output shaft from the bearing retainer tap shaft rearward. Remove the shims and spacer.
2. Remove the inner bearing from the output shaft.

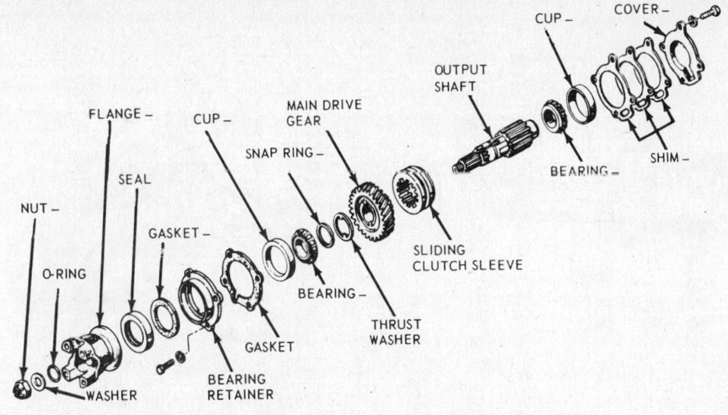

Front output shaft (© Ford Motor Co.)

3. Place the bearing retainer on a press and force out the outer cup, outer bearing and oil seal.
4. Using a soft drift, drive out the inner bearing cup.

Assembly

Front Output Shaft

Using an arbor press, force rear bearing on front output shaft.

Idler Shaft

1. Using a press, install rear idler bearing on the shaft.
2. Install snap-ring.

Rear Output Shaft

1. Press the inner bearing on the output shaft.
2. Using a soft-faced hammer, tap the inner bearing cup into the retainer.
3. Install the outer cup.
4. Place spacer and shims on the output shaft; then install the shaft in the bearing retainer housing.
5. Install the outer bearing on the shaft.
6. Place the bearing retainer and output shaft in a vise. Measure end-play with a dial indicator on end of the shaft. If not within specifications, adjust shim pack between the spacer and the front and rear bearing cones.
7. After setting correct end-play, install the bearing retainer seal.

Case

1. While holding the drive gear, sliding gear and thrust washer in the case, install the front output shaft, from the rear, through the gears and washer. Install the snap-ring.
2. Install the front output shaft rear bearing cup.
3. Place the front output shaft rear cover and shims on the case. After removing old sealant from all mating surfaces with thinner, apply gasket sealer to the attaching bolts and torque to specifications. With the cover installed, apply sealer to the outside edge of the adjusting shims, case and cover joints.
4. Install the front output shaft rear bearing on the shaft. Install the front bearing.
5. If the front bearing retainer oil seal was removed, install a new seal. Position the bearing retainer and gasket to the case and install attaching bolts.
6. Install the flange, new O-ring, washer and attaching nut on the front output shaft.
7. With a dial indicator on the front drive output shaft, check the end-play. If not within specified limits, increase or decrease the shim pack thickness at the front output shaft rear cover.
8. Place the idler gear in the case; then install the idler shaft through the gear. Install the front bearing.
9. Place the front and rear idler covers and gaskets on the case; then install attaching bolts.
10. Install a new shift rail seal.
11. Install the shift rail detent ball and spring in the top of the case.
12. Slide the shift rail into the case and position the fork on the rail as the rail enters the case. Depressing the detent ball and spring will allow the rail to pass. Secure the fork to the rail with the setscrew. Install the shift rail cap.
13. Position the rear output shaft and bearing retainer assembly to the case, then install the attaching bolts.
14. Install the flange, new O-ring, washer and attaching nut on the rear output shaft.
15. Place the top cover and gasket on the case, then install attaching bolts.
16. Fill the transfer case to the proper level with the recommended lubricant.

Specifications

END PLAY

Front Output Shaft	0.003-0.005"
Rear Output Shaft	0.003-0.005"

TORQUE LIMITS (FT. LBS.)

Transfer Case to Transmission Extension Bolts	20-30
Transfer Case to Transmission Output Shaft Nut	60-80
Front Output Shaft Rear Cover Bolts	25-32
Front Output Shaft Bearing Retainer Bolts	25-32
Idler Shaft Cover Bolts	25-32

Dana Model 24

Description

The Dana Model 24 is a two-speed gearbox that is manually controlled by a shift lever in the cab. The transfer case positions are: four-wheel-drive low (4L), neutral (N), two-wheel-drive high (2H) and four-wheel-drive high (4H).

Disassembly

1. Clean any dirt from the transfer case and remove the power take-off cover plate.
2. Remove both idler shaft bearing retainers.
3. Using a soft-faced hammer, tap the idler shaft and bearing to the rear until the bearing is free of the case.
4. Remove the idler shaft, two gears and spacer.
5. Remove the idler shaft front bearing.
6. Remove the flange retaining nuts from the front output shaft, the input shaft and the rear output shaft.
7. Remove the flanges and washers.
8. Remove the front output shaft

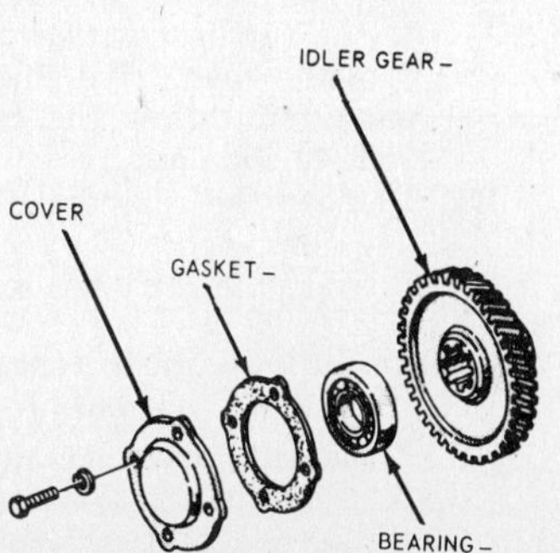

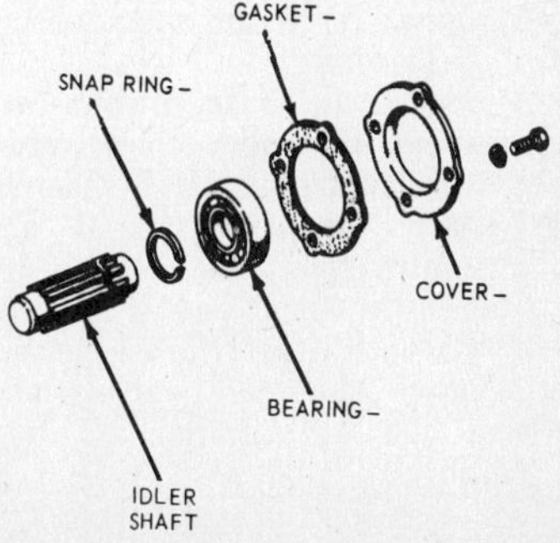

Idler shaft (© Ford Motor Co.)

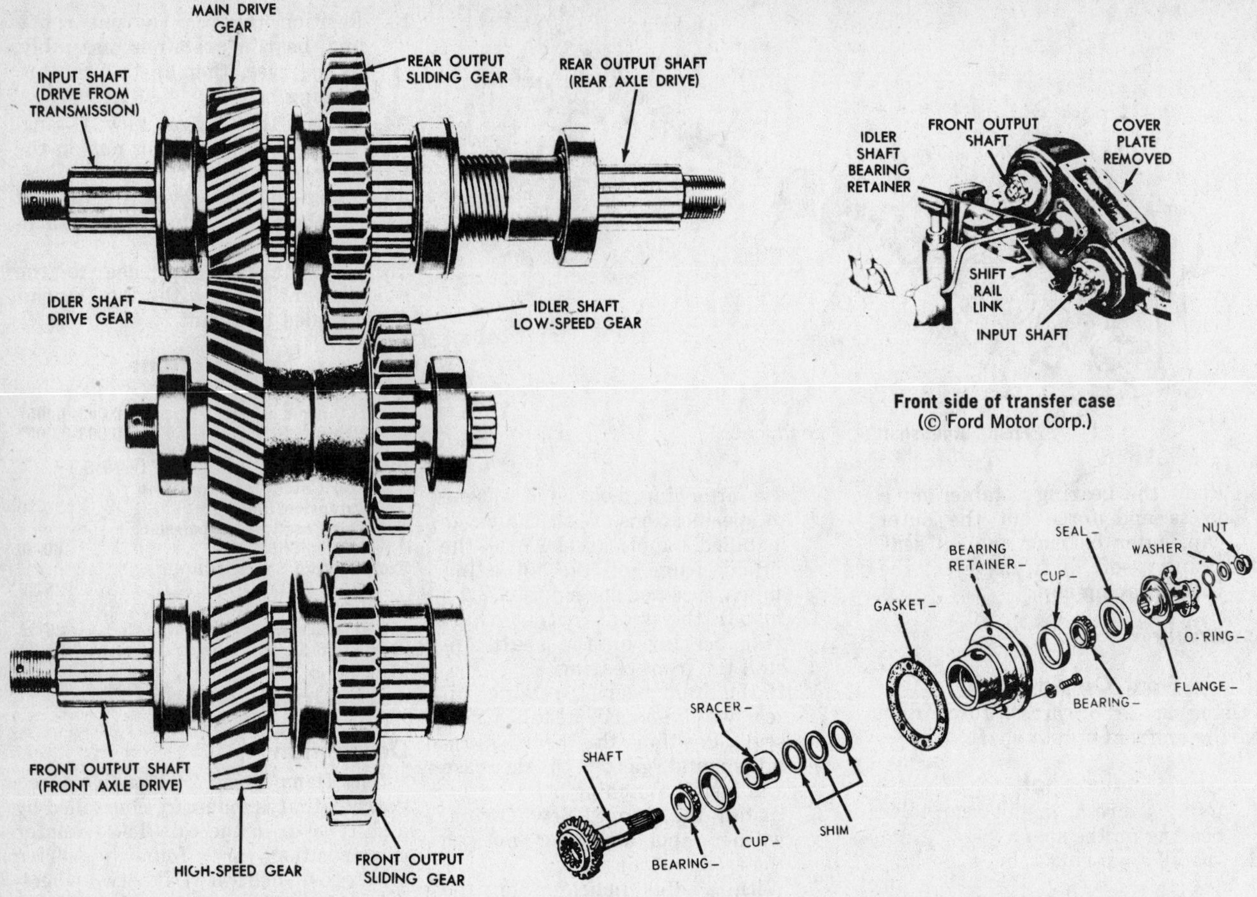

Dana model 24 transfer case gear train (© Ford Motor Co.)

Front side of transfer case (© Ford Motor Corp.)

Rear drive output shaft (© Ford Motor Co.)

front and rear bearing retainers.
9. Tap the front output shaft and rear bearing through the gears and case. Remove the high speed gear.
10. Remove the front output shaft front bearing and washer.
11. Remove the setscrew that retains the front drive shaft fork to the shift rail.
12. Remove the front output shaft sliding gear.
13. If the input shaft oil seal is to be replaced, remove it with a four-jaw puller and slide hammer.
14. Remove the input shaft bearing retainer.
15. If the output shaft bearing retainer oil seal is to be replaced, remove it with a puller and slide hammer.
16. Remove the rear output shaft bearing retainer; then remove the speedometer drive assembly.
17. Loosen the rear output shaft assembly from the case by driving on the front end of the input shaft with a soft-faced hammer.
18. Remove the rear output shaft and bearing retainer as an assembly.
19. Tap the input shaft through the front bearing, through the main drive gear, through the sliding gear and out of the case.
20. Lift the main drive gear out of the case and then drive out the input shaft front bearing.
21. Remove the setscrew that retains the rear drive shift fork to the shift rail.
22. Remove the rear output shaft sliding gear.
23. Remove the shift rail link from the two shift rails.
24. Remove the retaining plug, detent spring and ball which engage the front drive shift rail detent rod.
25. Remove the retaining plug detent spring and ball which engages the rear drive shift rail detent rod. Remove the front drive detent rod access hole plug.
26. Pull the front drive shift rail to the furthest outward position.
27. Pull the rear drive shift rail far enough to allow the two detent rods to slide out.
28. Remove the rear drive shift rail and fork.
29. Remove the shift rail seals.

Rear Output Shaft Disassembly and Assembly

1. Place the bearing retainer and rear output shaft assembly in a press and force out the shaft.
2. Remove the front bearing.
3. Install the front bearing.
4. Install the rear bearing and retainer.

Assembly

1. Slide the front drive shift rail all the way into the case and position the shift fork on the rail as the rail enters the case.
2. Install the two detent rods in the case.
3. Install the rear drive shift fork and hold the detent rods and the fork in place as the rear drive shift rail is pushed in as far as possible. NOTE: In steps 2 and 3, the shift rails should be inserted so that the detents are positioned as shown in illustration.
4. Pull the front drive shift rail out to its next detent. This will permit the rear drive shift rail to be pushed in to the full extent of its travel. After pushing the rear drive shift rail all the way in, push the front drive shift rail back to its extreme inward position.
5. Install the rear drive shift detent ball, spring and retaining plug; then install the access hole plug.
6. Install the front drive shift rail detent ball, spring and retaining plug.

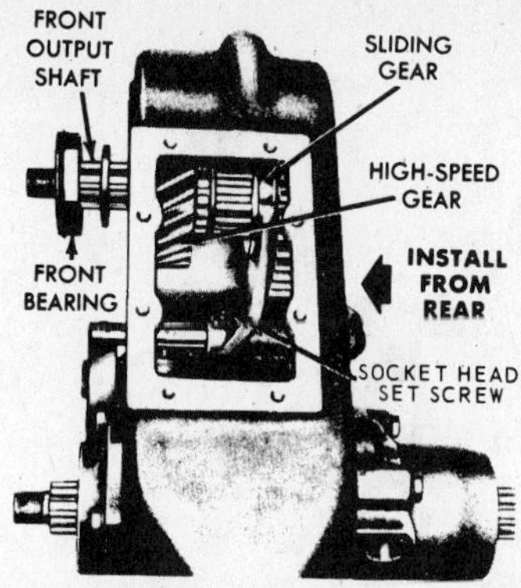

Removing or installing front output shaft
(© Ford Motor Corp.)

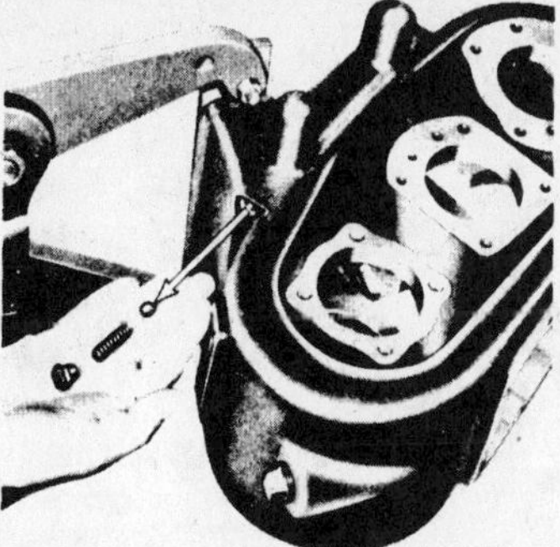
Front drive shift ball rail detent ball, spring and plug
(© Ford Motor Corp.)

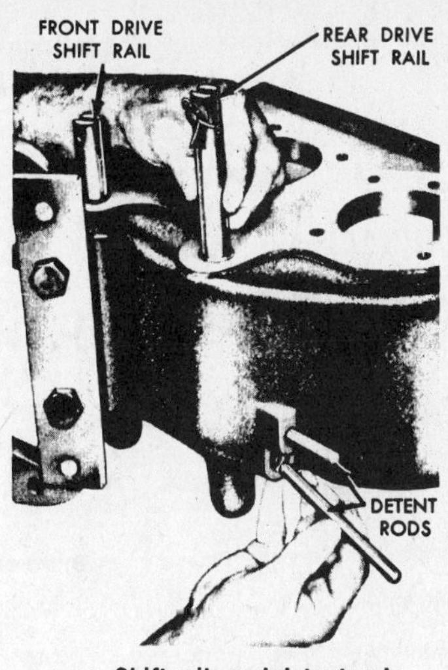

Shift rails and detent rods
(© Ford Motor Corp.)

7. Secure the shift rail link in the two shift rails.
8. Place the rear output sliding gear in the shift fork and secure the fork to the rear drive shift rail with the setscrew.
9. Install the input shaft front bearing and retainer assembly. Coat retainer and bolts with sealer.
10. Place the main drive gear in the case; then slide the input shaft into the rear of the case through the main drive gear and through the front bearing and retainer.
11. Install the roller bearings in the splined hub of the rear output shaft assembly with petrolatum or grease. Then install the shaft and bearing retainer assembly, making sure that the output shaft is aligned correctly with the input shaft. Coat the case, bearing retainer and bolts with sealer.
12. Position the front output sliding gear in the shift fork and secure the fork to the front drive shift rail with the setscrew.
13. While holding the sliding gear and high speed gear in position, install the front output shaft and rear bearing assembly through the two gears from the rear of the case.

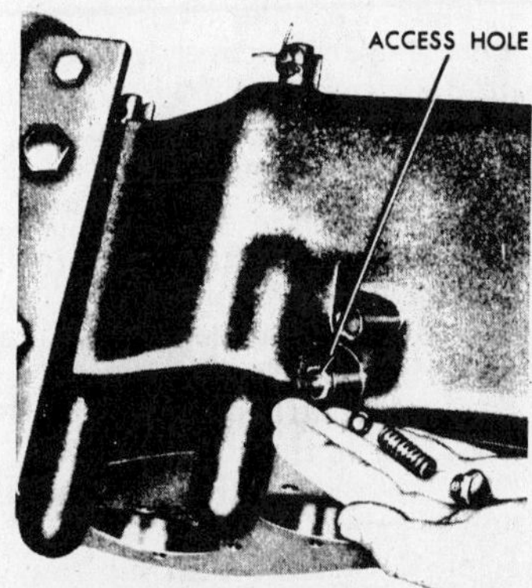

Rear drive shift rail detent ball, spring and plug
(© Ford Motor Corp.)

14. After coating with sealer, install the front output shaft rear bearing retainer and gasket.
15. Install the washer and bearing over the front output shaft at the front of the case and then install the front bearing retainer and gasket. Coat retainer with sealer.
16. Install the flange, washer, flange retaining nut and cotter key on each of the three shafts. Torque to specifications.
17. Place the idler shaft gears in the case and install the shaft and rear bearing assembly from the rear. After applying sealer to the plate and bolts, install the rear bearing retainer.
18. Position the spacer on the front end of the idler shaft and install the front bearing. Tap the bearing lightly with a mallet or soft-faced hammer.
19. Install the washer, retaining nut and cotter pin on the front end of the idler shaft.
20. After applying sealer to the plates and bolts, install the idler shaft front bearing retainer and the power take-off cover plate.

Specifications

END PLAY

Front Output Shaft	0.003-0.007″
Rear Output Shaft	0.003-0.007″

TORQUE LIMITS (FT. LBS.)

Transfer Case to Transmission Extension Bolts	20-30
Transfer Case to Transmission Output Shaft Nut	60-80
Front Output Shaft Rear Cover Bolts	25-32
Front Output Shaft Bearing Retainer Bolts	25-32
Idler Shaft Cover Bolts	25-32

New Process Model T200

Description

The New Process Model T200 transfer case is a 2-speed gearbox located under a frame crossmember near the center of the chassis. A short driveshaft connects power from the main transmission to the transfer case, which in turn transmits the power to the front and rear drive axles.

De-Clutch and Shift Rod Adjustment

1. Locate shift lever in HIGH SPEED position and de-clutch lever in DISENGAGED position.
2. Adjust shift rod clevis until there is a clearance of approximately ½″ between lever and end of floor slot.
3. Adjust de-clutch rod clevis until there is a minimum clearance of ½″ between protrusions on shift and de-clutch levers. CAUTION: A clearance of less than ½″ between lever protrusions may cause de-clutch lever to shift when applying parking brake.

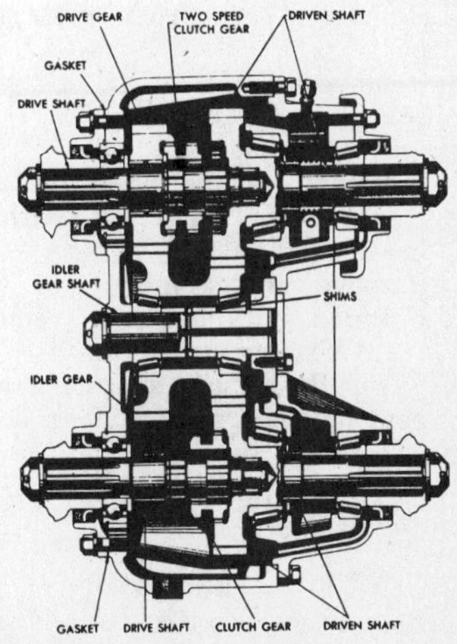

New process T-200 transfer case
(© Chrysler Corp.)

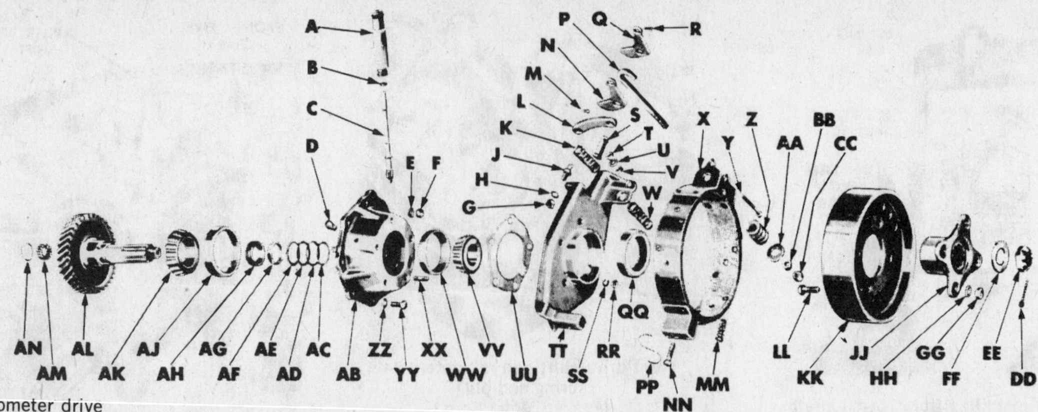

Brake output shaft bearing retainer assembly (© Chrysler Corp.)

A Speedometer drive pinion retaining nut
B Speedometer drive pinion oil seal
C Speedometer drive pinion
D Vent assembly
E Lock washer
F Nut
G Nut
H External teeth lock washer
J Brake spacer link stud
K Brake adjusting bolt compression spring
L Brake spacer link
M Cotter pin
N Brake cam lever
P Brake adjusting bolt
Q Brake cam lever
R Cotter pin
S Brake cam lever clevis pin
T Nut
U Lock washer
V Nut
W Brake adjusting bolt compression spring
X Brake band assembly with lining
Y Brake adjusting screw
Z Brake operating compression spring
AA Plain washer
BB Nut
CC Nut
DD Cotter pin
EE Slotted nut
FF Plain washer
GG Nut
HH Lock washer
JJ Companion yoke
KK Brake drum
LL Brake drum bolt
MM Anchor clip compression spring
NN Brake band anchor clip screw
PP Anchor clip screw lock wire
QQ Companion flange oil seal
RR Nut
SS Lock washer
TT Brake support
UU Brake support gasket
VV Rear bearing cone
WW Rear bearing cup
XX Stud
YY Screw
ZZ Lock washer
AB Bearing retainer
AC Bearing shim (.004 in.)
AD Bearing shim (.005 in.)
AE Bearing shim (.0125 in.)
AF Bearing shim (.015 in.)
AG Speedometer drive gear spacer
AH Speedometer drive gear
AJ Front bearing cup
AK Front bearing cone
AL Output shaft with integral gear
AM Output shaft rollers
AN Output shaft rollers snap ring

Disassembly

BRAKE OUTPUT SHAFT

1. Clean transfer case and drain lubricant.
2. Remove cotter pin and nut at end of brake output shaft. NOTE: Apply parking brake to keep shaft from turning.
3. Remove attaching cap screws, nuts and washers; then remove bearing retainer and gasket.
4. Remove brake drum, support and companion yoke.
5. Remove retaining nut and speedometer drive pinion.
6. Remove oil seal from brake support.
7. Remove shaft, rear bearing cone, shims, speedometer drive gear and spacer.
8. If bearing cups need replacement, drive them out with a brass drift.
9. Remove vent assembly.
10. Using a suitable puller, remove front bearing cone.
11. Carefully remove snap-ring and bearing rollers from gear bore.

NOTE: The brake output shaft and gear are serviced as a unit. *Do not remove gear from shaft.*

Rear Output Shaft

1. Remove yoke cotter pin and nut.
2. Remove companion yoke, then remove oil seal. NOTE: When removing companion yoke oil seal, use care not to damage bearing retainer.
3. Remove shaft, rear bearing cone, spacer and shims.
4. Remove front bearing cone, using a suitable puller.
5. Carefully remove snap-ring and bearing rollers from gear bore.

NOTE: Rear output shaft and gear are integral. *Do not remove gear from shaft.*

2-Speed Clutch Gear, Shifter Fork and Shaft

1. Remove safety wire and screw from shifter fork.
2. Remove screw, gasket, spring and poppet ball.
3. Remove shifter shaft, fork and 2-speed clutch gear.

Front Output Clutch Gear, Shifter Fork and Shaft

1. Remove safety wire and shift fork screw.
2. Remove screw, gasket, spring and poppet ball.
3. Remove shift shaft, fork and front output clutch gear.
4. Remove shift shaft oil seals.

Front Output Shaft

1. Remove cotter pin and yoke nut.
2. Remove plain washer and companion yoke.
3. Remove thrust washer and front output shaft.

Input Shaft

1. Remove cotter pin and yoke nut.
2. Remove washer and companion yoke.
3. Carefully remove input shaft and gear. Hold gear on shaft to retain bearing rollers.

Bearings and Retainers

1. Remove attaching nuts and lock washers, then remove gaskets and bearing retainers.
2. Remove companion yoke oil seals from case.
3. Using a brass drift, drive ball bearing assemblies out of case.

Idler Gear and Shaft

1. Remove cotter pin and slotted nut at end of idler shaft.
2. Remove screw, cover and gasket at other end of shaft.
3. Thread arbor tool (shown in illustration) on idler shaft. NOTE: Make sure arbor is firmly seated against shoulder on shaft.
4. Using a soft-faced hammer, drive idler shaft out of case.
5. Separate shaft and arbor, leaving arbor in the idler gear.
6. Remove idler gear (with arbor) and bearing.
7. Remove arbor, bearing cones, spacer and shims from gear.
8. If necessary to replace bearing cups, drive them out with a brass drift.

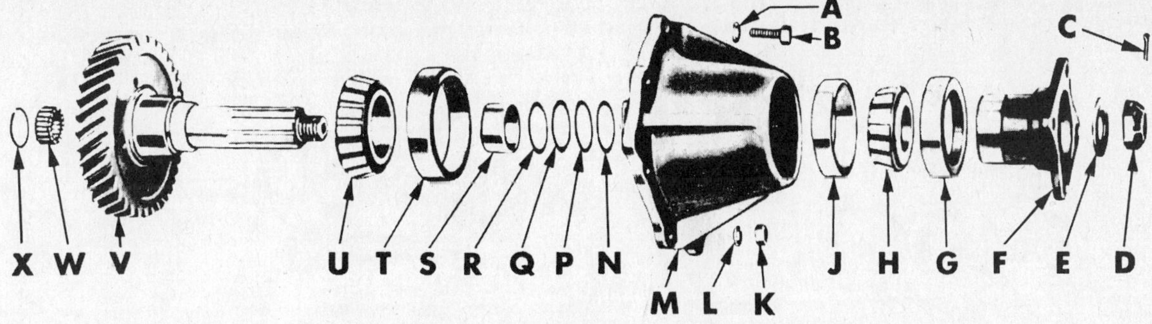

Rear axle output shaft bearing retainer assembly (© Chrysler Corp.)

A Lock washer
B Screw
C Cotter pin
D Slotted nut
E Plain wahser
F Companion yoke
G Companion yoke oil seal
H Rear bearing cone
J Rear bearing cup
K Nut
L Lock washer
M Bearing retainer
N Bearing shim (.004 in.)
P Bearing shim (.005 in.)
Q Bearing shim (.0125 in.)
R Bearing shim (.015 in.)
S Shaft spacer
T front bearing cup
U Output shaft with integral gear
W Output shaft rollers
X Output shaft rollers snap ring

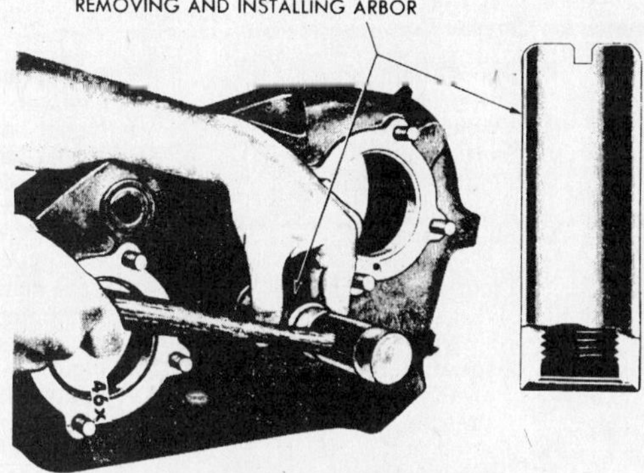

Removing or installing idler gear shaft with arbor tool (© Chrysler Corp.)

Assembly

Assembly of the transfer case is essentially a reversal of the disassembly procedure. However, items such as bearing preload, gasket preparation and oil seal installation must be accomplished before and during the assembly. The items listed below are of utmost importance and must be carefully considered in order to effect proper operation of the transfer case.

Brake Output Shaft

1. If new bearing cups are to be installed, remove any burrs, then carefully clean bores in retainer. Install bearing cups with an arbor press. NOTE: Make certain that cups seat firmly against shoulders in retainer bores.
2. Coat the 15 bearing rollers with gear lubricant and position them in gear bore. Secure with snapring.
3. If new shims are needed when assembling shaft and retainer, begin with a .0365 shim set. NOTE: The .0365 shim set consists of four different sized shims: .004″, .005″, .0125″ and .15″ (one of each).
4. To check bearing preload (after shaft and retainer assembly), position bearing retainer vertically in a soft-jawed vise, so that the shaft can rotate freely. Turn the shaft until the bearing rolls smoothly. Using an inch-pound torque wrench, measure bearing preload. NOTE: Make preload measurement with the wrench in motion.
5. Add or subtract shims as necessary to meet specifications. CAUTION: Incorrect preload will cause shortened bearing life, excessive noise and may promote oil leakage.
6. After setting correct bearing preload, remove slotted nut, washer and yoke. Coat outer surface of new oil seal with plastic type gasket cement. Install oil seal in brake support, then reassemble shaft.
7. When installing brake support on bearing retainer, make certain that studs are tight and that retainer oil drain holes, gasket cutout and support drain holes are all aligned.
8. Position speedometer drive pinion so that pilot at lower end of pinion engages hole in retainer boss.
9. When positioning retainer in transfer case, make certain that pad on retainer flange covers shift shaft opening.

Rear Output Shaft

1. If replacement of the bearing cups is necessary, follow procedure given in Step 1-Brake Output Shaft.
2. Measure bearing preload as described in Steps 3 and 4-Brake Output Shaft.
3. Position seal in bearing retainer with lip toward inside of case.

Idler Gear

1. The correct adjustment of the idler gear bearing is free rolling, but with no end-play. To achieve this, remove one shim at a time until a slight drag is felt when rotating shaft. Add a shim *just* thick enough to permit smooth roller operation.
2. Use special arbor shown in illustration to install idler gear and shaft in case.
3. When installing slotted nut at end of shaft, torque to specifications, then install cotter pin.

NOTE: Do not back off nut to align cotter pin hole. *Tighten,* if necessary.

Front Output Shaft

Position bearing retainer firmly against case, then measure clearance with a feeler gauge. Install a combination of gaskets approximately .006″ more than measured clearance.

NOTE: Gaskets are available in two thicknesses: .009″ and .013″.

Input Shaft

1. Install 70 bearing rollers with spacer in input shaft gear. Use a sleeve as shown in illustration to retain rollers.

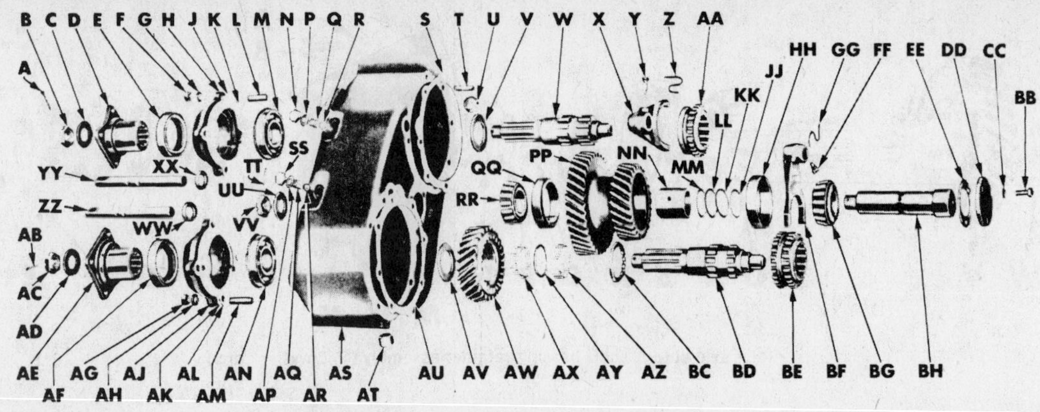

Transfer unit disassembled (© Chrysler Corp.)

A Cotter pin
B Slotted nut
C Plain washer
D Companion yoke
E Compression yoke oil seal
F Nut
G Lock washer
H Bearing retainer
J Bearing retainer gasket (.009 in.)
K Bearing retainer gasket (.013 in.)
L Bearing retainer stud
M Ball Bearing assembly
N Poppet ball screw
P Poppet ball screw gasket
Q Poppet ball spring
R Poppet ball
S Bearing retainer gasket
T Stud
U Pipe plug
V Front axle output shaft thrust washer
W Front axle output shaft
X Shifter fork
Y Shifter fork screw
Z Lock wire
AA Front axle clutch gear
CC Lock washer
BB Screw
DD Idler gear shaft cover
EE Idler gear shaft cover gasket
FF Shifter fork screw
GG Lock wire
HH Idler gear bearing cup
JJ Bearing shim (.004 in.)
KK Bearing shim (.005 in.)
LL Bearing shim (.0125 in.)
MM Bearing shim (.015 in.)
NN Idler gear bearing spacer
PP Idler gear
QQ Idler gear bearing cup
RR Idler gear bearing cone
SS Poppet ball screw
TT Cotter pin
UU Plain washer
VV Slotted nut
WW Shifter shaft oil seal
XX Shifter shaft oil seal
YY Front axle clutch gear shifter shaft
ZZ 2-speed clutch gear shifter shaft
AB Cotter pin
AC Slotted nut
AD Plain washer
AE Companion yoke
AF Companion yoke oil seal
AG Nut
AH Lock washer
AJ Bearing retainer
AK Bearing retainer gasket (.009 in.)
AL Bearing retainer gasket (.013 in.)
AM Bearing retainer stud
AN Ball bearing assembly
AP Poppet ball screw gasket
AQ Poppet ball spring
AR Poppet ball
AS Transfer case
AT Pipe plug
AU Bearing retainer gasket
AV Input shaft gear, outer thrust washer
AW Input shaft gear
AX Input shaft gear roller
AY Input shaft gear roller spacer
AZ Input shaft gear roller
BC Input shaft gear, inner thrust washer
BD Input shaft
BE 2-speed clutch gear
BF Shifter fork
BG Idler gear bearing cone
BH Idler gear shaft

2. Select bearing retainer gaskets as described under front output shaft.

Specifications

END PLAY

Idler Gear Bearing	Zero
Input Shaft	Approx. .006"
Front Output Shaft	Approx. .006"

BEARING PRELOAD (IN. LBS.)

Brake Output Shaft Bearing	15-30
Rear Output Shaft Bearing	15-30

TORQUE LIMITS (FT. LBS.)

Brake Output Shaft Yoke Nut	140-160
Rear Output Shaft Yoke Nut	140-160
Idler Shaft Nut	140-160
Bearing Retainer Cap Screws	30-35
Case Mounting Bolts	50-55

New Process Model T201

Description

The New Process Model T201 transfer case is a 2-speed gearbox which provides speed reduction and couples power to the front and rear driving axles.

CAUTION: Do not engage front driving axle when operating truck on hard surfaced roads at high speeds.

De-Clutch and Shift Rod Adjustment

NOTE: All adjustments must be made with the front axle engaged and the transfer case in low range.

1. Disconnect de-clutch and shift rods at shift levers.
2. Adjust de-clutch rod length until lever clears rear end of slot in cab underbody by 5/8". Secure adjusting yoke with locknut.
3. Adjust shift rod length until distance between protusions on shift and de-clutch levers is 1/4". Secure adjusting yoke with locknut.
4. Connect de-clutch and shift rods at shift levers and then road test vehicle.

Disassembly

Rear Output Shaft

1. Remove cotter pin and flange nut at rear output shaft.
2. Remove attaching bolts and nuts, then remove bearing retainer and gasket. Discard gasket.
3. Remove output shaft assembly from case.
4. Remove nut and washer at rear of shaft.
5. Remove brake drum by tapping on it lightly (if necessary).
6. Remove shaft and gear from bearing retainer.
7. Remove shims, spacer and speedometer drive gear. Tie shims together for reassembly.
8. Remove inner bearing cone, using a suitable puller.
9. Remove snap-ring and roller bearings from shaft gear bore. CAUTION: The rear output shaft and gear is serviced as an assembly. *Do not remove gear from shaft.*
10. Remove attaching nuts, brake support, bearing and oil seal. Discard seal.

Front Output Shaft

1. Remove attaching bolts and nuts, then remove rear bearing retainer and gasket. Discard gasket.
2. Remove cotter pin and nut at front output shaft.
3. Remove attaching nut, washer and companion flange.
4. Remove the front output shaft

1 Ball, shift bar poppet
2 Spring, shift bar poppet ball
3 Bar, front output shaft
4 Fork, shift
5 Screw, set
6 Clutch, front output sliding
7 Fork, shift
8 Gear, front output drive
9 Bearing, roller (70 req'd)
10 Spacer, bearing
11 Shaft, front output front gear
12 Washer, thrust
13 Bearing, ball
14 Retainer, lock
15 Nut, bearing retaining
16 Shaft, idler gear
17 Cone, idler gear bearing
18 Cup, idler gear bearing
19 Shim, set
20 Spacer, bearing
21 Shaft input
22 Ring, snap
23 Bearing, roller (15 req'd)
24 Gear, rear output drive w/shaft
25 Gear, speedometer drive
26 Spacer, speedometer drive gear
27 Clutch, two-speed sliding
28 Plug, pipe
29 Gasket, set
30 Bolt, hex head, w/lock washer
31 Retainer, front output shaft rear bearing
32 Bolt, hex head, w/lock washer
33 Washer, lock
34 Nut, hex
35 Breather
36 Cup, rear output shaft outer bearing
37 Cone, rear output shaft outer bearing
38 Support, hand brake
39 Seal, rear output shaft outer bearing oil
40 Stud
41 Retainer, rear output drive gear bearing
42 Plate, idler shaft cover
43 Cup, rear output shaft inner bearing
44 Cone, rear output shaft inner bearing
45 Case, transfer
46 Bolt w/washer
47 Bolt, hex head
48 Washer, lock
49 Cover, power take-off opening

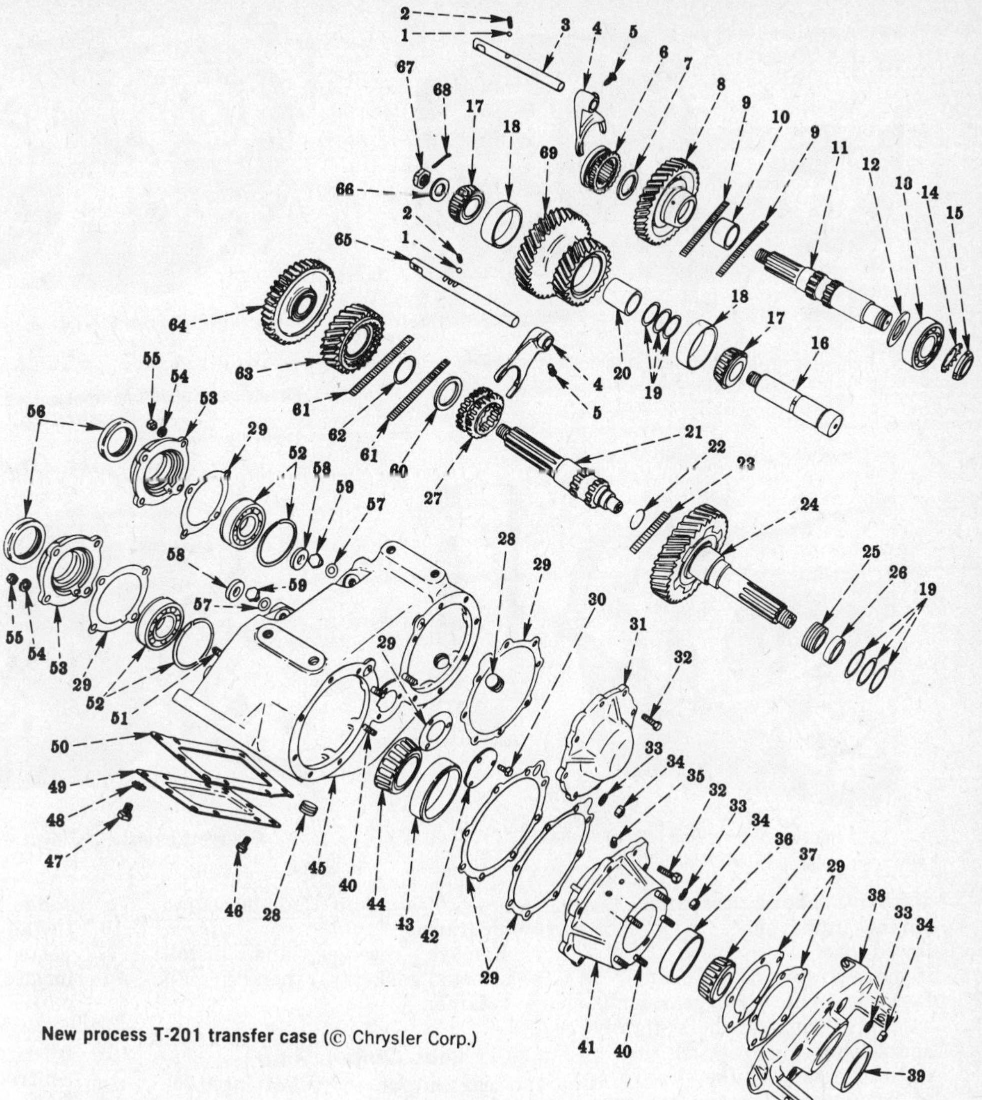

New process T-201 transfer case (© Chrysler Corp.)

50 Gasket, power take-off cover
51 Stud
52 Bearing, input and front output ball
53 retainer, input and front output bearing
54 Washer, lock
55. Nut, hex
56 Seal, input and front output bearing retainer oil
57 Gasket
58 Seal, front and rear output shift bar oil
59 Screw, poppet ball retainer
60 Washer, thrust
61 Bearing, roller (70 req'd)
62 Spacer, bearing
63 Gear, input drive
64 Gear, power take-off
65 Bar, two-speed shift
66 Washer
67 Nut, hex
68 Pin, cotter
69 Gear, Idler

assembly through the rear of the case.

5. Remove sliding clutch gear.
6. Position shaft assembly in a soft-jawed vise.
7. Remove lock retainer and bearing nut.
8. Using a suitable puller, remove bearing.
9. Remove front output shaft drive gear by lifting upward and holding the thrust washers against the hub to retain bearing rollers.
10. Carefully set aside thrust washers, then remove the two rows of bearing rollers and the spacer separating them.
11. Remove attaching nuts and bearing retainer with gaskets. Note number of gaskets used.

Idler Gear, Shift Bar and Fork

1. Remove safety wire and setscrews securing shift forks to shift bars.
2. Remove poppet ball retaining plugs, gaskets and poppet ball springs.
3. Pull shift bars out of the case, then remove shift forks and poppet balls.
4. Remove cotter pin, nut and washer from front end of shaft.
5. Remove attaching bolts, gasket and idler gear shaft cover plate.
6. Remove idler gear assembly. NOTE: When removing the idler gear assembly, use an arbor as shown in illustration and perform the following:

a. Install arbor on threaded end of shaft so that it seats against the shaft shoulder.
b. Drive arbor until shaft is free at rear of case.
c. Separate shaft and arbor.
d. Remove gear with arbor through front output shaft opening.
e. Remove arbor, shims, spacer and bearing cones. Tie shims together for reassembly.

Input Shaft

1. Remove cotter pin and input shaft flange nut.
2. Remove nut, flat washer and companion flange.
3. Remove input shaft assembly through rear output shaft opening in case. CAUTION: Make certain to retain power take-off

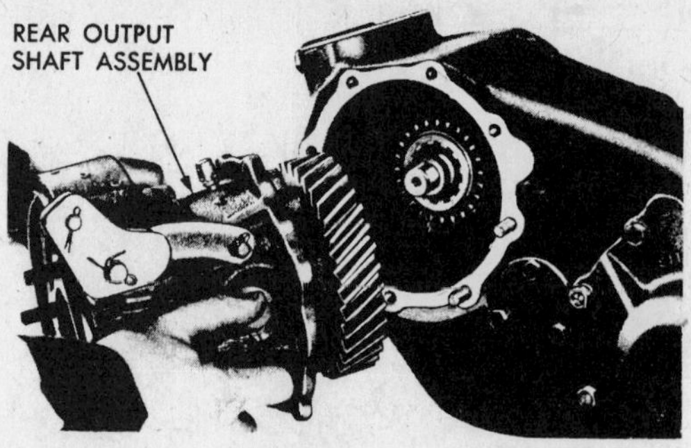

Removing or installing rear output shaft assembly
(© Chrysler Corp.)

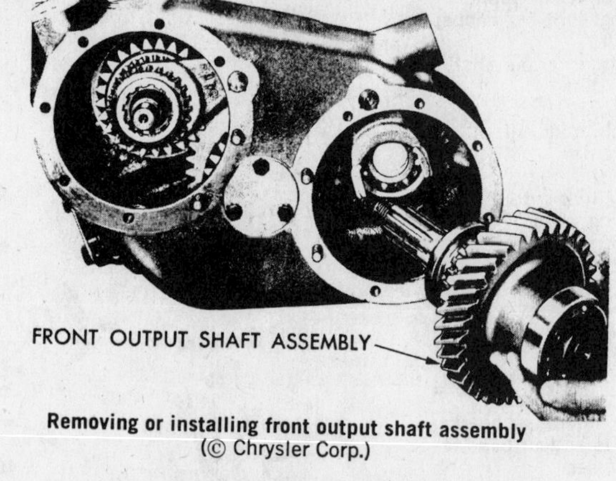

Removing or installing front output shaft assembly
(© Chrysler Corp.)

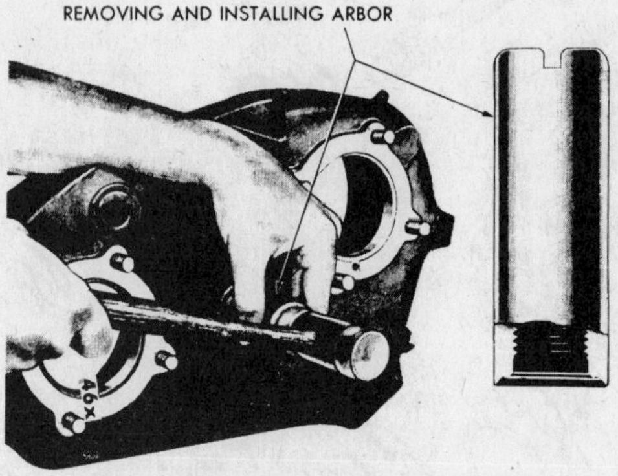

Removing or installing idler gear shaft
(© Chrysler Corp.)

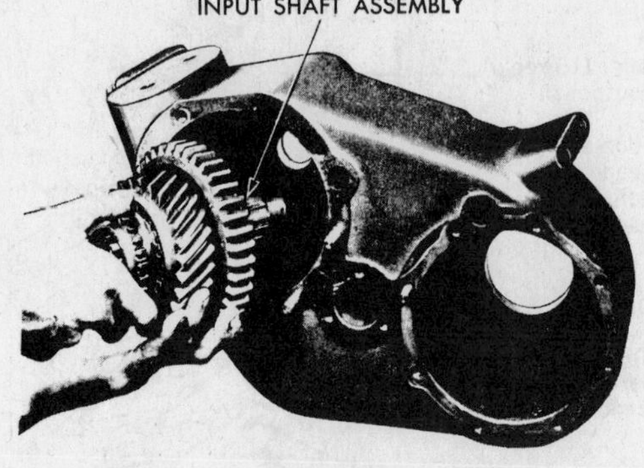

Removing or installing input shaft assembly
(© Chrysler Corp.)

and drive gear on the shaft.

4. Mount input shaft in a soft-jawed vise.
5. Remove power take-off gear.
6. Remove input drive gear while holding thrust washers tightly against hub.
7. Carefully remove the two rows of bearing rollers and the separating spacer.
8. Remove attaching nuts, bearing retainer, gaskets and oil seal. Note the number of gaskets used and discard the oil seal.

Assembly

The transfer case is assembled in the reverse order of disassembly. The following procedures, however, must all be completed before (or in some cases, during) installation of shaft and gear assemblies.

Input Shaft

1. The input shaft drive gear bearing consists of 70 rollers divided into two rows by a spacer.
2. Coat gear bore with grease, then position rollers and spacer.
3. Hold thrust washers against hub to retain rollers, then install gear on shaft.
4. Input shaft end-play is controlled by gasket thickness between case and bearing retainer.
5. Position retainer on case, then measure clearance with a feeler gauge.
6. Select gasket(s) with a thickness .005" more than measured clearance.
7. Remove retainer and install selected gasket(s), then reinstall retainer.

Rear Output Shaft

1. Rear output shaft bearing preload is set by shim set size selection.
2. Using an arbor press and suitable sleeve, install inner bearing cone on shaft. The cone should be firmly seated against gear.
3. Install speedometer drive gear, spacer and original bearing shim set.
4. Install rear output shaft in bearing retainer, then position outer bearing cone on shaft.
5. Install parking brake drum, flat washer and slotted nut. Torque nut to 125 ft. lbs.
6. Mount shaft and retainer assembly in a vise so that shaft is free to rotate.
7. Turn shaft until bearing rolls smoothly. Then, using an inch-pound torque wrench, measure bearing preload. Subtract or add shims as necessary to meet specifications. NOTE: Shims for adjusting bearing preload are available in four thicknesses.
8. After the final adjustment, remove slotted nut, washer and brake drum.
9. Install parking brake support and new support oil seal.
10. Install brake drum, washer and slotted nut. Torque nut to specifications.

Idler Gear

1. Idler gear bearing end-play is controlled by shim set size selection.
2. Clamp the idler gear shaft (large end) in a soft-jawed vise.
3. Install bearing cone against shoulder on shaft.
4. Install bearing spacer and original shim set.
5. Install idler gear (small end down) on shaft, then install other bearing cone.
6. Position spacer tool as shown in illustration, then install flat washer and nut. Torque nut to specifications.
7. Rotate gear until bearing rolls smoothly. Then using a dial indicator, measure idler gear bearing end-play. Add or subtract shims as necessary to meet specifications.
8. Disassemble idler gear shaft assembly. Tie newly selected shims together.
9. To install gear assembly in the case, position bearing cone in in the large end of the gear, then place gear (small end up) on a bench.
10. Install the same arbor used to remove idler gear shaft, a

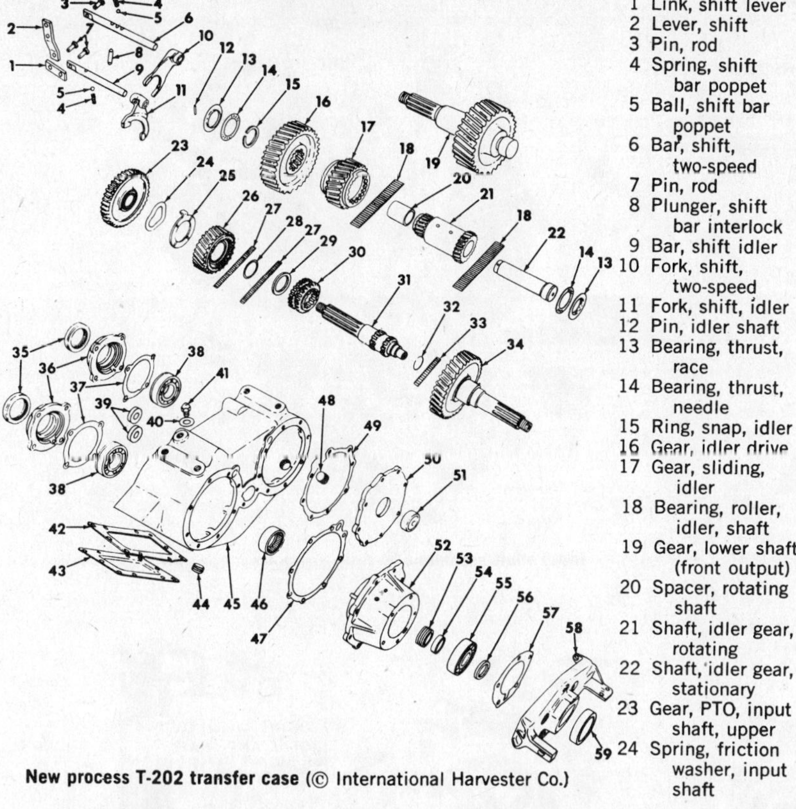

New process T-202 transfer case (© International Harvester Co.)

1 Link, shift lever
2 Lever, shift
3 Pin, rod
4 Spring, shift bar poppet
5 Ball, shift bar poppet
6 Bar, shift, two-speed
7 Pin, rod
8 Plunger, shift bar interlock
9 Bar, shift idler
10 Fork, shift, two-speed
11 Fork, shift, idler
12 Pin, idler shaft
13 Bearing, thrust, race
14 Bearing, thrust, needle
15 Ring, snap, idler
16 Gear, idler drive
17 Gear, sliding, idler
18 Bearing, roller, idler, shaft
19 Gear, lower shaft (front output)
20 Spacer, rotating shaft
21 Shaft, idler gear, rotating
22 Shaft, idler gear, stationary
23 Gear, PTO, input shaft, upper
24 Spring, friction washer, input shaft
25 Washer, friction, input shaft
26 Gear, drive, input shaft, upper
27 Bearing, roller, input shaft, front
28 Spacer, input shaft drive gear bearing
29 Washer, input shaft sliding clutch
30 Gear, clutch, input shaft, upper
31 Shaft, input
32 Ring, snap
33 Bearing, roller, drive gear
34 Gear, shaft, output drive
35 Seal, oil, input and output shaft, front
36 Retainer, bearing, input and output shaft, front
37 Gasket, bearing retainer
38 Bearing, input and output shaft, front
39 Seal, oil, shift bar
40 Gasket, shift bar poppet screw
41 Screw, shift bar poppet
42 Gasket, PTO cover
43 Cover, PTO opening
44 Plug, pipe
45 Case, transfer
46 Bearing, gear, output shaft, inner
47 Gasket, rear bearing retainer, upper
48 Plug, pipe
49 Gasket, rear bearing retainer, lower
50 Retainer, lower rear bearing (front output shaft)
51 Bearing, lower shaft, rear
52 Retainer, upper rear (output shaft) bearing
53 Gear, speedometer drive gear
54 Spacer, speedometer drive gear
55 Bearing, output shaft drive gear, outer
56 Spacer, brake drum flange
57 Gasket, brake drum support
58 Support, hand brake
59 Seal, oil, output shaft bearing, rear

spacer, new shims and other bearing cone in the idler gear.

11. Hold the idler gear assembly in the case with the small diameter gear facing rearward, then insert the shaft through the case (from rear) and thread it into the previously installed arbor.
12. Tap on the shaft until arbor extends through opposite side of case.
13. Remove arbor.

Two-Speed Clutch

When installing the two-speed clutch on the input shaft, make certain that the recessed side of the gear is toward the front of the case.

Front Output Shaft

1. The front output shaft drive gear bearing consists of 70 bearing rollers divided into two rows by a spacer.
2. Coat gear bore with grease, then position rollers and spacer.
3. Hold thrust washers against each hub to retain rollers, then install gear on shaft.
4. Shaft end-play is controlled by gasket thickness between case and bearing retainer.
5. Position retainer on case, then measure clearance with a feeler gauge.
6. Select gasket(s) with a thickness .005″ more than measured clearance.
7. Remove retainer and install selected gasket(s), then reinstall retainer.
8. When installing the front output shaft assembly in the case, locate front output shift bar as far toward rear of case as possible. This will make it possible to position shift fork in clutch gear collar and to align clutch gear splines on front output shaft.

Specifications

END PLAY

Input Shaft	Approx. 0.005″
Front Output Shaft	Approx. 0.005″
Idler Gear	0.000-0.002″

BEARING PRELOAD (IN. LBS.)

Rear Output Shaft Bearings	15-30

TORQUE LIMITS (FT. LBS.)

Front Retainer Nut	35-55
Poppet Screw	15-25
Idler Cover Screw	15-25
Drain and Filler Plugs	25-45
Top Cover	38-42
All Bearing Caps	38-42
Flange and Idler Shaft Nut	125
Input Shaft	300-400
Front Output Shaft	300-400
Rear Output Shaft	300-400
Idler Shaft Nut	140-160
Front Output Shaft Flange Nut	140-160
Input Shaft Flange Nut	140-160
Driveshaft Mating Flange Nuts	35
Breather	8-12
Brake Support Nut	25-45
Brake Retaining Screw	20-40
Brake Retainer Nut	25-45
Brake Drum	60-66
Brake Mounting	60-66
Brake Drum Nut	140-160
P.T.O. Screw	8-12
P.T.O. to Case	38-42
P.T.O. Bearing Cap	38-42
P.T.O. Top Cover	38-42
P.T.O. Shaft	300-400

New Process Model T202

Description

The New Process Model T202 transfer case is a two-speed gear box which is used to transmit power from the main transmission to a front driving axle, as well as to a conventional rear axle. Sliding clutch gears in the transfer case are controlled by a single lever to select various driving ranges. A separate control lever is provided for operating the power take-off assembly on units so equipped.

The transfer case should not be operated in four-wheel high range on dry, hard surface roads, as rapid tire wear will result.

CAUTION: Do not operate transfer case in neutral range for extended periods of time when power take-off assembly is disengaged.

Disassembly

NOTE: The following procedure covers a disassembly of the transfer case removed from the chassis and mounted in a suitable stand.

Rear (Upper) Output Shaft

1. Remove cotter pin from flange nut located at end of rear output shaft. Apply hand brake to prevent shaft from rotating; then break the torque on nut.
2. Remove hex head bolts and two nuts securing bearing retainer

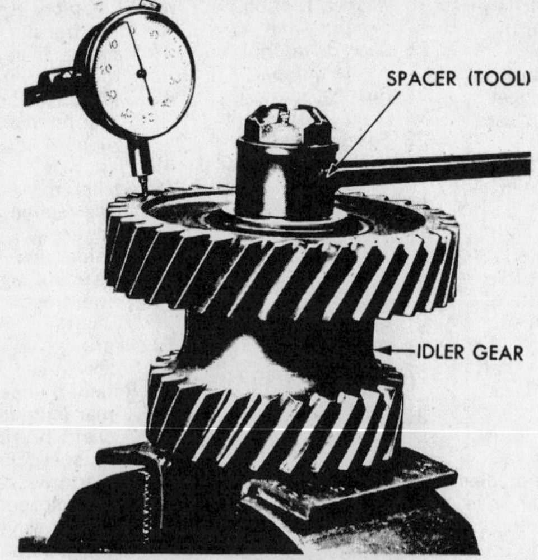

Checking idler gear bearing adjustment (© Chrysler Corp.)

Input shaft assembly (© International Harvester Co.)

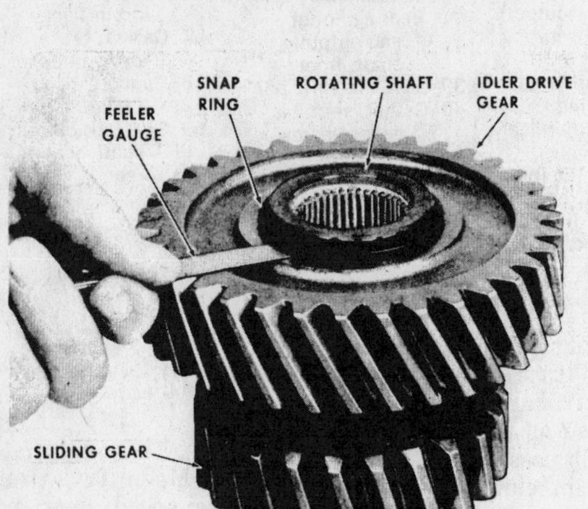

Idler gear assembly (© International Harvester Co.)

Front (lower) output shaft (© International Harvester Co.)

to case. Remove the rear output shaft assembly. Remove and discard gasket.

3. Place the output shaft assembly on a bench.
4. Remove the nut and flat washer at rear of shaft. Tap brake drum lightly and remove drum from shaft. Slide off brake drum flange spacer.
5. Remove output shaft with drive gear from upper rear bearing retainer. Slide off speedometer drive gear, spacer and drive gear inner bearing. Remove snap-ring and fifteen roller bearings.
6. Remove hex nuts and lock washers securing hand brake support to upper rear bearing retainer. Remove brake support and drive gear outer bearing. Remove oil seal and discard.

Input Shaft

1. Remove ten capscrews and lock washers attaching power take-off cover or assembly (if so equipped). Remove and discard gasket.
2. Remove shift bar poppet screw, spring and ball. Through the rear output shaft opening in case, remove roll pin securing two-speed shift fork on bar. Use a 5/32" diameter steel rod to drive out roll pin. NOTE: Where case interference prevents complete removal of roll pin, drive the pin until shift bar can be removed. Shift fork can then be moved toward input shaft clutch gear to provide clearance for removal of roll pin.
3. Position idler shift bar in four-wheel high drive position (shift bar to extreme rear in case). Simultaneously remove input shaft clutch gear and two-speed shift fork.
4. Remove cotter pin from nut at outer end of input shaft. Use a suitable flange holder to prevent shaft from turning; then break torque on nut. Remove the nut, flat washer and companion flange.
5. Move the input shaft and gear assembly toward rear of case by lightly tapping on the outer end of shaft. This will free shaft from bearing and permit shaft and power take-off gear to be removed. CAUTION: Hold input drive gear firmly against shoulder on shaft to retain roller bearings in bore of gear.
6. Place input shaft on a bench and remove drive gear, roller bearings, spacer and sliding clutch gear washer. Remove friction washer and washer spring from hub of power take-off gear.
7. Remove input shaft bearing retainer, gasket and bearing. If necessary, remove and discard oil seal from bearing retainer.

Front (Lower) Output Shaft

1. Remove cotter pin from nut at

outer end of front output shaft. Use a suitable flange holder to prevent shaft from turning; then break torque on nut. Remove nut, flat washer and flange.

2. Remove hex head bolts and nuts attaching input shaft rear bearing retainer to case. Lightly tap on end of shaft, moving it toward rear of case to displace shoulder on rear bearing retainer. Remove drive gear and shaft.
3. Press drive gear rear bearing from retainer. Remove front bearing retainer and bearing. If lubricant leakage is evident at the retainer, remove oil seal and discard.

Idler Shift Bar and Gear

1. Remove roll pin securing fork to idler shift bar. Use a 5/32" diameter steel rod to drive out pin. Withdraw shift bar and fork. NOTE: Spring tension on poppet ball will displace ball from case upon removing shift bar.
2. Remove shift bar interlock plunger and spring.
3. Remove roll pin from outer end of idler gear stationary shaft. Using a brass drift, drive the idler shaft toward rear of case. Remove shaft.
4. Remove idler gear rotating shaft assembly through the opening from which the rear output shaft assembly was removed. Place the gear assembly on a bench.
5. Remove thrust bearing and thrust bearing race at each end of rotating shaft. Remove individual roller bearing and spacer.
6. Remove snap-ring; then separate idler drive gear and shaft. Remove sliding clutch gear.

Assembly

Lubricate all bearings, bushings, spline shafts and shift bar forks at their contact surfaces during assembly. This will provide initial lubrication and avoid possible damage when the transfer case is first operated.

Idler Shift Bar and Gear

1. Place the idler gear rotating shaft in a vertical position with the large splined gear end resting on bench.
2. Position sliding clutch gear on shaft with the groove which receives idler shift fork, facing upward.
3. Position drive gear on shaft so that gear internal splines engage splines on shaft. CAUTION: The long shoulder side of drive gear must face sliding clutch gear to provide clearance with the inside face of case.
4. Install snap-ring and check for proper side clearance with drive gear. This is accomplished by inserting a feeler gauge between the ring and gear. Three different thicknesses of snap-rings are available for obtaining proper clearance. Select and install proper size. Refer to Specifications for recommended snap-ring side clearance. NOTE: Snap-ring side clearance must be maintained to prevent possible ring breakage.
5. Coat the bore of idler gear rotating shaft with Lubriplate No. 110; then assemble roller bearings and spacer. Apply Lubriplate to thrust bearing and bearing race; then assemble at each end of idler rotating shaft. Carefully place rotating shaft assembly in case. Align shaft with opening in front and rear of case for installing the stationary shaft. Install stationary shaft, making certain not to disturb roller bearing arrangement in bore of rotating shaft. Tap the shaft lightly until seated. Install roll pin in shaft at front of case.
6. Position poppet spring and ball in case. Hold the spring and ball in a compressed position and insert idler shift bar at front side of case. Place idler shift fork in position on sliding gear (shoulder on fork toward front of case) and install on shift bar. Secure fork to shift bar with roll pin.

NOTE: Side of shift bar employing only one detent must be facing upward.

Input Shaft

1. Place the input drive gear on a bench and assemble roller bearings and spacer. Coat the gear bore with Lubriplate No. 110 to retain bearing rollers.
2. Install sliding clutch washer; then carefully position drive gear with bearings on shaft. Place friction washer on shaft next to drive gear, with the tang opposite gear.
3. Assemble friction washer spring on hub of power take-off gear. NOTE: Install spring on recess side of gear.
4. Assemble input shaft with drive gear and power take-off gear in case. Hold the drive gear firmly to clutch gear washer to keep roller bearings in place. NOTE: Rotate friction washer until tang engages blind hole in power take-off gear.
5. With the idler shift bar in four-wheel high drive position (shift bar to extreme rear of case), insert interlock plunger in case.
6. Install two-speed shift bar in case so that side of bar with the single detent is facing the idler shift bar. Install sliding clutch gear and two-speed shift bar fork. Install roll pin to secure fork to shift bar.
7. Install input shaft bearing. CAUTION: Movement of input shaft toward rear of case while installing bearing will permit rollers to become displaced from bore of drive gear.
8. Position bearing retainer to case and install hex head bolts finger tight. Do not torque bolts at this time since gasket thickness must be determined following installation of rear output shaft assembly.

Front (Lower) Output Shaft

1. Install front output shaft bearing in face of case.
2. Install front output shaft and drive gear.
3. Press drive gear rear bearing in retainer. Install bearing with stamped end of bearing resting on press. Position gasket and retainer at rear face of case. Install hex head bolts with lock washers and tighten securely.
4. Install new oil seal in bearing retainer. Assemble retainer to front face of case and install hex head bolts finger tight. Do not torque bolts at this time.

Rear (Upper) Output Shaft

1. Support rear output shaft bearing retainer in a press; then install shaft inner bearing flush with outer surface of retainer.
2. Place bearing retainer on a bench and assemble drive gear and shaft. Position speedometer drive gear and spacer on shaft. Assemble outer bearing on shaft and install in upper rear bearing retainer. Install hand brake drum spacer.
3. Install new oil seal in hand brake support. Install gasket and brake support to upper rear bearing retainer.
4. Position gasket to bearing retainer and install the rear output assembly on case.

Input and Front Output Shaft Bearing Adjustment

The fit of the input and front output shaft bearing retainer to their respective bearings is controlled by gasket thickness. To determine the correct thickness or number of gaskets required, measure the clearance between retainer and case with a feeler gauge. Select gasket(s) which will give a bearing retainer fit within specified limits. See Specifications.

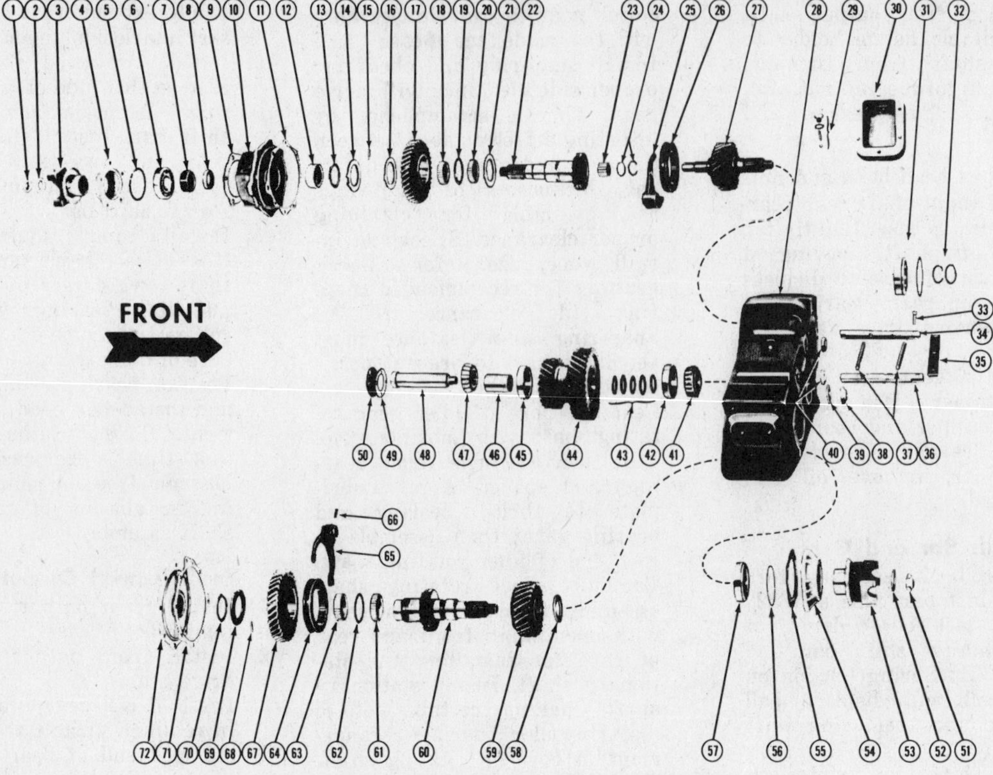

New process 205 transfer case (© G.M.C.)

1 Rear output shaft lock nut
2 Washer
3 Yoke
4 Bearing retainer and seal assembly
5 Snap ring
6 Bearing
7 Speedometer gear
8 Spacer
9 Gasket
10 Housing
11 Gasket
12 Bearing
13 Snap ring
14 Thrust washer
15 Thrust washer lock pin
16 Thrust washer (tanged)
17 Low speed gear
18 Needle bearings
19 Spacer
20 Needle bearings
21 Tanged washer
22 Rear output shaft
24 Washer and retainer
23 Needle bearings
25 Shift fork
26 Sliding clutch
27 Input shaft
28 Transfer case
29 Poppet plug, spring and ball
30 P.T.O. gasket and cover
31 Input shaft bearing and snap ring
32 Snap ring and rubber O-ring
33 Shift link clevis pin
34 Range shift rail
35 Shift rail connector link
36 Front wheel drive shift rail
37 Interlock pins
38 Rear idler lock nut
39 Washer
40 Shift rail seals
41 Idler shaft bearing
42 Bearing cup
43 Shims
44 Idler gear
45 Bearing cup
46 Spacer
47 Idler shaft bearing
48 Idler shaft
49 Cover gasket
50 Rear cover
51 Front output shaft lock nut
52 Washer
53 Yoke
54 Bearing retainer and seat
55 Gasket
56 Snap ring
57 Front bearing
58 Thrust washer
59 Front wheel high gear
60 Front output shaft
61 Needle bearings
62 Spacer
63 Needle bearing
64 Sliding clutch gear
65 Shift fork
66 Roll pin
67 Front output low gear
68 Thrust washer lock pin
69 Thrust washer
70 Snap ring
71 Rear cover gasket
72 Rear cover and bearing

Remove the retainer; then install selected gasket(s) and retainer.

Specifications

BEARING CLEARANCE

Input and Front Output Shaft Bearings .... 0.003-0.006"
Gasket Thickness Available .. 0.009-0.011"
0.0135-0.0165"

SNAP RING

Side Clearance .... 0.007-0.013"
Thickness Available .... 0.092-0.094"
0.095-0.097"
0.098-0.100"

POPPET BALL SPRING

Free Length .... 1.0"
Pressure @ 21/32" .... 30 Lbs.

TORQUE LIMITS (FT. LBS.)

Flange Nut .... Minimum 125

New Process Model 205

Description

The New Process Model 205 trans-

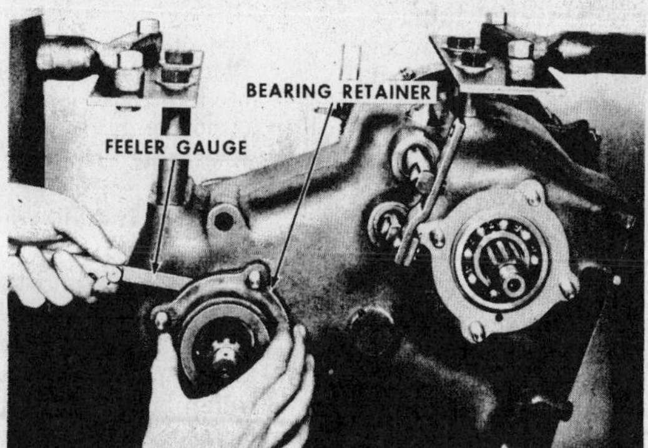

Input and front output shaft bearing adjustment (© International Harvester Co.)

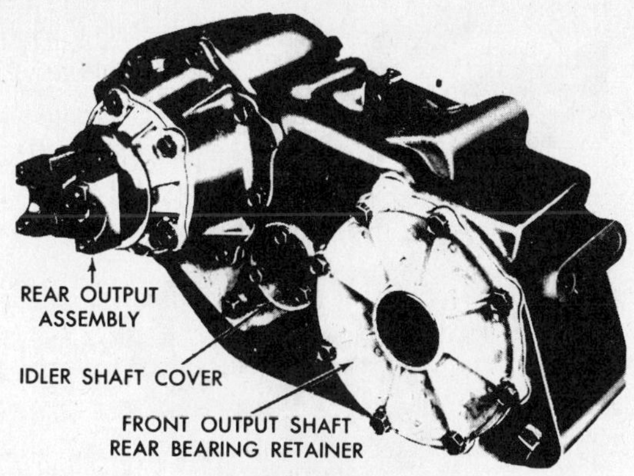

Rear view of transfer case
(© G.M.C.)

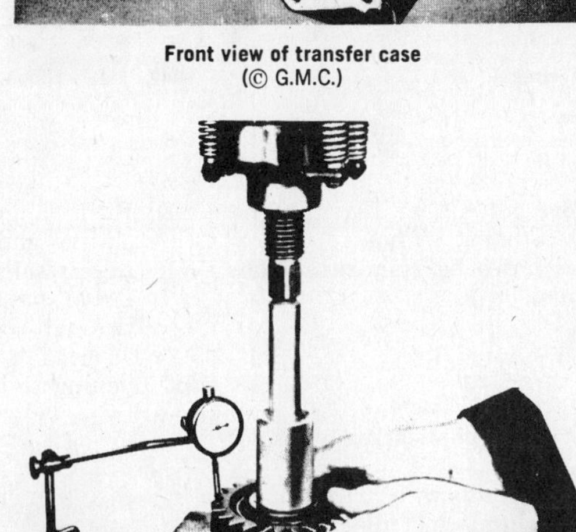

Front view of transfer case
(© G.M.C.)

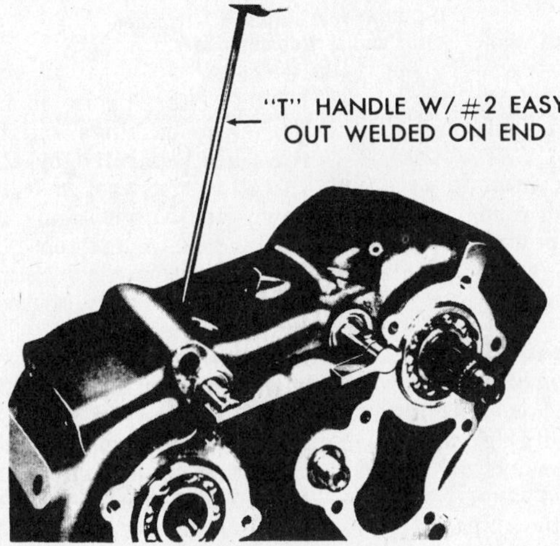

Removing shift fork pins
(© G.M.C.)

Checking idler gear end play
(© G.M.C.)

fer case is a two-speed gearbox mounted between the main transmission and the rear axle. The gearbox transmits power from the transmission and engine to the front and rear driving axles.

Disassembly

Rear Output Shaft and Yoke

1. Loosen rear output shaft yoke nut.
2. Remove shaft housing bolts, then remove the housing and retainer assembly.
3. Remove retaining nut and yoke from the shaft, then remove the shaft assembly.
4. Remove and discard snap ring.
5. Remove thrust washer and pin.
6. Remove tanged bronze washer. Remove gear needle bearings, spacer and second row of needle bearings.
7. Remove tanged bronze thrust washer.
8. Remove pilot rollers, retainer ring and washer.
9. Remove oil seal retainer, ball bearing, speedometer gear and spacer. Discard gaskets.
10. Press out bearing.
11. Remove oil seal from the retainer.

Front Output Shaft

1. Remove lock nut, washer and yoke.
2. Remove attaching bolts and front bearing retainer.
3. Remove rear bearing retainer attaching bolts.
4. Tap output shaft with a soft-faced hammer and remove shaft, gear assembly and rear bearing retainer.
5. Remove sliding clutch, gear, washer and bearing from output high gear.
6. Remove sliding clutch from the high output gear; then remove gear, washer and bearing.
7. Remove gear retaining snap-ring from the shaft, using large snap-ring picks. Discard ring.
8. Remove thrust washer and pin.
9. Remove gear, needle bearings and spacer.
10. Replace rear bearing, if necessary.

CAUTION: Always replace the bearing and retainer as an assembly. Do not try to press a new bearing into an old retainer.

Shift Rails and Forks

1. Remove the two poppet nuts, springs, and using a magnet, the poppet balls.
2. Remove cup plugs on top of case, using a 1/4" punch.
3. Position both shift rails in neutral, then remove fork pins with a long handled screw extractor.
4. Remove clevis pins and shift rail link.
5. Lower shift rails; upper rail first and then lower.
6. Remove shift forks and sliding clutch.
7. Remove the front output high gear, washer and bearing. Remove the shift rail cup plugs.

Input Shaft

1. Remove snap-ring in front of bearing. Tap shaft out rear of case and bearing out front of case, using a soft-faced hammer or mallet.
2. Tilt case up on power take-off and remove the two interlock pins from inside.

Idler Gear

1. Remove idler gear shaft nut.
2. Remove rear cover.
3. Tap out idler gear shaft, using a soft-faced hammer and a drift approximately the same diameter as the shaft.

Installing idler shaft
(© G.M.C.)

Installing rear output shaft spacer and speedometer gear
(© G.M.C.)

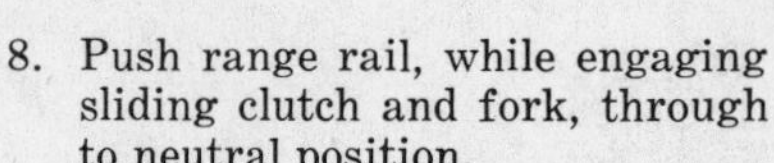

4. Remove idler gear through the front output shaft hole.
5. Remove two bearing cups from the idler gear.

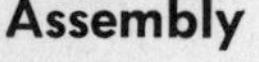

Assembly

Idler Gear

1. Press the two bearing cups in the idler gear.
2. Assemble the two bearing cones, spacer, shims and idler gear on a dummy shaft, with bore facing up. Check end-play.
3. Install idler gear assembly (with dummy shaft) into the case, large end first, through the front output shaft bore.
4. Install idler shaft from large bore side, driving it through with a soft-faced hammer or mallet.
5. Install washer and new locknut. Check for free rotation and measure end-play. Torque locknut to specifications.
6. Install idler shaft cover and new gasket. Torque cover bolts to specifications.

NOTE: Flat side of cover must be positioned towards front output shaft rear cover.

Shift Rails and Forks

1. Press the two rail seals into the case. NOTE: Install seals with metal lip outward.
2. Install interlock pins from inside case.
3. Insert slotted end of front output drive shift rail (with poppet notches up) into back of case.
4. While pushing rail through to neutral position, install shift fork (long end inward).
5. Install input shaft and bearing into case.
6. Install end of range rail (with poppet notches up) into front of case.
7. Install sliding clutch on fork, then place over input shaft in case.
8. Push range rail, while engaging sliding clutch and fork, through to neutral position.
9. Drive new lockpins into forks through holes at top of case.

NOTE: Tilt case on power take-off opening to install range rail lockpin.

Front Output Shaft and Gear

1. Install two rows of needle bearings in the front low output gear and retain with grease. NOTE: Each row consists of 32 needle bearings and the two rows are separated by a spacer.
2. Position front output shaft in a soft-jaw vise, with spline end down. Place front low gear over shaft with clutch gear facing down; then install thrust washer pin, thrust washer and new snap-ring. NOTE: Position snap ring gap opposite the thrust washer pin.
3. Place front drive high gear and washer in case. Install sliding clutch in the shift fork, then put fork and rail into 4-High position, meshing front drive high gear and clutch teeth.
4. Align washer, high gear and sliding clutch and bearing bore. Insert front output shaft and low gear assembly through the high gear assembly.
5. Install front output bearing and retainer with a new seal in the case.
6. Clean and grease rollers in front output rear bearing retainer. Install on case with one gasket and bolts coated with sealant. Torque bolts to specifications.
7. Install front output yoke, washer and locknut. Torque locknut to specifications.

Rear Output Shaft

1. Install two rows of needle bearings into the output low gear, retaining them with grease. NOTE: Each row consists of 32 needle bearings and the two rows are separated by a spacer.
2. Install thrust washer (with tang down in clutch gear groove) onto the rear output shaft.
3. Install output low gear onto shaft with clutch teeth facing downward.
4. Install thrust washer over gear with tab pointing up and away. Install washer pin.
5. Install large thrust washer over shaft and pin. Turn washer until tab fits into slot located approximately 90° away from pin.
6. Install snap-ring and measure shaft end-play.
7. Grease pilot bore and install needle bearings. NOTE: There are 15 pilot needle bearings.
8. Install thrust washer and new snap-ring in pilot bore.
9. Press new bearing into retainer housing.
10. Install housing on output shaft assembly.
11. Install spacer and speedometer gear. Install rear bearing.
12. Install rear bearing retainer seal.
13. Install bearing retainer assembly on housing, using one or two gaskets to achieve specified clearance. Torque attaching bolts to specifications.
14. Install yoke, washer and locknut on output shaft.
15. Position range rail in high, then install output shaft and retainer assembly on case. Torque housing bolts to specifications.

Case

1. Install power take-off cover and gasket. Torque attaching bolts to specifications.
2. Install cup plugs at rail pin holes. NOTE: After installing, seal the cup plugs.
3. Install drain and filler plugs. Torque to specifications.

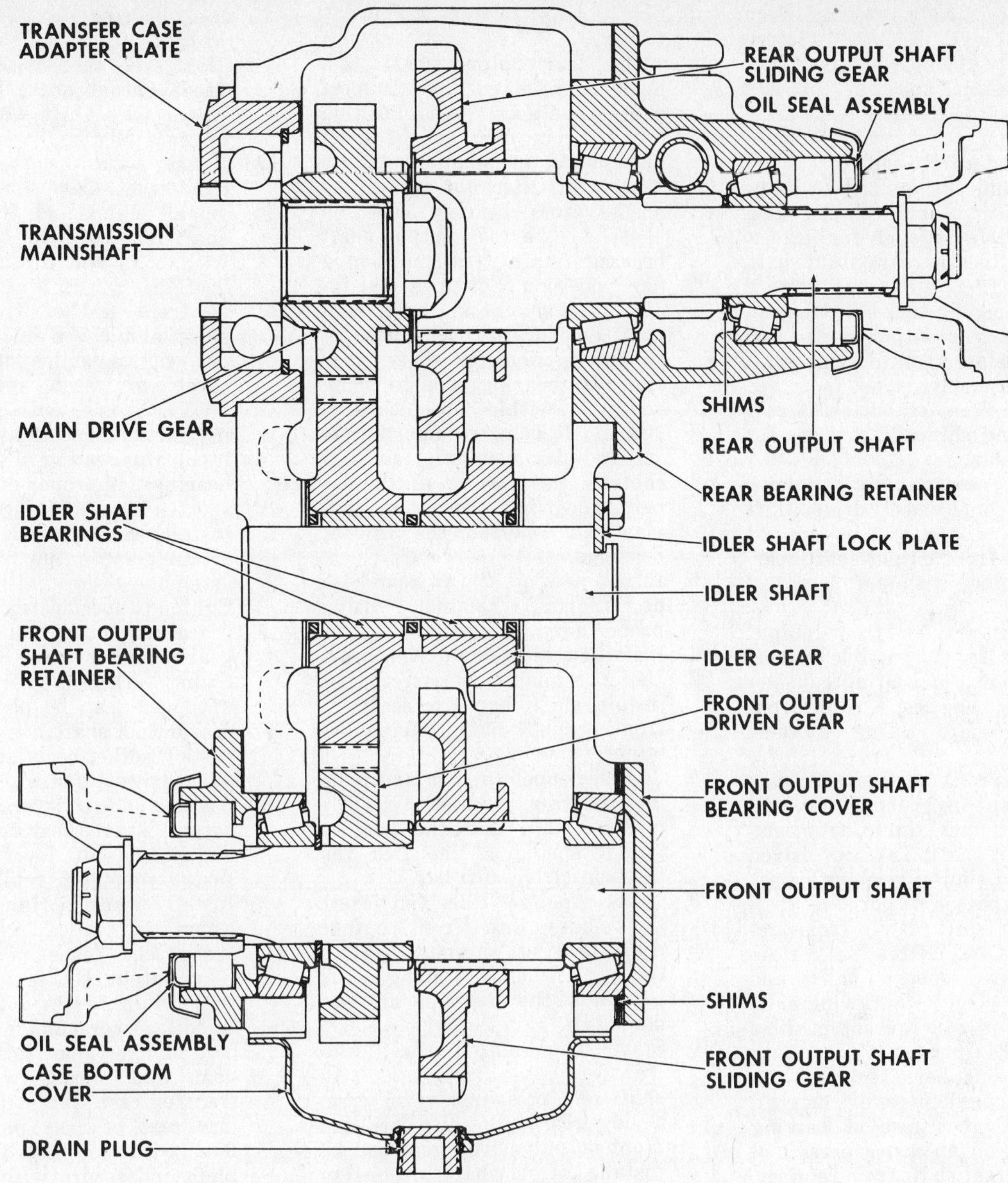

Spicer model 20 transfer case (© International Harvester Co.)

4. Install shift rail cross link, clevis pins and lock pins.

Specifications

END PLAY

Idler Gear	0.000-0.002″
Rear Output Shaft	0.002-0.027″

TORQUE LIMITS (FT. LBS.)

Idler Shaft Locknut	200
Idler Shaft Cover	18
Front Output Shaft Front Bearing Retainer	30
Front Output Shaft Yoke Locknut	200
Rear Output Shaft Bearing Retainer and Housing	30
Rear Output Shaft Yoke Locknut	30
P.T.O. Cover	15
Front Output Shaft Rear Bearing Retainer	30
Filler and Drain Plugs	30
Case to Frame	130
Case to Adapter	25
Adapter Mount	75
Case Bracket to Frame	
Upper	30
Lower	65
Adapter to Transmission	
Manual Transmission	22
Automatic Transmission	35

Spicer Model 20

Description

The Spicer Model 20 transfer case is essentially a two-speed gear box located at the rear of the standard transmission, which provides low and direct gear ranges. It also provides a means of connecting the power to the front axle.

Disassembly

1. Remove cover and gasket from bottom of transfer case.
2. Remove the front drive shift bar poppet spring access hole plugs from front output shaft bearing retainer. If necessary to remove shift bar lock plungers, remove the two expansion plugs from the housing.
3. Remove the idler gear shaft lock plate bolt and lock plate from rear of transfer case.
4. Using a hammer and brass drift, remove idler gear shaft, driving from the front end of the transfer case (opposite slotted end of shaft). As shaft passes thrust washers, remove washers. Remove idler gear with bearings and spacers as a sub-assembly. Remove bearings and spacer from bore of idler gear.
5. Remove end yoke retaining lock nuts from the front and rear output shafts. Using a suitable puller, remove the end yokes from both shafts.

6. Remove steady springs from shift levers. Remove setscrew securing shift lever pivot pin. Remove pin and lift out each lever as it is freed.
7. Remove socket-head setscrew from underdrive shift fork.
8. Move underdrive shift fork and rear output shaft sliding gear forward far enough for gear to clear splines on rear output shaft. Swing fork and gear toward cover opening and lift out gear.
9. Remove rear output shaft bearing retainer and output shaft as an assembly.
10. Remove front output shaft rear cover and shims. Tag shims for reassembly.
11. Remove socket-head setscrew from front wheel drive shift fork.
12. Remove front output shaft bearing retainer with shift bars and gasket.
13. Pull forward on front output shaft as far as possible to permit removal of bearing cup. Remove bearing cone from front output shaft, using suitable puller.
14. Remove front output shaft bearing snap-ring. Using a soft-faced hammer, tap on front end of output shaft. Take out driven gear and sliding gear with shift fork as shaft is withdrawn.
15. Remove shift bars from retainer. CAUTION: Be certain to secure poppet balls and springs when withdrawing shift bars. This will prevent possible personal injury.
16. Remove shift bar oil seals.
17. Remove speedometer driven gear.
18. Support inner face of bearing retainer on an arbor press and press output shaft from retainer.
19. Remove oil seal from retainer bore.
20. Remove tapered bearing cone and cup from rear bore of retainer. Remove tapered bearing cup from front bore. Remove O-ring seal.
21. Using a suitable puller, remove bearing cone from output shaft. Remove shims from shaft and tie together before laying aside. Remove speedometer drive gear.
22. Using a puller, remove bearing cone from front output shaft.

Assembly

1. Press bearing cone on rear end of front output shaft.
2. Install speedometer drive gear, shims and bearing cone on output shaft.
3. Position new O-ring seal in bore of rear output shaft bearing retainer. Install tapered bearing cup in front bore of retainer. Install other tapered bearing cup in rear bore of bearing retainer.
4. Place rear output shaft into bearing retainer and support shaft in an arbor press. Position bearing cone over end of shaft and using an adapter slightly larger in diameter than the shaft, press bearing cone on shaft. Locate rear output shaft bearing retainer assembly in a fixed position. Set up a dial indicator and check shaft end-play. Add or remove shims between speedometer drive gear and rear bearing cone to bring end-play within specifications. NOTE: It is very important to set end-play correctly, since it controls the seating of the tapered bearings. Incorrect end-play will shorten the life of bearings.
5. Install new oil seal in rear bore of bearing retainer, using proper adapter.
6. Install speedometer driven gear.
7. Using an adapter of correct size, install shift bar oil seals in front output shaft bearing retainer.
8. Install poppet springs and balls into bearing retainer. NOTE: make certain that the heavier loaded spring is installed for the front drive shift bar.
9. Depress poppet balls and insert shift bars into front output shaft bearing retainer. NOTE: Be sure when installing shift bars that the seal lips are not damaged.
10. Start front output shaft into transfer case from rear. As shaft emerges inside of case, sliding gear with shift fork and front output driven gear can be installed. Hold shaft in position and install bearing cup in rear bore of case. Install front output shaft bearing snap-ring.
11. Support rear end of front output shaft and using an adapter of correct diameter, tap bearing cone onto front end of shaft. With shaft held in position, install bearing cup in front bore of case.
12. Using a new gasket, install front output shaft bearing retainer with shift bars on front of transfer case.
13. Install socket-head setscrew in front wheel drive shaft fork.
14. Install shims and front output shaft rear cover on case. Secure with bolts and torque to specifications. Set up a dial indicator at front end of front output shaft and check end-play. Add or remove shims under rear cover to meet specifications. NOTE: It is essential to set end-play within specifications, since it controls seating of the tapered bearings. Improper end-play can shorten life of bearings.
15. Install rear output shaft bearing retainer and output shaft as an assembly. Secure with bolts and tighten to specifications.
16. Place rear output shaft sliding gear in underdrive shift fork. Swing fork and gear into case until gear can be positioned on rear output shaft.
17. Install socket-head setscrew in underdrive shift fork.
18. Position shift levers in front output shaft bearing retainer and install shift lever pivot pin. Install pivot pin retaining bolt. Install steady springs on shift levers.
19. Install end yokes on front and rear output shafts and secure with retaining lock nuts.
20. Install spacers and bearings in bore of idler gear. Position idler gear and thrust washers in transfer case. Insert idler shaft into rear of case until slot is flush with case face. Install lock plate and secure with retaining bolt. Tighten to specifications.
21. Install shift bar lock plungers and expansion plugs. Install shift bar poppet spring access hole plugs.
22. Position new gasket on bottom of transfer case and install

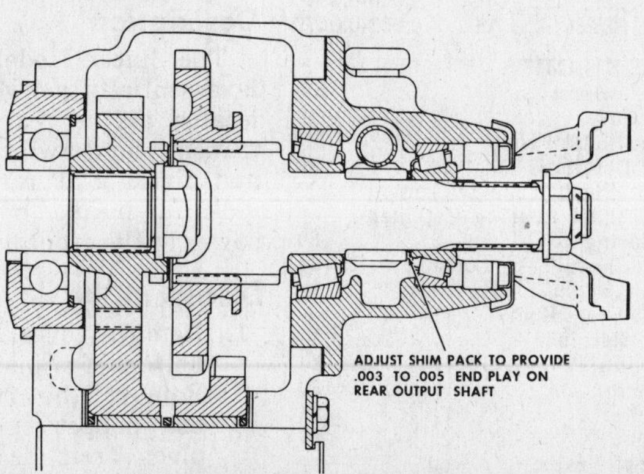

Rear output shaft end play adjustment
(© International Harvester Co.)

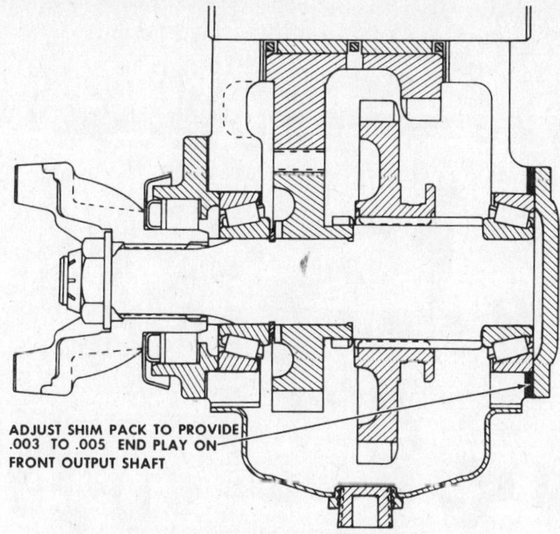

Front output shaft end play adjustment
(© International Harvester Co.)

cover. Secure with bolts and tighten to specifications.

Specifications

END PLAY

Rear Output Shaft	0.003-0.005″
Front Output Shaft	0.003-0.005″

BALL POPPET SPRING

Free Length	
Red	1.031″
Yellow	1.078″
Pressure @ Test Length	
Red @ 51/64″	20 Lbs.
Yellow @ 49/64″	12 Lbs.

TORQUE LIMITS (FT. LBS.)

Rear Output Shaft Bearing Retainer	30-40
Front Output Shaft Rear Bearing Cover	30-40
Front Output Shaft Front Bearing Retainer	30-40
Bottom Cover	15-20
Idler Shaft Lock Bolt	15-20
Companion Flange Nut	200-300

Timken Model 221

Description

The transfer case, mounted on frame and crossmember brackets behind the main transmission assembly, provides a means for transmitting power to the rear and/or front axles and power take-off. A single control rod, linked to the gearshift lever, is used to select desired gear in the transfer case.

Four-wheel-drive may be engaged or disengaged at any time without declutching when transfer case is in direct drive; however, in returning to two-wheel-drive from four-wheel-drive, the accelerator may have to be released momentarily, to relieve torque, while shift is being made.

Oil Seal Replacement

If it becomes necessary to replace oil seal in either the input or the front or rear output shafts, perform the following steps:

1. Drain lubricant from transfer case.
2. Disconnect applicable driveshaft.
3. Remove cotter pin and nut from U-joint yoke.
4. Use suitable puller and remove U-joint from shaft.
5. Remove cap screws attaching bearing cover; then remove cover and gasket.
6. Drive out old seal from bearing cover. Coat outer diameter of new seal with sealing compound and install it in bearing cover with lip facing inward.
7. Using new gasket, replace bearing cover. NOTE: Make sure oil passages are aligned when installing gasket and cover.
8. Drive U-joint yoke on shaft and replace nut and cotter pin.
9. Connect driveshaft. Replace lubricant.

Shift and Control Rod Adjustment

1. With crossbar disconnected, adjust both shift rod clevises to a distance of 2-9/32″ from center of pin hole to end of shift rod, then tighten jam nuts.
2. Connect shift rod clevises to crossbar with clevis and cotter pins.
3. Shift transfer case to 2-wheel drive position.
4. Disconnect shift control rod from lever at adjustable clevis.
5. Check clearance between crossbar and frame crossmember. If necessary, disconnect and readjust front drive shift rod clevis to obtain a minimum clearance of 3/16″. Connect shift rod clevis to crossbar.
6. Connect control rod to lever and shift transfer case to the "4-LO" position. Measure distance from center of clevis pin hole to bolt head. If necessary, disconnect and readjust shift control rod clevis to obtain a minimum clearance of 3-11/16″ (with 3-speed tranmission) or 1/4″ (with 4-speed transmission). Connect control rod clevis to shift lever.

Disassembly

Cover and Shift Rod

1. Mount transfer case on a suitable repair stand and drain lubricant.
2. Position transfer case shift rods in four-wheel low.
3. Remove nine cap screws attaching cover; then slide cover upward and lift to remove. NOTE: When removing cover, care should be taken not to lose detent balls and springs.
4. Remove detent balls and springs from holes in case and remove interlock pin from cover.
5. Cut lock wires; then remove shift fork set screws.
6. Using a brass drift, tap shift rods from case and lift out forks as each rod is removed. Remove oil seals.

Shaft Yokes and Deflector

1. Remove cotter pins and nuts from three U-joint yokes.
2. Using suitable puller, remove U-joint yokes.

Idler Shaft

1. Remove cap screws attaching front and rear idler shaft bearing caps to case; then remove caps, oil seal and adjusting shims. Attach shims to cap for reassembly. NOTE: Mark bearing cap with dye or prick punch for reassembly reference. They must be assembled to same location from which they were removed.
2. Press or drive idler shaft out of case. Remove input shaft constant mesh gear, spacer and low speed gear.
3. Remove bearing cone and bearing cup.

Front Output Shaft

1. Remove cap screws attaching front bearing cap; then remove cap, oil seal and gasket.
2. Pull front output shaft and bearing assembly from case. Remove bearing from shaft, using an arbor press.
3. Remove front sliding gear.
4. Remove cap screws attaching rear bearing cap; then remove cap and gasket.
5. Remove snap-ring from front output gear; then remove sliding spacer.
6. Drive output gear inward out of bearing; then lift out of case.
7. Remove bearing.

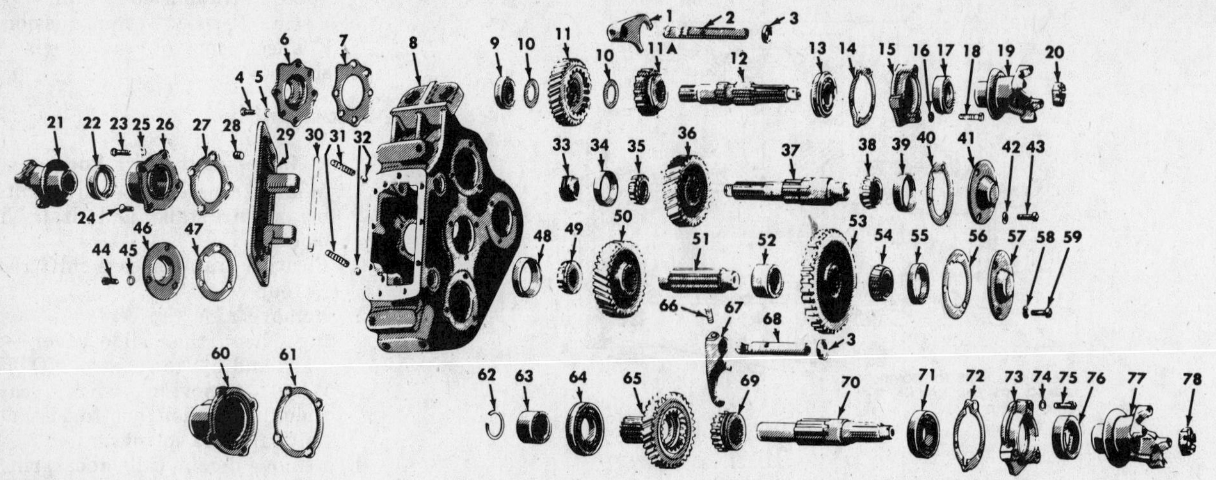

Timken model 221 transfer case (© G.M.C.)

1 Shift fork
2 Shift rod
3 Oil seal
4 Cap screw
5 Lock washer
6 Bearing cap
7 Gasket
8 Transfer case
9 Bearing
10 Washer
11 Direct drive gear
11A Input shaft gear
12 Input shaft
13 Bearing
14 Adjusting shims
15 Bearing cap
16 Lock washer
17 Oil seal
18 Cap screw
19 U-Joint yoke
20 Nut
21 U-Joint yoke
22 Oil seal
23 Cap screw
24 Flat cap screw
25 Lock washer
26 Bearing cap
27 Gasket
28 Breather
29 Cover
30 Interlock pin
31 Spring
32 Detent ball
33 Speedometer gear
34 Bearing cup
35 Bearing cone
36 Rear output gear
37 Rear output shaft
38 Bearing cone
39 Bearing cup
40 Adjusting shims
41 Bearing Cap
42 Lock washer
43 Cap screw
44 Cap screw
45 Lock washer
46 Bearing cap
47 Gasket
48 Bearing cup
49 Bearing cone
50 Input shaft gear
51 Idler shaft
52 Spacer
53 Low speed gear
54 Bearing cone
55 Bearing cup
56 Adjusting shims
57 Bearing cap
58 Lock washer
59 Cap screw
60 Bearing cap
61 Gasket
62 Snap ring
33 Spacer
64 Bearing
65 Front output gear
66 Set screw
67 Shift fork
68 Shift rod
69 Front sliding gear
70 Front output shaft
71 Bearing
72 Gasket
73 Bearing cap
74 Lock washer
75 Cap screw
76 Oil seal
77 U-Joint yoke
78 Nut

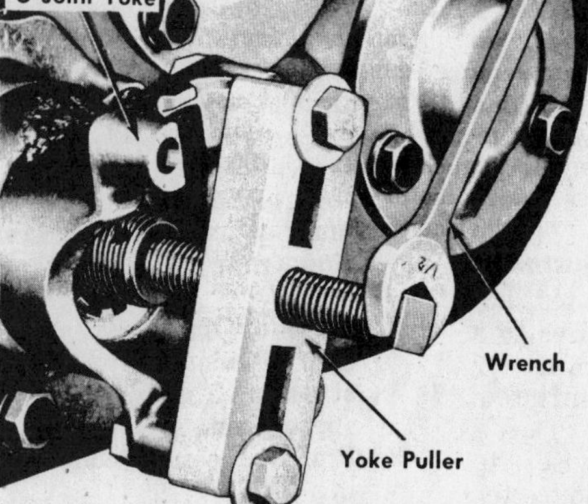

Removing U-Joint yoke (© G.M.C.)

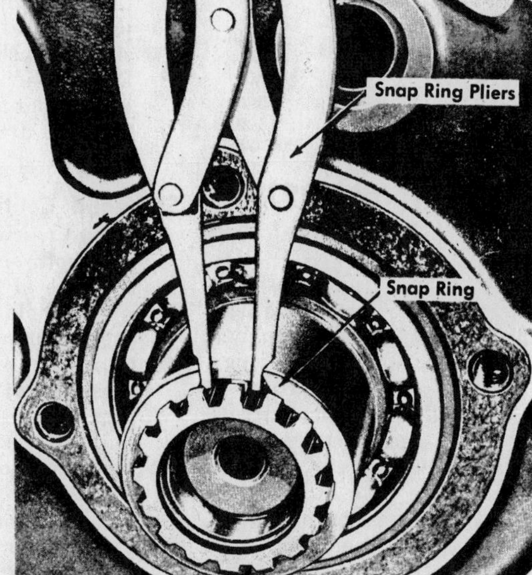

Removing snap-ring from front output gear (© G.M.C.)

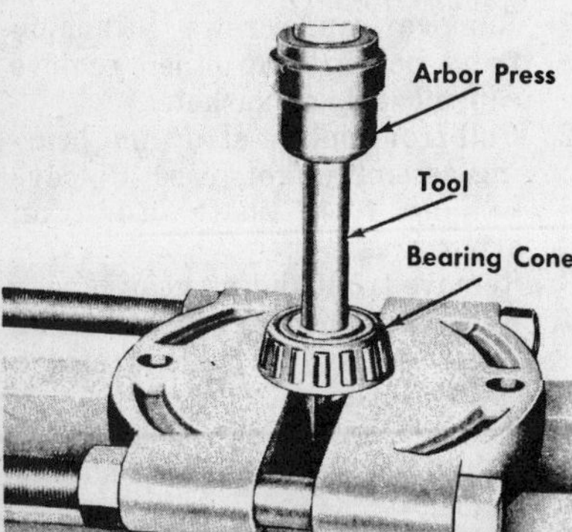

Removing bearing from idler shaft (© G.M.C.)

Rear Output Shaft

1. Remove cap screws attaching rear output bearing caps. Remove caps, gasket, oil seal and shims. Attach shims to cap for reassembly. NOTE: Mark bearing caps with dye or prick punch for reassembly reference. They must be assembled to same location from which they were removed.
2. Remove speedometer gear from rear output shaft; then press or drive shaft toward front of case until shaft and bearing can be removed. Lift out rear output shaft gear.
3. Remove bearing cone and bearing cup.

Input Shaft

1. Remove cap screws attaching

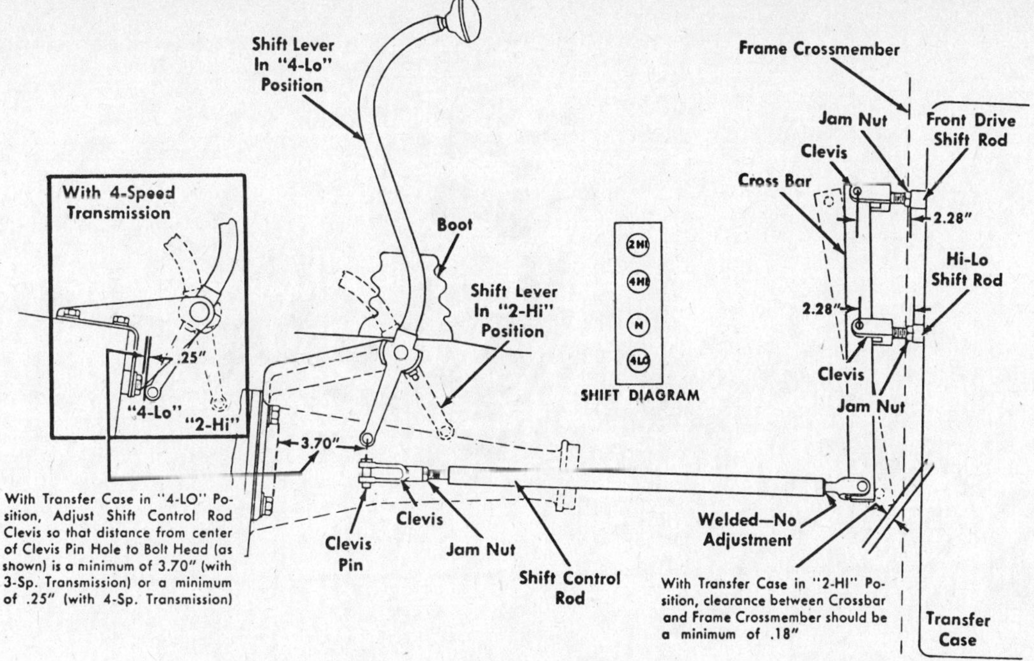

Shift and control rod adjustment (© G.M.C.)

rear bearing cap; then remove cap.
2. Remove cap screws attaching front bearing cap; then remove cap and shims. Attach shims to cap for reassembly.
3. Press or drive out input shaft toward front of case.
4. Remove direct drive gear, sliding gear and thrust washer from inside case.
5. Remove front bearing and washer. Remove other bearing from shaft.

Assembly

During assembly, it is important that all parts are cleaned and lubricated to prevent deterioration before unit is placed in service. Use new gaskets, oil seals, snap-rings and lock washers.

Input Shaft

1. Press front bearing onto shaft with shielded side of bearing toward shoulder on shaft.
2. Insert shaft through opening in front of case and as shaft is being moved into position, install sliding gear, washer, direct drive gear and washer. Install rear bearing on shaft with shielded side toward inside.
3. Install gasket and bearing cap at rear of case. Tighten cap screws securely.
4. At front of case, install bearing cap and shims. Use same thickness of shims as removed during disassembly.
5. Install U-joint yoke and nut. Tighten nut firmly and install cotter pin.

Rear Output Shaft

1. Press bearing cone onto rear output shaft.
2. Press or drive rear output shaft in case through shaft gear.
3. Press or drive bearing cup into case. Install bearing cap, using same thickness of shims that were removed. Tighten cap screws firmly.
4. At rear of shaft, press bearing cone onto shaft and bearing cup into case. Install speedometer drive gear.
5. Install new oil seal in bearing cap; then install gasket and cap with screws.
6. Install U-joint yoke and secure with nut. Tighten nut firmly and install cotter pin.
7. Check end play of shaft, using dial indicator. Remove or add adjusting shims as required until end play is as near zero as possible.

Front Output Shaft

1. Place front output gear inside case; then install bearing over gear hub and into position in case.
2. Press bearing onto output shaft.
3. As output shaft is installed through opening in front of case, sliding gear must be located on shaft as shaft is pushed into its proper position.
4. Install new oil seal in bearing cap; then install gasket and cap with screws.
5. Install spacer on gear; then install snap-ring.
6. Install gasket and bearing cap. Secure with cap screws.
7. Install U-joint yoke and secure with nut. Tighten nut securely and install cotter pin.

Idler Shaft

1. Press bearing cone onto front end of idler shaft.
2. Start idler shaft into front side of case and install low speed gear, spacer, constant mesh gear and bearing cone as shaft is pushed into position.
3. Press bearing cups into case and over bearing cones.
4. At rear of case, install bearing cap and gasket with cap screws.
5. At front of case, install bearing cap and adjusting shims with cap bolts. NOTE: Make sure adjusting shims used are same thickness as shims removed.
6. Check end play of shaft, using dial indicator. Subtract or add adjusting shims as required until end play is as near to zero as possible.

Cover and Shift Rod

1. Install oil seals in case.
2. Push shift rods into case with caution, so as not to damage oil seals.
3. Install shift forks on respective shift rods. Install set screws attaching forks to rods. Twist safety wire around shift rods and then through hole in set screw.
4. Insert detent balls and springs into holes in case.
5. Slide interlock pin into bosses on inner surface of cover. Install gasket on case with sealing compound. Press end of cover down; then slide cover upward and press into position. Secure with cap screws.

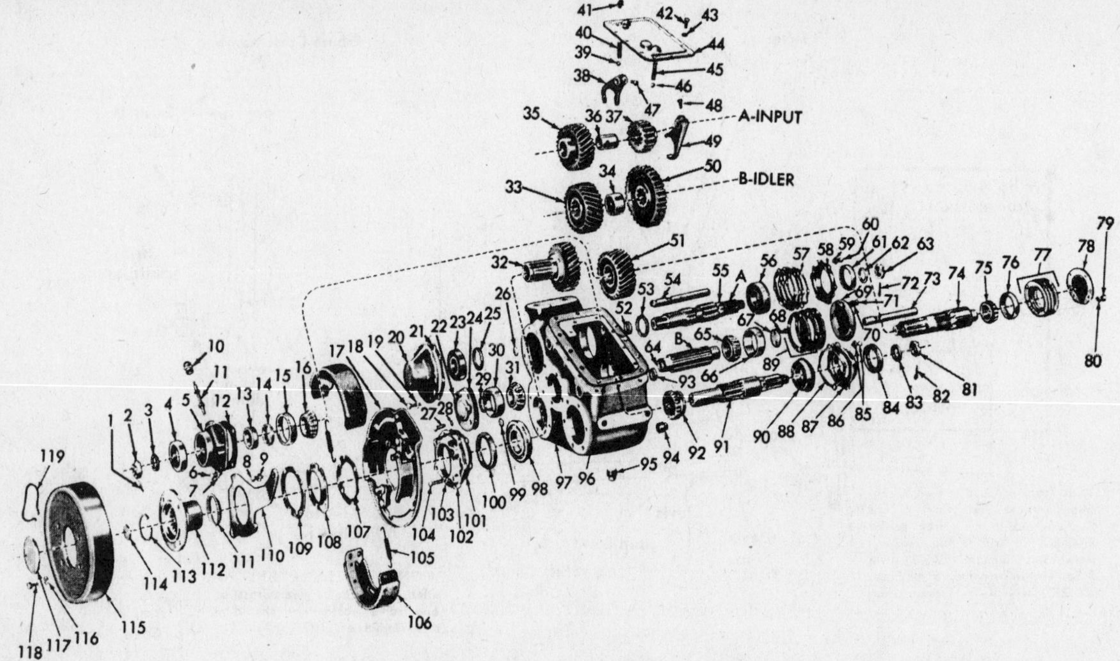

Timken model 223 transfer case (© Chrysler Corp.)

1 Cotter key
2 Nut
3 Washer
4 Oil seal
5 Rear output shaft rear bearing cap
6 Cap screw
7 Lock Washer
8 Cap screw
9 Lock washer
10 Speedometer driven gear bushing
11 Speedometer driven gear and shaft
12 Gasket
13 Speedometer drive gear
14 Spacer
15 Rear output shaft rear bearing cup
16 Rear output shaft rear bearing
17 Brake backing plate
18 Cap screw
19 Lock washer
20 Input shaft rear bearing cage
21 Gasket
22 Idler shaft rear bearing
23 Input shaft rear bearing
24 Gasket
25 Spacer
26 Shift shaft hole plug
27 Cap screw
28 Lock washer
29 Snap ring
30 Idler shaft rear bearing cup
31 Idler shaft rear bearing
32 Front output shaft
33 Idler shaft hi gear
34 Gear spacer
35 Direct drive gear
36 Direct drive gear bushing
37 Low speed sliding gear
38 Range shift fork
39 Detent ball
40 Detent spring
41 Beather
42 Cap screw
43 Washer
44 Housing cover
45 Detent spring
46 Detent ball
47 Shift fork set screw
48 Shift fork set screw
49 Front axle declutch shift fork
50 Idler shaft lo gear
51 Rear output shaft gear
52 Shift shaft oil seal
53 Direct drive gear spacing washer
54 Range shift shaft
55 Input shaft
56 Input shaft front bearing
57 Shims
58 Input shaft front bearing cap
59 Lock washer
61 Oil seal
62 Washer
63 Nut
64 Idler shaft
65 Idler shaft front bearing
66 Idler shaft front bearing cup
67 Bearing retainer plate
68 Cap screw
69 Idler shaft front bearing cap
70 Lock washer
71 Cap screw
72 Cotter key
73 Declutch shift shaft
74 Rear output shaft
75 Rear output shaft front bearing
76 Rear output shaft front bearing cup
77 Shims
78 Rear output shaft front bearing cap
79 Cap screw
80 Locker washer
81 Nut
82 Cotter key
83 Washer
84 Oil seal
85 Cap screw
86 Lock washer
87 Front output shaft front bearing cap
88 Gasket
89 Shims
90 Front output shaft front bearing (with snap ring)
91 Front output shaft
92 Declutch collar
93 Shift shaft oil seal
94 Oil filler plug (some units employ elbow arrangement)
95 Drain plug
96 Cover to housing gasket
97 Transfer case housing
98 Front output shaft rear bearing (with snap ring)
99 Shift shaft hole plug
100 Oil seal
101 Gasket
102 Front output shaft rear bearing cap
103 Washer
104 Cap screw
105 Brake shoe return spring
106 Brake shoe
107 Gasket
108 Oil deflector
109 Washer
110 Brake lever
111 Oil baffle
112 Brake hub
113 Snap ring
114 Small expansion plug
115 Brake drum
116 Lock washer
117 Large expansion plug
118 Cap screw
119 Lock wire

Specifications

END PLAY

Idler Shaft ..... As Near As Poss. To 0.0″
Rear Output Shaft .... As Near As Poss. To 0.0″

SHIMS

Type .... Selective Fit
Thickness Available .... 0.003″
0.005″
0.010″

COVER SPRING

Length .... 2.0″
Pressure @ 1.0″ ....50-60 Lbs.

Timken Model 223

Description

The Timken Model 223 is a 2-speed gearbox mounted behind the main transmission. An input shaft transmits power from the engine and transmission to an idler shaft and gear assembly, which in turn powers the front and rear output shafts.

It is recommended that front wheel drive be engaged only when necessary and not during highway driving at speed.

De-Clutch and Shift Rod Adjustment

NOTE: All adjustments must be made with front axle engaged and transfer case in low range.

1. Disconnect de-clutch and shift rods at the transfer case.
2. Adjust de-clutch rod length until lever clears rear end of slot in cab underbody by ½″. Secure adjusting yoke with locknut.
3. Adjust shift rod length until distance between protrusions on shift and de-clutch levers is ¼″.

Secure adjusting yoke with lock-nut.

4. Connect de-clutch and shift rods at transfer case and then road test vehicle.

Disassembly

Shift Cover

1. Remove attaching bolts and lift off case cover.
2. Remove shift rail detent springs and balls. A magnet will aid in removing detent balls.
3. Remove yoke nut cotter keys and yoke nuts.
4. Remove yokes, using a suitable puller.

Shift Shafts

1. Remove safety wire and lock-screws from gear and de-clutch shift shafts.
2. Using a brass drift, drive out both shafts through the rear of the case, while at the same time forcing out the expansion plugs.
3. Remove shift forks and de-clutch fork spacer.
4. Remove shift shaft seals.

Front Output Shaft

1. Remove attaching bolts and front output shaft front bearing cap.
2. Remove front output shaft and front drive declutch gear.
3. Drive out expansion plug in the output shaft gear, using a rod approximately 7/8" X 12".
4. Also remove plug in parking brake hub (if so equipped).

Idler Shaft and Gear

1. Remove attaching bolts and idler shaft front and rear bearing caps. Tie bearing adjusting shims together for reassembly.
2. Idler shaft bearings are a press fit; the shaft may either be driven or pressed out through the rear of the case.
3. Remove low speed gear, spacer and front bearing.
4. Remove the helical gear and tap out front bearing cup.
5. Remove snap-ring and then press rear bearing off shaft.

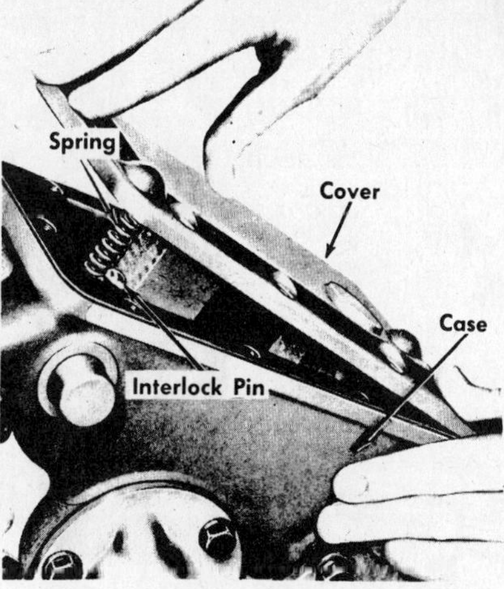

Installing case cover (© G.M.C.)

Front Output Gear

1. Remove rear bearing cap and gasket.
2. Remove bearing snap-ring and then tap gear into case. Lift gear and bearing out through cover opening.
3. Press off radial bearing.

Rear Output Shaft

1. Remove attaching bolts and front and rear output shaft bearing caps. Tie the bearing adjusting shims together for reassembly.
2. Remove speedometer drive gear and spacer.
3. Press rear output shaft and front bearing out of case. Remove gear and rear bearing through cover opening.
4. Using a suitable puller, remove the front bearing.

Input Shaft

1. Remove attaching bolts and input shaft front bearing cover and oil seal assembly. Tie adjusment shims together for reassembly.
2. Using a block of wood between sliding gear and case, press out input shaft and front bearing.
3. Remove sliding gear, drive gear and spacer.
4. Remove front bearing.

Assembly

Input Shaft

1. Using a suitable sleeve, install front bearing against shoulder at front end of input shaft. NOTE: Install with shielded side of bearing toward inside of case.
2. Install front bearing and input shaft into case. Mount sliding gear, spacer and drive gear, as shaft enters case.
3. Tap input shaft into position, using a suitable sleeve against the bearing inner race.
4. Install original shims plus 0.010". Install front cover and tighten cap screws.
5. Install thrust washer and rear bearing (shielded side toward inside of case).
6. Install a new gasket and cover or power take-off (if so equipped).
7. Using a dial indicator, measure shaft end-play. Remove enough shims so that end-play falls within specifications.

Pressing out rear output shaft (© Chrysler Corp.)

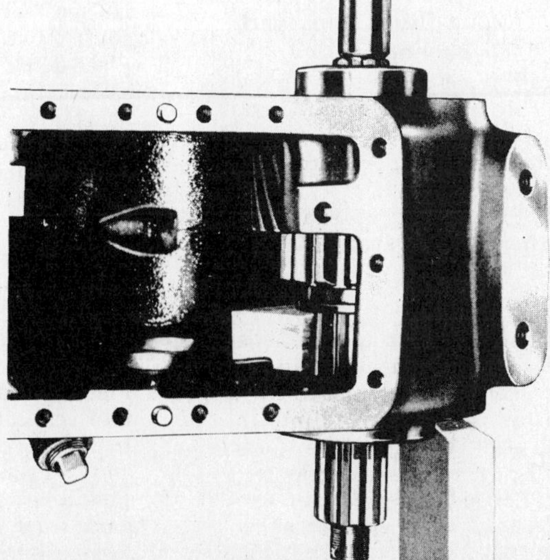
Pressing out input shaft (© Chrysler Corp.)

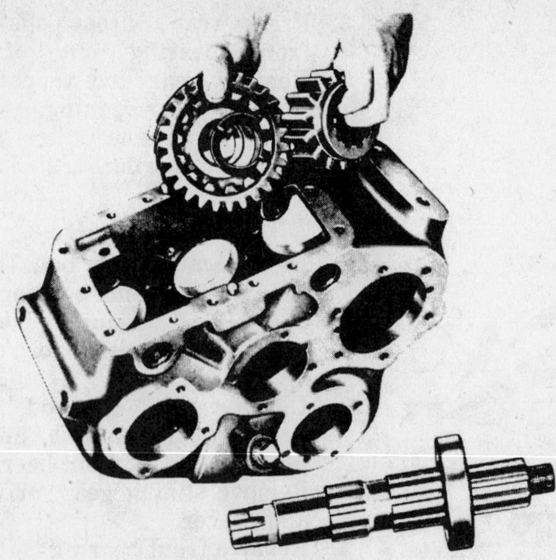

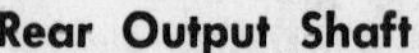

Removing or installing sliding gear, drive gear and spacer
(© Chrysler Corp.)

Checking input shaft end play
(© Chrysler Corp.)

Rear Output Shaft

1. Using a suitable sleeve, press front bearing on shaft.
2. Hold rear output gear in place inside case, then slide shaft into case and through gear.
3. Install front bearing cup and original shims plus 0.010″. Install bearing cover and lock washers, then tighten cap screws.
4. Using a suitable sleeve, press rear bearing on shaft. Tap bearing cup into case.
5. Install spacer and speedometer drive gear.
6. Place new gasket and bearing cap (with oil seal) over shaft. Install lock washers and cap screws.
7. Rotate shaft to seat the bearings.
8. Using a dial indicator, measure shaft end-play. Remove enough shims from under bearing cap so that end-play falls within specifications.

Front Output Shaft Gear and Bearing

1. Install front output shaft gear and bearing assembly through case bore.
2. Install snap-ring in groove on bearing outer race.

NOTE: Front output shaft gear and bearing must be installed before idler shaft and gear.

Idler Gear

1. Press rear bearing on idler shaft. Secure with snap-ring.
2. Hold helical gear inside case, then tap the idler shaft into the case and through the gear. NOTE: Install helical gear with short hub side toward rear.
3. Install low gear spacer and then install low gear. NOTE: Install low gear with long hub toward front of case.
4. Install rear bearing cup, new gasket and rear bearing cap, lockwashers and cap screws.
5. Drive front bearing onto idler shaft. CAUTION: Hold shaft rigid to avoid damaging rear bearing.
6. Install bearing retainer, capscrews and safety wire.
7. Tap front bearing cup into position.
8. Install adjusting shims.
9. Install front bearing cap, lockwashers and cap screws.
10. Using a dial indicator, measure shaft end-play. Remove enough shims to meet specifications.

Front Output Shaft

1. Install ball bearing on shaft with snap-ring toward outside.
2. Install sliding collar on shaft and then install shaft in case.
3. Install new gasket, bearing cap with oil seal, lockwashers and cap screws. Tighten cap screws to specifications.

Shift Shafts

1. If necessary, install new shift shaft oil seals.
2. Place de-clutch fork in collar.
3. Lubricate the de-clutch shift shaft and slide it into the case and through the fork. Install setscrew and safety wire.
4. Position range shift fork in sliding gear.
5. Slide range shift shaft through fork. Install setscrew and safety wire.
6. Install expansion plugs at rear of case.
7. Place detent balls and springs into position.
8. Install cover with a new gasket and cap screws.
9. Install power take-off with a new gasket (if so equipped). Install lockwashers and cap screws.
10. Install yokes or flanges and tighten nuts to specifications.

Specifications

END PLAY	
Input Shaft	0.003-0.005″
Idler Gear	0.003-0.005″
Rear Output Shaft	Zero Clearance Zero Preload

TORQUE LIMITS (FT. LBS.)	
Front Retainer Nut	35-55
Poppet Screw	15-25
Idler Cover Screw	15-25
Drain and Filler Plugs	25-45
Flange and Idler Shaft Nut	125
Top Cover	38-42
All Bearing Caps	38-42
Input Shaft	300-400
Front Output Shaft	300-400
Rear Output Shaft	300-400
Idler Shaft Nut	140-160
Input Shaft Flange Nut	140-160
Front Output Shaft Flange Nut	140-160
Driveshaft Mating Flange Nuts	35
Breather	8-12
Brake Support Nut	25-45
Brake Retainer Screw	20-40
Brake Retainer Nut	25-45
Brake Drum	60-66
Brake Mounting	60-66
Brake Drum Nut	140-160
P.T.O. Screw	8-12
P.T.O. to Case	38-42
P.T.O. Bearing Cap	38-42
P.T.O. Top Cover	38-42
P.T.O. Shaft	300-400

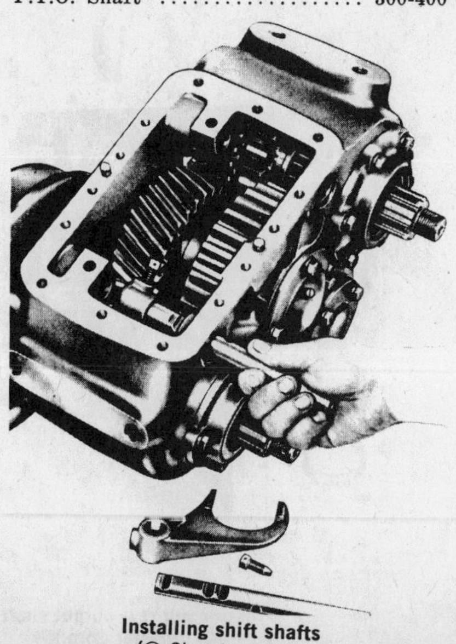

Installing shift shafts
(© Chrysler Corp.)

Manual Transmissions

Index

Diagnosis

Jumping out of High Gear

1. Misalignment of transmission case or clutch housing.
2. Worn pilot bearing in crankshaft.
3. Bent transmission shaft.
4. Worn high speed sliding gear.
5. Worn teeth in clutch shaft.
6. Insufficient spring tension on shifter rail plunger.
7. Bent or loose shifter fork.
8. End-play in clutch shaft.
9. Gears not engaging completely.
10. Loose or worn bearings on clutch shaft or mainshaft.

Sticking in High Gear

1. Clutch not releasing fully.
2. Burred or battered teeth on clutch shaft.
3. Burred or battered transmission main-shaft.
4. Frozen synchronizing clutch.
5. Stuck shifter rail plunger.
6. Gearshift lever twisting and binding shifter rail.
7. Battered teeth on high speed sliding gear or on sleeve.
8. Lack of lubrication.
9. Improper lubrication.
10. Corroded transmission parts.
11. Defective mainshaft pilot bearing.

Jumping out of Second Gear

1. Insufficient spring tension on shifter rail plunger.
2. Bent or loose shifter fork.
3. Gears not engaging completely.
4. End-play in transmission mainshaft.
5. Loose transmission gear bearing.
6. Defective mainshaft pilot bearing.
7. Bent transmission shaft.
8. Worn teeth on second speed sliding gear or sleeve.
9. Loose or worn bearings on transmission mainshaft.
10. End-play in countershaft.

Sticking in Second Gear

1. Clutch not releasing fully.
2. Burred or battered teeth on sliding sleeve.
3. Burred or battered transmission main-shaft.
4. Frozen synchronizing clutch.
5. Stuck shifter rail plunger.
6. Gearshift lever twisting and binding shifter rail.
7. Lack of lubrication.
8. Second speed transmission gear bearings locked will give same effect as gears stuck in second.
9. Improper lubrication.
10. Corroded transmission parts.

Jumping out of Low Gear

1. Gears not engaging completely.
2. Bent or loose shifter fork.
3. End-play in transmission mainshaft.
4. End-play in countershaft.
5. Loose or worn bearings on transmission mainshaft.
6. Loose or worn bearings in countershaft.
7. Defective mainshaft pilot bearing.

Sticking in Low Gear

1. Clutch not releasing fully.
2. Burred or battered transmission main-shaft.
3. Stuck shifter rail plunger.
4. Gearshift lever twisting and binding shifter rail.
5. Lack of lubrication.
6. Improper lubrication.
7. Corroded transmission parts.

Jumping out of Reverse Gear

1. Insufficient spring tension on shifter rail plunger.
2. Bent or loose shifter fork.
3. Badly worn gear teeth.
4. Gears not engaging completely.
5. End-play in transmission mainshaft.
6. Idler gear bushings loose or worn.
7. Loose or worn bearings on transmsision mainshaft.
8. Defective mainshaft pilot bearing.

Sticking in Reverse Gear

1. Clutch not releasing fully.
2. Burred or battered transmission main-shaft.
3. Stuck shifter rail plunger.
4. Gearshift lever twisting and binding shifter rail.
5. Lack of lubrication.
6. Improper lubrication.
7. Corroded transmission parts.

Failure of Gears to Synchronize

1. Binding pilot bearing on mainshaft, will synchronize in high gear only.
2. Clutch not releasing fully.
3. Detent springs weak or broken.
4. Weak or broken springs under balls in sliding gear sleeve.
5. Binding bearing on clutch shaft.
6. Binding countershaft.
7. Binding pilot bearing in crankshaft.
8. Badly worn gear teeth.
9. Scored or worn cones.
10. Improper lubrication.
11. Constant mesh gear not turning freely on transmission mainshaft. Will synchronize in that gear only.

Gears Spinning When Shifting into Gear from Neutral

1. Clutch not releasing fully.
2. In some cases an extremely light lubricant in transmission will cause gears to continue to spin for a short time after clutch is released.
3. Binding pilot bearing in crankshaft.

Cleaning of Transmission Components

Cleanliness of parts, tools, and work area is of the utmost importance. All transmission components (except bearing assemblies) should be cleaned in cleaning solvent and dried with compressed air before any inspection or work is begun. Great care should be taken when cleaning bearings. Bearings should always be cleaned separately from other parts in clean cleaning solvent and not gasoline. They must never be cleaned in a hot solution tank. It is advisable that they be soaked in cleaning fluid and then tapped against a block of wood in order to free any solidified lubricant that may be trapped inside. Rinse bearings thoroughly in clean solvent and then dry them with moisture-free compressed air being careful not to spin the bearings with the air stream. Rotate each bearing slowly and inspect rollers or balls for any signs of excessive wear, roughness, or damage. Those bearings not in excellent condition must be replaced. If they pass this inspection, they should be dipped in clean oil and wrapped in clean lintless cloth to protect them until installation.

Inspection of Transmission Components

All parts must be completely and carefully inspected and replaced for any signs of wear, stress, discoloration or warpage due to excessive heat. Whenever available, the magna flux process should be used on all parts except roller and ball bearings, to detect small cracks unseen by the eye. Inspect the breather assembly to see that it is not clogged or damaged and check all threaded parts for stripped or cross threads. Oil passages must be cleared of obstructions by the use of air pressure or brass rods and all gaskets, oil seals, lock wires, cotter pins, and snap rings are to be replaced. Small nicks or burrs in gears or splines can be removed with a fine abrasive stone. It is important that any housings or covers having cracks or other damage should be replaced and not welded. Synchronizers, not in excellent condition, must be replaced. The bronze synchronizer cone should be checked for wear or for any steel chips that may have become imbedded in it. Springs must be inspected for free length, compressed length, distortion, or collapsed coils.

IMPORTANT: The splines on many clutch gears, mainshafts, etc., are equipped with a machined relief called a "hopping guard". With the clutch gear engaged, the mating gear is free to slip into this notch, preventing the two gears from separating or "walking out of gear" under various load conditions. This is *not* a worn or chipped gear. Do not grind or discard the gear.

Check all shafts for spline wear or damage. If the mainshaft 1st and reverse sliding gear or clutch hub have worn into the sides of the splines, the shaft should be replaced. Shift forks, shift rods, interlock balls and pins must be replaced if scored, worn, distorted or damaged.

Clark 250V 5 Speed

Description

The Clark 250V is a medium duty transmission available with a direct drive fifth gear or an overdrive in fifth. Synchronizers are used only from fourth to fifth gear. Power take-off openings are located on both sides of the case. Lubricant capacity is 9 pints.

Disassembly of Transmission

1. Remove the gear shift housing, and shift the gears into two speeds at the same time. Remove the output shaft nut.
2. Remove the parking brake drum, spline flange, and brake shoe assembly.
3. Remove the output shaft bearing retainer and gasket. Slide the speedometer driving gear and spacer off the output shaft. Remove the oil seal from the output shaft bearing retainer.
4. Remove the low and reverse rocker arm and remove the shift rail lock plate at the rear of the case. When removing the first and reverse shift fork use a dummy shaft to prevent ejection of the ball and spring.
5. Insert the dummy shaft into the first and reverse shift fork, while removing the shift rail. Remove the fork from the transmission.
6. Carefully remove the dummy shaft, detent ball, and spring from the fork.
7. Remove the countershaft rear bearing cap and gasket.
8. Remove the snap-ring and tap the bearing from the output shaft.
9. Remove the input shaft bearing retainer, gasket, shaft and bearing assembly from the case. Remove the output shaft pilot bearing from the bore of the input shaft.
10. After removing the synchronizer, remove the output shaft assembly from the case. Remove the sliding gears.
11. Remove the reverse idler shaft retainer and reverse idler shaft. Life the reverse idler gear along with the bearings and spacer from the gear bore.
12. After removing the snap-ring from the countershaft, tap off the rear bearing.
13. Lift the countershaft assembly out of the case. Remove the countershaft front bearing from the case.

Disassembly of Sub-Assemblies

Output Shaft

1. Place the output shaft assembly (front end up), in a soft-jawed vise. Remove the snap-ring, the thrust washer and the fourth-speed gear for overdrive gear from the output shaft.
2. Remove the output shaft from the vise, and tap the forward end of the shaft on a block of wood. This will cause the weight of the third-speed gear to force the fourth-speed gear bushing off the output shaft.
3. Remove the bushing lock pin, the third-speed gear washer, and the third-speed gear. Remove the second-speed gear.

Input Shaft

If the input shaft bearing is to be replaced, remove the bearing retaining snap-rings from the input shaft and bearing.

Countershaft

1. Remove the snap-ring from the forward end of the countershaft.
2. Using a hydraulic press, press the drive gear off the countershaft.
3. Remove the key from the shaft, and press off remaining gears. Remove the remaining gear keys.

Gear Shift Lever Housing

1. Shift the cover into neutral.
2. Place the gear shift lever housing, bottom side up, in a vise, and remove the shift lever support spring and the spring seat. To remove the shift lever, push the lever up through the bottom of the housing.
3. Remove the pivot pin from the housing.

Gear Shift Housing

1. After clamping the cover upside down in a soft-jawed vise, knock out the three expansion plugs at the front. Remove the lockscrew from the low and reverse shifter shaft gates.
2. After making sure all the shifter shafts are in their neutral positions, cover the detent ball access hole in the front shifter shaft support to prevent the ball from popping out under spring tension. Then slide the low and reverse shifter shaft out of the front of the housing.
3. Remove the low and reverse shifter shaft detent ball and spring and the two interlocking balls from between the low and reverse shifter shaft and the 4-5 shifter shaft.
4. After removing the lock screw, slide out the 4-5 shaft. Cover the detent ball access hole in the front support.
5. Remove the interlocking pin from the 4-5 shifter shaft and the two interlocking balls installed between the 4-5 and 2-3 shifter shafts.
6. After removing the lock screws from the 2-3 shifter shaft gate and fork, slide out the shaft. Note the location of the spacer washer which is installed at the rear of the 2-3 fork. Cover the detent ball access hole in the front support.
7. Remove the 2-3 detent spring and ball.

Assembly of Sub-Assemblies

Gear Shift Housing

1. Install the low and reverse detent spring and ball (interlock

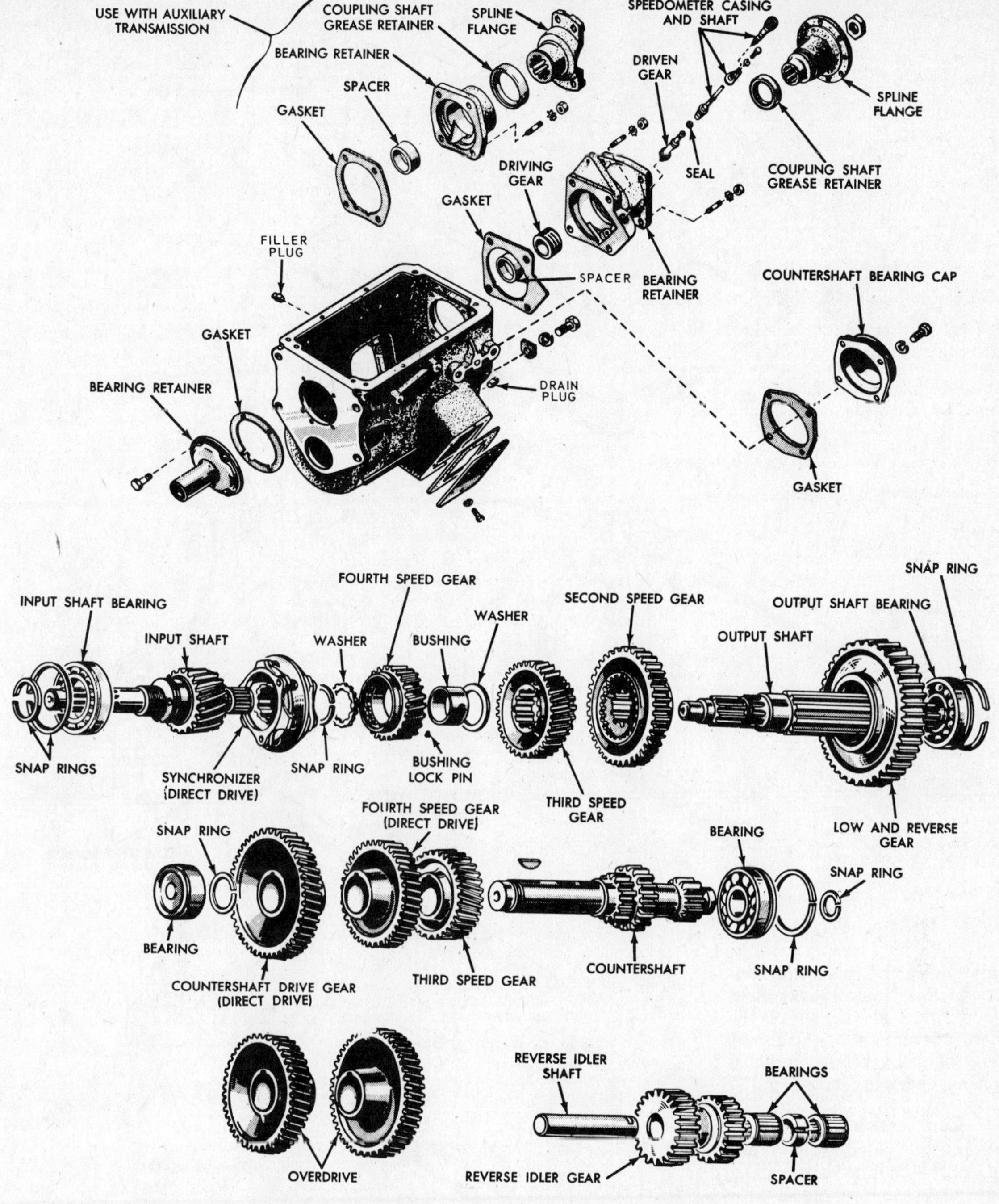

Clark 250V 5-speed transmission (© Clark Equipment Co.)

and detent balls are identical) and start the low and reverse shifter shaft into the housing.

2. With the three detent notches down and the interlocking detent notch toward the center of the cover, depress the ball and slide the shaft past the detent ball.
3. Slide the shift lever gate and then the low and reverse rocker arm gate onto the shifter shaft. Slide the shaft to the neutral detent and install the lock screws in the gates.
4. Working through the 4-5 shaft support hole, place two interlocking balls in the support boss.
5. After positioning the 4-5 detent spring and ball and the interlocking pin in the 4-5 shaft, depress the detent ball and slide the shaft past the ball.
6. Install the 4-5 fork and slide the shifter shaft to the neutral position. Leave the fork loose on the shaft.
7. Position the interlocking ball through the 2-3 shaft hole and against the 4-5 shaft. After positioning the 2-3 detent spring and ball, depress the ball and slide the 2-3 shaft past the ball.
8. Install the gate, fork, and spacer on the shaft.
9. After tightening the 4-5 fork lock screw, and installing the expansion plugs, check the movement and interlock in each position.
10. Install safety wire on all gate and fork locking screws.

Gear Shift Lever Housing

1. Install the gear shift lever pivot pin in the housing. Install the lever in the housing, engaging the lever fulcrum ball with the heel of the pivot pin.

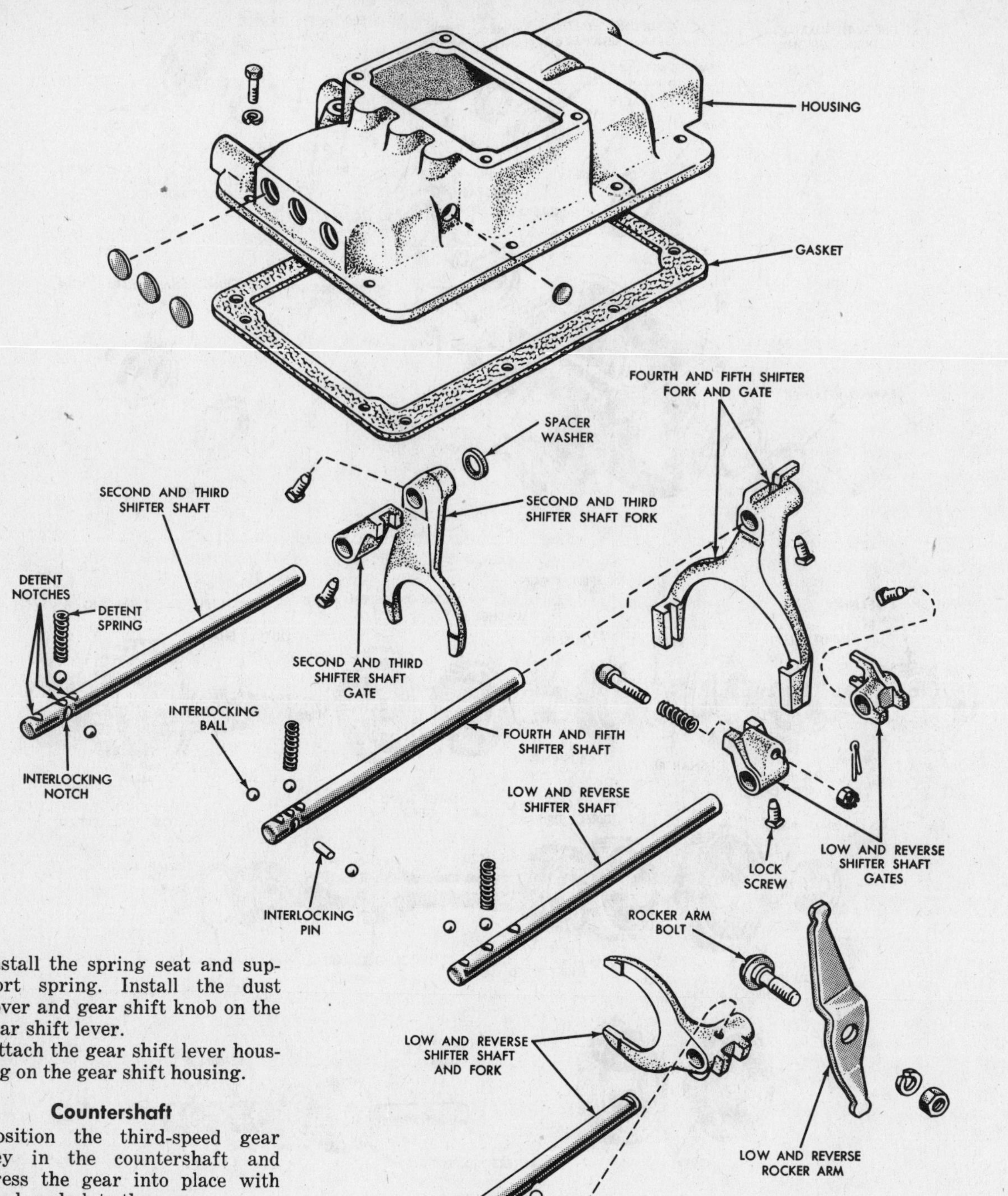

Gearshift housing components (© Clark Equipment Co.)

2. Install the spring seat and support spring. Install the dust cover and gear shift knob on the gear shift lever.
3. Attach the gear shift lever housing on the gear shift housing.

Countershaft

1. Position the third-speed gear key in the countershaft and press the gear into place with the long hub to the rear.
2. On the direct drive transmission, press the fourth-speed gear on the countershaft (long hub toward the front). (On the overdrive transmission, install the fifth-speed gear in the same manner).
3. Install the drive gear key in the shaft keyway.
4. Press the countershaft drive gear on the countershaft with the long hub toward the rear of the shaft. Install the snap-ring and washer on the countershaft.

Input Shaft

1. Press the bearing onto the input shaft with the snap-ring groove toward the forward end of the shaft. To prevent damage, apply pressure on the inner race of the bearing only.
2. Install two snap-rings—one on the input shaft and one in the bearing outer race.

Output Shaft

1. Place the output shaft (forward end up) in a soft-jawed vise.
2. Place the third-speed gear on the shaft, with the internal teeth down, and install the thrust washer. Place the lock pin in the washer. Place the lock pin in the fourth-speed gear bushing (fifth-speed gear bushing in the overdrive transmission), and position the bushing on the shaft, with the lock pin toward the upper end. Install the gear on the bushing, with the hub upward. Install the thrust washer and snap-ring.
3. End play of the fourth-speed gear must be 0.006-0.007 inch, if it isn't, replace the thrust

washer. This washer is available in the following thicknesses: 0.111-.113, 0.115-0.117, 0.119-0.121, 0.123-0.125 inch. To provide a tight stack-up between the fourth-speed locating washer, bushing, retaining washer and snap-ring, the following procedure should be followed. Before the fourth-speed gear is installed on the bushing, place the retaining washer on the shaft and hold it securely against the bushing. Holding the snap-ring parallel to the retaining washer, slip the snap-ring into the groove in the mainshaft. Select a washer that will assure a tight stack-up through the assembly. Remove the selected washer, and install the gear over the bushing. Place the selected washer in position and install the snap-ring on the shaft so that it is locked securely in the groove. (Minimum end play for fourth gear must be 0.006).

4. Remove the assembly from the vise. Install the second-speed gear on the shaft, with the internal teeth toward the front. Install the low and reverse gear, with the fork slot facing the front.

Assembly of Transmission

Coat all parts with transmission lubricant to prevent initial scoring.

1. Press the countershaft front bearing 3/64 inch below the front face of the case.
2. Lower the countershaft into the case and insert the shaft in the front bearing.
3. Place the rear bearing (snap-ring toward the rear) on the shaft.
4. Insert the two roller bearings and the spacer in the reverse idler gear bore. Place the gear assembly in position in the transmission case, with the small gear toward the rear of the case.
5. Insert the reverse idler shaft through the hole in the case, through the reverse idler gear, and into the forward support boss. Drive the reverse idler shaft into the case until the slot in the shaft is flush with the case. Install the retainer in the slot and secure with lock washer and bolt. Torque to specification.
6. Manipulate the output shaft assembly into position in the transmission case.
7. Position the synchronizer on the shaft, with the longer hub forward.
8. Place the output shaft rear bearing on the shaft with the snap-ring groove toward the rear. Install the snap-ring on the bearing. Tap the bearing onto the output shaft until the snap-ring is seated against the transmission case. Install the speedometer driving gear and spacer on the rear of the output shaft, and install the pilot bearing on the front end of the shaft.
9. Position the input shaft and bearing assembly in the forward end of the transmission case. Tap the front end of the shaft with a soft hammer until the snap-ring on the bearing is seated against the case. Install the input shaft bearing retainer and gasket. Be sure that the oil return holes in the retainer and gasket are aligned with those in the case.
10. Secure and torque the retainer onto the case.

Torque Chart

Nomenclature	*Torque Limits*
Bolt-reverse lockout plunger retainer	11/16—16 90-100
Bolt-clutch housing to engine block	7/16—14 40-50
Bolt-output shaft bearing retainer to trans. case	3/8—16 20-25 7/16—14 30-38 1/2—13 50-62 5/8—11 96-120
Bolt-gear shift lever tower to gearshift housing	3/8—16 20-25 5/16—18 11-16 7/16—14 30-35
Nut-drum parking brake to companion flange	3/8—24 35-45 7/16—20 50-70
Bolt—lever assy. to trans.	3/8—16 20-25
Nut-U-joint flange to trans. output shaft	1.00—20 90-125 1 1/4—18 225-275 1 1/2—18 275-350
Nut-countershaft bearing lock (5-speed extra heavy duty & 5-speed exclusive)	1 1/4—18 350-450
Bolt-gear shift housing trans. case	5/16—18 20-25 3/8—16 35-40
Bolt-clutch housing to trans. case	7/16—14 30-38 5/8—11 96-120 9/16—12 70-90
Bolt-parking brake to trans. bearing retainer	1/2—20 58-72 5/8—18 180-220 7/16—20 50-70
Nut-bellcrank to trans.	9/16—18 70-90
Bolt-countershaft & reverse idler shaft Retainer	1/2—13 60-70 5/16—18 25-30 3/8—16 25-37 3/8—16① 18-25① 7/16—14 40-45 1/2—13 80-85
Bolt-countershaft rear bearing retainer	5/16—18 25-30 3/8—16 35-40 7/16—14 45-55
Bolt-bellcrank to trans.	3/8—16 20-25
Bolt-gear shift housing trans. case (continued)	3/8—16② 30-35② 7/16—14 45-50
Bolt-bearing retainer to trans. (main w/o aux.)	1/2—13 50-62 5/8—11 96-120
Bolt-bearing retainer to trans. (main w/aux.)	5/8—11 96-120
Bolt-input shaft bearing retainer to trans. case	5/16—18 25-30 3/8—16 25-30 7/16—14 40-45
Bolt-countershaft front bearing retainer	5/16—18 25-30 3/8—16 25-35 7/16—14 50-55

11. Place the countershaft rear bearing cap and gasket on the case and torque to specification.
12. Install a new oil seal in the output shaft rear bearing retainer. Position the retainer and a new gasket on the case, and install the lockwashers and bolts. Torque the bolts to specification.
13. Install the detent ball and spring in the first and reverse shift fork socket and hold with the dummy shaft.
14. Engage the fork in the sliding gear groove. Insert the shift rail through the hole in the rear of the case and through the shift fork, pushing out the dummy shaft. Remove the dummy shaft, and drive the shift rail into the case until the edge of the lock slot is flush with the case. Install the shift rail lock plate, lockwasher, and cap screw.
15. Position the first and reverse rocker arm in the case, and install and torque the rocker arm pivot bolt, lockwasher, and nut.
16. Shift the gears into the neutral position. Place the gear shift housing and gasket on the case, making sure that the shift forks engage the slots in the gears and torque down the bolts.
17. Install the brake shoe assembly.
18. Install the U-joint spline flange an dthe brake drum on the output shaft splines, and install the flange nut. Shift the transmission into gear and torque the nut to specification. Install a new cotter pin on the nut and shaft.

Clark 265V 5 Speed

Description

The Clark 265V is a five-speed synchronized transmission with fifth speed being direct drive. Power take-off openings are provided on both sides of the transmission case. Lubricant capacity is 12 pints.

Disassembly of Transmission

1. Drain transmission assembly.
2. Remove control tower assembly and shift bar housing.
3. Shift transmission into two speeds at once and remove flange nut.
4. Remove brake band assembly, brake drum and flange assembly.
5. Remove mainshaft and countershaft rear bearing caps and gaskets.
6. While transmission is still locked in two speeds, remove countershaft rear bearing retaining nut.
7. Remove clutch release bearing and carrier assembly and clutch release yoke.
8. Remove drive gear bearing cap and gasket.
9. Remove main drive gear and bearing assembly from front of case. Proceed with caution as pilot bearing may be in pocket of drive gear, avoid dropping this bearing. If not in gear pocket, remove from end of mainshaft pilot.
10. Remove speedometer drive gear and spacer from mainshaft.
11. Rotate countershaft until flat on oil slinger is facing top of transmission.
12. Using a suitable puller, remove bearing from end of mainshaft.
13. Mainshaft assembly can now be removed from case.
14. Remove reverse idler shaft lock plate from rear of case.
15. Using a suitable puller, remove reverse idler shaft and gear.
16. Remove the two reverse idler bearings and bearing spacer from hub of gear.
17. Remove rear countershaft bearing from shaft and then remove countershaft assembly from case.
18. If countershaft front or pilot bearing is to be replaced, remove clutch housing from transmission.
19. Press pilot bearing from transmission case.

CAUTION: To prevent damage to the case bore, do not hammer or drive out bearing.

Disassembly of Sub-Assemblies

Mainshaft

1. Remove 1st and reverse sliding gears, and 4th and 5th synchronizer assembly from mainshaft.
2. Place mainshaft assembly (front

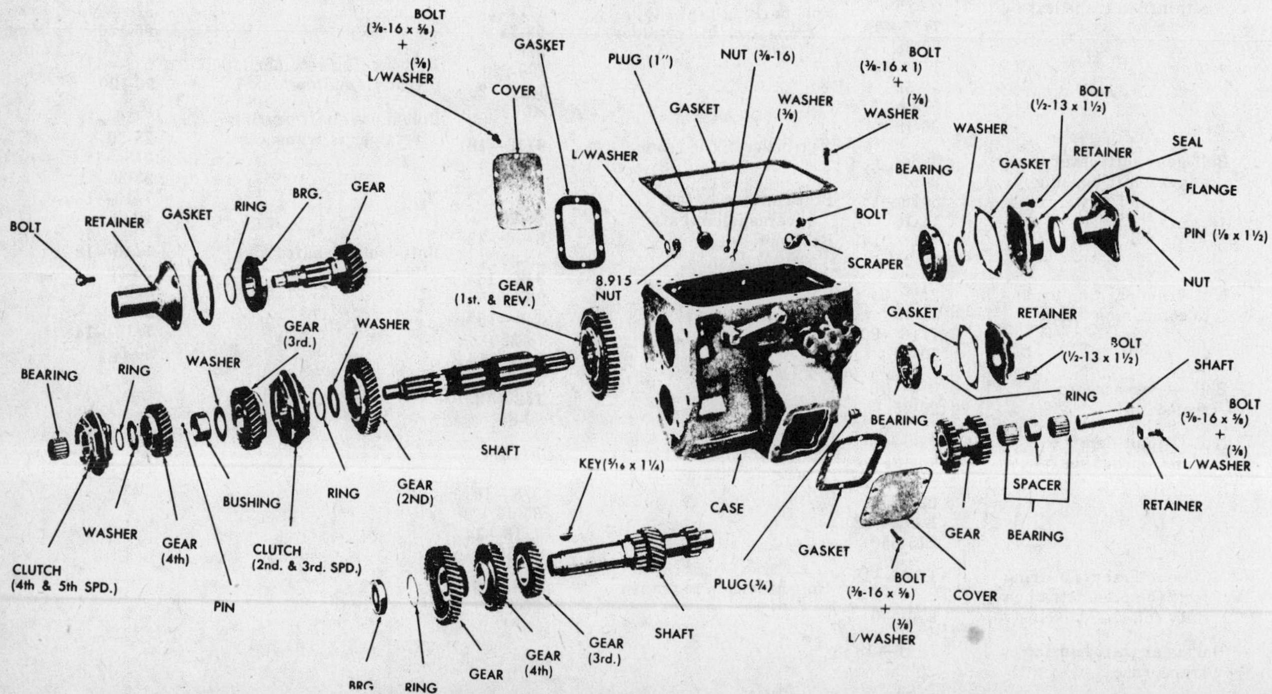

Clark 265V 5-speed transmission—exploded view (© G.M. Corp.)

end up) in a soft-jawed vise.
3. Remove snap-ring, fourth speed gear and washer from shaft.
4. Remove assembly from vise and, with front end down, pound slightly on block of wood, allowing the weight of the third-speed gear to force fourth speed gear bushing off of mainshaft. Remove this sleeve, locating pin and fourth speed gear locating washer from shaft. Care should be exercised not to lose this locating pin.
5. Third speed gear may now be removed from front shaft along with 2nd and 3rd synchronizer assembly.
6. Remove 2nd gear retaining ring and washer and 2nd speed gear.

Countershaft

1. Remove snap-ring at front end of countershaft.
2. Using an arbor press or suitable gear puller, remove countershaft drive gear, drive gear spacer, fourth speed gear and third speed gear.
3. Remove gear keys from shaft.

Clutch Release Bearing and Carrier

1. Using suitable puller or arbor press, remove clutch release bearing from carrier.

Main Drive Gear and Bearing

1. Place gear in a soft-jawed vise.
2. Remove drive gear bearing retainer ring and, using a puller, remove bearing.

Gear Shift Lever and Tower

1. Remove shift lever, support spring and washer.

Mainshaft Rear Bearing Cap

1. If replacement is necessary, press or drive out oil seal assembly.

Case and Bell Housing

1. Separate case and bell housing only if replacement of either part is necessary.

Shift Bar Housing

1. Remove welch plugs from forward openings in cover.
2. Shift all rails into neutral position and remove all shift rails and forks. CAUTION: Poppet holes should be covered when removing the poppet balls and springs since removal of the shifter shafts will cause these parts to be forcibly ejected.
3. Remove mesh locksprings and the four (4) interlock balls located in cross bore holes between 1st and reverse, 4th and 5th and 2nd and 3rd poppet holes of center rail support.
4. Remove lockscrews from 1st and reverse rocker lug and 1st and reverse shift lug.
5. Rocker arm may now be lifted from pivot pin.

Reverse Lug

1. Remove cotter key and nut from end of plunger.
2. Spring and plunger may now be removed from well in lug.

Reassembly of Sub-Assemblies

Mainshaft

1. Clamp mainshaft in soft-jawed vise with front end up.
2. Place 2nd speed gear on mainshaft with internal teeth facing up. Place 2nd gear retainer washer in position on shaft. Seat 2nd gear retainer ring in ring groove. (End play on 2nd gear must be a minimum of .006).
3. Place 2nd speed synchronizer on mainshaft with counterbore in shift hub down.
4. Place 3rd speed gear on shaft with toothed hub downward.
5. Drop 4th speed gear locating washer into position over shaft.
6. With lockpin in place in bushing, install bushing on shaft with lockpin toward upper end. Before pressing sleeve in place, center sleeve lock pin on spline. Failure to do this may shear pin and cause bushing seizure.
7. To insure a proper tight stack-up between the 4th speed locating washer, 4th speed bushing, 4th speed retaining washer and snap-ring, the following procedure should be followed: Before 4th speed gear is installed on bushing, place retaining washer on shaft and hold down securely against bushing. Holding snap-ring parallel to retaining washer, slip snap-ring into snap-ring groove in mainshaft. Select a variable thickness washer that will assure a tight stack-up through assembly. Remove selected washer, and install gear over bushing. Place selected washer in position and lock into shaft groove. (End play on 4th gear must be a minimum of .006.)
8. Remove assembly from vise and install sliding gears on shaft as follows:
   a. 4th and 5th synchronizer hub with lip on shift hub toward front.
   b. 1st and reverse gear with fork slot toward front.

Countershaft

1. Install woodruff keys in countershaft.
2. Press on 3rd speed gear with long hub toward rear.
3. Press on 4th speed gear with long hub toward front.
4. Press on countershaft drive gear with long hub toward rear followed by the retaining ring.

Main Drive Gear and Bearing Assembly

1. Assemble bearing on main drive gear with snap-ring toward pilot end of gear.
2. Install bearing retainer ring.

Mainshaft Rear Bearing Cap

1. Press new oil seal in bearing cap (lip of seal down).

Clutch Release Bearing and Carrier Assembly

1. Press clutch release bearing on bearing carrier.

Case and Bell Housing Assembly

1. If the countershaft front bearing is to be replaced, the following procedure must be followed.
2. Coat outer diameter of pilot bearing with non-hardening sealer.
3. Press pilot bearing in transmission case from clutch housing end of case. Open end of bearing facing rear of case.
4. Press bearing .007 below front face of case.
5. In order to obtain correct location of bell housing on case, it is recommended the following procedure be followed:
   a. Install drive gear and drive gear bearing assembly into case.

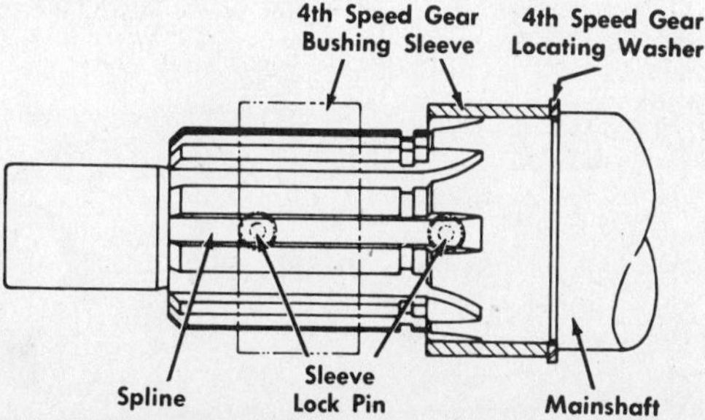

4th speed gear bushing sleeve and pin assembly
(© G.M.C.)

b. Install drive gear bearing cap over drive gear.
c. Secure bell housing to case.
d. Drive gear bearing cap, drive gear and bearing assembly must be removed from case after bell housing has been assembled so that countershaft assembly can be installed in case.

Shift Bar Housing Assembly

1. Install rocker arm on pivot pin.
2. Assemble 1st and reverse shift rail, lug and rocker lug in the following manner:
   a. Starting at left side of cover, push rail through opening in cover and slip 1st and reverse lug on rail. Push rail through two support bosses and through rocker lug.
   b. Install lockscrews in lugs and wire assembly.
   c. Shift into neutral position.
3. Install 4th and 5th shift rail and fork in following manner:
   a. Push rail through forward opening of cover.
   b. Install two (2) interlock balls between 1st and reverse, and 4th and 5th rails.
   c. Place mesh lock spring and then ball in position in well of forward rail support.
   d. Using suitable tool, compress spring and ball in such manner as to pass between guide fingers of 1st and reverse rocker lug if fingers are aligned.
   e. Slide 4th and 5th shift fork on rail with offset for lock screw toward rear of cover.
   f. Install lockscrew in fork and wire securely.
   g. Shift into neutral position.
4. Install 2nd and 3rd shift rail and fork in the following manner:
   a. Push rail through forward opening in cover.
   b. Install two (2) interlock balls between 2nd and 3rd and 4th and 5th poppet holes of forward rail support.
   c. Place mesh lock spring and ball in position in well of rail support and compress to allow rail to pass through support.
   d. Slide 2nd and 3rd shift fork onto rail, lockscrew and wire securely.
   e. Shift into neutral position.
5. Install welch plugs in forward openings.
6. Assemble 1st and reverse shift fork and rail in the following manner:
   a. Install mesh lock spring and ball in well of 1st and reverse shift fork and compress so that rail may pass through fork.
   b. Push rail through rear opening of cover.
   c. Holding fork in position on rocker arm (offset to rear), push rail through fork and into rail support.
   d. Install lockscrew in rail support and rail, then wire securely.
7. Check assembly of cover by shifting in and out of speeds. Then shift into 5th speed and attempt to shift into 1st, reverse, 2nd or 3rd at the same time. This provides a check on the proper assembly of interlock balls and pin. Cover should not shift into more than one speed at a time.
8. Return rail to neutral position.

Reassembly of Transmission

1. Position countershaft into case.
2. Press countershaft rear bearing into position on shaft with snap-ring toward rear.
3. Insert two roller bearings separated by spacer into hub of reverse idler gear and position in case. The gear with chamfered teeth should be toward rear of case.
4. Insert reverse idler shaft through hole in rear of case, through reverse gear and into forward support boss. Shaft should be driven in, until forward face of slot in shaft is flush with rear face of case and slot lined up to permit installation of locking plate.
5. Install locking plate in slot in end of shaft. Rotate countershaft until flat on oil slinger is toward top of transmission.
6. Install mainshaft assembly in transmission case.
7. Assemble mainshaft rear bearing over end of mainshaft with snap-ring in outer race facing toward the rear.
8. Install pilot bearing on mainshaft.
9. Install main drive gear and bearing assembly into case so that main drive gear engages

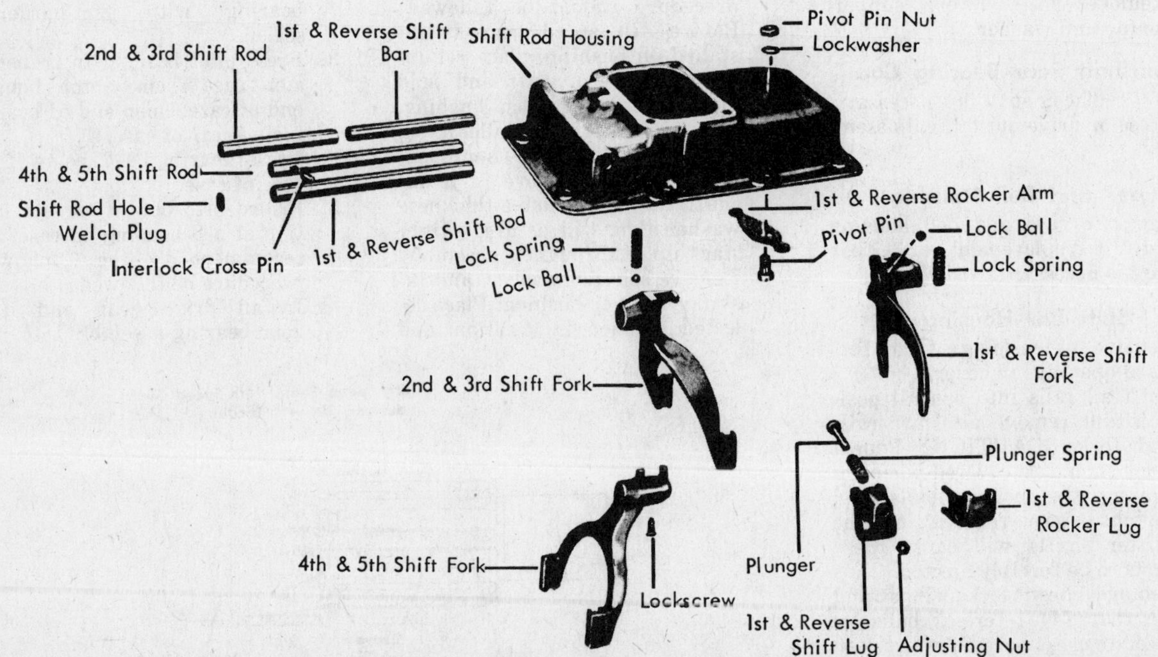

Shift bar housing assembly (© G.M. Corp.)

and meshes with countershaft gear.

10. Install main drive gear bearing cap and gasket. CAUTION: Be sure oil return hole in cap is lined up with oil return hole in case. This passage must be open and clear.
11. Clutch throwout bearing return spring clip should be installed under head of screw in assembly of bearing cap.
12. Install countershaft rear bearing retaining ring cap and gasket.
13. Install speedometer drive gear spacer and speedometer drive gear on mainshaft.
14. Install mainshaft rear bearing cap assembly and gasket.
15. Install brake drum and companion flange assembly.
16. Lock transmission in two speeds at same time and secure companion flange nut.
17. Assemble shift bar housing and gasket to case, making sure forks engage slots of gears.
18. Assemble gasket, gear shift lever and tower assembly to shift bar housing.

Clark Models 282 V 285 V 5 Speed

Description

The Clark models 282V and 285V have five forward speeds and one reverse with fifth speed being direct drive. Synchronizers aid shifting into all gears except first and reverse. All gears except first, reverse, and reverse idler are of helical design.

Gear Ratios—All Ratios Are (to 1)

Speed	*282V*	*285V*
1st	6.99	6.99
2nd	4.09	4.09
3rd	2.17	2.24
4th	1.17	1.47
5th	1.00	1.00
Reverse	5.89	5.89

Disassembly of Transmission

Cleanliness of working area, all parts, and tools cannot be overstressed. Overhaul of the transmission must not be made where dirt or other foreign particles are present. Before disassembling the transmission, the exterior of the case should be thoroughly cleaned to prevent the possibility of any dirt entering the internal mechanism.

NOTE: For more detailed information, consult the "cleaning and inspection" instructions at front of the transmission section.

IMPORTANT: On transmissions having a conventional gearshift lever, reinstall the control tower before cleaning the exterior of the transmission.

NOTE: The clutch housing should not be removed from the transmission case unless the housing, case, or countershaft front bearing needs replacement.

Removal of Mainshaft Assembly

See transmission components illustration.

1. Remove mainshaft rear bearing cap from case. Discard gasket.
2. Remove the speedometer drive gear from the mainshaft.
3. Remove the countershaft rear bearing cap and gasket.
4. Using snap-ring pliers, remove snap-ring that secures countershaft rear bearing.
5. Remove the main drive gear bearing cap from case.
6. Pull the main drive gear assembly from case being careful not to drop bearings into the bottom of the case.
7. Using bearing puller, move mainshaft assembly toward rear until rear bearing protrudes as far as possible from case. Remove bearing unit.
8. Tip front end of mainshaft upward (to prevent loss of components on shaft), and lift entire mainshaft assembly out of case.

Disassembly of Mainshaft

1. Remove 1st and reverse sliding gear from mainshaft. Set mainshaft in a soft-jawed vise. Remove 4th and 5th synchronizer assembly from other end of shaft. NOTE: 4th speed synchronizer cup may stay on mainshaft.
2. Pull the 4th and 5th shift hub sleeve retainer ring, sleeve and 4th speed gear off the mainshaft.
3. Remove 3rd gear retaining ring, locating washer, and 3rd gear from shaft.
4. Pull 2nd and 3rd synchronizer assembly off the mainshaft.
5. Now remove 2nd and 3rd hub sleeve retaining ring and sleeve from shaft. Remove other sleeve retaining ring.
6. Remove 2nd gear retaining ring, 2nd gear, and washer from the shaft.

Disassembly of Main Drive Gear

1. Remove bearing retaining ring.
2. Remove main drive gear bearing

Removing countershaft rear bearing retaining ring
(© Clark Equipment Co.)

Removing main drive gear
(© Clark Equipment Co.)

1 Shift rod cover screw
2 Shift rod cover screw lock washer
3 Shift rod cover
4 Control cover gasket
5 Mainshaft 5th speed synchronizer cup
6 Mainshaft 4th and 5th synchronizer assembly
7 Mainshaft 4th speed synchronizer cup
8 Mainshaft 4th and 5th shift hub sleeve retainer ring
9 Mainshaft 4th and 5th shift hub sleeve
10 Mainshaft 4th speed gear
11 Mainshaft 3rd gear retainer ring
12. Mainshaft 3rd gear locating washer
13 Mainshaft 3rd speed gear
14 Mainshaft gear synchronizer cup
15 Mainshaft 2nd and 3rd synchronizer assembly
16 Mainshaft 2nd and 3rd shift hub sleeve retainer ring
17 Mainshaft 2nd and 3rd shift hub sleeve
18 Mainshaft 2nd and 3rd shift hub sleeve retainer ring
19 Mainshaft 2nd speed gear
20 Mainshaft 2nd speed gear locating washer
21 Mainshaft 2nd speed gear retainer ring
22 Mainshaft
23 Mainshaft 1st speed gear
24 Countershaft rear bearing cap bolt
25 Countershaft rear bearing cap washer
26 Countershaft rear bearing cap
27 Countershaft rear bearing cap gasket
28 Countershaft rear bearing retainer ring
29 Countershaft rear bearing
30 Countershaft rear bearing oil slinger
31 Countershaft
32 Countershaft gear key
33 Countershaft 4th speed gear
34 Countershaft drive gear
35 Countershaft drive gear retainer ring
36 Filler plug
37 Magnetic drain plug
38 Flange nut
39 thru 43 Parking brake
44 Mainshaft rear oil seal
45 Mainshaft rear bearing cap screw
46 Mainshaft rear bearing cap screw lock washer
47 Mainshaft rear bearing cap with bushing
48 Mainshaft rear bearing cap gasket
49 Speedometer drive gear
50 Mainshaft rear bearing
51 Transmission case
52 P.T.O. cover plate gasket
53 P.T.O. cover plate
54 P.T.O. cover plate screw
55 Mainshaft rear bearing cap screw lock washer
56 Mainshaft rear bearing cap screw

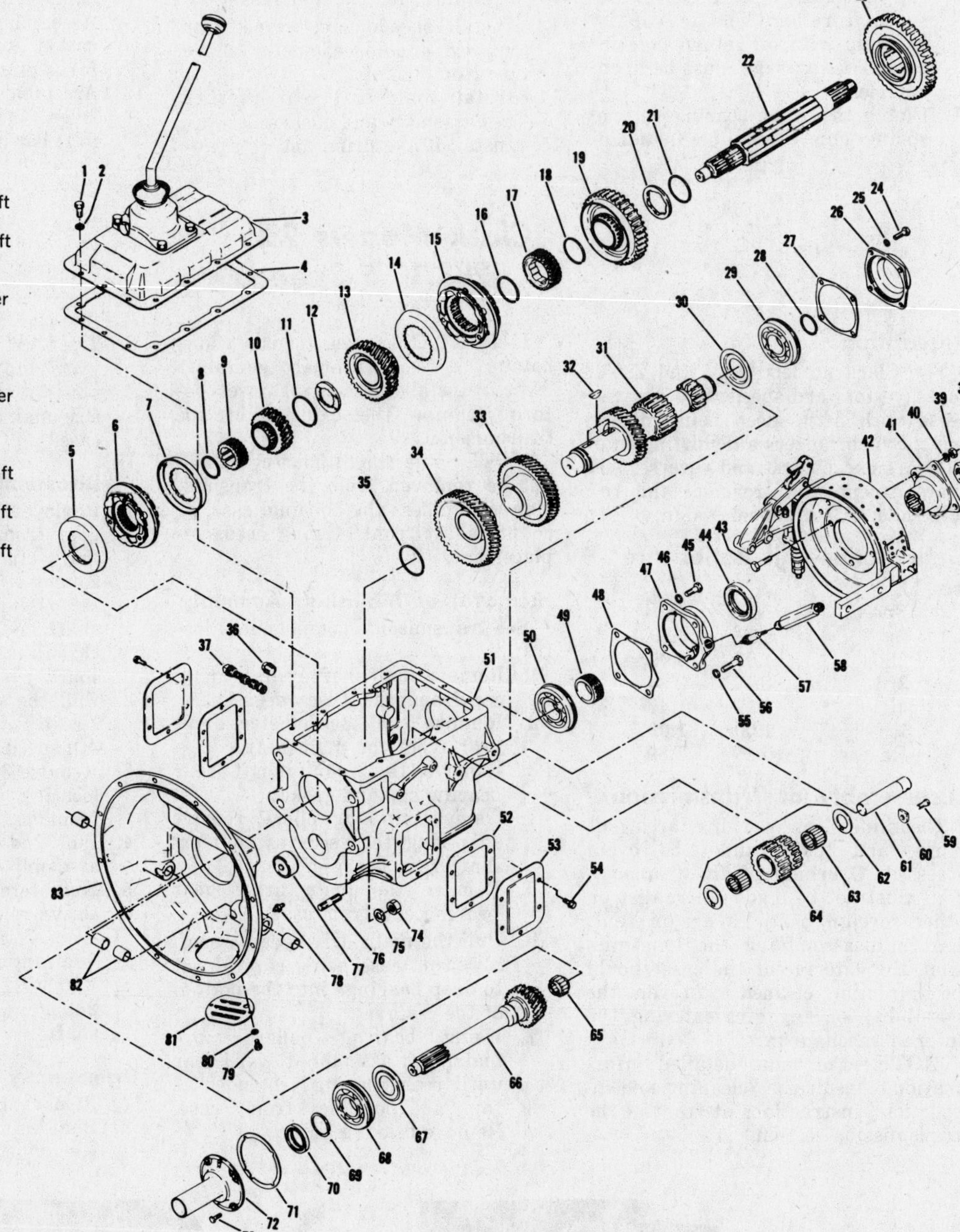

Transmission components (© Clark Equipment Co.)

57 Speedometer driven gear
58 Speedometer tube nut
59 Reverse idler shaft lock screw
60 Reverse idler shaft lock
61 Reverse idler shaft
62 Reverse idler thrust washer
63 Reverse idler bearing
64 Reverse idler gear
65 Mainshaft pilot bearing
66 Main drive gear
67 Main drive gear bearing oil slinger
68 Main drive gear bearing
69 Main drive gear bearing retainer ring
70 Main drive gear bearing cap oil seal
71 Main drive gear bearing cap gasket
72 Main drive gear bearing cap
73 Main drive gear bearing cap bolts
74 Clutch housing stud nut
75 Clutch housing stud nut lock washer
76 Clutch housing stud
77 Countershaft front bearing
78 Pedal shaft grease fitting
79 Clutch housing inspection plate bolt
80 Clutch housing inspection plate lock washer
81 Clutch housing inspection plate
82 Clutch pedal shaft bushing
83 Clutch housing

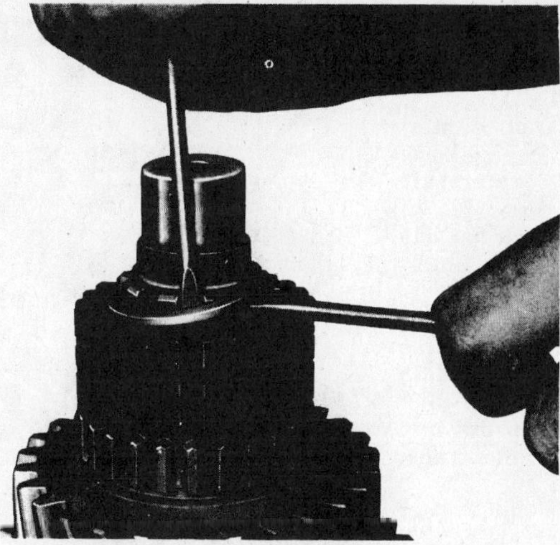

Removing shift hub sleeve retaining ring—4th and 5th speed
(© Clark Equipment Co.)

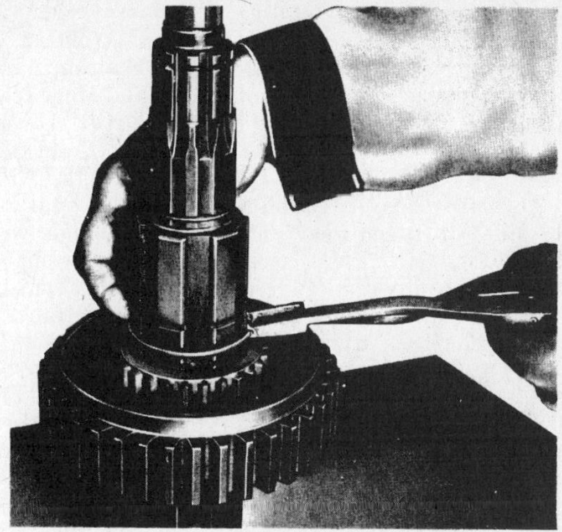

Removing 2nd gear retaining ring
(© Clark Equipment Co.)

and oil slinger from main drive gear.

3. Remove mainshaft pilot bearing.

Clutch Housing or Countershaft Front Bearing Replacement

1. If necessary to replace front countershaft bearing, remove clutch housing and drive front bearing from transmission case.
2. Lightly coat the outer diameter of the new bearing with non-hardening sealer. Install in transmission case with end of bearing 0.001 to 0.007-inch below face of case.
3. Reinstall clutch housing to front end of transmission case. Secure housing with four stud nut lock washers, and stud nuts.

Removal of Reverse Idler Gear

1. Remove reverse idler shaft lock screw and speedometer tube nut from case.
2. Using puller, pull reverse idler shaft out of case.
3. Remove shaft and reverse idler gear components including two thrust washers (one at each end of gear), gear, and two sets of roller bearings at the same time.

4th and 5th speed synchronizer assembly
(© Clark Equipment Co.)

Removal of Countershaft

1. Pry countershaft out until it is possible to remove snap-ring from bearing outer race. Using bearing puller, remove bearing from lower opening at rear of case.
2. Remove oil slinger from countershaft.
3. Raise forward end of countershaft assembly, and lift entire assembly out of case.

Disassembly of Countershaft

1. Remove retaining ring securing the countershaft 4th speed gear and the countershaft drive gear to the countershaft.
2. Remove drive gear and 4th speed gear from shaft.

CAUTION: Do not lose keys.

Assembly of Mainshaft

1. Position 2nd speed gear retaining ring and washer onto mainshaft, and install 2nd gear to shaft with gear's clutching teeth up.
2. Place one of the 2nd and 3rd shift hub sleeve retaining rings in position on mainshaft.
3. Install 2nd and 3rd shift hub sleeve onto shaft and secure with other sleeve retaining ring.
4. Install 2nd and 3rd synchronizer assembly along with cup onto shaft.
5. Place 3rd gear, clutching teeth down, along with locating washer onto shaft.
6. Install 3rd gear retaining ring to hold washer and gear onto shaft.
7. Position 4th gear on shaft with gear's clutching teeth up. Position 4th speed synchronizer cup on the clutching teeth of 4th gear before installing hub sleeve. Install 4th and 5th shift hub sleeve with chamfer down.
8. Install retaining ring to secure components on shaft.
9. Place 4th and 5th synchronizer assembly onto shift hub sleeve.

Removing shift hub sleeve retaining ring—2nd and 3rd speed
(© Clark Equipment Co.)

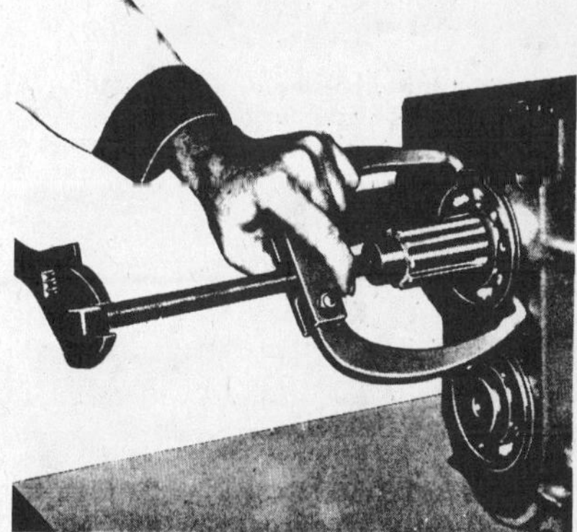

Removing mainshaft rear bearing
(© Clark Equipment Co.)

10. Position 1st and reverse sliding gear with shift fork slot down onto other end of mainshaft. This completes assembly of mainshaft.

Assembly of Countershaft

1. With keys in place on countershaft, slide 4th speed gear onto shaft.
2. Position the countershaft drive gear on the shaft. Secure gears on countershaft with retaining ring.

Assembly of Transmission

1. Coat front countershaft bearing rollers with heavy grease to hold in place until countershaft is installed.
2. Insert rear of countershaft through rear countershaft bearing bore. Move countershaft forward and into front bearing. CAUTION: Use extreme care while inserting countershaft into the countershaft front bearing to prevent loosening needle bearing rollers.
3. Position rear bearing oil slinger and start rear bearing.
4. Drive rear bearings on countershaft and into rear bearing bore. IMPORTANT: Countershaft drive gear must be supported on each side with a ¼-inch flat bar to prevent damage to countershaft front bearing. Install bearing retainer ring.
5. Use heavy grease on reverse idler thrust washers to hold in place. NOTE: Be sure the tang on each thrust washer fits into the slot provided in the transmission case.
6. Insert two reverse idler gear bearings in idler gear.
7. Install reverse idler gear and insert idler shaft through case and idler gear. NOTE: Idler shaft lock groove must line up with lock bolt hole. Drive shaft into position. Install shaft lock and bolt and torque at 20 to 25 foot-pounds torque.
8. Install mainshaft assembly into transmission case.
9. Assemble the pilot bearing in the main drive gear as follows:
a. A new pilot bearing comes from the factory with a plastic sleeve. Stand drive gear on end. Set bearing and sleeve over bearing pocket in drive gear. Slide bearing rollers and cage from plastic sleeve into bearing pocket.
b. If old pilot bearing is used, set rollers in bearing cage and hold in place with a rubber band. Slide bearing rollers and cage from rubber band into bearing pocket.
10. Install main drive assembly in transmission case. Clutching teeth on main drive gear must enter 5th speed synchronizer cup without binding.
11. Press oil seal (lip up) into drive gear bearing cap. Shellac a new gasket to bearing cap, being careful not to cover oil return groove in bearing cap.
12. With bearing cap oil return groove lined up with oil hole in transmission case install bearing cap and torque at 20 to 25 foot-pounds.
13. Install mainshaft rear housing.
14. Shellac a new gasket to countershaft bearing cap and tighten bolts 20 to 25 foot-pounds torque.
15. Install speedometer drive gear.
16. Press a new oil seal in mainshaft rear bearing cap with lip of seal down. Shellac gasket to bearing cap, being careful not to cover oil return grooves in bearing cap. Align oil grooves in cap with oil holes in case. Tighten bolts 20 to 25 foot-pounds torque.
17. Install four studs, washers, and nuts to secure entire brake and drum assembly to rear end of transmission case (when used). Tighten two bolts attaching brake assembly anchor bar on one side to 65 to 75 foot-pounds

Installing shift hub sleeve—4th and 5th
(© Clark Equipment Co.)

Installing countershaft front bearing
(© Clark Equipment Co.)

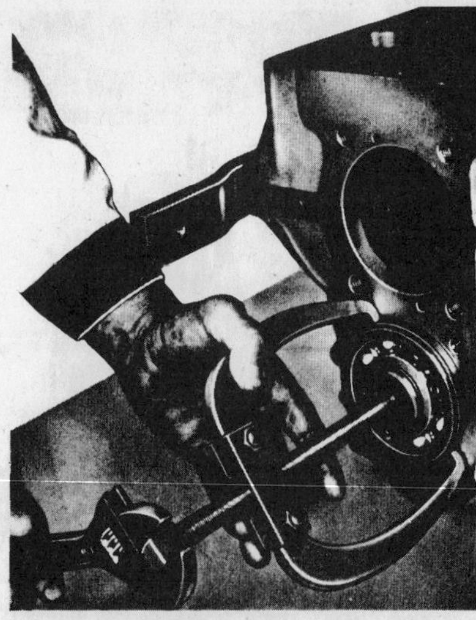

Removing countershaft rear bearing
(© Clark Equipment Co.)

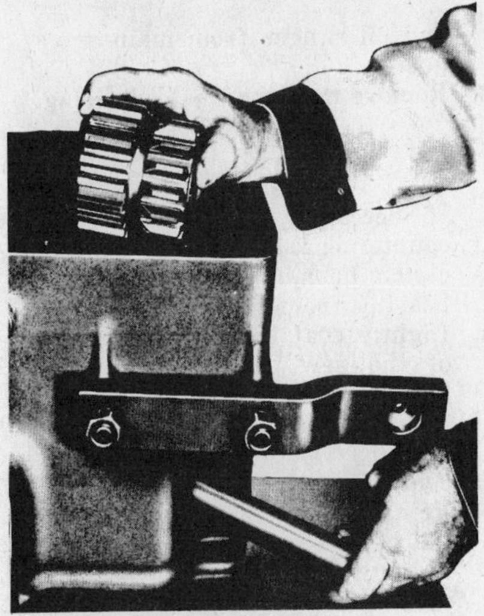

Removing idler gear
(© Clark Equipment Co.)

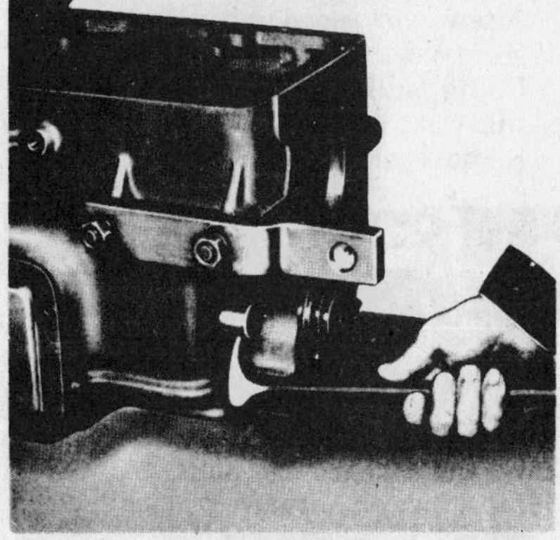

Removing reverse idler gear
(© Clark Equipment Co.)

torque. Tighten two bolts securing bracket on other side to 65 to 75 foot-pounds torque. With mainshaft flange or yoke installed, lock transmission in two gears. Install and tighten mainshaft nut to 400-450 foot-pounds torque.

18. With transmission shifted into neutral, install the shift rod control assembly with second and third, fourth and fifth shift forks set over shift hubs, first and reverse fork enters the slot on first and reverse gear. Tighten the four bolts securing shift rod support assembly 20 to 25 foot-pounds torque. Position three balls and springs.
19. Install the shift housing cover and torque the bolts to 20 to 25 foot-pounds.
20. Install the remote control assembly, or control tower assembly (depending on which one is used) to cover and tighten bolts 20 to 25 foot-pounds torque.

IMPORTANT: After overhauled unit has been in service for 3,000 miles the unit should be drained and refilled with recommended lubricant.

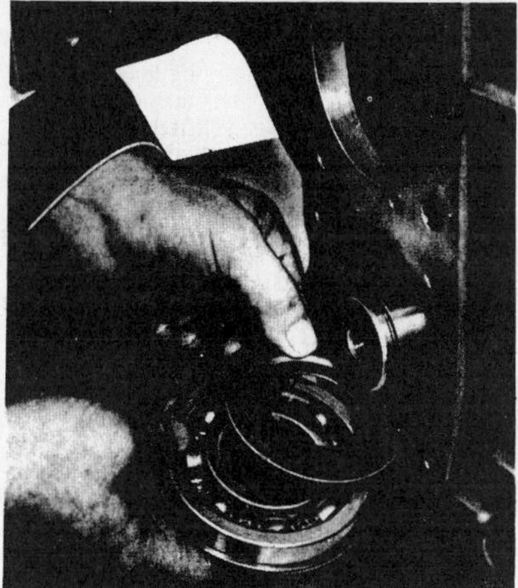

Assembly of rear bearing and oil slinger
(© Clark Equipment Co.)

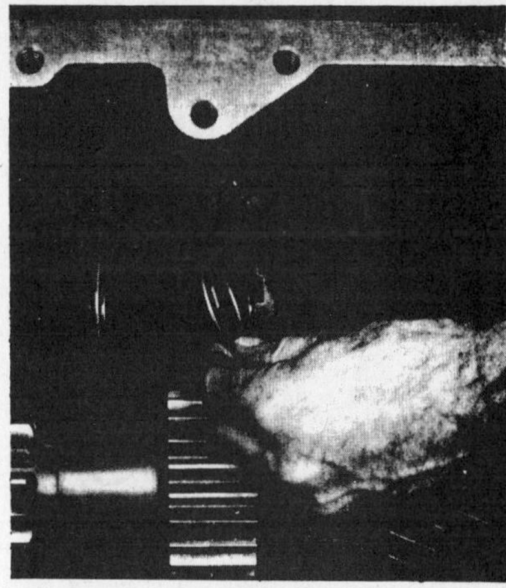

Positioning reverse idler thrust washers
(© Clark Equipment Co.)

Assembly of Remote Control Assembly

1. Position selector sleeve and ball assembly in remote control housing, then install washer and cap screw.
2. Position selector arm and shaft assembly and spacer in housing, then install washer and snapring.
3. Assemble reverse latch plunger,

Installing pilot bearing
(© Clark Equipment Co.)

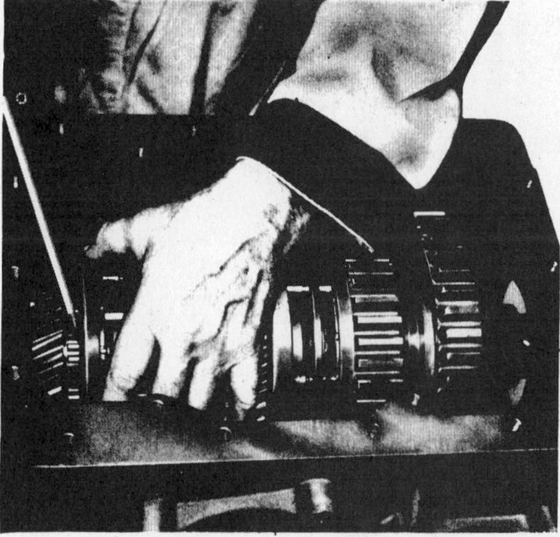

Main drive gear installed
(© Clark Equipment Co.)

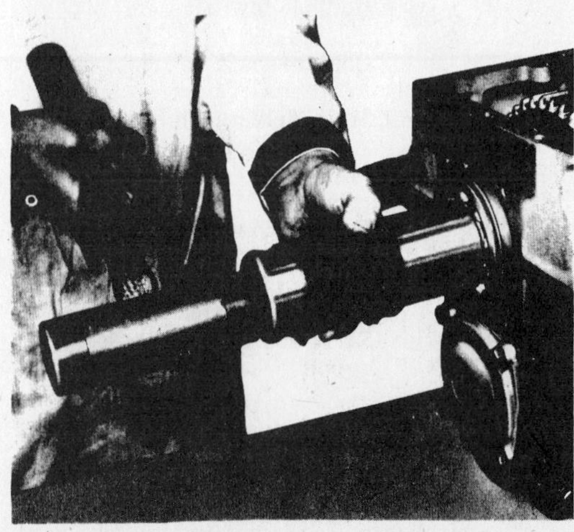

Installing mainshaft rear bearing
(© Clark Equipment Co.)

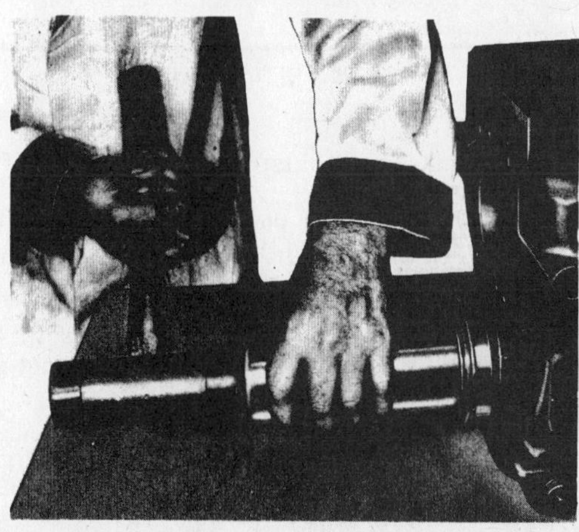

Using driver to install countershaft rear bearing
(© Clark Equipment Co.)

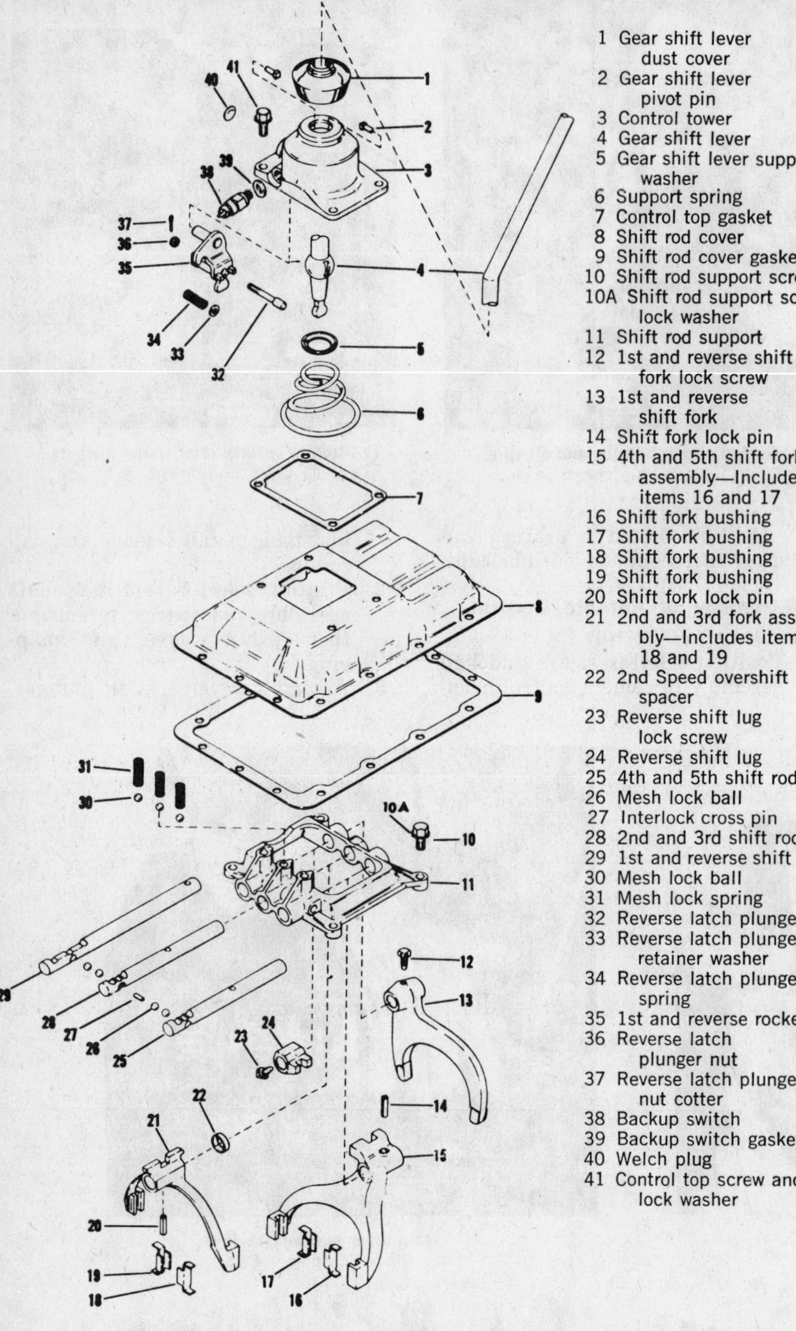

1 Gear shift lever dust cover
2 Gear shift lever pivot pin
3 Control tower
4 Gear shift lever
5 Gear shift lever support washer
6 Support spring
7 Control top gasket
8 Shift rod cover
9 Shift rod cover gasket
10 Shift rod support screw
10A Shift rod support screw lock washer
11 Shift rod support
12 1st and reverse shift fork lock screw
13 1st and reverse shift fork
14 Shift fork lock pin
15 4th and 5th shift fork assembly—Includes items 16 and 17
16 Shift fork bushing
17 Shift fork bushing
18 Shift fork bushing
19 Shift fork bushing
20 Shift fork lock pin
21 2nd and 3rd fork assembly—Includes items 18 and 19
22 2nd Speed overshift spacer
23 Reverse shift lug lock screw
24 Reverse shift lug
25 4th and 5th shift rod
26 Mesh lock ball
27 Interlock cross pin
28 2nd and 3rd shift rod
29 1st and reverse shift rod
30 Mesh lock ball
31 Mesh lock spring
32 Reverse latch plunger
33 Reverse latch plunger retainer washer
34 Reverse latch plunger spring
35 1st and reverse rocker
36 Reverse latch plunger nut
37 Reverse latch plunger nut cotter
38 Backup switch
39 Backup switch gasket
40 Welch plug
41 Control top screw and lock washer

Control tower components (© Clark Equipment Co.)

washer, spring, and nut to 1st and reverse rocker arm.

4. Adjust reverse latch plunger so rounded end is flush or slightly below the two flat ends of the 1st and reverse rocker arm. Using a cotter pin, lock adjusting nut in correct position.
5. Position shift finger and shifter shaft in housing, aligning splines of shaft with splines of selector sleeve and ball assembly, and hole in shaft with hole in finger.
6. Install shift finger screw, torque to 25 foot-pounds and secure with lockwire.
7. Install attaching parts that hold shifter shaft collar to shifter shaft.
8. Install attaching parts that hold shift lever assembly to shift lever mounting bracket and torque to 25-31 foot-pounds.
9. Install attaching parts that hold shift lever mounting bracket to housing. Be sure shift lever assembly is properly seated in slot of shifter shaft collar.
10. Place selector lever on selector arm and shaft assembly, so that the selector lever is perpendicular to the gasket side of the housing. Tighten nut firmly.
11. Place snap-ring on plunger and insert into housing. Thread back-up light switch into housing and tighten firmly.

Assembly of Control Tower

1. Insert shift lever through bottom of control tower.
2. Install washer and spring.
3. Assemble reverse latch plunger washer, spring, and nut to 1st and reverse rocker arm.
4. Adjust reverse latch plunger so rounded end is flush or slightly below the two flat ends of the 1st and reverse rocker arm. Secure adjusting nut with cotter pin.
5. Install reverse latch plunger assembly in control tower. Thread back-up light switch into control tower and tighten firmly.
6. Install dust cover and shift lever knob.

Torque Specifications

Location	*Foot-Pounds*
Companion flange or output yoke retaining nut	400-450
Brake anchor bar stud nuts	65-75
Brake drum bolts	50-60
Brake locating bracket nuts	65-75
Control tower assembly bolts	20-25
Countershaft bearing cap bolts	20-25
Main drive gear bearing cap bolts	20-25
Mainshaft rear bearing cap bolts	20-25
Remote control assembly bolts	20-25
Reverse idler lock and bolt	20-25
Shift rod cover bolts	20-25
Shift rod support assembly bolts	20-25

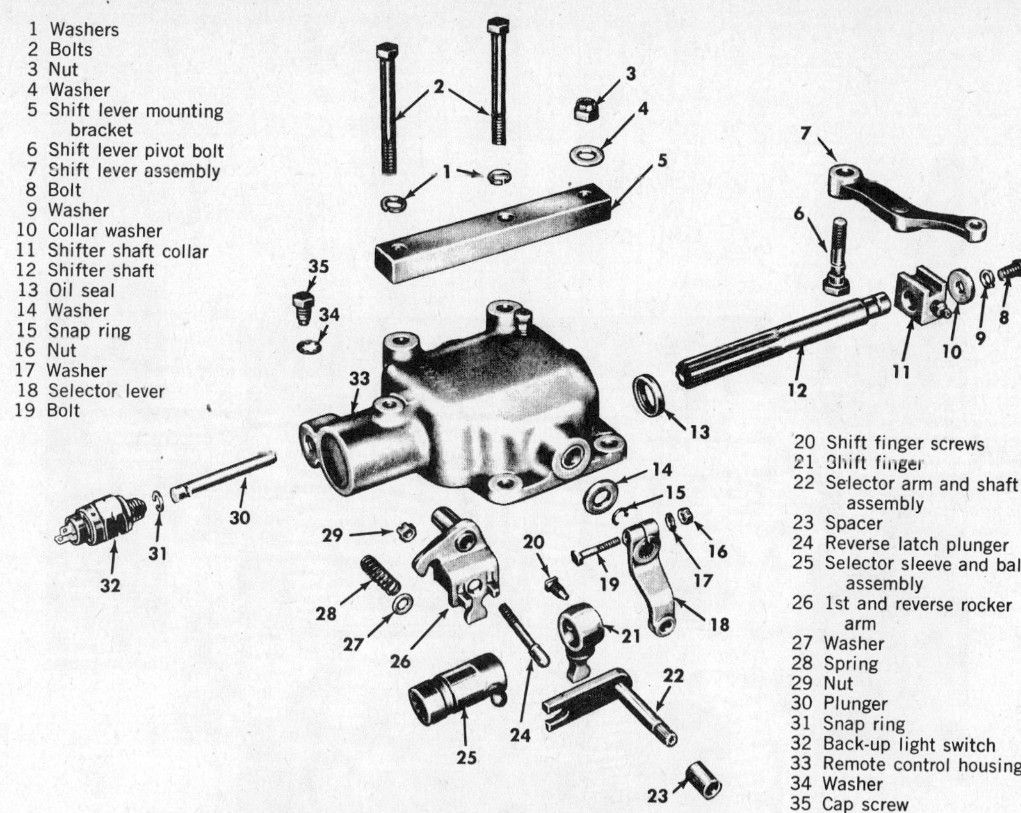

Remote control housing components (© Clark Equipment Co.)

Clark 300 V, 320 V, 380 V 5 Speed

Description

The Clark 300V, 320V, and 380V Series are 5-speed synchromesh transmissions with direct drive in fifth gear. The 320V and 380V Series transmissions can be identified by their serviceable shift fork wear pads. Lubricant capacity is 13 pints.

Disassembly of Transmission

1. Drain transmission assembly.
2. Remove control tower and shift bar housing assemblies.
3. Shifting by hand, engage transmission into two speeds at same time and remove mainshaft flange nut.
4. Remove brake band assembly.
5. Remove brake drum and flange assembly.
6. Remove mainshaft and countershaft rear bearing caps and gaskets.
7. While transmission is still locked in two speeds, remove countershaft rear bearing retaining nut.
8. Remove clutch release bearing, carrier assembly, and clutch release yoke.
9. Remove drive gear bearing cap and gasket.

Drive Gear and Bearing Removal—300 V Series

Remove main drive gear and bearing assembly from front of case. Proceed with caution as pilot bearing may be in pocket of drive gear, avoid dropping this bearing. If not in pocket of gear, remove from end of mainshaft pilot.

Drive Gear and Bearing Removal —320 V & 380 V Series

When removing the main drive gear from the mainshaft use caution as the pilot bearing, consisting of 12 rollers and a bearing cage, may fall in the transmission case.

10. Remove speedometer drive gear and spacer from mainshaft.
11. Using a suitable puller, remove bearing from end of mainshaft.
12. The mainshaft assembly can now be removed.
13. Remove reverse idler shaft lock plate.
14. Using a suitable puller, pull shaft and gear from case.
15. Remove the two reverse idler bearings and bearing spacer from hub of gear.
16. Push countershaft toward rear of case and remove rear countershaft bearing.
17. The countershaft assembly can now be removed from case.
18. If countershaft front or pilot bearing is to be replaced, remove clutch housing from transmission.
19. Press pilot bearing from transmission case. CAUTION: To prevent case bore damage do not hammer or drive out bearing.

Disassembly of Sub-Assemblies

Mainshaft

1. Remove 1st and reverse sliding gears, and 4th and 5th synchronizer assembly from mainshaft.
2. Place remainder of assembly in a soft-jawed vise with front end up.
3. Remove snap-ring, fourth speed gear and washer from shaft.
4. Remove assembly from vise and with front end pointed downward, pound slightly on block of wood, allowing the weight of the third speed gear to force fourth speed gear bushing off of main-

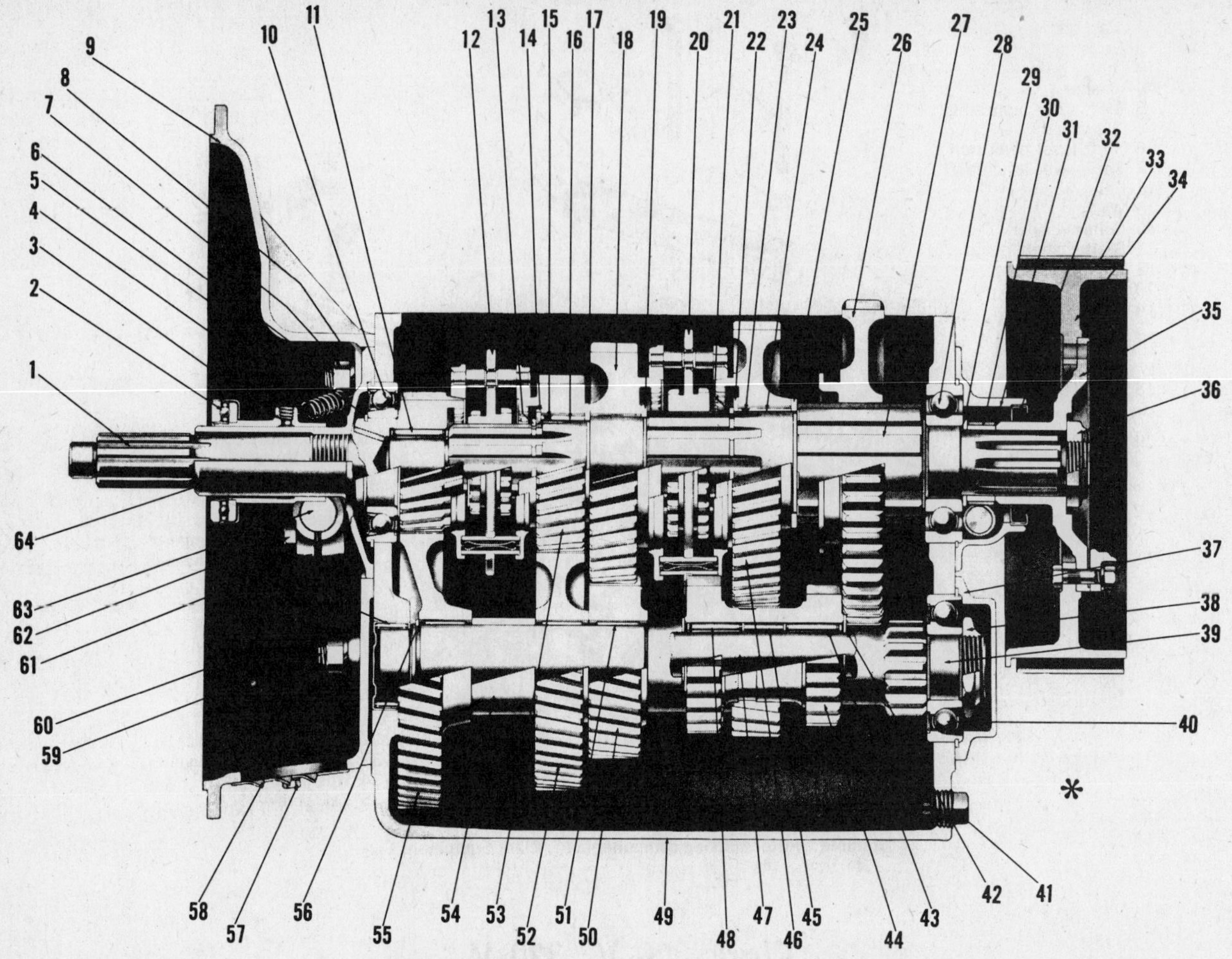

Clark 300V Series transmission (© Clark Equipment Co.)

1 Main drive gear
2 Clutch throw-out bearing
3 Clutch throw-out bearing carrier
4 Clutch release spring
5 Drive gear bearing retainer ring
6 Clutch housing to case stud
7 Clutch housing to case stud nut
8 Clutch housing to case stud nut lockwasher
9 Clutch housing
10 Drive gear bearing
11 Mainshaft pilot bearing
12 4th & 5th synchronizer assembly
13 Mainshaft 4th gear retainer ring
14 Mainshaft 4th gear retainer washer
15 Mainshaft 4th gear bushing sleeve pin
16 Mainshaft 4th gear bushing sleeve
17 Mainshaft 4th gear locating washer
18 Mainshaft 3rd gear & bushing assembly
19 Mainshaft 3rd gear thrust washer
20 2nd & 3rd synchronizer
21 Main shaft 2nd gear retainer ring
22 Mainshaft 2nd gear retainer washer
23 Mainshaft 2nd gear bushing sleeve pin
24 Mainshaft 2nd gear bushing sleeve
25 Mainshaft 2nd gear locating washer
26 Mainshaft 1st & reverse gear
27 Mainshaft
28 Mainshaft rear bearing
29 Speedometer drive gear spacer
30 Speedometer drive gear
31 Mainshaft rear bearing cap
32 Mainshaft rear bearing cap oil seal
33 Brake band
34 Brake drum
35 Companion flange
36 Companion flange nut
37 Countershaft rear bearing cap
38 Countershaft rear bearing retainer nut
39 Countershaft
40 Countershaft rear bearing
41 Magnetic drain plug
42 Thrust washer
43 Reverse idler bearing
44 Reverse idler gear
45 Reverse idler bearing spacer
46 Mainshaft 2nd gear
47 Reverse idler shaft
48 Reverse idler bearing
49 Transmission case
49D Filler plug
50 Countershaft 3rd gear
51 Countershaft gear key
52 Countershaft 4th gear
53 Mainshaft 4th gear
54 Countershaft drive gear spacer
55 Countershaft drive gear
56 Countershaft drive gear retainer ring
57 Clutch housing cover screw
58 Clutch housing cover
59 Clutch housing to case stud
60 Countershaft front bearing assembly
61 Clutch release yoke
62 Clutch release yoke screw
63 Clutch pedal shaft
64 Main drive gear bearing cap

shaft. When loose, remove sleeve and locating pin from shaft with fourth speed gear locating washer. Care should be exercised not to lose this pin.

5. Third speed gear may now be removed off front end of shaft.
6. Remove 2nd and 3rd synchronizer assembly.
7. Remove 2nd gear retaining ring and washer.
8. Remove 2nd speed constant mesh gear, bushing sleeve and locating washer from shaft.

Countershaft

1. Using an arbor press or suitable gear puller, remove countershaft drive gear, drive gear spacer, fourth speed gear and third speed gear.
2. Remove gear keys from shaft.

Clutch Release Bearing and Carrier

1. Using suitable puller or arbor press, remove clutch release bearing from carrier.

Main Drive Gear and Bearing

1. Place gear in soft-jawed vise.
2. Using suitable tool, remove retainer ring holding bearing on gear.

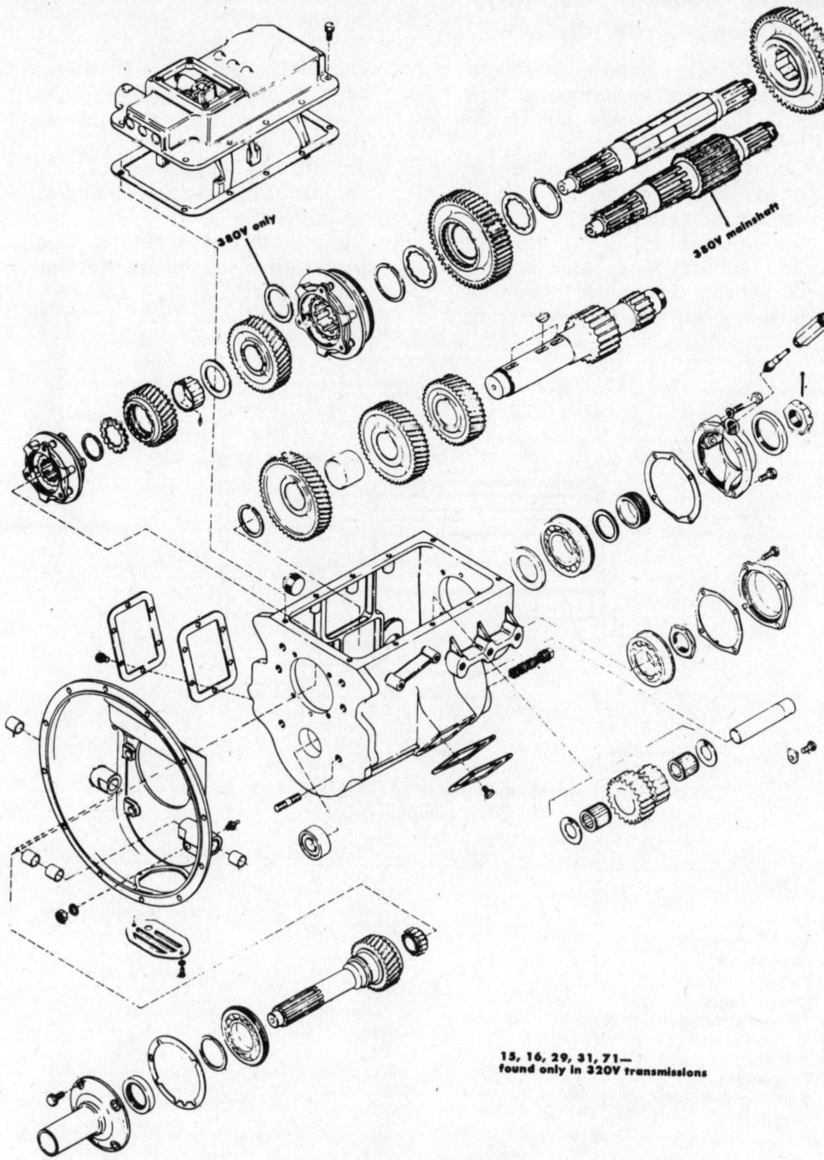

320V and 380V basic transmissions (© Clark Equipment Co.)

3. Using puller or arbor press, remove bearing from gear.

Gear Shift Lever and Tower

1. Remove gear shift knob and dust cover.
2. Remove shift lever, support spring and washer.

Mainshaft Rear Bearing Cap

1. If replacement is necessary, press or drive out oil seal assembly.

Case and Bell Housing

1. Separate case and bell housing. It is recommended that this be done only if replacement of either part is required.

Shift Bar Housing

1. Remove welch plugs from forward openings in cover.
2. Remove lockwires from shifter lugs and forks.
3. Shift all rails into neutral position.
4. Remove lockscrew from 2nd and 3rd shift fork and move rail toward rear of cover so lockscrew can be removed from lug.
5. Remove shift rails, lugs and forks from cover. CAUTION: Poppet holes should be covered when removing the poppet balls and springs since removal of the shifter shafts will cause these parts to be forcibly ejected.
6. Remove mesh locksprings and the four (4) interlock balls located in cross bore holes between 1st and reverse, 4th and 5th and 2nd and 3rd poppet holes of center rail support.
7. Remove lockscrew from 1st and reverse rocker lug, then move rail toward rear of cover so that lockscrew can be removed from 1st and reverse lug.
8. Rocker arm may now be lifted from pivot pin.

Reverse Lug

1. Remove cotter key and nut from end of plunger.
2. Spring and plunger may now be removed from well in lug.

Reassembly of Sub-Assemblies

Mainshaft Assembly

1. Clamp mainshaft (front end up) in a soft-jawed vice.
2. Install second gear locating washer onto shaft.
3. With lockpin in place in bushing sleeve, install bushing sleeve on shaft with lockpin toward upper end.
4. To insure a proper tight stack-up between the 2nd speed locating washer, 2nd speed bushing sleeve, 2nd speed retaining washer and snap-ring, the following procedure should be exercised. Before 2nd speed gear is installed on bushing sleeve, place retaining washer on shaft and hold down securely against bushing sleeve. Holding snap-ring parallel to retaining washer, slip snap-ring into groove in mainshaft. Select a washer that will assure a tight stack-up through assembly. Remove selected washer and install gear over bushing sleeve. Place selected washer in position and install snap-ring in the groove. (Minimum end play for 2nd gear—.006).
5. Place second and third synchronizer on splines of shaft and drop into position.
6. Drop third gear thrust washer and gear (toothed hub downward) on shaft.
7. Drop fourth speed gear locating washer into position over shaft.
8. With lockpin in place in bushing sleeve, install bushing sleeve on shaft with lockpin toward upper end. Before pressing sleeve in place, center sleeve lock pin in spline. Faiure to do this may shear pin and cause bushing seizure.
9. To insure a proper tight stack-up between the 4th speed locating washer, 4th speed bushing sleeve, 4th speed retaining washer and snap-ring, the following procedure should be exercised—Before 4th speed gear is installed on bushing sleeve, place retaining washer on shaft and hold down securely against bushing sleeve. Holding snap-ring parallel to retaining washer slip

snap-ring into groove in mainshaft. Select a washer that will assure a tight stack-up through assembly. Remove selected washer, and install gear over bushing sleeve. Place selected washer in position and install snap-ring. (End play on 4th gear must be a minimum of .006.)

10. Remove assembly from vise and install sliding gears on shaft as follows:
 a. 4th and 5th synchronizer hub with large end toward rear.
 b. 1st and reverse gear with fork slot toward front.

Countershaft Assembly

1. Install woodruff key in each key slot on countershaft except drive gear.
2. Press on 3rd speed gear and then 4th speed gear with long hubs toward rear.
3. Install drive gear spacer and drive gear key.
4. Press on countershaft drive gear with long hub toward rear.
5. Assemble retaining ring into position.

Main Drive Gear and Bearing Assembly

1. Assemble bearing on main drive gear with snap-ring toward pilot end of gear.
2. Install bearing retainer ring.

Mainshaft Rear Bearing Cap

1. Press new oil seal in bearing cap (Lip of seal down).

Clutch Release Bearing and Carrier Assembly

1. Press clutch release bearing on bearing carrier.

Case and Bell Housing Assembly

1. If the countershaft front bearing is to be replaced, the following procedure must be followed
2. Coat outer diameter of pilot bearing with non-hardening sealer.
3. Press pilot bearing in transmission case from clutch housing end of case. Open end of bearing toward rear of case.
4. Press bearing .007 below front face of case.
5. In order to obtain correct location of bell housing on case, it is recommended the following procedure be followed:
 a. Install drive gear, drive gear cap into case.
 b. Secure bell housing on case.
 c. Drive gear bearing cap, drive gear and bearing assembly must be removed from case after bell housing has been assembled in order that countershaft assembly can be installed in case.

Shift Bar Housing Assembly—300 V Series Transmission

1. Install rocker arm on pivot pin.
2. Assemble 1st and reverse shift rail, lug and rocker lug in the following manner:
 a. Starting at left side of cover, push rail through opening in cover and slip 1st and reverse lug on rail. Push rail through two support boss and holding rocker lug in position continue pushing rail through rocker lug.
 b. Install lockscrews in lugs and wire securely.
 c. Shift into neutral position.
3. Install 4th and 5th shift rail and fork in following manner:
 a. Push rail through forward opening of cover.
 b. Install two (2) interlock balls between 1st and reverse, and 4th and 5th rails.
 c. Place mesh lock spring and ball in position in well of forward rail support.
 d. Using suitable tool, compress

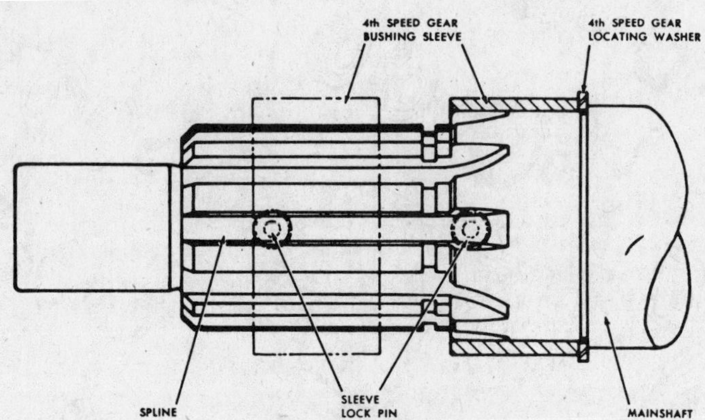

Proper installation of sleeve lock pins
(© Clark Equipment Co.)

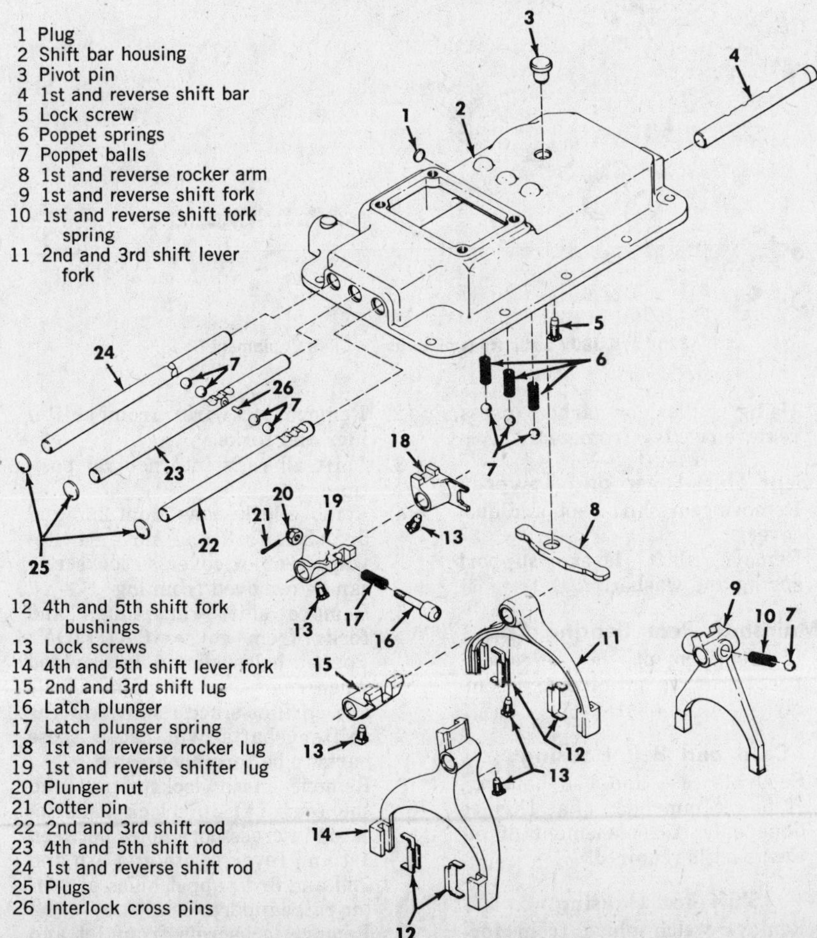

Shift bar housing components (© Clark Equipment Co.)

spring and ball in such manner as to pass between guide fingers of 1st and reverse rocker lug if fingers are aligned.

e. Slide 4th and 5th shift fork on rail with offset for lock screw toward rear of cover.

f. Install lockscrew in fork and wire securely.

g. Shift into neutral position.

4. Install 2nd and 3rd shift rail and fork in the following manner:

a. Push rail through forward opening in cover.

b. Install two (2) interlock balls between 2d and 3rd and 4th and 5th poppet holes of forward rail support.

c. Place mesh lock spring and ball in position in well of rail support.

d. Using suitable tool, compress spring and ball in such manner as to allow rail to pass through support.

e. Slide 2nd and 3rd shift fork onto rail with offset for lockscrew toward repairman.

f. Install lockscrew in fork and wire securely.

g. Shift into neutral position.

5. Install welch plugs in forward openings.

6. Assemble 1st and reverse shift fork and rail in the following manner:

a. Install mesh lock spring and ball in well of 1st and reverse shift fork.

b. Using suitable tool, compress ball and spring so that rail may pass through fork.

c. Push rail through rear opening of cover.

d. Holding fork in position on rocker arm and with offset to rear of cover, push rail through fork and into rail support.

e. Install lockscrew in rail support and rail, then wire securely.

7. Check assembly of cover by shifting in and out of speeds. Then shift into 5th speed and attempt to shift into 1st, reverse, 2nd or 3rd at the same time. This provides a check on the proper assembly of interlock balls and pin. Cover should not shift into more than one speed at a time.

8. Return rail to neutral position.

Torque Chart

Nomenclature	*Torque Limits*	*Nomenclature*	*Torque Limits*
Bolt-Reverse Lockout Plunger Retainer	11/16—16 90-100	Bolt-Parking Brake to Trans. Bearing Retainer	1/2—20C 45-55 5/8—18 180-220 7/16—20 50-70
Bolt-Clutch Housing to Engine Block	7/16—14 24-32 33-45	Nut-Bellcrank to Trans.	9/16—18 70-90 3/8—16C 20-25
Bolt-Output Shaft Bearing Retainer to Trans. Case	3/8—16 20-25 7/16—14 30-38 1/2—13 50-62 5/8—11 96-120	Bolt-Countershaft & Reverse Idler Shaft Retainer	1/2—13 60-70 5/16—18 25-30 3/8 16 25-37 3/8—16 18-25 7/16—14 40-45 1/2—13 80-85
Bolt-Gear Shift Lever Tower to Gearshift Housing	3/8—16 20 25 5/16—18 11-16 7/16—14 30-45	Nut-Countershaft Bearing Lock (5-Speed Extra Heavy Duty & 5-Speed Exclusive)	1 1/4—18 350-450
Nut-Drum Parking Brake to Companion Flange	3/8—24 37-50 7/16—20 40-55 1/2—20 74-86	Bolt-Gear Shaft Housing Trans. Case	5/16—18 20-25 3/8—16 35-40
Bolt—Lever Assy. to Trans.	3/8—16 20-25	Bolt-Clutch Housing to Trans. Case	7/16—14 30-38 5/8—11 96-120 9/16—12 70-90 5/8—18C 115-140 9/16—18C 81-102
Nut-Handbrake Anchor Bar to Trans. Case (except 5-Speed Extra-Heavy Duty)	9/16—18 100-110	Bolt—Gear Shift Housing Trans. Case	7/16—14 45-50
Nut Handbrake Anchor Bar to Trans. Case (5-Speed Extra-Heavy Duty only)	9/16—18 120-130	Nut-Countershaft Bearing Lock (5-Speed Exclusive Heavy Duty)	1 1/2—18 350-450
Nut-U-Joint Flange to Trans. Output Shaft	1.00—20 90-125 1 1/4—18 225-275 1 1/2—18 275-350	Bolt-Countershaft Front Bearing Retainer	5/16—18 25-30 3/8—16 25-35 7/16—14 50-55
Nut-Input Shaft Yoke to Aux. Trans.	1 1/4—18 275-350		
Bolt-Countershaft Rear Bearing Retainer	5/16—18 25-30 3/8—16 35-40 7/16—14 45-55 1/2—13 60-70		
Jam Nut—Adjusting Height Main Trans.	150-200		

Reassembly of Transmission

1. Install countershaft into case.

2. Install countershaft rear bearing with snap-ring onto shaft with snap-ring toward rear.

3. Insert two roller bearings separated by spacer into hub of reverse idler gear and lower into position in case. The gear with chamfered teeth should be toward rear of case. Insert idler thrust washers (2) on idler boss. (NOTE: Hold in place with grease while assembling.)

4. Insert reverse idler shaft through hole in rear of case, through reverse gear and into forward support boss. Shaft should be driven in, until forward face of slot in shaft is flush with rear face of case and slot lined up to permit installation of locking plate.

5. Install locking plate in position in end of shaft and secure with capscrew and lockwasher.

6. Install mainshaft assembly in transmission case.

7. Assemble mainshaft rear bearing over end of mainshaft with snap-ring in outer race facing toward the rear.

8. Install pilot bearing on mainshaft—300V only. 320 V and 380 V Series pilot bearing installation:

a. A new pilot bearing (if used) comes from the factory with a plastic sleeve. Stand drive gear on end. Set bearing and sleeve over bearing pocket in drive gear. Slide bearing rollers and cage from plastic sleeve into bearing pocker. NOTE: When new bearing is used, always install new bearing race on mainshaft.

b. If old pilot bearing is used, set rollers in bearing cage and hold in place with a rubber band. Slide bearing rollers and cage from rubber band into bearing pocket. Use caution when installing drive gear and pilot bearing on pilot end of mainshaft, and into transmission clutch housing.

9. Install main drive gear and bearing assembly into front case opening so that main gear engages and meshes with countershaft gear.
10. Install main drive gear bearing cap and gasket. CAUTION: Be sure oil return hole in cap is lined up with oil return hole in case. This passage must be open and clear.
11. Clutch throwout bearing return spring clip should be installed under head of screw in assembly of bearing cap.
12. Lock gears into two speeds at one time and install countershaft rear bearing retaining nut, drawing up tight and stake in position with punch.
13. Install countershaft rear bearing cap and gasket.
14. Install speedometer drive gear spacer and speedometer drive gear on mainshaft.
15. Install mainshaft rear bearing cap assembly and gasket.
16. Install brake drum and companion flange assembly.
17. Lock transmission in two speeds at same time and assemble companion flange nut and cotter pin.
18. Assemble shift bar housing and gasket to case, making sure forks engage gears.
19. Assemble gasket, gear shift lever and tower assembly to bar housing.

Clark 325 V & 327 V 5 Speed

Description

The Clark 325V and 327V transmissions are 5 speed synchromesh units with direct drive in fifth. 3rd, 4th, and 5th speed gears are of a helical design.

Gear Ratios—All Ratios Are (to 1)

Transmission Model	*325V*	*327V*
1st	7.01	6.27
2nd	3.97	3.55
3rd	2.34	1.89
4th	1.42	1.18
5th	1.00	1.00
Reverse	5.71	5.11

Disassembly of Transmission

Special care should be taken when overhauling the transmission. Unless this care is exercised, considerable damage may be done to the various parts of the transmission.

Overhaul should be made in a clean area, free from dirt and foreign particles. Before disassembling the transmission, the exterior of the case should be thoroughly cleaned to prevent the possibility of any dirt entering the internal mechanism.

IMPORTANT—On transmissions having a conventional gearshift lever, reinstall the control tower before cleaning the exterior of the transmission.

During the overhaul procedures, all parts should be thoroughly cleaned in cleaning solvent and then air dried. The use of wiping cloths or rags to dry parts should be avoided as they might leave a deposit of lint on the parts and cause future trouble. All parts not being worked on should be covered with clean paper.

When assembling the transmission or subassemblies during overhaul procedures, lubricate each moving part before that part is installed. Use new snap-rings, gaskets, and oil seals when assembling the transmission. Drain lubricant from transmission case if this was not done when the transmission was removed from vehicle. Old lubricants should be saved and examined for metal filings or other foreign particles as an aid in determining the cause of failure.

The transmission should be overhauled in the sequence outlined unless only one specific area is to be worked on.

Removal of Mainshaft Assembly

NOTE: See illustration of components

1. Remove companion flange nut from the rear end of mainshaft.
2. Remove the four bolts and lock washers holding mainshaft rear bearing cap. Remove the cap and gasket.
3. Remove the four bolt and lock washer assemblies holding countershaft rear bearing cap and remove the cap.
4. At the front end of transmission case, remove the clutch release bearing and support from extension of the drive gear bearing cap.
5. Remove the four bolts and lock washers attaching main drive gear bearing cap to case. Remove cap and its gasket.
6. Remove the main drive gear bearing and drive gear assembly from front of case being careful not to drop mainshaft bearing into bottom of case when pulling main drive gear assembly out.
   NOTE: Dropping bearings could damage them.

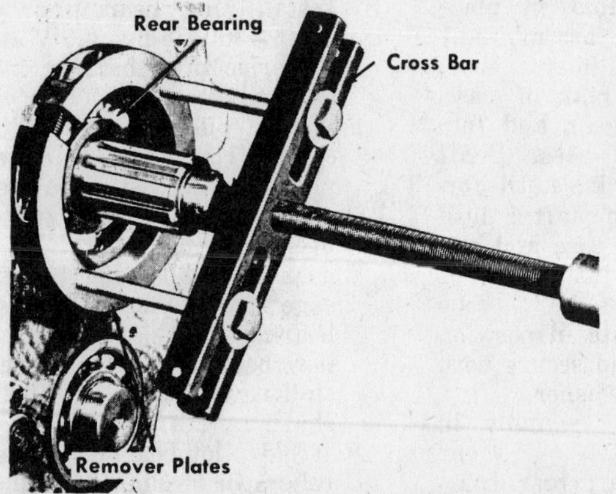

Removing mainshaft rear bearing
(© Clark Equipment Co.)

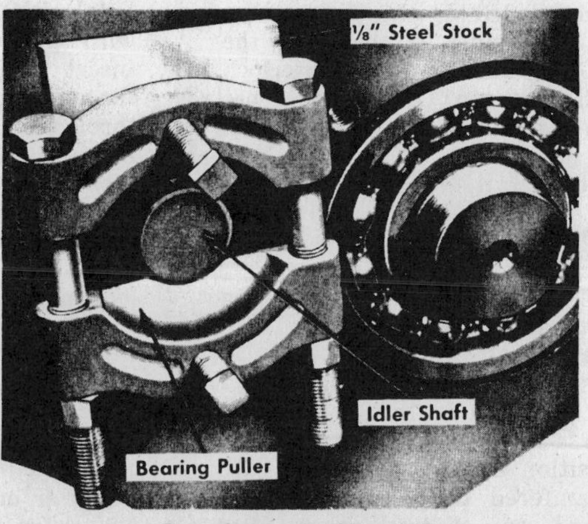

Removing reverse idler shaft
(© Clark Equipment Co.)

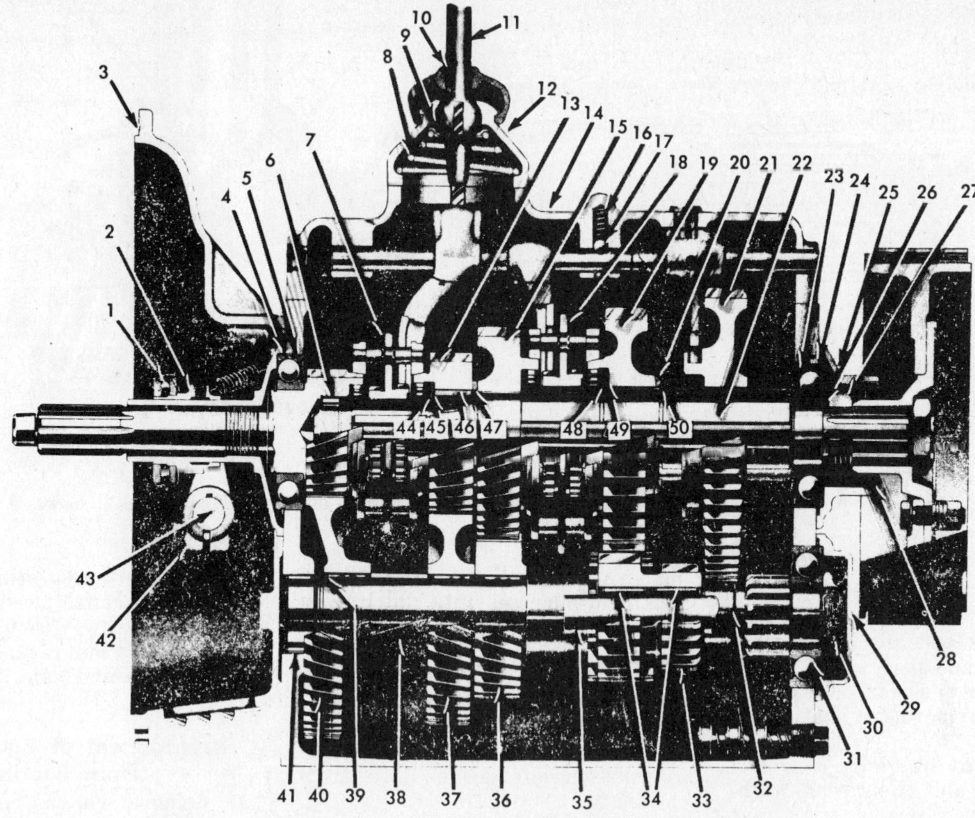

Clark 5-speed transmission—models 325V and 327V (© Clark Equipment Co.)

1 Clutch release bearing
2 Release bearing support
3 Clutch housing
4 Drive gear bearing retainer ring
5 Drive gear bearing
6 Mainshaft pilot bearing
7 4th and 5th synchronizer assembly
8 Gearshift lever spring
9 Spring seat washer
10 Dust cover
11 Gearshift lever
12 Control tower
13 Mainshaft 4th speed gear
14 Shift bar housing
15 Mainshaft 3rd speed gear
16 Poppet spring
17 Poppet ball
18 2nd and 3rd synchronizer assembly
19 Mainshaft 2nd speed gear
20 2nd gear locating washer
21 Mainshaft 1st and Reverse Gear
22 Mainshaft
23 Mainshaft rear bearing
24 Mainshaft rear bearing snap ring
25 Mainshaft rear bearing cap
26 Speedometer drive gear spacer
27 Speedometer drive gear
28 Rear bearing cap oil seal
29 Countershaft rear bearing cap
30 Countershaft rear bearing retainer nut
31 Countershaft rear bearing
32 Countershaft
33 Reverse idler gear
34 Reverse idler gear bearings
35 Reverse idler shaft
36 Countershaft 3rd speed gear
37 Countershaft 4th speed gear
38 Countershaft drive gear spacer
39 Snap ring
40 Countershaft drive gear
41 Countershaft front bearing
42 Clutch release yoke
43 Release yoke cross shaft
44 Snap ring
45 4th speed gear retainer washer
46 4th speed gear bushing sleeve
47 4th speed gear locating washer
48 Snap ring
49 2nd speed gear retainer washer
50 2nd speed gear snap ring

7. Remove the speedometer drive gear and spacer.
8. Push on front end of mainshaft assembly and force this entire assembly to the rear so that the rear mainshaft bearing completely clears rear facing of case. Remove snap-ring and use puller to remove the bearing from shaft.
9. Tilt the front end of mainshaft assembly upward in order to clear front end of transmission case. Lift assembly out of case.

Disassembly of Mainshaft Assembly

NOTE: See illustration of components.

1. Remove the 1st and reverse sliding gear from mainshaft.
2. Remove 4th and 5th synchronizer assembly from other end of shaft.
3. Place the entire remaining mainshaft assembly in soft metal (copper or bronze) vise (so shaft splines will not be damaged) with front end of shaft assembly pointing upward.
4. Use snap-ring picks to remove snap-ring from its position on shaft. Remove washer and 4th speed gear.
5. Remove mainshaft assembly from vise and, with the front end pointed down, lightly pound the assembly against a block of wood. This will cause weight of 3rd speed gear to force 4th speed gear bushing sleeve out of position on shaft. Remove bushing and locating washer from shaft, When bushing comes off shaft, locating pin should fall free.
6. Reposition mainshaft assembly in vise with front end again pointing upward. Remove 3rd gear, thrust washer, and 2nd and 3rd synchronizer assembly.
7. Remove snap-ring, retaining washer, and 2nd speed gear from shaft. Remove locating washer and snap-ring.

Disassembly of Main Drive Gear Assembly

1. Remove mainshaft pilot bearing from pocket in main drive gear.
2. Place main drive gear assembly into a soft metal vise (copper or bronze) so front end of assembly is pointing upward.
3. Remove drive gear bearing ring.
4. Use bearing remover plates with arbor press to force the gear

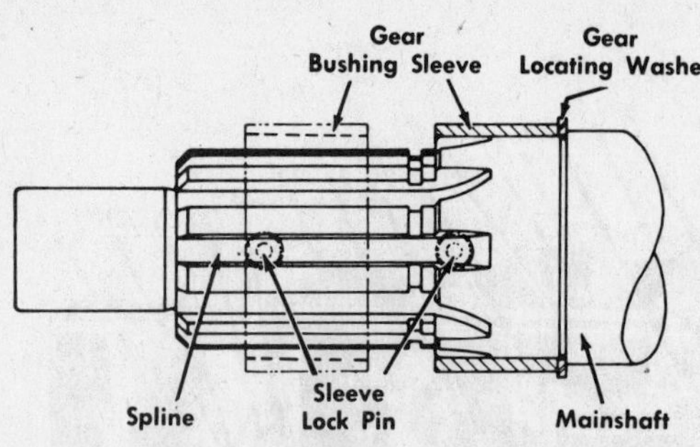

Proper installation of sleeve lock
(© Clark Equipment Co.)

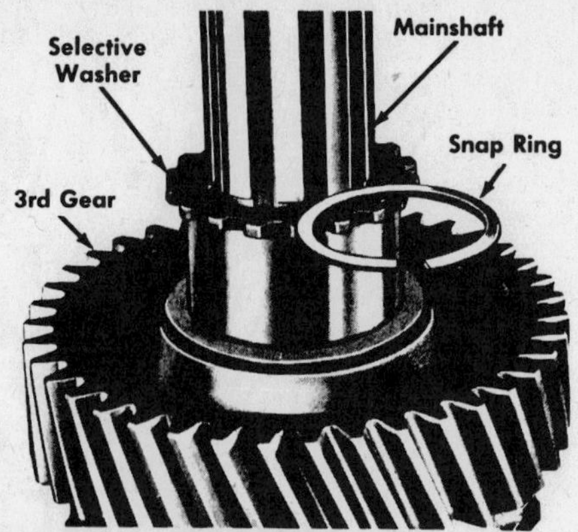

Selection of 4th speed gear retainer washer
(© Clark Equipment Co.)

bearing away from main drive gear.

Removal of Reverse Idler Gear Components

1. Remove the reverse idler gear shaft lock bolt and lock washer assembly and shaft lock.
2. Use puller in slot in reverse gear shaft to remove the shaft from the case.
3. Lift the reverse idler gear two bearings, and two thrust washers as an assembly from case and disassemble this subassembly into individual parts.

Removal of Countershaft Assembly

NOTE: See illustration of components

1. Push on front of countershaft to force entire assembly to the rear. This should bring countershaft rear bearing away far enough from rear facing of case so snap-ring can be removed from the bearing's outer race.
2. Use puller to remove the bearing.
3. Tilt front end of countershaft assembly upward, and lift it out of case.

NOTE: Front countershaft bearing unit cannot be removed for replacement purposes until clutch housing has been removed.

Disassembly of Countershaft

1. Remove snap-ring from its position on countershaft.
2. Use an arbor press and force countershaft drive gear from shaft.
3. Remove Woodruff key.
4. Remove countershaft drive gear spacer.
5. Use an arbor press and remove countershaft 4th speed gear and countershaft 3rd speed gear.
6. Remove the two remaining Woodruff keys.

Replacement of Mainshaft Rear Bearing Cap Oil Seal

1. If inspection shows that replacement is necessary, press or drive rear bearing cap oil seal assembly out of rear bearing cap.
2. Drive or press new oil seal into bore of bearing cap. Lip of oil seal goes in toward transmission case.

Replacement of Clutch Housing

1. Remove clutch housing.
2. Install new clutch housing on transmission case. Install lockwashers and nuts. Tighten nuts firmly.

Replacement of Countershaft Front Bearing

1. Remove clutch housing from case.
2. Using a crowfoot pry bar remove bearing from lower casebore.
3. When installing a new bearing, apply pressure only to outer race of bearing.

Replacement of Remote Control Oil Seal

1. Remove oil seal from remote control housing.
2. Press or drive new oil seal into bore of housing.

NOTE: Coat outer diameter of oil seal with a light coat of sealing cement prior to installation.

Removing countershaft rear bearing
(© Clark Equipment Co.)

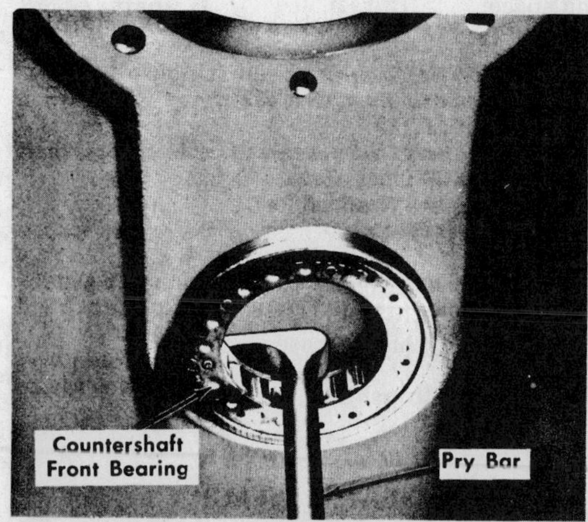

Removing countershaft front bearing
(© Clark Equipment Co.)

Assembly of Components

Assembly of Main Drive Gear

NOTE: See illustration of components

1. Lubricate main drive gear bearing and shaft. Press fit bearing onto shoulder of shaft; making sure that snap-ring on outer race of bearing unit is facing toward front end of main drive gear.
2. Place snap-ring into position on shaft.
3. Install pilot bearing to main drive gear in the following manner:
   a. If a new pilot bearing is used it comes from the factory with a plastic sleeve. Stand drive gear on end. Set bearing and sleeve over bearing pocket in drive gear. Slide bearing rollers and cage from plastic sleeve into bearing pocket.
   b. If old pilot bearing is used, set rollers in bearing cage and hold in place with a rubber band. Slide bearing rollers and cage from rubber band into bearing pocket.

Assembly of Countershaft

1. Install Woodruff keys in 3rd and 4th gear slots in countershaft.
2. Lubricate the countershaft and bore of each gear before installing gears on countershaft.
3. Press 3rd speed gear onto countershaft with the long hub facing the rear.
4. Install 4th speed gear in the same way with the long hub of gear to the rear.
5. Install drive gear spacer and drive gear key.
6. Press countershaft drive gear on countershaft with long hub toward rear. Install gear in same way used to install other gears.
7. Install snap-ring on countershaft making sure it is well seated and locked in groove.

1 Plug
2 Shift bar housing
3 Pivot pin
4 1st and reverse shift bar
5 Lock screw
6 Poppet springs
7 Poppet balls
8 1st and reverse rocker arm
9 1st and reverse shift fork
10 1st and reverse shift fork spring
11 2nd and 3rd shift lever fork
12 4th and 5th shift fork bushings
13 Lock screws
14 4th and 5th shift lever fork
15 2nd and 3rd shift lug
16 Latch plunger
17 Latch plunger spring
18 1st and Reverse rocker lug
19 1st and Reverse shifter lug
20 Plunger nut
21 Cotter pin
22 2nd and 3rd shift rod
23 4th and 5th shift rod
24 1st and reverse shift rod
25 Plugs
26 Interlock cross pins

Exploded view of shift bar housing (© Clark Equipment Co.)

Assembly of Mainshaft

NOTE: See illustration of components

1. Clamp the mainshaft in a soft jawed (copper or bronze) vise with shaft front end pointed upward.
2. Position 2nd speed gear snap-ring and retaining washer on shaft.
3. Before positioning 2nd speed gear onto shaft, place the retaining washer on shaft against 2nd speed gear.
4. Slip snap-ring into its proper groove on shaft. Check mainshaft components for snug fit.
5. With the large end of its hub toward the rear, place 2nd and 3rd synchronizer assembly over shaft splines and fit synchronizer into proper position.
6. Install 3rd speed gear and bushing sleeve on mainshaft with clutching hub facing rear of transmission.
7. Install the 4th gear locating washer to shaft. NOTE: When installing the 4th speed gear bushing sleeve and locking pin to the mainshaft, make sure that the pin is centered on a spline of the shaft before completely pressing bushing sleeve and pin assembly into place (also make sure pin is toward pilot or front end of shaft). It might be necessary to use a suitable sleeve and hammer to properly fit sleeve and pin assembly into place on shaft.
8. There are three thickness sizes of retaining washer from which to chose. Choose the thickest washer possible to assure the tightest fit of components.
9. Once a washer has been chosen that assures the tightest stacking fit on the shaft, remove the chosen washer and position 4th speed gear in place over bushing sleeve on shaft. Then again place selected washer into position, and secure assembly with snap-ring in proper groove on shaft. NOTE: If end play of 4th speed gear exceeds 0-.006 inch, the selected retainer washer is not thick enough, and a thicker one should be used.
10. Once 4th speed gear end play has been made, secure with snap-ring.

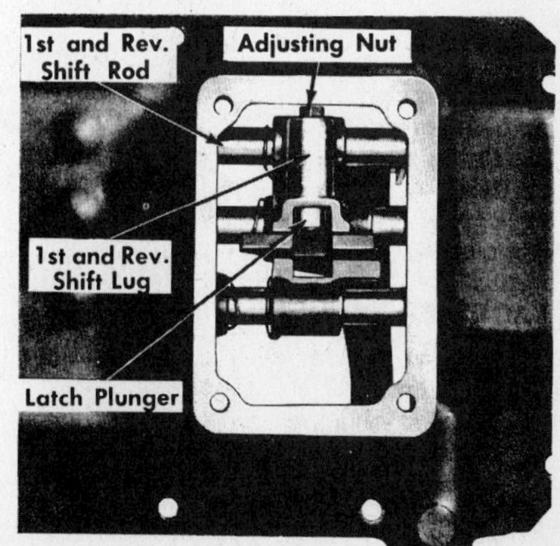

1st, and reverse shift lug and latch plunger (© Clark Equipment Co.)

11. Remove the entire mainshaft assembly from the vise, and fit the 4th and 5th speed synchronizer unit into place on the shaft making sure large hub end of synchronizer is facing rearward.
12. Place the 1st and reverse gear with its fork slot toward the front onto the other end of the mainshaft. This copletes the assembly of the mainshaft.

Assembly of Transmission

Installation of Countershaft

1. Make certain that the countershaft front bearing is installed in proper transmission case bore before installing countershaft assembly.
2. Position countershaft front bearing spacer on forward end of countershaft.
3. Manipulate countershaft assembly into transmission case.
4. Using suitable installer tool, install countershaft rear bearing. Be sure snap-ring is in position in groove of outer race of bearing. Press bearing into place on countershaft with snap-ring toward rear. Press bearing into transmission case until snap-ring contacts the case.
5. Hand-tighten countershaft rear bearing retainer nut.

Installation of Reverse Idler Gear Components

1. Insert one reverse idler gear bearing in reverse idler gear then install bearing spacer and the second bearing in bore of idler gear.
2. Install the reverse idler gear assembly in transmission case with chamfered teeth toward rear of case.
3. Insert reverse idler shaft through opening in rear of transmission case, into reverse idler gear and into forward support boss. Make sure groove for the retainer lock in rear of shaft. shaft is at bottom of shaft. Drive shaft in until inner edge of groove is flush with rear transmission case facing. Install retainer lock with bolt and lock washer and tighten securely.

Installation of Mainshaft

1. Install mainshaft assembly in case. Lower front end in line with pilot bearing opening. Carefully move mainshaft assembly forward into position.
2. Position mainshaft rear bearing over end of mainshaft with snap-ring in outer race of bearing facing the rear.
3. Drive mainshaft rear bearing on mainshaft and into transmission case until snap-ring on bearing contacts case.
4. Position main drive gear and bearing assembly into front of case so that drive gear engages and meshes with countershaft drive gear and snap-ring on bearing contacts transmission case. It may be necessary to use a suitable sleeve and hammer to drive gear and bearing into position.
5. Install main drive gear bearing cap and gasket on case and tighten firmly. IMPORTANT: Oil return hole in bearing cap must line up with oil hole in transmission cas
6. Install clutch throw-out bearing return spring clip under head of bolt when installing bearing cap.

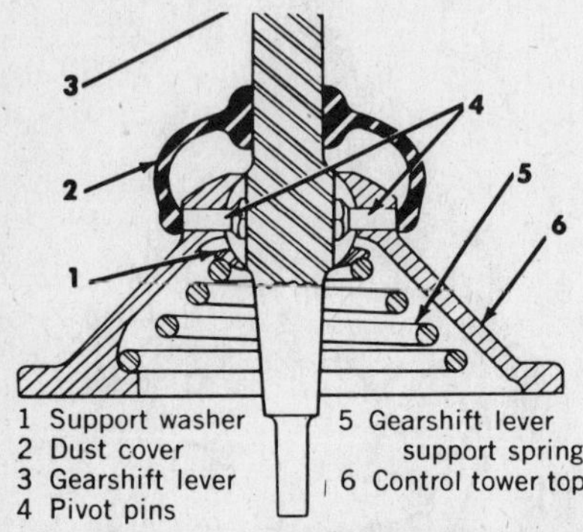

Control tower and gearshift lever assembly
(© Clark Equipment Co.)

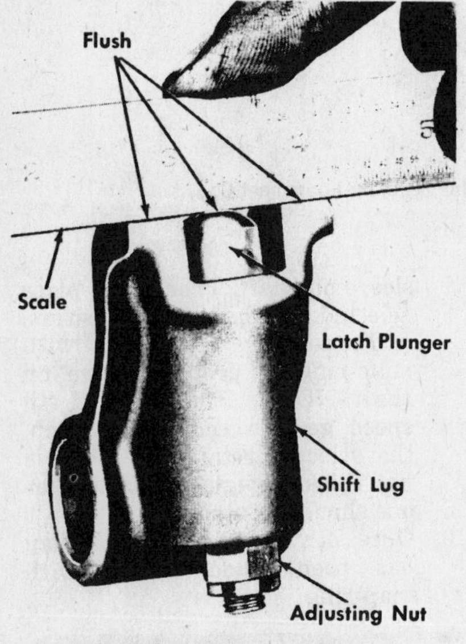

Adjusting latch plunger
(© Clark Equipment Co.)

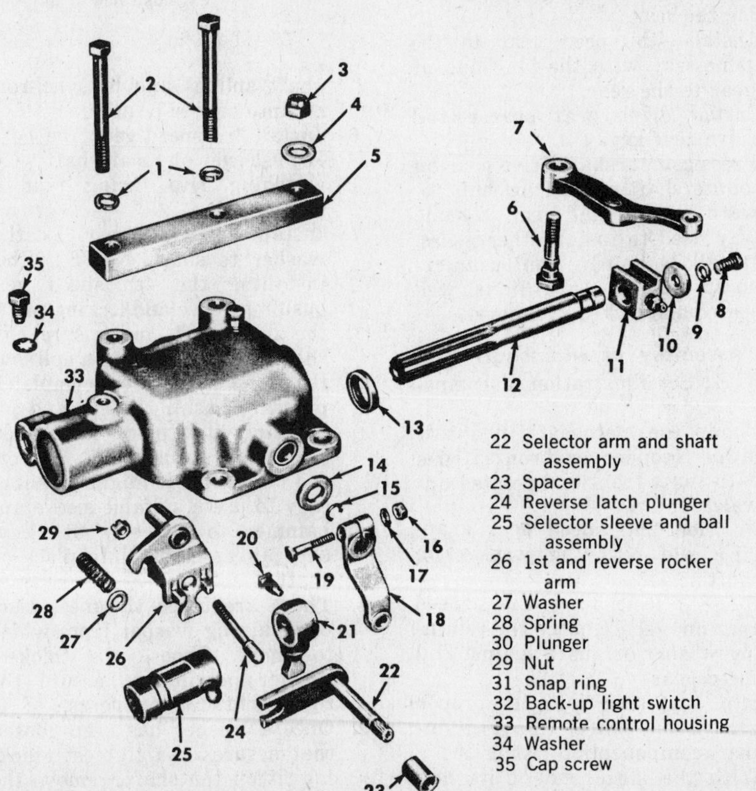

1 Washers
2 Bolts
3 Nut
4 Washer
5 Shift lever mounting bracket
6 Shift lever pivot bolt
7 Shift lever assembly
8 Bolt
9 Washer
10 Collar washer
11 Shifter shaft collar
12 Shifter shaft
13 Oil seal
14 Washer
15 Snap ring
16 Nut
17 Washer
18 Selector Lever
19 Bolt
20 Shift finger screws
21 Shift finger
22 Selector arm and shaft assembly
23 Spacer
24 Reverse latch plunger
25 Selector sleeve and ball assembly
26 1st and reverse rocker arm
27 Washer
28 Spring
30 Plunger
29 Nut
31 Snap ring
32 Back-up light switch
33 Remote control housing
34 Washer
35 Cap screw

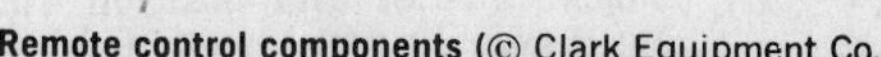

Remote control components (© Clark Equipment Co.)

7. Lock transmission gears into two speeds at the same time to lock up the transmission; then tighten countershaft rear bearing retaining nut. After nut is tightened, stake nut in position with punch and hammer.
8. Install countershaft rear bearing cap and new gasket. Tighten bolts firmly.
9. Install speedometer drive gear spacer and drive gear (if used) on mainshaft.
10. Install mainshaft rear bearing cap and new gasket. Tighten bolts firmly.
11. Install parking brake drum (if used) and companion flange on rear end of mainshaft.
12. With transmission still locked in two gears, install companion flange nut. Tighten nut to 250 foot-pounds torque and insert a new cotter pin.

Installation of Shift Bar Housing

1. With transmission in "Neutral," install shift bar housing and new gasket on transmission case. Be sure shift forks engage gear slots.
2. Install parking brake parts (if used).

Assembly of Control Tower Unit

NOTE: See illustration of control tower. On transmissions having conventional gearshift lever, complete the following procedures:

1. Install gearshift lever pivot pins in control tower, then insert gearshift lever through bottom of tower. Position shift lever so notch in ball position engages pivot pin heads.
2. Install spring seat washer (concave side against ball portion of lever). Install gearshift lever support spring against spring seat washer and control tower.
3. Place dust cover on gearshift lever.
4. Install gearshift lever knob.

Assembly of Remote Control Unit

NOTE: See illustration of components

1. Position selector sleeve and ball assembly in remote control housing, then install washer and cap screw. Tighten screw firmly.
2. Position selector arm and shaft assembly and spacer in housing, then install washer and snapring.
3. Assemble reverse latch plunger, washer, spring, and nut to 1st and reverse rocker arm.
4. Adjust reverse latch plunger so rounded end is flush or slightly below the two flat ends of the 1st and reverse rocker arm. Lock adjusting nut in proper position with a cotter pin.
5. Position shift finger in housing; then install shifter shaft in housing, aligning splines of shifter shaft with splines of selector sleeve and ball assembly and hole in shifter shaft with hole in shift finger.
6. Install shift finger screw, and torque to 25 foot-pounds and secure with lock wire.
7. Install attaching parts that hold shifter shaft collar to shifter shaft.
8. Install attaching parts that hold shift lever assembly to shift lever mounting bracket. Tighten nut to 25-31 foot-pounds torque.
9. Install attaching parts that hold shift lever mounting bracket to housing. Be sure shift lever assembly is properly seated in slot of shifter shaft collar.
10. Position selector lever on selector arm and shaft assembly, so that the selector lever is perpendicular to the gasket side of the housing. Tighten nut firmly.

Torque Wrench Specifications

Location	*Foot-Pounds*
Selector finger to shifter shaft screw	25
Companion flange or Yoke nut	400-450

Dodge A-230 3 Speed

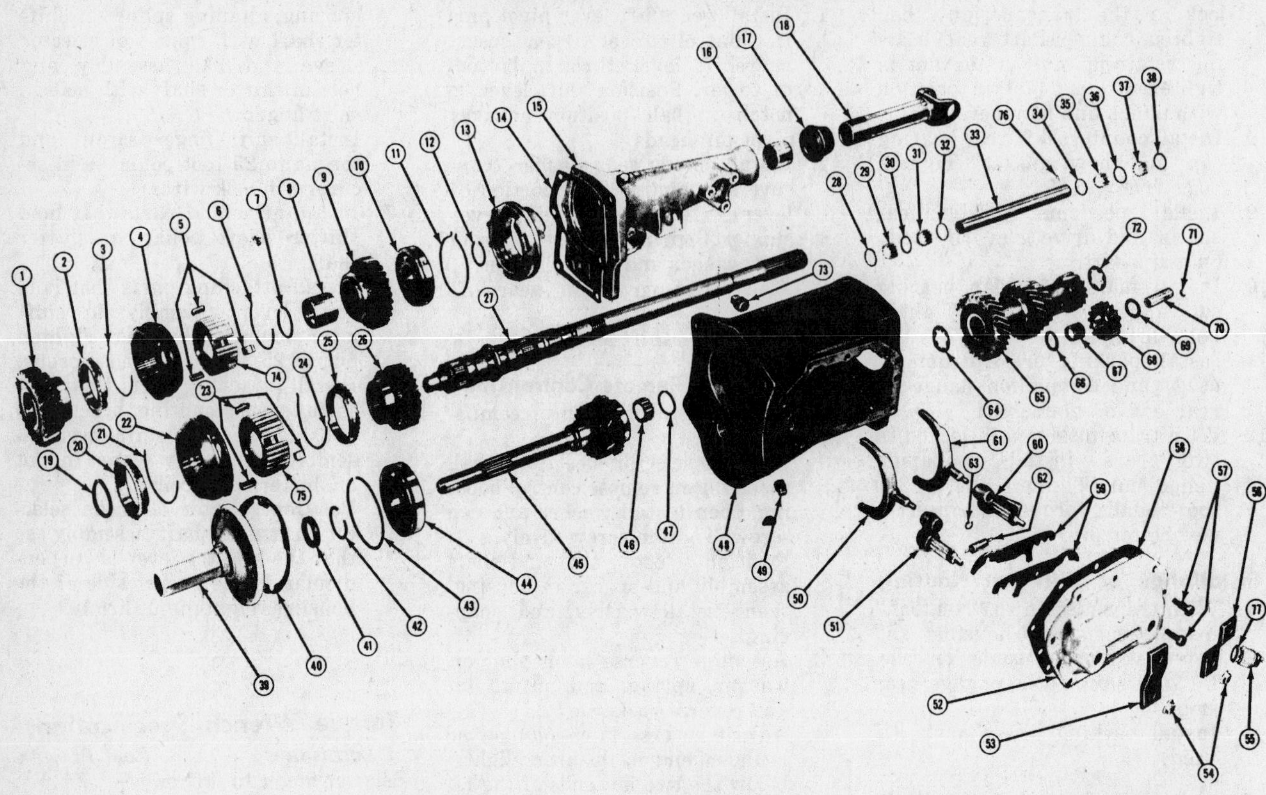

1 Gear first
2 Ring
3 Spring
4 Sleeve
5 Struts (3)
6 Spring
7 Snap ring
8 Bushing
9 Gear, reverse
10 Bearing
11 Snap ring
12 Snap ring
13 Retainer
14 Gasket
15 Extension
16 Bushing
17 Seal
18 Yoke
19 Snap ring
20 ring
21 Spring
22 Sleeve
23 Struts (3)
24 Spring
25 Ring
26 Gear, second
27 Shaft, output
28 Washer
29 Roller
30 Washer
31 Roller
32 Washer
33 Countershaft
34 Washer
35 Roller
36 Washer
37 Roller
38 Washer
39 Retainer
40 Gasket
41 Seal
42 Snap ring
43 Snap Ring
44 Bearing
45 Pinion, drive
46 Roller
47 Snap ring
48 Case
49 Plug, Drain
50 Fork
51 Lever
52 Housing
53 Lever
54 Nut, locking
55 Switch
56 Lever
57 Bolt
58 Gasket
59 Lever, interlock
60 Lever
61 Fork
62 Spring
63 Snap ring
64 Washer
65 Gear, countershaft
66 Washer
67 Roller
68 Gear, idler
69 Washer
70 Shaft
71 Key
72 Washer
73 Plug, filler
74 Gear, Clutch
75 Gear, clutch
76 Key
77 Gasket

A-230 3 speed transmission (© Chrysler Corp.)

Description

The Dodge A-230 is a three-speed transmission equipped with two synchonizer units to assist in the engagement of all forward gears. Lubricant capacity is 5 pints.

Disassembly of Transmission

Shift Housing and Mechanism

1. Shift to second gear.
2. Remove side cover. If shaft O-ring seals need replacement:
   a. Pull shift-forks out of shafts.
   b. Remove nuts and operating levers from shafts.
   c. Deburr shafts. Remove shafts.

Drive Pinion Retainer and Extension Housing

1. Remove pinion bearing retainer from front of transmission case. Pry off retainer oil seal. For clearance:
   a. With a brass drift, tap drive pinion as far forward as possible. Rotate cut away part of second gear next to countershaft gear. Shift second-third synchronizer sleeve forward.
   b. Remove speedometer pinion adapter retainer. Work adapter and pinion out of extension housing.
   c. Unbolt extension housing. Break housing loose with plastic hammer and carefully remove.

Idler Gear and Mainshaft

1. Insert dummy shaft in case to push reverse idler shaft and key out of case.
2. Remove dummy shaft and idler rollers.
3. Remove both tanged idler gear thrust washers.
4. Remove mainshaft assembly through rear of case.

Countershaft Gear and Drive Pinion

1. Using a mallet and dummy shaft, tap the countershaft rearward enough to remove key. Drive countershaft out of case, being careful not to drop the washers.
2. Lower countershaft gear to bottom of case.

3. Remove snap-ring from pinion bearing outer race (outside front of case).
4. Drive pinion shaft into case with plastic hammer. Remove assembly through rear of case.
5. If bearing is to be replaced, remove snap-ring and press off bearing.
6. Lift counter shaft gear and dummy shaft out through rear of case.

Mainshaft

1. Remove snap-ring from front end of mainshaft along with second gear stop ring and second gear.
2. Spread snap-ring in mainshaft bearing retainer. Slide retainer back off the bearing race.
3. Remove snap-ring at rear of mainshaft. Support front side of reverse gear. Press bearing off mainshaft.
4. Remove from press. Remove mainshaft bearing and reverse gear from shaft.
5. Remove snap-ring and first-reverse synchronizer assembly from shaft. Remove stop ring and first gear rearward.

Cleaning and Inspection

See "Cleaning and Inspection" instructions at front of transmission section.

Assembly of Transmission

Countershaft Gear

1. Slide dummy shaft into countershaft gear.
2. Slide one roller thrust washer over dummy shaft and into gear, followed by 22 greased rollers.
3. Repeat Step 2, adding one roller thrust washer on end.
4. Repeat steps 2 and 3 at other end of countershaft gear. There is a total of 88 rollers and 6 thrust washers.
5. Place greased front thrust washer on dummy shaft against gear with tangs forward.
6. Grease rear thrust washer and stick it in place in the case, with tangs rearward. Place countershaft gear assembly in bottom of transmission case until drive pinion is installed.

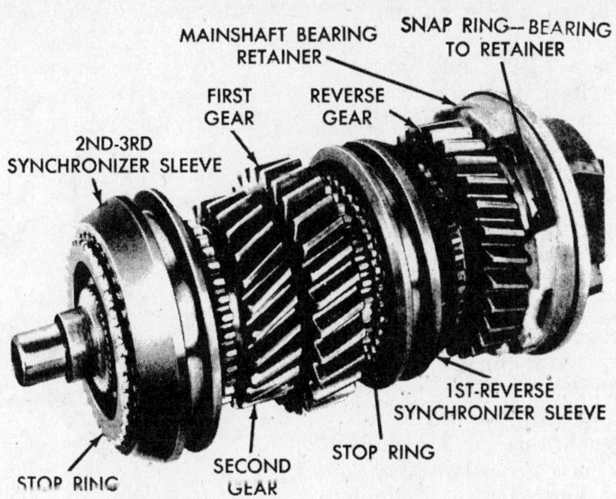

Mainshaft assembly (© Chrysler Corp.)

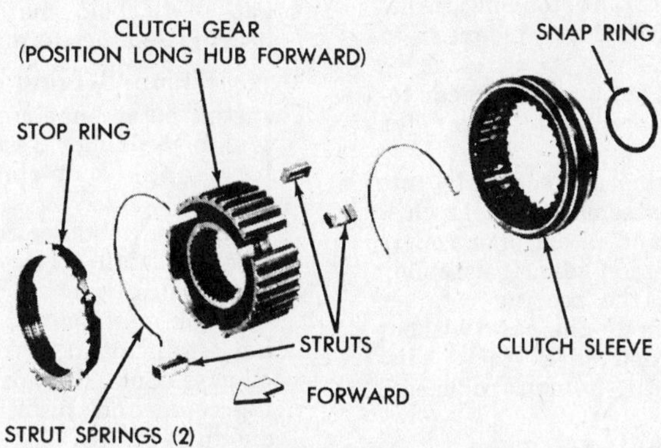

1st-reverse synchronizer (© Chrysler Corp.)

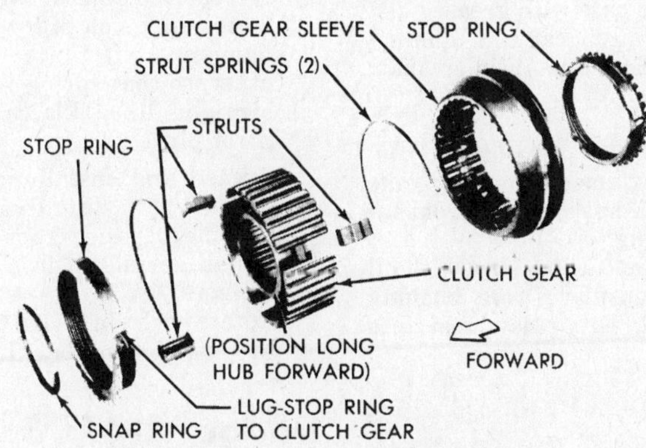

2nd-3rd synchronizer (© Chrysler Corp.)

Pinion Gear

1. Press new bearing on pinion shaft with snap-ring groove forward. Install new snap-ring.
2. Install 15 rollers and retaining ring in drive pinion gear.
3. Install drive pinion and bearing assembly into case.
4. Position countershaft gear assembly by positioning it and thrust washers so countershaft can be tapped into position. Be careful to keep the countershaft against the dummy shaft to keep parts from falling between them. Install key in countershaft.
5. Tap drive pinion forward for clearance.

Mainshaft

1. Place a stop ring flat on the bench. Place a clutch gear and a sleeve on top. Drop the struts in their slots and insert a strut spring with the tang inside on strut. Turn the assembly over and install second strut spring, tang in a different strut.
2. Slide first gear and stop ring over rear of mainshaft and against thrust flange between assembly over rear of mainshaft, first and second gears on shaft.
3. Slide first-reverse synchronizer indexing hub slots to first gear stop ring lugs.

4. Install first-reverse synchronizer clutch gear snap-ring on mainshaft.
5. Slide reverse gear and mainshaft bearing in place. Press bearing on shaft, supporting inner race of bearing. Be sure snap-ring groove on outer race is forward.
6. Install bearing retaining snap-ring on mainshaft. Slide snap-ring over the bearing and seat it in groove.
7. Place second gear over front of mainshaft with thrust surface against flange.
8. Install stop ring and second-third synchronizer assembly against second gear. Install second-third synchronizer clutch gear snap-ring on shaft.
9. Move second-third synchronizer sleeve forward as far as possible. Install front stop ring inside sleeve with lugs indexed to struts.
10. Rotate cut out on second gear toward countershaft gear for clearance.
11. Insert mainshaft assembly into case. Tilt assembly to clear cluster gears and insert pilot rollers in drive pinion gear. If assembly is correct, the bearing retainer will bottom to the case without force. If not, check for a misplaced strut, pinion roller, or stop ring.

Reverse Idler Gear

1. Place dummy shaft into idler gear. Insert 22 greased rollers.
2. Position reverse idler thrust washers in case with grease.
3. Position idler gear and dummy shaft in case. Install idler shaft and key.

Extension Housing

1. Remove extension housing yoke seal. Drive bushing out from inside housing.
2. Align oil hole in bushing with oil slot in housing. Drive bushing into place. Drive new seal into housing.

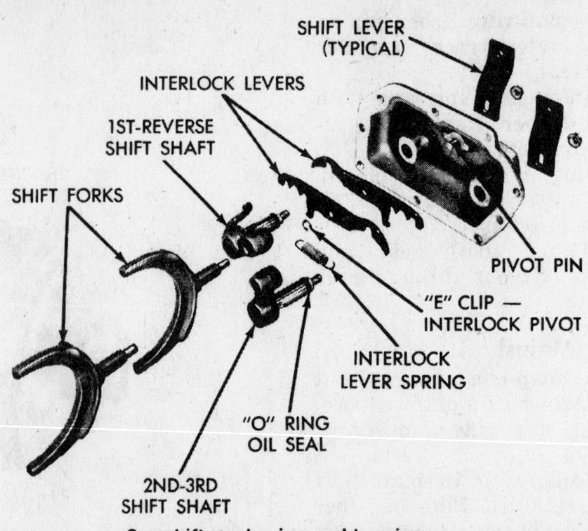

Gearshift mechanism and housing (© Chrysler Corp.)

3. Install extension housing and gasket to hold mainshaft and bearing retainer in place.

Drive Pinion Bearing Retainer

1. Install outer snap-ring on drive pinion bearing. Tap assembly back until snap-ring contacts case.
2. Using seal installer tool or equivalent, install a new seal in retainer bore.
3. Position main drive pinion bearing retainer and gasket on front of case. Coat threads with sealing compound, install bolts, torque to 30 ft. lbs.

Gearshift Mechanism and Housing

1. If removed, place two interlock levers in pivot pin with spring hangers offset toward each other, so that spring installs in a straight line. Place E-clip on pivot pin.
2. Grease and install new O-ring seals on both shift shafts. Grease housing bores and insert shafts.
3. Install spring on interlock lever hangers.
4. Rotate each shift shaft fork bore to straight up position. Install shift forks through bores and under both interlock levers.
5. Position second-third synchronizer sleeve to rear, in second gear position. Position first-reverse synchronizer sleeve to middle of travel, in neutral position. Place shift forks in the same positions.
6. Install gasket and gearshift mechanism. The bolt with the extra long shoulder must be installed at the center rear of the case. Torque bolts to 15 ft. lbs.
7. Install speedometer drive pinion gear and adapter. Range number on adapter, which represents the number of teeth on the gear, should be in 6 o'clock position.

Torque Chart

Manual A-203 3-Speed

	Foot-Pounds
Back up light switch	15
Extension housing bolts	50
Drive pinion bearing retainer bolts	30
Gearshift operating lever nuts	18
Transmission to clutch housing bolts	50
Transmission cover retaining bolts	12
Transmission drain plug	25

Dodge A-745 3 Speed

Description

The Dodge A-745 is a three-speed synchromesh transmission having helical type gears. Lubricant capacity is 3¼ pints.

Disassembly of Transmission

1. Remove output flange nut, then the drum and flange assembly, if so equipped. Remove parking brake assembly, if so equipped.
2. Remove case cover. Measure synchronizer float with a feeler gauge between the end of a synchronizer pin and the opposite synchronizer outer ring. A measurement from .050-.090 in. is acceptable for 1964-67 models. The measurement should be .060-.117 in. for 1968 and up models.
3. Remove the extension housing from the case.
4. Remove the mainshaft rear bearing, if it did not come off with the extension housing.
5. Remove transmission case cover and gasket.
6. Remove the drive pinion bearing retainer.
7. When removing the drive pinion and bearing assembly from the transmission case, slide the front inner stop ring from the short splines on the pinion as the assembly is being removed from the case.
8. Remove the main drive pinion bearing snap-ring.
9. Press bearing off pinion shaft and remove oil slinger.

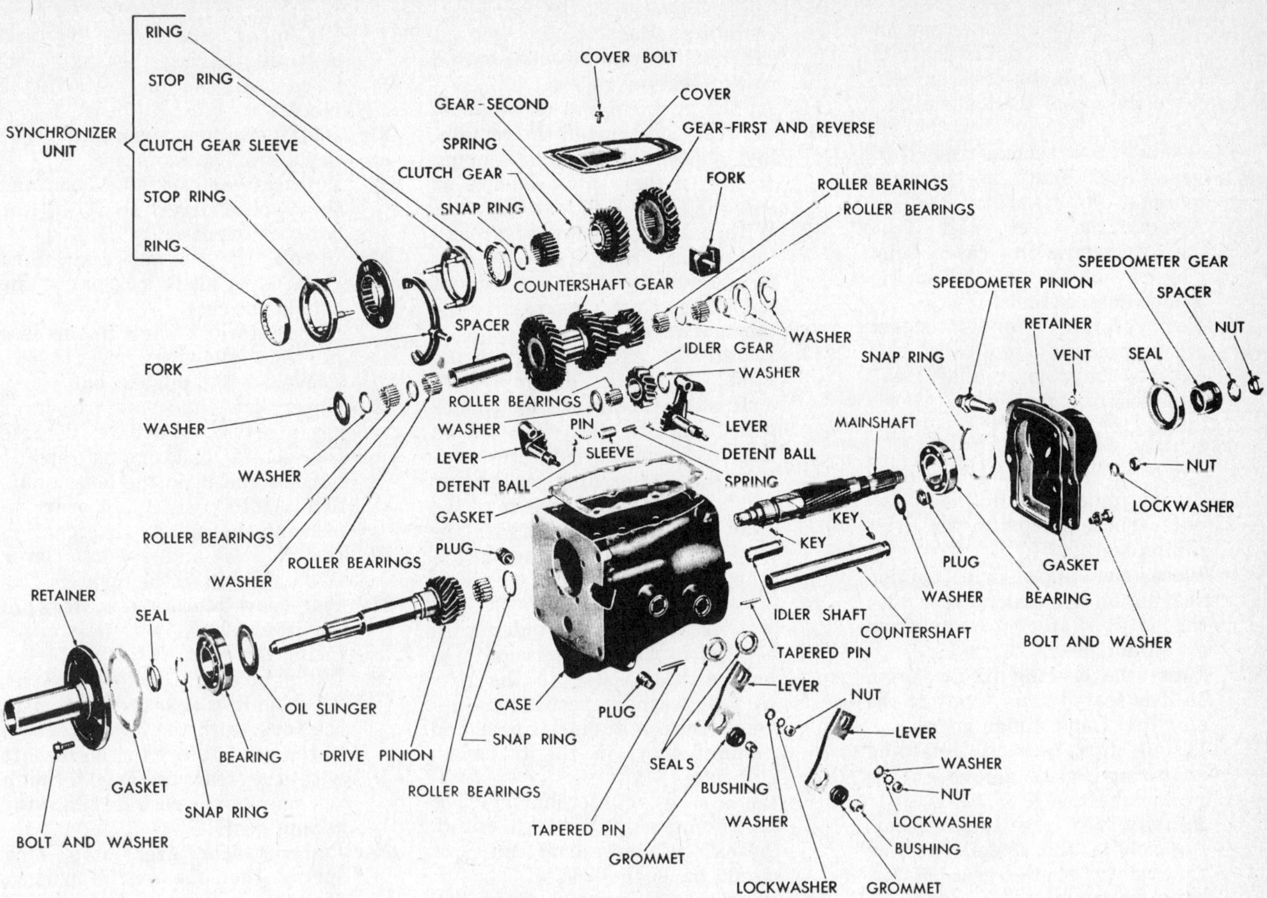

The A-745 transmission (© Chrysler Corp.)

10. Remove mainshaft pilot bearing snap-ring from the cavity of the pinion gear.
11. Remove the 15 pilot roller bearings.
12. Remove seal from pinion retainer.
13. Remove mainshaft rear bearing snap-ring from groove in mainshaft rear bearing bore in the case.
14. Remove the rear bearing snap-ring from groove in mainshaft rear bearing bore in the case.
14. Remove the rear bearing from the case by moving the mainshaft and rear bearing assembly to the rear.
15. Remove synchronizer assembly from case.
16. Remove second and third-speed shift fork.
17. Remove synchronizer clutch gear, snap-ring, clutch gear, second-speed gear, and first and reverse sliding gear from the mainshaft.
18. Withdraw mainshaft and bearing out through the rear of the case.
19. Remove the synchronizer clutch gear, second-speed gear, low and reverse sliding gear, and low and reverse shift fork from the case.
20. With a dummy shaft, drive the countershaft toward the rear of the case until the small key can be removed from the countershaft.
21. Remove the countershaft from the case.
22. Lift the cluster gear, the thrust washers and the dummy shaft assembly out of the case.
23. Dismantle the cluster gear, (88 rollers, four spacer rings and the center spacer from the cluster).
24. With a blunt drift, drive the reverse idler shaft toward the rear of the case far enough to remove the key from the shaft.
25. Completely remove the shaft from the case, then remove the idler gear.
26. Remove the thrust washers and 22 rollers.

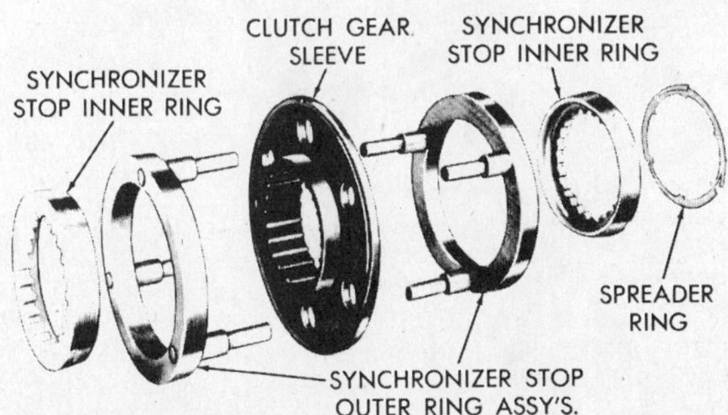

Synchronizer components (© Chrysler Corp.)

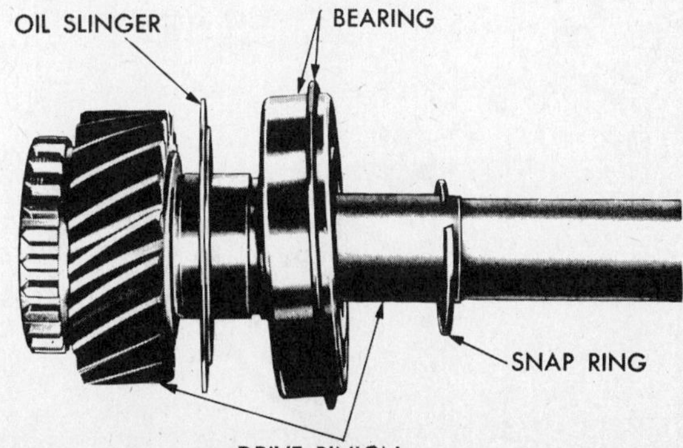

Drive pinion assembly (© Chrysler Corp.)

27. Wtih a small punch, remove low and reverse gear lever shaft tapered lock pin by driving it toward the top of the transmission case.
28. Remove the second and third gear lever shaft in the same manner.
29. Remove the lever shafts from the transmission case being careful not to lose the spring-loaded dentent balls.
30. Remove the interlock sleeve, spring pin and detent balls.
31. Remove both lever shaft seals and discard same.

Assembly of Transmission

1. Place oil slinger on the main drive pinion with the offset outer portion next to the drive pinion teeth.
2. Place the main drive pinion bearing on the pinion shaft with the outer snap-ring away from the pinion gear.
3. Press the bearing into position so it is seated firmly against the oil slinger and pinion gear.
4. Install the bearing retaining snap-ring in its groove on the pinion shaft.
5. Heavily grease the 15 pilot bearing rollers and install them in the cavity at the rear of the main drive pinion.
6. Install the snap-ring.
7. Place the bearing spacer in the center of the bore in the cluster gear and use the dummy shaft to assist in assembling the roller bearings.
8. Install a row of 22 rollers next to one end of the spacer, using heavy grease to hold them.
9. Place one of the four bearing spacer rings next to the row of rollers, and install another row of 22 rollers next to the spacer ring.
10. Install another spacer ring at the outside end of the second row of bearing rollers.
11. At the opposite end of the cluster gear bore, install the remaining spacer rings and bearing rollers in the same sequence as listed in Steps 8, 9, and 10.
12. With a small amount of grease, install the front thrust washer on the dummy shaft at the front end of the cluster gear, with the tabs outward.
13. Install the tabbed rear thrust washer onto the dummy shaft against the rear of the cluster gear with the tabs inserted in the cluster gear grooves.
14. Install the remaining rear thrust washer plate onto the rear of the gear and dummy shaft with the step in the washer facing upward, as viewed from the rear.
15. Align tabs of the front thrust washer vertically to index with notches in the transmission case and with the step in the rear thrust washer positioned upward. Insert the cluster gear and dummy shaft in the transmission case.
16. Using the countershaft, drive the dummy shaft forward, out of the case. Countershaft end play should be .0045-.028 in.
17. Position a dummy shaft in the reverse idler gear and, using heavy grease, install the 22 roller bearings into the gear.
18. Place the thrust washers at each end of the reverse idler gear, then place the assembly in the case with the chamfered end of the gear teeth toward the front.
19. Insert the reverse idler shaft into the rear case bore with the keyway to the rear, pushing the dummy shaft toward and out of the front of the transmission.
20. With the keyway in proper alignment, insert the key and continue driving the shaft forward until the key seats in the recess.
21. Install two new lever shaft seals in the transmission case.
22. Lubricate and install second and third-speed lever shaft in the bores of the case.
23. Install the second and third speed lever shaft lock pin in the hole in the case.
24. Place interlock parts in the case in the following order: ball, sleeve, spring, pin and ball.
25. Enter low and reverse lever shaft in the case bore, depress the detent ball against spring tension and push the lever shaft firmly into position, in order to prevent the ball from escaping.
26. Install low and reverse lever shaft lock pin in the case.
27. Place low and reverse fork in the lever shaft, with the offset facing the rear.
28. Whlie holding the low and reverse sliding gear in position in the fork, with the hub extension to the rear, insert the mainshaft with the rear bearing through the rear of the case and into the sliding gear.
29. Place synchronizer stop ring spring, then the rear stop ring, on the synchronizer splines of the second-speed gear. Install the second-speed gear onto the mainshaft. Synchronizer shims must be added if synchronizer float is more than the maximum in Step 2, disassembly. If float was less than minimum, the six pins must be shortened.
gear on the mainshaft with the
30. Install the synchronizer clutch shoulder to the front.
31. Select the thickest synchronizer clutch gear snap-ring that can be used, and install it in the

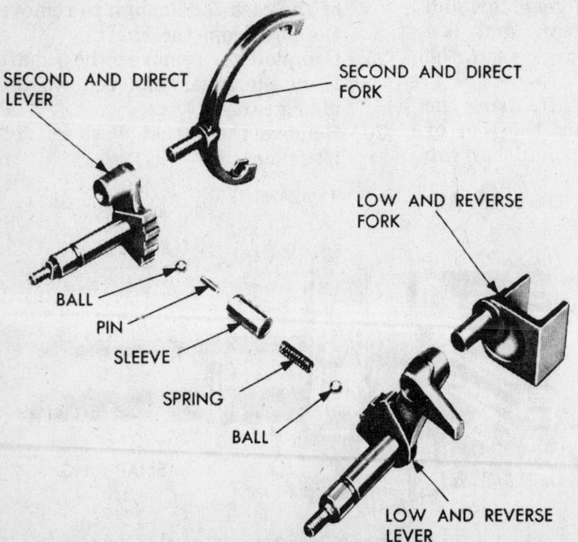

Shift fork assembly (© Chrysler Corp.)

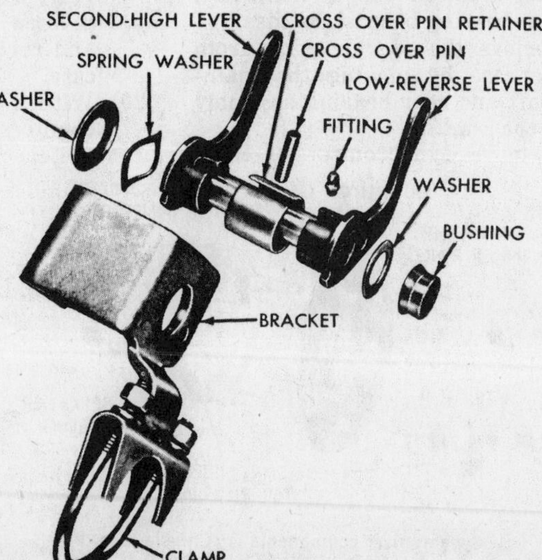

Gearshift controls (© Chrysler Corp.)

mainshaft groove.

32. Check to see that clearance between clutch gear and second-speed gear is .004-.014 in.
33. Hold the synchronizer clutch gear sleeve and two outer rings together with pins properly entered into the holes in the clutch gear sleeve and with the clutch gear sleeve engaged in the groove of the second- and third-speed shift fork, position the fork in the second- and third-speed lever shaft.
34. While holding the synchronizer parts and fork in position, slide the mainshaft forward, entering the synchronizer clutch gear into the clutch gear sleeve and simultaneously entering the mainshaft rear bearing in the case bore.
35. While still holding the synchronizer parts in position, tap the mainshaft forward until the rear bearing bottoms in the case bore.
36. Install the mainshaft rear bearing snap-ring into place in the case bore.
37. Install a new drive pinion retainer seal.
38. Place the synchronizer front inner ring in position in the front outer ring, and enter the main drive pinion through the case bore.
39. Engage the splines on the rear of the pinion with the inner stop ring, and tap the drive pinion into the case until the outer snap-ring on the pinion bearing is against the transmission case.
40. Place the drive pinion bearing retainer over the pinion shaft and against the transmission case. While holding the retainer against the transmission case, measure the clearance between the retainer and case and choose a gasket .003-.005 in. thicker than this reading.
41. Torque the front bearing retainer bolts to 30 ft. lbs.
42. Install a new extension housing seal.
43. Install extension housing and torque the bolts to 50 ft. lbs.
44. Install the parking brake assembly, on vehicles so equipped.
45. Install the parking brake drum (if so equipped) and flange assembly and torque to 175 ft. lbs.
46. Install the drain plug in the transmission case.
47. Install the gearshift operating levers, and torque to 12 ft. lbs.
48. Install the back-up light switch.
49. Install the speedometer cable and drive gear. Bring transmission to lubricant level.

Torque Chart

Gearshift rod and swivel assembly nuts	5/16-24	70 (in.-lbs.)
Backup light switch hole plug	9/16-18	15
Case drain plug	3/8	20
Case filler plug	1/2	30
Cast to clutch housing bolt	7/16-18	50
Drive pinion bearing retainer bolt	5/16-18	15
Extension bolt	3/8-16	30
Gearshift fork lock bolt	3/8-24	30
Gearshift housing lower bolt	5/16-18	15
Gearshift housing upper bolt	5/16-18	20
Gearshift operating lever nut	3/8-24	35
Gearshift selector ball spring bolt	1/2-20	25
Gearshift selector lever washer nut	5/16-24	20
Manual remote gearshift lever shaft bolt	1/4-20	10
Shaft flange nut	3/4-16	175

Dodge A-903 3 Speed

Description

The Dodge A-903 is a three-speed transmission having helical type gears. It is synchromesh to provide smooth shifting operation. Lubricant capacity is 6 pints.

Disassembly of Transmission

1. Remove output shaft yoke.
2. Remove the extension housing and housing oil seal.
3. Remvoe the transmission case cover. Measure synchronizer float with feeler gauges. This measurement is taken between the end of a synchronizer pin and the opposite synchronizer outer ring. A measurement from .050-.090 in. is acceptable for 1964-67 models. This measurement should be .060-.117 in. for 1968 and up models.
4. Remove the main drive pinion bearing retainer and assembly from the case. CAUTION: Be careful not to bind the inner synchronizer ring on the drive pinion clutch teeth.
5. Remove the snap-ring that locks the main drive pinion bearing onto the pinion shaft. Remove the bearing washer, press the shaft out of the bearing and remove the oil slinger.

Measuring the synchronizer float
(© Chrysler Corp.)

6. Remove the snap-ring from the drive pinion pilot bearing and remove the 14 rollers.
7. With transmission in reverse, remove the outer center bearing snap-ring, then partially remove the mainshaft.
8. Cock the mainshaft, then remove the clutch sleeve, the outer synchronizer rings, the front inner ring and the second-third shift box.
9. Remove clutch gear retaining snap-ring and clutch gear from the mainshaft.
10. Slide the second-speed gear, stop ring and synchronizer spring off the mainshaft.
11. Remove the low and reverse sliding gear and shift fork, as the mainshaft is completely withdrawn from the case.
12. Cluster gear end-play should be .005-.022 in. This measurement will determine thrust washer value at reassembly.
13. Remove the countershaft key and the countershaft.
14. Lift the gear cluster and thrust washers out of the case. Remove the needle bearings, (22 each end) and spacer from the clus-

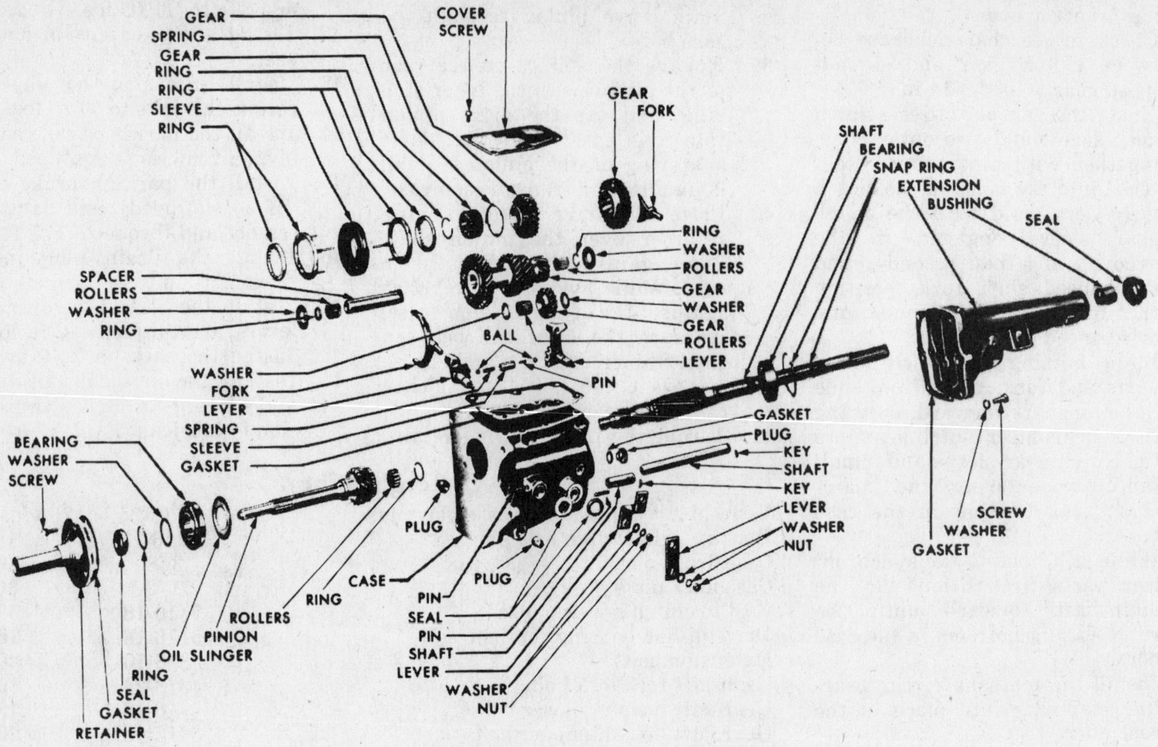

A-903 transmission (© Chrysier Corp.)

ter.

15. Remove the reverse idler shaft from the case. Remove key.
16. Lift the reverse idler gear, thrust washers and 22 needle bearings out of the case.
17. Remove gearshift operating levers from their respective shafts.
18. Drive out tapered retaining pin from either of the two lever shafts, then withdraw the shaft from the case. (The detent balls are spring-loaded, as the shaft is being withdrawn, the balls will fall to the bottom of the case.)
19. Remove the interlock sleeve, spring, pin and both balls from the case. Drive out the remaining tapered pin, then slide the lever shaft out of the transmission.
20. Remove the lever shaft seals.

Assembly of Transmission

1. Install two new shift lever shaft seals in the case.
2. Carefully insert low and reverse lever shaft into the rear of the case, through the seal and into position. Lock with a tapered pin. Turn lever until the center detent is in line with the interlock bore.
3. Install the interlock sleeve in its bore in the case, an interlock ball, spring and pin.
4. Place the remaining interlock ball on top of the interlock spring.
5. Depress the interlock ball and, simultaneously, install the second and high lever shaft into the fully seated position, with the center detent aligned with the detent ball. Secure the shaft with the remaining tapered pin.
6. Install the operating levers and secure to the shafts with nuts at 18 ft. lbs. of torque.

Countershaft (Cluster) Gear

1. Slide the dummy shaft and tubular spacer into the bore of the countergear.
2. Grease and install 22 bearing rollers into each end of the countergear bore in the area around the arbor. Install the bearing retaining rings at each end of the gear, covering the bearings.
3. Install a thrust washer at each end of the countergear and over the arbor. Install the countergear assembly in the case, making sure the tabs on the thrust washers slide into the grooves in the case. Correct cluster gear end-play is determined by the thrust washer thickness.

Reverse Idler Gear

1. Grease the reverse idler gear and slide dummy shaft into the bore, then install 22 bearing rollers in the bore and around the dummy shaft.
2. Install a new thrust washer at each end of the gear and over the arbor.
3. With the beveled end of the teeth forward, slide the gear into position in the case. Install the reverse idler shaft in its bore in the rear of the case. Install Woodruff key and align with the keyway in the case.
4. Drive the shaft into the case and idler gear until the key seats in recess.

Mainshaft

1. Install rear bearing on mainshaft and install selective fit snap-ring.
2. Hold low and reverse sliding gear in position with shift fork. Insert mainshaft with rear bearing through rear of case and into the sliding gear.
3. Place synchronizer spreader ring, and then rear stop ring, on synchronizer splines of second speed gear. Install second speed gear on mainshaft, with shims if required. Shims should be installed to correct excessive synchronizer float. If synchronizer float is below minimum, as measured on disassembly, shorten all six synchronizer pins.
4. Install synchronizer clutch gear and snap ring on mainshaft.
5. Install second and direct fork in lever shaft with offset toward rear of transmission. Hold synchronizer clutch gear sleeve and two outer rings together, with pins in holes in clutch gear sleeve. Engage second and direct fork with clutch year sleeve.
6. While holding synchronizer parts and fork in position, slide mainshaft forward, starting synchronizer clutch gear into clutch gear sleeve and mainshaft

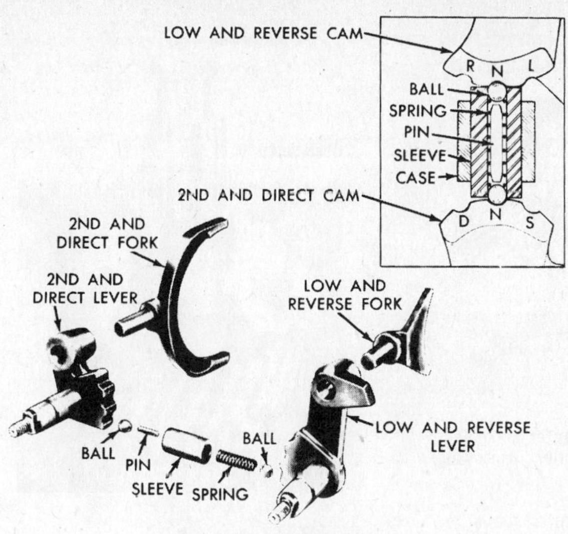

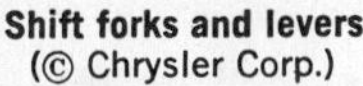
Shift forks and levers
(© Chrysler Corp.)

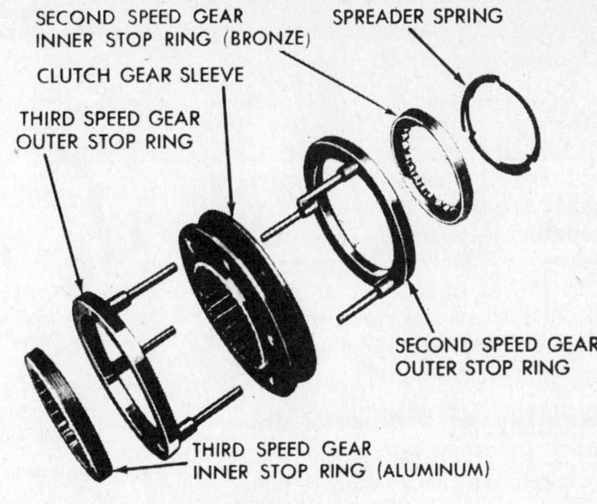

Synchronizer assembly
(© Chrysler Corp.)

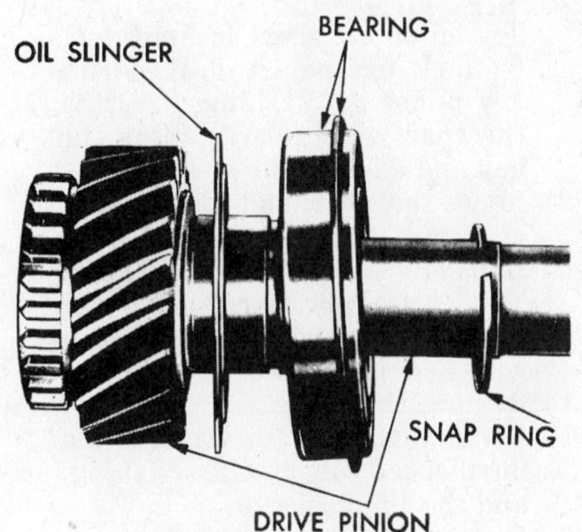

Drive pinion assembly
(© Chrysler Corp.)

rear bearing into the case bore. Synchronizer parts must be correctly positioned before mainshaft is positioned.

7. While holding synchronizer parts in position, tap mainshaft forward until rear bearing bottoms in the case bore.
8. Install mainshaft rear bearing selective fit snap-ring into case bore groove.

Drive Pinion (Clutch Shaft)

1. Slide the oil slinger over the pinion shaft against the gear.
2. Slide the bearing over the pinion shaft (ring groove away from the gear), then press to a firm seat against the oil slinger and gear.
3. Install the keyed washer, then the snap-ring. Four thicknesses of snap-ring are available to eliminate end-play. Install the large snap-ring onto the race of the ball bearing.
4. Install 14 greased bearing rollers in the bore of the pinion shaft gear. Install bearing roller retaining ring in the pinion gear bore.
5. Install third gear outer stop-ring and third gear inner stop-ring onto the mainshaft. Guide the drive pinion through the front of the case and engage the inner stop-ring with the clutch teeth, then seat the bearing so the large snap-ring is flush against the case.
6. Install a new bearing retainer seal and gasket.
7. Install the retainer and torque to 30 ft. lbs.

Extension Housing

1. Install a new rear mainshaft bushing, and a new oil seal.
2. Protect the oil seal with thimble-type seal protector, and with gasket attached, slide the extension against the case and torque to 50 ft. lbs.
3. Install flange assembly and secure with new washer and nut at 140 ft. lbs.
4. Grease the cover gasket, and install gasket on cover. Torque attaching bolts to 12 ft. lbs.
5. Install drain plug and back-up light switch (if so equipped) and tighten securely. Refill transmission to proper level.

Torque Chart

Transmission (Manual)	*Foot-Pounds*
Backup light switch hole plug	15
Case drain plug	20
Case filler plug	30
Case to clutch housing bolts	50
Drain plug	300 (in.-lbs.)
Drive pinion bearing retainer bolt	15
Extension bolt	30
Gearshift fork lock bolt	30
Gearshift lower bolt	15
Gearshift housing upper bolt	20
Gearshift operating lever nut	35
Gearshift rod and swivel assembly nuts	70 (in.-lbs.)
Gearshift selector ball spring bolt	25
Gearshift selector lever washer nut	20
Mainshaft flange nut	175
Manual remote gearshift lever shaft bolt	10
Operating lever retaining nuts	216
Pinion bearing retaining bolts	360
Transmission cover retaining bolts	144

Description

The Fuller 5H-74 is a constant mesh five-speed transmission having helical forward gears.

The forward speed gears on the mainshaft are in constant mesh with the countershaft gears. Power is transferred by locking the gear selected to the mainshaft by engaging the clutch teeth on the gears with the sliding gears on the mainshaft. Lubricant capacity is 22 pints.

Disassembly of Transmission

1. With the transmission in neutral, remove the gear shift housing.
2. Lock the transmission into two gears and remove the output shaft flange nut.
3. Remove the flange and brake drum as a unit, and disconnect the parking brake linkage.
4. Remove the brake shoe assembly.
5. Remove the output shaft rear bearing retainer and gasket, and remove the speedometer drive gear. Remove the oil seal from the retainer.
6. After removing the clutch release mechanism, remove the clutch housing.
7. Remove the input shaft bearing retainer and gasket, and then pull out the input shaft and bearing assembly. Remove the bearing retaining snap-ring from the case bore.
8. Mount the input shaft assembly in a soft—jawed vise and relieve the bearing nut peening. Remove the nut. This nut has a left-hand thread.
9. If the bearing is to be replaced, press or jar it from the shaft.
10. Remove the countershaft rear bearing adapter cap and gasket.
11. Remove the retainer plate from the rear end of the countershaft.
12. Remove the countershaft rear bearing adapter.
13. Drive the output shaft forward until it stops solidly, and then drive it to the rear until the rear bearing snap-ring is exposed.
14. Remove the bearing. If the bearing is to be replaced, remove the snap-ring.
15. Remove the output shaft and gears, except the sliding gears. Lift the sliding gears out of the case.
16. Remove the countershaft rear bearing cones, cups, and spacer from the retainer.
17. Remove the reverse idler shaft retainer and shaft. Remove the idler gear and bearings from the case.
18. Remove countershaft and gears from the case.

Fuller 5H-74 5 Speed

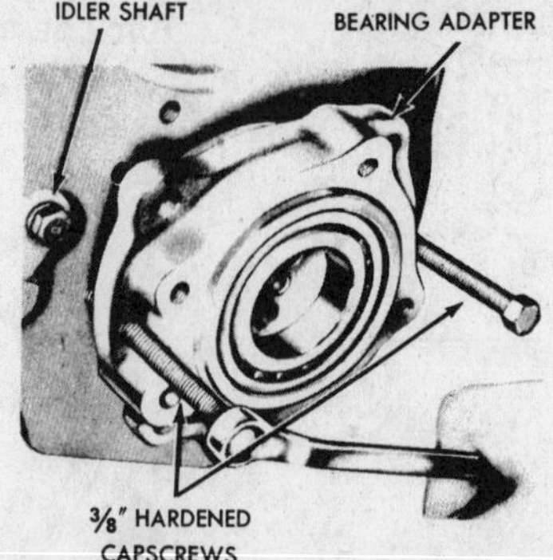

Countershaft bearing adapter removal
(© Eaton Yale & Towne, Fuller Trans. Div.)

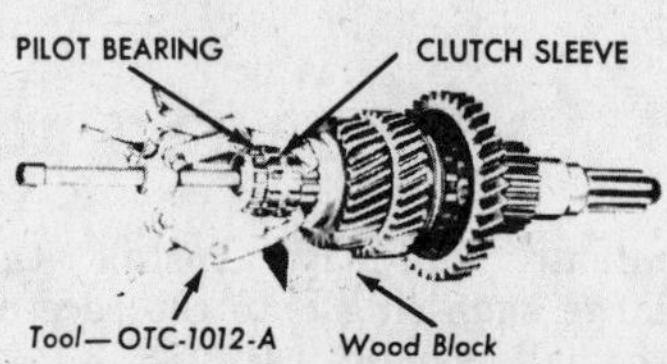

Output shaft pilot removal
(© Eaton Yale & Towne, Fuller Trans. Div.)

19. Remove the countershaft front bearing retainer, gasket, bearing, and spacer from the case.

Disassembly of Sub-Assemblies

Output Shaft

1. Remove the pilot bearing and the sliding clutch sleeve.
2. Pry the fourth speed gear washer key from its keyway between the shaft splines.
3. Align the fourth-speed gear washer with the output shaft grooves and then remove the gear and washer.
4. Press the shaft no more than 5/8 inch through the third-speed gear and the thrust washer.

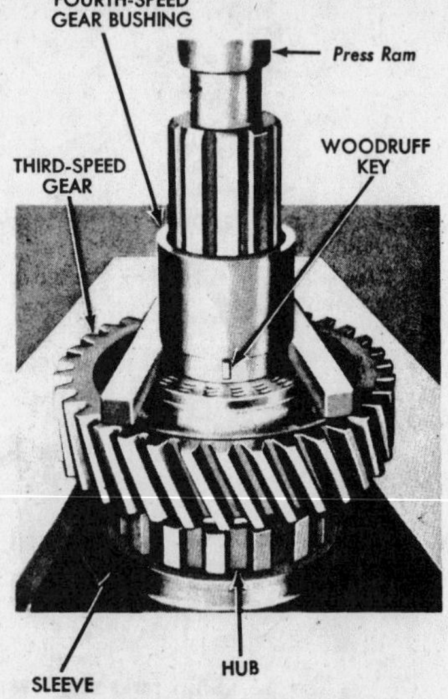

Fourth speed gear bushing key
(© Eaton Yale & Towne, Fuller Trans. Div.)

Travel of the shaft is limited to 5/8 inch by the small Woodruff key under the bushing. Pressing the shaft further will shear the key and damage the washer.

5. Move the gear and the washer rearward to their original positions against the shaft shoulder. Then with pry bars, move the bushing forward until the Woodruff key is completely exposed. Remove the key.
6. Remove the thrust washer, the third-speed gear, the bushing, and the clutch sleeve.
7. Press the output shaft through the third-speed gear bushing, the second-speed gear and the sleeve hub.
8. Remove the two remaining Woodruff keys.

Countershaft

When disassembling the countershaft, press the gears from the shaft

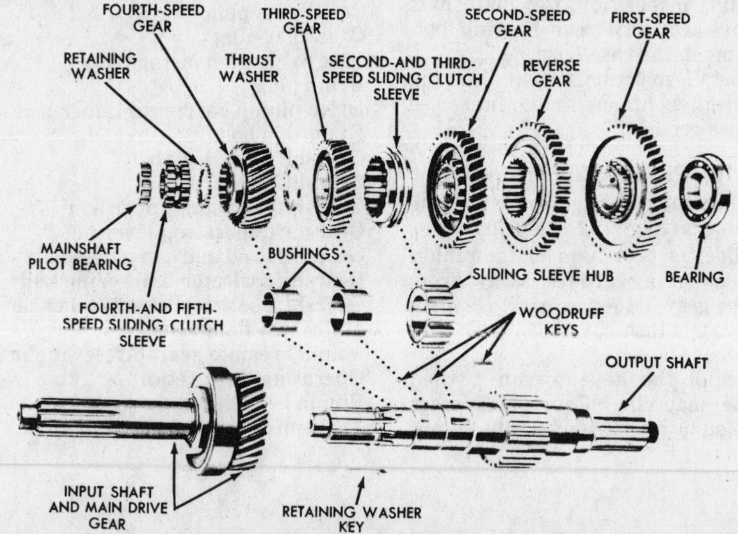

Input shaft and output shaft components
(© Eaton Yale & Towne, Fuller Trans. Div.)

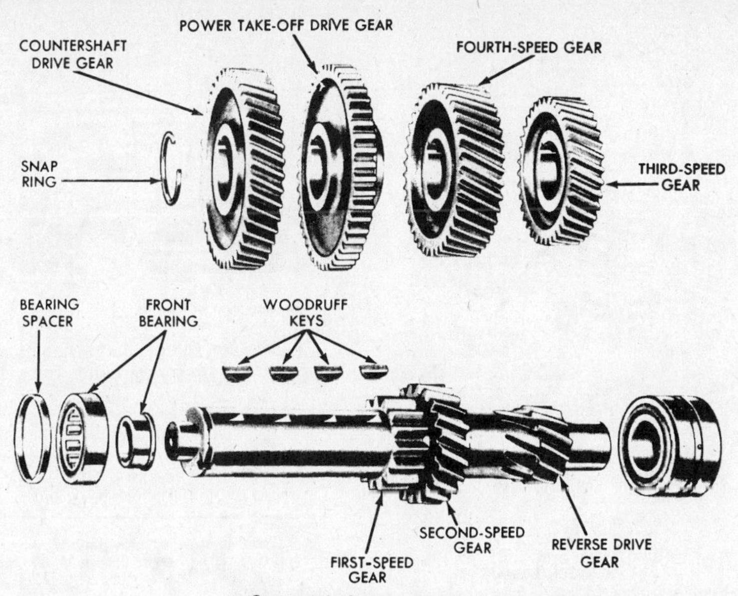

Countershaft components
(© Eaton Yale & Towne, Fuller Trans. Div.)

one at a time.

Gear Shift Housing

When disassembling the housing, remove the shift shafts one at a time, beginning with the rocker arm shaft and working down. Any shaft out of neutral position will lock the remaining shafts in the housing. Do not lose the interlock pin and balls as the low and reverse shaft is removed.

Assembly of Sub-Assemblies

Gear Shift Housing

1. Position the housing (left-hand side up) in a vise, and install the rocker arm and pivot pin.
2. Insert the rocker arm shift shaft through the webs and gates, install the set screws.
3. Insert the second-third shaft into the housing and through its fork. Install the set screw.
4. Position a 3/4 inch interlock ball in the housing opening between the second-third and the fourth-fifth shafts.
5. Insert the fourth-fifth shaft into the housing and through its fork. Insert the interlock pin into the shaft as the neutral notch enters the web. Install the lock screw.
6. Install the remaining 3/4 inch interlock ball.
7. Insert the low and reverse shaft through the housing, block, and fork. Install the set screws.
8. Lock-wire all set screws and the pivot pin retaining bolts.
9. Install the four 1/2 inch steel balls and the detent spring. Be sure all shifts are in neutral position so that the balls will fit into their slots.
10. Install the detent spring cover and a new gasket.
11. Install Welch plugs in the shift shaft openings of the housing.
12. Start the set screw and jam nut, tighten the screw until it bottoms; back it off one half turn, and tighten the jam nut.

Removing countershaft front bearing
(© Eaton Yale & Towne, Fuller Trans. Div.)

Countershaft

1. Install the Woodruff keys, and press on the gears, one at a time. Press the front bearing inner race on, and install the drive gear snap-ring.

Output Shaft

1. Install the Woodruff keys for the sleeve hub and the third-speed gear bushing.
2. Position the second-speed gear (clutching teeth to the front) on the output shaft, and then press the sleeve hub (recessed end to the front) tightly against the gear.
3. Press the third-speed gear bushing onto the shaft and aganist the sleeve hub. Position the clutch sleeve on its hub.
4. Position the third-speed gear (clutch teeth to the rear) on its bushing.
5. Install the thrust washer, chamfer to the rear, and install the remaining Woodruff key.
6. Press the fourth-speed gear (hub forward) and bushing onto the shaft.
7. Install the retaining washer, and measure the clearance between the fourth-speed gear and its

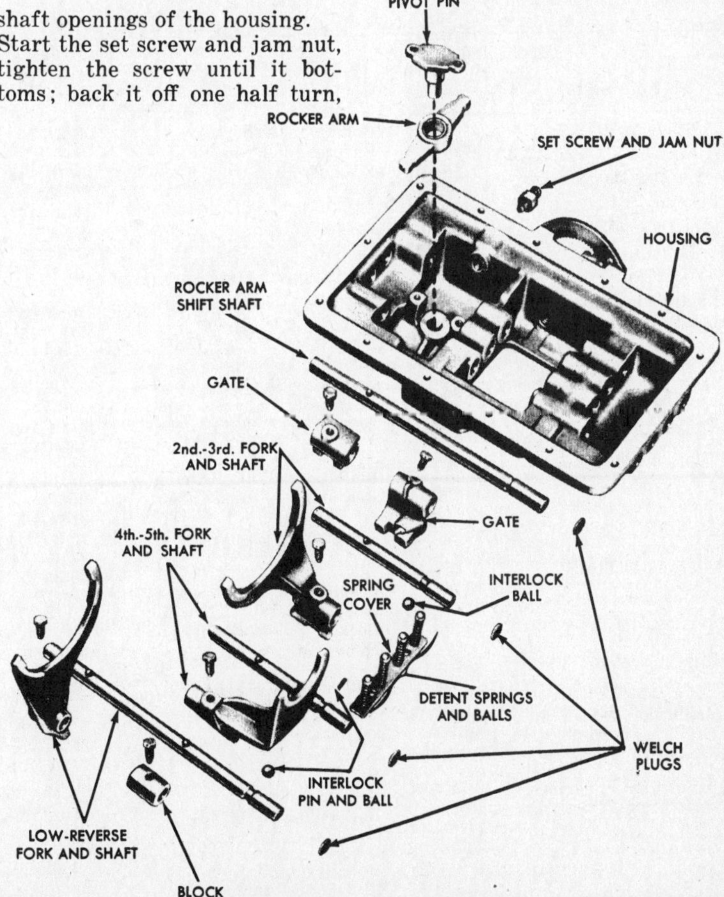

Gear shift housing components
(© Eaton Yale & Towne, Fuller Trans. Div.)

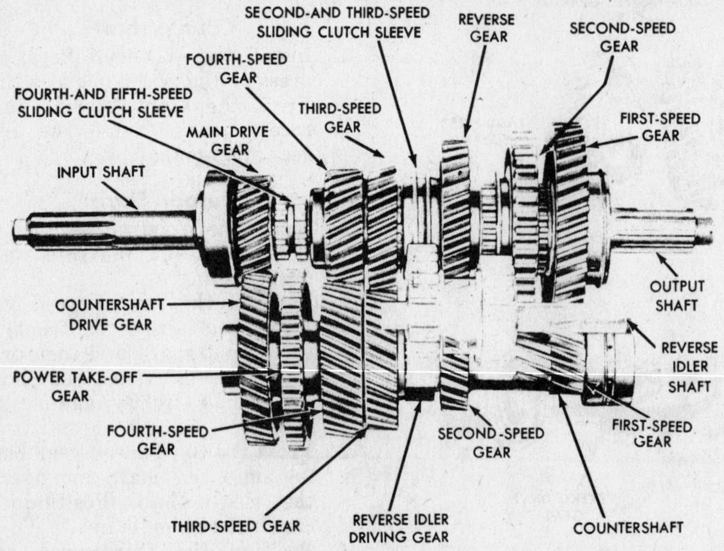

Gear train
(© Eaton Yale & Towne, Fuller Trans. Div.)

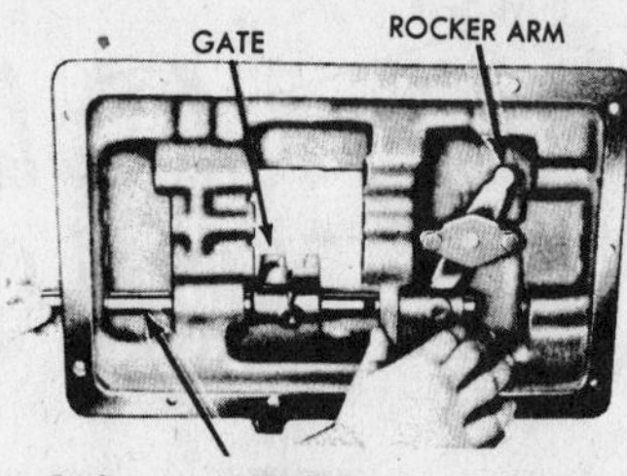

Rocker arm shifter shaft installation
(© Eaton Yale & Towne, Fuller Trans. Div.)

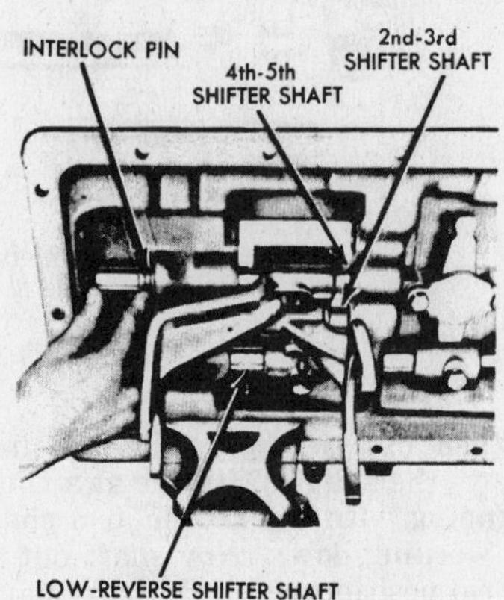

Installing fourth and fifth speed shifter shaft
(© Eaton Yale & Towne, Fuller Trans. Div.)

Torque Chart

Nomenclature	*Torque Limits*	*Nomenclature*	*Torque Limits*
Bolt-gear shift lever tower	3/8—16	Bolt-Countershaft Rear	5/16—18
to gearshift housing	20-25	Bearing Retainer	25-30
	5/16—18		3/8—16
	11-16		35-40
	7/16—14		7/16—14
	30-45		45-55
			1/2—13
Bolt-Clutch Housing to	7/16—14		60-70
Trans. Case	30-38		
	5/8—11	Bolt-Countershaft &	1/2—13
	96-120	Reverse Idler Shaft	60-70
	9/16—12	Retainer	5/16—18
	70-90		25-30
	5/8—18C		3/8—16
	115-140		25-37
	9/16—18C		3/8—16
	81-102		18-25
			7/16—14
Nut-U-Joint Flange to	1.00—20		40-45
Trans. Output Shaft	90-125		1/2—13
	1 1/4—18		80-85
	225-275		
	1 1/2—18	Bolt-Gear Shaft Housing	5/16—18
	275-350	Trans. Case	20-25
			3/8—16
Nut-Drum Parking Brake	3/8—24		35-40
to Companion Flange	37-50		
	7/16—20	Bolt-Input Shaft Bearing	5/16—18
	40-55	Retainer to Trans. Case	25-30
	1/2—20		3/8—16
	74-86		25-30
			7/16—14
Nut-Bellcrank to Trans.	9/16—18		40-45
	70-90		
	3/8—16C	Nut-Countershaft Bearing	1 1/2—18
	20-25	Lock (5-Speed Exclusive	
		Heavy Duty)	350-450
Bolt—Lever Assy. to	3/8—16		
Trans.	20-25	Bolt-Countershaft Front	5/16—18
Nut-Handbrake Anchor Bar	9/16—18	Bearing Retainer	25-30
to Trans. Case (5-Speed			3/8—16
Extra-Heavy Duty only)	120-130		25-35
			7/16—14
Bolt-Output Shaft Bearing	3/8—16		50-55
Retainer to Trans. Case	20-25	Bolt-Bellcrank to Trans.	3/8—16
	7/16—14		20-25
	30-38		
	1/2—13	Bolt-Reverse Lockout	11/16—16
	50-62	Plunger Retainer	90-100
	5/8—11		
	96-120		

thrust washer. If the clearance is not 0.006-0.012 inch, select the retaining washer to result in the specified end play.

8. Install the retaining washer key and the clutch sleeve (recessed end to the rear).
9. Install the pilot bearing.

Input Shaft

1. If the bearing was removed, install the new bearing, with its shield toward the shaft splines.
2. Install the bearing nut, and stake it at the milled slots.

Assembly of Transmission

1. Install the countershaft front bearing in the case bore.
2. Position the front bearing spacer and gasket, and install the retainer.
3. Position the countershaft assembly in the case and then tilt the case so that its rear face is up.
4. Position two wood or fiber blocks of equal thickness between the drive gear and the case.
5. Position the inner bearing outer race in the adapter, and then apply sealer to the adapter gasket.
6. Make sure the adapter oil return hole is aligned, and then install the gasket and the adapter.
7. Install the inner bearing cone.

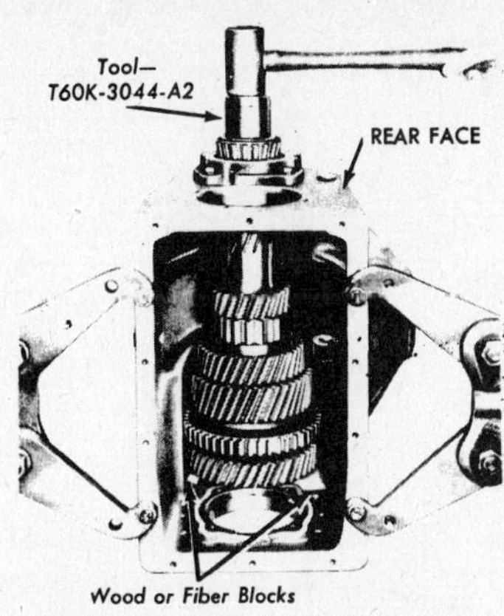

Countershaft rear bearing installation
(© Eaton Yale & Towne, Fuller Trans. Div.)

8. Position the spacer, and install the outer bearing cone. Position the outer bearing outer race.
9. Install the bearing lock plate and lock wire the bolts.
10. Apply sealer to the adapter cap gasket, and install the gasket and cap.
11. After tilting the case back to its normal position, install the idler gear and shaft. Be sure the flat on the shaft will align with the lock plate.
12. Install the lock plate.
13. Position the output shaft sliding gears in the case, and then position the output shaft assembly in the case. Check for proper gear engagement.
14. Install the rear bearing.
15. Install the input shaft bearing snap-ring in the case bore.
16. Position the input shaft assembly, and install the bearing retainer gasket and retainer, using a sealer.
17. Install the clutch housing and the speedometer drive gear.
18. Install a rear bearing retainer seal, gasket and retainer using a sealer.
19. Install the parking brake shoe assembly, and connect the brake linkage.
20. With the transmission locked in two gears, install the brake drum and flange and torque to specification.
21. Fill the transmission with lubricant.
22. Adjust the parking brake.
23. Install the gear shift housing, using a sealer on the gasket.

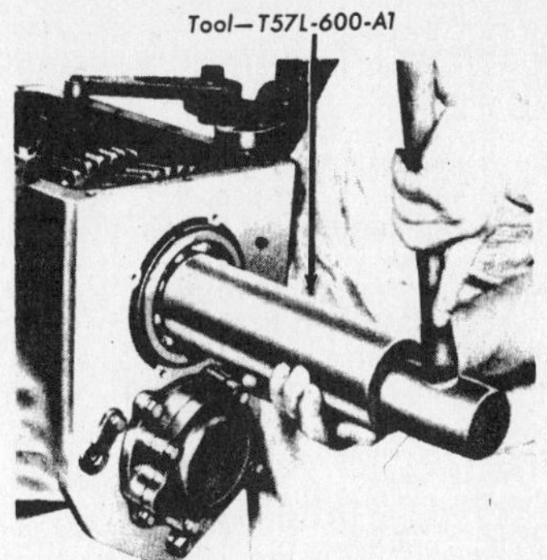

Installation of output shaft rear bearing
(© Eaton Yale & Towne, Fuller Trans. Div.)

Fuller 5W—430 5 Speed

Description

The Fuller SW-430 transmission has five speeds forward and one reverse.

In this transmission, second and third-speed ratios are engaged by a sliding clutch collar. The fourth and fifth-speed gears are engaged by a sliding clutch gear, also mounted on the mainshaft. A sliding gear on the mainshaft meshes with the countershaft low speed gear or reverse gear for gear engagement of these two speeds.

This transmission is designed so that all internal parts are continually bathed with oil circulated by the gear and shaft movement.

Specifications

Type	*Constant Mesh*	*Constant Mesh*
No. of speeds:		
Forward	5	5
Reverse	1	1
Ratios:		
Fifth	.825	1.000
Fourth	1.000	1.410
Third	1.890	2.460
Second	3.570	4.610
First	6.980	8.030
Reverse	6.950	8.000
Helical gears	2, 3, 4, 5	2, 3, 4, 5
Overdrive	Yes	No
Power-take-off:		
Openings	2	2
SAE Size	Large	Large
Location	Both Sides	Both Sides
Weight (Lbs.)	279	279
Lubricant capacity (Pts.)	19	19
Serial No. location	*	*

* Stamped above idler shaft on rear of case.

Precautions for Disassembly

1. The importance of cleanliness cannot be over stressed.
2. Do not remove the clutch housing unless absolutely necessary—either to replace the housing or case. If housing has been removed, be very careful when reassembling to maintain the 90° angularity between the machined face on the engine side of the housing and the centerline of the mainshaft bores in the case. Alignment of the pilot diameter of the clutch housnig with mainshaft bearing bores should also be carefully maintained within SAE tolerances.
3. Bearings should be carefully washed in solvent, relubricated and wrapped immediately after removal. Remove all bearings with bearing pullers. *Do not remove bearings with hammer and punch.*
4. Snap-rings removed with snap-ring pliers can be reused.
5. When removing components do so with restraint—do not force anything. Movement of some parts is restricted. *Use soft hammers and bars for all disassembly work.*

Disassembly of Sub-Assemblies

See exploded view of transmission.

Control Lever Housing

Shift transmission into neutral position. Remove and disassemble control lever housing.

Shift Bar Housing

With shift bar housing in a neutral position, lift housing from transmission.

During disassembly, lay out shift bars with corresponding forks and block in the same order as removed. This will facilitate reassembly.

Remove interlock ball cup from the front left side of housing.

Cut lockwires from shift block and shift fork setscrews and remove setscrews.

CAUTION: When removing the shift bars from the housing, use care not to lose the poppet balls and springs. Removal of these bars forcibly ejects the balls and springs from their bores at the front of the housing.

Using a curved soft bar, drive out upper shift bar and remove shift fork and poppet spring and ball. Keep other shift bars in housing in a neutral position or interlock parts will lock bars.

Using a curved soft bar, drive out the center and lower shift bars in the same manner as the upper shift bar,

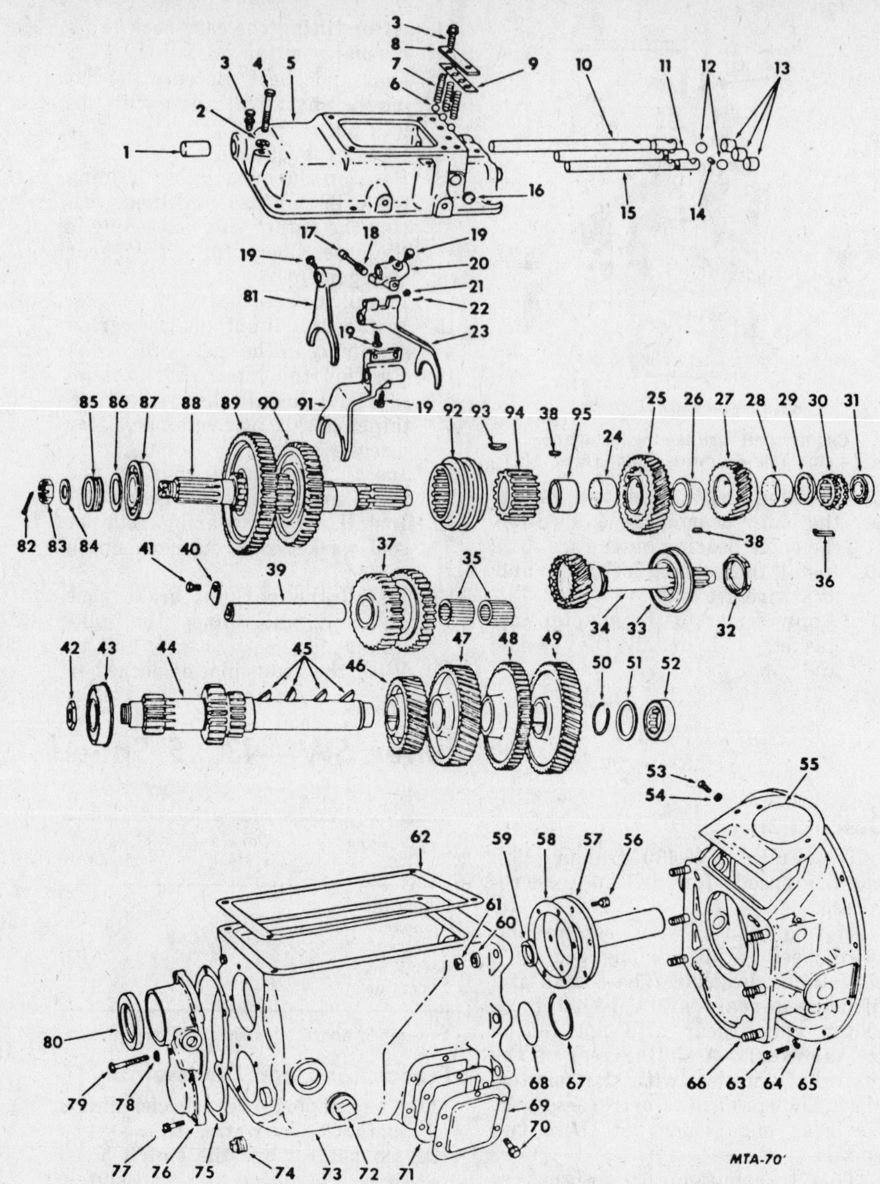

Transmission assembly components
(© Eaton Yale & Towne, Fuller Trans. Div.)

1 Cup, long
2 Washer, lock
3 Bolt
4 Bolt
5 Housing, shift bar
6 Ball, shift bar poppet
7 Spring, shift bar poppet ball
8 Cover, shift bar poppet
9 Gasket, shift bar poppet cover
10 Bar, first & reverse speed shift
11 Bar, fourth & fifth speed shift
12 Ball, shift bar interlock
13 Cup, short
14 Pin, shift bar interlock
15 Bar, second & third speed shift
16 Cup, interlock plunger
17 Plunger, shift bar interlock
18 Spring, shift block
19 Screw, shift block
20 Block, first & reverse speed shift
21 Nut, hex
22 Pin, cotter
23 Fork, fourth & fifth speed shift
24 Bushing, third speed gear
25 Gear, third speed
26 Sleeve, fourth & fifth speed gear
27 Gear
28 Bushing, fourth & fifth speed gear
29 Washer, mainshaft
30 Clutch, sliding
31 Bearing, mainshaft pilot
32 Nut, main drive gear bearing
33 Bearing, main drive
34 Gear, main drive
35 Bearing, reverse idler gear
36 Key, fifth speed gear washer
37 Gear, reverse idler
38 Key, woodruff
39 Shaft, reverse idler gear
40 Lock, reverse idler shaft
41 Bolt
42 Nut, countershaft rear bearing
43 Bearing, countershaft rear
44 Countershaft
45 Key, woodruff
46 Gear, countershaft third speed
47 Gear, countershaft
48 Gear, countershaft PTO
49 Gear, countershaft drive
50 Ring, countershaft gear snap
51 Washer, countershaft front brg.
52 Bearing, countershaft front
53 Bolt, hex-hd.
54 Washer, lock
55 Cover, bell housing
56 Bolt
57 Retainer, main drive gear brg.
58 Gasket, main drive gear brg. ret.
59 Seal, main drive gear ret.
60 Washer, lock
61 Nut, hex
62 Gasket, shift bar housing
63 Bolt, hex-hd.
64 Washer, lock
65 Housing, bell
66 Stud, bell housing
67 Ring, expansion plug snap
68 Plug, expansion
69 Cover, PTO opening
70 Bolt, hex-hd.
71 Gasket, PTO opening
72 Plug, pipe sq-hd.
73 Case, transmission
74 Plug, pipe sq-hd.
75 Gasket, rear bearing ret.
76 Retainer, mainshaft rear bearing
77 Bolt
78 Washer, lock
79 Bolt, hex-hd.
80 Seal, mainshaft oil
81 Fork, first & reverse speed shift
82 Pin, cotter
83 Nut, companion flange
84 Washer, companion flange nut
85 Gear, speedometer drive
86 Washer, mainshaft bearing
87 Bearing, mainshaft
88 Mainshaft
89 Gear, first speed
90 Gear, second speed
91 Fork, second & third speed shift
92 Collar, second third speed
93 Key, woodruff
94 Gear, second & third speed
95 Sleeve, mainshaft gear

remembering to keep the bars in the neutral position.

NOTE: When removing the center shift bar, be sure to extract the small interlock pin from the neutral notch of bar.

Companion Flange

Lock mainshaft by engaging two speeds with the sliding gears. Remove nut and companion flange from rear of mainshaft.

Countershaft rear bearing nut can also be removed at this time without the use of blocking. Remove rear bearing retainer and nut.

Main Drive Gear

Remove capscrews from main

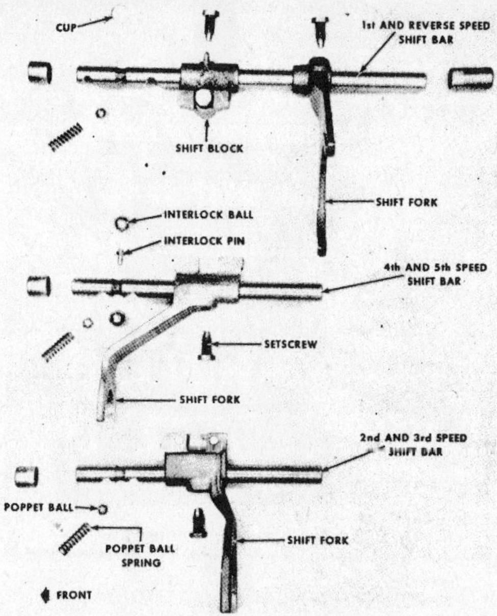

Shift bar housing components
(© Eaton Yale & Towne, Fuller Trans. Div.)

Withdrawing shift bar
(© Eaton Yale & Towne, Fuller Trans. Div.)

Removing shift bar, block and fork
(© Eaton Yale & Towne, Fuller Trans. Div.)

drive gear bearing retainer. Tap against main drive, gear from inside of case with soft bar to move assembly forward.

Remove retainer from shaft as main drive gear is moved forward.

Remove main drive gear assembly from front bore of case.

Mount main drive gear in a soft-jawed vise with pilot end up.

Remove main drive gear nut from shaft.

NOTE: Nut and shaft have a *left-hand thread*. Press main drive gear bearing off of shaft.

Replace bearing retainers that are worn or grooved from thrust of adjacent bearing outer race. Check oil rc turn threads in bearing retainers. If sealing action of threads has been destroyed by contact with input shaft or companion flange, replace retainer.

Mainshaft

Remove speedometer gear and mainshaft bearing washer from rear of mainshaft. Use a soft bar and mall aganist front of mainshaft to move assembly to the rear and to loosen rear bearing from case bore.

Remove mainshaft rear bearing from shaft.

Lift mainshaft assembly out of case leaving 1st and reverse-speed sliding gear inside of case. Remove 1st and reverse-speed sliding gear from case.

Mount mainshaft assembly in a soft-jawed vise. Remove pilot bearing from mainshaft. Using a puller tool behind the sliding clutch gear, remove the pilot bearing.

Remove sliding clutch gear from mainshaft.

Pry washer retaining key from between splines of mainshaft.

Remove fourth-speed gear and washer from mainshaft.

Press third-speed gear and fourth-speed gear sleeve from mainshaft.

Remove second and third-speed sliding clutch collar from clutch gear. Press second-speed gear, clutch gear and third-speed gear sleeve from mainshaft. Remove the three woodruff keys from mainshaft.

If replacing mainshaft gear bushings, use the proper size adapter. Clean bore of gear thoroughly and remove all burrs. Lubriplate new bushing, place gear on a flat surface and align oil hole in bushing with oil hole in gear. Using the proper adapter, press or drive bushing into gear.

NOTE: It is most important that bushing is installed straight and undamaged and that oil holes are in alignment.

Reverse Idler Gear

Remove reverse idler shaft lock and using a puller, remove reverse idler gear and the two thrust washers out of case. Remove the two needle bearings from the reverse idler gear bore.

Countershaft

If countershaft bearing nut has not been previously removed, relieve nut where it is peened into milled slot of shaft.

Place wood blocking between countershaft gears and case. Turn nut from shaft-right-hand thread.

Move countershaft assembly to rear to unseat rear bearing from case bore and shaft from front bearing. Pull rear bearing from shaft.

Lift countershaft assembly through top of case. Remove front bearing washer from countershaft or from case. Remove front bearing from case bore.

Remove snap-ring from front of

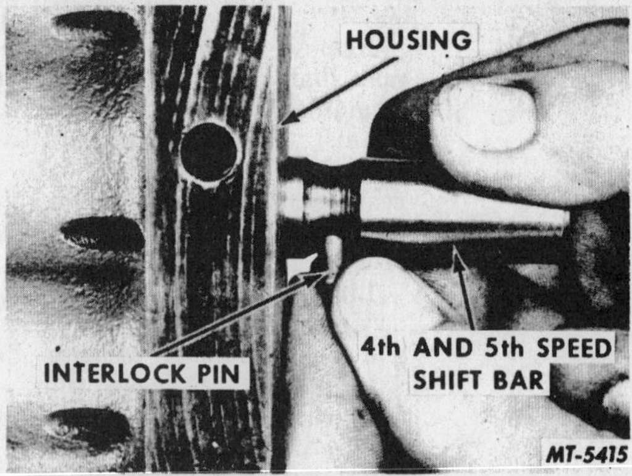

Removing interlock pin
(© Eaton Yale & Towne, Fuller Trans. Div.)

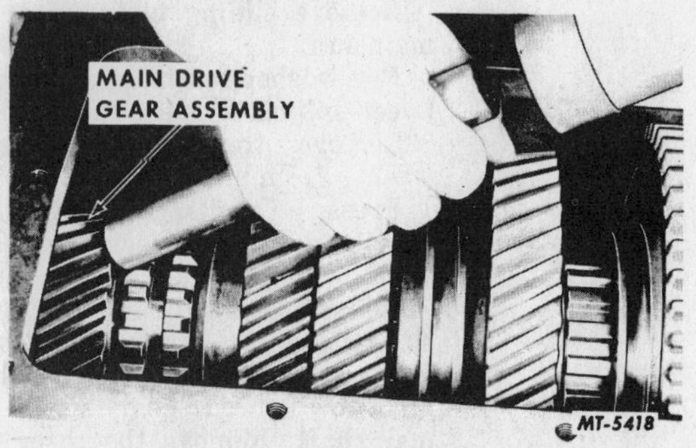

Moving maindrive gear assembly forward
(© Eaton Yale & Towne, Fuller Trans. Div.)

Unseating mainshaft rear bearing
(© Eaton Yale & Towne, Fuller Trans. Div.)

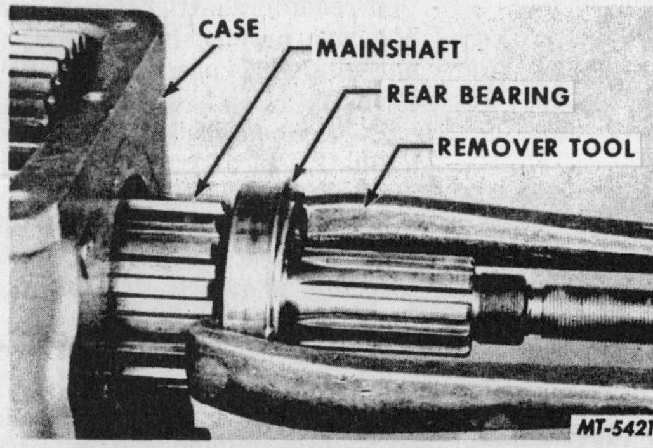

Rear bearing removal
(© Eaton Yale & Towne, Fuller Trans. Div.)

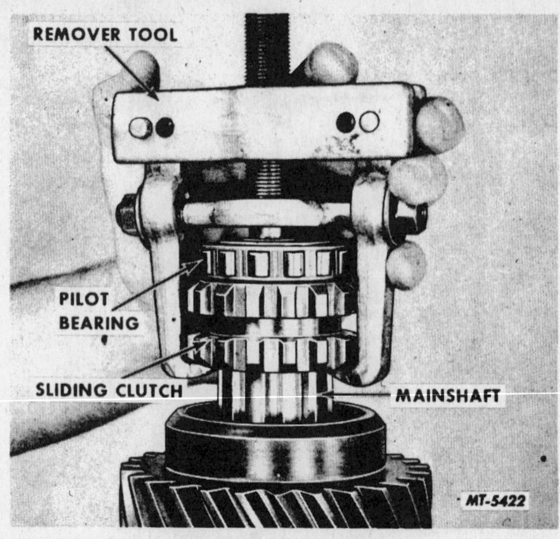

Pilot bearing removal
(© Eaton Yale & Towne, Fuller Trans. Div.)

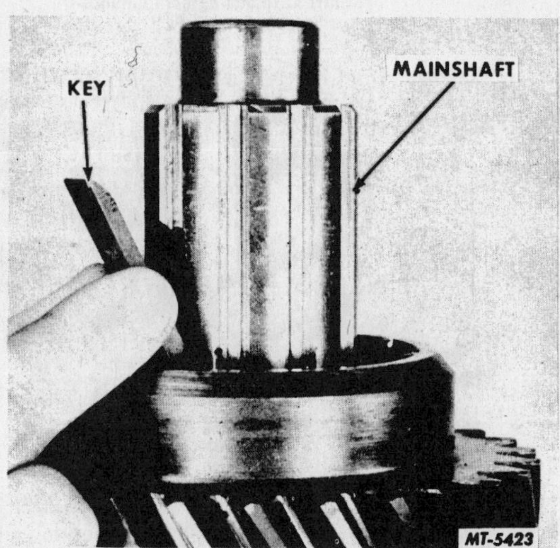

Removing key from mainshaft
(© Eaton Yale & Towne, Fuller Trans. Div.)

Pressing drive gear from countershaft
(© Eaton Yale & Towne, Fuller Trans. Div.)

countershaft.

Press drive gear from countershaft.

NOTE: Press gears from countershaft ONE AT A TIME.

Individually press power-take-off gear, fourth-speed gear, and third-speed from countershaft. Remove woodruff keys from countershaft.

Assembly of Sub-Assemblies

Install the four woodruff keys in countershaft. Press gears on counter shaft *one at a time*. Align third-speed gear keyway with countershaft keys. Press gear on shaft with long hub of gear seated tightly against integral gear of countershaft.

Align fourth-speed gear keyway with keys in countershaft. Press gear on shaft with long hub towards and tightly against PTO gear.

Line up keyway with keys and press power-take-off gear on countershaft with long hub seated tightly against fourth-speed gear. With keyway and keys aligned, press drive gear on countershaft with long hub tightly against PTO gear. Install snap-ring in groove at front of countershaft.

Install countershaft front bearing in case bore. Install washer on front of countershaft.

Insert front of shaft into front bearing. Be certain that washer has not moved from its place.

Install rear bearing on countershaft and into bore of case, shield to the inside. Seat bearing tightly against shoulder of shaft.

NOTE: Do not apply driving pressure to outer race of bearing.

Wedge a wood block between gears and case. Install countershaft bearing nut on rear of shaft and torque to specifications (see "Torque Chart"). This nut can also be tightened after the mainshaft has been installed and gears can be locked, thus eliminating the need for wood blocking.

Peen nut into milled slot in countershaft.

Reverse Idler Gear

Place the two needle bearings into bore of reverse idler gear. Insert reverse idler shaft through bore in case just enough to hold the rear thrust washer in position. Install washer on shaft.

Place front thrust washer in recess at front of reverse idler gear.

Place reverse idler gear with front thrust washer into case, large gear towards the front.

Install reverse idler shaft through washers and gear making sure that milled flat on end of shaft aligns with lock bolt hole and flush with case. Install reverse idler shaft lock and torque bolt to specifications.

Mainshaft

Position mainshaft in a soft-jawed vise with the pilot end up.

Install woodruff keys in the three keyways in the mainshaft. Install second-speed gear on mainshaft, clutching teeth towards pilot end.

Install pilot bearing on mainshaft, chamfered inner diameter to the rear.

Install first and reverse speed sliding gear on mainshaft with the shift fork slot facing front. Place gear on the extreme rear of mainshaft splines.

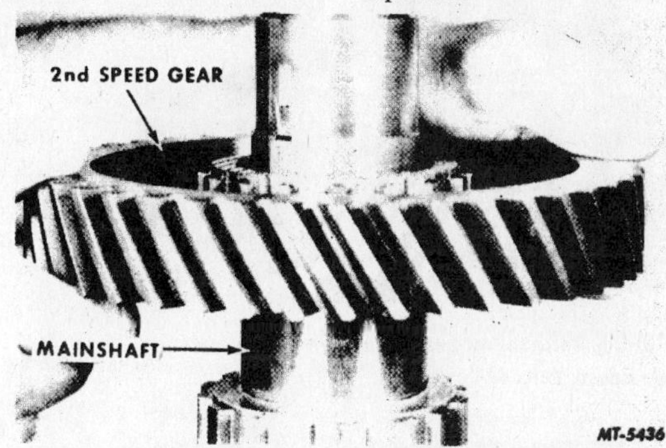

Second-speed gear installation
(© Eaton Yale & Towne, Fuller Trans. Div.)

Install clutch gear on mainshaft with the gear keyway aligned with the key in shaft. Fit tightly against shaft shoulder with chamfered ID towards second-speed gear.

Position mainshaft assembly in case. Place mainshaft rear bearing on shaft and into case bore, seating firmly against shoulder of shaft. Install speedometer gear washer on mainshaft against bearing. Install speedometer drive gear on rear of mainshaft and against washer.

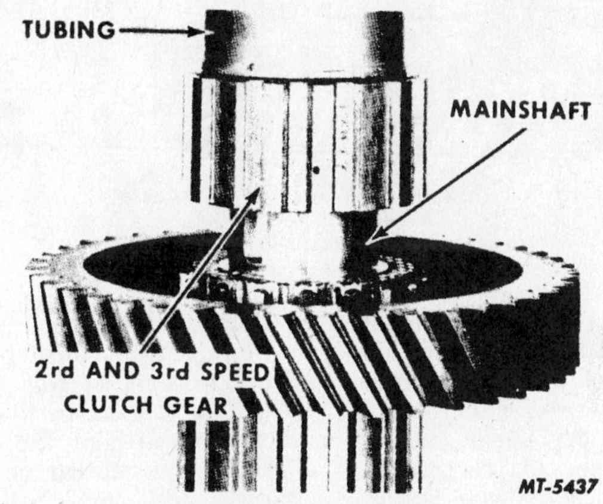

Clutch gear installation
(© Eaton Yale & Towne, Fuller Trans. Div.)

Install second and third-speed sliding clutch collar on clutch gear.

Align keyway in third-speed gear sleeve with key in mainshaft and install the sleeve on shaft, fitting tightly against clutch gear.

Install third-speed gear on sleeve with the clutching teeth facing rear of mainshaft and install sleeve on shaft, seating tightly against shoulder of shaft.

Install fourth-speed gear on sleeve, clutching teeth forward. Install washer in pocket of fourth-speed gear and in its groove or mainshaft, chamfer on ID towards gear.

Turn washer in its groove so that its lugs align with mainshaft splines. Install retaining key in keyway located between mainshaft splines.

Place fourth and fifth-speed sliding clutch on mainshaft with side marked *"front"* to the front.

Install mainshaft rear bearing retainer and gasket and torque bolts in a staggered sequence.

Main Drive Gear

Press main drive gear bearing tightly against shoulder of shaft with the snap-ring away from gear. Mount main drive gear in a soft-jawed vise with pilot end up. Apply a sufficient amount of metal to metal cement to threads of shaft and nut and torque down nut on shaft.

NOTE: Shaft and nut have a left-hand thread. Wipe off excess metal cement. Lock bearing nut by peening it into the two milled slots in mainshaft. Metal cement will harden sooner if placed under a heat lamp for 10 to 15 minutes.

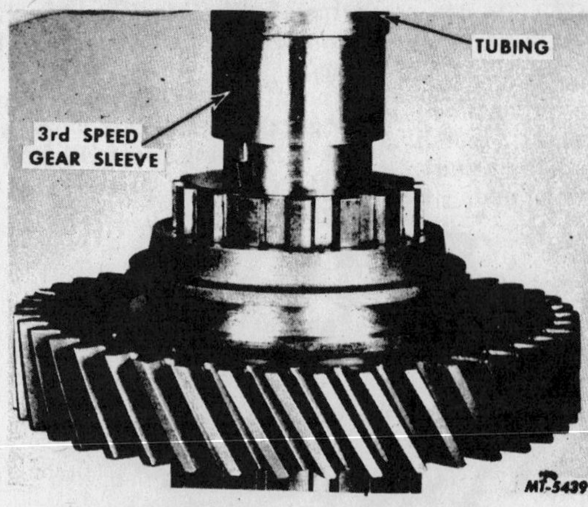

Installing third-speed gear sleeve on mainshaft
(© Eaton Yale & Towne, Fuller Trans. Div.)

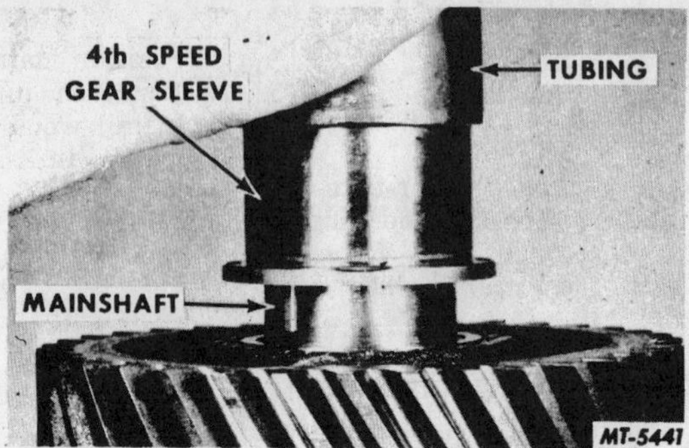

Installing fourth-speed gear sleeve on mainshaft
(© Eaton Yale & Towne, Fuller Trans. Div.)

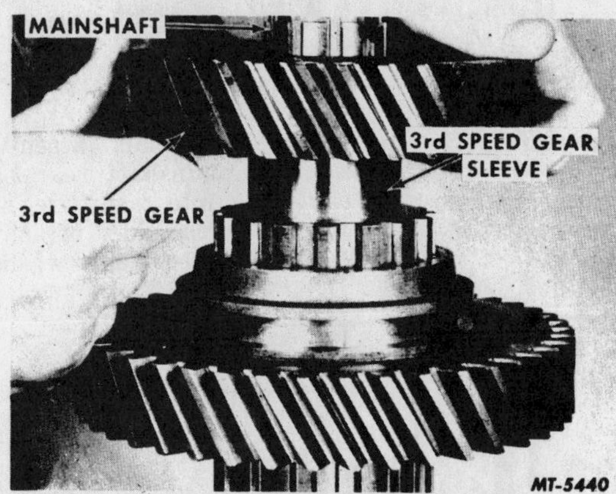

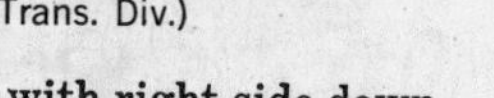

Third-speed gear installation
(© Eaton Yale & Towne, Fuller Trans. Div.)

Installing sliding clutch gear on mainshaft
(© Eaton Yale & Towne, Fuller Trans. Div.)

Install main drive gear assembly into case bore. Turn mainshaft during installation of drive gear to assure proper seating of pilot bearing in pocket of main drive gear.

Using the proper adapter, place a new seal in main drive gear bearing retainer, install the retainer and new gasket and torque bolts to specifications.

NOTE: Be certain that retainer is installed with oil channel to the bottom.

Companion Flange

Lock mainshaft by engaging two speeds with the sliding clutch gears. Install companion flange on mainshaft splines.

NOTE: Mainshaft rear bearing retainer must be perfectly aligned. Use companion flange as a gauge to see if retainer binds or rubs against companion flange when mainshaft is turned. If binding or rubbing takes place, loosen bolts, reposition retainer, and retorque bolts.

Install and torque companion flange nut on mainshaft. Install cotter pin.

Shift Bar Housing

Place shift lever housing in a vise with right side down.

Start 2nd and 3rd-speed shift bar through front, bottom bore in housing. This bar can be identified as the short one without the interlock pin bore in the neutral notch. As shift bar reaches poppet ball spring bore, insert spring and then ball into bore. Move shift bar into housing past ball.

Continue to push shift bar into housing and install the 2nd and 3rd-speed shift fork, making certain the legs of the fork are to the rear.

Install set screw in shift fork, tighten and wire securely.

Install ¾ interlock ball in opening in right side of housing. This ball rides between the 2nd and 3rd-speed shift bar and 4th and 5th-speed shift bar.

Enter the 4th and 5th-speed shift bar through front, center bore of housing.

This is the short bar with an interlock pin bore in the neutral notch. As shift bar reaches poppet ball spring bore, insert spring and ball in bore. Complete movement of bar into housing past ball and spring and install 4th and 5th-speed shift fork on bar

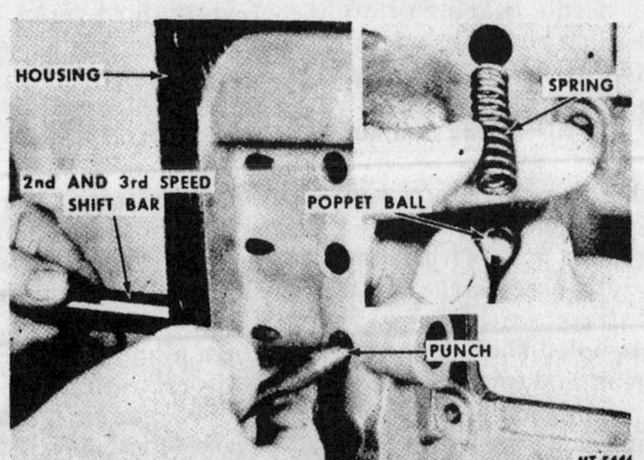

Installing shift bar, poppet ball and spring
(© Eaton Yale & Towne, Fuller Trans. Div.)

Installing 2nd and 3rd-speed shift fork
(© Eaton Yale & Towne, Fuller Trans. Div.)

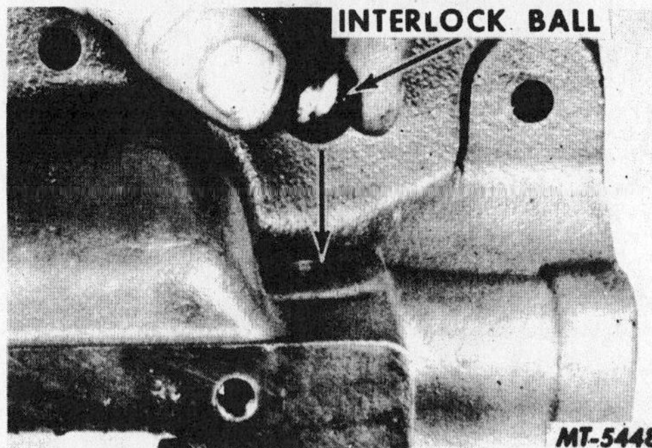

Installing interlock ball
(© Eaton Yale & Towne, Fuller Trans. Div.)

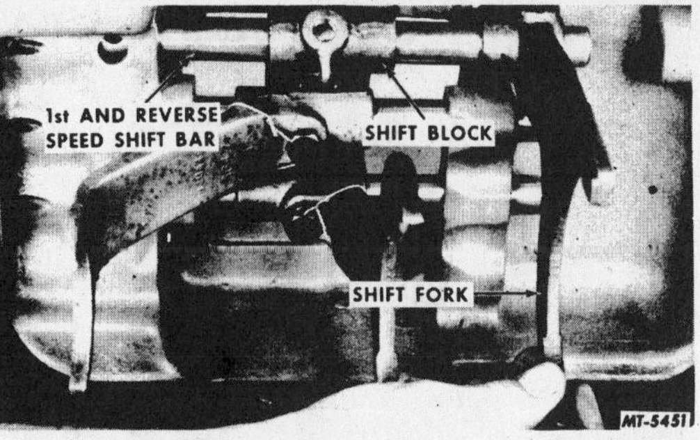

Installing first and reverse-speed shift fork and block
(© Eaton Yale & Towne, Fuller Trans. Div.)

Shift bars in neutral position
(© Eaton Yale & Towne, Fuller Trans. Div.)

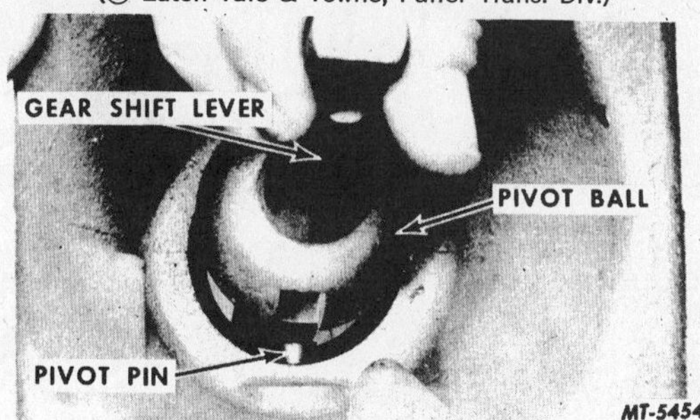

Gear shift lever installation
(© Eaton Yale & Towne, Fuller Trans. Div.)

with fork legs facing the front. Install interlock pin in neutral notch as notch enters housing.

Install setscrew in shift fork, tighten and wire securely.

Install ¾″ interlock ball in opening in right-side of housing. This ball rides between the 4th and 5th-speed shift bar and 1st and reverse-speed shift bar.

Start 1st and reverse-speed shift bar (the longest bar) through front top bore in housing. Insert spring and ball and push bar past them. Install shift block and 1st and reverse-speed shift fork on bar with long hub of fork towards front of housing.

Install shift fork and block setscrew. Tighten and wire securely. Recheck shift forks to assure correct position.

Install cup in interlock ball opening in right-side of housing. Install the longest cup in shift bar bore at rear of housing and place the other cups in the three shift bar bores at the front of the housing.

Make sure that transmission and shift bar housing assembly are in the neutral position.

Install shift bar housing and new gasket on transmission case and torque to specifications.

Control Lever Housing

Insert gear lever pivot pin in housing. Install lockwasher and nut on outer end of pivot pin.

Mount housing in a vise and place gear shift lever in housing. Align keyway in pivot ball with end of pivot pin.

Install tension spring washer and spring in housing. Depress spring until upper coil is held by lugs inside housing.

Remove assembly from vise and install rubber boot on gear shift lever. Install gear shift lever handle.

With shift bar housing assembly in neutral position, install new gasket and control lever housing entering lower end of lever in notches in shift forks and block. Install and torque bolts.

Lubrication

An initial oil change, flush and filter change (if so equipped) is recommended after the first 100 hours of use. After this initial service, do so every 10,000 miles or twice each year. This applies to normal usage of unit; however, for severe service, more frequent lubrication may be necessary. It is recommended that periodic checks be made for lubricant contamination to establish service periods for particular operations.

Do not overfill transmission. Overfilling will cause oil to be forced out of case through mainshaft openings.

Use straight mineral oil SAE-90 temperatures 0°F and up. Use SAE-80 for temperatures below 0°F.

Special Recommendations

Where temperature is consistently below 0°F and where parked vehicles are exposed to unusual cold for long periods, use SAE-75. Where temperatures are consistently above 90°F (unusually hot) use SAE-140 straight mineral oil.

See "Specifications Table" for lubricant capacity.

Torque Chart (Ft. lbs.)

Main drive gear bearing retainer to case	⅜-16 35-45
Shift bar housing to case	⅜-16 35-45
Rear bearing retainer to case	⅜-16 35-45
PTO or PTO cover to case	⅜-16 15-20
Companion flange to mainshaft	1¼-18 225-275
Reverse idler shaft lock bolt to case	⅜-16 15-20
Shift tower to shift cover	⅜-16 35-45
Main drive gear bearing nut	2⅛-16 250-300
Countershaft bearing nut	1¼-18 225-275

G.M. Corporation Model SM318 3 Speed

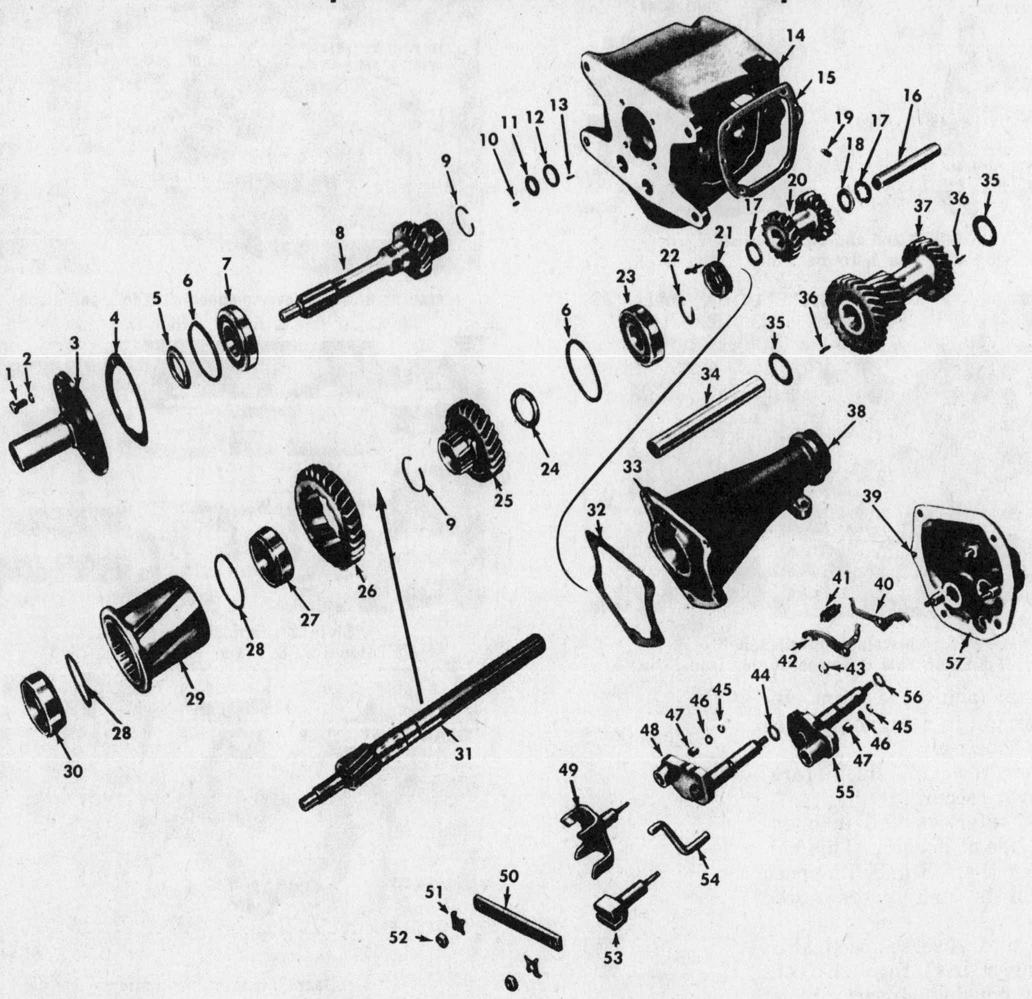

1 Bearing retainer bolt
2 Bearing retainer lock washer
3 Drive gear bearing retainer
4 Bearing retainer gasket
5 Drive gear bearing retaining nut
6 Drive gear bearing snap ring
7 Main drive gear bearing
8 Main drive gear
9 Energizing spring
10 Front pilot bearing rollers
11 Thrust washer
12 Thrust washer
13 Rear pilot bearing rollers
14 Transmission case
15 Side cover gasket
16 Reverse idler gear shaft
17 Thrust bearing washer
18 Thrust bearing
19 Reverse idler shaft pin
20 Reverse idler gear
21 Speedometer drive gear & clip
22 Snap ring
23 Mainshaft rear bearing
24 Thrust washer
25 Second speed gear
26 First & reverse sliding gear
27 Synchronizer ring
28 Synchronizer ring retainer
29 2nd and 3rd speed clutch
30 Synchronizer ring
31 Mainshaft
32 Extension gasket
33 Rear bearing snap ring groove
34 Countershaft
35 Thrust washer
36 Countershaft bearing rollers
37 Countergear
38 Transmission case extension
39 Cover locating pin
40 2nd and 3rd detent cam
41 Detent cam spring
42 1st and reverse detent cam
43 Detent cam retainer
44 1st and reverse shifter shaft O-ring
45 Shifter fork retainer
46 Shifter fork washer
47 Shifter fork roller
48 1st and reverse shifter shaft and plate assembly
49 1st and reverse shifter fork
50 Shifter interlock retainer
51 Interlock retainer stud nut lock
52 Interlock retainer stud nut
53 2nd and 3rd shifter fork
54 Shifter interlock
55 2nd and 3rd shifter shaft and plate assembly
56 2nd and 3rd shifter shaft O-ring
57 Side cover

Corporation Model SM318—exploded view (© G.M.C.)

Description

The G.M. Corporation Model SM318 (Muncie) is a synchromesh three speed transmission using helical gears. The countershaft gear is a cluster-type, mounted on needle roller bearings and supported on a steel countershaft which is press fit into the transmission case. The engagement of 2nd and 3rd gear is assisted by synchronizers.

General data	
Type	3-Speed
Synchromesh	2nd and 3rd Speeds
Model	SM318
Gear ratios	
1st Speed	2.94 to 1
2nd Speed	1.68 to 1
3rd Speed	1 to 1
Reverse	3.14 to 1

Disassembly

1. Remove the transmission side cover and gasket.
2. Pull the extension and mainshaft assembly out of the transmission case, leaving second and third-speed clutch and first and reverse sliding gear in the case.
3. Slide first and reverse gear from synchronizing clutch sleeve, then remove them separately through

side opening in transmission case.

4. Remove 24 rear and 14 larger front pilot bearing rollers from inside the main drive (clutch) gear.
5. Remove clutch gear bearing retainer.
6. Remove the countershaft by driving it from front to rear, using a dummy shaft. Lower the countergear to the bottom of the case.
7. Remove the clutch gear bearing snap-ring. Tap end of shaft to move gear and bearing assembly into case and remove through side of case.
8. Remove the counter gear with dummy, 50 rollers, and washers intact, from the case.
9. Drive the reverse idler shaft lock pin into the shaft. The pin is shorter than the diameter of the shaft.
10. With a drift, tap rear of reverse idler shaft to drive out plug ahead of the shaft.
11. Remove reverse idler gear, front thrust washer, radial roller thrust bearing and the rear thrust washer.
12. To remove the mainshaft from the extension, remove the speedometer driven gear from side of extension. Remove bearing snap-ring. Tap rear of shaft with a soft hammer to bring shaft, speedometer drive gear, second-speed gear and bearing as an assembly, forward and out of the extension.

Servicing the Mainshaft

1. Press speedometer drive gear off the main shaft.
2. Remove rear bearing-to-main shaft snap-ring and press bearing off shaft.
3. Remove second-speed gear thrust washer and second-speed gear.
4. Replace necessary parts and reassemble as follows:
   a. Slide second-speed gear on the shaft and install thrust washer with oil grooves toward the gear.
   b. Install new rear bearing, groove in outside of bearing toward second-speed gear.
   c. Select one of four available snap-rings so that end-play of bearing on shaft does not exceed .004 in.
   d. Start the speedometer drive gear on shaft with chamfered inside diameter of gear toward the bearing. Press the gear on the shaft until forward face of gear is 53/64 in. from rear face of bearing.

Servicing the Clutch Gear

1. With clutch gear in a soft-jawed vise, remove bearing retaining nut and oil slinger. The nut and oil slinger is a one piece steel casting with a left-hand thread and is staked in place on the clutch gear shaft.
2. To remove the bearing from the clutch gear, up-end the front of the transmission case on the bench. Install the gear and bearing in the front of the case with the snap-ring on the bearing.
3. Press the shaft out of the bearing and into the case.
4. Tap the bearing out of the case.
5. Press clutch gear bearing onto the clutch gear. Be sure the bearing locating ring groove is toward the front of the shaft.
6. Install clutch bearing retaining nut, tighten and stake securely.

Servicing the Synchronizer

1. Turn one synchronizer ring in the clutch (sleeve) until the ends of the ring retainer can be seen through the slot in the clutch sleeve.
2. Using a snap-ring expander, spread the retainer in the counterbore in the clutch sleeve, then withdraw the synchronizer ring.
3. Remove the other synchronizer ring in the same manner.
4. Lightly grease both synchronizer rings.
5. Install a synchronizer ring retainer in the counterbore at one end of the clutch sleeve.

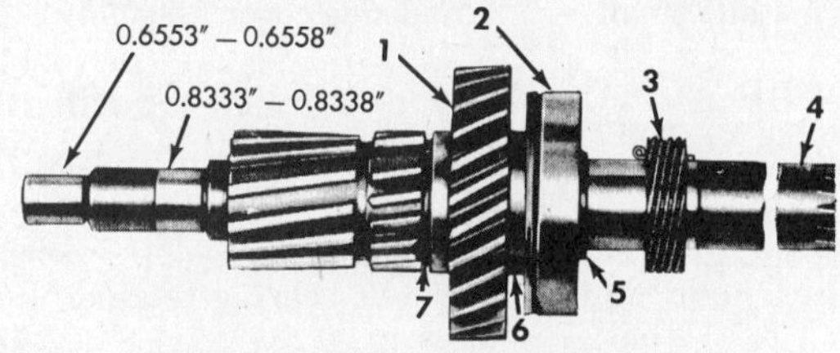

1 Second speed gear
2 Rear bearing
3 Speedometer drive gear
4 Mainshaft
5 Snap ring
6 Thrust washer
7 Energizing spring

Mainshaft assembly
(© G.M.C.)

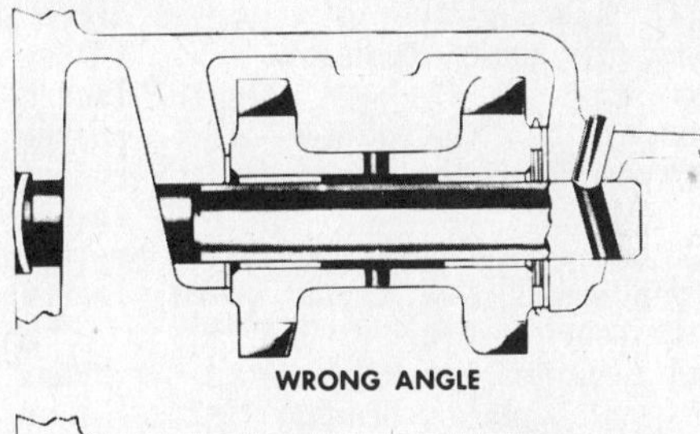

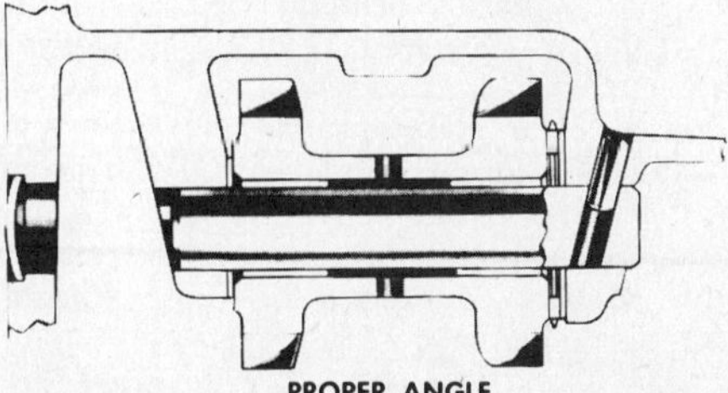

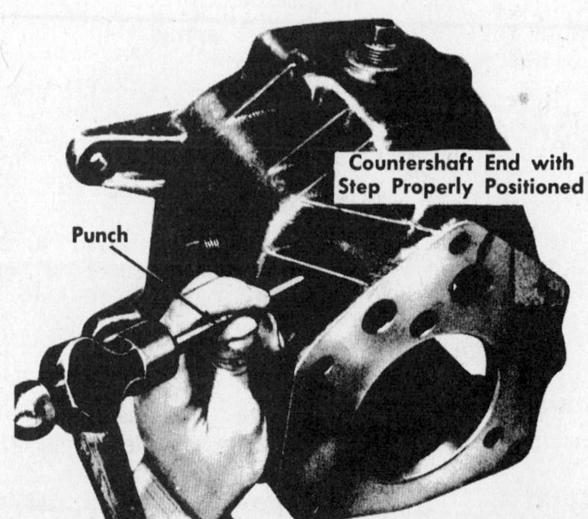

Proper position of countershaft end
(© G.M.C.)

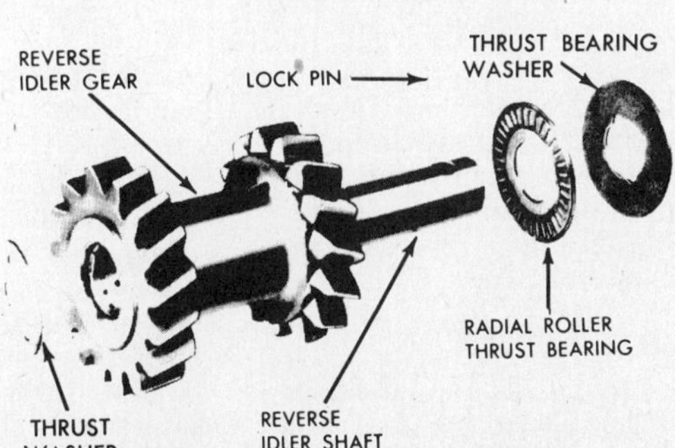

Reverse idler gear shaft and lock pin
(© G.M.C.)

6. Insert ring expander through slot in clutch sleeve and expand retainer in counterbore. Install ring in clutch sleeve.
7. Install other synchronizer ring in the same manner.

Transmission Assembly

1. Coat thrust washers and needle roller thrust bearing with grease.
2. Position the needle bearing against the rear of the gear (end with chamfered teeth) and position the large thrust washer against the bearing. Position small thrust washer at opposite end of gear.
3. From the rear of the case, install idler shaft, aligning lock pin hole in shaft with hole in case.
4. Position reverse idler gear in the cases of the radial roller thrust bearing is toward the rear of the case and the gear is lined up with the shaft. Tap shaft from rear until lock pin holes are lined up. NOTE: Replacement of gear bushings is not recommended. These bushings are bored to specifications using special boring tools and improper replacement can cause future problems. Bushing can be replaced only as a unit with the gear.
5. Coat new idler shaft pin with sealer and drive it in about 1/16 in. Penn the hole slightly.
6. Install new idler shaft expansion plug in front of case.
7. Grease both ends of the countergear bore and insert the dummy shaft.
8. Install 25 bearing rollers at each end of countergear.
9. Grease the bearing thrust washers and countergear thrust washers and place bearing thrust washers, followed by countergear thrust washers, at both ends of the countergear thrust washers and place bearing thrust washers, followed by countergear thrust washers, at both ends of the countergear, making sure that the tangs on the countergear thrust washers face out.
10. Let the gear, dummy shaft and washer assembly lie in the bottom of the case.
11. From inside the case, push clutch gear assembly through opening in front face of case and tap clutch gear assembly until clutch gear bearing locating ring groove is outside front of case.
12. Install snap-ring in bearing groove and tap clutch gear toward the rear until snap-ring is firm against the face of the case.
13. Install clutch gear bearing retainer and gasket.
14. Apply sealer to threads of bearing retainer bolts and torque to 12-15 ft. lbs.
15. Lift the countershaft into place and into alignment with the countershaft bore. Be sure that the thrust washers are in place.
16. Lubricate and start the countershaft into the case from the rear. Be sure the flat on the face of the shaft is horizontal and at the bottom to permit installation of case extension.
17. Push countershaft in and dummy shaft out until the flat on the end of the countershaft is flush with the rear face of the case.
18. Grease and install 14 large rollers in the pilot hole of the main drive gear, then install small I.D. spacer.
19. Insert the large I.D. front spacer, followed by the 24 small rollers.
20. Insert the large I.D. front spacer with chamfered side out.
21. Insert synchronizing clutch assembly, shoulder to front, through rear opening in case.
22. Line up two inner lugs of clutch sleeve synchronizing ring with two wide grooves in main drive gear and slide clutch assembly onto main drive gear.
23. Through side opening in the case, insert first and reverse sliding gear, with wide inner bevel and small round depression toward the rear. Pilot the first and reverse sliding gear onto the clutch.
24. Insert mainshaft assembly in the transmission case extension, and by spreading the mainshaft bearing snap-ring, tap front end of mainshaft until snap-ring seats in mainshaft bearing groove.
25. Affix new extension housing gasket to transmission case.
26. Align clutch splines on the mainshaft with clutch splines on second-speed gear so that they will receive the two inner lugs of the synchronizer ring of second and third-speed clutch. Mark for identification.
27. Insert mainshaft assembly through opening at rear of transmission case. Be sure the two inner lugs of the synchronizing ring engage the previously marked grooves of mainshaft and second speed gear.
28. Rotate extension housing to line up with case and finger tighten housing bolts with sealer on them.
29. Set transmission assembly top side up. Maneuver second and third speed clutch until extension housing fits flush against transmission case and torque to 40 to 45 ft. lbs.
30. Install speedometer driven gear, and side cover assembly.

Torque Wrench Specifications

	Foot-Pounds
Drain plug	24 to 35
Filler plug	25 to 35
Drive gear bearing retainer bolts	12 to 15
Transmission cover bolts	15 to 18
Transmission extension bolts	40 to 45
Shifter lever clamp bolt nuts	14 to 16
Shifter interlock retainer nuts	3 to 5
Drive gear bearing retainer nut	39 to 41

G.M. Corporation Model SM326 3 Speed

Description

The G.M. Corporation Model SM326 (Saginaw) is a synchromesh three-speed transmission using helical constant mesh gears. The engagement of all gears except reverse is assisted by synchronizers.

General data

Type 3-Speed

Synchromesh Gears 1st, 2nd, and 3rd

Model SM326 and SM326 w/Overdrive

Gear Ratios

1st Speed	2.85:1
2nd Speed	1.68:1
3rd Speed	1.00:1
Reverse	2.95:1

Transmission Disassembly

1. Remove side cover assembly and shift forks.
2. Remove clutch gear bearing retainer.
3. Remove clutch gear bearing to gear stem snap-ring. Pull clutch gear outward until a screwdriver can be inserted between bearing and case. Remove clutch gear bearing.
4. Remove speedometer driven gear and extension bolts.
5. Remove reverse idler shaft snap-ring. Slide reverse idler gear forward on shaft.
6. Remove mainshaft and extension assembly.
7. Remove clutch gear and third-speed blocker ring from inside

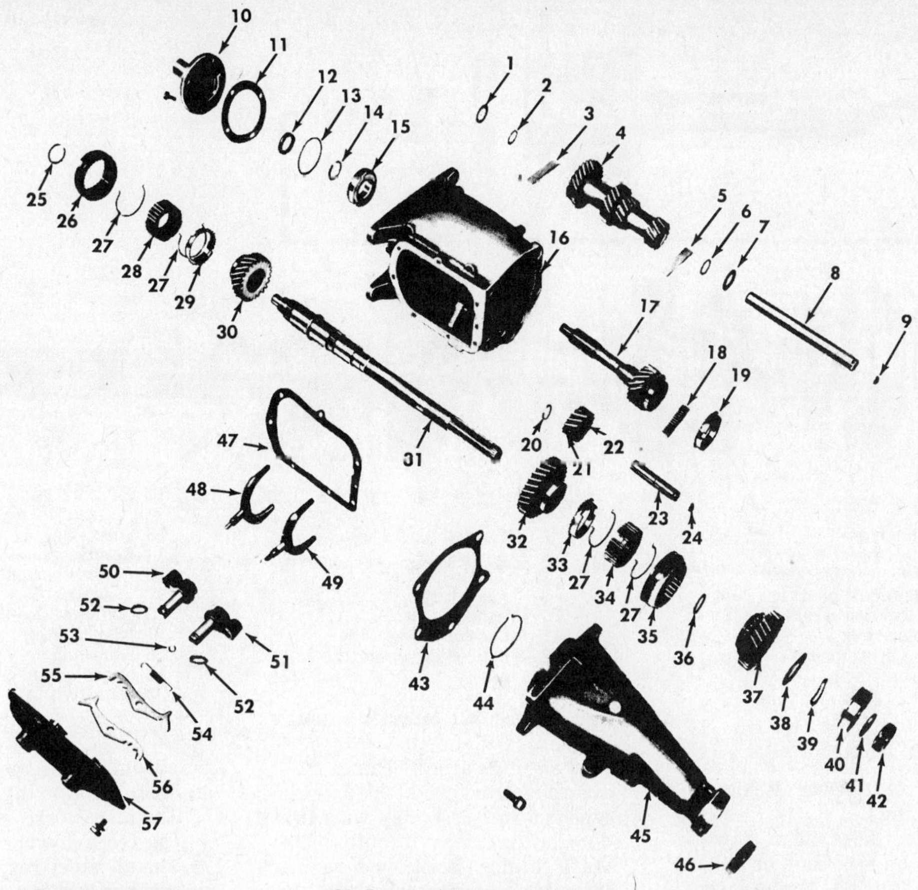

1 Thrust washer—front
2 Bearing washer
3 Needle bearings
4 Countergear
5 Needle bearings
6 Bearing washer
7 Thrust washer—rear
8 Countershaft
9 Woodruff key
10 Bearing retainer
11 Gasket
12 Oil seal
13 Snap ring—bearing to case
14 Snap ring—bearing to gear
15 Clutch gear bearing
16 Case
17 Clutch gear
18 Pilot bearings
19 3rd speed blocker ring
20 Retainer E-Ring
21 Reverse idler gear
22 Reverse idler gear bushing (not serviced separately)
23 Reverse idler shaft
24 Woodruff key
25 Snap ring—hub to shaft
26 2-3 synchronizer sleeve
27 Synchronizer key spring
28 2-3 Synchronizer hub assy.
29 2nd speed blocker ring
30 2nd speed gear
31 Mainshaft
32 1st speed gear
33 1st speed blocker ring
34 1st and reverse synchronizer hub assembly
35 1st and reverse synchronizer sleeve
36 Snap ring—hub to shaft
37 Reverse gear assy.
38 Thrust washer
39 Thrust washer
40 Rear bearing
41 Snap ring—bearing to shaft
42 Speedometer drive gear
43 Gasket
44 Snap ring—rear bearing to extension
45 Extension
46 Oil seal
47 Gasket
48 2-3 shift fork
49 1st and reverse shift fork
50 2-3 shifter shaft assembly
51 1st and reverse shifter shaft assembly
52 O-ring seal
53 Detent cam retainer ring
54 Spring
55 2nd and 3rd detent cam
56 1st and reverse detent cam
57 Side cover

SM326 transmission components (© G.M.C.)

case. Remove 14 roller bearings from clutch gear.

8. Expand the snap-ring which retains the mainshaft rear bearing. Remove the extension.
9. Usnig a dummy shaft, drive the countershaft and key out the rear of the case. Remove the gear, two tanged thrust washers, and dummy shaft. Remove bearing washer and 27 roller bearings from each end of countergear.
10. Use a long drift to drive the reverse idler shaft and key through the rear of the case.
11. Remove reverse idler gear and tanged steel thrust washer.

Mainshaft Disassembly

1. Remove second and third speed sliding clutch hug snap-ring from mainshaft. Remove clutch assembly, second speed blocker ring, and second speed gear from front of mainshaft.
2. Depress speedometer drive gear retaining clip. Remove gear. Some units have a metal speedometer drive gear which must be pulled off.
3. Remove rear bearing snap-ring.
4. Support reverse gear. Press on rear of mainshaft. Remove reverse gear, thrust washer, spring washer, rear bearing, and snap-ring. When pressing off the rear bearing, be careful not to cock the bearing on the shaft.
5. Remove first and reverse sliding clutch hub snap-ring. Remove clutch assembly, first speed blocker ring, and first gear.

Cleaning and Inspection

See "Cleaning and Inspection" instructions at front of transmission section.

Clutch Keys and Springs

Keys and springs may be replaced if worn or broken, but the hubs and sleeves are matched pairs and must be kept together.

1. Mark hub and sleeve for reas-

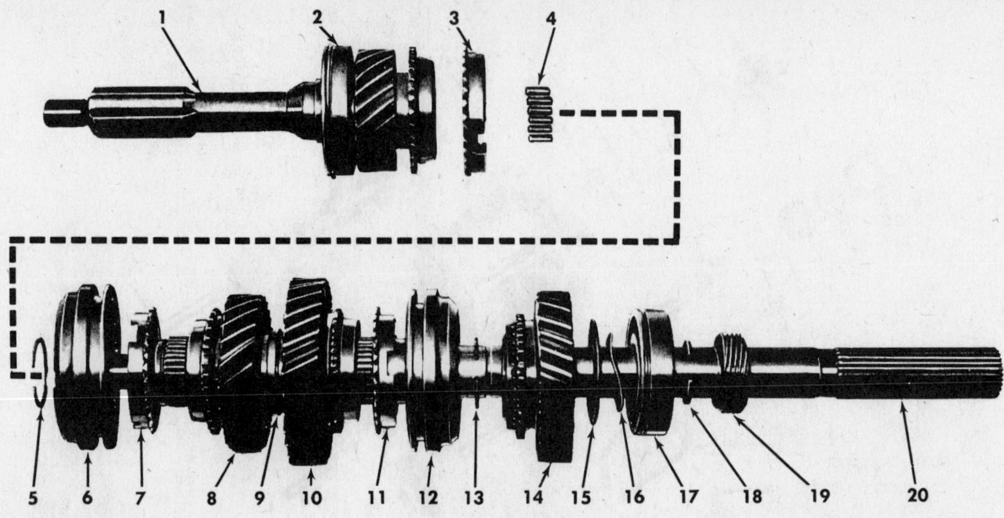

1 Clutch gear
2 Clutch gear bearing
3 3rd speed blocker ring
4 Mainshaft pilot bearings (14)
5 Snap ring
6 2-3 synchronizer assembly
7 2nd speed blocker ring
8 2nd speed gear
9 Shoulder (part of mainshaft)
10 1st speed gear
11 1st speed blocker ring
12 1st speed synchronizer assy.
13 Snap ring
14 Reverse gear
15 Reverse gear thrust washer
16 Spring washer
17 Rear bearing
18 Snap ring
19 Speedo drive gear
20 Mainshaft

Clutch gear and mainshaft assembly (© G.M.C.)

sembly.

2. Push hub from sleeve. Remove keys and springs.
3. Place three keys and two springs, one on each side of hub, in position, so all three keys are engaged by both springs. The tanged end of the springs should not be installed into the same key.
4. Slide the sleeve onto the hub, aligning the marks.

NOTE: A groove around the outside of the synchronizer hub marks the end that must be opposite the fork slot in the sleeve when assembled.

Extension Oil Seal and Bushing

1. Remove seal.
2. Using bushing remover and installer tool, or other suitable tool, drive bushing into extension housing.
3. Drive new bushing in from the rear. Lubricate inside of bushing and seal. Install new oil seal with extension seal installer tool or other suitable tool.

Clutch Bearing Retainer Oil Seal

1. Pry old seal out.
2. Install new seal using seal installer or suitable tool. Seat seal in bore.

Mainshaft Assembly

1. Turn front of mainshaft up.
2. Install second gear with clutching teeth up; the rear face of the gear butts against the flange on the mainshaft.
3. Install a blocker ring with clutching teeth down. All three blocker rings are the same.
4. Install second and third speed synchronizer assembly with fork slot down. Press it onto mainshaft splines. Both synchronizer assemblies are the same. Be sure that blocker ring notches align with synchronizer assembly keys.
5. Install synchronizer snap-ring. Both synchronizer snap-rings are the same.
6. Turn rear of shaft up.
7. Install first gear with clutching teeth up; the front face of the gear butts against the flange on the mainshaft.
8. Install a blocker ring with clutching teeth down.
9. Install first and reverse synchronizer assembly with fork slot down. Press it onto mainshaft splines. Be sure blocker ring notches align with synchronizer assembly keys.
10. Install snap-ring.
11. Install reverse gear with clutching teeth down.
12. Install steel reverse gear thrust washer and spring washer.
13. Press rear ball bearing onto shaft with snap-ring slot down.
14. Install snap-ring.
15. Install speedometer drive gear and retaining clip. Press on metal speedometer drive gear.

Transmission Assembly

1. Using dummy shaft load a row of 27 roller bearings and a thrust washer at each end of countergear. Hold in place with grease.
2. Place countergear assembly into case through rear. Place a tanged thrust washer, tang away from gear at each end. Install countershaft and key, making sure that tangs align with

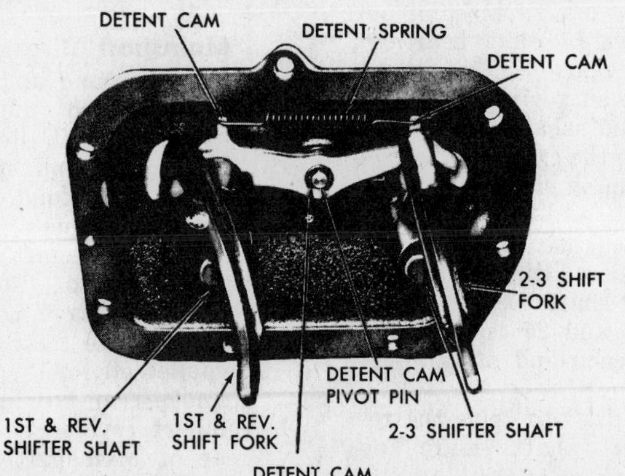

Side cover assembly (© G.M.C.)

notches in case.

3. Install reverse idler gear thrust washer, gear, and shaft with key from rear of case. Be sure thrust washer is between gear and rear of case with tang toward notch in case. NOTE: The reverse idler gear bushing may not be replaced separately—only as a unit with the gear.
4. Expand snap-ring in extension. Assemble extension over rear of mainshaft and onto rear bearing. Seat snap-ring in rear bearing groove.
5. Install 14 mainshaft pilot bearings into clutch gear cavity. Assemble third speed blocker ring onto clutch gear clutching surface with teeth toward gear.
6. Place clutch gear, pilot bearings, and third speed blocker ring assembly over front of mainshaft assembly. Be sure blocker rings align with keys in second-third synchronizer assembly.
7. Stick extension gasket to case with grease. Install clutch gear, mainshaft, and extension together. Be sure clutch gear engages teeth of countergear anti-lash plate. Torque extension bolts to 45 ft. lbs.
8. Place bearing over stem of clutch gear and into front case bore. Install front bearing to clutch gear snap-ring.
9. Install clutch gear bearing retainer and gasket. The retainer oil return hole must be at the bottom. Torque to 10 ft. lbs.
10. Install reverse idler gear shaft E-ring.
11. Shift synchronizer sleeves to neutral positions. Install cover, gasket, and forks, aligning forks with synchronizer sleeve grooves. Torque side cover bolts to 10 ft. lbs.
12. Install speedometer driven gear.

Torque Specifications

	Foot-Pounds
Extension to case attaching bolts	35-55
Drain and filler plugs	10-15
Side cover attaching bolts	18-24
Clutch gear retainer bolts	18-24

G.M. Corporation Model SM330 3 Speed

Description

The G.M. Corporation Model SM 330 (Muncie) is a three-speed transmission using helical constant mesh gears. The engagement of all gears except reverse is assisted by synchronizers.

General Data

Type	3-Speed
Synchromesh gears	1st, 2nd, and 3rd
Model	SM330 (Muncie)

Gear Ratios

1st Speed	3.03:1
2nd Speed	1.75:1
3rd Speed	1.00:1
Reverse	3.02:1

Transmission Disassembly

1. Remove side cover and shift forks.
2. Unbolt extension and rotate to line up groove in extension flange with reverse idler shaft. Drive reverse idler shaft and key out of case with a brass drift.
3. Move second-third synchronizer sleeve forward. Remove extension housing and mainshaft assembly.
4. Remove reverse idler gear from case.
5. Remove thirds peed blocker ring from clutch gear.
6. Expand snap-ring which holds mainshaft rear bearing. Tap gently on end of mainshaft to remove extension.
7. Remove clutch gear bearing retainer and gasket.
8. Remove snap-ring. Remove clutch gear from inside case by gently tapping on end of clutch gear.
9. Remove oil slinger and 16 mainshaft pilot bearings from clutch gear cavity.
10. Slip clutch gear bearing out front of case. Aid removal with a screwdriver between case and bearing outer snap-ring.
11. Drive countershaft and key out to rear.
12. Remove countergear and two tanged thrust washers.

Mainshaft Disassembly

1. Remove speedometer drive gear. Some speedometer drive gears, made of metal, must be pulled off.
2. Remove rear bearing snap-ring.
3. Support reverse gear. Press on rear of mainshaft to remove reverse gear, thrust washer, and rear bearing. Be careful not to cock the bearing on the shaft.
4. Remove first and reverse sliding clutch hub snap-ring.

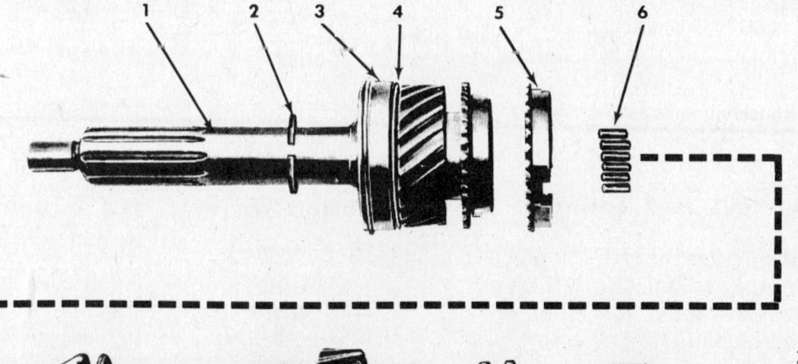

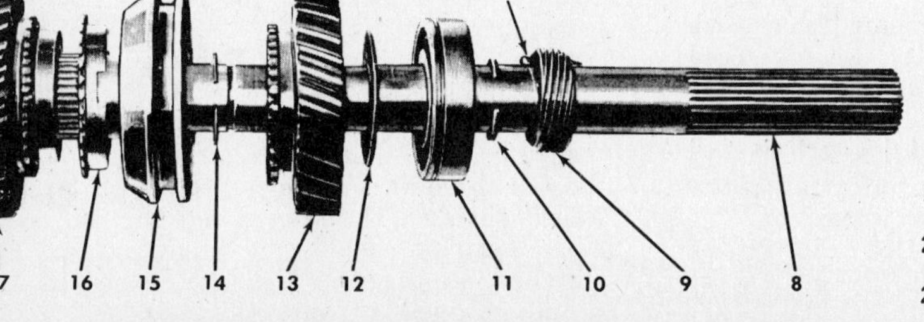

1 Main drive gear
2 Snap ring
3 Main drive gear bearings
4 Oil slinger
5 3rd speed blocker ring
6 Mainshaft pilot bearings
7 Speedometer retainer clip
8 Mainshaft
9 Speedometer drive gear
10 Snap ring
11 Rear bearing
12 Reverse gear thrust washer
13 Reverse gear
14 Snap ring
15 1st & reverse synchronizer assembly
16 First speed blocker ring
17 First speed gear
18 Shoulder (part of mainshaft)
19 Second speed gear
20 Second speed blocker ring
21 2nd and 3rd synchronizer assembly
22 Snap ring

Main drive gear and mainshaft assembly (© G.M.C.)

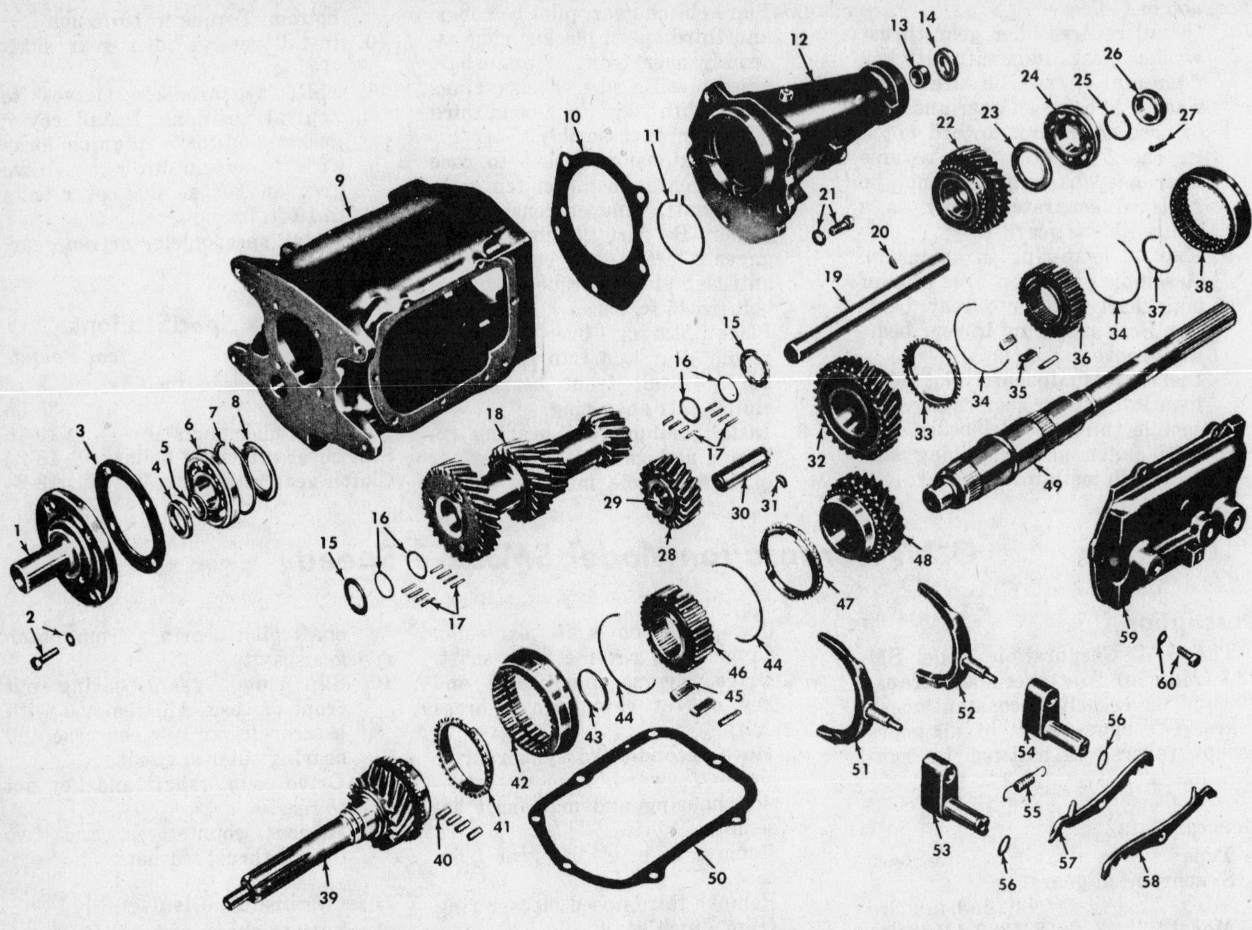

1 Bearing retainer
2 Bolt and lock washer
3 Gasket
4 Oil seal
5 Snap ring (bearing-to-main drive gear)
6 Main drive gear bearing
7 Snap ring bearing
8 Oil slinger
9 Case
10 Gasket
11 Snap ring (rear bearing-to-extension)
12 Extension
13 Extension bushing
14 Oil seal
15 Thrust washer
16 Bearing washer
17 Needle bearings
18 Countergear
19 Countershaft
20 Woodruff key
21 Bolt (extension-to-case)
22 Reverse gear
23 Thrust washer
24 Rear bearing
25 Snap ring
26 Speedometer drive gear
27 Retainer clip
28 Reverse idler gear
29 Reverse idler bushing
30 Reverse idler shaft
31 Woodruff key
32 1st speed gear
33 1st speed blocker ring
34 Synchronizer key spring
35 Synchronizer keys
36 1st and reverse synchronizer hub assembly
37 Snap ring
38 1st and reverse synchronizer collar
39 Main drive gear
40 Pilot bearings
41 3rd speed blocker ring
42 2nd and 3rd synchronizer collar
43 Snap ring
44 Synchronizer key spring
45 Synchronizer keys
46 2nd and 3rd synchronizer hub
47 2nd speed blocker ring
48 2nd speed gear
49 Mainshaft
50 Gasket
51 2nd and 3rd shifter fork
52 1st and reverse shifter fork
53 2-3 shifter shaft assembly
54 1st and reverse shifter shaft assembly
55 Spring
56 O-ring seal
57 1st and reverse detent cam
58 2nd and 3rd detent cam
59 Side cover
60 Bolt and lock washer

SM330 transmission components (© G.M.C.)

5. Support first gear. Press on rear of mainshaft to remove clutch assembly, blocker ring, and first gear.
6. Remove second and third speed sliding clutch hub snap-ring.
7. Support second gear. Press on front of mainshaft to remove clutch assembly, second speed blocker ring, and second gear from shaft.

Cleaning and Inspection

For more detailed information, see the "Cleaning and Inspection" instructions at front of transmission section.

1. Wash all parts in solvent.
2. Air dry.

Clutch Keys and Springs

Keys and sprnigs may be replaced if worn or broken, but the hubs and sleeves must be kept together as originally assembled.

1. Mark hub and sleeve for reassembly.
2. Push hub from sleeve. Remove keys and springs.
3. Place three keys and two springs, one on each side of hub, so all three keys are engaged by both springs. The tanged end of the springs should not be installed into the same key.
4. Slide the sleeve onto the hub, aligning the marks.

Extension Oil Seal and Bushing

1. Remove seal.
2. Using bushing remover and installer, or other suitable tool, drive bushing into extension housing.
3. Drive new bushing in from rear. Lubricate inside of bushing and seal. Install new oil seal with extension seal installer or suitable tool.

Clutch Bearing Retainer Oil Seal

1. Pry old seal out.
2. Install new seal using seal installer or suitable tool. Seat seal in bore.

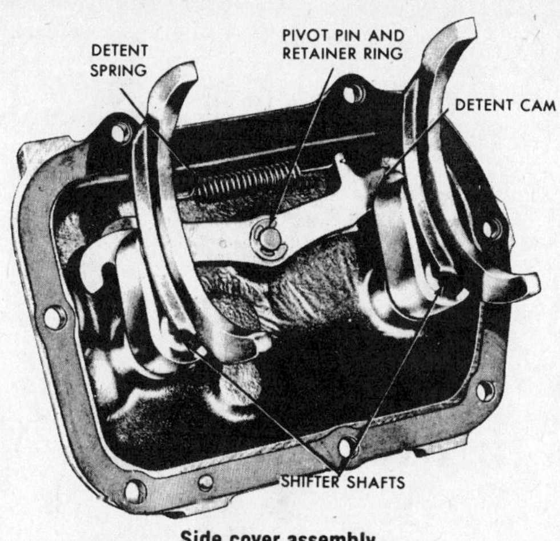

Side cover assembly
(© G.M.C.)

Mainshaft Assembly

1. Lift front of mainshaft.
2. Install second gear with clutching teeth up; the rear face of the gear butts against the mainshaft flange.
3. Install a blocking ring with clutching teeth downward. All three blocking rings are the same.
4. Install second and third synchronizer assembly with fork slot down. Press it onto mainshaft splines. Both synchronizer assemblies are identical but are assembled differently. The second-third speed hub and sleeve is assembled with the sleeve fork slot toward the thrust face of the hub; the first-reverse hub and sleeve, with the fork slot opposite the thrust face. Be sure that the blocker ring notches align with the synchronizer assembly keys.
5. Install synchronizer snap-ring. Both synchronizer snap-rings are the same.
6. Turn rear of shaft up.
7. Install first gear with clutching teeth upward; the front face of the gear butts against the flange on the mainshaft.
8. Install a blocker ring with clutching teeth down.
9. Install first and reverse synchronizer assembly with fork slot down. Press it onto mainshaft splines. Be sure blocker ring notches align with synchronizer assembly keys and synchronizer sleeves face front of mainshaft.
10. Install snap-ring.
11. Install reverse gear with clutching teeth down.
12. Install steel reverse gear thrust washer with flats aligned.
13. Press rear ball bearing onto shaft with snap-ring slot down.
14. Install snap-ring.
15. Install speedometer drive gear and retaining clip.

Transmission Assembly

1. Place a row of 29 roller bearings, a bearing washer, a second row of 29 bearings, and a second bearing washer at each end of the countergear. Hold in place with grease.
2. Place countergear assembly through rear case opening with a tanged thrust washer, tang away from gear, at each end. Install countershaft and key from rear of case. Be sure that thrust washer tangs are aligned with notches in case.
3. Place reverse idler gear in case. Do not install reverse idler shaft yet. NOTE: The reverse idler gear bushing may not be replaced separately—only as a unit.
4. Expand snap-ring in extension. Assemble extension over mainshaft and onto rear bearing. Seat snap-ring.
5. Load 16 mainshaft pilot bearings into clutch gear cavity. Assemble third speed blocker ring onto clutch gear clutching surface with teeth toward gear.
6. Place clutch gear assembly, without front bearing, over front of mainshaft. Make sure that blocker ring notches align with keys in second-third synchronizer assembly.
7. Stick gasket onto extension housing with grease. Assemble clutch gear, mainshaft, and extension to case together. Make sure that clutch gear teeth engage teeth of countergear antilash plate.
8. Rotate extension housing. Install reverse idler shaft and key.
9. Torque extension bolts to 45 ft. lbs.
10. Install oil slinger with inner lip facing forward. Install front bearing outer snap-ring and slide bearing into case bore.
11. Install snap-ring to clutch gear stem. Install bearing retainer and gasket and torque to 20 ft. lbs. Retainer oil return hole must be at 6 o'clock.
12. Shift both synchronizer sleeves to neutral positions. Install side cover, inserting shifter forks in synchronizer sleeve grooves.
13. Torque side cover bolts to 20 ft. lbs.

Torque Specifications

	Foot-Pounds
Extension to case attaching	45
Drain plug	30
Filler plug	15
Side cover attaching bolts	22
Main drive gear rètainer bolts	22
Transmission case to clutch Housing bolts	45

G.M. Corporation SM420 4 Speed

Description

The model SM420 synchromesh has four forward speeds and one reverse. Fourth speed is direct drive. All speeds except first and reverse use helicalgears.

General Data

Type	4-Speed Synchromesh
Model	SM420
Gear Tooth Design	
1st and Reserve	Spur
2nd and Third	Helical
Gear ratios	
1st Speed	7.05 to 1
2nd Speed	3.58 to 1
3rd Speed	1.71 to 1
4th Speed	1 to 1
Reverse	6.78 to 1

Disassembly of Transmission

See exploded view of transmission.

Shift Control Cover Removal

1. Remove gearshift lever from transmission cover using remover and replacer tool.
2. Remove transmission cover.
3. Remove nut lock and nut from reverse shifter lever eccentric. Drive eccentric out of transmission case and remove reverse shifter lever.

Clutch Drive Gear Removal

1. Remove drive gear bearing retainer and gasket.
2. Using a plastic hammer, remove the clutch drive gear from trans-

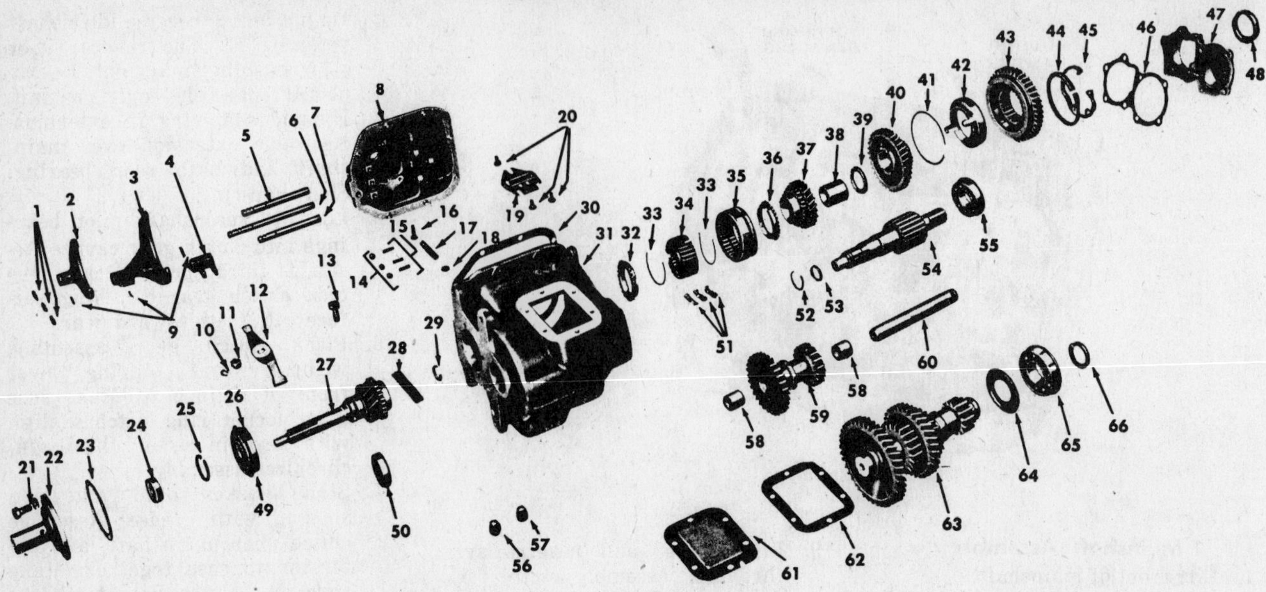

1 Hole plugs
2 3rd and 4th shift fork
3 1st and 2nd shift fork
4 Reverse shifter head
5 3rd and 4th speed shifter shaft
6 1st and 2nd speed shifter shaft
7 Reverse shifter shaft
8 Transmission cover
9 Taper pins
10 Nut Lock
11 Nut
12 Reverse shifter lever
13 Lever eccentric
14 Shifter shaft detent ball
15 Detent ball spring
16 Compression pin
17 Compression spring
18 Plug
19 Interlock Plate Assy.
20 Interlock Plate Pin
21 Retainer bolt
22 Drive gear bearing retainer
23 Retainer gasket
24 Seal
25 Bearing retainer ring
26 Drive gear bearing
27 Clutch drive gear
28 Mainshaft bearing rollers
29 Roller retainer
30 Cover gasket
31 Transmission case
32 Synchronizer cone (4th spd.)
33 Clutch key spring
34 Clutch hub
35 Clutch sleeve
36 Synchronizer cone (3rd spd.)
37 Mainshaft 3rd speed gear
38 3rd speed gear bushing
39 Thrust washer
40 Mainshaft 2nd speed gear
41 Synchronizer ring retainer
42 Synchronizer ring (2nd spd.)
43 Mainshaft 1st and reverse gear
44 Friction ring rubber strip
45 Friction ring (steel)
46 Rear bearing retainer gasket
47 Rear bearing retainer
48 Oil seal
49 Drive gear bearing snap ring
50 Countershaft front bearing
51 Clutch key
52 Clutch hub retainer ring
53 Bearing spacer
54 Mainshaft
55 Mainshaft rear bearing
56 Drain plug
57 Filler plug
58 Bushing
59 Reverse idler gear assy.
60 Idler gear shaft
61 P.T.O. opening cover
62 Cover gasket
63 Countershaft and gear assy.
64 Oil deflector
65 Countershaft rear bearing
66 Bearing retainer ring

Third and fourth speed synchronizing components (© G.M.C.)

mission. NOTE: Index cut-out section of clutch drive gear with countershaft driven gear to obtain clearance necessary for removal.

3. Remove drive gear synchronizer cone and mainshaft pilot bearing roller spacer from end of mainshaft.

Mainshaft Removal

1. Remove speedometer driven gear from rear bearing retainer.
2. Lock transmission into two gears at the same time.
3. Remove bolt, lock washer, and special washer or retaining nut; then remove universal joint front flange or yoke from mainshaft.
4. Remove rear bearing retainer and gasket.
5. Push mainshaft assembly to the rear and remove retaining ring from outer race of mainshaft rear bearing. Using bearing puller, pull bearing assembly from end of mainshaft.
6. With 1st and reverse sliding gear pushed forward, raise front of mainshaft and remove shaft from transmission.

Reverse Idler Gear Removal

1. Drive reverse idler gear shaft lock pin into the shaft. After pin has been driven into hole in shaft, shaft may be driven out of transmission case from front to rear with a brass drift and hammer.
2. Remove reverse idler gear assembly from case.

Countershaft Removal

1. Remove retainer ring from countershaft rear bearing.
2. Remove rear bearing snap-ring.
3. Engage grab edges of puller tool plate in ring grooves of countershaft rear bearing.
4. Using bearing puller, remove rear bearing assembly from rear end of countershaft.

1 Main drive gear
2 Bearing retainer snap ring
3 Bearing snap ring
4 Drive gear bearing
5 Direct drive synchronizer cone
6 Clutch sleeve key
7 Synchronizer cone
8 Mainshaft 3rd speed gear
9 Clutch sleeve
10 Key spring

Exploded view of transmission (© G.M.C.)

5. Raise front end of countershaft and remove from case.

NOTE: If transmission is equipped with power take-off, remove cover and gasket.

Disassembly of Subassemblies

See exploded view of transmission.

Shift Control Cover Disassembly

1. Remove reverse shifter head from shaft.
2. Remove shifter shafts and shift forks. NOTE: Remove shafts carefully so as not to lose detent balls and springs. There should be three of each.
3. Should it be necessary to remove the interlock plate assembly, cut the three attaching pins and remove assembly from transmission.
4. Remove expansion plug (caution—plug is under spring tension), compression spring, and reverse shifter compression pin from transmission cover.

Clutch Drive Gear Disassembly

1. Remove roller retainer and eighteen mainshaft pilot bearing rollers from rear end of clutch drive gear.
2. Remove bearing retaining snap-ring from clutch drive gear.
3. Position clutch drive gear in an arbor press and, using special tools, press drive gear assembly out of drive gear bearing.

Mainshaft Disassembly

1. Remove 3rd and 4th speed clutch hub retainer ring from pilot end of mainshaft.
2. Using an arbor press, press mainshaft out of gear cluster.
3. Remove 3rd and 4th speed clutch hub. Remove two clutch key springs from 3rd and 4th speed clutch hub. Remove 3rd and 4th speed clutch sleeve. Remove three clutch keys.
4. Remove 3rd speed gear synchronizer cone, 3rd speedgear and thrust washer.
5. Remove mainshaft 2nd speed gear, synchronizing ring retainer and synchronizer ring from mainshaft 1st and reverse gear.
6. Remove steel friction ring and rubber strip from splines of 1st and reverse gear.

Countershaft Disassembly

1. Remove snap-ring from front end of countershaft.
2. Using an arbor press, press countershaft out of stack of gears.

NOTE: Countershaft 1st speed gear is part of the countershaft.

Mainshaft Rear Bearing Retainer Oil Seal Replacement

1. Using a suitable sleeve, press or drive oil seal out of mainshaft rear bearing retainer.
2. Press or drive new oil seal into retainer until it bottoms. NOTE: Lightly coat outer diameter of oil seal with sealing cement. Wipe off excess cement. Lip of oil seal goes toward front of retainer.

Drive Gear Bearing Retainer Oil Seal Replacement

1. Pry old oil seal out of retainer.
2. Insert new oil seal on special tool with lip of seal toward flange on tool.
3. Support front surface of retainer in press and press seal into retainer until flange of tool bottoms on retainer.

Countershaft Front Bearing Replacement

1. If countershaft front bearing needs replacing, drive bearing out of transmission case.
2. Apply sealing cement to outer surface of new bearing and drive into case.

Reverse Idler Gear Bushing Replacement

1. If reverse idler gear bushings are scored or worn, use a suitable sleeve and press bushings out of gear.
2. Using installer tool, press new bushings into bore of idler gear. Press bushings into gear until 1 1/16-inch clearance is obtained between bushings and ends of gear.
3. Stake bushings in position using staking tool. NOTE: It is important that bushings be properly staked as they are of split type and may have a tendency to creep. Stake bushings approximately ¼-inch from split.
4. After bushings are installed they must be line reamed to size.

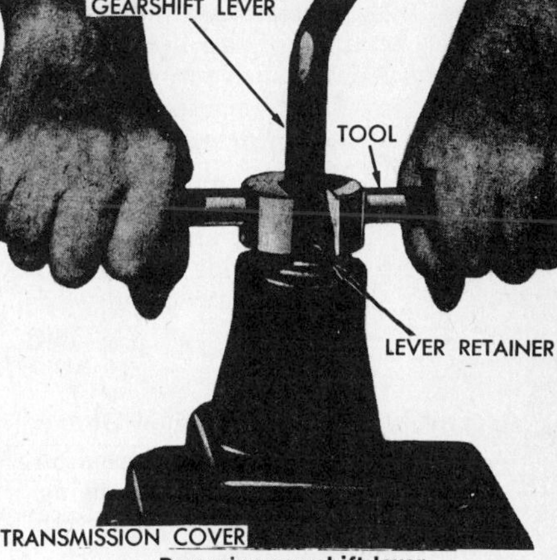

Removing gearshift lever
(© G.M.C.)

Assembly of Subassemlies

Assembly of Countershaft

1. Use new drive keys when assembling the countershaft. Position one new drive key in slot of countershaft. Using an arbor press install gears in the following order:
2. Using a suitable sleeve, press 2nd speed against shoulder on countershaft.
3. Press 3rd speed gear on the countershaft. Both sides of gear are identical so gear can be installed either way.
4. Press reverse gear on the countershaft so chamfered end of teeth face countershaft drive gear. Install spacer on countershaft.
5. Press drive gear on the countershaft.
6. After gears are pressed into po-

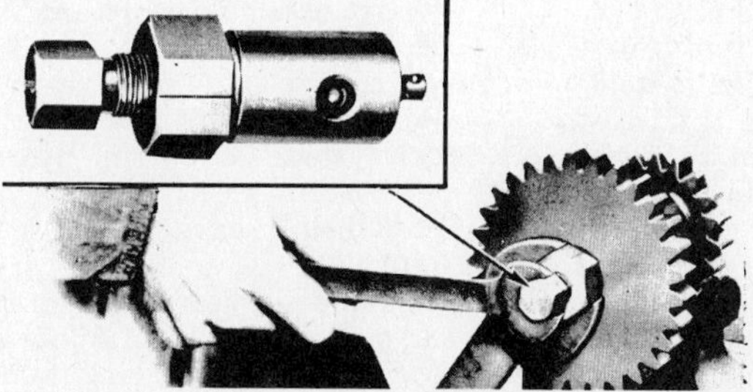
Staking reverse idler gear
(© G.M.C.)

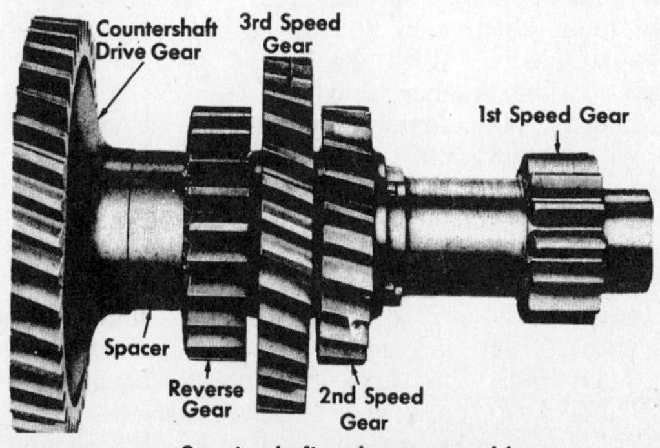

Countershaft and gear assembly
(© G.M.C.)

sition on countershaft, drive in the remaining three drive keys. Use a small punch to drive each key in 0.30″ maximum past front surface of drive gear.

7. Install snap-ring in groove of countershaft.

NOTE: Snap-ring is a selective type. Select a ring wide enough to completely fill space between edge of drive gear and front edge of ring groove.

Assembly of Clutch Drive Gear

1. Position drive gear bearing on drive gear shaft; then using press plate, press bearing onto drive gear.
2. Install retaining snap-ring on drive gear shaft.
3. Install snap-ring in drive gear bearing outer race.
4. Apply a small amount of grease to bearing surface in cavity at rear end of drive shaft. Install eighteen mainshaft pilot bearing rollers; then install bearing roller retainer.

NOTE: Purpose of installing roller retainer is to hold rollers in position when mainshaft is installed later. Mainshaft will force retainer forward from rollers into cavity at rear end of drive gear.

Assembly of Mainshaft

1. Assemble new friction ring rubber strip and then steel friction ring in groove in first and reverse sliding gear.
2. Assemble 2nd speed synchronizer ring to 1st and reverse sliding gear. Install retainer ring in groove of sliding gear. Retainer ring must be well seated in groove of gear.
3. Position 1st and reverse sliding gear assembly on splines of the mainshaft with synchronizer ring facing the front. NOTE: It may be necessary to pry against friction ring to engage all four spline engaging lugs.
4. Install 2nd speed gear on mainshaft with synchronizer springs toward synchronizer ring in 1st and reverse gear.
5. Install 2nd speed gear thrust washer.
6. Install 3rd speed gear bushing on mainshaft using special tool Bushing must bottom on 2nd speed gear thrust washer. With the bushing tight against washer, 2nd speed gear should have end play of 0.012-inch ± 0.003 inch.
7. Install 3rd speed gear over bushing and install synchronizer cone on tapered surface of 3rd speed gear.
8. Install clutch sleeve over clutch hub so long tapered surface on sleeve faces in same direction as long shoulder on hub. Place the three clutch keys into position. Install one clutch key spring on each side of clutch hub. Both clutch key springs must be installed in the same relative position to provide even tension on clutch keys.

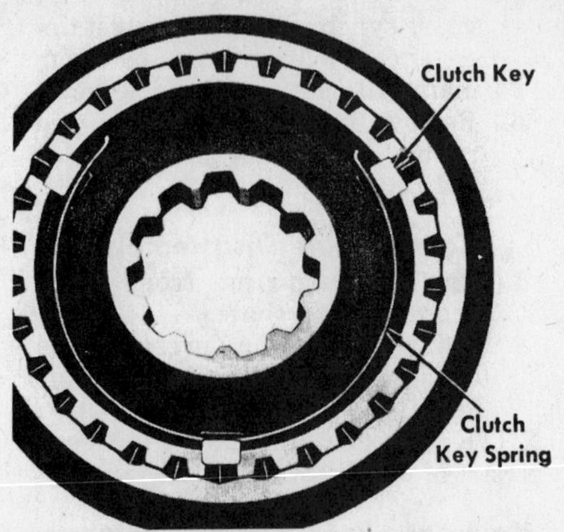

Clutch keys and spring location
(© G.M.C.)

9. Support mainshaft assembly in an arbor press; then install clutch hub assembly with tapered surface of clutch sleeve and long shoulder of clutch hub toward pilot on mainshaft. Press clutch hub assembly onto shaft until it bottoms. IMPORTANT: Make sure that slots in third speed gear synchronizer cone align with three clutch keys in clutch hub assembly.
10. 3rd speed gear end play of 0.012 inch ± 0.002 inch should exist when clutch hub is firmly seated against bushing.
11. Install clutch hub retainer ring.

NOTE: The retainer ring is a selective lock ring and should be checked carefully for proper thickness at assembly. There are four thicknesses available—0.083″, 0.087″, 0.091″ and 0.095″. Be sure to select a proper ring that will assemble to obtain 0.007-inch maximum end clearance.

To make ring selection, lay retainer ring outer edge in groove at forward side of clutch hub and check clearance.

Assembly of Shift Control Cover

NOTE: See picture of shifter shafts for proper installation.

1. Place shifter shaft detent ball springs and detent balls in position in transmission cover.
2. Depress detent ball and push 3rd and 4th shifter shaft into cover so that it passes over ball. Hold 3rd and 4th shift fork in position and push shaft on through fork until retainer pin hole in fork aligns with hole in shifter shaft. Install tapered pin.
3. Follow the above procedure and install 1st and 2nd speed shift shaft and shift fork and reverse shift shaft and reverse shifter head in transmission cover.
4. Install and stake shifter shaft hole expansion plugs in transmission cover.
5. Install new reverse shifter compression pin, spring, and expansion plug. Support cover in a vise and hold plug while staking.

NOTE: For initial lubrication and rust prevention, lubricate each moving part during assembly.

Installation of Countershaft

1. If countershaft front bearing was previously removed, apply sealing cement to outer surface of bearing; then drive in bearing until flush with front face of case.
2. Position countershaft assembly in transmission case with rear end of shaft extending through rear bearing hole.
3. Install oil deflector and rear bearing on countershaft assembly. Install bearing retainer ring in countershaft making sure it is well seated in groove of shaft.
4. Guide front end of shaft into front bearing. Rear bearing retainer snap-ring limits forward movement of countershaft.

Installation of Reverse Idler Gear

1. Position reverse idler gear assembly in transmission case; then install idler gear shaft into idler gear and transmission case from the rear. Be sure slot in rear end of shaft is in horizontal position.
2. Drive reverse idler gear shaft in until hole in shaft aligns with lock pin hole in transmission case. Drive new lock pin into shaft and case until pin is flush with case.

Installation of Mainshaft and Mainshaft Drive Gear

1. Position mainshaft assembly in case with rear of shaft extending out through rear bearing bore.
2. Using special tool, install mainshaft rear bearing assembly on rear end of mainshaft.
3. Install pilot bearing roller spacer on front end of mainshaft. Install drive gear synchronizer cone and move mainshaft assembly forward until clutch sleeve clears 3rd speed gear on countershaft assembly.
4. Align cut-out portion of clutch drive gear to obtain clearance with countershaft drive gear and install drive gear assembly into case.
5. Install drive gear bearing retainer and new gasket. Apply sealing cement to bearing retainer bolt threads and install with lock washers at 15-18 foot-pounds torque.
6. Enter mainshaft pilot end into bearing rollers in clutch drive

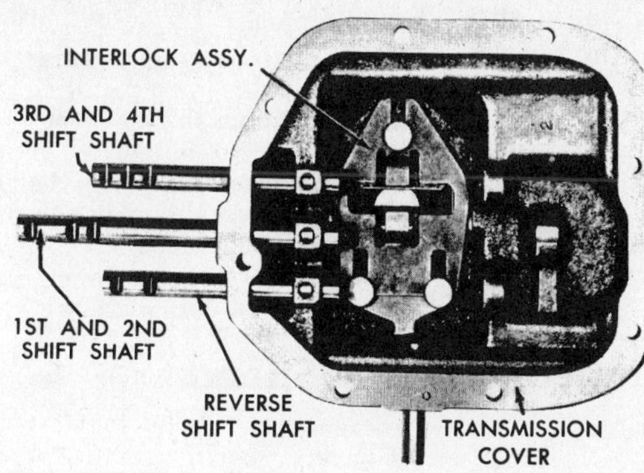

Shifter shaft positions
(© G.M.C.)

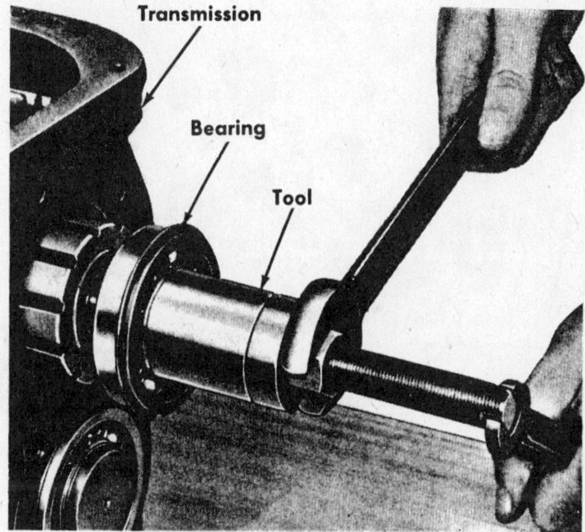

Installing rear bearing on mainshaft
(© G.M.C.)

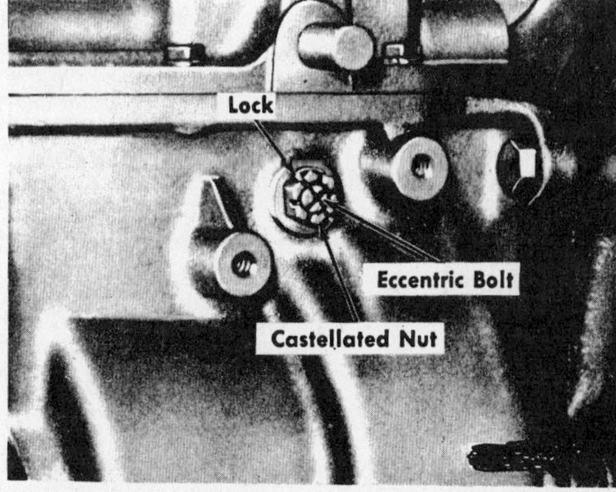

Reverse idler gear adjustment location
(© G.M.C.)

gear.

7. Attach puller tool to rear of case and press in mainshaft and bearing assembly. NOTE: Be sure the three cut-out sections of drive gear synchronizer cone align with the three clutch keys.
8. Install rear bearing retainer and gasket using a sealing cement on the bolts. Tighten bolts to 20-25 foot-pounds torque.
9. Position reverse shifter lever in transmission case with lower end engaged with groove in reverse idler gear.
10. Install lever eccentric at outer side of transmission case and torque nut to a minimum of 40 foot-pounds. NOTE: Nut-lock should not be installed until after reverse shifter lever is adjusted as described later.
11. On some transmissions, install output flange or yoke with attached speedometer drive gear, on the mainshaft. Lock transmission into two gears at one time and install special washer, lock washer, and bolt at a torque of 60-65 foot-pounds.
12. On other transmissions, install output flange or yoke on the mainshaft. Lock transmission into two gears at once and torque retaining nut to 95-120 foot-pounds.
13. If used, install parking brake parts, and adjust parking brake.
14. Install speedometer driven gear and adapter in rear bearing retainer. Tighten adapter firmly.

Installation of Shift Control Cover

1. Make sure all transmission gears are in "Neutral" position; then install transmission cover assembly and new gasket on transmission case. Be sure shift forks engage respective gears. Install attaching bolts and lock washers and torque to 20-25 foot-pounds.
2. On transmissions having a conventional gearshift lever, use special tool and install lever. Engage lugs of tool in open slot of retainer. Press down on tool and turn to the right to engage lugs on retainer. On transmissions having remote controls, install control linkage.
3. Use procedures described in the following text to make proper adjustment of reverse shifter lever:
   a. Position transmission in "Neutral." Loosen eccentric nut. Using a screwdriver in slot at outer end of eccentric, turn eccentric so that small round (dot) marks on slotted end of eccentric are toward rear of the transmission. This places reverse idler gear in its extreme rear position and will provide maximum engagement when transmission is shifted into reverse.
   b. Shift transmission into 2nd speed; then through the power take-off opening, check for interference between reverse idler gear and first and reverse gear. If interference exists, rotate eccentric counterclockwise to provide approximately 1/32-inch running clearance between gears.
   c. Shift transmission into reverse; then check for clearance between reverse idler gear and transmission case at the rear. If

necessary, rotate the eccentric an additional amount in a counterclockwise direction to obtain running clearance at this point.

d. Lock adjustment by tightening lock nut to 40 foot-pounds torque. Install nut lock.

4. Check operation of transmission by shifting into each gear and make sure drive gear can be rotated without binding in each position.
5. Install drain plug, filler plug, PTO cover (or unit, if used) and new gasket. Fill transmission with lubricant.

Torque Wrench Specifications

	Foot-Pounds
Drain plug	30 to 35
Drive gear bearing retainer bolts	15 to 18
Power take-off cover bolts	15 to 20
Rear bearing retainer bolts	20 to 25
Reverse shifter lever eccentric nut	40 ft.-lbs.
Transmission cover bolts	20 to 25
Universal joint flange nut (3500-4000)	95 to 120
Universal joint flange cap screw (1000-2500)	60 to 65

G.M. Corporation Model SM465 4 Speed

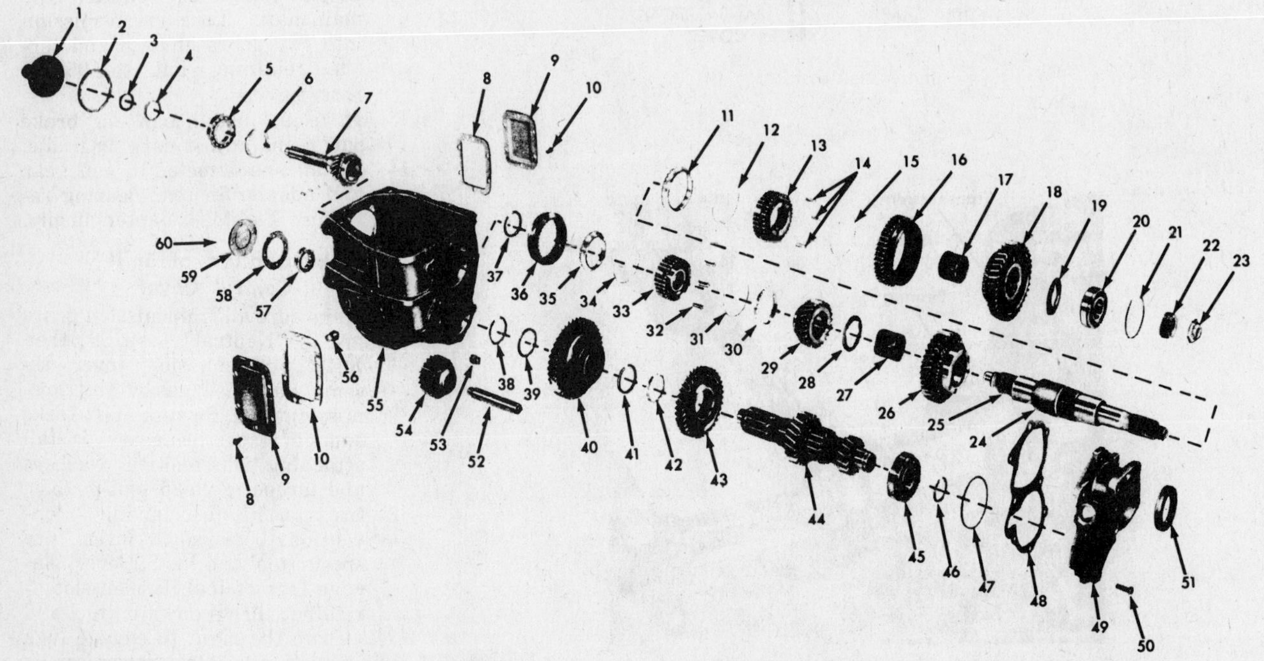

1 Clutch gear bearing retainer
2 Retainer gasket
3 Lip seal
4 Snap ring
5 Clutch gear bearing
6 Oil slinger
7 Clutch gear and pilot bearings
8 Power take-off cover gasket
9 Power take-off cover
10 Retaining screws
11 1st-2nd speed blocker ring
12 Synchronizer spring
13 1st-2nd speed synchronizer hub
14 Synchronizer keys
15 Synchronizer spring
16 Reverse driven gear
17 1st gear bushing
18 1st gear
19 Thrust washer
20 Rear main bearing
21 Bearing snap ring
22 Speedometer gear
23 Rear mainshaft lock nut
24 2nd speed bushing (on shaft)
25 Mainshaft
26 2nd speed gear
27 3rd gear bushing
28 Thrust washer
29 3rd speed gear
30 3rd speed blocker ring
31 Synchronizer spring
32 Synchronizer keys
33 3rd-4th synchronizer hub
34 Synchronizer spring
35 3rd-4th speed blocker ring
36 3rd-4th speed synchronizer sleeve
37 Snap ring
38 Snap ring
39 Thrust washer
40 Clutch countergear
41 Snap ring
42 Snap ring
43 3rd speed countergear
44 Countergear shaft
45 Countergear rear bearing
46 Snap ring
47 Bearing outer snap ring
48 Rear retainer gasket
49 Rear retainer
50 Retainer bolts
51 Retainer lip seal
52 Reverse idler shaft
53 Drain plug
54 Reverse idler gear
55 Case
56 Fill plug
57 Countergear front bearing
58 Gasket
59 Front cover
60 Cover screws

Transmission components (© G.M.C.)

Description

The G.M. Corporation Model SM465 (Muncie) transmission is a four speed transmission using helical gears. The action of all gears except reverse is aided by synchronizers.

Disassembly of Transmission

1. Remove transmission cover assembly. NOTE: Move reverse shifter fork so that reverse idler gear is partially engaged before attempting to remove cover. Forks must be positioned so rear edge of the slot in the reverse fork is in line with the front edge of the slot in the forward forks as viewed through tower opening.
2. Lock transmission into two gears. Remove the universal joint flange nut, universal joint front flange and brake drum assembly. NOTE: On 4-wheel drive models, use a special tool to remove mainshaft rear lock nut.
3. Remove parking brake and brake flange plate assembly on those vehicles having a driveshaft parking brake.
4. Remove rear bearing retainer and gasket.
5. Slide speedometer drive gear off mainshaft.
6. Remove clutch gear bearing retainers and gasket.
7. Remove countergear front bearing cap and gasket.
8. Using a screwdriver, pry off countershaft front bearing.
9. Remove countergear rear bear-

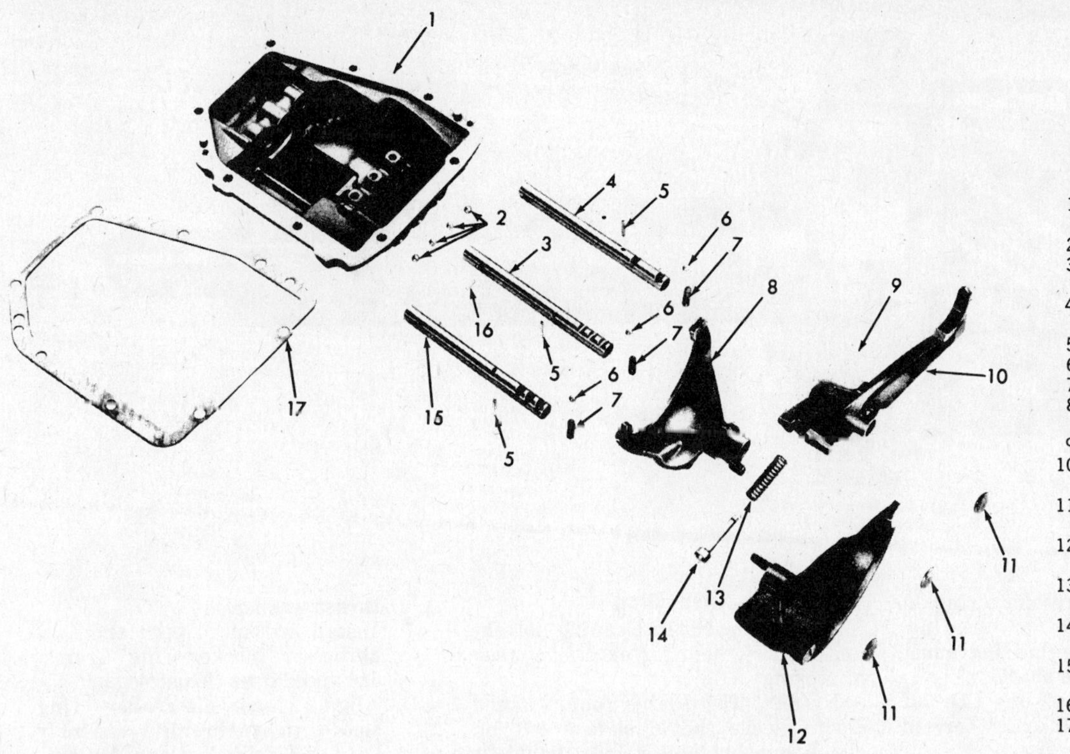

Shift cover assembly components (© G.M.C.)

ing snap-rings from shaft and bearing. Using special tool, remove countergear rear bearings.

10. Remove clutch gear bearing outer race to case retaining ring.
11. Remove clutch gear and bearing by tapping gently on bottom side of clutch gear shaft and prying directly opposite against the case and bearing snap-ring groove at the same time. Remove 4th gear synchronizer ring. CAUTION: Index cut out section of clutch gear in down position with countergear to obtain clearance for removing clutch gear.
12. Remove rear mainshaft bearing snap-ring and, using special tools, remove bearing from case. Slide 1st speed gear thrust washer off mainshaft.
13. Lift mainshaft assembly from case. Remove synchronizer cone from shaft.
14. Slide reverse idler gear rearward and move countergear rearward, then lift to remove from case.
15. To remove reverse idler gear, drive reverse idler gear shaft out of case from front to rear using a drift. Remove reverse idler gear from case.

Disassembly of Subassemblies

Transmission Cover Disassembly

1. Remove shifter fork retaining pins and drive out expansion plugs. NOTE: The third and fourth shifter fork must be removed before the reverse shifter head pin can be removed.
2. With shifter shafts in neutral position, remove shafts. CAUTION: Care should be taken when removing the detent balls and springs since removal of the shifter shafts will cause these parts to be forcibly ejected.
3. Remove retaining pin and drive out reverse shifter shaft.

Assembly

1. In reassembling the cover, care should be taken to install the shifter shafts in order—reverse, 3rd.-4th, and 1st.-2nd.
2. Place fork detent ball springs and balls in cover.
3. Start shifter shafts into cover and, while depressing the detent balls, push the shafts over the balls. Push reverse shaft through the yoke.
4. With the 3rd.-4th. shaft in neutral, line up the retaining holes in the fork and shaft. NOTE: Detent balls should line up with detents in shaft.
5. After 1st and 2nd fork is installed, place two inner-lock balls between the low speed shifter shaft and the high speed shifter shaft in the crossbore of the front support boss. Grease the interlock pin and insert it in the 3rd-4th shifter shaft hole. Continue pushing this shaft through cover bore and fork until retainer hole in fork lines up with hole in shaft.
6. Place two interlock balls in crossbore in front support boss between reverse, and 3rd and 4th shifter shaft. Then push remaining shaft through fork and cover bore, keeping both balls in position between shafts until retaining holes line up in fork and shaft. Install retaining pin.
7. Install 1st/2nd fork and reverse fork retaining pins. Install new shifter shaft hole expansion plugs.

Clutch Gear and Shaft Disassembly

1. Remove mainshaft pilot bearing rollers from clutch gear if not already removed, and remove roller retainer. Do not remove snap-ring on inside of clutch gear.
2. Remove snap-ring securing bearing on stem of clutch gear.
3. To remove bearing, position a special tool to the bearing and, with an arbor press, press gear and shaft out of bearing.

Assembly

1. Press bearing and new oil slinger onto clutch gear shaft using a special tool. Slinger should be located flush with bearing shoulder on clutch gear. CAUTION: Be careful not to distort oil slinger.
2. Install bearing snap-ring on clutch gear shaft.

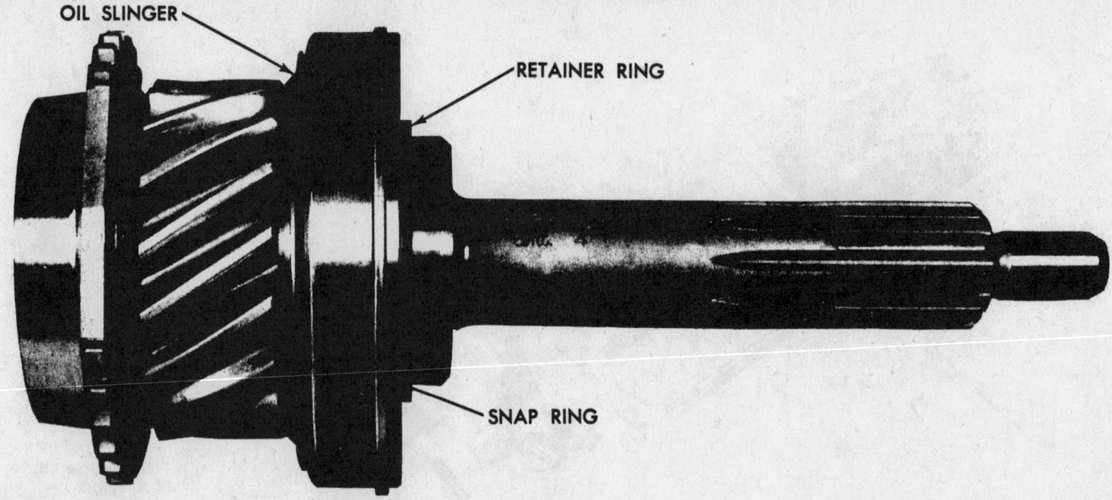

Clutch gear assembly (© G.M.C.)

3. Install bearing retainer ring in groove on O.D. of bearing. CAUTION: The bearing must turn freely on the shaft.
4. Install snap-ring on I.D. of mainshaft pilot bearing bore in clutch gear.
5. Lightly grease bearing surface in shaft recess, install transmission mainshaft pilot roller bearings and install roller bearing retainer.

NOTE: This roller bearing retainer holds bearings in position, and, in final transmission assembly, is pushed forward into recess by mainshaft pilot. Clutch Gear Bearing Retainer Oil Seal.

Bearing Retainer Oil Seal Replacement

1. Remove retainer and oil seal assembly and gasket.
2. Pry out oil seal.
3. Install new seal with lip of seal toward flange of tool.
4. Support front surface of retainer in press and drive seal into retainer.
5. Install retainer and gasket on case.

Mainshaft Disassembly

1. Remove first speed gear.
2. Remove reverse driven gear.
3. Press behind second speed gear to remove 3rd-4th synchronizer assembly, 3rd speed gear and 2nd speed gear along with 3rd speed gear bushing and thrust washer.
4. Remove 2nd speed synchronizer ring and keys.
5. Using a press, remove 1st speed gear bushing and 2nd speed synchronizer hub.
6. Without damaging the mainshaft, chisel out the 2nd speed gear bushing.

Inspection

Wash all parts in cleaning solvent and inspect them for excessive wear or scoring.

NOTE: Third and fourth speed clutch sleeve should slide freely on clutch hub but clutch hub should fit snugly on shaft splines.

Third speed gear must be running fit on mainshaft bushing and mainshaft bushing should be press fit on shaft.

First and reverse sliding gear must be sliding fit on synchronizer hub and must not have excessive radial or circumferential play. If sliding gear is not free on hub, inspect for burrs which may have rolled up on front end of half-tooth internal splines and remove by honing as necessary.

Mainshaft Assembly

1. Lubricate with E.P. oil and press onto mainshaft. CAUTION: 1st, 2nd and 3rd speed gear bushings are sintered iron, exercise care when installing.
2. Press 1st and 2nd speed synchronizer hub onto mainshaft with annulus toward rear of shaft.
3. Install 1st and 2nd synchronizer keys and springs.
4. Press 1st speed gear bushing onto mainshaft until it bottoms against hub. NOTE: Lubricate all bushings with E.P. oil before installation of gears.
5. Install synchronizer blocker ring and 2nd speed gear onto mainshaft and against synchronize hub. Align synchronizer key slots with keys in synchronizer hub.
6. Install 3rd speed gear thrust washer onto mainshaft inserting washer tang in slotted shaft. Then press 3rd speed gear bushing onto mainshaft against thrust washer.
7. Install 3rd speed gear and synchronizer blocker ring against 3rd speed gear thrust washer.
8. Align synchronizer key ring slots with synchronizer assembly keys and drive 3rd and 4th synchronizer assembly onto mainshaft. Secure assembly with snap-ring.
9. Install reverse driven gear with fork groove toward rear.
10. Install 1st speed gear against 1st and 2nd synchronizer hub. Install 1st speed gear thrust washer.

Countershaft Disassembly

1. Remove front countergear retaining ring and thrust washer. Do not re-use this snap-ring or any others.
2. Press countershaft out of clutch countergear assembly.
3. Remove clutch countergear and 3rd speed countergear retaining rings.
4. Press shaft from 3rd speed countergear.

Countershaft Assembly

1. Press the 3rd speed countergear onto the shaft. NOTE: Install gear with marked surface toward front of shaft.
2. Using snap-ring pliers, install new 3rd speed countergear retaining ring.
3. Install new clutch countergear rear retaining ring. CAUTION: Do not over stress snap-ring. Ring should fit tightly in groove with no side play.
4. Press countergear onto shaft against snap-ring.
5. Install clutch countergear thrust washer and front retaining ring.

Transmission Assembly

1. Lower the countergear into the

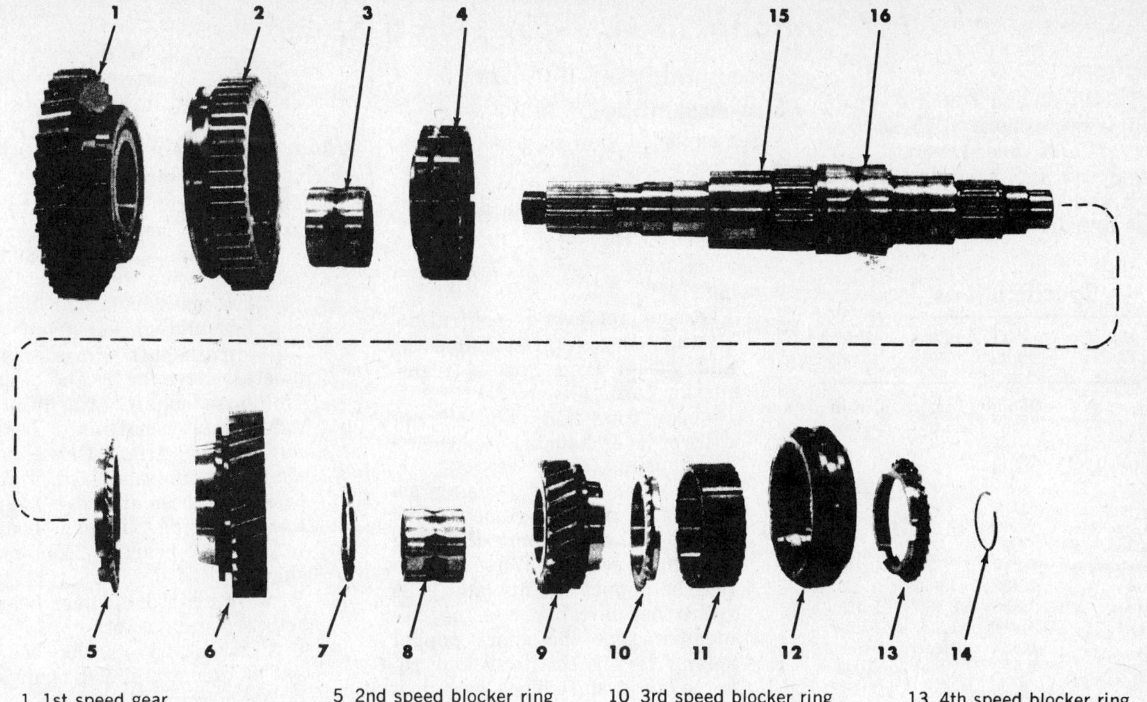

1 1st speed gear
2 Reverse driven gear
3 1st gear bushing
4 1st-2nd gear synchronizer hub assembly
5 2nd speed blocker ring
6 2nd speed gear
7 Thrust washer
8 3rd speed bushing
9 3rd speed gear
10 3rd speed blocker ring
11 3rd-4th speed synchronizer hub assembly
12 3rd-4th speed synchronizer sleeve
13 4th speed blocker ring
14 Snap ring
15 Mainshaft
16 2nd speed gear bushing

Mainshaft assembly (© G.M.C.)

case.

2. Place reverse idler gear in transmission case with gear teeth toward the front. Install idler gear shaft from rear to front, being careful to have slot in end of shaft facing down and flush with case.
3. Install mainshaft assembly into case with rear of shaft protruding out rear bearing hole in case. Rotate case onto front end. NOTE: Install 1st speed gear thrust washer on shaft, if not previously installed.
4. Install snap-ring on bearing O.D. and place rear mainshaft bearing on shaft. Drive bearing onto shaft and into case.
5. Install synchronizer cone on mainshaft and slide rearward to clutch hub. CAUTION: Make sure three cut-out sections of 4th speed synchronizer cone align with three clutch keys in clutch assembly.
6. Install snap-ring on clutch gear bearing O.D. Index cut out portion of clutch gear teeth to obtain clearance over countershaft drive gear teeth, and install into case.
7. Install clutch gear bearing retainer and gasket and torque to 15-18 ft. lbs.
8. Rotate case onto front end.
9. Install snap-ring on countergear rear bearing O.D., and drive bearing into place. Install snap-ring on countershaft at rear bearing.
10. Tap countergear front bearing assembly into case.
11. Install countergear front bearing cap and new gasket and torque to 20-30 in. lbs.
12. Slide speedometer drive gear over mainshaft to bearing.
13. Install rear bearing retainer with new gasket. Be sure snap ring ends are in lube slot and cut out in bearing retainer. Install bolts and tighten to 15-18 ft. lbs. Install brake backing plate assembly on those models having driveshaft brake. NOTE: On models equipped with 4-wheel drive, install rear lock nut and washer and torque to 120 ft. lbs. and bend washer tangs to fit slots in nut.
14. Install parking brake drum and/or universal joint flange. NOTE: Lightly oil seal surface.
15. Lock transmission in two gears at once. Install universal joint flange locknut and tighten to 90-120 ft. lbs.
16. Move all transmission gears to neutral except the reverse idler gear which should be engaged approximatly ⅜ of an inch (leading edge of reverse idler gear taper lines up with the front edge of the 1st speed gear). Install cover assembly and gasket. Shifting forks must slide into their proper positions on clutch sleeves and reverse idler gear. Forks must be positioned as in removal.
17. Install cover attaching bolts and gearshift lever and check operation of transmission.

Torque Chart

	Foot-Pounds
Rear bearing retainer	18
Cover bolts	25
Filler plug	35
Drain plug	35
Clutch gear bearing retainer bolts	18
Universal joint front flange nut	95
Power take off cover bolts	18
Parking brake	22
Countergear front cover screws	25
Rear mainshaft lock nut (4 wheel drive models)	95

International T-34, T-35, T-36 5 Speed

Description

The T-34, T-35 and T-36 are synchro-mesh transmissions with the exception of first and reverse gear. T-34 transmission have five speeds forward and one reverse. The fifth speed is overdrive. See specifications table.

Specifications

IH Model IH Code	T-34 13034	T-35 13035	T-36 13036
Type	OD. in 5th	Dir. in 5th	Dir. in 5th
No. of speeds:			
Forward	5	5	5
Reverse	1	1	1
Gear ratios:			
First (low)	6.210	7.170	6.210
Second	3.430	3.960	3.430
Third	1.810	2.365	2.050
Fourth	Direct	1.410	1.225
Fifth	0.823	Direct	Direct
Reverse	6.090	7.020	6.090
P.T.O. openings	2	2	2
Location	Both Sides	Both Sides	Both Sides
Weight (lbs.)	192	192	192
Lubricant cap. (pts.)	12	12	12
Serial no. Location	*	*	*

* Stamped above drain plug.

The Models T-35 and T-36 transmission have five speeds forward and one reverse. The fifth speed is direct. See shift diagrams.

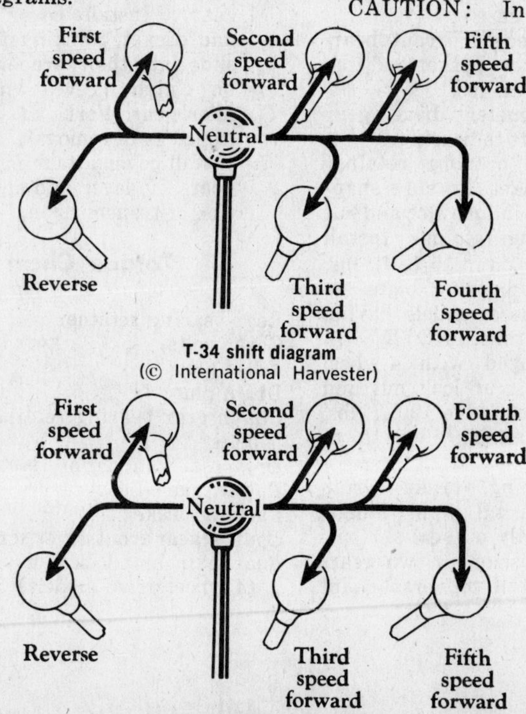

T-34 shift diagram (© International Harvester)

T-35, T-36 shift diagram (© International Harvester)

Disassembly of Sub-Assemblies

See exploded view of transmission. sion.

Control Lever and Shift Bar Housing

See exploded view of lever and housing.

1. Place control lever in neutral position. Remove shift bar housing and gasket from top of transmission case.
2. Remove four bolts and lift off control lever housing from shift bar housing.
3. Place control lever housing assembly in vise and remove shift handle and disassemble the lever housing assembly. When removing the poppet springs and balls from the shift bar housing, remember that the short poppet spring is for the first and reverse speed shift block and shift lock screws from first and reverse speed shitf block and shift forks. Drive fourth and fifth speed shift rail out toward the front of the shift bar housing, driving out shift rail thimble and remove shift fork.
4. Remove interlock ball and cross pin retainer thimble located on the left outside of the housing just below the poppet ball and spring housing, to release ball and pin. Remove first and reverse speed and second and third speed shift forks and shift rails. CAUTION: In reassembling controls. be certain to replace each part in its proper position.

Main Drive Gear and Mainshaft Removal

1. Lock the transmission into two gears and remove flange nut, washer and flange. Remove parking brake drum and band.
2. Remove mainshaft rear bearing retainer and gasket from case. Slide mainshaft slinger speedometer drive gear and washer from mainshaft. NOTE: Remove countershaft rear bearing nut at this time. Drive mainshaft assembly toward rear of case to expose its rear bearing and snap-ring. Using a bearing puller, pull bearing from mainshaft.
3. Remove main drive gear bearing retainer and gasket.
4. Lift main drive gear bearing and mainshaft pilot bearing out through front of case.
5. Lift mainshaft and gears out through top of case leaving the first and reverse speed gear in the case.
6. With the mainshaft assembly removed, lift the first and reverse speed gear out of the case. NOTE: During reassembly, "R" stamped on gear should face rear of case.

Synchronized Mainshaft Disassembly

1. Slide front (4th and 5th speed) synchronizer assembly off mainshaft.
2. Remove retainer ring and mainshaft clutch gear. NOTE: When reassembling mainshaft clutch gear, place oil grooves toward rear of mainshaft, or next to fourth speed gear. Slide fourth speed gear off mainshaft.
3. Remove mainshaft third speed gear retainer ring and thrust washer. NOTE: During reassembly of thrust washer, place oil grooves toward rear of mainshaft, or next to third speed gear. Slide mainshaft third speed gear off mainshaft.
4. Remove rear (2nd and 3rd speed) sychronizer assembly.
5. Slide mainshaft second speed retainer ring and thrust washer off the rear of the mainshaft. NOTE: When reassembling thrust washer, place oil grooves next to second speed gear. Slide mainshaft second speed gear off rear of mainshaft.

Countershaft and Reverse Idler Gear Removal

1. Remove lock plate from slot in reverse idler shaft and pull out

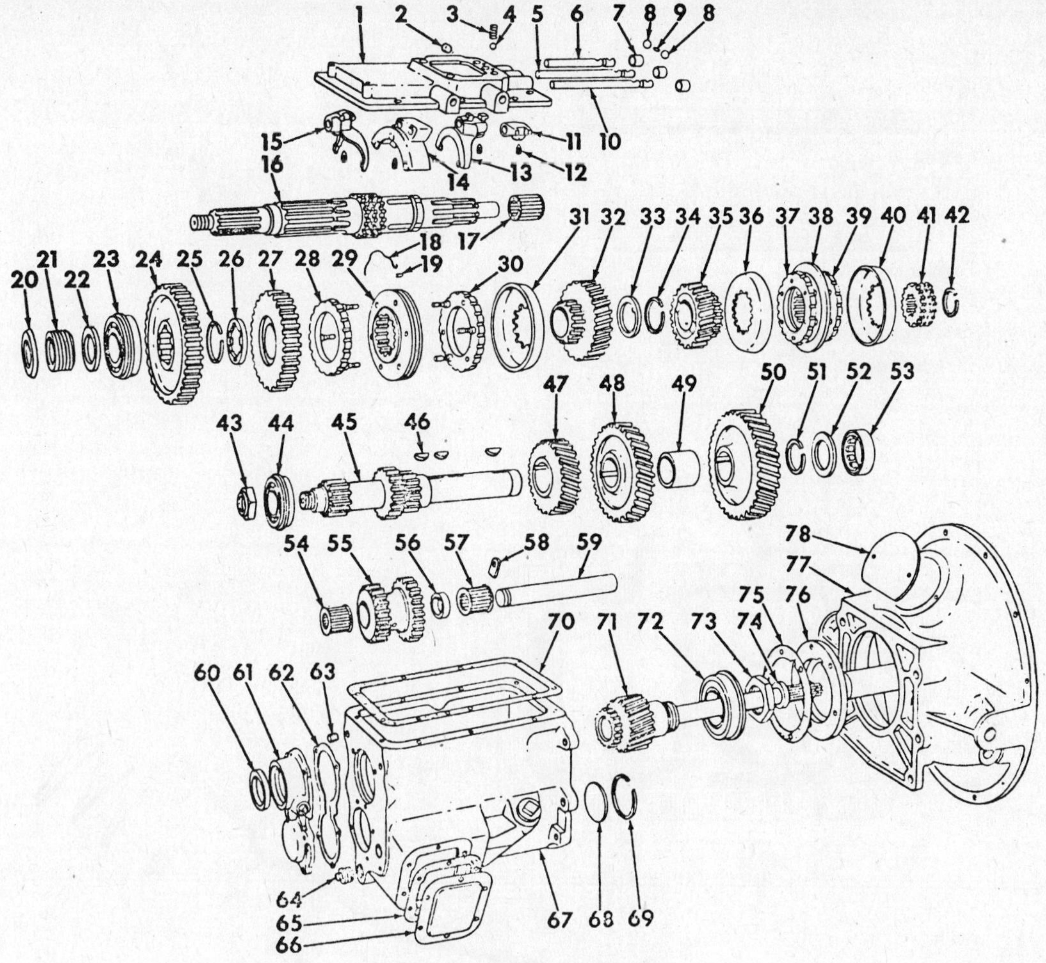

Transmission assembly components
(© International Harvester)

1 Housing, shift bar
2 Thimble, shift bar housing, side
3 Spring, poppet
4 Ball, poppet
5 Rail, 2nd & 3rd speed shift
6 Rail, 4th & 5th speed shift
7 Thimble, shift bar hsg. frt.
8 Ball, interlocking
9 Pin, cross interlocking
10 Rail, 1st & reverse speed shift
11 Block, 1st & rev. shift
12 Screw, locking
13 Fork, 4th & 5th speed shift
14 Fork, 1st & reverse speed shift
15 Fork, 2nd & 3rd speed shift
16 Mainshaft
17 Bearing, mashft. pilot
18 Spring
19 Pin, spring
20 Slinger, mainshaft
21 Gear, speedo. drive
22 Washer, mainshaft
23 Bearing, mashft. rear
24 Gear, 1st & rev. speed
25 Ring, retainer
26 Washer, thrust
27 Gear, mashft. 2nd
28 Ring, inner stop
29 Clutch, sliding
30 Ring, inner stop
31 Ring, outer stop
32 Gear, mashft. 3rd
33 Washer, thrust
34 Ring, retaining
35 Gear, mashft. 4th
36 Ring, outer stop
37 Ring, inner stop
38 Clutch, sliding
39 Ring, inner stop
40 Ring, outer stop
41 Gear, mashft. clutch
42 Ring, lock
43 Nut, ctshft. rear brg.
44 Bearing, ctshft. rear
45 Countershaft
46 Key, woodruff, ctshft.
47 Gear, ctshft. 3rd
48 Gear, ctshft. 4th
49 Spacer, ctshft. gear
50 Gear, ctshft. drive
51 Ring, snap, ctshft. gear
52 Washer, ctshft., frt. bearing thrust
53 Bearing, ctshft. frt. roller
54 Bearing, reverse idler gear
55 Gear, reverse idler
56 Spacer, reverse idler gear bearing
57 Bearing, reverse idler gear
58 Lock, reverse idler gear shaft
59 Shaft, reverse idler gear
60 Seal, mainshaft oil
61 Retainer, mainshaft rear bearing
62 Gasket, mainshaft rear bearing retainer
63 Plug, parking brake brkt. hole
64 Plug, drain, ctsk., pipe
65 Gasket, PTO opening cover
66. Cover, PTO opening
67 Case, transmission
68 Plug, expansion, ctshft.
69 Ring, snap, ctshft. expansion plug
70 Gasket, shift bar housing
71 Gear, main drive
72 Bearing, main drive gear
73 Nut, main drive gear bearing
74 Seal, oil, main drive gear bearing retainer
75 Gasket, main drive gear bearing retainer
76 Retainer, main drive gear bearing
77 Housing, bell
78 Cover, clutch hand hole

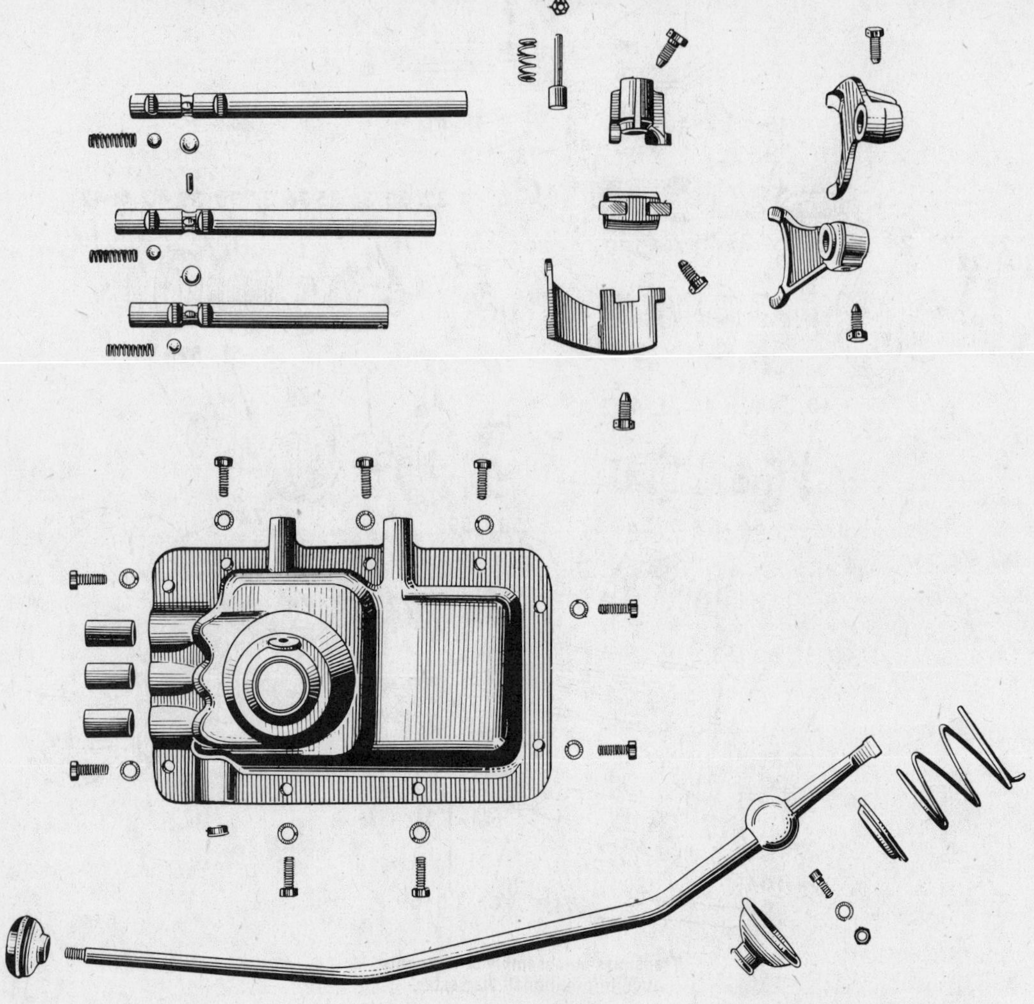

Control lever and housing components
(© International Harvester)

shaft with a puller.

2. Lift out reverse idler gear, bearings and thrust washers.
3. Drive countershaft assembly toward rear of case to expose rear bearing snap-ring. Using a puller, pull rear bearing from countershaft. Lift countershaft assembly and front bearing thrust washer from case. The countershaft front roller bearing is disassembled by removing the countershaft expansion plug snap-ring and driving the expansion plus from the case.
4. Drive countershaft front roller bearing from case with a brass drift.

Countershaft Disassembly

Remove snap-ring from countershaft. Using adapter plates, press countershaft drive gear, spacer, fourth speed gear and third speed gear from countershaft. Remove Woodruff keys from countershaft. NOTE: Use new snap-rings when reassembling.

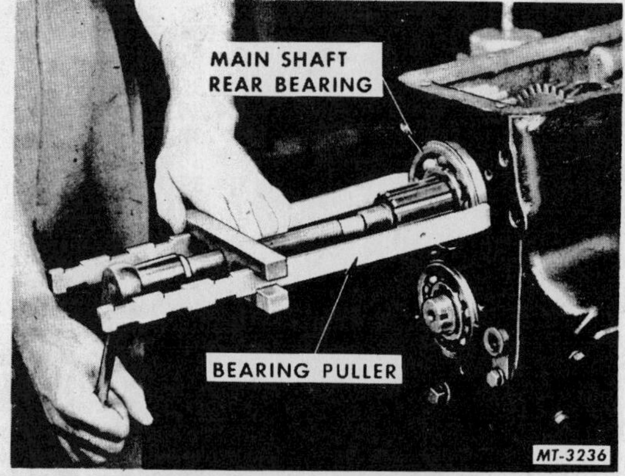

Mainshaft rear bearing removal
(© International Harvester)

Removing main drive gear bearing retainer
(© International Harvester)

Removing front synchronizer assembly
(© International Harvester)

Removing rear synchronizer assembly
(© International Harvester)

Removal of mainshaft fourth speed gear
(© International Harvester)

Removing mainshaft second speed gear
(© International Harvester)

Removal of mainshaft third speed gear
(© International Harvester)

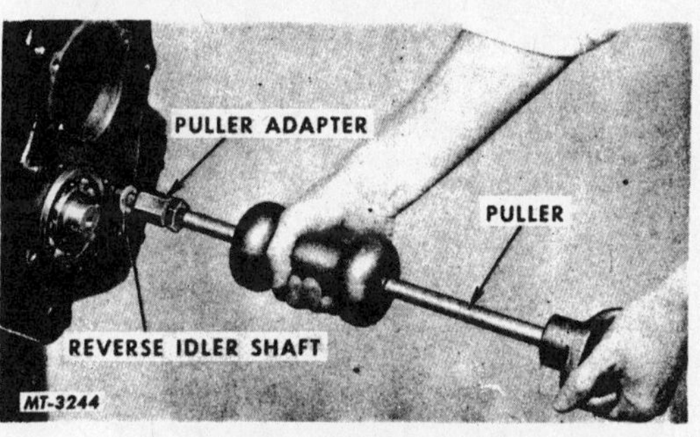

Reverse idler shaft removal
(© International Harvester)

Assembly of Sub-Assemblies

For reassembly, reverse the procedures for disassembly. See torque chart for tightening specifications.

Lubrication

Dip all roller bearings in transmission lubricant before reassembling. For initial filling, fill transmsision with proper lubricant until it runs out filler hole; then replace plug.

Check transmission oil level every 1,000 miles or at each lubrication. Fill as necessary. Drain and flush every 10,000 miles or twice each year, preferably in the spring and fall. Lubricant capacity is twelve pints.

Torque Chart (ft. lbs.)*

Drive gear bearing Retainer to case	3/8-16	30-40
Control lever housing to shift cover	7/16-14	50-70
Cover to case	3/8-16	30-40
Mainshaft rear bearing Retainer to case	3/8-16	30-40
Countershaft lock bolt to case	3/8-16	30-40
P.T.O. or P.T.O. cover to case	3/8-16	30-40
Companion flange to mainshaft	7/8-16	190-210

* Correct torque readings can be obtained only after the screw threads have been cleaned and lubricated.

New Process 420 4 Speed

Description

The four speed Model 420 transmission is a strong, exceptionally smooth, easy shifting transmission. All gears are of helical design except 1st and reverse which are spur type. The countershaft and all its gears are a single unit. Engagement of the 3rd and 4th gear is aided by pin type synchronizers. Lubricant capacity is 5½ pints. Power take-off outputs are located on both sides of the case.

Disassembly of Transmission

1. Shift gears into neutral.
2. Remove cover by turning it slightly counter-clockwise.
3. Check and record the amount of synchronizer end play for assembly reference.
4. Remove yoke and parking brake drum as an assembly. NOTE: The drum and yoke are balanced and, unless replacement of parts is required, it is recommended that drum and yoke be removed as a unit assembly.
5. Remove speedometer drive pinion and rear mainshaft bearing support.

Main Drive Gear Removal

1. Remove main drive gear bearing retainer.
2. Move synchronizer towards rear and, while slowly rotating main drive gear, tap on main drive gear shaft with a soft hammer and pull at the same time. A few of the clutch teeth on the main drive are missing to facilitate its removal past the cluster gears. This open space must be positioned at the bottom to allow withdrawal of the main drive gear from the transmission case.

Mainshaft Removal

1. Using a brass drift, drive mainshaft to rear making certain that the synchronizer assembly remains free on shaft.
2. Using a puller, remove rear bearing and speedometer gear (with spacer).
3. Remove sliding components of synchronizer separately.
4. Remove mainshaft assembly.

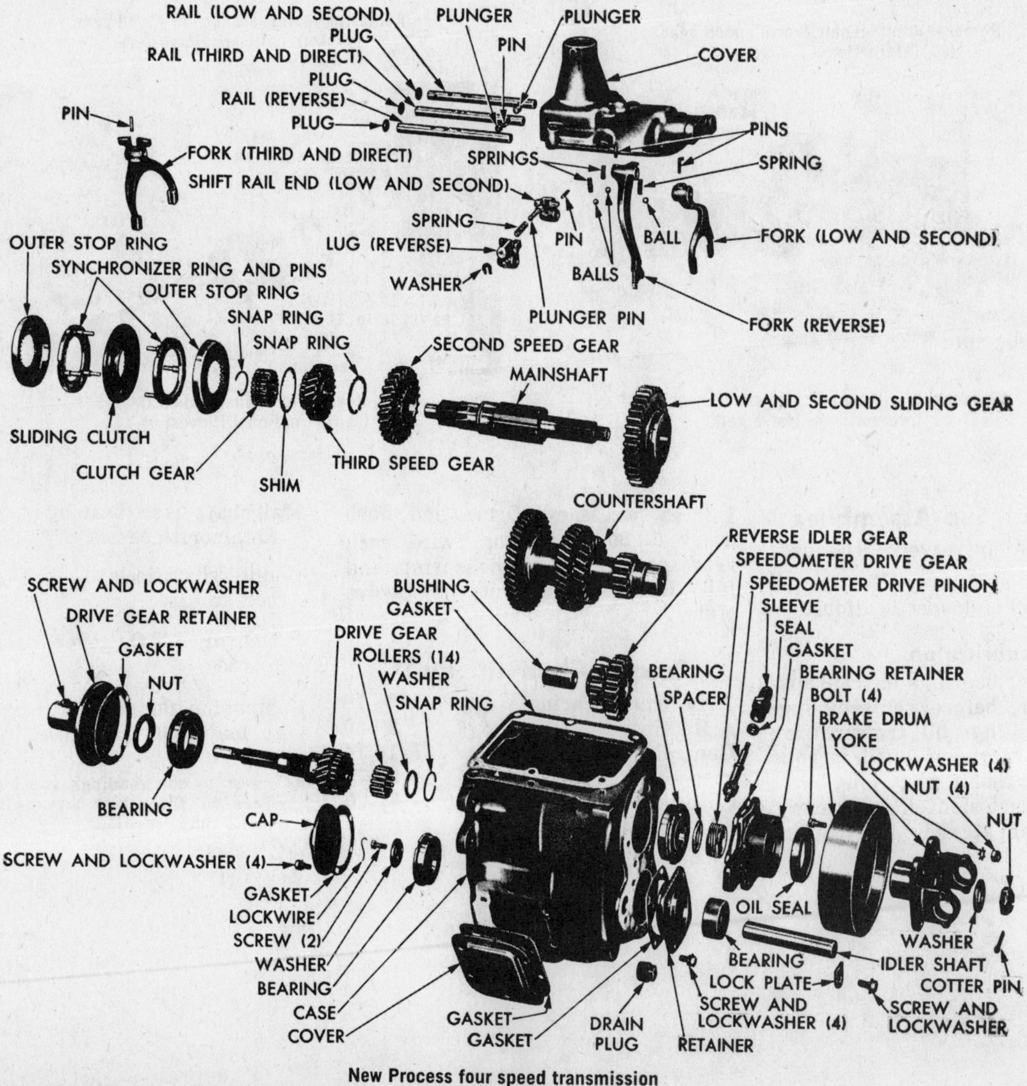

Removing cover
(© New Process Gear Div.)

RAIL (LOW AND SECOND)
PLUG
RAIL (THIRD AND DIRECT)
PLUG
RAIL (REVERSE)
PLUG
PLUNGER
PIN
PLUNGER
COVER
PIN
PINS
FORK (THIRD AND DIRECT)
SPRINGS
SPRING
SHIFT RAIL END (LOW AND SECOND)
SPRING
LUG (REVERSE)
WASHER
PIN
BALL
BALLS
FORK (LOW AND SECOND)
PLUNGER PIN
FORK (REVERSE)
OUTER STOP RING
SYNCHRONIZER RING AND PINS
OUTER STOP RING
SNAP RING
SNAP RING
SECOND SPEED GEAR
MAINSHAFT
LOW AND SECOND SLIDING GEAR
SLIDING CLUTCH
CLUTCH GEAR
SHIM
THIRD SPEED GEAR
COUNTERSHAFT
REVERSE IDLER GEAR
SPEEDOMETER DRIVE GEAR
SPEEDOMETER DRIVE PINION
SLEEVE
SEAL
GASKET
BEARING RETAINER
BOLT (4)
BRAKE DRUM
YOKE
LOCKWASHER (4)
NUT (4)
NUT
SCREW AND LOCKWASHER
DRIVE GEAR RETAINER
GASKET
NUT
BEARING
BUSHING
GASKET
DRIVE GEAR
ROLLERS (14)
WASHER
SNAP RING
BEARING
SPACER
CAP
SCREW AND LOCKWASHER (4)
GASKET
LOCKWIRE
SCREW (2)
WASHER
BEARING
CASE
COVER
GASKET
GASKET
DRAIN PLUG
RETAINER
OIL SEAL
BEARING
LOCK PLATE
SCREW AND LOCKWASHER (4)
IDLER SHAFT
WASHER
COTTER PIN
SCREW AND LOCKWASHER

New Process four speed transmission
(© New Process Gear Div.)

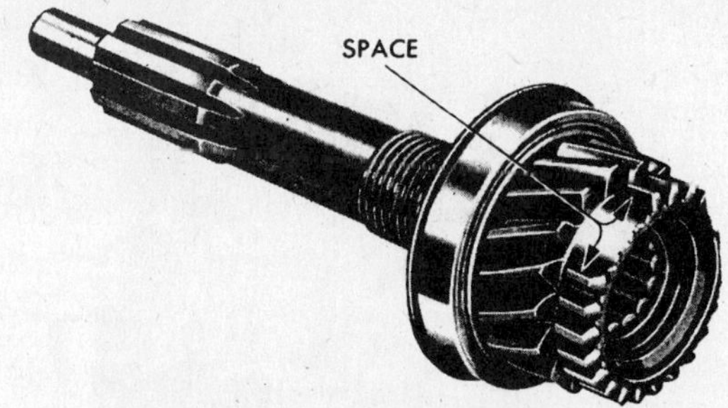

Main drive gear showing omitted clutch teeth
(© New Process Gear Div.)

Synchronizer removal
(© New Process Gear Div.)

Reverse Idler Gear Removal

Remove reverse idler lock screw and lock plate and lift idler shaft and gear from case.

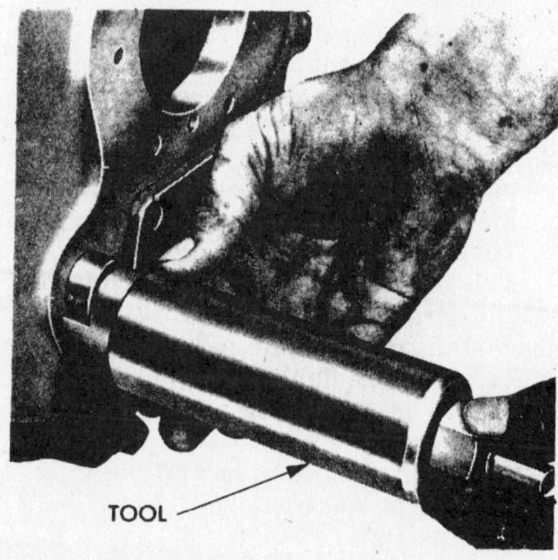

Idler shaft removal
(© New Process Gear Div.)

Countershaft Cluster Gear Removal

1. Remove bearing retainers at opposite ends of countershaft. The roller bearing assembly at rear end of shaft remains with the retainer.
2. Remove cluster gear assembly from case.
3. Remove front bearing.

Disassembling Sub-Assemblies

Mainshaft

1. Remove clutch gear snap-ring.
2. Remove clutch gear, synchronizer outer stop ring to 3rd speed gear shim (or shims) and 3rd speed gear.
3. Remove split lock ring and remove 2nd speed gear.
4. Remove low 2nd sliding gear.
5. Drive old seal from rear bearing support housing.

Countershaft

The cluster gears are integral with the shaft. The rear bearing and retainer are unserviceable items—they must be replaced if worn.

Reverse Idler

If necessary, press in a new bushing.

Cover and Shift Fork Assembly

1. Remove roll pin from 3rd and 4th speed fork (center rail) with an "easy out". NOTE: A square type or a closely wound spiral "easy out" mounted in a tap handle is preferable for this operation.
2. After removing pin, drive the rail to the rear and remove fork.
3. Continue driving rail to rear to remove rear expansion plug; being careful to catch poppet ball and spring. Also, note interlock pin and rail.
4. Remove remaining rails, lugs and shift forks in the same manner as center rail. NOTE: It is very seldom that the interlocks require removal from cover. However, to replace interlocks remove the plug from the interlock passage in the cover.
5. Remove the reverse spring loaded plunger from the lug (if required) by removing horse shoe lock from plunger shaft.

Main Drive Pinion

1. Secure main drive pinion gear in a soft jawed vise and remove bearing retaining lock nut. NOTE: Retaining nut has left hand thread.
2. Press bearing from shaft.
3. Remove lock ring, washer and pilot rollers from gear.

Assembling Sub-Assemblies

When assembling, use new expansion plugs, gaskets and seals. Lubricate all parts with transmission lubricant before assembly.

Mainshaft

1. Place mainshaft in a soft jawed vise with forward end up.
2. Install 2nd speed gear and lock in position with split lock ring.
3. Install 3rd speed gear with clutching teeth up.
4. Install spacer shim (or shims) and clutch gear (oil slots down).
5. Install clutch gear snap-ring; selecting the correct size to eliminate all clutch gear end play. Snap-rings are available in four thicknesses marked A, B, C and D. When installing the synchronizer assembly on the main shaft, the selection of third speed gear shims will depend upon the number of shims originally used and the amount of end play clearance recorded before disassembly. The number of shims necessary for correct end play clearance (.050 to .070), cannot be accurately measured until all the mainshaft components are in position and properly tightened.

Main Drive Pinion

1. Press bearing onto main drive gear pinion seating it against pinion shoulder.
2. Install retainer nut (left hand thread) and tighten securely.
3. Install large snap-ring on bearing race.
4. Lubricate roller bearings to hold rollers in place and insert in pocket of main drive gear.
5. Install washer and snap-ring.

Transmission Cover

1. Sight along the reverse rail bore in cover to be certain the interlock pin is clear of the hole. Enter the reverse rail into the bore at the rear of cover. Push it in further and install fork. Continue to push rail into cover until rail enters rail . pport containing cavity for poppet ball and spring.
2. Install spring and ball in support, compress spring, and push rail over ball.
3. Install lug on rail and install plug in cover.
4. Drive roll pins through lug, shift fork and rail.
5. Install 1st and 2nd speed rail assembly in same manner followed by 3rd and 4th speed rail assembly; being certain that interlock

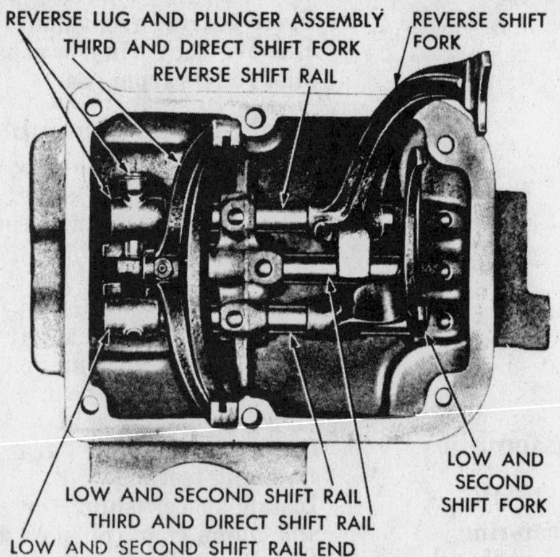

Cover and shift fork assembly
(© New Process Gear Div.)

FEELER GAUGES

Measuring synchronizer end play
(© New Process Gear Div.)

pin is in position in 3rd and 4th speed rail.

Installing Sub-Assemblies into Case

Countershaft

1. Lower countershaft assembly into case.
2. Install front bearing and front bearing washer, capscrews and lockwire and torque to 25-30 foot-pounds.
3. While holding gear assembly in alignment, install rear bearing support gasket and bearing assembly over front bearing opening in case. Install end cover and gasket.

Reverse Idler Assembly

1. Position reverse gear in case.
2. Align groove in idler shaft with lock plate.
3. Tap shaft into case far enough to start reverse gear.
4. While holding gear in position, tap shaft through case and gear.
5. Install lock plate, washer and cap screw.
6. Make sure gear turns freely on shaft.

Mainshaft and Main Drive Pinion

1. Install mainshaft and first speed gear through rear bearing opening in case.
2. With shaft assembly moved to rear of case install synchronizer components one at a time.
3. Install main drive pinion by tapping on outer bearing race while guiding main shaft pilot into roller bearing.
4. Make sure bearing snap-ring is flush against case.
5. Carefully drive rear bearing onto mainshaft and into case (snap-ring flush against case) using a suitable sleeve against inner race of bearing.
6. Install spacer and speedometer gear.
7. Install rear support and gasket.
8. Place front main drive pinion bearing retainer over pinion shaft without gasket.
9. Hold retainer tight against bearing and measure clearance between retainer and case with a feeler gauge.
10. Select a gasket approximately .005 inch thicker then measured clearance and install gasket and retainer.
11. End play should be .003 to .006 inch.
12. Check the synchronizer end play clearance (.050 to .070) after all mainshaft components are in position and properly tightened. If two sets of feeler gauges are used to measure this clearance, care should be used to keep gauges as close as possible to both sides of the mainshaft for best results. In some cases, it may be necessary to change the thickness of the shims to keep the end play clearance within the specified .050 to .070.
13. Install speedometer drive pinion.
14. Install yoke flange, drum and brake assembly.
15. Final tightening of nut may be made on truck, however, lock transmission to hold shaft for preliminary tightening.
16. Shift gears and/or synchronizer into all speed positions and check for free rotation. Be sure synchronizer pins are properly aligned.

Cover

1. Move gears into neutral position.
2. Carefully engage forks into proper gears and lower cover and new gasket into place.
3. Install one screw on each side of case and try gears for free rotation by shifting gears through cover tower with a long screwdriver and then install remaining screws.
4. Install transmission in truck and tighten yoke flange retaining nut before connecting universal joint.
5. Install gear shift lever and check for proper shifting operation.

Torque Chart

4-Speed Transmission 420

Cover screw	3/8-16	20-40
Drive gear retainer screw	5/16-18	15-25
Front countershaft retainer screw	5/16-18	15-25
Front countershaft bearing washer screw	5/16-24	12-22
Flange nut	7/8-16	125
Mainshaft rear retainer screw	5/16-18	15-25
Rear countershaft retainer screw	5/16-18	15-25
PTO cover screw	3/8-16	8-12
Filler and drain plug	3/4-14	25-45
Reverse idler shaft lock screw	3/8-16	20-40
Brake link shoulder screw	3/8-16	20-40

New Process 433, 435, 540, 541 Series 4 Speed and 5 Speed

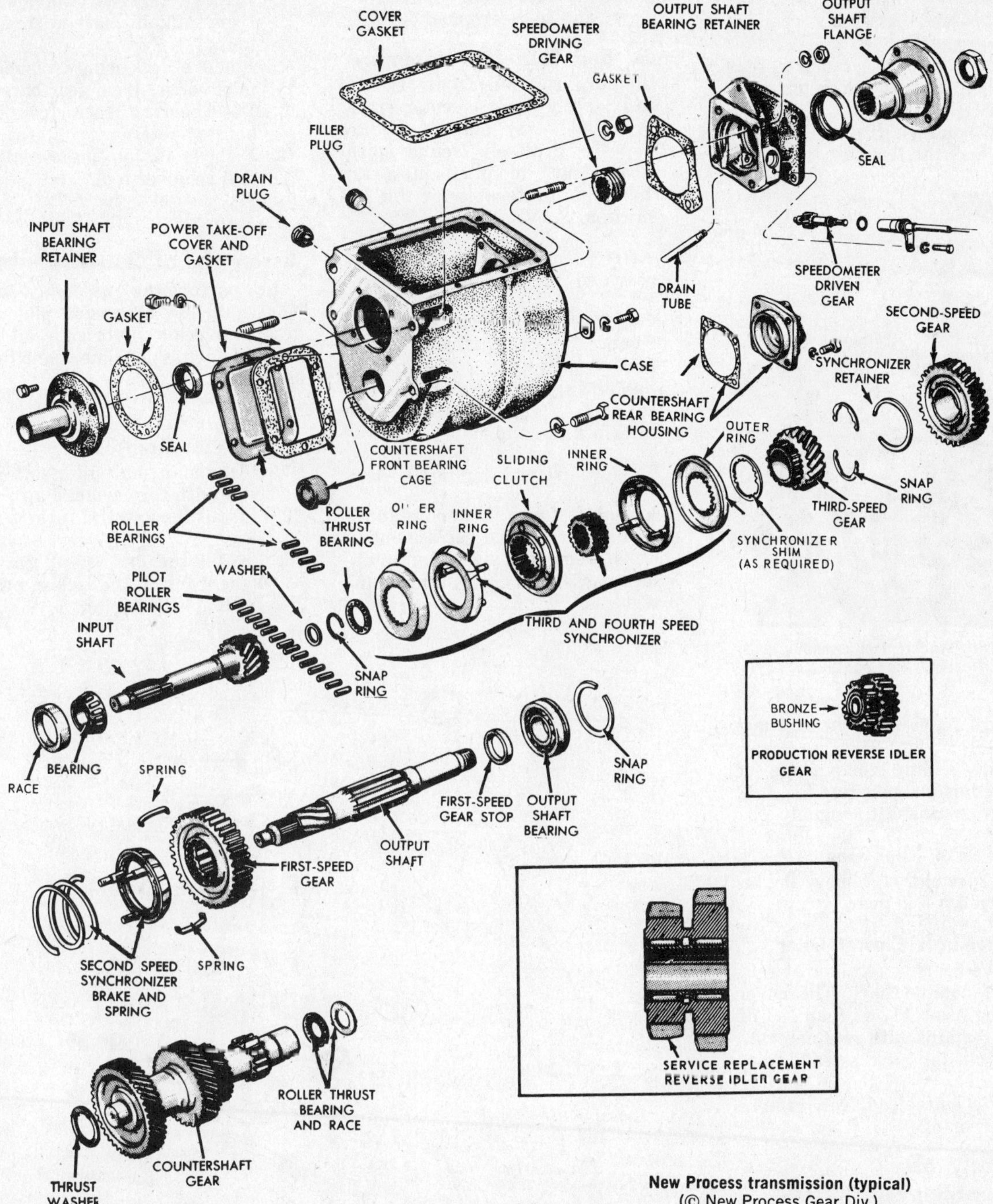

New Process transmission (typical)
(© New Process Gear Div.)

Description

This series is of a helical gear design except 1st and reverse which are spur type. The countershaft and all its gears are a single unit. The transmission is synchronized in 2nd, 3rd, and 4th gears. Lubricant capacity is 7 pints.

NOTE: The transmissions, although both four speed and 5 speed, are basically the same in construction. The four speed transmission is actually a five speed with the second speed gear and second speed synchronizer inner ring removed from the mainshaft and replaced by a spacer.

Removal of Sub-Assemblies

1. Shift gears into neutral.
2. Remove cover by rotating it slightly counter-clockwise to provide clearance to shifting forks. Check and record the amount of synchronizer end play for assembly reference.
3. Remove yoke and parking brake drum as an assembly. The drum and yoke are balanced and unless replacement of parts is required it is recommended that drum and yoke be removed as a unit assembly.
4. Remove speedometer drive pinion, and rear mainshaft bearing support.

Drive Pinion

Remove drive pinion bearing retainer and rotate the gear to align the notch in pinion gear clutch teeth with countershaft drive gear teeth. Remove drive pinion gear and tapered roller bearing from transmission.

Mainshaft

1. Using a brass drift, drive mainshaft to rear, making certain the synchronizer assembly remains free on shaft.
2. Using a puller, remove rear bearing and speedometer gear (with spacer).
3. Move mainshaft assembly to rear and tilt front of mainshaft

Removing synchronizer assembly
(© New Process Gear Div.)

up.

4. Remove roller type thrust bearing.
5. Remove sliding components of synchronizer separately.
6. Remove mainshaft assembly.

Reverse Idler Gear

Using a special tool, remove the reverse idler shaft and gear.

Countershaft Cluster Gear

1. Remove bearing retainer at rear end of countershaft. The roller bearing assembly at rear end of shaft remains with retainer.
2. Work cluster gear assembly out of case.
3. Using a suitable driver, remove front bearings.

Disassembly of Sub-Assemblies

Mainshaft

1. Remove clutch gear snap-ring.
2. Remove clutch gear, synchronizer outer stop ring to 3rd speed gear shim (or shims) and 3rd speed gear.
3. Remove special split lock ring with two screwdrivers and remove 2nd speed gear, and synchronizer.
4. Remove low 2nd sliding gear.
5. Drive old seal from rear bearing support housing.

Reverse Idler

1. Remove snap-ring and needle bearing retaining washer.
2. Remove bearings race.
3. Remove needle bearings (34 per row) and center washer.

Cover and Shift Fork Assembly

1. Remove roll pin from 3rd and 4th speed fork (center rail) with an "easy out." A square type or a closely wound spiral "easy out" mounted in a tap handle is preferable for this operation.
2. After removing pin, drive rail to rear and remove fork.
3. Continue driving rail to rear to remove rear expansion plug; being careful to catch poppet ball and spring as rail clears rail support in housing. Also, note interlock pin and rail.
4. Remove remaining rails, lugs and shift forks in same manner as center rail. To replace interlocks, remove plug from interlock passage in cover, remove interlocks.

Drive Pinion and Bearing Retainer

1. Remove tapered roller bearing from pinion shaft with special tool.
2. Remove lock ring washer and pilot rollers from gear bore.
3. Pull bearing race from front bearing retainer.
4. Remove pinion shaft seal, with seal remover tool.

Assembly of Sub-Assemblies

In performing assembly operations, use new expansion plugs, gaskets and seals. Lubricate all parts with transmission lubricant before assembly.

Mainshaft

1. Place mainshaft in a soft jawed vise with forward end up.
2. Install the low and reverse speed gear.
3. Install the 2nd speed gear and synchronizer and lock in position with split lock ring.

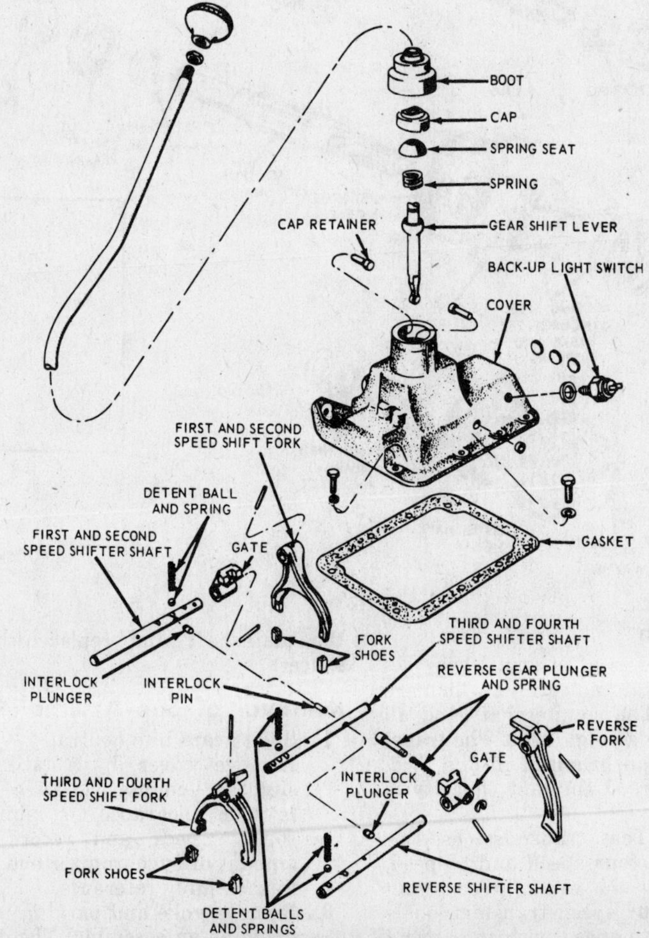

Gearshift cover components
(© New Process Gear Div.)

4. Install 3rd speed gear shim (or shims) and oil slots down.
5. Install clutch gear and a snap-ring that will eliminate all clutch gear end play. Snap rings are available in four thicknesses marked A, B, C and D.

When installing the synchronizer assembly on main shaft, the selection of shims on the 2rd speed gear, will be determined by the original number of shims and the amount of end play clearance recorded at this point during disassembly. The correct thickness of shims necessary to obtain proper end play clearance when unit is completely reassembled (.050 to .070), cannot be accurately measured until all the mainshaft components are in position and properly tightened.

Reverse Idler

1. Using a suitable grease, install needle bearings in reverse idler gear (34 per row) and center washer.
2. Install bearing race, retaining washer and snap-ring.

Drive Pinion and Bearing Retainer

1. Position drive pinion in arbor press.
2. Place a wood block on pinion gear and press into bearing until it contacts bearing inner race.
3. Insert lubricated roller bearings in pocket of drive gear.
4. Install washer and snap-ring.
5. Press in new bearing retainer seal with lip of seal toward mounting surface.
6. Press bearing race into retainer.

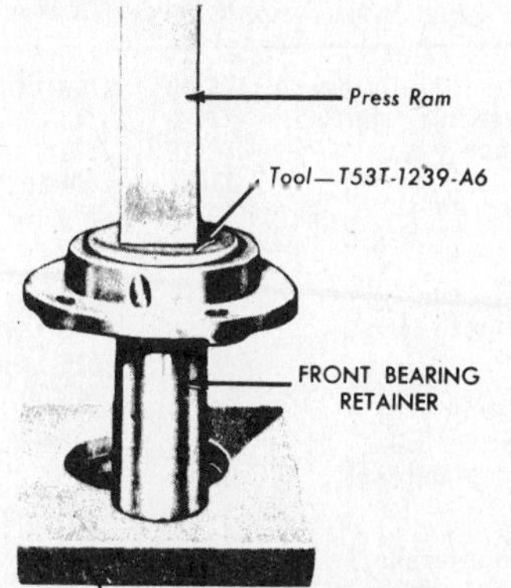

Installing front bearing race
(© New Process Gear Div.)

Transmission Cover

1. Sight along reverse rail bore in cover to be certain the interlock pin is clear of the hole. Start reverse rail through hole at rear of cover and position fork on rail. Continue to push rail into cover until rail enters rail support containing cavity for poppet ball and spring.

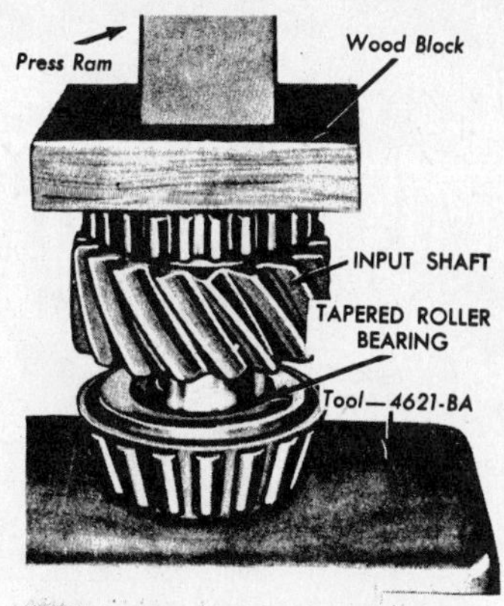

Installing input shaft bearing
(© New Process Gear Div.)

2. Install spring and ball in support and push rail over ball.
3. Install lug on rail and expansion plug in cover.
4. Drive roll pins through lug, shift fork and rail.
5. Install 1st and 2nd speed rail assembly in same manner followed by 3rd and 4th speed rail assembly; being certain that interlock pin is in position in 3rd and 4th speed rail.

Installing Sub-Assemblies

Countershaft

Lower countershaft assembly into case. Install rear bearing support gasket support and bearing assembly. Install end cover and gasket.

Reverse Idler Assembly

1. Position reverse gear in case.
2. Install lock plate on idler shaft.
3. Tap shaft through case and recap screw.
4. Install lock plate, washer and reverse gear.
5. Make sure gear turns freely on shaft.

Mainshaft and Drive Pinion

1. Lower rear end of mainshaft into case holding 1st speed gear on shaft and maneuver shaft through rear bearing opening.
2. Install synchronizer components one at a time.
3. Install roller type thrust bearing.
4. Carefully drive rear bearing onto shaft and into case (snap-ring flush against case) using a suitable sleeve against inner race of bearing.
5. Install drive pinion shaft and bearing assembly.
6. Install spacer and speedometer gear.
7. Install rear support and gasket.
8. Place drive pinion bearing retainer over pinion shaft without gasket.
9. Hold retainer tight against bearing and measure clearance between retainer and case with a feeler gauge.
10. Install a gasket shim pack .010-.015 inch thicker than this measured clearance to obtain the required 0.007 to 0.017 inch pinion shaft end play. Tighten front retainer bolts and recheck end play.
11. Check the synchronizer end play clearance (.050 to .070) after all mainshaft components are in position and properly tightened. Using two sets of feeler gauges, keep gauges as close as possible to both sides of the mainshaft for best results. In some cases, it may be necessary to change the shim thickness (A, B, C or D thickness) to keep the end play clearance within the specified (.050 to .070).
12. Install speedometer drive pinion.
13. Install yoke flange, drum and brake assembly.
14. Final tightening of nut may be performed on truck if transmission is locked into two gears.
15. Shift gears and/or synchronizer into all speed positions and check for free rotation. Be sure synchronizer pins are properly aligned.

Cover

1. Move gears into neutral position and lower cover and new gasket into place.
2. Install one screw on each side of case and try gears for free rotation by shifting gears through cover tower with a long screwdriver.
3. Install remaining cover screws.

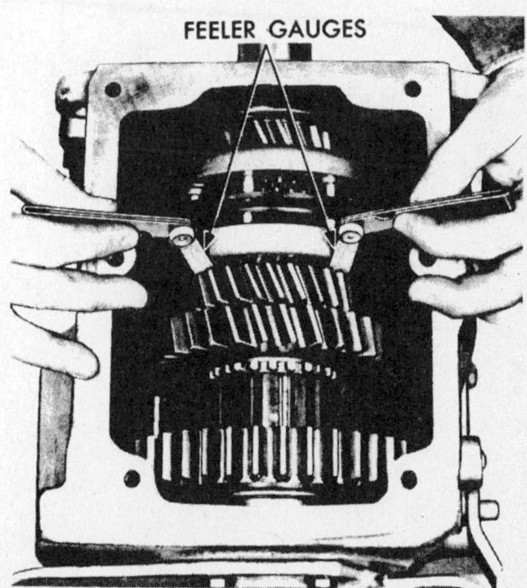

Measuring synchronizer end play
(© New Process Gear Div.)

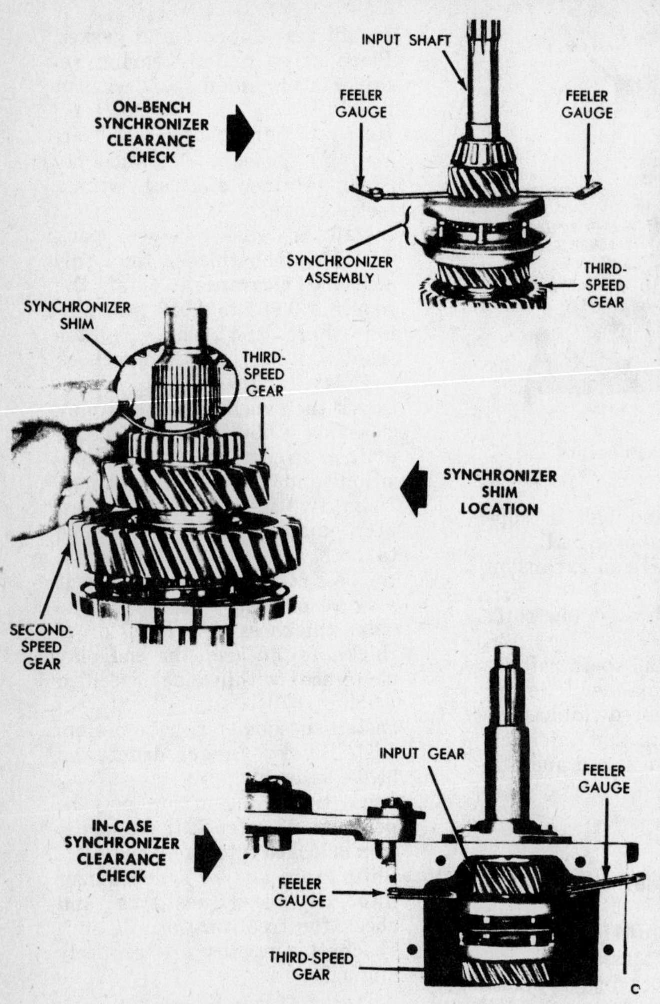

Measuring input shaft to synchronizer clearance
(© New Process Gear Div.)

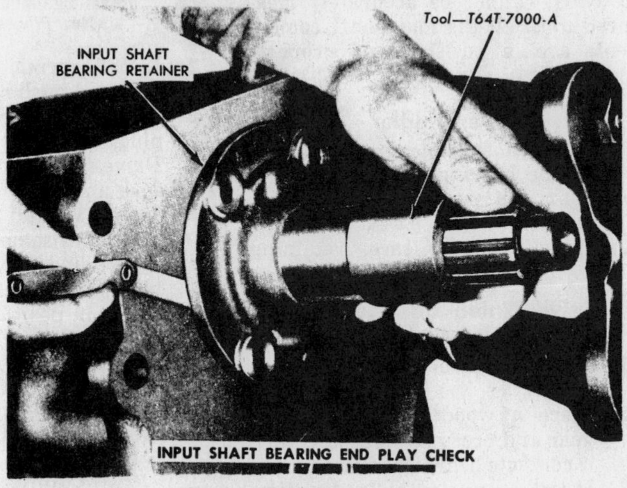

Checking input shaft end play
(© New Process Gear Div.)

Removing or installing cover
(© New Process Gear Div.)

Torque Chart

Nomenclature	*Nuts and/or Bolts and Torque Limits*		
Bolt—gear shift lever tower to gearshift housing	3/8-16 20-25	7/16-14 30-35	
Bolt—clutch housing to trans. case	7/16-14 30-38 5/8-11 96-120	9/16-12 70-90	
Nut—U-joint flange to trans. output shaft	1.00-20 90-125	1½-18 275-350	1¼-18 225-275
Nut—drum parking brake to companion flange	3/8-24 35-45	7/16-20 50-70	
Nut—bellcrank to trans.	9/16-18 70-90		
Bolt—lever assy. to trans.	3/8-16 20-25		
Nut—handbrake anchor bar to trans. case (5-speed extra-heavy duty only)	9/16-18 120-130		
Bolt—bellcrank to trans.	3/8-16 20-25		
Bolt—reverse lockout plunger retainer	11/16-16 80-100		
Bolt—countershaft rear bearing retainer	5/16-18 25-30 3/8-16 35-40	7/16-14 45-55 1/2-13 60-70	
Bolt—countershaft & reverse idler shaft retainer	5/16-18 25-30 3/8-16 25-37 3/8-16† 18-25†	7/16-14 40-45 1/2-13 80-85	
Bolt—gear shift housing to trans. case	5/16-18 20-25 3/8-16 35-40	3/8-16†† 30-35†† 7/16-14 45-50	
Bolt—power take off cover to trans. case	3/8-16 20-30		
Nut—countershaft bearing lock (5-speed extra H.D. & 5-speed exclusive)	1¼-18 350-450		
Nut—countershaft bearing lock (5-speed exclusive H.D.)	1½-18 350-450		
Bolt—Input shaft bearing retainer to trans. case	5/16-18 25-30 3/8-16 25-30	7/16-14 40-45	
Bolt—countershaft front bearing retainer	5/16-18 25-30 3/8-16 25-35	7/16-14 50-55	

Spicer 3000 & 5000 Series 5 Speed

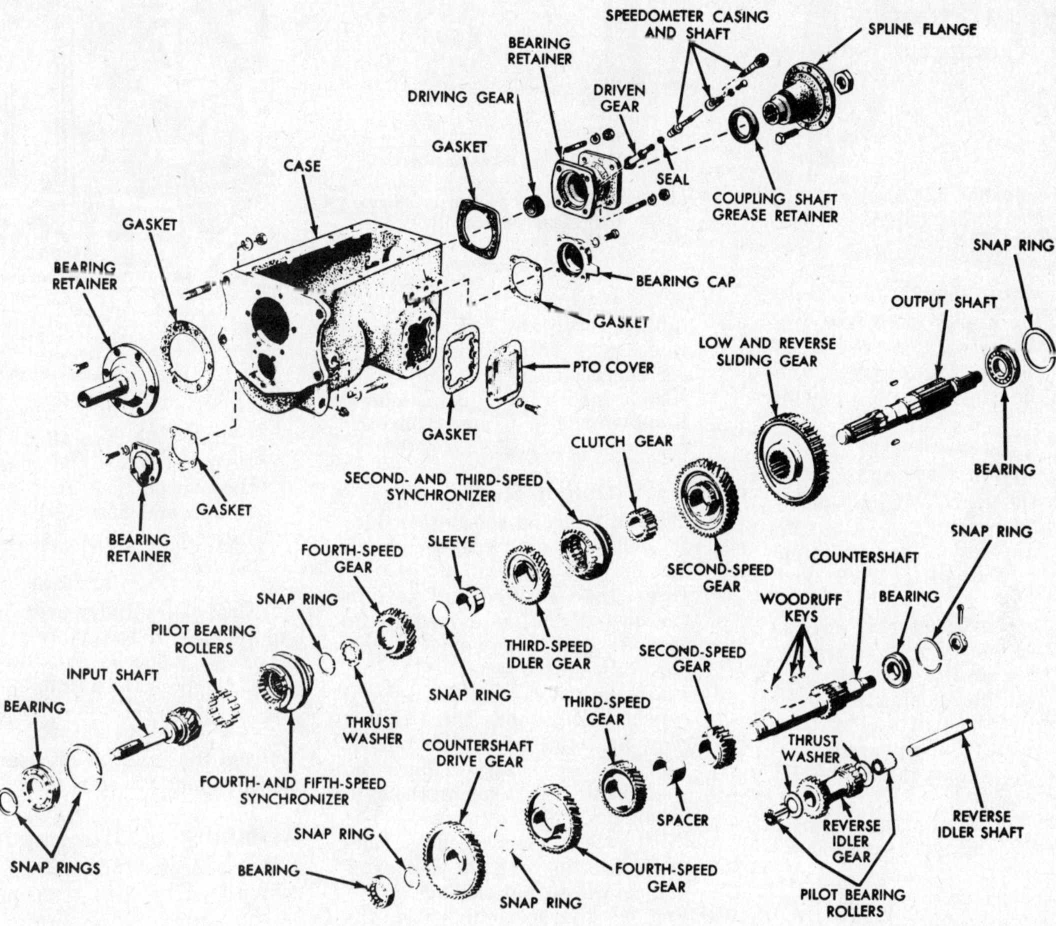

Spicer 5 speed transmission (© Dana Corp., Spicer Div.)

Description

The extra heavy-duty five-speed transmission (Spicer,) is a manually shifted, synchromesh, helical gear type. Fifth forward speed is direct drive. A power take-off is located on the right and left side of the transmission case.

Disassembly of Transmission

1. Remove the gear shift housing from the transmission case. Remove the detent balls from the housing and shift the transmission into two gears.
2. Remove the brake drum and spline flange.
3. Remove the brake shoe assembly, the output shaft bearing retainer, speedometer driving gear, and spacer.
4. Remove the countershaft rear bearing retainer, gasket, and countershaft nut.
5. Remove the left-side power take-off cover.
6. Remove the input shaft bearing retainer and gasket from the case. Using a soft drift, drive the input shaft and front bearing from the case. Remove the pilot rollers from the drive gear.
7. With a hardwood or fiber block placed against the front side of the second-speed gear, drive the input shaft assembly rearward until the output shaft bearing clears the case. Be careful not to hit the second-speed gear against the countershaft reverse gear. Remove the bearing from the output shaft.
8. When removing the output shaft from the case, slide off the first-speed gear.
9. Using a puller, remove the countershaft rear bearing.
10. Lift the countershaft assembly out of the case.
11. Remove the countershaft front bearing retainer, gasket and bearing from the front of the case.
12. Remove the reverse idler gear, and bearings from the gear bores.
13. Remove any of the 14 output shaft pilot rollers which may have dropped into the case.

Disassembly of Sub-Assemblies

Output Shaft

1. Remove the fourth and fifth speed synchronizer assembly snap-ring and thrust washer at the front of the fourth-speed gear. Remove the gear.
2. Remove the snap-ring at the front of the third-speed gear sleeve. The second and third-speed synchronizer can then be removed by bouncing the front of the output shaft on a block of wood.
3. Press the output shaft out of the second and third-speed synchronizer clutch gear and second-speed gear.

Countershaft

When replacing the countershaft or countershaft gear, press off one gear at a time. To remove the second-speed gear use special tool.

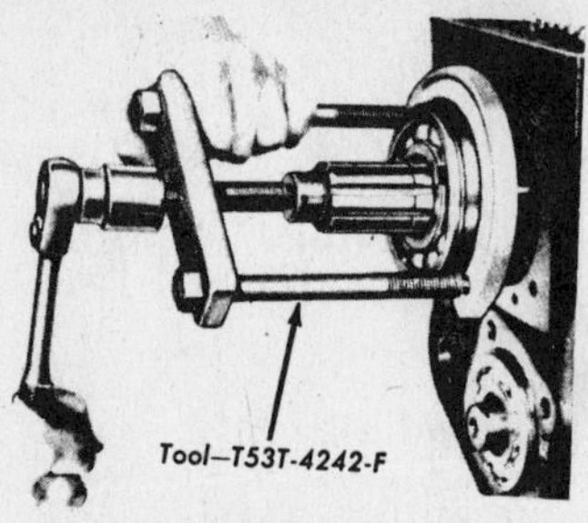

Removing output shaft bearing using special puller (© Dana Corp., Spicer Div.)

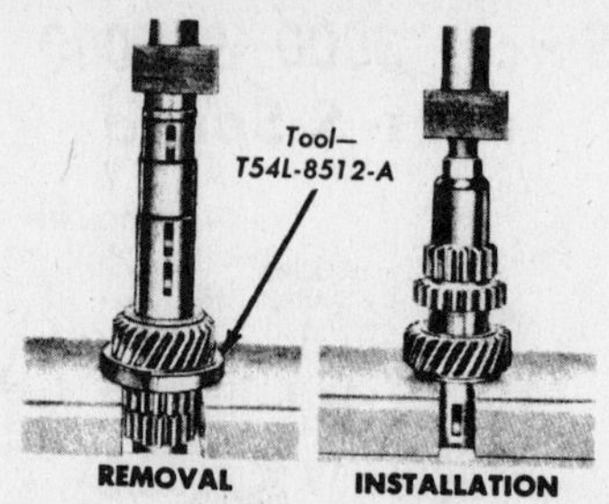

Replacing countershaft second speed gear (© Dana Corp., Spicer Div.)

Input Shaft

Remove the input shaft bearing only for replacement. Remove the retaining snap-ring, and press the bearing off the shaft.

Gearshift Housing

1. Attach the gear shift housing to the transmission case. Cut the lock wire from the retaining screws in the shifter forks and gates.
2. Mark the shifter forks, shafts, and gates for correct assembly. Shift the shafts into neutral. Drive out the housing plugs at the front of the shafts.
3. Remove the fourth and fifth speed-shaft from the front of the housing.
4. Remove the second and third-speed fork and shaft and interlocking pin.
5. Remove the low and reverse shifter shaft, fork, and gate. Remove the interlocking pin and plungers from the housing.

Assembly of Sub-Assemblies

Gearshift Housing

1. Place the low and reverse shifter gate and fork in the housing, and slide the shaft into the housing and through the gate and fork. Install the retaining screws in the gate and fork and hold with lock wire.
2. Install two plungers in the housing interlocking bore between the low and reverse and second and third shifter shaft bores. Install the interlock pin in the shaft and the second and third-speed fork in the housing. Slide the shaft into the housing and through the fork. Install the retaining screw, and lock wire.
3. Install the interlocking pin and plunger in the housing interlocking bore between the second and third-speed and fourth and fifth-speed shifter shaft guides. Install the fourth and fifth-speed shaft and fork. Install the retaining screw and lock wire.
4. Check the interlocking system for correct operation and, using sealer, install the housing plugs. Remove the housing from the transmission case.

Output Shaft

1. Place the second-speed gear onto the output shaft, with the clutch teeth facing forward.
2. Insert the two Woodruff keys in the output shaft and install the second and third-speed synchronizer clutch gear.
3. Place the second and third-speed synchronizer, and third speed gear and sleeve on the output shaft. Press the sleeve onto the shaft until it bottoms on the synchronizer clutch gear. The third-speed gear sleeve slots must line up with the Woodruff keys in the output shaft.
4. Remove the assembly from the press and install the snap-ring at the front of the third-speed gear sleeve.

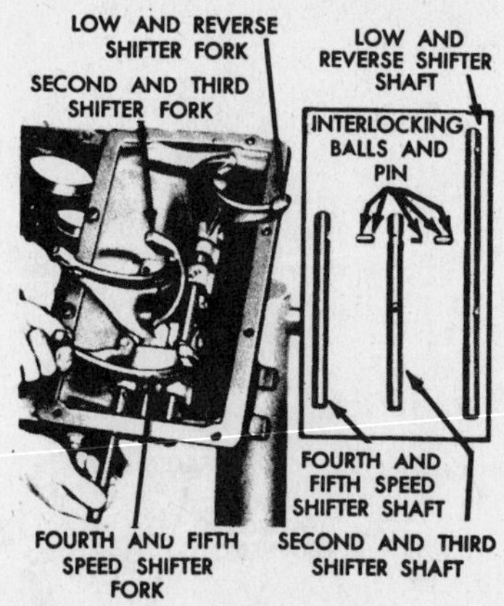

Gearshift housing (© Dana Corp., Spicer Div.)

5. Install the fourth-speed gear, thrust washer, and snap-ring on the output shaft. Install the fourth and fifth-speed synchronizer on the output shaft.

Countershaft

Install gears and spacer onto shaft and hold with the snap-rings. Each gear takes a specific Woodruff key, so install them one at a time.

Input Shaft

Press the input shaft bearing onto the shaft using special tool.

Assembly of Transmission

As a protection against scoring, coat all parts with transmission lubricant.

1. Tap the countershaft front bearing into the case and install retainer and new gasket. Line up

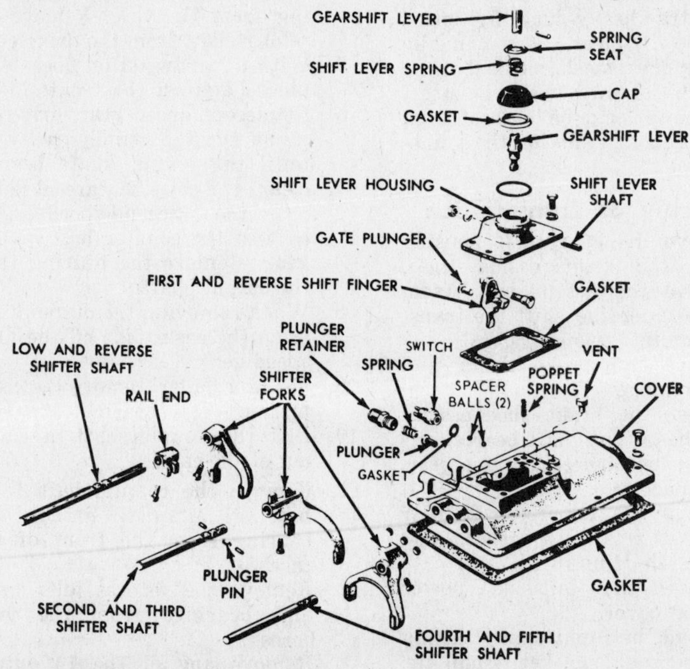

Gearshift housing components (© Dana Corp., Spicer Div.)

the oil return holes in the retainer, gasket and case and torque the 7/16" retainer bolts at 50-55 ft. lbs. (30 ft. lbs. for smaller bolts).

2. Place the assembled countershaft in the transmission case into the front bearing.
3. Drive the countershaft rear bearing onto the countershaft and into the case.
4. Install the idler gear bearings, and gear in the case. Drive the idler gear shaft into position, and install the power takeoff cover.
5. Tap the input shaft and bearing into the case. Place the pilot bearing rollers in the input shaft.
6. Install the input shaft bearing retainer without a gasket and tighten the bolts. With a feeler gauge, check the clearance between the bearing retainer and the case to determine gasket size.
7. Install the bearing retainer and gasket, making certain that the oil drain-hole is in line with the gasket and case holes. Torque retainer bolts to 30 ft. lbs., 40 ft. lbs. for 7/16" bolt.
8. Install the low and reverse gear on the output shaft and place the assembly in the case. Drive the output shaft bearing into position.
9. Shift the transmission into two gears. Install the countershaft nut and torque at 350-450 ft. lbs. Install the countershaft rear bearing retainer and torque the 7/16" bolts to 45 ft. lbs.
10. Install a new oil seal in the output shaft bearing retainer. Place the spacer and speedometer driving gear on the output shaft, and install the bearing retainer. Torque the bolts to specification.
11. Install the parking brake shoe assembly.
12. Install the brake drum and the spline flange. Torque the output shaft nut to specification.
13. Shift the transmission and gear shift housing into neutral, and install the gear shift housing and, using 7/16" bolts, torque to 45 ft. lbs.

Torque Chart

Nomenclature	*Nuts and/or Bolts and Torque Limits*		
Bolt-gear shift lever tower to gearshift housing	3/8-16 20-25	7/16-14 30-35	
Bolt-clutch housing to trans. case	7/16-14 30-38 5/8-11 96-120	9/16-12 70-90	
Nut-U-joint flange to trans. output shaft	1.00-20 90-125	1 1/2-18 275-350	1 1/4-18 225-275
Nut—drum parking brake to companion flange	3/8-24 35-45	7/16 20 50-70	
Nut—bellcrank to trans.	9/16-18 70-90		
Bolt—lever assy. to trans.	3/8-16 20-25		
Nut—handbrake anchor bar to trans. case (5-speed extra-heavy duty only)			
Bolt—bellcrank to trans.			
Bolt—reverse lock-out plunger retainer	11/16-16 80-100		
Bolt—countershaft rear bearing retainer	5/16-18 25-30 3/8-16 35-40	7/16-14 45-55 1/2-13 67-70	
Bolt—countershaft & reverse idler shaft retainer	5/16-18 25-30 3/8-16 25-37 3/8-16† 18-25†	7/16-14 40-45 1/2-13 80-85	
Bolt—gear shift housing to trans. case	5/16-18 20-25 3/8-16 35-40	3/8-16†† 30-35†† 7/16-14 45-50	
Bolt—power take off cover to trans. case	3/8-16 20-30		
Nut—countershaft bearing lock (5-speed extra h.d. & 5-speed exclusive)	1 1/4-18 350-450		
Nut—countershaft bearing lock (5-speed exclusive h.d.)			
Bolt—input shaft bearing retainer to trans. case	5/16-18 25-30 3/8-16 25-30	7/16-14 40-45	
Bolt—countershaft front bearing retainer	5/16-18 25-30 3/8-16 25-35	7/16-14 50-55	

Spicer 6000 Series 5 Speed

Description

This transmission is a 5-speed synchromesh helical gear design with direct drive in 5th speed on all models, except the 6853C, which has overdrive in 5th speed.

Engagement of all gears, except first and reverse, is aided by sleeve type synchronizers. All gears are of helical design, with the exception of first and reverse gears. Lubricant capacity is 17 pints.

General data

Make	Spicer
Type	5-Speed Synchromesh
Models	6852S, 6852K, 6852G, and 6853C
Clutch housing	S.A.E. #2

Gear ratios—all ratios are (to 1)

Transmission Model	6852G	6852K
1st	6.70	6.70
2nd	3.52	4.02
3rd	1.97	2.49
4th	1.17	1.57
5th	1.00	1.00
Reverse	6.72	6.72

Transmission Model	6852S	6853C
1st	5.71	5.71
2nd	3.20	3.00
3rd	1.89	1.78
4th	1.15	1.00
5th	1.00	0.85
Reverse	5.73	5.73

Disassembly of Transmission

Removal of Mainshaft

1. Remove clutch housing and clutch release mechanism as a unit.
2. Engage 2nd and 3rd synchronizer with mainshaft 2nd speed gear, and engage 4th and 5th synchronizer with mainshaft 4th speed or overdrive gear to lock transmission in two gears.
3. Remove companion flange or yoke retaining nut. Use puller to remove flange or yoke.
4. Remove speedometer driven gear and adapter (if used) from mainshaft rear bearing cap.
5. Remove mainshaft and countershaft rear bearing caps and gaskets.
6. Remove cotter pin and countershaft rear bearing nut.
7. Remove speedometer drive gear or spacer from rear end of mainshaft.
8. Remove mainshaft rear bearing snap-ring.
9. Using bearing puller, remove mainshaft rear bearing.
10. Remove mainshaft and gear assembly from the transmission case by clearing it from main drive gear and sliding assembly up and forward out of rear bearing bore.

Disassembly of Mainshaft

1. Remove the 1st and reverse sliding gear from mainshaft.
2. Remove 4th and 5th synchronizer.

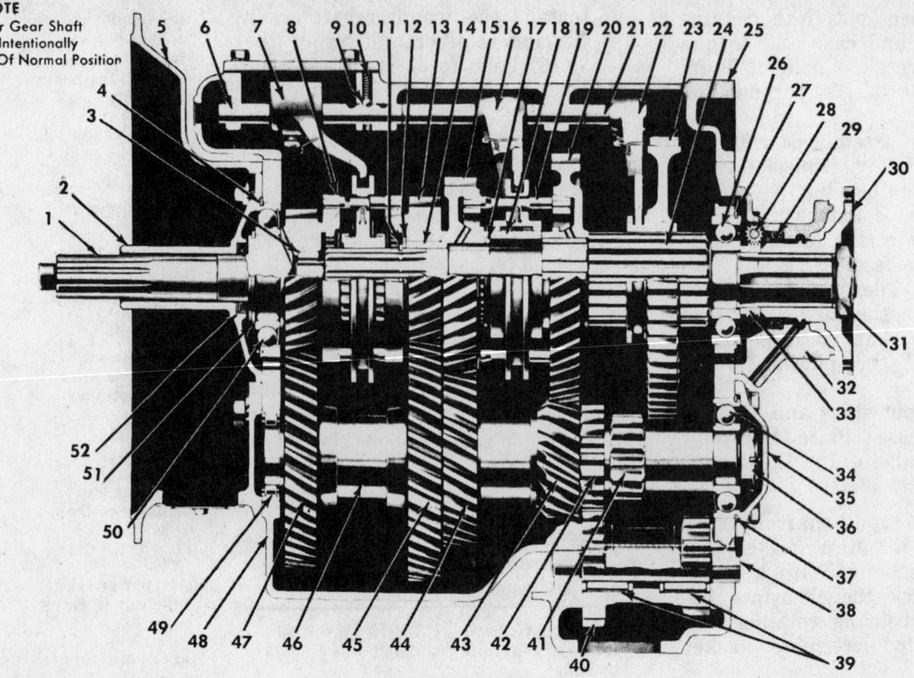

1 Main drive gear
2 Main drive gear bearing cap
3 Mainshaft pilot bearing rollers
4 Snap ring
5 Clutch housing
6 4th and 5th shift rod
7 4th and 5th shift fork
8 4th and 5th synchronizer
9 Poppet ball
10 Poppet spring
11 Snap ring
12 Thrust washer
13 Mainshaft 4th speed or overdrive gear
14 Mainshaft 4th speed or overdrive gear sleeve
15 Mainshaft 3rd speed gear
15 Mainshaft 3rd speed gear
16 2nd and 3rd shift fork
17 Snap ring
18 Mainshaft 2nd and 3rd speed clutch gear
19 2nd and 3rd synchronizer
20 Mainshaft 2nd speed gear
21 1st and reverse shift rod
22 1st and reverse shift fork
23 Mainshaft 1st and reverse sliding gear
24 Mainshaft
25 Shifter housing
26 Mainshaft rear bearing
27 Snap ring
28 Speedometer driven gear
29 Mainshaft rear bearing cap oil seal
30 Companion flange
31 Companion flange nut
32 Mainshaft rear bearing cap
33 Speedometer drive gear
34 Countershaft rear bearing
35 Countershaft rear bearing cap
36 Countershaft rear bearing nut
37 Snap ring
38 Reverse idler gear shaft
39 Reverse idler gear bearings
40 Reverse idler gear
41 Countershaft 1st gear teeth
42 Countershaft reverse gear teeth
43 Countershaft 2nd speed gear
44 Countershaft 3rd speed gear
45 Countershaft 4th speed or overdrive gear
46 Countershaft
47 Countershaft drive gear
48 Transmission case
49 Countershaft front bearing
50 Main drive gear bearing
51 Snap ring
52 Main drive gear bearing cap oil seal

Spicer 6000 Series 5 speed transmission (© Dana Corp., Spicer Div.)

3. Remove snap-ring and thrust washer.
4. Slide mainshaft 4th speed or overdrive gear from end of mainshaft.
5. Remove mainshaft 3rd speed gear and mainshaft 4th speed or overdrive gear sleeve. NOTE: If necessary to press off gear and sleeve, shift 2nd and 3rd synchronizer into engagement with mainshaft 2nd speed gear and support under 3rd speed gear. Be sure to remove sleeve pin from the inside of 4th speed or overdrive gear sleeve.
6. Slide 2nd and 3rd synchronizer from mainshaft.
7. Remove snap-ring from 2nd and 3rd speed clutch gear.
8. Support mainshaft 2nd speed gear under arbor press and press mainshaft out of 2nd and 3rd speed clutch gear and 2nd speed gear.

Removal of Maindrive Gear

1. Remove 14 mainshaft pilot bearing rollers which may have remained in cavity of main drive gear.
2. Remove main bearing cap and gasket.
3. Remove snap-ring from main drive gear bearing.
4. Remove main drive gear and bearing assembly from transmission case.

Disassembly of Main Drive Gear

1. Remove main drive gear bearing retaining snap-ring.
2. Using bearing remover plates with an arbor press, remove bearing from main drive gear.

Reverse Idler Gear Removal

IMPORTANT: When removing the reverse idler gear shaft, support the gear to prevent it from being damaged.

1. Using remover tool, remove reverse idler gear shaft, gear and bearings.

Removal of Countershaft

1. Using puller, remove countershaft rear bearing.
2. Lift the countershaft assembly out of transmission case.
3. Press or drive countershaft front bearing from bore of transmission case.

Disassembly of Countershaft

1. Support countershaft drive gear with parallel bars under hub and press countershaft free of gear.
2. Remove exposed countershaft gear key and snap-ring. Support 4th speed or overdrive gear and press countershaft free of gear.
3. Follow the same procedure and remove 2nd and 3rd speed gear.
4. Remove the remaining countershaft gear key.

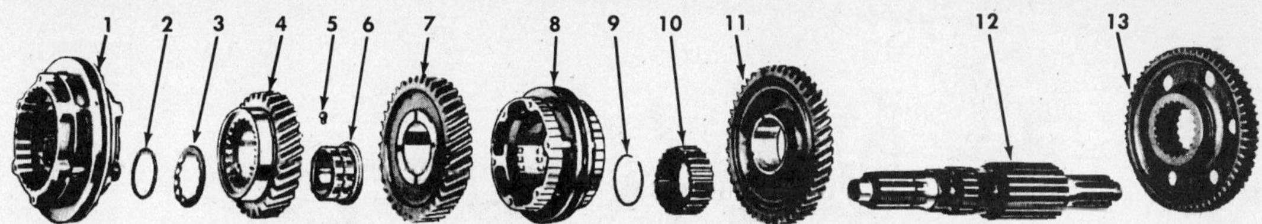

Mainshaft components (© Dana Corp., Spicer Div.)

1 4th and 5th speed synchronizer
2 Snap ring
3 Thrust washer
4 4th speed or overdrive gear
5 Sleeve pin
6 4th speed or over-drive gear sleeve
7 3rd speed gear
8 2nd and 3rd speed synchronizer
9 Snap ring
10 2nd and 3rd clutch gear
11 2nd speed gear
12 Mainshaft
13 1st and reverse sliding gear

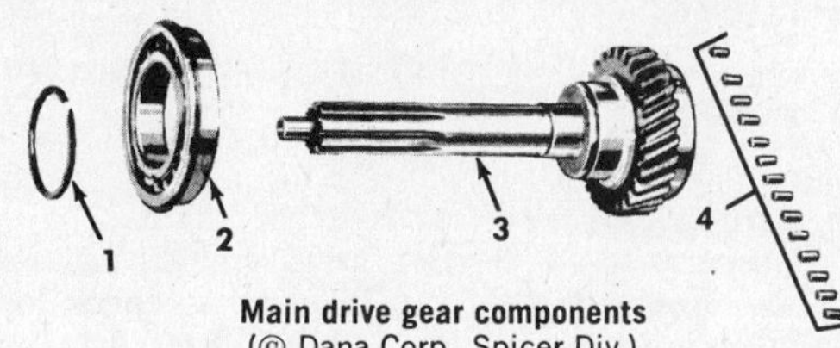

Main drive gear components (© Dana Corp., Spicer Div.)

1 Main drive gear bearing retainer ring
2 Main drive gear bearing
3 Main drive gear
4 Pilot bearing rollers

Using puller to remove mainshaft rear bearing (© Dana Corp., Spicer Div.)

Assembly of Subassemblies

Cleanliness is of the utmost importance. The transmission should be rebuilt in a clean working area. All parts, except those actually being worked on should be covered with clean lint-free paper. Avoid nicking, marring, or burring all surfaces.

IMPORTANT: Coat all thrust washers, splines of shafts, and bores of all gears with lubricant to provide initial lubrication thus preventing scoring or galling.

Assembly of Mainshaft

1. Position mainshaft in a soft-jawed vise, front end up. NOTE: Fit of new parts may require the use of an arbor press. If so, set up vertically and follow same procedure.
2. Position 2nd speed gear on mainshaft with clutch teeth and synchronizer cone facing up.
3. Using a suitable sleeve, press or drive 2nd and 3rd speed clutch gear on mainshaft. Install snap-ring in mainshaft groove. NOTE: Minimum end clearance between 2nd and 3rd speed clutch gear and 2nd speed gear should be 0.004″. Correct accordingly.
4. Slide 2nd and 3rd speed synchronizer on mainshaft until engaged with 2nd and 3rd speed clutch gear. IMPORTANT: The 2nd and 3rd speed synchronizer is often assembled backward on the mainshaft. Make sure that the long hub on synchronizer clutch gear faces the 2nd speed gear.
5. Place 3rd speed gear on mainshaft with clutch teeth and synchronizer cone facing downward.
6. Assemble sleeve pin to 4th speed or overdrive gear sleeve with head of pin inside sleeve, with flanged end of sleeve facing the 3rd speed gear, align sleeve pin with splines and press on the mainshaft.
7. Place 4th speed or overdrive gear on sleeve with clutch hub facing up and secure with thrust washer and snap-ring.

Assembly of Main Drive Gear

1. Press or drive main drive gear bearing onto main drive gear shaft and install snap-ring.

Assembly of Countershaft

1. Position first countershaft gear key in slot of countershaft. Press 2nd speed gear and, 2nd and 3rd gear spacer onto countershaft.
2. Install the remaining countershaft gear keys. It may be necessary to dress the keys with a file.
3. Press 3rd speed gear on the countershaft, followed by 4th speed gear, a snap-ring and drive gear secured by a snap-ring.

Assembly of Transmission

Installation of Mainshaft

1. Place mainshaft 1st and reverse sliding gear at an angle in the rear of the transmission case with shift fork collar facing toward front of case.
2. Place 4th and 5th synchronizer on mainshaft. Shift synchronizer clutch collar into engagement with mainshaft 4th speed or overdrive gear to help lock synchronizer in place during installation in case.
3. Lower rear of mainshaft into case, through 1st and reverse sliding gear and out mainshaft rear bearing bore. NOTE: There must be fourteen pilot bearing rollers in the main drive gear pocket.
4. Lower front of mainshaft to mesh with countershaft gears. Slide rear of mainshaft into pocket of main drive gear.
5. Slide rear bearing onto mainshaft with snap-ring facing the rear.
6. Tap bearing into case bore with its snap-ring flush with rear of case.
7. Press speedometer drive gear or spacer onto the mainshaft against bearing. NOTE: Install new oil seal in mainshaft rear bearing cap.
8. Install gasket with sealing cement and mainshaft rear bearing cap and torque cap screws to 35 to 40 foot-pounds. NOTE: Install speedometer driven gear (when used) through opening in mainshaft rear bearing cap.
9. Engage 2nd and 3rd synchronizer with mainshaft 2nd speed gear, and 4th and 5th synchronizer with mainshaft 4th speed or overdrive gear to lock transmission in two gears.
10. Install companion flange or yoke on mainshaft and secure with a washer and nut at a torque of 320 to 350 foot-pounds.
11. Remove rear bearing cap from countershaft and torque bearing nut to 320 to 350 foot-pounds and secure with cotter pin.
12. Install gasket and countershaft

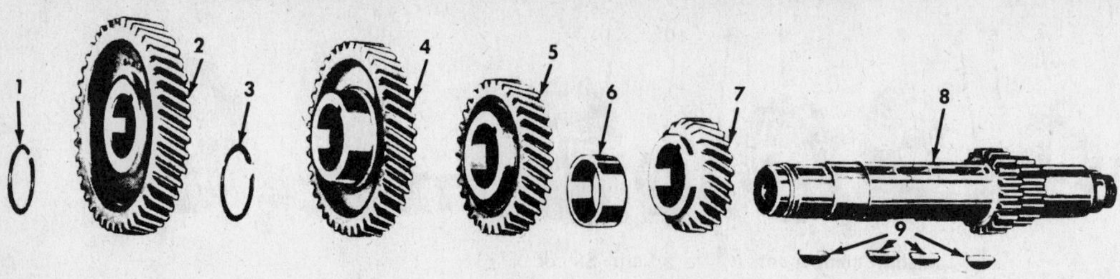

Countershaft components (© Dana Corp., Spicer Div.)

rear bearing (with sealing cement) and torque cap screws to 35 to 40 foot-pounds. NOTE: The projection on the countershaft rear bearing cap locks the reverse idler gear shaft into proper position.

13. Rotate main drive gear to check for free rotation of all gears and shafts.
14. Use pressure type oil can, filled with transmission lubricant (S.A.E. 50 engine oil of good quality) to force oil through holes and end slots of all mainshaft gears to open oil passageways. NOTE: Using the pressure type oil can, spray gear teeth with transmission lubricant to provide initial lubrication and to prevent corrosion.

Installation of Main Drive Gear

1. Install main drive gear and bearing from inside the transmission case, by tapping bearing through case bore.
2. Install snap-ring on outer race of bearing. Tap bearing rearward, so snap-ring is flush with case. NOTE: Install new oil seal in main drive gear bearing cap.
3. Install gasket (with sealing cement) and main drive gear bearing cap to transmission case and torque to 60 to 80 foot-pounds. IMPORTANT: Be sure the oil passages in the bearing cap, gasket and transmission case are all aligned.
4. Coat the pocket of main drive gear with Light Weight Ball and Roller Bearing Grease.
5. Place the fourteen pilot bearing rollers in main drive gear pocket.

Installation of Reverse Idler Gear

1. Install reverse idler gear bearings into gear and install in transmission case, with large gear on idler gear toward front of case. Mesh idler gear with countershaft and align bore of bearings with hole in transmission case.
2. Insert reverse idler gear shaft in rear of case, noting that "flat" on shaft is squared toward countershaft so that it can be locked by rear bearing cap.
3. Set countershaft rear bearing cap in place to check lock of reverse idler shaft. Finger-tighten bearing cap screws to prevent countershaft from moving during installation of mainshaft.

Installation of Countershaft

1. Press countershaft front bearing on front of countershaft.
2. Lower countershaft assembly into case, guiding rear end of shaft out through rear of case.
3. Guide countershaft front bearing into countershaft front bearing bore.
4. Place two strips of flat steel stock, approximately ⅜-inch thick, between countershaft drive gear and wall of case.
5. Seat bearing on shaft (should be tight fit) then remove the two steel strips and tap bearing into bore seating snap-ring against case.
6. Hand-tighten countershaft rear bearing nut.

Removal of Remote Control Assembly

NOTE: The Spicer 6000 transmission uses two different remote control assemblies: Prop shaft type and rod type.

1. Remove retainer, plunger pin spring, and plunger.
2. Remove remote control assembly from transmission as described below: IMPORTANT: Tilt the remote control assembly slightly to the left during removal to prevent the plunger from falling into the transmission.
3. Remove the plunger from the 1st and reverse shift finger.

Installation of Remote Control Assemblies

NOTE: The 6000 transmission is available with one of two different remote control assemblies but the installation procedures are the same for both.

1. Coat remote control assembly position on shifter housing.
2. Position plunger in 1st and reverse shift finger; then carefully install remote control assembly as shown, keeping the assembly slightly tilted to the left to prevent the plunger from falling into transmission.
3. Install plunger pin, plunger pin spring, and retainer.
4. Install remote control assembly-to-shifter housing attaching parts. Tighten cap screws firmly.

Installation of Control Tower

Install control tower as described below only when the transmission is going into storage.

1. Coat gasket with sealing cement and position on shifter housing.
2. Position plunger in 1st and reverse shift finger, then place the assembly and new gasket (with cement) on the shifter housing.
3. Install plunger, plunger spring, and plunger retainer and tighten down the tower with washers and capscrews.

Removal of Shifter Housing

NOTE: The Spicer 6000 transmission uses a forward control shifter housing and a center control shifter housing.

1. Remove shifter housing-to-transmission case attaching parts. NOTE: Carefully remove forward control shifter housing to prevent loss of the three poppet balls and springs.

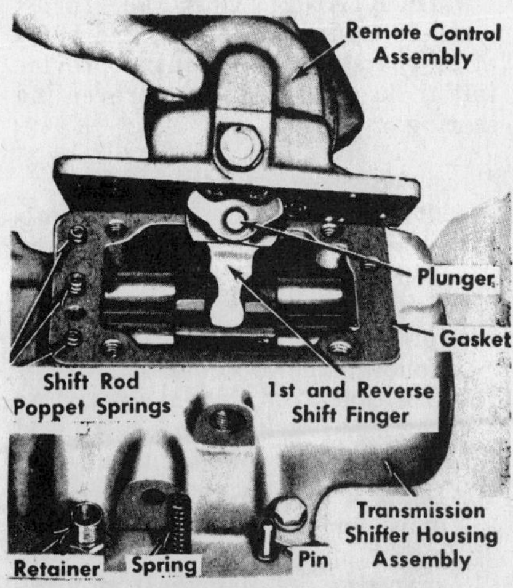

Replacing remote control assembly
(© Dana Corp., Spicer Div.)

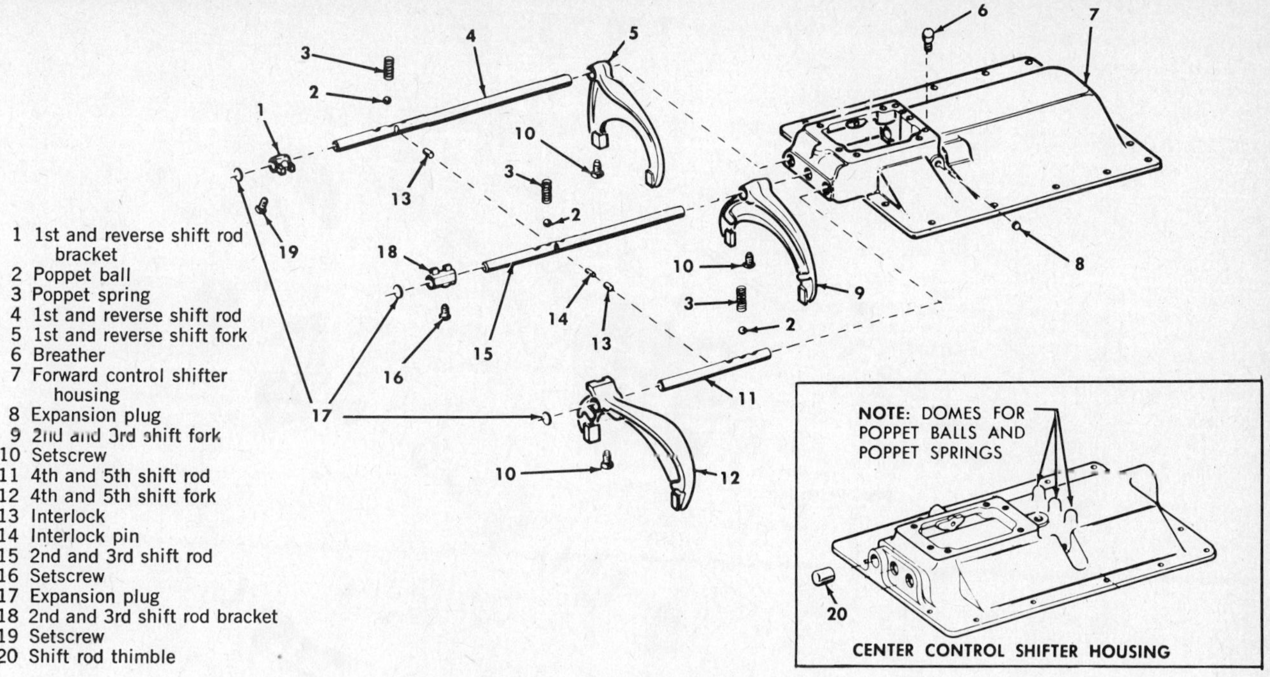

Shifter housing components (© Dana Corp., Spicer Div.)

2. Carefully remove shifter housing from the case.

Installation of Shifter Housing

NOTE: Make certain that shift forks and transmission clutch collars are in neutral position.

1. Carefully position shifter housing and gasket (use cement) on transmission case and make sure all three shift forks are in their corresponding shift collar and tighten down.
2. Use large screwdriver or small pry bar and check movement of each shift rod for proper shift action. Return shift rods to neutral position.

IMPORTANT: On transmissions using the forward control shifter housing, place the three poppet balls and springs in the shifter housing.

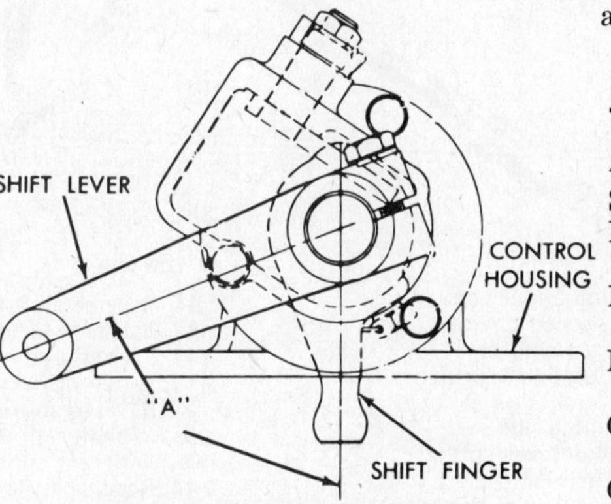

Rod type remote control adjustment
(© Dana Corp., Spicer Div.)

Torque Specifications

Location	*Foot-Pounds*
Shift fork set screws	45-50
Main drive gear bearing cap retaining cap screws	60-80
Mainshaft rear bearing cap retaining cap screws	35-40
Mainshaft flange or yoke retaining nut	320-350
Countershaft rear bearing retaining nut	320-350
Countershaft rear bearing cap retaining cap screws	35-40
Clutch housing retaining cap screws	90-95

Warner T-10 4 Speed

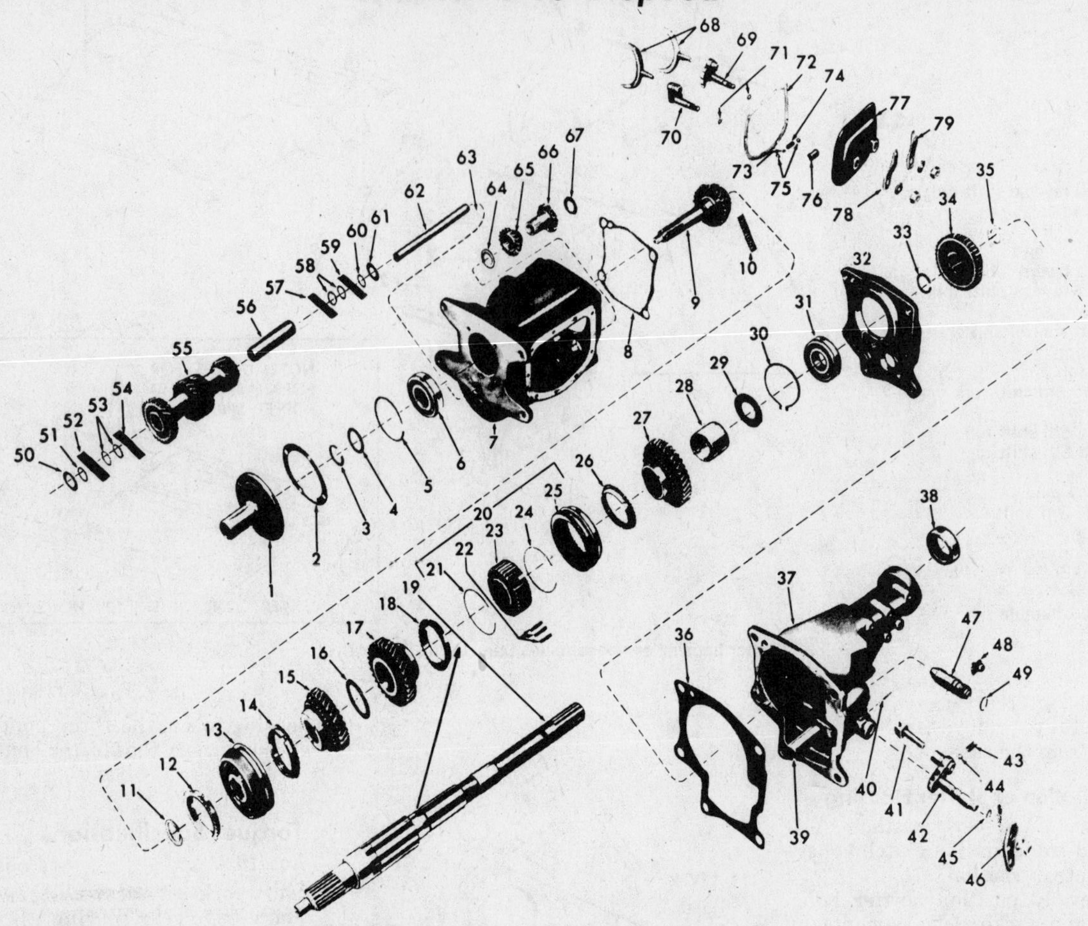

1 Bearing retainer
2 Gasket
3 Selective fit snap ring
4 Spacer washer
5 Bearing snap ring
6 Main drive gear bearing
7 Transmission case
8 Rear bearing retainer gasket
9 Main drive gear
10 Bearing rollers (14)
11 Snap ring (.086″ to .088″)
12 Fourth speed gear synchronizing ring
13 Third and fourth speed clutch sliding sleeve
14 Third speed synchronizing ring
15 Third speed gear
16 Second and third speed gear thrust washer (needle roller bearing)
17 Second speed gear
18 Second speed gear synchronizing ring
19 Mainshaft
20 First and second speed clutch assembly
21 Clutch key spring
22 Clutch keys
23 Clutch hub
24 Clutch key spring
25 First and second speed clutch sliding sleeve
26 First speed gear synchronizing ring
27 First speed gear
28 First speed gear bushing
29 First speed gear thrust washer
30 Rear bearing snap ring
31 Rear bearing
32 Rear bearing retainer
33 Selective fit snap ring
34 Reverse gear
35 Speedometer drive gear
36 Rear bearing retainer to case extension gasket
37 Case extension
38 Rear oil seal
39 Reverse idler shaft
40 Reverse shifter shaft lock pin
41 Reverse shift fork
42 Reverse shifter shaft and detent plate
43 Reverse shifter shaft ball detent spring
44 Reverse shifter shaft detent ball
45 Reverse shifter shaft "O" ring seal
46 Reverse shifter lever
47 Speedometer driven gear and fitting
48 Retainer and bolt
49 "O" ring seal
50 Tanged washer
51 Spacer (.050″)
52 Bearing rollers (20)
53 Spacer (2—.050″)
54 Bearing rollers (20)
55 Countergear
56 Countergear roller spacer
57 Bearing rollers (20)
58 Spacers (2—.050″)
59 Bearing rollers (20)
60 Spacer (.050″)
61 Tanged washer
62 Countershaft
63 Countershaft woodruff key
64 Reverse idler front thrust washer (flat)
65 Reverse idler gear (front)
66 Reverse idler gear (rear)
67 Tanged thrust washer
68 Forward speed shift forks
69 First and second speed gear shifter shaft and detent plate
70 Third and fourth speed gear shifter shaft and detent plate
71 "O" ring seals
72 Gasket
73 Interlock pin
74 Poppet spring
75 Detent balls
76 Interlock sleeve
77 Transmission side cover
78 Third and fourth speed shifter lever
79 First and second speed shifter lever

The Warner T-10 4-speed transmission—typical (© Borg Warner Corp.)

Description

The Warner T-10 is a fully synchronized four-speed transmission having a floor mounted shift lever. Lubricant capacity is 2½ pints.

Disassembly of Transmission

1. Drain transmission, mount in stand and remove side cover and shift controls.
2. Remove front bearing retainer and gasket.
3. Remove output shaft companion flange.
4. Drive out lock pin and pull reverse shift shaft out about ⅛ in. to disengage shifter fork from reverse gear.
5. Remove bolts and tap the case extension (with soft hammer) rearward. When idler gear shaft is out as far as it will go, move extension to the left so the reverse fork clears the reverse gear. Remove extension and gasket.
6. Remove rear bearing snap-ring from mainshaft.
7. Remove case extension oil seal.
8. Using a puller, remove speedometer drive gear.
9. Remove the reverse gear, reverse idler gear and tanged thrust washer.
10. Remove self-locking bolt holding the rear bearing retainer to transmission case.
11. Remove the entire mainshaft assembly.
12. Unload bearing rollers from main drive gear and remove fourth-speed synchronizer blocking ring.
13. Lift the front half of reverse idler gear and its thrust washer from the case.
14. Remove the main drive gear snap-ring and spacer washer.
15. With soft hammer, tap main drive gear out of front bearing.
16. From inside the case, tap out front bearing and snap-ring.
17. From the front of the case, tap out the countershaft with a dummy shaft.
18. Then lift out the countergear assembly with both tanged washers.
19. Dismantle the countergear, consisting of 80 rollers, six .050 in. spacers and a roller tubular spacer.
20. Remove mainshaft front snap-ring and slide third and fourth-speed clutch assembly, third-speed gear and synchronizer ring, second and third-speed gear thrust bearing, second-speed gear and second-speed synchronizer ring from front of mainshaft.
21. Press mainshaft out of retainer.
22. Remove the mainshaft rear snap-ring.
23. Support first and second-speed clutch assembly and press on rear of mainshaft to remove shaft from rear bearing, first-speed gear, and synchromesh ring, first and second-speed clutch sliding sleeve and first-speed gear bushing.

Assembly

Mainshaft

1. From the rear of the mainshaft, assemble first and second-speed clutch assembly to mainshaft (sliding clutch sleeve taper toward the rear, hub to the front) and press the first-speed gear bushing onto the shaft.
2. Install first speed gear synchronizing ring aligning notches in ring with keys in hub.
3. Install first-speed gear (hub toward front) and thrust washer with the washer grooves facing first-speed gear.
4. Press on the rear bearing, with the snap-ring groove toward the front of the transmission. Be sure the bearing is firmly seated against the shoulder on the mainshaft.
5. Install the selective fit snap-ring onto the mainshaft behind the rear bearing. Use the thickest ring that will fit between the rear face of the bearing and the front face of the snap-ring.
6. From the front of the mainshaft, install the second-speed gear synchronizing ring so that the ring notches correspond with the hub keys.
7. Install the second-speed gear (hub toward the back) and the second and third-speed gear thrust bearing.
8. Install third-speed gear (hub to front) and third-speed gear synchronizing ring (notches front).
9. Install third and fourth-speed gear clutch assembly (hub and sliding sleeve) with taper front, being sure keys in the hub correspond with notches in third-speed gear synchronizing ring.
10. Install snap-ring (.086-.088 in. thickness) into mainshaft groove in front of the third and fourth-speed clutch assembly.
11. Install rear bearing retainer plate. Spread the snap-ring on the plate to allow the snap-ring to drop around the rear bearing and press on the end of the mainshaft until the snap-ring engages the groove in the rear bearing.
12. Install reverse gear (shift collar to the rear).
13. Press speedometer drive gear onto the mainshaft so that there is a measurement of 4½ in. from the center of the gear to the flat surface of the rear bearing retainer.
14. Install special snap-ring into the groove at the rear of the mainshaft.

Countergear

1. Install countergear dummy and tubular roller bearing spacer into the countergear.
2. Using heavy grease to hold the rollers, install 20 bearing rollers in either end of the countergear, two spacers, 20 more rollers, then one spacer. Install the same combination of rollers and spacers in the other end of the countergear.
3. Set the countergear assembly in the bottom of the transmission case making sure the tanged thrust washers are in their proper position.

Main Drive Gear

1. Press bearing (snap-ring groove front) onto main drive gear until the bearing fully seats against the shoulder on the gear.
2. Install spacer washer and selective fit snap-ring in the groove in the main drive gear shaft.

NOTE: Variable thickness snap-rings are available to obtain a prescribed clearance of .000-.005 in. between the rear face of the snap-ring and the front face of the spacer washer.

Assembly of Transmission

1. Install main drive gear and bearing assembly through the side cover opening and into position in the transmission front bore. After assembly is in place, install front bearing snap-ring.
2. Lift countergear and thrust washers into place. Install Woodruff key into end of countershaft, then from the rear of the case, press the countershaft in until flush with rear of case and the dummy shaft is displaced. Maximum countergear end play is .025 in.
3. Install the 14 bearing rollers into the grease-coated end of the main drive gear.
4. Using heavy grease, position gasket on front face of rear bearing retainer. Install the fourth-speed synchronizing ring onto main drive gear with clutch key notches toward rear of transmission.
5. Position the reverse idler gear thrust washer on the machined face of the ear cast in the case for the reverse idler shaft. Position the front reverse idler gear on top of the thrust washer, hub facing toward rear of case.
6. Lower the mainshaft assembly

into the case, with the fourth-speed synchronizing ring notches aligning with the keys in the clutch assembly.

7. Install self-locking bolt, attach the rear bearing retainer to the transmission case and torque the bolt to 20-30 ft. lbs.
8. From the rear of the case, insert the rear reverse idler gear, engaging the splines with the portion of the gear within the case.
9. Place a greased gasket on the rear face of the rear bearing retainer.
10. Install remaining tanged thrust washer into place on reverse idler shaft, being sure the tang on the thrust washer is in the notch in the idler thrust face of the extension.
11. Place the two clutches in neutral position.
12. Pull reverse shifter shaft to left side of extension and rotate shaft to bring reverse fork to extreme forward position in the extension. Align forward and reverse idler gears.
13. Position the extension onto the transmission case by uniting the reverse idler shaft with the idler gears and engaging the shift fork with the reverse shift collar by turning the shifter shaft, the reverse gear will move rearward thus enabling installation of the extension.
14. Install three extension and retainer to case attaching bolts at 35-45 ft. lbs. and two extension to retainer attaching bolts (20-30 ft. lbs.). Use sealer on the lower, right bolt.
15. Align groove in reverse shift shaft with hole in boss and drive in lock pin.
16. Install the main drive gear bearing retainer and gasket aligning the oil well with the oil outlet hole and torque the sealer-coated bolts to 15-20 ft. lbs.
17. Install a shift fork into each clutch sleeve.
18. With both clutches in neutral, install side cover and gasket and torque to 10-20 ft. lbs. Use sealer on the lower right bolt.
19. Install first and second, and third and fourth shift levers.

Torque Chart

Part	*Location*	*Thread Size*	*Torque Ft. Lbs.*
Bolt	Front bearing retainer to transmission case	5/16-18	15-20
Bolt	Side cover bolts	5/16-18	15-20
Nut	Shift lever to shaft	5/16-18	12-18
Bolt	Transmission to flywheel housing	1/2-13	45-60
Bolt	Flywheel housing to engine	3/8-16	30-35

Warner T-14A, T-15A 3 Speed

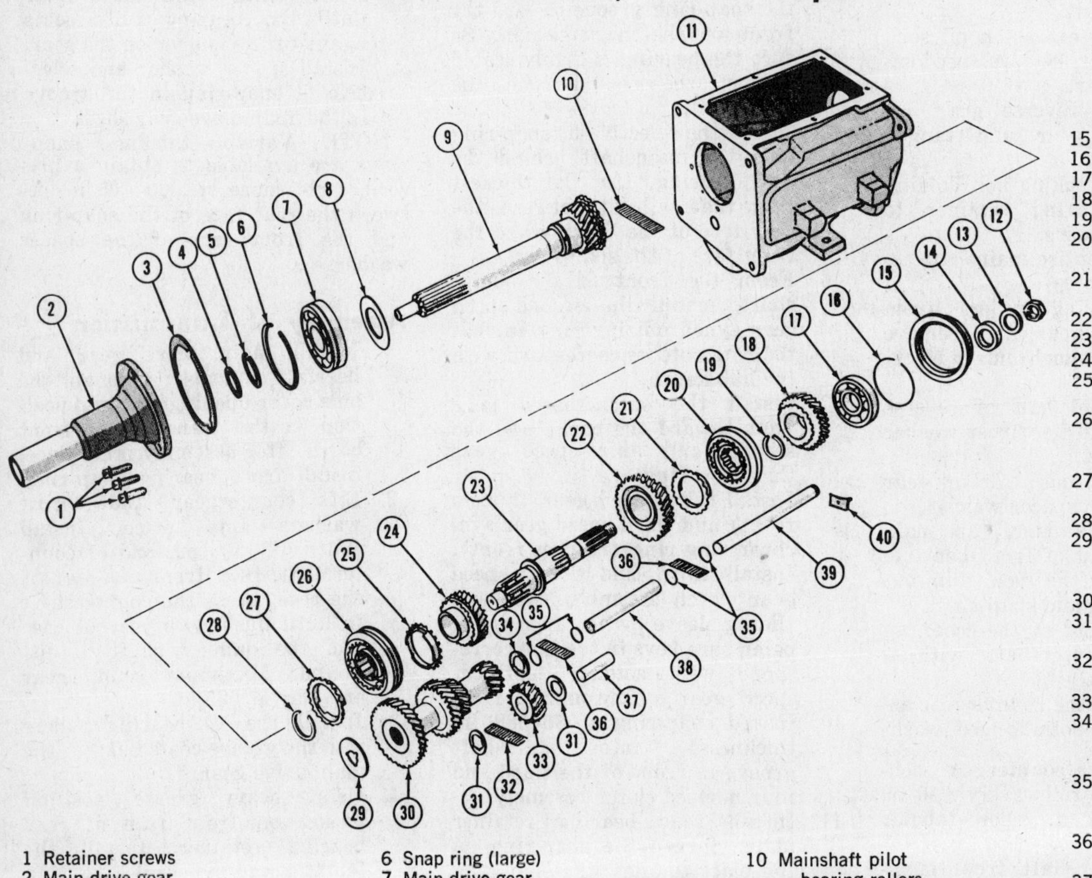

1 Retainer screws
2 Main drive gear bearing retainer
3 Retainer gasket
4 Oil seal
5 Snap ring (small)
6 Snap ring (large)
7 Main drive gear bearing
8 Oil retaining washer (slinger)
9 Main drive gear
10 Mainshaft pilot bearing rollers
11 Case
12 Nut
13 Flatwasher
14 Spacer
15 Bearing adapter
16 Snap ring
17 Mainshaft bearing
18 Reverse gear
19 Snap ring
20 Low synchronizer assembly
21 Synchronizer blocking ring
22 Low gear
23 Mainshaft
24 Second gear
25 Synchronizer blocking ring
26 Second-third synchronizer assembly
27 Synchronizer blocking ring
28 Snap ring
29 Countershaft front thrust washer (large)
30 Countershaft gear
31 Reverse idler gear bearing washer
32 Reverse idler gear roller bearings
33 Reverse idler gear
34 Countershaft rear thrust washer (small)
35 Countershaft bearing spacer washer
36 Countershaft roller bearings
37 Reverse idler shaft
38 Spacer
39 Countershaft
40 Lockplate

T-14A, T-15A three-speed transmission (© Borg Warner Corp.)

Description

The Warner T-14A, T-15A are fully synchronized three-speed transmissions having helical drive gears throughout. Lubricant capacity is 2½ pints.

Disassembly of Transmission

1. Separate transfer case from transmission by removing five capscrews.
2. Remove gearshift housing and disassembly by removing shift rails, poppet balls, springs, and shift forks.

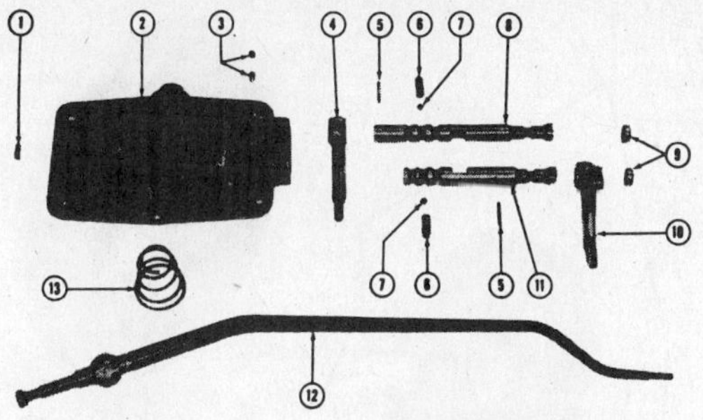

1 Control lever housing pin
2 Control housing
3 Interlock plunger and plug
4 Second-third shift fork
5 Shift fork pin
6 Poppet spring
7 Poppet ball
8 Second-third shift rail
9 Shift rail caps
10 Low-Reverse shift fork
11 Low-reverse shift rail
12 Shift lever
13 Shift lever support spring

Shift control assembly components
(© Borg Warner Corp.)

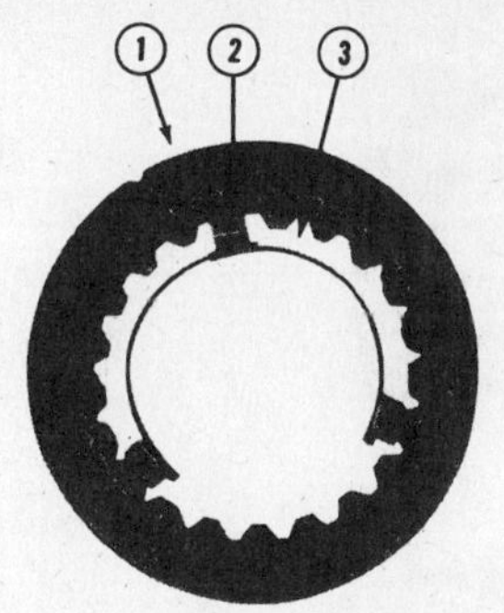

1 Clutch hub
2 Shifter plate
3 Synchronizer spring (1)
4 Clutch sleeve

Low synchronizer assembly
(© Borg Warner Corp.)

3. Remove nut, flat washer, transfer case drive gear, adapter, and spacer.
4. Remove main drive gear bearing retainer gasket.
5. Remove main drive gear and mainshaft bearing snap-rings and bearings.
6. Remove main drive gear and mainshaft assembly. NOTE: The T-15A transmission must be shifted into second gear to allow removal of the mainshaft and gear assembly.
7. On remote shift models, remove roll pins from lever shafts and housing. From inside case, slide levers and interlock assembly out. Remove forks and lever assemblies.
8. Remove lock plate from reverse idler shaft and countershaft.
9. Drive countershaft out to rear with dummy shaft. Remove countergear and two thrust washers. Remove spacer washers, rollers, and spacer from gear.
10. Drive reverse idler shaft out to rear. Remove gear, washers, and roller bearings.
11. Remove clutch hub snap-ring and second-third synchronizer assembly.
12. Remove second and reverse gears.
13. Remove clutch hub snap-ring and low synchronizer assembly.
14. Remove low gear.

Synchronizer Disassembly and Assembly

1. Remove springs. Low synchronizer has only one spring; second-third, two.
2. Mark sleeve and hub before separating.
3. Remove hub.
4. Remove three shifter plates from hub.
5. Inspect all parts for wear.
6. Assembly in reverse order of disassembly. On second-third unit, make sure that spring openings are 120 degrees from each other, with spring tension opposed.

NOTE: If a synchronized assembly is replaced on a floor shift unit, the shift fork operating the synchronizer being replaced must have the letter A just under the shaft hole on the side opposite the pin.

Inspection

1. Wash all parts in solvent.
2. Air dry but do not spin bearings with air pressure.
3. Check case bearing and shaft bores for cracks or burrs.
4. Check all gears and bronze blocking rings for cracks, and chipped, worn, or cracked teeth. If any gears are replaced, also replace the meshing gears.
5. Check all bearings and bushings for wear or damage.
6. Check that synchronizer sleeves slide freely on clutch hubs.

Assembly of Transmission

1. Place reverse idler gear with dummy shaft, roller bearing,

1 Reverse gear
2 Low synchronizer assembly
3 Low gear
4 Second gear
5 Second-Third synchronizer assembly
6 Main drive gear

Mainshaft assembly
(© Borg Warner Corp.)

1 Low-Reverse shift fork
2 Screwdriver
3 Second-Third interlock lever
4 Second-Third shift fork

Installing shifter forks
(© Borg Warner Corp.)

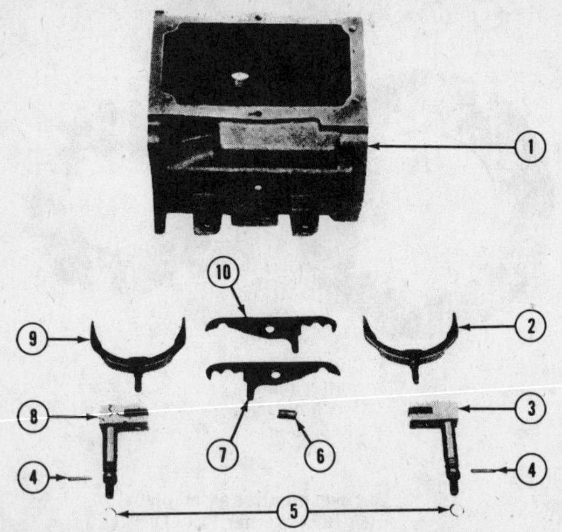

1 Case
2 Low-Reverse shift fork
3 Low-Reverse shift lever shaft
4 Tapered pin
5 O-ring
6 Poppet spring
7 Second-Third interlock lever
8 Second-Third shift lever shaft
9 Second-Third shift fork
10 Low-Reverse interlock lever

Shift bar housing components—remote control
(© Borg Warner Corp.)

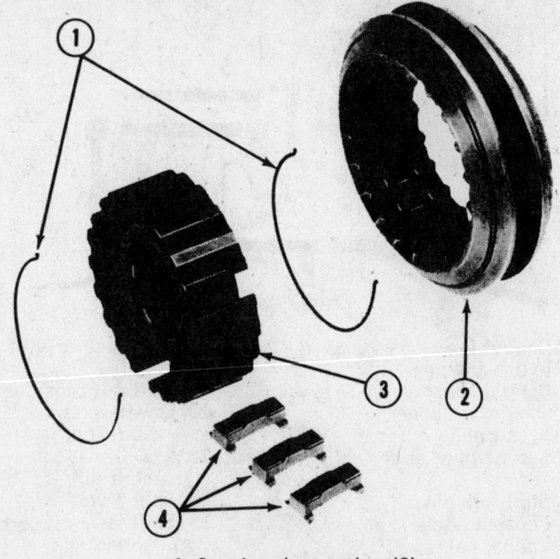

1 Synchronizer spring (2)
2 Clutch hub
3 Clutch sleeve
4 Shifter plate

Second—third synchronizer assembly
(© Borg Warner Corp.)

and thrust washers in case. Install reverse idler shaft.

2. Assembly countershaft center spacer, four bearing spacers, and bearing rollers in countershaft gear.
3. Install large countergear thrust washer in front of case. Position small thrust washer on countergear hub with lip facing groove in case. Holding countergear in position, push in countershaft from rear.
4. Install lock plate in slots of reverse idler shaft and countershaft.
5. Install to mainshaft:
   a. Low gear.
   b. Bronze blocking ring.
   c. Low synchronizer assembly.
   d. Largest snap-ring that fits in groove.
   e. Second gear.
   f. Bronze blocking ring.
   g. Second-third synchronizer assembly.
   h. Largest snap-ring that fits in groove.
   i. Reverse gear.
6. Install mainshaft assembly through top of case.
7. Install bronze blocking ring to second-third synchronizer assembly.
8. On remote shift units, install shifter shafts, with new O-rings, into case. NOTE: T-15 interlock levers are marked as to location. T-14 levers have no marks and are interchangeable.
9. Depress interlock lever while installing shift fork into shift lever and synchronizer clutch sleeve. Install poppet spring. Install tapered pins securing shafts in case.
10. Install main drive gear roller bearings.
11. Install main drive gear and oil slinger into case with cutaway portion of gear toward countergear. Install main drive gear to mainshaft.
12. Using bearing installer and thrust yoke tool, install main drive gear and mainshaft bearings and drive into position. The thrust yoke is needed to prevent damage to the synchronizer clutch.
13. Install main drive gear and mainshaft bearing snap-rings. The mainshaft bearing snap-ring is .010 thicker than main drive gear bearing snap-ring.
14. Install mainshaft rear bearing adapter, spacer, transfer case drive gear, flat washer, and nut. Torque nut to 130-170 ft. lbs.
15. Install main drive gear bearing retainer (with new oil seal) and gasket. Align oil drain holes in retainer and gasket.
16. Install case cover gasket. On remote shift units, install cover gasket with vent holes to left side.
17. Position gear train and floor-shift assembly in neutral. Insert shifter forks into clutch sleeves and torque to 8-15 ft. lbs.

General Information

Model	T14A
Make	Warner
Ratios:	
Low	3.100:1
Second	1.612:1
High	1.000:1
Reverse	3.100:1

Warner T-16 Fully Synchronized 3 Speed

Description

The Warner T-16 is a fully-synchronized 3-speed transmission. By using specially designed and proportioned helical gears, this transmission can operate at lower temperatures, provide higher torques, minimal frictional losses and produce a smoother, quieter operation.

General data	
Make	Warner
Type	3-Speed Synchromesh
Model	T-16D
Gear ratios	
1st Speed	2.86 to 1
2nd Speed	1.72 to 1
3rd Speed	1.00 to 1
Reverse	2.86 to 1

Gearshifting is performed from the steering column and transferred to the transmission by remote control rods.

Disassembly of Transmission

1. Clean outside of transmission.
2. Remove side cover assembly and

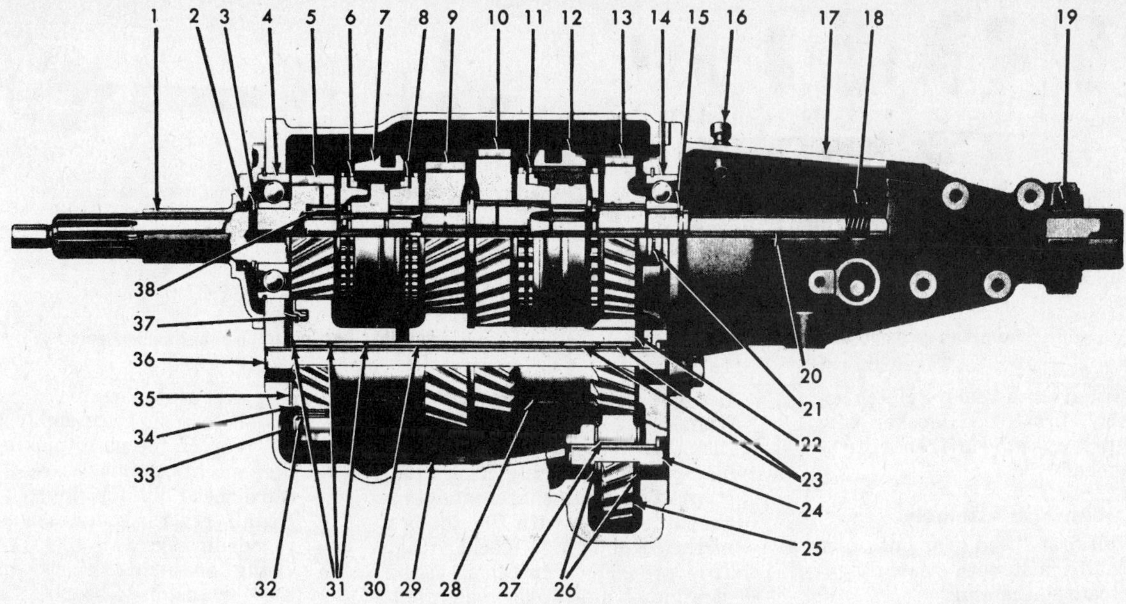

1 Bearing retainer
2 Lip oil seal
3 Snap ring and special washer
4 Clutch gear bearing
5 Clutch gear
6 3rd speed blocker ring
7 2-3 sliding clutch sleeve
8 2nd speed blocker ring
9 Second speed gear
10 First speed gear
11 1st speed blocker ring
12 1st and reverse sliding clutch sleeve
13 Reverse gear
14 Mainshaft rear bearing
15 Snap ring and special washer
16 Vent
17 Extension
18 Speedo drive gear
19 Extension oil seal
20 Mainshaft
21 Extension to bearing retainer ring
22 Countergear thrust washer
23 Roller bearings
24 Reverse idler shaft
25 Reverse idler gear
26 Thrust Washer
27 Roller bearings
28 Countergear
29 Magnet
30 Tube spacer
31 Washers (6)
32 Roll pin
33 Dampener plate
34 Spiral-Lox retainer
35 Countergear thrust washer
36 Countergear shaft
37 Dampener spring
38 Mainshaft pilot bearings

Warner T-16 cross section (© Borg Warner Corp.)

shift forks.

3. Loosen extension and rotate clockwise to expose reverse idler gear shaft.
4. Enter a long drift through the side cover opening and drive the reverse idler shaft and Woodruff key through the rear of the case.
5. Rotate the extension counterlockwise to expose countergear shaft and, with a brass drift, drive shaft and Woodruff key out the rear of case.
6. With the countergear dropped to the bottom of case, remove the mainshaft and extension assembly through the rear of case, remove the mainshaft pilot roller bearings from the clutch gear.
7. Remove snap-ring which retains mainshaft rear bearing and remove the extension from the rear bearing and mainshaft by tapping on end.
8. Remove the clutch gear bearing retainer and clutch gear bearing snap-ring and washer from the mainshaft.
9. Drvie the clutch gear through its bearing into the case and remove the bearing by tapping from inside the case.
10. Remove countergear and roller bearings, both countergear thrust washers, reverse idler gear and 25 roller bearings, and both idler gear thrust washers from the case.

Mainshaft Disassembly

1. Remove second and third-speed sliding clutch hub snap-ring from mainshaft. Then remove clutch assembly, second-speed blocker ring and second-speed gear from front of mainshaft.
2. Remove rear bearing snap-ring from mainshaft groove.
3. Press off reverse gear, rear bearing, special washer, snap-ring and the speedometer drive gear from rear of mainshaft.
4. Remove first and reverse sliding clutch hub snap-ring from the

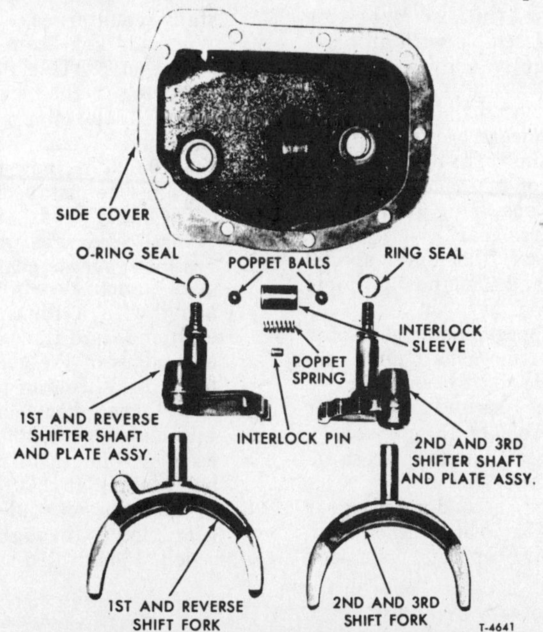

Transmission side cover and components
(© Borg Warner Corp.)

1 Snap ring
2 3rd speed blocker ring
3 2-3 clutch assembly
4 2nd speed blocker ring
5 2nd speed gear
6 Mainshaft
7 1st speed gear
8 1st speed blocker ring
9 1st reverse clutch assembly
10 Snap ring
11 Reverse gear
12 Rear bearing
13 Special washer
14 Snap ring
15 Speedo drive gear

Mainshaft assembly components
(© Borg Warner Corp.)

1 Retainer
2 Lip seal
3 Snap ring
4 Special washer
5 Snap ring
6 Clutch gear bearing
7 Clutch gear
8 Mainshaft pilot bearings
9 Bearing spacer

Clutch gear, bearing, retainer and components
(© Borg Warner Corp.)

mainshaft and remove clutch assembly, first-speed blocker ring and first-speed gear from rear of mainshaft.

Mianshaft Assembly

1. Install first-speed gear onto rear of mainshaft, with gear clutching teeth to the rear.
2. Install first-speed gear blocker ring over the first-speed gear tapered cone end (clutch key notches toward the rear).
3. Install first and reverse sliding clutch assembly over rear of mainshaft (be careful to engage the three keys with the notches of first-speed blocker ring). If properly installed, the straightest side of the clutch hub and the taper of the sliding sleeve will both be toward the rear of the mainshaft. NOTE: Synchronizer clutch hubs and sliding sleeves are selected units and should be kept together as originally assembled.
4. Install the first and reverse clutch hub snap-ring into the mainshaft groove. NOTE: There are three thicknesses of snap-rings. Use thickest snap-ring that will assemble with all parts stacked tightly, endwise.
5. Install reverse gear over rear of mainshaft, with the gear clutching teeth toward the front.
6. Press mainshaft rear bearing over rear of mainshaft, with its outer race snap-ring groove closest to reverse gear.
7. Install rear bearing special washer and snap-ring onto mainshaft.
8. Press the speedometer gear onto the rear of mainshaft until centered on the shaft boss.
9. Install the second-speed gear over the front of the mainshaft, with the gear clutching teeth toward the front.
10. Install the second-speed gear blocker ring over the second-speed gear tapered cone end (clutch key notches toward the front).
11. Install the second and third sliding clutch assembly over the front of the mainshaft, engaging the clutch keys with the notches of the second-speed blocker ring. If properly installed, the straightest side of the clutch hub should be toward the rear. The clutch sliding sleeve taper should be toward the front of the mainshaft.

NOTE: Snap-rings are available in four thicknesses. Use thickest snap-ring that will assemble with all parts stacked tightly, endwise.

Assembly of Transmission

1. Insert tube spacer in countergear. Install a spacer, 20 rollers, another spacer, 20 more rollers, then another spacer, at each end of countergear held in place with heavy grease and the dummy shaft.
2. Insert countergear assembly in case along with a tanged countergear thrust washer (tang away from the gear) at each end (large washer at front) and install countergear shaft and Woodruff key from the rear of the case. NOTE: Attach a dial indicator to the case and adjust it to determine countergear end-play. If end-play is greater than 0.025 in., new thrust washers must be installed.
3. With heavy grease, insert the 25 reverse idler gear bearing rollers into reverse gear bore. Place gear and bearing assembly, along with a thrust washer on each end, into the case. The beveled edges of the gear teeth face toward the front of the case.
4. Insert the pilot bearing rollers into clutch gear, and position in case. Do not install clutch gear ball bearing at this time.
5. Stand case on end with clutch gear down through a hole in bench. Place third-speed blocker ring over clutch gear.
6. Install mainshaft assembly from the rear of the case, picking up the spacers, pilot bearing and third-speed blocker rings.
7. Install reverse idler shaft and Woodruff key.
8. Using snap-ring pliers, install the extension-to-bearing snap-ring and then the extension and gasket over mainshaft and rear bearing. Be sure the snap-ring has started over the rear bearing. Install and tighten extension attaching bolts to 35-45 ft. lbs. Use graphite sealer on the two lower attaching bolts.
9. Tap on the front of clutch gear shaft to force rear bearing-to-extension snap-ring to seat in its groove.
10. With driving sleeve, drive the clutch gear ball bearing onto the clutch gear and into the case. Install washer and snap-ring onto input shaft. NOTE: Use thickest snap-ring (one of five thicknesses) that will assemble with all parts stacked tightly, endwise. Install snap-ring to outer race of clutch gear bearing. If bearing snap-ring groove is partially inside case opening, tap on inside bearing outer race with a long drift through side cover opening. NOTE: If mainshaft does not turn freely, check clutch sliding sleeves for neutral positions and that the blocker rings are free on their gear cone surfaces.
11. Install gaskets, clutch gear bearing retainer and lip seal assembly with oil drain passages at bottom and torque to 15-20 ft. lbs. Use graphite sealer on threads of retainer bolts. NOTE: Replace the original .025 in. gasket with two retainer-to-case gaskets (.010 and .015 in. thick).
12. Place the shift forks in the clutch sleeve grooves with the first and reverse fork hump to-

ward the bottom.

13. Install side cover and gasket and torque to 15-20 ft. lbs. NOTE: The two side cover-to-case retaining bolts have special oil sealing splines and must be used at these two through locations.

Torque Wrench Specifications

Clutch gear retainer to case bolts	20
Side cover to case bolts	20
Extension to Case bolts	40
Shift lever to shifter shaft nut	25
Lubrication filler and drain plugs	20
Transmission case to clutch housing bolts	55
Crossmember to frame nuts	25
Crossmember to mount bolts	40

Warner T-85N 3 Speed W/O.D.

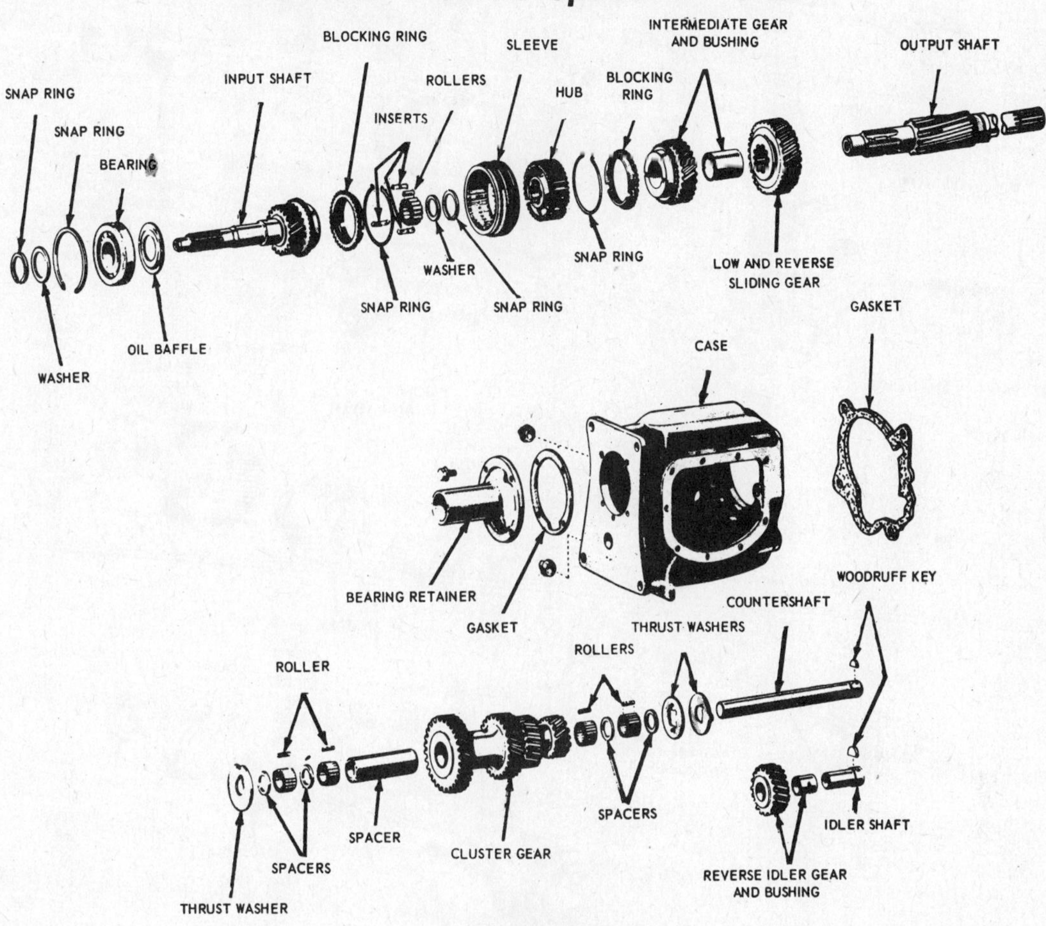

Warner 3-speed transmission
(© Borg Warner Corp.)

Description

The Warner T-85N overdrive is a synchronized 3 speed transmission with a 2 speed planetary gear transmission attached to the rear of the housing. An electrical control system automatically controls the overdrive shifts. Lubricant capacity is 4 pints.

Disassembly of Transmission

1. Mount the transmission in a vise.
2. Remove the gearshift housing assembly and gasket from the transmission.
3. Remove the shaft levers from the camshafts. Pull the shifter forks and cams out of the gearshift housing. With the cams removed, the interlock balls, sleeve, and spring will fall out of the housing.
4. Pull the shifter forks out of the cam and shaft assembly. Remove the oil seals from the camshafts.
5. Pull the solenoid body about ¼ turn, and remove it. Remove the governor.
6. With a sharp punch, pierce the snap-ring hole cover and remove the cover.
7. Remove the overdrive housing bolts, and the overdrive control shaft and lever pin.
8. Pull out the manual control shaft and lever as far as possible. Spread the snap-ring that retains the overdrive main shaft front bearing, and then remove the overdrive housing. It may be necessary to tap the overdrive main shaft to free the main shaft bearing from the housing.
9. Remove the overdrive main shaft from the assembly and the free-wheel unit rollers.
10. Remove the speedometer gear and drive ball. To install the main shaft bearing, press on the new bearing, and then install the thickest snap-ring that will fit. Snap-rings are available in the following sizes: 0.086-0.088, 0.0890-0.091, 0.092-0.094, and 0.095-0.097 inch.
11. Remove the free-wheel unit retainers. The free-wheel unit, planetary gear, sun gear, and shaft rail can now be removed.
12. Remove the snap-ring from the adapter, and then remove the plate and trough, balk ring and gear, and pawl.
13. Remove the input shaft bearing retainer and gasket and replace seal if necessary.
14. Rotate the overdrive adapter to expose the countershaft lock, and remove the lock.
15. With a drift, drive the counter-

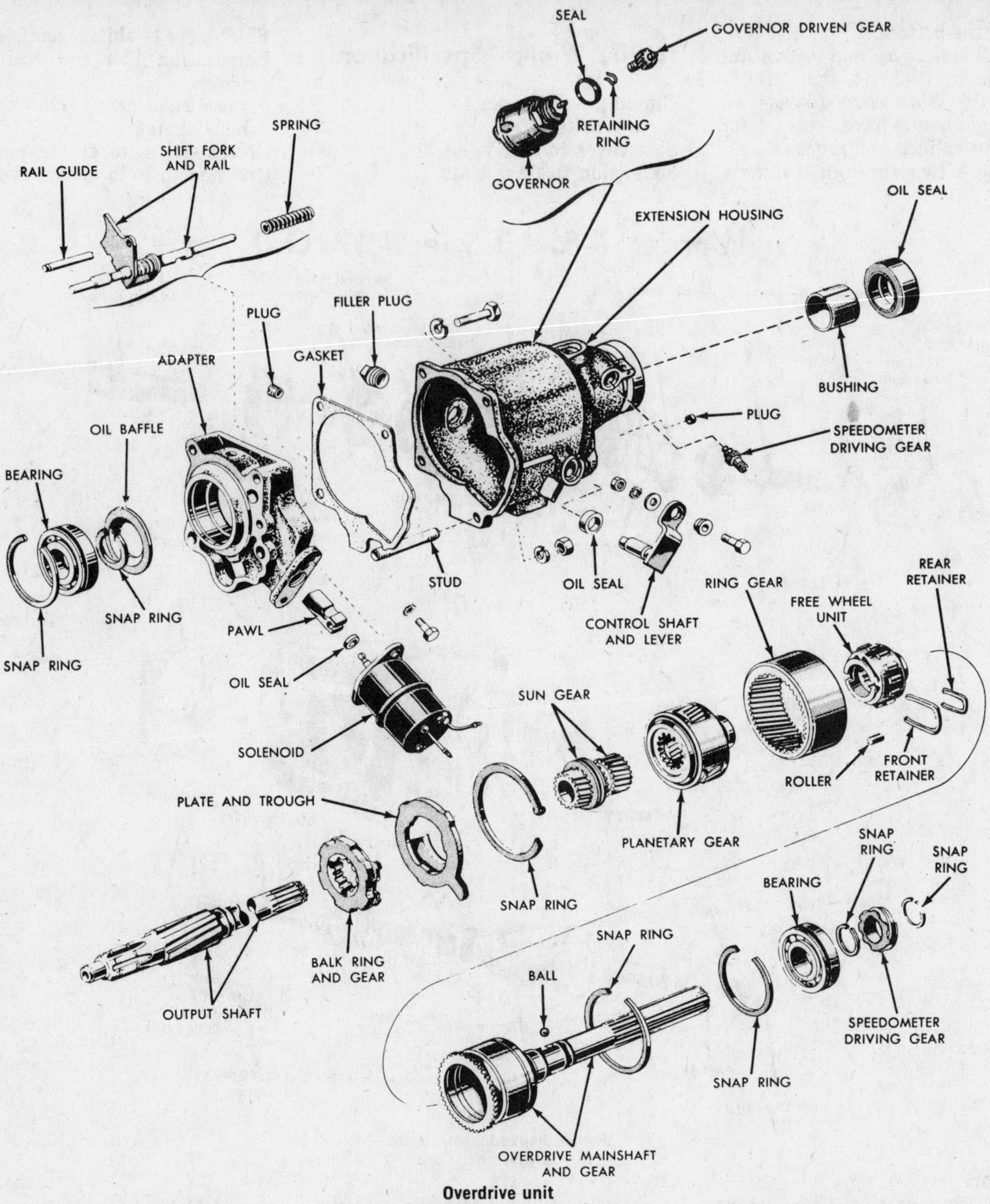

Overdrive unit
(© Borg Warner Corp.)

shaft toward the rear until it just clears the front case bore, and then push the countershaft out the rear with the tool shown.

16. Tap the input shaft and bearing out of the front of the case.
17. If the input shaft bearing is to be replaced, press off the bearing. The bearing baffle acts as a slinger, and must be installed so that it does not rub the bearing outer race as the shaft turns.
18. Remove the overdrive adapter and transmission output shaft as an assembly.
19. Remove the snap-ring at the front of the transmission output shaft, and then slide the synchronizer assembly, intermediate gear, and the sliding low and reverse gear off the shaft.

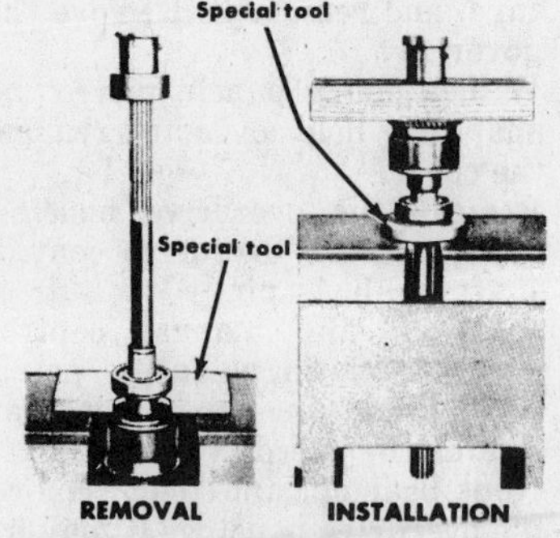

Mainshaft bearing removal or installation
(© Borg Warner Corp.)

20. Disassemble the synchronizer unit by sliding the intermediate and high sleeve off the hub. Remove the three inserts and two springs from the hub.

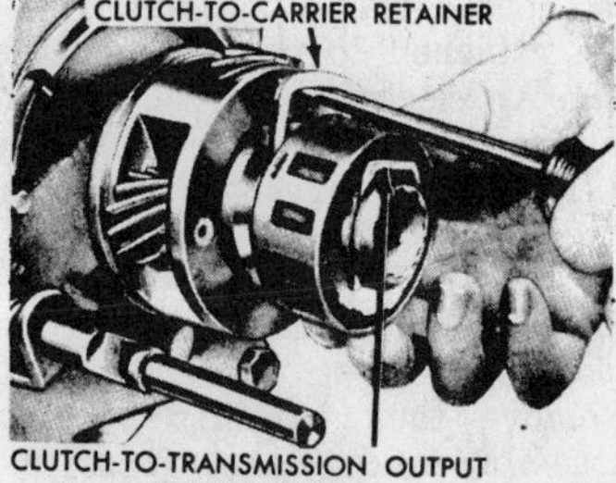

Removing free wheel unit retainer
(© Borg Warner Corp.)

21. Remove the snap-ring that holds the output shaft in the adapter and tap the bearing and shaft out of the adapter. Remove the baffle from the adapter.

Output shaft bearing replacement
(© Borg Warner Corp.)

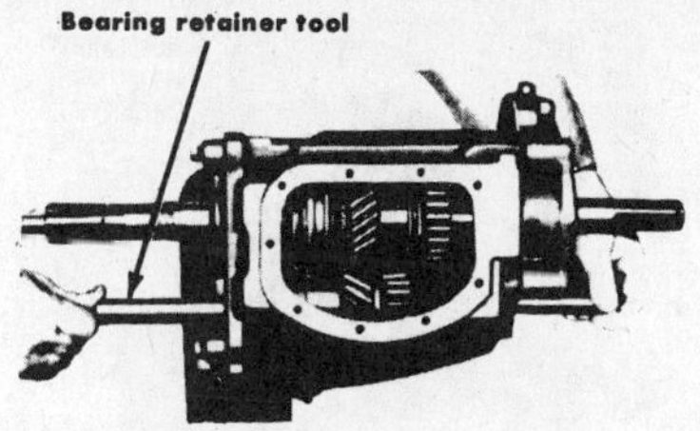

Removing countershaft—typical
(© Borg Warner Corp.)

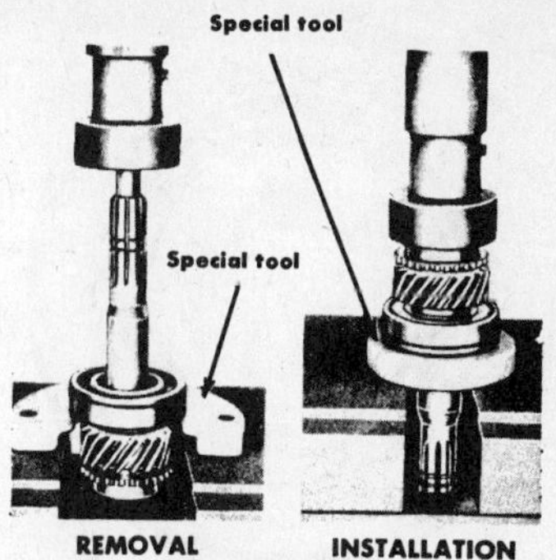

Input shaft bearing replacement
(© Borg Warner Corp.)

22. If the output shaft or bearing is to be replaced, press the old bearing off and the new bearing on and install the thickest snap-ring that will fit. Snap-rings are available in the following thicknesses: 0.0890-0.091, 0.092-0.094, 0.095-0.097, and 0.100-0.0102 inch.
23. While holding the washers and bearing retainer tool at the small end of the cluster gear to prevent the roller bearings and bearing retainer tool from falling out, lift the cluster gear assembly from the case.
24. Drive the reverse idler gear shaft out of the rear of the case.

Assembly of Transmission

Always use new gaskets and gasket cement during assembly. Put a thin coating of lubricant on all parts before installation.

1. Install new oil seals in the camshaft grooves. Place one cam and shaft assembly in position in the gearshift housing, and install the flat washer, lockwasher, and nut. Tighten the nut to specifications.
2. Assemble the interlock pin and balls in the interlock sleeve, and install the interlock assembly in the gearshift housing.
3. Place the other cam and shaft assembly in position and install the flat washer, lockwasher, and nut. Tighten the nut to specifications. Install the gearshift levers on the camshafts and the shifter forks to the cams.
4. Insert the bearing retainer tool in the cluster gear, and install the cluster gear bushings and spacer in the gear. Use cup grease to hold the bearings and bearing retainers in the cluster gear bore. After applying a thin coating of grease to the gear side of the thrust washers, properly position the washers at each end of the bearing retainer tool.
5. Position the cluster gear assembly in the transmission case. Install the countershaft, and check the clearance between the cluster gear front thrust washer and the case (0.004-0.018 inch). Remove the countershaft by installing the bearing retaining tool.
6. Position the reverse idler gear in the case, with the chamfered gear teeth ends toward the front.
7. Drive the reverse idler shaft into the case, with the locking notch aligned with the countershaft hole.
8. Place the output shaft bearing baffle in the overdrive adapter with the convex side toward the overdrive unit.
9. Install the output shaft bearing in the adapter, and install the snap-ring. Install the thickest snap-ring that will fit. Snap-rings are available in the following thicknesses: 0.086-0.088, 0.089-0.091, 0.092-0.094 and 0.095-0.097 inch.
10. Install the low and reverse sliding gear on the output shaft, with the shifter fork groove toward the front.
11. Install the intermediate gear on the output shaft, with the clutch teeth toward the front.
12. Assemble the synchronizer unit by installing the two springs on the hub, and placing the three inserts in the hub. Hook one spring end in an insert.
13. After lining up the etched marks on the sleeve and hub splines, slide the sleeve onto the hub.
14. Place a blocking ring on the intermediate gear, and install the synchronizer assembly on the transmission output shaft, with the hub thrust surface toward the rear.
15. Install the snap-ring that holds the synchronizer in place.
16. Position a new front gasket with gasket sealer on the overdrive adapter.
17. Position the overdrive adapter and transmission output shaft assembly in the transmission.
18. Seat the overdrive adapter squarely against the transmission case, and secure with a cap screw.
19. Insert the pilot roller bearings in the input shaft and hold with grease.
20. Place the blocking ring on the input shaft gear.
21. Tap the input shaft and bearing into the case while lining up the slots in the blocking ring with the synchronizer inserts.

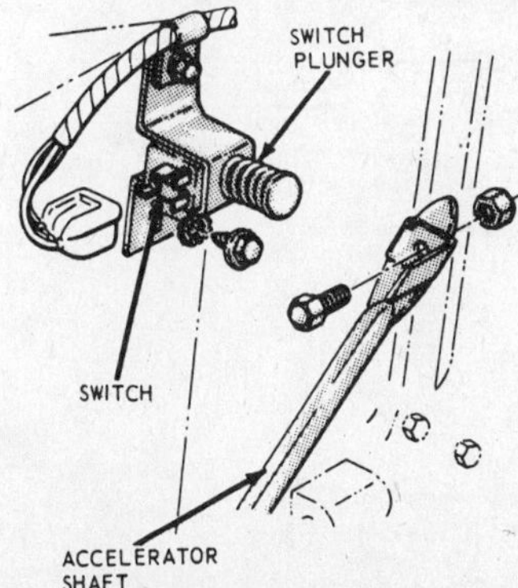

Kickdown switch adjustment
(© Borg Warner Corp.)

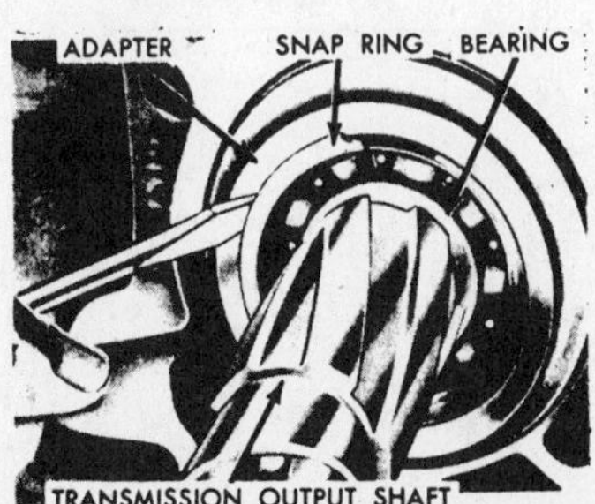

Removing output shaft bearing snap-ring
(© Borg Warner Corp.)

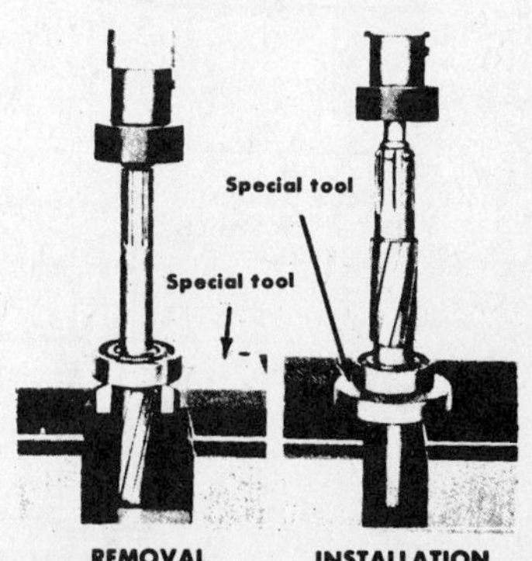

Removing adapter and output shaft
(© Borg Warner Corp.)

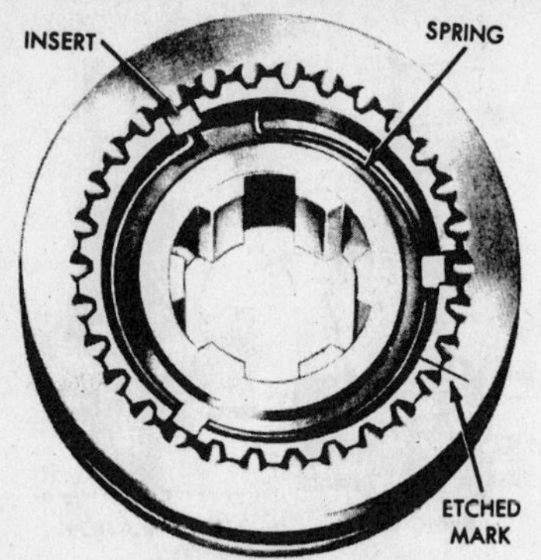

Synchronizer assembly
(© Borg Warner Corp.)

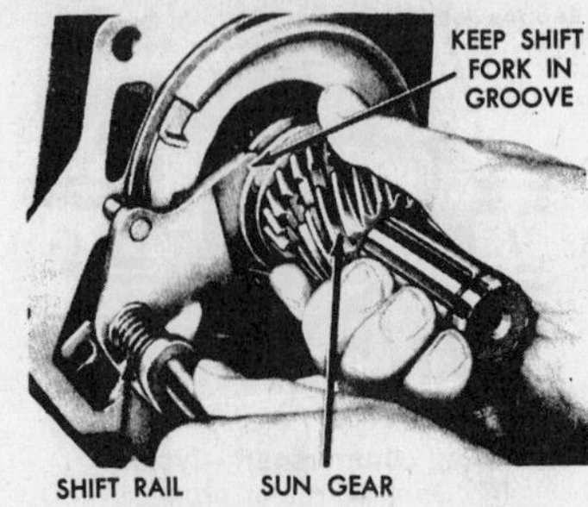

Installing sun gear and shift rail
(© Borg Warner Corp.)

Installing plate and trough
(© Borg Warner Corp.)

22. Position the input shaft bearing retainer without a gasket, and tighten the bolts to bottom the retainer on the bearing outer race snap-ring. Check the clearance between the retainer gasket surfaces and the case.
23. Select a gasket (or gaskets) which will seal the oil, and at the same time prevent end play between the bearing outer race snap-ring and the retainer. Gaskets are available in 0.010, 0.015, 0.020 and 0.025 inch thicknesses.
24. Install the input shaft bearing retainer on the transmission case. Torque the bolts to specification.
25. Pull out the adapter about ¼ inch, and rotate it to expose the countershaft hole.
26. Work the cluster gear into normal position by rotating the input and output shafts.
27. Push the countershaft into the case from the rear.
28. Align the slot in the countershaft with the slot in the reverse idler shaft, and install the lock plate.
29. Rotate the adapter to its normal position and seat it squarely against the transmission case. Check the block rings to make sure the slots are aligned with the synchronizer inserts.
30. Move the transmission so that the input shaft is pointing down.
31. Install the stud in the transmission case.
32. Place the balk ring gear assembly and pawl in the adapter.
33. Place the plate and trough assembly in the adapter and install its snap-ring.
34. Install the sun gear and shift rail.
35. Install the planet carrier and the clutch cam. Install the retainers.
36. Install the 12 free-wheel unit rollers and hold them in position with a strong rubber band.
37. Rotate the roller cage counterclockwise (from the rear) until the rollers are off the cam surfaces. The rubber band will hold them there.
38. Slide the overdrive main shaft carefully over the free-wheel unit rollers. The rubber band will not affect operation of the overdrive.
39. Align the shift rail spring with the holes in the overdrive housing.
40. Position a new rear gasket with gasket sealer on the overdrive adapter.
41. Position the overdrive housing over the overdrive main shaft and shift rail.
42. If the overdrive main shaft bearing snap-ring does not drop into its groove when the housing is seated squarely on the adapter, pry the overdrive main shaft bearing toward the rear, working through the snap-ring hole. Install the three bolts and one stud nut.
43. Engage the overdrive shaft lever by pushing it inward. The lever is correctly engaged when a spring load is apparent as the lever is pushed.
44. Install the retaining pin in the overdrive housing to hold the control shaft in place.
45. If necessary, replace the overdrive housing bushing.

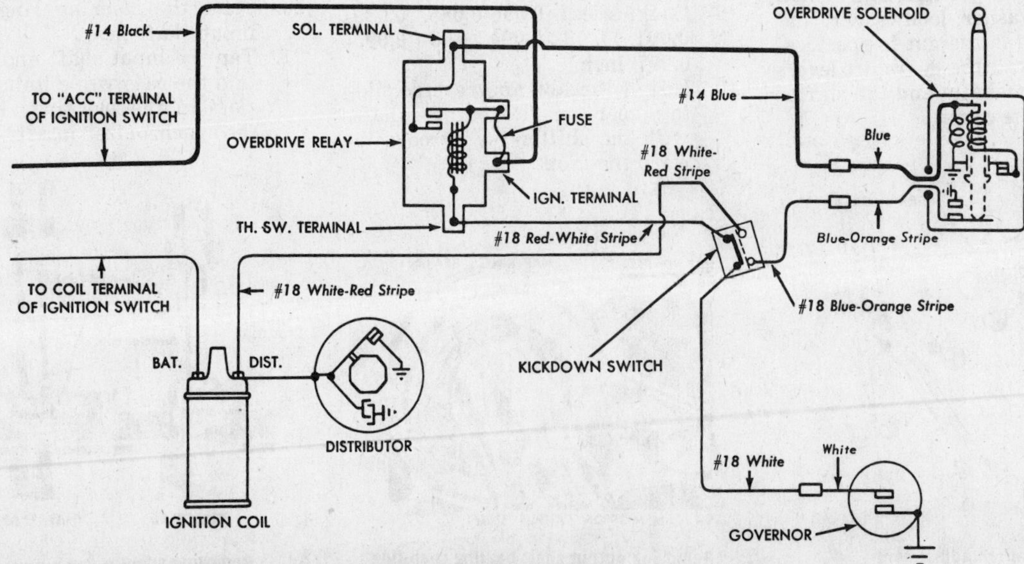

Overdrive electrical system (© Borg Warner Corp.)

46. Thread the governor into the overdrive housing.
47. With the cap drain hole at the bottom, rotate the solenoid ¼ turn from normal position, so that the half ball on the solenoid stem can engage the pawl. Install the two solenoid cap screws.
48. If the solenoid stem is properly engaged, the solenoid cannot be removed from the overdrive in its normal position. Any attempt to pull it out will merely compress the engaging spring in the solenoid.
49. Install a new gasket and the gearshift housing on the transmission. Be sure the shifter forks enter the grooves in the synchronizer and low and reverse sliding gear. Torque gearshift housing to transmission bolts to specifications.
50. Install the drain plugs in the transmission case and the overdrive housing.
51. Fill the transmission with the specified lubricant. This transmission should not be filled through the speedometer cable attachment opening like all other manual transmissions. Instead, pour ½ pint of lubricant in the speedometer cable attachment opening, one pint into the fill plug opening of the overdrive unit and, finally, 3 pints into the fill plug opening of the transmission case.

Torque Chart

Nomenclature	*Torque Limits*	*Nomenclature*	*Torque Limits*
Bolt-input shaft bearing retainer to trans. case	5/16-18 25-30 3/8-16 25-30 7/16—14 40-45	Nut-U-joint flange to trans. output shaft	1.00—20 90-125 1 1/4—18 225-275 1 1/2—18 275-350
Bolt-countershaft front bearing retainer	5/16—18 25-30 3/8—16 25-35 7/16—14 50-55	Bolt-bellcrank to trans.	3/8—16 20-25
Bolt-reverse lockout plunger retainer	11/16—16 90-100	Bolt-countershaft rear bearing retainer	5/16—18 25-30 3/8—16 35-40 7/16—14 45-55 1/2—13 60-70
Bolt-clutch housing to engine block	7/16—14 24-32 33-45	Nut-bellcrank to trans.	9/16—18 70-90 3/8—16C 20-25
Nut-drum parking brake to companion flange	3/8—24 37-50 7/16—20 40-55 1/2—20 74-86	Bolt-countershaft & reverse idler shaft retainer	1/2—13 60-70 5/16—18 25-30 3/8—16 25-37 3/8—16 18-25 7/16—14 40-45 1/2—13 80-85
Bolt-lever assy. to trans.	3/8—16 20-25	Bolt-gear shaft housing trans. case	5/16—18 20-25 3/8—16 35-40
Bolt-clutch housing to trans. case	7/16—14 30-38 5/8—11 96-120 9/16—12 70-90 5/8—18C 115-140 9/16—18C 81-102		

Warner T-85, T-89 3-Speed

Description

The Warner T-85 is a fully synchronized three-speed transmission controlled by a shift lever mounted on the steering column. Lubricant capacity is 4 pints.

Disassembly of Transmission

1. Remove the side cover assembly.
2. Rotate the rear bearing retainer extension to expose countershaft end and lock key.
3. Using a shaft dummy, drive countershaft to rear.
4. Work countershaft out of cluster, end spacers, rollers and roller bearing spacer.
5. Leave dummy shaft in the countershaft gear cluster to keep the bearings and spacers in location.
6. Lower countergear cluster down into bottom of case, then remove rear bearing retainer extension, gasket, and mainshaft assembly from transmission case.
7. Remove mainshaft front bearing rollers from inside the main drive gear.
8. Remove bearing spacing washer from front end of mainshaft.
9. Remove the main drive gear bearing retainer from front of case.
10. Remove main drive gear bearing snap-ring from front side of main drive gear bearing.
11. With transmission case front turned up, press main drive gear out of bearing.
12. Remove oil retainer from main drive gear.
13. Tap main drive gear bearing out through front of case and remove bearing snap-ring from shaft.
14. Using brass drift, drive reverse idler shaft to rear of case to clear lock key.
15. Remove lock key and, from rear of case, drive idler gear shaft into case, then remove idler gear and shaft from case.
16. Lift out countergear, dummy shaft, and washers from case.
17. Remove synchronizing ring from front side of second and third-speed clutch. Remove clutch hub retaining snap-ring from front end of mainshaft.
18. Remove second-and third-speed clutch sleeve from clutch hub, then remove hub from mainshaft.
19. Remove two clutch key springs and three clutch keys from clutch hub.
20. Remove rear synchronizer ring and second-speed gear from the mainshaft.
21. Remove first and reverse sliding gear from the mainshaft.
22. Remove speedometer driven gear lock plate.
23. Insert screwdriver in lock plate slot in fitting and pry fitting, gear and shaft from extension.
24. Remove mainshaft rear bearing front snap-ring from rear bearing retainer extension and tap mainshaft and rear bearing out of retainer extension.

25. Remove snap-ring from rear of speedometer drive gear.
26. Remove speedometer drive gear. Detent ball and speedometer gear front snap-ring.
27. Remove mainshaft rear bearing rear snap-ring.
28. Using a press, press mainshaft rear bearing from shaft.
29. Remove seal from rear bearing retainer.

Assembly of Transmission

1. Assemble by reversing the above procedure.

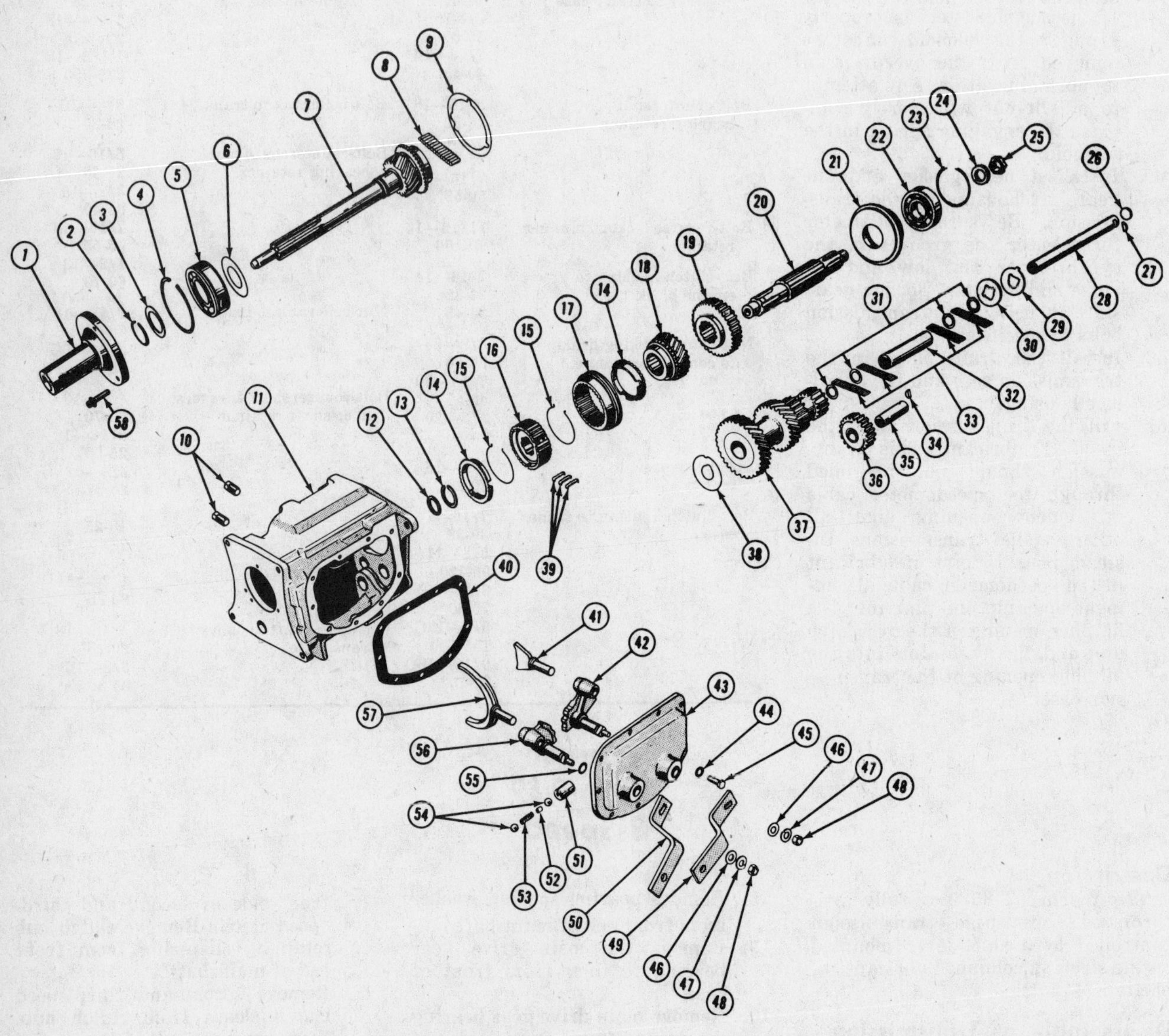

The Warner T-85 transmission (3-speed) (© Borg Warner Corp.)

1 Bearing retainer
2 Snap ring
3 Washer
4 Snap ring
5 Bearing
6 Washer
7 Main drive gear
8 Roller
9 Gasket
10 Pipe plug
11 Case
12 Spacer
13 Snap ring
14 Blocking ring
15 Synchronizer spring
16 Clutch hub, high and intermediate
17 Clutch sleeve, high and intermediate
18 Second speed gear
19 Sliding gear, low and reverse
20 Mainshaft
21 Bearing adapter
22 Bearing
23 Snap ring
24 Washer
25 Nut
26 Seal
27 Woodruff key
28 Countershaft
29 Thrust washer, steel
30 Thrust washer, rear
31 Washers
32 Spacer
33 Rollers
34 Woodruff key
35 Shaft
36 Reverse idler gear
37 Countershaft gears
38 Thrust washer, front
39 Synchronizer shifting plate
40 Gasket
41 Shift shoe, low and reverse
42 Shift lever, low and reverse
43 Side cover (Control Housing)
44 Lockwasher
45 Bolt
46 Washer
47 Lockwasher
48 Hex nut
49 Control lever, low and reverse
50 Control lever, high and intermediate
51 Interlock sleeve
52 Interlock pin
53 Poppet spring
54 Poppet ball
55 Oil seal
56 Shift lever, high and intermediate
57 Shift fork, high and intermediate
58 Cap screw

Warner T86, T-90
3 Speed

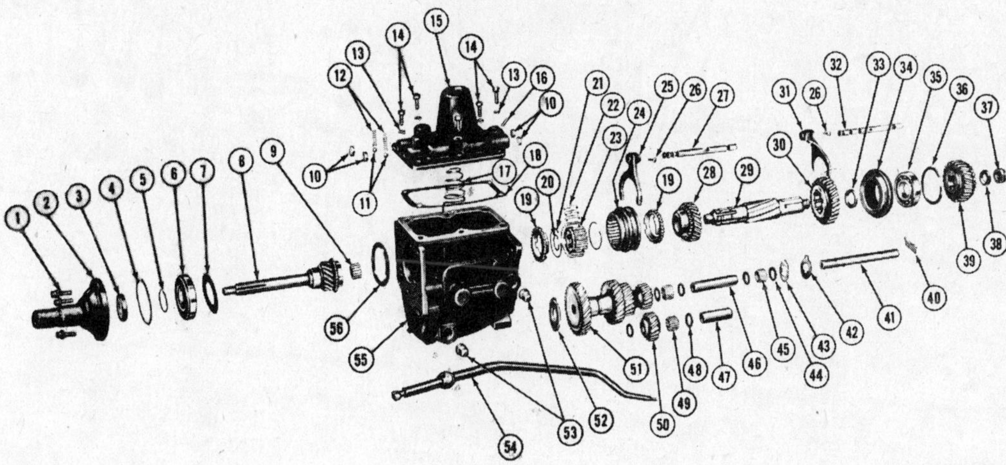

1 Bearing retainer screws
2 Main drive gear bearing retainer
3 Bearing retainer oil seal
4 Bearing snap ring
5 Main drive gear snap ring
6 Main drive gear bearing
7 Front bearing oil retaining washer
8 Main drive gear
9 Pilot roller bearing
10 Shift rail cap
11 Poppet ball
12 Poppet spring
13 Lock washer
14 Shift housing bolt
15 Control housing
16 Interlock plunger
17 Shift lever spring
18 Shift tower gasket
19 Blocking ring
20 Clutch hub snap ring
21 Synchronizer spring
22 Synchronizer plate
23 Clutch hub
24 Clutch sleeve
25 High and intermediate clutch fork
26 Shift fork pin
27 High and intermediate shift rail
28 Second speed gear
29 Main shaft
30 Low and reverse sliding gear
31 Low and reverse shift fork
32 Low and reverse shift rail
33 Bearing spacer
34 Rear bearing adapter
35 Rear bearing
36 Rear bearing snap ring
37 Nut
38 Washer
39 Transfer case drive gear
40 Lock plate
41 Countershaft
42 Rear Countershaft thrust washer (steel)
43 Rear countershaft thrust washer (bronze)
44 Countershaft bearing washer
45 Countershaft bearing
46 Countershaft center bearing spacer
47 Reverse idler gear shaft
48 Reverse idler gear bearing washer
49 Reverse idler gear roller bearings
50 Reverse idler gear
51 Countershaft gear
52 Countershaft front thrust washer
53 Plug
54 Shift lever
55 Transmission case
56 Retainer gasket

T-86 three-speed transmission—floor shift (© Borg Warner Corp.)

Description

The Warner T-86 and T-90 are synchronized three-speed transmissions having either a floor-mounted or a column-mounted shift lever.

Disassembly of Transmission

Except Jeep Models

1. Remove cover.
2. Remove front bearing cap, clutch shaft snap-ring and bearing lock-ring.
3. Remove the front bearing, using a bearing puller and a thrust yoke to prevent damaging synchronizer clutches.
4. Remove extension housing. Drive out seal from inside housing with oil seal remover and installer tool. Use bushing remover and installer tool to replace bushing.
5. Move mainshaft assembly back about ¾ in. Lower front end of clutch shaft, move mainshaft assembly over countergear and out of shift forks. Remove clutch shaft from front of case.
6. Check clutch shaft roller bearings for wear or damage.
7. Remove snap-ring, speedometer drive gear, and key.
8. Remove snap-ring, synchro-clutch assembly, second gear, friction ring, and low-reverse sliding gear. Press off rear bearing.
9. Remove shifter forks.
10. Remove shaft lock plate from rear of case.
11. Drive countershaft out to rear, using dummy shaft. Lower countergear to bottom of case.
12. Drive out reverse idler shaft. Remove reverse idler gear and countergear.
13. Remove outer shift levers and shifter shaft lock pins. Remove shifter shafts, two interlock ball bearings, sleeve and spring. Remove shaft oil seals from case.

Assembly of Transmission

1. Install new shift shaft oil seals.
2. Install low-reverse shift shaft, interlock sleeve, ball bearing, pin, and spring. Install second-high shift shaft and second ball bearing.
3. Shift mechanism into any gear position. With one end of interlock sleeve against shift shaft quadrant, clearance between opposite end of sleeve and quadrant on other shaft should be

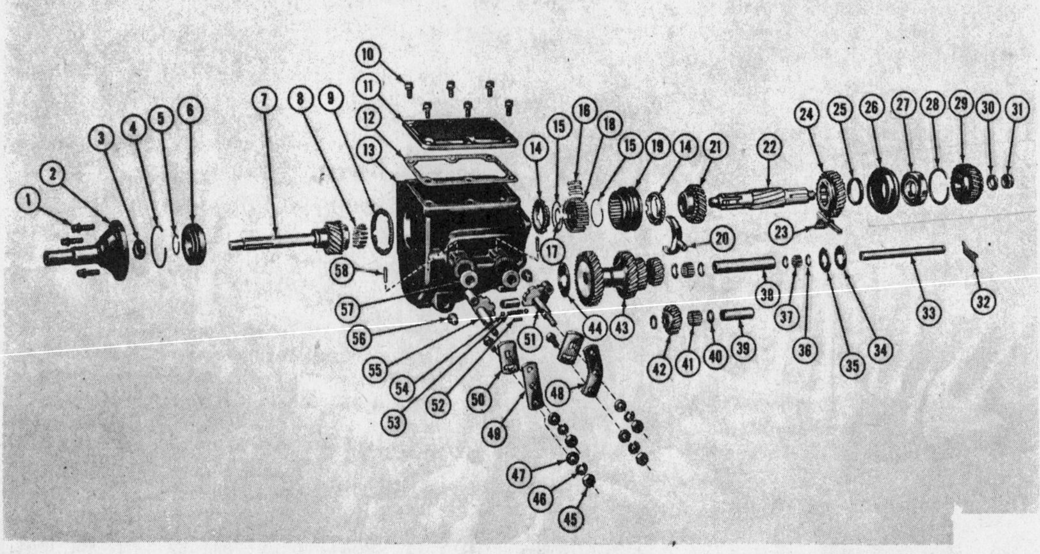

1 Retainer screws
2 Main drive gear retainer
3 Oil seal
4 Snap ring (large)
5 Snap ring (small)
6 Main drive gear bearing
7 Main drive gear
8 Main shaft bearing rollers
9 Retainer gasket
10 Cover bolt and lock washer
11 Case cover
12 Case cover gasket
13 Case
14 Blocking ring
15 Synchronizer spring
16 Shifting plate
17 Snap ring
18 Clutch hub
19 Clutch sleeve
20 Shift fork
21 Second speed gear
22 Main shaft
23 Shifting shoe
24 Sliding gear
25 Seal
26 Bearing adapter
27 Bearing
28 Snap ring
29 Transfer case drive gear
30 Washer
31 Nut
32 Locking plate
33 Countershaft
34 Washer (steel)
35 Washer (bronze)
36 Spacer
37 Needle bearings
38 Spacer washer
39 Reverse idler gear shaft
40 Spacer washer
41 Reverse idler gear roller bearings
42 Reverse idler gear
43 Countershaft gear
44 Countershaft front thrust washer
45 Nut
46 Lock washer
47 Control lever washer
48 Low and Reverse control lever (outer)
49 Intermediate and high control lever (outer)
50 Control lever (inner)
51 Low and reverse shift lever
52 Spacer
53 Spring
54 Ball
55 Intermediate and high shift lever
56 Plug
57 Oil seal
58 Taper pin

T-86 three-speed transmission—remote control (© Borg Warner Corp.)

.001-.007 in. Interlock sleeves are available in several sizes for adjustment.

4. Install lock pins and shift levers.
5. Install dummy shaft and bearings in countergear. Install thrust washers; the bronze front washer must index with the case.
6. Place countergear and dummy shaft in bottom of case.
7. Install reverse idler gear with chamfered side of teeth to front of case. Drive in shaft from rear.
8. Align slots in countershaft and reverse idler shaft. Position countergear and drive in countershaft. Install lock plate.
9. Install shifter forks.
10. Press rear bearing onto mainshaft. Install key, speedometer drive gear, and snap-ring.
11. Install low-reverse sliding gear on mainshaft with sliding collar to front. Gear should slide easily. Install second gear with tapered cone to front.
12. Install rear bearing snap-ring—the thickest possible.
13. Install synchro-clutch assembly and front snap-ring.
14. When synchro-clutch hub is pressed against snap-ring, there should be .003-.010 in. clearance between second gear and shoulder on mainshaft.
15. Install 14 greased rollers in clutch shaft.
16. Install front friction ring on clutch shaft and insert through top of case. Install mainshaft assembly through rear of case, moving to right to engage shifter forks in synchro-clutch collar and low-reverse sliding gear. Guide clutch shaft onto main shaft.
17. Install extension housing oil seal.
18. Install extension housing.
19. Install oil slinger, concave side to rear. Drive in front bearing using thrust yoke to prevent synchronizer damage.
20. Install thickest clutch shaft snap-ring that will fit in groove.
21. Install front bearing cap with new gasket. Choose thickness of gasket to give zero clutch shaft end play.
22. Clearance of friction rings should be .056-145 in.
23. Install cover and gasket.

Disassembly of Transmission

Jeep Models

1. Drain lubricant and flush out the case.
2. If a transfer case is involved, remove its rear cover.
3. If a power take-off is involved, remove the shift unit which replaces the cover.
4. Remove cotter pin, nut and washer and remove the transfer case main drive gear.
5. Remove the transmission shift cover.
6. Loop a piece of wire around the

Transfer case driving gear
(© Borg Warner Corp.)

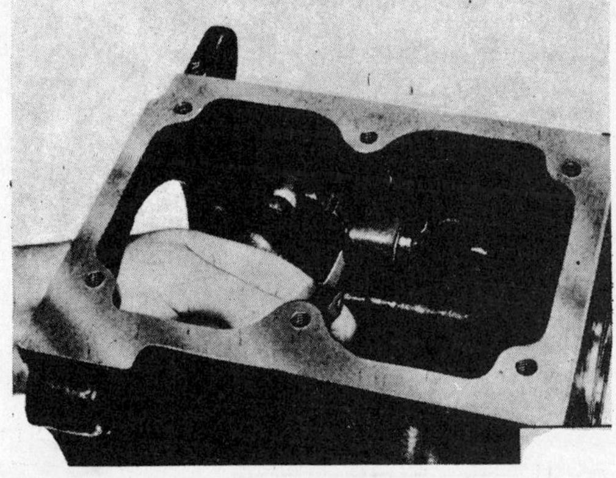
Interlock sleeve clearance
(© Borg Warner Corp.)

mainshaft just back of second-speed gear. Twist the wire and attach one end to the right front cover screw, the other end to the left cover screw. Tighten the wire to prevent the mainshaft from pulling out of the case when the transfer case is removed. Should the mainshaft come out, the synchronizer parts will drop into the bottom of the case.

7. Remove transfer case screws then tap lightly on the end of the transmission mainshaft to separate the two units. The transmission mainshaft bearing should slide out of the transfer case and stay with the transmission.
8. Remove front main drive gear bearing retainer and gasket.
9. Remove the oil collector hollow-head screws.
10. Remove lock plate from the reverse idler shaft and countershaft, at the rear of the case.
11. Drive the countershaft out the rear of the case with a dummy shaft and a brass drift.
12. Remove the mainshaft assembly through the case rear opening. Remove main drive gear.
13. Remove the countershaft gear set and three thrust washers from the bottom of the case, then dismantle the countershaft gear assembly.
14. Remove the reverse idler shaft and gear using a brass drift.
15. On column shift models, check clearance between ends of interlock sleeve and notched surface of each shift lever. The correct clearance is .001-.007 in. Several sizes of interlock sleeves are available for adjustment.

Assembly of Transmission

To assemble, reverse the disassembly procedures, giving the following points partciular attention:

1. The countershaft gear set, when assembled in the case, should have from .012-.018 in. end-play controlled by the thickness of the rear steel thrust washer.
2. Assemble the large bronze with the lip entered in the slot in the case.
3. The bronze-faced steel washer is placed next to the gear at the rear end, and the steel washer next to the case.
4. To assemble the countershaft bearing rollers, use a dummy shaft. Use grease and a loading sleeve to facilitate reassembly of the countershaft gear components.
5. In assembling the mainshaft gears, low and reverse gear is installed with the shift shoe groove toward the front.
6. In assembling the synchronizer unit, install the two springs in the high and intermediate clutch hub with spring tension opposed. Place the right lipped end of a spring in the hub slot and place the spring in the hub. Turn the hub around and make the same installation with the other spring, starting with the same slot. Install the three synchronizer shifting plates into the three slots in the hub, with the smooth sides of the plates out. Hold the plate in position and slip the second and direct clutch sleeve over the hub, with the long beveled edge toward the long part of the clutch hub. Install the completed assembly onto the mainshaft with the beveled edge of the clutch sleeve toward the front end of the shaft.
7. When installing the mainshaft, be sure the bearing rollers are in place in the pilot bore of the clutch gear.
8. Be sure that the countershaft and reverse idler shaft lock plate are in position and completely recessed into the indents of the transfer case.

Warner T-87 Series 3 Speed

Description

The T-87 is a three-speed synchronized transmission having helical design gears. The gearshift lever on most models, is located on the steering column and the shift is transferred to the transmission through remote control rods. On some models, shifting is performed with a floor mounted lever.

Disassembly of Transmission

Removal of Sub-Assemblies

1. Remove the gearshift housing cover from the case.
2. Remove the main drive gear bearing retainer from the shaft of the main drive gear.
3. Remove the brake assembly.
4. Remove the countershaft and reverse idler shaft lock plate and gasket from the transmission case.
5. Remove the rear bearing retainer and gasket.
6. Remove the cotter pin, nut, speedometer drive gear, and spacer from the main shaft.
7. Remove snap-ring holding main shaft bearing.
8. Pull bearing from main shaft

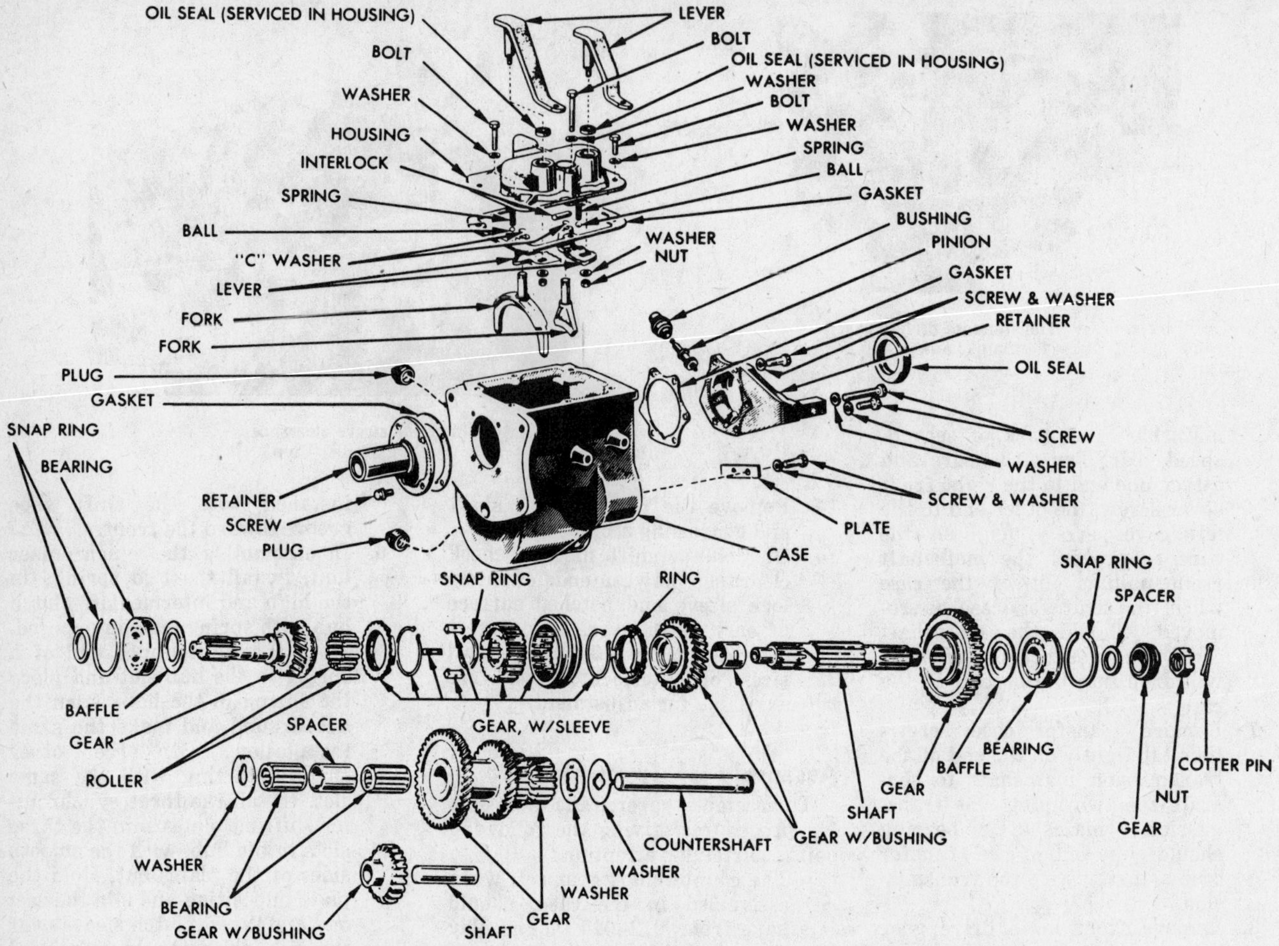

T-87 Series transmission—exploded view (© Borg Warner Corp.)

and remove oil baffle.

9. Drive the countershaft out through the rear of the case.
10. Pull the main drive gear as far forward as possible and lift the main shaft out of the case.
11. Remove the snap-ring from the main drive gear bearing. Tap lightly on front end of gear shaft until bearing is free. Place hand over rear end of gear to prevent loss of pilot bearing and lift the main drive gear assembly from case.
12. Remove the cluster gear assembly from the case, and remove the thrust washers from both ends.
13. Remove the two countershaft bearings and the spacer from inside the gear assembly.
14. Drive the reverse idler shaft forward until the shaft is free and lift the gear and shaft out of the case.

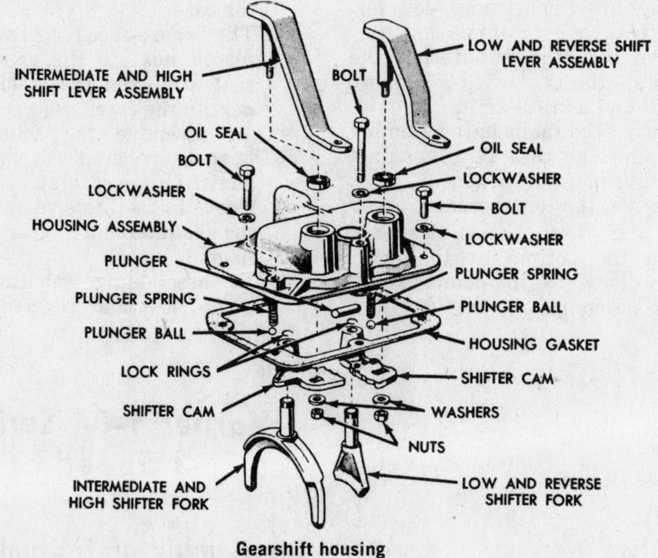

Gearshift housing
(© Borg Warner Corp.)

Disassembly of Sub-Assemblies

Main Shaft Disassembly

1. Slide sliding 1st and reverse gear from the main shaft.
2. Remove the snap-ring, and slide the synchronizer unit and 2nd speed gear off the shaft.
3. Remove the synchronizer stop ring from the 2nd speed gear.
4. Slide the synchronizer gear out of the sleeve.
5. Remove the snap-rings from each end of the hub and remove the three inserts.

NOTE: The stop rings used with

the synchronizer are removed separately. The rear stop ring is removed with the 2nd speed gear and the forward ring is removed with the main drive gear.

Main Drive Gear

1. Remove the synchronizer stop ring.
2. Remove the main shaft pilot bearing from inside the main drive gear.
3. Remove the snap-ring from the gear and pull or press the bearing off the gear.
4. Remove the oil baffle from the gear.

Gearshift Cover Disassembly

1. Remove the nuts and plain washers from the inner ends of the two gearshift levers.
2. Tap the inner ends of the levers until the shifter cams are forced off the lever shaft. Carefully remove the cams, gearshift cam balls and selector ball springs.
3. Slowly remove the levers and remove the interlock pin from the housing.
4. Remove the snap-rings and the gearshift forks.
5. Remove the gearshift lever oil seals from the top of the housing.

Assembly of Sub-Assemblies

Coat all parts with transmission lubricant to prevent scoring during initial operation.

Synchronizer Unit

Slide the three inserts into the synchronizer gear and install the two snap-rings on the ends of the gear. Slide the gear into the sleeve.

Main Shaft Assembly

1. Slide 2nd speed gear and bushing onto the front end of the main shaft.
2. Coat the synchronizer stop ring with grease and install on the shaft.
3. Install the synchronizer assembly on the shaft. Make sure the cut-outs on the stop ring coincide with inserts in the hub and install the snap-ring holding gear and synchronizer on the shaft.
4. Check the end play between the 2nd speed gear and shaft spline shoulder. If the end play exceeds 0.020 inch, replace any worn parts.
5. Install the sliding 1st and reverse gear on the rear end of the shaft.

Main Drive Gear

1. Install the oil baffle, bearing and small snap-ring on the main drive gear.
2. Grease the bore in the rear end of the shaft and install the main shaft pilot bearing in the bore.
3. Install the synchronizer stop ring on the rear end of the gear.

Countershaft and Gear Sub-Assembly

Install the spacer and two countershaft bearings in the cluster gear. Grease the thrust washers and position on ends of cluster gear.

Gearshift Cover Assembly

Reverse disassembly procedure.

Assembly in Case

Reverse Idler

1. Position the reverse idler gear and shaft in the transmission case. This shaft is driven in until the forward edge of the retainer notch in the shaft is flush with the rear face of the case.

2. Install the front cluster gear end washer with the washer tip hooked into the groove on the inside of the case. Position the cluster gear assembly in the case with the large gear toward the front. Make sure all end washers remain in position.

Main Drive Gear

1. Coat the forward synchronizer stop ring with grease and position on the rear end of the main drive gear.

2. Install the main drive gear in the transmission case.

3. Install the snap-ring on the outside of the main drive gear bearing. Make sure the snap-ring is flush with the face of the case.

4. Position a new gasket on the front of the transmission case.

5. Install the main drive gear retainer.

Main Shaft Assembly

1. Position the main shaft assembly in the transmission case and install the oil baffle on the shaft.

2. Install the snap-ring in the bearing groove and drive the bearing onto the shaft until the snap-ring is flush with face of the case.

3. Make sure that the synchronizer stop rings are free in the synchronizer assembly.

Countershaft

1. Raise the cluster gear assembly until the bearings in the assembly are aligned with the countershaft holes in the transmission case. Be sure the three washers are properly aligned.

2. Insert the countershaft into the hole in the rear of the case and push forward until the front edge of the notch in the shaft is flush with the rear face of the transmission case. The notch must also be aligned with the notch in the reverse idler shaft.

3. Install the countershaft and reverse idler shaft lock plate and gasket.

4. Install the rear bearing retainer and a new gasket.

5. Install the parking brake assembly on the rear bearing retainer.

Gearshift Cover Installation

1. Position a new gasket on top of the transmission case.

2. Place the gearshift forks in neutral position.

3. The reverse and first gearshift fork must be placed so that the smooth side of the fork is toward the gear. Otherwise the transmission will not shift into low gear.

4. Lower the housing assembly onto the transmission case seeing that the forks enter the proper channels in the sliding gear and the synchronizer sleeve.

5. Tighten the housing to case.

6. Install the drain plug.

7. Manually turn the projecting

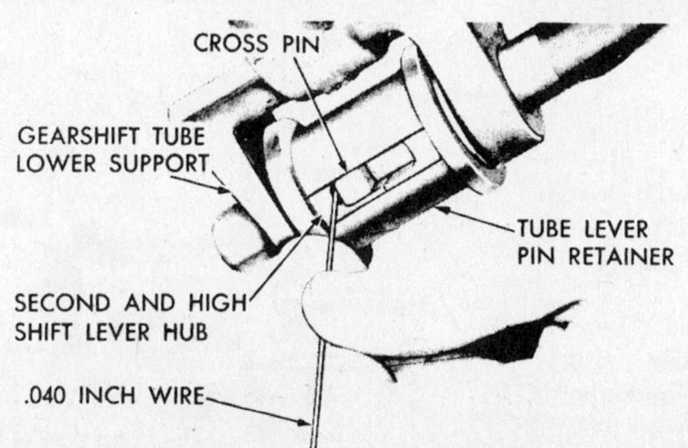

Gearshift crossover adjustment
(© Borg Warner Corp.)

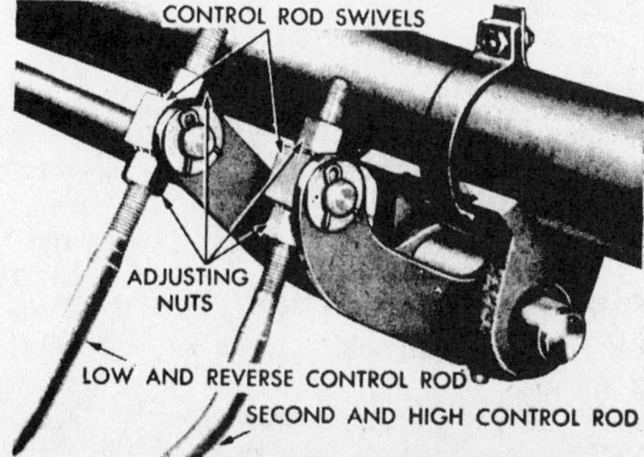

Gearshift lever adjustments
(© Borg Warner Corp.)

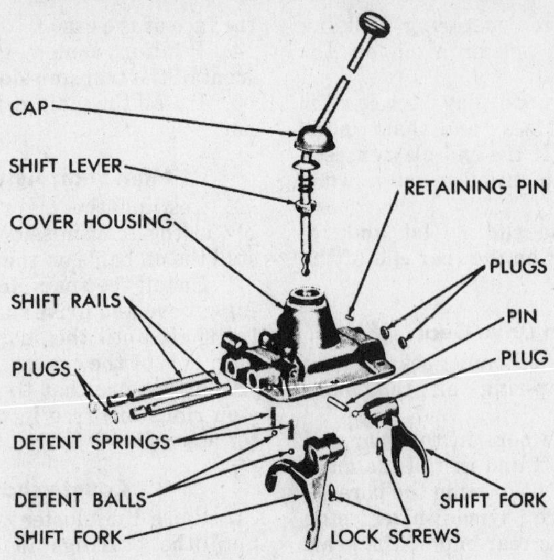

Gearshift housing assembly
(© Borg Warner Corp.)

shaft to make sure that the gears do not bind, and that the shifter forks are in the proper position.

Gearshift Control Adjustments

Crossover Adjustment

Before making the crossover adjustment, the gearshift lever shaft must be in its normal fully returned position in neutral.

1. After removing grease fitting from the tube lever pin retainer, rotate retainer until gearshift tube cross pin is exposed.
2. If a .040 inch feeler (round gauge) cannot be inserted between the gearshift tube cross pin and the bottom of the slot in the second—direct shift lever hub, then adjustment at the gearshift tube lower support must be made as follows:
3. Adjust support up or down to the .040 inch clearance. Torque support clamping screws to 70 inch-pounds.
4. Rotate tube lever pin retainer to original position and install the fitting at 70 inch-pounds torque. Failure to reinstall fitting will result in loss of gearshift tube cross pin.
5. Proper adjustment should provide equal up and down free travel of the gearshift lever in either high or 2nd gear position. Check crossover adjustment, at the manual lever, by making the crossover from 2nd—direct to low—reverse. Crossover movement should be free of interference. Crossover movement from low—reverse to 2nd—3rd likewise, should also be free of interference.

Control Rod Adjustment

Place transmission in neutral before making adjustment.

1. Loosen and back-off adjusting nut at the second—direct gearshift control rod swivel.
2. Turn both adjusting nuts in the direction required to locate lever, at steering wheel, with center spoke in true vertical plane. The gearshift lever should be directly under the right spoke of steering wheel.
3. Tighten adjusting nuts (70 inch-pounds torque) against the 2nd—direct control rod swivel block. Be sure transmission remains in neutral.
4. Loosen and back-off adjusting nut at low-reverse gearshift control rod swivel.
5. Position low—reverse gearshift lever in direct alignment with the 2nd—direct gearshift lever. Check by moving manual lever through crossover. Tighten adjusting nuts securely (70 inch-pounds torque) against swivel block. Don't lubricate swivel blocks. Incomplete engagement of gears can damage the transmission.

Gearshift Housing Assembly

NOTE: When disassembling the gearshift housing, place a cloth over shift rail to prevent loss of poppet ball and spring.

1. Install the low and reverse shift rail part way in the cover assembly, install the poppet ball and spring install the shift fork then drive the shift rail in remaining way.
2. Following the same procedure, install the intermediate and high shift rail and fork into the cover assembly.
3. Install the four expansion plugs, shift lever, cap and retaining pin.

Installation

Position transmission in neutral, install new gasket and cover assembly on transmission. Tighten the capscrews to 35 foot-pounds torque.

Torque Chart

Transmission	*Ft-lbs*
Transmission to flywheel housing	37-42
Transmission cover to case	14-19
Speedometer cable retainer to transmission extension	3-4.5
Transmission extension to case	40-50
Flywheel housing to engine	40-50
Filler plug	15-20
Drain plug	20-30

Warner T-89 Series 3 Speed

Description

The Warner T-89 is a fully synchronized three-speed transmission controlled by a column mounted shift lever.

Disassembly of Transmission

1. Install the transmission in a work stand.
2. Remove the gear shift housing.
3. Shift the transmission into two gears. Remove the output shaft nut and remove the parking brake assembly.
4. Remove the input shaft bearing retainer. Tap the input shaft and bearing toward the front as far as it will go.
5. Remove the output shaft bearing retainer bolts. Turn the retainer to expose the end of the countershaft.
6. Drive the countershaft toward the rear until it just clears the hole at the front of the case.

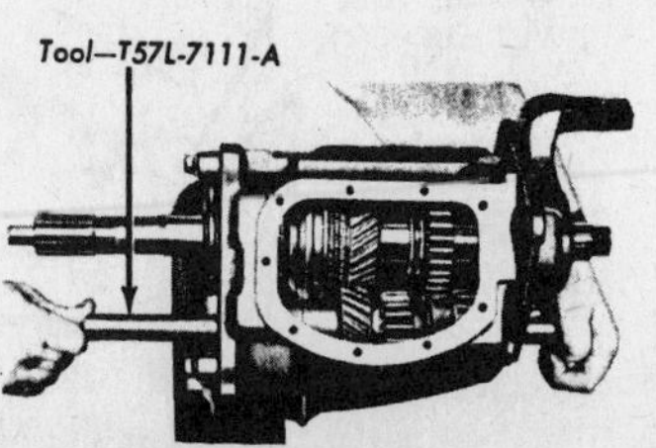

Removing countershaft
(© Borg Warner Corp.)

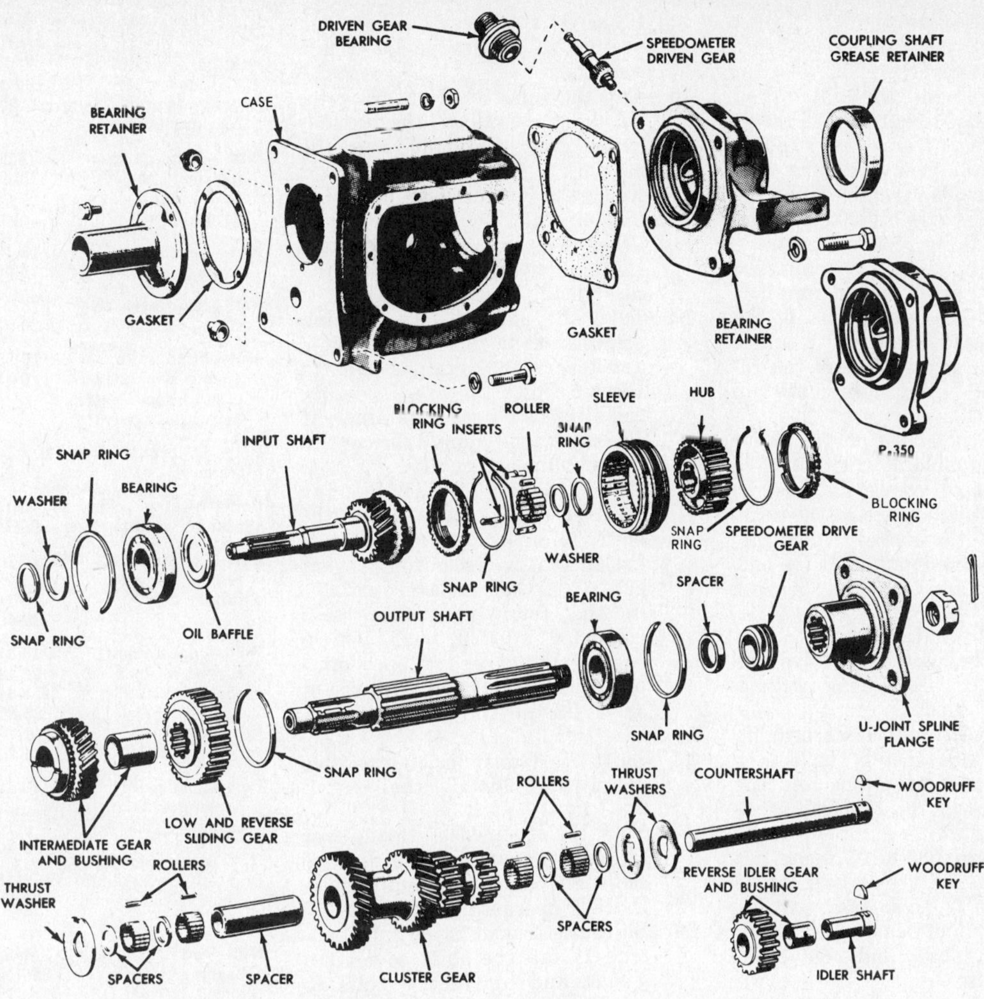

Warner T-89 series transmission—typical (© Borg Warner Corp.)

Push the counter shaft out of the rear of the case. Remove the Woodruff key from the countershaft.

7. Remove the output shaft assembly. Remove the pilot rollers from the rear of the input shaft.
8. Remove the bearing snap-ring and spacer washer from the input shaft. Drive the input shaft through the bearing. Remove the input shaft and bearing from the case.
9. Drive the reverse idler shaft out of the rear of the case.
10. Remove the cluster gear roller bearings and washers.
11. Remove the snap-ring at the front of the output shaft, and slide the synchronizer, intermediate gear, and low and reverse sliding gear off the shaft.
12. Remove the snap-ring that holds the outer race, and tap the output shaft bearing and shaft out of the bearing retainer casting and replace the bearing if worn.

Removing or installing output shaft (© Borg Warner Corp.)

Parts Repair or Replacement

Synchronizer

1. Slide the clutch sleeve off the hub and remove the three inserts and springs.
2. To assemble the synchronizer, align the index mark on the hub with the one on the sleeve.
3. Position the insert on the hub and slide the sleeve into place.
4. Install the insert springs.

cover.

Shift Cover

Check the condition of the shift levers and forks. If there is any binding or clashing of gears when the lever is operated, disassemble the cover.

Assembly

1. Install new seal rings in the shifter cam grooves.
2. Position one cam assembly in the gear shift cover.
3. Assemble the interlock spring and balls in the interlock, install the interlock assembly in the gear shift cover, and position the other cam assembly.
4. Install the gear shift levers and forks on the cams.

Assembly of Transmission

1. Position the cluster gear bearings and washers.
2. Position the cluster gear assembly in the case. The tang on the front thrust washer must be fitted into the slot in the case thrust surface. The tab on the rear steel washer must be up. Install the countershaft, and check

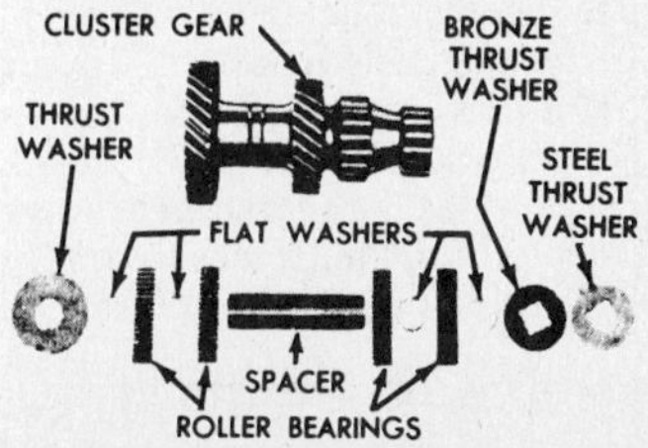

Cluster gear and components (© Borg Warner Corp.)

the cluster gear end play (0.006-0.020 inch).

3. Place the reverse idler gear in the case with the chamfered teeth ends toward the front. Drive the reverse idler shaft through the gear from the rear of the case. When the end of the shaft is nearly flush with the case install the Woodruff key.
4. Tap the input shaft bearing into the case until the snap-ring bottoms on the case. Install the input shaft bearing retainer without a gasket. Install the retainer and barely tighten the cap screws.
5. Position the baffle on the input shaft and hold it there with a light coat of grease. It must be installed at the rear of the bearing with the dished side away from the bearing so that the baffle does not rub the bearing outer race.
6. Place the input shaft (with baffle) in the case and drive the shaft into the bearing with a hardwood block.
7. Remove the input shaft bearing retainer, and install the spacer washer and snap-ring on the shaft. Install the thickest snap-ring that will fit. Snap-rings vary from 0.086-0.103 inch. Tap the input shaft and bearing as far to the front as they will go. Place the pilot bearing rollers in the input shaft and hold them with grease.
8. Install the output shaft and bearing in the bearing retainer casting. Install the thickest snap-ring that will fit. Assemble the low and reverse gear, intermediate gear and synchronizer assembly on the output shaft. Install the snap-ring at the front of the output shaft, and place the pilot bearing flat washer on the shaft.
9. Place a new gasket on the output shaft bearing retainer casting and install assembly in the case. Position the bearing retainer casting so that the countershaft hole is exposed.
10. Tap the input shaft bearing toward the rear until the bearing outer race snap-ring hits the case.
11. Raise the cluster gear assembly and install the countershaft. When the end of the countershaft is nearly flush with the case, install the Woodruff key.
12. Turn the output shaft bearing retainer to a normal position, and torque the retainer bolts to specification.
13. Install a new grease retainer, if necessary, and apply lubricant to the seal lips and cavity.
14. Install the input shaft bearing retainer and gasket. Torque the bolts to specification. Select a gasket that will seal and prevent end play. Gaskets are available in the following thicknesses: 0.010, 0.015, 0.020, 0.025 inch.
15. Install the spacer and speedometer driving gear on the output shaft. Install the parking brake assembly.
16. Shift the transmission into two gears and install the output shaft nut.
17. Pour the specified lubricant over the entire gear train to prevent scoring when the transmission is initially operated.
18. Shift the transmission into neutral. Install the shift cover and gasket and torque the bolts to specification.
19. Fill the transmission with the proper lubricant through the speedometer cable attachment opening.

Torque Chart

Nomenclature	*Nuts and/or Bolts and Torque Limits*		
Bolt—gear shift lever tower to gearshift housing	3/8-16 20-25		7/16-14 30-35
Bolt—clutch housing to trans. case	7/16-14 30-38 5/8-11 96-120		9/16-12 70-90
Nut-U-joint flange to trans. output shaft	1.00-20 90-125	1 1/2-18 275-350	1 1/4-18 225-275
Nut—drum parking brake to companion flange	3/8 24 35-45		7/16-20 50-70
Nut—bellcrank to trans.	9/16-18 70-90		
Bolt—lever assy. to trans.	3/8-16 20-25		
Nut—handbrake anchor bar to trans. case (5-speed extra-heavy duty only)	9/16-18 120-130		
Bolt—bellcrank to trans.	3/8-16 20-25		
Bolt—reverse lockout plunger retainer	11/16-16 80-100		
Bolt—countershaft rear bearing retainer	5/16-18 25-30 3/8-16 35-40		7/16-14 45-55 1/2-13 60-70
Bolt—countershaft & reverse idler shaft retainer	5/16-18 25-30 3/8-16 25-37 3/8-16† 18-25†		7/16-14 40-45 1/2-13 80-85
Bolt—gear shift housing to trans. case	5/16-18 20-25 3/8-16 35-40		3/8-16†† 30-35†† 7/16-14 45-50
Bolt—power take off cover to trans. case	3/8-16 20-30		
Nut—countershaft bearing lock (5-speed extra H.D. & 5-speed exclusive)	1 1/4-18 350-450		
Nut—countershaft bearing lock (5-speed exclusive H.D.)	1 1/2-18 350-450		
Bolt—input shaft bearing retainer to trans. case	5/16-18 25-30 3/8-16 25-30		7/16-14 40-45
Bolt—countershaft front bearing retainer	5/16-18 25-30 3/8-16 25-35		7/16-14 50-55

Warner T-98 Series T-18, T-19 4 Speed

Description

The Warner T-98, T-18, T-19 are four-speed fully synchronized transmissions having a floor-mounted shift lever and a power take-off opening on the right side of the case. The T-98, and T-18 first and reverse gears are spur gears while the others are helical. The T-19 has all helical gears.

Disassembly of Transmission

1. After draining the transmission and removing the parking break drum (or shoe assembly), lock the transmission in two gears and remove the U-joint flange, oil seal, speedometer driven gear and bearing assembly. Lubricant capacity is 6½ pints.
2. Remove the output shaft bearing retainer and the speedometer drive gear and spacer.
3. Remove the output shaft bearing snap-ring, and remove the bearing.
4. Remove the countershaft and

Removing countershaft
(© Borg Warner Corp.)

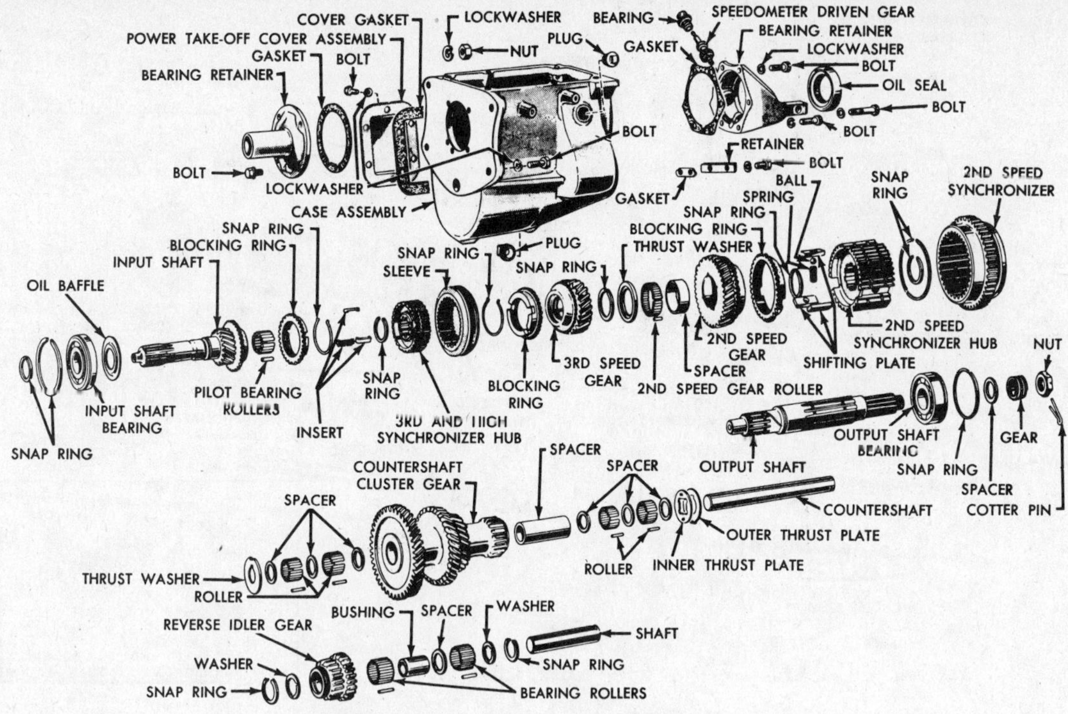

4-speed Warner T-98 series transmission (© Borg Warner Corp.)

idler shaft retainer and the power take-off cover.

5. After removing the input shaft bearing retainer, remove the snap-rings from the bearing and the shaft.
6. Remove the input shaft bearing and oil baffle.
7. Drive out the countershaft (from the front). Keep the dummy shaft in contact with the countershaft to avoid dropping any rollers.
8. After removing the input shaft and the synchronizer blocking ring, pull the idler shaft.
9. Remove the reverse gear shifter arm, the output shaft assembly, the idler gear, and the cluster gear. When removing the cluster, do not lose any of the rollers.

Disassembly of Sub-Assemblies

Output Shaft

1. Remove the third- and high-speed synchronizer hub snap-ring from the output shaft, and slide the third- and high-speed synchronizer assembly and the third-speed gear off the shaft. Remove the synchronizer sleeve and the inserts from the hub. Before removing the two snap-rings from the ends of the hub, check the end play of the second-speed gear (0.005-0.024 inch).
2. Remove the second-speed synchronizer snap-ring. Slide the

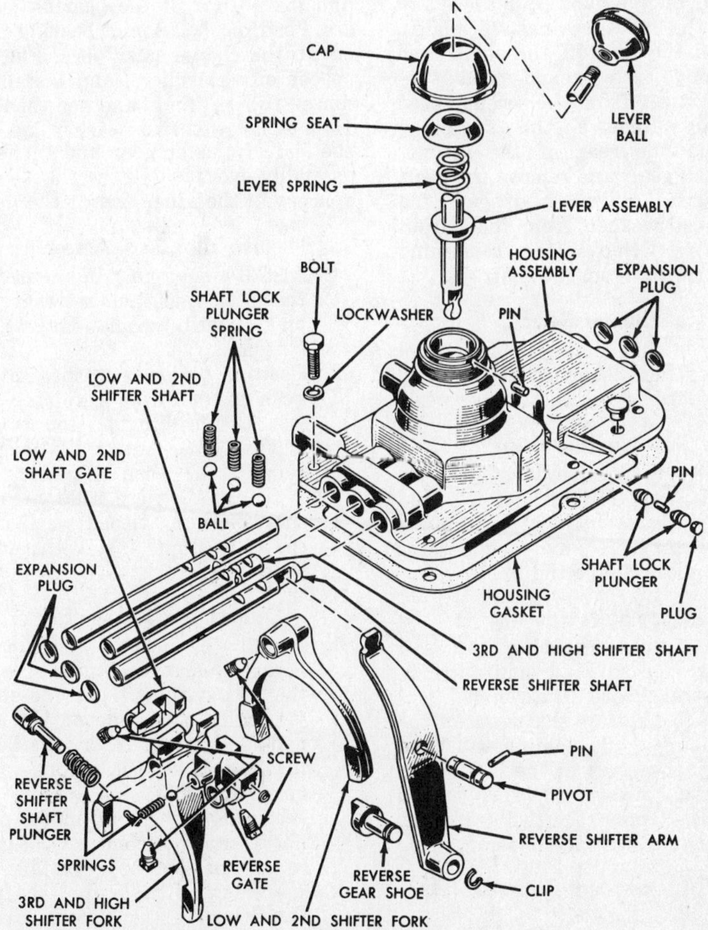

Conventional cab shift linkage (© Borg Warner Corp.)

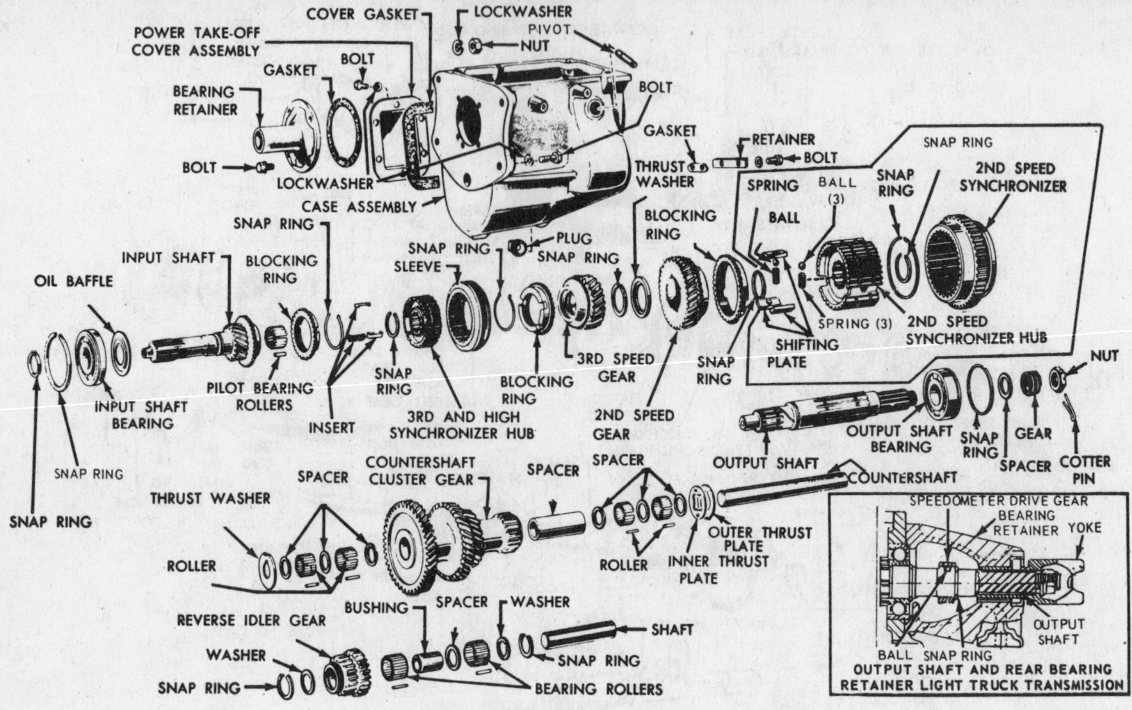

4-speed Warner T-18 transmission (© Borg Warner Corp.)

second-speed synchronizer hub gear off the hub. Do not lose any of the balls, springs, or plates. Pull the hub off the shaft, and remove the second-speed synchronizer from the second-speed gear. Remove the snap-ring from the rear of the second-speed gear, and remove the gear, spacer, roller bearings, and thrust washer from the output shaft. Remove the remaining snap-ring from the shaft.

Cluster Gear

Remove the dummy shaft, pilot bearing rollers, bearing spacers, and center spacer from the cluster gear.

Reverse Idler Gear

Rotate the reverse idler gear on the shaft, and if it turns freely and smoothly, disassembly of the unit is not necessary. If any roughness is noticed, disassemble the unit.

Gear Shift Housing

1. Remove the housing cap and lever. Be sure all shafts are in neutral before disassembly.
2. Tap the shifter shafts out of the housing while holding one hand over the holes in the housing to prevent loss of the springs and balls. Remove the two shaft lock plungers from the housing.

Assembly of Sub-Assemblies

Cluster Gear Assembly

Slide the long bearing spacer into the cluster gear bore, and insert the dummy shaft in the spacer. Hold the cluster gear in a vertical position, and install one of the bearing spacers. Position the 22 pilot bearing rollers in the cluster gear bore. Place a spacer on the rollers, and install 22 more rollers and another spacer. Hold a large thrust washer against the end of cluster gear and turn the assembly over. Install the rollers and spacers in the other end of the gear.

Reverse Idler Gear Assembly

1. Install a snap-ring in one end of the idler gear, and set the gear on end, wtih the snap-ring at the bottom.
2. Position a thrust washer in the gear on top of the snap-ring. Install the bushing on top of the washer, insert the 37 bearing rollers, and then a spacer followed by 37 more rollers. Place the remaining thrust washer on the rollers, and install the other snap-ring.

Output Shaft Assembly

1. Install the second speed gear thrust washer and snap-ring on the output shaft. Hold the shaft vertically, and slide on the second-speed gear. Insert the bearing rollers in the second-speed gear, and slide the spacer into the gear. (The T-18 model does not contain second speed gear rollers or spacer). Install the snap-ring on the output shaft at the rear of the second-speed gear. Position the blocking ring on the second-speed gear. Do not invert the shaft because the bearing rollers will slide out of the gear.
2. Press the second-speed synchronizer hub onto the shaft, and install the snap-ring. Position the shaft vertically in a soft-jawed vise. Position the springs and plates in the second-speed synchronizer hub, and place the hub gear on the hub.
3. With the T-19 model, press the first and second speed synchronizer onto the shaft and install the snap-ring. Install the first speed gear and snap-ring on the shaft and press on the reverse gear. For the T-19, ignore steps 2 and 4.
4. Hold the gear above the hub spring and ball holes, and position one ball at a time in the hub, and slide the hub gear downward to hold the ball in place. Push the plate upward, and insert a small block to hold the plate in position, thereby holding the ball in the hub. Follow these procedures for the remaining balls.
5. Install the third speed gear and synchronizer blocking ring on the shaft.
6. Install the snap-rings at both ends of the third and high-speed synchronizer hub. Stagger the openings of the snap-rings so that they are not aligned. Place the inserts in the synchronizer sleeve, and position the sleeve on the hub.
7. Slide the synchronizer assembly onto the output shaft. The slots in the blocking ring must be in

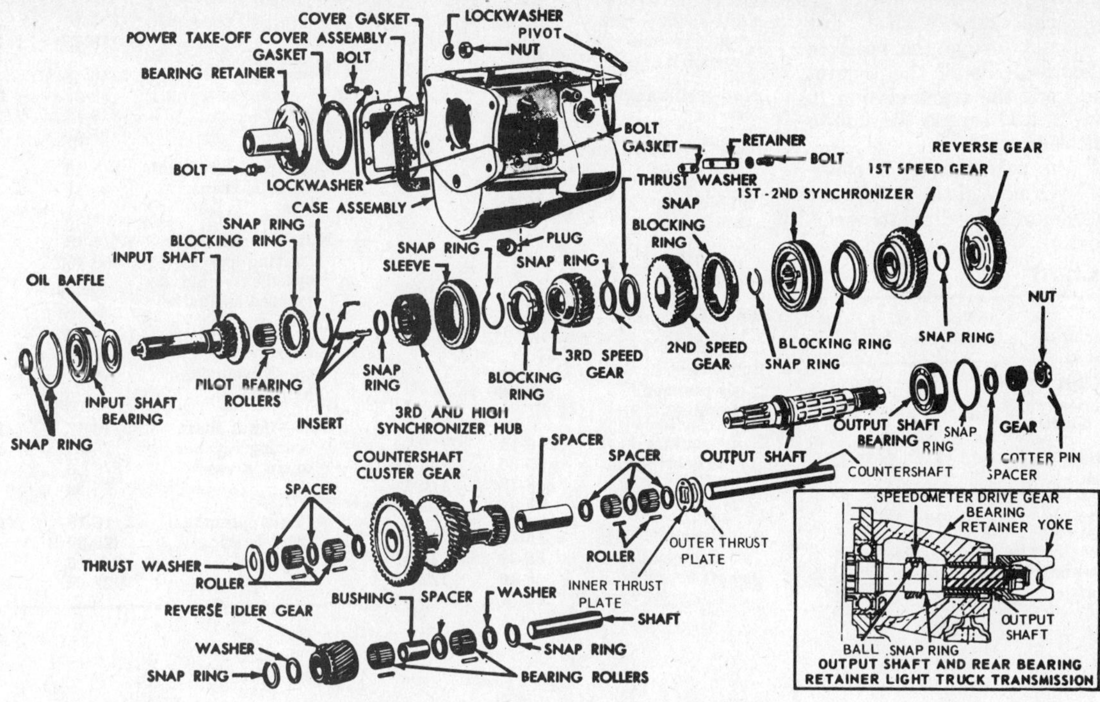

4-speed Warner T-19 transmission (© Borg Warner Corp.)

line with the synchronizer inserts. Install the snap-ring at the front of the synchronizer assembly.

Gear Shift Housing

1. Place the spring on the reverse gear shifter shaft gate plunger, and install the spring and plunger in the reverse gate. Press the plunger through the gate, and fasten it with the clip. Place the spring and ball in the reverse gate poppet hole. Compress the spring and install the cotter pin.
2. Place the spring and ball in the reverse shifter shaft hole in the gear shift housing. Press down on the ball, and position the reverse shifter shaft so that the reverse shifter arm notch does not slide over the ball. Insert the shaft part way into the housing.
3. Slide the reverse gate onto the shaft, and drive the shaft into the housing until the ball snaps into the groove of the shaft. Install the lock screw lock wire to the gate.
4. Insert the two interlocking plungers in the pockets between the shifter shaft holes. Place the spring and ball in the low and second shifter shaft hole. Press down on the ball, and insert the shifter shaft part way into the housing.
5. Slide the low and second shifter shaft gate onto the shaft, and install the corresponding shifter fork on the shaft so that the offset of the fork is toward the rear of the housing. Push the shaft all the way into the housing until the ball engages the shaft groove. Install the lock screw and wire that fastens the fork to the shaft. Install the third and high shifter shaft in the same manner. Check the interlocking system. Install new expansion plugs in the shaft bores.

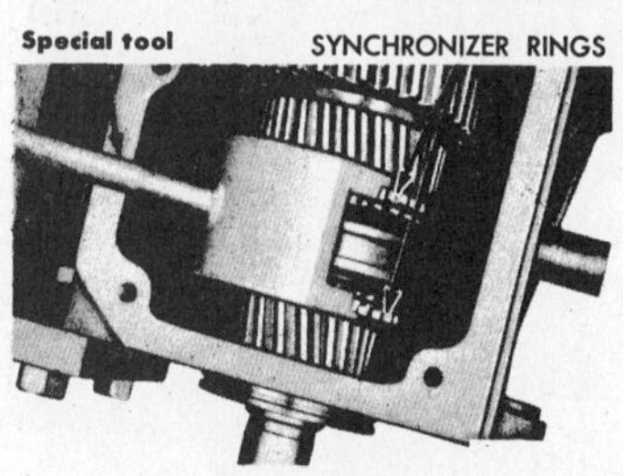

Stop yoke tool
(© Borg Warner Corp.)

Assembly of Transmission

1. Coat all parts, especially the bearings, with transmission lubricant to prevent scoring during initial operation.
2. Position the cluster gear assembly in the case. Do not lose any rollers.
3. Place the idler gear assembly in the case, and install the idler shaft. Position the slot in the rear of the shaft so that it can engage the retainer. Install the reverse shifter arm.
4. Drive out the cluster gear dummy shaft by installing the countershaft from the rear. Position the slot in the rear of the shaft so that it can engage the retainer. Use thrust washers as required to get 0.006 to 0.020 inch cluster gear end play. Install the countershaft and idler shaft retainer.
5. Position the input shaft pilot rollers and the oil baffle, so that the baffle will not rub the bearing race. Install the input shaft and the blocking ring in the case.
6. Install the output shaft assembly in the case, and use a special tool to prevent jamming the blocking ring when the input shaft bearing is installed.
7. Drive the input shaft bearing onto the shaft. Install the thickest select-fit snap-ring that will fit on the bearing. Install the input shaft snap-ring.
8. Install the output shaft bearing.
9. Install the input shaft bearing without a gasket, and tighten the bolts only enough to bottom the retainer on the bearing snap-ring. Measure the clearance between the retainer and the case, and select a gasket (or gaskets) that will seal in the oil and prevent end play between the retainer and the snap-ring. Torque the bolts to specification.
10. Position the speedometer drive gear and spacer, and install a new output shaft bearing retainer seal.
11. Install the output shaft bearing retainer. Torque the bolts to specification, and install safety wire.

12. Install the brake shoe (or drum), and torque the bolts to specification. Install the U-joint flange. Lock the transmission in two gears and torque the nut to specification.
13. Install the power take-off cover plates with new gaskets. Fill the transmission according to specifications.

Torque Chart

Nomenclature	*Nuts and/or Bolts and Torque Limits*		
Bolt—gear shift lever tower to gearshift housing	3/8-16 20-25	7/16-14 30-35	
Bolt—clutch housing to trans. case	7/16-14 30-38 5/8-11 96-120	9/16-12 70-90	
Nut—U-joint flange to trans. output shaft	1.00-20 90-125	1 1/2-18 275-350	1 1/4-18 225-275
Nut—drum parking brake to companion flange	3/8-24 35-45	7/16-20 50-70	
Nut—bellcrank to trans.	9/16-18 70-90		
Bolt—lever assy. to trans.	3/8-16 20-25		
Nut—handbrake anchor bar to trans. case (5-speed extra-heavy duty only)	9/16-18 120-130		
Bolt—belcrank to trans.	3/8-16 20-25		
Bolt—reverse lock-out plunger retainer	11/16-16 80-100		
Bolt—countershaft rear bearing retainer	5/16-18 25-30 3/8-16 35-40	7/16-14 45-55 1/2-13 60-70	
Bolt—countershaft & reverse idler shaft retainer	5/16-18 25-30 3/8-16 25-37	7/16-14 40-45 1/2-13 80-85	
	3/8-16† 18-25†		
Bolt—gear shift housing to trans. case	5/16-18 20-25 3/8-16 35-40	3/8-16†† 30-35†† 7/16-14 45-50	
Bolt—power take off cover to trans. case	3/8-16 20-30		
Nut—countershaft bearing lock (5-speed extra h.d. & 5-speed exclusive)	1 1/4-18 350-450		
Nut—countershaft bearing lock (5-speed exclusive h.d.)	1 1/2-18 350-450		
Bolt—input shaft bearing retainer to trans. case	5/16-18 25-30 3/8-16 25-30	7/16-14 40-45	
Bolt—countershaft front bearing retainer	5/16-18 25-30 3/8-16 25-35	7/16-14 50-55	

Automatic Transmissions

Index

Turbo Hydra-Matic

Warner

Diagnosis

This guide covers the most common symptoms and is an aid to careful diagnosis. The items to check arc listed in sequence to be followed for quickest results. Follow the checks in the order given for the particular transmission type.

Trouble Symptoms	Items to Check	
	In Truck	Out of Truck
Harsh N to D or N to R shift	CDEFGIJ	ab
Delayed shift—N to D	ACIHKJ	ca
Runaway on upshift and 3-2 kickdown	ABCDLIHK	b
Harsh upshift and 3-2 kickdown	BCDLIHJ	b
No upshift	ABCDLIHKM	b
No kickdown on normal downshift	ABNCDLIHKM	d
Erratic shifts	ABNCFOPQIKMJ	c
Slips in forward drive positions	ACIHK	abd
Slips in reverse only	CEGIK	
Slips in all positions	ACOIK	e
No drive in any position	ACOQIKJ	ca
No drive in forward positions	CDOLIHK	abd
No drive in reverse	CEGKMI	b
Drives in neutral	NIJ	a
Drags or locks	DELG	abfd
Noises	AORPMIJ	a
Hard to fill or blows out	AORSTQI	
Transmission overheats	ADEORTMI	abe
Unable to push-start truck (No rear pump after 1965)	ACEGI	g

Key to Checks

A. Oil Level	H. Accumulator	O. Regulator Valve and/or Spring	a. Front-Kickdown Clutch
B. Control Linkage	I. Valve Body Assembly	P. Output Shaft Bushing	b. Rear Clutch
C. Oil Pressure Check	J. Manual Valve Lever	Q. Strainer	c. Front Pump and/or Sleeve
D. Kickdown Band	K. Air Pressure Check	R. Converter Control Valve	d. Overrunning Clutch
E. Low-Reverse Band	L. K-D Servo Link	S. Breather Clogged	e. Converter
F. Improper Engine Idle	M. Governor	T. Cooler or Lines	f. Planetary
G. Servo Linkage	N. Gear Shift Cable		g. Rear Pump (Not after 1965)

General Information

This transmission is a hydraulically operated automatic transmission with six forward gear ratios and one reverse.

The transmission consists basically of a torque converter, a planetary gear train and a hydraulic control system for shifting gears.

The torque converter operates as a hydraulic torque multiplier and a fluid coupling between the engine and the gear train. The torque multiplying phase of the converter operates when the vehicle starts moving from a standstill and when a heavy load slows down the vehicle.

At certain speeds (when the action of the torque converter is no longer needed) an automatic lockup clutch in the converter locks the engine directly to the gear train for greater efficiency. The lockup clutch automatically disengages momentarily while shifts are being made.

A pedal operated hydraulic retarder assists the service brakes in controlling vehicle speed during long down hill braking and when slowing down in stop and go traffic.

Two separate fluid velocity type governors provide the fluid pressures needed to operate the hydraulic control system and make the shifts.

When the range selector lever is at D3-6 position the transmission can be operated in 3rd, 4th, 5th and 6th gears. The D3-4 position permits the use of only 3rd and 4th gears. When the lever is in the D3-5 position the vehicle can be operated in 3rd, 4th and 5th gears only. When the lever is at L1-2 (low range) the transmission will operate only in first and second gears. The reverse gear ratio is effective when the range selector is at R.

The gear ratios within the selected range are upshifted or downshifted automatically to meet changing road and load conditions. When the accelerator pedal is depressed to full throttle, each gear ratio shift point should occur at the highest speed for the shift. When the throttle is partly open, the shift points should occur at lower speeds.

A detent at the full throttle position of the accelerator pedal permits the driver to control certain shifts. When the pedal is pushed through the full throttle detent, the transmission will remain in the same gear ratio during acceleration or will immediately downshift to a lower gear to provide the best engine performance for the driving.

Adjustments

Range Selector Lever Linkage Adjustment

1. Place range selector lever in R (reverse) position.
2. Remove cotter pin from connection at transmission range selec-

tor lever. Move connector out of the way. Shift transmission lever all the way forward.

3. With the range selector lever in cab and transmission range selector lever in R (reverse) position, the pin in cable connector should be aligned with hole in transmission range selector lever.

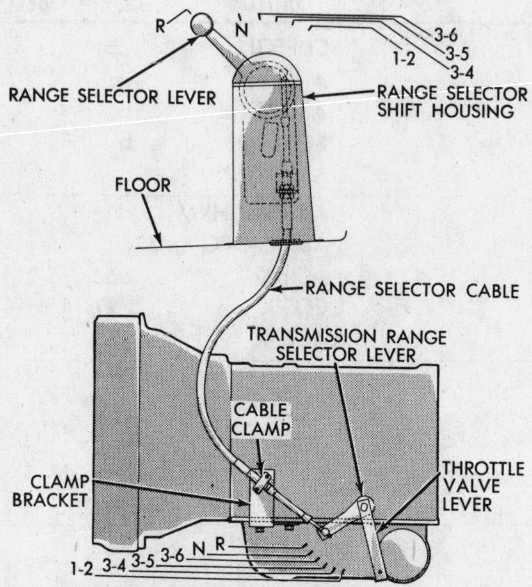

Range selector lever control adjustment
(© Chrysler Corp.)

4. If alignment is not correct, loosen jam nut at connector and turn connector in or out until alignment is obtained and connector pin can be installed easily.
5. Secure connector pin with cotter pin and tighten jam nut. Check operation of selector lever in all positions.

Neutral Safety Switch Adjustment

1. Check starter circuit at all range selector lever positions, by positioning lever and turning ignition switch to extreme clockwise position.
2. The engine should start only when the lever is in the N (neutral) position. If necessary to make an adjustment, first loosen neutral safety switch to bracket screws, and rotate switch clockwise so the starter circuit is closed when starter lever is set in N (neutral). Tighten switch mounting screws.
3. If engine fails to start with the range selector lever in N (neutral) position check switch lead wires and switch, by making a circuit check with a test lamp.

Throttle Linkage Adjustment

1. Remove throttle control spring and governor arm spring (if equipped).
2. At transmission, remove throttle control shift rod swivel cotter pin and remove swivel from TV lever.
3. Remove carburetor air cleaner.
4. Place carburetor throttle lever in idle position.
5. Adjust throttle control rod so that accelerator control bell crank stop is against bracket. Tighten nuts on throttle rod.
6. Move carburetor throttle lever to wide open position.
7. Wide open throttle stop bolt must be adjusted so that the bolt head contacts the bell crank when the throttle is in wide open position.

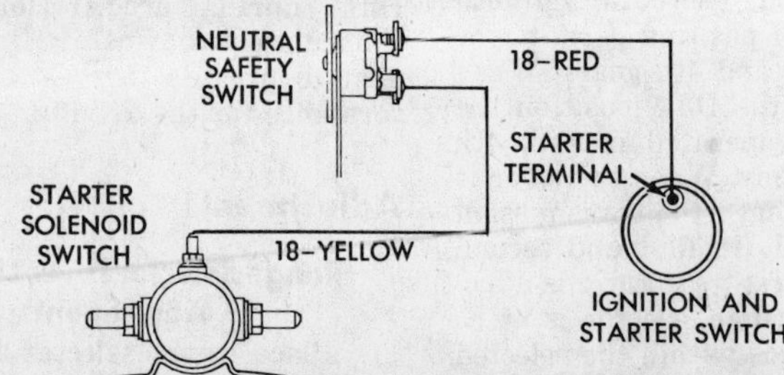

Neutral safety switch circuit diagram
(© Chrysler Corp.)

8. With throttle control shaft pushed upwards until travel of rod is stopped, at the transmission rotate the throttle control lever forward until the TV lever is firm against the internal stop. At this position the swivel pin should freely enter the lower hole in the transmission throttle valve control lever. Finger tighten front and rear adjusting nuts against swivel.
9. Back off the swivel three turns to back off valve, connect linkage tighten all nuts.
10. On all models the through detent pedal stop (located on throttle control bell crank) must be adjusted so that pedal forced cannot be applied to TV linkage. To do this adjust stop so that it contacts the bracket bolted to the engine at the same time the TV lever contacts the stop in the transmission. Then turn bolt 1/16″ turn further to eliminate any force being applied through the linkage from the stop in the transmission.

Retarder Linkage Adjustment

1. Adjust master cylinder push rod so there is a .010 inch free play (measured at pedal pad approximately 1/16 inch between push rod and master cylinder piston, when piston is in its fully returned position. The system must be free of air and master cylinder filled to ½″ of top.
2. Push rod on slave cylinder should travel ½ inch for full retarder action.

Maintenance

Checking Oil Level

1. The oil level should be checked every 1,000 miles and oil added when necessary.
2. The transmission oil should be at normal operating temperature 180° to 260° F.
3. The vehicle should be on level ground.
4. The parking brake and service brakes should be applied. CAUTION: Do not apply the hydraulic retarder while checking oil level. Applying the hydraulic retarder while in a stalled position will aerate the oil, making an accurate oil level check impossible.
5. Place range selector lever in N position and run engine at fast idle.
6. The oil should be at the "Full" mark on the dipstick. If not add oil till the proper level is obtained.

Changing Oil

1. Drain oil immediately while oil is still warm.

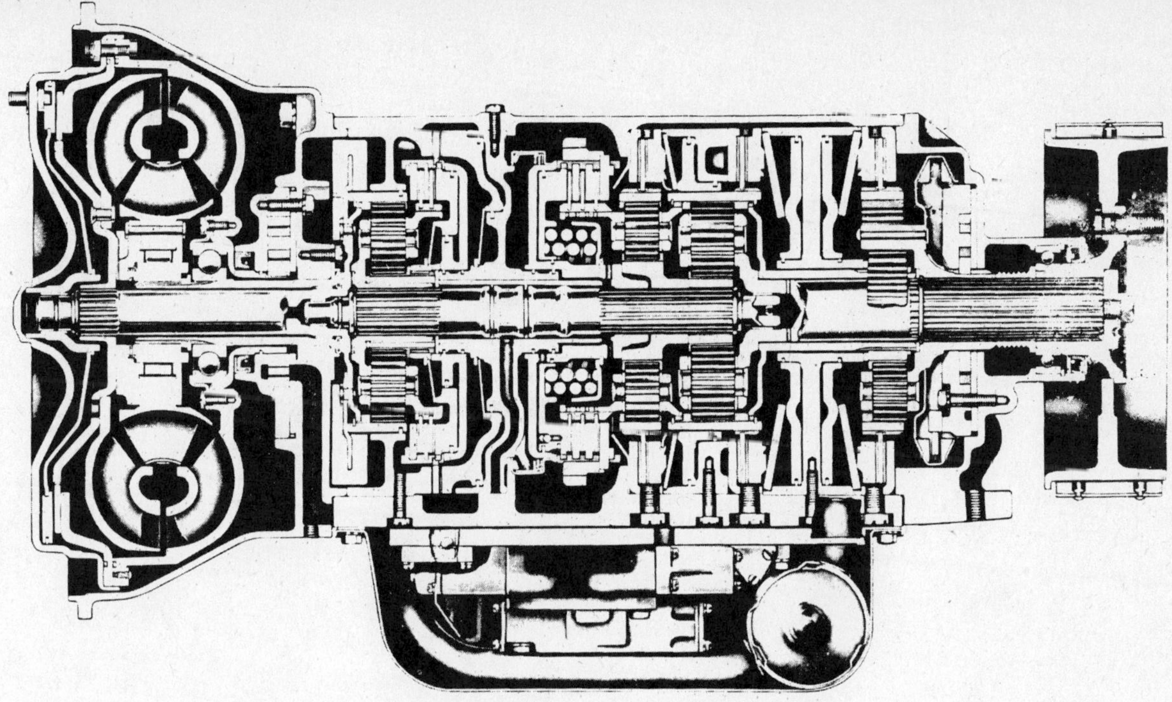

Transmission (Cross Section) Typical

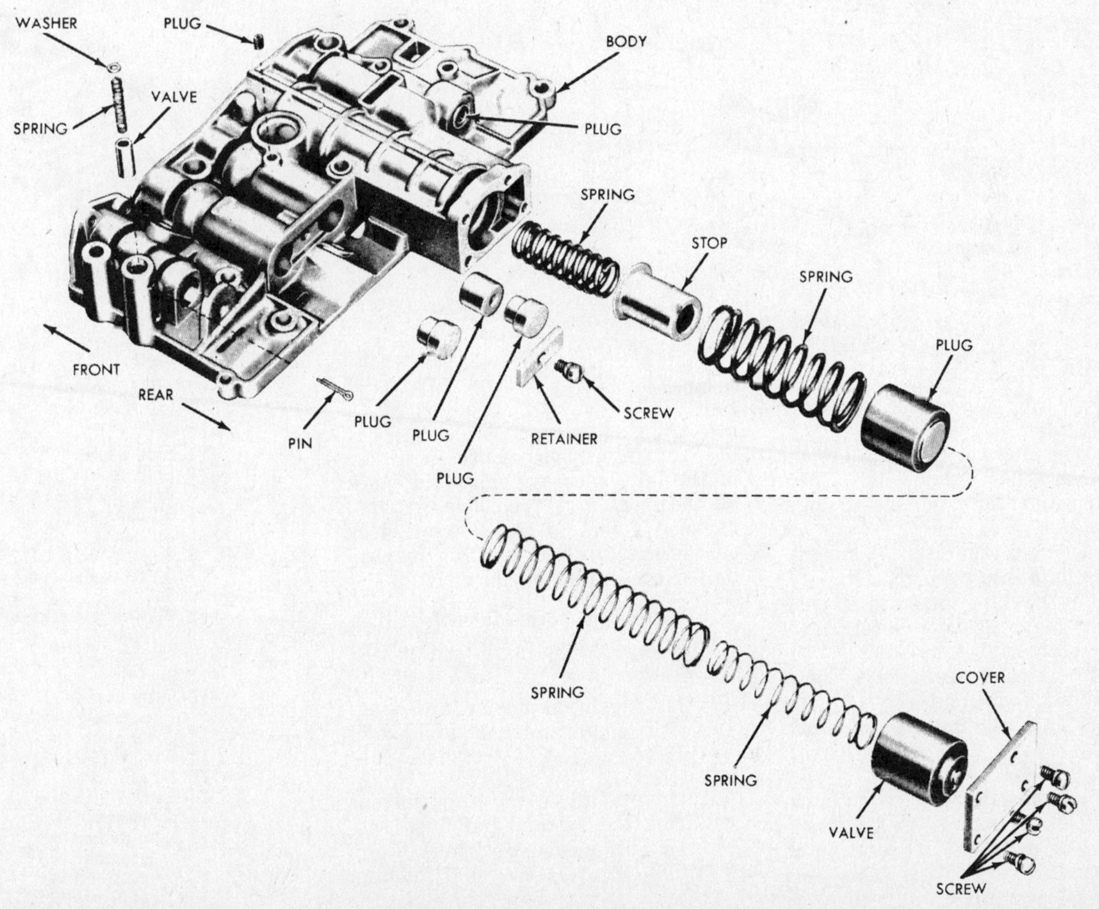

Exhaust Regulator Valve Body (Rear View)

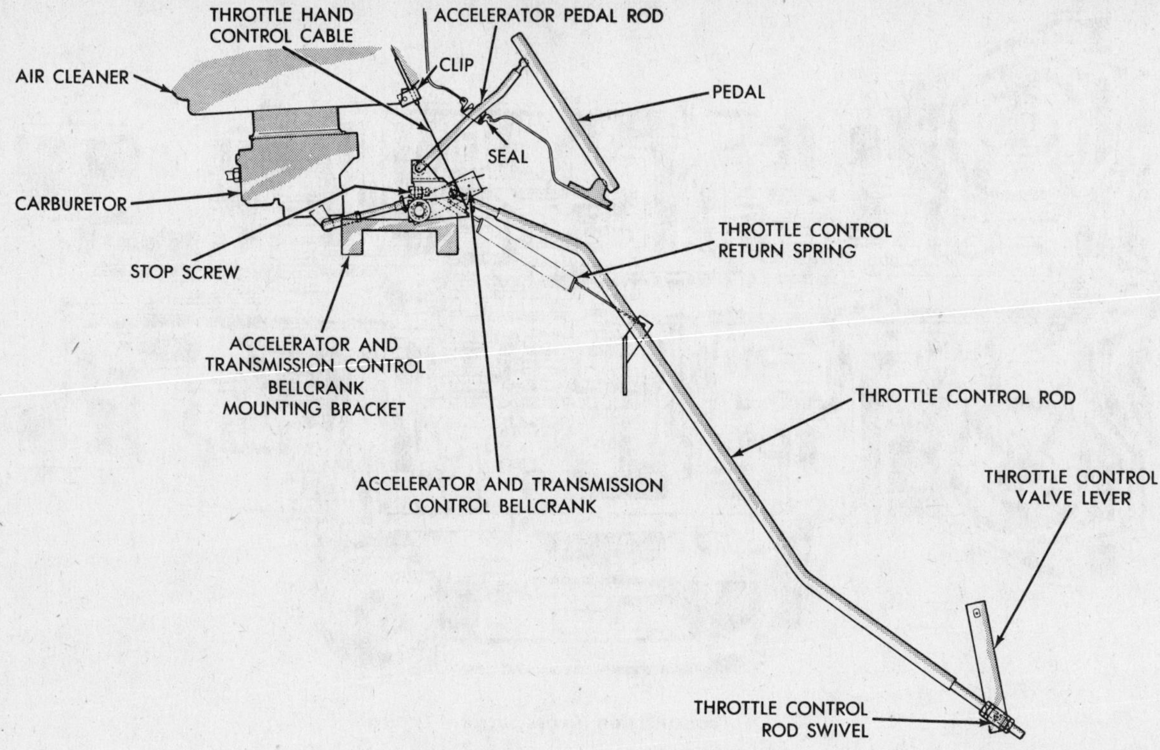

Throttle linkage assembly (© Chrysler Corp.)

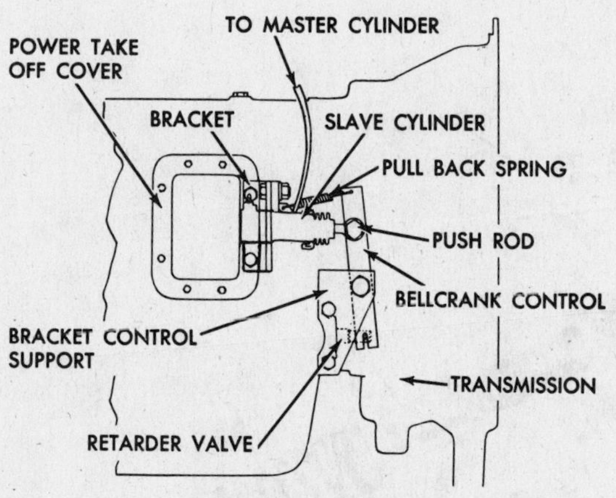

Retarder linkage adjustment
(© Chrysler Corp.)

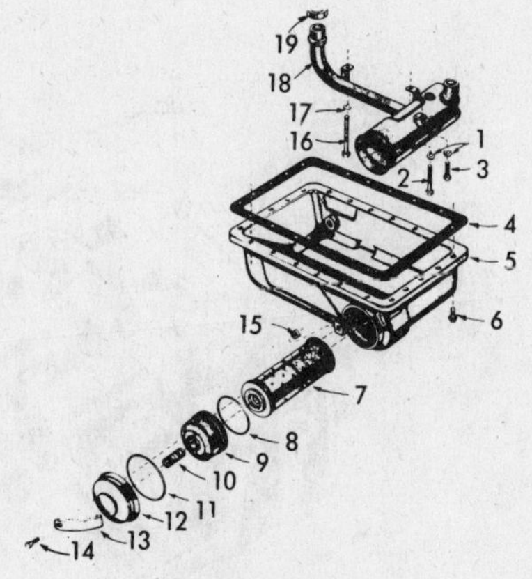

Oil filter assembly
(© Chrysler Corp.)

1 Lock washer
2 Bolt, ¼-20 x 3
3 Bolt, ¼-20 x 3
4 Oil pan gasket
5 Oil pan
6 Bolt, 5/16-18 x 1/2
7 Oil filter element
8 Seal ring
9 Oil filter element retainer
10 Spring
11 Seal ring
12 Filter cover assembly
13 Cover strap
14 Bolt, 5/16-24 x 1
15 Nut, 5/16-24
16 Bolt, ¼-20 x 1-⅛
17 Lockwasher
18 Oil filter can assembly
19 Oil suction tube seal ring

2. Loosen filter cover and allow oil to drain thoroughly.
3. Remove filter and install new one.
4. Pour eight quarts of transmission fluid into transmission.
5. Apply parking brake and position range selector lever in N and start engine.
6. Run engine at normal idle speed and add sufficient oil to bring level to "Full" mark on dipstick.

Oil Cooler

When clutch failure or other internal trouble has occured in the transmission any metal particles or clutch plate material that may have been carried into the oil cooler should be removed from the system by flushing the cooler before the transmission is put back into service. Foreign matter in the oil cooler system could block off the front pilot feed hole, get into various gears and clutches, or block off the output shaft bushing lubrication orifice in the splitter shaft.

1. Disconnect both oil cooler lines at hydraulic retarding valve body.
2. Back-flush oil cooler and lines with clean solvent and compressed air.
3. Remove all remaining solvent from the system and flush system with automatic transmission fluid. If after the final flushing there is no flow through the cooler or if it is restricted, replace oil filter.

Air Pressure Checks

Compressed air may be used to check operation of various clutches in the transmission and to find leaks that may be caused by broken, damaged or omitted seals. Be sure that air from source of supply is clean and dry.

1. To make air pressure checks, remove oil pan, valve body and oil transfer plate from transmission. Apply 85-100 psl (do not exceed 150 psl) air pressure at the appropriate holes in the mounting pad at bottom of transmission housing.
2. When air is applied as directed, listen for the noise that occurs when clutch is applied. If no clutch application noise is heard, a leak may exist in the hydraulic system.

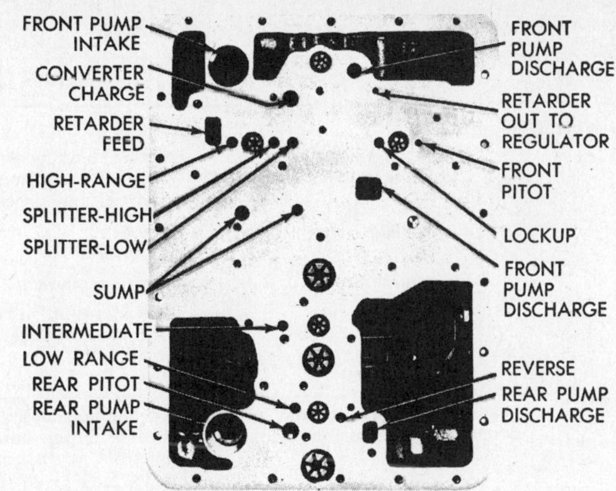

Fluid passages in transmission housing
(© Chrysler Corp.)

Clutches Air Pressure Check Chart

Check Passage	*Leak Location*	*Cause of Leak*
Low-splitter clutch	Between diaphragm and case	Bottom two anchor bolts loose, or not drawing diaphragm to case
	At piston id	Hook-type oil seal for id broken, or omitted
	At piston od	Seal at piston od broken, nicked or expander omitted
High-splitter clutch	Between diaphragm and case	Bottom two anchor bolts loose, or not drawing diaphragm to case
	At piston id	Hook-type oil seal for id broken, or omitted
	At piston od	Seal at piston od broken, nicked or expander omitted
	Lube hole in retarder valve body pad	Diaphragm front hub hook-type seal ring broken or omitted
	Retarder feed	Diaphragm rear hub hook-type seal ring broken or omitted
High-range clutch	Between diaphragm and case	Bottom two anchor bolts loose, or not drawing diaphragm to case
	At front-pilot hole or at lube in retarder valve body pad	Inner hook-type seal ring on rear hub broken or omitted
	At lube hole in retarder valve body pad	Rear hook-type seal ring on rear hub broken or omitted
	Around clutch piston spring	Hook-type seal ring for clutch piston id broken or omitted
	Around high-range clutch hub	Seal at piston od broken, nicked or expander omitted
Intermediate-range clutch	Between case and intermediate clutch piston housing	Anchor bolts loose, intermediate clutch housing not tight against hole in case
	At piston id	Hook-type ring broken or omitted
	Around low-range clutch plate	Same as above
	At piston return spring and piston od	Seal at piston od broken, nicked or expander omitted

Fluid Pressure Checks

Four 1/8" pipe plugs are provided in the transmission to check lockup, and governor pressures.

All four pressures can be checked without driving the truck on the road.

All gauge readings should be taken with the transmission fluid at normal operating temperature, and with the throttle and range selector linkages properly adjusted.

The test point for main pressure is pump outlet and the main pressure regulator valve. Since there is no check valve between the front pump and the main regulator valve a gauge installed at this point will read main pressure under all operating conditions. In normal operation, main pressure varies from 75 to 255 psl. Pressure vary with the converter and converter lockup operations, throttle positions and range selector valve positions. Refer to chart.

Main Pressure Check (Engine Idle)

1. With engine stopped connect pressure gauge at plug hole in converter housing.
2. Apply parking brake and start engine. The engine idle speed should be 475-500 rpm with range selector lever in neutral. With engine idling, read gauge in all selector lever positions.

Maximum Main Pressure Check

Converter Operation

1. Stop engine, remove transmission throttle control rod. Make certain swivel adjustment is not disturbed.
2. Move transmission throttle control lever to rear to insure throttle valve is fully closed.

Clutches Air Pressure Check Chart

Check Passage	*Leak Location*	*Cause of Leak*
Low-range clutch	Between case and low-reverse piston housing	Anchor bolt loose; low-reverse clutch housing not tight against case
	At piston id	Hook-type seal broken or omitted
	Around clutch id	Same as above
	At piston od	Seal at piston od broken, nicked or expander omitted
Reverse clutch	Between case and low-reverse piston housing	Anchor bolt loose; low-reverse clutch housing not tight against case
	At piston id	Hook-type seal broken or omitted
	Around clutch id	Same as above
	At piston od	Seal at piston od broken, nicked or expander omitted
Lockup clutch	At piston od	Seal broken, nicked, or omitted
	At od of converter cover	Seal between reaction plate and cover, or between plate and converter pump flange, damaged or omitted
	At turbine shaft	Broken or omitted hook-type rings at front end of turbine shaft, front end of splitter shaft, or center of splitter shaft

3. Start engine and apply service brakes. With hand throttle, set engine speed at 1,200 rpm, use a tachometer.

4. Read pressure gauge at all selector lever positions.

5. Return engine to idle speed before each shift. The readings represent the maximum pressure in convertor operation at closed transmission throttle valve.

6. Rotate transmission throttle control lever forward to its stop and fix lever in this position. Transmission throttle valve is now fully open.

7. With engine running at 1,200 rpm read pressure in all range selector positions.

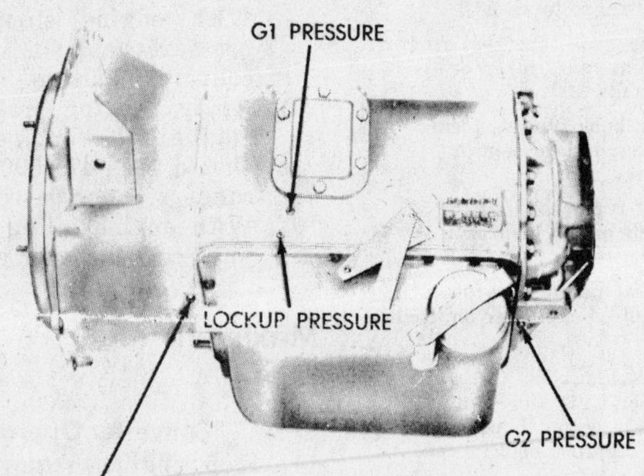

Fluid pressure test point locations
(© Chrysler Corp.)

Lockup Pressure Check (Closed Throttle)

To check converter lockup pressure in 2nd, 4th and 6th gears proceed as follows:

1. Remove propeller shaft and transmission throttle control rod, and move transmission lever rearward to fully close throttle valve. Release parking brake.

2. Start engine and move selector lever to L1-2, increase engine speed to 2,000 rpm and transmission will shift to second gear, then to lockup.

3. Read pressure gauge; it represents second gear converter lockup pressure at closed transmission throttle valve.

4. Move selector lever to D3-4, set engine speed at 2,000 rpm and read pressure gauge. This reading represents fourth gear converter lockup pressure at closed transmission throttle valve.

5. Move selector lever to D3-6, set engine speed at 2,000 rpm. Read the pressure gauge. This reading represents sixth gear converter lockup pressure at closed throttle.

Governor Pressure Check

1. Remove propeller shaft and transmission control rod; move lever rearward to fully close throttle valve. Release parking brake. Attach pressure gauge. At G-1 check point.

2. Start engine and increase speed to 2,800 rpm with selector lever at D3-6. Transmission will shift to sixth gear. Read gauge after pressure has stabilized.

3. To check G-2, stop engine and connect pressure gauge to G-2 checkpoint. Follow the same procedure as for G-1 pressure check.

Pressure Check Chart

Main Pressure Check—Engine Idle

Selector Lever Position	Gear	Clutches Applied	Engine rpm	Throttle Position at Transmission	Gauge Readings (psi) Minimum Main Pressure
N (Neutral)		Low Splitter	475-500	Closed	100
R (Reverse)	Third	Low Splitter, Reverse	Idle	Closed	50
D3-4, D3-5 or D3-6		Low Splitter, Intermediate Range	Idle	Closed	50
L1-2	First	Low Splitter, Low Range	Idle	Closed	50

Lockup Pressure Check—Operation (Maximum Throttle)

Selector Lever Position (Drive Shaft Disconnected)	Gear	Clutches Applied	Engine rpm	Throttle Position at Transmission	Gauge Readings (psi)
D3-5, D3-6	Third	Lockup, Low Splitter, Intermediate Range	2700	Maximum	107-125

Lockup Pressure Check (Closed Throttle)

Selector Lever Position (Drive Shaft Disconnected)	Gear	Clutches Applied	Engine rpm	Throttle Position at Transmission	Gauge Readings (psi)
L1-2	Second	Lockup, High Splitter, Low Range	2000	Closed	65-75
D3-4	Fourth	Lockup, High Splitter, Intermediate Range	2000	Closed	65-75
D3-5 D3-6	Sixth	Lockup, High Splitter, High Range	2000	Closed	65-75

Maximum Main Pressure Check—Converter Operation

Selector Lever Position	Engine rpm	Gauge Reading (psi) Closed Throttle	Full Throttle
N, R, D3-4, D3-5, D3-6 and L1-2	1200	155 (Minimum)	200 (Minimum)

Main Pressure Check—Hydraulic Retarder Operation

Selector Lever Position	Throttle Position at Transmission and Engine	Retarder Pedal Position	Minimum Main Pressure (psi)
N	Closed	At Stop	125

Governor Pressure Check G-1 and G-2

Selector Lever Position (Drive Shaft Disconnected)	Gear	Engine rpm	Throttle Position at Transmission	Gauge G-1 Limits	Reading (psi) G-2 Limits
D3-6	Sixth	2800	Closed	60-70	67-70

Oil Pan and Filter (Removal)

1. Remove oil filter cover and gasket, then remove retainer and filter element from transmission oil pan.
2. Remove oil pan and gasket, then remove seal rings from front pump pickup tubes.

Valve Bodies (Removal)

1. Remove the range selector valve body from oil transfer plate. *The shift valve steel detent ball and spring are free to fall out of the valve body when it is removed from the transfer plate.*
2. Remove downshift timing valve body from transfer plate.
3. Remove transfer plate and gasket from transmission housing. *Nylon ball in plate is free to fall when plate is removed.*
4. Remove retarder linkage and oil lines from retarder valve body.
5. Remove hydraulic retarder valve body and gasket. Remove nylon ball from housing.

Oil Transfer Plate

Disassembly

1. Remove converter lubrication supply cover. Do not remove valve seat unless it is bad.
2. Remove retainer, spring, seat and steel ball. *The low range clutch exhaust regulator valve is pressed into the oil transfer plate and should not be removed unless it is to be replaced.* An orifice cup is situated under this regulator valve. The cup serves to slow the exhaust of the low-range clutch when shifts occur between second and third gears.
3. Clean transfer plate and check valve operation. The valve should retain the cleaning solvent on side opposite spring for at least 15 seconds.

Assembly

1. Install lube supply valve seat (if removed) in lubrication supply cover and install cover.
2. Tighten screws from 24 to 36-inch-pounds. *The nylon ball is installed from the other side of oil transfer plate when plate is assembled to transmission housing.*
3. Assemble steel ball, seat, spring, and converter pressure regulator valve retainer to oil transfer plate. Torque screws at 24 to 36 inch-pounds.

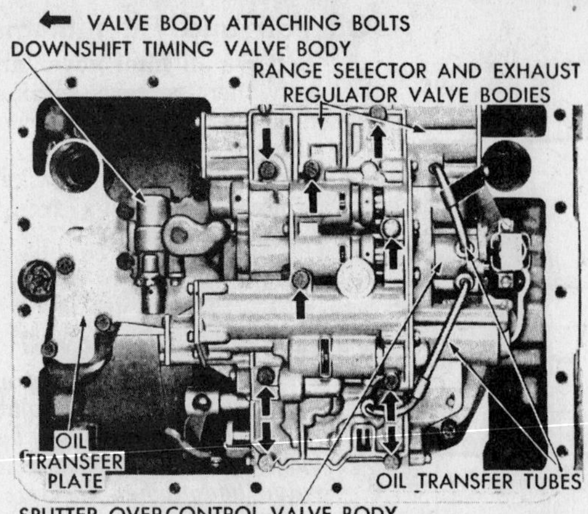

Valve bodies installed in transmission (© Chrysler Corp.)

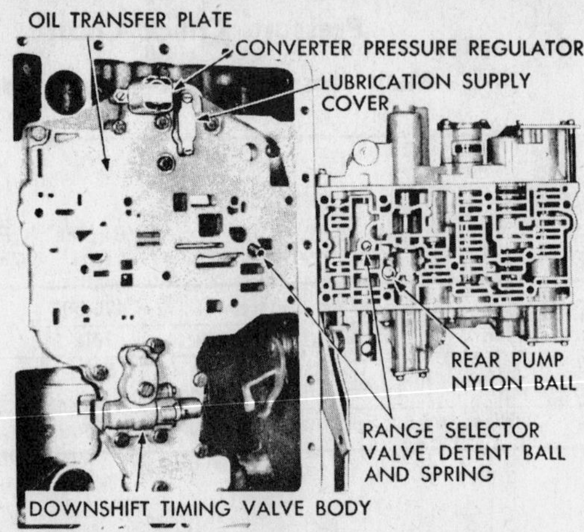

Removing control valve body from transfer plate (typical) (© Chrysler Corp.)

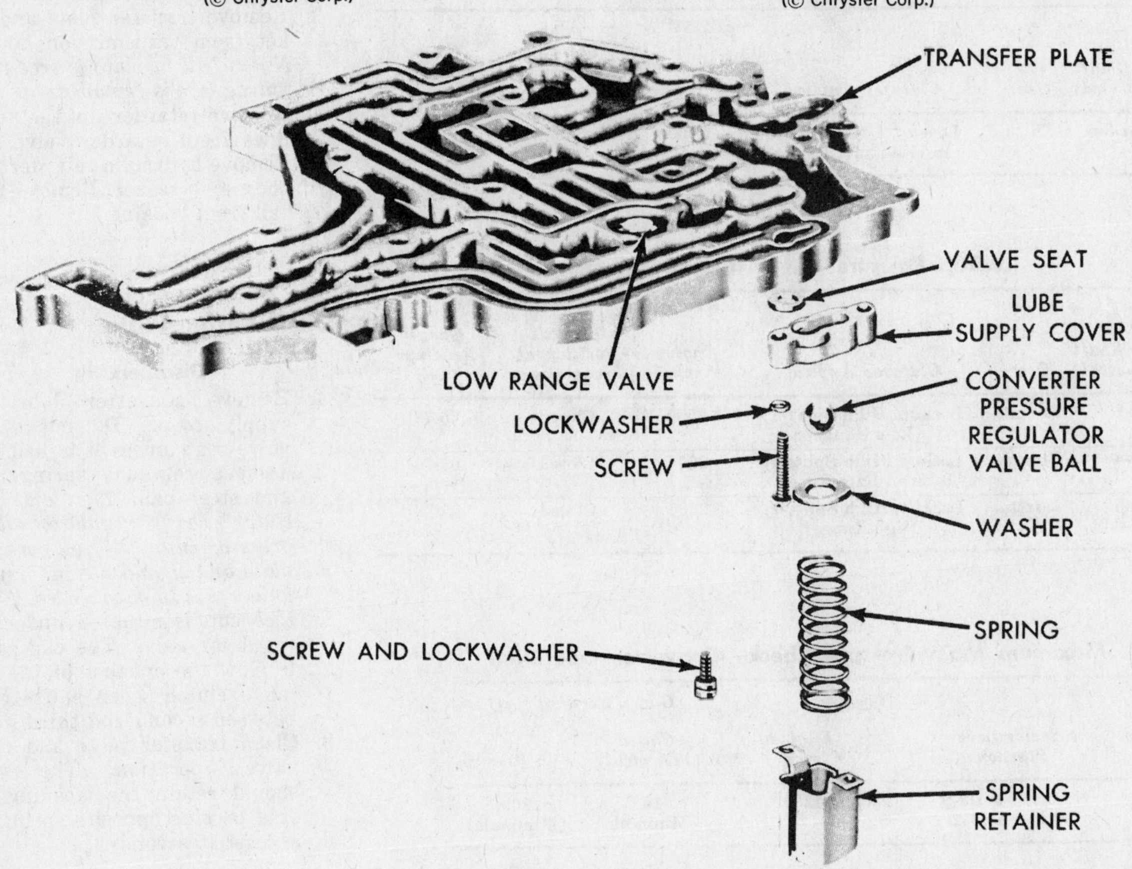

Oil transfer plate (© Chrysler Corp.)

Downshift Timing Valve

Disassembly

1. Remove downshift timing valve body from transfer plate.
2. Remove downshift timing valve cover.
3. Remove spring and downshift timing valve.

The oil passage orifice in valve body is .01875 to 0.1400 inch. In addition, the inside diameter at rear (closed end) of valve bore is approximately 0.04 inch. The diameter of the rear valve land is approximately 0.04 inch. Two coils at one end are painted blue.

Assembly

1. Insert valve in body and place spring on the stem of valve.
2. Install valve cover over spring and tighten screws from 24 to 36 inch-pounds.

Control Valve Body

Disassembly

Do not mix the various valve body springs.

1. Place the control valve body assembly with mating surface (oil transfer plate side) facing down.
2. Remove oil transfer tubes by pulling upward.
3. Remove exhaust regulator valve body.
4. Remove selector valve detent spring and lift valve body separator plate off the control valve body. Remove 3/8 inch steel detent ball from valve body.
5. Remove accelerator plug cover and plug.

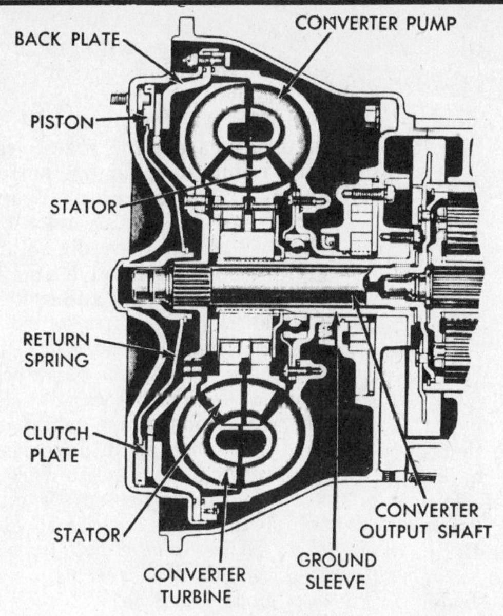

Torque Converter and Lock-Up Clutch (Cross Section)

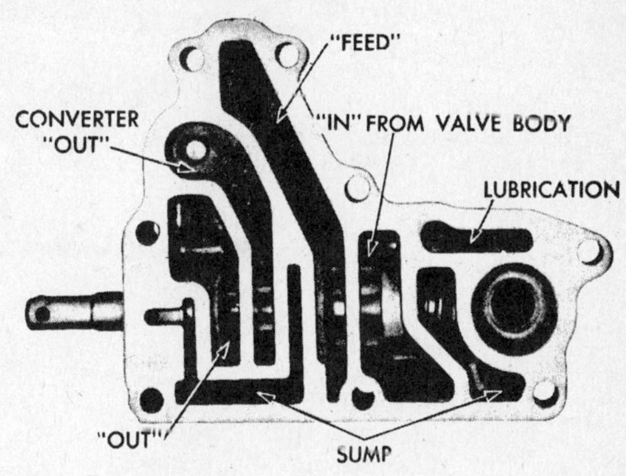

Oil Passages In Retarder Valve Body

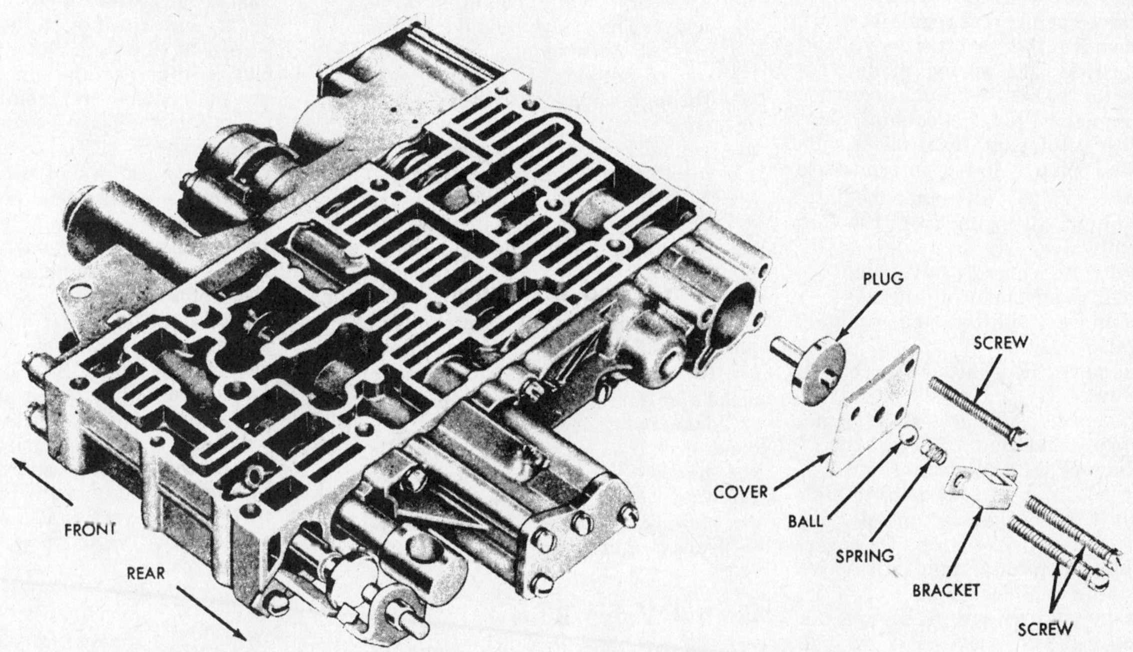

Accelerator Plug and Cover

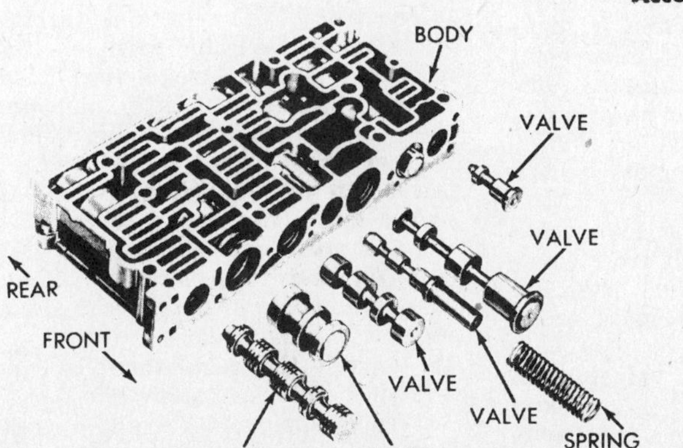

Control Valve Body Component Parts (Front)

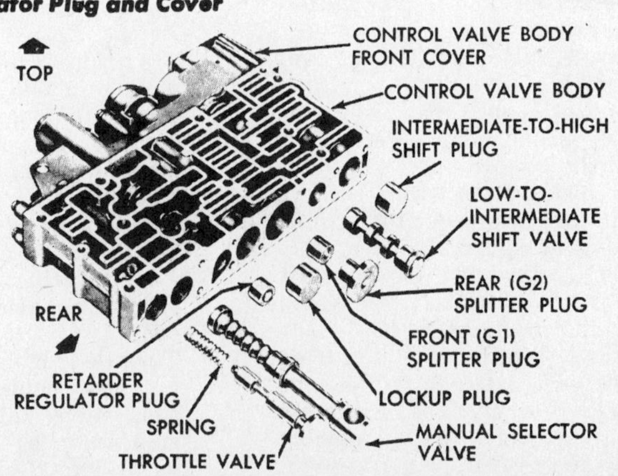

Rear of Control Valve Body

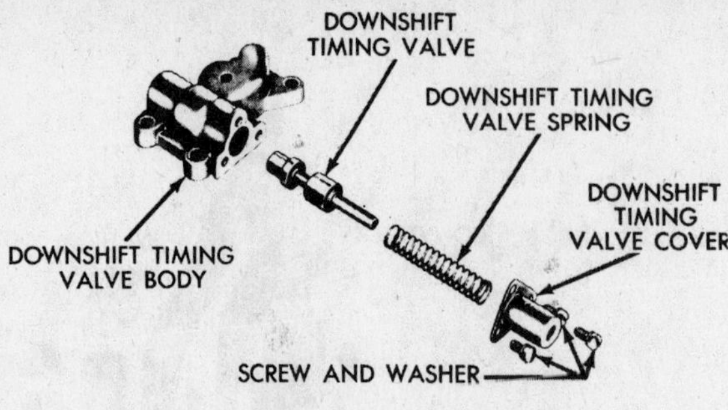

Downshift timing valve

6. Remove the regulator cover and lockup-knock-down plug, accumulator valve spring and accumulator valve.
7. Remove two screws and throttle valve retainer from valve body. Do not remove screw from retainer.
8. Remove valve body rear cover (spring loaded), then remove the low-to-intermediate shift valve spring, and regulator plug.
9. Remove the throttle valve and throttle valve spring, manual selector valve, hydraulic retarder regulator plugs, lock-up plug, rear pitot plug, front pitot spilter plug, low-to-intermediate shift valve, and intermediate-to-high shift plug from the control valve body.
10. Position control valve body on rear cover mounting surface.
11. Remove splitter over-control valve body.
12. Remove the splitter overcontrol valve.
13. Remove splitter shift plug spring and plug.
14. Remove the three screws attaching the intermediate-to-high shift valve cover to control valve body front cover. Remove cover, intermediate-to-high shift valve spring and blocker plug.
15. Remove three screws holding the valve body front cover to the control valve body. *Don't exert pressure on the cover because it is spring loaded.*
16. Remove valve body front cover assembly.
17. Remove ¼-inch ball which is freed when front cover is removed. Remove inhibitor valve and spring from cover. Remove main-pressure regulator spring, secondary spring, splitter relay valve spring and lockup shift valve spring which are exposed by removing front cover.
18. Remove throttle valve plug from valve body front cover. Remove retainer spring and withdraw pump overage valve assembly from front cover.
19. Remove the two overage valve spring retainers and spring from front cover. Remove throttle regulator valve, main-pressure regulator valve, lockup shift valve, splitter shift valve, splitter relay valve, and intermediate-to-high shift valve from front of control valve body.
20. Replace reverse-range clutch exhaust pressure regulator valve only if necessary. Check valve operation while cleaning valve body. The valve should retain solvent on side opposite spring for 15 seconds. If solvent leaks through sooner, valve is defective.
21. Do not remove reverse lockup inhibitor check valve retainer and 7/32-inch ball. If retainer, ball or valve body is defective, all three items must be replaced.

Cleaning and Inspection

Wash all parts in cleaning solvent and dry thoroughly with air. Check all parts and castings for cracks, nicks and burrs. Replace any cracked or damaged covers. Remove any nicks or burrs with a fine stone. *Do not sand or polish any radius on the valves or plugs. The valves and plugs are manufactured with a sharp edge to prevent dirt from sticking in the valve bore.*

Control Valve Body

1. *All valves and plugs should be installed dry and must move in the valve body bore by their own weight. Do not attempt to force any valves into the valve body bore, as it will damage the casting. If any valves or plugs stick, recheck for nicks or burrs. Remove the nicks or burrs with a fine stone.*
2. Position the range selector valve body with valve body front cover surface facing up and install the following parts in main valve body.
3. Throttle regulator valve, main pressure regulator valve, lockup shift valve, splitter shift valve, splitter relay valve, and intermediate-to-high shift valve. *The splitter relay valve should be installed with the widest land into control valve body first.*

Install the following parts in valve body front cover:

4. TV plug (hold in place with oil soluble grease), the main pressure regulator primary spring, and main pressure regulator secondary spring, ¼ inch nylon ball (hold in place with oil soluble grease), inhibitor valve and inhibitor valve spring and splitter relay spring.
5. Position the range selector valve body on its side, place valve body front cover against range selector valve body, front cover surface and push it into position, compressing the splitter relay valve and main pressure regulator springs. *Be careful to keep the 1/4 inch nylon ball in position. Install three screws, do not tighten at this time.*
6. Install the intermediate-to-high shift plug, spring and shift valve cover.
7. Install three screws to hold the cover but do not tighten the screws at this time.
8. Check the mating surface between front cover assembly and range selector body assembly. Be sure there is a tight seal and that none of the springs are caught between the housings. The front cover should not protrude above main valve body face since it assembles against the oil transfer plate.
9. Install splitter shaft plug into valve body front cover. Install overcontrol valve into overcontrol valve body. Install overcontrol valve body cover and hold with one screw (short). Install spring into recessed end of valve previously installed. Install complete overcontrol valve assembly on control valve body front cover, install the remaining two screws but do not tighten at this time.
10. Install the following parts in valve body rear cover side of the control valve body:

Throttle valve spring and throttle valve, manual selector valve, one hydraulic retarder regulator plug, lockup plug, front splitter plug and the rear splitter plug, low-to-intermediate shift valve, and intermediate-to-high shift plug. *All valves and plugs should be installed dry and must move in the valve body bore by their own weight. Do not force any valves or plugs, as the casting will be damaged.*

11. Install the regulator plug and the intermediate-to-low shift valve spring in valve body rear cover.
12. Install the three rear cover retaining screws. Install throttle valve retainer and screw, do not

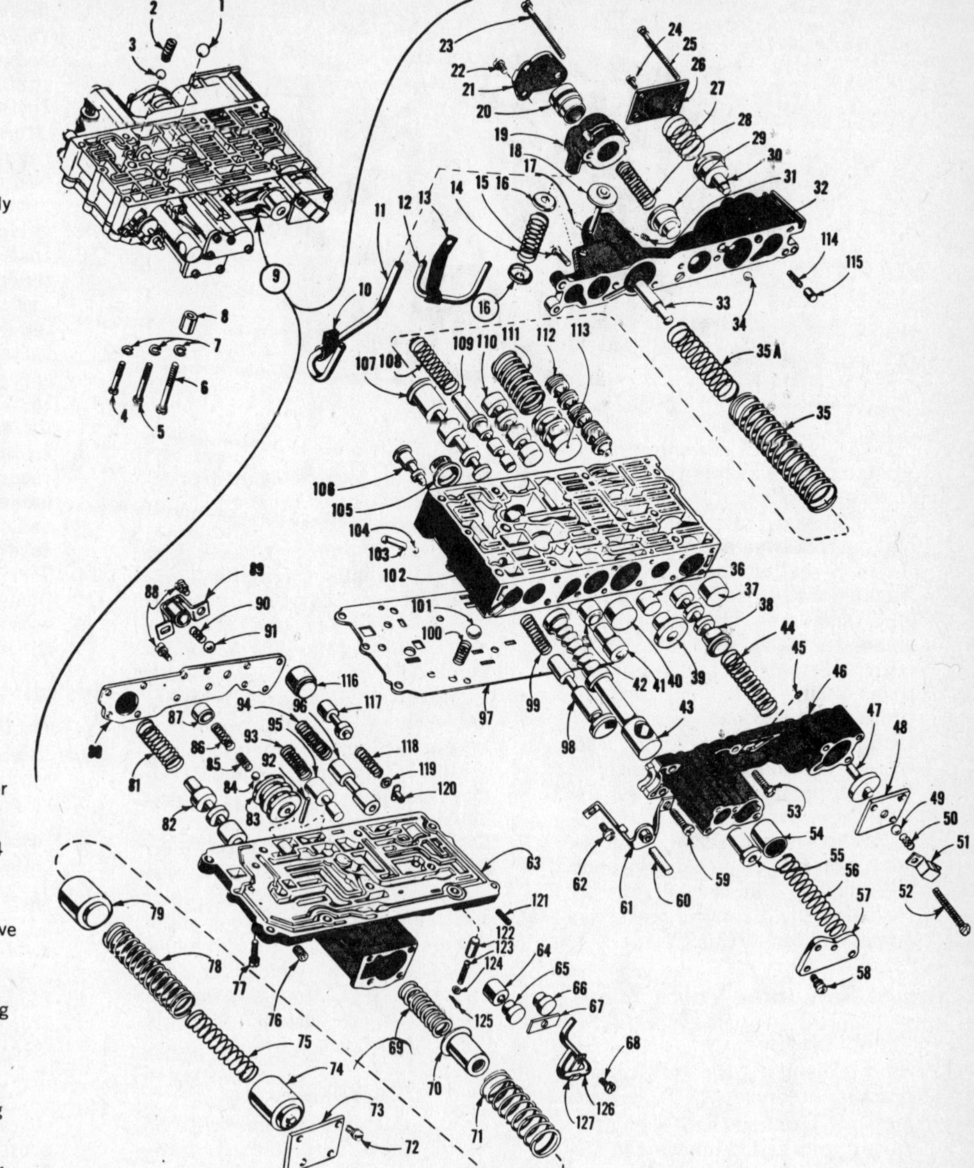

Oil Control valve body

1 Nylon ball, 1/2
2 Shift valve detent spring
3 Shift valve detent ball
4 Bolt, 1/4-20 x 2-3/4
5 Bolt, 1/4-20 x 3-1/4
6 Bolt, 1/4-20 x 3-3/4
7 Lock washer, 1/4
8 Valve body bolt sleeve
9 Control valve body assembly
10 Drive transfer tube clip
11 Drive transfer tube
12 High transfer tube
13 High transfer tube clip
14 Pump overage regulator spring
15 Screw and washer
16 Regulator spring retainer
17 Retainer spring
18 Pump overage regulator valve assembly
19 Overcontrol valve body
20 Overcontrol valve
21 Overcontrol valve cover
22 Screw and washer, 10-24 x 7/16
23 Screw and washer, 10-24 x 2-3/8
24 Screw and washer, 10-24 x 7/16
25 Screw and washer, 10-24 x 2-⅜
26 Intermediate-to-high shift valve cover
27 Intermediate-to-high shift valve spring
28 Splitter shift plug spring
29 Splitter shift plug
30 Intermediate-to-high blocker plug
31 Oval point setscrew, 10-24
31A Oval point setscrew, 10-24
32 Valve body front cover
33 Throttle valve plug
34 Nylon ball, 1/4
35 Main-pressure regulator valve spring (primary)
35A Main-pressure regulator valve spring (secondary)
36 Front splitter shift (G1) plug
37 Intermediate-to-high shift plug
38 Low-to-intermediate shift valve
39 Rear-splitter shift (G2) plug
40 Lockup plug
41 Regulator plug
42 Hydraulic retarder regulator plug
43 Manual selector valve
44 Intermediate-to-low shift valve spring
45 Oval point setscrew, 10-24
46 Valve body rear cover
47 Accelerator plug
48 Accelerator plug cover
49 Ball
50 Trimmer ball regulator spring
51 Valve guide bracket assembly
52 Screw and washer, 10-24 x 1-5/8
53 Screw and washer, 10-24 x 3/4
54 Accumulator valve
55 Lockup knockdown plug
56 Accumulator valve spring
57 Regulator cover
58 Screw and washer, 10-24 x 7/16
59 Screw and washer, 10-24 x 3/4
60 Throttle valve adjusting screw
61 Throttle valve retainer
62 Screw and washer, 10-24 x 3/8
63 Exhaust regulator valave body
64 Low-splitter exhaust regulator plug
65 Low-splitter exhaust regulator stop plug
66 Intermediate-exhaust regulator stop plug
67 Plug retainer
68 Screw and washer, 10-24 x 7/16
69 Trimmer secondary spring
70 Trimmer stop
71 Trimmer primary spring
72 Screw and washer, 10-24 x 7/16
73 Trimmer cover
74 Trimmer valve
75 Trimmer return inner spring
76 Pipe plug, 1/4
77 Screw and washer, 10-24 x 3/4
78 Trimmer return outer spring
79 Trimmer plug
80 Exhaust regulator valve cover
81 Lockup cutoff valve spring
82 Lockup cutoff valve
83 Extender valve body
84 Extender valve ball
85 Extender valve ball spring
86 Extender valve return spring
87 Extender valve
88 Screw and washer, 10-24 x 7/16
89 Valve guide bracket assembly
90 Trimmer ball regulator spring
91 Ball
92 Extender valve body roll pin
93 Low-splitter exhaust regulator valve spring
94 Inermediate exhaust regulator valve spring
95 Low-splitter exhaust regulator valve
96 Intermediate exhaust regulator valve
97 Valve body separator plate
98 Throttle valve
99 Throttle valve (TV) spring
100 Selector valve detent spring
101 Selector valve detent ball
102 Control valve body
103 Reverse lockup inhibitor check valve retainer
104 Nylon ball, 7/32
105 Reverse-range clutch exhaust regulator valve assembly
106 Throttle regulator valve
107 Main-pressure regulator valve
108 Lockup shift valve spring
109 Lockup shift valve
110 Splitter shift valve
111 Splitter relay valve spring
112 Intermediate-to-high shift valve
113 Splitter relay valve
114 6-5 inhibitor valve
116 Low inhibitor plug
117 Low inhibitor valve
118 3-2 inhibitor spring
119 Inhibitor spring retainer
120 Tee nut
121 Inhibitor spring adjusting screw
122 5-4 inhibitor valve
123 5-4 inhibitor spring
124 Spring retainer washer
125 Cotter pin
126 Signal tube
127 Signal tube clip

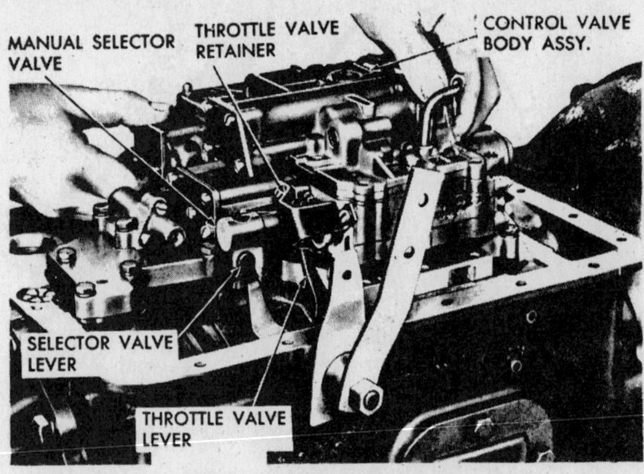

Control valve body (installed)

tighten screws at this time.

13. If throttle valve adjusting screw was removed from retainer, install at this time but do not lock. Refer to section on adjustments.
14. Install the lockup knockdown plug (small end first). Install accumulator valve. Install accumulator valve spring and regulator cover secure with four screws, tighten 24 to 36 inch-pounds.
15. Install accelerator plug and cover. On models which include the ball spring and bracket, install these parts at this time and secure with two screws but do not tighten. On models without ball, spring and bracket, install the three cover retaining screws, do not tighten at this time.

Exhaust Regulator Valve Body

Disassembly

1. On models using the valve guide bracket, remove two screws, bracket, trimmer ball regulator spring and ball. Remove the six remaining screws securing exhaust regulator valve body cover to exhaust regulator valve body on models which do not use the bracket assembly, remove eleven screws securing cover to valve body. *This cover is spring loaded and must be held while screws are being removed.* Remove cover.
2. Removal of exhaust regulator cover will expose the intermediate exhaust regulator valve spring, low-splitter valve spring and lockup cutoff valve spring. Remove these springs.
3. Remove intermediate exhaust regulator valve, lockup cutoff valve and low-splitter exhaust regulator valve.
4. Remove extender valve, extender valve spring and valve ball spring. Do not remove extender valve body and roll pin unless replacement is necessary. If replacement is necessary, remove roll pin and tap out extender valve body toward nearest opening (front) of exhaust regulator valve body.
5. Remove trimmer cover from fear of exhaust regulator valve body, remove cover. *This cover is spring loaded and must be held while screws are being removed.*
6. Remove trimmer valve, trimmer valve inner and outer springs, trimmer plug, trimmer primary spring, trimmer stop and trimmer secondary spring from exhaust regulator valve body.
7. Remove screw and retainer. Remove low-splitter exhaust regulator stop plug and low-splitter exhaust regulator plug. Remove intermediate exhaust stop plug from exhaust regulator valve body. *Models using the set screw on bottom of valve body do not use regulator plug.*

Assembly

1. Install intermediate exhaust regulator stop plug (small diameter first) into exhaust regulator valve body.
2. Install low-splitter exhaust regulator plug. *Some models do not use a plug in this location.*
3. Install low-splitter regulator stop plug, small diameter first.
4. Install signal tube, retainer, clip and screw. Tighten screw to 24-36 inch-pounds. *Tube must not protrude through body to interfere with separator plate to be installed later.*
5. Install trimmer secondary spring, trimmer stop, trimmer primary spring and trimmer plug.
6. Install trimmer inner and outer spring and trimmer valve. Install cover and four screws. Tighten screws to 24-36 inch-pounds.
7. Install the 5-4 inhibitor valve, inhibitor spring, flat washer and a new cotter pin into bottom of valve body.
8. Install extender valve body if removed previously, secure with roll pin. Press roll pin into valve body until slightly below flat surface of the body.
9. Install low-splitter exhaust regulator valve, intermediate exhaust regulator valve, low-splitter exhaust regulator spring and intermediate exhaust regulator valve spring.
10. Install extender valve ball, extender valve ball spring, extender valve return spring and extender valve, recessed end first.
11. Install lockup cutoff valve and spring.
12. Install inhibitor spring, inhibitor valve and inhibitor plug.
13. Install exhaust regulator cover, secure with nine screws. On models using bracket, spring and ball, install these parts and secure with two screws.
14. Tighten cover screws to 24 to 36 inch-pounds. Screw which secures drive transfer tube clip is not installed at this time.

Installation on Control Valve Body

1. Install range selector valve detent ball and spring in control valve body.
2. Install valve body separator plate on valve body assembly.
3. Install assembled exhaust regulator valve body and tighten screws 24-36 inch-pounds.
4. Place control valve body, flat (top) side down on a flat surface. Check to determine if the end covers project below the valve body. Tap valve body downward to correct any such projection. Tighten all screws at front and rear of valve body 24-36 inch-pounds. *This check is important. The valve body must seat tightly against the oil transfer plate.*
5. Assemble pump overage spring retainer to each end of pump valve spring. Compress spring and install between ribs on valve body front cover.
6. Install pump overage valve assembly and fasten with retainer spring. *Seat of valve assembly must protrude at least 0.005 inch beyond valve body mounting plane to assure seating of the valve against oil transfer plate.*
7. Install high transfer tube with clip. Install drive transfer tube with clip. Tighten screws 24 to 36 inch-pounds. *Signal tube installed previously is not to be depressed further at any time after separator plate is installed.*

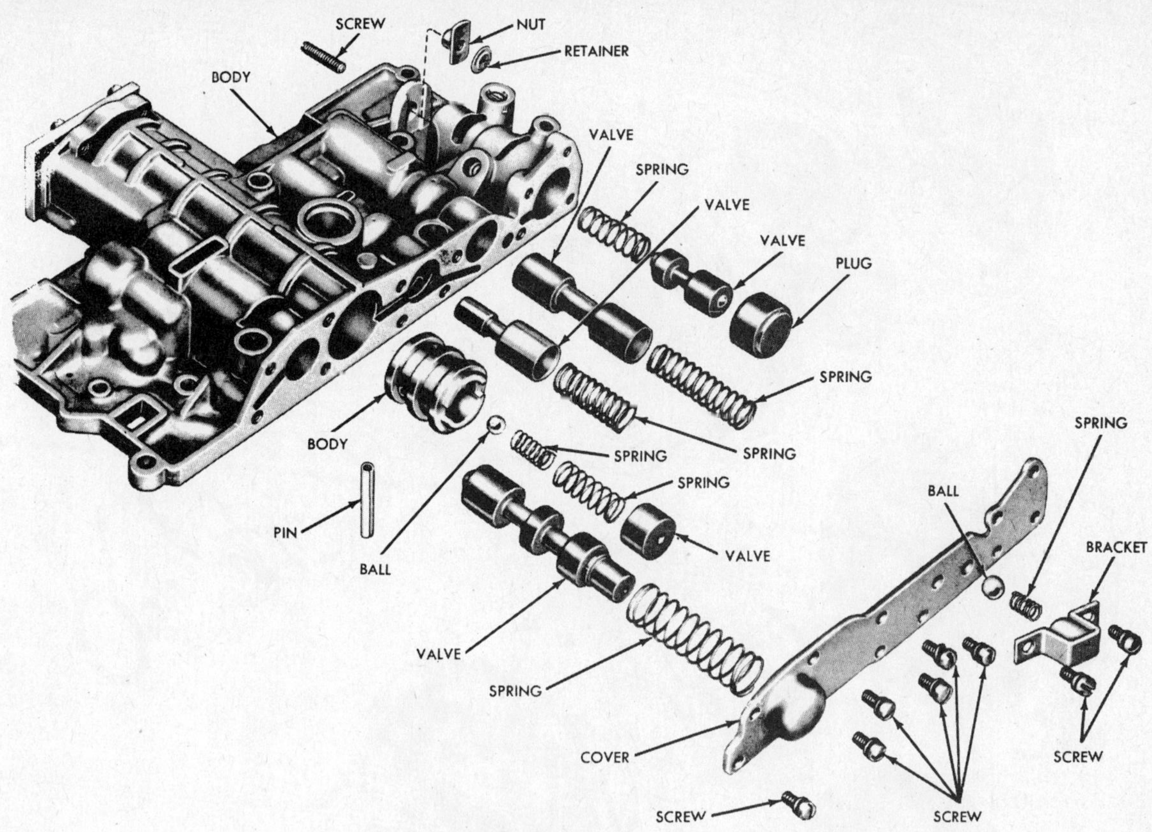

Exhaust regulator valve body (© Chrysler Corp.)

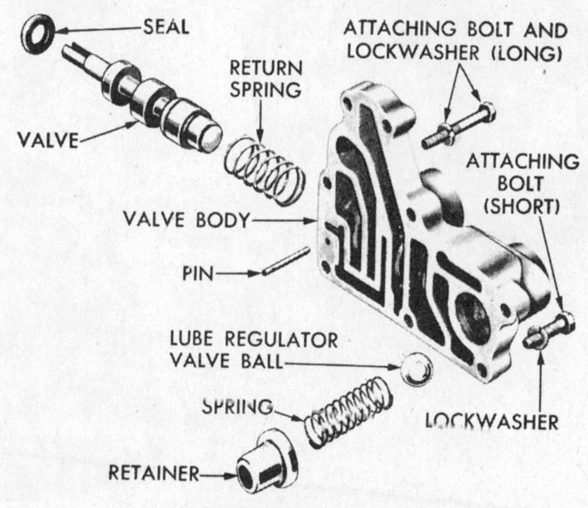

Hydraulic retarder valve body
(© Chrysler Corp.)

Hydraulic Retarder Control Valve Body

Disassembly

1. Place hydraulic retarder control valve body assembly on wood blocks or vise equipped with soft jaws (mounting surface downward).
2. Drive valve retaining pin out of valve body.
3. Place valve body on a wood surface (or vise equipped with soft jaws) with valve pointing upward. Using a soft hammer drive valve against spring in the body. The spring pressure will bounce valve back out and loosen the oil seal. *Remove any paint, dirt or burrs around seal to make seal removal operation easier.*
4. Remove seal, valve and spring from valve body. Loosen lubrication regulator valve retainer by tapping lightly around edge of retainer, then remove retainer, spring, and steel ball.

Assembly

1. Insert lubrication regulator valve steel ball in valve body and install lubrication regulator valve spring and retainer, starting the retainer straight in valve body.
2. Press retainer in until the large diameter is flush with mounting surface to .030 inch maximum below surface of valve body.
3. Insert the hydraulic retarder valve return spring in valve body bore, and insert valve against spring. The valve must move into the bore by its own weight.
4. Start valve retainer pin straight in body from mounting surface side of the body. Place valve body in a press so mounting surface is level and body is evenly supported. Hold valve in body against return spring and far enough to clear retaining pin holes, press pin into body.
5. Remove body from press and drive pin further to be sure it does not protrude above mounting surface of valve body.
6. Coat outer shell of a new valve oil seal with a suitable sealer and start seal straight into valve body. Press seal in until it is flush with valve body. *After assembly, valve must return to its normal position against retaining pin after actuation.*
7. Install hydraulic retarder valve body on transmission case transfer plate and range sele valve bodies in transmis

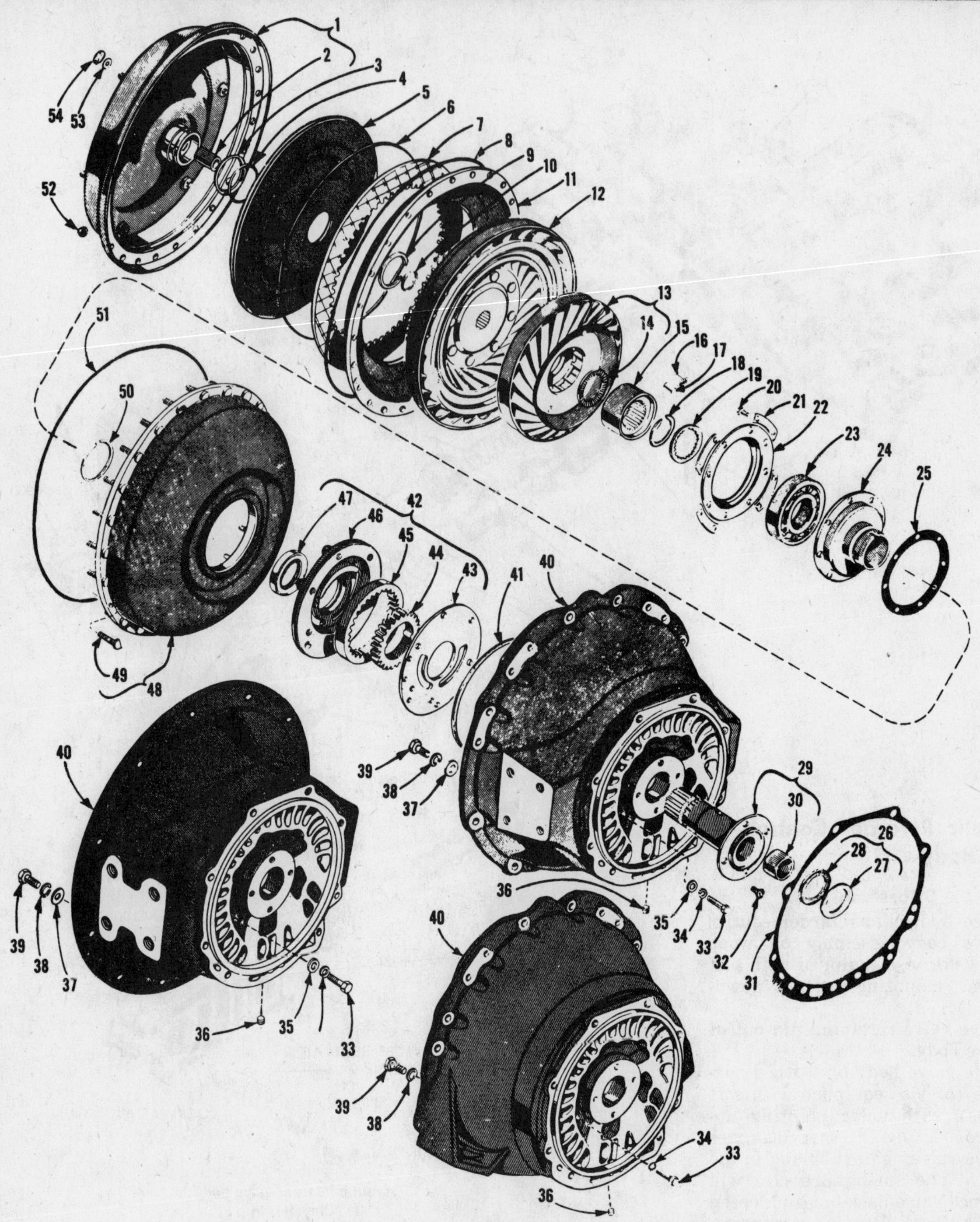

Torque converter, lock up clutch and front pump assemblies (© Chrysler Corp.)

1 Converter pump cover assembly
2 Bushing
3 Oil seal retainer
4 Oil seal
5 Lockup clutch piston assembly
6 Seal ring
7 Lockup clutch plate
8 Seal ring
9 Snap ring
10 Snap ring
11 Lockup clutch back plate
12 Turbine assembly
13 Stator and cam assembly
14 Thrust bearing assembly
15 Freewheel roller race
16 Freewheel roller spring
17 Freewheel roller
18 Snap ring
19 Spacer
20 Bolt, 1/4-20 x 5/8
21 Lock strip
22 Bearing retainer
23 Ball bearing
24 Converter pump hub
25 Converter pump hub gasket
26 Thrust bearing assembly
27 Needle thrust bearing race
28 Needle thrust bearing assembly
29 Converter ground sleever assembly
30 Bushing
31 Gasket
32 Self-locking bolt, 5/16-18 x 3/4
33 Bolt, 5/16-18 x1
34 Lock washer, 5/16
35 Plain washer, 5/16
36 Pipe plug, 1/8-27
37 Plain washer, 7/16
38 Lock washer, 7/16
39 Bolt, 7/16-14 x 2
40 Converter housing
41 Seal ring
42 Front oil pump assembly
43 Oil pump cover
44 Oil pump drive gear
45 Oil pump driven gear
46 Oil pump body
47 Seal
48 Converter pump assembly
49 Bolt, 5/16-24 x 1.30
50 Hook-type seal ring
51 Seal ring
52 Lock nut, 5/16-24
53 Spacer (AR)—
0.027 thk (gold)
0.045 thk (silver)
0.063 thk (copper)
0.081 thk (black)
0.099 thk (plain)
54 Retainer—0.015 thk

case. Make all necessary adjustments as outlined in adjustment section.

Servicing Torque Converter and Transmission out of Vehicle

Torque Converter Components

Removal

1. Drain oil from transmission.
2. Position transmission in a repair stand.
3. Remove pump cover assembly using a lifting strap and eye if necessary.
4. Remove lockup-clutch plate, seal ring and clutch back plate.
5. Remove hook-type seal ring, snap ring and seal ring.
6. Remove converter turbine assembly. Twist converter stator counterclockwise to lock it to the freewheel roller race and lift up while sliding fingers under the race end before it comes all the way off the shaft. Insert stator before releasing fingers.
7. Remove snap ring and converter pump spacer. Remove converter pump assembly. Remove converter housing.
8. Remove needle bearing assembly and needle bearing race, remove converter housing gasket.
9. Remove hydraulic retarder shaft and rotor assembly. Remove hook-type seal ring and thrust washer.

Oil Pan and Valve Body

Removal

1. Position transmission, bottom up and remove filter cover and seal ring.
2. Remove retainer, seal ring and filter element.
3. Remove oil pan.
4. Remove oil filter can assembly, remove seal ring from pipe.
5. Remove retarder valve body, 5/8 teflon ball and gasket.
6. Remove control valve body assembly, being very careful not to drop the two balls into the transmission case. Remove balls and spring.
7. Remove the downshift timing valve body assembly. Remove oil transfer plate assembly from case, being careful not to drop ball under plate into transmission case. Remove ball after plate is removed.

Rear Bearing Retainer

Removal

1. Position transmission with rear bearing retainer up. Remove speedometer drive (or plug).
2. Remove reverse, low and intermediate-range clutch reaction housing anchor bolt nuts, low

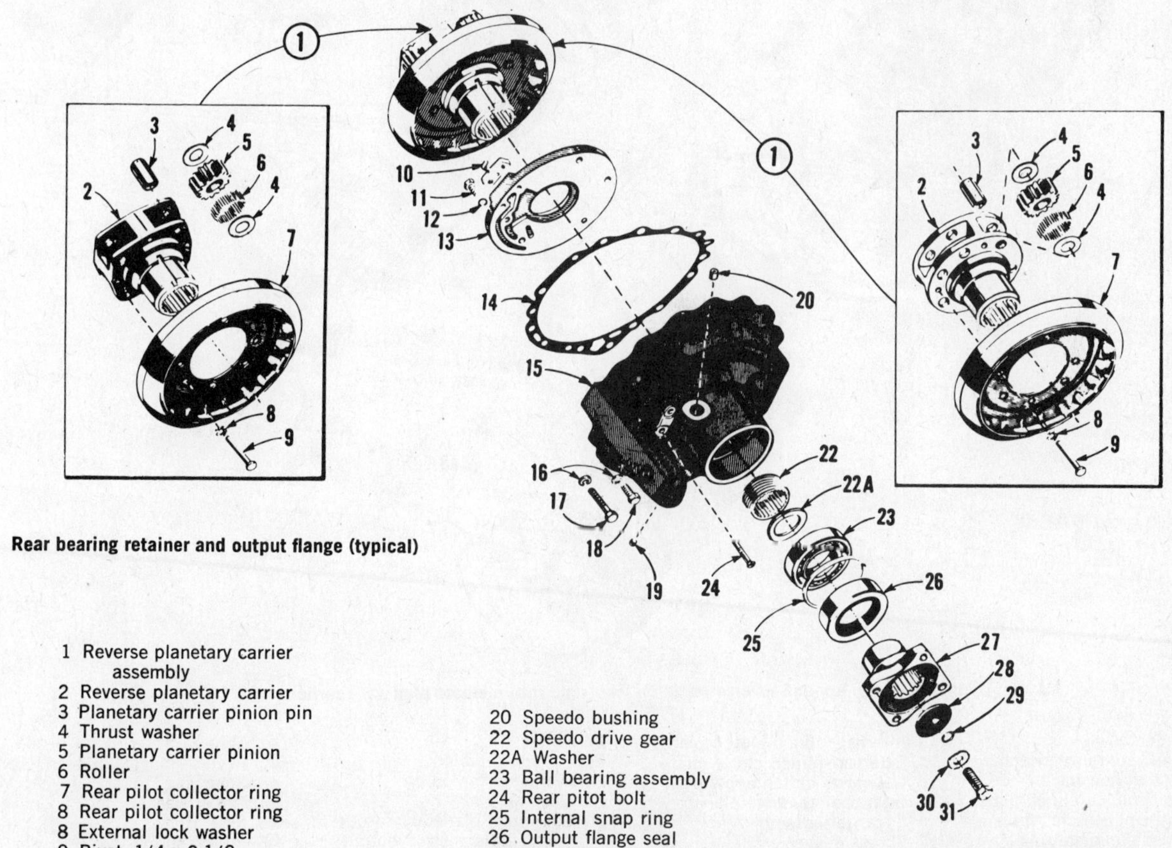

Rear bearing retainer and output flange (typical)

1 Reverse planetary carrier assembly
2 Reverse planetary carrier
3 Planetary carrier pinion pin
4 Thrust washer
5 Planetary carrier pinion
6 Roller
7 Rear pilot collector ring
8 Rear pilot collector ring
8 External lock washer
9 Rivet, 1/4 x 2-1/2
10 Rear pitot tube
11 Bolt, 5/16-18 x 1-3/8
12 Washer, 5/16 lock
13 Rear pitot adapter
14 Bearing retainer gasket (AR)—0.012 thk —0.016 thk —0.021 thk
15 Rear bearing retainer
16 Washer, 7/16 lock
17 Bolt, 7/16-14 x 2-1/2
18 Bolt, 7/16-14 x 1-3/8
19 Pipe plug, 1/8-27
20 Speedo bushing
22 Speedo drive gear
22A Washer
23 Ball bearing assembly
24 Rear pitot bolt
25 Internal snap ring
26 Output flange seal
27 Output flange
28 Flange retainer washer
29 Seal ring
30 Tab lock washer
31 Bolt, 1/2-20 x 1-1/2
36 Serrated shank bolt
37 Brake drum
38 Brake band assembly
39 Brake cam shoe
40 Brake adjusting bolt
41 Brake cam link
42 Cotter pin, 1/8 x 7/8
43 Clevis pin, 1/2 x 1-27/64
44 Lock washer, 1/4
45 Hexagon nut, 1/4-20
46 Brake cam
47 Brake release spring
48 Bolt
49 Brake bracket
52 Hexagon nut
53 Lock washer
55 Brake band anchor bolt spring
56 Clip screw
57 Lock wire

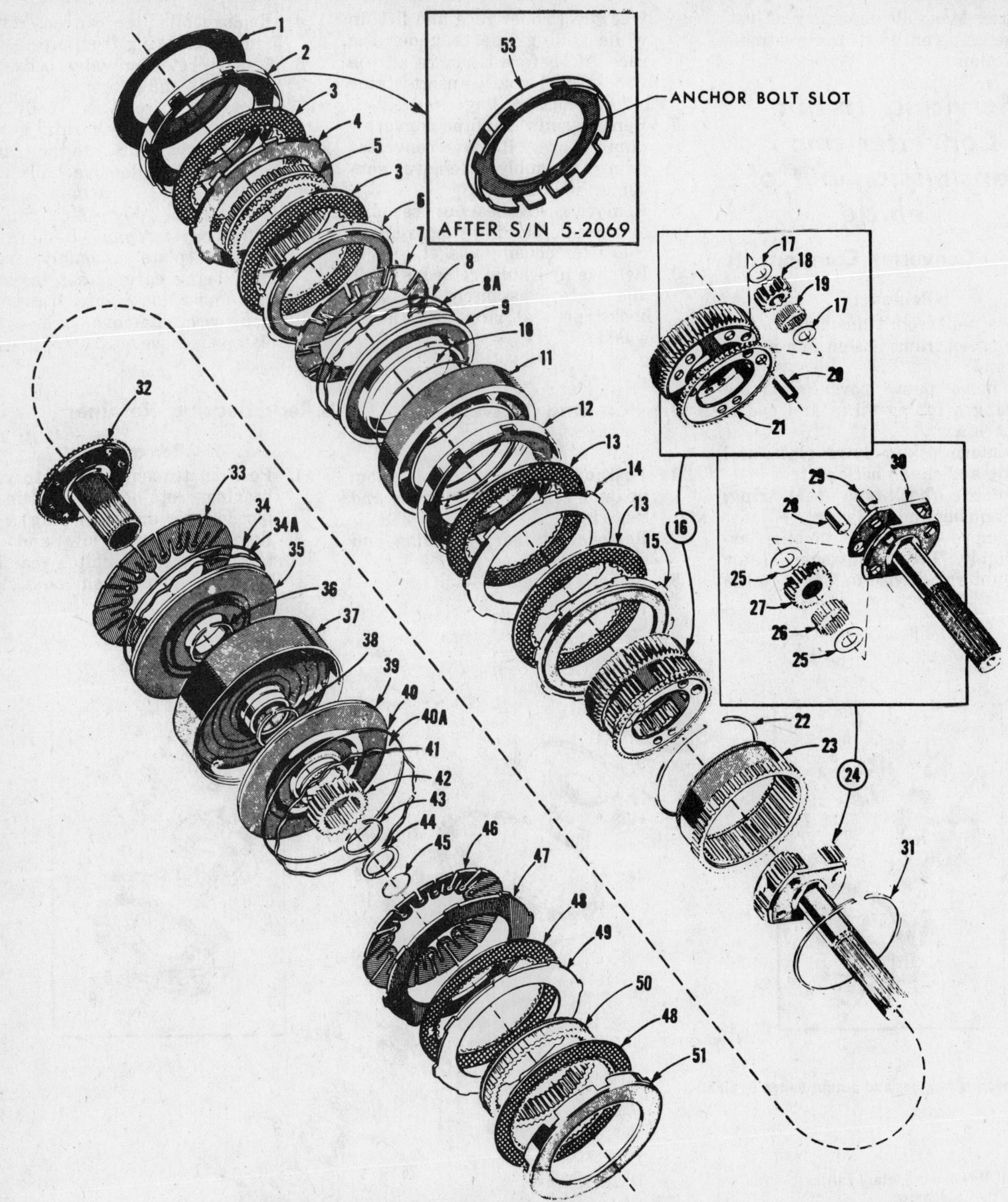

Intermediate, low and reverse range clutches and intermediate planetary carrier
(© Chrysler Corp.)

1 Oil collector
2 Intermediate-range clutch reaction housing
3 Internal-splined clutch plate
4 External-splined clutch plate
5 Intermediate-range ring gear assembly
6 Intermediate-range clutch apply plate
7 Intermediate-range clutch spring
8 Seal ring
8A Seal ring expander
9 Intermediate-range clutch piston
10 Hook-type seal ring
11 Intermediate-range piston housing
12 Low-range clutch reaction housing
13 Internal-splined clutch plate
14 External-splined clutch plate
15 Low-range clutch apply plate
16 Intermediate-range planetary carrier assembly
17 Thrust washer
18 Intermediate-range planetary pinion
19 Roller
20 Intermediate-range planetary pinion pin
21 Intermediate-range planetary carrier
22 Internal-snap ring
23 Low-range ring gear
24 Low-range planetary carrier and transmission output shaft assembly
25 Thrust washer
26 Roller
27 Planetary pinion
28 Planetary pinion pin
29 Bushing
30 Low-range planetary carrier and transmission output shaft
31 Internal-snap ring
32 Reverse-range sun gear shaft
33 Clutch spring
34 Seal ring
34A Seal ring expander
35 Low-range piston
36 Hook-type seal ring
37 Low and reverse-range piston housing
38 Hook-type seal ring
39 Reverse-range piston
40 Seal ring
40A Seal ring expander
41 Thrust washer
42 Reverse-range sun gear
43 Snap ring
44 Thrust washer
45 Snap ring
46 Clutch spring
47 Reverse-range clutch apply plate
48 Internal-splined clutch plate
49 External-splined clutch plate
50 Reverse-range ring gear assembly
51 Reverse-range clutch reaction housing
52 Clutch plate retaining ring
53 Clutch reaction housing (2, 12, 51)

and reverse-range piston housing anchor bolt and intermediate-range piston housing anchor bolt.
3. Remove rear bearing retainer from transmission housing.

Reverse Planetary Gearing and Clutch

Removal

1. Remove reverse-range planetary carrier assembly and thrust washer.
2. Lift out reverse-range clutch reaction housing with clutch plates and ring gear, place on a bench with plate up. Lift plates out of housing. *These parts have red markings and should not be intermixed with other clutches*
3. Lift out reverse-range clutch spring. Remove round wire snap ring, remove reverse-range reaction housing anchor bolt.
4. Using hoist and sling to release pressure from snap ring, remove snap ring from reverse-range sun gear shaft; disconnect slinge.
5. Remove reverse-range sun gear and internal splined reverse-range sun gear thrust washer.

Low and Intermediate-Range Gearing and Clutches

Removal

1. Working through openings in transmission housing, remove low and reverse-range piston housing assembly. *Keep fingers out of transmission housing.*
2. Lift out low-range clutch spring and low-range clutch apply plate. *Low-range clutch parts have green markings.*
3. Remove low-range clutch plates from transmission housing.
4. Remove internal snap ring from low-range ring gear and lift out reverse-range sun gear shaft.
5. Lift out transmsision output shaft assembly and the low-range ring gears and intermediate-range planetary assembly.
6. Remove low-range clutch reaction housing and anchor bolt.
7. Remove intermediate-range piston housing assembly from transmission.
8. Remove intermediate-range clutch spring and intermediate-range clutch apply plate from transmission housing. *Intermediate range clutch parts have yellow markings.*
9. Remove intermediate-range ring gear and clutch plates from intermediate-range clutch reaction housing. Remove intermediate range clutch reaction housing, anchor bolt and oil collector ring from transmission housing.

Splitter Mechanism, High-Range Clutch and Power Take-off Gear

Removal

1. Position transmission, converter end up. Remove low-splitter clutch reaction plate anchor bolt and the two high-range clutch diaphragm anchor bolts.
2. Remove low-splitter reaction plate from transmission housing. Remove high-range clutch diaphragm anchor bolt.
3. Install lifting eye into threaded hole in splitter output shaft. Hoist the entire splitter and high-range clutch section carefully from transmission housing.

Transmission and Component Parts Overhaul

Converter Pump Cover and Lockup Clutch

Disassembly

1. Remove lockup clutch back plate from converter pump cover, then lift out clutch plate. If necessary, tap edge of cover against a wooden block to remove back plate.
2. Remove seal ring from front flange of the back plate.
3. Remove snap ring from the lock-up clutch piston in pump cover, using compressor tool.
4. Remove piston from pump cover by tapping edge of cover against a wooden block.
5. Remove seal ring from outer groove in the piston.

Inspection

Clean all of the converter cover and lockup clutch parts and inspect for wear or damage. Replace all parts that are worn beyond the specified limits or that are damaged. (Consult Specifications).

Assembly

1. Install seal ring in outer groove in lockup clutch piston, then lightly oil the seal.
2. Install piston in converter pump cover so the dowel holes in piston engage dowels in the cover. *Be sure the balance marks on both parts are also aligned.* To align the parts correctly, place a heavy pencil mark in line with a dowel on bolt circle of the cover, then match this mark with another part on piston in line with a dowel hole on reverse side. *If dowels do not enter dowel holes, the lockup clutch will not disengage and the converter will not function.*
3. Install snap ring. If piston does not push far enough into pump cover to install the snap ring, use compressor tool to compress the piston.

Converter Pump

Disassembly

1. Remove seal ring from converter pump hub.
2. Tap out all damaged or worn converter pump bolts. Do not lose the positions of balance weights.
3. Flatten lock strip tabs and remove the four strips and eight bolts from bearing retainer. Remove retainer from pump.
4. Tap hub from the pump.
5. Remove the polyacrylate seal ring from the pump and the gasket ring from the hub.
6. Drive bearing from the hub, using a soft drift.

Assembly

1. If any converter pump bolts were removed, press new ones into place.
2. Install balance weights in their proper position.
3. Install a new polyacrylate seal ring in outer groove of pump face just inside bolt circle.
4. Install new seal ring on hub mounting surface groove of the pump.
5. Install bearing in pump hub and position hub in the pump.
6. Install gasket in pump hub.
7. Install bearing retainer on hub, align mounting holes and install the four locking strips and retainer-to-converter pump bolts. Torque bolts at 9 to 11 foot-pounds.

Converter Stator

Disassembly

Remove springs or rollers from stator.

Inspection

Check the stator for cracks or excessive wear. Check the springs and rollers for nicks, burrs, or other damage. Replace parts if necessary.

Assembly

1. Apply oil soluble grease in stator cam pockets, then place the overrun roller springs in openings with open ends facing stator bore.
2. Compress springs to allow roller to be inserted in shallow end of each cam pocket. Install one spring and roller in each of the ten pockets in the stator. When all springs and rollers have been installed, press them into the cam pockets to make room for the freewheel race.

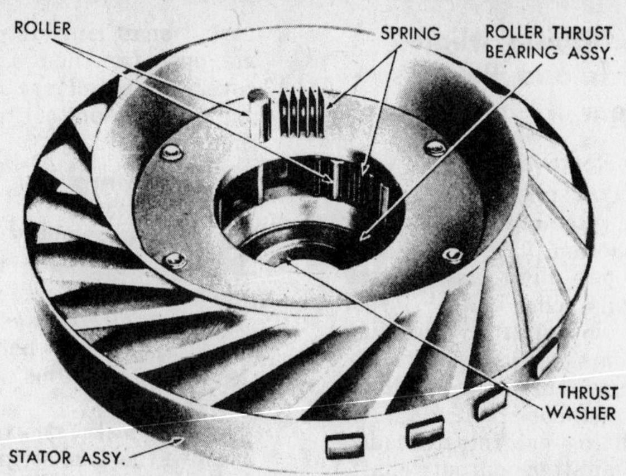

Converter stator

3. Install freewheel roller race. (counterbored side facing away from the stator), into the stator and cam assembly. Rotate freewheel roller race in a clockwise direction while installing it. When it is fully seated, twist it firmly in the opposite direction to lock it into the stator and cam assembly. Place stator and cam assembly so freewheel roller race is upward until installation.

Converter Housing and Front Pump

Disassembly

1. Remove bolts and lock washers that retain the front pump to the housing and remove pump body and gears.
2. Lift front pump cover and seal ring out of housing.
3. Remove gears from pump body and drive seal ring out of the front of pump body.
4. Remove bolts holding ground sleeve assembly to converter housing. Using a wood block drive shaft from housing.

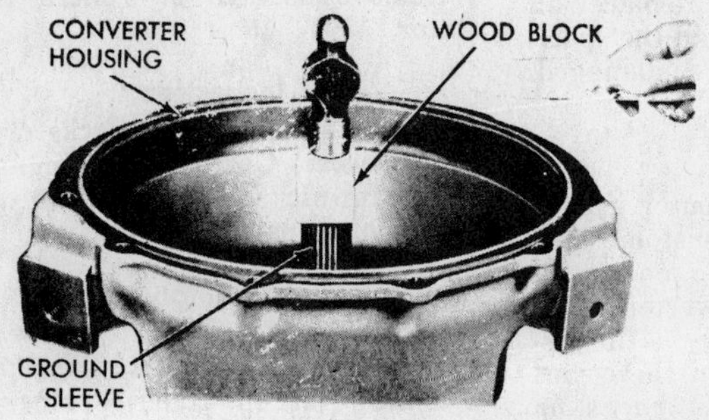

Removing converter ground sleeve

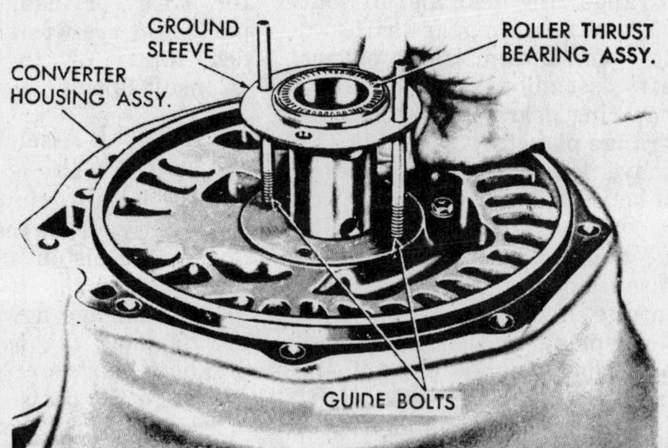

Positioning torque converter ground sleeve in housing

Assembly

1. Align holes in ground sleeve with holes in converter housing by installing two headless guide bolts. *The bolt holes are off-set and shaft cannot be rotated after it is driven into place.*
2. Place shaft through rear of housing and, using a wood block against rear of shaft, drive shaft tight against housing.
3. Replace the two headless bolts with retaining bolts and tighten to 17 to 20 foot-pounds.
4. Coat the outer diameter of a new front pump seal with sealing material. Start seal into front bore of pump body. Support the machined rear face of the pump body on a flat surface and drive seal into body, using driver.
5. The distance from surface of seal to the rear machined surface of pump body is 1.595-1.605 inches.
6. Place pump gears in pump body. Install the square section "O" type seal ring around pump cover.
7. Place pump in front of converter housing and install four bolts with lockwashers through rear of converter housing into the pump body.
8. Tighten the two remaining bolts with lock washers from 15 to 18 foot-pounds. Using oil soluble grease (to hold needle roller thrust bearing assembly in place), position bearing assembly in rear of ground sleeve.

Reverse and Intermediate Range Clutch Plates and Ring Gears

Disassembly

1. Straighten and remove clutch plate retainer ring at either side of plate.
2. Lift plate off the gear, then straighten and remove other ring.

Assembly

1. Engage the internal splines of clutch plate with external splines of ring gear, and position plate between the two grooves cut around outside diameter of ring gear.
2. Place a new clutch plate retainer ring in one of the two grooves and crimp the ring at five evenly spaced intervals around gear. *Do not crimp retainer ring at points where cutouts are in friction facings.*
3. Turn assembly over and install a second new retainer ring in the same manner as first ring.

Low Range and Reverse or Intermediate Range Piston Housing

Disassembly

1. Tap housing on a wood block to loosen and remove pistons.
2. Remove the polyacrylate seal ring from outer groove of piston and the hook type seal ring from housing, or from piston in the case of intermediate range piston.

Assembly

For assembly, reverse the disassembly procedure.

Stone chamfered edge of piston

housing to prevent cutting new piston seals. Lightly coat seals with oil and carefully install pistons.

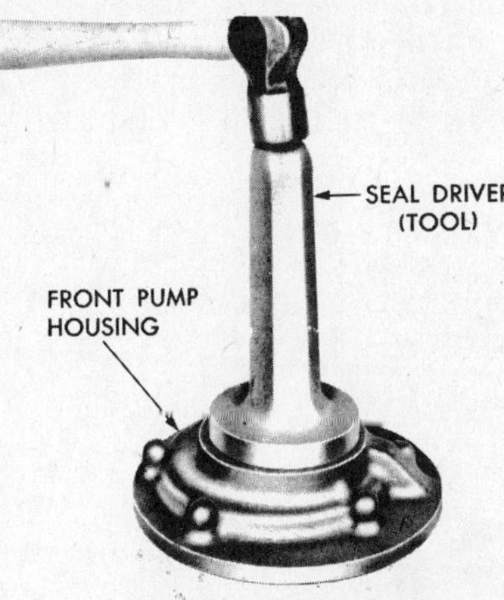

Installing front pump oil seal

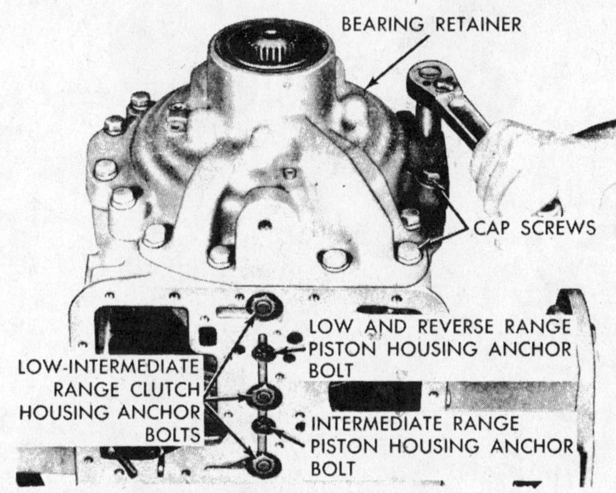

Anchor bolt locations

Low Range Ring Gear and Intermediate Range Planetary Carrier

Disassembly

1. Remove the snap ring that locks reverse range sun gear shaft to low range ring gear (if not previously done).
2. Remove internal snap ring from low range ring gear.
3. Remove intermediate range planetary carrier.

Assembly

1. Mesh external teeth of planetary carrier wtih internal teeth of ring gear and push carrier into ring gear.
2. Install internal snap ring to hold assembly together. *Refer to Paragraph "Procedure for Checking Range Clutch Clearances Before Installation."*

Splitter Mechanism, High Range Clutch and Power Take-off Gear

Shaft and Rotor Disassembly

1. Remove hook-type seal ring from groove in gear outside diameter of hydraulic retarder shaft and rotor assembly.
2. If bushing needs replacement, remove from large end of shaft.

Assembly

To assemble, reverse disassembly procedures.

Clutch Package Disassembly

Splitter Planetary Carrier

1. Remove splitter output shaft snap ring.
2. Remove splitter planetary carrier assembly and bronze splitter washer.
3. Do not disassemble carrier assembly. If there is evidence of excessive wear or damage, replace carrier assembly as a unit.

Splitter Clutches

1. Lift off splitter clutch assembly and place it flat side down. Lift off bronze thrust washer. (On models having an 8 tanged, low-splitter clutch plate, remove plate at this time.)
2. Remove high-splitter clutch reaction plate.
3. Remove one high-splitter clutch, internal splined plate, one external splined plate and the other internal splined plate.
4. Place splitter clutch housing assembly in a press and using a remover and installing sleeve, depress the high-splitter clutch piston return spring to remove pressure against snap ring. Remove snap ring and piston return spring.
5. Remove high-splitter clutch piston, seal ring and expander if used from piston outside diameter.
6. Remove hook-type seal ring from high-splitter clutch housing.
7. Replace splitter sun gear bushing if necessary.

High-Range Clutch Diaphragm

1. Remove the two hook-type seal rings from hub of high-range clutch diaphragm assembly.
2. Turn the diaphragm and high-range clutch assembly over so the rear end of splitter output shaft is up. *When turning assembly over, grip all components together to prevent damage to the pitot tube.*
3. Remove snap ring from rear end of splitter output shaft. Remove the low and intermediate-range sun gears.
4. Turn diaphragm and high-range clutch over, placing low-splitter clutch piston up. *When turning assembly over, grip all components together to prevent damage to the pitot tube.*
5. Remove splitter output shaft assembly, the two hook-type seal rings and two wire type snap rings. *Do not remove oriface plug in end of shaft.*
6. Place assembly in a press and using remover and installer sleeve, depress the low-splitter piston return spring to reline pressure on snap ring. Remove snap ring.
7. Remove low-splitter clutch piston, seal ring and seal expander if used from piston outside diameter.
8. Remove hook-type seal ring from hub of diaphragm.
9. Lift off high-range clutch diaphragm and remove the two hook-type seal rings from hub. Remove pitot tube.

High-Range Clutch and Piston

1. Turn high-range clutch over and remove internal snap ring from clutch housing.
2. Remove high-range clutch reaction plate.
3. On 5-plate clutch assemblies, remove three internal-splined and two external-splined high-range clutch plates. The 7-plate clutch assemblies have four internal-splined and three external-splined clutch plates. Remove power take-off gear (on those models which use a separate gear).
4. Block up the assembly so that no weight will be on the governor oil collector ring and use a press and a remover and installer sleeve to compress high-range

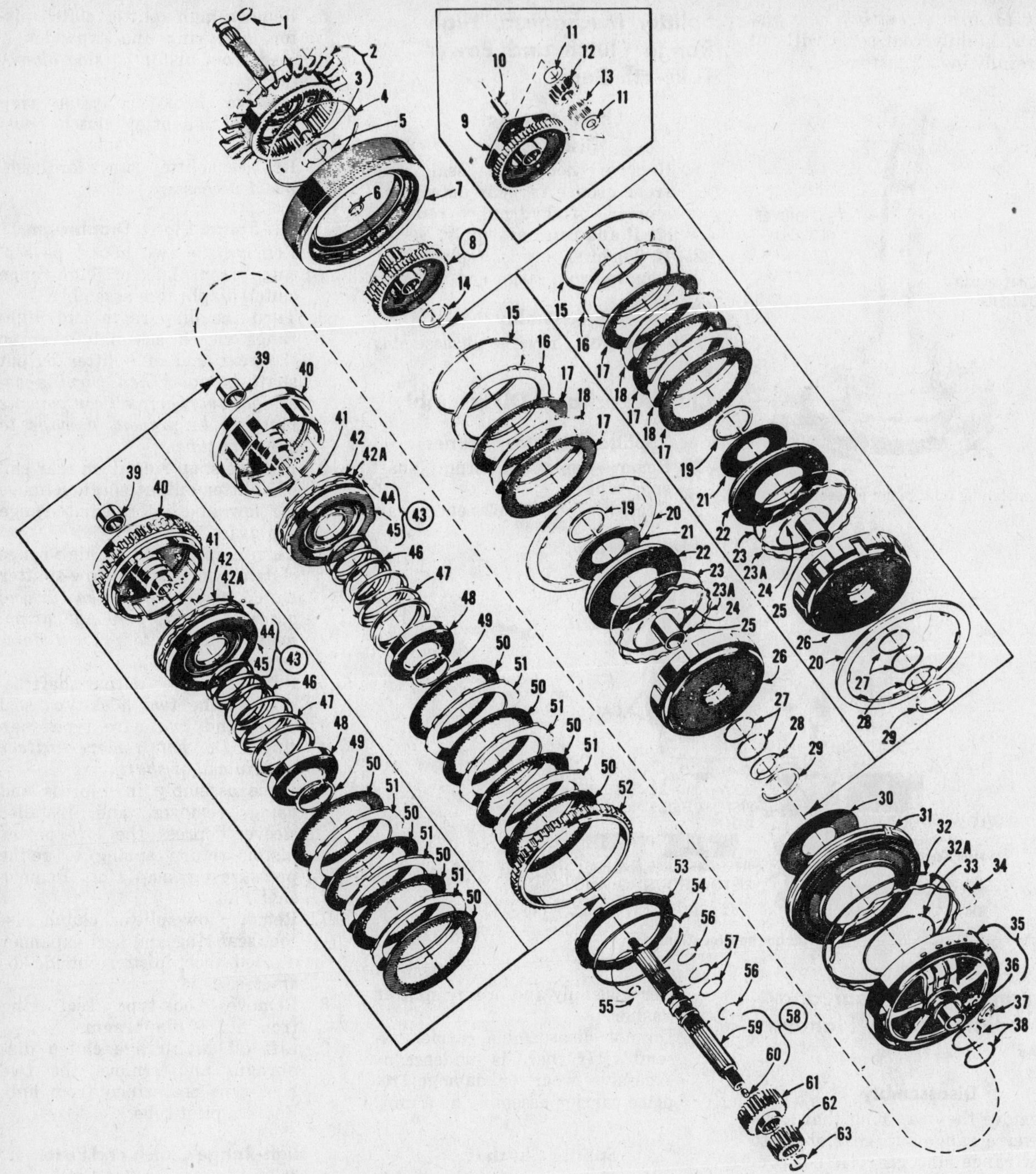

Splitter mechanism, hydraulic retarder and high range clutch (© Chrysler Corp.)

1 Hook-type seal ring
2 Turbine shaft and hydraulic retarder rotor assembly
3 Bushing
4 Hook-type seal ring
5 Thrust washer
6 Snap ring
7 Low-splitter clutch reaction plate
8 Splitter planetary carrier assembly
9 Splitter planetary carrier
10 Splitter planetary pin
11 Thrust washer
12 Splitter planetary pinion
13 Roller
14 Thrust washer
15 Internal-snap ring
16 High-splitter clutch reaction plate
17 Internal-splined clutch plate
18 External-splined clutch plate
19 Snap ring
20 Low-splitter clutch plate
21 Piston return spring
22 High-splitter piston
23 Seal ring
23A Seal ring expander
24 Hook-type seal ring
25 Bushing
26 High-splitter housing and gear assembly
27 Hook type seal ring
28 Thrust washer
29 Snap ring
30 Piston return spring
31 Low-splitter clutch piston
32 Seal ring
32A Seal ring expander
33 Hook-type seal ring
34 Screw and washer, 10-32 x 5/8
35 Diaphragm assembly
36 Sleeve
37 Front pitot tube
38 Hook-type seal ring
39 Bushing
40 High-range clutch housing assembly
41 Hook-type seal ring
42 Seal ring
42A Seal ring expander
43 High-range clutch piston assembly
44 Ball, 1/4 Dia.
45 High-clutch piston
46 Inner spring
47 Outer spring
48 High-range clutch spring retainer
49 Snap ring
50 Internal-splined clutch plate
51 External-splined clutch plate
52 Power take off gear
53 High-range clutch reaction plate
54 Snap ring
55 Hook-type seal ring
56 Wire-type snap ring
57 Hook-type seal ring
58 Splitter output shaft assembly
59 Splitter output shaft
60 Lube orifice plug
61 Intermediate-range sun gear
62 Low-range sun gear
63 Snap ring

clutch piston return springs. Remove snap ring. *Do not attempt to remove snap ring without a press.*

5. Remove the high-range clutch piston return spring retainer and two springs.
6. Tap rear of high-range clutch housing assembly on wood blocks to loosen piston. Remove high-range clutch piston seal ring (and expander, if used) from piston outside diameter. Remove hook-type seal ring from hub of high-range clutch housing.
7. Replace high-range clutch housing bushing (or needle bearing) if necessary.

Clutch Package Assembly

Splitter Clutches

1. If splitter sun gear bushing was removed from a high-splitter clutch housing, use a press and bushing installer to replace it.
2. Install hook-type seal ring on hub of high-splitter clutch housing assembly.
3. Install seal ring expander (if used) and seal ring in groove in high-splitter piston outside diameter and install piston in high-splitter clutch housing. On models which have external tangs on high-splitter piston, align the tangs with any opposite pair of slots in high-splitter housing. On models having dowels in high-splitter housing, be sure they are inserted in high-splitter piston recesses.
4. Using a press and installer sleeve, install the high-splitter piston return spring, concave side down, install snap ring. *Depress spring only enough to install snap ring.*
5. On models using a 6-tanged plate, install the low-splitter, internal tanged clutch plate, making sure that tangs are not in the same slots as piston tangs. *Low-splitter clutch failure will result if piston tangs and clutch tangs are in the same slot.*
6. In 3-plate clutch assemblies, install an internal-splined plate, the external-splined and the other internal-splined plate. In 5-plate assemblies, install another external-splined plate and another internal-splined plate.
7. Install high-splitter clutch reaction plate with smooth side facing clutch plates. Install snap ring.

High-Range Clutch and Piston

1. If the high-range clutch housing bushing was removed from the housing, install a new bushing. Press bushing flush to 0.010 below surface. On models using a needle bearing at this location, install new needle bearing numbered end out. Using a suitable tool, press against bearing shell and square with bore, press bearing flush to 0.010 below surface.
2. Install hook-type seal ring on hub of high-range clutch housing.
3. Install seal ring expander (if used) and seal ring in groove in outside diameter of high-range clutch piston and install high-range clutch piston in housing, smooth side first. *On models using pistons with external tangs, tangs must be engaged in slots in housing. On models using dowels in housing, dowels must engage recesses in piston.*
4. Install the two high-range clutch piston return springs and place cup of retainer over spring.
5. Place the assembly in a press keeping governor oil collector ring off the bench. Compress springs and install snap ring.
6. On the 5-clutch plate model, install an internal-splined, high-range clutch plate first, then install an external-splined plate, another internal-splined plate, another external-splined plate and a third internal-splined

Installing high range clutch housing bushing
(© Chrysler Corp.)

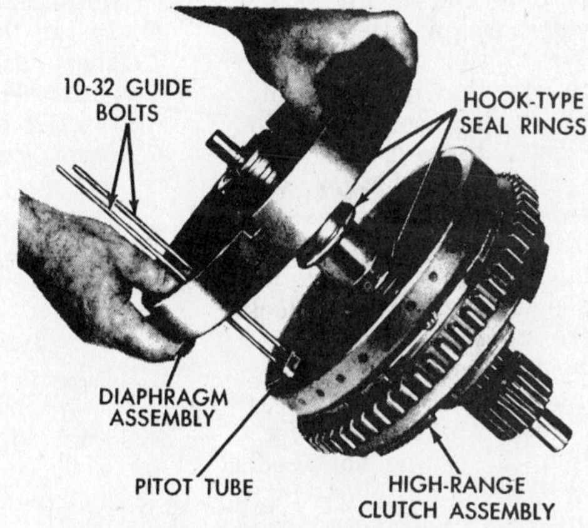

Installing high range clutch diaphram assembly
(© Chrysler Corp.)

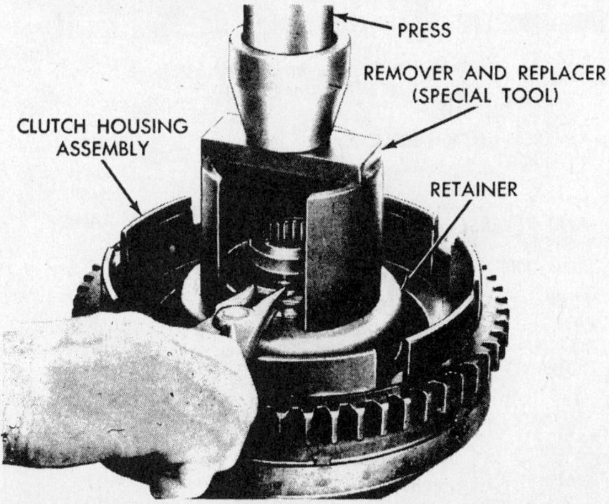

Installing high range clutch spring retainer snap ring
(© Chrysler Corp.)

plate. For the 7-plate model, install a third external-splined plate and a fourth internal-splined plate.

7. Install power take-off gear with end slots up (on models using a separate gear).
8. Install high-range clutch reaction plate so the two longer tangs engage slots in power take-off gear. Install internal snap ring. See paragraph on "checking range clutch clearances" using clearance tolerance of 0.040-0.050.

Splitter and High-Range Clutch Package

1. Install a wire type snap ring in groove around spline on ends of splitter output shaft. Install two hook-type seal rings in seal ring grooves near center of shaft. Install shaft into high-range clutch housing orifice end first.
2. Install intermediate and low-range sun gears (chamfered end out) on output shaft, orifice end.
3. Install snap ring on orifice end of splitter output shaft.
4. Install two hook-type seal rings on long hub end of high-range clutch diaphragm assembly. Install two 10-32 guide bolts in front pitot tube with tube center oil hole facing bolts. Position guide bolts through the high-range clutch diaphragm with pitot tube tip toward outside diameter. Guide the pitot tube into oil slinger trough and carefully slide sleeve over the two hook-type seal rings on splitter shaft and the two hook seal rings on diaphragm hub into high-range clutch hub. Diaphragm sleeve end enters a bushing (or needle bearing) in clutch hub. Replace the guide bolts with screws and washers and torque to 30-48 inch-pounds.
5. Install hook-type seal ring on hub diaphragm. Install seal ring expander (if used) with ends down toward piston, and seal ring in groove in outside diameter of low-splitter clutch piston.
6. Install low-splitter clutch piston into diaphragm assembly. Install piston return spring with inside cone up. Seat snap ring against spring with hammer and drift.
7. Install two hook-type rings on hub of diaphragm assembly. Grease and install bronze thrust washer in bore of splitter clutch housing.
8. On models using the 8-tanged low-splitter clutch plate, install the plate on the assembled high-splitter clutch engaging the 8 slots on outside of housing. (Six tang plate is installed at time of high splitter plate installation). Install the assembled splitter clutch on diaphragm hub using care as hook-type seal enter housing.
9. Install a greased bronze thrust washer in hub of splitter planetary carrier.
10. Install splitter planetary carrier assembly into clutch housing. Install snap ring.

Range Selector and Throttle Control Levers

1. Install a new "O" type seal ring on range selector lever shaft and insert shaft (from inside transmission) through transmission housing.
2. Install range selector valve lever (external) on shaft so that both lever and shaft arms point approximately toward bottom of transmission.
3. Install range selector lever washer and nut and tighten nut from 14 to 17 foot-pounds. *Bend washer against a flat on nut.*
4. Install a new "O" type seal ring on throttle control lever shaft and insert shaft through range selector shaft from inside transmission.
5. Install throttle external lever on shaft so that both lever and shaft arms point approximately toward bottom of transmission.
6. *Bend washer against a flat on nut and tighten from 14 to 17 foot-pounds.*

Procedure for Checking Range Clutch Clearances Before Installation

If any pistons, piston housings, apply plates, reaction housings, cushion springs or clutch plates have been replaced in the low-intermediate or reverse range clutches, clutch clearances must be checked. This can be done prior to assembly in transmission housing, by using a fixture tool.

1. Place intermediate range clutch reaction housing (coded yellow) in fixture tool with four of the housing lots adjacent to the four posts of the tool. Various clutch parts are color coded. These parts should be assembled in the same location when transmission is serviced to insure proper fitting. Parts coded with yellow are for intermediate range clutch, those coded green are for low range clutch, and red marking identifies reverse range clutch parts.
2. Place intermediate range clutch plate and ring gear in intermediate range reaction housing, long part of ring gear down.
3. Install intermediate range clutch plate. Install intermediate range clutch cushion spring with convex side up.
4. Install intermediate range clutch piston and piston housing (piston down).
5. Install low range clutch reaction

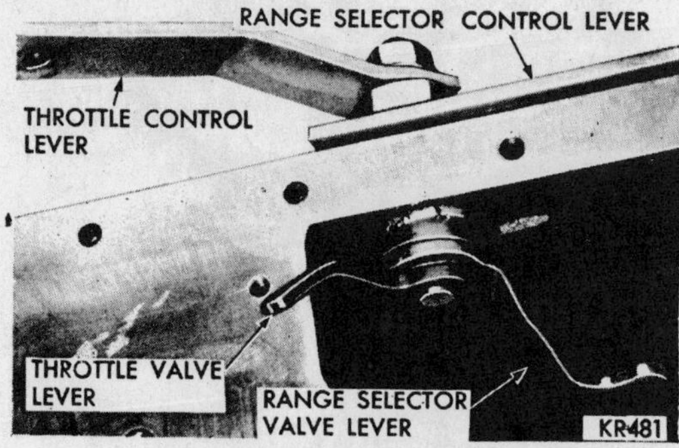

Internal control lever identification
(© Chrysler Corp.)

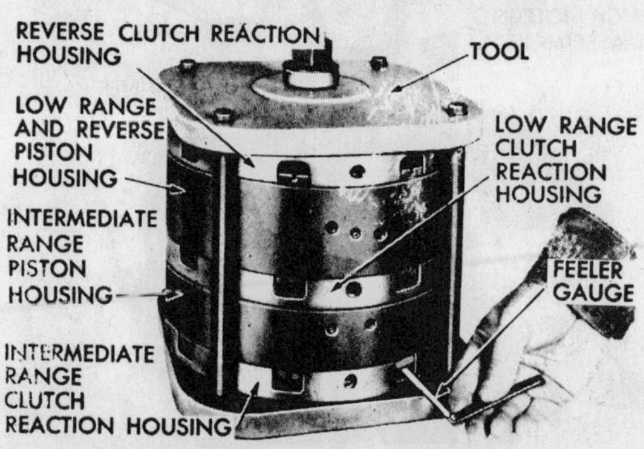

Checking range clutch clearance using fixture
(© Chrysler Corp.)

housing (slots up).

6. Install low range clutch plate (flat side down). Install low range cushion spring with convex side up.
7. Install low and reverse range piston and housing assembly with red marking up. Install reverse range cushion spring with convex side down.
8. Install the reverse range clutch plate (flat side up). Install reverse range clutch reaction housing (slots down). Place top plate of fixture tool on clutch stack.
9. Install top to tool and tighten nut to 30 foot-pounds. *Make certain cushion springs and other components are all concentric as pressure is applied.*
10. Using a feeler gauge, measure clearances between clutch friction plates and clutch plates of reverse range clutch. Repeat this procedure for low range clutch.
11. Clearance should be .010 to .015 inches for reverse range and low range clutch. The intermediate range clutch should show a clearance of .020 to .030 inches.
12. If clutches do not meet specified clearances, it will be necessary to change the apply plates. Apply plates are available for reverse, low, and intermediate ranges in three thicknesses for each clutch. The thicknesses are: .458 inch to .462, .465 inch to .469 inch, and .472 inch to .476 inch.
13. By measuring the maximum thickness of the apply plate from clutch stack, and by considering the clearance measurement taken while stack is assembled, the correct plate (required to bring the clearance to specifications) may be chosen.
14. When the correct clutch clearances for three ranges have been made, remove clutch pack from fixture and place on a bench in reverse order. In this way, each part may be selected in correct order for assembly in transmission.

Installation of Subassemblies in Transmission Housing

All clutch plates must be soaked in specified transmission oil for 2 minutes before being installed. All thrust surfaces, gears, bushings and bearings must be oiled as they are installed.

Splitter Mechanism, High Range Clutch and Power Take-off Gear

Installation

1. Using a lifting eye, install the splitter section and high range clutch assembly. The three anchor bolt holes in the high range clutch diaphragm assembly must align with three holes in transmission housing (two holes in the bottom and one hole in the top of housing).
2. Install the three anchor bolts (the shorter bolt is installed at top of transmission). Tighten the two bottom bolts to 17-20 foot-pounds. *Do not tighten the top bolt at this time. Failure to tighten the bolts in the correct sequence may result in internal oil leakage.*

Hydraulic Retarder

Installation

1. Install low splitter clutch reaction plate with *vanes toward front of housing and the anchor bolt hole in line with hole in bottom of housing.*
2. Install reaction plate anchor bolt and tighten to 17-20 foot-pounds. Tighten the support anchor bolt (at the top of the transmission) to 17-20 foot-pounds.
3. Install the hook type seal ring around splitter ring gear of turbine shaft and hydraulic retarder rotor.

Installing low splitter clutch reaction plate
(© Chrysler Corp.)

4. Make sure thrust washer is in front of the splitter planetary carrier assembly and the hook type seal ring is in the groove at front of splitter output shaft assembly. Oil the thrust washer and hook type seal ring, then install turbine shaft and hydraulic retarder rotor assembly. *Be careful to avoid damaging the hook type seal ring at the front of the splitter output shaft.*

Torque Converter Components

Installation

1. Place converter housing gasket on transmission housing. Tape rotor shaft for protection, remove tape after stator is installed.
2. Check needle roller thrust bearing assembly to be sure that it is being held in place at rear of reaction shaft by oil soluble grease.
3. Install converter housing on transmission housing assembly and tighten the 10 mounting bolts and lock washers from 42 to 50 foot-pounds.
4. Install the hook type seal ring on converter pump hub.
5. Install converter pump in converter housing. Make sure the slots in the hub mate with the front pump drive lugs and the hook type seal ring on hub passes through front pump seal without damage to seal ring or seal.
6. Install seal in groove just inside the bolt circle.
7. Install the overrun race spacer on reaction shaft with concave side up.
8. Install a new snap ring to hold the spacer.
9. Carefully install the assembled stator and roller race. *The stator when installed, should overrun in the direction of the arrow on the converter pump and should lock when turned in the opposite direction.*
10. Install torque converter turbine on turbine shaft.
11. Install snap ring and hook type seal ring on turbine shaft. Install the polyacrylate seal ring in groove just inside the bolt circle on front of the lockup clutch back plate. *Be sure the seal is in place inside the bolt circle of converter pump.*
12. Install back plate. *If inked balance marks are found on back plate, converter pump lockup piston and pump cover, assemble the parts with marks aligned.*
13. Install lockup clutch plate on back plate with integral teeth engaging the turbine splined ring.
14. Install converter pump cover assembly on converter pump stud. If balance marks are on cover and pump align balance marks.

15. Install four nuts at 90 degree intervals and tighten alternately to 10 foot-pounds to prevent the polyacrylate seal from being forced out of its groove. Install the remaining nuts and tighten all nuts from 19 to 23 foot-pounds.

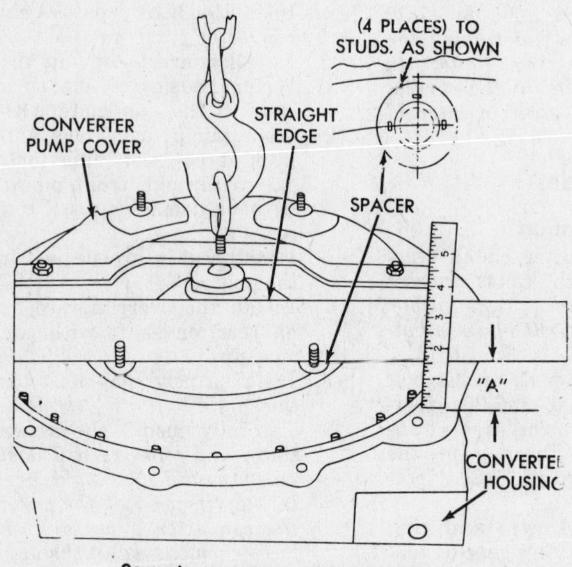

Converter pump cover shim selector

16. If any of the parts listed below are replaced in the course of transmission assembly, the dimension indicated by "A" must be checked. The required dimension is 1.572-1.592 inches. Parts replacement which may affect dimension "A" are: the converter pump cover assembly, lockup clutch reaction plate, converter pump, converter pump hub, converter reaction shaft assembly or the converter housing.
17. Dimension "A" may be checked by fastening a sling or strap to two opposite converter pump cover studs and applying a pull of 100 pounds or more to remove all end play. While the pull is applied, measure distance "A". If the dimension is not within 1.572-1.592 inch, install or remove converter stack control spacers at the pump cover studs as needed.
18. The correct dimension should be established at each of the six stud positions. The spacers are furnished as follows:

Thickness	*Color Code*
.027-inch	Gold
.045-inch	Silver
.063-inch	Copper
.081-inch	Black
.099-inch	Plain

When the correct dimension is established, stake the spacers to the studs.

Low-Intermediate Range Clutches, Gearing and Low Range and Reverse Clutch Piston Housing

Installation

1. Position transmission rear end up. Install oil collector with the conical portion facing toward front of the housing.
2. Install the intermediate range clutch reaction housing so threaded anchor bolt hole is aligned with anchor hole in the bottom of the transmission housing.
3. Install anchor bolt (do not tighten) *Refer to disassembly procedure for the color coding of the clutch components.*
4. Install the intermediate range ring gear .296 inch to .300 inch thick with the longer section of gear toward front of transmission and toward reaction plate.
5. Install the intermediate range clutch apply plate. Install the intermediate range clutch spring *with convex side toward rear of transmission. Make sure the spring is centered perfectly on the clutch apply plate on which it seats so the intermediate range piston housing will seat properly around it.*
6. Install the intermediate range piston housing, and with taped hole in piston housing in line with the corresponding anchor bolt hole in bottom of transmission housing.
7. Install (but do not tighten) the intermediate range clutch piston housing anchor bolt.
8. Install the low range clutch reaction housing, aligning taped hole in the plate with its corresponding anchor bolt hole in bottom of transmission housing.
9. Install the low range ring gear and intermediate range planetary carrier. Rotate assembly until planetary pinion teeth engage internal teeth of the intermediate range ring gear.

Installing oil connector ring

10. Install (but do not tighten) the reaction housing anchor bolt.
11. Install clutch plate and clutch apply plate.
12. Install transmission output shaft assembly, engaging the planetary pinion teeth with the internal teeth of the low range ring gear.
13. Install the reverse sun gear shaft over the output shaft. Mesh teeth on flange with internal teeth of the low range ring gear.
14. Install a new snap ring in the internal groove of low range ring gear, then install low range clutch spring *with convex side toward rear of transmission.* Make sure the spring is centered on the clutch apply plate so low range reverse clutch piston housing will seat around it.
15. Install assembled low range and reverse clutch piston housing, aligning tapped hole in piston housing with corresponding anchor bolt hole in bottom of transmission housing. *Refer to disassembly procedure for correct color code. Do not install the anchor bolt at this time.*

Reverse Range Planetary Gearing and Clutch

Installation

1. Install splined thrust washer and sun gear on reverse range sun gear shaft.

Using hoist to install snap ring

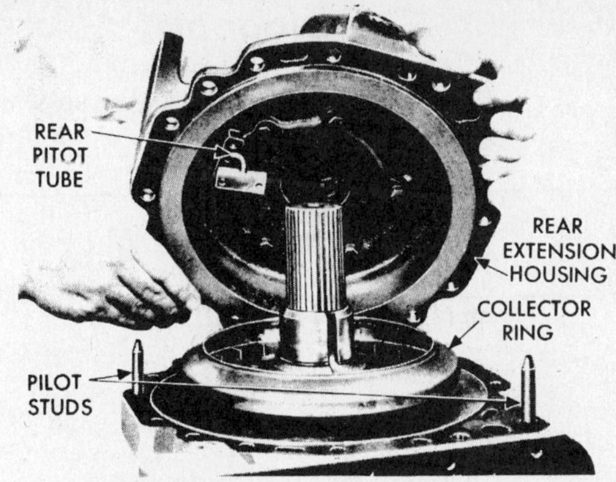

Pilot tube alignment and extension housing installation

2. Place snap ring on transmission output shaft, using a hoist, raise the output shaft and sun gear shaft until snap ring groove in sun gear shaft clears sun gear. Install snap ring.
3. Lift transmission output shaft and install snap ring.
4. Press low and reverse range piston housing into transmission housing and finger tighten anchor bolt. Install reverse range clutch spring with concave side up, center spring carefully. Depress spring edge and install anchor bolt through hole from inside transmission.
5. Place clutch apply plate on a bench with flat surface up. Position the reverse ring gear and clutch plate assembly on the apply plate with longer section of ring gear (external teeth up). Over these two parts, position reverse reaction housing with slots down so slots engage clutch apply plate tangs.
6. Install this assembly in transmission housing aligning anchor bolt slot in reaction housing with anchor bolt head previously installed in transmission housing. Anchor bolt nut, finger tighten.
7. Install reverse planetary carrier and rear pitot collector ring on the output shaft. *Make sure the planetary pinions mesh with the sun gear and internal teeth of reverse ring gear.*

Rear Bearing Extension and Output Flange

Installation

1. Install the rear bearing retainer (without a gasket) on rear of transmission housing. Install four retainer mounting bolts at 90° intervals and tighten the bolts to 7 foot-pounds. Draw bearing retainer down evenly.
2. Check clearance between bearing retainer and rear surface of transmission housing near the points bolts. This clearance will determine which gaskets to use.
3. Gaskets are available in .012, .016 and .021 inch thicknesses. If the gaskets are not clearly marked, measure each with a micrometer. If clearance is .005-.015 inch, use the .012 gasket. If clearance is .015-.021 inch use the .016 gasket. If clearance is .022-.027 inch use the .021 gasket. For clearance of .028-.029 inch, use one .012 and one .016 gasket.
4. Install but do not tighten the low range reverse clutch piston housing and reverse clutch reaction housing anchor bolts.
5. Remove the bearing retainer. Tighten the five anchor bolts to 10-foot-pounds at this time.
6. Install the previously selected rear bearing retainer gasket.
7. Install two guide bolts in the rear pitot tube. Make sure the open (drilled port) side of the pitot tube is toward the bolts.
   To make a guide bolt, thread one end of a 6 inch by ¼ inch diameter brazing rod. Use a ¼ inch—28 die and thread for a distance of ⅜ inch. Round off the unthreaded end.
8. Swing the pitot tube toward the center of bearing retainer so that it will clear the pitot collector ring when the retainer is installed, install retainer.
9. Turn pitot tube to its normal position and start the other mounting bolt. Leave 1/16 inch or more of the mounting bolts protruding at rear of retainer.
10. Place the pitot tube in the rear pitot collector ring with tube portion toward the vanes and guide bolts toward rear of transmission. Carefully lower the rear bearing retainer over the output shaft while guiding the ends of the guide bolts through the pitot tube mounting bolt holes in the retainer. *Do not remove the pitot tube guide bolts at this time. Do not turn the output shaft until the output flange retaining bolt is installed. Otherwise, damage to the pitot tube or governor vanes may result.*
11. Install the rear bearing retainer bolts and lock washers. Tighten from 42-50 foot-pounds. Tighten the two anchor bolts to 17 to 20 foot pounds. Tighten the three self locking anchor bolt nuts to 35 to 40 foot-pounds.
12. Replace the two guide bolts with pitot tube bolts and tighten to 8-10 foot-pounds.
13. Install the output flange. *Do not turn the output shaft while installing flange.. If shaft is turned, damage to the pitot tube or governor may result.*
14. Install the "O" type seal ring, tab lock washer and output flange bolt. Tighten bolt from 83 to 100 foot-pounds.
15. Install the speedometer fitting in rear bearing extension housing.

Diagnosis

This guide covers the most common symptoms and is an aid to careful diagnosis. The items to check are listed in sequence to be followed for quickest results. Follow the checks in the order given for the particular transmission type.

TROUBLE SYMPTOMS	Items to Check In Truck	Items to Check Out of Truck
Harsh N to D or N to R shift	CDEFGIJ	ab
Delayed Shift—N to D	ACIHKJ	ca
Runaway on upshift and 3-2 kickdown	ABCDLIHK	b
Harsh upshift and 3-2 kickdown	BCDLIHJ	b
No upshift	ABCDLIHKM	b
No kickdown on normal downshift	ABNCDLIHKM	d
Erratic shifts	ABNCFOPQ IKMJ	c
Slips in forward drive positions	ACIHK	abd
Slips in reverse only	CEGIK	
Slips in all positions	ACOIK	e
No drive in any position	ACOQIKJ	ca
No drive in forward positions	CDOLIHK	abd
No drive in reverse	CEGKMI	b
Drives in neutral	NIJ	a
Drags or locks	DELG	abfd
Noises	AORPMIJ	a
Hard to fill or blows out	AORSTQI	
Transmission overheats	ADEORTMI	abe
Unable to push-start car (No rear pump after 1965)	ACEGI	g

Key to Checks

A. Oil level
B. Control linkage
C. Oil pressure check
D. Kickdown band
E. Low-reverse band
F. Improper engine idle
G. Servo linkage
H. Accumulator
I. Valve body assembly
J. Manual valve lever
K. Air pressure check
L. K-D servo link
M. Governor
N. Gear shift cable
O. Regulator valve and/or spring
P. Output shaft bushing
Q. Strainer
R. Converter control valve
S. Breather clogged
T. Cooler or lines

a. Front-kickdown clutch
b. Rear clutch
c. Front pump and/or sleeve
d. Overrunning clutch
e. Converter
f. Planetary
g. Rear pump (not after 1965)

General Information

The Torqueflite transmission combines a torque converter with a fully automatic three-speed gear system. The converter housing and transmission case are combined into one aluminum casting. The transmission consists of two multiple-disc clutches, an overrunning clutch, two servos and bands, and two planetary gear sets. This provides three forward speeds and one reverse.

The torque converter is driven by the crankshaft, through a bolted-on, flexible driving plate. Cooling of the converter-transmission assembly is controlled by circulating the transmission fluid through a cooler core, located in the radiator lower tank. The torque converter assembly is a sealed unit, impractical to service in the field, except for cleaning.

For information relative to application, such as linkage adjustments, and unit removal and replacement, refer to the truck section.

Starting in 1966, the rear pump has been eliminated from the Torqueflite transmission assembly.

Operating differences are essentially, that the governor receives oil from the manual control valve rather than from the rear pump, then distributes it to the shift valves, according to the pressures supplied to the governor.

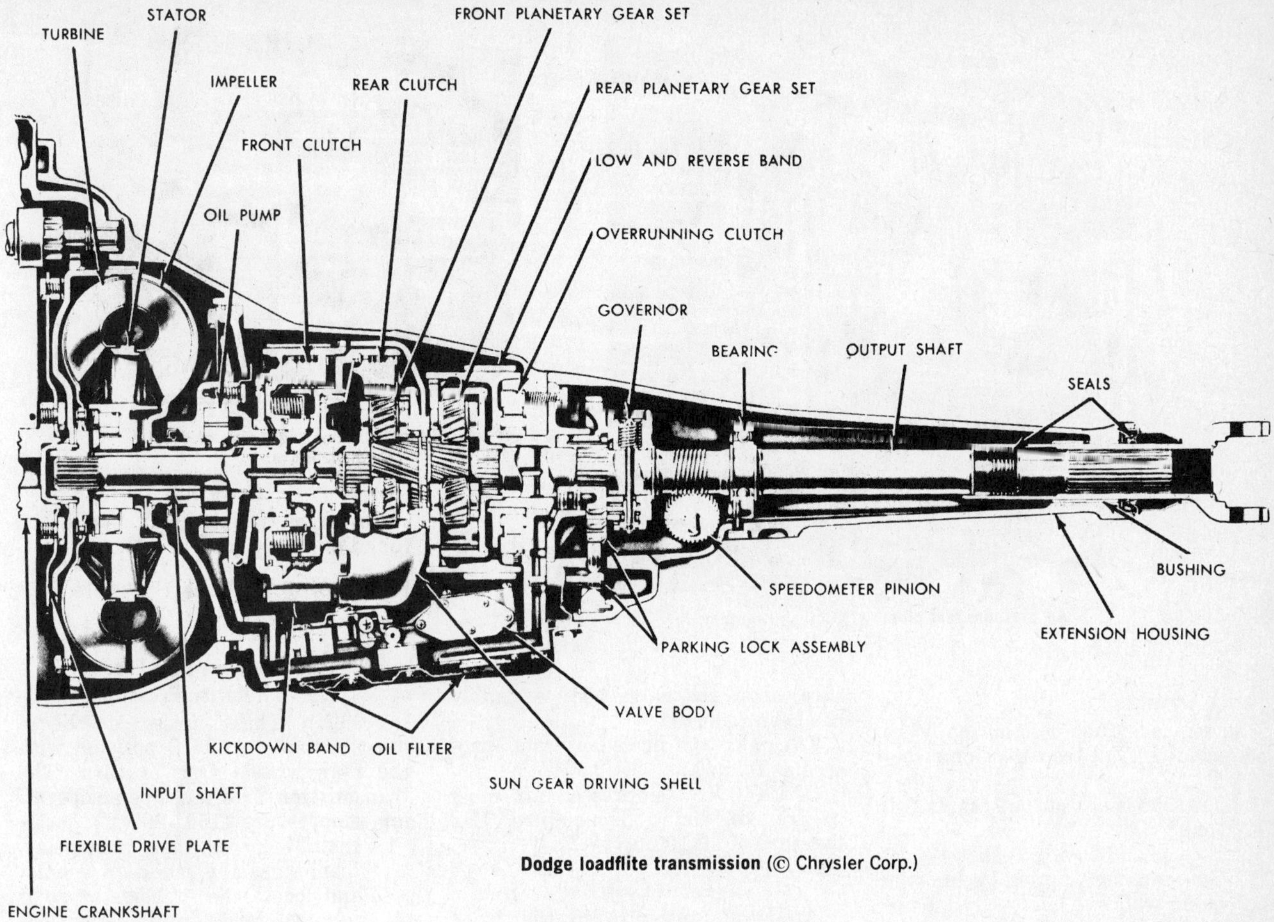

STATOR
TURBINE
FRONT PLANETARY GEAR SET
IMPELLER
REAR CLUTCH
REAR PLANETARY GEAR SET
FRONT CLUTCH
LOW AND REVERSE BAND
OIL PUMP
OVERRUNNING CLUTCH
GOVERNOR
BEARING
OUTPUT SHAFT
SEALS
BUSHING
SPEEDOMETER PINION
EXTENSION HOUSING
PARKING LOCK ASSEMBLY
VALVE BODY
KICKDOWN BAND
OIL FILTER
SUN GEAR DRIVING SHELL
INPUT SHAFT
FLEXIBLE DRIVE PLATE
ENGINE CRANKSHAFT

Dodge loadflite transmission (© Chrysler Corp.)

Band Adjustments

Kickdown Band

The kickdown band adjusting screw is located on the left-hand side of the transmission case near the throttle lever shaft.

1. Loosen the locknut and back off about five turns. Be sure the adjusting screw is free in the case.
2. Using wrench, tool C-3380 with adapter C-3790, or similar tools, torque the adjusting screw to 47-50 in. lbs. If adapter is not used, tighten adjusting screw to 72 in. lbs. which is the true torque.
3. Back off the adjusting screw, exactly to specification. Keep the screw from turning, and torque the locknut to specification.

Kickdown Band Adjustments

A-727 sixes and V8	2 turns
A-727 kickdown adjusting screw torque	29 ft. lbs.

Low and Reverse Band

Access to the low and reverse band requires oil pan removal.

1. Raise the truck, drain transmission and remove the transmission oil pan.
2. Loosen the band adjusting screw locknut and back off the nut about five turns. Be sure the adjusting screw turns freely in the lever.
3. With the same tools as used on the kickdown band adjustment (C-3380 and C-3790), tighten the adjusting screw to 47-50 in. lbs. If adapter is not used, torque to 72 in. lbs. the true torque.
4. Back off the adjusting screw exactly to specification. Keep the screw from turning and torque the locknut to specification.
5. Reinstall oil pan, using new gasket, and torque the pan bolts to 150 in. lbs.
6. Refill transmission to prescribed level.

Low and Reverse Band Screw Adjustment

A-727

1964-66	3 turns
1967 and up	2 turns

Adjustment screw torque 35 ft. lbs.

LOW AND REVERSE BAND ADJUSTING SCREW
BOLTS (10)
FLUID FILTER
PARKING LOCK CONTROL ROD
NEUTRAL FINGER
LINE PRESSURE ADJUSTMENT
NEUTRAL STARTING SWITCH
PARK FINGER

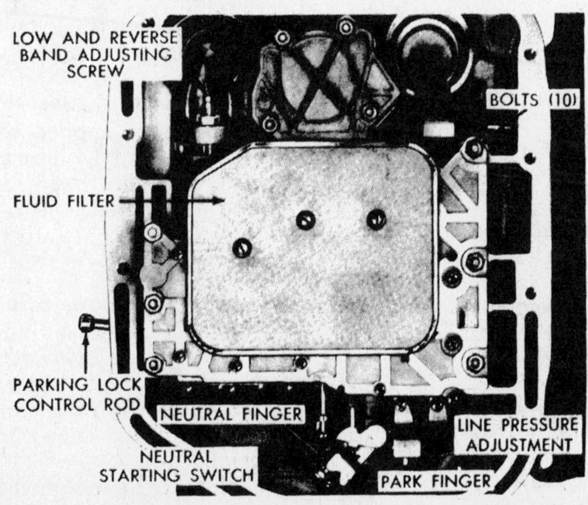

Bottom view of transmission (pan removed)
(© Chrysler Corp.)

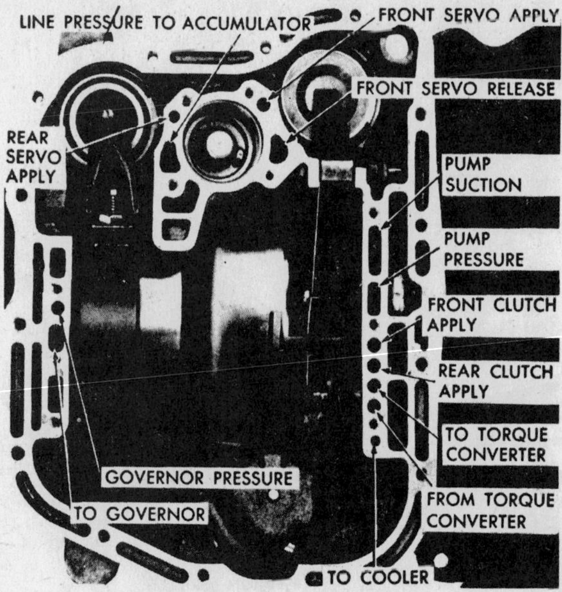

Air pressure test points (© Chrysler Corp.)

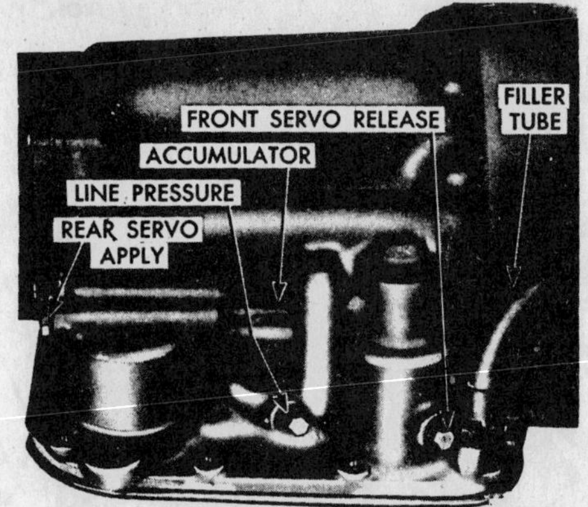

Pressure test locations (right side of case) (© Chrysler Corp.)

Fluid Leaks

Some leaks that can normally be corrected without transmission removal are:

1. Transmission output shaft oil seal.
2. Extension housing gasket.
3. Speedometer pinion seal and cable seal.
4. Oil filter tube seal.
5. Oil pan gasket and drain plug.
6. Gearshift control cable seal.
7. Throttle shaft seal.
8. Neutral starting switch seal.
9. Oil cooler line fittings and pressure take-off plugs.

Oil found inside the converter housing should be positively identified as transmission oil before any major transmission work is performed.

Leaks Requiring Transmission Removal

1. Fractures or sand holes in transmission case.
2. Sand hole or fracture in front oil pump.
3. Front pump housing retaining screws or damaged sealing washers.
4. Front oil pump housing seal (on outside diameter of pump housing).
5. Converter assembly and impeller shaft oil seal (located in front pump housing).

Tests

Air Pressure Tests

The front clutch, rear clutch, kickdown servo and low and reverse servo may be checked with air pressure, after the valve body assembly has been removed.

To make air pressure tests, proceed as follows:

CAUTION: Compressed air must be free of dirt and moisture. Use pressure of 30-100 psi.

Front Clutch

Apply air pressure to the front clutch apply passage and listen for a dull thud. This will indicate operation of the front clutch. Hold the air pressure at this point for a few seconds and check for excessive oil leaks.

NOTE: If a dull thud cannot be heard in the clutch, place finger tips on clutch housing and again apply air pressure. Movement of piston can be felt as clutch is applied.

Rear Clutch

Apply air pressure to the rear clutch apply passage and proceed in an identical manner as that described in the previous paragraph.

Kickdown Servo

Air pressure applied to the kickdown servo apply passage should tighten the front band. Spring tension should be sufficient to release the band.

Low and Reverse Servo

Direct air pressure into the low and reverse servo apply passage. Response of the servo will result in a tightening of the rear band. Spring tension should be enough to release the band.

If clutches and servos operate properly, no upshift or erratic shift conditions existing, trouble exists in the control valve body assembly.

Governor

Governor troubles can usually be found during a road or pressure test.

Hydraulic Control Pressure Checks

Line Pressure and Front Servo Release Pressure

NOTE: These pressure checks must be made in the D position with the rear wheels free to turn. The transmission fluid must be at operating temperature (150°-200°F).

1. Install an engine tachometer, then, raise the truck on a hoist and locate the tachometer so it can be read from under the truck.
2. Connect two 0-100 psi pressure gauges (tool C-3292 or other good gauges) to pressure takeoff points at the top of the accumulator and at the front servo release.
3. With the selector in D position, increase engine speed gradually until the transmission shifts into High. Reduce engine speed slowly to 100 rpm. The line pressure must be 54-60 psi with front servo release having no more than a 3 psi drop.
4. Disconnect throttle linkage from transmission throttle lever and more throttle lever gradually to full throttle position. Line pressure must rise to maximum of 90-96 psi just before or at kickdown into low gear. Front servo repressure must follow line pressure up to kickdown point and should not be more than 3 psi below line pressure. If pressure is not 54-60 psi at 1000 rpm, adjust line pressure.

If line pressure is not as above, adjust the pressure as outlined under the heading: Hydraulic Control Pressure Adjustments—"Line Pressure."

If front servo release pressures are less than specified, and line pressures are within limits, there is excessive leakage in the front clutch and/or front servo circuits.

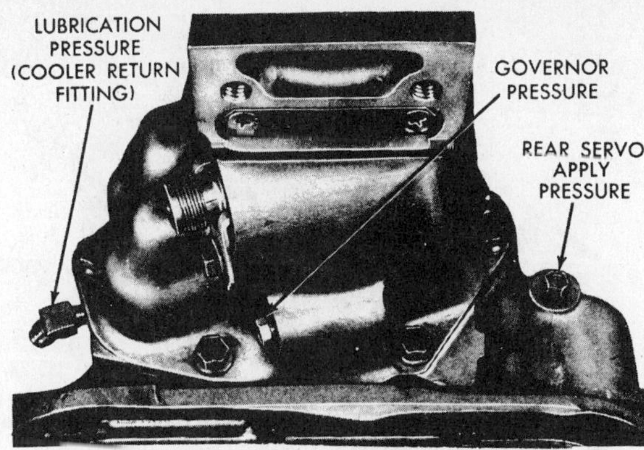

Pressure test locations (right side of case) (© Chrysler Corp.)

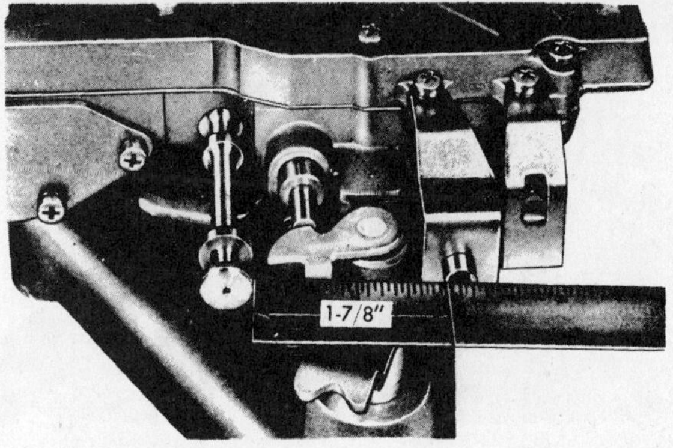

Measuring spring retainer location (© Chrysler Corp.)

Lubrication Pressures

A lubrication pressure check should be made when line pressure and front servo release pressures are checked.

1. Install a T fitting between the cooler return line fitting and the fitting hole in the transmission case at the rear left side of the transmission. Connect a 0-100 psi pressure gauge to the T-fitting.
2. At 1000 engine rpm, with throttle closed and transmission in High, lubrication pressure should be 5-15 psi. Lubrication pressure will approximately double as throttle is opened to maximum line pressure.

Rear Servo Apply Pressure

1. Connect a 0-300 psi pressure gauge, tool C-3293 or its equivalent, to the apply pressure take off point at the rear servo.
2. With the control in the R position, and the engine running at 1600 rpm, the reverse servo apply pressure should be 230-280 psi.

Governor Pressure

1. Connect a 0-100 psi gauge (same as the one used for line pressure and front servo release pressure) to the governor pressure takeoff point. This location is at the lower left rear corner of the extension mounting flange.
2. Governor pressure should fall within limits in chart.

Pressure should change smoothly with truck speeds.

If governor pressures are incorrect at the prescribed speeds, the governor valve and/or weights are probably sticking.

Hydraulic Control Pressure Adjustments

Line Pressure

An incorrect throttle pressure setting will cause incorrect line pressure even though line pressure adjustment is correct. Always inspect and correct throttle pressure adjustment before adjusting line pressure.

NOTE: Before adjusting line pressure, measure distance between manual valve (valve in 1-low position and line pressure adjusting screw. This measurement must be 1⅞ in. Correct by loosening spring retainer screws and repositioning spring retainer. The regulator valve may cock and hang up in its bore if spring retainer is out of position.

If line pressure is not correct remove valve body assembly to adjust. The correct adjustment is 1-5/16 in. measured from valve body to inner edge of adjusting nut. Vary adjustment slightly to obtain specified line pressure.

One complete turn of the adjusting screw (Allen head) changes closed throttle line pressure about 1.66 psi. Turning the screw counterclockwise increases pressure, clockwise decreases pressure.

Throttle Pressure

Because throttle pressures cannot be checked, exact adjustments should be checked and made correct whenever the valve body is disturbed.

1. Remove the valve body assembly, as outlined in a succeeding coverage entitled, Valve Body Assembly and Accumulator Piston.
2. Loosen throttle lever stop screw locknut and back off the screw about five turns.
3. Insert gauge pin of tool C-376 between the throttle lever cam and the kickdown valve.
4. Push on the tool and compress the kickdown valve against its spring, so that the throttle valve is completely bottomed inside the valve body.
5. As the spring is being compressed, finger tighten the throttle lever stop screw against the throttle lever tang, with the lever cam touching the tool and the throttle valve bottomed. (Be sure the adjustment is made with the spring fully compressed and the valve bottomed in the valve body.)
6. Remove the tool and secure the stop screw locknut.

Service Operations in Truck

Some sub-assemblies can be removed for repairs without removing the transmission from the truck. Detailed reconditioning of sub-assemblies is covered further in the text.

Speedometer Pinion

Removal and Installation 1964-65

1. Remove screw and retainer which holds the cable to the extension housing. Carefully work the pinion and sleeve out of the housing.
2. Replace the pinion and/or oil seal by prying the clip off the pinion and sliding the pinion and seal assembly from the cable.
3. If transmission fluid is found in the cable housing, replace the seal inside the pinion bore, then, slide the pinion over the end of the cable and secure it with the spring clip.
4. To install, push the pinion and sleeve into the extension housing as far as possbile, then install the retainer screw. Tighten to 150 in. lbs.

Removal and Installation 1966 and Up

Rear axle gear ratio and tire size determine pinion gear size.

1. Remove bolt and retainer securing speedometer pinion adapter in extension housing.
2. With cable housing connected, carefully work adapter and pinion out of extension housing.
3. If transmission fluid is found in cable housing, replace seal in

Line pressure adjustments (© Chrysler Corp.)

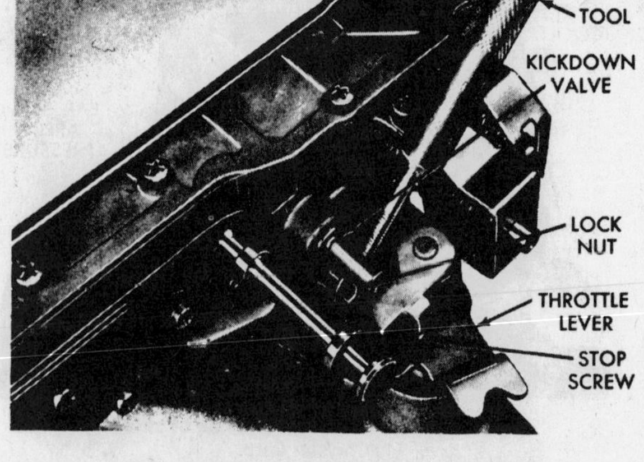

Throttle pressure adjustment (© Chrysler Corp.)

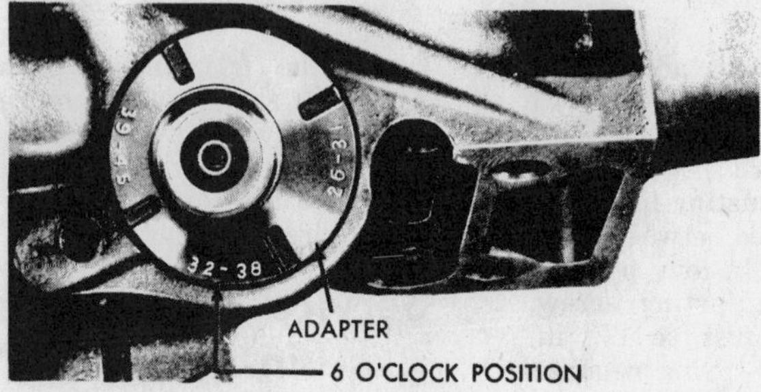

Speedometer pinion and adapter installed (© Chrysler Corp.)

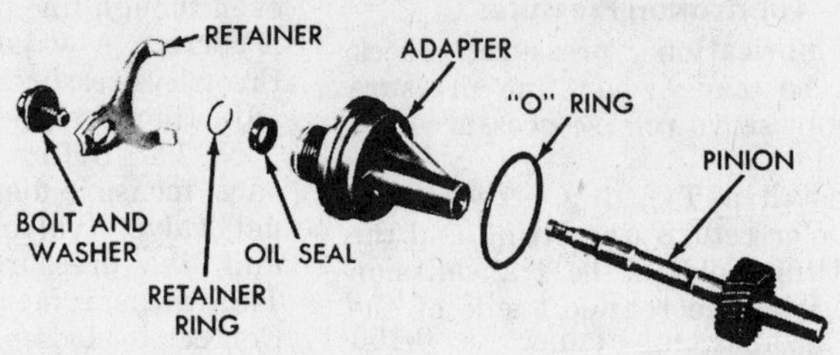

Speedometer drive (© Chrysler Corp.)

adapter. Start seal and retainer ring in adapter, then push them into adapter with Tool C4004 or equivalent until tool bottoms. CAUTION: Before installing pinion and adapted assembly make sure adapter flange and mating area on extension housing are perfectly clean. Dirt or sand will cause misalignment and speedometer pinion gear noise.
4. Note number of gear teeth and install pinion gear into adapter.
5. Rotate pinion gear and adapter assembly so that number on adapter corresponding to number of teeth on gear is in six o'clock position as assembly is installed.
6. Install retainer and bolt with retainer tangs in adapter positioning slots. Tap adapter firmly into extension housing and tighten retainer bolt to 100 in. lbs.

Output Shaft Oil Seal

Replacement—1964-65 A-727

1. Disconnect driveshaft at rear universal joint. Carefully pull shaft out of transmission exte shaft out of transmission extension housing. Be careful not t scratch or nick ground surface on sliding spline yoke.
2. Cut boot off seal, then screw taper threaded end of Tool C-748 or equivalent into seal. Tighten screw of tool to remove seal. If tool is not available, remove by gently tapping out around circumference of seal with slide hammer. Take care not to engage slide hammer or tail shaft bearing.
3. To install new seal, place seal in opening of extension and drive it into housing with Tool C-3972 or suitable drift.
4. Carefully guide front universal joint into extension housing and onto output shaft splines. Connect driveshaft to rear axle pinion shaft yoke.

Replacement—1966 and Up

1. Mark parts for reassembly. Disconnect driveshaft at rear universal joint. Carefully pull shaft yoke out of transmission extension housing. Be careful not to scratch or nick ground surface of sliding spline yoke.
2. Remove extension housing yoke seal with Tool C-3994 or C-3985 or equivalent. If tools are not available, remove by gently tapping out around circumference of seal with slide hammer.
3. To install new seal, place seal in opening of extension housing and drive it into housing with Tool C-3995 or C-3972 or suitable drift.
4. Carefully guide front universal joint yoke into extension housing and onto the mainshaft splines. Align marks made at removal and connect driveshaft to pinion shaft yoke.

Extension Housing Removal 1964-65

1. Remove the speedometer drive pinion and sleeve assembly.
2. Disconnect front universal joint at companion flange.
3. Drain about two quarts of fluid from the transmission.
4. Loosen parking lock cable clamp bolt where cable enters housing cover. Tap end of clamp bolt lightly to release its hold on the cable. Remove housing cover lower plug. Insert screwdriver through hole. While exerting pressure against projecting portion of cable lock-spring, withdraw lock cable.
5. Remove two bolts securing extension housing to crossmember insulator.
6. Raise transmission slightly with service jack to clear crossmember. Remove crossmember attaching bolts and remove cross member, insulator, and spring assembly.
7. Remove extension housing to transmission bolts, tap housing lightly with soft mallet to break it loose from transmission, and remove housing.

1966 and Up

1. Mark parts for reassembly. Disconnect driveshaft at rear universal joint. Carefully pull shaft out of extension housing.
2. Remove speedometer pinion and adapted asembly. Drain approximately two quarts of fluid from

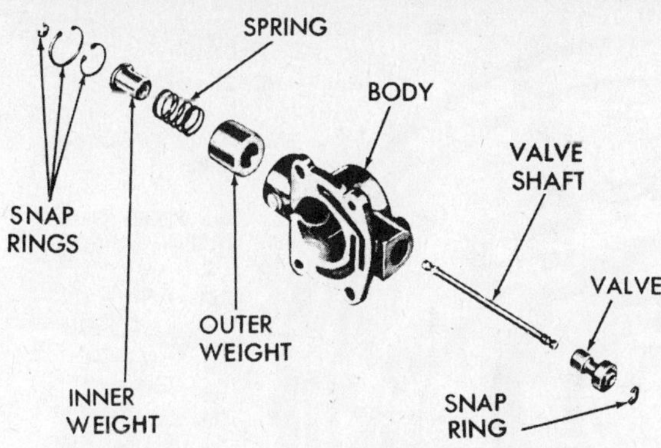

Governor assembly (© Chrysler Corp.)

transmission.

3. Remove bolts securing extension housing to crossmember. Raise transmission slightly with service jack and remove center crossmember and support assembly.
4. Remove extension housing to transmission bolts. On console shifts, remove two bolts securing gearshift torque shaft lower bracket to extension housing. Swing bracket out of way. NOTE: Gearshift lever must be in 1-low position so that parking lock control rod can be engaged or disengaged with parking lock sprag.
5. Remove two screws, plate, and gasket from bottom of extension housing mounting pad.
6. Spread large snap ring from output shaft bearing with Tool C-3301 or equivalent.
7. With snap ring spread as far as possible tap extension housing gently off output shaft bearing.
8. Carefully pull extension housing rearward to bring parking lock control rod knob past parking sprag and remove housing.

Governor

Removal

1. Remove extension housing. NOTE. Remove output shaft support bearing if so equipped.
2. With a screwdriver, carefully pry the snapring from the weight end of governor valve shaft. Slide the valve and shaft assembly out of the governor housing.
3. Remove the large snap-ring from the weight end of the governor housing and lift out the governor weight assembly.
4. Remove snap-ring from inside governor weight, remove inner weight and spring from the outer weight.
5. Remove the snap-ring from behind the governor housing, then slide the governor housing and support assembly from the output shaft. If necessary, remove the four screws and separate the governor housing from the support.

Cleaning and Inspection

The primary cause of governor operating trouble is sticking of the valve or weights. This is brought about by dirt or rough surfaces. Thoroughly clean and blow dry all of the governor parts, crocus cloth any burrs or rough bearing surfaces and clean again. If all moving parts are clean and operating freely, the governor may be reassembled.

Installation

1. Assemble the governor housing to the support, then finger oil passage of the governor housing aligns with the passage in the support.
2. Align the master spline of the support with the master spline on the output shaft, slide the assembly into place. Install the snap-ring behind the governor housing. Torque bolts to 100 in lbs.
3. Assemble the governor weights and spring fasten with snap-ring inside of large governor weight. Place the weight assembly in the governor housing shaft retaining snap-ring. Install output shaft support bearing if so equipped.
4. Place the governor valve on the valve shaft, insert the assembly into the housing and through the governor weights. Install the shaft retaining snap-ring. Install output shaft support bearing if so equipped.
8. Install the extension housing. Connect the propeller shaft.

Rear Oil Pump, Through 1965

Removal

1. Remove extension housing.
2. Remove governor and support.
3. Unscrew the rear oil pump cover retaining bolts and remove the pump cover.
4. Draw a line across the face of the inner and outer pump rotors (with dye) so that they may be reinstalled in the same position.
5. Slide off the inner rotor, (don't drop the small driving ball). Remove the outer rotor from the pump body..

NOTE: If replacement of the pump body is necessary, the transmission must be dismantled to allow driving the pump body out (rearward) with a wood block.

Inspection

Clean and blow dry all pump parts and examine contacting surfaces for evidence of wear, burrs or other damage. With the parts cleaned and reassembled, place a straightedge across the face of the rotors an pump body. With a feeler gauge, check clearance between the straightedge and the face of the rotors. Clearance limits are at front of section.

Installation

1. Place the outer rotor in the pump body.
2. Rotate the output shaft so that the inner rotor driving ball (or

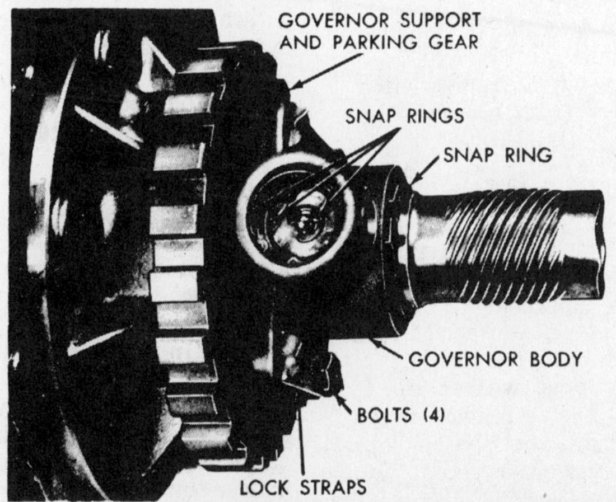

Governor shaft and weight snap-rings
(© Chrysler Corp.)

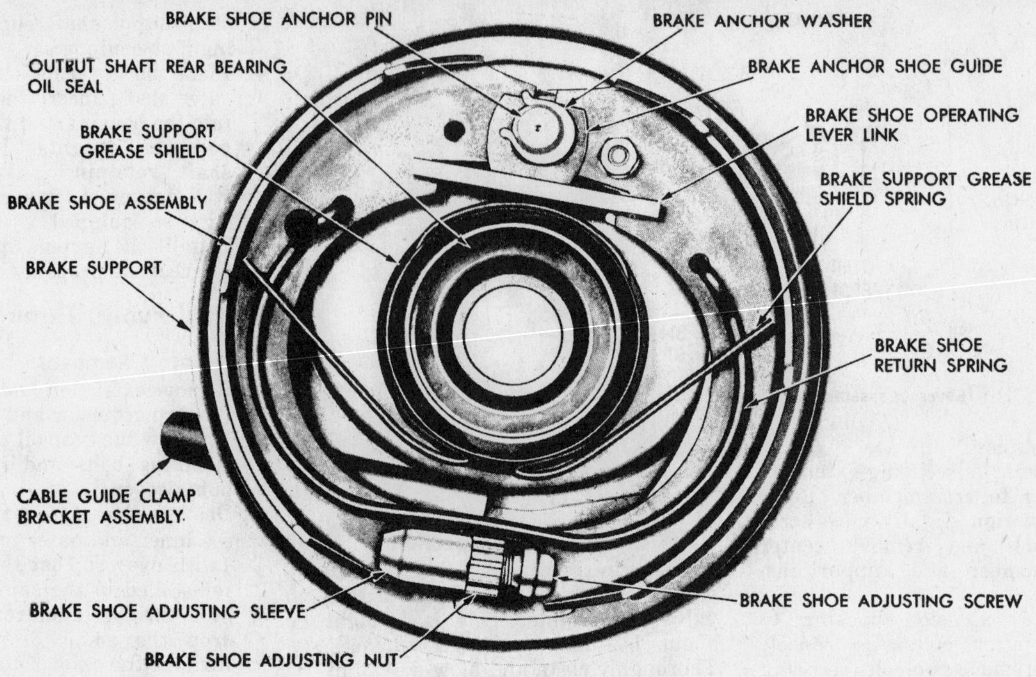

Internal expanding parking brake (drum removed) (© Chrysler Corp.)

ball key) pocket is up. Drop the ball into the pocket and slide the inner rotor onto the output shaft, in alignment with the ball.

3. Position the outer rotor to align its dye mark with the mark on the inner rotor.
4. Install the pump cover with the attaching bolts turned in a few threads. Slide the aligning fixture, tool C-3762 all the way in until it bottoms against the rotor.
5. Install the governor and support.
6. Install extension housing, brake assembly and connect the propeller shaft.
7. Connect the parking brake cable (drum-type).

Neutral Starting Switch

Removal

1. Drain about two quarts of transmission fluid.
2. Disconnect wire from switch and unscrew from transmission case.

Installation and Test

1. With the proper control cable adjustment assured, and the N selector depressed, make sure the switch operating lever is aligned in the center of the switch opening in the case.
2. Place the cupped washer and O ring over the threads of the switch. Screw the switch into the transmission case a few turns.
3. Connect one lead of a test lamp to battery current and the other lead to the switch terminal. Screw into the transmission case until the lamp lights. Now, tighten the switch an additional one-third to one-half turn. NOTE: The switch must be tight enough to prevent oil leaks. If not, add a thin washer and readjust the switch.
4. Remove test lamp and reattach the regular wire to the switch.
5. Bring transmission fluid to correct level.

Valve Body Assembly and Accumulator Piston

Removal 1964-65

1. Loosen pan bolts and drain all of the fluid from the transmission.
2. Remove the oil pan and gasket.
3. Loosen the clamp bolt and lift the throttle lever, washer and seal from the transmission throttle lever shaft.
4. Shift the manual control into 1 (Low) position to expose the nut holding the cable adapter to the manual lever. Remove the nut and disengage the adapter from the lever.
5. With a drain pan under the transmission, remove the ten hex-head valve body to transmission case bolts. Hold the valve body in position while removing bolts.
6. Lower the valve body assembly. Be careful not to cock the throttle lever shaft in the case hole or lose the accumulator spring.
7. Insert tool C-434 inside the accumulator piston and remove the piston from the transmission case. Inspect the piston assembly for scoring, broken rings and wear. Replace as required.

NOTE: Servicing the valve body is outlined later in the text.

Installation 1964-65

1. All mating surfaces must be clean and free of burrs.
2. Install accumulator piston into the transmission case.
3. Position accumulator spring on the valve body.
4. Position the valve body assembly in place in the transmission and start all the retaining bolts.
5. Snug the bolts down evenly then torque to 100 in. lbs.
6. Connect the control cable adapter to the manual lever and install retaining nut.
7. Install seal, flat washer and throttle lever onto the throttle shaft. Tighten the clamp bolt.
8. Install clean oil pan with new gasket.
9. Add fluid to correct level.

Removal 1966 and Up

1. Raise vehicle on hoist and loosen oil pan bolts, tap pan to break it loose, allowing fluid to drain.
2. Remove pan and gasket.
3. Disconnect throttle and gear shift linkage from levers on transmission. Loosen clamp bolts and remove levers.
4. Remove E clip securing parking lock rod to valve body manual lever.
5. Remove backup light and neutral start switch.
6. Place drain pan under transmission, remove ten hex

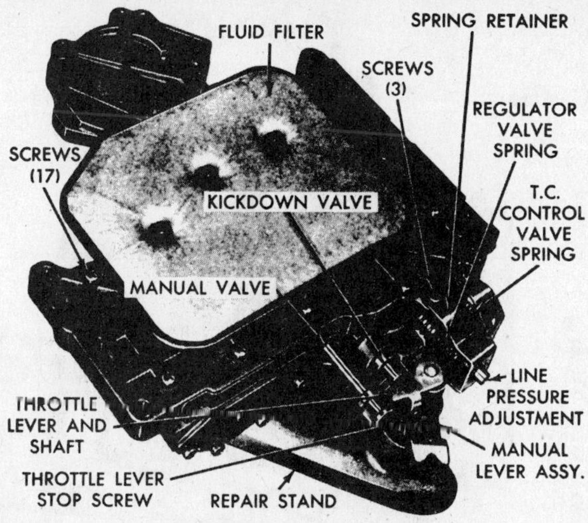

Valve body and control assembly
(© Chrysler Corp.)

head valve body to transmission case bolts. Hold valve body in position while removing bolts.

7. While lowering valve body down out of transmission case, disconnect parking lock rod from lever. To remove rod pull if forward out of case. If necessary rotate driveshaft to align parking gear and sprag to permit knob on end of control rod to pass sprag.
8. Withdraw accumulator piston from transmission case. Inspect piston for scoring, and rings for wear or breakage.
9. If valve body manual lever shaft seal requires replacement, drive it out of case with punch.
10. Drive new seal into case with 15/16 in. socket and hammer.

Installation
1966 and Up

1. If parking lock rod was removed, insert it through opening in rear of case with knob positioned against plug and sprag. Move front end of rod toward center of transmission while exerting rearward pressure on rod to force it past sprag. Rotate driveshaft if necessary.
2. Install accumulator piston in transmission case.
3. Place accumulator spring on valve body.
4. Place valve body manual lever in low position. Lift valve body into its approximate position, connect parking lock rod to manual lever and secure with E clip. Place valve body in case, install retaining bolts finger tight.
5. With neutral start switch installed, place manual lever in neutral position. Shift valve body if necessary to center neutral finger over neutral switch plunger. Snug bolts down evenly. Torque to 100 in. lbs.
6. Install gearshift lever and tighten clamp bolt. Check lever shaft for binding by moving lever through all detends. If lever binds, loosen valve body bolts and re-align.
7. Make sure throttle shaft seal is in place, install flat washer and lever and tighten clamp bolt. Connect throttle and gearshift linkage and adjust as required.
8. Install oil pan using new gasket. Add transmission fluid to proper level.

Detailed Unit Reconditioning

The following reconditioning data covers the removal, disassembly, inspection, repair, assembly and installation procedures for each subassembly in detail.

NOTE: In the event that any part has failed in the transmission, the converter should be thoroughly flushed to insure the removal of fine particles that may cause damage to the reconditioned transmission.

Oil Pan Removal

1. Secure transmission in a repair stand.
2. Unscrew attaching bolts and remove oil pan and gasket.

Valve Body Removal

1964-65

1. Unscrew nut and remove control cable adapter from valve body manual lever.
2. Remove (ten) hex-head valve body-to-transmission case bolts. (Hold the valve body in position while removing bolts.)
3. Lift the valve body out of the transmission case, don't cock the throttle lever shaft.

1966 and Up

1. Loosen clamp bolts and remove throttle and gearshift levers from transmission.
2. Remove backup light and neutral start switch.
3. Remove ten hex head valve body to transmission bolts. Remove E clip securing parking lock rod to valve body manual lever.
4. Whie lifting valve body upward out of transmission case, disconnect parking lock rod from lever.

Accumulator Piston and Spring

Removal

1. Lift the spring from the accumulator piston and withdraw the piston from the case.

Checking Drive Train End-Play

1. Attach a dial indicator to the extension housing and seat the plunger on the end of the output shaft.
2. Pry the output shaft out and tap it in to register the extreme shaft end-play.
3. Record this reading for possible future use. Correct end play is found at front of section.

Governor and Support Removal

1. Remove the snap-ring from the weight end of the governor valve shaft. Slide the valve and shaft assembly from the governor housing.

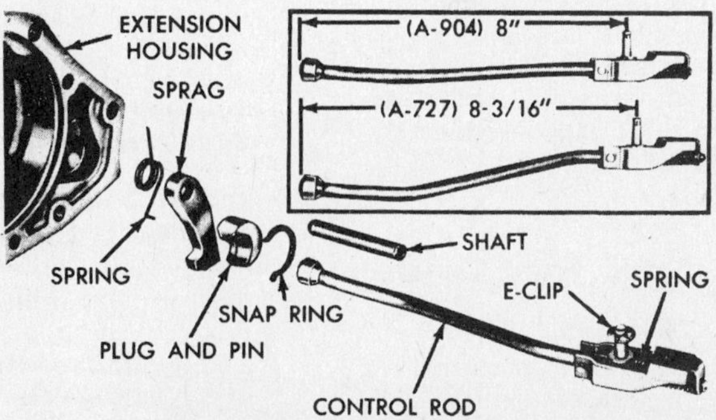

Parking lock components (© Chrysler Corp.)

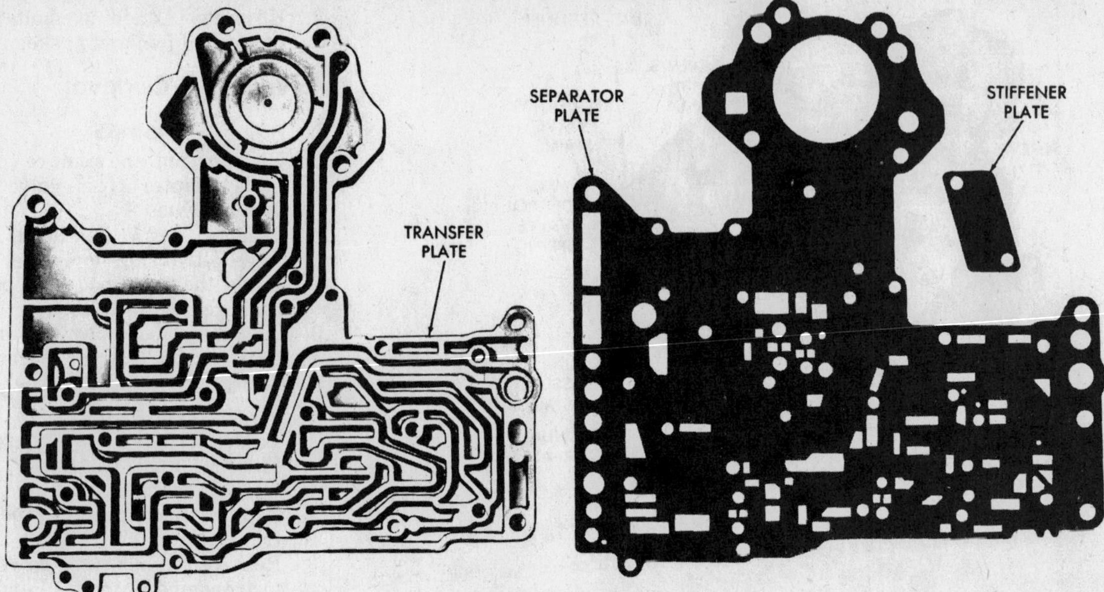

Transfer and separator plate (© Chrysler Corp.)

2. Remove the snap-ring from behind the governor housing, then slide the governor housing and support from the output shaft.

Rear Oil Pump Through 1965

Removal

1. Unscrew the rear oil pump cover retaining bolts and remove the cover.
2. Mark the face of the inner an outer pump rotor (with dye) so they may be reassembled in the same relationship.
3. The inner rotor is keyed to the output shaft by a small ball. Remove outer rotor from pump body.

NOTE: If the rear oil pump body is to be replaced, drive it rearward, out of the case (with a wood block), after the transmission case has been stripped.

Front Oil Pump and Reaction

Shaft Support Removal

1. Remove front pump housing retaining bolts.
2. Attach a tool to the pump housing flange, using the eleven and four o'clock hole locations.
3. Bump outward, evenly, with the tool to withdraw oil pump and reaction shaft support assembly from the case.

Front Band and Front Clutch

Removal

1. Loosen the front band adjuster, remove the head strut and slide the band from the case.
2. Slide the front clutch assembly from the case.

Input Shaft and Rear Clutch

Removal

Grasp the input shaft and slide the shaft and rear clutch assembly out of the case.

NOTE: Don't lose the thrust washer located between the rear end of the input shaft and the front end of the output shaft.

Planetary Gear Assemblies, Sun Gear, Driving Shell, Low and Reverse Drum Removal

While hand-supporting the output shaft and driving shell, carefully slide the assembly forward and out of the case.

Rear Band and Low-Reverse Drum Removal

Remove low-reverse drum, loosen rear band adjuster, remove band strut and link, and remove band from case.

Overrunning Clutch Removal

1. Notice the established position of the overrunning clutch rollers and springs before disassembly.
2. Slide out the clutch hub and remove rollers and springs.
3. Remove low and reverse drum thrust washer from inside the overrunning clutch case on 1964-65 transmissions.

Kickdown Servo Removal

1. Compress kickdown servo spring using engine valve spring compressor. Then remove snap ring.
2. Remove the rod guide, spring and piston rod from the case. Don't damage the piston rod or guide during removal.
3. Withdraw piston from the transmission case.

Low and Reverse Servo Removal

1. Using a suitable tool, depress the piston spring retainer and remove the snap ring.
2. Remove the spring retainer, spring, servo piston and plug assembly from the case.

Flushing the Torque Converter

1. Connect the converter assembly to the crankshaft mounting plate. Remove one drain plug and empty the converter of transmission fluid.
2. Insert a screwdriver into the converter and turn the stator hub (large splined hub) counterclockwise until one of the 1/8 x 3/8 in. slots of this assembly is visible, at the top. A second opening, directly below, provides an ample opening for the kerosene flush (if poured slowly).
3. Slowly pour two quarts of new, clean kerosene into the torque converter. Wipe dry and close the hub opening with masking tape.
4. Disconnect the coil wire, then rotate the converter for about ten seconds by cranking the engine.
5. Drain the converter and repeat the operation at least once, but as many times as is required to thoroughly flush all of the flakes and dirt from the unit.
6. Now, with both plugs removed, rotate the converter several times; this should further remove pocketed solvent and dirt. Replace the plugs and remove the converter assembly from its mounting plate.

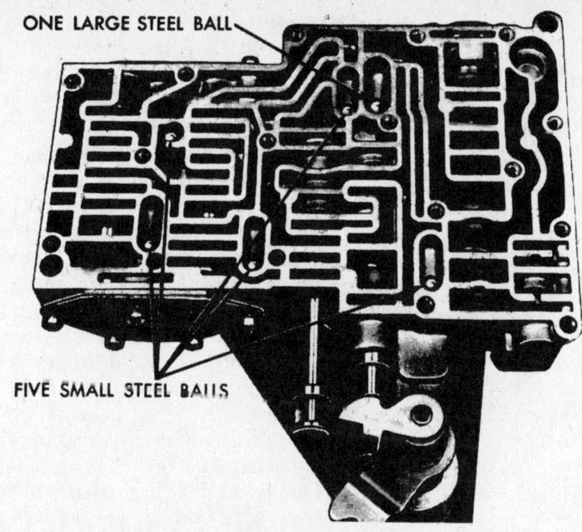

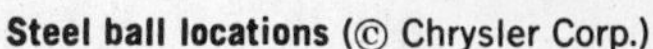

Steel ball locations (© Chrysler Corp.)

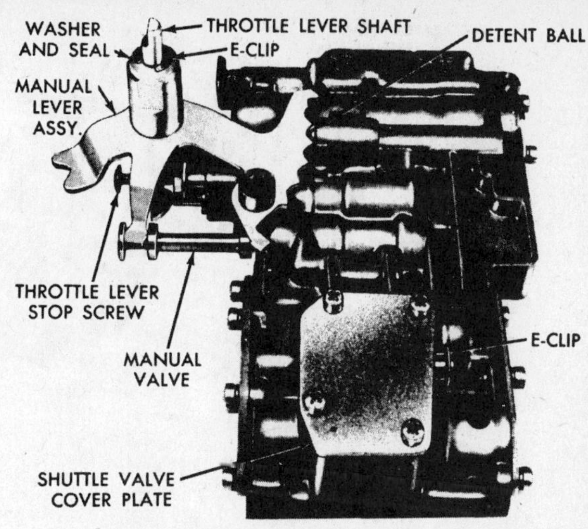

Valve body controls (© Chrysler Corp)

Before removing any of the transmission sub-assemblies, thoroughly clean the exterior of the unit, preferably by steam. When disassembling, each part should be washed in a suitable solvent, and either set aside to drain or dried with compressed air. Do not wipe with sop towels. All of the transmission parts require extremely careful handling to avoid nicks and other damage to the accurately machined surfaces.

Sub-Assembly Reconditioning

The following procedures cover the disassembly, inspection, repair and assembly of each sub-assembly as removed from the transmission.

The use of crocus cloth is permissible but not encouraged as extreme care must be used to avoid rounding off sharp edges of valves. The edge portion of valve body and valves is very important to proper functioning.

NOTE: Use all new seals and gaskets, and coat each part with automatic transmission fluid, type A, suffix A, during assembly.

Valve Body

Disassembly

NOTE: This area is extremely critical, and sensitive to distortion. Never champ any portion of the valve body or transfer plate in a vise. Clean with new solvent and dry with compressed air. Start all valves into their respective chambers with a twisting motion, seeing that they are well lubricated with automatic transmission fluid.

1. With the valve body in a clean repair stand, remove three attaching screws and the oil screen.
2. Hold the spring retainer bracket against spring tension, remove the three bracket retaining screws.
3. Remove spring bracket, torque converter valve spring, and the regulator valve spring with line pressure adjusting screw assembly. NOTE: Do not alter the setting of the line pressure adjusting screw and nut. The nut has an interference thread and does not turn easily on the screw.
4. Slide the regulator valve and spring retainer ring from the valve body. Slide torque converter control valve from the valve body.
5. Remove the (14) transfer plate retaining screws. Lift the transfer plate and steel plate assembly off the valve body.
6. Invert the transfer plate assembly and remove the stiffener plate. Remove the remaining screws securing the steel plate to the transfer plate, and lift off the steel plate.
   Remove rear pump check valve and spring on 1964-65 transmissions.
7. On 1964-65 transmissions, remove reverse blocker valve cover and lift out spring and valve.
8. On 1964-68 transmissions, note location of six steel balls in valve body. On 1969 and up transmission, note location of seven steel balls. (One of them is larger than the others and is in the larger chamber). Remove the steel balls, front pump check valve and spring.
9. On 1964-65 transmissions, invert valve body and lay it on clean paper. Remove E-clip from the throttle lever shaft. While holding manual lever detent ball and spring in their bore with tool C-3765, or similar tool, slide manual lever from the throttle shaft. Remove detent ball and spring.
10. Remove manual valve from valve body.
11. Remove throttle lever and shaft from body.
12. Remove shuttle valve cover plate. Remove E-clip from the exposed end of shuttle valve.
13. Remove throttle lever stop screw, being careful not to disturb the setting.
14. Remove kickdown detent, kickdown valve, throttle valve spring and throttle valve.
15. Remove governor plug and end plate. Tip up the valve body to allow the shuttle valve throttle plug, spring, shuttle valve and the shift valve governor plugs to slide out. NOTE: The first-second valve plug has a longer stem.
16. Remove the shift valve end plate and slide out the two springs and valves.
17. Remove the regulator valve end plate. Slide the regulator valve line pressure plug, sleeve, and the regulator valve throttle pressure plug from the body.

Cleaning and Inspection

Inspect all components for scores, loose or bent levers, burrs and warping. Don't straighten bent levers; renew them. Loose levers may be silver soldered at the shaft. Burrs and minor nicks may be carefully removed with crocus cloth. Check for valve body warping or distortion with a surface plate (plate glass will do) and a feeler gauge. Do not attempt to service a distorted plate or valve body, this is a very critical area.

Check all springs for distortion or fatigue. Check valves for scores and freedom of movement in the bores, they should fall of their own weight, in and out of the bore. The front and rear pump check valves are provided with a controlled leakage path. This keeps the rear pump primed.

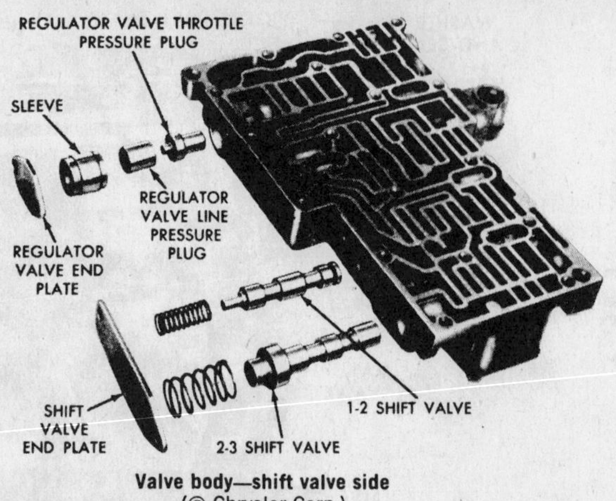

Valve body—shift valve side
(© Chrysler Corp.)

Assembly

1. On 1964-65 transmissions, insert the rear pump check valve and spring into the transfer plate. Position the steel plate on pump check valve in its bore with a thin steel scale and install four steel plate to transfer plate retaining screws. Torque these screws evenly to 28 in. lbs. Check rear pump check valve for free movement in the transfer plate. Install stiffener plate and tighten retaining screw to 28 in. lbs.
2. On 1964-65 transmissions, turn transfer plate over and install reverse blocker valve spring and valve. Rotate valve until it seats through the steel plate. Hold the valve down and install blocker valve cover plate. Torque the two retaining screws to 28 in. lbs. On 1966-70 transmissions, place separator plate on transfer plate. Install stiffener plate and retaining screws exactly as shown. Make sure all bolt holes are aligned. Tighten stiffener plate screws to 28 in. lbs.
3. Insert the first-second and second-third shift valve governor plugs into their respective bores. Install shuttle valve, valve spring and shuttle valve throttle plug. Install governor plug end plate and torque the four retaining screws to 28 in. lbs.
4. Install E-clip onto end of shuttle valve. Install shuttle valve cover plate and torque the three retaining screws to 28 in. lbs.
5. Install the first-second and second-third shift valves and springs. Install shift valve and plate and torque the three retaining screws to 28 in. lbs.
6. Insert regulator valve throttle pressure plug, sleeve (with the undercut on the sleeve toward the end plate), and the line pressure plug. Install regulator valve end plate and torque the two retaining screws to 28 in. lbs.
7. Insert throttle valve and spring. Slide the kickdown detent onto kickdown valve (with counterbore side of detent toward valve), then insert the assembly in the valve body.
8. Install throttle lever stop screw and tighten locknut finger tight.
9. Insert manual valve into the valve body.
10. Install throttle lever and shaft on the valve body. Insert detent spring and ball into its bore in the valve body. Depress ball and spring and slide manual lever over throttle shaft so that it engages manual valve and detent ball. Install the retaining E-clip onto the throttle shaft.
11. Position the valve body assembly on the bench or holding stand.
12. Place six steel balls in the valve body chambers (with large ball in the large chamber). Place the front pump check valve and spring in the valve body. On 1969-70 transmissions, install spring and 3/8 in. high pressure relief valve ball.
13. Position transfer plate assembly on the valve body. Hold front pump check valve in its bore with a thin steel scale. Install the (14) retaining screws, starting at the center and working outward. Torque screws to 28 in. lbs.
14. Install the torque converter

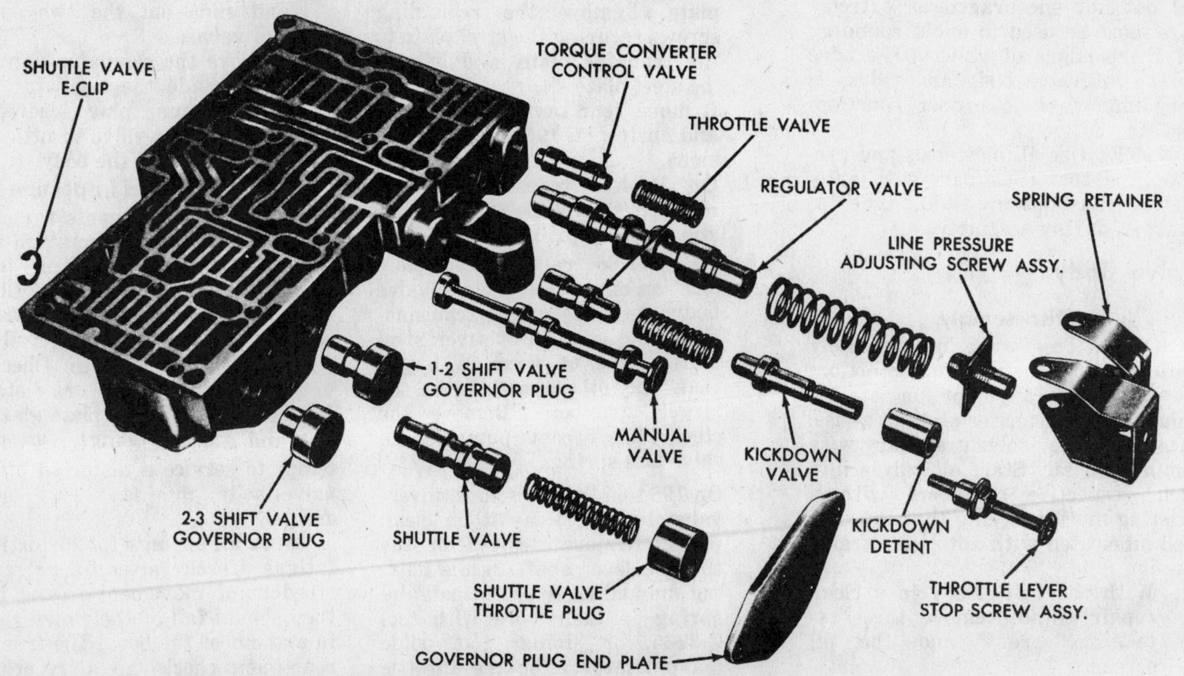

Valve body—lever side (© Chrysler Corp.)

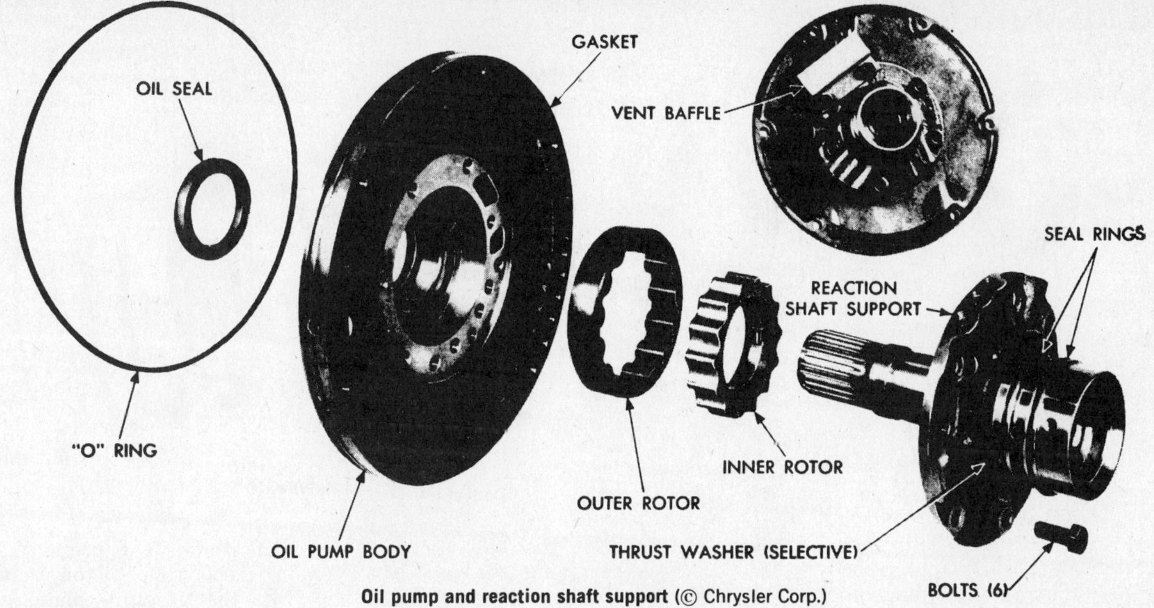

Oil pump and reaction shaft support (© Chrysler Corp.)

valve, regulator valve and spring retainer ring.

15. Place the torque converter valve spring over the ends of their respective valves. Place line pressure adjusting screw assembly on the end of the regulator valve spring, with the long dimension of the nut at right angles to the valve body.
16. Install spring retainer bracket (make sure the converter valve spring is engaged on the tang in the bracket). Torque the three bracket retaining screws to 28 in. lbs.
17. Install oil strainer and torque the three retaining screws to 28 in. lbs.

IMPORTANT: After reconditioning the valve body, adjust the throttle and line pressure How ever, if line pressure was satisfactory before disassembly, do not change this adjustment.

Accumulator Piston and Spring

Inspect both seal rings for wear and freedom in the piston grooves. Check the piston for scores, burrs, nicks and wear. Check the piston bore for corresponding damage and check piston spring for distortion and fatigue. Replace parts as required.

Governor

Disassembly

1. Remove the large snap-ring from the weight end of governor housing and lift out the governor weight assembly.
2. Remove the snap-ring from in side the governor weight. remove the inner weight and spring from the outer weight.

NOTE: Thoroughly clean all parts in a suitable and clean solvent. Check for damage and free movement before assembly.

3. If lugs on support gear are damaged, remove four bolts and separate support from governor body.

Assembly

1. If support was separated from governor body, assemble and tighten bolts finger tight.
2. Assemble the governor weights and spring, then secure with snap-ring inside large governor weight.
3. Place the weight assembly in the governor housing and install snap-ring.

Rear Oil Pump, through 1965, Inspection

Clean and inspect oil pump body and cover for wear, gouging or any other type of damage. Inspect rotors for scoring or pitting. With rotors cleaned and assembled in the pump body, apply a straightedge across the face of rotors and pump body. With a feeler gauge, check clearance between straightedge and face of rotors.

Front Pump and Reaction Shaft Support

Disassembly

The illustration shows the front oil pump and reaction shaft support disassembled.

1. Remove bolts from rear side of reaction shaft support and life support from the pump.
2. Dye-spot the face of the inner and outer rotors so they may be reinstalled in their original relationship, then remove the rotors.
3. Remove the rubber seal ring from front pump body flange.
4. Drive out the oil seal with blunt punch.

Inspection

Clean and inspect interlocking seal rings on the reaction shaft support for wear or broken interlocks, be sure they turn freely in their grooves. Check all machined surfaces of pump body and reaction shaft support for scuff marks and burrs. Inspect pump rotors for scores and pits. With rotors clean and installed into the pump body, apply a straightedge across the face of the rotors and pump body. With a feeler gauge check straightedge to rotor face clearance.

Assembly

1. Place reaction shaft support in assembling tool C-3759 and place it on the bench, with the support hub resting on the bench. Screw two pilot studs, tool C-3283, or satisfactory substitutes, into threaded holes of reaction shaft support flange.
2. Assemble rotors with dye marks aligned, place rotors in center of the support. The two driving lugs inside rotor must be next to the face of the reaction shaft support.
3. Lower pump body over pilot studs, insert tool C-3756 or substitute through pump body and engage pump inner rotor. Turn the rotors, with the tool, to enter them into pump body. With the pump body firmly against the reaction shaft support, tighten ring squeezer or clamping tool securely.
4. Invert the front pump and reaction shaft support assembly,

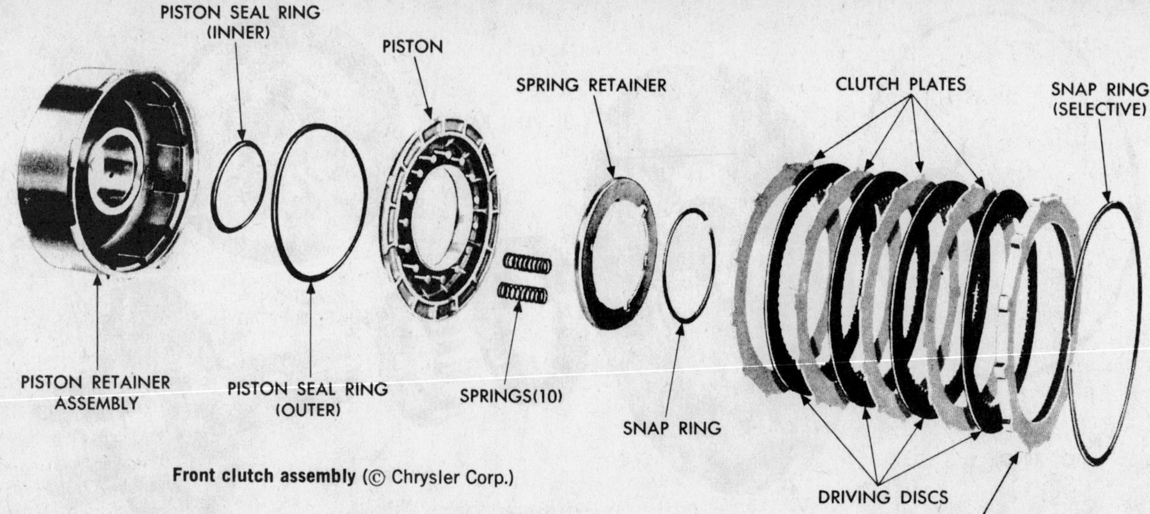

Front clutch assembly (© Chrysler Corp.)

with the clamping tool intact. Install support to pump body bolts. Remove clamping tool, pilot studs and rotor aligning studs.

5. Insert new oil seal into opening of front oil pump housing (with lip of seal facing inward). Drive seal into housing.

Front Clutch

Disassembly

Exploded view of front clutch assembly is illustrated.

1. With screwdriver or pick, remove large snap-ring, which holds the pressure plate in the clutch piston retainer. Lift pressure plate and clutch plates out of the retainer.
2. Install compression tool C-3863 for A-727 transmissions, or similar tool, over piston spring retainer (see illustration). Compress spring and remove snap-ring, then, slowly release tool until the spring retainer is free of the hub. Remove the compressor, retainer and spring.
3. Turn the clutch retainer upside down and bump on a wooden block to remove the piston. Remove seal rings from the piston and clutch retainer hub.

Inspection

Inspect clutch discs for evidence of burning, glazing and flaking. A general method of determining clutch plate breakdown is to scratch the lined surface of the plate with a finger nail. If material collects under the nail, replace all driving discs. Check driving splines for wear or burrs. Inspect steel plates and pressure plate surfaces for discoloration, scuffing or damaged driving lugs. Replace if necessary.

Check steel plate lug grooves in clutch retainer for smooth surfaces. Plate travel must be free. Inspect band contacting surface of clutch retainer, being sure the ball moves freely. Check seal ring surfaces in clutch retainer for scratches or nicks, light annular scratches will not interfere with the sealing of neoprene rings.

Inspect inside bore of piston for score marks. If light marks exist, polish with crocus cloth. Check seal ring grooves for nicks and burrs. Inspect neoprene seal rings for deterioration, wear and hardness. Check piston spring, retainer, and snap-ring for distortion and fatigue.

Assembly

1. Lubricate and install inner seal ring onto hub of clutch retainer. Be sure that lip of seal faces down and is properly seated in the groove.
2. Lubricate and install outer seal ring onto clutch piston, with lip of seal toward the bottom of the clutch retainer. Place piston assembly in retainer and, with a twisting motion, seat the piston in the bottom of the retainer.
3. Place spring on the piston hub and position spring retainer and snap-ring on spring. Compress spring with tool, or suitable ring compressor, and seat snap-ring in the hub groove. Remove compressor.
4. Lubricate all clutch plates, then, install a steel plate, followed by a lined plate, until all plates are installed. Install the pressure plate and snap-ring. Be sure the snap-ring is correctly seated.
5. With front clutch assembled, insert a feeler gauge between the pressure plate and snap-ring. The clearance should be to specification. If not, install a snap-ring of proper thickness.

Rear Clutch

Disassembly

1. With a small screwdriver or pick, remove the large snap-ring that secures the pressure plate in the clutch piston retainer. Lift the pressure plate, clutch plates, and inner pressure plate from the retainer.
2. On 1964-65 A-727 transmissions, remove piston ring snap ring and remove spring. On 1966-70 transmissions, carefully pry one end of wave spring out of its groove in clutch retainer and remove wave spring, spacer ring and clutch piston spring.
3. Remove compressor tool and piston spring. Turn clutch retainer assembly upside down and bump on a wood block to remove the piston. Remove seal rings from the piston.

Inspection

Inspect driving discs for indication of damage; handle as previously outlined under front clutch inspection.

Assembly

1. Lubricate, then install inner and outer seal rings onto the clutch piston. Be sure the seal lips face toward the head of the clutch retainer and seals are properly seated in the piston grooves.
2. Place piston assembly in retainer and, with a twisting motion, seat piston in bottom of retainer.
3. On 1964-65 A-727 transmissions, place spring over piston with outer edge of spring positioned below snap ring groove. Start one end of snap ring in groove. Make sure spring is exactly centered on piston. Progressively tap snap ring into groove. Be sure snap ring is fully seated in groove. On 1966-70 transmissions, place clutch piston spring and spacer ring on top of piston in clutch retainer. Make sure spring and spacer ring are placed in retainer recess. Start one end of wave spring in retainer groove. Progressively push

Removing front clutch retainer snap-ring
(© Chrysler Corp.)

Front clutch piston return springs
(© Chrysler Corp.)

or tap spring into place making sure it is fully seated in groove.

4. Install inner pressure plate into clutch retainer, with raised portion of plate resting on the spring.
5. Lubricate all clutch plates, then install one lined plate, followed by a steel plate, until all plates are installed. Install outer pressure plate and snap-ring.
6. With rear clutch completely assembled, insert a feeler gauge between the pressure plate and snap-ring. The clearance should be to specification. If not, install snap-ring of proper thickness to obtain the required clearance.

NOTE: Rear clutch plate clearance is very important to obtaining satisfactory clutch performance. Clearance is influenced by the use of various thickness outer snap-rings.

Planetary Gear Train

Disassembly

Refer to illustrations for assembly and disassembly of these units.

1. Remove thrust washer from forward end of output shaft.
2. Remove snap-ring from forward end of output shaft, then, slide front planetary assembly from the shaft.
3. On A-727 transmissions, slide front annulus gear off planetary gear set. Remove thrust washer from rear side of planetary gear set.
4. Slide the sun gear, driving shell, and rear planetary assembly, with low and reverse drum, from the output shaft.
5. Remove sun gear and driving shell from the rear planetary assembly. On A-727 transmissions, remove thrust washer from inside driving shell. On all transmissions, remove snap-ring and steel washer from sun gear (rear side of driving shell). Slide sun gear out of driving shell, then remove snap-ring and steel washer from opposite end of sun gear, if necessary.
6. Remove thrust washer from forward side of rear planetary assembly. Remove snap-ring from front side of low and reverse drum, then slide rear planetary assembly out of drum. If necessary, remove snap-ring from rear of annulus gear in order to separate the support from the annulus gear.

Inspection

Inspect output shaft bearing surfaces for burrs or other damage. Light scratches or burrs may be polished out with crocus cloth or a fine stone. Check speedometer drive gear for damage, and make sure all oil passages are clear.

Check bushings in the sun gear for wear or scores. Replace sun gear assembly if bushings show wear or other damage. Inspect all thrust washers for wear and scores. Replace

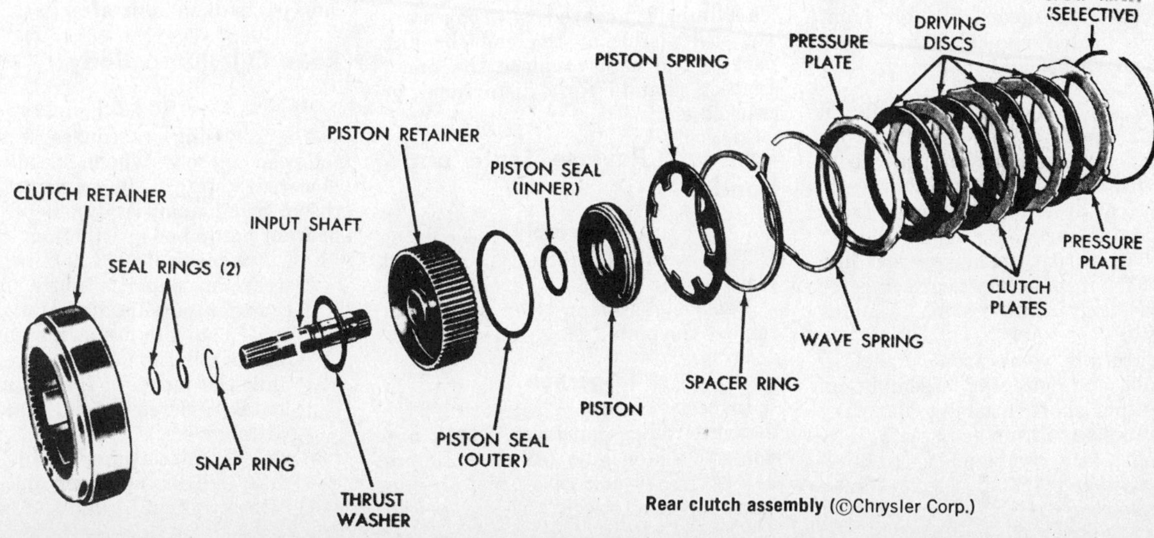

Rear clutch assembly (©Chrysler Corp.)

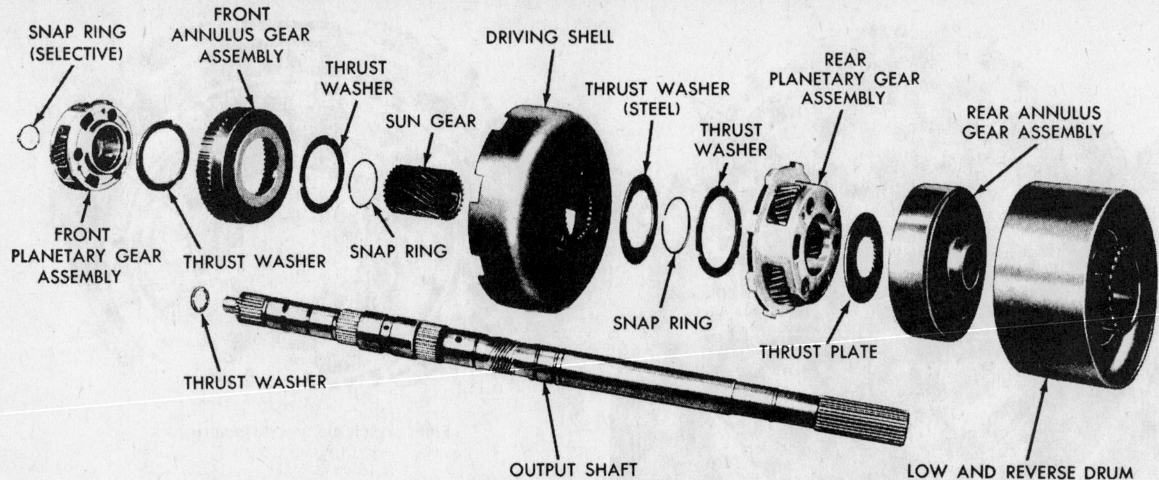

Planetary gear train and output shaft assembly (© Chrysler Corp.)

if necessary. Check lock rings for distortion and fatigue. Inspect annulus gear and driving gear teeth for damage. Inspect planetary gear carrier for cracks and the pinions for broken or worn gear teeth.

Assembly—A-727

1. On 1964-65 transmissions, place rear planetary gear assembly in rear annulus gear. Place thrust washer on front side of planetary gear assembly. Insert output shaft in rear opening of rear annulus gear. Carefully work shaft through annulus gear and planetary gear assembly. Make sure shaft splines are fully engaged in splines of annulus gear.
2. On 1966-70 transmissions, install rear annulus gear on output shaft. Apply thin coat of grease on thrust plate, place it on shaft, and in annulus gear making sure teeth are over shaft splines. Position rear planetary gear assembly in rear annulus gear. Place thrust washer on front side of planetary gear assembly.
3. Install snap ring in front groove of sun gear (long end of gear). Insert sun gear through front side of driving shell. Install rear steel washer and snap ring.
4. Carefully slide driving shell and sun gear assembly on output shaft, engaging sun gear teeth with rear planetary pinion teeth. Place thrust washer inside front driving shell.
5. Place thrust washer on rear hub of front planetary gear set. Slide assembly into front annulus gear.
6. Carefully work front planetary and annulus gear assembly on output shaft, meshing planetary pinions with sun gear teeth.
7. With all components properly positioned, install selective snap ring on front end of output shaft. Measure end play of assembly. Adjust end play with selective snap rings.

Overrunning Clutch Inspection

Inspect clutch rollers for smooth round surfaces, they must be free of flat spots, chipped edges and flaking. Inspect roller contacting surfaces on both cam and race for pock marks and roller wear-marks. Check springs for distortion and fatigue and inspect low and reverse drum thrust. On 1966-70 A-727 transmissions, inspect cam set screw for tightness.

Kickdown Servo and Band

Inspection

See illustration for an exploded view of the kickdown servo.

Inspect piston and guide seal rings for wear, and be sure of their freedom in grooves. It is not necessary to remove seal rings, unless circumstances warrant. Inspect piston for scores, burrs or other damage. Check fit of guide on piston rod. Check piston for distortion and fatigue. Inspect band lining for wear and fit of lining material to the metal band. This lining is grooved; if grooves are not still visible at the ends or any part of the band, replace the band. Inspect band for distortion or cracked ends.

Low and Reverse Servo and Band

Disassembly

The illustration shows an exploded view of the low and reverse servo.

Remove snap-ring from piston and remove the piston plug and spring.

Inspection

Inspect neoprene seal ring for damage, rot, or hardness. Check piston and piston plug for nicks, burrs, scores and wear. The piston plug must operate freely in the piston. Check the piston bore in the case for scores or other damage. Examine springs for distortion and fatigue.

Check band lining for wear and the fit of the lining to the metal band. This lining has a grooved surface; if the grooves are worn away at the ends or at any part of the band, replace the band. Inspect the band for distortion or cracked ends.

Assembly

Lubricate and insert the piston plug and spring into the piston, and secure with the snap-ring.

Sub-Assemblies Installation

The following assembly procedures include the installation of sub-assemblies into the transmission case and adjustment of the drive train end-play. Do not use force to assemble any of the mating parts. Always use new gaskets during the assembly operations.

NOTE: Use only automatic transmission fluid, type A, suffix A, or fluid of equivalent chemical structure, to lubricate automatic transmission parts during, or after, assembly.

Rear Oil Pump Body

1964-65

The following procedures should be followed closely when installing a new rear pump body, or reinstalling the original pump body, in order to prevent pump body distortion.

1. Cut a piece of .002-.003 in. thick wrapping paper, slightly smaller than the outside diameter of the outer rotor, to use as a shim during installation.
2. Chill the pump body to approximately 0°F. in a deep freeze, or with dry ice.
3. Quickly place pump body in the case, and install inner and outer rotors. Smear a daub of grease on the face of the rotors, center

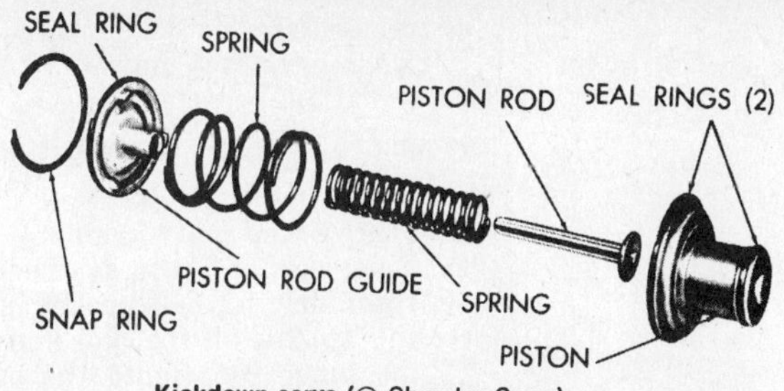

Kickdown servo (© Chrysler Corp.)

Low and reverse servo (© Chrysler Corp.)

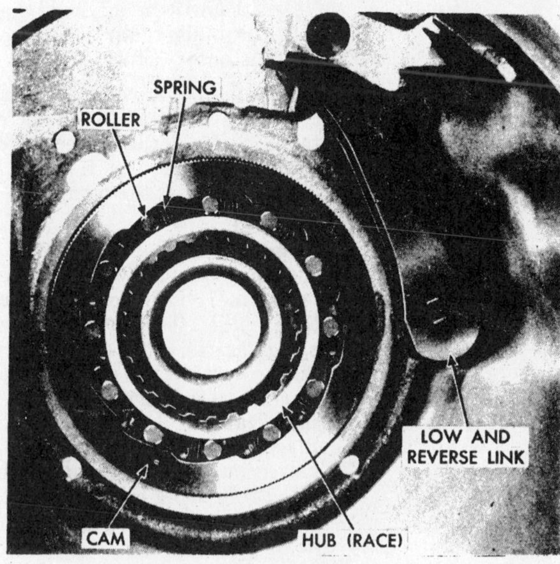

Overrunning clutch, low and reverse band link (© Chrysler Corp.)

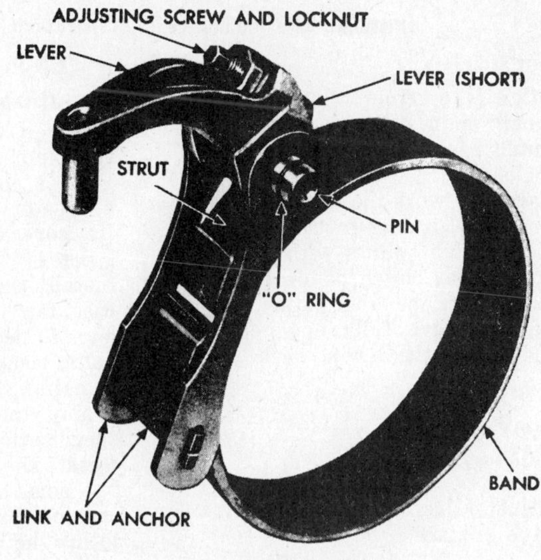

Low and reverse band and linkage (© Chrysler Corp.)

the paper shim on face of rotors, then install pump cover and tighten retaining bolts firmly.

4. After the pump body has warmed to room temperature, remove the pump cover, paper shim and rotors.

Overrunning Clutch

1964-65

1. With the transmission case positioned upright, place low and reverse drum thrust washer in overrunning clutch housing, then, place the clutch hub (race) on the thrust washer.
2. Install springs and rollers.

1966 and Up

With transmission case in upright position, insert clutch hub inside cam, install overrunning clutch rollers and springs as shown in figure.

Low and Reverse Servo and Band

1. Carefully work servo piston assembly into the case with a twisting motion. Place spring, retainer and snap-ring over the piston.
2. Using the screw portion of tool C-3322, or suitable substitute, depress the spring and install the snap-ring.
3. Position rear band in the case, install the short strut, then connect the long lever and strut to the band. Screw in band adjuster just enough to hold struts in place. Install low-reverse drum. On 1966-70 A-727 transmissions, be sure long link and anchor assembly is installed to provide running clearance for low-reverse drum.

Kickdown Servo

1. Carefully insert servo piston into case bore. Install piston rod, two springs and guide. Depress guide and install snap-ring.

NOTE: Maximum performance A-727 transmissions use only one small spring.

Planetary Gear Assemblies, Sun Gear, Driving Shell, Low and Reverse Drum

1. While supporting the assembly in the case, insert output shaft through the overrunning clutch hub. Carefully work the assembly rearward, engaging the drum splines with splines of the overrunning clutch hub. CAUTION: Be careful not to damage the ground surfaces of the output shaft during installation.
2. Apply a daub of grease to the selective thrust washer and install washer on the front end of the output shaft.

NOTE: If the drive train end-play was not within specifications when checked (Checking Drive Train End-Play), replace the thrust washer with one of proper thickness.

Input Shaft and Rear Clutch

1. Turn transmission in an upright position, with the output shaft pointing downward.
2. Align the rear clutch plate inner splines, then lower the input shaft and clutch assembly into position in the case.
3. Carefully work the clutch assembly, in a circular motion, to engage the clutch splines with the splines of the kickdown annulus gear support.
4. Daub one side of the fiber thrust washer with heavy grease, then position washer in the recess on the front face of the rear clutch retainer.

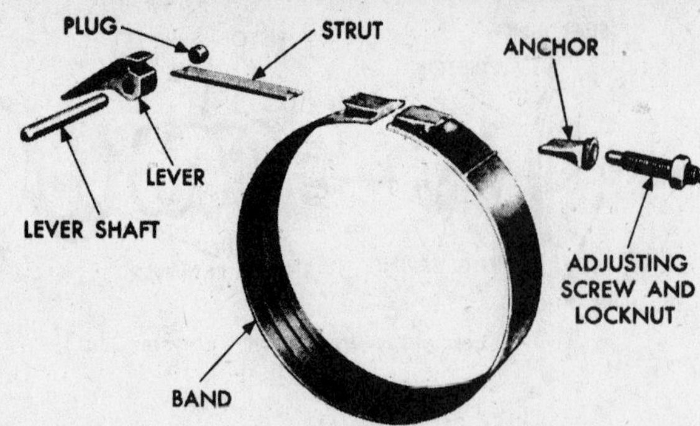

Kickdown band and linkage (© Chrysler Corp.)

Front Clutch

1. Align the front clutch plate inner splines, then lower the clutch assembly into position in the case.
2. Carefully work the clutch assembly, in a circular motion, to engage clutch splines with splines of the rear clutch piston retainer. Be sure the front clutch driving lugs are fully engaged in the slots of the driving shell.

Front Band

1. Slide the band over the front clutch assembly.
2. Install band strut, screw in the adjuster just enough to hold the band in place.

Front Oil Pump and Reaction Shaft Support

1. Screw (two) pilot studs into front pump opening in the case.
2. Place a new rubber seal ring in groove on outer flange of pump. Be sure the seal ring is not twisted.
3. Install the assembly into the case, tap lightly with a soft mallet if necessary. Install four bolts, remove pilot studs, install remaining bolts and pull down evenly, then, torque the bolts to specification.
4. Rotate the pump rotors until the two small holes in the handle of the tool are vertical. This is to locate the inner rotor so the converter impeller shaft will engage the inner rotor lugs during installation.

Torque Reference

	Foot-Pounds	*Inch-Pounds*
Kickdown band adjusting screw locknut (eight cylinder cars)	29	—
Kickdown band adjusting screw locknut (six cylinder cars)	—	—
Kickdown lever shaft plug	25	150
Reverse band adjusting screw locknut (eight cylinder cars)	35	—
Reverse band adjusting locknut (six cylinder cars)	20	—
Cooler line fitting 1964-68	—	75
1969 and up		110
Control cable adjusting wheel bolt		
Converter drive plate to crankshaft bolt	—	40
Converter drive plate to torque converter bolt	55	—
Extension housing to transmission case bolt	—	270
Extension housing to insulator mounting bolt	24	—
1964-67	35	—
1968 and up	40	—
Extension housing—crossmember to frame bolt	75	—
Front oil pump housing to transmission case bolt	—	150
Governor body to parking sprag bolt	—	100
Neutral starter switch	25-30	—
Oil pan bolt	—	150
Output shaft flange nut 1964-65 only	175	—
Overrunning clutch cam set screw	—	40
Reaction shaft support to front oil pump bolt		
1964-67 all and 1968-69 A-727	—	150
1968-69 A-904	—	125
1970 all	—	160
Rear oil pump cover bolt 1964-65 only	—	140
Transmission to engine bolt	25-30	—
Valve body screw 1964-67	—	28
1968 and up	—	35
Valve body to transmission case bolt	—	100

Rear Oil Pump Through 1965

1. Place outer rotor in pump body.
2. Turn output shaft so the inner rotor driving ball pocket is facing up. Install the ball and slide the inner rotor onto the output shaft, in alignment with the ball
3. Position the outer rotor so the dye marks will be aligned, then push the inner rotor into mesh with the outer rotor.
4. Install the pump cover, with the retaining bolts threaded a few turns. Slide aligning sleeve, tool C-3762, all the way in, until it bottoms against the rotors.

Governor

1. Align the master spline of the governor support with the master spline on the output shaft, then slide the assembly into place. Install snap-ring behind the governor housing. Torque housing-to-support screws to specification.
2. Place the governor valve on the valve shaft, insert the assembly into the housing and through the governor weights. Install the valve shaft retaining snap-ring.

Extension Housing

1964-65

1. Using new gasket, slide extension housing into place. Install retaining bolts and washers, and tighten bolts to 25 ft. lbs.
2. Install transmission output shaft flange. Install washer with its three projections toward flange and install nut with its convoluted surface contacting washer. Hold flange so that it does not move and torque nut to 175 ft. lbs. Torque reading must be taken as nut passes over hump.

1966 and Up

1. Install snap ring in front groove on output shaft.
2. Install bearing on shaft with its outer race ring groove toward front. Press or tap bearing tight against front snap ring.
3. Install rear snap ring.
4. Place new extension housing gasket on transmission case.
5. Place output shaft bearing retaining snap ring in extension housing. Spread ring as far as possible, then carefully tap extension housing into place. Make sure snap ring is fully seated in bearing groove.
6. Install and torque extension housing bolts to specification.
7. Install gasket, plate, and two screws on bottom of extension housing mounting pad.
8. Install speedometer pinion and adapter assembly.

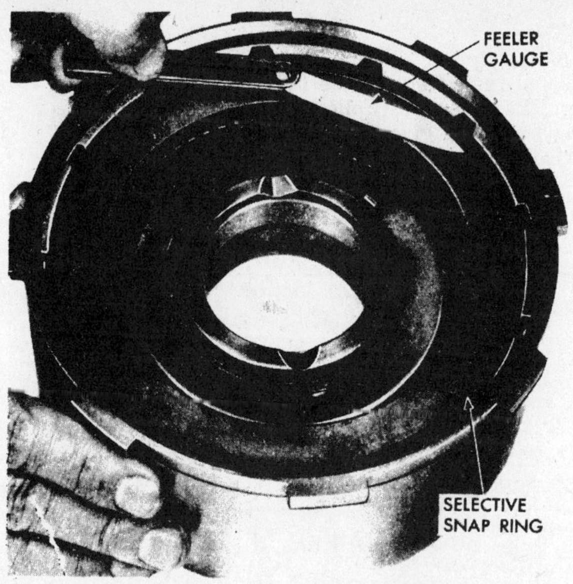

Measuring Front Clutch Plate Clearance

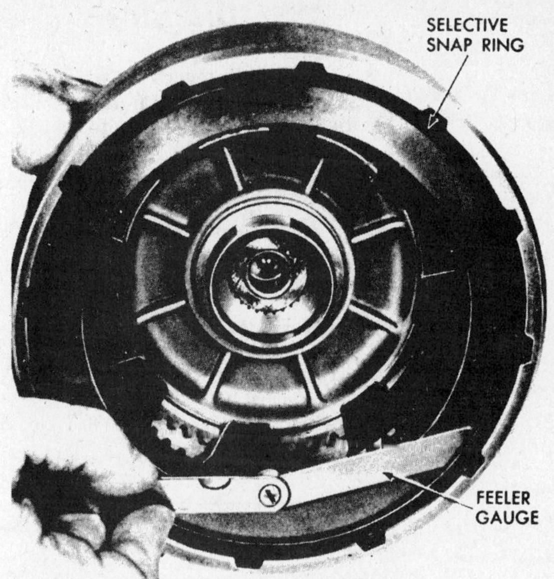

Measuring Rear Clutch Plate Clearance

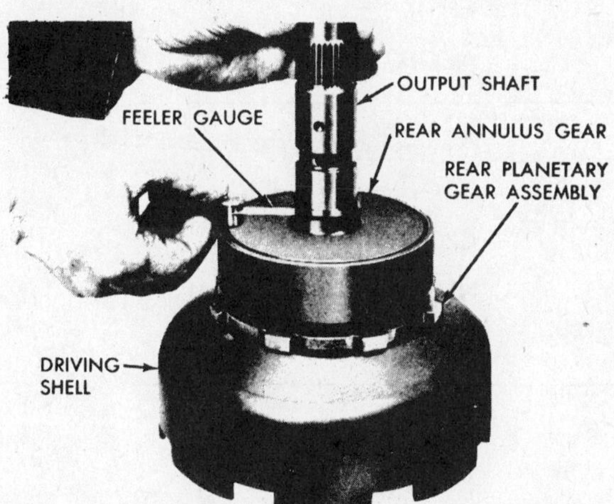

Measuring End Play of Planetary Gear Assemblies

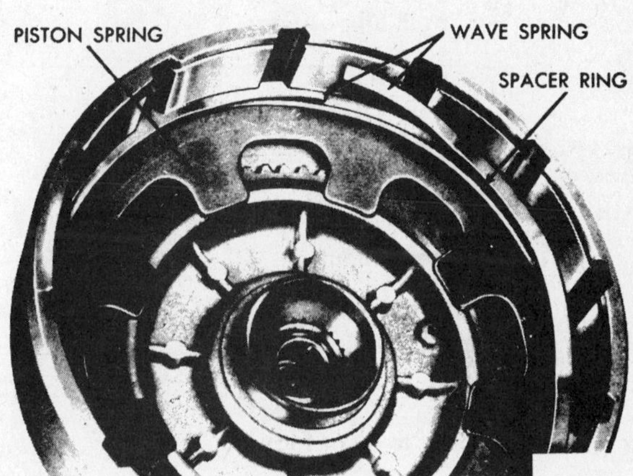

Installing Rear Clutch Spring, Spacer Ring and Wave Spring

Overrunning Clutch Cam Stake Locations

Diagnosis

This guide covers the most common symptoms and is an aid to careful diagnosis. The items to check are listed in sequence to be followed for quickest results. Follow the checks in the order given for the particular transmission type.

TROUBLE SYMPTOMS	Items to Check In Truck	Items to Check Out of Truck
Harsh N to D or N to R shift	CDEFGIJ	ab
Delayed Shift—N to D	ACIHKJ	ca
Runaway on upshift and 3-2 kickdown	ABCDLIHK	b
Harsh upshift and 3-2 kickdown	BCDLIHJ	b
No upshift	ABCDLIHKM	b
No kickdown on normal downshift	ABNCDLIHKM	d
Erratic shifts	ABNCFOPQ IKMJ	c
Slips in forward drive positions	ACIHK	abd
Slips in reverse only	CEGIK	
Slips in all positions	ACOIK	e
No drive in any position	ACOQIKJ	ca
No drive in forward positions	CDOLIHK	abd
No drive in reverse	CEGKMI	b
Drives in neutral	NIJ	a
Drags or locks	DELG	abfd
Noises	AORPMIJ	a
Hard to fill or blows out	AORSTQI	
Transmission overheats	ADEORTMI	abe
Unable to push-start car (No rear pump after 1965)	ACEGI	g

Key to Checks

A. Oil level
B. Control linkage
C. Oil pressure check
D. Kickdown band
E. Low-reverse band
F. Improper engine idle
G. Servo linkage
H. Accumulator
I. Valve body assembly
J. Manual valve lever
K. Air pressure check
L. K-D servo link
M. Governor
N. Gear shift cable
O. Regulator valve and/or spring
P. Output shaft bushing
Q. Strainer
R. Converter control valve
S. Breather clogged
T. Cooler or lines

a. Front-kickdown clutch
b. Rear clutch
c. Front pump and/or sleeve
d. Overrunning clutch
e. Converter
f. Planetary
g. Rear pump (not after 1965)

General Information

Check the Fluid Level Every 1,000 Miles

If the transmission is at room temperature, having engine idling and transmission in Neutral, the "L" mark on the dipstick is then the correct level. However, if transmission is at operating temperature, the oil level, with transmission in Neutral and engine idling, should be at the "F" mark. Add Automatic Transmission Fluid Type A to bring to proper mark. Be careful not to overfill.

Drain and refill every 20,000 Miles, Oftener in Severe Service

Remove plate from bottom of torque converter housing and turn converter to bring drain plug into reach. Remove converter drain plug and transmission drain plug. When reinstalling plugs check that gaskets are good. Tighten torque converter drain plug to 50 ft. lbs. Tighten oil pan drain plug to 25 ft. lbs.

Pour 5 qts of Type A fluid thru filler tube at right of engine into transmission. Start engine and while

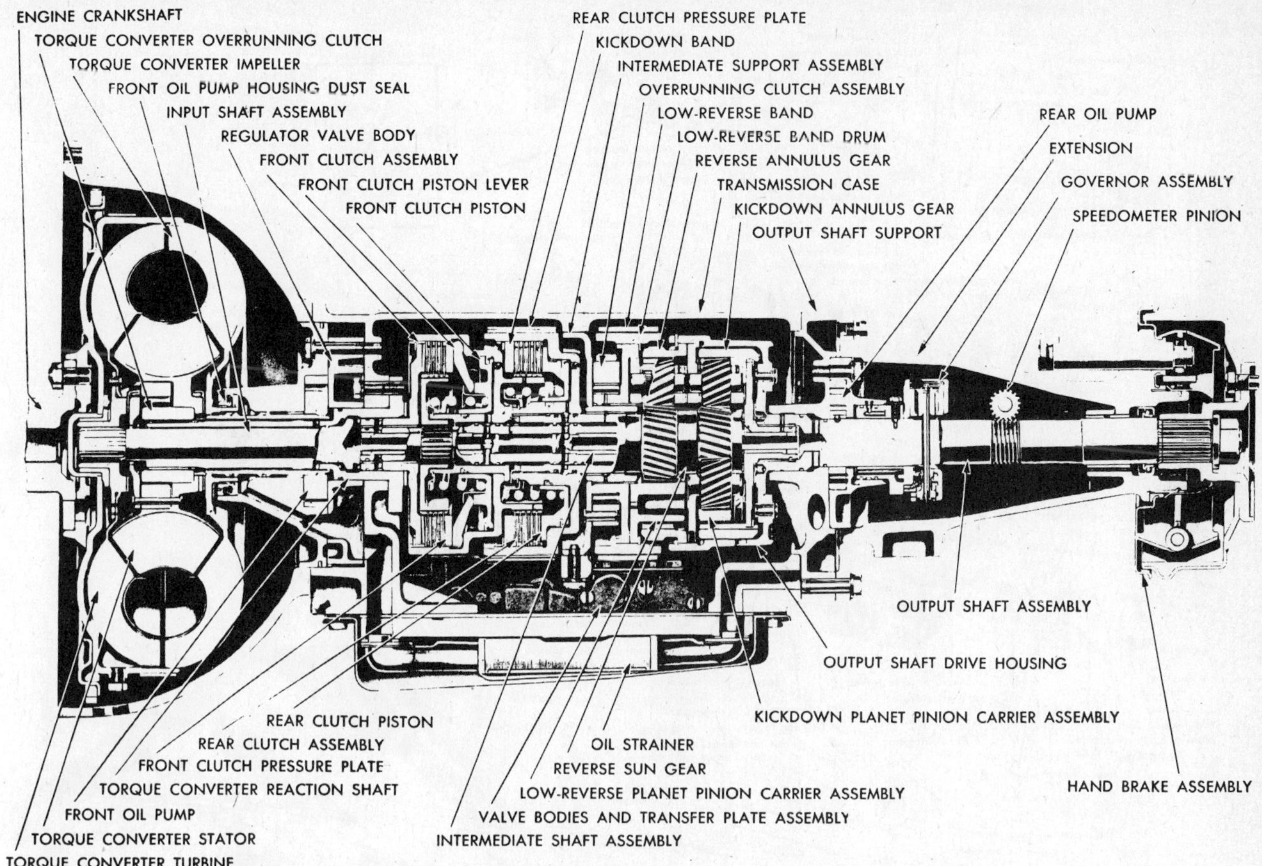

Typical loadflite transmission and torque converter (© Chrysler Corp.)

it idles with transmission in Neutral add enough fluid to bring level to the "L" mark on the dipstick. This will be about 3 qts.

Cold Weather Operation

If weather temperatures are low enough to require 5W oil in the engine the Type A fluid in the transmission may be diluted with one quart of kerosene. Drain 1 qt. from trainsmission and then add kerosene. Check level.

When weather gets warmer, the kerosene will evaporate and the level can be kept constant by adding Type A fluid as required.

Starting the Engine Without use of the Starter

Push the truck to start it. Towing a truck with an automatic transmission to start the engine is likely to result in the towed truck ramming the towing truck.

With the "1" button pushed in, push the truck. At a speed above 15 mph the transmission will operate and the engine will turn.

Towing Truck Equipped with Torque-Flite

If transmission is undamaged and can be placed in Neutral the truck can be towed at moderate speed. Chrysler says that distance towed with transmission turning should not exceed 100 miles.

Using Engine as a Brake on Hills

The "1" button must be pushed in for this transmission to get maximum effect of engine braking on hills. Pushing in the "2" button will allow partial engine braking.

Use of Reverse

If the "R" button is pushed in at any speed above 10 mph a blocker valve in the transmission will move the manual control to Neutral. When the truck speed drops below 10 mph the "R" button must be pushed in again.

Checking for Oil Leaks

Leaks Repaired Without Removing Transmission

Rear bearing oil seal
Rear extension gasket
Speedometer drive gasket
Transmission oil pan gasket
Regulator Valve and Converter Control Valve spring-retainer gaskets
Control cable housing seal and gasket
The pressure test plugs
Neutral starter safety switch
Oil cooler and its lines and fittings

NOTE: Oil cooler can be checked like any other radiator. Do not use over ten pounds of air pressure. On 1957 models cooler is part of radiator.

Leaks Requiring Removal of Transmission

Sand holes in case or pumps
Front oil pump screws, sealing washers, dust seal
Seal on outside diameter of front oil pump
Torque converter seals

Band Adjustment

Both bands are adjusted in the same way. The front (kickdown) band is on the left side of the transmission. The rear (Low-Reverse) band is on the right side of the transmission. On either band use a ¾ inch wrench to back off the lock nut. Check that the band adjusting screw turns freely, then tighten to 70-75 inch pounds (5½-6 foot pounds). Now back off the adjusting screw exactly: 3½ turns for the Front (Kickdown) band; 2¼ turns for the Rear (Low) Band. Tighten the locknut to 35-40 ft. lbs.

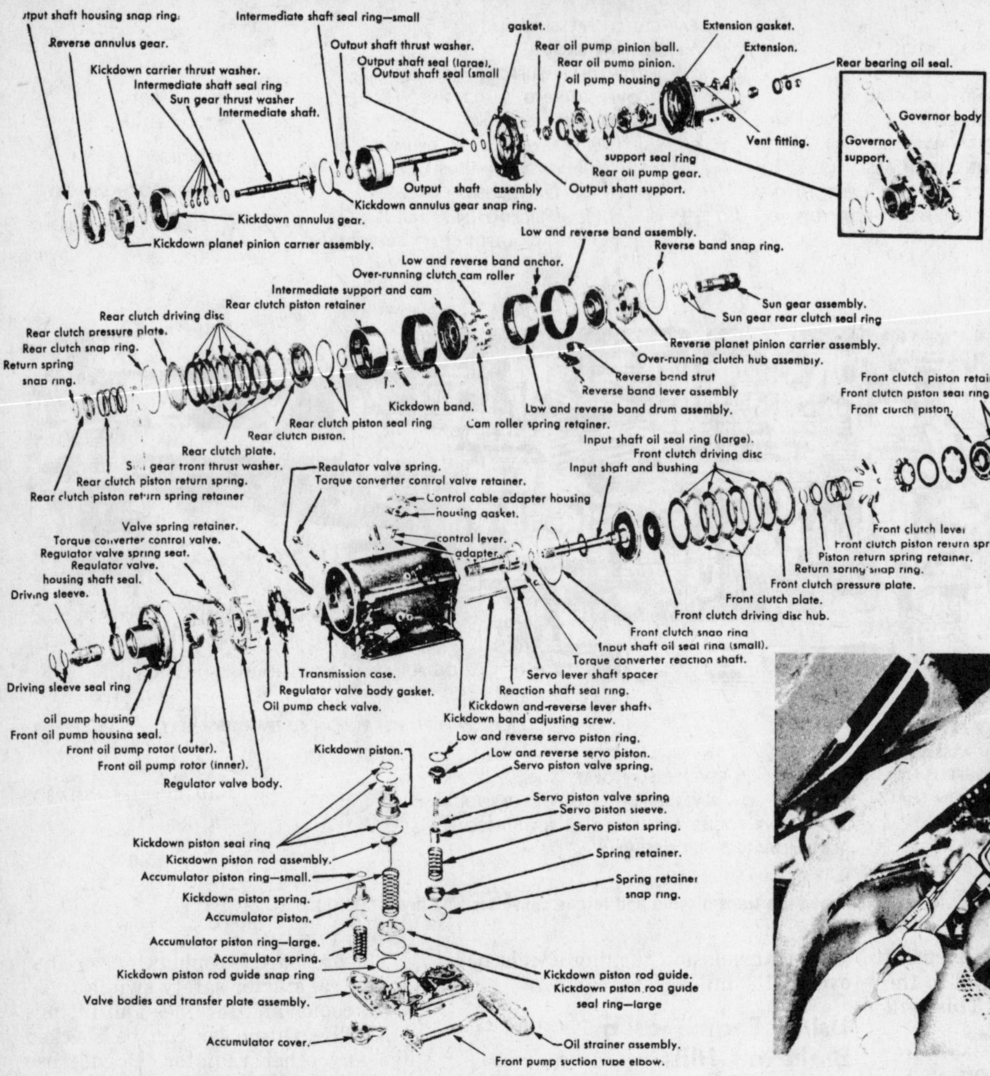

Exploded view of loadflite transmission (© Chrysler Corp.)

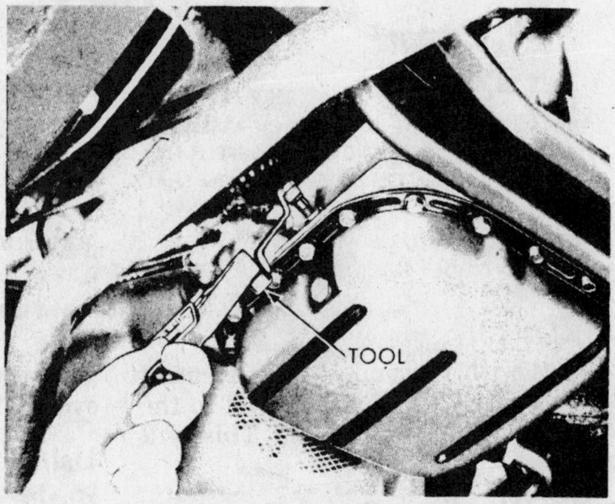

Adjusting front band (© Chrysler Corp.)

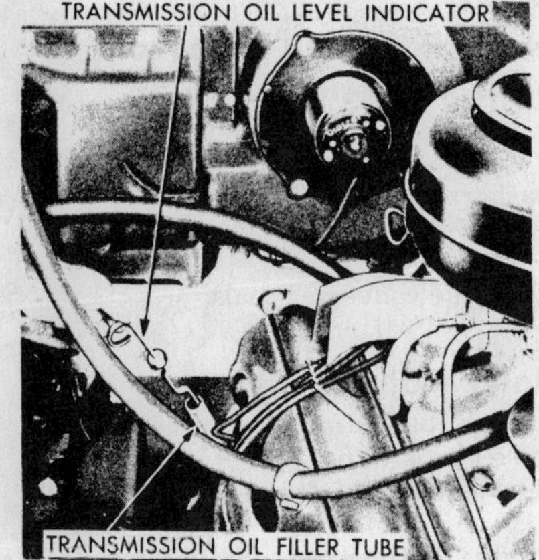

Oil level indicator—total capacity about 8 qts. (© Chrysler Corp.)

Fluid Pressure Checks

Use a fluid pressure gauge capable of measuring from 0 to 300 psi.

Line Pressure

Connect the gauge in place of the 1/8 in. pipe plug at the Line Pressure Take-Off on the forward portion of the left side of the transmission case. With the brakes on and the engine running at 800 rpm, the pressure should read 90 psi as the buttons: 1, 2, D and N are pushed in.

Jack up the rear of the truck to take the rear wheels off the floor. Set engine speed at 1600 rpm and push in the "R" button. Pressure should be 225 psi. Failure to reach this pressure shows trouble may be defective front pump or regulator valve.

Governor Pressure

Connect the guage in the place of the 1/8 in. pipe plug at the Governor Pressure Take-Off on the lower left side of the output shaft support. Jack the rear wheels off the floor and with them free to turn push in the "D" button. Run the engine to show 8 mph on the speedometer. Pressure should read 2-3 psi. When speedometer reads 27 mph, pressure should be 27-32 psi. When speedometer reads 38 mph, pressure should read 44-47 psi. When speedometer reads 75 mph, pressure should read 75-82 psi. Failure to reach these pressures indicates trouble in the governor or the rear pump.

Lubrication Pressure

Connect the gauge in the place of the 1/8 pipe plug on the Lubrication Pressure Take-Off on left side toward the front of the transmission case just above the line pressure take-off plug. With engine running at 800 rpm, pressure should be 10-30 psi. If pressure is incorrect the trouble can be in the regulator valve or the converter control valve. If the pressure is extremely high the lubrication passages are clogged.

Front Servo Release and Rear Clutch Apply Pressure

Connect the gauge in place of the 1/8 in. pipe plug on the Front Servo Release and Rear Clutch Apply Pressure Take-Off located on the lower

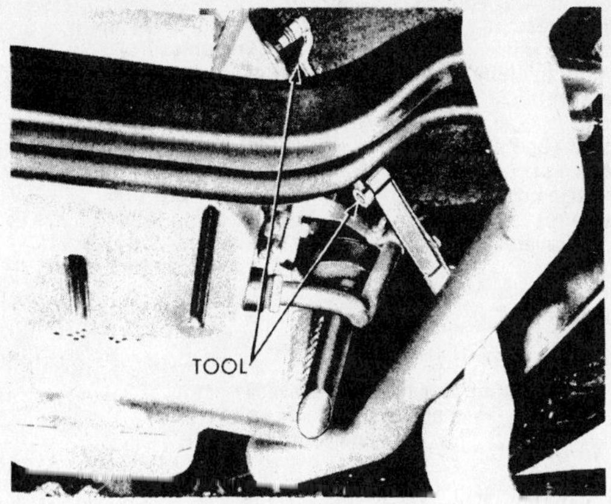

Adjusting rear band
(© Chrysler Corp.)

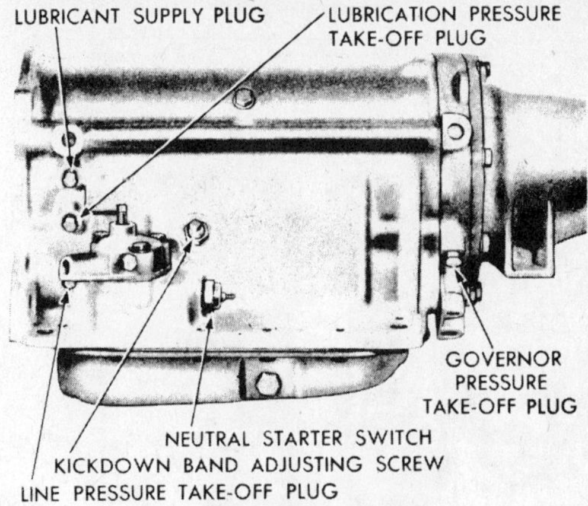

View of left side of transmission
(© Chrysler Corp.)

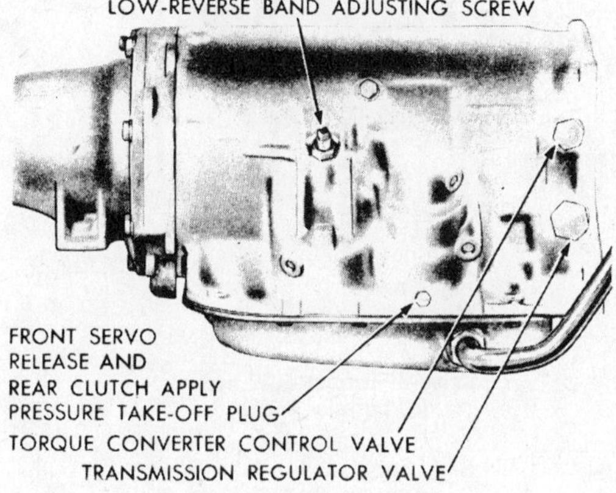

View of right side of transmission
(© Chrysler Corp.)

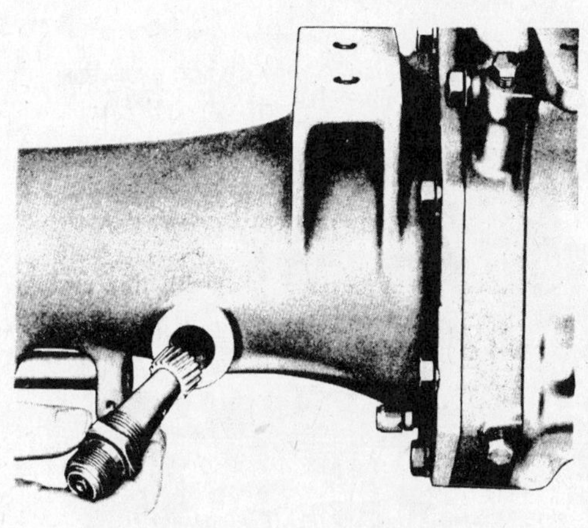

Removing speedometer drive pinion
(© Chrysler Corp.)

right side of the transmission case. The pressure reading should not be more than 15 psi below the line pressure reading with truck in Direct Drive (High).

Air Pressure Checks

1. The Front Clutch Passage

Located slightly toward the center of the transmission from the accumulator. Listen for dull thud to indicate clutch is operating.

2. The Rear Clutch Passage

Located near center of rear edge of transmission. Listen for dull thud to indicate rear clutch is operating.

3. Kickdown (Front) Servo Line Apply Passage

Located toward center of case and to the front of the servo. Observe operation of servo, linkage and front band.

4. Kickdown (Front) Servo Throttle-Compensated Apply Passage

Located toward center of case and to rear of servo. Observe operation of servo.

5. Low-Reverse (Rear) Servo Apply Passage

Located toward center of case and to the front of servo. Observe operation of the servo, the linkage, the rear band.

6. Line Pressure To Governor Passage

Located in left rear corner of transmission case lower surface. Rotate the propeller shaft slightly. Listen for a click to indicate that flyweight has operated.

In Truck Services

Speedometer Pinion

Located on left side of rear extension.

Disconnect speedometer cable and sheath from the drive pinion and sleeve assembly. Unscrew pinion and sleeve assembly from the extension. When reinstalling, tighten pinion and sleeve assembly to 45 ft, lbs. before reconnecting cable and sheath.

Neutral Safety (Starter) Switch

Located on left side of transmission. It is screwed into the manual control cable housing. Two quarts of fluid should be drained from the transmission before the switch is removed from the control cable housing. Note that the switch uses a gasket. Tighten to 15-20 ft. lbs. Do not neglect to refill transmission to proper level.

Valve Bodies and Transfer Plate Assembly

Push in button marked "1". Remove oil pan. Disconnect throttle rod from throttle lever at transmission; be careful not to change adjustment. Loosen the screw holding transmission throttle lever and remove the lever. Clean up control cable housing and remove flat washer and felt seal from throttle lever shaft. Remove clip screw, lock washer and clip holding control cable sheath to housing. Remove plug in side of housing and working thru this opening with a screwdriver release the spring lock and pull the cable free. Now use screwdriver to push the manual control lever rearward to the last detent which is reverse. Remove the three screws and dished washers to release control cable housing and gasket. Note that the manual valve is located on its shaft just 7/32 in. above surface to

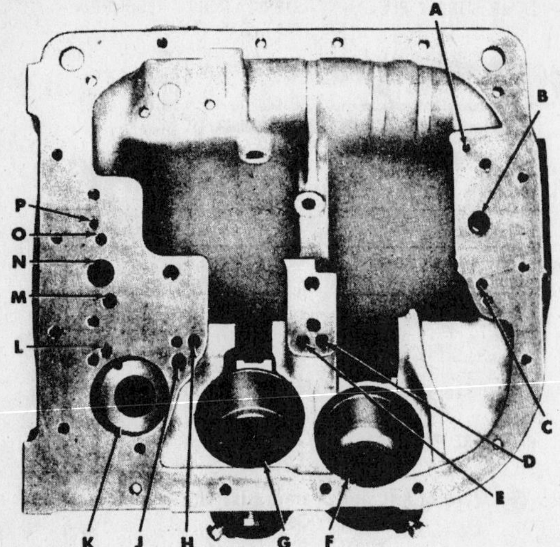

A Governor pressure
B Rear pump inlet
C Rear clutch 'apply' (line pressure)
D Low and reverse servo 'apply' (line pressure)
E Kickdown servo 'apply' (throttle compensated pressure)
F Low and reverse servo (location)
G Kickdown servo (location)
H Kickdown servo 'apply' (line pressure)
J Kickdown servo 'release' (line pressure)
K Accumulator (location)
L Front clutch and accumulator 'apply' (line pressure)
M Line pressure
N Front pump inlet
O Reverse upset (reverse blocker 'apply') (line pressure)
P Line pressure gauge

Use air pressure on passages shown to check operation of units (© Chrysler Corp.)

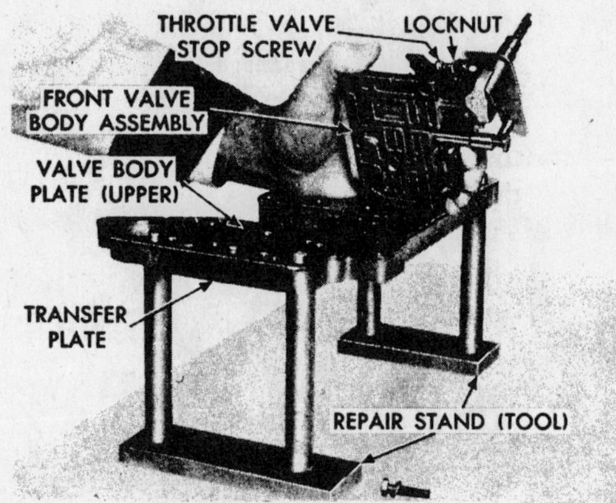

Removal of front valve body (© Chrysler Corp.)

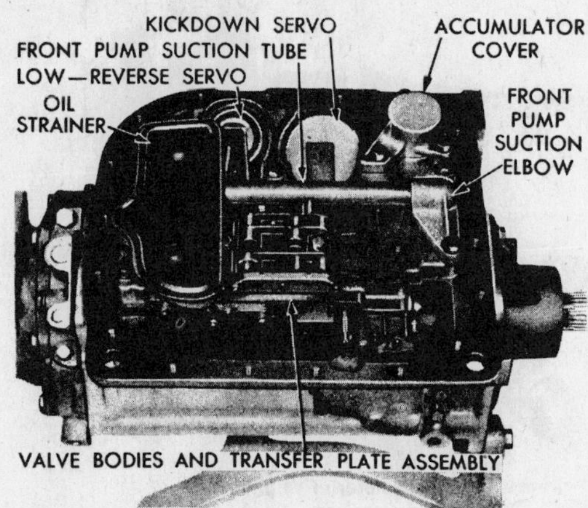

Strainer and valve bodies installed (© Chrysler Corp.)

which housing was attached. Loosen clamp screw and slide lever from shaft.

Remove the two front pump suction elbow screws and dished washers. Note that the dish is always away from the head. Remove oil strainer assembly.

The accumulator is spring loaded. Use care when removing the three screws and removing the accumulator cover and spring.

Unscrew five transfer plate bolts and dished washers and so remove valve bodies and transfer plate assembly.

Front (Kickdown) Servo Piston

After the valve bodies and the transfer plate assembly have been removed, the front band adjusting screw should be loosened to permit removal of the front band anchor and strut. A special tool is now required to compress the servo piston into its bore so that the snap ring can be removed. Removal of the snap ring permits removal of the piston rod guide, piston spring, piston rod and the piston.

Inspect riveting of piston rod, inspect guide contacting surface for nicks or burrs. Check that seal ring turns freely in groove. Inspect the three rings, two are interlocking, on the piston for wear and broken locks. They should turn freely in their grooves. It is not necessary to remove rings. Check surface of the piston for surface smoothness. Check the spring and snap ring for distortion.

Accumulator Piston

Remove valve bodies and transfer plate assemblies. Using pliers, remove accumulator piston from transmission case.

Lubricate seal rings and place accumulator piston into position. Compress outer seal ring and tap lightly into transmission case. Install valve bodies and transfer plate assembles.

Output Shaft Rear Bearing Oil Seal

Disconnect the front universal joint. Apply the hand brake and remove the propeller shaft flange nut and dished washer. Release hand brake and install puller (if necessary). Remove the propeller shaft flange and brake drum assembly. Remove the transmission brake support grease shield spring (small one). Remove brake support grease shield from extension. If screwdriver or sharp instrument is used in performing this operation, care must be exercised not to damage the neoprene sealing surface at bottom of shield. Install puller, and remove the transmission output shaft rear bearing oil seal.

Using driver, install new output shaft rear bearing oil seal (metal portion of seal facing in) until driver bottoms on extension. Install brake support grease shield on extension. Indent on grease shield must match groove in extension for correct positioning. Also, shield must be located on extension far enough to permit installation of spring. Install brake support grease shield spring (opening in spring toward adjusting sleeve). Make sure spring is properly seated in groove. Install propeller shaft flange, dished washer, and nut. Apply hand brake and torque the propeller shaft flange nut to 200 ft. lbs. Connect front universal joint and torque nuts to 33-37 ft. lbs. Check fluid level.

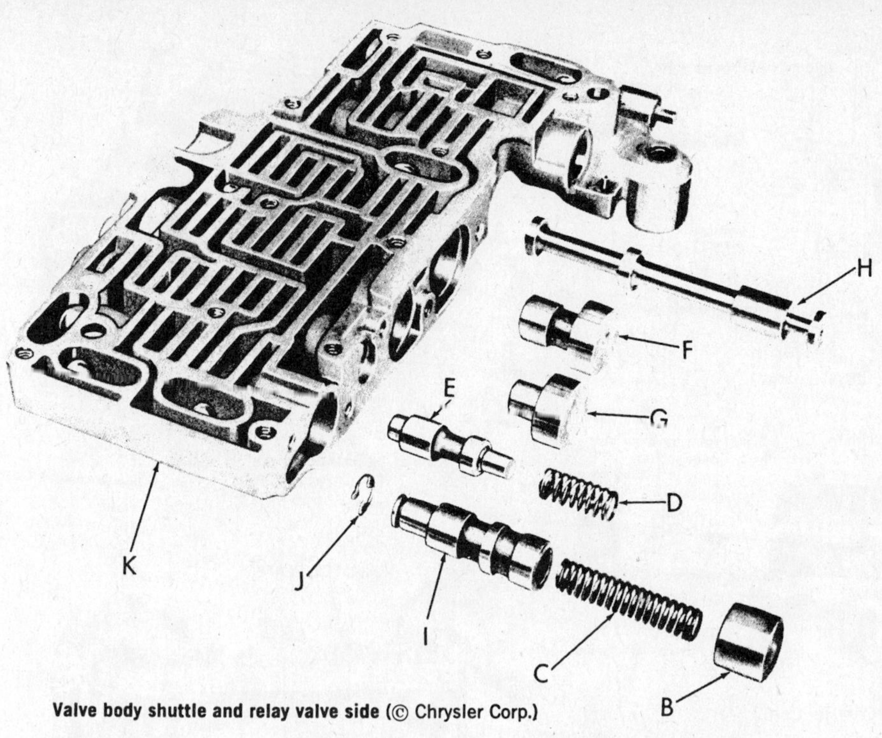

Valve body shuttle and relay valve side (© Chrysler Corp.)

A Shuttle valve and governor plug cover
B Shuttle valve plug
C Shuttle valve spring
D 1-2 relay valve spring
E 1-2 relay valve

F 1-2 shift valve governor plug
G 2-3 shift valve governor plug
H Manual valve
I Shuttle valve
J Shuttle valve snap ring
K Valve body

L Shift valve cover plate
M 1-2 shift valve spring
N 2-3 shift valve spring
O 1-2 shift valve
P 2-3 shift valve
Q Throttle compensating valve spring
R Throttle compensating valve
S Throttle valve cover
T Throttle valve
U Throttle valve spring
V Kickdown valve
W Kickdown valve detent

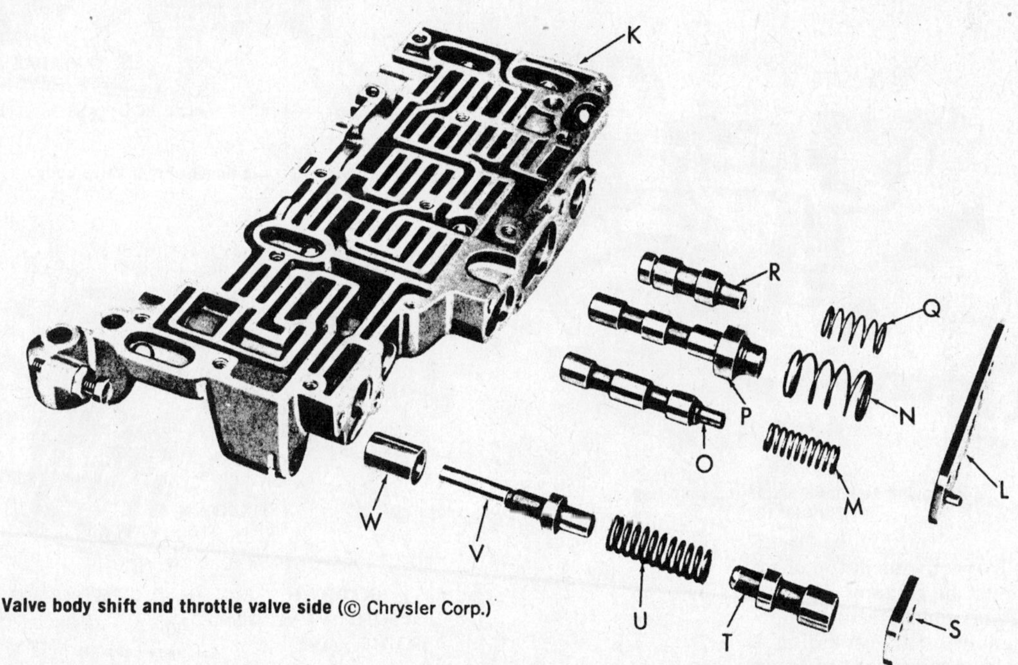

Valve body shift and throttle valve side (© Chrysler Corp.)

Rear Extension and Output Shaft Bearing

Drain approximately two quarts of fluid from transmission. Disconnect front universal joint. Apply hand brake and remove propeller shaft flange nut and dished washer. Release hand brake and using puller (if necessary), remove the propeller shaft flange and drum assembly. Remove brake adjusting screw cover plate and loosen cable clamp bolt on hand brake support. Disengage the ball end of the cable from operating lever and remove cable from brake support.

Disconnect speedometer cable and housing at transmission extension and remove speedometer drive pinion and sleeve assembly. Remove the two nuts and lock washers that hold engine rear support insulator to the crossmember, leaving insulator attached to extension. Remove the two top transmission extension to case screws and lock washers. Using suitable jack and extreme care (to prevent damage to oil pan), raise transmission sufficiently for insulator on extension to clear crossmember. Remove four of the remaining extension to case screws and lock washers and install guide studs.

Due to interference of the insulator, it will be necessary to remove the bottom extension to case screw with the extension; that is, back screw out as far as possible and slide extension back and continue loosening of screw.

CAUTION: Do not remove the one output shaft support to transmission case screw.

Remove extension and hand brake as one assembly. Remove extension gasket. If care is used, it is not necessary to remove hand brake support and shoe assemblies from extension to replace output shaft rear bearing.

Inspect extension for cracks in casting and remove burrs from gas-

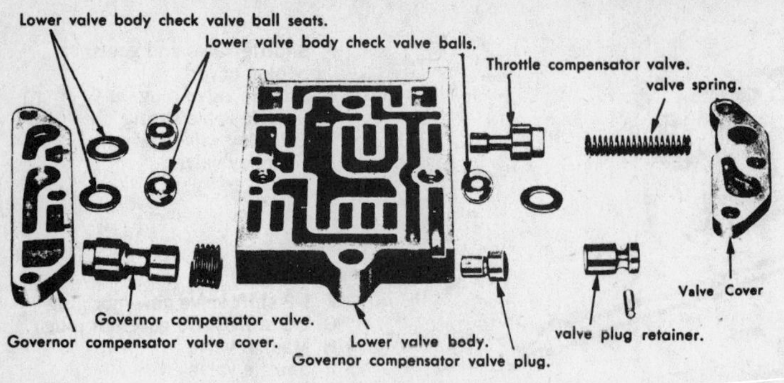

Lower valve body (© Chrysler Corp.)

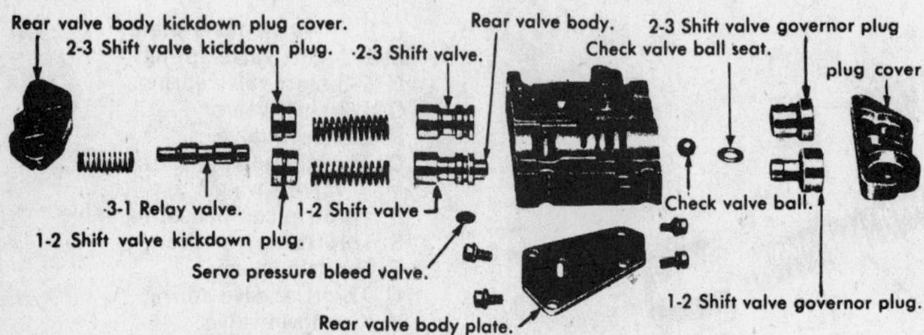

Rear valve body (© Chrysler Corp.)

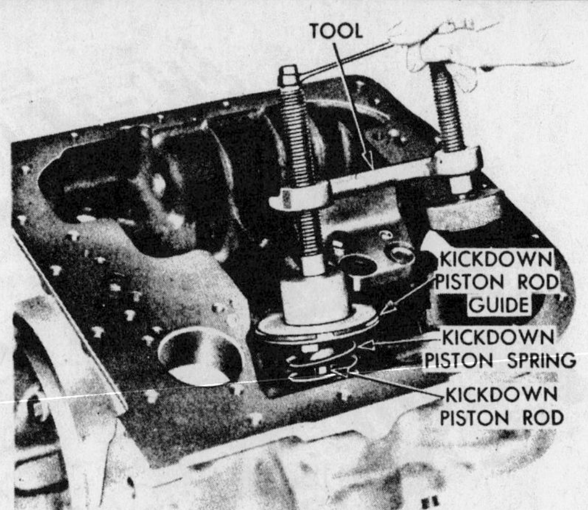

Removing kickdown piston spring (© Chrysler Corp.)

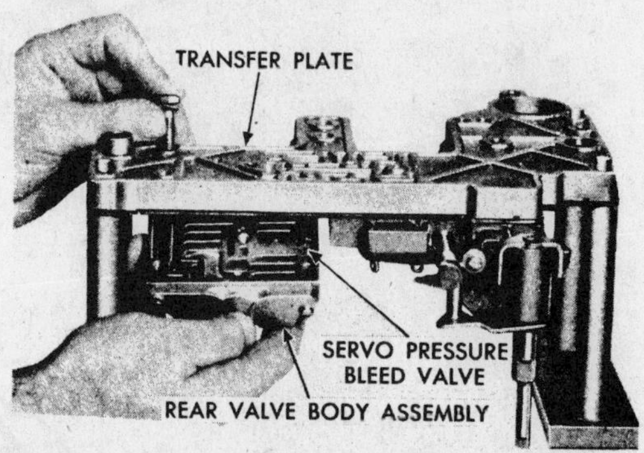

Removal of rear valve body (© Chrysler Corp.)

Removing kickdown piston-rod snap-ring (© Chrysler Corp.)

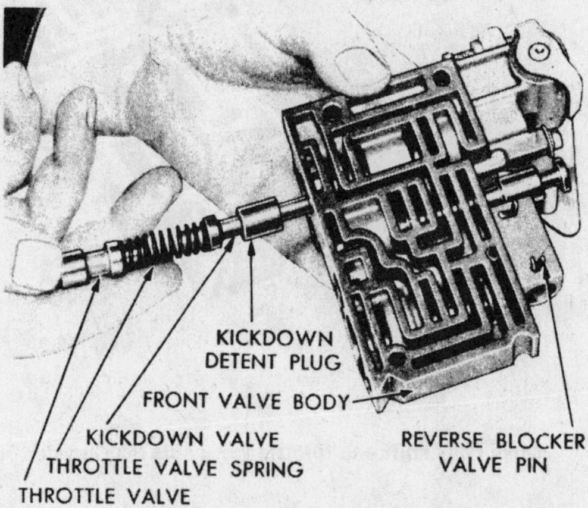

Removing throttle and kickdown valves from front valve body (© Chrysler Corp.)

ket surface. Inspect vent in top of extension. It must be clear of dirt, under-coating, and such. Besides allowing air to enter as transmission is drained this vent takes care of fumes and oil expansion due to heat. Clean the output shaft rear bearing with compressed air but do not spin it. If bearing is rough, remove the oil seal and then the bearing snap ring. Note that snap ring has a beveled edge. Drive bearing out the rear of the extension. When new bearing is properly seated install the snap ring. It should be firmly seated in its groove with bevel side out.

With guid studs installed in transmission case, install a new extension gasket over guide studs and into position against output shaft support. Do not use sealing material on gasket. Using extreme care, place extension and hand brake assembly over output shaft and on guide studs. Due to interference of the insulator, it will be necessary to start the bottom extension to case screw as the extension is pushed into position against support.

Do not attempt to pull extension in with the aid of screws; otherwise, damage to extension may result. The propeller shaft flange and drum assembly may be used to force bearing in extension on output shaft. Do not use hammer.

Remove guide studs install the six remaining extension to case screws and lock washers. Draw down evenly and tighten from 25 ft. lbs. After screws have been properly torqued, turn output shaft to make sure it turns freely. Lower transmission and at the same time align mounting studs in insulator with holes in crossmember. Install the two nuts and lock washers that hold the rear engine support insulator and torque from 30-35 ft. lbs. Engage ball end of hand brake cable in operating lever

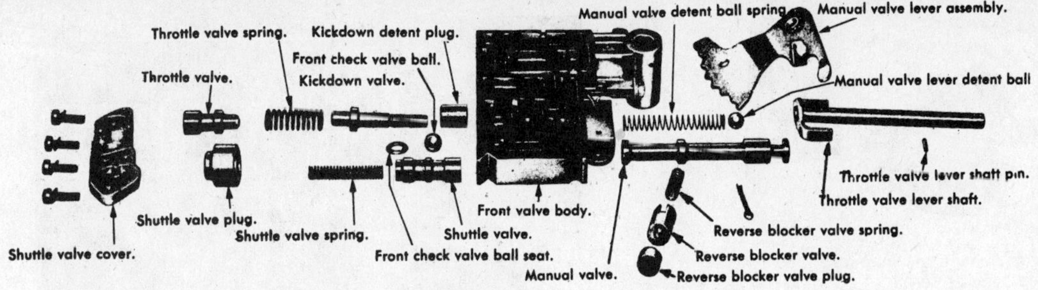

Front valve body arrangement (© Chrysler Corp.)

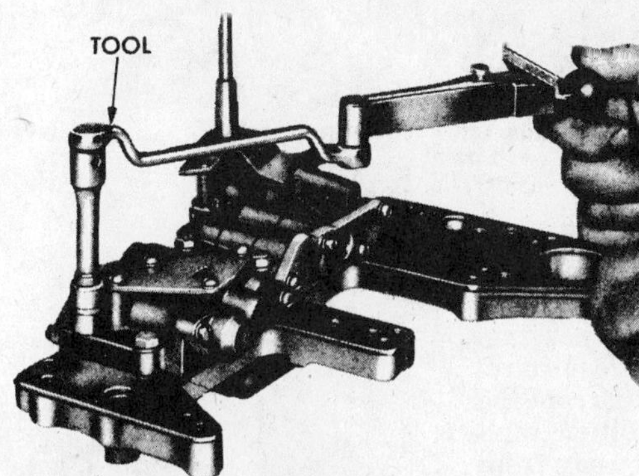

Tighten valve body screws to 50-60 inch lbs. (© Chrysler Corp.)

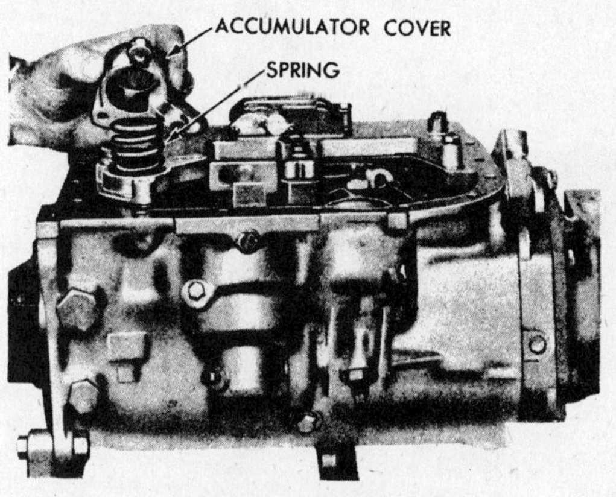

Removing accumulator cover (© Chrysler Corp.)

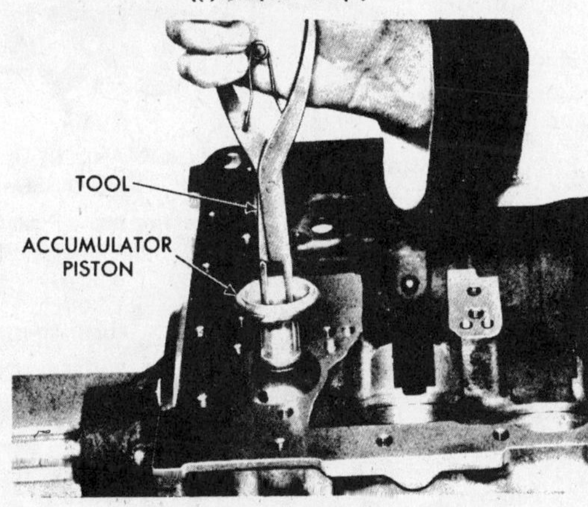

Removing accumulator piston (© Chrysler Corp.)

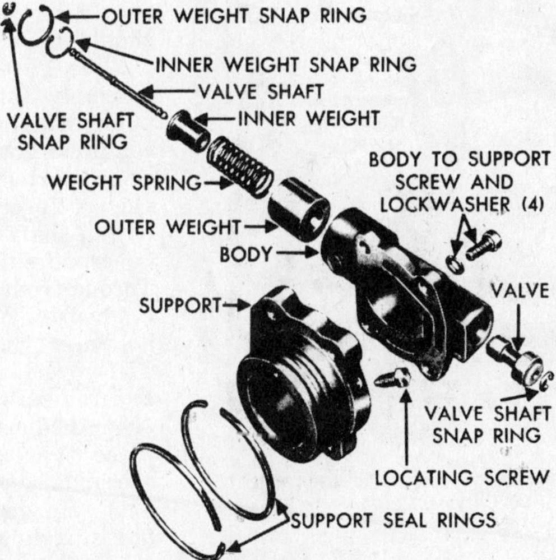

Exploded view of a governor (© Chrysler Corp.)

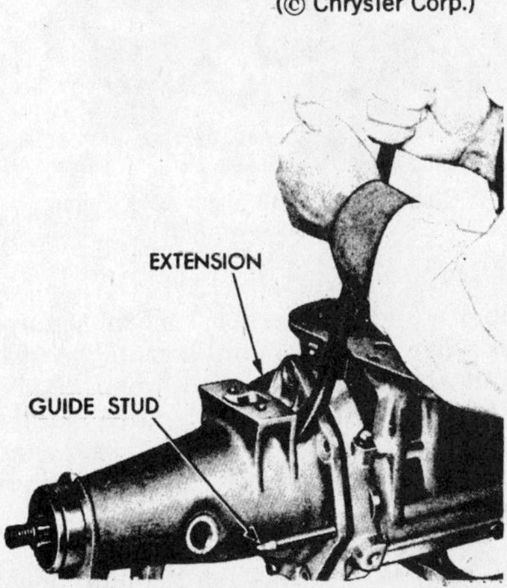

Removing rear case extension (© Chrysler Corp.)

and tighten cable clamp bolt. Apply hand brake and tighten Universal Joint Flange Nut to 200 ft. lbs. Install adjusting screw cover plate on hand brake support. Connect front universal joint and torque nuts from 33-37ft. lbs. Install speedometer pinion and sleeve assembly. Torque from 40-45 ft. lbs. and connect speedometer cable housing. Refill transmission to proper level with a good grade of Automatic Transmission Fluid.

Governor

Refer to Extension Removal. Using a screwdriver, remove the governor valve shaft snap ring (small) from the weight assembly end. Remove governor valve shaft and valve from governor body assembly. Using pliers remove governor weight assembly snap ring (large) and remove governor weight assembly from valve body.

The primary cause of governor operating failures is due to improper operation of governor valve which may be sticking in housing or travel restricted by chips or other foreign matter. If inspection reveals that it is necessary for further governor serv-

Removing governor shaft snap-ring (© Chrysler Corp.)

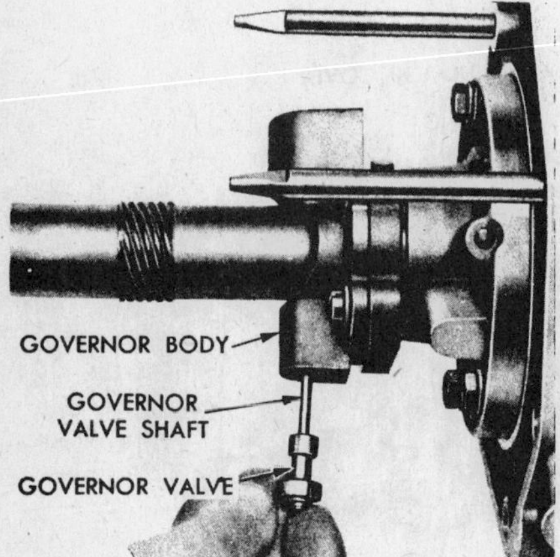

Removing governor valve and shaft assembly (© Chrysler Corp.)

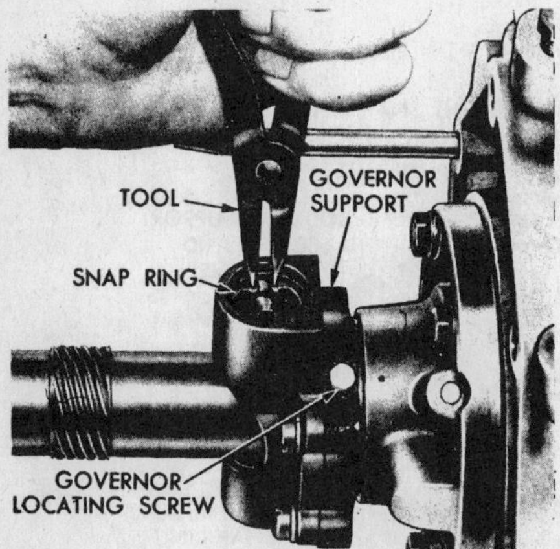

Removing snap-ring to release governor weight (© Chrysler Corp.)

Removal of governor weight (© Chrysler Corp.)

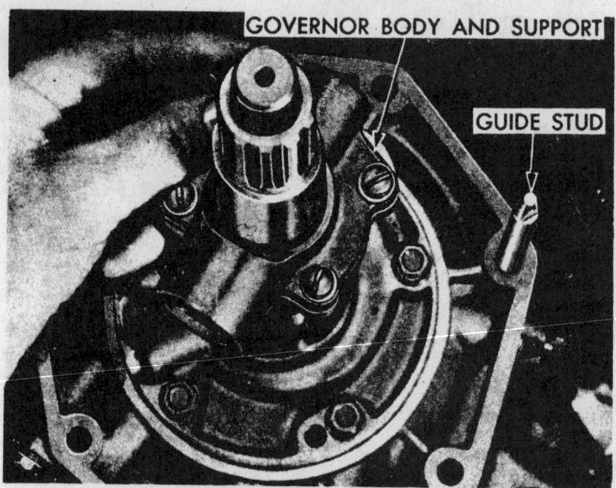

Remove locating screw to release governor assembly (© Chrysler Corp.)

icing, then remove governor support locating screw, using a 5/16 in. socket, and remove governor and support assembly from rear oil pump housing. Normal servicing does not require removal of the governor body from the governor support. If condition warrants removal of governor body from governor support, when reassembling, do not tighten governor body screws until governor body support is located on output shaft.

Inspect all parts for burrs and wear. Inspect oil passages; they should be clean. Valves and weights should move freely.

Slide governor body and support assembly into position in rear oil pump housing. Using extreme care, compress governor support seal rings as support enters oil pump housing. Do not force. Align locating hole in output shaft to locating screw hole in governor support and install screw. Torque from 5-7 ft. lbs. Holes can be aligned by turning output shaft and holding governor body.

If governor body has been removed and reinstalled, torque the four governor body screws from 6-8 ft. lbs. Place governor weight assembly (secondary weight snap ring facing out) into governor body; and using pliers install snap ring. Make sure snap ring seats properly. With the governor valve (small end up) on governor valve shaft, slide shaft into governor body through the output shaft and governor weight assembly; at the same time, position valve in body. Install the governor valve shaft snap ring. Replace snap ring if distorted. After snap ring installation apply sufficient pressure to both ends of valve shaft to force snap rings to outer portion of snap ring grooves Check operation of governor weight assembly and valve by turning output shaft. Both should fall freely in body. Install transmission extension.

Rear Oil Pump

Apply paragraphs on "Rear Extension" and "Governor." Then remove the five rear oil pump housing to output shaft support screws and dished washers, and install guide studs. Remove pump housing, gear, and governor assembly from output shaft.

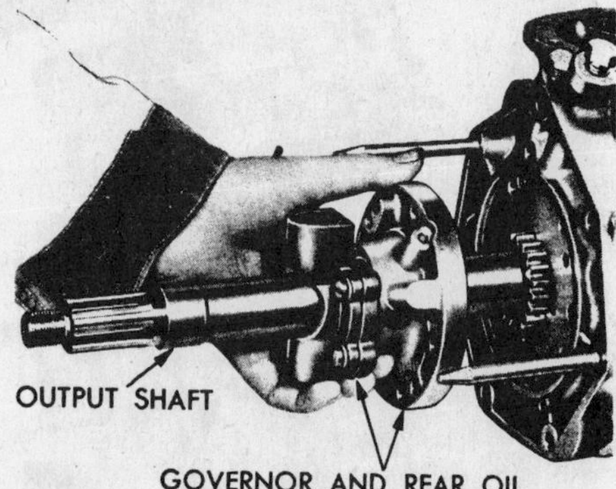

Removing rear oil pump (© Chrysler Corp.)

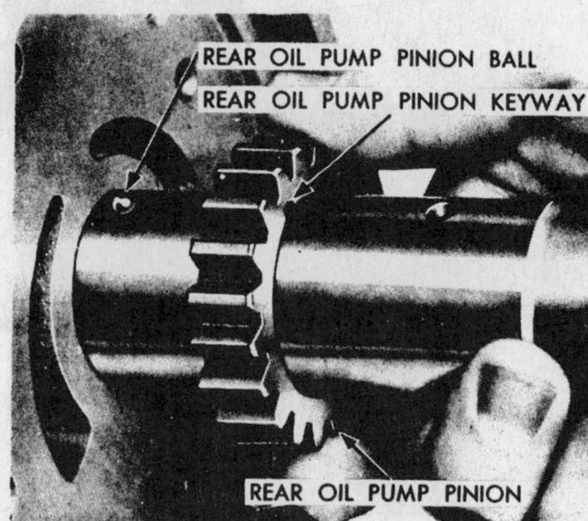

Removing rear oil pump drive pinion (© Chrysler Corp.)

Use Prussian blue and mark both pump gears in relation to pump housing face. Do not use scribe. Oil pump pinion is keyed to output shaft by a small ball. Use care when removing pinion so as not to lose ball. Remove

Removal of front pump drive sleeve
(© Chrysler Corp.)

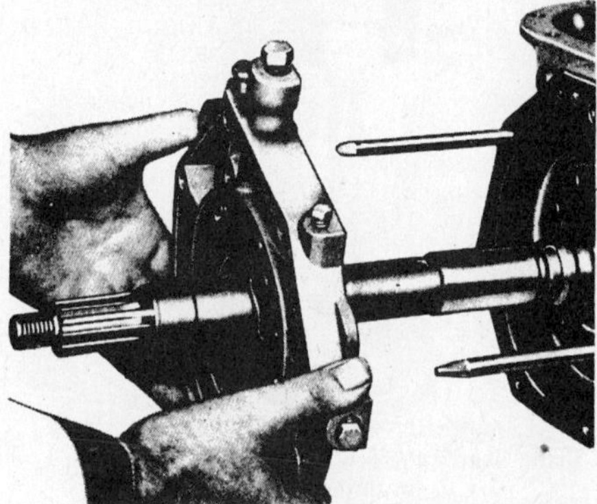

Removal of output shaft support
(© Chrysler Corp.)

Removing front pump
(© Chrysler Corp.)

output shaft support.

Front Pump Drive Sleeve

Removal of the transmission permits removal of the front pump drive sleeve. It slips out of the front pump housing. Inspect the neoprene seal ring for nicks, deterioration, hardness. Inspect the interlocking seal ring for wear or broken locks; check that it turns freely in the groove. Check the driving lugs at each end for excessive wear. Check bearing surface for nicks, burrs, scratches.

Front Oil Pump

Remove the Transmission Regulator and Converter Control Valves.

Remove the seven front oil pump to transmission case screws and washers. The washers are made of aluminum and should be discarded if distorted. Tap pump housing gently with a plastic hammer and so remove front pump from transmission case. Mark the pump gears with Prussian blue (do not scribe) so that they may be reassembled with the faces out.

Inspect the dust shield in the front of the pump housing and if need be drive the seal out the front. Put metal portion of new seal down on front of pump and drive on new seal until it bottoms.

Inspect inner surface of housing that contacts the seal rings of the drive sleeve. Surface should be smooth. If bushing in housing is worn, replace housing assembly. Bushing is not sold separately.

Check the oil pump gears for scratches or grooving. Check that passages in housing are free and clear.

Using a straight edge and feeler gauge, check that clearance is .0010 to .0025 inch. If clearance between lobes is greater than .010 inch, or the clearance between outer edge of outer gear and housing is greater than .010 inch, the gears or pump housing should be renewed.

Replace the gears in the housing as marked at disassembly: that is, be sure counterbore in pinion gear faces front of truck.

Check the outer "O" ring seal on the pump body for nicks or deterioration. With inner and outer seals lubricated and pump gears is position, place oil pump housing over guide pins as shown in illustration. Start five of the screws with aluminum washers and draw the housing down evenly until it is seated in transmission case. Remove guide pins, install the two remaining screws and washers and tighten all evenly to 14-16 ft. lbs.

Lubricate and install the front pump drive sleeve bearing surface first. Turn sleeve to check that oil pump gears turn freely.

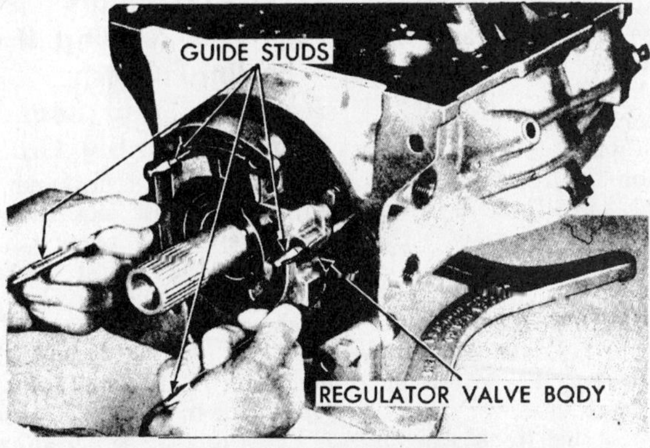

Removing regulator valve body
(© Chrysler Corp.)

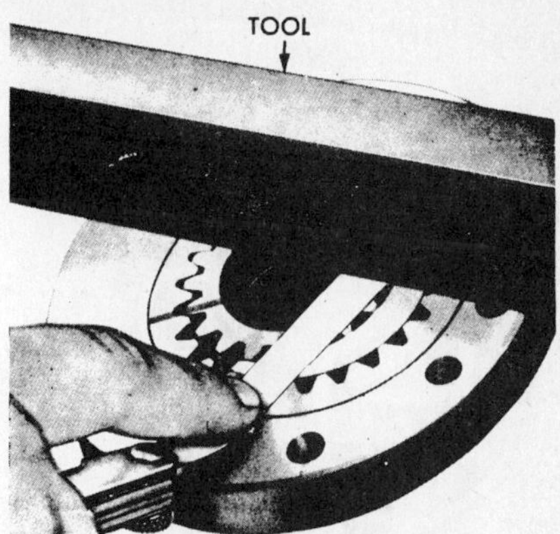

End clearance of pump gears should be .0010" .0025". Not markings on gears.
(© Chrysler Corp.)

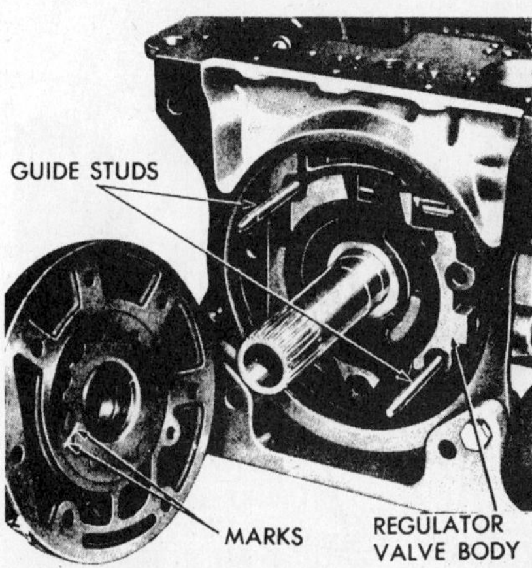

Installing front pump. Note match marks. Counterbore in pinion gees toward front of car.
(© Chrysler Corp.)

Regulator Valve Body

Remove the front pump, the torque converter control valve, and the transmission regulator valve.

Install guide pins thru valve body into case and, using threaded holes provided in valve body, thread in two screws and use as handles to pull valve body from the case. The valve body is made of aluminum and must be carefully handled. Removal of the body permits removal of regulator valve body to transmission case gasket.

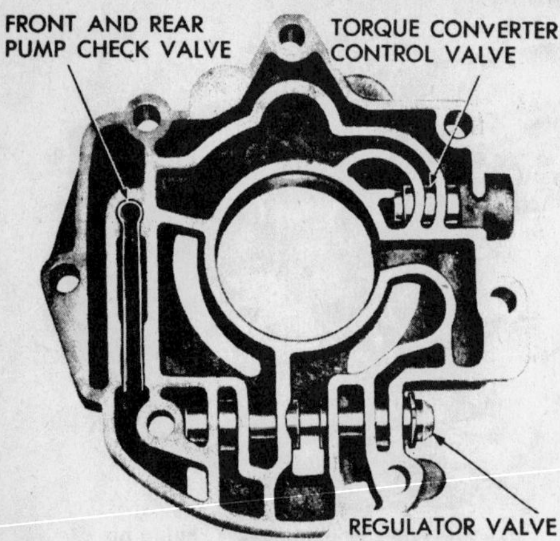

Rear view of regulator valve body
(© Chrysler Corp.)

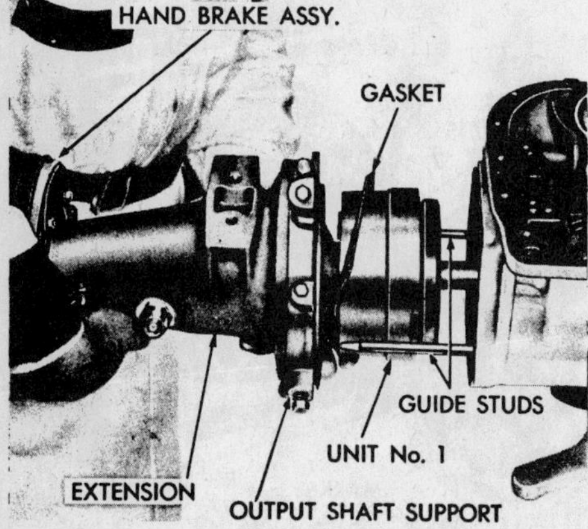

Removing unit no. 1 complete with handbrake and rear extension assemblies
(© Chrysler Corp.)

Clean the valve body and valves in solvent and dry with compressed air. Check that valves move freely in their bores.

The inner bore of the valve body must be smooth where it contacts the neoprene seal on the reaction shaft. The reaction shaft is a force fit in the transmission case and unless the splines are worn there is no need to mess with it.

If it does have to be pressed out, use heat lamps to heat transmission case to 170-190 deg. F. before attempting to reinstall.

Be sure that guide pins are in place and then install regulator valve body gasket into position against the transmission case. Check that neoprene seal ring is properly positioned on reaction shaft. Install valve body.

Power Train Units

There are three power trains units in the transmission; these are numbered 1, 2 and 3 with No. 1 the rear-most but first-out unit. The units are removed, disassembled, and assembled in the order of 1, 2, 3. Installation in the transmission goes in the order of 3, 2, 1.

Unit No. 1: Output Shaft, Kickdown (2nd Speed) Planet Pinion Carrier, Intermediate Shaft

Unit No. 1 is easily removed af removal of rear extension, governor and rear oil pump as covered earlier in this section.

Remove Unit No. 1 by sliding unit out rear of transmission case. Support assembly as much as possible to prevent damage to seal rings on intermediate shaft. The unit can also be removed as one piece with the rare extension.

Use the hand brake drum and the front half of the front universal joint as a holding fixture.

Unit: No. 2: Low-reverse, also kickdown, Sun Gear Assembly; Low-Reverse Planetary Gear Set; Over-Running (Free Wheeling) Clutch Assembly; and Rear Clutch Assembly Group

Loosen both front and rear band adjusting screw lock nuts and back the screws out about three turns. Remove the three intermediate-support locating screws and lock washers. Two are outside the case. One is inside. Match mark intermediate support to the inside locating screw hole to facilitate reassembly.

Keeping unit centered and holding

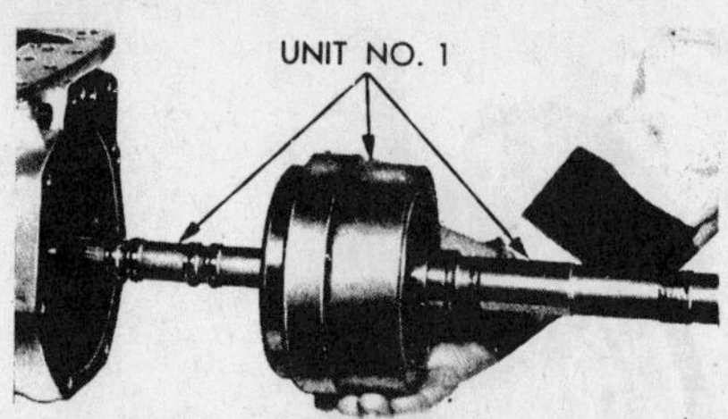

Removal of power train thru rear of case
(© Chrysler Corp.)

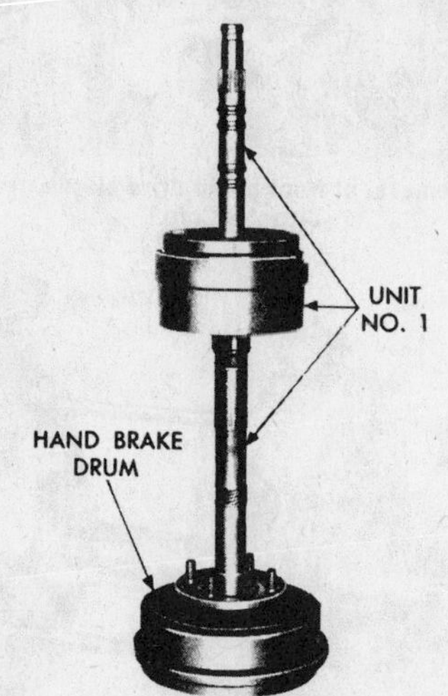

Using handbrake drum as holding fixture for unit no. 1
(© Chrysler Corp.)

Clearance between snap-ring and intermediate shaft should be near zero
(© Chrysler Corp.)

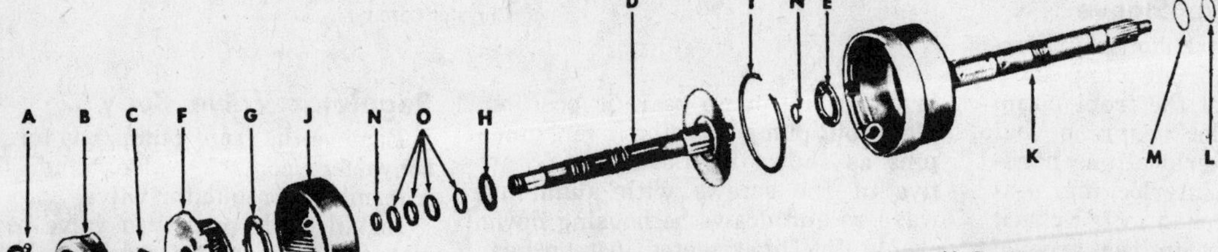

A Output shaft drive housing snap ring
B Reverse annulus gear
C Thrust plate
D Intermediate shaft
E Output shaft thrust washer
F Kickdown planet pinion carrier assembly
G Kickdown carrier thrust washer
H Sun gear thrust washer
I Kickdown annulus gear snap ring
J Kickdown annulus gear
K Output shaft assembly
L Output shaft seal ring—small
M Output shaft seal ring—large
N Intermediate shaft seal ring—small
O Intermediate shaft seal ring—large

Exploded view of unit no. 1. Note that "G" the roller type washer, is the sun gear rear thrust washer (© Chrysler Corp.)

Installing unit no. 2
(© Chrysler Corp.)

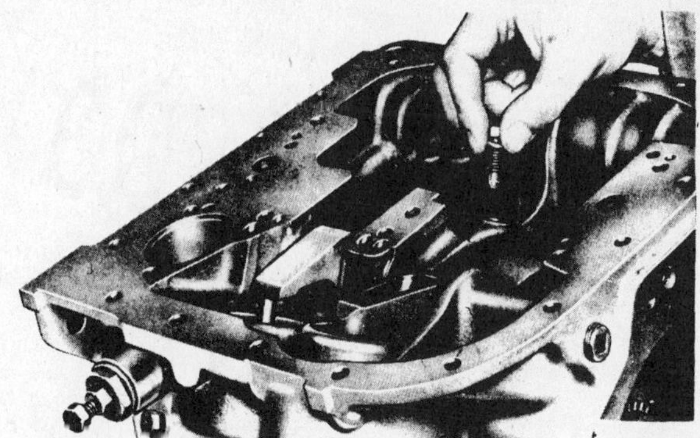

Match mark intermediate support to locating screw hole for easier installation (© Chrysler Corp.)

front clutch assembly forward remove Unit No. 2 from case. Illustration shows rear clutch group sequence.

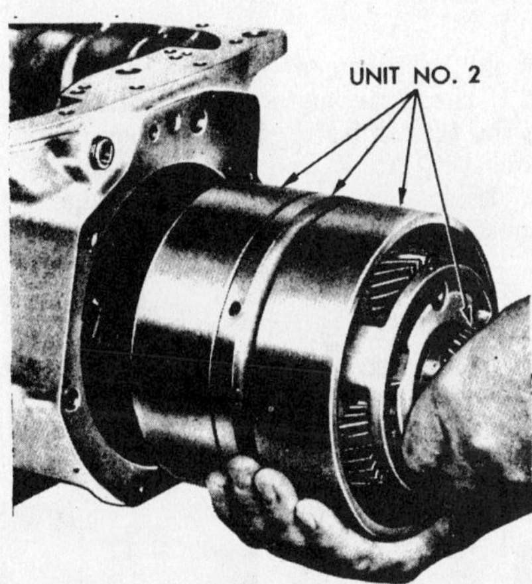

Removal of power train unit no. 2 thru rear of case (© Chrysler Corp.)

Unit No. 3: Input Shaft Assembly and Front Clutch Assembly Group

Keep unit centered as much as possible and remove from transmission case. Be careful to prevent the seal rings on the input shaft gouging the aluminum sealing surface in the reaction shaft. Illustration shows front clutch group sequence.

Transmission End Play

The end clearance of the front clutch assembly is critical in that too much will result in a clunking noise while too little will damage the thrust washers and clutches. The end play can be checked with the transmission in the truck.

The fibre input shaft thrust washer is the control thrust washer for end play in the transmission. The required thickness of this washer is determined both before disassembly of the transmission and after reassembly.

Install a dial indicator. Pry the front clutch forward by inserting a

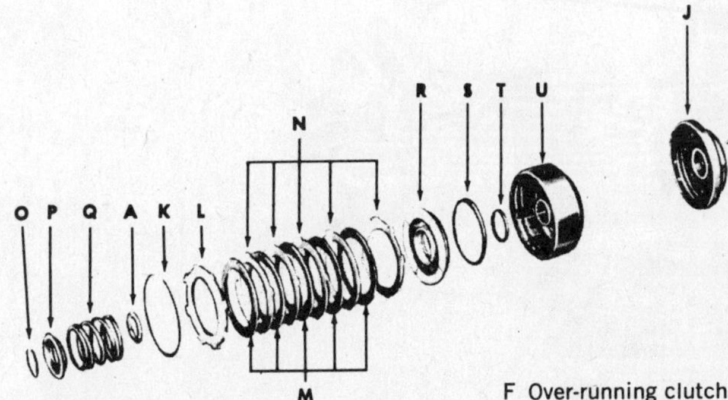

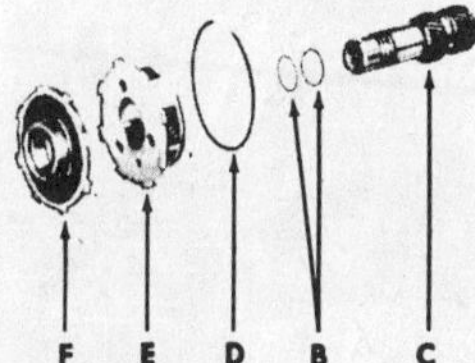

A Sun gear thrust washer (same as output shaft thrust washer)
B Sun gear rear clutch seal ring
C Sun gear assembly
D Reverse band snap ring
E Reverse planet pinion carrier assembly
F Over-running clutch hub assembly
G Low and reverse band drum
H Over-running clutch cam roller spring
I Over-running clutch cam roller
J Intermediate support and cam assembly
K Rear clutch snap ring
L Pressure plate
M Driving disc
N Clutch plate
O Piston return spring snap ring
P Return spring retainer
Q Return spring
R Piston
S Piston seal ring—outer
T Piston seal ring—inner
U Piston retainer assembly

Exploded view of unit no. 2 (©Chrysler Corp.)

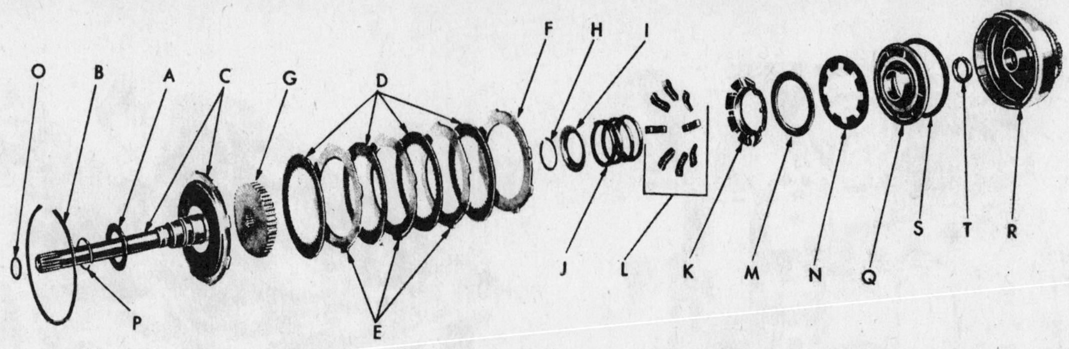

Exploded view of unit no. 3. Note that fibre thrust washer controls front clutch end play (© Chrysler Corp.)

H Spring retainer snap ring
I Spring retainer
J Return spring
K Lever retainer
L Levers
M Cushion spring washer
N Cushion spring

O Small oil seal ring
P Large oil seal ring
Q Piston
R Piston retainer
S Outer piston seal ring
T Inner piston seal ring

A Input shaft thrust washer
B Input shaft snap ring
C Input shaft
D Driving discs
E Clutch plates
F Pressure plate
G Driving disc hub

screwdriver between the front and rear clutch assemblies. While so holding front clutch forward, set dial indicator on zero. Now pry the front clutch assembly toward the rear and take indicator reading. The reading should be between .020 in. and .050 in. If the clearance is not within limits the transmission must be removed from the truck and the input-shaft to trogue-converter reaction-shaft thrust washer changed. Measure the thickness of the old washer and select a thicker or thinner one to give the correct clearance. There are three available: Natural color—.115-.117; black—.097-.099; red—.078-.080.

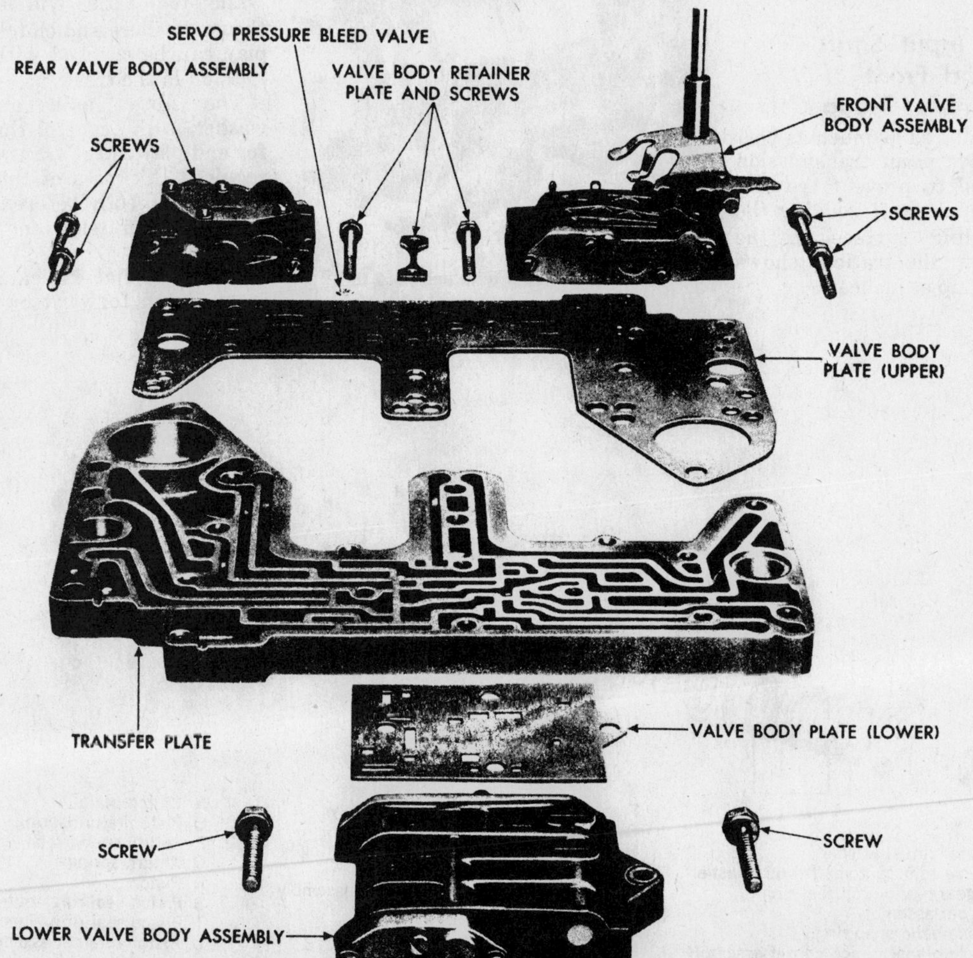

Valve Bodies and Transfer Plate (Separated)

Diagnosis

This diagnosis guide covers the most common symptoms and is an aid to careful diagnosis. The items to check are listed in the sequence to be followed for quickest results. Thus, follow the checks in the order given for the particular transmission type.

TROUBLE SYMPTOMS	Items to Check	
	In Truck	Out of Truck
Rough initial engagement in D1 or D2	KBUFEG	a
1-2 or 2-3 shift points incorrect or erratic	ABLCDUER	
Rough 1-2 shifts	BJGUEF	
Rough 2-3 shifts	BJUFGER	bl
Dragged out 1-2 shift	ABJUGEFR	c
Engine overspeeds on 2-3 shift	CABJUEFG	bl
No 1-2 or 2-3 upshift	CLBDUEGJ	bc
No 3-1 shift in D1 or 3-2 shift in D2	DE	
No forced downshift	LEB	
Runaway engine on forced downshift	UJGFEB	c
Rough 3-2 or 3-1 shift at closed throttle	KBJEF	
Shifts 1-3 in D1 and D2	GJBEDR	
No engine braking in first gear—manual low	CHIEDR	
Creeps excessively	KW	
Slips or chatters in first gear, D1	ABUFE	acg
Slips or chatters in second gear	ABJGUFER	ac
Slips or chatters in R	ABHUIFER	bcl
No drive in D1	ACUER	g
No drive in D2	ACUJER	cg
No drive in L	ACUEIR	cg
No drive in R	ACHUIER	bcl
No drive in any selector position	ACUFER	cd
Lockup in D1		bec
Lockup in D2	HI	becg
Lockup in L	GJ	bec
Lockup in R	GJ	aec
Parking lock binds or does not hold	C	e
Transmission overheats	OFBU	j
Maximum speed too low, poor acceleration	VW	j
Transmission noisy in N and P	AF	df
Transmission noisy in any drive position	AF	fadg
Fluid leaks	AMNOPQSTBIJX	hik
Car moves forward in N	C	a

Key to Checks

A. Fluid level
B. Vacuum diaphragm unit or tube
C. Manual linkage
D. Governor
E. Valve body
F. Pressure regulator
G. Intermediate band
H. Reverse band
I. Reverse servo
J. Intermediate servo
K. Engine idle speed
L. Downshift linkage—inner lever position
M. Converter drain plug
N. Oil pan and/or filler tube gaskets/seals
O. Oil cooler and/or connections
P. Manual or downshift lever shaft seal
Q. Pipe plug, side of case
R. Perform air pressure checks
S. Extension housing-to-case gasket or washers
T. Extension housing rear oil seal
U. Make control pressure test
V. Engine performance
W. Vehicle brakes
X. Speedometer driven gear adaptor seal

a. Forward clutch
b. Reverse—high clutch
c. Hydraulic system leakage
d. Front pump
e. Parking brake linkage
f. Planetary assembly
g. Planetary one-way clutch
h. Engine rear oil seal
i. Front oil pump seal
j. Converter oneway clutch
k. Front pump-to-case seal or gasket
l. Reverse—high clutch piston air bleed valve

General Information

This section provides instructions for testing, inspecting, adjusting, and repairing the Ford C4 automatic and C4S semi-automatic transmissions. Where there are differences in procedures or specifications, these differences will be given.

The Ford C4 automatic transmission (see illustration) is a three speed unit that provides automatic upshifts and downshifts through three forward gear ratios and also

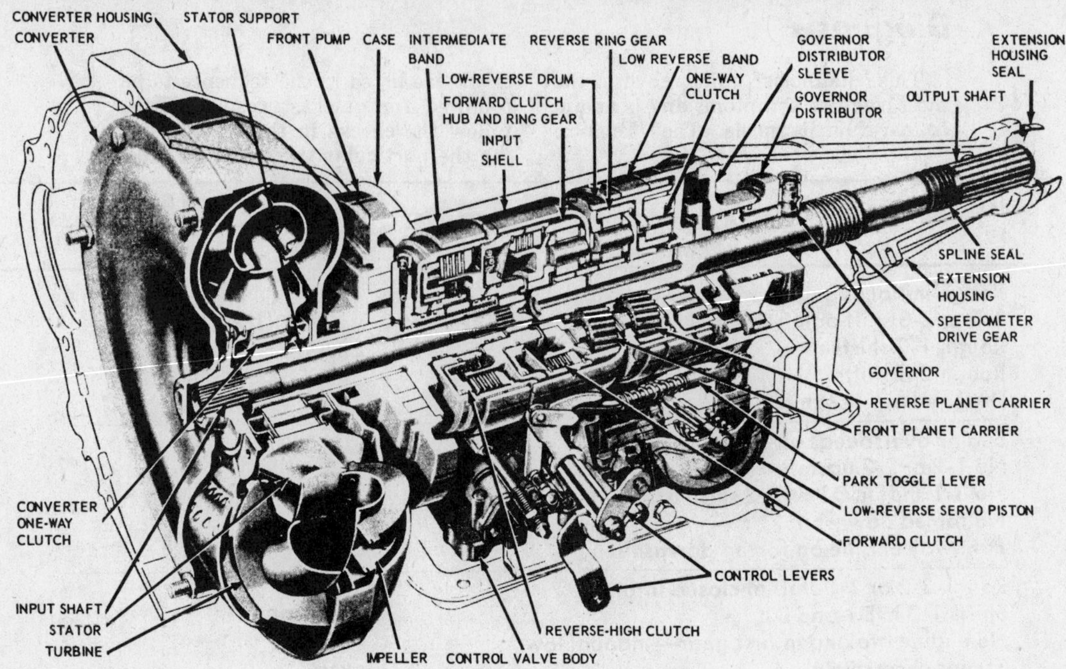

C-4 automatic transmission (© Ford Motor Co.)

provides manual selection of first and second gears.

The Ford C4S semi-automatic transmission is a manually operated power shift transmission which does not require a clutch pedal. The transmission is similar to the C4 automatic transmission except for differences in the control valve body and there is no vacuum diaphragm, throttle rod, governor, and the inner and outer downshift lever assemblies.

Both transmissions consist of a torque converter, planetary gear train, two multiple disc clutches, a one-way clutch, and a hydraulic control system. The only adjustments necessary on these transmissions during normal maintenance are band adjustments on the intermediate and low-reverse bands. The transmission fluid is cooled through an oil cooler core in the radiator lower tank when a steel converter is used. If an aluminum converter is used, the transmission fluid is air-cooled.

Towing

If a disabled truck is to be towed a short distance, it may be towed safely by placing the selector lever in the Neutral position and releasing the parking brake. The driver of the towed truck should be careful to maintain a safe stopping distance behind the towing behicle. The towing speed should not exceed 30 mph.

If the disabled truck must be towed a long distance, or the transmission cannot be put into Neutral gear, or there is no driver for the disabled truck, raise the rear of the truck until the wheels clear the ground and tow the truck backwards.

Starting the Engine Without the Starter

The transmission may be used to start an engine when the starter cannot be used by moving the disabled truck at a road speed of about 25 mph while in neutral gear and then placing the transmission in Low gear with the ignition switch on. The transmission will turn the engine over fast enough to start and the truck will move under its own power. Extreme care must be taken to prevent the truck from rushing forward so fast that it hits another truck or obstacle. Also, if the disabled truck is being pushed, the rear truck must drop back before the start is attempted to avoid hitting the front truck when it stops moving forward momentarily.

Transmission Checks

Before doing any of the tests and adjustments given in this section, the following preliminary checks should be done.

Transmission Fluid Level Check

1. Position the truck on a level place and firmly apply the parking brake. NOTE: on trucks equipped with a vacuum brake release, disconnect the release line and plug the end of the line. If this is not done, the parking brake will not hold the truck when the transmission is in any drive gear.
2. Start the engine and run at normal idle speed. If the transmission fluid is cold, the engine should idle at a fast idle speed (about 1200 rpm) until the fluid is warm. When the transmission fluid reaches its normal operating temperature, slow the engine to normal idle speed.
3. Shift the transmission through all drive positions briefly and then put it in the Park position. Do not shut off the engine during the fluid level check.
4. Locate the transmission fluid dipstick and clean all dirt and grease from the cap before removing it. On some trucks, the dipstick is located in the right rear corner of the engine compartment. On other trucks, the dipstick is located under the front floor-mat to the right of center.
5. Pull the dipstick out of the filler tube, wipe it clean, and reinsert it into the filler tube until it is fully seated.
6. Pull the dipstick out again and see where the fluid level is on the dipstick. The correct level is between the ADD and FULL marks on the dipstick. If necessary, add enough fluid through the filler tube to raise the fluid level to the correct level. *Do not overfill the transmission.* Replace the dipstick in the filler tube.
7. If a vacuum brake release line was disconnected, reconnect it and test for proper operation.

Fluid Aeration Check

If the transmission is overfilled with too much fluid, the fluid will be whipped up into a foamy or aerated condition. This condition will cause

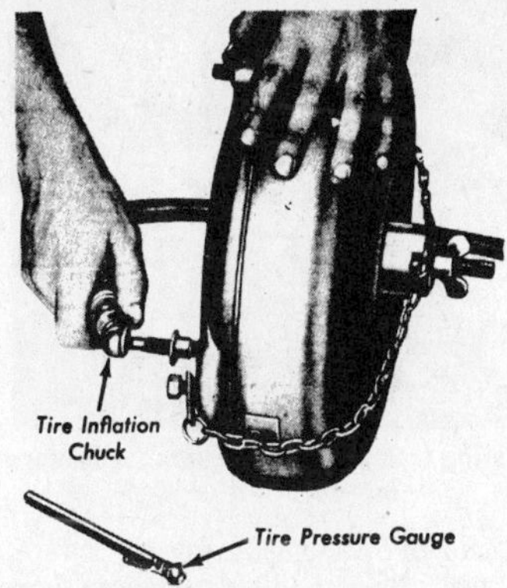

Converter leak checking tool installed
(© Ford Motor Co.)

low control pressure and the fluid may be forced out of the vent or through ruptured seals.

Check the transmission fluid level for low level conditions that may indicate leaks or cause poor operation.

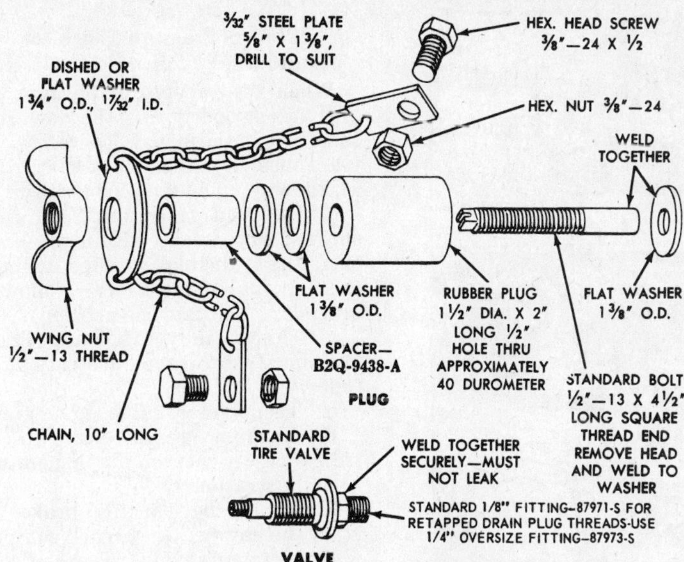

Converter leak checking tool (© Ford Motor Co.)

Transmission Fluid Leakage Checks

Make the following checks if a leakage is suspected from the transmission case:

1. Clean all dirt and grease from the transmission case.
2. Inspect the speedometer cable connection at the extension housing of the transmission. If fluid is leaking here, disconnect the cable and replace the rubber seal.
3. Inspect the oil pan gasket and attaching bolts for leaks. Tighten any bolts that appear loose to the proper torque (10-13 ft-lbs) Recheck for signs of leakage. If necessary, remove the pan attaching bolts and old pan gasket and install new gasket and reinstall the pan and its attaching bolts.
4. Check filler tube connection at the transmission for signs of leakage. If tube is leaking, tighten the connection to stop the leak. If necessary, disconnect the filler tube, replace the O-ring, and reinstall the filler tube.
5. Inspect all fluid lines between the transmission and the cooler core in the lower radiator tank. Replace any lines or fittings that appear to be worn or damaged. Tighten all fittings to the proper torque.
6. Inspect the engine coolant for signs of transmission fluid in the radiator. If there is transmission fluid in the engine coolant, the oil cooler core is probably leaking. The oil cooler core may be tested further by disconnecting all lines to it and applying 50-75 psi air pressure through the fittings. Remove the radiator cap to relieve any pressure buildup outside the cooler core. If air bubbles appear in the coolant or if the cooler core will not hold pressure, the oil cooler core is leaking and must be replaced. Oil cooler core repair and replacement is discussed in the section on Cooling Systems in this manual.
7. Inspect the openings in the case where the downshift control lever shaft and the manual lever shaft are located for leaks. If necessary, replace the defective seal.
8. Inspect all plugs or cable connections in the transmission for signs of leakage. Tighten any loose plugs or connectors to the proper torque according to the specifications.
9. Remove the lower cover from the front of the bellhousing and inspect the converter drainplugs for signs of leakage. If there is a leak around the drainplugs, loosen the plug and coat the threads with a sealing compound and tighten the plug to the proper torque.

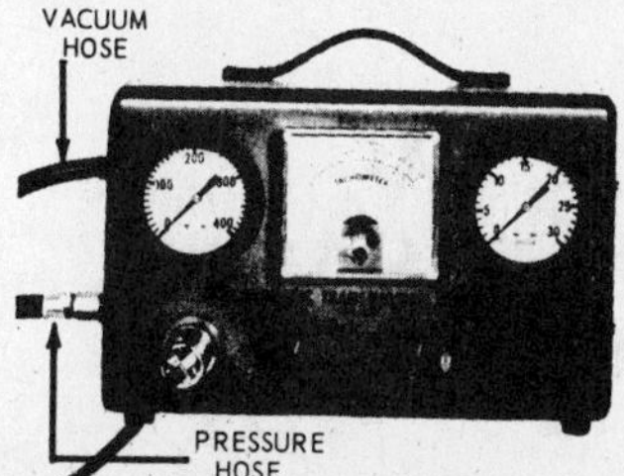

Automatic transmission tester
(© Ford Motor Co.)

NOTE: fluid leaks from around the converter drainplug may be cause of the leak before beginning rerear main bearing or from the oil gallery plugs. To determine the exact cause of the leak before beginning repair procedures, an oil-soluble aniline or fluorescent dye may be added to the transmission fluid to find the source of the leak and whether the transmission is leaking. If a fluorescent dye is used, a black light must be used to detect the dye.

If further converter checks are necessary, remove the transmission from the truck and the converter from the transmission. The converter cannot be disassembled for cleaning or repair. If the converter is leaking, it must be replaced with a new unit. The converter may be cleaned by using the Rotunda Automatic Transmission Torque Converter and Cooler Cleaner. To further check the converter for leaks, assemble and install the converter leak checking tool shown and fill the converter with 20 psi air pressure. Then, place the converter in a tank of water and watch for air bubbles. If no air bubbles are seen, the converter is not leaking.

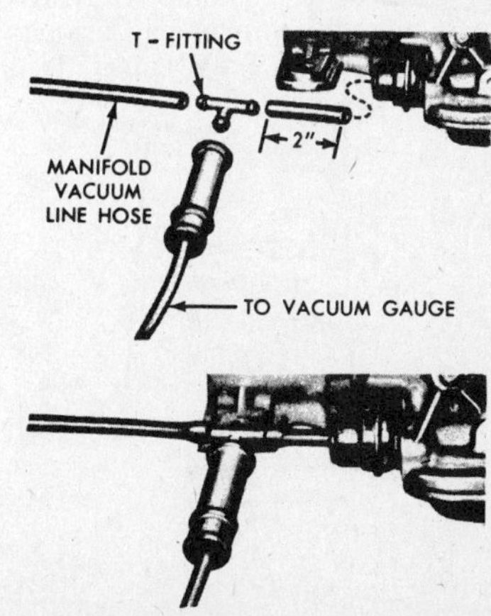

Typical vacuum test line connections
(© Ford Motor Co.)

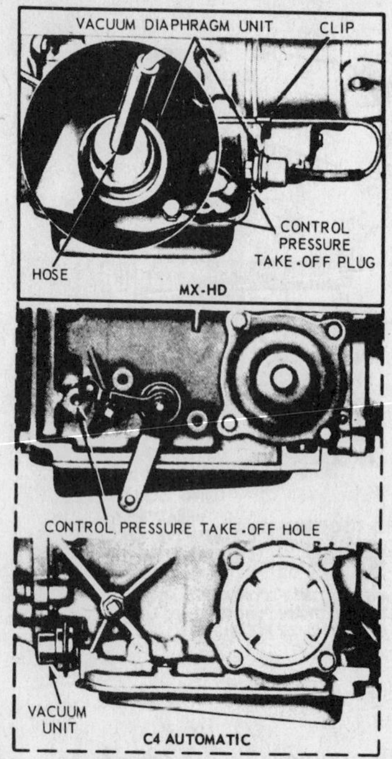

Typical vacuum diaphragm and control pressure connecting point (© Ford Motor Co.)

Engine Idle Speed Check

Check the idle speed of the engine and adjust it at the carburetor using the procedure given in the Fuel System section. Too slow an idle speed will cause the engine to run roughly; and too fast an idle speed will cause the car to creep while the transmission is in a Drive position, shift harshly, and downshift roughly.

Anti-Stall Dashpot Clearance Check

After properly adjusting the engine idle speed, check the clearance of the anti-stall dashpot using the procedure given in the Truck Section.

Manual Linkage Checks

Correct manual linkage is necessary for the proper operation of the manual valve which helps control fluid pressure to various transmission components. Improperly adjusted manual linkage may cause fluid leaks if not corrected.

Control Pressure Check for Automatic Transmissions (C4)

When the vacuum diaphragm unit operates properly and the downshift linkage is adjusted correctly, all transmission shifts (automatic and kickdown) should occur within the specified road speed limits. If these shifts do not occur within the limits or if the transmission slips during a shift point, perform the following procedure to locate the problem:

1. Connect the Automatic Transmission Tester (see illustration) as follows:
   a. Tachometer cable to engine
   b. Vacuum gauge hose to the transmission vacuum diaphragm unit (see illustration)
2. Apply the parking brake and start the engine. On a truck equipped with a vacuum brake release, disconnect the vacuum line or use the service brake since the parking brake will release automatically when the transmission is put in any Drive position.
3. Check engine idle speed and throttle and downshift linkage for correct operation. Check the transmission diaphragm unit for leaks.

Control Pressure Check for Semi-Automatic Transmissions (C4S)

If the shifts do not occur within the proper road speeds or the transmission slips during a shift point, do the following procedure to find the possible trouble:

1. Connect the tachometer of the automatic transmission tester to the engine.
2. Attach the pressure gauge to the control pressure outlet at the transmission.
3. Firmly apply the parking brake and start the engine. If the truck is equipped with a vacuum brake release, disconnect the line and plug the end so the parking brake will hold.
4. Adjust the engine idle speed to the correct rpm. If the engine idle speed cannot be adjusted to the proper range by the carburetor idle speed adjustment screw, check the throttle linkage for binding conditions.

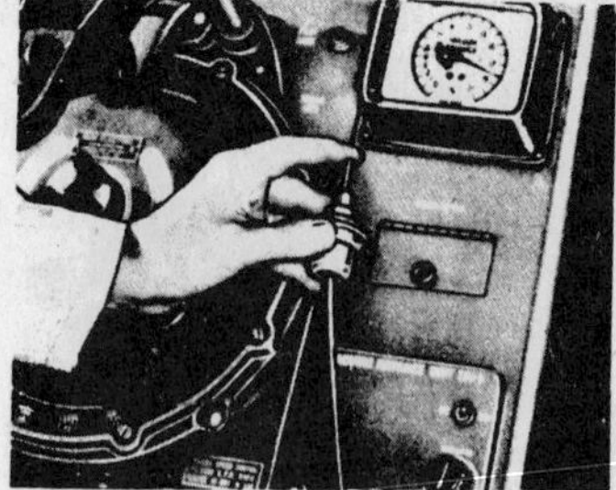

Testing transmission vacuum for leakage (© Ford Motor Co.)

Vacuum Diaphragm Unit Check—Non-Altitude Compensating Type

1. Remove the vacuum diaphragm unit from the transmission after disconnecting the vacuum hose.
2. Connect the vacuum hose to the vacuum diaphragm unit and note the reading on the vacuum gauge. If the reading is 18 inches of vacuum, the vacuum diaphragm unit is good. While removing the vacuum hose from the vacuum diaphragm unit, hold a finger over the end of the control rod. As the vacuum is released, the internal spring of the vacuum diaphragm unit will push the control rod out.

Vacuum Diaphragm Unit Check—Altitude-Compensating Type

The vacuum diaphragm unit may be checked for damaged or ruptured bellows by doing the procedure below:

1. Remove the diaphragm and the throttle valve rod from the transmission.
2. Insert a rod into the diaphragm unit until it is seated in the hole. Make a reference mark on the rod where it enters the diaphragm (see illustration).
3. Place the diaphragm unit on a weighing scale with the end of the rod resting on the weighing pan and gradually press down

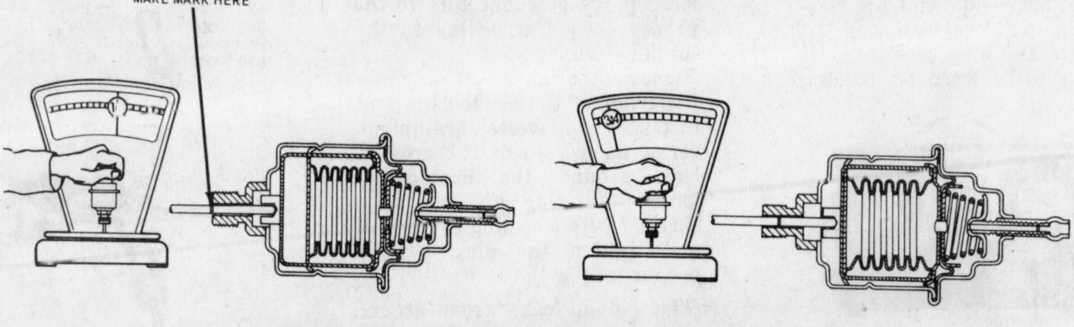

Checking vacuum unit bellows (© Ford Motor Co.)

on the diaphragm unit.

4. Note the force (in pounds) at which the reference mark on the rod moves into the diaphragm. If the reference mark is still visible at 12 pounds of pressure on the scale, the diaphragm bellows is good. But if the reference mark on the rod disappears before four pounds of force, the diaphragm bellows are damaged and the diaphragm unit must be replaced.

Shift Point Checks for Automatic Transmissions

To determine if the transmission is shifting at the proper road speeds, do the following procedure:

1. Check the minimum throttle upshifts by placing the transmission selector lever in the Drive position and noting the road speeds at which the transmission shifts from first gear to second gear to third gear. All shifts should occur within the specified limits.
2. While driving in third gear, depress the accelerator pedal past the detent (to the floor). Depending on vehicle speed, the transmission should downshift from third gear to second gear or from second gear to first gear.
3. Check the closed-throttle downshift from third gear to first gear by coasting down from about 30 mph in third gear. This downshift should occur at the specified road speed. NOTE: when the transmission selector lever is at 2, the transmission will operate only in second gear. Manually move the selector lever to either D or 1 to shift gears automatically.
4. With the transmission in third gear and the car moving at a road speed of 25 mph, the transmission should downshift to second gear when the selector lever is moved from D to 2 to 1. This check will determine if the governor pressure and shift control valves are operating properly. If the transmission does not shift within the specified limits or certain gear ratios cannot be obtained, refer to the Trouble diagnosis chart at the beginning of this section.

Air Pressure Checks

If the truck will not move in one or more ranges, or, if it shifts erratically, the items at fault can be determined by using air pressure at the indicated passages.

Drain the transmission and remove the oil pan and the control valve assembly.

NOTE: oil will spray profusely during this operation.

Front Clutch

Apply sufficient air pressure to the front clutch input passage. (See illustration.) A dull thud can be heard when the clutch piston moves. Check also, for leaks.

Governor

Remove the governor inspection cover from the extension housing. Apply air to the front clutch input passage. (See illustration). Listen for a sharp click and watch to see if the governor valve snaps inward as it should.

valve assemblies, which should be disassembled, cleaned and inspected.

If operation of the clutches is not normal; that is, if both clutches apply from one passage or if one fails to move, the aluminum sleeve (bushing) in the output shaft is out of position or badly worn. (See illustration.)

Use air pressure to check the passages in the sleeve and shaft, and also check the passages in the primary sun gear shaft.

If the passages in the two shafts and the sleeve are clean, remove the clutch assmblies, clean and inspect the parts.

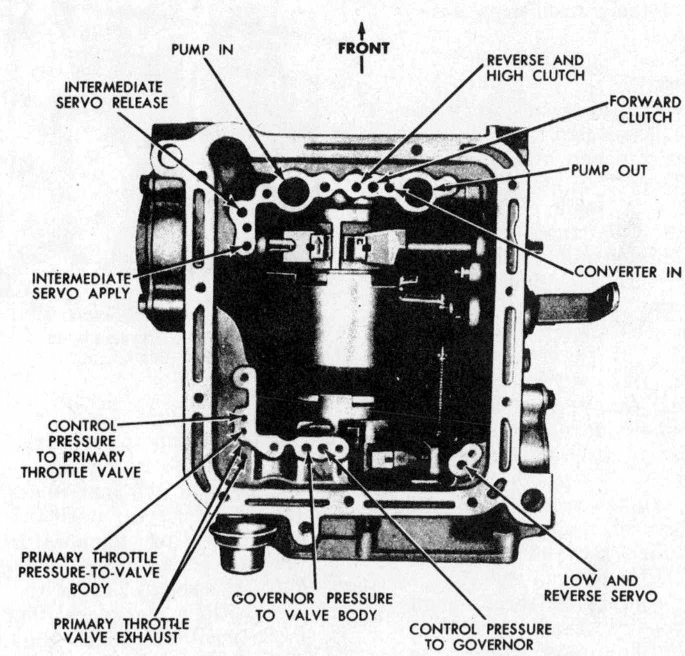

Case fluid passage hole identification (© Ford Motor Co.)

Rear Clutch

Apply air to the rear clutch passage (See illustration) and listen for the dull thud that will indicate that the rear clutch piston has moved. Listen also for leaks.

Front Servo

Apply air pressure to the front servo apply tube (See illustration.) and note if front band tightens. Shift the air to the front servo release tube, which is next to the apply tube, and watch band release.

Rear Servo

Apply air pressure to the rear servo apply passage. The rear band should tighten around the drum.

Conclusions

If the operation of the servos and clutches is normal with air pressure, the no-drive condition is due to the control valve and pressure regulator

Erratic operation can also be caused by loose valve body screws. When reinstalling the valve body be careful to tighten the control valve body screws as specified in the Torque Limits table.

In-Vehicle Adjustments and Repairs

The adjustments and repairs presented in this part of the section on transmissions may be done without removing the entire transmission from the truck. Some of these procedures will require the use of special tools and instruments.

Transmission Fluid Drain and Refill

Normal maintenance and lubrication requirements do not include periodic changes of transmission fluid. Only when it is necessary to remove the pan for major repairs or adjustments will it be necessary to replace the transmission fluid. At this time the converter, oil cooler core, and flushed out to remove any dirt or deposits that might clog these units later.

When filling a completely dry (no fluid) transmission and converter, install five quarts of transmission fluid and then start the engine. Shift the selector lever through all positions briefly and set at Park position. Check the fluid level and add enough fluid to raise the level to between the ADD and FULL marks on the dipstick. *Do not overfill the transmission.*

The procedure for a partial drain and refill of the transmission fluid is given below:

1. Raise the truck on a hoist or jack stands.
2. Place a drain pan under the transmission pan.
3. Loosen the pan attaching bolts to allow the fluid to drain. NOTE: on some models of the C4 and C4S transmissions, the transmission fluid is drained by disconnecting the fluid filler tube from the transmission fluid pan.
4. When the fluid has stopped draining to level of the pan flange, remove the pan bolts starting at the rear and along both sides of the pan, allowing the pan to drop and drain gradually.
5. When all the transmission fluid has drained, remove the pan and the fluid filter and clean them. Discard the old pan gasket.
6. After completing the transmission repairs or adjustments, install the fluid filter screen, a new pan gasket, and the pan on the transmission. Tighten the pan attaching bolts to the proper torque (12-16 ft-lbs).
7. Install three quarts of transmission fluid through the filler tube. If the filler tube was removed to drain the transmission, install the filler tube using a new O-ring.
8. Start and run the engine for a few minutes at low idle speed and then at the fast idle speed (about 1200 rpm) until the normal operating temperature is reached. *Do not race the engine.*
9. Move the selector lever through all positions and place it at the Park position. Check the fluid level, and add fluid till the level is between the ADD and FULL marks on the dipstick. *Do not overfill the transmission.*

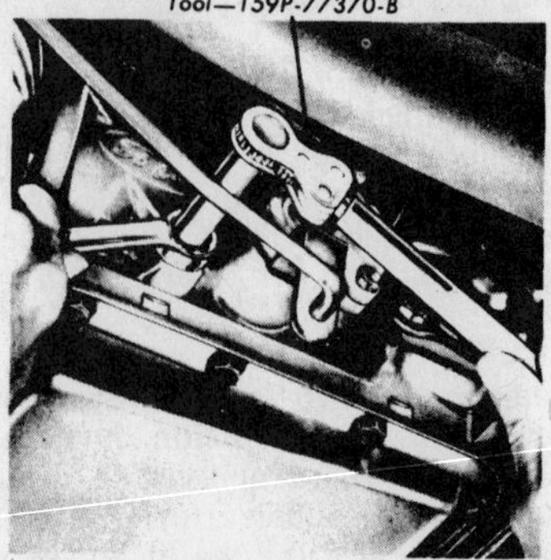

Adjusting intermediate band
(© Ford Motor Co.)

Adjusting low-reverse band
(© Ford Motor Co.)

Band Adjustments

Intermediate Band

1. Clean all the dirt from the adjusting screw and remove and discard the locknut.
2. Install a new locknut on the adjusting screw. Using the tool shown in the illustration, tighten the adjusting screw until the wrench clicks and breaks at 10 ft-lbs. torque.
3. Back off the adjusting screw *Exactly* 1¾ turns.
4. Hold the adjusting screw steady and tighten the locknut to the proper torque.

Low-Reverse Band

1. Clean all dirt from around the band adjusting screw, and remove and discard the locknut.
2. Install a new locknut on the adjusting screw. Using the tool shown in the illustration, tighten the adjusting screw until the wrench clicks and breaks at 10 ft-lbs torque.
3. Back off the adjusting screw *Exactly 3 full turns.*
4. Hold the adjusting screw steady and tighten the locknut to the proper torque.

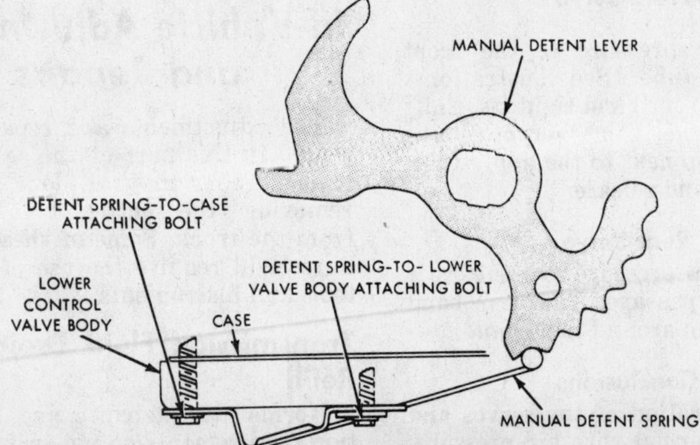

Control valve body detent spring installed (© Ford Motor Co.)

Transmission Component Removal and Installation

The components that may be removed from and installed in the transmission while it is in the truck are discussed in this part of the C4 and C4S transmission section. Only procedures for removing and installing these components are given here. Disassembly and repair of the units is given in a later part.

To avoid repetition, the following tasks should be done before proceeding with the removal and installation of components.

1. Raise the truck so the transmission is accessible from under the truck.
2. Drain the fluid from the transmission. Some models are drained by removing the filler tube from the transmission oil pan. Others are drained by removing the oil pan attaching bolts gradually from the rear of the pan. If the same fluid is to be reused, filter it through a 100 mesh screen. Reuse the fluid only if it is in good condition.
3. Remove the oil pan attaching bolts, the oil pan, and the old gasket. Discard gasket.
4. Be sure to have a good tranmission jack available and a holding device for the transmission if it is removed from the truck later

Oil Pan and Control Valve Removal and Installation

1. Do all the preliminary operations given at the beginning of this section.
2. On 1970 model C4 transmissions only, shift the transmission to Park position and remove the

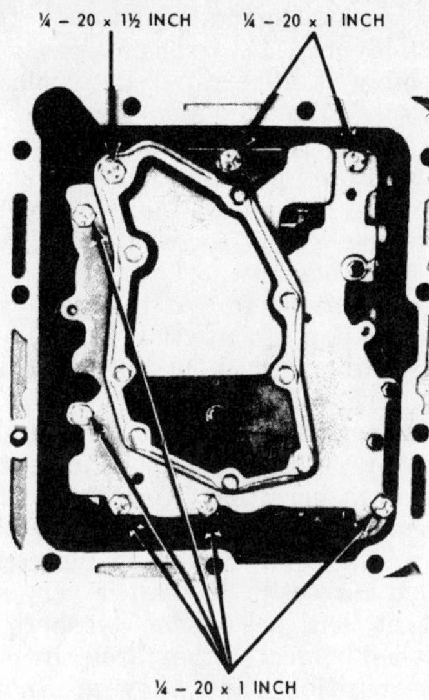

Control valve body attaching bolts
(© Ford Motor Co.)

two bolts holding the manual detent spring to the control valve body and case.

3. Remove all the valve body-to-case attaching bolts. Hold the manual valve in place and remove the valve body from the case. If the manual valve is not held in place, it could be bent or damaged.
4. Refer to the Component Disassembly and repair section for control valve body repair procedures.
5. Thoroughly clean the old gasket material from the case and remove the nylon shipping plug from the oil filler tube hold. This nylon plug is installed before shipment and should be discarded when the transmission oil pan is removed.
6. Be sure the transmission is in the Park position (manual detent lever is in P detent position). Install the valve body in the case. Position the inner downshift lever between the downshift lever stop and the downshift valve. Be sure the two lands on the end of the manual valve engage the actuating pin on the manual detent lever.
7. Install seven valve body attaching bolts but do not tighten them.
8. Place the detent spring on the lower valve body and install the spring-to-case bolt finger tight.
9. While holding the detent spring roller in the center of the manual detent lever, install the detent spring-to-lower valve body bolt and tighten it to 80-120 in-lbs. torque.
10. Tighten the remainder of the control valve body attaching bolts to 80-120 in-lbs. torque.
11. Put a new gasket on the oil pan, install pan in place, and install and tighten all the pan attaching bolts to the proper torque.
12. If the filler tube was removed, reinstall it and tighten securely. If necessary, replace the oil seal around the filler tube to prevent leakage.
13. Lower the truck and fill the transmission with enough fluid to bring the level up to the FULL mark on the dipstick. Check for fluid leaks at this time.

Intermediate Servo Removal and Installation

1. Raise the truck and remove the four servo cover attaching bolts (right-hand side of case). Remove the cover and identification tag (*do not lose tag*).
2. Remove the gasket, piston, and piston return spring.
3. Install the piston return spring in the case. Place a new gasket on the cover. Install the piston and cover in the transmission case, using two 51/6-18 x 1¼ bolts 180 degrees apart to align the cover against the case.
4. Install the transmission identification tag and two attaching bolts. Remove the two 1¼ bolts and install the other two cover attaching bolts. Tighten all cover attaching bolts to the proper torque.
5. Adjust the intermediate band. Lower the truck and fill the transmission with enough fluid to raise the fluid level to the FULL mark on the dipstick.
6. If the intermediate band cannot be adjusted correctly, remove the oil pan and control valve body and see if the struts are installed correctly. Adjust the struts and reinstall the control valve body and oil pan with a new gasket. Refill the transmission with fluid.

Low-Reverse Servo Piston Removal and Installation

1. Raise the truck on a hoist.
2. Loosen the reverse band adjusting screw locknut and tighten the adjusting screw to 10 ft-lbs torque. This operation will hold the band strut against the case and prevent it from falling when the reverse servo piston is removed.
3. Remove the four servo cover attaching bolts and remove the servo cover and seal from the case.
4. Remove the servo piston from the case. *The piston and piston seal are bonded together and must be replaced together.*
5. Install the servo piston assembly into the case. Place a new cover seal on the cover and position them by installing two 51/6-18 bolts, 1¼ in. long, at 180 degrees apart on the case. Install two cover attaching bolts with the identification tag.
6. Remove the two positioning bolts and install the other two cover bolts. Tighten all the cover attaching bolts to the proper torque.
7. Adjust the low-reverse band. Lower the truck and fill the transmission with enough fluid to raise the fluid level to the FULL mark on the dipstick.
8. If the low-reverse band cannot be adjusted properly, the transmission must be drained and the oil pan and valve body removed. Check the alignment of the band struts. Reinstall the valve body and the oil pan with a new gasket, and refill the transmission with fluid.

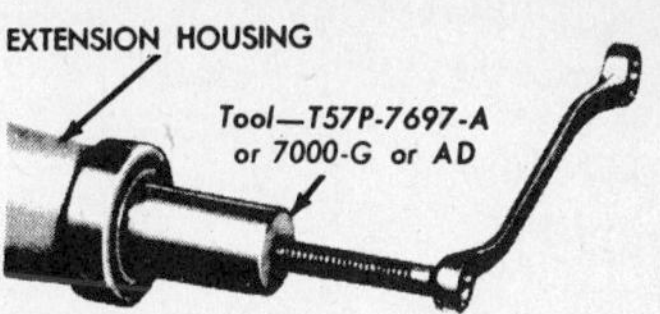

Removing extension housing bushing
(© Ford Motor Co.)

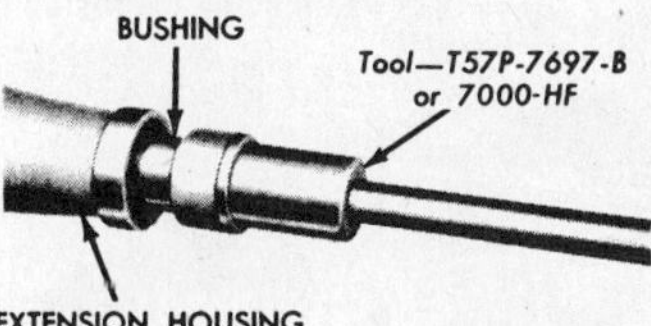

Installing extension housing bushing
(© Ford Motor Co.)

Extension Housing Bushing and Rear Seal Removal and Installation

1 Disconnect the drive shaft from the transmission.
2. If only the rear seal needs replacing, carefully remove it with a tapered chisel or use the tools shown in the illustration. Remove the bushing as shown. Be careful not to damage the spline seal with the bushing remover.
3. Install the new bushing, using the special tool shown.
4. Before installing a new rear seal, inspect the sealing surface of the universal joint yoke for scores. If the universal joint yoke is scored, replace the yoke.
5. Inspect the housing counterbore for burrs and remove them with crocus cloth if necessary.
6. Install the new rear seal into the housing, using the tool shown in the illustration. The seal should be firmly seated in the housing. Coat the inside diameter of the fiber portion of the seal with lu-

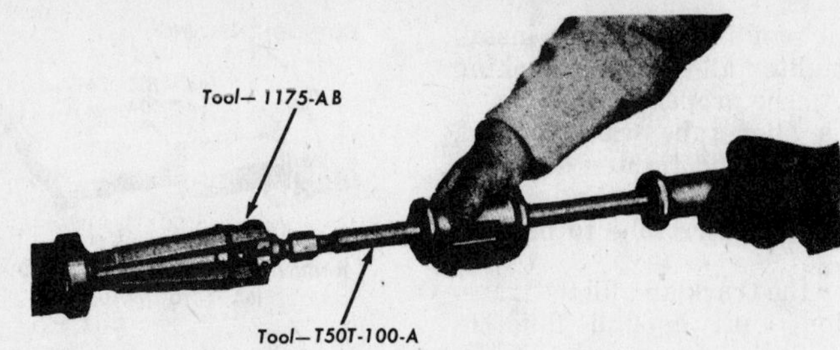

Removing extension housing seal (© Ford Motor Co.)

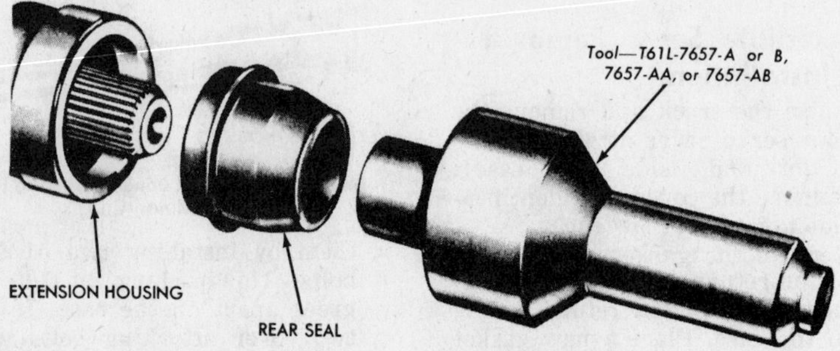

Installing extension housing seal (© Ford Motor Co.)

bricant.

7. Coat the front universal joint spline with lubricant and install the drive shaft.

Extension Housing Removal and Installation

1. Raise the truck on a hoist.
2. Remove the drive shaft. Place a transmission jack under the transmission for support.
3. Remove the speedometer cable from the extension housing.
4. Remove the extension housing-to-crossmember mount attaching bolts. Raise the transmission and remove the mounting pad between the extension housing and the crossmember.
5. Loosen the extension housing attaching bolts to drain the transmission fluid.
6. Remove the six extension housing attaching bolts and remove the extension housing.
7. To install the extension housing, reverse the above removal instructions. Install a new extension housing gasket. When the extension housing has been installed and all parts have been secured, lower the truck and fill the transmission with the correct amount of fluid. Check for fluid leaks around the extension housing area.

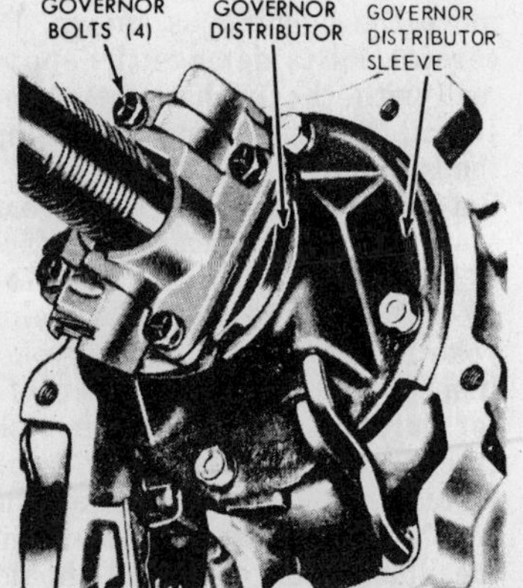

Governor location (© Ford Motor Co.)

Governor Removal and Installation (C4 Automatic only)

1. After removing the extension housing according to the instructions above, remove the governor housing-to-governor distributor attaching bolts. Remove the governor housing from the distributor.
   Refer to the Component Disassembly and Repair section for instructions on repairing the governor assembly.
2. Install the governor housing on the governor distributor and tighten the attaching bolts to the proper torque.
3. Install the extension housing with a new gasket according to the instructions above.
4. When the extension housing has been installed and all bolts have been tightened to the proper torque, lower the truck and fill the transmission with fluid to the proper level. Check around the extension housing area for leaks.

Transmission Overhaul Procedures

The transmission overhaul procedures presented here are the checks and repairs that must be done with the transmission out of the truck. Disassembly of each transmission subassembly is illustrated by exploded views of the subassembly showing how the individual parts fit together. Reassembly of the subassembly is often the reverse of the disassembly procedure except for alignment, special tolerances, etc.

Procedures for removing the transmission from the truck and reinstalling it back in the truck are given in the Truck Section.

During the transmission disassembly and reassembly operations, ten thrust washers that are installed between the subassemblies of the gear train must be removed and reinstalled correctly. Since it is very important that these thrust washers be installed correctly, they are shown in their positions and they are numbered for further identification. The No. 1 thrust washer is located at the front pump, and the No. 10 thrust washer is located at the packing pawl ring gear.

During all repairs to the transmission subassemblies, the following instructions must be followed:

1. Be sure that no dirt or grease gets in the transmission. All parts must be clean. *Remember—a little dirt can disable a transmission completely if it gets in a fluid passage.*
2. Handle all transmission parts carefully to avoid burring or nicking bearing or mating surfaces.
3. Lubricate all internal parts of the transmission with clean transmission fluid before assembling. *Do not use any other lubricants except on gaskets or thrust washers which may be coated lightly with vaseline to ease assembly.*
4. Always use new gaskets when assembling the parts of the transmission.
5. Tighten all bolts and screws to the recommended torque limits

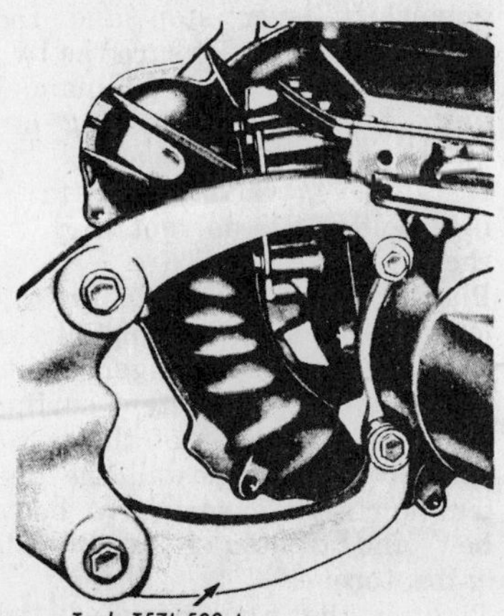

Transmission mounted in holding fixture (© Ford Motor Co.)

using a torque wrench.

Transmission Disassembly

Disassemble the transmission by following the procedures below:

1 Thoroughly clean the outside of the transmission to prevent dirt or grease from getting inside the mechanism. *Do this before removing any subassembly.*
2. Place the transmission in the transmission holder. See illustration.

Removing or installing vacuum unit
(© Ford Motor Co.)

3. Remove the converter from the transmission front pump and converter housing.
4. On a C4 automatic transmission, remove the transmission vacuum unit with the tool shown in the illustration. Remove the vacuum unit gasket and the control rod.
5. On a C4 automatic transmission, remove the primary throttle valve from the opening at the rear of the case.

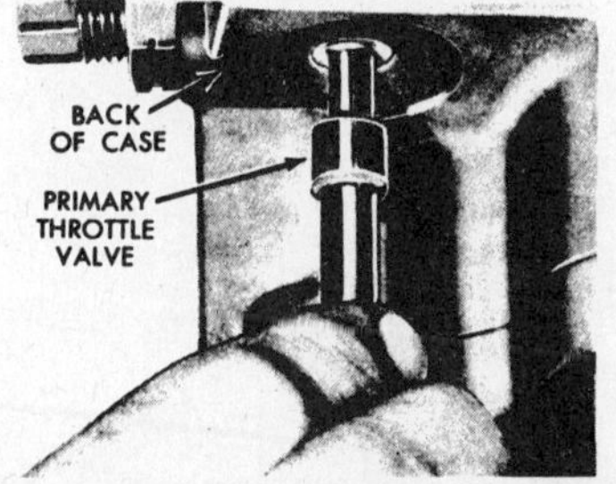

Removing or installing primary throttle valve
(© Ford Motor Co.)

6. Remove the transmission pan attaching bolts, oil pan, and gasket.
7. Remove the control valve body attaching bolts and then lift the control valve body from the case.
8. Loosen the intermediate band adjusting screw and remove the intermediate band struts from the case. Loosen the low-reverse band adjusting screw and remove the low-reverse band struts.

Transmission End-Play Check

1. Remove one of the converter housing attaching bolts and mount the dial indicator support tool in the hole. Mount a dial indicator on the support so that a contact rests on the end of the input shaft. See illustration.

Layout of band struts
(© Ford Motor Co.)

Checking gear train end play
(© Ford Motor Co.)

2. Install the extension housing seal replacer tool on the output shaft to provide support and alignment for the shaft.
3. Using a screwdriver, move the input shaft and the gear train to the rear of the case as far as possible. Set the dial indicator at zero while holding a slight pressure on the screwdriver.
4. Remove the screwdriver and insert it behind the input shell. Move the input shell and the front part of the gear train forward.
5. Record the dial reading for later reference during transmission reassembly. The end play reading should be from 0.008 to 0.042 in. If the end play reading is not within this range, selective thrust washers must be used to obtain the proper reading. The selective thrust washers to be used are listed in the table shown.
6. Remove the dial indicator, its support bar, and the extension housing seal replacer tool.

Removal of Case and Extension Parts

1. Rotate the transmission in the holding fixture until it is in a vertical position with the converter housing up.
2. Remove the five converter housing attaching bolts and remove the converter housing from the transmission case.

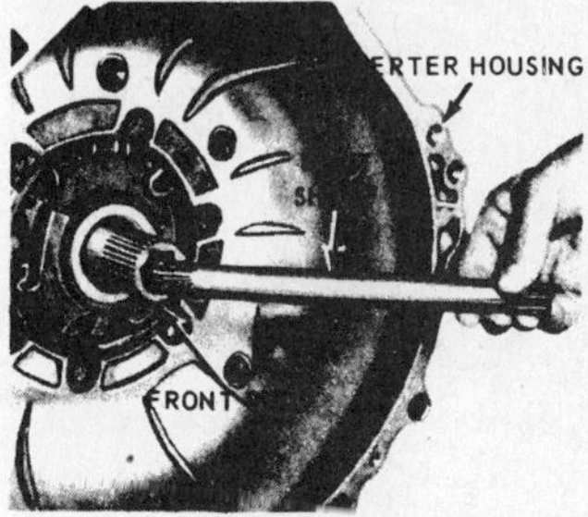

Removing or installing input shaft
(© Ford Motor Co.)

3. Remove the seven front pump attaching bolts. Remove the front pump by inserting a screwdriver behind the input shell and pushing it forward until the front pump seal is above the edge of the case. Remove the front pump and gasket from the case. If the selective thrust washer No. 1 did not come out with the front pump, lift it from the top of the reverse-high clutch.

Removing front pump
(© Ford Motor Co.)

4. Remove the intermediate and low-reverse adjusting screws from the case. Rotate the intermediate band to align the band ends with the clearance hole in the case. Remove the intermediate band from the case.
5. Using a screwdriver between the input shell and the rear planet carrier (see illustration), lift the input shell upward and remove the forward part of the gear train as an assembly.
6. Place the forward part of th^ gear train in the holding fixture shown.
7. With the gear train in the holding fixture, remove the reverse-high clutch and drum from the forward clutch. If thrust washer No. 2 did not come out with the front pump, remove the thrust washer from

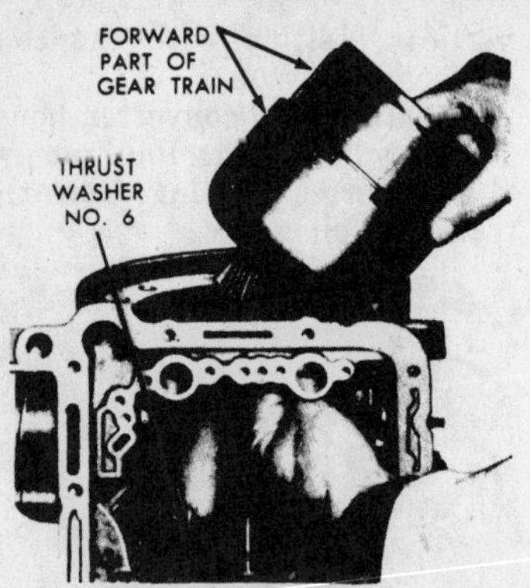

Removing or installing forward part of gear train
(© Ford Motor Co.)

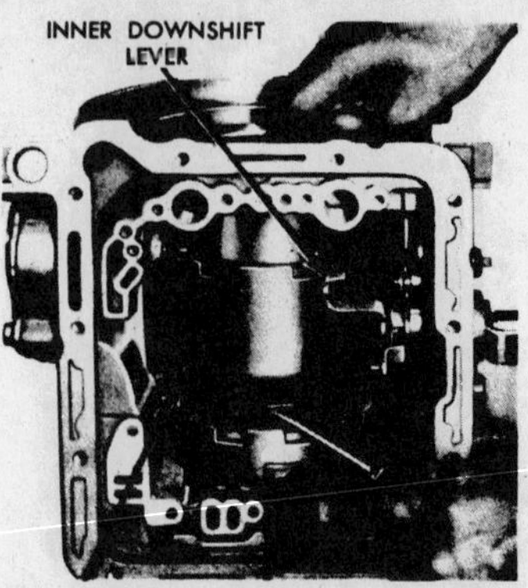

Lifting input shell and gear train
(© Ford Motor Co.)

Forward part of gear train in holding fixture
(© Ford Motor Co.)

the forward clutch cylinder. If a selective spacer was used, remove the spacer. Remove the forward clutch from the forward clutch hub and ring gear.

8. If the thrust washer No. 3 did not come out with the forward clutch, remove the thrust washer from the forward clutch hub and lift the forward clutch hub and ring gear from the front planet carrier.
9. Remove thrust washer No. 4 and the front planet carrier from the input shell.
10. Remove the input shell, sun gear and thrust washer No. 5 from the holding fixture.
11. From inside the transmission case, remove thrust washer No. 6 from the top of the reverse planet carrier. Remove the reverse planet carrier and thrust washer No. 7 from the reverse ring gear and hub.
12. Move the output shaft forward and, with the tool shown in the illustration, remove the reverse ring gear and hub from the output shaft. Remove the thrust washer No. 8 from the low and reverse drum.
13. Remove the low-reverse band from the case. Remove the one-way clutch inner race by rotating the race clockwise as it is removed.
14. Remove the 12 one-way clutch rollers, springs and the spring retainer from the outer race. *Do not lose or damage any of the 12 springs or rollers. The outer race of the one-way clutch cannot be removed from the case*

Position of intermediate band for removal or installation
(© Ford Motor Co.)

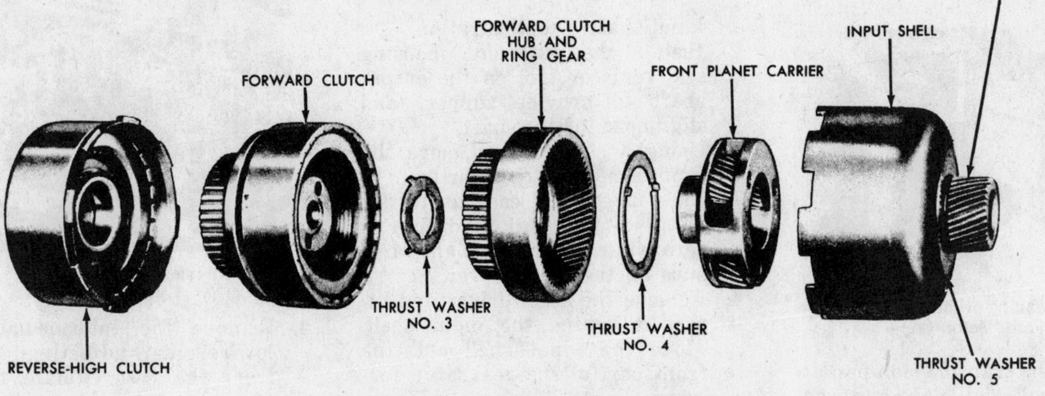

Forward part of gear train disassembled (© Ford Motor Co.)

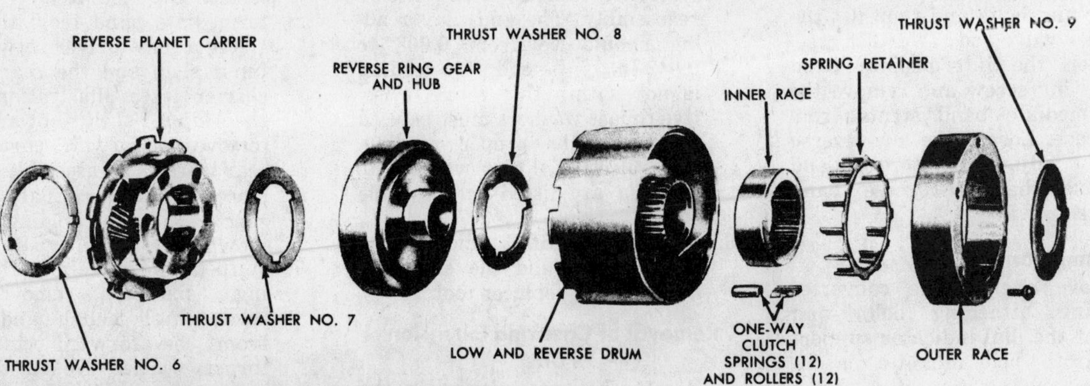

Lower part of gear train disassembled (© Ford Motor Co.)

Reverse ring gear retaining ring-removal (© Ford Motor Co.)

Removing low-reverse band (© Ford Motor Co.)

until the extension housing, output shaft and governor distributor sleeve are removed.

15. Remove the transmission from the holding fixture. Place the transmission on the bench in a vertical position with the extension housing up. Remove the four extension housing attaching bolts, the extension housing, and the gasket from the case.
16. Pull outward on the output shaft and remove the output shaft and governor distributor assembly (if so equipped) from the governor distributor sleeve.
17. On a C4 automatic transmission, remove the governor distributor lock ring from the output shaft. Remove the governor distributor from the output shaft.
18. Remove the four distributor sleeve attaching bolts and the distributor sleeve from the case. *Do not bend or distort the fluid tubes as the tubes are removed from the case with the distributor sleeve.*
19. Remove the parking pawl return spring, pawl, and pawl retaining pin from the case.
20. Remove the parking gear and thrust washer No. 10 from the case.

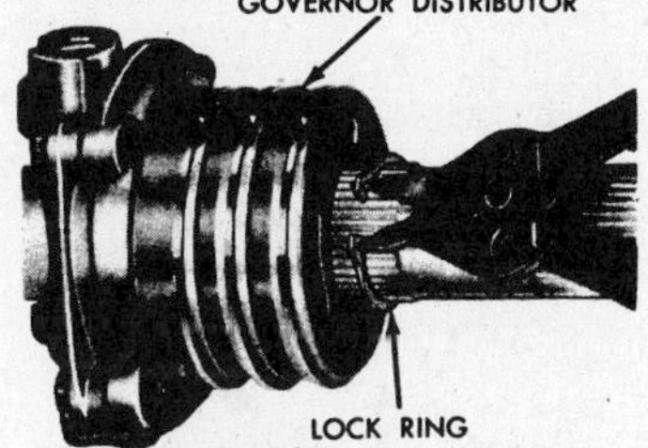

Removing governor snap-ring (© Ford Motor Co.)

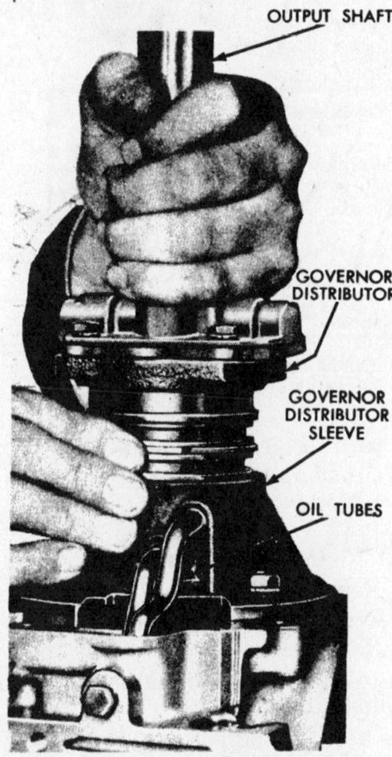

Removing or installing output shaft and governor distributor (© Ford Motor Co.)

21. Remove the six one-way clutch outer race attaching bolts with the tool shown. As the bolts are removed, hold the outer race that is located inside the case in position. Then, remove the outer race and thrust washer No. 9 from the case.

Component Disassembly and Assembly

To avoid repetition, the following rules should be followed during examination, repairs or replacement and reassembly:

1. Avoid dirt and damage due to careless handling.
2. Lubricate all internal parts, before assembly, with transmission fluid. Use no other fluids, except on gaskets and thrust washers, which may be coated with petrolatum as a temporary adhesive to facilitate assembly.
3. Always use new gaskets and seals.
4. Torque all bolts to specifications.

Low-Reverse Servo

1. Remove the four servo cover-to-case retaining bolts. Remove transmission identification tag, vent tube and retaining clip from the case.
2. Remove the servo cover, cover seal, servo piston, and piston return spring from the case. See illustration.

Removing one way clutch outer race retaining bolts (© Ford Motor Co.)

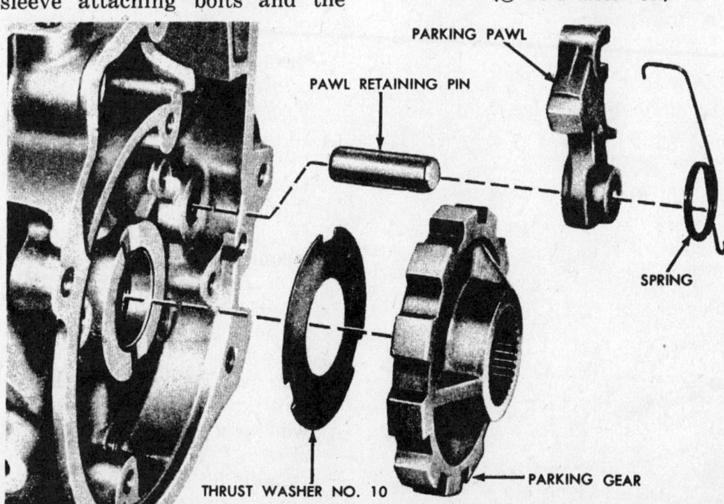

Parking pawl, disassembled (© Ford Motor Co.)

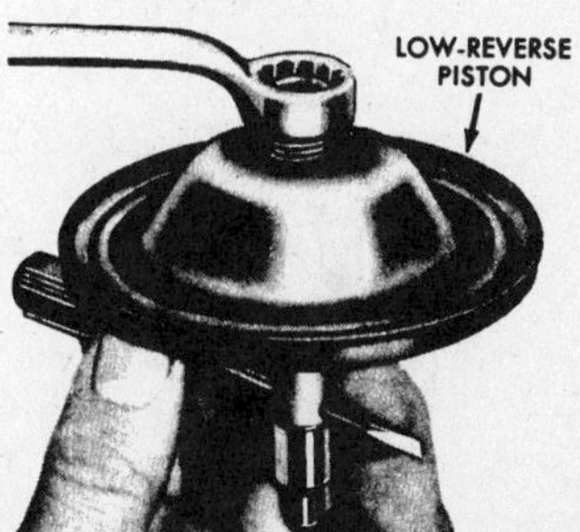

Low-reverse servo piston-removal (© Ford Motor Co.)

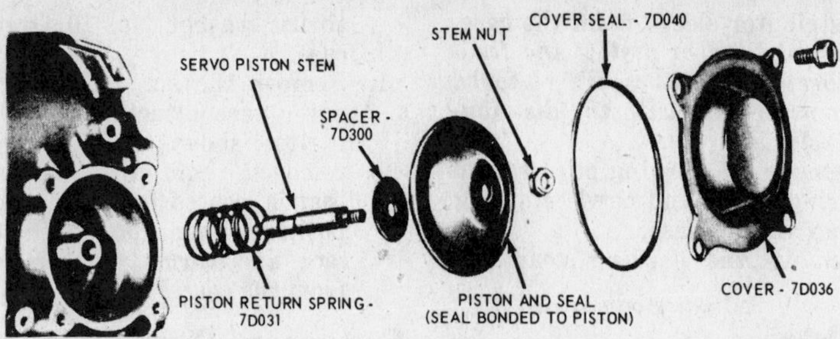

Low-reverse servo disassembled (© Ford Motor Co.)

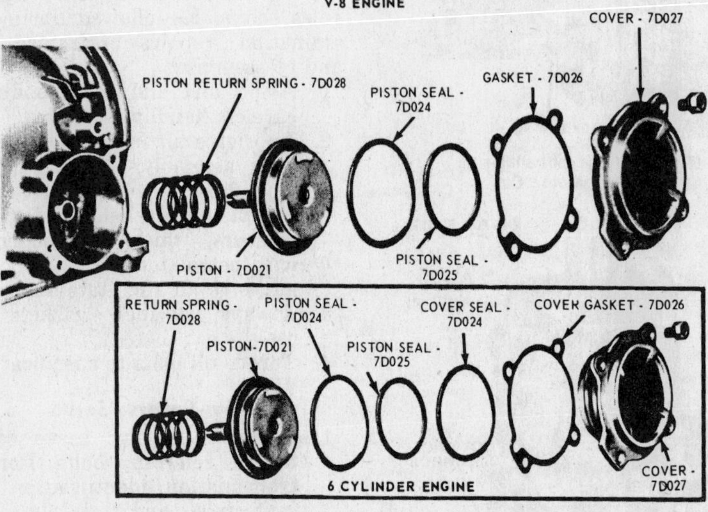

Intermediate servo-disassembled (© Ford Motor Co.)

3. The piston seal is bonded to the piston. If the seal is bad, replace piston and seal assembly.
4. Disassemble piston from piston rod.
5. Install (See illustration) new servo piston and torque the nut to specifications.
6. Place piston return spring in the servo bore of the case. Lubricate piston and seal, then, install it in bore of case.
7. Place new seal on cover and install cover on case. Install identification tag, vent tube, and retaining clip. Install the four cover bolts and torque to specifications.

Intermediate Servo

1. Remove the four servo cover-to-case retaining bolts.
2. Remove the cover, gasket, piston and piston return spring. See illustration.
3. On a transmission used with six cylinder engines, remove the intermediate servo piston from the cover by forcing air pressure into the pressure hole in the cover.
4. Remove seal rings from the piston and cover.
5. Install new seal on the cover and servo piston. Lubricate and install the piston into the cover.
6. Install the piston return spring into the servo bore of the case.
7. With a new gasket in place, position the piston and cover assembly in the case.

NOTE: use two 5/16-18 x 1¼ in. bolts, 180° apart, to position the cover on the case. Install two cover attaching bolts. Remove the two pilot bolts, then, install the regular bolts and torque all of the retaining bolts to specifications.

Downshift and Manual Linkage

1. Downshift outer and inner levers have been removed from the case during removal and disassembly procedures. From inside the case, remove the upper retaining ring and the flat washer from the manual lever link. Remove the upper end of the lever link from the case retaining pin.
2. From the back of the transmission case, remove the upper retaining ring and flat washer from the parking pawl link. Remove the pawl link and spacer from the case retaining pin.
3. From the back of the transmission case, remove the parking pawl link, toggle rod, and the manual lever link as an assembly.
4. Remove the rear parking pawl link lower retaining ring, flat washer and link from the toggle rod.
5. Remove the manual lever link lower retaining ring, flat washer, and link from the toggle rod.

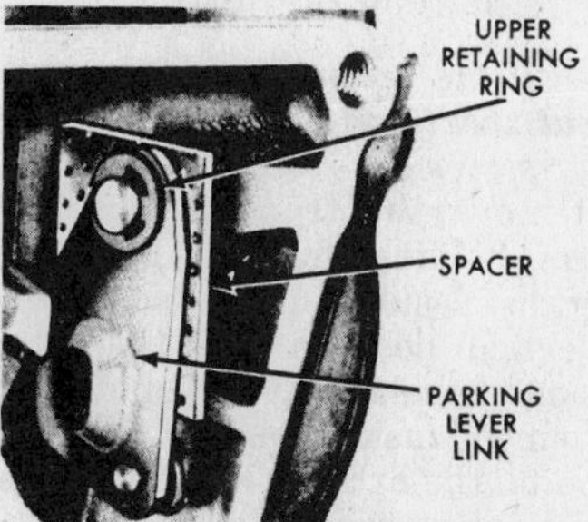

Parking lever pawl link and spacer (© Ford Motor Co.)

Parking pawl toggle rod (© Ford Motor Co.)

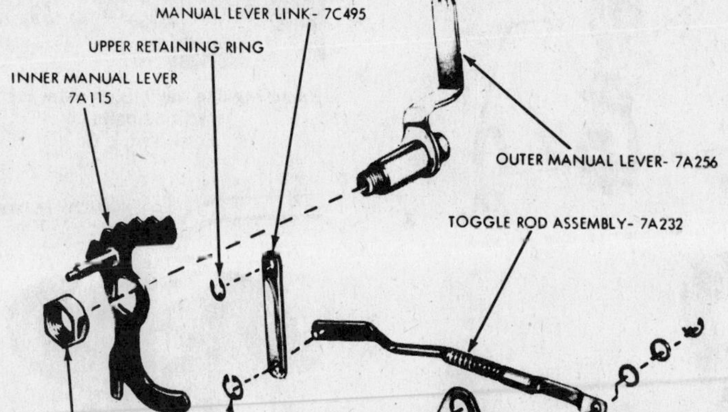

Transmission case internal linkage (© Ford Motor Co.)

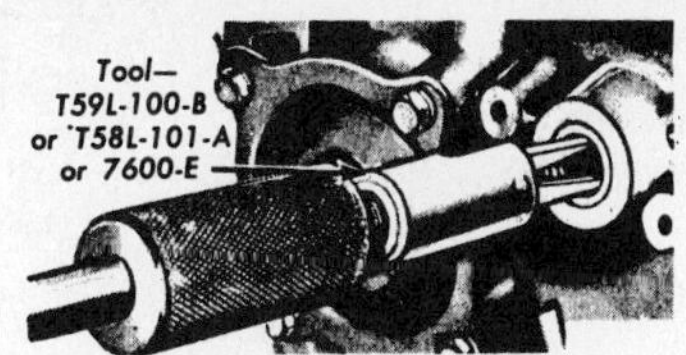

Removing manual lever seal
(© Ford Motor Co.)

6. Install manual and parking pawl links, flat washers and retaining rings to the toggle rods.
7. Remove the inner manual lever retaining nut and lever. Remove the outer manual lever from the case. Remove manual lever seal.
8. Install new seal onto manual lever.
9. Install outer manual lever into the case. Install inner manual lever and retaining nut. Torque nut to specifications.
10. From back of the transmission case, install parking toggle rod and link into the case. Install parking pawl link spacer onto the case retaining pin. Dimpled side of the spacer should be facing the center of the transmission case.
11. Install the parking pawl link onto the case retaining pin. Install flat washer and retaining ring.
12. Position inner manual lever behind the manual lever link, with the cam on the lever contacting the lower link pin.
13. Install the upper end of the manual lever link onto the case retaining pin. Install flat washer and retaining ring.
14. Operate the manual lever and check for correct linkage operation.

Control Valve Body Disassembly and Assembly

Disassembly and assembly procedures are given for all models of the C4 and C4S automatic transmission control valve bodies. Where there are differences in construction, they are given. Refer to the illustrations of the different control valve bodies that show how they fit together while doing these procedures.

1970 Control Valve Body Disassembly

1. Remove the screws attaching the oil screen to the valve body and remove the oil screen. Be carefu not to lose the throttle pressure limit valve and spring when separating the oil screen from the valve body.
2. Remove the attaching screws from the lower valve body and separate the upper and lower valve bodies, the gasket, separator plate and the hold-down plate. Be careful not to lose the upper valve body shuttle valve and check valve when separating the upper and lower valve bodies.
3. Slide the manual valve out of the body.
4. Pry the low servo modulator valve retainer from the body and remove the retainer plug, spring, and valve from the valve body. While working in the same bore, pry the retainer, spring, and the downshift valve from the valve body (see illustration).
5. Depress the throttle booster plug and remove the retaining pin. Then, remove the plug, valve, and spring from the valve body.
6. Remove the cover over the cut-back valve and the transition valve from the valve body.
7. Remove the cut-back valve and the transition valve spring, transition valve, 2-3 back-out valve, and spring from the valve body.
8. Remove the cover from over the 1-2 shift valve and the 2-3 shift valve. Remove the 2-3 shift valve, spring, and the throttle modulator valve from the valve body. Remove the 1-2 shift valve, D-2 valve, and spring from the valve body.
9. Remove the retaining pin from the retainer after depressing the intermediate servo accumulator valve. Remove the retainer, intermediate servo accumulator valve, and spring from the valve body.

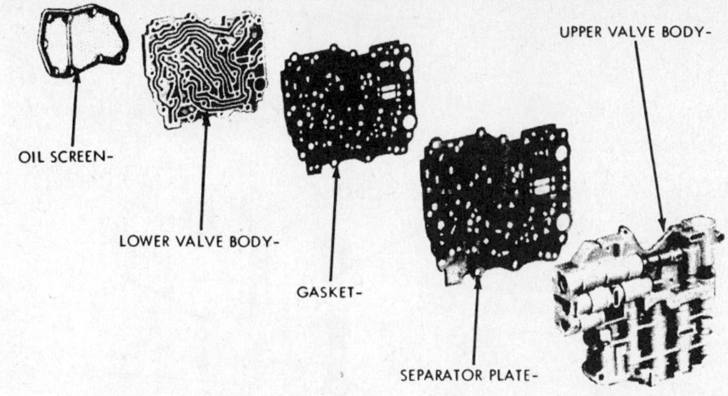

Upper & lower valve bodies 1970 C-4S (© Ford Motor Co.)

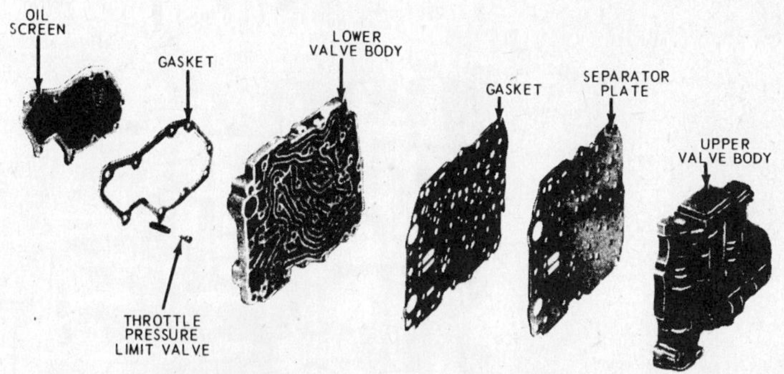

Upper & lower valve bodies C-4 (© Ford Motor Co.)

10. Depress the main oil pressure booster valve and remove the retaining pin. Remove the main oil pressure booster valve, sleeve, springs, retainer, and main oil pressure regulator valve from the valve body.
11. Remove the line coasting boost valve retaining clip, the spring, and line coasting boost valve from the valve body.

1970 Control Valve Body Assembly

Assembly procedures are the reverse of the disassembly procedures given above. The shuttle valves should be installed in the lower valve body and the separator plate fastened securely before proceeding with the upper valve body. All valves should move freely in the bores and any burrs or scoring should be carefully removed with crocus cloth. Tighten all screws to the proper torque.

1970 Control Valve Body Disassembly (C4S Semi-Automatic)

1. Remove the attaching screws from the oil screen on the lower valve body and remove the oil screen.
2. Remove the attaching screws from the underside of the lower valve body and the two attaching screws from the topside of the upper valve body and separate the valve bodies. Be careful not to lose the rubber ball shuttle valve when separating

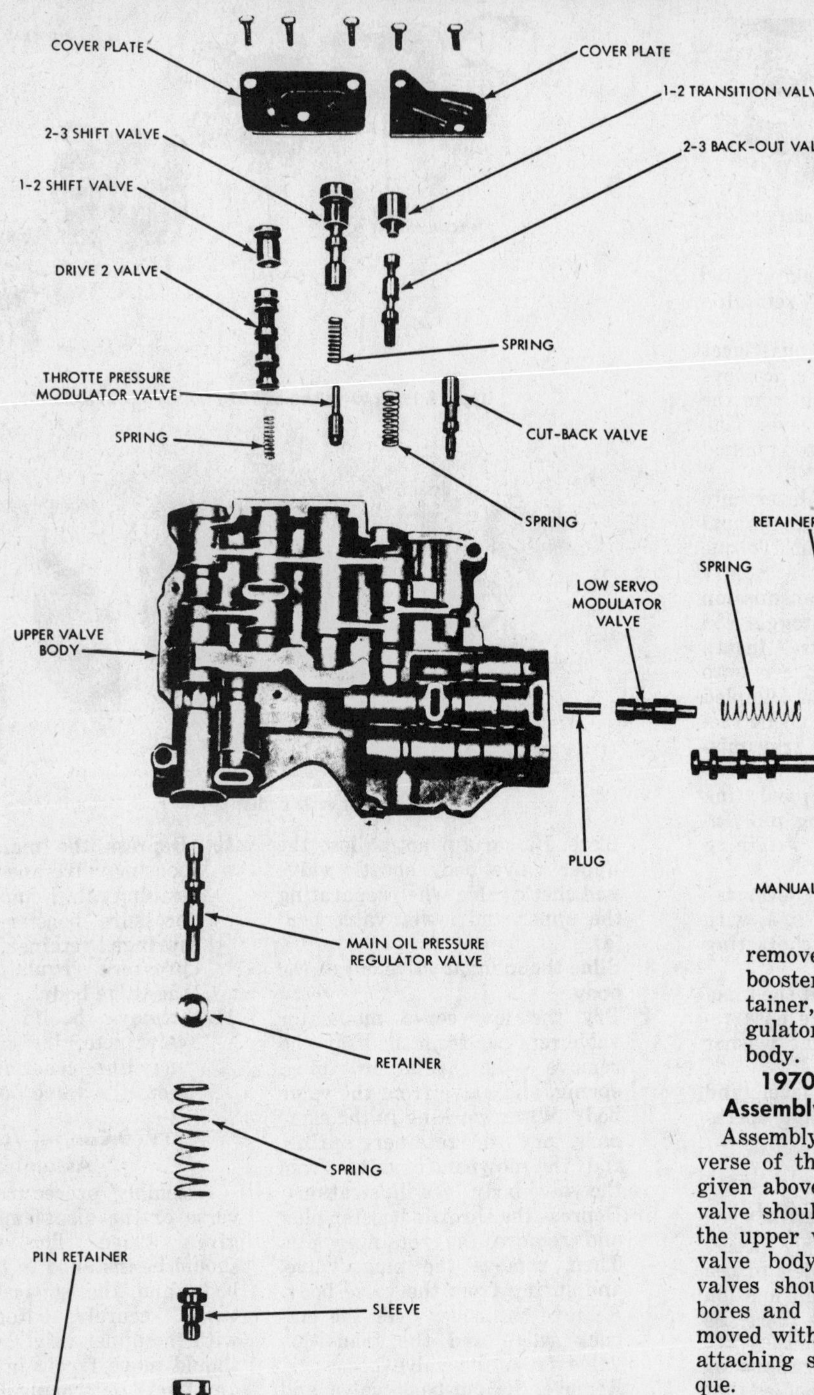

Upper valve body-disassembled C-4S (© Ford Motor Co.)

the upper and lower valve bodies.

3. Slide the manual valve from the valve body. Remove the retainer clip, plug, spring, low servo modulator valve, and plug from the valve body.
4. Remove the cover over the cut-back, 1-2 transition, and 2-3 back-out valves. Remove the cut-back valve and the 1-2 transition and the 2-3 back-out valves and the spring from the valve body.
5. Remove the cover plate from over the 2-3 shift valve, throttle pressure modulator valve, 1-2 shift valve, and drive 2 valve. Remove the 2-3 shift valve, spring, and the throttle pressure modulator valve. Then, remove the 1-2 shift valve. Drive 2 valve, and spring from the valve body.
6. Depress the main oil pressure booster valve inward and remove the retaining pin. Then, remove the main oil pressure booster valve, sleeve, spring, retainer, and main oil pressure regulator valve from the valve body.

1970 Control Valve Body Assembly (C4S Semi-Automatic)

Assembly procedures are the reverse of the disassembly procedures given above. The rubber ball shuttle valve should be placed as shown in the upper valve body and the lower valve body fastened in place. All valves should move freely in their bores and any burrs or scoring removed with crocus cloth. Tighten all attaching screws to the proper torque.

1967-69 Control Valve Body Disassembly and Assembly (C4 Automatic)

The procedures for the disassembly and assembly of the 1967-1969 control valve bodies are the same as those given for the 1970 control valve body. The same control valve body is used for transmissions made in those years.

1965-66 Control Valve Body Disassembly and Assembly (C4 Automatic)

The disassembly and assembly procedures for the 1965-66 control valve bodies are similar to those

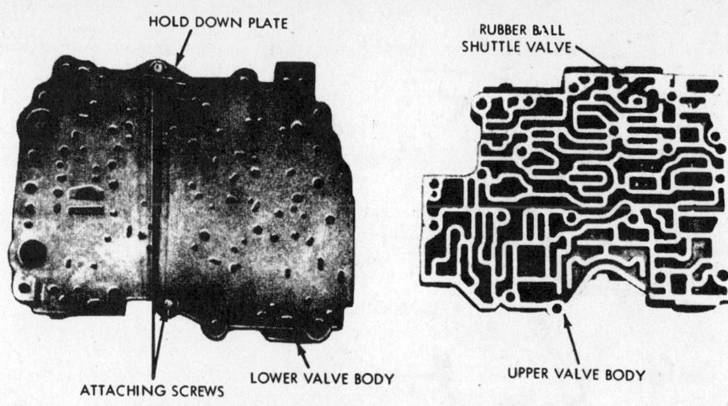

Upper & lower valve bodies C-4S 1970 (© Ford Motor Co.)

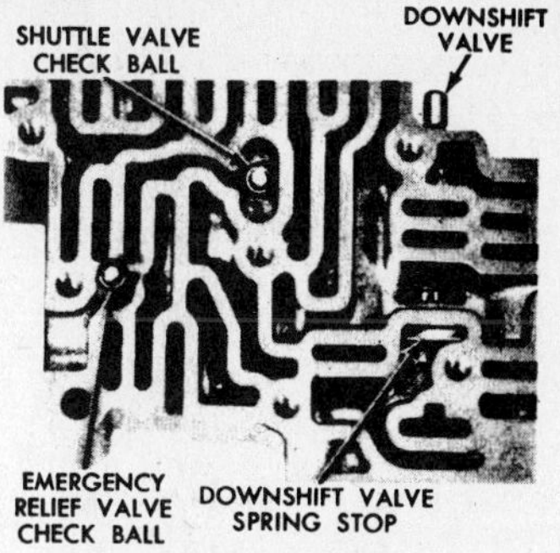

Upper valve body check ball and spring location (© Ford Motor Co.)

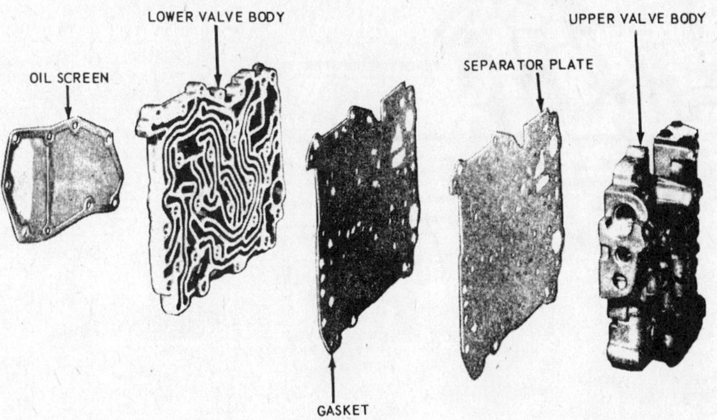

Upper & lower valve bodies 1966 (© Ford Motor Co.)

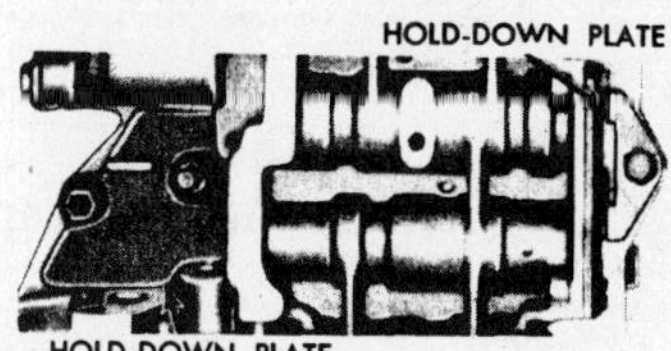

Hold down plate location (© Ford Motor Co.)

given for the 1970 control valve body (C4 automatic). There are some differences in construction between these control valve bodies which may be seen in the illustrations. The assembly instructions are the reverse of the disassembly instructions.

1964 Control Valve Body Disassembly and Assembly (C4 Automatic)

The 1964 control valve body is disassembled according to instructions given for the 1970 control valve body and as shown in the disassembled views of the control valve body. The assembly instructions are the reverse of the disassembly instructions. Install the valves and springs as shown and be sure they move freely in their bores. Any burrs or scoring should be removed with crocus cloth. Tighten all screws to the proper torque.

Front Pump Disassembly

1. Remove the four seal rings from the stator support and, in 1964-67 models, the O-ring seal from the pump housing.
2. Remove the five bolts that secure the stator support to the front pump housing. Remove stator support from pump housing.
3. Replace the stator bushings if they are worn or damaged. Use a cape chisel to cut the bushing through. Then, pry up the loose ends of the bushing with an awl and remove the bushing. Press a new bushing in the stator support.

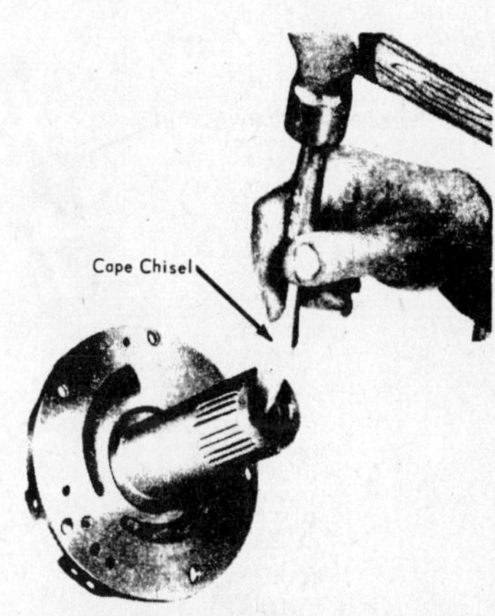

Removing stator support bushings (© Ford Motor Co.)

4. Replace the bushing in the pump housing with the tools shown, making sure the slot and groove are toward the rear of the body and 60 degrees below the center line.

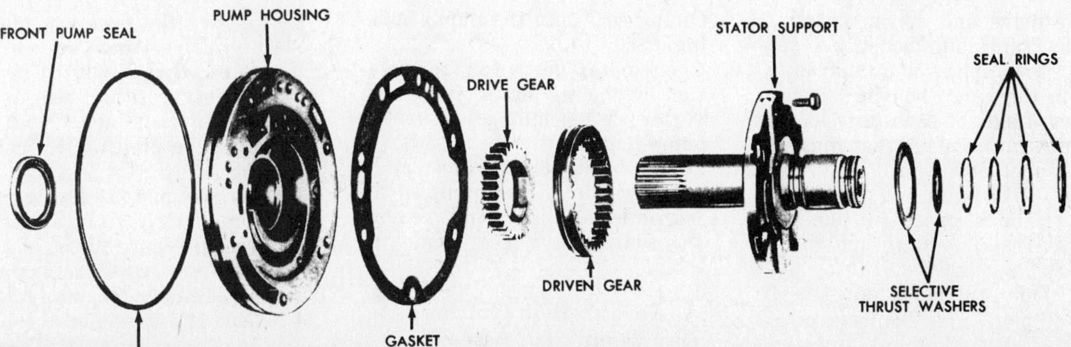

Typical front pump and stator support (© Ford Motor Co.)

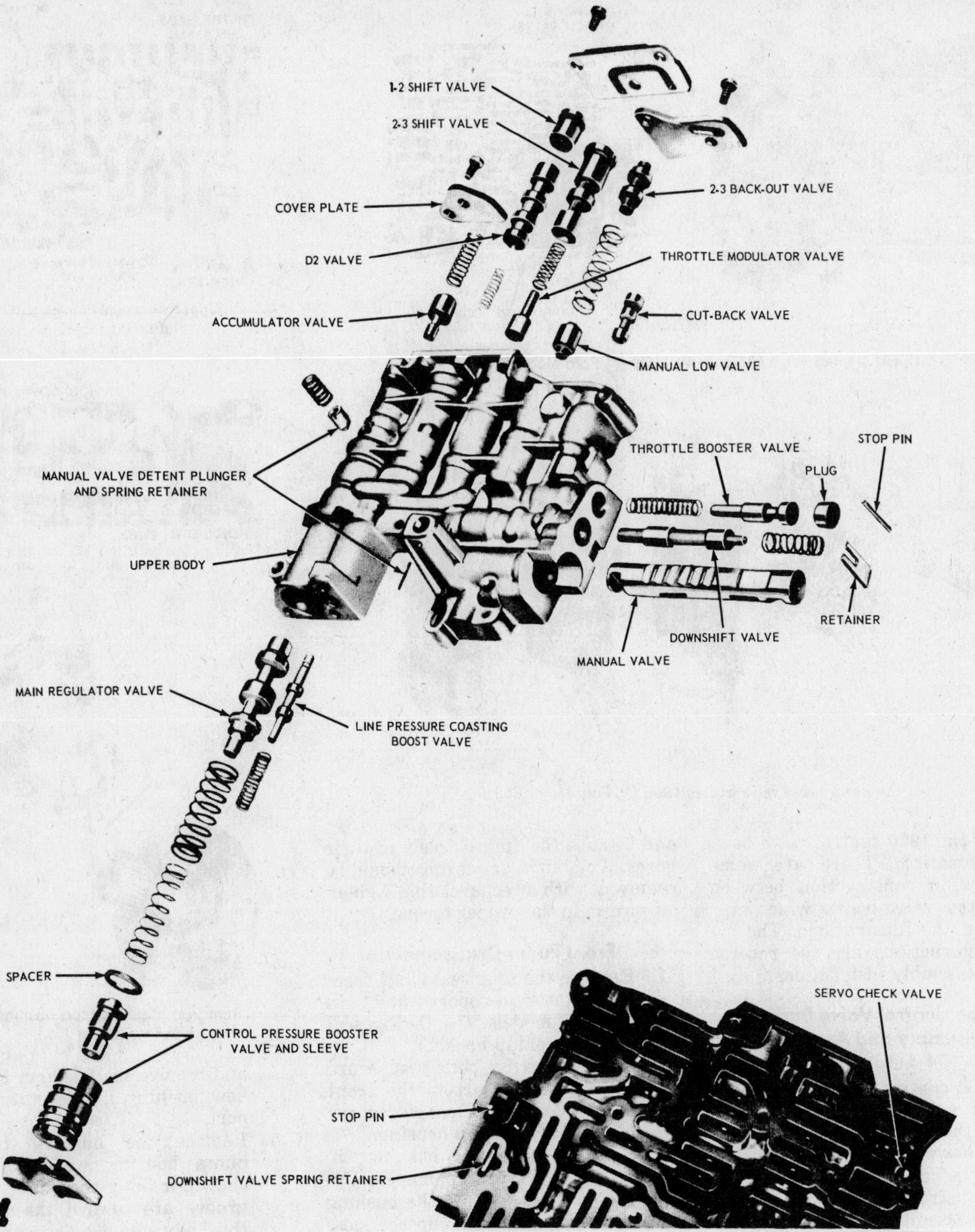

Upper valve body disassembled 1965 C-4 (© Ford Motor Co.)

5. Remove drive and driven gears from the front pump housing.
6. Install the drive and driven gears in the pump housing. The chamfered side of each gear has an identification mark that must be positioned downward, against the face of the pump housing.
7. Place stator support in pump housing. Install and torque the five retaining bolts.
8. Install four seal rings onto the stator support. The two large oil rings are assembled first, in the oil ring grooves toward the front of the stator support. Install the O-ring seal onto the pump housing.
9. Check pump gears for free rotation by placing pump on the converter drive hub and turning pump housing.
10. If the front pump seal must be replaced, mount the pump in the transmission case and remove the seal with a seal removing tool.

Reverse-High Clutch Disassembly and Assembly

1. Remove pressure plate retaining snap-ring.
2. Remove the pressure plate, and the drive and driven clutch plates. CAUTION: Use no detergent or other cleaning solution on the lined clutch plates. Wipe the plates with a lint-free cloth.
3. Remove piston spring retainer snap ring by applying arbor press pressure to the clutch hub. Compress piston return springs, then, remove the snap ring.
4. Back off press pressure, remove the retainer and ten piston return springs.
5. Remove the piston by applying

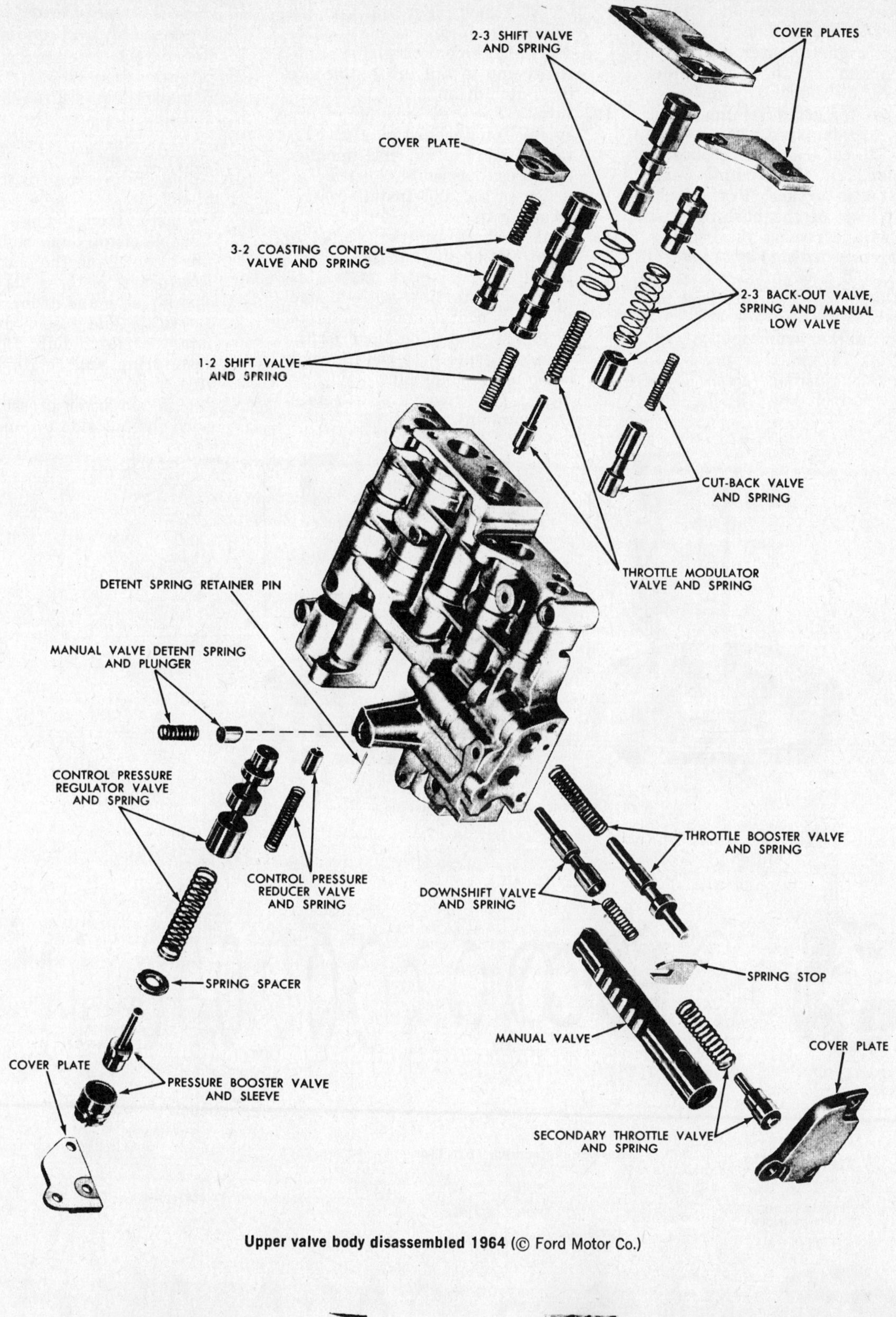

2-3 SHIFT VALVE AND SPRING
COVER PLATES
COVER PLATE
3-2 COASTING CONTROL VALVE AND SPRING
2-3 BACK-OUT VALVE, SPRING AND MANUAL LOW VALVE
1-2 SHIFT VALVE AND SPRING
CUT-BACK VALVE AND SPRING
THROTTLE MODULATOR VALVE AND SPRING
DETENT SPRING RETAINER PIN
MANUAL VALVE DETENT SPRING AND PLUNGER
CONTROL PRESSURE REGULATOR VALVE AND SPRING
THROTTLE BOOSTER VALVE AND SPRING
CONTROL PRESSURE REDUCER VALVE AND SPRING
DOWNSHIFT VALVE AND SPRING
SPRING STOP
SPRING SPACER
MANUAL VALVE
COVER PLATE
COVER PLATE
PRESSURE BOOSTER VALVE AND SLEEVE
SECONDARY THROTTLE VALVE AND SPRING

Upper valve body disassembled 1964 (© Ford Motor Co.)

Tool—1175-AB
Tool—T50T-100-A

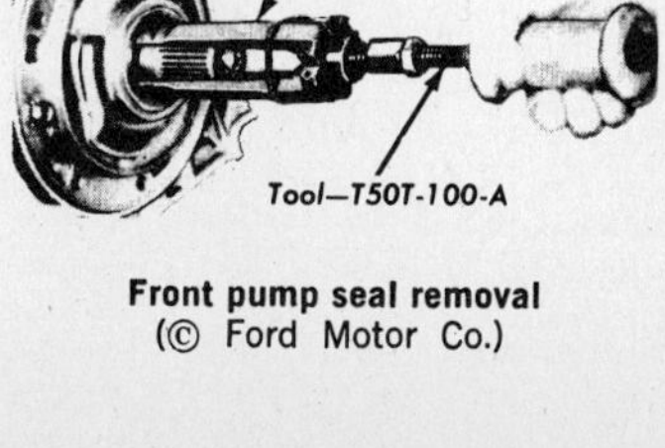

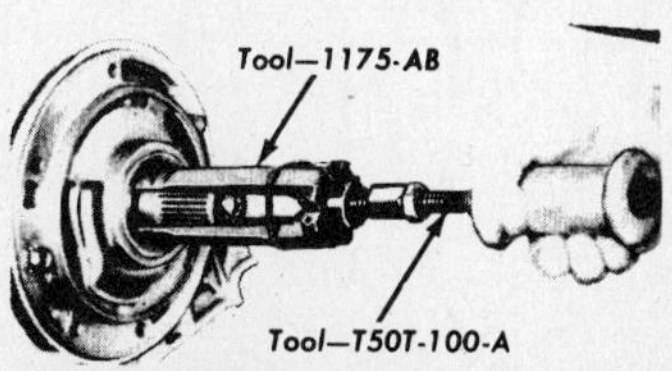

Front pump seal removal
(© Ford Motor Co.)

Tool—T63L-77837-A or 77837-A

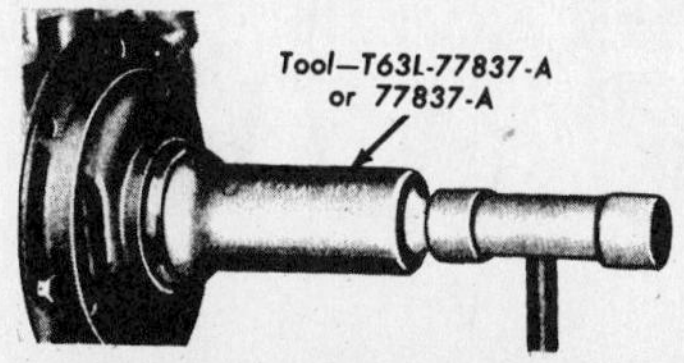

Installing front pump seal
(© Ford Motor Co.)

air pressure to the piston apply hole of the clutch hub.

6. Remove piston outer seal from the piston and the piston inner seal from the clutch drum.
7. Remove the drum bushing if it is worn or damaged. Use a cape chisel to cut a shallow groove ¾ in. long in the bushing seam until it is broken. Pry up the loose ends of the bushing with an awl and remove the bushing. *To prevent leakage at the stator support O-rings, do not nick or damage the hub surface with the chisel.*
8. Position the drum and a new bushing in an arbor press and press the bushing into the drum with the tool shown in the illustration.
9. Install a new inner seal into the clutch drum and a new outer seal onto the clutch piston. Lubricate and install the piston into the clutch drum.
10. Locate the ten piston return springs on the piston. Place retainer on top of the springs. Compress assembly with an arbor press, and install the retainer snap-ring.
11. Soak new composition plates in transmission fluid before installation. Install clutch plates, alternately, starting with a steel plate, then a composition plate. The last plate installed is the pressure plate with the internally-chamfered side up.
12. Install the pressure plate retaining snap-ring.

Forward Clutch Disassembly and Assembly

1. Remove the clutch pressure plate retaining snap ring.
2. Remove the pressure plate, drive and driven plates from the hub.
3. Remove the disc spring retaining snap-ring.
4. Apply air pressure to the clutch piston pressure hole to remove the piston from the hub.
5. Remove piston outer seal and the inner seal from the clutch hub.
6. Install new piston seals onto the clutch piston and drum.
7. Lubricate and insert the piston into the clutch hub. Install the disc spring and retaining snap-ring.
8. Install the lower pressure plate, with the flat side up and the ra-

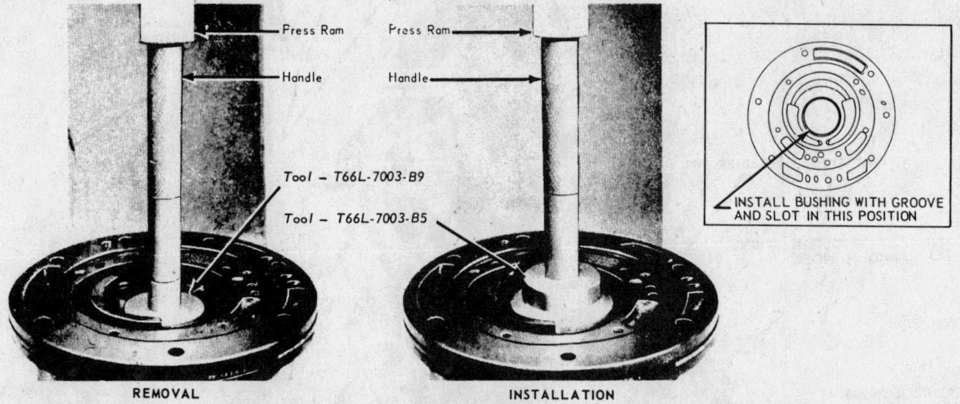

Removing front pump housing bushing (© Ford Motor Co.)

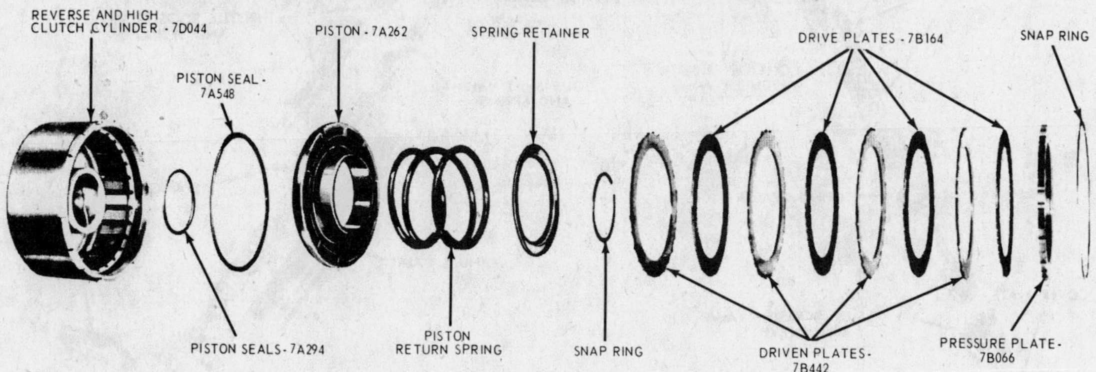

Reverse-high clutch 1970 C-4 (© Ford Motor Co.)

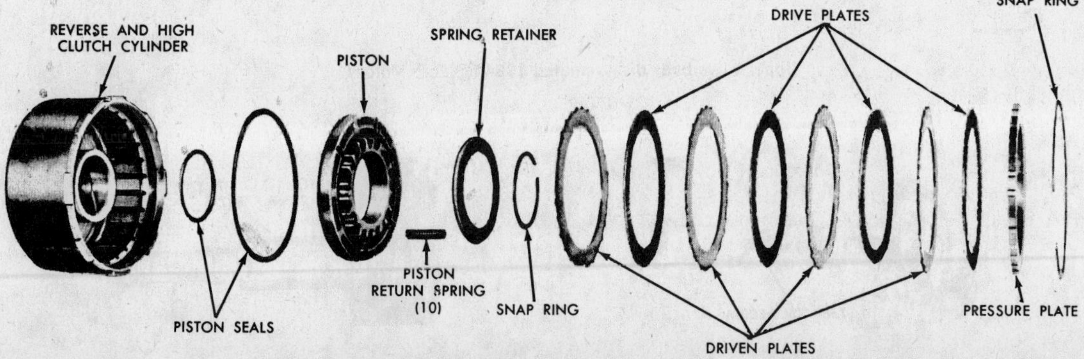

Reverse-high clutch 1970 C-4 (© Ford Motor Co.)

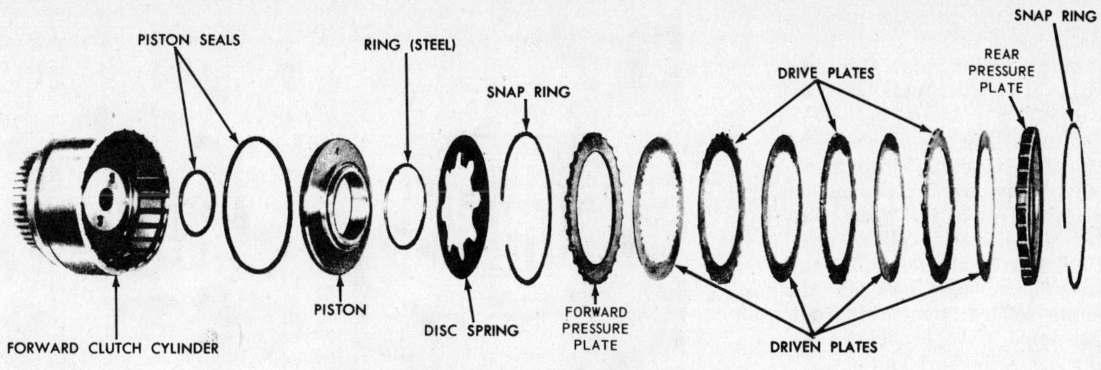

Forward clutch-disassembled (© Ford Motor Co.)

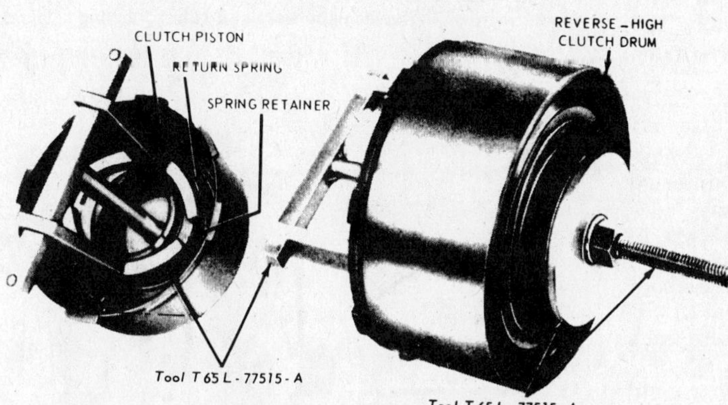

Removing or installing clutch piston retainer snap-ring (© Ford Motor Co.)

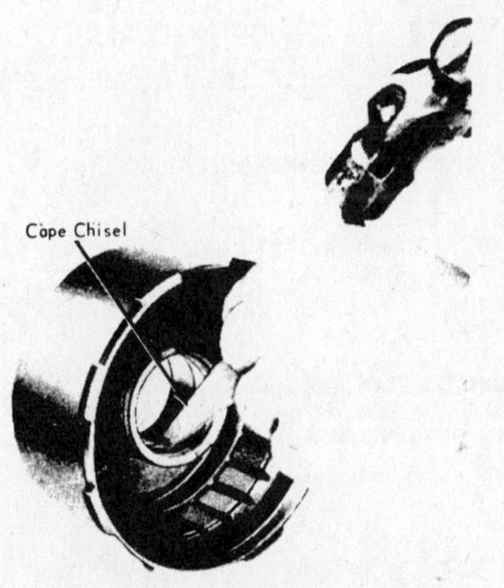

Removing reverse-high clutch bushing (© Ford Motor Co.)

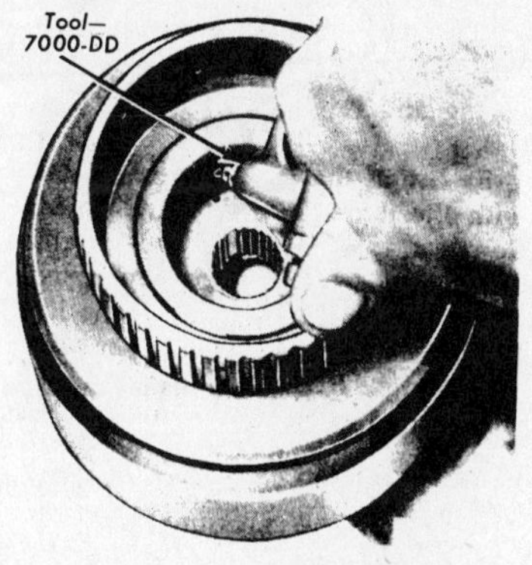

Removing forward clutch piston (© Ford Motor Co.)

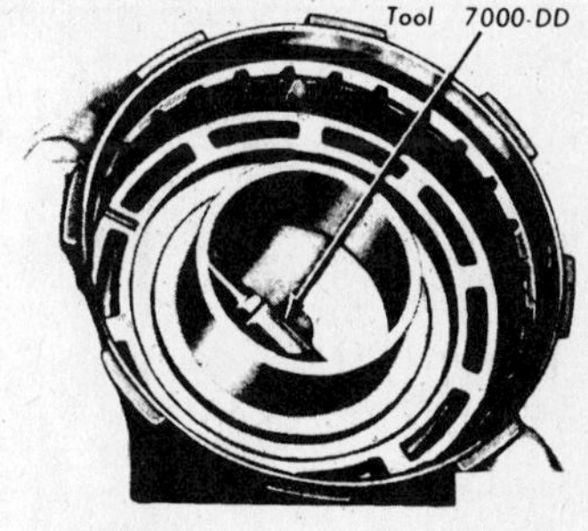

Removing reverse-high clutch piston (© Ford Motor Co.)

diused side downward. Install one composition clutch plate and alternately install the drive and driven plates. The last plate to be installed will be the upper pressure plate, with the internally-chamfered side up.

9. Install pressure plate retaining snap-ring.
10. With a feeler gauge, check clearance between the snap ring and the pressure plate. Downward pressure on the plate should be used when making this check. Clearance should be 0.025-0.050 in.
11. If clearance is not within specifications, selective snap-rings are available in the following thicknesses: 0.050-0.054, 0.064-0.068, 0.078-0.082, and 0.092-0.096 in. Install the most correct size and recheck the clearance.

Forward Clutch Hub and Ring Gear Disassembly and Assembly

1. Remove forward clutch hub retaining snap-ring.
2. Separate clutch hub from ring gear.
3. Press the bushing from the clutch hub.
4. Install a new bushing into the clutch hub as shown.
5. Install clutch hub into ring gear.
6. Install hub retaining snap-ring.

Forward Planet Carrier Disassembly and Assembly

1. With a small punch inserted into the end of the planet gear retaining pin hole, force the shaft retaining pins outward. With side cutters, remove retaining pins.
2. Remove three planet gear pins, three gears, thrust washers and spacers.
3. Remove outer race, thrust bearing, and the inner race.
4. Install the inner race, thrust bearing and outer race.
5. Install 21 bearing rollers into each planet gear. Hold rollers in place with petrolatum. Position

gears, spacers, and washers in the carrier.
6. Install gear pins and align retaining pin holes. Install retaining pins.
7. When only the thrust bearing and races have to be removed, remove only two of the planet gear pins. Move the gears outward far enough to allow removal of the thrust bearing and races. This will prevent the bearing rollers from falling out. Reassemble the thrust bearing and races, two gears and pins.

Input Shell and Sun Gear Disassembly and Assembly

1. Remove external snap-ring from sun gear.
2. Remove thrust washer No. 5 from input shell and sun gear.
3. From inside the shell, remove the sun gear. Remove internal snap-ring from sun gear.
4. If the sun gear bushings are to be replaced, use the tool shown in the illustration and press both bushings through the gear.
5. Press a new bushing into each end of the sun gear.
6. Install internal snap-ring onto sun gear. Install sun gear into the input shell.
7. Install thrust washer No. 5 onto sun gear and input shell.
8. Install external snap-ring onto sun gear.

Replacing sun gear bushing (© Ford Motor Co.)

Reverse Ring Gear and Hub Disassembly and Assembly

1. Remove hub retaining snap-ring from reverse ring gear.
2. Remove the hub from reverse ring gear.
3. Install hub into reverse ring gear.
4. Install snap-ring into reverse ring gear.

Governor and Oil Distributor Disassembly (C4 Automatic Only)

1. Remove the oil rings from the governor oil distributor.

Replacing forward clutch hub bushing (© Ford Motor Co.)

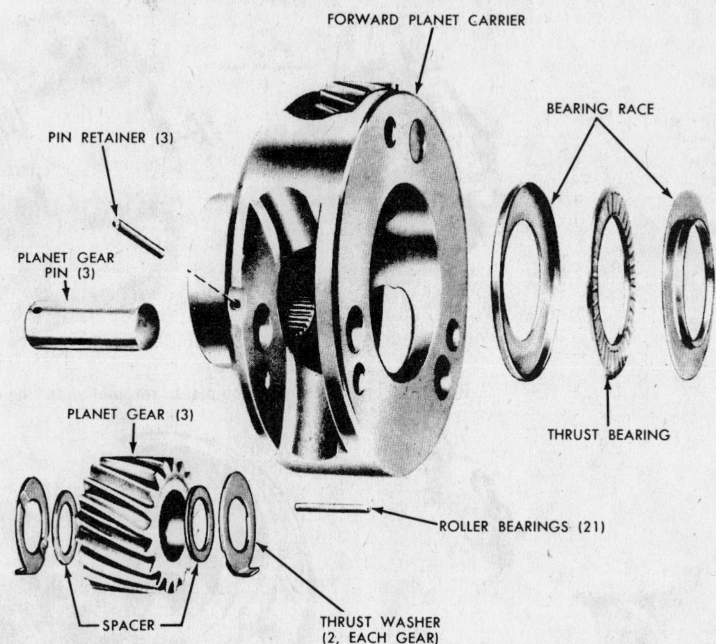

Forward planet carrier-disassembled (© Ford Motor Co.)

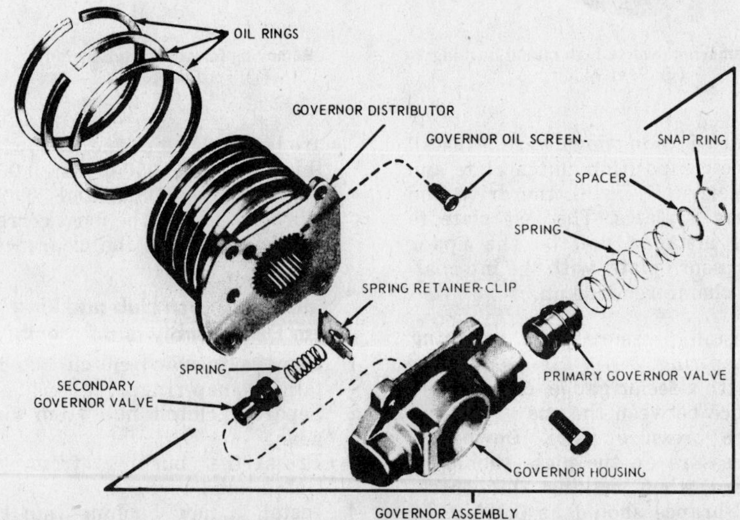

Governor and oil distributor (© Ford Motor Co.)

2. Remove the governor housing attaching bolts and remove the governor assembly from the distributor. Remove the governor oil screen. NOTE: in 1964 models only, the governor assembly was made in two parts and they were removed separately.
3. Remove the primary governor valve retaining ring. Remove the washer, spring, and primary governor valve from the housing.
4. Remove the secondary governor valve retaining clip, spring, and governor valve from the housing.
5. After cleaning and inspecting all governor parts, install the secondary governor valve in its housing. Install the spring and spring retaining clip with its small concave area facing downward.

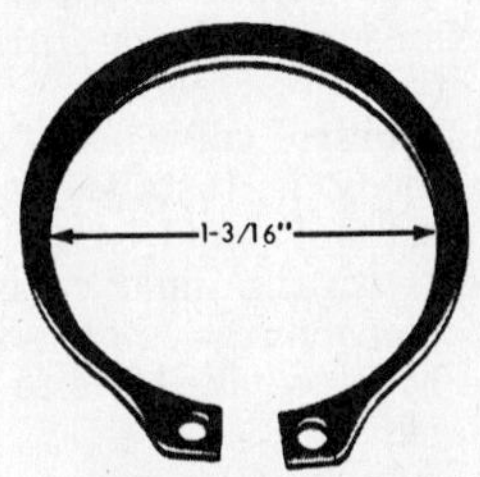

RETAINS REVERSE RING GEAR AND HUB TO OUTPUT SHAFT

1-1/4"

RETAINS GOVERNOR DISTRIBUTOR TO OUTPUT SHAFT

Governor and reverse ring gear and hub identification
(© Ford Motor Co.)

6. Install tho primary govcrnor valve in the housing. Install the spring, washer, and retaining clip. Be sure the washer is centered in the housing on the fully seated in the ring groove in fully seated in the ring groove ni the housing.
7. Install the oil rings on the governor distributor. Install the governor oil screen and mount the governor assembly on the distributor, tightening the attaching bolts to the proper torque.

Transmission Assembly

1. Install thrust washer No. 9 inside the transmission case.
2. Place the one-way clutch outer race inside the case. From the rear of the case, install the six outer race-to-case retaining bolts. Torque to specifications.
3. Stand the transmission case on end (rear end up). Install parking pawl retaining pin.
4. Install parking pawl on the case retaining pin. Install pawl return spring.
5. Install thrust washer No. 10 onto the parking pawl gear. Place gear and thrust washer on back face of case.
6. Place two oil distributor tubes in the governor distributor sleeve. Install the sleeve onto the case. As the distributor sleeve is installed, the oil tubes have to be inserted into the two holes in the case and the parking pawl retaining pin has to be inserted in the alignment hole in the distributor.
7. Install the four governor distributor sleeve-to-case retaining bolts and torque to specifications.
8. Install governor distributor assembly onto the output shaft. Install the distributor retaining snap-ring.
9. Check oil rings in the governor distributor for clearance. Install the output shaft and governor distributor into the distributor sleeve.
10. With a new gasket in place on the extension housing, install the extension housing, vacuum tube clip and the extension housing to case retaining bolts. Torque bolts to specifications.
11. Rotate transmission case so that front end is up, making sure that thrust washer No. 9 is in position at the bottom of the case.
12. On the bench, install the 12 one-way clutch springs onto the spring retainer.
13. Place the one-way clutch spring retainer, with springs installed, into the outer race, located inside the transmission.
14. Check the position of each spring on the spring retainer. Install the inner race inside the spring retainer and 12 springs
15. Starting at the back of the one-way clutch outer race, install the 12 clutch rollers. Each spring will be partially compressed as the roller is installed between the outer and inner race.
16. After the clutch has been assembled, rotate the inner race clockwise to center the rollers and springs Install low and roverso drum. The splines of the drum must engage the splines of the one-way clutch inner race. Check the clutch operation by rotating the low and reverse drum. The drum should rotate clockwise but should not rotate counterclockwise.
17. Install thrust washer No. 8 on top of the low and reverse drum. Install the low and reverse band into the case, with the end of the band for the small strut toward the low-reverse servo.
18. Install the reverse ring gear and hub onto the output shaft.
19. Move the output shaft forward and install the reverse ring gear hub-to-output shaft retaining ring.
20. Place thrust washers Nos. 6 and 7 on the reverse planet carrier. Install planet carrier into the reverse ring gear and engage the tabs of the carrier with the slots in the low-reverse drum.
21. From inside the transmission case, install the inner downshift lever.

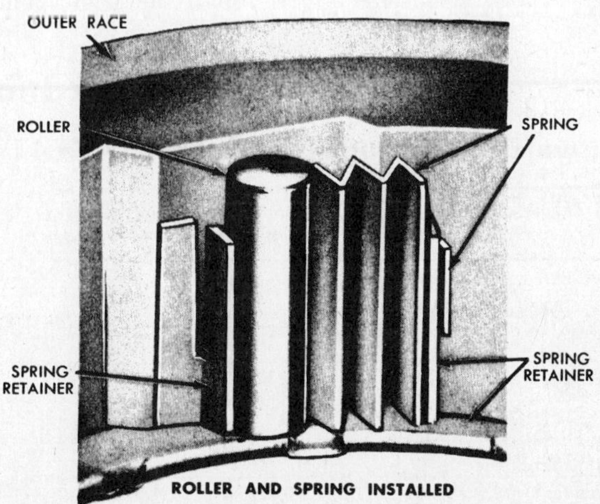

One way clutch installation (© Ford Motor Co.)

22. On the bench, install the forward clutch into the reverse-high clutch by rotating the units to mesh the reverse-high clutch plates with the splines of the forward clutch. Using the end-play check reading obtained during the transmission disassembly, determine which No. 2 steel thrust washer is necessary to get the proper end-play reading and proceed as follows:
   a. Place the stator support vertically on the bench and install the correct No. 2 thrust washer or washer and saucer as required to bring the end-play within the correct range.
   b. Install the reverse-high clutch and the forward clutch on the stator support.
   c. Invert the complete assembly making sure the intermediate brake drum bushing is seated on the forward clutch mating surface. Select the thickest fiber washer (No. 1) that can be inserted between the stator support and the intermediate brake drum thrust surfaces and still maintain a slight clearance. Do not select a washer that must be forced between the stator support and the intermediate brake drum.
   d. Remove the intermediate brake drum and forward clutch unit from the stator support.
   e. Install the selected No. 1 and No. 2 thrust washers on the front pump stator support using enough vaseline to hold the thrust washers in place while installing the front pump.
23. Install thrust washer No. 3 onto the forward clutch.
24. Install forward clutch hub and ring in the forward clutch by rotating the units to mesh the forward clutch plates with the splines on the forward clutch hub.
25. Install thrust washer No. 4 on the front planet carrier into the forward clutch hub and ring gear.
26 Install input shell and sun gear onto the gear train. Rotate the input shell to engage the drive lugs of the reverse-high clutch. If the drive lugs will not engage the outer race inside the forward planet carrier is not centered in the end of the sun gear inside the input shell. Center the thrust bearing race and install the input shell.
27. Hold the gear train together and install the forward part of the gear train assembly into the case. The input shell sun gear must mesh with the reverse pinion gears. The front planet carrier internal splines must mesh with the splines of the output shaft.
28. Install intermediate band through front of case. The side of the band with the anchor tabs goes toward the back of the transmission. If using a new band, soak in transmission fluid.
29. Install a new front pump gasket onto the case. Using the end-play check readings that were obtained during disassembly, install the correct selective thrust washers Nos. 1 and 2 onto the front pump stator support. Use vaseline to hold the washers in place.
30. Lubricate the front pump O-ring with transmission oil, then install the front pump stator support into the reverse-high clutch. Align the pump to the case and install two front pump to case retaining bolts, 180° apart. Alternately tighten the two bolts until the pump is properly seated in the case. Remove the two front pump retaining bolts.
31. Install the converter housing onto the front pump and case. Install the six converter housing to case retaining bolts. Torque bolts to specifications.
32. Install input shaft. Place transmission in horizontal position, then check transmission end play. If end-play is not within limits, either the wrong selective thrust washers were used, or one of the 10 thrust washers is improperly positioned.
33. Remove the dial indicator used for checking end play and install the one converter housing to case retaining bolt. Torque the bolt to specifications.
34. Install the intermediate and low-reverse band adjusting screws into the case. Install the struts for each band.
35. Adjust intermediate and low-reverse band.
36. Install a universal joint yoke onto the output shaft. Rotate the input and output shafts in both directions to check for free rotation of the gear train.
37. Install control valve body. As the valve body is installed, engage the manual and down-shift valves with the inner control levers. Torque the eight control valve body-to-case bolts to specifications.
38. With a new oil pan gasket in place, install the oil pan and torque the eleven attaching bolts to specifications.
39. Install the extension housing-to-case retaining bolts and torque to specifications.
40. Install primary throttle valve into the transmission case.
41. Install vacuum unit, gasket and control rod into the case.
42. Make sure the input shaft is properly installed in the front pump, stator support and gear train. Install the converter into the front pump and the converter housing.

Specifications

Control Pressure at Zero Output Shaft Speed—1964

Engine Speed	*Throttle*	*Manifold Vac. —Ins. Hg.*	*Selector Lever Position*	*Control Pressure (P.S.I.)*
Idle	Closed	*Above 18	P, N, D1, D2, L	55-62
			R	55-96
As required	As required	17.5-16.5	D1, D2, L	Pressure starts to increase
As required	As required	10	D1, D2, L	95-110
As required	As required	3	D1, D2, L	138-148
			R	213-227

*Vehicles checked at high altitudes

At altitudes above sea level it may not be possible to obtain 18" of vacuum at idle. For idle vacuums of less than 18" refer to following table to determine idle speed pressure specification in forward driving ranges (D1, D2, or L).

Engine Vacuum	*Control Pressure (PSI)*
17	55-65
16	55-71
15	55-77
14	55-83
13	55-89
12	55-95
11	55-101

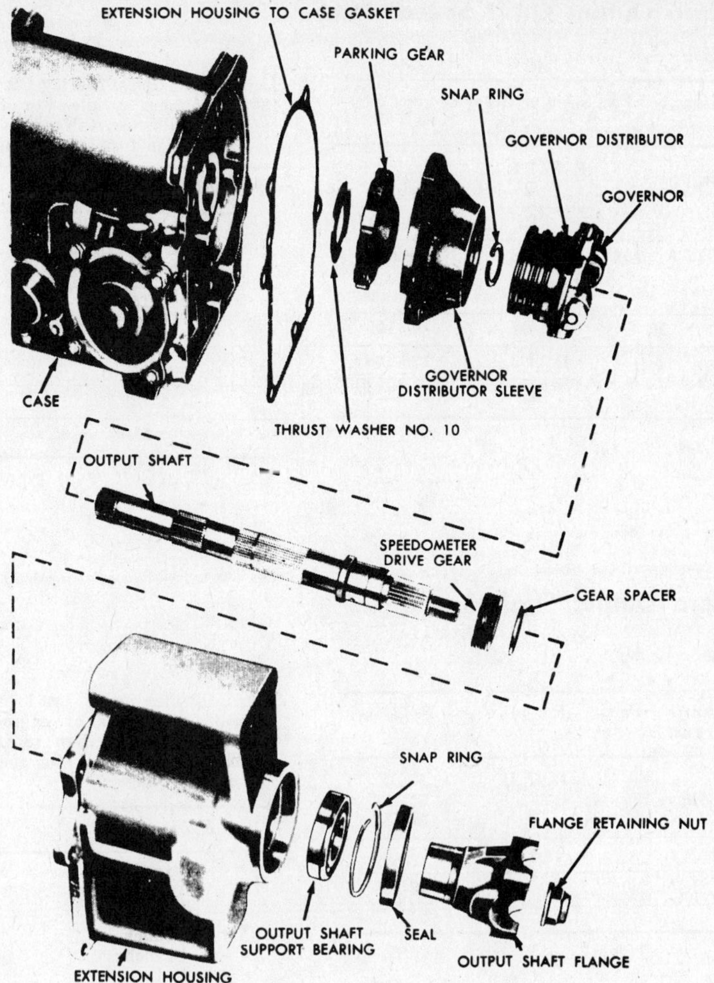

Extension Housing and Output Shaft Related Parts

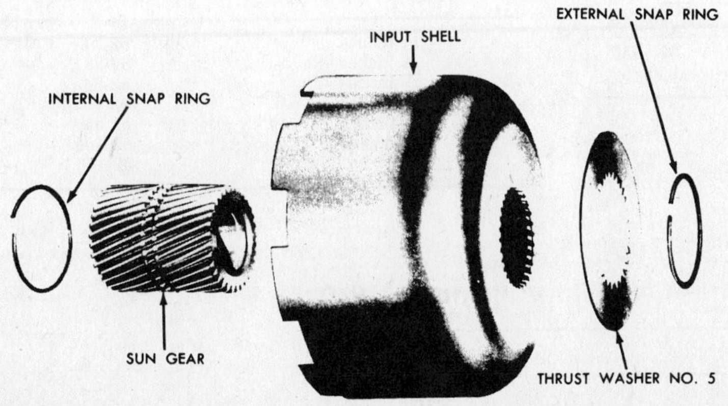

Input Shell and Sun Gear Disassembled

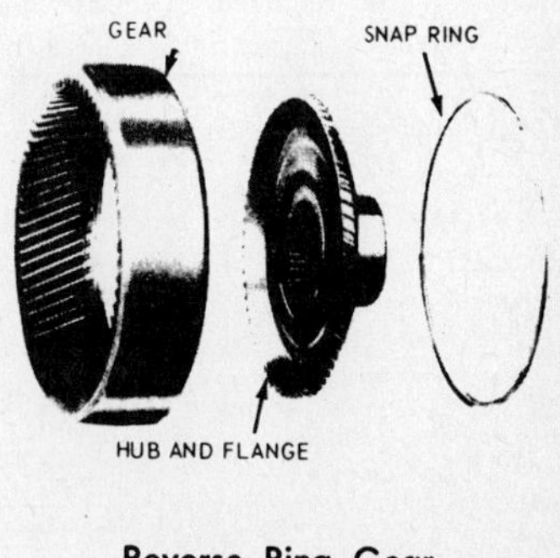

Reverse Ring Gear and Hub Disassembled

Control Pressure at Zero Output Shaft Speed—1965, 1966, 1967

Engine Speed	*Throttle*	*Manifold Vac. Ins. Hg.*	*Selector Lever Position*	*Control Pressure (P.S.I.)*
Idle	Closed	*Above 18	P, N, D1, D2, L	55-62
			R	55-100
As required	As required	17 Approx.	D1, D2, L	Pressure starts to increase
As required	As required	10	D1, D2, L	96-105
As required	As required	3	D1, D2, L	138-148
			R	215-227

*Vehicles checked at high altitudes

At altitudes above sea level it may not be possible to obtain 18" of vacuum at idle. For idle vacuums of less than 18" refer to following table to determine idle speed pressure specification in forward driving ranges (D1, D2, or L).

Engine Vacuum	*Control Pressure (PSI)*
17	55-62
16	55-68
15	55-74
14	55-80
13	55-87
12	55-93
11	55-99

Control Pressure at Zero Output Shaft Speed C4 Transmission—1968, 1969

Engine Speed	*Throttle*	*Manifold Vac. Ins. Hg*	*Range*	*P.S.I.*
Idle	Closed	Above 18①	P, N, D, 2, 1 R	55-61 55-102 55-182
As required	As required	10	D, 2, 1	93-101
As required	Wide open	Below 1.0	D, 2, 1 R	142-150 254-268

① At altitudes above sea level, it may not be possible to obtain 18 inches of engine vacuum at idle. For idle vacuums of less than 18 inches, refer to the following table to determine idle speed pressure specifications in D driving range.

Engine Vacuum	*Line Pressure*
17 inches	55-66
16 inches	55-71
15 inches	55-76
14 inches	55-81
13 inches	55-86
12 inches	55-91
11 inches	55-96

Control Pressure at Zero Output Shaft Speed—1970

Engine Speed	*Throttle*	*Manifold Vac. Ins. Hg.*	*Range*	*P.S.I.*
Idle	Closed	① Above 18	P. N. D. 2, 1 R	52-69 80-110 100-180
As required	As required	10	D, 2, 1	96-110
As required	As required	3.0	D, 2, 1 R	135-155 220-250

① At altitudes above sea level, it may not be possible to obtain 18 inches of engine vacuum at idle. For idle vacuums of less than 18 inches, refer to the following table to determine idle speed pressure specification in D driving range.

Engine Vacuum	*Line Pressure*
17 inches	52-74
16 inches	52-78
15 inches	52-84
14 inches	52-90
13 inches	52-95
12 inches	52-100
11 inches	52-106

Control Pressure—C4S Semi-Automatic—1970

Engine Speed	*Throttle*	*Range*	*P.S.I.*
Idle	Closed	P, N, H1, 2, 1 R	70-130 70-260
1400 rpm	As required	H1, 2, 1	110-130
1400 rpm	As required	R	210-260

Checks and Adjustments—1964

Operation	*Specification*
Transmission end play check	0.008-0.042 inch *Selective thrust washers available
Turbine and stator end play check	0.060 inch (maximum)
Intermediate band adjustment	Adjust screw to 10-foot-pounds torque, and back off 1½ turns
Low-reverse band adjustment	Adjust screw to 10-foot-pounds torque, and back off 3 turns
Forward clutch pressure plate to snap ring clearance	0.022 to 0.042 inch Selective snap ring thicknesses 0.092-0.088 0.078-0.074 0.064-0.060

*Selective Thrust Washers (No. 1 and 2 used in pairs)

Thrust Washer No. 1		*Thrust Washer No. 2*	
Composition Thrust Washer	*Color of Washer*	*No. Stamped on Washer*	*Metal Thrust Washer*
.108-.104	Blue	5	.109-.107
.091-.087	Yellow	4	.092-.090
.074-.070	Black	3	.075-.073
.057-.053	Tan	2	.058-.056
.042-.038	Green	1	.043-.041

Checks and Adjustments—1965

Operation	*Specification*
Transmission end play check	0.008-0.042 inch Selective thrust washers available
Turbine and stator end play check	0.060 inch (maximum)
Intermediate band adjustment	Adjust screw to 10-foot-pounds torque, and back off 1¾ turns
Low-reverse band adjustment	Adjust screw to 10-foot-pounds torque, and back off 3 turns
Forward clutch pressure plate to snap ring clearance	0.022 to 0.042 inch Selective snap ring thicknesses 0.092-0.088 0.078-0.074 0.064-0.060
Reverse-high clutch pressure plate to snap ring clearance	0.060-0.080 inch Selective snap ring thicknesses 0.102-0.106 0.092-0.088 0.078-0.074 0.064-0.060

Selective Thrust Washers (No. 1 and 2)

Thrust Washer No. 1		*Thrust Washer No. 2*	
Composition Thrust Washer	*Color of Washer*	*No. stamped on Washer*	*Metal Thrust Washer*
.138-.142	Purple		
.121-.125	Red		
.108-.104	Blue	5	.109-.107
.091-.087	Yellow	4	.092-.090
.074-.070	Black	3	.075-.073
.057-.053	Tan	2	.058-.056
.042-.038	Green	1	.043-.041

Checks and Adjustments—1966, 67

Operation	*Specification*	
Transmission end play	0.008-0.042 inch Selective thrust washers available	
Turbine and stator end play check	0.060 inch (maximum)	
Intermediate band adjustment	Adjust screw to 10 ft-lbs torque, then back off 1¾ turns and tighten locknut to spec.	
Low-reverse band adjustment	Adjust screw to 10 ft-lbs torque, then back off 3 turns and tighten locknut to spec.	
Forward clutch pressure plate-to-snap ring clearance	*No. of Composition Plates in Clutch*	*Clearance Specification*
	4	0.020-0.036 in.
	5	0.026-0.042 in.
	Selective snap ring thicknesses 0.102-0.106 0.088-0.092 0.074-0.078 0.060-0.064	
Reverse-high clutch pressure plate-to-snap ring clearance	0.050-0.066 inch Selective snap ring thicknesses 0.102-0.106 0.088-0.092 0.074-0.078 0.060-0.064	

Selective Thrust Washers (No. 1 and 2)

Thrust Washer No. 1		*Thrust Washer No. 2*	
Composition Thrust Washer	*Color of Washer*	*No. Stamped on Washer*	*Metal Thrust Washer*
.138-.142	Purple		
.121-.125	Red		
.108-.104	Blue	5	.109-.107
.091-.087	Yellow	4	.092-.090
.074-.070	Black	3	.075-.073
.057-.053	Tan	2	.058-.056
.042-.038	Green	1	.043-.041

Checks and Adjustments C4 Transmission—1968

Operation	*Specification*
Transmission end play	0.008-0.042 inch (selective thrust washers available)
Turbine and stator end play	New or rebuilt 0.023 max. Used 0.040 max.
Intermediate band adjustment	Adjust screw to 10 ft-lbs torque, then back off 1¾ turns.
Low-reverse band Adjustment	Adjust screw to 10 ft-lbs torque, then back off 3 turns.
Selective snap ring thickness	.102-.106, .088-.092, .074-.078, .060-.064

Selective Thrust Washers

Nylon Thrust Washer W/Tangs	*Color of Washer*	*No. Stamped On Washer*	*Metal Thrust Washer*
.053-.0575	Red		
.070-.074	Green	5	.109-.107
.087-.091	Natural	4	.092-.090
.104-.108	Black	3	.075-.073
.121-.125	Yellow	2	.058-.056
.138-.142	Blue	1	.043-.041

Checks and Adjustments C4 Transmission—1969

Operation	*Specification*
Transmission end play	0.008-0.042 inch (selective thrust washers available)
Turbine and stator end play	Model PEB—New or rebuilt 0.044 max., used 0.060 max.
	Model PEE, PEA new or rebuilt 0.023 max., used 0.040 max.
Intermediate band adjustment	Remove and discard lock nut. Adjust screw to 10 ft-lbs torque, then back off 1¾ turns. Install new lock nut and torque to specification.
Low-reverse band adjustment	Remove and discard lock nut. Adjust screw to 10 ft-lbs torque, then back off 3 turns. Install new locknut and torque to specification.
Selective snap ring thickness	.102-.106, .088-.092, .074-.078, .060-.064

Selective Thrust Washers

Thrust Washer No. 1		*Thrust Washer No. 2*	
Nylon Thrust Washer W/Tangs	*Color of Washer*	*No. Stamped On Washer*	*Metal Thrust Washer*
.053-.0575	Red	1	.041-.043
.070-.074	Green	2	.056-.058
.087-.091	Natural (White)	3	.073-.075
.104-.108	Black	4	.090-.092
.121-.125	Yellow	5	.107-.109

Checks and Adjustments C4—1970

Operation	*Specification*
Transmission end play	0.008-0.042 inch (selective thrust washers available)
Turbine and stator end play	Model PEB, PEG—new or rebuilt 0.044 max. Used 0.060 max.
	Model PEE, PEA, PEF—New or rebuilt 0.023 max. Used 0.040 max.
Intermediate band adjustment	Remove and discard lock nut. Adjust screw to 10 ft-lbs torque, then back off 1¾ turns. Install new lock nut and torque to specification.
Low-reverse band adjustment	Remove and discard lock nut. Adjust screw to 10 ft-lbs torque, then back off 3 turns. Install new lock nut and torque to specification.
Selective snap ring thickness	.050-.054, .064-.068, .078-.082, .092-.096

Selective Thrust Washers

Thrust washer No. 1		Thrust Washer No. 2	
Nylon Thrust Washer W/Tangs	*Color of Washer*	*No. Stamped On Washer*	*Metal Thrust Washer*
.053-.0575	Red	1	.041-.043
.070-.074	Green	2	.056-.058
.087-.091	Natural (White)	3	.073-.075
.104-.108	Black	Spacer	.032-.036①
.121-.125	Yellow		

① This is a selective spacer. The spacer must be installed next to the stator support to obtain correct end play.

Control Valve Body Spring Identification—1964

Spring	*Total Coils*	*Free Length*	*O.D.*	*Wire Diameter*	*Lbs. Load*	*Length*
Main oil pressure reducer valve	19	1.42	.281	.035	3.012	.887
Cut back control valve	19	1.00	.200	.020	1.05	.59
Manual valve detent	10	.74	.300	.047	8.0	.601
3-2 coasting control valve	10	.83	.285	.023	1.0	.476
Line pressure relief	17	1.15	.198	.041	7.0	.80
Secondary throttle valve	14	1.581	.350	.026	1.728	.565
2-3 backout control valve	11½	1.26	.45	.032	1.47	.580
Main oil pressure regulator valve	16	1.92	.48	.049	9.09	.876
Throttle pressure modulator valve	19	1.29	.29	.029	2.15	.620
Control 1-2 shift valve	14	1.58	.26	.026	1.7	.70
Throttle downshift valve	12	.79	.24	.023	1.15	.48
2-3 shift valve	6½	1.18	.53	.031	1.38	.39
Throttle pressure booster valve	16¾	1.589	.311	.035	4.80	.84

Control Valve Body Spring Identification—1965

Spring	*Total Coils*	*Free Length*	*O.D.*	*Wire Diameter*	*Lbs. Load*	*Length*
Manual valve detent	9	.74	.295	.045	7.5	.601
Line pressure coasting boost	15	1.12	.287	.032	3.5	.620
2-3 backout control valve	11½	1.26	.45	.032	1.47	.580
Main oil pressure regulator valve	9.75	1.86	.615	.047	6.2	.208
Throttle pressure modulator valve	15	1.513	.292	.0286	3.573	.620
Control 1-2 shift valve	13	.95	.230	.019	1.0	.450
Throttle downshift valve	9	1.042	.360	.031	3.0	.476
Throttle pressure booster valve	15	.458	.243	.036	5.25	.84
Line pressure boost (Inner)	12.5	2.055	.450	.032	2.98	.564
Intermediate band accumulator valve	12.5	1.107	.325	.025	1.10	.551

Control Valve Body Spring Identification—1966, 1967

Spring	Total Coils	Free Length	O.D.	Wire Diameter	Lbs. Load	Length
Manual valve detent	9	.74	.295	.045	7.5	.601
2-3 backout control valve	10	1.515	.450	.026	1.353	.580
Main oil pressure regulator valve	9.75	1.86	.615	.047	6.200	.608
Throttle pressure modulator	15	1.513	.292	.286	3.675	.620
Control 1-2 shift valve	13	.950	.230	.019	1.00	.450
Throttle downshift valve	9	1.042	.360	.031	3.0	.476
Throttle pressure booster valve	15	1.421	.326	.036	5.250	.730
Control pressure booster valve	23.5	.965	.290	.032	1.00	.715
Intermediate band accumulator valve	12.5	1.107	.325	.025	1.100	.551

Control Valve Body Spring Identification C4 Transmission—1968

Spring	Total Coils	Free Length	O.D.	Wire Dia.	Lbs. Load	Length	Color Code
Manual valve detent	9	0.74	0.295	0.045	7.5	0.601	None
2-3 backout control valve	10	1.515	0.450	0.026	1.353	0.580	White
Main oil press. reg. valve	12	2.53	0.615	0.047	7.24	0.716	Pink
Throttle press. modulator	15	1.513	0.292	0.028	3.675	0.620	Yellow
Drive 2 valve	10	0.735	0.230	0.019	0.80	0.450	Gray
Throttle downshift valve	9	0.962	0.380	0.034	3.44	0.440	Dk. Green
Throttle press. booster valve	15	1.39	0.249 I.D.	0.036	5.250	0.730	Purple
Control press. booster valve	12.8	1.66	0.350	0.028	1.63	0.696	None
Inter. band accumulator valve	11	1.38	0.375 I.D.	0.024	1.00	0.400	White
Line coasting boost valve	10	1.03	0.346	0.034	4.42	0.464	White

Control Valve Body Spring Identification C4 Transmission—1969

Spring	Total Coils	Free Length	O.D.	Wire Dia.	Lbs. Load	Length	Color Code
Manual valve detent all except PEC-EI	10	.764	.295	.44	6.5	.601	White
Model PEC-EI	9	.74	.295	.045	7.5	.601	None
2-3 backout control valve	10	1.515	.450	.026	1.353	.580	White
Main oil press. reg. valve	12	2.53	.615	.047	7.24	.716	Pink
Throttle press. modulator	15	1.513	.292	.028	3.675	.620	Yellow
Drive 2 valve	10	.735	.230	.019	.80	.450	Gray

Control Valve Body Spring Identification C4 Transmission—1969

Spring	Total Coils	Free Length	O.D.	Wire Dia.	Lbs. Load	Length	Color Code
Throttle downshift valve	9	.962	.380	.034	3.44	.440	Dk. Green
Throttle press. booster valve	15	1.39	.249 I. D.	.036	5.250	.730	Purple
Control press. booster valve	12.8	1.66	.350 I. D.	.028	1.63	.696	None
Inter. band accumulator valve ①	11	1.38	.375 I. D.	.024	1.0	.400	Purple
Inter. band accumulator valve ②	10	1.293	.375 I. D.	.0258	1.25	.400	None
Line press coasting boost valve	10	1.03	.346	.034	4.42	.464	White

① Used on models PEA-A2, MI, NI,
② Used on models PEB-B2, C2, PEE

Control Valve Body Spring Identification C4 Automatic—1970

Spring	Total Coils	Free Length	O.D.	Wire Dia.	Lbs. Load	Length	Color Code
Manual valve detent			Leaf Type		7.25	.542	None
2-3 backout valve	13	1.345	.345	.0258	1.45	.620	Gray
1-2 transition valve:	12	1.150	.330	.023	.95	.480	Dk. Green
Throttle downshift valve	10	0.816	.280	.0301	3.00	.500	None
Low servo modulator valve	12	1.270	.380	.0268	1.54	.553	Orange
Throttle pressure booster valve all except PEE-AC1, AH1, M1, V1, PEF	15	1.109	.281	.0332	4.50	.620	None
model PEE-AC1, AH1, M1, V1, PEF	15	1.39	.285	.036	5.25	.730	Purple
Throttle pressure limit valve	14	1.192	.295	.0379	6.25	.770	Brown
Throttle pressure modulator valve	15	1.513	.292	.0286	3.575	.620	Yellow
Line pressure coast boost valve	10	1.023	.340	.0332	4.10	.494	Dk. Blue
Drive 2 valve	13	.950	.230	.019	1.00	.450	Violet
Int. servo accumulator valve Model PEE-AC1, AH1, M1, V1, AG1	9	.680	.300	.0244	1.00	.390	Orange
model PEA-A3, PEE-AD1, AE1, AF1, PEB, PEF	8	.680	.300	.0258	1.50	.390	Lt. Green
model PEA-M2, N2	9	.845	.300	.258	2.00	.390	None
Main oil pressure reg., valve inner	11	1.40	.407	.0286	1.49	.739	None
Main oil pressure reg. valve outer	9	1.667	.668	.0507	7.30	.586	Pink

Control Valve Body Spring Identification C4S Semi-Automatic—1970

Spring	*Total*	*Free Length*	*O.D.*	*Wire Dia.*	*Length*	*Lbs. Load*
2-3 backout control valve	10	1.031	.356	.034	4.44	.464
Main oil press reg. valve	9	1.667	.671	.0507	7.30	.586
Throttle press modulator	15	1.24	.297	.034	4.50	.740
Drive 2 valve	9.3	.594	.230	.030	3.0	.450
Low servo modulator valve	12	1.412	.380	.028	1.89	.553

Torque Limits—C4 and C4S Automatic Transmissions—Ft. Lbs.

Item	*Ft-lbs* 1964	1965	1966	1967	1968	1969	1970
Converter to flywheel	20-30	20-30	20-30	20-30	20-30	23-28	23-28
Converter hsg. to trans.	28-40	28-40	28-40	28-40	28-40	28-40	28-40
Front pump to trans. case	28-40	28-40	28-40	28-40	28-40	28-40	28-40
Outer race to case	13-20	13-20	13-20	13-20	13-20	13-20	13-20
Oil pan to case	12-16	12-16	12-16	12-16	12-16	12-16	12-16
Rear servo cover to case	12-20	12-20	12-20	12-20	12-20	12-20	12-20
Stator support to pump	12-20	12-20	12-20	12-20	12-20	12-20	12-20
Converter cover to converter hsg.	10-13	10-13	10-13	10-13	12-16	12-16	12-16
Intermediate servo cover to case	12-20	12-20	12-20	12-20	16-22	16-22	16-22
Extension hsg. to case	28-40	28-40	28-40	28-40	28-40	28-40	28-40
Converter drain plug	20-30	20-30	20-30	20-30	20-30	20-30	20-30
Pressure gauge tap	9-15	9-15	9-15	9-15	9-15	9-15	9-15
Manual control lever nut	35-45	35-45	30-40	30-40	30-40	8-12	8-12
Downshift lever to case	12-20	12-20	12-16	12-16	12-16	12-16	12-16
Filler tube to engine	20-25	20-25	20-25	20-25	20-25	20-25	20-25
Filler tube to pan						32-42	32-42
Diaphragm assy to case	15-23	15-23	15-23	15-23	15-23	15-23	15-23
Distributor sleeve to case	12-20	12-20	12-20	12-20	12-20	12-20	12-20
Reverse servo piston to rod	12-20	12-20	12-20	12-20	*	*	*
Transmission to engine			40-50	40-50	40-50	40-50	40-50
Transmission to engine: Falcon and Mustang						23-33	23-33
Cooler bracket & oil pan to case			12-16	12-16			
Band adjust stop to case	35-45	35-45	35-40	35-40	35-45	35-45	35-45
Yoke to output shaft						60-80	60-80

* Tighten to 10 ft-lbs and back off ⅝ turn.

Torque Limits—C4 and C4S Automatic Transmissions—In. Lbs.

Item	1964	1965	1966	1967	1968	1969	1970
End plate to valve body screw	20-35	20-35	20-35	20-35	20-35	20-35	20-35
Lower to upper valve body bolts	20-35	20-35	40-55	40-55	40-50	40-55	40-55
Screen to valve body screws	20-35	20-35	40-55	40-55	40-55	40-55	40-55
Neutral switch to case screws	30-45	30-45	55-75	55-75		55-75 *	55-75 *
Neutral switch to column						20	20
Screen & valve body to case bolts	80-120	80-120	80-120	80-120	80-120	80-120	80-120
Screen to valve body bolts	80-120	80-120	80-120	80-120	80-120	80-120	80-120
Governor body to distributor (collector) body bolts	80-120	80-120	80-120	80-120	80-120	80-120	80-120
Cooler line fittings	80-120	80-120	80-120	80-120	80-120	80-120	80-120
Reinforcement plate to body					40-55	40-55	40-55
Accumulator plate to body					80-120	50-90	50-90
Inner downshift lever stop					40-55	40-55	40-55

* Mustang and Cougar only

Diagnosis

This diagnosis guide covers the most common symptoms and is an aid to careful diagnosis. The items to check are listed in the sequence to be followed for quickest results. Thus, follow the checks in the order given for the particular transmission type.

TROUBLE SYMPTOMS	Items to Check In Truck	Out of Truck
No drive in D, 2 and 1	CWER	ac
Rough initial engagement in D or 2	KBWFE	a
1-2 or 2-3 shift points incorrect or erratic	ABLCDWER	
Rough 1-2 upshifts	BJGWEF	
Rough 2-3 shifts	BJWFGER	br
Dragged out 1-2 shift	ABJWGEFR	c
Engine overspeeds on 2-3 shift	CABJWEFG	br
No 1-2 or 2-3 shift	CLBDWEGJ	bc
No 3-1 shift in D	DE	
No forced downshifts	LEB	
Runaway engine on forced 3-2 downshift	WJGFEB	c
Rough 3-2 or 3-1 shift at closed throttle	KBJEF	
Shifts 1-3 in D	GJBEDR	
No engine braking in first gear—1 range	CHEDR	
Creeps excessively	K	
Slips or chatters in first gear, D	ABWFE	aci
Slips or chatters in second gear	ABJGWFER	ac
Slips or chatters in R	ABHWFER	bcr
No drive in D only	CWE	i
No drive in 2 only	ACWJER	c
No drive in 1 only	ACWER	c
No drive in R only	ACHWER	bcr
No drive in any selector lever position	ACWFER	cd
Lockup in D only		gc
Lockup in 2 only	H	bgci
Lockup in 1 only		gc
Lockup in R only		agc
Parking lock binds or does not hold	C	g
Transmission overheats	OFBW	ns
Maximum speed too low, poor acceleration	YZ	n
Transmission noisy in N and P	AF	d
Transmission noisy in first, second, third or reverse gear	AF	hadi
Fluid leak	AMNOPQS UXBJ	jmp
Car moves forward in N	C	a

Key to Checks

A. Fluid level
B. Vacuum diaphragm unit or tubes restricted—leaking—adjustment
C. Manual linkage
D. Governor
E. Valve body
F. Pressure regulator
G. Intermediate band
H. Low-reverse clutch
J. Intermediate servo
K. Engine idle speed
L. Downshift linkage—including inner level position
M. Converter drain plugs
N. Oil pan gasket, filler tube or seal
O. Oil cooler and connections
P. Manual or downshift lever shaft seal
Q. ⅛ inch pipe plugs in case
R. Perform air pressure check
S. Extension housing-to-case gasket
U. Extension housing rear oil seal
W. Perform control pressure check
X. Speedometer driven gear adapter seal
Y. Engine performance
Z. Vehicle brakes
a. Forward clutch
b. Reverse-high clutch
c. Leakage in hydraulic system
d. Front pump
g. Parking linkage
h. Planetary assembly
i. Planetary one-way clutch
j. Engine rear oil seal
m. Front pump oil seal
n. Converter one-way clutch
p. Front pump to case gasket or seal
r. Reverse-high clutch piston air bleed valve
s. Converter pressure check valves

General Information

The C6 automatic transmission is a three-speed unit that provides automatic upshifts and downshifts through the three forward gear ratios and also provides manual selection of first and second gears. The converter housing and the fixed splines which engage the splined OD of the low-reverse clutch steel plates are both cast integrally into the case.

Only one band (intermediate) is used in the C6 transmission. This band, along with the forward clutch, is used to obtain intermediate gear. Only the adjustment of the intermediate band can be done without major disassembly.

The C6 automatic transmission is very similar to the C4 automatic transmission, and most of the maintenance and overhaul procedures given for the C4 transmission will apply to the C6 transmission with some modifications of certain components. One important difference between the C6 and the C4 transmissions is that the C6 transmission uses a low-reverse clutch in place of the

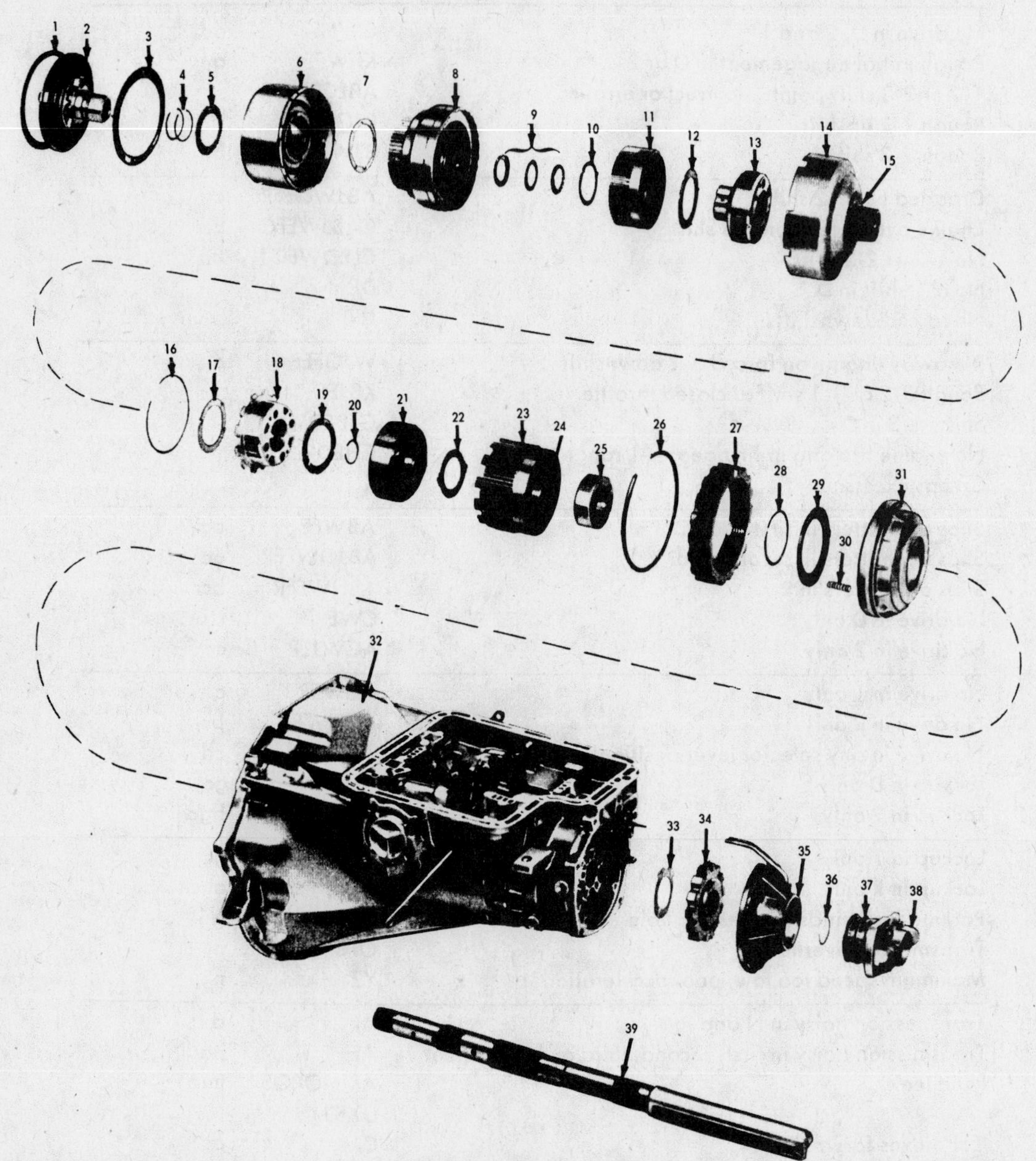

Drive train disassembled (© Ford Motor Co.)

1 Front pump seal ring
2 Front pump
3 Gasket
4 Seal
5 Number 1 thrust washer (selective)
6 Reverse—high clutch assembly
7 Number 2 thrust washer
8 Forward clutch assembly
9 Number 3 thrust washer
10 Number 4 thrust washer
11 Forward clutch hub assembly
12 Number 5 thrust washer
13 Forward planet assembly
14 Input shell and sun gear assembly
15 Number 6 thrust washer
16 Snap ring
17 Number 7 thrust washer
18 Reverse planet assembly
19 Number 8 thrust washer
20 Reverse ring gear and hub retaining ring
21 Reverse ring gear and hub
22 Number 9 thrust washer
23 Low—reverse clutch hub
24 One-way clutch
25 One-way clutch inner race
26 Snap ring
27 Low—reverse clutch
28 Snap ring
29 Low—reverse piston return spring retainer
30 Return spring
31 Low—reverse piston
32 Case
33 Number 10 thrust washer
34 Parking gear
35 Governor distributor sleeve
36 Snap ring
37 Governor distributor
38 Governor
39 Output shaft

low-reverse band used in the C4 transmission. Otherwise, the gear trains are the same, as are the clutch combinations. The hydraulic control systems are very similar, except for minor differences in design. All components which are different from the C4 components are illustrated and the procedures to repair them are given.

There is no drain plug in the transmission pan. To drain the transmission oil, remove all of the oil pan attaching bolts, except the two at the front; loosen these, and let the pan tilt and drain.

Intermediate Band Adjustment

1. Raise the truck on a hoist or place on jack stands.
2. Clean threads of the intermediate band adjusting screw.
3. Loosen adjustment screw locknut.
4. Tighten band adjustment until torque wrench T59P-77370-B overruns itself. Then, back off the screw one complete turn. Tighten the adjusting screw locknut to 35-45 ft. lbs.

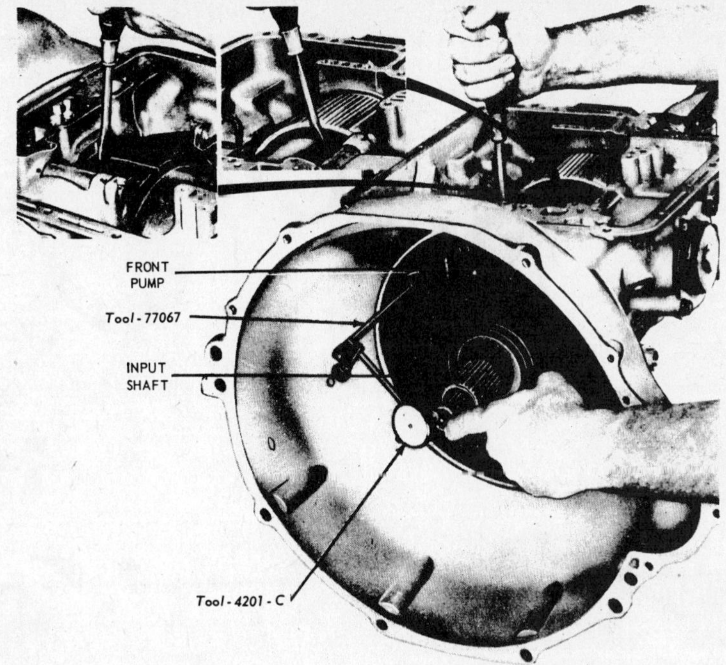

Checking gear train end play (© Ford Motor Co.)

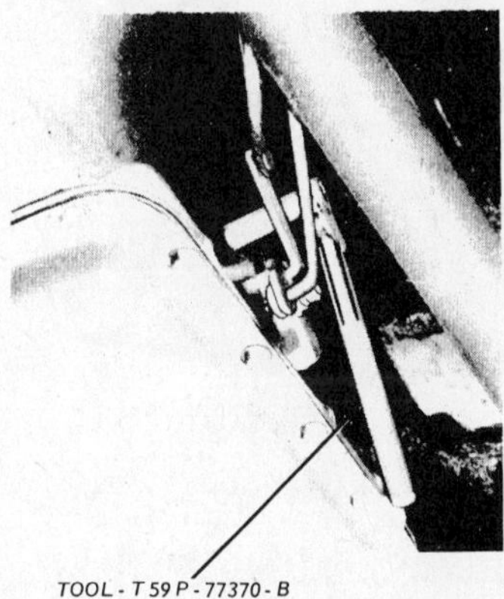

Adjusting intermediate band
(© Ford Motor Co.)

Transmission Disassembly

1. Thoroughly clean outside of transmission to prevent possible contamination during reassembly.
2. If one is available, secure the unit in a repair stand. Drain the oil.
3. Remove converter from the unit.
4. Remove oil pan attaching bolts, oil pan and gasket.
5. Remove valve body attaching bolts and the valve body.
6. Attach a dial indicator to the front pump. Install tool T61L-7657-B into the extension housing to center the shaft.
7. Pry the gear train to the rear of the case and, at the same time, press the input shaft inward until it bottoms. Set the dial indicator to read zero.
8. Pry the gear train forward and note the amount of gear train end-play. Record the end-play to simplify assembly. Remove the dial indicator from the pump and the tool from the extension housing.
9. Slip the input shaft out of the front pump. Remove the vacuum diaphragm, rod and primary throttle valve from the case.
10. Remove the front pump attaching bolts. Pry the gear train forward to remove the pump.
11. Loosen the band adjusting screw and remove the two struts.
12. Rotate the band 90°, counterclockwise, to align the ends with the slot in the case. Slide the band off the reverse-high clutch drum.
13. Remove the forward part of the gear train as an assembly.
14. Remove the large snap-ring that holds the reverse planet carrier in the low-reverse clutch hub. Lift the planet carrier from the drum.
15. Remove the snap-ring that holds the reverse ring gear and hub on the output shaft. Slide the ring gear and hub from the shaft.
16. Rotate the low-reverse clutch hub, in a clockwise direction, and, at the same time, withdraw it from the case.
17. Remove the low-reverse snap-ring from the case, then remove the clutch discs, plates and pressure plate from the case.
18. Remove the extension housing bolts and vent tube from the case. Remove the extension housing and gasket.
19. Slide the output shaft assembly from the transmission case.
20. Remove the distributor sleeve attaching bolts and remove the sleeve parking gear and the thrust washer.
21. Compress the low-reverse clutch piston release spring with tool T-65P-77515-A. Remove the snap-ring. Remove the tool and spring retainer.
22. Remove the one-way clutch inner race attaching bolts from the rear of the case. Remove the inner race from the inside of the case.
23. Remove the low-reverse clutch piston from the case.

Component Disassembly and Assembly

NOTE: For component services, see Component Disassembly and Assembly, in the (C-4 dual range) 3-speed aluminum transmission, immediately preceding this coverage. The exceptions are the following, in the area of the low-reverse clutch.

Output Shaft Hub and Ring Gear Disassembly

1. Remove the hub retaining snap-ring from the ring gear.
2. Lift hub from ring gear.

Output Shaft Hub and Ring Gear Assembly

1. Position the hub in the ring gear.
2. Secure the hub with the retaining snap-ring. Make sure the snap-ring is fully engaged with the groove.

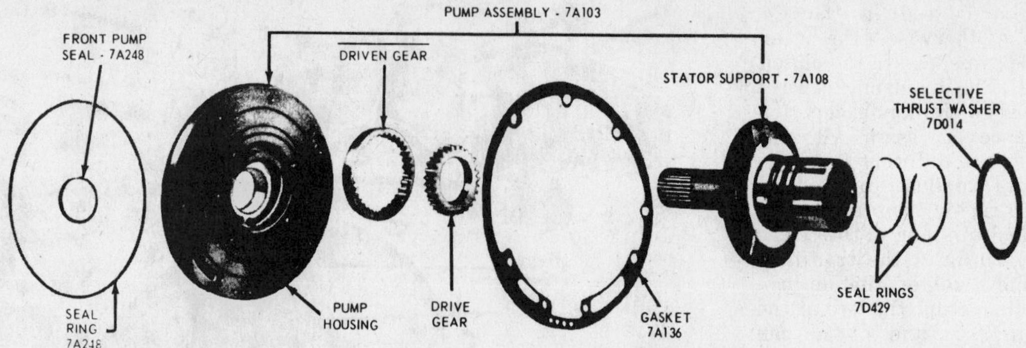

Front pump disassembled (© Ford Motor Co.)

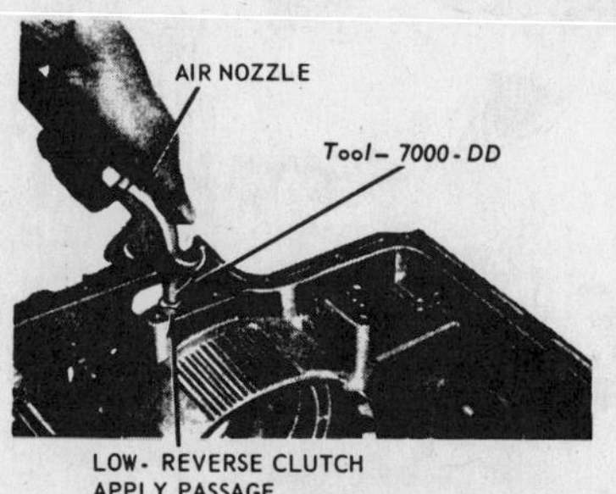

Removing reverse clutch piston (© Ford Motor Co.)

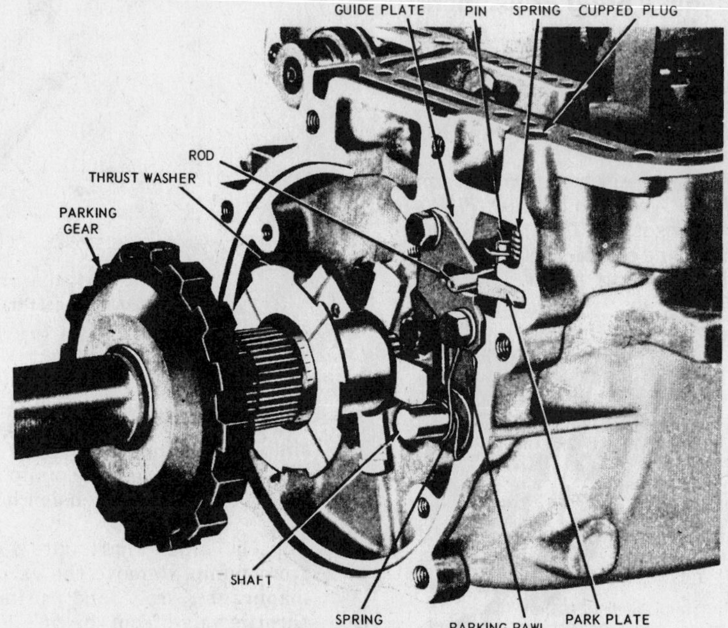

Parking pawl mechanism (© Ford Motor Co.)

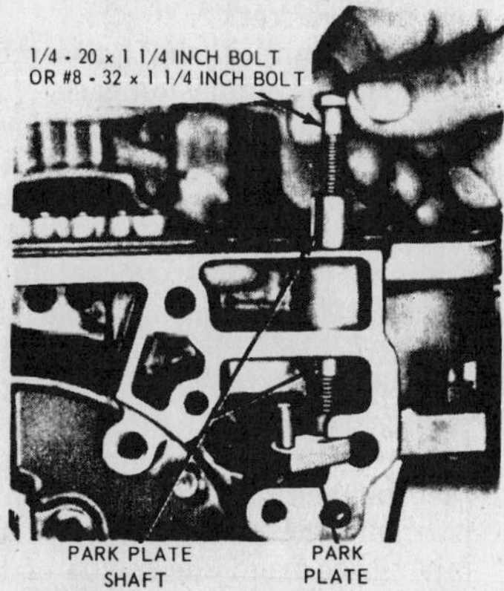

Removing park plate shaft (© Ford Motor Co.)

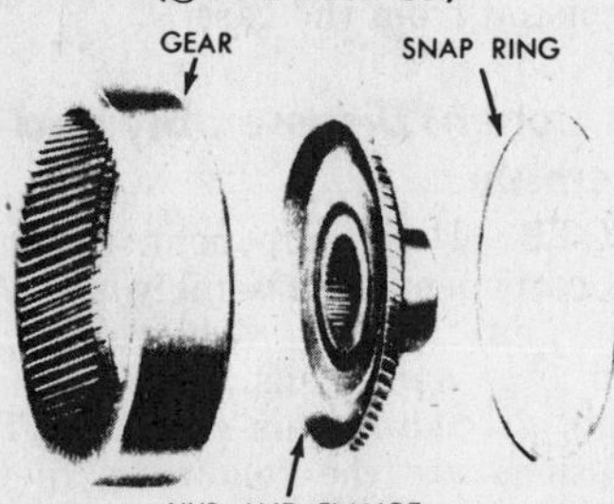

Output shaft hub and ring gear (© Ford Motor Co.)

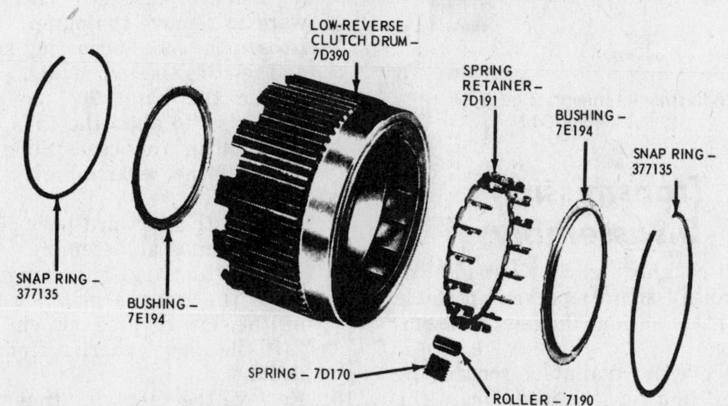

One way clutch—disassembled (© Ford Motor Co.)

One-Way Clutch Disassembly

1. Remove the snap-ring and rear bushing from the rear of the low-reverse clutch hub.
2. Remove the springs and rollers from the spring retainer and lift the spring retainer from the hub.
3. Remove the remaining bushing and snap-ring from the hub.

One-Way Clutch Assembly

1. Install a snap-ring in the forward snap-ring groove of the low-reverse clutch hub.
2. Place the low-reverse clutch hub on the bench with the forward end down as shown.
3. Place the forward clutch bushing against the snap-ring with the flat side up. Install the one-way clutch spring retainer on top of the bushing. Be sure to install the retainer in the hub so that the springs load the rollers in a counterclockwise direction when looking down at the unit.
4. Install a spring and roller into each of the spring retainer com-

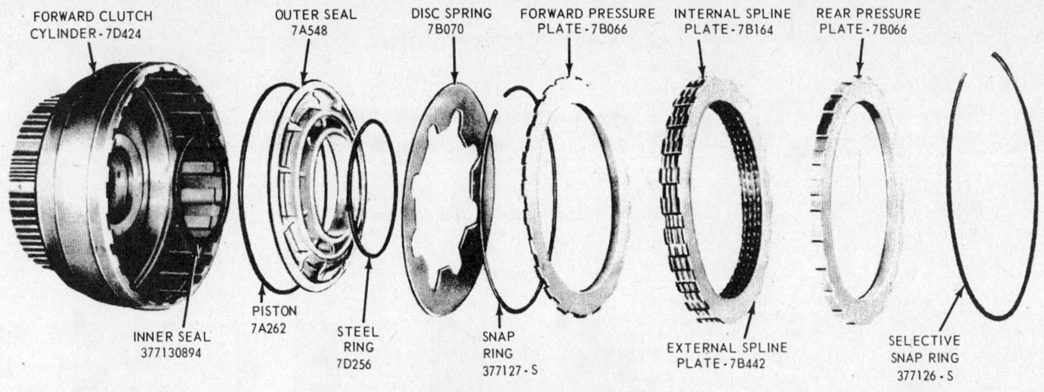

Forward clutch disassembled (© Ford Motor Co.)

partments by slightly compressing each spring and placing the roller between the spring and the spring retainer.

5. Install the rear bushing on top of the retainer with the flat side down.
6. Install the remaining snap-ring at the rear of the low-reverse clutch hub to secure the assembly.

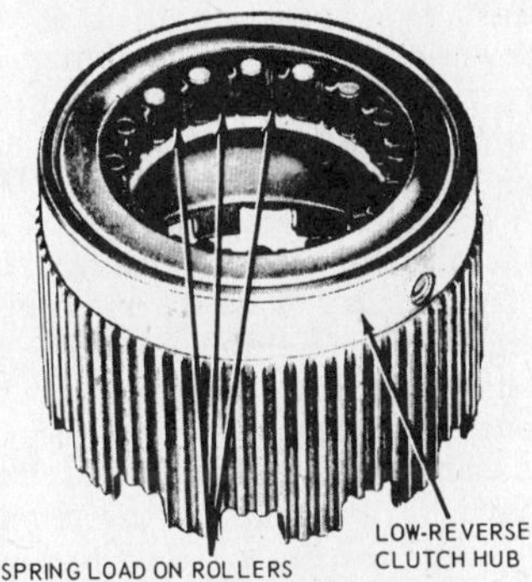

Installing one-way clutch (© Ford Motor Co.)

Servo Disassembly

1. Apply air pressure to the port in the servo cover in order to remove the piston and stem.
2. Remove the seals from the piston.
3. Remove the seal from the cover.

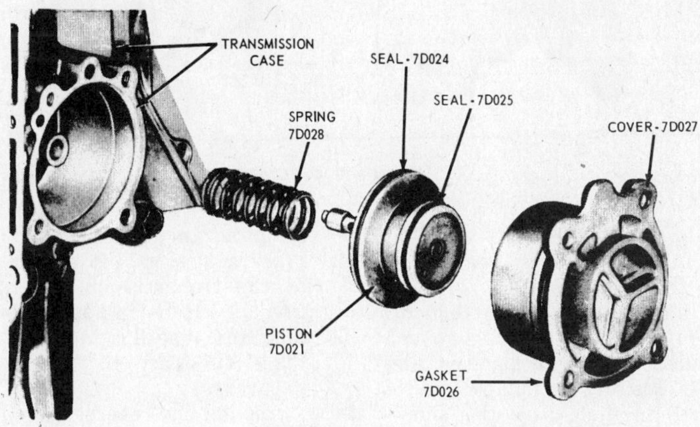

Servo—disassembled (© Ford Motor Co.)

Servo Assembly

1. Dip the new seals in transmission fluid.
2. Install the new seals onto the piston.
3. Install the new seal into the cover.
4. Dip the piston in transmission fluid and install it into the cover.

Low-Reverse Clutch Piston Disassembly

1. Remove the inner and outer seals from the low-reverse clutch piston.

Low-Reverse Clutch Piston Assembly

1. Dip the new seals in clean transmission fluid and install onto the piston.

Output Shaft Disassembly

1. Remove the governor attaching bolts and the governor.
2. Remove the snap-ring that secures the governor distributor onto the output shaft and slide it off the front of the shaft.
3. Remove the seal rings from the distributor.

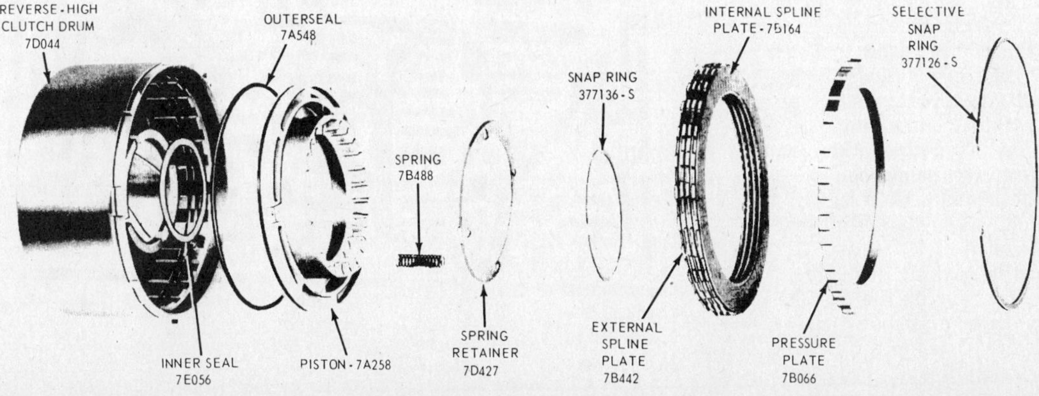

Reverse high clutch disassembled (© Ford Motor Co.)

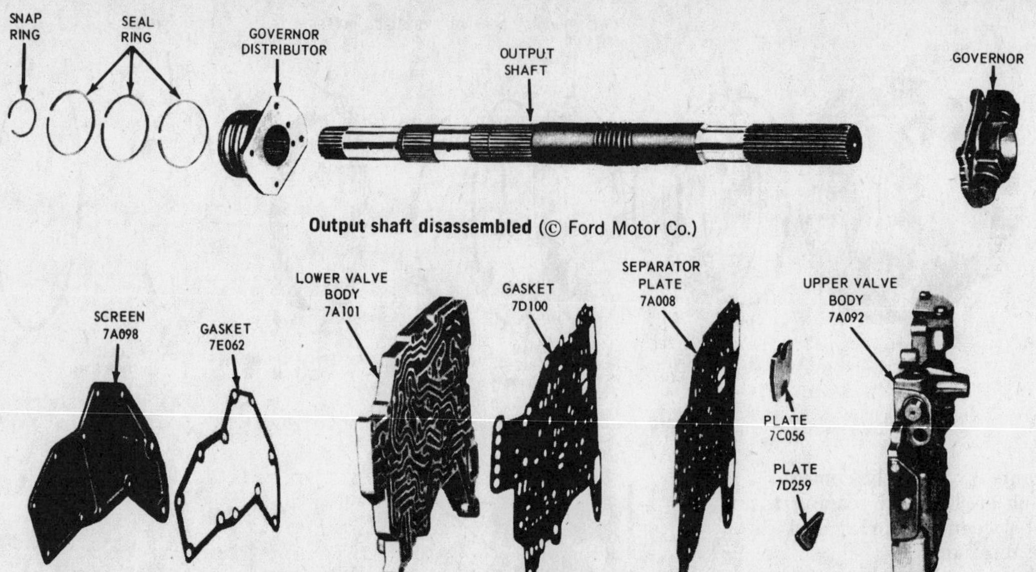

Output shaft disassembled (© Ford Motor Co.)

Upper and lower valve bodies—disassembled (© Ford Motor Co.)

Output Shaft Assembly

1. Carefully install new seal rings onto the distributor.
2. Working from the front end of the output shaft, slide the governor distributor into place on the shaft. Install the snap-ring to secure it. Make sure the snap-ring is seated in the groove.
3. Position the governor on the distributor and secure with attaching screws.

Transmission Assembly

1. Place transmission case in a holding fixture.
2. Tap the reverse clutch piston into place in the case with a clean rubber hammer.
3. Hold the one-way clutch inner race in position, then install and torque attaching bolts.
4. Install a low-reverse clutch return spring into each pocket of the reverse clutch piston. Press the springs firmly into the piston to prevent their falling out.
5. Position the spring retainer over the springs and position the retainer snap-ring in place on the one-way inner race.
6. Install the compressing tool and compress the springs just enough to install the low-reverse clutch piston retainer snap-ring.
7. Install the snap-ring, then remove the compressing tool.
8. Place the transmission case on the bench, with the front end facing downward.
9. Position the parking gear thrust washer and gear on the case.
10. Position the oil distributor sleeve and tubes in place on the rear of the case. Install and torque the attaching bolts.
11. Install the output shaft and governor as an assembly.
12. Place a new gasket on the rear of the transmission case. Position the extension housing on the case and install attaching bolts.
13. Place the case in the holding fixture.
14. Align the low-reverse clutch hub and one-way clutch with the inner race at the rear of the case. Rotate the low-reverse clutch hub clockwise, while applying pressure to seat it on the inner race.
15. Install the low-reverse clutch plates. Start with a steel plate and follow with friction and steel plates, alternately. If new composition (friction) plates are being used, soak them in new transmission fluid for 15 minutes before installation. Install the pressure plate and snap-ring. Test the operation of the low-reverse clutch by applying air pressure at the clutch pressure apply hole in the case. A six-plate clutch pack is used in PDE-A model transmissions.
16. Install the reverse planet ring gear thrust washer, ring gear and hub assembly. Insert the snap-ring into its groove in the output shaft.
17. Assemble the front and rear thrust washers onto the reverse planet assembly. Retain them with vaseline, then insert the assembly into the ring gear. Install the snap-ring into the ring gear.
18. Place the reverse-high clutch on

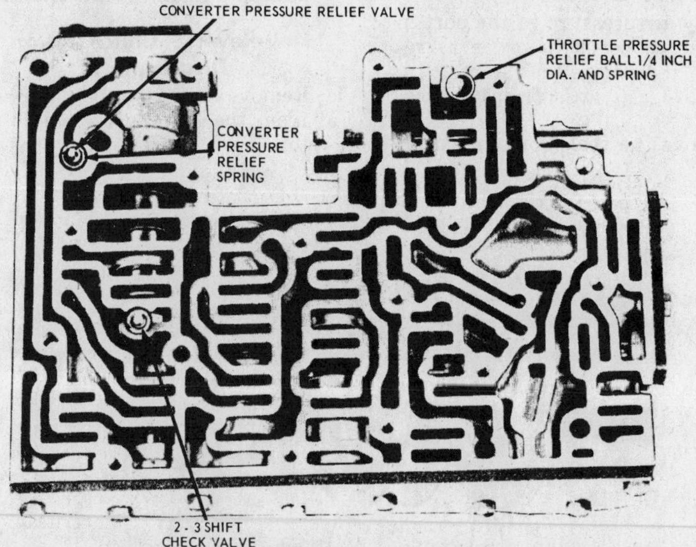

Converter pressure relief valve, throttle pressure relief valve and 2-3 shift check valve locations (© Ford Motor Co.)

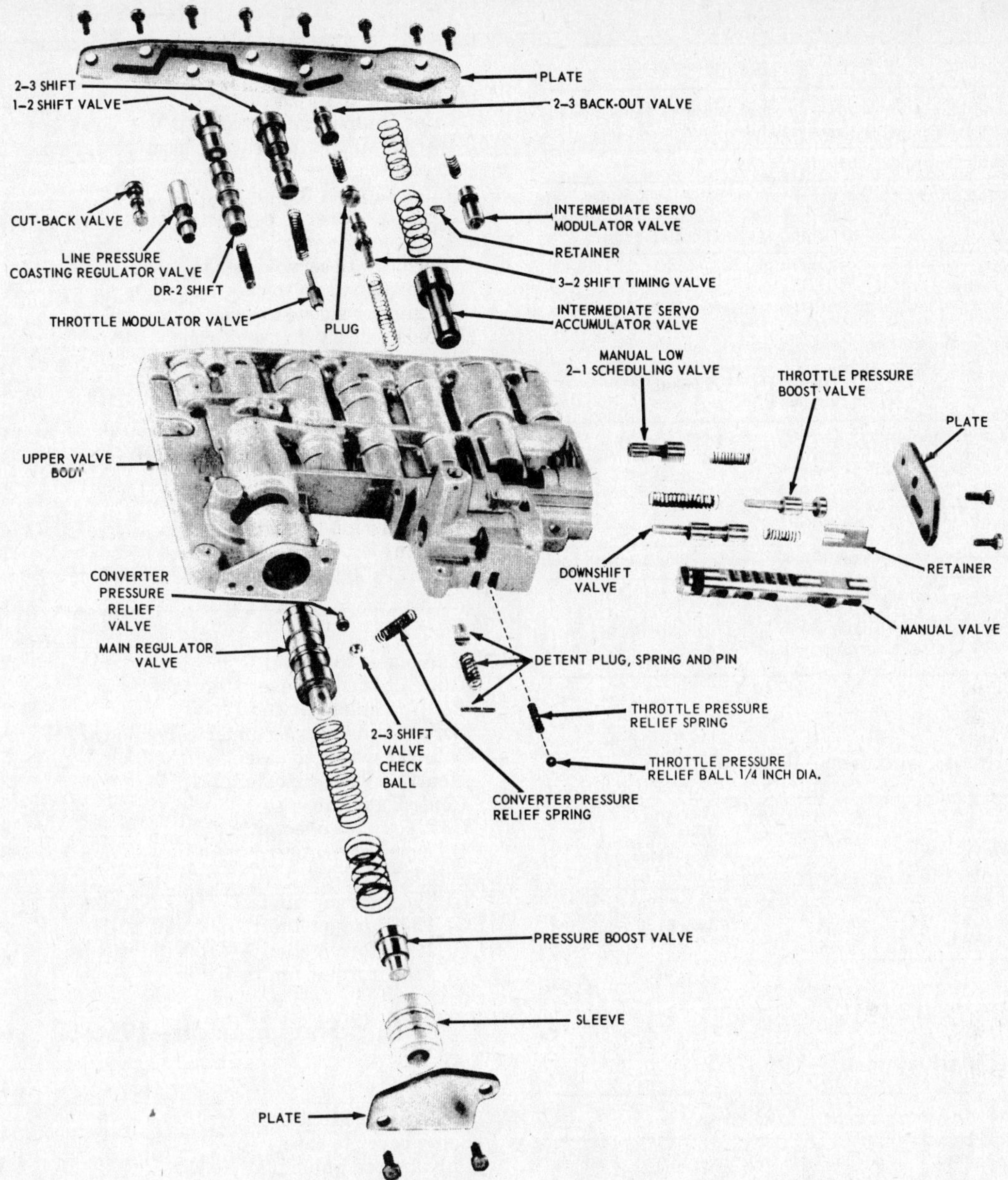

Upper control valve body—disassembled (© Ford Motor Co.)

the bench, with the front end facing down. Install the thrust washer onto the rear end of the reverse-high assembly. Retain the thrust washer with vaseline and insert the splined end of the forward clutch into the open end of the reverse-high clutch so that the splines engage the reverse-high clutch friction plates.

19. Install the thrust washer, retaining it with vaseline, onto the front end of the planet ring gear and hub. Insert the ring gear into the forward clutch.
20. Install the thrust washer onto the front end of the forward planet assembly. Retain the washer with vaseline and insert the assembly into the ring gear. Install the input shell and sun gear assembly.
21. Install the reverse-high clutch, forward clutch, forward planet assembly and input shell and sun gear, as an assembly, into the transmission case.
22. Insert the intermediate band into the case around the reverse and high clutch cylinder, with the narrow band end facing toward the servo apply lever. Install the struts and tighten the band adjusting screw just enough to retain the band.
23. Place a selective thickness bronze thrust washer on the rear shoulder of the stator support and retain it with vaseline. Lay a new gasket on the rear mounting face of the pump and position it on the case, being careful not to damage the O-ring. Install six of the seven mounting bolts.
24. Adjust the intermediate band as previously stated in Intermediate Band Adjustment. Then, install the input shaft.
25. Install the tool (4201-C dial indicator) at the seventh mounting bolt and check the transmission end-play. Remove the tool, then install the remaining bolt.
26. Install the control valve into the case, making sure that the levers engage the valves properly.
27. Install the primary throttle valve, rod, and the vacuum diaphragm into the case.
28. Install a new oil pan gasket, and the oil pan.
29. Install the converter assembly.
30. Install the transmission into the car.

Checks and Adjustments—1966-67

Operation	*Specification*	
Transmission end play	0.008-0.044 inch selective thrust washers available	
Turbine and stator end play	0.060 in.	
Intermediate band adjustment	Adjust screw to 10 ft-lbs torque, then back off one full turn and tighten lock nut to specification.	
Forward clutch pressure plate-to-snap ring clearance	0.048-0.061 in.	
Selective snap ring thicknesses	0.065-0.069 in. 0.074-0.078 in.	0.083-0.087 in.
Reverse-high clutch pressure plate-to-snap ring clearance	*Transmission Models*	
	PDD—B, C, K, T, U, S and W	PDD—D, L, F, H and N
	0.022-0.036 Inch	0.027-0.043 Inch
Selective snap ring clearances	0.065-0.069 in. 0.074-0.078 in.	0.083-0.087 in.

Selective Thrust Washers—1966-70

Identification No.	*Thrust Washer Thickness—Inch*	*Identification No.*	*Thrust Washer Thickness—Inch*
1	0.056-0.058	4	0.103-0.105
2	0.073-0.075	5	0.118-0.120
3	0.088-0.090		

Checks and Adjustments—1968-70

Operation	*Specification*
Transmission end play	0.008-0.044 (selective thrust washers available)
Turbine and stator end play	New or rebuilt 0.021 in. max. Used 0.030 in. max. ①
Intermediate band adjustment	Remove and discard lock nut. Adjust screw to 10 ft-lbs torque, then back off 1 turn, install new lock nut and tighten lock nut to specification.
Forward clutch pressure plate-to-snap ring clearance	0.031-0.044
Selective snap ring thicknesses	0.056-0.060 in., 0.065-0.069 in., 0.074-0.078 in., 0.083-0.087 in., 0.092-0.096 in.
Reverse-high clutch pressure plate-to-snap ring clearance	*Transmission Models*
	PGA, PJA 0.022-0.036 in.
	PGB-AF2, F3, G3, PJB, PJC-A, B, E, F, PJD 0.027-0.043 in.
Selective snap ring thicknesses	0.065-0.069 in., 0.074-0.078 in, 0.083-0.087 in.

① To check end play, exert force on checking tool to compress turbine to cover thrust washer wear plate. Set indicator at zero.

Torque Limits—1968-70

	Ft-Lbs
Converter to flywheel	20-30
Front pump to trans. case	12-20
Overrunning clutch race to case	18-25
Oil pan to case	12-16
Stator support to pump	12-16
Converter cover to converter hsg.	12-16
Guide plate to case	12-16
Intermediate servo cover to case	10-14
Diaphragm assy. to case	15-23
Distributor sleeve to case	12-16
Extension assy. to trans. case	25-30
Pressure gauge tap	9-15
Band adj. screw locknut to case	35-45
Cooler tube connector lock	25-35
Converter drain plug	14-28
Manual valve inner lever to shaft	30-40①
Downshift lever to shaft	12-16
Filler tube to engine	20-25
Transmission to engine	40-50
Steering col. lock rod adj. nut	10-20
Neutral start switch actuator lever bolt	6-10
	In-Lbs
End plates to body	20-30
Inner downshift lever stop	20-30
Reinforcement plate to body	20-30
Screen and lower to upper valve body	50-60②
Neutral switch to case	55-75
Neutral switch-to column	20
Control assy. to case	90-125③
Gov. body to collector body	80-120④
Oil tube connector	80-145

① 1969 torque limits— 8-12 ft.-lbs.
② 1968 torque limits— 40-50 ft.-lbs.
③ 1968 torque limits—100-120 ft.-lbs.
④ 1968 torque limits—100-120 ft.-lbs.

Torque Limits—1966-67

	Ft-Lbs
Pressure gauge tap	9-15
Servo cover to case	10-14
Parking rod guide plate to case	12-16
Outer downshift lever to shaft	12-16
Distributor sleeve to case	12-16
Support assy. to pump body	12-16
Oil pump to case	12-16
Oil pan to case	12-16
Conv. hsg. lower cover to trans.	12-16
Converter drain plugs	14-28
Diaphragm assy. to case	15-23
One-way clutch race to case	18-25
Flywheel to converter	20-30
Extension hsg. to case	25-30
Connector assy. to case	25-35
Manual lever to shaft	30-40
Band adj stop to case	35-45
Transmission to engine	40-50
	In-Lbs
Plate to control assy.	20-30
Lower to upper valve body	40-50
Upper to lower valve body	40-50
Screen & lwr v.b. to upper v.b.	40-50
Neutral switch assy. to case	55-75
Control assy. to case	100-120
Governor to collector	100-120

Control Pressure at Zero Governor RPM—1968-70

Engine speed			Idle			As required		As required		
Throttle			Closed			As required		As required		
Manifold vacuum (inches Hg)			Above 18 ①			10		Below 1.0		
Range			Control Pressure (psi) P, N, D, 2, 1	R	TV Pressure (psi)	Control Pressure (psi) D, 2, 1	TV Pressure (psi)	Control Pressure (psi) D, 2, 1	R	TV Pressure (psi)
	Barometric Pressure in Inches HG	Nominal Altitude (Feet)								
psi @ Barometric Pressure ②	29.5	Sea Level	56-62	71-86	7-10	100-115	40-44	160-190	240-300	77-84
psi @ barometric pressure ③	28.5	1000	49-59	65-80	4-7	99-114	37-41	158-176	233-290	74-80
	27.5	2000	49-56	60-75	2-5	96-111	35-39	156-174	228-284	72-78
	26.5	3000	49-56	56-71	0-3	91-106	32-36	151-169	222-277	69-75
	25.5	4000	49-56	56-65	0	88-103	30-34	146-164	215-269	66-72
	24.5	5000	49-56	56-65	0	84-98	27-31	143-161	211-264	64-70
	23.5	6000	49-56	56-65	0	80-95	25-29	138-156	204-256	61-67

Manifold Vacuum	Barometric Pressure at 29.5 Inches ② T.V.	Cont.	Barometric Pressure at 24.5 Inches ④ T.V.	Cont.
17	11-14	56-69	0-1	49-56
16	15-18	56-75	2-5	49-56
15	20-22	56-84	7-9	49-61
14	23-26	56-92	10-13	56-67
13	28-31	56-98	15-18	56-75
12	32-35	56-105	19-22	56-84
11	36-40	56-111	23-27	56-92

① It may not be possible to obtain 18 inches of engine vacuum at idle. For idle vacuums of less than 18 inches the following table provides idle speed pressure specifications in D range:

② These specifications (with altitude compensating diaphragm) apply at observed barometric pressure of 29.5 inches (nominal sea level)

③ Specifications for barometric pressures of less than 29.5 inches.

④ At barometric pressures between 29.5 inches and 24.5 inches idle, pressures should fall between the values shown.

Control Pressure at Zero Output Shaft Speed—Altitude Compensating Type Vacuum Diaphragm—1966-67

Engine speed			Idle			As required		As required		As required		
Throttle			Closed			As required		As required		Open through detent		
Manifold vacuum (inches Hg)			Above 17			15		10		Below 1.0		
Range			Control Pressure (psi) P, N, D1, D2, L	R	TV Pressure (psi)	Control Pressure (psi) D1, D2, L	TV Pressure (psi)	Control Pressure (psi) D1, D2, L	TV pressure (psi)	Control Pressure (psi) D1, D2, L	R	TV Pressure (psi)
	Barometric pressure in inches HG	Nominal altitude (feet)										
psi @ barometric pressure	29.5	Sea Level	51-66	72-108	0-13	70-78	20-22	98-109	40-44	157-172	230-252	80-84
	28.5	1000	51-59	72-104	0-11	67-75	18-20	94-105	38-41	149-163	220-242	77-81
	27.5	2000	51-59	72-99	0-8	63-71	15-17	91-101	36-38	145-159	215-236	74-78
	26.5	3000	51-59	72-99	0-5	59-67	12-14	87-97	33-36	142-157	211-231	72-76
	25.5	4000	51-59	72-92	0-3	57-64	10-12	85-94	31-33	139-154	207-227	70-74
	24.5	5000	51-59	72-83	0	51-60	7-9	81-90	28-31	136-151	202-222	67-72
	23.5	6000	51-59	72-83	0	51-60	5-7	78-87	26-28	132-147	198-217	64-68

Diagnosis

This diagnosis guide covers the most common symptoms and is an aid to careful diagnosis. The items to check are listed in the sequence to be followed for quickest results. Thus, follow the checks in the order given for the particular transmission type.

TROUBLE SYMPTOMS	Items to Check: In Truck	Items to Check: Out of Truck
Rough initial engagement in D1 or D2	KBWFEG	
1-2 or 2-3 shift points incorrect or erratic	ABCDWEL	
Rough 2-3 shifts	BGFEJ	
Engine overspeeds on 2-3 shift	BGEF	m
No 1-2 or 2-3 upshift	DECJG	bcf
No 3-1 shift	KBE	
No forced downshift	LWE	
Runaway engine on forced downshift	GFEJB	c
Rough 3-2 or 3-1 shift at closed throttle	KBE	
Creeps excessively	KZ	
Slips or chatters in first gear, D1	ABWFE	acfi
Slips or chatters in second gear	ABGWFEJ	ac
Slips or chatters in R	AHWFEIB	bcf
No drive in D1	CE	i
No drive in D2	ERC	acf
No drive in L	CER	acf
No drive in R	HIERC	bef
No drive in any selector position	ACWFER	cd
Lockup in D1	CIJ	bgc
Lockup in D2	CHI	bgci
Lockup in L	GJE	bjc
Lockup in R	GJ	agc
Parking lock binds or does not hold	C	g
Transmission overheats	OFG	l
Engine will not push-start	ACFE	ec
Maximum speed too low, poor acceleration	Y	l
Transmission noisy in N and P	F	ad
Noisy transmission during coast 30-20 mph with engine stopped		e
Transmission noisy in any drive position	F	hbad
Fluid leaks	MNOPQSTUX	jkl

Key to Checks

A. Fluid level
B. Vacuum diaphragm unit or tubes
C. Manual linkage
D. Governor
E. Valve body
F. Pressure regulator
G. Front band
H. Rear band
I. Rear servo
J. Front servo
K. Engine idle speed
L. Downshift linkage
M. Converter drain plug
N. Oil pan, filler tube and/or seals
O. Oil cooler and/or connections
P. Manual or throttle shaft seals
Q. Pipe plug, side of case
R. Perform air pressure checks
S. Extension housing-to-case gasket or washer
T. Center support bolt lock washer
U. Extension housing rear oil seal
W. Make control pressure check
X. Speedometer drive gear adaptor seal
Y. Engine performance
Z. Vehicle brakes

a. Front clutch
b. Rear clutch
c. Hydraulic system leakage
d. Front pump
e. Rear pump
f. Fluid distributor sleeve—output shaft
g. Parking linkage
h. Planetary assembly
i. Planetary oneway clutch
j. Engine rear oil seal
k. Front oil pump seal
l. Front pump-to-case seal or gasket
m. Rear clutch piston air bleed valve

General Information

This section provides procedures for testing, inspecting, adjusting, and repairing the FMX 3-speed automatic transmission. Where there are differences in procedures or specifications for various model changes, these differences will be outlined.

The Ford FMX 3-speed automatic transmission is a three-speed unit that provides automatic upshifts and downshifts through three forward gear ratios and also provides manual selection of first and second gears. The transmission consists of a torque converter, planetary gear assembly, two multiple disc clutches, and a hydraulic control system.

The FMX transmission cools its transmission fluid through a cooler core in the radiator lower tank when a steel converter is used. If an aluminum converter is used, the transmission fluid is air-cooled.

Towing

If the disabled truck is to be towed a short distance, it may be towed safely by placing the selector lever in the Neutral position and releasing the parking brake. The driver of the towed truck should be careful to maintain a safe distance behind the towing vehicle. The towing speed should not exceed 30 mph.

If the disabled truck is to be towed a long distance, or the transmission cannot be put in the Neutral gear, or if there is no driver for the towed truck, raise the truck so the rear wheels clear the ground and tow the truck backwards.

Starting the Engine without the Starter

The transmission may be used to start an engine when the starter cannot be used by moving the disabled truck at a road speed of about 25 mph while in Neutral and then placing the transmission in Low gear while the ignition is on. The resultant turning over of the engine will start the engine and the truck may move under its own power. The disabled truck may be towed or pushed but extreme care must be taken not to lose control of the truck's motion and cause a collision. When the engine starts, the truck will move forward quickly and must be slowed enough to avoid a collision. If the disabled truck is being pushed, the rear truck must drop back before the transmission is engaged to avoid hitting the front car.

Transmission Checks

Before performing any of the tests and adjustments given in this part of this section, the following preliminary checks should be done:

Transmission Fluid Level Check

1. Position the truck on a level place and firmly apply the parking brake.

NOTE: on trucks equipped with a vacuum brake release, disconnect the release line and plug the end of the line. Otherwise, the parking brake will not hold the truck in any drive gear of the transmission.

2. Start the engine and run at normal idle speed. If the transmission fluid is cold, the engine should idle at a fast idle speed (about 1200 rpm) until the fluid is warm. When the transmission fluid reaches its normal operating temperature, slow the engine to normal idle speed.
3. Shift the transmission selector lever through all drive positions briefly and then put it in the Park position. Do not shut off the engine during the fluid level check.
4. Locate the transmission fluid dipstick and clean all dirt and grease from the cap before removing it. On some trucks the dipstick is located in the right rear corner of the engine compartment. On other trucks, the dipstick is located under the front floormat to the right of center.
5. Pull the dipstick out of the filler tube, wipe it clean, and reinsert it into the filler tube until it is fully seated.
6. Pull the dipstick out again and see where the fluid level is on the dipstick. The correct level is between the ADD and FULL marks on the dipstick. If necessary, add enough fluid through the filler tube to raise the fluid to the correct level. *Do not overfill the transmission.* Replace the dipstick in the filler tube.
7. If a vacuum brake release line was disconnected, reconnect it and test for proper operation.

Fluid Aeration Check

If the transmission is overfilled with too much fluid, the fluid will be whipped up into a foamy or aerated condition. This condition will cause low control pressure and the fluid may be forced out of the vent or through ruptured seals.

Check the transmission fluid level for low level conditions that may indicate fluid leaks or, at the very least, poor operation.

Transmission Fluid Leakage Checks

Make the following checks if a leakage is suspected from the transmission case:

1. Clean all dirt and grease from the transmission case.
2. Inspect the speedometer cable connection at the extension housing of the transmission. If fluid is leaking here, disconnect the cable and replace the rubber seal.
3. Inspect the oil pan gasket and attaching bolts for leaks. Tighten any bolts that appear loose to the proper torque (10-13 ft. lbs.). Recheck for signs of leakage. If necessary, remove the pan attaching bolts and old pan gasket and install new gasket and reinstall the pan and its attaching bolts.
4. Check filler tube connection at the transmission for signs of leakage. If tube is leaking, tighten the connection to stop the leak. If necessary, disconnect the filler tube, replace the O-ring, and reinstall the filler tube.
5. Inspect all fluid lines between the transmission and the cooler core in the lower radiator tank. Replace any lines or fittings that appear to be worn or damaged. Tighten all fittings to the proper torque.
6. Inspect the engine coolant for signs of transmission fluid in the radiator. If there is transmission fluid in the engine coolant, the oil cooler core is probably leaking.

NOTE: the oil cooler core may be tested further by disconnecting all lines to it and applying 50-75 psi air pressure through the fittings. Remove the radiator cap to relieve any pressure build-up outside the cooler core. If air bubbles appear in the coolant or if the cooler core will not hold pressure, the oil cooler core is leaking and must be replaced.

7. Inspect the openings in the case where the downshift control lever shaft and the manual lever shaft are located for leaks. If necessary, replace the defective seal.
8. Inspect all plugs or cable connections in the transmission for signs of leakage. Tighten any loose plugs or connectors to the proper torque according to the specifications.
9. Remove the lower cover from the front of the bellhousing and inspect the converter drainplugs for signs of leakage. If there is a leak around the drainplugs, loosen the plug and coat the threads with a sealing compound and tighten the plug to the proper torque.

NOTE: fluid leaks from around the converter drainplug may be caused by engine oil leaking past the rear main bearing or from the oil

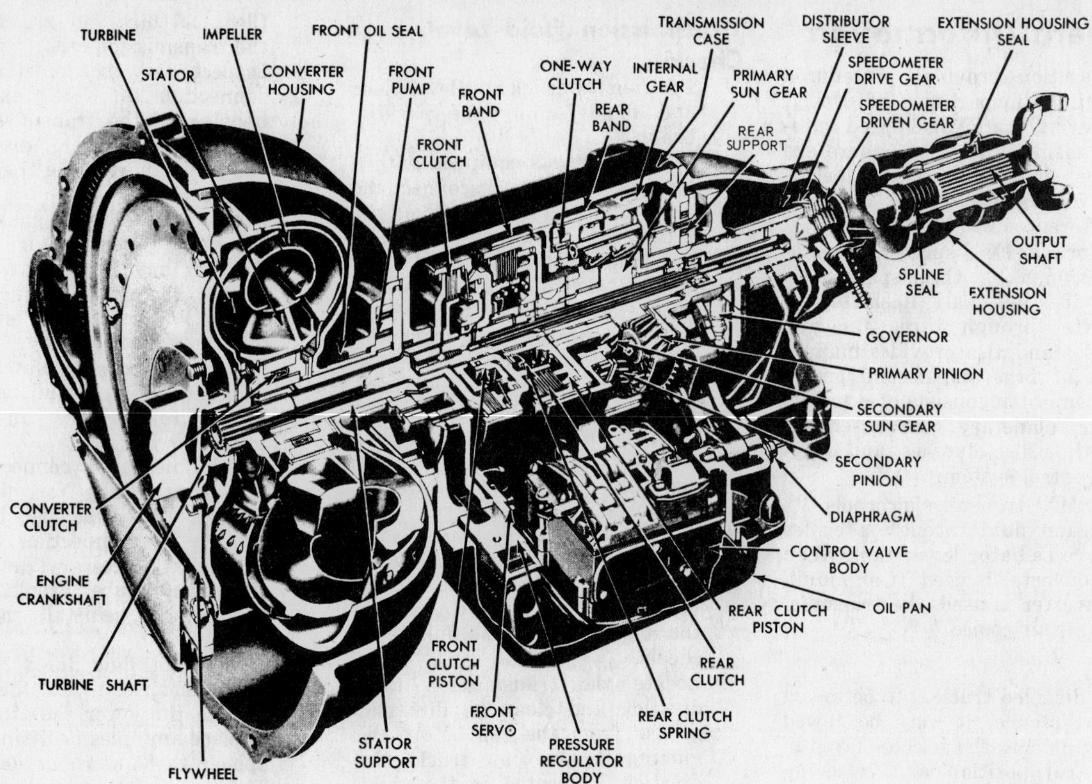

Typical MX—H.D. transmission (© Ford Motor Co.)

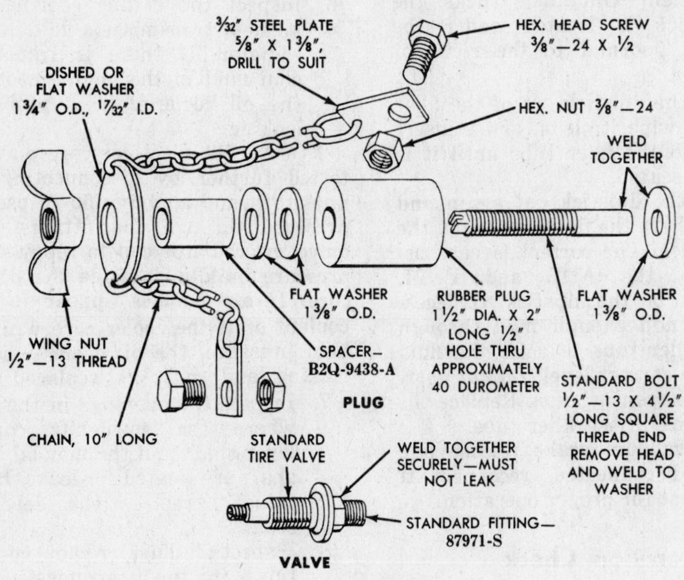

Converter leak checking tool (© Ford Motor Co.)

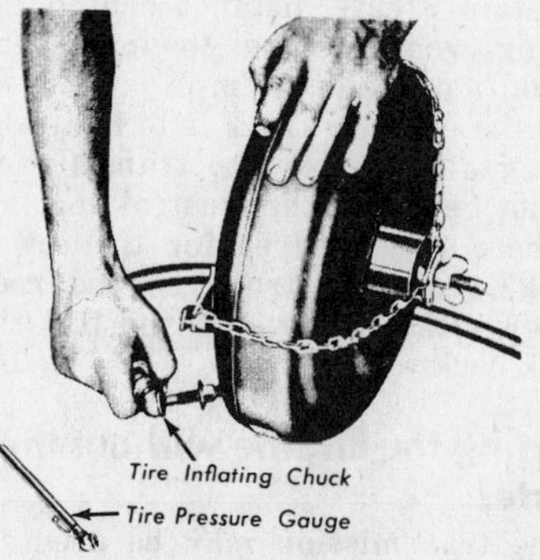

Typical converter leak checking tool (© Ford Motor Co.)

gallery plugs. To determine the exact cause of the leak before beginning repair procedures, an oil-soluble aniline or fluorescent dye may be added to the transmission fluid to find the source of the leak and whether the transmission is leaking. If a fluorescent dye is used, a black light must be used to detect the dye.

If further converter checks are necessary, remove the transmission from the truck and the converter from the transmission. The converter cannot be disassembled for cleaning or repair. If the converter is leaking, it must be replaced with a new unit. The converter may be cleaned by using the Rotunda Automatic Transmission Torque Converter and Cooler Cleaner LRE-60081. To further check the converter for leaks, assemble and install the converter leak checking tool shown and fill the converter with 20 psi air pressure. Then, place the converter in a tank of water and watch for air bubbles. If no air bubbles are seen, the converter is not leaking.

Engine Idle Speed Check

Check the idle speed of the engine and adjust it at the carburetor. Too slow an idle speed will cause the engine to run roughly; and too fast an idle speed will cause the truck to creep while the transmission is in a Drive position, shift harshly, and downshift roughly.

Anti-Stall Dashpot Clearance Check

After properly adjusting the engine idle speed, check the clearance of the anti-stall dashpot.

Manual Linkage Checks

Correct manual linkage is necessary for the proper operation of the manual valve which helps control fluid pressure to various transmission components. Improperly adjusted manual linkage may cause fluid leaks if not corrected.

Control Pressure Check for Automatic Transmissions

When the vacuum diaphragm unit operates properly and the downshift linkage is adjusted correctly, all transmission shifts (automatic and kickdown) should occur within the specified road speed limits. If these shifts do not occur within the limits or if the transmission slips during a shift point, perform the following procedure to locate the problem:

1. Connect the Automatic Transmission Tester as follows:
   a. Tachometer cable to engine.
   b. Vacuum gauge hose to the transmission vacuum diaphragm unit.

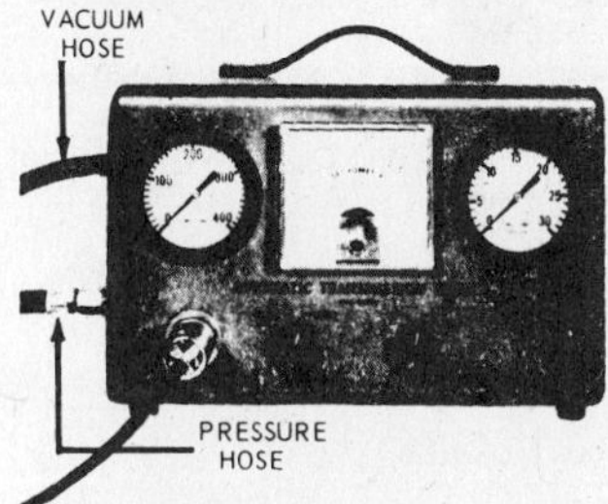

Rotunda are—
29-05 automatic transmission tester
(© Ford Motor Co.)

   c. Pressure gauge to the control pressure outlet on the transmission.
2. Apply the parking brake and start the engine. On a truck equipped with a vacuum brake release, disconnect the vacuum line or use the service brakes since the parking brake will release automatically when the transmission is put in any Drive position.
3. Check engine idle speed and throttle and downshift linkage for correct operation. Check the transmission diaphragm unit for leaks.

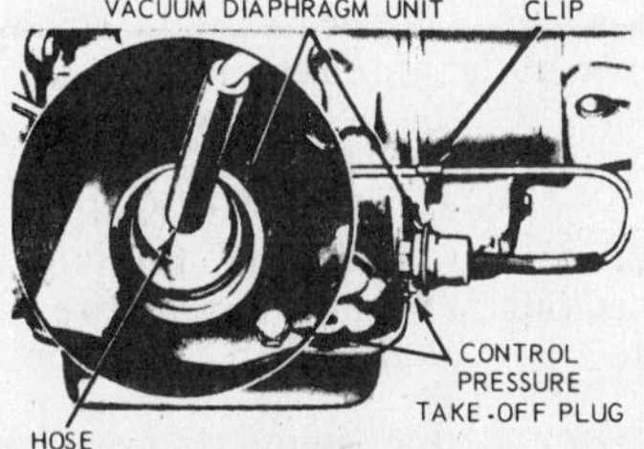

Typical control pressure connecting points
(© Ford Motor Co.)

Vacuum Diaphragm Unit Check

Non-Altitude Compensating Type

1. Remove the vacuum diaghragm unit from the transmission after disconnecting the vacuum hose.

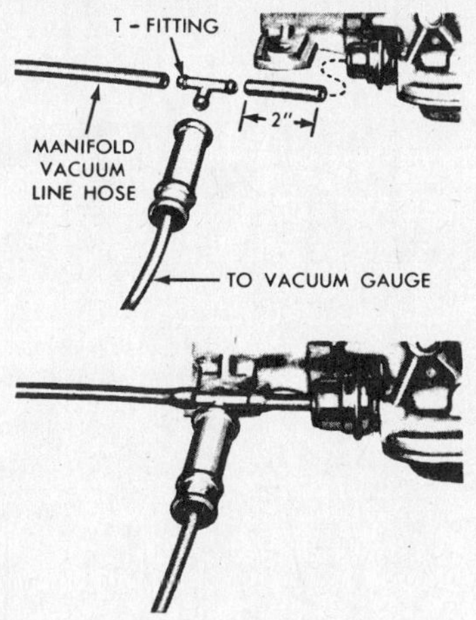

Typical vacuum test line connections
(© Ford Motor Co.)

2. Adjust a distributor tester equipped with a vacuum pump until the vacuum gauge shows 18 inches with the vacuum hose blocked.

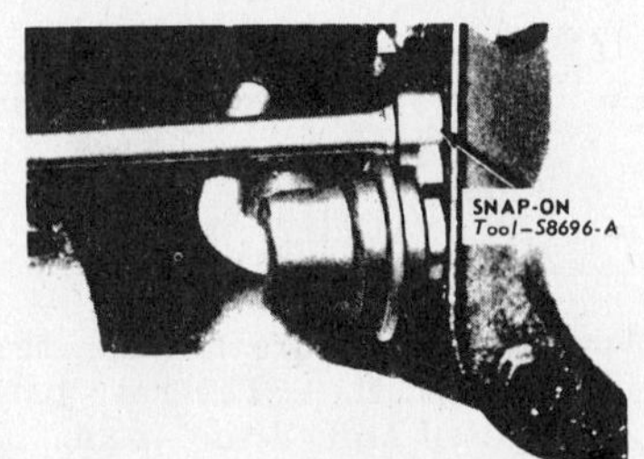

Removing or installing vacuum diaphragm
(© Ford Motor Co.)

3. Connect the vacuum hose to the vacuum diaphragm unit and note the reading on the vacuum gauge. If the reading is 18 inches of vacuum, the vacuum diaphragm unit is good. While removing the vacuum hose from the vacuum diaphragm unit, hold a finger over the end of the control rod. As the vacuum is released, the internal spring of the vacuum diaphragm unit will push the control rod out.

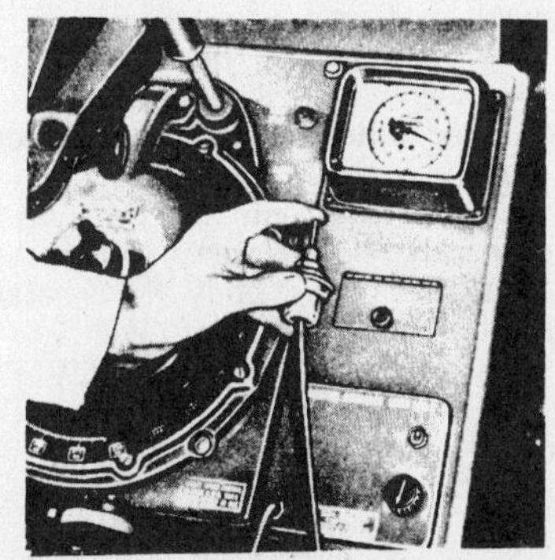

Testing transmission vacuum unit for leakage
(© Ford Motor Co.)

Altitude-Compensating Type

The vacuum diaphragm unit may be checked for damaged or ruptured bellows by doing the procedure below:

1. Remove the diaphragm and the throttle valve rod from the transmission.
2. Insert a rod into the diaphragm unit until it is seated in the hole. Make a reference mark on the rod where it enters the diaphragm.
3. Place the diaphragm unit on a weighing scale with the end of the rod resting on the weighing pan and gradually press down on the diaphragm unit.
4. Note the force (in pounds) at which the reference mark on the rod moves into the diaphragm. If the reference mark is still visible at 12 pounds of pressure on the scale, the diaphragm bellows is good. But if the reference mark on the rod disappears before four pounds of force, the diaphragm bellows are damaged and the diaphragm unit must be replaced.

Shift Point Checks for Automatic Transmissions

To determine if the transmission is shifting at the proper road speeds, do the following procedure:

1. Check the minimum throttle upshifts by placing the transmission selector lever in the Drive position and noting the road speeds at which the transmission shifts from first gear to second gear to third gear. All shifts should occur within the specified limits.
2. While driving in third gear, depress the accelerator pedal past the detent (to the floor). Depending on vehicle speed, the transmission should downshift from third gear to second gear or from second gear to first gear.
3. Check the closed-throttle downshift from third gear to first gear by coasting down from about 30 mph in third gear. This downshift should occur at the specified road speed.

NOTE: when the transmission selector lever is at 2, the transmission will operate only in second gear. Manually move the selector lever to either D or 1 to shift gears automatically.

4. With the transmission in third gear and the truck moving at a road speed of 35 mph, the transmission should downshift to second gear when the selector lever is moved from D to 2 to 1. This check will determine if the governor pressure and shift control

valves are operating properly. If the transmission does not shift within the specified limits or certain gear ratios cannot be obtained, refer to the Trouble Diagnosis chart at the beginning of this section.

Air Pressure Checks

If the truck will not move in one or more ranges, or, if it shifts erratically, the items at fault can be determined by using air pressure at the indicated passages.

Drain the transmission and remove the oil pan and the control valve assembly.

NOTE: oil will spray profusely during this operation.

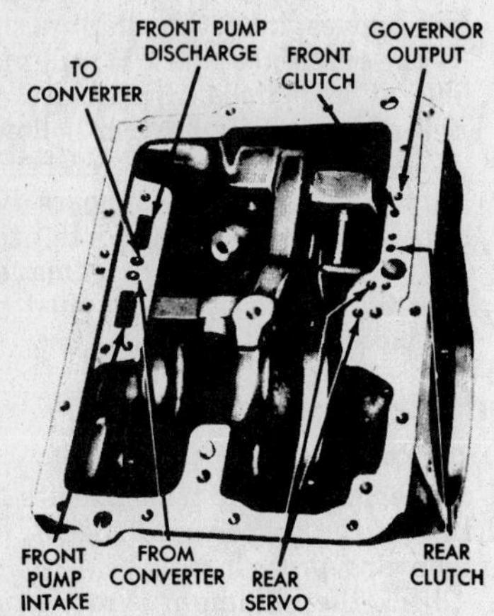

Case fluid hole identification (© Ford Motor Co.)

Front Clutch

Apply sufficient air pressure to the front clutch input passage. A dull thud can be heard when the clutch piston moves. Check also, for leaks.

Governor

Remove the governor inspection cover from the extension housing. Apply air to the front clutch input passage. (See illustration). Listen for a sharp click and watch to see if the governor valve snaps inward as it should.

Rear Clutch

Apply air to the rear clutch passage (See illustration) and listen for the dull thud that will indicate that the rear clutch piston has moved. Listen also for leaks.

Front Servo

Apply air pressure to the front servo apply tube and note if front band tightens. Shift the air to the front servo release tube, which is next to the apply tube, and watch band release.

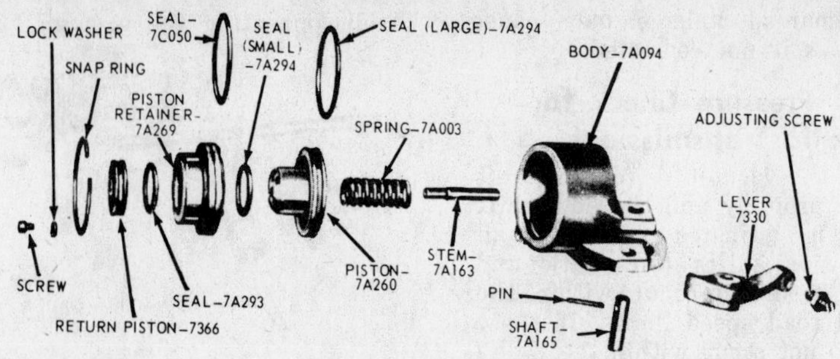

Front servo disassembled (© Ford Motor Co.)

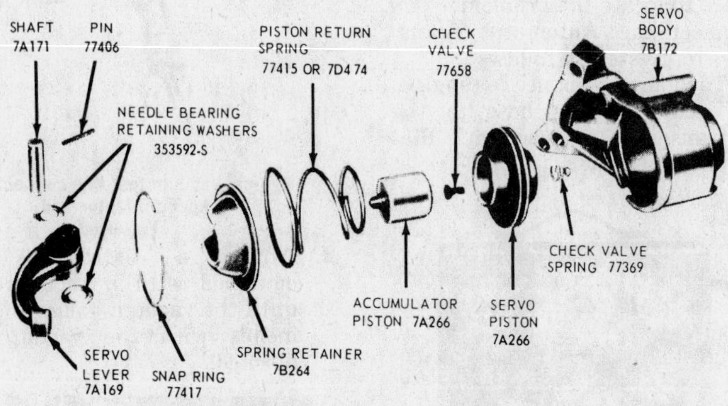

Rear servo disassembled (© Ford Motor Co.)

Rear Servo

Apply air pressure to the rear servo apply passage. The rear band should tighten around the drum.

Conclusions

If the operation of the servos and clutch is normal with air pressure, the no-drive condition is due to the control valve and pressure regulator valve assemblies, which should be disassembled, cleaned and inspected.

If operation of the clutches is not normal; that is, if both clutches apply from one passage or if one fails to move, the aluminum sleeve (bushing) in the output shaft is out of position or badly worn. (See illustration.)

Use air pressure to check the passages in the sleeve and shaft, and also check the passages in the primary sun gear shaft.

If the passages in the two shafts and the sleeve are clean, remove the clutch assemblies, clean and inspect the parts.

Erratic operation can also be caused by loose valve body screws. When reinstalling the valve body be careful to tighten: the pressure regulator valve to case bolts to 17-22 ft. lbs., the pressure regulator valve cover screws to 20-30 in. lbs., the control valve body screws to 20-30 in. lbs., the 1/4-20 capscrew (lower to upper valve body) to 4-6 ft. lbs., and the control valve body to case bolts to 8-10 ft. lbs.

In-Vehicle Adjustments and Repairs

The adjustments and repairs presented in this part of the section on FMX transmissions may be done without removing the entire transmission from the truck. Some of these procedures will require the use of special tools and instruments.

Transmission Fluid Drain and Refill

Normal maintenance and lubrication requirements do not include periodic changes of transmission fluid. Only when it is necessary to remove the pan for major repairs or adjustments will it be necessary to replace the transmission fluid. At this time the converter, oil cooler core, and cooler lines should be thoroughly flushed out to remove any dirt or deposits that might clog these units later.

When filling a completely dry (no fluid) transmission and converter, install five quarts of transmission fluid and then start the engine. Shift the selector lever through all positions briefly and set at Park position. Check the fluid level and add enough fluid to raise the level to between the ADD and FULL marks on the dipstick. *Do not overfill the transmission.*

The procedure for a partial drain and refill of the transmission fluid is given below:

1. Raise the truck on a hoist or jack stands.
2. Place a drain pan under the transmission pan.
3. Loosen the pan attaching bolts to allow the fluid to drain.

NOTE: on FMX Transmissions (also called Cruise-O-Matic and Merc-O-Matic) used in 1968 and earlier models of Ford, the transmission fluid is drained by disconnecting the fluid filler tube from the transmission fluid pan.

4. When the fluid has stopped draining to level of the pan flange, remove the pan bolts starting at the rear and along both sides of the pan, allowing the pan to drop and drain gradually.
5. When all the transmission fluid has drained, remove the pan and the fluid filter and clean them. Discard the old pan gasket.
6. After completing the transmission repairs or adjustments, install the fluid filter screen, a new pan gasket, and the pan on the transmission. Tighten the pan attaching bolts to the proper torque (10-13 ft. lbs.).
7. Install three quarts of transmission fluid through the filler tube. If the filler tube was removed to drain the transmission, install the filler tube using a new O-ring.
8. Start and run the engine for a few minutes at low idle speed and then at the fast idle speed (about 1200 rpm) until the normal operating temperature is reached. *Do not race the engine.*
9. Move the selector lever through all positions and place it at the Park position. Check the fluid level, and add fluid till the level is between the ADD and FULL marks on the dipstick. *Do not overfill the transmission.*

Band Adjustments

Front Band Adjustment

When it is necessary to adjust the front band of the transmission, perform the following procedure:

1. Drain the transmission fluid and remove the oil pan, fluid filter screen, and clip. The same transmission fluid may be reused if it is filtered through a 100-mesh screen before being installed. Only transmission fluid in good condition should be used.
2. Clean the pan and filter screen and remove the old gasket.
3. Loosen the front servo adjusting screw locknut.

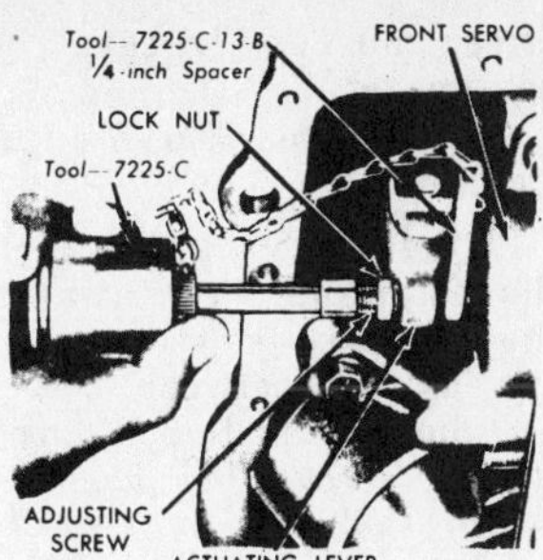

Front band adjustment—typical
(© Ford Motor Co.)

NOTE: special band adjusting wrenches are recommended to do this operation correctly and quickly.

4. Pull back the actuating rod and insert a ¼ in. spacer bar between the adjusting screw and the servo piston stem. Tighten the adjusting screw to 10 in. lbs. torque. Remove the spacer bar and tighten the adjusting screw an additional ¾ turn. Hold the adjusting screw fast and tighten the locknut securely (20-25 ft. lbs.).
5. Install the transmission fluid filter screen and clip. Install the pan with a new pan gasket.
6. Refill the transmission to the FULL mark on the Dipstick. Start the engine, run for a few minutes, shift the selector lever through all positions, and place it in Park. Recheck the fluid level again and add fluid to proper level if necessary.

Alternate Front Band Adjustment

An alternate method of adjusting the front band is presented here. The method is the same as the one given above except for the tools that are used. The procedure is as follows:

1. Drain the transmission and remove and clean the pan and fluid filter. Discard the old gasket.
2. Loosen the front servo adjusting screw locknut two full turns with a 9/16 in. wrench. Check that the adjusting screw rotates freely.
3. Pull the actuating lever back and insert the ¼ in. spacer bar between the servo piston stem and the adjusting screw. Install the socket drive handle on the 9/16 in. socket.
4. Insert the T-handle extension through the socket handle and put the screwdriver socket on the T-handle extension.
5. Put the assembled adjusting tool on the adjusting screw so that the screwdriver socket is on the screw and the 9/16 in. socket is on the adjusting screw locknut.
6. Put a torque wrench on the T-handle extension and tighten the adjusting screw to 10 in. lbs. torque.
7. Remove the ¼ in. spacer bar and tighten the adjusting screw an additional ¾ turn. Hold the adjusting screw steady and tighten the locknut to 20-25 ft. lbs. torque.
8. Install the fluid filter screen, clip, and pan with a new gasket on the transmission. Refill the transmission as given earlier.

Rear Band Adjustments

The rear band of the FMX transmission may be adjusted by any of the methods given below. On most truck the basic external band adjustment is satisfactory. The internal band adjustment procedure may be done when the external adjustment procedure cannot be done correctly. On trucks with a console floor shift, the entire console and shift lever and linkage will have to be removed to gain access to the rear band external adjusting screw.

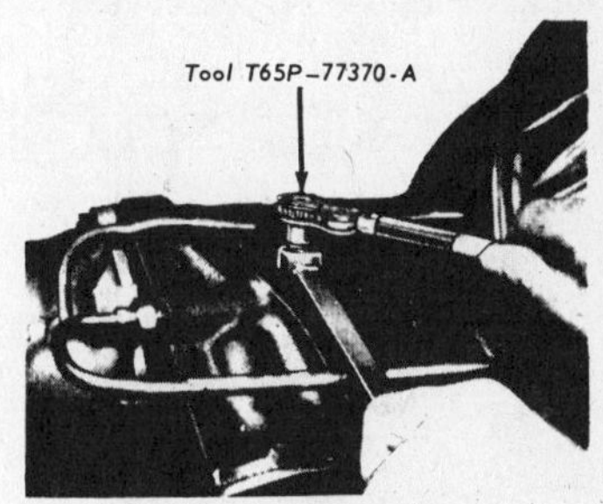

Rear band adjustment
(© Ford Motor Co.)

Rear Band External Adjustment

The procedure for adjusting the rear band externally is as follows:

1. Locate the external rear band adjusting screw on the transmission case, clean all dirt from the threads, and coat the threads with light oil.

NOTE: the adjusting screw is located on the upper right side of the transmission case. Access is often through a hole in the front floor to the right of center under the carpet.

2. Loosen the locknut on the rear band external adjusting screw. On 1970 Cougar and Mustang cars, use the special tool illustrated to loosen the locknut.
3. Using the special preset torque wrench shown, tighten the adjusting screw until the handle clicks at 10 ft. lbs. torque. If the adjusting screw is tighter than 10 ft. lbs. torque, loosen the adjusting screw and retighten to the proper torque.
4. Back off the adjusting screw 1½ turns. Hold the adjusting screw steady while tightening the locknut to the proper torque (35-40 ft. lbs.). *Severe damage may re-*

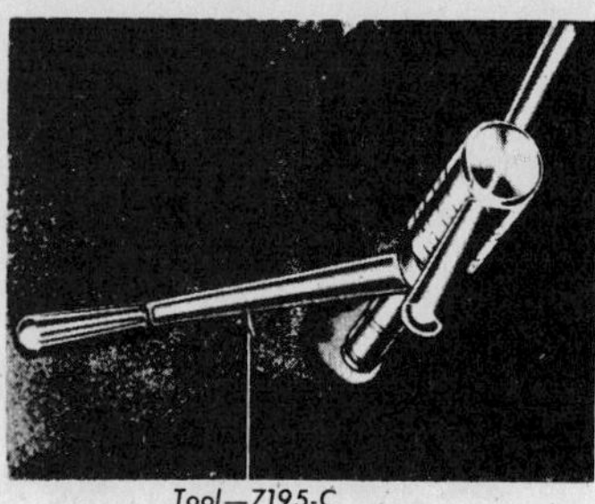

Adjusting rear band
(© Ford Motor Co.)

sult if adjusting screw is not backed off exactly 1½ turns.

Alternate Rear Band External Adjustment

The alternate method of adjusting the rear band is basically the same as the procedure given above. The difference between the two methods is that the alternate procedure uses the band adjusting tool shown in the illustration. The tool is assembled as given below and adjusted according to the instructions given above.

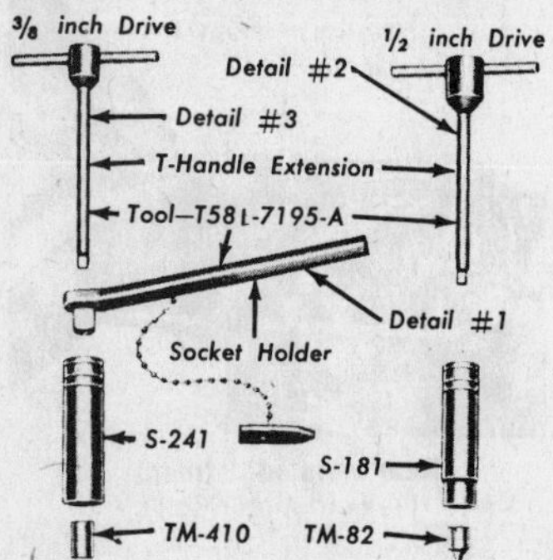

Front and rear band adjusting tools
(© Ford Motor Co.)

1. Put the socket holder on the ¾ in. socket. Insert the ⅜ in. drive T-handle extension through the socket holder and socket. Put the 5/16 in., 8-point socket on the extension. Place a torque wrench on the T-handle extension.
2. Place the assembled adjusting tool on the adjusting screw so that it engages the adjusting screw and locknut and do the procedure given above.
3. After adjusting the rear band correctly, hold the adjusting screw steady and tighten the locknut securely.

Rear Band Internal Adjustment

The rear band is adjusted internally by doing the following procedure:

1. Drain the transmission fluid. If it is to be reused, pour the fluid through a 100-mesh screen as it drains from the transmission. Reuse the transmission fluid only if it is in good condition.
2. Remove and clean the pan, fluid filter, and clip. Discard the old pan gasket.
3. Loosen the rear servo adjusting locknut.
4. Pull the adjusting screw end of the actuating lever away from the servo body and insert the spacer tool between the servo accumulator piston and the adjusting screw. *Be sure the flat surfaces of the tool are placed squarely between the adjusting screw and the accumulator piston. Tool must not touch servo piston and the handle must not touch the servo piston spring retainer.*
5. Using a torque wrench with an Allen head socket, tighten the adjusting screw to 24 in. lbs. torque.
6. Back off the adjusting screw exactly 1½ turns. Hold adjusting screw steady and tighten the locknut securely. Remove the spacer tool.
7. Install the fluid filter, clip, and pan with a new gasket.
8. Fill the transmission with the correct amount of fluid.

Transmission Component Removal and Installation

The various components of the FMX transmission that may be removed while the transmission is in the truck are given in this part of the FMX transmission section. Installation is often the reverse of the removal instructions except for adjustment and alignment.

Governor Assembly Removal and Installation

The governor assembly may be removed from transmissions built before 1968 through an extension housing access or inspection plate. On 1968 and later models of the FMX transmission, the extension housing must be removed with all attaching parts to remove the governor assembly from the output shaft. It may be necessary to remove the entire transmission from the truck to do this removal procedure.

The removal procedure for the governor assembly is as follows:

1. Remove the governor inspection plate from the right side of the extension housing (see Illustration), and rotate the driveshaft until the governor appears in the opening.
2. Remove the two screws holding the governor body to the counter weight sleeve. Be careful not to drop the screws or the valve into the extension housing.

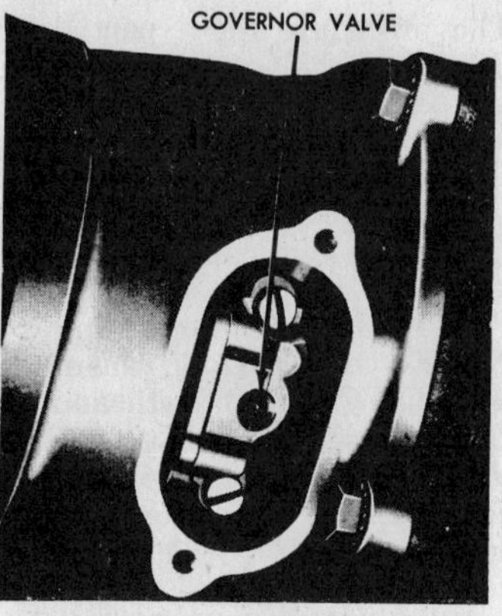

Governor valve
(© Ford Motor Co.)

3. Disassemble the governor by removing the two screws holding the side plate. Inspect the governor valve for scoring and free movement in its bore. Be sure the spring, sleeve, and plug are not damaged. Blow valve body passages clear of obstructions.
4. Reassemble the governor assembly (see illustration), aligning the passages in the sleeve and body. Tighten the valve body cover screws with 20-30 in. lbs. torque.

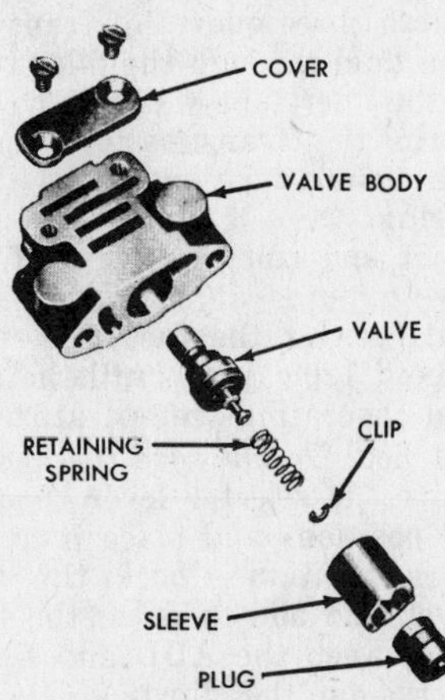

Governor disassembled
(© Ford Motor Co.)

5. Install the governor assembly on the counterweight sleeve, tightening the mounting screws with 50-60 in. lbs. torque. Replace the governor inspection plate on the extension housing.

Extension Housing Removal and Installation

1. Raise the truck high enough for easy access to the extension housing.
2. Drain the transmission.
3. Disconnect the driveshaft from the rear axle and slide the front yoke from the extension housing.
4. Disconnect the speedometer cable from the extension housing.

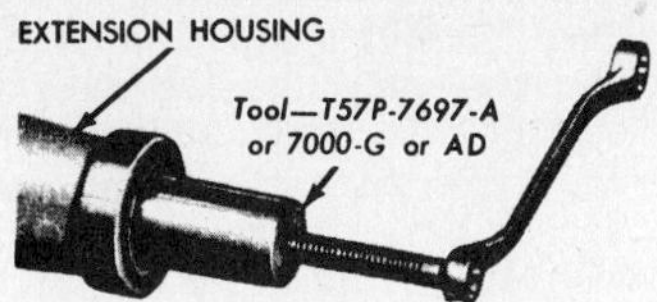

Removing extension housing bushing (© Ford Motor Co.)

5. Remove the rear engine support nuts. Place a transmission jack under the transmission and raise it enough to clear the crossmember.

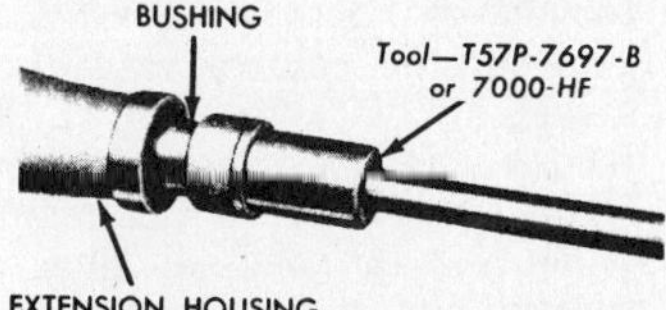

Installing extension housing bushing (© Ford Motor Co.)

6. Remove the bolts and nuts securing the crossmember to the side rails of the frame. Move the crossmember out of the way.
7. Remove the attaching bolts holding the engine rear support to the extension housing and remove the rear support from the extension housing.
8. Remove all the extension housing attaching bolts, slide the housing off the output shaft, and discard the gasket.
9. Installation is the reverse of the removal procedures. Tighten the housing attaching bolts to 30-40 ft. lbs. torque. Check that the output shaft rotates freely by hand. If it binds or feels tight, check the needle bearing and race for correct position.

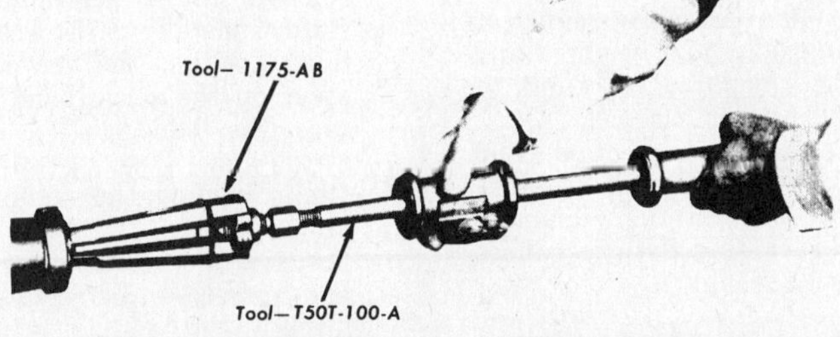

Removing extension housing seal (© Ford Motor Co.)

Extension Housing Bushing and Rear Seal Removal and Installation

1. Disconnect the driveshaft from the extension housing.
2. Carefully remove the rear seal from the housing.
3. Remove the extension housing bushing using the bushing remover tool (see illustration). *Be careful not to damage the spline seal.*

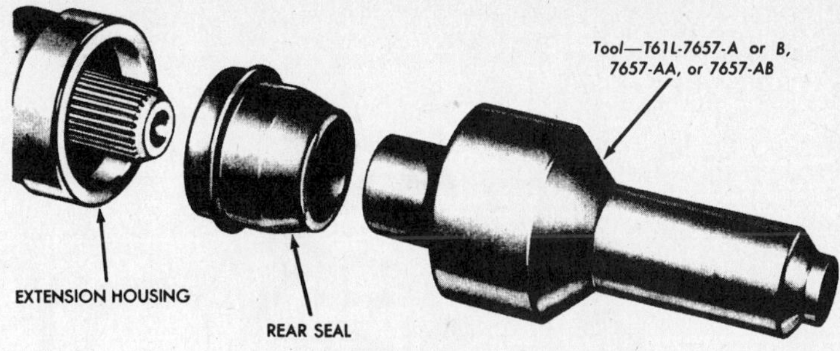

Installing extension housing seal (© Ford Motor Co.)

4. Install new bushing in the extension housing using the special tool
5. Inspect the universal joint yoke sealing surface for scoring or gouges. Replace the yoke if damaged.
6. Inspect the housing counterbore for burrs and, if necessary, smooth with crocus cloth.
7. Using a special tool, install the new rear seal into the end of the extension housing. Check that the seal is firmly seated.

Control Valve Body and Oil Pan Removal and Installation

1. Raise the truck on a hoist or jackstands and place a drain pan under the transmission.
2. Loosen the pan attaching bolts so that the transmission fluid drains down to the level of the pan flange. Then, starting at the rear of the pan and working forward along the sides, remove the pan attaching bolts until all the fluid has drained.
3. Remove the oil pan, fluid filter screen, and clip and clean them thoroughly. Discard the old pan gasket.
4. Remove the vacuum diaphragm assembly using the special tool required (Snap-On tool S8696-A or FCO-24). *Do not use pliers, pipe wrenches, etc. to remove the vacuum diaphragm unit. Do not let any solvents enter the vacuum diaphragm unit.* Remove the push rod and the fluid screen and its retaining clip.
5. Remove the small compensator pressure tube.

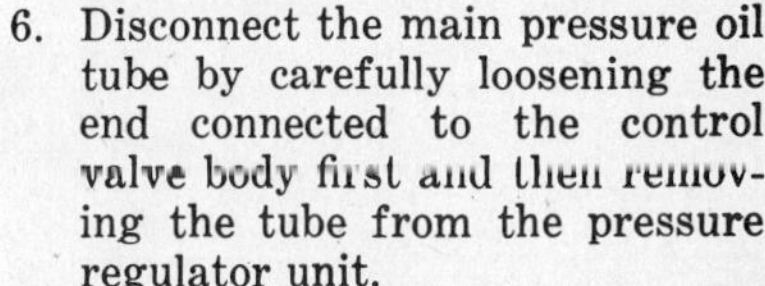

6. Disconnect the main pressure oil tube by carefully loosening the end connected to the control valve body first and then removing the tube from the pressure regulator unit.

CAUTION: be sure to remove the tube in this manner. Otherwise, the tube could be kinked or bent causing improper fluid pressures and possible damage to the transmission.

7. Loosen the front servo attaching bolts about three turns.
8. Remove the three control valve body attaching bolts and carefully lower the valve body, sliding it off the front servo tubes. *Do not damage the valve body or the tubes.*
9. Disassemble the control valve body into the various parts as shown in the illustration in the major repair section.
10. When installing the control valve body, align the front servo tubes with the holes in the valve body. Shift the manual lever to the 1 detent and place the inner downshift lever between the downshift lever stop and the downshift valve. Be sure the manual lever engages the actuating pin in the manual detent lever.
11. Loosely install the control valve body attaching bolts and move the control valve body toward the center of the transmission case until there is a clearance of 0.050 in. between the manual valve and the actuating pin on the manual detent lever.
12. Tighten the attaching bolts to 8-10 ft. lbs. torque. Ensure that the rear fluid filter retaining clip is installed under the valve body.
13. Install the main pressure oil tube, connecting the end to the pressure regulator unit first and then connecting the other end to the main control valve assembly by gently tapping it with a soft-faced hammer.
14. Install the compensator pressure tube on the pressure regulator and control valve body.
15. Check the manual lever for free motion in each detent position

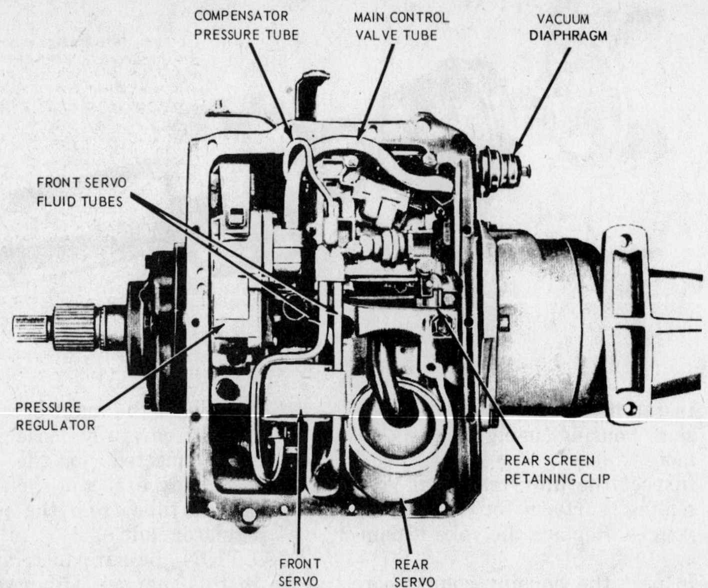

Typical hydraulic control system (© Ford Motor Co.)

by rotating it one full turn. If the manual lever binds in any detent position, loosen the valve body attaching bolts and move the valve body away from the center of the transmission case until the binding is relieved. Retighten the attaching bolts according to step 12.

16. Place the pushrod in the bore of the vacuum diaphragm unit and insert the other end of the pushrod into the threaded opening in the case. Install the vacuum diaphragm unit and tighten it to 20-30 ft. lbs. torque.
17. Tighten the front servo attaching bolts to 30-35 ft. lbs. torque.
18. Adjust the front band.
19. Install the fluid filter and its retaining clip.
20. Install the oil pan with a new pan gasket, tightening the pan attaching bolts to 10-13 ft. lbs. torque.
21. Adjust the rear band. If necessary to adjust the rear band internally, do the adjustment immediately after the front band adjustment.
22. Fill transmission with fluid. Start and run engine for a few minutes and check the fluid level after shifting the transmission through all positions. *Do not overfill the transmission.*
23. Check the adjustment of the transmission control linkage.

Pressure Regulator Removal and Installation

The pressure regulator unit may be removed from the transmission while it is in the truck.

1. Drain the transmission of fluid and remove the pan, fluid filter screen, and its retaining clip. Discard the used pan gasket.
2. Remove the compensator pressure tube from between the control valve body and the pressure regulator. See illustration for location of components.
3. Remove the main pressure oil tube by gently prying off the end connected to the control valve first and then disconnect the other end from the pressure regulator. *Be sure to remove the tube in this order to prevent kinking or bending it.*
4. Loosen the spring retainer clip and carefully release the spring tension on the pressure springs. Remove the valve springs, retainer and valve stop, and the valves from the pressure regulator body.
5. Remove the pressure regulator attaching bolts and washers and take the regulator body out of the transmission case.
6. After cleaning, inspection, and reassembly, install the pressure regulator unit in the transmission by reversing the procedures in steps 1 through 5.

Front Servo Removal and Installation

1. Drain the transmission fluid from the transmission case and remove the pan, fluid filter screen, and its retaining clip.
2. Remove the vacuum diaphragm unit.
3. Loosen the three control valve body attaching bolts.
4. Remove the front servo attaching bolts, hold the band strut steady with the fingers, and remove the front servo unit.
5. After repairing the front servo unit, install it by first positioning the front band forward in the transmission case with the end of the band facing downward. Be sure the front servo anchor pin is placed in the case web. Align the large end of the servo strut with the servo actuating lever, and align the small end with the band end.
6. Rotate the band, strut, and servo to align the anchor end of the band with the anchor in the case. Push the servo unit onto the control valve body tubes.
7. Install the attaching bolts and tighten them to 30-35 ft. lbs. torque.
8. Tighten the control valve body attaching bolts to 8-10 ft. lbs. torque. Check the clearance (0.050 in.) between the manual valve and the manual lever actuating pin.
9. Adjust the front band.
10. Install the vacuum diaphragm unit and its pushrod.
11. Install the fluid filter screen, its retaining clip, and the pan with a new pan gasket.
12. Fill the transmission with fluid.
13. Adjust the downshift and manual shift linkage.

Rear Servo Removal and Installation

1. Drain the transmission fluid from the transmission, and remove the pan, fluid filter screen, and its retaining clip.
2. Remove the vacuum diaphragm unit (see Vacuum Diaphragm Removal procedure).
3. Remove the control valve body and the two front servo tubes.
4. Remove the rear servo attaching bolts, hold the actuating and anchor struts with the fingers, and remove the rear servo unit.
5. Before installing the rear servo unit, position the servo anchor strut on the servo band and rotate the band to engage the strut.
6. While holding the servo anchor strut in place with the fingers, position the actuating lever strut and install the rear servo unit in place.
7. Loosely install the rear servo attaching bolts, with the longer bolt in the inner bolt hole.
8. Move the rear servo unit towards the center of the transmission case against the attaching bolts. While holding the servo in this position, tighten the attaching bolts to 40-45 ft. lbs. torque.
9. Install the two front servo tubes and the control valve body. Check for proper clearance (0.050 in.) between the manual valve and the manual actuating pin.

10. Adjust the rear band using the procedures given in the Rear Band Adjustments.
11. Install the fluid filter screen, its retaining clip, and the oil pan with a new gasket. Fill the transmission with fluid.

Parking Pawl Removal and Installation

The parking pawl assembly may be removed from the transmission while it is in the truck.

1. Raise the truck and drain the fluid from the transmission. *Do not remove the pan.*
2. Place the special engine support bar (T65E-6000J) under the converter housing.
3. Remove the driveshaft from the rear axle and slide the front yoke out of the extension housing.
4. Remove the two nuts securing the engine rear support to the crossmember.
5. Place a transmission jack under the transmission and raise the engine and transmission enough to take the weight off the crossmember.
6. Remove the bolts and nuts securing the crossmember to the frame side rails and slide the crossmember out of the way. Lower the jack slowly until the engine and transmission are resting on the special engine support bar.
7. Remove the two rear support-to-extension housing bolts and remove the rear support.
8. Disconnect the speedometer cable from the extension housing.
9. Remove the pan, fluid filter screen, and its retaining clip.
10. Loosen the rear band adjusting screw locknut and tighten the adjusting screw to 24 in. lbs. torque.

NOTE: the rear band will tighten around the planet carrier and hold the planet carrier and clutch assemblies in position during repair operations on the parking pawl.

11. Remove the small compensator pressure tube from the pressure regulator and control valve body.
12. Remove the main pressure oil tube from between the main control valve body and the pressure regulator. Be sure to disconnect the end of the tube connected to the control valve body first to avoid kinking or bending the tube.
13. Disconnect the vacuum diaphragm unit after removing the vacuum hose.
14. Loosen the front servo attaching bolts.
15. Remove the three control valve body attaching bolts and lower the valve body while carefully pulling it off the front servo tubes.
16. Remove the rear servo attaching bolts and the rear servo unit.
17. Remove the extension housing attaching bolts and housing.
18. Remove the output shaft and rear support assembly.
19. Remove the parking pawl pin from the case with a magnet.
20. Working from inside the case, tap the shoulder of the toggle lever pin to move the retaining plug part way out of the case. Remove the plug with pliers.
21. Loosen and remove the toggle lever pin by alternately sliding the toggle lever from side to side and pushing outward at the same time until it is loose. Lift the pawl and toggle lever from the case as one assembly.
22. After replacing worn or damaged parts, reinstall the new parking pawl and link assembly with the toggle lever pin and plug.
23. Secure the pawl to the case with the pawl pin.
24. Install the rear support and output shaft after putting a new gasket on the rear support and the thrust washer is in place. Make sure the pressure tubes are positioned properly in the case.
25. Position a new gasket on the extension housing and secure the extension housing to the transmission case by tightening the attaching bolts.
26. Install the rear servo and struts.
27. Install the main control valve body assembly as given in the procedure on *Oil Pan and Control Valve Body Removal and Installation.*
28. Tighten the front servo attaching bolts to 30-35 ft. lbs. torque.
29. Install the main pressure oil tube and the small compensator pressure tube to the control valve body and the pressure regulator.
30. Adjust the front band.
31. Adjust the rear band.
32. Install the vacuum control rod, the vacuum diaphragm unit, and attach the vacuum hose.
33. Install the fluid filter screen, retaining clip, and pan with a new gasket.
34. Connect the speedometer cable to the extension housing.
35. Secure the engine rear support to the extension housing with the two attaching bolts.
36. Place transmission jack under the transmission and raise the transmission and engine high enough to position and secure the rear support crossmember to the frame side rails. Tighten the attaching bolts and nuts to the specified torque.
37. Lower the transmission jack till the transmission and engine are resting on the rear support crossmember. Install and tighten to specified torque the nuts securing the rear support to the crossmember. Remove the transmission jack and the engine support bar.
38. Adjust the transmission control linkage.
39. Install the driveshaft and lower the car.
40. Fill the transmission with correct amount of fluid.

Transmission Overhaul Procedures

The transmission overhaul procedures presented here are the checks and repairs that must be done with the transmission out of the truck. Disassembly of each transmission subassembly is illustrated by exploded views of the subassembly showing how the individual parts fit together. Reassembly of the subassembly is often the reverse of the disassembly procedure except for alignment, special tolerances, etc.

During all repairs to the transmission subassemblies, the following instructions must be followed:

1. Be sure that no dirt or grease gets in the transmission. All parts must be clean. *Remember—a little dirt can disable a transmission completely if it gets in a fluid passage.*
2. Handle all transmission parts carefully to avoid burring or nicking bearing or mating surfaces.
3. Lubricate all internal parts of the transmission with clean transmission fluid before assembling. *Do not use any other lubricants except on gaskets or thrust washers which may be coated lightly with vaseline to ease assembly.*
4. Always use new gaskets when assembling the parts of the transmission.
5. Tighten all bolts and screws to the recommended torque limits using a torque wrench.

Transmission Disassembly

1. Thoroughly clean the outside of the transmission to prevent dirt or grease from getting inside the mechanism. *Do this before removing any subassembly.*
2. Place the transmission in the transmission holder.
3. Remove the transmission oil pan, gasket, and fluid filter retaining clip.

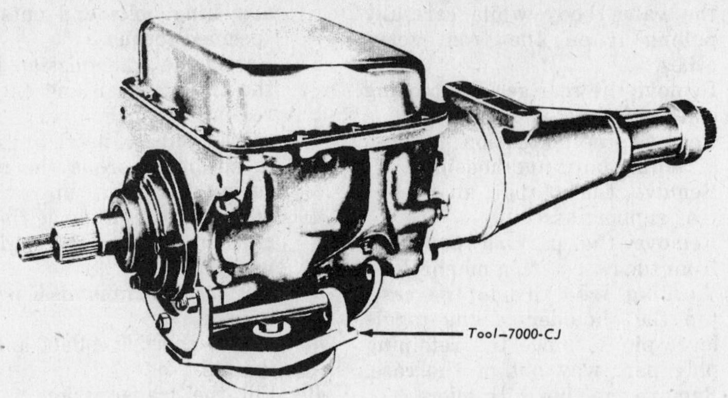

Transmission mounted in holding fixture (© Ford Motor Co.)

4. Lift the fluid filter screen off the forward tube, and then off the rear tube.
5. Remove the spring seat from the pressure regulator. *Maintain constant pressure on the spring seat and release slowly to prevent spring distortion and personal injury.*
6. Remove the pressure regulator springs and pilots but do not remove the valves yet.
7. Loosen but do not remove the pressure regulator attaching bolts.
8. Remove the small compensator pressure tube from the pressure regulator and the control valve body.
9. Remove the main pressure oil tube from the pressure regulator and the main control valve body assembly. Gently pry off the end connected to the main control valve body first and then remove the tube from the pressure regulator. *Failure to do this may kink or bend the tube causing damage to the transmission later.*
10. Loosen the front and rear servo band adjusting screws five turns. Loosen the front servo attaching bolts three turns.
11. Remove the vacuum diaphragm unit and pushrod.
12. Remove the control valve body attaching bolts and align the levers to allow removal of the valve body. Lift the valve body up and pull it off the servo tubes. Place the valve body on a clean surface.
13. Remove the pressure regulator from the case. Keep the control pressure valve and the converter pressure valve in the regulator body to avoid damaging the valves.
14. Remove the front servo apply, accumulator, and release tubes by twisting and pulling at the same time. Remove the front servo attaching bolts. While holding the front servo strut with the fingers, lift the front servo from the case.
15. Remove the rear servo attaching bolts. While holding the actuating and anchor struts with the fingers, lift the rear servo from the case.

Transmission End-Play Check

The transmission end play check is done as given below:

1. Remove one of the front pump attaching bolts and mount the dial indicator support tool in the hole. Mount a dial indicator on the support so that a contact rests on the end of the turbine shaft.

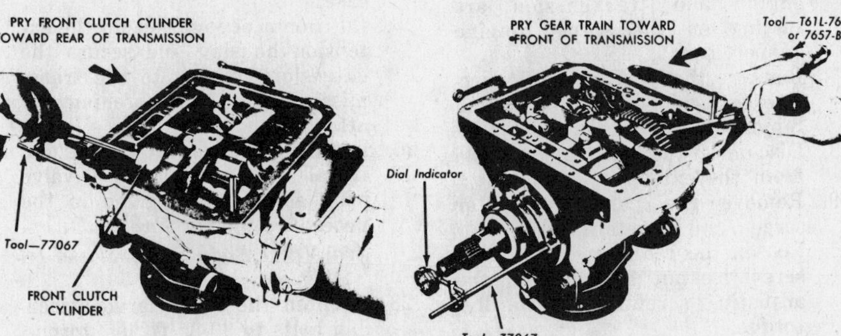

Transmission end play check (© Ford Motor Co.)

2. Install the extension housing seal replacer on the output shaft to provide support for the shaft.
3. Using a screwdriver, move the front clutch cylinder to the rear of the transmission case as far as possible. Set the dial indicator to zero while holding a slight pressure on the screwdriver.
4. Remove the screwdriver. Insert it between the large internal gear and the case and move the front clutch cylinder to the front of the case.
5. Record the indicator reading for later use during transmission reassembly. The end-play reading should be between 0.010-0.029 in. If the reading is not within these limits, a new selective thrust washer must be used when reassembling the transmission.
6. Remove the dial indicator, its support tool, and the extension housing seal replacer.

Case and Extension Housing Parts Removal

1. Remove the remaining front pump attaching bolts and the front pump assembly from the case. If necessary, tap the cap screw bosses to loosen the front pump from the case.
2. Remove the five case-to-extension housing attaching bolts. These bolts also hold the rear pump in the case. While holding the rear pump in position remove the housing carefully.
3. Remove the output shaft assembly (see illustration). To aid in removing the assembly, insert a screwdriver between the output shaft ring gear and the pinion carrier and move the assembly rearward. Be careful not to bend the pressure tubes between the rear support or distributor sleeve and the case as they are removed.

NOTE: on output shaft assemblies used in 1964 to 1966 transmissions, the speedometer drive gear is removable. The nylon speedometer drive gear may be replaced by removing the snap-ring securing it on the shaft, prying the oil distributor sleeve both rearward and forward on the shaft, and then, tapping the drive gear loose from the output shaft with a hammer and a small drift. The speedometer drive gear drive ball should fall out of its place in the output shaft, but it may need to be picked out. See the accompanying illustrations.

4. Remove the four seal rings from the output shaft using the fingers to prevent breaking them.
5. Remove the governor snap-ring from the output shaft. With a soft-faced hammer, tap the governor assembly off the output shaft. Remove the governor drive ball (see illustration).
6. Pull the rear support and gasket from the output shaft. Take the needle bearings and race from

the rear support.

7. Remove the selective thrust washer from the rear of the pinion carrier and then remove the pinion carrier.
8. Remove the primary sun gear rear thrust bearing and races from the pinion carrier.

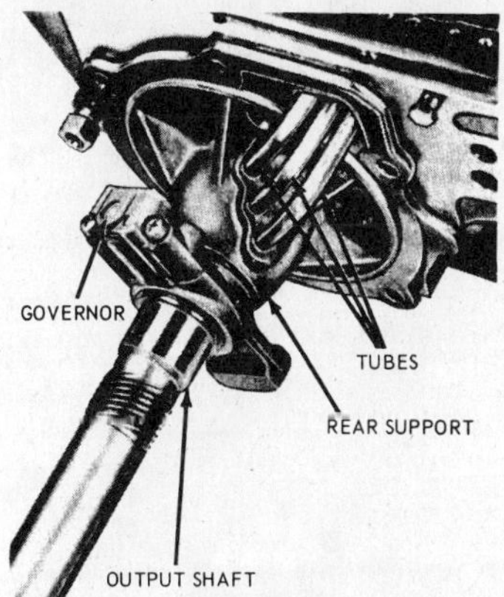

Rear support and output shaft installed
(© Ford Motor Co.)

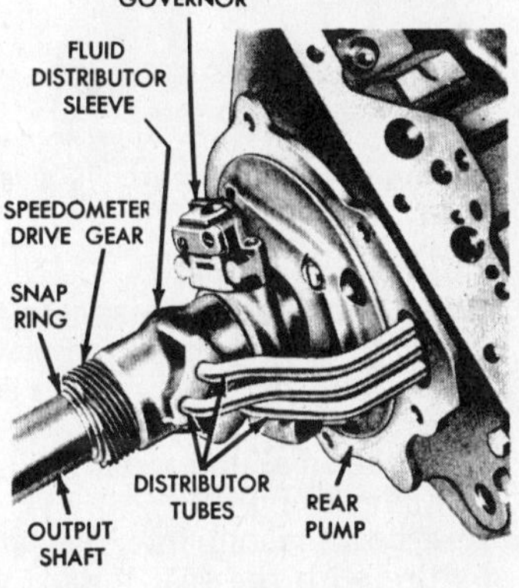

Output shaft and rear pump installed
(© Ford Motor Co.)

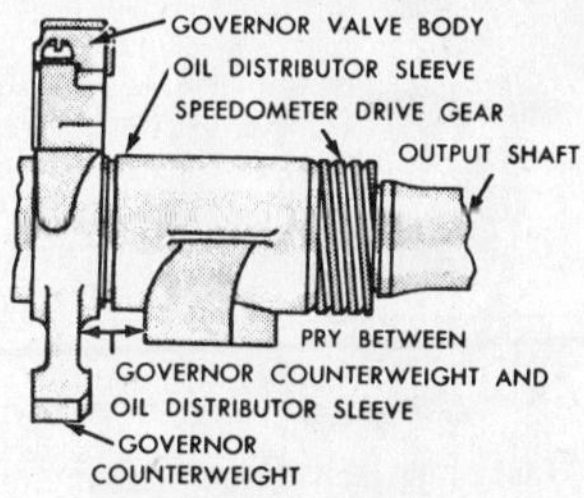

Pressure apply area for removing speedometer gear
(© Ford Motor Co.)

9. Note the position of the band for later reference during assembly. Use the depression in the band end next to the adjusting screw for a reference. Squeeze the ends of the rear band together, tilt the band to the rear, and remove the band from the case.
10. Remove the two center support outer bolts (one on each side) from the case.
11. Hold the end of the input shaft in tight enough to hold the clutch units together and pull the center support and the front and rear clutch assemblies from the case as one unit

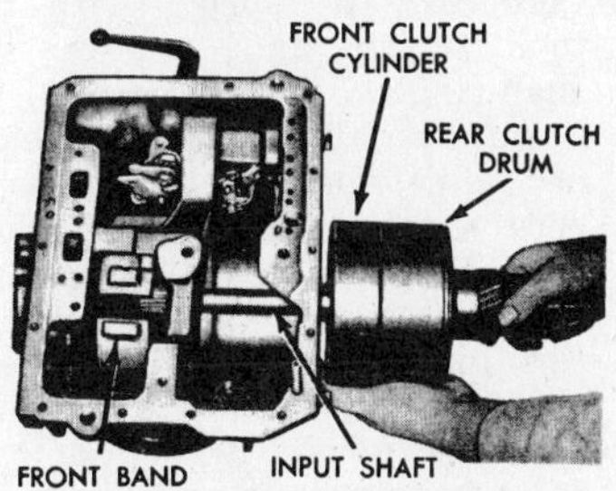

Removing input shaft and clutch
(© Ford Motor Co.)

12. Install the clutch assemblies.
13. Remove the thrust washer from the front of the input shaft.
14. To remove the front band, position the band ends between the case webbing and tilt the bottom of the band rearward. Then, squeeze the ends of the band together and remove from the rear of the case.

Installing output shaft bushing
(© Ford Motor Co.)

15. Lift the front clutch assembly from the primary sun gear shaft.
16. Remove the bronze and the steel thrust washers from the rear clutch assembly. Wire the thrust washers together to assure correct installation.
17. Remove the front clutch seal rings from the primary sun gear shaft.
18. Lift the rear clutch assembly from the primary sun gear shaft.
19. Remove the rear clutch seal rings from the primary sun gear shaft. *Do not break the seal rings.*
20. Remove the primary sun gear shaft front thrust washer.

Rear Brake Drum Support Bushing Removal and Installation

If the rear brake drum support bushing is to be replaced, press the bushing from the support as shown in the illustration. Then, press a new bushing into the brake drum support with the tool shown.

Output Shaft Bushing Removal and Installation

1. Remove the worn bushing by using a cape chisel to break through the bushing wall.
2. Pry the loose ends of the bushing up with an awl and remove the bushing.
3. Install a new bushing on the output shaft hub by pressing it on with the installation tool.

Primary Sun Gear Shaft Seal Ring Replacement

1. Place the primary sun gear shaft in the clutch bench fixture.
2. Check the fit of the seal rings in their respective bores. If equipped with cast iron seal rings, there should be a clearance of 0.002-0.009 in. between the ends. If equipped with teflon

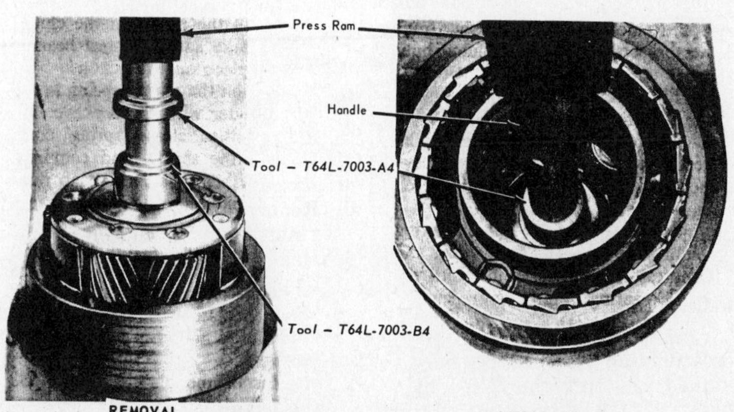

Replacing rear brake drum support bushing (© Ford Motor Co.)

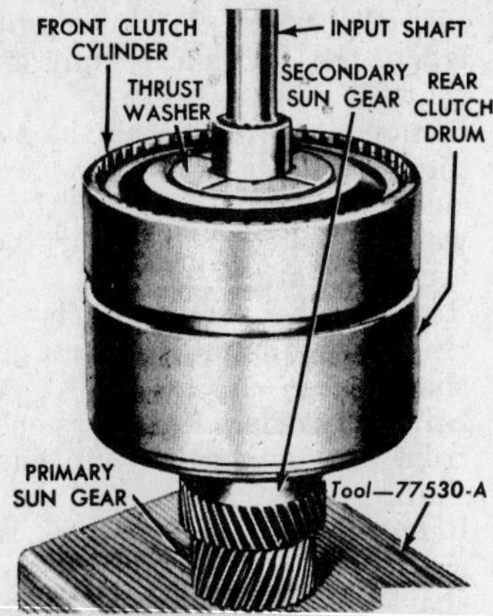

Input shaft and clutch mounted in holding fixture (© Ford Motor Co.)

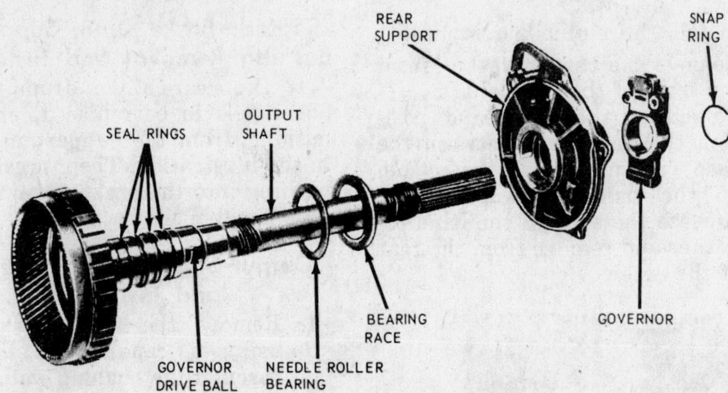

Output shaft disassembled (© Ford Motor Co.)

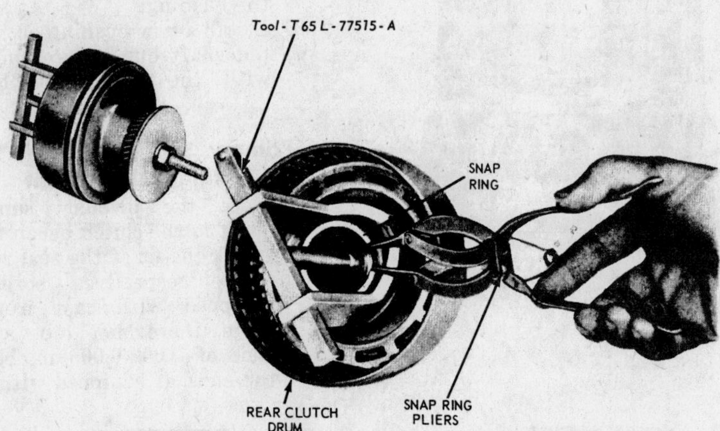

Removing rear clutch spring snap-ring (© Ford Motor Co.)

seals that are worn or damaged, cut the seals from the shaft with a sharp knife. Do not score the ring grooves.

3. Replace the teflon seals with cast iron seal rings, and check for free movement in the groove.

Rear Clutch Disassembly and Assembly

The rear clutch may be removed and installed by doing the following procedure:

1. Remove the clutch pressure plate snap-ring and the pressure plate from the drum. Also, remove the waved cushion spring and the composition and steel plates.

NOTE: in 1967-70 transmissions, composition plates replaced bronze plates and a waved cushion spring was added.

2. Compress the spring with the tool shown and remove the snap-ring with snap-ring pliers.
3. Carefully guide the spring retainer while releasing spring pressure so that the retainer does not lock in the snap-ring grooves.
4. Position the primary sun gear shaft in the rear clutch. Place an air hose nozzle in one of the holes in the shaft and block the other hole. Force the clutch piston out of the clutch drum with air pressure. *Hold one hand over the piston to prevent damaging it.*
5. Remove the inner and outer seal rings from the clutch piston.
6. Remove the rear clutch sun gear bushing if it is worn or damaged by cutting it out with a cape chisel. See illustration. When the bushing is cut through, pry the ends up with an awl and remove the bushing.
7. Install a new rear clutch sun gear bushing
8. Install new inner and outer seal rings on the piston.

Removing rear clutch sun gear bushing (© Ford Motor Co.)

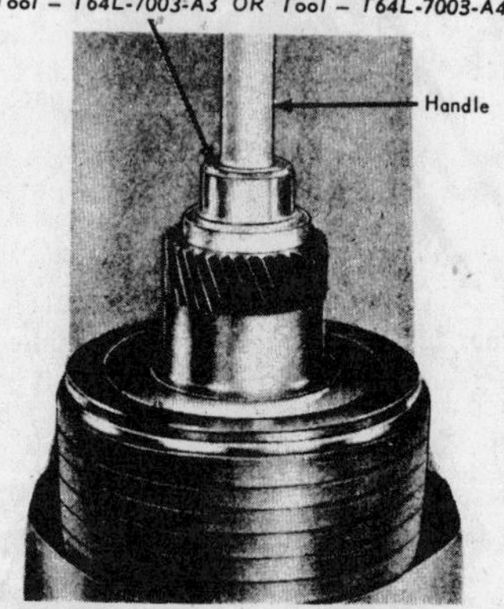

Installing rear clutch sun gear bushing (© Ford Motor Co.)

9. When installing the piston in the clutch drum, lubricate the piston seals and the tools with clean transmission fluid.
10. Push the small fixture down over the cylinder hub.
11. Insert the piston into the large fixture with the seal toward the thin-walled end. See illustration.

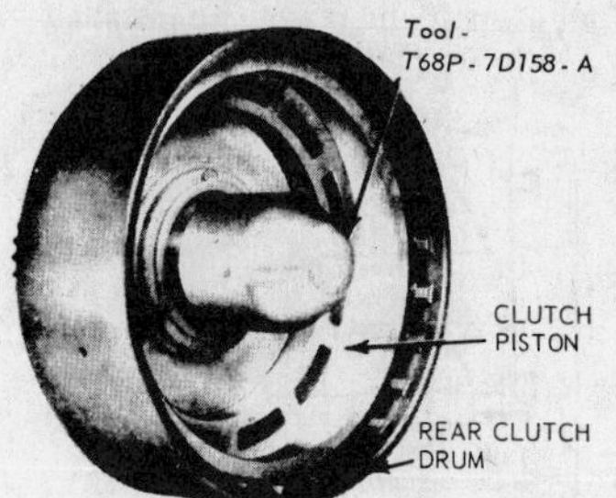

Installing rear clutch piston (© Ford Motor Co.)

12. Hold the piston and large fixture and insert as one unit into the cylinder. Push down over the small fixture until the large tool stops against the shoulder in the cylinder; then push the piston down, out of the tool, until it bottoms in the cylinder. Remove the tools.
13. Install the clutch release spring and position the retainer on the spring.
14. Install the spring compressor retainer and install the snap-ring.

While compressing the spring, guide the retainer to avoid catching on the snap-ring groove. Be sure the snap-ring is fully seated in the groove.

15. Install the composition and steel clutch plates. If new plates are installed, soak them in clean transmission fluid for 15 minutes before assembling them.
16. Install a steel clutch plate and the waved cushion spring. Then, install steel and composition friction plates alternately starting with a steel plate.
17. Install the clutch pressure plate with the bearing surface down. Then install the snap-ring, being sure the snap ring is fully seated in its groove.
18. Check the free pack clearance between the pressure plate and the snap-ring with a feeler gauge. The clearance should be 0.030-0.055 in. If the clearance is not within this range, install a selective snap-ring with one of the following thicknesses: 0.060-0.064, 0.074-0.078, 0.088-0.092, 0.102-0.106 in. Insert the correct snap-ring and recheck the clearance.
19. Install the thrust washer on the primary sun gear shaft. Lubricate all parts with transmission fluid and install the two center seal rings.
20. Install the rear clutch on the primary sun gear shaft. *Be sure all loose needle bearings are in the hub correctly.* Install the two seal rings in the front grooves.
21. Install the steel and the bronze thrust washers on the front of the secondary sun gear assembly. If the steel washer is chamfered, place the chamfered side down.

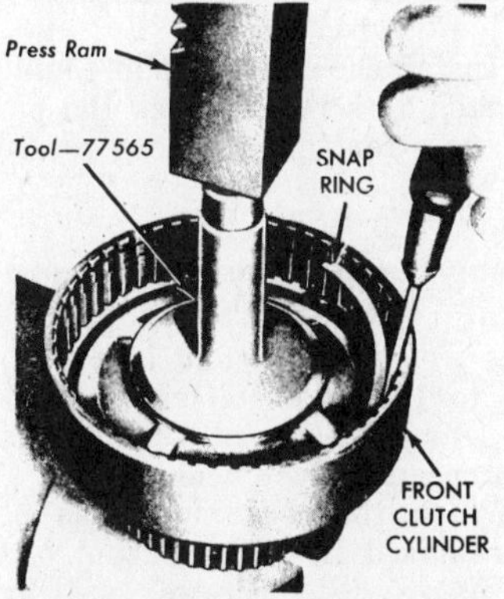

Removing front clutch snap-ring
(© Ford Motor Co.)

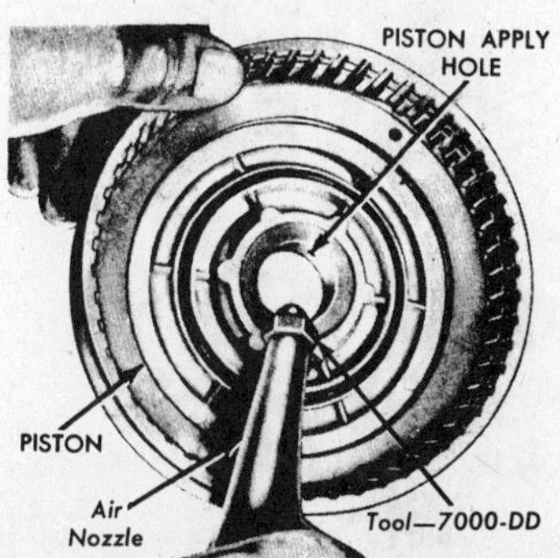

Removing front clutch piston
(© Ford Motor Co.)

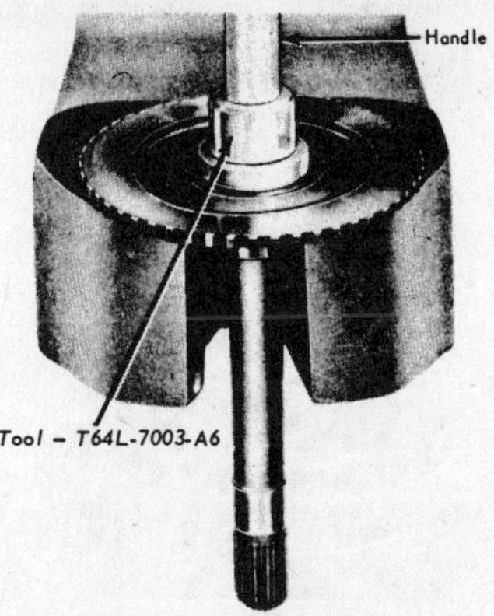

Installing input shaft bushing
(© Ford Motor Co.)

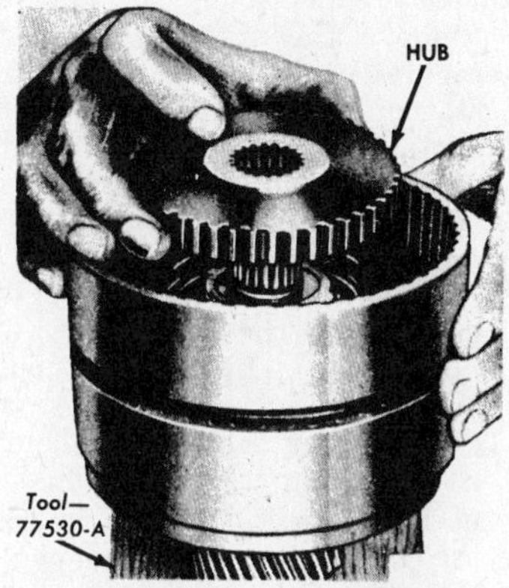

Installing front clutch hub
(© Ford Motor Co.)

Installing pressure plate
(© Ford Motor Co.)

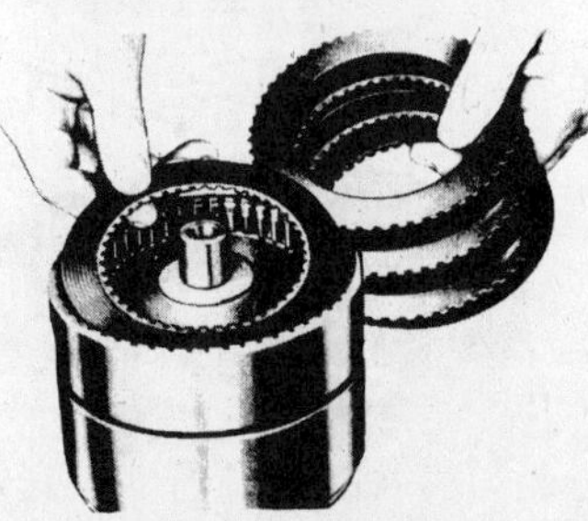
Installing clutch plates
(© Ford Motor Co.)

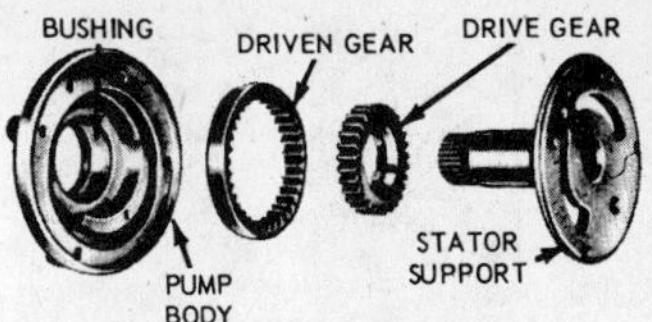

Front pump disassembled
(© Ford Motor Co.)

Front Clutch Disassembly and Assembly

1. Remove the clutch cover snap-ring by prying it up with a screwdriver, and remove the input shaft from the clutch drum.
2. Remove the thrust washer from the thrust surface of the clutch hub. Lift the clutch hub straight up to remove it from the clutch drum.
3. Remove the composition and the steel clutch plates and the pressure plate from the clutch drum.
4. Place the front clutch spring compressor on the release spring, position the clutch drum on the bed of an arbor press, and compress the release spring with the arbor press until the release spring snap-ring can be removed (see illustration).
5. Remove the clutch release spring from the clutch drum.
6. Using the special air nozzle shown in the illustration, place the air nozzle against the clutch apply hole in the front clutch housing and force the piston out of the housing.
7. Remove the piston inner seal from the clutch housing and remove the piston outer seal from the groove in the piston.
8. Remove the input shaft bushing if it is worn or damaged. Use a cape chisel and cut along the bushing seam until the chisel breaks through the bushing wall. Pry up the loose ends of the bushing with an awl and remove the bushing.
9. Put a new bushing over the end of the installation tool and position the tool and bushing over the bushing hole. Then, press the bushing into the input shaft.

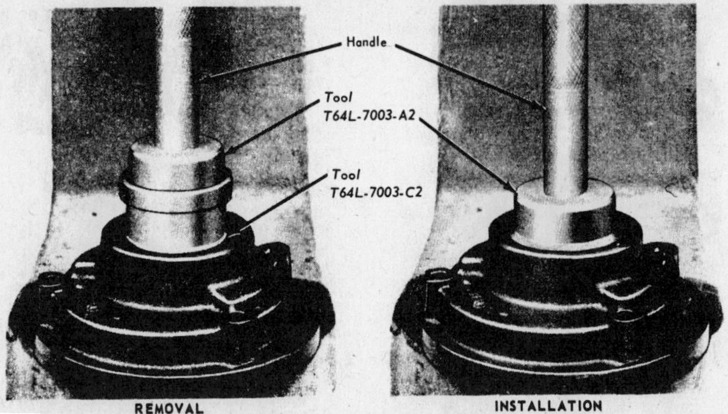

Replacing front pump housing bushing (© Ford Motor Co.)

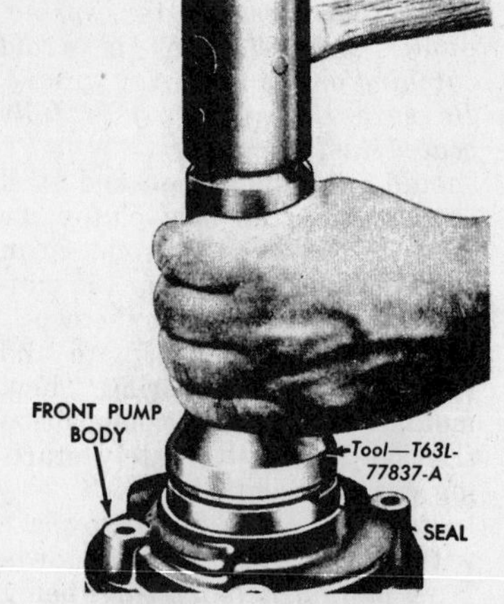

Installing front pump seal (© Ford Motor Co.)

10. Install a new piston inner seal ring in the clutch cylinder and a new piston outer seal in the groove in the piston. Lubricate all parts with transmission fluid before installation.
11. Install the piston in the clutch housing. *Be sure the steel bearing ring is in place on the piston.*
12. Place the release spring in the clutch cylinder with the concave side up. Put the release spring compressor on the spring and compress the spring with an arbor press. Then, install the snap-ring in the groove in the piston.
13. Install the front clutch housing on the primary sun gear shaft by rotating the clutch units to mesh the rear clutch plates with the serrations on the clutch hub. *Do not break the seal rings.*
14. Install the clutch hub in the clutch cylinder with the deep counterbore down. Install the thrust washer on the clutch hub.
15. Install the pressure plate in the clutch cylinder with the bearing surface up (see illustration). Install the composition and the steel clutch plates alternately, starting with a composition plate (see illustration). Lubricate all the plates with transmission fluid before installing. The last friction plate is selective in thickness. Select the thickest plate that will be a minimum of 0.010 in. below the input shaft shoulder in the cylinder. All other plates should be the thinnest available.
16. Install the turbine shaft in the clutch cylinder, and then install the snap-ring in the groove in the piston.
17. Install the thrust washer on the turbine shaft.

Front Pump Disassembly and Assembly

The front pump is disassembled and reassembled according to the procedure below:

1. Remove the stator support attaching screws and remove the stator support. Mark the top surface of the pump driven gear with Prussian blue to assure correct assembly. *Do not scratch the pump gears.*
2. Remove the drive and driven gears from the pump body (see illustration). Inspect the pump body housing, gear pockets and crescent for scoring and burrs.
3. If the pump housing bushing needs replacing, press it from the front housing as shown in the illustration. Press a new bushing into the pump housing with the tools shown.
4. If any parts other than the stator support or bushings are defective, replace the pump as a unit. Minor burrs and scores may be removed with crocus cloth. The stator support is serviced separately.
5. Bolt the front pump to the transmission case with capscrews. Install the oil seal remover and pull the front seal from the pump body. See illustration.
6. Clean and inspect the counterbore, smoothing any rough spots with crocus cloth.
7. Remove the pump body from the transmission case.
8. Coat the new seal with a good sealing compound. Then place the seal in the pump body and drive the seal into the pump body with the tool shown in the illustration. The tool may be reworked to install the latest type of seal if necessary.
9. Place the pump driven gear in the pump body with the mark facing down. Install the drive gear in the pump body with the chamfered side of the flats facing down.
10. Install the stator support and attaching screws. Check the pump gears for free and easy rotation.

Rear Pump Disassembly and Assembly

The rear pump that is found in 1964 to 1967 transmissions may be disassembled and reassembled using the procedure given below:

1. When the rear pump has been removed from the output shaft, remove the screws and lockwashers holding the pump cover to the pump body (see illustration). Remove the pump cover.

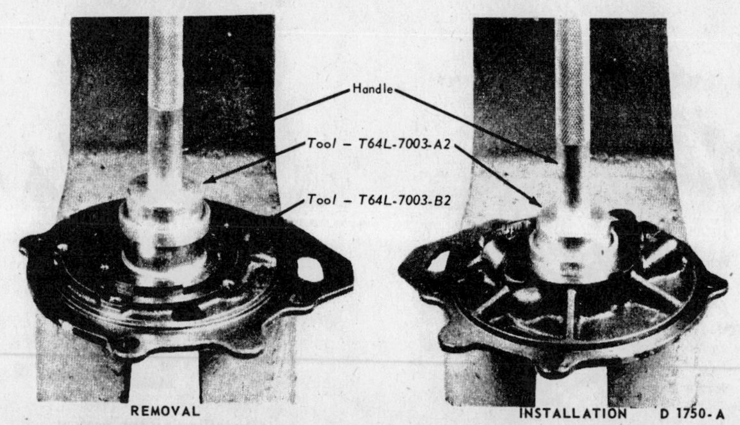

Replacing rear support housing bushing (© Ford Motor Co.)

REGULATOR BODY
CONTROL PRESSURE VALVE
VALVE STOP
CONVERTER PRESSURE VALVE
RETAINER
CONVERTER PRESSURE VALVE SPRINGS
RETAINER
SEPARATOR PLATE
COVER

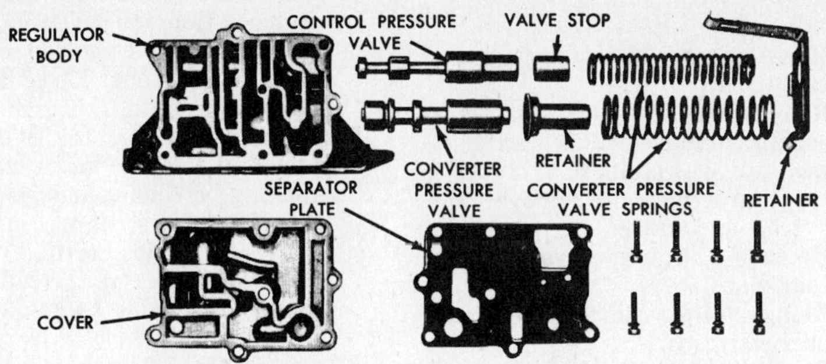

Pressure regulator assembly (© Ford Motor Co.)

COVER
CHECK BALL AND SPRING
PLATE
3-2 KICKDOWN CONTROL VALVE
1-2 SHIFT ACCUMLATOR LOCKOUT VALVE
1-2 SHIFT ACCUMLATOR VALVE
SPRING RETAINER
SEPARATOR PLATE
VALVE INHIBITOR
SIDE PLATE
1-2 SHIFT VALVE
LOWER BODY
TRANSITION VALVE
2-3 SHIFT VALVE
2-3 SHIFT DELAY VALVE
2-3 DELAY AND THROTTLE REDUCING VALVE SLEEVE
LOW SERVO MODULATOR VALVE
LOW SERVO LOCKOUT VALVE
SEPARATOR PLATE
END PLATE
FRONT PLATE
THROTTLE REDUCING VALVE
COMPENSATOR SLEEVE AND PLUG
DOWNSHIFT VALVE
MANUAL VALVE
THROTTLE BOOST SHORT VALVE AND SLEEVE
SPRING RETAINER
2-1 SCHEDULING VALVE
THROTTLE BOOST VALVE
UPPER BODY
COMPENSATOR VALVE
COMPENSATOR CUT-BACK VALVE
REAR PLATE
SEPARATOR
PLUG
THROTTLE VALVE
THROTTLE VALVE BODY

Control valve—disassembled (© Ford Motor Co.)

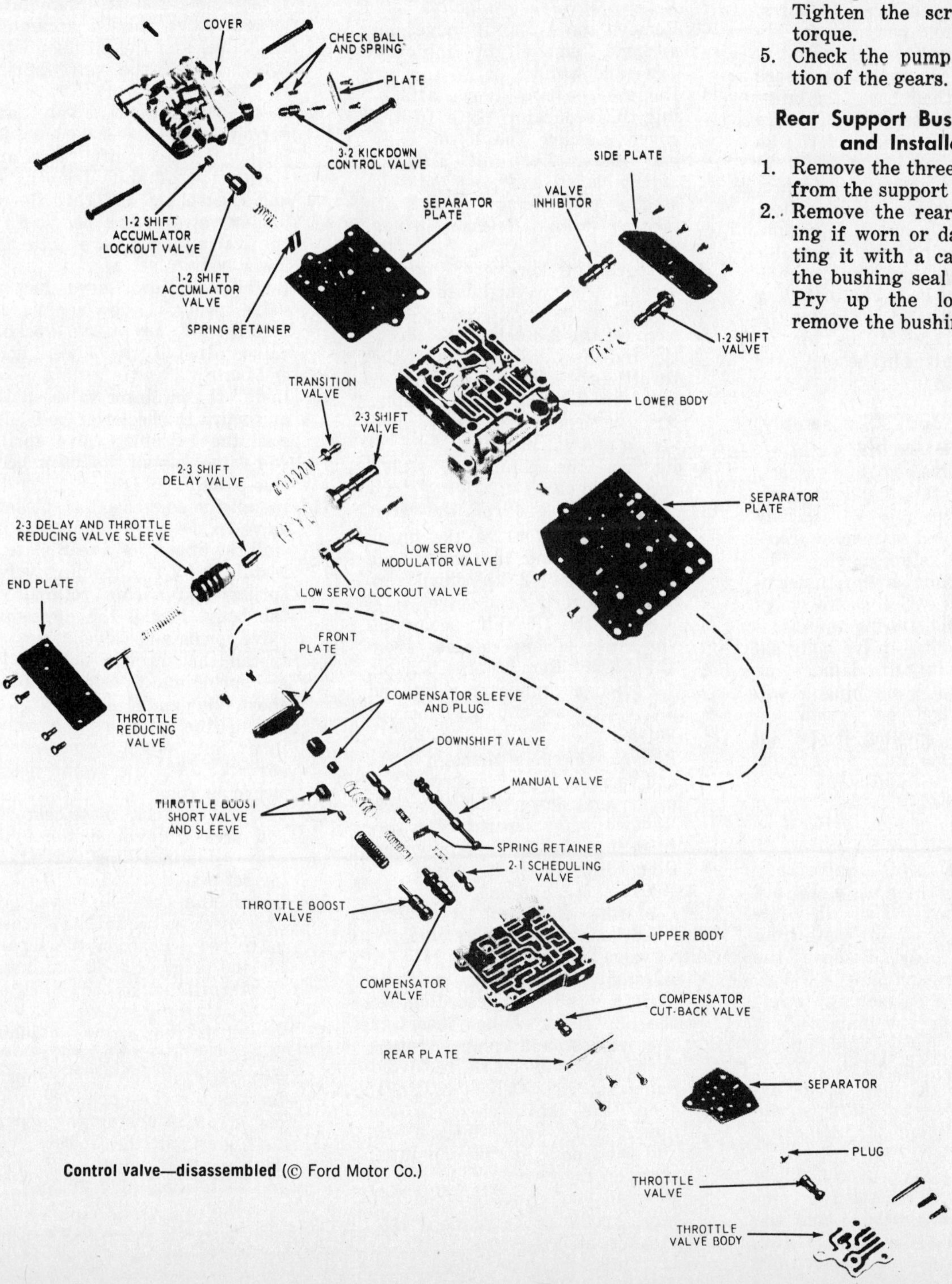

2. Mark the top faces of the pump drive and the pump driven gears with Prussian blue for realignment during assembly. *Do not scratch or gouge the pump gears.*
3. Remove the drive and driven gears from the pump body.
4. After cleaning and inspection, place the pump drive gear in the body with the mark facing up. Place the pump driven gear in the body with its mark facing up and in line with the drive gear mark. Install the pump cover, attaching screws and lockwashers. Tighten the screws to proper torque.
5. Check the pump for free rotation of the gears.

Rear Support Bushing Removal and Installation

1. Remove the three pressure tubes from the support housing.
2. Remove the rear support bushing if worn or damaged by cutting it with a cape chisel along the bushing seal until it breaks. Pry up the loose ends and remove the bushing.

3. Press a new bushing into the support housing with the tool shown in the illustration.
4. Install the pressure tubes.

Pressure Regulator Disassembly and Assembly

1. Remove the valves from the regulator body.
2. Remove the regulator body cover attaching screws, and remove the cover (see illustration).
3. Remove the separator plate.
4. Clean all parts in solvent and dry with dry compressed air.
5. Inspect the regulator body and cover mating surfaces for burrs. Check the fluid passages for obstructions. Inspect the control pressure and converter pressure valves and their bores for burrs and scoring. Remove all burrs carefully with crocus cloth. Be sure the valves move freely in their bores when dry. Inspect the valve springs for distortion.
6. Reassemble the pressure regulator by placing the separator plate and the regulator cover on the regulator body and installing the attaching screws. Tighten the screws to 20-30 in. lbs. torque. Insert the valves in the regulator body.

Control Valve Body Disassembly and Assembly

The control valve body is disassembled according to the procedure given below. The reassembly is basically the reverse of the disassembly procedure but careful reference should be made to the accompanying illustration showing the entire control valve body disassembled. During the disassembly of the control valve body assembly, be careful not to damage the valves and keep everything clean. Place the valve body on a clean surface while disassembling it. *Do not separate the upper and lower valve bodies and cover until after the valves have been removed.*

1. Remove the manual valve (see illustration).
2. Remove the throttle valve body and the separator plate. Do not lose the check valve when removing the separator plate from the valve body. Remove the throttle valve and plug.
3. Remove one attaching screw from the separator plate holding it to the lower valve body. Remove the upper body front plate. *Since the plate is spring-loaded, hold the plate steady while removing the attaching screws.*
4. Remove the compensator sleeve and plug, and remove the compensator valve springs and the compensator valve.
5. Remove the throttle boost short valve and sleeve. Remove the throttle boost valve spring and valve.
6. Remove the downshift valve and spring. Remove the 2-1 scheduling valve retainer from the valve body and remove the spring and valve.
7. Remove the upper valve body rear plate.
8. Remove the compensator cut-back valve.
9. Remove the lower body side plate. *This plate is spring-loaded and must be held steady while removing the attaching screws. Release springs gradually.*
10. Remove the 1-2 shift valve and spring. Remove the inhibitor valve and spring.
11. Remove the two screws attaching the separator plate to the cover. Remove the lower body end plate. *The end plate is spring-loaded and must be held steady while removing the attaching screws. Release springs gradually.*
12. Remove the low servo lockout valve, low servo modulator valve and spring.
13. Remove the 2-3 delay and throttle reducing valve sleeve, the throttle reducing valve, spring, and the 2-3 shift delay valve. Also, remove the 2-3 shift valve spring and valve.
14. Remove the transition valve spring and valve.
15. Remove the plate from the valve body cover. Remove the check ball spring and the check ball. Remove the 3-2 kickdown control valve spring and valve.
16. Remove the 1-2 shift accumulator valve spring retainer from the cover. Remove the spring, 1-2 shift accumulator valve and 1-2 shift accumulator lockout valve.
17. Remove the long through bolts and screws and separate the upper and lower valve bodies. Remove the separator plates from the valve bodies and cover. Do not lose the check valves.

After cleaning and inspecting the parts of the disassembled control valve body assembly, reassemble the control valve body as follows:

1. Arrange all the parts in their correct positions according to the illustration. When inserting the valves and plugs, rotate them in their bores to avoid damaging the soft body castings.
2. Place the check valve in the upper body (see illustration) and then position the separator plate on the body.
3. Position the lower body on the upper body and loosely install the attaching screws.
4. Put the check valve in the cover and position the cover and separator plate on the lower body. Install the four long through bolts.
5. Align the separator with the upper and lower valve body attaching bolt holes and install the attaching bolts, tightening them to 48-72 in. lbs. torque. *Excessive tightening of the bolts may distort the valve bodies, causing valves or plugs to stick.*
6. Install the 3-2 kickdown control valve and spring and the check ball and spring in the cover. Install the plate.
7. Insert the 1-2 shift accumulator lockout valve, the 1-2 accumulator valve, and the spring in the cover. Install the valve spring retainer.
8. Install the transition valve and spring in the lower body. Also install the 2-3 shift valve and spring, the 2-3 shift delay valve, and the spring and throttle reducing valve in the sleeve. Slide the valve and sleeve into the lower body.
9. Install the low servo lockout valve spring, the low servo modulator, and low servo lockout valves. Install the lower body end plate.
10. Install the inhibitor valve spring and valve in the lower body. Install the 1-2 shift valve spring and valve. Install the lower body side plate.
11. Install the compensator cut-back valve in the upper body and install the upper body rear plate.
12. Install the 2-1 scheduling valve, spring, and spring retainer in the body. Install the downshift valve spring and valve.
13. Install the throttle boost valve and spring and the throttle boost short valve and sleeve.
14. Install the compensator valve, inner and outer compensator springs and the compensator sleeve and plug.
15. Position the front plate correctly and press it against the upper body while installing the attaching screws.
16. Install the throttle valve, plug and check valve in the throttle valve body. Position the separator on the upper body and install the throttle valve body with the three attaching screws.
17. Install the four screws attaching the cover to the lower body, the two screws attaching the separator plate to the upper body, and one screw attaching the separator plate to the lower body. Tighten the cover and body screws to the proper torque.

Front Servo Disassembly and Assembly

The front servo is disassembled and reassembled according to the procedure given below. Refer to the disassembled view of the front servo to identify the parts.

1. Remove the servo piston retainer snap-ring. Since the servo piston is spring-loaded, hold the piston steady while removing the snap-ring and release the spring pressure gradually.

2. Remove the servo piston retainer, servo piston, and the return piston from the servo body. It may be necessary to tap the piston stem lightly with a soft-faced hammer to separate the piston retainer from the servo body.

3. On PHD models, remove the screw and washer from the end of the piston stem and separate the piston retainer, return piston, and the servo piston.

4. Remove all seal rings and the spring from the servo body.

5. Inspect the servo body for cracks and the piston bore and the servo piston stem for scores. Check all fluid passages for obstructions.

6. Check the actuating lever for free movement and wear. If it is necessary to replace the actuating lever shaft, remove the retaining pin and push the shaft out of the bracket. If the shaft is not held in place by a retaining pin, it is held in place by serrations on one side and it is a press-fit. To remove this type of shaft, press on the end opposite the serrations. Inspect the adjusting screw threads and the threads in the lever.

7. Check the servo spring and servo band strut for distortion.

8. Inspect the servo band lining for excessive wear and bonding to the metal. Replace the lining if it is worn so much that the grooves are not clearly seen. Inspect the band ends for cracks and check the band for distortion.

9. Lubricate all parts of the front servo by soaking in transmission fluid to ease assembly.

10. Install the inner and outer seal rings on the piston retainer. Install new O-rings on the return piston and the servo piston. See the illustration and accompanying table for the servo components used in each model of the FMX transmission.

11. On PHD models, tap the piston stem into the servo piston. Insert the servo piston in the piston retainer. Tap the return piston onto the piston stem and into the piston retainer. Be sure the dished side of the return piston is toward the servo piston. Fasten the return piston to the stem with a screw and plain washer.

12. Place the servo piston release spring in the servo body. Install the servo piston, retainer, and return piston in the servo body as an assembly. Compress this assembly into the body and secure it with the snap-ring. *Be sure the snap-ring is fully seated in the groove.*

13. Install the adjusting screw and locknut in the actuating lever if they were removed.

Rear Servo Disassembly and Assembly

1. Remove the servo actuating lever shaft retaining pin with a 1/8-inch punch. Remove the shaft and actuating lever needle bearings and thrust washers. See illustration.

2. Press down on the servo spring retainer and remove the snap ring, releasing the pressure on the retainer slowly to prevent the spring from flying out.

3. Remove the retainer and the servo spring.

4. Force the servo piston out of the body with air pressure, holding one hand over the piston to prevent damage.

5. Remove the accumulator piston from the servo piston.

6. On transmissions from 1964 to 1967 a piston seal ring must be removed. FMX transmissions in 1968 to 1970 do not have this seal ring.

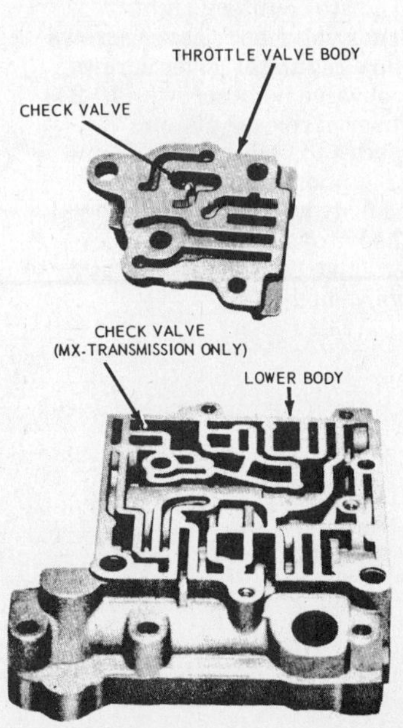

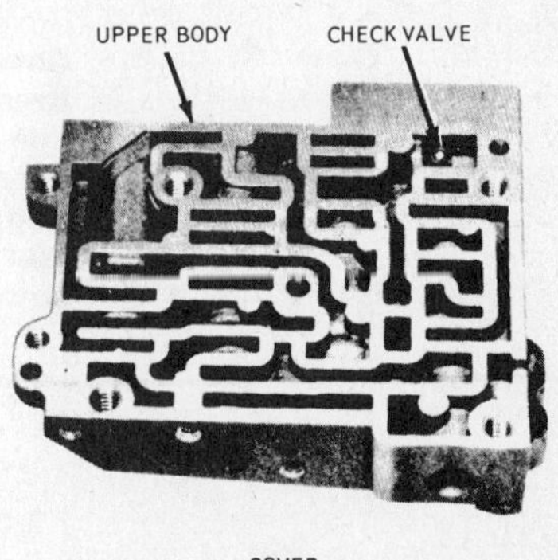

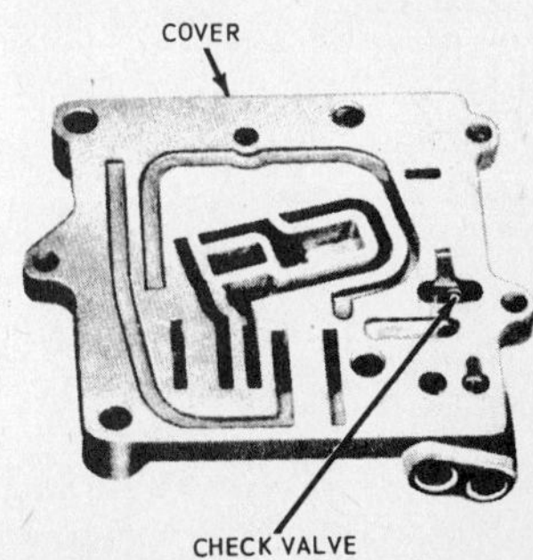

Check valve locations (© Ford Motor Co.)

7. On those transmissions that have a seal ring, install a new seal ring in the servo piston.

8. Install the accumulator piston in the servo piston. Install the servo piston in the servo body. Install the servo spring with the small coiled end against the servo piston. *Be sure to lubricate all parts with transmission fluid to aid assembly.*

9. Install the spring retainer, compressing the spring with a C-clamp. Then, install the snap-ring in the groove.

10. Install the needle bearings in the actuating lever. Then, install the actuating lever and thrust washers with the socket in the lever bearing on the piston stem. Install the actuating lever shaft, aligning the retaining pin holes, and install the pin.

11. Check the actuating lever for free movement.

Torque Limits

When assembling the various components of the FMX automatic transmission, the bolts and nuts must be tightened within a specified range to prevent damage to the bolts, nuts or the transmission conponents. The torque limits for the FMX and C6 automatic transmissions are listed below in the accompanying tables.

Torque Limits for FMX Automatic Transmission

	Ft. Lbs.
Converter to flywheel	23-28
Converter hsg. to trans. case	40-50
Front pump to trans. case	17-22
Front servo to trans. case	30-35
Rear servo to trans. case	40-45
Upper valve body to lower valve body	4-6
Oil pan to case	10-13
Converter cover to converter hsg.	12-16
Regulator to case	17-22
Planetary support to trans. case	20-25
Control valve body to trans. case	8-10
Diaphragm assy. to case	20-30
Cooler return check valve	9-12
Extension assy. to trans. case	30-40
Pressure gauge tap	7-15
Converter drain plug	15-28
Rear band adjusting screw to case	35-40
Front band adjusting screw locknut	20-25
Manual valve inner lever to shaft	20-30
Downshift lever to shaft	17-20
Filler tube to engine	20-25
Transmission to engine	40-50
Neutral start switch actuator lever bolt	6-10
Steering col. lock rod adj. nut	10-20
	In. Lbs.
Governor to counterweight	50-60
Governor valve body cover screws	20-30
Pressure regulator cover screws	20-30
Control valve body screws (10-24)	20-30
Front servo release piston	20-30
End plates to body	20-30
Stator support to pump	25-35
Lower body and cover plate to valve body	20-30
T.V. body to valve body	20-30
Lower valve body cover and plate to valve body	48-72

Diagnosis

This diagnosis guide covers the most common symptoms and is an aid to careful diagnosis. The items to check are listed in the sequence to be followed for quickest results. Thus, follow the checks in the order given for the particular transmission type.

TROUBLE SYMPTOMS	Items to Check	
	In Truck	Out of Truck
Car will not move in any selector position	ABC	cab
Engine speed flares, as slipping clutch	ABDFE	def
Engine speed flares on upshift	ADBG	ghi
Transmission will not upshift	HIJ	klm
Harsh upshift	JDGK	
Harsh deceleration downshift	DLMNG	
No downshift	MHI	
Clutch failure, burnt plates	DAHO	hi
Excessive creep in drive	JL	
Car creeps in neutral	J	hd
No drive in reverse	J	jng
Improper shift points	JIH	l
Unable to push-start car		m
Oil leaks	PQG	oa
Oil forced out at filler tube	AQ	p

Key to Checks

A. Oil level
B. Oil screen
C. Pressure regulator valve
D. Band adjustment
E. Servo seal
F. Servo blocked
G. Vacuum modulator or line
H. Governor
I. Throttle valve
J. Throttle linkage
K. Hydraulic modulator valve
L. Too high idle speed
M. Valves malfunctioning
N. Make pressure tests
O. Driving too fast in low
P. Oil leaks at external points
Q. Oil cooler or lines
a. Front pump
b. Input shaft
c. Front pump priming valve
d. Low band
e. Low band linkage
f. Converter stator
g. Clutch feed blocked
h. High clutch
i. Front clutch relief valve
j. Reverse clutch relief valve
k. Low clutch valve stuck
l. Rear pump priming valve
m. Rear pump or drive
n. Low clutch
o. Front pump attaching bolts
p. Pump circuit leakage

General Description

The Powerglide transmission is a two speed unit with a one piece aluminum case and an aluminum case extension.

Driving ranges are low, high and reverse, with a throttle controlled downshift to low range available for sudden acceleration.

The oil pump is the gear type; the pump housing is used as the front bulkhead of the transmission. The torque converter is a three element welded unit bolted to the engine flywheel; it drives through a two speed planetary gearset. Low range uses a band clutch; drive and reverse ranges use disc clutches. The valve body assembly is bolted to the bottom of the transmission case; the modulator valve bore is in the upper part of the valve body assembly. The governor is mounted to the output shaft, inside the case extension.

Transmission removal and installation, shift linkage adjustment, low band adjustment in the truck, neutral safety switches, and transmission downshift linkages are covered in the truck section.

Fluid Change Schedule

For 1964-66 models, it is not necessary to change the automatic transmission fluid except when the transmission is removed. For 1967 models, the manufacturer recommends draining the transmission sump every 12,000 miles; for 1968-70 models, every 24,000 miles; 2 quarts to all models. The fluid level should then be rechecked. This should be done with the engine idling, the selector lever in Neutral, and the transmission at operating temperature.

Transmission Disassembly

Extension, Governor and Rear Oil Pump—1964-66 Models

1. Place transmission in a holding fixture, if possible.
2. Remove converter holding tool, then lift off the converter.
3. If replacement is necessary, remove speedometer driven gear. Loosen cap screw and retainer clip and remove gear from extension.
4. Remove transmission extension by removing five attaching bolts. Note seal ring on rear pump body.
5. Remove speedometer drive gear from output shaft.
6. Remove C-clip from governor shaft of the weight side of governor, then remove the shaft and governor valve from the opposite side of the governor assembly and the two belleville springs.
7. Loosen the governor drive screw and slide the governor over the end of the output shaft.
8. Remove four bolts holding the rear oil pump to the transmission case and remove the pump body, drain back baffle, extension seal ring, drive and driven gears.
9. Remove oil pump drive pin. (This is of extreme importance.)
10. Remove the rear pump wear plate.

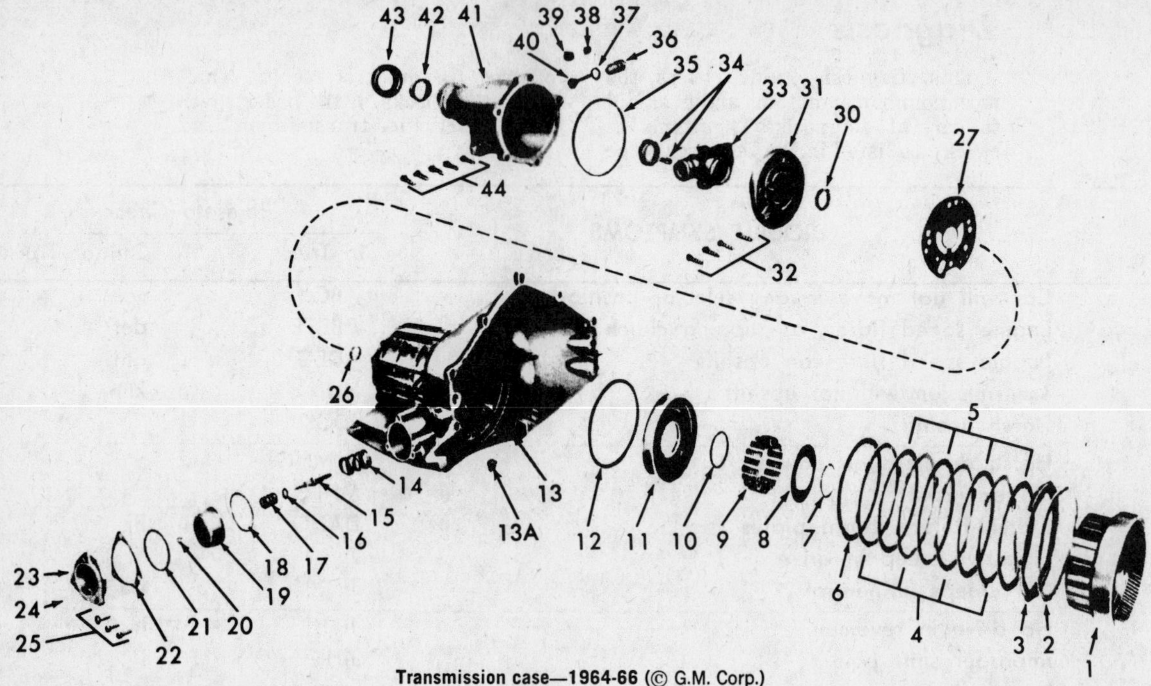

Transmission case—1964-66 (© G.M. Corp.)

1 Reverse ring gear
2 Reverse clutch pack snap ring
3 Reverse clutch pressure plate
*4 Reverse clutch reaction plates
*5 Reverse clutch drive plates
6 Reverse clutch cushion spring
7 Reverse clutch piston return spring retainer snap ring
8 Reverse clutch piston return spring retainer
9 Reverse clutch piston return springs
10 Reverse clutch piston inner seal
11 Reverse clutch piston
12 Reverse clutch piston outer seal
13 Transmission case
*V-283 models use 5 plates each
V-327 & V-409 use 6 plates each
14 Servo piston return spring
15 Servo piston rod
16 Servo piston apply spring seat
17 Servo piston apply spring
18 Servo piston seal ring
19 Servo piston
20 Servo piston rod spring retainer
21 Servo cover seal
22 Servo cover gasket
23 Servo cover
24 Servo cover plug
25 Servo cover bolts
26 Transmission case bushing
27 Rear pump wear plate
28 Rear pump drive gear
29 Rear pump driven gear
30 Rear pump body bushing
31 Rear pump body
32 Rear pump assembly to case attaching bolts
33 Governor assembly
34 Speedometer drive gear
35 Rear pump seal
36 Speedometer shaft fitting
37 Speedometer shaft fitting oil seal
38 Lock plate attaching screw
39 Lock plate
40 Speedometer driven gear
41 Transmission extension
42 Extension bushing
43 Extension oil seal
44 Extension to case attaching screws

Transmission Internal Components

11. Rotate holding fixture, or turn the transmission, until the front end is pointing up. Then remove the seven front oil pump bolts. (The bolt holes are of unequal spacing to prevent incorrect location upon installation.)
12. Remove the front oil pump and stator shaft assembly and the selective fit thrust washer using an inertia puller or substitute.
13. Release tension on the low band adjustment, then with transmission horizontal, grasp the transmission input shaft and carefully work it and the clutch drum out of the case. Be careful not to lose the low sun gear bushing from the input shaft. The low sun gear thrust washer will probably remain in the planet carrier.
14. The low brake band and struts may now be removed.
15. Remove the planet carrier and the output shaft thrust caged bearing from the front of the transmission.
16. Remove reverse ring gear if it did not come out with the planet carrier.
17. With a large screwdriver, remove the reverse clutch pack retainer ring and lift out the reverse clutch plates and the cushion spring.
18. Install reverse piston spring compressor through rear bore of the case, with the flat plate on the rear face of the case, and turn down wing nut to compress the rear piston spring retainer and springs. Then remove the snap ring. A spring compressor may be made up from a suitable length bolt and large flat washers.
19. Remove the compression tool, the reverse pistol spring retainer, and the 17 piston return springs.
20. Remove the rear piston by applying air pressure to the reverse port in the rear of the transmission case. Remove inner and outer seals.
21. Remove the three servo cover bolts, servo cover, piston and spring.

Oil Pan and Valve Body

NOTE: the oil pan and valve body may be serviced without removing the extension, and internal components, covered in the preceding steps.

22. Rotate the transmission until the unit is upside down (oil pan on top). Remove oil pan attaching bolts, oil pan, and gasket.
23. Remove vacuum modulator and gasket, and vacuum modulator plunger, dampening spring, and valve.

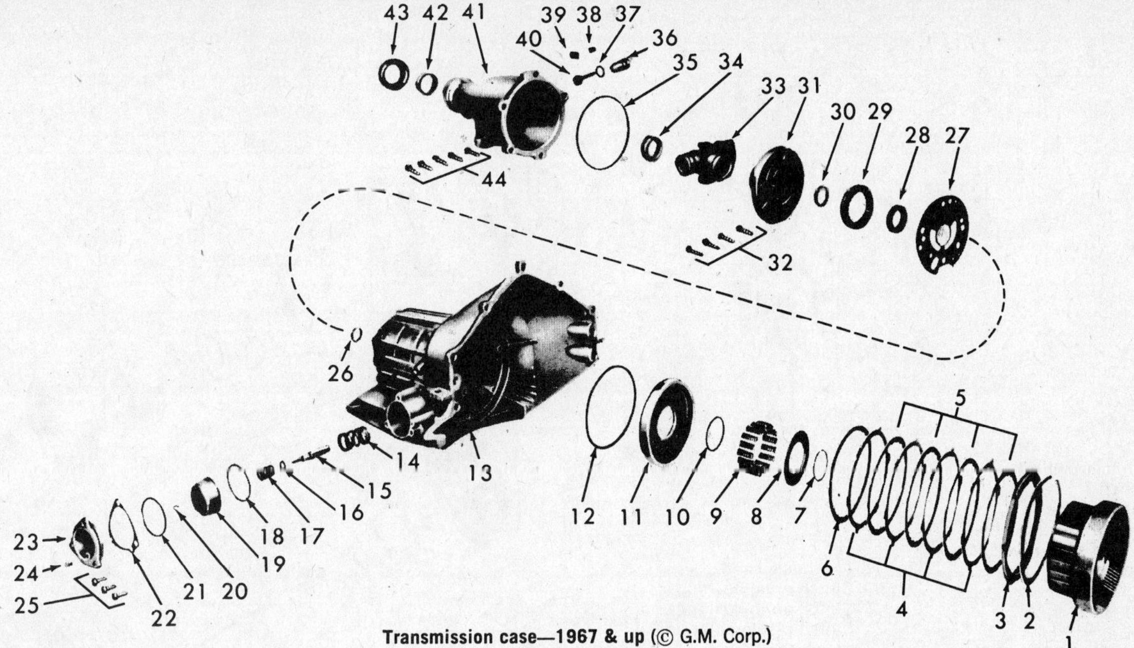

Transmission case—1967 & up (© G.M. Corp.)

1 Reverse ring gear
2 Reverse clutch pack snap ring
3 Reverse clutch pressure plate
4 Reverse clutch reaction plates
5 Reverse clutch drive plates
6 Reverse clutch cushion spring
7 Reverse clutch piston return spring retainer snap ring
8 Reverse clutch piston return spring retainer
9 Reverse clutch piston return springs
10 Reverse clutch piston inner seal
11 Reverse clutch piston
12 Reverse clutch piston outer seal
13 Transmission case
13A Transmission case screen
14 Servo piston return spring
15 Servo piston rod
16 Servo piston apply spring seat
17 Servo piston apply spring
18 Servo piston seal ring
19 Servo piston
20 Servo piston rod spring retainer
21 Servo cover seal
22 Servo cover gasket
23 Servo cover
24 Servo cover plug
25 Servo cover bolts
26 Transmission case bushing
27 Gasket
30 Governor support bushing
31 Governor support
32 Governor support to case attaching bolts
33 Governor assembly
34 Speedometer drive gear and clip
35 Seal
36 Speedometer shaft fitting
37 Speedometer shaft fitting oil seal
38 Lock plate attaching screw
39 Lock plate
40 Speedometer driven gear
41 Transmission extension
42 Extension bushing
43 Extension oil seal
44 Extension to case attaching screws

24. Remove two bolts holding the detent guide plate to the valve body and the transmission case. Remove the guide plate and the range selector detent roller spring.
25. Remove the remaining valve body-to-transmission case attaching bolts and lift out the valve body and gasket. Disengage the servo apply tube from the transmission case as the valve body is removed.
26. If necessary, the throttle valve, shift and parking actuator levers and the parking pawl and bracket may be removed.

Unit Assembly Overhaul

Converter and Stator

The converter is a welded assembly and no internal repairs are possible. Check the seams for stress or breaks and replace the converter if necessary.

Front Pump

Seal Replacement

If the front pump seal requires replacement, remove the pump from the transmission, pry out and replace the seal. Drive new seal into place. Then, if no further work is needed on the front pump, reinstall it into the case. (The outer edge of the seal should be coated with non-hardening sealer before installation.)

Disassembly

1. Remove pump cover-to-body attaching bolts and the cover.
2. Remove pump gears from body.
3. Remove rubber seal from pump body.

Inspection

1. Wash all parts in solvent. Blow out all oil passages.
2. Inspect pump gears for nicks or damage.
3. Inspect body and cover faces for nicks or scoring. Inspect cover hub outside diameter for nicks .010 in. below the surface.
9. With all parts clean and dry, install pump gears and check:
   a. clearance between outside diameter of driven gear and body should be .0035-.0065 in.
   b. clearance between inside diameter of driven gear and crescent should be .003-.009 in.

Removing rear oil pump drive pin (© G.M. Corp.)

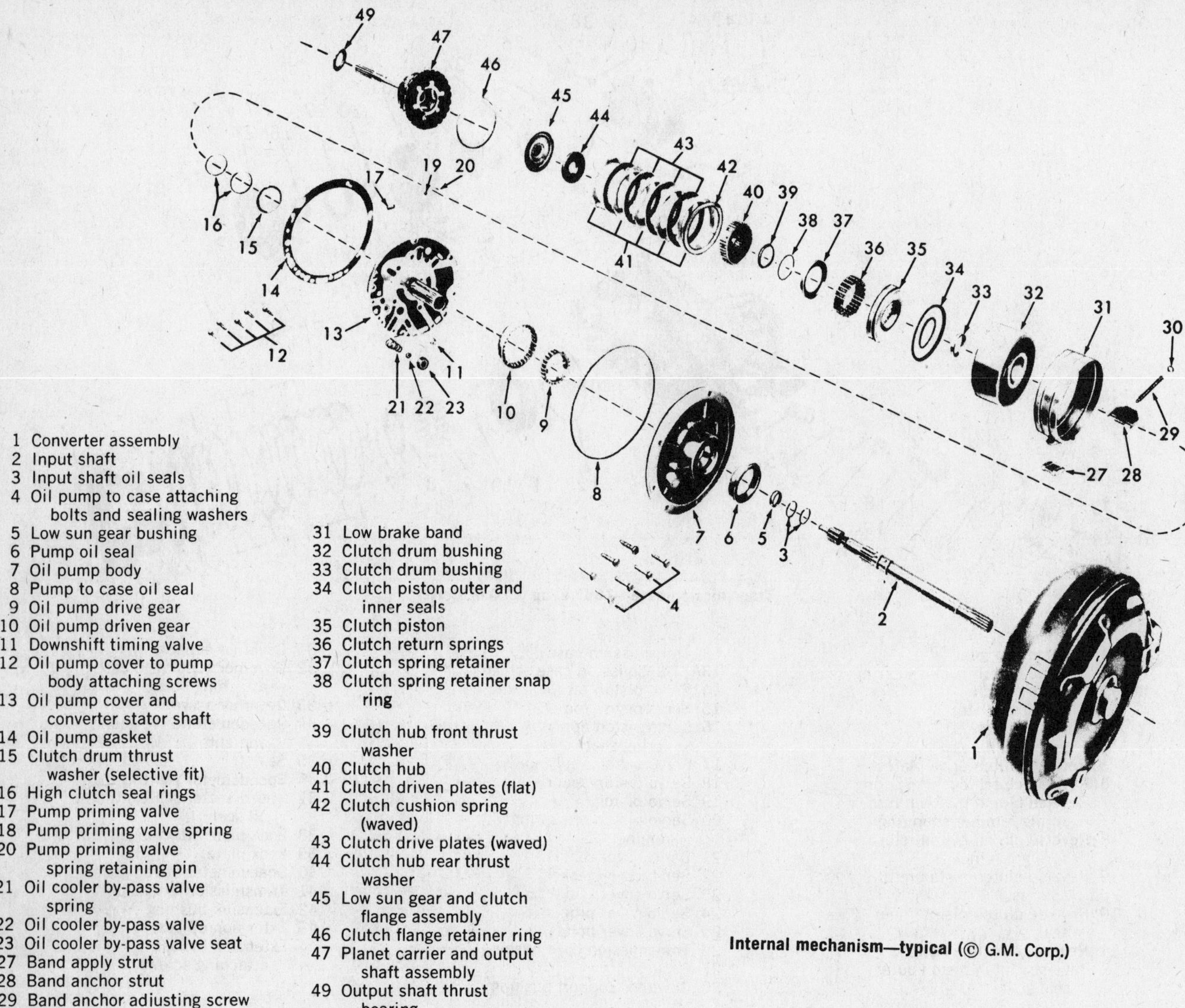

Internal mechanism—typical (© G.M. Corp.)

c. gear end clearance should be .0005-.0015 in.

or burrs.

4. Check for free operation of priming valve. Replace if necessary.
5. Inspect body bushing for galling or scoring. Check clearance be tween body bushing and converter pump hub. Maximum clearance is .005 in. If the bushing is damaged, replace the pump body.
6. Inspect converter housing hub outside diameter for nicks or burrs. Repair or replace.
7. If oil seal is damaged or leaking, pry out and drive in a new seal.
8. Check condition of oil cooler bypass valve. Replace if leaking. An "Easy-Out" type remover may be used to remove the valve. Tap new valve seat into place with a soft hammer or brass drift so that it is flush or up to

Assembly

1. Remove the input shaft, clutch drum, low band and struts as outlined under "Transmission Disassembly."
2. Install downship timing valve, conical end out, into place in the pump cover to a height of 17/32 in. measured from shoulder of valve assembly to face of pump cover.
3. Oil the drive and driven gears and install them into the pump body.
4. Set pump cover in place over the body and loosely install two attaching bolts.
5. Place pump assembly, less the rubber seal ring, upside down into the pump bore of the case. Install remaining attaching bolts and torque to 20 ft. lbs.
6. Remove pump assembly from case bore. Replace the clutch drum and input shaft, low band and struts as described under "Transmission Assembly."
7. Renew rubber seal ring in its groove in the pump body and install the pump assembly in place in the case bore, using a new gasket. Be sure that the selective fit thrust washer is in place.
8. Install attaching bolts. (Use new bolt sealing washers if necessary.)

Rear Pump—1964-66 Models

The rear pump is removed as described in the "Transmission Disassembly" procedures earlier in this section. Inspection procedures are the same as for the front pump. Assembly of the rear pump is described in the "Transmission Assembly" procedures later in this section.

Clutch Drum

Disassembly

CAUTION: When working with the clutch drum, use extreme care

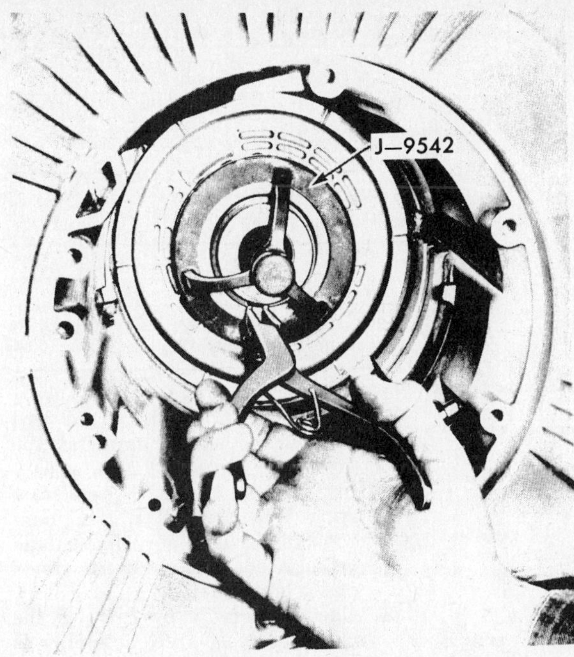

Removing rear piston spring retainer snap-ring
(© G.M. Corp.)

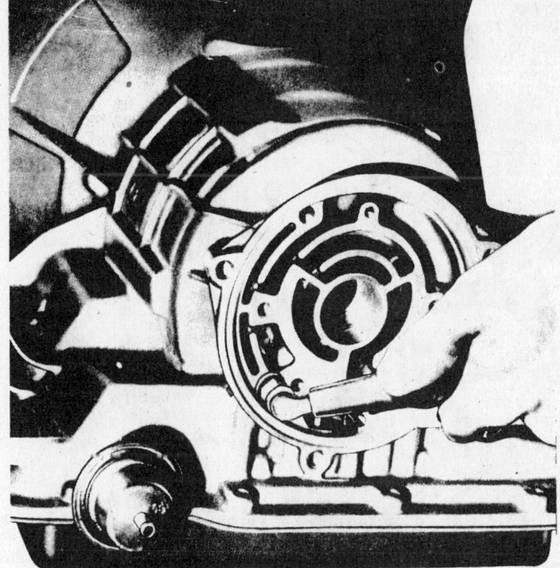
Applying air pressure to remove rear piston
(© G.M. Corp.)

that the machined face on the front of the drum not be scratched, scored, nicked, or otherwise damaged. This machined face must be protected whenever it is brought to bear on a press or tool of any sort.

1. Remove retainer ring, low sun gear and clutch flange assembly from the clutch drum.
2. Remove the hub rear thrust washer.
3. Lift out clutch hub, then remove clutch pack and hub front thrust washer. Note the number and sequence of plates.
4. Remove spring retainer. Compress the springs with a spring compressor or an arbor press enough to permit removal of the retainer snap-ring. Then, releasing pressure on the springs, remove retainer and the 24 springs.
5. Lift up on the piston with a twisting motion to remove it from the drum, then remove inner and outer seals.

Inspection

1. Wash all parts in solvent, blow out all passages, and air dry. Do not use rags to dry parts.
2. Check drum bushing for scoring or excessive wear.
3. Check steel ball relief valve in clutch drum. Be sure that it is free to move and that orifice in front face of drum is open. If ball is loose enough to come out, or not loose enough to rattle, replace drum. Do not attempt replacement or restaking of ball.
4. Check fit of low sun gear and clutch flange assembly in clutch drum slots. There should be no appreciable radial play.
5. Check low sun gear for nicks or burrs. Check gear bore for wear.
6. Check clutch plates for burring, wear, pitting, or metal pick-up. Faced plates should be a free fit over clutch hub; steel plates should be a free fit in clutch drum slots.
7. Check condition of clutch hub splines and mating splines of clutch faced plates.
8. Check clutch pistons for cracks or distortion.

Clutch Drum Bushing Replacement

If replacing drum bushing, carefully press out the old bushing. Then press (don't hammer) the new bushing into place from the machined face side of the drum. Press only far enough to bring the bushing flush with the clutch drum. Do not force the tool against the clutch drum machined face.

Assembly

1. Install new piston inner seal into hub of clutch drum with seal lip toward front of transmission.
2. Install new piston seal into clutch piston. Seal lips must be pointed toward the clutch drum, (front of transmission). Lubricate the seals and install piston into clutch drum with a twisting motion.
3. Place 24 springs in position on the piston, then place the retainer on the springs.
4. Depress the retainer plate and springs far enough to permit installation of the spring retainer snap-ring into its groove on the clutch drum hub.
5. Install the hub front washer with its lip toward the clutch drum, then install the clutch hub.
6. Install cushion spring if used. Install the steel reaction plates and drive (faced) plates alternately, beginning with a steel reaction plate.

NOTE: the number and sequence of plates varies with the power and torque requirements of the car model involved. On some models, the first driven plate is a selective fit. See the clutch assemblies chart for details.

Clutch Assemblies

Up to 1968 Models	*L-4 & 230 L-6 Pass. Cars.*	*307 V-8; Pass. Car; 250 L-6 Pass. Cars (exc. Taxi & Hvy. Duty Chassis) 327V-8 Pass. Cars*	*250L-6 Taxi & Hvy. Duty Chassis; 396V-8 Pass. Cars.*	*350V-8 396V-8*
Drive plate	3	4	5	5
Driven plate	4	5	6	6
Cushion spring	1	1	None	1

Models 1969-70	*L-4 & 230L-6 Pass. Cars*	*307V-8; 230L-6 Truck; 250-L-6 Exc. Taxi & Hvy. Duty Chassis 292 L-6 Truck*	*250L-6 Taxi & Hvy. Duty Chassis; 350 V-8 Truck*	*350V-8*
Drive plate	3	4	5	5
Driven plate	4	5	6	6
Cushion Spring	1	1	None	1

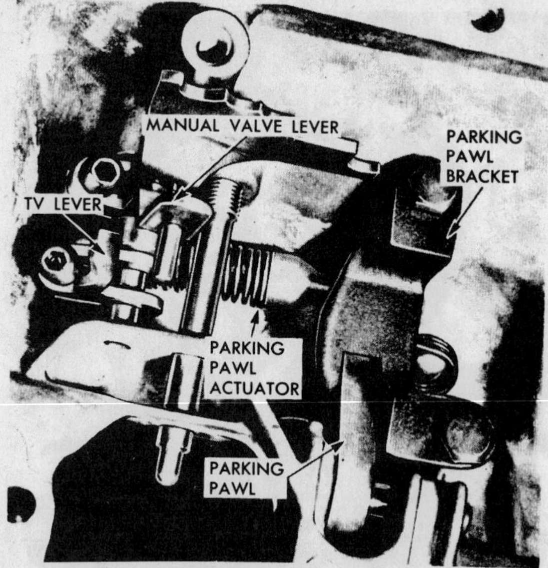

Inner control levers, parking pawl and bracket (© G.M. Corp.)

Checking gear end play (© G.M. Corp.)

TORQUE DRIVE

1969-70 Models	*L-4 L-6*
Drive plate	5
Driven plate	6
Cushion spring	1

350 and 396 V-8 Selective Driven Plate Chart

Plate Stack Height (Less Selective Plate)	*Plate Part Number*	*Color Code*	*Plate Thickness*
.903-.872	3883903	Orange	.060±.0025
.872-.798	3883904	Blue	.090±.0025

7. Install the rear hub thrust washer with its flange toward the low sun gear, then install the low sun gear and flange assembly and secure with retaining ring. When installed, the openings in the retainer ring should be adjacent to one of the lands of the clutch drum.
8. Check assembly by turning the clutch hub. If free, assembly is OK.

Low Band

Due to band design and transmission characteristics, this band should require very little attention. However, while the transmission is disassembled, the bands hould be thoughly cleaned, then replaced if any trace of scoring, burning, cracks, or excessive wear or damage is found.

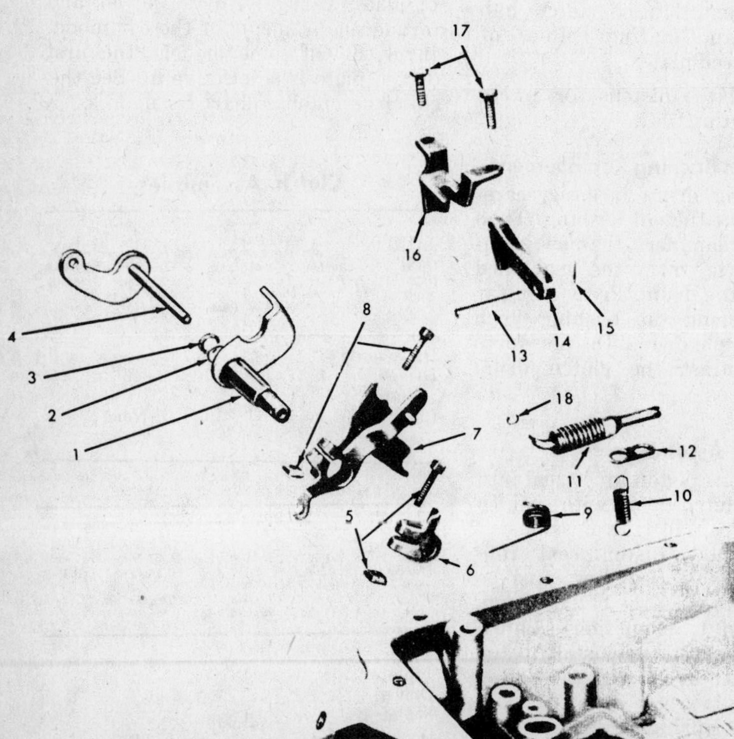

1 Park lock and range selector outer lever and shaft
2 Throttle valve control shaft oil seal
3 Throttle valve control shaft washer
4 Throttle valve control lever and shaft
5 Throttle valve control inner lever to control shaft attaching screw and nut
6 Throttle valve control inner lever
7 Park lock and range selector inner lever
8 Park lock and range selector inner lever attaching screw and nut
9 Park lock pawl disengaging spring
10 Range selector detent roller spring
11 Park lock actuator assembly
12 Range selector detent roller spring retainer
13 Park lock pawl shaft
14 Park lock pawl
15 Park lock pawl shaft retaining ring
16 Park lock pawl reaction bracket
17 Park lock pawl reaction bracket attaching bolts
18 Park lock actuator to park lock and range selector inner lever retaining clip

Manual levers—typical (© G.M. Corp.)

Checking planet gear end clearance (© G.M. Corp.)

Planet Assembly and Input Shaft

Inspection

1. Wash planet carrier and input shaft in cleaning solvent, blow out all passaes, and air dry. Do not use rags to dry parts.
2. Inspect planet pinions for nicks or other tooth damage.
3. Check end clearance of planet gears. The clearance should be .006-.030 in.
4. Check input sun gear for tooth damage. Check thrust washer for damage.
5. Inspect output shaft bearing surface and input pilot bushing for nicks or scoring.
6. Inspect input shaft splines for nicks or damage. Check fit in clutch hub, input sun gear, and turbine hub.
7. Check oil seal rings for damage; rings must be free in input shaft ring grooves. Remove rings and insert in stator support bore. Check to see that hooked ring ends have clearance. Replace rings on shaft.

Repairs

NOTE: some large planet carrier assemblies have the pinion shafts flared at each end for retention in the carrier. No overhaul of this type of carrier assembly should be attempted. If inspection shows excessive wear or damage, replace the entire carrier assembly.

1. Place the planet carrier assembly in a padded vise so that the front (parking lock gear end) of the assembly is up.
2. Using a prick punch, mark each pinion shaft and the carrier assembly so that, when reassembling, each shaft will be returned to its original location.
3. Remove pinion shaft lock plate screws and rotate plate counterclockwise far enough to remove it.
4. Starting with a short planet pinion, drive the lower end of the pinion shaft up until the shaft is above the press fit area of the output shaft flange. Feed a dummy shaft into the short planet pinion from the lower end, pushing the planet pinion shaft ahead of it until the tool is centered in the pinion and the pinion shaft is removed.
5. Remove short planet pinion.
6. Remove dummy shaft, needle and bearing spacers from short pinion. NOTE: twenty needle bearings are used in each end of each gear and are separated by a bearing spacer in the center.
7. By following Steps 4, 5, and 6, remove the adjacent long planet pinion that was paired, by thrust washers, to the short pinion now removed.
8. Remove upper and lower thrust washers.
9. Remove and disassemble remaining planet pinions, in pairs, as above.
10. Remove low sun gear needle thrust bearing, input sun gear, and thrust washer.
11. Wash all parts in solvent and blow dry, then inspect.
12. Inspect input shaft bushing in base of output shaft. If damaged, it may be removed by using a slide hammer. New bearing can be installed by using pilot end of input shaft as press tool.
13. Using dummy shaft, assemble needle bearings and spacer (20 rollers in each end) in one of the long planet pinions. Use petroleum jelly to aid in holding the rollers in position.
14. Position long planet gear, with dummy shaft centered in the pinion and with thrust washers at each end, in the planet carrier. Oil grooves on thrust washers must be toward the gears. NOTE: long pinions are located opposite the closed portions of the carrier and short pinions are located in the openings.
15. Feed a second dummy shaft in from the top, picking up the upper thrust washer and the pinion and pushing the already installed dummy shaft out the lower end. As the first dummy is pushed down, be sure that it picks up the lower thrust washer.
16. Select the correct pinion shaft, as marked in Step 2, lubricate the shaft and install it from the top, pushing the assembling tools (dummy) ahead of it.
17. Turn the pinion shaft so that the slot or groove at the upper end faces the center of the assembly.
18. With a brass drift, drive the shaft in until the lower end is flush with the lower face of the planet carrier.
19. Following the same procedure as outlined in Steps 13 through 18, assemble and install a short planet pinion into the planet carrier adjacent to the long pinion now installed. NOTE: the thrust washers, already installed with the long planet pinion, also serve for this short planet pinion, because the two pinions are paired together on one set of thrust washers.
20. Install the input sun gear thrust washer, input sun gear, and low sun gear needle thrust bearing.
21. Assemble and install the remaining planet pinions, in pairs, as previously explained.
22. Check end clearance of planet gears. This clearance should be .006-.030 in.
23. Place the shaft lock plate in position. Then, with the extended portions of the lock plate aligned with slots in the planet pinion shafts, rotate the lock plate clockwise until the three attaching screw holes are accessible.
24. Install lock plate attaching screws and torque to 2½ ft. lbs.

Governor

The governor assembly is a factory balanced unit. If body replacement is needed, the two sections must be replaced as a unit.

Disassembly

NOTE: the governor valve and shaft were removed in Step 6 of "Transmission Disassembly" procedures.

1. Remove the outer weight by sliding toward center of body.
2. Remove smaller inner weight retaining snap-ring and remove inner weight and spring.
3. Remove the four body assembly bolts and separate the body, hub and gasket. Remove the two seal rings.

Inspection

1. Clean all parts in solvent and air dry.
2. Check all parts. Replace all bent, scored, or otherwise damaged parts. Body and hub must be replaced as a unit.

Assembly

1. Reassemble governor weights and install into body bore. Replace seal ring on hub.
2. Slide hub into place on output shaft and lock into place with drive screw. Install gasket and governor body over output shaft, install governor shaft, line up properly with output shaft and install body attaching bolts. Torque bolts to 6-8 ft. lbs.
3. Check governor weight for free fit in body after the four attaching bolts are torqued. If the weight sticks or binds, loosen the bolts and retorque.

Valve Body

Removal

Remove valve body, as described under "Transmission Disassembly". If performing the operation on the truck, the vacuum modulator valve, oil pan and gasket, guide detent plate and range selector detent roller spring must be removed in order to remove the valve from the transmission.

Disassembly

1. Remove manual valve, suction screen and gasket.
2. Remove cover bolts, then remove

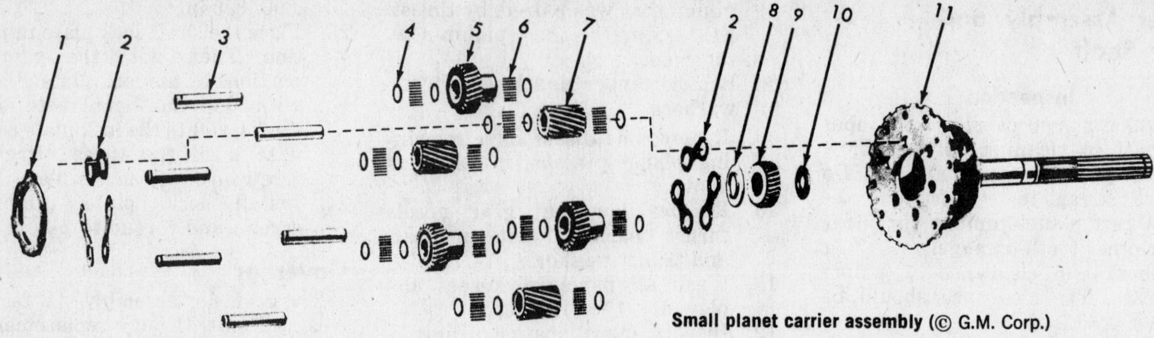

Small planet carrier assembly (© G.M. Corp.)

1 Pinion shaft lock plate
2 Pinion thrust washer
3 Pinion shaft
4 Needle bearing washer
5 Short planet pinion gear
6 Needle bearings
7 Long planet pinion gear
8 Low sun gear thrust bearing
9 Input sun gear
10 Input sun gear thrust washer
11 Carrier and output shaft

lower valve body and transfer plate from upper valve body. Discard gaskets.

3. Remove the front and rear pump check valves and springs from 1964-66 models.
4. From the upper valve body, remove the throttle valve and detent valve and the downshift timing valve as follows:
   A. Throttle Valve and Detent Valve—Remove the retaining pin by wedging a thin screw-driver between its head and the valve body, then removing the detent valve assembly and throttle spring. Tilt valve body to allow the throttle valve to fall out. If necessary, remove the C clip and disassemble the detent valve assembly. NOTE: do not change adjustment of hex nut on the detent valve assembly. This is a factory setting and should not normally be changed. However, some adjustment is possible if desired. See "Throttle Valve Adjustment," in later text.
   B. Downshift Timing Valve — Drive out the roll pin, remove valve spring and downshift timing valve.
5. From the lower valve body, remove the low-drive shift valve and the pressure regulator valve as follows:
   A. Low-Drive Shift Valve—Remove the snap-ring and tilt valve body to remove low-drive regulator valve sleeve and valve assembly, valve spring seat, valve springs and the shifter valve.
   B. Pressure Regulator Valve—Remove the snap-ring, then tilt valve body to remove the hydraulic modulator valve sleeve and valve, pressure regulator valve spring seat, spring, damper valve, spring seat and valve.

Inspection

1. Clean all parts in solvent; air dry. Use no rags.
2. Check all valves and valve bores for burrs or other deformities which could cause valve hang-up.

Assembly

NOTE: see the valve body illustration for identification of upper and lower valve body gaskets for 1964-66 models. For 1967-70 models, the gaskets are identical.

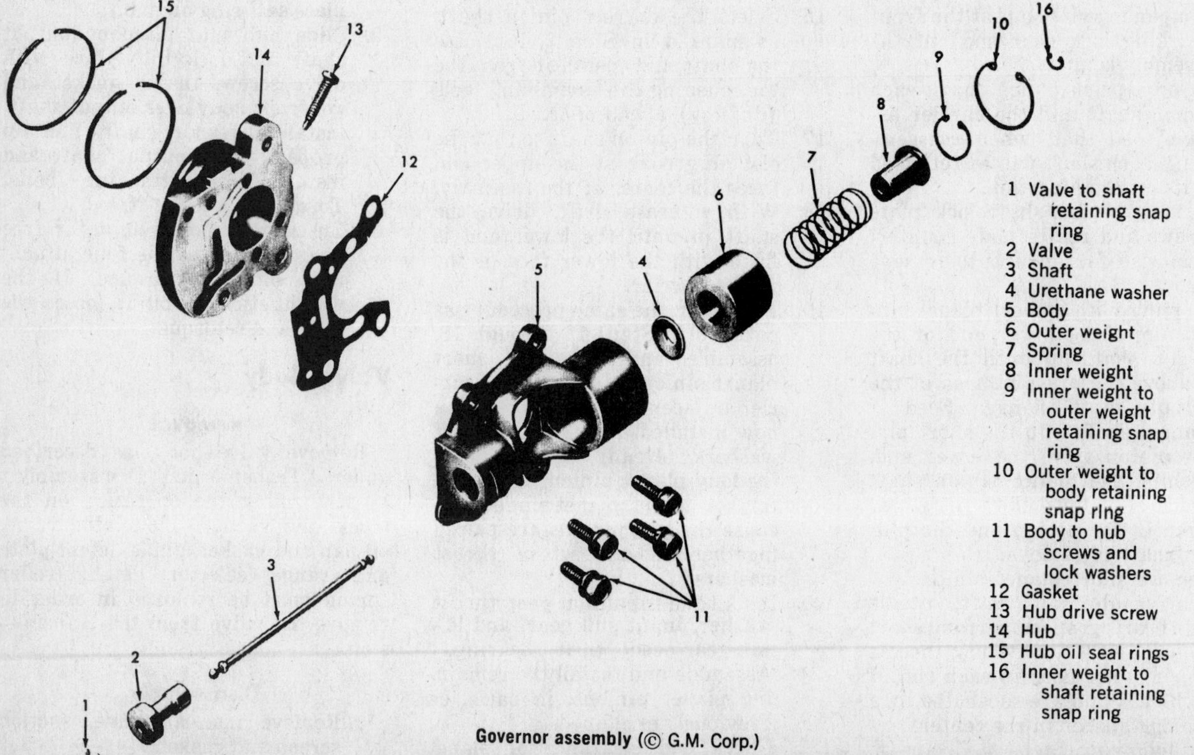

Governor assembly (© G.M. Corp.)

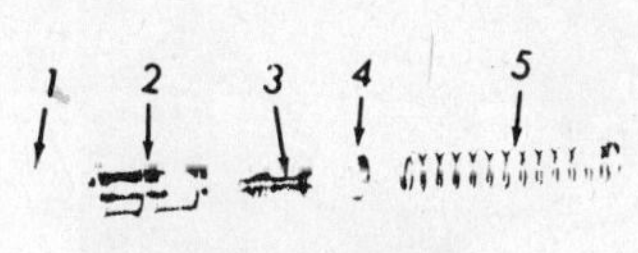
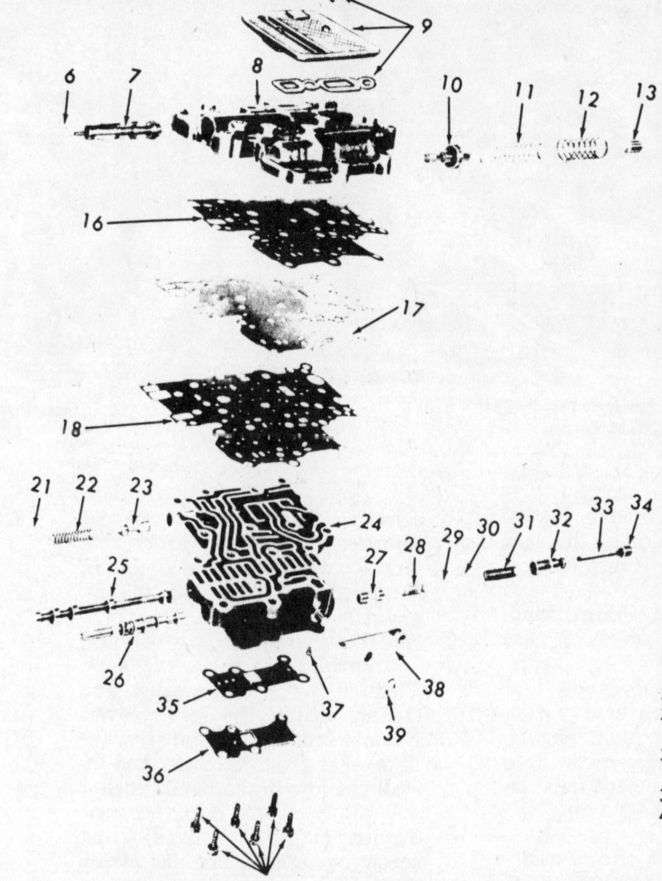

Valve body assembly sequence (© G.M. Corp.)

1. Replace valve components in proper bores, reversing the steps of disassembly outlined above.
2. Place front and rear pump check valves and springs into place in upper valve body on 1964-66 models only. Install the gasket and transfer plate.
3. Install lower valve body and gasket and install attaching bolts. Torque to 15 ft. lbs.
4. Install valve body onto transmission, as outlined under "Transmission, Assembly" in later text.

Vacuum Modulator

The vacuum modulator is mounted on the left rear of the transmission and can be serviced from beneath the truck.

Removal

1. Remove vacuum line at the modulator.
2. Unscrew the modulator from the transmission with a thin 1 in. tappet-type wrench.
3. Remove vacuum modulator valve.

Inspection

1. Check the vacuum modulator plunger and valve for nicks and burrs. If such damage cannot be repaired with a stone, replace the part.
2. Check the vacuum modulator for leakage with a vacuum source. If the modulator leaks, replace the assembly.

Installation

Reverse removal procedure.

Transmission Assembly

NOTE: if removed, assemble manual linkage to case, as described in Steps 1-7.

1. Install parking lock pawl and shaft and insert a new E-ring retainer.
2. Install parking lock pawl pull-back spring over its boss at rear of pawl. The short leg of the spring should locate in the hole in the pawl.
3. Install parking pawl reaction bracket with its two bolts.
4. Fit the actuator assembly between the parking pawl and the bracket.
5. Insert outer shift lever into the case. Pick up inner shift lever and parking lock assembly. Tighten Allen-head lock.
6. Insert outer throttle valve lever and shaft, special washer, and O-ring into case and pick up inner throttle valve lever. Tighten Allen-head lock.
7. Thread low band adjusting screw into case.

NOTE: to prevent possible binding between throttle lever and range selector controls, allow .010-.020 clearance between inner throttle valve lever and inner shift lever.

Transmission Internal Components

8. Install inner and outer rear piston seals onto reverse piston and, (with lubrication) install piston into the case.
9. With transmission case facing up, install the 17 reverse piston springs and their retainer ring.
10. Install spring compressing tool. Compress the return springs, allowing the retaining ring snap-ring to be installed. Remove the ring to be installed. Remove the compressor.
11. Install the cushion spring.
12. Lubricate and install reverse clutch pack, beginning with a reaction spacer plate and alternating with the faced plates until all plates are installed.

NOTE: the number and sequence of plates varies with the power and torque requirements of the truck model involved.

The notched lug on each reaction plate is installed in the groove at the seven o'clock position in the case. Then, install the thick pressure plate

Installing clutch plates—typical
(© G.M. Corp.)

Installing detent guide plate
(© G.M. Corp.)

which has a dimple in one lug to align with the same slot in the case as the notched lugs on the other reaction plates.

13. Install clutch plate retainer ring.
14. Turn rear of transmission case down.
15. Align the internal lands and grooves of the reverse clutch pack faced plates, then engage the reverse ring gear with these plates. This engagement must be made by feel while turning the ring gear.
16. Place output shaft thrust bearing over the output shaft and install the planetary carrier and output shaft into the transmission case.
17. Move transmission to horizontal position.
18. The two input shaft seal rings should be in place on the shaft. Install clutch drum (machined face first) onto the input shaft and install the low sun gear bushing against shoulder.
19. Install clutch drum and input shaft assembly into case, aligning thrust washer on input shaft and indexing low sun gear with the short pinions on the planet carrier.
20. Remove rubber seal ring from the front pump body and install front pump, gasket and selective fit thrust washer into case. Install pump-to-case bolts.
21. To check for correct thickness of the selective fit thrust washer, move transmission so that output shaft points down and proceed as follows:
    A. Mount a dial indicator so that the indicator plunger is resting on the end of the input shaft. Zero the indicator.
    B. Push up on the output shaft and watch the total dial movement.
    C. The indicator should read .028-.059 in. If reading is not within specifications, remove front pump change to a thicker or thinner selective thrust washer. Repeat above checking procedure. NOTE: washers are available in thicknesses of .061, .078, .092 in. and .106 in.
22. Install servo piston, piston ring, and spring into the servo bore. Then, using a new gasket and O-ring, install the servo cover.
23. Remove front pump and selective fit washer from the case, and install the low brake band, anchor and apply struts into the case. Tighten the low band adjusting screw enough to prevent struts from falling out of case.
24. Place the seal ring in the groove around front pump body and the two seal rings on the pump cover extension. Install the pump, gasket and thrust washer into the case. Install all pump bolts. Torque bolts to 15 ft. lbs.

Extension Governor and Rear Oil Pump—1964-66 Models

25. Turn transmission so that output shaft points upward.
26. Install governor support and gasket, drain back baffle, and support to case attaching bolts.
27. Install governor over output shaft. Install governor shaft and valve, urethane washer, and retaining C clips. Center shaft in output shaft bore and tighten governor hub drive screw.
28. Install speedometer gear to output shaft.
29. Place extension seal ring over governor support. Install transmission extension and five retaining bolts.
30. Replace speedometer driven gear.

Extension, Governor and Governor Support—1967-70 Models

25. Turn transmission so that output shaft points upward.
26. Install governor support and gasket, drain back baffle, and support to case attaching bolts.
27. Install governor over output shaft. Install governor shaft and valve, urethane washer, and retaining C clips. Center shaft in output shaft bore and tighten governor hub drive screw.
28. Install speedometer gear to output shaft.
29. Place extension seal ring over governor support. Install transmission extension and five retaining bolts.
30. Replace speedometer driven gear.

Oil Pan and Valve Body

31. With transmission upside down, the manual linkage and the selector lever detent roller installed, install the valve body with a new gasket. (Carefully guide the servo apply line into its boss in the case as the valve body is set in place.) Position the manual valve actuating lever fully forward to more easily pick up the manual valve. Install six mounting bolts and the range selector detent roller spring. On 1967-70 models, install new gasket and suction screen to valve body.
32. Install the guide plate. Install attaching bolts.
33. Install vacuum modulator valve, the vacuum modulator and the gasket.
34. Install oil pan, using a new gasket, then the pan attaching bolts.
35. Install the converter and safety holding strap.

Throttle Valve TV Adjustment

No provision is made for checking TV pressures. However, if operation of the transmission is such that some adjustment of the TV is indicated, pressures may be raised or lowered by adjusting the position of the jam nut on the throttle valve assembly. To raise TV pressure 3 psi, back off

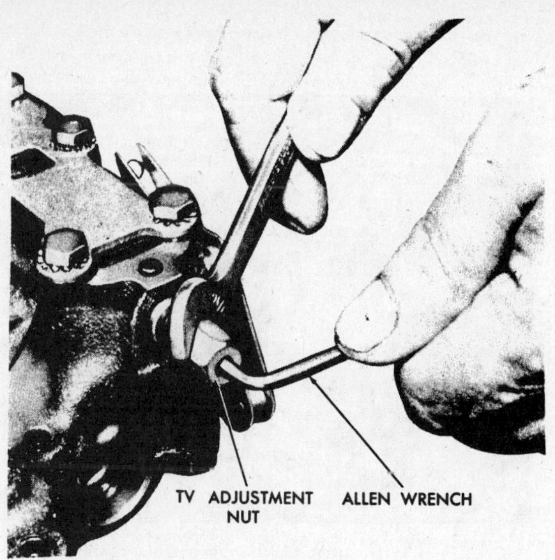

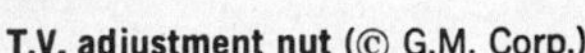
T.V. adjustment nut (© G.M. Corp.)

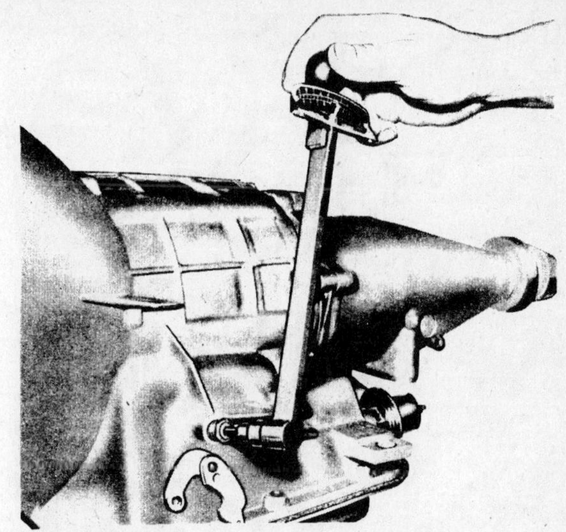
Low band adjustment (© G.M. Corp.)

the jam nut one full turn.

Conversely, tightening the jam nut one full turn, lowers TV pressure 3 psi. A difference of 3 psi in TV pressure will cause a change of about 2-3 mph in the wide open throttle upshift point. The end of the TV adjusting screw has an Allen head so the screw may be held stationary while the jam nut is locked.

NOTE: use care in changing this adjustment, as no pressure tap is provided to check TV pressure.

Low Band Adjustment

Tighten the low servo adjusting screw to 40 in. lbs. for 1964-66 models; 70 in. lbs. for 1967-70 models. The input and output shaft must be rotated simultaneously to properly center the low band on the clutch drum. Then, back off four complete turns for a band which has been in use for 6,000 miles or more, or three turns for one in use less than 6,000 miles, and tighten the locknut.

CAUTION: The amount of back-off is very critical. Back off exactly three or four turns.

Torque References

	Foot-Pounds	
	1964-66 Models	*1967-70 Models*
Transmission case to engine	25-30	35
Oil pan to case	7-10	7-10
Extension to case	20-30	20-30
Servo cover to case	15-20	20
Front pump to case	13-17	13-17
Front pump cover to body attaching bolts	15-20	20
Pinion shaft lock plate attaching screws	2-3	2-3
Governor body to hub	6-8	6-8
Governor hub drive screw	6-8	6-8
Rear pump or governor support to case	8-11	8-11
Valve body to case	8-11	15
Suction screen attaching screws	2-3	2-3
Upper valve body plate	3-5	5
Lower to upper valve body	13-15	15
Inner control lever allen head locks	6-8	2½
Low band adjusting locknut	13-17	13-17
Converter to engine	15-20	35

Removing Oil Pump

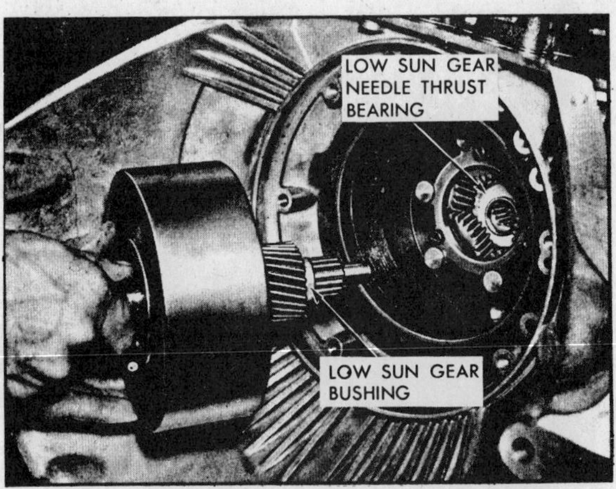

Removing Clutch Drum and Input Shaft

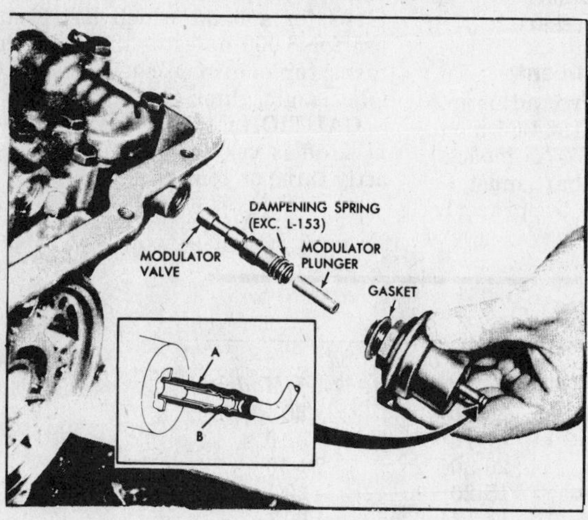

Vacuum Modulator, Dampening Spring, Plunger and Valve

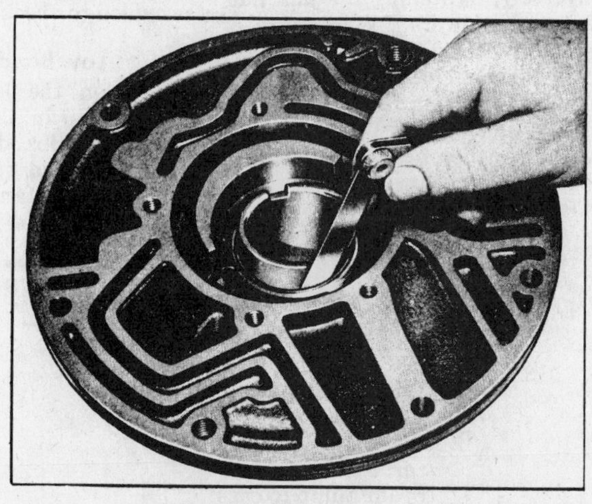

Checking Pump Body Bushing to Converter Pump Hub Clearance

Checking Driven Gear to Pump Body Clearance

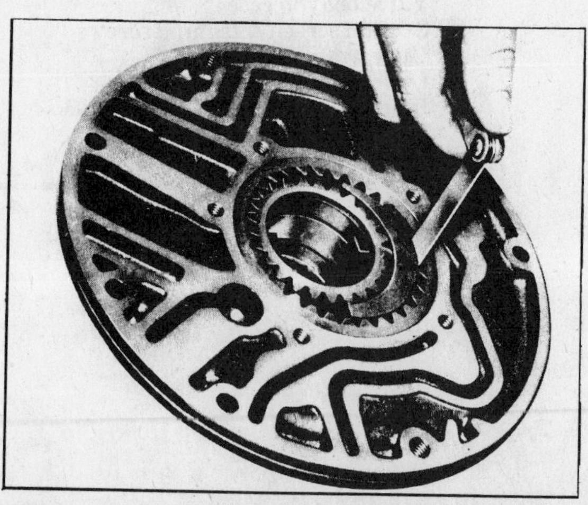

Driven Gear to Crescent Clearance

Diagnosis

This diagnosis guide covers the most common symptoms and is an aid to careful diagnosis.

TROUBLE SYMPTOMS	Items to Check In Truck	Out of Truck
Car will not move in any selector position	ABC	cab
Engine speed flares, as slipping clutch	ABDFE	def
Engine speed flares on upshift	ADBG	ghi
Transmission will not upshift	HIJ	klm
Harsh upshift	JDGK	
Harsh deceleration downshift	DLMNG	
No downshift	MHI	
Clutch failure, burnt plates	DAHO	hi
Excessive creep in drive	JL	
Car creeps in neutral	J	hd
No drive in reverse	J	jng
Improper shift points	JIH	l
Unable to push-start car		m
Oil leaks	PQG	oa
Oil forced out at filler tube	AQ	p

Key to Checks

A. Oil level
B. Oil screen
C. Pressure regulator valve
D. Band adjustment
E. Servo seal
F. Servo blocked
G. Vacuum modulator or line
H. Governor
I. Throttle valve
J. Throttle linkage
K. Hyraulic modulator valve
L. Too high idle speed
M. Valves malfunctioning
N. Make pressure tests
O. Driving too fast in low
P. Oil leaks at external points
Q. Oil cooler or lines

a. Front pump
b. Input shaft
c. Front pump priming valve
d. Low band
e. Low band linkage
f. Converter stator
g. Clutch feed blocked
h. High clutch
i. Front clutch relief valve
j. Reverse clutch relief valve
k. Low clutch valve stuck
l. Rear pump priming valve
m. Rear pump or drive
n. Low clutch
o. Front pump attaching bolts
p. Pump circuit leakage

General Information

This type transmission is identified by a cast iron case. It uses a 3-element converter. The clutch plates are waved in place of dished. These plates are identified by an "O" and must be stacked in one direction.

Oil Level Check

Check the level every 1000 miles, with transmission at operating temperature and the selector in neutral. With engine idling oil should not be above the "full" mark and added to when below the "add 1 quart" mark.

Be careful not to overfill, to avoid aerating and foaming.

Oil Change Schedule

Starting with 1961 do not change except at overhaul.

Drain and Refill Procedure

With engine at operating temperature, remove drain plug at rear of transmission. To refill replace plug and with engine idling, add $4\frac{1}{2}$ quarts of approved type "A" fluid. Continue idling until oil is hot and recheck level as above.

Now is a good time for visual inspection of cooler core and lines for leaks and proper heat flow.

Towing the Truck

When the hand lever is in Neutral the car may be towed. When the rear wheels are on the ground Neutral is the ONLY position that can be used for towing.

Speed in Tow should never exceed 45 mph.

To place the transmission in Neutral when the hand lever is inoperative:

1. Remove the cotter pin and disconnect the long control rod at the bell crank on the left side of the transmission case.
2. Push the bell crank as far rearward as it will go. (This will be Reverse.) Now move it forward to the third detent which will be Neutral. Naturally if the Transmission is locked up the truck must not be moved on its rear wheels unless the drive shaft is disconnected at the universal joint.

Band Adjustment

Reverse Band

The adjustment screw for the reverse band is hidden behind the Servo Cover on the right side of the case. On all models the cover can be removed without disturbing the transmission.

Do not remove the servo pistons while the transmission is in the truck for to do so will permit the band struts to drop down into the transmission case.

Release the reverse band adjusting screw lock nut and tighten the adjusting screw up snug. From up snug back the adjusting screw out two and three-quarters turns. Tighten the lock nut to 20-25 ft lbs. Tighten reverse band adjusting screw to 5 to 7 ft. lbs. and back off $2\frac{1}{2}$ turns.

Reinstall the servo cover and the modulator.

Low Band Adjustment

The low band adjusting screw is hidden under a protective cap on the left side of the transmission case. Working under the truck remove the cover to expose the adjusting screw and the lock nut.

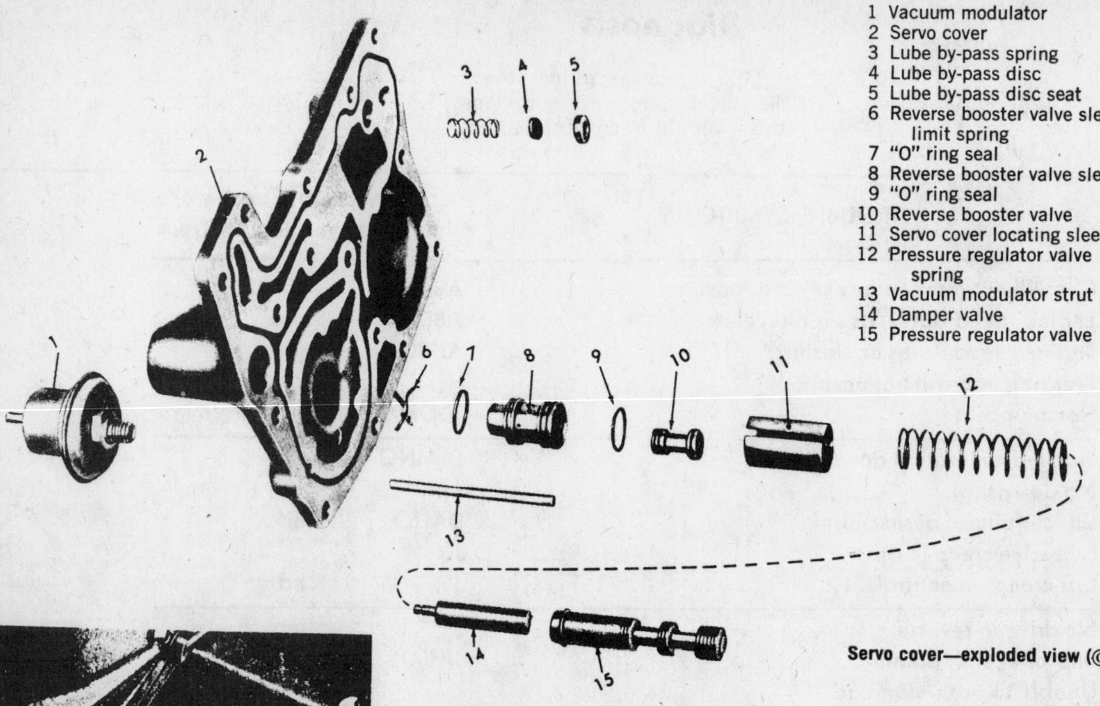

Servo cover—exploded view (© G.M. Corp.)

Adjusting low band (© G.M. Corp.)

Tighten the adjusting screw to 5 to 7 ft. lbs. and back off exactly four turns. Tighten lock knut to 20-25 ft. lbs.

Basic Pressure Checks

With transmission at normal operating temperature connect gauge at low servo apply clutch release side of low servo throttle valve and governor test points. The gauges should be in truck away from driver's feet, with lines along steering jacket, past the jacket seal.

Wide open throttle upshift 82-90 psi with V-8 and 68-74 psi with 6-cylinder.

After up-shift pressure on low servo supply and high clutch should be alike. If pressures are alike and slippage is felt mechanical trouble in clutch is indicated. Leakage in high clutch line between low and drive valve body and high clutch is indicated if pressures vary more than 5 psi.

Idle Pressure in "Drive" Range

Low servo apply, 60-71 psi with V-8 and 55-65 psi with 6-cylinder.

Manual "Low" Range

Low servo apply at 1000 rpm, 114-127 psi with V-8 and 70-80 psi with 6-cylinder.

Drive Range Coast Pressure

Coasting in drive at 20-25 mph, low servo apply pressure 47-53 psi with either engine.

Throttle Valve and Governor

Throttle valve pressure varies with accelerator position, 0-63 psi with V-8 and 0-50 with 6-cylinder. Governor pressure is relative to truck speed.

Reverse Pressure

With brakes applied and lever in "Reverse" at 1000 rpm, 240-275 psi with V-8 and 167-191 psi with 6-cylinder.

Match Points

The following points should be marked on disassembly.

Flywheel to Primary Pump Cover
Primary Pump Cover to Primary Pump
Pinion Shaft to Pinion Carrier
Front Portion of Carrier to Rear Portion of Carrier
Bands to Case

Disassembly of Transmission

Oil Pump Suction Pipe and Screen

(This operation can be performed with the transmission still in the truck.)

Unbolt the right side cover of the bell housing. Remove cover and gasket. Unbolt the suction pipe retainer and lift out the pipe retainer and screen.

Wash the assembly in solvent. Blow with compressed air to dry.

Reverse removal procedure to replace. Use a new seal on the pipe ahead of the retainer. Install in the cover a new "O" ring seal for the filler tube. Use a new cover to case gasket.

Transmission Throttle Valve

(This operation can be performed with the transmission still in the truck.)

Unbolt the left side cover and remove the cover and throttle valve as an assembly. Remove cover to case gasket. Do not unbolt the outer lever as it acts to hold the inner lever in place on the assembly.

NOTE: If it becomes necessary to disassemble the throttle valve, be careful not to disturb the adjustment. It is preset to 62 psi (plus or minus 1 psi) at the factory.

It is more than likely that trouble with this assembly can be cleared by a thorough cleaning.

Remove the low-and-drive-valve-body to side cover attaching bolts and lock-washers. Remove the throttle valve outer lever and catch the inner lever and shaft seal.

Hold the low and drive valve body in one hand and with a soft faced hammer tap on the inner side of the side cover until it is free of the locating pins.

CAUTION: Exert pressure on the detent valve when separating valve body from the cover to keep the parts from falling out. A clip can easily be

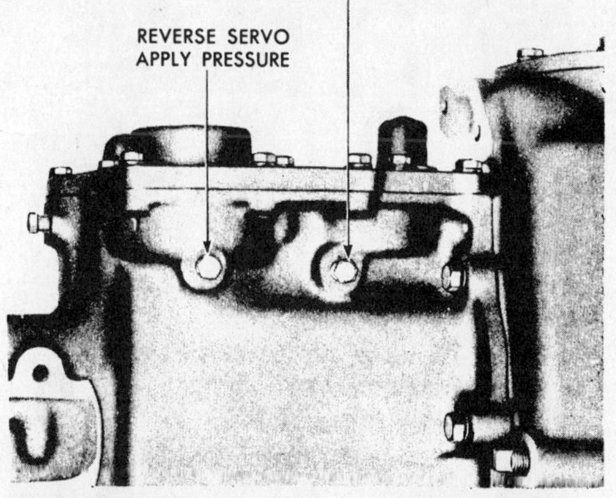

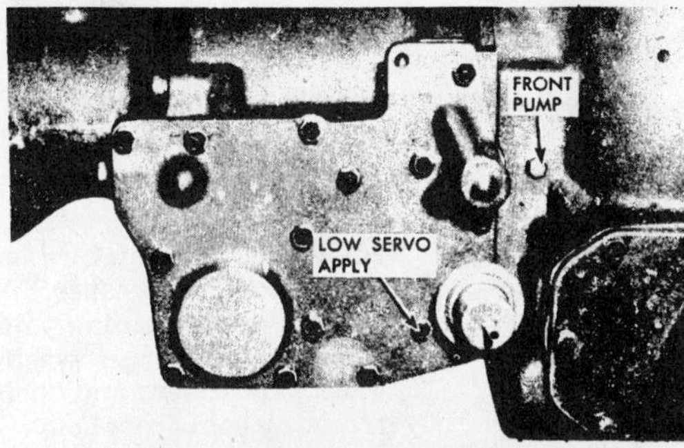

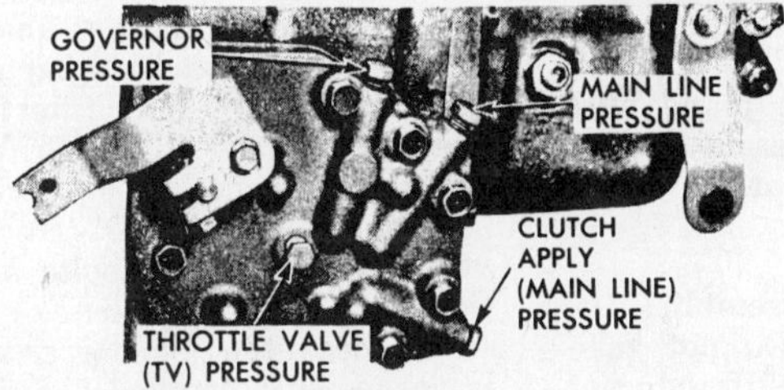

Pressure check points (© G.M. Corp.)

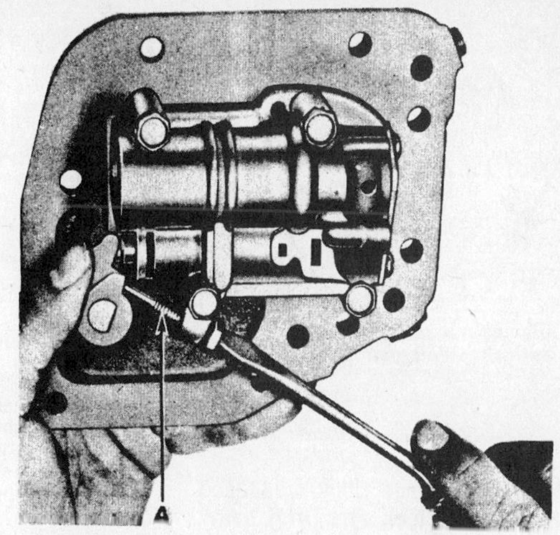

Throttle valve inner lever adjustment
(© G.M. Corp.)

made that retains the detent valve in its bore during disassembly and assembly to cover.

If during disassembly a new detent valve, throttle valve, or spring, is installed the throttle valve inner lever should be adjusted.

Hold the lever so it just contacts the face of the detent valve. Turn the adjusting screw "A" until it touches the flat surface of the lever's step. Back off one complete turn and tighten the adjusting screw lock.

If there is a screw in the lower end of the throttle valve inner lever, hold the lever as described above and turn this lower screw in to touch the thread of the adjusting screw.

Rear Oil Pump

(This operation can be performed with Powerglide in the truck.)

Set the hand lever in Park.

Remove the speedometer drive shaft and gear unit from the left rear of the transmission case.

Mark the rear oil pump body with reference to the case for easier installation.

Remove the four bolts holding the rear oil pump to the case.

Drop the propeller shaft assembly down out of the way.

1 Low and drive regulator valve cap retainer ring
2 Low and drive regulator valve cap
3 Low and drive regulator valve sleeve
4 Low and drive regulator valve
5 Low and drive valve inner spring
6 Low and drive valve outer spring
7 Low and drive valve
8 Detent valve
9 Detent valve spring
10 Detent valve spring seat
11 Throttle valve spring regulator assembly
12 Low and drive valve body
13 Throttle valve inner lever adjusting screw and lock nut
14 Throttle valve spring
15 Throttle valve and retainer clip
16 Low and drive body end plate gasket
17 Attaching screws and lock washers

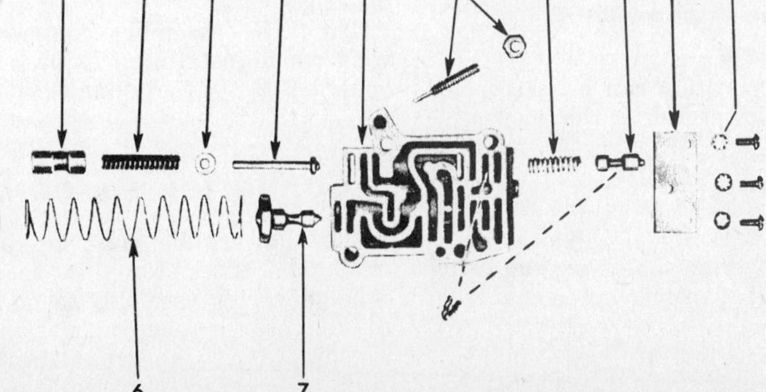

Low and drive valve body—exploded view (© G.M. Corp.)

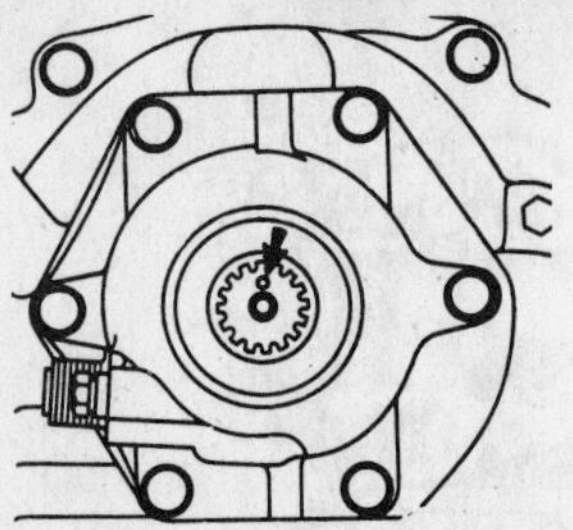

Aligning rear pump drive pin with slot in oil pump cover (© G.M. Corp.)

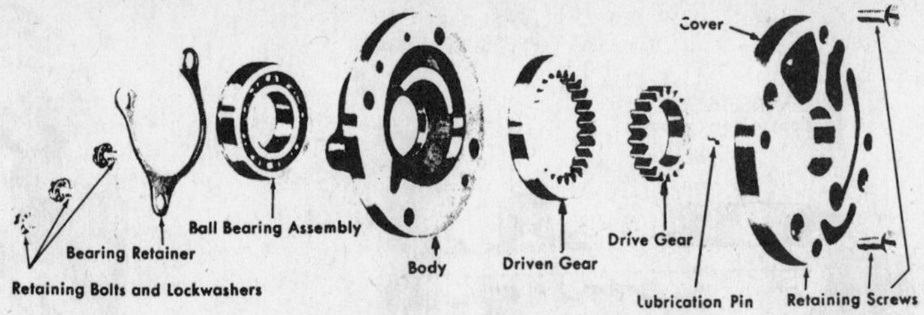

Rear pump (© G.M. Corp.)

1 Governor sleeve
2 Governor valve
3 Governor weight assemblies
4 Governor thrust cap
5 Governor weight pins

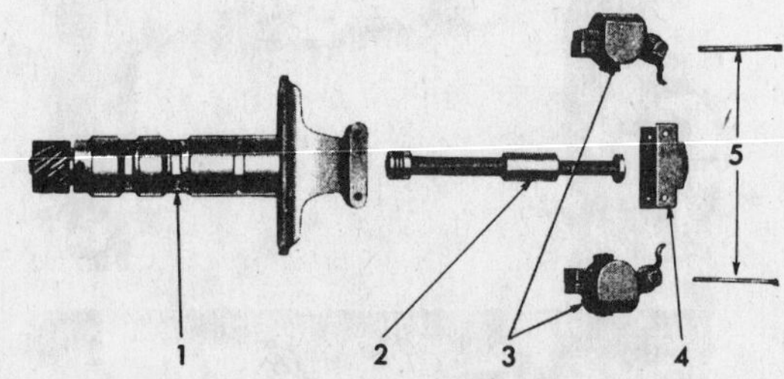

Governor—exploded view (© G.M. Corp.)

Remove the three lock-washered bolts holding the lock ring and bearing in the pump body.

Install three long bolts in these holes (they are blind holes) and, using them as points of leverage, ease the oil pump out of the case.

NOTE: On late models the oil pump is driven by a loose fitting pin in the output shaft.

There is an "O" stamped on the end of the shaft to show the location of the pin. When this "O" is toward the top of the transmission the pin is aligned with a slot in the rear oil pump front cover. This permits removal of the planetary carrier and output shaft assembly thru the front of the case.

CAUTION: When assembling the rear pump, be sure that the Lubrication Hole Pin is installed correctly. The headed end should be installed toward the pump body plate.

If this pin is omitted, or installed incorrectly, leaks may result due to over lubrication in the transmission extension cavity.

The bearing lock plate was not used on all models. Install one on any units found to be not already so equipped.

The bearing is a tight fit on the output shaft. If when using this procedure the pump refuses to move, the transmission will have to be removed from the truck and disassembled.

On no condition exert forward pressure on the output shaft with the transmission assembled.

Governor Assembly All Models

(This operation can be performed with the Powerglide in the truck.)

Removal

Unbolt and remove the governor cover and gasket.

Turn governor clockwise and bring it out of the transmission case.

Disassembly

All the parts of the governor except the oil seal rings on the sleeve are selected fits and individually calibrated. Parts for the governor are not sold separately but only as a unit.

Therefore if anything is needed other than the oil seal rings, a whole new governor assembly must be installed.

For cleaning, the unit may be taken apart.

Cut off one end of each of the governor weight pins and remove the pins. Measure and record their diameter, for the same gage piano wire must be used when reassembling to preserve the unit's calibration.

Overhaul

Inspect the weight assemblies for distortion or damage. Do not take apart. Check that the weights do not bind in their retainers.

Insert the rings in the bore in the case and check that the hooked ends have clearance.

Reinstall

Reinstall the oil seal rings on the sleeve.

Reinstall the valve, wider end in.

Reassemble the thrust cap to the weight to the old ones. Crimp the pins. Be sure new pins are similar in weight to the old ones. Crimp the ends of both pins and check the weight assemblies that they aren't binding.

Turn the assembly counterclockwise when installing. Tighten cover bolts to 6½-8½ foot pounds.

Converter Assembly

The Powerglide must be removed from the truck for this operation. The converter assembly is no longer retained to the reactor shaft and may be slipped off the input shaft as a unit.

Remove the primary pump retaining cover to the primary pump.

With a small punch drive out the cover locating dowels.

Remove turbine, stator, and converter pump thrust washer.

Remove cam retaining snap ring and front stator thrust washer, stator race, cam rollers and springs and overrunning cam from body.

Next remove rear cam snap ring and rear stator thrust washer.

Thoroughly clean all parts. Do not use rags as lint may interfere with operation. Make thorough inspection and replacements.

Always use new "O" ring on converter cover. Cover bolts should be tightened to 15-20 ft. lbs.

To check that converter assembly is properly installed, measure as shown in illustration the distance from the machined front face of the bell housing to the front surface of a converter drive lug. The distance should be no more than 9/16". Temporarily fasten the converter to the bell housing so it won't fall out of place.

Bell Housing

Removal

Remove the transmission from the truck.

Remove the converter assembly from the transmission.

Remove the oil screen, the modulator assembly, the servo cover assembly and the throttle valve assembly.

Be sure that the pressure regulator valve is out of the case and safely put out of the way.

Remove the low band adjusting screw cover, loosen the lock nut and tighten the adjusting screw to hold the clutch assembly in place. A ¼" Allen wrench is required for this operation.

Remove the one bolt running from the inside of the bell housing into the transmission case.

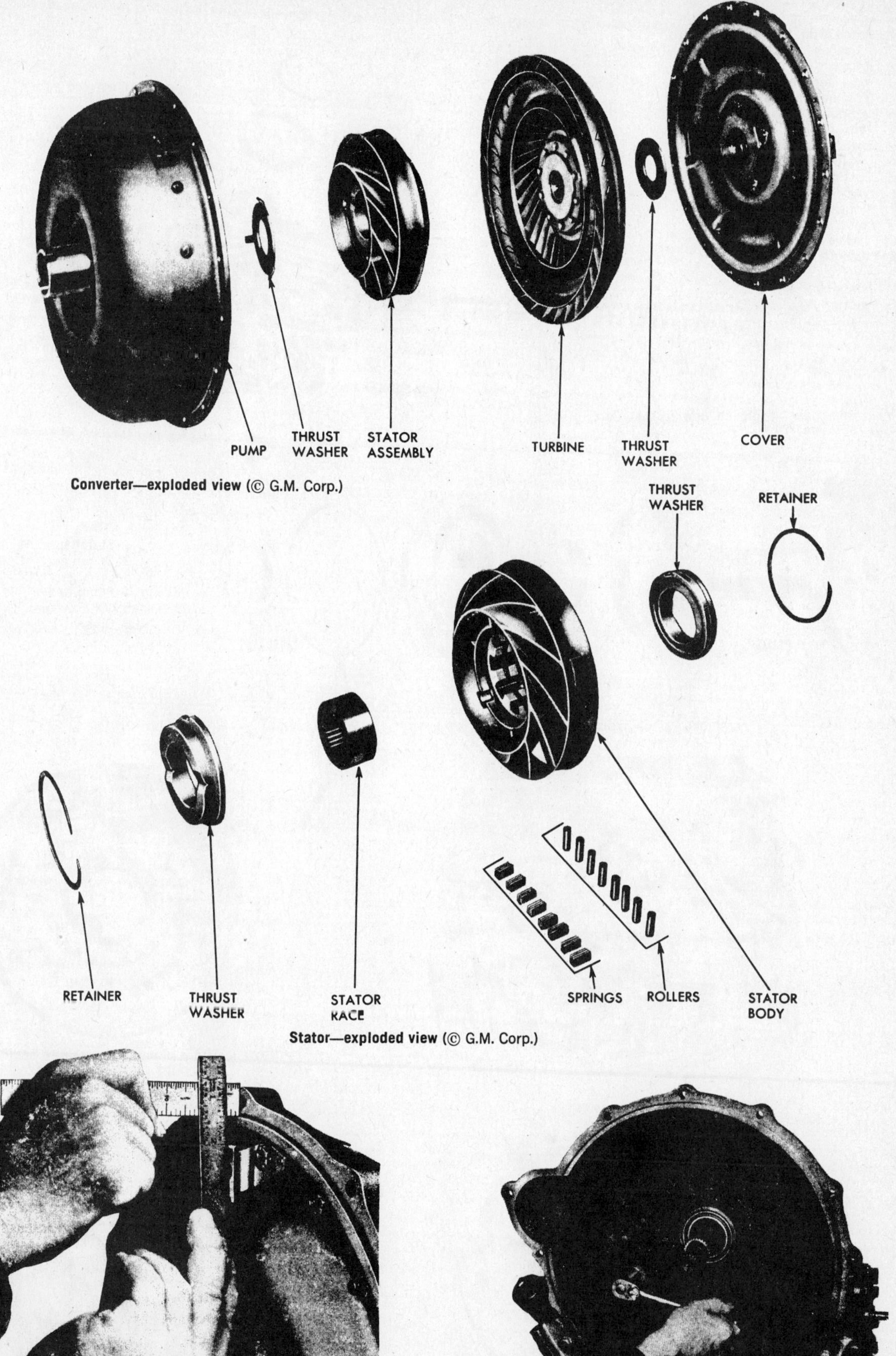

Converter—exploded view (© G.M. Corp.)

Stator—exploded view (© G.M. Corp.)

Checking converter pump hub engagement (© G.M. Corp.)

Removing housing to transmission case self locking bolt (© G.M. Corp.)

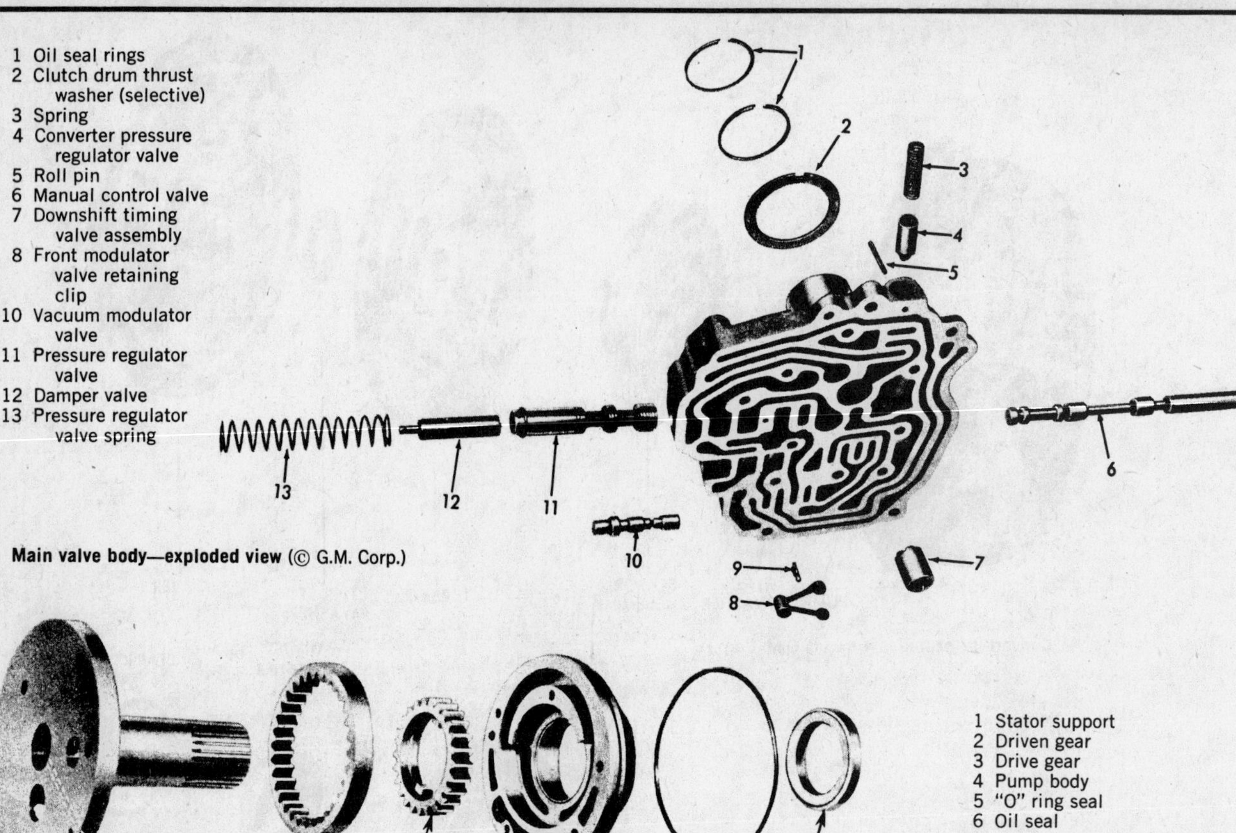

Main valve body—exploded view (© G.M. Corp.)

Front pump—exploded view (© G.M. Corp.)

Valve body attaching bolts (© G.M. Corp.)

Clearance front pump driven gear to body .002"—.0055" (© G.M. Corp.)

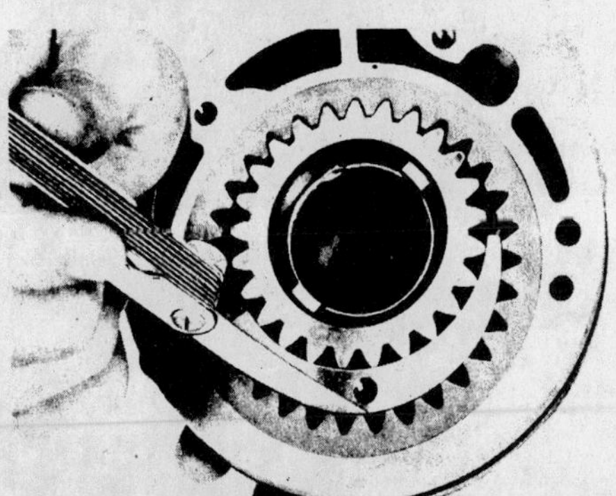

Clearance between the inner diameter of the driven gear and the crescent (© G.M. Corp.)

Checking gear and clearance .005"—.0015" (© G.M. Corp.)

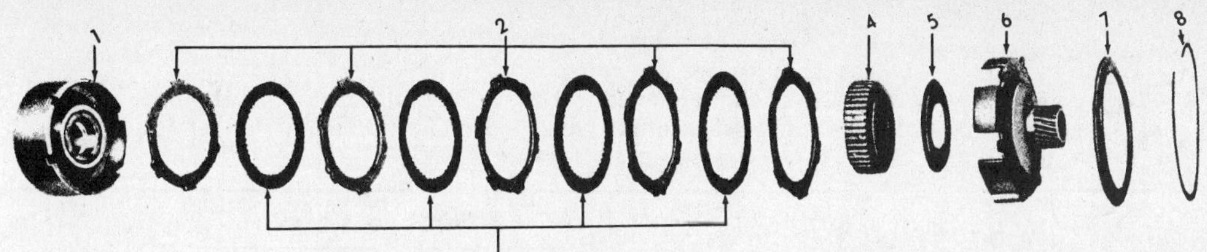

Clutch assembly—exploded view (© G.M. Corp.)

1 Clutch drum assembly
2 Clutch driven plate
3 Clutch drive plate
4 Clutch hub
5 Clutch hub thrust washer
6 Low sun gear and clutch flange assembly
7 Clutch flange retainer
8 Retainer ring

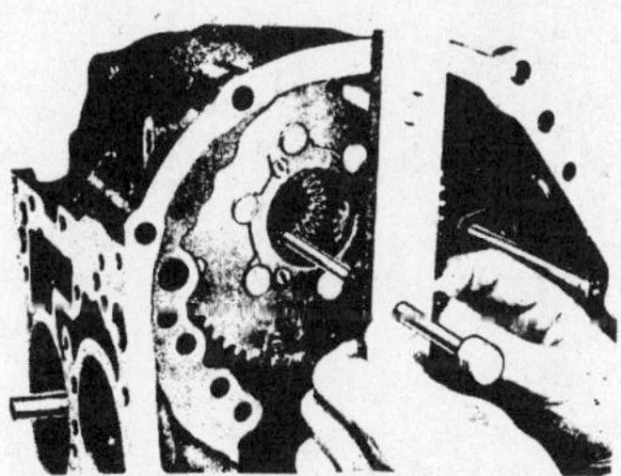

Measuring sun gear depth (© G.M. Corp.)

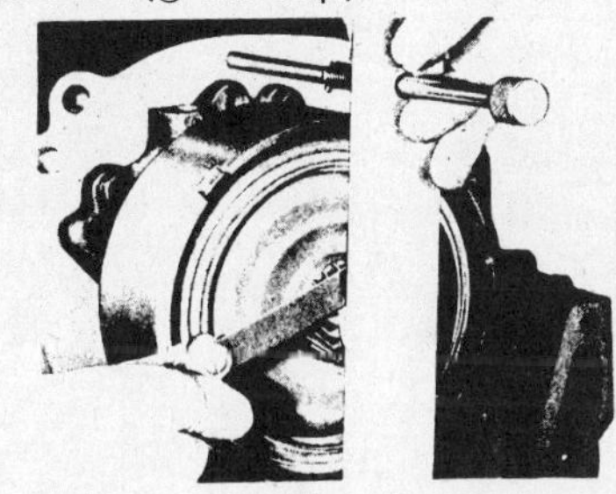

Measuring low to reverse sun gear clearance (© G.M. Corp.)

Remove the transmission case to bell housing bolts and lock washers.

Carefully separate the bell housing from the transmission case.

Note that there are two (2) gaskets, one between the bell housing, the valve body, and the transmission case, and another smaller crescent moon shaped one between the valve body and the case.

Note that there is a bronze thrust washer on the oil delivery sleeve of the valve body to intervene between the clutch assembly and the valve body.

On late models this thrust washer is the one controlling transmission endplay.

Reinstall Bell Housing

The valve should extend 11/16″ in low position.

Install new crescent valve body to case gasket.

Raise the manual valve outer lever to top detent position, which is reverse.

The connecting lever inside the case is called the reaction lever. It is now set to engage the inner lever in the bell housing. The fact that they properly engage can be observed through the opening occupied by the throttle valve assembly.

Valve Body and Front Oil Pump Assembly

With the transmission out of the truck and lying on the bench remove the manual control valve and wrap it in protective material.

Remove the bolts and lock-washers attaching the valve body to the bell housing and the front pump.

Remove the valve body and its gasket. Wrap the valve body so it is protected.

Drive the front oil pump and reactor shaft assembly out of the bell housing to the rear.

With oil pumps disassembled check for galling or scoring and check for proper clearances.

Clutch

Remove retainer ring and flange retainer. Remove low sun gear and flange from drum. Now remove thrust washer hub and plates.

Compress spring to remove snap ring and slowly release seat and spring.

Rap the drum sharply on block of wood to remove piston.

Carefully inspect both seals, piston, drum, bushings and plates. Be sure the relief valve ball is free and that it seats properly.

In reassembling coat all parts with transmission oil to prevent sticking and scoring.

When installing plates start with a steel plate. The three, thick .090″ plates must be in center of pack.

Reassembly

As planetary parts, with clutch, drums and bands are reassembled, check clearances as indicated in illustration. Various thickness washers are available to place in front of clutch drum to obtain a clearance of .007″ to .035″.

Illustration shows measuring to obtain clearance between low and reverse sun gears. Select proper washer to obtain clearance of .025″ to .050″.

Diagnosis

This diagnosis guide covers the most common symptoms and is an aid to careful diagnosis. The items to check are listed in the sequence to be followed for quickest results. Thus, follow the checks in the order given for the particular transmission type.

TROUBLE SYMPTOMS	Items to Check	
	In Truck	Out of Truck
No drive in D range	ABCD	abc
No drive in R or slips in reverse	ABCEGHIJL	efa
Drive in neutral	B	a
First speed only—no 1-2 shift	KG	g
1-2 shift at full throttle only	MNG	
First and second speeds only—no 2-3 shift	MNG	f
Slips in all ranges	ACEFG	dfahc
Slips—1-2 shift	ACELGO	gh
Rough 1-2 shift	CELGJOGJ	hi
Slips 2-3 shift	ACELG	fh
Rough 2-3 shift	CELO	
Shifts occur—too high or too low car speed	CKEMGL	
No detent downshifts	NMG	
No part throttle downshift (heavy-duty model "OE" only)	CEG	
No engine braking—super range—second speed	O	i
No engine braking—low range—first speed	GJ	ik
Park will not hold	BPQ	
Poor performance or rough idle—stator not functioning	RS	lo
Noisy transmission	TF	dafgn

Key to Checks

A. Oil level
B. Manual linkage (external)
C. Check oil pressure
D. Manual control disconnected inside
E. Modulator and/or lines
F. Clogged strainer or intake leaks
G. Valves, body and/or leaks
H. Reverse feed passages
I. Valve check balls
J. Rear servo and accumulator
K. Governor and/or feed line seals
L. Pump regulator and boost valve
M. Detent solenoid
N. Detent switch
O. Front servo and accumulator
P. Internal linkage
Q. Parking pawl and/or link
R. Stator switch
S. Valve body-stator section
T. Cooler or lines
a. Front clutch
b. Clutch feed seals and gaskets
c. Low sprags
d. Front pump
e. Rear band
f. Direct clutch
g. Intermediate clutch
h. Pump-to-case gasket
i. Intermediate check valve ball in case
j. Front band
k. Rear band
l. Turbine shaft
m. Converter assembly
n. Planetary assembly

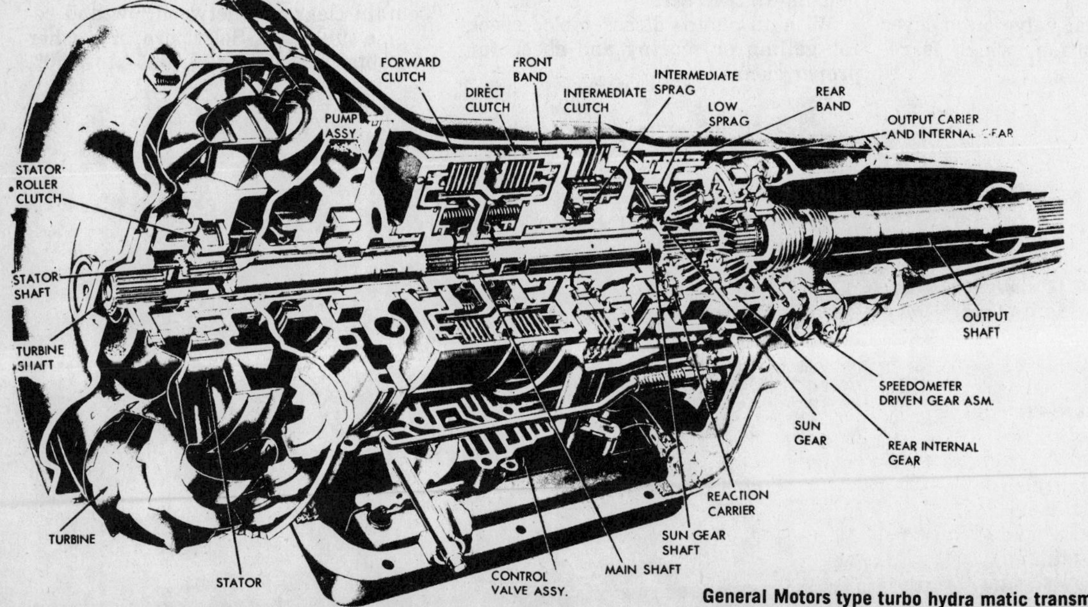

General Motors type turbo hydra matic transmission (© G.M. Corp.)

The illustration is typical. While design and repair procedures are similar, components vary with truck application and should not be considered interchangeable.

General Information

The General Motors type 400 transmission is a fully automatic unit consisting of a three element torque converter and a three speed and reverse planetary gear set. Three multiple disc clutches, one sprag, one roller clutch, and two bands control the planetary gear set operation.

The torque converter consists of a driving member, a driven member, and a stator assembly. The stator has a roller clutch which allows it to turn in one direction only. As the speed of the driving member increases, the roller clutch allows the stator to free-wheel on its shaft. This causes the torque converter to cease its torque multiplication function and to operate as a fluid coupling with a drive ratio of approximately one to one.

Fluid Specifications

Oil capacity, transmission and converter
Approx. 22 pints
Capacity between marks on dip stick
1 pint
Type of oil
Automatic transmission fluid Type A
Drain and refill
24,000

Draining and Refilling

The transmission fluid should be drained and refilled at 24,000 mile intervals. To do this:

1. Drain transmission oil.
2. Remove oil pan attaching screws.
3. Remove oil pan and gasket.
4. Remove strainer or filter.
5. Thoroughly clean oil strainer or filter and oil pan in solvent. Blow dry with air.
6. Renew oil strainer gasket and oil pan gasket.
7. Install oil strainer or filter.
8. Install oil pan. Torque attaching screws to 10-12 ft. lbs.
9. Add about five pints of transmission fluid.
10. Start engine. Do not race engine. Move selector lever slowly through each range. Check fluid level.
11. With transmission cold, add enough fluid to bring level to 1/4 in. below the Add mark. With the transmission at normal temperature, add enough fluid to bring the level to the Full mark. About fifteen miles of highway driving is required to bring the transmission to normal temperature.
12. In case of transmission overhaul, proceed as in Steps 9-11. Start with five pints of fluid if converter has not been replaced; eight pints if it has been replaced. Total capacity is about 22 pints, but correct level is determined by the mark on the dipstick rather than by amount of fluid added.

Transmission Disassembly

Clean outside of the unit thoroughly to prevent dirt from entering the unit.

1. With transmission in a work cradle or on a clean bench, lift the converter straight off the transmission input shaft.
2. With transmission bottom-up, remove modulator assembly attaching screw and retainer, then remove the modulator assembly and O-ring seal.

Governor, Speedometer Driven Gear, Oil Pan, Strainer and Intake Pipe Removal

1. Remove attaching screws, governor cover and gasket, then withdraw governor from the case.
2. Remove speedometer driven gear attaching screw and retainer, then withdraw the driven gear assembly.
3. Remove oil pan attaching screws, then the oil pan. Discard gasket.
4. Remove pump intake pipe and strainer assembly, then the pipe-to-case O-ring seal.

Control Valve Assembly, Governor Pipes and Detent Spring Assembly Removal

1. Disconnect the lead wire from the pressure switch assembly. Remove the switch assembly from the valve body, if necessary. This switch is installed on 1970 models only.

Transmission in holding fixture
(© G.M. Corp.)

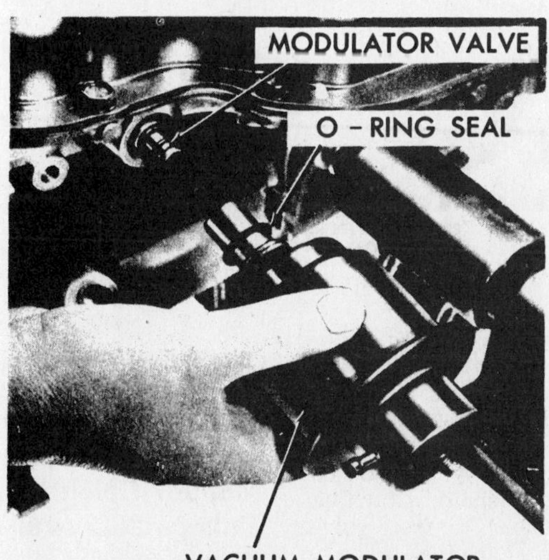

Removing vacuum modulator and valve
(© G.M. Corp.)

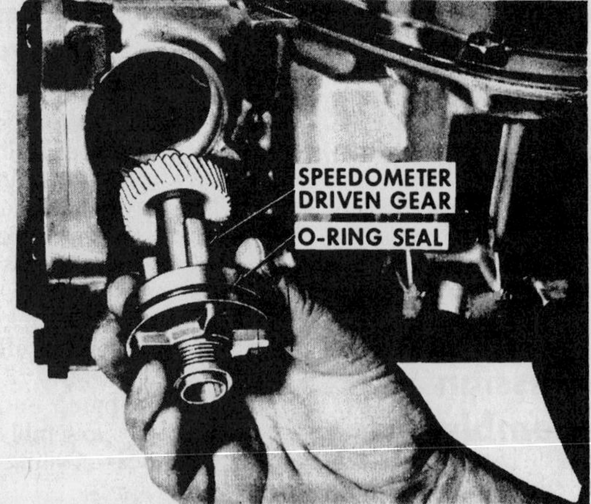

Removing speedometer drive gear and sleeve
(© G.M. Corp.)

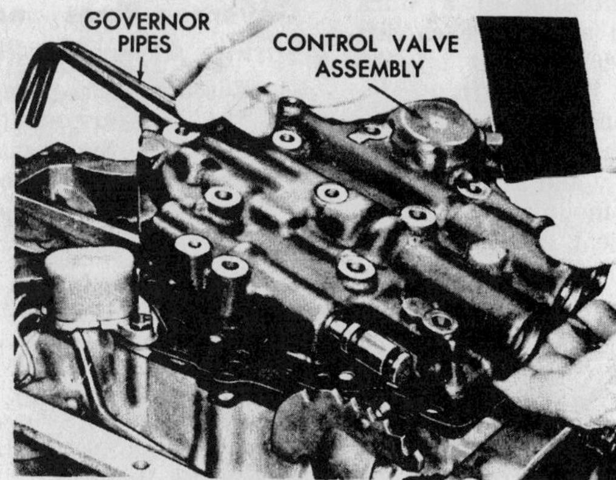

Removing control valve assembly and governor pipes from case
(© G.M. Corp.)

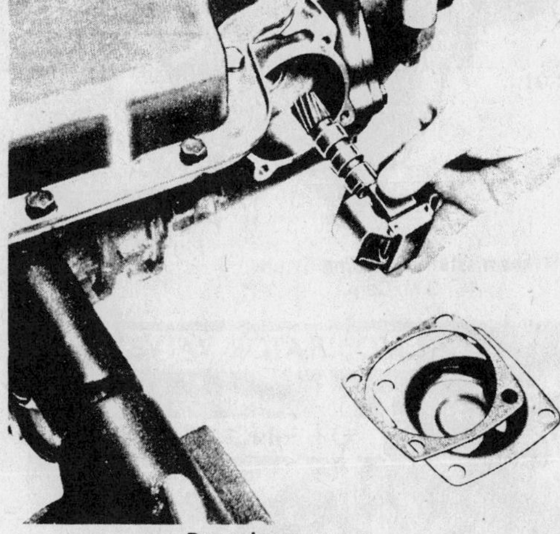

Removing governor
(© G.M. Corp.)

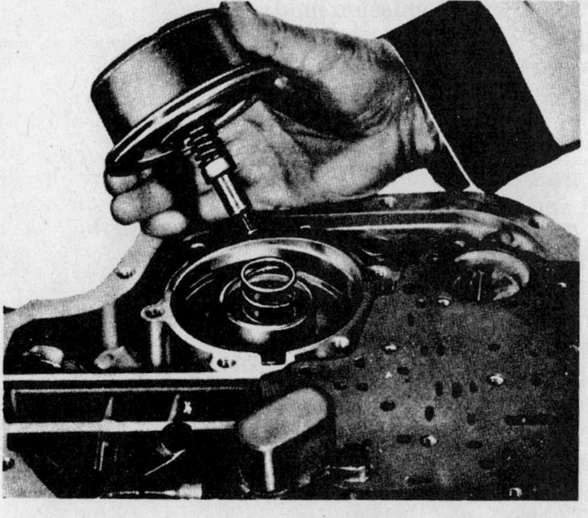

Removing rear servo
(© G.M. Corp.)

2. Remove control valve body attaching screws and detent roller and spring assembly. NOTE: do not remove solenoid attaching screws. Remove control valve body and governor pipes.
3. Remove the governor pipes from valve body. Then remove valve body-to-spacer gasket.

Rear Servo, Solenoid, Valve Body Spacer, Front Servo, Manual Detent and Parking Linkage Removal

1. Remove rear servo cover attaching screws, the cover and gasket, then the rear servo assembly from the case.
2. Remove servo accumulator springs.
3. Disconnect the solenoid leads from connector terminal. Withdraw connector and O-ring seal.
4. Remove solenoid attaching screws, solenoid and gasket.
5. Remove valve body spacer plate and gasket.
6. Remove six check balls from cored passages in transmission case.
7. Remove the front servo assembly.
8. Loosen the jam nut which holds the detent lever to the manual shaft. Then remove detent lever from manul shaft and remove manual shaft.
9. Remove parking actuator rod and detent lever assembly. Then remove detent lever E-ring and the detent lever.
10. Remove attaching screws and park bracket; then the parking pawl return spring.
11. Remove parking pawl shaft retainer, then the parking pawl shaft, O-ring and pawl.

Rear Oil Seal and Extension Housing Removal

1. Pry rear oil seal from extension housing.
2. Remove housing attaching bolts, then remove extension housing and housing-to-case oil seal.

Oil Pump, Forward Clutch and Gear Unit Removal

1. Pry front seal from the pump. Then remove pump attaching bolts.
2. With slide hammers attached, remove pump from transmission case. Discard pump-to-case seal

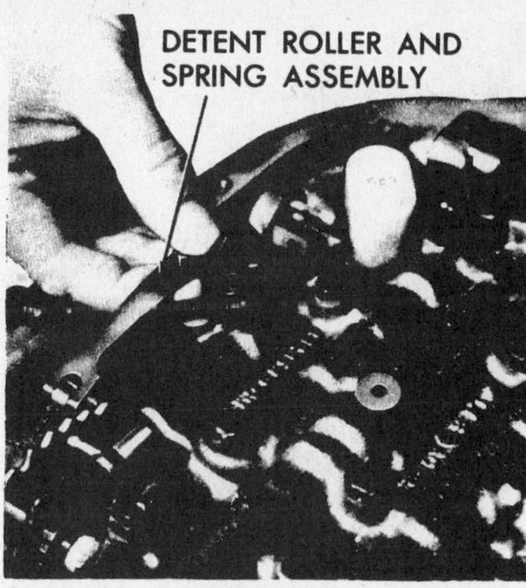

Removing detent roller and spring assembly
(© G.M. Corp.)

Removing detent solenoid and gasket
(© G.M. Corp.)

Removing front pump using slide hammers
(© G.M. Corp.)

ring. Discard pump-to-case gasket.
3. Remove turbine shaft from transmission.
4. Remove forward clutch assembly. Be sure that the bronze thrust washer came out with the clutch housing assembly.
5. Remove the direct clutch assembly. Remove front band and sun gear shaft.
6. Remove the case center support-to-case bolt and center support locating screw. 1969-70 models have no locating screw.
7. Remove intermediate clutch backing plate-to-case snap-ring. Then remove the backing plate, three composition, and three steel clutch plates.
8. Remove the center support to-case retaining snap-ring.
9. Remove the entire gear unit assembly.
10. Remove the output shaft-to-case thrust washer from the rear of the output shaft, or from inside the case.
11. Remove rear unit selective washer from transmission case.
12. Remove rear band assembly.
13. Remove support to case spacer from inside case.

Component Disassembly, Inspection, and Assembly

Governor

All components of the governor, except the driven gear, are a select fit and so calibrated. Therefore, service this unit as an assembly.

Clean and inspect all parts for wear or other damage. Check valve opening at feed port with a feeler gauge, holding the governor with the weights extended completly outward. Check valve opening at exhaust port, holding governor with weights completely inward. If either opening is less than .020 in., replace governor assembly.

If a new governor drive gear is installed, a new pin hole must be drilled 90 degrees from the original hole.

Front Servo Inspection

1. Inspect servo pin for admage.
2. Inspect servo piston for damaged oil ring groove, cracks, or porosity. Check freedom of oil seal ring in groove.
3. Check fit of servo pin in piston.

Rear Servo Disassembly

1. Remove E-ring which holds the servo piston to band apply pin.
2. Remove servo piston and seal from band apply pin. Remove second washer from band apply pin.
3. Remove washer, spring, and retainer.

Rear Servo Inspection

1. Check freedom of accumulator rings in piston.
2. Check fit of band apply pin in servo piston. Inspect pin for scores or cracks.
3. Inspect accumulator and servo pistons for cracks or porosity.

Rear Servo Assembly

1. Install spring retainer, spring,

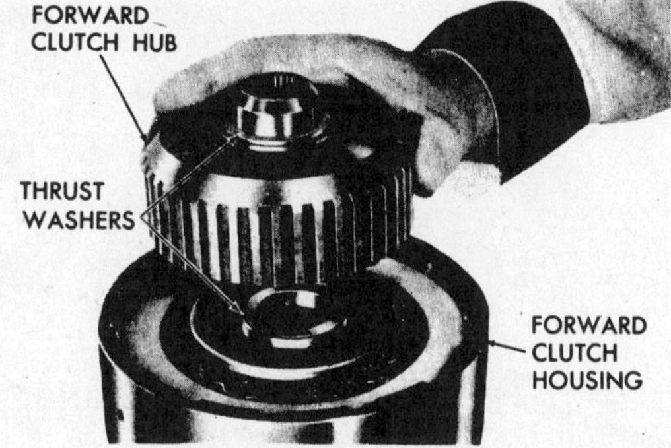

Removing forward clutch
(© G.M. Corp.)

and washer on band apply pin.
2. Install band apply pin, retainer, spring, and washer into bore of servo piston and secure with E-ring.
3. Install oil seal on servo piston. Install outer and inner oil seal rings on accumulator piston and assembly into bore of servo piston.

Control Valve Body Disassembly

When disassembling control valve body, be careful to identify springs so that they can be replaced in their proper locations.

1. Position valve assembly with cored face up and accumulator pocket on bottom.
2. Remove manual valve from upper bore.
3. Compress accumulator piston spring and remove E-ring retainer. Remove accumulator piston and spring.
4. Press out retaining pin from upper right bore. Remove 1-2 modulator bushing, 1-2 regulator valve and spring, 1-2 detent valve, and 1-2 shift valve. 1-2 regulator valve and spring may

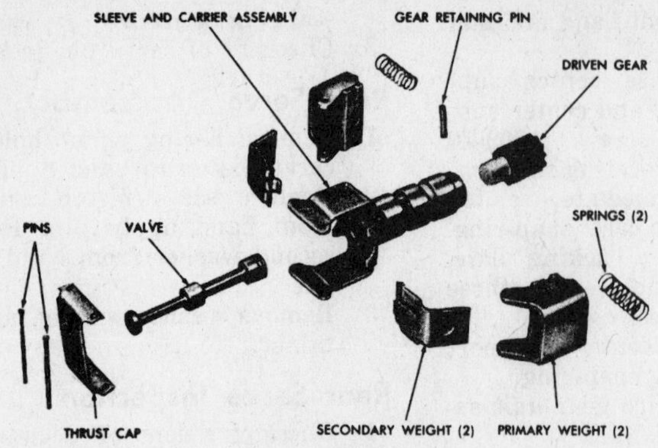

Governor assembly
(© G.M. Corp.)

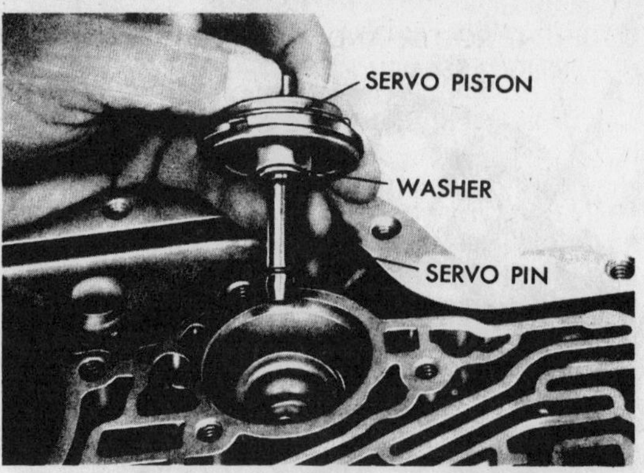

Removing front servo piston, washer and pin
(© G.M. Corp.)

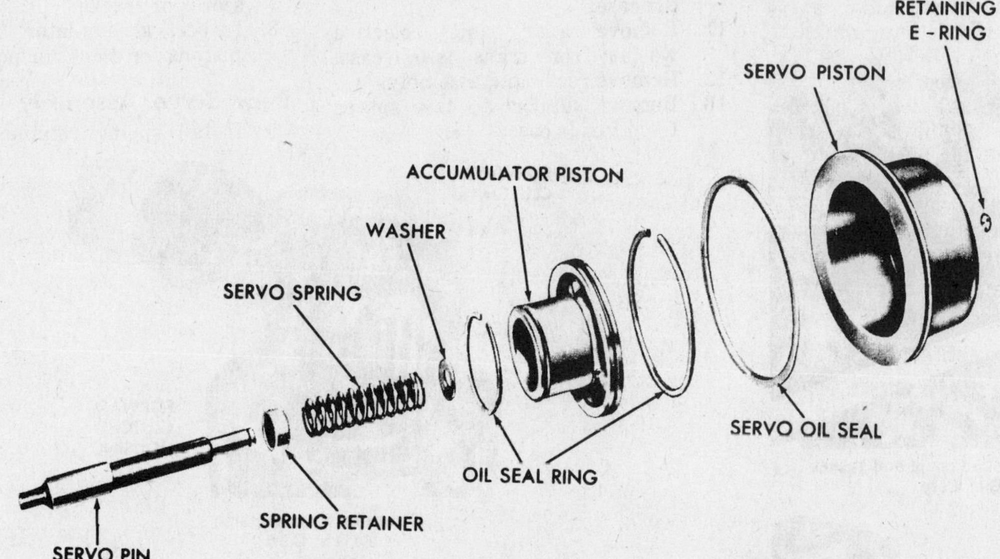

Exploded view of rear servo and accumulator (© G.M. Corp.)

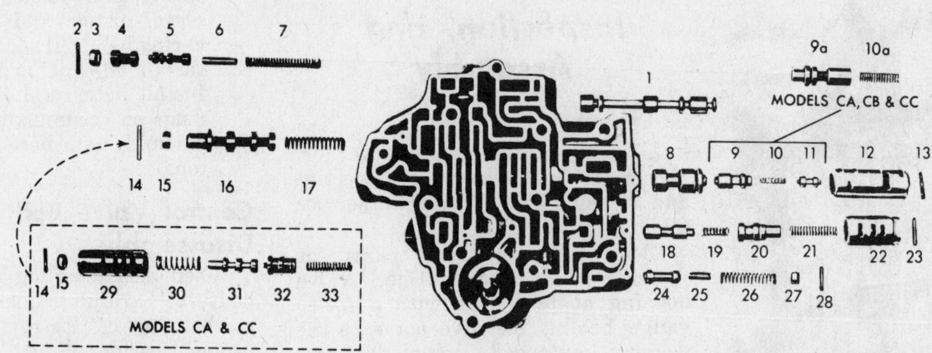

1 Manual valve
2 Retaining pin
3 Bore plug
4 Detent valve
5 Detent regulator valve
6 Spacer pin
7 Detent regulator spring
8 1-2 shift valve
9 1-2 Dentent valve
9a 1-2 modulator valve
10 1-2 regulator spring
10a 1-2 modulator spring
11 1-2 regulator valve
12 1-2 modulator bushing
13 Retaining pin
14 Grooved retaining pin
15 Bore plug
16 1-2 accumulator valve
17 1-2 accumulator spring
18 2-3 shift valve
19 3-2 intermediate spring
20 2-3 modulator valve
21 2-3 valve spring
22 2-3 modulator bushing
23 Retaining pin
24 3-2 valve
25 Spacer pin
26 3-2 valve spring
27 Bore plug
28 Retaining pin
29 1-2 accumulator bushing
30 1-2 accumulator secondary spring
31 1-2 accumulator valve
32 1-2 primary accumulator valve

Control valve body layout (© G.M. Corp.)

be inside of 1-2 modulator bushing.

5. Press out retaining pin from center right bore. Remove 2-3 modulator bushing, 2-3 shift valve spring, 2-3 modulator valve, 3-2 intermediate spring, and 2-3 shift valve. 2-3 modulator valve will be inside of 2-3 modulator bushing.
6. Press out retaining pin from lower right bore. Hold hand over bore, as plug may pop out. Remove plug, 3-2 valve spring, spacer, and 3-2 valve.
7. Holding hand over bore, press out retainer pin from upper left bore. Remove bore plug, detent valve, detent regulator valve, spacer, and detent regulator valve spring.
8. Pry out grooved retainer ring from lower left bore with long nose pliers. Remove bore plug, 1-2 accumulator bushing, 1-2 accumulator valve, secondary spring, primary 1-2 accumulator valve, and spring.
9. Remove governor oil feed screen from oil feed hole in valve body.

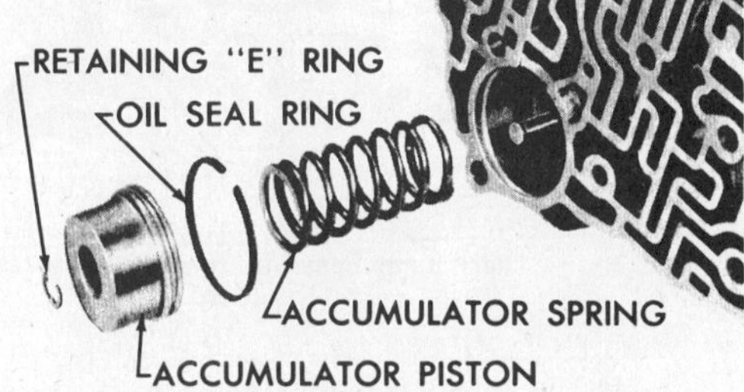

Removing front accumulator piston and spring
(© G.M. Corp.)

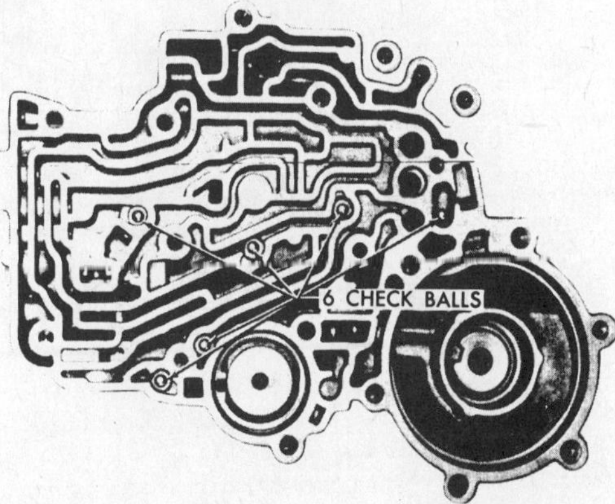

Location of check bills
(© G.M. Corp.)

Control Valve Body Inspection

1. Wash control valve body, valves and other parts in solvent. Do not allow valves to bump together. Air dry parts and blow out all passages.
2. Inspect all valves and bushings carefully. Burrs may be removed with a fine stone or fine crocus cloth and light oil. Be careful not to round off shoulders of valves.
3. Test all valves and bushings for free movement in their bores. All valves should fall freely of their own weight.
4. The manual valve is the only valve that can be serviced separately. If any of the other valves are defective or damaged, install a new control valve assembly.
5. Inspect body for cracks or scored bores. Check all springs for distortion or collapsed coils.

Control Valve Body Assembly

1. Replace front accumulator spring and piston into valve body. Compress spring and piston, assuring that piston pin is correctly aligned with hole in piston and that oil seal ring does not catch on lip of bore when installing piston. Secure piston and spring with E-ring retainer.
2. Install 1-2 accumulator primary spring, 1-2 primary valve, and 1-2 accumulator bushing into lower left bore. Place 1-2 accumulator secondary valve, stem end out, into the 1-2 accumulator bushing. Place 1-2 accumulator secondary spring over stem end of valve. Replace bore plug and retaining pin.
3. Install detent regulator valve spring and spacer into upper left bore, making certain that spring seats in bottom of bore. Compress spring and hold with a small screwdriver between end of spring and wall on cored side of valve body. Insert detent regulator valve, stem end out, and detent valve, small land first. Insert bore plug, press inward, remove screwdriver, and install retaining pin.
4. Insert 3-2 valve in bottom right bore. Place spacer inside 3-2 valve spring and insert spacer and spring in bore. Install bore plug and retaining pin.
5. Install 3-2 intermediate spring on stem end of 2-3 shift valve. Install valve and spring, valve first, into center right bore. Be sure that valve seats in bottom of bore. Place 2-3 modulator valve, hole end first, into 2-3 modulator bushing. Install valve and bushing in bore. Install 2-3 shift valve spring into hole in 2-3 modulator valve. Secure with retaining pin.
6. Seat 1-2 shift valve, stem end out, in bottom of upper right bore. Install 1-2 regulator valve, larger stem first, and spring and 1-2 detent valve, hole end first, into 1-2 modulator bushing. Align spring in bore of 1-2 detent valve. Install assembly into upper right bore of control valve body. Install retaining pin.
7. Replace governor oil feed screen assembly in governor oil feed hole.
8. Install manual valve with detent pin groove to the right.

Oil Pump Disassembly

1. Place the pump over a hole in the bench, shaft down, cover up.
2. Compress regulator boost valve bushing against the pressure regulator spring and remove the snap-ring.
3. Remove the boost valve bushing and valve, then the spring.
4. Remove valve spring retainer and spacer/s, if present, and regulator valve.
5. Remove pump cover to body attaching bolts, then remove the cover.
6. Remove the retaining pin and bore plug from the pressure regulator bore.
7. Remove the two hook-type oil rings from the pump cover.
8. Remove pump to forward clutch housing selective washer.
9. Mark drive and driven gears for reassembly, then remove the gears.

Oil Pump Inspection

1. Inspect drive gear, driven gear, gear pocket, and crescent for scoring, galling, or other damage.
2. Replace pump gears in pump and check pump body face to

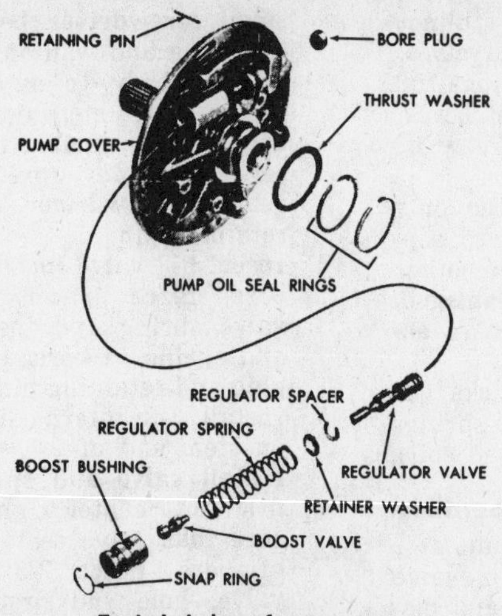

Exploded view of pump cover
(© G.M. Corp.)

Installing pump drive gear
(© G.M. Corp.)

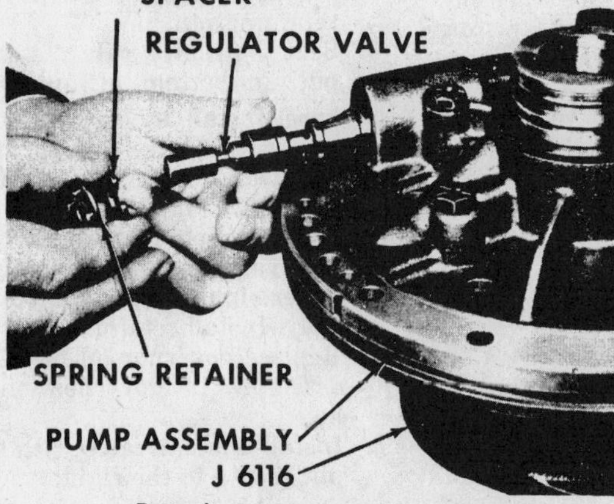

Removing pressure regulator valve
(© G.M. Corp.)

Check pump body face to gear clearance
(© G.M. Corp.)

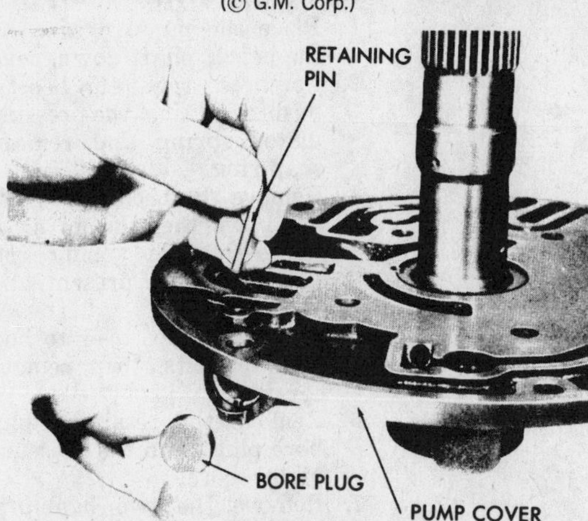

Installing pressure regulator regaining pin and´bore, lug
(© G.M. Corp.)

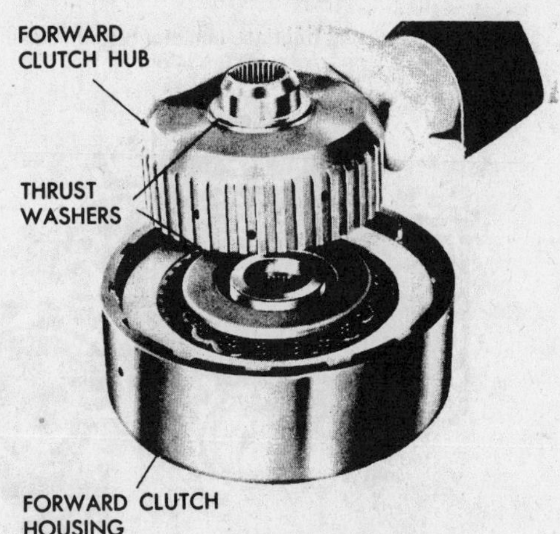

Removing forward clutch hub and thrust washers
(© G.M. Corp.)

face gear clearance. The clearance should be .0008-.0035 in.

3. Check pump body face for scoring or nicks. Check oil passages in pump body for roughness or obstructions. Check condition of cover bolt attaching threads. Check for flatness of pump body face. Check pump body bushing, for scores or nicks. If a new bushing is installed, drive it in flush to .010 in. below the gear pocket face.
4. Replace pump attaching bolt seals if necessary.
5. Check pump cover face for flatness. Check for scoring or chips in pressure regulator bore. Check that all passages are unobstructed. Check for scoring or damage at pump gear face. Check that breather hole in pump cover is open.
6. Check condition of stator shaft splines and bushings.
7. Check oil ring grooves for damage or wear. Check selective thrust washer for wear.
8. Make sure that pressure regulator valve and boost valve operate freely.

Oil Pump Assembly

1. Install drive and driven gears into the pump body, alignment marks up and in proper index, (drive gear with drive tangs up).
2. Install pressure regulator spring spacer/s if required, retainer and spring into the pressure regulator bore.
3. Install pressure regulator valve from the opposite end of the bore, stem end first.
4. Install boost valve into bushing, stem end out, and install both parts into the pump cover by compressing the bushing against the spring. Install the snap-ring.
5. Install the regulator valve bore plug and retaining pin into opposite end of bore.
6. Install the front unit selective thrust washer over the pump cover delivery sleeve.
7. Install two hook-type oil seal rings.
8. Assemble pump cover to pump body with attaching bolts. (Leave bolts one turn loose at this time.)
9. Place pump aligning strap over pump body and cover, then tighten tool.
10. Install pump cover bolts. Remove clamp and install pump-to-case O-ring seal and gasket.

Forward Clutch Disassembly

1. Remove forward clutch housing-to-direct clutch hub snap-ring.
2. Remove direct clutch hub.
3. Remove forward clutch hub and thrust washers.
4. Remove five composition and five steel clutch plates. Press out the turbine shaft.
5. Compress the spring retainer and remove the snap-ring.
6. Remove the compressor, snap-ring, spring retainer and 16 release springs, then lift out the piston.
7. Remove inner and outer piston seals.
8. Remove center piston seal from the forward clutch housing.

Forward Clutch Inspection

1. Inspect clutch plates for burning, scoring, or wear.
2. Inspect springs for collapsed coils or distortion.
3. Check clutch hubs for worn splines, thrust faces, and open lubrication holes.
4. Check piston for cracks.
5. Check clutch housing for wear, scoring, open oil passages, and free operation of ball check.
6. Inspect turbine shaft for:
   a. Open lubrication passages at each end.
   b. Spline damage.
   journals.
   c. Damage to ground bushing
   d. Cracks or distortion of shaft.

Air checking forward clutch
(© G.M. Corp.)

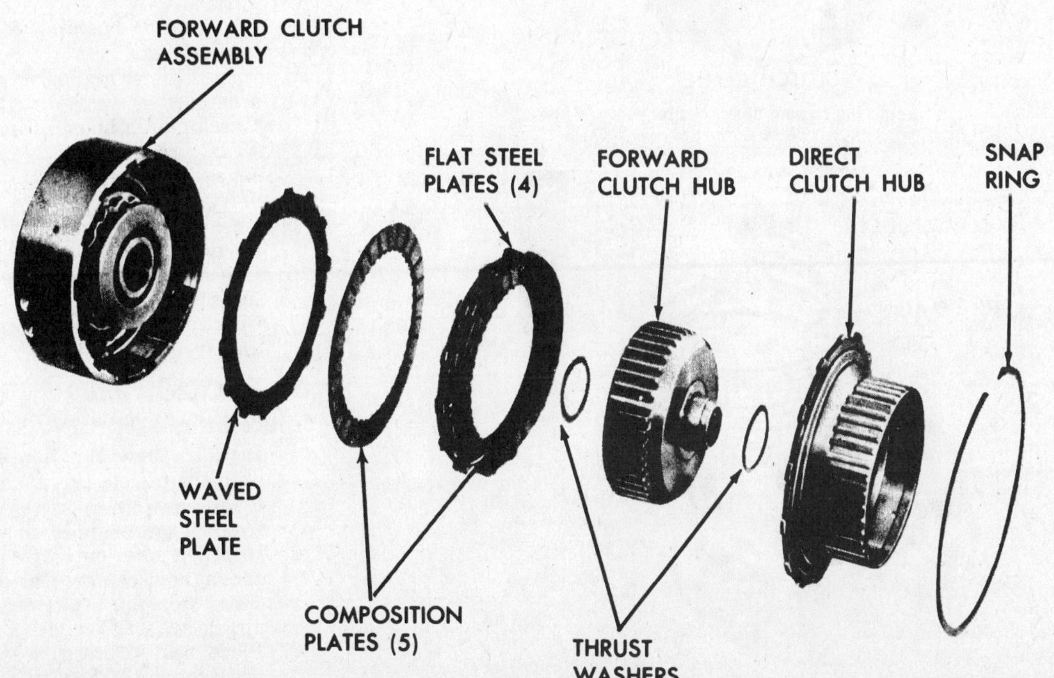

Exploded view of forward clutch (© G.M. Corp.)

Forward Clutch Assembly

1. Place new inner and outer oil seals on clutch piston, lips away from spring pockets.
2. Place a new center seal on the clutch housing, lip faces up.
3. Place a seal protector (thimble) tool into clutch drum and install the piston.
4. Install 16 clutch release springs into pockets in the piston.
5. Lay the spring retainer and the snap-ring on the springs.
6. Compress springs using compressor, and install snap-ring. Press in turbine shaft.
7. Install the direct clutch hub washers; retain with petroleum jelly.
8. Place forward clutch hub into forward clutch housing.
9. Lubricate with transmission oil and install the clutch pack, five composition, and five steel plates, starting with steel and alternating steel and composition.
10. Install clutch hub and retaining snap-ring.
11. Place forward clutch housing on pump delivery sleeve and air-check clutch operation.

Direct Clutch and Intermediate Sprag Disassembly

1. Remove intermediate clutch retainer snap-ring, then the retainer.
2. Remove clutch outer race, bushings and sprag assembly.
3. Invert the unit and remove backing plate to clutch housing snap-ring.
4. Remove direct clutch backing plate, five composition, and five steel plates.
5. Using clutch compressor tool compress the spring retainer and remove the snap-ring.
6. Remove retainer and 16 piston release springs.
7. Remove direct clutch piston, then remove the outer and inner seals from the piston.
8. Remove center piston seal from the direct clutch housing.

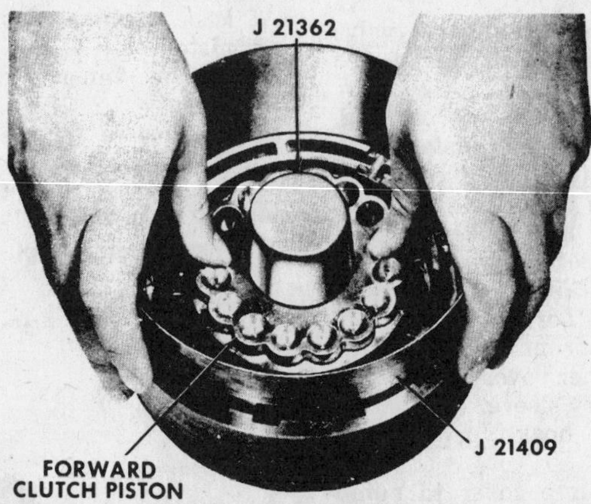

Installing forward clutch piston
(© G.M. Corp.)

Removing forward clutch center seal
(© G.M. Corp.)

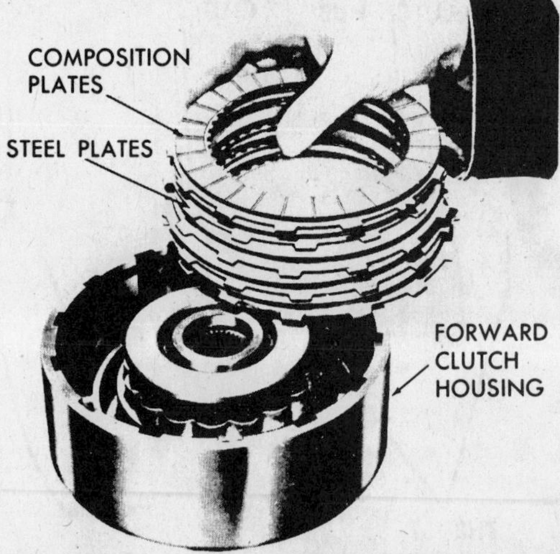

Installing forward clutch composition and steel plates
(© G.M. Corp.)

Direct Clutch and Intermediate Sprag Inspection

1. Check for popped or loose sprags.
2. Check sprag bushings for distortion or wear.
3. Inspect inner and outer races for scratches or wear.
4. Check clutch housing for cracks, wear, proper opening of oil passages, and wear on clutch plate drive lugs.
5. Check clutch plates for wear or burning.
6. Check backing plate for scratches or damage.
7. Check clutch piston for cracks and free operation of ball check.

Direct Clutch and Intermediate Sprag Assembly

1. Install a new clutch piston seal onto the piston, lips facing away from spring pockets. Apply transmission fluid to oil seals.
2. Install a new outer piston seal, and a new center seal onto the clutch housing, lip of seal facing up.
3. Place seal protectors over hu' and clutch housing, then install piston.
4. Install 16 springs into piston,

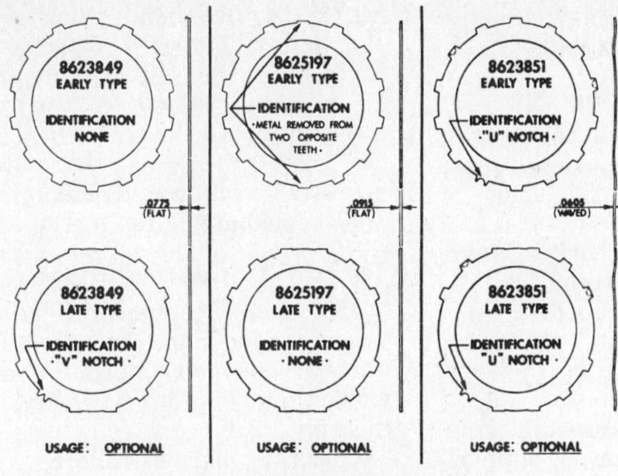

Clutch plate identification
(© G.M. Corp.)

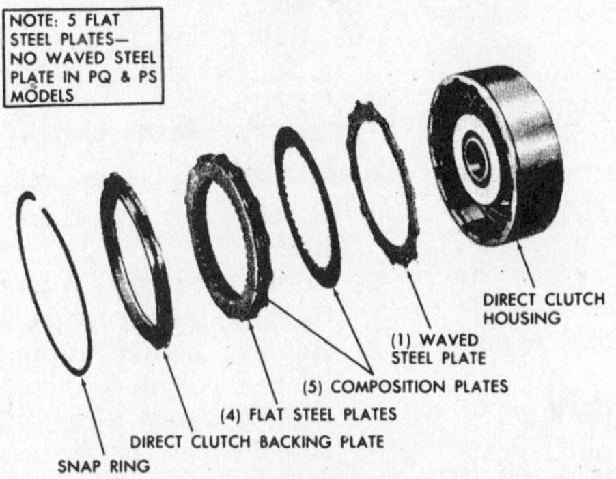

Layout of direct clutch
(© G.M. Corp.)

Removing direct clutch assembly
(© G.M. Corp.)

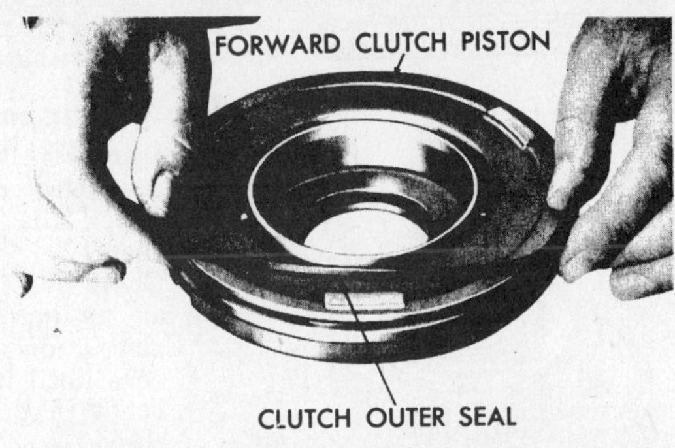

Removing or installing forward clutch piston outer seal
(© G.M. Corp.)

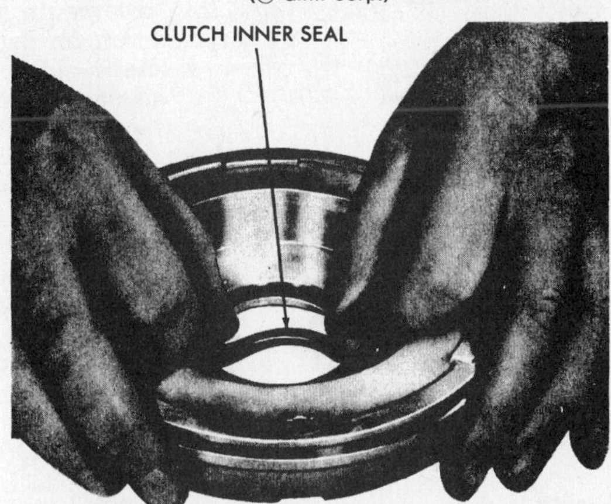

Installing direct clutch inner seal
(© G.M. Corp.)

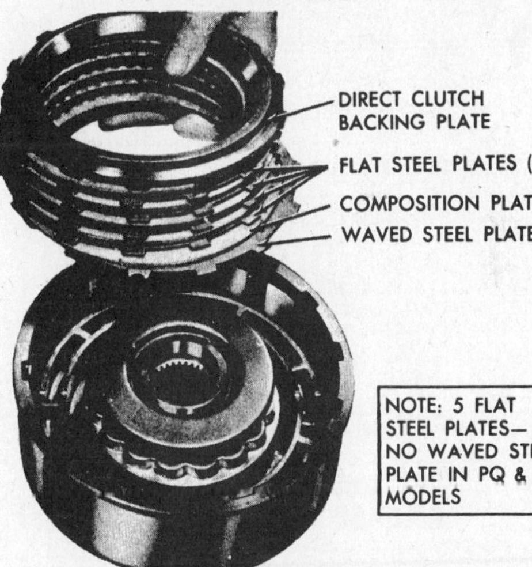

Installing direct clutch backing plate, and clutches
(© G.M. Corp.)

place retainer and snap-ring on retainer.

5. With clutch compressor, compress the clutch and install snap-ring.
6. Install five composition and five steel clutch plates, starting with steel and alternating composition and steel.
7. Install clutch backing plate, then install the backing plate snap-ring.
8. Invert the unit and install one sprag bushing, cup side up, over the inner race.
9. Install sprag assembly into outer race.
10. With ridge on inner cage facing down, start sprag and outer race over inner race with clockwise turning motion. NOTE: outer race should not turn counterclockwise.
11. Install sprag bushing over sprag cup side down.
12 Install clutch retainer and snap-ring.
13. Place direct clutch assembly over center support and air check operation of direct clutch.

NOTE: it is normal for air applied to reverse passage to escape from direct clutch passage. Air applied to direct clutch passage should move direct clutch.

Center Support Disassembly

1. Remove four hook-type oil rings from center support.
2. Using clutch fingers, compress the spring retainer and remove the snap-ring.
3. Remove spring retainer and 12 clutch release springs.
4. Remove intermediate clutch piston.
5. Remove inner piston seal. NOTE: do not remove the three screws holding the roller clutch

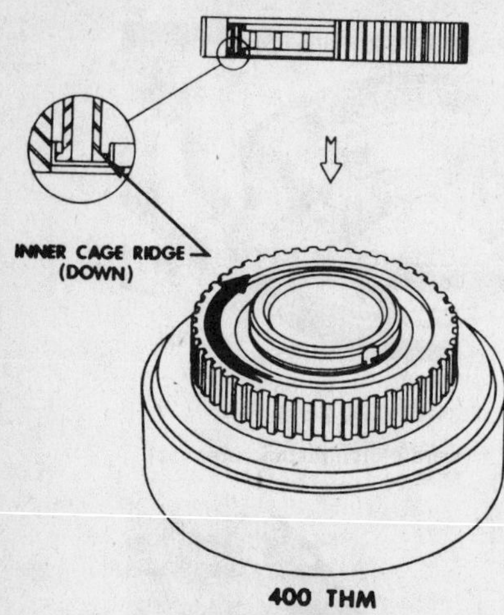

Correct sprag rotation
(© G.M. Corp.)

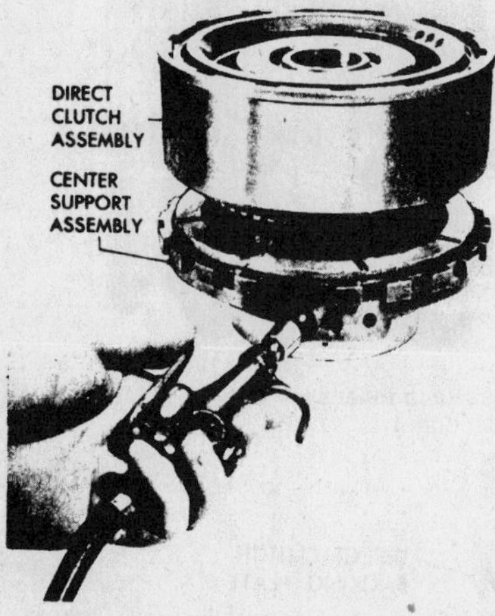

Air checks direct clutch assembly
(© G.M. Corp.)

inner race to the center support.

6. Remove outer piston seal.

Center Support Inspection

1. Inspect roller clutch inner race for scratches or identations. Check that lubrication hole is open.
2. Check bushing for scoring, wear, or galling. If bushing is replaced, drive new bushing into bore until it is flush to .010 in. below the top of the oil delivery sleeve.
3. Check oil seal rings and ring grooves in the center support tower for damage.
4. Make air pressure check of oil passages to be sure they are not interconnected.
5. Inspect piston sealing surfaces for scratches. Inspect piston seal grooves for damage. Check piston for cracks or porosity.
6. Check release springs for distortion or collapsed coils.
7. Check support to case spacer for burrs or raised edges. Repair with a stone or fine sand paper.

Center Support Assembly

1. Install new inner and outer seals on the piston, lip on inner seal facing away from the spring pocket.
2. Install inner spring protector tool onto the center support hub; lubricate the seal and install the piston.
3. Install 12 release springs into the piston.
4. Place spring retainer and snap-ring over the springs.
5. Using the clutch spring compressor, compress the springs and install the snap-ring.
6. Install four hook-type oil rings.
7. Air check the operation of intermediate clutch piston.

Torque Converter Inspection

The torque converter is a welded assembly and must be serviced as a unit. If converter output shaft has more than .050 in. end-play, renew the unit.

Check for leaks as follows:

A. Install converter leak test fixture and tighten.
B. Fill converter with air, 80 psi.
C. Submerge in water and check for bubbles.

Planetary Gear Unit Disassembly

1. Remove center support assembly.
2. Remove center support to reaction carrier thrust washer.
3. Remove center support to sun gear races and thrust bearing. One race may already have been removed with the center support.
4. Remove reaction carrier and roller clutch assembly.
5. Remove front internal gear ring from output carrier assembly.
6. Remove sun gear.
7. Take off reaction carrier to output carrier thrust washer.
8. Turn carrier assembly over.

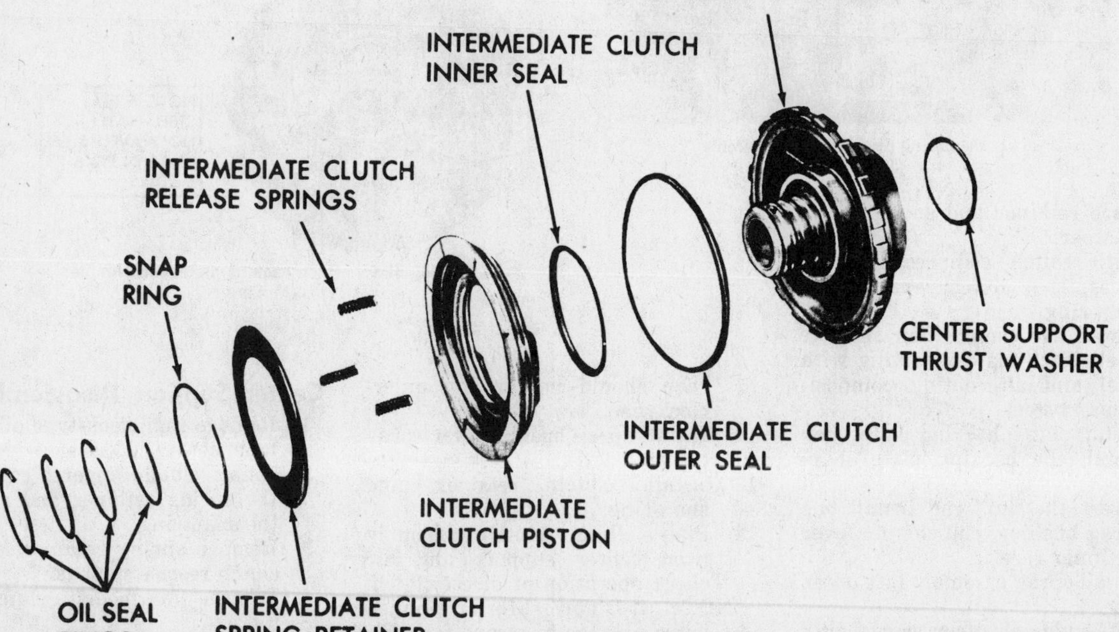

Center support assembly—layout (© G.M. Corp.)

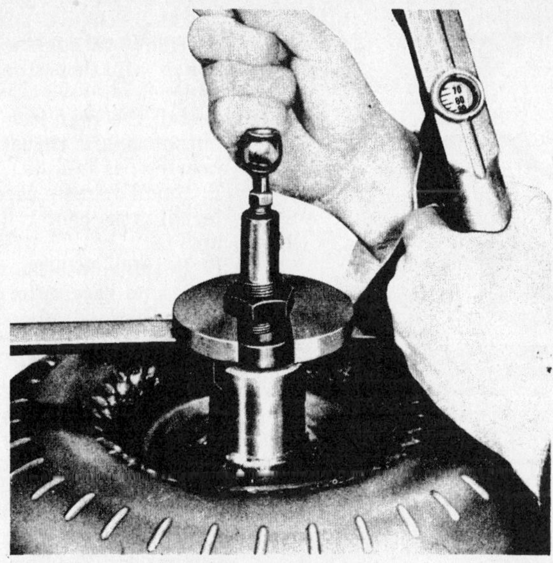
Air checking converter
(© G.M. Corp.)

Remove output shaft to output carrier snap ring.
9. Output shaft may now be removed.
10. Measure to determine speedometer drive gear location with relation to the end of the shaft for reassembly. Remove nylon speedometer drive gear by depressing retaining clip and sliding gear off output shaft. Remove steel speedometer drive gear with a suitable puller.
11. Remove output shaft to rear internal gear thrust bearing and two races.
12. Remove rear internal gear and mainshaft. Remove rear internal gear to sun gear thrust bearing and two races. Remove rear internal gear to mainshaft snap ring. Remove mainsahft.

Inspection of Reaction Carrier, Roller Clutch, and Output Carrier Assembly

1. Insert band surface reaction carrier for burring or scoring.
2. Check roller clutch outer race for scoring or wear. Check thrust washer for wear.
3. Check bushing for damage. If bushing is damaged, replace reaction carrier.
4. Check reaction carrier pinions for damage, rough bearings, or excessive tilt. Check pinion end play. It should be .009-.024 in. Pinions may be replaced if necessary.
5. Check roller clutch for damaged members. Check roller clutch cage for damage.
6. Inspect front internal gear (out-put carrier) for damaged teeth. Inspect output carrier pinions, for damage, rough bearings, and excessive tilt. Check pinion end play. It should be .009-.024 in.
7. Inspect parking pawl lugs for cracks or damage. Inspect output locating splines for damage.
8. Check front internal gear ring for flaking.

Planetary Gear Unit Assembly

1. Install rear internal gear onto end of mainshaft, then install the snap-ring.
2. Install sun gear to internal gear thrust races and bearings against inner face of rear internal gear as follows:
   a. Place large race against the internal gear, with flange facnig up.
   b. Place thrust bearing against race.
   c. Place small race against the bearing, with inner flange facing the bearing, or down.
3. Install the output carrier over the mainshaft so that the pinions mesh with the rear internal gear.

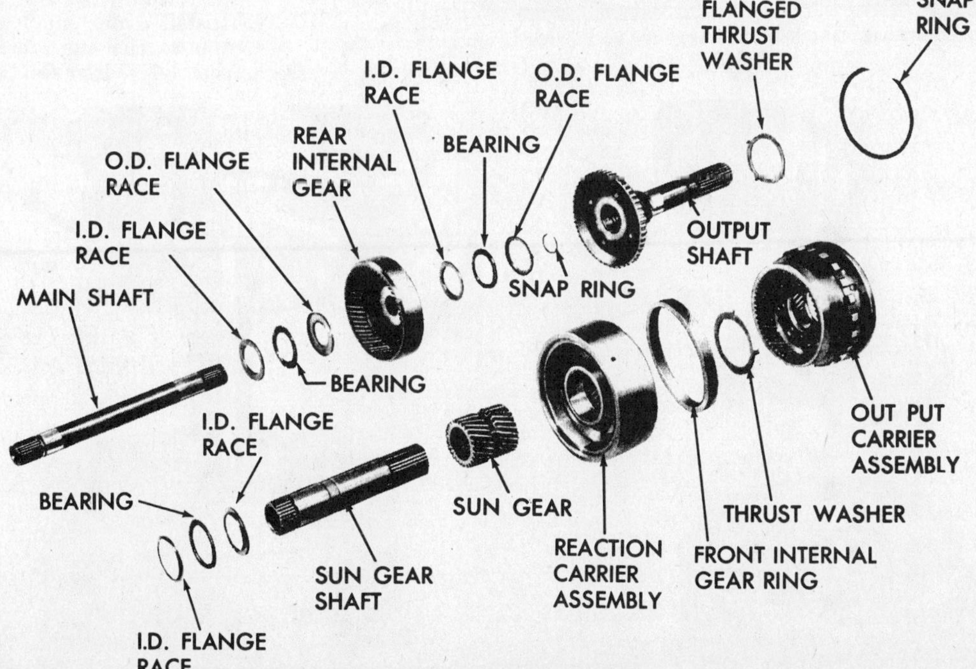

Gear unit—layout (© G.M. Corp.)

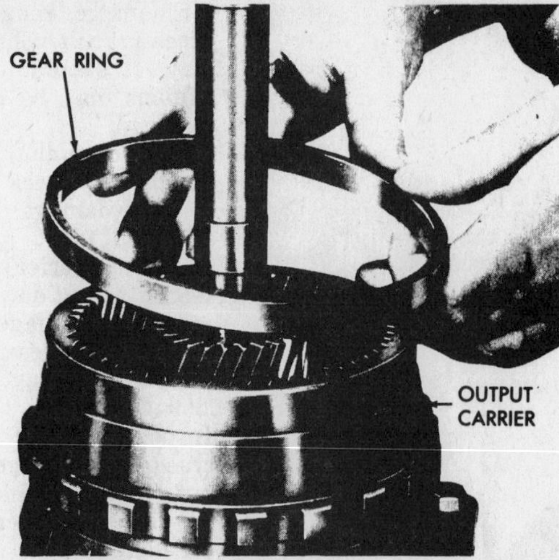

Installing front internal gear ring to output carrier
(© G.M. Corp.)

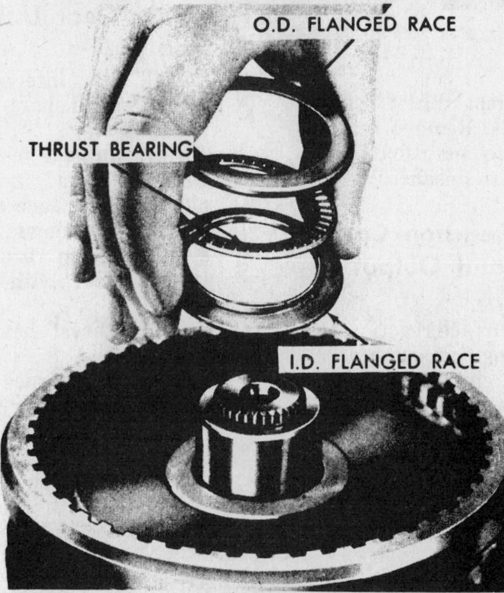

Installing rear internal gear to output shaft bearing and races
(© G.M. Corp.)

4. Place the above portion of the assembly through a hole in the bench so that the mainshaft hangs downward.
5. Install the rear internal gear to output shaft thrust races and bearings as follows:
   a. Small diamete race against internal gear, center flange facing up.
   b. Bearing onto the race.
   c. Second race onto the bearing, outer flange cupped over the bearing.
6. Install output shaft into the output carrier assembly.
7. Install output shaft to output carrier snap-ring.
8. Turn assembly over and support it so that the output shaft hangs downward.
9. Install the reaction carrier to output carrier thrust washer, tabs facing down and in their pockets.
10. Install sun gear, splines, chamfer down. Install gear ring over output carrier.
11. Install sun gear shaft, then the reaction carrier.
12. Install the center support to sun gear thrust races and bearing as follows:
    A. Install the large race, center flange up over the sun gear shaft.
    B. Install thrust bearing.
    C. Install the second race, center flange up.
13. Install roller clutch to reaction carrier outer race. Install the center support to reaction carrier thrust washer into the recess in the support. Retain with petroleum jelly.
14. Install center support into reaction carrier and roller clutch assembly. With reaction carrier

Installing output shaft
(© G.M. Corp.)

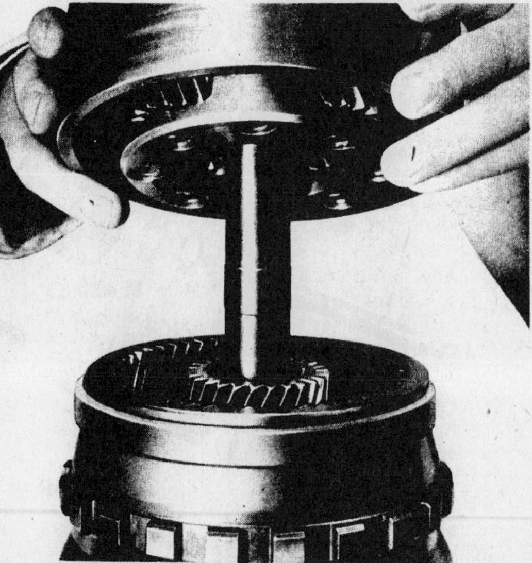
Installing reaction carrier and roller assembly
(© G.M. Corp.)

held, center support should only turn counterclockwise.

15. Install a gear unit assembly holding tool to hold units in place. Install output shaft to case thrust washer tabs in pockets and retain with petroleum jelly.

Transmission Assembly

Parking Mechanism, Rear Band and the Complete Gear Assembly Installation

1. Install O-ring seal onto parking pawl shaft, then install parking pawl, tooth toward inside of case.
2. Install the pawl shaft retaining clip and the return spring, square-end hooked on the pawl.
3. Install parking brake bracket guides over pawl, using two attaching bolts.

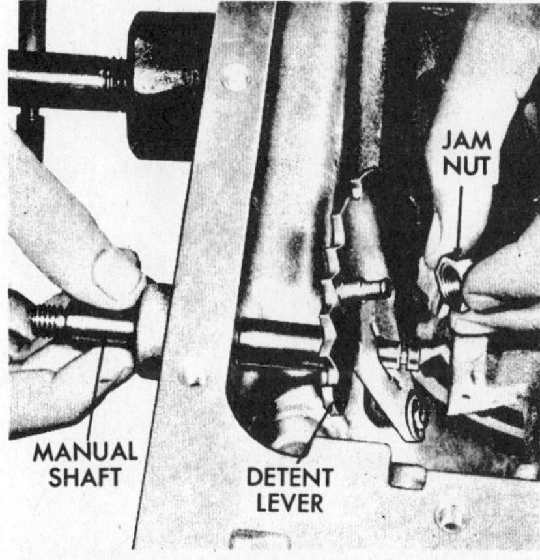

Installing dent lever and jam nut to manual shaft (© G.M. Corp.)

4. Install rear band assembly so that the two lugs index with the two anchor pins. Install support to case spacer with ring gap adjacent to band anchor pin.
5. Install rear selective washer into slots provided inside rear of transmission case. Dip washer in transmission fluid.
6. Install the complete gear unit assembly into the case.
7. Lubricate and install center support to case snap-ring. Install bevel side up. NOTE: the support to case spacer is .040 in. thick and is flat on both sides. The center support to case snap-ring has one side beveled. The intermediate clutch backing plate to case snap ring is .093 in. thick and is flat on both sides.
8. On 1964-1968 models, install the case to center support locating screw and torque to 5 ft. lbs. Lubricate and install case to center support bolt and torque to 22 ft. lbs. Remove the locating screw. On 1969-70 models, install the case to center support bolt by placing a center support locating tool or equivalent tool into case direct clutch passage with handle of tool pointing to right as viewed from front of transmission and parallel to bell housing mounting face. Apply pressure downward on tool handle to hold the center support firmly against the case splines. Torque the case to center support bolt to 22 ft. lbs.

Installing direct clutch assembly (© G.M. Corp.)

9. Install three steel and three composition clutch plates. Alternate the plates, starting with steel.
10. Install the backing plate, ridge up, then the snap-ring. Locate snap-ring gap opposite band anchor pin.
11. Check rear end-play as follows:
    A. Install a threaded rod or a long bolt into an extension hous- attaching bolt hole.
    B. Mount dial indicator on the rod and index it with the end of the output shaft.
    c. Move the output shaft in and out. Read the end-play. End-play should be .007-.019 in. The selective washer controlling the end-play is the steel washer, having three lugs, that is located between the thrust washer and the rear face of the transmission case.

If a different washer thickness is required to obtain proper end-play, it can be selected from the following chart.

1964-67

Thickness	*Notches*
.078-.082 in.	None
.086-.090 in.	1 tab side
.094-.098 in.	2 tabs side
.102-.106 in.	1 tab O.D.
.110-.114 in.	2 tabs O.D.
.118-.122 in.	3 tabs O.D.

1968-70

Thickness	*Notches and/or*	*Numeral*
.074—.078 in.	None	1
.082—.086 in.	1 Tab Side	2
.090—.094 in.	2 Tabs Side	3
.098—.102 in.	1 Tab O.D.	4
.106—.110 in.	2 Tabs O.D.	5
.114—.118 in.	3 Tabs O.D.	6

Front Band, Direct Clutch and Forward Clutch Installation

1. Install front band, with band anchor hole placed over the band anchor pin, and apply lug facing the servo hole.
2. Install the direct clutch and intermediate sprag assembly. (Removal of direct clutch plates may help.)
3. Install forward clutch hub to direct housing bronze thrust washer onto the forward clutch hub. Retain with petroleum jelly.
4. Install forward clutch assembly, indexing the direct clutch hub so the end of the mainshaft will be flush with the end of the forward clutch hub. Use turbine shaft as a tool.
5. Install turbine shaft; end with the short spline goes into the forward clutch housing.
6. Install pump-to-case gasket onto the case face and install the front pump assembly and all but one attaching bolt and seal. Torque to 18 ft. lbs. NOTE: if turbine shaft cannot be rotated as pump is being pulled into place, forward or direct clutch housing has not been properly installed to index with all clutch plates. This condition must be corrected before pump is fully pulled into place.
7. Drive in a new front seal.
8. Check front unit end-play as follows:
    A. Install one rod of slide hammer, with 5/16-18 in. thread, into the empty pump assembly attaching bolt hole.
    B. Mount dial indicator on the rod and adjust the indicator probe to contact end of turbine shaft.
    C. Hold output shaft forward while pushing turbine shaft rearward to its stop.
    D. Set dial indicator to zero.
    E. Pull turbine
    F. Read end-play, as registered on dial. The reading should be .003-.024 in.

The selective washer controlling this end-play is located between the pump cover and the forward clutch housing. If more, or less, washer thickness is required to bring end-play within specifications, make selection from the thickness-color chart.

Installing front band
(© G.M. Corp.)

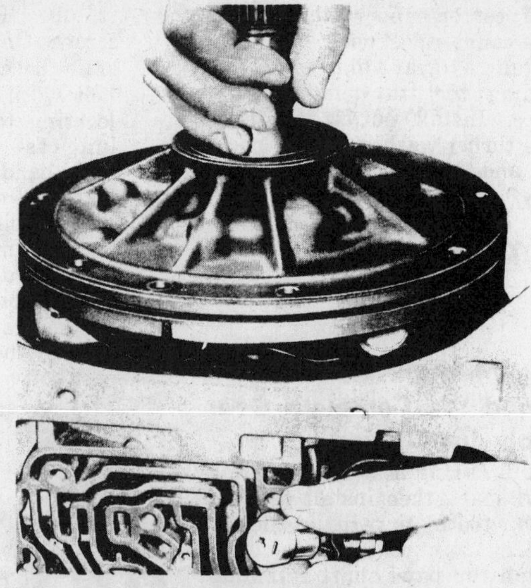
Installing pump assembly
(© G.M. Corp.)

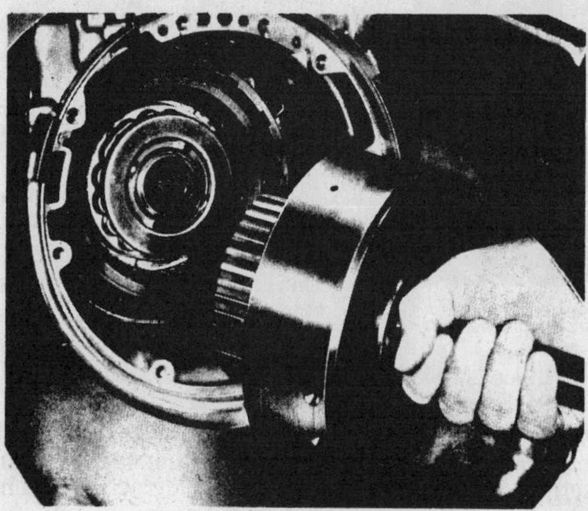
Installing forward clutch assembly
(© G.M. Corp.)

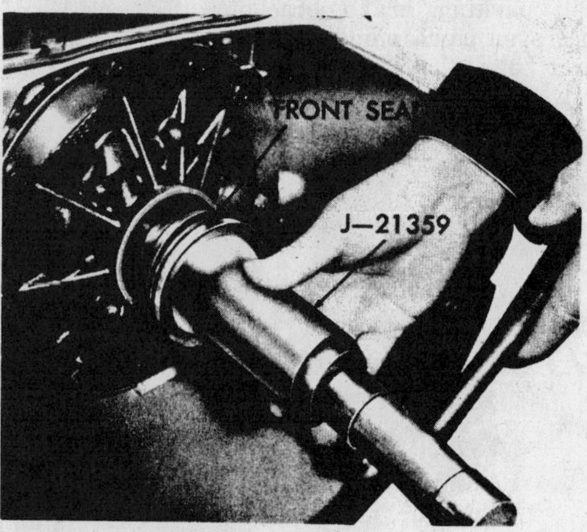

Installing front pump oil seal
(© G.M. Corp.)

Checking front unit end play
(© G.M. Corp.)

Thickness	*Color*
.060-.064 in.	Yellow
.071-.075 in.	Blue
.082-.086 in.	Red
.093-.097 in.	Brown
.104-.108 in.	Green
.115-.119 in.	Black
.126-.130 in.	Purple

9. Remove dial indicator and install the remaining front pump attaching bolt and seal. Torque to 18 ft. lbs.

Rear Extension Housing Assembly Installation

1. Install extension housing-to-case O-ring seal onto extension housing.
2. Attach extension housing to transmission case. Torque to 22 ft. lbs.
3. Drive in a new extension housing rear seal.

Manual Linkage Installation

1. Install new manual shift shaft seal into the case.
2. Insert actuator rod into the manual detent lever from the side opposite the pin.
3. Install actuator rod plunger under the parking bracket and over the pawl.
4. Install manual lever and shaft through the case and detent lever, then lock with hex nut on

the manual shift shaft. (Be sure detent retaining nut is tight.) Install retaining pin.

Check Balls, Front Servo Gaskets, Spacer and Solenoid Installation

1. Install front servo spring and retainer into transmission case.
2. Install flat washer on front servo pin, on end opposite taper. Install pin and washer into case so that tapered end of pin is contacting band.
3. Install oil seal ring on front servo piston, and install on apply pin so that identification numbers on shoulders are exposed. Check freeness of piston in bore.
4. Install six check balls into transmission case pockets.
5. Install valve body spacer to case gasket and spacer plate. Install detent solenoid and gasket, with connector facing outer edge of case. Do not tighten bolts at this time.
6. Install O-ring seal on electrical connector. Lubricate and install electrical connector with locator tab in notch on side of case. Connect detent wire and lead wire to electrical connector. Be sure to install electrical wire clip.

Rear Servo Installation

1. Before installing the rear servo assembly, check the band apply pin, using rear band apply fixture as follows:
   A. Attach band apply pin selection gauge, to the transmission case with attaching screws.
   B. Apply 25 ft. lbs. torque and select proper servo pin to be used from scale on the tool.
   C. Remove tool and make note of proper pin to be used during assembly.

There are three selective pins: The identification consists of a ring located on the band lug end of the pin. Selecting the proper pin is equivalent to adjusting the band.

2. Install rear accumulator spring.
3. Install servo assembly, then the gasket and cover. Torque bolts to 18 ft. lbs.

Control Valve and Governor Pipe Installation

1. Install control valve-to-spacer gasket, then install governor pipes into the control valve body assembly.
2. Install two guide pins, then install the control valve body and governor pipe assembly into the transmission. NOTE: be sure the manual valve is properly indexed with the pin on the manual detent lever.
3. Remove guide pins and install valve assembly attaching bolts and manual detent and roller assembly.
4. Tighten detent solenoid and control valve attaching bolts to 8 ft. lbs. torque.
5. On 1970 models, install the pressure switch assembly and torque to 8 ft. lbs. Connect pressure switch assembly lead wire.

Strainer and Intake Pipe Installation

1. Install case-to-intake pipe O-ring onto strainer and intake pipe assembly.
2. Install strainer and pipe assembly. Install new filter on models so equipped.
3. Install new pan gasket, then install the pan. Torque to 12 ft. lbs.
4. Install modulator shield and all pan attaching screws. Torquc pan attaching screws.

Modulator Assembly Installation

1. Install modulator valve into the case, stem end out.
2. Install O-ring seal onto the vacuum modulator, then install assembly into the case.
3. Install modulator retainer and attaching bolt. Torque to 18 ft. lbs.

Governor and Speedometer Driven Gear Installation

1. Install governor assembly.
2. Attach governor cover and gasket with four bolts. Torque to 18 ft. lbs.
3. Install speedometer driven gear assembly. Install retainer and attaching bolt.

Converter Installation

1. Place transmission in cradle or portable jack.
2. Install converter assembly to pump assembly, making certain that the converter hub drive slots are fully engaged with the pump drive gear tangs and that the converter is installed all the way toward the rear of the transmission.

Torque Specifications

Foot-Pounds

	Foot-Pounds
Pump cover bolts	18
Parking pawl bracket bolts	18
Center support bolt	22
Pump-to-case attaching bolts	18
Extension-to-case attaching bolts	22
Rear servo cover bolts	18
Detent solenoid bolts	8
Control valve body bolts	8
Bottom pan attaching screws	12
Modulator retainer bolt	18
Governor cover bolts	18
Manual lever-to-manual shaft nut	20
Linkage swivel clamp screw	20
Transmission-to-engine mounting bolts	40
Rear mount-to-transmission bolts	40
Oil cooler line	16
Filter retainer bolt	10
Pressure switch assembly	8

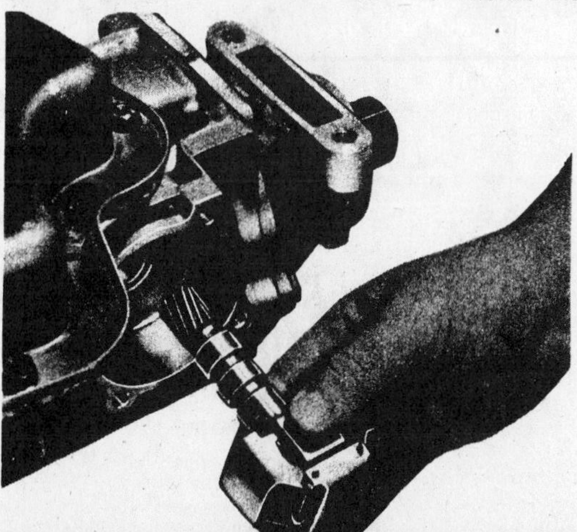

Installing governor assembly
(© G.M. Corp.)

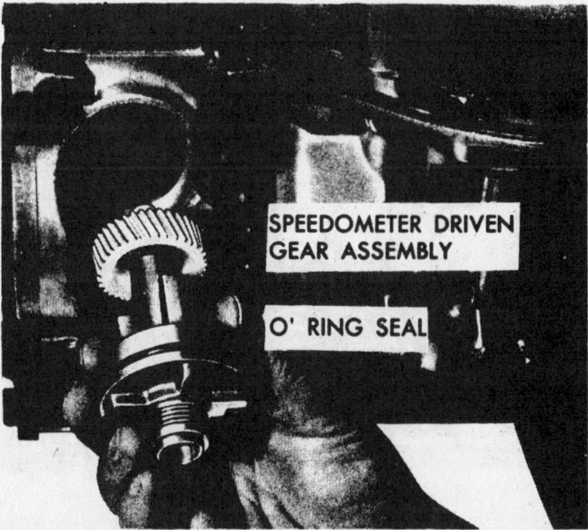

Installing speedometer driven gear and sleeve
(© G.M. Corp.)

Checking Rear Band Pin

Installing Rear Servo Cover and Gasket

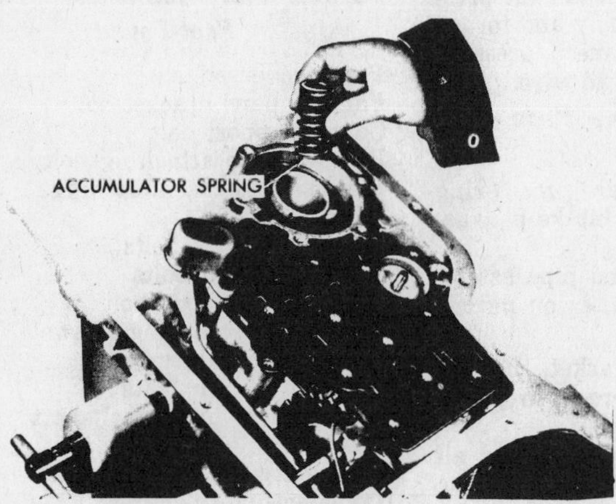

Installing Rear Accumulator Spring

Installing Control Valve Assembly and Governor Pipes

Installing Rear Servo Assembly

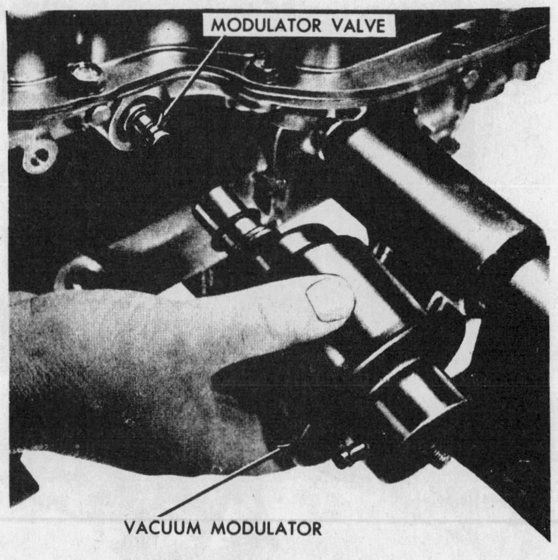

Installing Vacuum Modulator and Valve

Diagnosis

This diagnosis guide covers the most common symptoms and is an aid to careful diagnosis. The items to check are listed in the sequence to be followed for quickest results. Thus, follow the checks in the order given for the particular transmission type.

TROUBLE SYMPTOMS		Items to Check	
		In Truck	Out of Truck
Engagement	Harsh	BCDLQ	cf
	Delayed forward	ABCDKLQ	a
	Delayed reverse	ACDFKLQ	a
	None	ABCJKLQ	ajkln
	No forward D1	ACKLQ	abi
	No forward D2	ABCKLQ	ab
	No reverse	ABCFEOKQ	aeh
	No neutral	CLQ	c
Upshifts	No 1-2	ACEMKLNQ	aw
	No 2-3	ACELNQ	aerw
	Points too high	ABCELQ	a
	Points too low	ABELQ	a
	1-2 delayed followed closely by 2-3 shift	ABCEMKLNQ	abg
	2-3 slips	ABCEKLNQ	aegr
	1-2 harsh	ABCEMLQ	b
	2-3 harsh	ABCEMLQ	f
	1-2 ties up	AFLQ	fk
	2-3 ties up	ACMN	
Downshifts	No 2-1 in D-1	ABCELQ	iw
	No 2-1 in L range	ABCELOQ	hw
	No 3-2	ABELNQ	gw
	Points too high	ABCELQ	a
	Points too low	ABCELQ	a
Forced Downshifts	2-1 slips	ABCQ	bi
	3-2 slips	ABCMKLNQ	aegr
	3-1 shifts above 55-66 MPH	CEKLNQ	ag
	2-1 harsh		abi
	3-2 harsh	ABCMLNQ	ef
Reverse	Slips or chatters	ABCFOKLQ	acehr
	Tie up	AMNLQ	ac
Line pressure	Low idle	ACDEKLQ	al
	High idle	ABLQ	
	Low stall	ABEKLQ	alw
	High stall	ABLQ	
Stall speed	Too low (200 RPM or more)	H	n
	Too high D-1	ABCJKLQ	jbabins
	Reverse too high	ABCFJKLOQ	jnhest
Others	No push start	A	m
	Poor acceleration	H	nw
	Noisy in neutral	Q	fndo
	Noisy in Park	Q	ndo
	Noisy in all gears	Q	noq
	Noisy in 1 and 2 only		oqu
	Park does not hold	CP	p
	Oil surges out breather	AGEKL	amv
	Oil surges out filler tube	AGIK	amv
	Ties up in low, 1st or D-1 1st	MKLNQ	fa
	Ties up in D-1 or D-2 2nd gear	FCLOQ	fai
	Ties up in D-1 or D-2 3rd gear	FCMKLNOQ	fai

Key to Checks

I—With Pan and Oil In

A. Oil level
B. Check Oil Pressure
C. Manual Linkage Adjustment
D. Engine Idle Speed
E. Governor
F. Rear Band Adjustment
G. Check Dip Stick Length and Graduation
H. Engine Tune-up
I. Breather Restricted
J. Propellor Shaft or Axle Shaft

II—With Oil Drained and Pan Off

K. Missing or Damaged Oil Tubes
L. Valve Body Attaching Bolts Loose or Missing
M. Front Band Adjustment
N. Front Servo
O. Rear Servo
P. Parking Linkage
Q. Control Valve and/or Loose Screws

III—Out of Truck

a. Missing or Damaged Sealing Rings
b. Front Clutch Parts Slipping, Worn or Faulty
c. Front Clutch Parts Seized or Distorted
d. Front Hub Thrust Washer Missing (Noticed in N, P or R only)
e. Rear Clutch Parts Slipping, Worn or Faulty
f. Rear Clutch Parts Seized or Distorted
g. Front Band
h. Rear Band
i. One-Way Spray Clutch Slipping or Assembled in Reverse Position
j. Broken Input Shaft
k. Front Pump Drive or Converter Hub Broken
l. Front Pump Worn
m. Rear Pump
n. Converter
o. Front Pump
p. Parking Linkage
q. Planetary Assembly
r. Rear Clutch Ball Check Leaks
s. Broken Output Shaft
t. Broken Gears
u. Forward Sun Gear Thrust Washer Missing
v. Breather Baffle Missing
w. Output Shaft Plug Missing (6-cyl.)

General Information

The transmission consists of a hydraulically-controlled planetary gear box with torque converter. The torque converter is a sealed unit and cannot be serviced separately.

Transmissions equipped with D-1 start in low, shift to intermediate, and then to direct.

When equipped with D only, they start in intermediate and then shift to direct. Drive in low is through the L position only.

Checking Fluid Level

Check fluid at least every 4,000 miles. Check at operating temperature, after moving control through all positions, engine idling. Use care never to overfill.

Draining and refilling are not recommended except during major repairs. In all cases, use automatic transmission fluid type A, AQ-ATF +suffix A. capacity—type A cast iron, 22 pints; type B aluminum, 18 pints.

Towing

Truck may be towed in N for short distance if transmission is not damaged. With damaged transmission or for longer distances, raise rear of truck or remove drive line.

To start by pushing, place in neutral then, at about 30 mph, shift to D or D-1.

In-Truck Repairs

Band Adjustment—Front

Loosen locknut on adjusting screw and insert .25 in. gauge block between end of adjusting screw and servo rod. Tighten screw to 10 in. lbs. and tighten locknut to 20-25 ft. lbs.

Rear Band Adjustment

Loosen locknut and adjust screw to

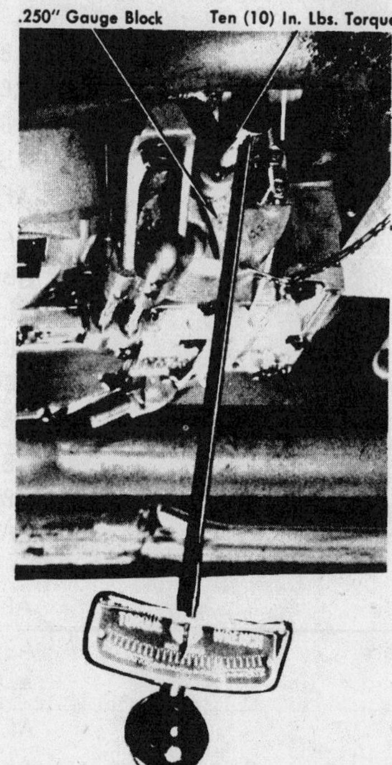

Adjusting front servo
(© American Motor Corp.)

10 ft. lbs. Mark adjusting screw for reference and back off screw one and one-half turns. Tighten locknut to 35-40 ft. lbs.

Testing

Stall Test

With engine at normal operating temperature and transmission in D or D-1, apply parking brake and foot brake if necessary. Accelerate engine (Type A) for not over 15 seconds. If engine will not reach more than 1400-1450 rpm, poor engine performance is indicated. If it goes above 1650-1700 rpm, converter or transmission slippage is indicated. Under 1300 (Type B) indicates poor engine performance, and above 1500 repm, indicates converter or transmission

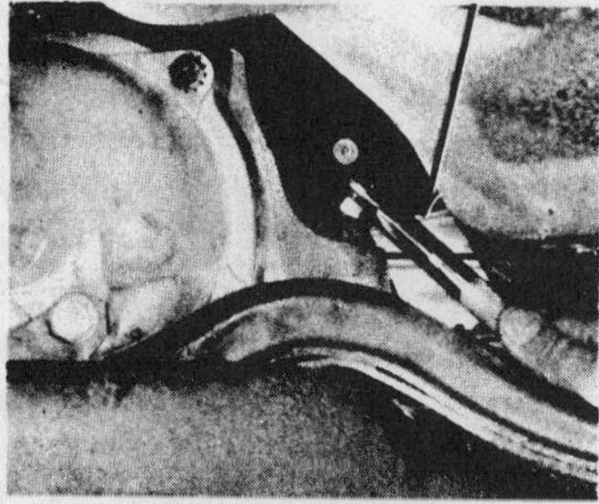

Adjusting rear band
(© American Motor Corp.)

slippage.

Air Pressure Test

With oil pan and control valve removed, make sure servo attaching screws are tight and front servo tubes in place. To prevent over-spray it is well to hold clean towel over transmission opening.

Front Clutch—Apply air pressure to front clutch passage. A dull thud indicates clutch is operating. Hold air pressure for a short time to check for leaks in this circuit.

Rear Clutch—Apply air pressure to rear clutch passage. A dull thud indicates clutch is operating. Hold air pressure to check for leaks in this circuit.

Front and rear Bands and Servos—Apply pressure to indicated passage and note band applications.

Governor Valve—Remove governor inspection cover. Apply air pressure to front clutch passage. Listen for a click and note that valve snaps inward.

Pressure Tests

Jeep	*1963-69*
6 & V8	6 & V8
idle	stall
closed	—
R,L,D,	D
14-16	—
55-65	130-160

* NOTE: In some cases the vacuum may be low due to altitude or a new engine. Here, an external vacuum source must be used. To utilize this vacuum source, disconnect engine vacuum line, connect external source to control unit, and adjust source to specified amount. Then, test transmission pressure.

Oil Pressure Test

With Vacuum and Solenoid Control

1. A preliminary setting for the vacuum control unit is 23/64 in. between back of case and front of unit. With pressure and vacuum gauges connected, as in illustration, start and warm up engine to normal operating temperature and place transmission control in N.
2. To obtain pressures as specified in the charts, turn unit into transmission to raise pressure and out of transmission to reduce pressure.
3. If proper vacuum cannot be obtained, a leaky diaphragm in unit is indicated. (Note: fluctuation of pressure gauge at idle in N is a normal condition.) Shorten the linkage to obtain the pressures as specified in the charts.

Components

Pressure Regulator Valve Removal and Installation

1. Remove oil pan and screen.
2. Maintain pressure on spring retainer and remove retainer tabs.
3. Remove spring and pilots and pull regulator valve (smaller valve) out about ½ in. to release oil in converter.
4. Remove pipe from valve assembly and rear pump.
5. Remove large control pressure tube.
6. Remove regulator valve assembly.
7. Reverse above for installation.

Control Valve Removal and Installation

1. Remove oil pan and screen, large and small pressure tubes.
2. Loosen front servo retaining screw, then remove vacuum and solenoid unit.
3. Remove control valve retaining screws, disengage front servo pressure tube and remove control valve from case.
4. Reverse above for installation.

Front and Rear Servo Removal and Installation

1. Remove attaching screws. With one hand hold the strut and lift

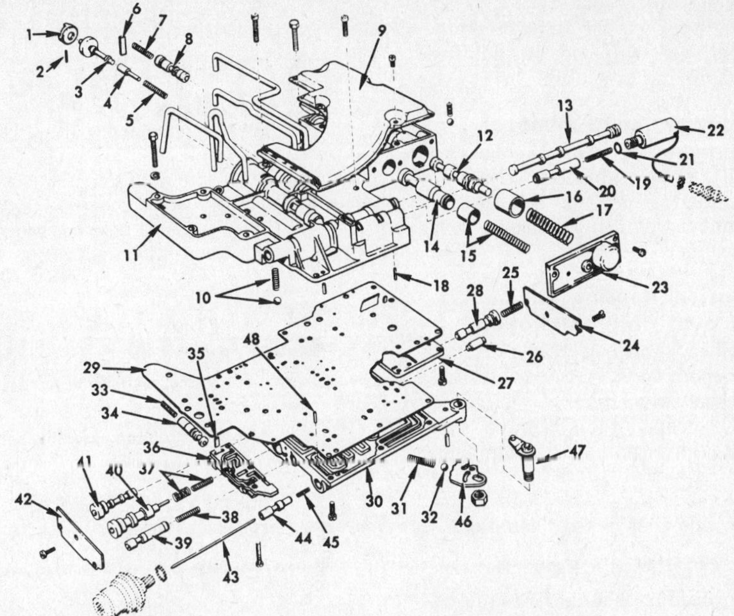

1 Modulator valve spacer
2 Dowel pin
3 Modulator valve
4 Modulator valve plug
5 Modulator valve spring
6 Servo orifice control valve stop
7 Servo orifice control valve spring
8 Servo orifice control valve
9 Oil screen
10 2-3 shift valve circuit ball and spring
11 Lower valve body
12 Primary regulator valve
13 Manual valve
14 Secondary regulator valve
15 Secondary regulator valve spring
16 Primary regulator valve sleeve
17 Primary regulator valve spring
18 Solenoid retaining pin
19 Down-shift valve return spring
20 Down-shift valve
21 "O" ring
22 Downshift solenoid
23 Lower valve body end
24 Front end plate
25 1-2 shift valve spring
26 2-3 shift valve plunger
27 Oil tube plate
28 1-2 shift valve plunger
29 Separator plate
30 Upper valve body
31 Detent spring
32 Detent ball
33 Front clutch orifice control valve spring
34 Front clutch orifice control valve
35 Front clutch orifice control valve stop
36 Range control valve body
37 2-3 shift valve spring
38 Range control valve spring
39 1-2 shift valve
40 2-3 shift valve
41 Range control valve
42 Rear end plate
43 Throttle valve control rod
44 Throttle valve
45 Throttle valve spring
46 Detent lever
47 Manual control valve lever
48 Throttle valve retaining pin

Control valve assembly sequence (© American Motors Corp.)

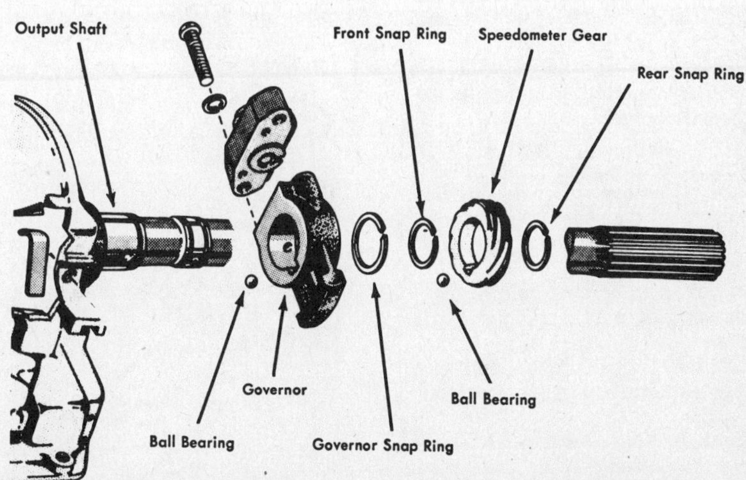

Speedometer drive gear and governor assembly (© American Motors Corp.)

servo from case.
2. Reverse above for reinstallation. Lubriplate will aid in holding strut during assembly.

Governor Body Removal

1. Remove inspection hole cover.
2. Rotate shaft to place governor in alignment.
3. Remove retaining screws and governor.

Extension Housing Oil Seal Removal and Installation

1. Remove torque tube, if so equipped.
2. Remove driveshaft.
3. With proper tool, remove seal, using care not to damage seal mating surface.
4. Reverse above for installation. Felt side goes next to housing.

End-Play Check

This procedure should be made before any of the main units are disturbed in the transmission.

1. Remove one front pump retaining screw and mount dial indicator so that contact rests against input shaft.
2. With front clutch assembly pried toward rear of case, set dial indicator to zero. Now, pry between parking gear and case to move units toward front of case. Note dial indicator reading. Limits should be .010-.029 in. (.015 in. preferred.)

Internal Part Removal

1. Remove front pump.
2. Remove rear housing.
3. Remove oil distributor.
4. Remove sleeve, four seal rings and governor snap-ring, then slide off governor. (Do not lose drive ball.)
5. Remove rear pump inlet and outlet tubes and slide rear pump, gasket and drive key from shaft.
6. While holding carrier in position, slide shaft and internal gear toward rear.
7. Remove thrust washer. (This is washer controlling end-play, recorded above.)
8. While holding sun gear in position, slide pinion carrier toward rear. Remove thrust washer from inside carrier. (Note position of cone on inner diameter of washer.)
9. Remove cap screws holding center support and remove support from case.
10. Remove both clutches and sun gear as a unit. Remove the front washer.
11. Remove thrust washer and contour washer from between clutches.
12. Remove front band by tilting through bottom of case.

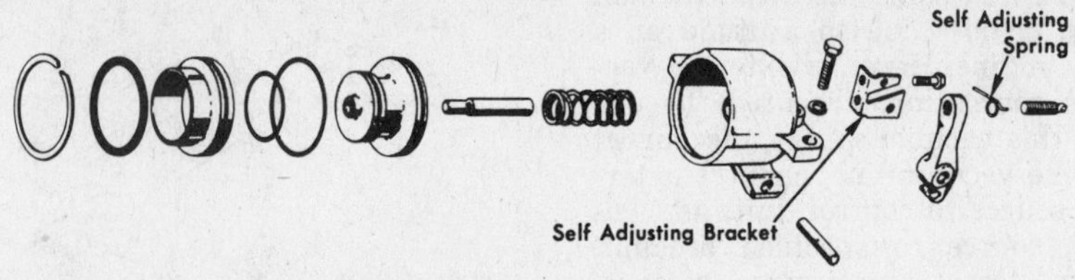

Front servo components (© American Motors Corp.)

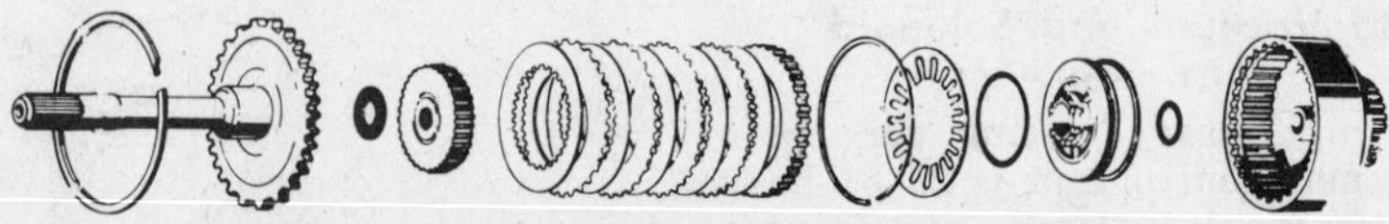
Front clutch assembly sequence (© American Motors Corp.)

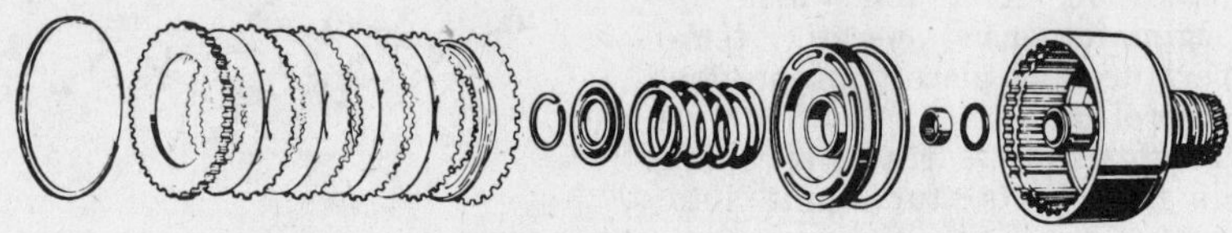
Rear clutch components (© American Motors Corp.)

Pump components (© American Motors Corp.)

Component Reconditioning

Front Clutch Disassembly and Assembly

1. Remove cover, snap-ring, then input shaft and fiber washer from hub.
2. Remove the driven and drive plates, pressure plate, and hub from the drum.
3. Force the piston from drum bore by applying air pressure to the clutch apply hole.
4. The outer seal and inner O-ring may now be removed.
5. Check all parts and replace as needed. The lined plates should be replaced when the grooves in the lining are no longer visible or the plates are warped.
7. Lubricate all parts in reassembly with transmission fluid. Replace the outer seal and O-ring and reassemble in reverse of disassembly procedure.

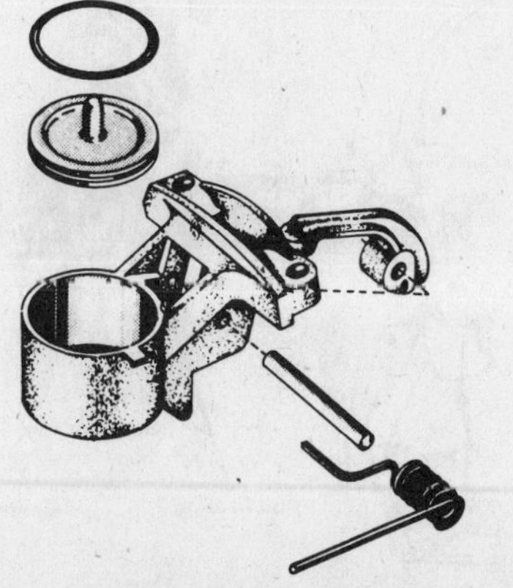
Rear servo assembly
(© American Motor Corp.)

Rear Clutch Assembly

1. Lubricate all rear clutch parts with transmission oil before reassembly.
2. Check the steel plates for proper

dish. This dish should be .010-.020 in., when measured on a flat plate.

3. Install piston. Press spring and retainer into position and install snap-ring.
4. Install the drive and driven plates and the pressure plate, then install the snap-ring. NOTE: the dished plates are installed with the dished side up and the pressure plate with the smooth side down.
5. Follow the assembly procedure in reverse of the removal procedure.

Front and Rear Pumps

Normal disassembly and inspections are required for scratches, scores and excessive wear. See illustrations for reassembly sequences.

To reassemble components follow disassembly instructions of preceding sections in reverse order.

Torque Specifications

	Foot-Pounds
Converter to drive plate	23-28
Transmission case to converter housing	40-45
Front pump to transmission case	17-22
Front servo to transmission case	30-35
Rear servo to transmission case	40-45
Planetary center support to transmission case	20-25
Upper to lower valve body	4-6
Control valve body to transmission case	8-10
Pressure regulator to transmission case	17-22
Extension to transmission case	23-38
Oil pan to transmission case	10-20

Rear Axle Section

Index

REAR AXLE SERVICE DIAGNOSIS

Condition	*Possible Cause*	*Correction*
Rear Wheel Noise	(1) Wheel loose.	(1) Tighten loose nuts.
	(2) Faulty, brinelled wheel bearing.	(2) Faulty or brinelled bearings must be replaced. Check rear axle shaft end play.
	(3) Excessive axle shaft end play.	(3) Readjust axle shaft end play.
Rear Axle Drive Shaft Noise	(1) Misaligned axle housing.	(1) Inspect rear axle housing, alignment. Correct as necessary.
	(2) Bent or sprung axle shaft.	(2) Replace bent or sprung axle shaft.
	(3) End play in drive pinion bearings.	(3) Refer to Pinion Bearing Pre-load.
	(4) Excessive gear lash between ring gear and pinion.	(4) Check adjustment of ring gear and pinion. Correct as necessary.
	(5) Improper adjustment of drive pinion shaft bearings.	(5) Adjust pinion bearings.
	(6) Loose drive pinion companion flange nut.	(6) Tighten drive pinion flange nut to torque specified.
	(7) Improper wheel bearing adjustment.	(7) Check axle shaft end play. Readjust as necessary.
	(8) Scuffed gear tooth contact surfaces.	(8) If necessary, replace scuffed gears.
Rear Axle Drive Shaft Breakage	(1) Improperly adjusted wheel bearings.	(1) Replace broken shaft and readjust end play.
	(2) Misaligned axle housing.	(2) Replace broken shaft after correcting rear axle housing alignment.
	(3) Vehicle overloaded.	(3) Replace broken shaft. Avoid excessive weight on vehicle.
	(4) Abnormal clutch operation.	(4) Replace broken shaft, after checking for other possible causes. Avoid erratic use of clutch.
	(5) Grabbing clutch.	(5) Replace broken shaft. Inspect clutch and make necessary repairs or adjustments.
	(6) Normal fatigue.	(6) Replace broken shaft. Inspect to determine causes or damage.
Differential Case Breakage	(1) Improper adjustment of differential bearings.	(1) Replace broken case; examine gears and bearings for possible damage. At reassembly, adjust differential bearings.
	(2) Excessive ring gear clearance.	(2) Replace broken case; examine gears and bearings for possible damage. At reassembly, adjust ring gear and pinion backlash.
	(3) Vehicle overloaded.	(3) Replace broken case; examine gears and bearings for possible damage. Avoid excessive weight on vehicle.
	(4) Erratic clutch operation.	(4) Replace broken case. After checking for other possible causes, examine gears and bearings for possible damage. Avoid erratic use of clutch.
Differential Side Gear Broken at Hub	(1) Excessive axle housing deflection.	(1) Replace damaged gears. Examine other gears and bearings for possible damage. Check rear axle housing alignment.
	(2) Misaligned or bent axle shaft.	(2) Replace damaged gears. Check axle shafts or alignment. Examine other gears and bearings for possible damage.
	(3) Worn thrust washers.	(3) Replace damaged gears. Examine other gears and bearings for possible damage. Replace thrust washers that are badly worn.
Scoring of Differential Gears	(1) Insufficient lubrication.	(1) Replace scored gears. Scoring marks on the pressure face of gear teeth or in the bore are caused by instantaneous fusing of the mating surfaces. Scored gears should be replaced. Fill rear axle to required capacity with proper lubricant.
	(2) Improper grade of lubricant.	(2) Replace scored gears. Inspect all gears and bearings for possible damage. Clean out and refill axle to required capacity with proper lubricant.
	(3) Excessive spinning of one wheel.	(3) Replace scored gears. Inspect all gears, pinion bores and shaft for scoring, or bearings for possible damage. Service as necessary.
Tooth Breakage (Ring Gear and Pinion)	(1) Overloading.	(1) Replace gears. Examine other gears and bearings for possible damage. Replace parts as needed. Avoid overloading of vehicle.
	(2) Erratic clutch operation.	(2) Replace gears, and examine remaining parts for possible damage. Avoid erratic clutch operation.
	(3) Ice-spotted pavements.	(3) Replace gears. Examine remaining parts for possible damage. Replace parts as required.
	(4) Normal fatigue.	(4) Replace gears. Examine broken parts to determine cause of normal fatigue.
	(5) Improper adjustment.	(5) Replace gears. Examine other parts for

REAR AXLE SERVICE DIAGNOSIS

possible damage. Make sure ring gear and pinion backlash is correct.

Condition	Possible Cause	Correction
Rear Axle Noise	(1) Insufficient lubricant.	(1) Refill rear axle with correct amount of the proper lubricant. Also check for leaks and correct as necessary.
	(2) Improper ring gear and pinion adjustment.	(2) Check ring gear and pinion tooth contact.
	(3) Unmatched ring gear and pinion.	(3) Remove unmatched ring gear and pinion. Replace with a new matched gear and pinion set.
	(4) Worn teeth on ring gear or pinion.	(4) Check teeth on ring gear and pinion for contact. If necessary, replace with new matched set.
	(5) Loose drive pinion bearings.	(5) Adjust drive pinion bearings.
	(6) Loose differential gear bearings.	(6) Adjust differential gear bearings.
	(7) Misaligned or sprung ring gear.	(7) Check ring gear for runout.
	(8) Loose carrier housing bolts.	(8) Tighten carrier housing nuts to Specifications. Also, check for oil leaks and correct as necessary.
Loss of Lubricant	(1) Lubricant level too high.	(1) Drain excess lubricant by removing filler plug and allow lubricant to level at lower edge of filler plug hole.
	(2) Worn axle shaft oil seals.	(2) Replace worn oil seals with new ones. Prepare new seals before replacement.
	(3) Cracked rear axle housing.	(3) Repair or replace housing as required.
	(4) Worn drive pinion oil seal.	(4) Replace worn drive pinion oil seal with a new one.
	(5) Scored and worn companion flange.	(5) Replace worn or scored companion flange and oil seal.
Overheating of Unit	(1) Lubricant level too low.	(1) Refill rear axle.
	(2) Incorrect grade of lubricant.	(2) Drain, flush and refill rear axle with correct amount of the proper lubricant.
	(3) Bearings adjusted too tightly.	(3) Readjust bearings.
	(4) Excessive wear in gears.	(4) Check gears for excessive wear or scoring. Replace as necessary.
	(5) Insufficient ring gear to pinion clearance.	(5) Readjust ring gear and pinion backlash and check gears for possible scoring.

Nominal Assembly Dimension and Adapter Disc Chart

Axle Model	*Nominal Assembly Dimension*	*Adapter Disc Tool Number*
44	2.625"	SE-1065-9-SS
60	3.125"	SE-1065-9-Y
1618-9	4.125"	SE-1065-9-G
		SE-1065-9-I
1790A-1A	4.2190"	SE-1065-9-CC
		SE-1065-9-E
G161	3.551"	SE-1065-9-E
H140	3.551"	SE-1065-9-E
H162	3.719"	SE-1065-9-F
13800	3.6244"	SE-1065-9-G
		SE-1065-9-E
16802-3	4.125"	SE-1065-9-G
		SE-1065-9-I
17800-1	4.4062"	SE-1065-9-M
		SE-1065-9-G
G361	2.625"	SE-1065-9-PP
		SE-1065-9-O
H340	2.625"	SE-1065-9-PP
		SE-1065-9-O
H362	2.937"	SE-1065-9-R
		SE-1065-9-PP
28M	3.4725"	SE-1065-9-D

General Axle Service Section

Axle Shaft Removal

Procedure for axle shaft removal is the same with axle assembly removed or installed in the vehicle.

Flanged Type

1. Remove stud nuts. Strike center of flange to loosen split tapered dowels, then remove dowels.
2. Using puller screws, remove flange and gasket.

Splined Type

1. Remove cap and gasket at hub.
2. Thread adapter into tapped hole in axle shaft and attach slide hammer to adapter. Use slide hammer to pull axle shaft.

Installation

1. Install new gasket against hub.
2. Dip splined end of shaft in axle lubricant, and insert shaft through hub.
3. Turn shaft as necessary to mesh shaft splines with differential side gear splines.
4. As shaft is pushed inward, align with hub studs or hub splines.
5. On splined type, install cap, gasket, and cap screws, then tighten cap screws.
6. On flanged type, install split tapered dowels and nuts at studs.
7. Clearance should exist between nut and flange; if not, this indicates excessive wear at studs, dowels, or flange holes. Replace worn parts.

Cleaning

All component parts of an axle should be thoroughly cleaned in a cleaning fluid, using a stiff brush to remove dirt.

Cleaning Bearings

Proper bearing cleaning is important. Bearings should always be cleaned separately from other rear axle parts.

1. Soak all bearings in clean kerosene or Diesel fuel oil. CAUTION: Ordinary gasoline should not be used. Bearings should not be cleaned in a hot solution tank.
2. Slush bearings in cleaning solution until all oil lubricant is loosened. Brush bearings with soft bristled brush until ALL dirt has been removed. Remove loose particles of dirt by striking flat against a wood block.
3. Rinse bearings in clean fluid. While holding races to prevent rotation, blow dry with compressed air. *Do not spin bearings while drying.*
4. After bearings have been inspected, lubricate thoroughly with regular axle lubricant; then wrap each bearing in clean cloth until ready to use.

Cleaning Parts

Immerse all parts in suitable cleaning fluid and clean thoroughly. Use a stiff bristle brush as required to remove foreign deposits. Clean all lubricant passages or channels in pinion cage, carrier, caps and retainers. Make certain that interior of housing is thoroughly cleaned. Clean vent plugs and breathers.

Small parts such as cap screws, bolts, studs, nuts etc., should be cleaned thoroughly.

Inspection

Magna Flux all steel parts, except ball and roller bearings, to determine presence of wear and cracks.

Bearings

Rotate each bearing slowly, and replace if rough, damaged, defective or worn. Replace bearing if cups or cages are damaged.

Gears

Examine drive gear and drive pinion, differential pinions and differential side gears carefully, for damaged teeth, worn spots in surface hardening, distortion and where drive gear is attached to differential case with rivets, inspect rivets for looseness, replace loose rivets. Check radial clearances between differential side gears and differential case. Check fit of differential pinions on spider.

Differential Case

Inspect case for cracks, distortion or damage, if in good condition, thoroughly clean case and cover; then assemble case with bolts and mount in lathe centers of "V" block stand. If lathe is not available, install diffe-

Checking drive gear run-out
(© G.M.C.)

rential side bearings and mount case in differential carrier. Install dial indicator and check differential case run out.

Differential case with drive gear installed is checked in the same manner, except that dial indicator reading must be taken at rear instead of at case flange.

Whenever run-out exceeds limits, it may be corrected as later described under "Repair" in this section. However, the support case used in the 2-speed axle cannot be repaired and should be replaced with new case.

Axle Shafts

Examine splined end of axle shaft for twisted or cracked splines, twisted shaft, and worn dowel holes in flange. Install new shafts if necessary.

Install axle shaft assembly in lathe centers and check shaft run-out with dial indicator, if run-out exceeds limits, replace shaft. Place dial indicator so that indicator shaft end contacts inner surface of flange near outer edge of flange and check flange run-out.

Gaskets

With the exception of Timken axles, replace all gaskets with new ones. The use of gaskets on Timken axles at pinion cages, cross shaft covers and cages, where adjusting shims are also used, is being discontinued. In service, replace gasket with a shim pack approximately .015″ thick, which will maintain same bearing preload and gear adjustment as when gasket was used.

Shims

Carefully inspect shims for uniform thickness. Where various thickness of shims are used in a pack, it is recommended that the thickest shims be used between the thin shims.

Thrust Washers

Replace all thrust washers.

Spider

Carefully inspect spider arms for wear or defects.

Differential Pinion Bushings

Examine bushings (when used) for excessive wear, looseness, or damage. Check fit of gears on spider for excessive clearance. See "repair" paragraph for directions on bushing replacement.

Axle Housing Sleeves

Sleeves showing damaged threads, wear, or other damage should be replaced if hydraulic press is available, otherwise replace housing.

Housing Check

Before Removal

A check for bent axle housing can be made with unit in vehicle; however, conventional alignment instruments can be used if available.

1. Raise rear axle with a jack until wheels clear floor. Block up axle under each spring seat.
2. Check wheel bearing adjustment and adjust if necessary, then check wheels for looseness and tighten wheel nuts if necessary.
3. Place a chalk mark on outer side wall of tires at bottom. Measure across tires at chalk marks with a toe-in gauge.
4. Turn wheels half-way around so that chalk marks are positioned at top of wheel. Measure across tires again. If measurement at top is 1/8″ or more, smaller than measurement at bottom of wheels, axle housing has sagged and is bent. If measurement at top exceeds bottom dimension by 1/8″ or more, axle housing is bent at ends.
5. Turn chalk marks on both wheels so that marks are level with axle and at rear of vehicle. Take measurement with toe-in gauge at chalk marks; then turn both chalk marks to front and level with axle and take another measurement. If measurement at front exceeds rear dimension by 1/8″ or more, axle is bent to the rear. If the measurement condition is the reverse, the axle is bent forward.

After Removal

After axle assembly has been completely disassembled, housings may be checked for bent condition in following manner:

1. Temporarily install wheel hubs, and adjust wheel bearings so that hubs will just turn. Do not lock adjustment.
2. After axle shafts have been inspected as previously described, install shafts and draw stud nuts up tight.
3. Indicators can be made locally from 3/16″ drill rod to dimensions shown. Remove any burrs from splines; then use hose clamps to hold indicators to shafts.
4. Each indicator must be positioned at right angle to its shaft. Both indicators must be in alignment with one another. There should be a slight gap between the points. Measure and note dimensions of this gap.
5. Rotate shafts simultaneously and measure gap at four points, 90 degrees apart. If gap at any point exceeds original gap by more than 1/16″, axle housing is bent.

General Repair

Differential Case

Excessive run-out on differential case may be corrected by machining flange at gear side of case. Exceptions to this practice are noted under specific axle procedures. Remove just enough metal (cut on a true plane) from flange to correct run-out.

Drive Gear Replacement

These instructions apply to all riveted type drive gears.

1. Mark exact center of rivet heads with center punch on gear side of case. Drill heads off of rivets

with drill slightly smaller than diameter of rivets. Drive rivets out with drift pin.

2. After cleaning differential case thoroughly, position drive gear on case and fasten with two bolts installed opposite one another and tighten firmly. NOTE: When a new bevel gear or differential case is installed the differential case and bevel gear holes must be line reamed and full size rivets used.
3. Install rivets using riveting fixture. After rivets are installed, remove temporary bolts and install rivets in their place. Check each rivet thoroughly.
4. When the correct rivet and set is used, the head being formed will be at least 1/8" larger in diameter than the rivet hole. The head will also be approximately the same height as the preformed head. The formed head should not be more than 1/16" less than the preformed head.

Oil Seal Contact Surfaces

Surface of parts, contacted by oil seals must be free of corrosion, pits and grooves. When abrasive cleaning fails to clean up the seal contact surface and restore smooth finish, a new part must be installed.

Differential Pinion Bushing

Some axles use a differential pinion which is fitted with a bushing. These bushings are replaceable.

Removal

1. Place pinion in a soft-jawed vise.
2. Using a hacksaw, split bushing at two places and remove halves.
3. Remove burrs or sharp edges from pinion bore before installing new bushings.

Installation

A bushing replacing and burnishing kit is available. Kit consists of bar, anvil, adapters and 6 balls.

1. Place pinion on tubular anvil, then position bushing in inner end of pinion bore.
2. Select proper size adapter, then press bushing into pinion.
3. Select burnishing ball that is approximately .005" larger than spider arm diameter.
4. Press burnishing ball through bushing, using round bar against ball. This burnishing ball will force bushing metal into groove inside pinion bore thereby locking it in place. Inside diameter of bushing is sized to provide correct clearance between bushing and spider arm.

Oil Seal Removal

Oil seals can be removed with a drift pin. When removing seal, be careful that it does not become cocked and result in damage to the retainer. Clean surface of retainer carefully, so that seal will seat properly in retainer.

Installation

Coat outer surface of seal retainer with a light coat of sealer, to prevent lubricant leaks. Carefully start seal in retainer. Cutting, scratching, or curling of lip of seal seriously impairs its efficiency and usually results in premature replacement. Lip of seal should be coated with a high temperature grease containing zinc oxide to help prevent scoring and damage to parts during installation.

Seals must always be installed so that seal lip is toward the lubricant.

Pinion Bearing Adjustments (Pre-Load)

Pinion bearing must be adjusted for pre-load before assembly is installed in carrier.

Do not install oil seal until after adjustment is made—installation of seal would produce false rotating torque.

Cage Type

1. With pinion bearings, and adjusting spacers (or shims) installed in cage, check bearing contact by rotating cage.
2. Using a press, apply pressure (25,000 lbs.) to outer bearing.
3. Wrap soft wire around cage and pull on horizontal line with spring scale. Rotating (not starting) torque should be within limits recommended by manufacturer. NOTE: Method of determining inch-pounds torque with scale is to determine radius of cage. Multiply radius in inches by pounds pull required to rotate cage to determine inch-pounds torque. Example: An 8-inch diameter divided by 2 equals 4-inch radius. Multiply 4-inch (radius) by 5 pounds (pull) equals 20 inch pounds torque.
4. If press is not available, check preload torque by installing propeller shaft yoke, washer, and nut and torque to specifications; then check as previously explained. Remove yoke after correct adjustment is obtained.

Bevel Gear Shaft Bearing Adjustment

Bevel gear shaft bearings must be adjusted for pre-load before pinion and cage assembly and differential assembly are installed in carrier.

1. Wrap several turns of soft wire around gear teeth on cross shaft, then pull on a horizontal line with spring scale. Rotating (not starting) torque should be used. NOTE: Method of determining inch-pounds torque with scale is to determine radius. Multiply radius in inches by pounds pull required to rotate shaft to determine inch-pounds torque. Example: An 8-inch diameter divided by 2 equals 4-inch radius times 5 pounds (pull) equals 20 inch-pounds torque.
2. Remove or add shims from under cage or cap opposite bevel gear to obtain specified bearing pre-load.
3. When making bevel gear and pinion tooth contact or backlash adjustments it is sometimes necessary to remove or add shims from one side. *Always remove or add an equal thickness to the opposite side so to maintain correct pre-load.*

Gear Tooth Contact and Backlash

Method of adjusting pinion and bevel gear to obtain proper gear tooth contact and backlash varies with the axle type. Therefore, the fol-

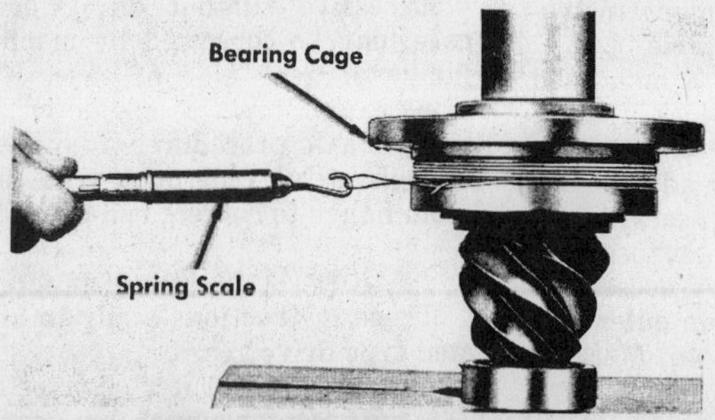

Checking pinion bearing pre-load (© G.M.C.)

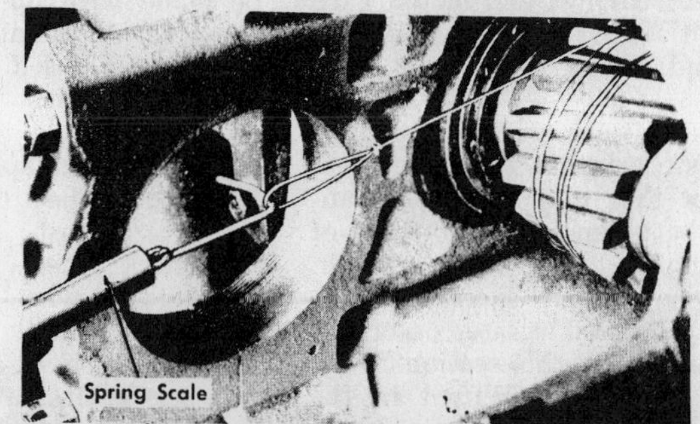

Checking pre-load on bevel gear cross shaft (© G.M.C.)

lowing instructions cover all types of axles, except as noted. Proper gear tooth contact can be determined by using red lead on gear teeth, or by using a pinion setting gauge.

When using the gauge method, backlash is established after the pinion has been properly set. With red lead method, backlash is obtained first, then proper tooth contact is established.

Pinion Setting Gauge Method

The pinion setting gauge is a direct reading micrometer mounted in arbor. Adapter discs, which fit in differential bores are mounted in sleeves that fit over the arbor. The "Nominal Assembly Dimension" chart lists the proper adapter discs to be used for the various axle models. The proper discs hold the gauge assembly so that center line of arbor coincides with centerline of carrier bores.

Terms Used

Certain dimensions must be determined when using the pinion setting gauge:

1. *Nominal Assembly Dimension.* This dimension (varying with axle model) is the distance between the center line of the drive gear (or differential carrier bore) and the end of the drive pinion. This dimension may be marked on the pinion or listed on the "Nominal Assembly Dimension and Adapter Disc" chart.
2. *Individual Variation Distance,* This dimension is a plus or minus variation of the *Nominal Assembly Dimension* on each individual pinion which may be caused by manufacturing variations.
3. *Corrected Nominal Dimension.* This dimension is the *Nominal Assembly Dimension* plus or minus the *Individual Variation Distance.*
4. *Corrected Micrometer Distance* is the *Corrected Nominal Dimension* less the thickness of the gauge set step plate (0.400″) mounted on end of pinion.
5. *Initial Micrometer Reading* is the dimension taken by micrometer to the gauge step plate.
6. *Shim Pack Correction* is determined by the difference between the *Corrected Micrometer Distance* and the *Initial Micrometer Reading,* and represents the amount of shim pack to be added or removed as later explained.

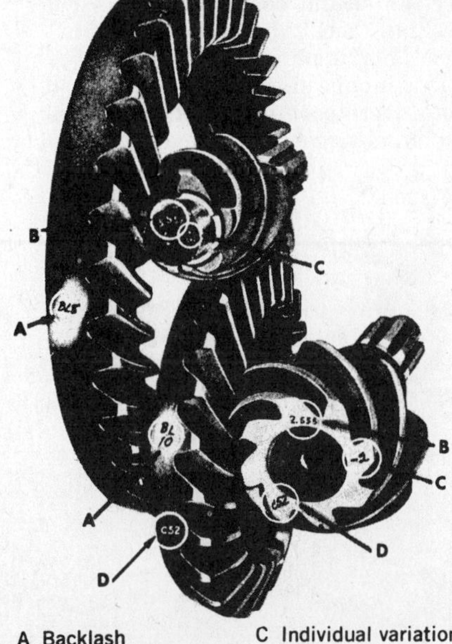

A Backlash
B Nominal assembly dimension
C Individual variation distance
D Gear and pinion matching number

Pinion and bevel gear markings (typical) (© G.M.C.)

Markings on Pinion and Drive Gear

Nominal Assembly Dimension

The Nominal Assembly Dimension, is etched on the end of pinion on Timken axles and shown is *"Nominal Assembly Dimension and Adapter Disc"* chart. On Eaton axles, this dimension must be obtained from the chart.

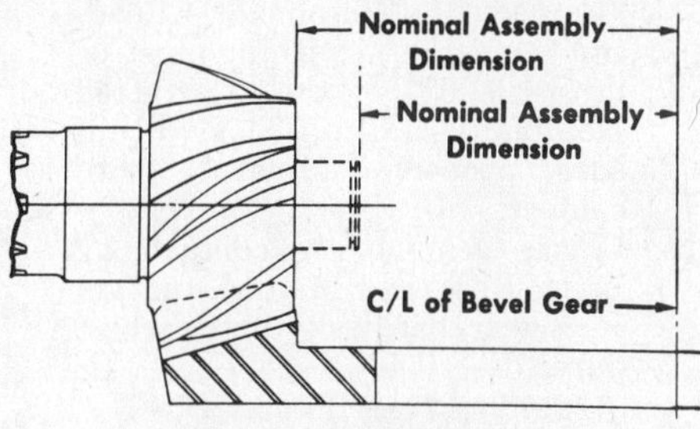

Nominal assembly dimension (© G.M.C.)

Individual Variation Distance

The *Individual Variation Distance* is a plus (+) or minus (−) dimension representing thousandths of an inch, and is etched on end of pinion on Timken axles.

On some Eaton axles, the dimension is etched on end of pinion or may be found on the outside diameter of pinion splines.

Other Markings

All other markings on pinion or drive gear should not be confused with *Nominal Assembly Dimension* or *Individual Variation Distance* markings.

Pinion Setting Procedures

1. Determine the *Nominal Assembly Dimension* from the pinion marking or from chart. Also note *Individual Variation Distance* from marking on pinion.
2. When the nominal assembly dimension is greater than the micrometer span, add the 1″ or 2″ extension as required to micrometer. Be sure parts are clean and securely attached.
3. Locate the assembled micrometer in master gauge using the proper checking block. The micrometer should be accurate within 0.0005″.
4. Remove any nicks or burrs from carrier bores with crocus cloth.
5. Install pinion and cage assembly in carrier. *Using the original shim pack,* be sure that shims are clean and properly aligned with oil passages in cage and carrier. Install cap screws or stud nuts and *tighten to recommended torque.*
6. Install gauge set step plate clamp assembly tightly to carrier with clamp screw at center of pinion. On some axles clamp can be secured to carrier by using bracket.

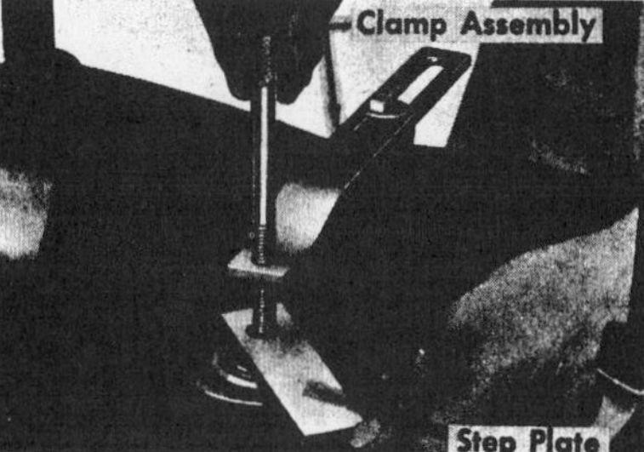

Installing clamp and step plate (© G.M.C.)

7. With step plate clamp assembly securely attached to carrier, install gauge set step plate.
8. After determining the *Nominal Assembly Dimension,* select the proper adapter disc from the chart. In some instances, two identical discs are used, and in other instances two different slightly tapered discs are used. When tapered discs are used, assemble the discs and sleeves to the arbor with smaller outside diameter of discs toward out side. Tighten the sleeve nuts.
9. Retract micrometer and install the assembled gauge in carrier.
10. Subtract from or add to the *Nominal Assembly Dimension,* the *Individual Variation Dimension* to arrive at the *Corrected Nominal Dimension.*
11. Subtract the thickness (0.400″) of the step plate (mounted on pinion end), from *Corrected Nominal Dimension* to get the *Corrected Micrometer Distance.*
12. Run Micrometer thimble down to measure distance from center of carrier bores (drive gear center) to step plate on pinion. This is the *Initial Micrometer Reading.*

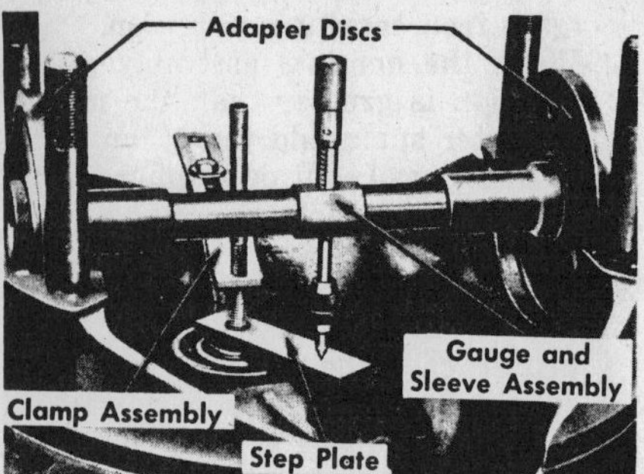

Position of pinion setting gauge
(© G.M.C.)

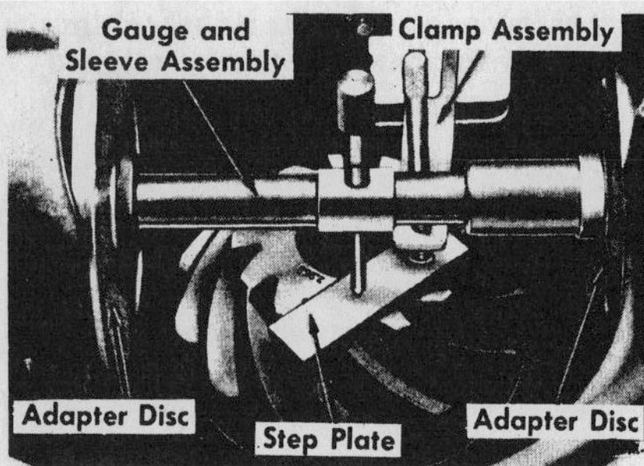

Installation of pinion gauge (Timken 2-speed)
(© G.M.C.)

13. The difference between the *Corrected Micrometer Distance and* the *Initial Micrometer Reading* determines the thickness of shim pack to be removed or added.

NOTE: When adjusting shims are located at pinion bearings instead of between pinion cage and carrier it will be necessary to remove instead of adding shims (paragraph a) or add, instead of remove (paragraph b), shims.

a. When the "corrected micrometer distance" is more than the "initial micrometer reading," shim pack thickness equal the difference must be added. As an example:

	In.
Nominal assembly dimension	3.551
Individual variation distance	+0.008
Corrected nominal dimension	3.559
Deduct step plate thickness	0.400
Corrected micrometer distance	3.159
Subtract initial micrometer reading	3.139
Shim pack to be added	0.020

b. When the "corrected micrometer distance" is less than the "initial micrometer reading," shim pack thickness equal the difference must be removed. As an example:

	In.
Nominal assembly dimension	2.656
Individual variation distance	−0.002
Corrected nominal dimension	2.654
Deduct step plate thickness	0.400
Corrected micrometer distance	2.254
Initial micrometer reading	2.274
Subtract 2.254" from 2.274 = the amount of shim pack to be removed	0.020

14. Remove gauge and discs and step plate.
15. Remove pinion and cage assembly as instructed in respective axle assembly.
16. Add to or remove from original pinion cage to carrier adjusting shim pack as determined by calculations in paragraph 13.
17. Install shim pack pinion and cage assembly as described in separate axle sections. Recheck in manner described above. The "Corrected Micrometer Reading" must be within plus or minus 0.002" of the "Corrected Nominal Distance." This will insure properly adjusted tooth contact.
18. Check gear tooth contact by using Red Lead Method and adjust gear backlash. Both procedures described later.

Setting New Pinion (Without Gauge)

Whenever a pinion setting gauge is not available, the approximate thickness of the pinion shim pack at the rear pinion bearing cup, change the sign of the marking (individual variation distance) on the *new* pinion (plus to minus or minus to plus), then add the variation of the old pinion (sign unchanged) which will determine the amount the original shim pack must be changed when installing a new pinion.

On those types of axles where the shims are located between the pinion cage and differential carrier, change the sign of the marking (individual variation distance) on the *old* pinion (plus to minus or minus to plus), then add variation of the new pinion (sign unchanged) which will determine how much the original shim pack must be altered when installing a new pinion.

When the approximate thickness of shim pack has been determined, final check of gear tooth contact must be made using Red Lead Method.

Gear Tooth Contact (Red Lead)

Gear tooth contact cannot be successfully accomplished until pinion and bevel gear bearings are in proper adjustment and gear backlash is within specified limits.

Check for proper tooth contact by painting a few teeth of bevel gear with oiled red lead. Turn pinion in direction of normal rotation, then check tooth impression on bevel gear.

Gear Backlash

Gears that have been in extended service, form running contacts due to wear of teeth; therefore the original shim pack (between pinion cage and carrier) should be maintained when checking backlash. If backlash exceeds maximum tolerance, reduce backlash only in the amount that will avoid overlap of worn tooth section.

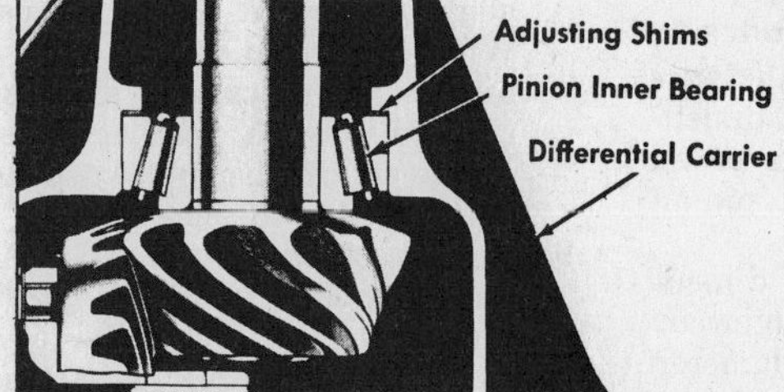

Pinion Markings Old Pinion	New Pinion	Difference Between Markings
+5	+8	−3 Remove .003" Shim
+8	+5	+3 Add .003" Shim
−3	−5	+2 Add .002" Shim
−5	−3	−2 Remove .002" Shim
−3	+4	−7 Remove .007" Shim
+2	−4	+6 Add .006" Shim

The sign of the new pinion is changed and then added algebraically to the old pinion sign.

Determining pinion shim pack thickness (if shim pack is located at rear pinion bearing cup)
(© G.M.C.)

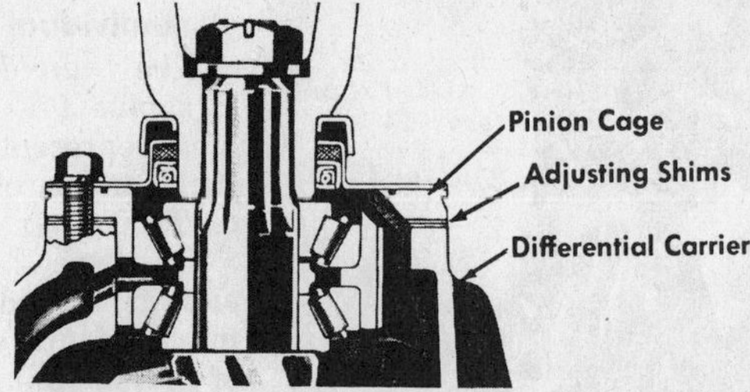

Pinion Markings Old Pinion	New Pinion	Difference Between Markings
+8	+6	−2 Remove .002" Shims
+6	−2	−8 Remove .008" Shims
−4	+4	+8 Add .008" Shims
+2	+6	+4 Add .004" Shims
−7	−4	+3 Add .003" Shims
−2	−6	−4 Remove .004" Shims

The sign of the old pinion is changed and then added algebraically to the new pinion sign.

Determining pinion shim pack thickness (if shims are located between pinion cage and differential carrier)
(© G.M.C.)

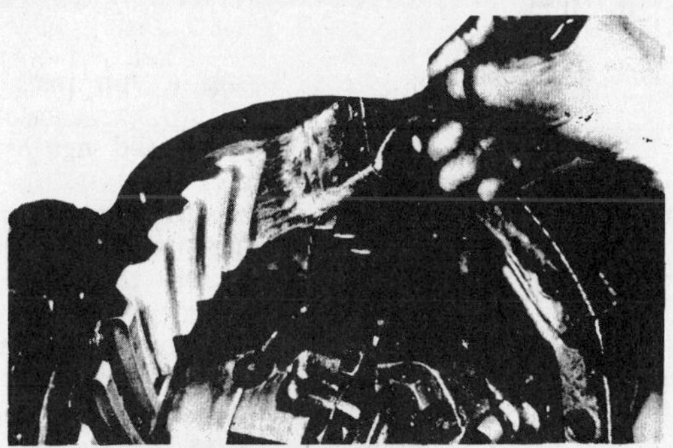

PAINTING GEAR TEETH

CORRECT TYPE TOOTH CONTACT

A HIGH NARROW CONTACT is not desirable. If gears are permitted to operate with an adjustment of this kind, noise, galling and rolling over of top edge of teeth will result. To obtain correct contact, move pinion toward bevel gear. This lowers contact area to proper location. This adjustment will decrease the backlash which may be corrected by moving bevel gear away from pinion.

A LOW NARROW CONTACT is not desirable. If gears are permitted to operate with an adjustment of this type, galling, noise and grooving of teeth will result. To obtain correct contact, move pinion away from drive gear. This will raise contact area to proper location. A correct backlash is obtained by moving bevel gear toward pinion.

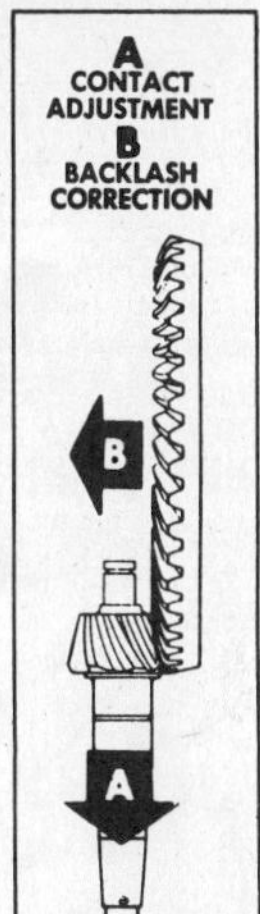

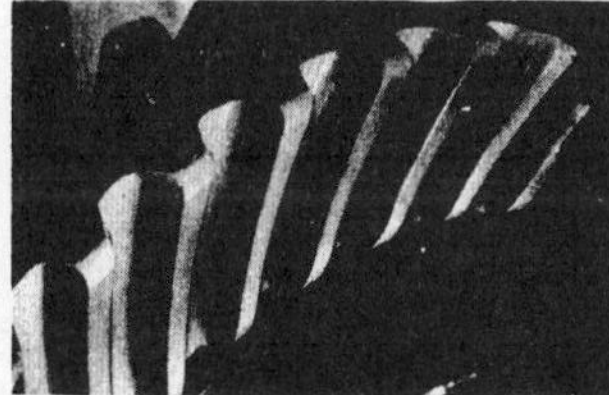

A SHORT TOE CONTACT is not desirable. If gears are permitted to operate with an adjustment of this type, chipping at tooth edges and excessive wear due to small contact area will result. To obtain correct contact, move drive gear from pinion. This will increase the lengthwise contact and move contact toward heel of tooth. Correct backlash is obtained by moving pinion toward bevel gear.

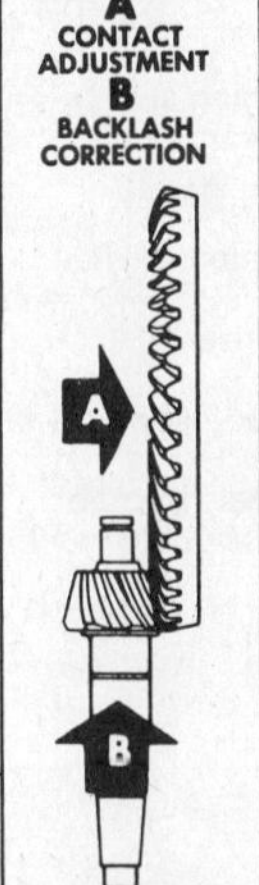

A SHORT HEEL CONTACT is not desirable. If gears are permitted to operate with an adjustment of this type, chipping, excessive wear and noise will result. To obtain correct contact, move drive gear toward pinion to increase lengthwise contact and move contact toward toe. A correct backlash is obtained by moving pinion away from drive gear.

Gear tooth contact chart (© G.M.C.)

Smoothness and roughness can be noted by rotating bevel gear.

If a slight overlap is present at worn tooth section, rotation will be rough.

If new gears are installed, check backlash with dial indicator.

Backlash is increased by moving bevel gear away from pinion, and may be decreased by moving bevel gear toward pinion.

When the drive gear is attached to the differential, backlash is accomplished at differential bearing adjusting rings. It should be remembered that when one ring is tightened, the opposite ring must be loosened an equal amount to maintain previously established bearing adustment.

On axles where the bevel gear is supported by cross shaft, backlash is accomplished by adding or removing shims under bearing cages.

Checking gear backlash (bevel gear) (© G.M.C.)

Chevrolet Semi-Floating Single Speed with Removable Carrier

½ Ton Trucks Thru 1962

Differential Carrier Disassembly

1. Mount the carrier assembly in a bench vise or holding fixture.
2. Mark the bearing caps and carrier for reasssembly in the same position. Remove the differential adjusting nut locks and bearing cap bolts and lockwashers.
3. Remove the bearing caps and adjusting nuts by tapping on the bosses of the caps until free.
4. Remove the differential and ring gear assembly from the carrier.
5. Remove the pinion shaft lock screw, pinion shaft and axle shaft spacer, then roll out the pinions and remove the side gears.
6. Hold the pinion flange from turning and remove the pinion flange nut and washer, then remove the pinion flange.
7. Remove the drive pinion by tapping on the front with a soft faced hammer.
8. Remove the pinion flange oil seal, pinion front bearing and bearing spacer from the carrier. NOTE: Some axles may have a 1/16" shim behind the spacer. This is a production item and should be discarded.
9. Thoroughly clean and inspect all parts and replace as necessary.

Pinion and/or Bearing Replacement

1. If necessary to replace the pinion bearings, tap the old cups out of the carrier using a brass drift.
2. Position the new cup in the carrier, thick edge of the cup toward the shoulder of the carrier. Using a cup installer, tap the cup into the carrier until it is fully seated against the shoulder.
3. Press the rear bearing cone and roller assembly from the pinion and note the shim between the bearing cone and pinion head.
4. When the ring gear and pinion or the pinion rear bearing assembly are replaced, the correct

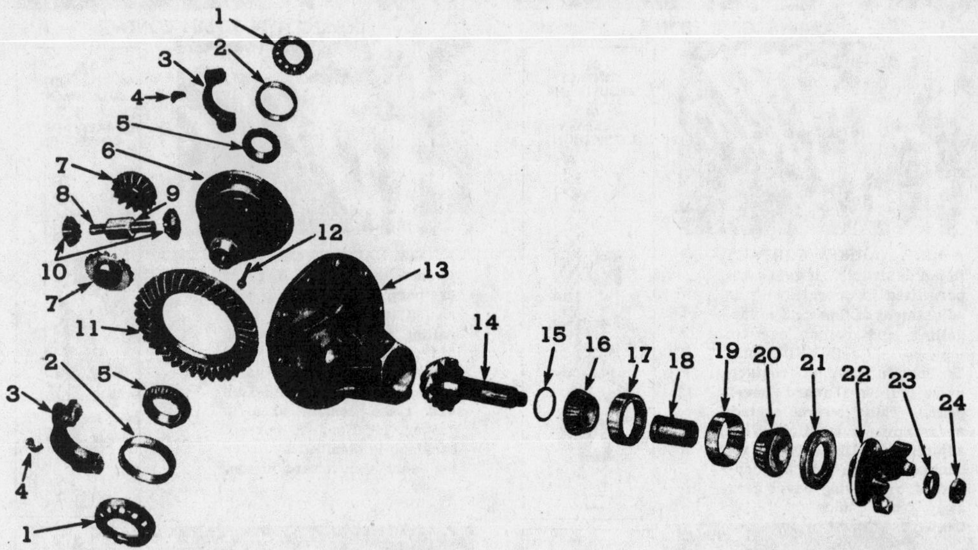

1 Differential bearing adjusting nut
2 Differential bearing outer race
3 Differential bearing caps
4 Differential bearing adjusting nut lock
5 Differential bearing cone and roller assembly
6 Differential case
7 Differential side gear
8 Differential pinion shaft
9 Axle shaft spacer
10 Differential pinion
11 Ring gear
12 Differential pinion shaft lock
13 Differential carrier
14 Drive pinion
15 Pinion depth adjusting shim
16 Rear pinion bearing cone and roller assembly
17 Rear pinion bearing outer race
18 Pinion bearing spacer
19 Front pinion bearing outer race
20 Front pinion bearing cone and roller assembly
21 Pinion flange oil seal
22 Pinion flange
23 Special washer
24 Self locking nut

Single speed rear axle—exploded view (© Chevrolet Div., G.M. Corp.)

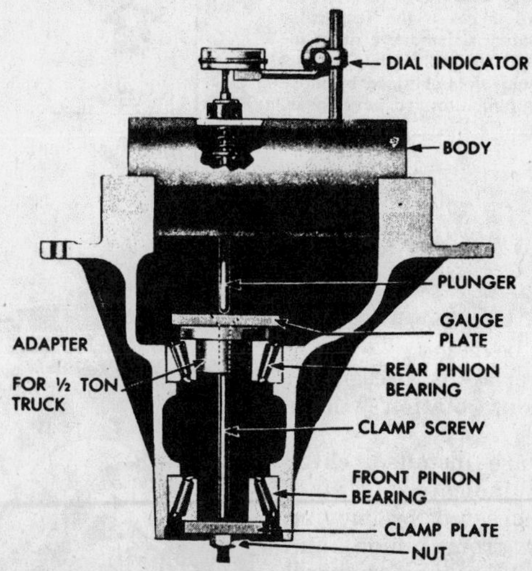

Differential carrier with pinion setting gauge installed
(© Chevrolet Div., G.M. Corp.)

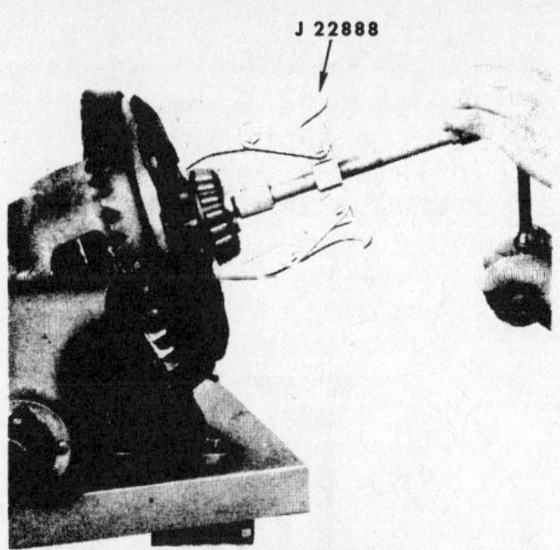

Differential bearing removal
(© Chevrolet Div., G.M. Corp.)

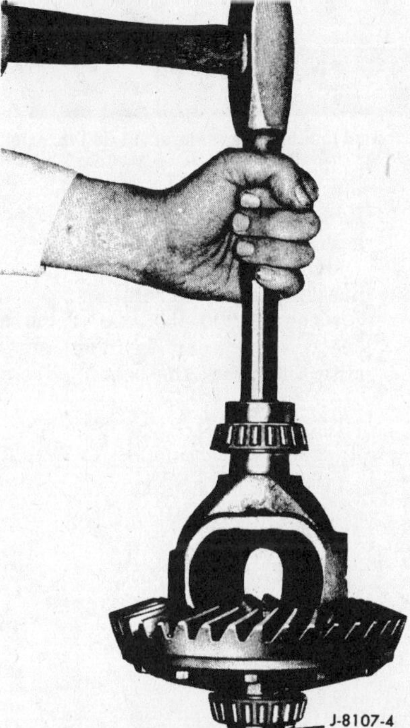

Differential bearing installation
(© Chevrolet Div., G.M. Corp.)

shim thickness must be determined by using special gauges or by the trial and error method according to tooth pattern.

5. Position the shim selected on the pinion shaft against the pinion head.
6. Press the new cone and roller assembly on the pinion.

Differential Bearing Replacement

1. Using a bearing puller, remove the bearings from the case.
2. Place the new bearing on the hub of the case, thick side of inner race toward case. Using a bearing driver, drive the bearing into place.

Ring Gear Replacement

1. Remove the ring gear bolts and lockwashers.
2. With a soft hammer tap the ring gear off the case.
3. Install five guide pins, made from 3/8" - 24x1½" long cap screws with the heads cut off and ends slotted, to the ring gear.
4. Position the ring gear on the case. Install every other ring gear bolt and lockwasher, then draw them up evenly and snugly so that the ring gear back face is tight against the case flange.
5. Remove the guide pins and install the remaining bolts, torque all bolts to 40-60 ft. lbs.

Differential Carrier Reassembly

1. Lubricate the pinion bearings and install the pinion in the carrier.
2. Install a new pinion bearing spacer, large end toward the gear.
3. Install the front pinion bearing cone and roller assembly on the pinion shaft.
4. Soak the new seal in light engine oil before installation. Wipe the outside of the seal and coat the outside with sealer. Using a seal driver, install the seal so the top of the seal is 3/16" from the front face of the differential carrier.
5. Install the pinion flange, special washer and new self-locking nut.
6. Holding the pinion flange, tighten the pinion flange nut until torque required to turn the pinion is 15 to 25 inch pounds for new bearings and seal, or 5 to 15 inch pounds when reinstalling used parts.
7. Lubricate the hubs of the side gears and install in the differential case. Roll the two pinions into place and insert the axle shaft spacer, pinion shaft and lock screw to hold the gears in place.
8. Install the differential assembly in the carrier and install the outer races and adjusting nuts.
9. Install the bearing caps, aligning the marks on the cap with the marks on the carrier.
10. Install and tighten the cap screws until the lockwashers just flatten out.

Ring Gear and Pinion Adjustment

1. Loosen the right hand adjusting nut and tighten the left hand adjusting nut while turning the ring gear. Continue tightening the left hand nut until all lash is removed, then back off the left hand nut one or two notches to a locking position.

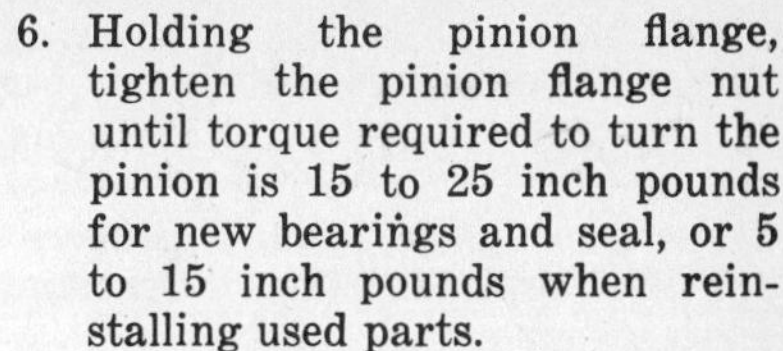

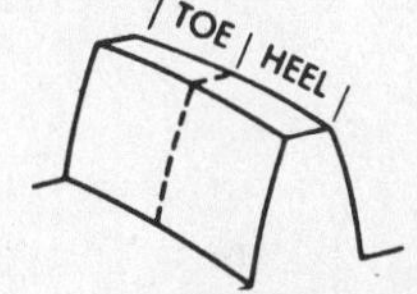

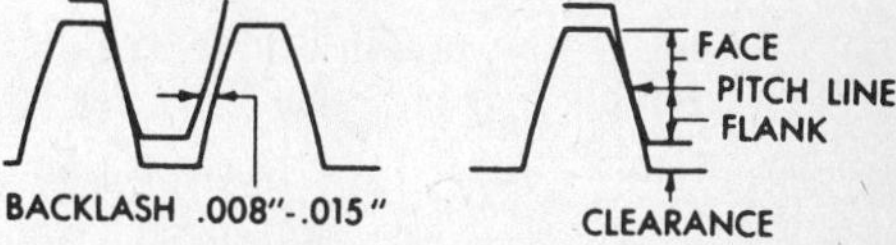

Gear tooth nonemclature
(© Chevrolet Div., G.M. Corp.)

2. Tighten the right hand nut to force the left bearing firmly into contact with the left adjusting nut. Then loosen the right nut and again tighten snugly against the bearing. NOTE: This position may be determined by feeling movement in the right hand

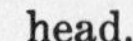

B-TOE CONTACT

C-HEEL CONTACT

D-FACE CONTACT

A-CORRECT TOOTH CONTACT

E-FLANK CONTACT

Gear tooth contact patterns (© Chevrolet Div., G.M. Corp.)

differential bearing outer race when contact is made.

3. Tighten the right hand nut an additional two or three notches to a locking position. This operation preloads the differential bearings.
4. Mount a dial indicator on the carrier and check the back lash between the ring gear and pinion. The back lash should be from .003″-.010″ with .005″-.008″ preferred. This is changed by moving each adjustment nut an equal

lash.

5. Tighten the bearing cap bolts to 115-135 ft. lbs. Recheck the back lash and install both adjusting nut locks.

amount in the same direction to retain preload and change back

Chevrolet Full Floating Single Speed

Differential Carrier Disassembly

1. Mount the carrier assembly in a bench vise or holding fixture.
2. On axles so equipped, loosen the ring gear thrust pad lock nut and remove the thrust pad.
3. Remove the differential adjusting nut locks and bearing cap bolts and lockwashers.
4. Mark the bearing caps and carrier for reassembly in the same position. Remove the bearing caps and adjusting nuts by tapping on the bosses of the caps until free from the dowels.
5. Remove the differential and ring gear assembly from the carrier.
6. Remove the bolts which attach the pinion bearing retainer to the carrier.
7. Remove the pinion and bearing assembly from the carrier.

NOTE: It may be necessary to drive this unit from the carrier. Use a brass drift against the pilot end of the pinion.

8. On all axles except the 11,000 lb. from 1967, remove shims from inside the carrier housing making note of the number and total thickness of shims removed.
9. On all axles except the 11,000 lb., the pinion rear bearing outer race and roller assembly is pressed into the carrier. Remove the assembly by driving it from its seat using a soft drift or punch.

Pinion and/or Bearing Replacement

1. Clamp the pinion drive flange in a bench vise.
2. Remove the cotter pin, nut and washer from the end of the pinion.

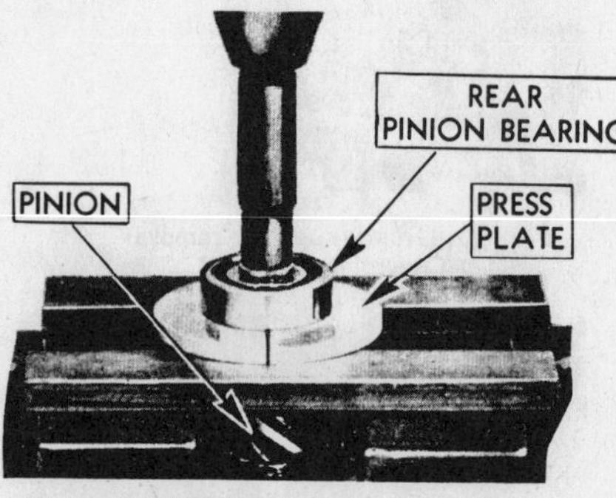

Pinion rear bearing removal (11,000 lb. axle) (© Chevrolet Div., G.M. Corp.)

3. Remove the drive flange and bearing retainer assembly.
4. Drive the oil seal, and packing if present, from the retainer.
5. On the 11,000 lb. axle, remove the pinion rear bearing snap ring and press the bearing from

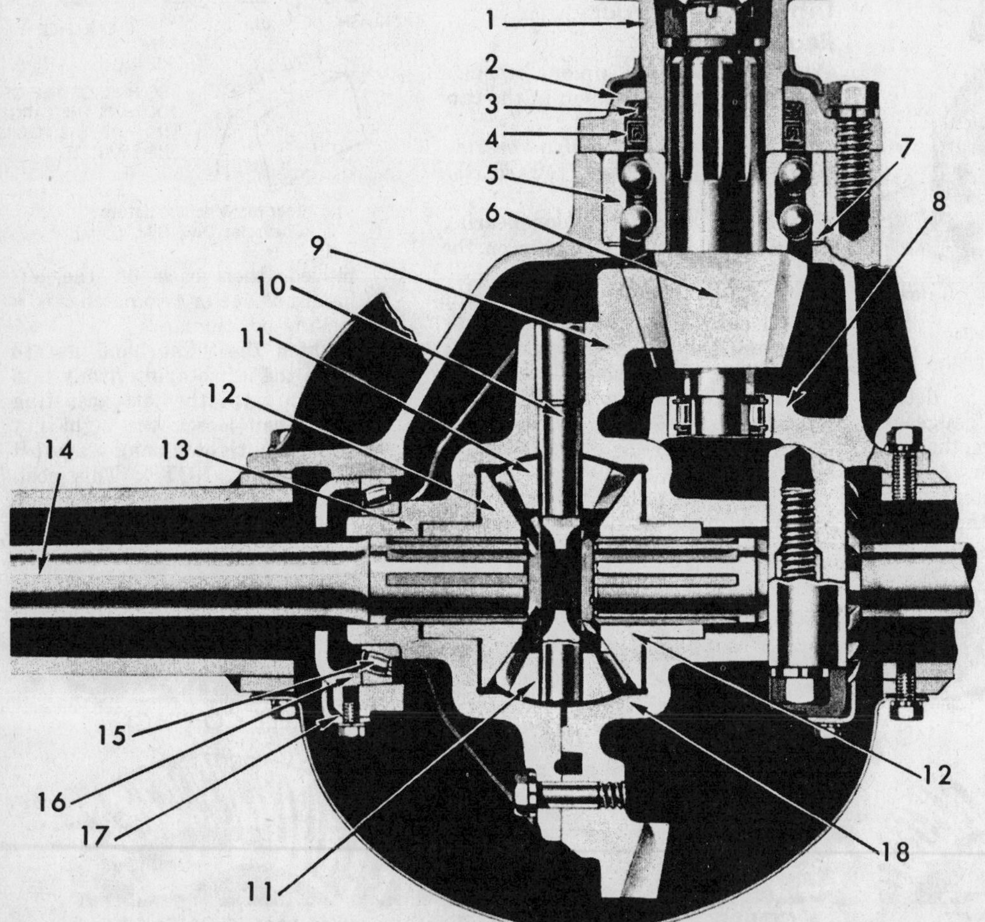

1 Universal joint yoke
2 Pinion bearing retainer and oil seal
3 Oil seal packing
4 Oil seal
5 Front pinion bearing
6 Drive pinion
7 Pinion bearing shim
8 Rear pinion bearing
9 Ring gear
10 Differential spider
11 Differential pinion (spider) gear
12 Differential side gear
13 Differential case—left half
14 Axle shaft
15 Differential bearing
16 Differential bearing adjusting nut
17 Adjusting nut lock
18 Differential case—right half

5200 and 7200 lb. axle—cross section (© Chevrolet Div., G.M. Corp.)

1 Universal joint yoke
2 Pinion bearing and oil seal retainer
3 Oil seal
4 Gasket
5 Front pinion bearing
6 Drive pinion
7 Pinion Bearing shim
8 Rear pinion bearing
9 Ring gear thrust pad
10 Ring gear
11 Differential spider
12 Differential pinion (spider) gear
13 Differential side gear
14 Differential case—left half
15 Axle shaft
16 Differential bearing
17 Differential bearing adjusting nut
18 Adjusting nut lock
19 Differential case—right half

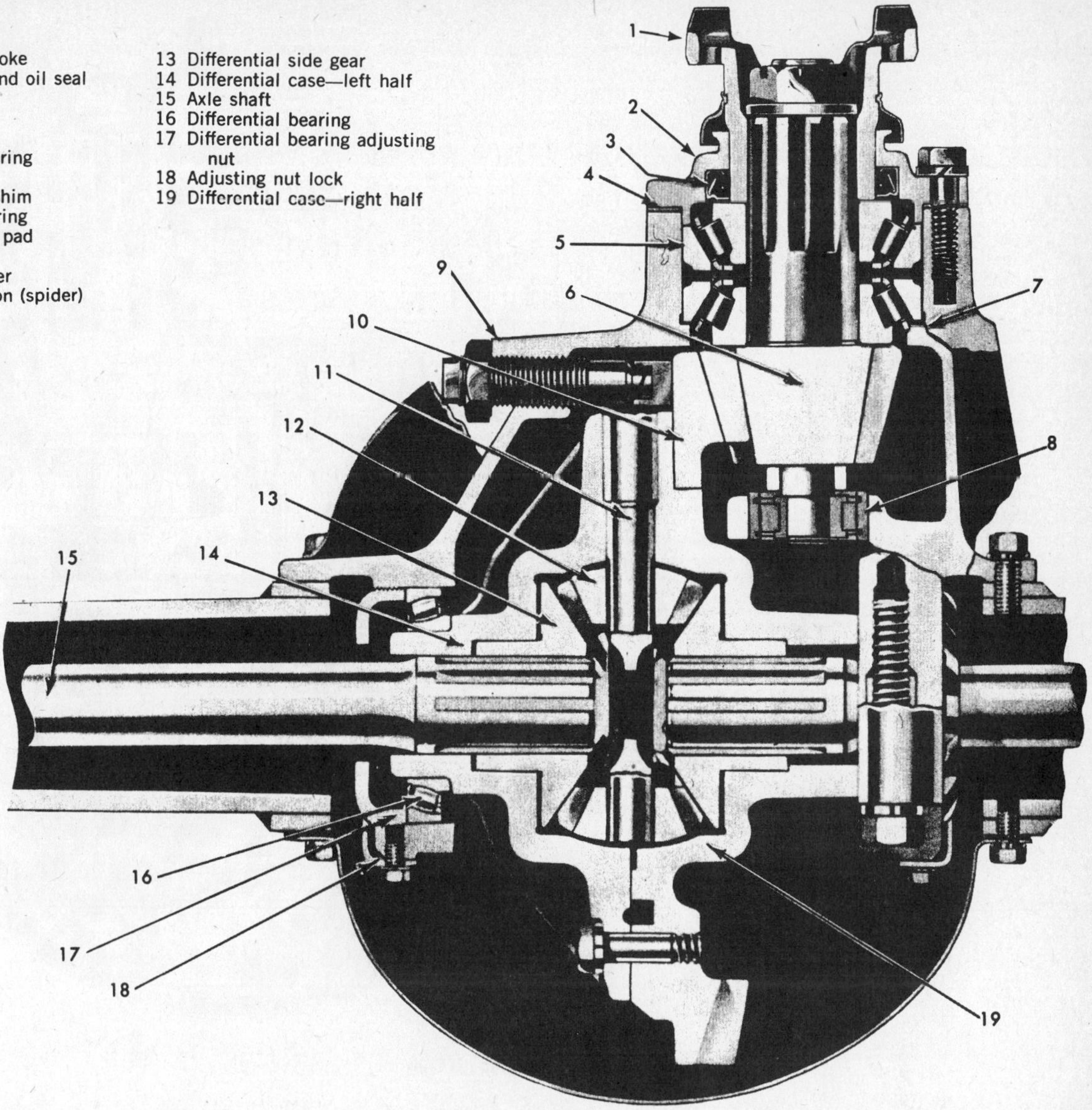

5200 and 7200 lb. axle—with adjusting screw (© Chevrolet Div., G.M. Corp.)

Pinion rear bearing removal—exc. 11,000 lb. axle (© Chevrolet Div., G.M. Corp.)

Pinion inner bearing inner race removal (13,500-15,000 and 17,000 lb. axles) (© Chevrolet Div., G.M. Corp.)

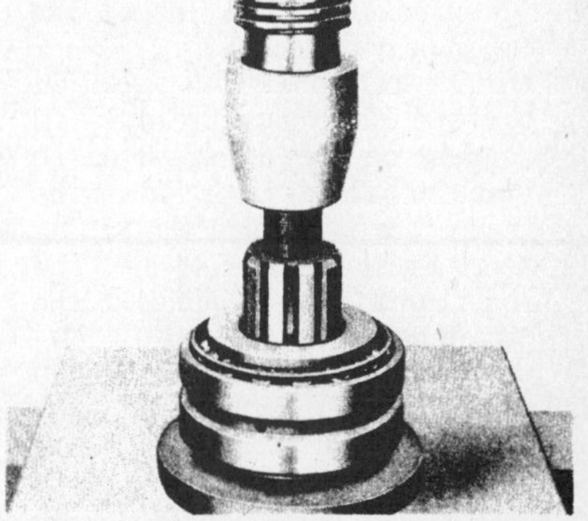

Drive pinion front bearing removal—typical (© Chevrolet Div., G.M. Corp.)

the pinion.

6. On the 13,500, 15,000 and 17,000 lb. axles press the inner race of the rear bearing from the pinion.
7. On the 5200 and 7200 lb. axles press the pinion from the bearing.
8. On the 11,000 lb. axle, press the front bearing from the pinion.
9. On the 13,500, 15,000 and 17,000 lb. axles press the front bearing from the pinion.
10. Soak the new oil seal (and packing) in engine oil. Install the felt packing, if so equipped, in the bottom of the retainer. Press the oil seal into the retainer.
11. On the 5200, 7200, 13,500, 15,000 and 17,000 lb. axles, lubricate the pinion rear bearing and press it into the carrier. Then install the inner race on the 13,500, 15,000 and 17,000 lb. axle pinion shaft.
12. On the 11,000 lb. axle, install the pinion rear bearing on the pin-

1 Universal joint yoke
2 Pinion bearing retainer and oil seal
3 Oil seal packing
4 Oil seal
5 Front pinion bearing
6 Drive pinion
7 Rear pinion bearing
8 Ring gear thrust pad
9 Ring gear
10 Differential spider
11 Differential pinion (Spider) gear
12 Differential side gear
13 Differential case—left half
14 Axle shaft
15 Differential bearing
16 Differential bearing adjusting nut
17 Adjusting nut lock
18 Differential case—right half

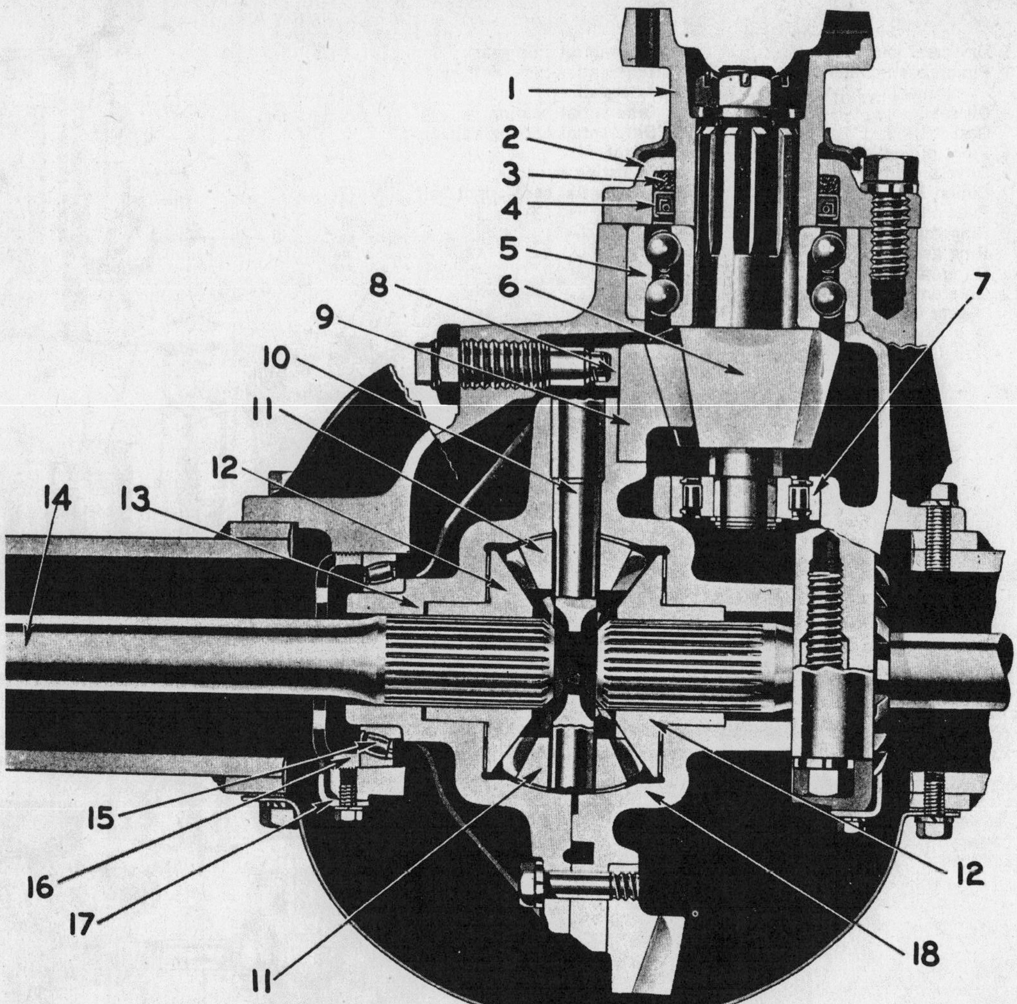

11000 lb. axle cross section (© Chevrolet Div., G.M. Corp.)

ion shaft making sure that the chamfered side of the inner race seats against the shoulder on the pinion shaft. Then install the pinon bearing lock ring.

13. On the 11,000 lb. axle, position the one piece double row ball bearing on the pinion shaft so that the extended portion of the inner race is toward the pinion head. Press the bearing onto the shaft until it seats against the pinion head.
14. On the 5200, 7200, 13,500, 15,000 and 17,000 lb. axles, place one cone and roller assembly on the pinion shaft so that the large end of bearing is toward the pinion. Then position the outer race, spacer and cone and roller assembly on the pinion shaft. Press the bearing until it seats against the pinion head.
15. Slide the oil seal retainer on the pinion shaft, then tap the flange onto the splines.
16. Clamp the drive flange in a bench vise and install the flange washer and nut. Torque the nut to 220 ft. lbs. and install the cotter pin without backing off on the nut.

Pinion rear bearing inner race installation (13,500 15,000 and 17,000 lb. axles) (© Chevrolet Div., G.M. Corp.)

Differential Disassembly

1. Check the differential case to make sure that the two halves are marked so they may be reassembled in the same relation.
2. Remove the bolts holding the case and cover together.
3. Separate the cover from the case and remove the differential side gears and thrust washers, pinion gears with thrust washers and differential spider.
4. Remove the ring gear from the case by tapping the back of the gear with a soft faced hammer.

Differential Reassembly

1. Install two guide pins (made from cap screws with the heads cut off and ends slotted) to the new gear opposite each other.
2. Start the guide pins through the case flange and tap the ring gear on the case.
3. Lubricate the differential side gears, pinions and thrust washers.
4. Place the differential pinions and thrust washers on the spider.
5. Assemble the side gears and pinions and thrust washers to the left half of the case.
6. Assemble the case halves being sure to line up the marks on the two halves.
7. Install the differential to ring gear bolts and lock washers and tighten evenly until the ring gear is flush with the case

1 Universal joint yoke
2 Pinion bearing retainer
3 Oil seal
4 Shims
5 Pinion bearing assembly
6 Drive pinion
7 Rear pinion bearing
8 Ring gear thrust pad
9 Ring gear
10 Differential spider
11 Differential pinion (spider) gear
12 Differential side gear
13 Differential case (left half)
14 Axle shaft
15 Differential bearing
16 Differential bearing adjusting nut
17 Adjusting nut lock
18 Differential case (right half)

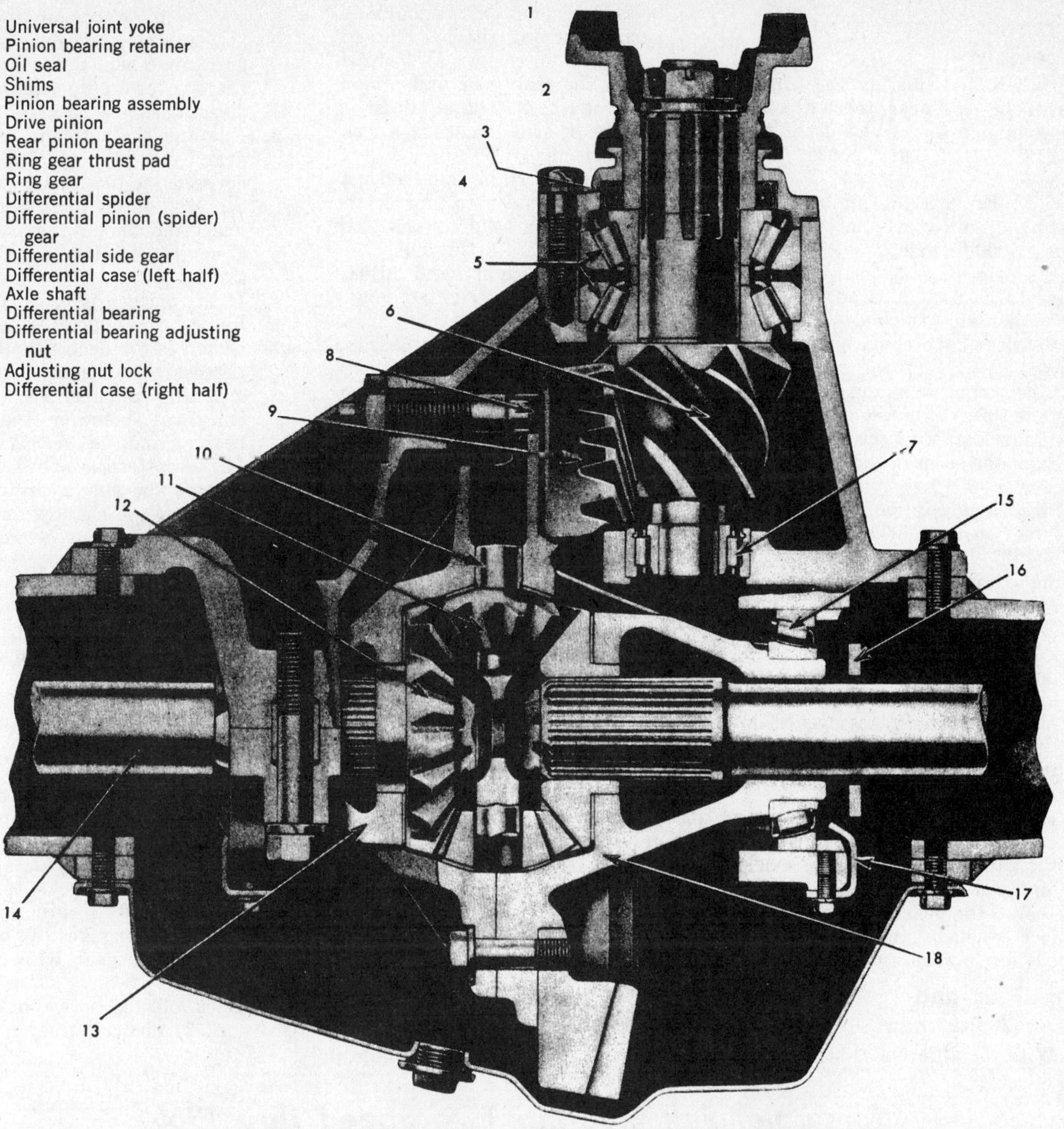

13,500, 15,000 and 17,000 lb. axle—cross section (© Chevrolet Div., G.M. Corp.)

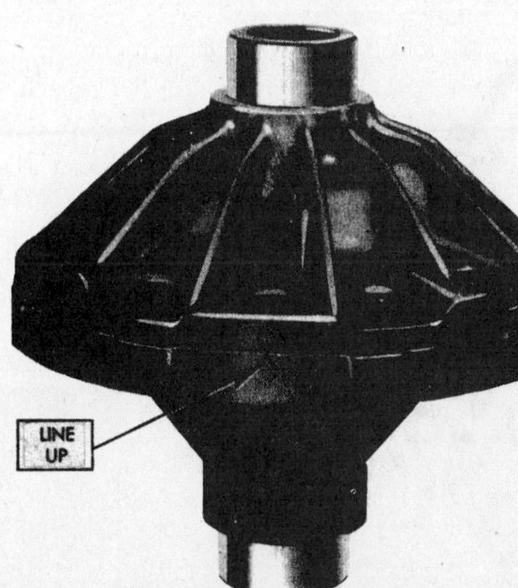

Differential case line up marks
(© Chevrolet Div., G.M. Corp.)

flange.

8. Remove the two guide pins and install the remaining two bolts.
9. Torque all bolts to specifications:
   Thru 1966—85-95 ft. lbs.
   From 1967
   Except below—110 ft. lbs.
   15,000 lb. and 17,000 lb. axles—160 ft. lbs.

Differential Bearing Replacement

1. Using a bearing puller, remove the bearings from the case.
2. Place the new bearing on the hub of the case, thick side of inner race toward case. Using a bearing driver, drive the bearing into place.

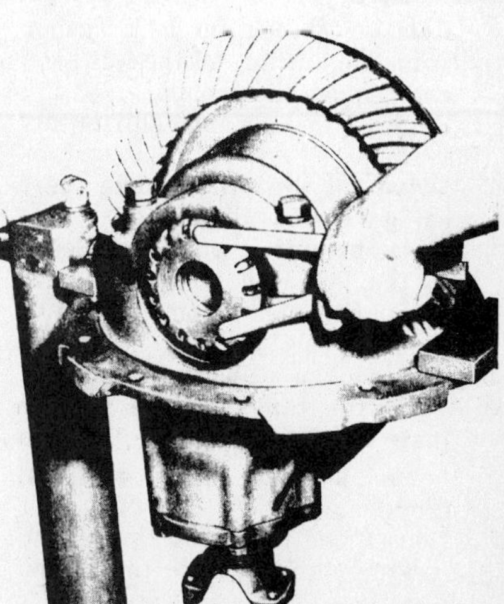

Ring gear and pinion adjustment
(© Chevrolet Div., G.M. Corp.)

Differential Carrier Reassembly

To facilitate adjusting the pinion depth in the ring gear, there are five shims available for service use. They are .012″, .015″, .018″, .021″ and .024″.

NOTE: From 1967, pinion depth adjustment shims are not required for the 11,000 lb. axle.

If the original ring gear and pinion are to be used it is advisable to replace the same thickness of shims in the carrier counter bore that were removed.

If a new ring gear and pinion are used, one .021″ shim should be used as a standard starting set up.

1. Place the shim in the bore in the carrier.
2. Place a new pinion bearing retainer gasket on the retainer and install the pinion assembly in the carrier.
3. Install and tighten the pinion bearing retainer bolts and lock washers.
4. Lubricate the differential bearing rollers with engine oil and place the outer races over them.
5. Install the differential assembly in the carrier and install the adjusting nuts.
6. Install the differential bearing caps making sure the marks on the caps line up with the marks on the carrier.
7. Install the bearing cap bolts and lock washers and tighten until the lock washers just flatten out.

Ring Gear and Pinion Adjustment

1. With the differential bearing cap bolts loosened just enough to permit turning the bearing adjusting nuts, remove all lash between the ring gear and pinion.
2. Back off the left hand adjusting nut one or two notches to a locking position.
3. Tighten the right hand adjusting nut firmly to force the differential in solid contact with the left hand adjusting nut.
4. Back off the right hand adjusting nut and again tighten snugly against the bearing.
5. Tighten the right hand adjusting nut from one to two additional notches to a locking position. NOTE: This method of adjustment provides for proper preload of the bearings.
6. Mount a dial indicator on the carrier and check the backlash between the ring gear and pinion Backlash should be .003″ to .012″ (.005″ to .008″ preferred). If the backlash is more than .012″ loosen the right hand adjusting nut one notch and tighten the left hand adjusting nut one notch. If the backlash is less than .003″ loosen the left hand adjusting nut one notch and tighten the right hand adjusting nut one notch.
7. Tighten the bearing cap bolts to specifications.
   Except below—
   205 ft. lbs.
   5200 and 7200 lb. axles—
   100 ft. lbs.
8. Install the side bearing adjusting nut locks.

Checking Pinion Depth

1. Coat the ring gear teeth lightly and evenly with a mixture of red lead and oil to produce a contact pattern. Then turn the pinion shaft several revolutions in both directions.
2. Examine the pattern on the ring gear teeth. If the pinion depth is correct, the tooth pattern will be centered on the pitch line and toward the toe of the ring gear. (See Illustration in this section).
3. If the pattern is below the pitch line on the ring gear teeth, the pinion is too deep and it will be necessary to remove the pinion assembly and increase the shim thickness between the pinion bearing and the carrier.
4. If the pattern is above the pitch line on the ring gear teeth, the pinion is too shallow and it will be necessary to decrease the shim thickness.
5. Changing the pinion depth will make some change in the backlash; therefore, it will be necessary to readjust the backlash.

Ring Gear Thrust Pad Adjustment

On axles equipped with a thrust pad, inspect the bronze tip of the thrust pad and if worn install a new one.

1. Install the thrust pad and tighten the screw until the bronze tip engages the back face of the ring gear while rotating the gear.
2. Back off the screw one-twelfth (1/12) turn and tighten the locknut.

Chevrolet Full Floating Two Speed thru 1965

Differential Carrier Disassembly

1. Remove the bolt and lock washer from the anchor, on the left side, and remove the anchor.
2. Remove the vacuum shifter assembly.
3. Drive out the shifter yoke shaft using a drift and hammer.
4. Slide the shifter yoke and sleeve to the left removing the sleeve and shifter yoke from the end of the sun gear.
5. Remove the adjusting nut locks.
6. Bend the tangs on the locking plate down and remove the two bolts, locking plate, and oil trough.
7. Loosen the ring gear thrust pad lock nut and remove the thrust pad.
8. Remove the bearing cap bolts then remove the bearing caps and adjusting nuts by tapping

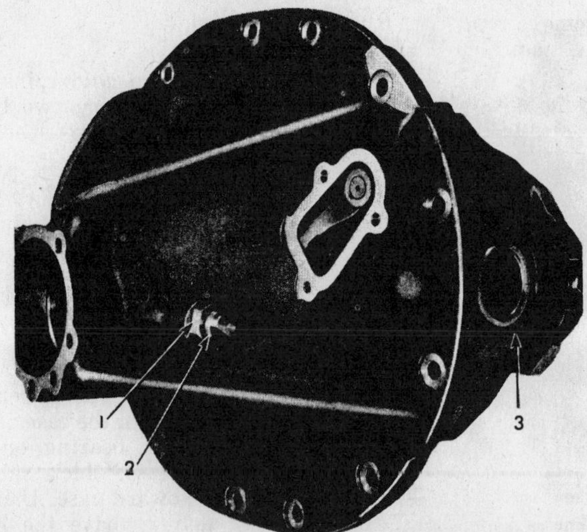

Thrust pad and anchor
(© Chevrolet Div., G.M. Corp.)

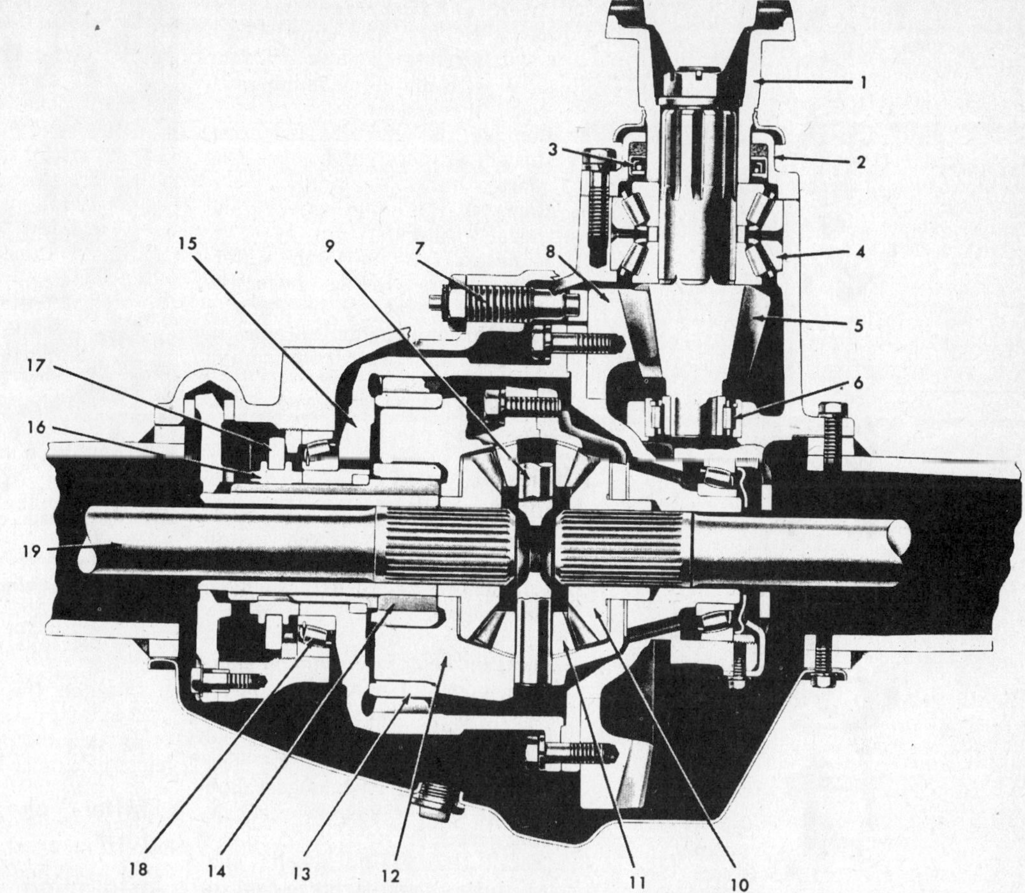

Two speed axle—cross section (15,000 and 17,000 lb. capacity (© Chevrolet Div. G.M. Corp.)

on the bosses of the caps until free from the dowels.

9. Remove the differential and planet assembly from the housing.

Pinion Disassembly

1. Loosen the pinion bearing oil seal retainer bolts and lockwashers.
2. Tap on the flange, driving out the pinion assembly gradually while continuing to loosen the bolts. NOTE: Remove the shims from the carrier housing and note the amount.
3. Remove the rear pinion bearing from the carrier housing.
4. Place the pinion flange in a vise and remove the cotter pin, nut, flat washer, and pinion flange.
5. Remove the pinion bearing oil seal retainer and remove the seal.
6. Press the double thrust bearing off the pinion.
7. Press the inner race off the pinion.

Pinion Assembly

1. Install the rear inner race on the pinion.
2. Lubricate and install the double thrust bearing on the pinion.
3. Install a new seal in the pinion bearing oil seal retainer.
4. Install the rear pinion bearing in the differential carrier housing.
5. Install the oil seal retainer on the pinion.
6. Place the pinion flange in a vise and install the pinion on the flange.
7. Install the flat washer and nut on the pinion, torque the nut to 160-280 ft. lbs., and install the cotter pin.
8. Install the pinion bearing shim in the carrier housing, then place the pinion assembly in the carrier housing by tapping on

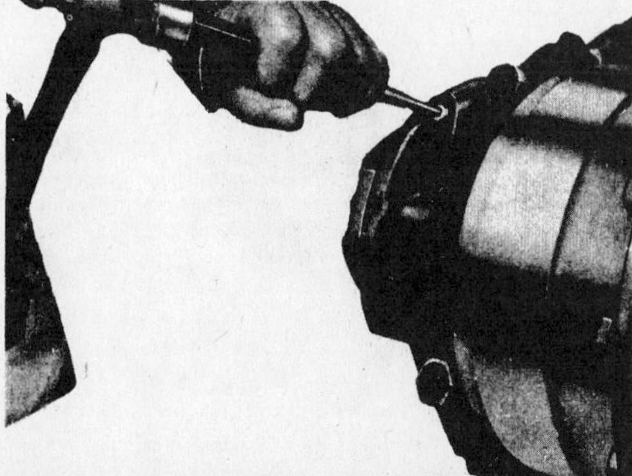

Removing shifter yoke shaft
(© Chevrolet Div., G.M. Corp.)

Removing sleeve and yoke
(© Chevrolet Div., G.M. Corp.)

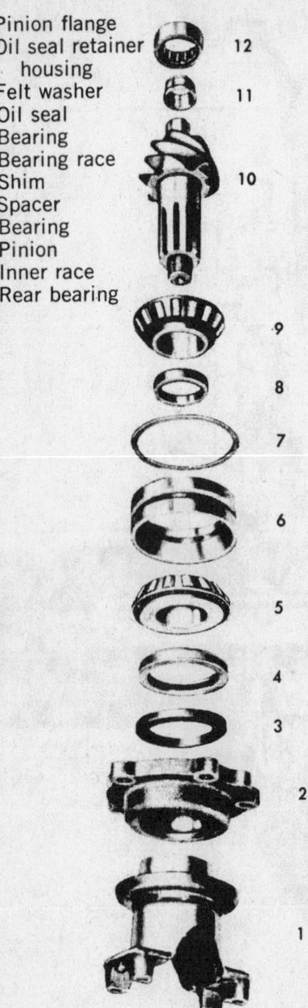

Exploded view of pinion assembly
(© Chevrolet Div., G.M. Corp.)

the pinion flange until the assembly is in far enough to start the bolts. Torque the bolts to 90-100 ft. lbs. CAUTION: If i· is possible to measure any amount of "in and out" movement of the pinion assembly at this point, remove the pinion assembly and check the following:

a. Pinion nut drawn to 160-280 ft. lbs.
b. Pinion bearing preload (15-25 inch pounds for new bearing, 5-15 inch pounds for used parts).

9. Pinion bearing depth shim installed.

Differential and Planet Disassembly

1. Mark the ring gear, support case and case cover for alignment.
2. Remove the bolts and lockwashers retaining the ring gear to the planet support case and cover assembly and remove the cover.
3. Remove the sun gear and planet gears, and mark the gears.
4. Lift the differential and planet support assembly off the case cover.
5. Remove the bolts and lockwashers from the planet support and cover and separate the two parts. NOTE: The support and cover are stamped on all four sides with matching numbers to assist in reassembly.
6. Remove the spider, gears and thrust washers, and mark the gears.
7. Remove the side gears and thrust washers.
8. If necessary, remove the differential side bearings from the case and cover by inserting a drift through the drilled holes in the case and cover and tapping off the bearings.
9. Inspect all parts for damage or excessive wear.

Differential and Planet Assembly

1. Using a bearing driver, install the differential side bearings.
2. Lubricate the thrust washers, side gears, spider and differential gears and assemble the parts in the differential and planet support. Place the support cover in position so that the identification marks line up, and install the cover. NOTE: The side gear with the longest hub belongs on the side nearest the ring gear.
3. Install the retaining bolts and lockwashers and tighten them to 70-110 ft. lbs.
4. Install the four planet gears, with the large chamfer on the I.D. of the gear toward the base of the journal.
5. Install the sun gear in the planet gears.
6. Using guide pins installed in the ring gear, assemble the ring gear, support case cover, differential and planet assembly and support case. Make sure the marks line up.
7. Install the retaining bolts and lockwashers and torque to 85-95 ft. lbs.

Differential Carrier Reassembly

1. Install the assembled differential and planet assembly in the carrier housing then install the bearing races on both sides.
2. Install the differential bearing adjusting nuts.
3. Install the bearing caps on the dowels. Install the cap bolts and lock washers and tighten them until the lockwashers just flatten out.

Ring Gear and Pinion Adjustment

For procedures see Chevrolet Full Floating Single Speed Axle in this section.

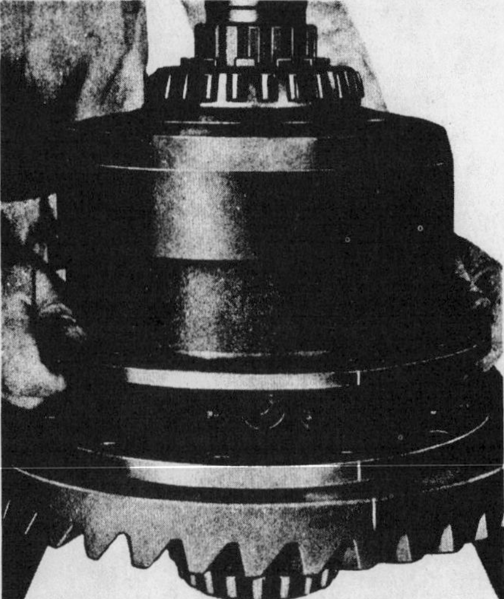
Alignment marks on ring gear case and cover
(© Chevrolet Div., G.M. Corp.)

Checking Pinion Depth

For procedures see Chevrolet Full Floating Single Speed Axle in this section.

Tighten the bearing cap bolts to 190-220 ft. lbs.

Install the oil trough with sufficient clearance to the ring gear.

Shifter Yoke, Sleeve and Shaft

Installation

1. Install the shifter yoke on the shifter sleeve and install the assembled parts on the sun gear. NOTE: Install the splined end of the shifter yoke to the rear of the differential.
2. Install the shifter lever and shaft through the housing into the shifter yoke mating the two parts. CAUTION: The end of the shift lever shaft must be flush with lever hub to avoid binding when the vacuum shifter assembly is installed.

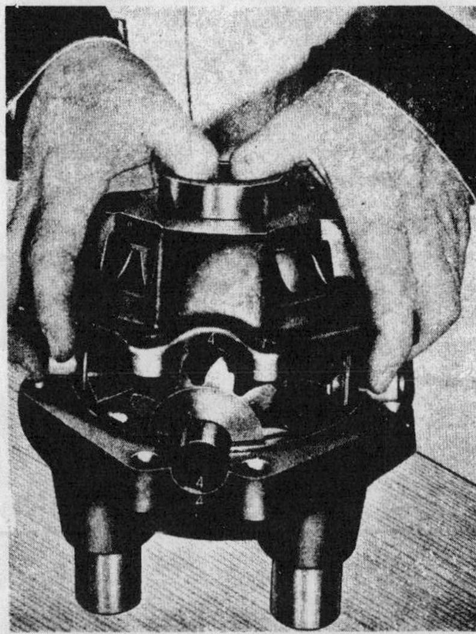
Separating support and cover
(© Chevrolet Div., G.M. Corp.)

Chevrolet Full Floating Two Speed from 1966

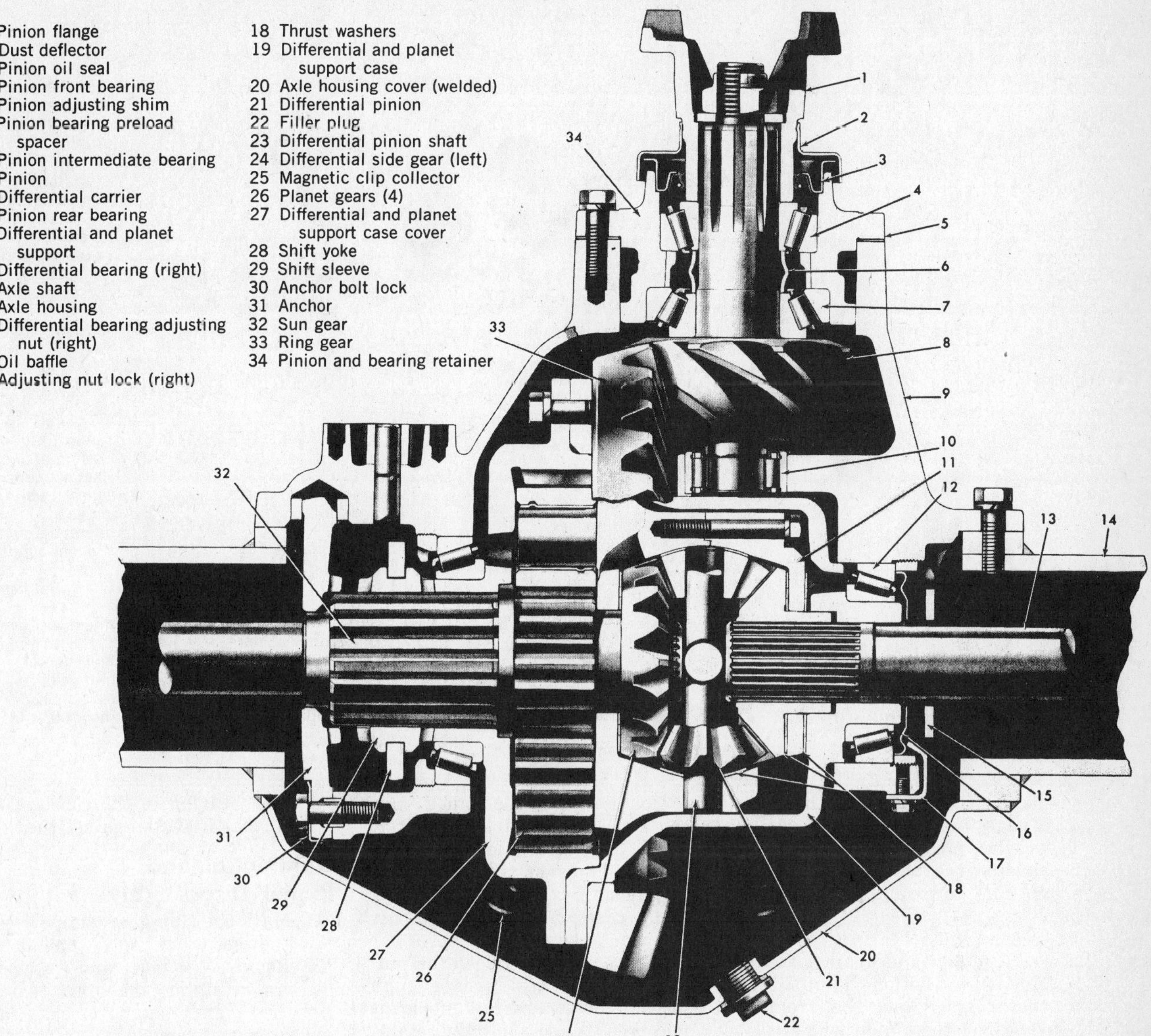

Two speed axle—cross section (© Chevrolet Div., G.M. Corp.)

Differential Carrier Disassembly

1. Place the differential carrier assembly in a repair stand or large vise.
2. Hold the flange and remove the drive pinion nut and washer. Discard the nut and use a new nut for reassembly.
3. Remove the flange from the pinion by tapping on the flange with a brass drift and hammer.
4. Remove the cap screws securing the pinion bearing retainer to the carrier. Rap the retainer sharply with a soft faced hammer to loosen the retainer from the carrier.
5. Withdraw the retainer and pinion from the carrier and remove the shims from between the carrier and retainer. Save the shims to facilitate adjustment during reassembly.
6. Remove the bolts retaining the shifter assembly to the carrier and remove the shifter assembly.
7. Remove the bolt and bolt lock from the shift yoke anchor, then remove the anchor from the carrier.
8. Drive out the shifter yoke shaft, using a drift and hammer.
9. Slide the shifter yoke and sleeve to the left, removing the sleeve and shifter yoke from the end of the sun gear.
10. Remove the adjusting nut locks.
11. Remove the retaining bolts and withdraw the oil trough.
12. Remove the bearing cap bolts, then remove the bearing caps and adjusting nuts by tapping on the bosses of the caps until free from the dowels.
13. Remove the differential and planet assembly from the housing.

Pinion Disassembly

1. Pry the pinion oil seal from the retainer.
2. Press the pinion out of the retainer.
3. Press the bearings and races from the pinion and retainer.
4. Remove the pinion rear bearing from the carrier by tapping on the outer race with a brass drift to unseat the bearing.
5. Clean all parts and check for damage and excessive wear.

Pinion Assembly

1. Using a driver, install the front and intermediate bearing races

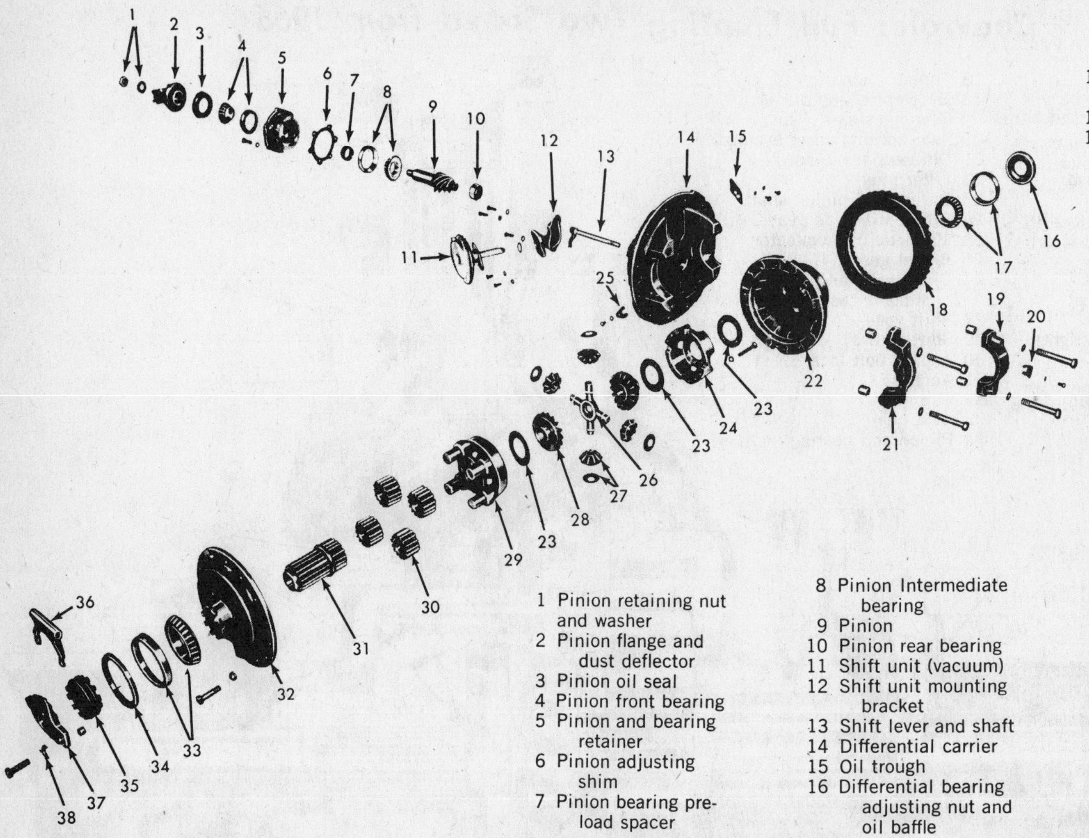

1 Pinion retaining nut and washer
2 Pinion flange and dust deflector
3 Pinion oil seal
4 Pinion front bearing
5 Pinion and bearing retainer
6 Pinion adjusting shim
7 Pinion bearing pre-load spacer
8 Pinion Intermediate bearing
9 Pinion
10 Pinion rear bearing
11 Shift unit (vacuum)
12 Shift unit mounting bracket
13 Shift lever and shaft
14 Differential carrier
15 Oil trough
16 Differential bearing adjusting nut and oil baffle
17 Differential bearing (right)
18 Ring gear
19 Differential bearing cap (right)
20 Adjusting nut lock (right)
21 Differential bearing cap (left)
22 Differential and Planet support case
23 Thrust washer
24 Differential and planet support cover
25 Adjusting nut lock (left)
26 Differential pinion shaft
27 Differential pinion and thrust washer (4)
28 Differential side gear (2)
29 Differential and planet support
30 Planet gears (4)
31 Sun gear
32 Differential and planet support case cover
33 Differential bearing (left)
34 Differential bearing adjusting nut (left)
35 Shift sleeve
36 Shift yoke
37 Shift anchor
38 Anchor bolt lock

Exploded view of carrier (© Chevrolet Div., G.M. Corp.)

in the bearing retainer with the thick edges facing each other.

2. Press the pinion intermediate bearing on the pinion with the thick end toward the pinion head.
3. Place the pinion bearing spacer over the pinion and against the bearing, then position the pinion in the retainer and the front bearing over the pinion with the thin edge of the bearing toward the spacer.
4. Press the front bearing on the pinion so that the inner race contacts the bearing spacer. CAUTION: The pilot end of the pinion serves as an inner race for the pinion rear bearing, exercise care so as not to damage this machined surface.
5. Pack the cavity between the pinion oil seal lips with a high melting point bearing lubricant and press the seal into the retainer bore until it bottoms against the internal shoulder.
6. Using a driver, install the pinion rear bearing in the carrier bore so that it seats against the stop.

Differential and Planet Disassembly

1. Mark the ring gear, support case and case cover for alignment.
2. Remove the bolts and lockwashers retaining the ring gear to the planet support case and cover and remove the cover.
3. Mark all gears for reassembly, then remove the sun gear and planet gears.

Removing pinion rear bearing
(© Chevrolet Div., G.M. Corp.)

Separating support case and cover
(© Chevrolet Div., G.M. Corp.)

4. Lift the differential and planet support assembly from the support case.
5. Remove the bolts and lockwashers from the planet support and cover, then separate the two parts.
6. Mark all parts for reassembly, then remove the spider, pinion gears and thrust washers.
7. Remove the side gears and thrust washers.
8. Remove the differential bearings from the support case and cover by inserting a drift through the holes in the case and cover and tapping off the bearings.
9. Clean all parts and check for damage and excessive wear.

Differential and Planet Reassembly

1. Replace the differential side bearings by using an appropriate driver.
2. Lubricate the thrust washers, side gears, spider and pinion gears. Assemble the parts in the planet support, using reference marks made at disassembly. NOTE: The side gear with the longest hub should be positioned in the support cover.
3. Align and install the cover, torque the retaining bolts to 70 ft. lbs.
4. Install the planet gears on the support journals, then position the sun gear in the planet gears.
5. Using guide pins installed in ring gear, assemble the ring gear, support case cover, differential and planet assembly and support case. Make sure the marks line up.
6. Install the retaining bolts and lockwashers and torque to 140 ft. lbs.

Differential Carrier Reassembly

1. Position the differential outer races on the bearings, then place the differential into the carrier.
2. Install the differential adjusting nuts.
3. Position the bearing caps in the carrier making sure that the adjusting nuts properly engage the threads in the caps.
4. Tighten the cap bolts evenly until the adjusting nuts turn freely in the threads.
5. Install the shims on the carrier.
6. Guide the pinion and bearing retainer assembly into the carrier bore.
7. Install bearing retainer to carrier bolts and lockwashers and torque the bolts to 95 ft. lbs.
8. Install the pinion flange on the pinion.
9. Install the washer and new self-locking nut, and holding the flange, tighten the pinion nut to seat the flange and preload the pinion bearings.
10. Tighten the nut until the flange, bearings and spacer are all firmly seated then measure the torque required to rotate the pinion 25-35 inch pounds for new bearings or 5-15 inch pounds when used bearings are reinstalled.

Ring Gear and Pinion Adjustment

For procedures, see Chevrolet Full Floating Single Speed Axle in this section.

Checking Pinion Depth

For procedures, see Chevrolet Full Floating Single Speed Axle in this section.

NOTE: The pinion bearing shims are located between the pinion bearing retainer and the carrier.

Tighten the bearing cap bolts to 205 ft. lbs.

Install the oil trough to the carrier, adjust the trough to ring gear so that the clearance .03″-.09″.

Shifter Yoke, Sleeve and Shaft Installation

1. Position the shifter yoke in the radial groove of the shifter sleeve.
2. Slide the shifter sleeve over the sun gear. NOTE: The splined end of the shifter yoke must be toward the rear of the differential.
3. Install the shift lever and shaft assembly through the housing into the shifter yoke mating splines. CAUTION: The end of the shift lever must be flush with the end of the shift lever shaft to prevent binding with the shifter assembly.
4. Install the shifter to carrier retaining bolts.

Single-Speed, Single Reduction Eaton

Description

This is a full-floating axle having spiral bevel drive gear and pinion, and using a four-pinion differential assembly. The pinion has three roller bearings—two in front of the pinion teeth and one behind.

Disassembly

1. Remove thrust block screw.
2. Punch mark carrier leg, bearin cap and bearing adjusting nut to aid in reassembly.
3. Remove bearing caps and adjusting nuts.
4. Lift assembly out of carrier housing.
5. Punch mark differential case halves for correct alignment. Separate case halves.
6. Remove pinion shaft pinions, side gears, thrust washers and bearing cones.
7. Separate drive gear from cage.
8. Remove pinion shaft yoke.
9. Using a drift, drive pinion and cage assembly from carrier. CAUTION: Support bearing cage when driving assembly from carrier.
10. Wire bearing cage shim pack together to facilitate reassembly.
11. Lift bearing cage from pinion and remove cork seal. Remove pinion drive yoke washer and front bearing cone from cage.
12. Remove pinion bearing spacer washer, spacer, inner bearing cone and pilot bearing from pinion shaft.
13. Remove pinion cage bearing cups.
14. Clean all parts thoroughly in a suitable solvent and blow dry with compressed air. The bearings should be immersed in clean solvent and rotated by hand until clean. After cleaning, blow dry with compressed air. Do not spin bearings with air pressure, as they might score due to absence of any lubrication. Inspect all parts for wear or imperfections. The thrust shoulders must be flat, so that bearing cups will seat properly. Install a new case if cracked or distorted. (For further details, see "cleaning" and "inspection" in the "General Axle Service" section).

Staking pinion shaft with bearing ball
(© Eaton Yale & Towne Inc.)

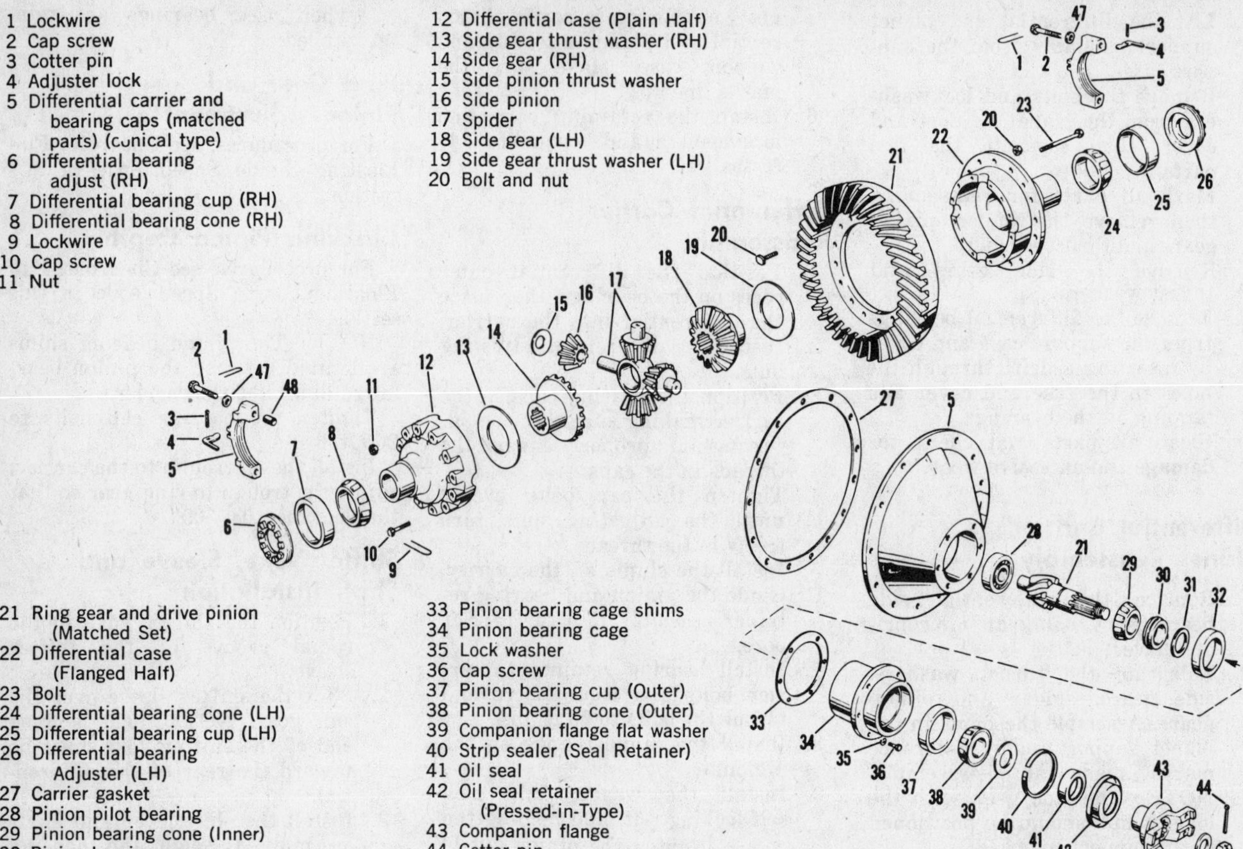

Eaton single-speed, single reduction rear axle (© Eaton Yale & Towne Inc.)

Assembly

1. Press drive pinion inner bearing cone and rear pilot bearing firmly against pinion shoulder.
2. Stake pilot bearing in at least four places. Install pinion cage bearing cups.
3. Place bearing spacer and washer on pinion shaft. Lubricate bearing cone with SAE 90 oil and position bearing cage on bearing. Lubricate and press outer bearing on pinion shaft. Rotate cage to assure normal bearing contact. If a press is not available, install pinion yoke washer and nut and torque to specifications.
4. While the assembly is in the press under pressure or pinion nut torqued to specifications, check pinion bearing pre-load. The correct pressures and torques for preload are:

Pinion Shaft Thread Size and Number of Threads Per Inch	*Required Pressure to Obtain Correct Pre-Load lbs.*	*Required Torque to Obtain Correct Pre-Load ft. lbs.*
⅞ in. x 16	10,000	200-325
1⅛ in. x 18	12,000	325-450
1¼ in. x 12	15,000	400-600

5. Wrap a soft wire around cage and pull on horizontal line with pound scale. Measure diameter of pinion cage. Assuming cage diameter is 6 inches, pulling radius would be 3 inches; therefore, 6 pounds pull on scale would equal 18 inch-pounds preload.
6. Use rotating torque, not starting torque. If rotating torque is not within 15 to 35 inch-pounds, use thinner spacer to increase preload or thicker spacer to decrease pre-load. Torque must be near low limit inch-pounds with

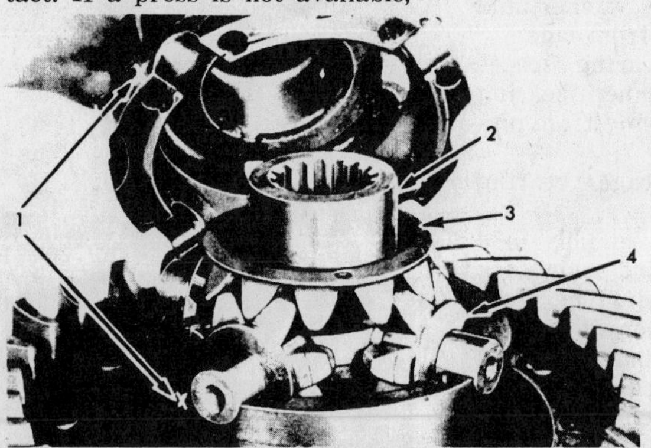

1 Alignment marks
2 Side gear
3 Thrust washer
4 Thrust washer

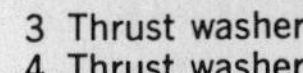

Separating differential case halves
(© Eaton Yale & Towne Inc.)

Removing thrust block screw
(© Eaton Yale & Towne Inc.)

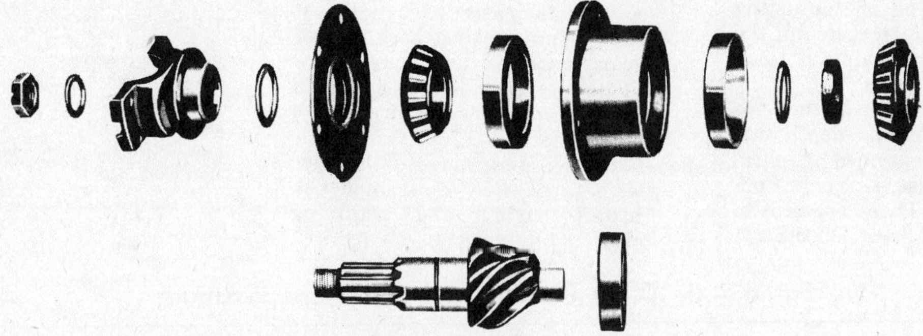

Pinion and cage assembly components (© Eaton Yale & Towne Inc.)

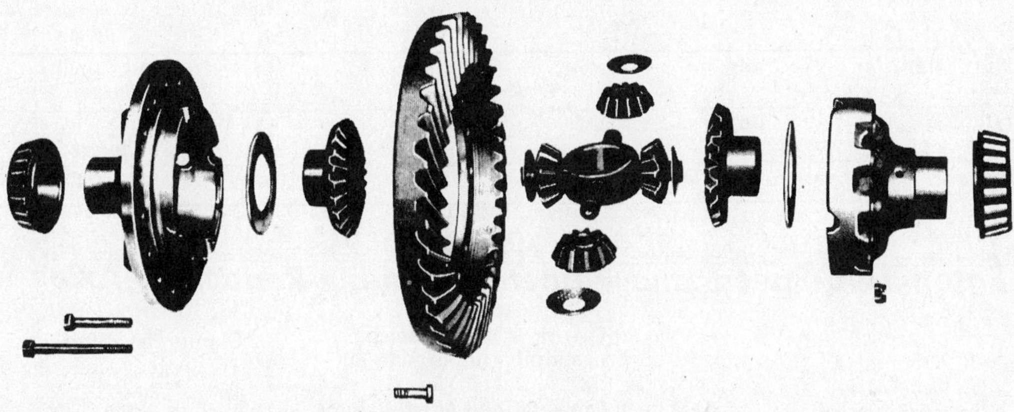

Differential assembly components (© Eaton Yale & Towne Inc.)

original pinion bearings and near high limit when using new bearings.

7. Upon obtaining correct preload, install a new pinion oil seal assembly. Install pinion yoke spacer, yoke and nut, and torque nut to specifications. Install a new cork seal on pinion cage.
8. Place original shim pack on carrier, tap pinion and cage assembly into place with a soft mallet. Make sure oil passages in cage and carrier align. Install lock washers and bolts at 100-125 foot-pounds. See the "General Axle Service" section if a new pinion is being installed and follow the "Pinion Setting Procedures" (Depth Gauge Method) for adjusting pinion location.
9. Position drive gear on differential case, install and torque bolts.
10. Lubricate differential case inner walls and all parts with rear axle gear lubricant during assembly.
11. Install thrust washer and side gear in drive gear half of case. Assemble pinions and thrust washers on pinion shaft, and place in case. Place other side and thrust washer on four pinions.
12. Align mating marks and install other case half. Draw case down evenly with four bolts. Check for free rotation of differential gears and correct if necessary. Install remaining bolts at 80-100 foot-pounds and install lock wire.
13. Press differential bearings squarely and firmly on differential case halves.
14. Thread drive gear thrust block screw in carrier far enough to install thrust block. Coat thrust block with heavy grease and place it on end of screw.
15. Lubricate differential bearings and cups with rear axle lubricant. Place cups over bearing and position assembly in carrier housing. Hand-tighten adjusting nuts against bearing cups.
16. Install bearing caps in correct location and tap lightly into position, making sure they are not cross-threaded. Make certain that some backlash is present between drive gear and pinion. Install bearing cap bolts snugly with allowance for turning adjusting nuts.
17. Attach a dial indicator to the carrier with the pointer resting against back face of drive gear. Eliminate all end play by turning right adjusting nut clockwise.
18. Tighten adjusting nuts, one notch each, to pre-load differential bearings. Align notches for installation of adjusting nut locks.
19. Position dial indicator so that

the pointer rests against face of one of the drive gear teeth. Check backlash between drive gear and pinion at 90 degree intervals of rotation.

20. Adjust backlash to .008-.015 inch (.008 preferred, especially on new gears.) When adjusting backlash, back off one adjusting nut and advance opposite nut the same amount to maintain bearing pre-load.
21. If the Depth Gauge Method for adjusting the pinion depth was not used as mentioned in paragraph 8, then use the Tooth Contact Method. Then proceed to step 22. See "General Axle Service" section. If pinion was adjusted by the Depth Gauge Method go directly to step 22.
22. Tighten bearing cap bolts, to 175-200 foot-pounds. Install the adjusting nut locks and lock wires.
23. Tighten thrust block adjusting screw sufficiently to locate thrust block firmly against back face of gear. Back off adjusting screw ¼ turn to provide .010-.015 inch clearance and lock securely with nut.
24. Place oil distributor in carrier with taper side of scoop down, install spring and retaining plug.

Torque Chart

Carrier to housing bolt or stud nut	7/16-14	50-70
	1/2-13	80-100
	5/8-11	150-175
Differential case bolt	7/16-14	50-70
	1 2-13	80-100
Differential bearing cap bolt	5/8-11	150-175
	11/16-11	175-200
	13/16-10	225-250
Differential bearing adjuster lock bolt	9/16-12	100-125
	5/8-11	150-175
Electric shift unit (mounting)	7/16-20	50-70
Pinion cage bolt	9/16-12	100-125
Pinion shaft yoke nut	7/8-16	200-325
	1-1/8-18	325-450
	1-1/4-12	400-600

Eaton Axle Drive Pinion Adjustment Specifications

		Specifications for Drive Pinion Bearing Preload Adjustment				*Drive Pinion Position Adjustment*	
	Axle Models	*Pinion Bearing Spacer Thickness*	*Drive Pinion Nut Torque Setting (ft.-lbs.)*	*Arbor Press Preload Pressure Setting (tons)*	*Spring Scale Reading (pounds) To obtain 15 to 35 in.-lbs. Torque*	*Pinion Bearing Cage Shim Pack*	*Depth Gauge Setting*
Single	17101, 17121	0.639	400-600	7-8	6-14	0.030 + 0.125 Spacer	4.2187
Reduction	18101, 18121	0.639	400-600	7-8	6-14	0.030 + 0.125 Spacer	4.2187
Axles	19121	0.185	550-850	10-11	5-11	0.024	4.600

Eaton Two-Speed and Planetary Double Reduction Axles

Description

The two-speed axle is a full-floating type with bevel drive gear and pinion, and uses a four-pinion differential assembly. The pinion has three roller bearings—two tapered bearings in front of the pinion teeth and one straight roller bearing behind the teeth. An oiling system provides lubrication to the pinion bearings, differential bearings and planetary unit. The planetary double reduction axle combines the ring and pinion and the planetary unit in one axle housing. Procedures for disassembly are the same as the two-speed except the double reduction axle has no shift mechanism and, instead of a sliding clutch gear, it uses a sun gear.

Differential Carrier

Disassembly

1. Inspect the carrier before disassembly. (See "cleaning" and "inspection" paragraph in the "General Axle Service" section).
2. After removing the oil distributor plug, pull the oil distributor and spring out of the differential carrier.
3. Remove the shift fork shaft plugs, and shaft.
4. Remove the shift fork seal and the shift fork from the housing. Pull the sliding clutch gear out of the differential carrier.
5. Punch the right and left bearing adjusters to aid in relocating the adjustment when reassembling. Remove the differential bearing cap bolts. Back off one bearing adjusting nut to relieve the bearing preload.
6. Remove the right and left bearing caps, bearing adjusters, and locks.
7. Lift the differential and planetary assembly out of the differential side bearing cups.
8. Mark the right and left support cases so that they can be reassembled in the same relative position. Remove the bolts which hold the ring gear to the gear support cases.
9. Clamp the differential assembly (ring gear end up) in a soft-jawed vise.
10. Tap the ring gear with a soft hammer on the gear tooth side until the gear is free of the flange on the right support case.
11. Lift the left support case, thrust washer, oil collector drum, and ring gear from the right support case.
12. Using a soft hammer, remove the high-speed clutch plate from the differential case.
13. Remove the planetary gears and gear pins.
14. Lift the differential assembly and the thrust washer out of the right support case. Mark the two pieces of the differential case for proper assembly.
15. Separate the right and left

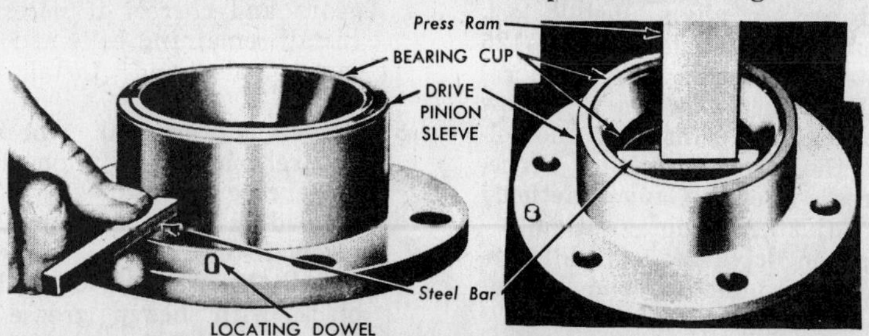

Removal or installation of pinion bearing cup
(© Eaton Yale & Towne Inc.)

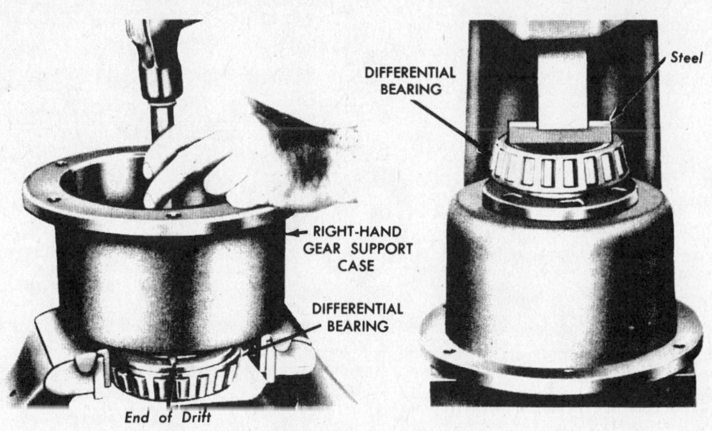

Removing or Installing Differential Bearing

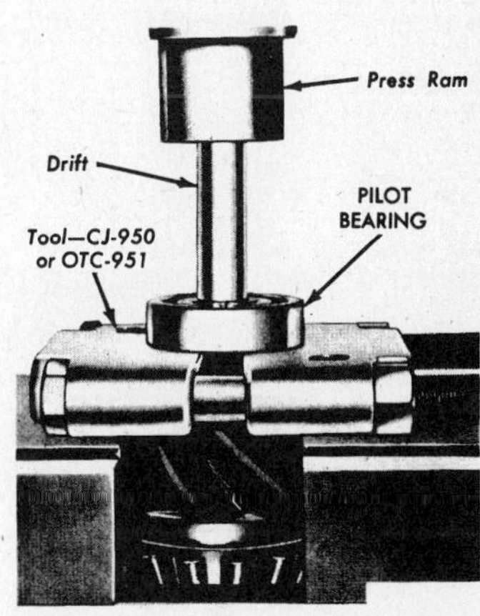

Removing Pinion Pilot Bearing

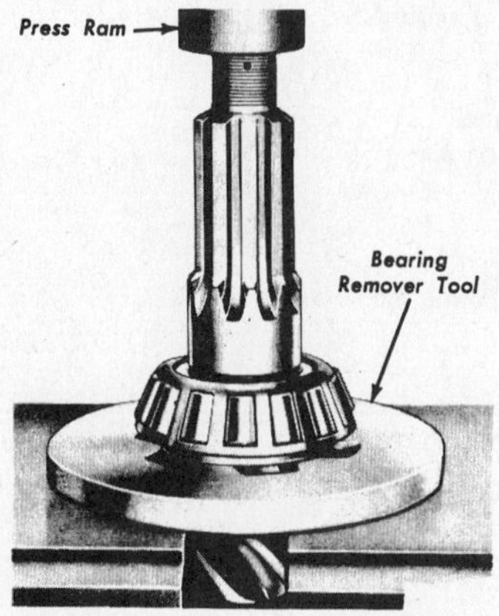

Removing Pinion Rear Bearing Cone

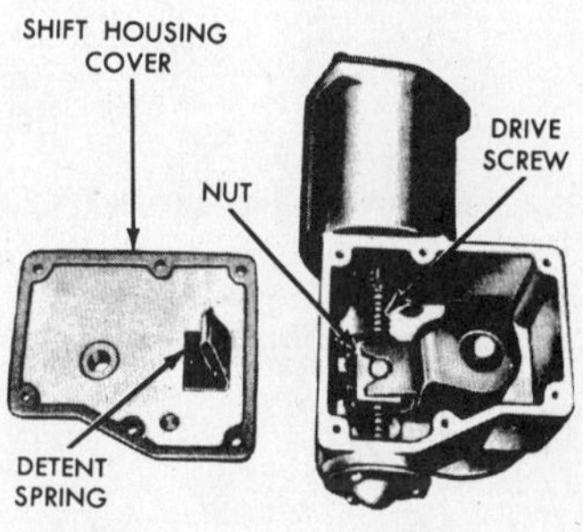

Drive Screw Nut in Center Position

Removing Drive Screw Bearing

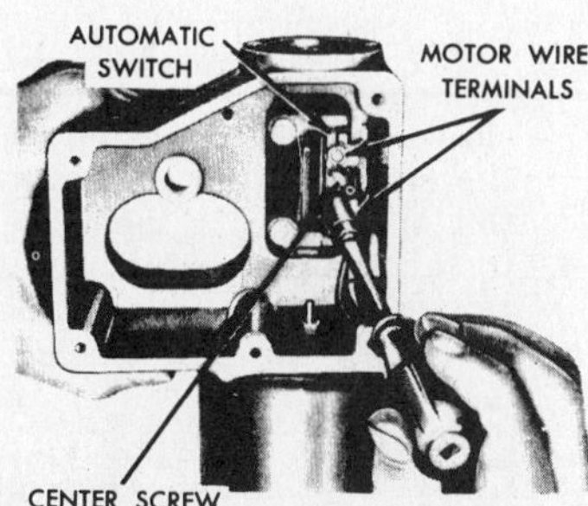

Removing Motor Wire

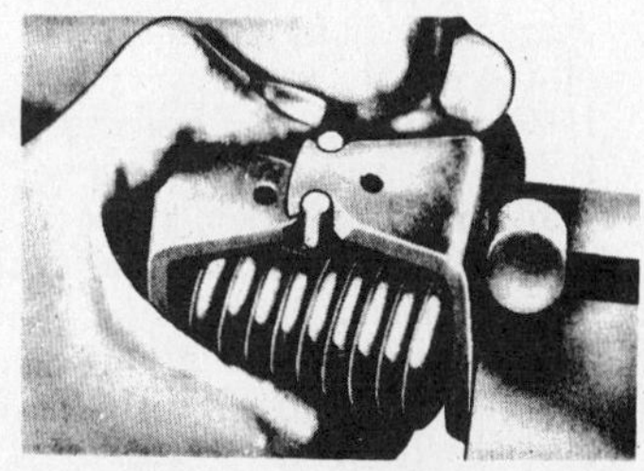

Disassembly Torsion Spring

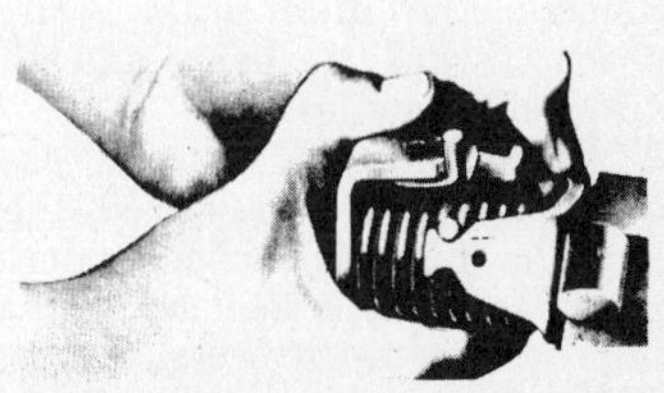

Assembling Torsion Spring

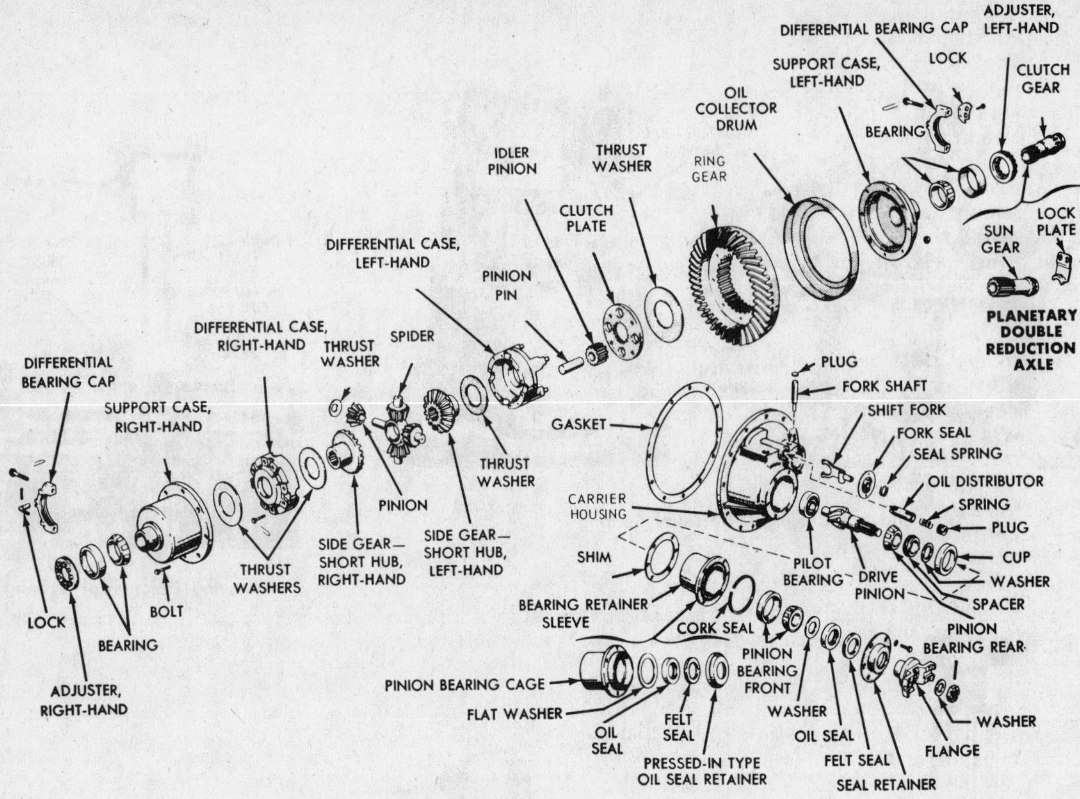

Eaton planetary two-speed or double reduction axle (© Eaton Yale & Towne Inc.)

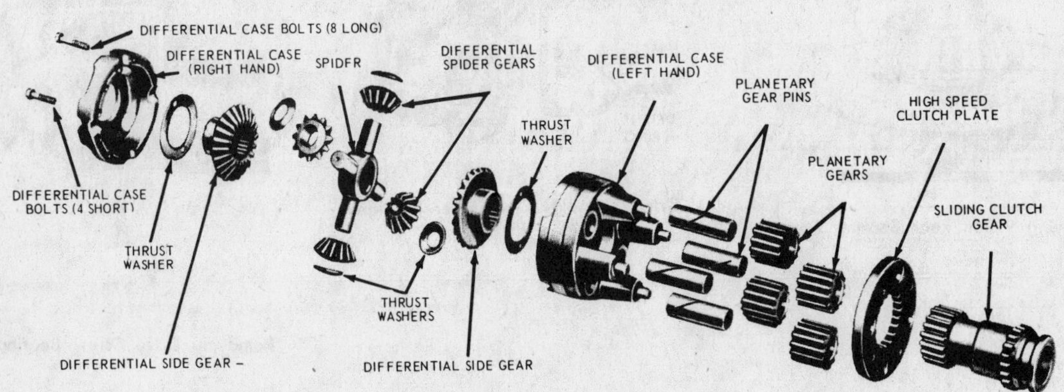

Planetary and differential assembly (© Eaton Yale & Towne Inc.)

differential cases. Remove the differential side gears and thrust washers.

16. Remove the differential spider gears, thrust washers, and the differential spider.
17. If the differential support case bearings are to be replaced, they may be removed with a drift. Press on the new bearing so that the ram pressure is against the bearing inner race and not against the roller cage.
18. Hold the pinion shaft flange and remove the pinion shaft nut.
19. Remove the bolts that attach the pinion bearing sleeve to the carrier housing. With a drift, drive the pinion assembly out of the front of the carrier housing.
20. Press the pinion shaft out of the shaft flange and pinion shaft front bearing cone. Remove the bearing preload spacer from the pinion shaft.
21. If the pinion rear bearing cone is to be replaced, remove the pilot bearing, then remove the pinion rear bearing cone with a bearing remover tool.
22. If the pinion bearing cups are to be replaced they may be removed with a small steel bar.

Assembly

1. Press the pilot bearing on the pinion shaft and stake the pinion shaft end at 4 points.
2. Press the pinion rear bearing onto the shaft until seated.
3. To install a new bearing cup, place the pinion bearing retainer sleeve in a press and, using a steel bar, press the cup in the sleeve until it is seated against the recess in the sleeve. Repeat this operation for the other cup.
4. Install the pinion in the bearing retainer sleeve. Place the old spacer on the pinion shaft and install the spacer washer and the pinion front bearing.
5. Check and adjust the pinion bearing preload (see "General Axle Service" section).
6. Install a new oil seal in the seal retainer or bearing sleeve.
7. Press the universal joint flange on the pinion shaft. Install the flat washer and nut and torque to specifications.
8. If the pinion and ring gear are being replaced, adjust the shim

pack between the pinion bearing sleeve and carrier housing as explained in the "General Axle Service" section.

9. Install a new gasket in the pinion bearing sleeve, if so equipped.
10. Place the shim pack on the bearing sleeve and install the pinion and sleeve assembly in the carrier housing. Install the sleeve to housing bolts and lock washers and torque to specifications.
11. Place the left half of the differential support case in a vise with the planetary side facing downward. Place one of the differential side gear thrust washers in position in the case. Place the differential left-hand side gear (with the short hub) in position in the case.
12. Install the four differential pinions and thrust washers on the differential spider, then place the spider in the differential case. Place the right side gear and thrust washer on the differential pinions.
13. Place the right half of the differential case in position over the differential spider, then install and torque the case bolts.
14. Insert the four planetary gear pins in the holes in the differential case.
15. Place the four planetary gears on the planetary gear pins. Position the high speed clutch plate on the planetary gear pins with the chamfered teeth facing the planetary gears. Tap the plate in place with a brass hammer.
16. Position the gear support thrust washer in the right gear support case.
17. Place the differential assembly in the gear support case with the planetary end facing upward. Place the ring gear (teeth facing down) over the differential assembly, and engage the planetary gears with the internal teeth on the ring gear.
18. Align the ring gear bolt holes with those in the gear support case. Place the oil collector drum on the ring gear (open side facing gear) with the notches between the bolt holes in the ring gear.
19. Apply oil to each side of the high-speed clutch plate thrust washer and position on the high-speed clutch plate. Place the left gear support case on the ring gear, and line up the bolt holes in the ring gear and both gear support cases.
20. Install the 6 bolts through the gear support cases with the bolt heads against the flange of the right gear support case. Install and torque the nuts and secure with lock wire.
21. Install the differential assembly in the carrier housing and adjust backlash and preload (see "General Axle Service" section).
22. Check and adjust the gear tooth contact pattern.
23. Install the sliding clutch gear and attach the shift fork to it. Install the shift fork shaft through the hole in the differential carrier and into the shift fork. Install the shift fork shaft plugs. Place the shift fork seal and retainer on the shift fork. Shift the axle into the low range.
24. Place the oil distributor and spring in the carrier. Install the oil distributor plug and gasket.

Drive Pinion Adjustment Specifications

Axle Models		*Specifications for Drive Pinion Bearing Preload Adjustment*				*Drive Pinion Position Adjustment*	
		Pinion Bearing Spacer Thickness	*Drive Pinion Nut Torque Setting (ft.-lbs.)*	*Arbor Press Preload Pressure Setting (tons)*	*Spring Scale Reading (pounds) To obtain 15 to 35 in.-lbs. Torque*	*Pinion Bearing Cage Shim Pack*	*Depth Gauge Setting*
	13802, 15201	0.530	225-350	4-5	7-16	0.040 + 0.250	3.6244
2-speed	16802, 16244	0.528	325-450	5-6	7-16	0.043	4.125
Axles	17201, 17221	0.638	400-600	7-8	6-14	0.037	4.062
	18201, 18221	0.638	400-600	7-8	6-14	0.037	4.4062
	19221	0.188	600-800	10-11	5-11	0.025	4.7812
Planetary Double Reduction Axles	18301	0.638	400-600	7-8	6-14	0.037	4.4062

Torque Chart

Description		*Ft.-Lbs.*
Differential bearing adjuster lock	Cap screw 9/16-12 (Grade 5)	115-125
	Cap screw 5/8-11 (Grade 5)	160-175
	Cap screw 3/4-10 (Grade 5)	275-300
Differential bearing cap to carrier	Cap screw 5/8-11 (Grade 7)	150-170
	Cap screw 11/16-11 (Grade 7)	210-250
	Cap screw 13/16-10 (Grade 7)	350-425
	Cap screw 7/8-9 (Grade 7)	425-500
Differential carrier to axle housing	Cap screw 7/16-14 (Grade 5)	45-55
	Cap screw 1/2-13 (Grade 5)	75-85
	Cap screw 5/8-11 (Grade 5)	160-175
	Stud nut 1/2-20 (Grade 8)	110-130
	Stud nut 5/8-18 (Grade 8)	220-240
Differential case (axle)	Cap screw 7/16-14 (Grade 7)	55-65
	Cap screw 1/2-13 (Grade 7)	90-105
	Cap screw 9/16-12 (Grade 7)	135-155
Ring gear support case	Bolt/nut 7/16-20 (Grade 7)	60-80
	Bolt/nut 1/2-20 (Grade 7)	90-100
	Bolt/nut 9/16-18 (Grade 7)	130-150
	Bolt/nut 5/8-18 (Grade 7)	190-210
	Locknut 5/8-18	165-190

Description		*Ft.-Lbs.*
Drive pinion	Nut 1-20	225-350
	Nut 1-1/8-18	325-450
	Nut 1-1/4-12	400-600
	Nut 1-1/2-18	500-700
	Nut 1-3/4-12	600-800
Drive pinion bearing cage to carrier	Cap screw 9/16-12 (Grade 5)	115-125
	Cap screw 9/16-12 (Grade 7)	135-155
	Cap screw 5/8-11 (Grade 5)	160-175
	Cap screw 5/8-11 (Grade 7)	170-190
Inspection cover to axle housing	Cap screw 7/16-14 (Grade 3)	35-50
	Cap screw 7/16-14 (Grade 5)	45-55
Shift units to carrier (2-speed)	Stud nut 7/16-20 (Grade 5)	35-45
	Stud nut 1/2-20 (Grade 5)	85-95
Cover plate to carrier (pdr) (At shift unit opening)	Cap screw 7/16-14 (Grade 5)	45-55
	Cap screw 1/2-13 (Grade 5)	75-85
Oil pickup through to carrier	Nylock screw 1/4-20 (Grade 5)	35-50 in.-lbs.

Single-Speed, Single Reduction Timken (Rockwell-Standard)

Description

This rear axle is a full-floating type with a hypoid drive gear and pinion, and uses a four-pinion differential assembly. The straddle mounted pinion has two tapered roller bearings in front of the pinion teeth and a straight roller bearing behind the pinion teeth. The differential carrier assembly can be removed while the axle remains in the truck.

Differential Carrier Assembly

Removal

1. Remove axle shafts.
2. Drain lubricant. Disconnect propeller shaft at pinion shaft yoke.
3. Remove carrier from axle housing and clean thoroughly.

Disassembly

1. Punch mark carrier leg, bearing cap, and bearing adjusting nut to assist in reassembly.
2. Remove screws, adjusting nut locks, bearing caps and adjusting nuts.
3. Loosen lock nut and back off drive gear thrust block adjusting screw.
4. Lift differential out of carrier and remove thrust block from end of adjusting screw inside of carrier.
5. Punch mark differential case halves for correct reassembly alignment and separate case halves.
6. Remove pinion shaft, pinions, side gears, thrust washers and differential bearing cones.
7. To remove drive gear, carefully center punch each rivet in center of rivet head. Use a drill 1/32 inch smaller than the body of rivet to drill through the rivet head. Press out rivets.
8. Remove pinion shaft nut, washer and yoke. Driving yoke off will cause runout.
9. Remove pinion bearing cover and oil seal assembly and, using puller screws, remove bearing cage. Using a pinch bar to remove cage will damage shims. Driving pinion from inner end with a drift will damage bearing lock ring groove.
10. Wire bearing cage shim pack together to facilitate adjustment when reassembling.
11. Tap pinion shaft out of cage with soft mallet or press shaft from cage. Remove bearing from cage.
12. Remove spacers and inner bearing from shaft.
13. Remove pinion shaft rear pilot bearing lock ring; and then bearing.
14. Remove oil seal assembly from bearing cover.
15. Clean all parts thoroughly in a suitable solvent and blow dry with compressed air. Do not spin bearings with air pressure as they might score due to absence of any lubrication.

Inspect all parts for wear or roughness and replace if necessary. (For details, see "cleaning" and "inspection" in "General Axle Service" section).

Inspect all machined surfaces for nicks, burrs or scratches.

Assembly

1. Press drive pinion inner bearing cone firmly against pinion shoulder.
2. Press rear pilot bearings firmly against pinion shoulder and install lock ring into pinion shaft groove.
3. Press bearing cups firmly against bearing cage shoulders.
4. Lubricate pinion bearings with SAE 90 oil and insert pinion and bearing assembly into pinion cage.
5. Place original spacers on pinion shaft, and install front bearing and press firmly against spacers. Rotate cage several revolutions

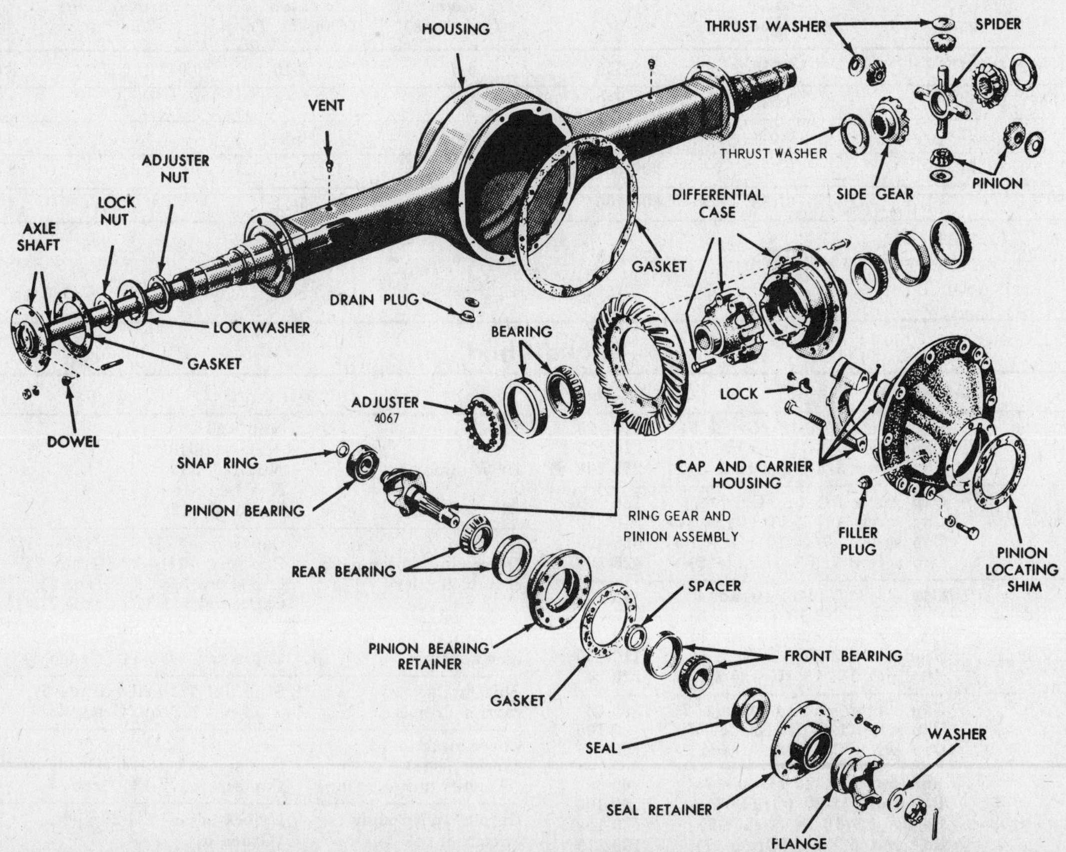

Timken single-speed, single reduction rear axle (© Ford Motor Co.)

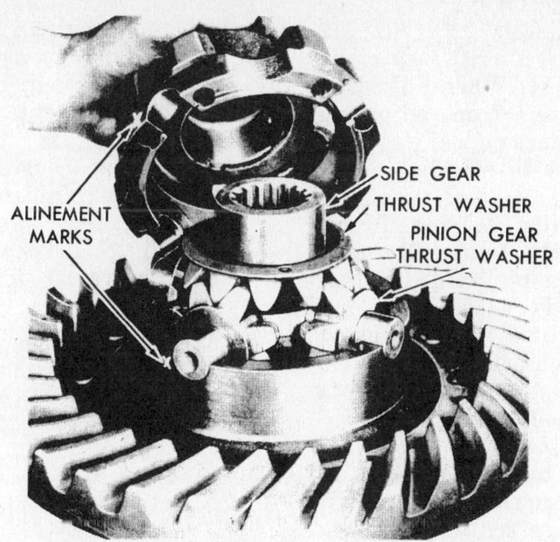

Differential case alignment marks (© G.M.C.)

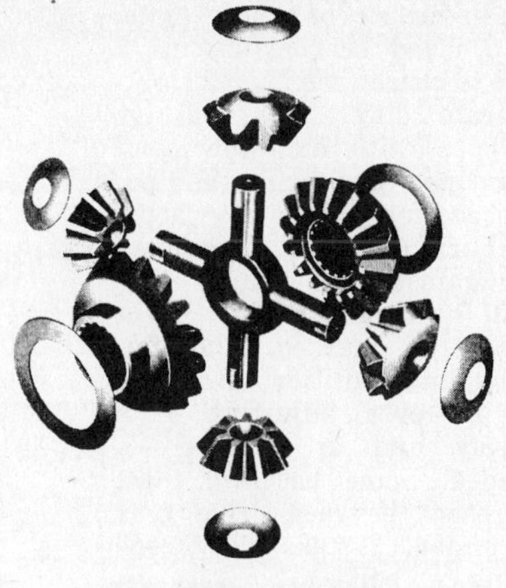
Exploded view of side gear and pinion assembly (© Chrysler Corp.)

to assure normal bearing contact. If a press is not available, install pinion yoke and nut and torque to specifications.

6. While the assembly is in the press under pressure or pinion nut torqued to specifications, check pinion bearing pre-load. The correct pressures and torque for checking pre-load are:

Pinion Shaft Thread Size and Number of Threads Per Inch	*Required Pressure to Obtain Correct Pre-Load lbs.*	*Required Torque to Obtain Correct Pre-Load ft. lbs.*
1 in. x 20	12,000	300- 400
1¼ in. x 18	22,000	700- 900
1½ in. x 12	28,000	800-1100
1½ in. x 18	28,000	800-1100
1¾ in. x 12	28,000	800-1100

7. Wrap a soft wire around cage and pull on horizontal line with pound scale when determining pinion bearing pre-load, first measure diameter of the pinion cage. Assuming cage diameter is 6 inches, the pulling radius would be 3 inches; therefore, 5 pounds pull on the scale would equal 15 inch-pounds pre-load.
8. Use rotating torque, not starting torque. If rotating torque is not within 5 to 15 inch-pounds, use thinner spacer to increase pre-load or thicker spacer to decrease pre-load. Torque must be near low limit inch-pounds with original pinion bearings and near high limit when using new bearings. Remove yoke and install new oil seal.
9. Lubricate pinion shaft oil seal and lightly coat outer edge of seal body with non-hardening sealing compound. Press seal against cover shoulder. Install new gasket and bearing cover.
10. Install pinion yoke, washer and nut. Place pinion and cage assembly over carrier studs, hold yoke and tighten nut to specified torque. Install cotter key without backing off nut to align cotter key holes.
11. Place original shim pack on carrier studs with thin shims on both sides to create maximum sealing. Position pinion and cage assembly over studs and tap into position with soft mallet. Install lock washers and nuts. Tighten nuts to specified torque. If a new pinion is being installed, consult the "General Axle Service" section for correct procedure.
12. Rivet drive gear to differential case using new rivets. Rivets should not be heated, but always upset cold. When correct rivet is used, head being formed will be at least ⅛ inch larger in diameter than rivet hole and approximately the same height as performed head. Avoid excessive pressure as it might distort case holes and cause gear eccentricity. Unless shops are equipped to do cold upsetting of rivets properly, replacement bolts should be used.
13. Lubricate differential case inner walls and all component parts with rear axle gear lubricant during assembly.
14. Install thrust washer and side gear in drive gear half of case. Assemble pinions and thrust washers on pinion shaft and position this assembly in the case. Place other side gear and thrust washer in position on the four pinions.
15. Install other case half with mating marks aligned. Draw case down evenly with four bolts. Check for free rotation of differential gears and correct if necessary. Install and torque remaining bolts and then lock wire.
16. Press differential bearings squarely and firmly on differential case halves. Differential bearing cup fit in the pedestal bores should be checked before installing assembly in carrier.
17. Temporarily install bearing cups, threaded adjusting nuts or split ring and bearing caps. Tighten cap bolts to specified torque. Bearing cups must be of a hand push fit in the bores; if not, the bores must be enlarged

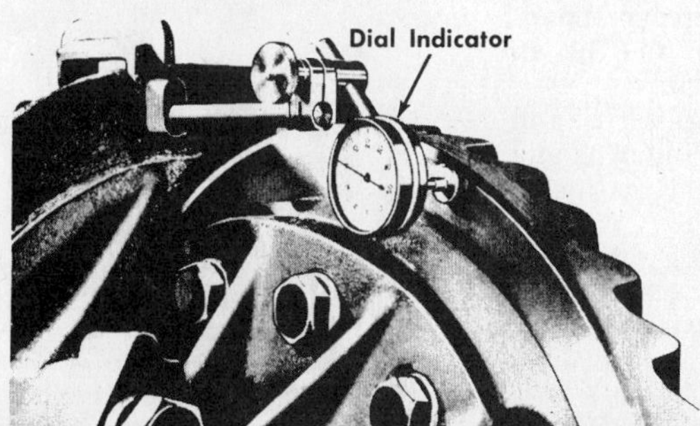

Making check of drive gear run-out (© G.M.C.)

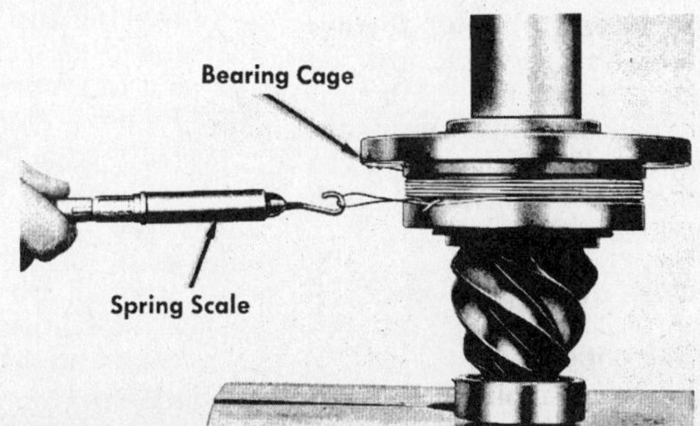

Checking pinion bearing pre-load (© G.M.C.)

with a scraper or emery cloth. Use a blued bearing cup as a gauge to check each fit.

18. Lubricate differential bearings and cups with axle lubricant. Place cups over bearings and position assembly in carrier housing. Turn adjusting nuts hand tight against bearing cups.
19. Install bearing caps in correct location as marked, and tap lightly into position. Be sure caps fit over adjusting nuts properly and are not cross-threaded. Some backlash must be present between drive gear and pinion. Install and torque bearing cap bolts.
20. Attach a dial indicator to the carrier with the pointer resting against back face of drive gear. Eliminate all end play by turning right adjusting nut clockwise. Rotate drive gear and check runout. If runout exceeds .008 inch, remove differential and check the cause.
21. Tighten adjusting nuts, one notch each, to pre-load differential bearings.
22. Position dial indicator so the pointer rests against face of one of the drive gear teeth. Check backlash between drive gear and pinion at 90 degree intervals of rotation.
23. Adjust backlash to .006-.012 inch (.006 preferred, especially on new gears). When adjusting backlash, back off one adjusting nut and advance opposite nut the same amount to maintain bearing pre-load.
24. If the "Pinion Setting Procedures" (Depth Gauge Method) for adjusting pinion depth (see "General Axle Service" section) was not used, adjust gears using the Tooth Contact Method. Then proceed to step 25. If Depth Gauge Method was used, go directly to step 25.
25. Torque bearing cap bolts and install and torque adjusting nut locks and cap screws and lock wire.
26. Hold drive gear thrust block on rear face of gear with heavy grease, rotate gear until hole in thrust block aligns with adjusting screw hole in carrier. Install adjusting screw and lock nut, tighten screw enough to locate thrust block firmly against back face of gear. Back off adjusting screw ¼ turn to create .010-.015 inch clearance and lock securely with nut. Recheck to assure minimum clearance of .010 inch during full rotation of drive gear.

Installation

1. Install a new gasket on axle housing flange. Start carrier into clean housing and hold in place with four equally spaced washers and nuts. Tighten nuts alternately to draw carrier evenly into housing. Install and torque carrier flange lock washers and nuts.
2. Install axle drive shafts and connect universal joint at pinion flange.
3. Fill axle housing to proper level and road test vehicle.

Torque Chart

Carrier to housing screw or stud nut	1/2-20	94-102
	5/8-18	186-205
	3/4-16	325-360
Differential case bolt	1/2-20	94-102
	9/16-18	132-145
	5/8-18	186-205
	3/4-16	325-360
Differential bearing cap bolt	5/8-11-18	127-140
	3/4-10-16	230-250
	7/8-9	345-370
	7/8-14	375-415
	1-12	555-615
Differential bearing adjuster lock bolt	5/16-18	15-17
	1/2-13	85-91
	9/16-12	120-129
	5/8-11	168-180
Pinion shaft yoke nut	1-20	300-400
	1-1/4-18	700-900
	1-1/2-18	800-1100
	1-1/2-12	800-1100
	1-3/4-12	800-1100
Shaft flange stud	7/16-20	52-58

Timken Bearing Preload

Axle Model	*Pinion Shaft Nut-Thread Size and Torque Limits (Foot-Pounds)*		*Press Ram Pressure for Preload Check (Tons)*	*Pinion and Cross Shaft Bearing Preload (Inch-Pounds)*	*Backlash Limits (Inches)*	*Differential Bearing Preload Adjusting Nut Notches Tighten from Zero End Play (each Adjusting Nut)*
Single-speed Single reduction	1-20	300-400	6	5-15	0.005-0.015	1
	1¼ x 18	700-900	11	5-15	0.005-0.015	1
	1¼ x 18	800-1100	14	5-15	0.005-0.015	1
	1½ x 12	800-1100	14	5-15	0.005-0.015	1
	1½ x 18	800-1100	14	5-15	0.005-0.015	1

Timken (Rockwell- Standard) Single-Speed Double Reduction Axles

Description

This axle includes a hypoid helical drive and a two-step gear reduction. The first reduction is through the hypoid pinion and ring gears with the second reduction through the helical gears. The helical pinion gear engages with the helical drive gear. The axle housings are one-piece with full-floating axle shafts.

Disassembly of Rear Axle

Differential Carrier

1. Before disassembling, inspect the unit as described in the "cleaning" and "inspection" paragraph of the "General Axle Service" section.
2. Punch-mark one differential bearing cap and the corresponding carrier leg. This will be an aid to proper reassembly.
3. Remove the locking wires and bolts from both bearing caps and remove both bearing adjuster nuts.
4. Back off both bearing adjusters one full turn to reduce bearing pre-load. Remove both bearing caps and adjusters and wire together.
5. Lift the differential out of the carrier.

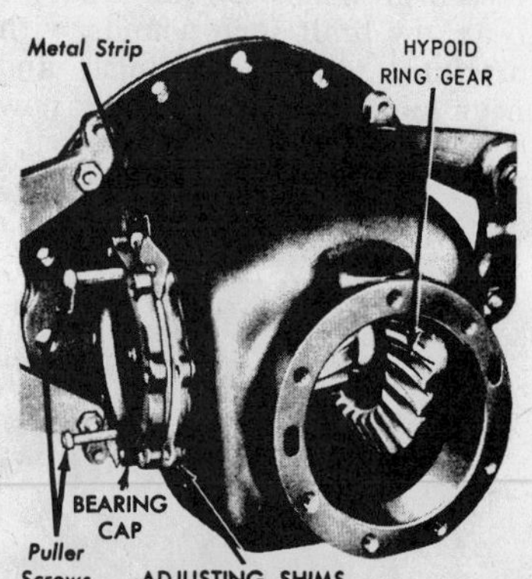

Removing cross shaft bearing cap and positioning metal strips (© Rockwell Stand. Div.)

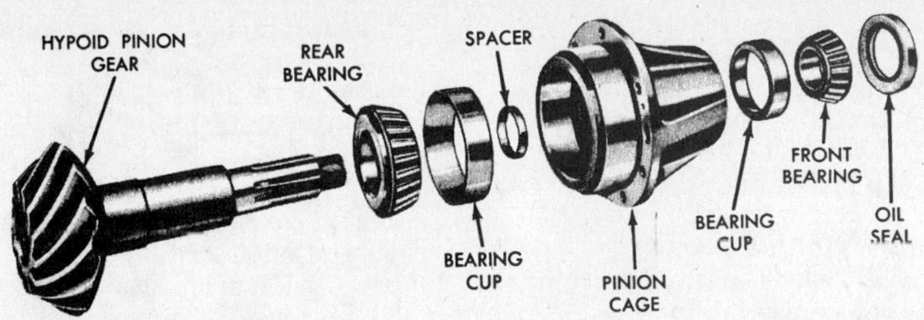

Hypoid pinion gear and cage (exploded view)
(© Rockwell Stand. Div.)

6. Remove the U-joint flange nut and then remove flange with a rawhide mallet. If this is unsuccessful, the flange can be pressed off when the hypoid pinion cage is being disassembled.
7. Using two 3 inch 38—16 puller screws, remove the cage and pinion gear from the carrier.
8. Remove the pinion adjusting shims from the carrier and re-use if the same hypoid gear set is to be used again when the carrier is assembled.
9. Place a wooden block under the helical pinion gear to support the cross shaft. Then remove the bolts from the cross shaft bearing cap mounted on the differential carrier—opposite the hypoid ring gear.
10. Force the bearing cap out of the carrier about ¼ inch by prying the hypoid ring gear away from the side of the carrier.
11. Place metal strips under both puller screw holes in the bearing cap and, using puller screws, hold them in place against the adjusting shims. Do not tighten the screws directly onto the adjusting shims.
12. Tighten the puller screws evenly against the metal strips, and remove the bearing cap and the adjusting shims from the carrier.
13. Carefully remove the hypoid ring gear and cross shaft from the carrier.
14. Replace either cross shaft bearing cup if necessary. Remove the damagod or worn cup from the bearing cap with a suitable puller. To operate the cup in the bearing cap, tap the cap out of the carrier about ¼ inch with a soft drift and remove from the carrier.

Cross Shaft

1. Remove the locking wire, two screws, and the bearing retaining plate from the hypoid ring gear end of the cross shaft.
2. Press the cross shaft out of the ring gear and the bearing next to the gear. Remove the Woodruff key that holds the gear on the shaft.
3. Press the remaining bearing from the cross shaft.

Differential Gear and Case

1. Mount the differential in a soft-jawed vise. Then, if necessary, remove both differential side bearings.
2. Punch-mark each case half to aid proper assembly.
3. Separate the helical drive gear and the two case halves. If rivets are binding these parts, center—punch the head of each rivet followed by a ⅛ inch pilot hole at each punch-mark, and then a ½ inch hole drilled ½ inch deep and complete by pressing out all the rivets with a ½ inch punch. *Do not attempt to remove the rivets with a hammer and chisel.*
4. Remove the spider, pinion gears, thrust washers, and side gears.

Pinion Cage

1. Press the hypoid pinion gear shaft out of the pinion cage, and then remove the bearing preload spacer from the shaft.
2. Press the rear bearing from the shaft and pull the rear bearing cup from the pinion cage.
3. Press the front bearing cup and the oil seal from the pinion cage and clean and inspect all parts as explained in the "General Axle Service" section.

Assembly of Rear Axle

Pinion Cage

1. Install the rear bearing on the hypoid pinion gear shaft against the gear shoulder. Use a 3 inch sleeve about one inch long under the bearing race so that the press ram won't damage roller cage.
2. Press the rear bearing cup *firmly against the shoulder in the pinion cage.*
3. Install the front bearing cup in the pinion cage making sure that the cup seats firmly against the shoulder in the cage.
4. Coat the pinion rear bearing with axle lubricant, and position the pinion gear in the cage.
5. Position the original bearing preload spacer on the pinion gear shaft and press the pinion front bearing onto the shaft against the spacer. Use a 3 inch sleeve about 5 inches long over

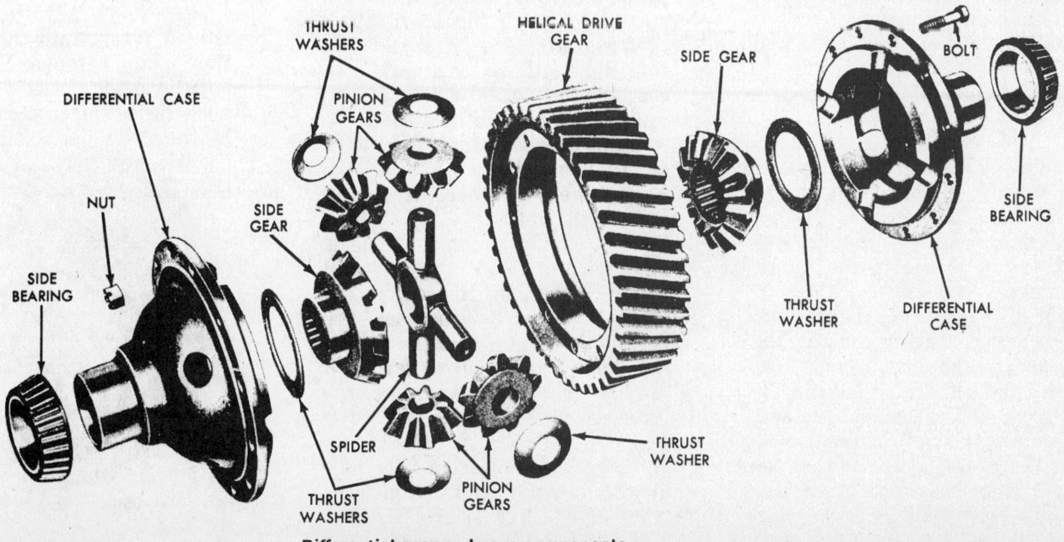

Differential gear and case components
(© Rockwell Stand. Div.)

the bearing race so that the press ram doesn't damage the bearing roller cage.

6. Rotate the pinion cage several times to be sure that the bearings are properly seated. Then check the pinion bearing preload as explained in the "General Axle Service" section. If the preload is too low, install a thinner spacer under the front bearing. To decrease the preload, install a thicker spacer under the bearing.
7. When the preload is correct, install the oil seal in the pinion cage.

Differential Gear and Case

1. Check the mating surfaces of the differential case halves and the helical drive gear to be sure they are clean and free of burrs. Then coat all differential parts and the inner walls of the case, with axle lubricant.
2. Install the differential side bearings, making sure they are properly seated. Use a 3¼ inch sleeve about one inch long over the bearing race so that the force of the press ram doesn't damage the bearing roller cage.
3. Position a thrust washer and a side gear in one of the differential case halves. Then place the spider, the pinion gears, and their thrust washers in position. Install the remaining side gear and thrust washer in the case.
4. Position the helical drive gear and install the other case half, aligning the marks on both halves.
5. Install 6 bolts in alternate holes around the case on the side of the gear having the smaller offset. Tighten the bolts and nuts enough to draw the gear and both case halves together. Then check the rotation of the side gears and pinion gears.
6. Install the remaining 6 bolts and nuts, and torque them evenly to specifications and lock wire.

Cross Shaft

1. Place the Woodruff key (tapered end toward pinion gear) in the cross shaft. Then press the hypoid ring gear on the shaft—seating it against the shaft shoulder.
2. Carefully press the shaft into the bearing, seating the bearing against the shoulder.
3. Install the remaining bearing on the other end of the shaft. Use a 3 inch sleeve about one inch long over the bearing race so that the press ram won't damage the bearing roller cage.
4. Install the bearing retaining plate and torque and wire the screws.
5. Press the cross shaft bearing cups into the bearing caps. Be sure that the cups are properly seated against the shoulders in the cap bores.

Differential Carrier

1. Coat all parts with axle lubricant before assembly.
2. Position the original shim pack on the right cross shaft bearing

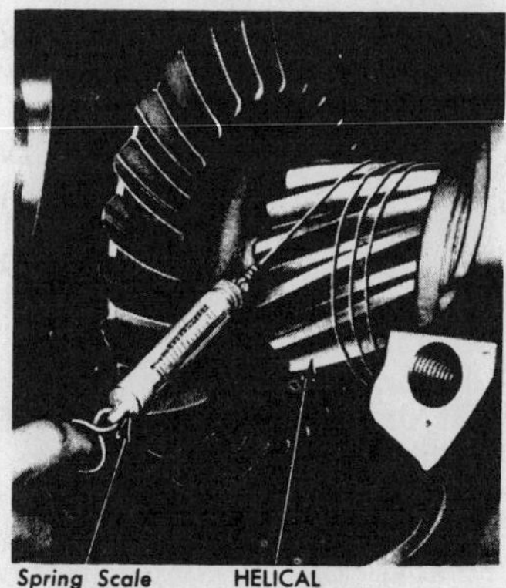

Checking cross shaft bearing preload
(© Rockwell Stand. Div.)

cap and install and torque the cap on the differential carrier.

3. Install the cross shaft in the carrier so that the end of the shaft opposite the hypoid ring gear enters the bore of the left bearing cap. The right bearing should enter and seat in its bearing cap. Place a wooden block under the helical pinion gear to support the cross shaft.
4. Position the original shim pack on the left cross shaft bearing cap and install and torque the cap on the differential carrier.
5. Rotate the cross shaft to test for normal bearing contact. Then check the cross shaft bearing preload. *Do not read the pull required to start the cross shaft rotating. Read only the steady rotating pull on the scale.* To change the scale reading into in-lbs. torque, multiply the scale reading by one-half the diameter of the helical pinion gear at the point where the cord is wound around the gear.
6. If the bearing preload torque is not within 5-15 in-lbs., add shims to decrease the preload, or remove shims to increase the preload. *To prevent changing the hypoid ring gear backlash setting, change shims only at the bearing cap opposite the ring gear.*
7. Install the pinion cage-filler hole at top. Install and torque the bolts and lock washers. Use the original shim pack between the pinion cage and the differential

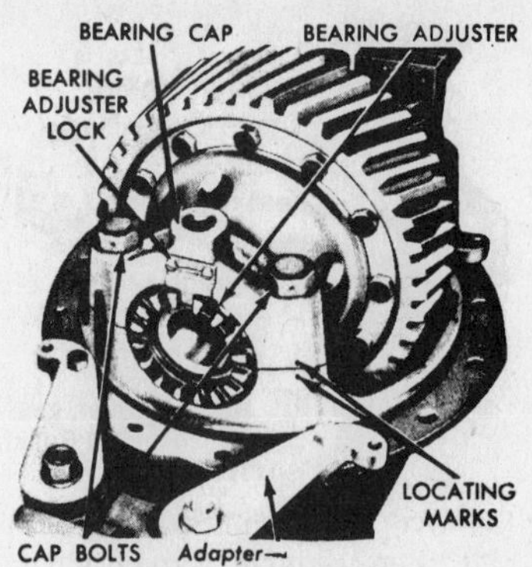

Installation of bearing caps
(© Rockwell Stand. Div.)

carrier if the original hypoid gears (ring gear and pinion set) are used. If new hypoid gears are installed, follow the shim selection procedure in the "General Axle Service" section.

8. Install the U-joint flange, torque the nut and install cotter pin.
9. The backlash can be adjusted by transferring shims from one cross shaft bearing cap to the other. To move the hypoid ring gear away from the hypoid pinion gear, transfer shims from the right cap to the left cap. To move the ring gear closer to the pinion gear, transfer shims from left to right. For each 0.010 inch movement of the ring gear, the backlash changes about 0.008 inch. Adjust backlash to 0.010 inch and check the gear tooth contact pattern. After obtaining a good pattern at 0.010 backlash, increase backlash to 0.020-0.026 inch regardless of the backlash marking on the ring gear.
10. Check and adjust the tooth contact pattern (see the "General Axle Service" section).
11. Check the fit of the differential side bearing cups and the bearing adjusters in the bearing caps. The adjusters should thread freely into the caps, and they should move the bearing cups into the bores with the cap bolts tightened to normal torque. If the cups do not move when

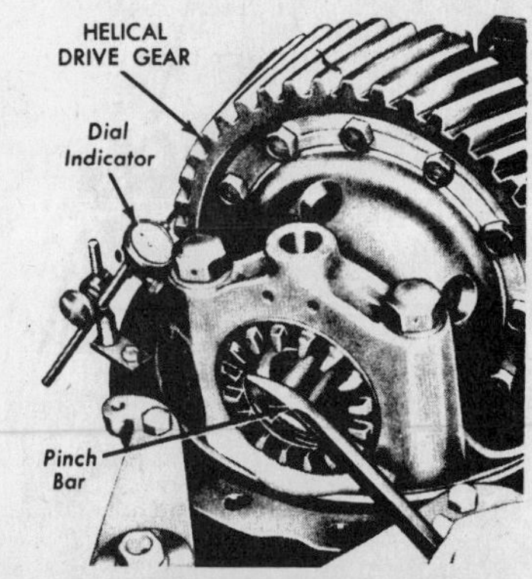

Determining differential end play
(© Rockwell Stand. Div.)

the adjusters are hand tightened, remove the caps and clean the bearing surfaces.

12. Position a bearing cup on each differential side bearing. Then place the differential on the carrier so that the bearing cups rest in the carrier legs centering the drive gear on the helical pinion gear.
13. Place the bearing adjusters on the threads in the carrier legs, and position the bearing caps on the carrier leg with the matching marks aligned. Check to see that the threads in the caps and legs are matched if so, install and torque the cap bolts.
14. Hand tighten the bearing adjusters until they just touch the bearing cups. Then install a dial indicator and check the differential end play using a pinch bar to move the differential away from indicator. Then tighten the bearing adjuster opposite the dial indicator until there is no side-to-side movement of the differential, and the dial indicator shows no end play.
15. After obtaining the correct end play, adjust the differential bearing preload by tightening the bearing adjusters an additional ¾-2½ notches (total for both adjusters).
16. Install the bearing adjuster locks and cap screws.
17. Install locking wires on the lock cap screws and bearing cap bolts.

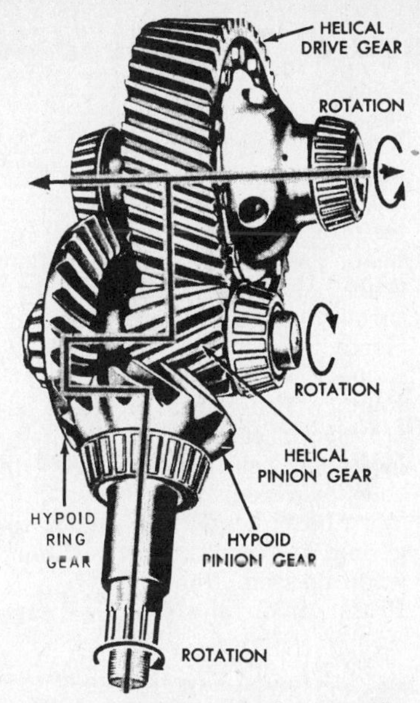

Single-speed, double reduction power flow
(© Rockwell Stand. Div.)

Bearing Preload

Axle Model	*Pinion Shaft Nut-Thread Size and Torque Limits (Foot-Pounds)*		*Press Ram Pressure for Preload Check (Tons)*	*Pinion and Cross Shaft Bearing Preload (Inch-Pounds)*	*Backlash Limits (Inches)*	*Differential Bearing Preload Adjusting Nut Notches Tighten from Zero End Play (each Adjusting Nut)*
Single-Speed	1¼ x 18	700-900	11	5-15	0.020-0.026	1
Double Reduction	1½ x 12	800-1100	14	5-15	0.020-0.026	1
	1½ x 18	800-1100	14	5-15	0.020-0.026	1

Torque Chart

Location	*Cap Screws or Stud Nuts* *Diameter*	*Threads per. in.*	*Torque-Lb. Ft. Min.-Max.*
These torques are	3/8	24	38-49
given according	3/8	16	33-43
to diameter and	7/16	14	53-77
threads per inch.	7/16	20	53-67
The torque will	1/2	13	81-104
be the same for	1/2	20	81-104
a specific size	9/16	12	116-149
no matter where	9/16	18	116-149
the bolt or cap	5/8	11	160-205
screw is used	5/8	18	160-205
on the axle	3/4	10	290-370
except for those	3/4	16	290-370
listed below.	7/8	9	470-595
	7/8	14	510-655
	1	14	580-745
Adjusting nut lock	5/16 1/2	18 13	16-20 75-96
Inspection cover	3/8	16	.27-35
Shift unit (mounting) Shift unit lock nut, set screw and clamp screw	3/8 3/8 7/16	16 16 14	27-35 30-33 30-33
Shift unit travel limiting screws	1/2 5/8	13 11	40-45 30-33

Torques given apply to parts coated with machine oil; for dry (as received) parts increase torques 10%; for parts coated with multi-purpose gear oil decrease torques 10%. Nuts on studs to use same torque as for driving the stud.

Timken (Rockwell- Standard) Two-Speed Double Reduction Axles

Description

This is a full-floating rear axle having a hypoid drive gear and pinion and using a four-pinion differential assembly. The pinion and cross shaft are each mounted on two tapered roller bearings.

Disassembly

1. Punch-mark one carrier leg and bearing cap for reassembly reference.
2. Remove differential and gear assembly.
3. Punch-mark case halves for correct alignment when assembling.
4. Separate differential case halves. Remove side gears, thrust washers, pinions and pinion shaft.
5. Remove differential side bearing.
6. Separate gears from case. Center-punch rivets in center of head. Use drill 1/32 inch smaller than body of rivet to drill through head, and then press out rivets.
7. Remove pinion shaft yoke.
8. Remove pinion bearing cage assembly. If cage is not free, tap loose, or use puller screws in holes provided.
9. Wire bearing cage shim pack together to facilitate adjustment when reassembling.
10. Press pinion shaft out of cage and remove adjusting spacers from shaft. Remove rear bearing from pinion shaft.
11. Press front bearing and pinion shaft oil seal from pinion cage.
12. Remove two bearing cups from pinion cage.
13. Remove shift fork shaft and shift fork.
14. Tap sleeve from carrier *with a soft mallet*. Wire shim pack together to facilitate reassembly.
15. Remove screws and force out bearing cage by using a small pinch bar between back of hypoid gear and carrier housing. Wire shim pack together to facilitate reassembly.
16. Remove cross shaft and hypoid gear assembly.
17. Remove cap screws and press cross shaft from bearing and hypoid gear (ring gear). Slide off high speed pinion and remove shift collar, plungers and springs. Precautions should be taken when removing shift collar as the plungers and springs will fly out. Reinstall shift collar and press shaft through low speed pinion and bearing.
18. Remove cross shaft bearing cups. If cross shaft bearing cover is removed (hypoid gear side), be sure to wire shim pack together.
19. Clean all parts thoroughly in a suitable solvent and blow dry

Differential carrier on stand
(© Rockwell Stand. Div.)

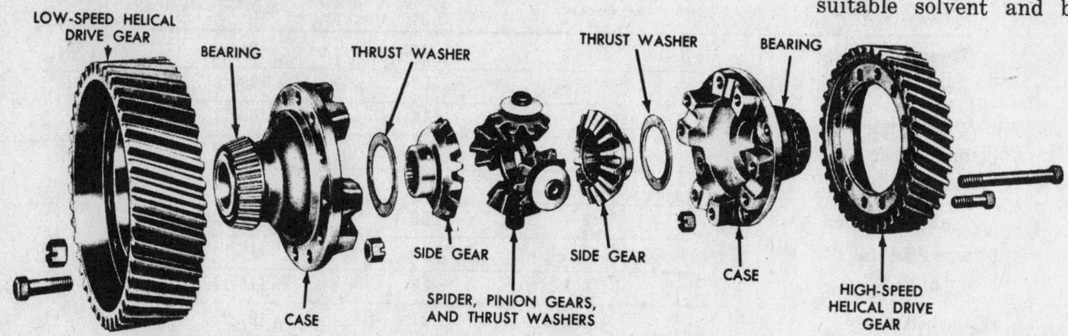

Differential gears and case (exploded view)
(© Rockwell Stand. Div.)

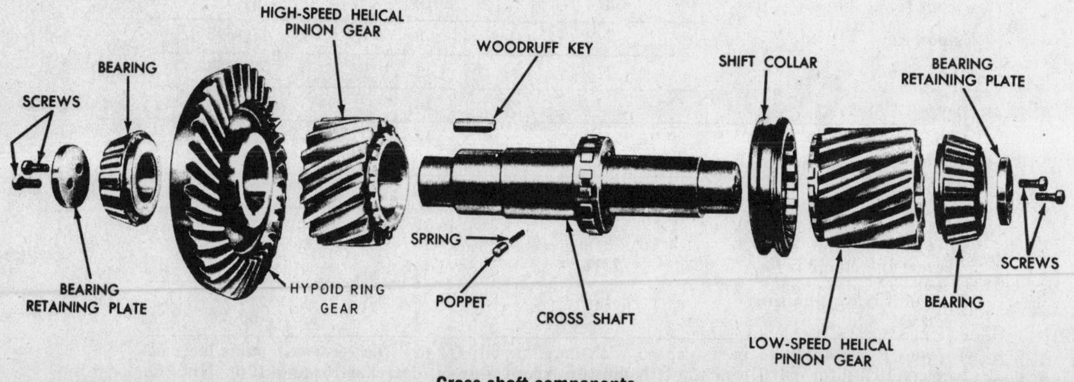

Cross shaft components
(© Rockwell Stand. Div.)

with compressed air. Remove any foreign material from carrier housing. The bearings should be submerged in clean solvent and rotated by hand until clean. After cleaning, blow dry with compressed air. *Do not spin bearings with air pressure, as they might score due to absence of any lubrication.* See the "General Axle Service" section for details on cleaning and inspection.

Assembly

1. Press drive pinion rear bearing cone firmly against pinion shoulder.
2. Press pinion cage bearing cups squarely and firmly against cage shoulder.
3. Place bearing spacer on pinion shaft with bevel side toward front bearing. Lubricate bearing cone with axle lubricant and position bearing cage on shaft. Lubricate and press front bearing on pinion shaft. Rotate cage to assure normal bearing contact. If a press is not available, install pinion yoke and nut and torque to specifications.
4. While assembly is in the press under pressure or pinion nut torqued to specifications, check pinion bearing pre-load. The correct pressures and torques for checking pre-load are:

Pinion Shaft Thread Size and Number of Threads Per Inch	*Required Pressure to Obtain Correct Pre-Load lbs.*	*Required Torque to Obtain Correct Pre-Load ft. lbs.*
1 in. x 20	12,000	300- 400
1¼ in. x 18	22,000	700- 900
1½ in. x 12	28,000	800-1100

5. Wrap a soft wire around cage and pull on horizontal line with pound scale. When determining pinion bearing pre-load, first measure diameter of pinion cage. Assuming cage diameter is 6 inches, pulling radius would be 3 inches; therefore, 4 pounds pull on scale would equal 12 inch-pounds pre-load.
6. Use rotating torque, not starting torque. If rotating torque is not within 5 to 15 inch-pounds, use thinner spacer to increase pre-load or thicker spacer to decrease pre-load. Torque must be near low limit inch-pounds with original pinion bearings and near high limit when using new bearings.
7. Lubricate a new pinion oil seal and install in pinion cage. Install pinion yoke, washer and nut, tighten to specified torque. Pinion and cage assembly is not installed until after cross shaft and hypoid gear installation. However, if pinion depth gauge tool is being used, install pinion assembly with original shims, then refer to "Pinion Setting Procedures" ("General Axle Service" section). After pinion depth is established, remove pinion and cage assembly.
8. Lubricate inner bearing surfaces on low and high speed pinions with axle lubricant. On some axles (H341, L345), the low speed (small) pinion is located next to the hypoid gear. On the others (Q345, RT340) the high speed (large) pinion is next to the hypoid gear.
9. Position correct pinion on hypoid gear end of cross shaft, with splined row of teeth toward center of cross shaft. Install key in shaft and start cross shaft into hypoid gear in line with keyway, then press shaft into hypoid gear. Insert feeler gauge between end of helical pinion and thrust surface on cross shaft must be .010-.025 inch.
10. Coat the three plungers and springs with axle lubricant, and install in cross shaft. Align the three tapered splines in shift collar with the three plungers, slide collar over plungers with side of collar marked LOW SIDE toward low speed (small) pinion.
11. Install remaining pinion on cross shaft with splined row of teeth toward center of shaft. Press cross shaft bearing firmly against cross shaft shoulder. Pinion end play must be .010 to .026 inch.
12. Install bearing retaining washers and torque cap screws to 42-45 foot-pounds and install lock wire.
13. Press bearing cups firmly against shoulder in the bearing covers.
14. Install cross shaft bearing cover (hypoid gear side) in carrier housing with original shim pack. Torque cap screws.
15. Lubricate bearing cones with axle lubricant, then position cross shaft assembly in bearing cup in carrier. If a front mounted shift unit is used, position shift fork and install shift shaft through its bearings in the carrier and fork. Align hole in fork with detent in shaft. Torque lock screw and install lock-wire. Start the other bearing cover and original shim pack in carrier housing (side opposite hypoid gear). Tap cover into position and torque down cap screws. Rotate cross shaft and gear assembly several times to assure normal bearing contact.
16. Lock low speed pinion and cross shaft with shift collar. Wrap a soft wire around the pinion and pull horizontally with a pound scale. To calculate cross shaft bearing pre-load, first measure diameter of pinion gear. Assuming pinion diameter is 4 inches, pulling radius would be 2 inches; therefore, 7 pounds pull on scale would equal 14 inch-pound pre-load.
17. Use rotating torque, not starting torque. If rotating torque is not within 5 to 15 inch-pounds, use thinner shim under bearing cover (side opposite hypoid gear) to increase pre-load or thicker shim to decrease pre-load.
18. Install drive pinion and cage assembly using corrected shim pack if pinion setting gauge was used, or original shim pack if gauge was not used. Install lock washers and torque cap screws.
19. Attach a dial indicator to the carrier with the pointer resting against face of one of the drive gear teeth and adjust backlash temporarily to .010 inch.

To increase backlash, remove sufficient shims from under cross shaft bearing cover (opposite hypoid gear), and insert shims of equal thickness under opposite bearing cover. To decrease backlash, reverse procedure. Following this method,

Determining cross shaft preload
(© Rockwell Stand. Div.)

Determining shift fork clearance
(© Rockwell Stand. Div.)

cross shaft bearing pre-load will be retained.

With backlash temporarily set at .010 inch, check gear tooth pattern. Refer to "Gear Tooth Contact" in the "General Axle Service" section. After correct tooth contacts have been made, readjust backlash to measure .020 to .026 inch.

20. If axle has a side mounted shift unit, tap shaft unit sleeve into carrier housing with original shim pack. Install lock washers and tighten nuts to 26-29 foot-pounds.

If electric shift unit is used, hold shift fork in the collar, lubricate and slide shift shaft through sleeve and into collar. Install and tighten lock screw. Tighten lock nut to 30-35 foot-pounds and install lock wire. Install shift unit.

Check clearance of shift fork pads in shift collar. The clearance should be .010 minimum on each side of fork in both high and low speed positions. Add or remove shims to achieve correct adjustment.

Shift unit adjustment
(© Rockwell Stand. Div.)

Check Operation of Shift Unit

If air shift control is used, hold shift fork in position in the collar, lubricate and slide air shift unit shaft through the sleeve and into the fork. Install lock screw. Tighten lock nut to 30-35 foot-pounds and install lockwire.

21. On those axles with a front mounted air shift unit, shift both shift unit and shift fork in HI position using no gaskets. Position the shaft unit and bell-crank assembly in slot of shift shaft. Install lock washers and nut and torque to specifications.

With collar and fork shifted to engage helical pinion next to hypoid gear, adjust Allen screw and nut in top of carrier to center the fork in the collar within .005".

With collar and fork shifted to engage the helical pinion away from hypoid gear, adjust hex head bolt and lock nut in cross shaft cage to center the fork in the collar within .005". (When checking shift fork clearance, make certain collar is flush with end face of pinion being engaged.)

Check Shift Unit Operation

22. Install high and low speed helical gears on their respective differential case halves. If rivets are used, install them cold. Instead of rivets, bolts can be used but must be tightened to specified torque.
23. Lubricate case inner walls and all parts with axle lubricant.
24. Install thrust washer and side gear in one of case halves. Assemble pinions and thrust washers on pinion shaft (spider) and install assembly. Engage the other side gear and thrust washer with pinions.
25. Aligning mating marks, unite case halves with four of the long bolts equally spaced. Check assembly for free rotation of gears and correct if necessary. Torque remaining bolts and install lock wire.
26. Press differential side bearings squarely and firmly on case halves.
27. Temporarily install bearing cups, threaded adjusting nuts or split ring and bearing caps. Torque cap bolts. Bearing cups must be hand pushed into the bores; or enlarged with a scraper or emery cloth until a hand push fit is obtained. Use a blued bearing cup as a gauge to check fit. If split rings cannot be turned by hand, reduce their O.D. slightly with a fine mill file.
28. Lubricate side bearings with axle lubricant. Place bearing cups in the cones, then position differential assembly between grooves in carrier legs.
29. Insert thin split rings in carrier leg grooves, making certain there is clearance betwen bearing cup faces and the rings.
30. Attach a dial indicator to the carrier housing with its pointer resting against side surface of one of the drive gears. With a pair of small pinch bars, manipulate assembly back and forth between the split rings and

Adjusting differential bearing preload
(© Rockwell Stand. Div.)

measure the end play.

31. Remove and measure split ring thickness. To the total thickness of the two thin rings, add the end play figure, plus another .017 to .022 inch to obtain total thickness of two thicker rings required to obtain proper bearing pre-load. For example: If necessary thin rings were .290 inch each for a total of .580 inch, and the end play is .005 inch, then .580 inch plus .005 inch equals .585 inch. Adding an additional .020 inch for a total of .605 inch thickness for the two split rings would provide .020 inch pre-load on the bearings. The .605 inch may be divided between the two rings such as .300 and .305 inch.
32. Insert one split ring in carrier leg groove and move differential assembly tightly against ring. Install opposite split ring (with gap upward) by tapping it into the groove with a blunt drift.
33. Tap bearing caps into correct location. Torque cap bolts and install lock wire.

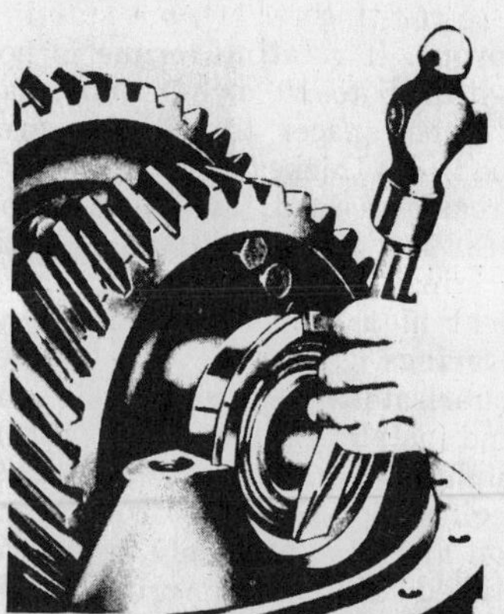
Split ring installation
(© Rockwell Stand. Div.)

Torque Chart

Item	Size	Torque
Carrier to housing bolt or stud nut	7/16-14-20	54-58
	1/2-13-20	85-91
	5/8-11-18	168-180
Cross shaft bearing cage and cover screw	1/2-13-20	85-91
	9/16-12-18	120-129
	5/8-11	168-180
Cross shaft bearing lock screw	7/6-14	42-45
	9/16-12	92-101
Differential case bolts	3/8-16	34-37
	7/16-14	54-58
	1/2-20	94-102
	9/16-18	132-145
	5/8-18	186-205
	3/4-16	325-360
Differential bearing cap bolt	5/8-11-18	127-140
	3/4-10-16	230-250
	7/8-9-14	345-370
	7/8-14	375-415
	1-14	375-415
Pinion cage bolt	3/8-16	34-37
	7/16-14-20	54-58
	1/2-13-20	85-91
	9/16-12-18	120-129
	5/8-11	168-180
Pinion shaft yoke nut	7/8-20	175-250
	1-20	300-400
	1-1/4-18	700-900
	1-1/2-12-18	800-1100
	1-3/4-12	800-1100

Bearing Preload

Axle Model	*Pinion Shaft Nut-Thread Size and Torque Limits (Foot-Pounds)*		*Press Ram Pressure for Preload Check (Tons)*	*Pinion and Cross Shaft Bearing Preload (Inch-Pounds)*	*Backlash Limits (Inches)*	*Differential Bearing Preload Adjusting Nut Notches Tighten from Zero End Play (each Adjusting Nut)*
2-Speed	1¾ x 12	800-1100	14	5-15	0.020-0.026	1
Double Reduction	1 x 20	300-400	6	5-15	0.020-0.026	1
	1¼ x 18	700-900	11	5-15	0.020-0.026	1
	1½ x 12	800-1100	14	5-15	0.020-0.026	1

Spicer Single Reduction Models 27, 30, 44, 44-1, 53, 60, 60-35, 70

1 Nut
2 Washer
3 Pinion flange
4 Outer bearing shims
5 Drive pinion
6 Inner bearing shims
7 Lock pin
8 Differential gear
9 Thrust washer
10 Axle shaft
11 Differential bearing cone
12 Differential bearing cup
13 Bearing cap
14 Differential bearing adjusting shims
15 Differential pinion
16 Thurst washer
17 Cover
18 Pinion shaft
19 Ring gear
20 Differential case
21 Differential bearing adjusting shims
22 Differential bearing cap
23 Differential bearing cone
24 Differential bearing cup
25 Cover bolt
26 Gasket
27 Axle shaft
28 Axle shaft guide (front axle only)
29 Oil seal (front axle only)
30 Thrust washer
31 Ring gear bolt
32 Oil slinger (front axle only)
33 Differential carrier
34 Inner bearing cone
35 Inner bearing cup
36 Outer bearing cup
37 Outer bearing cone
38 Oil slinger
39 Oil seal and gasket

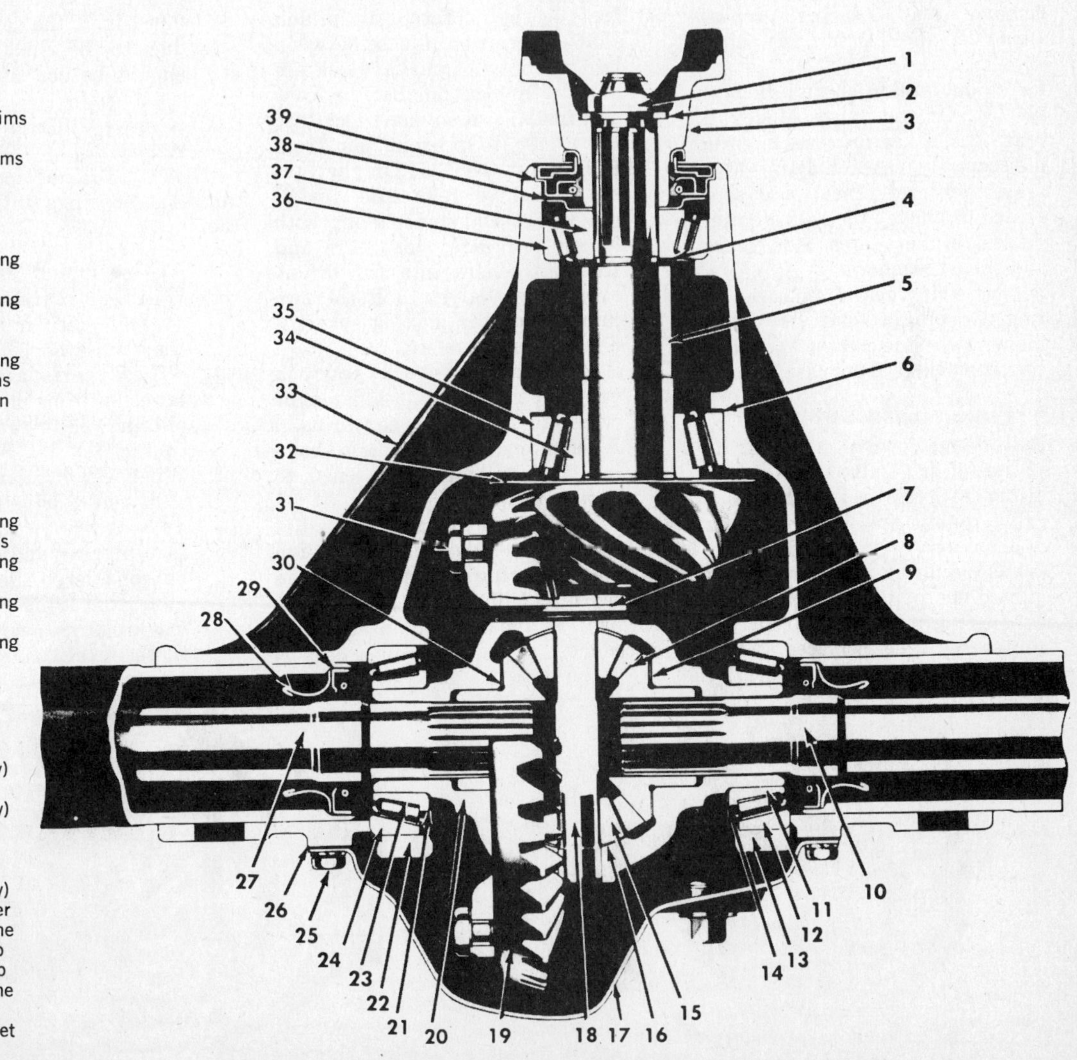

Axle differential assembly (© Dana Corp., Spicer Div.)

Differential Removal

1. Drain lubricant.
2. Remove cover and gasket. NOTE: Attached to a cover bolt is a metal tag which shows the number of teeth on pinion and ring (drive) gear.
3. Remove bearing cap screws. Note the matching marks on cap and carrier and make sure caps are reassembled to correct markings.
4. Using a spreader tool, spread carrier a maximum of 0.020 inch and meausre amount of spread with a dial indicator. IMPORTANT: Carrier may be permanently damaged if spread more than 0.020 inch. Do not attempt differential removal without using a spreader.
5. Carefully lift differential assembly out of carrier.

Differential Disassembly

1. Remove and label the two bearing cups.
2. Use a suitable type puller to remove the bearing cones. Remove and label adjusting shims.
3. Drive out pinion shaft lock pin. NOTE: On the Spicer Model 70 rear axle, punch-mark the differential case halves (for reassembly reference) and separate. Remove the differential spider, pinion gears, side gears and thrust washers.
4. Separate ring gear from case.
5. Remove pinion shaft, two pinions, two side gears, and four thrust washers from case.

Drive Pinion Disassembly

1. Pull flange (yoke) from shaft splines of drive pinion.
2. Using a press or soft hammer, drive pinion and inner bearing cone assembly out of carrier.
3. Remove and tag shim pack from splined end of pinion. NOTE: If either ring (drive) gear or pinion are to be replaced, write down markings (+), (–), or (0) located at face end of pinion for reassembly reference.
4. Remove oil seal assembly from carrier bore. This frees oil seal gasket, oil slinger, and bearing cone.
5. If replacement of the pinion tapered bearings is necessary, the bearing cups should be removed from carrier as follows:
   a. Use remover with a driver or slide hammer to remove inner bearing cup from carrier. This frees shim pack. Remove and tag shims for reassembly.
   b. Remove outer bearing cup.
6. Use remover set to separate bearing cone from drive pinion.
7. Separate oil slinger from pinion. NOTE: This oil slinger is only found on some axle models.

Differential Assembly

1. Place side gears with new thrust washers in position inside case.
2. Place pinions and thrust washers in position in case.
3. Install the differential pinion shaft in position in case between two pinions. Align shaft lock pin hole with lock pin hole in case and install pinion shaft lock pin. Peen hole to prevent pin from falling out. NOTE: On the Spicer Model 70 rear axle, install the differential spider along with its pinion gears, side gears and thrust washers into the differential case halves. Bolt the two halves together making sure the punch-marks line up.
4. Place ring (drive) gear in proper position against flange of case and bolt ring gear to case. Alternately tighten these bolts until all bolts are tightened to proper torque.

NOTE: Do not install differential cones or shim packs until pinion depth and bearing preload have been checked out. Differential bearing adjustment is a part of axle assembly procedure.

Differential Bearing Adjustment

1. Press fit bearing cones tightly against shoulders on case. IMPORTANT: Do not install shims at this time.
2. Install bearing cups.
3. Install spreader tool and dial indicator, and spread carrier as described in "Differential Removal."
4. Place differential assembly into carrier.
5. Install bearing caps using their respective cap screws. Make sure caps are assembled to their correct markings. Hand tighten bearing cap screws.
6. Install dial indicator at carrier with indicator button contacting back of ring (drive) gear. Rotate ring gear and check run-out.
7. If run-out exceeds 0.002-inch, remove the differential assembly and remove ring gear from the case.
8. Reinstall differential assembly without ring gear and check run-out of differential case flange. If run-out still exceeds 0.002-inch, the defect is probably due to bearings or case, and should be corrected before proceeding.
9. Remove differential from carrier.

NOTE: Do not install shims behind the bearings until final installation.

Drive Pinion Installation

1. If either drive pinion or ring (drive) gear must be replaced, they must be installed as a set. (These parts are matched and lapped at time of manufacture to obtain the correct gear tooth contact.)
2. Whenever it is necessary to install a new drive pinion, the plus (+) or minus (–) marking on face of rear end of pinion must be considered. Select a new pinion and ring gear set with markings as near as possible to those on old pinion. If marking

Installation of spreader and dial indicator
(© Dana Corp., Spicer Div.)

Mark locations on carrier and caps
(© Dana Corp., Spicer Div.)

on both old and new pinion is the same, do not change thickness of shim pack.

3. The approximate difference between markings on old and new drive pinion is the adjustment that will have to be made in the shim packs.
4. In the first listing below note that the new pinion is a plus eight (+8) while the old pinion is a plus five (+5). Making a difference of plus three (+3). This means that the thickness of each shim pack must be decreased by 0.003-inch. Other examples are:

Pinions New Pinion	*Old Pinion*	*Difference Between Markings*	*Amount To Change Each Shim Pack (in.)*
+8	+5	+3	Dec. 0.003
+5	+8	−3	Inc. 0.003
−5	−3	−2	Inc. 0.002
−3	−5	+2	Dec. 0.002
+5	−3	+8	Dec. 0.008
−4	+2	−6	Inc. 0.006

5. Once proper adjustment in shim packs has been made, place oil slinger, if so equipped, over pinion shaft. Install pinion inner bearing cone over shaft, and use bearing installer and an arbor press to press bearing onto pinion shaft. Bearing must be seated tightly against shoulder or oil slinger.
6. Use pinion front bearing cup installer to install outer bearing cup into carrier bore.
7. Install the selected inner shim pack in carrier. Then use pinion rear bearing cup installer to install inner bearing cup.
8. Insert pinion, oil slinger (when used) and inner bearing cone assembly into carrier and place the selected shim pack into position on outer end of pinion shaft.
9. Place outer bearing cone over pinion shaft, then use installer to seat bearing tight against shim pack.
10. Install pinion flange (yoke), washer and nut. Hold flange while tightening nut to proper torque.

NOTE: Install oil slinger and oil seal only after pinion depth and pinion bearing preload have been checked out.

Checking Pinion Depth Adjustment

1. A pinion depth gauge and correct adapter, which gives a micrometer reading, should be used to determine pinion depth. The actual pinion depth setting can be determined by adding gauge reading to thickness of step plate and comparing result with the nominal dimension of 2.625-inch (models 44/60-35) or 3.125-inch (model 60).
2. If the pinion setting is within minus (−) 0.001-inch to plus (+) 0.003-inch of this nominal dimension, the pinion position can be considered satisfactory.
3. If pinion setting exceeds these limits, it must be corrected by adjusting thickness of shim pack behind the pinion inner bearing cup.

Pinion Bearing Preload Adjustment

1. Use a torque wrench to check pinion bearing preload.
2. Rotating torque of pinion should be from 15 to 30 inch-pounds.
3. Add or remove shims from pack just behind outer bearing cone to bring preload within these torque limits.

Differential Installation

1. Use dial indicator and spreader tool as described in "Differential Removal," to spread carrier a maximum of 0.020-inch.
2. Install bearing cups and place differential assembly in carrier. Rotate differential and, with a soft hammer, tap ring (drive) gear to assure a proper bearing seating.
3. Reinstall bearing caps in their proper locations as indicated by marks made during the removal procedure. Finger tighten cap screws. Relieve the spreader tool pressure, and tighten cap screws to 70-90 foot-pounds.
4. Move differential assembly tightly against drive pinion.
5. Install dial indicator securely to carrier, then set button at zero and against back of drive gear.
6. Move the differential toward the dial indicator and note the reading. For accuracy, repeat this operation several times.
7. Remove the differential assembly from carrier. Install a shim pack behind differential bearing cone at drive gear side, equal to the dimension indicated by dial indicator.
8. Subtract the indicator reading from the reading previously obtained in paragraph "Differential Bearing Adjustment."
9. To the above result should be added 0.015 to 0.020-inch in shims to provide bearing preload.
10. Install the above shim pack behind differential bearing cone at side opposite to drive gear.
11. Spread differential carrier, using spreader tool.
12. Install differential bearing cups then locate differential assembly in carrier.
13. Rotate differential assembly, tapping gear to seat bearings.
14. Install differential bearing caps in their correct location as indicated by marks made upon disassembly. Finger tighten cap screws.
15. Remove differential carrier spreader tool. Tighten differential bearing cap screws to proper torque.
16. Install dial indicator and check drive gear to drive pinion backlash at four equally spaced points around the drive gear. Backlash must be held to 0.003 to 0.006-inch and must not vary more than 0.002-inch between positions checked.
17. Whenever backlash is not within limits, differential bearing shim pack should be corrected.

Axle Shaft Installation

Procedures for installation of axle shafts remain the same with axle assembly removed or installed on the vehicle.

Spicer Power-Lok Differential

Description

Unlike the standard differential, the locking differential equally divides the torque load between the driving wheels. The vehicle equipped with the locking differential can be operated on any surface (sand, snow, etc.) with a minimum of slippage through one wheel and provides the greatest power to the wheel getting traction. The vehicle with the standard differential provides power to the wheel that's easiest to turn—that is, the one experiencing the poorest traction while the other wheel may be gripping well.

When negotiating a turn, the locking differential allows the outer wheel to turn faster than the inner. When traveling in a straight direction, and the vehicle loses traction over a rough or slippery road, the clutches will lock up and neither wheel will spin. A specified lubricant must be used for locking differentials.

Disassembly

1. Remove and tag differential bearing cups and cones.

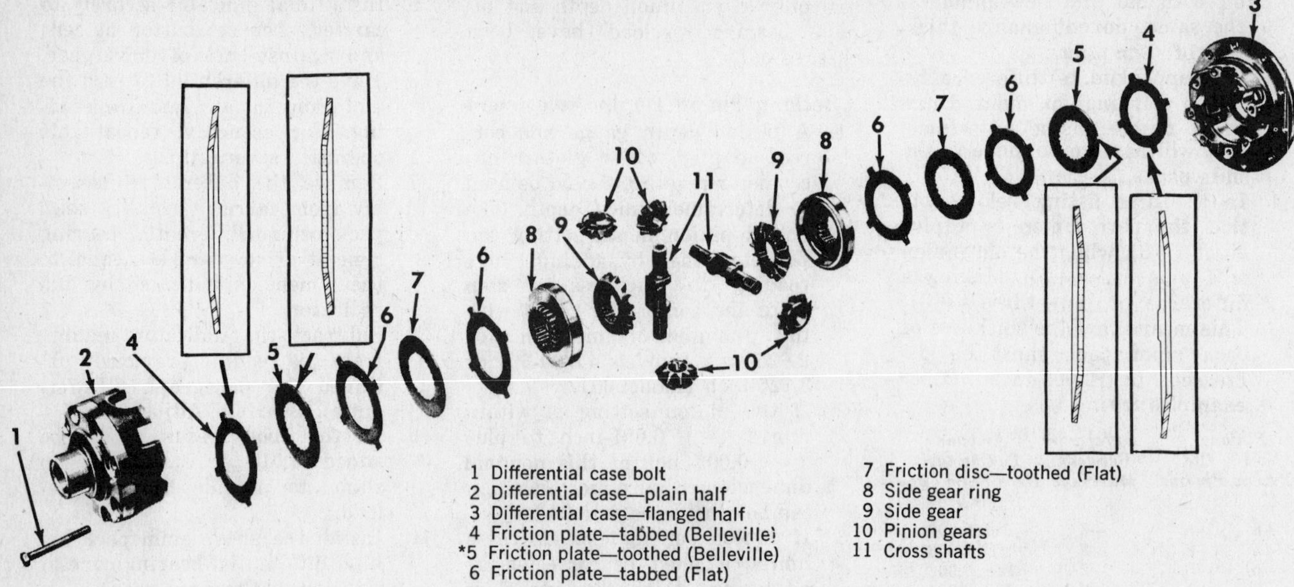

1 Differential case bolt
2 Differential case—plain half
3 Differential case—flanged half
4 Friction plate—tabbed (Belleville)
*5 Friction plate—toothed (Belleville)
6 Friction plate—tabbed (Flat)
7 Friction disc—toothed (Flat)
8 Side gear ring
9 Side gear
10 Pinion gears
11 Cross shafts

Powr-Lok differential (exploded view) (© G.M.C.)

2. Tag each bearing cone and shims and punch-mark differential halves for re-location reference.
3. Separate differential case halves.
4. Remove five plates and discs from side gear ring. IMPORTANT: Carefully observe the order in which the plates are used, since they must be replaced in the same order.
5. Remove side gear ring and side gear.
6. Remove two cross shafts and pinion gears.
7. Remove side gear, side gear ring, and five plates and discs from the opposite side and tag them for reassembly.

Cleaning and Inspection

1. Check cross shafts and pinions for scoring, wear, pitting, etc. If the center lands of either cross shaft are worn, inspect axle shaft ends to determine if the axle shaft is rubbing against cross shaft. This rubbing condition may cause a whine or howl that is similar to a pinion bearing noise, at 40 to 50 mph. This can be corrected by grinding 1/32" off the end of the axle shaft.
2. Inspect clutch discs and plates for wear, cracked, or distorted condition.
3. Inspect side gear rings, side gears, and differential cases for worn, cracked, or distorted condition. For further information on cleaning and inspection, see "General Axle Service" section.

Assembly

During assembly operations, lightly coat all parts with the correct lubricant.

1. Place tabbed Belleville friction plate in flanged differential case, being extremely careful that convex (bulged) side is toward the case.
2. Assemble remaining plates and discs to splines of side gear ring, being sure they are assembled in the same order of removal. The convex (bulged) side of the Belleville friction disc should be toward the case and it should nest into the Belleville friction plate. CAUTION: Do not attempt to operate the Powr-Lok with only one wheel on a jack. This might cause the vehicle to jump off the jack. Both wheels must be elevated from the ground.
3. Place assembled side gear ring with plates and discs in flanged half of differential case.
4. Install side gear and cross shafts

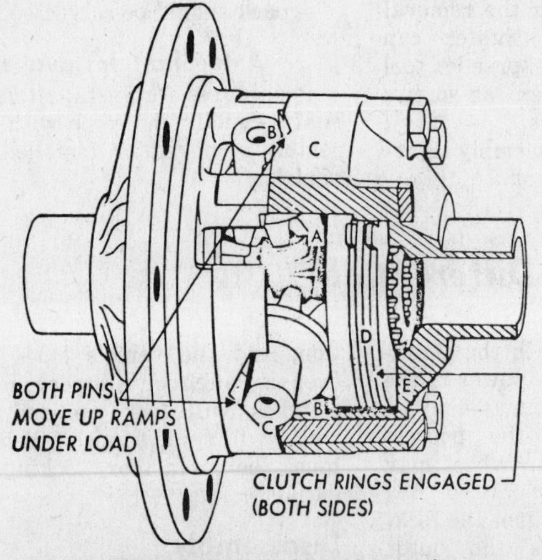

Location of cross pins with vehicle moving in a straight forward direction (Powr-Lok)
(© International Harvester Co.)

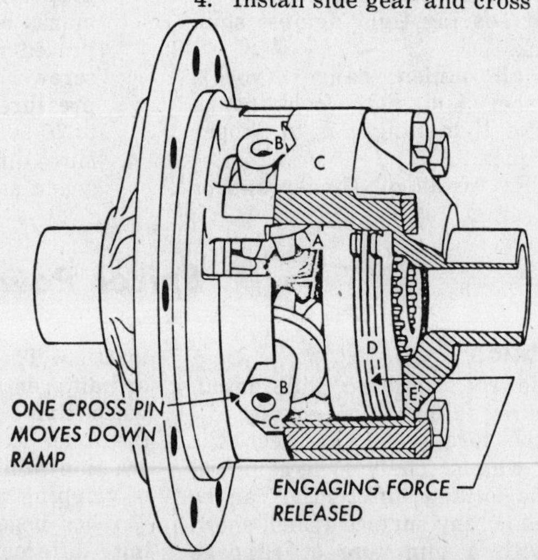

Location of cross pins with vehicle making a left hand turn (Powr-Lok)
(© International Harvester Co.)

with pinions.

5. In the order listed install the following: side gear, side gear ring, flat plate with tabs, flat disc with teeth, flat plate with tabs, Belleville disc with convex (bulged) side up, or toward case, Belleville plate, with convex (bulged) side up, or toward case.
6. Position plain half of differential case over previously assembled parts with punch marks on both halves aligned.
7. Install but do not tighten, differential case bolts.
8. Before tightening bolts, use axle shafts and align splines of the side gear and side gear ring, on each side. Tighten bolts evenly and alternately. Remove axle shafts.
9. Re-check components for proper assembly. Each pinion cross shaft can be tight on its ramp or if there is clearance it should be only a few thousands, and it should be equal at all four cross shaft ends.

Testing Procedure

The Powr-Lok can be effectively tested for correct operation by placing one rear wheel on good dry pavement and the other on ice, snow, mud, gravel, grease, etc.

It can easily be determined whether or not the non-slipping wheel is providing pulling power. This procedure should be repeated with the opposite wheels on the dry and slippery surfaces.

If suspected that the unit is not operating properly, it can be checked by the following procedure.

Place transmission in neutral. Raise one wheel off the floor and place a block in the front and rear of the opposite wheel. Install a special tool across two wheels studs and a torque wrench to special tool. Disregard breakaway torque and observe only the torque required to continuously turn the wheel smoothly.

If the torque reading is less than 40 foot-pounds, the unit should be disassembled and repairs made.

Ford Traction-Lok Limited Slip Differential

Disassembly

1. Remove the ring gear and separate the case halves.
2. Press the ring gear from the case.
3. Place the differential case in a press to load the case at the bearing journals so that the pre-load of the springs is overcome (approx. 1,500 lbs.). If a press is not available, use two 7/16 inch bolts and nuts in the ring gear mounting holes (one on each side) to compress the case halves together and overcome pre-load spring tension. With case under pressure, loosen the two Allen or Phillips head screws which hold the case halves together until one or two threads of the screws remain engaged. Remove case from press, tap on the cover to loosen it; then, remove both screws.
4. With the cover facing down, lift off the case. Remove the pre-load spring plate and four pre-load springs.
5. Remove the side gear, four clutch plate ear guides, clutch hub, friction and steel clutch plates and shim(s).
6. Drive out the pinion shaft lock pins and long pinion shaft from the case.
7. Remove the two short pinion shafts. Lift out the center block, then remove the pinion gears, thrust washers and side gear and thrust washer.
8. If removed, the differential bearings can be installed in one of the following ways:
   a. With the differential case and cover completely assembled.
   b. On the case or cover when disassembled. However, when pressing the bearing on the cover, a block of wood must be used to prevent cover damage.

Assembly

1. Lubricate all parts with recommended lubricant during assembly.
2. Mount the differential case in a soft jaw vise and place a side gear thrust washer and side

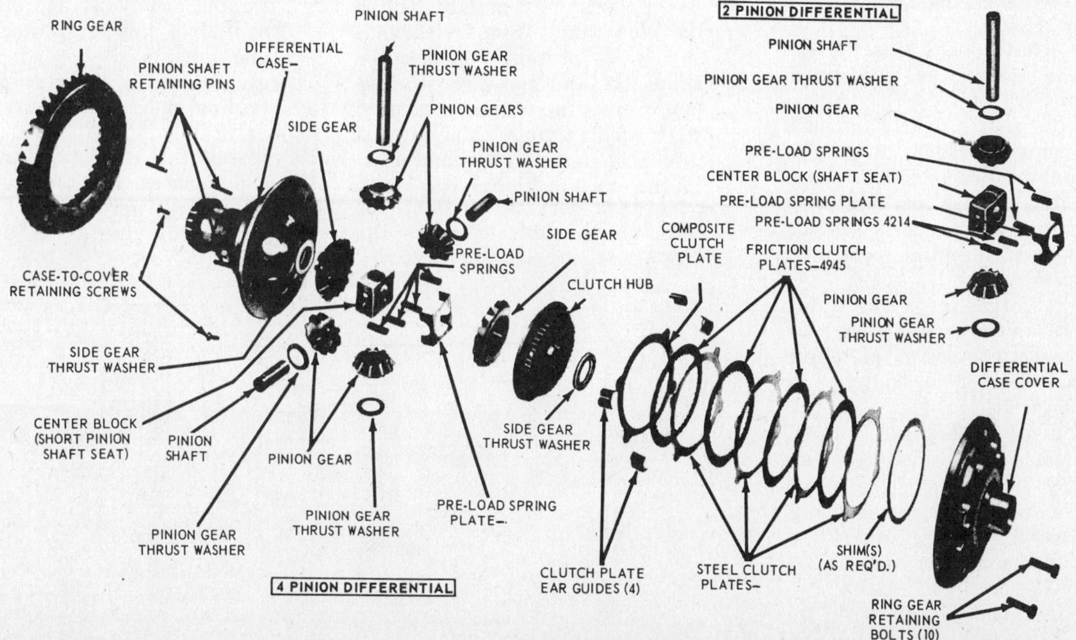

Ford Traction-Lok differential (exploded view) (© Ford Motor Co.)

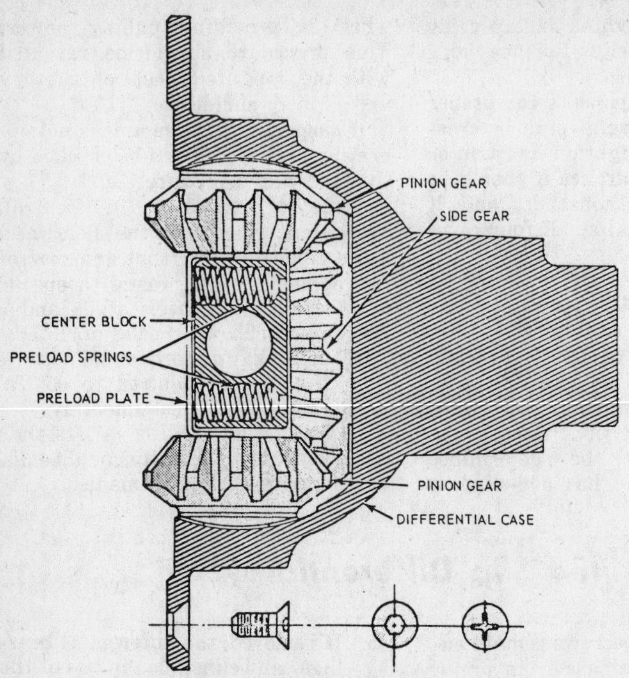

Center block and pre-load springs installation (Traction-Lok)
(© Ford Motor Co.)

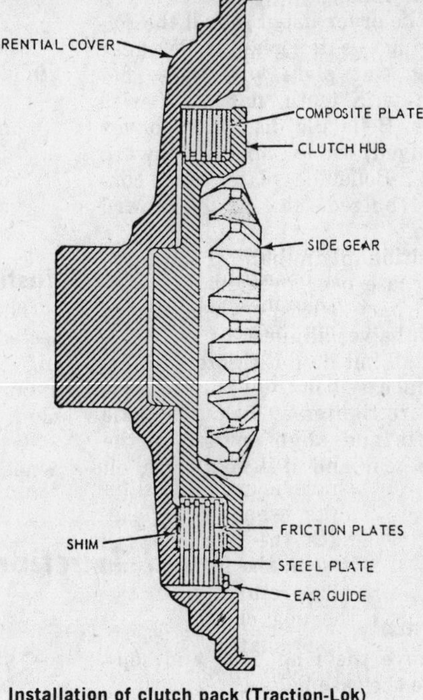

Installation of clutch pack (Traction-Lok)
(© Ford Motor Co.)

gear in the counterbore.

3. Install the pinion thrust washers and place the pinion gears on the side gear aligning the holes in the washers and gears with those in the case.
4. Install the center block. The center block has two machined sides and two rough sides.
5. Drive in the long pinion shaft aligning the lock pin holes in the shaft with the case holes. The center block should be positioned so the long shaft is driven through the rough side and short shafts driven through the machined side.
6. Install shaft lock pins. Make sure the pinion and side gears move freely.
7. Place the four pre-load springs in the center block.
8. Position the pre-load plate over the seated springs, making sure the springs are properly seated.
9. Mount the differential cover in a soft-jawed vise.
10. Insert shim(s) of 0.050 total thickness in the cover cavity.
11. Install the composite plate on the back side of the clutch hub with the friction side against the hub; next, install a friction plate, then steel, friction, steel, friction, steel, friction, and lastly a steel plate. When using new clutch plates, soak the plates in hypoid lubricant for 30 minutes before installation.
12. Place the clutch hub with the clutch plates into the clutch ear cavities in the differential cover. Make sure that the splines on the last friction plate are engaged on the hub.
13. Obtain a 5/8 inch x 2½ inch or 9/16 inch x 2½ inch bolt, nut and two 1½ inch outside diameter flat washers approx. ⅛ inch in thickness. These parts are necessary to compress the clutch pack in order to obtain the proper shim selection. Insert a bolt and washer through the clutch hub and place a flat washer on the bolt and then install the nut and torque to 10 or 15 ft. lbs.
14. Place the shim template tool in the clutch hub. Some clearance should be present between the shim tool and the cover-to-case mating surface and measured with a feeler gauge. A shim pack thickness chart (see manufacturer's specifications) will indicate the correct amount of shim(s) to subtract from the 0.050 shim originally installed.
15. After determining shim size, remove the bolt, nut and flat washers. If necessary to change the shim thickness, remove the clutch hub and clutch plates.
16. Install the selected shim(s) in the cover cavity, re-install the components as outlined in Steps 11 and 12.
17. Install the four steel clutch ear guides and side gear.
18. Press the two halves together; then, insert the two Allen head or Phillips head screws, and tighten evenly. If a press is not available, any two stock bolts and nuts may be used opposite each other in the ring gear retaining holes to compress both halves.
19. Install the ring gear and bolts and washers. Tighten evenly and alternately across the diameter of the ring gear at 65-80 ft. lbs.

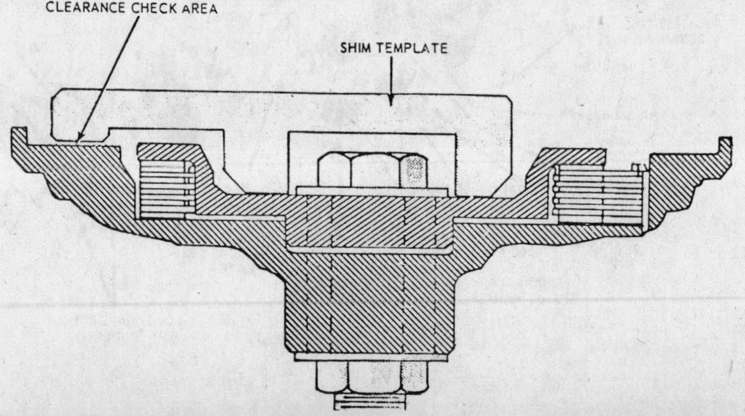

Shim template tool application (Traction-Lok) (© Ford Motor Co.)

20. Before installing the differential into a vehicle, a bench torque check must be made. Check the torque required to rotate one side gear while the other is held stationary. The initial break-away torque may exceed 250 ft. lbs. The rotating torque required to keep the side gear turning with new clutch plates is 100 to 250 ft. lbs. (The torque may fluctuate 10-40 ft. lbs.).

No-Spin Differential

Description

The No-Spin differential is a locking differential operating through a system of dog clutches and cams. In the No-Spin unit the rear wheels are locked together at the axle shafts by dog clutches. The limited slip differential has conventional gearing with a system of clutches serving to slow down the normal differential action. When the vehicle is turning, differentiation results when a series of cams disengages the dog clutch on the side turning in the largest circle. When the vehicle returns to straight line travel, the dog clutches engage and lock the axle shafts together at the differential case. In the No-Spin differential, the inside wheel turns at the same speed as the ring gear because it is locked up to the differential case. On the other hand, a geared differential system averages the power to the rear wheels, so that the inside wheel may turn slower than the ring gear.

The main difference between the silent type and the standard type is that the silent type contains a hold out ring placed between the driven clutch and the spider. When the vehicle is turning (outside wheel unlocked) the driven clutch on that side walks around the spider creating a clicking noise in the standard type. The in-and-out motion of the driven clutch creates this noise. The silent type limits this in-and-out motion until the moment the wheels return to straight-ahead movement.

Disassembly

1. Punch-mark differential case halves. CAUTION: The No-Spin differential is assembled under spring tension and held together with a retaining bolt and washers. If this bolt is not available, use a ½-13x6" bolt with nut and washers. If a retainer bolt is not used, hold differential case halves firmly to prevent sudden spring release.
2. Remove differential case and

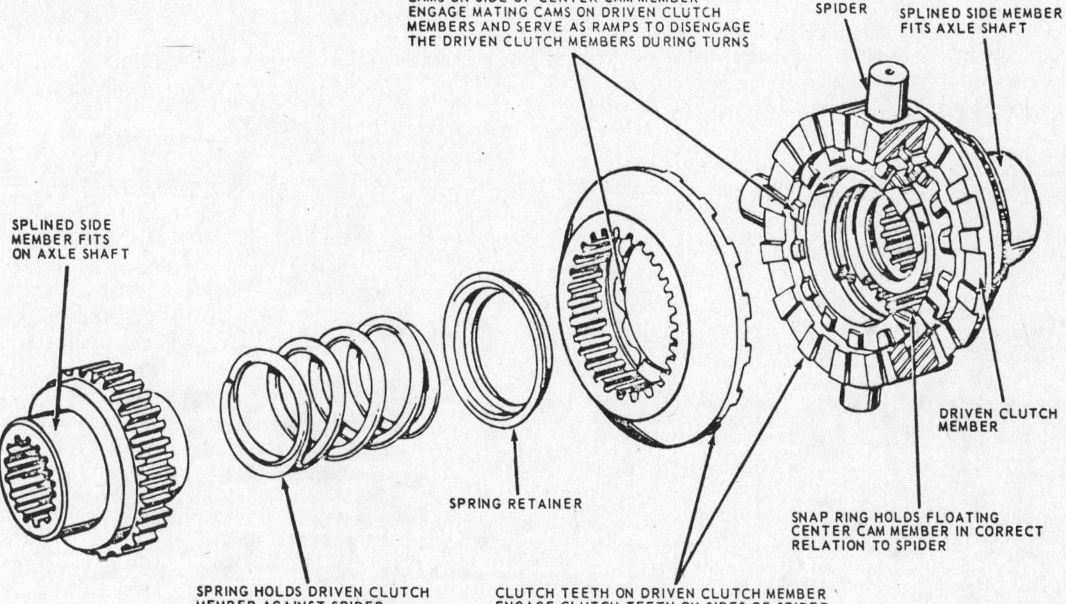

Standard No-Spin differential (exploded view) (© Ford Motor Co.)

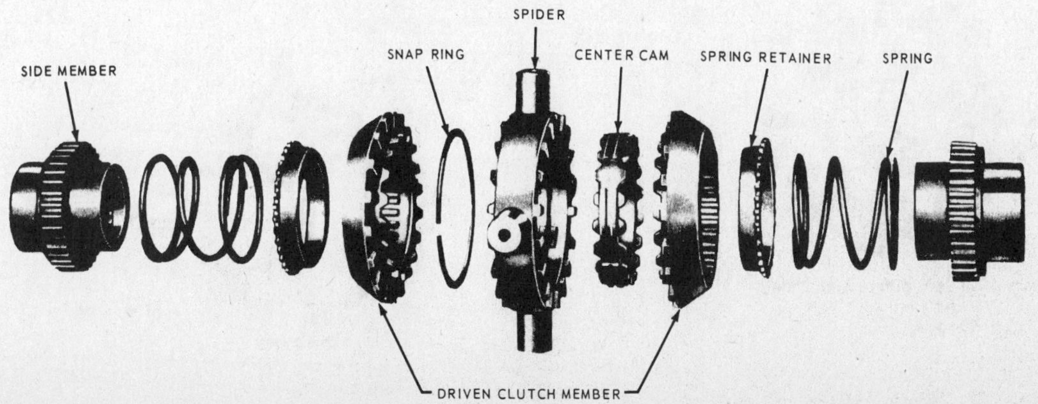

No-Spin differential-standard type (© Ford Motor Co.)

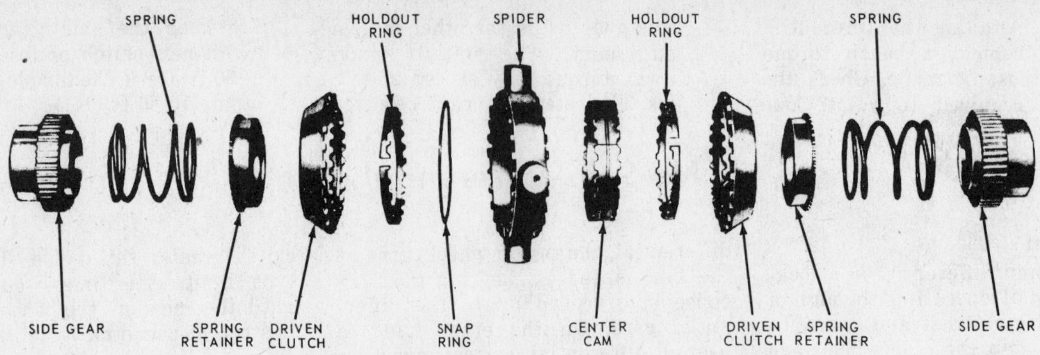

No-Spin differential-silent type (no case) (© Ford Motor Co.)

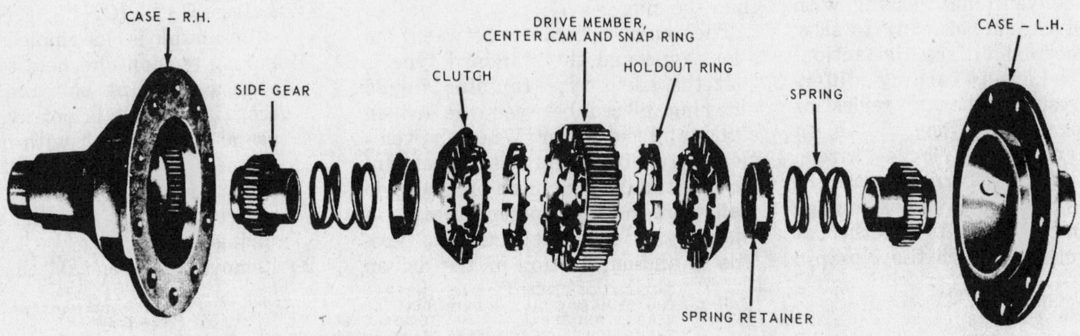

No-Spin differential—silent type (splined drive member with case) (© Ford Motor Co.)

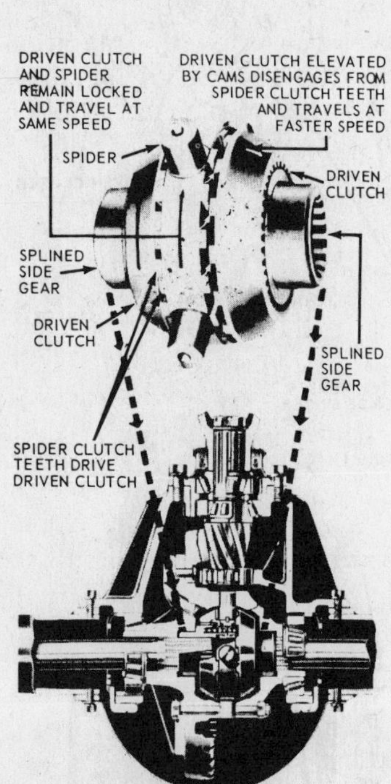

Position of No-Spin differential when installed
(© Ford Motor Co.)

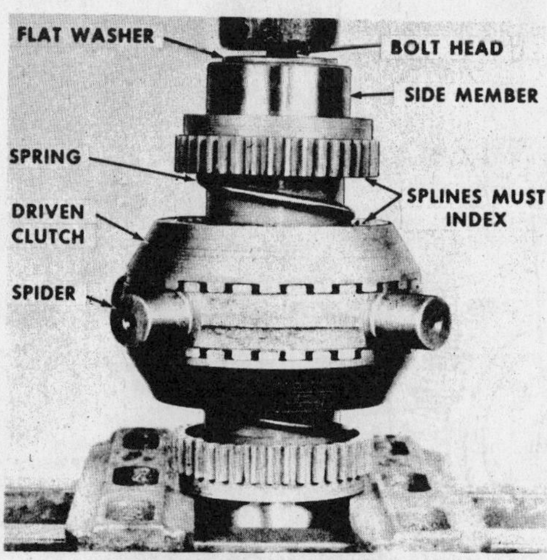

Releasing spring pressure (No-Spin)
(© International Harvester Co.)

Inserting assembly retaining bolt (No-Spin)
(© International Harvester Co.)

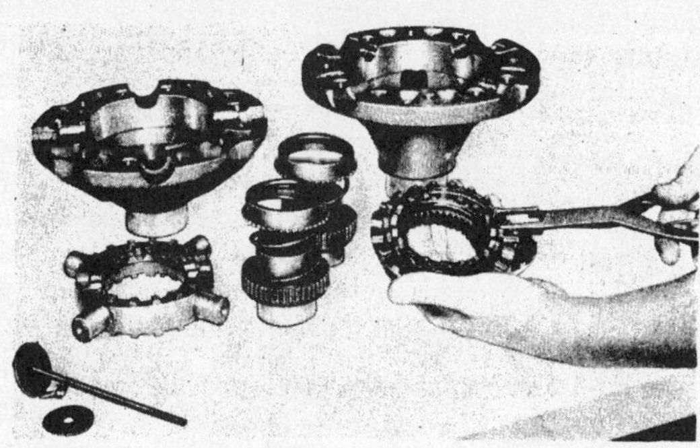

Holdout ring removal (No-Spin)
(© G.M. Corp.)

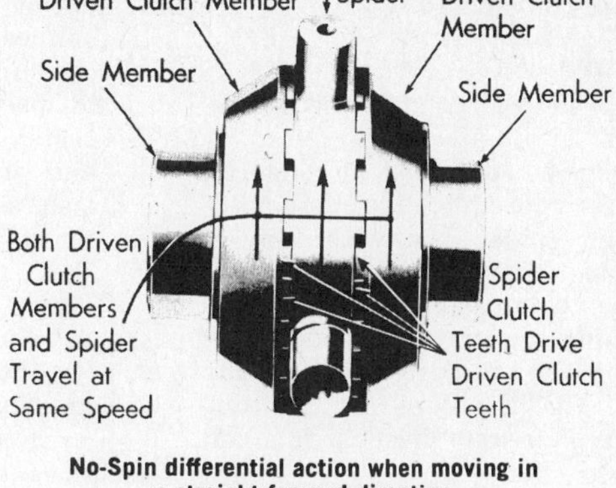

No-Spin differential action when moving in a straight forward direction
(© International Harvester Co.)

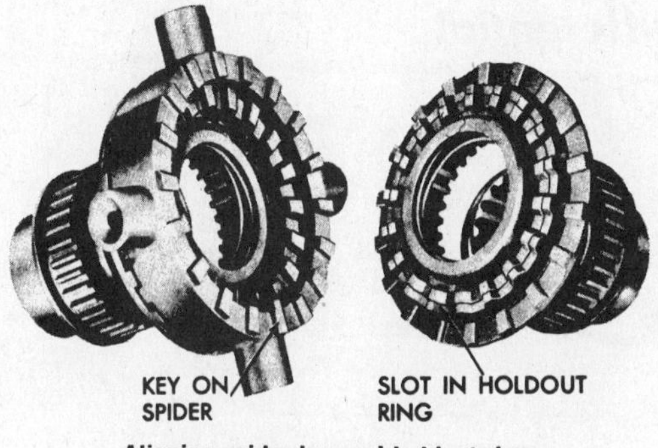

Aligning spider key and holdout ring (No-Spin)
(© G.M. Corp.)

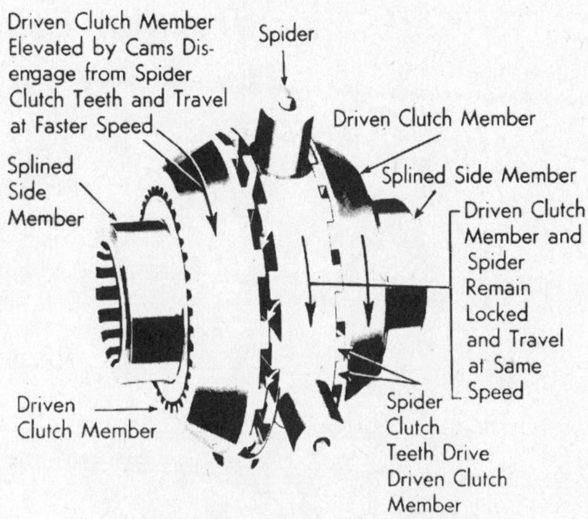

No-Spin differential action when making a right hand turn in a rearward direction
(© International Harvester Co.)

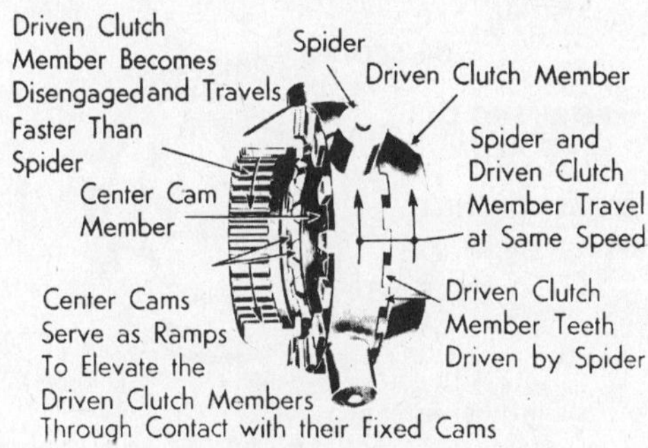

No-Spin differential action when making a forward right hand turn
(© International Harvester Co.)

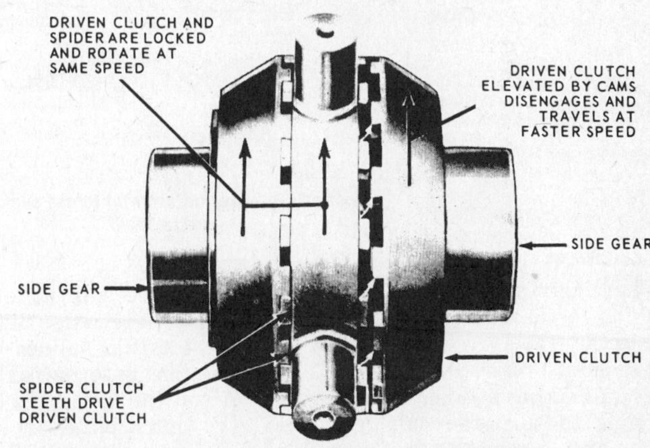

No-Spin operation when making a left hand turn (© Ford Motor Co.)

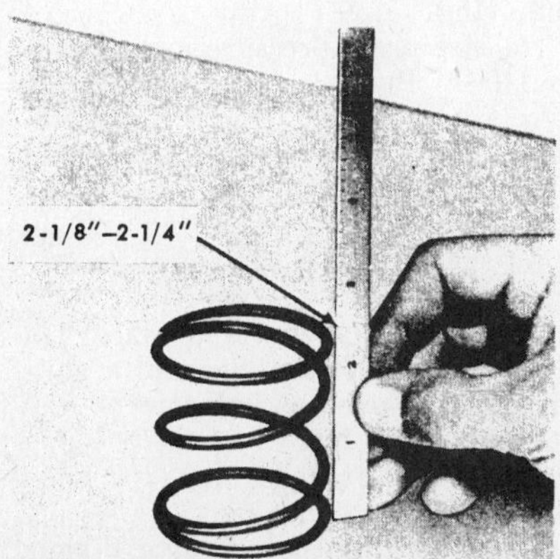

Measuring spring free height (No-Spin)
(© G.M. Corp.)

No-Spin.

3. Remove side gears, springs and retainers and driven clutches.
4. Remove split holdout rings.

NOTE: Do not disassemble spider, center cam and snap-ring assembly as they are not serviced separately.

Cleaning and Inspection

1. Using a solvent, thoroughly clean all parts.
2. Check side gear and driven clutch splines for excessive wear or fracture.
3. Check spider, center cam, holdout ring and driven clutch teeth for excessive chipping or burring. Minor chips or burrs may be dressed down with a fine stone. NOTE: Replace holdout rings or cams in pairs only.
4. Check spring retainer seat and

splines for fractures.

5. Measure spring height. Free height should be 2⅛"-2¼".

Assembly

1. Lubricate all clutch teeth and cams before assembly.
2. Assemble split holdout rings to center cam and spider assembly. Align spider key with slot in holdout ring.
3. Assemble driven clutches, spring retainers, springs and side gears to spider and center cam assembly. NOTE: Carefully position spring seats inside retainer cups.
4. Compress assembly with retainer bolt if available. If not available, install No-Spin in differential case, rotate to engage splines, and hold tightly until case and cover bolts are torqued to specifications.
5. Install No-Spin unit in carrier and adjust bearings and backlash as outlined previously for the standard differential unit.
6. Test operation of unit as follows:
   A. Raise both rear wheels off the floor.
   b. Shift transmission into gear.
   c. Rotate both rear wheels as far forward as possible.
   d. With assistant holding left wheel forward, rotate the right wheel to the rear, checking for free rotation.
   e. Rotate both wheels as far to the rear as possible.
   f. While holding the left wheel to the rear, rotate the right wheel forward and check for free rotation.
   g. Repeat Steps c-f, holding the right wheel and rotating the left wheel for left side forward and rearward operation check.
   h. If wheels cannot be rotated freely in this manner, remove and inspect the unit.

Traction Equalizer Differential

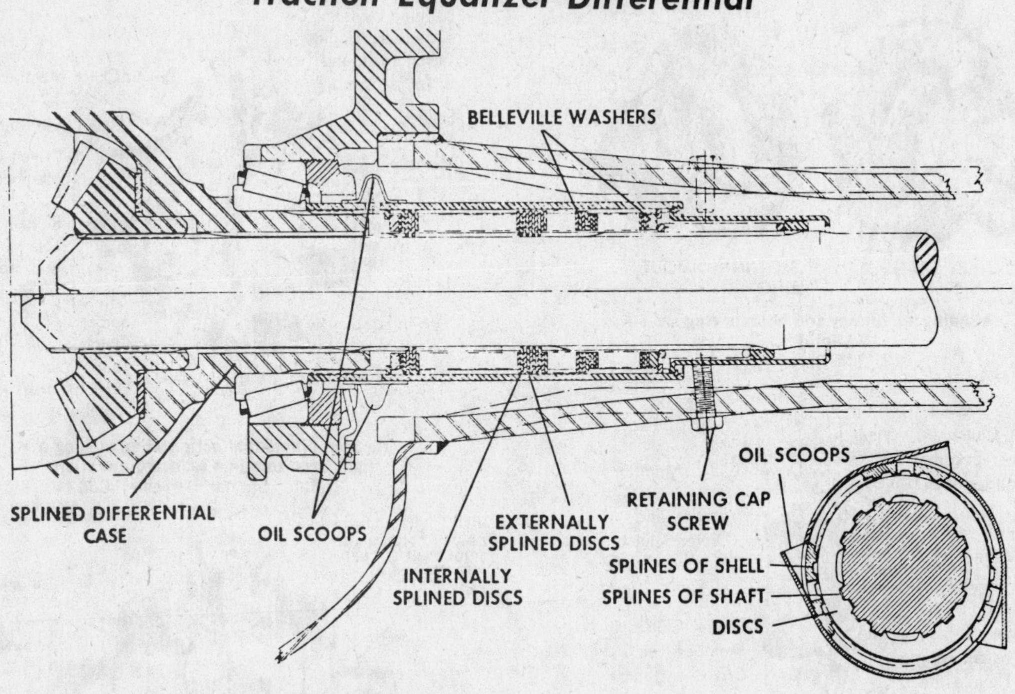

Traction Equalizer differential (cross section) (© International Harvester Co.)

Description

When driving straight ahead or straight to the rear, drive torque is sent to the wheels in the same way as on a standard rear axle.

When making a turn, the differential acts to turn the outside wheel faster and further than the inside wheel. While differentiation takes place, the outer wheel ground traction overpowers the clutch pack friction and the clutch plates rotate. This action takes place constantly in both units mounted on the axle shafts as the vehicle deviates minutely from a straight forward or straight rearward drive.

The Traction Equalizer consists of an internally splined cartridge which mates with the externally splined differential case extension. The shell contains a series of clutch plates which are splined alternately on the inside and outside diameters to match the internal splines of the cartridge and the external axle shaft splines. A constant pressure is maintained on the clutch plates by several Belleville spring washers. Oil scoops automatically pick up the standard axle lubricant.

Disassembly

Place cartridge assembly under press with oil scoop end down. Apply light pressure to the retainer assembly to compress the spring and permit removal of outer snap-ring. Remove the snap-ring, retainer spring and axle shaft collar.

Replace cartridge under press, oil scoop end down. Insert mandrel with flange end up. Compress Belleville springs with a light pressure (2-3 tons) and remove washer retaining snap-ring.

Release press pressure and remove mandrel. Place cartridge assembly over a post or bar (this will keep internal parts in original order). Hold internal parts down with a sleeve and lift off cartridge shell. Clean and inspect shell and snap-ring at oil scoop end.

Wire internal parts together in their original order, clean in a suitable solvent such as kerosene or diesel fuel oil. *Do Not Use Gasoline.* Dry immediately after cleaning with soft, clean, lintless wiping rags.

Clean housing thoroughly and blow dry with compressed air.

Inspect housing for cracks, nicks, and burrs at machined surfaces and

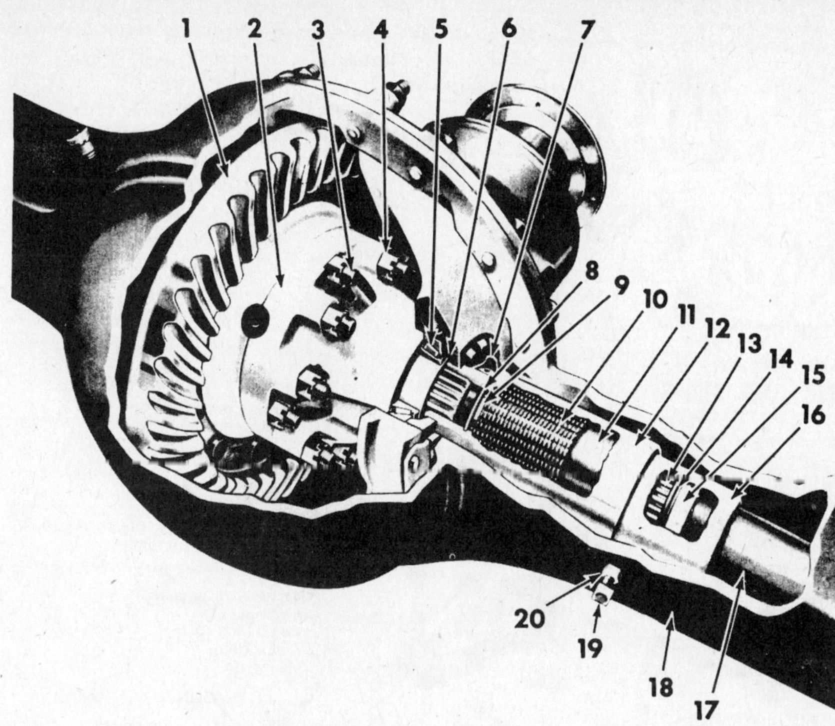

Traction Equalizer differential (© International Harvester Co.)

if present, remove with small file or stone. Make all necessary repairs before reassembling.

Reassembly

Install snap-ring at oil scoop end.

Place cartridge shell with oil scoop end down over mandrel.

Starting with a thick washer followed by discs and Belleville springs, remove and oil (axle lubricant) internal parts from post, one at a time. Install parts in shell over mandrel.

NOTE: Install discs alternately, starting with an externally splined disc. Belleville springs are to be installed in alternating groups of four, starting with concave side down (toward last disc which is to be an externally splined disc). If discs bind in the cartridge, tap (do not force) into position.

Carefully remove mandrel and insert at top of cartridge, with flange end up. Position a sleeve against the washer at bottom of assembly.

Using a press, compress (2-3 tons pressure) Belleville springs and install the retaining snap-ring.

Release the press pressure and mount a dial indicator with its stem against the top of the mandrel flange.

Apply a 2 to 3 ton press pressure and read dial indicator for movement required to compress discs and springs. Compression should be between .120″ to .160″, if more, add one or more splined discs (discs are approximately .040″ thick).

NOTE: Last disc must be an externally splined disc.

Release press pressure and remove mandrel. Install axle shaft collar (chamfered edge up) and retainer.

Compress spring with a slight amount of press pressure and install snap-ring.

CAUTION: When working on a truck equipped with a differential locking device, raise BOTH rear wheels off the ground. If only one wheel is raised, power will be transferred to the other wheel and the truck will force itself off its supports.

Lubrication

The Traction Equalizer assembly is lubricated with the same lubricant that is used in conventional differentials.

Check level at each chassis lubrication or 1,000-mile interval.

Drain and flush differential carrier every 10,000 miles or twice a year, preferably in the spring and fall.

Sure-Grip Differential

CAUTION: When working on vehicles equipped with sure-grip axles, raise BOTH rear wheels while engine is running. These axles can exert significant driving force with one wheel.

Using Proper Lubricant

If an axle assembly produces a chatter or moan, change the lubricant before attempting to disassemble it. The wrong lubricant can produce these noises and result in scoring of clutch plates and discs. Operate vehicle to increase lubricant temperature and, with a suction pump, withdraw old lubricant. Refill axle with special sure-grip lubricant and road-test for 100 miles to determine if noise condition has been corrected—if not, disassemble unit and repair.

Removal and Disassembly of Differential

NOTE: For details on removing and installing differential, refer to the Spicer single reduction axle section and "General Axle Service" section.

1. Place carrier and tube assembly in a vise.
2. Remove carrier cover and drain lubricant.
3. Clean components and dry with compressed air.
4. In preparing to measure drive gear back face runout (provided no side play was found) mount a dial indicator on pilot stud, and load the indicator stem slightly when plunger is at right angles to back face of drive gear.

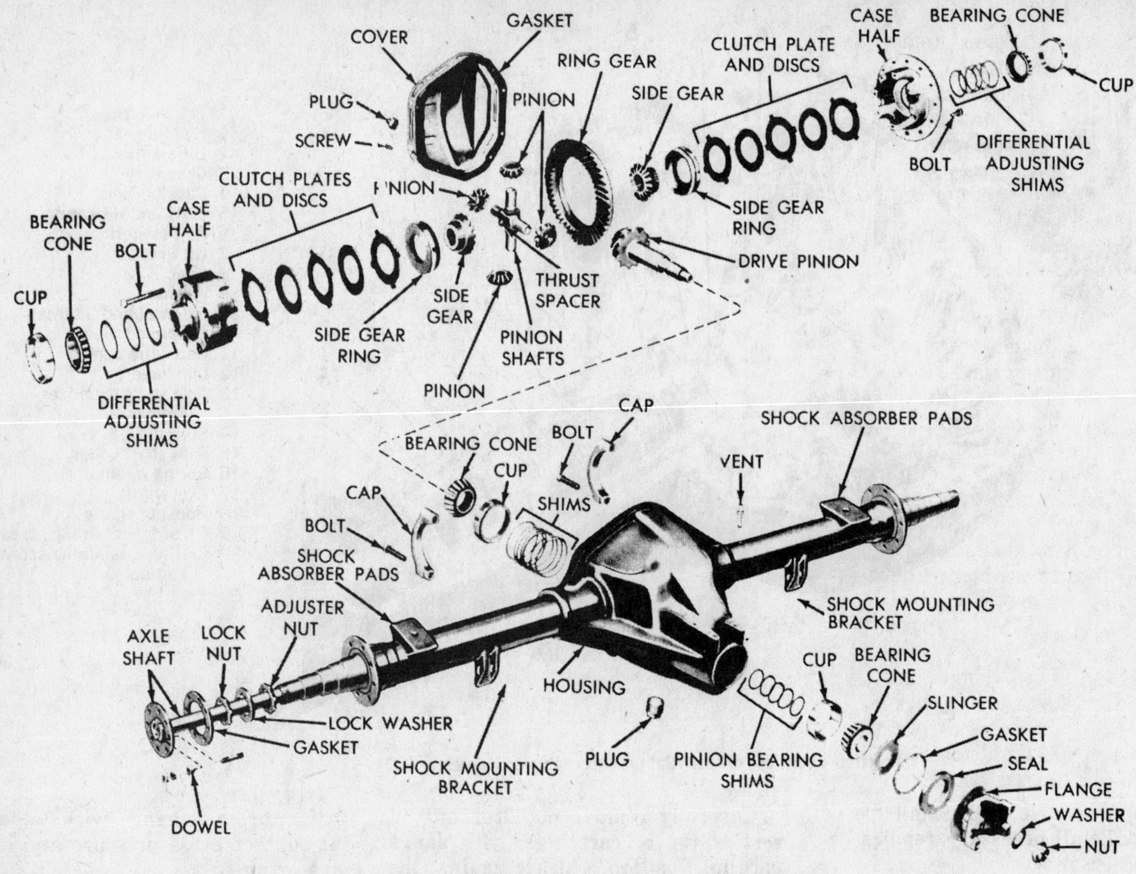

Spicer 60 Sure-Grip rear axle assembly (© Chrysler Corp.)

5. Measure drive gear back face runout by making several rotations of drive gear and reading dial indicator. Mark drive gear and differential case at point of maximum runout, this will be very helpful later in checking differential case runout. Total indicator readings in excess of .006 inch might indicate possible loose drive gear or damaged differential case.
6. Check the clearance between the differential bearing cap and bearing cup by trying to insert a .003 inch feeler gauge between them. If gauge enters, then there is excessive clearance possibly caused by bearing cup having turned in carrier.
7. Note identifying letters stamped on bearing caps and face of carrier housing seal surface. Letters stamped on left side are in horizontal position while right side are in vertical position. Always match identifying letters for proper reassembly.
8. Remove the differential bearing caps and locate spreader tool in locating holes of axle housing and turn tight at this time.
9. Install pilot stud on left side of axle housing. Attach dial indicator and load indicator stem slightly against opposite side of axle housing.
10. Tighten spreader tool nut enough to create .015 inch movement of dial indicator so that differential case and ring gear assembly can be removed. *Do not spread over .020 inch as it will result in permanent damage to carrier casting.*
11. Remove dial indicator and differential case and ring gear assembly from housing. Using a screwdriver, carefully lift out differential case and ring gear. Keep respective bearing cups

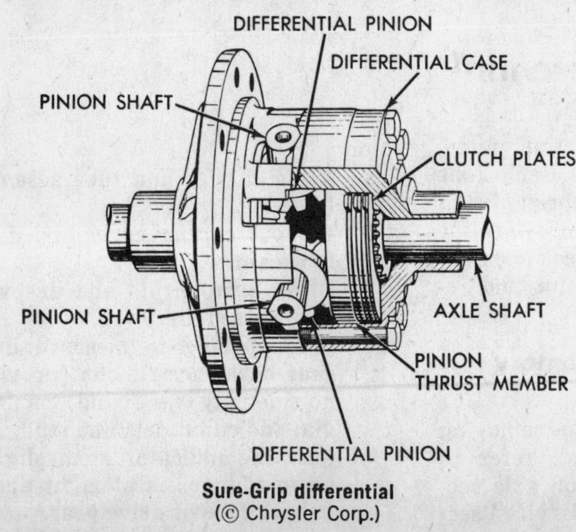

Sure-Grip differential
(© Chrysler Corp.)

Identifying bearing caps (Sure-Grip)
(© Chrysler Corp.)

with bearing cones unless they need replacement.

12. Place the differential case in a soft-jawed vise and remove and discard the drive gear screws. Using a fiber mallet, tap the drive gear loose from the differential case pilot.
13. If the drive gear runout exceeded .006 inch in step 5, differential case flange runout should be remeasured. Install differential case with respective bearing cups into axle housing. Remove spreader tool. Install bearing caps and tighten snugly. Mount dial indicator in contact with flange face of differential case, and measure runout as described in Step 5. Total maximum runout should be .003 inch. It is often possible to reduce excessive runout by positioning drive gear 180 degrees from point of maximum runout when reassembling ring gear on differential case.
14. Position carrier and tube assembly in vise. Remove drive pinion nut and washer and drive pinion flange.
15. Remove drive pinion oil seal, slinger, gasket, front pinion bearing cone and preload shim pack. Record the thickness of the shims in case they should be lost.
16. Press out the drive pinion stem and rear bearing cone assembly.
17. Drive out the front and rear pinion bearing cups from housing. Remove the shim from behind the rear bearing cup and record the thickness of shim pack.
18. Remove rear bearing cone from drive pinion stem.
19. Remove differential bearing cones from differential case hubs. Be careful that bearing remover adapters are located so as not to pull on bearing cage.
20. Remove the shims located behind each bearing and record thickness to aid in reassembly.

Determining runout on drive gear mounting flange face (Sure-Grip)
(© Chrysler Corp.)

Disassembling the Differential Case

1. Remove the axle drive gear. Measure runout of the drive gear mounting flange and replace both case halves if more than .003 inch.

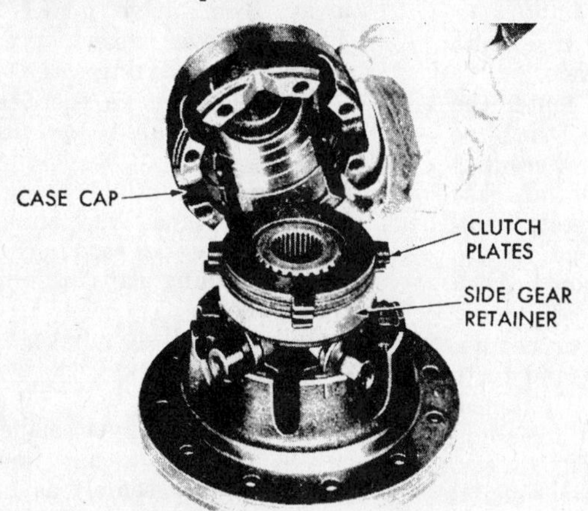

Removing or installing differential case cap (Sure-Grip)
(© Chrysler Corp.)

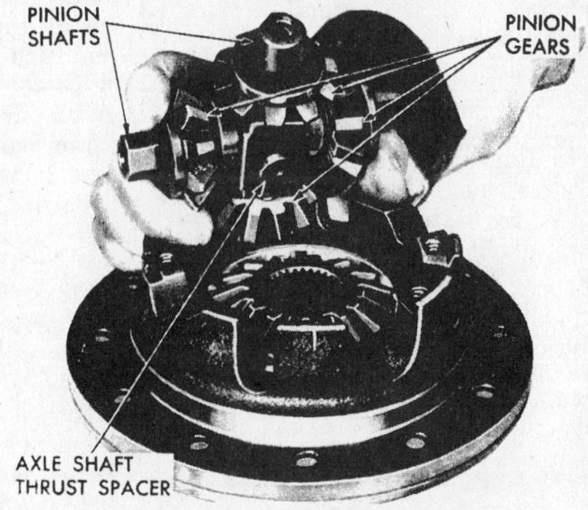

Installing pinion shafts and gears (Sure-Grip)
(© Chrysler Corp.)

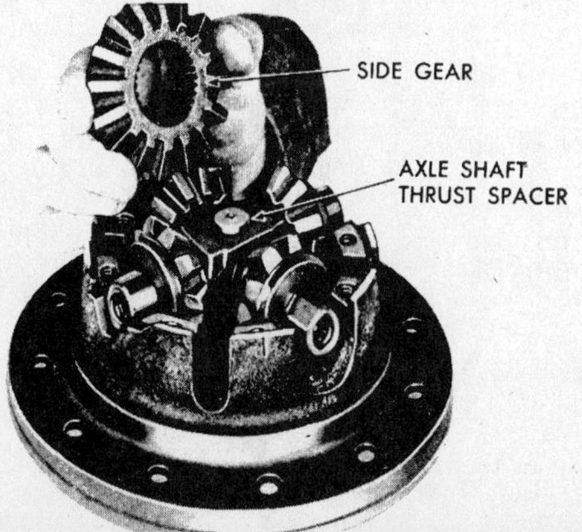

Removing or installing side gear (Sure-Grip)
(© Chrysler Corp.)

Side gear installation (Sure-Grip)
(© Chrysler Corp.)

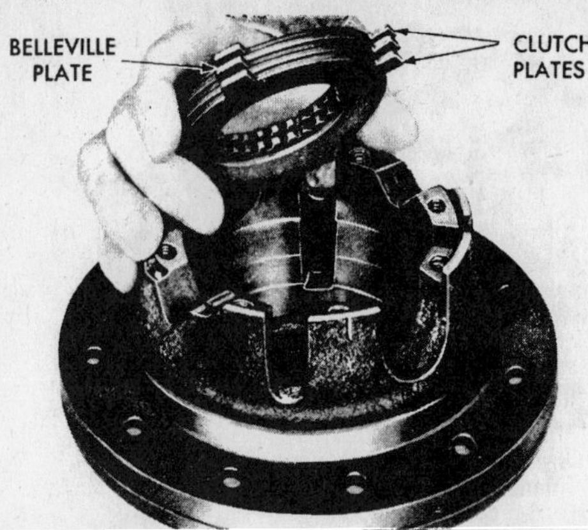

Installing clutch plates and discs (Sure-Grip)
(© Chrysler Corp.)

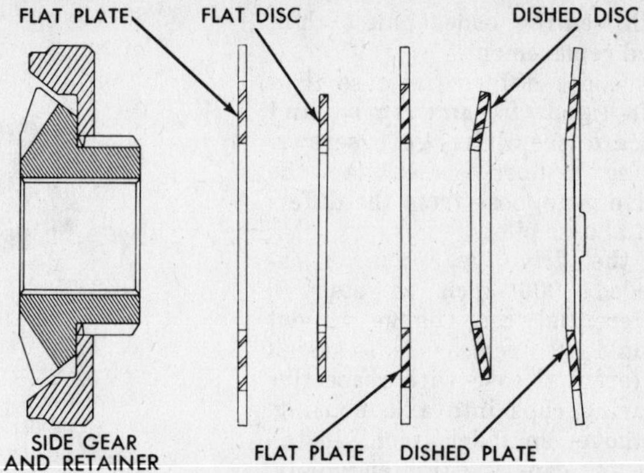

Proper sequence of plates and discs on the Sure-Grip
(© Chrysler Corp.)

2. Punch-mark case halves for realignment reference. Remove case cap and clutch plates.
3. Remove side gear retainer and side gear.
4. Remove pinion shafts with pinion gears.
5. Remove remaining side gear, side gear retainer and clutch plates.

Cleaning and Inspection

1. Clean all parts in cleaning solvent and, with the exception of bearing cones, dry with compressed air.
2. All machined contact surfaces should be smooth and free of any burrs. Raised metal on shoulders of bores caused by cup removal should be flattened with a flat nosed punch.
3. Check differential bearings and pinion bearing cone and cup assemblies for any defects. When replacing bearings, always replace the cup and cone in a set only.
4. Clean and inspect all differential parts for wear, nicks and burrs. The inner and outer flat clutch plates and outer flat clutch disc should be replaced if worn or distorted. Replace both case halves if one is worn. See "Cleaning and Inspection" in "General Axle Service" section for further details.

Assembling the Differential Case

1. Position clutch plates and discs in each case half.
2. Place side gears in their retainers and insert retainer splines through the splines of clutch discs.
3. Place aligning pin through one axle shaft thrust spacer. Assemble pinion shafts on aligning pin.
4. Place pinion gears on shafts and install assembly in drive gear half of case.
5. Place the cap half of case on drive-gear half and align the punch-marks.
6. Install the differential case bolts and turn in a few threads.
7. With shafts installed, center the cross shafts between the two ramp surfaces in differential case. Tighten differential case bolts evenly by alternately turning opposite bolts to 45 ft. lbs. To keep side gear and clutch plate splines in exact alignment during the tightening procedure, move axle shafts back and forth as bolts are being tightened. After assembly, slight misalignments of the splines can be corrected by moving axle shafts back and forth until free. Remove axle shafts.

Installation of Case and Drive Gear

The contacting surfaces of the drive gear and differential case flange must be clean and free of all burrs.

1. Position drive gear on differential case pilot, aligning threaded holes in drive gear and differential case flange.
2. Insert drive gear screws through case flange and into drive gear. After all cap screws are properly started, tap drive gear against differential case flange with a leather or rubber mallet.
3. Clamp unit in a brass jaw vise and alternately tighten each cap screw to 100-200 foot-pounds.
4. Position each differential bearing cone on hub of differential case (without shims), small end away from drive gear. CAUTION: Never exert pressure against the bearing cage, since this would damage the bearing and make it unfit for further use.
5. Position differential bearing cups on their respective cones and insert differential case in carrier. Install bearing caps and finger tighten bolts.
6. Install dial indicator fixture with pointer contacting back face of drive gear.
7. Insert a screwdriver blade between bearing cup and housing and pry case assembly as far as possible to one side of housing. Set dial indicator at zero. Using screwdriver, pry case to opposite side of housing and record the reading. This reading indicates the amount of shims needed to take up the clearance between the differential bearing cups and the case.
8. Remove dial indicator, and remove bearing caps. Remove differential assembly from housing.

Dana Positraction Differential

Disassembly

1. Remove ring gear and install spring compresser tool.
2. Compress and remove springs and spring cups.
3. Rotate differential side gear with axle shaft until pinions align with case opening. Remove pinions and thrust washers by prying clutch pack away from pinion.
4. Remove clutch packs and side gears. NOTE: The clutch pack is

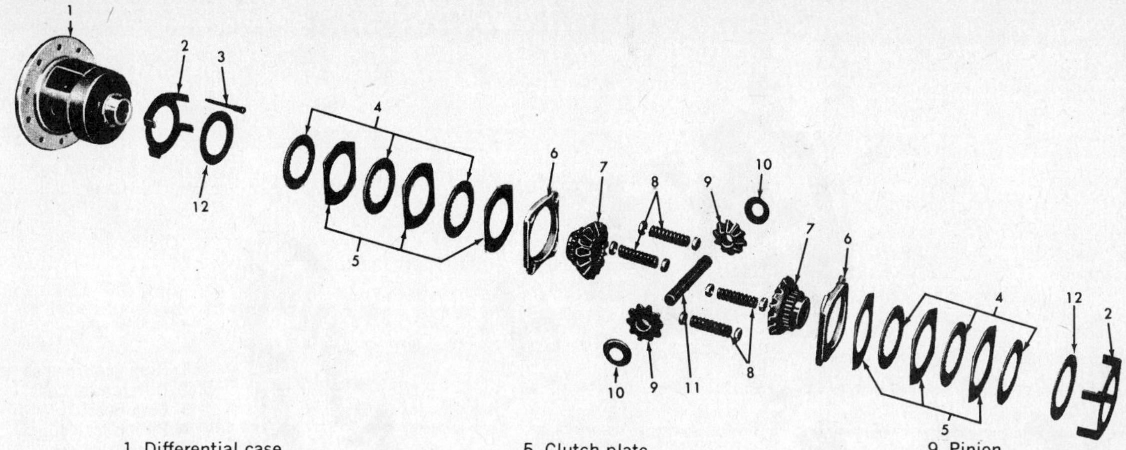

1 Differential case
2 Cage
3 Lock pin
4 Clutch disc
5 Clutch plate
6 Spring seat
7 Side gear
8 Spring and spring cups
9 Pinion
10 Thrust washer
11 Pinion shaft
12 Shim

Dana positraction (exploded view) (© G.M. Corp.)

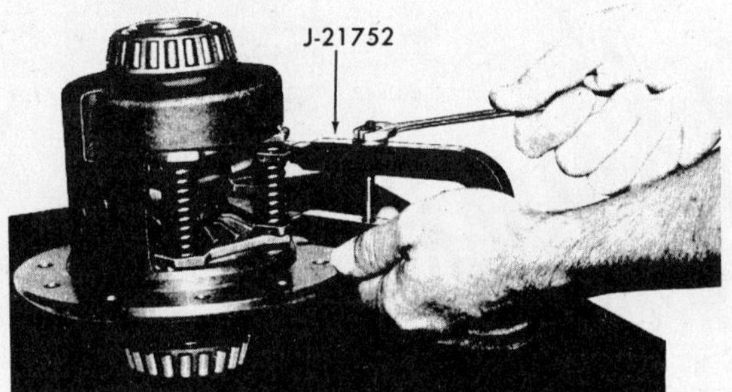

Removing positraction spring
(Dana) (© G.M. Corp.)

Determining positraction rotating torque
(Dana) (© G.M. Corp.)

Clutch pack installation
(Dana) (© G.M. Corp.)

assembled to a predetermined height of .552″ ± .002″, therefore make sure that clutch pack components are removed and kept together as a unit. Do not mix plates, discs or shims from one pack with those of another pack.

5. Pry clutch pack cage out of differential case.

Inspection

1. Clean and inspect components for excessive wear and replace where necessary.
2. Inspect clutch pack for excessive wear or overheating and replace as a unit if necessary.
3. If plates and discs are suitable for reinstallation, measure the clutch pack thickness (including shim). Total thickness should be .552″ ± .002″, replace shims as required to maintain this height. Shims are available in thickness of .016″, .020″, .024″, .026″ and .028″.

Reassembly

1. Place clutch pack cages into case with side tabs up and flat sides parallel with flat sides in case.
2. Place aluminum spring seat plate over side gear.
3. Alternately place clutch plate and clutch disc on side gear until pack is complete. Make sure clutch discs align with side gear teeth, then place shim over last clutch disc.
4. Install clutch pack and side gear assemblies in case.
5. Place pinion gear between differential side gears through large opening in case. Rotate side gears and install second pinion and thrust washers directly opposite first.
6. Place spring cup in bore and, using the spring compressor, install spring, and spring cup into spring seats. Repeat for remaining springs.
7. Install ring gear on case.
8. Place differential in carrier and adjust bearings and backlash (see "General Axle Service" section).
9. Test unit as follows:
   a. Raise rear of vehicle until both rear wheels are off the ground, and remove one wheel and tire assembly.
   b. Attach an adapter to axle shaft flange and install a ½-13 bolt into adapter.
   c. With wheel and tire assembly still on vehicle held firmly to prevent turning, measure torque required to rotate opposite axle shaft with a 0-150 lb. torque wrench attached to an adapter. Torque required to rotate axle shaft should be no less than 40 ft. lbs.

Eaton Positraction Differential

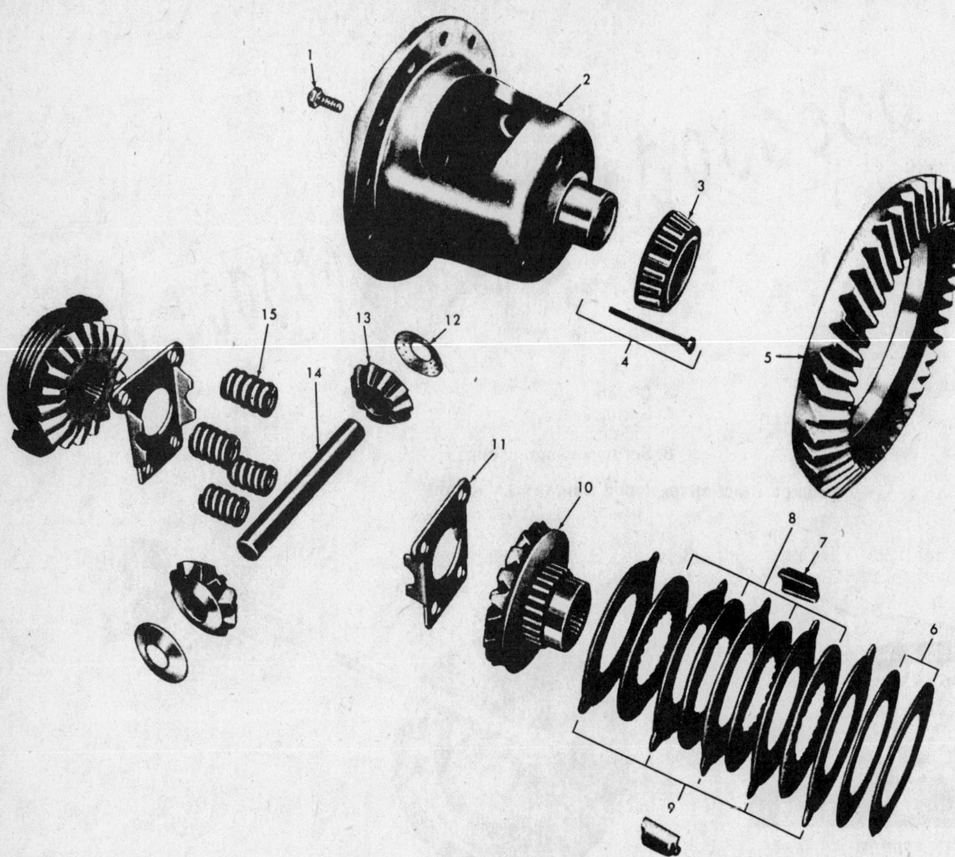

Eaton positraction (© G.M. Corp.)

Disassembly

1. Remove ring gear and side bearings.
2. Remove pinion shaft from the case.
3. Remove the preload spring retainer and springs by tapping on the spring retainer. Drive the spring retainer from the case sufficiently to allow insertion of a ¼ inch bolt and nut in each of the two front springs.
4. Continue to drive out spring retainer until enough is exposed to permit installation of bar stock and "C" clamp. Center the bar stock over the axle shaft hole in the spring retainer, then compress "C" clamp and withdraw spring pack.
5. Place spring pack in vise and remove bolts and relieve pressure.
6. Remove the pinion thrust washers from behind the pinion gears.
7. Remove pinion gears from case by rotating them in one direction only. Rotate differential case clockwise to remove the first gear, then rotate case counter-clockwise to remove the second gear. To remove second gear, it may be necessary to assist pinion gear upon its seat by prying on gear through observation hole in case.
8. Remove side gear, clutch pack, shims and guides from case and tap assembly from case. Repeat removal on opposite gear.
9. Separate clutch pack assembly

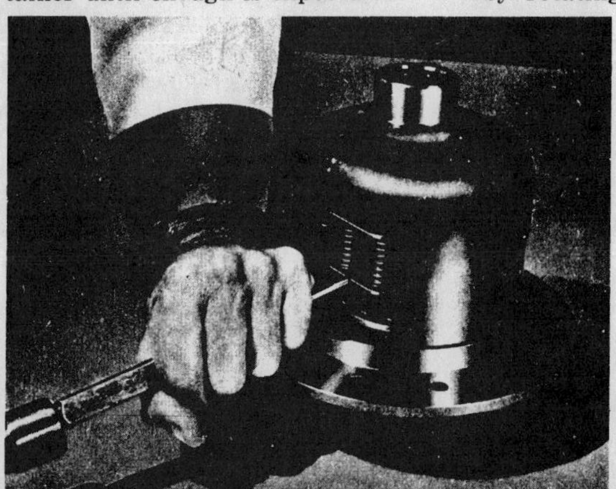

Removing pre-load spring pack
(Eaton) (© G.M. Corp.)

Position of "C" clamp and bar stock for spring removal
(Eaton) (© G.M. Corp.)

from side gear. Retain clutch pack assembly with original side gear.

Inspection

1. Replace worn or scored clutch plates and discs. NOTE: Clutch plates and discs are not serviced separately, if replacement is necessary, entire clutch pack must be replaced.
2. Inspect preload springs for defects.
3. Replace any weak springs.
4. Examine spring retainer for alignment between the retainer halves and for excessive wear at spring seats.

Reassembly

1. Lubricate clutch plates and discs with special positraction lubricant.
2. Alternately position clutch plate and disc on side gear, beginning and ending with clutch plate, until clutch pack is complete.
3. Install clutch pack guides on the clutch plate lugs. Make sure that the clutch disc lugs engage with side gear teeth.
4. Select shims of equal thickness as those removed from the case, or if old shims are suitable, reinstall them over the side gear hub.
5. Lubricate and assemble opposite side gear as above.
6. Install one side gear, clutch pack assemby and shim(s) in the differential case.
7. Position pinion gears and thrust washers on side gears. Install pinion shaft through case and gears.
8. Install dial indicator with button against pinion gear.
9. Compress clutch pack and move the pinion gear to obtain a tooth clearance.
10. Remove side gear assembly and repeat tooth clearance procedure for opposite side gear.
11. Remove pinion shaft, gears and thrust washers.
12. Install remaining side gear, clutch pack assembly and shims in case.
13. Install pinion gears and thrust washers (installation is reversal of removal).
14. Assemble springs in spring retainer and clamp assembly in vise. Install "C" clamp and bar stock on spring retainer then install a 1/4 inch bolt and nut in each front spring.
15. Position spring pack between side gears and remove bar stock and "C" clamp.
16. Drive spring pack into side gears sufficiently to retain front springs, then remove bolts from springs. Drive spring pack into position.
17. Install the pinion shaft and torque lock screw.
18. Check alignment of spring retainer with side gears and change if necessary.
19. Install side bearings and ring gear to case (same procedure as conventional differential).
20. Place differential in carrier and adjust bearings and backlash as outlined for the conventional differential.
21. Check operation of unit as follows:
    a. Raise rear of vehicle with *Both* rear wheels off ground, and remove one wheel and tire assembly.
    b. Attach Adapter to axle shaft flange and install a 1/2-13 bolt into adapter.
    c. With wheel and tire assembly still on vehicle held firmly to prevent turning, measure torque required to rotate opposite axle shaft with a 0-150 lb. torque wrench attached to adapter. Torque required to rotate axle shaft should be minimum of 40 ft. lbs.

Determining clearance of pinion gear tooth
(Eaton) (© G.M. Corp.)

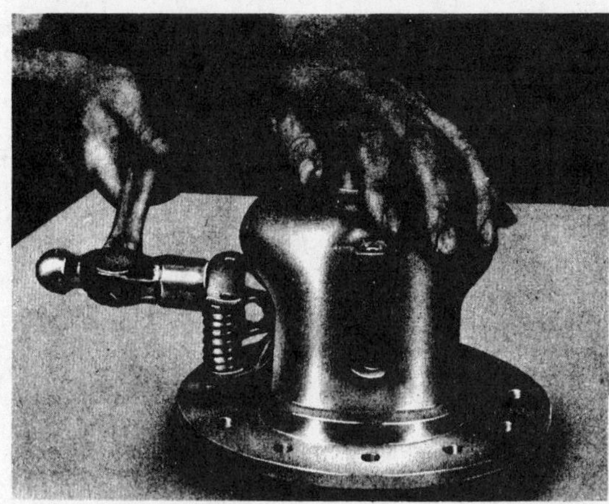

Spring pack installation
(Eaton) (© G.M. Corp.)

Measuring positraction rotating torque
(Eaton) (© G.M. Corp.)

Electric Shift System

Two-Speed Axle Electric Shift System

Description

The electric shift control system consists of a control switch, speedometer adapter, shift units, and interconnecting wiring harness.

The shift unit and automatic switch assembly, mounted on differential carrier, shifts the axle into "low" or "high", determined by the position of the control switch situated on the shift lever. The speedometer adapter (12 volts), attached to the back of speedometer, is electrically connected to the control switch. When in "low" range, an electromagnet shifts the adapter to compensate for gear reduction difference between "high" and "low." When in "high" range, current is released from electro-magnet and a spring holds the adapter in "high" range. Shift mechanism will not function if ignition switch is off. If an electrical short occurs, a circuit breaker is present to protect the system.

Cleaning and Inspection

Clean all parts except motor in cleaning solvent. The automatic switch, drive screw, and electric motor are each serviced as an assembly. The drive screw should turn freely when the nut is held. When the nut gets to either end of the screw, the screw should continue to turn, but the nut should not jam or run off the ends.

The motor is reversible. With the motor housing connected to one battery terminal, and either one of the two motor wires connected to the other battery terminal the motor will run in one direction and in the opposite direction if the other motor wire is connected.

Maintenance and Troubleshooting of System

The only general maintenance necessary on the shift control system is periodic lubrication of unit. Fill to level of filler plug with refrigerant machine oil.

Troubleshooting

A test light consisting of a 12-volt bulb with two wires a few feet long with small battery clip ends can be used for testing the system. Test in the following sequence:

1. Disconnect two wires from shift unit at rear axle. Place ignition switch in "ON" position, and control switch on shift lever in "hi" position.
2. Connect one lead of test light to ribbed wire and other lead to a ground and make the following checks. For the "lo" position, place switch in "low" and move the test lead from the ribbed wire to the smooth wire and make the following checks:
   a. Should light come on and stay on, the circuit is good and the trouble will probably be in the shift unit.
   b. If the light fails to come on this indicates that the circuit is open between the control switch and the shift unit and further tests will be necessary.
   c. If the light comes on intermittently, this indicates that there is a short between the control or ignition switch and shift unit, and further test will be required.
3. Connect one lead of test light to control switch side of circuit breaker and other lead to ground. If light comes on, and stays on, the circuit is satisfactory. However, if the light fails to come on, the circuit between the control switch and circuit breaker is either open or shorted.
4. Connect one test lead to load side of circuit breaker and opposite lead to ground. Should light come on, and stay on, the circuit breaker is good. However, if the light fails to come on the circuit breaker is faulty.
5. At chassis junction, remove both wires, then test circuit through red wire with white stripe. Reconnect both wires to terminal.
6. At chassis junction, remove wire from terminal. Place axle shift lever switch in "lo" position and test circuit and then make same test in "hi" position.

The control or ignition switch can be best tested by substituting a new unit.

If the vehicle shifts normally, but the speedometer adapter fails to operate, make the test to determine if the adapter is getting current range. If current is present, replace the adapter. When the trouble is traced to the shift unit, it should be replaced.

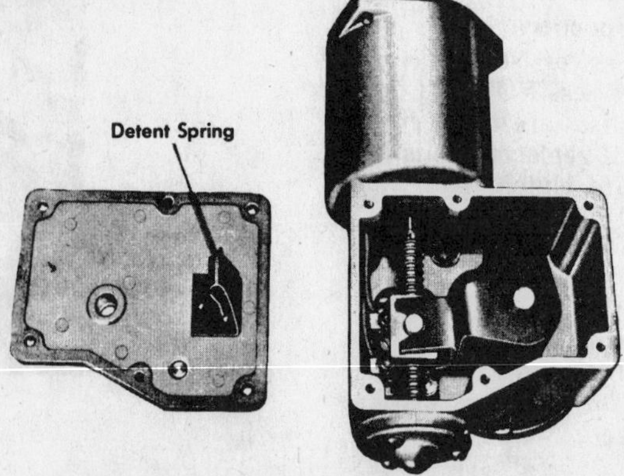

Position of drive nut when disassembling
(© G.M.C.)

POSITION IN HIGH

POSITION IN LOW

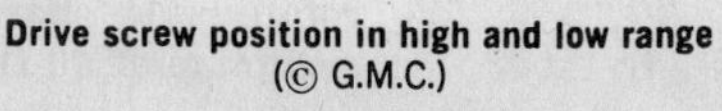

Drive screw position in high and low range
(© G.M.C.)

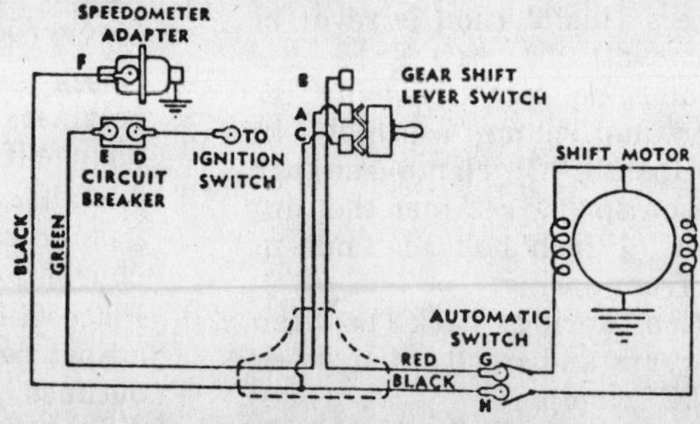

Electric shift wiring diagram
(© Chrysler Corp.)

Disassembly of the Eaton and GMC Unit

1. Remove housing cover and gasket and drain housing.
2. By turning drive screw, run nut to the center of the screw. IMPORTANT: This is essential to prevent damage to drive nut contact bumper, and is also necessary in assembly.
3. Remove shift fork actuating lever, torsion spring, and spring winding lever as an assembly by pulling shaft up and remove from housing.
4. Remove bearing cover and gasket.
5. Push down on drive screw assembly until bearing assembly is free of housing.
6. Insert screwdriver in screw, then remove bearing lock nut and bearing with snap-ring. Drive screw assembly can then be lifted out of housing.
7. Remove the motor wires.
8. Remove three screws and lock washers which attach motor cover to housing. Pull out motor with cover attached. Remove grommet.
9. Remove two jam nuts and fiber washers from outside of housing. On inside remove automatic switch.
10. Do not disassemble the shift fork actuating lever, torsion spring, and spring winding lever unless necessary to replace one of the parts. If necessary to disassembly, turn spring winding lever clockwise and pull to separate.

Assembly of the Eaton and GMC Unit

1. Install automatic switch assembly into housing with a flat head screw. On outside of housing, install two bushings, fiber washers, and jam nuts over switch terminal screws. Tighten nuts firmly.

Drive screw bearing removal (© G.M.C.)

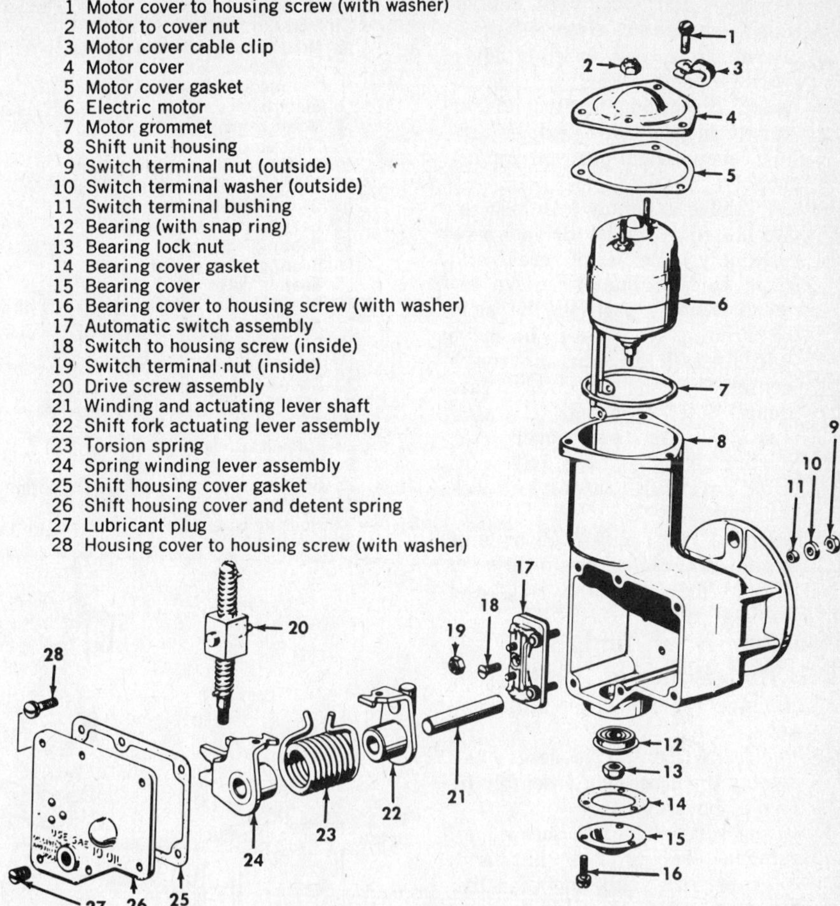

Eaton and GMC electric shift motor components (© G.M.C.)

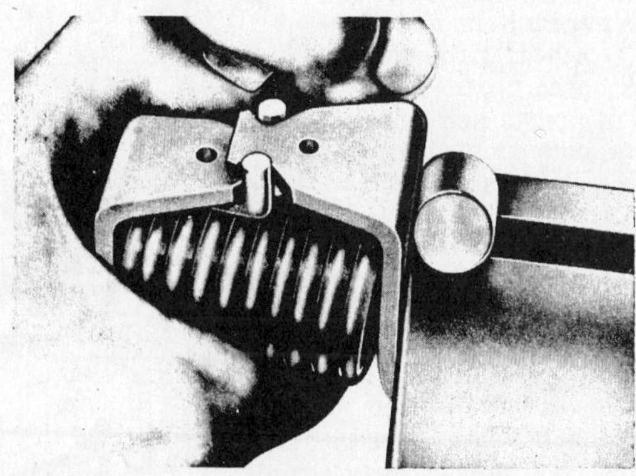
Separating torsion spring from lever (© G.M.C.)

2. Install motor assembly grommet and gasket on housing. Install motor and cover into housing. Install three screws and lock washers and two stop nuts. Install motor cover cable clip under outer screw. Tighten screws and nuts firmly.
3. Attach motor wires to switch terminals. The red or longer wire attaches to bottom terminal. Tighten inside terminal nuts firmly.
4. With a screwdriver inserted into drive screw, install bearing on end of screw with shielded side of bearing toward inside. Hold bearing with bearing lock nut.
5. Run nut to center of screw, then insert slotted end of screw into housing, meshing slotted end with armature shaft. NOTE: Fiber bumper contacts on drive nut must be toward switch.
6. Install gasket and cover with three screws and lock washers.
7. If the assembly consisting of shift fork actuating lever, torsion spring, and spring winding lever has been separated, reas-

semble. With shift fork actuating lever in vise, assemble parts. Turn the spring winding lever with one end of spring, in clockwise direction until end of spring is past shift fork actuating lever; then push in on assembly.

8. Dip above assembly in lubricant. With drive nut on drive screw assembly in center of screw, and fiber contact bumper down toward switch, position the slots of winding lever over the drive nut. Install the shaft through center of the assembly into depression in housing.
9. Install gasket and cover with spring detent against drive nut. Hold cover with screws and lock washers.
10. Remove oil plug. With unit standing with motor up fill with refrigerant machine oil and reinstall plug.

Disassembly of Timken (Rockwell-Standard) Unit

1. Remove bearing cover and gasket.
2. Push down on drive screw assembly until bearing assembly is free of housing.
3. Insert screwdriver in screw and remove bearing lock nut and bearing with snap ring then lift out drive screw assembly.
4. Remove the motor wires.
5. Remove three screws and lock washers which attach motor cover to housing. Pull out motor with cover attached. Grommet can then be removed.
6. Remove two jam nuts and fiber washers from outside of housing. On inside, remove automatic switch.
7. Do not disassemble torsion spring, and spring winding lever unless necessary to replace one of the parts. If neccessary to disassemble, place assembly in vise. Place a short piece of rod in hub of spring winding lever as a safety factor to prevent injury should torson spring slip out of control. Place two pieces of tubing over spring ends, pull spring ends apart, then raise spring above spring winding lever. To assemble, reverse this procedure.

1 Motor cover to housing screw (with washer)
2 Motor to cover nut
3 Motor cover cable clip
4 Motor cover
5 Motor cover gasket
6 Electric motor
7 Motor grommet
8 Shift unit housing
9 Switch terminal nut (outside)
10 Switch terminal washer (outside)
11 Switch terminal bushing
12 Bearing (with snap ring)
13 Bearing lock nut
14 Bearing cover gasket
15 Bearing cover
16 Bearing cover to housing screw (with washer)
17 Automatic switch assembly
18 Switch to housing screw (inside)
19 Switch terminal nut (inside)
20 Drive screw assembly
21 Winding and actuating lever shaft
22 Spring winding lever
23 Torsion spring
24 Shift housing cover gasket
25 Shift housing cover and detent spring
26 Lubricant plug
27 Housing cover to housing screw (with washer)
28 Housing to carrier seal

Timken (Rockwell-Standard) electric shift motor components (© G.M.C.)

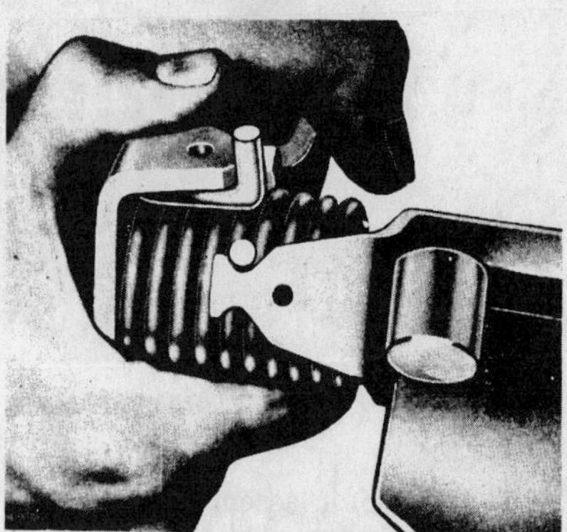

Assembling torsion spring and levers (Eaton) (© G.M.C.)

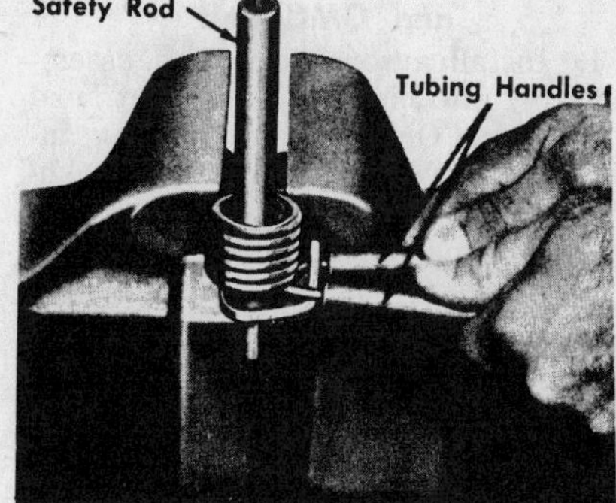

Torsion spring removal (Timken) (© G.M.C.)

Assembly of Timken (Rockwell-Standard) Unit

1. Install automatic switch assembly into housing. On outside of housing, install two bushings, fiber washers, and jam nuts over switch terminal screws.
2. Install motor assembly grommet, then install gasket on housing. Install motor and cover into housing. Install three screws and lock washers and two stop nuts. Install motor cover cable clip under outer screw. Tighten screws and nuts firmly.
3. Attach motor wires to switch teminals. The red or longer wire attaches to bottom terminal.
4. With a screwdriver inserted into drive screw, install bearing on end of screw with shielded side of bearing toward inside.
5. Run nut to center of screw, then insert slotted end of screw into housing, meshing slotted end with armature shaft. NOTE: Fiber bumper contact on drive nut must be toward switch.
6. Install gasket and cover.

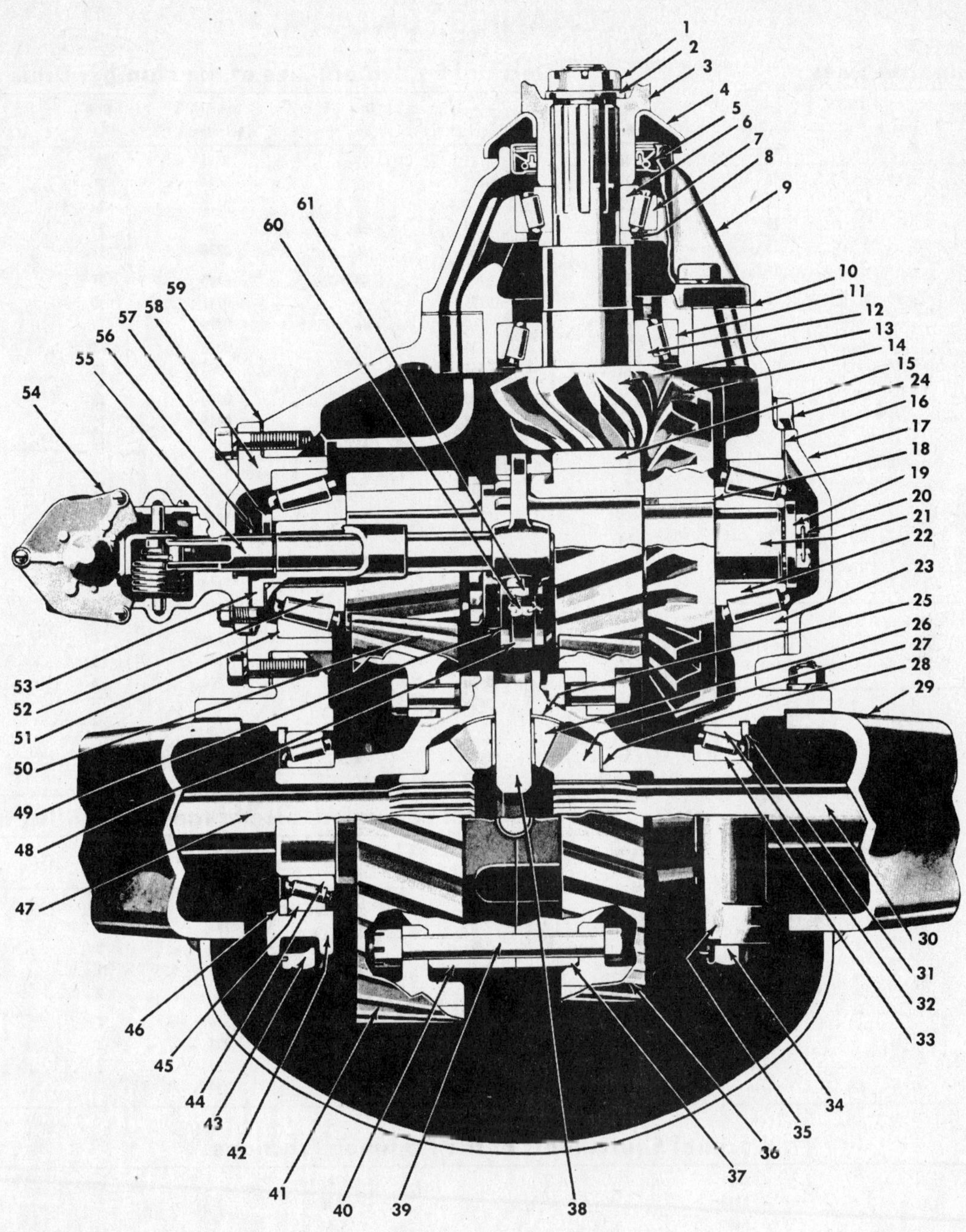

Sectional View of Rear Axle (Electric Shift Shown)

1. Yoke Nut
2. Nut Washer
3. Propeller Shaft Yoke
4. Dust Deflector
5. Oil Seal
6. Bearing Cone - Outer
7. Bearing Cup - Outer
8. Adjusting Spacer
9. Pinion Cage
10. Adjusting Shims
11. Bearing Cup - Inner
12. Bearing Cone - Inner
13. Drive Pinion
14. Bevel Gear
15. Drive Gear
16. Adjusting Shims
17. Bearing Cap
18. Gear Key
19. Retaining Washer
20. Retaining Screw
21. Crosss Shaft
22. Bearing Cone
23. Bearing Cup
24. Cap Screw
25. Pinion Thrust Washer
26. Differential Pinion
27. Differential Side Gear
28. Side Gear Thrust Washer
29. Housing
30. Axle Shaft - Right
31. Adjusting Spacer - Right
32. Bearing Cup - Right
33. Bearing Cone - Right
34. Cap Screw
35. Bearing Cap - Right
36. Driven Gear
37. Differential Case - Right
38. Differential Spider
39. Differential Case Bolt
40. Differential Case - Left
41. Driven Gear
42. Bearing Cap - Left
43. Cap Screw
44. Bearing Cone - Left
45. Bearing Cup - Left
46. Adjusting Spacer - Left
47. Axle Shaft - Left
48. Shift Yoke
49. Shift Clutch
50. Drive Gear
51. Bearing Cup
52. Bearing Cone
53. Shift Shaft Sleeve
54. Electric Shift Unit
55. Shifter Shaft
56. Retaining Screw
57. Retaining Washer
58. Bearing Cage
59. Adjusting Shims
60. Set Screw
61. Lock Nut

MECHANICS' DATA

Tap Drill Sizes

National Coarse or U.S.S.

Screw & Tap Size	Threads Per Inch	Use Drill Number
No. 5	40	39
No. 6	32	36
No. 8	32	29
No. 10	24	25
No. 12	24	17
1/4	20	8
5/16	18	F
3/8	16	5/16
7/16	14	U
1/2	13	27/64
9/16	12	31/64
5/8	11	17/32
3/4	10	21/32
7/8	9	49/64
1	8	7/8
1 1/8	7	63/64
1 1/4	7	1 7/64
1 1/2	6	1 11/32

National Fine or S.A.E.

Screw & Tap Size	Threads Per Inch	Use Drill Number
No. 5	44	37
No. 6	40	33
No. 8	36	29
No. 10	32	21
No. 12	28	15
1/4	28	3
5/16	24	I
3/8	24	Q
7/16	20	W
1/2	20	29/64
9/16	18	33/64
5/8	18	37/64
3/4	16	11/16
7/8	14	13/16
1 1/8	12	1 3/64
1 1/4	12	1 11/64
1 1/2	12	1 27/64

Decimal Equivalent Size of the Number Drills

Drill No.	Decimal Equivalent	Drill No.	Decimal Equivalent	Drill No.	Decimal Equivalent
80	.0135	53	.0595	26	.1470
79	.0145	52	.0635	25	.1495
78	.0160	51	.0670	24	.1520
77	.0180	50	.0700	23	.1540
76	.0200	49	.0730	22	.1570
75	.0210	48	.0760	21	.1590
74	.0225	47	.0785	20	.1610
73	.0240	46	.0810	19	.1660
72	.0250	45	.0820	18	.1695
71	.0260	44	.0860	17	.1730
70	.0280	43	.0890	16	.1770
69	.0292	42	.0935	15	.1800
68	.0310	41	.0960	14	.1820
67	.0320	40	.0980	13	.1850
66	.0330	39	.0995	12	.1890
65	.0350	38	.1015	11	.1910
64	.0360	37	.1040	10	.1935
63	.0370	36	.1065	9	.1960
62	.0380	35	.1100	8	.1990
61	.0390	34	.1110	7	.2010
60	.0400	33	.1130	6	.2040
59	.0410	32	.1160	5	.2055
58	.0420	31	.1200	4	.2090
57	.0430	30	.1285	3	.2130
56	.0465	29	.1360	2	.2210
55	.0520	28	.1405	1	.2280
54	.0550	27	.1440		

Decimal Equivalent Size of the Letter Drills

Letter Drill	Decimal Equivalent	Letter Drill	Decimal Equivalent	Letter Drill	Decimal Equivalent
A	.234	J	.277	S	.348
B	.238	K	.281	T	.358
C	.242	L	.290	U	.368
D	.246	M	.295	V	.377
E	.250	N	.302	W	.386
F	.257	O	.316	X	.397
G	.261	P	.323	Y	.404
H	.266	Q	.332	Z	.413
I	.272	R	.339		

Decimal Equivalents of the Common Fractions

Fraction	Decimal	Fraction	Decimal	Fraction	Decimal
1/64	.0156	21/64	.3281	43/64	.6719
1/32	.0313	11/32	.3438	11/16	.6875
3/64	.0469	23/64	.3594	45/64	.7031
1/16	.0625	3/8	.3750	23/32	.7188
5/64	.0781	25/64	.3906	47/64	.7344
3/32	.0938	13/32	.4063	3/4	.7500
7/64	.1094	27/64	.4219	49/64	.7656
1/8	.1250	7/16	.4375	25/32	.7813
9/64	.1406	29/64	.4531	51/64	.7969
5/32	.1563	15/32	.4688	13/16	.8125
11/64	.1719	31/64	.4844	53/64	.8281
3/16	.1875	1/2	.5000	27/32	.8438
13/64	.2031	33/64	.5156	55/64	.8594
7/32	.2188	17/32	.5313	7/8	.8750
15/64	.2344	35/64	.5469	57/64	.8906
1/4	.2500	9/16	.5625	29/32	.9063
17/64	.2656	37/64	.5781	59/64	.9219
9/32	.2813	19/32	.5938	15/16	.9375
19/64	.2969	39/64	.6094	61/64	.9531
5/16	.3125	5/8	.6250	31/32	.9688
		41/64	.6406	63/64	.9844
		21/32	.6563		

LIGHT UP FOR SAFETY

Federal standard for vehicle lights and reflectors applies to all new vehicles—trucks, tractors, trailers, semi-trailers, buses and cars.

The department of Transportation's Federal Motor Vehicle Safety Standard No. 108 sets lighting and reflector requirements for:

- Trucks, tractors, trailers, semi-trailers and buses 80 in. or more wide manufactured after Dec. 31, 1967 and for . . .
- All vehicles—trucks, tractors, trailers, semi-trailers, buses and passenger cars manufactured after Dec. 31, 1968 regardless of width.

Diagrams illustrate number, color and approximate location of lights and reflectors for all vehicles falling under Standard No. 108. Mounting instructions are outlined on p. 165. Exceptions, additions, and special rulings are included on p. 166.

TRUCKS, BUSES, CARS LESS THAN 80 IN. WIDE

WHITE HEADLIGHTS
AMBER PARKING LIGHTS
AMBER TURN SIGNALS
RED TAIL LIGHTS
AMBER OR RED TURN SIGNALS
AMBER OR RED STOP LIGHTS
RED REFLECTORS
WHITE LICENSE PLATE LIGHT
WHITE BACK-UP LIGHT
AMBER REFLECTOR
AMBER SIDEMARKER
RED REFLECTOR
RED SIDEMARKER

TRUCKS, BUSES, CARS 80 IN. WIDE OR MORE

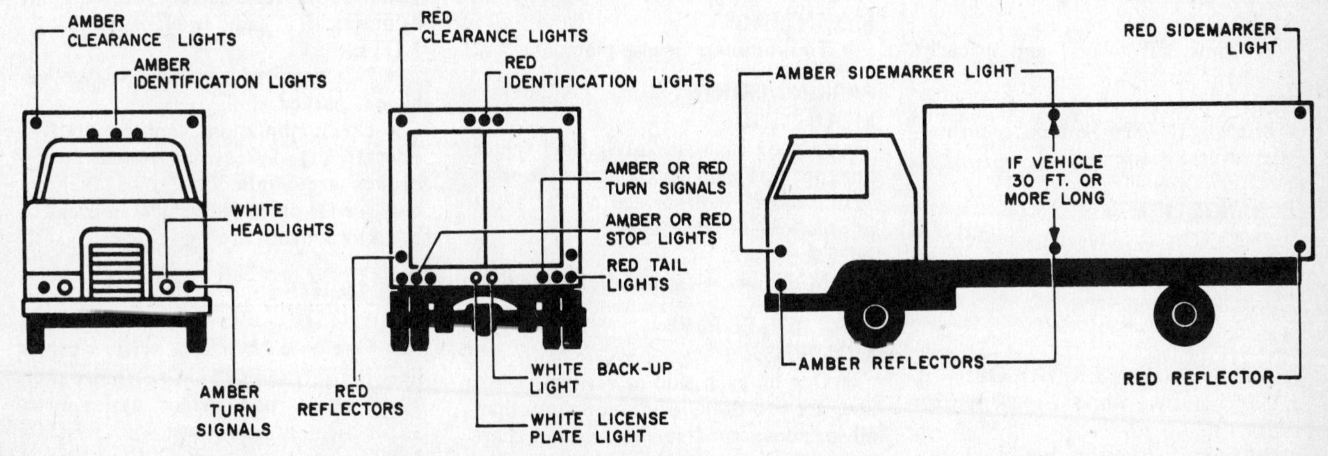

TRAILERS, SEMI-TRAILERS LESS THAN 80 IN. WIDE

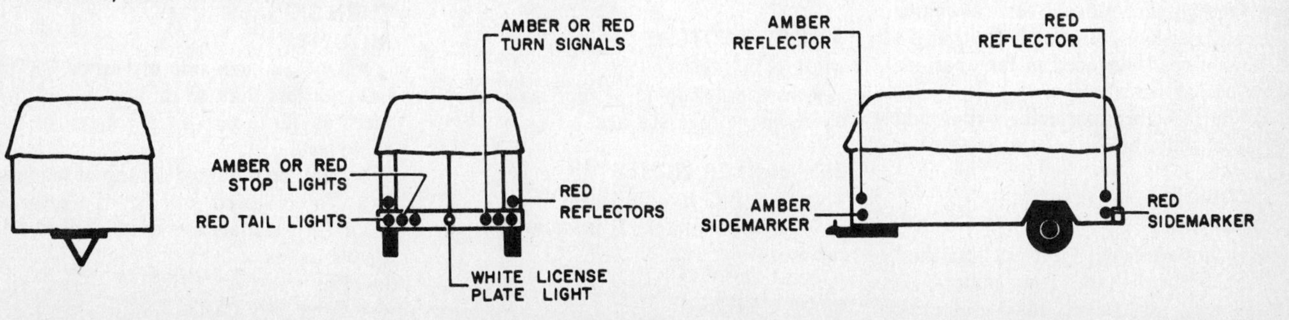

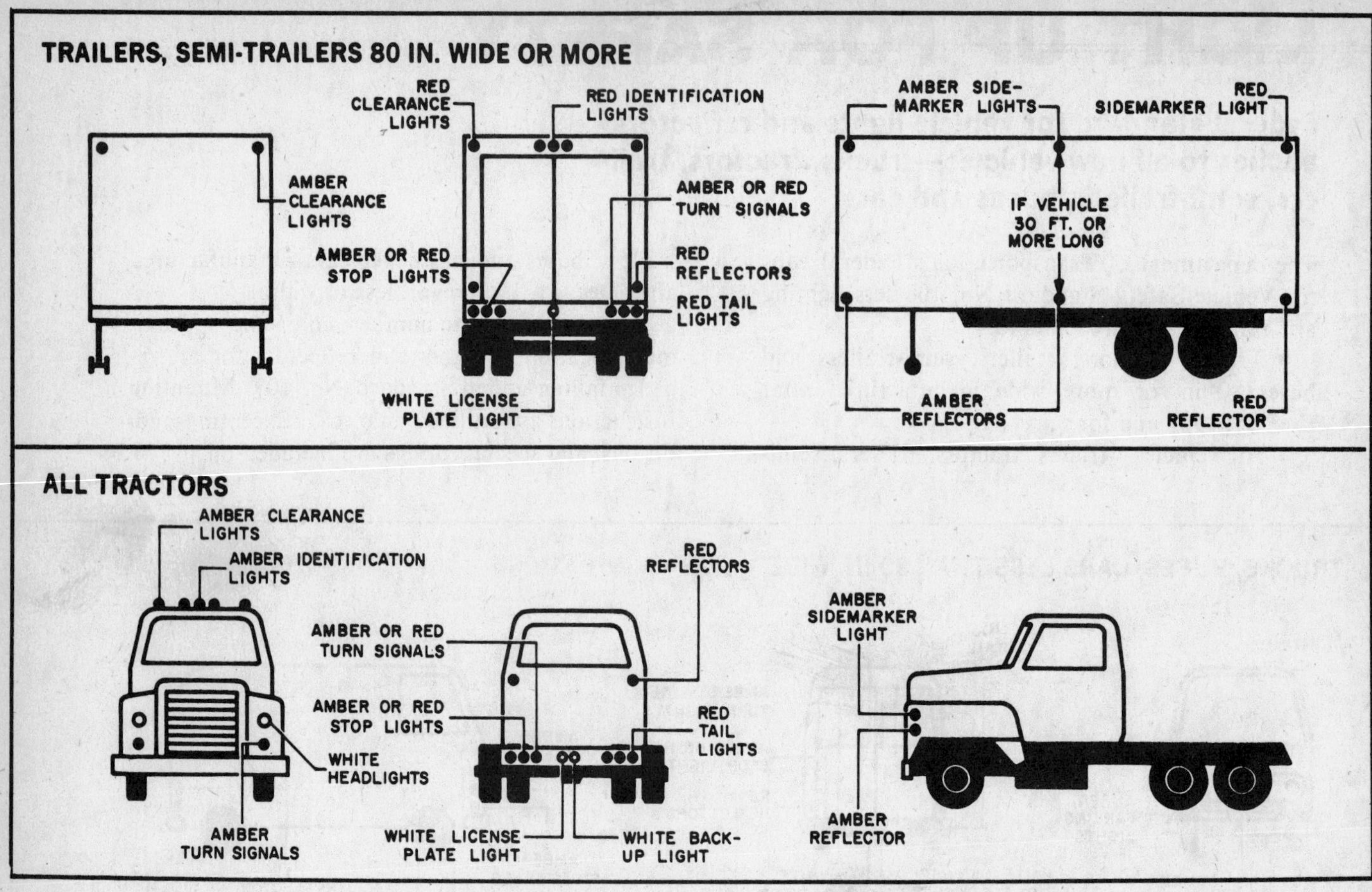

MOUNTING AND SPECIAL INSTRUCTIONS

BACK-UP LIGHT

MOUNTING:

- To show 3 ft to rear and to each side.

NOTE:

- Must light when ignition is turned on and reverse gear engaged.

CLEARANCE LIGHTS

MOUNTING:

- As close as practical to upper left and right edges.

HEADLIGHTS

LOCATION, NUMBER, COLOR:

- On front, two, white, 7-in., Type 2, or . . .
- On front, two, white, 5 ¾-in., Type 1, plus two, white, 5 ¾-in., Type 2.

MOUNTING:

- One on each side of vertical center line not less than 24 in. or more than 54 in. above road surface, as far apart as practical, at same level.
- High-low beam selector switch and indicator required.

IDENTIFICATION LIGHTS

MOUNTING:

- In horizontal row on not less than 6-in. nor more than 12-in. centers, as close as practical to vertical center line.
- Not to extend below top of windshield in front.
- May be mounted at top of body.

LICENSE PLATE LIGHT

MOUNTING:

- To illuminate license plate.

PARKING LIGHTS

MOUNTING:

- One on each side of vertical center line, not less than 15 in. nor more than 72 in. above road surface, as far apart as practical, at same level.

NOTE:

- Must light when headlights are lit.

REAR REFLECTORS

MOUNTING:

- One on each side of vertical center line, not less than 15 in., nor more than 60 in. above road surface, as far apart as practical, at same level.
- May be mounted on back of cab on tractors.

SIDE REFLECTORS

MOUNTING:

- Not less than 15 in. nor more than 60 in. above road surface.

SIDEMARKER LIGHTS

MOUNTING:

- Not less than 15 in. above road surface.

STOP LIGHTS

MOUNTING:

- One on each side of vertical center line, not less than 15 in. nor more than 72 in. above road surface, as far apart as practical, at same level.

NOTE:

- Not required to operate when vehicle is parked.
- On combinations, not required to operate (1) on towing vehicle when brakes are applied on towed vehicle only, or (2) on towed vehicle in event of breakaway from towing vehicle.

TAIL LIGHTS

MOUNTING:

- One on each side of vertical center line, not less than 15 in. nor more than 72 in. above road surface, as far apart as practical, at same level.

NOTE:

- Must light when headlights are lit.

TURN SIGNALS

MOUNTING:

- One on each side of vertical center line, not less than 15 in. above road surface, as far apart as practical, at the same level.
- May be mounted on top of fenders.
- Not required on rear of tractor, if front turn signals are double-faced and visible to rear.

NOTE:

- Four-way flasher required.
- Must be operable with ignition turned off.
- Must include driver indicator.

NOTES

NOTES

NOTES

NOTES